LONGMAN
ACTIVE
STUDY
DICTIONARY
OF ENGLISH

NEW EDITION

Editorial Director
Susan Maingay

Managing Editor
Sheila Dignen

Co-ordinating Editor
Alison Steadman

Senior Lexicographer
Fiona McIntosh

Lexicographers
Deborah Brewer
Janet Hilsdon
Gillian Lazar
Fred McDonald
Susan Morris
Carole Owen
Jocelyn Potter
Valerie Smith
and Denise Beall
   Judy Bowles

Pronunciation Editor
Dinah Jackson

Production
Clive McKeough

Design
Ken Brooks
Paul Price-Smith

Usage and study notes
Donald Adamson
Susan Maingay
Carole Owen

Exercises
Nick Dawson

Cover
Geoff Sida
Margaret Camp

Illustrators
Garry Benfield
Biz Hull
Hard Lines
Tony Richards
Larry Rostant
Chris Ryley

D1192002

Thanks are also due to Valerie Bevan and Jane Walsh.

The publishers would like to thank the many students who have contributed samples of their work to the Longman Learner's Corpus.

The publishers and editorial team gratefully recognize the contribution of the lexicographers and editors on the first edition.

Addison Wesley Longman Limited
Edinburgh Gate
Harlow
Essex
CM20 2JE
England
and Associated Companies throughout the world.

First published 1991
16 15 14

Set in 6.5/6.75 Nimrod
Printed and bound in Great Britain by
Caledonian International Book Manufacturing Ltd,
Glasgow

ISBN 0-582-06329-9

Contents

Guide to the Dictionary

SPELLING

Different spelling

> **judg·ment** /ˈdʒʌdʒmənt/ *n* (also **judgement**) **1** [C] an official decision given by a judge or a court of law: *The judgment was given yesterday.* **2** [C] an opinion formed after careful thought: *In my judgment, the plan is unlikely to succeed.* **3** [U] the ability to make sensible, wise decisions: *a man of sound judgment*

Alternative spellings are shown in brackets like this —see page 14

British and American spelling

> **col·our¹** /ˈkʌlərʲ/ *n* (**color** *AmE*) **1** [U] the quality which allows you to see the difference between, for example, a red flower and a blue flower when they are both the same size and shape: *an insect that can change colour | colour television | a colour film*

American spellings are shown in brackets like this —see page 14

Irregular plurals

> **mouse** /maʊs/ *n* **1** [plural is **mice** /maɪs/] a small furry animal with a long tail that lives in houses and in fields: *a field mouse | I think we've got mice in the kitchen.* **2** [plural is **mouses**] a small box connected to a computer by a wire which you move around on a surface in order to work the computer —see picture on page 539

If the plural of a noun is irregular, it is shown like this —see page 13

> **po·ta·to** /pəˈteɪtəʊ/ *n* **potatoes** [C;U] a round white vegetable with a thin brown or yellow skin, that is cooked and served in many different ways: *I've peeled the potatoes. | baked potatoes | Is there any mashed potato left?*

Irregular verbs

> **hope¹** /həʊp/ *v* **hoped, hoping 1** [I; + (that)] to want something to happen and have some confidence that it probably will happen: *I hope he comes tomorrow. | She hopes to go to college next year. | We're hoping for a big order from the Middle East. | "Is she coming?" "I hope so." | I hope not.*

Does the spelling change? We show the different forms like this —see page 14

SOUND/PRONUNCIATION

Sound

> **ap·ple** /ˈæpəl/ *n* **1** a hard round fruit with white juicy flesh and red, green, or yellow skin

The pronunciation of each word is shown like this —see page 21

Stress

> **a·bil·i·ty** /əˈbɪlɪti/ *n* **abilities** [C;U] skill and power to do something: *She has the ability to think and write clearly. | a person of great musical ability | a job more suited to his abilities*

Do you say a̲bility or abi̲lity? —see page 21

For more information on pronunciation turn to the inside of the back cover of the dictionary.

MEANING

Definitions

> **egg**[1] /eg/ n **1** [C;U] a rounded object with a hard shell, which can contain a baby bird, insect, or snake; eggs are often eaten as food: *Each female lays five or six eggs.* | *I never eat bacon and egg* | *A dozen eggs, please.*

> **cock·le** /ˈkɒkəl ‖ ˈkɑː-/ n a small SHELLFISH

Word meanings are simply explained and easy to understand. Words that you may not know are written IN CAPITAL LETTERS LIKE THIS; you can find all these words in the dictionary —see page 11

More than one meaning

> **a·cute** /əˈkjuːt/ adj **1** very great or severe (used of bad situations): *She was in acute pain.* | *an acute lack of food* **2** showing an ability to understand things clearly and deeply: *an acute analysis of the political situation* **3** able to notice small differences: *Dogs have an acute sense of smell.* **4** tech less than 90 degrees (used of an angle) –compare OBTUSE –**acutely** adv : *acutely embarrassing* –**acuteness** n [U]

Many words have more than one meaning. The first meaning is often the commonest, but don't forget to check the others too —see page 12

Examples

> **lat·er** /ˈleɪtəʳ/ adv **1** after some time: *I can't do it now, but I'll do it later.* | *At first they said 32 people had died, but later they said it was 15.* | *She had a cup of coffee and read for a while. Later that afternoon she took a walk down to the beach.*

Many helpful examples show you how to use the word —see page 12

GRAMMAR

Parts of speech

> **age**[1] /eɪdʒ/ n **1** [C;U] the number of years that a person has lived: *He is 10 years of age.* | *At your age you should know better.* | *She died at the age of 79.* | *What ages are your children?*
> **age**[2] v **aged, aging** or **ageing** [I;T] to become older and weaker or make someone seem older and weaker: *After his wife's death he aged quickly.* | *The illness has aged him.*

The letters tell you whether a word is a noun or verb etc. —see page 15

Word families

> **ea·ger** /ˈiːgəʳ/ adj having a strong desire to do something or a strong interest in something: *I was very eager to meet him.* | *He's eager for success.* | *crowds of eager tourists*
> □ USEFUL PATTERNS be eager to do something; be eager for something –**eagerly** adv –**eagerness** n [U]

Words which are part of the same word family but which have different parts of speech are shown like this —see page 9

Countable and uncountable nouns

lace¹ /leɪs/ n 1 [U] a very fine cloth with a lot of holes in it, which is used to decorate clothes and other things: *lace curtains* 2 [C] a string or cord which goes through two holes on the edges of clothes or shoes in order to fasten them together

These letters tell you whether the noun can be used in the plural.
[C] means it can, [U] means it cannot
—see page 15

Transitive and intransitive verbs

ar·rive /əˈraɪv/ v arrived, arriving [I] 1 to reach a place: *What time does the plane arrive in New York?* | *The train arrived late at the station.* 2 to happen: *At last our holidays arrived.*

ar·rest¹ /əˈrest/ v [T] 1 to catch someone and declare that they are believed to be guilty of a crime: *He was arrested for stealing a car.* 2 *fml* to stop the growth or development of something: *Doctors successfully arrested the growth of the disease.*

These letters tell you whether a verb is followed by a direct object.
[I] means it is never followed by an object, [T] means it is always followed by an object
—see page 16

Verbs followed by prepositions

ab·scond /əbˈskɒnd, æb- ‖ æbˈskɑːnd/ v [I] *fml* to run away suddenly and secretly, usually because you have done something wrong: *He absconded* **with** *all the money.* | *They absconded* **from** *the police station.*

The words in bold type show you the prepositions which typically follow the verb —see page 18

Verbs followed by other grammatical patterns

care·ful /ˈkeəfəl ‖ ˈkeər-/ adj 1 taking care: *We were careful not to mention it to his wife.* | *You should be more careful* **with** *your money.* | *a careful driver* | *Be careful crossing the road.* | *Do be careful how you carry those eggs!*
□ USEFUL PATTERNS to be careful (not) to do something; to be careful with something; to be careful doing something...; to be careful where/ who/ what/how...

The useful patterns note shows you the grammatical patterns which usually follow the word —see page 18

Phrasal verbs

arrive at sthg *phr v* [T] to reach a situation or decision: *After many hours' talk, the committee arrived at a decision.*

This tells you that the objects always follows the preposition when you use *arrive at*.

thrash sthg ↔ **out** *phr v* [T] to reach agreement about a problem or produce a decision by talking about it in detail: *After a long argument we thrashed out a plan.* | *We need to thrash this out.*

The arrow means that you can say *thrash the plan out* or *thrash out the plan* —see page 10

Choosing the right word

kid¹ /kɪd/ *n* **1** [C] *infml* a child or young person: *My kids are two and six.* | *college kids* | *It's immoral putting kids in uniform and sending them to fight a war.*

Formal and informal
Would it be correct
to use this word in
a school essay?
—see page 19

Usage Notes

much² *det. pron. n* **more, most 1** used in questions asking about the amount of something that there is: *How much cheese have we got left?* | *How much does it cost.* **2** *fml* a large amount: *I have much pleasure in welcoming you today.* | *Much of what he says is true.*
■ USAGE **Much** is not usually used in simple statements. Instead use **a great deal of** or **a lot of**: *She's got* **a lot of** *money.* | *We've already collected* **a great deal of** *information.* | **a lot of** *trouble* | **a great deal of** *discomfort*

The usage note
gives extra
information about
words and explains
the meaning and
use of similar words
—see page 13

Opposites

hap·py /ˈhæpi/ *adj* **happier, happiest 1** feeling, expressing, or giving pleasure and satisfaction: *a happy child* | *You look very happy.* | *a happy marriage* | *I'm not very happy about their decision.* —opposite **unhappy**

This shows a word
with the opposite
meaning

Related words

a·the·ist /ˈeɪθi-ɪst/ *n* a person who does not believe in the existence of God —compare AGNOSTIC —**atheistic** /ˌeɪθiˈɪstɪk/ *adj*

This shows a word
which is related or
which might be
confused

Idioms

hab·it /ˈhæbɪt/ *n* **1** [C;U] something you do regularly, often without thinking: *She has the annoying habit of biting her fingernails.* | *He smokes only out of habit.* | *I can't get him to break the habit.* **2** [C] a special set of clothes worn by members of some religious groups **3 be in the habit of doing something** to do something regularly: *We're in the habit of meeting for lunch on Fridays.* [RELATED PHRASES **get into the habit of; make a habit of:** *Make a habit of cleaning your teeth after meals.*]

Idioms and set
phrases are shown
like this. Similar or
alternative phrases
are shown as
RELATED
PHRASES

Using your dictionary

This workbook section contains information and exercises to help you use the dictionary.

The easy exercises are marked *. Start with these exercises and then move on to the ones marked**. The answers to the exercises are on page 774.

This dictionary tells you a lot about English words and how to use them – in writing and speaking as well as in reading and listening. You can use this dictionary to:

check the spelling of a word
find the meaning of a word
find out how to use a word correctly in a sentence
find out how to use a word appropriately in context
find the correct pronunciation of a word

This dictionary contains a lot of information. In order to use it properly, you need to be able to find the information you want quickly and easily.

Finding a word quickly

SPELLING

This dictionary contains about 45,000 words and phrases, listed in alphabetical order. The English alphabet has 26 letters. The order of the letters is this:-

A B C D E F G H I J K L M N O P Q R S T U V W X Y Z
a b c d e f g h i j k l m n o p q r s t u v w x y z

Exercise 1*
Put these words in alphabetical order:

animal   well   queen   jug   happy   zoo

1 ....   4 ....

2 ....   5 ....

3 ....   6 ....

If two words begin with the same letter, you must look at the second letter, then the third, and so on.
Exercise 2*
Put these words in alphabetical order:

animal   actor   absent   address   about   abacus

1 ....   4 ....

2 ....   5 ....

3 ....   6 ....

OPENING THE DICTIONARY AT THE RIGHT PLACE

Close your dictionary and look at the side. You
will see that there are marks on the edges of the
pages. These can help you to open the dictionary
at the right place. It is useful to remember that:
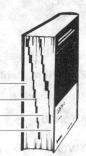
   a-d are in the first quarter of the dictionary
   e-l are in the second quarter of the dictionary
   m-r are in the third quarter of the dictionary
   s-z are in the last quarter of the dictionary

FINDING THE RIGHT PAGE

When you open the dictionary you will see that a word appears in bold type
at the top of each page. The word at the top of the left hand page is the first
word on that page, and the word at the top of the right hand page is the last
word on that page. If you know the order of the alphabet, you will know at a
glance whether you need to go forwards or backwards to find the word you
need to look up.

FINDING A WORD WHEN YOU DON'T KNOW THE SPELLING

The spelling of English words is
sometimes difficult. This dictionary
has special Spelling Notes to
help you. These can be found at
the bottom of some of the pages
and look like this:-

> **SPELLING NOTE**
> Words with the sound / k /, like **cut**, may be spelt
> **k-**, like **key**, or **qu-**, like **queen**.
> Words with the sound / s /, like **city**, may be spelt
> **s-**, like **soon**, or **ps-**, like **psychology**.

Exercise 3*
The words below have all been misspelt. Can you correct the spellings using
the spelling notes to help you?

fotograph	....	**sinema**	....
kalendar	....	**jentleman**	....
nife	....	**riter**	....
sircle	....	**shauffeur**	....

FINDING RELATED WORDS

Some words are made from other words. These do not always have their own
entries; instead, they are given in the entry for the word from which they come.
For example, the noun **agility** comes from the adjective **agile**, so it is given
at the same entry. Similarly, the adverb **enjoyably** is found within the entry
for **enjoyable**.

Exercise 4*
These words do not have separate entries in the dictionary. Where would you expect to find them?

1 **admirer**	....	5 **hijacking**	....
2 **craftsmanship**	....	6 **kind-heartedly**	....
3 **exploration**	....	7 **liveliness**	....
4 **forcibly**	....	8 **poisoner**	....

TWO WORD ENTRIES

Sometimes words are joined together with a hyphen, like **middle-aged**, and sometimes they are written as two words, like **ice cream**. All these expressions are listed alphabetically as though they were only one word.

Exercise 5*
Look up these two word entries in the dictionary. Write down the word which comes before and after each one. The first one has been done for you.

adamant
....

Adam's apple
adept
....

crown prince
....

....

....

eagle-eyed
....

half-term
....

....

....

personal computer
....

semi-detatched
....

PHRASAL VERBS

In English there are many verbs which are made up of two or three words. These are called "phrasal verbs" (see Study Note on page 475). Phrasal verbs may have a completely different meaning from that of the main verb. They can be found at the end of the entry for the main verb, like this:

> **dry²** *v* **dried, 1** [I] to become dry: *They laid the clothes out to dry in the sun.* **2** [T] to make something dry: *I need a towel to dry my hair.* | *Shall I dry the dishes?*
>
> **dry up** *phr v* **1** [I;T **dry** sthg ↔ **up**] to make or become completely dry: *The river dries up in the hot season.* **2** [I] to come to an end: *Sources of ivory have dried up following the international ban on the trade.*

Exercise 6*

Put these words and phrasal verbs in the order you would expect to find them in the dictionary:

> **picnic   pickpocket   pick-me-up   pick out**
> **pick   pianist   pick up   picket**

1 .... 4 ....

2 .... 5 ....

3 .... 6 ....

IDIOMS

An idiom is a phrase which means something different from the meanings of the separate words. This dictionary lists common idioms under the first important word, unless that word is one of the following, in which case the idiom will be listed under the entry for the second important word.

be	go	pass
bring	have	put
come	hold	run
do	keep	set
get	let	take
give	make	

Exercise 7**

The phrases below are all idioms. Where would you expect them to be listed? Underline the word where you think you would find them.

1. **have a hand in**

2. **keep an eye on**

3. **teach someone a lesson**

4. **have a field day**

5. **be sold on something**

6. **put someone's back up**

Understanding meaning

This dictionary shows the meanings of words in definitions, examples, and sometimes "usage notes".

DEFINITIONS

You should always start by looking at the definition of a word. The definitions in the dictionary have all been written using a limited defining vocabulary of

2000 common words, the same as in the Longman Dictionary of Contemporary English. This means that the definitions of even the most difficult words are simply explained and easy to understand.

Exercise 8*
Look at the definitions of the words below:

air terminal air force air hostess airport airline

Now put the correct word in the spaces in each of these sentences.

1 *The .... is closed because of fog.*

2 *The .... gave the passengers a meal and a cup of coffee.*

3 *My uncle was a fighter pilot in the .... during the war.*

4 *My flight was delayed so I waited in the ....*

5 *The .... is in trouble because of the high cost of fuel.*

EXAMPLES

The dictionary gives many examples of words in use. These examples give you more information about a word and how it is used.

Exercise 9**
Look at the definitions and examples for the words written in bold in the questions below. Then try to answer the questions.

1 *Who might give you an **accolade**?* ....

2 *Name something that can **capsize**.* ....

3 *Name three things that can **fascinate** you.* ....

4 *What sort of day is it if the weather is **gusty**?* ....

5 *What can you **inherit**?* ....

6 *What sort of items are **perishable**?* ....

MORE THAN ONE MEANING

Many words in English have more than one meaning. The dictionary shows this by giving each different meaning a number. When you look at an entry in the dictionary you must always read all the different meanings to make sure that you have found the right one.

Exercise 10**
Read the dictionary entry for **tight¹** and look at the sentences below. All the
sentences include the word **tight**, but it has a different meaning in each one.
In the box beside each sentence, write the number of the dictionary definition
which best explains what **tight** means.

1 *a tight dress* ☐

2 *security was tight* ☐

3 *stretch the fabric tight* ☐

4 *a tight fit* ☐

5 *she's so tight with money ...* ☐

6 *marching in tight formation* ☐

Usage notes give you more
information about how to use
words, and often show you
alternative words too. They can be
found at the end of some of the
entries, and look like this:

> **ac·com·mo·da·tion** /əˌkɒməˈdeɪʃən ‖ əˌkɑː-/ *n* [U]
> somewhere to live, for example a room, flat, house
> or hotel room: *The high cost of accommodation
> makes life difficult for students in London.*
> ■ USAGE In British English the word **accommo-
> dation** is uncountable and is not, therefore, used
> in the plural: *The university offers excellent* **accom-
> modation** *for summer visitors.* | *The school pro-
> vides* **accommodation** *for all its students.* (Note
> that it may be used in the plural in American
> English.)

Choosing the right form

IRREGULAR PLURALS

Most nouns make their plural forms
by adding **-s** or **-es**. If a word has
an irregular plural, the dictionary
shows you the correct form.

> **po·ta·to** /pəˈteɪtəʊ/ *n* **potatoes** [C;U] a round white
> vegetable with a thin brown or yellow skin, that is
> cooked and served in many different ways: *I've
> peeled the potatoes.* | *baked potatoes* | *Is there any
> mashed potato left?*

Exercise 11*
Write the correct plural form of these words:

abacus	....	**cargo**	....
grouse	....	**index**	....
phenomenon	....	**sky**	....
tomato	....	**wife**	....

COMPARATIVE AND SUPERLATIVE FORMS OF ADJECTIVES

Most adjectives with one syllable make the comparative and superlative
forms by adding **-er** and **-est** (*rich, richer, richest*). Many adjectives with two
or more syllables make the comparative form with **more** and **less** (*more*

comfortable, less expensive). The superlative forms are made with **the most** and **the least** (*the most beautiful flower, the least ambitious worker*). Some adjectives do not follow this pattern. For these words, the dictionary will show you what the comparative and superlative forms are. For more information, see the Study Note on page 99.

PARTS OF VERBS

Most regular verbs add **-ed** to form the past tense form and the past participle (*I work/I worked/I have worked*). They make the present participle by adding **-ing** (*I am working*). Irregular verbs make their past tense, past participle and present participle in unpredictable ways. This dictionary gives you the past tense and past participle of irregular verbs at the entries, and also in a table on page 782. The table will also show you what the present participle is if that too is irregular. The past tenses and past participle forms of irregular verbs are also listed as separate entries.

> **fly**¹ /flaɪ/ *v* **flew** /fluː/, **flown** /fləʊn/ **1** [I] to move through the air: *A small bird flew up into the tree.* | *This plane is due to fly to New York this evening.*

> **flew** /fluː/ the past tense of FLY

> **flown** /fləʊn/ the past participle of FLY

ALTERNATIVE SPELLINGS

If you look up the word **judgment** in the dictionary, you will see that it has two different spellings. Both of them are correct, but **judgment** is the more common, so it is written first.

If you look up the word **colour**, you will see that it has two different spellings; **color**, used in American English, and **colour**, used in British English. In this dictionary, British and American spelling differences are shown like this: the British spelling is given first, and the usual American spelling is given in brackets with the label *AmE*.

> **judg·ment** /ˈdʒʌdʒmənt/ *n* (also **judgement**) **1** [C] an official decision given by a judge or a court of law: *The judgment was given yesterday.* **2** [C] an opinion formed after careful thought: *In my judgment, the plan is unlikely to succeed.* **3** [U] the ability to make sensible, wise decisions: *a man of sound judgment* | *Her decision shows a lack of political judgment.*

> **col·our**¹ /ˈkʌləʳ/ *n* (**color** *AmE*) **1** [U] the quality which allows you to see the difference between, for example, a red flower and a blue flower when they are both the same size and shape: *an insect that can change colour* | *colour television* | *a colour film*

Using words correctly

GRAMMAR

This dictionary tells you a lot about the grammar of words and how to use them in sentences.

Word classes or "parts of speech"

Sometimes a word may belong to more than one word class. For example, the word **fly** can be a noun or a verb. Each part of speech has its own entry. If you see a small raised number after a word, this means that it has more than one entry, and you will have to look at all of them to be sure you have found the one you want.

Exercise 12*
Look up these words in the dictionary. How many different word classes does each one belong to? Write the word classes in the spaces below.

1 **above** ....   4 **pilot** ....

2 **cause** ....   5 **sharp** ....

3 **in** ....   6 **through** ....

Grammar codes

If you look inside the front cover of the dictionary, you will see an explanation of all the grammar codes which are used. It is useful for you to understand all these codes. In this section we will only deal with the most commonly used grammar codes.

Countable [C] and uncountable [U] nouns

If the word you look up is a noun, the dictionary shows you whether it has a plural form or not. Most nouns in English have a plural. They are known as "countable" nouns. In this dictionary nouns do not have a grammar code if they are countable in all their meanings. Nouns which have no plural form are generally known as "uncountable" nouns and are shown in the dictionary by the grammar code [U].

Exercise 13*
Tick the words from the list below which can be used in the plural.

    attack ☐   **rice** ☐

    apple ☐   **furniture** ☐

    information ☐   **adventure** ☐

Some nouns are countable in some meanings but uncountable in others. Look at the entry for **acid** below. You will see that it is marked [C;U]. This means that it is countable in one meaning but uncountable in its other meaning.

For example, in the sentence:
How much acid is there in the bottle? **acid** is uncountable because we are thinking about the quantity of liquid in the bottle.

ac·id[1] /ˈæsɪd/ *n* **1** [C;U] a chemical substance which may destroy things it touches: *The acid burnt a hole in the carpet.* | *nitric acid*

In the sentence:
The scientists found three different acids in the water, **acid** is countable because we are thinking about the number of different acids. See the Study Note on page 178 for further information.

Using verbs with countable and uncountable nouns

Countable nouns like **apple** are followed by a verb in the singular when there is only one of them; e.g. *The apple is red.* and by a verb in the plural when there is more than one: e.g. *Those three apples are red.* Uncountable nouns like furniture are followed by a singular verb e.g. *That furniture is very expensive.* | *All furniture is expensive.*

A few nouns referring to groups of people can take both singular and plural verbs. For example, both of these sentences are correct:

The football team is going to Spain. The football team are going to Spain. The dictionary shows you when this is the case by coding the word [+ sing/pl verb].

team[1] /tiːm/ *n* [+sing/pl verb] **1** a group of people who work together or play a game or sport together: *He's in the school cricket team.* | *A team of management consultants has been called in to advise us.* | *Do you enjoy team games?* **2** two or more animals pulling the same vehicle: *a team of horses*

Transitive [T] and Intransitive [I] verbs

If the word you look up is a verb, this dictionary tells you a lot about how to use it. First it tells you whether the verb is transitive or intransitive (see Study Note on page 589 for more information). Transitive verbs like **absorb** are followed by a noun or noun phrase as a direct object.

SUBJECT	VERB	DIRECT OBJECT
The sponge	*absorbed*	*the water*

Intransitive verbs like **arrive** are never followed by a noun or noun phrase as a direct object. They may, however, be followed by some kind of complement.

SUBJECT	VERB	COMPLEMENT
		at the hotel
My friends	*arrived*	*on time*
		by car

Sometimes, as with the verb **smile**, the complement can be missed out completely.

SUBJECT	VERB	NO COMPLEMENT
She	*smiled*	

Some verbs like **smell** can be intransitive in one meaning and transitive in another.

I can smell smoke! [T + direct object]
That flower smells nice. [I + complement]

Exercise 14**
Look up the verbs in the sentences below. Are they being used correctly or incorrectly? Mark the sentences with a tick or a cross. Then rewrite the incorrect sentences, making the necessary corrections.

1 *My father arrived the station.* ....

2 *They arrived at half past ten.* ....

3 *The telephone rang.* ....

4 *I enjoyed the meal.* ....

5 *They opened.* ....

6 *The car stopped.* ....

Verbs like 'be' and 'seem'
A few verbs are not marked with [T] or [I]. Instead they are marked [+ complement]. This means that they must be followed by a complement which is usually an adjective or a noun, as in these sentences:

The flowers are pretty.
She looks angry.
She became prime minister.

See the Study Note on page 589 for more information.

Verbs followed by a clause beginning with 'that'
The sentences below all show verbs which are often followed by a clause beginning with **that**.

They claimed that they were innocent.
I think that he will be late.

This is shown in the dictionary by the code [+ that].
If the word **that** is in brackets
[+ (that)] it can be left out.
  I believe that we will win or
  I believe we will win

claim¹ /kleɪm/ *v* ..... **2** [+(that)] to say that something is true, even if there is no proof: *He claims to be rich.* | *She claimed that she was the true Queen.*

Verbs followed by other grammatical patterns

Look at these sentences:

I enjoy cooking. ✓   *I want to go home.* ✓
I enjoy to cook. ✗   *I want going home.* ✗

The second sentence in each pair is incorrect. This dictionary can prevent you from making this type of mistake by showing you the sentence patterns which typically follow such words. At the end of some entries you will find a section called USEFUL PATTERNS. In this section you will find the grammatical patterns which usually follow the word.

See the Study Note on page 269 for more information.

> **en·joy** /ɪnˈdʒɔɪ/ *v* [T] **1** to get pleasure from things and experiences: *I enjoyed the film very much.* | *He thoroughly enjoyed his day out.* | *She enjoys listening to music.*
> □ USEFUL PATTERNS to enjoy something; to enjoy doing something

Exercise 15**

Complete the sentences below using the correct form of the verb in brackets. The USEFUL PATTERNS notes at the entries for the words in bold type will help you.

1 *He **accused** his wife .... an affair.* (have)

2 *She's very **fond** of .... to the cinema.* (go)

3 *I **hope** .... you again.* (see)

4 *The regulations do not **permit** customers .... on the premises.* (drink)

5 *The witness saw (**see**) the man .... the car.* (steal)

Words followed by prepositions

Look up **abscond** in the dictionary. In the examples you will see that the prepositions **with** and **from** are printed in bold type. This tells you that those are the the prepositons which most frequently follow abscond. The examples also tell you that you say "abscond **with** something" (money, jewels etc.) but that you say "abscond **from** somewhere".

Exercise 16**

Put the correct prepositions in these sentences. The examples in your dictionary will help you.

1 *She was afflicted .... deafness.*

2 *You must concentrate .... the matter in hand.*

3 *He was freed .... all his responsibilities.*

4 *He has to liaise closely .... his colleagues.*

5 *She rifled .... her desk looking for the missing document*

See the Study Note on page 759 for further information.

Objects of phrasal verbs

The dictionary helps you to decide the correct position of the object when you are using a phrasal verb. In some phrasal verbs, the object always follows the preposition. The dictionary shows this type of verb in this way:

> **arrive at** sthg *phr v* [T] to reach a situation or decision: *After many hours' talk, the committee arrived at a decision.*

In other phrasal verbs, the object can either follow the preposition, or come between the parts of the verb. The dictionary shows this by placing a double headed arrow next to the object as in the entry for **hand over** opposite:

> **hand over** *phr v* **1** [T **hand** sbdy/sthg ↔ **over**] to give someone or something to a person: *Come on, hand over the money.* | *He was handed over to the police.* **2** [I;T **hand** sthg ↔ **over**] to give power or responsibility to someone else: *The old government will hand over to the new one next week.* | *The captain refused to hand over command of his ship to anyone else.*

You will notice that the dictionary also shows you whether the object can be a person, a thing, or both, by using **sbdy**, **sthg** or **sbdy/ sthg**.

Style

Nearly all the words in the dictionary can be found and used in most types of speech and writing. However, there are some words in the dictionary which are not used in all situations. These words have labels such as *AmE, BrE, fml, infml, dialect, slang* etc. to show you where and when they can be used. You will find a full list of all the labels used inside the front cover of the dictionary.

Exercise 17*
Look up the words in bold in the following sentences and write down the style label(s) you find there.

1 *His hunger **abated** after he drank some soup.* ....

2 *She's always **grousing** about something!* ....

3 *The annual **jamboree** was always very successful.* ....

4 *Are you feeling **lonesome**?* ....

5 *Please place your litter in the **receptacle** provided.* ....

6 *The party was a **shambles** from start to finish!* ....

Exercise 18*

Some of the words in the list below would not be suitable for a school essay because they are either too formal or too informal. Tick the boxes alongside the words that you could use in your essay:

adorn ☐   **seek** ☐

begin ☐   **succinct** ☐

commence ☐   **telly** ☐

erroneous ☐   **television** ☐

look for ☐   **wrong** ☐

Syllables and hyphenation

SYLLABLES

Exercise 19*

Look at the definition of syllable in the dictionary. Now write these words in the correct column.

alphabet   and   animal   axe   address   angry

1 syllable	2 syllables	3 syllables
....	....	....
....	....	....

HYPHENATION

When you are writing or typing, you sometimes have to divide a word at the end of a line by using a hyphen. In English, you can only divide a word at the break between two syllables. The boundaries between the syllables are shown in the dictionary by dots:

> **la·bor·a·tory** /ləˈbɒrətri ‖ ˈlæbrətɔːri/ *n* **laboratories** (also **lab** *infml*) a building or room which contains scientific apparatus and in which a scientist works

You should only divide a word at the boundary between two syllables, and you should never divide a one-syllable word or carry over just one letter to the next line.

Exercise 20*

Look at the sentences below. Which words have been hyphenated correctly?

The English alp-habet has 26 let-ters.

An Indian ele-phant is a use-ful animal.

Later, she bec-ame the Presid-ent of her cou-ntry.

Pronunciation

STRESS

If a word has two or more syllables, one of those syllables is always stressed. That means that we say it with more force. Look at the first line of the entry for alphabet.

> **al·pha·bet** /ˈælfəbet/ n the set of letters used in writing any language, arranged in order

> *This mark comes immediately before the first syllable and shows that we put the stress on the first syllable: that is: we say alphabet.*

Exercise 21*
Look at these pairs of words and circle the correct stress pattern.

| above | above | accept | accept |
| action | action | address | address |

When you looked at the pronunciation of **address** did you notice that some speakers of American English say address?

NOUNS WITH DIFFERENT STRESS

Read these sentences aloud:

> *I bought a new record today.*
> *The band went to the studio to record their new song.*

Did you say record correctly in the two sentences? The pronunciations given at the entries in the dictionary will show you that the noun **record** is pronounced record, while the verb **record** is pronounced record.

Exercise 22*
Many words in English like **record** can be stressed in two different ways. Look up the words **increase** and **permit** in the dictionary, and underline the part of the word that is stressed in each example:

1 a *The number of students at the school will increase next year.*
  b *There will be an increase in the number of students next year.*

2. a *This card will permit you to enter the building.*
  b *You need a permit to enter the building.*

See page 784 for more information on stress.

CONSONANTS AND VOWELS

This dictionary uses a phonetic alphabet (the IPA) to show you how to pronounce words. You will find the symbols used inside the back cover of the dictionary. The phonetic alphabet isn't difficult to learn: start by learning the consonant symbols, then learn the vowel symbols. Each dictionary entry is followed by a phonetic representation between sloping lines, like this: apple /'æpəl/.

Exercise 23**
All the words below have one of these vowel sounds:

/iː/ as in t<u>ea</u>m   /e/ as in b<u>e</u>d   /ɒ/ as in p<u>o</u>t   /uː/ as in d<u>o</u>

Put each word in one of the lists under the correct vowel sound. Use your dictionary for any words you don't know how to pronounce.

bed, blue, boot, bread, bury, cough, do, field, friend, group, key, move, people, pot, said, scene, sheep, shoe, team, watch.

/iː/	/e/	/ɒ/	/uː/
....	....	....	....
....	....	....	....
....	....	....	....
....	....	....	....
....	....	....	....

Now check the sounds with the list inside the back cover and practise saying the words in the lists. Did you notice that the words bed, bread, bury, friend and said all contain the same /e/ sound, even though they are spelt differently?

BRITISH AND AMERICAN PRONUNCIATIONS

This dictionary shows both the standard British English pronunciation and, after the two vertical lines, the parts of the pronunciation which differ in standard American.

porce-lain /'pɔːslɪn ‖ 'pɔːrsəlɪn/ *n* [U] a thin shiny substance made of baked clay which is used to make fine quality cups and dishes

A, a

A, a /eɪ/ **A's, a's** or **As, as** the 1st letter of the English alphabet

A¹ a note in Western music

a /ə/ *strong* eɪ/ *indefinite article, det* (also **an** before a vowel sound) **1** one: *There was a man standing by the door.* | *She's an artist.* **2** used before some words of quantity: *a few weeks* | *a lot of people* | *a little water* **3** every: *A bicycle has two wheels.* **4** every or each: *six times a day* | *£3 a packet* | *We're paid ten pounds an hour.* **5** used before someone's name when you do not know the person: *There's a Mr Robinson on the telephone for you.* –see AN (USAGE) **6** when you have several points you want to make, you can order them and show where each one starts by using "a", "b", "c", etc.; teachers and speakers on technical subjects do this, and some people use them in conversation: *There are two reasons why the plant has failed to flower: a, it hasn't had enough light and, b, the temperature hasn't been sufficiently high.* | *"Do you think he'll get the job?" "Well, I don't really because, a, he hasn't got the qualifications and, b, he hasn't got much experience."*

ab·a·cus /ˈæbəkəs/ *n* **abacuses** a frame holding wires on which small balls can be moved, used for counting

a·ban·don /əˈbændən/ *v* [T] **1** to leave someone or something for a long time or for ever: *The sailors abandoned the sinking ship.* | *He abandoned his wife.* | *an abandoned building* **2** to stop an activity without finishing it or getting the result you want: *The search was abandoned when night came.* **3** **abandon yourself to** to allow yourself to be completely controlled by a feeling: *He abandoned himself to despair.* –**abandonment** *n* [U]

a·base /əˈbeɪs/ *v* **abased, abasing** *fml* **abase yourself** to behave in a way that makes you lose pride or respect for yourself

a·bashed /əˈbæʃt/ *adj* uncomfortable or ashamed in the presence of others: *He looked suitably abashed as his mistakes were pointed out.*

a·bate /əˈbeɪt/ *v* **abated, abating** [I] *fml* to become less strong: *The ship waited in the harbour until the storm abated.*

ab·at·toir /ˈæbətwɑːʳ/ *n* BrE a building in which animals are killed for meat

ab·bess /ˈæbʲs, ˈæbes/ *n* a woman who is the head of a religious establishment for women called a CONVENT

ab·bey /ˈæbi/ *n* a building in which nuns (NUN) or monks (MONK) live or lived

ab·bot /ˈæbət/ *n* a man who is the head of a religious establishment for men called a MONASTERY

ab·bre·vi·ate /əˈbriːvieɪt/ *v* **abbreviated, abbreviating** [T] to make something shorter, usually a word, a talk or a piece of writing

ab·bre·vi·a·tion /ə,briːviˈeɪʃən/ *n* a short form of a word, usually used in writing; for example, 'adj.' is an abbreviation for 'adjective'

ab·di·cate /ˈæbdɪkeɪt/ *v* **abdicated, abdicating 1** [I] to officially give up the position of king or queen: *The King abdicated in favour of his son.* **2** **abdicate responsibility** to refuse to be responsible for something any longer –**abdication** /,æbdɪˈkeɪʃən/ *n* [C;U]

ab·do·men /ˈæbdəmən, æbˈdəu-/ *n tech* a part of your body below your chest, that includes your stomach and bowels –**abdominal** /æbˈdɒm₃nəl ‖ -ˈdɑː-/ *adj* : *abdominal pains*

ab·duct /æbˈdʌkt, əb-/ *v* [T] to take someone away unlawfully, often by force: *The police think the missing woman may have been abducted.* –**abduction** /-ˈdʌkʃən/ *n* [C;U]

a·bet /əˈbet/ *v* -tt- [T] **aid and abet** to help someone to do something wrong or dishonest

a·bey·ance /əˈbeɪəns/ *n fml* **in abeyance** not in use at the moment: *These rules are temporarily in abeyance.* | *an old custom that has fallen into abeyance*

ab·hor /əbˈhɔːʳ, æb-/ *v* -rr- [T; not in progressive forms] to hate something very much: *Most people abhor cruelty to children.*

ab·hor·rent /əbˈhɒrənt ‖ -ˈhɔːr-/ *adj* hateful or unacceptable: *The idea of killing animals for food is abhorrent to many people.* | *I find his behaviour abhorrent.* –**abhorrence** *n* [U]

a·bide¹ /ˈʲəˈbaɪd/ *v* **abided, abiding** [T] **can't abide** to dislike something very much: *I can't abide noisy children.* | *He never could abide queuing.* see BEAR² (USAGE)

abide by sthg *phr v* [T] to follow or obey rules, agreements, and decisions: *If you join the club you must abide by its rules.*

abide² *v* **abode** /əˈbəʊd/, **abided, abiding** to stay or live somewhere (a word which is no longer used in modern English)

a·bid·ing /əˈbaɪdɪŋ/ *adj* lasting for a long time: *The experience left me with an abiding hatred of dogs.*

a·bil·i·ty /əˈbɪlᵻti/ *n* **abilities** [C;U] skill and power to do something: *She has the ability to think and write clearly.* | *a person of great musical ability* | *a job more suited to his abilities*

ab·ject /ˈæbdʒekt/ *adj* **1** **abject poverty** extreme poverty, deserving great pity **2** **an abject apology** an apology showing lack of pride or self-respect

a·blaze /əˈbleɪz/ *adj* [never before a noun] **1** on fire: *The wooden house was quickly ablaze.* **2** very bright: *The village was ablaze with light.*

a·ble /ˈeɪbəl/ *adj* **1** **able to do something** having enough power, skill, knowledge, time, or money to do something: *Will you be able to come?* | *We might be able to afford a new car next year.* | *I was only able to do three questions in the exam.* | *I wasn't able to contact him.* | *At last I was able to get the door open.* **2** clever or skilled at doing something: *a very able student*

a·bly /ˈeɪbli/ *adv* with skill: *She organized the meeting very ably.*

ab·norm·al /æbˈnɔːməl ‖ -ˈnɔːr-/ *adj* different from what is usual or expected and so worrying in some way: *She was afraid the child was abnormal.* | *abnormal levels of radiation* –**abnormally** *adv* : *He was behaving abnormally.* | *It was abnormally hot.* –**abnormality** /,æbnɔːˈmælᵻti ‖ -nər-/ *n* **abnormalities** [C;U]

a·board /əˈbɔːd ‖ əˈbɔːrd/ *adv,prep* [never before a noun] on or into a ship, aircraft, train or bus: *The boat is ready to leave. All aboard!* | *The plane crashed, killing everyone aboard.*

a·bode /əˈbəʊd/ *n fml* your home, or the place where you live: *She has the right of abode in the U.K.* | *a person of no fixed abode*

a·bol·ish /ə'bɒlɪʃ ‖ ə'bɑː-/ v [T] to bring something to an end by law: *Slavery was abolished in England in the 19th century.* –**abolition** /ˌæbə'lɪʃən/ n [U]: *the abolition of the death penalty*

a·bom·i·na·ble /ə'bɒmɪnəbəl, -mənə- ‖ ə'bɑː-/ adj extremely bad, unpleasant, or shocking: *The judge said it was the most abominable crime he had ever heard of.* –**abominably** adv

ab·o·rig·i·nal /ˌæbə'rɪdʒɪnəl◄/ adj belonging to or concerning the people who have lived in a place from the earliest times

ab·o·rig·i·ne /ˌæbə'rɪdʒɪni/ n (also **Aborigine**) a member of one of the tribes living in Australia when European people arrived

a·bort /ə'bɔːt ‖ ə'bɔːrt/ v 1 [I;T] to end a PREGNANCY, usually intentionally, when the baby is still too small to live: *The doctor had to abort the baby.* | *Many women abort spontaneously in the early weeks of pregnancy.* 2 [T] to end a plan or process before it has been finished: *The space flight had to be aborted because of difficulties with the computer.*

a·bor·tion /ə'bɔːʃən ‖ ə'bɔːr-/ n [C;U] the intentional ending of a PREGNANCY when the baby is still too small to live: *She was advised to have an abortion.* | *a debate on the question of abortion*

a·bor·tive /ə'bɔːtɪv ‖ ə'bɔːr-/ adj unsuccessful (used of actions or plans): *an abortive attempt by the army to take power*

a·bound /ə'baʊnd/ v [I] fml 1 to exist in large numbers: *Rumours abound on the subject of his marriage.* 2 to contain large numbers of: *The rivers abound with fish.*

a·bout¹ /ə'baʊt/ prep 1 on a particular subject: *We talked about the weather.* | *a book about birds* | *I haven't had time to think about your idea yet.* 2 in a place: *He's somewhere about the house.* | *There were books lying about the room.* 3 **about someone** in someone's appearance, or their way of behaving: *There was something mysterious about him.* 4 **what about, how about: a** a phrase used when you are introducing a new idea into a conversation: *Yes, but what about animals? They have rights as well, don't they?* **b** a phrase used when you are suggesting that someone could do something, or inviting them to do it: *How about a drink?* | *How about coming round for a meal later?*

about² adv 1 in a place, often not doing very much: *People were lying about in the sun.* | *We spent the morning just sitting about.* 2 in a place and able to be used or obtained: *Is there a pair of scissors about?* | *Is your mother about?* | *I'm afraid there's no one about to deal with your query at the moment.* 3 near to a particular amount: *There were about 50 people there.* | *He arrived about ten minutes later.* 4 **be about to do something** to be just going to do something: *We were about to leave when the phone rang.* | *They're about to move house.*

a·bove /ə'bʌv/ adv,prep 1 adv,prep higher than something or over it: *The sky above us was clear and blue.* | *flying just above the surface of the water* | *We could hear shouting coming from the flat above.* | *Birds were circling high up above.* –see picture on page 540 2 adv,prep more than a particular number or amount: *Don't let your overdraft rise above £1000.* | *The temperature had risen to above freezing.* | *children aged seven and above* 3 adv,prep higher in rank or power than someone else: *He's just above me in the hierarchy.* | *Anybody of the rank of captain and above will be invited.* 4 adv on an earlier page or higher up on the same page: *The figures given above show that pollution is still*

increasing in an alarming way. 5 **above something, above doing something** too good, too honest, or too proud to do something: *I'm sure he's above stealing.* 6 **above all** most important of all; you use this when you are coming to your most important point: *For this job, you need to be reliable and you need to be good with people but, above all, you need a sense of humour.*

a·bove-board /ə,bʌv'bɔːd◄,ə'bʌvbɔːd ‖ ə'bʌvbɔːrd/ adj [never before a noun] open and honest: *His part in the affair was quite aboveboard.*

a·bra·sive /ə'breɪsɪv/ adj 1 rough (used to describe a substance which will make a surface smooth and clean) 2 rather rude and offensive: *Her manner is particularly abrasive.*

a·breast /ə'brest/ adv [never before a noun] 1 side by side and facing the same direction: *lines of soldiers marching five abreast* 2 **keep/be abreast of** to know the most recent facts about something: *She read the papers to keep abreast of the latest developments.*

a·bridge /ə'brɪdʒ/ v **abridged, abridging** [T] to make a speech or a piece of writing shorter by taking parts out: *This book is an abridged version of Dickens' original novel.* –**abridgment** n

a·broad /ə'brɔːd/ adv [never before a noun] to or in another country: *He lived abroad for many years.* | *Are you going abroad this summer?*

a·brupt /ə'brʌpt/ adj 1 sudden and unexpected: *The train came to an abrupt halt.* 2 rough and rather rude in the way you speak or behave: *She had a rather abrupt manner.* –**abruptly** adv –**abruptness** n [U]

ab·scess /'æbses/ n a swelling on or in your body containing a thick yellowish liquid called PUS

ab·scond /əb'skɒnd, æb- ‖ æb'skɑːnd/ v [I] fml to run away suddenly and secretly, usually because you have done something wrong: *He absconded with all the money.* | *They absconded from the police station.*

ab·sence /'æbsəns/ n 1 [C;U] the state or time of not being in a place, or of being away: *Please look after the house during my absence.* | *Absence makes the heart grow fonder.* 2 [U] non-existence or lack: *The biggest problem facing the police is the absence of reliable information.*

ab·sent¹ /'æbsənt/ adj 1 not present: *Four students are absent from class today.* 2 [only before a noun] showing lack of attention to what is happening: *an absent look on his face*

ab·sent² /əb'sent, æb- ‖ æb-/ v fml **absent yourself** to stay away: *He absented himself from the meeting.*

ab·sen·tee /ˌæbsən'tiː◄/ n a person who stays away: *There are fewer absentees in the summer because the children are healthier.* | *an absentee landlord*

ab·sen·tee·is·m /ˌæbsən'tiːɪzəm/ n [U] the act of staying away from school or from your place of work with no good reason: *The level of absenteeism in this factory is much too high.*

ab·sent·ly /'æbsəntli/ adv in a manner showing lack of attention

absent-mind·ed /ˌ·· '··◄/ adj forgetful or too concerned with your thoughts to notice what is happening or what you are doing –**absent-mindedly** adv –**absent-mindedness** n [U]

ab·so·lute /'æbsəluːt/ adj 1 complete and total: *a man of absolute honesty* | *That's absolute nonsense!* 2 having limitless power: *the power of an absolute monarch* 3 not depending on or measured by comparison with other things: *In absolute terms, wages* *have risen, but not in comparison with the cost of living.* –compare RELATIVE

ab·so·lute·ly /ˈæbsəluːtli, ˌæbsəˈluːtli/ *adv* **1** completely: *It's difficult to cross the desert by car, but not absolutely impossible.* | *I'm absolutely exhausted.* **2** a word used to show that you completely agree with someone: *"Do you think so?" "Absolutely!"*

ab·so·lu·tion /ˌæbsəˈluːʃən/ *n* [U] forgiveness given by the Christian church for an offence against a religious law

ab·solve /əbˈzɒlv ‖ -ɑːlv/ *v* **absolved, absolving** [T] to free someone from a responsibility or duty, or from having to be punished for a wrong: *The report absolved her from all blame.*

ab·sorb /əbˈsɔːb, əbˈzɔːb ‖ -ɔːrb/ *v* [T] **1** to take in heat, light, or a liquid: *The drug is absorbed through the skin.* **2** to understand or take in information: *We are constantly absorbing new ideas.* **3** to accept or deal with something easily, without any serious effects: *The company has been able to absorb these extra costs.* **4** to take all someone's interest or attention: *The new baby absorbs all her energy.* **5** to gain control over a smaller group or company: *The company has absorbed all its rivals.* –**absorption** /-ˈɔːpʃən ‖ -ɔːr-/ *n* [U]

ab·sorbed /əbˈsɔːbd, -ˈzɔːbd ‖ -ɔːrbd/ *adj* giving all your attention to something: *He was soon absorbed in his book.* | *She is absorbed by her own problems.*

ab·sor·bent /əbˈsɔːbənt, -ˈzɔː- ‖ -ɔːr-/ *adj* able to take in liquids

ab·sorb·ing /əbˈsɔːbɪŋ, -ˈzɔː- ‖ -ɔːr-/ *adj* very interesting: *I find my new course absorbing.*

ab·stain /əbˈsteɪn/ *v* [I] **1** to intentionally not do something you enjoy doing: *Jack was advised to abstain from alcohol for a few days.* **2** to not vote, rather than voting for or against something: *I couldn't decide who to vote for, so in the end I abstained.*

ab·sten·tion /əbˈstenʃən/ *n* [C;U] an act of not voting rather than voting for or against something: *50 votes for, 35 against, and 7 abstentions*

ab·sti·nence /ˈæbstɪnəns/ *n* [U] the act of keeping away from things you enjoy

ab·stract¹ /ˈæbstrækt/ *adj* **1** general, and not related to a particular situation: *an abstract argument about justice* | *abstract thought* **2** not trying to represent objects as they would be seen by a camera (used of works of art): *an abstract painting*

abstract² /ˈæbstrækt/ *n* **1** a shortened form of a speech or piece of writing **2** something that does not try to represent an object as it would be seen by a camera (used of works of art): *a large abstract by Picasso*

ab·stract³ /əbˈstrækt, æb-/ *v* [T] to separate out important pieces of information from a speech or piece of writing

ab·stract·ed /əbˈstræktɪd, æb-/ *adj* lost in thought, and so not noticing what is happening –**abstractedly** *adv*

ab·strac·tion /əbˈstrækʃən, æb-/ *n* **1** [U] a state in which you are thinking deeply and do not notice what is happening around you **2** [C] an idea which is general and not related to the material world: *A good judge must consider all the facts of a case as well the abstraction "justice".*

ab·struse /əbˈstruːs, æb-/ *adj fml* difficult to understand: *a rather abstruse argument*

ab·surd /əbˈsɜːd, -ˈzɜːd ‖ -ɜːrd/ *adj* foolish or senseless: *It's absurd not to wear a coat in such cold weather.* –**absurdly** *adv* –**absurdity** /əbˈsɜːdʌti, -ˈzɜː- ‖ -ɜːr-/ *n* **absurdities** [C;U]

a·bun·dance /əˈbʌndəns/ *n* **1** an abundance of a very great quantity of: *The country has an abundance of skilled workers, but not enough jobs.* **2** in abundance in large numbers or great quantity: *There was food and drink in abundance.*

a·bun·dant /əˈbʌndənt/ *adj* existing in great quantity: *abundant supplies of oil and gas* –**abundantly** *adv*

a·buse¹ /əˈbjuːz/ *v* **abused, abusing** [T] **1** to say very rude or cruel things to someone **2** to treat someone cruelly or violently: *She had been beaten and sexually abused.* **3** to use something badly or wrongly: *He had abused his power.*

a·buse² /əˈbjuːs/ *n* **1** [U] rude or cruel words: *He greeted me with a stream of abuse.* **2** [U] cruel or violent treatment of someone: *physical abuse of children* **3** [C;U] wrong or bad use of something: *the problem of drug abuse* | *This is an abuse of your position.*

a·bu·sive /əˈbjuːsɪv/ *adj* using unkind, rude, or cruel language: *an abusive letter* –**abusively** *adv*

a·bys·mal /əˈbɪzməl/ *adj* very bad: *The food was abysmal.*

a·byss /əˈbɪs/ *n* **1** a deep hole which appears to have no bottom **2** a strong feeling that there is no hope: *an abyss of despair*

A/C an abbreviation for ACCOUNT¹ (5)

a·ca·cia /əˈkeɪʃə/ *n* **acacias** *or* **acacia** a tree found mainly in hot countries

ac·a·dem·ic¹ /ˌækəˈdemɪk◂/ *adj* **1** concerning the teaching or studying of subjects taught to provide skills for the mind, especially in a college or university: *academic subjects* | *academic qualifications* **2** not practical or useful: *What car to buy is a purely academic question for me, because I can't afford one at all!*

academic² *n* a college or university teacher

a·cad·e·my /əˈkædəmi/ *n* **academies 1** a society of people interested in encouraging art, science, or literature **2** a school for training in a special art or skill: *a military academy* | *an academy of music*

ac·cede /əkˈsiːd, æk-/ *v* **acceded, acceding** *fml* **accede to something: a** to agree to do or accept something: *He finally acceded to our request.* **b** to take a high post or position after someone has left it

ac·cel·e·rate /əkˈseləreɪt/ *v* **accelerated, accelerating 1** [I] to move faster: *The car accelerated.* | *Jack accelerated to overtake the bus.* **2** [T] to make something happen more quickly: *a plan to accelerate the growth of tourism* –**acceleration** /əkˌseləˈreɪʃən/ *n* [U]

ac·cel·e·ra·tor /əkˈseləreɪtəʳ/ *n* the piece of apparatus in a motor vehicle which is used to increase speed –see picture on page 49

ac·cent¹ /ˈæksənt ‖ ˈæksent/ *n* **1** a particular way of speaking, usually connected with a country, area, or class: *He speaks with a strong Welsh accent.* **2 the accent** particular importance given to something: *The accent of the report is on safety.* **3** importance given to a word or part of a word by saying it with more force: *The accent in the word "important" is on the second syllable.* **4** the mark used above a part of a word in writing or printing to show what kind of sound is needed when it is spoken: *Some people write "café" with an acute accent on the "e".*

ac·cent² /əkˈsent ‖ ˈæksent/ *v* [T] to pronounce a word or a part of a word with more force

ac·cen·tu·ate /ək'sentʃueɪt/ v **accentuated, accentuating** [T] to make something more important or noticeable: *The dark frame accentuates the brightness of the picture.* –**accentuation** /ək,sentʃu'eɪʃən/ n [U]

ac·cept /ək'sept/ v **1** [I;T] to agree to receive something: *I'm delighted to accept this gift.* | *The Unions accepted the company's offer.* **2** [I;T] to agree to do or use something: *He asked her to marry him, and she accepted.* | *I never believed that the government would accept free and fair elections.* | *They refuse to accept new technology.* **3** [T; + that] to agree that something is true: *I accept that it's dangerous, but I want to try.* | *He refused to accept the fact that he was getting old.* ◻ USEFUL PATTERNS to accept that…; to accept the fact that… **4** [T] to let someone join a course or organization: *The college only accepts local students.* **5** [T] to suffer something unpleasant or difficult without trying to prevent it or change it: *He accepted the situation for years.* **6 accept responsibility** to agree that you are responsible for something

ac·cep·ta·ble /ək'septəbəl/ adj satisfactory: *Your work is not acceptable.* | *This solution was acceptable to everyone involved.* –opposite **unacceptable** –**acceptably** adv –**acceptability** /ək,septə'bɪlɪti/ n [U]

ac·cept·ance /ək'septəns/ n [U] **1** agreement to receive something or someone: *The Unions recommended acceptance of the offer.* | *Two weeks after applying for the job I received a letter of acceptance.* **2** agreement that something is true: *their acceptance of the theory* **3** the act of suffering something unpleasant or difficult, without trying to prevent it or change it: *his acceptance of defeat* **4 gain acceptance, win acceptance** to become popular or liked: *The idea is gaining acceptance.*

ac·cess /'ækses/ n **1** [C] a way to reach or enter a building: *The only access to that building is along a muddy track.* **2** [U] the ability or right to obtain or use something: *Students need easy access to books.* | *Do you have access to that information?* **3** [U] the right to see someone: *The court gave him access to his child at weekends.*

ac·ces·si·ble /ək'sesɪbəl/ adj **1** possible to reach: *The island is accessible only by boat.* **2** easy to understand and enjoy (used of a book or work of art) –opposite **inaccessible** –**accessibility** /ək,sesɪ'bɪlɪti/ n [U]

ac·ces·sion /ək'seʃən/ n [U] fml the act of taking up a high position: *her accession to the throne*

ac·ces·so·ry /ək'sesəri/ n **accessories 1** something which is not a necessary part of something larger but which makes it more useful, effective or beautiful: *Accessories for this car include a roof rack and a radio.* **2 accessories** things such as hats, shoes, and gloves, which you wear or carry and which often match your clothes: *a black dress with matching accessories* **3** law a person who helps another in doing something criminal

ac·ci·dent /'æksɪdənt/ n **1** something unpleasant, undesirable, or damaging that happens without intention or by chance: *There's been a serious accident on the motorway.* | *He was killed in a climbing accident.* | *She had an accident with the tin opener and cut her hand.* | *Don't be angry with me – it was an accident.* **2 by accident** by chance: *He opened her letter by accident.* | *We met by accident.*

ac·ci·den·tal /,æksɪ'dentl◂/ adj happening by chance, not by plan or intention –**accidentally** adv

accident-prone /'·· ·/ adj more likely to have accidents than most people

ac·claim¹ /ə'kleɪm/ v [T] to praise publicly: *The new drug has been acclaimed as the most important discovery for years.*

acclaim² n [U] strong expressions of approval and praise: *The book received considerable acclaim.*

ac·cla·ma·tion /,æklə'meɪʃən/ n [C;U] loud sounds of approval and praise

ac·cli·ma·tize /ə'klaɪmətaɪz/ v **acclimatized, acclimatizing 1** [I;T] to become accustomed to the general weather conditions in a new part of the world: *It took several days to get acclimatized to the atmosphere in Mexico City.* **2 acclimatize yourself to something** to become accustomed to something: *He can't acclimatize himself to working at night.* –**acclimatization** /ə,klaɪmətaɪ'zeɪʃən ‖ -tə-/ n [U]

ac·co·lade /'ækəleɪd/ n strong praise and approval: *His new book received the highest accolade from the critics.*

ac·com·mo·date /ə'kɒmədeɪt ‖ ə'kɑː-/ v **accommodated, accommodating** [T] **1** to provide someone with a place in which to live or stay **2** to have enough space for something or someone: *enough shelves to accommodate all our books* **3** fml to change things to help someone or to do what someone wants: *We will make every effort to accommodate the needs of our clients.*

ac·com·mo·dat·ing /ə'kɒmədeɪtɪŋ ‖ ə'kɑː-/ adj willing to help, by changing things if necessary

ac·com·mo·da·tion /ə,kɒmə'deɪʃən ‖ ə,kɑː-/ n [U] somewhere to live, for example a room, flat, house or hotel room: *The high cost of accommodation makes life difficult for students in London.* ■ USAGE In British English the word **accommodation** is uncountable and is not, therefore, used in the plural: *The university offers excellent* **accommodation** *for summer visitors.* | *The school provides* **accommodation** *for all its students.* (Note that it may be used in the plural in American English.)

ac·com·pa·ni·ment /ə'kʌmpənimənt/ n **1** something which is used or provided with something else **2** music played to support singing or another instrument

ac·com·pa·nist /ə'kʌmpənɪst/ n a person who plays a musical accompaniment

ac·com·pa·ny /ə'kʌmpəni/ v **accompanied, accompanying** [T] **1** fml to go with someone, especially on a journey: *The Governor was accompanied to the palace by a military escort.* **2** to appear with someone or something: *A series of colour photographs accompanies the text.* **3** to make supporting music for someone: *The singer was accompanied by a famous pianist.*

ac·com·plice /ə'kʌmplɪs ‖ ə'kɑːm-, ə'kʌm-/ n a person who helps someone to carry out a crime

ac·com·plish /ə'kʌmplɪʃ ‖ ə'kɑːm-, ə'kʌm-/ v [T] to succeed in doing something: *We tried to arrange a meeting but accomplished nothing.*

ac·com·plished /ə'kʌmplɪʃt ‖ ə'kɑːm-, ə'kʌm-/ adj good at something: *an accomplished singer*

ac·com·plish·ment /ə'kʌmplɪʃmənt ‖ ə'kɑːm-, ə'kʌm-/ n **1** [U] the act of finishing work completely and successfully: *When he had finished, he felt a real sense of accomplishment.* **2** [C] a skill: *Being able to play the piano well is just one of his accomplishments.*

ac·cord¹ /əˈkɔːd ‖ -ɔːrd/ v [I] *fml* to agree: *The evidence of the second witness does not accord with that of the first.*

accord² n **1** [C;U] agreement: *The two governments are completely in accord on the question of preserving peace.* | *accords between neighbouring states* **2 of your own accord** without being asked **3 with one accord** with everybody agreeing

ac·cord·ance /əˈkɔːdəns ‖ -ɔːr-/ n **in accordance with** in agreement with or in obedience to: *Seat belts must be worn, in accordance with the law.*

ac·cord·ing·ly /əˈkɔːdɪŋli ‖ -ɔːr-/ adv **1** *fml* for the reason just given: *We see that you have an income of less than £2000 a year. Accordingly, we have decided to grant you free tuition.* –see Study Note on page 508 **2** in a suitable way: *Some events are very formal. Others are very informal. You have to dress accordingly.* | *If you change your address, please notify the office accordingly.*

according to /·ˈ··· ·/ prep **1** as said by someone or shown by something: *According to our records, you still have six of our desks.* | *According to George, she's a really good teacher.* **2** in a way that agrees with something: *We will be paid according to the amount of work we do.*

■ USAGE **1** Do not use **according to** when giving your own opinion. Instead use phrases such as, **in my opinion**.... **2** Do not use **according to** with words like **opinion** or **view**. Compare: **According to** *the government*.... | *In the government's* view/opinion....

ac·cor·di·on /əˈkɔːdiən ‖ -ɔːr-/ n a musical instrument like a box; you play it by pressing both sides in and out to force air through it while working the keys with your fingers

ac·cost /əˈkɒst ‖ əˈkɔːst, əˈkɑːst/ v [T] to go up to and speak to someone, especially a stranger, often in a threatening manner or with the offer of sex

ac·count¹ /əˈkaʊnt/ n **1** [C] a written or spoken report: *Give us an account of what happened.* | *There was an account of the train crash in the paper.* **2** [C] a sum of money kept in a bank which may be added to and taken from: *I've got an account with First City Bank.* | *My salary is paid directly into my bank account.* **3 accounts** [pl] a record or statement of money received and paid out by a bank, business, person or group: *The accounts show that business is beginning to improve.* | *She does the accounts for a London firm.* **4** [C;U] an arrangement which allows you to take goods away and then pay for them later: *I'll pay for the shirt now, but could you put the shoes on my account, please.* | *Could I take them on account?* **5** [C] a statement of money owed: *Please pay your account immediately.* **6 by all accounts** according to what everyone says **7 of great account** of great importance **8 of no account** of no importance **9 on account of** because of **10 on no account, not on any account** not for any reason: *He must not go there on any account.* | *On no account must he go there.* **11 on someone's account** out of consideration for someone's wishes: *Don't stay up late on my account.* **12 put/turn something to good account** to really make the best use of something, often unexpectedly **13 take something into account, take account of something** to give proper consideration to something when making a judgment or decision: *You must take her illness into account.*

account² v **account for something** to give an explanation or reason for something: *He can't account for his mistake.* | *How do you account for the fact that you've arrived late every day this week?*

ac·coun·ta·ble /əˈkaʊntəbəl/ adj [never before a noun] responsible and prepared to give an explanation for your actions: *I am not accountable to you for my decisions.* –**accountability** /əˌkaʊntəˈbɪləti/ n [U] : *demands for an increase in police accountability*

ac·coun·tan·cy /əˈkaʊntənsi/ n (**accounting** *AmE*) [U] the work or job of an accountant

ac·coun·tant /əˈkaʊntənt/ n a person whose job is to keep and examine the money accounts of businesses or people

ac·cu·mu·late /əˈkjuːmjǝleɪt/ v **accumulated, accumulating** [I;T] to make or become greater in quantity or size: *We've accumulated a large number of books over the years.* –**accumulation** /əˌkjuːmjǝˈleɪʃən/ n [C;U] : *an accumulation of work while I was ill*

ac·cu·ra·cy /ˈækjǝrəsi/ n [U] exactness or correctness –opposite **inaccuracy**

ac·cu·rate /ˈækjǝrət/ adj exactly correct: *Give me an accurate report of what happened.* | *Is the station clock accurate?* –opposite **inaccurate** –**accurately** adv

ac·cu·sa·tion /ˌækjǝˈzeɪʃən/ n [C;U] a statement saying that someone has done something wrong or criminal: *We were shocked by the accusation that he'd stolen the money.* | *She's made some pretty serious accusations* **against** *the director.* | *accusations* **of** *fraud*

ac·cuse /əˈkjuːz/ v **accused, accusing** [T] to say that someone has done something wrong or has broken the law: *He was accused of murder.* | *Are you accusing me of cheating?* | *Her teacher accused her of stealing the books.* | *an accusing look*

□ USEFUL PATTERNS **to accuse someone of something; to accuse someone of doing something** –**accuser** n

ac·cused /əˈkjuːzd/ n *fml* **the accused** a person charged with a crime: *The accused pleaded not guilty.*

ac·cus·tom /əˈkʌstəm/ v [T] to make someone used to something: *He had to accustom himself to the cold weather of his new country.*

ac·cus·tomed /əˈkʌstəmd/ adj **1 get accustomed to something** *fml* to become used to something: *It took ages to get accustomed to living abroad.* [RELATED PHRASE **be accustomed to something**] **2** [only before a noun] usual: *sitting in her accustomed place at the table*

ace /eɪs/ n **1** a playing card that has a single mark on it and usually has the highest or the lowest value **2** *infml* a person of the highest class or skill in something: *an ace skier*

ache¹ /eɪk/ v **ached, aching** [I] **1** to have or suffer a continuous, but not violent, pain: *I'm aching all over.* | *My head aches.* **2 be aching to do something** *infml* to have a strong wish to do something: *She was aching to go to the party, but her parents wouldn't let her.*

ache² n a continuous, dull pain: *He's always complaining about his aches and pains.* | *a headache*

■ USAGE **1 Backache, headache, stomachache, toothache** are the most common nouns formed from **ache**. **2 Headache** is always countable: *I've got a* **headache**. The other nouns are usually uncountable: *I've got* **toothache**, but some people treat them as countable, especially when they are talking about a sharp, sudden pain: *The meal gave me* **stomachache**/a **stomachache**.

a·chieve /ə'tʃiːv/ v achieved, achieving [T] 1 to succeed in doing something: *He will never achieve anything if he doesn't work harder.* | *We were all exhausted, but felt we had achieved quite a lot.* 2 to get something as the result of action or effort: *As a result of advertising, we've achieved a big increase in sales this year.* –**achievable** *adj*

a·chieve·ment /ə'tʃiːvmənt/ n 1 [U] the successful finishing or gaining of something: *Passing the exam gave her a real sense of achievement.* 2 [C] something successfully finished or gained, especially through skill and hard work: *a remarkable achievement* | *He has broken two world records in one day, which is quite an achievement.*

ac·id¹ /'æsɪd/ n 1 [C;U] a chemical substance which may destroy things it touches: *The acid burnt a hole in the carpet.* | *nitric acid* 2 [U] *slang* the drug LSD 3 **acid test** a test or trial which will prove whether something is as valuable as it is supposed to be: *It looks good, but will it work? That's the acid test!*

acid² *adj* 1 having an unpleasantly sour taste 2 unkind or hurtful: *an acid remark*

acid rain /ˌ·· '·/ n rain which damages trees and plants because it contains acid put out into the air by industry –see picture on page 246

a·cid·i·ty /ə'sɪdəti/ n [U] the quality of being acid

ac·knowl·edge /ək'nɒlɪdʒ ‖ -'nɑː-/ v acknowledged, acknowledging 1 [T; + that] to accept something and be prepared to admit it: *When the results were announced, the Prime Minister acknowledged defeat.* | *He finally acknowledged that they had been defeated.* | *She acknowledged having made a mistake.*
□ USEFUL PATTERNS to acknowledge something; to acknowledge that…; to acknowledge doing something
2 [T] to accept something as being legal or real, or as having value: *The terrorists refused to acknowledge the court.* | *She is acknowledged as an expert on the subject.* | *She is acknowledged to be their best tennis player.*
□ USEFUL PATTERNS to acknowledge something; to acknowledge someone or something as; to acknowledge someone or something to be
3 [T] to state that you have received something: *We must acknowledge his letter.* 4 [T] to show that you recognize someone, for example by smiling or waving: *He walked right past me without even acknowledging me.*

ac·knowl·edg·ment /ək'nɒlɪdʒmənt ‖ -'nɑː-/ n (also **acknowledgement**) 1 [U] the act of accepting or admitting something: *the Prime Minister's acknowledgment of defeat* 2 [C] something given, done, or said as a way of thanking or of showing that something has been received: *I wrote to them three weeks ago, and I haven't had an acknowledgement yet.* 3 **in acknowledgement of** in recognition of: *He was given a gold watch in acknowledgement of his services.*

ac·ne /'ækni/ n [U] a condition, common among young people, in which spots appear on the face and neck

a·corn /'eɪkɔːn ‖ -ɔːrn, -ərn/ n the fruit of the OAK tree

a·cous·tic /ə'kuːstɪk/ adj 1 of sound or the sense of hearing 2 making its natural sound, not helped by electrical apparatus: *an acoustic guitar*

a·cous·tics /ə'kuːstɪks/ n 1 [U] the scientific study of sound 2 [pl] the qualities of a place, especially a hall, which make it good or bad for hearing music and speeches: *The acoustics of this concert hall are excellent.*

ac·quaint·ance /ə'kweɪntəns/ n 1 [C] a person who you know, especially through work or business, but who is not a close friend 2 [sing;U] knowledge obtained through personal experience rather than careful study: *I have some acquaintance with the language.* 3 **make someone's acquaintance** *fml* to meet someone for the first time

ac·quainted /ə'kweɪntɪd/ adj fml 1 **be acquainted with something** to be familiar with something: *I am already acquainted with the facts.* 2 **be acquainted with someone** to be slightly known to someone socially: *We are already acquainted.* 3 **get/become acquainted with someone** to get to know someone

ac·qui·esce /ˌækwi'es/ v acquiesced, acquiescing [I] *fml* to agree, often unwillingly but without arguing: *He acquiesced in the plans his parents had made for him.* –**acquiescence** n [U] –**acquiescent** adj

ac·quire /ə'kwaɪər/ v acquired, acquiring [T] 1 *fml* to get something, especially by your own work, skill, or action: *I managed to acquire two tickets for the concert.* | *The company has recently acquired a new office building in central London.* | *Typing is a skill well worth acquiring.* 2 **acquired taste** something that you may learn to like after a while: *Some alcoholic drinks are an acquired taste.*

ac·qui·si·tion /ˌækwɪ'zɪʃən/ n 1 [U] the act of acquiring something 2 [C] something that you have acquired: *This car is my latest acquisition.* | *Intel is the latest acquisition of this American computer company.*

ac·quis·i·tive /ə'kwɪzɪtɪv/ adj keen on getting and possessing things (a word used to express disapproval): *He's very acquisitive and has filled his house with things.* –**acquisitiveness** n [U]

ac·quit /ə'kwɪt/ v [T] 1 to give a decision in a court of law that someone is not guilty of a crime: *They acquitted him of murder.* | *He was acquitted.* –opposite **convict** 2 **acquit yourself well/badly** *fml* to perform well or badly: *She acquitted herself rather well in the exam.*

ac·quit·tal /ə'kwɪtl/ n [C;U] the act of declaring someone to be not guilty, or the condition of being found not guilty in a court of law –opposite **conviction**

a·cre /'eɪkər/ n a unit for measuring land, equal to 4,840 square yards or about 4,047 square metres: *The total area of a football field is about two acres.*

a·cre·age /'eɪkərɪdʒ/ n [U] the area of a piece of land measured in acres

ac·rid /'ækrɪd/ adj stinging your eyes and nose: *the acrid smell of burning wood*

ac·ri·mo·ny /'ækrɪməni ‖ -məʊni/ n [U] bitter feeling between people, often strongly expressed –**acrimonious** /ˌækrɪ'məʊniəs/ adj –**acrimoniously** adv

ac·ro·bat /'ækrəbæt/ n a person skilled in performing difficult physical actions, such as walking on their hands or on the high wire, especially at a CIRCUS (2) –**acrobatic** /ˌækrə'bætɪk◄/ adj

ac·ro·bat·ics /ˌækrə'bætɪks/ n [pl;U] the art or tricks of an acrobat

a·cross /ə'krɒs ‖ ə'krɔːs/ adv,prep 1 adv,prep from one side of something to the other side: *We walked across the bridge.* | *She stood up and marched across the room.* | *He drew a straight line across the page.* | *We got to the river, and then realized that we had no way of getting across.* | *The stream measures six* *metres across.* **2** *prep* on the other side of a road or river: *They live just across the road from us.* –see picture on page 540

act¹ /ækt/ *v* **1** [I] to do something: *The council must act before more people are killed on that road.* | *He had to act swiftly.* **2** [I] to behave: *The report said that the doctor had acted correctly.* | *She's acting very strangely these days.* **3** [I;T] to represent a character, especially in a play or film: *Jerome Flynn is acting* **in** *Shakespeare's "As You Like It".* | *He's acting the part of Orlando.* | *I can't take her seriously because she always seems to be acting.* **4** [I] to produce an effect: *Does the drug take long to act?* | *It acts* **on** *the nervous system.* **5 act as: a** to do a job which is not your usual one, sometimes for only a short time: *She's acting as caretaker while the real one is on holiday.* | *His wife's fed up with acting as an unpaid secretary.* **b** to operate as: *The electric wire acts as a fence to keep the animals in.* **6 act for** to represent another person in legal or business affairs: *the solicitor acting for the buyer* **7 act on** to take action according to advice, suggestions, or information: *They acted on our advice.*

act sthg ↔ **out** *phr v* [T] to express thoughts and feelings in actions and behaviour rather than in words

act up *phr v* [I] *infml* to behave or perform badly: *His car is acting up again.*

act² *n* **1** *fml* something that someone has done: *a foolish act* | *an act of cruelty* **2** (also **Act**) a law: *Parliament has passed an act banning the drug.* | *the Gun Control Act* **3** (also **Act**) one of the main divisions of a play: *Hamlet kills the king in Act 5, Scene 2.* | *at the end of the first act* **4** one of a number of short events in a television show or a theatre or CIRCUS (2) performance: *The next act will be a snake charmer.* **5** *infml* an example of insincere behaviour used to influence people's feelings: *He doesn't really mean it. It's just an act.* **6 get in on the act** *infml* to get a share of an activity, and especially any advantages that may come as a result

act·ing¹ /ˈæktɪŋ/ *n* [U] the art of representing a character, especially in a play or film

acting² *adj* [only before a noun] appointed to carry out the duties of an office or position for a short time: *Our director is in hospital, but the acting director can see you.*

ac·tion /ˈækʃən/ *n* **1** [U] doing things for a purpose: *We're tired of talking about the problem – now is the time for action!* | *What's your plan of action?* | *The police had to take firm action to deal with the protestors.* **2** [C] something that you do: *His prompt action saved her life.* | *a very kind action* | *The baby watched all its mother's actions.* **3** [C] effect: *Photographs are produced by the action of light on film.* **4** [U] fighting or a fight between armies and navies: *the results of military action* | *Her husband was killed in action.* **5** [C] a charge or matter for consideration by a court of law: *If he doesn't pay us soon we'll have to bring an action against him.* | *a libel action* **6 the action** the main events in a play or book: *The action takes place in a mountain village.* **7** [C] the way in which something moves or works: *The horse had a fine jumping action.* | *studying the action of the heart* **8 action-packed** full of exciting action **9 action replay** the showing again, usually more slowly, of a piece of a film in which you see a particularly interesting part of a sports event **10 in action** doing a typical activity: *He's a very good tennis player: you ought to see him in action.* **11 out of action** unable to move or operate: *Can I borrow your car? Mine's out of action.* **12 put into action** to begin to use a plan or idea: *The government is now putting the new policy into action.*

ac·tiv·ate /ˈæktɨveɪt/ *v* **activated, activating** [T] to make something start working: *This button activates the heating system.* –**activation** /ˌæktɨˈveɪʃən/ *n* [U]

ac·tive¹ /ˈæktɪv/ *adj* **1** doing things or always ready or able to do things: *Although he is over 70 he is still active.* | *an active member of the club, who goes to every meeting* | *an active volcano* | *an active chemical* –opposite **inactive** **2** *tech* relating to or containing a verb which has the person or thing doing the action as the subject; in the sentence "The boy kicked the ball", "kicked" is an active verb –opposite **passive**¹ (2) –**actively** *adv*

active² *n* [sing] *tech* **the active** the active part or form of a verb

ac·tiv·ist /ˈæktɨvɨst/ *n* a person taking an active part in a political movement

ac·tiv·i·ty /ækˈtɪvɨti/ *n* **activities** **1** [U] movement or action: *a day full of activity* | *There's been a lot of activity in the town centre today.* | *political activity* | *economic activity* –opposite **inactivity** **2** [C] something done for pleasure, interest or education: *Among her activities are swimming and photography.* | *classroom activities* **3** [pl] things done by a group, often one opposed to the government, to advance their aims: *the activities of the New National Party* | *terrorist activities*

ac·tor /ˈæktəʳ/ *n* a person who acts in a play or film or on television

ac·tress /ˈæktrɨs/ *n* a woman who acts in a play or film or on television

ac·tu·al /ˈæktʃuəl/ *adj* [only before a noun] **1** existing as a real fact, and not existing just as an idea: *The actual cost of the repairs was a lot less than we had expected.* **2** really; you use this expression when you are saying something which is not what people might expect from the last thing you said: *I did my best to encourage her, but in actual fact, I don't think she's got much chance.*

ac·tu·al·ly /ˈæktʃuəli, -tʃəli/ *adv* **1** a word used to show that you are giving the real information about something: *We didn't actually go up the Eiffel Tower, though we saw it.* | *The people who actually have power are the owners of big industries.* **2** a word used to correct the wrong idea in a polite way: *It isn't expensive. Actually, it's very cheap.* | *"He's in his office." "Actually, he's at lunch."* **3** you use "actually" when you are politely correcting someone, or giving an opinion which is different from theirs, or telling them something unexpected: *"You can really taste the butter in this cake." "Well, actually, I used margarine."* | *"You've finished that letter, haven't you?" "Well, no, I haven't, actually."*

■ USAGE Do not use **actually** when you mean "at the present time." Instead use phrases such as, **at present, currently, at the moment, nowadays**: *Where are you working* **at the moment**? | *She is* **currently** *directing her third film.*

ac·u·men /ˈækjɵmən, əˈkjuːmən/ *n* [U] *fml* ability to think and judge quickly and well: *Her business acumen has made her very successful.*

ac·u·punc·ture /ˈækjɵˌpʌŋktʃəʳ/ *n* [U] the method of stopping pain and curing diseases by pricking certain parts of the body with needles, used especially in China

a·cute /əˈkjuːt/ *adj* **1** very great or severe (used of bad situations): *She was in acute pain.* | *an acute lack of food* **2** showing an ability to understand things clearly and deeply: *an acute analysis of the political situation* **3** able to notice small differences: *Dogs have an acute sense of smell.* **4** *tech* less than 90 degrees (used of an angle) –compare OBTUSE –**acutely** *adv* : *acutely embarrassing* –**acuteness** *n* [U]

AD /ˌeɪ ˈdiː/ since the birth of CHRIST; an abbreviation for the Latin phrase **anno domini**; you use AD when you are giving dates: *a battle in 1649 AD*

ad /æd/ *n infml* an advertisement

ad·age /ˈædɪdʒ/ *n* an old wise phrase

ad·a·mant /ˈædəmənt/ *adj fml* determined not to change your mind: *He's absolutely adamant.* | *She's adamant that she won't go.* –**adamantly** *adv*

Ad·am's ap·ple /ˌædəmz ˈæpəl ‖ ˈ·· ·/ *n* the part at the front of the throat that is seen to move when a person, especially a man, talks or swallows

a·dapt /əˈdæpt/ *v* **1** [T] to make something suitable for a new need or purpose: *He adapted an old car engine to use in his boat.* | *The author is adapting his novel for television.* | *The car has been specially adapted for use by the handicapped.* | *We must adapt our methods to the new circumstances.* | *Some birds are well adapted to life on water.* **2** [I] to change your behaviour or ideas to fit a new situation: *The children have adapted well to life in the country.*

a·dapt·a·ble /əˈdæptəbəl/ *adj* able to change your behaviour or ideas so as to manage well in a new situation (a word used to express approval) –opposite **unadaptable** –**adaptability** /əˌdæptəˈbɪlɪti/ *n* [U]

ad·ap·ta·tion /ˌædæpˈteɪʃən/ *n* [C;U] something adapted or the process of adapting: *a new adaptation of the book for television* | *Darwin explained the adaptation of living things to their environment.*

a·dapt·or /əˈdæptər/ *n* (also **adapter**) a PLUG that makes it possible to use more than one piece of electrical machinery from a single SOCKET

add /æd/ *v* **1** [T] to put something together with something else: *Mix the flour and salt. Add the water.* | *Add a few more names to the list.* | *The tower was added in 1232.* **2** [T] to put numbers or amounts together and calculate the total: *If you add 5 and 3 you get 8.* | *Add 5 to 3.* | *Add the travel costs and the hotel bill together.* **3** [T; + that] to say something else when speaking: *"Susan's left home," she said. "I don't understand why," she added.* | *Have you anything to add, John?* | *I should like to add that we are pleased with the result.* **4 add insult to injury** to make a bad situation even worse: *He helped himself to my dinner and then, to add insult to injury, asked me to wash up.*

add sthg ↔ **on** *phr v* [T] to join on: *We're going to add another room on to our house.*

add to sthg *phr v* [T] to increase something: *The rise in electricity costs has added to our difficulties.*

add up *phr v* **1** [I;T **add** sthg ↔ **up**] to put numbers or amounts together and calculate the total: *Add the costs up.* | *He's not fit to work in a bank. He can barely add up.* **2** [I] *infml* to make sense: *His story just didn't add up.*

add up to sthg *phr v* [T] **1** *infml* to result in: *What it adds up to is that she won't let me go.* **2** to result in a particular total: *This adds up to 1,000 miles.*

ad·ded /ˈædɪd/ *adj* [only before a noun] further: *It's cheap, and it has the added advantage of being much faster.*

added to *prep* in addition to something: *It's cheap, added to which it's much faster.*

ad·den·dum /əˈdendəm/ *n* **addenda** /əˈdendə/ *tech*

something that is added at the end of a speech or piece of writing

ad·der /ˈædər/ *n* a small poisonous snake found in northern Europe and northern Asia

ad·dict /ˈædɪkt/ *n* a person who is unable to free themselves from a harmful habit, especially of taking drugs: *a drug addict*

ad·dict·ed /əˈdɪktɪd/ *adj* unable to stop taking or using something: *addicted to heroin* | *My children are hopelessly addicted to television.*

ad·dic·tion /əˈdɪkʃən/ *n* [C;U] a strong need which makes you dependent on something bad, for example drugs: *the growing problem of heroin addiction among young people*

ad·dic·tive /əˈdɪktɪv/ *adj* making you addicted to something: *This drug is highly addictive.*

ad·di·tion /əˈdɪʃən/ *n* **1** [U] the addition together of several numbers **2** [C] something added: *A newly born child is often called an addition to the family.* **3 in addition** besides; you use this expression when you add another thing to what you have already mentioned: *Candidates should fill in and return the form. In addition, they should enclose a recent, passport-size photograph.* | *In addition to giving a general introduction to computers, the course also provides practical experience.*

ad·di·tion·al /əˈdɪʃənəl/ *adj* added to something already there: *An additional charge is made for heavy bags.* –**additionally** *adv*

ad·di·tive /ˈædɪtɪv/ *n* a substance added in small quantities to something else so as to improve the quality, or add colour or taste

ad·dress¹ /əˈdres/ *v* [T] **1** to write a name and address on an envelope or parcel **2** *fml* to direct what you say to a person or group: *The queen addressed the crowd.* | *Address your remarks to the chairperson, please.* **3 to address yourself to something** *fml* to consider something carefully so that you can decide what should be done about it: *We must address ourselves to the problem of drugs among young people.*

ad·dress² /əˈdres ‖ əˈdres, ˈædres/ *n* **1** details of where someone works or lives, including the number of the building, name of the street and town: *I can't read the address on this letter.* **2** a formal speech

ad·ept /ˈædept, əˈdept ‖ əˈdept/ *adj* highly skilled: *Be careful when you play cards with him – he's very adept at cheating.* –**adeptly** *adv*

ad·e·quate /ˈædɪkwət/ *adj* enough for the purpose, and no more: *The city's water supply is no longer adequate for its growing population.* | *A teacher's salary is barely adequate to support a family.* –opposite **inadequate** –**adequately** *adv* –**adequacy** *n* [U]

ad·here /ədˈhɪər/ *v* **adhered, adhering** [I] **1** to stick firmly: *Glue makes one surface adhere to another.* **2 adhere to something** to firmly support an idea or belief: *She adhered to the view that a broad education was important.*

ad·her·ence /ədˈhɪərəns/ *n* [U] firm support for certain beliefs or ideas: *his strict adherence to his religious beliefs*

ad·her·ent /ədˈhɪərənt/ *n* a person who supports a particular idea, opinion, or political party

ad·he·sion /ədˈhiːʒən/ *n* [U] the state or action of one thing sticking to another

ad·he·sive /ədˈhiːsɪv/ *n* a substance, such as GLUE, that can make things stick together –**adhesive** *adj*

ad hoc /ˌæd ˈhɒk, -ˈhəʊk ‖ -ˈhɑːk, -ˈhəʊk/ adj made or arranged for a particular purpose: *an ad hoc committee set up to deal with the water shortage*

a·dieu /əˈdjuː ‖ əˈduː/ n **adieus** or **adieux** lit /əˈdjuːz ‖ əˈduːz/ goodbye

ad·ja·cent /əˈdʒeɪsənt/ adj fml very close or next to: *The two families live in adjacent streets.* | *His office is adjacent to mine.*

ad·jec·tive /ˈædʒəktɪv/ n a word which describes a noun: *The word "black" in the phrase "a black car" is an adjective.* **–adjectival** /ˌædʒəkˈtaɪvəl◂/ adj : *an adjectival phrase* –see Study Note on page 687

ad·join /əˈdʒɔɪn/ v [I;T] fml to be next to something: *Our house adjoins theirs.* | *The two buildings adjoin.* | *the adjoining room*

ad·journ /əˈdʒɜːn ‖ -ɜːrn/ v [I;T] to stop a meeting or a trial for a short time or until a slightly later date: *This trial has been adjourned until next week.* | *The committee adjourned for an hour.* **–adjournment** n [C;U] : *The court met again after an adjournment of two weeks.*

ad·ju·di·cate /əˈdʒuːdɪkeɪt/ v **adjudicated, adjudicating** [I;T] fml to judge or make an official decision: *She's been asked to adjudicate a singing competition.* | *The union needs someone to adjudicate on the dispute.* **–adjudicator** n

ad·junct /ˈædʒʌŋkt/ n something that is added or joined to something else but is not a necessary part of it

ad·just /əˈdʒʌst/ v **1** [T] to correct or slightly change the position of something: *He adjusted his tie.* **2** [I] to change to suit a particular situation or new conditions: *He adjusted quickly to the heat of India.* **–adjustable** adj: *an adjustable chair* **–adjustment** n [C;U]: *I've had to make a lot of adjustments.*

ad lib¹ /ˌæd ˈlɪb◂/ adj spoken or performed without preparation: *ad lib remarks* **–ad lib** adv : *She spoke ad lib.*

ad lib² /ˌ· ˈ·/ v **-bb-** [I;T] infml to say something or play music without preparation or planning: *The actress forgot her lines but ad libbed very amusingly.*

ad·min·is·ter /ədˈmɪnəstəʳ/ v [T] **1** to direct or control the affairs of a country, company or organization: *Mr Jones administers the company's accounts.* **2** fml to give a drug to someone: *She administered the medicine to the sick woman.* **3** to make sure a law or test is used properly: *The courts administer the law.*

ad·min·is·tra·tion /ədˌmɪnəˈstreɪʃən/ n **1** [U] the control or direction of affairs, for example in a country or business: *You will need some experience in administration.* **2 the Administration** the national government of the U.S.A.: *the Bush Administration*

ad·min·is·tra·tive /ədˈmɪnəstrətɪv ‖ -streɪtɪv/ adj to do with the control or direction of affairs in a country or business: *His responsibilities are mainly administrative.* **–administratively** adv

ad·min·is·tra·tor /ədˈmɪnəstreɪtəʳ/ n a person who controls or directs the affairs of a country or business

ad·mi·ra·ble /ˈædmərəbəl/ adj considered worthy of praise and respect: *an admirable attempt*

ad·mi·ral /ˈædmərəl/ n [C] an officer who holds a very high rank in a navy

Ad·mi·ral·ty /ˈædmərəlti/ n BrE **the Admiralty** the government department which controls the navy

ad·mi·ra·tion /ˌædməˈreɪʃən/ n [U] a feeling of pleasure and respect: *I was filled with admiration for his courage.*

ad·mire /ədˈmaɪəʳ/ v **admired, admiring** [T] **1** to approve of and respect someone or something: *We all admired her for the way she saved the children from the fire.* **2** to look at someone or something with pleasure: *Stop looking in the mirror admiring yourself!* | *They admired the garden.* –see WONDER (USAGE) **–admirer** n : *He is one of her many admirers.*

ad·mis·si·ble /ədˈmɪsəbəl/ adj acceptable or allowed: *admissible behaviour* | *facts admissible in court* –opposite **inadmissible**

ad·mis·sion /ədˈmɪʃən/ n **1** [U] permission given to enter a building or a country, or join a school or club: *They campaigned for the admission of women to the club.* | *the admission of refugees into France* **2** [U] the cost of entering: *Admission £1* **3** [C] a statement saying that something bad or unpleasant is true: *His admission of guilt surprised everyone.*

ad·mit /ədˈmɪt/ v **-tt-** **1** [I;T; + (that)] to agree, often unwillingly, that something bad or unpleasant is true: *Few politicians admit their mistakes.* | *She'll never admit that she is wrong.* | *The prisoner admitted to the murder.* | *John admitted breaking the window.* | *"You're right," she admitted.* ◻ USEFUL PATTERNS **to admit that...; to admit (to) something; to admit (to) doing something 2** [T] to allow someone or something to enter a place: *There were no windows to admit air.* **3** [T] to allow someone to join a club or organization **4 be admitted** to be taken in to hospital until you are better: *He was admitted to hospital suffering from burns.*

ad·mit·tance /ədˈmɪtəns/ n [U] **1** the right to enter a place **2 gain admittance** to be allowed to enter a place: *Journalists were unable to gain admittance.* –see ADMISSION (USAGE)

ad·mit·ted·ly /ədˈmɪtɪdli/ adv you use "admittedly" when you allow that there are facts which do not support your idea: *I don't know why you're so against him. Admittedly, he's rather odd, but he's a very kind person.* | *I think this is the best bed we're going to find. It's not very cheap, admittedly, but I think we won't regret spending the money on it.*

ad·mon·ish /ədˈmɒnɪʃ ‖ -ˈmɑː-/ v [T] fml to warn someone gently that they have done something wrong: *The witness was admonished by the judge for failing to answer the question.* **–admonition** /ˌædməˈnɪʃən/ n [C;U]

a·do /əˈduː/ n **without more ado/without further ado** with no further delay

ad·o·les·cent /ˌædəˈlesənt◂/ n a boy or girl in the period between being a child and being a grown person –see CHILD (USAGE) **–adolescent** adj

a·dopt /əˈdɒpt ‖ əˈdɑːpt/ v [T] **1** to take someone else's child into your family and make it legally your child: *He was adopted as a baby.* –compare FOSTER **2** to begin to have or use an idea, plan, or way of doing something: *We adopted the new method of production.* | *The government is adopting a tougher approach to crime.* **3** to formally approve and accept something: *The committee adopted her suggestions.*

a·dop·tion /əˈdɒpʃən ‖ əˈdɑːp-/ n [C;U] the act of adopting a child: *If you cannot have children of your own, why not consider adoption?*

a·dop·tive /əˈdɒptɪv ‖ əˈdɑːp-/ adj [only before a noun] fml having adopted a child (used of parents): *her adoptive parents*

a·dor·a·ble /ə'dɔːrəbəl/ adj attractive, charming, and worthy of love: *What an adorable child!*

ad·o·ra·tion /ˌædə'reɪʃən/ n [U] deep love and respect

a·dore /ə'dɔːr/ v **adored, adoring** [T; not in progressive forms] **1** to love someone deeply and respect them very much: *an adoring look* | *He adores his elder brother.* **2** *infml* to like something very much: *She adores the cinema.* | *She adores going to the cinema.*

a·dorn /ə'dɔːn ‖ -ɔːrn/ v [T] to decorate something and make it attractive: *a Christmas tree adorned with lights* –see DECORATE (USAGE)

a·dorn·ment /ə'dɔːnmənt ‖ -ɔːr-/ n **1** [U] the act of adorning something **2** [C] something that improves the beauty of something else

a·dren·a·lin /ə'drenəl-ɪn/ n [U] a chemical substance made by your body when you are feeling anger, fear, or anxiety, which gives you more strength to take action

a·drift /ə'drɪft/ adv **1** not tied to anything, and moved about by the sea or wind (used of boats) **2** **have gone adrift** to no longer be working as intended: *Our plans seem to have gone adrift.*

a·droit /ə'drɔɪt/ adj quick and skilful in thought or action: *a journalist adroit* at *asking questions* –**adroitly** adv –**adroitness** n [U]

ad·u·la·tion /ˌædʒʊ'leɪʃən/ n [U] praise that is more than is necessary or deserved

ad·ult /'ædʌlt, ə'dʌlt/ n a fully grown person or animal –**adult** adj : *an adult lion*

a·dul·ter·ate /ə'dʌltəreɪt/ v **adulterated, adulterating** [T] to make a substance weaker or of poorer quality by adding something else to it: *wine adulterated with water* –**adulteration** /ə,dʌltə'reɪʃən/ n [U]

a·dul·ter·er /ə'dʌltərər/ n a married man who has sexual relations with someone who is not his wife

a·dul·ter·ess /ə'dʌltr-ɪs/ n a married woman who has sexual relations with someone who is not her husband

a·dul·ter·y /ə'dʌltəri/ n [U] sexual relations between a married person and someone to whom they are not married –**adulterous** adj

ad·vance[1] /əd'vɑːns ‖ əd'væns/ v **advanced, advancing 1** [I] to improve in understanding or development: *Scientists have advanced greatly in their knowledge of physics.* **2** [T] to help or support a cause: *This policy will do nothing to advance world peace.* **3** [I] to move forward in position, usually in order to attack someone: *Napoleon's army advanced* on *Moscow.* –compare RETREAT **4** [T] to bring something forward to an earlier date or time: *The date of the meeting was advanced.* **5** [T] to provide money earlier than the usual or proper time: *The company will advance you £200 until your salary is paid.* **6** [T] to introduce or suggest something: *The report advances the idea that safety standards should be improved.*

advance[2] n **1** [C] forward movement: *the advance of the enemy* **2** [C;U] improvement or progress: *There have been great advances in medicine in the last 50 years.* **3** [C] money that is paid or lent before the proper time: *Some authors are given an advance* on *their books.* **4 in advance** before a date or time: *We always pay the rent in advance.* **5 make advances to someone** to try to become someone's friend or start a sexual relationship with them

advance[3] adj happening before something else: *We were given no advance warning of his arrival.*

ad·vanced /əd'vɑːnst ‖ əd'vænst/ adj **1** having a very developed industry: *the advanced industrial nations of the world* **2** at a high level of knowledge or skill: *advanced studies* | *an advanced child*

ad·vance·ment /əd'vɑːnsmənt ‖ əd'væns-/ n [U] **1** improvement or development: *the advancement of science* **2** being moved to a more important position or job: *He's very concerned about his own advancement at work.*

ad·van·tage /əd'vɑːntɪdʒ ‖ əd'væn-/ n **1** [C] something that may help you to be successful or to get something that you want: *Her experience gave her a big advantage* over *the other applicants.* **2** [C;U] a favourable condition resulting from something: *Is there any advantage in getting there early?* | *This method has the advantage of saving fuel.* | *the advantages of living in the country* **3 to your advantage** useful or favourable for you: *It's to your advantage to contact him.* **4 take advantage of** to make use of someone or something, sometimes unfairly: *I'll take advantage of your offer.* | *I'm afraid he's just taking advantage of your generosity.* –opposite **disadvantage**

ad·van·ta·geous /ˌædvən'teɪdʒəs, ˌædvæn-/ adj helpful to a particular aim –opposite **disadvantageous** –**advantageously** adv

ad·vent /'ædvent/ n fml **the advent of** the start of an important event, period, or invention: *People are much better informed since the advent of television.*

ad·ven·ture /əd'ventʃər/ n [C;U] a journey, activity, or experience that is strange, exciting, and often dangerous: *her exciting adventures in the Himalayas* | *a life of adventure*

ad·ven·tur·er /əd'ventʃərər/ n a person who has or looks for adventures

ad·ven·tur·ous /əd'ventʃərəs/ adj **1** eager to take risks and try new things **2** exciting and full of danger: *an adventurous life* –opposite **unadventurous** –**adventurously** adv

ad·verb /'ædvɜːb ‖ -ɜːrb/ n a word which describes or adds to the meaning of a verb, an adjective, another adverb, or a sentence, and which answers such questions as how? when? or where?: *In the sentences "He ran slowly" and "It was very beautiful", "slowly" and "very" are adverbs.* –see Study Note on page 687 –**adverbial** /əd'vɜːbiəl ‖ -ɜːr-/ n,adj

ad·ver·sa·ry /'ædvəsəri ‖ 'ædvərseri/ n **adversaries** fml an enemy or someone you are competing against

ad·verse /'ædvɜːs ‖ -ɜːrs/ adj fml unfavourable to you: *The proposal has attracted a lot of adverse comment.* | *adverse weather conditions* –**adversely** adv

ad·ver·si·ty /əd'vɜːsɪti ‖ -ɜːr-/ n **adversities** [C;U] difficulties or problems: *A good friend will not desert you in time of adversity.* | *He met with many adversities.*

ad·ver·tise /'ædvətaɪz ‖ -ər-/ v **advertised, advertising 1** [I;T] to tell the public about something, such as an event, service, or article for sale, for example in a newspaper or on television: *I advertised my house in the "Daily News".* | *a poster advertising shampoo* **2** [I] to ask for someone or something by placing a notice somewhere like a newspaper or shop window: *We should advertise* **for** *someone to look after the garden.* –**advertiser** n

ad·ver·tise·ment /əd'vɜːtɪsmənt ‖ ˌædvər'taɪz-/ n (also **ad, advert** infml) something used for advertising things, such as a notice on a wall or in a newspaper, or a short film shown on television

ad·ver·tis·ing /ˈædvətaɪzɪŋ ‖ -ər-/ n [U] the business of encouraging people to buy goods through advertisements

ad·vice /ədˈvaɪs/ n [U] an opinion given by one person to another on how that other should behave or act: *I asked the doctor for her advice.* | *On her advice I am staying in bed.* | *Let me give you a piece of advice.*

■ USAGE The word **advice** is uncountable and is not, therefore, used in the plural: *She gave me a lot of good* **advice**. | *Ask your teacher for* **advice**. | *a piece of excellent* **advice**

ad·vis·ab·le /ədˈvaɪzəbəl/ adj [never before a noun] sensible or wise: *It is advisable always to wear a safety belt when you're driving.* –opposite **inadvisable** –**advisability** /ədˌvaɪzəˈbɪlⰓti / n [U]

ad·vise /ədˈvaɪz/ v advised, advising 1 [T] to tell someone what you think they should do: *The doctor advised me to take more exercise.* | *I advised him that he should join a union.* | *Can you advise me where to stay?*

☐ USEFUL PATTERNS to advise someone; to advise someone to do something; to advise someone that they should do something; to advise someone how, where, when… etc.
2 **advise against something, advise someone against something** to warn someone not to do something: *Lawyers advised against signing the contract.* | *He advised me against giving up my job.* 3 [I;T] to act as a professional adviser to someone: *the experts who advise the President* | *She advises on legal matters.* 4 [T] fml to inform someone about something: *We wish to advise you that you now owe the bank £500.*

ad·vis·er /ədˈvaɪzəʳ/ n (also **advisor** AmE) a person whose job is to give advice, especially to a government or business: *the President's special adviser on foreign affairs*

ad·vi·so·ry /ədˈvaɪzəri/ adj having the power or duty to advise people

ad·vo·cate[1] /ˈædvəkeɪt/ v advocated, advocating [T] to suggest or support an idea, plan, or action, often in public: *The opposition party advocates an immediate reduction in transport costs.*

ad·vo·cate[2] /ˈædvəkⰓt, -keɪt/ n 1 law a lawyer who speaks in favour of someone or against them in court 2 a person who publicly supports an idea or way of life: *He is a strong advocate of prison reforms.*

aer·i·al[1] /ˈeəriəl/ n a wire put up on top of a building or a car to receive radio or television broadcasts –see pictures on pages 49 and 441

aerial[2] adj [only before a noun] from the air or happening in the air: *aerial photographs* | *an aerial battle*

aer·o·bics /eəˈrəʊbɪks/ n [U] a form of very active physical exercise which is usually done in a class to music, and is intended to strengthen your heart and lungs: *She does aerobics twice a week.* | *an aerobics class*

aer·o·drome /ˈeərədrəʊm/ n (**airfield** AmE) a small airport

aer·o·dy·nam·ics /ˌeərəʊdaɪˈnæmɪks/ n [U] the scientific study of objects moving through the air –**aerodynamic** adj : *aerodynamic laws*

aer·o·plane /ˈeərəpleɪn/ n (**airplane** AmE) a flying vehicle that has wings, and is driven by at least one engine –see picture on page 735

aer·o·sol /ˈeərəsɒl ‖ -sɑːl/ n a small container from which liquid can be forced out in the form of a fine mist

aes·thet·ic /iːsˈθetɪk, es- ‖ es-/ adj (also **esthetic** AmE) related to a sense of beauty, especially in art: *The building is functional but has little aesthetic interest.* –**aesthetically** /-kli/ adv

aes·thet·ics /iːsˈθetɪks, es- ‖ es-/ n (also **esthetics** AmE) [U] the study or science of beauty, especially in art

a·far /əˈfɑːʳ/ adv lit **from afar** from a great distance

af·fa·ble /ˈæfəbəl/ adj friendly and easy to talk to –**affably** adv –**affability** /ˌæfəˈbɪlⰓti / n [U]

af·fair /əˈfeəʳ/ n 1 [C] an event or set of connected events: *The meeting was a noisy affair.* | *the Watergate affair* 2 **affairs** [pl] matters needing attention or connected with a particular subject: *The minister deals with important affairs of state.* | *foreign affairs* 3 [C] a sexual relationship between two people not married to each other, especially when one of them is married to someone else

af·fect /əˈfekt/ v [T] 1 to influence or to cause a result or change in something: *The nurses' strike affects all hospitals.* | *How was the village affected by the storm?* 2 to cause feelings of sorrow, anger, or love: *She was deeply affected by the news of his death.*

■ USAGE Compare **affect** and **effect**. **Affect** is usually a verb: *The new law will* **affect** *all of us.* **Effect** is usually a noun: *The new law will have an* **effect** *on all of us.* The verb **effect** is very formal and means "to cause or produce": *to* **effect** *a change in government policy*

af·fec·ta·tion /ˌæfekˈteɪʃən/ n [C;U] behaviour which is not natural and which aims to make people admire you: *All that talk about art is just an affectation. She doesn't really know the first thing about it.*

af·fect·ed /əˈfektⰓd/ adj not real, natural, or sincere: *She has a really affected voice on the phone.* –opposite **unaffected**

af·fec·tion /əˈfekʃən/ n [U] a feeling of love or fondness

af·fec·tion·ate /əˈfekʃənⰓt/ adj showing love or fondness towards people –**affectionately** adv

af·fil·i·ate[1] /əˈfɪlieɪt/ v **affiliated, affiliating** [I] (of an organization) to join or have a close connection with a larger organization: *We hope that other groups will affiliate* **with** *the Party.* –**affiliated** adj: *a group of affiliated companies* | *a medical centre affiliated* **to** *the University* –**affiliation** /əˌfɪliˈeɪʃən/ n. *He never tried to hide his political affiliations.*

af·fil·i·ate[2] /əˈfɪliⰓt/ n an organization which is joined to a larger organization: *The firm is an affiliate of a major company.*

af·fin·i·ty /əˈfɪnⰓti/ n **affinities** [C;U] 1 close similarity or connection 2 strong attraction or feeling of shared interests: *He feels a strong sense of affinity* **with** *this village.* | *She has a natural affinity* **with** *other women.*

af·firm /əˈfɜːm ‖ -ɜːrm/ v [T; + that] fml to declare, often for the second or third time, that something is true: *The minister affirmed the government's intention to reduce taxes.* –**affirmation** /ˌæfəˈmeɪʃən ‖ ˌæfər-/ n [C;U]

af·fir·ma·tive /əˈfɜːmətɪv ‖ -ɜːr-/ adj fml 1 showing agreement or giving the answer 'yes': *an affirmative answer* 2 **answer in the affirmative** to answer 'yes' –opposite **negative** –**affirmatively** adv

af·fix /əˈfɪks/ v [T] fml to fix, fasten, or stick: *A stamp should be affixed to the envelope.*

af·flict /əˈflɪkt/ v [T] to cause severe suffering or

pain: *He was afflicted* **with** *blindness.* | *afflicted* **by** *terrible wounds*

af·flic·tion /ə'flɪkʃən/ *n* [C;U] *fml* something causing suffering or pain

af·flu·ent /'æfluənt/ *adj* having plenty of money or other possessions –**affluence** *n* [U]

af·ford /ə'fɔːd ‖ -ɔːrd/ *v* [T] **1** to have enough money to do or buy something without difficulty: *Can you afford £35,000 for a house?* | *Since she lost her job, she can no longer afford to go on holiday.* □ USEFUL PATTERNS to afford something; to afford to do something **2** to be able to do something or let something happen without risk or damage to yourself: *You can't afford to lose their support.* | *She can afford to be rude to her neighbours now she's moving.* | *We can't afford any more trouble.* **3** *fml* to provide with: *The tree afforded us shelter from the rain.*

af·front /ə'frʌnt/ *n* an act or remark that is rude to someone or hurts their feelings

a·field /ə'fiːld/ *adv* **far afield** far away: *Don't go too far afield or we might lose you.* | *We get a lot of tourists from Europe, and some from even further afield.*

a·flame /ə'fleɪm/ *adj* [never before a noun] on fire

a·float /ə'fləʊt/ *adj* [never before a noun] **1** floating on water **2 stay afloat, keep afloat** to stay or keep out of debt

a·foot /ə'fʊt/ *adj* [never before a noun] being prepared or already happening: *There is a plan afoot to pull down the old building.*

a·fraid /ə'freɪd/ *adj* [never before a noun] **1** worried or frightened about something that might happen: *She looked lonely and afraid.* | *He was afraid of being bitten.* | *I was afraid of upsetting her.* | *My aunt was afraid that she might catch a cold.* | *He was afraid the plane would crash.* □ USEFUL PATTERNS be afraid of something; be afraid of doing something; be afraid that… **2 afraid of someone/something** frightened because someone or something is unpleasant or will hurt you: *The child is afraid of the dark.* | *He's afraid of Bill.* **3 afraid to do something** nervous or unwilling to do something because you are worried about what might happen: *She was afraid to go out alone at night.* **4 I'm afraid** a phrase used to show that you are sorry about something or to disagree politely with someone: *I can't come to the party, I'm afraid.* | *"Is Richard there?" "I'm afraid not."* | *I'm afraid that these facts are incorrect.* **5 afraid for** worried or concerned about someone or something: *During the flood she was afraid for her father and his house.*

a·fresh /ə'freʃ/ *adv fml* again from the beginning: *We decided to close down the business and start afresh.*

Af·ri·can¹ /'æfrɪkən/ *adj* connected with Africa or coming from Africa

African² *n* a person from Africa

af·ter¹ /'ɑːftəʳ ‖ 'æf-/ *prep* **1** in the time following something: *We'll leave after breakfast.* | *I'll phone you some time after six o'clock.* **2 day after day, week after week, etc.** every day, every week, etc.: *I hated having to sit in a classroom day after day.* **3** following someone or something: *"P" comes after "O" in the alphabet.* | *I ran after her.* **4** because of something that has happened: *After the way he treated me I never want to see him again.* **5** looking for someone or trying to catch them: *The police are after me.* **6** trying to get something: *I think he's only*

after your money! **7 be named/called after someone** to be given the same name as someone: *He was named Jack, after his father.* **8 after all:** a in spite of things which had been done or thought earlier: *There are two r's in "earring". You see, I was right after all.* | *I was feeling a bit tired, but then David said he was going, so I decided to go after all.* **b** don't forget; a phrase used when you are giving force to your opinion with good reasons: *You can't expect him to understand. After all, he's only six years old.*

■ USAGE Do not use the phrase **after all** to refer to the time when something happens. **After all** has two main uses. **1** To show that something is true in spite of what has been done or said before: *She said she wasn't going to come, but she turned up* **after all.** | *I didn't believe you, but you were right* **after all!** | *I've changed my mind, I think I'll have a coffee* **after all.** In this use **after all** usually comes at the end of a sentence. **2** To introduce an idea that explains or supports what you are saying: *It's not his fault. He's only obeying orders* **after all.** | *Don't be too hard on her.* **After all** *she's only a child.* | *Of course he can afford it.* **After all** *he is a millionaire!* **9 after that:** a you use "after that" when you move on to the next stage in a story that you are telling: *They mixed the clay and sand, and then added some water. After that, they rolled the mixture into a ball.* **b** you use "after that" when you give the next in a group of instructions: *Mix the clay and sand. Then add the water. After that, roll the mixture into a ball.* **c** you use "after that" when you go on to the next stage of a process you are describing: *The letters are taken to the sorting office and sorted. After that, they are sent out to the main postal towns, where they are sorted again.*

after² *adv,conj* later than someone or something else: *I went to live in France, and soon after I met my wife.* | *John came last Tuesday, and I arrived the day after.* | *Soon after he'd left I realized that he'd left his coat.*

af·ter·ef·fect /'ɑːftərɪˌfekt ‖ 'æf-/ *n* an unpleasant effect or result: *the after-effects of the new drug*

af·ter·life /'ɑːftəlaɪf ‖ 'æftər-/ *n* [sing] the life that is thought by some people to follow death

af·ter·math /'ɑːftəmæθ ‖ 'æftər-/ *n* [sing] the period following an unpleasant event such as an accident, storm, or war: *There was confusion in the aftermath of the accident.*

af·ter·noon /ˌɑːftə'nuːn ‖ ˌæftər-/ *n* the period which begins at about midday and ends at about six o'clock: *on Tuesday afternoons* | *I like to sleep in the afternoon.* | *an afternoon walk* | *in the late afternoon*

af·ter·wards /'ɑːftəwədz ‖ 'æftərwərdz/ *adv* (also **afterward**) later, after something else has happened: *She had her supper and then went to bed soon afterwards.*

a·gain /ə'gen, ə'geɪn ‖ ə'gen/ *adv* **1** once more: *Could you explain it again, please?* | *I'd love to go to Africa again.* | *We had to listen to his jokes yet again!* **2** you use "again" when you are going to make another point of the same kind as your last one: *Let's now compare this screen with the last one we looked at. Again, we see that colour is very important.* **3** back to the same place or same condition as before: *She was ill for a long time, but she's well again now.* | *I can't wait to be home again.* **4 again and again** repeatedly many times: *The government keeps coming out with the same excuses again and again.* **5 then again, there again** on the other hand: *He might get the job, but then again he might not have the right qualifications.*

a·gainst /ə'genst, ə'geɪnst ‖ ə'genst/ *prep* **1** in opposition to someone or something: *We discussed the arguments for and against capital punishment.* | *The government have threatened to use force against the rebels.* | *We're playing against a team from the North next week.* | *It is important that we win the battle against inflation.* **2** touching something or pressing on it: *He leaned his bike against the wall.* | *The rain was beating against the window.* –see picture on page 540 **3** as a defence or protection from something: *We're insured against burglary.* **4 against the law** not allowed by the law: *It's against the law to sell alcohol to children under 18.* **5** in the opposite direction to the wind or to the movement of water: *trying to sail against the wind* | *We had to row against the current.*

age¹ /eɪdʒ/ *n* **1** [C;U] the number of years that a person has lived: *He is 10 years of age.* | *At your age you should know better.* | *She died at the age of 79.* | *What ages are your children?* **2** [U] one of the periods of life: *You don't get your pension until you reach retirement age.* | *Who will look after you in old age?* **3** [U] the state of being old: *His back was bent with age.* **4** [C] a particular period of history: *the history of painting through the ages* | *the age of television* **5 an age, ages** a long time: *I haven't seen her for ages.* **6 come of age** to become an adult in law and be allowed to vote and get married [RELATED PHRASE **be of age**] **7 over age** too old to do a particular thing because the rules do not allow it **8 under age** not legally old enough to do something

age² *v* **aged, aging** *or* **ageing** [I;T] to become older and weaker or make someone seem older and weaker: *After his wife's death he aged quickly.* | *The illness has aged him.*

aged¹ /'eɪdʒd/ *adj* [never before a noun] a word used to say how old someone is: *a man aged 40*

ag·ed² /'eɪdʒɪd/ *adj* **1** very old: *an aged man* **2 the aged** very old people: *care of the sick and the aged*

age·less /'eɪdʒləs/ *adj* never showing signs of growing old

a·gen·cy /'eɪdʒənsi/ *n* **agencies** a business that arranges services for people: *I got this job through an employment agency.*

a·gen·da /ə'dʒendə/ *n* **1** a list of the subjects to be talked about at a meeting **2 on the agenda** being considered and talked about: *Protecting the environment is very much on the agenda.*

a·gent /'eɪdʒənt/ *n* **1** someone who represents the business affairs of another person or of a firm: *Our agent in Rome deals with all our Italian business.* **2** someone who works for a government and tries to find out the secrets of other governments: *a secret agent* **3** something that causes a particular result: *Soap is a cleansing agent.*

ag·gra·vate /'ægrəveɪt/ *v* **aggravated, aggravating** [T] **1** to make a problem worse or more serious: *The lack of rain aggravated the already serious lack of food.* **2** to annoy someone: *His little habits really aggravate me!* | *an aggravating way of interrupting people* –**aggravation** /ˌægrə'veɪʃən/ *n* [U]

ag·gre·gate /'ægrɪgət/ *n* [C;U] a total

ag·gres·sion /ə'greʃən/ *n* [U] angry or violent behaviour in which you attack someone: *an act of aggression* | *feelings of aggression*

ag·gres·sive /ə'gresɪv/ *adj* **1** always ready to argue with people or attack them: *He has a very aggressive manner.* **2** forceful, and determined to succeed: *If you want to succeed in business you must be aggressive.* | *an aggressive marketing campaign* –**aggressively** *adv*

ag·gres·sor /ə'gresər/ *n fml* a person or country that begins a fight or war without a good reason

ag·grieved /ə'griːvd/ *adj fml* feeling angry and upset because you have been treated unfairly

a·ghast /ə'gɑːst ‖ ə'gæst/ *adj* [never before a noun] suddenly filled with surprise, fear, and shock

ag·ile /'ædʒaɪl ‖ 'ædʒəl/ *adj* **1** able to move quickly and easily **2** able to think quickly (used of someone's mind) –**agility** /ə'dʒɪlɪti / *n* [U]

ag·i·tate /'ædʒɪteɪt/ *v* **agitated, agitating 1** [T] to make someone feel worried **2** [I] to argue strongly in public for or against political or social changes: *people agitating for political reforms*

ag·i·ta·tion /ˌædʒɪ'teɪʃən/ *n* [U] **1** a strong feeling of worry **2** public argument or actions for or against political or social changes

ag·i·ta·tor /'ædʒɪteɪtər/ *n* a person who tries to encourage political or social changes by public argument or actions

a·glow /ə'gləʊ/ *adj* [never before a noun] *lit* bright with colour and warmth

ag·nos·tic /æg'nɒstɪk, əg- ‖ -'nɑː-/ *n* someone who believes that it is not possible to know whether there is a God or whether there is life after death –compare ATHEIST –**agnostic** *adj* –**agnosticism** /-tɪsɪzəm/ *n* [U]

a·go /ə'gəʊ/ *adv* in the past: *He left ten minutes ago.* | *How long ago did she die?* | *That all happened a long time ago.*

■ USAGE **1** We nearly always use **ago** with the past tense of verbs, but not with perfect forms (formed from **have**). Compare, *I came here a year* **ago** and *I have been here for a year/*since *1990.* **2** When we want to show the difference between a time in the past and a time even further back we use **before (that)** or **previously** instead of **ago**: *My grandfather died five years* **ago**; *my grandmother had already died three years* **before (that)***/three years* **previously**.

a·gog /ə'gɒg ‖ ə'gɑːg/ *adj* [never before a noun] *infml* excited about something, and keen to know what will happen next

ag·o·nize /'ægənaɪz/ *v* **agonized, agonizing** (also **agonise** *BrE*) [I] *infml* to spend a lot of time worrying about something or trying to make a decision: *Nina has been agonizing over whether to take the job abroad.*

ag·o·nized /'ægənaɪzd/ *adj* (also **agonised** *BrE*) showing great pain or suffering: *an agonized cry*

ag·o·niz·ing /'ægənaɪzɪŋ/ *adj* (also **agonising** *BrE*) causing great pain or worry: *an agonizing decision*

ag·o·ny /'ægəni/ *n* **agonies** [C;U] very great pain or suffering in your mind or body: *He lay in agony until the doctor arrived.* | *She was suffering agonies of doubt.*

a·grar·i·an /ə'greəriən/ *adj* concerning farmland or its ownership

a·gree /ə'griː/ *v* **agreed, agreeing 1** [I; + (that)] to have the same opinion about something: *She agreed with me.* | *We agreed that the government should do more to protect the environment.* | *We agreed on a price for the car.* | *I agree with you about this.* **2 agree to something, agree to do something** to say that you will do something that someone else has suggested: *The government will never agree to the plan.* | *She agreed to look after the cat for the weekend.* **3 be agreed** to have reached the same decision about something: *We were all agreed that* *the government has not done enough to tackle this problem.* **4 agree with something** to believe that something is right: *I don't agree with hitting children.* **5 not agree with someone** *infml* to make someone ill: *Strawberries don't agree with me.* **6** [I] to be in accordance with something or be the same as something: *The two statements agree in everything except the smallest details.*

a·gree·a·ble /ə'griːəbəl/ *adj* **1** pleasant, enjoyable, or acceptable: *The weather was very agreeable.* –opposite **disagreeable 2 agreeable to something** willing to do or accept something

a·gree·a·bly /ə'griːəbli/ *adv* pleasantly: *I was agreeably surprised.*

a·gree·ment /ə'griːmənt/ *n* **1** [U] the state of having reached the same opinion or feeling about something: *They finally reached agreement after long discussions.* –opposite **disagreement 2** [U] the act of showing that you accept something: *The committee needs your agreement.* **3 in agreement** having the same opinion about something as someone else: *We are all in agreement about the need to tackle inflation.* **4** [C] an arrangement or promise made between people or countries: *an arms-control agreement* | *You have broken our agreement.*

ag·ri·cul·ture /'ægrɪ,kʌltʃəʳ/ *n* [U] the practice of farming, especially of growing crops –**agricultural** /,ægrɪ'kʌltʃərəl◂/ *adv*

a·ground /ə'graund/ *adv* **run aground, go aground** (of a ship) to touch the bottom of a sea or lake and be unable to move

ah /ɑː/ *interj* a word used to express surprise, pity, pain, or pleasure: *Ah! I hurt my foot on that stone.* | *Ah, there you are!*

a·ha /ɑː'hɑː/ *interj* a word used to express surprise, satisfaction, or understanding: *Aha, so it's you hiding there!*

a·head /ə'hed/ *adv,adj* **1** *adv* in front of you: *There were quite a few cars on the road ahead.* | *He ran ahead to see what was happening.* | *There was a roadblock straight ahead* of *us.* **2** *adv* into the future: *We must look ahead and try to plan for the future.* | *It's important to plan ahead.* **3** *adv,adj* more advanced than someone else or winning in a competition against them: *Our team was ahead at half time.* | *We're ahead* of *all the other companies in this field.* | *I think we might finish the project ahead of schedule.*

a·hoy /ə'hɔɪ/ *interj* a greeting shouted on a boat

aid¹ /eɪd/ *v* [T] to help or give support to someone –see HELP¹ (USAGE)

aid² *n* **1** [U] help that is given to someone: *I managed to go up the mountain with the aid of a guide.* **2** [U] money, food, and services given to people who need them: *They are sending aid to the victims of the disaster immediately.* | *overseas aid* **3** [C] a thing that helps you do something: *A dictionary is an important aid in learning a new language.* **4 in aid of** in support of: *What is the money in aid of?* **5 go to someone's aid** to help someone: *He went to the aid of the injured man.*

aide /eɪd/ *n* a person employed to help a government minister

AIDS /eɪdz/ a very serious disease, which destroys the body's defences against infection; an abbreviation for **Acquired Immune Deficiency Syndrome**

ail /eɪl/ *v* [I;T] *old fash* to become ill and grow weak

ail·ing /'eɪlɪŋ/ *adj* ill or weak, and not getting better or stronger: *his ailing mother* | *the country's ailing economy*

ail·ment /'eɪlmənt/ *n* an illness that is not serious

aim¹ /eɪm/ *v* **1** [I;T] to point or direct a weapon towards an object you want to hit: *He aimed the gun carefully.* | *He aimed it* **at** *the bottles.* **2 aim to do something, aim at doing something** to direct your efforts and plans towards making something happen: *The company aims to increase sales overseas.* | *I'm aiming at getting a good job in advertising.* **3** [T] to direct something at someone in order to influence them: *an advertising campaign aimed* **at** *young people*

aim² *n* **1** [U] the act of pointing a weapon: *Her aim was very good.* **2 take aim** to point a weapon at something: *He took aim, then fired.* **3** [C] the thing that you are trying to do or get: *The project was set up with the aim of helping young unemployed people.*

aim·less /'eɪmləs/ *adj* without any clear purpose: *His life was aimless.* –**aimlessly** *adv*

ain't /eɪnt/ *v* short for "am not", "is not", "are not", "has not", and "have not"; many people do not consider this to be correct English: *We ain't coming.* | *They ain't got it.*

air¹ /eəʳ/ *n* **1** [U] the mixture of gases which surrounds the Earth and which we breathe: *She opened the window to get some fresh air.* **2 the air** the space around you above the ground: *She threw the ball into the air.* **3** [sing] a general appearance or feeling: *There was an air of excitement in the stadium.* | *He had an air of sadness about him.* | *The city had a depressing air.* **4 by air** by plane: *We decided to go by air.* **5 air travel** travel by plane **6 disappear into thin air** to disappear completely **7 give yourself airs, put on airs** to behave as if you are more important than you really are **8 on the air** broadcasting on the radio or television [RELATED PHRASE **off the air**]

air² *v* **1** [I;T] to dry in a place that is warm and has plenty of dry air: *You should always air clothes thoroughly.* | *Hang those shirts up to air.* **2** [T] to make a room fresh by letting in air: *I'll open the windows to air the room.* **3** [T] to make your ideas known to other people: *The discussion will give everyone a chance to air their views.* –**airing** *n* [always **an airing**] : *Let's give the room a good airing.*

air·borne /'eəbɔːn ‖ 'eərbɔːrn/ *adj* **1** carried about by the air (used of seeds) **2** flying in the air (used of aircraft)

air·bus /'eəbʌs ‖ 'eər-/ *n* a plane for carrying large numbers of passengers on short flights

air-con·di·tion·ing /'·· ·,···/ *n* [U] the system that uses machines to keep air in a building cool –**air-conditioned** *adj*

air·craft /'eəkrɑːft ‖ 'eərkræft/ *n* [plural is **aircraft**] a plane of any type, with or without an engine

aircraft car·ri·er /'··,···/ *n* a warship that carries aircraft and has a large flat surface where they can take off and land

air·field /'eəfiːld ‖ 'eər-/ *n* an open area, smaller than an airport, where aircraft may land and take off

air force /'eəfɔːs ‖ 'eərfɔːrs/ *n* the part of the military organization of a country that is concerned with fighting in the air

air·host·ess /'eə,həustɪs ‖ 'eər-/ *n* a woman who looks after passengers in a plane

airing cup·board /'·· ,··/ *n* a warm dry cupboard used for airing clothes

air·less /ˈeələs ‖ ˈeər-/ adj without fresh air: *The room was hot and airless.*

air·lift /ˈeəˌlɪft ‖ ˈeər-/ n the carrying of a lot of people or supplies by aircraft, often to or from a place that is difficult to get to –**airlift** v [T]

air·line /ˈeəlaɪn ‖ ˈeər-/ n a business that runs a regular service for carrying passengers and goods by air

air·lin·er /ˈeəˌlaɪnəʳ ‖ ˈeər-/ n a large plane used for carrying passengers

air·lock /ˈeəlɒk ‖ ˈeərlɑːk/ n 1 the air blocking the flow of a liquid in a tube or pipe 2 an enclosed space through which air cannot accidentally pass, for example in a spacecraft

air·mail /ˈeəmeɪl ‖ ˈeər-/ n [U] the system of sending letters and parcels by air

air·man /ˈeəmən ‖ ˈeər-/ n airmen -mən/ a person of low rank in a country's air force

air·miss /ˈeəˌmɪs ‖ ˈeər-/ n airmisses a situation in which two planes very nearly hit each other in the air

air·plane /ˈeəpleɪn ‖ ˈeər-/ n the usual American word for AEROPLANE

air·port /ˈeəpɔːt ‖ ˈeərpɔːrt/ n a place you arrive at or leave from when travelling by plane –see picture on page 735

air raid /ˈ· ·/ n an attack by military aircraft

air·ship /ˈeəˌʃɪp ‖ ˈeər-/ n an old type of aircraft containing gas to make it lighter than air and with an engine to make it move

air·sick /ˈeəˌsɪk ‖ ˈeər-/ adj sick because of the movement of an aircraft

air·space /ˈeəspeɪs ‖ ˈeər-/ n [U] the sky above a country, regarded as the property of that country

air·strip /ˈeəˌstrɪp ‖ ˈeər-/ n a small stretch of land used by aircraft to take off and land

air ter·mi·nal /ˈ· ˌ···/ n a building at an airport where passengers wait before getting on their plane

air·tight /ˈeətaɪt ‖ ˈeər-/ adj not allowing air to pass in or out: *airtight containers*

air·waves /ˈeəweɪvz ‖ ˈeər-/ n on the airwaves on radio or television

air·wor·thy /ˈeəˌwɜːði ‖ ˈeərˌwɜːrði/ adj safe to fly (used of aircraft) –**airworthiness** n [U]

air·y /ˈeəri/ adj airier, airiest 1 having plenty of fresh air inside (used of buildings): *The room was large and airy.* 2 not based on facts or not very practical: *his airy plans | airy schemes to become a millionaire* 3 joking and not seeming to care about things that should be taken seriously: *She dismissed my objection with an airy wave of her hand.* –airily /ˈeərɪli/ adv

aisle /aɪl/ n a passage between rows of seats in a church, theatre, or cinema, or between rows of shelves in a large shop

a·jar /əˈdʒɑːʳ/ adj [never before a noun] not quite closed (used of a door)

a·kin /əˈkɪn/ adj fml akin to something similar to something

à la carte /ˌæ lə ˈkɑːt, ˌɑː lɑː- ‖ -ɑːrt/ adj,adv French choosing food from a list where each dish has its own separate price: *We ate à la carte. | an à la carte menu*

a·lac·ri·ty /əˈlækrɪti/ n [U] fml great willingness

a·larm¹ /əˈlɑːm ‖ əˈlɑːrm/ n 1 [U] sudden fear and anxiety when there is the possibility of danger: *There is no need for any alarm – you are quite safe.*

2 [C] something such as a bell, noise, or light which is used to give a warning 3 raise the alarm, sound the alarm to warn people of danger, especially by shouting

alarm² v [T] to make someone feel afraid and anxious: *Parents are very alarmed at the amount of violence on television.*

alarm clock /·ˈ· ·/ n a clock that can be set to make a noise at a certain time to wake you up

a·larm·ing /əˈlɑːmɪŋ ‖ əˈlɑːr-/ adj very worrying: *There has been an alarming increase in violent crime.*

a·larm·ist /əˈlɑːmɪst ‖ əˈlɑːr-/ n a person who warns other people of danger unnecessarily –**alarmist** adj

a·las /əˈlæs/ interj lit a word used to express sadness

al·be·it /ɔːlˈbiːɪt/ conj fml although: *It was a very important, albeit small, mistake.*

al·bi·no /ælˈbiːnəʊ ‖ ælˈbaɪ-/ n a person or animal born with very white skin and hair, and pink eyes

al·bum /ˈælbəm/ n 1 a book used for collecting things such as photographs or stamps 2 a record which plays for about 20 minutes on each side

al·bu·men /ˈælbjʊmɪn ‖ ælˈbjuː-/ n [U] the white or colourless part of an egg

al·che·my /ˈælkəmi/ n [U] the science of trying to find a way to turn metals into gold –**alchemist** /-ɪst/ n

al·co·hol /ˈælkəhɒl ‖ -hɔːl/ n [U] 1 the colourless liquid present in drinks such as wine and beer; alcohol can make people drunk 2 drinks containing this liquid: *I never drink alcohol.*

al·co·hol·ic¹ /ˌælkəˈhɒlɪk◄ ‖ -ˈhɔː-/ adj containing alcohol or related to alcohol –opposite non-alcoholic

alcoholic² n a person who cannot stop the habit of drinking too much alcohol

al·co·hol·is·m /ˈælkəhɒlɪzəm ‖ -hɔː-/ n [U] the disease caused by the continued drinking of a lot of alcohol

al·cove /ˈælkəʊv/ n a partly enclosed space in the wall of a room where you can put furniture or shelves

al·der·man /ˈɔːldəmən ‖ -dər-/ n aldermen /-mən/ a local government officer

ale /eɪl/ n [U] a type of beer, especially one that is pale in colour

a·lert¹ /əˈlɜːt ‖ -ɜːrt/ adj 1 quick to notice what is happening 2 alert to something knowing about a danger or problem: *We were alert to the dangers of the plan.* –**alertness** n [U]

alert² n 1 a situation in which people are ready and watching for danger 2 on the alert ready and watching for danger

alert³ v [T] to warn someone of a danger or problem: *We must alert young people to the dangers of smoking.*

A lev·el /ˈeɪ ˌlevəl/ n the higher of the two standards of examination formerly taken at most British schools; an abbreviation for Advanced Level

al·gae /ˈældʒiː, -giː/ n [pl] very small, simple plants that live in or near water

al·ge·bra /ˈældʒɪbrə/ n [U] a branch of MATHEMATICS in which signs and letters are used to represent numbers –**algebraic** /ˌældʒɪˈbreɪ-ɪk◄/ adj

al·go·rith·m /ˈælgərɪðəm/ n a list of instructions to a computer which are carried out in a fixed order

a·li·as[1] /ˈeɪliəs/ n a false name, especially one used by a criminal

alias[2] prep a word used when you are giving someone's alias: *The police are looking for Stephen Smith, alias Edward Ball.*

al·i·bi /ˈælɨbaɪ/ n proof that a person was in another place at the time of a crime and so could not have done it: *He didn't have an alibi for the night of the murder.*

a·li·en[1] /ˈeɪliən/ adj 1 belonging to another country or race 2 different and strange: *an alien environment* | *Their ideas are quite alien to our way of thinking.*

alien[2] n 1 a foreigner who is not a citizen of the country where he or she is living 2 a creature from another world

a·li·en·ate /ˈeɪliəneɪt/ v **alienated, alienating** [T] to make someone stop feeling friendly or sympathetic: *The government has alienated a lot of people with this new policy.*

a·li·en·a·tion /ˌeɪliəˈneɪʃən/ n [U] a feeling of not belonging to or not being part of your surroundings: *The increasingly dull nature of many industrial jobs has led to the alienation of many workers.*

a·light[1] /əˈlaɪt/ v [I] fml 1 to get off a vehicle at the end of a journey –see TRANSPORT (USAGE) 2 (of a bird) to come down from the air onto a surface

alight[2] adj [never before a noun] burning: *The fire was still alight.*

a·lign /əˈlaɪn/ v [T] 1 to arrange something into a straight line, or into the same line as something else: *The pictures were all aligned perfectly.* 2 **align yourself with someone, be aligned with someone** to come into agreement with someone else because you have the same aims: *They aligned themselves with the workers in the struggle for freedom.*

a·lign·ment /əˈlaɪnmənt/ n 1 [U] a position in which something is in a straight line 2 [U] the act of forming into a group with other people who have the same aims 3 [C] a group of people who have the same aims: *new political alignments forming before the election*

a·like[1] /əˈlaɪk/ adj [never before a noun] similar: *The two brothers are very much alike.*

alike[2] adv 1 in a similar way: *She treats all her children alike.* 2 equally: *a training course for employed and unemployed alike*

al·i·men·ta·ry /ˌælɨˈmentəri/ adj tech concerning food and the way it is treated in your body

al·i·mo·ny /ˈælɨməni ‖ -məʊni/ n [U] money that someone has to pay regularly to their former partner after they have been divorced (DIVORCE)

a·live /əˈlaɪv/ adj [never before a noun] 1 living and not dead: *Is he still alive?* | *We want to keep the debate alive.* 2 active and full of life: *She's so alive!* 3 **alive to something** having full knowledge of something: *He was alive to the dangers of the work.* 4 **alive with** covered with or full of living things: *The place was alive with people.* 5 **come alive** to become interesting and full of life

al·ka·li /ˈælkəlaɪ/ n **alkalies** or **alkalies** [C;U] tech a substance that forms chemical salts when combined with acids –**alkaline** /-laɪn ‖ -lɨn/ adj

all[1] /ɔːl/ det, predeterminer, pron 1 the whole of something: *He ate all his food.* | *He ate it all.* | *We walked all the way into town.* | *We worked hard all last year.* 2 every one of: *I've invited all the people in the office.* | *All children like toys.* | *Are you all

hungry?* | *There are twenty questions on the paper. Please answer them all.* | *We invited thirty people, but not all of them came.* 3 **all in** with everything included: *an all-in price of £50.* 4 **all out** using all your strength or making as much effort as you can: *an all-out attack on the enemy* 5 **not at all** not in any way: *I'm afraid I don't agree with you at all.* | *He's not at all shy.*

all[2] adv 1 completely: *She sat all alone.* | *I got all dirty.* 2 for each side: *The final result of the match was three all.* 3 **all but** almost: *We've all but finished here.* | *It's all but impossible.* 4 **all over** everywhere in a place: *We've been looking all over for you.* | *They've travelled all over Europe.* 5 **all the same** even so: *Sometimes young children can be so difficult, but they're lovely all the same.*

Al·lah /ˈælə/ n the Muslim name for God

al·lay /əˈleɪ/ v [T] fml to make a feeling like fear, anger, or doubt less strong

all clear /ˌ ˈ/ n a signal telling you that a danger has passed

al·le·ga·tion /ˌælɨˈɡeɪʃən/ n fml a statement suggesting that someone has done something bad or criminal, but which is not supported by proof: *These allegations of cruelty must be investigated.*

al·lege /əˈledʒ/ v **alleged, alleging** [T; +that] fml to state that something is true before giving proof: *The police allege that the man was murdered.*

al·leged /əˈledʒd/ adj suggested, but not proved to be true: *The alleged crimes took place last month.* –**allegedly** /əˈledʒɨdli/ adv : *He had allegedly committed several other crimes.*

al·le·giance /əˈliːdʒəns/ n [C;U] loyalty and support given to a leader, a country, or an idea: *We had to swear allegiance to our country.*

al·le·go·ry /ˈælɨɡəri ‖ -ɡɔːri/ n [C;U] a story, poem, or painting in which the characters and actions represent good and bad qualities –**allegorical** /ˌælɨˈɡɒrɪkəl ‖ -ˈɡɔː-, -ˈɡɑː-/ adj

al·le·lu·ia /ˌælɨˈluːjə/ n, interj see HALLELUJA

al·ler·gic /əˈlɜːdʒɪk ‖ -ɜːr-/ adj having an allergy or caused by an allergy: *He is allergic to cats.* | *an allergic rash*

al·ler·gy /ˈælədʒi ‖ -ər-/ n **allergies** a condition in which your body is very sensitive to something that you eat or breathe so that it makes you feel ill or suffer in some way

al·le·vi·ate /əˈliːvieɪt/ v **alleviated, alleviating** [T] to make suffering or an unpleasant situation less severe –**alleviation** /əˌliːviˈeɪʃən/ n [U]

al·ley /ˈæli/ n a narrow street between buildings in a town

al·li·ance /əˈlaɪəns/ n 1 [C;U] a close agreement between countries or groups for a shared purpose: *We are hoping for an alliance between government and industry.* 2 [C+sing/pl verb] a group of people or countries formed to look after the interests of its members: *the Western alliance*

al·lied /ˈælaɪd, əˈlaɪd/ adj 1 joined by a political agreement: *the allied nations* 2 related or connected in some way

al·li·ga·tor /ˈælɨɡeɪtər/ n a large animal with a long body and a hard skin that lives on land and in rivers in parts of America and China

al·lit·er·a·tion /əˌlɪtəˈreɪʃən/ n [U] the appearance of the same sound at the beginning of two or more words that are close to each other (as in "Round the rocks runs the river")

al·lo·cate /ˈæləkeɪt/ v **allocated, allocating** [T] to keep or give something for a particular purpose: *That space has already been allocated for building a new hospital.* | *the amount of money allocated to the National Health Service*

al·lo·ca·tion /ˌæləˈkeɪʃən/ n **1** [U] the allocating of things for a particular purpose **2** [C] a share of something, such as money, that is allocated to a particular person or for a particular purpose

al·lot /əˈlɒt ‖ əˈlɑːt/ v -tt- [T] to give something to someone as their share: *Two rooms had been allotted to me.*

al·lot·ment /əˈlɒtmənt ‖ əˈlɑːt-/ n **1** a share of something such as money that is given to someone **2** a small piece of land rented out by a town council in Britain for growing vegetables

al·low /əˈlaʊ/ v **1** [T] to give permission for someone to do something or have something: *We don't allow smoking in our offices.* | *They allow us four weeks holiday a year.* | *As a child, I was never allowed to stay up late.*
□ USEFUL PATTERNS to allow something; to allow someone something; to allow someone to do something
2 [T] to let someone go somewhere: *Dogs are not allowed in the children's play area.* | *I'm afraid you're not allowed in.* **3** [T] to make it possible for something to happen: *We must not allow inflation to rise any further.*
□ USEFUL PATTERN to allow something to happen
4 [T] to keep or give an amount of time or money for a particular purpose: *Allow ten days for delivery.* | *I've allowed myself three weeks to get the job finished.*
□ USEFUL PATTERNS to allow an amount; to allow yourself an amount
5 allow for something to take something into consideration so that you can deal with it if it happens **6** [+ that] *fml* to admit that something is true: *I allow that there may have been some mistake.*

al·low·a·ble /əˈlaʊəbəl/ adj acceptable and so permitted

al·low·ance /əˈlaʊəns/ n **1** an amount of money that is given to someone regularly: *an allowance of £5,000 a year* | *a travelling allowance* **2 make allowances for something** to take facts into consideration when making a decision or judgment

al·loy /ˈælɔɪ ‖ ˈælɔɪ, əˈlɔɪ/ n a metal made by mixing together two or more different metals

all right¹ /ˌ· ˈ·/ adj [never before a noun] **1** safe, unharmed, or healthy: *Is the driver all right after the accident?* **2** satisfactory and acceptable: *Is the food all right?*

all right² adv **1** in an acceptable or satisfactory way: *Is John getting on all right at University?* **2** a word used when you are agreeing to do something: *"Will you help me?" "All right."* –see ALRIGHT (USAGE)

all-round /ˈ· ·/ adj [only before a noun] having ability in many things –**all-rounder** /ˌ· ˈ··/ n

al·lude /əˈluːd/ v **alluded, alluding** *fml* **allude to something** to speak about something in an indirect way

al·lure /əˈljʊər ‖ əˈlʊər/ n [sing] attraction or charm

al·lur·ing /əˈljʊərɪŋ ‖ əˈlʊər-/ adj very attractive

al·lu·sion /əˈluːʒən/ n [C;U] *fml* an act of speaking about something in an indirect way: *He made several allusions to my failure.*

al·lu·vi·al /əˈluːvɪəl/ adj made of soil put down by rivers, lakes, or floods

al·ly¹ /əˈlaɪ ‖ ˈælaɪ, ˈælaɪ/ v **allied, allying** [T] **ally yourself with someone** to join with someone and support them politically: *They allied themselves with America during the war.*

al·ly² /ˈælaɪ ‖ ˈælaɪ, əˈlaɪ/ n **allies** a person or country that helps or supports another one, especially in war

al·ma·nac /ˈɔːlmənæk ‖ ˈɔːl-, ˈæl-/ n a book giving a list of the days of a year, and also information about the movement of the sun, the moon, and the sea

al·might·y /ɔːlˈmaɪti/ adj **1 Almighty** having the power to do anything (used of God): *God Almighty* **2** *infml* very big or loud: *There was an almighty crash.*

al·mond /ˈɑːmənd ‖ ˈɑː-, ˈæ-, ˈæl-/ n a kind of nut

al·most /ˈɔːlməʊst ‖ ˈɔːlməʊst, ɔːlˈməʊst/ adv very nearly but not quite: *I lived in India for almost two years.* | *She's been very ill, but she's almost better now.* | *I almost forgot that it was his birthday today.* | *Almost everybody who was invited came.*

alms /ɑːmz ‖ ɑːmz, ɑːlmz/ n [pl] money, food, or clothes given to poor people (a word which is no longer used in modern English)

a·loft /əˈlɒft ‖ əˈlɔːft/ adv [never before a noun] high up in the air

a·lone /əˈləʊn/ adv,adj **1** without other people: *He lives alone.* | *I was alone in the room.* | *She had never been on holiday alone.* | *She alone knew his real identity.* **2** [only after a noun] only
■ USAGE **Alone** is neither good nor bad: *She lives on tea and cake when she's alone.* **Solitary** and **lone**, when used of things, mean that there is only one: *a solitary/ lone tree in the garden*, but used of people they may show sadness, like **lonely** or (especially in American English) **lonesome**: *Come over and see me; I'm feeling a bit lonely/lonesome.*

a·long¹ /əˈlɒŋ ‖ əˈlɔːŋ/ prep moving or positioned on a road, river, etc: *She walked along the road.* | *I love driving along narrow country lanes.* | *There were trees all along the river bank.* | *Their house is just a bit further along this road.* –see picture on page 540

along² adv **1** forward: *She was cycling along, singing to herself.* | *I walked along behind him.* **2** to a place: *You go straight to the restaurant. I'll come along later.* | *The others will be along soon.* **3** with you: *Is it all right if I bring the children along?* **4 all along** during the whole of a period of time: *I'd known all along that the idea wouldn't work.* **5 along with** with: *Along with many other people, I'm very worried about the situation.*

a·long·side /əˌlɒŋˈsaɪd ‖ əˌlɔːŋ-/ prep,adv **1** next to and in line with the edge of something: *We brought our boat alongside theirs.* | *We saw their car and pulled up alongside.* **2** together with something or someone else: *Scientists are working alongside the police to discover the cause of the explosion.*

a·loof /əˈluːf/ adj apart and distant from other people, or not joining in and doing things with other people: *He kept himself aloof from the others.* –**aloofness** n [U]

a·loud /əˈlaʊd/ adv (also **out loud**) **1** in a voice that people can hear: *The teacher asked her to read the poem aloud.* **2** in a loud voice: *The pain caused him to cry aloud.*

al·pha /ˈælfə/ n the first letter (α) in the Greek alphabet

al·pha·bet /ˈælfəbet/ n the set of letters used in writing any language, arranged in order

al·pha·bet·i·cal /ˌælfəˈbetɪkəl◂/ adj arranged in the order of the alphabet: *The names are listed in alphabetical order.* –**alphabetically** /-kli/ adv

al·pine /ˈælpaɪn/ adj concerning or existing in high mountains

al·read·y /ɔːlˈredi/ adv **1** before a particular time, or before expected: *He had already left by the time I got there.* | *The meeting doesn't start for another half hour, but quite a few people are already here.* **2** before: *"Would you like to have lunch with us?" "No thank you, I've already eaten."* –see JUST² (USAGE)
■ USAGE **1** Compare **already** and **yet**. We use **already** mainly in positive sentences: *I've already asked her.* We use **yet** mainly in questions and negatives: *Have you asked her yet?* | *I haven't asked her yet.* **2** Compare **already** and **all ready**. *We're all ready* means that all of us are ready.

al·right /ɔːlˈraɪt/ adv all right
■ USAGE In the past, people considered **all right** the only correct form, but **alright** is very common now.

a·lso /ˈɔːlsəʊ/ adv as well: *She speaks German and French, and also Spanish.* | *I've seen his latest film, and I've also seen a few of his earlier ones.* | *It was not only cold and windy, but also raining!* | *"The Moon, the Moon" is available on CD. It's also available as a cassette.* –see Study Note on page 508

al·tar /ˈɔːltər/ n a table used in a religious ceremony

al·ter /ˈɔːltər/ v [I;T] to change in some way: *It's still the same book. Only the cover has been altered.* | *The government's policy on this hasn't altered.*

al·ter·a·tion /ˌɔːltəˈreɪʃən/ n **1** [C] a change in something: *The Bill went through Parliament with only a few minor alterations.* **2** [U] the act of changing something

al·ter·ca·tion /ˌɔːltəˈkeɪʃən ‖ -tər-/ n fml a noisy quarrel

al·ter·nate¹ /ɔːlˈtɜːnət ‖ ˈɔːltɜːr-, ˈɑːl-/ adj [only before a noun] **1** happening in a regular way, first one thing and then the other thing: *a week of alternate rain and sunshine* **2 alternate days, alternate weeks,** etc. every second day, week, etc.: *He works on alternate days.*

al·ter·nate² /ˈɔːltəneɪt ‖ -tər-/ v alternated, alternating **1** [I] to follow regularly, with first one thing happening and then the other: *Her moods alternated between cheerfulness and despair.* | *Periods of heavy rain alternated with periods of drought.* **2** [T] to do first one thing and then the other: *We alternated periods of work and rest.* –**alternation** /ˌɔːltəˈneɪʃən ‖ -tər-/ n [C;U]

al·ter·na·tive¹ /ɔːlˈtɜːnətɪv ‖ ɔːlˈtɜːr-, æl-/ adj [only before a noun] **1** able or suitable to be used or done instead of something else: *When traffic is bad use the alternative route.* **2** different from what is usual or accepted: *alternative technologies* | *alternative medicine*

alternative² n something that can be used or done instead of something else: *We had to fight: there was no alternative.* | *Many farmers are now growing maize as an alternative to wheat.*

al·ter·na·tive·ly /ɔːlˈtɜːnətɪvli ‖ ɔːlˈtɜːrn-, æl-/ adv a word used when you are suggesting an alternative to the first suggestion: *I could pick you up on my way into town or, alternatively, we could meet in town.*

al·though /ɔːlˈðəʊ/ conj **1** in spite of something: *I recognized her at once, although I hadn't seen her for*

ten years. | *Although it was raining we decided to go for a walk.* **2** but: *I think she's going to apply for the job, although I'm not sure.*

al·ti·tude /ˈæltɪtjuːd ‖ -tuːd/ n [C;U] the distance that something is above sea level: *They were flying at a low altitude.*

al·to /ˈæltəʊ/ n a singing voice that is quite high for a man and quite low for a woman

al·to·geth·er /ˌɔːltəˈgeðər◂/ adv **1** completely: *It's not altogether a bad idea.* | *We've now stopped making this product altogether.* | *This is an altogether different problem.* | *What he's saying is not altogether true.* **2** considering all things: *It will look very ugly and cost a lot of money. Altogether, I'm not too keen on the idea.*

al·tru·is·m /ˈæltruːɪzəm/ n [U] concern for the happiness of other people rather than your own –**altruistic** /ˌæltruˈɪstɪk◂/ adj : *His motives were entirely altruistic.*

al·u·min·i·um /ˌæljuˈmɪniəm, ˌælə-/ n (**aluminum** /əˈluːmɪnəm/ AmE) [U] a silver-coloured metal that is light and easily shaped

al·ways /ˈɔːlwʌz, -weɪz/ adv **1** all the time or every time: *We've always lived here.* | *The sun always rises in the east.* | *She's always late!* | *He's always criticizing me!* **2** for ever: *I shall always love you.* **3 can always, could always** a phrase used when you are suggesting what someone could do: *If she's not in the office, you could always try phoning her at home.*

am /m, əm; strong æm/ the first person singular present tense of BE: *I am living in London now.* –see 's (USAGE)

AM /ˌeɪ ˈem/ a system of broadcasting by radio in which the strength of the sound waves varies; an abbreviation for **amplitude modulation**

a.m. /ˌeɪ ˈem/ letters which follow numbers to show that a time is before midday: *the 8 a.m. train from London* | *We arrived at 11 a.m.* –compare P.M.

a·mal·gam·ate /əˈmælɡəmeɪt/ v **amalgamated, amalgamating** [I] (of businesses or organizations) to join together to form a larger business or organization: *The two companies amalgamated two years ago.* –**amalgamation** /əˌmælɡəˈmeɪʃən/ n [C;U]

a·mass /əˈmæs/ v [T] to collect things such as money or facts in very large amounts

am·a·teur¹ /ˈæmətər, -tʃʊər, -tʃər, ˌæməˈtɜːr/ n **1** a person who does something for enjoyment and not as their job: *Only amateurs may compete in the Olympic Games.* **2** a person without much experience or skill in a particular activity: *Those builders were really only amateurs.*

amateur² adj **1** done for enjoyment and not as a job: *amateur football* | *an amateur detective* **2** not very skilfully done: *The performance was rather amateur.* –**amateurism** n [U]

am·a·teur·ish /ˈæmətərɪʃ, ˌæməˈtjʊərɪʃ, -ˈtɜːrɪʃ ‖ ˌæməˈtʊr-, -ˈtɜːr-/ adj not very skilfully done

a·maze /əˈmeɪz/ v amazed, amazing [T] to make you feel very surprised: *It amazed me to hear that you were leaving.* –**amazed** adj : *Everyone looked amazed when he walked in.* –**amazement** n [U]

a·maz·ing /əˈmeɪzɪŋ/ adj very surprising and causing pleasure or admiration: *What an amazing film!* | *It's so fast – it's amazing!*

am·bas·sa·dor /æmˈbæsədər/ n an important official representing his or her country in the capital city of another country: *the British Ambassador to Spain*

am·ber /ˈæmbəʳ/ adj,n [U] **1** a hard yellowish-brown clear substance used for making jewellery: *clear amber beads* **2** a yellowish-brown colour

am·bi·dex·trous /ˌæmbɪˈdekstrəs/ adj able to use either hand with equal skill

am·bi·ence /ˈæmbɪəns/ n (also **ambiance** AmE) [U] the character or feeling of a place: *The restaurant has a pleasant ambience.*

am·big·u·ous /æmˈbɪgjuəs/ adj not clear, and able to be understood in more than one way: *an ambiguous reply* –**ambiguity** /ˌæmbɪˈgjuːti/ n ambiguities [C;U] : *There were several ambiguities in her statement.*

am·bi·tion /æmˈbɪʃən/ n **1** [U] strong desire to obtain success, power, or riches: *a politician full of ambition* **2** [C] something that you very much want to do or obtain: *His main ambition is to be famous.*

am·bi·tious /æmˈbɪʃəs/ adj **1** having a strong desire to be successful, powerful, or rich: *an ambitious young man* **2** daring and difficult to do successfully: *This is the most ambitious project I've ever taken on.*

am·biv·a·lent /æmˈbɪvələnt/ adj not clear in your mind about whether you like or dislike something: *I have a very ambivalent attitude towards giving to charity.* –**ambivalence** n [U]

am·ble /ˈæmbəl/ v ambled, ambling [I] to walk slowly because you are not in a hurry: *He was ambling along by the riverside*

am·bu·lance /ˈæmbjʊləns/ n a motor vehicle for carrying sick or wounded people to hospital

am·bush /ˈæmbʊʃ/ v [T] to attack someone after hiding and waiting for them –**ambush** n

a·me·li·o·rate /əˈmiːliəreɪt/ v ameliorated, ameliorating [T] fml to make a situation better or less difficult –**amelioration** /əˌmiːliəˈreɪʃən/ n [U]

a·men /ɑːˈmen, eɪ-/ interj a word said by Christians at the end of a prayer: *for ever and ever, Amen*

a·me·na·ble /əˈmiːnəbəl/ adj willing to be guided or influenced by something: *I've always found him very amenable.* | *She is amenable to reason.*

a·mend /əˈmend/ v [T] to make changes to something that has been written or said: *The law has been amended recently.*

a·mend·ment /əˈmendmənt/ n [C;U] a change made to something that has been written: *The government is proposing several amendments to the Bill.*

a·mends /əˈmendz/ n make amends to do something for someone to show that you are sorry about something harmful or unkind that you did to them: *How can I ever make amends for such unkindness?*

a·me·ni·ty /əˈmiːnɪti ‖ əˈme-/ n amenities a public place where people can go for pleasure or entertainment: *Local amenities include parks and swimming pools.*

A·mer·i·can /əˈmerɪkən/ adj belonging to or connected with the United States of America: *the American dollar*

American foot·ball /·,···‖·/ n (football AmE) [U] an American ball game similar to football –see picture on page 637

A·mer·i·can·is·m /əˈmerɪkənɪzəm/ n a word or phrase of English that is used in the United States

am·e·thyst /ˈæmɪθɪst/ n [C;U] a purple stone used in jewellery

a·mi·a·ble /ˈeɪmiəbəl/ adj fml pleasant and friendly: *She proved to be a most amiable companion.* –**amiability** /ˌeɪmiəˈbɪlɪti/ n [U]

am·i·ca·ble /ˈæmɪkəbəl/ adj pleasant and without argument: *We reached an amicable agreement.* –**amicably** adv

a·mid /əˈmɪd/ prep (also **amidst** /əˈmɪdst/) fml in the middle of a lot of things: *Amid all the noise and excitement, suddenly I heard a voice that I knew.*

a·miss /əˈmɪs/ adj fml **1** something is amiss = something is wrong: *I knew that there was something amiss.* **2** take something amiss to be angry about something or feel hurt because you have understood it wrongly

am·mo·ni·a /əˈməʊniə/ n [U] a strong gas or liquid with a sharp unpleasant smell, used in cleaning substances

am·mu·ni·tion /ˌæmjʊˈnɪʃən/ n [U] **1** bullets and explosives fired from a weapon **2** information that can be used against someone: *The tax increases will be used as ammunition by the opposition.*

am·ne·si·a /æmˈniːziə ‖ -ʒə/ n [U] med loss of memory

am·nes·ty /ˈæmnəsti/ n amnesties an official declaration of forgiveness given by a state to political criminals: *The President granted an amnesty on Independence Day.*

a·mok /əˈmɒk ‖ əˈmʌk/ run amok to run around in a wild and uncontrolled way, often destroying things or killing people

a·mong /əˈmʌŋ/ prep (also **amongst** /əˈmʌŋst/) **1** in the middle of a lot of people or things: *He stood among the bricks and rubble that had been his home.* | *My purse is somewhere among all this mess.* | *She loves being among a lot of people.* **2** in a particular group of people or concerning a particular group of people: *Unemployment is especially high among young men under 25.* | *There is a lot of anger among women about this new law.* | *There has been much discussion about this among politicians.* | *Just talk among yourselves for a few minutes.* **3** between three or more people: *The money was divided equally among them.* –see BETWEEN (USAGE) **4** among other things a phrase used when you are giving just one thing as an example: *He was, among other things, a poet and a painter.*

a·mor·al /eɪˈmɒrəl, æ- ‖ eɪˈmɔː-, -ˈmɑː-/ adj not caring whether something is right or wrong

am·o·rous /ˈæmərəs/ adj concerning sexual love or wanting sexual love: *He was giving me amorous looks.*

a·mor·phous /əˈmɔːfəs ‖ -ɔːr-/ adj having no fixed form or shape: *an amorphous blob of jelly*

a·mount¹ /əˈmaʊnt/ n a quantity of something: *Large amounts of money were spent on the bridge.*

amount² v amount to something: **a** to mean something without stating it directly: *His words amounted to a refusal.* **b** to make a total of a particular amount: *His debts amount to over £1,000.*

amp /æmp/ n **1** (also **ampere** /ˈæmpeəʳ ‖ ˈæmpɪər/ fml) a measure of a quantity of electricity: *a 10 amp fuse* **2** see AMPLIFIER

am·phet·a·mine /æmˈfetəmiːn, -mɪn/ n a drug which makes people feel very excited: *Amphetamine abuse can lead to physical exhaustion.*

am·phib·i·an /æmˈfɪbiən/ n an animal that is able to live both on land and in water –**amphibious** /æmˈfɪbiəs/ adj

am·phi·thea·tre /ˈæmfɪθɪətəʳ/ n (amphitheater AmE) a large open area with rows of seats around it, used for performing plays

am·ple /ˈæmpəl/ adj **1** enough of something and some more: *Don't hurry. We have ample time.* **2** large: *a garden of ample proportions*

am·pli·fi·er /ˈæmplɪfaɪəʳ/ n (also **amp** infml) an instrument used in radios and record players (RECORD PLAYER) that makes sounds or signals louder –see picture on page 442

am·pli·fy /ˈæmplɪfaɪ/ v amplified, amplifying [T] **1** to increase sound from electrical instruments **2** to explain something in greater detail: *This statement needs to be amplified.* –amplification /ˌæmplɪfɪˈkeɪʃən/ n [U]

am·pu·tate /ˈæmpjʊteɪt/ v amputated, amputating [I;T] to cut off a part of someone's body for medical reasons: *She had to have a leg amputated.* –amputation /ˌæmpjʊˈteɪʃən/ n [C;U]

a·muse /əˈmjuːz/ v amused, amusing [T] **1** to make someone laugh or smile: *We were very amused by her comments.* **2** to keep someone happy and prevent them from losing interest: *It's a toy which will amuse children for hours.* | *The children amused themselves by playing games.*

a·muse·ment /əˈmjuːzmənt/ n **1** [U] the feeling that you have when you are amused by something: *I listened in amusement.* **2** [C] something which gives people pleasure or entertainment: *Big cities have theatres, football matches, and many other amusements.*

a·mus·ing /əˈmjuːzɪŋ/ adj making you laugh or smile: *an amusing story*

an /ən; *strong* æn/ indefinite article, det see A
■ USAGE The choice of **a** or **an** before a set of letters like *UN* or *FM* depends on how we say the first letter, not on whether the letter itself is a vowel or a consonant. Put **a** if we say the letter with a consonant sound: **a** *UN official.* Put **an** if we say the letter with a vowel sound: **an** *FM radio.*

a·nach·ro·nis·m /əˈnækrənɪzəm/ n a thing which is no longer suitable because it belongs to the past –anachronistic /əˌnækrəˈnɪstɪk◄/ adj

a·nae·mi·a /əˈniːmiə/ n (also **anemia** AmE) [U] the unhealthy condition of not having enough red cells in your blood –anaemic /əˈniːmɪk/ adj

an·aes·the·si·a /ˌænəsˈθiːziə ‖ -ʒə/ n (also **anesthesia** AmE) [U] the use of pain-killing drugs in medicine

an·aes·thet·ic /ˌænəsˈθetɪk/ n (also **anesthetic** AmE) [C;U] a drug which stops feelings of pain; an anaesthetic is given either in a limited area (**local anaesthetic**) or in the whole body (**general anaesthetic**), when a patient becomes unconscious during a medical operation

a·naes·the·tist /əˈniːsθətɪst ‖ əˈnes-/ n (also **anesthetist** AmE) a person who gives an anaesthetic to a patient before a medical operation

a·naes·the·tize /əˈniːsθətaɪz ‖ -ˈnes-/ v anaesthetized, anaesthetizing (also **anaesthetise** BrE, **anesthetize** AmE) [T] to make someone unable to feel pain by giving them an anaesthetic

an·a·gram /ˈænəgræm/ n a word or phrase made by changing the order of the letters in another word or phrase, for example 'silent' is an anagram of 'listen'

a·nal /ˈeɪnəl/ adj involving or connected with a person's ANUS

an·al·ge·sic /ˌænəlˈdʒiːzɪk/ n tech a drug which stops you from feeling pain –analgesic adj

a·nal·o·gous /əˈnæləgəs/ adj fml analogous to something similar to something else in certain ways

a·nal·o·gy /əˈnælədʒi/ n analogies **1** [C] a degree of similarity: *He drew an analogy between the way water moves and the way light travels.* **2** [U] **by analogy** by comparing something with another similar thing

an·a·lyse /ˈænəl-aɪz/ v analysed, analysing (also **analyze** AmE) [T] to examine something carefully in order to find out about it: *The chemicals were analysed in our laboratories.* | *This problem needs to be analysed in detail.*

a·nal·y·sis /əˈnæləsɪs/ n analyses /-siːz/ [C;U] a careful examination of something which helps you to understand and explain it: *His analysis of the accident showed what had happened.*

an·a·lyst /ˈænəl-ɪst/ n **1** a person who makes an analysis of a subject and gives opinions about it: *political analysts* **2** see PSYCHOANALYST

an·a·lyt·ic /ˌænəlˈlɪtɪk◄/ adj (also **analytical** /-kəl/) using reason or able to use reason

an·ar·chis·m /ˈænəkɪzəm ‖ -ər-/ n [U] the political belief that society should have no government or laws, but people in society should work together and help each other –anarchist n

an·ar·chy /ˈænəki ‖ -ər-/ n [U] a state of complete disorder and confusion, when no-one is in control and no-one follows any rules or laws –anarchic /æˈnɑːkɪk ‖ -ɑːr-/ adj

a·nath·e·ma /əˈnæθəmə/ n fml [sing;U] something that you hate very much: *Those opinions are an anathema to me.*

a·nat·o·my /əˈnætəmi/ n anatomies **1** [U] the scientific study of the bodies of living things and the way their parts fit together **2** [C] the way that the parts of a living thing or a body fit together: *the anatomy of a rabbit* –anatomical /ˌænəˈtɒmɪkəl ‖ -ˈtɑː-/ adj

an·ces·tor /ˈænsəstəʳ, -ses- ‖ -ses-/ n a person from whom someone is descended: *My ancestors came from Spain in the eighteenth century.* –ancestral /ænˈsestrəl/ adj [only before a noun]

an·ces·try /ˈænsəstri, -ses- ‖ -ses-/ n ancestries [C;U] the people from whom someone is descended: *British citizens of Indian ancestry*

an·chor¹ /ˈæŋkəʳ/ n a heavy hooked metal object that is dropped into the water to stop a boat moving away

anchor² v **1** [I] to stop sailing and lower the anchor: *We anchored just off Cape Town.* **2** [T] to fix something firmly into a place or a position

an·chor·age /ˈæŋkərɪdʒ/ n a place where ships may stop and lower their anchor

an·cho·vy /ˈæntʃəvi ‖ ˈæntʃəʊvi/ n anchovies a small fish with a strong, salty taste

an·cient /ˈeɪnʃənt/ adj **1** belonging to times long ago: *ancient Rome* | *ancient ruins* **2** very old: *That car's ancient!*

an·cil·la·ry /ænˈsɪləri ‖ ˈænsɪləri/ adj fml or tech providing help or support for the people who work in an organization

and /ənd, ən, *strong* ænd/ conj **1** used to join two words or expressions: *I need a knife and fork.* | *my mother and father* | *He was cold and hungry.* | *She started shouting and screaming.* | *Three hundred and fifty people were there.* **2** used to show that two things happen at the same time or almost at the same time: *I looked at the book and realized that it* *was not the one I wanted.* | *I woke up and got out of bed.*

an·ec·dote /ˈænɪkdəʊt/ *n* a short amusing story about something that has happened –**anecdotal** /ˌænɪkˈdəʊtl◂/ *adj*

a·ne·mi·a /əˈniːmiə/ *n* see ANAEMIA

a·nem·o·ne /əˈneməni/ *n* **1** a garden plant with red, white, or blue flowers **2** a small sea animal with a jelly-like body

an·es·the·si·a /ˌænɪsˈθiːziə || -ʒə/ *n* see ANAESTHESIA

anesthetic *n* see ANAESTHETIC

anesthetist *n* see ANAESTHETIST

anesthetize *v* see ANAESTHETIZE

a·new /əˈnjuː || əˈnuː/ *adv lit* in a new or different way: *beginning life anew after retirement*

an·gel /ˈeɪndʒəl/ *n* **1** a messenger from God, usually represented as a person with wings and dressed in white **2** a person who is very kind and cares for others –**angelic** /ænˈdʒelɪk/ *adj*

an·ger¹ /ˈæŋgəʳ/ *n* [U] a strong feeling of displeasure that you feel when someone has behaved in a cruel or unkind way towards you :*She returned, full of anger at the way she had been treated.* | *I can feel nothing but anger at your behaviour.*

anger² *v* [T] to make someone feel angry: *His attitude had angered me.*

an·gle¹ /ˈæŋgəl/ *n* **1** the space between two lines that meet or cross each other, measured in degrees: *The roads join at an angle of 90 degrees.* **2** at an angle sloping, and not upright or straight: *The plant was growing at an angle.* **3** a point of view: *We need to tackle this problem from a different angle.*

angle² *v* **angled, angling** [T] **1** to represent something from a particular point of view: *She angles her reports to suit the reader.* **2** be angling for something to be trying to make someone offer something to you without asking for it directly

an·gler /ˈæŋgləʳ/ *n* someone who fishes with a hook and line

An·gli·can /ˈæŋglɪkən/ *n* a member of a branch of the Christian religion –**Anglican** *adj*

an·gli·cize /ˈæŋglɪsaɪz/ *v* **anglicized, anglicizing** (also **anglicise** *BrE*) [T] to make something sound or appear English

an·gling /ˈæŋglɪŋ/ *n* [U] the activity of fishing with a hook and line: *angling equipment* –**angling** *v* [I; only in progressive forms] : *I really enjoy angling.*

An·glo-Sax·on /ˌæŋgləʊ ˈsæksən/ *n* a member of the people who lived in England from about 600 to 1066 AD –**Anglo-Saxon** *adj*

an·gry /ˈæŋgri/ *adj* **angrier, angriest** very annoyed: *He gets angry at the slightest thing.* | *It really makes me feel angry.* | *I'm very angry with him.* –**angrily** *adv*

■ USAGE Do not use **angry** to describe a person's character. Instead, use words like **quick-tempered** (fairly weak) or **bad-tempered** (stronger).

an·guish /ˈæŋgwɪʃ/ *n* [U] very great grief or pain: *She suffered great anguish.* –**anguished** *adj* : *anguished cries*

an·gu·lar /ˈæŋgjɪləʳ/ *adj* **1** having sharp corners **2** very thin (used of people): *her thin angular face*

an·i·mal¹ /ˈænɪməl/ *n* a living creature; "animal" is sometimes used for all living creatures, sometimes for all creatures except humans, and sometimes just for mammals (MAMMAL): *The forest is full* of wild animals. | Of all the animals, we are the cleverest.

animal² *adj* **1** connected with animals or made from animals: *animal fats* **2** concerning only your body, not your mind or spirit: *We are told to suppress our animal instincts.*

an·i·mate¹ /ˈænɪmɪt/ *adj* having life –**opposite inanimate**

an·i·mate² /ˈænɪmeɪt/ *v* **animated, animating animate someone's face** to make someone look excited and full of life: *Laughter animated his face for a moment.*

an·i·ma·ted /ˈænɪmeɪtɪd/ *adj* full of life and excitement: *an animated debate*

an·i·ma·tion /ˌænɪˈmeɪʃən/ *n* [U] **1** excitement and interest: *They were full of animation as they talked of their holiday.* **2** the making of films in which people and things that are drawn seem to move and talk

an·i·mos·i·ty /ˌænɪˈmɒsɪti || -ˈmɑː-/ *n* **animosities** [C;U] a feeling of hatred and anger: *There was a lot of animosity between the two countries.*

an·i·seed /ˈænɪsiːd/ *n* [U] the strong-tasting seeds of a plant; aniseed is used in sweets, medicines, and alcoholic drinks

an·kle /ˈæŋkəl/ *n* the part of your body where your foot joins your leg

an·nals /ˈænəlz/ *n* [pl] *fml* a record of the past events of a nation or society, written year by year: *She has an important place in the annals of British politics.*

an·nex /əˈneks || əˈneks, ˈæneks/ *v* [T] to take control of land or property without permission: *The country was annexed at the beginning of the war.* –**annexation** /ˌænekˈseɪʃən/ *n* [C;U] : *the annexation of Austria*

an·nexe /ˈæneks/ *n* (**annex** *AmE*) a building joined to or positioned near the main building: *a hospital annexe*

an·ni·hi·late /əˈnaɪəleɪt/ *v* **annihilated, annihilating** [T] to destroy something or defeat someone completely: *The city had been virtually annihilated.* –**annihilation** /əˌnaɪəˈleɪʃən/ *n* [U]

an·ni·ver·sa·ry /ˌænɪˈvɜːsəri || -ɜːr-/ *n* **anniversaries** a date which is remembered because it is an exact number of years after an event: *Today is the tenth anniversary of the country's independence.* | *our wedding anniversary*

An·no Dom·i·ni /ˌænəʊ ˈdɒmɪnaɪ || -ˈdɑː-/ *fml* see AD

an·no·tate /ˈænəteɪt/ *v* **annotated, annotating** [T] *fml* to add notes to a book in order to explain certain parts of it: *an annotated text* –**annotation** /ˌænəˈteɪʃən/ *n* [C;U]

an·nounce /əˈnaʊns/ *v* **announced, announcing 1** [T; + that] to state something publicly: *He suddenly announced that he was leaving.* | *The winner of the competition will be announced later today.* | *The election results were announced to the waiting crowd.* | *"John's dead," she announced.*

☐ USEFUL PATTERNS to announce something; to announce something to someone; to announce that...

2 [T] to introduce people when they arrive at a formal occasion: *The guest of honour was announced.*

an·nounce·ment /əˈnaʊnsmənt/ *n* **1** [C] a public statement: *I've got an important announcement to make.* **2** [U] the act of saying something publicly: *the announcement of the trade figures*

an·nounc·er /əˈnaʊnsəʳ/ n a person who gives information to people, especially on radio or television

an·noy /əˈnɔɪ/ v [T] to make someone feel rather angry: *He was beginning to annoy me.*

an·noy·ance /əˈnɔɪəns/ n 1 [U] the feeling of being annoyed: *He showed signs of annoyance.* 2 [C] something which annoys you: *The noisy traffic is a continual annoyance.*

an·noy·ing /əˈnɔɪ-ɪŋ/ adj making you feel angry: *an annoying delay*

an·nu·al¹ /ˈænjuəl/ adj 1 happening or done every year or once a year: *an annual holiday | the annual meeting* 2 calculated over a period of one year: *What's his annual income?* –**annually** adv

annual² n 1 a plant that lives for only one year or one season 2 a book or magazine for children which appears once each year

an·nu·i·ty /əˈnjuːɪ̣ti ‖ əˈnuː-/ n **annuities** a fixed sum of money paid each year to a person for a stated number of years or until they die

an·nul /əˈnʌl/ v -ll- [T] tech to declare officially that a marriage, agreement, or law no longer exists –**annulment** n [C;U]

an·ode /ˈænəʊd/ n tech the part of an electrical instrument such as a BATTERY which collects electrons (ELECTRON); the anode is often a rod or wire shown as (+)

a·noint /əˈnɔɪnt/ v [T] to put oil or water onto a person's head as part of a religious ceremony

a·nom·a·ly /əˈnɒməli ‖ əˈnɑː-/ n **anomalies** fml a person, thing, or fact that is different from what is usual and which may be impossible to explain –**anomalous** /əˈnɒmələs ‖ əˈnɑː-/ adj : *anomalous results*

a·non¹ /əˈnɒn ‖ əˈnɑːn/ adv lit or infml soon: *See you anon.*

anon² a word written at the end of a piece of writing to show that it is not known who wrote it; an abbreviation for ANONYMOUS

a·non·y·mous /əˈnɒnɪ̣məs ‖ əˈnɑː-/ adj done, made, or given by someone whose name is not known: *an anonymous letter | an anonymous gift* –**anonymously** adv

an·o·nym·i·ty /ˌænəˈnɪmɪ̣ti/ n [U] 1 the condition of not having your name known: *The author prefers anonymity.* 2 the condition of not having any interesting and different qualities: *the anonymity of hotel rooms*

an·o·rak /ˈænəræk/ n BrE a short coat with a cover for your head –see picture on page 50

an·o·rex·ic /ˌænəˈreksɪk/ adj suffering from a disease which makes you very afraid of becoming fat, and so afraid to eat

an·oth·er /əˈnʌðəʳ/ det, pron 1 one more of the same kind: *Would you like another biscuit? | I had one drink, then decided that I needed another.* 2 a different one: *This car's falling to bits. We must get another one. | We were glad the war was happening in another country. | The women were in one room, the men in another.*

an·swer¹ /ˈɑːnsəʳ ‖ ˈæn-/ n 1 [C;U] a reply to what someone says, asks, or does: *He rang the doorbell but there was no answer. | She can't give us an answer yet. | I think I know the answer to your problem. | Her only answer to their threat was to laugh.* 2 **in answer to something** as a reply to what someone says, asks, or does: *In answer to your previous question: I don't think so.* 3 [C] a result

which you get when calculating with numbers: *The answer is 255.* 4 [C] an action which gets rid of a problem: *There is no easy answer to the problem of unemployment.*

answer² v 1 [I;T;+that] to reply to something someone has said or asked: *You didn't answer his question. | Why didn't you answer? | Answer your mother, John! | I answered with a smile. | He asked her why, but she answered that she didn't know. | "I don't know," she answered.*
□ USEFUL PATTERNS to answer; to answer someone; to answer a question; to answer that…: "…" she answered
2 **answer the telephone** to pick up the telephone when it rings 3 **answer the door** to open the door when someone knocks on it 4 **answer a description, answer to a description** to fit a description: *The police have seen a man answering to his description.*
■ USAGE Compare **answer, reply, respond.** 1 **Answer** and **reply** are both common verbs for answering questions, but **reply** is a little more formal. **Respond** is very formal. 2 With an object we must use *to* after **reply** and **respond**, but not after **answer**. Compare *They did not* **answer** *my question* and *They did not* **reply to/respond to** *my enquiry.*
answer back phr v [I;T **answer** sbdy **back**] infml to reply rudely: *Don't answer me back!*
answer for phr v 1 [T **answer for** sbdy/sthg] to state that someone has certain qualities: *I can answer for his honesty.* 2 [T **answer for** sthg] to be punished for an action: *One day you will have to answer for this.* 3 **have a lot to answer for** to have done a lot of things that have had bad results: *Town-planners have a lot to answer for.*

an·swer·a·ble /ˈɑːnsərəbəl ‖ ˈæn-/ adj **answerable to someone, answerable for something** having to explain your actions to someone: *He is answerable to the Managing Director. | We should be answerable for all our actions.*

ant /ænt/ n a small insect which lives on the ground in large groups

an·tag·o·nis·m /ænˈtægənɪzəm/ n [U] active opposition or hatred between people or groups: *The two men felt a strong antagonism* **towards** *each other.*

an·tag·o·nist /ænˈtægənɪ̣st/ n an opponent in a fight or competition

an·tag·o·nis·tic /æn͵tægəˈnɪstɪk/ adj showing opposition or hatred towards someone

an·tag·o·nize /ænˈtægənaɪz/ v **antagonized, antagonizing** (also **antagonise** BrE) [T] to make someone feel angry with you: *I wouldn't antagonize him, if I were you.*

Ant·arc·tic /ænˈtɑːktɪk ‖ -ɑːr-/ n **the Antarctic** the very cold most southern part of the world

an·te·ced·ent /ˌæntɪ̣ˈsiːdənt/ n fml a person, thing, or event that comes before something related to it

an·te·date /ˈæntɪdeɪt, ˌæntɪˈdeɪt/ v **antedated, antedating** [T] fml to come before something else in time

an·te·lope /ˈæntɪ̣ləʊp ‖ ˈæntəl-/ n a graceful animal like a deer, able to run very fast

an·te·na·tal /ˌæntɪˈneɪtl◂/ adj [only before a noun] tech of the period of time before a woman gives birth: *an antenatal clinic*

an·ten·na /ænˈtenə/ n 1 [plural is **antennae** /-niː/] one of two long thin sensitive organs on the heads of some insects 2 [plural is **antennas**] AmE the AERIAL of a radio or television

an·ter·i·or /æn'tɪəriəʳ/ adj 1 fml earlier in time 2 tech nearer the front

an·them /'ænθəm/ n a religious song of praise written for a special occasion

an·thol·o·gy /æn'θɒlədʒi ‖ æn'θɑː-/ n anthologies a collection of works by different writers in one book: an anthology of poetry

an·thro·poid /'ænθrəpɔɪd/ adj like a human: anthropoid apes

an·thro·pol·o·gy /ˌænθrə'pɒlədʒi ‖ -'pɑː-/ n [U] the scientific study of the human race, including its different beliefs, customs, and social habits –anthropologist n –anthropological /ˌænθrəpə-'lɒdʒɪkəl ‖ -'lɑː-/ adj

an·ti·bi·ot·ic /ˌæntɪbaɪ'ɒtɪk ‖ -'ɑː-/ n a drug such as PENICILLIN, which is used to destroy harmful bacteria and to cure infections in a person's body

an·ti·bod·y /'æntɪˌbɒdi ‖ -ˌbɑː-/ n antibodies a substance produced in the blood which fights infection

an·tic·i·pate /æn'tɪsɪˌpeɪt/ v anticipated, anticipating 1 [T; +that] to expect something: He's anticipating trouble when the factory opens again. | We anticipate that there will be a lot of opposition to the plan. | I anticipated meeting a few problems.
☐ USEFUL PATTERNS to anticipate something; to anticipate doing something; to anticipate that... 2 [T; +that] to see what is likely to happen and taken action in order to be ready: I tried to anticipate the kind of questions they might ask me at the interview. | We had anticipated that the enemy would try to cross the river and had destroyed the bridge.
☐ USEFUL PATTERNS to anticipate something; to anticipate that... –anticipation /æn,tɪsɪ'peɪʃən/ n [U] –anticipatory /æn,tɪsɪ'peɪtəri ‖ æn'tɪsə-pətɔːri/ adj

an·ti·cli·max /ˌæntɪ'klaɪmæks/ n something unexciting, ordinary, or disappointing, which comes after something exciting: Coming home again was a bit of an anticlimax.

an·ti·clock·wise /ˌæntɪ'klɒkwaɪz ‖ -'klɑːk-/ adj,adv (counterclockwise AmE) in the opposite direction to the movement of the hands of a clock: Turn it anticlockwise.

an·tics /'æntɪks/ n [pl] odd behaviour, usually intended to amuse people

an·ti·cy·clone /ˌæntɪ'saɪkləʊn/ n tech an area of high air pressure, causing either hot or cold settled weather conditions

an·ti·dote /'æntɪdəʊt/ n 1 a substance that stops or controls a poison working inside a person's body: The poison has no known antidote. 2 something which helps you to change a difficult situation: We need an antidote to our present political troubles.

an·ti·freeze /'æntɪfriːz/ n [U] a chemical substance put in water to stop it from freezing; antifreeze is used especially in car engines

an·tip·a·thy /æn'tɪpəθi/ n [U] a strong feeling of dislike or hatred: the President's well-known antipathy to trade unions –antipathetic /ˌæntɪpə'θetɪk/ adj

an·ti·quat·ed /'æntɪˌkweɪtɪd/ adj belonging to the past and not suited to modern needs or conditions: antiquated laws | an antiquated machine –see OLD (USAGE)

an·tique /æn'tiːk/ n an old object, such as a piece of jewellery or furniture, which is rare and valuable

an·tiq·ui·ty /æn'tɪkwɪti/ n antiquities 1 [C] a building, ruin, or work of art from the ancient world, especially from ancient Rome or Greece 2 [U] ancient times: the temples of antiquity 3 [U] great age: a building of great antiquity

an·ti-Sem·i·tis·m /ˌæntɪ 'semɪtɪzəm/ n [U] hatred of the Jewish people –anti-Semitic /-sɪ'mɪtɪk/ adj

an·ti·sep·tic /ˌæntɪ'septɪk◂/ n [C; U] a chemical substance able to prevent infection in a wound by killing harmful bacteria

an·ti·so·cial /ˌæntɪ'səʊʃəl/ adj 1 causing annoyance by showing no concern for other people: It's antisocial to play your radio so loud at this time of the night. 2 not liking to mix with other people: Jane's very friendly, but her husband's rather antisocial.

an·tith·e·sis /æn'tɪθəsɪs/ n antitheses /-siːz/ the exact opposite of something: The antithesis of death is life.

ant·ler /'æntləʳ/ n one of the long horns with branches on the head of a male deer

an·to·nym /'æntənɪm/ n tech a word opposite in meaning to another word; for example, "hot" is the antonym of "cold".

a·nus /'eɪnəs/ n tech the opening through which solid food waste leaves your bowels

an·vil /'ænvɪl/ n an iron block on which hot metals are hammered and shaped

anx·i·e·ty /æŋ'zaɪəti/ n anxieties [C;U] 1 a feeling of fear and worry about something uncertain: I sensed her anxiety. | Sometimes it helps to talk about your fears and anxieties. 2 great eagerness to do something and worry that you might not be able to do it

anx·ious /'æŋkʃəs/ adj 1 nervous or troubled: I was rather anxious about the children when they didn't come home from school. | an anxious wait for our examination results 2 very eager to do something: She was anxious not to offend her guests. | We were anxious that everyone should know the truth. | He was anxious for news.
☐ USEFUL PATTERNS be anxious to do something; be anxious that someone should do something; be anxious for something –see NERVOUS (USAGE) –anxiously adv

an·y¹ /'eni/ det, pron 1 no matter which one or no matter what kind: They're all free – take any you like. | Any child would know that. | Any help would be welcome. 2 [used only in negatives and questions] some: Have you got any money? | He hasn't got any imagination. | Are there any letters for me? I never seem to get any. –see SOME (USAGE)

any² adv [used only in negatives and questions] at all: I can't stay any longer. | Do you feel any better?

an·y·bod·y /'eni,bɒdi, 'enibədi ‖ -,bɑːdi/ pron (also anyone) 1 any person or people, no matter who: Anybody can cook if they try. | He thinks he's cleverer than anyone else. 2 [used only in negatives and questions] any person: Is there anybody there? | There wasn't anyone in the building. | If anybody asks for you, I'll tell them you've gone out. –see EVERYBODY (USAGE)

an·y·how /'enihaʊ/ adv 1 carelessly, not in a regular or ordered way: His clothes had been thrown down just anyhow. 2 see ANYWAY

an·y·one /'eniwʌn/ pron see ANYBODY
■ USAGE Compare anyone and any one. Anyone refers to a person: I don't want anyone to know my secret. Any one can refer to a person or thing and it is often followed by of: There are three possible answers and I can accept any one of them.

an·y·thing /'eniθɪŋ/ pron 1 [used only in negatives and questions] any thing: There wasn't anything in the cupboard. | You can't believe anything she says. |

Would you like anything to eat? **2** any thing or things, no matter what: *Surely anything's better than a war!* | *He'll do anything for a quiet life.* **3 anything but** not at all: *She's anything but poor!* **4 not anything like** not at all: *It isn't anything like as cold as it was yesterday.* **5 as easy as anything, as fast as anything,** etc. very easy, fast, etc.: *The exam was as easy as anything.* **6 or anything** a phrase used to say that there are other possibilities: *Would you like a biscuit or anything?*

an·y·way /ˈeniweɪ/ *adv* (also **anyhow**) **1** used when you are saying something which supports something else that you have just said: *I don't think he's the right person for the job, and he hasn't got any qualifications anyway.* **2** used when you are saying that something is true in spite of something else: *It wasn't quite the right colour, but I bought it anyway.* **3** used when you are continuing with a story or changing the subject: *Anyway, I must go now, so I'll talk to you later.*

an·y·where /ˈeniweəʳ/ *adv* **1** in or to any place, no matter where: *Sit anywhere you like.* | *I'd be willing to go and work anywhere in the world.* **2** [used only in negatives and questions] in or to any place: *Did you go anywhere yesterday?* | *We didn't go anywhere on holiday this year.*

a·part /əˈpɑːt ‖ -ɑːrt/ *adv* **1** separated by a distance: *She was standing a little apart from the others.* | *The two buildings are three miles apart.* | *He and his wife are living apart.* **2** into parts: *He took the clock apart to repair it.* | *I'm afraid the chair has fallen apart.* **3 apart from: a** except for: *a good piece of work, apart from a few slight faults* **b** in addition to: *The Government has plenty of problems to deal with, apart from inflation.* **4 tell apart** to be able to see the difference between things: *I can't tell the two boys apart.*

a·part·heid /əˈpɑːtheɪt, -teɪt, -taɪt, -taɪd ‖ -ɑːrt-/ *n* [U] the political separation by law of people of different races, especially the separation of black and white people in South Africa

a·part·ment /əˈpɑːtmənt ‖ -ɑːrt-/ *n* **1** the usual American word for FLAT⁴ –see HOUSE¹ (USAGE) **2** a large or splendid room: *the Royal Apartments*

apartment house /·ʹ··· ·/ *AmE* a large building containing many apartments

ap·a·thet·ic /ˌæpəˈθetɪk◄/ *adj* not interested in anything: *This year's students are a rather apathetic bunch.* –**apathetically** /-kli/ *adv*

ap·a·thy /ˈæpəθi/ *n* [U] lack of interest, or lack of desire to do something: *There is a sense of public apathy about the government's latest policies.*

ape¹ /eɪp/ *n* an animal like a monkey, but larger and without a tail; a GORILLA is a kind of ape

ape² *v* **aped, aping** [T] to try to copy a person's behaviour, manners, or speech

a·per·i·tif /əˌperəˈtiːf/ *n* an alcoholic drink that people have before a meal

ap·er·ture /ˈæpətʃəʳ ‖ ˈæpərtʃʊər/ *n* a hole, crack, or other narrow opening

a·pex /ˈeɪpeks/ *n* the top or highest point of something: *the apex of a triangle* | *the apex of his career*

a·phid /ˈeɪfɪd, ˈæfɪd/ *n* a small insect that lives by sucking the juices of plants

aph·o·ris·m /ˈæfərɪzəm/ *n* a short and clever saying that expresses something that people believe to be true

aph·ro·dis·i·ac /ˌæfrəˈdɪziæk/ *n* a medicine or drug that causes sexual excitement

a·piece /əˈpiːs/ *adv old fash* each: *The apples cost sixpence apiece.*

a·pol·o·get·ic /əˌpɒləˈdʒetɪk◄ ‖ əˌpɑː-/ *adj* saying that you are sorry for doing something wrong or causing trouble: *was very apologetic.* | *He wrote me an apologetic letter.* –**apologetically** /-kli/ *adv*: *He smiled apologetically.*

a·pol·o·gize /əˈpɒlədʒaɪz ‖ əˈpɑː-/ *v* **apologized, apologizing** (also **apologise** *Br E*) [I] to say that you are sorry for doing something wrong or causing trouble: *I'll apologize to her tomorrow.* | *He apologized for being late.* | *She didn't even apologize!*

a·pol·o·gy /əˈpɒlədʒi ‖ əˈpɑː-/ *n* **apologies** **1** [C;U] a statement saying that you are sorry for doing something wrong or causing trouble: *That is completely untrue – I demand an immediate apology.* | *Please accept our apologies for any inconvenience we have caused.* | *She can't come; she sends her apologies.* | *I wrote a letter of apology.* **2 an apology for** something *infml* a very bad example of something

ap·o·plex·y /ˈæpəpleksi/ *n* [U] *old fash* a serious illness in which you suddenly lose the ability to move or feel anything –**apoplectic** /ˌæpəˈplektɪk◄/ *adj*

a·pos·tle /əˈpɒsəl ‖ əˈpɑː-/ *n* **1** one of the 12 men chosen by Jesus Christ to teach his message **2** a person who believes strongly in certain ideas and tries to spread them

a·pos·tro·phe /əˈpɒstrəfi ‖ əˈpɑː-/ *n* the sign (') used in writing **a** to show that one or more letters or figures have been left out (as in *don't* for *do not* and *'47* for *1947*) **b** before or after *s* to show possession or relation (as in *John's coat, James' coat, St James's Park, lady's coat, ladies' coats, children's coats*) **c** before *s* to show the plural of letters and figures (as in *There are 2 f's in "off"* and *Your 8's look like S's*.)

ap·pal /əˈpɔːl/ *v* **appalled, appalling** (**appall** *AmE*) [T] to shock someone so deeply that they are very upset: *We were appalled to hear that she had been murdered.* | *People were appalled by reports of the famine.* | *I was appalled at how old she looked.*

ap·pal·ling /əˈpɔːlɪŋ/ *adj* **1** shocking and terrible **2** *infml* very bad: *an appalling waste* | *an absolutely appalling play* –**appallingly** *adv*

ap·pa·ra·tus /ˌæpəˈreɪtəs ‖ -ˈræ-/ *n* [C;U] a set of instruments, machines, tools, or materials needed for a particular purpose: *a piece of apparatus in a gym* | *The television men set up their apparatus ready to film.*

ap·par·el /əˈpærəl/ *n* [U] clothes worn on an important occasion (a word no longer used in modern English)

ap·par·ent /əˈpærənt/ *adj* **1** clearly seen or understood: *Her anxiety was apparent to everyone.* | *The reasons for his anger soon became apparent.* **2** seeming to be real or to exist: *I was shocked by his apparent lack of concern for other people.*

ap·par·ent·ly /əˈpærəntli/ *adv* **1** a word used when you do not know something for certain, but have heard that it is true: *I wasn't there, but apparently she tried to drown him.* | *"Did she succeed?" "Apparently not."* **2** seeming to be but not necessarily so: *She looked up and smiled, apparently pleased to see him.*

ap·pa·ri·tion /ˌæpəˈrɪʃən/ *n* a dead person that you think you see appearing as a spirit

ap·peal¹ /əˈpiːl/ *n* **1** [C;U] a strong request for something: *His appeal for help went unanswered.* | *Local* *people are launching an appeal for money to build a new hall.* **2** [U] the power to make you feel attracted or interested: *Films of that sort have lost their appeal.* **3** [C;U] a request to a higher court to change the decision of a lower court: *You have the right of appeal.* | *His appeal was turned down by the High Court.*

appeal² *v* [I] **1** to make a strong request for something: *The government is appealing to everyone to save water.* | *The charity appealed for more money.* **2 appeal to someone** to please, attract, or interest someone: *Does the idea of working abroad appeal to you?* | *His books don't appeal to me at all.* **3** to request a higher law court to change the decision of a lower court

ap·peal·ing /ə'piːlɪŋ/ *adj* **1** showing that you want something: *He gave me an appealing look.* **2** attractive or interesting: *The idea of a free holiday is rather appealing.* –opposite **unappealing** (for sense 2) –**appealingly** *adv*

ap·pear /ə'pɪə^r/ *v* **1** [I] to come into view: *A ship appeared on the horizon.* **2** [I] to begin to be seen or used: *Several new products have recently appeared on the market.* | *Credit cards first appeared about 20 years ago.* **3** [I;+complement] to seem: *She appeared upset at the news.* | *He appears to be very happy.* | *People appear to like this new product.* □ USEFUL PATTERNS **to appear to be something; to appear to do something; to appear + adj** **4 it appears that…** a phrase used when you are saying that something seems to be true, although you find it surprising: *It appears that he no longer works for the company.* | *It appears that I was wrong.* **5** [I] to be printed and put on sale: *His first novel appeared last month.* **6** [I] to be present in a court when you have been accused of a crime: *He appeared in court, charged with attempted murder.* **7** [I] to perform publicly in a play, show, or film: *He's currently appearing in "Hamlet" at the National Theatre.*

ap·pear·ance /ə'pɪərəns/ *n* **1** [sing] coming into view or arrival: *The thieves ran off at the appearance of the police.* | *His sudden appearance shocked everyone.* **2** the time when something is first present or first used: *Television viewing has increased since the appearance of satellite TV.* **3** the way you look to other people: *Her pale appearance worried her mother.* | *He gave the appearance of being bored.* **4** a public performance in a play, show, or film: *His first public appearance was at the age of 5.* **5** the official presence of a person in court when they have been accused of a crime **6 keep up appearances** to continue to behave in your usual way because you are too proud to admit to other people that you have suffered a loss of money or social position **7 put in an appearance** to go to an event for a short time: *I suppose I'd better put in an appearance at the party.* **8 to all appearances** a phrase used when you are saying that something seems to be true: *To all appearances he seems happy.*

ap·pease /ə'piːz/ *v* **appeased, appeasing** [T] to make someone calm or less angry by giving them what they want –**appeasement** *n*

ap·pend /ə'pend/ *v* [T] *fml* to write something at the end of a longer piece of writing: *I append a list of those shops which sell our products.*

ap·pend·age /ə'pendɪdʒ/ *n* something that is joined to something larger or more important

ap·pen·di·ci·tis /ə,pendɪ'saɪtɪs/ *n* [U] a painful condition caused when your appendix becomes infected

ap·pen·dix /ə'pendɪks/ *n* **appendixes** or **appendices** /-dɪsiːz/ **1** a small tube in your body which is closed at one end and joined to your bowel at the other end **2** additional information which is placed at the end of a book

ap·per·tain /,æpə'teɪn ‖ -ər-/ *v* *fml* **appertain to something** to belong or be related to something: *the responsibilities appertaining to the leadership*

ap·pe·tite /'æpɪtaɪt/ *n* [C;U] a strong physical desire for something, especially food: *Don't eat any sweets before dinner or you'll spoil your appetite.* | *I completely lost my appetite while I was ill.* –see DESIRE² (USAGE)

ap·pe·tiz·er /'æpɪtaɪzə^r/ *n* something small which you eat or drink before a meal

ap·pe·tiz·ing /'æpɪtaɪzɪŋ/ *adj* looking and smelling good and therefore making you feel hungry (used of food) –opposite **unappetizing**

ap·plaud /ə'plɔːd/ *v* [I;T] **1** to show that you liked a play, actor, or performance by hitting your hands together **2** to express strong approval of someone or something: *We must applaud the council's decision not to close the hospital.*

ap·plause /ə'plɔːz/ *n* [U] loud praise for a performance or performer, in which people hit their hands together repeatedly

ap·ple /'æpəl/ *n* **1** a hard round fruit with white juicy flesh and red, green, or yellow skin –see picture on page 344 **2 be the apple of your eye** *infml* to be the person or thing that you love the most: *He was the apple of his father's eye.*

ap·pli·ance /ə'plaɪəns/ *n* a machine that does a particular job in your home: *electrical appliances such as dishwashers and washing machines* –see MACHINE¹ (USAGE)

ap·pli·ca·ble /ə'plɪkəbəl, 'æplɪkəbəl/ *adj* suitable for or relating directly to a particular person or situation: *This rule is not applicable to foreigners.*

ap·pli·cant /'æplɪkənt/ *n* a person who makes a formal, written request, for example for a job or university place

ap·pli·ca·tion /,æplɪ'keɪʃən/ *n* **1** [C] a formal written request for something: *I wrote five applications for jobs but got nothing.* | *Do I have to fill in an application form?* **2 on application** by making a formal written request: *Details will be sent on application.* **3** [C;U] the putting of something to practical use: *Let's see if the results of the survey have a practical application.* **4** [C;U] the process of putting something onto a surface: *a second application of paint* **5** [U] careful and continuous attention or effort: *He worked with great application to learn a new language.*

ap·plied /ə'plaɪd/ *adj* able to be used in a practical way: *applied mathematics* –opposite **pure**

ap·ply /ə'plaɪ/ *v* **applied, applying** **1** [I] to request something, especially in writing: *I'll apply for the job today.* **2** [T] to use something such as a method or a law: *Apply as much force as is necessary.* | *to apply a new method* **3** [T] to put something onto a surface: *Apply some medicine to the wound.* **4** [I] to have an effect on something or to be directly related to it: *This rule doesn't apply.* | *This question applies only to married men.* **5 apply yourself, apply your mind** to work hard with careful attention: *He applied himself to his work.*

ap·point /ə'pɔɪnt/ *v* [T] **1** to choose someone formally for a position or job: *We must appoint a new teacher soon.* | *They appointed him to be chairman.*

2 *fml* to arrange or decide a time or day on which to do something: *Let's appoint a day for our next meeting.* –**appointed** *adj* : *She wasn't there at the appointed time.*

ap·point·ment /ə'pɔɪntmənt/ *n* **1** [C] an arrangement to meet someone at a particular time and place, especially a formal or official meeting: *I have an appointment* with *the doctor.* | *Make an appointment to see your dentist as soon as possible.* | *I'm afraid I won't be able to keep my appointment.* **2** by appointment by arranging to meet at a particular time: *The doctor will only see you by appointment.* **3** [U] the choosing of someone for a position or job: *He is responsible for the appointment of all new staff.* **4** [C] a job: *I've applied for a teaching appointment in London.*

ap·por·tion /ə'pɔːʃən ‖ -ɔːr-/ *v* [T] *fml* to divide something and share it out: *It was difficult to apportion the blame for the accident.* | *He apportioned his possessions among his children.*

ap·praise /ə'preɪz/ *v* appraised, appraising [T] *fml* to judge the value, quality, or condition of something: *The students' work is carefully appraised.* –**appraisal** *n*

ap·pre·cia·ble /ə'priːʃəbəl/ *adj* enough to be felt, noticed, or considered important: *an appreciable difference* –**appreciably** *adv*

ap·pre·ci·ate /ə'priːʃieɪt/ *v* appreciated, appreciating **1** [T] to understand and enjoy the good qualities or value of something: *They don't appreciate good wine.* | *I appreciate your help.* **2 I would appreciate it if…** a rather formal phrase used to ask someone to do something: *We would appreciate it if you would provide further information.* **3** [T; + that] to understand something: *I do appreciate the fact that the project will be very expensive.* | *We*

appreciate that the task will not be easy. **4** [I] to increase in value over time: *Houses in this area have all appreciated in value since the new road was built.* –**appreciation** /ə‚priːʃi'eɪʃən/ *n* [C;U]

ap·pre·cia·tive /ə'priːʃətɪv/ *adj* feeling or showing understanding, admiration, or gratefulness –**appreciatively** *adv*

ap·pre·hend /‚æprɪ'hend/ *v* [T] *fml* to take a person who breaks the law into police control

ap·pre·hen·sion /‚æprɪ'henʃən/ *n* **1** [U] anxiety or fear about the future: *She waited for news with great apprehension.* **2** [C;U] *fml* the act of seizing a person who breaks the law

ap·pre·hen·sive /‚æprɪ'hensɪv/ *adj* worried or anxious about what might happen –**apprehensively** *adv*

ap·pren·tice /ə'prentɪs/ *n* a person who has agreed to work for a skilled employer for a fixed period and usually for low wages, in order to learn a skill

ap·pren·tice·ship /ə'prentɪsʃɪp/ *n* [C;U] the time you spend as an apprentice: *I've got to serve a three year apprenticeship.*

ap·proach¹ /ə'prəʊtʃ/ *v* **1** [I;T] to move nearer to something or someone: *We approached the house.* | *I moved out of the way as the procession approached.* | *Inflation is approaching 10%.* **2** [I;T] to come nearer in time: *The day was fast approaching when we would have to leave.* **3** [T] to speak to someone about something for the first time, especially to ask for something or offer something: *Did he approach you about lending him some money?* **4** [T] to begin to consider something: *He approached the difficulty with great thought.*

approach² *n* **1** [U] the act of moving nearer to something or someone: *At our approach, the*

CAR

Exercise 1

There are 10 mistakes in this passage. Change the words in bold type to correct the mistakes.

Mr Sampson opened the **bonnet** and put his briefcase on the back seat of the car. Then he got in, put his key in the **glove compartment** and started the engine. He put his foot on the **brake pedal** and moved the gear lever into first gear. Before driving off, he adjusted the **heater** so that he could see the traffic behind him. It was still dark so Mr Sampson switched on his **reversing light** so that he could see the road in front of him.

As he approached the town he looked at the **mileometer** and noticed that he was running out of petrol. There was a filling station on the left so Mr Sampson switched on his **windscreen wipers** to show that he was going to turn left. Then he put his foot on the **accelerator** because he wanted to slow down.

He stopped beside a petrol pump and took off the **hub cap** so that the attendant could fill the petrol tank. "Perhaps I need some oil as well," thought Mr Sampson "I'd better check." So he opened the boot and looked inside. "That's strange," he thought "I'm sure I had an engine when I left home!"

What mistake has Mr Sampson made?

Exercise 2

Think of your own car or a car you know well. How many of these things has it got?

wheels	windscreen wipers
steering wheel	indicator lights
aerial	rear view mirror
door mirrors	seat belts
wings	gears

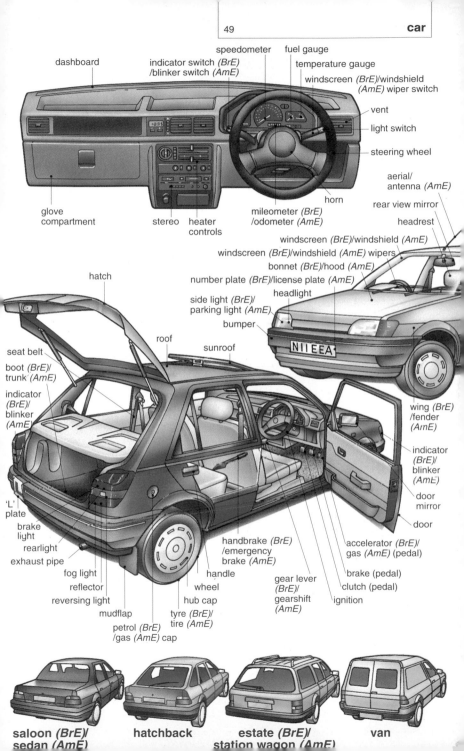

dashboard

speedometer

fuel gauge

indicator switch *(BrE)*/blinker switch *(AmE)*

temperature gauge

windscreen *(BrE)*/windshield *(AmE)* wiper switch

vent

light switch

steering wheel

aerial/antenna *(AmE)*

rear view mirror

headrest

horn

glove compartment

stereo

heater controls

mileometer *(BrE)*/odometer *(AmE)*

windscreen *(BrE)*/windshield *(AmE)*

windscreen *(BrE)*/windshield *(AmE)* wipers

bonnet *(BrE)*/hood *(AmE)*

number plate *(BrE)*/license plate *(AmE)*

hatch

side light *(BrE)*/parking light *(AmE)*

headlight

bumper

roof

sunroof

seat belt

boot *(BrE)*/trunk *(AmE)*

indicator *(BrE)*/blinker *(AmE)*

NIIEEA

wing *(BrE)*/fender *(AmE)*

indicator *(BrE)*/blinker *(AmE)*

door mirror

door

'L' plate

brake light

rearlight

exhaust pipe

fog light

reflector

reversing light

mudflap

petrol *(BrE)*/gas *(AmE)* cap

handbrake *(BrE)*/emergency brake *(AmE)*

handle

wheel

hub cap

tyre *(BrE)*/tire *(AmE)*

gear lever *(BrE)*/gearshift *(AmE)*

accelerator *(BrE)*/gas *(AmE)* (pedal)

brake (pedal)

clutch (pedal)

ignition

saloon *(BrE)*/sedan *(AmE)*

hatchback

estate *(BrE)*/station wagon *(AmE)*

van

knickers *(BrE)*/underpants *(AmE)*

nightdress/
night gown

bra

shorts

vest *(BrE)*
undershirt
(AmE)

tights

cuff

t-shirt

underp

waistcoat
(BrE)
vest
(AmE)

turban

jumper *(BrE)*
/sweater *(AmE)*

jear

sweatshirt

braces *(BrE)*
suspenders
(AmE)

zip *(BrE)*
zipper *(AmE)*

collar

lapel

tie

jacket

shirt

sari

anorak *(BrE)*
/parka *(AmE)*

glove

pyjamas *(BrE)*
/pajamas *(AmE)*

sandals

slipper

boots

suit

scarf

leggings

socks

sleeve

button

coat

plimsoll *(BrE)*
tennis shoe *(AmE)*

skirt

pocket

cardigan

tracksuit *(Br*
sweats *(Am.*

brim

dress

watch

raincoat

belt

ring

hat

heel

trousers

shoes

woolly hat *(BrE)*/stocking cap *(AmE)*

buckle

mitten

earring

(shoe)
lace

necklace

bracelet

brooch

trainers *(BrE)*/
running shoes
(AmE)

animals fled. **2** [U] the fact of coming nearer in time: *At the approach of winter the weather grew colder.* **3** [C] a road or path leading to a place: *All approaches to the town were blocked by snow.* **4** [C] a way of doing something or considering something: *a new approach to teaching English* **5** [C] an act of speaking to someone for the first time, usually because you want something from them: *They have made several approaches to that company with a view to doing business.*

ap·proa·cha·ble /ə'prəʊtʃəbəl/ *adj* **1** friendly and easy to talk to –opposite **unapproachable** **2** able to be reached in a particular way: *That village is only approachable on foot.*

ap·pro·ba·tion /ˌæprə'beɪʃən/ *n* [U] *fml* praise or approval

ap·pro·pri·ate¹ /ə'prəʊprɪ‑ɬt/ *adj* correct or suitable: *His clothes were not appropriate for the occasion.* | *The ambassador will be provided with facilities appropriate to his status.* | *You should complain to the appropriate authorities.* –opposite **inappropriate** –**appropriately** *adv* –**appropriateness** *n* [U]

ap·pro·pri·ate² /ə'prəʊprɪeɪt/ *v* **appropriated, appropriating** [T] *fml* to steal or take something for your own use: *He was accused of appropriating government money.*

ap·prov·al /ə'pruːvəl/ *n* [U] **1** favourable opinion or judgment: *I hope this plan meets with your approval.* **2** official permission: *We have to wait for the council's approval before we can start to build.* **3 have/get something on approval** to buy something and take it home with an agreement that you can take it back to the shop if you decide that you do not want it

ap·prove /ə'pruːv/ *v* **approved, approving 1 approve of** to believe that something or someone is good or acceptable: *I don't approve of smoking.* | *My parents don't approve of my friends.* | *I approve of your decision.* **2** [T] to agree to something officially: *The Council hasn't approved the plans yet.*

ap·prox·i·mate¹ /ə'prɒksɬmɬt ‖ ə'prɑːk‑/ *adj* nearly correct but not exact: *Can you give me an approximate price for the job?* –**approximately** *adv* : *We've got approximately £300.*

ap·prox·i·mate² /ə'prɒksɬmeɪt ‖ ə'prɑːk‑/ *v* **approximated, approximating: approximate something, approximate to something** to be very similar to something

ap·prox·i·ma·tion /ə‚prɒksɬ'meɪʃən ‖ ə‚prɑːk‑/ *n* **1** a number or calculation that is not exact but is good enough **2** something which is not correct in every detail, but which is near enough

a·pri·cot /'eɪprɬkɒt ‖ 'æprɬkɑːt/ *n* a small soft yellow fruit with a furry outside and a single large stone inside

A·pril /'eɪprɬl/ *n* (also **Apr** *abbreviation*) the 4th month of the year

April fool /ˌ··'·/ *n* a person who has been deceived by a trick played on the morning of April 1st, which is called **April Fools' Day**

a·pron /'eɪprən/ *n* a piece of cloth or plastic that you put over the front of your clothes to keep them clean, for example while you are cooking

apt /æpt/ *adj* **1 apt to do something** likely to do something or having a tendency to do it: *This kind of shoe is apt to slip on wet ground.* | *She is apt to forget.* **2** exactly suitable: *an apt remark* –**aptly** *adv* : *He was aptly punished for his behaviour.*

CLOTHES

Exercise 1

We wear different clothes for different activities. These people have each made one mistake. What is it?

1 Mr Collins is in a business meeting. He is wearing a dark suit, a red t-shirt, black socks and black shoes.

2 Mrs Stanford is climbing a mountain. She is wearing blue jeans, a red sweat-shirt, a blue scarf, a red anorak, black socks and green slippers.

3 Sandra is dancing with her boyfriend in a disco. She is wearing a red sweater, a white blouse, a brown skirt, brown tights, red shoes and a blue raincoat.

4 Mandy is jogging in the park. She is wearing a yellow track suit, blue trainers, a red dressing gown and a blue hat.

5 Frank is getting ready to go to bed. He is wearing red and white striped pyjamas, a red tie, a brown dressing gown and brown slippers.

Exercise 2

How often do these clothes have these things? Put a tick (✔) for always, a cross (✗) for never, and a question mark (?) for sometimes.

	belt	collar	sleeves	pockets	lapels	buttons
jeans	?	✗	✗	✔	✗	✔
raincoat						
nightdress						
tracksuit						
waistcoat						
gloves						
sandals						
scarf						

ap·ti·tude /ˈæptɪtjuːd ‖ -tuːd/ n a natural ability to learn something quickly and to do it well: *She has a real aptitude for maths.*

a·quar·i·um /əˈkweəriəm/ n **aquariums** or **aquaria** /-riə/ a glass container for fish and other water animals, or a building with many of these

A·quar·i·us /əˈkweəriəs/ n one of the signs of the ZODIAC

a·quat·ic /əˈkwætɪk, əˈkwɒ- ‖ əˈkwæ-, əˈkwɑː-/ adj living or happening in or on water: *aquatic plants | Aquatic sports include swimming and rowing.*

aq·ue·duct /ˈækwɪdʌkt/ n a bridge built to carry water across a valley

aq·ui·line /ˈækwɪlaɪn ‖ -laɪn, -lɪn/ adj fml long and curving (used of someone's nose)

Ar·a·bic nu·me·ral /ˌærəbɪk ˈnjuːmərəl ‖ ˈnjuː--/ n one of the signs used for numbers in the English and many other alphabets such as 1, 2, 3, 4

ar·a·ble /ˈærəbəl/ adj used for growing crops or suitable for growing crops: *arable land*

ar·bi·tra·ry /ˈɑːbɪtrəri ‖ ˈɑːrbɪtreri/ adj not decided by rules or reason but by chance or a person's personal opinion: *an arbitrary selection of books | arbitrary decisions which make no sense* –**arbitrarily** /ˈɑːbɪtrərəli ‖ ˌɑːrbɪˈtreərɪli/ adv

ar·bi·trate /ˈɑːbɪtreɪt ‖ ˈɑːr-/ v **arbitrated, arbitrating** [I;T] to act as a judge in an argument especially at the request of both sides

ar·bi·tra·tion /ˌɑːbɪˈtreɪʃən ‖ ˌɑːr-/ n go to arbitration to ask a third person to settle an argument between two people: *The men agreed to go to arbitration to settle their pay claim.*

arc /ɑːk ‖ ɑːrk/ n part of a circle or any curved line

ar·cade /ɑːˈkeɪd ‖ ɑːr-/ n a covered passage, especially with an arched roof, with shops on one or both sides: *a shopping arcade*

arch¹ /ɑːtʃ ‖ ɑːrtʃ/ n **1** the top curved part over a doorway, window, or bridge **2** the raised part of the bottom of your foot

arch² v [I;T] to form something into the shape of an arch: *The cat arched her back in anger.*

ar·chae·ol·o·gy /ˌɑːkiˈɒlədʒi ‖ ˌɑːrkiˈɑː-/ n (also **archeology**) [U] the study of ancient times by examining the buried remains of buildings and tools –**archaeologist** n –**archaeological** /ˌɑːkiə-ˈlɒdʒɪkəl ‖ ˌɑːrkiəˈlɑː-/ adj –**archaeologically** /-kli/ adv

ar·cha·ic /ɑːˈkeɪ-ɪk ‖ ɑːr-/ adj belonging to the past and no longer used: *archaic language*

arch·bish·op /ˌɑːtʃˈbɪʃəp◂ ‖ ˌɑːrtʃ-/ n a priest of very high rank in some branches of the Christian church, responsible for the churches in a large area

ar·cher /ˈɑːtʃəʳ ‖ ˈɑːr-/ n a person who shoots with a BOW³ (1) and ARROW, usually for sport

ar·cher·y /ˈɑːtʃəri ‖ ˈɑːr-/ n [U] the sport of shooting with a BOW³ (1) and ARROW

ar·chi·pel·a·go /ˌɑːkɪˈpeləgəʊ ‖ ˌɑːr-/ n **archipelagoes** or **archipelagos** a group of small islands

ar·chi·tect /ˈɑːkɪtekt ‖ ˈɑːr-/ n a person who plans new buildings and who is responsible for making sure that they are built properly

ar·chi·tec·ture /ˈɑːkɪtektʃəʳ ‖ ˈɑːr-/ n [U] **1** the art and science of building, including its planning, making, and decoration **2** the style or manner of building: *the architecture of ancient Greece | Gothic architecture* –**architectural** /ˌɑːkɪˈtektʃərəl ‖ ˌɑːr-/ adj –**architecturally** adv

ar·chives /ˈɑːkaɪvz ‖ ˈɑːr-/ n [pl] **1** a collection of old papers, reports, letters, and photographs of a particular group or country, kept for historical interest **2** a place for storing such historical material

Arc·tic /ˈɑːktɪk ‖ ˈɑːr-/ n **the Arctic** the very cold, most northern part of the world –**arctic** adj: *arctic weather conditions*

ar·dent /ˈɑːdənt ‖ ˈɑːr-/ adj having strong feelings of admiration or love for something or someone: *an ardent supporter of government policies | her ardent admirers* –**ardently** adv

ar·dour /ˈɑːdəʳ ‖ ˈɑːr-/ n (**ardor** AmE) [U] fml a strong feeling of excitement, admiration, or love: *patriotic ardour*

ar·du·ous /ˈɑːdjuəs ‖ ˈɑːrdʒuəs/ adj needing hard and continuous effort: *an arduous climb | arduous work* –**arduously** adv

are /əʳ; strong ɑːʳ/ the present tense plural of BE

ar·e·a /ˈeəriə/ n **1** the size of a flat surface measured by multiplying the length by the width: *What's the area of the front garden?* **2** a particular place or division of a town, a country, or the world: *I was born in a very poor area of London. | The Sahara desert is one of the driest areas in the world.* **3** a particular space or surface: *a room with a dining area at one end | a parking area* **4** a subject or activity: *developments in the area of language teaching | What area do you work in?*

a·re·na /əˈriːnə/ n an enclosed area used for sports or public entertainments

aren't /ɑːnt ‖ ˈɑːrənt/ **1** short for "are not": *They aren't here. | Aren't you coming?* **2** used in questions as a short form of "am not": *I'm your friend, aren't I?*

ar·gu·a·ble /ˈɑːgjuəbəl ‖ ˈɑːr-/ adj **1** able to be questioned or doubted: *The government claim that their policies will help the unemployed, but that's arguable.* **2** it is arguable that… a phrase used when you are giving your opinion about something: *It is arguable that the government has no right to interfere in this matter.* –**arguably** adv

ar·gue /ˈɑːgjuː ‖ ˈɑːr-/ v **argued, arguing** **1** [I] to fight or disagree with someone using words: *Do what you are told and don't argue with me. | They're always arguing about money.* **2** [I;T, + that] to provide reasons for or against something, especially in a clear order: *He argues well. | It could be argued that sending men to the moon is a waste of money. | She argued her case very well. | Ministers argued for and against the proposals.*

ar·gu·ment /ˈɑːgjəmənt ‖ ˈɑːr-/ n **1** [C] an unfriendly disagreement, often with people shouting at each other: *They're always having arguments about money.* **2** [C] a reason given to support or disprove something: *We listened to all the arguments for and against the plan.* **3** [U] the use of reason to decide something: *We should try to settle this affair by argument, not by fighting.*

ar·gu·men·ta·tive /ˌɑːgjʊˈmentətɪv ‖ ˌɑːr-/ adj often disagreeing or arguing with people

a·ri·a /ˈɑːriə/ n a song that is sung by only one person in an OPERA

ar·id /ˈærɪd/ adj **1** having very little rain and so very dry: *arid soil | an arid region* **2** without interest or imagination: *arid theories | an arid existence*

Ar·ies /ˈeəriːz, ˈæri-iːz/ n one of the signs of the ZODIAC

a·rise /əˈraɪz/ v **arose** /əˈrəʊz/, **arisen** /əˈrɪzən/, **arising** [I] **1** to happen or appear: *New difficulties are constantly arising as we do the work.* **2** lit to get up

ar·is·toc·ra·cy /ˌærɪˈstɒkrəsi ‖ -ˈstɑː-/ n aristocra-cies the people of the highest social class, people from noble families and with titles of rank

ar·is·to·crat /ˈærɪˌstəkræt, əˈrɪ- ‖ əˈrɪ-/ n a member of the highest social class –**aristocratic** /ˌærɪˌstə-ˈkrætɪk◄, əˌrɪ- ‖ əˌrɪ-/ adj

a·rith·me·tic¹ /əˈrɪθmətɪk/ n [U] the science of cal-culation by numbers –compare MATHEMATICS

ar·ith·met·ic² /ˌærɪθˈmetɪk/ adj (also **arithmetical** /-ɪkəl/) connected with the science of calculation by numbers –**arithmetically** /-kli/ adv

arm¹ /ɑːm ‖ ɑːrm/ n 1 [C] one of your two upper limbs: *She carried the box under her arm.* | *He was shot in his left arm.* 2 [C] something that is shaped like an arm or moves like an arm: *the arm of a chair* | *the arm of a record player* | *a narrow arm of the sea* 3 **arms** [pl] weapons used in war 4 **arm in arm** with arms joined together: *They walked arm in arm.* 5 **be up in arms** to be very angry and ready to argue or fight about something: *The women are up in arms over their low rate of pay.* 6 **welcome someone with open arms** to show that you are pleased to see someone by holding your arms out towards them to take hold of them 7 **welcome something with open arms** to be very pleased that something has happened

arm² v [T] to supply someone with weapons: *The country armed itself in preparation for war.*

ar·ma·da /ɑːˈmɑːdə ‖ ɑːr-/ n lit a collection of armed ships

ar·ma·ments /ˈɑːməmənts ‖ ˈɑːr-/ n [pl] weapons and other fighting apparatus used in a war

arm·band /ˈɑːmbænd ‖ ˈɑːrm-/ n a band of material that you wear round your arm to show that you have an official position; people sometimes wear black armbands to show that someone has just died

arm·chair /ˈɑːmtʃeəʳ, ˌɑːmˈtʃeəʳ ‖ ˈɑːrm-, ˌɑːrm-/ n a chair with supports for your arms – see picture on page 442

armed /ɑːmd ‖ ɑːrmd/ adj 1 carrying a weapon or weapons: *Both men were armed.* 2 **armed robbery** a crime in which a person steals something and in which they are carrying a weapon, usually a gun 3 **armed with something** having or knowing something useful: *I went to the meeting armed with various facts and figures.* 4 **armed to the teeth** carrying a lot of weapons

armed forc·es /ˌ·· ˈ··/ n [pl] the military forces of a country, usually the army, navy, and air force

arm·ful /ˈɑːmful ‖ ˈɑːrm-/ n all that a person can hold in one or both arms: *She was carrying an armful of books.*

ar·mi·stice /ˈɑːmɨstɨs ‖ ˈɑːrm-/ n an agreement made during a war to stop fighting, usually for a limited period of time

ar·mour /ˈɑːməʳ ‖ ˈɑːr-/ n (**armor** *AmE*) [U] 1 strong metal or leather protection that men and horses used to wear in battle 2 strong metal pro-tection on fighting vehicles, ships, and aircraft

ar·moured /ˈɑːməd ‖ ˈɑːrmərd/ adj (**armored** *AmE*) protected by a hard metal covering: *an armoured car*

ar·mour·y /ˈɑːməri ‖ ˈɑːr-/ n armouries (**armory** *AmE*) a place where weapons are stored

arm·pit /ˈɑːmˌpɪt ‖ ˈɑːrm-/ n the hollow place under your arm at your shoulder

ar·my /ˈɑːmi ‖ ˈɑːr-/ n armies [+ sing/pl verb] 1 the military forces of a country trained to fight on land 2 a large group of people, especially one that is organized for a purpose: *An army of workers are building the Channel Tunnel.*

a·ro·ma /əˈrəumə/ n a strong pleasant smell from food and drink: *the aroma of fresh coffee* –**aromatic** /ˌærəˈmætɪk◄/ adj : *Aromatic herbs are often used in cooking.*

a·rose /əˈrəuz/ v the past tense of ARISE

a·round /əˈraund/ adv,prep 1 adv,prep moving or positioned in a circle: *She spun the wheel around.* | *He put a belt around his waist.* | *We sat around the table.* | *People were standing around the fire.* | *The children gathered around to listen to the story.* | *a large tree measuring three metres around the trunk* 2 adv so as to face the other way: *Turn the clock around so that I can see it.* | *He swung around to look at me.* 3 adv,prep visiting all the parts of a place, or a lot of different places: *They've been travelling around together.* | *We're driving around France this summer.* | *A guide showed us around the castle.* 4 prep near a place: *A lot of the people who live around here work in London.* 5 adv to someone's house: *He invited us around to his house for a meal.* 6 **around a corner** turning a corner or past a corner: *He dis-appeared around the corner.* | *The post office is just around that corner.* 7 **this way around, the other way around, the right way around, etc.** a phrase used to say which way something is facing or in which order things are placed: *You've got that hat on the wrong way around.* | *Those two numbers should be the other way around.* 8 adv in a place and able to be used or obtained: *Is there any paper around?* | *I'm afraid there's no-one around to deal with your query at the moment.* 9 prep about: *There were around 50 people at the meeting.*

a·rouse /əˈrauz/ v aroused, arousing [T] 1 to wake someone up: *Aroused from a deep sleep, he was rather short tempered.* 2 to make someone have a particular feeling: *Her behaviour aroused the suspicions of the police.* 3 to make someone sexu-ally excited

ar·raign /əˈreɪn/ v [T] tech to call or bring someone before a court of law to face a charge

ar·range /əˈreɪndʒ/ v arranged, arranging 1 [T;+that] to make plans for something to happen and to agree with other people that it will happen: *I've arranged the meeting for 2 pm.* | *He didn't ar-range to come with me.* | *Can you arrange for a taxi to collect us?* | *I arranged that we should meet at the station.*
□ USEFUL PATTERNS to arrange something; to arrange to do something; to arrange for someone to do something; to arrange that…
2 [T] to put things in a certain order or position so that they are neat or attractive: *The food was ar-ranged beautifully on the plates.* 3 [T] to set out a piece of music in a certain way, for example for different instruments 4 **an arranged marriage** a marriage in which parents choose a partner for their children

ar·range·ment /əˈreɪndʒmənt/ n 1 **arrangements** [pl] plans and preparations for something to hap-pen: *He's making arrangements for the wedding.* | *travel arrangements* 2 [C] an agreement with someone to do something: *I have an arrangement with my boss to do some of my work at home.* 3 by arrangement arranged in advance 4 [C] a group of things that have been put in an attractive or neat order: *a beautiful flower arrangement* 5 [U] putting into position or order: *The arrangement of furni-ture in the office is being changed.* 6 [C] the setting of a piece of music

ar·ray¹ /əˈreɪ/ v [T] fml 1 to place soldiers in order

ready for battle: *The soldiers were arrayed on the opposite hill.* **2** to dress someone in fine clothes: *Arrayed in all her finery, she felt ready to meet the world.*

array² *n* **1** an attractive show or collection: *There was an impressive array of film stars at the premiere.* **2** *lit* clothes for a special occasion

ar·rears /əˈrɪəz ‖ əˈrɪərz/ *n* [pl] **1** money that is owed and should have been paid: *There were huge arrears to be paid.* **2** **be in arrears** to be behind in a payment and so owe someone money: *Sally was two months in arrears with her rent.*

ar·rest¹ /əˈrest/ *v* [T] **1** to catch someone and declare that they are believed to be guilty of a crime: *He was arrested for stealing a car.* **2** *fml* to stop the growth or development of something: *Doctors successfully arrested the growth of the disease.* **3** **arrest someone's attention** to make someone notice something

arrest² *n* **1** [C;U] the act of arresting someone: *The police made several arrests at the football match.* **2** **under arrest** not allowed to go free because you have been arrested

ar·riv·al /əˈraɪvəl/ *n* **1** [U] the act of arriving: *The arrival of Flight 208 from Singapore has been delayed.* | *On my arrival home I was greeted by my parents.* **2** [C] a person that has arrived: *The new arrivals waited in the reception area.*

ar·rive /əˈraɪv/ *v* **arrived, arriving** [I] **1** to reach a place: *What time does the plane arrive in New York?* | *The train arrived late at the station.* **2** to happen: *At last our holidays arrived.*

arrive at sthg *phr v* [T] to reach a situation or decision: *After many hours' talk, the committee arrived at a decision.*

ar·ro·gant /ˈærəgənt/ *adj* proud and self-important in an unpleasant way: *Elizabeth thought he was an arrogant, selfish man.* | *arrogant behaviour* –**arrogantly** *adv* –**arrogance** *n* [U] : *His arrogance made him unpopular.*

ar·row /ˈærəʊ/ *n* **1** a thin straight stick with a point at one end and feathers at the other, which is used as a weapon or in sport **2** a sign like an arrow (→) used to show the direction or position of something: *Follow the arrows for the footpath.*

ar·se·nal /ˈɑːsənl ‖ ˈɑːr-/ *n* a store of weapons and explosives: *The police found an arsenal of guns and explosives in the terrorists' house.*

ar·se·nic /ˈɑːsənɪk ‖ ˈɑːr-/ *n* [U] a very strong poison

ar·son /ˈɑːsən ‖ ˈɑːr-/ *n* [U] the crime of setting fire to property in order to cause damage –**arsonist** *n*

art /ɑːt ‖ ɑːrt/ *n* **1** [U] the skill of drawing or painting: *Tania is going to study art in Italy.* **2** [U] objects such as paintings that are considered to be beautiful: *an art collection* **3** [U] the production of things like painting, music, or literature: *She devoted her life to her art.* **4** [sing] something which needs a lot of skill: *the art of making friends* **5 the arts** [pl] the production or performing of things like music, plays, or films: *The government provides a lot of financial support for the arts.* **6 arts** [pl] subjects, especially those taught at university, that are not considered a part of science: *There is heavy competition for places on courses leading to arts degrees.*

ar·te·fact /ˈɑːtɪfækt ‖ ˈɑːr-/ *n* see ARTIFACT

ar·te·ry /ˈɑːtəri ‖ ˈɑːr-/ *n* **arteries 1** a blood vessel that carries blood from your heart to the rest of your body **2** *tech* a main road, railway, or river –**arterial** /ɑːˈtɪəriəl ‖ ɑːr-/ *adj* [only before a noun]: *arterial roads leading into the capital*

art·ful /ˈɑːtfəl ‖ ˈɑːr-/ *adj* clever and skilful, often in a way that is not completely honest: *an artful attempt to gain our sympathy*

ar·thri·tis /ɑːˈθraɪtɪs ‖ ɑːr-/ *n* [U] a disease causing pain and swelling in the joints of your body –**arthritic** /ɑːˈθrɪtɪk ‖ ɑːr-/ *adj,n*

ar·ti·choke /ˈɑːtɪtʃəʊk ‖ ˈɑːr-/ *n* **1** (also **globe artichoke**) a plant with a leafy kind of flower that can be eaten as a vegetable **2** (also **Jerusalem artichoke**) a plant with a potato-like root that can be eaten as a vegetable

ar·ti·cle /ˈɑːtɪkəl ‖ ˈɑːr-/ *n* **1** a particular thing or object, especially one of a group: *Burglars stole several articles of value from the house.* **2** a piece of writing in a newspaper or magazine: *an article on unemployment* | *I've read an article about her.* **3** *tech* the words "a" or "an" (**indefinite article**) and "the" (**definite article**)

ar·tic·u·late¹ /ɑːˈtɪkjʊlɪt ‖ ɑːr-/ *adj* expressing or able to express thoughts and feelings clearly: *She is a very bright and articulate child.* –**articulately** *adv*

ar·tic·u·late² /ɑːˈtɪkjʊleɪt ‖ ɑːr-/ *v* **articulated, articulating** [I;T] to speak clearly and effectively: *He articulated each word carefully.* –**articulation** /ɑːˌtɪkjʊˈleɪʃən ‖ ɑːr-/ *n* [U]

ar·tic·u·la·ted /ɑːˈtɪkjʊleɪtɪd ‖ ɑːr-/ *adj* consisting of two parts that are joined together by a metal bar (used of vehicles): *a huge articulated lorry*

ar·ti·fact /ˈɑːtɪfækt ‖ ˈɑːr-/ *n* (also **artefact**) a tool or other small object made by a person

ar·ti·fice /ˈɑːtɪfɪs ‖ ˈɑːr-/ *n fml* **1** [C] a clever trick **2** [U] the use of clever tricks and deceit

ar·ti·fi·cial /ˌɑːtɪˈfɪʃəl◂ ‖ ˌɑːr-/ *adj* **1** not natural but made by people: *artificial flowers* | *This drink contains no artificial colours.* **2** not real or sincere: *She welcomed me with a rather artificial smile.* –**artificially** *adv*

artificial res·pi·ra·tion /ˌ····· ··ˈ··/ *n* [U] the forcing of air into the lungs of a person who has stopped breathing by pressing their chest and blowing air into their mouth

ar·til·le·ry /ɑːˈtɪləri ‖ ɑːr-/ *n* [U] **1** large guns either on wheels or fixed in one place **2** the part of the army that uses large guns

ar·ti·san /ˌɑːtɪˈzæn ‖ ˈɑːrtɪzən/ *n* a person who does skilled work with their hands

art·ist /ˈɑːtɪst ‖ ˈɑːr-/ *n* **1** a person who paints, draws, or produces pieces of art **2** see ARTISTE

ar·tiste /ɑːˈtiːst ‖ ɑːr-/ *n* (also **artist**) a professional singer, actor, or dancer

ar·tis·tic /ɑːˈtɪstɪk ‖ ɑːr-/ *adj* **1** concerning or typical of art or artists: *artistic freedom* **2** having or showing imagination and skill in art: *All the children in the family are artistic.* –**artistically** /-kli/ *adv*

art·ist·ry /ˈɑːtɪstri ‖ ˈɑːr-/ *n* [U] the skill of someone like an artist, musician, or actor: *His artistry is admired all over the world.*

art·less /ˈɑːtləs ‖ ˈɑːr-/ *adj* simple and natural, without any deceit: *an artless village child* | *an apparently artless question* –**artlessly** *adv*

art·y /ˈɑːti ‖ ˈɑːrti/ *adj* **artier, artiest** trying to appear artistic or stylish (a word used to show disapproval) –**artiness** *n* [U]

as¹ /əz; *strong* æz/ *adv,prep* **1** used when you are comparing things, or saying that they are like each other in some way: *He's not as old as me.* | *She's the same age as me, but not as clever.* | *We must get to the hospital as quickly as possible.* **2** being or considered to be a particular thing: *He was trying to make his living as a painter.* | *He's working as a window cleaner at the moment.* | *I had been to Ireland many times as a child.* | *As a writer, I need to spend a lot of time observing people.* | *She regarded me as an enemy.* | *They treated the whole thing as a joke.* –see LIKE³ (USAGE)

as² *conj* **1** used when you are comparing things, or saying that they are like each other in some way: *He's not quite as brilliant as his brother is.* | *She can run just as fast as I can.* | *She failed the exam, just as I had done the year before.*

■ USAGE In negative comparisons, we can use **not** as or **not so**: *He's not as old/not so old as you.*

2 while something is happening: *As I was getting onto the bus, I realized that I had left my purse at home.* | *He called to me as I walked past.* | *I talked to each of the guests as they arrived.* **3** because: *As it was now November, it was getting quite cold.* | *I didn't bother to stop and chat to Sarah, as I had spoken to her earlier that day.* | *As you're so clever, perhaps you can sort out this problem for us!* **4** though: *Tired as I was, I was determined to get the job finished.* **5 as it is** in fact: *I hoped things might get better, but as it is they seem to be getting worse!* **6 as it were** a phrase used when you are saying that something is true in a certain way: *He is my best friend, my brother, as it were.* **7 as well** also: *Dick came up to London with us. Judy came as well.*

as for /ˈ···/ *prep* used when you are starting to talk about a new subject: *We've got a spare bed for you, but as for the children, I'm afraid they'll have to sleep on the floor.* | *Alison hasn't been much help. As for George, he's quite useless.*

as if /·ˈ·/ (also **as though**) *conj* in a way that suggests that something is true: *She looked as if she'd been crying.* | *He stared at me blankly, as if he didn't believe me.* | *He shook his head as if to say no.*

as of /ˈ··/ *prep* (also **as from**) from a particular time: *As of today you are in charge.*

as regards /ˌ·ˈ·/ *prep* concerning or regarding a particular thing: *As regards your recent enquiry, I am sorry to inform you that we have no job vacancies at the moment.*

as to /ˈ··/ *prep* concerning or regarding a particular thing: *He's very uncertain as to whether it's the right job for him.* | *We had been given no guidance as to what was expected of us.*

a.s.a.p. /ˌeɪ es eɪ ˈpiː, ˈeɪsæp/ a written abbreviation for **as soon as possible**

as·bes·tos /æsˈbestəs/ *n* [U] a solid substance which does not burn and which is used as protection against fire or heat

as·cend /əˈsend/ *v* [I;T] *fml* to move upwards or move to the top of something: *The plane ascended rapidly after take-off.* –opposite **descend**

as·cen·dan·cy /əˈsendənsi/ *n* (also **ascendency**) [U] *fml* power or influence over someone

as·cent /əˈsent/ *n* **1** [C] moving or climbing upwards: *The team hope to make a successful ascent of the mountain.* **2** [U] the process by which someone develops and becomes more advanced: *a rapid ascent to a position of power* **3** [C] a path or road which slopes upwards

as·cer·tain /ˌæsəˈteɪn ‖ ˌæsər-/ *v* [T; +that] *fml* to discover or get to know something: *The police are trying to ascertain the facts.*

as·cet·ic /əˈsetɪk/ *n* a person whose simple, often religious way of life allows no physical pleasures –**ascetic** *adj fml*

as·cribe /əˈskraɪb/ *v* **ascribed, ascribing** [T] **ascribe something to** to believe that something is the result of a particular thing or the work of a particular person: *He ascribes his success to skill and hard work.*

ash /æʃ/ *n* [U] (also **ashes** [pl]) **1** the soft grey powder that remains after something has been burnt: *cigarette ash* | *The house burnt to ashes.* **2 ashes** [pl] the remains of a dead person after burning: *Her ashes were scattered over the sea.* **3** [C;U] a type of forest tree, or its wood

a·shamed /əˈʃeɪmd/ *adj* [never before a noun] feeling shame, guilt, or sorrow about something: *He felt ashamed of his old clothes.* | *I was ashamed to admit what I had done.* | *You should be ashamed of yourself.*

□ USEFUL PATTERNS to be ashamed of someone/something; to be ashamed to do something –**ashamedly** /əˈʃeɪmˌdli/ *adv*

ash·en /ˈæʃən/ *adj* very pale because of shock or fear (used of a person's face)

a·shore /əˈʃɔːʳ/ *adv* on or onto the shore or land from the sea: *We came ashore at Dover.*

ash·tray /ˈæʃtreɪ/ *n* a small dish for cigarette ash

Ash Wednes·day /ˌ·ˈ··/ *n* the first day of LENT

A·sian /ˈeɪʃən, ˈeɪʒən ‖ ˈeɪʒən, ˈeɪʃən/ *n* (also **A·si·at·ic** /ˌeɪʃiˈætɪk, ˌeɪzi-, ˌeɪʒi- ‖ ˌeɪʒi-, ˌeɪzi-/) a person from Asia –**Asian** *adj*

a·side¹ /əˈsaɪd/ *adv* to the side or out of the way: *She stepped aside to let them pass.* | *He put his work aside for a time.*

aside² *n* a remark in a low voice not intended to be heard by everyone present

ask /ɑːsk ‖ æsk/ *v* **1** [I;T] to make a request for someone to tell you something: *Can I ask a question?* | *She asked me several difficult questions.* | *I think I'd better ask him who he is.* | *We need to ask where to go next.* | *He asked me if I would like a drink.* | *"How old are you?" she asked.*

□ USEFUL PATTERNS to ask a question; to ask someone a question; to ask (someone) who, where, why, how, etc.; "...?" he asked

2 ask someone to do something to say to someone that you would like them to do something for you: *She asked me to lend her some money.* | *I needed someone to sort out my money for me, so I asked Jim.* **3 ask for something, ask someone for something** to say to someone that you would like them to give you something: *I sat down at a table and asked for a cup of tea.* | *She's never asked me for money.* **4 ask for someone** to say that you would like to talk to someone on the telephone: *I phoned the office and asked for Jane.* **5 ask someone somewhere** to invite someone somewhere: *I asked her in for a drink.* | *He hadn't been asked to the party.* **6 ask after someone** to ask whether someone is well: *I met Mark in town, and he asked after you.* **7 be asking for trouble** to be behaving in a way which will cause trouble for you

■ USAGE Compare **ask, inquire, question**. **Ask** is the usual verb for questions: *"When were you born?" he* **asked**. | *He* **asked** *me the time.* **Enquire** (or **inquire**) is more formal: *"What is your date of birth?" he* **enquired**. But we cannot use **enquire** before a pronoun object (*me, you, him, her, us, them*). The verb **question** means "to ask a person a lot of questions": *The police* **questioned** *the suspect for several hours.*

a·skew /əˈskjuː/ *adv* [never before a noun] not straight or level: *He wore his hat askew.*

a·sleep /ə'sliːp/ *adj* [never before a noun] **1** sleeping: *Be quiet! The baby is asleep.* **2 fast asleep, sound asleep** sleeping very deeply **3** unable to feel anything (used of an arm or a leg that has been in one position for too long) **4 fall asleep** to go into a state of sleep

as·par·a·gus /ə'spærəgəs/ *n* [U] a plant whose young green stems are eaten as a vegetable

as·pect /'æspekt/ *n* **1** a particular side or characteristic of a situation: *The training course covers every aspect of the job.* **2** the direction in which a window, room, or front of a building faces: *The house has a southerly aspect.* **3** *lit* appearance: *Her face wore a melancholy aspect.*

as·per·sion /ə'spɜːʃən, -ʒən ‖ -ɜːr-/ *n fml* **cast aspersions on** to suggest that someone is not very good at something (a phrase which is often used in a humorous way): *She cast aspersions on my driving.*

as·phalt /'æsfælt ‖ 'æsfɔːlt/ *n* [U] a hard black substance that is used to make the surface of roads

as·phyx·i·ate /æs'fɪksieɪt, əs-/ *v* **asphyxiated, asphyxiating** [T] *fml* to kill someone by making them unable to breathe: *She was asphyxiated by the smoke.* –**asphyxiation** /æs,fɪksi'eɪʃən, əs-/ *n* [U]

as·pi·rant /ə'spaɪərənt, 'æspɪrənt/ *n fml* a person who hopes for and tries to get something important

as·pi·ra·tion /,æspɪ'reɪʃən/ *n* a strong desire to have or do something, especially something important: *He has aspirations to become a great writer.*

as·pire /ə'spaɪəʳ/ *v* **aspired, aspiring, aspire to something, aspire to do something** to have a strong desire to do something and aim to do it: *She aspires to be prime minister.* –**aspiring** *adj* : *an aspiring young actress*

as·pi·rin /'æsprɪn/ *n* [C;U] a common medicine that reduces pain and fever: *She took two aspirins.* | *a bottle of aspirin*

ass /æs/ *n* an animal like a horse but smaller and with longer ears

as·sail /ə'seɪl/ *v* [T] *fml* **1** to attack someone violently: *The police were assailed with rocks.* **2 be assailed by** to be worried or troubled by problems: *Tom was assailed by doubts.*

as·sai·lant /ə'seɪlənt/ *n fml* an attacker

as·sas·sin /ə'sæsɪn/ *n* a person who murders someone for political reasons

as·sas·sin·ate /ə'sæsɪneɪt ‖ -əneɪt/ *v* **assassinated, assassinating** [T] to murder an important person for political reasons –see KILL¹ (USAGE) –**assassination** /ə,sæsɪ'neɪʃən ‖ -sən'eɪ-/ *n* [C;U]

as·sault¹ /ə'sɔːlt/ *n* [C;U] a violent attack, often on a person: *a vicious assault on an old lady* | *The captain led an assault against the castle.* | *He was sent to prison for assault.*

assault² *v* [T] to attack someone violently

as·sem·ble /ə'sembəl/ *v* **1** [I;T] to gather or collect together: *The schoolchildren assembled in the hall to listen to the headmaster.* | *The books are assembled on the shelves in alphabetical order.* **2** [T] to put the different parts of something together: *It was easy to assemble the bookcase myself.*

as·sem·bly /ə'sembli/ *n* **assemblies** [C;U] the meeting of a group of people for a particular purpose: *School assembly will begin at nine o'clock.*

assembly line /·'·· ,·/ *n* a production process in a factory where each worker does one particular job and then the work is passed on a moving band to the next worker

as·sent /ə'sent/ *v* [I] *fml* to agree to something: *The committee would not assent to the proposal.* –opposite **dissent** –**assent** *n* : *The director has given her assent.*

as·sert /ə'sɜːt ‖ -ɜːrt/ *v* **1** [T;+that] to state an opinion forcefully: *The lawyer asserted his belief in his client's innocence.* **2** [T] to behave in a determined way in order to make other people recognize something: *She asserted her independence by going out alone.* **3 assert yourself** to behave in a strong and determined way so that people take notice of you

as·ser·tion /ə'sɜːʃən ‖ -ɜːr-/ *n* [C;U] a forceful statement or claim: *He repeated his assertions that he was not guilty.*

as·ser·tive /ə'sɜːtɪv ‖ -ɜːr-/ *adj* behaving in a confident, determined way so that people take notice of you: *You must be more assertive if you want people to listen to you.* –**assertively** *adv* –**assertiveness** *n* [U]

as·sess /ə'ses/ *v* [T] **1** to think carefully about a situation or problem, and make a judgment about it: *We must assess the political situation carefully.* **2** to judge the quality, amount, or value of something: *Teachers have to assess their students' work regularly.* | *It's difficult to assess exactly how much damage was caused.* –**assessment** *n* [C;U]

as·set /'æset, 'æsɪt/ *n* **1** [C] something that is useful and helpful: *A sense of humour is a great asset.* **2 assets** [pl] *fml* the property of a person or a company which can be sold to pay off debts

as·sid·u·ous /ə'sɪdjuəs ‖ -dʒuəs/ *adj* working hard or paying great attention to detail –**assiduously** *adv*

as·sign /ə'saɪn/ *v* [T] **1** to give something to someone to use: *They have assigned me a small room.* ☐ USEFUL PATTERNS to assign someone something; to assign something to someone **2** to give someone a job to do: *Guards were assigned to watch the hotel day and night.* **3** to send someone to a place, usually to do a job: *He was assigned to Tokyo.*

as·sign·ment /ə'saɪnmənt/ *n* **1** [C] a job which you are given to do: *The newspaper is sending her on a special assignment to India.* **2** [U] the act of giving someone a job to do

as·sim·i·late /ə'sɪmɪleɪt/ *v* **assimilated, assimilating** **1** [I;T] to make an accepted part of or become an accepted part of a group or country: *America has assimilated many people from Europe.* | *They assimilated easily into their new jobs.* **2** [T] to understand something properly: *You have to assimilate the facts, not just remember them.* –**assimilation** /ə,sɪmɪ'leɪʃən/ *n* [U]

as·sist /ə'sɪst/ *v* [I;T] *fml* to help or support someone: *Two nurses assisted the doctor in performing the operation.* –see HELP¹ (USAGE)

as·sist·ance /ə'sɪstəns/ *n* **1** [U] help and support: *Our organization needs more financial assistance.* **2 come to someone's assistance** to help someone

as·sist·ant /ə'sɪstənt/ *n* a person who helps someone in a job, and is under that person's direction: *This is my assistant, Sally.* | *He is an assistant cook.*

as·so·ci·ate¹ /ə'səʊʃieɪt, -sieɪt/ *v* **associated, associating** **1** [I;T] to join or be connected with someone or something: *He associates with some very strange people.* | *I am not associated with any political group.* **2** [T] to connect ideas in your mind: *I don't associate the two ideas.* | *She associates summer with holidays.*

as·so·ci·ate² /ə'səʊʃiɪt, -ʃit/ n a person connected with another person, especially in work: *He's not a friend, just a business associate.*

as·so·ci·a·tion /ə,səʊsi'eɪʃən, ə,səʊʃi-/ n **1** [C] an organization of people joined together for a particular purpose: *an association to help blind people* | *the Association of Scientific Workers* **2 in association with** together with someone or something else: *The council is working in association with the Department of Education.* **3** [U] the act of connecting things in the mind

as·sort·ment /ə'sɔːtmənt ‖ -ɔːr-/ n a group of mixed things or of various kinds of the same thing: *An assortment of strange objects lay on her desk.* | *an assortment of biscuits* **–assorted** *adj* : *a bag of assorted sweets*

as·sume /ə'sjuːm ‖ ə'suːm/ v assumed, assuming **1** [T;+that] to believe that something is true without any real proof: *If he's not here in five minutes, we'll assume he isn't coming.* | *Assuming it rains tomorrow, what shall we do?* | *I assumed that she was American but she was actually Canadian.* **2** [T] to begin to use or have something, sometimes without the right to do so: *He will assume responsibility for the new staff.* | *The army has assumed control of the government.* **3** to pretend to have a quality or way of behaving: *He assumes a well-informed manner, but in fact he knows very little.* **–assumption** /ə'sʌmpʃən/ n [C;U] : *Our assumption that we would win was mistaken.*

as·sur·ance /ə'ʃʊərəns/ n **1** [C] a firm statement or promise: *He gave repeated assurances that he would finish the work.* | *an assurance of your loyalty* **2** [U] (also **self-assurance**) strong belief in your own ability and powers: *The new teacher lacks assurance in the classroom.* **3** [U] BrE insurance against events that are certain rather than possible: *life assurance*

as·sure /ə'ʃʊəʳ/ v assured, assuring [T] **1** to tell someone that something is certainly true, in order to make them feel more confident: *I assure you that this medicine cannot harm you.* | *I can assure you of his good intentions.*
□ USEFUL PATTERNS to assure someone of something; to assure someone that…
2 to make someone feel certain of having something: *Our clients are assured of a trouble-free holiday.* | *We can assure you a carefree retirement.*
□ USEFUL PATTERNS to assure someone of something; to assure someone something

as·sured /ə'ʃʊəd ‖ -ərd/ adj **1** (also **self-assured**) confident in your own abilities: *He has an assured and relaxed manner.* **2** having or showing certainty: *Her success as a singer looks assured.* **–assuredly** /ə'ʃʊəʳdli/ adv

as·te·risk /'æstərɪsk/ n **1** a mark like a star (*), used to make you look at a note at the bottom of a page **2** a mark like a star (*), often used in grammar to show that something is incorrect

as·te·roid /'æstərɔɪd/ n one of many small planets (PLANET) between MARS and JUPITER

asth·ma /'æsmə ‖ 'æzmə/ n [U] a disease which makes breathing very difficult at times **–asthmatic** /æs'mætɪk ‖ æz-/ adj,n : *He is asthmatic.*

as·ton·ish /ə'stɒnɪʃ ‖ ə'stɑː-/ v [T] to fill someone with great surprise: *Kate's memory for names and faces astonishes me.* **–astonished** adj : *I was astonished to find out how rich they are.* **–astonishing** adj : *Her performance in the play was astonishing.*

as·ton·ish·ment /ə'stɒnɪʃmənt ‖ ə'stɑː-/ n [U] great surprise

as·tound /ə'staʊnd/ v [T] to fill someone with shock and surprise: *He was astounded when he heard he had won.* **–astounding** adj

a·stray /ə'streɪ/ adv **1 go astray** to go off the right path and get lost **2 lead someone astray** to introduce someone to bad habits: *The attractions of the big city soon led the young man astray.*

a·stride /ə'straɪd/ adv,prep with a leg on each side of something: *He was sitting astride his horse.*

as·trin·gent /ə'strɪndʒənt/ adj **1** able to tighten up someone's skin or stop bleeding **2** severe and bitter: *an astringent remark*

as·trol·o·gy /ə'strɒlədʒi ‖ ə'strɑː-/ n [U] the art of understanding the supposed influence of the stars and planets (PLANET) on events and on people's character **–astrological** /,æstrə'lɒdʒɪkəl ‖ -'lɑː-/ adj **–astrologically** /-kli/ adv **–astrologer** /ə'strɒlədʒəʳ ‖ ə'strɑː-/ n

as·tro·naut /'æstrənɔːt ‖ -nɔːt, -nɑːt/ n a person who travels in a spacecraft

as·tro·nom·i·cal /,æstrə'nɒmɪkəl ‖ -'nɑː-/ adj **1** concerning the study of the stars **2** infml extremely large: *Astronomical sums of money will be needed for this plan.* **–astronomically** /-kli/ adv

as·tron·o·my /ə'strɒnəmi ‖ ə'strɑː-/ n [U] the scientific study of the sun, moon, and stars **–astronomer** n

as·tute /ə'stjuːt ‖ ə'stuːt/ adj clever and quickly able to see something that is to your advantage **–astutely** adv **–astuteness** n [U]

a·sy·lum /ə'saɪləm/ n **1** [U] protection and shelter, especially when it is given by a government to people who have left their country for political reasons: *The refugees were granted political asylum.* **2** [C] old fash a hospital which treats illnesses of the mind

at /ət; strong æt/ prep **1** in a particular place: *He was standing at the door.* | *I'll be at home this afternoon* | *I bumped into Mary at the post office.* | *The children are all at school.* | *We spent five hours waiting at the airport.* | *They live at number 24 Bridge Street.* –see picture on page 540 **2** when it is a particular time: *I'll see you at two o'clock.* | *We got home at midnight.* | *I got up at dawn.* | *He died at Christmas.* **3** towards someone or something: *He picked up a stone and threw it at me.* | *There's no need to shout at me!* | *He shot at the bird, but missed.* | *She looked at me and smiled.* **4** because of something: *I was very surprised at the outcome of the discussions.* | *We all laughed at his jokes.* **5 good at something, bad at something,** etc. able to do something well, badly, etc.: *She's not very good at tennis.* | *I'm very bad at cooking.* **6** used to show the cost, speed, age, or rate of something: *The book is being sold at £3.95.* | *We were driving along at sixty miles per hour.* | *He left school at sixteen.* | *Unemployment is increasing at an alarming rate.*

ate /et, eɪt ‖ eɪt/ the past tense of EAT
■ USAGE Most British people say /et/, though some of them say /eɪt/. Most Americans say /eɪt/, and many Americans consider that /et/ is incorrect.

a·the·is·m /'eɪθi-ɪzəm/ n [U] disbelief in the existence of God

a·the·ist /'eɪθi-ɪst/ n a person who does not believe in the existence of God –compare AGNOSTIC **–atheistic** /,eɪθi'ɪstɪk/ adj

ath·lete /'æθliːt/ n a person who is very good at sports, and is physically strong and active

ath·let·ic /æθ'letɪk, əθ-/ *adj* **1** connected with athletes or athletics **2** physically strong and active, and good at sports

ath·let·ics /æθ'letɪks, əθ-/ *n* [U] sports demanding strength and speed, such as running and jumping –see picture on page 637

at·las /'ætləs/ *n* a book of maps

at·mo·sphere /'ætməsfɪəʳ/ *n* **1** the mixture of gases that surrounds the Earth, or any other PLANET **2** the air, especially in a room: *a smoky atmosphere* **3** the general character or feeling of a place: *Since the bomb exploded in the hotel, the atmosphere has been tense.*

at·mo·spher·ic /ˌætməs'ferɪk◂/ *adj* **1** [always before a noun] of or concerning the Earth's atmosphere: *atmospheric pressure* **2** beautiful and full of mystery: *atmospheric music*

at·oll /'ætɒl ‖ 'ætɔːl, 'ætɑːl/ *n* a ring-shaped island made of CORAL

at·om /'ætəm/ *n* the smallest piece of a substance that can exist alone or can combine with other substances to form a chemical chain

atom bomb /'··· ·/ (also **atomic bomb** /·ˌ·· '·/) *n old fash* a bomb that uses the explosive power made by splitting atoms

a·tom·ic /ə'tɒmɪk ‖ ə'tɑː-/ *adj* **1** of or concerning an atom or atoms **2** working on or moving by the power made by splitting atoms –**atomically** /-kli/ *adv*

atomic en·er·gy /·ˌ··'···/ *n* [U] the power made by splitting atoms; it is used to make electricity, and in NUCLEAR weapons

a·tone /ə'təʊn/ *v* **atoned, atoning atone for something** to make repayment for something bad that you have done: *He tried to atone for his sins by a life of prayer.* –**atonement** *n* [U]

a·tro·cious /ə'trəʊʃəs/ *adj* **1** extremely cruel and shocking: *atrocious crimes* **2** *infml* very bad: *an atrocious meal* –**atrociously** *adv*

a·troc·i·ty /ə'trɒsɪti ‖ ə'trɑː-/ *n* **atrocities** an act of great evil or cruelty: *Many atrocities were committed during the war.*

at·tach /ə'tætʃ/ *v* [T] **1** to fix, fasten, or join one thing to another: *Please attach a photograph to the application form.* | *There's a health club attached to the hotel.* **2 be attached to** to be connected to a group or organization, especially for a short time: *I was attached to the art department for three months during my training.* **3 be attached to someone** to be fond of someone: *I am very attached to her.* **4 attach importance to something** to think that something is important

at·tach·ment /ə'tætʃmənt/ *n* **1** [C] something that can be fixed to something else: *This machine has a special attachment for cutting metal.* **2** [C;U] fondness or friendship

at·tack¹ /ə'tæk/ *v* **1** [I;T] to use violence against someone or against a place especially with weapons: *The enemy attacked at night.* | *She was attacked on her way home.* **2** [T] to speak or write strongly against someone: *The minister has been strongly attacked by the newspapers for his comments.* **3** [T] to harm or damage something, especially by a continuing action: *This disease attacks most crops.* **4** [T] to begin to deal with something with determination: *We should attack the problem at once.* –**attacker** *n*

attack² *n* **1** [C;U] an act of violence intended to harm: *There has been an attack on the president's*

life. | *vicious attacks* | *nuclear attack* **2** [C] a piece of writing that is strongly against someone or something: *The article contained an attack on government policy.* **3** [C] a sudden and severe period of illness: *an attack of malaria* **4 come/be under attack** to suffer violence or strong disapproval: *The city is under attack.* | *The headmaster came under attack for his views.*

at·tain /ə'teɪn/ *v* [T] to succeed in gaining something, especially after effort: *He attained the position of company director.* –**attainable** *adj* –**attainment** *n*

at·tempt¹ /ə'tempt/ *v* [T] to make an effort to do something which may be difficult: *The second question was so difficult I didn't even attempt it.* | *I attempted to speak but was told to be quiet.*
□ USEFUL PATTERNS to attempt something; to attempt to do something

attempt² *n* **1** an effort made to do something: *I passed my driving test at the second attempt.* | *It was his attempt at humour, but nobody laughed.* | *He made several attempts to escape.*
□ USEFUL PATTERNS an attempt at something; an attempt to do something
2 an attempt on someone's life an effort made to kill someone: *The President has survived two attempts on his life.*

at·tend /ə'tend/ *v* **1** [I;T] to be present at an event: *I shall be attending the meeting.* | *How many children attend the school?* | *Unfortunately, I was unable to attend.* **2** [I] *fml* to give your attention to something: *Are you attending to what I am saying?* **3** [T] *fml* to go with someone in order to look after them: *The Queen was attended by her bodyguard.*
■ USAGE People who **attend** a play or concert are the **audience**; people who **attend** a religious service are the **congregation**; people who **attend** a game, such as football, are **spectators**. But an **attendant** is someone whose job is to look after a public place: *a swimming-pool attendant.*

attend to sbdy/sthg *phr v* [T] to deal with something or look after someone: *I have an urgent matter to attend to.* | *She's attending to the baby.*

at·tend·ance /ə'tendəns/ *n* **1** [C;U] the act of being present, especially regularly: *Attendance at school is required by law.* | *Church attendances have fallen in recent years.* **2** [sing] the number of people present at an event: *The public meeting attracted a large attendance.* **3 in attendance on** *fml* going or being with someone in order to help them: *A doctor is in attendance on the Queen.*

at·tend·ant /ə'tendənt/ *n* a person who looks after a place or person: *a museum attendant* –see ATTEND (USAGE)

at·ten·tion /ə'tenʃən/ *n* [U] **1** the act of fixing your mind on something, especially by watching or listening carefully: *I felt I had her full attention.* | *He likes to be the centre of attention.* | *Your request will receive our full attention.* **2 pay attention** to listen carefully and give your full thought to something: *The teacher told the students to pay attention.* | *I didn't pay attention to what she said.* **3 attract/ catch someone's attention** to make someone notice something: *I tried to attract the waiter's attention.* **4** particular care or notice: *Old cars often need a lot of attention to keep them working.* **5 at/to attention** standing straight and still like a soldier

at·ten·tive /ə'tentɪv/ *adj* **1** taking careful notice of things: *The class was very attentive and quiet.* **2** kind and helpful: *He was very attentive to his grandmother and did everything for her.* –opposite inattentive –**attentively** *adv* –**attentiveness** *n* [U]

at·tic /ˈætɪk/ n the room at the top of a house just below the roof

at·tire /əˈtaɪəʳ/ n [U] fml clothes

at·ti·tude /ˈætɪtjuːd ‖ -tuːd/ n 1 a way of feeling, thinking, or behaving: I found her attitude very unfriendly. | She has a very odd attitude to money. | His attitude towards me was always rather cold. | Attitudes have changed since I was young. 2 fml the position in which someone is standing or sitting

at·tor·ney /əˈtɜːni ‖ -ɜːr-/ n the usual American word for LAWYER

at·tract /əˈtrækt/ v [T] 1 to make someone like or admire someone or something: She was attracted by his smile. | I've always been attracted to tall women. 2 attract attention to be noticed and receive attention: Her novel has attracted a lot of attention. 3 to cause interest, or make something come near: Flowers attract bees. | I am not attracted to city life.

at·trac·tion /əˈtrækʃən/ n 1 [U] the ability to attract people: The idea of travelling to the moon holds little attraction for me. | physical attraction 2 [C] something which people admire and are interested in: The main attraction of this town is its excellent theatre. | tourist attractions

at·trac·tive /əˈtræktɪv/ adj 1 causing interest or pleasure: The idea is very attractive. 2 pretty or HANDSOME (used of a person): an attractive man 3 pleasant to look at: The garden looks very attractive. –see BEAUTIFUL (USAGE) **–attractively** adv **–attractiveness** n [U]

at·tri·bute /ˈætrɪbjuːt/ n a quality forming part of the nature of a person or thing: Kindness is one of his many attributes.

at·trib·ute /əˈtrɪbjuːt ‖ -bjət/ v **attributed, attributing attribute something to** to believe something to be the result or work of: Jim attributes his success to hard work. | This song is usually attributed to J. S. Bach.

at·tuned /əˈtjuːnd ‖ əˈtuːnd/ adj **be attuned to something** to be used to or ready for something: I'm not really attuned to his way of thinking yet.

au·ber·gine /ˈəʊbəʒiːn ‖ -bər-/ n [C;U] BrE a large fruit with a purple skin that is eaten as a vegetable

au·burn /ˈɔːbən ‖ -ərn/ adj reddish-brown (used especially of hair) –see picture on page 245

auc·tion¹ /ˈɔːkʃən/ n 1 a public meeting to sell goods to the person who offers the most money: a furniture auction 2 **by auction, at auction** at an auction: The paintings will be sold by auction.

auction² v [T] to sell something at an auction

auc·tio·neer /ˌɔːkʃəˈnɪəʳ/ n a person who is in charge of an auction

au·da·cious /ɔːˈdeɪʃəs/ adj fml willing to be daring and take risks **–audaciously** adv

au·dac·i·ty /ɔːˈdæsəti/ n [U] behaviour which is daring and often disrespectful

au·di·ble /ˈɔːdəbəl/ adj loud enough to be heard –opposite **inaudible**: His reply was barely audible. **–audibly** adv **–audibility** /ˌɔːdəˈbɪləti/ n

au·di·ence /ˈɔːdɪəns ‖ ˈɔː-, ˈɑː-/ n [+sing/pl verb] 1 the people listening to or watching a performance, speech, or television show: The audience was very excited. | a radio audience of 10 million | a member of the audience | Cinema audiences have declined. 2 a formal meeting between somebody powerful and somebody less important: He had an audience with the Pope.

au·di·o /ˈɔːdi-əʊ/ adj [always before a noun] tech connected with or used in the broadcasting or receiving of sound radio signals

au·di·o-vis·u·al /ˌ...ˈ...◂/ adj using pictures and sound in educational materials: The school's audio-visual equipment includes videos and cassettes.

au·dit /ˈɔːdɪt/ v [T] to make an official examination of the accounts of a business **–auditor** n

au·di·tion¹ /ɔːˈdɪʃən/ n a performance given by a singer, actor, or dancer as a test of their ability for a particular job

audition² v [I;T] to give or make someone give an audition

au·di·to·ri·um /ˌɔːdɪˈtɔːriəm/ n the space in a theatre where people sit when listening to or watching a performance

aug·ment /ɔːgˈment/ v [I;T] fml to make something become bigger by adding to it: He augments his income by working in the evenings.

au·gur /ˈɔːgəʳ/ v **augur well/ill** lit to be a sign of good or bad things in the future: This rain augurs well for the farmers.

au·gust /ɔːˈgʌst/ adj lit noble and grand

Au·gust /ˈɔːgəst/ (also **Aug**) n the 8th month of the year

aunt /ɑːnt ‖ ænt/ (also **aunt·ie, aunt·y** /ˈɑːnti ‖ ˈænti/ infml) n the sister of your father or mother, or the wife of your uncle: Take me swimming, Auntie Jane! | My aunt lives in the country. –see picture on page 343

au pair /ˌəʊ ˈpeəʳ/ n (also **au pair girl** /ˈ· ˈ· ˌ·/) a young foreign woman who lives with a family in order to learn their language, in return for doing light work in the house

au·ra /ˈɔːrə/ n an effect or feeling that seems to surround and come from a person or place: There was an aura of decay in the village.

au·ral /ˈɔːrəl/ adj tech of or related to the sense of hearing: aural skills

aus·pic·es /ˈɔːspɪsəz/ n [pl] **under the auspices of** fml with the support and approval of: This conference has been arranged under the auspices of the United Nations.

aus·pi·cious /ɔːˈspɪʃəs/ adj fml promising or showing signs of future success: We are gathered here on this auspicious occasion... **–auspiciously** adv

aus·tere /ɔːˈstɪəʳ, ɒ- ‖ ɔː-/ adj 1 without comfort or enjoyment: Life in the monastery was austere. 2 very serious: an austere manner 3 plain and without decoration **–austerely** adv **–austerity** /ɔːˈsterəti, ɒ- ‖ ɔː-/ n [U]

au·then·tic /ɔːˈθentɪk/ adj known to have been made, painted, or written by a particular person or at a particular time and known not to be a copy: This is an authentic Roman coin. **–authenticity** /ˌɔːθenˈtɪsəti/ n [U]

au·then·tic·ate /ɔːˈθentɪkeɪt/ v **authenticated, authenticating** [T] to prove that something is authentic and not a copy **–authentication** /ɔːˌθentɪˈkeɪʃən/ n [U]

au·thor /ˈɔːθəʳ/ n 1 the writer of a book, article, play, poem, or any piece of writing 2 the person who produces an idea or plan

au·thor·i·tar·i·an /ɔːˌθɒrɪˈteəriən ‖ ɔːˌθɑː-, əˌθɔː-/ adj demanding that rules and laws must always be obeyed, and that personal freedom is not important: an authoritarian style of government **–authoritarian** n : He's a strict authoritarian. **–authoritarianism** n [U]

au·thor·i·ta·tive /ɔːˈθɒrɪtətɪv, ə- ‖ əˈθɑːrəteɪtɪv, əˈθɔː-/ adj **1** having or showing power and the ability to command or control others: *an authoritative voice* **2** that can be completely trusted: *an authoritative dictionary* –**authoritatively** adv

au·thor·i·ty /ɔːˈθɒrɪti, ə- ‖ əˈθɑː-, əˈθɔː-/ n **authorities 1** [U] the power or right to control and command people: *She enjoys exercising her authority over her staff.* | *Young people have no respect for authority these days.* **2 in authority** having power over other people: *She has no respect for people in authority.* **3** [U] the right to do a particular thing: *I do not have the authority to sign any contracts.* **4** [C] a person or group with the power or right to control and command people: *The government is the highest authority in the country.* | *the local education authority* **5 the authorities** the government or a government department: *The authorities have refused to allow him to enter the country.* **6** [U] the ability to influence people: *Although she has no official position in the party, she has a lot of authority.* **7** [C] a person who knows a lot about a subject and is respected: *She is an authority on Roman history.*

au·thor·ize /ˈɔːθəraɪz/ v **authorized, authorizing** (also **authorise** BrE) [T] to give permission: *Who is authorized to sign these invoices?* | *I cannot authorize payment of this bill until it has been checked.*
□ USEFUL PATTERNS to authorize something; to authorize someone to do something –**authorization, authorisation** /ˌɔːθəraɪˈzeɪʃən ‖ ˌɔːθərə-/ n [C;U]

au·to·bi·og·ra·phy /ˌɔːtəbaɪˈɒgrəfi ‖ -baɪˈɑː-/ n **autobiographies** a book written by someone about their own life –compare BIOGRAPHY –**autobiographical** /ˌɔːtəbaɪəˈgræfɪkəl/ adj –**autobiographically** /-kli/ adv

au·toc·ra·cy /ɔːˈtɒkrəsi ‖ ɔːˈtɑː-/ n **autocracies** [C;U] rule by one person with unlimited power

au·to·crat /ˈɔːtəkræt/ n **1** a ruler with unlimited power **2** a person who gives orders without considering the wishes of other people –**autocratic** /ˌɔːtəˈkrætɪk◄/ adj –**autocratically** /-kli/ adv

au·to·graph¹ /ˈɔːtəgrɑːf ‖ -græf/ n a famous person's name, written in their own handwriting: *We asked the singer for her autograph.*

autograph² v [T] to sign something with your own name: *I've got an autographed copy of her book.*

au·to·mate /ˈɔːtəmeɪt/ v **automated, automating** [T] to make something work by machinery and without the work of people: *The factory is now fully automated.*

au·to·mat·ic /ˌɔːtəˈmætɪk◄/ adj **1** able to work or move by itself without needing the operation of a person (of a machine): *The heating system here has an automatic temperature control.* | *This washing machine is fully automatic.* **2** done without thinking, especially as a habit: *The movements needed to ride a bicycle soon become automatic.* **3** certain to happen, without the need for further action: *You will get an automatic pay increase every year.* –**automatically** /-kli/ adv

au·to·ma·tion /ˌɔːtəˈmeɪʃən/ n [U] the use of machines that need little or no human control

au·to·mo·bile /ˈɔːtəməbiːl ‖ -məu-/ n fml, AmE a car: *the automobile industry*

au·ton·o·mous /ɔːˈtɒnəməs ‖ ɔːˈtɑː-/ adj having autonomy: *Catalonia is an autonomous region of Spain.* –**autonomously** adv

au·ton·o·my /ɔːˈtɒnəmi ‖ ɔːˈtɑː-/ n [U] the right of self-government or management of your own affairs, usually of a state or group within a country

au·top·sy /ˈɔːtɒpsi ‖ -taːp-/ n **autopsies** an examination of a dead body to discover the cause of death

au·tumn /ˈɔːtəm/ n (also **Autumn**) [C;U] the season between summer and winter: *I left England last autumn.* –**autumnal** /ɔːˈtʌmnəl/ adj

aux·il·i·a·ry /ɔːgˈzɪljəri, ɔːk- ‖ ɔːgˈzɪljəri, -ˈzɪləri/ adj giving help or additional support: *auxiliary workers* –**auxiliary** n **auxiliaries**

auxiliary verb /·,···¹·/ n tech a verb that is used with another verb to show differences such as person and tense; in English the auxiliary verbs are **be**, **do**, and **have** (e.g. in *"I am running"*, *"I didn't climb"*, *"they have heard"*)

a·vail¹ /əˈveɪl/ n lit **to no avail** without success: *We tried and tried, but it was all to no avail.*

avail² v **avail yourself of** fml to make use of a chance to do something: *You should avail yourself of every opportunity to improve your English.*

a·vai·la·ble /əˈveɪləbəl/ adj **1** able to be obtained or used: *I'm sorry, Madam, those shoes are only available in small sizes.* | *When will the paperback edition be available?* **2** free to see or talk to someone: *The doctor is not available just now.* | *I will be available on Monday.* –opposite **unavailable** –**availability** /ə,veɪləˈbɪlɪti/ n [U]

av·a·lanche /ˈævəlɑːnʃ ‖ -læntʃ/ n **1** a large mass of rocks or snow and ice crashing down the side of a mountain **2** a lot of things happening or coming at the same time: *An avalanche of letters landed on the doormat.*

a·vant-garde /ˌævɒŋ ˈgɑːd ‖ ˌævɑːŋ ˈgɑːrd/ adj based on the newest and most modern ideas in music, theatre, and literature: *an avant-garde painter*

av·a·rice /ˈævərɪs/ n [U] fml extreme desire for wealth –**avaricious** /ˌævəˈrɪʃəs◄/ adj

Ave n a written abbreviation for AVENUE

a·venge /əˈvendʒ/ v **avenged, avenging** [T] fml to do harm to someone in return for something bad that they have done: *He avenged his brother's death by burning the house.* –**avenger** n

av·e·nue /ˈævɪnjuː ‖ -nuː/ n **1** a wide road in a town, often between two rows of trees: *My address is 11 Carlton Avenue, Bristol.* **2** a way of getting something done: *They explored every avenue but could not find a solution.*

av·e·rage¹ /ˈævərɪdʒ/ n **1** [C] the amount found by adding together several quantities and then dividing by the number of quantities: *The average of 3, 8, and 10 is 7.* | *The price of cars has increased by an average of 6%.* **2** [U] a level or standard regarded as usual or ordinary **3 above average** better than average: *Tanya is good at maths – well above average.* [RELATED PHRASE **below average**] **3 on average** usually: *On average babies start walking at a year old.*

average² adj [only before a noun] **1** calculated by making an average of a number of quantities: *What is the average rainfall for July?* **2** regarded as usual or ordinary: *The average British family has two children.* | *I am of average weight.* **3** neither good or bad in quality: *The film was just average – nothing special.*

average³ v **averaged, averaging** [T] to do or have something regularly, usually, as an average: *Our company averages 20 enquiries a day.*

average out phr v [I] infml to come to an average quantity or standard over a period of time: *My hours of work average out at about 35 a week.*

a·verse /ə'vɜːs ‖ -ɜːrs/ adj **averse to** opposed to: *I don't drink usually, but I am not averse to the occasional glass of champagne.*

a·ver·sion /ə'vɜːʃən ‖ ə'vɜːrʒən/ n [sing] a strong dislike for something: *She has an aversion to cats.*

a·vert /ə'vɜːt ‖ -ɜːrt/ v [T] **1** to prevent something unpleasant from happening: *An accident was only averted by her quick thinking.* **2** *fml* to turn away: *He quickly averted his gaze.*

a·vi·a·ry /'eɪviəri ‖ 'eɪvieri/ n **aviaries** a large cage or enclosure for keeping birds in

a·vi·a·tion /ˌeɪvi'eɪʃən ‖ ˌeɪ-, ˌæ-/ n [U] **1** the development and production of aircraft **2** the business of operating aircraft

a·vi·a·tor /'eɪvieɪtər ‖ 'eɪ-, 'æ-/ n old fash the pilot of an aircraft

av·id /'ævɪd/ adj doing something a lot because you enjoy it: *Liz is an avid reader.* **–avidly** adv

av·o·ca·do /ˌævə'kɑːdəʊ◄/ (also **avocado pear** /ˌ... '◄/) n a green tropical fruit with a large stone and smooth oily flesh

a·void /ə'vɔɪd/ v [T] **1** to make an effort not to do something or to stop something from happening: *A healthy diet will help you avoid heart disease.* | *She avoided answering most of my questions.* | *He left the room to avoid having to speak to her.*
□ USEFUL PATTERNS to avoid something; to avoid doing something
2 to keep away from a person, place, or thing: *Turn right here to avoid the city centre.* | *The doctor's told me to avoid alcohol.* **–avoidable** adj **–avoidance** n [U] : *tax avoidance*

a·vow /ə'vaʊ/ v [T;+that] fml to state or admit something openly **–avowal** n [C;U]

a·vowed /ə'vaʊd/ adj [only before a noun] openly declared or admitted: *an avowed Communist*

a·wait /ə'weɪt/ v [T] fml **1** to wait for something: *I am awaiting their reply.* **2** to be ready for someone: *A warm welcome awaits you.*

a·wake[1] /ə'weɪk/ adj [never before a noun] **1** not asleep: *She lay awake for hours, thinking.* | *I'm not really awake until I've had a cup of coffee.* **2 awake to something** fml conscious of something: *He is awake to the difficulties he faces.* **3 wide awake** not at all sleepy

awake[2] /ə'weɪk/ v **awoke** /ə'wəʊk/ or **awaked**, **awaked** or **awoken** /ə'wəʊkən/, **awaking** (also **awaken**) fml **1** [I;T] to stop sleeping: *I awoke to the sound of birds singing.* | *The noise awoke me.* **2 awake to something** to become conscious of something: *Suddenly they awoke to the danger.*

a·wak·en·ing /ə'weɪkənɪŋ/ n **1** the beginning of a feeling or activity: *There has been an awakening of concern for the environment.* **2 a rude awakening** a shock felt when you find out or suddenly understand something unpleasant

a·ward[1] /ə'wɔːd ‖ ə'wɔːrd/ v [T] to officially give a prize or money to someone for a special reason: *He was awarded the Nobel Prize for Literature.* | *The judge awarded a large sum of money to the families of the dead.*
□ USEFUL PATTERNS to award something to someone; to award someone something

award[2] n a prize or money, given by an organization for a special reason: *the award for Best Actress* | *The University sometimes gives awards to students with financial difficulties.*

a·ware /ə'weər/ adj having knowledge or understanding: *Women are often more aware of their feelings than men.* | *Are you aware that there is a problem?* | *I'm quite aware of how you must feel.* | *She is very politically aware.*
□ USEFUL PATTERNS be aware of something; be aware that... –opposite **unaware** **–awareness** n [U]

a·wash /ə'wɒʃ ‖ ə'wɔːʃ, ə'wɑːʃ/ adj [never before a noun] **1** covered with water: *The river flooded, and soon the streets were awash.* **2 awash with something** infml having too much of something: *The office is awash with computers but there's no money for new staff.*

a·way[1] /ə'weɪ/ adv **1** moving from a place: *He got into the car and drove away.* | *She walked away from the house.* | *Go away!* –see picture on page 540 **2** distant from a place: *Is your house far away?* | *They live three miles away.* **3** not at home or at your usual place of work: *She's away on holiday at the moment.* | *He had to go away on business.* **4** in a safe place: *I'll put the plates away.* **5** so as to be gone: *The water had all boiled away.* **6** all the time or continuously: *They worked away all day.*

away[2] adj [only before a noun] played at the sports field of your opponent: *We've got an away match next week.*

awe /ɔː/ n [U] **1** a feeling of respect mixed with fear or admiration: *I watched the powerful ocean with awe.* **2 in awe of someone** having feelings of respect and fear for someone: *He is in awe of his father.*

awe-in·spir·ing /'··ˌ··/ adj causing feelings of awe

awe·some /'ɔːsəm/ adj causing feelings of awe: *an awesome account of the terrors of war* | *an awesome responsibility*

awe·struck /'ɔːstrʌk/ adj fml filled with awe: *We sat in awestruck silence after hearing the truth at last.*

aw·ful /'ɔːfəl/ adj **1** very unpleasant and shocking: *The pain was awful.* | *That's awful news.* **2** infml not very well: *I feel awful.* **3** infml not very pleasant: *What an awful day!* | *The food tasted awful.* **4 an awful lot** infml very many or very much: *I've got an awful lot of things to do.* | *Big dogs need an awful lot of food.* | *Babies cry an awful lot!*

aw·ful·ly /'ɔːfəli/ adv infml very: *It's awfully cold in here.* | *That's an awfully good idea.*

a·while /ə'waɪl/ adv fml for a short time

awk·ward /'ɔːkwəd ‖ -ərd/ adj **1** lacking skill in moving your body easily or confidently: *He is rather awkward with his hands.* **2** difficult to use or do: *an awkward size* | *This machine is awkward to clean.* **3** causing difficulty or uncomfortable feelings: *Our visitors came at an awkward time.* | *She asked me some very awkward questions.* | *an awkward silence* **4** unwilling to help: *Stop being so awkward!* **–awkwardly** adv **–awkwardness** n [U]

aw·ning /'ɔːnɪŋ/ n a covering made of strong cloth, used as protection from sun or rain

a·woke /ə'wəʊk/ the past tense of AWAKE

a·wok·en /ə'wəʊkən/ the past participle of AWAKE

axe[1] /æks/ n **axes** /'æksɪz/ (also **ax** AmE) a tool with a heavy metal blade on the end of a long handle, used to cut wood –see picture on page 638

axe[2] v **axed**, **axing** (also **ax** AmE) [T] to reduce costs, plans, or services or to stop them completely: *The new school project was axed by the government.*

ax·i·om /'æksiəm/ n a statement that is accepted as true by most people **–axiomatic** /ˌæksiə'mætɪk◄/ adj

ax·is /ˈæksɪ̣s/ n **axes** /ˈæksiːs/ **1** the imaginary line around which something moves: *The Earth turns on its axis.* **2** a line at the side (X-axis) or bottom (Y-axis) of a GRAPH, along which things are measured

ax·le /ˈæksəl/ n a bar with a wheel on each end

aye /aɪ/ adv dialect yes: *Aye, aye, sir.*

az·ure /ˈæʒəʳ, ˈæʒjʊəʳ, ˈæzjʊəʳ ‖ ˈæʒər/ adj bright blue: *the azure sky*

B,b

B, b /biː/ *B's, b's or* **Bs, bs** **1** the 2nd letter of the English alphabet **2** when you have several points you want to make, you can order them and show where each one starts by using "a", "b", "c", etc; teachers and speakers on technical subjects do this, and some people use them in conversation: *There are two reasons why the plant has failed to flower: a, it hasn't had enough light and, b, the temperature hasn't been sufficiently high.* | *"Do you think he'll get the job?" "Well, I don't really because, a, he hasn't got the qualifications and, b, he hasn't got much experience."*

b. a written abbreviation for BORN: *b. 1885*

BA /ˌbiː ˈeɪ/ **1** an abbreviation for BACHELOR OF ARTS: a first university degree not in a scientific subject: *He has a BA.* **2** a person who has a BA: *John Stephens, BA*

baa /baː/ *n* the sound that a sheep or lamb makes

bab·ble /ˈbæbəl/ *v* **babbled, babbling** [I] **1** to talk quickly and foolishly, or in a way that is hard to understand: *What are you babbling on about?* **2** to make continuous sounds like a stream: *a babbling stream* | *The baby babbled away for hours.* –**babble** *n*

babe /beɪb/ *n* **1** *old fash* a baby **2** *AmE slang* a woman, usually a young one

ba·boon /bəˈbuːn ‖ bæ-/ *n* a large monkey

ba·by /ˈbeɪbi/ *n* **babies** **1** a very young child, usually one who has not yet learnt to speak: *It's a baby girl.* | *a tiny baby* –see CHILD (USAGE) **2** a very young animal or bird: *a baby monkey* **3** something younger or smaller than others like it: *She's the baby of the class.* **4** *infml* something that is the special responsibility of a particular person: *You'd better ask Peter about that – it's his baby.* **5** *AmE slang* a word used to address someone you love

baby car·ri·age /ˈ··· ˌ··/ *n* the usual American word for PRAM

ba·by·hood /ˈbeɪbihʊd/ *n* [U] the period of time when you are a baby

ba·by·ish /ˈbeɪbi-ɪʃ/ *derog* **1** like a baby: *They told him it was babyish to cry.* **2** suitable for a baby: *That toy's too babyish for a six-year-old.*

baby-mind·er /ˈ··· ˌ··/ *n BrE* a person who looks after your baby

baby-sit /ˈ··· ·/ *v* **baby-sat, baby-sat, baby-sitting** [I] to look after children while their parents are out: *I'm baby-sitting for Mrs Davis tonight.* –**baby-sitter** *n*: *We couldn't go out because we couldn't get a baby-sitter.*

bach·e·lor /ˈbætʃələr/ *n* an unmarried man

Bachelor of Arts /ˌ··· · ˈ·/ *n* –see BA

Bachelor of Sci·ence /ˌ··· · ··/ *n* –see BSC

back¹ /bæk/ *n* **1** the part of your body that is behind you, opposite your chest, and goes from your neck to your bottom: *He was lying on the floor on his back.* | *She was carrying a baby on her back.* –see PAIN (USAGE) **2** **the back** the part of something that is opposite the front: *Please write your address on the back of the cheque.* | *The index is at the back of the book.* | *We couldn't hear very well because we were right at the back of the hall.* **3** the part of a chair that you lean on when you are sitting **4** **be glad to see the back of** to be glad when you do not have to see someone or something any more **5** **behind someone's back** in a way that is unknown to the person concerned: *The decision was taken behind my back.* | *They've been talking about me behind my back.* **6** **put someone's back up** to annoy someone **7** **the back of beyond** a place that is far away from other places **8** **turn your back on someone** to refuse to help or see someone

back² *adv* **1** in the direction that is behind you: *She stepped back to look at the painting.* | *He turned round and looked back towards the town.* **2** where someone or something was before: *I put the book back on the shelf.* | *We'll be back home tomorrow.* **3** away from a person or thing: *Stand back from the fire.* **4** in someone's possession again: *She gave the book back to me.* | *I don't know if I'll ever get my money back.* **5** in reply: *I'll phone you back later.* | *I wrote to her but she never wrote back.* **6** towards or in an earlier time: *This law was brought in back in 1968.*

back³ *adj* [only before a noun] **1** at the back: *I always use the back door.* | *the back wheels of the car* **2** owed from an earlier time: *The company owes me £500 in back pay.* **3** **back road, back street** a small road in a town or city

back⁴ *v* **1** [I] to move backwards: *He backed out of the room.* | *The car backed out of the garage.* **2** [T] to make a vehicle move backwards: *She backed the car down the drive.* **3** [T] to support someone, often by giving them money: *We persuaded a couple of firms to back the project.* **4** [T] to put money on a person or animal in a race: *I backed three horses and they all lost!*

back away *phr v* [I] to move away from someone or something because you are frightened

back down *phr v* [I] to admit that you were wrong about something

back onto sth *phr v* [T] (of a building) to have something at the back: *The house backs onto open fields.*

back out *phr v* [I] to decide that you will not do something that you had agreed to do: *They backed out of the deal at the last minute.*

back sbdy/sth **↔ up** *phr v* [T] to support someone or something, especially by showing that they are telling the truth: *The evidence seems to back up what you are saying.*

back·bit·ing /ˈbækbaɪtɪŋ/ *n* [U] unkind talk about someone who is not present

back·bone /ˈbækbəʊn/ *n* **1** [C] the row of bones in the centre of your back **2** [sing] the part of a group that provides the main support: *Small farmers form the backbone of our nation!* **3** [U] strength of character: *"No backbone," said the old man. "That's the trouble with young people today!"*

back·break·ing /ˈbækbreɪkɪŋ/ *adj* very hard and needing a lot of effort: *backbreaking work*

back·date /ˌbækˈdeɪt/ *v* **backdated, backdating** [T] to make something come into operation from an earlier date: *The increase in pay agreed in June will be backdated to January.*

back·drop /ˈbækdrɒp ‖ -drɑːp/ (also **backcloth** /-klɒθ ‖ -klɔːθ/) *n* a situation in which something happens: *The events of the 1930s provided the backdrop for the film.*

back·er /ˈbækər/ *n* someone who supports a plan or a person with money

back·fire /ˌbækˈfaɪər ‖ ˈbækfaɪər/ *v* **backfired, backfiring** [I] **1** to make a loud noise as a result of an explosion in the engine which comes too soon (used of a motor vehicle) **2** to have an effect opposite to the effect intended: *His plan to get rich back-fired and he lost all his money.*

back·gam·mon /ˈbækgæmən/ *n* [U] a game for two players, using round wooden pieces and DICE on a special board

back·ground /ˈbækgraʊnd/ *n* **1** [C] the scenery or ground behind the main objects or people in view, a picture, or a photograph: *This is a photo of my house; in the background you can see the mountains.* **2** [C;U] the conditions that exist when something happens and that help to explain it: *The election took place against a background of widespread unemployment.* | *I'll need a bit more background information before I can help you.* **3** [C] a person's family, experience, and education: *She's from a rather disturbed background.* **4 in the background** not noticed very much: *She's got a lot of power, but she likes to remain in the background.*

back·hand /ˈbækhænd/ *n* a stroke in tennis made with the back of the hand turned in the direction of movement: *He's got an excellent backhand.* –compare FOREHAND

back·hand·ed /ˌbækˈhændɪd◀ | ˈbækhændɪd/ *adj* **backhanded compliment** a remark about someone that sounds pleasant but is usually not intended kindly

back·hand·er /ˈbækhændər/ *n infml* money given to someone in order to influence their actions or decisions

back·ing /ˈbækɪŋ/ *n* **1** [U] help or support, especially by giving money: *The plan has plenty of backing, and will probably succeed.* **2** [C;U] any kind of material that is put on the back of an object to protect it: *a cardboard backing* **3** [C] the music or singing that helps and supports the main singer or musician

back·lash /ˈbæklæʃ/ *n* **1** a strong but usually delayed feeling by many people against a growing belief or practice, especially towards a political or social development **2** a sudden violent backward movement

back·log /ˈbæklɒg | -lɔːg, -lɑːg/ *n* a lot of things needing to be done that were not done at the proper time: *After his holiday, he had a large backlog of work to deal with.*

back·pack /ˈbækpæk/ *n AmE* a special type of bag that you carry on your back –**backpacker** *n* –**backpacking** *n* [U]

back·ped·al /ˌbækˈpedl | ˈbækˌpedl/ *v* **-ll-** (**-l-** *AmE*) **1** to PEDAL backwards, on a bicycle **2** *infml* to do or say something differently from the way you were going to do or say it

back seat /ˌ·ˈ·◀/ *n* **1** a seat at the back of a car **2 take a back seat** to take a less important position: *She won't take a back seat to anyone.*

back·side /ˈbæksaɪd/ *n infml* the part of your body on which you sit

back·stage /ˌbækˈsteɪdʒ/ *adv* **1** behind the stage in a theatre **2** secretly

back street /ˈ··/ *n* a street away from the main streets of a town or city

back·stroke /ˈbækstrəʊk/ *n* [sing;U] a swimming stroke done on your back

back·track /ˈbæktræk/ *v* [I] **1** to go back over the same path **2** to change a promise or intention and say or do something different

back·up /ˈbækʌp/ *n* [U] help which you have in addition to, or instead of, other support **2 backup**

copy a copy of information stored on a computer which you keep separate in case the main copy is lost: *Make a backup copy, just in case you lose the file.*

back·ward /ˈbækwəd | -ərd/ *adj* **1** in the direction that is behind you: *He gave a backward glance to see if he was being followed.* **2** slow to learn things: *a backward child* **3** not having modern factories or a modern way of life: *a backward country*

back·wards /ˈbækwədz | -ərdz/ *adv* (also **backward** *AmE*) **1** in the direction that is behind you: *He stepped backwards to let him past.* **2** towards the past: *We must look forwards, not backwards.* | *He described the new law as a step backwards.* **3** in the opposite way to the way that is usual: *Can you say the alphabet backwards?* **4 backwards and forwards** first in one direction and then in the opposite direction **5 know something backwards** to know something perfectly

back·wa·ter /ˈbækwɔːtər | -wɔː-, -wɑː-/ *n* **1** a part of a river where the water does not move **2** a place not influenced by outside events or new ideas: *There's nothing for young people in this village; it's a real backwater.*

back·woods /ˈbækwʊdz/ *n* **the backwoods** uncleared land far away from towns

back·yard /ˌbækˈjɑːd | -ˈjɑːrd◀/ *n* **1** *BrE* a yard behind a house, covered with a hard surface **2** *AmE* an area of ground behind a house, usually covered with grass

ba·con /ˈbeɪkən/ *n* [U] salted or smoked meat from the back or sides of a pig –see picture on page 344 –see MEAT (USAGE)

bac·te·ri·a /bækˈtɪəriə/ *n* [pl] very small living things, some of which cause disease; they exist in water, soil, air, plants, and the bodies of people and animals

bad /bæd/ *adj* **worse** /wɜːs | wɜːrs/, **worst** /wɜːst | wɜːrst/ **1** not good or unpleasant: *a bad smell* | *The boys were punished for their bad behaviour.* | *I have some bad news for you, I'm afraid.* **2** not very skilful or of a low standard: *She is a bad teacher.* | *I'm bad at maths.* **3** unwell or hurt: *She's got a bad leg.* **4** damaging or harmful: *Smoking is bad for your health.* | *Pollution is having a bad effect on plants and animals.* **5** serious or severe: *a bad cold* | *The winter's been bad this year.* **6** not fit to eat: *This fish has gone bad.* **7 bad language** offensive language **8 bad debt** a debt that is unlikely to be paid **9 feel bad** to feel ashamed or sorry: *I do feel bad about missing your birthday.* **10 have a bad name** to have lost people's respect: *That car has a bad name among motorists.* **11 in a bad way** very ill or in serious trouble **12 it's too bad, that's too bad** *infml* I'm sorry: *It's too bad you couldn't come last night.* **13 not bad** *infml* quite good: *"How are you?" "Not bad, thanks."* | *This cake isn't at all bad.* –**badness** *n* [U]

bade /bæd, beɪd/ the past tense and past participle of BID

badge /bædʒ/ *n* anything, especially a piece of metal or plastic, worn to show a person's job, rank, or membership of a group

bad·ger¹ /ˈbædʒər/ *n* an animal which has black and white fur, lives in holes in the ground, and is active at night

badger² *v* [T] to persuade someone by asking them again and again: *The children badgered me to take them to the cinema.*

bad·ly /ˈbædli/ *adv* **1** in a bad way: *badly made clothes* | *The book was badly written.* | *I played very* *badly today.* –opposite **well** **2** very much: *They want money badly.* | *He is badly in need of help.* | *The whole area has been badly affected by snow storms.*

badly-off /ˌ··ˈ·/ *adj* **worse-off, worst-off** [never before a noun] poor

bad·min·ton /ˈbædmɪntən/ *n* [U] a game like tennis played by two or more people who hit a small feathered object called a SHUTTLECOCK over a high net

bad-tem·pered /ˌ·ˈ···◂/ *adj* feeling angry and dissatisfied: *Why are you so bad-tempered this afternoon?*

baf·fle /ˈbæfəl/ *v* **baffled, baffling** [T] to confuse someone greatly: *I was completely baffled by his remark.* –see ANGRY (USAGE) –**bafflement** *n* [U] –**baffling** *adj* : *a baffling question*

bag¹ /bæg/ *n* **1** a container made of material such as paper, plastic, or leather, used to carry things in: *a shopping bag* | *a polythene bag* –see picture on page 148 **2** a woman's handbag: *Where's my bag?* **3** the things in a bag: *Tom ate a whole bag of cherries.* **4 bags of** lots of: *bags of ideas* **5 have bags under your eyes** to look very tired **6 in the bag** *infml* certain to be won: *The contract is in the bag.*

bag² *v* **-gg-** [T] **1** to put things into bags **2** to get the right to do or have something which a lot of other people might like: *She's bagged us a couple of seats in the front row.*

bag·gage /ˈbægɪdʒ/ *n* [U] all the cases and bags you take when you travel

bag·gy /ˈbægi/ *adj* **baggier, baggiest** *infml* hanging loosely (used of clothes): *His trousers were baggy at the knees.*

bag·pipes /ˈbægpaɪps/ *n* [pl] a musical instrument in which air stored in a bag is forced out through pipes to produce the sound: *to play the bagpipes*

bail¹ /beɪl/ *n* **1** [U] money left with a court of law so that a prisoner can be set free until they are tried: *The prisoner was released on bail.* | *The judge granted bail.* **2 stand/go bail for someone** to pay money so that someone may be set free in this way **3** [C] either of two small pieces of wood laid on top of the stumps (STUMP¹) in cricket

bail² *v*
  bail out *phr v* **1** [T **bail** sbdy ↔ **out**] to obtain someone's freedom by paying money called bail to show that you are sure that they will appear in court later: *Clark was charged with robbing the bank. His family paid £5000 to bail him out.* **2** [T **bail** sbdy ↔ **out**] to help someone out of a difficult situation which they have got into, usually through their own fault **3** [I;T **bail** sthg ↔ **out**] to remove water from a boat to prevent it sinking: *Quick – start bailing out!* **4** [T **bail** sbdy/sthg ↔ **out**] to help a person or a business out of difficulties by providing money **5** [I] to escape from an aircraft by PARACHUTE: *The pilot bailed out of the burning plane.*

bai·liff /ˈbeɪlɪf/ *n* **1** *law* an official, especially one who takes possession of goods or property when money is owed **2** a person who looks after land for the owner

bait¹ /beɪt/ *n* **1** [U] food used to attract and catch fish, animals, or birds: *The fisherman put the bait on the hook.* **2** [C;U] something you use to attract someone when you want them to do something

bait² *v* [T] **1** to put bait on a hook to catch fish or in a trap to catch animals **2** to make someone angry intentionally

baize /beɪz/ *n* [U] thick green cloth used to cover tables on which certain games are played

bake /beɪk/ *v* **baked, baking** [I;T] **1** to cook in an OVEN: *to bake bread* | *The bread is baking.* **2** to make something hard by heating it: *In former times, bricks were baked in the sun.* –see COOK¹ (USAGE)

baked beans /ˌ·ˈ·/ *n* [pl] small white beans cooked with tomatoes (TOMATO); people usually buy them in tins

bak·er /ˈbeɪkəʳ/ *n* **1** a person who bakes bread and cakes, especially professionally **2 baker's** a shop which sells bread and cakes: *The baker's has got Christmas cakes already.* | *I'm just going to the baker's.*

bak·er·y /ˈbeɪkəri/ *n* bakeries a place where bread and cakes are baked or sold

bal·ance¹ /ˈbæləns/ *v* **balanced, balancing** **1** [I;T] to get into a steady position and not allow to fall to one side or the other, especially when this is difficult: *She balanced the cup on top of a huge pile of books.* | *When you learn to ride a bicycle, you have to learn to balance.* **2** [T] to give equal importance to two or more things: *They have to balance the demand for a better service with the need to keep costs down.* **3** [I;T] to prevent something from becoming too unequal: *His imagination is balanced by great practicality.* **4** [T] to consider one thing in relation to another: *You have to balance the advantages of living in the country against the disadvantages.* **5 balance the books** to show that the money that has been paid out is equal to the money that has been paid in **6 balance the budget** to make sure that your income will be as much as you intend to spend

balance² *n* **1** [sing;U] a condition of being steady and not falling over: *He's got something wrong with his ears, and his balance isn't very good.* **2 keep your balance** to stay in a steady position without falling to one side or the other, even when it is difficult [RELATED PHRASE **lose your balance**: *As she reached out from the ladder, she lost her balance and fell.*] **3 off balance** in an unsteady physical position: *The blow knocked him off balance, and he fell.* **4** [C;U] a steady state in which everything has equal power or is in the right relationship to everything else: *The balance of nature is being upset by intensive agriculture.* **5 strike a balance** to find a middle way between two things: *If you want your children to grow up well, you have to strike a balance* **between** *firmness and affection.* **6** [C] an amount that remains: *My bank balance is only £72.* | *The accountant said that the balance at the end of the last financial year was £97,000.* **7** [U] fairness in reporting different views on a subject: *the need for balance in the reporting of political affairs* **8** [U] a state of mind in which you are calm and reasonable: *It's no use getting worked up at every small crisis. You need to keep a sense of balance.* **9 on balance** taking everything into consideration: *I think on balance I preferred the old system.* **10 in the balance** in a state of uncertainty where the result could be good or bad: *The future of the nation is in the balance.*

bal·anced /ˈbælənst/ *adj* **1** fair: *a balanced judgment* | *a balanced account* **2** good because everything is in the correct relationship to everything else: *a balanced diet* | *a balanced budget* **3** having a firm sensible mind: *She's very well balanced.* –opposite **unbalanced** (for sense 3)

balance of pay·ments /ˌ···ˈ·ˌ·/ *n* [sing] (also **balance of trade**) the amount of money coming into a country in comparison with the amount going out

balance of pow·er /₁···'··/ n [sing] **1** a position in which power, especially political or military power, is evenly balanced on all sides: *The growth of the new political party upset the balance of power.* **2 hold the balance of power** to be able to make one side more powerful than the other by giving it your support

bal·co·ny /'bælkəni/ n **balconies** **1** a place for people to stand or sit on, built out from the upper part of a building: –see picture on page 441 *You can see the sea from our balcony.* **2** the seats upstairs in a theatre

bald /bɔːld/ adj **1** with little or no hair on the head –see picture on page 245 **2** stated directly with no attempt to soften the unpleasant truth: *a bald statement of the facts* –**baldness** n [U]

bald·ing /'bɔːldɪŋ/ adj becoming bald: *a balding man*

bald·ly /'bɔːldli/ adv spoken plainly, and sometimes even cruelly: *The doctor told her baldly she was going to die.*

bale¹ /beɪl/ n a large mass of soft material, tightly tied so that it can be moved: *a bale of cotton* | *a bale of straw*

bale² v **baled, baling**
bale out phr v **1** [I] to escape from an aircraft by PARACHUTE: *The pilot baled out of the burning plane.* **2** [I;T] **bale** sthg ↔ **out**] to remove water from a boat to prevent it sinking: *Quick! Start baling out!*

bale·ful /'beɪlfəl/ adj full of hate and desire to do harm: *a baleful look* –**balefully** adv

balk /bɔːk, bɔːlk/ v see BAULK

ball /bɔːl/ n **1** a round object used in a game or sport: *to throw a ball* | *The ball bounced into the road.* **2** anything of a similar shape: *a ball of string* | *a snowball* **3** a rounded part of the body: *the ball of the foot* | *an eyeball* **4 on the ball** infml showing up-to-date knowledge and an ability to think and act quickly: *That new secretary is really on the ball.* **5 play ball** infml to COOPERATE **6 keep the ball rolling** to continue something **7 start the ball rolling** to begin something **8** a large formal occasion for social dancing **9 have a ball** infml to have a very good time

bal·lad /'bæləd/ n a simple song or poem which tells a story

bal·last /'bæləst/ n [U] **1** heavy material which is carried in a ship to keep it steady **2** broken stone used as a bed for railway lines or as the bottom part of a road

ball bear·ing /₁·'··/ n **ball bearings** metal balls moving in a ring round a bar in a machine so that the bar may turn more easily

ball·cock /'bɔːlkɒk / -kɑːk/ n an apparatus for opening and closing a hole through which water passes, worked by a hollow floating ball which rises and falls with the level of the water

bal·le·ri·na /₁bælə'riːnə/ n a female ballet dancer

bal·let /'bæleɪ ‖ bæ'leɪ, 'bæleɪ/ n **1** [C] a kind of dance in which a story is told without speech or singing **2** [U] the art of doing such dances: *She has studied ballet for six years.* **3** [C + sing/pl verb] a group of ballet dancers who work together: *The Bolshoi Ballet is coming to London.*

bal·lis·tics /bə'lɪstɪks/ n [U] the scientific study of the movement of objects that are thrown or forced through the air, such as bullets fired from a gun

bal·loon¹ /bə'luːn/ n **1** a small bag made of rubber or a similar material that can be blown up, used as a toy or to decorate your house when you have a party **2** a bag of strong light material filled with gas or heated air so that it can float in the air; some balloons carry people in a basket under them

balloon² v [I] to get bigger and rounder: *Her skirt ballooned out in the wind.*

bal·loon·ing /bə'luːnɪŋ/ n [U] the sport of flying in a balloon –**ballooning** v [only in progressive forms]

bal·lot¹ /'bælət/ n **1** the action or system of secret voting: *The ballot is an important part of the democratic process.* | *Let's have a ballot on it.* **2 at the ballot box** by secret voting: *The issue will be decided at the ballot box.*

ballot² v [T] to find out what people think by a secret vote: *The General Workers' Union balloted its members on the issue of safety.* | *Balloting took place last Thursday.*

ball·point /'bɔːlpɔɪnt/ n a pen which has a ball at the end that rolls ink onto the paper

ball·room /'bɔːlrʊm, -ruːm/ n **1** a large room for formal social dancing

balm /bɑːm ‖ bɑːm, bɑːlm/ n **1** [C;U] oily liquid with a strong but pleasant smell, used as medicine or to lessen pain **2** [U] something which comforts you after your feelings have been hurt

balm·y /'bɑːmi ‖ 'bɑːmi, 'bɑːlmi/ adj soft and warm (used of air)

bal·us·trade /₁bælə'streɪd ‖ 'bæləstreɪd/ n a row of upright pieces of stone or wood with a bar along the top, guarding the outer edge of any place from which people might fall

bam·boo /₁bæm'buː·/ n [U] a tall plant of the grass family, or its hard, hollow, jointed stems, often used for making furniture

bam·boo·zle /bæm'buːzəl/ v **bamboozled, bamboozling** infml **bamboozle someone into doing something** to trick someone into doing something

ban¹ /bæn/ v **-nn-** [T] to forbid, especially by law: *He was banned from driving for three months.* | *All strikes have been banned.*
□ USEFUL PATTERNS to ban something; to ban someone from doing something

ban² n an order banning something: *a ban on smoking* | *The union has imposed a ban on overtime.*

ba·nal /bə'nɑːl, bə'næl/ adj very ordinary, and not interesting: *a banal remark* –**banality** /bə'nælɪti/ n [C;U]

ba·na·na /bə'nɑːnə ‖ -'næ-/ n **1** a long tropical fruit, with a yellow skin and a soft inside –see picture on page 344 **2 bananas** mad or stupid: *Just stop that noise! You're driving me bananas.*

band¹ /bænd/ n **1** a thin flat narrow piece of material, often circular; a band can be used for fastening things together or it can be part of a piece of clothing or machinery: *a rubber band* **2** [+ sing/pl verb] a group of people formed for a common purpose and often with a leader: *a band of armed men* **3** [+ sing/pl verb] a group of musicians: *a jazz band* | *The band is touring the country next month.* **4** a line of a colour or pattern different from that of the area on either side of it: *There was an orange band on the snake's back.* **5** one of the parts of the whole range of something: *people in the $60,000–$80,000 income band*

band² v
band together phr v [I] to get together in a group, usually with some special purpose

ban·dage[1] /ˈbændɪdʒ/ (**gauze** AmE) n a long narrow piece of material, for binding round a wound or round a part of the body that has been hurt

bandage[2] v **bandaged, bandaging** [T] to tie a bandage round a part of someone's body: The doctor bandaged his broken ankle.

B & B /ˌbiː ən ˈbiː/ an abbreviation for bed and breakfast, a service offered by a guesthouse or other place where you can stay the night; you get a bed for the night and breakfast, but no other meals

ban·dit /ˈbændʌt/ n an armed robber, usually working in a group, who attacks travellers in wild places

band·stand /ˈbændstænd/ n a raised place, open at the sides but with a roof, where a band plays

ban·dy[1] /ˈbændi/ adj **1** curved outwards at the knees (used to describe legs) **2 bandy-legged** /ˌ··ˈ·◂ ‖ ˈ···/ having bandy legs

bandy[2] v **bandied, bandied, bandying**
bandy sthg ↔ **about/around** phr v [T] to say things to other people carelessly, without thinking about them properly: Several different figures have been bandied about, but these are the correct ones.

bane /beɪn/ n **the bane of your life** the greatest cause of continual trouble to you

bang[1] /bæŋ/ n **1** a sudden loud noise: The door shut with a bang. **2** a sharp blow: a bang on the head **3 go off with a bang** (of a social occasion) to be very successful

bang[2] v **1** [T] to hit something sharply: He fell and banged his knee. **2** [T] to move something violently and with a loud noise: She banged the chair against the wall. **3** [I] to move violently and with a loud noise: Somewhere a door was banging in the wind. | There's someone banging about upstairs.

bang[3] interj a word used to represent a loud noise: Bang! Another firework flew into the air.

bang[4] adv infml **1** directly or exactly: The sales figures are bang on target. | The lights went out bang in the middle of Act 2. **2 bang on** exactly correct **3 Bang goes**... a phrase you use when something you would like or the chance of it suddenly disappears: Bang goes our free time this weekend.

bang·er /ˈbæŋəʳ/ n infml **1** a SAUSAGE **2** a noisy FIREWORK

ban·gle /ˈbæŋgəl/ n a band worn round the arm or ankle as a decoration

bangs /bæŋz/ n [P] the usual American word for a FRINGE[1] (1)

ban·ish /ˈbænɪʃ/ v [T] to send someone away, usually from their own country, as a punishment: banished by the government. –**banishment** n [U]

ban·is·ter /ˈbænʌstəʳ/ n a row of upright pieces of wood or metal with a bar along the top guarding the outer edge of stairs

ban·jo /ˈbændʒəʊ/ n a stringed musical instrument with a long neck, and a body like a drum, used to play popular music

bank[1] /bæŋk/ n **1** an organization which performs services connected with money, and which usually has local offices in which money is kept for customers and paid out on demand: I drew some money out of the bank. **2** a place where something is stored, especially products of human origin for medical use: Hospital blood banks have saved many lives. **3** land along the side of a river or lake **4** a long pile of earth which is heaped up in a field or garden **5** a mass of a substance such as snow or mud: The banks of dark cloud promised rain. **6** a SANDBANK

bank[2] v [I;T] to put or keep money in a bank: Who do you bank with? | Did you bank that cheque?
bank on sbdy/sthg phr v [T] to depend on: I'm banking on you to help me with the arrangements. | "I do hope the weather will be good on Saturday." "Don't bank on it."
bank up phr v [I;T **bank** sthg ↔ **up**] to form into a mass or heap: The wind had banked the snow up against the wall.

bank ac·count /ˈ·· ·ˌ·/ n an arrangement for someone to keep money in a bank and take it out when they want to: How much money have you got in your bank account?

bank·er /ˈbæŋkəʳ/ n a person who owns a bank or who shares in the control of a bank: International bankers are gathering in Rome.

bank hol·i·day /ˌ· ˈ···/ n in the United Kingdom, an official public holiday, not a Saturday or Sunday, when the banks are closed

bank·ing /ˈbæŋkɪŋ/ n [U] the business of a bank or a banker: a career in banking | the international banking system

bank note /ˈ·· ·/ n a piece of paper money printed for the national bank of a country for public use

bank·rupt[1] /ˈbæŋkrʌpt/ adj **1** unable to pay your debts **2 go bankrupt** to become unable to pay your debts

bankrupt[2] v [T] to make someone bankrupt or very poor

bank·rupt·cy /ˈbæŋkrʌptsi/ n **bankruptcies** [C;U] the state of being bankrupt: The company is threatened with bankruptcy. | Bankruptcies increased during the last quarter of 1990.

bank state·ment /ˈ·· ·ˌ··/ n a list of payments into and out of your bank account; the bank sends you statements regularly

ban·ner /ˈbænəʳ/ n **1** a long piece of cloth on which a sign or message is painted, usually carried by people: The marchers' banners said "We want work." **2** lit a flag

banns /bænz/ n [pl] a public declaration in church of an intended marriage

ban·quet /ˈbæŋkwʌt/ n a formal dinner for many people in honour of a special person or occasion, especially one at which speeches are made

ban·ter /ˈbæntəʳ/ v [I] to speak playfully or jokingly –**banter** n [U]: The actress exchanged banter with reporters.

bap·tis·m /ˈbæptɪzəm/ n [C;U] a Christian religious ceremony in which someone becomes a member of the Church –**baptismal** /bæpˈtɪzməl/ adj

Bap·tist /ˈbæptʌst/ n a member of a branch of the Christian church which believes that baptism should be only for people old enough to understand its meaning

bap·tize /bæpˈtaɪz/ v **baptized, baptizing** (also **baptise** BrE) [T] to perform the ceremony of baptism

bar[1] /bɑːʳ/ n **1** something solid that is long and straight: an iron bar | a bar of chocolate **2** a long piece of wood or metal across a door, gate, or window that keeps it shut or prevents movement through it: There were metal bars across the windows of the prison. **3** one of the rooms in a building called a PUB where people can buy and drink alcohol **4** a room in a hotel, theatre, or other public building where people can buy and drink alcohol **5** the high table where drinks are served in a bar **6** a place where food and drink are sold: a snack bar | a coffee bar **7** in America, a place where people buy and drink alcohol **8** a group of notes in music: *She sang the first three bars of the song.* **9** a bank of sand or stones under the water **10 behind bars** in prison **11 prisoner at the bar** the person being tried in a court of law

bar² *v* -rr- [T] **1** to close something firmly with a bar: *to bar the door* **2** to keep in or out by barring something: *They barred themselves in.* **3** to block something: *to bar the way to the city* **4** to forbid something, or forbid someone from doing something: *Smoking has been barred in the office.* | *The protesters were barred* from *entering the building.*

bar³ *prep* except: *The whole group was at the party, bar John.*

bar·bar·i·an /ba:ˈbeəriən ‖ ba:r-/ *n* an uncivilized person, especially one who is rude and wild in behaviour: *The barbarians conquered Rome.* –**barbaric** /ba:ˈbærɪk ‖ ba:r-/ *adj* : *barbaric people* | *a barbaric punishment* –**barbarism** /ˈba:bərɪzəm ‖ ˈba:r-/ *n* –**barbarous** /ˈba:bərəs ‖ ˈba:r-/ *adj*

bar·bar·i·ty /ba:ˈbærɪti ‖ ba:r-/ *n* **barbarities** [C;U] cruelty of the worst kind: *The barbarities of the last war must not be repeated.*

bar·be·cue¹ /ˈba:bɪkju: ‖ ˈba:r-/ *n* **1** a metal frame on which you cook meat and other food over an open fire outdoors **2** an outdoor party with food cooked on a barbecue

barbecue² *v* **barbecued, barbecuing** [T] to cook meat and other food on a barbecue

barbed /ba:bd ‖ ba:rbd/ *adj* **1** with one or more sharp points **2** intended to hurt someone and make them feel upset: *a barbed remark*

barbed wire /ˌ·ˈ·/ *n* [U] wire with short sharp points in it: *a barbed-wire fence to keep the animals in*

bar·ber /ˈba:bəʳ ‖ ˈba:r-/ *n* **1** a person, usually a man, who cuts men's hair **2 barber's** the place where a barber works: *He's gone to the barber's.* | *You can get them in the barber's.*

bar·bi·tu·rate /ba:ˈbɪtʃjrɪt ‖ ba:rˈbɪtʃjrɪt,-reɪt/ *n* [C] *tech* a drug that makes people calm and sends them to sleep

bard /ba:d ‖ ba:rd/ *n lit* a poet

bare¹ /beəʳ/ *adj* **1** not covered by anything: *bare feet* | *bare floorboards* **2** empty: *The cupboard was completely bare.* **3 with your bare hands** using only your hands, but no tools or weapons: *He killed her with his bare hands.* **4** [only before a noun] the most basic, with nothing added: *the bare facts of a case* –**bareness** *n* [U]

bare² *v* **bared, baring** [T] to uncover something so that it can be seen: *The animal bared its teeth in anger.*

bare·back /ˈbeəbæk ‖ ˈbeər-/ *adj,adv* riding without a SADDLE: *a bareback rider*

bare·faced /ˌbeəˈfeɪst◂ ‖ ˈbeərfeɪst/ *adj* shameless: *a barefaced lie*

bare·foot /ˈbeəfʊt ‖ ˈbeər-/ *adj,adv* not wearing any shoes

bare·head·ed /ˌbeəˈhedɪd◂ ‖ ˈbeərhedɪd/ *adj,adv* not wearing a hat

bare·ly /ˈbeəli ‖ ˈbeərli/ *adv* only just: *We have barely enough money to last the weekend.* | *I can barely understand what he's talking about.* –see HARDLY (USAGE)

bar·gain¹ /ˈba:gɪn ‖ ˈba:r-/ *n* **1** an agreement, especially one to do something in return for something else: *He made a bargain with his wife: "You do the shopping and I'll do the cooking."* **2** something that is both cheap and good value: *These shoes were a real bargain.* | *bargain prices* **3 drive a hard bargain** to get an agreement very much in your own favour **4 into the bargain** a phrase used when you are stating forcefully that something is true in addition to everything else you have said: *She had to look after a house, her sick mother – and four children into the bargain.*

bargain² *v* [I] **1** to talk about the conditions of a sale, agreement, or contract: *We bargained with her about the price.* | *They were bargaining over a horse.* **2 he hadn't bargained for/on**… he had not expected that something would happen and did not include it in his plans: *I hadn't bargained for such heavy rain, and I got very wet.*

barge¹ /ba:dʒ ‖ ba:rdʒ/ *n* a boat with a flat bottom used mainly for carrying heavy goods on a CANAL or river

barge² *v* **barged, barging** [I] (also **barge your way**) to move rudely and ungracefully, often hitting against things: *He barged onto the bus before everyone else.* | *She barged her way into the room.* **barge in** *phr v* [I] to rush in rudely or interrupt: *The door burst open and the children barged in.*

bar·i·tone /ˈbærɪtəʊn/ *n* a singing voice lower than a TENOR and higher than a BASS

bark¹ /ba:k ‖ ba:rk/ *v* **1** [I] to make the loud, sharp sound of a dog or fox: *The dog always barks at the postman.* **2** [T] to shout something in a sharp voice: *The officer barked an order at us.* **3 bark up the wrong tree** *infml* to try to do something based on a mistaken idea

bark² *n* **1** [C] the loud, sharp sound made by a dog or fox **2 his bark is worse than his bite** *infml* = he seems more unpleasant or difficult than he really is **3** [U] the strong outer covering of a tree

bar·ley /ˈba:li ‖ ˈba:rli/ *n* [U] a grain plant like grass grown for food and also used in the making of beer

bar·man /ˈba:mən ‖ ˈba:r-/ *n* **barmen** /-mən/ a man who serves drinks in a BAR¹; a woman who does this is called a **barmaid** /ˈba:meɪd ‖ ˈba:r-/

bar·my /ˈba:mi ‖ ˈba:rmi/ *adj infml* foolish or a little mad: *You must be barmy to play football in this weather.*

barn /ba:n ‖ ba:rn/ *n* a large farm building where crops are stored or animals are kept

barn·yard /ˈba:nja:d ‖ ˈba:rnja:rd/ *n* a yard on a farm with barns and other buildings round it

ba·rom·e·ter /bəˈrɒmɪtəʳ ‖ -ˈra:-/ *n* an instrument which measures the air pressure; you use it to judge probable changes in the weather

bar·on /ˈbærən/ *n* **1** a British nobleman of the lowest rank **2** a very powerful businessman: *an oil baron* | *a press baron* –**baronial** /bəˈrəʊniəl/ *adj*

bar·on·ess /ˈbærənɪs/ *n* **1** a woman who is the wife of a baron **2** a British noblewoman of the lowest rank

bar·on·et /ˈbærənɪt, -net/ *n* a British nobleman with the rank of KNIGHT¹ (2) whose title passes on to his son when he dies

bar·rack /ˈbærək/ *v* [I;T] *infml* to interrupt someone giving a speech by shouting at them: *They barracked the speaker throughout the meeting.*

bar·racks /ˈbærəks/ *n* [plural is **barracks**] a building or group of buildings that soldiers live in: *The barracks is in Kingsdown Road.*

bar·rage¹ /ˈbæra:ʒ ‖ ˈba:rɪdʒ/ *n* **1** a pile of earth or stones built across a river, usually to control the level of the water

barrage² /ˈbæra:ʒ ‖ bəˈra:ʒ/ *n* **1** the continuous firing of a number of heavy guns **2** a large number of questions or complaints which are made very quickly one after the other: *a barrage of criticism*

bar·rel /'bærəl/ *n* **1** a round metal, plastic, or wooden container with a flat top and bottom: *a beer barrel* –see picture on page 148 **2** the long part of a gun that looks like a tube: *a rifle barrel*

bar·ren /'bærən/ *adj* **1** unable to produce a good crop (used of land) **2** not able to produce young (used of female animals) **3** useless or producing no result: *a barren argument* –compare FERTILE, FRUITFUL –**barrenness** *n* [U]

bar·ri·cade[1] /'bærɪˌkeɪd, ˌbærɪ'keɪd/ *n* a quickly-built wall of vehicles or heavy objects put across a road or passage to block the advance of the enemy

barricade[2] *v* **barricaded, barricading** [T] **1** to put a barricade across something: *Demonstrators had barricaded the street.* **2 barricade yourself in** to shut yourself in a room or building and put something heavy against the door in order to protect yourself against your enemy: *The terrorists barricaded themselves in the embassy.*

bar·ri·er /'bæriəʳ/ *n* **1** something used to keep people or things apart and prevent or control their movement: *The police put up barriers to control the crowd.* | *The cream acts as a barrier* **against** *infection.* **2** something which prevents people from talking to each other, agreeing with each other, or succeeding in their aims: *the language barrier* | *Lack of confidence is the biggest barrier* **to** *investment in this industry.*

bar·ring /'bɑːrɪŋ/ *prep* **1** except for: *The whole group was at the party, barring John.* **2** if the thing mentioned does not happen: *Barring any unexpected problems, we'll finish the job tonight.*

bar·ris·ter /'bærɪstəʳ/ *n* a lawyer in England who has the right to speak and argue in the higher courts of law

bar·row /'bærəʊ/ *n* **1** a small cart with a roof made of material from which fruit and vegetables are sold in the street **2** a WHEELBARROW

bar·ter /'bɑːtəʳ/ *v* [I;T] to exchange goods for other goods: *They bartered farm products for machinery.* | *bartering for food* –**barter** *n* [U]

base[1] /beɪs/ *n* **1** the lowest part of something, especially the part on which it stands: *a lamp with a heavy base* | *leaves at the base of the stem* **2** a centre from which something is controlled and plans are made: *Our company's base is in London, but we have branches all round the world.* | *a military base* **3** the original part from which something develops or from which other things are made: *A knowledge of human biology is a useful base for training as a nurse.* **4** the part of something where it is joined to something else: *the base of the leaf* **5** a chemical substance which combines with an acid to form a salt **6** any of the four points which a baseball player must touch in order to make a run

base[2] *v* **based, basing be based** to have a centre for your work or an activity: *They're based in Birmingham, but they travel all over the West Midlands.* | *a London-based firm*

base sthg on sthg *phr v* [T] **1** to make or develop something using something else as a starting point: *You should always base your opinions on facts.* | *The film is based on the book by D. H. Lawrence.*

base·ball /'beɪsbɔːl/ *n* [U] a game played with a BAT and a ball called a baseball between two teams of nine players each, on a large field with four bases; baseball is popular in America: *a baseball player/a baseball team*

base·ment /'beɪsmənt/ *n* a room or rooms in a house which are below street level –see picture on page 441

bash[1] /bæʃ/ *v* [T] *infml* to hit something or someone hard, so as to break it or hurt them: *He bashed her over the head with a brick.* | *I've just bashed my head on the door.*

bash[2] *n infml* **1** a hard blow: *He gave him a bash on the nose.* **2 have a bash** to try to do something even though you might not succeed: *I'll have a bash* **at** *rowing the boat, although I've never done it before.*

bash·ful /'bæʃfəl/ *adj* lacking confidence, especially when talking to people you do not know: *a bashful smile* | *bashful teenagers* –**bashfully** *adv* –**bashfulness** *n* [U]

ba·sic /'beɪsɪk/ *adj* **1** more necessary and important than anything else: *the basic rules of good driving* **2** simple and having only the things which are really necessary: *The accommodation is very basic.*

basic *n* **1** BASIC (also **Basic**) a very commonly used computer language **2 basics** [pl] the simplest and most important things: *When you get down to basics, love counts for more than possessions.* | *She did a short course to learn the basics of carpentry.*

ba·sic·ally /'beɪsɪkli/ *adv* a word used when you are giving a fact or statement which you think is the most important one: *Basically, he's a nice person, but he doesn't always show it.* | *He's basically nice.* | *Basically, we need more money.*

ba·sin /'beɪsən/ *n* **1** a round container for holding liquids or mixing foods **2** a WASHBASIN **3** an area of land from which water runs down into a river: *the Amazon Basin*

ba·sis /'beɪsɪs/ *n* **bases** /'beɪsiːz/ **1** the most important principle or fact from which something is made or developed: *What is the basis* **for** *your opinion?* | *The lectures formed the basis of a new book.* **2** an agreed arrangement: *She works for us on a part-time basis.*

bask /bɑːsk ‖ bæsk/ *v* **1** [I] to lie or sit in pleasant warmth, usually from the sun: *I was lying on the sand, basking* **in** *the sunshine.* **2 bask in someone's approval** to enjoy the fact that someone likes you or approves of you

bas·ket /'bɑːskɪt ‖ 'bæ-/ *n* **1** a container made from narrow pieces of wood or plastic woven together: *a shopping basket* | *a wastepaper basket* –see picture on page 148 **2** a basket and the things it contains: *a basket of apples* **3** an open net fixed to a metal ring high up off the ground, through which players try to throw the ball in the game of basketball

bas·ket·ball /'bɑːskɪtbɔːl ‖ 'bæs-/ *n* **1** [U] an indoor game between two teams of five players each, in which each team tries to throw a large ball through the other team's basket –see picture on page 637 **2** [C] the ball used in this game

bass[1] /beɪs/ *adj* deep or low in sound (used of a male singing voice or a musical instrument): *He has a fine bass voice.* | *a bass drum*

bass[2] /beɪs/ *n* **1** the lowest male singing voice **2** the lowest range of sounds in written music **3** –see DOUBLE BASS

bas·soon /bə'suːn/ *n* a wooden musical instrument which makes a deep sound and is played by blowing

bas·tard /'bæstəd, 'bɑː- ‖ 'bæstərd/ *n* **1** a child of unmarried parents **2** *slang* a person who has behaved very badly to another person *You bastard! How* *could you do this to me!* **3** *slang* a person you feel fond of or sorry for: *You lucky bastard!*

baste /beɪst/ v **basted, basting** [T] **1** to join pieces of cloth together in long loose stitches **2** to pour melted fat over meat that is cooking

bas·ti·on /ˈbæstiən ‖ -tʃən/ n something that strongly defends a particular principle or activity: *His club doesn't allow women members. It's one of the last bastions of male chauvinism.*

bat¹ /bæt/ n **1** a specially shaped wooden stick used for hitting the ball in various games –see BASEBALL, CRICKET², TABLE TENNIS **2** a flying animal that looks like a mouse and is active at night **3 off your own bat** *infml* without being told or forced to: *Have you done all this work off your own bat?*

bat² v -**tt**- **1** [T] to hit a ball with a bat **2** [I] to have a turn to hit the ball in a game of cricket or BASE-BALL: *Who's batting now?* **3 not bat an eyelid** *infml* to show no feeling or surprise: *She heard the news without batting an eyelid.*

batch /bætʃ/ n a number of things or people to be dealt with at one time: *a batch of bread/the next batch of students* | *The prisoners were released in batches of 20.*

bat·ed /ˈbeɪtɪd/ adj **with bated breath** with a great desire to know: *He waited for the news with bated breath.*

bath¹ /bɑːθ ‖ bæθ/ n **baths** /bɑːðz, bɑːθs ‖ bæðz, bæθs/ **1** (**bathtub** *AmE*) a container in which you sit to wash your whole body **2 baths** a public swimming pool **3 have a bath, take a bath** to sit in a bath and wash your body

bath² v **1** [T] to give a bath to someone: *He's bathing the baby.* **2** [I] to sit in a bath and wash your body: *She baths every morning.*

■ USAGE **1** When talking about what you do to get clean say **have a bath/take a bath**: *I have a bath every morning.* **2** When talking about swimming in the sea or a river use the verb **bathe** or the expression **go for a bathe**: *Further along the beach we saw some people bathing.* | *Let's go for a bathe.* (Do NOT use **have/take a bath** with this meaning.) **3** When talking about lying in the sun use the verb **sunbathe**: *They spent the afternoon sunbathing.* | *A week of swimming and sunbathing will do you the world of good.* (Do NOT use **have/take a bath** with this meaning.)

bathe¹ /beɪð/ **bathed, bathing** v **1** [I] to swim for pleasure: *I like to bathe in the sea.* **2** [T] to cover or wash something gently with water or other liquid: *Bathe your ankle twice a day.* **3** [I] *AmE* to sit in a bath and wash your body **4 be bathed in light** to be covered in light: *The fields were bathed in sunlight.* –see BATH² (USAGE) –**bathing** n [U]: *Bathing is dangerous near the rocks.* | *a bathing suit*

bathe² n **have a bathe, go for a bathe** to swim for pleasure

bath·er /ˈbeɪðəʳ/ n a swimmer

bath·robe /ˈbɑːθrəʊb ‖ ˈbæθ-/ n **1** a loose piece of clothing that you wear before and after you have a bath or swim **2** the usual American word for DRESS-ING GOWN

bath·room /ˈbɑːθrʊm, -ruːm ‖ ˈbæθ-/ n **1** a room containing a BATH and usually a TOILET **2** the usual American word for a TOILET: *Can I use your bathroom, please?*

bath·tub /ˈbɑːθtʌb ‖ ˈbæθ-/ n –see BATH¹

bat·man /ˈbætmən/ n **batmen** /-mən/ an officer's personal servant in the armed forces

bat·on /ˈbætɒn, -tn ‖ bæˈtɑːn, bə-/ n **1** a short thin stick used by a CONDUCTOR to show the beat of the

music **2** a short thick stick used as a weapon by a policeman

bats·man /ˈbætsmən/ n **batsmen** /-mən/ the player in cricket who tries to hit the ball with a BAT¹(1)

bat·tal·ion /bəˈtæljən/ n a group of 500–1000 soldiers made up of four or more companies(COMPANY(5)): *The second battalion is going abroad.*

bat·ter¹ /ˈbætəʳ/ v **1** [T] to hit a person repeatedly: *She had been battered by her drunken husband.* | *battered to death* **2** [I;T] to hit or beat against something repeatedly: *Someone was battering on the door.* | *The ship was battered against the rocks.* | *a battered old car* | *They battered the door down.*

batter² n [U] **1** a mixture of flour, eggs, and milk, beaten together and used in cooking **2** a person who bats (BAT² (2))

bat·tered /ˈbætəd ‖ -ərd/ adj **1** knocked and worn: *a battered copy of "Treasure Island"* | *a battered teddy bear* | *a battered old car* **2** repeatedly beaten: *a refuge for battered wives*

bat·ter·ing /ˈbætərɪŋ/ n repeated beating which results in damage: *The house took a real battering in the 1987 gales.*

bat·ter·ing ram /ˈ··· ·/ n a large heavy log used in the past during war for breaking through the doors and walls of castles and towns

bat·ter·y /ˈbætəri/ n **batteries 1** a small apparatus which provides electrical power, which you put inside something such as a radio **2** a number of big guns fixed in a warship or fort **3** a line of small boxes in which hens are kept and specially treated so that they will lay eggs frequently: *battery hens* | *She won't buy battery eggs. She'll only have free-range ones.* **4** a set of things of the same kind that happen together or are kept together: *They gave her a whole battery of tests to try to find out what she's allergic to.*

bat·tle¹ /ˈbætl/ n **1** a fight between enemies or opposing groups: *the Battle of Waterloo* | *It was one of the worst battles of the First World War.* **2** a struggle to obtain something or prevent something: *a battle for power in the government* | *the battle against inflation* | *the battle against cancer* –compare WAR

battle² v **battled, battling** [I] to struggle in order to do or obtain something: *Firemen are still battling to get the fire under control.*

bat·tle·field /ˈbætlfiːld/ n a place at which a battle is fought

bat·tle·ground /ˈbætlɡraʊnd/ n **1** a place at which a battle is fought **2** a subject about which people disagree strongly

bat·tle·ments /ˈbætlmənts/ n [pl] a low wall round the top of a castle or fort, with spaces to shoot through

bat·tle·ship /ˈbætlʃɪp/ n the largest kind of warship, with the biggest guns and heaviest armour

bau·ble /ˈbɔːbəl/ n a cheap, bright decoration or piece of jewellery

baulk /bɔːk, bɔːlk/ v (also **balk**) **baulk at something** to be unwilling to face or agree to something difficult or unpleasant: *Sally baulked at the idea of doing the exam again.*

bawd·y /ˈbɔːdi/ adj mentioning sex in a rude and amusing way: *bawdy jokes*

bawl /bɔːl/ v [I;T] to shout or cry in a loud hard voice: *The baby bawled all night.* | *He bawled an order at me.*

bay /beɪ/ n **1** a part of the sea or of a large lake

enclosed in a curve of the land: *the Bay of Biscay* | *We went swimming in the bay.* **2** any one of the parts into which a building or space is divided: *This parking bay is reserved for staff only.* **3** hold some-one **or** something **at bay, keep someone or something at bay** to keep someone or something a safe distance away: *He kept me at bay with a knife.* **4** a horse whose colour is reddish-brown

bay win·dow /ˌ· ·ˈ··/ n a window that sticks out from a building and is built up from the ground

bay·o·net /ˈbeɪənˌt, -net/ n a long knife fixed to the end of a soldier's gun

ba·zaar /bəˈzɑːʳ/ n **1** a marketplace or a group of shops, especially in the Middle East **2** a sale to collect money in order to help a person or organization: *a church bazaar*

BBC /ˌbiː biː ˈsiː◄/ n [U] the British radio and television broadcasting company that is paid for by public money; an abbreviation for **British Broadcasting Corporation**: *She's a producer at the BBC.* | *It's on BBC tonight.*

BC /ˌbiː ˈsiː/ adv before the birth of CHRIST; you use BC when giving dates: *Rome was founded in 753 BC.*

be – see box below

beach¹ /biːtʃ/ n a shore of a sea or lake covered by sand or small stones –see SHORE¹ (USAGE)

beach² v [T] to push or drive a boat or large animal onto the shore

bea·con /ˈbiːkən/ n **1** a fire on a hill, tower, or pole, used as a signal **2** a light or radio signal used as a guide or warning to sailors or pilots **3** an encouraging example that shows how something worthwhile can be done

bead /biːd/ n **1** a small ball of glass or other material with a hole through it, often threaded on a string and worn as jewellery: *She was wearing a string of green beads.* **2** a small drop of liquid: *beads* of sweat

bead·y /ˈbiːdi/ adj **beady eyes** small, round, and shining eyes

beak /biːk/ n the hard horny mouth of a bird

bea·ker /ˈbiːkəʳ/ n **1** *BrE* a drinking cup with no handle –see picture on page 148 **2** a small glass cup shaped for pouring, as used in a chemical LABORATORY

beam¹ /biːm/ n **1** a long heavy bar of wood, especially one of the main ones used to support the roof of a building **2** a line of light shining out from some bright object: *a moonbeam* | *a laser beam* **3** radio waves sent out along a narrow path in one direction only, often to guide aircraft **4** a bright look or smile: *"How nice to see you!" she said, with a beam of welcome.* **5 off beam** *infml* not exactly correct

beam² v **1** [I] (used of the sun and other shining objects) to send out light: *The sun beamed down.* **2** [I;T] to smile brightly and happily: *He beamed a cheerful welcome.* **3** [T] to send a radio signal out in a certain direction: *The signal is beamed to a satellite.*

bean /biːn/ n **1** a seed of a plant, grown for food: *beans are usually sold dried or tinned: baked beans* **2** a seed container of the bean plant with the seeds inside it, eaten as a fresh vegetable: *green beans* –see picture on page 344 **3** a seed of certain other plants, from which food or drink can be made: *coffee beans* | *cocoa beans* **4 full of beans** *infml* full of life and eagerness

bear¹ /beəʳ/ n a large, heavy animal with thick, rough fur

bear² v bore /bɔːʳ/, **borne** /bɔːrn/ [T] **1** to carry something from one place to another: *The seeds are*

---

be /bi; *strong* biː/ v

present tense
   I **am**, I'm
   You **are**, you're
   He / she / it **is**, he's / she's / it's
   We **are**, we're
   You **are**, you're
   They **are**, they're

past tense
   I **was**
   You **were**
   He / she / it **was**
   We **were**
   You **were**
   They **were**

past participle
   been
present participle
   being
negative short forms
   aren't, isn't, wasn't, weren't

For the pronunciation of these forms look them up in the dictionary at their own place.

1 [auxiliary verb] used to form the continuous tenses of verbs:
Where are you going? | *She was reading a book.* | *We're leaving tomorrow.* | *I'm working at the moment.*

2 [auxiliary verb] used to form the passive of verbs:
He was attacked by three men. | *The building was decorated last year.* | *Has the telephone been repaired yet?*

3 [auxiliary verb] used to show what will happen or what must happen:
He's to meet the president next week. | *You're to get this finished by tomorrow morning.*

4 [auxiliary verb] used to show what might happen:
If you were to invest your money wisely, you could make quite a nice profit.

5 [+complement] used to give the name, date or position of something, or to describe it in some way:
This is Mr Stevenson | *"What's that?" "It's a hammer."* | *Today is Monday.* | *She's a doctor.* | *The book is on the table.* | *The concert was last night.* | *January is the first month of the year.* | *This house is very old.* | *He's a very clever man.*

6 there is, there are, etc. a phrase used to say that something or someone exists, or to say where they are:
Suddenly there was a loud scream. | *There were three people in the room.* | *There is a possibility that he will arrive late.*

borne long distances by the wind. | *They arrived bearing gifts for us.* **2** to support the weight of something: *I don't think that branch will bear your weight.* **3** to have or show a mark or sign: *The letter bore his signature.* | *All the furniture bears the family's coat of arms.* **4** to suffer and accept something unpleasant without complaining: *He bore the pain bravely.* | *This last disappointment was almost more than I could bear.*

■ USAGE Compare **abide, bear, endure, stand, tolerate 1** We use *can't* with **abide, bear, endure** and **stand** to show great dislike. *Can't* **stand** is very common: *I can't* **stand** *him/his attitude!* We use **abide** mainly with people: *I can't* **abide** *that man!* We use **bear** and **endure** for really serious things: *He couldn't* **bear/endure** *listening to reports of the disaster.* **2** We use **bear, endure** and **stand** with things that are painful or uncomfortable. **Endure** suggests pain that lasts for a long time: *Try to* **bear/stand** *the pain as long as you can.* | *She* **endured** *great pain for many years.* **3** We use **tolerate** with people or behaviour, but not with pain: *I won't* **tolerate** *your rudeness!*

5 can't bear to dislike someone or something very much: *I can't bear travelling.* | *I can't bear that man!* **6** *lit* to give birth to a child: *She had borne three children.* | *He wanted her to bear him a son.* **7** to produce fruit or flowers: *It's an old tree and hasn't borne any fruit for years.* **8 bear the brunt of something** to suffer the worst effects of something: *As always, it's the poor who will bear the brunt of the economic recession.* | *These two cities bore the brunt of the fighting.* **9 bear a grudge** to continue to feel angry with someone for a long time after they have done something to hurt you: *I was furious at the time, but I don't bear him any grudge.* **10 bear left, bear right** to turn left or right: *Bear left at the next roundabout.* **11 bear something in mind** to consider something when you are making a decision or a judgement: *Please bear in mind that there are a lot of other people interested in buying the property.* **12 it doesn't bear thinking about** = it is too terrible to think about **13 bear no relation/ resemblance to something** to be very different from something: *His story bears no relation to the truth.* **14 bear witness to something** to show that something is true or exists: *His latest film bears witness to his great acting ability.*

bear down on sbdy/sthg *phr v* [T] to move nearer to someone or something quickly and in a threatening way: *We tried to row away as the ship bore down on us.*

bear sthg ↔ **out** *phr v* [T] to show that something is true: *His story was borne out by several witnesses.*

bear up *phr v* [I] to show courage and remain cheerful when you have a lot of difficulties

bear with sbdy *phr v* [T] to be patient with someone: *If you'll just bear with me for a few minutes, I will explain everything.*

bear·a·ble /ˈbeərəbəl/ *adj* able to be suffered or accepted: *The pain was just bearable.* | *His salary increase made life more bearable.* –opposite **unbearable**

beard /bɪəd ‖ bɪərd/ *n* hair on a man's chin and cheeks: *Not all men have beards.* | *John no longer wears a beard.* –see picture on page 245 –compare MOUSTACHE **bearded** *adj* : *a tall, bearded man* | *a grey-bearded old man*

bear·er /ˈbeərəʳ/ *n* **1** *fml* a person who brings or possesses something such as an official letter: *Please help the bearer of this document.* **2** a person

who helps to carry something: *The bearers carried the coffin to the grave.* | *the flagbearer*

bear·ing /ˈbeərɪŋ/ *n* **1** [sing] someone's way of holding or moving their body, especially when this shows their behaviour or character: *her proud, upright bearing* **2** [C] *tech* the part of a machine which holds another part so that it can turn or move more easily **3** [C] *tech* a direction or angle as shown by a compass: *We need to take a bearing* **4 have a bearing on something** to have a connection with or an influence on something: *What you said has no bearing on the matter.* **5 lose your bearings** to become confused: *In all this mass of details I'm afraid I've rather lost my bearings.* [RELATED PHRASE **get your bearings**]

beast /biːst/ *n* **1** *lit* an animal **2** a person or sometimes a thing that you think is very unpleasant: *a beast of a job* | *Her husband was a real beast.* | *You beast!* –**beastly** *adj* : *beastly weather* –**beastliness** *n* [U]

beat¹ /biːt/ *v* **beat, beaten** /ˈbiːtn/ **1** [T] to defeat someone or do better than they: *She beat Holly Wilson in the finals.* | *She's hoping to beat the world 1000 metre record.* –see WIN¹ (USAGE) **2** [T] to hit someone repeatedly, usually with a hard object: *The students were beaten by the police.* **3** [I;T] to hit something hard and continuously: *The rain was beating against the windows.* | *The police beat the door down.* | *They beat the drums.* **4** [I;T] to move regularly: *You can hear its heart beating.* | *The bird beat its wings rapidly.* **5** [T] to mix something well with regular movement of a fork or spoon: *Beat two eggs and add them to the mixture* **6 beat about the bush** to delay talking about or answering questions about the most important part of a subject **7 Beat it!** *slang* Go away! **8 beat someone at their own game** to use successfully against someone a method which they use themselves **9 beat someone to it** to do something before someone else **10 beat time** to make regular movements or noises with your hands and feet at the same speed as a piece of music **11 it beats me** *infml* I can't understand it

beat down *phr v* **1** [I] (of the sun) to be very hot and bright **2** [I] (of the rain) to come down very hard **3** [T **beat** sbdy ↔ **down**] to persuade someone to reduce a price: *He wanted £50 for the dress, but I beat him down to £40.*

beat sbdy/sthg **off** *phr v* [T] to prevent an attacker from succeeding: *He managed to beat the dogs off.*

beat sthg ↔ **out** *phr v* [T] **1** to make sounds by beating: *The drummers beat out their music.* **2** to put out a fire by beating

beat sbdy **to** sthg *phr v* [T] to defeat someone by being the first to do something: *They had hoped to win a big contract in Japan, but they were beaten to it by a German company.*

beat sbdy ↔ **up** *phr v* [T] *infml* to hurt someone badly by hitting: *The boys robbed the old man and then beat him up.*

beat² *n* **1** [C] a single movement or blow, especially as part of a group: *one beat of the drum every 60 seconds* **2** [sing] a regular sound produced by or as if by repeated beating: *the beat of the drum* **3** [Sing] a regular timing in music or poetry: *Every member of the band must follow the beat.* | *music with a strong beat* **4** [C] the usual area for which someone, especially a policeman, is responsible in their job

beat³ *adj* [never before a noun] **1** *infml* very tired: *I'm dead beat after all that work!* **2** defeated: *I had to admit that I was beat.*

beat·en¹ /ˈbiːtn/ the past participle of BEAT

beat·en² adj **1** shaped by beating, e.g. with a hammer or by people's feet: *a plate made of beaten gold* | *We followed a well-beaten path through the forest.* **2** off the beaten track not often visited: *Every year they go camping somewhere off the beaten track.*

beat·er /ˈbiːtəʳ/ n **1** a tool used in the kitchen to mix eggs and other things: *an egg beater* **2** a tool used for beating floor coverings: *a carpet beater*

beat·ing /ˈbiːtɪŋ/ n **1** an act in which one person hits another hard many times, usually with something such as a stick; a beating is sometimes given as a punishment: *The child had been given a severe beating.* **2** a bad defeat, especially in a game or competition: *Our team took quite a beating. The score was five–nil.* **3** take some beating be so good that it will be difficult for anything else to be better: *Your chocolate puddings take some beating.*

beat-up /ˌ·ˈ·◂/ infml adj in very bad condition because used so much or treated so badly: *a beat-up old car*

beau·ti·cian /bjuːˈtɪʃən/ n a person who gives beauty treatments to your face or nails

beau·ti·ful /ˈbjuːtɪfəl/ adj giving great pleasure to your mind or senses: *a beautiful girl* | *a beautiful sunset* –**beautifully** adv
■ USAGE **1 Beautiful** is quite a strong word to describe a person's appearance. **Pretty, handsome, good-looking** or **attractive** may be more suitable words. **2** We use **beautiful** and **pretty** to describe women, children and things, but usually not men: *a beautiful girl* | *a beautiful house* | *a pretty child* | *a pretty picture.* We use **good-looking** to describe men and women, but not things. We use **handsome** to describe men, or women who are **good-looking** in a strong, healthy way. We use **attractive** to describe men, women and things: *an attractive young man* | *an attractive pattern.*

beau·ti·fy /ˈbjuːtɪfaɪ/ v **beautified, beautifying** [T] to make something beautiful

beau·ty /ˈbjuːti/ n **beauties 1** [U] the quality of being attractive to look at or hear, or pleasing to the mind: *a poem of great beauty* | *the beauty of the scenery* **2** [C] someone beautiful, usually a woman, or something beautiful: *She is a great beauty.* | *the beauties of nature* **3** [C] infml someone or something very good or very bad: *That apple is a real beauty.* | *That black eye is a real beauty!* **4** the beauty of the advantage of: *The beauty of my idea is that it would cost so little!*

beauty spot /ˈ··· ·/ n a place known for the beauty of its scenery

bea·ver /ˈbiːvəʳ/ n a water and land animal of the rat family with a broad flat tail which builds walls across streams

be·calmed /bɪˈkɑːmd ‖ -ˈkɑːmd, -ˈkɑːlmd/ adj unable to move forward because of lack of wind (used of a sailing ship)

be·cause /bɪˈkɒz, bɪˈkəz ‖ bɪˈkɔːz, bɪˈkəz/ conj a word you use when you are giving a reason for something: *"Why can't I go?" "Because you're too young!"* | *We couldn't go out because it was too cold.* **because of** prep for the reason given: *The event was called off because of the rain.*

beck /bek/ n be at someone's **beck and call** to always have to be ready to do everything someone asks

beck·on /ˈbekən/ v [I;T] to show someone with a movement of the finger or hand that you want them to move nearer: *She's beckoning to you.* | *She beckoned me to follow her.*

be·come /bɪˈkʌm/ v became /bɪˈkeɪm/, become, becoming **1** [+ complement] to begin to be something: *He became king in 1938.* | *The weather became warmer.* **2** [T] fml to be right or suitable for: *That sort of behaviour does not become a person in your position.*
become of sbdy/sthg phr v [T] to happen to somebody or something, often in a bad way: *Whatever became of that nice girl you used to share a flat with?*
■ USAGE **Become** is not always the best word when you describe a change in a person or thing. To describe a change in colour you can use **turn,** or **go** if it is a temporary change: *The leaves are turning brown.* | *His face turns/goes red when he is angry.* We can use **go** or **become** in these expressions: *to go/become deaf* | *to go/become blind.* People **go** mad; meat **goes** bad.

be·com·ing /bɪˈkʌmɪŋ/ adj old fash (a word which is sometimes used in a humorous way) **1** looking very good on the wearer: *Blue always looks very becoming on her.* **2** proper or suitable: *His laughter was not very becoming on such a solemn occasion.* –opposite **unbecoming**

bed¹ /bed/ n **1** [C;U] an article of furniture to sleep on: *a room with two beds* | *a comfortable bed for the night* | *It's time for bed.* | *She's gone to bed.* | *She's in bed.* | *He helped me into bed.* **2** make a bed to make bed ready to sleep in: *When I've done the washing up, I'll make the beds.* **3** [C] a surface that forms the base or bottom of something: *The hut rests on a bed of cement.* | *I served the chicken on a bed of lettuce.* | *the bed of the river* | *the seabed* **4** [C] a piece of ground in which plants grow in a garden: *a flowerbed* **5** [C] a band of rock of a certain kind lying above or below others: *The building stands on a bed of rock.* **6** bed and breakfast a service offered by a guesthouse or other place where you can stay the night; you get a bed for the night and breakfast, but no other meals **7** a bed of roses infml a happy comfortable state **8** he got out of bed on the wrong side infml = he's in a bad temper **9** go to bed with someone to have sexual relations with someone: *He tried to get her to go to bed with him.*

bed² v -dd- [T] to fix on a base or beneath the surface: *The machine is bedded in cement.*
bed down phr v [I + adv/prep] to make yourself comfortable for the night when you have not got a proper bed

bed·clothes /ˈbedkləʊðz, -kləʊz/ n [pl] the sheets and covers that you put on a bed

bed·ding /ˈbedɪŋ/ n [U] **1** sheets and other things which you use to make your bed **2** something soft on which a person or animal can sleep

be·deck /bɪˈdek/ v [T] fml to decorate something: *The cars were all bedecked with flowers for the ceremony.*

be·dev·il /bɪˈdevəl/ v -ll- BrE ‖ -l- AmE [T] to cause problems to someone continually

bed·lam /ˈbedləm/ n [U] infml a wild noisy place or activity

bed·pan /ˈbedpæn/ n a low wide vessel used by a sick person for emptying their bowels without getting out of bed

be·drag·gled /bɪˈdrægəld/ adj with the clothes and hair in disorder: *a bedraggled appearance*

bed·rid·den /ˈbedˌrɪdn/ adj unable to get out of bed because of illness or old age

bed·room /ˈbedrʊm, -ruːm/ n a room for sleeping in

bed·side /ˈbedsaɪd/ n the side of a bed: *He was called to the bedside of his sick father.* | *a bedside lamp*

bed-sit·ter /ˌ·ˈ··/ (also **bed-sit** /ˈ· ˌ·/ *infml*) n a room used for both living and sleeping in –see HOUSE¹ (USAGE)

bed-spread /ˈbedspred/ n a decorative cloth cover for a bed

bee /biː/ n **1** a black and yellow insect that makes HONEY and buzzes (BUZZ) **2 a bee in your bonnet** *infml* a fixed idea: *He has a bee in his bonnet about health foods.*

beech /biːtʃ/ n **1** [C] a tree with a smooth grey trunk, spreading branches, and green leaves **2** [U] the wood of this tree

beef¹ /biːf/ n [U] the meat of farm cattle –see MEAT (USAGE)

beef² v **beef about something** *infml* to complain continually about something: *Stop beefing about your pay and do some work!*

beef·y /ˈbiːfi/ adj beefier, beefiest *infml* big, strong, and perhaps fat (used of a person)

bee·hive /ˈbiːhaɪv/ n see HIVE (1)

bee·line /ˈbiːlaɪn/ n **make a beeline for something** *infml* to go quickly and directly towards something: *The children made a beeline for the swings.*

been /biːn, bɪn ‖ bɪn/ v **1** the past participle of BE: *They've been photographed.* **2** gone and come back from: *Have you ever been to India?* **3** arrived and left: *I see the postman hasn't been yet.* –see GO¹ (USAGE)

beer /bɪəʳ/ n **1** [U] a bitter alcoholic drink made from MALT and hops (HOP³): *Do you like beer?* **2** [C] a drink of beer: *We had several beers.* **3** [U] any of several kinds of drink, usually non-alcoholic, made from roots or plants: *ginger beer* –**beery** adj : *unpleasant beery breath*

bees·wax /ˈbiːzwæks/ n [U] wax made by bees, used for making furniture polish and candles

beet /biːt/ n **1** [C;U] (also **sugar beet**) a plant with a thick root underground, used as a vegetable or made into sugar. **2** the usual American word for BEETROOT

bee·tle /ˈbiːtl/ n an insect with hard wing coverings

beet·root /ˈbiːtruːt/ (**beet** AmE–) n beetroot or beetroots [C;U] a plant with a large round red root, which is cooked and eaten as a vegetable: *beetroot salad* –see picture on page 344

be·fall /bɪˈfɔːl/ v befell /bɪˈfel/, befallen /bɪˈfɔːlən/ [I;T] *fml* (usually used of something bad) to happen to someone as if by fate: *Some misfortune must have befallen them.*

be·fore¹ /bɪˈfɔːʳ/ adv at an earlier time or on an earlier occasion: *Haven't I seen you somewhere before?* | *He had never been to London before.*

before² prep **1** earlier than: *We must leave before lunch time.* | *They got there before us.* **2** ahead of someone or something: *Her name comes before mine on the list.* **3** in front of someone of something: *She had to give evidence before a magistrate.* **4** in a more important position: *Your family should come before everything else.* **5 before that** you use "before that" when you are showing what order events happen in: *In five minutes' time we'll have the news, but before that let's go over to the London Weather Centre for the weather forecast.*

before³ conj earlier than the time when something happens: *I'd like to talk to you before you go.* | *We must consider all the facts before we make a decision.*

be·fore·hand /bɪˈfɔːh d ‖ -ˈfɔːr-/ adv before something else happens: *If you knew what was going to happen, why didn't you warn us beforehand?*

be·friend /bɪˈfrend/ v [T] *fml* to act as a friend to someone who needs your help: *He befriended me when I was young.*

beg /beg/ v **-gg- 1** [I;T] to ask people in the street to give you money or food: *He lives by begging.* | *She sat at the station begging for money.* **2** [I;T] to ask for something with great eagerness or anxiety: *to beg for forgiveness* | *Could I beg a favour of you* | *He begged me to stay.*
□ USEFUL PATTERNS to beg for something; to beg someone to do something
3 [I] (of a dog) to sit up with its front legs held against its chest **4 going begging** *infml* able to be taken or used **5 I beg your pardon** you use this expression when you are saying that you are sorry, or when you did not hear what someone said and you want them to say it again **6 beg the question: a** to treat as true something that is not yet proved **b** to avoid answering a question

beg·gar¹ /ˈbegəʳ/ n **1** a person who lives by begging **2** *infml* a person, especially a man: *So you're off to Hong Kong tomorrow, you lucky beggar!* **3 beggars can't be choosers** *infml* poor people have to take anything they can get and must not hope to get exactly what they want

beggar² v [T] *fml* to make someone very poor

be·gin /bɪˈgɪn/ v began /bɪˈgæn/, begun /bɪˈgʌn/, beginning **1** [I] to start: *Tell me when to begin.* | *Work on the new railway will begin in 1995.* | *The story began with a plane crash.* | *I began by explaining the situation.* **2** [T] to start something: *They're beginning a new serial on BBC 2 next week.* | *It's beginning to rain.* | *She began learning English last year.*
□ USEFUL PATTERNS to begin something; to begin to do something; to begin doing something
3 [I] to come into existence: *The war began in 1979.* **4 to begin with: a** firstly; when you are speaking or writing and you have several points you want to make, you can order them and introduce them with expressions such as "to begin with," and "secondly,": *It can't be done. To begin with, there's no time to plan it, and secondly, we haven't got enough men.* **b** at first: *To begin with the weather was dreadful, but it improved later in the week.* –see START¹ (USAGE)

be·gin·ner /bɪˈgɪnəʳ/ n a person who is just beginning to do or learn something

be·gin·ning /bɪˈgɪnɪŋ/ n [C;U] the starting point or origin: *She knows that book from beginning to end.* | *at the beginning of the month*
■ USAGE **1** Note the use of the preposition at in the phrase **at the beginning**: *As I mentioned at the* **beginning** *of my letter...* | *He arrived at the beginning of the lunch hour.* | *at the* **beginning** *of the century* **2** When you want to contrast an early time with a later time use **at first**: *At first we thought it was a joke but then we realized it was true.* | *Nobody liked her at first but she soon became quite popular.*

be·grudge /bɪˈgrʌdʒ/ v begrudged, begrudging [T] **1** to feel angry about doing something that you do not want to do: *I begrudge spending so much money on train fares.* **2 begrudge someone something** to feel angry that someone should have something: *We shouldn't begrudge him his success.*

be·guile /bɪˈgaɪl/ v beguiled, beguiling [T] *fml* **1** to charm someone: *Her eyes and voice beguiled me.* **2 beguile someone into doing something** to deceive or cheat someone into doing something *He*

beguiled me into lending him my bicycle.
-beguiling *adj*

be·half /bɪˈhɑːf ‖ bɪˈhæf/ *n* **on behalf of** (also **in behalf of** *AmE*) for someone or in someone's interests: *The President can't be here today, so I'm going to speak on his behalf.* | *On behalf of everyone here, I'd like to thank you both very much for coming.*

be·have /bɪˈheɪv/ *v* **behaved, behaving** **1** [I + adv/prep] to act in a particular way: *She behaved with great courage.* | *He's been behaving very oddly lately.* | *My car has been behaving well since it was repaired.* **2** [I] to act in a socially acceptable or polite way: *He'll have to learn how to behave.* **3** **behave yourself** to act in a socially acceptable or polite way: *Just stop being naughty and behave yourself!* **4** **behaved** behaving in the stated way: *a very badly behaved child*

be·hav·iour /bɪˈheɪvjəʳ/ *n* (**behavior** *Am E*) [U] **1** a way of behaving: *It was very odd behaviour for a policeman.* **2** **be on your best behaviour** to be very polite

be·head /bɪˈhed/ *v* [T] to cut someone's head off

be·hind[1] /bɪˈhaɪnd/ *adv,prep* **1** *adv,prep* at the back of something: *A stream runs behind the house.* | *She ran out from behind a tree.* | *a house with a large garden behind* -see picture on page 540 **2** *adv* late or slow: *We're a month behind with the rent.* **3** *adv,prep* less successful than someone else: *We finished three points behind the leaders.* **4** *adv* where something or someone was before: *The others went for a walk but I stayed behind.* | *I had left my handbag behind.* **5** *prep* causing something: *I think that John is behind all this.* **6** *prep* supporting someone: *The country is firmly behind the prime minister.*

behind[2] *n old fash* the part of your body that you sit on

be·hind·hand /bɪˈhaɪndhænd/ *adj,adv fml* late: *We're a month behindhand with the rent.*

be·hold /bɪˈhəʊld/ *v* **beheld** /bɪˈheld/, **beheld** [T] *lit* to see someone or something

beige /beɪʒ/ *n,adj* [U] a pale dull yellowish brown -see picture on page 147

be·ing /ˈbiːɪŋ/ *n* **1** **come into being** to begin to exist: *When did the club first come into being?* **2** [C] a creature: *a human being* | *a being from outer space*

be·la·bour /bɪˈleɪbəʳ/ *v* (**belabor** *AmE*) [T] to talk about something for too long: *He kept belabouring the point until we were all absolutely fed up with it.*

be·lat·ed /bɪˈleɪtɪd/ *adj* delayed or arriving too late: *a belated apology* **-belatedly** *adv*

belch /beltʃ/ *v* **1** [I] to pass gas noisily from your stomach out through your throat **2** [T] to throw something out with force or in large quantities: *chimneys belching smoke*

bel·fry /ˈbelfri/ *n* **belfries** a tower for a bell, for example on a church

be·lie /bɪˈlaɪ/ *v* **belied, belied, belying** *fml* [T] to give a false idea of something: *Her smile belied her feelings of displeasure.*

be·lief /bɪˈliːf/ *n* **1** [sing;U] the feeling that something is true or that something really exists: *belief in God* | *my belief that he is right* **2** [sing;U] trust or a feeling that someone or something is good or can be depended on: *her misplaced belief in her husband* | *The failure of the operation has shaken my belief in doctors.* **3** [C] an idea which is considered true, often one which is part of a system of ideas: *my religious beliefs* | *strongly-held beliefs* **4** **beyond**

belief: a too strange to be believed: *His story is beyond belief.* **b** very great

be·lie·va·ble /bɪˈliːvəbəl/ *adj* that seems real and can be believed **-opposite unbelievable** **-believably** *adv*

be·lieve /bɪˈliːv/ *v* **believed, believing** [*not in progressive forms*] **1** [T + (that)] to think that something is true: *I don't believe these figures.* | *You can't believe anything she says.* | *It's hard to believe that she's only 25.* **2** [T + (that)] to have an opinion: *I believe that she will win the next election.* | *70% of the people asked believe the government's policies are right.* | *The jury believed her to be innocent.* **3** [T] to think that someone is telling the truth: *I believe her.* | *The police don't believe him.* **4** **believe it or not** you use this expression when you are surprised or you think that the person you are talking to will be surprised: *I asked for an extra week's holiday and, believe it or not, she agreed!* **5** **believe me** you use this expression to add force to what you are saying: *I don't like it any more than you do, believe me.* **6** **would you believe it** you use this expression when you are surprised or shocked: *"He was back again only two days later." "Well! Would you believe it!"* **7** **make believe** to pretend: *He's making believe he's really ill. He just wants your sympathy.*

believe in *phr v* **1** [T **believe in** sthg] to think that something exists: *Do you believe in fairies?* **2** [**believe in** sbdy] to have faith or trust in someone: *Christians believe in Jesus.* **3** [**believe in** sthg] to have confidence in the value of something: *Jim believes in going for a run every morning.*

be·liev·er /bɪˈliːvəʳ/ *n* **1** someone who believes in God **2** someone who believes in something: *He's a great believer in the benefits of exercise.*

be·lit·tle /bɪˈlɪtl/ *v* **belittled, belittling** [T] *fml* to make something seem small or unimportant and not very good: *Don't belittle yourself.* | *You mustn't belittle your efforts.*

bell /bel/ *n* a round hollow metal object, which makes a ringing sound when struck or when a movable hanging part hits the inside: *a bicycle bell* | *a doorbell*

bel·lig·er·ent /bɪˈlɪdʒərənt/ *adj* angry and ready to fight: *I felt tired and belligerent.*

bel·low /ˈbeləʊ/ *v* **1** [I] to make the loud deep hollow sound typical of a BULL [1] (1) **2** [I;T] to shout something in a loud, deep voice: *"Go away!" he bellowed.* **-bellow** *n*

bel·ly /ˈbeli/ *n* **bellies** **1** *infml* the part of the human body, between the chest and the legs, which contains the stomach and bowels **2** a surface or object curved or round like this part of your body: *the belly of the plane*

bel·ly·ache /ˈbeli-eɪk/ *v* **bellyached, bellyaching** [I] *infml* to complain repeatedly, especially about something unimportant: *Stop bellyaching about the colour and get on with the job!*

belly but·ton /ˈ··, ··/ *n infml* your NAVEL

bel·ly·ful /ˈbeliful/ *n infml* **a bellyful of something** too much of something: *I've had a bellyful of your complaints.*

be·long /bɪˈlɒŋ ‖ bɪˈlɔːŋ/ *v* [I] to be in the right place: *That chair belongs in the other room.* | *I don't really feel I belong here.*

belong to *phr v* **1** [T **belong to** sbdy] to be owned by someone: *That dictionary belongs to me.* **2** [T

belong to sthg] to be a member of a group or to be connected with a group: *Which party do you belong to?*

be·long·ings /bɪˈlɒŋɪŋz ‖ bɪˈlɔːŋ-/ n [pl] the things which belong to you: *She lost all her belongings in the fire.*

be·lov·ed /bɪˈlʌvɪd/ n [sing] *fml* a person you love very much: –**beloved** *adj*

be·low /bɪˈləʊ/ *adv,prep* 1 *adv,prep* lower than something: *He lives in the flat below me.* | *We could hear shouting coming from the room below.* | *miners who work below ground* –see picture on page 540 2 *adv,prep* lower in rank: *I have four people working below me.* | *the rank of captain and below* 3 *adv* further on in a piece of writing: *More details are given below.* | *See page 82 below.* 4 *prep* less than a particular amount: *children below the age of seven* | *We must get inflation down to below 10%.*

belt¹ /belt/ n 1 a band of cloth or leather that you wear around your waist: *a dress with a matching belt* –see picture on page 50 2 a moving band of rubber used for driving a machine or for carrying things along: *Put your suitcases on the moving belt.* 3 an area where a particular thing is common or where a particular type of person lives: *the corn belt of the USA* | *the commuter belt*

belt² v 1 [T] to fasten something with a belt 2 [T] *infml* to hit someone or something: *Shut up or I'll belt you!* 3 [I+adv/prep] *infml* to move or travel very fast: *We absolutely belted down the motorway.* 4 **belt up** *infml* = shut up: *Belt up, will you!*

belt sthg ↔ **out** *phr* v [T] to shout or sing something loudly: *The Sergeant Major belted out the orders.*

be·moan /bɪˈməʊn/ v [T] *fml* to express deep sorrow about something: *He bemoaned his fate.*

be·mused /bɪˈmjuːzd/ *adj* confused, as if you do not know what is happening: *She looked totally bemused.*

bench /bentʃ/ n 1 a long seat made of wood or stone for two or more people: *a park bench* 2 a long strong work table 3 **the bench** the seat where a judge sits in court, or the judge: *What is the opinion of the bench?*

bend¹ /bend/ v bent /bent/, **bent, bending** 1 [I] (also **bend down, bend over**) to move the top part of your body down towards the ground: *He bent down to pick up a book.* –see picture on page 736 2 [I] to move into a curved position: *I can't get this wire to bend.* 3 [T] to force something into a curved position: *You've bent your fork.* | *Bend your knees a bit more.* 4 **be bent on something** to be determined to do something: *She is bent on getting into publishing.* 5 **bend over backwards** to make every effort to help someone 6 **bend the rules** to allow yourself or someone else to do something which is really against the rules

bend² n 1 a curved part of a road or river: *Slow down, this is quite a sharp bend.* 2 **round the bend** *infml* mad: *He really drives me round the bend!*

be·neath /bɪˈniːθ/ *adv,prep* 1 *fml* under or below: *She could feel the warm sand beneath her feet.* | *We looked down from the hills at the valley beneath.* 2 **beneath someone** not worthy of someone: *He considered that manual work was beneath him.*

ben·e·fac·tor /ˈbenɪˌfæktəʳ/ n a person who helps other people by giving money; a woman who does this is called a **benefactress** /-trɪs/

be·nef·i·cent /bɪˈnefɪsənt/ *adj fml* kind and generous

ben·e·fi·cial /ˌbenɪˈfɪʃəl/ *adj* having a good effect: *These measures should prove beneficial to the economy.*

ben·e·fi·cia·ry /ˌbenɪˈfɪʃəri ‖ -ˈfɪʃieri/ n **beneficiaries** 1 a person who receives something and is helped by it 2 a person who is left money or property by someone who has died

ben·e·fit¹ /ˈbenɪfɪt/ n 1 [C] something which helps you in some way: *Modern technology has brought many benefits.* 2 **have the benefit of something** to have something which is useful or helpful to you: *She had the benefit of a good education.* 3 **of benefit to someone, to someone's benefit** useful or helpful to someone: *The money was of great benefit to me.* 4 **for someone's benefit** in order to help someone: *I did it for your benefit.* 5 [U] money which is given by the government to people who need it: *You should be able to claim unemployment benefit.* 6 **give someone the benefit of the doubt** to accept that someone is telling the truth, even though you do not necessarily believe them

benefit² v 1 [T] to be useful or helpful to someone: *These changes in the law will benefit many people.* 2 **benefit from something, benefit by something** to gain as a result of something: *Who would be most likely to benefit from the old man's death?*

be·nev·o·lent /bɪˈnevələnt/ *adj* kind and helpful –**benevolence** n [U] –**benevolently** *adv*

be·nign /bɪˈnaɪn/ *adj* 1 kind and gentle 2 favourable (used of the weather) 3 not dangerous (used of a disease or TUMOUR) –**benignly** *adv*

bent¹ /bent/ the past tense and past participle of BEND

bent² *adj BrE infml* 1 dishonest (used of people in official positions) 2 HOMOSEXUAL

bent³ n a natural ability and interest: *She's got an artistic bent.*

be·queath /bɪˈkwiːð, bɪˈkwiːθ/ v [T] *fml* to leave money, property, or ideas to other people after you die: *My aunt bequeathed me her gold watch.* –**bequest** /bɪˈkwest/ n : *He left a bequest of £5,000 to his children.*

be·reaved /bɪˈriːvd/ *adj fml* having suffered the death of a close friend or relative: *The Prime Minister has sent letters of condolence to the bereaved families.* –**bereavement** n [U]

be·reft /bɪˈreft/ *adj* **bereft of something** completely without something: *She was bereft of all hope.*

be·ret /ˈbereɪ ‖ bəˈreɪ/ n a flat, round cap with a tight headband, usually made of wool

ber·ry /ˈberi/ n **berries** a small soft fruit with seeds; berries grow on bushes or trees

ber·serk /bɜːˈsɜːk, bə- ‖ bərˈsɜːrk, ˈbɜːrsɜːrk/ *adj* **go berserk** to lose control, especially to become very angry and violent

berth¹ /bɜːθ ‖ bɜːrθ/ n 1 a place where a ship can be tied up in a harbour 2 a bed in a ship, train, or aircraft 3 **give someone/something a wide berth** *infml* to avoid someone or something dangerous or unpleasant

berth² v [I;T] to come or be brought into a port to be tied up: *The ship berthed next to the quay.*

be·seech /bɪˈsiːtʃ/ v besought /bɪˈsɔːt/ *or* beseeched, besought *or* beseeched *lit* [T] to ask someone to do something in an urgent and anxious way: *I beseech you to pardon him.* **beseechingly** *adv*

be·set /bɪˈset/ v beset, beset, besetting [T] to cause

severe problems or difficulties to someone or something: *the difficulties which beset the project* | *He was beset by doubts.*

be·side /bɪ'saɪd/ *prep* **1** next to someone or something: *He came and stood beside me.* –see picture on page 540 **2** compared to something or someone: *This year's profits don't look very good beside last year's.* **3 beside yourself** unable to control yourself because you feel so strongly, usually anger or grief: *He was beside himself with rage.*

be·sides[1] /bɪ'saɪdz/ *adv* in addition; you use this word when you make another point or give another reason that you have just thought of: *I don't think I'm going to Scotland for Christmas. It's such a long way. Besides, I haven't got much money left.* –see Study Note on page 508

besides[2] *prep* in addition to something: *There were three other people at the meeting besides Mr Day.*
■ USAGE **Besides** means "as well as" but **except** means "leaving out; but not". So *All of us passed* besides *John* means that John passed too, but *All of us passed* except *John* means that John did not pass.

be·siege /bɪ'siːdʒ/ *v* **besieged, besieging** [T] **1** to surround a place with armed forces: *The castle was besieged in the last century.* **2 besieged with, besieged by** to have a lot of demands made on you all at once: *The police have been besieged by people wanting information about the accident.*

be·sot·ted /bɪ'sɒtɪd ‖ bɪ'sɑː-/ *adj* so fond of someone or something that you are unable to think or behave sensibly: *He's completely besotted with her.*

best[1] /best/ *adj* [superlative of GOOD] **1** the most good: *She is the best tennis player in the world.* | *She's my best friend.* | *I want to do what is best for the children.* **2 the best part of something** most of something: *We spent the best part of a year in London.*

best[2] *adv* [superlative of WELL] **1** most well: *Which picture do you like best?* | *I asked how I could best help them.* | *Tuesday would suit me best.* **2 as best you can** as well as you can: *Just answer the questions as best you can.* **3 had best** a phrase you use when you are telling someone that they should do something: *You had best tell her straight away.*

best[3] *n* [sing] **1 the best** the thing or person that is most good or most successful: *Only the best is good enough for him.* | *We all want the best for our children.* **2 your best** your greatest effort: *I did my best to finish it on time.* | *We'll try our best to get there by lunch time.* **3 at your best** full of life and looking attractive: *I'm not at my best at six o'clock in the morning!* **4 all the best** an expression you use to give someone your good wishes when you are leaving them or they are leaving you **5 at best** if the best thing happens: *At best we'll only make a small profit this year.* **6 make the best of something** to accept something that is not very good, and use it or enjoy it in the best way that you can: *I couldn't afford to give up my job, so I just had to make the best of it.*

bes·ti·al /'bestiəl ‖ 'bestʃəl/ *adj fml* cruel and behaving like an animal (used of a person's behaviour): *bestial cruelty* –**bestiality** /ˌbesti'æləti ‖ ˌbestʃi-/ *n* [U]

best man /ˌ· '·/ *n* the friend and attendant of a man who is getting married

be·stow /bɪ'stəʊ/ *v fml* **bestow something on/ upon someone** to give something to someone: *Many gifts were bestowed on them.* –**bestowal** *fml n* [sing]

best·sel·ler /ˌ· '··/ *n* a book that sells in very large numbers

bet[1] /bet/ *n* **1** an agreement to risk money on the result of a future event: *I won my bet.* | *I've got a bet with my father that the Conservatives won't win the next election.* | *I think I'll put a bet on that horse.* **2 your best bet** = the best thing that you can do: *Your best bet is to say nothing about it.*

bet[2] *v* **bet, bet, betting** **1** [T] to risk money on the result of a future event: *I'll bet you £5 that they'll win the next election.* | *I never bet money on horse races.* **2** I bet *infml* = I'm sure: *I bet it will rain tomorrow!*

be·tray /bɪ'treɪ/ *v* [T] **1** to be disloyal or unfaithful to someone: *I never believed that he would betray us.* **2** *fml* to tell people secret information: *He betrayed the plan to a rival company.* **3** to show your real feelings or intentions: *Her face betrayed her nervousness.*

be·tray·al /bɪ'treɪəl/ *n* [C;U] the act of betraying someone or something: *a betrayal of my principles*

be·troth·al /bɪ'trəʊðəl/ *n old fash* a promise to marry someone

be·trothed /bɪ'trəʊðd/ *adj old fash* having promised to marry someone

bet·ter[1] /'betər/ *adj* **1** [comparative of GOOD] more good: *She's much better at maths than I am.* | *This film is better than his last one.* **2** improved in health: *I'm feeling a little better today.* | *When you're better you must come and visit us.* **3 your better half** your husband or wife; an expression that is usually used humorously **4 the better part of something** more than half of something: *We haven't seen her for the better part of a year.*

better[2] *adv* [comparative of WELL] **1** in a better way: *She swims much better than she used to.* **2** to a greater degree: *He knows the town better than I do.* | *I like this picture better than the other one.* **3 had better** a phrase you use when you are telling someone that they should do something: *You'd better go home now.* | *I'd better not tell him what happened.*
■ USAGE **1 Had better/'d better** are used in conversation when giving firm advice about what a person should do, especially to avoid a problem: *You'd better go now or you'll be late.* | *We'd better take out medical insurance for our holiday.* | *I think I'd better phone to say I'll be late.* **2** Note that **you'd better** is a very direct way of giving advice which can also be used to give an order: *Look,* **you'd better** *ring me tonight.* | *Hadn't you better apologize?* | **You'd better not** *show your face here again.* For this reason, do NOT use **you'd better** if you want to make a polite suggestion. Instead use phrases such as, **Why don't you**...? **Why not**...? **It might be a good idea to**.... **3** Note that **had better/'d better** are followed by the infinitive WITHOUT 'to'.

better[3] *n* **1 change for the better** to change and become better: *Let's hope that things will soon change for the better.* **2 get the better of someone** to defeat someone or make them seem foolish: *She always manages to get the better of me.*

better[4] *v* [T] to improve on something: *We made record profits last year, and we're hoping to better them this year.*

be·tween /bɪ'twiːn/ *adv,prep* **1** *adv,prep* (also in between) in the space in the middle of two things or people: *a village somewhere in between London and Oxford* | *I was sitting between my parents.* –see picture on page 540 **2** *adv,prep* (also in between) in the time after one thing has finished and before another thing has begun: *I'll phone you between five and six this evening.* | *I ate breakfast and lunch, but nothing in between.* **3** *prep* above one amount and below another: *children aged between eight and ten years* **4** *prep* done or shared by two people: *The bonds between them are very strong.* | *The money was divided between the two sons.* **5 between you and me** a phrase you use when you are telling someone something that is secret: *Between you and me, I think she's pregnant.* **6 few and far between** rare or infrequent: *Good managers are few and far between.*

■ USAGE Compare **between** and **among**. Use **between** when you are talking about only two people or things: *I divided the chocolates between the two children.* Use **among** when you are talking about more than two people or things: *I divided the chocolates among all the children.*

bev·er·age /ˈbevərɪdʒ/ *n fml* a drink, for example tea, coffee or wine

be·ware /bɪˈweər/ *v* [I only in infinitive and imperative form] a word used to warn someone to be careful about something: *Beware of signing any agreement without studying it carefully.* | *He warned us to beware.*

be·wil·der /bɪˈwɪldər/ *v* [T] to make you feel confused: *His attitude bewildered me.* –**bewildered** *adj*: *She looked completely bewildered.* –**bewilderment** *n* [U]

be·witch /bɪˈwɪtʃ/ *v* [T] **1** to produce a magic, often harmful, effect on someone **2** to attract someone's complete attention, as if by magic: *She had a bewitching smile.*

be·yond /bɪˈjɒnd ‖ bɪˈjɑːnd/ *adv,prep* **1** *adv,prep* on or to the further side of something: *He wouldn't travel with us beyond the border.* | *He said he would come with us as far as the river but not beyond.* **2** *prep* more than or further than: *The level of inflation has now risen beyond 10%.* **3** *prep* except: *I know nothing beyond what I've already told you.* **4 beyond you** too difficult for you to understand

bi·as¹ /ˈbaɪəs/ *n* [C;U] **1** a tendency to be either for or against something or someone: *His plays show a definite left wing bias.* | *She was accused of political bias.* **2** a tendency to be good at particular things: *Her scientific bias showed itself in early childhood.*

bias² *v* -s- *or* -ss- [T] to influence someone so that they have either a favourable or unfavourable opinion about something although they do not necessarily know all the facts about it: *His background biases him* **against** *foreigners.* | *I admit I'm rather biased* **in favour of** *our candidate.* | *He described the report as biased and inaccurate.*

bib /bɪb/ *n* a cloth tied under a child's chin to protect its clothes when it is eating

bi·ble /ˈbaɪbəl/ *n* the holy book of the Christians –**biblical** /ˈbɪblɪkəl/ *adj*

bib·li·og·ra·phy /ˌbɪbliˈɒɡrəfi ‖ -ˈɑːɡ-/ *n* **bibliographies** a list at the end of a book which names all the books and articles which the writer used to help them write their book

bi·car·bon·ate /baɪˈkɑːbənɪt, -bəneɪt ‖ -ˈkɑːr-/ *n* (also **bicarbonate of soda** /·,··· ·'··/, **bicarb** /ˈbaɪkɑːb‖-kɑːrb/ *infml*) [U] a white chemical powder used in baking or as a medicine for your stomach

bi·cen·te·na·ry /ˌbaɪsenˈtiːnəri ‖ -ˈtenəri, -ˈsentəneri/ *n* **bicentenaries** the day or year exactly 200 years after a particular event: *The company's bicentenary was in 1974.*

bi·cen·ten·ni·al /ˌbaɪsenˈteniəl/ *n* the usual American word for BICENTENARY

bi·ceps /ˈbaɪseps/ *n* [plural is **biceps**] the large muscle on the front of your upper arm

bick·er /ˈbɪkər/ *v* [I] to argue with someone about something unimportant: *Stop bickering will you!* | *They're always bickering about money.*

bi·cy·cle /ˈbaɪsɪkəl/ *n* (also **bike**) **1** a vehicle with two wheels which you move by pushing its pedals (PEDAL) round and round with your feet: *She's learning to ride a bicycle.* **2 by bicycle** travelling on a bicycle: *Let's go by bicycle.* –see TRANSPORT (USAGE)

bid¹ /bɪd/ *n* **1** an offer to pay a certain price for something that is being sold: *I made a final bid of £20.* **2** an offer to do some work at a certain price: *Bids for building the bridge were invited from British and American firms.* **3** a chance to make a declaration in certain card games of the number of games that you think you will win **4** an attempt to do or get something: *The criminal made a bid* **for** *freedom by trying to run away.* | *a bid to overthrow the government*

bid² *v* **bid, bid, bidding** [I;T] **1** to offer to pay a certain price for something that is being sold: *I can afford to bid £50, but no more.* | *Who will bid £10* **for** *this beautiful plate?* **2** to make a bid in a game of cards –**bidder** *n* : *The buildings will be sold to the highest bidder.*

bid³ *v* **bade** /bæd, beɪd/ *or* **bid, bidden** /ˈbɪdn/ *or* **bid, bidding** *lit* **1** bid someone good morning to say good morning: *He bid me good morning as he passed.* **2** [T] to order or tell someone to do something: *She would never do as she was bidden.* | *She bade him come.*

bid·ding /ˈbɪdɪŋ/ *n* **do something at someone's bidding, do someone's bidding** to do something that someone has asked you to do

bide /baɪd/ *v* **bided, biding bide your time** to wait, usually for a long time, until the right moment

bi·det /ˈbiːdeɪ ‖ bɪˈdeɪ/ *n* a kind of small low bath which you can sit on to wash your bottom

bi·en·ni·al¹ /baɪˈeniəl/ *adj* happening once every two years: *The city's biennial jazz festival begins next week.* –**biennially** *adv*

biennial² *n* a plant which lives for two years and produces seed in the second year

bier /bɪər/ *n lit* a movable frame like a table, used for supporting a dead body at a funeral

bi·fo·cals /baɪˈfəʊkəlz ‖ ˈbaɪfəʊ-/ *n* [pl] glasses which have an upper part made for looking at distant objects, and a lower part made for reading –see PAIR¹ (USAGE)

big /bɪɡ/ *adj* **bigger, biggest 1** of more than average size, amount, or importance: *There's a big parcel for you.* | *The biggest ship that's ever been built* | *There's been a big rise in house prices this year.* | *The big question is what to do next.* **2** used when asking the size, amount, or importance of something: *How big is their house?* | *We need to find out just how big the problem is.* **3 too big for your boots** *infml* believing yourself to be more important than you really are

big·a·my /ˈbɪɡəmi/ *n* [U] the crime of being married to two people at the same time: *He was charged with bigamy.* –**bigamist** *n* –**bigamous** *adj*

Big Broth·er /ˌ· ˈ··/ n a government or political leader who has too much power over society and limits your freedom

big·ot /ˈbɪɡət/ n someone who thinks, unreasonably, that their own opinions are correct, especially about matters of religion, race, or politics, and doesn't pay attention to the opinions of other people –**bigoted** adj : He was arrogant and bigoted.

big·ot·ry /ˈbɪɡətri/ n [U] the holding of strong, unreasonable opinions, and unwillingness to pay attention to the opinions of other people

big·wig /ˈbɪɡwɪɡ/ n infml a person with a high position in an organization

bike /baɪk/ n (also **bicycle**) a vehicle with two wheels that you ride by pushing its pedals (PEDAL) round and round with your feet

bi·ki·ni /bɨˈkiːni/ n a garment in two pieces which women wear for swimming

bi·lat·er·al /baɪˈlætərəl/ adj including or concerning two people or two countries: a bilateral agreement –**bilaterally** adv

bil·ber·ry /ˈbɪlbəri ‖ -beri/ n bilberries a low bushy plant which grows in Northern Europe and produces small dark blue fruit

bile /baɪl/ n [U] a bitter liquid produced in your LIVER¹ which helps your body to DIGEST food

bilge /bɪldʒ/ n [U] infml foolish talk: Don't give me that bilge!

bi·lin·gual /baɪˈlɪŋɡwəl/ adj 1 spoken or written in two languages: a bilingual dictionary 2 able to speak two languages equally well: a bilingual secretary

bil·i·ous /ˈbɪliəs/ adj feeling sick and having a headache: Fatty food makes some people bilious. –**biliousness** n [U]

bill¹ /bɪl/ n 1 a list of things bought or services supplied and their price: She paid the bill and left the restaurant. | the gas bill 2 a plan for a law, written down for the government to consider: M.P.s rejected the bill by 240 votes to 138. 3 AmE a piece of paper money a five-dollar bill 4 the beak of a bird

bill² v [T] 1 to send a bill to someone: They've forgotten to bill me for the wine. 2 to advertise someone who is going to appear in a show: She was billed to appear in a new play in London.

bill·board /ˈbɪlbɔːd ‖ -ɔːrd/ n a large board in a public place, on which notices are put

bil·let /ˈbɪlɨt/ v [T] to provide lodging for soldiers in a private house, especially for a short time: The soldiers were billeted in private houses.

bil·li·ards /ˈbɪljədz ‖ -ərdz/ n [U] a game played by two people on a cloth-covered table called a **billiard table**; the players use long sticks to knock balls into pockets at the sides of the table

bil·lion /ˈbɪljən/ det, n, pron **billion** or **billions** 1 the number 1,000,000,000 2 BrE old fash the number 1,000,000,000,000 –**billionth** det, n, pron, adv

bil·low¹ /ˈbɪləʊ/ n a rolling mass of smoke or mist: Billows of smoke rose from the chimney.

billow² v [I] 1 (of smoke) to rise and roll in a large mass: Smoke billowed out of the burning building. 2 to fill with air and move about in the wind: Her skirt billowed in the wind. –**billowing** adj : billowing sails

billy goat /ˈ·· ·/ n a male goat

bi·month·ly /baɪˈmʌnθli/ adv, adj 1 appearing or happening every two months: a bimonthly magazine 2 happening twice a month: a bimonthly meeting

bin /bɪn/ n a large container, usually with a lid, used for storing things in or putting waste in

bi·na·ry /ˈbaɪnəri/ adj tech 1 consisting of two things or two parts 2 **binary system** a number system using the two numbers, 0 and 1, as a base, used especially with computers

bind¹ /baɪnd/ v [T] **bound** /baʊnd/, **bound** 1 to tie something firmly: His hands and feet had been bound. 2 to strengthen or decorate something with a binding: The book hasn't been bound yet. | You'll have to bind the edges of the rug. 3 to make substances stick together in a mass: Add a beaten egg to bind the mixture. 4 to unite people: They are bound together by their religious beliefs. 5 to force someone to do something: The agreement bound him to secrecy.

bind sbdy over phr v [T] BrE law (of a court of law) to order someone to cause no more trouble for a certain period of time

bind² n infml a bind something that is difficult or annoying: It's a real bind not having a telephone.

bind·er /ˈbaɪndəʳ/ n 1 a machine or person that binds things, especially books: Your book is still at the binder's. 2 a hard cover with metal rings inside for holding sheets of paper together

bind·ing¹ /ˈbaɪndɪŋ/ n 1 [C] a book cover: a book with a beautiful leather binding 2 [U] a band of material that is sewn or stuck along the edge of something in order to make it stronger or more attractive

binding² adj having the legal power to force someone to obey a promise or an agreement: a binding agreement

binge /bɪndʒ/ n a period of drinking a lot of alcohol

bin·go /ˈbɪŋɡəʊ/ n [U] a game of chance played for prizes, in which players mark numbers on cards as the numbers are called out to them

bi·noc·u·lars /bɨˈnɒkjɨləz, baɪ- ‖ -ˈnɑːkjɨlərz/ n [pl] a pair of glasses used for making distant objects look nearer: Shall we take the binoculars? There might be some interesting birds to look at. –see PAIR¹ (USAGE)

bi·o·chem·is·try /ˌbaɪəʊˈkemɨstri/ n [U] the scientific study of the chemical processes that take place in living things

bi·o·de·gra·da·ble /ˌbaɪəʊdɨˈɡreɪdəbəl/ adj able to decay naturally by the action of bacteria: biodegradable substances such as paper and wood

bi·og·ra·pher /baɪˈɒɡrəfəʳ ‖ -ˈɑːɡ-/ n a writer who writes biographies

bi·og·ra·phy /baɪˈɒɡrəfi ‖ -ˈɑːɡ-/ n **biographies** [C;U] an account of a person's life written by someone else: Boswell wrote a famous biography of Dr. Johnson. | a writer specialising in biography –**biographical** /ˌbaɪəˈɡræfɪkəl/ adj

bi·o·log·ic·al /ˌbaɪəˈlɒdʒɪkəl ‖ -ˈlɑː-/ adj 1 relating to biology, or to the way in which living things live and behave 2 using living things such as bacteria as weapons: biological warfare | biological weapons 3 using natural chemicals called ENZYMES in order to clean things: biological washing powder

bi·ol·o·gy /baɪˈɒlədʒi ‖ -ˈɑːl-/ n [U] the scientific study of living things: human biology | She has a degree in biology. | a biology lesson –**biologist** n

bi·on·ic /baɪˈɒnɪk ‖ -ˈɑːn-/ adj infml having greater powers than those of ordinary human beings, for example greater strength or speed

bi·par·tite /baɪˈpɑːtaɪt ‖ -ˈpɑːr-/ adj agreed or shared by two groups: a bipartite agreement

bi·ped /ˈbaɪped/ n tech an animal with two feet

bi·plane /ˈbaɪpleɪn/ n an aircraft with two sets of wings, one above the other

birch /bɜːtʃ ‖ bɜːrtʃ/ n 1 a tree with smooth wood and thin branches 2 the birch a wooden rod used in the past for punishing people

bird /bɜːd ‖ bɜːrd/ n 1 a creature with wings and feathers which can fly 2 BrE infml a young woman (a word which is considered offensive to women) 3 early bird infml a person who gets up early or arrives early 4 kill two birds with one stone infml to get two good results from one action

bird of prey /ˌ· · ˈ·/ n a bird that kills other birds and small animals for food

bird's-eye view /ˌ· · · ˈ·/ n a general view seen from high up: a bird's-eye view of Paris

bi·ro /ˈbaɪərəʊ/ n [C;U] tdmk a pen with a small metal ball at the end: a black biro | a short note written in biro

birth /bɜːθ ‖ bɜːrθ/ n 1 [C;U] the act, time, or process of being born: the birth of her first baby | Last year there were more births than deaths. | She weighed eight pounds at birth. 2 give birth to have a baby: She gave birth to a fine healthy baby. 3 [U] your family origin: He was of noble birth. 4 by birth because of where you were born: She was French by birth. 5 the birth of something the beginning or origin of something: the birth of television | the birth of a nation

birth con·trol /ˈ· ·ˌ·/ n [U] the act of limiting the number of children born, for example by CON-TRACEPTION: More and more third world countries are encouraging birth control.

birth·day /ˈbɜːθdeɪ ‖ ˈbɜːr-/ n the day in each year which is the date on which someone was born: Happy birthday! | a birthday party

birth·mark /ˈbɜːθmɑːk ‖ ˈbɜːrθmɑːrk/ n an unusual coloured mark which someone has on their body when they are born

birth·place /ˈbɜːθpleɪs ‖ ˈbɜːr-/ n the place where you were born

birth·rate /ˈbɜːθreɪt ‖ ˈbɜːr-/ n the number of births for every 100 or every 1000 people in a particular area during a given time: a birthrate of three per 100

bis·cuit /ˈbɪskət/ n BrE 1 a small flat cake, usually sweetened 2 take the biscuit infml to be the best, worst, most surprising or most annoying thing you have ever seen or heard of: He's done some stupid things before, but this really takes the biscuit!

bi·sect /baɪˈsekt ‖ ˈbaɪsekt/ v [T] tech to divide something into two equal parts –bisection /baɪˈsekʃən ‖ ˈbaɪsek-/ n [U]

bi·sex·u·al /baɪˈsekʃuəl/ adj 1 sexually attracted to both men and women 2 possessing both male and female sexual parts: a bisexual plant –bisexuality /baɪˌsekʃuˈæləti/ n [U]

bish·op /ˈbɪʃəp/ n 1 a Christian priest in charge of the churches and priests in a large area 2 one of the pieces in a game of CHESS

bish·op·ric /ˈbɪʃəprɪk/ n the area for which a bishop is responsible

bi·son /ˈbaɪsən/ n a large wild animal like a cow

bis·tro /ˈbiːstrəʊ/ n a place where you can eat and drink, especially in France; bistros are usually small and quite cheap

bit¹ /bɪt/ n 1 a small piece or quantity of something: Would you like another bit of cake? | I've been doing a bit of Christmas shopping. | We need a bit of good luck. 2 a metal bar that is put in a horse's mouth and used for controlling its movements 3 a part of a tool for cutting or making holes 4 a bit slightly: This coffee's a bit cold. | I'm a bit tired. 5 a bit of a phrase you use when you are saying what something is, but want to make it seem less strong: We've got a bit of a problem with the computer. | This rain's a bit of a nuisance. 6 for a bit for a short time: I'm just going out for a bit. 7 not a bit not at all: He wasn't a bit embarrassed. 8 bits and pieces small things of various kinds: I went home to pick up a few bits and pieces that I needed for the weekend. 9 bit by bit, a bit at a time gradually: We're getting the house sorted out bit by bit. 10 every bit as just as: She's every bit as clever as her brother. 11 to bits into small pieces: Her dress was all torn to bits. | The bridge was blown to bits by the explosion.
■ USAGE Use a bit before adjectives: I'm a (little) bit tired; and a bit of before nouns: a bit of money | a bit of a problem.

bit² the past tense of BITE

bitch¹ /bɪtʃ/ n 1 a female dog 2 a woman who is unkind and bad-tempered You bitch!

bitch² v [I] infml to complain about other people in a nasty way: She's always bitching about the children, but they're not really naughty.

bitch·y /ˈbɪtʃi/ adj bitchier, bitchiest saying unkind things about other people (used of women): She made a few bitchy remarks about her flatmate. –bitchily adv –bitchiness n [U]

bite¹ /baɪt/ v bit /bɪt/, bitten /ˈbɪtn/, biting 1 [I;T] to cut, crush, or seize something with your teeth: He bit into the apple. | I was afraid the dog might bite me. 2 [T] (of some insects) to prick your skin painfully: I've been bitten by a mosquito. 3 [I] (of fish) to take food on a fisherman's hook and so get caught: The fish aren't biting today. 4 [I] (of a piece of machinery) to touch a surface firmly or move against a surface without slipping: The ice on the road was so hard that the car wheels would not bite. 5 [I] to begin to have an unpleasant effect: The economic sanctions are really beginning to bite. 6 bite someone's head off infml to speak to someone rudely and angrily 7 bite the dust infml to be killed or defeated
bite sthg. ↔ back phr v [T] infml to prevent yourself from saying something

bite² n 1 take a bite, have a bite to bite something that you are going to eat: She took a large bite of the cake. 2 have a bite to eat infml to eat a small meal 3 a wound caused by biting: His arm was covered in insect bites. 4 the act of a fish taking food on a fisherman's hook and so getting caught
■ USAGE We can use the word bite (verb and noun) when talking about many kinds of insect: They had been bitten all over by mosquitoes/fleas/red ants. | They were covered in mosquito bites. For some insects, however, we use the word sting: He had been stung by an angry wasp/bee/scorpion. | His eye was swollen from a particularly bad bee sting.

bit·ing /ˈbaɪtɪŋ/ adj 1 very cold: a biting wind 2 cruel: He made some biting remarks.

bit·ten /ˈbɪtn/ the past participle of BITE

bit·ter¹ /ˈbɪtəʳ/ adj **1** having a sharp, unpleasant taste: *The coffee tasted bitter.* **2** angry and unhappy: *He feels very bitter about the way he was treated.* **3** making you feel very angry and unhappy: *The result was a bitter disappointment to me.* **4** filled with hate or caused by hate: *They are bitter enemies.* | *The bitter fighting continued for several years.* **5** very cold (used of the wind or weather): *a bitter winter wind* **6 do something to the bitter end** to continue to do something to the end, even though it is unpleasant or difficult –**bitterly** adv –**bitterness** n [U]

bitter² n [U] BrE a type of beer: *A pint of bitter, please.*

bit·ty /ˈbɪti/ adj consisting of a lot of small parts or pieces which do not seem to go together very well: *a rather bitty collection of short stories*

bi·tu·men /ˈbɪtjʊmɪn ‖ bəˈtuː-/ n [U] a black sticky substance used in road-making

biv·ou·ac¹ /ˈbɪvu·æk/ n a soldiers' camp in which the soldiers sleep in the open without tents

bivouac² v **bivouacked, bivouacking** [I] to spend the night in the open without tents

bi·zarre /bəˈzɑːʳ/ adj very strange or unusual: *He had a bizarre appearance and manner.* –**bizarrely** adv

blab /blæb/ v **-bb-** [I] infml to tell people something that should be a secret

black¹ /blæk/ adj **1** of the colour of night: *She wore a black dress.* | *black clouds* –see picture on page 147 **2** without cream or milk (used of tea and coffee): *Two black coffees, please.* **3** belonging to a race of people with dark skins: *the problems of black people living in Britain* **4** very bad (used of situations): *Things were beginning to look very black for us.* **5 black and blue** covered in dark marks as the result of being hit: *He was black and blue all over.* **6 black and white** containing only the colours black, white, and grey: *a black and white photograph* **7 in black and white** in writing: *I want this agreement in black and white.* **8 black eye** an area of dark skin around someone's eye caused by being hit **9 black hole** an area in outer space into which everything near it, including light itself, is pulled **10 a black look** an angry look: *She gave me a black look.* **11 black magic** magic that is used for evil purposes **12 black market** the system by which goods are bought and sold unlawfully at a time when such trade is controlled: *They bought butter on the black market during the war.* –**blackness** n [U]

black² n **1** [U] the colour of night: *old ladies dressed in black* **2** [C] a person of a race which has dark skin (a word which is considered offensive by some people) **3 in the black** having money in a bank account: *Our account is in the black this month.*

black³ v [T] **1** to make something black by covering it with a black substance: *They blacked their faces.* **2** to refuse to work with particular goods or people: *The trade union blacked a firm that refused to pay proper wages.* **3 black someone's eye** to hit someone on or near their eye, causing the skin round their eye to become dark
black out phr v [I] **1** to faint: *I must have blacked out, because I don't remember anything about the accident.*

black·ber·ry /ˈblækbəri ‖ -beri/ n **blackberries** a dark sweet fruit which grows wild or is grown in gardens –see picture on page 344

black·bird /ˈblækbɜːd ‖ -ɜːrd/ n a common European bird of which the male is black with a yellow beak

black·board /ˈblækbɔːd ‖ -ɔːrd/ n a dark smooth board used in schools for writing or drawing on with chalk

black·cur·rant /ˌblækˈkʌrənt◂ ‖ -ˈkɜːr-/ n a garden fruit with small round black berries

black disc /ˌ·ˈ·/ n a record: *The album is available on compact disc and black disc.*

black·en /ˈblækən/ v [T] **1** to make something black: *The walls had been blackened by smoke.* **2** to make something appear bad: *They tried to blacken the party's reputation.*

black·head /ˈblækhed/ n a small, black spot on someone's skin

black·jack /ˈblækdʒæk/ n **1** [U] a card game usually played for money **2** [C] AmE a short stick used as a weapon

black·leg /ˈblækleg/ n BrE a person who continues to work when other people have stopped working to demand more money or better conditions (a word used to express disapproval)

black·list /ˈblækˌlɪst/ n a list of people who are not approved of for some reason or who are to be punished: *He had been placed on a blacklist.* –**blacklist** v [T]: *They had been blacklisted for non-payment of debts.*

black·mail¹ /ˈblækmeɪl/ n [U] the crime of obtaining money from someone by threatening to make known something unpleasant

black·mail² v [T] to obtain money from someone by blackmail: *Don't think you can blackmail me.* –**blackmailer** n

black·out /ˈblækaʊt/ n **1** a period when a place is made completely dark, either during wartime or when the electric power supply fails **2** a loss of consciousness for a short time: *He had had a blackout after the accident and could not remember what happened.*

black·smith /ˈblækˌsmɪθ/ n a person who makes and repairs things made of iron, such as horseshoes

blad·der /ˈblædəʳ/ n **1** a bag of skin inside your body, in which waste liquid called URINE collects before it is passed out **2** a bag of skin, leather, or rubber which can be filled with air or liquid

blade /bleɪd/ n **1** the flat cutting part of a knife, sword, or other cutting tool **2** the flat wide part of an OAR or a PROPELLER **3** a long flat leaf of grass

blame¹ /bleɪm/ v **blamed, blaming** [T] **1** to believe or state that someone is responsible for something bad: *He always tries to blame other people when things go wrong.* | *Opposition parties have blamed the government for the rise in inflation.* | *The failure of the talks was blamed on the British government's unwillingness to compromise.*
□ USEFUL PATTERNS to blame someone; to blame someone for something; to blame something on someone
2 be to blame for something to be responsible for something bad: *They were not to blame for the accident.* **3 don't blame, can't blame** a phrase used when you are saying that you understand why someone has done something and you do not think that they were wrong to do it: *You can't really blame him for putting his own interests first.* | *I've finally given up my job.' 'I don't blame you!'*

blame² n [U] **1** responsibility for something bad: *No one is entirely free from blame in this affair.* **2 lay/put the blame on someone** to state that

someone is responsible for something bad **3 take/bear the blame for something** to accept that you are responsible for something bad: *We were ready to take the blame for what had happened.*
■ USAGE 1 The following sentences have a similar meaning, but note how the nouns **blame** and **fault** are used in different ways: *They were* not to blame *for the accident.* | *The accident was* not their fault. 2 In conversation **fault** is more commonly used than **blame** to say that someone is (or is not) responsible for something bad which has happened: *It's all* your fault*!* *I should never have listened to you.* | *Don't blame me! It's not* my fault *you were late.*

blame·less /ˈbleɪmləs/ *adj* free from blame or guilt: *She had led a blameless life.* –**blamelessly** *adv*

blame·wor·thy /ˈbleɪm,wɜːði || -ɜːr-/ *adj fml* deserving blame

blanch /blɑːntʃ || blæntʃ/ *v* **1** [T] to put fruit or vegetables into boiling water for a very short time: *Blanch the almonds to remove the skin.* **2** [I] to become pale with fear or cold: *She blanched when she saw me.*

blanc·mange /bləˈmɒnʒ, -ˈmɒndʒ || -ˈmɑː-/ *n* [C;U] a sweet dish made with flour, sugar, and milk, and eaten cold

bland /blænd/ *adj* **1** without much taste: *I find her food very bland.* **2** showing no strong feelings or opinions so as to avoid offending people: *He criticized television's bland coverage of the election.* –**blandly** *adv* –**blandness** *n* [U]

blank¹ /blæŋk/ *adj* **1** having nothing on, for example no writing or no sound: *a blank page* | *a blank cassette* | *Please write your name in the blank space at the top of the page.* **2** without expression, interest, or understanding: *I tried to explain, but he just gave me a blank look.* | *She looked completely blank.* **3 blank cheque** a signed cheque on which the amount of money has not yet been written **4 blank verse** poetry that does not RHYME –**blankly** *adv* –**blankness** *n* [U]

blank² *n* **1** an empty space on a piece of paper: *In this exercise you have to fill in each blank with one word.* **2 my mind was a complete blank** = I couldn't remember or think of anything **3** (also **blank cartridge**) a CARTRIDGE that contains an explosive but no bullet

blan·ket /ˈblæŋkɪt/ *n* **1** [C] a thick woollen covering used especially on beds to protect you from the cold: *We might need an extra blanket tonight.* **2** [C] a thick covering of something over an area: *The valley was covered with a blanket of snow.* **3** [only before a noun] including all people or all cases: *We are introducing a blanket ban on smoking in the building.*

blare /bleər/ *v* **blared, blaring** [I] to make a loud, unpleasant noise: *blaring car horns* –**blare** *n* [U]: *the blare of a brass band*
blare out *phr v* [I;T **blare** sthg ↔ **out**] to make a loud, unpleasant noise or loud, unpleasant music: *The radio blared out the news.* | *Loud music was blaring out.*

bla·sé /ˈblɑːzeɪ || blɑːˈzeɪ/ *adj* not feeling excited about something because you have experienced it many times before: *You're being very blasé about it: aren't you glad you won the prize?*

blas·pheme /blæsˈfiːm/ *v* **blasphemed, blaspheming** [I] to speak without respect about God or holy things: *He can hardly speak without blaspheming against God.* –**blasphemous** /ˈblæsfɪməs/ *adj* : blasphemous talk

blas·phe·my /ˈblæsfɪmi/ *n* **blasphemies** [C;U] disrespectful language about God or holy things: *Their conversation was full of blasphemies.*

blast¹ /blɑːst || blæst/ *n* **1** a sudden strong movement of wind or air: *the icy blasts of the north wind* | *a blast of hot air from the oven* **2** an explosion: *The windows were shattered by the blast.* **3** a very loud and usually unpleasant sound of a brass wind instrument: *He blew several loud blasts on his horn.* **4 at full blast** playing as loud as possible: *She had the radio on at full blast.*

blast² *v* [T] to make a hole in something by using an explosion: *They've blasted a tunnel through the mountain.*
blast off *phr v* [I] (of a space vehicle) to rise up into the air

blast³ *interj* a word used to express anger: *Oh blast! I forgot to phone John.*

blast·ed /ˈblɑːstɪd || ˈblæstɪd/ *adj* [only before a noun] a word used to express anger and give force to what you are saying: *Make that blasted dog keep quiet!*

blast fur·nace /ˈ· ˌ··/ *n* a steel container where iron is separated from iron ORE by the action of heat

blast-off /ˈ· ·/ *n* the moment when a space vehicle leaves the ground and moves up into the air

bla·tant /ˈbleɪtənt/ *adj* very noticeable and without shame (a word used to express disapproval): *his blatant disregard for the law* | *a blatant lie* –**blatantly** *adv*

blaze¹ /bleɪz/ *v* **blazed, blazing** [I] **1** to burn with a bright flame: *A fire was blazing in the corner of the room.* **2** (of light) to be very bright: *Lights blazed in every room.* **3 his eyes blazed with anger** = he looked very angry **4 blaze a trail** to do something new and exciting which other people can copy or follow

blaze² *n* **1** a large fire: *Firemen soon brought the blaze under control.* **2 a blaze of light, a blaze of colour** a bright show of light or colour **3 a blaze of publicity** a sudden large amount of attention given to someone or something

blaz·er /ˈbleɪzər/ *n* a short coat often with the special sign of a school or club on it

blaz·ing /ˈbleɪzɪŋ/ *adj* **1** very hot (used of the sun or the weather): *the blazing heat of the sun* | *It was a blazing hot day.* **2 blazing row** a very angry and loud argument

bleach¹ /bliːtʃ/ *v* [T] to make something white or lighter in colour: *His hair had been bleached by the sun.*

bleach² *n* [U] a strong substance used to clean things or to make things lighter in colour

bleak /bliːk/ *adj* **1** cold, unattractive, and without trees or flowers: *The landscape was bleak and uninviting.* **2** cold, dull, and grey (used of the weather): *a bleak winter's day* **3** without hope: *Our future looks very bleak.*

blear·y /ˈblɪəri/ *adj* unable to see well because of tiredness or crying (used of someone's eyes): *He sat rubbing his bleary eyes.* –**blearily** *adv* : *She looked at me blearily.*

bleat /bliːt/ *v* [I] **1** to make the sound that a sheep or goat makes **2** to speak or say something in a weak, complaining voice: *"I don't want to go," he bleated.* –**bleat** *n*

bled /bled/ the past tense and past participle of BLEED

bleed /bliːd/ *v* **bled** /bled/, **bled** [I] to lose blood from your body: *Your nose is bleeding.*

bleep¹ /bliːp/ n a short, high, repeated sound sent out by an electrical apparatus

bleep² v **1** [I] (of a machine) to make a short, high sound **2** [T] to call someone using a bleeper: *Bleep Doctor Rice – it's an emergency!*

bleep·er /'bliːpər/ n a small machine which you carry in your pocket, and which bleeps when you are needed somewhere

blem·ish¹ /'blemɪʃ/ v [T] to spoil the beauty or perfection of something: *His reputation had been severely blemished by the scandal.*

blemish² n a mark that spoils the appearance of something

blend¹ /blend/ v **1** [T] to mix things together thoroughly: *Blend the cocoa with the milk and water. | Blend the sugar, flour, and eggs together.* **2** [I] to go well together: *Their voices blend well with each other.*

blend in phr v [I] to be similar to surrounding things, and so be not easily seen or noticed: *These houses seem to blend in well with their surroundings. | Chameleons can change their colour to blend into their surroundings.*

blend² n something produced by blending or mixing several things together: *my favourite blend of coffee | His manner was a blend of friendliness and respect.*

blend·er /'blendər/ ‖ n a small electric machine used for making solid foods into a smooth liquid

bless /bles/ v blessed or blest /blest/, blessed or blest [T] **1** to ask for God's favour and protection for something: *The priest blessed the ship before it left port.* **2** to make something holy: *The bread and wine had been blessed by the priest.* **3 be blessed with something** to be lucky enough to have something such as a skill or good quality: *We were both blessed with good health.* **4 Bless you!** a phrase that you say to someone who has just sneezed (SNEEZE)

bless·ed /'blesɪd/ adj **1** fml holy and favoured by God: *Blessed are the peacemakers.* **2** very nice, and giving a rest from something unpleasant: *a few moments of blessed silence*

bless·ing /'blesɪŋ/ n **1** an act of asking for or receiving God's help and protection: *The blessing of the Lord be upon you all.* **2 your blessing** your approval or encouragement: *The government has given its blessing to the new plan. | The agreement was made with the President's blessing.* **3 a blessing in disguise** something which seems unpleasant at first but is really the best thing that could have happened: *Failing my exams turned out to be a blessing in disguise.*

blew /bluː/ the past tense of BLOW

blight¹ /blaɪt/ n [sing] something which damages or spoils things

blight² v fml [T] to spoil something: *Her life was blighted by ill health.*

blind¹ /blaɪnd/ adj **1** unable to see: *She had been blind from birth.* **2** not reasonable or not controlled: *He was in a blind panic. | Love is blind.* **3 blind to something** not conscious of something: *Is the government blind to the needs of the elderly?* **4 blind corner** a corner that is difficult to see round when you are driving **5 blind drunk** extremely drunk **6 blind spot** a part of the road behind you that you cannot see when you are driving **7 as blind as a bat** completely blind **8 not take a blind bit of notice** to take no notice at all: *I've told*

her a hundred times, but she never takes a blind bit of notice. **9 turn a blind eye to something** to pretend not to notice something: *You girls shouldn't be in here, but I'll turn a blind eye to it, just this once.* –**blindly** adv –**blindness** n [U]

blind² v [T] **1** to make someone unable to see something: *He was blinded by the smoke.* **2** to stop someone from being conscious of something: *The government's optimistic words must not blind us to the dangers of rising inflation.*

blind³ n a piece of cloth or other material which can be pulled down to cover a window

blind al·ley /ˌ· '··/ n a road with no way out at the other end

blind date /ˌ· '·/ n infml an occasion arranged for someone to meet a person of the opposite sex whom they have never met before, with the intention of forming a relationship with them: *We met on a blind date.*

blind·fold¹ /'blaɪndfəʊld/ v [T] to cover someone's eyes with a piece of material to prevent them from seeing

blindfold² n a piece of material that covers someone's eyes to prevent them from seeing: *He tore off his blindfold.*

blink¹ /blɪŋk/ v **1** [I;T] to open and shut your eyes quickly, several times: *She blinked as she came into the light. | Blink your eyes to get the grit out.* **2** [I] (of a light) to flash rapidly on and off

blink² n **1** an act of blinking **2 on the blink** infml not working properly (used of a machine)

blink·er /'blɪŋkər/ n the usual American word for the INDICATOR on a car

blink·ered /'blɪŋkəd ‖ -ərd/ adj **1** wearing blinkers **2** unable to understand or accept anything except ideas that are familiar to you already: *The Prime Minister is completely blinkered in her opinions.*

blink·ers /'blɪŋkəz ‖ -ərz/ n [pl] a pair of leather pieces that are fixed beside a horse's eyes so that it can only see straight ahead

blip /blɪp/ n a short, regular sound or image produced by an electrical machine

bliss /blɪs/ n [U] complete happiness

bliss·ful /'blɪsfəl/ adj making you feel extremely happy: *We spent a blissful two weeks on our own.* –**blissfully** adv

blis·ter¹ /'blɪstər/ n **1** a painful watery swelling under your skin: *New shoes always give me blisters.* **2** a small swelling on the surface of paint or rubber

blister² v [I;T] to form blisters: *My hands blister very easily. | The heat blistered the paint on the door.*

blis·ter·ing /'blɪstərɪŋ/ adj **1** very hot (used of the sun or the weather) **2** expressing great anger: *a blistering attack on the government*

blithe /blaɪð ‖ blaɪð, blaɪθ/ adj done without careful thought: *a blithe remark* –**blithely** adv

blitz /blɪts/ n **1 the Blitz** the attacking of British cities from the air during the second world war **2** a period during which you make a great effort and do a job quickly

bliz·zard /'blɪzəd ‖ -ərd/ n a severe storm with strong winds and snow –see WEATHER (USAGE)

bloat·ed /'bləʊtɪd/ adj **1** unpleasantly swollen: *the bloated body of a drowned animal* **2** infml very full of food

blob /blɒb ‖ blɑːb/ n a drop of a thick liquid: *There was a blob of paint on the floor.*

bloc /blɒk ‖ blɑːk/ *n* [+sing/pl verb] a group of people or nations that take action together: *The Eastern bloc is gathering next week in Berlin.*

block[1] /blɒk ‖ blɑːk/ *n* **1** a solid piece of something such as wood or stone: *The floor was made of wooden blocks.* | *a block of ice* **2** a large building divided into separate parts: *a block of flats* | *an office block* **3** a large building or a group of buildings built between two streets in a town or city: *She lives two blocks from here.* | *I'm going for a walk round the block.* **4** a quantity of things considered as a single unit: *He had bought a block of shares in the business.* **5 a mental block** an inability to understand: *I'm afraid I've got a real mental block about computers.* **6 the block** a large piece of wood on which people's heads were cut off in the past

block[2] *v* [T] **1** to prevent things from moving through or along something: *Something's blocking the pipe.* | *My nose is blocked and I can't breathe properly.* | *Quite a lot of roads are blocked.* **2** to prevent something from happening: *The government have blocked our plans.*
   block sthg ↔ **out** *phr v* [T] **1** to try very hard not to think about something **2** to stop light or a signal from reaching somewhere
   block sthg ↔ **up** *phr v* [T] to prevent things from moving through or along something: *The sink's got blocked up again.*

block·ade /blɒˈkeɪd ‖ blɑː-/ *v* **blockaded, blockading** [T] to prevent goods from reaching a place by the use of military power: *Ships have blockaded all the major ports.* –**blockade** *n*

block·age /ˈblɒkɪdʒ ‖ ˈblɑː-/ *n* something that prevents movement through a pipe or tube

block let·ters /ˌ· ˈ··/ *n* *BrE* (also **block capitals** /ˌ· ˈ····/) [pl] letters that are written in their CAPITAL form: *He wrote her name in block letters, MARY.*

bloke /bləʊk/ *n* *BrE* *infml* a man

blond /blɒnd ‖ blɑːnd/ *adj* **1** light yellow in colour (used of hair) –see picture on page 245 **2** having light-coloured hair and skin (used of a man)

blonde[1] /blɒnd ‖ blɑːnd/ *adj* having light-coloured hair and skin (used of a woman) –see picture on page 245

blonde[2] *n* a woman with light-coloured hair and skin

blood /blʌd/ *n* [U] **1** the red liquid which flows through your body: *She had lost a lot of blood, and was very weak.* **2** a person's family background: *a woman of noble blood* **3 be in your blood** to be a skill or quality that you have naturally, and that other members of your family also have: *Her family have been farmers for hundreds of years, so farming is in her blood.* **4 make your blood boil** to make you extremely angry: *His attitude to women really makes my blood boil sometimes!* **5 make your blood run cold** to make you very afraid

blood·bath /ˈblʌdbɑːθ ‖ -bæθ/ *n* the violent killing of many people

blood·cur·dling /ˈblʌdˌkɜːdlɪŋ ‖ -ɜːr-/ *adj* very frightening (used of something that you hear): *bloodcurdling cries of pain*

blood·hound /ˈblʌdhaʊnd/ *n* a large hunting dog with a very good sense of smell

blood·less /ˈblʌdləs/ *adj* **1** very pale (used of someone's skin): *her bloodless cheeks* **2** without killing or violence: *a bloodless coup*

blood poi·son·ing /ˈ· ˌ···/ *n* [U] a serious illness caused by an infection in your blood

blood pres·sure /ˈ· ˌ···/ *n* [U] the force with which blood travels through your body: *He's got high blood pressure.*

blood·shed /ˈblʌdʃed/ *n* [U] fighting in which people are violently killed or hurt: *The authorities are trying to prevent further bloodshed.*

blood·shot /ˈblʌdʃɒt ‖ -ʃɑːt/ *adj* red (used of someone's eyes)

blood sport /ˈ· ·/ *n* a sport in which a bird or animal is killed: *I am against all blood sports.*

blood·stain /ˈblʌdsteɪn/ *n* a mark where blood has fallen on something –**bloodstained** *adj*: *bloodstained clothing*

blood·stream /ˈblʌdstriːm/ *n* the blood as it flows around your body: *The poison has entered her bloodstream.*

blood·thirst·y /ˈblʌdˌθɜːsti ‖ -ɜːr-/ *adj* having too much interest in violence

blood ves·sel /ˈ· ˌ··/ *n* one of the tubes in your body through which your blood flows

blood·y[1] /ˈblʌdi/ *adj* **bloodier, bloodiest 1** covered with blood: *a bloody nose* **2** with a lot of wounding and killing: *a bloody battle* **3** [only before a noun] *BrE infml* used for giving force to what you are saying (a word which some people consider not to be polite): *Don't be a bloody fool!*

bloody[2] *adv* *BrE infml* a word used for giving force to what you are saying (a word which some people consider not to be polite): *It's bloody cold in here!*

bloody-mind·ed /ˌ·· ˈ···◂/ *adj* *BrE infml* intentionally being unhelpful and making difficulties for other people –**bloody-mindedness** *n* [U]

bloom[1] /bluːm/ *n* **1** a flower: *What beautiful blooms!* **2 in bloom** fully open (used of a flower)

bloom[2] *v* [I] **1** to produce flowers: *The roses are blooming.* **2** to look very healthy and well: *Jane is positively blooming with health these days.*

blos·som[1] /ˈblɒsəm ‖ ˈblɑː-/ *n* **1** [C;U] the flowers of a fruit tree: *apple blossom* **2 in blossom** with its flowers fully open (used of a tree)

blossom[2] *v* [I] **1** (of a tree) to produce flowers **2** to develop in a pleasing way: *a blossoming friendship* | *Sally is blossoming into a beautiful girl.*

blot[1] /blɒt ‖ blɑːt/ *n* **1** a drop of a liquid which has fallen onto something and made a mark: *a blot of ink* **2** something that spoils something **3 blot on the landscape** something that spoils the appearance of a place: *That new building is a real blot on the landscape.*

blot[2] *v* **-tt-** [T] **1** to dry a surface with a soft cloth or paper **2 blot your copybook** *infml* to do something to spoil your good record
   blot sthg ↔ **out** *phr v* [T] **1** to make something difficult or impossible to see: *The mist blotted out the sun.* **2** to destroy a memory or a thought, so that you no longer think about it: *She had tried to blot out the memory of that terrible day.*

blotch /blɒtʃ ‖ blɑːtʃ/ *n* a coloured mark on something, especially a large and irregular mark –**blotchy** *adj*

blot·ter /ˈblɒtər ‖ ˈblɑː-/ *n* a large piece of blotting paper on which paper with writing on can be pressed to dry the ink

blotting pa·per /ˈ·· ˌ··/ *n* [U] thick soft paper used to dry writing in wet ink

blouse /blaʊz ‖ blaʊs/ *n* a shirt worn by a woman or girl

blow¹ /bləʊ/ v blew /bluː/, blown /bləʊn/ **1** [I] to send air out through your mouth: *She put her lips to the whistle and blew.* **2** [I] (of the wind) to move and cause a current of air: *The wind had been blowing all night.* **3** [T+adv/prep] (of the wind or an explosion) to move something or make it fall: *The wind was so strong that it blew several trees down.* | *His hat was blown off.* | *Both his legs were blown off in the blast.* **4** [I+adv/prep] to move or fall because of the wind or a current of air: *I was afraid of the roof might blow off.* | *leaves blowing about in the wind* **5** [T] to make something such as a horn or whistle make a sound by blowing into it or forcing air through it: *The referee blew his whistle.* **6** [I] (of something such as a horn or a whistle) to make a sound: *Car horns were blowing behind me.* | *They were still losing 4-3 when the whistle blew.* **7 blow a fuse** to cause an electrical FUSE to stop working suddenly **8 a fuse has blown** = an electrical FUSE has stopped working suddenly **9** [T] *infml* to spend a lot of money, often foolishly: *We blew all our savings on a holiday.* **10** [T] *infml* to lose a good chance to do something: *I had the chance to go to the United States this summer, but I've blown it!* **11 blow hot and cold** to keep changing your mind about something or someone, sometimes seeming very keen and sometimes seeming not at all keen **12 blow your nose** to force air out through your nose in order to clear it, for example when you have a cold **13 blow your own trumpet** to speak too proudly about good or clever things that you have done **14 blow your top** *infml* to become very angry: *When he saw the figures he blew his top.*

blow sthg ↔ **out** *phr v* [T] to blow air onto a flame or candle so that it stops burning

blow over *phr v* [I] (of a storm or an argument) to stop: *We didn't dare go out until the storm had blown over.* | *They had an enormous row, but it'll probably blow over within a day or two.*

blow up *phr v* **1** [T **blow** sthg ↔ **up**] to destroy something by means of an explosion: *The bridge was blown up by terrorists.* **2** [I] to explode: *The plane blew up as it was taking off.* **3** [T **blow** sthg ↔ **up**] to fill something such as a tyre with air: *Make sure you blow up the tyres before setting off.* | *blowing up balloons* **4** [T **blow** sthg ↔ **up**] to make a photograph larger: *I want to have the picture blown up so that I can put it on the wall.* **5** [I] (of a storm) to begin: *I think there's a storm blowing up.*

blow² *n* **1** an act of hitting someone hard with your hand or with a weapon: *He had received a severe blow to the head.* **2** a shock or disappointment: *The news was a terrible blow to us all.* **3 a blow for something** something which helps a system or an idea: *striking a blow for freedom of speech* **4** an act of blowing: *Give your nose a good blow.* | *Give a big blow.* **5 blow-by-blow account** an account of something which gives details of everything that happened **6 come to blows** to start fighting: *I'm sure they're going to come to blows one of these days.*

blow³ *interj old fash* a word used to show anger

blow-dry /ˈ·ˌ·/ v [T] to dry hair with an electric dryer held in your hand –**blow-dry** *n*: *They charge £10 for a cut and blow-dry.*

blow-lamp /ˈbləʊlæmp/ *n* a lamp which gives a small, very hot flame, used for example for burning off paint

blown /bləʊn/ the past participle of BLOW

blow-out /ˈbləʊaʊt/ *n* **1** the bursting of a tyre: *He had a blowout on the motorway.* **2** *infml* a very big meal

blow-pipe /ˈbləʊpaɪp/ *n* a tube used for blowing small stones or poisoned arrows used as a weapon

blub-ber /ˈblʌbəʳ/ *n* [U] the fat of sea animals, especially whales (WHALE), from which oil is obtained

blud-geon /ˈblʌdʒən/ *v* [T] **1** to hit someone repeatedly with something heavy **2 bludgeon someone into something** to force someone to do something, often by threatening them

blue¹ /bluː/ *adj* **bluer, bluest 1** of the colour of the clear sky or of the deep sea on a fine day: *She was wearing a dark blue dress.* | *He painted the door blue.* | *My hands were blue with cold.* –see picture on page 147 **2** *infml old fash* sad and without hope **3** *infml* concerned with sex: *blue films* **4 blue blood** the quality of being born into a noble family: *He's convinced he's got blue blood in his veins.* **5 do something till you are blue in the face** to do something for ever; without ever being successful: *You can telephone her till you're blue in the face but she'll never come.*

blue² *n* **1** [U] the colour that is blue: *a woman dressed in blue* | *A light blue would be nice for the door.* **2 out of the blue** very suddenly and unexpectedly: *John arrived, completely out of the blue.* **3 the blues** a type of slow, sad music from the Southern US: *a well-known blues singer*

blue-bell /ˈbluːbel/ *n* a blue bell-shaped flower

blue-ber-ry /ˈbluːbəri ‖ -beri/ *n* **blueberries** a small bush which grows in North America and produces small dark blue fruit

blue-bot-tle /ˈbluːˌbɒtl ‖ -ˌbɑːtl/ *n* a large blue fly

blue-col-lar /ˌ· ˈ···◄/ *adj* [only before a noun] relating to workers who do hard or dirty work with their hands: *a blue-collar union*

blue-print /ˈbluːˌprɪnt/ *n* **1** a plan for making a machine or building a house **2** a description of a plan or an idea, saying how it will work: *The report is a blueprint for the reform of the whole tax system.*

bluff¹ /blʌf/ *v* [I] to try and make someone think that you are in a stronger position than you really are, often by pretending to be very confident: *I knew that he was only bluffing.*

bluff² *n* [sing;U] the action of bluffing: *He threatened to dismiss me from my job, but it's all bluff.* | *We all thought his threats were just a bluff.*

bluff³ *adj* rough, cheerful, and direct, perhaps without considering the feelings of other people

blun-der¹ /ˈblʌndəʳ/ *n* a stupid unnecessary mistake

blunder² *v* **1** [I] to make a stupid unnecessary mistake **2** [I+adv/prep] to move awkwardly or unsteadily, because you cannot see: *He blundered through the dark forest.*

blun-der-buss /ˈblʌndəbʌs ‖ -ər-/ *n* an old kind of gun which has a barrel with a wide mouth

blunt¹ /blʌnt/ *adj* **1** not sharp: *This knife's blunt.* **2** telling the truth directly, without trying to be polite or kind: *To be quite blunt, I think you've made an awful mess of things.* –**bluntness** *n* [U]

blunt² *v* [T] **1** to make something blunt **2** to make a feeling weaker: *The bad weather has rather blunted their enthusiasm for going camping.*

blunt-ly /ˈblʌntli/ *adv* said in a rough, direct way without trying to be polite or kind: *To put it bluntly, there's no way you're going to pass this exam.*

blur¹ /blɜːʳ/ *n* [sing] something that you cannot see clearly, or that you cannot remember clearly: *The*

houses appeared as a blur in the mist. | *My memory of the accident is only a blur.*

blur² *v* -rr- [T] **1** to make something difficult to see clearly or difficult to see through: *Tears blurred my eyes.* | *a very blurred photograph* **2** to make something less clear: *The article tries to blur the distinction between race and religion.*

blurt /blɜːt ‖ blɜːrt/ *v*

blurt sthg ↔ **out** *phr v* [T] to say something which you should not say, suddenly and without thinking: *Peter blurted out the news before we could stop him.*

blush /blʌʃ/ *v* [I] to become red in the face, from shame or because people are looking at you: *Stop it! You're making me blush!* | *He blushed* **with** *shame.* –**blush** *n* : *His remarks brought a blush to my cheeks.*

blus·ter /ˈblʌstəʳ/ *v* [I] to speak loudly, roughly, and angrily –**bluster** *n* [U]

blus·ter·y /ˈblʌstəri/ *adj* rough and windy (used of the weather)

BO /ˌbiː ˈəʊ/ *n* [U] an unpleasant smell coming from a person's body; an abbreviation for **body odour**

bo·a /ˈbəʊə/ *n* (also **boa constrictor**) a large South American snake that kills animals by crushing them

boar /bɔːʳ/ *n* **1** a male pig that is kept for breeding **2** a wild pig

board¹ /bɔːd ‖ bɔːrd/ *n* **1** [C] a long thin flat piece of cut wood **2** [C] a flat piece of wood or plastic used for a particular purpose: *She pinned the list up on the notice board.* | *a chess board* **3** [C] a group of people who have responsibility for a particular organization or activity: *the school's board of governors* | *the English Tourist Board* | *a board of examiners* **4** [C+sing/pl verb] (also **board of directors**) a committee of the directors of a company which is responsible for the management of the company: *He's joined the board of Intel.* | *The Board is meeting the union today.* **5** [U] the cost of meals: *I pay £50 a week for board and lodging.* **6 above board** completely honest and known about by everyone **7 across the board** for all groups or all the members of a group: *a wage increase of 10% across the board* **8 go by the board** (of a plan) to be no longer possible or practical: *We had intended to get a new car, but that's gone by the board now that I've lost my job.* **9 on board** in or on a ship or public vehicle: *Get on board!* | *I went on board, but felt sick almost immediately.* **10 take something on board** to understand or accept something fully: *I don't think he's really taken her objections on board.*

board² *v* **1** [T] to get onto a ship or into a public vehicle: *Passengers should board the train now.* **2** [I] (of a plane) to be ready for passengers to get in: *Flight 387 for New York is now boarding at Gate 15.* **3 board with someone** to live in someone's house and receive meals there in return for payment

board·er /ˈbɔːdəʳ ‖ ˈbɔːr-/ *n* **1** a pupil who lives at his or her school **2** a person who pays to live in another person's house and receive meals there: *Mrs Brown takes in boarders, I think.*

boarding card /ˈ·· ·/ *n* (also **boarding pass**) an official card which allows you to get on a plane or ship

boarding house /ˈ·· ·/ *n* a private lodging house, not a hotel, that supplies meals

boarding school /ˈ·· ·/ *n* [C;U] a school at which the pupils live: *My son goes to boarding school.*

board·room /ˈbɔːdruːm, -rʊm ‖ ˈbɔːrd-/ *n* a room in which the directors of a company hold meetings

board·walk /ˈbɔːdwɔːk ‖ ˈbɔːrd-/ *n AmE* a footpath made of wooden boards, usually by the sea

boast¹ /bəʊst/ *v* **1** [I;+that] to talk too proudly about something that you have got or something that you have done: *She's boasting* **about** *the fact that she's just passed her driving test.* | *He boasted* **of** *his many achievements.* | *Don't believe him; he's just boasting.* | *They boasted that they'd won every match they'd played this season.* **2** [T] to have something that is unusual and desirable: *It's a tiny village but it boasts three shops.*

boast² *n* an act of talking too proudly about something that you have got or something that you have done

boast·ful /ˈbəʊstfəl/ *adj* expressing too much pride in yourself or in things that you have done –**boastfully** *adv* –**boastfulness** *n* [U]

boat /bəʊt/ *n* **1** a vehicle for travelling across water, usually a small one: *a fishing boat* | *a sailing boat* | *They crossed the river in a boat.* **2 by boat** in a boat or ship: *We're going by boat.*

■ USAGE A **boat** is usually smaller than a **ship**, or travels shorter distances: *a fishing boat/a boat across the English Channel.* But in ordinary speech we sometimes use **boat** even for a a large passenger ship, travelling a long distance: *There were over 2000 passengers on the* **boat/ship** *going to America.*

boat·swain /ˈbəʊsən/ *n* see BOSUN

boat train /ˈ· ·/ *n* a train that takes people to or from a ship

bob¹ /bɒb ‖ bɑːb/ *v* -bb- **1** [I] to move quickly and repeatedly up and down on water: *The small boat was bobbing up and down on the rough sea.* **2 bob a curtsy** to bend your knees and bend your body forwards as a sign of respect

bob² *n* **1** a woman's hairstyle in which the hair is cut short to the same length all round **2** [plural is **bob**] *infml* a former British coin, worth 5p

bob·bin /ˈbɒbən ‖ ˈbɑː-/ *n* a small roller on which thread is wound, for example in a sewing machine

bob·ble /ˈbɒbəl ‖ ˈbɑː-/ *n* a small woolly ball for decorating clothes, especially woolly hats

bob·by /ˈbɒbi ‖ ˈbɑːbi/ *n* **bobbies** *BrE infml* a policeman

bob·sleigh /ˈbɒbsleɪ ‖ ˈbɑːb-/ *n* a small vehicle that runs on metal blades, and is used for sliding down snowy slopes

bode¹ /bəʊd/ *v* **boded, boding** *lit* **bode ill** to be a sign of bad things in the future: *Their current unpopularity bodes ill for the Nationalists' chances in the next election.* [RELATED PHRASE: **bode well**]

bode² the past tense of BIDE

bod·ice /ˈbɒdɪs ‖ ˈbɑː-/ *n* the part of a woman's dress above the waist

bod·i·ly¹ /ˈbɒdɪli ‖ ˈbɑː-/ *adj* [only before a noun] relating to your body: *He likes his bodily comforts.*

bodily² *adv* taking hold of someone's whole body: *She refused to move, so her mother picked her up bodily and carried her to bed.*

bod·y /ˈbɒdi ‖ ˈbɑːdi/ *n* **bodies** **1** [C] the physical parts of a person as opposed to their mind or soul; sometimes "body" means all the physical parts of a person, and sometimes just the main, central part, without the arms and legs: *Her body was covered from head to toe in painful red spots.* | *They buried the body in an unmarked grave.* | *He had a wound on his leg and two more on his body.* **2** [C] the main part of something: *We sat in the body* **of** *the hall.* **3** [C] a large amount of something: *a substantial body* **of** *opinion that rejects this theory* | *We have collected a large body of data.* **4** [C;sing/pl verb] a group of people who do something together in a planned way: *The House of Commons is an elected body.* | *The governing body of the college meet every Thursday.* **5** [U] good strong taste that wine has: *I like a wine with plenty of body.* **6** [U] strength and firmness that your hair has: *Use a conditioner to give your hair more body.* **7** [C] *tech* a physical object **8 -bodied** having a certain kind of body: *a wide-bodied plane* | *a full-bodied wine* **9 keep body and soul together** to have enough money and food to live on **10 over my dead body** a phrase used to show your determination that something will not happen: *You'll come into this house over my dead body!*

body build·ing /'··ˌ··/ *n* [U] doing regular special exercises to make your muscles bigger and stronger

bod·y·guard /'bɒdigɑːd ‖ 'bɑːdigɑːrd/ *n* a man or group of men whose duty is to guard an important person

bod·y·work /'bɒdiwɜːk ‖ 'bɑːdiwɜːrk/ *n* [U] the main outside parts of a motor vehicle, as opposed to the engine and wheels

bog /bɒg ‖ bɑːg, bɔːg/ *n* [C;U] a large area of soft wet ground into which your feet sink when you try to walk on it **–boggy** *adj*

bo·gey /'bəʊgi/ *n* (also **bogy, bogie**) **1** (also **bogey man**) an imaginary evil spirit, often used to frighten children **2** a cause of fear, especially an imaginary one **3** a piece of dry MUCUS in your nose

bog·ged down /ˌbɒgəd 'daʊn ‖ ˌbɑːgd-, ˌbɔːgd-/ *adj* unable to move forward or advance: *The car got bogged down in the mud.* | *The talks with the staff are bogged down on the question of working hours.*

bog·gle /'bɒgəl ‖ 'bɑː-/ *v* **the mind boggles** = something is very surprising or difficult to understand: *The mind boggles at the idea of underwater football.*

bo·gus /'bəʊgəs/ *adj* false, but pretending to be real

bo·he·mi·an /bəʊ'hiːmiən, bə-/ *n old fash* a person, especially an artist, who lives in a very informal way and does not follow the usual rules of social life **–bohemian** *adj*

boil[1] /bɔɪl/ *v* **1** [T] to cause a liquid to reach the temperature at which liquid changes into a gas: *Make sure you boil the water for at least five minutes.* | *Shall I boil the kettle?* **2** [I] (of a liquid) to reach this temperature: *Is the milk boiling yet?* **3** [T] to cook food in water at 100°C: *Boil the potatoes for 20 minutes.* | *a boiled egg* **4 boil dry** to boil until there is no liquid left : *Don't let the pan boil dry.* –see COOK[1] (USAGE) **5 make someone's blood boil** to make someone very angry: *It made my blood boil to see someone treat a child like that.*

boil away *phr v* [I] **1** to be reduced to nothing by boiling: *The water had all boiled away and the pan was burned.* **2** to boil continuously: *The kettle was boiling away merrily on the stove.*

boil down to sthg *phr v* [T] a phrase used when you are stating what something really is or really means: *It's a very complex situation, but basically it boils down to a power struggle between the trade union and the directors.*

boil over *phr v* [I] to boil and flow over the sides of a container: *Turn off the gas. The milk is boiling over.*

boil[2] *n* **1** [sing] an act or state of boiling: *Give the clothes a good boil to get them white.* **2 bring something to the boil** to heat liquid until it boils **3 on the boil** boiling: *Heat the mixture until it is just on the boil.* [RELATED PHRASE: **off the boil**] **4** [C] a painful infected swelling under your skin

boil·er /'bɔɪləʳ/ *n* a large container in which water is boiled to provide heat, for example in a house

boiler suit /'···ˌ·/ *n* a piece of clothing like a pair of trousers and a shirt made in one piece; boiler suits are worn for doing dirty work

boil·ing /'bɔɪlɪŋ/ *adj* **1** very hot: *I'm boiling.* | *It's boiling in the sun.* **2 boiling hot** extremely hot **3 boiling with rage/anger** extremely angry: *I was absolutely boiling with rage when I came out of the interview.*

boiling point /'··ˌ·/ *n* **1** [C;U] the temperature at which a liquid boils: *Water has a boiling point of 100°C.* | *Heat the milk until it reaches boiling point.* **2** [U] the point at which high excitement or anger breaks into action

bois·ter·ous /'bɔɪstərəs/ *adj* noisy, cheerful, and rough: *a group of boisterous children* **–boisterously** *adv*

bold /bəʊld/ *adj* **1** brave, confident, and willing to take risks: *The council has announced its bold, new plans for the city centre.* **2** clear and strong (used of the appearance of something): *the bold shape of the cliffs* | *bold colours* **–boldly** *adv* **–boldness** *n* [U]

bol·lard /'bɒləd, -lɑːd ‖ 'bɑːlərd/ *n* a short thick post used to mark the edge of a road

bol·shie /'bɒlʃi ‖ 'bəʊlʃi, 'bɒːl-, 'bɑːl-/ *adj BrE infml* (also **bolshy**) bad-tempered, and unwilling to do what people tell you to do

bol·ster[1] /'bəʊlstəʳ/ *v* [T] (also **bolster** sthg ↔ **up**) to give necessary support and encouragement to something: *Let's hope this achievement will bolster her confidence.* | *The government is introducing measures to bolster up the economy*

bolster[2] *n* a long round PILLOW

bolt[1] /bəʊlt/ *n* **1** a metal bar that slides across to fasten a door or window **2** a screw with no point, which fastens into a piece of metal called a NUT to hold things together **3 bolt of lightning** a flash of lightning **4 make a bolt for it** to run away suddenly **5 bolt from the blue** a piece of news that is unexpected and very surprising

bolt[2] *v* **1** [I] to run away suddenly, often because you are afraid: *He bolted for the door.* | *The horse bolted and threw me in the mud.* **2** [T] (also **bolt** sthg ↔ **down**) to eat something very quickly: *Don't bolt your food!* | *I bolted down a couple of sandwiches.* **3** [T] to fasten something with a bolt: *I bolted the two parts together.* | *She bolted the door.*

bolt[3] *adv* **bolt upright** standing or sitting very straight and stiffly: *He heard the strange noise again, and sat bolt upright in bed.*

bomb[1] /bɒm ‖ bɑːm/ *n* **1** a container filled with explosive: *A bomb had been planted in the hotel.* | *the bomb* NUCLEAR bombs in general: *How many countries have got the bomb now?* **3 go like a bomb** *BrE infml* to go very well: *The party went like a bomb.*

bomb[2] *v* **1** [I;T] to attack a place with bombs, especially by dropping them from aircraft: *London was very badly bombed during the war.* | *a bombing raid* **2** [I+adv/prep] *infml* to travel very quickly: *bombing along the motorway*

bom·bard /bɒm'bɑːd ‖ bɑːm'bɑːrd/ *v* [T] **1** to attack a place heavily with gunfire: *The warships bombarded the port.* **2** to aim or direct a lot of something at someone: *The speaker was bombarded with questions.* **–bombardment** *n* [C;U]

bomb·er /'bɒməʳ ‖ 'bɑː-/ *n* **1** an aircraft that carries and drops bombs **2** a person who puts bombs into buildings and other places

bomb·shell /ˈbɒmʃel ‖ ˈbɑːm-/ n infml a piece of unpleasant news that comes unexpectedly and is a great surprise: *The news of the defeat came as an absolute bombshell to us.*

bo·na fi·de /ˌbəʊnə ˈfaɪdi◄ ‖ ˈbəʊnə faɪd/ adj real, not just pretending: *The hotel car park is only for bona fide guests.*

bo·nan·za /bəˈnænzə, bəʊ-/ n something that makes you very rich suddenly and unexpectedly

bond¹ /bɒnd ‖ bɑːnd/ n 1 [C] something that joins people together, such as a shared feeling: *the bond between mother and child | two countries united in the bonds of friendship* 2 [C] an official paper in which a government or an industrial firm promises to pay back with interest money that has been lent: *National Savings bonds* 3 [sing] a state of being stuck together: *This new glue makes a firmer bond.* 4 bonds [pl] lit ropes used for tying up a prisoner

bond² v [T] 1 to stick things firmly together: *Bond the rubber to the wood.* 2 to make people feel close and united

bond·age /ˈbɒndɪdʒ ‖ ˈbɑːn-/ n [U] lit the condition of being a slave or a prisoner

bone¹ /bəʊn/ n 1 [C;U] the hard parts of your body, which are covered by flesh and skin: *He broke a bone in his leg. | a dog gnawing a bone | fragments of bone* 2 **bone of contention** something that causes argument: *That island has been a bone of contention between our two countries for years.* 3 **have a bone to pick with someone** to have something to complain about to someone: *I've got a bone to pick with you.* 4 **make no bones about doing something** to feel no doubt or shame about doing something: *She made no bones about telling me what she thought of me.*

bone² v **boned, boning** [T] to take the bones out of a piece of meat or fish: *Could you bone the meat for me, please?* –**boned** adj

bone-dry /ˌ· ˈ·◄/ adj completely dry

bone-i·dle /ˌ· ˈ···◄/ adj extremely lazy

bone·less /ˈbəʊnləs/ adj without bones

bon·fire /ˈbɒnfaɪəʳ ‖ ˈbɑːn-/ n a large fire built outside, either for pleasure or to burn unwanted things

bon·go /ˈbɒŋgəʊ ‖ ˈbɑːŋ-/ n **bongos** or **bongoes** (also **bongo drum** /ˈ·· ·/) a small drum that you play with your hands

bon·ho·mie /ˈbɒnəmi ‖ ˌbɑːnəˈmiː/ n lit [U] cheerful and easy friendliness

bon·kers /ˈbɒŋkəz ‖ ˈbɑːŋkərz/ adj [never before a noun] BrE infml mad: *You're completely bonkers.*

bon·net /ˈbɒnʌt ‖ ˈbɑː-/ n 1 a soft hat that is tied under the chin, usually worn by babies: *a pink, knitted bonnet* 2 BrE a metal lid over the engine of a car: *Can you open up the bonnet?* –see picture on page 49

bon·ny /ˈbɒni ‖ ˈbɑːni/ adj **bonnier, bonniest** pretty and healthy: *a bonny baby*

bo·nus /ˈbəʊnəs/ n 1 an additional payment made to people who work for a business: *The workers got a Christmas bonus.* 2 a pleasant thing that is in addition to what you expect: *It's a real bonus that my mother lives so near our new house.*

bon·y /ˈbəʊni/ adj **bonier, boniest** 1 very thin (used of a person or a part of their body): *long, bony fingers* 2 full of bones (used of fish or meat)

boo¹ /buː/ interj, n **boos** a shout of disapproval or strong disagreement

boo² v **booed, booing** [I;T] to show that you do not like someone, or that you disagree with them, by shouting "Boo!": *The crowd booed the speaker. | He was booed off the stage.*

boob¹ /buːb/ v [I] infml to make a foolish mistake

boob² /buːb/ n 1 a foolish mistake 2 **boobs** infml a woman's breasts

boo·by prize /ˈbuːbi praɪz/ n a prize given as a joke for the worst performance in a competition

booby trap /ˈ··· ·/ n a hidden bomb: *Watch out! There may be a booby trap.* –**booby trap** v [T] -**pp-**: *They were afraid that the room might be booby trapped.*

book¹ /bʊk/ n 1 a collection of sheets of paper fastened together in a strong paper cover; you use books for reading or for writing in: *a book about gardening | Open your book on page six.* 2 **books** [pl] written records of money or names kept by an organization: *How many names have you on your books?* 3 any collection of things fastened together between cardboard or plastic covers: *a book of stamps | a book of matches* 4 **by the book** according to the rules 5 **in someone's bad books** infml not liked very much by someone because you have done something which annoyed them [RELATED PHRASE: **in someone's good books**]

book² v 1 [I;T] to arrange in advance to have something: *I've booked a table for two. | Be sure to book in advance to make sure of getting a seat.* 2 **be fully booked, be booked up** to have no places free because they have all been booked in advance: *I'm sorry, we're completely booked up this week.* 3 [T] infml enter someone's name officially in police records, with the charge made against them: *He was booked on a charge of speeding.*
  book in phr v 1 [I;T **book** sbdy ↔ **in**] to have a place kept for someone at a hotel: *I've booked you in at the Grand Hotel. | We've all booked in at the same hotel. | I booked into a small hotel in the town centre.* 2 [I] to report your arrival at a hotel desk, airport etc: *We booked in at 3 o'clock.*

book·a·ble /ˈbʊkəbəl/ adj able to be booked in advance: *All seats in the theatre are bookable.*

book·case /ˈbʊk-keɪs/ n a piece of furniture with shelves for putting books on –see picture on page 442

book·ends /ˈbʊkendz/ n supports to hold up a row of books

book·ing /ˈbʊkɪŋ/ n BrE an arrangement that you make in advance to have something such as a theatre seat or a hotel room kept for you: *All bookings must be made at least three weeks in advance.*

book·keep·ing /ˈbʊkˌkiːpɪŋ/ n [U] the activity of keeping the accounts of a business or organization –**bookkeeper** n

book·let /ˈbʊklʌt/ n a small book giving information

book·mak·er /ˈbʊkˌmeɪkəʳ/ n (also **bookie** /ˈbʊki/infml) a person who takes money that people risk on the result of competitions or races, and who pays the winners

book·mark /ˈbʊkmɑːk ‖ -ɑːrk/ n something put between the pages of a book so that you can find a particular page easily

book·stall /ˈbʊkstɔːl/ n a table or small shop open at the front, where books and magazines are sold

book to·ken /ˈ· ˌ··/ n a card that can be exchanged for books: *He gave me a £5 book token for my birthday.*

book·worm /'bʊkwɜːm ‖ -ɜːrm/ n a person who is very fond of reading

boom¹ /buːm/ v [I] **1** to make a loud deep hollow sound: *The guns boomed.* **2** to grow rapidly in value: *Business is booming.*
boom out *phr v* [I;T **boom** sthg ↔ **out**] to say something in a loud, deep voice: *His answer boomed out.* | *He boomed out his answer.*

boom² n a rapid growth or increase in something: *There has been a boom in exports this year.* | *a population boom*

boo·mer·ang /'buːməræŋ/ n a curved stick which comes back to you when you throw it into the air, used for hunting by Australian ABORIGINES

boon /buːn/ n a thing which is a great help or comfort to people: *A car is a real boon when you live in the country.*

boor /bʊəʳ/ n an extremely rude person –**boorish** *adj*

boost¹ /buːst/ v [T] **1** to increase something: *to boost prices* | *plans to boost production by 30% next year* **2** to improve: *Let's try to boost his self-confidence.*

boost² n **1** an increase in amount: *a boost in share prices* **2** an action that brings help or encouragement: *Pay increases would give a boost to teachers' low morale.*

boost·er /'buːstəʳ/ n **1** a machine which provides additional power or force: *a booster rocket* **2** a substance that increases the effectiveness of a drug or medicine: *Children have the measles injection at 18 months and need a booster at 5 years.*

boot¹ /buːt/ n **1** a shoe that covers your whole foot and ankle: *army boots* | *wellington boots* –see picture on page 50 **2** *BrE* an enclosed space at the back of a car for bags and boxes –see picture on page 49 **3 get the boot, be given the boot** *infml* to be dismissed from your job: *If he keeps behaving so badly, he'll soon get the boot.* **4 the boot is on the other foot** *infml* the situation has now changed completely and someone else has power or control **5 lick someone's boots** *infml* to try to gain someone's favour by being too polite and too obedient **6 put the boot in** *BrE infml* to kick someone hard, usually when they are already on the ground **7 to boot** *fml* a phrase used when you are adding something to what you have just said: *He is dishonest, and a coward to boot.* **8 too big for your boots** *infml* having too high an opinion of yourself

boot² v *infml* [T] to kick: *He booted the ball up the field.*
boot sbdy ↔ **out** *phr v* [T] *infml* to send someone away rudely and forcefully or dismiss them from a job: *They booted him out for being drunk at work.*

boot·ee /'buːtiː, buː'tiː/ n a baby's soft woollen boot

booth /buːð ‖ buːθ/ **booths** /buːðz/ n **1** a small building put up for a short time where goods are sold or games are played **2** an enclosed place big enough for one person at a time: *a telephone booth* | *a voting booth*

boot·leg /'buːtleg/ v **-gg-** [I;T] to make, carry, or sell alcoholic drink unlawfully: *bootlegging smuggled whisky*

boot·y /'buːtiː/ n [U] valuable goods taken from a place by a victorious army

booze¹ /buːz/ v **boozed, boozing** [I] *infml* to drink a lot of alcohol: *He spends every night boozing with his friends.*

booze² n [U] *infml* alcoholic drink

booz·er /'buːzəʳ/ n *infml* **1** a person who drinks a lot of alcohol **2** *BrE* a PUB

booze-up /'· ·/ n *BrE infml* a party at which a lot of alcohol is drunk

bor·der¹ /'bɔːdəʳ ‖ 'bɔːr-/ n **1** the dividing line between two countries: *soldiers guarding the border* | *He lives near the Malawi border.* **2** a band of something round the edge of an object for decoration: *a green mat with a white border* **3** a thin piece of land with flowers in it, usually round the edge of an area of grass

border² v [T] **1** to be along the edge of something: *fields bordered by woods* **2** to have a common border with: *the area where Finland borders Russia*
border on sthg *phr v* [T] to be almost like something: *His remarks bordered on rudeness.*

bor·der·line¹ /'bɔːdəlaɪn ‖ 'bɔːrdər-/ n the point at which two states or conditions are very close together and very similar to each other: *the borderline between madness and genius*

borderline² *adj* [only before a noun] not belonging clearly to one type or group: *I'm not sure whether he'll pass the exam – he's very much a borderline case.*

bore¹ /bɔːʳ/ v **bored, boring** **1** [I;T] to make a deep round hole in something: *This drill can bore through solid rock.* | *They bored a well for the villagers.* **2** [T] to make someone feel uninterested: *Politics bore me nowadays.* **3 her eyes bored into me** = she looked hard at me

bore² n **1** a person who talks in an uninteresting way: *He's such a bore!* **2 a bore** *BrE infml* something which is uninteresting and annoying: *It's a bore having to go to school when the weather's so lovely.* **3** a measurement of the width of a gun barrel or pipe

bore³ v the past tense of BEAR²

bored /bɔːd ‖ bɔːrd/ *adj* **1** tired and uninterested: *The students all looked bored.* | *She was bored with her job.* **2 bored to tears** extremely bored

bore·dom /'bɔːdəm ‖ 'bɔːr-/ n [U] the feeling of being bored: *She didn't try to hide her boredom.*

bor·ing /'bɔːrɪŋ/ *adj* dull and not interesting: *a boring film*

born /bɔːn ‖ bɔːrn/ *adj* **1** [never before a noun] brought into existence at the beginning of your life: *He was born in 1964.* **2** [only before a noun] able to do something easily and well: *a born teacher* **3 born and bred** having grown up from birth in a place: *She was born and bred in Yorkshire.* **4 -born** born in the place mentioned: *an American-born writer*

borne /bɔːn ‖ bɔːrn/ **1** the past participle of BEAR² **2 -borne** carried as stated: *Some plants have wind-borne seeds.*

bo·rough /'bʌrə ‖ -rəʊ/ n a town, or an area of a large town, with powers of government: *the London Borough of Islington*

bor·row /'bɒrəʊ ‖ 'bɑː-, 'bɔː-/ v [T] **1** to take something for a certain time, intending to return it: *Can I borrow your dictionary for a moment?* | *I borrowed £5 from my mother.* **2** to take or copy words or ideas: *English has borrowed words from many languages.*

bos·om /'bʊzəm/ n **1** a woman's breasts: *She held the child to her bosom.* **2 a bosom friend** a very close friend

boss[1] /bɒs ‖ bɔːs/ n infml an employer: I'm my own boss. | Where's the boss?

boss[2] v [T] (also **boss** sbdy **about/around**) to tell someone what to do: She's always bossing me about.

boss·y /'bɒsi ‖ 'bɔːsi/ adj **bossier, bossiest** enjoying giving orders too much: a bossy school captain –**bossiness** n [U]

bo·sun /'bəʊsən/ n (also **boatswain**) a chief seaman on a ship

bot·a·ny /'bɒtni ‖ 'baː-/ n [U] the scientific study of plants –**botanical** /bə'tænɪkəl/ adj [only before a noun] : botanical gardens

botch /bɒtʃ ‖ baːtʃ/ v [T] infml (also **botch** sthg ↔ **up**) to do a job badly or in an awkward way: You've really botched that up! –**botch** n (also **botch up**) : I've made a terrible botch of mending the car.

both /bəʊθ/ predeterminer, det, pron **1** the one as well as the other: Both the contestants were given a prize. | Both of my children are at school now. | Both suggestions are good. | We both enjoy dancing. | They were both embarrassed by his praise. | He's had two wives, and divorced them both. **2 both... and...** not only... but also...: We visited both New York and Washington. | I felt both excited and apprehensive.

both·er[1] /'bɒðər ‖ 'baː-/ v **1** [T] to annoy or worry someone: Does the heat bother you? | I'm busy: don't bother me now. | I could tell that something was bothering him. | It doesn't bother me what you do. **2 not bother** not to make the effort to do something: Don't bother to return it. | He never even bothered to say goodbye. | Don't bother about the washing up. □ USEFUL PATTERNS not bother to do something; not bother doing something; not bother about something
3 I can't be bothered = I am not going to do something because I do not want to make the effort: I can never be bothered to make my bed in the morning.

bother[2] n **1** [U] trouble or inconvenience: We had a lot of bother finding our way here. | It was no bother. **2 a bother** something or someone that is annoying or difficult: I'm sorry to be such a bother.

bother[3] interj a word used to show annoyance: Bother! I've lost my keys.

bot·tle[1] /'bɒtl ‖ 'baːtl/ n **1** a glass or plastic container for liquids –see picture on page 148 **2** the quantity held by a bottle: Add half a bottle of wine.

bottle[2] v **bottled, bottling** [T] to put something into bottles: After making the mint jelly, she bottled it in small jars.
bottle sthg ↔ **up** phr v [T] to keep your troubles or worries to yourself, without telling other people about them: She had bottled up her fears for too long.

bottle bank /'··· ·/ n a place where members of the public can leave bottles so that the glass can be used again

bot·tle·neck /'bɒtlnek ‖ 'baː-/ n **1** a place where a road becomes narrow and where the traffic must slow down **2** something that makes activity slower: a serious bottleneck in production

bot·tom /'bɒtəm ‖ 'baː-/ n **1** [C] the lowest part of something: at the bottom of the stairs | some tea left at the bottom of your cup **2 the bottom** the ground under the sea, a lake, or a river: They sent the enemy ship to the bottom of the sea. **3 the bottom** the least important or powerful part of something: I'm no good at maths – I'm always at the bottom of the class. | He started life at the bottom but quickly worked his way up. **4 the bottom** the far end: I'll walk with you to the bottom of the road. | at the bottom of the garden **5** [C] the part of your body on which you sit: He fell on his bottom. **6 at the bottom of something** the cause of something: Who is at the bottom of all this trouble? **7 get to the bottom of something** to find the cause of something **8** [only before another noun] lowest or last: the bottom rung of the ladder –compare TOP[1]

bot·tom·less /'bɒtəmləs ‖ 'baː-/ adj **1** very deep: a bottomless pit **2** having no limit: The supply of money seemed bottomless.

bough /baʊ/ n lit a main branch of a tree

bought /bɔːt/ past tense and participle of BUY[1]

boul·der /'bəʊldər/ n a large stone or rock

boule·vard /'buːlvaːd ‖ 'buːləvaːrd, 'bʊ-/ n a wide street with trees on each side

bounce[1] /baʊns/ v **bounced, bouncing 1** [I] to spring back or up again after hitting a surface: The ball bounced several times. **2** [T] to throw something, for example a ball, against a surface so that it bounces: bouncing a ball against a wall **3** [I + adv/prep] to walk quickly because you are happy: She bounced into the room. **4** [I] (of a cheque) to be returned by a bank as worthless

bounce[2] n [C;U] the act or action of bouncing: The ball gave a high bounce. | The ball has plenty of bounce.

bounc·ing /'baʊnsɪŋ/ adj **a bouncing baby** a healthy, active baby

bounc·y /'baʊnsi/ adj **1** full of life and eager for action: She was bouncy and cheerful. **2** able to bounce well: a bouncy ball

bound[1] /baʊnd/ adj **1 bound to** a phrase you use to say that you think someone will certainly do something, or something will certainly happen: She's bound to pass her driving test. | That tree's bound to fall over next time there's a strong wind. | In a group as big as this, you're bound to get occasional disagreements. | I knew that he was bound to have told her about our plans. **2** [never before a noun] having a legal or moral duty to do something: The government is bound by its agreement with the unions. | I felt bound to tell you. **3** (of a book) fastened within covers: a small book bound in leather **4 bound up in something** very busy with something or very interested in something: She's very bound up in her work at the moment. **5 bound up with something** closely connected with something: His future is closely bound up with that of the company. **6** intending to go in a particular direction or to a particular place: She got on a boat bound for Ireland.

bound[2] v **1** [I+adv/prep] to move with large jumps: The animals bounded away. **2** [T] to mark the boundaries or edges of a place: The village was bounded by trees.

bound[3] n **1** a large jump: With one bound he was over the wall. **2 bounds** [pl] the limits beyond which it is impossible or undesirable to go: His suggestions go beyond the bounds of reason and possibility. | His greed for power knows no bounds. **3 out of bounds** (of a place) forbidden: The pub is definitely out of bounds to us.

bound[4] the past tense and past participle of BIND

bound·a·ry /'baʊndəri/ n **boundaries 1** the dividing line between surfaces, spaces, or countries: A

river forms the boundary **between** *the two counties.*
2 the outer limit of something: *the boundaries* **of**
human knowledge

bound·less /'baʊndləs/ *adj* without limits: *He has*
boundless energy and enthusiasm.

boun·te·ous /'baʊntiəs/ *adj lit* giving or given
freely: *bounteous gifts*

boun·ti·ful /'baʊntɪfəl/ *adj lit* in large quantities: *a*
bountiful supply

boun·ty /'baʊnti/ *n lit* [U] generosity: *a rich lady*
famous for her bounty to the poor

bou·quet /bəʊ'keɪ, buː-/ *n* **1** a bunch of flowers
given to someone or carried at a formal occasion:
The bride carried a wonderful bouquet **of** *roses.* **2**
the smell of a wine: *a rich bouquet*

bour·bon /'bʊəbən ‖ 'bɜːr-/ *n* [C;U] a type of
American WHISKY

bour·geois /'bʊəʒwɑː ‖ bʊər'ʒwɑː/ *adj old fash* of
or typical of the MIDDLE CLASS

bour·geoi·sie /ˌbʊəʒwɑː'ziː ‖ ˌbʊər-/ *n* the **bour-**
geoisie the MIDDLE CLASS

bout /baʊt/ *n* a short period of great activity or
illness: *a bout* **of** *fever*

bou·tique /buː'tiːk/ *n* a small fashionable shop

bo·vine /'bəʊvaɪn/ *adj tech* relating to a cow or ox:
bovine tuberculosis

bow¹ /baʊ/ *v* **1** [I;T] to bend your head or the top part
of your body forward, often as a sign of respect:
Everyone bowed as the Queen walked into the room. |
He bowed his head in shame. **2** to accept or
obey something: *I bow to your greater experience.*
bow out *phr v* [I] to stop doing something or leave
in order to let someone else take your place: *He*
bowed out of the competition to let the younger
members take part.

bow² /baʊ/ *n* **1** a bending forward of the upper part
of the body, or the head, to show respect: *He moved*
aside for her with a polite bow. **2** **take a bow** to
come on stage to receive praise at the end of a performance **3** the front part of a ship –compare
STERN

bow³ /bəʊ/ *n* **1** a piece of wood held in a curve by a
tight string and used for shooting arrows **2** a long
thin piece of wood with a tight string fastened along
it, used for playing musical instruments that have
strings **3** a knot with two circles and two loose ends
used for tying up shoes and for decorations: *She tied*
the ribbon in a loose bow.

bowed /baʊd/ *adj* curved or bent: *bowed legs*

bow·els /'baʊəlz/ *n* [pl] **1** tubes from your stomach
which carry the waste matter out of your body **2**
the deep inner part of something: *deep in the bowels*
of *the earth*

bow·er /'baʊəʳ/ *n lit* a pleasant, shaded shelter
under the trees

bowl¹ /bəʊl/ *n* **1** [C] a deep uncovered container: *a*
washing-up bowl | *a flower bowl* | *a sugar bowl* –see
picture on page 148 **2** [C] the contents of a bowl: *a*
bowl of sugar **3 bowls** [U] a game in which people
roll big wooden balls as near as possible to a smaller
ball

bowl² *v* [I;T] to throw or roll a ball to a player in a
game such as cricket. **2 bowl** to accept or
bowl sbdy ↔ **over** *phr v* [T] **1** to knock someone or
something down: *Someone ran round the corner*
and nearly bowled me over. **2** to give a pleasant

surprise to someone: *Your news has completely*
bowled me over.

bow-legged /ˌbəʊ'legd, -'legɪd◄/ *adj* having legs
which curve outwards at the knee

bowl·er /'bəʊləʳ/ *n* **1** a person who bowls in a game
of cricket **2** (also **bowler hat** /ˌ·· '·/*BrE*) a man's
round black hard hat, worn especially by British
businessmen

bowl·ing /'bəʊlɪŋ/ *n* a game in which balls are rolled
in order to knock down a group of sticks or other
objects –**bowling** *v* [U] : *tenpin bowling*

bow tie /ˌbəʊ 'taɪ/ *n* a tie fastened at the front with
a knot in the shape of a BOW³ (3)

box¹ /bɒks ‖ bɑːks/ *n* **1** a container with stiff sides
and often with a lid, usually made of cardboard or
wood: *a box of matches* | *a shoebox* –see picture on
page 148 **2** the contents of a box: *He's eaten a whole*
box of chocolates. **3** a small room or enclosed space:
a box at the theatre | *the witness box in a law-court* |
the signal box on a railway line | *a telephone box* **4**
the box *BrE infml* television: *They show old films*
on the box every night.

box² *v* **1** [T] to put things in a box or boxes: *The*
oranges were quickly boxed and sent off. **2** [I;T] to
fight someone with your hands –see BOXING
(USAGE) **3 box someone's ears** *infml* to hit someone on their ears, especially as a punishment
box sbdy/sthg ↔ **in** *phr v* [T] to enclose in a small
space: *She feels completely boxed in living in that*
tiny flat.

box·car /'bɒkskɑːʳ ‖ 'bɑːks-/ *n AmE* a roofed railway carriage that carries goods

box·er /'bɒksəʳ ‖ 'bɑːk-/ *n* a person who boxes,
especially professionally: *a heavyweight boxer*

box·ing /'bɒksɪŋ ‖ 'bɑːk-/ *n* [U] the sport of fighting
with tightly closed hands –see picture on page 637

Boxing Day /'·· ·/ *n* [C;U] a public holiday in England and Wales, on the first day after Christmas
that is not a Sunday

box num·ber /'· ˌ··/ *n* a number used as a mailing
address, especially in replying to newspaper advertisements

box of·fice /'· ˌ··/ *n* a place in a theatre, cinema, or
concert hall, where tickets are sold: *I'll wait for you*
at the box office.

boy¹ /bɔɪ/ *n* **1** a young male person: *Our new baby*
is a boy. | *The school is for both girls and boys.* **2** a
son, especially a young one: *My little boy's hurt him-*
self. **3 the boys** *infml* a man's male friends: *He's*
having a night out with the boys.

boy² *interj AmE infml* an expression used to show
a strong feeling, like excitement: *Boy, what a game!*

boy·cott /'bɔɪkɒt ‖ -kɑːt/ *v* [T] to refuse to do business with someone or take part in something as a
way of showing your disapproval: *They're boycot-*
ting the shop because the people who work there
aren't allowed to join a union. | *to boycott a meeting*
–**boycott** *n*

boy·friend /'bɔɪfrend/ *n* a male friend of a girl or
woman who she likes very much, and with whom
she may sometimes have a sexual relationship:
This is my boyfriend, Jim.

boy·hood /'bɔɪhʊd/ *n* [C;U] the state or time of being
a boy: *a happy boyhood*

boy·ish /'bɔɪ-ɪʃ/ *adj* like a boy: *his boyish laughter* |
her boyish figure –**boyishly** *adv* –**boyishness** *n* [U]

boy scout /ˌ· '·‖ '··/ *n* a SCOUT² (2)

BR /ˌbiː ˈɑːʳ ◂/ an abbreviation for British Rail (the British railway system)

bra /brɑː/ n (also **brassiere** fml) a piece of clothing worn by women under their clothes to support their breasts –see picture on page 50

brace¹ /breɪs/ n **1** something used for supporting or strengthening something **2** a wire worn inside the mouth, usually by children, to straighten their teeth **3** [plural is **brace**] a pair of birds or animals: *three brace of pheasants* **4 braces** [pl] BrE bands, often made of elastic, worn over the shoulders to hold up trousers –see picture on page 50 –see PAIR (USAGE)

brace² v **braced, bracing** [T] **1** to make something stronger: *We had to brace the walls when we put the new roof on.* **2 brace yourself** to prepare yourself, usually for something unpleasant or difficult: *Brace yourself for a shock!*

brace-let /ˈbreɪslɪt/ n a band, usually of metal, that you wear round your wrist or arm for decoration –see picture on page 50

brac-ing /ˈbreɪsɪŋ/ adj fresh and health-giving (used especially of air): *the bracing sea air*

brack-en /ˈbrækən/ n [U] a plant which grows in forests and becomes a rich red-brown in autumn

brack-et¹ /ˈbrækɪt/ n **1** a piece of metal or wood fixed to a wall to support something: *The shelf rested on two strong brackets.* **2** (also **square bracket**) either of the pair of signs [ ] used around a word or sentence in a piece of writing to enclose information **3** (also **round bracket**) either of the pair of signs ( ) around a word or sentence in a piece of writing **4** a group of people who share a similar income or age: *This product is aimed at people in the 16–25 age bracket.*

bracket² v [T] **1** to enclose something in brackets **2** to consider certain people or things as similar: *Don't bracket me and my friends together with those idiots!*

brack-ish /ˈbrækɪʃ/ adj not pure (used of water) –**brackishness** n [U]

brag /bræg/ v **-gg-** [I;T] to talk too proudly about yourself, or your possessions: *Don't brag!* | *He bragged of having won first prize.* | *He bragged about his family background.*

braid¹ /breɪd/ v [T] the usual American word for PLAIT²

braid² n **1** [U] threads of silk or other material twisted to form a narrow decorative border: *gold braid* **2** [C] the usual American word for a PLAIT¹

braille /breɪl/ n [U] a way of printing with raised round marks which blind people can read by touching

brain¹ /breɪn/ n **1** the organ of your body in the upper part of your head, which controls thought, feeling, and physical activity: *The brain is extremely delicate.* | *He suffered brain damage in the accident.* **2** the ability to think clearly and intelligently: *a good business brain* | *He's nice, but he hasn't got much of a brain.* | *You were born with a brain – use it!* **3** infml a person with a very good mind: *Some of the best brains in the country are here tonight.* **4 be the brains of something** infml to be the person who organizes something, such as a business: *Speak to Sheila – she's the real brains behind the outfit.* **5 have something on the brain** to think about something continually, often when you do not want to: *I've got that stupid tune on the brain.* | *You're terrible – you've got sex on the brain!*

brain² v [T] infml to hit someone on the head very hard

brain-child /ˈbreɪntʃaɪld/ n [sing] infml someone's idea or invention, especially if it is successful: *This scheme was the brainchild of the town's mayor.*

brain drain /ˈ· ·/ n a movement of large numbers of skilled people from their own country to other countries where they can earn more money

brain-less /ˈbreɪnləs/ adj silly and stupid –**brainlessly** adv

brain-storm /ˈbreɪnstɔːm ‖ -stɔːrm/ n infml **1** BrE a sudden inability to think clearly: *I don't know why I forgot those papers: I must have had a brainstorm.* **2** the usual American word for a BRAINWAVE

brain-storm-ing /ˈbreɪnstɔːmɪŋ ‖ -stɔːr-/ n [U] a method of finding answers to problems in which all the members of a group think very quickly of as many ideas as they can

brain-wash /ˈbreɪnwɒʃ ‖ -wɔːʃ, -wɑːʃ/ v [T] to make someone change their beliefs by very strong persuasion: *Don't let all those advertisements brainwash you into buying that soap.* | *The new regime attempted to brainwash the masses.* –**brainwashing** n [U]

brain-wave /ˈbreɪnweɪv/ n BrE infml a sudden clever idea: *I've just had a brainwave!*

brain-y /ˈbreɪni/ adj **brainier, brainiest** infml clever

braise /breɪz/ v **braised, braising** [T] to cook meat or vegetables slowly in liquid in a covered dish –see COOK¹ (USAGE)

brake¹ /breɪk/ n **1** the part of a vehicle which makes it go slower or stop: *Always check the brakes before going on a journey.* –see picture on page 49 **2 put the brakes on something** to slow down or stop something: *The government has put the brakes on spending by increasing interest rates.*

brake² v **braked, braking** [I] to make something slow or stop by or as if by using a brake: *She braked suddenly to avoid hitting the car in front.*

bram-ble /ˈbræmbəl/ n a common wild bush of the rose family, especially the wild BLACKBERRY

bran /bræn/ n [U] the crushed skin of wheat and other grain, separated from the flour

branch¹ /brɑːntʃ ‖ bræntʃ/ n **1** the part of a tree which grows from the trunk: *an overhanging branch* **2** a part of something larger which can be separated from it and is usually less important: *a branch railway* **3** a division of an organization, group, or subject: *Which branch of medicine are you studying?* | *Our firm has branches in most major cities.*

branch² v [I] to become divided into or form branches: *Turn off where the road branches to the right.*

branch off phr v [I] to leave a main road or a planned course of action:

branch out phr v [I] to add to the range of your activities: *The bookshop has decided to branch out into selling tapes and records.*

brand¹ /brænd/ n **1** a class of goods which is the product of a particular firm or producer: *What is your favourite brand of soap?* **2** a mark made by burning, usually to show ownership: *These cattle have a particularly distinctive brand.* **3** a particular quality or way of acting: *his unique brand of journalism* | *a peculiar brand of humour*

brand² v [T] **1** to mark something by burning it, usually to show who owns it: *Our cattle are branded with the letter B.* **2 brand someone as something** to say that someone has a bad character of a particular kind: *The newspapers have branded all football supporters as troublemakers.*

bran·dish /ˈbrændɪʃ/ v [T] to wave something about in a violent or excited way: *He stormed into the house brandishing an axe.*

brand name /ˈ· ˌ·/ n the name given to a product by its maker

brand-new /ˌ· ˈ·◄/ adj new and completely unused

bran·dy /ˈbrændi/ n brandies [C;U] a strong alcoholic drink made from wine

brash /bræʃ/ adj too confident often because of lack of experience –**brashly** adv –**brashness** n [U]

brass /brɑːs ‖ bræs/ n [U] 1 a very hard bright yellow metal, a mixture of COPPER and ZINC: *a brass curtain ring* 2 [+ sing/pl verb] the set of musical instruments made of brass and played by blowing them: *a brass band* 3 **get down to brass tacks** *infml* to come to the really important facts or business

bras·si·ere /ˈbræziəʳ ‖ brəˈzɪəʳ/ n see BRA

brass·y /ˈbrɑːsi ‖ ˈbræsi/ adj brassier, brassiest 1 like brass in colour 2 loud and unpleasant in sound 3 *infml* shameless and too self-confident in manner or appearance (used of women to express disapproval)

brat /bræt/ n a badly-behaved child

bra·va·do /brəˈvɑːdəu/ n [U] the showing of courage or confidence to make other people think you are brave

brave[1] /breɪv/ adj courageous and ready to suffer danger or pain: *brave soldiers | a brave attempt at a smile* –**bravely** adv: *"I'll try," she said bravely.* –**bravery** /ˈbreɪvəri/ n [U] : *an act of outstanding bravery*

brave[2] n a young North American Indian man

brave[3] v braved, braving [T] to face danger or difficulties without showing fear: *She braved her parents' displeasure by marrying him.*

bra·vo /ˈbrɑːvəu, brɑːˈvəu/ interj, n a word used to show your approval when someone, especially a performer, has done well

brawl /brɔːl/ n a noisy quarrel or fight, often in a public place –**brawl** v [I]

brawn /brɔːn/ n [U] muscle –**brawny** adj: *his brawny arms*

bray /breɪ/ v [I] 1 to make the sound that a donkey makes 2 to make a loud, unpleasant noise: *He brayed with laughter.* –**bray** n

bra·zen[1] /ˈbreɪzən/ adj without shame: *a brazen lie* –**brazenly** adv

brazen[2] v **brazen it out** to face trouble or blame with confidence and without shame even when you have done something wrong

bra·zi·er /ˈbreɪziəʳ ‖ -ʒəʳ/ n a metal container for burning coal

breach /briːtʃ/ n 1 [C;U] an act of breaking or not fulfilling a law, a promise, or a custom: *Your action is a breach of our agreement.* 2 [C] an opening, especially one made in a wall by attackers 3 **a breach of confidence** the action of telling people things that you should not tell anyone 4 **a breach of the peace** fighting in a public place 5 **in breach of** not fulfilling: *You are clearly in breach of your contract.* –**breach** v [T]

bread /bred/ n [U] 1 a common food made of baked flour: *a loaf of bread | a slice of bread | bread and cheese | brown bread* –see picture on page 344 2 food considered as a means of staying alive: *our daily bread* 3 *slang* money 4 **bread and butter:** a bread spread with butter b *infml* a way of earning money: *He doesn't just write for fun: it's his bread and butter.* 5 **know which side your bread is buttered** *infml* to know what will be of most gain to yourself

bread-crumb /ˈbredkrʌm/ n a very small bit of bread

bread-line /ˈbredlaɪn/ n **on the breadline** extremely poor

breadth /bredθ, bretθ/ n [C;U] 1 the distance from one side of something to the other: *He travelled the length and breadth of the country.* – compare LENGTH (1) 2 a wide range: *His book showed the great breadth of his learning.*

bread·win·ner /ˈbred wɪnəʳ/ n the person who works to earn most of the family's money: *My mother is the breadwinner in our family.*

break[1] /breɪk/ v broke /brəuk/, broken /ˈbrəukən/ 1 [I] to separate into pieces suddenly or violently: *I dropped the glass and it broke. | Suddenly the rope broke. | A piece of the branch had broken off. | The box fell and broke open.* 2 [T] to cause something to separate into pieces by hitting it or dropping it: *Be careful you don't break that dish. | He fell and broke a bone in his leg.*

■ USAGE Compare **break, tear, cut, smash, crack, burst.** You cannot **break** soft things like cloth or paper, but you can **tear** them, which means "pull apart so as to leave rough edges", or **cut** them, which means "divide by using a sharp edge": *He tore the letter into pieces. | I cut the cake with a knife.* Things made of glass or china may **break** (or **be/get broken**) or **smash**, which means "break suddenly into small pieces": *The dish smashed on the floor.* **Crack** means "break without the parts becoming separated": *You've cracked the window, but luckily you haven't broken it.* **Burst** means "break suddenly by pressure from inside": *She blew up the paper bag until it burst.*

3 [I] (of a machine) to stop working: *We used to have an electric lawn mower, but it broke.* 4 [T] to cause a machine to stop working: *Don't keep switching the kettle on and off like that-you'll break it.* 5 [T] to fail to keep a law or a promise: *I'm afraid you're breaking the law. | She had no intention of breaking her promise.* 6 [T] to destroy someone's ability and do termination to continue doing something: *They'll never break her spirit. | They beat him up and tortured him, and in the end they broke him.* 7 [I] to have a rest from doing something: *Let's break for lunch.* 8 [T] to cause something to end: *We need to have talks to try to break the deadlock. | She drinks a lot, but she's trying to break the habit. | A loud crash broke the silence.* 9 [I] (of a boy's voice) to become deeper: *He was still young, and his voice had not yet broken.* 10 **break a journey** to have a rest in the middle of a journey 11 **break someone's fall** to stop someone from falling too far or hurting themselves too much: *Fortunately some of the lower branches broke his fall.* 12 **break a record** to beat a record by doing something better or faster than anyone else: *He won the 100 metres and broke the world record.* 13 **break a code** to manage to understand a secret way of talking or writing 14 **break someone's serve** to win a game when someone else is serving in a game of tennis: *She has to break her opponent's serve now if she wants to win this match.* 15 **break news to someone** to tell someone something: *My father came and broke the bad news to me.* 16 **news breaks** = news becomes known: *I remember I was sitting in the garden when news of war broke.* 17 **day breaks** = it begins to get light: *Day was just breaking as I got up.* 18 **a storm breaks** = a storm begins 19 **a wave breaks** = a wave comes onto the shore: *We sat on the beach watching the waves breaking on the shore.* 20 **break the back of something** to finish the main part or the

worst part of a job: *I think we've broken the back of the painting now.* **21 break cover** to run out from a hiding place **22 break even** to end up h~ving gained as much money as you have spen.: *We reckon the company should break even by next year.* **23 break free, break loose** to become free from someone or something: *He managed to break free and escape.* **24 break new ground** to do something new: *This research is really breaking new ground.* **25 break the ice** to make people feel more comfortable with each other at a social event: *We need to have a few drinks to help break the ice.*

break away *phr v* [I] to move away from someone, or escape from them: *Two policemen were holding him, but he managed to break away.*

break down *phr v* **1** [T **break** sthg ↔ **down**] to make something such as a door fall to the ground by hitting or kicking it: *When the police arrived they had to break down the door.* **2** [I] (of a machine) to stop working: *The car broke down on the motorway.* **3** [I] to fail: *The peace talks have broken down.* | *Finally his resistance broke down.* **4** [I] to lose control and start laughing or crying: *He broke down and wept when his mother died.* **5** [T **break** sthg ↔ **down**] to separate something into different parts or change it into a different form: *Fats cannot easily be broken down by the body.*

break in *phr v* **1** [I] to enter a building by force, for example in order to steal something: *Somebody had broken in and taken everything of value.* –see THIEF (USAGE) **2** [I] to interrupt when someone is speaking: *Sorry to break in on you like this.* | *"Don't tell them that," she broke in angrily.* **3** [T **break** sbdy ↔ **in**] to make someone familiar with a new job or a new situation: *There's a lot to learn, but we'll try to break you in gently.* **4** [T **break** sthg ↔ **in**] to wear something new so that it becomes more comfortable: *These shoes are quite new, so I'm still breaking them in.*

break into sthg *phr v* [T] **1** to enter a building by force: *Thieves had broken into the house through an upstairs window.* **2** to begin to do something suddenly: *She broke into song.* | *We all broke into laughter.* | *He broke into a run.* **3** to use a part of something that you had been keeping: *We had to break into our savings to pay for the repairs.*

break sbdy **of** sthg *phr v* [T] to cure someone of a bad habit: *He still smokes 40 cigarettes a day, but we're trying to break him of the habit.*

break off *phr v* **1** [T **break** sthg ↔ **off**] to remove a part of something by breaking it: *We broke off a few branches.* **2** [I] to become separated from the main part of something by being broken: *I dropped the teapot and the handle broke off.* **3** [T **break** sthg ↔ **off**] to end a relationship or an agreement: *The government has said that it will not break off diplomatic relations.* | *They've broken off their engagement.* **4** [I] to stop saying or doing something suddenly: *She started talking, then broke off when the telephone rang.*

break out *phr v* [I] **1** (of something bad) to start suddenly: *We're all hoping that war won't break out.* | *A fire broke out at the factory.* **2 break out in spots** to become covered in spots suddenly: *Her face had broken out in spots.* | *He broke out in a rash.* **3** to escape from a prison: *Three prisoners broke out of a top security prison last night.*

break through *phr v* **1** [T **break through** sthg] to force your way through something: *Some members of the crowd managed to break through the police barrier.* **2** [I] to suddenly become seen: *The day started off cloudy, but later the sun broke through.*

break up *phr v* **1** [I;T **break** sthg ↔ **up**] to break or separate into smaller pieces: *The car was broken up for scrap.* | *Police were called in to break up the crowd.* | *The ice started to break up when the warm weather came.* **2** [I;T **break** sthg ↔ **up**] to end: *The meeting broke up after only half an hour.* | *Demonstrators managed to get in and break up the council meeting.* **3** [I] to end a marriage or other relationship: *Their marriage broke up after two years.* | *The relationship wasn't working, so we decided to break up.* **4** [I] to stop going to school or college because the holidays are starting: *When do we break up?* | *We broke up last Friday.*

break with sbdy/sthg *phr v* [T] to end a friendship, relationship, or connection with someone or something: *He broke with the Labour party and stood for parliament as an independent.* | *breaking with the old traditions*

break² *n* **1** a hole or opening in something where it has broken or split: *There was a break in the cable.* | *a break in the clouds* **2** a short pause when you rest from an activity: *I think it's time for a coffee break.* | *We worked for four hours without a break.* **3** an act of ending a friendship, relationship, or connection with someone or something: *After her break with the Conservative party, she joined the Social Democrats.* | *a break with the past* **4 break of day** the time of day when it first starts to get light **5** a lucky chance to do something: *This job could give me the break I've been waiting for.*

break·age /'breıkıdʒ/ *n* **1** [C] the action of breaking something: *All breakages must be paid for.* **2** [U] *fml* the act of breaking something: *The vase is insured against accidental breakage.*

break·a·way /'breıkəweı/ *adj* [only before a noun] separate from a larger group: *a breakaway faction within the political party*

break·down /'breıkdaʊn/ *n* **1** a failure in the operation of a machine or system: *The trip took longer than we expected because our car had a breakdown.* | *a breakdown of law and order* **2** a failure in agreement or understanding: *a breakdown in the talks* **3** (also **nervous breakdown**) a medical condition of being unable to manage because of anxiety or worry **4** a detailed description of something so that you can understand it better: *I'd like a breakdown of these figures, please.*

break·er /'breıkə^r/ *n* a large wave that rolls onto the shore

break·fast /'brekfəst/ *n* [C;U] the first meal of the day: *He has breakfast at seven o'clock.* | *She ate a hearty breakfast.* | *She likes eggs for breakfast.* –**breakfast** *v* [I] : *We breakfasted on orange juice and eggs.*

break-in /'· ·/ *n* the illegal entering of a building using force: *£7000 was stolen in the break-in.*

break·neck /'breıknek/ *adj* **at breakneck speed** extremely fast and usually dangerously

break·through /'breıkθru:/ *n* an important discovery or advance, often made suddenly and after earlier failures: *Scientists have made a major breakthrough in their treatment of the disease.* | *a scientific breakthrough*

break·up /'breıkʌp/ *n* **1** the coming to an end of a relationship or an organization: *the breakup of a marriage* | *the breakup of the alliance* **2** a division into smaller parts: *the breakup of the large farms*

break·wa·ter /'breık,wɔ:tə^r ‖ -,wɔ:-, -,waı-/ *n* a thick wall built out into the sea to lessen the force of the waves near a harbour

breast /brest/ *n* **1 breasts** the two parts of a woman's body that produce milk **2** the upper front part of the body between the neck and the stomach: *a bird with an orange breast* **3** the part of your body where your feelings are supposed to come from: *He felt a surge of pride in his breast.* **4 make a clean breast of something** to admit the truth about something bad you have done

breast·stroke /ˈbrest-strəʊk/ *n* [U] a way of swimming on your front, pulling your arms back from your head and kicking your legs outwards

breath /breθ/ *n* **1** [U] air taken into and breathed out of your lungs: *He gabbled out his story, scarcely pausing for breath.* **2** [C] a single act of breathing air in and out: *Take a deep breath and start again from the beginning.* **3 a breath of fresh air** a little clean, pure air: *Let's step outside a moment for a breath of fresh air.* **4 out of breath** having difficulty in breathing easily, for example after running **5 get your breath back** to be able to breathe easily again: *Hang on a minute – let me get my breath back!* **6 hold your breath** to stop breathing deliberately: *She can hold her breath for over a minute.* **7 take someone's breath away** to surprise or shock someone very much: *The way he spoke to his boss fairly took my breath away.* **8 under your breath** in a low voice or whisper

breath·a·lyze /ˈbreθə-laɪz/ *v* **breathalyzed, breathalyzing** (also **breathalyse**) [T] (of the police) to measure the amount of alcohol that the driver of a car has drunk with a special apparatus called a **breathalyzer**

breathe /briːð/ *v* **breathed, breathing 1** [I;T] to take air into your lungs and let it out again: *Get off! I can't breathe.* | *He was breathing very heavily.* | *Don't breathe those fumes!* **2 breathe something over someone** to send something out of your mouth towards someone: *Don't stand so close; you're breathing garlic all over me.* **3** [T] to say something softly: *"Shh," he breathed.* **4 not breathe a word of something** to say nothing about something: *Don't breathe a word of this to anyone!* **5 breathe again, breathe more easily, breathe a sigh of relief** to feel calm again after feeling anxious **6 breathe new life into something** to make something become more exciting or full of life **7 breathe down someone's neck** to watch someone extremely closely –**breathing** *n* [U] : *machines monitoring her breathing*

breathe in *phr v* [I;T **breathe** sthg ↔ **in**] to take air into your lungs: *Breathe in slowly.* | *They breathed in the scent of the roses.*

breathe out *phr v* [I;T **breathe** sthg ↔ **out**] to let air or gas out of your lungs: *"Hold your breath," said the doctor. "Now breathe out."*

breath·er /ˈbriːðəʳ/ *n infml* a short pause for a rest

breathing space /ˈ·· ·/ *n* [sing; U] a short period when you are free from work or worry

breath·less /ˈbreθləs/ *adj* **1** breathing heavily or with difficulty **2** causing you to stop breathing because of being excited or afraid: *a breathless pause* –**breathlessly** *adv*

breath·tak·ing /ˈbreθˌteɪkɪŋ/ *adj* very exciting or shocking –**breathtakingly** *adv* : *breathtakingly beautiful*

bred /bred/ the past tense and past participle of BREED

breech·es /ˈbrɪtʃɪz/ *n* (**britches** *AmE*) [pl] trousers which go to your knees

breed¹ /briːd/ *v* **bred** /bred/, **bred, breeding 1** [I] (of animals) to produce young: *They won't breed if you keep them in a cage.* **2** [T] to keep animals or plants for the purpose of producing young animals or developing new plants: *He's bred a new variety of rose.* | *The winning horse was bred in Ireland.* **3** [T] to cause a condition or feeling to develop: *Flies and dirt breed disease.* | *Don't hit them back; violence breeds violence.*

breed² *n* [+sing/pl verb] **1** a particular class of animal or plant **2** a particular kind of person or object: *the first of a new breed of lasers*

breed·er /ˈbriːdəʳ/ *n* a person who breeds animals or plants

breed·ing /ˈbriːdɪŋ/ *n* [U] **1** the producing of young by animals or plants **2** the business of keeping animals or plants in order to obtain new and better kinds, or young for sale: *good breeding stock* **3** training in good manners, often thought to be related to high social position: *a person of excellent breeding*

breeding ground /ˈ·· ·/ *n* **1** a place where animals go to produce their young **2** a place where something can develop easily: *These village wells are the breeding ground of disease.*

breeze¹ /briːz/ *n* a light gentle wind: *A cool breeze was blowing.* –see WIND¹ (USAGE)

breeze² *v* **breezed, breezing** [I +adv/prep] to go quickly and in a carelessly confident way: *He just breezed in and sat down, without even apologizing!*

breez·y /ˈbriːzi/ *adj* **1** having fairly strong but gentle winds blowing: *a fine breezy morning* **2** cheerful and carelessly confident: *a breezy manner*

breth·ren /ˈbreðrən/ *n* [pl] a word used when you are talking to people in church, or talking about the members of a religious group

brev·i·ty /ˈbrevɪ̯ti/ *n* [U] **1** shortness in time: *the brevity of the meeting* **2** the quality of expressing things in very few words: *the wonderful brevity of her writing style*

brew /bruː/ *v* **1** [I;T] to make beer **2** [T] to mix something with hot water to prepare a drink **3** [I] to become ready for drinking after being mixed with hot water and left for a few minutes (used of tea): *We let the tea brew for five minutes.* **4 be brewing** (of something bad) to be starting to develop: *Trouble's brewing.* | *A storm was brewing.* –**brew** *n* : *a strong brew of beer*

brew·er /ˈbruːəʳ/ *n* a person or company that produces beer

brew·er·y /ˈbruːəri/ *n* a place where beer is made

bri·ar /ˈbraɪəʳ/ *n* [C;U] see BRIER

bribe¹ /braɪb/ *v* **bribed, bribing** [T] to persuade or influence someone in a position of power by giving them gifts or favours: *He bribed the police officer.* | *I bribed her into giving me the documents.*

bribe² *n* something offered or given when bribing someone: *The official was accused of taking bribes from local businessmen.*

brib·er·y /ˈbraɪbəri/ *n* [U] the giving or taking of bribes: *He was charged with bribery.*

bric-a-brac /ˈbrɪk ə ˌbræk/ *n* [U] small objects of various kinds, for decoration in a house

brick¹ /brɪk/ *n* **1** [C;U] a hard piece of baked clay used for building: *They used yellow bricks to build the house.* | *The house is made of brick.* **2** [C] something in the shape of a brick: *a brick of ice cream*

brick² *v*

brick sthg ↔ **up** *phr v* [T] to fill something completely with bricks: *They've bricked up the windows in the old house.*

brick·lay·er /ˈbrɪkˌleɪəʳ/ *n* a workman who builds walls with bricks –**bricklaying** *n* [U]

bride /braɪd/ *n* a girl or woman who is about to be married, or is just married: *The bride wore a beautiful white dress.*

bride-groom /ˈbraɪdɡruːm, -ɡrʊm/ *n* (also **groom**) a man who is about to be married, or just married

brides-maid /ˈbraɪdzmeɪd/ *n* an unmarried girl or woman, usually one of several, who helps the bride on the day of the marriage ceremony –compare BEST MAN

bridge¹ /brɪdʒ/ *n* **1** [C] something built to take a road or railway over a river, road, or railway: *We crossed the river there because it was the only bridge for miles.* | *a railway bridge* | *a bridge over the Thames* **2 the bridge** the part of a ship on which the captain and other officers stand when they are controlling it **3** [U] a card game for four players **4 the bridge of the nose** the bony upper part of your nose, between your eyes

bridge² *v* **bridged, bridging** [T] **1** to build a bridge across something: *to bridge a river* **2 bridge the gap** to reduce the difference between two things: *an attempt to bridge the gap between different cultures*

bri-dle¹ /ˈbraɪdl/ leather bands put on a horse's head to control its movements

bridle² *v* **bridled, bridling 1** [T] to put a bridle on a horse **2** [I] to show anger or displeasure, especially by making a proud upward movement of your head and body: *He bridled at my request.*

brief¹ /briːf/ *adj* **1** not lasting for very long: *I'll just have a brief look at the newspaper.* **2** using only a few words and not describing or talking about things in detail: *a brief letter* | *I'll try to be brief.* **3 in brief** using only a few words and giving only general points rather than details: *Here is the news in brief.* | *In brief, he says "no".* –**briefly** *adv* : *She spoke briefly.*

brief² *n* **1** a set of instructions about someone's duties or jobs: *His brief was to improve the company's sales figures.* **2 briefs** [pl] men's UNDER-PANTS or women's KNICKERS

brief³ *v* [T] to give instructions or necessary information to someone: *The officer briefed his men on what tactics to use.* –**briefing** *n* [C;U]: : *Before the meeting, let me give you a briefing.*

brief-case /ˈbriːfkeɪs/ *n* a flat case for carrying papers or books

bri-er /ˈbraɪəʳ/ *n* (also **briar**) [C;U] a wild bush covered with prickles, especially the wild rose bush

bri-gade /brɪˈɡeɪd/ *n* [+ sing/pl verb] **1** a part of an army, of about 5000 soldiers **2 the Fire Brigade** the organization responsible for putting out fires

brig-a-dier /ˌbrɪɡəˈdɪəʳ◂/ *n* an army officer of high rank

bright /braɪt/ *adj* **1** full of light or shining strongly: *What a bright sunny day!* | *a bright light* **2** cheerful: *You look very bright and cheerful this morning.* | *bright eyes* **3** strong, clear, and easily seen (used to describe a colour): *bright blue* **4** quick at learning things: *a very bright child* **5 a bright idea** a clever idea **6** showing hope or signs of success: *You have a bright future ahead of you.* –**brightly** *adv* –**brightness** *n* [U]

bright-en /ˈbraɪtn/ *v* [I;T] to make or become brighter (also **brighten up; brighten** sthg ↔ **up**) *The weather is brightening.* | *She brightened up when she heard the good news.* | *A few flowers should brighten up the room.*

bril-liant /ˈbrɪljənt/ *adj* **1** very bright or splendid in appearance: *a brilliant blue sky* | *brilliant light* **2** very clever: *a brilliant student* | *a brilliant idea* –**brilliance** *n* [U] –**brilliantly** *adv*

brim¹ /brɪm/ *n* **1** the top edge of a container: *The glass was full to the brim.* **2** the bottom part of a hat which turns outwards to give shade, or protection against rain **3 -brimmed** having a brim (used of hats): *a wide-brimmed hat*

brim² *v* **-mm-** [I] to be very full: *a brimming cup of coffee* | *His eyes brimmed* **with** *tears.*

brim over *phr v* **1** [I] to be very full of a liquid, so that the liquid comes out **2 be brimming over with** to be full of a pleasant feeling, and show it in the way that you behave: *He was brimming over with joy.*

brim-ful /ˈbrɪmˌfʊl/ *adj* [never before a noun] full to the top or overflowing

brine /braɪn/ *n* [U] water containing salt, used for preserving food

bring /brɪŋ/ *v* **brought** /brɔːt/, **brought 1** [T] to carry something to or towards a place: *Bring your books with you when you come.* | *I've brought a present for you.* | *She brought me some flowers.* | *Can I bring a friend to the party?*
□ USEFUL PATTERNS to bring something; to bring something for someone; to bring someone something
2 [T+adv/prep] to move something somewhere: *He brought his hand down onto the table.* **3** [T] to cause something to happen or start: *Money doesn't necessarily bring happiness.* | *The scene brought tears to my eyes.* **4** [T+adv/prep] to cause or persuade someone to come to a place: *The noise brought several people out of their houses to see what was going on.* | *The fair brings a lot of tourists to the town.* **5** [T+adv/prep] to cause someone or something to be in a particular state: *That brings the total to £200.* | *Let's hope that we can soon bring this war to an end.* | *The club brought me into contact with a lot of people.* | *This dispute must be brought to an end.* **6 can't bring yourself to do something** to be unable do something because it is so unpleasant: *I couldn't bring myself to kill the poor creature.* **7 bring a charge against someone** to say officially to someone that it is believed that they have done something illegal: *He was arrested, and a charge of murder was brought against him.* **8 bring a child into the world** to give birth to a child

bring sthg ↔ **about** *phr v* [T] to cause something to happen: *This crisis has been brought about by the stupidity of our politicians.*

bring sthg/sbdy ↔ **along** *phr v* [T] to bring someone or something with you to a place: *Please come to the party, and bring a few friends along if you like.*

bring back *phr v* **1** [T **bring** sbdy/sthg ↔ **back**] to bring someone or something with you when you return to a place: *If you're going to the shop, could you bring back a few things for me?* | *We'll take you to the concert, and we can also bring you back.* **2** [T **bring** sthg ↔ **back**] to cause something to return: *Those songs certainly bring back a lot of memories.* | *a campaign to bring back the death penalty*

bring down *phr v* **1** [T **bring** sthg ↔ **down**] to cause something to come down to a lower place or a lower level: *Gunmen shot at the plane and brought it down.* | *The government is determined to bring down inflation.* **2** [T **bring** sbdy/sthg ↔ **down**] to cause a person or a government to lose their position of power: *This latest crisis could well bring down the government.*

bring sthg ↔ **forward** *phr v* [T] **1** to introduce or suggest a new idea: *Several new proposals have been brought forward.* **2** to decide that something will take place at an earlier time than had been planned: *The meeting has been brought forward to Tuesday.*

bring in *phr v* **1** [T **bring** sthg ↔ **in**] to introduce something: *The government is bringing in new laws to protect children.* **2** [T **bring** sbdy ↔ **in**] to ask someone to take part in something, especially in order to help with a problem: *We need to bring in a few experienced people to get the job finished on time.* **3** [T **bring** sthg ↔ **in**] to earn a particular amount of money: *She's bringing in £200 a week. | This new tax will bring in a lot of extra money for the government.* **4 bring in a verdict** to give a particular VERDICT in a court of law: *The jury brought in a verdict of guilty.*

bring sthg ↔ **off** *phr v* [T] to succeed in doing something difficult: *It will be a great achievement if they manage to bring it off.*

bring on *phr v* **1** [T **bring** sbdy/sthg ↔ **on**] to cause someone or something to grow, develop, or improve: *The shock nearly brought on a heart attack. | He was given special coaching to bring him on.* **2 bring something on yourself** to cause something unpleasant to happen to you

bring out *phr v* **1** [T **bring** sthg ↔ **out**] to produce a new product: *The company has just brought out a new range of cosmetics.* **2 bring out the best in someone** to make someone behave very well: *The crisis brought out the best in everyone.* [RELATED PHRASE: **bring out the worst in someone**] **3** [T **bring** sbdy **out**] to encourage someone to talk to other people and feel at ease with other people

bring sbdy ↔ **round** *phr v* [T] **1** to cause someone to regain consciousness: *We tried everything we could think of to bring her round.* **2** to persuade someone to change their opinion so that it is the same as your opinion

bring sbdy ↔ **to** *phr v* [T] to cause someone to regain consciousness

bring up *phr v* **1** [T **bring** sbdy ↔ **up**] to educate and care for a child: *I think that both parents should be involved in bringing up the children. | She was a polite and well brought up child.* –see RAISE¹ (USAGE) **2** [T **bring** sthg ↔ **up**] to introduce a subject during a conversation: *I didn't dare bring up the question of money. | All these problems were brought up at the last meeting.* **3** [T **bring** sthg ↔ **up**] to be sick: *He ate his dinner and then promptly brought it all up again.*

brink /brɪŋk/ *n* **be on the brink of something** to be about to do or experience something wonderful or terrible: *Scientists say they are on the brink of a major discovery.* [RELATED PHRASE **come/bring someone to the brink of something**]

brisk /brɪsk/ *adj* quick and active: *a brisk walk* –**briskly** *adv* –**briskness** *n* [U]

bris·tle¹ /ˈbrɪsəl/ *n* [C;U] short stiff coarse hair: *His chin was covered with bristles.*

bristle² *v* **bristled, bristling** [I] (of hair or fur) to stand up stiffly: *The cat's fur bristled.*
  bristle with sthg *phr v* [T] to be full of something: *The market place bristled with activity.*

Brit /brɪt/ *n infml* a British person

britch·es /ˈbrɪtʃɪz/ *n* [pl] –see BREECHES

Brit·ish /ˈbrɪtɪʃ/ *adj* from or connected with Britain

brit·tle /ˈbrɪtl/ *adj* hard but easily broken or damaged: *brittle glass*

broach /brəʊtʃ/ *v* **broach a subject** to introduce as a subject of conversation: *At last he broached the subject of the new contract.*

broad /brɔːd/ *adj* **1** wide: *He was tall, with broad shoulders. | the broad horizon* **2** used in giving measurements: *four metres broad* **3** not limited, but including a lot of different things or people: *The course appeals to a broad range of people.* **4** general, and not including a lot of details: *Give me a broad idea of your plans.* **5 in broad daylight** during the day, when it is light: *The raid took place in broad daylight.* **6** showing clearly where the speaker comes from: *She spoke broad Scots.*

broad bean /ˌ· ˈ· ‖ ˈ· ·/ *n* a large flat bean

broad·cast¹ /ˈbrɔːdkɑːst ‖ -kæst/ *n* something sent out by radio or television: *The broadcast suffered from technical problems.* –**broadcast** *adj* : *broadcast news*

broadcast² *v* **broadcast, broadcast 1** [I;T] to send out something on radio or television: *The BBC broadcasts to all parts of the world. | The BBC will broadcast the news at 10 o'clock.* **2** [T] to make something widely known: *He broadcast the news of his pay rise.* –**broadcaster** *n* –**broadcasting** *n* [U]

broad·en /ˈbrɔːdn/ *v* **1** [I;T] (also **broaden out;** **broaden** sthg ↔ **out**) to make or become wider: *The river broadens out here. | plans to broaden the road* **2** [T] to make something less limited: *We need to broaden our campaign.* **3 broaden someone's mind** to make someone more willing to accept different ideas or customs: *Travel broadens the mind.*

broad·ly /ˈbrɔːdli/ *adv* in general: *Broadly, I agree with you.*

broad·mind·ed /ˌbrɔːdˈmaɪndɪd◄/ *adj* willing to respect the opinions or actions of others even if they are very different from your own –opposite **narrow-minded** –**broadmindedness** *n* [U]

broad·side /ˈbrɔːdsaɪd/ *n* a strong spoken or written attack: *She delivered a broadside against government policies.*

bro·cade /brəˈkeɪd ‖ brəʊ-/ *n* [U] decorative cloth usually of silk, often with a raised pattern of gold or silver threads

broc·co·li /ˈbrɒkəli ‖ ˈbrɑː-/ *n* [U] a vegetable whose young green flower heads are eaten

bro·chure /ˈbrəʊʃəʳ, -ʃʊəʳ ‖ brəʊˈʃʊəʳ/ *n* a small book giving instructions or the details of a service: *a holiday brochure*

brogue /brəʊg/ *n* **1** a way of speaking **2 brogues** [pl] strong shoes with a pattern made in the leather –see PAIR (USAGE)

broil /brɔɪl/ *v* [I;T] the usual American word for GRILL

broke¹ /brəʊk/ past tense of BREAK¹

broke² *adj* [never before a noun] *infml* **1** completely without money: *I'm always broke by the end of the week.* **2 go broke** to lose so much money that you have to close your business

bro·ken¹ /ˈbrəʊkən/ past participle of BREAK¹

broken² *adj* **1** damaged, spoilt, or made useless by breaking: *Be careful of the broken glass. | a broken leg | a broken clock* **2** interrupted: *a broken journey | broken sleep* **3** without hope: *a broken spirit | a broken man* **4** destroyed by the separation of a husband and wife: *a broken marriage | a broken home* **5** not kept: *a broken law | a broken promise* **6** imperfectly spoken or written: *broken English*

broken-down /ˌ·· ˈ·◄/ *adj* needing repair (used to describe cars and machines)

broken-heart·ed /ˌ·· ˈ·◄/ *adj* filled with grief: *He was broken-hearted when his son died.*

bro·ker /ˈbrəʊkəʳ/ n a person who does business for someone else, for example in buying and selling shares or foreign money

brol·ly /ˈbrɒli ‖ ˈbrɑːli/ n **brollies** BrE infml an UMBRELLA

bron·chi·tis /brɒŋˈkaɪtɪs ‖ brɑːŋ-/ n [U] an illness of the two tubes connecting the WINDPIPE with the lungs; it causes severe coughing

bronze¹ /brɒnz ‖ brɑːnz/ adj **1** made of bronze **2** **bronze medal** a piece of bronze that you win when you come third in a race or competition **3** the colour of bronze

bronze² n **1** [U] a metal made mainly of copper and tin **2** [C] a bronze medal **3** [U] a dark yellowish-brown colour

bronzed /brɒnzd ‖ brɑːnzd/ adj made attractively brown by the sun: *handsome young men bronzed by the sun*

brooch /brəʊtʃ/ n a decoration worn on women's clothes, fastened on with a pin –see picture on page 50

brood¹ /bruːd/ n a family of young birds

brood² v [I] **1** to sit on eggs as a hen does **2** to think about something angrily or sadly for a long time: *Don't just sit there brooding – do something!*

broody /ˈbruːdi/ adj **1** wanting to sit on eggs (used of hens) **2** wanting to have a baby (used of women)

brook /brʊk/ n a stream

broom /bruːm, brʊm/ n a large brush which has a long handle and is used for sweeping

broom·stick /ˈbruːmˌstɪk, ˈbrʊm-/ n the long thin handle of a broom

broth /brɒθ ‖ brɔːθ/ n [U] thin soup made by cooking meat and vegetables in water and then removing them: *chicken broth*

broth·el /ˈbrɒθəl ‖ ˈbrɑː-, ˈbrɔː-/ n a house where men can pay women to have sex

broth·er /ˈbrʌðəʳ/ n **1** a male relative with the same parents: *John and Peter are brothers.* | *John is Peter's brother.* –see picture on page 343 **2** a male member of a religious group, especially a MONK: *a Christian brother* | *Evening prayers will be read by Brother John.*

broth·er·hood /ˈbrʌðəhʊd ‖ -ər-/ n **1** [U] the feeling of being united with other people as if you were brothers: *the brotherhood of man* **2** [C] a society of men living a religious life

brother-in-law /ˈ··· ·ˌ·/ n **brothers-in-law** **1** the brother of your husband or wife **2** the husband of your sister –see picture on page 343

broth·er·ly /ˈbrʌðəli ‖ -ər-/ adj kind and typical of a brother: *brotherly advice*

brought /brɔːt/ the past tense and past participle of BRING

brow /braʊ/ n fml **1** an EYEBROW **2** your FOREHEAD **3** **the brow of a hill** the upper part of a hill

brow·beat /ˈbraʊbiːt/ v **browbeat, browbeaten** /biːtn/, **browbeating** [T] to force someone to obey by using fierce looks or words: *Don't let them browbeat you into doing all the dirty work.*

brown¹ /braʊn/ adj of the colour of earth, wood, or coffee: *brown shoes* | *He's very brown after his holiday.* | *brown rice* | *brown paper* –**brown** n [C;U]: *We chose brown.* | *a dark brown* –see picture on page 147

brown² v [I;T] to make or become brown: *First, brown the meat in hot fat.*

browse /braʊz/ v **browsed, browsing** [I] **1** to feed on the leaves and young parts of bushes and trees **2** to look at things, especially books, without any particular purpose, for enjoyment: *I enjoy browsing through old magazines.* –**browse** n : *While you were out I had a good browse through your books.*

bruise¹ /bruːz/ n a discoloured place where the skin of a person or fruit has been damaged by a blow or fall

bruise² v **bruised, bruising** [T] to cause one or more bruises on something: *She fell and bruised her knee.* | *a bruised finger*

brunch /brʌntʃ/ n [C;U] infml a meal combining breakfast and the meal eaten in the middle of the day called **lunch**, and eaten in the middle of the morning

bru·nette /bruːˈnet/ n (also **brunet** AmE) a woman of a fair-skinned race with dark hair –see picture on page 245

brunt /brʌnt/ n **bear the brunt** to suffer the heaviest part of something unpleasant: *I had to bear the brunt of his anger.*

brush¹ /brʌʃ/ n **1** [C] a thing consisting of hairs on a handle that you use for things like putting paint on something, cleaning dirt off, or making your hair tidy: *a dustpan and brush* | *a clothes brush* | *a toothbrush* | *a paintbrush* **2** [C] an act of brushing: *I'll just give my hair a quick brush.* **3** [U] (also **brushwood**) small branches of trees or bushes **4** [U] small rough trees and bushes, or land covered by these **5** **have a brush with someone** infml to have a short and unpleasant meeting or argument with someone: *I've just had a brush with the law.*

brush² v [T] **1** to clean something or make something tidy with a brush: *Have you brushed your teeth?* | *I brushed my hair.* **2** to pass lightly over something: *The wind gently brushed his cheek.* **3** **brush past someone, brush by someone** to move past someone, perhaps carelessly or angrily, so that you touch them

brush sbdy/sthg ↔ **aside** phr v [T] to refuse to consider something seriously: *He brushed the difficulties aside.*

brush sbdy/sthg ↔ **away** phr v [T] **1** to refuse to consider something seriously: *She brushed his arguments away.* **2** to remove something with a brushing movement: *She brushed away a tear.* | *He brushed away a fly.*

brush ↔ **up** phr v [T] to study a subject again in order to relearn what you have forgotten: *I must brush up my French before I go to Paris.*

brush-off /ˈ· ·/ n **give someone the brush-off** infml to refuse to be friendly or to listen to someone: *I wanted to ask her out to dinner but she gave me the brush-off.*

brusque /bruːsk, brʊsk ‖ brʌsk/ adj quick and rather impolite: *He had a rather brusque manner.* –**brusquely** adv –**brusqueness** n [U]

brus·sels sprout /ˌbrʌsəlz ˈspraʊt/ n (also **sprout**) a green vegetable that is a small tight ball of leaves

bru·tal /ˈbruːtl/ adj **1** rough, cruel, and insensitive: *a brutal attack* **2** **the brutal truth** a fact that is true but unpleasant –**brutally** adv –**brutality** /bruːˈtælɪti/ n [C;U]: *the brutality of war*

bru·tal·ize /ˈbruːtəlaɪz/ v **brutalized, brutalizing** (also **brutalise** BrE) [T] **1** to make someone brutal

Comparative and superlative forms of adjectives are used to show an increase in quality, quantity, or degree.

Comparatives and superlatives are formed in various ways.

*The girls are all quite **tall**. Meg is **taller than** Gill. Sue is **the tallest** of the three.*

*These rings are **expensive**. The gold ring is **more expensive than** the silver one. The diamond ring is **the most expensive** of all.*

1. Adjectives of one syllable

By adding **-er** or **-est** to the end of the word;

tall   taller   tallest

rich   richer   richest

If the adjective already ends in **-e** you only need to add **-r** or **-st**

nice   nicer   nicest

rare   rarer   rarest

Sometimes, when the adjective ends in a single consonant, you need to double the final consonant before forming the comparative and superlative. The dictionary tells you when you need to do this:

big /bɪg/ *adj* **bigger, biggest**

big   bigger   biggest

fat   fatter   fattest

2. Adjectives of two syllables

If the word ends in **-y**, change the **-y** to **-i** and then add **-er** or **-est**. The dictionary tells you when you need to do this:

heav·y /ˈhevi/ *adj* **heavier, heaviest**

heavy   heavier   heaviest

happy   happier   happiest

If the adjective does NOT end in **-y**, then form the comparative and superlative using **more** and **most**:

useful   more useful   most useful

famous   more famous   most famous

3. Adjectives of three syllables or more

Form the comparative and superlative using **more** and **most**.

expensive   more expensive   most expensive

comfortable   more comfortable   most comfortable

4. 'Irregular' Comparatives and Superlatives

Some adjectives use a completely different word for the comparative and superlative forms. You can find these 'irregular' forms in the dictionary·

good¹ /gʊd/ *adj* **better, best**

good   better   best

bad   worse   worst

NOTE·

There are some exceptions to these general rules. The most important to remember are:

For adjectives which are formed from a verb and end in **-ed** or **-ing**, always use **more** and **most** for the comparative and superlative:

bored   more bored   most bored

boring   more boring   most boring

Adjectives which start with the negative prefix **un-** can use **-er** and **-est** even if they have three syllables:

unhappy   unhappier   unhappiest

2 to treat someone in a brutal manner –**brutalization** /ˌbruːtəl-aɪˈzeɪʃən ‖ -tələ-/ n [U]

brute /bruːt/ n **1** a rough, cruel, and insensitive person: *Her husband is a real brute.* **2** an animal, especially a large one (a word used to express disapproval) **3 brute force, brute strength** force used without any intelligence: *In the end I had to use brute force to open the box.*

brut·ish /ˈbruːtɪʃ/ adj very cruel: *Their life is nasty, brutish, and short.*

BSc /ˌbiː es ˈsiː/ (also **BS** AmE) **1** an abbreviation for BACHELOR OF SCIENCE, a first university degree in a science subject: *He has a BSc in Chemistry.* **2** someone who has a BSc: *Mary Jones, BSc*

bub·ble¹ /ˈbʌbəl/ n a hollow ball of liquid containing air or gas: *The water's boiling; look at the bubbles.* | *soap bubbles* | *to burst a bubble*

bubble² v **bubbled, bubbling** [I] **1** to form bubbles or rise as bubbles: *The gas bubbled to the surface of the water.* **2** to make the sound of bubbles rising in liquid: *We could hear the pot bubbling away quietly on the fire.* **3 bubble over with joy** to show great happiness

bubble gum /ˈ·· ·/ n [U] CHEWING GUM that can be blown into bubbles

bub·bly¹ /ˈbʌbli/ adj **1** full of bubbles **2** full of life: *a bubbly personality*

bubbly² n [U] old fash infml CHAMPAGNE

buck¹ /bʌk/ n **1** a male deer or rabbit **2** AmE infml an American dollar

buck² v **1** [I] (especially of a horse) to jump up and kick with the back legs **2** [T] to throw a rider off by doing this: *The horse bucked its first rider off.* **buck up** phr v **1** [I] to hurry up or make more effort **2** [I;T **buck** sbdy ↔ **up**] to make or become more cheerful

buck·et /ˈbʌkɪt/ n **1** a round plastic, metal, or wooden container with a handle, for carrying liquids –see picture on page 48 **2** (also **bucketful**) the contents of a bucket: *Give each tree a bucket of water.* **3 the rain came down in buckets** = it rained very hard

bucket² v **bucket down** phr v [I] BrE infml to rain very hard

buck·le¹ /ˈbʌkəl/ n a metal fastener for joining the ends of a belt or for decoration: *The buckle's come off my sandal.* –see picture on page 50

buckle² v **buckled, buckling 1** [I;T] to fasten with a buckle: *He buckled his belt tightly.* | *The straps buckled up easily.* | *The two ends buckle together at the back.* | *He buckled on his sword.* **2** [I;T] to make or become bent through heat, shock, or pressure: *The wheel of my bicycle was buckled in the accident.*| *The wheel buckled.* **buckle down** phr v [I] infml to begin to work seriously: *She buckled down to work.*

bud¹ /bʌd/ n **1** a young flower or leaf before it opens **2 come into bud** to form buds: *My roses are just coming into bud.* **3** AmE BUDDY (2)

bud² v -**dd**- [I] to produce buds

Bud·dhis·m /ˈbʊdɪzəm ‖ ˈbuː-, ˈbʊ-/ n [U] a religion of east and central Asia growing out of the teaching of Buddha and teaching that pureness of spirit is the answer to suffering –**Buddhist** n, adj

bud·ding /ˈbʌdɪŋ/ adj [only before a noun] beginning to develop: *a budding poet*

bud·dy /ˈbʌdi/ n **buddies** infml **1** a good friend

(usually used of a male friend of a man): *They're real buddies.* **2** AmE a way of talking to someone, especially a man, who you are angry with: *Get out of my way, buddy!*

budge /bʌdʒ/ v **budged, budging** [I;T] **1** to move a little: *I can't budge this rock.* | *This rock won't budge at all.* **2** to change a publicly stated position: *The union refused to budge on its demand for an 8% rise.*

bud·ger·i·gar /ˈbʌdʒərigɑːʳ/ n (also **budgie** infml) a small brightly coloured bird, often kept in a cage in British houses

bud·get¹ /ˈbʌdʒɪt/ n **1** a plan of how to arrange private or public spending: *the family budget* | *In his annual budget the Chancellor announced a rise in income tax.* **2** the quantity of money stated in these plans: *a budget of £10,000,000* | *running the Council on a very tight budget*

budget² v [I] to plan private or public spending within the limits of a certain amount of money: *We're having to budget very carefully at the moment.* | *She budgeted for a new car.* –**budgetary** adj

budget³ adj cheap and good value: *a budget buy* | *budget holidays*

bud·gie /ˈbʌdʒi/ n infml –see BUDGERIGAR

buff¹ /bʌf/ adj pale brown: *a buff envelope*

buff² v [T] (also **buff** sthg ↔ **up**) to polish metal with something soft, so that it shines

buff³ n infml a person who is very interested in and knows a lot about the stated subject: *a film buff* | *He's a bit of a wine buff.*

buf·fa·lo /ˈbʌfələʊ/ n **buffaloes** or **buffalos** any of several kinds of cattle with long flattish curved horns, found mainly in Asia, Africa, and North America

buff·er /ˈbʌfəʳ/ n **1** one of a pair of plates on springs fixed to a railway carriage or engine, or to the end of the railway track, which reduce the shock if the train hits anything **2** protection: *The Prime Minister's popularity in the country acted as a buffer against criticism from his colleagues.*

buf·fet¹ /ˈbʌfɪt/ v [T] to push or throw something repeatedly with great force: *We were buffeted by the wind and rain.*

buf·fet² /ˈbʊfeɪ ‖ bəˈfeɪ/ n **1** a meal, often laid out on a long table, and usually consisting of cold food, which people serve for themselves and eat standing up or sitting down near by **2** an informal restaurant which serves meals to travellers

buffet car /ˈbʊfeɪ ˌkɑː ‖ bəˈfeɪ ˌkɑːr/ n a part of a train where you can buy food and drink

buf·foon /bəˈfuːn/ n a rough and noisy fool –**buffoonery** n [U]

bug¹ /bʌg/ n **1** an insect, especially one which does damage or which people do not like: *The bed was full of bugs.* **2** a small living thing causing disease: *There are some nasty bugs going around at the moment.* | *He picked up a bug on his travels.* **3** something wrong with a piece of ELECTRONIC apparatus, especially a computer: *We'll have to iron out the bugs in that new program.* **4** an apparatus for listening secretly to other people's conversations: *The police tested the room for bugs.* **5** infml a very strong but often not lasting interest in something: *She's been bitten by the travel bug.*

bug² v -**gg**- [T] **1** to fit a place with a secret listening apparatus: *The embassy was bugged.* **2** infml to annoy someone: *What's bugging you?*

bug·gy /ˈbʌgi/ n **buggies** a seat on wheels used for

pushing a young child; buggies fold and are light so that you can carry them

bu·gle /ˈbjuːgəl/ n a brass musical instrument, played by blowing, used especially for army calls –**bugler** n

build¹ /bɪld/ v **built** /bɪlt/, **built**, **building** 1 [I;T] to make things like houses, factories, or ships: *They're building a new bridge.* | *The house was built of honey-coloured stone.* 2 [T] to develop something gradually: *It's our party's aim to build a better society.* | *to build confidence between the two countries* 3 **build on something** to use one success to gain another one: *He hopes to build on the increase in productivity by opening new factories.*
build sthg ↔ **in** phr v [T] to form something as a fixed part of something else and not add it on afterwards
build on phr v 1 [T **build** sthg ↔ **on**] to add another part to a building: *The garage was built on to the west end of the house in the 1930s.* 2 [T **build on** sthg] to use something as a base for further development: *Her new job will allow her to build on her previous experience in marketing.*
build up [I;T **build** sthg ↔ **up**] to make or become greater in quantity: *After four o'clock the traffic begins to build up.* | *She built the business up from nothing.* | *to build up your strength.*

build² n [C;U] the shape and size of the human body: *a tall man with a powerful build* | *We are of the same build.*

build·er /ˈbɪldər/ n a person whose job is building, especially someone who owns a building company: *a local firm of builders*

build·ing /ˈbɪldɪŋ/ n 1 [C] something with a roof and walls, such as a house, a factory, or an office block: *The World Trade Center is one of the world's tallest buildings.* | *historic buildings* 2 [U] the process or business of making buildings

building so·ci·e·ty /ˈ··· ·,···/ n building societies an organization in Britain into which people pay money in order to save it and gain interest, and which lends money to people who want to buy houses

build-up /ˈbɪld-ʌp/ n a gradual increase: *a military buildup* | *the buildup of traffic on the road*

built /bɪlt/ 1 the past tense and past participle of BUILD 2 **-built** formed in the stated way: *a heavily-built man*

built-in /ˌ·ˈ·◄/ adj planned as part of something and fixed into it: *a built-in washing-machine*

built-up /ˌ·ˈ·◄/ adj covered with buildings: *a built-up area*

bulb /bʌlb/ n 1 the round root of certain plants; bulbs grow leaves and flowers once a year, often in the spring 2 any object of this shape, especially the glass part of an electric lamp: *a light bulb*

bul·bous /ˈbʌlbəs/ adj fat and round with a narrow top: *a bulbous nose*

Bulgarian¹ /bʌlˈgeəriən/ adj from or connected with Bulgaria

Bulgarian² n 1 [C] a person from Bulgaria 2 [U] the language of Bulgaria

bulge¹ /bʌldʒ/ n a swelling of a surface caused by pressure: *a bulge in the wall*

bulge² v **bulged**, **bulging** [I] to swell out: *a bulging stomach* | *His pockets were bulging* **with** *money.*

bulk /bʌlk/ n 1 [U] great size or quantity, often combined with inconvenient shape 2 **the bulk of** the greater part of: *The bulk of the work has already*

been done. 3 **in bulk** in large quantities and not packed in separate containers: *We buy the goods in bulk.*

bulk·y /ˈbʌlki/ adj **bulkier**, **bulkiest** large and of an inconvenient shape: *a bulky parcel*

bull /bʊl/ n 1 the male of the cow, kept on farms to be the father of young cattle 2 **a bull in a china shop** infml a rough careless person in a place where skill and care are needed 3 **take the bull by the horns** infml to face difficulties in spite of fear

bull·dog /ˈbʊldɒg ‖ -dɔːg/ n a fierce dog of English origin, with a short neck and short thick legs

bull·doze /ˈbʊldəʊz/ v **bulldozed**, **bulldozing** [T] 1 to force objects and earth out of the way with a bulldozer 2 **bulldoze someone into doing something** to force someone into doing something

bull·doz·er /ˈbʊldəʊzər/ n a heavy machine used to make the surface of the ground level

bul·let /ˈbʊlɪt/ n a small piece of metal with a rounded or pointed end, fired from a gun

bul·le·tin /ˈbʊlətɪn/ n 1 a short official notice or news report intended to be made public without delay: *Here is the latest bulletin about the President's health.* 2 a short printed newspaper produced by an organization or group

bulletin board /ˈ··· ·/ n the usual American word for NOTICEBOARD

bull·fight /ˈbʊlfaɪt/ n a form of entertainment in Spain, Portugal, and Latin America in which a man fights, and usually kills, a BULL –**bullfighter** n –**bullfighting** n [U]

bul·lion /ˈbʊljən/ n [U] large pieces of gold or silver: *gold bullion*

bul·lock /ˈbʊlək/ n a young BULL which has had its sex organs removed so that it cannot breed

bull·ring /ˈbʊlˌrɪŋ/ n a circular place surrounded by rows of seats where bullfights take place

bull's-eye /ˈ· ·/ n the middle of a round board with circles on it which people try to hit when shooting: *Congratulations! It's a bull's-eye!*

bul·ly /ˈbʊli/ v **bullied**, **bullying** [I;T] to use your strength to hurt or frighten people who are not as strong as you are: *He had been bullied at school.* | *The older boys bullied us* **into** *stealing for them.* –**bully** n **bullies**

bul·rush /ˈbʊlrʌʃ/ n a tall grasslike plant that grows beside rivers

bul·wark /ˈbʊlwək ‖ -ərk/ n a strong wall built for defence or protection

bum¹ /bʌm/ n 1 BrE infml the part of your body on which you sit 2 AmE infml someone who has no home and lives by begging 3 infml someone who is considered worthless, lazy, or unable to do their job

bum² v **-mm-** [T] infml to ask for something without waiting for someone to offer it to you: *Can I bum a cigarette off you?*
bum about/around phr v [I] to travel around to different places for pleasure, usually with very little money

bum·ble /ˈbʌmbəl/ v **bumbled**, **bumbling** [I] infml to speak without making much sense, or so that the words are hard to hear clearly: *What are you bumbling on about now?*

bum·ble·bee /ˈbʌmbəlbiː/ n a large hairy bee which makes a loud noise when flying

bum·bling /ˈbʌmblɪŋ/ adj moving or behaving in a confused or disorganized way: *You bumbling idiot!*

bump¹ /bʌmp/ v 1 [I;T] to hit or knock something

by accident: *Mummy, I've bumped my head.* | *I bumped my knee against the wall.* | *Those cars are going to bump into each other.* **2** [I+adv/prep] to move along in an uneven way because the ground is not smooth: *We bumped along the track to the farm.*

bump into sbdy *phr v* [T] *infml* to meet someone by chance: *Guess who I bumped into this morning?*

bump sbdy ↔ **off** *phr v* [T] *infml* to murder someone

bump sbdy ↔ **up** *phr v* [T] *infml* to increase something: *You need a good result to bump up your average.*

bump² *n* **1** the sound of something hitting something else: *We heard a bump in the next room.* **2** a car accident which is not very serious: *I've just had a bump in the car.* **3** a raised round swelling on your body, often caused by someone hitting you: *He had a nasty bump on his head.* **4** an uneven part of a flat surface: *bumps in the road*

bum·per¹ /ˈbʌmpəʳ/ *n* **1** a bar fixed on the front and back of a car to protect it if it knocks against something –see picture on page 49 **2 bumper-to-bumper** very close together and not moving very fast (used of traffic)

bumper² *adj* [only before a noun] larger or greater than usual: *a bumper crop of potatoes*

bump·y /ˈbʌmpi/ *adj* **bumpier, bumpiest** not smooth: *a bumpy road* | *a bumpy ride*

bun /bʌn/ *n* **1** a small round sweet cake **2** hair fastened into a tight round shape at the back of your head: *She wears her hair in a bun.*

bunch¹ /bʌntʃ/ *n* **1** a number of things of the same kind fastened, held, or growing together at one point: *I gave her a bunch of flowers.* | *a bunch of bananas* | *a bunch of keys* **2** *infml* a group of people who are similar in some way: *They're all nice in my department, but John is the best of the bunch.* | *My students are quite a nice bunch.*

bunch² *v* [T] to form into close groups: *The leaders are bunched together a long way ahead of the other runners.*

bun·dle¹ /ˈbʌndl/ *n* **1** a number of things tied together or wrapped up so that you can carry them easily **2 a bundle of nerves** extremely nervous: *I'm a bundle of nerves.*

bundle² *v* **bundled, bundling** [I+adv/prep; T+adv/prep] to move or hurry in a rather quick and rough manner: *The police bundled him into a car and drove away.* | *We all bundled into the bus.* | *They bundled the children off to school.*

bundle sthg ↔ **up** *phr v* [T] to collect things together quickly and untidily: *She bundled up her knitting and went to answer the phone.*

bung¹ /bʌŋ/ *n* a round piece of rubber, wood or other material used to close the hole in a container

bung² *v* [T + adv/prep] *BrE infml* to put, push, or throw something somewhere quickly and carelessly: *Bung the butter in the fridge, will you?*

bung sthg ↔ **up** *phr v* [T] *infml* to block something: *My nose is bunged up.*

bun·ga·low /ˈbʌŋgələʊ/ *n* a house which is built on one level –see HOUSE (USAGE) –see picture on page 44

bun·gle /ˈbʌŋgəl/ *v* **bungled, bungling** [I;T] to do something badly: *He'll bungle the job.* **–bungler** *n*

bun·ion /ˈbʌnjən/ *n* a painful swelling on your big toe

bunk /bʌŋk/ *n* **1** [C] a narrow bed fixed to a wall on a ship or train **2** [C] (also **bunk bed**) one of two beds

placed one above the other, often for children **3** [U] *infml* nonsense: *That's a load of bunk.* **4 do a bunk** *BrE infml* to leave without telling anyone

bun·ker /ˈbʌŋkəʳ/ *n* **1** a place to store coal, usually on a ship or outside a house **2** a shelter, usually built underground, for protection against military attack **3** a large hole on a GOLF COURSE

buoy¹ /bɔɪ ‖ ˈbuːi, bɔɪ/ *n* a floating object fastened to the bottom of the sea which shows ships where there are rocks or where it is safe to go

buoy² *v* [T] **1** to keep something at a high level **2** to keep someone cheerful: *Her spirits were buoyed up by hopes of success.*

buoy·an·cy /ˈbɔɪənsi ‖ ˈbɔɪənsi, ˈbuːjənsi/ *n* [U] **1** the tendency of an object to float or the power of a liquid to make something float: *the buoyancy of light wood* **2** the ability of prices or business to return to a high level after a problem: *the buoyancy of the American market* **3** the ability to remain cheerful or to recover quickly from disappointment –**buoyant** *adj* : *The financial markets are still buoyant.*

bur·ble /ˈbɜːbəl ‖ ˈbɜːr-/ *v* **burbled, burbling** [I] **1** to make a sound like a stream flowing over stones **2** to talk quickly but in a way that makes little sense: *He burbled on for hours.*

bur·den¹ /ˈbɜːdn ‖ ˈbɜːr-/ *n fml* **1** something heavy that you have to carry **2** something which continually worries you or is difficult to bear: *the burden of responsibility*

burden² *v* [T] *fml* **1** to give someone a lot of heavy things to carry: *Burdened with so much equipment, I climbed with difficulty.* **2 burden someone with something** to cause someone a lot of worry or trouble: *I won't burden you with my problems.*

bu·reau /ˈbjʊərəʊ/ *n* **bureaux** /ˈbjʊərəʊz/ **1** *BrE* a large desk or writing-table with a wooden cover which slides over the top to close it **2** the usual American word for a CHEST OF DRAWERS **3** a division of a government department **4** an office where a particular kind of work is done: *an information bureau*

bu·reauc·ra·cy /bjʊəˈrɒkrəsi ‖ -ˈrɑː-/ *n* **bureaucracies 1** [C;U] a system of government by many officials who are appointed rather than elected; **bureaucracy** sometimes means these officials **2** [U] a system of doing things officially which is annoying, unnecessarily difficult to understand, and usually ineffective

bu·reau·crat /ˈbjʊərəkræt/ *n* an official who works in a government department and who follows all the rules carefully, perhaps too carefully

bu·reau·crat·ic /ˌbjʊərəˈkrætɪk◂/ *adj* taking a long time to do things because there are lots of official rules: *bureaucratic procedures*

bur·ger /ˈbɜːgəʳ ‖ ˈbɜːr-/ *n* small pieces of meat made into a round flat shape and fried before eating

bur·glar /ˈbɜːgləʳ ‖ ˈbɜːr-/ *n* someone who gets into a house or shop illegally in order to steal things –see THIEF (USAGE)

burglar a·larm /ˈ··· ·ˌ·/ *n* an apparatus that makes a loud warning noise when a thief breaks into a building

bur·glar·y /ˈbɜːgləri ‖ ˈbɜːr-/ *n* **burglaries** [C;U] the crime of entering a building by force with the intention of stealing things

bur·gle /ˈbɜːgəl ‖ ˈbɜːr-/ *v* **burgled, burgling** (also **burglarize** /ˈbɜːgləraɪz ‖ ˈbɜːr-/ *AmE*) [I;T] to break into a building and steal from it: *I was burgled while I was out last night.*

bur·i·al /ˈberɪəl/ *n* [C;U] the act or ceremony of putting a dead body into a grave

bur·ly /ˈbɜːli ‖ ˈbɜːrli/ *adj* big and strong (used of a person) **–burliness** *n* [U]

burn[1] /bɜːn ‖ bɜːrn/ *v* **burnt** /bɜːnt ‖ bɜːrnt/ *or* **burned** /bɜːnd ‖bɜːrnd/, **burnt** *or* **burned** **1** [I] to be on fire: *It looked as if the whole city was burning.* | *The wood was damp, so didn't burn easily.* **2** [T] to damage, hurt, or destroy something by means of heat or fire: *You should burn all those old papers.* | *I burnt my hand on the iron.* | *Careful you don't burn the meat.* | *If you go out in this hot sun you'll get burned.* **3** [I] (of food) to be spoilt by being cooked too much or too quickly: *Oh no, the potatoes have burnt.* **4** [T] to use something for power, heating, or lighting: *This boiler will burn oil or coal.* **5** [I] to be or feel very hot: *My face was burning.* **6 burning with** full of a strong feeling: *She was burning with desire.* **7 be burning to do something** to be very eager to do something: *I was burning to tell everyone the news.* **8 burn your boats/bridges** to do something which means that you will not be able to change your mind and do something different later: *We must be careful not to burn our boats.*

burn away *phr v* [I] to disappear by being burnt: *The wood had burnt away to nothing.*

burn down *phr v* **1** [I] (of a building) to be destroyed by being burnt: *The cinema burnt down last year.* **2** [T **burn** sthg ↔ **down**] to destroy a building by burning it: *The school was burnt down by vandals.*

burn sthg ↔ **off** *phr v* [T] to remove something by burning: *He was badly injured in the accident, and all his hair was burnt off.*

burn out *phr v* **1** [I] to stop working because of damage caused by heat: *The engine had burned out.* **2 the fire burned out, the fire burned itself out** the fire stopped burning because there was nothing left to burn **3 burn yourself out** to become ill or very tired by working too hard

burn up *phr v* **1** [I] to be destroyed by being burned: *The rocket burnt up when it re-entered the earth's atmosphere.* **2** [I] (of a fire or a flame) to burn more brightly or more strongly **3** [T **burn** sthg ↔ **up**] to use a lot of fuel: *This engine really burns up petrol!*

■ USAGE In British English **burned** is used as the past tense or past participle of **burn** only if the verb is intransitive: *The fire* **burned** *brightly*. But if the verb is transitive **burnt** is more usual: *She* **burnt** *his letters.*

burn[2] *n* a place on your skin where you have been burned: *Many of the victims suffered severe burns.*

burn·ing /ˈbɜːnɪŋ ‖ ˈbɜːr-/ *adj* **1** being on fire: *a burning house* **2** very hot: *a burning fever* **3** [only before a noun] very important or urgent: *The environment is one of the burning issues of our time.* **4** [only before a noun] powerful or very strong (used of feelings): *a burning desire* | *a burning ambition*

bur·nished /ˈbɜːnɪʃ ‖ ˈbɜːr-/ *adj* polished with something hard and smooth (used of metal)

burnt /bɜːnt ‖ bɜːrnt/ the past tense and past participle of BURN[1]

burnt-out /ˌ· ˈ·◄/ *adj* **1** completely destroyed by fire **2** very tired and possibly ill from too much hard work

burp /bɜːp ‖ bɜːrp/ *v infml* **1** [T] to help a baby to get rid of stomach gas, usually by rubbing or gently striking its back **2** [I] to make a noise as stomach gas suddenly rises to your mouth **–burp** *n*

bur·row[1] /ˈbʌrəʊ ‖ ˈbɜːrəʊ/ *n* a hole in the ground made by an animal such as a rabbit, in which it lives or hides

burrow[2] *v* **1** [I+adv/prep] to move in a particular direction by digging: *They burrowed under the fence.* **2** [I;T] to press close to someone or under something as if looking for warmth, safety, or love: *He burrowed under the bedclothes.*

bur·sar /ˈbɜːsəʳ ‖ ˈbɜːr-/ *n* someone in a college or school who is responsible for the accounts

bur·sa·ry /ˈbɜːsəri ‖ ˈbɜːr-/ *n* a sum of money given to a student to help pay for a course of study

burst[1] /bɜːst ‖ bɜːrst/ *v* **burst, burst, bursting** **1** [I;T] to break open or apart suddenly because of too much pressure inside, causing the contents to come out: *Don't drive over those nails – you'll burst a tyre.* | *Help! I've got a burst water pipe!* | *That balloon will burst if you leave it in the sun.* **2 be bursting with** to be very full of something: *The town is bursting with tourists.* –see BREAK (USAGE) **3 burst open** to open violently and suddenly: *The door burst open and the police stormed in.* **4** [I + adv/prep] to move suddenly and quickly in a way that is noticed: *He burst angrily into the room.* **5 bursting to do something** extremely keen to do something: *She's bursting to tell you her news.* **6** [I] to make a sudden loud noise: *A cheer burst from the crowd.* **7 burst into flames** suddenly to begin to burn

burst in on sbdy *phr v* [T] to interrupt someone suddenly and noisily: *They burst in on me while I was working.*

burst into sthg *phr v* [T] to start doing something, for example, crying, laughing, or singing: *She burst into tears.* | *We burst into fits of laughter.*

burst out *phr v* **1 burst out laughing/crying** to begin laughing or crying suddenly **2** [I] to say suddenly and with strong feeling: *"I don't believe it!" he burst out.*

burst[2] *n* **1** the result of something which has burst: *a burst in the water pipes* **2** a sudden short period of great activity, loud noise, or strong feeling: *a burst of laughter* | *a burst of machine-gun fire*

bur·y /ˈberi/ *v* **buried, buried, burying** [T] **1** to put a dead body into a grave: *She was buried next to her late husband.* **2** to cover something up either intentionally or accidentally: *The dog has buried a bone in the garden.* | *His glasses were buried under a pile of newspapers.* **3 bury yourself in something** to work very hard at something on your own: *After his wife's death, he buried himself in his business.* **4 bury the hatchet** *infml* to become friends again after a quarrel

bus[1] /bʌs/ *n* **1** a large motor vehicle which takes people from one place to another: *I hope she catches the bus.* | *You're going to miss the bus.* –see picture on page 735 **2 by bus** travelling in a bus: *Let's go by bus.* –see TRANSPORT (USAGE)

bus[2] *v* **-ss-** [T] to move people by bus: *The village children are bussed to the school in the nearest town.*

bus con·duc·tor /ˈ· ·ˌ··/ *n* someone on a bus who is in charge of selling tickets

bush /bʊʃ/ *n* **1** a low woody plant, smaller than a tree and with many stems: *a rose bush* –see picture on page 441 **2 the bush** uncleared wild country in Australia or Africa

bush·y /ˈbʊʃi/ *adj* **bushier, bushiest** growing thickly (usually used of hair): *a bushy beard* | *a bushy tail* **–bushiness** *n* [U]

bus·i·ly /ˈbɪzᵻli/ *adv* in an active way: *She bustled around busily.*

busi·ness /'bɪznɪs/ n 1 [U] the work you do as a job to earn money: *I'm in the insurance business.* | *He's here on business, not for pleasure.* 2 [U] the production, buying, and selling of goods and services: *She wants to go into business when she leaves college.* | *He set up in business as a property developer.* 3 **do business with someone** to buy something from someone, or sell something to them: *It's a pleasure to do business with you.* 4 [U] the amount or value of trade being done: *"How's business?"* | *Business is booming.* 5 [C] an organization which provides a service or buys and sells something: *He runs a small travel business in town.* | *It's a very profitable business.* 6 [U] your responsibility or concern: *What I do with the money is none of your business.* 7 [sing; U] a situation, event, or matter for talking about together: *Let's get down to the main business of the meeting.* | *It's a strange business.* | *Investing in shares is a risky business.* 8 **have no business to do something, have no business doing something** to have no right to do something 9 **get down to business** to start dealing with the most important subject 10 **out of business** no longer able to operate as a business: *These big increases in rent could put a lot of small shops out of business.*

busi·ness·like /'bɪznɪs-laɪk/ adj acting quickly, calmly, and with common sense: *Kate conducted the meeting in a businesslike way.*

busi·ness·man /'bɪznɪsmən/ n **businessmen** /-mən/ 1 a man who works in business, for example as the owner, director, or manager of a company 2 a man who knows how to make money from good deals: *You won't be able to knock the price down. He's a very good businessman.*

busi·ness·wom·an /'bɪznɪswʊmən/ n **businesswomen** /-'wɪmɪn/ 1 a woman who works in business, for example as the owner, director, or manager of a company 2 a woman who knows how to make money from good deals

bus·ker /'bʌskər/ n a person who plays music in the street for money

bus stop /'· ·/ n a fixed place where buses stop for passengers: *I saw him waiting at the bus stop.*

bust¹ /bʌst/ v **busted** or **bust**, **busted** or **bust** [T] *infml* 1 to break something: *I bust my watch this morning.* 2 (of the police) to take someone to a police station because they have done something wrong: *He was busted for possessing marijuana.* 3 (of the police) to enter a place without warning to look for something illegal
bust up phr v *infml* 1 [I] to quarrel and end a relationship: *I've bust up with my boyfriend.* 2 [T **bust sthg ↔ up**] to spoil something and make it come to an end: *"Why are the police here?" "Apparently Greenpeace are planning to bust up the meeting."*

bust² n 1 a piece of SCULPTURE showing someone's head, shoulders, and chest 2 a woman's breasts 3 a measurement round a woman's breasts and back: *She's got a 34-inch bust.*

bust³ adj *infml* 1 broken: *My watch is bust.* 2 **go bust** (of a business) to fail because it cannot pay the money that it owes, so that it has to close: *I'm not surprised he went bust, considering the risks he took.*

bus·tle¹ /'bʌsəl/ v **bustled**, **bustling** [I] to move in a hurried and determined way because you are very busy: *She bustled about the house.* –**bustling** adj : *a bustling market town*

bustle² n [U] excitement, noise, and great activity: *the bustle of a big city*

bust-up /'· ·/ n *infml* 1 a fight: *There was quite a bust-up last night outside the cinema.* 2 the end of a relationship, usually following a serious quarrel: *the bust-up of their marriage*

bus·y¹ /'bɪzi/ adj **busier**, **busiest** 1 having a lot of work or other things to do so that you are not free for anything else: *She's busy now. Can you come back later?* | *I was too busy working to notice the time.* | *a busy man* 2 full of work or activity: *a busy day* | *one of the busiest airports in the world* 3 in use (used of telephones): *I'm sorry, sir, the line is busy.* –**busily** adv

busy² v **busied**, **busied**, **busying: busy yourself with something** to give yourself something to do: *He busied himself with answering letters.*

bus·y·bod·y /'bɪzi,bɒdi ‖ -,bɑːdi/ n someone who takes too much interest in other people's affairs and may try to give advice which is not wanted

but¹ /bət; *strong* bʌt/ conj 1 a word you use when you are saying something which is opposite to or different from something else that you have just said: *I'd like to go, but I can't.* | *It costs a lot of money, but it's well worth it.* | *We were going to come and see you, but it rained so we stayed at home.* | *The house was small but pleasant.* | *He won not one but two prizes!* 2 a word you use when you are surprised by what someone else has just said, and are also pleased, shocked, angry, etc: *"They've decided to close the school down." "But that's ridiculous!"* | *"Mary's leaving tomorrow." "But she only arrived yesterday!"* | *"He's finally managed to get a job." "But that's wonderful news!"* 3 a word you use when you are introducing a new subject: *Later in the programme we'll be discussing the progress of the war. But first here are the news headlines.* | *I'm sure there's a lot more that could be said on this subject, but let's move on to our next question.* 4 used after expressions such as "I'm sorry" and "excuse me": *I'm sorry, but could you repeat that, please?* | *Excuse me, but haven't I met you somewhere before?* 5 **but then** an expression you use when you are adding something that shows that a fact is not surprising: *It's not a very sophisticated computer, but then it only cost a few hundred pounds.*

but² prep 1 except: *There's no one here but me.* | *All but one of the ships were destroyed.* 2 **but for** except for the efforts of a particular person or the effects of a particular thing: *But for her, I would have drowned.* | *But for his help, I would probably still be stranded there now.* 3 **the next but one** the one after the next one 4 **the last but one** the one before the last one

butch /bʊtʃ/ adj BrE *infml* dressing and behaving too much like a big strong man (used of women)

butch·er¹ /'bʊtʃər/ n 1 someone who works in or owns a shop which sells meat 2 **butcher's** a shop which sells meat: *I'm just going to the butcher's to get something for dinner.*

butcher² v [T] 1 to kill animals for their meat 2 to kill people in a cruel way –see KILL (USAGE)

but·ler /'bʌtlər/ n the chief male servant of a house

butt¹ /bʌt/ v [I;T] to hit or push against something with the head or horns
butt in phr v [I] *infml* to interrupt a conversation when you have not been asked for your opinion: *I wish you wouldn't keep butting in on us.*

butt² n 1 the thick end of a tool or weapon: *a rifle butt* 2 the small piece of a cigarette which is left when you have finished smoking 3 someone that people make fun of: *Poor John was the butt of all* *their jokes.* **4** *infml* the part of your body that you sit on: *Get off your butt and do some work.*

but·ter¹ /ˈbʌtəʳ/ *n* [U] **1** a fairly solid yellow fat made from cream and spread on bread or used in cooking –see picture on page 344 **2 butter wouldn't melt in his mouth** *infml* =he looks as if he would never do anything wrong but this is never really so –**buttery** *adj*

butter² *v* [T] to spread something with butter: *Shall I butter your bread for you?*

butter sbdy ↔ **up** *phr v* [T] *infml* to praise or please someone because you want them to do something for you

but·ter·cup /ˈbʌtəkʌp ‖ -ər-/ *n* a small plant with yellow flowers which grows in fields

but·ter·fly /ˈbʌtəflaɪ ‖ -ər-/ *n* **butterflies 1** [C] a delicate insect which has large beautifully-coloured wings **2 have butterflies in your stomach** *infml* to feel very nervous before doing something **3** [U] (also **butterfly stroke**) a way of swimming on your front in which you move both your arms together over your head

but·ter·scotch /ˈbʌtəskɒtʃ ‖ -ərskɑːtʃ/ *n* [U] a sweet food made from sugar and butter boiled together

but·tock /ˈbʌtək/ *n* **buttocks** the two fleshy parts of your body on which you sit

but·ton¹ /ˈbʌtn/ *n* **1** a small hard object, usually fixed to one part of a piece of clothing and passed through a hole in another part to join them together: *Do your buttons up, Mary.* –see picture on page 50 **2** a small object or piece of apparatus that is pressed to start a machine: *Which button do I press first?*

button² *v* [T] to close or fasten something with buttons: *Button your coat! It's cold outside.*

button sthg ↔ **up** *phr v* [T] **1** to close or fasten something with buttons **2** *infml* to complete something successfully: *The new contract is all buttoned up now.*

but·ton·hole¹ /ˈbʌtnhəʊl/ *n* **1** a hole for a button to be put through to fasten a shirt or coat **2** *BrE* a flower to wear in a buttonhole or pinned to your coat or dress

buttonhole² *v* **buttonholed, buttonholing** [T] *infml* to stop someone and force them to listen to you: *She buttonholed me in the corridor and asked me for another pay rise.*

but·tress¹ /ˈbʌtrɪs/ *n* a support for a wall

buttress² *v* **1** to support something with a buttress **2** *fml* to support or strengthen something: *Buttressed by its past profits, the company managed to survive for another five years.*

bux·om /ˈbʌksəm/ *adj* attractively healthy-looking, usually with large breasts (an old-fashioned word which is now usually used humorously)

buy¹ /baɪ/ *v* **bought** /bɔːt/, **bought, buying 1** [I;T] to obtain something by paying money: *We bought the flat for £50,000.* | *Let me buy you a drink.* | *They bought the car secondhand from their neighbours.* | *When prices are low, I buy.*
□ **USEFUL PATTERNS:** to buy something for someone; to buy someone something; to buy something + adjective
2 [T] *infml* to be willing to believe something: *The police will never buy a story like that.* **3 buy time** *infml* to delay an action or decision that seems to be coming too soon: *He tried to buy time by doing a lot of talking.*

buy sbdy ↔ **off** *phr v* [T] to pay someone money so that they do not carry out a threat or cause trouble

buy sbdy ↔ **out** *phr v* **1** [T] to gain control of a business by buying all the shares which you do not already own **2 buy yourself out** to pay money so that you can leave the army before you should: *He bought himself out of the army.*

buy sthg ↔ **up** *phr v* [T] to buy all of something that it is possible to buy: *All the suitable building land has been bought up by property developers.*

buy² *n* *infml* something bought, especially something of value at a low price: *It's a good buy at that price!*

buy·er /ˈbaɪəʳ/ *n* **1** someone who chooses and buys things to be sold in a large shop **2** someone who is buying: *We've got a buyer for our flat!*

buzz¹ /bʌz/ *v* **1** [I] to make the continuous sound that bees make **2** [I] to be full of people talking excitedly: *The room buzzed* **with** *excitement.* **3** [I;T] to call someone by using a buzzer: *She buzzed for her secretary.* **4 buzz off** *BrE infml* go away: *Buzz off and stop bothering me.*

buzz² *n* **1** the sound of bees **2** a feeling of excitement **3 give someone a buzz** *infml* to telephone someone: *I'll give you a buzz tomorrow.*

buz·zard /ˈbʌzəd ‖ -ərd/ *n* a large brown bird that kills and eats other creatures

buz·zer /ˈbʌzəʳ/ *n* a piece of electrical machinery that makes a buzzing sound

by¹ /baɪ/ *prep* **1** near: *He was standing by the window.* –see picture on page 540 **2** past: *She rushed by me.* **3** through using or doing something: *The burglars got in by an open window.* | *He makes his living by writing.* **4** used to show who did something or what caused something: *The house was built by my father.* | *a play by Shakespeare* | *The school was damaged by fire.* **5** no later than a particular time: *I've got to get this finished by Friday.* **6** in accordance with something: *By law employers have to make sure that their machinery is safe.* | *He never plays by the rules.* **7** used in measurements and numbers: *a room 15 feet by 20 feet* | *Divide the total by three.* | *What's seven multiplied by eight?*

by² *adv* **1** past: *She moved aside to let me get by.* **2 by and by** *infml* a little bit later **3 by and large** in general: *By and large I agree with you.*

bye /baɪ/ *interj infml* (also **bye-bye**) a word used when you leave someone or someone leaves you

by-e·lec·tion /ˈ· ·ˌ··/ *n* a special election held when a Member of Parliament suddenly dies or leaves his or her position

by·gone /ˈbaɪɡɒn ‖ -ɡɔːn/ *adj* [only before a noun] of a time long ago: *relics of a bygone age*

by·gones /ˈbaɪɡɒnz ‖ -ɡɔːnz/ *n* **let bygones be bygones** *infml* to forgive and forget the bad things in the past

by·pass¹ /ˈbaɪpɑːs ‖ -pæs/ *n* **1** a road around a busy town: *the Oxford bypass* **2** a way of directing blood through new tubes to avoid the part of someone's heart which is not working properly

bypass² *v* [T] to avoid something: *Can we bypass Derby?* | *I bypassed the usual complaints procedure by writing directly to the owner of the company.*

by-prod·uct /ˈ· ˌ··/ *n* **1** something additional which is produced when making or doing something else: *Silver is often obtained as a by-product during the separation of lead from rock.* **2** an additional result, sometimes unexpected or unintended

by·stand·er /ˈbaɪˌstændəʳ/ *n* someone standing near, but not taking part in what is happening: *The*

police asked bystanders about the accident. | *I was just an innocent bystander.*

byte /baɪt/ *n tech* a unit of computer information

by·way /'baɪweɪ/ *n* a small road or path which is not much used or known

by·word /'baɪwɜːd ‖ -ɜːrd/ *n* a person, place, or thing that is taken as representing some quality: *The general's name had become a byword for cruelty in war.*

C,c

C,c /siː/ **C's, c's** or **Cs, cs** – **1** the 3rd letter of the English alphabet **2** when you have several points you want to make, you can order them and show where each one starts by using "a", "b", "c", etc.; teachers and speakers on technical subjects do this: *There are three factors which have contributed to the plant's failure to flower: a, the day length has been too long; b, the temperature has not been sufficiently high; and, c, the growing medium has been too acid.*

c 1 a written abbreviation for CENT **2** a written abbreviation for CIRCA: *c 1834*

C an abbreviation for CENTIGRADE or CELSIUS: *100°C*

cab /kæb/ n **1** a taxi: *Shall we walk or take a cab?* **2** **by cab** travelling in a cab: *Let's go by cab.* **3** the part of a bus or railway engine in which the driver sits or stands **4** a horse-drawn carriage for hire in former times

cab·a·ret /'kæbəreɪ ‖ ˌkæbə'reɪ/ n [C;U] entertainment, usually singing and dancing, in a restaurant or club at night

cab·bage /'kæbɪdʒ/ n [C;U] a large round vegetable with thick green leaves –see picture on page 344

cab·in /'kæbɪn/ n **1** a small room on a ship usually used for sleeping **2** a small roughly built wooden house: *a log cabin* **3** the enclosed space at the front of an aircraft in which the pilot sits

cab·i·net /'kæbɪnɪt, 'kæbnɪt/ n **1** a piece of furniture, with shelves or drawers, used for storing or showing things: *She keeps her most expensive china in a glass cabinet.* | *a medicine cabinet* **2** [+ sing/pl verb] the most important ministers of the government, who meet as a group to make decisions or to advise the head of the government: *The cabinet meets next week to discuss education.*

ca·ble¹ /'keɪbəl/ n **1** [C;U] thick, heavy rope usually made of wire, used on board ships and to support bridges **2** [C;U] a set of wires which carry electricity, television signals, or telephone messages: *a cable connecting the printer to the computer* | *an underwater telephone cable* **3** [C] *fml* a TELEGRAM **4** [U] CABLE TELEVISION

ca·ble² v **cabled, cabling** [I;T] to send something by TELEGRAM: *He cabled the news to London.* | *I cabled him some money.*

cable car /'··· ·/ n a vehicle which is supported in the air by a cable, used for carrying people to the tops of mountains

cable tel·e·vi·sion /ˌ··· ···'···/ n [U] a system of broadcasting television by cable, usually paid for by the user

cack·le /'kækəl/ v **cackled, cackling** [I] **1** to make the noise made by a hen **2** to laugh loudly and unpleasantly with a sound like this: *The old man cackled with amusement.*

cac·tus /'kæktəs/ n **cactuses** or **cacti** /taɪ/ a desert plant protected by sharp prickles, with thick fleshy stems and leaves

ca·dav·er /kə'deɪvəʳ, kə'dæ- ‖ kə'dæ-/ n *fml* a dead human body

ca·dence /'keɪdəns/ n **1** a regular beat of sound **2** the rise and fall of the human voice

ca·det /kə'det/ n a person studying to become an officer in one of the armed forces or the police

cadge /kædʒ/ v **cadged, cadging** [I;T] *infml* to get or try to get something by asking, often seeming to be taking advantage of someone: *He cadged 50p for cigarettes from me yesterday.*

cae·sar·e·an /sɪˈzeəriən/ n (also **cesarean**) an operation in which a woman's body is cut open to allow the baby to be taken out, when an ordinary birth may be difficult or dangerous

ca·fe /'kæfeɪ ‖ kæ'feɪ, kə-/ n (also **café**) a small restaurant where drinks and light meals are served

caf·e·te·ri·a /ˌkæfɪ'tɪəriə/ n a restaurant, often in a factory or college, where people collect their own food and drink and carry it to a table

caf·feine /'kæfiːn ‖ kæ'fiːn/ n [U] a chemical substance found in coffee and tea which makes people feel more active

cage /keɪdʒ/ n an enclosure made of a framework of wires or bars, used especially for keeping animals or birds in –**caged** adj : *a caged bird*

cag·ey /'keɪdʒi/ adj infml secretive or unwilling to give information: *She's very cagey about her past life.* –**cagily** adv

ca·jole /kə'dʒəʊl/ v **cajoled, cajoling** [T] to persuade someone to do something by using false praise or deceit: *I was cajoled into taking the job.*

cake /keɪk/ n **1** [C;U] a sweet food made by baking flour, eggs, fat, and sugar: *a birthday cake* | *Would you like a piece of cake?* **2** [C] a flat shaped piece of something: *a fish cake* | *a cake of soap* **3** **be a piece of cake** infml to be very easy: *That exam was a piece of cake!* **4** **have your cake and eat it** infml to have both the choices that are offered: *You spend all you money on beer and then complain about being poor. You can't have your cake and eat it.* **5** **go/sell like hot cakes** to be sold very quickly: *Those pictures are going like hot cakes.*

caked /keɪkt/ adj thickly covered or formed into a hard mass: *My boots were caked with mud.*

ca·lam·i·ty /kə'læmɪti/ n calamities [C;U] a sudden terrible event that causes great loss and suffering: *It would be an absolute calamity for these villages if the river flooded again.*

cal·ci·um /'kælsiəm/ n [U] a silver-white metallic ELEMENT found in bones, teeth, and chalk

cal·cu·late /'kælkjʊleɪt -kjə-/ v **calculated, calculating** [I;T;+(that)] to find out or make a firm guess about something, often by using numbers: *Have you calculated the total yet?* | *The experts have calculated that the market for these computers will expand by 200% next year.* | *We'll have to calculate how much we can spend on advertising.* □ USEFUL PATTERNS to calculate something; to calculate (that)...; to calculate when, how much....

cal·cu·lat·ed /'kælkjʊleɪtɪd/ adj **1** intentionally planned to gain a particular result: *a calculated threat* **2** **a calculated risk** something you decide to do although you know that it may have bad results: *I took a calculated risk when I bought those shares.*

cal·cu·lat·ing /'kælkjʊleɪtɪŋ/ adj making careful plans to get what you want, without considering the effects on other people (a word used to express disapproval): *a cold, calculating killer*

cal·cu·la·tion /ˌkælkjʊˈleɪʃən/ *n* [C;U] the result of using numbers to work out an amount: *The calculations are based on the latest statistics.*

cal·cu·la·tor /ˈkælkjʊˌleɪtəʳ/ *n* a small machine which can perform calculations: *a pocket calculator* –see picture on page 539

cal·cu·lus /ˈkælkjʊləs/ *n* [U] a way of making calculations in MATHEMATICS about quantities which are continually changing, such as the speed of a falling stone or the slope of a curved line

cal·dron /ˈkɔːldrən/ *n* see CAULDRON

cal·en·dar /ˈkælɪndəʳ/ *n* 1 a list showing the days and months of the year: *a desk calendar | According to the calendar, Christmas falls on a Monday this year.* –see picture on page 539 2 a system for fixing the beginning, length and divisions of a year and putting the days, weeks and months in a particular order: *the Muslim calendar* 3 a calendar month one of the 12 divisions of the year: *From January 1st to February 1st is one calendar month.*

calf /kɑːf ‖ kæf/ *n* calves /kɑːvz ‖ kævz/ 1 the young of the cow or of other large animals such as the elephant –see MEAT (USAGE) 2 the fleshy back part of your leg between your knee and your ankle

cal·i·bre /ˈkælɪbəʳ/ *n* (also caliber *AmE*) 1 [*sing*;U] the quality of something or someone: *This work is of a very high calibre.* 2 [C] the size of a bullet or the inside size of a gun

cal·i·co /ˈkælɪkəʊ/ *n* [U] a heavy cotton cloth

call¹ /kɔːl/ *v* 1 [I;T] to say something in a loud voice because you want someone to hear you: *She called to her friends. | I heard someone call my name. | "Hello," she called. | He called for help.* 2 be called to have a particular name: *She was engaged to a man called Fred Emmerson. | What's your dog called? | Her latest novel is called "The Lonely City".* 3 [T] to give something or someone a name: *What are you going to call the baby? | If I had a son, I'd call him Joshua. | Her full name is Patricia, but her friends all call her Pat.* 4 [T] to say that someone or something has a particular quality or is a particular thing: *Are you calling me a liar? | She called me stupid and incompetent.* 5 [T] to ask someone to come to where you are, either by shouting to them, or by telephoning them or sending them a message: *My mother was calling me. | He called me over to his desk. | The minister has called union leaders to a meeting. | I'd better call a doctor.* 6 [I;T] to telephone someone: *I picked up the phone and called my office. | I just called to ask how you were.* 7 [T] to arrange for something to take place: *The president called an election. | The prime minister has called an emergency meeting of the Cabinet to discuss the crisis.* 8 [I] to make a short visit to someone: *I'll call to collect the money tomorrow. | I called at my aunt's on my way home.* 9 [I] (of an animal) to make its usual cry: *I could hear doves calling in the woods.* 10 call a halt to something to make something stop 11 call something to mind to remember something: *He did tell me his name, but I can't call it to mind now.*

SPELLING NOTE

Words with the sound /k/, like cut, may be spelt k-, like key, or qu-, like queen.
Words with the sound /s/, like city, may be spelt s-, like soon, or ps-, like psychology.

---

call back *phr v* 1 [T call sbdy ↔ back] to call someone so that they return towards you: *I was about to leave when my secretary called me back.* 2 [I] to make another visit to someone: *I asked the salesman if he could call back later.* 3 [I;T call sbdy ↔ back] to telephone someone who you tried to telephone earlier, or who tried to telephone you earlier: *It's engaged, so I'll call back later. | Mrs Evans is busy at the moment – shall I get her to call you back?* –see TELEPHONE¹ (USAGE)

call for *phr v* 1 [T call for sthg] to demand something: *Opposition leaders have called for a public enquiry.* 2 [T call for sbdy] to collect someone: *I'll call for you at eight o'clock.*

call in *phr v* 1 [T call sbdy ↔ in] to ask someone to come in: *I think we'd better call in a doctor.* 2 [I] to make a short visit to someone: *I'll call in to see you this afternoon. | Call in on us if you're in town.*

call sthg ↔ **off** *phr v* [T] 1 to say that something will not take place: *The match was called off because of the bad weather.* 2 to order a dog or other animal to keep away from someone: *Call your dog off!*

call on sbdy *phr v* [T] 1 to visit someone: *I called on my uncle while I was in London.* 2 (also call upon sbdy) to ask someone to do something: *Opposition groups have called on the government to change the tax laws.*

call sbdy ↔ **out** *phr v* [T] 1 to order someone to come and help: *The army was called out to help the police clear the streets.* 2 to order someone to stop work: *The union immediately called the men out on strike.*

call sbdy ↔ **up** *phr v* [T] 1 to order someone to join the armed forces: *All men aged between 18 and 30 were called up.* 2 to telephone someone: *I'll call you up this evening.*

call² *n* 1 a demand for something to be done: *There have been many calls for a ceasefire in the war.* 2 a conversation on the telephone, or an attempted conversation: *I had a call from the managing director this morning. | There's a call for you.* –see TELEPHONE¹ (USAGE) 3 a cry made by a bird or an animal: *We heard the familiar call of the cuckoo.* 4 make a call, pay a call to visit someone: *I'm hoping to pay a call on my parents while I'm in London.* 5 no call for no need for; a phrase you use when you disapprove of something that someone has done: *There was no call for you to say those unpleasant things to her.* 6 on call ready to work if you are needed: *Which doctor is on call tonight?*

call box /ˈ·· ·/ *n* a small hut or enclosure containing a public telephone

call·er /ˈkɔːləʳ/ *n* 1 a person making a telephone call, especially when spoken to by the OPERATOR: *I'm sorry, caller, the number is engaged.* 2 a person who makes a short visit: *John's a regular caller here.*

call girl /ˈ·· ·/ *n* a PROSTITUTE who makes her arrangements by telephone

call·ing /ˈkɔːlɪŋ/ *n* 1 a strong desire to do a particular job, especially one which helps other people 2 *fml* a profession

cal·li·pers /ˈkælɪpəz ‖ -ərz/ *n* (also calipers *AmE*) [pl] metal supports fixed to the legs to help a person with weak legs to walk

cal·lous /ˈkæləs/ *adj* cruel and having no sympathy for the sufferings of other people –callously *adv* –callousness *n* [U]

cal·low /ˈkæləʊ/ *adj* young and without experience (a word used to express disapproval): *a callow youth*

cal·lus /ˈkæləs/ *n* an area of thick hard skin: *He had calluses on his hands.*

calm¹ /kɑːm ‖ kɑːm, kɑːlm/ *adj* **1** quiet and not worried or excited: *The police chief advised his men to stay calm and not to lose their tempers.* **2** not windy: *It became calm after the storm.* **3** smooth and still: *The sea was calm.* –**calmly** *adv*

calm² *n* [sing;U] **1** a time of peace and quiet without excitement or worry **2** an absence of wind or rough weather

calm³ *v* [T] to make someone less excited, worried, or angry: *She tried to calm the baby by giving it some milk.*
calm down *phr v* [I;T **calm** sbdy ↔ **down**] to become or make someone less angry, excited, or worried: *For goodness sake, calm down! | It was difficult to calm my brother down.*

cal·o·rie /ˈkæləri/ *n* **1** a measure used for the amount of heat or ENERGY (3) that a food will produce: *One thin piece of bread has 90 calories. | I can only eat 1500 calories a day on this diet.* **2** a measure of heat

calves /kɑːvz ‖ kævz/ the plural of CALF

cam·ber /ˈkæmbər/ *n* [C;U] a slight downward curve on both sides of a road which causes water to run off

cam·cord·er /ˈkæmˌkɔːdər ‖ -ˌkɔːr-/ *n* a machine which you carry around and use to take films on a VIDEO CASSETTE

came /keɪm/ the past tense of COME

cam·el /ˈkæməl/ *n* a large long-necked animal with one or two large humps (HUMP) on its back, used for riding or carrying goods in desert countries

cam·e·o /ˈkæmi-əʊ/ *n* **1** a short piece of writing describing a character or situation, or a small part in a film or play acted by a well-known actor **2** a piece of jewellery consisting of a raised shape on a background of a different colour stone

cam·e·ra /ˈkæmərə/ *n* **1** an apparatus for taking photographs or making films **2 in camera** *fml* in secret: *The court met in camera*

cam·e·ra·man /ˈkæmərəmæn/ *n* **cameramen** /-men/ a person who operates a camera for films or television

cam·ou·flage /ˈkæməflɑːʒ/ *v* **camouflaged**, **camouflaging** [T] to hide something, especially a military object, by covering it with branches, paint, or nets so that it looks like part of the surroundings –**camouflage** *n* [C;U]

camp¹ /kæmp/ *n* **1** [C;U] a place where people live in tents or huts usually for a short time: *a military camp | It was getting dark, so we pitched camp beside the stream. | Let's go back to camp.* **2** [C] a group of people who share the same ideas, especially in politics: *This is the policy favoured by the anti-nuclear camp.*

camp² *v* [I] **1** to stay in a place for a short time and sleep in a tent: *We camped down by the river.* **2 go camping** to go on a holiday in which you sleep in a tent: *We're going camping in France next year.*
camp out *phr v* [I] to sleep outdoors in a tent – **camping** *n* [U] : *Camping doesn't appeal to me at all. | Where can I buy camping equipment?*

cam·paign¹ /kæmˈpeɪn/ *n* a set of organized military, political, or business actions intended to obtain a particular result: *a successful election campaign | an advertising campaign | a campaign against smoking*

campaign² *v* [I] to lead or take part in a campaign: *Sally is campaigning for women's right to equal pay.* –**campaigner** *n*

camp bed /ˌ· ˈ·/ *n* a light narrow bed that folds flat and can be easily carried

camp·er /ˈkæmpər/ *n* **1** a person who camps **2** a motor vehicle big enough to live in while you are on holiday

camp·site /ˈkæmpsaɪt/ *n* a place like a field where you can have a holiday in a tent

cam·pus /ˈkæmpəs/ *n* [C;U] the grounds of a university, college, or school: *Do you live on campus?*

can¹ /kən; *strong* kæn/ *v past tense* **could** /kʊd/ *negative short forms* **can't**, **cannot**, **couldn't** [modal verb] **1** to be able to do something or know how to do something: *Can you swim? | I can't hear very well. | Can you see those people over there? | She can speak French fluently. | I can't remember where I put it. | We couldn't afford a holiday last year. | I can't stop and chat – I'm in a hurry.* **2** to be allowed to do something: *You can't play football here. | You can wait in here if you like. | He said that I could borrow his car.* **3** [only in negatives] used when you are saying that something is impossible: *It can't be true! | "There's Steven over there." "But it can't be – he's in Australia." | Things can't go on as they are. The situation must get better soon.* **4 can you** a polite way of asking someone to do something: *Can you help me carry this box, please? | Can you tell me the way to the railway station?* **5 can I, can we,** etc a polite way of asking someone if they will let you do something: *Can I borrow your pen, please?* **6 can't you** a way of telling someone angrily to do something: *Can't you keep quiet for a minute?* –see Study Note on page 392

can² /kæn/ *v* **-nn-** [T] to preserve food by putting it in a closed metal container in which there is no air: *The fish is brought ashore and canned immediately.| canned sardines*

can³ /kæn/ *n* **1** a small closed metal container in which food or drink is preserved: *He opened a can of beans. | a can of beer | The park was littered with empty beer cans.* –see picture on page 148 **2** a container with a lid used for holding liquids such as oil or petrol

ca·nal /kəˈnæl/ *n* a long, narrow bit of water made for boats to travel along or to bring or remove water from an area: *the Panama Canal*

ca·nar·y /kəˈneəri/ *n* **canaries** a small yellow bird usually kept as a pet for its singing

can·cel /ˈkænsəl/ *v* **-ll-** (**-l-** *AmE*) [T] **1** to state or decide that something will not happen: *My mother's not well so I've cancelled my trip to New York. | We regret to announce that the 11.05 train to Bristol has been cancelled.* **2** to inform someone that you no longer want something: *I've cancelled my subscription to that magazine.* **3 cancel a cheque** to draw a line through a cheque so that it can no longer be used
cancel sthg ↔ **out** *phr v* [T] to be exactly equal but opposite to something else and therefore to produce no effect: *Our profits overseas are cancelled out by our losses at home.*

can·cel·la·tion /ˌkænsəˈleɪʃən/ *n* [C;U] a decision not to do something or to stop something being done for you or sent to you *The flight is fully booked, but if there are any cancellations we'll let you know.| The cancellation of the order led to the closure of the factory.*

can·cer /ˈkænsəʳ/ n 1 [C;U] a serious disease in which the body's cells increase too fast, producing a growth which may cause death: *lung cancer* | *He's got cancer of the throat.* **2 Cancer** one of the signs of the ZODIAC

can·cer·ous /ˈkænsərəs/ adj having the disease of cancer

can·did /ˈkændɪd/ adj directly truthful, even when telling the truth is uncomfortable or unwelcome: *Go on, give me your candid opinion.* **–candidly** adv : *She talked quite candidly about her unhappy marriage.*

can·di·da·cy /ˈkændɪdəsi/ n (also **canditature** BrE) [C;U] the fact of being a candidate, usually for a political office: *He announced his candidacy for the next presidential election.*

can·di·date /ˈkændɪdət ‖ -deɪt, -dət/ n 1 a person who wants to be chosen for a job, or for a position given as the result of an election: *Her supporters have nominated her as a candidate for the post of union representative.* | *a presidential candidate* 2 a person taking an examination

can·dle /ˈkændl/ n 1 a round stick of WAX containing a length of string, which gives light when it burns **2 can't hold a candle to** *infml* to be not nearly as good as something **–candlelight** n [U]

can·dle·stick /ˈkændlˌstɪk/ n a holder for one or more candles

can·dour /ˈkændəʳ/ n (**candor** AmE) [U] the quality of being sincerely honest and truthful

can·dy /ˈkændi/ n **candies** AmE [C;U] a shaped piece of boiled sugar or chocolate

cane¹ /keɪn/ n 1 [C;U] the hard smooth often hollow stem of certain plants such as BAMBOO: *cane furniture* | *We need some canes to support the raspberry bushes in the garden.* 2 [C] a stick used to help you while walking or used to hit someone as a punishment: *My brother was given the cane for fighting at school.*

cane² v **caned, caning** [T] to punish someone by hitting them with a cane

ca·nine /ˈkeɪnaɪn, ˈkæ- ‖ ˈkeɪ-/ adj tech of or like a dog

can·is·ter /ˈkænɪstəʳ/ n a metal container used for holding a dry substance or a gas

can·ker /ˈkæŋkəʳ/ n [C;U] an area of soreness caused by a disease which attacks the flesh, especially the mouth and ears, of animals and people and the wood of trees

can·na·bis /ˈkænəbɪs/ n [U] a drug made from the dried leaves of the HEMP plant, often smoked to give a feeling of pleasure, but whose use is illegal in many countries

canned /kænd/ adj preserved in a tin (used of food)

can·ni·bal /ˈkænɪbəl/ n an animal or person that eats the flesh of its own kind **–cannibalism** n [U]

can·ni·bal·ize /ˈkænɪbəlaɪz/ v **cannibalized, cannibalizing** (also **cannibalise** BrE) [T] to take a machine to pieces in order to use the parts in other machines

can·non¹ /ˈkænən/ n **cannons** or **cannon** a big gun, fixed to the ground or on wheels: *a 15th century cannon*

SPELLING NOTE

Words with the sound / k /, like **cut**, may be spelt **k-**, like **key**, or **qu-**, like **queen**.
Words with the sound / s /, like **city**, may be spelt **s-**, like **soon**, or **ps-**, like **psychology**.

---

cannon² v **cannon into** to run into someone or something violently: *He came running round the corner and cannoned into me.*

cannon ball /ˈ··· ·/ n a heavy iron ball fired from a cannon

can·not /ˈkænɒt, -nɒt ‖ -nɑːt/ fml can not: *Mr Smith is sorry that he cannot accept your kind invitation to dinner.* –compare CAN'T

can·ny /ˈkæni/ adj clever and not easily deceived especially in money matters

ca·noe¹ /kəˈnuː/ n a long light narrow boat, pointed at both ends, and moved by a PADDLE held in the hands

canoe² v **canoed, canoeing** [I] 1 to travel in a canoe **2 go canoeing** to go out in a canoe on the sea or a river for sport or pleasure **–canoeing** n [U] : *Canoeing is hard work on the arms.* **–canoeist** n

can·on /ˈkænən/ n 1 an established law of the Christian Church **2** fml a generally accepted standard of behaviour or thought **3** a Christian priest with special duties in a CATHEDRAL **–canonical** /kəˈnɒnɪkəl ‖ -ˈnɑː-/ adj

can·on·ize /ˈkænənaɪz/ v **canonized, canonizing** (also **canonise** BrE) [T] to declare a dead person to be a SAINT: *Joan of Arc was canonized in 1920.*

can o·pen·er /ˈ· ˌ···/ n see TIN OPENER

can·o·py /ˈkænəpi/ n **canopies** a cover fixed over a seat or bed, used either for decoration or for shelter

canst /kənst; strong kænst/ **thou canst** biblical (when talking to one person) you can

cant /kænt/ n [U] insincere talk about religion or morals

can't /kɑːnt ‖ kænt/ short for **can not**: *I can't come with you: I'm busy.* | *You can swim, can't you?* –compare CANNOT

can·tan·ker·ous /kænˈtæŋkərəs/ adj bad-tempered **–cantankerously** adv

can·teen /kænˈtiːn/ n 1 a place in a factory, school, or office where people go to eat and drink: *I always have lunch in the canteen.* **2** a small container in which water or other drink is carried **3** BrE a box which contains a set of knives, forks, and spoons

can·ter /ˈkæntəʳ/ n the movement of a horse which is faster than a TROT but slower than a GALLOP: *We set off at a canter.* **–canter** v [I]

can·vas /ˈkænvəs/ n 1 [U] strong rough cloth used to make tents, sails, or bags **2** [C;U] strong rough cloth used by artists for oil paintings: *She showed me her canvases.* **3 under canvas** in a tent: *It's fun sleeping under canvas.*

can·vass /ˈkænvəs/ v [I;T] 1 to try and persuade people in a certain area that they should support or vote for a particular political party: *I'm canvassing for votes tonight.* **2** to try and find out what people think about a particular subject: *Let's canvass opinion before beginning the campaign.*

can·yon /ˈkænjən/ n a deep and narrow valley often with a river flowing through it: *the Grand Canyon*

cap¹ /kæp/ n 1 a soft flat hat with a curved part sticking out at the front worn by men or boys, or as part of a uniform: *a schoolboy's cap* **2** the top or end of an object which is used to protect it: *Put the cap back on the bottle.* **3** a small round object fitted inside a woman to allow her to have sex without having children **4 go cap in hand** to go without pride to someone in order to ask for something: *He went cap in hand to the director to ask for more money.*

cap² v -pp- [T] **1** to cover something: *Clouds capped the hills.* **2** to improve on what someone has said or done: *He capped my story by telling a better one.* **3** to cap it all in addition to everything else: *His wife left him, his car was stolen, then to cap it all he lost his job!*

ca·pa·bil·i·ty /ˌkeɪpə'bɪlɪti/ n **capabilities** [C;U] the quality of being able to do something: *Could you explain the machine's technical capabilities to me?* | *Do you think the super powers will use their nuclear capability?*

ca·pa·ble /'keɪpəbəl/ adj **1** skilful and effective: *a very capable doctor* | *Don't worry, she's very capable.* **2** capable of something, capable of doing something having the power, skill, or other qualities needed to do something: *Don't annoy her: she's capable of making life very difficult for people she dislikes.* | *Would you say he is capable of murder?* **3** capable of fml able to be: *a remark capable of being misunderstood* –opposite **incapable** –**capably** adv

ca·pac·i·ty /kə'pæsɪti/ n **capacities 1** [sing;U] the amount that something can hold, produce, or carry: *The seating capacity of this theatre is 500.* | *The machine is working at full capacity.* | *This factory has a productive capacity of 200 cars a week.* | *The seating area was filled to capacity, so we had to stand.* **2** [C;U] an ability to do something: *He has a great capacity for enjoying himself.* | *Her capacity to remember facts is remarkable.* **3** [C] a position of responsibility: *I'm speaking in my capacity as minister of trade.* | *They took him on in an advisory capacity.*

cape /keɪp/ n **1** a loose covering for the top part of your body without separate arm-coverings: *A bicycle cape will protect you in wet weather.* **2** a piece of land going out into the sea: *the Cape of Good Hope*

ca·per /'keɪpəʳ/ v [I] old fash to jump about or dance in a happy way: *We watched the lambs capering in the fields.*

ca·pil·la·ry /kə'pɪləri || 'kæpəleri/ n **capillaries** a very fine hairlike tube which carries blood around your body

cap·i·tal¹ /'kæpɪtl/ n **1** [C] the most important city in a country or area: *Paris is the capital of France.* | *the financial capital of Europe* **2** [U] a sum of money, especially one used to produce more money or to start a business: *The bank put up the capital for his new enterprise.* | *a successful firm that offers investors a high return on capital* **3** [C] (also **capital letter**) a letter which is written or printed in its large form, used especially at the beginning of a word or sentence

capital² adj **1** [only before a noun] punishable by death: *Murder can be a capital offence.* **2** [only before a noun] concerned with wealth in the form of money or property: *We need a big programme of capital investment to modernize the railways.* **3** old fash excellent: *What a capital idea!*

cap·i·tal·is·m /'kæpɪtl-ɪzəm/ n [U] a political system in which trade and industry belong mostly to private people rather than to the government –compare COMMUNISM

cap·i·tal·ist /'kæpɪtl-ɪst/ n a person or country that uses or supports capitalism –**capitalist** adj : *the capitalist countries of the West*

cap·i·tal·ize /'kæpɪtl-aɪz/ v **capitalized, capitalizing, capitalize on something** to use something in order to gain an advantage: *She capitalized on his mistake and won the game.*

capital pun·ish·ment /ˌ··· '···/ n [U] a legal punishment which says that a person who is guilty of a serious crime, such as a murder, should be put to death

ca·pit·u·late /kə'pɪtʃʊleɪt/ v **capitulated, capitulating** [I] **1** to stop fighting the enemy and agree to their conditions **2** to accept someone else's demands unwillingly: *The hijackers capitulated to the government's threat.* –**capitulation** /kəˌpɪtʃʊ'leɪʃən/ n [C;U]

ca·price /kə'priːs/ n [C;U] a sudden often foolish change of mind or behaviour without any real cause

ca·pri·cious /kə'prɪʃəs/ adj often changing without warning: *We can't go camping while the weather is so capricious.*

Cap·ri·corn /'kæprɪkɔːn || -ɔːrn/ n one of the signs of the ZODIAC

cap·size /kæp'saɪz || 'kæpsaɪz/ v [I;T] **capsized, capsizing** [I;T] to turn upside down in the water, or to make a boat turn upside down in the water: *The yacht capsized in the storm, but luckily it didn't sink.* | *a capsized boat*

cap·sule /'kæpsjuːl || -səl/ n **1** a very small object containing medicine which you swallow **2** the part of a space vehicle in which the people live and work

cap·tain¹ /'kæptən/ n **1** the leader of a team or group: *the captain of the football team* **2** the person in command of a ship or aircraft: *Are we ready to sail, Captain?* **3** an officer of middle rank in the armed forces

captain² v [T] to be the leader or commander of a group of people: *When I was at school I captained the hockey team.*

cap·tion /'kæpʃən/ n words written above or below a picture to say what it is about: *I didn't understand the drawing until I read the caption.*

cap·ti·vate /'kæptɪveɪt/ v **captivated, captivating** [T] to charm and excite someone so that it is difficult for them to think of anything else: *I was captivated by the city's beauty.* –**captivating** adj

cap·tive¹ /'kæptɪv/ adj **1** kept as a prisoner: *captive animals* | *We were held captive for three months.* **2** a captive audience a person or people who cannot easily leave and must therefore listen: *Lying in my hospital bed, I was a captive audience for her boring stories.*

captive² n **1** a person kept as a prisoner especially in war **2** take someone captive to take someone as a prisoner

cap·tiv·i·ty /kæp'tɪvɪti/ n [U] the state of being kept as a prisoner: *Many animals do not breed in captivity.*

cap·tor /'kæptəʳ/ n fml a person who keeps someone as a prisoner: *I soon escaped from my captors.*

cap·ture¹ /'kæptʃəʳ/ v **captured, capturing** [T] **1** to take a person or animal as a prisoner: *He was captured as he tried to escape from the country.* **2** to take control of something often by force: *They've captured a large share of the market.* | *The speech captured our attention.* **3** to preserve something through pictures or words: *The photographs captured the evening sunlight.* **4** tech to put something into a form that can be used by a computer

capture² n [U] the act of taking or being taken by force: *He was released six months after his capture.*

car /kɑːʳ/ n **1** a road vehicle with wheels and an engine which is used as a means of travel for a small number of people: *You can't park your car here.* **2**

by car travelling in a car: *Shall we go by car?* **3** a carriage or vehicle used on railways: *Does this train have a restaurant car? | a sleeping car*

ca·rafe /kə'ræf, kə'rɑːf/ *n* a bottle with a wide neck for serving wine or water at a meal

car·a·mel /'kærəməl, -mel/ *n* **1** [U] burnt sugar used for giving food a special taste and colour **2** [C] a sticky sweet made with sugar, butter, and milk

car·at /'kærət/ *n* (also **karat** *AmE*) a unit which measures the purity of gold or the weight of a jewel: *a 22-carat gold ring*

car·a·van /'kærəvæn/ *n* **1** a vehicle with wheels which can be pulled by a car, and which people can cook and sleep in on holiday **2** a covered horse-drawn cart in which people such as gipsies (GIPSY) live or travel **3** a group of people with animals travelling together for protection through desert areas: *a caravan of merchants*

car·a·van·ning /'kærəvænɪŋ/ *v* go **caravanning** to go on holiday taking a caravan to cook and sleep in: *My parents always go caravanning in September.* –**caravanning** *n* [U]

car·bo·hy·drate /ˌkɑːbəʊ'haɪdreɪt, -drət ‖ ˌkɑːr-/ *n* [C;U] a substance found in food that provides the body with heat and strength: *Bread is full of carbohydrate.*

car·bon /'kɑːbən ‖ 'kɑːr-/ *n* [U] **1** a chemical substance found in a pure form as diamonds or GRAPHITE or in an impure form as coal or petrol **2** (also **carbon paper**) a sheet of thin paper coloured on one side which is used between sheets of typing to make copies

carbon di·ox·ide /ˌ·· ·'··/ *n* [U] the gas produced when humans and animals breathe out, or when carbon is burned in air

carbon mo·nox·ide /ˌ·· ·'··/ *n* [U] a poisonous gas produced when carbon, such as petrol, is burnt in air

car·bun·cle /'kɑːbʌŋkəl ‖ 'kɑːr-/ *n* a large painful infected swelling under the skin

car·bu·ret·tor /ˌkɑːbjʉ'retəʳ, -bə- ‖ 'kɑːrbəreɪtəʳ/ *n* (**carburetor** *AmE*) the part in a car engine where air and petrol mix and produce an explosive gas which provides the power

car·cass /'kɑːkəs ‖ 'kɑːr-/ *n* (also **carcase** *BrE*) the body of a dead animal, especially one which is ready to be cut up as meat

card /kɑːd ‖ kɑːrd/ *n* **1** [C] (also **playing card**) one of a set of 52 small pieces of stiff paper with pictures or numbers on them used for various games: *It's my turn to deal the cards. | a pack of cards* **2 cards** [pl] games played with cards: *Let's play cards. | I hate people who cheat at cards.* **3** [C] a piece of stiff paper, usually with a picture on the front and a message inside, sent or given to a person on special occasions: *a birthday card | a Christmas card | I sent her a get-well card when she was in hospital.* **4** [C] a POSTCARD **5** [C] a small sheet of stiff paper or plastic with information printed on it and having various uses: *a credit card | a business card | an identity card | a cheque card* **6** [U] strong, stiff paper **7 have a card up your sleeve** *infml* to have a secret,

usually effective plan **8 lay/put your cards on the table** to be completely open and honest about your position or plans **9 on the cards (in the cards** *AmE*) *infml* probable: *They say another price rise for petrol is on the cards.*

card·board /'kɑːdbɔːd ‖ 'kɑːrdbɔːrd/ *n* [U] a sort of thick, stiff paper often used for making boxes

car·di·ac /'kɑːdi·æk ‖ 'kɑːr-/ *adj* [only before a noun] *tech* connected with the heart or with heart disease: *a cardiac patient | a cardiac arrest*

car·di·gan /'kɑːdɪgən ‖ 'kɑːr-/ *n* a woollen piece of clothing which is fastened at the front with buttons and worn on the top half of your body –see picture on page 50

car·di·nal¹ /'kɑːdənəl ‖ 'kɑːr-/ *n* a ROMAN CATHOLIC priest of high rank

cardinal² *adj fml* most important: *a cardinal sin*

cardinal num·ber /ˌ··· '··/ *n* any of the numbers 1, 2, 3, etc., that show quantity rather than order –compare ORDINAL

card in·dex /'· ˌ··/ *n* a number of cards each with a particular piece of information and arranged in a special order, usually alphabetical

card·phone /'kɑːdfəʊn ‖ 'kɑːr-/ *n* a public telephone where you pay for your call with a telephone card and not money

care¹ /keəʳ/ *n* **1** [U] the process of looking after someone or something that needs attention: *The clinic provides a high standard of medical care. | The children are disabled and need special care. | advice on hair care* **2** [U] the responsibility for looking after someone or dealing with something: *We left the baby in the care of our neighbour.* **3** [U] serious attention and effort: *Try to do your work with a bit more care.* **4** [U] paying attention that you do not damage or hurt someone or something: *Glass: handle with care!* **5** [C;U] a feeling of worry, concern, or unhappiness: *freedom from care | without a care in the world* **6 care of** (also **c/o**) at the address of a particular person **7 take care** be careful: *Take care not to drop that vase.* **8 take care of** to be responsible for someone or deal with something: *I'll take care of the baby while you're out. | Don't worry about your ticket–it's all been taken care of.* **9 take someone into care** to take a young person into a home run by the government or a local council

■ USAGE **1** If you want to talk about being responsible for someone or something, use **take care of** or **look after**: *She asked me to* **take care of**/**look after** *her cat while she was away. | Who will* **take care of**/**look after** *the children when I'm at work? | My secretary will* **take care of**/**look after** *the travel arrangements.* **2** If you are talking about somebody who is ill, you can also use **care for** but this is a rather literary use: *She devoted 20 years of her life to* **caring for** *her elderly parents.* (It would be more usual to use **take care of** or **look after** here too.) **3** If you want to tell someone to be careful, use **take care (of)**: *Take care of that money I gave you! Don't leave it lying around. | Take care of yourself! | Bye! Take care!* **4** If you want to talk about something being important (or not important) use **care (about)**: *He cares too much about other people's opinions. | I* **don't care about** *him – what about me?| I* **don't care** *what you think. | "You'll get into trouble." "I* **don't care!**"

care² *v* **cared, caring 1** [I;T] to be worried, concerned about, or interested in someone or something: *When his dog died Alan didn't seem to care at*

all. | *The only thing she cares* about *is money.* | *"We'll be late." "I don't care." | He doesn't care if he puts on weight. | He doesn't seem to care where he works.*
☐ USEFUL PATTERNS to care; to care about something; to care if…; to care where, why, who…
2 care to do something to choose to do something: *It was a failure, whichever way you care to look at it.* **3 would you care to** *fml* = would you like to: *Would you care to wait here a moment, sir?*

care for sbdy/sthg ↔ *phr v* [T] **1** to nurse or look after someone or something: *He's very good at caring for sick animals.* **2** [usually used in negatives and questions] to like something: *Would you care for a drink? | I don't much care for coffee.*

ca·reer¹ /kəˈrɪəʳ/ *n* **1** a job or profession in a particular area of work for which you are trained and in which you get more responsibility and earn more money as time goes on: *a career* in *law | From this point his career really took off. | She has good career prospects.* **2** the part of your life when you are working: *She spent most of her career as a teacher in London.*

career² *adj* [only before a noun] regarding your job as a career for a long time: *a career woman | a career diplomat*

career³ *v* [I + adv/prep] to go at full speed as if out of control: *The car careered down the hill and nearly hit an old lady.*

care-free /ˈkeəfriː ‖ ˈkeər-/ *adj* happy and without worry: *The long summer days ahead made her feel quite carefree.*

care-ful /ˈkeəfəl ‖ ˈkeər-/ *adj* **1** taking care: *We were careful not to mention it to his wife. | You should be more careful* with *your money. | a careful driver | Be careful crossing the road. | Do be careful how you carry those eggs!*
☐ USEFUL PATTERNS to be careful (not) to do something; to be careful with something; to be careful doing something…; to be careful where/who/what/how…
2 Be careful! a phrase used when the person you are speaking to faces a possible danger: *Be careful you don't fall off that ladder.* **3** showing concern and giving attention to details: *The doctor made a careful examination.* **–carefully** *adv : Drive carefully!* **–carefulness** *n* [U]

care-less /ˈkeələs ‖ ˈkeər-/ *adj* **1** not taking enough care: *He's a very careless driver | It was very careless of you to lose her books.* **2** not showing enough concern about detail: *This is careless work. Do it again!* **–carelessly** *adv* **–carelessness** *n* [U]

car·er /ˈkeərə/ *n* someone who has to stay at home to look after an old or sick person, usually for several years, but who is not paid any money

ca·ress¹ /kəˈres/ *n* a loving touch or kiss

caress² *v* [T] to touch or kiss someone lovingly: *He caressed her long black hair.*

care·tak·er /ˈkeəteɪkəʳ ‖ ˈkeər-/ a person employed to look after a large public building, such as a school, and to be responsible for small repairs and cleaning

caretaker gov·ern·ment /ˌ··· ˌ···/ *n* a government which is in control for a usually short period between the end of one government and the appointment of a new government

car·go /ˈkɑːgəʊ ‖ ˈkɑːr-/ *n* **cargoes** *or* **cargos** [C;U] the things which are taken from one place to another in a ship, plane, or other vehicle: *We sailed from Newcastle with a cargo of coal.*

Car·ib·be·an /ˌkærɪˈbiːən◂ ‖ kəˈrɪbiən/ *adj* from or connected with a country in the West Indies

car·i·ca·ture /ˈkærɪkətʃʊəʳ/ *n* [C;U] a drawing or description of a person which is made so that the appearance or character seem more odd or amusing than they really are: *Have you seen the caricature of the Prime Minister in the paper today?* **–caricature** *v* **caricatured, caricaturing** [T]

car·ing /ˈkeərɪŋ/ *adj* providing care and support: *the caring professions, such as nursing*

car·nage /ˈkɑːnɪdʒ ‖ ˈkɑːr-/ *n* [U] *fml* the killing and wounding of large numbers of people, especially in war: *The battlefield was a scene of terrible carnage.*

car·nal /ˈkɑːnl ‖ ˈkɑːrnl/ *adj* [only before a noun] *fml* relating to sexual desires and feelings (a word used to express disapproval): *carnal pleasures*

car·na·tion /kɑːˈneɪʃən ‖ kɑːr-/ *n* a sweet-smelling white, pink, or red flower

car·ni·val /ˈkɑːnɪvəl ‖ ˈkɑːr-/ *n* [C;U] a public entertainment with processions and dancing on a special occasion, or a period of time when this takes place: *carnival time in Rio de Janeiro*

car·ni·vore /ˈkɑːnɪvɔːʳ ‖ ˈkɑːr-/ *n* an animal that eats meat: *Lions are carnivores; rabbits are not.* **–carnivorous** /kɑːˈnɪvərəs ‖ kɑːr-/ *adj*

car·ol /ˈkærəl/ *n* a religious song of joy and praise sung at Christmas

ca·rouse /kəˈraʊz/ *v* **caroused, carousing** [I] *llt* to have some noisy fun after drinking a lot of alcohol

car·ou·sel /ˌkærəˈsel/ *n* (also **carrousel**) a moving belt at an airport from which passengers collect their bags and cases

carp¹ /kɑːp ‖ kɑːrp/ *v* [I] *infml* to find faults and complain continuously about things that are not important: *I wish you'd stop carping* about *the way I dress.*

carp² *n* a large fish that lives in lakes, pools, and slow-moving rivers

car park /ˈ· ·/ *n* a place where you can leave your car sometimes for a small payment: *I managed to park in a multistorey car park.*

car·pen·ter /ˈkɑːpɪntəʳ ‖ ˈkɑːr-/ *n* a person who is skilled at making and repairing wooden objects

car·pen·try /ˈkɑːpɪntri ‖ ˈkɑːr-/ *n* [U] the art or work of a carpenter

car·pet¹ /ˈkɑːpɪt ‖ ˈkɑːr-/ *n* **1** [C;U] thick, heavy floor covering for floors or stairs, usually made of wool: *a lovely Persian carpet | We'll put carpet down in the hall.* –see picture on page 442 **2** [C] anything which covers a large area of ground: *a carpet* of *flowers*

carpet² *v* [T] to cover something with a carpet

car phone /ˈ· ·/ *n* a private telephone in someone's car

car·riage /ˈkærɪdʒ/ *n* **1** *BrE* [C] one of the parts of a train where passengers sit: *I'll be sitting in the third carriage from the front of the train.* –see picture on page 735 **2** [C] a wheeled vehicle which is pulled by a horse **3** [U] the cost of moving goods from one place to another: *The price includes carriage.* **4** [C] a movable part of a machine: *The carriage of a typewriter which holds and moves the paper.* **5** [sing;U] *fml* the way a person holds their head and body when standing or walking

carried a·way /ˌ··· ·ˈ·/ *adj* [never before a noun] filled with strong feelings or excitement, especially so that you behave unreasonably: *I'm afraid my husband got rather carried away; he's very sorry.*

car·ri·er /ˈkæriəʳ/ n **1** a person or thing that carries goods or passengers from one place to another **2** a person or thing that does not suffer any of the effects of a disease but carries it and passes it to other people

carrier bag /ˈ··· ·/ (**shopping bag** AmE) n a cheap strong paper or plastic bag with handles, for carrying away from a shop

car·rot /ˈkærət/ n **1** [C;U] a long, thin, orange vegetable: Have some more carrots. | carrot juice –see picture on page 344 **2** [C] infml a reward that you are promised for doing something: My boss dangled a carrot by saying he'd give me a pay rise if I helped him over the weekend.

car·ry /ˈkæri/ v carried, carried, carrying **1** [T] to hold something and take it with you: I had to carry my suitcases all the way to the hotel. | The police don't usually carry guns. | These pipes carry the oil across the desert. –see picture on page 736 **2** [T] to have a disease and spread it to other people: Some mosquitoes carry malaria. | Rats are dirty and can carry diseases. **3** [T] (of a newspaper or magazine) to contain a particular picture or article: Several newspapers carried pictures of the scene of the accident. | The paper carries an article about the dangers of smoking. **4** [T] to have something as a usual or necessary result: The crime of murder carries the death penalty in many countries. | The job carries certain risks. **5** [I] (of a sound) to be able to reach a certain distance: Her voice didn't carry to the back of the hall. | The sound carried for miles. **6 be carried** to be approved: The motion was carried by 310 votes to 306. **7 be carrying a child** lit to be PREGNANT **8 carry weight** to be respected and believed by people: His opinions carry a lot of weight. **9 be/get carried away** to be too excited: I got carried away and bought three pairs of shoes instead of one. **10 carry something too far** to do something too much or for too long: It was funny at first, but she carried the joke too far.

carry sthg ↔ **forward** phr v [T] to move a number from the bottom of one row of figures to the top of the next row, in order to add it to the next row

carry sthg ↔ **off** phr v [T] **1** to succeed in doing something: It's a risky venture, and I'm not sure they'll be able to carry it off. **2** to win a prize: Jean carried off all the prizes.

carry on phr v **carry on with something, carry on doing something** to continue doing something: We carried on with our discussion. | He carried on talking in spite of the noise.

carry sthg ↔ **out** phr v [T] to complete a job or put into practice a plan or order: This research has been carried out at the University of Leeds. | Our planes carried out a bombing raid on enemy targets. | He never carried out his threat to resign. | They were only carrying out their orders.

carry through phr v **1** [T **carry** sthg ↔ **through**] to put into practice a plan or order: The government managed to carry through the reforms despite fierce opposition. **2** [T **carry** sbdy **through** sthg] to help someone to manage when they are ill or having difficulties: Her great courage carried her through the illness.

car·ry·cot /ˈkærikɒt ‖ -kɑːt/ n an object shaped like a box in which a baby sleeps and can be carried about

cart¹ /kɑːt ‖ kɑːrt/ n **1** a vehicle made of wood and pulled by hand or by animals, used for example on a farm to carry heavy things **2 put the cart before the horse** to do unimportant things before the really important ones

cart² v [T; +adv/prep] infml **1** to carry something heavy: I've been carting this suitcase around the town all afternoon. **2** to take or remove someone, often disrespectfully, carelessly, or using force: They carted him off to the police station. | She carts the kids around with her wherever she goes.

carte blanche /ˌkɑːt ˈblɑːnʃ ‖ ˌkɑːrt-/ n [U] freedom to do exactly what you want to: My parents gave me carte blanche to organize the party.

car·tel /kɑːˈtel ‖ kɑːr-/ n a combination of companies, often international ones, intended to limit fair competition and increase their profits

cart·horse /ˈkɑːthɔːs ‖ ˈkɑːrthɔːrs/ n a powerful horse used for heavy work on farms

car·ti·lage /ˈkɑːtəlɪdʒ ‖ ˈkɑːr-/ n [C;U] a strong elastic substance found round your joints

car·tog·ra·phy /kɑːˈtɒɡrəfi ‖ kɑːrˈtɑː-/ n [U] the science or art of making maps

car·ton /ˈkɑːtn ‖ ˈkɑːrtn/ n a box made from stiff paper, usually used for holding food or drink: a carton of milk –see picture on page 148

car·toon /kɑːˈtuːn ‖ kɑːr-/ n **1** a humorous drawing, often dealing with something of interest in the news in an amusing way **2** a set of drawings in a newspaper or magazine telling the story of particular characters **3** a film made by photographing drawings: a Mickey Mouse cartoon –**cartoonist** n

car·tridge /ˈkɑːtrɪdʒ ‖ ˈkɑːr-/ n **1** a tube containing explosive and shot for a gun **2** a small case in a record player containing the needle that picks up sound signals from a record **3** a thin tube with ink in it which you put inside a pen

cart·wheel /ˈkɑːt·wiːl ‖ ˈkɑːrt-/ n a movement in which a person turns over by putting their hands on the ground and moving their legs sideways in the air –**cartwheel** v [I]

carve /kɑːv ‖ kɑːrv/ v **carved, carving 1** [T] to cut a special shape out of wood or stone: The sculptor carved a bird from the block of stone. | They carved their initials on the tree. **2** [I;T] to cut cooked meat: Shall I carve you another slice of chicken? **3 carve something out for yourself** to make or get something by working hard: She has managed to carve out a career for herself as a comic actress.

carve sthg ↔ **up** phr v [T] to divide something into smaller pieces: They carved up the profits between them.

carv·ing /ˈkɑːvɪŋ ‖ ˈkɑːr-/ n **1** [C] something made by carving **2** [U] the work, art, or skill of a person who carves

carving knife /ˈ·· ˌ·/ n a long sharp knife used for cutting large pieces of meat

cas·cade¹ /kæˈskeɪd/ n **1** a small waterfall falling through rocks **2** lit anything that seems to flow downwards in a mass: Her hair fell over her shoulders in a cascade of curls.

cascade² v [I +adv/prep] to fall fast and in great quantities: I watched the rainwater cascading down the window.

case /keɪs/ n **1** [C] a single example of something: Doctors have reported several cases of malaria. | We are seeing more and more cases of children being neglected and abused. | This is a typical case of the government's stupidity and lack of understanding. **2** [C] a set of events that needs to be studied and understood by someone, for example by the police or in a court of law: *Hundreds of police are working on this case.* | *a very difficult murder case* | *The case will be heard in court next week.* **3** [C] the facts and arguments that support what someone is saying: *There is a very good case for reducing taxes immediately.* | *For years he has argued the case against government control.* | *The police have a very good case against her.* **4** [C;U] the form of a word, usually a noun, which shows its relationship with the other words in a sentence; for example, "me" is the object case of "I" **5** [C] a large box in which goods can be stored or moved: *a case of wine* **6** [C] a large bag for carrying your clothes and other things in, for example when you go on holiday: *He offered to carry my case to my room.* **7 a case in point** a good example of something that you are saying: *More and more children are suffering the effects of divorce. Sarah is a case in point; her parents split up when she was three and she has lived with her grandmother since then.* **8 in any case** a phrase you use when you are stating forcefully that something is true: *The cost might turn out to be lower than we thought, but in any case it will still be a substantial amount of money.* | *Tim's not coming to the concert. He says he's too busy. He hasn't got any money, in any case.* –see Study Note on page 508 **9 in that case, in which case** as this is true: *"I'm afraid I won't be able to give you a lift after all." "Well in that case I'll just have to walk."* **10 in case, just in case** because something might happen: *I've brought some sandwiches in case we get hungry.* | *I brought my key just in case you forgot yours.* **11 in case of** if or when something happens: *In case of fire, sound the alarm and leave the building immediately.*

■ USAGE Note the tenses of the verbs following **in case** in these sentences: *Take your umbrella in case it rains.* | *I'll give you the front door key in case I am out.* | *She took lots of warm clothes in case the weather turned cold.*

12 the case true or correct: *It is the case that fewer crimes are committed by women than by men.* **13 lower case** small letters of the alphabet: *The computer commands should all be written in lower case.* | *a lower case "e"* **14 upper case** the CAPITAL letters of the alphabet: *an upper case "E"*

case·ment win·dow /ˈkeɪsmənt ˈwɪndəʊ/ *n* (also **casement**) a window that opens like a door

cash¹ /kæʃ/ *n* [U] **1** money in coins and notes: *I haven't got any cash on me – can I pay by cheque?* **2** *infml* money in any form: *Denis is always short of cash.* **3 cash on delivery** see C.O.D.

cash² *v* [T] to exchange something such as a cheque for cash: *Can you cash these traveller's cheques for me?*

cash in on sthg *phr v* [T] to take full advantage of a situation: *The company cashed in on the difficulties of its rivals.*

cash card /ˈ· ·/ *n* a special plastic card used for obtaining money from a machine at a bank

cash crop /ˈ· ·/ *n* a crop produced for sale rather than for use by the grower

cash desk /ˈ· ·/ *n* the desk in a shop where payments are made

ca·shew /ˈkæʃuː, kəˈʃuː/ *n* a small curved nut

cash flow /ˈ· ·/ *n* [sing; U] the movement of money into and out of a company: *We've got serious cash flow problems.*

cash·ier /kæˈʃɪəʳ/ *n* a person that people pay in places like shops, banks, or hotels

cash·mere /ˈkæʃmɪəʳ ‖ ˈkæʒ-, ˈkæʃ-/ *n* [U] a kind of fine soft wool

cash reg·is·ter /ˈ· ˌ···/ *n* a machine used in places like shops to show how much people have to pay

cas·ing /ˈkeɪsɪŋ/ *n* a protective covering: *This wire has a rubber casing.*

ca·si·no /kəˈsiːnəʊ/ *n* **casinos** a place where people play cards or other games for money

cask /kɑːsk ‖ kæsk/ *n* a barrel-shaped container for holding and storing liquids

cas·ket /ˈkɑːskɪt ‖ ˈkæs-/ *n* **1** a small container for holding valuable things like letters or jewellery **2** the usual American word for COFFIN

cas·se·role /ˈkæsərəʊl/ *n* **1** [C] a deep dish with a cover in which food can be cooked and served –see picture on page 148 **2** [C;U] the food cooked in a casserole, usually a mixture of meat and vegetables: *a beef casserole*

cas·sette /kəˈset/ *n* **1** a small flat container with TAPE inside it, used to record or play sounds **2** a container of photographic film which can be put complete into a camera **3 cassette recorder** a machine containing a cassette that records and plays back sounds

cast¹ /kɑːst ‖ kæst/ *v* **cast, cast** [T] **1** to give a part in a play or a film to an actor: *She was cast in the role of Ophelia.* **2** to throw something: *fishermen casting their nets into the sea* **3** *lit* to throw light or shadows: *The trees cast a shadow across the lawn.* **4** to make an object by pouring metal or plastic into a shaped container: *a bell cast in bronze* **5 be cast away** to be left somewhere after your ship has sunk **6 cast an eye over something** to look at something, especially quickly **7 cast a spell** to say magic words in order to make something happen **8 cast a vote** to express your choice in an election usually by marking a piece of paper or raising your hand **9 cast light on something** to help to explain something: *You know her better than I do; can you cast any light on her behaviour?*

cast about/around for sthg *phr v* [T] to look for something in all directions

cast off *phr v* [I;T **cast** sthg ↔ **off**] to untie a boat or a ship: *We're ready – cast off!*

cast² *n* **1** [+ sing/pl verb] the actors in a play or film: *The cast is ready to start.* **2** a hard protective covering for holding a broken bone in place while it gets better

cas·ta·nets /ˌkæstəˈnets/ *n* [pl] a musical instrument made of two pieces of wood which you hold in your hand and strike against each other

cast·a·way /ˈkɑːstəweɪ ‖ ˈkæst-/ *n* a person who escapes when their ship is sunk and reaches the shore of a strange country or lonely island

caste /kɑːst ‖ kæst/ *n* [C;U] the Hindu system of dividing people into different classes of society according to their birth or their job

cast·er /ˈkɑːstəʳ ‖ ˈkæs-/ *n* (also **castor**) a wheel fixed to the base of a piece of furniture so that it can be easily moved

caster sug·ar /ˈ·· ˌ··/ *n* (also **castor sugar**) [U] very fine white sugar often used in cooking

cas·ti·gate /ˈkæstɪgeɪt/ *v* **castigated, castigating** [T] *fml* to express strong disapproval of someone

cast·ing /ˈkɑːstɪŋ ‖ ˈkæstɪŋ/ *n* [U] the choosing of actors for a play or film

casting vote /ˌ·· ˈ·/ *n* a deciding vote used by a chairman when both sides have an equal number of votes

cast i·ron /ˌ· ˈ···/ *n* [U] a hard but easily breakable type of iron

cast-iron /ˌ· ˈ···/ *adj* **1** made of cast iron **2** hard and strong: *a cast-iron stomach* **3** impossible to doubt: *a cast-iron alibi*

cas·tle /ˈkɑːsəl ‖ ˈkæ-/ *n* **1** a large strongly-built building or set of buildings made in the past to give protection from attack **2** one of the powerful pieces in the game of CHESS

cast-off /ˈkɑːstɒf ‖ ˈkæstɔːf/ *n infml* an unwanted article of clothing: *She gave her castoffs to her younger sister.*

cast·or /ˈkɑːstəʳ ‖ ˈkæs-/ *n* see CASTER

castor oil /ˌ·· ˈ·◂/ *n* [U] a thick yellow oil taken for medical reasons

castor sug·ar *n* [U] see CASTER SUGAR

cas·trate /kæˈstreɪt ‖ ˈkæstreɪt/ *v* **castrated**, **castrating** [T] to remove all or part of the sex organs of a male animal or person −**castration** /kæˈstreɪʃən/ *n* [C;U]

cas·u·al /ˈkæʒuəl/ *adj* **1** not showing much interest: *His casual manner annoyed her.* **2** informal (used of clothes): *casual wear* **3** [only before a noun] not serious or thorough: *The casual newspaper reader doesn't read articles on politics every day.* **4** employed only to do a job lasting a short time: *casual labour* **5** resulting from chance: *a casual meeting* −**casually** *adv* : *casually dressed*

cas·u·al·ty /ˈkæʒuəlti/ *n* **casualties** **1** [C] a person hurt in an accident or killed in battle: *Two buses collided outside the British Museum today. There were no casualties.* | *Their army suffered heavy casualties.* **2** [U] (also **casualty department**) a place in a hospital where people hurt in accidents are taken: *They rushed her to casualty.* **3** [C] a person or thing that suffers as a result of an action: *The new school was never finished; it was a casualty* **of** *the recent spending cuts.*

cat /kæt/ *n* **1** a small animal with soft fur often kept as a pet or in buildings to catch mice and rats **2** any animal related to the cat, for example a lion or a tiger **3 let the cat out of the bag** *infml* to tell a secret, usually unintentionally

cat·a·clys·m /ˈkætəklɪzəm/ *n fml* a sudden and violent event or change −**cataclysmic** /ˌkætəˈklɪzmɪk/ *adj*

cat·a·comb /ˈkætəkuːm ‖ -kəʊm/ *n* an underground burial place made up of many passages and rooms

cat·a·logue /ˈkætəlɒg ‖ -lɔːg, -lɑːg/ *n* (**catalog** *AmE*) **1** a book containing information about goods that may be bought in a shop or sent by post **2** a book with a list of all the objects in a place, for example a MUSEUM

catalogue² *v* **catalogued** or **cataloged**, **cataloguing** or **cataloging** (**catalog** *AmE*) [T] **1** to make a list for a special purpose: *You need to catalogue all the items in the house for valuation purposes.* **2** to put information into a catalogue

cat·a·lyst /ˈkætl-ɪst/ *n* **1** a substance which, without itself changing, causes chemical activity to go faster **2** something that causes something important to happen: *The First World War served as a catalyst* **for** *major social changes in Europe.*

cat·a·pult¹ /ˈkætəpʌlt, -pʊlt/ *n* **1** a small Y-shaped stick with a rubber band fastened between the forks, used by children to shoot small stones **2** a

machine for throwing heavy stones or balls, used as a weapon in the past

catapult² *v* [T; + adv/prep] to throw something suddenly: *A car crashed into the pram and the baby was catapulted into the road.*

cat·a·ract /ˈkætərækt/ *n* **1** a growth on a person's eye causing a slow loss of sight **2** a large waterfall

ca·tarrh /kəˈtɑːʳ/ *n* [U] a condition causing a flow of thick liquid in your nose and throat when you have a cold

ca·tas·tro·phe /kəˈtæstrəfi/ *n* a sudden, unexpected event that causes great suffering, misfortune, or ruin: *The flood was a terrible catastrophe in which many people died.* −**catastrophic** /ˌkætəˈstrɒfɪk◂ ‖ -ˈstrɑː-/ *adj*

catch¹ /kætʃ/ *v* **caught** /kɔːt/, **caught** **1** [T] to hold and stop something that is moving in the air: *The dog caught the ball in its mouth.* | *Here, I've found your key. Catch!* −see picture on page 736 **2** [T] to trap something, especially after chasing or hunting it: *Cats like to catch mice.* | *The police are sure they will catch the thief.* **3 catch someone in the act of, catch someone redhanded** to suddenly find someone doing something that they should not be doing: *I caught him reading my diary.* **4** [T] to discover something: *The chances of a cure are very good, if the disease is caught early.* **5** [T] to be in time for something: *If we go home now, we'll just catch the 10 o'clock news.* | *Hurry up − we've got a train to catch!* **6** [T] to get an illness: *Put your coat on, or you'll catch a cold.* **7** [I;T] to become or to cause something to be accidentally held, fastened, or stuck: *My coat caught in the door.* | *I caught my dress on a nail.* **8 catch someone's attention** to make someone notice something suddenly **9 catch someone's imagination** to interest someone so that they start thinking about an idea **10 catch sight of** to notice someone or something: *I caught sight of my old friend in town today.* **11 not catch something** to not hear something clearly: *I didn't quite catch what you said.* **12** [I;T] (also **catch fire**) to start to burn: *The leaves caught quickly.* | *The house caught fire.* **13 catch someone's eye** to make someone notice you: *See if you can catch the waiter's eye.*

catch on *phr v* [I] **1** to become popular: *The new fashion really caught on.* **2** to understand something: *He finally caught on* **to** *what they were doing.*

catch sbdy ↔ **out** *phr v* [T] to show that someone is wrong or is doing something wrong

catch up *phr v* **1** [I;T **catch** sbdy/sthg **up**] to come up from behind and reach the same point as someone: *She's slower than her sister, but catching up fast.* | *We are catching up* **with** *Japan in industrial production.* | *You carry on walking and I'll catch you up in a minute.* **2** [I] to bring or come up to date: *I have to catch up* **on** *writing letters tonight so I can't come out.* **3 be caught up in** included in something, often against your wishes: *The government seems to have got caught up in the argument between Russia and America.*

catch² *n* **1** the action of seizing and holding a ball: *That was a good catch!* **2** something that has been caught, usually a quantity of fish: *The fishermen got a good catch last night.* **3** a hook or other apparatus for fastening something or holding it shut: *The catch on this door is broken.* **4** *infml* a hidden difficulty: *That house is very cheap; there must be a catch in it somewhere!*

catch-22 /ˌ·ˈ··ˈ·/ *n* [U] a situation that you cannot escape from because of something that is part of the situation itself: *The report complained of the catch-22 situation facing homeless people − that to register* *for a council house they must first have an address.*

catch·ing /ˈkætʃɪŋ/ adj [never before a noun] infml infectious (used of a disease)

catch·ment ar·e·a /ˈkætʃmənt ˌeəriə/ n the area from which a school gets its pupils, or from which people go to a particular hospital, etc.

catch-phrase /ˈ··/ n a phrase, often with little meaning, which becomes fashionable and widely used for a time

catch·word /ˈkætʃwɜːd ‖ -ɜːrd/ n a word or phrase repeated regularly by a particular person or political party

catch·y /ˈkætʃi/ adj easy to remember: a catchy song

cat·e·gor·i·cal /ˌkætɪˈgɒrɪkəl ‖ -ˈgɔː-, -ˈgɑː-/ adj completely certain (used of a statement): a categorical denial **–categorically** /-kli/ adv : I asked her several times to come, but she categorically refused.

cat·e·go·rize /ˈkætɪɡəraɪz/ v **categorized, categorizing** (also **categorise** BrE) [T] to put someone or something in a group with similar people or things: He was categorized as a trouble-maker.

cat·e·go·ry /ˈkætɪɡəri ‖ -ɡɔːri/ n **categories** a group of similar people or things

ca·ter /ˈkeɪtəʳ/ v **1** [I] to provide and serve food and drinks for a large group of people: Who's catering at your daughter's wedding? **2 cater for someone** to provide what is wanted or needed by someone: a holiday company that caters mainly for older people **3 cater to** to try to please someone's desires or needs, usually of a bad kind: a paper that caters to the lowest tastes of the reading public

cat·er·pil·lar /ˈkætəˌpɪləʳ ‖ -tər-/ n a small wormlike creature with many legs that feeds on the leaves of plants

ca·the·dral /kəˈθiːdrəl/ n an important large church

cath·o·lic /ˈkæθəlɪk/ adj **1** fml including many different things (used to describe interests): catholic opinions **2 Catholic** relating to the Roman Catholic Church: Catholic children | Catholic schools

Catholic n someone who follows the Roman Catholic religion: She's a practising Catholic. **–Catholicism** /kəˈθɒlɪsɪzəm ‖ kəˈθɑː-/ n [U]

cat·nap /ˈkætnæp/ n infml a very short light sleep

cat's eye /ˈ··/ n a small object fixed in the middle of a road which shines when lights shine on it

cat·tle /ˈkætl/ n [pl] male and female cows kept on a farm

cat·ty /ˈkæti/ adj infml unpleasant and unkind: a catty remark

caught /kɔːt/ v the past tense and past participle of CATCH

caul·dron /ˈkɔːldrən/ n (**caldron** AmE) a large round metal pot for boiling liquids over a fire

cau·li·flow·er /ˈkɒlɪˌflaʊəʳ ‖ ˈkɔː-, ˈkɑː-/ n [C;U] a garden vegetable with green leaves around a large white head of undeveloped flowers –see picture on page 344

cause¹ /kɔːz/ n **1** [C] a person or thing that makes something happen –see REASON (USAGE) **2** [U] reason: Don't give him any cause for complaint. **3** [C] a principle or movement which people fight for: She's committed to the cause of nuclear disarmament.

cause² v **caused, causing** [T] to make something happen: What caused the accident? | His illness caused him to miss the game. | This car has caused me a lot of trouble. | The disaster was caused by poor planning.

□ USEFUL PATTERNS to cause something; to

cause someone to do something; to cause someone something

cause·way /ˈkɔːzweɪ/ n a raised road or path across wet ground or water

caus·tic /ˈkɔːstɪk/ adj **1** able to burn by chemical action: caustic soda **2** very unpleasant (used of remarks): his caustic comments

cau·tion¹ /ˈkɔːʃən/ n **1** [U] care taken to avoid danger: You must exercise great caution when operating the machine. **2** [C] a spoken warning given by a policeman

caution² v [T] to warn someone: The policeman said, "I must caution you that anything you say may be used against you."

cau·tion·ar·y /ˈkɔːʃənəri ‖ -neri/ adj fml giving advice or a warning

cau·tious /ˈkɔːʃəs/ adj taking care to avoid danger: a very cautious driver **–cautiously** adv: I opened the door cautiously. **–cautiousness** n [U]

cav·al·cade /ˌkævəlˈkeɪd, ˈkævəlkeɪd/ n a procession of people, riders, or vehicles

cav·a·lier /ˌkævəˈlɪəʳ ◄/ adj showing no consideration for the feelings of other people: I'm annoyed at your cavalier treatment of him.

cav·al·ry /ˈkævəlri/ n [U + sing/pl verb] **1** soldiers trained to fight using horses **2** part of the army that uses vehicles

cave¹ /keɪv/ n a large natural hole below ground or in the side of a cliff or hill

cave² v **caved, caving**
cave in phr v [I] **1** to fall inwards: The roof of the old house caved in. **2** to suddenly stop opposing something

cave·man /ˈkeɪvmæn/ n **cavemen** /-men/ a person who lived in a cave in very ancient times

cav·ern /ˈkævən/ n a large deep cave **–cavernous** adj : the lion's cavernous mouth

cav·i·ar /ˈkæviɑːʳ/ n (also **caviare**) [U] the salted eggs of fish, eaten as food

cav·i·ty /ˈkævɪti/ n **cavities** a hole or hollow space in a solid mass: a cavity in a tooth

ca·vort /kəˈvɔːt ‖ -ɔːrt/ v [I] infml to jump or dance about noisily

caw /kɔː/ n the loud rough cry of various large birds **–caw** v [I]

cc /ˌsiː ˈsiː/ a unit used for measuring how much something can contain; an abbreviation for **cubic centimetre**: a 250cc engine

CD /ˌsiː ˈdiː/ n an abbreviation for COMPACT DISC

cease /siːs/ v **ceased, ceasing** [I;T] fml to stop: Disputes with the management must cease immediately. | The law will cease to be valid from midnight tonight. | They have ceased trading in that part of the world.

□ USEFUL PATTERNS to cease; to cease to do something; to cease doing something

cease-fire /ˈ··/ n a formal agreement between both sides to stop fighting

cease·less /ˈsiːsləs/ adj going on without stopping for a long time: I'm fed up with all this ceaseless arguing. **–ceaselessly** adv

ce·dar /ˈsiːdəʳ/ n [C;U] a tall tree that does not lose its leaves in winter

cede /siːd/ v **ceded, ceding** [T] fml to give something, usually land, to another country or person, often after losing a war: In 1871 France ceded Alsace–Lorraine to Germany.

cei·ling /ˈsiːlɪŋ/ n **1** the inner surface of the top of a room –compare ROOF¹ (1) **2** an official upper limit on things like wages or rents

cel·e·brate /ˈselɪbreɪt/ v **celebrated, celebrating**
1 [I;T] to do something special because of a particular event or special occasion: *You got the job! Let's*
celebrate. | *We celebrated the New Year with a party.*
2 [T] *fml* to praise someone in speech or writing **3**
[T] (of a priest) to perform a religious ceremony

cel·e·brat·ed /ˈselɪbreɪtɪd/ adj famous: *a celebrated*
painter | *Venice is celebrated for its beautiful*
buildings.

cel·e·bra·tion /ˌselɪˈbreɪʃən/ n **1** [C] a special occasion because something good has happened or
because it is an occasion like a birthday: *We enjoyed*
a quiet celebration on our own. **2** [U] *fml* the showing of praise and pleasure: *in celebration of his mag-*
nificent achievement

ce·leb·ri·ty /sɪˈlebrɪti/ n **celebrities** a famous
person

cel·e·ry /ˈseləri/ n [U] a vegetable with greenish-
white stems: *I only had a stick of celery for lunch.*
–see picture on page 344

ce·les·ti·al /sɪˈlestiəl ‖ -tʃəl/ adj fml relating to the
sky or heaven

cel·i·bate /ˈselɪbət/ adj never taking part in sexual
activity, especially for religious reasons –**celibacy**
/-bəsi/ n [U]

cell /sel/ n **1** a small room in a prison or police station where prisoners are kept **2** the smallest part
of an animal or plant that can exist on its own: *Plant*
cells reproduce by dividing. **3** a small room with little furniture where a member of a religious organization lives

cel·lar /ˈselər/ n an underground room, often used
for storing things: *a wine cellar*

cel·list /ˈtʃelɪst/ n a person who plays the cello

cel·lo /ˈtʃeləʊ/ n **cellos** (also **violincello** fml) a musical instrument with four strings, like the VIOLIN
but larger and producing a deeper sound; you hold
it between your knees

cel·lo·phane /ˈseləfeɪn/ n [U] tdmk thin transparent
material used for wrapping up food

cel·lu·lar /ˈseljʊlər/ adj relating to the cells in a plant
or an animal

cel·lu·loid /ˈseljʊlɔɪd/ n [U] tdmk a plastic substance
made mainly from cellulose, used in the past to
make film

cel·lu·lose /ˈseljʊləʊs/ n [U] the material from which
the cell walls of plants are made, used in making
paper, plastic, and many man-made materials

Cel·si·us /ˈselsiəs/ n a scale of temperature at which
water freezes at 0° and boils at 100°: *a temperature*
of 10° Celsius

Cel·tic /ˈkeltɪk, ˈseltɪk/ adj connected with the peo-
ple, culture, or language of the Celts, an ancient
European people whose descendants live in Wales,
Scotland, Ireland, and Britanny

ce·ment[1] /sɪˈment/ n [U] **1** a grey powder used in
building, which becomes hard like stone when
mixed with water and allowed to dry **2** a type of
glue

cement[2] v [T] **1** to strengthen a relationship: *Our*
holiday together cemented our friendship. **2** to cover
something with cement

SPELLING NOTE

Words with the sound /k/, like **cut**, may be spelt
k-, like **key**, or **qu-**, like **queen**.
Words with the sound /s/, like **city**, may be spelt
s-, like **soon**, or **ps-**, like **psychology**.

---

cem·e·tery /ˈsemɪtri ‖ -teri/ n a place where dead
people are buried

cen·sor /ˈsensər/ n an official who examines books,
plays, or films and has the power to remove anything offensive –**censor** v [T]: *Prisoners' letters are*
usually censored. –**censorship** n [U]

cen·sure /ˈsenʃər/ n fml [U] the expressing of strong
disapproval: *The opposition passed a vote of censure*
on the government. –**censure** v **censured, censur-**
ing [T] fml

cen·sus /ˈsensəs/ n an official count of all the people in a country, including details of where they
live and the jobs they do

cent /sent/ n a unit of money used in the US; there
are 100 cents in a dollar

cen·te·na·ry /senˈtiːnəri ‖ -ˈte-, ˈsentəneri/ n the day
or year exactly 100 years after a particular event

cen·ten·ni·al /senˈteniəl/ n the usual American word
for CENTENARY

cen·ter /ˈsentər/ n,v see CENTRE

Cen·ti·grade /ˈsentɪɡreɪd/ n a scale of temperature
at which water freezes at 0° and boils at 100°

cen·ti·me·tre /ˈsentɪˌmiːtər/ n (**centimeter** AmE)
a unit for measuring length, equal to 0·01 metres
or about 0·4 INCHES

cen·tral /ˈsentrəl/ adj **1** [only before a noun] at or
forming the centre of a place, object, or system: *the*
mountains of central Europe | *computers linked to*
a central database **2** [never before a noun] convenient because of being near the centre: *Our house*
is very central for the shops and theatres. **3** [only before a noun] the most important: *The central aim of*
this government is social equality.

central heat·ing /ˌ·· ˈ··/ n [U] a system of heating
buildings in which heat is produced at a single
point and carried to parts of the building by pipes

cen·tral·ize /ˈsentrəlaɪz/ v **centralized, centraliz-**
ing (also **centralise** BrE) [T] to place something
under central control: *Some countries are really too*
big for centralized government. –**centralization**
/ˌsentrəlaɪˈzeɪʃən ‖ -lə-/ n [U]

cen·tre[1] /ˈsentər/ n (**center** AmE) **1** the exact middle part or point: *Although London is Britain's cap-*
ital it is not at the centre of the country. | *chocolates*
with soft centres **2** a place or building used for a par-
ticular activity: *a shopping centre* | *a leisure centre*
3 a place where something is very important or
very active: *He likes to be the centre of attention.* | *the*
centre of the nation's shipbuilding industry **4** the
centre a position that is not extreme in politics: *the*
parties of the centre –see MIDDLE[2] (USAGE)

centre[2] v **centred, centring** (**center** AmE) **1** [T]
to place something in or at the centre: *The picture*
would look better if you centred it between the two
other pictures. **2 centre on something, centre**
around something to have something as the most
important subject: *Our thoughts centred on the girl*
who had died.

centre of grav·i·ty /ˌ··· ˈ···/ n the point in an object
on which it will balance

cen·tu·ri·on /senˈtʃʊəriən ‖ -ˈtʊ-/ n an army officer
of ancient Rome, commanding about 100 men

cen·tu·ry /ˈsentʃəri/ n **centuries 1** a period of 100
years **2** (also **Century**) one of the 100-year periods
used in giving dates: *the twentieth century*

ce·ram·ics /sɪˈræmɪks/ n [pl] objects produced by
shaping bits of clay and baking them until they are
hard –**ceramic** adj

ce·re·al /ˈsɪəriəl/ n **1** [C] a plant such as wheat
grown to produce grain: *cereal crops* **2** [C;U] food

made from grain, eaten at breakfast in some countries

cer·e·bral /ˈserᵻbrəl ‖ səˈriː-, ˈserᵻ-/ *adj tech* connected with the brain

cer·e·mo·ni·al /ˌserᵻˈməʊniəl/ *adj* belonging to a ceremony **–ceremonially** *adv*

cer·e·mo·ni·ous /ˌserᵻˈməʊniəs/ *adj* very formal and polite –opposite **unceremonious –ceremoniously** *adv*

cer·e·mo·ny /ˈserᵻməni ‖ -məʊni/ *n* **ceremonies** **1** [C] a formal, solemn, and well-established action or set of actions used for marking an important public, social, or religious event: *the wedding ceremony* **2** [U] the special order and formal behaviour demanded by custom on particular occasions: *The queen was crowned with proper ceremony.* **3** **without ceremony** without waiting or treating something as very important

cer·tain¹ /ˈsɜːtn ‖ ˈsɜːrtn/ *adj* **1** having no doubts about something: *I'm absolutely certain that it was him I saw.* | *She felt certain that she would get the job.* | *I'm not certain where he lives.* | *We'll win the competition–I'm certain of that.* □ USEFUL PATTERNS be certain of something; be certain that...; be certain how, why, when, etc **2** clearly proved to exist or to be true: *There is no certain cure for this illness.* **3** sure to happen: *It is almost certain that the government will lose the next election.* | *The army claim that they are heading for certain victory.* –see SURE¹ (USAGE) **4 be certain to do something** to be sure or very likely to do something: *She's certain to pass her exams.* | *Whatever I do, he's certain to criticize it.* **5 make certain** to do something in order to be sure about something: *We need to make certain that these policies are implemented.* **6 know something for certain** to know something without any doubt: *I don't know for certain how old she is.* **7** [only before a noun] quite small in amount or degree: *He makes a certain amount of profit from the business, but he'll never be rich.* | *I agree with you to a certain extent.* **8** [only before a noun] present and noticeable, but difficult to describe in detail: *He has a certain charm.* **9 a certain** used before someone's name when you do not know the person: *A certain Mr Robinson phoned you today.*

certain² *determiner,pron* a word you use to talk about one or more people or things, without saying exactly which ones they are: *There are certain reasons why this information cannot be made public.* | *When the water reaches a certain level, the pump switches itself off.* | *Certain coastal areas are most at risk from flooding.* | *Certain of these questions have never been answered.*

cer·tain·ly /ˈsɜːtnli ‖ ˈsɜːr-/ *adv* **1** without doubt: *"I read a lot." "You've certainly got a lot of books!"* | *Inflation will almost certainly rise this year.* **2** a word used when you are agreeing with something or when you want to make your answer seem strong: *"Will you help me?" "Certainly I will."* | *"Can I use your phone?" "Certainly. Go ahead."* **3 certainly not** a strong way of answering a question in the negative: *"Will you lend me your comb?" "Certainly not!"*

cer·tain·ty /ˈsɜːtnti ‖ ˈsɜːr-/ *n* **certainties 1** [U] the quality of being sure: *I can't say with certainty what my plans are.* **2** [C] a clearly established fact: *It's an absolute certainty that this horse will win.* –opposite **uncertainty**

cer·tif·i·cate /səˈtɪfɪkət ‖ sər-/ *n* an important paper containing information that an official person says is true: *a birth certificate*

cer·ti·fy /ˈsɜːtᵻfaɪ ‖ ˈsɜːr-/ *v* **certified, certifying** [T] **1** to declare that something is correct or true: *The bank certified my accounts.* **2** to provide someone with an official paper to show they have completed a course of training for a particular profession: *a certified teacher* **3** to declare someone mad: *His parents had tried to get him certified insane.*

cer·ti·tude /ˈsɜːtᵻtjuːd ‖ ˈsɜːrtᵻtuːd/ *n fml* [U] the quality of being sure

cer·vix /ˈsɜːvɪks ‖ ˈsɜːr-/ *n tech* the narrow opening into a woman's WOMB **–cervical** /ˈsɜːvɪkəl ‖ ˈsɜːr-/ *adj*

ce·sar·e·an /sᵻˈzeəriən/ *n* see CAESAREAN

ces·sa·tion /seˈseɪʃən/ *n fml* stopping: *a cessation of hostilities*

cess·pit /ˈsesˌpɪt/ *n* (also **cesspool** /-puːl/) an underground container or hole where household waste water is collected, especially SEWAGE

cf a word used in writing which tells the reader to compare something else; an abbreviation for the Latin word **confer "compare"**

chafe /tʃeɪf/ *v* **chafed, chafing 1** [I;T] to make or become sore, painful, or uncomfortable by rubbing: *Her skin chafes easily.* | *Her shoes chafed the skin on her feet.* **2** [I] to become impatient or annoyed: *He chafed at the delay.*

chaff /tʃɑːf ‖ tʃæf/ *n* [U] the outer part of a seed of grain

chain¹ /tʃeɪn/ *n* **1** [C;U] rings of metal fitted together: *The bridge was supported by heavy iron chains hanging from the two towers.* | *She had a gold chain round her neck.* | *Have you got any chain?* **2** [C] a number of things connected in some way: *Mr Patel runs a chain of launderettes.* | *an unfortunate chain of events* **3 in chains** kept in prison or as a slave

chain² *v* [T; + adv/prep] to limit the freedom of someone or something with a chain: *It's time the dogs were chained up for the night.* | *The protesters chained themselves to the gate of the nuclear power plant.*

chain mail /ˈ· ·/ *n* [U] a type of armour made by joining small metal rings together

chain re·ac·tion /ˌ· ·ˈ··/ *n* a number of events or chemical changes related to each other in such a way that each causes the next

chain-smoke /ˈ· ·/ *v* **chain-smoked, chain-smoking** [I;T] to smoke cigarettes continually **–chain-smoker** *n*

chain store /ˈ· ·/ *n* one of a group of similar shops owned by one person or organization

chair¹ /tʃeəʳ/ *n* **1** a piece of furniture on which one person can sit, which usually has a back, a seat, and four legs **2** the person in charge of a meeting: *Please address your remarks to the chair.* **3** the position of PROFESSOR: *She holds the chair of chemistry in that university.* **4 the chair** *infml* the ELECTRIC CHAIR

chair² *v* [T] to be the chairman of a meeting

chair·man /ˈtʃeəmən ‖ ˈtʃeər-/ *n* **chairmen** /-mən/ **1** a person who is in charge of a meeting or who directs the work of a committee or organization: *one of our most experienced chairmen* **2** the person in charge of a large organization or company: *the chairman of IBM*

chair·man·ship /ˈtʃeəmənʃɪp ‖ ˈtʃeər-/ *n* the rank, position, or period in office of chairman

chair·per·son /ˈtʃeəˌpɜːsən ‖ ˈtʃeərˌpɜːrsən/ *n* **chairpersons** someone who is in charge of a meeting or a committee

chair·wom·an /ˈtʃeəˌwʊmən ‖ ˈtʃeər-/ *n* **chair-**

women /-,wimin/ a woman who is in charge of a meeting or a committee

chal·et /ˈʃæleɪ ‖ ʃæˈleɪ/ n a small house, usually made of wood and with a steep roof

chal·ice /ˈtʃælɪs/ n a gold or silver decorated cup, used to hold wine in Christian religious services

chalk¹ /tʃɔːk/ n **1** [U] a soft white rock: *chalk hills* **2** [C;U] chalk that has been made into sticks and used for writing or drawing **3 as different as chalk and cheese** *infml* completely unlike each other −**chalky** *adj*

chalk² v [I;T] to write, mark, or draw with chalk **chalk** sthg ↔ **up** *phr* v [T] *infml* to succeed in getting something, especially points in a competition: *Our team has chalked up another victory.*

chal·lenge¹ /ˈtʃæləndʒ/ v challenged, challenging [T] **1** to invite someone to compete against you or to test their abilities: *I challenged him to a game of tennis.* | *I challenge you to climb that rock!*
□ USEFUL PATTERNS to challenge someone to something; to challenge someone to do something **2** to question whether something is right: *She challenged the justice of the new law.* −**challenger** n

challenge² n **1** [C] an invitation to compete in a fight or match: *He accepted his friend's challenge to swim across the river.* **2** [C;U] something difficult or exciting that needs a great effort: *To build a bridge in a month was a real challenge.* −**challenging** *adj*: *a challenging job*

cham·ber /ˈtʃeɪmbər/ n **1** a room used for a special purpose like a formal meeting: *Everyone wanted to hear the new Chairman speak and the Council chamber was full.* **2** a group of people elected or appointed to make laws or govern a country: *The upper chamber votes on the proposals put forward in the lower chamber.* **3** an enclosed space, in the body or in a machine: *The gun has six chambers for bullets.* **4** *old fash* a room, especially a bedroom **5 chambers** [pl] offices used by lawyers who work at court

cham·ber·maid /ˈtʃeɪmbəmeɪd ‖ -ər-/ n a woman employed to clean and tidy bedrooms, especially in a hotel

chamber mu·sic /ˈ·· ,··/ n music written for a small group of instruments and suitable for performance in a private home or small hall

cha·me·le·on /kəˈmiːliən/ n a small animal with a long tail, which can change its colour to match its surroundings

champ¹ /tʃæmp/ v [I] to bite noisily

champ² n *infml* see CHAMPION

cham·pagne /ʃæmˈpeɪn/ n [U] a French white wine containing a lot of bubbles, often drunk on special occassions

cham·pi·on¹ /ˈtʃæmpiən/ n **1** (also **champ** *infml*) a person or animal that has won competitions of courage, strength, or skill: *a tennis champion* **2** a person who fights for a special cause: *a champion of women's rights*

champion² v [T] to fight for or defend a principle, a movement, or a person

cham·pi·on·ship /ˈtʃæmpiənʃɪp/ n **1** a competition held to find the champion **2** the position, title, rank, or period of being the champion: *Do you think*

SPELLING NOTE
Words with the sound / ʃ /, like **chauffeur**, may be spelt **sh-**, like **shop**.

anyone can take the championship from him?

chance¹ /tʃɑːns ‖ tʃæns/ n **1** [U] the force that seems to make things happen without cause or reason, and that cannot be controlled by humans: *Chance plays an important part in many card games.* | *It happened quite by chance.* **2** [C;U] a possibility: *You'd have more chance of catching the train if you got a bus to the station.* | *Is there any chance that he'll be coming to Paris this week?* | *She doesn't stand a chance of winning.* | *"What are the chances of seeing the director today?" "No chance!"* **3 a chance in a million** *infml* extremely lucky, or extremely unlucky: *I never thought I'd find it again; it was a chance in a million!* **4 be in with a chance** to have a slight chance of doing or getting something desirable **5** [C] a situation that is good for something: *I never miss a chance of playing football.* | *I haven't had a chance to sit down all day!* | *You'd better do it now − you may not get a second chance.* **6** [C] a risk: *The rope might break, but that's a chance I'll have to take!* **7 by any chance** a very polite phrase used in a question when you think the answer will be "no": *You haven't got a spare stamp by any chance?* **8 on the off chance** in the slight hope that something might happen: *We heard the theatre was full, but we went on the off chance of getting seats.*

■ USAGE Compare **chance**, **opportunity**, **occasion**. **1** You can use **chance** or **opportunity** when by good luck you have time to do something: *I'll speak to Professor Smith at the conference, if I get the* **chance**/the **opportunity**. **2** When you are talking about possibility alone, use **chance**, not **opportunity**: *There's a slight* **chance** (= possibility) *that this plane will crash.* **3** We usually use **occasion** to refer to a time when something happens: *He met the president on several* **occasions**.

chance² v chanced, chancing [not in progressive forms] **1** [T] to take a chance with something: *You shouldn't chance all your money at once.* **2** [I] *fml* to happen without being planned: *She chanced to be in the park when I was there.* **3 chance it** *infml* to take a risk
chance on sbdy/sthg *phr* v [T] *old fash* to meet someone or find something by chance

chance³ *adj* [only before a noun] unplanned: *a chance meeting*

chan·cel·lor /ˈtʃɑːnsələr ‖ ˈtʃæn-/ n (also **Chancellor**) **1** the head of government, in some countries: *the West German chancellor* **2** the head of a university **3 the Chancellor of the Exchequer** the government minister who deals with taxes and government spending in Britain

chanc·y /ˈtʃɑːnsi ‖ ˈtʃænsi/ *adj infml* risky or uncertain: *That was a chancy thing to do. You could have been killed.*

chan·de·lier /ˌʃændəˈlɪər/ n a large decorative holder for lights or candles, hanging from the CEILING

change¹ /tʃeɪndʒ/ v changed, changing **1** [I] to become different: *In autumn the leaves change* from green *to* brown. | *He's changed a lot since I last saw him.* **2** to make something or someone different: *The discovery of oil there has changed the whole character of the area.* **3** [T] to put something in place of something else: *Can I change this red jumper for a blue one?* | *She changed her books at the library.* | *She's changed her job − she's a hairdresser now.* | *He changed trains in Paris.* | *I don't like talking about the divorce. Let's change the subject.* **3** [I;T] to put on different clothes: *She changed out of her new dress and into something more comfortable.* | *I must change these shoes before we go out.* |

I'll be ready in five minutes. I've just got to change.
4 change a baby, change a baby's nappy to put a new NAPPY on a baby **5 change a bed, change the sheets** to put new coverings on a bed **6** [T] to give money in exchange for money of a different type: *Where can I change my English money for dollars?* | *Can you change a pound into tenpenny pieces?* **7 change hands** to become someone else's property: *This house has changed hands three times in the last two years.* **8 change your mind** to form a new opinion or wish: *We were going to go to Paris this weekend, but we've changed our minds.* **9 change your tune** to act in a different way because you have discovered something new: *He said he didn't like black-haired women, but when he saw my friend Debbie he soon changed his tune!*

change into *phr v* **1** [T **change into** sbdy/sthg] to become something different: *The next morning, the water had changed into ice.* **2** [T **change** sbdy/sthg **into** sbdy/sthg] to cause to become something different: *You can't change iron into gold.*

change over *phr v* [I] to make a complete change: *In 1971 Britain changed over from pounds, shillings, and pence to the new decimal money system.*

change² *n* **1** [C;U] the act or result of changing: *We need a change of leadership.* | *There was little change in his condition.* **2 make a change** to be something different from usual and for that reason enjoyable: *We eat a lot of potatoes, so rice makes a nice change.* **3 for a change** as something different from usual: *We always go to French restaurants. Let's go to an Italian restaurant for a change.* **4** [C] something different: *She's on holiday; she needed a change.* **5** [C] something new and fresh used in place of something else: *He took a change of clothes with him.* | *Your car needs an oil change.* **6** [U] the money returned to you in a shop when you have paid more than the price of something: *Don't forget your change!* **7** [U] small coins, rather than notes: *Can you give me change for a pound?*

■ USAGE **1** If you want to say that one thing is put in the place of another, use **change of**: *There'll be a change of government at the next election.* | *I need a change of job.* **2** If you are talking about changes which happen to something or somebody, use **change(s) in**: *There's been a subtle change in his attitude to women.* | *some interesting changes in the structure of society* | *recent changes in government policy* | *a change in the weather*

change·a·ble /ˈtʃeɪndʒəbəl/ *adj* likely to change (used especially of the weather) –**changeability** /ˌtʃeɪndʒəˈbɪlɪti/ *n* [U]

change·o·ver /ˈtʃeɪndʒˌəʊvəʳ/ *n* a change from one activity or system to another

chang·ing room /ˈ··· ·/ *n* a room in a clothes shop, swimming pool, or sports centre where you change your clothes

chan·nel¹ /ˈtʃænl/ *n* **1** a particular television station: *It's on channel 10.* | *What's on the other channel?* **2** a narrow sea passage: *The English Channel separates England and France.* **3** a way or passage along which liquid flows: *There's a channel in the middle of the old street to help rainwater flow away.* **4** a part of a river which is safe for ships travelling along it **5** the line of travel which ships travelling across the sea should use **6 channels** a way to arrange for something to be done: *I'm afraid I can't help you – you'll have to go through the official channels.*

channel² *v* **-ll-** (also **-l-** *AmE*) [T] **1** to direct something in a particular way: *I decided to channel my energies into something useful.* **2** to form a

channel in something, or to take something such as water somewhere by means of a channel

chant /tʃɑːnt ‖ tʃænt/ *n* **1** a religious song with words sung on very few notes **2** a group of words repeated many times: *a football chant* –**chant** *v* [I;T]

cha·os /ˈkeɪ-ɒs ‖ -ɑːs/ *n* [U] a state of complete disorder and confusion: *After the earthquake the city was in chaos.*

cha·ot·ic /keɪˈɒtɪk ‖ -ˈɑːtɪk/ *adj* in a state of complete disorder and confusion: *a chaotic muddle* –**chaotically** /-kli/ *adv*

chap /tʃæp/ *n infml* a man or boy

chap·el /ˈtʃæpəl/ *n* **1** a part of a church, prison, hospital, college, or school where people pray and where small services can be held **2** a church used by nonconformists (NONCONFORMIST), people who do not belong to the Church of England or the Roman Catholic church

chap·er·one¹ /ˈʃæpərəʊn/ *n* an older woman who goes with a young unmarried woman to social events and is responsible for her behaviour

chaperone² *v* **chaperoned, chaperoning** [I;T] to act as a chaperone to someone

chap·lain /ˈtʃæplɪn/ *n* a religious minister who works for a club, a college, part of the armed forces

chapped /tʃæpt/ *adj* sore and cracked (used of your skin): *chapped lips*

chap·ter /ˈtʃæptəʳ/ *n* **1** one of the main divisions of a book or long article: *Please turn to Chapter Five.* **2** a particular period in someone's life or in history: *the finest chapter in American history* **3 chapter and verse** giving all the exact details

char /tʃɑːʳ/ *n old fash* see CHARWOMAN

char·ac·ter /ˈkærɪktəʳ/ *n* **1** [C;U] the qualities which make a person or place different from another: *I know what he looks like, but what about his character?* **2** [U] qualities which make someone or something attractively different: *a woman of great character* | *The old house had a lot of character.* **3** [C] a person in a book or play: *The main character is a young student.* **4** [C] *infml* a person who has a particular quality which is described: *He's a strange character.* **5** [C] *infml* an unusual or humorous person: *He's a real character* **6** [C] a letter or written sign: *The characters in Chinese writing look like small pictures.* **7 be out of character** to be unlike someone's usual nature [RELATED PHRASE **be in character**]

char·ac·ter·is·tic¹ /ˌkærɪktəˈrɪstɪk◂/ *adj* typical of a person's character: *With characteristic generosity, she gave them £100.* –**characteristically** /-kli/ *adv*

characteristic² *n* a special and easily recognized quality of someone or something: *A characteristic of the camel is its ability to live for a long time without water.*

char·ac·ter·ize /ˈkærɪktəraɪz/ *v* **characterized, characterizing** (also **characterise** *BrE*) [T] **1** to be typical of someone or something: *His books are characterized by long and detailed descriptions of the countryside.* **2** to describe the character of a person or thing: *She characterized him as lazy and selfish.* –**characterization** /ˌkærɪktəraɪˈzeɪʃən ‖ -rə-/ *n* [C;U]

cha·rade /ʃəˈrɑːd ‖ ʃəˈreɪd/ *n* **1** a false or foolish activity which pretends to be serious: *The management went through a charade of negotiating with the union leaders.* **2 charades** [pl] a game in which people have to guess the word that is being acted out

char·coal /ˈtʃɑːkəʊl ‖ ˈtʃɑːr-/ *n* [U] black material used for burning and drawing

charge¹ /tʃɑːdʒ ‖ tʃɑːrdʒ/ v **charged, charging** **1** [I;T] to ask for an amount of money in payment: *How much do you charge for your eggs?* | *The hotel charged me £50 for the room.* **2** [T] to add the cost of something to someone's bill: *Charge the drinks to my account.* **3** [I] to run very fast, often in order to attack someone: *The children charged out of school.* | *The elephant suddenly charged.* **4** [T] to say officially to someone they have done something against the law: *He was charged with stealing the jewels.* **5** [T] *fml* to give someone the responsibility for doing something: *The chief engineer is charged with maintaining safety throughout the railway system.* **6** [T] to pass an electric current through something so that it stores electricity: *I need to charge my car battery.*

charge² n **1** [C] the price asked for something: *The charge for cleaning the curtains was £13.* | *What are the charges like in that hotel?* **2 free of charge** costing nothing: *Delivery is free of charge.* **3 in charge** in a position of responsibility: *I don't know. Ask Mr Davis – he's in charge.* **4 take charge** to take control: *She took charge of the business when her father died.* **5 have charge of** be responsible for: *He has charge of the children while his wife is at work.* **6** [C] a statement accusing a person of a crime or an offence: *He was arrested on a charge of murder.* | *He faces a charge of murder.* | *The President's policy leaves him open to charges of favouring the rich.* **7 bring a charge against someone** to say formally to someone that someone has done something wrong **8** [C] a rushing forceful attack **9** [C] an explosive put into a gun or weapon **10** [C] electricity put into an electrical apparatus **11** [C] *fml* a person or thing for which someone is responsible

■ USAGE Compare **charge** and **cost**. **Cost** is the more general word for the amount of money you need to pay in order to do something or to have something done: *The government claim the cost of providing an adequate health service has greatly increased.* | *What would be the cost of a week in a London hotel?* | *The company has agreed to pay the cost of my trip to Paris.* **Charge** is the word for the amount of money you are asked to pay for a particular service: *A 10% service charge is included.* | *The hotel provides breakfast free of charge.* | *There will be a small charge for the use of the telephone.*

charged /tʃɑːdʒd ‖ -ɑːr-/ adj causing strong feelings or argument: *an emotionally charged atmosphere*

char·i·ot /ˈtʃæriət/ n a horse-drawn vehicle with 2 wheels, used in ancient times in battles and races –**charioteer** /ˌtʃæriəˈtɪəʳ/ n

cha·ris·ma /kəˈrɪzmə/ n [U] the special ability to charm or attract other people –**charismatic** /ˌkærɪzˈmætɪk◂/ adj

char·i·ty /ˈtʃærɪti/ n **charities** **1** [C] an organization that gives money and help to people who are poor, sick, or in difficulty: *The Red Cross is an international charity.* **2** [U] money or help given to people in need: *too proud to accept charity.* | *They make regular donations to charity.* **3** [U] sympathy and kindness –**charitable** adj : *a charitable act* –**charitably** adv

char·la·tan /ˈʃɑːlətən ‖ ˈʃɑːr-/ n a person who pretends to have a special knowledge or skill (a word

---

SPELLING NOTE
Words with the sound /ʃ/, like **chauffeur**, may be spelt **sh**, like **shop**.

---

used to express disapproval): *I'm not going to that doctor again – the man's a complete charlatan!*

charm¹ /tʃɑːm ‖ tʃɑːrm/ n **1** [C;U] the ability to please or delight other people: *You'll have to use all your charm to talk him into it.* | *This town has a charm you couldn't find in a big city.* **2** [C] an object worn as a decoration or to bring good luck: *a charm bracelet* | *a lucky charm*

charm² v [T] **1** to please or delight other people: *She can charm everyone with her smiles.* **2** to control something as if by magic: *He charmed the snake with his music.* –**charmer** n

charm·ing /ˈtʃɑːmɪŋ ‖ -ɑːr-/ adj very pleasing and delightful: *What a charming young man!* –**charmingly** adv

charred /tʃɑːd ‖ tʃɑːrd/ adj black from having been burned: *There was nothing left but a few charred remains.*

chart¹ /tʃɑːt ‖ tʃɑːrt/ n **1** a table showing information in the form of a picture: *a weather chart* **2** a detailed map of the sea or stars **3 the charts** a list of the most popular records: *It's gone straight into the charts.*

chart² v [T] to show or record something on a chart

char·ter¹ /ˈtʃɑːtəʳ ‖ -ɑːr-/ n **1** [C] a statement by the government or ruler which gives rights and freedoms to the people: *a charter of human rights* **2** [U] the practice of hiring buses or planes for private use: *charter flights*

charter² v [T] to hire a bus or plane for private use

chartered ac·coun·tant /ˌ··· ·ˈ··/ n an ACCOUNTANT who has completed training

char·wom·an /ˈtʃɑːˌwʊmən ‖ ˈtʃɑːr-/ n **charwomen** /-ˌwɪmɪn/ old-fash (also **char**) a woman who works as a cleaner in a house or office

char·y /ˈtʃeəri/ adj fml **be chary of** to be careful about what you do or believe: *He's chary of spending too much on transport.* –**charily** adv

chase¹ /tʃeɪs/ v **chased, chasing** **1** [I;T] to follow someone or something rapidly in order to catch them: *a cat chasing a mouse* | *Chase after them and remind them about the party.* **2** [I;T] to try very hard to get something: *We had a hundred people chasing only three jobs!* **3** [T + adv/prep] to make someone or something leave or run away: *They chased the dog out of the kitchen.* | *people chased from their homelands* **4** [I + adv/prep] to run about in a hurry: *The children are always chasing in and out.* | *I've been chasing all over town to buy his present.*

chase² n **1** an act of chasing something: *an exciting car chase in the film* **2 give chase** to run after someone in order to catch them: *She saw the thief and gave chase.*

chasm /ˈkæzəm/ n **1** a deep crack in the surface of the earth or ice **2** a big difference between two ideas or groups of people: *a political chasm between the two countries*

chas·sis /ˈʃæsi/ n (plural is **chassis** /ˈʃæsiz/) the framework on which the body of a vehicle is built

chaste /tʃeɪst/ adj old fash not having sex with anyone, or not having sex with anyone except your husband or wife (a word used to express approval) –**chastely** adv

chas·ten /ˈtʃeɪsən/ v [T] fml to make someone feel sorry about their bad or foolish behaviour: *He was chastened by the accident.*

chas·tise /tʃæˈstaɪz/ v **chastised, chastising** [T] fml to punish or blame someone severely

chas·ti·ty /ˈtʃæstɪti/ n [U] the state of not having sex with anyone, or not having sex with anyone except your husband or wife (a word used to express approval): *Chastity before marriage is still demanded in some societies.*

chat /tʃæt/ *v* -tt- [I] to talk in a friendly and informal way: *They like to get together and chat about the old days.* –**chat** *n*: *I had a chat with Mrs Bennett about her son's problems.*

chat sbdy ↔ **up** *phr v* [T] *infml* to talk to someone with the idea of attracting them and perhaps having sex with them

chat·line /'tʃætlaɪn/ *n* a way of talking to people by telephone; you ring a number and can have a conversation with several different people at the same time.

chat show /'· ·/ *n* a television or radio show in which well-known people talk to each other and are asked questions

chât·eau /'ʃætəʊ ‖ ʃæ'təʊ/ *n* **chateaus** *or* **chateaux** /'ʃætəʊz ‖ ʃæ'təʊz/ a castle or large country house in France

chat·ter¹ /'tʃætəʳ/ *v* [I] **1** to talk rapidly, usually about something unimportant: *The children were chattering happily.* **2 my teeth chattered** = my teeth knocked together because of cold or fear

chatter² *n* [U] **1** informal and unimportant conversation **2** a rapid knocking sound made by teeth or machines: *the chatter of machine-gun fire*

chat·ter·box /'tʃætəbɒks ‖ -tərbɑːks/ *n infml* a person who talks a lot

chat·ty /'tʃæti/ *adj* **chattier, chattiest** *infml* friendly and fond of talking

chauf·feur /'ʃəʊfəʳ, ʃəʊ'fɜːʳ/ *n* a person employed to drive someone's car –**chauffeur** *v* [I;T]

chau·vin·is·t /'ʃəʊvɪnᵻst/ *n* **1** a person who believes that their country is always right and better than all others **2** a man who believes that men are better than women and who treats women badly –**chauvinism** *n* [U] : *his appalling chauvinism* –**chauvinist, chauvinistic** /ˌʃəʊvɪˈnɪstɪk◂/ *adj*

cheap /tʃiːp/ *adj, adv* **1** low in price and good value for money: *Fresh vegetables are very cheap in the summer.* **2** low in price and of poor quality: *a cheap-looking suit* **3** not valuable: *Five hundred years ago human life was considered very cheap.* **4** unfair and unkind: *a cheap victory | a cheap joke* **5 get something cheap** to buy something for less money than it is worth **6 on the cheap** cheaply and, for that reason, not very well –**cheaply** *adv* : *a cheaply-furnished room*

cheap·en /'tʃiːpən/ *v* [T] **1** to make someone, especially yourself, less good or honourable: *Don't cheapen yourself by bothering to reply to his insults.* **2** to make something cheaper: *The dollar's increase in value has cheapened imports.*

cheat¹ /tʃiːt/ *v* **1** [I] to act dishonestly in order to win or gain something: *He always cheats at cards. | They were caught cheating in the exam.* **2** [T] to take something unfairly or dishonestly from someone: *He cheated the old woman out of her money. | They were cheated of victory.* **3** [I] to do something in a way which is not the way it should be done, but which is easier

cheat² *n* **1** a person who cheats **2** a person who is lazy and does something an easy way instead of the proper way

check¹ /tʃek/ *v* **1** [I;T;+(that)] to examine something, or make sure that everything is correct or as you expect it to be: *I'm just going to check this money. | You'll need to check on the quality. | I don't think she's in the office today. I'll just go and check. |*

Please check that he's done it properly before he leaves. | Can you check **with** *the police that we're allowed to enter the area?* **2** [T] to find out: *He checked the temperature every morning. | Check whether the papers have come.* **3** [T] to control or hold back: *The illness checked her progress.*

check in *phr v* [I] to report your arrival at a hotel desk, an airport, etc.: *You must check in an hour before your plane leaves.*

check out *phr v* **1** [I] to pay the bill and leave a hotel: *We checked out of the Hilton at 10 o'clock.* **2** [T **check** sthg ↔ **out**] *infml* to inquire about something to find out whether it is true or correct: *The police checked out his story.*

check up on sbdy/sthg *phr v* [T] to make thorough inquiries about someone or something: *She heard the police were checking up on her.*

check² *n* **1** [C] an examination to make sure that something is correct or as you want it to be: *a security check at the airport | a check on the quality of factory goods | I'll just have a quick check to see if he's asleep.* **2 in check** under control: *We've kept smallpox in check for ten years now.* **3** [C] the usual American word for a RECEIPT: *I've lost the check for my coat.* **4** [C] the usual American word for a bill at a restaurant **5** [C] the usual American word for a CHEQUE **6** [C;U] a pattern of coloured squares: *a blue and white check shirt* **7** [U] a situation in a game of CHESS when one player's king is under direct attack

checked /tʃekt/ *adj* having a pattern of coloured squares: *a checked tablecloth* –see picture on page 147

check·er·ed /'tʃekəd ‖ -ərd/ *adj* see CHEQUERED

check·ers /'tʃekəz ‖ -ərz/ *n* [sing] the usual American word for DRAUGHTS

check-in /'· ·/ *n* the place where you report your arrival at a hotel, an airport, etc.

checking ac·count /'··· ·ˌ·/ *n* the usual American word for a CURRENT ACCOUNT

check·list /'tʃekˌlɪst/ *n* a complete list of things that you must get or do or check, which you use to make sure you do not forget anything

check·mate¹ /'tʃekmeɪt/ *n* [C;U] the attack and defeat of a king in CHESS

checkmate² *v* **checkmated, checkmating** [T] **1** to win a CHESS game with a checkmate **2** to stop or completely defeat someone

check·out /'tʃek-aʊt/ *n* a desk in a self-service shop where you pay for goods

check·point /'tʃekpɔɪnt/ *n* a place where an examination is made of people, traffic, or goods: *You have to go through checkpoints on the border.*

check·up /'tʃek-ʌp/ *n* a medical examination: *I've got to have a checkup for my new job.*

ched·dar /'tʃedəʳ/ *n* (also **Cheddar**) [U] a hard smooth yellowish cheese

cheek¹ /tʃiːk/ *n* **1** [C] the fleshy part of your face below your eyes: *plump red cheeks* **2** [U] *infml* disrespectful rude behaviour: *She had the cheek to tell me to mind my own business.*

cheek² *v* [T] to behave disrespectfully or rudely towards someone

cheek·bone /'tʃiːkbəʊn/ *n* the bone just below your eye

cheek·y /'tʃiːki/ *adj* **cheekier, cheekiest** *infml* disrespectful, though sometimes in an attractive way: *Don't be so cheeky! | a cheeky smile* –**cheekiness** *n* [U]

cheep /tʃiːp/ *v* [I] (of birds) to make a weak high noise –**cheep** *n*

cheer¹ /ˈtʃɪəʳ/ n **1** [C] a shout of approval and encouragement: *the cheers of the crowd* **2** [U] *old fash* happiness and good spirits: *Christmas, the season of good cheer*

cheer² v [I] to shout in approval and support: *Every time a goal was scored the crowd cheered wildly.*
  cheer sbdy ↔ **on** *phr v* [T] to encourage someone by shouting approval: *The crowd cheered the home team on.*
  cheer up *phr v* **1** [I] to become happier: *Cheer up! The news isn't too bad.* **2** [T **cheer** sbdy ↔ **up**] to make someone happier: *His friends tried to cheer him up.*

cheer·ful /ˈtʃɪəfəl ‖ -ər-/ adj **1** tending to laugh and smile and be full of life: *Despite all her problems, she's always cheerful.* **2** likely to cause happy feelings: *cheerful music* –**cheerfully** adv : *"It doesn't matter," he said cheerfully.* –**cheerfulness** n [U]

Cheer·i·o /ˌtʃɪəriˈəʊ/ interj infml a word used when you leave someone or someone leaves you

cheer·less /ˈtʃɪələs ‖ ˈtʃɪər-/ adj dull and sad: *a cheerless rainy day*

cheers /tʃɪəz ‖ tʃɪərz/ interj infml **1** a word used to express good wishes just before people drink alcohol **2** thank you: *"Here's that £5 I owe you." "Oh, cheers."* **3** a word used when you leave someone or someone leaves you

cheer·y /ˈtʃɪəri/ adj **cheerier, cheeriest** smiling and cheerful: *a cheery greeting* –**cheerily** adv –**cheeriness** n [U]

cheese /tʃiːz/ n [C;U] solid food made from milk: *We need some cheese for the sandwiches.* | *They sell a good range of French cheeses.* –see picture on page 344

cheese·cake /ˈtʃiːzkeɪk/ n [C;U] cake made with creamy cheese, and sometimes fruit on top

chee·tah /ˈtʃiːtə/ n a large animal of the cat family, able to run very fast

chef /ʃef/ n the chief cook in a restaurant

chem·i·cal¹ /ˈkemɪkəl/ adj relating to chemistry or made by chemistry: *A chemical change takes place when the acid is added.* –**chemically** /-kli/ adv

chemical² n any substance used in or produced by chemistry

chem·ist /ˈkemɪst/ n **1** a scientist specializing in chemistry who works in industry or at a university: *a research chemist* **2** a person who makes up drugs and medicines in a shop **3 chemist's** (also **drugstore** *AmE*) a shop where medicines and other goods are sold: *I got some skin cream at the chemist's.*

chem·is·try /ˈkemɪstri/ n [U] the study of the substances which make up the universe and the way in which they change and combine with each other: *She's got a degree in chemistry.*

cheque /tʃek/ n (**check** *AmE*) a form instructing a bank to pay money to someone: *I'd like to pay by cheque, please.* | *He wrote out the cheque.*

cheque card /ˈ· ·/ n a plastic card given to people by a bank, promising that the bank will pay out the money written on their cheques up to a certain amount: *I'm afraid we can't accept cheques without a cheque card.*

chequ·er·ed /ˈtʃekəd ‖ -ərd/ adj (**checkered** *AmE*)

SPELLING NOTE

Words with the sound / ʃ /, like **chauffeur**, may be spelt **sh-**, like **shop**.

---

1 covered with a pattern of different coloured squares: *a chequered flag* **2** varied, with good and bad parts: *He'd had a chequered past.*

cher·ish /ˈtʃerɪʃ/ v [T] fml to care for something or someone in a tender, loving way: *He cherished the memory of his dead wife.*

cher·ry /ˈtʃeri/ n **cherries** a small round fruit with red or black skin –see picture on page 344

cher·ub /ˈtʃerəb/ n **1** [plural **cherubs** or **cherubim**] an ANGEL shown in a painting as a young child with wings **2** a sweet and pretty child –**cherubic** /tʃəˈruːbɪk / adj

chess /tʃes/ n [U] a game for two players, played on a board of black and white squares, in which each player tries to move his or her pieces to trap the other player's king

chest /tʃest/ n **1** the upper front part of your body: *He was suffering from chest pains.* –see PAIN (USAGE) **2** a large strong box with a lid: *an old oak chest* **3 get something off your chest** to talk about something you are worrying about so that you feel better: *It's obvious something's bothering you. Come on, get it off your chest!*

chest·nut¹ /ˈtʃesnʌt/ n **1** a tree which produces smooth brown nuts in prickly cases **2** a smooth brown nut in a prickly case

chestnut² adj,n [U] reddish-brown (usually used of hair and horses)

chest of drawers /ˌ· · ˈ·/ n **chests of drawers** a piece of furniture with several drawers

chest·y /ˈtʃesti/ adj suffering from a disease of the chest

chew¹ /tʃuː/ v [I;T] to crush food with your teeth before swallowing it
  chew sth ↔ **over** *phr v* [T] infml to think about a question or a problem: *Let me chew it over for a few days and let you know.*

chew² n [sing] the act of chewing

chewing gum /ˈ· ·/ n [U] (also **gum**) a type of sweet made to be chewed but not swallowed

chew·y /ˈtʃuːi/ adj needing to be chewed: *a chewy toffee*

chic /ʃiːk/ adj fashionable and having a good idea of style: *I think your hat is rather chic.* –**chic** n [U]

chick /tʃɪk/ n a young chicken or other bird

chick·en¹ /ˈtʃɪkɪn/ n **1** [C] a bird kept for its meat and eggs: *a huge shed for 2000 chickens* | *He keeps chickens in his garden.* **2** [U] the meat of this bird: *chicken pie* –see MEAT (USAGE) –see picture on page 344

chicken² v
  chicken out *phr v* [I] infml to decide not to do something because you are afraid: *I chickened out of telling him at the last minute.*

chick·en·feed /ˈtʃɪkɪnfiːd/ n [U] infml a small unimportant amount of money

chicken pox /ˈ· · ·/ n [U] a disease which causes fever and spots on the skin

chic·o·ry /ˈtʃɪkəri/ n [U] a plant with bitter-tasting leaves

chide /tʃaɪd/ v **chided, chiding** [I;T] lit to speak angrily to someone who has done something wrong

chief¹ /tʃiːf/ n a leader of a group or organization: *The president is chief of the armed forces.*

chief² adj [only before a noun] **1** highest in rank: *the chief clerk* **2** most important: *Rice is the chief crop in this area.*

chief·ly /ˈtʃiːfli/ adv mainly: *The accident happened chiefly because you were careless.*

chief·tain /ˈtʃiːftɪn/ n the leader of a tribe

chif·fon /'ʃɪfɒn ‖ ʃɪ'fɑːn/ n [U] a soft transparent silky material used for scarves (SCARF) and evening dresses

chil·blain /'tʃɪlbleɪn/ n a red painful swelling on your hand or foot, caused by being cold

child /tʃaɪld/ n **children** /'tʃɪldrən/ **1** a young person, not yet fully grown: *We've known each other since we were children.* **2** a son or daughter: *We have five children but they're all grown-up now.* **3** child's play something that is very easy to do: *Riding a bicycle will be child's play when you've had some practice.*
■ USAGE Compare **child** with **baby, infant, toddler, teenager, adolescent, youth, kid**. A very young child is a **baby**, or an **infant** (rather formal). A child who has just learned to walk is a **toddler**. People aged 13 to 19 are **teenagers**. A younger teenager may be called an **adolescent**. This word is rather formal, or it may show disapproval: *Some adolescents were telling silly jokes.* A **youth** is an older teenager, usually male. This word may also show disapproval: *The police arrested several youths.* British people use **kids** as an informal word for **children**: *Let's take the kids to the park.* Americans use **kids** as an informal word for all young people: *We met a group of college kids.*

child a·buse /·· ·,·/ n [U] the physical or sexual mistreatment of children

child·bear·ing /'tʃaɪld,beərɪŋ/ n [U] the process of giving birth to children: *worn out with childbearing* | *a woman of childbearing age*

child·birth /'tʃaɪldbɜːθ ‖ -ɜːrθ/ n [U] the act of giving birth to a child

child·hood /'tʃaɪldhʊd/ n [C;U] the time when you are a child: *He had a very happy childhood.*

child·ish /'tʃaɪldɪʃ/ adj **1** of or for a child: *The girl spoke in a high childish voice.* **2** in a silly manner unsuitable for someone who is not a child: *a childish remark* – compare CHILDLIKE **–childishly** adv **–childishness** n [U]

child·less /'tʃaɪldləs/ adj not having any children: *a childless couple*

child·like /'tʃaɪldlaɪk/ adj having the natural lovable quality of a child: *She looked at me with childlike trust.* –compare CHILDISH (2)

child·min·der /'tʃaɪldmaɪndəʳ/ n someone who looks after other people's children, for example when the parents are at work **–childminding** n [U]

chil·dren /'tʃɪldrən/ n the plural of CHILD –see picture on page 343

chill¹ /tʃɪl/ v [I;T] to make or become cold, but not freezing: *This wine needs to be chilled. I'll pop it in the fridge.* | *After ten minutes in that cold wind I felt thoroughly chilled.*

chill² n **1** a cold with a fever: *I think I've caught a chill.* **2** [sing] a feeling of coldness: *There was a chill in the air this morning.*

chill³ adj unpleasantly cold (used of weather): *a chill wind*

chil·li /'tʃɪli/ n chillis or chillies **1** [C;U] a small red or green vegetable, used to give a very hot taste to food: *red chillies* | *chilli sauce* **2 chilli con carne** a dish in which small pieces of meat are cooked with beans in a liquid with chillis in it **3 chilli powder** a powder made from chillis and used to give a very hot taste to food

chil·ling /'tʃɪlɪŋ/ adj making you feel very frightened or worried: *a chilling murder story*

chill·y /'tʃɪli/ adj **chillier, chilliest 1** quite cold: *a chilly morning* | *I feel chilly without a coat.* **2**

unfriendly: *She gave me a chilly stare.* **–chilliness** n [sing; U]

chime¹ /tʃaɪm/ n a clear ringing sound of a bell or of a clock: *the chime of wedding bells* | *the chimes of Big Ben*

chime² v **chimed, chiming 1** [I;T] to make musical bell-like sounds: *The church bells were chiming.* **2** [T] to show the time by the sound of bells: *The clock chimed one o'clock.*
chime in phr v [I] *infml* to interrupt or join in a conversation suddenly: *"I want to come too,"* Sally *chimed in.*

chim·ney /'tʃɪmni/ n a hollow pipe which allows smoke and gases from a fire to go up and out of a building: *The factory chimneys poured smoke into the air.* –see picture on page 441

chim·ney·pot /'tʃɪmnɪpɒt ‖ -pɑːt/ n a pipe at the top of a chimney –see picture on page 441

chim·ney·sweep /'tʃɪmni-swiːp/ n (also **sweep** *infml*) a person whose job is cleaning the insides of chimneys

chim·pan·zee /,tʃɪmpæn'ziː, -pən-/ n (also **chimp** /tʃɪmp/ *infml*) an African APE with dark hair

chin /tʃɪn/ n **1** the front part of your face below your mouth **2 Chin up!, Keep your chin up!** *infml* a phrase used to someone in a difficult situation to encourage them to be cheerful

chi·na /'tʃaɪnə/ n [U] **1** a hard white substance made by baking fine clay **2** plates, cups, and dishes made from very fine clay: *She always puts out the best china for visitors.*

Chi·nese¹ /,tʃaɪ'niːz◂/ adj from or connected with China: *a Chinese restaurant*

Chinese² n **1** the Chinese the people of China **2** [U] the language of China

chink /tʃɪŋk/ n **1** a narrow crack or opening: *He watched the meeting secretly, through a chink in the wall.* **2 chink of light** a narrow beam of light shining through a crack **3** a short ringing sound: *the chink of coins in his pocket*

chintz /tʃɪnts/ n [U] cotton cloth with brightly coloured patterns and a shiny surface: *chintz curtains*

chip¹ /tʃɪp/ n **1 chips** long thin pieces of potato cooked in deep fat: *fish and chips* **2** (also **microchip, silicon chip**) a very small piece of SILICON containing a set of ELECTRONIC parts and their connections, used especially in computers **3** a small piece broken off an object: *a chip of wood* **4** a crack or mark left when a small piece is broken off an object: *This cup's got a chip in it.* **5** the usual American word for CRISP³ **6** a flat plastic object used for representing money in certain games **7 a chip off the old block** *infml* a person very like one of their parents in character (a phrase used to express approval) **8 have a chip on your shoulder** *infml* to be angry because you feel unfairly treated: *He's got a chip on his shoulder about not having gone to university.* **9 when the chips are down** *infml* when there is a serious situation

chip² v **-pp-** [I;T] to cause something to lose a small piece from its surface or edge: *This rock chips easily.* | *Oh dear! Someone's chipped one of the cups.* | *a chipped cup* | *I've chipped a piece off my tooth!*
chip sthg ↔ **away** phr v [T] to remove or destroy something by gradually breaking small pieces off it
chip away at sthg phr v [T] to break small pieces off something: *He was chipping away at the rock with a hammer.*

chip in phr v infml **1** [I] to interrupt or join in a conversation suddenly: *Of course John had to chip in and upset everybody.* | *Sheila chipped in with a few sensible comments.* **2** [I;T **chip in** sthg] to add your share of money, goods, or activity: *If we all chip in a few pounds we can get her something really nice.* | *Brian chipped in with a couple of bottles of wine.*

chi·rop·o·dist /kɪˈrɒpədɪst,ʃɪ- ‖ -ˈrɑː-/ n a person who looks after people's feet –**chiropody** n [U]

chirp /tʃɜːp ‖ tʃɜːrp/ n the short high sound of small birds or some insects –**chirp** v [I]

chirp·y /ˈtʃɜːpi ‖ ˈtʃɜːrpi/ adj **chirpier, chirpiest** infml cheerful and happy: *You seem very chirpy today.* –**chirpily** adv –**chirpiness** n [U]

chis·el¹ /ˈtʃɪzəl/ n a metal tool with a sharp edge at the end of a blade, used for cutting into or shaping wood, stone, or metal. –see picture on page 638

chisel² v **-ll-** (**-l-** AmE) [I;T] to cut or shape something with a chisel: *He chiselled a hole in the door.*

chit /tʃɪt/ n a short note showing a sum of money that someone owes or has paid

chit·chat /ˈtʃɪt-tʃæt/ n [U] infml informal conversation

chiv·al·rous /ˈʃɪvəlrəs/ adj fml showing polite behaviour and good manners towards women (used of men) –**chivalrously** adv –**chivalry** n [U]: *"The age of chivalry is not dead", he said, opening the door for her.*

chives /tʃaɪvz/ n [pl] a plant related to the onion, often eaten uncooked in salads

chlo·ri·nate /ˈklɔːrɪˌneɪt/ v **chlorinated, chlorinating** [T] to disinfect water by putting chlorine in it – **chlorination** /ˌklɔːrɪˈneɪʃən/ n [U]

chlo·rine /ˈklɔːriːn/ n [U] a greenish-yellow gas that has a strong smell and is used to disinfect water

chlor·o·form /ˈklɒrəfɔːm, ˈklɔː- ‖ ˈklɔːrəfɔːrm/ n [U] a poisonous liquid that has a strong smell, formerly used in medicine to make people unable to feel anything

chlo·ro·phyll /ˈklɒrəfɪl, ˈklɔː- ‖ ˈklɔːr-/ n [U] the green substance in the stems and leaves of plants

chock /tʃɒk ‖ tʃɑːk/ n a shaped piece of wood placed under something to prevent it from moving: *Put some chocks behind the wheels or it will roll back.*

chock-a-block /ˌtʃɒk əˈblɒk◂ ‖ ˈtʃɑːk əˌblɑːk/ adj (also **choc-a-bloc**) [never before a noun] infml very crowded and completely full: *The road was chock-a-block with cars again today.*

chock-full /ˌ◂ ˈ◂/ adj infml completely full

choco·late /ˈtʃɒklɪt ‖ ˈtʃɑːkəlɪt, ˈtʃɔːk-/ n **1** [U] a sweet, hard, brown food made from crushed COCOA beans: *Would you like a piece of chocolate?* | *a bar of chocolate* **2** [C] a small sweet covered with chocolate: *a box of chocolates* **3** [C;U] a drink made from hot milk, and sometimes water, mixed with powdered chocolate: *A hot chocolate, please.* | *a tin of drinking chocolate*

choice¹ /tʃɔɪs/ n **1** [C] the act or result of choosing: *I'm sure he's made the right choice.* | *the people's choice for president* **2** [C;U] the power or chance of

choosing: *She gave me a choice between looking after the baby or cleaning the kitchen.* | *I have no choice but to do as he tells me.* **3** [C] a variety of different things from which you can choose: *There's a wide choice of apples in the shops these days.* **4 of your choice** that you prefer: *the dish of your choice* **5 from choice, by choice** if you had the power to choose: *I wouldn't drive at night from choice.*

choice² adj high quality (used of food and drink): *choice apples*

choir /kwaɪəʳ/ n [+sing/pl verb] a group of people who sing together especially during religious services: *The church choir is singing tonight.*

choke¹ /tʃəʊk/ v **choked, choking 1** [I] to struggle to breathe or stop breathing because your breathing passages are blocked: *Water went down his throat and he started to choke.* **2** [T] to make someone choke: *She choked him to death.* **3** [T] to fill something up completely and block it: *The pipe was choked with leaves.*

choke sthg ↔ **back** phr v [T] to control a strong feeling and not show it more than you can help: *They choked back the tears.*

choke² n **1** the act or sound of choking **2** an apparatus that controls the amount of air going into a car engine; you switch the choke on when the engine is cold

chol·e·ra /ˈkɒlərə ‖ ˈkɑː-/ n [U] a dangerous infectious disease which attacks the stomach and bowels

cho·les·te·rol /kəˈlestərɒl ‖ -rəʊl/ n [U] a substance which helps to carry fats in the body, too much of which is thought to be bad for the arteries (ARTERY)

choose /tʃuːz/ v **chose** /tʃəʊz/, **chosen** /ˈtʃəʊzən/, **choosing** [I;T] **1** to pick out one thing from a greater number of things: *Would you like to choose the wine?* | *The cakes all looked so good, I didn't know which to choose.* | *Choose a cake for me.* | *They chose her as their leader.* | *They chose her to represent them.* | *Have you chosen where we should go to eat?* | *There are ten to choose from.* | *I had to choose between staying with my parents and going abroad.* | *"Which one shall we buy?" "You choose."* **2** choose **to do something** to decide to do something: *Many women choose to go on working after the birth of their first child.* | *He chose not to go home until later.* **3** there's not much to choose between them, there's little to choose between them = they are very much alike

choos·y /ˈtʃuːzi/ adj **choosier, choosiest** difficult to please: *Jean's very choosy about what she eats.*

chop¹ /tʃɒp ‖ tʃɑːp/ v **-pp-** [T] **1** (also **chop** sthg ↔ **up**) to cut something into very small pieces: *Chop the onions.* | *They chopped the branches up.* **2** to cut something by repeatedly hitting with a sharp tool, such as an AXE: *She chopped the block of wood in two.* | *We tried to chop a path through the thick forest.* **3 chop and change** to keep changing your opinion: *Make your mind up – don't keep chopping and changing!*

chop sthg ↔ **down** phr v [T] to chop at a tree near the bottom until it falls

chop² n **1** a quick short cutting blow **2** a small piece of meat, usually containing a bone: *pork chops* –see picture on page 344 **3 for the chop** infml soon going to be stopped: *It looks as if the scheme is for the chop.* **4 get the chop** infml to be dismissed from work

chop·per /ˈtʃɒpəʳ ‖ ˈtʃɑː-/ n **1** a heavy sharp-ended tool for cutting wood or meat **2** infml a HELICOPTER

SPELLING NOTE

Words with the sound / ʃ /, like **chauffeur**, may be spelt **sh-**, like **shop**.

chop·py /'tʃɒpi ‖ 'tʃɑːpi/ adj **choppier, choppiest** covered with many small waves (used of water): a choppy sea

chop·sticks /'tʃɒp-stɪks ‖ 'tʃɑːp-/ n a pair of narrow sticks used in East Asian countries for eating food; you hold them between your thumb and fingers

cho·ral /'kɔːrəl/ adj related to or sung by a CHOIR or CHORUS: a choral society | choral music

chord /kɔːd ‖ kɔːrd/ n **1** a combination of several musical notes sounded at the same time **2** tech a straight line joining two points on a curve

chore /tʃɔːr/ n **1** a small regular job in the house, for example the washing-up: I spent the morning doing household chores. **2** an unpleasant and uninteresting job

chor·e·og·ra·phy /ˌkɒri'ɒɡrəfi, ˌkɔː- ‖ ˌkɔːri'ɑːɡ-/ n [U] the art of dancing or the organization of dance steps to be performed on the stage –**choreographer** n

chor·is·ter /'kɒristər ‖ 'kɔːr-, 'kɑːr-/ n a member of a CHOIR, especially a boy

chor·tle /'tʃɔːtl ‖ 'tʃɔːrtl/ n a laugh of pleasure or satisfaction –**chortle** v **chortled, chortling** [I]

cho·rus¹ /'kɔːrəs/ n **1** [C+sing/pl verb] a group of people who sing together: The chorus was very good today. **2** [C] a piece of music for a chorus **3** [C] a piece of music played or sung after each part of a song **4** [sing] something said by a lot of people at the same time: His announcement was greeted by a chorus of disapproval.

chorus² v [T] to say something together at the same time

chose /tʃəʊz/ the past tense of CHOOSE

cho·sen /'tʃəʊzən/ the past participle of CHOOSE

Christ /kraɪst/ n (also **Jesus Christ, Jesus**) the man who established Christianity

chris·ten /'krɪsən/ v [T] **1** a Christian ceremony which makes someone a member of the church by giving them a name: The baby was christened by the priest. | We christened our baby John. **2** to name an object officially: The ship was christened the Queen Mary.

chris·ten·ing /'krɪsənɪŋ/ n the Christian ceremony for naming a person, usually a baby

Chris·tian¹ /'krɪstʃən, -tiən/ n a person who believes in the religious teachings of Jesus Christ

Christian² adj **1** relating to Christianity a Christian nation | the Christian philosophy **2** kind and forgiving **3 Christian name** a person's first name: What's his Christian name? –see FIRST NAME (USAGE)

Chris·ti·an·i·ty /ˌkrɪsti'ænəti/ n [U] the religion based on the life and teachings of Jesus Christ: Do you believe in Christianity?

Christ·mas /'krɪsməs/ n [C;U] the period of time around the Christian holy day on December 25th: Christmas cards | Happy Christmas! | Did you have a nice Christmas?

Christmas Day /ˌ·· '·/ n [C;U] the Christian holy day on December 25th in honour of the birth of Jesus Christ

Christmas Eve /ˌ·· '·/ n the day before Christmas Day: We sing carols on Christmas Eve.

Christmas tree /'·· ·/ n a real or plastic FIR tree with lights and decorations on it, used to decorate people's homes at Christmas

chrome /krəʊm/ n [U] (also **chromium** /-ɪəm/) a hard, shiny, silver-coloured metal: There's less chrome and more plastic on modern cars.

chro·mo·some /'krəʊməsəʊm/ n tech a very small part of a cell in a plant, animal, or human that controls its nature

chron·ic /'krɒnɪk ‖ 'krɑː-/ adj **1** lasting a very long time (used of an illness): a chronic cough **2** [only before a noun] suffering from an illness or other problem over a long period: a chronic alcoholic | a chronic invalid **3** infml very bad: a chronic example of bad management –**chronically** /-kli/ adv : chronically depressed

chron·i·cle /'krɒnɪkəl ‖ 'krɑː-/ n a record of historical events, which are arranged in order of time –**chronicle** v **chronicled, chronicling** [T] : a book which chronicles the nation's history

chron·o·log·i·cal /ˌkrɒnə'lɒdʒɪkəl◄ ‖ ˌkrɑːnə'lɑː-/ adj arranged according to the order of time: a list of World Cup winners in chronological order. –**chronologically** /-kli/ adv

chrys·a·lis /'krɪsəlɪs/ n **chrysalises** /-siːz/ an insect at an early stage of its development, before it can fly

chry·san·the·mum /krɪ'sænθəməm, -'zæn-/ n a garden plant with large brightly-coloured flowers in autumn

chub·by /'tʃʌbi/ adj **chubbier, chubbiest** pleasantly fat (used especially of children) –see picture on page 245 –**chubbiness** n [U]

chuck /tʃʌk/ v [T] infml to throw something with a short, quick movement: Chuck me an apple will you?.

chuck out sthg ↔ **away** phr v [T] infml to get rid of something: "Do you want this polythene bag?" "No, chuck it away."

chuck out phr v infml **1** [T **chuck** sbdy ↔ **out**] to force a person to leave a place: The barman threatened to chuck us out of the pub if we got drunk. **2** [T **chuck** sthg ↔ **out**] to throw something away: I'll chuck out all my old school books and make some more room.

chuck sthg ↔ **in** phr v [T] infml to leave a job, often because you are unhappy with it: She hated her boss so much that she chucked in her job.

chuck·le /'tʃʌkəl/ v **chuckled, chuckling** [I] to laugh quietly: I could hear him chuckling to himself as he read his book. –**chuckle** n : He gave a quiet chuckle.

chug /tʃʌg/ v **-gg-** [I+adv/prep] (of an engine or vehicle) to make a heavy beating noise while moving slowly along: The little boat chugged along the river. | The old steam engine chugged slowly up the hill. –**chug** n : the chug of the engine

chum /tʃʌm/ n old-fash infml a good friend: They are old school chums.

chum·my /'tʃʌmi/ adj old-fash infml friendly

chump /tʃʌmp/ n infml a fool

chunk /tʃʌŋk/ n a solid piece or lump: a chunk of cheese

chunk·y /'tʃʌŋki/ adj **1** thick and heavy: chunky jewellery | a chunky sweater **2** attractive to women because big, with a broad chest and strong appearance (used of men)

church /tʃɜːtʃ ‖ tʃɜːrtʃ/ n **1** [C;U] a building for public Christian worship: the church on the hill **2** [U] the religious services held in a church: I'm going to church today. | I'll see you after church. **3** [C] any of the separate religious groups within the Christian religion: She was a loyal member of the Catholic Church.

Church of Eng·land /ˌ· · ·'··/ n the Church of England the state religion in England, with the King or Queen as its head

church-go·er /'·ˌ···/ n a person who goes to church regularly

church·yard /'tʃɜːtʃjɑːd ‖ 'tʃɜːrtʃjɑːrd/ n an open space around a church in which dead people are buried

churl·ish /'tʃɜːlɪʃ ‖ -ɜːr-/ adj rude because you do not admit the generosity of other people –**churlish·ness** n [U]

churn[1] /tʃɜːn ‖ tʃɜːrn/ n 1 a container in which milk is shaken until it becomes butter 2 BrE a metal container like a very large bottle in which milk is stored or carried from the farm –see picture on page 148

churn[2] v [T] 1 to make butter using a churn 2 (also **churn** sth ↔ **up**) to move about violently: The ship churned up the water as it passed. 3 **make your stomach churn** infml to make you so nervous or excited that you feel sick: The thought of my driving test made my stomach churn.

churn sth ↔ **out** phr v [T] infml to produce something in large numbers without caring about the quality: She churns out about three new books every year.

chute /ʃuːt/ n a long, narrow, steep slope, used for getting things to a lower level: an emergency chute | a rubbish chute

chut·ney /'tʃʌtni/ n [U] a strong-tasting sweet and sour mixture of fruit or vegetables which is eaten with cheese or meat

CIA /ˌsiː aɪ 'eɪ/ n a government body in the US which gathers secret information about other countries; an abbreviation for **Central Intelligence Agency**: a member of the CIA

CID /ˌsiː aɪ 'diː/ n a special branch of the UK police force; an abbreviation for **Criminal Investigation Department**

ci·der /'saɪdəʳ/ n [C;U] an alcoholic drink made from apple juice: Two ciders and a beer, please.

ci·gar /sɪ'gɑːʳ/ n a brown tube-shaped roll of uncut tobacco leaves for smoking

cig·a·rette /ˌsɪgəˈret ‖ ˌsɪgəˈret, 'sɪgəret/ n a thin white paper tube of finely cut tobacco for smoking: She lit a cigarette but stubbed it out immediately.

cinch /sɪntʃ/ n infml a cinch something that you can do very easily: My exam was a cinch. I passed with top marks.

cin·der /'sɪndəʳ/ n all that is left of a piece of coal or other material after it has been burnt: All that was left of the fire was the grey cinders. | The toast was burnt to a cinder.

cin·e·ma /'sɪnɪˌmə/ n BrE 1 a theatre in which films are shown for entertainment: Which cinema is it at? 2 **the cinema** the art or industry of making films: She's worked in the cinema all her life. 3 **go to the cinema** to go to see a film

cin·na·mon /'sɪnəmən/ n [U] a sweet-smelling light brown powder used for giving a special taste to food such as fruit or cakes

ci·pher /'saɪfəʳ/ n (also **cypher**) 1 a secret system

of writing: The government uses a secret cipher for its official messages. 2 a person of no importance

cir·ca /'sɜːkə ‖ 'sɜːr-/ prep fml (also **c**) a word you use to say that something happened in about the year stated: born circa 50 BC

cir·cle[1] /'sɜːkəl ‖ 'sɜːr-/ n 1 a flat, round area enclosed by a curved line, so that everywhere is equally distant from the centre 2 an object or area which has the general shape of a circle: Let's sit in a circle. | a circle of chairs 3 a group of people who meet regularly because they share a common interest: a large circle of friends | I belong to the Literary Circle. 4 an upper floor in a theatre: Are we going to go to the circle or in the stalls? 5 **come full circle** to go through several changes or developments and end up back at the starting point: I tried everything I could think of, but ended up coming full circle. 6 **go round in circles** to make no progress 7 **run round in circles** to be very busy without making much progress

circle[2] v **circled, circling** 1 [T] to draw a circle around something: The teacher circled their spelling mistakes in red ink. 2 [I;T] to move in a circle around something: The plane circled the airport before landing.

cir·cuit /'sɜːkₐt ‖ 'sɜːr-/ n 1 the closed path of an electric current: The lights went out because of a sudden break in the circuit. 2 a path in the shape of a ring: We made a circuit of the old city walls. | a racing circuit 3 a regular journey from place to place for a particular event or purpose: the tennis circuit

cir·cu·i·tous /sɜː'kjuːₐtəs ‖ sɜːr-/ adj fml going a long and difficult way round: the river's circuitous course | a circuitous route –**circuitously** adv

cir·cu·lar[1] /'sɜːkjᵿləʳ ‖ 'sɜːr-/ adj 1 shaped like a circle: a circular area 2 moving in a direction which leads you back to where you started: a circular journey | a circular argument –**circularity** /ˌsɜːkjᵿˈlærₐti ‖ ˌsɜːr-/ n [U] : She seemed unaware of the circularity of her argument.

circular[2] n a printed advertisement, paper, or notice sent to a large number of people: Did you see that circular from the new theatre?

cir·cu·late /'sɜːkjᵿleɪt ‖ 'sɜːr-/ v **circulated, circulating** 1 [I;T] to move in a circular direction within a closed space: Blood circulates **round** the body. | The heart circulates blood round the body. 2 [I] infml to move about freely and without difficulty: He circulated at the party, talking to lots of people. | The new roundabout has helped the traffic to circulate better. 3 [I;T] to spread information to a large group of people: I'll circulate the report at the meeting. | Jokes were circulating about him. –**circulatory** /ˌsɜːkjᵿˈleɪtəri, 'sɜːkjᵿlətəri ‖ 'sɜːrkjᵿləˌtɔːri/ adj

cir·cu·la·tion /ˌsɜːkjᵿˈleɪʃən ‖ ˌsɜːr-/ n 1 [C;U] the movement of blood through your body: Bad circulation can cause tiredness. 2 [C] the number of copies of a newspaper, magazine, or book that are sold over a period of time: This magazine has a circulation of 400,000. 3 **in circulation: a** in use in a society and passing from one person to another: The government has reduced the number of £5 notes in circulation. **b** enjoying an active social life: He was soon back in circulation after his spell in hospital. [RELATED PHRASE **out of circulation**]

cir·cum·cise /'sɜːkəmsaɪz ‖ 'sɜːr-/ v **circumcised, circumcising** [T] to cut off the skin at the end of a man's PENIS or a woman's CLITORIS in a religious ceremony –**circumcision** /ˌsɜːkəmˈsɪʒən ‖ ˌsɜːr-/ n [C;U]

SPELLING NOTE

Words with the sound / k /, like **cut**, may be spelt **k-**, like **key**, or **qu-**, like **queen**.
Words with the sound / s /, like **city**, may be spelt **s-**, like **soon**, or **ps-**, like **psychology**.

cir·cum·fer·ence /sə'kʌmfərəns ‖ sər-/ n [C;U] the length around the outside edge of a round object: *The Earth's circumference is more than 40,000 kilometres.* | *The tower is 20 metres in circumference.*

cir·cum·scribe /'sɜːkəmskraɪb ‖ 'sɜːr-/ v **circumscribed, circumscribing** [T] to keep something within narrow limits: *His activities have been severely circumscribed since his illness.*

cir·cum·spect /'sɜːkəmspekt ‖ 'sɜːr-/ adj careful and avoiding risk: *You won't catch Kidd making a rash statement. He's always very circumspect.* –**circumspection** /ˌsɜːkəm'spekʃən ‖ ˌsɜːr-/ n [U]

cir·cum·stance /'sɜːkəmstæns, -stəns ‖ 'sɜːr-/ n **1** a face or condition which influences a situation: *We can't judge what he did till we know all the circumstances.* | *Circumstances forced me to accept a very low price.* **2 circumstances** fml the amount of money you have **3 in no circumstances, under no circumstances, not under any circumstances** never: *I will not vote for him under any circumstances.* **4 in the circumstances, under the circumstances** as a result of a particular situation: *The weather was terrible. In the circumstances, I decided to postpone my journey.*

cir·cum·stan·tial /ˌsɜːkəm'stænʃəl◀ ‖ ˌsɜːr-/ adj indirect, and not proving that something is true (used of evidence): *We've only got circumstantial evidence.*

cir·cum·vent /ˌsɜːkəm'vent ‖ ˌsɜːr-/ v [T] fml to avoid a rule or law: *The company has opened an office abroad in order to circumvent British tax laws.* –**circumvention** /-'venʃən/ n [U]

cir·cus /'sɜːkəs ‖ 'sɜːr-/ n **1** a group of travelling entertainers and animals who perform various acts of skill and daring **2** a performance by these people **3** a round open area where a number of streets join together: *Oxford Circus*

cis·sy /'sɪsi/ n **cissies** see SISSY

cis·tern /'sɪstən ‖ -ərn/ n a container for storing water, especially for a TOILET

cit·a·del /'sɪtədəl, -del/ n a castle or fort built to be a place of safety and defence in time of war

ci·ta·tion /saɪ'teɪʃən/ n **1** a short passage taken from something written or spoken **2** an official statement that someone has been very brave

cite /saɪt/ v **cited, citing** [T] fml **1** to mention something as an example or proof in a formal way: *The minister supported his argument by citing the latest crime figures.* **2** to call someone to appear before a court of law: *He was cited in a divorce case.*

cit·i·zen /'sɪtɪzən/ n **1** a person who lives in a particular city or town and can vote there: *the citizens of Rome* **2** a person who belongs to a particular country by birth or NATURALIZATION, and who expects protection from it: *She's a British citizen but lives in India.*

cit·i·zen·ship /'sɪtɪzənʃɪp/ n [U] having the official rights and duties of a citizen: *After eight years in the country he obtained American citizenship.*

cit·rus /'sɪtrəs/ n any of the trees of the orange family grown in warm countries for their juicy fruit

cit·y /'sɪti/ n **cities 1** a place which is more important than a town and has a larger population: *Many industrial cities are experiencing serious unemployment.* **2 the City** the centre of business and money matters in London

civ·ic /'sɪvɪk/ adj relating to a city or its citizens: *the civic centre* | *civic duties*

civ·il /'sɪvəl/ adj **1** concerning the state as opposed to the army or the church: *a civil marriage* | *civil*

defence 2 dealing with the legal rights of private citizens: *Civil law is different from criminal law.* **3** polite enough, without being friendly: *Try to be civil to him, even if you don't like him.* –**civilly** /'sɪvəl-i/ adv

ci·vil·ian /sɪ'vɪljən/ n a person who is not a member of the armed forces: *Innocent civilians suffered in the attack.*

ci·vil·i·ty /sɪ'vɪləti/ n **civilities 1** [U] behaviour which is polite but not friendly **2 civilities** [pl] expressions which are polite but not very friendly

civ·i·li·za·tion /ˌsɪvəl-aɪ'zeɪʃən ‖ -vəl-ə'zeɪ-/ n (also **civilisation** BrE) **1** [U] a high level of social organization with developed systems of art, science, religion, and government: *The survival of civilization as we know it depends on many environmental factors.* **2** [C] a civilized society of a particular time or place: *Compare the civilizations of ancient China and Japan.*

civ·i·lize /'sɪvəl-aɪz/ v **civilized, civilizing** (also **civilise** BrE) [T] to educate and improve a society or nation: *The Romans hoped to civilize all the tribes of Europe.*

civ·i·lized /'sɪvəl-aɪzd/ adj (also **civilised** BrE) **1** having a high level of social organization: *a very civilized part of the world* **2** pleasant, charming, and without roughness of manner or style: *a very civilized person* | *This place looks more civilized now that we've painted it.*

civil rights /ˌ·· '·/ n [pl] rights such as freedom and equality which belong to all citizens without regard to their race, religion, colour, or sex: *the civil rights movement*

civil ser·vant /ˌ·· '··/ n a person employed in the civil service

Civil Ser·vice /ˌ·· '··/ n **the Civil Service** all the various national government departments: *She is a member of the civil service.* | *The Civil Service has a great deal of power.* –see OFFICER (USAGE)

civil war /ˌ·· '·/ n [C;U] a war between opposing groups of people who live in the same country: *the American Civil War*

clad /klæd/ adj [never before a noun] lit **clad in** a wearing or covered: *The old lady was clad in a fur coat.* | *The mountain was clad in mist.*

claim¹ /kleɪm/ v **1** [I;T] to say that something belongs to you as a right: *Old people are able to claim a special heating allowance from the government.* | *Did you claim on the insurance after your car accident?* | *You are entitled to claim for your travelling expenses.* **2** [+(that)] to say that something is true, even if there is no proof: *He claims to be rich.* | *She claimed that she was the true Queen.* □ USEFUL PATTERNS to claim to be something; to claim to have done something; to claim that... **3 claim lives** (of a natural event such as a flood) to kill people: *The earthquake claimed hundreds of lives.*

claim² n **1** a demand for something as a right: *The government would not even consider his claim for money.* | *She put in a claim for her travelling expenses.* **2** a right to something: *He has a rightful claim to the property – it was his mother's.* **3** a statement that something is true, especially one that other people disagree with: *His claim about the number of people killed in the war was clearly mistaken.* | *His claim to be the richest man in England has been disputed.* **4 claim to fame** a reason for being famous: *The town's only claim to fame is that it has the biggest car park in the country.* **5 lay**

claim to something to say that something belongs to you as a right **–claimant** n

clair·voy·ant /kleə'vɔɪənt ‖ kleər-/ n a person who says that they are able to see what will happen in the future **–clairvoyant** adj : clairvoyant powers **–clairvoyance** n [U]

clam¹ /klæm/ n a kind of SHELLFISH

clam² v -mm-
clam up phr v [I] infml to become silent, especially because of fear or unwillingness to give information

clam·ber /ˈklæmbəʳ/ v [I + adv/prep] to climb over something with difficulty, using both your hands and your feet: Their wretched children wouldn't stop clambering over my furniture.

clam·my /ˈklæmi/ adj unpleasantly warm and sticky: clammy hands | clammy weather

clam·our¹ /ˈklæməʳ/ n (**clamor** AmE) **1** [sing] a loud confused noise or shouting: a clamour of voices **2** [U] a continuous strong demand or complaint made by a large number of people: ignoring the public clamour for lower taxes

clamour² v (**clamor** AmE) [I;T] to express a strong demand for something, often noisily: The children were clamouring to be fed. | They are clamouring for radical changes in the organization.

clamp¹ /klæmp/ n an apparatus for fastening or holding things firmly together: The police are using wheel clamps to stop cars from parking here.

clamp² v [T] to fasten something with a clamp: He clamped the two pieces of wood together.
clamp down phr v [I] to become firmer in order to control a situation: The police are going to clamp down on parking in this area.

clamp·down /ˈklæmpdaʊn/ n infml a sudden official effort to control a particular activity: The Government has decided to have a clampdown on drunken driving.

clan /klæn/ n **1** especially in Scotland, a large group of families all related to one another and having the same name **2** a large group of people related in some way (a word which is often used in a humorous way)

clan·des·tine /klæn'destɪn/ adj fml existing or done secretly, and often illegal: a clandestine organization

clang /klæŋ/ v [I;T] to make a loud, metallic ringing noise: The prison gate clanged shut. **–clang** n [sing] : The iron gate shut with a heavy clang.

clang·er /ˈklæŋəʳ/ n infml **drop a clanger** to make a very noticeable mistake or an unfortunate remark: She dropped a clanger when she mentioned his ex-wife.

clank /klæŋk/ v [I;T] to make a loud metallic sound: The prisoner's chains clanked as he walked.

clap¹ /klæp/ v **-pp- 1** [I;T] to bring your open hands together with a quick movement and loud sound, especially to show approval or excitement: The teacher clapped her hands to attract the class's attention. | The audience had enjoyed the play, and clapped loudly. **2** **clap someone on the back** to hit someone lightly on the back with your open hand

in a friendly manner because you are pleased **3** **not clap eyes on someone** infml not to see someone at all for a period: She went off with my money, and I haven't clapped eyes on her since. **4** [T + adv/prep] to put or place something into a particular place or position: She immediately realised she had said the wrong thing and clapped her hand over her mouth. **5** **clap someone in prison** to put someone in prison

clap² n **1** a sudden loud explosive sound: a clap of thunder **2** **clap on the back** a light friendly hit on the back with an open hand: He gave me a clap on the back **3** **give someone a clap** to clap someone's performance: Come on, everyone, give him a clap! **4** **the clap** slang the disease GONORRHEA

clap·per /ˈklæpəʳ/ n the small metal object hung inside a bell which strikes it to make it ring

clap·trap /ˈklæptræp/ n [U] infml silly or insincere remarks that should not be believed: What a load of claptrap!

clar·i·fy /ˈklærɪ̩faɪ/ v **clarified, clarifying** [T] to make something easier to understand by explaining it more fully: When will the government clarify its position on equal pay for women? **–clarification** /ˌklærɪfɪˈkeɪʃən/ [C;U] : He asked for clarification of the government's position.

clar·i·net /ˌklærɪ̩'net/ n a tube-like musical instrument made of wood that you play by blowing:

clar·i·ty /ˈklærɪti/ n [U] **1** the quality of speaking or thinking clearly: He possesses great clarity of mind. | She put forward her argument with great clarity. **2** the ability to be seen or heard clearly: the clarity of the painter's brush-strokes | the clarity of her voice

clash¹ /klæʃ/ v **1** [I] to come into opposition with someone or something: The violent mob clashed with the police. | Our suggestions tend to clash. **2** [I] (of two colours or styles) not to look nice together: Her orange blouse clashes with her pink lipstick. **3** [I] (of two or more events) to happen, inconveniently, at the same time: I couldn't go to their wedding as it clashed with my holiday. **4** [I;T] to make a loud noise by hitting metal objects against each other:

clash² n **1** a fight or struggle: The government has reported clashes on its border. **2** an argument or disagreement: a clash of interests **3** a loud metallic noise: a clash of cymbals

clasp¹ /klɑːsp ‖ klæsp/ n **1** a small metal fastener for holding two things together or for shutting something: the clasp on a belt **2** a tight firm hold, by the hand or in your arms

clasp² v [T] **1** to hold something firmly: He clasped the money in his hands. **2** to fasten something with a clasp

class¹ /klɑːs ‖ klæs/ n **classes 1** [C+sing/pl verb] a group of pupils or students who are taught together: a class of 30 children | Our class is reading "Macbeth" at the moment. **2** [C;U] a period of time during which pupils or students are taught: What time does the next class begin? | Don't talk in class! **3** [U] the way that a society is divided into different social groups: Class differences can divide a nation. | Is education class-based? **4** [C] (also **classes** pl]) a group of people whose members are similar socially and politically: Most of the middle class now take their holidays abroad. | the working class | the upper class | the ruling classes **5** [C] a group of things which have similar characteristics: four main word-classes: nouns, verbs, adjectives, and adverbs **6** [C] a level of quality for people and things: *"What class is your degree?" "I got a third."* | *A first-class ticket to Birmingham, please.* **7 be in a class of your own** to be special and different **8 have class** to have a stylish quality that attracts admiration: *She dresses beautifully. She's got real class.*

class² *v* [T] to state that someone or something belongs in a particular group or type: *British women are classed as senior citizens when they are sixty.*

class-con-scious /ˌ· ˈ··/ *adj* **1** conscious of the importance of social class **2** very conscious of your own position in society and, usually, thinking that the upper classes are better than the lower classes

clas-sic¹ /ˈklæsɪk/ *adj* **1** having the highest quality and being of lasting importance: *It's a classic film – I can't wait to see it again.* **2** belonging to a simple and formal style: *a classic dress* | *a classic building* **3** of a very typical and well-known kind: *She is a classic example of a good teacher.*

classic² *n* **1** a highly-praised work of literature of lasting importance: *That book is one of the classics of English literature.* | *a modern classic* **2** *infml* the best example of something: *That joke's a classic. It really is funny!* **3 classics** [pl] the languages, literature, and history of ancient Greece and Rome

clas-si-cal /ˈklæsɪkəl/ *adj* **1** (also **Classical**) in the style of ancient Greek or Roman models in literature or art: *classical literature* **2** written with serious artistic intentions and having lasting value (used of music): *I prefer pop music to classical music.* **3** based on an old or established system of principles and methods: *Galileo challenged the classical views on the solar system.*

clas-si-fi-ca-tion /ˌklæsɪfɪˈkeɪʃən/ *n* **1** [U] the act of classifying people or things into groups: *The classification of all the library books took longer than we'd expected.* **2** [C] a division within a group

clas-si-fied /ˈklæsɪfaɪd/ *adj* **1** officially secret (used of government, especially military, information) **2** divided or arranged in classes **3 classified ad** a small advertisement placed in a newspaper by a person wishing to sell or buy something

clas-si-fy /ˈklæsɪfaɪ/ *v* **classified, classifying** [T] to arrange or place people or things into groups or types: *Whales are classified as mammals, not fish.*

class-room /ˈklɑːs-rʊm, -ruːm ‖ ˈklæs-/ *n* a room in a school or college in which a class meets for a lesson

class-y /ˈklɑːsi ‖ ˈklæsi/ *adj* **classier, classiest** *infml* stylish and fashionable, especially in an upper-class way

clat-ter /ˈklætəʳ/ *v* [I;T] to make a number of short, loud sounds by knocking things against each other: *The metal dish clattered down the stone stairs.* –**clatter** *n* [sing;U] : *the clatter of the printing machines* | *a clatter of pots and pans*

clause /klɔːz/ *n* **1** in grammar, a group of words containing a subject and a FINITE verb, usually forming only part of a sentence. In "She came home when she was tired", "She came home" and "when she was tired" are two separate clauses. –compare PHRASE, SENTENCE **2** a separate part or division of a written legal agreement

claus-tro-pho-bi-a /ˌklɔːstrəˈfəʊbiə/ *n* [U] fear of being enclosed in a small closed space: *I suffer from claustrophobia.* –**claustrophobic** *adj*

claw¹ /klɔː/ *n* **1** a sharp curved nail on the foot of an animal or bird **2** a limb of certain insects and sea animals such as CRABS, used for attacking and holding objects

claw² *v* [I;T] to tear, seize, or pull with a sharp movement: *The cat clawed at the leg of the table.* | *He clawed a hole in my tights.*
claw sth ↔ back *phr v* [T] to get something back with great difficulty or effort

clay /kleɪ/ *n* [U] heavy grey or red earth which becomes hard when baked at a high temperature and is used for making pots

clean¹ /kliːn/ *adj* **1** free from dirt: *Are your hands clean?* | *clean clothes* **2** not yet used: *a clean piece of paper* **3** morally or sexually pure: *He led a clean life.* | *a clean joke* **4** not disobeying rules or laws: *a clean fight* | *a clean driving licence* **5** having a smooth even edge or surface: *a clean cut* | *the aircraft's clean lines* **6 clean sweep:** **a** a complete removal or change: *He was anxious to make a clean sweep of all the old ideas.* **b** a complete victory in which the winner wins every part of a competition: *Germany has made a clean sweep of the swimming events.* **7 come clean** *infml* to admit your guilt and tell the unpleasant truth: *Why don't you come clean and tell us your real plans?*

clean² *v* [I;T] to make something free from dirt: *I shall have to clean the windows. I can hardly see out!* –**clean** *n* [sing] : *I must give the windows a good clean.* –**cleaning** *n* [U] : *We have a lady to do the cleaning for us.*
clean out *phr v* **1** [T **clean** sthg ↔ **out**] to make something thoroughly clean and tidy **2** [T **clean** sbdy ↔ **out**] *infml* to take all the money belonging to a person **3** [T **clean** sthg ↔ **out**] to steal everything from a place: *The thieves cleaned out the store.*
clean up *phr v* **1** [I;T **clean** sthg ↔ **up**] to make something clean or tidy: *It's your turn to clean up.* | *Can you clean up those pieces of broken bottle.* **2** [T **clean** sthg ↔ **up**] to make a place free from crime: *The police have begun a campaign to clean up the inner cities.*
clean up after sbdy *phr v* [T] to clean and put away things that someone else has made dirty or untidy: *If you're a housewife, you seem to spend your whole life cleaning up after other people.*

clean³ *adv infml* completely: *The bullet went clean through his arm.* | *I clean forgot his birthday.*

clean-cut /ˌ· ˈ·◂/ *adj* neat and clean in appearance

clean-er /ˈkliːnəʳ/ *n* **1** a person whose job is to clean the inside of a building **2** a person whose job is to clean a particular thing: *a window cleaner* **3** a machine or substance used for cleaning: *a vacuum cleaner* **4 cleaner's** a shop where you can have clothes or material cleaned with chemicals instead of water **5 take someone to the cleaner's** *infml* to make someone lose all their money, especially by dishonesty

clean-li-ness /ˈklenlinəs/ *n* [U] the habit of keeping clean

clean-ly /ˈkliːnli/ *adv* in a neat way, without making any mess: *The knife cut cleanly through the cake.*

cleanse /klenz/ *v* **cleansed, cleansing** [T] *fml* to make a cut or wound free from dirt

cleans-er /ˈklenzəʳ/ *n* [C;U] a substance used for cleaning your skin

clean-shav-en /ˌ· ˈ··◂/ *adj* having no hair on the lower part of your face

clear¹ /klɪəʳ/ *adj* **1** easy to see through: *clear glass* **2** free from anything that marks or darkens: *a clear sky* | *clear skin* **3** free from anything that blocks or covers: *a clear view* | *The road's clear of snow now.* **4** free from other planned activity: *I see that next*

week is clear. Let's meet then. **5** easy to hear, read, or understand: *a clear speaker | a clear style of writing | The instructions aren't very clear.* **6 get something clear** to come to understand something: *I'll go on to the second point if everybody's got the first point clear.* **7 make something clear** to tell someone something or explain it to them so that they understand it **8** able to think and understand quickly and well: *a clear thinker | Don't drink too much. You want to keep a clear head for your interview.* **9** impossible to doubt, question, or be mistaken about: *a clear case of murder | She's made her feelings quite clear. | It's becoming clear to most people that the Government was wrong. | It isn't yet clear whether these changes have had any effect.* **10** [never before a noun] feeling certain: *She seems quite clear about her plans. | I'm still not clear how it works.* **11** free from guilt or blame: *a clear conscience* **12 do I make myself clear?** = do you understand? (a phrase you use when you are annoyed with someone) **–clearness** *n* [U]

clear² *adv* **1** out of the way, so as to be no longer inside or near: *She jumped clear of the train.* **2** completely: *The prisoner got clear away.*

clear³ *v* **1** [I] to become clear: *After the storm the sky cleared.* **2** [T] to make something clear: *This soap should help clear your skin.* **3** [T + adv/prep] to remove something that is not wanted: *Will you clear the plates away? | Whose job is it to clear snow from the road? | I'll just clear all these papers off the table.* **4** [T] to declare someone to be free from blame: *He was cleared of murder, but found guilty of dangerous driving.* **5** [T] to give someone official permission for something: *The plans for the new school have not yet been cleared by the council.* **6 clear something with someone** to get official permission for something from someone: *You can't begin until you've cleared it with the headmaster.* **7** [T] to pass by or over something without touching it: *The horse easily cleared every fence.* **8** [T] to repay a debt in full: *You ought to clear your debts before thinking about another holiday.* **9 clear the air** to remove doubt and bad feeling by honest explanation **10 clear your throat** to cough, often in order to get attention

clear away *phr v* [I;T **clear** sthg ↔ **away**] to make an area tidy by removing things to their proper places: *Has everybody finished eating? Can I clear away?*

clear off *phr v* [I] *infml* to leave a place, often quickly: *Clear off, you boys!*

clear out *phr v* **1** [I] *infml* to leave a place: *cleared out of the house* **2** [T **clear** sthg ↔ **out**] to collect and throw away unwanted objects: *I decided to clear out all the old clothes that we never wear.* **3** [T **clear** sthg ↔ **out**] to empty something of unwanted objects: *I'm going to clear out my desk.*

clear up *phr v* **1** [I;T **clear** sthg ↔ **up**] to tidy up or put things in order: *Can you clear up before he arrives please? | I've lots of work to clear up by the weekend.* **2** [T **clear** sthg ↔ **up**] to find an answer to something: *to clear up the mystery | Let's try and clear up the misunderstanding.* **3** [I] (of a situation) to get better: *I hope the weather clears up before Sunday. | My cold has cleared up at last.*

SPELLING NOTE

Words with the sound /k/, like **cut**, may be spelt **k-**, like **key**, or **qu-**, like **queen**.
Words with the sound /s/, like **city**, may be spelt **s-**, like **soon**, or **ps-**, like **psychology**.

---

clear⁴ *n* **in the clear** *infml*: **a** not in danger **b** not to be blamed or thought guilty: *He's got an alibi, so he's in the clear.*

clear·ance /ˈklɪərəns/ *n* **1** [U] the removal of things that are not wanted: *a programme of slum clearance* **2** [C;U] the act or result of getting permission or approval: *The ship sailed as soon as it got clearance from the port authority.* **3** [C;U] the distance between one object and another one passing beneath or beside it: *The clearance between the bridge and the top of the bus was only ten centimetres.* **4** [C;U] a sale of goods at lower prices: *a shop clearance*

clear-cut /ˌ·ˈ·◄/ *adj* **1** clear in meaning: *We now have clear-cut plans for future action.* **2** having a smooth and regular shape

clear-head·ed /ˌ·ˈ···◄/ *adj* able to think clearly and sensibly

clear·ing /ˈklɪərɪŋ/ *n* a small area of land that has been cleared of trees inside a larger area of trees

clear·ly /ˈklɪəli ‖ ˈklɪərli/ *adv* **1** in a clear manner: *He spoke very clearly. I could hear every word. | The bottle was clearly labelled.* **2** without any doubt: *That's clearly a mistake. | Clearly, he's getting too old for this job.*

clear-sight·ed /ˌ·ˈ···◄/ *adj* able to make good judgments

cleav·age /ˈkliːvɪdʒ/ *n* **1** the space between a woman's breasts, especially that which can be seen when she is wearing a low-cut dress **2** *fml* a division or disagreement between people: *a sharp cleavage in society between rich and poor*

cleave /kliːv/ *v* **cleaved** *or* **cleft** /kleft/ *or* **clove** /kləʊv/, **cleaved** *or* **cleft** *or* **cloven** /ˈkləʊvən/, **cleaving** [T] *lit* to divide or separate something by a cutting blow

cleav·er /ˈkliːvər/ *n* an tool like an AXE, used especially for cutting up large pieces of meat

clef /klef/ *n* a special sign put at the beginning of a line of written music to show how high or low the notes should be played

cleft /kleft/ the past tense and past participle of CLEAVE

clem·en·cy /ˈklemənsi/ *n fml* [U] mercy, especially when shown in making punishment less severe

clench /klentʃ/ *v* [T] to close or hold tightly: *She clenched her teeth. | He clenched his money in his hand. | a clenched fist*

cler·gy /ˈklɜːdʒi ‖ -ɜːr-/ *n* [pl] priests, especially in the Christian church, who are allowed to perform religious services: *the power of the clergy*

cler·gy·man /ˈklɜːdʒimən ‖ -ɜːr-/ *n* **clergymen** /-mən/ a member of the clergy –see PRIEST (USAGE)

cler·i·cal /ˈklerɪkəl/ *adj* **1** relating to the work of an office clerk: *We're looking for a new clerical assistant.* **2** relating to or concerning the clergy

clerk /klɑːk ‖ klɜːrk/ *n* **1** a person employed to keep records and accounts, and to do general office work **2** an official in charge of the records of a court, town council, etc.

clev·er /ˈklevər/ *adj* **1** having a quick and able mind: *a clever student | a clever worker* **2** showing that someone has a quick and able mind: *a clever idea* **3** showing ability or skill with your hands or body: *He's very clever with his hands.* **–cleverly** *adv*: **–cleverness** *n* [U]

cli·ché /ˈkliːʃeɪ ‖ kliːˈʃeɪ/ *n* an idea or expression used so commonly that it has lost much of its meaning and effectiveness (a word used to express disapproval)

click[1] /klɪk/ *n* a short sharp sound, such as the noise of a key turning in a lock

click[2] *v* 1 [I;T] to make a short sharp sound: *The door clicked shut.* | *She clicked her fingers to get the waiter's attention.* 2 [I] *infml* suddenly to become clear to someone: *Her joke suddenly clicked and we all laughed.* 3 [I] *infml* to find that you like someone: *They clicked immediately.*

cli·ent /'klaɪənt/ *n* a person who pays a professional person or organization for help and advice –see CUSTOMER (USAGE)

cliff /klɪf/ *n* a high very steep face of rock on a coast: *the white cliffs of Dover*

cliff·hang·er /'klɪf,hæŋəʳ/ *n infml* a story or competition which is exciting because the result is in doubt until the very end: *The game was a real cliffhanger.*

cli·mac·tic /klaɪ'mæktɪk/ *adj* forming the most exciting part of something

cli·mate /'klaɪmɨt/ *n* 1 the average weather conditions at a particular place: *a tropical climate* 2 the state of affairs or general feeling at a particular time: *The present political climate makes an election unlikely.* | *They live in a climate of fear.*

cli·mat·ic /klaɪ'mætɪk/ *adj* relating to the climate of a place: *The climatic conditions were good.*

cli·max[1] /'klaɪmæks/ *n* 1 the most exciting or important part of a story or some action, usually happening near the end: *the climax of the film* | *the climax of her career* 2 the highest point of sexual pleasure

climax[2] *v* [I] to reach the most exciting or important part: *a life of service to the nation, climaxing in her appointment as President*

climb[1] /klaɪm/ *v* 1 [I;T] to move towards the top of something such as a hill or tree: *Do you think you can climb that tree?* | *He climbed up the ladder.* see picture on page 736 2 [I] to rise: *The plane climbed quickly.* | *The road climbed steeply up the hill.* 3 [I; + adv/prep] to move with difficulty, especially into or out of a small space: *She climbed into the car.* | *He climbed out of the window.* | *We managed to climb down the cliff.*

climb down *phr v* [I] *infml* to admit that you were wrong about something

climb[2] *n* 1 a journey upwards made by climbing: *It was a two-hour climb to the top.* 2 a steep slope: *There was a steep climb on the road out of town.*

climb·er /'klaɪməʳ/ *n* 1 a person who climbs mountains: *a famous mountain climber* 2 a plant that climbs

clinch /klɪntʃ/ *v* [T] 1 *infml* to settle an agreement: *The two businessmen clinched the deal quickly.* 2 to cause someone to reach a clear decision: *That clinches it – I'm not going.*

cling /klɪŋ/ *v* **clung** /klʌŋ/, **clung** [I] 1 to hold tightly to something or someone: *The child was clinging to its mother.* 2 to stick firmly to something: *The wet shirt clung to his body.* 3 **cling to something** to continue to believe that something is true or right because you want to believe it: *She still clings to the belief that her son is alive.*

cling·film /'klɪŋfɪlm/ *n* [U] thin transparent plastic put round food to keep it fresh

cling·ing /'klɪŋɪŋ/ *adj* 1 fitting or sticking tightly to your body (used of clothes): *a clinging shirt* 2 too dependent upon the presence of another person: *a clinging child*

clin·ic /'klɪnɪk/ *n* 1 a building or part of a hospital where specialized medical treatment and advice is given: *The clinic is near the station.* | *the ear, nose, and throat clinic* 2 a regular period of time when you can go to a hospital for a particular kind of treatment or advice: *The ante-natal clinics are held on Tuesdays and Thursdays.*

clin·i·cal /'klɪnɪkəl/ *adj* 1 connected with practical medical treatment rather than medical ideas: *clinical analysis* 2 showing little or no personal feeling: *He seemed to have a rather clinical view of the breakup of his marriage.* –**clinically** /-kli/ *adv*

clink /klɪŋk/ *v* [I;T] to make a sound like the sound of pieces of glass or metal lightly hitting each other –**clink** *n* [sing]

clip[1] /klɪp/ *n* 1 a small object, usually made of plastic or metal, for holding things tightly together or in place: *a paper clip* | *a hair clip* 2 a short quick blow: *She gave him a clip around the ears.* 3 the act of cutting something, especially to make it neater 4 a short piece of a film or television show, shown separately

clip[2] *v* -**pp**- 1 [I;T] to put a clip on things to hold them firmly together or to keep them in place: *Clip these sheets of paper together please.* | *The lamp clips on to the front of the bicycle.* 2 [T] to cut something, especially in order to cut some parts off or to make it neater: *I think I'd better clip the hedge.* 3 to hit someone with a short quick blow

clip clop /ˌklɪp 'klɒp ‖ -'klɑːp/ *n* the sound made by a horse walking on hard ground

clip·pers /'klɪpəz ‖ -pərz/ *n* [pl] a sharp instrument, often like scissors, used for clipping things: *nail clippers* | *hedge clippers* –see PAIR (USAGE)

clip·ping /'klɪpɪŋ/ *n* 1 **clippings** [pl] pieces cut off or out of something: *nail clippings* 2 a piece of writing that has been cut out of a newspaper or magazine: *Have you saved that newspaper clipping about my friend?*

clique /kliːk/ *n* a small closely united group of people who are part of a larger group and who are often unfriendly to other groups (a word used to express disapproval) –**cliquey** *adj*

clit·o·ris /'klɪtərɨs/ *n* a small front part of the female sex organ which is a centre of sexual excitement

cloak[1] /kləʊk/ *n* 1 a loose outer garment worn like a coat but which has no separate coverings for your arms 2 something used to hide the truth: *a cloak of secrecy*

cloak[2] *v* [T] *lit* to cover something or hide it: *The hills were cloaked in mist.*

cloak-and-dag·ger /ˌ··'··/ *adj* [only before a noun] full of violence and mystery (used especially of plays, films, and stories)

cloak·room /'kləʊkrʊm, -ruːm/ *n* 1 a room in a public building where hats, coats, and bags may be left for a short time 2 *BrE* a LAVATORY especially in a public building

clob·ber /'klɒbəʳ ‖ 'klɑː-/ *v* [T] *infml* 1 to hit someone hard: *I'll clobber you if you don't do what you're told.* 2 to defeat someone easily: *The socialists were clobbered in the last election.*

clock[1] /klɒk ‖ klɑːk/ *n* 1 an instrument for measuring or showing time, not worn like a watch: *According to the station clock, the train's late.* –see picture on page 442 2 an instrument in a car which tells you how many miles or kilometres a car has travelled 3 **around/round the clock** all day and night, without stopping: *We worked around the clock to finish the job.* **4 put the clock back** to move the hands of a clock to show an earlier time: *In Italy they put the clock back two hours every October.* **5 put the clock forward** to move the hands of a clock to show a later time **6 put the clock back, turn the clock back** to return to older ideas or methods

clock² *v* [T] to measure how long something takes: *I clocked his progress for the first mile.*

clock off *phr v* [I] to record the time at which you leave work, especially in a factory

clock on *phr v* [I] to record the time at which you arrive at work, especially in a factory

clock sthg ↔ **up** *phr v* [T] to record the number of miles or kilometres travelled, the number of points won, etc.: *It's a new car, but we've already clocked up 1000 miles.*

clock·wise /'klɒk-waɪz ‖ 'klɑːk-/ *adj,adv* in the direction in which the hands of a clock move: *Turn the handle clockwise to lock the door.* –opposite **anticlockwise**

clock·work /'klɒk-wɜːk ‖ 'klɑːk-wɜːrk/ *n* [U] **1** machinery that can be wound up with a key, and that is used especially in clocks and toys: *clockwork toys.* **2 like clockwork** *infml* easily and without problems: *The whole conference ran like clockwork.*

clod /klɒd ‖ klɑːd/ *n* a lump of clay or earth

clog /klɒg ‖ klɑːg/ *v* -**gg**- [I;T] (also **clog up**; **clog** sthg ↔ **up**) to block something or to become blocked: *You've clogged the sink with those cabbage leaves.* | *These roads clog up with heavy lorries.*

clogs /klɒgz ‖ klɑːgz/ *n* shoes made of wood or with wooden SOLES

clois·ter /'klɔɪstəʳ/ *n* a covered passage in a religious building, which has open archways on one side

clois·tered /'klɔɪstəd ‖ -ərd/ *adj* living apart from the life of others that surrounds you: *a cloistered university life*

clone¹ /kləʊn/ *n tech* the descendant of a single plant or animal, produced scientifically to have exactly the same form as the parent

clone² *v* **cloned, cloning** [T] to produce a plant or an animal that is a clone

close¹ /kləʊz/ *v* **closed, closing 1** [T] to shut something: *She closed the door quietly.* | *The company has decided to close its London branch.* **2** [I] to shut: *What time does the library close this evening?* **3** [T] to bring something to an end: *This conversation is now closed.*

close down *phr v* **1** [T **close** sthg ↔ **down**] to stop all work at a factory or business: *The steelworks will be closed down next month.* **2** [I] (of a factory or business) to stop working: *The toy factory closed down last year.*

close in *phr v* [I] **1** to surround someone and gradually move nearer to them: *His enemies were gradually closing in on him.* **2 the days are closing in** = the days are becoming shorter because winter is coming

close² *n* **1** the end of something: *The long strike has finally drawn to a close.* | *At the close of play, the*

score was three all. **2** the area around a large important church

close³ /kləʊs/ *adj* **1** [never before a noun] near: *The shops are quite close.* | *Our house is quite close to the town centre.* **2** [only before a noun] near in relationship: *I haven't got many close relatives.* **3** [only before a noun] thorough or careful: *We kept a close watch on the children.* **4** too warm and with no wind: *The weather was close and humid.* **5** decided by only a very small difference: *We won, but the game was very close.* **6 close at hand** near: *The shops are quite close at hand.* **7 close call, close shave, close thing** something bad that nearly happened but did not happen: *That was a close shave!* –see NEAR (USAGE)

close⁴ *adv* **1** near: *They were sitting very close together.* | *Don't come too close!* **2 close on** *infml* almost: *It happened close on 50 years ago.*

closed /kləʊzd/ *adj* **1** shut: *The door is closed.* **2** not open to the public: *The shop is closed on Thursdays.* | *The Post Office is closed for lunch.* **3** not open to everyone: *a club with a closed membership* **4** not allowing outside influence: *a closed prison* **5 closed book** something which you know nothing about: *Fishing is a closed book to me.* **6 closed shop** a factory or other establishment in which the workers must belong to one particular trade union **7 closed circuit television** a television system used inside a building: *We used closed circuit television at the shop to prevent shoplifting.*

close-knit /ˌkləʊs ˈnɪt◂/ *adj* (also **closely-knit**) closely bound together by sharing similar beliefs and activities: *a close-knit community*

close sea·son /ˈkləʊs ˌsiːzən/ *n* (also **closed season**) the period of each year when certain animals, birds, or fish may not be killed for sport by law

close-set /ˌkləʊs ˈset◂/ *adj* placed very near to each other (used of eyes)

clos·et¹ /'klɒzət ‖ 'klɑː-, 'klɔː-/ *n AmE* a tall cupboard built into the wall of a room

closet² *v* **be closeted with someone** to be talking privately to someone

closet³ *adj* [only before a noun] not shown or admitted openly: *a closet alcoholic*

close-up /'kləʊs ʌp/ *n* a photograph or film showing a lot of detail taken very near to the subject

clo·sure /'kləʊʒəʳ/ *n* [C;U] the closing of something such as a factory or business: *The present economic situation has led to the closure of a lot of companies.* | *campaigning against hospital closures*

clot¹ /klɒt ‖ klɑːt/ *n* **1** a thickened mass or sticky lump, formed when blood dries up: *a blood clot* **2** *BrE infml* a stupid person

clot² *v* -**tt**- [I] to become thick and form lumps: *clotted cream*

cloth /klɒθ ‖ klɔːθ/ *n* **1** [U] material made from wool, nylon, or cotton, and used for making things such as clothes and coverings: *I'll need 3 metres of cloth for that dress.* **2** [C] a piece of material used for a particular purpose: *a cloth for cleaning the windows* | *two new dish cloths*

■ USAGE Do not use **cloth** (klɒθ ‖ klɔːθ) or **cloths** (klɒθs ‖ klɔːθs) to mean "the things that people wear". Instead use **clothes** (kləʊðz, kləʊz): *a clothes shop* | *The guests all wore casual clothes.*

clothe /kləʊð/ *v* **clothed, clothing** [T] **1** to provide clothes for someone: *They have to work hard to feed and clothe their family.* **2 clothed in** *fml* dressed in: *She was clothed in green.*

clothes /kləʊðz, kləʊz/ n [pl] garments, such as trousers, dresses, or shirts, that you wear: *I need some new clothes.*

■ USAGE Note that **clothes** is a plural noun and cannot be used in the singular. Use it to talk in general about the things that people wear: *He bought a lot of new* **clothes**. | *I need some smart* **clothes** *for the wedding.* If you need to talk about a single article of clothing you can use the rather formal word **garment**: *Customers are allowed to take a maximum of three* **garments** *into our fitting rooms.* Usually, however, you will be able to use a more exact word: *She bought three* **sweaters** *and a* **pair of trousers**.

clothes·horse /ˈkləʊðzhɔːs, ˈkləʊz- ‖ -ɔːrs/ n BrE a framework on which clothes are hung to dry indoors

clothes peg /ˈ· ·/ n a small wooden or plastic instrument for holding washing on a line to dry

cloth·ing /ˈkləʊðɪŋ/ n [U] clothes that people wear: *warm winter clothing* | *These people need food, clothing, and shelter.*

cloud¹ /klaʊd/ **1** [C;U] a white or grey mass of very small drops of water floating in the sky: *Black rainclouds are gathering.* | *There's a lot of cloud today.* **2** [C] a mass of smoke or dust: *They drove off in a cloud* **of** *dust.* **3 a cloud of** a large number of small things moving in a mass: *a cloud of mosquitos* **4** [C] something that causes unhappiness or fear: *The clouds of war were gathering* **5 under a cloud** not approved of or trusted: *He left his job under a cloud.* **6 on cloud nine** *infml* extremely happy: *He was on cloud nine when he heard he'd got the job.*

cloud² v **1** [I;T] to make something less easy to see through, or to become less easy to see through: *The glass was dirty and clouded.* **2** [T] to make something unclear: *The explanations given seem to cloud the issues even more.* **3** [T] to make a situation unhappy or unpleasant: *His suspicions clouded their relationship.*

cloud over phr v [I] **1** (of someone's face) to begin to look unhappy or angry: *His face clouded over when I told him the news.*

cloud·burst /ˈklaʊdbɜːst ‖ -ɜːrt-/ n a sudden very heavy fall of rain

cloud·y /ˈklaʊdi/ adj **cloudier, cloudiest 1** full of clouds: *a cloudy day* | *a cloudy sky* **2** not transparent: *This beer looks cloudy to me.* **3** unclear: *a cloudy memory of what happened*

clout¹ /klaʊt/ n *infml* **1** [C] a blow or knock given with your hand **2** [U] influence

clout² v [T] *infml* to hit someone with your hand

clove¹ /kləʊv/ n **1** the dried flower of a tropical Asian plant, used in cooking **2** a small piece of the GARLIC root: *a clove of garlic*

clove² the past tense of CLEAVE

clo·ven¹ /ˈkləʊvən/ the past participle of CLEAVE

cloven² adj **cloven hoof** a foot divided into two parts, like that of a sheep or goat

clo·ver /ˈkləʊvər/ n [U] **1** a small plant with pink, purple, or white flowers **2 in clover** *infml* living in comfort

clown¹ /klaʊn/ n **1** a performer who wears funny clothes and tries to make people laugh by jokes, tricks, or doing silly things **2** someone who tries to make people laugh by saying or doing silly things

clown² v [I] to behave stupidly or foolishly in order to make people laugh: *Stop clowning around!*

club¹ /klʌb/ n **1** a society of people who join together

for a certain purpose, for example sport or amusement: *We belong to the golf club.* **2** the building where they meet: *The Cricket Club is closed.* **3** a group of people who pay a regular sum of money for something: *a book club* **4** a heavy stick, suitable for use as a weapon **5** a specially shaped stick for hitting the ball in a game of GOLF **6 clubs** a set of playing cards with one or more three-leafed figures printed in black

club² v **-bb-** [T] to beat or hit someone with a heavy stick: *He was clubbed to death.*

club together phr v [I] to share the cost of something with others: *We clubbed together to buy her a present.*

cluck /klʌk/ n the noise that a hen makes –**cluck** v [I]

clue /kluː/ n **1** something that helps you to find an answer to a problem: *a clue to his disappearance* | *I don't know the answer. Give me a clue.* **2 not have a clue** *infml* not to have any idea: *I haven't a clue what time it starts.*

clued up /ˌ· ˈ·/ adj *infml* very well-informed: *He's quite clued up about music.*

clump¹ /klʌmp/ n **1** a group of trees, bushes, or plants growing together **2** a heavy solid lump or mass of dirt, soil, or mud

clump² v [I + adv/prep] to walk with slow heavy noisy footsteps: *Listen to him clumping around upstairs.*

clum·sy /ˈklʌmzi/ adj **clumsier, clumsiest 1** awkward and ungraceful in movement: *Look where you're going, you clumsy boy!* **2** awkward, careless or insensitive in the things that you say or do: *a clumsy remark* | *a clumsy attempt to deal with the situation* **3** difficult to use or control: *Those boots are too clumsy for long walks.* –**clumsily** adv –**clumsiness** n [U]

clung /klʌŋ/ the past tense and past participle of CLING

clus·ter¹ /ˈklʌstər/ n a number of things of the same kind close together in a group: *a cluster of stars* | *The men were standing* **in** *a cluster at the back.*

cluster² v [I;T] to gather or grow in a group: *The boys clustered round the fire and sang songs.*

clutch¹ /klʌtʃ/ v **1** [T] to hold something tightly: *The mother clutched her baby in her arms.* **2 clutch at** to try to take hold of something: *She clutched at the bannister as she began to fall.* **3 clutch at straws** to try anything to help you to get out of a difficult situation

clutch² n **1** a tight hold on something usually because you are afraid: *His clutch was not tight enough and he fell from the branch.* **2** an apparatus in a car which allows working parts of an engine to be connected or disconnected: *Press the clutch and change gear.* –see picture on page 49 **3 in the clutches of** in the control or possession of someone: *Once he was in the clutches of the enemy he knew he'd never escape.*

clut·ter¹ /ˈklʌtər/ v [T] (also **clutter** sthg ↔ **up**) to make something untidy or fill it with unnecessary objects: *Don't clutter up your room.* | *The room was cluttered with furniture.*

clutter² n [U] a lot of things scattered about in a disorderly manner: *a room full of clutter*

cm a written abbreviation for CENTIMETRE(S)

c/o used when you are sending a letter to someone by sending it to another person who will keep it for them; an abbreviation for **care of**: *Send it to John Smith c/o The Post Office, Cambridge.*

Co.¹ a written abbreviation for COUNTY: *Sunderland, Co. Durham*

Co.² /kəʊ/ an abbreviation for COMPANY: *James Smith & Co.*

coach¹ /kəʊtʃ/ *n* **1** *BrE* a bus used for long-distance travel or touring **2 by coach** travelling in a coach: *We're going by coach.* **3** a railway passenger carriage **4** a person who trains sportsmen and sportswomen: *a football coach* **5** a large enclosed carriage with four wheels pulled by horses

coach² *v* [I;T] to train or teach a person or a group of people: *I coach people for English examinations.* | *He's being coached for the Olympic Games.*

co·ag·u·late /kəʊˈægjʊleɪt/ *v* **coagulated, coagulating** [I;T] to change from a liquid into a solid or very thick mass: *Blood coagulates when it meets air.* –**coagulation** /kəʊˌægjʊˈleɪʃən/ *n* [U]

coal /kəʊl/ *n* **1** [U] a black mineral which is dug from the earth and which can be burned to give heat: *Put some more coal on the fire, please.* | *a coal miner* **2 coals** [pl] burning pieces of coal **3 haul someone over the coals** *infml* to speak very angrily to someone who has done something wrong

co·a·lesce /ˌkəʊəˈles/ *v* **coalesced, coalescing** [I] *fml* to grow together or unite so as to form one group or system –**coalescence** *n* [U]

co·a·li·tion /ˌkəʊəˈlɪʃən/ *n* a union of separate political parties or people for a special purpose, usually for a limited period of time: *The three parties joined together to form a coalition.* | *a coalition government*

coal·mine /ˈkəʊlmaɪn/ *n* a mine from which coal is dug

coarse /kɔːs ‖ kɔːrs/ *adj* **1** not fine or smooth: *a coarse woollen garment* | *coarse grains of sand* **2** rough and rather rude in manner: *coarse behaviour* | *a coarse joke* –**coarsely** *adv* –**coarseness** *n* [U]

coars·en /ˈkɔːsən ‖ ˈkɔːr-/ *v* **1** [T] to make something coarse: *The wrong kind of soap can coarsen the skin.* **2** [I;T] to make or become rude and rough in manner: *She had coarsened since leaving home.* | *The army had coarsened him.*

coast¹ /kəʊst/ *n* **1** the land next to the sea: *a trip to the coast* | *the north coast of Scotland* | *the Pacific coast* –see SHORE¹ (USAGE) **2 the coast is clear** *infml* all danger has gone: *Leave now, while the coast is clear!*

coast² *v* [I] to keep moving without additional power: *She switched off the car engine and coasted down the hill.*

coast·guard /ˈkəʊstɡɑːd ‖ -ɑːrd/ *n* **1 the coastguard** a naval or police organization intended to watch for ships in danger and prevent unlawful activity at sea **2** [C] a member of this organization

coast·line /ˈkəʊstlaɪn/ *n* the edge of a coast, as seen from the sea or on a map

coat¹ /kəʊt/ *n* **1** a piece of clothing with long sleeves (SLEEVE) that you wear over your other clothes to keep you warm outdoors –see picture on page 50 **2** an animal's fur, wool, or hair **3** a covering of something spread over a surface: *a coat of paint*

coat² *v* [T] to put a thin covering of something on the surface: *The table was coated* **with** *dust.*

coat hang·er /ˈ· ˌ··/ *n* –see HANGER

coat of arms /ˌ· · ˈ·-/ *n* **coats of arms** a set of patterns or pictures, used by a person or an organization as their special sign

coax /kəʊks/ *v* [T] **1** to persuade someone by kind or patient words: *I coaxed him* **into** *going to school.* **2** to obtain something by gentle persuasion: *I coaxed a kiss* **from** *the little girl.* **3** to use patience to make something work: *She coaxed the machine* **into** *action.*

cob /kɒb ‖ kɑːb/ *n* the long hard central part of an ear of MAIZE, which can be cooked and eaten: *corn on the cob*

cob·bled /ˈkɒbəld ‖ ˈkɑː-/ *adj* covered with cobblestones (used of roads): *old cobbled streets*

cob·bler /ˈkɒblər ‖ ˈkɑː-/ *n old fash* a person who repairs shoes

cob·ble·stones /ˈkɒbəlstəʊn ‖ ˈkɑː-/ *n* (also **cobbles**) [pl] stones with a rounded upper surface used for covering the surface of roads in former times

co·bra /ˈkəʊbrə/ *n* an African or Asian poisonous snake

cob·web /ˈkɒbweb ‖ ˈkɑːb-/ (also **spiderweb** *AmE*, **web**) *n* a very fine network of sticky threads made by a SPIDER to catch insects

Co·ca-Co·la /ˌkəʊkə ˈkəʊlə/ *n tdmk* (also **Coke** /kəʊk/) **1** [U] a FIZZY non-alcoholic dark-coloured drink **2** [C] a bottle or glass of Coca-Cola: *Two Cokes, please.*

co·caine /kəʊˈkeɪn, kə-/ *n* (also **coke** /kəʊk/ *infml*) [U] a drug used for preventing pain, or taken illegally for pleasure: *Police have seized cocaine with a street value of £8m.*

cock¹ /kɒk ‖ kɑːk/ *n* **1** a fully-grown male bird **2** a fully-grown male chicken

cock·a·too /ˌkɒkəˈtuː ‖ ˈkɑːkətuː/ *n* an Australian bird with large feathers on the top of its head

cock·crow /ˈkɒk-krəʊ ‖ ˈkɑːk-/ *n* [U] *lit* the time of day when light first appears

cock·e·rel /ˈkɒkərəl ‖ ˈkɑː-/ *n* a young male chicken

cock·eyed /ˌkɒkˈaɪd◂ ‖ ˌkɑːk-/ *adj infml* **1** stupid and not likely to succeed: *a cockeyed idea* **2** not straight: *That picture's all cockeyed.*

cock·le /ˈkɒkəl ‖ ˈkɑː-/ *n* a small SHELLFISH

Cock·ney /ˈkɒkni ‖ ˈkɑːkni/ *n* **1** a person born and living in the poorer parts of London especially one from the East End **2** the speech of people who live in the East End of London

cock·pit /ˈkɒkˌpɪt ‖ ˈkɑːk-/ *n* the part of a plane or a racing car in which the pilot or driver sits

cock·roach /ˈkɒk-rəʊtʃ ‖ ˈkɑːk-/ *n* (**roach** *AmE*) a large black insect which lives especially in old or dirty houses

cock·sure /ˌkɒkˈʃʊər◂ ‖ ˌkɑːk-/ *adj* too sure of yourself (a word used to express disapproval)

cock·tail /ˈkɒkteɪl ‖ ˈkɑːk-/ *n* **1** a mixed alcoholic drink **2** a small dish of mixed food eaten at the start of a meal: *a prawn cocktail*

cock-up /ˈ· ·/ *n BrE slang* a mistake that prevents something from being done successfully (a rude word)

cock·y /ˈkɒki ‖ ˈkɑːki/ *adj* **cockier, cockiest** *infml* too sure of yourself (a word to express disapproval): *I don't like him. He's far too cocky.* –**cockiness** *n* [U]

co·coa /'kəʊkəʊ/ n 1 [U] a dark brown powder used to make chocolate 2 [C;U] a hot drink made from this powder and milk or water: *a cup of cocoa*

co·co·nut /'kəʊkənʌt/ n 1 [C] a very large nut with hard white flesh and a centre filled with a milky juice 2 [U] the flesh of this nut eaten raw or used in cooking

co·coon /kə'kuːn/ n a protective case of silky threads round an insect at the PUPA stage

co·cooned /kə'kuːnd/ adj 1 wrapped up warmly or tightly: *He was cocooned in his sleeping bag.* 2 protected and cut off from problems in life: *He accused them of being cocooned by the welfare state.*

cod /kɒd/ n [plural is **cod**] [C;U] a large sea fish

C.O.D. /ˌsiː əʊ 'diː/ a system where you pay for something when it is delivered; an abbreviation for **cash on delivery** *You can order the goods C.O.D.*

code¹ /kəʊd/ n 1 [C;U] a system of words, letters, or numbers used instead of ordinary writing, to send secret messages: *The message was in code.* 2 [C;U] a system of signals used instead of letters and numbers in a message that is broadcast: *a telegraphic code* 3 [C] a part of a telephone number, for a village, town or country: *The code for Nottingham is 0602.* | *local dialling codes* 4 [C] a system of laws or rules: *the Napoleonic code* | *the highway code* 5 [C] a set of ideas which a society shares: *the accepted code of behaviour* 6 **code of practice** the formal rules of correct behaviour for a profession: *The Solicitors' Association has recently drawn up a new code of practice.*

code² v **coded, coding** [T] to translate a message into a code

co·ed¹ /ˌkəʊ'ed◂ ‖ 'kəʊed/ adj BrE infml an abbreviation for COEDUCATIONAL

coed² /'kəʊed/ n AmE infml a female student in a college or university open to both sexes

co·ed·u·ca·tion·al /ˌkəʊedjʊ'keɪʃənəl ‖ -dʒə-/ adj educating boys and girls together: *a co-educational school* –**coeducation** n [U]

co·erce /kəʊ'ɜːs ‖ -'ɜːrs/ v **coerced, coercing** [T] fml to force someone to do something: *The defendant claimed that he had been coerced into making a confession.* –**coercion** /kəʊ'ɜːʃən ‖ -'ɜːrʒən/ n [U]

co·ex·ist /ˌkəʊɪg'zɪst/ v [I] 1 to exist together peacefully in spite of having different opinions or different political systems: *Now the war has ended, the two countries will have to learn to coexist.* –**coexistence** n [U]: *peaceful coexistence*

C of E /ˌsiː əv 'iː/ an abbreviation for CHURCH OF ENGLAND

cof·fee /'kɒfi ‖ 'kɔːfi, 'kɑːfi/ n 1 [U] a brown powder made by crushing the beans of the coffee tree 2 [U] a hot brown drink made from this powder: *Would you like a cup of coffee?* 3 [C] a cup of coffee: *Two coffees, please!*

coffee bar /'·· ·/ n BrE a place where light meals, cakes, and non-alcoholic drinks are served

coffee ta·ble /'·· ˌ··/ n a small low table –see picture on page 442

cof·fer /'kɒfər ‖ 'kɔː-, 'kɑː-/ n a large strong box for holding money, jewels, or other valuable objects

cof·fin /'kɒfɪn ‖ 'kɔː-/ n the box in which a dead person is buried

cog /kɒg ‖ kɑːg/ n 1 a tooth round the edge of a wheel that causes it to move or be moved by another wheel in a machine 2 **a cog in the machine** an unimportant person in a large organization

co·gent /'kəʊdʒənt/ adj having the power to make someone believe a reason or argument –**cogently** adv –**cogency** n [U]

cog·i·tate /'kɒdʒɪteɪt ‖ 'kɑː-/ v **cogitated, cogitating** [I] fml to think carefully and seriously about something

co·gnac /'kɒnjæk ‖ 'kəʊ-, 'kɑː-/ n [C;U] a strong alcoholic drink made in France

co·hab·it /ˌkəʊ'hæbɪt/ v [I] fml (of two unmarried people) to live together as though married –**cohabitation** /kəʊˌhæbɪ'teɪʃən/ n [U]

co·her·ent /kəʊ'hɪərənt/ adj 1 clear and easy to understand: *a coherent argument* 2 able to put ideas or words together clearly: *As he recovered from the shock, he gradually became more coherent.* –**coherently** adv –**coherence** n [U]

co·he·sion /kəʊ'hiːʒən/ n [U] 1 the act or state of sticking together tightly: *We need greater cohesion in the party if we want to win the election.* 2 tech connection in ideas between different parts of a sentence or between one sentence and another –**cohesive** /-'hiːsɪv/ adj

coif·fure /kwɒ'fjʊər ‖ kwɑː-/ n fml a style of arranging or cutting a woman's hair

coil¹ /kɔɪl/ v [I;T] to wind or twist into a continuous circular shape: *The snake coiled itself round the tree.* **coil sthg ↔ up** phr v [T] to wind something into a continuous circular shape: *Now coil up the rope.* | *The snake coiled itself up again.*

coil² n 1 one of a connected set of rings or twists into which something such as a rope or wire can be wound: *a coil of rope* | *a loose coil of hair* 2 tech an apparatus made by coiling a length of wire, used for carrying an electric current 3 **the coil** a small metal or plastic object fitted inside a woman's body to prevent her having a baby

coin¹ /kɔɪn/ n 1 a piece of money made of metal: *I changed £5 at the bank, because I needed some coins for the ticket machine.*

coin² v [T] 1 to make coins from metal: *The government has decided to coin more 50-pence pieces.* 2 to invent a new word: *Who coined the word "nuke"?* 3 **to coin a phrase** a phrase used for excusing yourself when you have just used an expression which is used far too much: *"Do you come here often?...to coin a phrase!"*

coin·age /'kɔɪnɪdʒ/ n [U] the system of coins used in a country: *decimal coinage*

co·in·cide /ˌkəʊɪn'saɪd/ v **coincided, coinciding** [I] 1 to happen at the same time or in the same place: *Unfortunately, our holidays don't coincide this year.* | *Her eighteenth birthday is going to coincide with the final exam.* 2 (of ideas or opinions) to be in agreement

co·in·ci·dence /kəʊ'ɪnsɪdəns/ n [C;U] a combination of events, happening by chance which are often surprising: *What a coincidence that I was in London at the same time as you!* –**coincidental** /kəʊˌɪnsɪ'dentl/ adj –**coincidentally** adv

coke /kəʊk/ n 1 [U] the solid substance that remains after gas has been removed from coal by heating, used for producing heat by burning 2 **Coke** see COCA-COLA 3 [U] see COCAINE

col·an·der /'kʌləndər, 'kɒ- ‖ 'kʌ-, 'kɑː-/ n a bowl-shaped pan with holes in it, used for separating food from liquid

cold¹ /kəʊld/ adj 1 having a low temperature or one that is lower than it should be: *a cold wind* | *It's a cold day for July, isn't it?* | *I'm cold.* | *My coffee's gone cold.* 2 showing a lack of friendly feelings: *a cold smile* | *She seemed cold and uncaring.* 3 cooked but not eaten hot (used of food): *cold meats* 4 **out cold**

unconscious, especially as the result of a severe blow to the head **5 cold comfort** little or no help in a bad situation **6 cold sweat** a condition of great fear or nervousness: *I broke out in a cold sweat.* **7 cold turkey** the unpleasant sick feeling caused by the sudden stopping of the use of a drug **8 cold war** a state of severe political struggle, but without actual fighting, between countries with opposed political systems **9 get cold feet, have cold feet** to become worried about doing something as the time to do it comes near: *She told me she was getting cold feet about getting married.* **10 in cold blood** in a planned and heartless way: *They killed the old man in cold blood!*

cold² *n* **1** an illness of the nose or throat, which is common in winter and may cause headaches, coughing, and slight fever: *He's got a bad cold.* | *Be careful you don't catch a cold.* | *She's had two or three colds this winter.* **2 the cold** a low temperature or cold weather: *Don't go out into the cold without a coat!* **3 out in the cold** *infml* unwanted or not considered: *He was left out in the cold at school because he didn't like sports.*

cold-blood·ed /ˌ·ˈ··/ *adj* **1** having a body temperature that changes according to the temperature of the surroundings: *Snakes are cold-blooded.* **2** cruel and showing complete lack of feeling: *a cold-blooded murder*

cold-heart·ed /ˌ·ˈ··/ *adj* lacking sympathy: *a cold-hearted refusal to help* –**cold-heartedly** *adv* –**cold-heartedness** *n* [U]

cold·ly /ˈkəʊldli/ *adv* without friendly feelings: *He looked at me coldly without a smile.*

cold·ness /ˈkəʊldnəs/ *n* [U] **1** the state of being cold **2** lack of friendly feelings

col·ic /ˈkɒlɪk/ ‖ /ˈkɑː-/ *n* [U] a severe pain in the stomach and bowels of babies

col·lab·o·rate /kəˈlæbəreɪt/ *v* **collaborated, collaborating** [I] **1** to work together for a special purpose: *Turner collaborated with Leech on the marine biology project.* **2** to help an enemy country which has taken control of your own country (a word used to express disapproval): *He was accused of collaborating with the enemy.* –**collaborator** *n* –**collaboration** /kəˌlæbəˈreɪʃən/ *n* [U] : *The two companies are working in close collaboration.*

col·lage /ˈkɒlɑːʒ/ ‖ /kəˈlɑːʒ/ *n* **1** [U] the art of making pictures by sticking various materials onto a surface **2** [C] a picture made in this way

col·lapse¹ /kəˈlæps/ *v* **collapsed, collapsing** **1** [I] to fall down or inwards suddenly: *The bridge collapsed under the weight of the train.* **2** [I] to fall down in a helpless or unconscious condition: *This man's collapsed. Please can you get a doctor?* **3** [I] to fail suddenly and completely: *All opposition to the government collapsed because of the war.* **4** [I;T] to fold into a shape that takes up less space: *This table collapses, so I can store it easily when I'm not using it.*

collapse² *n* **1** [U] the act of falling down or inwards: *The storm caused the collapse of the entire building.* **2** [U] a failure: *The peace talks were on the verge of*

collapse. **3** [C;U] the sudden and complete loss of strength or will: *a state of near collapse* | *He suffered a nervous collapse.*

col·lap·si·ble /kəˈlæpsəbəl/ *adj* able to be folded up for easy storing: *a collapsible bicycle*

col·lar¹ /ˈkɒləʳ/ ‖ /ˈkɑː-/ *n* **1** the part of a shirt, dress, or coat that fits round your neck –see picture on page 50 **2** a band put round an animal's neck

collar² *v* [T] *infml* to catch and hold someone: *The police collared him as he was getting on the boat.*

col·lar·bone /ˈkɒləbəʊn/ ‖ /ˈkɑːlər-/ *n* either of a pair of bones going from the base of your neck to your shoulders

col·lat·e·ral /kəˈlætərəl/ *n* [U] *fml* property or money that you promise to a person in case you cannot pay back a debt: *He offered his house as collateral for the loan.*

col·league /ˈkɒliːg/ ‖ /ˈkɑː-/ *n* a person who works with you, especially in a profession

col·lect /kəˈlekt/ *v* **1** [I;T] to gather together: *Collect the books and put them on my desk.* | *A crowd of people had collected at the scene of the accident.* | *The government could save money by improving the way it collects taxes.* | *"Has she got a hobby?" "Yes, she collects foreign coins."* | *They are collecting data on family size.* **2** [T] to come to take someone or something away: *He collected the children from school.* **3** [I;T] to get money from people to help others: *I'm collecting for the blind.* | *How much did you collect?* **4 collect your thoughts** to try to order your ideas and feel calm before you do something

col·lect·ed /kəˈlektɪd/ *adj* **1** put together in one book or as a collection: *the collected works of Shakespeare* **2** **cool, calm, and collected** in full control of yourself

col·lec·tion /kəˈlekʃən/ *n* **1** [U] the act of collecting something: *What time is the next collection from this post box?* | *Your shoes are ready for collection.* **2** [C] a group of things that has gathered together, or has been gathered together: *an odd collection of people* | *a new collection of poems* | *She has a very good collection of foreign stamps.*

col·lec·tive¹ /kəˈlektɪv/ *adj* [only before a noun] shared by all the members of a group together: *the collective opinion of the governments of Western Europe* | *collective ownership* –**collectively** *adv*

collective² *n* a business or farm owned and controlled by the people who work in it

col·lec·tor /kəˈlektəʳ/ *n* **1** a person employed to collect things: *a ticket collector* | *a rent collector* **2** a person who collects things such as stamps or coins for pleasure

col·lege /ˈkɒlɪdʒ/ ‖ /ˈkɑː-/ *n* **1** [C;U] a place, sometimes part of a university, for education after leaving school or for preparing for a particular type of job: *The art college is next to the station.* | *He starts college in January.* **2** [C] a body of teachers and students considered as a whole: *The college proposes certain changes of policy.*

col·lide /kəˈlaɪd/ *v* **collided, colliding** [I] **1** to crash violently into something: *Two buses have collided in the town centre.* | *His car collided with a lorry.* **2** to come into strong opposition with someone: *The President collided with Congress over his budget plans.*

col·lie·ry /ˈkɒljəri/ ‖ /ˈkɑːl-/ *n* **collieries** *BrE* a mine for coal and the buildings and machinery connected with it

col·li·sion /kə'lɪʒən/ n **1** a violent crash: *Many people were hurt in the collision* between *a bus and a car.* | *a head-on collision* **2** a strong disagreement: *a collision of interests* **3** a **collision course** a path or course of action likely to result in problems: *The government and the trades unions are on a collision course.*

col·lo·qui·al /kə'ləʊkwiəl/ adj used in ordinary informal conversation: *Don't put these colloquial expressions in your examination essay.* –**colloquially** adv

col·lo·qui·al·ism /kə'ləʊkwiəlɪzəm/ n an expression used in ordinary informal conversation

col·lu·sion /kə'luːʒən/ n [U] *fml* secret agreement between two or more people with the intention of cheating or deceiving others

co·lon /'kəʊlən/ n **1** the mark (:) used in writing to introduce a list, examples, or an explanation **2** part of the large tube which takes waste matter down from your stomach

colo·nel /'kɜːnl ‖ 'kɜːr-/ n an officer of middle rank in an army or air force

co·lo·ni·al /kə'ləʊniəl/ adj related to countries ruled by a more powerful, distant country: *The African people have successfully fought against colonial rule.*

co·lo·ni·al·is·m /kə'ləʊniəlɪzəm/ n [U] the system of colonizing other countries: *British colonialism led to the establishment of a large empire.* –**colonialist** adj, n

col·o·nize /'kɒlənaɪz ‖ 'kɑː-/ v colonized, colonizing (also **colonise** *BrE*) [I;T] to make a country or area into a colony: *The British first colonized Australia in the 18th century.* –**colonization** /ˌkɒlənaɪ'zeɪʃən ‖ ˌkɑːlənə-/ n [U]

col·on·nade /ˌkɒlə'neɪd ‖ ˌkɑː-/ n a row of upright stone posts supporting a roof or a row of arches

col·o·ny /'kɒləni ‖ 'kɑː-/ n colonies **1** a country or area under the control of a more powerful distant country and often settled by people from that country **2** a group of people from the same country or with the same interests, living together: *a nudist colony* **3** a group of the same kind of animals or plants living or growing together: *a colony of ants*

col·or /'kʌlər/ n –see COLOUR

col·ored /'kʌləd ‖ -ərd/ adj,n –see COLOURED

col·or·ful /'kʌləfəl ‖ -ər-/ adj –see COLOURFUL

col·or·ing /'kʌlərɪŋ/ n –see COLOURING

col·or·less /'kʌlələs ‖ 'kʌlər-/ adj –see COLOURLESS

co·los·sal /kə'lɒsəl ‖ kə'lɑː-/ adj extremely large: *a colossal building* | *spending on a colossal scale*

co·los·sus /kə'lɒsəs ‖ kə'lɑː-/ n colossuses *or* colossi /-saɪ/ a person or thing of very great size, importance, or ability: *China is a colossus compared to Hong Kong.*

col·our¹ /'kʌlər/ n (**color** *AmE*) **1** [U] the quality which allows you to see the difference between, for example, a red flower and a blue flower when they are both the same size and shape: *an insect that can change colour* | *colour television* | *a colour film* **2** [C] red, blue, green, black, brown, yellow, white, etc.: *What colour is your car?* | *They come in different colours.* | *a sort of reddish colour* **3** [C;U] a paint or a coloured pencil: *His paintbox only holds six colours.* | *I must sharpen my colours.* **4** [U] the general appearance of someone's skin, especially when related to how healthy they look: *The cold wind brought colour to her cheeks.* **5** [U] details or behaviour of a place, thing, or person, that are interesting and excite the imagination: *She loved the life, noise, and colour of the market.* **6 in colour** printed or shown in all colours not just black and white: *I thought the film would be in colour but it was an old black and white one.* **7 off colour** *infml* a little ill
■ USAGE Notice how we use **is** in this question and answer: *"What colour is it?" "It's red."*

colour² v (**color** *AmE*) **1** [T] to cause something to have colour, especially a picture or something in a picture: *His younger sister was colouring a picture.* | *Why don't you colour the dog brown?* **2** [I] to gain or change colour: *He coloured with embarrassment.* **3** [T] to influence your opinion about something: *Personal feelings coloured his judgment.* **colour** sthg ↔ **in** *phr* v [T] to colour a drawing using coloured pencils: *You haven't coloured the dog in.*

colour bar /'·· ·/ n the set of laws or customs in some places which prevent black people from mixing freely with white people

colour-blind /'·· ·/ adj unable to see the difference between certain colours –**colour blindness** n [U]

col·oured¹ /'kʌləd ‖ -ərd/ adj (**colored** *AmE*) **1** having colour, not just black or white: *coloured sheets* | *The sea was green-coloured.* **2** belonging to a race that does not have a white skin or, especially in South Africa, of mixed race (a word that is considered offensive by many people) **3** full of unfair opinion and not completely honest

coloured² (**colored** *AmE*) n a person in South Africa who is of mixed race

col·our·ful /'kʌləfəl ‖ -ər-/ adj (**colorful** *AmE*) **1** having bright colours: *a bird with colourful wings* **2** full of interest, often because of a lot of variety or detail: *a colourful period of history* | *He's a colourful character.*

col·our·ing /'kʌlərɪŋ/ n (**coloring** *AmE*) **1** [C;U] a substance used for giving a colour to food: *This product contains no artificial colouring.* **2** [U] the colour of your hair and skin: *People with fair colouring should cover up in the sun.*

col·our·less /'kʌlələs ‖ 'kʌlər-/ adj (**colorless** *AmE*) **1** without colour: *Water is a colourless liquid.* **2** lacking interest: *a colourless existence*

colour prej·u·dice /·· ˌ···/ n unreasonable dislike of people of other colours

colour sup·ple·ment /'·· ˌ···/ n a free colour magazine often given with British Sunday newspapers

colt /kəʊlt/ n a young male horse

col·umn /'kɒləm ‖ 'kɑː-/ n **1** a tall solid stone post, used in a building as a support or for decoration **2** anything tall and narrow: *a column of smoke* | *Add up that column of figures, will you?* **3** a group of people moving in a long line: *a column of soldiers* **4** one of the long narrow divisions into which print is arranged in a book or on a newspaper page: *This page is arranged in two columns.* **5** an article by a particular writer, that regularly appears in a newspaper or magazine: *his weekly column in the local paper*

col·umn·ist /'kɒləmʒst, -ləmnʒst ‖ 'kɑː-/ n a person who writes a regular article for a newspaper or magazine

co·ma /'kəʊmə/ n a state like sleep, of long unnatural deep unconsciousness, from which it is difficult to wake up: *After the accident she went into a coma.*

co·ma·tose /'kəʊmətəʊs/ adj **1** *tech* deeply unconscious **2** sleepy and slow to do anything (a word which is often used in a humorous way)

comb[1] /kəʊm/ *n* **1** a flat piece of plastic or metal with a row of thin teeth, which you use to tidy your hair **2** a decoration used in a woman's hair **3** the red fleshy growth on the head of a male chicken

comb[2] *v* [T] **1** to tidy your hair with a comb: *Comb your hair before you go out.* **2** to search a place thoroughly: *The police combed the woods for the missing boy.*

com·bat[1] /ˈkɒmbæt ‖ ˈkɑːm-/ *n* [C;U] a fight or struggle between two people, groups, armies, or ideas: *These troops have very little experience of actual combat.* | *killed in combat*

com·bat[2] /ˈkɒmbæt, kəmˈbæt ‖ kəmˈbæt, ˈkɑːmbæt/ *v* -tt- (also -t- *AmE*) [T] *fml* to fight or struggle against something: *As a doctor, he spent his life combatting disease.* | *The police are now using computers to help combat crime.*

com·ba·tant /ˈkɒmbətənt ‖ kəmˈbætənt/ *n* a person who takes part in fighting in a war

com·bi·na·tion /ˌkɒmbɨˈneɪʃən ‖ ˌkɑːm-/ *n* **1** [C] a mixture of separate people or things that are joined together to form a single unit: *A combination of parties formed the new government.* | *I felt a strange combination of shock and amusement.* **2** [U] **in combination** being joined together: *The dancers and singers worked well in combination.* **3** [C] a set of special numbers or letters needed to open a special lock

com·bine[1] /kəmˈbaɪn/ *v* **combined, combining** [I;T] to join two or more things together: *The two parties have combined to form a government.* | *We'll have our meeting over dinner and combine business with pleasure.*

com·bine[2] /ˈkɒmbaɪn ‖ ˈkɑːm-/ *n* **1** a group of businesses joined together **2** (also **combine harvester**) a large machine which cuts corn and separates and cleans the grain

com·bus·ti·ble /kəmˈbʌstɨbəl/ *adj* able to catch fire and burn easily: *Petrol is highly combustible.* –combustible *n*

com·bus·tion /kəmˈbʌstʃən/ *n* [U] *fml* the act of catching fire and burning

come /kʌm/ *v* **came** /keɪm/, **come, coming** [I] **1** to move towards a place, especially the place where the speaker is: *He got up and came towards me.* | *The train came into the station.* | *She came running into the room.* | *I'm afraid I won't be able to come to the party.* | *You must come and visit us some time.* | *He came to see what was going on.* **2** to arrive: *Everyone else is here but we're still waiting for John to come.* | *Spring has come at last!* | *I think the time has come to abolish this law.* **3** to reach a place: *We walked on until we came to a village.* | *They came to a little bridge over a stream.* | *The water came to my waist.* | *Her hair comes down to her waist.* | *The thick mud came up to my ankles.* **4** to be in a particular place or position: *I came last in the race.* | *What letter comes after "p"?* **5** to become: *My shoelaces have come undone.* | *The label's come off, so I don't know what's inside.* | *One of the wheels had come loose.* **6** to be produced or offered in a particular way: *The bag comes in three different colours, red, blue, or*

---

yellow. | *Cars come in all shapes and sizes these days.* **7 come and go** to change often and quickly: *These fashions and crazes come and go very rapidly.* **8 come to do something: a** to happen to do something: *How did you come to be invited to the party?* **b** to begin to do something: *I came to enjoy our little chats.* | *I'm sure you'll come to enjoy the work in time.* **9 come to think of it** a phrase you use when you have just remembered something: *Come to think of it she still owes me £20.* **10 come unstuck** to meet with difficulties and failure: *I think the government might finally come unstuck over the economy.* **11 how come?** *infml* a phrase you use when you are asking how something happened: *How come she got that job so easily, when she hasn't got any qualifications?* **12 to come** in the future: *I'm afraid we might see unemployment rise even further in the weeks and months to come.*

come about *phr v* [I] to happen: *How did this crisis come about?* | *This situation should never have come about.*

come across *phr v* **1** [T **come across** sthg/sbdy] to meet someone or discover something by chance: *I came across an old friend I hadn't seen for years.* | *I came across some old books in the attic.* **2** [I] to have a particular effect on the people listening: *His speech came across very well.* | *She came across as being vain and silly.*

come along *phr v* [I] **1** to advance or improve: *How's your work coming along?* **2** to happen or arrive by chance: *I got the job because I came along at just the right time.* **3 Come along!** a phrase you use to tell someone to hurry up or make an effort to do something: *Come along, or we'll be late.*

come apart *phr v* [I] to break into pieces: *I picked up the book and it just came apart in my hands.*

come at sbdy *phr v* [T] to move towards someone in a threatening way: *She came at me with a knife.*

come away *phr v* [I] to become loose or disconnected from something: *The handle came away in my hands.*

come back *phr v* [I] **1** to return: *I'm sure she'll come back home eventually.* **2** to become fashionable or popular again: *Bright colours are coming back this year.* **3 come back to something** to talk about something again later: *I'll come back to that question later.* **4 come back to you** to return into your mind: *I can't think of his name, but it'll probably come back to me in a minute.*

come between *phr v* **come between people** to cause trouble between people: *We tried not to let our financial difficulties come between us.*

come by sthg *phr v* [T] to obtain something: *How did you come by all that furniture?* | *Jobs are hard to come by at the moment.*

come down *phr v* [I] **1** to fall down: *Several trees came down in the storm.* **2** to become less: *Hopefully, inflation will start to come down now.* **3 come down in favour of someone, come down on someone's side** to decide to support someone: *The industrial court came down on the side of the unions.*

come down on sbdy *phr v* [T] to punish someone severely, or show strong disapproval of them: *The courts are going to come down heavily on young offenders.*

come down to sthg *phr v* [T] to have something as the most important fact: *What it comes down to is a choice between cutting wages or reducing staff.*

come down with sthg *phr v* [T] *infml* to catch an illness: *He came down with flu.*

come forward *phr v* [I] to offer to help in some way: *No one has come forward with information about the murder.*

come from sthg *phr v* [T] to have something as a place of origin: *Milk comes from cows.* | *Where do you come from?* | *I come from Newcastle but I've spent most of my life in London.*

come in *phr v* [I] **1** (of information) to be received: *Reports are just coming in of a train crash in the South East.* **2** to be elected: *The Socialists came in three years ago.* **3** to become fashionable or popular: *Ethnic clothes started coming in the early sixties.* **4** have money coming in to be earning money: *We haven't got much money coming in at the moment.* **5** come in handy, come in useful to be useful: *Don't throw those bottles away – they might come in handy one day.*

come in for sthg *phr v* [T] to receive blame or disapproval: *The committee has come in for a lot of criticism recently.*

come in on sthg *phr v* [T] to take part in something: *They were very keen to come in on the plan.*

come into sthg *phr v* [T] **1** to gain money because someone has left it to you when they died: *She came into a lot of money when her mother died.* **2 come into your own** to show your abilities fully: *He came into his own when he was put in charge of the department.*

come of sthg *phr v* [T] **1** to result from something: *I don't think that any good will come of all this.* **2 come of age** to reach the age of 18 or 21, when you are considered to be an adult

come off *phr v* **1** [I;T **come off** sthg] to become unfastened or disconnected: *A button's come off my coat.* | *The door handle came off in my hand.* **2** [I] to happen successfully: *The wedding came off as planned.* | *I hope the deal comes off.* **3 come off** well to be in a good position as the result of something: *Most schools should come off well from the reorganization.* [RELATED PHRASE: **come off badly**] **4 Come off it!** a phrase you use when you do not believe what someone is saying: *Come off it! They must have known what was going on!*

come on *phr v* [I] **1 be coming on** *infml* to be starting: *I could feel a headache coming on.* **2** to advance or improve: *His French has come on very nicely this term.* **3 Come on!** a phrase you use to tell someone to hurry up or make an effort to do something: *Come on, let's get going.*

come on to sthg *phr v* [T] to begin to talk about something: *I'll come on to the question of money a bit later.*

come out *phr v* [I] **1** to appear in the sky: *It was getting dark and the stars were coming out.* **2** to be produced and become available for people to buy: *When's your new book coming out?* **3** (of information) to become known: *It has now come out that many people suffered severe side effects from the drug.* | *The truth will come out one day.* **4** (of a photograph) to be produced successfully: *I took a lot of photos on holiday but only a few came out.* **5** (of a mark) to disappear: *I've washed this shirt three times but the stain still hasn't come out.* **6** to declare your opinion publicly: *The American government has come out against the plan.* | *Many leading politicians have come out in favour of the war.*

come out in sthg *phr v* [T] to become covered in marks or spots: *He came out in a rash.*

come out with sthg *phr v* [T] to say something suddenly or unexpectedly: *He came out with some ridiculous ideas.*

come over *phr v* **1** [I] to come to a place: *When did you first come over to England?* | *You must come over and see us some time.* **2** [I] to have a particular effect on the people listening: *His speech came over very well.* **3** [T **come over** sbdy] (of a strong feeling) to suddenly have an effect on someone: *A feeling of dizziness came over me.* | *I don't know what came over him.*

come round *phr v* [I] **1** to become conscious again: *He came round after a few minutes.* **2** to change your mind and accept an idea: *He'll come round to our way of thinking sooner or later.* **3** to happen as a regular event: *Christmas will soon be coming round again.* **4** to visit someone: *You must come round for a drink one evening.*

come through *phr v* **1** [I] (of official information or an official document) to arrive: *Have your exam results come through yet?* | *I'm still waiting for my visa to come through.* **2** [T **come through** sthg] to successfully come to the end of something difficult or unpleasant: *Only a few companies have managed to come through the recession.* | *We don't know whether he'll come through the operation.*

come to *phr v* **1** [**come to** sthg] to reach something: *It has come to my notice that some money is missing.* | *The present government came to power in 1990.* **2** [**come to** sthg] to make a particular amount as a total: *The bill came to £15.* | *Our total savings now come to over £7000.* **3** [**come to** sbdy] to come into your mind: *Suddenly the words of the song came to me.* | *When did the idea for this book first come to you?* **4** [I] to become conscious again: *I wanted to be there when he came to after the operation.* **5 when it comes to...** = as far as a particular thing is concerned: *When it comes to politics I know very little.* **6 come to pass** *fml* to happen

come under sthg *phr v* [T] **1** to be governed or controlled by someone: *This committee will come under the Education Department.* **2** to receive something unpleasant: *We came under heavy gunfire.* | *The government has come under severe criticism for these policies.* **3** to be found in a particular place in a system for storing information: *What section does this come under?*

come up *phr v* [I] **1** to be talked about or discussed: *Your question came up at the meeting.* **2** to happen: *I'll let you know if anything comes up.* | *Something's come up – I'll have to go home.* | *Her wedding's coming up soon.* **3** to come near to someone: *He came up and asked me the time.* | *A woman came up to me in the street.* **4** to appear in the sky: *The snow started to melt as the sun came up.*

come up against sthg *phr v* [T] to meet a problem or difficulty: *We've come up against a serious problem.*

come upon sbdy/sthg *phr v* [T] to meet someone or something by chance: *A bit later I came upon a group hikers out for a walk.*

come up to sthg *phr v* [T] **be coming up to** be getting near to a time: *The time is now coming up to six o'clock.*

come up with sthg *phr v* [T] to think of or suggest an idea: *He couldn't come up with an answer.* | *No one has come up with an alternative.*

come-back /ˈkʌmbæk/ *n* a return to a former position of strength or importance: *We just managed to make a comeback in the second half of the match.* | *Mini-skirts are making a comeback.*

co·me·di·an /kəˈmiːdiən/ *n* a person whose job is telling jokes or making people laugh

co·me·di·enne /kəˌmiːdiˈen/ *n* a female comedian

come-down /ˈkʌmdaʊn/ *n infml* a fall in importance: *It's a bit of a comedown to get a good pass in the exams and then not get a job.*

com·e·dy /ˈkɒmɪdi ‖ ˈkɑː-/ n comedies 1 [C] a funny play, film, or other work –compare TRAGEDY: *Her last three films have been comedies.* | *One of Shakespeare's most famous comedies* 2 [U] the humorous quality of something, either in a play or film or in real life: *We all laughed at the comedy of the situation.* | *an actor with a real flair for comedy*

come·ly /ˈkʌmli/ adj lit attractive (used of women) –comeliness n [U]

com·et /ˈkɒmɪt ‖ ˈkɑː-/ n a very bright object like a star with a long tail, that moves round the sun

com·fort[1] /ˈkʌmfət ‖ -ərt/ n 1 [U] the state of being free from anxiety, pain, or unhappiness: *This car is built for comfort.* | *They live a life of great comfort.* | *His words gave me some comfort.* 2 a comfort someone or something that gives you encouragement or strength: *My husband was a great comfort to me when I was ill.* 3 [C] something which makes life easier and more enjoyable: *The comforts of modern civilization*

comfort[2] v [T] to make someone feel less worried or unhappy: *I tried to comfort Jean after her mother's death.* –comforter n

com·for·ta·ble /ˈkʌmftəbəl, ˈkʌmfət- ‖ ˈkʌmfərt-, ˈkʌmft-/ adj (also comfy ˈkʌmfi/ infml) 1 providing physical comfort: *a comfortable chair* | *I love these shoes – they're so comfortable!* 2 not experiencing too much physical pain: *I'm quite comfortable in this chair.* 3 feeling happy and confident, with no worries: *I never feel comfortable when he's around.* 4 providing a pleasant way of life without worries about money: *a comfortable income* | *We're not rich but we're fairly comfortable.* –comfortably adv

com·ic[1] /ˈkɒmɪk ‖ ˈkɑː-/ adj funny or humorous: *a comic performance* | *a comic actress*

comic[2] n 1 (also comic book /·· ·/ AmE) a magazine for children containing pictures which tell a story 2 infml a person who is funny or amusing, especially a person who entertains people by making them laugh

com·i·cal /ˈkɒmɪkəl ‖ ˈkɑː-/ adj odd or strange in a way that is amusing: *She looked so comical with the bucket on her head.*

comic strip /·· ·/ n a set of drawings telling a short story

com·ing[1] /ˈkʌmɪŋ/ n 1 [sing] fml arrival: *With the coming of winter, days get shorter.* 2 comings and goings acts of arriving and leaving: *We saw the comings and goings of the visitors from our bedroom window.*

coming[2] adj [only before a noun] going to come or happen soon: *The coming months are going to be hard.*

com·ma /ˈkɒmə ‖ ˈkɑːmə/ n the mark (,) used in writing for separating different parts of a sentence or things in a list

com·mand[1] /kəˈmɑːnd ‖ kəˈmænd/ v [T] 1 to order someone to do something: *She commanded us to leave the city.* | *"Don't move," she commanded.* □ USEFUL PATTERN to command someone to do something

2 to have control over armed forces: *General Carter commands this regiment.* 3 to deserve and get: *He commands a lot of respect.* –see ORDER[2] (USAGE)

command[2] n 1 [C] an order: *All his commands were quickly obeyed.* 2 [U] control: *The army is under the king's direct command.* | *She took command when her husband died.* 3 in command having power or control over someone or something 4 command of something knowledge of something or ability to use it: *He has good command of spoken French.* | *His command of advanced mathematics is very impressive.*

com·man·dant /ˌkɒmənˈdænt ‖ ˈkɑːməndænt/ n the chief officer in charge of a military organization

com·man·deer /ˌkɒmənˈdɪər ‖ ˌkɑː-/ v [T] 1 to seize private property for military use without asking permission or giving payment 2 to take something from someone less important or powerful: *The boss has commandeered my desk again.*

com·mand·er /kəˈmɑːndər ‖ kəˈmæn-/ n 1 an officer in charge of a military or police organization 2 BrE an officer in the Royal Navy

com·mand·ing /kəˈmɑːndɪŋ ‖ kəˈmæn-/ adj 1 commanding officer the officer who is in charge 2 deserving or expecting respect and obedience: *She spoke in a loud, commanding voice.* | *We've lost our commanding position in the business world.*

Com·mand·ment /kəˈmɑːndmənt ‖ kəˈmænd-/ n any of the ten laws in the Bible which God says that people should obey

com·man·do /kəˈmɑːndəu ‖ kəˈmæn-/ n commandos or commandoes a member of a small military unit specially trained for making surprise attacks in enemy areas

com·mem·o·rate /kəˈmeməreɪt/ v commemorated, commemorating [T] to exist in order to make people remember an important person or event: *This statue commemorates those who died in the war.* –commemoration /kəˌmeməˈreɪʃən/ n [U]

com·mence /kəˈmens/ v commenced, commencing [I;T] fml to begin or start: *As it's already two o'clock shall we commence?* | *Should we commence the attack?*
□ [USEFUL PATTERNS: to commence; to commence something; to commence doing something] –commencement n

com·mend /kəˈmend/ v [T] fml 1 to praise someone formally: *She was highly commended for her efficiency.* 2 to tell someone that something is very good: *This restaurant was commended to me.*

com·men·da·ble /kəˈmendəbəl/ adj worthy of praise: *commendable efforts* –commendably adv

com·men·da·tion /ˌkɒmənˈdeɪʃən ‖ ˌkɑː-/ n an official prize or honour given to someone because they have done something very good: *She was given a commendation for bravery.*

com·men·su·rate /kəˈmenʃərɪt/ adj fml equal to something or suitable for it: *He was given a job commensurate with his age and experience.*

com·ment[1] /ˈkɒment ‖ ˈkɑː-/ n [C;U] 1 an opinion about something or a judgment about it: *I asked the minister if she had any comments about the election.* | *He was making rude comments about the other people in the room.* | *The director was not available for comment.* | *a fair comment* 2 no comment a phrase used by people in public life when they do not want to give an opinion or explanation about something

---

SPELLING NOTE

Words with the sound / k /, like **cut**, may be spelt **k-**, like **key**, or **qu-**, like **queen**.
Words with the sound / s /, like **city**, may be spelt **s-**, like **soon**, or **ps-**, like **psychology**.

comment² *v* [I; + that] to make a remark or give an opinion: *The teacher refused to comment on the examination results.* | *Jean commented that she thought it was time for a new government.*

com·men·ta·ry /ˈkɒməntəri ‖ ˈkɑːmənteri/ *n* **commentaries 1** [C] a description of an event which is broadcast on radio or television usually while the event is happening: *His spirited commentary makes a match very interesting even on the radio.* | *a football commentary* **2** [C;U] a written collection of opinions, explanations or judgments, on a book, event, or situation: *political commentaries*

com·men·tate /ˈkɒmənteɪt ‖ ˈkɑː-/ *v* **commentated, commentating** [I] to describe and talk about an event while it is being broadcast on radio or television –**commentator** *n*

com·merce /ˈkɒmɜːs ‖ ˈkɑːmɜːrs/ *n* [U] the buying and selling of goods: *Our country has grown rich because of its commerce with other nations.* | *The recession will hit both industry and commerce.*

com·mer·cial¹ /kəˈmɜːʃəl ‖ kəˈmɜːr-/ *adj* **1** related to or used in the buying and selling of goods: *Our commercial laws changed when we joined the EEC.* **2** [only before a noun] producing or likely to produce profit: *The film was a commercial success.* | *a commercial radio station* –**commercially** *adv*

commercial² *n* an advertisement on television or radio

com·mer·cial·ized /kəˈmɜːʃəlaɪzd ‖ kəˈmɜːr-/ *adj* (also **commercialised** *BrE*) too concerned with making profits: *I find Christmas too commercialized these days.*

commercial ve·hi·cle /·,·· ˈ···/ *n* a vehicle used for carrying goods from place to place along roads

com·mis·e·rate /kəˈmɪzəreɪt/ *v* **commiserated, commiserating** [I] to express sympathy or pity for someone after something unpleasant has happened to them: *I commiserated with her over her failure.*

com·mis·e·ra·tion /kə,mɪzəˈreɪʃən/ *n* [U] an expression of sympathy or pity for someone

com·mis·sion¹ /kəˈmɪʃən/ *n* **1** [C;U] an amount of money that is paid to a salesman when he or she sells something: *His salary is quite small, but he earns a lot on commission.* | *My commission on this sale should be £100.* **2** [C] a particular job or duty given to a person, usually to build something or produce a work of art: *He was glad to be given the commission for the design of a new theatre.* **3** [C + sing/pl verb] a group of people specially appointed to perform certain duties: *She established a commission to suggest improvements in the educational system.* | *The Commission meet twice a week.* **4** [C] an official paper appointing someone to a high rank in the armed forces

commission² *v* [T] **1** to officially ask someone to do something, especially to produce a work of art: *He was commissioned to paint portraits of the royal family.* | *The Government has commissioned a report on the Health Service.* **2** to give someone a commission in the armed forces

com·mis·sion·aire /kə,mɪʃəˈneəʳ/ *n BrE* an attendant at the door of a cinema, theatre, or hotel

com·mis·sion·er /kəˈmɪʃənəʳ/ *n* an official in charge of a certain government department or other organization: *the Church commissioners* | *the British High Commissioner*

com·mit /kəˈmɪt/ *v* -tt- [T] **1** to do something wrong, bad, or unlawful: *There has been a rise in the amount of crime committed.* | *She committed suicide.* | *He*

denied that he had committed the murder. **2** to order someone to be placed in a prison or in a MENTAL hospital: *He was found guilty and committed to prison.* **3** to set money or time apart for something: *They committed all their resources to the project.* **4** **commit yourself to something** to promise to do or support something: *The government has committed itself to improving the National Health Service.* **5** **not commit yourself** to not give your true opinion about something: *He won't commit himself on the issue of women's rights.* **6** **commit something to memory** to learn something so that you can remember it: *He committed the address to memory.*

com·mit·ment /kəˈmɪtmənt/ *n* **1** [C] a responsibility which takes a lot of your time regularly: *We must honour our commitments to smaller nations.* | *family commitments.* **2** [U] a deep belief in a system or idea: *I've never doubted her commitment to feminism.*

com·mit·tal /kəˈmɪtl/ *n* [C;U] the act of sending a person to prison or to a MENTAL hospital

com·mit·ted /kəˈmɪtɪd/ *adj* very loyal to a particular aim, job, or way of life: *Jean's a very committed teacher.* | *We are very committed to equal rights for women.*

com·mit·tee /kəˈmɪti/ *n* [+ sing/pl verb] a group of people chosen to study a particular problem or take particular decisions: *He's on a lot of committees.* | *The committee believe that the hospital must be improved.*

com·mod·i·ty /kəˈmɒdɪti ‖ kəˈmɑː-/ *n* **commodities** a product, especially a mineral or farm product, that is bought and sold: *agricultural commodities*

com·mo·dore /ˈkɒmədɔːʳ ‖ ˈkɑː/ *n* an officer of middle rank in the navy

com·mon¹ /ˈkɒmən ‖ ˈkɑː-/ *adj* **1** usual or frequent: *Rabbits and foxes are common in Britain.* | *It is now quite common for women to become managers.* **2** [only before a noun] ordinary and not special: *the common people* | *Common salt is very cheap.* | *There is no cure for the common cold.* **3** belonging to or shared by two or more people or things: *We share a common language.* | *This feature is common to all the new machinery.* **4** having a coarse, rough way of speaking or behaving **5** **the Commons** the HOUSE OF COMMONS **6** **for the common good** in order to help or be to the advantage of people in general **7** **common ground** a subject about which people agree: *When it comes to politics, we are on common ground.* **8** **common knowledge** something known by most people **9** **common law** the unwritten law of England, based on custom and court decisions rather than on laws made by Parliament **10** **common-law husband/wife** a man or woman you have lived with for some time without having married, and who is considered to be your husband or wife. **11** **the Common Market** the EEC **12** **common noun** a noun that is not the name of a particular person, place, or thing; "book" and "sugar" are common nouns **13** **common sense** practical good sense and judgment: *He's got no common sense!* **14** **have something in common** to share the same quality, or interest: *John and I have nothing in common.*

common² *n* an area of grassland which all people are free to use

com·mon·er /ˈkɒmənəʳ ‖ ˈkɑː-/ *n* a person who is not a member of a noble family or does not have a title

com·mon·ly /ˈkɒmənli ‖ ˈkɑː-/ *adj* usually or generally: *He's commonly known as "Joe".*

common-or-gar·den /ˌ·· ·ˈ···◄/ adj [only before a noun] BrE infml ordinary: They've got a common-or-garden house just like anyone else.

com·mon·place /ˌkɒmənˈpleɪs◄ ‖ ˌkɑː-/ adj very common or ordinary and so not very interesting: Soon it will be commonplace for people to travel to the moon.

Com·mon·wealth /ˈkɒmənwelθ ‖ ˈkɑː-/ n the Commonwealth an organization of independent states which were formerly parts of the British Empire, established to encourage trade and friendly relations among its members

com·mo·tion /kəˈməʊʃ∂n/ n [sing; U] noisy confusion or excitement: The imprisonment of the union leaders caused a commotion in Parliament. | What's all the commotion about?

com·mu·nal /ˈkɒmjʊn∂l, kəˈmjuːnl ‖ ˈkɑː-/ adj shared by or used by all the members of a group: communal land | communal ownership of property

com·mune¹ /kəˈmjuːn/ v communed, communing lit commune with to have a close relationship with: I often walk by the sea to commune with nature.

com·mune² /ˈkɒmjuːn ‖ ˈkɑː-, kəˈmjuːn/ n a group of people who live and work as a team for the general good He's joined a commune.

com·mu·ni·ca·ble /kəˈmjuːnɪkəb∂l/ adj fml able to be passed easily from one person to another (used of ideas and diseases)

com·mu·ni·cate /kəˈmjuːn‿keɪt/ v communicated, communicating **1** [I] to share or exchange ideas or information with someone by speaking, writing, or using other means: We managed to communicate with each other by using sign language. | The two ships communicated by radio. **2** [T] to make an idea or piece of information known and understood: Radio and television were widely used to communicate government policy. | He doesn't communicate his ideas very clearly to the students.

com·mu·ni·ca·ting /kəˈmjuːn‿keɪtɪŋ/ adj joined together by a door: communicating bedrooms

com·mu·ni·ca·tion /kəˌmjuːn‿ˈkeɪʃ∂n/ n **1** [U] the act of communicating: Communication with France was difficult during the telephone and postal strike. | Radio and television are important means of communication. **2** [C] fml a letter or message: This communication is secret; no one but you must see it. **3** communications [pl] the various ways of communicating, and sending information between places by means of roads, railways, radio, telephone, or television: Moscow has excellent communications with all parts of the Soviet Union. | communications networks

com·mu·ni·ca·tive /kəˈmjuːn‿kətɪv/ adj very willing to talk or give information

com·mu·nion /kəˈmjuːnjən/ n **1** [U] the sharing or exchange of feelings, beliefs or ideas: communion with nature | communion between man and God **2** Communion [C;U] the religious service in churches in which bread and wine are shared in a solemn ceremony

com·mu·ni·qué /kəˈmjuːn‿keɪ ‖ kəˌmjuːn‿ˈkeɪ/ n an official report or declaration to the public or newspapers: In its latest communiqué the government suggests that both sides will soon reach an agreement.

com·mu·nis·m /ˈkɒmjʊnɪzəm ‖ ˈkɑː-/ n [U] the political system in which the state controls the means of production and there is no private property – compare SOCIALISM

com·mu·nist /ˈkɒmjʊnɪst ‖ ˈkɑː-/ n a person who believes in communism

com·mu·ni·ty /kəˈmjuːn‿ti/ n communities [+ sing/pl verb] a group of people who live in the same area or who have the same interests, religion, or nationality: The job of a politician is to serve the community. | They have done a lot for the local community. | The black community are very worried by these recent events.

com·mute /kəˈmjuːt/ v commuted, commuting **1** [I] to travel regularly a long distance between your home and work: She commutes from Cambridge to London every day. **2** [T] fml to make a punishment less severe: His punishment was commuted from death to life imprisonment.

com·mut·er /kəˈmjuːtəʳ/ n a person who regularly travels a long distance to work

com·pact¹ /kɒmˈpækt, ˈkɒmpækt ‖ kəmˈpækt/ adj **1** firmly and closely packed together: The trees grew in a compact mass. **2** taking up very little space: The flat was tidy and compact. | This computer is more compact than most.

com·pact² /ˈkɒmpækt ‖ ˈkɑːm-/ n a small flat container for a woman's face powder and a mirror

compact disc /ˌ·ˌ ·ˈ·, ˌ··ˈ· ‖ ˌ·ˌ ·ˈ·/ n a type of record with very high quality sound played on a special machine – see picture on page 442

com·pact·ed /kəmˈpæktɪd/ adj pressed together firmly and closely: a compacted mass

com·pan·ion /kəmˈpænjən/ n someone who you spend time with, either as a friend or because you are travelling with them: He was my only companion during the war. | My fellow travellers were good companions.

com·pan·io·na·ble /kəmˈpænjənəb∂l/ adj friendly and likely to be a good companion

com·pan·ion·ship /kəmˈpænjənʃɪp/ n [U] friendly company: He missed the companionship he'd enjoyed in the navy.

com·pa·ny /ˈkʌmpəni/ n companies **1** [C + sing/pl verb] an organization of people who work together in business or trade: a bus company | Which company do you work for? | Robinson and Company | My company sell computers. **2** [C + sing/pl verb] a group of entertainers who work together: The theatre company tour the country every summer. **3** [U] friendship from people with whom you spend time: I was grateful for Jean's company on the train. **4** [U] one or more guests: No, you can't go out tonight; we're expecting company. **5** [C] a group of about 120 soldiers **6 keep someone company** to spend time with someone so that they are not alone: If you're going for a walk, I'll come too to keep you company. **7 in company** in the presence of a group of people: Don't swear in company! **8 part company** to go your own separate ways

com·pa·ra·ble /ˈkɒmpərəb∂l ‖ ˈkɑːm-/ adj fml similar and of equal size or quality, and so able to be compared: A comparable car would cost far more abroad. | This job is not comparable to any other. | His poetry is hardly comparable with Shakespeare's! – **comparably** adv

---

SPELLING NOTE

Words with the sound /k/, like **cut**, may be spelt **k-**, like **key**, or **qu-**, like **queen**.
Words with the sound /s/, like **city**, may be spelt **s-**, like **soon**, or **ps-**, like **psychology**.

com·par·a·tive[1] /kəm'pærətɪv/ *adj* **1** showing the differences and similarities between things of the same kind: *a comparative study of European languages* **2** measured or judged when compared with something of the same kind: *the comparative wealth of the south of England* **3** related to the form of adjectives or adverbs expressing an increase in quality, quantity, or degree; for example, "bigger" is the comparative form of "big"

comparative[2] *n tech* **the comparative** the comparative form of an adjective or adverb –see Study Note on page 99

com·par·a·tive·ly /kəm'pærətɪvli/ *adv* compared with others: *Man is a comparatively new creature on the face of the earth.*

com·pare /kəm'peəʳ/ *v* **compared, comparing** [T] **1** to examine or judge one thing against another in order to show how they are the same or how they are different: *If you compare the two cars you'll find that yours is better designed.* | *Researchers compared living conditions in London* with *those in other cities.* | *We've been comparing notes on our trips to India.* **2** to say that two things are similar in some way: *She has often been compared to her mother.* **3 compared with, compared to** a phrase used when you are saying how things are different: *Their prices are low compared to those in other shops.* **4 cannot compare with, does not compare with =** is not as good as: *Living in a town can't compare with living in the country.*

com·par·i·son /kəm'pærɪsən/ *n* **1** [C;U] the act of judging two things and saying whether they are similar or different: *He made a comparison of of housing conditions in different parts of the country.* | *We looked at the prices of goods in one shop, then looked in other shops for comparison.* **2 in comparison, by comparison** a phrase used when you are comparing things: *The driver's injuries were trivial in comparison* with *those of the passengers.* **3 there is no comparison** a phrase used when you are saying that one thing is very much better than another: *There is no comparison* between *frozen and fresh food.*

com·part·ment /kəm'pɑːtmənt ‖ -ɑːr-/ *n* **1** one of the small rooms in a railway carriage: *We sat in a second-class compartment.* **2** a special part of a container used for keeping certain things in: *This fridge hasn't got a compartment for frozen foods.*

com·part·men·tal·ize /ˌkɒmpɑːt'mentl-aɪz ‖ kəmˌpɑːrt-/ *v* **compartmentalized, compartmentalizing** (also **compartmentalise** *BrE*) [T] to divide something into separate parts

com·pass /'kʌmpəs/ *n* **1** an instrument for showing direction, usually consisting of a freely-moving MAGNETIC needle which always points to the north **2 compasses** [pl] a V-shaped instrument used for drawing circles or measuring distances on maps **3 the compass of something** *fml* the range of something: *To help the old is well within the compass of the government's social responsibility.*

com·pas·sion /kəm'pæʃən/ *n* [U] pity or sympathy for people who are suffering: *The world's main religions all teach us to have compassion* for *the poor and hungry.*

com·pas·sion·ate /kəm'pæʃənɪt/ *adj* showing pity or sympathy for other people –**compassionately** *adv*

com·pat·i·ble /kəm'pætɪbəl/ *adj* able to live, exist, or be used together without difficulty or danger: *Is your computer compatible* with *this equipment?* | *Do you think that religion is compatible with science?* | *Their marriage ended because they were simply not compatible.* –opposite **incompatible** –**compatibly** *adv*

com·pat·ri·ot /kəm'pætriət ‖ -'peɪt-/ *n* a person from the same country as another person

com·pel /kəm'pel/ *v* **-ll-** [T] **1** to make someone do something by force: *My father compelled us to stay indoors.* **2** *fml* to make someone feel something through persuasion: *His great skill compels our admiration.*

com·pel·ling /kəm'pelɪŋ/ *adj* **1** making you believe something: *This is a very compelling argument.* **2** very exciting and interesting: *a very compelling book*

com·pen·di·um /kəm'pendiəm/ **compendiums** or **compendia** *n fml* a book containing a short but detailed account of facts or information

com·pen·sate /'kɒmpənseɪt ‖ 'kɑːm-/ *v* **compensated, compensating 1** [T] to give someone money for a loss, damage, or inconvenience: *He was compensated* for *his loss of earnings.* **2 compensate for something** to remove the bad effects of something: *Her intelligence more than compensates for her lack of experience.*

com·pen·sa·tion /ˌkɒmpən'seɪʃən ‖ ˌkɑːm-/ *n* **1** [U] money paid to someone to pay for loss or damage: *He lost his job, but got no compensation.* **2** [C] something which makes a situation seem less bad: *There are some compensations* for *the power cuts.*

com·pen·sa·to·ry /ˌkɒmpən'seɪtəri ‖ kəm'pensə-ˌtɔːri/ *adj* **1 compensatory payment** a payment of money made to compensate someone **2** made to help people with special needs or problems: *compensatory education*

com·pere /'kɒmpeəʳ ‖ 'kɑːm-/ *n BrE* a person whose job is to introduce acts in a stage or television show –**compere** *v* **compered, compering** [T]: *Who compered last night's show?*

com·pete /kəm'piːt/ *v* **competed, competing** [I] to try to win or gain something in competition with someone else: *John competed* for *a place at the school, but didn't get in.* | *Although there were only four horses competing it was an exciting race.* | *The two companies have to compete* against *each other for customers.* | *I don't want to compete* with *you.*

com·pe·tent /'kɒmpɪtənt ‖ 'kɑːm-/ *adj* **1** having the ability or skill to do something effectively: *He's a very competent driver.* –opposite **INCOMPETENT 2** satisfactory and showing ability or skill: *She did a competent job.* –**competence** *n* [U] –**competently** *adv*

com·pe·ti·tion /ˌkɒmpɪ'tɪʃən ‖ ˌkɑːm-/ *n* **1** [U] a situation in which two or more people are trying to win or gain the same thing: *There was keen competition* between *the journalists to get the story first.* | *The two firms were in competition* with *each other.* | *There was a lot of competition* for *the job.* **2** [C] an event in which many people try to do the same thing, to find out who is the best: *a dancing competition*

com·pet·i·tive /kəm'petɪtɪv/ *adj* **1** related to or decided by competition: *the competitive nature of British society* | *competitive sports* **2** eager to appear better or more successful than other people: *He's extremely competitive.* **3** able to sell or be sold successfully because the price charged is reasonable: *British industry is not competitive enough.* | *Their prices are very competitive.* –**competitively** *adv* –**competitiveness** *n* [U]

com·pet·i·tor /kəm'petɪtər/ n a person, team, or firm competing with another or others: *There were 10 competitors in the race.* | *Last year our company sold many more computers than our competitors.*

com·pi·la·tion /ˌkɒmpɪ'leɪʃən ‖ ˌkɑːm-/ n 1 [C] a book or other work that contains a collection of smaller works 2 [U] the act of compiling something

com·pile /kəm'paɪl/ v compiled, compiling [T] to make a report or book from facts and information found in various places: *It takes years of hard work to compile a good dictionary.* | *The programme was compiled by members of the medical research team.* –compiler n

com·pla·cent /kəm'pleɪsənt/ adj too pleased or satisfied with yourself, and feeling that you do not need to worry about something: *After winning six times we became complacent and thought we'd never lose.* –complacency n [U] : *I see no reason for the government's complacency.* –complacently adv

com·plain /kəm'pleɪn/ v [I;T; + that] 1 to express feelings of annoyance or unhappiness about something: *Mary is always complaining about something.* | *He complained that he couldn't find a job anywhere.* | *Our neighbour said he'd complain to the police if we made any more noise.*
□ USEFUL PATTERNS to complain; to complain about something to someone; to complain that… 2 complain of something to say that you have a pain or illness: *He had been complaining of a pain in his chest.*

com·plaint /kəm'pleɪnt/ n 1 [C] a statement expressing annoyance or unhappiness about something: *The police received several complaints about the noise from our party.* | *I'm really tired of his endless complaints!* | *He made a complaint against his former employers.* | *We handed in a list of our complaints.* 2 [C] an illness in one part of your body: *a serious liver complaint.* 3 [U] the act of complaining: *I'm going to write a letter of complaint.* | *You have no cause for complaint.*

com·ple·ment[1] /'komplɪmənt ‖ 'kɑːm-/ n 1 something that completes something else by adding what is lacking: *A fine wine is a complement to a good meal.* 2 a full complement the total quantity needed to make something complete: *The school's English department has its full complement of teachers.* 3 a word or a phrase, especially a noun or adjective, that follows a verb and describes the subject of the verb; for example, in "She is American", "American" is the complement.

com·ple·ment[2] /'komplɪment ‖ 'kɑːm-/ v [T] to make something better or nicer by adding something that was lacking: *This wine complements the food perfectly.* | *The bus and train services complement each other very well.*

com·ple·men·ta·ry /ˌkɒmplɪ'mentəri◄ ‖ ˌkɑːm-/ adj making something better or nicer by adding something that was lacking

com·plete[1] /kəm'pliːt/ adj 1 having all the parts or people that are necessary or usual: *John's birthday did not seem complete without his father there.* | *a complete set of the works of Shakespeare* –opposite **incomplete** 2 finished or ended: *When will work on the new railway be complete?* 3 [only before a noun] a word used to add force to what you are saying: *It was a complete surprise to see you on the bus yesterday.* | *He's a complete idiot!* 4 complete with including or containing something additional: *We bought the house complete with furniture.* –completeness n [U] –completion /kəm'pliːʃən/ n

complete[2] v completed, completing [T] 1 to add

COLOURS

Colours are often associated with particular things or ideas. Read the dictionary entries for the colours in the box. Also read the entries for words associated with the colour (red carpet, blue collar etc.). Now look at the eight lists of words below. Which colour is connected with the ideas in each list?

black
green
pink
white
blue
grey
red
yellow

[1]	[2]	[3]	[4]
shame	butter	dull	good health
anger	gold	fear	
debt	age	worry	
unneccessary rules		heavy	
communist		lack of knowledge	
danger			

[5]	[6]	[7]	[8]
sky	nature	night	with milk or cream
sea	environment	very bad	official
cold	jealous	angry	very hot
nobility	young	having money	
manual	inexperienced	refuse to work with	
sudden and	permission	evil	
unexpected		unlawful	

Do these colours have different meanings in your own language? Which ideas are associated with these colours?

barrel

crate

bucket

flask *(BrE)*/thermos *(AmE)*

drum

bottle

churn *(BrE)*/pail *(AmE)*

box

carton

ca

bag

packet *(BrE)*/package *(AmE)*/box

tin/can

tub

j

jug *(BrE)*/pitcher *(AmE)*

kettle

casserole

saucepan

frying pan

vase

plant pot *(BrE)*/flower pot *(AmE)*

pot

cup & saucer

mug

glass

teapot

bowl

dish

sachet *(BrE)*/packet *(AmE)*

tube

waste bin *(BrE)*/waste paper basket

basket

beaker *(BrE)*/glass

what is missing or needed to something to form a finished whole: *I need one more stamp before my collection is completed.* | *Seeing her parents again completed her happiness.* **2** to finish something or bring it to an end: *When will work on the new road be completed?*

com·plete·ly /kəmˈpliːtli/ *adv* totally: *The army made a completely successful attack on the enemy capital.* | *I completely forgot about it.*

com·plex¹ /ˈkɒmpleks ‖ ˌkaːmˈpleks◄/ *adj* **1** difficult to understand, explain, or deal with: *Her political ideas were too complex to get support from ordinary people.* | *This is a very complex problem.* **2** consisting of many closely connected parts: *There is a complex network of roads connecting Glasgow and Edinburgh.* –**complexity** /kəmˈpleksti/ *n* **complexities** [C;U]

com·plex² /ˈkɒmpleks ‖ ˈkaːm-/ *n* **1** a group of buildings or one large building used for a particular purpose: *a sports complex* | *a shopping complex* **2** a group of unconscious fears or feelings which influence someone's behaviour and cause problems for them: *He's got a terrible guilt complex.* | *He's got a complex about his success.*

com·plex·ion /kəmˈplekʃən/ *n* **1** the natural colour and appearance of someone's skin, especially on their face: *a pale complexion* **2** the complexion of something the general character or nature of something: *The dismissal of the Minister for Foreign Affairs has changed the whole complexion of the government.*

com·pli·ance /kəmˈplaɪəns/ *n* [U] *fml* obedience to a rule or law: *Compliance with the law is expected of all citizens.* **2** willingness to agree too easily with the wishes and demands of other people: *I was surprised at her compliance with all our suggestions.*

com·pli·ant /kəmˈplaɪənt/ *adj* very willing to do what people ask you to do: *I don't respect people who are too compliant.*

com·pli·cate /ˈkɒmplɪkeɪt ‖ ˈkaːm-/ *v* **complicated, complicating** [T] to make something difficult to understand or deal with: *It is a serious problem, complicated by the fact that we have no experience in this area.* | *Do you always have to complicate matters by forgetting to bring something?*

com·pli·cat·ed /ˈkɒmplɪkeɪtɪd ‖ ˈkaːm-/ *adj* very difficult to understand or deal with: *Don't ask me such complicated questions.* | *a complicated machine*

com·pli·ca·tion /ˌkɒmplɪˈkeɪʃən ‖ ˌkaːm-/ *n* **1** something that adds new difficulties: *The union's demand for higher wages was a complication that the government had not expected.* **2 complications** [pl] a new illness that happens during the course of another illness: *He seemed to be getting better, but I'm afraid there are now complications.*

com·plic·i·ty /kəmˈplɪsti/ *n* [U] the act of taking part with another person in something wrong or illegal

com·pli·ment¹ /ˈkɒmplɪmənt ‖ ˈkaːm-/ *n* **1** an expression of praise, admiration, or respect: *"You look lovely." "Oh, thanks for the compliment."* | *Her boss paid her the compliment of promoting her.* **2 compliments** a word used to express respect or good wishes: *My compliments to the chef!*

com·pli·ment² /ˈkɒmplɪment ‖ ˈkaːm-/ *v* [T] to say something to someone expressing praise, admiration, or respect: *John complimented Jean on her latest novel.*

com·pli·men·ta·ry /ˌkɒmplɪˈmentəri◄ ‖ ˌkaːm-/ *adj* **1** expressing admiration, praise, or respect **2** given free: *He gave me some complimentary tickets for the theatre.*

CONTAINERS

Exercise 1

Complete this passage by filling in the blanks. There is one dash for each missing letter.

From cow to cup of tea

Farmer Brown milked his cows at four o'clock this morning. He collected the milk in a ¹b _ _ _ _ _. Then he poured it into a ²c _ _ _ _ and sent it to the dairy. The people at the dairy put the milk into ³b _ _ _ _ _ s which they then put into ⁴c _ _ _ _ s. The milkman collected the milk from the dairy and delivered it to the houses in the town.

Mrs Savage wanted two pints of milk today because her friend, Mrs Rolls, was coming to tea. Mrs Savage boiled some water in the ⁵k _ _ _ _ _ and poured it over the tea leaves which she had put in her best silver ⁶t _ _ _ _ _. Then she put two ⁷c _ _ s and two ⁸s _ _ _ _ s on a tray. After that, she poured some milk into a small ⁹j _ _ and put it on the tray.

"Would you like some milk in your tea?" she asked Mrs Rolls.

"No thank you" Mrs Rolls replied "Have you got any lemon?"

Exercise 2

What are these containers made of? Put a tick (✔) for often, a cross (✗) for never and a question mark (?) for sometimes.

	wood	plastic	glass	china	paper	metal
bag	✗	✔	✗	✗	✔	✗
bottle						
crate						
cup						
saucepan						
box						
jug						
vase						
tube						

com·ply /kəm'plaɪ/ v **complied, complying** [I] *fml* to do what is demanded by an order, a rule, or a person with power: *People who refuse to comply* **with** *the law will be punished.*

com·po·nent /kəm'pəʊnənt/ n any of the parts that make up a whole machine or system

com·pose /kəm'pəʊz/ v **composed, composing** 1 [I;T] to write music, especially a piece of music or poetry: *He plays the piano beautifully, and he composes his own music.* | *I'm trying to compose a letter to the newspaper.* 2 **compose yourself** to make yourself calm and quiet after being angry or upset: *Please try to compose yourself!* 3 **be composed of** to be formed from different parts: *Water is composed of hydrogen and oxygen.*

com·pos·er /kəm'pəʊzəʳ/ n a person who writes music

com·pos·ite /'kɒmpəzɪt ‖ kɑːm'pɑː-/ adj fml made up of a number of different parts or substances –**composite** n

composition /ˌkɒmpə'zɪʃən ‖ ˌkɑːm-/ n 1 [C;U] a piece of music or poetry that you have written: *a piece of music of her own composition* | *one of Mozart's last compositions* 2 [C;U] the different parts of which something is made up: *Who decided the composition of the committee?* | *the chemical composition of plants* 3 [C] a short piece of writing done as an educational exercise: *We had to do a composition on the problem of crime.* 4 [C] a mixture of various substances: *a composition of different chemicals*

com·post /'kɒmpɒst ‖ 'kɑːmpəʊst/ n [U] a mixture of decayed plant matter, such as cut grass or leaves, used for making the soil richer

com·po·sure /kəm'pəʊʒəʳ/ n [U] calmness and complete control over your feelings: *Keep calm: don't lose your composure.*

com·pound¹ /kəm'paʊnd/ v fml [T] 1 to add to or increase a problem or difficulty: *His lack of confidence was compounded by losing his job.* 2 **be compounded of** to be formed by mixing different things together

com·pound² /'kɒmpaʊnd ‖ 'kɑːm-/ n 1 something consisting of a combination of two or more parts: *a chemical compound* 2 an area enclosed by a wall or fence which contains a group of buildings: *the prison compound*

compound³ adj consisting of a combination of two or more parts: *a compound leaf*

com·pre·hend /ˌkɒmprɪ'hend ‖ ˌkɑːm-/ v [I;T; + that] fml to understand something: *The judge said that it was difficult to comprehend the actions of the police in this matter.*

com·pre·hen·si·ble /ˌkɒmprɪ'hensəbəl ‖ kɑːm-/ adj easily understood: *You often find a writer's books more comprehensible if you know about his life.* –**comprehensibly** adv –**comprehensibility** /ˌkɒmprɪhensəˈbɪlɪti ‖ kɑːm-/ n [U]

com·pre·hen·sion /ˌkɒmprɪ'henʃən ‖ ˌkɑːm-/ n 1 [U] the act of understanding or the ability to understand –opposite **incomprehension** 2 [C;U] a reading or listening exercise to test how well a student understands written or spoken language

---

SPELLING NOTE

Words with the sound / k /, like **cut**, may be spelt **k-**, like **key**, or **qu-**, like **queen**.
Words with the sound / s /, like **city**, may be spelt **s-**, like **soon**, or **ps-**, like **psychology**.

---

com·pre·hen·sive¹ /ˌkɒmprɪ'hensɪv ‖ ˌkɑːm-/ adj including everything that is necessary: *The government gave a comprehensive explanation of its plans for industrial development.* –**comprehensively** adv

comprehensive² n BrE (also **comprehensive school** /ˌ··'·· ·/) a SECONDARY school where pupils of all abilities are taught

com·press /kəm'pres/ v [T] 1 to force a substance into a smaller space 2 to express thoughts, ideas, or information in fewer words: *The report's been compressed into three pages.* –**compressed** adj : *compressed air* –**compression** /-preʃən/ n [U]

com·prise /kəm'praɪz/ v **comprised, comprising** [T] 1 to include or be made up of: *The school staff comprises ten teachers.* | *The United Kingdom comprises England, Wales, Scotland and Northern Ireland.* 2 to form a part of a larger group: *Women teachers comprise 15% of the teaching staff.*

com·pro·mise¹ /'kɒmprəmaɪz ‖ 'kɑːm-/ n [C;U] an agreement in which both sides accept that they cannot have exactly what they want: *It is better to settle arguments by compromise, not with threats.* | *We eventually reached a compromise.*

compromise² v **compromised, compromising** 1 [I] to settle an argument by reaching an agreement in which both sides accept that they cannot have exactly what they want: *We couldn't agree whether to go to a restaurant or a café, so we compromised and went to the pub.* 2 **compromise yourself** to do something which shows that you are not completely honest or sincere: *She claimed the politician had compromised himself in his private life.* –**compromising** adj

com·pul·sion /kəm'pʌlʃən/ n 1 [U] force or strong influence that makes a person do something: *I will pay nothing under compulsion.* 2 [C] a strong unreasonable desire to do something: *Her compulsion to drink is causing serious problems.*

com·pul·sive /kəm'pʌlsɪv/ adj [only before a noun] very difficult to stop or control: *compulsive gambling* | *a compulsive desire to eat all day long* –**compulsively** adv

com·pul·so·ry /kəm'pʌlsəri/ adj which must be done by law: *Is military service compulsory in your country?* –compare VOLUNTARY –**compulsorily** adv

com·punc·tion /kəm'pʌŋkʃən/ n fml [U] an awkward feeling of guilt that stops you doing something: *That woman had no compunction about telling me a lie.*

com·pute /kəm'pjuːt/ v **computed, computing** fml [T] to calculate a result or answer

com·put·er /kəm'pjuːtəʳ/ n a machine that can store and recall information and make calculations at very high speeds: *a personal computer* | *computer software*

com·put·er·ize /kəm'pjuːtəraɪz/ v **computerized, computerizing** (also **computerise** BrE) [T] 1 to arrange for a computer to do a lot of the work: *The firm has decided to computerize its wages department.* 2 to store information in a computer: *They have computerized their criminal records.* –**computerized** adj –**computerization** /kəmˌpjuːtəraɪˈzeɪʃən ‖ -rə-/ n [U]

com·put·ing /kəm'pjuːtɪŋ/ n [U] the activity or skill of using a computer

com·rade /'kɒmrɪd, -reɪd ‖ 'kɑːmræd/ n 1 fml a close companion 2 someone who belongs to the same union or left wing group. *Comrades, please support this motion*

com·rade·ship /ˈkɒmrɪdʃɪp, -reɪd- ‖ ˈkɑːmræd-/ *n* [U] *fml* friendship

con /kɒn ‖ kɑːn/ *v* **-nn-** *infml* [T] to trick someone by telling them things that are not true: *They've conned me out of £5. | He conned me into doing all his work for him.*

con·cave /ˌkɒnˈkeɪv◂, kən- ‖ ˌkɑːnˈkeɪv◂, kən-/ *adj* curved inward, like the inside surface of a hollow ball: *a concave mirror* –opposite **convex**

con·ceal /kənˈsiːl/ *v* [T] *fml* to hide something: *She concealed her feelings. | He concealed his debts from his wife. | She tried to conceal how she felt.*

con·cede /kənˈsiːd/ *v* **1** [T; + that] to admit unwillingly that something is true or correct: *I'll concede that particular point, but I still think your basic argument is wrong. | The bank conceded that they had made a mistake.* **2** [T] to allow someone to have something: *After the First World War, Germany conceded a lot of land to her neighbours. | As there was no chance of winning he conceded the match.* **3** **concede defeat** to accept and state that you have lost: *The government conceded defeat as soon as the election results were known.*

con·ceit /kənˈsiːt/ *n* (also **conceitedness** ˈkənˈsiːtɪdnəs/) [U] too high an opinion of your own abilities and importance: *showing signs of conceit and selfishness*

con·ceit·ed /kənˈsiːtɪd/ *adj* too proud of your abilities or the things that you have done: *He was an arrogant, conceited man.*

con·cei·va·ble /kənˈsiːvəbəl/ *adj* able to be believed or imagined: *It is just conceivable that he'll win, but not really very likely.* –**conceivably** *adv*

con·ceive /kənˈsiːv/ *v* **1** [T] to form an idea of something or imagine it: *Scientists first conceived the idea of the atomic bomb in the 1930s. | It's difficult to conceive of living without electricity.* **2** [I;T] to become PREGNANT with a child: *The baby was conceived in March and born in December. | My wife was unable to conceive.*

con·cen·trate¹ /ˈkɒnsəntreɪt ‖ ˈkɑːn-/ *v* **concentrated, concentrating** [I;T] **1** to direct all your thoughts, efforts, or attention towards something: *I can't concentrate on anything when I'm hungry. | He concentrated on finding somewhere to live. | Be quiet. I'm trying to concentrate.* **2** to come or bring together in or around one place: *Industrial development is being concentrated in the south of the country. | The crowds concentrated round the palace.*

concentrate² *n* [C;U] a substance which has been made stronger by having liquid removed from it: *orange juice concentrate*

con·cen·trat·ed /ˈkɒnsəntreɪtɪd ‖ ˈkɑːn-/ *adj* **1** increased in strength by removing some of the liquid **2** [only before a noun] using a lot of attention or effort: *He has made a concentrated effort to improve his work.*

con·cen·tra·tion /ˌkɒnsənˈtreɪʃən ‖ ˌkɑːn-/ *n* **1** [U] direction of attention and hard thought: *This book will need all your concentration.* **2** [C] a large amount of something at a particular place: *There is a concentration of industry in the south of the country.* **3** the **concentration** *tech* the amount of a substance contained in a liquid

concentration camp /ˌ··ˈ·· ·/ *n* a prison camp where people are kept during a war

con·cen·tric /kənˈsentrɪk/ *adj tech* having the same centre: *concentric circles*

con·cept /ˈkɒnsept ‖ ˈkɑːn-/ *n* a general idea or principle: *It's difficult to grasp the concept of infinite space.*

con·cep·tion /kənˈsepʃən/ *n* **1** [C] a general understanding or idea: *You've no conception of what it was like to be there.* **2** [U] the act of forming an idea or plan: *The robbery was very imaginative in conception.* **3** [U] the process by which a woman becomes PREGNANT: *There are nine months between conception and birth.*

con·cep·tu·al /kənˈseptʃuəl/ *adj fml* connected with the forming of ideas in your mind –**conceptually** *adv*

con·cern¹ /kənˈsɜːn ‖ -ɜːrn/ *v* [T] **1** to be about: *This story concerns a person who lived in Russia a long time ago.* **2** to be of importance or interest to someone: *The marriage of a queen concerns all the people who live in her country. | This concerns all of you.* **3** to worry you: *This is a problem which concerns all parents.* **4 concern yourself with something** to take an interest in something: *She concerned herself with looking after the old people in her area.* **5 to whom it may concern** a phrase used at the beginning of a letter which anyone may read

concern² *n* **1** [C] a matter that is of interest or importance to someone: *It's your work I want to talk about. Your private life isn't my concern. | the concerns of ethnic minorities* **2** [U] worry or anxiety: *There is no cause for concern. | There is some concern about his health.* **3 of concern to** important to: *The problem of unemployment is of great concern to everyone.* **4** [C] a business or firm: *The restaurant is a family concern.* **5 a going concern** a business which is making a profit

con·cerned /kənˈsɜːnd ‖ -ɜːr-/ *adj* **1** anxious or worried: *I was very concerned about my mother's illness. | She was concerned for their safety.* **2** having an active personal interest: *I am concerned for their happiness. | He's very concerned to help.* **3** [only after a noun] having something to do with an event or activity: *I'll pass on your comments to the people concerned.* **4 as far as I'm concerned** – in my opinion **5 be concerned with** to be about: *This story is concerned with a Russian family in the nineteenth century.* **6 where something is concerned, as far as something is concerned** in matters that have an effect on something: *Where work is concerned, I always try to do my best.*

con·cern·ing /kənˈsɜːnɪŋ ‖ -ɜːr-/ *prep fml* in connection with: *Concerning your letter, I am pleased to inform you that your plans are quite acceptable to us. | a story concerning a beaver and an otter*

con·cert /ˈkɒnsət ‖ ˈkɑːnsərt/ *n* **1** a performance given by a number of musicians **2 in concert** *fml* working together: *The various governments decided to act in concert over this matter.*

con·cert·ed /kənˈsɜːtɪd ‖ -ɜːr-/ *adj* [only before a noun] **1** planned or done together by agreement: *a concerted attempt by all governments to stop crime* **2 concerted effort** a very big attempt: *She has made a concerted effort to improve her work.* –**concertedly** *adv*

con·cer·ti·na /ˌkɒnsəˈtiːnə ‖ ˌkɑːnsər-/ *n* a small musical instrument that you hold in your hands and play by pressing in from each side

con·cer·to /kənˈtʃɜːtəʊ ‖ -ˈtʃertəʊ/ *n* a piece of music for one or more instruments playing with an ORCHESTRA

con·ces·sion /kənˈseʃən/ *n* **1** something allowed unwillingly or after an argument: *The firm's* promise to increase our pay was a concession to union demands. **2** a right given by a government or owner of land to do something special: *oil concessions in the North Sea*

con·cil·i·ate /kən'sɪlieɪt/ v **conciliated, conciliating** *fml* [T] to reach an agreement with someone after an argument or disagreement –**conciliation** /kən,sɪli'eɪʃən/ n [U] : *The government ignored the union's attempts at conciliation.*

con·cil·i·a·to·ry /kən'sɪliətəri ‖ -tɔːri/ adj trying to end a disagreement: *a conciliatory gesture* | *a conciliatory tone*

con·cise /kən'saɪs/ adj expressing a lot in a few clear words: *a concise speech* | *a concise dictionary* –**concisely** adv –**conciseness** /kən'saɪsnəs/ n [U]

con·clude /kən'kluːd/ v **1** [I;T] *fml* to come or bring to an end: *We concluded the meeting at eight o'clock.* | *"So I had to walk," he concluded.* | *We concluded by giving him a vote of thanks.* **2** [+ (that)] to decide that something is true or reach a decision based on known facts: *The judge concluded that the prisoner was guilty.* **3** [T] *fml* to arrange or settle something after a lot of talking

con·clu·sion /kən'kluːʒən/ n **1** a judgment or decision that you reach after some thought: *What conclusions did you draw from his behaviour?* | *I came to the conclusion that I should accept the job.* **2** the end: *I found the conclusion of her book rather difficult to understand.* **3** the settling of something like a business deal: *the conclusion of a peace treaty* **4 in conclusion** a phrase used when you are ending a speech or piece of writing: *In conclusion, I'd just like to thank you all for coming.*

con·clu·sive /kən'kluːsɪv/ adj proving that something is true: *The police have conclusive proof of his guilt.* –opposite **inconclusive** –**conclusively** adv

con·coct /kən'kɒkt ‖ -'kɑːkt/ v [T] **1** to make something by combining things which are not usually put together: *Jean concocted a splendid meal from the leftovers.* **2** to invent something false: *He always manages to concoct some new excuse for being late.* –**concoction** /-'kɒkʃən ‖ -'kɑːk-/ n

con·com·i·tant /kən'kɒmɪtənt ‖ -'kɑː-/ n *fml* something that often goes or happens with something else: *Deafness is a frequent concomitant of old age.* –**concomitant** adj : *We lived through the war with all its concomitant sufferings.*

con·cord /'kɒŋkɔːd ‖ 'kɑːŋkɔːrd/ n [U] *fml* peaceful and friendly relations: *The two tribes had lived in concord for many centuries.*

con·course /'kɒŋkɔːs ‖ 'kɑːŋkɔːrs/ n a large hall or open place where crowds of people can gather: *the airport concourse*

con·crete¹ /'kɒŋkriːt ‖ kɑːn'kriːt/ adj *fml* **1** existing as something real or solid rather than something in the mind: *I prefer paintings of concrete objects that I can recognize.* **2** clear: *Have you got any concrete thoughts on what we should do next?* –**concretely** adv

con·crete² /'kɒŋkriːt ‖ 'kɑːŋ-/ n [U] a building material made by mixing sand, very small stones, cement, and water: *a concrete floor* –**concrete** v **concreted, concreting** : *The path has been concreted.*

SPELLING NOTE

Words with the sound / k /, like **cut**, may be spelt **k-**, like **key**, or **qu-**, like **queen**.
Words with the sound / s /, like **city**, may be spelt **s-**, like **soon**, or **ps-**, like **psychology**.

---

con·cur /kən'kɜːʳ/ v -rr- *fml* [I;+that] to agree: *The two judges concurred with one another.* | *We have studied your proposal and we all concur.*

con·cur·rent /kən'kʌrənt ‖ -'kɜːr-/ adj **1** existing or happening at the same time: *He is serving two concurrent prison sentences.* **2** *fml* in agreement: *My opinions are concurrent with yours in this matter.* –**concurrently** adv –**concurrence** n [C;U]

con·cus·sion /kən'kʌʃən/ n [U] a medical condition in which you become unconscious or feel confused after a heavy blow to your head: *He's suffering from concussion after falling off his bicycle.* –**concuss** v [T] : *Don't worry; she's only concussed.*

con·demn /kən'dem/ v [T] **1** to express strong disapproval of someone or something: *Most people are willing to condemn violence of any sort.* **2** to give a serious punishment to someone who is guilty in a court of law: *He was condemned to death.* **3** to force someone into an unpleasant situation: *His bad leg has condemned him to a wheelchair.* **4** to declare a building officially unfit for use: *The house has been condemned by the Council.* –**condemnation** /,kɒndəm'neɪʃən, -dem- ‖ ,kɑːn-/ n [C;U]

con·den·sa·tion /,kɒndən'seɪʃən, -dən- ‖ ,kɑːn-/ n [U] **1** drops of liquid formed when steam or hot air touches a cold surface: *There was condensation on the windows.* **2** the reduction of an account of something into a shorter form

con·dense /kən'dens/ v **1** [T] to make an account of something shorter while still including all the important parts: *a condensed report* **2** [I;T] to cool something so that it becomes liquid or solid **3** [T] to make a liquid thicker by removing some of the water: *cans of condensed soup*

con·de·scend /,kɒndɪ'send ‖ ,kɑːn-/ v **1** condescend to do something to agree to do something although you think that you are too important to do it: *Do you think the directors will actually condescend to have lunch with us in the canteen?* **2** [I] to behave as though you are better or more important than other people –**condescending** adj : *Don't be so condescending!* –**condescension** n [U]

con·di·ment /'kɒndᵻmənt ‖ 'kɑːn-/ n *fml* a powder or liquid used for giving a special taste to food; for example, salt and pepper are condiments

con·di·tion¹ /kən'dɪʃən/ n **1** [U] the state that something is in: *The car is in excellent condition.* **2** [U] someone's state of health: *Her condition is improving.* **3 out of condition** not very fit and healthy: *I'm a bit out of condition at the moment.* **4** [C] an illness of a part of your body, which continues for a long time: *She has a heart condition.* **5** [C] something that is needed to make something else possible: *We had to satisfy several conditions before we were allowed to join the club.* **6 on one condition, on condition that** phrases used when you are saying that something will only happen if something else happens: *She'll join us on one condition: that we don't discuss divorce.* | *I'll come on condition that John is invited too.* **7 conditions** [pl] the general situation or state of affairs at a particular time or place: *Their working conditions were terrible.* | *Housing conditions have improved in this area.* | *Even under the best conditions, we couldn't get there in less than three days.*

condition² v [T] **1** to train someone to behave in a certain way or to have certain beliefs: *Most people are conditioned to believe what they read in newspapers.* **2 be conditioned by** to be controlled by something else: *The amount of money I spend is conditioned by the amount I earn.*

con·di·tion·al /kən'dɪʃənəl/ *adj* depending on something else happening: *His agreement to buy our house was conditional on us leaving all the furniture in it.* –**conditionally** *adv*

con·di·tion·er /kən'dɪʃənəʳ/ *n* a substance which you put on your hair after you have washed it, to help it remain in good condition

con·di·tion·ing /kən'dɪʃənɪŋ/ *n* [U] the process by which someone is trained to behave in certain ways or to hold certain beliefs

con·do·lence /kən'dəʊləns/ *n* [U;pl] an expression of sympathy for someone when one of their friends or relatives has died: *Please accept my condolences.* | *a letter of condolence*

con·dom /'kɒndəm ‖ 'kɑːn-, 'kʌn-/ *n* a rubber covering which a man wears over his PENIS when he is having sex; it is used as a means of birth control or for protection against disease

con·do·min·i·um /ˌkɒndə'mɪniəm ‖ ˌkɑːn-/ *n AmE* (also **condo** *infml*) **1** a block of flats, each of which is owned by the people who live in it **2** a single flat in one of these blocks

con·done /kən'dəʊn/ *v* **condoned, condoning** [T] to regard bad behaviour as acceptable: *We would never condone the use of violence.*

con·du·cive /kən'djuːsɪv ‖ -'duː-/ *adj fml* **conducive to** likely to result in something or to make something possible: *Smoking a whole packet of cigarettes a day is not exactly conducive to good health.*

con·duct¹ /kən'dʌkt/ *v* **1** [T] to take someone somewhere, often as a guide: *He conducted us on a tour of the castle.* **2 conducted tour** a visit to a place in which a guide goes with you and shows you all the interesting things **3** [T] to carry something out: *British Rail is conducting an enquiry into safety standards on trains.* **4 conduct yourself** *fml* to behave in a certain way: *Servants were expected to conduct themselves in a decorous manner.* **5** [I;T] to stand in front of musicians and direct their music: *Who's conducting tonight?* | *Lyons will be conducting the symphony orchestra.* **6** [T] to act as a path for electricity or heat: *Rubber won't conduct electricity.*

con·duct² /'kɒndʌkt, -dəkt ‖ 'kɑːn-/ *n* [U] **1** *fml* behaviour: *I'm glad to see your conduct at school has improved.* **2** the direction of the course of a business or similar activity: *We are not satisfied with the conduct of the negotiations.*

con·duc·tor /kən'dʌktəʳ/ *n* **1** a person who directs the playing of a group of musicians while standing in front of them **2** a person employed to collect payments from passengers on a bus or train: *a bus conductor* **3** something that acts as a path for electricity or heat: *Wood is a poor conductor of heat.*

cone /kəʊn/ *n* **1** a hollow or solid object with a round base and a point at the top **2** something you can eat which is shaped like a cone and which has ice-cream inside: *an ice-cream cone* **3** the fruit of a PINE or FIR tree

con·fec·tion·e·ry /kən'fekʃənəri/ *n* [U] sweet cakes, ice-cream, or sweets –**confectioner** *n*

con·fed·e·ra·cy /kən'fedərəsi/ *n* **confederacies** *fml* a union of people, parties, or states for political purposes or trade

con·fed·e·rate /kən'fedərɪt/ *n* **1** a member of a confederacy **2** a person who helps you with something secret or dishonest

con·fed·e·ra·tion /kənˌfedə'reɪʃən/ *n* an organization of groups or firms for political or business purposes

con·fer /kən'fɜːʳ/ *v* **-rr-** *fml* **1** [I] to talk about opinions or views: *The ministers are still conferring on this matter.* | *The Prime Minister is conferring with her advisors.* **2** [T] to give a title or honour to someone: *An honorary degree was conferred on him by the university.*

con·fe·rence /'kɒnfərəns ‖ 'kɑːn-/ *n* **1** a meeting held so that opinions and ideas on a subject can be exchanged: *a conference of European states* | *a conference on environmental issues* **2 in conference** having a meeting with someone: *I'm afraid Mrs Pike is in conference until three o'clock.*

con·fess /kən'fes/ *v* **1** [I;T;+(that)] to admit to a fault or crime: *It's time to confess.* | *He has confessed to the murder.* | *She confessed all her crimes.* | *Jean confessed that she'd eaten all the cakes.*
□ USEFUL PATTERNS to confess something; to confess something; to confess to something; to confess to doing something; to confess that...
2 I must confess a phrase used when you are being honest and admitting something: *I must confess I've never liked him very much.* **3** [I;T] *tech* to admit your faults to a priest or to God

con·fessed /kən'fest/ *adj* admitted by the person concerned to be true: *Mrs Jones is a confessed alcoholic.*

con·fes·sion /kən'feʃən/ *n* **1** [C;U] a statement admitting your crime or faults: *I'd like to make a confession.* **2** [U] *tech* a meeting with a priest at which you tell him what you have done wrong: *Are you going to confession?*

con·fet·ti /kən'feti/ *n* [U] small pieces of coloured paper thrown about at weddings

con·fi·dant /'kɒnfɪdænt, ˌkɒnfɪ'dænt ‖ 'kɑːnfɪdænt/ *n fml* someone you talk to about your secrets or personal matters; a woman who you talk to in this way is called a **confidante**

con·fide /kən'faɪd/ *v* [T; + that] to tell your secrets to someone you trust not to tell anyone else: *He confided to me that he had once been in prison.* | *She confided that her illness was getting worse.* | *She confided her worries to me.*
□ USEFUL PATTERNS to confide something to someone; to confide that...; to confide to someone that...
confide in sbdy *phr v* [T] to talk freely to someone about your secrets: *John felt he could confide in his brother.*

con·fi·dence /'kɒnfɪdəns ‖ 'kɑːn-/ *n* **1** [U] belief that a person or thing will perform as you hope and expect: *We have complete confidence in you.* **2** [U] a calm, unworried feeling, based on a strong belief in yourself: *She's a good musician, but she lacks confidence.* **3** [U] trust: *How can I win his confidence?* **4 in confidence, in strict confidence** trusting the person being told to keep the matter a secret: *I'm telling you all this in confidence.* **5 take someone into your confidence** to tell someone something secret or private because you trust them **6** [C] *old fash* a secret: *They exchanged confidences about their boyfriends.*

con·fi·dent /'kɒnfɪdənt ‖ 'kɑːn-/ *adj* **1** certain that things will happen as you want them to: *The government is confident of winning the next election.* | *He*

is confident that he'll pass the exam. **2** feeling or expressing a strong belief in yourself: *a calm and confident young man* | *a confident smile*

con·fi·den·tial /ˌkɒnfɪˈdenʃəl‖ ˌkɑːn-/ *adj* intended to be kept secret and not talked about openly: *This report is still confidential.* | *I think he's been passing confidential information to our competitors.* –**confidentially** *adv*

con·fid·ing /ˈkɒnfaɪdɪŋ/ *adj* trusting other people with your own private affairs: *her confiding nature* –**confidingly** *adv*

con·fine /kənˈfaɪn/ *v* **confined, confining** [T] **1** to keep a person or thing in a small, enclosed space: *The animal was confined in a very small cage.* | *A bad cold confined John to bed for a week.* **2** to keep something within limits: *Please confine your remarks to the subject under discussion.* **3** **confine yourself to** to limit yourself to something: *I'll confine myself to talking about this one project.* –**confinement** *n*: *They were kept in confinement for a year, until their trial.*

con·fines /ˈkɒnfaɪnz‖ ˈkɑːn-/ *n* [pl] limits or borders: *This is outside the confines of human knowledge.* | *You may not leave the confines of the university.*

con·firm /kənˈfɜːm‖ -ɜːrm/ *v* [T; + that] **1** to show or state that something is certainly true or will definitely happen: *The extra evidence confirmed our suspicions.* | *The Prime Minister confirmed that the election would be on June 20th.* **2 be confirmed** *tech* to be admitted to full membership of a Christian church

con·fir·ma·tion /ˌkɒnfəˈmeɪʃən‖ ˌkɑːnfər-/ *n* **1** [U] something that shows other things to be true: *There has still been no official confirmation of the number of deaths.* **2** [C;U] *tech* a religious service in which a person is made a full member of a Christian church

con·firmed /kənˈfɜːmd‖ -ɜːr-/ *adj* [only before a noun] unwilling to change a habit or way of life: *He's a confirmed bachelor.*

con·fis·cate /ˈkɒnfəskeɪt‖ ˈkɑːn-/ *v* **confiscated, confiscating** [T] to take private property away from someone when you have the right to do so and wish to punish them: *I had my radio confiscated by our chemistry teacher today.* –**confiscation** /ˌkɒnfəˈskeɪʃən‖ ˌkɑːn-/ *n*

con·fla·gra·tion /ˌkɒnfləˈgreɪʃən‖ ˌkɑːn-/ *n fml* a large fire that destroys buildings or forests

con·flict¹ /ˈkɒnflɪkt‖ ˈkɑːn-/ *n* [C;U] **1** a serious disagreement between different people or principles: *It will lead to conflict between Unions and Management.* | *Personal and political conflicts among ministers are increasingly common.* **2 come into conflict** to argue or disagree: *We came into conflict over money.* | *Town planners are coming into conflict with farmers as cities expand.* [RELATED PHRASES: **be in conflict; bring people into conflict**] **3** war or fighting: *Armed conflict is now unavoidable.*

con·flict² /kənˈflɪkt/ *v* [I] to disagree: *Do British laws conflict with any international laws?* | *Our job is to make sense of all this conflicting evidence.*

SPELLING NOTE

Words with the sound / k /, like **cut**, may be spelt **k-**, like **key**, or **qu-**, like **queen**.
Words with the sound / s /, like **city**, may be spelt **s-**, like **soon**, or **ps-**, like **psychology**.

---

con·flu·ence /ˈkɒnfluəns‖ ˈkɑːn-/ *n fml* the place where two or more rivers flow together

con·form /kənˈfɔːm‖ -ɔːrm/ *v* [I] *fml* **1** to follow established rules or patterns: *This piece of equipment does not conform to the official safety standards.* **2** to behave like most other people: *There is great pressure on school-children to conform.* –**conformity** *n* [U]

con·form·ist /kənˈfɔːmɪst‖ -ɔːr-/ *adj, n* a person who follows the established rules, values, and customs of a group or of society (a word often used to express disapproval)

con·found /kənˈfaʊnd/ *v* [T] to confuse and surprise someone by being unexpected: *The results confounded all our expectations.*

con·front /kənˈfrʌnt/ *v* [T] **1** to face someone boldly or threateningly: *I was confronted by two men demanding money.* **2 confront someone with something** to show someone something in order to say with reason that they are guilty: *When she was confronted with video recordings, she had to admit she was involved.* **3** to try to deal with something that you cannot avoid: *You'll have to confront the problem sometime.* **4** to cause problems for someone: *A number of difficulties now confronted me.*

con·fron·ta·tion /ˌkɒnfrənˈteɪʃən‖ ˌkɑːn-/ *n* [C;U] a situation of open disagreement: *We must avoid confrontation with the government.*

con·fuse /kənˈfjuːz/ *v* **confused, confusing** [T] **1** to make someone feel uncertain about what to think or do: *John's account is just confusing me.* **2** to make a situation harder to understand: *Stop trying to confuse matters and listen!* **3** to find it difficult to tell the difference between people or things: *I'm always confusing John with his twin brother.* –**confused** *adj*: *I thought I knew what to do, but now I'm confused.* –**confusedly** /kənˈfjuːzɪdli/ *adv* –**confusing** *adj*: *His explanation was really confusing.*

con·fu·sion /kənˈfjuːʒən/ *n* [U] **1** a situation in which people are uncertain about what to think or do: *There was some confusion as to whether we had won.* **2** a situation in which it is difficult to tell the difference between two people or things: *To avoid confusion, the teams wore different colours.* **3** a state of great disorder: *The announcement caused panic and confusion.*

con·geal /kənˈdʒiːl/ *v* [I;T] to become thick or solid: *The liquid congealed.* | *congealed blood*

con·ge·ni·al /kənˈdʒiːniəl/ *adj fml* pleasing or interesting to you: *I find both the work and the people congenial.* –**congenially** *adv*

con·gen·i·tal /kənˈdʒenɪtl/ *adj tech* existing at or from your birth (used of diseases): *congenital deafness* –**congenitally** *adv*

con·ges·ted /kənˈdʒestɪd/ *adj* **1** blocked by heavy traffic: *The streets of London are increasingly congested.* **2** blocked with liquid (used of parts of the body): *My head hurts and my nose is congested.* –**congestion** /-ˈdʒestʃən/ *n* [U]: *traffic congestion* | *congestion of the lungs*

con·glom·e·rate /kənˈglɒmərət‖ -ˈglɑː-/ *n* a large business firm producing goods of very different kinds

con·glom·e·ra·tion /kənˌglɒməˈreɪʃən‖ -ˌglɑː-/ *n* a collection of many different things gathered together: *It was a strange conglomeration of shops, flats, and government offices.*

con·grat·u·late /kənˈgrætʃ‍ɡleɪt/ v **congratulated, congratulating** [T] to express your pleasure or admiration for a happy event or success: *I was just phoning to congratulate you on your exam results.* –**congratulation** /kənˌgrætʃ‍ɡˈleɪʃən/ n [U] –**congratulatory** /kənˌgrætʃ‍ɡˈleɪtəri ‖ -ˈɡrætʃ‍ɡlətɔːri/ adj : *a congratulatory telegram*

con·grat·u·la·tions /kənˌgrætʃ‍ɡˈleɪʃənz/ interj,n [pl] an expression of pleasure or admiration for someone's success or good fortune: *You got the job? Congratulations!* | *Congratulations* on *your engagement.*

con·gre·gate /ˈkɒŋɡrɪɡeɪt ‖ ˈkɑːŋ-/ v **congregated, congregating** [I] to come together in a large group: *Crowds congregated in the town square to hear the President.*

con·gre·ga·tion /ˌkɒŋɡrɪˈɡeɪʃən ‖ ˌkɑːŋ-/ n a group of people gathered together in a church for religious worship

con·gress /ˈkɒŋɡres ‖ ˈkɑːŋɡrɪs/ n **1 Congress** the highest law-making body of the US, consisting of the SENATE and the House of Representatives: *Congress has approved the new education budget.* **2** (also **Congress**) a formal meeting of representatives of organizations or countries to exchange information and opinions: *We're attending a medical congress.* | *the Congress of Vienna* –**congressional** /kənˈgreʃənəl/ adj : *congressional elections*

con·i·cal /ˈkɒnɪkəl ‖ ˈkɑː-/ adj shaped like a CONE(1): *a conical hat* | *huts with conical roofs*

co·ni·fer /ˈkəʊnɪfəʳ, ˈkɒ- ‖ ˈkɑː-/ n a tree on which brown cones (CONE (3)) grow and which usually keeps its leaves in winter –**coniferous** /kəˈnɪfərəs/ adj

con·jec·ture¹ /kənˈdʒektʃəʳ/ n [C;U] a guess based on the little information that you have: *Whether or not the President knew will always be a matter for conjecture.*

conjecture² v **conjectured, conjecturing** [I; + that] to guess

con·ju·gal /ˈkɒndʒ‍ɡəl ‖ ˈkɑːn-/ adj [only before a noun] fml concerning the relationship between husband and wife: *the conjugal bed*

con·ju·gate /ˈkɒndʒ‍ɡeɪt ‖ ˈkɑːn-/ v **conjugated, conjugating** [T] tech to give in a particular order the various forms of a verb that show number, person, and time: *All I remember from my schooldays is how to conjugate Latin verbs.* –**conjugation** /ˌkɒndʒ‍ɡˈeɪʃən ‖ ˌkɑːn-/ n

con·junc·tion /kənˈdʒʌŋkʃən/ n **1** a word such as "but" or "and" that connects words, phrases, or parts of sentences –see Study Note on page 687 **2 in conjunction with** together with: *The army is acting in conjunction with the police in the hunt for terrorists.*

con·jure /ˈkʌndʒəʳ ‖ ˈkɑːn-/ v **conjured, conjuring** [I;T] to make something appear as if by magic: *The magician conjured a rabbit out of his hat.* | *Paul's very good at conjuring.*

conjure sthg ↔ **up** phr v [T] **1** to give an image or idea of something **2** to make something appear as if by magic

con·jur·er /ˈkʌndʒərəʳ ‖ ˈkɑːn-/ n (also **conjuror**) a professional entertainer who does conjuring tricks to amuse others

con·nect /kəˈnekt/ v **1** [T] (also **connect** sthg ↔ **up**) to join two or more places or things: *The railway line connects London and Edinburgh.* | *The plumber connected up all the pipes and turned on the water.* | *The tape recorder is connected to a loudspeaker.* **2** [T] to suggest that two or more things are related: *There is no evidence to connect her with the crime.* **3** [T] to join two people by telephone: *Could you connect me with a number in Indonesia, please?* **4** [T] to join something to an electricity supply: *Make sure the machine's connected properly.* **5** [I] to be planned so that passengers arrive in time to catch another train, bus, or plane and continue on their journey: *The ten o'clock plane connects with a flight to Paris.* –opposite **disconnect** (for senses 3, 4)

con·nect·ed /kəˈnektɪd/ adj related to someone or something else: *Is your decision to leave connected with anything I said?* –opposite **unconnected**

con·nec·tion /kəˈnekʃən/ n (also **con·nex·ion** BrE) **1** [U] the joining of two or more things: *I'm waiting for the connection of the new pipes to the water supply.* –opposite **disconnection** **2** [C] a relationship between things: *Do you know that there's a connection between smoking and heart disease?* **3** [C] a plane, train or bus arranged for a time which allows passengers to continue on the next part of their journey: *There are connections in Paris for all European capitals.* **4** [C] something that joins two places or things: *There are excellent road and railway connections between major cities.* | *The machine won't work because of a faulty connection.* **5 connections** [pl] people known to someone through their family or through business: *She's English but has Irish connections.* | *We have connections with a firm in Zurich.* **6 in connection with** fml concerning: *I am writing in connection with your recent request for information about the department.*

con·nive /kəˈnaɪv/ v **connived, conniving** [I] **1** fml to work secretly for some wrong or illegal purpose: *She connived with her friend to cheat in the examination.* **2 connive at something** to make no attempt to stop something that you know is wrong: *I believe you connived at the man's escape because you felt sorry for him.*

con·nois·seur /ˌkɒnəˈsɜːʳ ‖ ˌkɑː-/ n someone who has a good knowledge and understanding of subjects such as art or music, and whose judgments are respected: *a connoisseur of fine wines*

con·no·ta·tion /ˌkɒnəˈteɪʃən ‖ ˌkɑː-/ n an idea suggested by a word rather than the actual meaning of the word: *The word "peasant" has negative connotations in English.*

con·quer /ˈkɒŋkəʳ ‖ ˈkɑːŋ-/ v **1** [I;T] to win land or defeat an enemy by fighting: *The Normans conquered England in 1066.* | *a conquering army* **2** [T] to gain control over something difficult: *The mountain was finally conquered by climbers in 1982.* –**conqueror** n

con·quest /ˈkɒŋkwest ‖ ˈkɑːŋ-/ n **1** [U] the defeat or control of something: *the conquest of Britain by invading armies* | *The conquest of this rare disease has always been her aim.* **2** [C] land won as a result of fighting: *French conquests in Asia* **3** [C] a person of the opposite sex whose admiration or love has been won (a word which is often used in a humorous way): *She's coming to dinner with her latest conquest. (I think his name's Pete.)*

con·science /ˈkɒnʃəns ‖ ˈkɑːn-/ n **1** an inner sense that tells you whether you are doing something right or wrong: *Vote according to your conscience.* | *He's behaving like a man with a guilty conscience.*

2 have a clear conscience to know that you have done nothing wrong **3 conscience-stricken** feeling very guilty about something you have or have not done **4 have something on your conscience** to feel guilty about something that you have or have not done **5 in all conscience** doing what you know is right: *I couldn't in all conscience stop him seeing his father.*

con·sci·en·tious /ˌkɒnʃiˈenʃəs ‖ ˌkɑːn-/ *adj* careful to do everything very carefully and well: *a conscientious worker | a conscientious piece of work* –see CONSCIOUS (USAGE) –**conscientiously** *adv* –**conscientiousness** *n* [U]

con·scious /ˈkɒnʃəs ‖ ˈkɑːn-/ *adj* **1** [never before a noun] awake and able to think: *He is badly hurt but still conscious.* –opposite **unconscious 2** [never before a noun] knowing and understanding: *Peter isn't conscious of his bad manners. | I was conscious that he was ill at ease.* **3** [only before a noun] intentional: *a conscious decision | a conscious effort* –**consciously** *adv*

■ USAGE 1 The usual opposite of **conscious** is **unconscious**: *He's still* **unconscious** *after the accident.* But in psychology, both **unconscious** and **subconscious** are used: *the* **unconscious/subconscious** *mind.* **2** Do not confuse **conscious** with **conscientious** which means "very careful in the way you do your job".

con·scious·ness /ˈkɒnʃəsnəs ‖ ˈkɑːn-/ *n* [sing; U] **1** all the ideas and opinions held by a person or a group of people about a particular subject: *You can see his political consciousness developing.* **2** feeling or understanding: *a consciousness that someone else was in the room* **3 lose consciousness** to fall into a state like sleep so that you cannot think or understand what is happening [RELATED PHRASE **regain consciousness**]

con·script /kənˈskrɪpt/ *v* [T] to make someone serve in one of the armed forces: *My son was conscripted into the navy during the war.* –**conscript** /ˈkɒn-skrɪpt ‖ ˈkɑːn-/ – : *He's a conscript.* –**conscription** /kənˈskrɪpʃən/ *n* [U]

con·se·crate /ˈkɒnsɪˌkreɪt ‖ ˈkɑːn-/ *v* **consecrated, consecrating** [T] to declare something to be holy in a special ceremony: *The church will be consecrated by the bishop.* –**consecration** /ˌkɒnsɪˈkreɪʃən ‖ ˌkɑːn-/ *n* [U]

con·sec·u·tive /kənˈsekjʊtɪv/ *adj* following one after the other: *I saw him on three consecutive days.* –**consecutively** *adv*

con·sen·sus /kənˈsensəs/ *n* [sing; U] general agreement: *What is the consensus of opinion? | We must come to a consensus quickly.*

con·sent¹ /kənˈsent/ *v* [I] to agree to something: *Her father reluctantly consented to her marriage.* –compare DISSENT¹

consent² *n* [U] **1** agreement or permission: *We need your parents' written consent.* **2 by common consent, by general consent** by the agreement of most people

con·se·quence /ˈkɒnsɪˌkwəns ‖ ˈkɑːnsɪˌkwens/ *n* **1** the result of an action or situation: *Teacher shortages are a consequence of low pay. | If you get caught,*

you'll have to face the consequences. **2 of little/no consequence** not important

con·se·quent·ly /ˈkɒnsɪˌkwəntli ‖ ˈkɑːn-/ *adv fml* therefore: *No candidate succeeded in obtaining a majority of the votes. Consequently new elections were held.*

con·ser·va·tion /ˌkɒnsəˈveɪʃən ‖ ˌkɑːnsər-/ *n* [U] **1** protection from damage or destruction: *the conservation of our limited supplies of water* **2** the protection of natural things: *I am involved in wild life conservation.* –**conservationist** *n* : *Conservationists are protesting about plans for a new motorway.*

con·ser·va·tism /kənˈsɜːvətɪzəm ‖ -ɜːr-/ *n* [U] **1** dislike of change, especially sudden change: *We are seeing a new conservatism among young people.* **2** (also **Conservatism**) the political beliefs of the Conservative Party, which say that any change to the established order of society should be slow and carefully considered

con·ser·va·tive¹ /kənˈsɜːvətɪv ‖ -ɜːr-/ *adj* **1** unwilling to change your ideas about things: *He is very conservative in his views of women.* **2** not very modern in style, taste, or manners: *She dresses in a rather conservative way.* **3** careful, and probably less than the true amount: *The figure of three million unemployed is a conservative estimate based on government statistics.* **4 Conservative** concerned with or belonging to the Conservative Party: *Conservative voters* –**conservatively** *adv*

conservative² *n* **1 Conservative** a member of the Conservative Party **2** someone who does not like change

Conservative Par·ty /·ˈ··· ˌ··/ *n* the political party in Britain which tends to be against sudden changes in the way that society is organized, and is against state control of industry

con·ser·va·to·ry /kənˈsɜːvətəri ‖ -ˈsɜːrvətɔːri/ *n* **1** a room, mainly of glass, which is joined to a house and where plants are often grown **2** a school where people are trained in music

con·serve /kənˈsɜːv ‖ -ɜːrv/ *v* **conserved, conserving** [T] to keep something from being damaged, wasted, or destroyed: *Conserve your energy! | methods of conserving electricity*

con·sid·er /kənˈsɪdə/ *v* **1** [I;T] to think about something carefully: *I'm considering changing my job. | We need some time to consider.*
□ USEFUL PATTERNS: to consider something; to consider doing something
2 [T; +(that)] to think of someone or something in a particular way: *I consider him to be a good musician.*
□ USEFUL PATTERNS to consider someone to be something; to consider that…
3 [T; +(that)] to take something into account: *If you consider that she's only been studying English a year, she speaks it very well. | All things considered, it would be better to resign.*

con·sid·e·ra·ble /kənˈsɪdərəbəl/ *adj* fairly large (used of the amount of something): *a considerable length of time | a considerable number of people* –**considerably** *adv* : *Our house is considerably smaller than theirs.*

con·sid·er·ate /kənˈsɪdərət/ *adj* thoughtful about other people's rights or feelings: *It was very considerate of you to tell us you would be late.* –opposite **inconsiderate** –**considerately** *adv*

con·sid·e·ra·tion /kənˌsɪdəˈreɪʃən/ *n* **1** [U] thought for other people's feelings: *You show no consideration for anyone but yourself!* **2** [U] careful thought and attention: *We shall give your request careful consideration.* **3** [C] a fact that needs to be considered when making a decision: *Local facilities are an important consideration when you buy a house.* **4 take something into consideration** to consider something when making a judgment: *Your illness will be taken into consideration by the examiners.*

con·sid·ered /kən'sɪdəd ‖ -ərd/ *adj* **1** [only before a noun] reached after careful thought: *It is my considered opinion that you are wrong.* **2 all things considered** when you consider everything: *All things considered, I think we did very well.*

con·sid·er·ing /kən'sɪdərɪŋ/ *prep, conj* taking into account: *He did very well in his examinations, considering how little work he had done.*

con·sign /kən'saɪn/ *v* [T] *fml* **1** to send something to a person or place for sale: *The goods were consigned to you by rail.* **2** *fml* to put a person or thing into a particular place or situation: *My mother consigned me to my uncle's care.* | *All those papers have been consigned to the dustbin.*

con·sign·ment /kən'saɪnmənt/ *n* **1** [C] a number of goods sent together: *The whole consignment of bananas was rotten.* **2** [U] the act of sending someone or something to another place

con·sist /kən'sɪst/ *v* **1 consist of something** to be made up of a number of things: *The city of New York consists of five boroughs.* | *a delivery of supplies, consisting mainly of food and medicines* **2 consist in something** to be really: *For me, the pleasure of the meal consisted entirely in the conversation – the food was terrible.*

con·sis·ten·cy /kən'sɪstənsi/ *n* **consistencies 1** [U] behaviour which always follows the same principles or pattern: *We need greater consistency in the advice we give to the public.* **2** [C;U] the degree of thickness: *Mix the butter and sugar to the consistency of thick cream.*

con·sis·tent /kən'sɪstənt/ *adj* **1** always following the same principles or patterns of behaviour: *He's been a consistent supporter of women's rights.* **2 consistent with** in agreement with: *That statement is not consistent with what you said earlier.* –**consistently** *adv*

con·so·la·tion /ˌkɒnsə'leɪʃən ‖ ˌkɑːn-/ *n* [C;U] a person or thing that gives comfort during a time of sadness or disappointment: *The only consolation was that I hadn't spent any money.*

con·sole¹ /kən'səʊl/ *v* **consoled, consoling** [T] **1** to give comfort or sympathy to someone in times of disappointment or sadness: *Nothing will console her for the loss of her dog.* | *She tried to console me with a cup of tea.* **2 console yourself** to make yourself feel better: *Console yourself with the thought that he didn't get the job either!* –**consolatory** /kən'sɒlətəri, -'səʊl ‖ -'səʊlətɔːri, -'sɑːl-/ *adj*

con·sole² /'kɒnsəʊl ‖ 'kɑːn-/ *n* a flat surface containing the controls for a machine

con·sol·i·date /kən'sɒlˌdeɪt ‖ -'sɑː-/ *v* **consolidated, consolidating** [I;T] **1** to increase in strength or effectiveness: *Britain is trying to consolidate her position in Europe.* **2** to join together: *Several small businesses have recently consolidated to form a single large company.* –**consolidation** /kənˌsɒlˌ'deɪʃən ‖ -ˌsɑː-/ *n* [C;U]

con·som·mé /kən'sɒmeɪ, 'kɒnsəmeɪ ‖ ˌkɑːnsə'meɪ/ *n* [U] thin, clear soup: *chicken consommé*

con·so·nant /'kɒnsənənt ‖ 'kɑːn-/ *n* **1** a speech sound made by partly or completely stopping the flow of air as it goes through your mouth **2** any of the letters of the English alphabet except a, e, i, o, u

con·sort¹ /'kɒnsɔːt ‖ 'kɑːnsɔːrt/ *n fml* the wife or husband of a ruler

con·sort² /kən'sɔːt ‖ -ɔːrt/ *v* **consort with somebody** to spend time in the company of someone who is disapproved of: *He is said to consort with known criminals.*

con·sor·ti·um /kən'sɔːtiəm ‖ -ɔːr-/ *n* **consortiums** *or* **consortia** a number of companies or businesses working together: *The banks have formed a consortium.*

con·spic·u·ous /kən'spɪkjuəs/ *adj* easily noticed: *She felt very conspicuous in a men's club.* | *That hat makes him even more conspicuous than usual.* –**conspicuously** *adv*

con·spi·ra·cy /kən'spɪrəsi/ *n* **conspiracies** [C;U] the secret planning of an illegal act by a number of people: *She was found guilty of conspiracy to murder.* | *Details of the conspiracy have just been made public.*

con·spi·ra·tor /kən'spɪrətər/ *n* a member of a group who make a secret plan to do something illegal –**conspiratorial** /kənˌspɪrə'tɔːriəl/ *adj* : *a conspiratorial whisper* –**conspiratorially** *adv*

con·spire /kən'spaɪər/ *v* **conspired, conspiring** [I] **1** to plan together secretly to do something illegal: *The four men conspired to rob a bank.* **2** *fml* to happen at the same time, leading to a particular bad result: *Events conspired to make the policies impossible to carry out.* | *I felt as though everything was conspiring against me.*

con·sta·ble /'kʌnstəbəl ‖ 'kɑːn-/ *n* a British police officer of the lowest rank

con·stab·u·la·ry /kən'stæbjʊləri ‖ -leri/ *n* **constabularies** the police force of a particular area or country

con·stant /'kɒnstənt ‖ 'kɑːn-/ *adj* **1** fixed or unchanging: *a constant speed* **2** happening all the time: *I dislike these constant arguments.* **3** loyal to a person or idea: *my constant companion* –**constantly** *adv*

con·stel·la·tion /ˌkɒnstˌ'leɪʃən ‖ ˌkɑːn-/ *n* a group of stars in a fixed pattern

con·ster·na·tion /ˌkɒnstə'neɪʃən ‖ ˌkɑːnstər-/ *n* [U] great shock and worry: *He looked at me in consternation.*

con·sti·pa·tion /ˌkɒnstˌ'peɪʃən ‖ ˌkɑːn-/ *n* [U] inability to empty your bowels for a period of time –**constipated** /'kɒnstˌ'peɪtˌd ‖ 'kɑːn-/ *adj*

con·sti·tu·en·cy /kən'stɪtʃuənsi/ *n* **constituencies** an area of a country, represented in the government by a Member of Parliament

con·sti·tu·ent /kən'stɪtʃuənt/ *n* **1** a voter in a particular area of a country: *Constituents can see their MP by appointment.* **2** any of the parts that make up a whole: *the constituents of an atom* –**constituent** *adj*

con·sti·tute /'kɒnstˌtjuːt ‖ 'kɑːnstˌtuːt/ *v* **constituted, constituting** *fml* [+ complement; not in progressive forms] **1** to form something: *the 50 states that constitute the USA* **2** to be considered the same as something: *This constitutes an important breakthrough in medical knowledge.*

con·sti·tu·tion /ˌkɒnstɪ̩'tjuːʃən ‖ ˌkɑːnstɪ̩'tuː-/ n 1 the system of laws and principles according to which a country is governed: *Are you reading about the American constitution?* 2 the general condition of a person's body: *He's always had a weak constitution.* 3 the way in which something is put together: *I'm concerned about the constitution of the new committee.*

con·sti·tu·tion·al /ˌkɒnstɪ̩'tjuːʃənəl ‖ ˌkɑːnstɪ̩'tuː-/ adj 1 allowed or limited by a political constitution: *There are severe constitutional limits on the queen's power.* 2 related to a political constitution: *a constitutional crisis* 3 related to a person's general physical condition –**constitutionally** adv

con·strain /kən'streɪn/ v [T] fml to make someone behave in a certain way by limiting their freedom to decide: *I am constrained by the need to care for my mother.*

con·strained /kən'streɪnd/ adj 1 awkward and unnatural: *a constrained manner* 2 **feel constrained to do something** to feel that you have to do something

con·straint /kən'streɪnt/ n [C;U] something that limits your freedom of action, often by the use of threat or force: *Teachers have to work within the constraints of the system.* | *We acted under constraint.*

con·strict /kən'strɪkt/ v [T] 1 to make something narrower 2 to limit someone's freedom of action –**constricting** adj –**constriction** /-'strɪkʃən/ n [U]

con·struct /kən'strʌkt/ v [T] to build or make something: *a bridge constructed of metal and concrete*

con·struc·tion /kən'strʌkʃən/ n 1 [U] the business or work of building: *I work in the construction industry.* 2 [C] something that is built: *The conference centre is an enormous construction in the city centre.* 3 **under construction** being built: *Five new hotels are under construction.*

con·struc·tive /kən'strʌktɪv/ adj helping to improve or develop something: *She has a very constructive attitude to local problems.* –**constructively** adv

con·strue /kən'struː/ v construed, construing fml [T] to understand something in a certain way: *My comments were construed as criticism.*

con·sul /'kɒnsəl ‖ 'kɑːn-/ n an official who lives in a foreign city and works to help citizens of his or her own country there –**consular** /-sjₐləʳ ‖ -sələr/ adj

con·su·late /'kɒnsjₐlₐt ‖ 'kɑːnsələ̩t/ n the official building in which a consul lives or works

con·sult /kən'sʌlt/ v [T] 1 to go to a person or book for information or advice: *Have you consulted a doctor about your illness?* | *We need to consult a map.* 2 **consult with someone** to exchange opinions or information with someone: *I'll need to consult with my partner before making a decision.*

con·sul·tant /kən'sʌltənt/ n 1 an important hospital doctor who gives specialist advice 2 a person who gives specialist professional advice to others: *an industrial relations consultant* –**consultancy** n **consultancies** [C; U] : *He runs a computer consultancy firm.*

SPELLING NOTE

Words with the sound / k /, like **cut**, may be spelt **k-**, like **key**, or **qu-**, like **queen**.
Words with the sound / s /, like **city**, may be spelt **s-**, like **soon**, or **ps-**, like **psychology**.

---

con·sul·ta·tion /ˌkɒnsəl'teɪʃən ‖ ˌkɑːn-/ n 1 [C] a meeting held to exchange opinions and ideas: *We held a hurried consultation in the corridor.* 2 [U] an exchange of opinions or ideas: *The decision was made in consultation with the local police.* 3 [U] a search for information, usually in a book: *Dictionaries are available for consultation.*

con·sume /kən'sjuːm ‖ -'suːm/ v consumed, consuming [T] fml 1 to eat or drink something 2 to use something that cannot then be used again: *Arguing consumed too many hours of the committee's time.* | *The country produces far less than it consumes.* 3 (of a fire) to destroy something: *The buildings were consumed by flames.* 4 to fill the thoughts or feelings of someone continuously, especially in a damaging way: *She was consumed by guilt.*

con·sum·er /kən'sjuːməʳ ‖ -'suː-/ n a person who buys goods and uses services: *More laws are needed to protect consumers.*

con·sum·ing /kən'sjuːmɪŋ ‖ -'suː-/ adj [only before a noun] so strong that nothing else has the same importance: *Her consuming ambition is to be an opera singer.*

con·sum·mate¹ /kən'sʌmₐt/ adj fml extremely skilful: *He won the race with consummate ease.* | *a consummate liar*

con·sum·mate² /'kɒnsəmeɪt ‖ 'kɑːn-/ v consummated, consummating [T] fml 1 to make a marriage or relationship complete by having sex 2 to make something complete: *to consummate a business deal* –**consummation** /ˌkɒnsə'meɪʃən ‖ ˌkɑːn-/ n [C;U]

con·sump·tion /kən'sʌmpʃən/ n [U] 1 the act of eating or drinking something: *The food was declared unfit for human consumption.* 2 the use of something: *The nation's consumption of coal increased again last year.* 3 TUBERCULOSIS (a word no longer used in modern English)

cont. a word written at the bottom of a page to show that something continues on the next page; an abbreviation for **continued**

con·tact¹ /'kɒntækt ‖ 'kɑːn-/ n 1 [U] the state of touching or being close to a person or thing: *Have the other children been in contact with the disease?* | *The fire started when two wires came into contact.* 2 [U] the state of giving a message to someone or exchanging information and ideas: *The desert people have little contact with the outside world.* | *Have you been in contact with your lawyer recently?* | *He's trying to make contact with the ship by radio.* 3 [C] infml a person you know who can help you in some way: *I've got a contact in the tax office who I can phone.* 4 [C] a part that completes an electrical CIRCUIT when it touches another part

contact² v [T] to get a message to someone: *Do you know where I can contact him?*

contact lens /'·· ·/ n a very small plastic LENS which you put on your eye instead of wearing glasses

con·ta·gious /kən'teɪdʒəs/ adj 1 spread by touch (used of a disease) 2 spread quickly among people: *Her laughter was contagious.*

con·tain /kən'teɪn/ v [T] 1 to have something inside that may or may not be a part of it: *This bottle contains enough water for all of us.* | *a book containing all the information I needed* | *fertilizers containing nitrogen* 2 to keep something under control: *I tried to contain my anger.* | *Drastic measures are required to contain the disease.*

con·tain·er /kən'teɪnə^r/ n **1** a box, bottle, barrel, or any other object used for holding something **2** an extremely large metal box used for carrying goods by road, by sea, or on the railway

con·tam·i·nate /kən'tæm̩neɪt/ v **contaminated, contaminating** [T] to make something impure by mixing it with an unclean substance: *All our drinking water has been contaminated.* **–contamination** /kən₁tæm̩'neɪʃən/ n [U]: *radioactive contamination*

contd. a word written at the bottom of a page to show that something continues on the next page; an abbreviation for **continued**

con·tem·plate /'kɒntəmpleɪt ‖ 'kɑːn-/ v **contemplated, contemplating 1** [I;T] to consider something carefully for a long time: *He's contemplating his next move.* **2** [T] to consider doing something: *Have you ever contemplated leaving him?* □ USEFUL PATTERNS to contemplate something; to contemplate doing something **3** [T] *fml* to look thoughtfully at a person or thing

con·tem·pla·tion /₁kɒntəm'pleɪʃən ‖ ₁kɑːn-/ n [U] deep thought: *She spent an hour in quiet contemplation.* **–contemplative** /kən'templətɪv, 'kɒntəmpleɪtɪv ‖ kən'templətɪv, 'kɑːntəm₁pleɪtɪv/ adj: *He has a quiet, contemplative nature.*

con·tem·po·ra·ry¹ /kən'tempərəri, -pəri ‖ -pəreri/ adj **1** happening at the present time: *contemporary art* **2** belonging to the same time as something else that is mentioned: *I'm reading contemporary accounts of the war.*

contemporary² n **contemporaries** a person living or working at the same time as someone else: *Susan was a contemporary of mine at college.*

con·tempt /kən'tempt/ n [U] **1** total lack of respect for someone or something: *She gave me a look of utter contempt.* **2 beneath contempt** too unimportant or unworthy to think about at all: *Don't worry about what those boys say to you; they are completely beneath contempt.*

con·temp·ti·ble /kən'temptᵻbəl/ adj deserving a total lack of respect: *That was a contemptible trick to play on a friend!* **–contemptibly** adv

con·temp·tu·ous /kən'temptʃuəs/ adj feeling or expressing a total lack of respect for a person or thing: *She gave a contemptuous laugh.* **–contemptuously** adv

con·tend /kən'tend/ v **1** [T; + that] to claim that something is true: *The lawyer contended that she had not returned home until 11.00.* **2 contend with something** to deal with a problem: *I felt I had enough difficulties to contend with, without taking on someone else's problems.* **3** [I] to compete for something: *They are contending with each other for the party leadership.*

con·tend·er /kən'tendə^r/ n a person who takes part in a competition

con·tent¹ /kən'tent/ adj [never before a noun] satisfied and happy: *Dad seems really content since he retired.* | *She was content to let him deal with all the arrangements.* | *I'm very content with what I've got.*

content² v [T] **1** to make someone feel happy or satisfied **2 content yourself with something** to limit yourself to something and be satisfied with it: *John contented himself with one glass of wine.*

con·tent³ /'kɒntent ‖ 'kɑːn-/ n **1** [U] the subject matter of something: *It's not the style of the book I object to; it's the content.* **2** [sing] the amount of a

substance contained in something: *Oranges have a high water content.* **3 contents** [pl] the things that are contained in something: *The police emptied her bag and examined the contents.* | *He drank the entire contents of the bottle.* | *Check the chapter headings on the contents page.*

con·tent·ed /kən'tentᵻd/ adj satisfied and happy: *My father seems contented at last.* **–contentedly** adv **–contentment** n [U]

con·ten·tion /kən'tenʃən/ n **1** [U] argument and lack of agreement about something: *This is no time for contention.* **2** [C] a claim or opinion: *It is my contention that the plan will never succeed.* **3 in contention** competing to win

con·ten·tious /kən'tenʃəs/ adj fml likely to cause argument: *His proposal is rather contentious.*

con·test¹ /'kɒntest ‖ 'kɑːn-/ n **1** a competition or game: *a contest of skill* | *a beauty contest* **2** a struggle or fight: *the contest for leadership of the party*

con·test² /kən'test/ v [T] **1** to compete for something: *How many people are contesting this seat on the council?* **2** to argue about a decision: *I intend to contest the judge's decision in another court.*

con·tes·tant /kən'testənt/ n someone who is competing: *There are 50 contestants in the next race.*

con·text /'kɒntekst ‖ 'kɑːn-/ n **1** the words before and after a word or phrase: *You should be able to tell the meaning of this word from its context.* **2** the situation in which something happens: *You need to see the dispute in its political context.* **3 in context** in relation to the whole situation [RELATED PHRASE **out of context**: *My words were quoted out of context.*] **–contextual** /kən'tekstʃuəl/ adj

con·ti·nent /'kɒntᵻnənt ‖ 'kɑːn-/ n **1** any of the main large land masses on the earth: *the continent of Africa* **2 the Continent** BrE Europe without the British Isles: *You can't buy these on the Continent.* **–continental** /₁kɒntᵻ'nentl ‖ ₁kɑːn-/ adj

con·tin·gen·cy /kən'tɪndʒənsi/ n **contingencies** a possibility that might cause problems in the future: *We must be prepared for all contingencies.* | *contingency plans*

con·tin·gent¹ /kən'tɪndʒənt/ n [+ sing/pl verb] **1** a group of soldiers or police gathered together to help a larger force **2** a group of people who represent a country or organization: *Has the Scottish contingent arrived yet?*

contingent² adj fml **contingent on** dependent on something uncertain: *Our arrival time is contingent on the weather.*

con·tin·u·al /kən'tɪnjuəl/ adj repeated and frequent: *He has continual arguments with his father.* **–continually** adv

■ USAGE Compare **continual** and **continuous**. **Continual** usually describes repeated actions. These may be annoying actions: *Stop that continual hammering!* | *I'm tired of your continual complaints.* **Continuous** describes things that continue without a break: *I was exhausted after six hours of continuous driving.*

con·tin·u·a·tion /kən₁tɪnju'eɪʃən/ n **1** [U] the act of continuing something: *They voted against the continuation of this tax system.* **2** [C] something which follows something else and seems a part of it: *Her second book is a continuation of her autobiography.*

con·tin·ue /kən'tɪnjuː/ v **continued, continuing** [I;T] **1** to go on over a long period, without stopping: *The fighting continued for two days.* | *The company is hoping sales will continue at their present*

rate. | *He continued* **with** *his painting.* | *She continued to look at them in silence.* | *We continued washing the car.*

□ USEFUL PATTERNS to continue something; to continue with something; to continue to do something; to continue doing something

2 to start again after an interruption: *The play will continue in 15 minutes.* | *Are you going to continue gardening after dinner?*

□ USEFUL PATTERNS to continue something; to continue to do something; to continue doing something

3 to go further in the same direction: *This road continues on down the valley.*

con·tin·u·ous /kən'tɪnjuəs/ *adj* continuing without stopping: *The brain needs a continuous supply of blood.* –see CONTINUAL (USAGE) **–continuously** *adv* : *It rained continuously.* **–continuity** /ˌkɒntʃ'nju:ʃti ‖ ˌkɑːntʃ'nu:-/ *n* [U]

con·tort /kən'tɔːt ‖ -ɔːrt/ *v* [I;T] to twist violently out of shape: *Her face was contorted with anger.* **–contortion** /-'tɔːʃən ‖ -'tɔːr-/ *n* [C;U]

con·tour /'kɒntʊər ‖ 'kɑːn-/ *n* **1** (also **contours** (pl)) the shape of an area: *the contours* **of** *the British coast* **2** (also **contour line**) a line drawn on a map joining points of equal height

con·tra·band /'kɒntrəbænd ‖ 'kɑːn-/ *n* [U] goods brought into or out of a country illegally: *to trade in contraband*

con·tra·cep·tion /ˌkɒntrə'sepʃən ‖ ˌkɑːn-/ *n* [U] the practice of preventing sex from resulting in the woman becoming PREGNANT, and the methods for doing this: *Which method of contraception do you use?*

con·tra·cep·tive /ˌkɒntrə'septɪv ‖ ˌkɑːn-/ *n* a drug or object used as a means of preventing an act of sex from resulting in the woman becoming PREGNANT **–contraceptive** *adj*

con·tract[1] /'kɒntrækt ‖ 'kɑːn-/ *n* a formal legal agreement between people, usually in writing: *My lawyer is drawing up a contract which we should both sign.* **–contractual** /kən'træktʃuəl/ *adj* : *You have a contractual obligation to finish the building this month.* **–contractually** *adv*

con·tract[2] /kən'trækt/ *v* **1** [I;T] to make or become smaller or shorter: *Metal contracts as it becomes cool.* | *In conversational English "is not" often contracts to "isn't".* **2** [I;T] to arrange something by formal agreement: *They have contracted to build the new tunnel by 1997.* | *Have you contracted* **with** *a local builder?* | *I've been contracted to do the job.* **3** [T] to get a serious illness: *My son's contracted malaria.*

contract *sthg* ↔ **out** *phr v* [T] to employ another person or firm to do a job: *The work has been contracted out to a private company.*

con·trac·tion /kən'trækʃən/ *n* **1** [U] the process of getting smaller or shorter: **2** [U] the act of making something smaller or shorter **3** [C] the shortened form of a word or words; for example, "won't" is a contraction of "will not"

SPELLING NOTE

Words with the sound / k /, like **cut**, may be spelt **k-**, like **key**, or **qu-**, like **queen**.
Words with the sound / s /, like **city**, may be spelt **s-**, like **soon**, or **ps-**, like **psychology**.

---

con·trac·tor /kən'træktər ‖ 'kɑːntræk-/ *n* a person or business that works for other people or businesses: *a building contractor*

con·tra·dict /ˌkɒntrə'dɪkt ‖ ˌkɑːn-/ *v* **1** [I;T] to correct something that someone has said which you believe is wrong: *Don't contradict me!* **2** [T] to be in opposition or disagreement with something else so that one of the two must be false: *This report contradicts everything we've been told.* **–contradictory** *adj*

con·tra·dic·tion /ˌkɒntrə'dɪkʃən ‖ ˌkɑːn-/ *n* **1** [C;U] a difference between two facts, opinions, or qualities which means that they cannot both be true: *There is no contradiction* **between** *the Prime Minister's views and my own.* **2** [U] the act of saying that something is wrong or that the opposite is the truth: *I think I can say, without fear of contradiction, that this is of vital importance to all of us.* **3 a contradiction in terms** an impossible combination of words: *To say that he is an evil benefactor is a contradiction in terms.*

con·tral·to /kən'træltəʊ/ *n* **contraltos** the lowest female singing voice

con·trap·tion /kən'træpʃən/ *n* a strange machine or piece of apparatus: *I don't understand how this contraption works.*

con·tra·ry[1] /'kɒntrəri ‖ 'kɑːntreri/ *n* **1** **the contrary** *fml* the opposite: *They say he is guilty, but I believe the contrary.* **2** **on the contrary** a phrase used to express a strong opposite to what has just been said: *"I hear you like your new job." "On the contrary, it's rather boring."* **3** **to the contrary** that something else is true: *You may be right; there's no evidence to the contrary.*

■ USAGE Compare **on the contrary**, **on the other hand**, **in contrast**. We use **on the contrary** to show that an idea which came before is completely wrong: *"Tom is a good student, isn't he?" "On the contrary, he's lazy and stupid."* We use **on the other hand** to add an idea which is different but is part of a single general picture: *"Dick did badly in the examination. On the other hand, his classwork is excellent."* We use **in contrast** to show that two people or things are completely, and surprisingly, different: *"Harry's work is poor, but in contrast, his sister's work is excellent."*

contrary[2] *adj* **1** opposing: *contrary opinions* **2** **contrary to** a phrase used to state that something is not true before expressing an opposite view which is true: *Contrary to popular belief, the sun does sometimes shine in Britain!*

con·trar·y[3] /kən'treəri/ *adj* unreasonable (used of a person): *Don't be so contrary!*

con·trast[1] /'kɒntrɑːst ‖ 'kɑːntræst/ *n* **1** [C;U] difference between people or things that are compared: *I've never seen such a contrast* **between** *brother and sister.* **2** **by contrast**, **in contrast** when compared with something else in order to show the difference: *The Labour Party supports state control of key services. The Conservative Party, by contrast, has decided to privatize them.* –see CONTRARY[1] (USAGE)

con·trast[2] /kən'trɑːst ‖ -'træst/ *v* **1** [T] to compare two people or things so that differences are made clear: *In this book the writer contrasts two views of management.* | *Compare and contrast Mrs Thatcher's policies* **with** *those of Mr Major.* **2** [I] to show a difference when compared: *His attitudes contrast sharply* **with** *my own.*

con·tra·vene /ˌkɒntrəˈviːn ‖ ˌkɑːn-/ v **contravened, contravening** [T] to break a law or a rule: *Your behaviour contravened the laws of the country.* –**contravention** /-ˈvenʃən/ n [C;U]

con·trib·ute /kənˈtrɪbjuːt/ v **contributed, contributing 1** [I;T] to join with others in giving money for a person or cause: *Everybody contributed a pound towards Jane's present.* | *Would you like to contribute?* **2** [I] to help cause something: *Luck and a good family background contributed to his success.* **3** [I;T] to write something for a magazine or newspaper –**contribution** /ˌkɒntrɪˈbjuːʃən ‖ ˌkɑːn-/ [C;U] n : *Would you like to make a contribution to our funds?* | *Everyone acknowledges his contribution to Russian literature.* –**contributor** /kən ˈtrɪbjətəʳ/ n : *a regular contributor to our magazine*

con·trib·u·to·ry /kənˈtrɪbjətəri ‖ -tɔːri/ adj **1** [only before a noun] helping to bring about a result: *a contributory factor in his downfall* **2** paid for by the workers as well as by the employer (used of a PENSION or insurance plan)

con·trite /ˈkɒntraɪt ‖ ˈkɑːn-/ adj old fash or lit showing guilt or sorrow for your actions: *a contrite apology* –**contritely** adv –**contrition** /kənˈtrɪʃən/ n [U]

con·trive /kənˈtraɪv/ v **contrived, contriving 1 contrive to do something** to succeed in doing something in spite of difficulty: *She finally contrived to escape.* **2** [T] to succeed in making something happen in spite of difficulty: *He actually contrived a meeting with the Queen!*

con·trived /kənˈtraɪvd/ adj unnatural and forced: *Her smile was polite, but rather contrived.*

con·trol¹ /kənˈtrəʊl/ v **-ll-** [T] to have direct influence or power over something: *The pressure of steam in the engine is controlled by this button.* | *He wasn't a bad teacher, but he couldn't control his class.* | *I realize that you are angry, but please try to control yourself.*

control² n **1** [U] the power to command or influence: *Which party has control of the town council?* | *Don't worry; I am in full control of the situation.* | *He lost control of the steering and his car ran into a tree.* | *George took control of the business when his father died.* **2** [C;U] a method or system used to direct or influence something in a particular way: *Where's the volume control on this radio?* | *government control over industry* | *price controls* **3** [C] the place from which a machine or system is controlled: *Passport control is to your left.* **4 in control** in command: *Who's in control here?* **5 out of control** in a state in which no proper direction is possible: *The car went out of control and crashed.* **6 under control** made to behave properly after being in a dangerous or confused state: *The firemen finally got the fire under control.* | *It took the teacher months to bring her class under control.* **7** [C] a standard against which scientific results are compared –**controller** n

con·tro·ver·sial /ˌkɒntrəˈvɜːʃəl◂ ‖ ˌkɑːntrəˈvɜːrʃəl/ adj causing a lot of argument or disagreement: *a controversial decision* –**controversially** adv

con·tro·ver·sy /ˈkɒntrəvɜːsi, kənˈtrɒvəsi ‖ ˈkɑːntrəvɜːrsi/ n -**controversies** [C;U] a lot of argument and disagreement about something: *The new proposal has caused an enormous amount of controversy.* | *I am referring to recent controversies over the tax system.*

co·nun·drum /kəˈnʌndrəm/ n a confusing and difficult problem

con·ur·ba·tion /ˌkɒnɜːˈbeɪʃən ‖ ˌkɑːnɜːr-/ n a number of towns that have spread and joined together into one area, often with a large city as its centre

con·va·lesce /ˌkɒnvəˈles ‖ ˌkɑːn-/ v **convalesced, convalescing** [I] to spend time getting well after an illness: *We're sending Nan to the seaside to convalesce.*

con·va·les·cence /ˌkɒnvəˈlesəns ‖ ˌkɑːn-/ n [sing;U] the period of time you spend getting well again after an illness

con·va·les·cent /ˌkɒnvəˈlesənt ‖ ˌkɑːn-/ n a person spending time getting well again after an illness –**convalescent** adj : *a convalescent nursing home*

con·vec·tion /kənˈvekʃən/ n [U] the movement caused by warm gas or liquid rising, and cold gas or liquid sinking: *a convection heater* | *Warm air rises by convection.*

con·vene /kənˈviːn/ v **convened, convening** fml **1** [I] to meet: *The ministers convened for an emergency session.* **2** [T] to call a group or committee to a meeting: *The chairman has convened a meeting for next Wednesday.*

con·ve·ni·ence /kənˈviːniəns/ n **1** [U] qualities which make something right for a particular purpose: *We bought this house for its convenience.* **2** [C] something which makes things easy or comfortable for the user: *This kitchen has every modern convenience.* **3** [U] personal comfort or advantage: *He thinks only of his own convenience.* **4 at your convenience** at a time which is suitable for you

convenience food /·ˈ··· ˌ·/ n [C;U] food which is very easy to prepare and can be used at any time, like a whole meal in one packet

con·ve·ni·ent /kənˈviːniənt/ adj **1** suited to your needs or to the situation: *What's a convenient time for you?* **2** usefully near: *Our house is very convenient for the shops.* –opposite **inconvenient** –**conveniently** adv

con·vent /ˈkɒnvənt ‖ ˈkɑːnvent/ n a place where religious women called nuns (NUN) live or teach

con·ven·tion /kənˈvenʃən/ n **1** [C;U] the generally accepted way of doing things, especially with regard to social behaviour: *It is a matter of convention rather than a strict rule.* | *He ignores stylistic conventions when he writes.* –see HABIT (USAGE) **2** [C] a meeting of people with a shared purpose: *a teachers' convention* **3** [C] a formal agreement between countries: *Britain has agreed to sign the convention.*

con·ven·tion·al /kənˈvenʃənəl/ adj **1** following accepted customs and standards, sometimes too closely: *He's an old-fashioned man with conventional ideas.* | *conventional Western medicine* –opposite **unconventional 2** not NUCLEAR (used of weapons) –**conventionally** adv

con·verge /kənˈvɜːdʒ ‖ -ɜːr-/ v **converged, converging** [I] to come together towards the same point: *The roads converge just before the station.* | *Crowds are converging on the stadium.* –**convergent** adj –**convergence** n [C;U]

con·ver·sant /kənˈvɜːsənt ‖ -ɜːr-/ adj fml **conversant with** familiar with: *I'm not conversant with the rules yet.*

con·ver·sa·tion /ˌkɒnvəˈseɪʃən ‖ ˌkɑːnvər-/ n [C;U] **1** an informal talk in which people exchange news, feelings, and thoughts: *a private conversation* | *a telephone conversation* | *How can I make polite*

conversation with someone I dislike? **2 in conversation with** *fml* talking to someone –**conversational** *adj* : *conversational English* –**conversationally** *adv*

con·verse /kən'vɜːs ‖ -ɜːrs/ *v* **conversed, conversing** [I] *fml* to talk informally

con·ver·sion /kən'vɜːʃən ‖ -'vɜːrʒən/ *n* [C;U] **1** a change from one purpose or system to another: *the conversion of a house* **into** *flats* | *He did a quick conversion from yards into metres.* **2** a change in which a person accepts a new religion or belief completely: *His conversion* **to** *Islam was unexpected.*

con·vert[1] /kən'vɜːt ‖ -ɜːrt/ *v* [I;T] **1** to change into another form, state or system: *Coal can be converted* **to** *gas.* | *This seat converts* **into** *a bed.* | *I want to convert some dollars into pounds.* | *They are living in a converted barn.* **2** to accept, or persuade another person to accept, a particular religion, belief, or opinion: *Anne has converted* **to** *Christianity* | *John was converted to Buddhism by a Thai priest.* | *My son has finally converted me to pop music.*

con·vert[2] /'kɒnvɜːt ‖ 'kɑːnvɜːrt/ *n* a person who has been persuaded to accept a particular religion or belief

con·ver·ti·ble[1] /kən'vɜːtɪbəl ‖ -ɜːrt-/ *adj* **1** able to be changed into another form: *This bed is easily convertible* **into** *a sofa.* **2** able to be freely exchanged (used of types of money): *The local currency is not convertible, so you'd better take some dollars.*

convertible[2] *n* a car with a roof that can be folded back

con·vex /ˌkɒn'veks◂, kən- ‖ ˌkɑːn'veks◂, kən-/ *adj tech* curved outwards: *a convex mirror* –opposite **concave**

con·vey /kən'veɪ/ *v* [T] **1** *fml* to take or carry something from one place to another: *We were conveyed to the palace in a fleet of Jaguars.* **2** to make your feelings, ideas or thoughts known to other people: *I can't convey how angry I feel.*

con·vey·er belt /·'·· ·/ *n* (also **conveyor belt**) an endless moving belt that carries objects from one place to another

con·vict[1] /kən'vɪkt/ *v* [T] to declare that someone is guilty of a crime after a trial in a court: *They were convicted* **of** *murder.* | *He's a convicted criminal.*

con·vict[2] /'kɒnvɪkt ‖ 'kɑːn-/ *n* a person who has been declared guilty of a crime and sent to prison, especially for a long time: *an escaped convict*

con·vic·tion /kən'vɪkʃən/ *n* [C;U] **1** the act of finding someone guilty of a crime after a trial in a court: *After conviction, he appealed to a higher court.* | *This was her third conviction for stealing.* **2** very firm and sincere belief: *a man of strong convictions* | *She was speaking from conviction.*

con·vince /kən'vɪns/ *v* **convinced, convincing** [T] **1** to make someone believe something: *It took them hours to convince me* **of** *his guilt.* | *It was hard to convince the children that we couldn't afford to keep a pet.*

☐ USEFUL PATTERNS to convince someone of something; to convince someone that…

2 be convinced that to be completely certain about something: *I was absolutely convinced he was telling the truth.*

■ USAGE **Compare convince and persuade.** These are normally used in different ways. **Convince** means "make someone believe something" and it does not have **to** after it: *The politician con- vinced me that his party was the best.* **Persuade** means "make someone willing to do something" and it often has **to** after it: *The politician* **persuaded** *me to join him his party.* **2 Convince** is sometimes used in a similar way to **persuade**, though some people consider that this is incorrect: *They finally con- vinced me to leave my job.*

con·vinc·ing /kən'vɪnsɪŋ/ *adj* so good that you feel something must be true: *a convincing explanation* –opposite **unconvincing** –**convincingly** *adv*

con·viv·i·al /kən'vɪviəl/ *adj fml* pleasantly merry and friendly: *a very convivial evening* –**conviv- iality** /kənˌvɪvi'ælɨti / *n* [U]

con·vo·lut·ed /'kɒnvəluːtɨd ‖ 'kɑːn-/ *adj fml* difficult to understand: *convoluted arguments*

con·voy /'kɒnvɔɪ ‖ 'kɑːn-/ *n* [+ sing/pl verb] **1** a group of ships or vehicles travelling together: *The convoy was attacked by rebels.* **2 in convoy** travel- ling together: *They were travelling in convoy.*

con·vulse /kən'vʌls/ *v* **convulsed, convulsing** *fml* [I;T] to shake violently: *We were convulsed with laughter.*

con·vul·sion /kən'vʌlʃən/ *n* an unnaturally violent and sudden movement caused by illness: *She occa- sionally has terrible convulsions.* –**convulsive** /-sɪv/ *adj*

coo /kuː/ *v* [I] **1** to make a sound like the low soft cry of a DOVE or PIGEON **2** to make soft, loving noises: *She cooed over the new baby.*

cook[1] /kʊk/ *v* **1** [I;T] to prepare food for eating by us- ing heat: *I enjoy cooking.* | *He's cooking dinner for me tonight.* | *Shall we cook the vegetables or eat them raw?* **2** [I] to be prepared by using heat (used of food): *Make sure this meat cooks for at least an hour.* **3 be cooking** *infml* to be being planned without your knowledge –**cooking** *n* [U] : *Do you like En- glish cooking?*

■ USAGE We can **cook** food in several different ways. We can **bake** bread using dry heat in an **oven**. We can **roast** meat in an oven or over an open fire. We can **grill** pieces of meat, or **toast** thin, flat pieces of bread under direct heat (from a **grill**). We can **boil** potatoes or **stew** meat using a pot filled with water. If the food boils very slowly it **simmers**. We can **braise** meat and vegetables by cooking them slowly in a covered pot with fat and water. We can **steam** vegetables by cooking them over water in a raised container so that the water does not touch them directly. We can **fry** eggs, meat and potatoes by cooking them in hot fat or oil.

cook sthg ↔ **up** *phr v* [T] *infml* **1** to invent some- thing that is not true: *She cooked up an excuse about her parents being ill.* **2** to plan something which is often secret and not completely honest: *He's cooked up a scheme to get rich quickly.*

cook[2] *n* a person who prepares and cooks food: *My mother's a wonderful cook.*

cook-chill /ˌ· '·◂/ *adj* **cook-chill food** food which is prepared in advance; it is cooked, made cool very quickly, and then warmed up when you want to eat it

cook·er /ˈkʊkəʳ/ n BrE an apparatus on which food is cooked

cook·e·ry /ˈkʊkəri/ n [U] the art or activity of preparing food: *cookery lessons* | *a cookery book*

cook·ie /ˈkʊki/ n (also **cooky**) **1** the usual American word for a BISCUIT **2** AmE infml a person of a particular type: *a clever cookie*

cool¹ /kuːl/ adj **1** slightly cold: *a cool day* **2** pleasantly cold: *a cool drink* | *It was lovely and cool in the shade.* **3** calm and unexcited: *Keep cool and do your best.* **4** not as friendly as usual: *Charles has been very cool towards me recently.* **5** **keep a cool head** to stay calm so that you can think clearly –**coolly** /ˈkuːl-li/ adv –**coolness** n [U]

cool² v [I;T] **1** to become or to make something slightly colder: *Leave the mixture to cool.* | *Cool your forehead with a damp cloth.* **2 cool it** infml keep calm

cool down phr v [I:T **cool** sbdy/sthg ↔ **down**] to become calmer, or to make someone calmer: *Cool down and we'll discuss it later.* | *Try and cool her down before she does anything stupid.*

cool off phr v [I] to become less hot: *I need to cool off in the shade.*

coop¹ /kuːp/ n a cage for hens: *a chicken coop*

coop² v

coop sbdy/sthg ↔ **up** phr v [T] to shut into a small space: *We were cooped up in that tiny room for days.*

co·op·e·rate /kəʊˈɒpəreɪt ‖ -ˈɑːp-/ v **cooperated, cooperating** (also **co-operate**) [I] **1** to work or act together for a shared purpose: *The British cooperated with the French in building the tunnel.* **2** to do what someone wants you to do: *I needed help, but he simply wouldn't cooperate.*

co·op·e·ra·tion /kəʊˌɒpəˈreɪʃən ‖ -ˌɑːp-/ n (also **co-operation**) [U] **1** the act of working together for a shared purpose: *The film was produced in cooperation with the BBC.* **2** willingness to work together: *Thank you for your cooperation.*

co·op·e·ra·tive¹ /kəʊˈɒpərətɪv ‖ -ˈɑːp-/ adj (also **co-operative**) **1** willing to help: *The teacher thanked them for being so cooperative.* –opposite **uncooperative 2** done or owned by people working together: *a cooperative farm* –**cooperatively** adv

cooperative² n a firm, farm, or shop owned and operated by people working together: *The business has become a cooperative.*

co-opt /ˌkəʊ ˈɒpt ‖ -ˈɑːpt/ v [T] to choose someone to join a committee by the votes of existing members: *I've been co-opted onto the board of governors.*

co·or·di·nate¹ /kəʊˈɔːdɪneɪt ‖ -ˈɔːr-/ v **coordinated, coordinating** [T] to organize people or things so that they work together effectively: *We need to coordinate our efforts.*

co·or·din·ate² /kəʊˈɔːdɪn̩t ‖ -ˈɔːr-/ n tech one of a set of numbers or letters that give the exact position of a point on a map

co·or·di·na·tion /kəʊˌɔːdɪˈneɪʃən ‖ -ˌɔːr-/ n [U] **1** the organization of people or things so that they work together effectively **2** the way in which muscles work together when performing a movement: *Dancers need good coordination.*

coot /kuːt/ n a small black water bird with a white spot on its forehead

cop¹ /kɒp ‖ kɑːp/ n infml a police officer

cop² v **-pp-**

cop out phr v [I] infml to avoid doing something that

you should do: *He promised to help and now he's trying to cop out of it!* –**cop-out** /ˈ··/ n : *Writing instead of phoning is a real cop-out!*

cope /kəʊp/ v **coped, coping** [I] to deal successfully with something: *Can you cope with all this work?* | *She has so many problems, it's no wonder she can't cope.*

co·pi·ous /ˈkəʊpiəs/ adj a lot of something: *He takes copious notes.* –**copiously** adv

cop·per /ˈkɒpəʳ ‖ ˈkɑː-/ n **1** [U] a soft reddish metal **2** [U] a reddish-brown colour **3** [C] BrE infml a coin of low value made of brown metal: *Can you lend me a few coppers?* **4** [C] infml a police officer

copse /kɒps ‖ kɑːps/ n a small wood of trees or bushes

cop·u·late /ˈkɒpjᵿleɪt ‖ ˈkɑːp-/ v **copulated, copulating** [I] fml to have sex –**copulation** /ˌkɒpjᵿˈleɪʃən ‖ ˌkɑːp-/ n [U]

cop·y¹ /ˈkɒpi ‖ ˈkɑːpi/ n **copies 1** [C] something that is made to look exactly like something else: *I need four copies of this letter.* | *That's a good copy of a Picasso.* **2** [C] a single example of a magazine, book, or newspaper: *Have you seen my copy of "The Times"?* **3** [U] tech written material to be printed: *All copy must reach the editor by tomorrow at the latest.* | *advertising copy* | *a copy editor*

copy² v **copied, copying 1** [T] to make something that looks exactly like something else: *Could you copy these documents?* **2** [T] to do something or behave like someone else: *Jean always copies the way I dress.* **3** [I;T] to cheat by writing exactly the same thing as someone else: *He was caught copying in the maths test.*

copy sthg ↔ **down** phr v [T] to write down exactly what someone has said

copy sthg ↔ **out** phr v [T] to write something exactly as it is written elsewhere: *I want you to copy out the graph in your exercise books.*

cop·y·right /ˈkɒpiraɪt ‖ ˈkɑː-/ n [C;U] the right in law to produce or sell a book, play, film, or record for a fixed period of time: *Who owns the copyright on your book?*

cor·al /ˈkɒrəl ‖ ˈkɔː-, ˈkɑː-/ n [U] a white, pink, or reddish substance formed from the bones of very small sea animals, often used for making jewellery

cord /kɔːd ‖ kɔːrd/ n **1** [C;U] a piece of thick string or thin rope **2** [C;U] a piece of wire with a protective covering, for connecting electrical apparatus to the electricity supply **3** [C] a part of the body which looks like a piece of string: *the spinal cord* | *her vocal cords* **4 cords** [pl] infml trousers made from corduroy

cor·di·al¹ /ˈkɔːdiəl ‖ ˈkɔːrdʒəl/ adj fml friendly: *a cordial welcome* | *a cordial invitation* –**cordiality** /ˌkɔːdiˈælᵻti ‖ ˌkɔːrdʒiˈæ-, ˌkɔːrˈdʒæ-/ n [U] –**cordially** adv

cor·di·al² n [C;U] fruit juice to which water is added before drinking: *lime cordial*

cor·don /ˈkɔːdn ‖ ˈkɔːrdn/ n a line or ring of police, soldiers, or military vehicles placed around an area to protect or enclose it

cordon sthg ↔ **off** phr v [T] to enclose an area with a line or ring of police, soldiers, or military vehicles: *The whole area has been cordoned off.*

cor·du·roy /ˈkɔːdʒᵿroɪ, -djᵿ- ‖ ˈkɔːrdərɔɪ/ n [U] thick, strong cotton cloth with raised lines on one side: *a corduroy jacket* | *a pair of corduroy trousers*

core¹ /kɔːʳ/ n **1** the hard central part of certain fruits, which contains the seeds: *Throw away that old apple core.* **2** the central part of something: *the*

earth's core **3 to the core** completely: *She's American to the core.* **4** the most important part of something: *the core of the problem*

core² *v* **cored, coring** [T] to remove the hard central part from a fruit

cork¹ /kɔːk ‖ kɔːrk/ *n* **1** [U] a light material which forms the outer skin of a particular tree trunk and is used for making things like table mats **2** [C] a round piece of this material which is put into the neck of a bottle, especially one containing wine, to close it tightly

cork² *v* [T] to close a bottle tightly by putting a cork in the top of it −opposite **uncork**

cork·screw /ˈkɔːkskruː ‖ ˈkɔːrk-/ *n* a tool made of twisted metal with a handle, used for pulling corks out of bottles −see picture on page 638

corn /kɔːn ‖ kɔːrn/ *n* **1** [U] *BrE* the seed of any of various types of grain plants, especially wheat **2** [U] *AmE* (also **maize, sweet corn** *BrE*) the seed of a tall plant grown, especially in America and Australia, for its ears of yellow seeds −see picture on page 344 **3** [C] a painful area of hard, thick skin on your foot, usually on or near a toe

cor·ner¹ /ˈkɔːnəʳ ‖ ˈkɔːrn-/ *n* **1** the point at which two lines, surfaces, or edges meet: *in the corner of the room* | *in the bottom left-hand corner of the page* | *He fell and banged his head on the corner of the table.* | *How many corners does a hexagon have?* **2** the place where two roads, paths, or streets meet: *I'll meet you on the corner of Smith Street and Beach Road.* | *She waited for him on the corner.* **3** a distant part of the world: *People came from all corners of the earth to hear her sing.* **4** (also **corner kick** /ˈ··· ·/) a kick taken from the corner of the field in football **5 in a tight corner** in a difficult or threatening situation from which it is hard to escape

corner² *v* **1** [T] to force a person or animal into a difficult situation from which it is hard to escape: *He was cornered behind the bicycle shed.* **2 corner the market** to gain control of the buying, selling, or production of goods: *They have now cornered the market in leather goods.* **3** [I] (of a vehicle or driver) to turn a corner: *My car corners well, even on wet roads.*

cor·ner·stone /ˈkɔːnəstəʊn ‖ ˈkɔːrnər-/ *n* **1** a stone set at one of the bottom corners of a building, often as part of a special ceremony **2** something important on which something else depends: *Free speech is the cornerstone of democracy.*

cor·net /ˈkɔːnɪt ‖ kɔːrˈnet/ *n* **1** a small, brass, musical instrument like a TRUMPET **2** *BrE* (also **cone**) a thin container for ICE-CREAM which is pointed at one end and is eaten with its contents

corn·flakes /ˈkɔːnfleɪks ‖ ˈkɔːrn-/ *n* [pl] breakfast food made from crushed corn and usually eaten with milk and sugar

corn·flour /ˈkɔːnflaʊəʳ ‖ ˈkɔːrn-/ *n* [U] a fine flour made from crushed corn or other grain and used in cooking to thicken liquids

cor·nice /ˈkɔːnɪs ‖ ˈkɔːrn-/ *n* a decorative border along the top edge of the front of a building or PILLAR or round the top of the walls in a room

---

SPELLING NOTE

Words with the sound / k /, like **cut**, may be spelt **k-**, like **key**, or **qu-**, like **queen**.
Words with the sound / s /, like **city**, may be spelt **s-**, like **soon**, or **ps-**, like **psychology**.

---

corn·y /ˈkɔːni ‖ ˈkɔːrni/ *adj* **cornier, corniest** *infml* too familiar, simple, or old-fashioned to be interesting: *a corny joke* | *a corny film*

co·rol·la·ry /kəˈrɒləri ‖ ˈkɔːrəleri, ˈkɑː-/ *n* **corollaries** *fml* a statement or course of action that is a direct result of another one

cor·o·na·ry¹ /ˈkɒrənəri ‖ ˈkɔːrəneri, ˈkɑː-/ *adj* [always before a noun] *tech* related to the heart

coronary² *n* **coronaries** (also **coronary thrombosis** *fml*) a HEART ATTACK caused when the blood supply to your heart is blocked

cor·o·na·tion /ˌkɒrəˈneɪʃən ‖ ˌkɔː-, ˌkɑː-/ *n* the ceremony at which a person officially becomes king or queen

cor·o·ner /ˈkɒrənəʳ ‖ ˈkɔː-, ˈkɑː-/ *n* an official who inquires into the causes of an accidental or unexpected death

cor·o·net /ˈkɒrənɪt ‖ ˌkɔːrəˈnet, ˌkɑː-/ *n* a small decorative covering worn on the heads of princes or members of noble families

cor·po·ral¹ /ˈkɔːpərəl ‖ ˈkɔːr-/ *n* a person of low rank in the army or airforce

corporal pun·ish·ment /ˌ··· ·ˈ···/ *n* physical punishment, usually hitting someone: *Corporal punishment is no longer permitted in schools.*

cor·po·rate /ˈkɔːpərɪt ‖ ˈkɔːr-/ *adj* **1** belonging to or shared by all the members of a group: *corporate responsibility* | *a corporate effort* **2** belonging to or related to a corporation −**corporately** *adv*

cor·po·ra·tion /ˌkɔːpəˈreɪʃən ‖ ˌkɔːr-/ *n* **1** a large business organization: *John works for a large American chemical corporation.* | *the British Broadcasting Corporation* **2** [+ sing/pl verb] *BrE* a group of people elected to govern a town: *The corporation is in financial trouble.*

corps /kɔːʳ/ *n* [plural is **corps** /kɔːz ‖ kɔːrz/] **1** (also **Corps**) a trained army group with special duties: *the medical corps* **2** a group of people united in the same activity: *the president's press corps* | *the diplomatic corps*

corpse /kɔːps ‖ kɔːrps/ *n* a dead body

cor·pu·lent /ˈkɔːpjʊlənt ‖ ˈkɔːrp-/ *adj* *fml* very fat −**corpulence** *n* [U]

cor·pus /ˈkɔːpəs ‖ ˈkɔːr-/ *n* **corpora** /ˈkɔːpərə ‖ ˈkɔːr-/ or **corpuses** a collection of all the writings of a special kind: *the corpus of Shakespeare's works*

cor·pus·cle /ˈkɔːpəsəl, kɔːˈpʌ- ‖ ˈkɔːrpə-/ *n* any of the red or white cells in your blood

cor·ral /kɒˈrɑːl, kə- ‖ kəˈræl/ *n* an enclosed area where cattle or horses are kept, especially in the US

cor·rect¹ /kəˈrekt/ *adj* **1** without mistakes: *a correct answer* | *correct spelling* **2** following proper standards of manners: *correct behaviour* −opposite **incorrect** −**correctly** *adv* −**correctness** *n* [U]

correct² *v* [T] to make something right or better: *Correct my spelling if it's wrong.* | *She'll need glasses to correct her eyesight.*

cor·rec·tion /kəˈrekʃən/ *n* **1** [C] a change that makes something right or better: *I'll show you the mistakes, but I want you to make the corrections.* **2** [U] the activity of making something right or better: *speech correction* **3** [U] *old fash* punishment −**corrective** /-tɪv/ *adj* : *corrective surgery*

cor·re·la·tion /ˌkɒrɪˈleɪʃən ‖ ˌkɔː-, ˌkɑː-/ *n* a relationship in which two things happen together and may have an effect on each other: *a high correlation between unemployment and crime* –**correlate** /ˈkɒrəleɪt ‖ ˈkɔː-, ˈkɑː-/ *v* **correlated, correlating** [I;T]

cor·re·spond /ˌkɒrɪˈspɒnd ‖ ˌkɔːrɪˈspɑːnd, ˌkɑː-/ *v* [I] **1** to be in agreement with something: *These goods don't correspond with the list of the ones I ordered.* | *These two lists don't correspond.* **2** to be equal to something: *An M.A. in Scotland corresponds to a B.A. from an English university.* **3** to exchange letters regularly: *Janet and Bob corresponded for many years.* | *I haven't corresponded with any of my old school friends for years.*

cor·re·spon·dence /ˌkɒrɪˈspɒndəns ‖ ˌkɔːrɪˈspɑːn-, ˌkɑː-/ *n* [sing;U] **1** the activity of writing or exchanging letters: *I need a secretary to help with my correspondence.* **2** the letters exchanged between people: *The library bought all the correspondence between Queen Victoria and her daughters.* **3** agreement or similarity between particular things: *There is little correspondence between her public statements and reality.* **4 correspondence course** a course of lessons that you receive by post and do at home

cor·re·spon·dent /ˌkɒrɪˈspɒndənt ‖ ˌkɔːrɪˈspɑːn-, ˌkɑː-/ *n* **1** a person with whom another person exchanges letters regularly **2** someone employed by a newspaper or by television to report news from a distant area or on a particular subject: *a war correspondent* | *our correspondent in Rome*

cor·re·spon·ding /ˌkɒrɪˈspɒndɪŋ◂ ‖ ˌkɔːrɪˈspɑːn-, ˌkɑː-/ *adj* [only before a noun] similar or related: *Profits for the first three months are 50% higher than in the corresponding period last year.* –**correspondingly** *adv*

cor·ri·dor /ˈkɒrɪdɔːʳ ‖ ˈkɔːrɪdər, ˈkɑː-/ *n* **1** a passage between two rows of rooms: *Room 101 is at the end of the corridor.* **2** a narrow piece of land that passes through a foreign country

cor·rob·o·rate /kəˈrɒbəreɪt ‖ kəˈrɑː-/ *v* **corroborated, corroborating** [T] to support an opinion or claim with additional information or proof: *Several people who saw the accident corroborated the driver's statement.* –**corroborative** *adj : corroborative evidence* –**corroboration** /kəˌrɒbəˈreɪʃən ‖ kəˌrɑː-/ *n* [U]

cor·rode /kəˈrəʊd/ *v* **corroded, corroding** [I;T] to destroy or be destroyed slowly, especially by chemicals: *Acid causes metal to corrode.* | *Acid corrodes metal.* –**corrosive** /-sɪv/ *adj*

cor·ro·sion /kəˈrəʊʒən/ *n* [U] **1** the process of becoming slowly destroyed by chemicals **2** a substance, such as RUST, which is produced as a result of this process: *corrosion on the body of a car*

cor·ru·ga·ted /ˈkɒrəgeɪtɪd ‖ ˈkɔː-, ˈkɑː-/ *adj* formed in rows of folds that look like waves: *a corrugated iron roof*

cor·rupt¹ /kəˈrʌpt/ *adj* **1** dishonest and prepared to receive money to do things that are wrong or illegal: *a corrupt judge* **2** immoral or bad: *a corrupt political system* **3** containing mistakes and having less value than the original: *They spoke a corrupt form of French.* | *a corrupt computer disk* –**corruptly** *adv* –**corruptness** *n* [U]

corrupt² *v* [T] **1** to cause a person to become dishonest or immoral: *He has been corrupted by power.* **2** to change the original form of something so that it has less value: *Our language has been corrupted by the introduction of foreign words.* –**corruptible** *adj* –**corruptibility** /kəˌrʌptɪˈbɪlɪti / *n* [U]

cor·rup·tion /kəˈrʌpʃən/ *n* [U] **1** the act or process of making someone dishonest or immoral **2** dishonest or immoral behaviour: *the corruption of the ancient Roman court*

cor·set /ˈkɔːsɪt ‖ ˈkɔːr-/ *n* a very tight-fitting undergarment worn by women to give shape to their body –**corseted** *adj*

cor·tege cortège /kɔːˈteɪʒ ‖ kɔːrˈteʒ/ *n fml* a procession of attendants, especially at a funeral

cosh /kɒʃ ‖ kɑːʃ/ *n BrE infml* a short hard stick which is used as a weapon

cos·met·ic¹ /kɒzˈmetɪk ‖ kɑːz-/ *n* a substance such as a cream or powder, which is intended to make a woman's skin more beautiful: *They sell lipsticks, eye shadow, and a whole range of other cosmetics.*

cosmetic² *adj* **1** intended to make your skin or body more beautiful: *a cosmetic cream* | *cosmetic surgery* **2** dealing only with the appearance of something rather than what is really important: *cosmetic changes to the law*

cos·mic /ˈkɒzmɪk ‖ ˈkɑːz-/ *adj* belonging or related to the whole universe –**cosmically** /-kli/ *adv*

cos·mo·naut /ˈkɒzmənɔːt ‖ ˈkɑːz-/ *n* a Soviet ASTRONAUT

cos·mo·pol·i·tan /ˌkɒzməˈpɒlɪtən ‖ ˌkɑːzməˈpɑː-/ *adj* **1** consisting of people from many different parts of the world: *London is a very cosmopolitan city.* **2** showing wide experience of different people and places: *a cosmopolitan outlook on life*

cos·mos /ˈkɒzmɒs ‖ ˈkɑːzməs/ *n* **the cosmos** the universe considered as an ordered system

cos·set /ˈkɒsɪt ‖ ˈkɑː-/ *v* [T] to pay a great deal of attention, sometimes too much, to making a person comfortable and contented

cost¹ /kɒst ‖ kɔːst/ *n* **1** [C] the amount of money paid or needed to buy, do, or produce something: *Think about the cost of bringing up a child!* | *The students are given £100 a year to cover the cost of books and stationery.* | *Our production costs are rising faster than we can increase prices.* **2** [sing] something needed, given, or lost in order to obtain something: *War is never worth the terrible cost in human life.* **3 at all costs, at any cost** no matter what the cost or result might be: *We must avoid war at all costs.* **4 to someone's cost** from your own unpleasant experience: *Drinking dirty water can be very dangerous, as I found out to my cost.*

■ USAGE Compare **cost** and **price**. **Cost** often means the money you pay for a service: *the cost of having a car repaired* but we can also use it for very general things: *the cost of living*. **Price** usually means the money you pay for a particular object: *What is the price of this watch?*

cost² *v* **cost, cost, costing 1** [T no passive] to be able to be bought or made at a certain price: *These shoes cost £25.* | *How much does that dress cost?* | *This jacket cost me £100.*

□ USEFUL PATTERNS to cost something; to cost someone something

2 It'll cost you! *infml* = It'll be expensive for you: *You can go by air, but it'll cost you.* **3** [T] to result in the loss of something: *The expedition cost him his life.* | *Her marriage cost her her career.* **4** [T past tense and past participle **costed**] to calculate the price to be charged for a job or service: *The builder costed the job at £450.* **5 cost an arm and a leg, cost the earth, cost a bomb** *infml* to be extremely expensive

co·star /ˈkəʊ stɑːʳ/ *n* a famous actor or actress who appears with another famous actor or actress in a film or play

cost·ef·fec·tive /ˈ··ˌ··/ *adj* bringing the best possible profits or advantages at the lowest possible cost: *They discovered it was more cost-effective to change from electricity to gas.*

cost·ly /ˈkɒstli ‖ ˈkɔːstli/ *adj* **costlier, costliest** **1** costing a lot of money **2** using a lot of important things which are then lost: *The war was costly in terms of both human lives and national pride.*

cost of liv·ing /ˌ·· ˈ··/ *n* **the cost of living** the cost of buying the goods and services you need to live at an average standard of comfort

cos·tume /ˈkɒstjʊm ‖ ˈkaːstuːm/ *n* [C;U] **1** clothes or a garment typical of a certain period, country, activity, or profession: *dancers in national costume* | *actors in 18th century costume* | *a swimming costume* | *a costume drama*

co·sy¹ /ˈkəʊzi/ *adj* **cosier, cosiest** (also **cozy** *AmE*) warm and comfortable: *a cosy little house* | *a cosy evening by the fire* **–cosily** *adv* **–cosiness** *n* [U]

cosy² *n* **cosies** a covering put over a boiled egg or teapot to keep the contents warm: *a tea cosy*

cot /kɒt ‖ kaːt/ *n BrE* a small bed with high, movable sides, for a young child

cot·tage /ˈkɒtɪdʒ ‖ ˈkaː-ːdʒ/ *n* a small house, especially in the country –see HOUSE (USAGE) –see picture on page 441

cottage cheese /ˌ···ˈ· ‖ ˈ··· ·/ *n* [U] soft, lumpy, white cheese made from sour milk

cot·ton¹ /ˈkɒtn ‖ ˈkaːtn/ *n* [U] **1** a tall plant which produces soft white hair used for making thread or cloth **2** thread or cloth made from the cotton plant: *a cotton dress* | *a reel of blue cotton*

cotton² *v*
cotton on *phr v* [I] *infml* to understand something: *It was a long time before I cottoned on to what he meant.*

cotton wool /ˌ···ˈ·/ *n* [U] *BrE* a soft mass of cotton, used especially for cleaning your skin or wounds

couch¹ /kaʊtʃ/ *n* a long piece of furniture, usually with a back and arms, on which more than one person can sit or lie

couch² *v* **be couched in** to be expressed in a certain way: *The government's refusal was couched in friendly terms.*

cough¹ /kɒf ‖ kɔːf/ *v* **1** [I] to push air out from your throat with a sudden rough sound, especially because of discomfort in your lungs or throat as a result of a cold or other infection: *She was coughing and sneezing all day.* **2** [T] (also **cough** sthg ↔ **up**) to clear something from your throat by coughing: *I knew she was seriously ill when she began to cough blood.* **3** [I] to make a sound like a cough: *The engine coughed once or twice, but would not start.*
cough up *phr v* [I;T **cough up** sthg] *infml* to produce money or information unwillingly

cough² *n* **1** a sudden rough noise caused by someone pushing air out of their throat: *She gave a nervous cough.* **2** a medical condition marked by frequent coughing: *John had a bad cough all last week.*

could /kəd; *strong* kʊd/ *v* negative short form

SPELLING NOTE
Words with the sound / k /, like **cut**, may be spelt **k-**, like **key**, or **qu-**, like **queen**.
Words with the sound / s /, like **city**, may be spelt **s-**, like **soon**, or **ps-**, like **psychology**.

---

couldn't [modal verb] **1** the past tense of CAN: *I can't sing now, but I could when I was young.* | *They asked me if I could dance.* | *She said that she couldn't come to the party.* | *He asked if he could smoke.* | *I said that he could borrow my car.* **2** used to show that something might be possible: *He could lose his job if he's not careful.* | *I could come tomorrow if you like.* | *That could be my handbag over there.* | *If we could leave by six o'clock, we'd be in London by eight.* | *He was lucky – he could have been killed.* –see Study Note on page 392 **3 could you** a polite way of asking someone to do something: *Could you help me lift this box, please?* | *Could you just move your chair out of the way, please?* **4 could I, could we,** etc a polite way of asking someone if they will let you do something: *Could I use your telephone, please?* | *Could we leave our bags here, please?* **5 I could** *infml* = I would like to: *I could just eat bacon and eggs now!* **6 you could** *infml* = you should: *You could tell me when you're going to be late home!* | *You could have washed up your plate!* **7 couldn't you** *infml* a way of trying to persuade someone to do something that they do not want to do: *Couldn't you just spare five minutes to look at this for me?*

couldn't /ˈkʊdnt/ *v* short for "could not": *"Couldn't you see anything?" "No, I couldn't."*

could've /ˈkʊdəv/ *v* an abbreviation for **could have**: *"I could've gone with you."*

coun·cil¹ /ˈkaʊnsəl/ *n* [+sing/pl verb] a group of people appointed or elected at a local or organizational level to make laws or decisions or to give advice: *the Security Council of the United Nations* | *We applied to the town council for permission to build a hotel.*

council² *adj* [only before a noun] *BrE* owned and controlled by the local council (used of houses or flats): *We live in a council house in East London.*

coun·cil·lor /ˈkaʊnsələʳ/ *n* a member of a council: *What do you think, Councillor Evans?* | *I've been a city councillor for years.*

coun·sel¹ /ˈkaʊnsəl/ *n* **1** [C;U] *law* the lawyer speaking for someone in a court of law: *counsel for the defence* | *the counsel for the prosecution* **2** [U] *old fash* advice

counsel² *v* **-ll-** *BrE* **(-l-** *AmE*) [T] *fml* to advise someone: *We were counselled against travelling at night.* | *the counselling service for new students*

coun·sel·lor /ˈkaʊnsələʳ/ *n* (**counselor** *AmE*) **1** an adviser: *a marriage guidance counsellor* **2** *AmE* a lawyer

count¹ /kaʊnt/ *v* **1** [I;T] to say the numbers in order, one by one or by groups: *I can count up to 20 in Arabic.* | *Count from one to ten and then open your eyes.* **2** [T] to calculate the total number of things in a group: *We counted the paintings and found that one was missing.* | *Have the votes been counted yet?* **3** [T] to include someone or something: *There are six people in my family, counting my parents.* **4** [I;T] to consider a person or thing or to be considered of a particular type or quality: *It doesn't count as a crime.* | *I count you as one of my best friends.* **5 count yourself** to consider yourself: *Count yourself lucky to have escaped!* **6** [I not in progressive forms] to have value or importance: *It is not how much you read but what you read that counts.* | *He has no experience in this field, so his opinion doesn't count.* **7 count against someone** to help cause someone to lose or fail in something: *Jeans will count against you at the interview.* **8 count the cost** to calculate or suffer the bad effects of something you have done **9 count your blessings** think of all the things you have that make you happy: *Stop complaining and count your blessings.* **10 don't count your chickens before they are hatched** don't think that it is certain that you will get something, or that things will happen in the way you hope they will

count down *phr v* [I] to count backwards in seconds to zero, especially before sending a spacecraft into space

count in *phr v* [T count sbdy in] *infml* to include someone: *If you're planning a trip to London, count me in.*

count on sbdy/sthg *phr v* [T] **1** to depend on someone or something: *She can always be counted on for support.* | *You can't count on the weather being fine.* | *We can count on him to come.* **2** to expect someone to do something or something to happen: *I didn't count on John arriving so early.*

count out *phr v* **1** [T **count** sthg ↔ **out**] to put things down in turn while counting them: *He counted out ten £5 notes.* **2** [T **count** sbdy ↔ **out**] to declare a BOXER who fails to rise from the floor after ten seconds to be the loser of a fight **3** [T **count** sbdy **out**] *infml* to leave someone out: *If you're playing football in this weather you can count me out!*

count² *n* **1** an act of counting or the total reached by counting: *At the last count, I'd visited 15 countries.* **2 lose count** to fail to know the exact number: *I've lost count of how many times he's said he's leaving her.* [RELATED PHRASE **keep count**] **3** (also **Count**) the title of a European nobleman with a rank of a British EARL **4 be out for the count** to be unconscious for a period of ten seconds during a BOXING match

count·a·ble /ˈkaʊntəbəl/ *adj* **1** able to be counted **2 countable noun** *tech* a noun that has both singular and plural forms and that can be used with numbers and with words such as **many**, or **few**, or with **a** or **an**; in this dictionary, countable nouns are often marked [C] −opposite **uncountable** −see Study Note on page 178

count·down /ˈkaʊntdaʊn/ *n* [C;U] an act of counting backwards in seconds to zero, especially before sending a spacecraft into space: *Prepare for countdown: ten, nine, eight, seven ...*

coun·te·nance¹ /ˈkaʊntⁱnəns/ *n fml* the appearance of your face or its expression: *an angry countenance*

countenance² *v* [T] *fml* to allow something or to approve of it: *We will never countenance violence.*

coun·ter¹ /ˈkaʊntəʳ/ *n* **1** a narrow table or flat surface in a shop or bank where you go to be served **2 over the counter** obtainable directly from a shop: *Those pills are available over the counter now.* **3 under the counter** secretly, and often not legally: *During the war you could only get cigarettes under the counter.* **4** a small object used to show a player's position on the board in some games; it is often made of plastic and looks like a coin

counter² *v* [I;T] to do or say something which opposes a person or an idea: *My employer countered my request for more money by threatening to dismiss me.* | *I countered by pointing out that statistics are often unreliable.*

counter³ *adv* **run counter to something** to be opposed to something: *ideas that ran counter to everything I believed was right*

coun·ter·act /ˌkaʊntərˈækt/ *v* [T] to reduce or change the effect of something by doing something

that has the opposite effect: *This drug should counteract the poison.*

coun·ter·at·tack /ˈkaʊntərətæk/ *n* an attack on an enemy who has attacked you −**counterattack** *v* [I;T]

coun·ter·bal·ance /ˈkaʊntəˌbæləns ‖ -tər-/ *n* a weight or force that acts as a balance for another weight or force −**counterbalance** /ˌkaʊntəˈbæləns ‖ -tər-/ *v* **counterbalanced, counterbalancing** [T]: *He used his weight to counterbalance the load.*

coun·ter·clock·wise /ˌkaʊntəˈklɒkwaɪz ‖ -tər ˈklɑːk-/ *adj,adv* −see ANTICLOCKWISE

coun·ter·feit /ˈkaʊntəfɪt ‖ -tər-/ *v* [T] to make a copy of something so that people will think it is the real thing: *It is against the law to counterfeit money.* −**counterfeit** *adj* : *a counterfeit coin* −**counterfeiter** *n*

coun·ter·foil /ˈkaʊntəfɔɪl ‖ -tər-/ *n* a part of a cheque that you keep to show what the cheque was for

coun·ter·mand /ˌkaʊntəˈmɑːnd, ˈkaʊntəmɑːnd ‖ ˈkaʊntərmænd/ *v* [T] to give an order which means that one given earlier must not be carried out

coun·ter·part /ˈkaʊntəpɑːt ‖ -ərpɑːrt/ *n* a person or thing that serves the same purpose or has the same position as another: *British police officers are working with their French counterparts to catch the terrorists.*

coun·ter·sign /ˈkaʊntəsaɪn ‖ -ər-/ *v* [T] to sign something that someone else has signed: *I can sign cheques, but my boss has to countersign them.*

coun·tess /ˈkaʊntⁱs/ *n* the title of the wife of an EARL or COUNT, or a woman of the same rank

count·less /ˈkaʊntləs/ *adj* [only before a noun] very many: *She succeeded only after countless failures.*

coun·try¹ /ˈkʌntri/ *n* **countries 1** [C] a nation or state with its land or population: *Have you visited this country before?* **2** [C] the people of a nation or state: *Our country has always been peace-loving.* −see FOLK¹ USAGE **3 the country** the land outside cities or towns: *We're going to spend a few days in the country.* **4** [U] land with a special nature or character: *good farming country*

country² *adj* [only before a noun] in or related to the land outside cities or towns: *country life* | *a country house*

country and west·ern /ˌ··· ·ˈ··/ *n* (also **country music** /ˌ··· ˈ··/) [U] popular music in the style of the southern and western US

coun·try·man /ˈkʌntrimən/ *n* **countrymen** /-mən/ a person from your own country

coun·try·side /ˈkʌntrisaɪd/ *n* [U] land outside the cities and towns, used for farming or left unused

coun·ty /ˈkaʊnti/ *n* **counties** a large area of land in Britain, Ireland, and the US which has its own government to deal with local matters

coup /kuː/ *n* **coups** /kuːz/ **1** a coup d'état **2** a clever and successful action: *Getting the contract was quite a coup.*

coup d'é·tat /ˌkuːdeɪˈtɑː ‖ -deˈtɑː/ *n* **coups d'état** (*same pronunciation*) (also **coup**) the sudden or violent seizing of power in a state by a small group of people who have not been elected

cou·pé /ˈkuːpeɪ ‖ kuːˈpeɪ/ *n* (also **coupe** /kuːp/) a car with two doors and a sloping back

cou·ple¹ /ˈkʌpəl/ *n* **1** two things considered together: *I've got a couple of steaks for lunch.* **2** two people, usually a man and a woman, who are married, live together, or have a very close

couple

relationship: *We've invited three other couples to dinner.* **3** *infml* a small number: *I'll just have a couple of drinks.*

couple² *v* **coupled, coupling 1** [T] to join two vehicles together, especially parts of a train: *The engine was coupled to the carriages, and the train pulled out.* **2 coupled with** together with: *Low salaries, coupled with a shortage of cheap housing, make it difficult for young people to leave home.*

cou·pon /ˈkuːpɒn ‖ -pɑːn/ *n* **1** a piece of paper giving you the right to obtain something free or more cheaply than usual: *a coupon for ten pence off a packet of soap* | *Collect six coupons for a free bracelet.* **2** a printed form, for example in a newspaper, on which you can order goods, ask for information, or enter a competition

cour·age /ˈkʌrɪdʒ ‖ ˈkɜːr-/ *n* [U] **1** the quality that makes you able to control your fear and do something dangerous or difficult: *It took courage to stand up to him like that.* | *I couldn't be a soldier, I haven't got the courage.* **2 have the courage of your convictions** to be brave enough to do or say what you think is right

cou·ra·geous /kəˈreɪdʒəs/ *adj* brave: *a courageous action* | *a courageous person* –**courageously** *adv*

cour·gette /kʊəˈʒet ‖ kʊr-/ *n* a small green MARROW cooked and eaten as a vegetable

cou·ri·er /ˈkʊriər/ *n* **1** a tourist guide who stays with and looks after groups of travellers **2** someone who carries important or urgent papers, parcels, or messages

course¹ /kɔːs ‖ kɔːrs/ *n* **1** a movement from one point to another in space or time: *During the course of the flight we shall be serving drinks.* **2** the direction of movement taken by someone or something: *Our course is directly south.* | *the course of a stream* **3** a set of lessons or studies: *a French course* | *an evening course* | *a four-year history course* **4** *BrE* a plan, especially for medical treatment, with a number of steps: *a course of exercises* | *You must finish the whole course of tablets, even if your symptoms have gone.* **5** one of the parts of a meal: *We had a three-course dinner.* | *The first course was soup.* **6** an area of land or water on which a race is held or certain types of sport played: *a golf course* **7** action you can take in a particular situation: *There are several courses of action we could take.* | *Your best course would be to own up before they find out.* **8 of course** certainly: *Of course I'll still love you when you're old.* | *"Were you glad to leave there?" – "Of course not!"* **9 on course** going the right way: *The ship is on course.* | *She's on course for a gold medal.* [RELATED PHRASE **off course**]

course² *v* **coursed, coursing** [I] *lit* (of liquid) to flow or move rapidly: *Tears coursed down his cheeks.*

court¹ /kɔːt ‖ kɔːrt/ *n* **1** [C;U] a room or building in which law cases can be heard and judged: *He appeared in court today charged with attempted murder.* | *The court was full of people interested in the case.* | *Silence in court!* **2 the court** the people gathered together to hear and judge a law case: *The court stood when the judge entered.* **3** [C;U] a specially prepared and marked area in which

---

SPELLING NOTE

Words with the sound / k /, like **cut**, may be spelt **k-**, like **key**, or **qu-**, like **queen**.
Words with the sound / s /, like **city**, may be spelt **s-**, like **soon**, or **ps-**, like **psychology**.

---

certain ball games, such as tennis, are played: *Are the players on court yet?* | *She knocked the ball right out of the court.* **4** [C] used as the name of a large building, especially a block of flats: *They lived in Westbury Court.* **5** [C;U] the place where the king or queen lives and carries out his or her formal duties, or the people who spend time in this place: *The British court is in London.* **6 take someone to court** to start an action in law against someone

court² *v* **1** [T] to pay attention to an important person so that they will like you or help you in some way **2 court disaster** to risk danger or failure by behaving foolishly or without thinking **3** [I] *old fash* to spend time together with the intention of marrying: *when your mother and I were courting*

cour·te·ous /ˈkɜːtiəs ‖ ˈkɜːr-/ *adj fml* polite and respectful to others –**opposite discourteous** –**courteously** *adv*

cour·te·sy /ˈkɜːtʲsi ‖ ˈkɜːr-/ *n fml* [U] polite behaviour –**opposite discourtesy**

court·ier /ˈkɔːtiər ‖ ˈkɔːr-/ *n* a noble who spent time at the court of a king or other ruler in former times

court-mar·tial¹ /ˌ‖ ˈ-ˌ-/ *n* **courts-martial** *or* **court martials 1** a military court that tries people for offences against military law **2** a trial by a military court

court-martial² *v* **-ll-** (also **-l-** *AmE*) [T] to try someone in a military court for an offence against military law

court·ship /ˈkɔːtʃɪp ‖ ˈkɔːrt-/ *n lit* [U] the process of courting, or the time during which a man and a woman are courting (COURT²)

court·yard /ˈkɔːtjɑːd ‖ ˈkɔːrtjɑːrd/ *n* a flat space enclosed by walls or buildings, next to or within a castle, large house, or other large building

cous·in /ˈkʌzən/ *n* the child of your uncle or aunt –see picture on page 343

cove /kəʊv/ *n* a small sheltered opening in the coastline

cov·en /ˈkʌvən/ *n* a group or gathering of witches (WITCH)

cov·e·nant /ˈkʌvənənt/ *n* **1** a formal solemn agreement between two or more people or groups **2** a written promise to pay a certain amount of money to someone regularly for a certain number of years

Cov·en·try /ˈkʌvəntri, ˈkɒv- ‖ ˈkʌv-, ˈkɑːv-/ *n* **send someone to Coventry** to refuse to speak to someone as a sign of disapproval or as a punishment: *His mates sent him to Coventry for working during the strikes.*

cov·er¹ /ˈkʌvər/ *v* [T] **1** to place or spread something over something else to protect it or hide it: *She covered her ears to shut out the noise.* | *Cover the table with a cloth.* –opposite **uncover 2** to lie over a particular surface or area: *furniture covered in dust* | *The town covers five square miles.* **3** to include or deal with something: *His talk covered British history between the wars.* **4** to travel a certain distance: *I want to cover 100 miles before it gets dark.* **5** to report the details of an event for a newspaper: *Our best reporter covered the trial.* **6** to be enough money to pay for something: *Will £10 cover the cost of a new skirt?* **7** to protect someone from loss, especially through insurance *I'm covered against all accidents.* **8** to aim a gun at a person or a place in order to protect someone from attack or to prevent someone from escaping **9** to watch and stay close to an opponent or an area in a game such as football **10 cover for someone** to act in place of someone who is absent: *John's ill today so will you cover for him, Jean?*

cover sthg ↔ **up** *phr v* [T] **1** to place something over something else to protect it or hide it: *Cover the furniture up before you start painting.* **2** to prevent something from being noticed: *She tried to cover up her nervousness.*

cover up for sbdy *phr v* [T] *infml* to hide something wrong or shameful to save someone else from punishment or blame: *He says he did it, but I think he's trying to cover up for a friend.*

cover² *n* **1** [C] anything that protects something by covering it, especially a piece of material, lid, or top: *Put a cover on the chair before the cat sits on it.* | *a cushion cover* **2** [C] the outside of a magazine or book: *the photograph on the front cover* **3** [U] shelter or protection: *The flat land gave the soldiers no cover from enemy fire.* **4** [U] insurance against loss or damage: *Make sure you have adequate insurance cover.* **5** [C] something that hides something or keeps it secret: *This business is a cover for drug-dealing.* **6 break cover** to come out of hiding **7 take cover** to shelter or hide from something **8 under cover of darkness** while it is dark and no-one can see you **9 under separate cover** in a separate envelope or parcel: *This is a receipt. The goods will be sent later under separate cover.*

cov·er·age /ˈkʌvərɪdʒ/ *n* [U] the amount of time and space given by television or a newspaper to report a particular piece of news or an event

cov·er·ing /ˈkʌvərɪŋ/ *n* something that covers or hides something else: *Put a covering over the hole.*

covering let·ter /ˌ···ˈ··/ *n* a letter or note containing an explanation or more information, sent with a parcel or another letter

cov·ert /ˈkʌvət, ˈkəʊvɜːt ‖ ˈkəʊvərt/ *adj* secret, hidden, or not openly shown: *covert political activities* –opposite **overt** –**covertly** *adv*

cov·er-up /ˈ···-/ *n* an attempt to prevent people knowing about something shameful or criminal

cov·et /ˈkʌvɪt/ *v* [T] *lit* to have a strong desire to possess something (a word used to express disapproval) –**covetous** *adj*

cow¹ /kaʊ/ *n* **1** a large female animal kept on farms to provide milk **2** a male or female animal of this kind: *a field full of cows* **3** the female form of the elephant and certain other large sea and land animals: *a cow elephant* **4** an unpleasant woman: *She's a real cow.* –see MEAT (USAGE)

cow² *v* [T] to make someone afraid or control them by violence or threats: *The people were cowed into submission.*

cow·ard /ˈkaʊəd ‖ -ərd/ *n* a person who is not brave (a word used to express disapproval): *Jump, you coward; you won't hurt yourself!* | *I'm such a coward about injections.* –**cowardly** *adj*

cow·ard·ice /ˈkaʊədɪs ‖ -ər-/ *n* [U] lack of courage

cow·boy /ˈkaʊbɔɪ/ *n* **1** a man employed to look after cattle, especially in North America **2** a person who is careless or dishonest in their work or business: *cowboy builders*

cow·er /ˈkaʊəʳ/ *v* [I] to bend low and move back because you feel afraid: *The children were cowering in a corner.*

cow·pat /ˈkaʊpæt/ *n* a lump of cow DUNG

cow·slip /ˈkaʊslɪp/ *n* a wild plant with small yellow flowers

cox /kɒks ‖ kɑːks/ *n* a person who controls the direction and speed of a rowing boat, especially in races

–**cox** *v* [T] : *She'll cox the Oxford boat again next season.*

coy /kɔɪ/ *adj* pretending to be quiet and modest in order to attract attention: *She gave a coy little smile and looked away.* | *We all know how well you did. There's no need to be coy about it.* –**coyly** *adv*

coy·ote /ˈkɔɪ-əʊt, kɔɪˈəʊti ‖ ˈkaɪ-əʊt, kaɪˈəʊti/ *n* a wild dog that looks like a large fox; coyotes live in North America

coy·pu /ˈkɔɪpuː/ *n* **coypus** a large water rat from South America; it is kept for its valuable fur

co·zy /ˈkəʊzi/ *adj,n* see COSY

crab /kræb/ *n* **1** [C] a sea animal with a broad flat shell and five pairs of legs **2** [U] the flesh of a crab cooked as food –see picture on page 344

crab·by /ˈkræbi/ *adj infml* bad-tempered

crack¹ /kræk/ *v* **1** [I] to break so that lines appear on the surface: *Don't pour hot water into the glass or it will crack.* –see BREAK (USAGE) **2** [T] to break something so that lines appear on its surface: *I dropped a plate and cracked it.* **3** [I;T] to make a sudden explosive sound or to cause something to make such a sound: *He cracked his whip and rode off.* | *Thunder cracked and rumbled.* **4** [T] to hit a part of your body against something and hurt it: *The boy fell and cracked his head against the wall.* **5** [I] to lose control under pressure: *His voice cracked with emotion.* | *He'd been overworking for weeks when he cracked.* **6 crack a joke** *infml* to tell people a joke **7** [T] to succeed in dealing with a problem: *We must crack this problem.* **8 crack open a bottle** *infml* to open a bottle of wine, beer, etc.

crack down *phr v adv* [I] to become more severe: *The military government decided to crack down on all political activity.*

crack up *phr v adv* **1** [I] to lose control and be unable to deal with things under pressure **2 not all it's cracked up to be** *infml* not as good as people say it is

crack² *n* **1** a thin line or narrow split on the surface of something or between two things. *a crack in the window* | *a crack in the floorboards* **2** an explosive sound: *a crack of thunder* | *the crack of the guns* **3** a sudden sharp blow: *a crack on the head.* **4 have a crack at something** *infml* to attempt to do something **5** a joke or funny remark: *He's always making cracks about my big feet.* **6 the crack of dawn** the first light of day

crack³ *adj* [only before a noun] **1** of high quality or very good ability: *a crack commando unit* **2** a **crack shot** someone who is very good at shooting

crack·down /ˈkrækdaʊn/ *n* action taken to stop or discourage bad behaviour: *a crackdown on drunken driving*

crack·er /ˈkrækəʳ/ *n* **1** a thin unsweetened BISCUIT: *cheese and crackers* **2** a small cardboard tube covered with coloured paper and containing a small present; crackers are often pulled open at CHRISTMAS

crack·le /ˈkrækəl/ *v* **crackled, crackling** [I] to make small sharp sounds: *The fire crackled.* –**crackle** *n* : *the crackle of burning logs* | *a loud crackle*

crack·ling /ˈkræklɪŋ/ *n* [U] **1** the hard brown skin of cooked PORK **2** the sound of something that crackles: *the crackling of the fire*

crack·pot /ˈkrækpɒt ‖ -pɑːt/ *n infml* a person with very strange, foolish, or mad ideas –**crackpot** *adj* : *a crackpot scientist*

cra·dle[1] /'kreɪdl/ n 1 a small bed for a baby, especially one that can be moved gently from side to side 2 the place where something began: *Greece was the cradle of Western civilization.* 3 a framework used for supporting something being built or repaired, or for doing certain jobs: *Window cleaners are pulled up and down tall buildings on cradles.*

cradle[2] v **cradled, cradling** [T] to hold and support someone gently: *John cradled the baby in his arms.*

craft /krɑːft ‖ kræft/ n 1 a job or trade needing skill, especially with your hands: *the jeweller's craft* 2 [plural is **craft**] a boat, especially a small one: *The harbour was full of sailing craft.*

crafts·man /'krɑːftsmən ‖ 'kræ-/ n **craftsmen** -mən/ a highly skilled worker, especially one who works with their hands: *furniture made by the finest craftsmen* –**craftsmanship** n [U]

craft·y /'krɑːfti ‖ 'kræf-/ adj cleverly deceitful: *The politician was too crafty.* –**craftily** adv –**craftiness** n [U]

crag /kræg/ n a high steep rough rock or mass of rocks

crag·gy /'krægi/ adj 1 steep and rocky 2 rough, with deep lines: *his craggy features*

cram /kræm/ v **-mm-** 1 [T] to force people or things into a small space: *We were all crammed in with hardly room to breathe.* 2 **be crammed with, be crammed full of** to be very full of things: *a bag crammed with clothes* 3 [I] to prepare for an examination by working very hard for a short time: *He sat up all night cramming.*

cramp[1] /kræmp/ n [C;U] severe pain from the sudden tightening of a muscle, which makes it difficult to move: *stomach cramps | I've got cramp in my leg.*

cramp[2] v 1 [T] to prevent the natural growth or development of something 2 **cramp someone's style** infml to prevent someone from behaving in the way in which they would like to behave

cramped /kræmpt/ adj 1 limited in space: *a cramped little flat* 2 **cramped handwriting** writing with the letters too closely together

cran·ber·ry /'krænbəri ‖ -beri/ n **cranberries** a small red sour-tasting berry

crane[1] /kreɪn/ n a machine for lifting heavy objects by means of a very strong rope or wire fastened to a movable arm

crane[2] v **craned, craning** [I;T] to stretch out your neck in order to see something: *Jane craned her neck to look for her friend in the crowd.*

cra·ni·um /'kreɪniəm/ n **craniums** or **crania** /'-niə/ tech the part of your SKULL that covers your brain –**cranial** adj

crank /kræŋk/ n 1 an apparatus, such as a handle fixed at right angles to a rod, which changes movement in a straight line into circular movement. 2 infml a person with very peculiar ideas: *a religious crank*

craps /kræps/ n [U] 1 an American game played with two DICE for money 2 **shoot craps** to play this game

---

SPELLING NOTE

Words with the sound / k /, like **cut**, may be spelt **k-**, like **key**, or **qu-**, like **queen**.
Words with the sound / s /, like **city**, may be spelt **s-**, like **soon**, or **ps-**, like **psychology**.

---

crash[1] /kræʃ/ v 1 [I;T] to have an accident to a vehicle, or to cause a vehicle to have an accident: *The car crashed into a tree. | He crashed my car.* 2 [I; + adv/prep] to fall or move noisily: *The plates crashed to the floor.* 3 [I] to make a sudden loud noise: *The lightning flashed and thunder crashed.* 4 [I] (of a business or an organization concerned with money) to fail suddenly: *The New York stock exchange crashed in 1929.* 5 (of a computer system) to stop working suddenly

crash[2] n 2 a sudden loud noise: *a crash of thunder | the crash of breaking glass* 1 a violent accident involving vehicles: *All the passengers were killed in the plane crash.* 3 a sudden severe business failure: *the crash of the Metropolitan Bank.*

crash[3] adj 1 **crash course** a course of study in which you try to learn things very quickly 2 **crash diet** a diet intended to help you lose weight very quickly

crash bar·ri·er /'· ˌ···/ n a strong fence built to prevent accidents

crash hel·met /'·ˌ··/ n a strong HELMET worn by racing car drivers and motorcycle riders to protect their heads in an accident

crash-land /'· ·/ v [I] to land a plane in dangerous conditions so that as little damage as possible is done –**crash landing** /ˌ· '··/ n [C;U]

crass /kræs/ adj 1 stupid, unfeeling, or coarse: *crass behaviour | a crass remark* 2 very great (used of stupidity or foolishness): *crass stupidity | crass ignorance* –**crassly** adv –**crassness** n [U]

crate /kreɪt/ n a large wooden box for carrying or storing things: *a milk crate | a crate of apples* –see picture on page 148

cra·ter /'kreɪtəʳ/ n 1 the round bowl-shaped mouth of a VOLCANO 2 a rough round hole in the ground: *a bomb crater | craters on the moon's surface*

cra·vat /krə'væt/ n BrE a wide piece of material that men wear tied round their neck inside their shirt collar

crave /kreɪv/ v **craved, craving** [I;T] to have a very strong desire for something: *Sometimes I crave for a piece of chocolate. | She craves admiration.*

cra·ven /'kreɪvən/ adj completely lacking courage

crav·ing /'kreɪvɪŋ/ n a very strong desire: *a craving for drugs* –see DESIRE[2] (USAGE)

crawl[1] /krɔːl/ v [I] 1 to move slowly on your hands and knees or with your body close to the ground or other surface: *The baby crawled across the room. | There's an insect crawling up your back!* –see picture on page 736 2 to move slowly and with difficulty: *The traffic was crawling through the centre of town.* 3 **be crawling with** to be full of people or insects: *The room was crawling with flies. | The town was crawling with soldiers.* 4 infml to be very nice to someone in order to get something for yourself (a word used to express disapproval): *She got her promotion by crawling to the boss.* 5 **make your skin crawl** to cause a very unpleasant feeling often of terror: *Snakes make my skin crawl.*

crawl[2] n [sing] 1 a very slow movement or the action of crawling 2 a rapid way of swimming on your stomach, moving first one arm and then the other over your head, and kicking your feet up and down: *I can do the crawl now.*

cray·fish /'kreɪˌfɪʃ/ n **crayfish** or **crayfishes** a small animal with a shell, which lives in rivers and streams and can be eaten

cray·on /ˈkreɪən, -ɒn ‖ -ɑːn, -ən/ n a stick of coloured WAX, or a pencil containing coloured wax, used for writing or drawing on paper –**crayon** v [I;T]

craze /kreɪz/ n a very popular fashion for a very short time: *This diet is the latest craze in America.*

crazed /kreɪzd/ adj very angry or mad

cra·zy /ˈkreɪzi/ adj 1 mad or foolish: *He's crazy to go out in this weather! | a crazy idea | a crazy old man* 2 **be crazy about** infml to be very keen on something or someone: *She's crazy about dancing. | He's crazy about her.* 3 **drive someone crazy** infml to make someone angry: *This noise is driving me crazy.* 4 **like crazy** infml very actively: *You'll have to work like crazy to get this finished.* –**crazily** adv –**craziness** n [U]

creak /kriːk/ v [I] to make a sound like that of a badly-oiled door opening: *The stairs creaked under his weight.* –**creak** n

creak·y /ˈkriːki/ adj making a creaking sound: *a creaky door* –**creakily** adv –**creakiness** n [U]

cream[1] /kriːm/ n 1 [U] the thick fatty yellowish liquid taken from milk, which is eaten or drunk with other foods: *Have some cream in your coffee. | a cream cake | whipped cream | sour cream* 2 [C;U] something similar to cream or containing cream: *a chocolate cream | cream of chicken soup* 3 [C;U] a thick substance that you put on your skin: *face cream | Put some of this cream on that burn.* 4 **the cream** of the best part of a group: *the cream of society* 5 [U] a yellowish white colour: *You look nice in cream.*

cream[2] adj a yellowish-white colour: *She wore a cream dress.* –see picture on page 147

cream[3] v [T] to mix or beat butter and sugar together until the mixture is thick and soft
cream sbdy/sthg ↔ **off** phr v [T] to remove the best: *We cream off the cleverest pupils and send them to a special school.*

cream·y /ˈkriːmi/ adj **creamier, creamiest** 1 containing cream or like cream in taste or feel: *creamy coffee | creamy soap* 2 yellowish-white –**creaminess** n [U]

crease[1] /kriːs/ n 1 a line made intentionally or accidentally on cloth or paper by folding, ironing, or crushing it: *You've got a crease in your dress where you've been sitting. | Be careful when you iron your trousers to get the creases straight.* 2 a line marked on a cricket ground to show where a player should stand to hit the ball

crease[2] v creased, creasing [I;T] to put or get creases in something: *She wanted to wear her black dress but it was too creased. | cloth that creases easily* **crease up** phr v [I] infml to begin to laugh a lot

cre·ate /kriˈeɪt/ v created, creating [T] 1 to cause something to exist: *God created the world. | The new road will create a lot of traffic. | Her bad behaviour is creating a lot of problems.* 2 to produce or invent something new: *creating paintings and sculptures | The designers and technicians together created a new computer system.* 3 to appoint someone to a special rank or position: *The Queen's son was created Prince of Wales.*

cre·a·tion /kriˈeɪʃən/ n 1 [U] the act of creating something: *the creation of jobs by the government* 2 [C] something produced by invention or imagination: *an artist's creation* 3 [U] the universe, world, and all living things: *Man is the lord of creation. | God's creation*

cre·a·tive /kriˈeɪtɪv/ adj 1 producing new and original ideas and things: *creative thinking | creative*

writing | *They're a creative couple; she paints and he writes novels.* 2 producing results based on newness of thought or imagination: *useful and creative work* –**creatively** adv –**creativity** /ˌkriːeɪˈtɪvəti/ (also **creativeness**) /kriˈeɪtɪvnəs/ n [U] : *Someone with creativity is needed for this job.*

cre·a·tor /kriˈeɪtə[r]/ n 1 a person who creates: *Unusually, small businesses are the creators of much of this country's wealth.* 2 **the Creator** God: *She gave thanks to her Creator.*

crea·ture /ˈkriːtʃə[r]/ n 1 an animal or being of some kind: *all God's creatures | creatures from outer space | The crocodile is a strange-looking creature.* 2 a person of a particular kind (a word often used to express disapproval, pity, or some other feeling) *You stupid creature! You've spoilt all my plans. | The poor creature had no family at all.* 3 **a creature of habit** a person who always does things in the same way or at a regular time

crèche /kreʃ ‖ kreʃ, kreɪʃ/ n BrE a place where babies and young children are cared for while their parents work

cre·dence /ˈkriːdəns/ n fml **give credence to something** to show that you believe that something is true: *The newspapers are giving no credence to his latest statements.*

cre·den·tials /krɪˈdenʃəlz/ n [pl] 1 a letter or other written proof of a person's official position or good character 2 anything that proves a person's abilities or their suitability for something: *His credentials are excellent. He has all the qualifications and experience we need.*

cred·i·bil·i·ty /ˌkredəˈbɪləti/ n [U] the quality that something has which makes people trust it or believe it: *The Chernobyl accident has undermined the credibility of the nuclear power industry.*

cred·i·ble /ˈkredəbəl/ adj deserving to be believed, trusted, or taken seriously: *This news hardly seems credible. | a credible defence policy* –**credibly** adv

cred·it[1] /ˈkredət/ n 1 [U] the system of buying things and paying for them later: *You can buy the furniture on credit* 2 [U] money you are allowed to owe, or the period of time you are allowed to pay, for things you have bought: *up to £50 credit | six months' credit* 3 [C] an amount of money in or put into someone's account, for example at a bank: *Last month's credits exceeded debits by £5.* 4 [U] the quality of being likely to repay debts: *His credit is good. You can trust him.* 5 [U] public approval or praise for doing something good: *I got no credit for my invention. | Her boss claimed all the credit for her hard work.* 6 [sing;U] someone who brings honour or respect: *You're a real credit to your team. | Those children are a credit to their parents.* 7 [U] belief or trust: *This theory is gaining credit among scientists.* 8 [C] a part of a course completed by a student, especially at a university in the US 9 **do someone credit** to bring someone honour or respect: *Our army does us credit.* 10 **in credit** containing money (used of a bank account) 11 **to someone's credit**: a in someone's favour: *It is to the workers' credit that they opposed the establishment of a military government.* b successfully finished: *She's not yet 30, and already she has five books to her credit!*

cred·it[2] v [T] 1 to believe something: *Do you really credit the government's statement?* 2 to put an amount of money in an account: *Please credit £10 to my account. | Credit my account with £10.*
credit sbdy **with** sthg phr v [T] to believe that somebody has a particular good quality: *Please credit me with some sense!*

cred·i·ta·ble /ˈkredɪtəbəl/ *adj* deserving praise, honour, or approval: *a creditable effort to establish peace* –**creditably** *adv*

credit card /ˈ···/ *n* a card which allows you to obtain goods and services without using coins or notes; the cost is added to your account and you pay it later

cred·i·tor /ˈkredɪtəʳ/ *n* a person or firm that someone owes money to

cred·u·lous /ˈkredjʊləs ‖ -dʒə-/ *adj* too willing to believe things, especially without real proof –**credulously** *adv* –**credulity** /krɪˈdjuːlɪti ‖ -ˈduː-/ *n* [U]

creed /kriːd/ *n* a system of beliefs or principles, especially religious ones

creek /kriːk/ *n AmE* a small narrow stream or river

creep /kriːp/ *v* **crept** /krept/, **crept** [I] **1** to move carefully and quietly, so that no one will notice you: *The cat crept silently towards the mouse.* | *We crept upstairs because we didn't want to wake the baby.* **2** to move with your body close to the ground: *The dog crept under the bed.* **3** to try to win someone's favour by being too nice to them (a word used to express disapproval) **4** to move very slowly: *The tide crept up the beach.* | *cars creeping along the icy roads*
creep in *phr v* [I] to begin to appear: *Mistakes are creeping in which could have been avoided.* | *More and more foreign words are creeping into the language.*
creep up on sbdy/sthg *phr v* [T] to gradually get nearer to someone or something, without being noticed: *They crept up on the sentry and overpowered him.* | *Old age is creeping up on me.*

creep·er /ˈkriːpəʳ/ *n* a plant which climbs up trees and walls or grows along the ground

creeps /kriːps/ *n infml* **give someone the creeps** to make someone feel fear or strong dislike: *The old castle gives me the creeps.*

creep·y /ˈkriːpi/ *adj* **creepier, creepiest** *infml* creating an unpleasant feeling of fear: *a creepy old house* –**creepily** *adv* –**creepiness** *n* [U]

cre·mate /krɪˈmeɪt ‖ ˈkriːmeɪt/ *v* **cremated**, **cremating** [T] to burn a dead person at a funeral ceremony –**cremation** /krɪˈmeɪʃən/ *n* [C;U]

crem·a·to·ri·um /ˌkreməˈtɔːriəm ‖ ˌkriː-/ *n* **crematoriums** *or* **crematoria** /-riə/ (also **crematory** /ˈkremətəri ‖ ˈkriːmətɔːri/) a building in which dead people are cremated

cre·ole /ˈkriːəʊl/ *n* (also **Creole**) **1** [C;U] a language which is formed by the combination of a European language with one or more others and is the native language of its speakers; creole languages are common in the Caribbean **2** [C] a person of mixed European and African race who comes from the West Indies –**creole** *adj*

cre·o·sote /ˈkriːəsəʊt/ *n* [U] thick brown oily liquid used for preserving wood

crepe /kreɪp/ *n* (also **crêpe**) **1** [U] a light cloth with a slightly rough surface made from cotton, silk, or wool **2** [U] (also **crepe rubber** /ˌ· ˈ··/) tightly

---

SPELLING NOTE
Words with the sound / k /, like **cut**, may be spelt **k-**, like **key**, or **qu-**, like **queen**.
Words with the sound / s /, like **city**, may be spelt **s-**, like **soon**, or **ps-**, like **psychology**.

---

pressed rubber used especially for the bottoms of shoes **3** [C] a very thin PANCAKE

crept /krept/ *v* the past tense and past participle of CREEP

cre·scen·do /krɪˈʃendəʊ/ *n* **crescendos** *or* **crescendoes** **1** a gradual increase in the loudness of a piece of music **2** a point of greatest excitement or urgency: *The demands for an election rose to a crescendo.*

cres·cent /ˈkresənt/ *n* **1** a curved shape like the moon during its first and last quarters, when it forms less than half a circle: *a crescent-shaped sword* | *a crescent moon* **2** a curved row of houses or a curved street: *48 Woodside Crescent* **3** (also **Crescent**) the sign of the Muslim religion: *a war between Cross and Crescent*

cress /kres/ *n* [U] a very small plant whose stems and leaves are eaten raw

crest /krest/ *n* **1** a growth of feathers on top of a bird's head **2** the top of a hill or wave **3** a special picture used as a sign of a family or organization

crest·fal·len /ˈkrest₁fɔːlən/ *adj* disappointed or sad

cret·in /ˈkretɪn ‖ ˈkriːtn/ *n* **1** *infml* a very stupid person: *You silly cretin!* **2** a person whose development of mind and body has stopped in early childhood

cre·vasse /krɪˈvæs/ *n* a deep open crack, especially in thick ice

crev·ice /ˈkrevɪs/ *n* a narrow crack or opening, especially in rock

crew /kruː/ *n* [+ sing/pl verb] **1** all the people working on a ship, plane, or space vehicle: *The crew is waiting for the captain's instructions.* | *The crew have gone ashore.* **2** a group of people working together for a particular purpose: *a television crew* | *the repair crew*

crib¹ /krɪb/ *n AmE* a bed with movable sides for a baby or small child **2** an open box or wooden framework holding food for animals

crib² *v* **-bb-** [I;T] *infml* to copy something dishonestly from someone else: *I didn't know the answers so I cribbed them off John.*

crick /krɪk/ *n* a painful stiffening of the muscles, especially in your back or neck, making movement difficult –**crick** *v* [T] : *I cricked my neck playing tennis.*

crick·et /ˈkrɪkɪt/ *n* **1** an outdoor game popular in Britain, played with a ball, BAT, and wickets (WICKET) by two teams of 11 players each –see picture on page 637 **2** a small brown insect which jumps; the male makes loud noises by rubbing its wings together

cried /kraɪd/ *v* the past tense and past participle of CRY¹

cries /kraɪz/ *v* the 3rd person singular present tense of CRY¹

crime /kraɪm/ *n* **1** [C] an action which is punishable by law: *Drug-smuggling is a serious crime.* | *She had committed a terrible crime.* **2** [U] illegal activity in general: *It is the job of the police to prevent crime.* | *the crime rate* | *crime statistics* **3** [C] a pity or shame: *It's a crime to waste all this food.*

crim·i·nal¹ /ˈkrɪmɪnəl/ *adj* **1** [only before a noun] related to crime or its punishment: *a specialist in criminal law* | *a criminal offence* **2** wrong, but not illegal: *a criminal waste of money* –**criminally** *adv*

criminal² *n* a person who is guilty of crime: *These men are criminals and must be punished!*

crim·son /ˈkrɪmzən/ *n* [U] a deep purplish red colour –**crimson** *adj* –see picture on page 147

cringe /krɪndʒ/ *v* **cringed, cringing** [I] **1** to bend and move back especially because of fear: *She cringed when he came in.* **2** to have an uncomfortable feeling of shame: *I cringed with embarrassment when she was rude to my teacher.*

crin·kle /ˈkrɪŋkəl/ *v* **crinkled, crinkling** [I;T] to make many fine lines or folds in something: *My clothes were all crinkled from being in the suitcase.* | *His face crinkled, and then he laughed out loud.* –**crinkle** *n* –**crinkly** *adj* : *chocolates in crinkly paper cases*

crip·ple¹ /ˈkrɪpəl/ *n* a person who is unable to use their body properly, especially their legs, because of illness or accident (an old fashioned word which many people consider to be offensive)

cripple² *v* **crippled, crippling** [T] **1** to hurt or wound a person or an animal so that they cannot move properly **2** to weaken or damage a system or organization: *The economy was crippled by the war.* | *crippling debts*

cri·sis /ˈkraɪsɪs/ *n* **crises** /-siːz/ **1** a situation of great danger, difficulty, or uncertainty, often resulting from political disagreements: *a governmental crisis* | *the crisis in Southern Africa* **2** a situation where people lack what they need: *a housing crisis* **3** a feeling of great suffering about a problem in your life: *His doctor gave him some pills after his last emotional crisis.*

crisp¹ /krɪsp/ *adj* **1** hard and dry (used of food): *crisp bacon* | *Keep the biscuits in a tin so they stay crisp.* **2** firm, fresh, or stiff: *a crisp apple* | *crisp vegetables* | *a crisp new bank note* | *crisp white sheets* **3** quick and clear (used of speech or writing): *a crisp reply* **4** cold, dry, and fresh (used of weather or air): *a crisp winter's day* | *the crisp autumn wind* –**crisply** *adv* –**crispness** *n* [U]

crisp² *n* (also **potato crisp** *BrE*) a thin piece of potato cooked in very hot fat, dried, and usually sold in packets

criss·cross¹ /ˈkrɪskrɒs || -krɔːs/ *adj* having a number of crossing straight lines: *a crisscross design*

crisscross² *v* [I;T] to form a crisscross pattern on something: *Train tracks crisscross the country.*

cri·te·ri·on /kraɪˈtɪəriən/ *n* **criteria** /-riə/ or **criterions** an established standard or principle on which a judgment is based: *What criteria do you use when judging a student's work?*

crit·ic /ˈkrɪtɪk/ *n* **1** a person who makes judgments about works of art, music, or literature, and writes about them, especially as a job **2** a person who dislikes and expresses strong disapproval of someone or something: *He's one of her strongest critics.*

crit·i·cal /ˈkrɪtɪkəl/ *adj* **1** judging someone or something severely: *Why are you so critical of the government?* **2** very serious, important, or dangerous: *a critical stage of the illness* | *The elections will be critical for the country's future.* **3** [only before a noun] providing careful judgment of the good or bad qualities of something: *critical writings on art* | *a critical analysis of the education system* –**critically** /-kli/ *adv*

crit·i·cis·m /ˈkrɪtɪsɪzəm/ *n* [C;U] **1** the act of forming judgments about the good or bad qualities of anything, especially artistic work **2** unfavourable judgment or disapproval: *Your criticisms seem to*

have offended him. | *Everything the government does seems to attract criticism.*

crit·i·cize /ˈkrɪtɪsaɪz/ *v* (also **criticise** *BrE*) [I;T] **1** to judge someone or something severely: *The minister criticized my decision.* | *The workers were strongly criticized for going on strike.* **2** to make careful judgments about the good and bad qualities of someone or something

cri·tique /krɪˈtiːk/ *n* an article or book which examines and makes careful judgment of a situation or someone's work: *a critique of Marx's writings*

croak /krəʊk/ *v* [I] **1** to make a deep low noise like a FROG makes **2** to speak with a rough voice as if you have a sore throat –**croak** *n*: *the croak of a frog*

cro·chet /ˈkrəʊʃeɪ || krəʊˈʃeɪ/ *n* [U] **1** a way of making clothes or tablecloths by using wool and a special hooked needle **2** things made by using crochet **3 crochet hook** the needle used in crochet –**crochet** *v* [I;T]: *I'll crochet a dress for a baby.*

crock /krɒk/ *n* a heavy clay pot used in the kitchen

crock·er·y /ˈkrɒkəri || ˈkrɑː-/ *n* [U] cups, plates, and dishes that you eat or drink from: *the sink was full of dirty crockery.*

croc·o·dile /ˈkrɒkədaɪl || ˈkrɑː-/ *n* **1** [C] a large meat-eating animal with a long body, a hard skin, and sharp teeth, which lives in or near rivers in hot countries **2** [U] the skin of this animal used as leather

cro·cus /ˈkrəʊkəs/ *n* **crocuses** a small plant with purple, yellow, or white flowers which open in early spring

crois·sant /ˈkrwɑːsɒŋ || krwɑːˈsɔːŋ/ *n* a piece of light buttery pastry, shaped in a curve and often eaten for breakfast

cro·ny /ˈkrəʊni/ *n* **cronies** a friend or companion (a word often used to express disapproval): *The minister's always doing favours for his cronies.*

crook¹ /krʊk/ *n* **1** *infml* a dishonest person, often a thief **2 the crook of your arm** the inside part of your elbow where it bends

crook² *v* [T] to bend your arm or finger: *crooking her finger to beckon us*

crook·ed /ˈkrʊkɪd/ *adj* **1** twisted or bent: *a crooked street* | *a crooked back* **2** *infml* dishonest –**crookedness** *n* [U]

croon /kruːn/ *v* [I;T] to sing gently in a low soft voice

crop¹ /krɒp/ *n* **1** a plant or plant product such as grain, fruit, or vegetables grown by a farmer: *Wheat is a widely grown crop in Britain.* | *The crops were badly damaged in the storm.* **2** the amount of such a product produced and collected in a single season or place: *India had the biggest cotton crop ever this year.* **3** a group of similar things or people that appear at the same time: *a whole new crop of students*

crop² *v* **-pp-** **1** [T] (of an animal) to eat the tops of grass or plants: *The sheep cropped the grass short.* **2** [T] to cut a person's hair short: *She looks like a prisoner with her cropped hair.* **3** [I] (of a plant) to produce a crop: *Pears are cropping well this year.* **crop up** *phr v* [I] *infml* to happen or appear unexpectedly: *A problem has cropped up at work so I'll be late home tonight.*

cro·quet /ˈkrəʊkeɪ, -ki || krəʊˈkeɪ/ *n* [U] a game played on grass in which players knock balls through small metal arches with a hammer

cross¹ /krɒs || krɔːs/ *n* **1** a shape (× or +) with four equal arms that meet in the centre **2** a mark often used as a sign of where something is or should be, for example on a map, or as a sign that something is incorrect, for example in pupils' work **3** (also **Cross**) a shape like an upright post with a bar across it near the top which is a sign of the Christian religion: *the sign of the Cross* **4** an object or picture in the shape of a cross which is used for decoration or as a sign of the Christian religion, or worn as an honour for bravery: *She wore a gold cross | The graves were marked by wooden crosses.* | *He won the George Cross during the war.* **5** a person or situation which causes sorrow or suffering and tests your patience or goodness: *Everyone has his own cross to bear in this life.* **6** a combination of two different things: *The drink tasted like a cross between coffee and hot chocolate.* | *a cross between a horse and a donkey*

cross² *v* **1** [T] to go, pass, or travel from one side of something to another: *The soldiers took three days to cross the desert.* | *Be careful when you're crossing the road.* | *We crossed the border at dawn.* | *The railway line crosses the country from coast to coast.* **2** [I;T] to pass across each other: *I'll meet you where the paths cross.* **3** [T] to make someone angry because you oppose their plans or wishes: *Anne hates being crossed so don't argue with her.* **4 cross yourself** to move your hand in the shape of a cross and on the top part of your body as a sign of the Christian religion: *She crossed herself as she left the church.* **5** [T] to cause an animal or plant to breed with one of another kind: *Is it possible to cross a tiger with a lion?* **6** [T] to put one leg or arm on top of the other: *Jean crossed her legs.* **7 cross swords** to be opposed to someone, especially in an argument: *The management crossed swords with the union over the pay formula.*

cross sbdy/sthg ↔ **off** *phr v* [T] to remove something from a list by drawing a line through it: *If you don't want to come, cross your name off.*

cross sthg ↔ **out** *phr v* [T] to draw a line through written words, because they are wrong or not to be read: *Cross it out and write it again correctly.*

cross³ *adj* angry or bad-tempered: *The old man was really cross when Jane broke his window.* –**crossly** *adv* –**crossness** *n* [U]

cross·bar /ˈkrɒsbɑːʳ/ ‖ /ˈkrɔːs-/ *n* **1** a bar joining two upright posts: *He almost scored a goal, but the ball hit the crossbar.* **2** the top bar of the frame of a man's bicycle

cross·bow /ˈkrɒsbəʊ/ ‖ /ˈkrɔːs-/ *n* a powerful type of BOW³ that is fired like a gun

cross·breed /ˈkrɒsbriːd/ ‖ /ˈkrɔːs-/ *n* an animal or plant which is a mixture of breeds –**crossbred** /-bred/ *adj* : *a crossbred horse*

cross·check /ˌkrɒsˈtʃek/ ‖ /ˌkrɔːs-/ *v* [T] to make certain that a calculation or answer is right by using a different method

cross·coun·try /ˌ·ˈ··◄/ *adj,adv* across the fields or open country: *a cross-country race* | *cross-country skiing*

cross·ex·am·ine /ˌ·· ·ˈ··/ *v* **cross-examined, cross-examining** [I;T] to question somebody, especially a witness, very carefully, usually in order to compare the answers with other answers they have given before –**cross-examination** /ˌ·· ···ˈ··/ *n* [C;U]

SPELLING NOTE

Words with the sound / k /, like **cut**, may be spelt **k-**, like **key**, or **qu-**, like **queen**.
Words with the sound / s /, like **city**, may be spelt **s-**, like **soon**, or **ps-**, like **psychology**.

---

cross-eyed /ˌ·ˈ·◄ ‖ ˈ··/ *adj* having eyes which look in towards your nose

cross·fire /ˈkrɒsfaɪəʳ ‖ ˈkrɔːs-/ *n* [U] one or more lines of gunfire coming from different places, but directed at the same point

cross·ing /ˈkrɒsɪŋ ‖ ˈkrɔː-/ *n* **1** a journey across the sea **2** a place where two railway lines or tracks cross or where a road crosses the railway **3** a place at which a road, river, or railway line may be crossed safely

cross-legged /ˌkrɒs ˈlegd◄ ‖ ˌkrɔːs ˈlegʌd◄/ *adj,adv* sitting with your knees wide apart and your ankles crossed

cross·piece /ˈkrɒspiːs ‖ ˈkrɔːs-/ *n* a piece of anything lying across something else

cross-pur·pos·es /ˌ·ˈ···/ *n* **at cross-purposes** talking about different things without being conscious of it, and so not understanding each other: *I think we're talking at cross-purposes.*

cross-re·fer /ˌ·· ·ˈ·/ *v* **-rr-** [I;T] to direct the reader from one place in a book to another place in the same book: *In this dictionary* CAPITAL *letters are used to cross-refer* **from** *one word* **to** *another.*

cross-ref·er·ence /ˌ·· ˈ·· ‖ ˈ·· ˌ··/ *n* a note in a book telling the reader to look at another place in the same book in order to find more information

cross·roads /ˈkrɒsrəʊdz ‖ ˈkrɔːs-/ *n* [plural is **crossroads**] **1** a place where two or more roads cross each other –see picture on page 735 **2** an important point, especially one where you have to take an important decision

cross-sec·tion /ˈ·ˌ·ˌ··/ *n* **1** a drawing of something showing what you would see if you cut across it, especially at right angles to its length: *a cross-section of a plant stem* **2** a number of different people who, together, seem to be typical of society: *A cross-section of the public were interviewed by market researchers.*

cross·word /ˈkrɒsˌwɜːd ‖ ˈkrɔːsˌwɜːrd/ *n* (also **crossword puzzle** /ˈ·· ˌ··/) a printed word game which you do by fitting words guessed from questions and information (called CLUES) into a pattern of numbered squares going down and across

crotch /krɒtʃ ‖ krɑːtʃ/ *n* (also **crutch**) the part of your body between the tops of your legs, or the part of a pair of trousers that covers this

crotch·et·y /ˈkrɒtʃ ʌti ‖ ˈkrɑː-/ *adj infml* bad-tempered and hard to please

crouch /kraʊtʃ/ *v* [I] to lower your body close to the ground by bending your knees and back: *We crouched down behind the wall to shelter from the wind.* | *The tiger crouched, ready to spring.* –see picture on page 736

crou·pi·er /ˈkruːpɪəʳ/ *n* a person who collects the money lost and pays out the money won at a table where games such as ROULETTE are played

crow¹ /krəʊ/ *n* **1** a large shiny black bird with a loud cry **2 as the crow flies** measuring a distance in a straight line from one point to another: *We're twenty kilometres from town as the crow flies, but nearly thirty by road.* **3** the loud high cry of a fully-grown male chicken

crow² *v* [I] **1** to make the loud high cry of a fully-grown male chicken **2** *infml* to speak proudly (a word used to express disapproval): *I wish John would stop crowing about his examination results.*

crow·bar /ˈkrəʊbɑːʳ/ *n* an iron bar used to force something open or to force two things apart

crowd¹ *v* 1 [I; + adv/prep] to gather together and in large numbers: *People crowded* **round** *the scene of the accident.* | *Screaming fans crowded* **around** *the film star.* 2 [T] to fill a place so that it is not easy to move: *Shoppers crowded the streets.* 3 [I; T; + adv/prep] to press tightly into a small place: *They all crowded* **into** *the taxi.* | *There were six of us, all crowded* **into** *a tiny flat.*

crowd² /kraʊd/ *n* 1 a large number of people gathered together for a particular purpose: *a crowd gathered to watch the parade* | *There were crowds* **of** *people at the theatre.* | *a football crowd* | *They vanished into the crowd.* 2 *infml* a particular group of friends or a social group: *I don't like the college crowd.* 3 **follow the crowd, go with the crowd** *infml* to be easily influenced and to do what most people do in a particular situation: *He does what he wants – he doesn't just follow the crowd.*

crowd·ed /ˈkraʊdᵻd/ *adj* completely full or filled with people: *a crowded room* | *The beach gets so crowded in August.*

crown¹ /kraʊn/ *n* 1 a circular decoration usually made of gold with jewels in it, which a king or queen wears on their head as a sign of royal power 2 something which looks like or represents this often given to someone as a prize: *a crown of flowers for the Carnival Queen* 3 the top or highest part of your head, a hat, or a hill 4 **the Crown** the governing power of a kingdom: *land belonging to the Crown*

crown² *v* [T] 1 to place a crown solemnly on the head of a person as a sign of royal power or victory 2 *lit* to cover the top of something: *Trees crowned the hill.* 3 to complete something in the most perfect way: *The government's record was crowned by its success in the peace talks.* 4 **to crown it all** a phrase used when you went to show that the last thing or event in a list is the best or worst thing to happen: *His house burnt down, his car was stolen, and to crown it all he lost his job.*

crown jew·els /ˌ· ˈ··/ *n* [pl] the crown and jewels which belong to the Crown and are worn or used on great state occasions

crown prince /ˌ· ˈ·◂/ *n* the man who has the lawful right to be king after the death of the present king or ruling queen; if this person is a woman she is called the **crown princess**

cru·cial /ˈkruːʃəl/ *adj* of the greatest importance: *at a crucial moment* | *Speed is crucial* **to** *our success.* –**crucially** *adv*

cru·ci·fix /ˈkruːsᵻfɪks/ *n* a cross with a figure of Christ on it

cru·ci·fix·ion /ˌkruːsᵻˈfɪkʃən/ *n* 1 [C;U] the act of crucifying someone 2 **the Crucifixion** the death of Christ on the Cross, or a picture or other representation of it

cru·ci·fy /ˈkruːsᵻfaɪ/ *v* **crucified, crucifying** [T] 1 to kill someone by nailing them to a cross and leaving them to die 2 to be cruel or unpleasant to someone, especially publicly: *He was crucified by public opinion because his book offended so many people.*

crude /kruːd/ *adj* 1 in a natural state or untreated: *crude oil* | *crude rubber* 2 rude or lacking sensitive feeling: *Do you have to be so crude?* 3 too simply or unskilfully made, expressed, or calculated: *a crude shelter in the forest* | *crude ideas* | *crude statistics* –**crudely** *adv*

cru·di·ty /ˈkruːdᵻti/ *n* **crudities** (also **crudeness** /ˈkruːdnᵻs/) [C;U] the quality of being crude, or an example of crude language or behaviour

cru·el /ˈkruːəl/ *adj* **crueller, cruellest** 1 without pity; and enjoying causing pain and suffering: *The soldiers were very cruel* **to** *their prisoners.* 2 causing suffering, pain, or hardship: *a cruel punishment* | *a cruel remark* | *Dog-fighting is cruel.* –**cruelly** *adv*

cru·el·ty /ˈkruːəlti/ *n* **cruelties** 1 [U] the quality of being cruel: *cruelty to animals* 2 [C] an example of cruel behaviour

cru·el·ty-free /ˌ··· ˈ·◂/ *adj* made without being tested on animals (used of products such as soaps)

cru·et /ˈkruːᵻt/ *n* a set of containers for pepper, salt, and other substances to add to your food, put on the table at meals

cruise¹ /kruːz/ *v* [I] 1 to sail for pleasure in an unhurried way 2 (of a car or plane) to move at a steady, unhurried speed, especially on a long journey: *a cruising speed of 60 miles an hour*

cruise² *n* a sea voyage for pleasure

cruise con·trol /ˈ· ·ˌ·/ *n* a special part in a car which allows you to use less petrol when you are travelling steadily at high speed

cruis·er /ˈkruːzəʳ/ *n* 1 a boat with places to sleep and eat 2 a large fast warship

crumb /krʌm/ *n* 1 a very small piece of dry food, especially bread or cake: *Sweep up the crumbs from under the table.* 2 a very small amount: *We managed to pick up a few crumbs of knowledge.*

crum·ble /ˈkrʌmbəl/ *v* **crumbled, crumbling** 1 [T] to make something break into very small pieces: *He crumbled the bread in his fingers.* 2 [I] to break into small pieces, often because of age: *As the years passed, the old church crumbled.* 3 [I] to end or fail: *After centuries the Roman Empire crumbled.*

crum·bly /ˈkrʌmbli/ *adj* easily crumbled

crum·pet /ˈkrʌmpᵻt/ *n* a small round breadlike cake with holes in one side usually eaten hot and spread with butter

crum·ple /ˈkrʌmpəl/ *v* **crumpled, crumpling** [I;T] to make something become full of irregular folds by pressing or crushing it: *Don't sit on that shirt – you'll crumple it!* | *The front of the car crumpled as it crashed into the wall.*

crunch¹ /krʌntʃ/ *v* 1 [I;T] to crush food noisily with your teeth: *The dog was crunching* **on** *a bone.* 2 [I] to make noise like something being crushed: *Our feet crunched on the snow.* | *The stones crunched under the car tyres.* –**crunchy** *adj* **crunchier, crunchiest**

crunch² *n* 1 a crunching sound 2 **the crunch** *infml* a difficult moment at which an important decision must be made 3 **if/when it comes to the crunch, when the crunch comes** if you reach the point where you have to act or decide

cru·sade¹ /kruːˈseɪd/ *n* 1 **the Crusades** any of the Christian wars to win back Palestine from the Muslims 800 years ago 2 a set of activities to support or fight against something that you feel strongly about: *a crusade* **against** *crime* | *a crusade* **for** *better prison conditions*

cru·sade² *v* **crusaded, crusading** [I] to take part in a crusade: *She's always crusading* **for** *women's rights.* –**crusader** *n*

crush¹ /krʌʃ/ *v* 1 [T] to press something with great force so as to break or destroy its natural shape: *The tree fell on top of the car and crushed it.* | *Wheat is crushed to make flour.* 2 [I; + adv/prep] (of people) to press tightly and uncomfortably into a place: *The* *crowd crushed through the gates.* **3** [T] to destroy an army or an organization: *The revolt was crushed by the army.*

crush² *n* **1** [sing] uncomfortable pressure caused by a great crowd of people: *There was such a crush on the train!* **2** [U] a drink made by crushing fruit: *orange crush* **3 have a crush on someone** *infml* to have a strong, foolish, and short-lived love for someone, often an older person: *I had a terrible crush on my teacher.*

crust /krʌst/ *n* [C;U] **1** the hard outer surface of baked bread **2** baked pastry **3** a hard outer covering: *the earth's crust* | *a thin crust of ice*

crus·ta·cean /krʌˈsteɪʃən/ *n* any of a group of animals, mostly sea animals, with several pairs of legs and a hard outer shell; a CRAB is a crustacean

crust·y /ˈkrʌsti/ *adj* **1** having a hard well-baked crust: *a crusty loaf* **2** bad-tempered and impatient: *a crusty old man*

crutch /krʌtʃ/ *n* **1** a stick with a piece that fits under your arm, for supporting a person who has difficulty in walking: *When he broke his leg he had to walk on crutches.* **2** –see CROTCH

crux /krʌks/ *n* **the crux** the central part of a problem: *The crux of the matter is ...*

cry¹ /kraɪ/ *v* **cried, cried, crying 1** [I] to produce tears from your eyes usually, as a sign of sadness: *She cried when she heard of her friend's death.* | *The children cried for their father.* **2** [I] to speak loudly or shout, usually with fear or excitement: *"Run, run!" he cried.* | *"That's wonderful!" she cried.* **3** [I] to make the natural sound of certain animals and birds: *Listen to the seabirds crying.* **4 cry your eyes out, cry your heart out** to cry a lot for a long time: *When her dog died my daughter cried her eyes out.* **5 cry over spilt milk** to waste time feeling sorry about something that cannot be changed for the better

cry off *phr v* [I] *infml* to fail to fulfil a promise or agreement: *He said he'd help, but then he cried off.*
cry out *phr v* [I] to shout loudly, usually with fear or pain: *He cried out in pain.*
cry out against sthg *phr v* [T] to complain or express your disapproval of something very strongly
cry out for sthg *phr v* [T] to be in great need of something: *The garden is crying out for rain.*

cry² *n* **cries 1** any loud sound expressing a strong feeling like fear or pleasure: *a cry of anger* **2** a loud shout, often to attract attention: *a cry of "Stop, thief!"* **3** [sing] a period of crying: *You'll be better after you've had a good cry.* **4** the natural sound of certain animals or birds **5** a general public demand: *a national cry for lower taxes*

cry·ing /ˈkraɪ-ɪŋ/ *adj infml* **1 a crying need** an urgent need **2 a crying shame** *infml* a very great shame *It's a crying shame, the way she hits that child.*

crypt /krɪpt/ *n* an underground room beneath a church

cryp·tic /ˈkrɪptɪk/ *adj* mysterious or with hidden meaning: *a cryptic message* | *a cryptic remark* –**cryptically** /-kli/ *adv*

SPELLING NOTE
Words with the sound / k /, like **cut**, may be spelt **k-**, like **key**, or **qu-**, like **queen**.
Words with the sound / s /, like **city**, may be spelt **s-**, like **soon**, or **ps-**, like **psychology**.

---

crys·tal /ˈkrɪstl/ *n* **1** [U] a transparent natural mineral that looks like ice **2** [U] colourless glass of very high quality: *a crystal wine glass* **3** [C] a small regular shape formed naturally by a chemical substance when it becomes solid: *sugar and salt crystals*

crys·tal·lize /ˈkrɪstəlaɪz/ *v* (also **crystallise** *BrE*) [I;T] **1** to make a substance form crystals: *At what temperature does sugar crystallize?* **2** (of thoughts or opinions) to become clear or fixed: *She's trying to crystallize her ideas into a practical plan.* | *Their attitude has crystallized.* –**crystallization** /ˌkrɪstəlaɪˈzeɪʃən‖-lə-/ *n* [U]

cu. an abbreviation for CUBIC

cub /kʌb/ *n* **1** a young bear, lion, tiger, or fox **2 the cubs** (also **Cub Scouts**) a division of the SCOUTS for younger boys

cube¹ /kjuːb/ *n* **1** a solid object with six equal square sides **2** the number made by multiplying a number by itself twice: *The cube of 3 is 27.* (3×3×3=27)

cube² *v* **cubed, cubing** [T] **1** to cut something into cubes **2** to multiply a number by itself twice: *3 cubed* (written 3³) *is 27.*

cu·bic /ˈkjuːbɪk/ *adj* related to a way of measuring space when the length of something is multiplied by the width and height of it: *a cubic centimetre* | *cubic capacity*

cu·bi·cle /ˈkjuːbɪkəl/ *n* a very small enclosed division of a larger room, such as one used for undressing at a swimming pool

cuck·oo /ˈkuku‖ˈkuːku:, ˈkʊ-/ *n* a bird that lays its eggs in another bird's nest; it has a call that sounds like its name

cu·cum·ber /ˈkjuːkʌmbəʳ/ *n* [C;U] a long, thin, round vegetable with a dark green skin and light green watery flesh, which is eaten raw –see picture on page 344

cud·dle¹ /ˈkʌdl/ *v* **cuddled, cuddling** [I;T] to put your arms around someone or something lovingly: *He was sitting cuddling the baby.*
cuddle up *phr v* [I] to lie close and comfortably with someone: *The children cuddled up to each other in the dark.*

cuddle² *n* [sing] an act of cuddling someone: *My daughter came to me for a cuddle.*

cud·dly /ˈkʌdli/ *adj* lovable, soft, and slightly fat: *a cuddly baby*

cud·gel /ˈkʌdʒəl/ *n* a short thick heavy stick used as a weapon

cue /kjuː/ *n* **1** a signal for the next person to speak or act in a play: *The actor missed his cue and came onto the stage late.* **2 on cue** exactly when expected: *And right on cue he walked through the front door.* **3** a long straight wooden rod used for pushing the ball in BILLIARDS or SNOOKER

cuff¹ /kʌf/ *n* **1** the end of a shirt SLEEVE –see picture on page 50 **2** *AmE* the TURN-UP of a pair of trousers **3 off the cuff** without preparation: *I'm afraid I can't answer your question off the cuff.* **4** an act of hitting someone lightly with your open hand

cuff² *v* [T] to hit someone lightly with your open hand

cui·sine /kwɪˈziːn/ *n* [U] a style of cooking: *French cuisine*

cul-de-sac /ˈkʌl də ˌsæk, ˈkʊl-‖ˌkʌl də ˈsæk, ˌkʊl-/ *n* **cul-de-sacs** or **culs-de-sac** /kʌl, kʊl/ a street which is closed at one end

cul·i·na·ry /'kʌlɟnəri ‖ 'kʌlɟneri, 'kjuːl-/ adj fml related to the kitchen or cooking: culinary delights | culinary skills

cull /kʌl/ v [T] to kill the weakest of a group of animals –**cull** n : a seal cull

cul·mi·nate /'kʌlmɟneɪt/ v fml **culminate in something** to end in something: minor clashes culminating in a full-scale war

cul·mi·na·tion /ˌkʌlmɟ'neɪʃən/ n [U] the last and highest point of something, especially after a long period of development: The discovery was the culmination of his life's work.

cu·lottes /kjuː'lɒts ‖ kjuː'lɑːts/ n [pl] women's trousers, reaching below the knee, which are cut to look like a skirt

cul·pa·ble /'kʌlpəbəl/ adj fml deserving blame –**culpability** /ˌkʌlpə'bɪlɟti/ n [U]

cul·prit /'kʌlprɟt/ n the person guilty of a crime or offence

cult /kʌlt/ n **1** a religious group with beliefs considered unusual: The Moonies' cult is widespread in America. | an ancient tribal cult **2** a particular fashion or style, especially among a small number of people: Her books have a certain cult following.

cul·ti·vate /'kʌltɟveɪt/ v **cultivated, cultivating** [T] **1** to prepare land to grow crops on **2** to plant, grow, and raise a crop **3** to develop your mind through study: to cultivate a knowledge of art **4** to encourage the friendship of someone you regard as useful to know: John always tries to cultivate people who might be able to help his career.

cul·ti·vat·ed /'kʌltɟveɪtɟd/ adj **1** used for growing plants or crops **2** showing good education and manners: He's an extremely cultivated man.

cul·ti·va·tion /ˌkʌltɟ'veɪʃən/ n [U] the growing of plants or crops: to bring new land under cultivation

cul·tu·ral /'kʌltʃərəl/ adj **1** relating to the art, beliefs, and customs of a particular society **2** relating to things like art, music, and theatre: The city is trying to promote cultural activities. –**culturally** adv

cul·ture /'kʌltʃəʳ/ n **1** [C;U] the art, beliefs, and customs of a particular society: ancient Greek culture | a tribal culture **2** [U] things like art, music, and theatre: Paris is a good city for anyone who is interested in culture. | a man of little culture **3** [C;U] the growing of bacteria for scientific use **4** [U] tech the practice of raising animals and growing plants: bee culture

cul·tured /'kʌltʃəd ‖ -ərd/ adj **1** showing good education, good manners, and an interest in art and music: a cultured mind –opposite **uncultured 2** grown or produced by people: a cultured pearl

cum·ber·some /'kʌmbəsəm ‖ -bər-/ adj **1** heavy and awkward to carry or wear: I hate wearing this cumbersome diving gear. **2** lengthy and difficult: Getting a passport can be a cumbersome process.

cu·mu·la·tive /'kjuːmjɟlətɪv ‖ -leɪtɪv/ adj increasing steadily in quantity: Interest on that loan will be cumulative. | The cumulative effect of air pollution. –**cumulatively** adv : At first, the drug does no harm, but cumulatively its effects are bad.

cun·ning /'kʌnɪŋ/ adj clever at deceiving people: I knew I would have to be cunning if I wanted to get my own way. –**cunning** n [U] : He showed great cunning when he was planning his escape. –**cunningly** adv

cup¹ /kʌp/ n **1** a small round container, usually with a handle, from which hot liquids are drunk:

a cup and saucer –see picture on page 148 **2** the contents of a cup: a cup of tea | Add one cup of flour to half a cup of sugar. **3** a prize in a competition which is often a silver cup on a flat base: Which team do you think will win the cup this year? **4** something shaped like a cup: the cup of a flower **5 someone's cup of tea** infml the sort of thing that someone likes: Football's not really my cup of tea.

cup² v **-pp- cup your hands** to form your hands into the shape of a cup: She cupped her cold hands round the mug of hot tea.

cup·board /'kʌbəd ‖ -ərd/ n a piece of furniture with shelves and a door where clothes, plates, or food may be stored

cup·ful /'kʌpfʊl/ n **cupfuls** as much of a substance as a cup will hold: a cupful of sugar | Add two cupfuls of milk.

cu·rate /'kjʊərɟt/ n a priest who helps the main priest in a PARISH

cu·ra·tor /kjʊ'reɪtəʳ/ n the person in charge of an important collection of books, paintings, or other objects: chief curator of the British Museum

curb¹ /kɜːb ‖ kɜːrb/ n **1** a tight control: Keep a curb on your anger. **2** –see KERB

curb² v [T] to control something undesirable like bad temper

curds /kɜːdz ‖ kɜːrdz/ n [U] the thick soft substance that separates from milk when it becomes sour

cur·dle /'kɜːdl ‖ 'kɜːrdl/ v **curdled, curdling** [I;T] to turn sour and thick: The milk has curdled in the coffee.

cure¹ /kjʊəʳ/ v **cured, curing** [T] **1** to bring health to someone who is ill: This medicine cured me of my cold. **2** to get rid of an illness or a problem: The only way to cure backache is to rest. | government action to cure unemployment **3** to preserve food, tobacco, or skin by drying it, hanging it in smoke, or covering it with salt

cure² n **1** a medicine that cures an illness or disease: There is still no cure for the common cold. **2** a return to health after illness: This drug should bring about a cure. **3** something that ends a problem: There is no easy cure for high inflation.

cur·few /'kɜːfjuː ‖ 'kɜːrf-/ n a time during which everyone must stay indoors: The government imposed a curfew from sunset to sunrise.

cu·ri·o /'kjʊəriəʊ/ n a small object, valuable because it is rare, old, or beautiful

cu·ri·os·i·ty /ˌkjʊəri'ɒsɟti ‖ -'ɑːs-/ n **curiosities 1** [sing;U] the desire to know something or learn about something: There was intense curiosity about their wedding plans. **2** [C] something that is strange, interesting, or rare: My great-aunt's cottage is full of curiosities.

cu·ri·ous /'kjʊəriəs/ adj **1** [never before a noun] eager to know something or to learn about something: We were curious to know where she'd gone. | I'm very curious about our new neighbours **2** odd or strange: We heard a curious noise upstairs. –**curiously** adv : Curiously enough, we had met before.

curl¹ /kɜːl ‖ kɜːrl/ n **1** a piece of hair that curves round: a mass of blonde curls **2** something with the shape of a curl: a curl of smoke

curl² v [I;T] **1** to form a curl or curls: I don't like my hair straight so I'm having it curled. **2** to move round and round: The ivy curled itself round the branches of the tree. | The smoke curled upwards.

Countable nouns

apple and **chair** are both COUNTABLE nouns, because they are things we can count; there can be more than one of them:

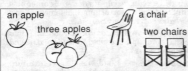

an apple
three apples
a chair
two chairs

These nouns can be used in the plural and can be used with **a** or **an** when they are singular.

In the dictionary, [C] means countable, and [U] means uncountable. If a noun does not have a [C] or a [U] printed by it, this means that is always countable.

Uncountable nouns

sand and **water** are UNCOUNTABLE nouns, because they are substances which cannot be counted:

sand
water

These nouns are not usually used in the plural.

There are some nouns, like **love** and **beauty** (ABSTRACT nouns) which cannot be counted because they are not physical things like apples and chairs. These are uncountable nouns too.

For more information on countable and uncountable nouns turn to page 15.

---

nouns that are both countable and uncountable

Some nouns, like **light** and **coffee**, can be [C] (countable) in one meaning and [U] (uncountable) in another. When they are [C] they can become plural. When they are [U] they cannot. For example:

[U] *the* **light** *of the sun*

[C] *Turn on the* **lights**

[U] *a jar of* **coffee**   [U] *a pot of* **coffee**

[C] Three ***coffees*** *please*

plural and singular nouns

Some nouns, like **trousers** are used only in the plural, i.e. they take a plural verb. These nouns are marked [pl] in the dictionary.

> **trou·sers** /ˈtraʊzəz ‖ -ərz/ *n* [pl] an outer garment covering your body from the waist down, with one part for each leg: *a pair of blue trousers*

Some nouns, like **feel**, are usually used only in the singular. These nouns are used with **a** and **an,** and are marked [sing] in the dictionary:

> **feel**[2] *n* [sing] **1** the sensation that you experience when you touch and feel something: *The skin has a rough feel.*

more and less

The list below show you which words to use with [C] and [U] nouns to show quantity. They answer questions like *How many?* and *How much?*

all

How many
(use with [C] nouns)

every, all
Every *student /* **all** *the students came to the meeting.*

most
Most *of my friends came to the party.*

many, a lot of
Many *people walk to school every day. I spoke to* **a lot of** *people.*

some, several
Some *of these apples taste sour.* **Several** *people were waiting for the bus.*

not many, only a few
There are **not many** */* **only a few** *tickets left.*

not ... any, no, none
He couldn't answer **any** *of the exam questions. There are* **no** *eggs left;* **none** *at all.*

How much
(use with [U] nouns)

all
He ate **all** *the bread.*

most
He spends **most** *of his time reading.*

much, a lot of, a great deal of
Much *of what he says is true. He ate* **a lot of** *bread. She did* **a great deal of** *work.*

some
There's **some** *bread in the cupboard.*

little, not much
There's only **a little** */* **not much** *room left.*

not ... any, no, none
He didn't give me **any** *help. There's* **no** *petrol in the car,* **none** *at all*

---

some and any

any is usually used insted of **some** in questions and sentences with *not*:
Have you got **any** *eggs/milk?*
No, I haven't got **any** *eggs/milk.*

It is also possible to use **some** in a question, especially when you expect the answer to be *yes*:
Could you spare **some** *eggs/milk, please?*
Would you like **some** *more coffee?*

Some common mistakes with uncountable nouns

If a noun is marked [U] do NOT use it in the plural. If a particular meaning of a noun is marked [U] do not use it in the plural with this meaning:
– *We need some more informations.*
– *They've just bought a lot of new furnitures.*
– *I must wash my hairs tonight.*

If a noun, or a meaning of a noun, is marked [U] do NOT use it with **a** or **an** in sentences like these:
– *The hotel is surrounded by a beautiful scenery.*

– *We are having a really fine weather at the moment.*
– *She gave me a very good advice.*

Remember that uncountable nouns are used WITHOUT an article in general statements like these:

– *The crime is a problem in most big cities.*
– *She wrote an article about the role of women in the society.*
– *He is studying the medicine.*

curl up _phr v_ [I] **1** to lie comfortably with your arms and legs pulled up close to your body: _She curled up in front of the fire with a good book._ **2** to bend at the edges with age: _The leaves became brown and curled up._

curl·y /ˈkɜːli ‖ ˈkɜːrli/ _adj_ having curls: _curly hair_ –see picture on page 245 –**curliness** _n_ [U]

cur·rant /ˈkʌrənt ‖ ˈkɜːr-/ _n_ **1** a small dried seedless GRAPE, sometimes used in cakes **2** a small black, red, or white juicy fruit that grows in bunches on certain bushes

cur·ren·cy /ˈkʌrənsi ‖ ˈkɜːr-/ _n_ **currencies 1** [C;U] the particular type of money in use in a country: _The different currencies of Europe_ | _the need to earn foreign currency to pay for imports_ | _changing traveller's cheques for the local currency_ **gain currency** (of an idea) to become accepted

cur·rent¹ /ˈkʌrənt ‖ ˈkɜːr-/ _adj_ **1** belonging to the present time: _The work would cost £2000 at current prices._ **2** in general use: _That word is no longer in current use._ –**currently** _adv_

current² _n_ **1** [C] a continuously moving mass of liquid or gas, especially one flowing through a slower-moving liquid or gas: _The current is strongest in the middle of the river._ | _hot air currents_ **2** [C;U] a flow of electricity: _Turn off the current before you change the bulb._ **3** [C] a general movement towards a particular opinion: _The current of public opinion is against the government._

current ac·count /ˈ·· ·ˌ·/ _n_ a bank account from which money can be taken out by cheque or by using a card; it is meant for ordinary spending money, not for the money you want to save

cur·ric·u·lum /kəˈrɪkjʊləm/ _n_ **curricula** /-lə/ _or_ **curriculums** all the courses of study offered in a school, college, or university: _Computer studies is now on the curriculum._

curriculum vi·tae /kə‚rɪkjʊləm ˈviːtaɪ/ _n BrE fml_ a short written account of your education and past employment, used especially when you are looking for a new job

cur·ry /ˈkʌri ‖ ˈkɜːri/ _n_ **curries** [C;U] an Indian dish of meat, vegetables, or fish, cooked in a thick hot-tasting liquid and usually eaten with rice: _I like vegetable curry._ | _I'll have a chicken curry._ **curry** _v_ **curried, currying** [T] : _curried chicken_

curse¹ /kɜːs ‖ kɜːrs/ _n_ **1** something said which expresses anger or hate, or which uses swear words **2 put a curse on someone** to make a solemn wish that with the help of God or some magical power, something unpleasant will happen to someone **3** a cause of trouble and harm: _Foxes can be a curse to farmers._

curse² _v_ **cursed, cursing 1** [T] to wish that something unpleasant will happen to someone: _She cursed him for ruining her life._ **2** [I;T] to swear at someone or something: _cursing the car because it wouldn't start_ | _He hit his thumb with the hammer and cursed loudly._ **3 be cursed with** to have something bad that you can't get rid of: _She was cursed with a stammer all her life._

cur·so·ry /ˈkɜːsəri ‖ ˈkɜːr-/ _adj_ done quickly without

---

attention to details: _Even a cursory glance at the report showed that our situation was serious._ –**cursorily** _adv_

curt /kɜːt ‖ kɜːrt/ _adj_ saying very little and therefore appearing rude: _a curt reply_ | _a curt manner_ –**curtly** _adv_ –**curtness** _n_ [U]

cur·tail /kɜːˈteɪl ‖ kɜːr-/ _v_ [T] _fml_ to reduce or limit something: _The government hopes to curtail public spending._ –**curtailment** _n_ [C;U]

cur·tain¹ /ˈkɜːtn ‖ ˈkɜːrtn/ _n_ **1** a piece of hanging cloth that can be pulled across to cover a window or door: _I'll draw the curtain as it's getting dark._ | _a shower curtain_ | _a pair of curtains_ –see picture on page 442 **2** a piece of heavy material that can be lowered across the front of the stage in a theatre

curtain² _v_ [T] to provide a room with a curtain **curtain sthg** ↔ **off** _phr v_ [T] to separate something from the rest of the room with a curtain: _a bedroom with a wash-basin curtained off in one corner_

curt·sy /ˈkɜːtsi ‖ ˈkɜːr-/ _n_ **curtsies** (also **curtsey**) a woman's act of respect to someone of higher rank, done by bending her knees and lowering her head and shoulders –**curtsy** _v_ **curtsied, curtsying** [I]

cur·va·ture /ˈkɜːvətʃəʳ ‖ ˈkɜːr-/ _n_ [C;U] the degree to which something is curved: _the curvature of the earth's surface_

curve¹ /kɜːv ‖ kɜːrv/ _v_ **curved, curving** [I;T] to bend in the shape of a curve: _The road curved to the right._

curve² _n_ a line of which no part is straight and which contains no angles: _a curve in the road_

cush·ion¹ /ˈkʊʃən/ _n_ **1** a bag filled with a soft substance on which you can lie, sit, or rest comfortably: _He lay on the floor with a cushion under his head._ –see picture on page 442 **2** something like this in shape or purpose: _A hovercraft rides on a cushion of air._

cushion² _v_ [T] to reduce the force or unpleasant effects of something: _When his wife died nothing could cushion the blow._ | _His savings should cushion him against the problems of old age._

cush·y /ˈkʊʃi/ _adj_ **cushier, cushiest** _infml_ easy in a way that makes other people jealous (used of a job or style of life) –**cushiness** _n_ [U]

cus·tard /ˈkʌstəd ‖ -ərd/ _n_ [U] _BrE_ a thick sweet yellow liquid made of milk, eggs, and flour, and poured over sweet foods

cus·to·di·an /kʌˈstəʊdiən/ _n_ a person who takes care of someone or something officially: _the custodian of the royal library_ | _custodians of public morality_

cus·to·dy /ˈkʌstədi/ _n_ [U] **1** the right given in a court of law to look after someone: _After the divorce the mother was given custody of the children._ **2 in custody** guarded by the police: _The stolen car is now in police custody._ | _The criminal was taken into custody._

cus·tom /ˈkʌstəm/ _n_ **1** [C;U] an activity or ceremony that is part of the way of life of a particular group of people: _Social customs vary greatly from country to country._ | _an ancient tribal custom_ **2** [C] something you usually do: _It was his custom to shout at lazy pupils._ –see HABIT (USAGE) **3** [U] _fml_ regular support given to a shop by those who buy things from it: _We lost a great deal of custom when that new shop opened._

cus·tom·a·ry /ˈkʌstəməri ‖ -meri/ _adj_ usual: _It is customary to give people gifts on their birthdays._ –**customarily** /-mərəli ‖ ‚kʌstəˈmerəli/ _adv_

custom-built /ˌ··ˈ·◂/ adj (also **custom**-made) made specially for a particular person

cus·tom·er /ˈkʌstəmər/ n someone who buys goods or services from a shop or business regularly: *The new shop across the road has taken away most of my customers.*

■ USAGE Compare **customer, shopper, client, patient, guest.** When you buy goods from a particular shop you are a **customer** of that shop: *Mrs Low can't come to the telephone – she's serving a* **customer.** When you go out to buy goods from shops you are a **shopper:** *a busy street full of* **shoppers.** When you pay for a service from a professional person such as a lawyer you are a **client,** but when you go to a doctor you are a **patient.** When you pay for a room in a hotel you are a **guest.**

Cus·toms /ˈkʌstəmz/ n [pl] (also **customs**) a place where your belongings are searched when you leave or enter a country, and where you have to pay tax on certain goods: *As soon as I'd got through customs I jumped into a taxi.*

cut¹ /kʌt/ v cut, cut, **cutting** 1 [I;T] to press a sharp object such as a knife into something, with the result that a part of it is removed or it is damaged: *She cut the meat into small pieces. | I cut my finger on a piece of broken glass. | Be careful you don't cut yourself with that knife. | He cut the cake into slices. | These scissors don't cut very well. | He cut a hole in the wood.* –see BREAK (USAGE) 2 [T] to make someone's hair or nails shorter by using scissors: *You ought to cut your fingernails. | I must get my hair cut.* 3 [T] to remove a part of a film, a television broadcast, or a piece of writing: *Some of the most violent scenes were cut from the film.* 4 [T] to reduce something: *Government spending will have to be cut next year. | Bus services in the area have been cut.* 5 **cut a tooth** to grow a tooth: *Most babies cut their first tooth at about six months old.* 6 **cut the cards** to divide a pile of playing cards in two before giving them out to the players 7 **cut corners** to do something in a less than perfect way in order to save time or money 8 **cut it fine** to leave yourself very little time or money to do something 9 **cut your losses** to stop taking part in a business that is failing, before you lose too much money

cut across sthg *phr v* [T] 1 to go across something in order to arrive somewhere more quickly: *Go down to the stream, then cut across the field to the main road.* 2 to go across the limits of a group or subject, and so include or have an effect on more than one group or subject: *This is an important moral issue which cuts across party lines.*

cut back *phr v* 1 [T cut sthg ↔ **back**] to cut a plant close to its stem so that it will grow better next year 2 [I;T cut sthg ↔ **back**] to reduce something: *All local services will have to be cut back. | We need to cut back on our expenditure.*

cut down *phr v* 1 [T cut sthg ↔ **down**] to make something fall to the ground by cutting it: *Hundreds of trees have been cut down.* 2 [I;T cut sthg ↔ **down**] to reduce something: *You smoke too much – you ought to cut down. | I'm trying to cut my drinking down. | We'll have to cut down on our spending.*

cut in *phr v* [I] to interrupt someone when they are talking: *Mr Davies cut in to ask if anyone would like a drink. | I continued with my story, but she cut in on me again.*

cut off *phr v* 1 [cut sthg ↔ **off**] to remove something by cutting it: *She cut off a few of the branches.* 2 [cut sthg ↔ **off**] to disconnect a supply of something: *The gas has been cut off.* 3 [T cut sbdy ↔ **off**] to disconnect a telephone line while people

are talking: *We were cut off half way through the conversation.* 4 [T cut sbdy/sthg ↔ **off**] to separate a person or place from the other people or places around: *Several villages have been cut off by the snow. | I felt terribly isolated and cut off when we moved to a new town.*

cut out *phr v* 1 [T cut sthg ↔ **out**] to remove something by cutting it: *She cut the advertisement out of the newspaper.* 2 [T cut sthg ↔ **out**] to stop doing something: *I'm trying to cut out smoking altogether.* 3 [I] (of an engine) to stop suddenly: *Every time I slowed down the engine cut out.* 4 **cut it out** *infml* a phrase you use to tell someone to stop doing something 5 **not cut out for something, not cut out to do something** not well-suited for something: *I'm not cut out for acting. | She's not cut out to teach.*

cut sthg ↔ **short** *phr v* [T] to bring something to an end before the proper time: *Our holiday had to be cut short because the weather was so bad.*

cut up *phr v* 1 [T cut sthg ↔ **up**] to cut something into pieces: *Cut the meat and vegetables up into small pieces.* 2 **be cut up** to feel very upset: *He was really cut up when his wife died.*

cut² n 1 an opening or wound caused by cutting: *There were several small cuts in the cloth. | How did you get that cut on your hand?* 2 a piece of meat to be cooked in one piece: *A leg of lamb is one of the most expensive cuts you can buy.* 3 a reduction: *We are all hoping for tax cuts. | There have been massive cuts in government spending.* 4 *infml* a share in something: *I had been promised my cut of the profits.* 5 **a cut above** *infml* of better quality than most other things or people: *She thinks she's a cut above the rest of us.*

cut-and-dried /ˌ··ˈ·◂/ adj already decided: *cut-and-dried opinions*

cut·back /ˈkʌtbæk/ n a planned decrease: *The government is planning more cutbacks in public expenditure.*

cute /kjuːt/ adj delightfully pretty and often small: *What a cute little baby!* –**cutely** adv –**cuteness** n [U]

cut glass /ˌ·ˈ·◂/ n [U] glass with patterns cut on it: *a cut-glass bowl*

cu·ti·cle /ˈkjuːtɪkəl/ n an outer covering of hard skin round the lower edges of the nails on your toes and fingers

cut·lass /ˈkʌtləs/ n a short sword with a slightly curved blade

cut·le·ry /ˈkʌtləri/ n [U] knives, forks, and spoons used for eating

cut·let /ˈkʌtlɪt/ n a small piece of meat with a bone: *lamb cutlets*

cut·out /ˈkʌtaʊt/ n 1 something that disconnects a motor or an electrical CIRCUIT, especially if there is too much load on it 2 a figure cut out of paper, wood, or cardboard

cut-price /ˌ·ˈ·◂/ adj [only before a noun] sold at reduced prices: *cut-price petrol*

cut·ter /ˈkʌtər/ n 1 a small fast boat 2 an instrument used for cutting: *a hedge-cutter | a pair of wire-cutters*

cut·ting¹ /ˈkʌtɪŋ/ n 1 a stem or leaf cut from a plant and put in soil or water to form roots and grow into a new plant 2 *BrE* an article cut out from a newspaper or magazine 3 a passage cut through a hill for a road or railway

cutting² adj 1 unkind (used of something that someone says): *The teacher was unpopular because*

he was always making cutting remarks. **2** uncomfortably strong and cold (used of the wind) –**cuttingly** *adv*

CV /ˌsiː ˈviː/ *n* an abbreviation for CURRICULUM VITAE

cwt *n* **cwts** a written abbreviation for HUNDREDWEIGHT

cy·a·nide /ˈsaɪənaɪd/ *n* [U] a very strong poison

cyc·la·men /ˈsɪkləmən/ *n* a plant with white, purple, pink, or red flowers

cy·cle¹ /ˈsaɪkəl/ *n* **1** a number of related events happening in a regularly repeated order: *the cycle of the seasons* | *the cycle of boom and slump* **2** the period of time needed for this to be completed: *a 50-second cycle* **3** a number of connected poems or songs written about someone or something **4** a bicycle: *a cycle shop* | *cycle racing*

cy·cle² *v* **cycled, cycling** [I] to ride a bicycle – see picture on page 637

cy·clic /ˈsaɪklɪk/ *adj* (also **cyclical** /ˈsɪklɪkəl, ˈsaɪk-/) happening again and again in a regular pattern

cy·clist /ˈsaɪklɪst/ *n* someone who rides a bicycle

cy·clone /ˈsaɪkləʊn/ *n* a very violent tropical wind moving rapidly in a circle round a calm central area

cyg·net /ˈsɪgnɪt/ *n* a young SWAN

cyl·in·der /ˈsɪlɪndər/ *n* **1** a hollow or solid shape with a circular base and straight sides **2** the tube within which a PISTON moves backwards and forwards in an engine

cy·lin·dri·cal /səˈlɪndrɪkəl/ *adj* in the shape of a cylinder

cym·bal /ˈsɪmbəl/ *n* a musical instrument which is like a round thin metal plate; it is struck, sometimes against another, to make a loud ringing noise –**cymbalist** *n*

cyn·ic /ˈsɪnɪk/ *n* someone who thinks that people only do things which will help them in some way: –**cynical** *adj*: *She was very cynical about his reason for coming to see her.* –**cynically** /-kli/ *adv* –**cynicism** /-nˌsɪzəm/ *n* [U]: *There was a mood of general cynicism in the country about the forthcoming elections.*

cy·press /ˈsaɪprəs/ *n* a tree with dark green leaves and hard wood, that does not lose its leaves in winter

cyst /sɪst/ *n* an enclosed hollow growth in or on your body, containing liquid

czar /zɑːr/ *n* – see TSAR

Czech¹ /tʃek/ *adj* of or connected with Czechoslovakia

Czech² *n* **1** [C] a person from Czechoslovakia **2** [U] a language spoken in Czechoslovakia

D,d

D,d /diː/ **D's, d's** *or* **Ds, ds** the 4th letter of the English alphabet

-'d **1** short for WOULD: *I asked if he'd go.* **2** short for HAD: *I asked if he'd gone.* –see 's (USAGE)

d an abbreviation for **died:** *d 1937*

d' short for DO: *D'you like it?*

dab¹ /dæb/ n **1** a quick or light touch: *He made a few dabs at the fence with the paintbrush, but that was all.* **2** a small amount of a substance: *a dab of paint*

dab² v **-bb-** [I;T] to touch something lightly and quickly, usually several times: *She dabbed her eyes with her handkerchief.* | *He dabbed at the wound with a wet cloth.*

dab·ble /ˈdæbəl/ v **dabbled, dabbling 1** [I] to work at or study something without serious intentions: *He likes dabbling in politics.* **2** [T] to move your hands or feet playfully about in water: *She dabbled her toes in the river.* –**dabbler** n

dab hand /ˌ· '·/ n someone who is very good at something: *She's a dab hand at cards.*

dachs·hund /ˈdækshʊnd, -sənd/ n a small dog with short legs and a long body

dad /dæd/ n infml father: *Can we go now, Dad?* | *Is your dad at home?*

dad·dy /ˈdædi/ n father (used by and to small children)

daf·fo·dil /ˈdæfədɪl/ n a yellow flower seen in early spring

daft /dɑːft ‖ dæft/ adj infml silly or foolish: *That was a daft thing to do.* | *Don't be so daft!*

dag·ger /ˈdægər/ n **1** a short pointed knife used in the past as a weapon **2 at daggers drawn** angry, and ready to fight: *They've been at daggers drawn ever since her promotion was announced.* **3 look daggers at someone** to look very angrily at someone: *She looked daggers at me as I spoke.*

dai·ly¹ /ˈdeɪli/ adj,adv every day, or every working day: *daily meetings* | *The mail is delivered twice daily.*

daily² n **dailies 1** (also **daily newspaper** /ˌ·· '····/) a newspaper printed and sold every day except Sunday **2** (also **daily help** /ˌ·· '·/) infml a woman who comes to your house every day to do housework

dain·ty¹ /ˈdeɪnti/ adj **daintier, daintiest** small, pretty, and delicate: *a dainty child* | *dainty movements* –**daintily** adv –**daintiness** n [U]

dainty² n **dainties** a nice piece of food, especially a small cake

dair·y /ˈdeəri/ n **dairies 1** a place on a farm where milk is kept and butter and cheese are made **2** a shop where milk, butter, cheese, and eggs are sold, or a place from which these products are sent to shops –**dairy** adj : *dairy products*

dairy cat·tle /ˈ·· ˌ··/ n [pl] cattle kept for milk rather than for meat

da·is /ˈdeɪɪs, deɪs/ n a raised part of the floor at one end of a hall, for speakers to stand on

dai·sy /ˈdeɪzi/ n **daisies** a very common small flower, white around a yellow centre

dale /deɪl/ n dialect a valley

dal·ly /ˈdæli/ v **1** [I] to be slow or waste time: *Don't dally over your food.* **2 dally with** to think about

something, but not very seriously: *They dallied with the idea of buying a larger house.*

dal·ma·tian /dælˈmeɪʃən/ n a large white dog with black spots

dam¹ /dæm/ n a wall or bank built across a river to keep back water: *The dam burst after weeks of heavy rain.*

dam² v **-mm-** [T] to build a dam across a river to block it: *They're damming the river.*
dam up phr v [T **dam** sthg ↔ **up**] **1** to build a dam across a river to block it **2** to control a feeling so that it does not show: *Don't dam up your anger – tell him how you feel.*

dam·age¹ /ˈdæmɪdʒ/ n [U] **1** harm done to something: *The storm caused extensive damage.* | *This new law has done a lot of damage to the government's popularity.* **2 damages** [pl] law money that someone must pay to another person for hurting them, or causing harm, or loss: *The court ordered the newspaper to pay me £500 in damages.*

damage² v **damaged, damaging** [T] to harm something

dam·ask /ˈdæməsk/ n [U] a heavy cloth with a pattern woven into it

dame /deɪm/ n **1** AmE slang a woman: *What a dame!* **2 Dame** a British title given to a woman to honour her work: *Dame Ellen Terry was a famous actress.*

damn¹ /dæm/ v [T] **1** (of God) to send someone to HELL after their death **2 damn it, damn you** an expression of anger or disappointment

damn² adj inf [only before a noun] a word used for giving force to an expression, good or bad (a word which some people consider not to be polite): *He's a damn fool.*

damn³ adv infml **1** a word used for giving force to an expression, good or bad (a word which some people consider not to be polite): *Don't be so damn foolish.* | *He ran damn fast.* **2 damn well** a phrase used for giving force to a verb, usually about something bad: *Don't lie to me – you knew damn well what was happening!*

damn⁴ interj infml an expression of anger or disappointment

damn⁵ n infml **I don't care/give a damn** = I don't care at all: *I don't care a damn what you do.*

dam·na·tion /dæmˈneɪʃən/ n [U] **1** an expression of anger or disappointment **2** the state of being sent to HELL after death

damned /dæmd/ adj **1** a word used for giving force to a statement: *I'm damned sure I gave him the money.* **2 well I'm damned, I'll be damned** = I'm very surprised **3 be damned if** to refuse to do something because you think it is unreasonable: *I'm damned if I'm going to give up my one free day of the week to help him.*

damn·ing /ˈdæmɪŋ/ adj strongly suggesting guilt: *Some damning information against them was discovered.*

damp¹ /dæmp/ adj rather wet, often in an unpleasant way: *The room felt cold and damp.* –**damp, dampness** n [U] –**damply** adv

damp² v
damp sthg ↔ **down** phr v [I] to make a fire burn more slowly: *Damp down the fire before you go to bed.*

damp·en /ˈdæmpən/ v [T] **1** to make something damp: *The rain hardly dampened the ground.* **2** to make feelings of happiness or excitement less strong *Nothing can dampen my spirits on such a nice day!*

dam·sel /ˈdæmzəl/ n *lit* a young unmarried woman, especially of noble birth

dam·son /ˈdæmzən/ n a type of PLUM tree, or its purple fruit

dance¹ /dɑːns ‖ dæns/ v **danced, dancing 1** [I] to move your body, especially your feet and hands, at the speed of the music: *She loves dancing.* | *I can't dance to this music.* | *Will you dance with me?* **2** [T] to perform a dance: *Can you dance the quickstep?* **3** [I;T] to move quickly up and down or around: *The words on the page were dancing in front of my eyes.* | *He danced round the room.* | *She danced her little sister in her lap.*

dance² n **1** [C] an act of dancing: *Let's just have one more dance.* **2** [C] a particular set of movements, usually performed to music: *The waltz is a beautiful dance.* **3** [C] a social meeting for dancing: *My parents are going to a dance tonight.* **4** [U] the art of dancing: *I'm not very keen on modern dance.* **–dancer** n

dan·de·li·on /ˈdændⱼlaɪən/ n a wild bright yellow flower

dan·druff /ˈdændrəf, -drʌf/ n [U] small pieces of dead, white skin that can sometimes be seen in a person's hair

dan·ger /ˈdeɪndʒəʳ/ n **1** [U] the possibility of harm: *"Danger! Falling rocks".* | *a danger signal* | *a place where children can play without danger* | *She's been very ill, but now she's out of danger.* | *I think his life's in danger.* **2 in danger of doing something** likely to do something: *He's in danger of losing his job.* **3** [C] a possible cause of harm: *the dangers of smoking*

dan·ger·ous /ˈdeɪndʒərəs/ adj able or likely to harm people: *a dangerous criminal* | *a dangerous drug* | *The situation is potentially dangerous.* **–dangerously** adv : *He's driving very dangerously.*

dan·gle /ˈdæŋgəl/ v **dangled, dangling 1** [I;T] to hang or swing loosely: *keys dangling from a chain* | *He sat on the edge of the table dangling his legs.* **2 dangle something in front of someone** to offer something as an attraction, usually because you want someone to do something

dank /dæŋk/ adj unpleasantly wet and cold (used of buildings or parts of buildings): *a dank cellar* | *the dank stone walls of his prison cell*

dap·per /ˈdæpəʳ/ adj small and with a neat appearance (used especially of men)

dap·pled /ˈdæpəld/ adj marked with spots of colour, or of sun and shadow: *a dappled horse*

dare¹ /deəʳ/ v negative short form **daren't 1 dare to do something, dare do something** to be brave enough to do something: *I daren't tell you any more.* | *We all knew she was wrong, but none of us, dared to tell her.* | *I want to ask for a pay rise, but I daren't.* | *I dare not be late home again.* | *If you dare tell anyone about this, I'll never speak to you again!* –see Study Note on page 392 **2 dare someone to do something** to try to persuade someone to do something dangerous so that they can show how brave they are: *He dared me to jump.* **3 don't you dare** a phrase you use to tell someone angrily not to do something: *Don't you dare talk to me like that!* **4 how dare you** a phrase you use when you are very angry about something that someone has done: *How dare you take my car without asking me?*

dare² n an invitation to someone to do something dangerous in order to show how brave they are

daren't /deənt ‖ deərnt/ short for **dare not**: *I daren't ask him.*

dare·say /ˌdeəˈseɪ◂ ‖ ˈdeərseɪ/ v **I daresay** = I suppose: *I daresay you're right.* | *It will come, I daresay.*

dar·ing /ˈdeərɪŋ/ adj very brave: *a daring attempt to save the children from the fire* | *a daring crime* **–daring** n [U] : *He showed great daring.*

dark¹ /dɑːk ‖ dɑːrk/ adj **1** without enough light to see clearly: *It's too dark to read.* | *In winter it gets dark here early.* **2** black or nearly black in colour: *dark hair* | *a dark blue shirt* | *a man wearing a dark suit* –see picture on page 147 **3** sad and without hope: *dark thoughts* | *You always look on the dark side of things.* **4** unpleasant and frightening: *There's a dark side to his character.* | *He gave me a dark look.* **5 keep something dark** to keep something secret **–darkly** adv :*He spoke darkly of trouble to come.* **–darkness** n [U]

dark² n **1 the dark** the absence of light: *Can cats see in the dark?* | *Some children are afraid of the dark.* **2 before dark** before night has begun: *Make sure you get home before dark.* [RELATED PHRASE **after dark**: *We're not allowed out after dark.* **3 keep someone in the dark** to keep something a secret from someone: *The public were kept in the dark about the government's plans.*

dark·en /ˈdɑːkən ‖ ˈdɑːr-/ v **1** [I;T] to make or become dark: *The sky darkened and the rain began to fall.* **2** [I] (of someone's face) to show anger: *His face darkened with anger.*

dark glas·ses /ˌ· ˈ··/ n [pl] glasses with dark glass in them to protect your eyes from the sun

dark horse /ˌ· ˈ·/ n someone who tends to keep their activities, feelings, or intentions secret, and who may have unexpected qualities or abilities

dar·ling¹ /ˈdɑːlɪŋ ‖ ˈdɑːr-/ n a word used when you speak to or about someone you like or love: *Hurry up, darling!* | *My granddaughter is a little darling.*

darling² adj [only before a noun] dearly loved: *my darling child*

darn¹ /dɑːn ‖ dɑːrn/ v [I;T] to repair a hole in cloth or a garment by weaving threads across the hole: *Can you darn socks?* | *I hate darning.* **–darn** n

darn² adj,adv (also **darned**) a word used to express anger or disappointment: *It's a darn nuisance.*

dart¹ /dɑːt ‖ dɑːrt/ n **1** [C] a small object with a sharp point which can be thrown or shot: *a poisoned dart* **2** [C] a quick sudden movement: *He made a dart for the door.* **3** [C] a fold sewn into a garment, to make it fit better **4 darts** [U] a game in which people throw darts at a special circular board called a **dartboard**

dart² v **1** [I + adv/prep] to move suddenly and quickly: *He darted towards the door.* | *She darted across the street.* **2 dart a look at someone** to look at someone suddenly and quickly: *She darted an angry look at her husband.*

dash¹ /dæʃ/ v **1** [I] to move with sudden speed: *I'm late – I must dash!* | *He dashed across the road.* **2** [I + adv/prep; T + adv/prep] to throw or hit something with great force: *The waves dashed against the rocks.* | *She dashed the books to the ground.* **3 dash someone's hopes** to destroy someone's hopes completely: *The accident dashed John's hopes of playing in the football team.*

dash² n **1 make a dash for** to run a short distance very quickly: *I made a dash for the door.* **2** [C] a small amount of something: *a dash* **of** *pepper* | *a dash of colour* **3** [C] a mark (–) used in writing and printing **4** [U] a combination of bravery and a stylish manner: *a man of great dash and spirit*

dash·board /'dæʃbɔːd ‖ -bɔːrd/ *n* the instrument board in a car, where many of the controls are –see picture on page 49

dash·ing /'dæʃɪŋ/ *adj* attractive and stylish: *a dashing young officer*

da·ta /'deɪtə, 'dɑːtə/ *n* [pl;U] facts or information: *What does the data tell us?* | *We can't give you the results until we've looked at all the data.*
■ USAGE Although plural in its Latin form, **data** is now often used as an uncountable [U] noun.

da·ta·base /'deɪtə,beɪs/ *n* a large collection of information that is stored in a computer system in such a way that it can easily be found by a computer user

date¹ /deɪt/ *n* **1** a particular time that can be shown by a number, for example the number of a day or the number of a year: *What's the date today? It's the third of August.* | *The date on the coin is 1921.* **2** an arrangement to meet at a particular time and place: *They made a date to meet soon.* **3** *infml* an arrangement to meet a girlfriend or boyfriend: *I've got a date with Jane this evening.* **4** *AmE infml* girlfriend or boyfriend: *Of course you can bring your date to my party.* **5** a small brown sweet fruit with a long stone, which grows on trees in hot countries **6 out of date** no longer fashionable, or no longer able to be used: *Her clothes are about 20 years out of date.* | *This ticket is out of date.* **7 to date** until now: *We've had few responses to date.* **8 up to date** modern, well informed, or at the point where you should be: *The equipment here is really up to date.* | *Keep me up to date with the news, will you?* | *I'm up to date with my homework now.*

date² *v* **dated, dating** **1** [T] to guess or show the age of something: *Archeologists can't date this pot exactly.* | *This dress dates me, doesn't it!* **2** [T] to write the date on something: *a letter dated 15th June* **3** [I] to seem no longer fashionable: *This type of music is beginning to date.* **4** [I;T] *AmE infml* to have or meet a girlfriend or boyfriend: *They've been dating for months.* | *He's dating Susan.* **5 date back to something, date from something** to have begun or been made at a particular date or time: *This church dates back to 1173.* | *The building dates from 1626.*

dat·ed /'deɪtɪd/ *adj* no longer fashionable: *These ideas seem rather dated now.*

date of birth /ˌ· · '·/ *n* the exact date on which you were born: *"What's your date of birth?" "10th May 1960."*

daub /dɔːb/ *v* [T] to put a substance onto a surface carelessly: *His clothes were daubed* **with** *mud.* | *He daubed paint* **on** *the wall.*

daugh·ter /'dɔːtəʳ/ *n* someone's female child: *Mr and Mrs Jones have three daughters.* –see picture on page 343

daughter-in-law /'··· · ·/ *n* **daughters-in-law** the wife of your son –see picture on page 343

daunt /dɔːnt/ *v* [T] to make someone afraid that they will not be able to do something: *We were daunted by the amount of work we had to do.* –**daunting** *adj*: *a daunting task*

daunt·less /'dɔːntləs/ *adj* brave –**dauntlessly** *adv*

daw·dle /'dɔːdl/ *v* **dawdled, dawdling** *infml* [I] to waste time by acting or moving slowly: *Stop dawdling or we'll be late.* –**dawdler** *n*

dawn¹ /dɔːn/ *n* **1** [C;U] the time of day when light first appears: *We got up at dawn.* | *the stillness of a summer dawn* **2 dawn is breaking** = light is just beginning to appear **3 the dawn of** the time when something is just beginning to develop: *the dawn of civilization*

dawn² *v* **1 the day dawned, the morning dawned** = it began to grow light: *The morning dawned fresh and clear after the storm.* **2 dawn on, upon** somebody to become clear to someone: *It suddenly dawned on me that I had caught the wrong train.*

day /deɪ/ *n* **1** [C] a period of 24 hours: *There are seven days in a week.* | *Christmas Day* –see USAGE **2** [C;U] the time between sunrise and sunset: *I'm usually out during the day.* | *It rained all day.* **3** [C] a period of work within a 24-hour period: *She works an eight-hour day.* | *They're demanding a four-day week.* **4 days** [pl] a period in history or someone's life: *in the days before the revolution* | *He began his days in a village.* **5 in my day** = when I was young: *Things were different in my day.* **6 these days, in this day and age** now, as opposed to the past: *People don't seem so polite these days.* **7 one day, some day** at some time in the future **8 to this day** until now: *To this day we haven't heard the whole story.* **9 have had your day** not to be popular or successful any longer: *Trade Unions have had their day.* **10 call it a day** *infml* to finish working for the day **11 make someone's day** to make someone very pleased or happy **12 the other day** recently: *I saw Geoff the other day.*

day·break /'deɪbreɪk/ *n* [U] the time of day when light first appears

day·dream /'deɪdriːm/ *n* a lot of pleasant thoughts, especially about things that you would like to happen –**daydream** *v* [I] : *She's always daydreaming.* –**daydreamer** *n*

day·light /'deɪlaɪt/ *n* [U] **1** the light of day: *There's more daylight in summer.* | *The house was burgled in broad daylight.* **2** the time of day when it begins to get light

day off /ˌ· '·/ *n* a day when you do not have to go to work

day re·turn /ˌ· ·'·/ *n* a ticket for a bus or train journey when you want to go and come back on the same day

day·time /'deɪtaɪm/ *n* [sing; U] the time between sunrise and sunset: *I can't sleep in the daytime.* | *Daytime flights are always more expensive.*

day-to-day /ˌ· ·'·◂/ *adj* [only before a noun] happening every day as a regular part of life: *life's day-to-day routine*

daze /deɪz/ *n* **in a daze** unable to think or feel clearly

dazed /deɪzd/ *adj* unable to think or feel clearly, for example because of a blow or shock: *She was dazed after the accident.* | *The news left him dazed.*

daz·zle /'dæzəl/ *v* **dazzled, dazzling** [T] **1** to make someone unable to see by throwing a strong light in their eyes: *The lights of the car dazzled me.* **2** to fill someone with admiration: *The whole family was dazzled by her success.* –**dazzle** *n* [sing] : *the dazzle of the bright lights* | *the dazzle of her smile*

DC /ˌdiː 'siː/ a flow of electricity that moves in one direction only; an abbreviation for **direct current** –compare **AC**

DDT /ˌdiː diː 'tiː/ *n* [U] a chemical used to kill insects

dea·con /'diːkən/ *n* a religious official in various Christian churches; a woman deacon is called a **deaconess**

dead¹ /ded/ adj **1** no longer alive: a dead man | a dead body | That plant is dead. –see USAGE **2** without the necessary power to work properly: The phone went dead. **3** without life, movement, or activity: The whole place seems dead. **4** no longer in use: a dead language | dead issues **5** infml very tired: I'm absolutely dead. **6** complete or exact (a word used before a noun for emphasis): We came to a dead stop. | dead silence **7** dead to the world very deeply asleep **8** wouldn't be seen dead infml = would refuse to do something or go somewhere: I wouldn't be seen dead wearing that hat. | She wouldn't be seen dead at any event organized by Bob. ■ USAGE If you are thinking about the fact that somebody is no longer alive, use the adjective **dead**: My grandfather has been dead for several years. | When I approached the bed, I realised the patient was dead. | Shakespeare and Dickens are dead, but we still read their works. If you are thinking about the moment or the action of dying, use the verb **die**: My grandfather died in 1985. | I realised the patient had died in the night. | When did Dickens die?

dead² n **1 in the dead of night, at dead of night** in the middle of winter or in the middle of the night when everything is quiet and still **2 the dead** a person who has died or people who have died

dead³ adv **1** infml completely or extremely: I'm dead tired. **2** infml exactly: The police station is dead ahead. **3 stop dead** to stop suddenly and completely

dead·en /'dedn/ v [T] to make a sound or feeling less strong: The drugs deadened the pain. | Thick walls deaden noise.

dead end /ˌ· '·◂/ n **1** a street with no way out at one end **2** a situation or position which cannot change or develop any more: It's a dead end job.

dead·line /'dedlaɪn/ n a date or time before which something must be done: Next Friday's the deadline for this report.

dead·lock /'dedlɒk ‖ -lɑːk/ n [C;U] a situation in which a disagreement cannot be settled: The talks ended in deadlock.

dead·ly¹ /'dedli/ adj **deadlier, deadliest 1** very dangerous and likely to cause death: a deadly disease | deadly weapons **2** very effective in hurting someone: a deadly remark | a deadly insult **3** complete and total in an unpleasant way: They are deadly enemies. | There was a deadly silence. **4** infml very dull: The party was deadly. –**deadliness** n [U]

deadly² adv very: He was being deadly serious.

dead·pan /'dedpæn/ adj showing no feeling and appearing to be serious even when you are joking: deadpan humour | a deadpan expression

dead weight /'ded ˌweɪt/ n [sing] something that is very heavy and difficult to lift

deaf /def/ adj **1** unable to hear: a special school for deaf children | Speak up, I'm a bit deaf. **2 be deaf to something, turn a deaf ear to something** to refuse to listen to something: She was deaf to all my requests. **3 fall on deaf ears** not to be listened to: His warnings fell on deaf ears. –**deafness** n [U]

deaf·en /'defən/ v [T] to make it difficult for you to hear anything: We were deafened by the noise. –**deafening** adj: a deafening noise

deal¹ /diːl/ v **dealt** /delt/, **dealt 1** [I;T] (also **deal out; deal** sth ↔ **out**) to give out playing cards to players in a card game: It's my turn to deal. | He dealt out the cards. | I dealt three cards to each player. | I dealt them four cards each. **2 deal someone a blow** to hit someone hard, or to do someone or something sudden harm: She dealt him a blow on the side of his face. | This policy dealt a severe blow to British industry.

deal in sth phr v [T] to buy and sell things: This shop deals in men's clothing.

deal with sbdy/sthg phr v [T] **1** to take the necessary action to find an answer to a problem: How would you deal with this situation? **2** to be about: This book deals with the troubles in Ireland. **3** to do business with a company or person: I've dealt with Jones and Taylor for 20 years.

deal² n **1** an arrangement or agreement, especially in business: We did quite well out of the deal. | Perhaps we can do a deal with our competitors. | It's a deal! **2 a great deal, a good deal** a lot: A great deal of money has been spent on the new hospital. | You'll have to work a good deal faster. **3** [C] someone's turn to give out cards to players in a card game: Is it my deal? **4 a bad deal, a raw deal** infml unfair or unpleasant treatment: Working nights again! I always get a raw deal from this company. ■ USAGE Remember that **a great deal of** is usually used with uncountable [U] nouns: **a great deal of** effort/money/kindness. Do NOT use it with countable [C] nouns. Instead you can say: **a great many** people/countries/activities or, more informally, **a lot of** people/countries/activities.

deal·er /'diːləʳ/ n **1** a person who buys and sells a particular type of thing: a used-car dealer | a dealer in stolen goods **2** a person who is dealing in a game of cards

deal·ing /'diːlɪŋ/ n **1** [U] the buying and selling of things: There's a lot of drug dealing in this area. **2** [U] a way of behaving towards other people: I'm in favour of plain honest dealing. **3 dealings** [pl] personal or business relations with someone: I've never had any dealings **with** him.

dealt /delt/ the past tense and past participle of DEAL

dean /diːn/ n **1** a priest of high rank in some Christian churches, who is in charge of a large church **2** an official of high rank in some universities

dear¹ /dɪəʳ/ adj **1** much loved, or very important to you: He's a dear friend of mine. | The house is very dear **to** her. **2** a word used before a name or title at the beginning of a letter: Dear Jane | Dear Sir | Dear Mrs Jones **3** expensive: That coat's too dear, I'm afraid.

dear² n a word used when talking to or about someone you like or love: Did you have a good day at work, dear? | She's a real dear.

dear³ interj a word used for expressing surprise, disappointment, or slight anger: Oh dear! I've lost my pen. | Dear! dear! What will he do next?

dear·ly /'dɪəli ‖ 'dɪərli/ adv **1 love someone dearly** to love someone very much: He loves his wife dearly. **2 would dearly like, would dearly love** = would very much like: I'd dearly love to see what he keeps in that box. **3 pay dearly** to suffer a lot as the result of something that you have done: He paid dearly **for** his mistake.

dearth /dɜːθ ‖ dɜːrθ/ n a lack: There's a dearth of good secretaries in the firm.

death /deθ/ n **1** [C;U] the end of life: His mother's death was a great shock to him. | Car accidents cause many deaths. **2** [U] the end of something: a defeat that meant the death of all my hopes **3 to death** until no longer alive: He was beaten to death. **4 put to death** to kill someone, especially with official permission: The prisoners were all put to death. **5 at**

death's door *infml* extremely ill **6 catch your death of cold** *infml* to become very ill with a cold: *If you go out dressed like that, you'll catch your death of cold.* **7 frightened to death, worried to death** very frightened or worried

death·blow /ˈdeθbləʊ/ *n* an act or event that destroys or ends something: *His refusal to help us dealt a deathblow to our plans.*

death·ly /ˈdeθli/ *adj, adv* as quiet, as cold, or as pale as someone who is dead: *a deathly silence* | *She looked deathly pale.*

death trap /ˈ· ·/ *n* something, usually a building or vehicle, which is very dangerous and could cause the death of people in it: *That old car is a real death trap.*

death war·rant /ˈ· ˌ··/ *n* a written official order to kill someone

de·bar /dɪˈbɑːʳ/ *-rr- v* [T] *fml* **debar someone from something** to officially prevent someone from doing something: *He's been debarred from using the library.*

de·base /dɪˈbeɪs/ *v* **debased, debasing 1** [T] to reduce the quality or value of something **2 debase yourself** to behave in such a way that people have less respect for you –**debasement** *n* [C;U]

de·ba·ta·ble /dɪˈbeɪtəbəl/ *adj* perhaps not true: *They say their policies have not caused unemployment, but I think that's debatable.*

de·bate¹ /dɪˈbeɪt/ *n* **1** [C] a formal and often public meeting in which speakers express different arguments in relation to the same subject: *a long debate in Parliament* **2** [C; U] the process of talking about a question: *After much debate, the committee decided to close the school.* **3 open to debate** perhaps not true

debate² *v* **debated, debating 1** [I;T] to talk about something quite formally with another person or other people, usually in an effort to persuade them: *Ministers are debating the future of the health service today.* **2** [T] to consider possibilities: *I'm seriously debating whether to change jobs next year.*

de·bauched /dɪˈbɔːtʃt ‖ dɪˈbɔːtʃt, dɪˈbɑːtʃt/ *adj* behaving badly, especially in relation to sex and alcohol: *His behaviour was thoroughly debauched.*

de·bauch·er·y /dɪˈbɔːtʃəri ‖ -ˈbɔː-, -ˈbɑː-/ *n* [U] behaviour which is not socially acceptable, especially in relation to sex and alcohol

de·bil·i·tate /dɪˈbɪlɪteɪt/ *v* **debilitated, debilitating** [T] to make someone or something weak: *This heat debilitates most Europeans.* | *a debilitating disease*

de·bil·i·ty /dɪˈbɪlɪti/ *n* [U] *fml* weakness, especially as the result of illness

deb·it¹ /ˈdebɪt/ *n* a record in your bank account of money that you have spent or that you owe –compare CREDIT

debit² *v* [T] to take money from someone's bank account: *Would you just debit my account, please.* –compare CREDIT

deb·o·nair /ˌdebəˈneəʳ/ *adj old fash* charming, well-dressed, and confident (used of men): *a debonair young man*

de·brief /ˌdiːˈbriːf/ *v* [T] to obtain information from someone who has just done something which is important to you, by asking very detailed questions: *All returning diplomats are debriefed.*

deb·ris /ˈdebriː, ˈdeɪ- ‖ dəˈbriː, deɪ-/ *n* [U] the remains of something broken to pieces or destroyed: *A lot of debris has been lying around since the war.*

debt /det/ *n* **1** [C;U] something that you owe to someone else: *If I win, I'll pay all my debts.* | *I owe you a real debt of gratitude for everything you've done.* **2 a bad debt** money which is owed but which will probably never be repaid **3 in debt** owing money to someone: *She's always in debt.* | *I'm worried that we're running into debt.* [RELATED PHRASE **out of debt**] **4 in someone's debt** grateful to someone: *After all the help you've given me, I'm forever in your debt.*

debt·or /ˈdetəʳ/ *n* a person who owes money

de·bunk /ˌdiːˈbʌŋk/ *v infml* [T] to point out the truth about a wrong idea, or make it seem less important

de·but /ˈdeɪbjuː, ˈdebjuː ‖ deɪˈbjuː, dɪ-/ *n* a person's first public appearance: *The singer made his debut as Mozart's Don Giovanni.*

deb·u·tante /ˈdebjʊtɑːnt/ *n* a girl who has just formally entered upper-class society

Dec. *n* a written abbreviation for DECEMBER

dec·ade /ˈdekeɪd, deˈkeɪd/ *n* a period of 10 years: *Prices have risen steadily during the past decade.*

dec·a·dent /ˈdekədənt/ *adj* having falling standards, especially moral standards: –**decadence** *n* [U]

de·caf·fein·at·ed /diːˈkæfɪneɪtɪd/ *adj* having had the CAFFEINE removed from it (used of tea or coffee)

de·cant /dɪˈkænt/ *v* [T] to pour liquid, especially wine, carefully from one container into another

de·cant·er /dɪˈkæntəʳ/ *n* a container, usually a glass bottle, from which you serve wine or certain other drinks

de·cap·i·tate /dɪˈkæpɪteɪt/ *v* **decapitated, decapitating** [T] to cut off someone's head –**decapitation** /dɪˌkæpɪˈteɪʃən/ *n* [C;U]

de·cay¹ /dɪˈkeɪ/ *v* **1** [I;T] to destroy something or be destroyed very slowly through chemical and other changes: *Sugar can decay your teeth.* | *a decayed body* **2** [I] to become weaker and less influential, while social standards probably also fall: *It seems that all great civilizations decay in time.*

decay² *n* [U] the process, state, or result of decaying: *dental decay* | *This material is tough, and resistant to decay.*

de·ceased /dɪˈsiːst/ *n law* **the deceased** a person who has died or people who have died: *The deceased left a large sum of money to his wife.* –**deceased** *adj* : *the deceased woman*

de·ceit /dɪˈsiːt/ *n* [U] speech or action which is intended to make someone believe something that is not true for a dishonest purpose

de·ceit·ful /dɪˈsiːtfəl/ *adj* intending to make someone believe something that is not true –**deceitfully** *adv* –**deceitfulness** *n* [U]

de·ceive /dɪˈsiːv/ *v* **deceived, deceiving 1** [T] to make someone believe something that is not true for a dishonest purpose: *He deceived her from their first meeting, when he told her he was single.* **2 deceive yourself** not to allow yourself to think that something is true, although you know really that it is true: *When are you going to stop deceiving yourself and face up to reality?* –**deceiver** *n*

De·cem·ber /dɪˈsembəʳ/ *n* (also **Dec.**) the 12th and last month of the year

de·cen·cy /ˈdiːsənsi/ *n* [U] **1** socially acceptable behaviour **2 have the decency to do something** to have the good manners to do something: *Her work was terrible, but at least she had the decency not to ask for payment.*

de·cent /ˈdiːsənt/ adj 1 socially acceptable: *Surely that skirt's too short to be decent!* 2 acceptable or good: *You can get quite a decent meal there.* | *a decent salary* 3 honest and good (used of people): *Decent people just can't feel safe around here any more.* 4 kind: *It's very decent of you to drive me to the station.* –**decently** adv

de·cen·tral·ize /ˌdiːˈsentrəlaɪz/ v **decentralized, decentralizing** (also **decentralise** BrE) [I;T] (of a company or a government department) to move from one big place to several smaller places –**decentralization** /ˌdiːsentrəlaɪˈzeɪʃən ‖ -lə-/ n [U]

de·cep·tion /dɪˈsepʃən/ n [C;U] an action or behaviour which is intended to make someone believe something that is not true

de·cep·tive /dɪˈseptɪv/ adj making you believe something that is not true: *Appearances can be deceptive.* –**deceptively** adv –**deceptiveness** n [U]

dec·i·bel /ˈdesɪbel/ n tech a measure of the loudness of sound

de·cide /dɪˈsaɪd/ v 1 [I;T; +(that)] to make a choice or judgment: *I don't know which one to take – I'll let you decide.* | *I've decided to resign.* | *Let's decide where to go!* | *They decided on Spain.* | *The court decided in his favour.* | *I decided that it would cost too much.* □ USEFUL PATTERNS to decide where, when, how, whether…; to decide on something; to decide to do something; to decide that… 2 [T] to make someone arrive at a choice or judgment: *His illness finally decided me; I could not leave.* 3 [T] to bring something to a clear or certain end: *A goal in the last minute decided the match.*

de·cid·ed /dɪˈsaɪdɪd/ adj very clear or definite: *a decided change for the better* –**decidedly** adv

de·cid·u·ous /dɪˈsɪdʒuəs/ adj having leaves that fall off in autumn: *deciduous trees* –compare EVERGREEN

dec·i·mal¹ /ˈdesɪməl/ adj based on the number 10: *decimal currency*

decimal² n (also **decimal fraction**) a number such as .5, .375, or .06

dec·i·mal·ize /ˈdesɪməlaɪz ‖ ˈdesəmə-/ v **decimalized, decimalizing** (also **decimalise** BrE) [I;T] to change to a decimal system of money, or counting –**decimalization** /ˌdesɪməlaɪˈzeɪʃən ‖ ˌdesəmələ-/ n [U]

decimal point /ˌ··· ˈ·/ n the dot at the left of a decimal fraction

dec·i·mate /ˈdesɪmeɪt/ v **decimated, decimating** [T] fml to destroy a large part or a large number of something: *Disease decimated the population.* –**decimation** /ˌdesɪˈmeɪʃən/ n [U]

de·ci·pher /dɪˈsaɪfər/ v [T] to find meaning in something that is difficult to read or understand: *Your writing is almost impossible to decipher.*

de·ci·sion /dɪˈsɪʒən/ n 1 [C;U] a choice of one out of a number of possibilities: *Who made the decision to go there?* | *Whose decision was it?* | *They expect to reach a decision soon.* | *The moment of decision had arrived.* 2 [U] the quality of being able to make choices quickly

de·ci·sive /dɪˈsaɪsɪv/ adj 1 having or showing the ability to make decisions quickly: *We need a strong, decisive leader.* 2 leading to a certain result: *a decisive battle* –**decisively** adv –**decisiveness** n [U]

deck¹ /dek/ n 1 a level of a ship or bus: *Smoking is only allowed on the top deck.* 2 **on deck** on the place around the top of a ship in the open air: *Shall we go up on deck?* 3 the usual American word for a PACK¹ (4) of playing cards

deck² v
  deck sbdy/sthg ↔ out phr v [T] to make something or someone more attractive: *The street was decked out with flags.*

deck·chair /ˈdektʃeər/ n a folding chair usually used outdoors

de·claim /dɪˈkleɪm/ v fml [I;T] to speak loudly and clearly like an actor –**declamatory** /dɪˈklæmətəri ‖ -tɔːri/ adj

dec·la·ra·tion /ˌdekləˈreɪʃən/ n a written or spoken statement, giving information in an official manner: *Please make a written declaration of all the goods you bought abroad.* | *a declaration of war*

de·clare /dɪˈkleər/ v 1 [T; + (that)] to make something public or official, according to rules or custom: *Our government has declared war on Ruritania.* | *Jones was declared the winner.* | *I declare Mr B. Schiff elected!* 2 [T; + (that)] to state something clearly and forcefully: *He declared his support for the terrorists.* | *She declared that she knew nothing about the robbery.* | *He declared himself to be a member of their party.*
  □ USEFUL PATTERNS to declare something; to declare that…; to declare yourself to be…. 3 [T] to state the value of goods which you have bought abroad and on which you may have to pay tax: *Have you anything to declare?*

de·cline¹ /dɪˈklaɪn/ v **declined, declining** 1 [I] to move from a better to a worse position, or from higher to lower: *As his health has declined, so has his influence.* 2 [I;T] fml to refuse something, usually politely: *We invited them, but they declined.* | *They declined our invitation.* | *The minister declined to make a statement.* –see REFUSE (USAGE)
  □ USEFUL PATTERNS to decline something, to decline to do something

decline² n 1 [C;U] a change to something worse, smaller, or lower: *There has been a sharp decline in interest in farming.* | *The government's popularity is in decline.* 2 **on the decline, falling into decline** becoming weaker or less important: *The car industry in Britain is falling into decline.*

de·code /ˌdiːˈkəʊd/ v [T] **decoded, decoding** to discover the meaning of something expressed in a CODE¹(1)

de·com·pose /ˌdiːkəmˈpəʊz/ v **decomposed, decomposing** [I;T] to decay –**decomposition** /ˌdiːkɒmpəˈzɪʃən ‖ -kɑːm-/ n [U]

dé·cor /ˈdeɪkɔːr ‖ deɪˈkɔːr/ n [U] the decoration and furnishing of a place, house, or stage: *The food at the restaurant is good but the décor is awful.*

dec·o·rate /ˈdekəreɪt/ v **decorated, decorating** 1 [I;T] to make something more attractive by adding something beautiful or by putting paint or paper on the walls of a house: *The streets were decorated with flags.* | *We spent the weekend decorating.* 2 [T] to give someone an official mark of honour, such as a MEDAL: *He was decorated for outstanding bravery in the last war.*

dec·o·ra·tion /ˌdekəˈreɪʃən/ n 1 [U] the act or art of decorating, or the process of being decorated 2 [C;U] something that is added to make something more attractive: *Christmas decorations* | *simple architectural designs with no decoration* 3 [C] something, such as a MEDAL, which is given as a sign of honour

dec·o·ra·tive /ˈdekərətɪv ‖ ˈdekərə-, ˈdekəreɪ-/ adj attractive, or used to make something else more attractive: *a decorative gold table* –**decoratively** adv

dec·o·ra·tor /ˈdekəreɪtəʳ/ n a person who paints houses inside and out

dec·o·rous /ˈdekərəs/ adj fml correct and respectful (used of behaviour or appearance) –**decorously** adv

de·co·rum /dɪˈkɔːrəm/ n [U] correct and respectful behaviour or appearance

de·coy /ˈdiːkɔɪ/ n something which is used for leading a person or bird into a trap –**decoy** v [T]

de·crease /dɪˈkriːs/ v **decreased, decreasing 1** [I] to become less or to make something less in size, number, strength, or quality: *Our sales have been decreasing.* **2** [T] to make something less in size, number, strength, or quality: *The company may need to decrease its workforce.* –opposite **increase** –**decrease** /ˈdiːkriːs/ n [C;U] : *a decrease in sales*

de·cree¹ /dɪˈkriː/ n an official command or decision

decree² v [T; + that] to state or order something officially: *The new governor has decreed that all this fighting should end.*

de·crep·it /dɪˈkrepɪt/ adj old and in bad condition

de·cry /dɪˈkraɪ/ v [T] fml to say that you do not approve of something

ded·i·cate /ˈdedɪkeɪt/ v **dedicated, dedicating** [T] to declare that a place is holy, often with a solemn ceremony: *The new church will be dedicated on Sunday.*

dedicate sthg to sbdy/sthg phr v [T] to declare a book or performance to be in honour of someone: *Tonight's performance is dedicated to the memory of Lord Olivier.* **2** to give time to a particular purpose: *She dedicated herself to the fight for equal rights.* | *He dedicated his life to the needs of his country.* **3** to declare a formal association between something and a particular person or people: *This monument is dedicated to the earthquake victims.*

ded·i·cat·ed /ˈdedɪkeɪtɪd/ adj working very hard for a particular purpose, or being very interested in something: *She's very dedicated to her work.* | *a dedicated doctor*

ded·i·ca·tion /ˌdedɪˈkeɪʃən/ n **1** [C;U] the giving of something to a particular purpose **2** [U] the quality of being very interested in or working very hard and unselfishly for something: *She worked with great dedication to find a cure for the disease.* **3** [C] the words at the beginning of a book or a piece of music where writers express their love, respect, or thanks to people

de·duce /dɪˈdjuːs ‖ dɪˈduːs/ v **deduced, deducing** [T; + that] to decide that something must be true by using information that you already know is true: *...and from this I deduce that he was killed by his ex-wife.* –**deducible** adj

de·duct /dɪˈdʌkt/ v [T] to take away an amount or a part from a total: *Don't forget to deduct travel expenses from your earnings.* –**deductible** adj

de·duc·tion /dɪˈdʌkʃən/ n **1** [C;U] an idea which you reach about the truth of something by using information that you already know is true, or the process of reaching that idea: *Her deduction that he was now dead was correct.* | *His powers of deduction are impressive.* **2** [C] an amount which is taken away from a total, or the act of taking it away: *After deductions, she earns £180 a week.*

deed /diːd/ n **1** lit an action: *a good deed* | *evil deeds* **2** law a written paper that is an official record of an agreement

deem /diːm/ v [T] fml to consider: *I would deem it an honour if you would accompany me.*

deep /diːp/ adj,adv **1** going far down from a surface: *The river is very deep here.* | *a deep wound* **2** used in giving measurements to show how far from the outside edge something is: *a shelf 30 cm deep and 120 cm long* | *a mine two kilometres deep* | *How deep is the river here?* **3** strong and dark (used of colour): *The sky was deep blue.* **4** strongly felt: *I have a deep suspicion that he's not telling us the truth.* | *deep feelings of hatred* **5** difficult to understand: *deep scientific principles* **6 deep sleep** a sleep from which it is difficult to wake up **7 deep thinker** someone who thinks about things in a very serious way **8 go off the deep end** slang to lose your temper suddenly or violently **9 in deep trouble, in deep water** in serious trouble **10 thrown in at the deep end** having to begin with the most difficult part of something –**deeply** adv –**deepness** n [U]

deep·en /ˈdiːpən/ v [I;T] to make or become deeper: *We'll have to deepen the well if we want more water.* | *The colour of the sky deepened as the sun went down.*

deep freeze /ˌ·ˈ· ‖ ˈ· ·/ n a container for keeping food at very low temperatures

deep-seat·ed /ˌ·ˈ··◂/ adj strong and established some time ago: *a deep-seated dislike of foreigners*

deer /dɪəʳ/ n [plural is **deer**] a large grass-eating animal which can run fast; the males usually have wide branching horns –see MEAT (USAGE)

de·face /dɪˈfeɪs/ v **defaced, defacing** [T] to spoil the appearance of something, for example by writing or making marks on it –**defacement** n [U]

de·fame /dɪˈfeɪm/ v **defamed, defaming** [T] fml to damage the good opinion held about someone by saying something bad about them –**defamatory** /dɪˈfæmətəri ‖ -tɔːri/ adj –**defamation** /ˌdefəˈmeɪʃən/ n [U]

de·fault¹ /dɪˈfɔːlt/ v [I] to fail to fulfil an agreement, contract, or duty: *He defaulted on his payments for support of the child.*

default² n **1** [U] failure to fulfil an agreement or legal duty **2 by default** because something that might have made the situation different did not happen: *Her opponent was ill, so she won by default.*

de·feat¹ /dɪˈfiːt/ v [T] **1** to win a victory over someone: *Scotland defeated Wales by three goals to one.* | *The British army was finally defeated in 1783.* **2** to make something fail: *It was lack of money that defeated their plan.* **3** to be too difficult to do successfully: *This task defeats me!*

defeat² n **1** [U] victory over someone or something: *Superior air defence contributed to their defeat of the enemy.* **2** [C;U] failure to win or to succeed: *The team has suffered several defeats recently.* | *He'll never admit defeat.*

de·feat·is·m /dɪˈfiːtɪzəm/ n [U] expectation of failure –**defeatist** n

def·e·cate /ˈdefɪkeɪt/ v **defecated, defecating** fml [I] to send waste matter out of your bowels –**defecation** /ˌdefɪˈkeɪʃən/ n [U]

de·fect¹ /ˈdiːfekt, dɪˈfekt/ n something which is lacking or not right: *There's a defect in each of those machines.* | *Your plan has one serious defect.*

de·fect² /dɪˈfekt/ v [I] to leave a group or your country, especially for political reasons, and go to an opposing one –**defector** n –**defection** /-ˈfekʃən/ n [C;U]

de·fec·tive /dɪˈfektɪv/ adj lacking something necessary and so not working well: *defective machinery* –**defectively** adv –**defectiveness** n [U]

de·fence /dɪˈfens/ n (also **defense** AmE) **1** [U] the act of protecting someone or something from attack: *the defence of one's country* | *He spoke in defence of justice.* **2** [C;U] something that is used for protection: *Trees are a defence against the wind.* **3** [U] the weapons and armed forces that a country has to protect itself from attack: *The government has increased its spending on defence.* **4** [sing] arguments that you use to defend yourself in court: *She said in her defence that she had not seen the "No Parking" sign.* **5 the defence** someone who has been charged with a crime, together with their lawyers, in court. –**defenceless** adj

de·fend /dɪˈfend/ v **1** [T] to protect someone or something from attack: *We can't defend the port from attack by land and sea.* | *I don't like having to defend my beliefs.* **2** [I;T] to protect a position in sports so as to stop an opponent advancing, gaining points, or winning: *Tonight he will be defending his lightweight boxing title.* | *He defended with skill.* **3** [T] to act as a lawyer for someone who has been charged with a crime –**defensible** adj

de·fen·dant /dɪˈfendənt/ n law a person who has been charged with a crime in a court case

de·fen·sive /dɪˈfensɪv/ adj **1** used or intended for protection: *defensive weapons* | *a defensive position* **2** seeming to expect disapproval or attack (used of a person or behaviour): *She became very defensive when I asked her how much the car had cost.* –**defensively** adv –**defensiveness** n [U]

de·fer /dɪˈfɜːr/ v **-rr-** **1** [T] to delay something until a later date: *Let's defer any action for a few weeks.* | *His military service was deferred until he finished college.* **2 defer to someone** to accept the wishes or opinions of another person, usually because you respect them: *I shall, of course, defer to your better judgment.*

def·er·ence /ˈdefərəns/ n [U] fml respect that you show to someone because of their higher position or greater power –**deferential** /ˌdefəˈrenʃəl◄/ adj

de·fi·ant /dɪˈfaɪənt/ adj showing lack of respect or a refusal to obey someone –**defiance** n [U] –**defiantly** adv

de·fi·cien·cy /dɪˈfɪʃənsi/ n **deficiencies** [C;U] a condition in which something is lacking or not good enough: *Can't you see the deficiencies in this plan?* | *vitamin deficiency.*

de·fi·cient /dɪˈfɪʃənt/ adj not having any or enough of something which is necessary: *They tend to eat food deficient in iron.*

def·i·cit /ˈdefɪsɪt/ n an amount, especially of money, which is the difference between what you have and what you need or expected to have: *The directors have reported a deficit of £2.5 million.*

de·file /dɪˈfaɪl/ v **defiled, defiling** [T] to make something less clean or pure: *The animals defiled the water.* –**defilement** n [U]

de·fine /dɪˈfaɪn/ v **defined, defining** [T] to show or explain what something is or means, or what its limits are: *"Hope" is a hard word to define.* | *This book defines the position of the national government in city affairs.* | *The issue hasn't been clearly defined.*

def·i·nite /ˈdefɪnət, ˈdefənət/ adj clear and certain: *We demand a definite answer.* | *a definite success*

definite ar·ti·cle /ˌ··· ˈ···/ n in English the word THE

def·i·nite·ly /ˈdefɪnətli, ˈdefənətli/ adv certainly or clearly: *That answer is definitely true.* | *That was definitely the best play I've seen all year.* | *He is definitely coming.* | *"Will you be inviting Sarah?" "No, definitely not!"*

def·i·ni·tion /ˌdefɪˈnɪʃən/ n **1** [C] a statement which explains the exact meaning of a word or phrase **2** [U] clearness of shape, colour, or sound: *This photograph lacks definition.*

de·fin·i·tive /dɪˈfɪnɪtɪv/ adj **1** providing a firm decision that cannot be questioned: *a definitive answer* **2** showing the highest standard as compared with other similar things: *She's written the definitive history of Vienna.* –**definitively** adv

de·flate /ˌdiːˈfleɪt, dɪ-/ v **deflated, deflating** [I;T] **1** to become smaller or make something smaller through loss of air or gas: *The tyre deflated.* | *After the party they deflated the balloons.* **2** to make someone lose confidence: *I felt utterly deflated by her laughter.* **3** to reduce a country's supply of money, leading to less demand for goods and less industrial activity, and usually resulting in lower prices –**deflation** /-ˈfleɪʃən/ n [C;U]

de·flect /dɪˈflekt/ v **1** [I; T] to cause something to change direction: *One of their players deflected the ball into his own goal.* **2** [T] to turn an attack away from yourself: *I tried to deflect his criticism by changing my account of the incident.*

de·form /dɪˈfɔːm ‖ -ɔːrm/ v [T] to spoil the form or appearance of someone or something: *a face deformed by disease*

de·for·mi·ty /dɪˈfɔːmɪti ‖ -ɔːr-/ n **deformities** [C;U] an imperfection of the body caused by damage or illness: *Lack of essential minerals can cause deformity in unborn children.*

de·fraud /dɪˈfrɔːd/ v [T] to get something from someone by unfair means: *They have been charged with intent to defraud their employers.*

de·frost /ˌdiːˈfrost ‖ -ˈfrɔːst/ v [I;T] to remove ice from something that has been frozen: *I should really defrost the refrigerator.* | *Don't let the meat defrost too quickly.*

deft /deft/ adj quick and skilful: *a deft catch* –**deftly** adv –**deftness** n [U]

de·funct /dɪˈfʌŋkt/ adj no longer in existence or working

de·fuse /ˌdiːˈfjuːz/ v **defused, defusing** [T] **1** to remove the FUSE from something explosive so as to prevent an explosion: *The expert defused the bomb just in time.* **2 defuse a situation** to remove the nervousness or possible harm from a situation

de·fy /dɪˈfaɪ/ v **defied, defying** [T] **1** to refuse to obey someone or something: *In not paying this tax, they are defying the law.* **2 defy someone to do something** to ask someone to do something which is considered impossible: *I defy you to give me one good reason for believing you.* **3** to make something impossible: *The untidiness of his room defies description.*

de·gen·e·rate¹ /dɪˈdʒenəreɪt/ v **degenerated, degenerating** [I] to become worse in character, quality, or appearance: *a fine young man who has degenerated under the influence of alcohol* | *The wide road degenerated into a narrow bumpy track.* –**degeneration** /dɪˌdʒenəˈreɪʃən/ n [U]

de·gen·e·rate² /dɪˈdʒenərɪt/ adj showing a low standard of morals or behaviour: *a group of degenerate young men*

de·grade /dɪˈɡreɪd/ v **degraded, degrading** [T] to reduce respect for someone: *It was very degrading to be punished in front of the whole class.* | *Pornography degrades women.* –**degradation** /ˌdeɡrəˈdeɪʃən/ n [U]

de·gree /dɪˈɡriː/ n **1** [C] tech a unit of measurement: *an angle of 90 degrees (90°)* | *It's 84 degrees in the* shade. | *a temperature of 21 degrees Celsius* **2** [C;U] level or amount, especially of ability or progress: *The students have different degrees of ability.* | *To what degree can he be trusted?* | *He can be trusted to some degree.* | *He is getting better by degrees.* **3** [C] a course of study at a university or POLYTECHNIC, or the title you get if you complete this: *To do the job, you must have a degree in history.* | *a chemistry degree*

de·hy·drate /ˌdiːˈhaɪdreɪt/ *v* **dehydrated, dehydrating 1** [T] to remove all the water from something, often in order to preserve it **2** [I] to lose water from the body –**dehydration** /ˌdiːhaɪˈdreɪʃən/ *n* [U]: *He was suffering from dehydration.*

de·i·fy /ˈdiːɪfaɪ, ˈdeɪ-/ *v* **1** [T] to consider something or someone as a god to be worshipped –**deification** /ˌdiːɪfɪˈkeɪʃən, ˌdeɪ-/ *n* [U]

deign /deɪn/ *v* **deign to do something** to lower yourself to do something you consider unimportant: *They wrote to their headmaster, but he didn't even deign to reply.*

de·i·ty /ˈdiːɪti, ˈdeɪ-/ *n* **deities** a god or goddess

dé·jà vu /ˌdeɪʒɑːˈvjuː, -ˈvuː/ *n* [U] the feeling that you have already experienced in the past what is actually happening at the present moment

de·jec·ted /dɪˈdʒektɪd/ *adj* sad and disappointed: *a dejected look* –**dejectedly** *adv* –**dejection** /dɪˈdʒekʃən/ *n* [U]

de·lay¹ /dɪˈleɪ/ *v* **1** [T] to do something later than planned: *We decided to delay our holiday until next month.* | *Could you delay giving her the news until we've seen her?*
☐ USEFUL PATTERNS to delay something; to delay doing something
2 [I;T] to slow something down or cause it to be late: *They're trying to delay until help arrives.* | *My train was delayed for an hour.*

delay² *n* [C;U] a period of time during which an action or event does not happen as it is supposed to: *Delays of two hours or more were reported on the roads this morning.* | *Do it without delay!*

de·lec·ta·ble /dɪˈlektəbəl/ *adj* very pleasing

del·e·gate¹ /ˈdelɪɡət/ *n* a person chosen to represent a group of people

del·e·gate² /ˈdelɪɡeɪt/ *v* **delegated, delegating 1** [I;T] to give someone part or all of your power, rights, or duties for a certain time: *Part of the art of management is knowing when to delegate.* | *I have delegated my command to Captain Roberts.* **2** [T] to appoint someone to do a particular job: *I've been delegated to organize the weekly meetings.*

del·e·ga·tion /ˌdelɪˈɡeɪʃən/ *n* **1** [U] the giving to someone of part or all of your power, rights, or duties **2** [C + sing/pl verb] a group of people chosen to represent others: *A delegation from the United Nations has just arrived.*

de·lete /dɪˈliːt/ *v* **deleted, deleting** [T] to cross out and remove something that has been written down: *Delete his name from the list.* –**deletion** /dɪˈliːʃən/ *n* [C;U]

de·lib·e·rate¹ /dɪˈlɪbərət/ *adj* **1** intentional: *The car crash wasn't an accident – it was a deliberate attempt to kill him!* **2** slow and careful (used of speech, thought, or movement): *He stood up in a very deliberate way and left the room.* –**deliberately** *adv*

de·lib·e·rate² /dɪˈlɪbəreɪt/ *v* **deliberated, deliberating** [I;T] *fml* to consider something carefully before making a decision: *The judges are deliberating.* | *They are deliberating what to do.*

de·lib·e·ra·tion /dɪˌlɪbəˈreɪʃən/ *n* **1** [U] careful consideration **2 deliberations** [pl] careful consideration or discussions about something **3** [U] the quality of being slow and unhurried in speech, thought, or movement

del·i·ca·cy /ˈdelɪkəsi/ *n* **delicacies 1** [U] the quality of being delicate: *She admired the delicacy of the lace table-cloth* | *a matter of some delicacy* **2** [C] something good to eat that is considered rare or costly: *Caviar is a great delicacy.*

del·i·cate /ˈdelɪkət/ *adj* **1** easy to damage and therefore needing to be handled carefully: *Be careful with those wine glasses – they're very delicate.* **2** needing careful consideration in order to avoid failure or trouble: *Don't mention his divorce – it's rather a delicate subject.* | *The negotiations are at a delicate stage.* **3** pleasant though not very noticeable: *a delicate taste* | *a delicate smell* | *a delicate shade of pink* **4** sensitive: *A delicate instrument can record even very slight changes in temperature.* **5** small, careful, and controlled: *a delicate movement* **6** often ill: *a very delicate child* –**delicately** *adv*

del·i·ca·tes·sen /ˌdelɪkəˈtesən/ *n* a shop that sells unusual and often expensive foods, for example cheeses and cold meats from foreign countries

de·li·cious /dɪˈlɪʃəs/ *adj* tasting or smelling very pleasant: *Thank you for the delicious meal.* –**deliciously** *adv*

de·light¹ /dɪˈlaɪt/ *v* [I;T] to give a great feeling of pleasure: *a book that is certain to delight* | *He delighted them with his witty performance.*
delight in sth *phr v* [T] to get great pleasure from something: *She delights in making me look stupid.*

delight² *n* **1** [C;U] great pleasure or satisfaction: *the delights of London's night life* | *a shriek of delight* **2 take delight in something** to enjoy something

de·light·ed /dɪˈlaɪtɪd/ *adj* very pleased or satisfied: *Thank you for your invitation – I'd be delighted to come.* | *We were absolutely delighted with his progress.*
☐ USEFUL PATTERNS be delighted with something; be delighted to do something

de·light·ful /dɪˈlaɪtfəl/ *adj* very pleasing and attractive: *a delightful little girl* –**delightfully** *adv*

de·lin·quen·cy /dɪˈlɪŋkwənsi/ *n* [U] behaviour which is neither socially nor legally acceptable: *the problem of juvenile delinquency*

de·lin·quent /dɪˈlɪŋkwənt/ *n* a young person who does socially unacceptable things or who breaks the law –**delinquent** *adj* : *delinquent behaviour*

de·lir·i·ous /dɪˈlɪəriəs/ *adj* in an excited dreamy state in which you cannot think clearly, for example because of a fever: *He was so ill he became delirious.* | *delirious with joy* –**deliriously** *adv* : *deliriously happy* –**delirium** /-riəm/ *n* [U]

de·liv·er /dɪˈlɪvə⁰/ *v* [T] **1** to take things to people's houses or places of work: *Letters are delivered every day.* | *Yes, we deliver newspapers.* | *The parcel was delivered to my door.* **2** to give something that has been promised or is hoped for: *Do you think the government will deliver the promised tax cuts?* **3 deliver a baby** to help in the birth of a baby **4** to speak or read aloud in public: *He delivered his speech effectively.* **5** *fml* to set someone free from something unpleasant **6 deliver a blow** to hit someone hard

de·liv·er·ance /dɪˈlɪvərəns/ *n* [U] *fml* the act of saving someone from harm or danger or the state of being saved from danger

de·liv·er·y /dɪ'lɪvəri/ n **deliveries** **1** [C;U] the act of taking something to someone: *The next postal delivery is at 2 o'clock.* **2** [C;U] the things that are taken to someone: *I signed for a large delivery of coal.* **3** [C] the birth of a child: *The mother had an easy delivery.* **4** [C;U] the act or style of speaking in public **5** [C;U] the act or style of throwing a ball in a game: *a good delivery*

del·ta /'deltə/ n **1** the fourth letter of the Greek alphabet (Δ δ) **2** an area of low land shaped like a Δ where a river divides into branches before entering the sea, especially the Nile Delta in Egypt

de·lude /dɪ'luːd/ v **deluded, deluding** [T] to make someone believe in something that is not true: *Don't delude yourself about her ability to do the job.| They were deluded into thinking that their investment would be safe.*

del·uge¹ /'deljuːdʒ/ n **1** a great flood **2** very heavy rain **3** a very large number of things which happen at the same time: *a deluge of questions*

deluge² v **deluged, deluging** [T] to have to deal with a large number of things happening at the same time: *The minister was deluged with questions.*

de·lu·sion /dɪ'luːʒən/ n a false belief which is usually strongly held: *She was under the delusion that he would marry her. | She's suffering from delusions of grandeur.*

de luxe /dɪ 'lʌks ‖ -'lʊks/ adj of especially good quality and more expensive than other similar products: *I bought the deluxe model.*

delve /delv/ v **delved, delving** [I] to search thoroughly in order to find something: *She delved into her handbag for her keys.*

dem·a·gogue /'deməɡɒɡ ‖ -ɡɑːɡ/ n a political leader who has gained power by exciting people's feelings rather than by reasoned argument (a word used to express disapproval)

de·mand¹ /dɪ'mɑːnd ‖ dɪ'mænd/ v **1** [T; + that] to ask for something firmly and not be willing to accept a refusal: *The workers are demanding more money. | I demanded to know the truth. | They demanded that he should be dismissed.* □ USEFUL PATTERNS to demand something; to demand to do something; to demand that... **2** [T] to ask someone firmly to tell you something: *"Where have you been all night?" she demanded.* **3** [T] to need attention, effort, or hard work: *Work of this kind demands total commitment.*

demand² n **1** [C] an extremely firm request or claim: *The government had to give in to the terrorists' demands. | the workers' demand for a 10% pay rise* **2 on demand** able to be obtained as soon as it is wanted: *machines which dispense cash on demand* **3** [U] a need or wish of people generally for particular goods or services: *There's not much demand for hats these days.* **4 in demand, in great demand** wanted by a lot of people: *You seem to be in great demand today!* **5 make demands on someone** to take up a lot of someone's time and effort: *The school makes heavy demands on its teachers.*

de·mand·ing /dɪ'mɑːndɪŋ ‖ dɪ'mæn-/ adj needing a lot of effort or attention: *a very demanding baby*

de·mar·ca·tion /ˌdiːmɑː'keɪʃən ‖ -ɑːr-/ n [sing;U] an imaginary line which separates two areas or activities: *There is a clear demarcation between the jobs of editor and sub-editor.*

de·mean /dɪ'miːn/ v **demean yourself** fml to make people have less respect for you: *Don't demean yourself by taking such a badly paid job.*

de·mea·nour /dɪ'miːnəʳ/ n fml (**demeanor** AmE) someone's manner and behaviour towards other people

de·ment·ed /dɪ'mentᵻd/ adj mad or showing an unbalanced mind –**dementedly** adv

de·mise /dɪ'maɪz/ n [U] **1** the failure of something or someone that used to be successful: *the demise of the record player* **2** law the death of a person

de·mo·bi·lize /diː'məʊbᵻlaɪz/ v **demobilized, demobilizing** fml (also **demobilise** BrE) [T] to let someone leave the armed forces –**demobilization** /dɪˌməʊbɪlaɪ'zeɪʃən ‖ -bələ-/ n [U]

de·moc·ra·cy /dɪ'mɒkrəsi ‖ dɪ'mɑː-/ n **democracies** **1** [U] a system of government which is made up of representatives who have been elected by the people **2** [C] a country which has this system of government: *Britain is an example of a parliamentary democracy.*

dem·o·crat /'deməkræt/ n **1** a person who believes in the principles of democracy **2 Democrat** a member or supporter of a particular political party: *A Liberal Democrat* **3 the Democrats** one of the two largest political parties of the US

dem·o·crat·ic /ˌdemə'krætɪk◂/ adj **1** favouring and practising democracy: *a democratic system of government* **2** being fair to different sides: *Let's be democratic about this and take a vote.* –**democratically** /-kli/ adv

de·mol·ish /dɪ'mɒlɪʃ ‖ dɪ'mɑː-/ v [T] **1** to knock something down or destroy it: *They're finally going to demolish that old building.* **2** to prove that an idea or an argument is wrong: *We've demolished all her objections to the plan.*

dem·o·li·tion /ˌdemə'lɪʃən/ n [C;U] the action of knocking something down or destroying it

de·mon /'diːmən/ n an evil spirit –**demonic** /dɪ'mɒnɪk ‖ dɪ'mɑː-/ adj

de·mon·stra·ble /dɪ'mɒnstrəbəl, 'demən- ‖ dɪ'mɑːn-/ adj fml able to be shown or proved to be true: *a demonstrable fact* –**demonstrably** adv

dem·on·strate /'demənstreɪt/ v **demonstrated, demonstrating** **1** [T; + that] to prove something by reasoning: *Galileo demonstrated that objects of different weight fall at the same speed.* **2** [T; + that] to explain something by showing clearly: *Please demonstrate how the machine works. | She demonstrated the correct way to put a bandage on.* **3** [T] to show a particular skill or quality: *He demonstrated extraordinary courage.* **4** [I] to take part in a public show of opposition or support for something: *They demonstrated against the new law.* –**demonstrator** n

dem·on·stra·tion /ˌdemən'streɪʃən/ n **1** [C;U] the act of showing how something works: *Can you give us a demonstration?* **2** [C;U] the act of proving something **3** [C] a public show of opposition or support for something, often with marching: *Some students are holding a demonstration against nuclear weapons.*

de·mon·stra·tive /dɪ'mɒnstrətɪv ‖ dɪ'mɑːn-/ adj showing your feelings openly: *a demonstrative person*

de·mor·al·ize /dɪ'mɒrəlaɪz ‖ dɪ'mɔː-, dɪ'mɑː-/ v **demoralized, demoralizing** (also **demoralise** BrE) [T] to make someone lose confidence or courage: *The army was demoralized by defeat.* –**demoralization** /dɪˌmɒrəlaɪ'zeɪʃən ‖ dɪˌmɔːrələ-, -ˌmɑːr-/ n [U]

de·mote /dɪˈməʊt/ v demoted, demoting [T] to lower someone in rank or position, often as a punishment –**demotion** /dɪˈməʊʃən/ n [C;U]

de·mur /dɪˈmɜːʳ/ v -rr- [I] fml to show a lack of eagerness for a plan or a suggestion: I demurred at the prospect of a whole evening alone with him.

de·mure /dɪˈmjʊəʳ/ adj quiet and polite (used especially of women and children): a demure young lady –**demurely** adv

den /den/ n **1** the home of a wild animal, such as a lion or a fox **2** a place where people are busy with a secret activity: a den of thieves

de·ni·al /dɪˈnaɪəl/ n [C;U] **1** the act of saying that something is not true: He has made a public denial of the story in the newspapers. **2** a refusal to give something which people feel is deserved: a denial of justice

den·im /ˈdenɪm/ n **1** [U] a strong cotton cloth which is often blue, used to make clothes: denim jeans **2** **denims** [pl] trousers made of denim –see PAIR (USAGE)

de·nom·i·na·tion /dɪˌnɒmɪˈneɪʃən ‖ dɪˌnɑː-/ n a particular religious group which has slight differences in belief from other similar groups –**denominational** adj

de·note /dɪˈnəʊt/ v denoted, denoting [T; + that] to be a sign for something: A smile usually denotes pleasure. | The sign "=" denotes that two things are equal.

de·nounce /dɪˈnaʊns/ v denounced, denouncing [T] to make a spoken or written attack against someone in public: The minister's action was denounced in the newspapers. | They denounced him to the police as a criminal.

dense /dens/ adj **1** closely packed or crowded together: a dense crowd | dense traffic **2** difficult to see through: a dense fog **3** infml slow to understand things: He's really dense! –**densely** adv : a densely populated area

den·si·ty /ˈdensɪti/ n densities **1** [U] the amount to which an area is filled with people or things: This area has a very high population density. **2** [C;U] tech the relationship of the amount of matter in something to the space into which the matter is packed: the density of a gas

dent /dent/ n **1** a small hollow in the surface of something as a result of being hit: a bad dent in the side of my car **2** a dent in, a dent to a reduction in or to something: Only getting third prize was a terrible dent to her pride. | The holiday has made a big dent in our savings. –**dent** v [T] : I'm afraid I've dented the car.

den·tal /ˈdentl/ adj related to your teeth: dental decay | in need of dental treatment

den·tist /ˈdentɪst/ n a person professionally trained to examine and treat people's teeth **2 go to the dentist's** the place where you go to have your teeth looked after by the dentist: I can't come to the meeting; I've got to go to the dentist's this afternoon. –**dentistry** n [U]

den·tures /ˈdentʃəz ‖ -ərz/ n [pl] a set of specially made teeth worn by someone who has lost all or most of their natural teeth

de·nude /dɪˈnjuːd ‖ dɪˈnuːd/ v denuded, denuding fml [T] to remove the covering from something: Rain has denuded the mountainside of soil.

de·nun·ci·a·tion /dɪˌnʌnsiˈeɪʃən/ n [C;U] the act of making a spoken or written attack against someone in public

de·ny /dɪˈnaɪ/ v denied, denying **1** [T; + (that)] to say that something is untrue: He has denied all the stories in the newspapers. | She denied that she had ever agreed to marry him. | They denied telling his mother.
☐ USEFUL PATTERNS to deny something; to deny doing something; to deny that...
2 [T] to refuse to accept something: Can you deny the truth of his statement? **3** [T] to refuse to allow someone to have or do something: I was denied the chance of going to university.
☐ USEFUL PATTERNS to deny something to someone; to deny someone something
4 fml to say that you have no connection with someone or something: He has denied his country and his principles!

de·o·do·rant /diːˈəʊdərənt/ n [C;U] a chemical substance that is used to prevent unpleasant body smells

de·part /dɪˈpɑːt ‖ -ɑːrt/ v fml [I] to go away from somewhere, especially when starting a journey: The 9.30 train to Leeds will depart from platform 6. **2 depart from something** fml to turn away from a previous course of action or way of thinking: I'd like to depart from the main subject of my speech for a few moments.

de·part·ed /dɪˈpɑːtɪd ‖ -ɑːr-/ adj **1** gone for ever: her departed youth **2** fml dead

de·part·ment /dɪˈpɑːtmənt ‖ -ɑːr-/ n a division in an organization, such as a hospital, university, large shop, or business: the History Department | the toy department | the casualty department of the local hospital –**departmental** /ˌdiːpɑːtˈmentl◂ ‖ -ɑːr-/ adj : a departmental meeting

department store /·ˈ··· ·/ n a large shop divided into departments which sell different types of goods

de·par·ture /dɪˈpɑːtʃəʳ ‖ -ɑːr-/ n **1** [C;U] the act of going away from somewhere: What is the departure time of the flight to New York? **2** [C] the act of doing something which is different from usual: The new system is a radical departure from our old methods.

de·pend /dɪˈpend/ v **that depends, it depends** = I am not completely sure: "How much do you want to spend?" "I don't know. It depends. I'd like to see what the choice is first."
depend on sbdy/sthg phr v [T] **1** to need someone a great deal for help or support: His family depend on him. **2** to trust that someone will help you when you need them to: We're depending on you to finish the job by Friday. | You can depend on me. **3** to be decided by someone or something: The amount you pay depends on where you live.

de·pen·da·ble /dɪˈpendəbəl/ adj able to be trusted –**dependability** /dɪˌpendəˈbɪləti/ n [U]

de·pen·dant /dɪˈpendənt/ n (also **dependent**) a person who depends on someone else for money: Please state on the document whether you have any dependants.

de·pen·dence /dɪˈpendəns/ n [U] **1** the regular need for someone else's help or support: his dependence on his mother **2** the regular need for something: our increasing dependence on oil | drug dependence

de·pen·dent /dɪˈpendənt/ adj **1** in need of someone or something: a dependent child | a country heavily dependent on foreign aid **2 dependent on** decided by a particular thing or fact: The success of the show is always dependent on the weather.

de·pict /dɪˈpɪkt/ v fml [T] **1** to represent something in a picture: This painting depicts the Battle of Waterloo. **2** to describe someone as a certain kind of person: The author depicts her as a mean old woman. –**depiction** /dɪˈpɪkʃən/ n [C;U]

de·plete /dɪˈpliːt/ v depleted, depleting fml [T] to reduce the amount of something: *Unexpected expenses have left us with severely depleted savings.* –depletion /dɪˈpliːʃən/ n [U]

de·plore /dɪˈplɔːr/ v deplored, deploring fml [T] to express feelings of extreme disappointment or shock at something: *The teacher deplored the appalling behaviour of her pupils.* –deplorable adj : *a deplorable waste of money* –deplorably adv : *She behaved deplorably.*

de·ploy /dɪˈplɔɪ/ v [T] to organize things so that they can be used without delay, especially for military action: *They deployed all the light aircraft that were available.* –deployment n [U]

de·port /dɪˈpɔːt/ ‖ -ɔːrt/ v [T] to send a foreigner out of a country because they do not have a legal right to be there –deportation /ˌdiːpɔːˈteɪʃən ‖ -pɔːr-/ n [C;U]

de·port·ment /dɪˈpɔːtmənt ‖ -ɔːr-/ n old fash [U] the way a young lady behaves, especially the way she stands and walks

de·pose /dɪˈpəʊz/ v deposed, deposing [T] to remove someone from a high official position: *The head of state was deposed by the army.*

de·pos·it¹ /dɪˈpɒzɪt ‖ dɪˈpɑː-/ v [T] **1** to leave something or to put something down: *The truck deposited its load of sand.* **2** (of a natural process) to leave something in a place: *Every surface was covered in dust deposited by desert winds.* **3** to officially put money or valuable articles in a safe place, especially a bank: *He's deposited quite a lot of money recently.*

deposit² n **1** something left in a place by a natural process: *There are rich deposits of gold in those hills.* **2** a payment of part of the money owed for something, made so that the seller will not sell the goods to anyone else: *We put down a deposit on a new car today.* **3** an act of officially putting money or valuable articles in a safe place: *I'd like to make a deposit please.* **4** money which you pay when you hire or rent something and which you get back if you do not damage what you have rented

deposit ac·count /·ˈ·· ·,·/ n a bank account which earns interest; you have to tell the bank in advance if you want to take money out

dep·ot /ˈdepəʊ ‖ ˈdiːpəʊ/ n **1** a place where goods are stored **2** a large area where buses or trains are kept when they are not being used **3** AmE a bus or railway station

de·praved /dɪˈpreɪvd/ adj evil: *The judge described the murderer as a depraved and vicious man.*

de·prav·i·ty /dɪˈprævɪti/ n depravities [C;U] an evil state or action

de·pre·ci·ate /dɪˈpriːʃieɪt/ v depreciated, depreciating [I] to fall in value –depreciation /dɪˌpriːʃiˈeɪʃən/ n [U]

de·press /dɪˈpres/ v [T] **1** to make you feel very sad: *The bad news depressed me.* **2** to reduce the amount or value of something: *The threat of war has depressed business activity.*

de·pressed /dɪˈprest/ adj **1** very sad **2** suffering from low levels of business activity: *depressed areas of the country*

de·press·ing /dɪˈpresɪŋ/ adj making you feel very sad: *a depressing piece of news* –depressingly adv

de·pres·sion /dɪˈpreʃən/ n **1** [C;U] a feeling of sadness and hopelessness: *He's suffering from depression.* **2** [C] a period of reduced business activity

and high unemployment: *the great depression of the 1930s* **3** [C] a part of a surface lower than the other parts: *The rain collected in depressions on the ground.*

de·prive /dɪˈpraɪv/ v deprived, depriving deprive someone of something to take something away from someone: *They deprived their prisoner of his rights.* –deprivation /ˌdeprɪˈveɪʃən/ n [C;U]

de·prived /dɪˈpraɪvd/ adj without food, money, or good living conditions: *a deprived childhood*

dept. n a written abbreviation for DEPARTMENT

depth /depθ/ n [C;U] **1** the distance from the surface to the bottom of something or from the front to the back: *What is the depth of the shelves?* | *They dived to a depth of 30 feet.* **2** The amount that someone knows, feels, or understands: *I was surprised by the depth of his feelings.* **3** the seriousness of a situation: *the depth of the crisis* **4 in depth** in detail: *We'll have to examine the problem in depth.* | *an in-depth study* **5 out of your depth: a** in water deeper than your height **b** unable to understand something: *I'm completely out of my depth in this argument.* **6 the depths** the deepest, most central, or worst part of something: *She lives in the depths of the country.* | *the depths of depression*

dep·u·ta·tion /ˌdepjʊˈteɪʃən/ n a group of people who are sent somewhere as representatives of a larger group: *The minister agreed to receive a deputation from the railwaymen's union.*

dep·u·tize /ˈdepjʊtaɪz/ v deputized, deputizing (also deputise BrE) [I] to act as a deputy

dep·u·ty /ˈdepjʊti/ n deputies **1** the person in the second most powerful position in an organization: *the deputy leader of the party* **2** a person given the power to act for someone else: *Jean will be my deputy while I am away.* **3** a member of the lower house of parliament in certain countries

de·rail /ˌdiːˈreɪl, dɪ-/ v [T] to make a train come off the railway line –derailment n [C;U]

de·ranged /dɪˈreɪndʒ/ adj seriously ill in the mind: *That poor woman is completely deranged.* –derangement n [U]

der·e·lict /ˈderəlɪkt/ adj not used and falling into decay (used of buildings): *a derelict old house*

de·ride /dɪˈraɪd/ v derided, deriding [T] fml to laugh at something you consider to be worthless

de·ri·sion /dɪˈrɪʒən/ n [U] the action of laughing unkindly at something considered worthless: *They greeted his suggestion with shouts of derision.* –derisive /dɪˈraɪsɪv, -zɪv/ adj : *derisive laughter* –derisively adv

de·ri·so·ry /dɪˈraɪsəri/ adj **1** very small and so not worth considering seriously: *a derisory offer of £10 for something worth £100* **2** showing a total lack of respect

der·i·va·tion /ˌderɪˈveɪʃən/ n the origin from which something comes: *What is the derivation of the word "television"?*

de·riv·a·tive¹ /dɪˈrɪvətɪv/ n something coming from something else: *French is a derivative of Latin.*

derivative² adj not original or new: *a rather derivative piece of music*

de·rive /dɪˈraɪv/ v derived, deriving **1** [T] fml to get something from someone or from something else: *Maria derives great pleasure* from *playing the piano.* **2** [I;T] to come from: *The word "French" derives* from *both Greek and Latin.* | *This word is derived from Latin.*

der·ma·ti·tis /ˌdɜːməˈtaɪtɪs ‖ ˌdɜːr-/ n [U] a disease of your skin, marked by redness, swelling, and pain

de·rog·a·to·ry /dɪˈrɒgətəri ‖ dɪˈrɑːgətɔːri/ *adj fml* showing lack of respect for someone: *derogatory remarks about the government*

der·rick /ˈderɪk/ *n* a CRANE¹ for lifting and moving heavy weights, for example into or out of a ship

de·scend /dɪˈsend/ *v fml* [I;T] to go down: *The sun descended behind the hills.* | *The Queen descended the stairs.* **2 descend on/upon someone** to arrive suddenly to visit or stay with someone: *The whole family descended on us at Christmas.* **3 descend to something** to behave in a way that is below your usual standards: *He eventually descended to cheating.*

de·scen·dant /dɪˈsendənt/ *n* a person or animal that has the stated person or animal as their grandfather or grandmother, great-grandfather, etc.: *He is a descendant of Queen Victoria.* –compare ANCESTOR

de·scend·ed /dɪˈsendɪd/ *adj* **descended from someone** having the stated person or animal as their grandfather or grandmother, great-grandfather, etc.: *She claims to be descended from George Washington.*

de·scent /dɪˈsent/ *n* **1** [C;U] the process of going or coming down: *The road makes a sharp descent just past the lake.* | *his descent into a life of crime* **2** [U] your family origins: *She is of German descent.*

de·scribe /dɪˈskraɪb/ *v* **described, describing** [T] to say what something is like: *The police asked me to describe the man.* | *Try to describe exactly what happened.* | *Would you describe your mother as a nervous woman?* ☐ USEFUL PATTERNS to describe something; to describe what/how/where...; to describe someone or something as....

de·scrip·tion /dɪˈskrɪpʃən/ *n* **1** [C;U] an account of what someone or something is like or how something happened: *Terry gave a detailed description of everything that had taken place.* | *I recognized the man from the description in the newspaper.* **2** [C] a sort or kind: *The hull was packed with people of every description.* –**descriptive** /-tɪv/ *adj* : *descriptive writing* –**descriptively** *adv*

des·e·crate /ˈdesɪkreɪt/ *v* **desecrated, desecrating** [T] to spoil something holy, or to use it for purposes which are not holy –**desecration** /ˌdesɪˈkreɪʃən/ *n* [U]

des·ert¹ /ˈdezət ‖ -ərt/ *n* a large area of land, often covered with sand, where there is very little rain and so very few plants: *the Sahara Desert* | *a hot desert wind*

de·sert² /dɪˈzɜːt ‖ -ɜːrt/ *v* **1** [T] to leave a place so that it becomes empty: *The weather changed and the holidaymakers deserted the beach.* **2** [T] to leave someone completely or for the last time: *John's friends deserted him when he was accused of murder.* **3** [I;T] (of someone in the armed forces) to leave a place without permission: *The soldier deserted his post.*

de·sert·ed /dɪˈzɜːtɪd ‖ -ɜːr-/ *adj* with no people present: *a deserted village*

de·sert·er /dɪˈzɜːtər ‖ -ɜːr-/ *n* a person who leaves military service without permission

de·ser·tion /dɪˈzɜːʃən ‖ -ɜːr-/ *n* [C;U] the act of leaving, especially with the intention of never returning

de·serve /dɪˈzɜːv ‖ -ɜːrv/ *v* **deserved, deserving** [T not in progressive forms] to be worthy of a particular thing: *You've been working all morning – you deserve a rest.* | *She deserved to win.*

☐ USEFUL PATTERNS to deserve something; to deserve to do something

de·serv·ed·ly /dɪˈzɜːvɪdli ‖ -ɜːr-/ *adv* rightly, because someone is worthy of something: *He's made a lot of money, and deservedly so.*

de·serv·ing /dɪˈzɜːvɪŋ ‖ -ɜːr-/ *adj* **1** worthy of support and help: *We should give the money to a deserving cause.* **2 deserving of** *fml* worthy of: *deserving of the highest praise*

des·ic·cate /ˈdesɪkeɪt/ *v* **dessicated, dessicating** [I;T] to make or become dried up

de·sign¹ /dɪˈzaɪn/ *v* [T] **1** to make a drawing or plan so that someone can make or build something: *Who designed the Sydney Opera House?* **2** to develop something for a certain purpose or use: *a book designed mainly for use in colleges* | *These coins were designed to help blind people identify their money.* –**designer** *n* : *She's a dress designer.* | *an aircraft designer*

design² *n* **1** [C] a drawing showing how something is to be made **2** [U] the art of making drawings or patterns showing how something is to be made: *a school of dress design* | *the importance of good design* **3** [C] a decorative pattern, especially one that is not repeated: *a carpet with a floral design in the centre* **4** [C] a plan in your mind **5 have designs on something** to have the intention of getting something, especially cleverly or dishonestly: *Watch out for Ted – I think he has designs on your job.*

des·ig·nate¹ /ˈdezɪgneɪt/ *v* **designated, designating** [T] **1** to call something by a particular name because it fulfils a special purpose: *The wood was designated an area of special scientific interest.* | *designated as a conservation zone* **2** to appoint someone formally to do a particular job: *She was designated as the Minister of Education.* | *designated to take over the position of Chairman* –**designation** /ˌdezɪgˈneɪʃən/ *n* [C;U]

des·ig·nate² /ˈdezɪgnət, -neɪt/ *adj* [only after a noun] a person appointed to a job who has not yet started work: *The Director designate was invited to attend the meeting.*

de·sir·a·ble /dɪˈzaɪərəbəl/ *adj* worth having, doing, or wanting: *a desirable job* –compare UNDESIRABLE –**desirability** /dɪˌzaɪərəˈbɪləti/ *n* [U]

de·sire¹ /dɪˈzaɪər/ *v* **desired, desiring** [T not in progressive forms] **1** *fml* to wish or want something very much: *We all desire happiness.* **2** to be sexually attracted to someone **3 leave a lot to be desired** to be not very satisfactory: *The standard of cooking here leaves a lot to be desired.*

desire² *n* [C;U] **1** a strong wish: *filled with a sudden desire for fame* | *I haven't the slightest desire to see my family again.* **2** a strong wish for sexual relations with someone: *Antony's desire for Cleopatra* ■ USAGE Compare **desire, appetite, craving, lust**. You can have a **desire** for anything: *a desire for success* | *a desire to help someone* **Appetite** is most often used for things of the body, especially food: *The baby has a good* **appetite**. A **craving** is a strong desire, especially for things that people think are bad: *a craving for cigarettes*. **Lust** is a very strong and usually derogatory word: *the lust for power/sex*

de·sir·ous /dɪˈzaɪərəs/ *adj fml* [never before a noun] having a strong wish: *people desirous of fame*

de·sist /dɪˈzɪst, dɪˈsɪst/ *v fml* [I] to stop doing: *The judge told the man to desist from threatening his wife.*

desk /desk/ *n* **1** a table, often with drawers, at which you read, write, or work –see picture on page 539 **2** an area where particular work is done: *I left a message at the reception desk.*

des·o·late /ˈdesələt/ *adj* sad and lonely: *the desolate Arctic wastes* –**desolation** /ˌdesəˈleɪʃən/ *n* [U]: *a sense of utter desolation*

de·spair¹ /dɪˈspeəʳ/ *v* [I] to lose all hope: *Don't despair: things will get better soon!* | *Sometimes I despair of ever passing my driving test!* –**despairingly** *adv*

despair² *n* [U] complete loss of hope: *Defeat after defeat filled us with despair.*

de·spatch /dɪˈspætʃ/ *n,v* – see DISPATCH

des·per·ate /ˈdespərɪt/ *adj* **1** wanting or needing something very much: *He's desperate for work.* | *They're desperate to escape.*
□ USEFUL PATTERNS be desperate for something; be desperate to do something
2 violent and not caring about danger, especially because you have lost hope: *a desperate criminal* **3** dangerous, and done when everything else has failed: *a last desperate effort to win* **4** very difficult and dangerous (used of a situation): *The country is in a desperate state.* –**desperately** *adv*

des·per·a·tion /ˌdespəˈreɪʃən/ *n* [U] the state of being desperate: *He kicked at the locked door in desperation.*

des·pic·a·ble /dɪˈspɪkəbəl, ˈdespɪ-/ *adj* deserving to be despised: *That was a despicable thing to do!* –**despicably** *adv* : *You behaved despicably!*

de·spise /dɪˈspaɪz/ *v* **despised, despising** [T not in progressive forms] to consider something to be worthless or extremely bad

de·spite /dɪˈspaɪt/ *prep* **1** in spite of: *Despite the bad weather we had a lovely time.* **2** **despite yourself** in spite of the fact that you did not really want to do something: *I found myself apologizing despite myself.*

de·spon·dent /dɪˈspɒndənt ‖ dɪˈspɑːn-/ *adj* feeling very unhappy and without hope –**despondently** *adv* –**despondency** *n* [U]

des·pot /ˈdespɒt, -ət ‖ ˈdespət, -ɑːt/ *n* a person who has great power and uses it unjustly or cruelly –**despotic** /dɪˈspɒtɪk, de- ‖ -ˈspɑː-/ *adj* –**despotism** /ˈdespətɪzəm/ *n* [U]

des·sert /dɪˈzɜːt ‖ -ɜːrt/ *n* [C;U] sweet food served at the end of a meal: *We had cake for dessert.*

des·sert·spoon /dɪˈzɜːtspuːn ‖ -ɜːr-/ *n* **1** a spoon between a TEASPOON and a TABLESPOON in size **2** (also **dessertspoonful**) as much as a dessertspoon will hold

des·ti·na·tion /ˌdestɪˈneɪʃən/ *n* a place where you are going or where something is sent: *The parcel was sent to the wrong destination.*

des·tined /ˈdestɪnd/ *adj* **1** intended by fate for some special purpose: *Robert is destined for a career in the army.* | *The plan was destined not to succeed.*
□ USEFUL PATTERNS be destined for something; be destined to do something
2 **destined for** going to a particular place: *a ship destined for Bombay*

des·ti·ny /ˈdestɪni/ *n* **destinies 1** [C] something which must happen: *It would be her destiny to lead her country.* **2** [U] (also **Destiny**) the force which, some people believe, decides what will happen to us

des·ti·tute /ˈdestɪtjuːt ‖ -tuːt/ *adj* without things like food and clothing, or the money to buy them: *jobless and destitute, sleeping in doorways and begging for food* –**destitution** /ˌdestɪˈtjuːʃən ‖ -ˈtuː-/ *n* [U]

de·stroy /dɪˈstrɔɪ/ *v* [T] **1** to ruin something: *The fire destroyed most of the building.* | *All hopes of a peaceful settlement were destroyed by his violent speech.* **2** to kill an animal because it is unwanted or in pain: *The horse broke its leg and had to be destroyed.*

de·stroy·er /dɪˈstrɔɪəʳ/ *n* **1** a person or thing that destroys something **2** a small fast warship

de·struc·tion /dɪˈstrʌkʃən/ *n* [U] destroying something or being destroyed: *The enemy bombs caused widespread destruction.* | *the destruction of the forest by fire*

de·struc·tive /dɪˈstrʌktɪv/ *adj* causing great damage: *a destructive storm* | *These emotional scenes are very destructive.* –**destructiveness** *n* [U]

des·ul·to·ry /ˈdesəltəri, ˈdez- ‖ -tɔːri/ *adj fml* lacking organization and purpose

de·tach /dɪˈtætʃ/ *v* [T] to separate something from another thing –**detachable** *adj* : *a detachable shoulder-strap*

de·tached /dɪˈtætʃt/ *adj* **1** not connected on any side with any other building (used of a house) –see picture on page 441 **2** not influenced by personal feelings (used of a person or an opinion)

de·tach·ment /dɪˈtætʃmənt/ *n* **1** a state where personal feelings have no influence: *The journalist viewed the situation with total detachment.* **2** [C] a group of soldiers, sent from the main group on special duty

de·tail /ˈdiːteɪl ‖ dɪˈteɪl/ *n* **1** [C;U] a small point or fact: *Everything in her story is correct, down to the smallest detail.* | *He has a good eye for detail –he notices everything.* **2** **in detail** thoroughly: *I haven't read the report in detail yet.* **3** **go into detail** to give all the information **4** **details** [pl] information or the facts about something: *Send for details of our range of sportswear.* –**detailed** *adj* : *a detailed account*

de·tain /dɪˈteɪn/ *v* [T] *fml* to make someone stay somewhere: *The police have detained two men for questioning.* | *I mustn't detain you, I know you're very busy.*

de·tect /dɪˈtekt/ *v* [T] to find or notice something: *Small quantities of poison were detected in the dead man's stomach.*

de·tec·tion /dɪˈtekʃən/ *n* [U] **1** the work of finding out all the information about a crime, especially who was responsible: *the art of detection* | *His crime escaped detection for many years.* **2** noticing or being noticed: *The plane penetrated enemy airspace without detection.*

de·tec·tive /dɪˈtektɪv/ *n* a person, often a member of the police force, whose special job is to find out information about criminals

de·tec·tor /dɪˈtektəʳ/ *n* any instrument for finding out if something is present: *a metal detector*

dé·tente /ˈdeɪtɒnt, deɪˈtɒnt ‖ -ɑːnt/ *n* (also **detente**) [U] calmer political relations between countries

de·ten·tion /dɪˈtenʃən/ *n* [U] the act of preventing a person from leaving a place like a school, police station, or prison, or the state of being prevented from leaving: *Political opponents were subject to detention without trial.* | *I'm in detention tomorrow for not doing my homework.*

de·ter /dɪˈtɜːʳ/ *v* -rr- [T] *fml* to discourage someone from doing something: *new airport security measures to deter drug smugglers* | *High fares and poor service deter people from travelling by train.*

de·ter·gent /dɪ'tɜːdʒənt ‖ -ɜːr-/ *n* [C;U] a chemical product used for cleaning things like clothes and dishes

de·te·ri·o·rate /dɪ'tɪəriəreɪt/ *v* deteriorated, deteriorating [I] to become worse: *His deteriorating health forced him to retire.* –**deterioration** /dɪˌtɪəriə'reɪʃən/ *n* [U]

de·ter·mi·na·tion /dɪˌtɜːmɪ'neɪʃən ‖ -ɜːr-/ *n* [U] 1 a firm intention to succeed in doing something: *The police chief spoke of his determination to catch the killers.* 2 the act of deciding what something is or will be

de·ter·mine /dɪ'tɜːmɪn ‖ -ɜːr-/ *v* determined, determining [T] *fml* 1 to find something out: *to determine the rights and wrongs of the case* 2 to decide: *He determined to go at once.* | *an event which determined his future*

de·ter·mined /dɪ'tɜːmɪnd ‖ -ɜːr-/ *adj* having a strong will; or a strong intention to do something: *a very determined woman* | *I am absolutely determined to go.*
☐ USEFUL PATTERN be determined to do something

de·ter·min·er /dɪ'tɜːmɪnəʳ ‖ -ɜːr-/ *n* a word that limits the meaning of a noun and comes before adjectives that describe the same noun: *In the phrase "his new car", the word "his" is a determiner.*

de·ter·rent /dɪ'terənt ‖ -'tɜːr-/ *n* something which stops people doing something because they are afraid of what might happen: *Do you think the death penalty acts as a deterrent to murderers?* | *the nuclear deterrent* –**deterrent** *adj*

de·test /dɪ'test/ *v* [T not in progressive forms] to hate someone or something: *I detest people who tell lies.* –**detestable** *adj* : *a detestable child*

det·o·nate /'detəneɪt/ *v* detonated, detonating [I;T] to explode or make something explode: *Land-mines can be detonated by vehicles driving over them.* –**detonation** /ˌdetə'neɪʃən/ *n* [U]

de·tour /'diːtuəʳ/ *n* a longer journey than necessary: *a detour to avoid the town centre*

de·tract /dɪ'trækt/ *v* detract from something to make something seem less good: *His later work was poor, and this detracted from his reputation.*

det·ri·ment /'detrɪmənt/ *n fml* 1 to the detriment of causing damage to something: *actions that may be to the detriment of the company's reputation* 2 without detriment to without damaging something –**detrimental** /ˌdetrɪ'mentl◂/ *adj*

deuce /djuːs ‖ duːs/ *n* [U] 40 points to each player in a game of tennis

de·val·u·a·tion /diːˌvæljuˈeɪʃən/ *n* [U] a reduction in the value of something, especially the exchange value of money

de·val·ue /diːˈvæljuː/ *v* devalued, devaluing [T] to reduce the value of something, especially the exchange value of money: *The currency was devalued by ten per cent.*

dev·a·state /'devəsteɪt/ *v* devastated, devastating [T] to damage something so badly that very little is left –**devastation** /ˌdevəˈsteɪʃən/ *n* [U]

dev·a·stat·ed /'devəsteɪtɪd/ *adj* shocked and sorrowful: *When our son was killed, we were devastated.*

dev·a·stat·ing /'devəsteɪtɪŋ/ *adj* 1 damaging something so badly that very little is left: *a devastating storm* 2 *infml* making you feel very upset: *The news was devastating.* –**devastatingly** *adv*

develop /dɪ'veləp/ *v* 1 [I] to grow: *The fighting could easily develop into a full-scale war.* | *This flower developed from a tiny seed.* 2 [T] to improve something or make it grow: *a campaign to develop the local economy* 3 [T] to get an illness, a fault, or a characteristic: *She developed cancer at the age of 30.* | *The machine developed a fault.* | *He had developed a taste for fast food.* 4 [T] to invent or produce a new product or idea: *The Romans developed the technique of glass-blowing.* | *Several companies are currently developing AIDS drugs.* 5 [T] to build houses and factories on a piece of land: *Much of the land in the south-east of the county has now been developed.* 6 [I] (of a country) to start to have modern industries: *The government agreed to spend more on helping developing countries.* 7 [T] to produce pictures from a photographic film: *I must get my holiday photos developed.*

de·vel·op·er /dɪ'veləpəʳ/ *n* a person who makes money by buying land and building houses or factories on it

de·vel·op·ment /dɪ'veləpmənt/ *n* 1 [C] a new event: *There has been an important new development in the political situation.* 2 [C] a new invention, or an improvement to an existing machine or process: *recent developments in the treatment of cancer* 3 [U] the growth or improvement of something: *the rapid development of the oil industry* | *the country's economic development programme* 4 [U] the building of houses and factories on land: *Plans were being submitted for the development of this site.* 5 [C] a group of new buildings: *a new housing development on the edge of town* 6 [U] the invention or production of new products and ideas: *the development of two experimental aircraft* | *We should encourage companies to spend more on research and development.* 7 [U] the process by which a poor country starts to have modern industries: *The government has given 32 million pounds in food and development aid.* | *the minister for overseas development*

de·vi·ant /'diːviənt/ *adj* different from what is accepted (a word used to express disapproval) –**deviant** *n* : *criminals and other deviants*

de·vi·ate /'diːvieɪt/ *v* deviated, deviating [I] deviate from something to be or become different from what is normal or acceptable

de·vi·a·tion /ˌdiːviˈeɪʃən/ *n* [C;U] a noticeable difference from what is expected, particularly from accepted standards of behaviour: *sexual deviation* | *a deviation from the norm*

de·vice /dɪ'vaɪs/ *n* 1 a thing invented to fulfil a special purpose: *a device for measuring stress* –see MACHINE (USAGE) 2 a way of achieving a particular purpose: *a device for avoiding income tax* 3 leave someone to their own devices to leave someone to do something alone, and not give them any help or advice

dev·il /'devəl/ *n* 1 the Devil the most powerful evil spirit 2 an evil spirit 3 a high-spirited or troublesome person, especially a child: *He's good at school, but he's a little devil at home.* 4 *infml* a word used for a person: *You lucky devil!* | *The poor devils lost everything in the floods.*

dev·il·ish /'devəlɪʃ/ *adj* evil and cruel

de·vi·ous /'diːviəs/ *adj* 1 not going in the straightest or most direct way: *a devious route* 2 not direct or honest: *a devious plan* | *He's very devious.* –**deviously** *adv*

de·vise /dɪ'vaɪz/ *v* devised, devising [T] to plan or invent something: *He devised a plan for winning the game.*

de·void /dɪ'vɔɪd/ adj fml **devoid of something** completely without something, especially a quality: He is devoid of human feeling!

de·vo·lu·tion /ˌdiːvə'luːʃən/ n [U] the giving of governmental power to a smaller group

de·volve /dɪ'vɒlv ‖ dɪ'vɑːlv/ v **devolved, devolving devolve on someone** (of power or work) to be passed to another person or group

de·vote /dɪ'vəʊt/ v **devoted, devoting devote yourself to something, devote your time to something** to give your time and effort to something: He has devoted his life to helping blind people. | We shouldn't devote any more time to this question.

de·vot·ed /dɪ'vəʊtɪd/ adj loving someone or something very much and giving them time and attention: a devoted father | He is devoted to his wife. –**devotedly** adv

dev·o·tee /ˌdevə'tiː/ n a person who admires someone or something: a devotee of everything Italian

de·vo·tion /dɪ'vəʊʃən/ n [U] **1** the act of giving a lot of attention to something **2** great fondness for someone **3** strong religious feeling

de·vour /dɪ'vaʊər/ v [T] to eat something quickly and hungrily

de·vout /dɪ'vaʊt/ adj having strong religious beliefs: a devout Hindu –**devoutly** adv

dew /djuː ‖ duː/ n [U] the small drops of water which form on cold surfaces during the night

dew·y /'djuːi ‖ 'duːi/ adj wet with dew

dex·ter·i·ty /dek'sterəti/ n [U] the quality of cleverness and skill, for example in the use of your hands

dex·ter·ous /'dekstərəs/ adj (also **dextrous**) clever and skilful with your hands

di·a·be·tes /ˌdaɪə'biːtiːz, -tɪs/ n [U] a disease in which a person cannot control the level of sugar in their blood

di·a·bet·ic /ˌdaɪə'betɪk◂/ n a person suffering from diabetes –**diabetic** adj : She became diabetic at the age of 25. | diabetic foods

di·a·bol·i·cal /ˌdaɪə'bɒlɪkəl ‖ -'baː-/ adj infml very unpleasant and annoying: What diabolical weather! –**diabolically** /-kli/ adv

di·ag·nose /'daɪəgnəʊz ‖ -nəʊs/ v **diagnosed, diagnosing** [T] to discover the nature of a disease or problem: The doctor diagnosed my illness as a rare bone disease.

di·ag·no·sis /ˌdaɪəg'nəʊsɪs/ n **diagnoses** /-siːz/ [C;U] the act of finding out what is wrong and describing it: What's your diagnosis of the situation? | a diagnosis of rheumatism –**diagnostic** /-'nɒstɪk ‖ -'naː-/ adj : modern diagnostic techniques

di·ag·o·nal /daɪ'ægənəl/ adj **1** running in a sloping direction (used of straight lines) **2** joining opposite corners of a square –**diagonal** n –**diagonally** adv

di·a·gram /'daɪəgræm/ n a simple drawing which shows how something works –**diagrammatic** /ˌdaɪəgrə'mætɪk/ adj –**diagrammatically** /-kli/ adv

dial[1] /'daɪəl/ n **1** the face of an instrument, such as a clock, which shows information by means of a pointer or figures **2** the wheel on a telephone with numbered holes for the fingers, which you move round when you make a telephone call

dial[2] v -**ll**- (-**l**- AmE) [I;T] to press the buttons or move the dial on a telephone in order to make a telephone call: How do I dial Paris? | Put in the money before dialling. –see TELEPHONE (USAGE)

di·a·lect /'daɪəlekt/ n [C;U] a variety of a language spoken in one part of a country: the Yorkshire and Lancashire dialects | a poem written in Scottish dialect –**dialectal** /ˌdaɪə'lektl/ adj

di·a·lec·tic /ˌdaɪə'lektɪk/ n (also **dialectics** /ˌdaɪə-'lektɪks/) [U] tech the art or method of arguing according to certain rules of question and answer –**dialectical** adj

di·a·logue /'daɪəlɒg ‖ -lɔːg, -lɑːg/ n (**dialog** AmE) [C;U] **1** a written conversation in a book or play: a short dialogue between Hamlet and his mother | She's good at writing dialogue. **2** a conversation which examines differences of opinion between leaders or groups of people: At last there is hope of dialogue between the two sides.

di·am·e·ter /daɪ'æmɪtər/ n a straight line from one side of a circle to the other side, passing through the centre of the circle

di·a·met·ri·cally /ˌdaɪə'metrɪkli/ adv **be diametrically opposed** to be completely different: The two ideas are diametrically opposed.

di·a·mond /'daɪəmənd/ n **1** [C] a hard, bright precious stone used for jewellery and industrial purposes: a diamond ring **2** [C] a figure with four straight sides of equal length that stands on one of its points **3 diamonds** a set of playing cards with one or more diamonds in red: the four of diamonds

di·a·per /'daɪəpər ‖ 'daɪpər/ n the usual American word for NAPPY

di·a·phragm /'daɪəfræm/ n **1** the muscle that separates your lungs from your stomach **2** a round rubber object that a woman puts inside her VAGINA to allow her to have sex without having children

di·ar·rhoea /ˌdaɪə'rɪə/ n (also **diarrhea**) [U] an illness in which a person empties their bowels too often and in a very liquid form

di·a·ry /'daɪəri/ n **diaries 1** a daily record of the events in a person's life, often contained in a book: He recorded all the day's events in his diary. | Nowadays many people don't bother to keep a diary. **2** BrE a book in which you keep a record of things to be done in the future: "Can you come on Wednesday?" "I'll just look in my diary to see if I'm free." –see picture on page 539

dice[1] /daɪs/ n [plural is **dice**] a small block of wood or plastic, with six sides and a different number of spots from one to six on the various sides, used in games of chance

dice[2] v **diced, dicing 1** [T] to cut food into small square pieces: The meat should be finely diced. **2 dice with death** to take a great risk

dic·ey /'daɪsi/ adj **dicier, diciest** infml risky and uncertain

di·chot·o·my /daɪ'kɒtəmi ‖ -'kɑː-/ n **dichotomies** fml a division into two parts or groups which are very different or have very different opinions: the dichotomy between opponents and supporters of nuclear weapons

dic·tate /dɪk'teɪt ‖ 'dɪkteɪt/ v **dictated, dictating** [I;T] **1** to say words for someone else to write down or for a machine to record: She was dictating a letter to her secretary. | Don't interrupt me while I'm dictating. **2** to state conditions that you have the power to force people to accept: We're now in a position to dictate terms to our employers.

dic·ta·tion /dɪk'teɪʃən/ n **1** [U] the act of dictating or writing down what is dictated: a secretary taking dictation **2** [C] something dictated to test your ability to hear and write a language correctly: The teacher gave us two French dictations today.

dic·ta·tor /dɪk'teɪtər‖ 'dɪkt,eɪtər/ *n* a ruler who has complete power over a country especially after gaining power by force

dic·ta·to·ri·al /ˌdɪktə'tɔːriəl/ *adj* 1 relating to a dictator or like a dictator 2 behaving or giving orders in a forceful way, without regard for people's feelings: *He's very dictatorial and won't listen to anyone else's opinion.* –**dictatorially** *adv*

dic·ta·tor·ship /dɪk'teɪtəʃɪp ‖ -'teɪtər-/ *n* 1 [C;U] government by a dictator 2 [C] a country ruled by a dictator

dic·tion /'dɪkʃən/ *n* [U] the way in which a person pronounces words: *Actors need training in diction.*

dic·tion·a·ry /'dɪkʃənəri ‖ -neri/ *n* **dictionaries** a book that gives a list of words in alphabetical order, with their meanings in the same or another language

did /dɪd/ the past tense of DO

di·dac·tic /daɪ'dæktɪk/ *adj fml* meant to teach, especially to teach a moral lesson

did·n't /'dɪdnt/ short for "did not": *You saw him, didn't you?*

die¹ /daɪ/ *v* **died, died, dying** /'daɪ-ɪŋ/ [I] 1 to stop living: *He died at the age of 102.* | *Her mother was dying of cancer.* 2 **die a ... death** to die in a particular way: *She died a natural death.* 3 **be dying for something** to want something very much: *I was dying for something to eat.* [RELATED PHRASE: **be dying to do something.**]
die away *phr v* [I] (of sound, wind, or light) to become less and less and then stop
die down *phr v* [I] to become less strong or violent: *The fire is dying down.* | *The excitement died down.*
die off *phr v* [I] to die one by one: *As she got older and older, her relatives all died off.*
die out *phr v* [I] to disappear completely and so no longer exist: *Most of the old customs have now died out.* | *Several species have died out already.*

die² *n* a metal block used for shaping metal or plastic

die·sel en·gine /'diːzəl ,endʒɪn/ *n* (also **diesel**) a type of oil-burning engine often used for buses and trains

di·et¹ /'daɪət/ *n* 1 [C;U] a person's usual food or drink: *Proper diet and exercise are both important for health.* | *living on a diet of fast food* 2 [C] a limited list of food and drink that one is allowed: *This diet only allows you to eat fresh fruit.* | *a high-fibre diet* 3 **be on a diet, go on a diet** to be trying to lose weight by eating a limited amount of food

di·et² *v* [I] to try to lose weight by eating a limited amount of food: *No sugar in my coffee, please –I'm dieting.*

dif·fer /'dɪfər/ *v* [I] 1 to be different: *Nylon differs from silk in origin and cost.* 2 to have different opinions: *The two brothers often differ.* | *He differed with his brother on how to look after their parents.*

dif·fer·ence /'dɪfərəns/ *n* 1 [C;U] a way in which things are unlike each other: *There are many differences between living in a city and living in the country.* | *There is not much difference in size between them.* 2 [C] the amount by which two numbers or quantities are different: *The difference between 5 and 11 is 6.* 3 **make no difference, not make any difference** to have no effect on a situation 4 **make all the difference** to be very important and help you in some way 5 **have your differences** to have a slight disagreement with someone: *We've had our differences, but we're still good friends.*

dif·fe·rent /'dɪfərənt/ *adj* not the same: *The two sisters are quite different.* | *This new drug is quite different from all the others available.* | *My opinions are very different to yours.* | *We met a lot of different people at the party.* –**differently** *adv*

■ USAGE Some people consider that **different from** is the only correct form, and so you will always be right if you use it. Note, however, that **different to** is also very common in British English. **Different than** is also used in American English.

dif·fe·ren·tial /ˌdɪfə'renʃəl◄/ *n* the amount of difference between things, especially difference in wages between workers at different levels in the same industry

dif·fe·ren·ti·ate /ˌdɪfə'renʃieɪt/ *v* **differentiated, differentiating** [I;T] to see, express, or make a difference: *This company does not differentiate between men and women – it employs both on equal terms.* –**differentiation** /ˌdɪfərenʃi'eɪʃən/ *n* [C;U]

dif·fi·cult /'dɪfɪkəlt/ *adj* 1 not easy to do or understand: *The exam questions were all very difficult.* | *It's difficult to understand her ideas.* | *It's quite difficult for me to get to your house.*
□ USEFUL PATTERNS **be difficult to do** something, **be difficult for** someone **to do** something 2 not helpful and not easy to please (used of people): *a difficult child* | *She's being very difficult at the moment.*

dif·fi·cul·ty /'dɪfɪkəlti/ *n* **difficulties** 1 something which causes a problem: *Our main difficulty is lack of money.* | *There were some difficulties in reaching an agreement.* 2 **have difficulty doing** something, **have difficulty in doing something** to be unable to do something easily: *I had difficulty hearing the speaker.* | *He had no difficulty in understanding her.* 3 **with difficulty** not easily: *His English was very bad and he spoke with difficulty.* [RELATED PHRASE: **without difficulty**] 4 **be in difficulties, be in difficulty** to have problems: *A lot of people are in difficulties with their mortgage repayments.* | *He went to help her with her car as she was obviously in difficulty.* [RELATED PHRASE: **get into difficulty**]

dif·fi·dent /'dɪfɪdənt/ *adj* unable to speak or act with confidence: *He is diffident about expressing his opinions.* –opposite **confident** –**diffidently** *adv* – **diffidence** *n* [U]

dif·fuse¹ /dɪ'fjuːs/ *adj fml* 1 widely spread: *a diffuse population scattered about the island* 2 using too many words and not expressing ideas clearly –**diffusely** *adv*

dif·fuse² /dɪ'fjuːz/ *v* **diffused, diffusing** [I;T] *fml* to spread something out or become spread out in a lot of different directions or to a lot of different people: *to diffuse knowledge* | *diffused light* –**diffusion** /-'fjuːʒən/ *n* [U]

dig¹ /dɪɡ/ *v* **dug** /dʌɡ/, **dug, digging** [I;T] 1 to break up and move earth: *I spent two hours digging the vegetable garden.* | *The dog has been digging in that corner for half an hour.* | *They dug a tunnel through the mountain.* 2 to push or be pushed into something: *A nail from my shoe was digging into my foot.* | *The cat dug its claws into the mouse.*
dig at sbdy *phr v* [T] to make unpleasant remarks about someone: *The teacher is always digging at me.*
dig sthg ↔ **out** *phr v* [T] 1 to find something that has been hidden for a long time: *Look at those red trousers that I dug out from the back of the cupboard.* 2 to get something out after it has been

buried: *It snowed last night and we had to dig the car out.*

dig sthg ↔ **up** *phr v* [T] **1** to make a hole by taking away earth: *They are digging up the road outside the house.* **2** to take something out of the ground: *My neighbour dug up some gold coins in the garden.* **3** to discover facts that had been hidden: *Journalists managed to dig up some surprising facts about the minister's past.*

dig² *n* **1** *infml* a quick push: *John's falling asleep, just give him a dig.* **2** an unpleasant remark: *Sally keeps making digs about my work.* **3** a place where ARCHAEOLOGISTS are digging to find information about the past which is buried in the ground **4** digs [pl] *BrE infml* lodgings: *When his family left London, Tom moved into digs.*

di·gest¹ /dai'dʒest, dɨ-/ *v* **1** [T] to change food into a form that the body can use: *Babies can't digest cow's milk.* **2** [T] to think about something carefully and understand it: *I heard her speech, but I haven't digested it yet.* –**digestible** *adj*

di·gest² /'daidʒest/ *n* a short account of a piece of writing which gives the most important facts: *a digest of Roman laws*

di·ges·tion /dai'dʒestʃən, dɨ-/ *n* [C;U] the act of digesting or the ability to digest food: *Digestion is more difficult for old people.* | *I've always had a good digestion.*

di·ges·tive /dai'dʒestiv, dɨ-/ *adj* **1** relating to the digestion of food: *digestive juices* **2** **digestive biscuit** *tdmk* a type of sweet biscuit

di·git /'didʒɨt/ *n* **1** any of the numbers from 0 to 9: *The number 2001 contains four digits.* **2** *fml* a finger or toe

di·gi·tal /'didʒɨtl/ *adj* **digital watch, digital clock** a watch or clock that has no hands and shows the time by means of numbers

dig·ni·fied /'dignɨfaid/ *adj* proud, calm, and making people feel respect for you: *a dignified old man* –opposite **undignified**

dig·ni·ta·ry /'dignɨtəri ‖ -teri/ *n* **dignitaries** *fml* a person who has an important position in public life: *Many of the local dignitaries attended the mayor's funeral.*

dig·ni·ty /'dignɨti/ *n* [U] **1** qualities of character or appearance which make people feel respect: *He always acted with great dignity.* **2** formal and grand behaviour: *The dignity of the occasion was lost when he fell down the steps.*

di·gress /dai'gres/ *v* [I] *fml* to stop what you are saying and begin to talk about something else: *I'll tell you a funny story, if I may digress for a moment.* –**digression** /-'greʃən/ *n* [C;U]

dike /daik/ *n* –see DYKE

di·lap·i·dat·ed /dɨ'læpɨdeitɨd/ *adj* old, broken, and falling to pieces: *a dilapidated old car* | *The house looked a bit dilapidated.* –**dilapidation** /dɨ,læpɨ'deiʃən/ [U]

di·late /dai'leit/ *v* dilated, dilating *fml* [I] (of your eyes) to become bigger: *Her eyes dilated with terror.* –**dilation** /-'leiʃən/ *n* [U]

di·lem·ma /dɨ'lemə, dai-/ *n* a difficult situation in which you have to choose between two possible actions: *She was in a dilemma as to whether to stay at school or get a job.*

dil·i·gent /'dilɨdʒənt/ *adj* showing steady, careful effort: *Though he's not clever he's a diligent worker and should do well in the exams.* –**diligently** *adv* –**diligence** *n* [U]

di·lute¹ /dai'lu:t/ *v* diluted, diluting [T] to make a liquid weaker or thinner by mixing another liquid with it: *He diluted the paint with water.* –**dilute** /,dai'lu:t◄/ *adj* : *dilute acid* –**dilution** /-'lu:ʃən/ *n* [C;U]

dim¹ /dim/ *adj* -mm- **1** not bright or clear: *The light is too dim for me to read easily.* | *the dim shape of an animal in the mist* **2** *infml* stupid and foolish –**dimly** *adv*

dim² *v* -mm- [I;T] to make or become less bright: *The lights in the theatre began to dim.* | *You can use this switch to dim the lights.*

dime /daim/ *n* a coin of the US and Canada, worth ten cents

di·men·sion /dai'menʃən, dɨ-/ *n* **1** a measurement in any one direction: *Length is one dimension, and width is another.* **2** one side of a problem or subject: *There is another dimension to this problem which you haven't mentioned.* **3** **dimensions** [pl] the measurements or size of something: *What are the dimensions of the room?* | *The true dimensions of the problem have only just been recognized.* **4** **-dimensional** having the stated number of dimensions: *A three-dimensional object has length, depth, and height.*

di·min·ish /dɨ'miniʃ/ *v* [I;T] *fml* to become or make something smaller or less important: *Children's enthusiasm for noisy games never seems to diminish.* | *The government's diminishing popularity is worrying for the Prime Minister.*

dim·i·nu·tion /,dimɨ'nju:ʃən ‖ -'nu:-/ *n* [C;U] the condition of diminishing or being diminished

di·min·u·tive /dɨ'minjɨtiv/ *adj fml* extremely small

dim·ple /'dimpəl/ *n* a little hollow place especially one that forms in your cheek when you smile

din /din/ *n* a loud, continuous, confused, and unpleasant noise

dine /dain/ *v fml* dined, dining [I] to eat dinner: *We dined at the Ritz last night.* | *They dined on lobster and champagne.*

dine out *phr v* [I] to eat dinner in a restaurant or at a friend's home

din·er /'dainər/ *n* **1** someone who is having a meal in a restaurant **2** *AmE* a small restaurant beside the road **3** *AmE* a carriage on a train where food is served

ding-dong /,diŋ'dɒŋ◄ ‖ 'diŋdɔ:ŋ/ *n* **1** [U] the noise made by a bell **2** [sing] *infml* a noisy argument: *I had a bit of a ding-dong with my mother last night.*

din·ghy /'diŋgi, 'diŋi/ *n* **dinghies** **1** a small open boat carried on a larger boat to take passengers to the shore **2** a small sailing or rowing boat

din·gy /'dindʒi/ *adj* **dingier, dingiest** dirty and dull in colour (used of things and places): *a dingy little room* –**dingily** *adv* –**dinginess** *n* [U]

dining room /'··· ·/ *n* a room where meals are eaten in a house or hotel

din·ner /'dinər/ *n* **1** [C;U] the main meal of the day, eaten either at midday or in the evening: *What time do you usually have dinner?* | *It's dinner time* | *We're having fish for dinner.* | *My husband's cooking dinner tonight.* **2** [C] a formal occasion in the evening when this meal is eaten: *The firm are giving a dinner in honour of her retirement.*

■ USAGE If **dinner** is at midday, the evening meal is usually called **tea** or (especially later in the evening) **supper**. If **dinner** is in the evening, the midday meal is usually called **lunch**.

dinner jack·et /ˈ·· ˌ··/ n a man's JACKET which is usually black and worn with a white shirt, black BOW TIE, and trousers on formal occasions

di·no·saur /ˈdaɪnəsɔːr/ n a very large animal that lived in very ancient times and which no longer exists

di·o·cese /ˈdaɪəsɪs/ n the area of a country which a BISHOP is responsible for

dip¹ /dɪp/ v -pp- **1** [T] to put something into a liquid for a moment: *I dipped my pen in the ink.* **2** [I;T] to move downwards: *The sun dipped below the horizon.* | *I wish people would dip their headlights when they meet another car at night.* | *The road dips just around the corner.*
dip into sthg *phr v* [T] **1** to read or study something for a short time: *I haven't read that book properly –I've only dipped into it.* **2** to use up money that has been saved: *I've had to dip into my savings quite a lot recently.*

dip² n **1** a slope down or slight drop in height: *a dip in the road* **2** *infml* a quick swim **3** a thick liquid food into which vegetable pieces can be dipped: *a cheese dip* | *an avocado dip*

diph·ther·i·a /dɪfˈθɪəriə, dɪp-/ n [U] a serious infectious disease of the throat which makes breathing difficult

diph·thong /ˈdɪfθɒŋ, ˈdɪp- ‖ -θɔːŋ/ n *tech* a vowel sound made by pronouncing two vowels quickly one after the other

di·plo·ma /dɪˈpləʊmə/ n a course of study or examination at a particular level and the official piece of paper to show that you have been successful in it: *She got her teaching diploma last year.* | *I'm doing a diploma in engineering.*

di·plo·ma·cy /dɪˈpləʊməsi/ n [U] **1** the management of good relations between countries and government **2** skill at dealing with people and difficult situations successfully: *The lawyers handled the divorce with great diplomacy.*

dip·lo·mat /ˈdɪpləmæt/ n someone employed by their government to represent their country in another country, for example an AMBASSADOR

dip·lo·mat·ic /ˌdɪpləˈmætɪk ◂/ adj **1** [only before a noun] related to the management of good relations between countries: *Nigel joined the diplomatic service.* **2** good at dealing with people in a way which causes no bad feeling: *Try to be diplomatic when you refuse her invitation.* **–diplomatically** /-kli/ adv

dire /daɪər/ adj **1** very great or terrible: *in dire need of food* | *a dire warning* **2 in dire straits** in a seriously difficult position

di·rect¹ /dɪˈrekt, daɪ-/ v **1** [T +adv/prep] to send or aim something at a particular person or thing: *Most of the money will be directed towards medical research.* | *civil unrest directed against the white community* | *Please direct your complaints to the manager.* **2** [T] *fml* to tell someone the way to a place: *Can you direct me to the station?* **3** [T] to control the way something is done: *He directed the building of the new bridge.* | *Who directed that play on television last night?* **4** [T] *fml* to order: *The policeman directed the crowd to move back.* **–see** LEAD (USAGE)

direct² adj **1** going from one point to another without stopping or turning aside: *Which is the most direct way to London?* | *a direct flight from London to Los Angeles* | *She scored a direct hit.* **2** with no other person or thing being included: *He was asked to leave school as a direct result of his*

behaviour. | *We need the chairman's direct intervention.* **3** honest and easily understood: *He refused to give a direct answer to my question.* | *I've always found her direct and open.* **4** [only before a noun] exact: *He's the direct opposite of his brother.* **–direct** *adv* : *The next flight goes direct to Rome.*

di·rec·tion /dɪˈrekʃən, daɪ-/ n **1** [C] the place or point towards which a person or thing moves, faces or is aimed: *Which direction does the house face?* | *We travelled in an easterly direction for some time.* | *When the first shot was fired, the protesters ran off in all directions.* **2 in the direction of** towards: *They drove off in the direction of London.* **3** [U] control, guidance, or advice: *The choir is under the direction of Mr Butler.* | *That boy needs firmer direction from his parents.* **4 directions** [pl] instructions on how to get somewhere or how to do something: *She gave me directions to the station.* | *Just follow the directions on the packet.*

di·rec·tive /dɪˈrektɪv, daɪ-/ n *fml* an official order

di·rect·ly¹ /dɪˈrektli, daɪ-/ adv **1** exactly: *He lives directly opposite the church.* | *in the flat directly above ours* **2** honestly and openly: *She answered me very directly.* **3** at once or very soon: *He should be here directly.*

directly² *conj* as soon as: *I came directly I got your message.*

di·rec·tor /dɪˈrektər, daɪ-/ n **1** a person who controls or manages an organization or company **2** someone who directs a play or film, deciding how it is performed and filmed

di·rec·to·ry /dɪˈrektəri, daɪ-/ n **directories** a book or list of names, numbers or other facts, arranged in alphabetical order

dirge /dɜːdʒ ‖ dɜːrdʒ/ n a slow sad song sung at a funeral

dirt /dɜːt ‖ dɜːrt/ n [U] **1** an unclean substance, such as mud or dust: *Wash the dirt off your hands.* | *The floor is covered with dirt.* **2** soil or loose earth: *The children were outside playing happily in the dirt.*

dirt·y¹ /ˈdɜːti ‖ ˈdɜːr-/ adj **dirtier, dirtiest 1** not clean: *dirty hands* | *Repairing cars is a dirty job.* **2** concerned with or thinking about sex in rather an unacceptable way: *a dirty joke* | *You've got a dirty mind.* | *a dirty old man* **3** unpleasant or dishonest: *a dirty trick* **4** disapproving or unacceptable: *He gave me a dirty look.* | *"Empire" is a dirty word these days.*

dirty² v **dirtied, dirtying** [T] to make something unclean: *Don't dirty your hands.*

dis·a·bil·i·ty /ˌdɪsəˈbɪləti/ n **disabilities 1** [U] the state in which you cannot use your body properly: *She gets a disability pension from the government.* **2** [C] something that makes you unable to use your body properly: *Blindness is a very serious disability.*

dis·a·bled /dɪsˈeɪbəld/ adj **1** unable to use your body properly: *He's been disabled since the war, when he lost his arm.* **2 the disabled** people who have a physical problem or illness of the mind which influences the way they live

dis·ad·van·tage /ˌdɪsədˈvɑːntɪdʒ ‖ -ˈvæn-/ n something that makes progress or success difficult: *The main disadvantage of the project is the cost.* | *Not being able to speak Spanish could put you at a disadvantage.* | *The lack of good training facilities will be to your disadvantage.* **–opposite advantage** **–disadvantageous** /ˌdɪsædvənˈteɪdʒəs, -væn-/ adj

dis·ad·van·taged /ˌdɪsədˈvɑːntɪdʒd ‖ -ˈvæn-/ adj coming from a poor social background: *More* *financial help is needed for the disadvantaged sections of the community.*

dis·a·gree /ˌdɪsəˈgriː/ v **disagreed, disagreeing** [I] **1** to have or express different opinions or to quarrel: *We always disagree* **about** *everything.* | *They disagreed over who should drive.* | *I'm afraid I disagree* **with** *you.* **2** to be different from each other: *These reports disagree on many important points.* **3** disagree **with** you *infml* to make you feel ill: *Onions always disagree with me.*

dis·a·gree·a·ble /ˌdɪsəˈgriːəbəl/ adj unpleasant: *a disagreeable job* | *a disagreeable person* –opposite **agreeable** –**disagreeably** adv

dis·a·gree·ment /ˌdɪsəˈgriːmənt/ n [C;U] the action or the state of having a different opinion about something from someone else: *We have been having a few disagreements lately.* | *I am in total disagreement with you over this.*

dis·al·low /ˌdɪsəˈlaʊ/ v [T] *fml* to refuse officially to accept something: *The referee has disallowed that goal.*

dis·ap·pear /ˌdɪsəˈpɪər/ v [I] **1** to move so that you cannot see or find it: *Several top-secret files have mysteriously disappeared.* | *By the time the police arrived the rioters had disappeared.* **2** to stop existing: *Dinosaurs disappeared millions of years ago.* **3** disappear **into thin air** to go out of sight suddenly and with no explanation –**disappearance** n [C;U] :*Her disappearance was very worrying.*

dis·ap·point /ˌdɪsəˈpɔɪnt/ v [T] to cause someone to feel disappointed: *I'm sorry to disappoint you, but I can't come after all.*

dis·ap·point·ed /ˌdɪsəˈpɔɪntɪd/ adj unhappy because something or someone is not as good as you hoped they would be, or something has not happened as you hoped it would: *I'm very disappointed* **in** *him.* | *Are you disappointed* **at** *losing the race?* | *I was disappointed to hear you'd failed your driving test.* –**disappointedly** adv

dis·ap·point·ing /ˌdɪsəˈpɔɪntɪŋ/ adj making you unhappy because something is not as good as you hoped it would be: *Your examination marks are rather disappointing.* | *disappointing news* –**disappointingly** adv

dis·ap·point·ment /ˌdɪsəˈpɔɪntmənt/ n **1** [U] the state of being disappointed: *To his great disappointment, she wasn't on the train.* **2** [C] someone or something which is not as good as you hoped it would be: *Our son has been a disappointment* **to** *us.* | *The film was a bit of a disappointment – we expected it to be much better.*

dis·ap·prov·al /ˌdɪsəˈpruːvəl/ n [U] a feeling or opinion that someone else is behaving badly: *He spoke with disapproval of your behaviour.* | *She shook her head in disapproval.* –opposite **approval**

dis·ap·prove /ˌdɪsəˈpruːv/ v [I] to think that something is wrong or immoral: *We strongly disapprove of the firm's new policy.* –opposite **approve** –**disapprovingly** adv

dis·arm /dɪsˈɑːm/ v **1** [T] to take weapons away from someone: *The police disarmed the criminal.* **2** [I] to reduce the size and strength of the armed forces in a country: *Unless both sides disarm, neither will feel safe.* **3** [T] to make someone less angry and more friendly: *I didn't trust him at first but his smile completely disarmed me.*

dis·ar·ma·ment /dɪsˈɑːməmənt/ n [U] the act of reducing a country's weapons or armed forces: *new plans for nuclear disarmament*

dis·ar·range /ˌdɪsəˈreɪndʒ/ v **disarranged, disarranging** [T] to make something untidy

dis·ar·ray /ˌdɪsəˈreɪ/ n *fml* **in disarray** very untidy or not organized: *After the fighting, the army was in disarray.*

dis·as·so·ci·ate /ˌdɪsəˈseʊʃieɪt, -sieɪt/ v **disassociated, disassociating** –see DISSOCIATE

di·sas·ter /dɪˈzɑːstər‖dɪˈzæ-/ n [C;U] **1** a sudden event which causes great loss or harm: *The earthquake was one of the worst natural disasters the country has ever suffered.* **2** *infml* a failure: *The party was a disaster.*

di·sas·trous /dɪˈzɑːstrəs‖dɪˈzæ-/ adj very bad or ending in failure: *a disastrous mistake* | *The results were disastrous.* –**disastrously** adv

dis·band /dɪsˈbænd/ v [I;T] to stop existing as an organisation: *The club has disbanded.*

dis·be·lief /ˌdɪsbɪˈliːf/ n [U] a feeling that something is not true or doesn't exist: *He shook his head in disbelief.*

dis·be·lieve /ˌdɪsbɪˈliːv/ v **disbelieved, disbelieving** [T] to think that someone is not telling the truth: *I see no reason to disbelieve his story.*

■ USAGE **disbelieve** is a strong and formal word which suggests there are good reasons for not accepting that a story or statement is true. It is not the usual opposite of **believe** especially when **believe** means "approve of". Instead say: *I* **don't believe** *you.* | *I* **don't believe** *in letting children do what they want.*

disc /dɪsk/ n (**disk** *AmE*) **1** something round and flat: *a metal disc* **2** a record for playing on a RECORD PLAYER **3** a flat piece of CARTILAGE between the bones of your back: *The pain was caused by a slipped disc.*

dis·card /dɪsˈkɑːd‖-ɑːrd/ v [T] to get rid of something as being useless: *Discard the outside leaves of the lettuce.* | *He discarded his old friends when he got rich.*

di·scern /dɪˈsɜːn‖-ɜːrn/ v [T] *fml* to see, notice, or understand something by looking or thinking about it carefully: *He was just able to discern the road in the dark.* –**discernible** adj –**discernibly** adv

di·scern·ing /dɪˈsɜːnɪŋ‖-ɜːr-/ adj able to make good judgments in matters of style, fashion, or beauty: *The paper has a discerning readership.*

dis·charge¹ /dɪsˈtʃɑːdʒ‖-ɑːr-/ v **discharged, discharging** [T] **1** to allow a person to go or send them away: *She's been discharged from hospital.* **2** to send, pour, or let out liquid or gas: *The wound discharged pus.* | *Smoke was discharged into the atmosphere.* **3** to perform a duty or promise **4** to pay a debt completely **5** to unload something: *The ship discharged its cargo onto the dock.* **6** to fire a gun

dis·charge² /dɪsˈtʃɑːdʒ, ˈdɪstʃɑːdʒ‖-ɑːr-/ n **1** [U] the action of sending someone or something away: *After my discharge from the army I went into business.* **2** [C;U] a substance that comes out of something else: *There's still some discharge from the wound.*

di·sci·ple /dɪˈsaɪpəl/ n **1** a follower of a religious teacher, especially one of the 12 first followers of Christ **2** a follower of any great leader or teacher

dis·ci·pli·nar·i·an /ˌdɪsəplɪˈneəriən/ n someone who believes people should obey rules and who makes them do this

dis·ci·pline¹ /ˈdɪsəplɪn/ n **1** [C;U] the training of someone's mind and body to produce **obedience**

and self-control: *military discipline* | *Learning poetry is a good discipline for the memory.* **2** [U] control gained as a result of this training: *Good discipline in the classroom makes it easier to work.* **3** [U] punishment or firm control intended to produce obedience: *That child needs discipline.* –**disciplinary** /ˈdɪsɪ̭plɪnəri, ˌdɪsɪ̭ˈplɪ- ‖ ˈdɪsɪ̭plɪ̭neri/ *adj* : *Those who break the rules will face disciplinary action.*

discipline² *v* **disciplined, disciplining** [T] **1** to train someone to behave or act in a certain way: *You must learn to discipline yourself at university.* | *They never discipline their children.* **2** to punish someone: *Offenders will be severely disciplined.*

disc jock·ey /ˈ· ˌ·-/ *n* –see DJ

dis·claim /dɪsˈkleɪm/ *v* [T] **disclaim responsibility** to say that you are not responsible for something that has happened: *He disclaimed all responsibility for the accident.*

dis·close /dɪsˈkləʊz/ *v* **disclosed, disclosing** [T] to show or tell someone something: *He refused to disclose his name and address to the police.*

dis·clo·sure /dɪsˈkləʊʒəʳ/ *n* [C;U] a fact which is no longer kept secret or the act of telling people this fact: *She made several surprising disclosures about her past life.*

dis·co /ˈdɪskəʊ/ *n* **discos** (also **discotheque** *fml*) a place or party where people dance to records

dis·col·our /dɪsˈkʌləʳ/ *v* (also **discolor** *AmE*) [I;T] to change and spoil the colour of something: *His teeth were discoloured from smoking.* –**discolour·ation** /dɪsˌkʌləˈreɪʃən/ *n* [C;U]

dis·com·fort /dɪsˈkʌmfət ‖ -ərt/ *n* **1** [U] slight pain or an unpleasant feeling: *Your injury isn't serious, but may cause some discomfort.* | *His ex-wife's presence caused him a lot of discomfort.* **2** [C] something that makes you uncomfortable: *the discomforts of travel*

dis·con·cert /ˌdɪskənˈsɜːt ‖ -ɜːrt/ *v* [T] to make someone feel doubt and anxiety: *She was disconcerted to see that she was being watched.* –**disconcertingly** *adv*

dis·con·nect /ˌdɪskəˈnekt/ *v* [T] to break the connection of something, for example, a telephone line or electricity supply: *My phone's been disconnected because I didn't pay the bill.* –**opposite connect** –**disconnection** /-ˈnekʃən/ *n* [C;U]

dis·con·nect·ed /ˌdɪskəˈnektɪ̭d/ *adj* not well planned or put together (used of thoughts and ideas): *a few disconnected remarks*

dis·con·so·late /dɪsˈkɒnsələt ‖ -ˈkɑːn-/ *adj fml* very unhappy or disappointed –**disconsolately** *adv*

dis·con·tent /ˌdɪskənˈtent/ *n* (also **discontentment** /-mənt/) [U] the feeling of not being happy or satisfied –**discontented** *adj*

dis·con·tin·ue /ˌdɪskənˈtɪnjuː/ *v* **discontinued, discontinuing** [T] to stop or end something: *That bus service has been discontinued.* | *We can't replace those cups; the pattern's been discontinued.*

dis·cord /ˈdɪskɔːd ‖ ˈdɪskɔːrd/ *n* **1** [U] *fml* disagreement between people **2** [C] a lack of agreement heard when musical notes are played which do not sound pleasant together –**discordant** /dɪsˈkɔːdənt ‖ -ɔːr-/ *adj*

dis·co·theque /ˈdɪskətek/ *n fml* –see DISCO

dis·count¹ /ˈdɪskaʊnt/ *n* **1** a reduction made to the usual price of something: *a ten percent discount for cash* **2 at a discount** below the usual price

dis·count² /dɪsˈkaʊnt ‖ ˈdɪskaʊnt/ *v* [T] to regard something as unlikely to be true or important: *Experts have discounted the possibility of a second earthquake in the area.*

dis·cour·age /dɪsˈkʌrɪdʒ ‖ -ˈkɜːr-/ *v* **discouraged, discouraging** [T] **1** to make someone less confident about something or less willing to do something: *Don't be discouraged by your results.* | *The bad weather discouraged people from attending the parade.*
□ USEFUL PATTERNS to discourage someone; to discourage someone from doing something
2 to persuade someone not to do something: *His mother tried to discourage him from joining the navy.*
□ USEFUL PATTERNS to discourage someone; to discourage someone from doing something –opposite **encourage** –**discouragingly** *adv* dis·**couragement** *n* [C;U]

dis·cour·te·ous /dɪsˈkɜːtiəs ‖ -ɜːr-/ *adj fml* showing bad manners –opposite **courteous** –**discourteously** *adv*

dis·cov·er /dɪsˈkʌvəʳ/ *v* **1** [T] to find or learn about something for the first time: *Columbus discovered America in 1492.* | *The stolen goods were discovered in their garage.* **2** [T; +(that)] to find out a fact, or the answer to a question: *Did you ever discover who sent you the flowers?* | *Scientists have discovered that this disease is carried by rats.* –see INVENT (USAGE)
□ USEFUL PATTERNS to discover something; to discover who, why, where, etc.; to discover that… –**discoverer** *n*

dis·cov·er·y /dɪsˈkʌvəri/ *n* **discoveries 1** [U] the action of finding something: *The discovery of oil on their land made the family rich.* **2** [C] something that is found out: *He made an important archaeological discovery.*

dis·cred·it¹ /dɪsˈkredɪ̭t/ *v* [T] to stop people believing in or having respect for something: *a deliberate attempt to discredit the government.*

discredit² *n* **1** [U] loss of belief, trust, or the good opinion of others: *Their disgraceful behaviour has brought discredit to the school.* **2 to your discredit** making people lose their respect for you: *To her discredit, she refused to help.*

dis·cred·i·ta·ble /dɪsˈkredɪ̭təbəl/ *adj* shameful

di·screet /dɪˈskriːt/ *adj* careful about what you say and do: *a discreet silence* | *It wasn't very discreet of you to ring me up at the office.* –opposite **indiscreet** –**discreetly** *adv*

di·screp·an·cy /dɪˈskrepənsi/ *n* **discrepancies** [C;U] difference between things that should be the same: *There is some discrepancy between their two descriptions.* | *How do you explain the discrepancies in the accounts?*

di·screte /dɪˈskriːt/ *adj fml* separate: *The examination tests discrete items of language.*

di·scre·tion /dɪˈskreʃən/ *n* [U] **1** the quality of being careful about what you say and do –opposite **indiscretion 2** the ability to decide what is the best thing to do: *I can't tell you how long to stay. I'll leave that to your discretion.* **3 at someone's discretion** according to someone's judgment: *Promotion is at the manager's discretion.* –**discretionary** *adj*

di·scrim·i·nate /dɪˈskrɪmɪ̭neɪt/ *v* **discriminated, discriminating** [I] **1** to see or make a difference between things or people: *You must try to discriminate between facts and opinions.* **2** to treat a person or group differently, usually worse: *That law discriminates against immigrants.* | *Many employers still discriminate in favour of men.*

dis·crim·i·na·tion /dɪˌskrɪmɪˈneɪʃən/ n [U] **1** the treating of one group of people differently from another: *racial discrimination | sex discrimination* **2** the ability to see small differences between things, usually showing good taste and judgment −**discriminating** /dɪˈskrɪmɪˌneɪtɪŋ/ adj

dis·cus /ˈdɪskəs/ n a heavy object shaped like a plate which is thrown as far as possible as a sport

dis·cuss /dɪˈskʌs/ v [T] to talk about the details of something with someone else: *We discussed what to do and where we should go. | I wanted to discuss my plans with my father.*
■ USAGE Remember that the verb **discuss** is transitive and is NOT, therefore, followed by a preposition. (The noun **discussion** may sometimes be followed by the preposition **about**). Compare: *We were discussing our holiday plans. | We were having a discussion about our holiday plans.*

dis·cus·sion /dɪˈskʌʃən/ n **1** [C] a talk about the details of something with someone else: *The chairman wants to have a discussion about training with us.* **2** [U] the act of talking about the details of something: *After much discussion the matter was settled.* **3 under discussion** being talked about

dis·dain¹ /dɪsˈdeɪn/ n [U] fml the feeling that someone or something is worthless or not important enough to deserve your attention −**disdainful** adj

disdain² v [T not in progressive forms] fml **1** to regard something as worthless: *Why do you disdain my offer of friendship?* **2 disdain to do something** to refuse to do something because you think it is not worth your attention: *She disdained to answer.*

dis·ease /dɪˈziːz/ n [C;U] an illness caused by infection or a disorder in the body or mind, not by an accident: *Insects can cause disease. | an infectious disease | a rare plant disease* −**diseased** adj: *a diseased bone | a diseased plant*
■ USAGE Compare **disease** and **illness**. A **disease** is a particular medical condition with a particular cause. It is often serious and long-lasting: *AIDS is one of the most alarming diseases of modern times.* **Illness** is a more general word for the state of being unwell, and an **illness** is not always serious: *At this time of year some children are always absent from school because of illness.*

dis·em·bark /ˌdɪsɪmˈbɑːk ‖ -ɑːrk/ v [I;T] to put or go on shore from a ship, or land from an aircraft −**disembarkation** /ˌdɪsembɑːˈkeɪʃən ‖ -ɑːr-/ n [U]

dis·em·bod·ied /ˌdɪsɪmˈbɒdid ‖ -ˈbɑː-/ adj (only before a noun) **1** existing without a body: *disembodied spirits of the dead* **2** coming from someone who cannot be seen: *disembodied voices in the darkness*

dis·en·chant·ed /ˌdɪsɪnˈtʃɑːntɪd ‖ -ˈtʃæntɪd/ adj no longer liking or believing in the value of something: *I'm disenchanted with my job.* −**disenchantment** n [U]

dis·en·gage /ˌdɪsɪnˈɡeɪdʒ/ v **disengaged, disengaging** [I;T] fml **1** to disconnect or separate: *Disengage the gears when you park the car.* **2** (of military or naval forces) to stop fighting

dis·en·tan·gle /ˌdɪsɪnˈtæŋɡəl/ v **disentangled, disentangling** [T] **1** to free something which is knotted or mixed up: *Can you disentangle this piece of string for me?* **2** to free from a position it is difficult to escape from: *I finally managed to disentangle myself from the barbed wire.*

dis·fa·vour (**disfavor** AmE) /dɪsˈfeɪvər/ n [U] fml **1** dislike or disapproval: *His behaviour was viewed with great disfavour.* **2** the state of being disliked: *John seems to have fallen into disfavour with his boss.*

dis·fig·ure /dɪsˈfɪɡər ‖ -ˈfɪɡjər/ v **disfigured, disfiguring** [T] to spoil the appearance of: *The disease left his face disfigured.* −**disfigurement** n [C;U]

dis·grace¹ /dɪsˈɡreɪs/ n **1** [sing;U] a cause of shame or loss of honour and respect: *Being poor is no disgrace. | Doctors like that are a disgrace to our hospitals. | That old suit of yours is a disgrace.* **2 be in disgrace** to be regarded with disapproval because of something you have done wrong

disgrace² v **disgraced, disgracing** [T] **1** to behave badly and so cause shame to someone: *He disgraced himself last night by drinking too much.* **2 be disgraced** to be disapproved of and to lose respect because of something you have done wrong: *Most corrupt leaders are publicly disgraced in the end.*

dis·grace·ful /dɪsˈɡreɪsfəl/ adj completely unacceptable: *His behaviour was disgraceful!*

dis·grun·tled /dɪsˈɡrʌntld/ adj annoyed and disappointed: *When Mr Simpson was promoted the other supervisors were very disgruntled.*

dis·guise¹ /dɪsˈɡaɪz/ v **disguised, disguising** [T] **1** to change the usual appearance of someone or something in order to hide the truth: *She disguised herself as a man. | He was disguised as a football supporter.* **2** to hide the real situation: *We cannot disguise the fact that business is bad.*

disguise² n [C;U] something that you wear to hide who you really are: *He wore a false beard and thick glasses as a disguise. | They crossed the border in disguise.*

dis·gust¹ /dɪsˈɡʌst, dɪz-/ n [U] a strong feeling of dislike and disapproval, sometimes making you feel sick: *His dirty habits filled her with disgust. | After waiting for their food for an hour they left the restaurant in disgust.*

disgust² v [T] to make you feel strong dislike and disapproval, and sometimes physically ill: *We're all disgusted at the way his wife has treated him. | What a disgusting smell!*

dish¹ /dɪʃ/ n **1** a large container, not very deep, from which food is put onto people's plates: *a vegetable dish | a serving dish* −see picture on page 148 **2** cooked food of a particular kind: *a wonderful dish of salmon baked in the oven* **3 dishes** [pl] all the plates, cups, knives, and forks that have been used for a meal: *Let's wash the dishes. | We'll do the dishes.* **4** −see SATELLITE DISH

dish² v
dish something ↔ out phr v [T] infml to give something out to people: *to dish out the soup | He's always dishing out advice.*
dish up phr v [I;T **dish** sthg ↔ **up**] to put the food for a meal onto plates: *Help me dish up the dinner, will you? | Wash your hands quickly, I'm just about to dish up.*

dis·heart·en /dɪsˈhɑːtn ‖ -ɑːr-/ v [T] to make someone lose hope and confidence: *She was disheartened by her lack of progress.*

di·shev·elled /dɪˈʃevəld/ adj very untidy (used of a person or their clothes or hair)

dis·hon·est /dɪsˈɒnɪst ‖ -ˈɑːn-/ adj not honest or truthful: *a dishonest politician | to get money by dishonest means* −**dishonestly** adv −**dishonesty** n [U]

dis·hon·our /dɪsˈɒnər ‖ -ˈɑː-/ n fml (**dishonor** AmE) [sing;U] something or someone that brings shame and loss of respect: *His desertion from the army brought dishonour on his family.* −**dishonour** v [T] −**dishonourable** adj

dish·y /ˈdɪʃi/ adj dishier, dishiest infml having sexual charm: I agree, he is rather dishy!

dis·il·lu·sion /ˌdɪsɪˈluːʒən/ v [T] to correct a belief that someone has that is wrong: I hate to disillusion you but we're not going to get a pay rise this year. –disillusionment n [U]

dis·il·lu·sioned /ˌdɪsɪˈluːʒənd/ adj feeling bitter and unhappy because you have learnt the truth about someone or something that you formerly admired: He's very disillusioned with the present government.

dis·in·clined /ˌdɪsɪnˈklaɪnd/ adj [never before a noun] unwilling: I feel disinclined to go out in this weather. –disinclination /ˌdɪsɪnklɪˈneɪʃən/ n [sing;U] fml

dis·in·fect /ˌdɪsɪnˈfekt/ v [T] to clean something with a chemical that can destroy bacteria –disinfection /-ˈfekʃən/ n [U]

dis·in·fec·tant /ˌdɪsɪnˈfektənt/ n [C;U] a chemical used to destroy bacteria

dis·in·her·it /ˌdɪsɪnˈherɪt/ v [T] to stop someone from receiving your money and property after your death by changing your WILL³

dis·in·te·grate /dɪsˈɪntəɡreɪt/ v disintegrated, disintegrating [I] 1 to break up into small pieces: The box was so old it just disintegrated when he picked it up. 2 (of an arrangement or organization) to come to an unsuccessful end: The project disintegrated owing to lack of support in the community. –disintegration /dɪsˌɪntəˈɡreɪʃən/ n [U]

dis·in·terest·ed /dɪsˈɪntrəstɪd/ adj able to judge a situation fairly because you will not get an advantage from it: As a disinterested observer, who do you think is right? –disinterestedly adv
■ USAGE 1 Compare **disinterested** and **uninterested**. You are **disinterested** if you have nothing to gain personally from agreeing with one side or another in an argument: We must get someone who is disinterested to decide which of us is right. You are **uninterested** in something if you find it boring or if you do not usually give it your attention: I'm afraid I'm completely uninterested in football. 2 Although **disinterested** is sometimes used to mean "not interested" many people feel that this is not correct.

dis·joint·ed /dɪsˈdʒɔɪntɪd/ adj not following naturally (used of words or ideas): He gave a rather disjointed account of his holiday. –disjointedly adv

disk /dɪsk/ n 1 the usual American spelling of DISC 2 a flat circular piece of plastic used for storing computer information

disk drive /ˈ· ·/ n a piece of electrical equipment used for passing information to and from a computer disk –see picture on page 539

dis·like¹ /dɪsˈlaɪk/ v disliked, disliking [T] to think that something is unpleasant: I dislike big cities. | I dislike being spoken to like that.

dis·like² /ˌdɪsˈlaɪk/ n [C;U] 1 a feeling that someone or something is unpleasant: He has a strong dislike for anything to do with politics. 2 take a dislike to to begin to dislike: She took an instant dislike to him.

dis·lo·cate /ˈdɪsləkeɪt ‖ -ləʊ-/ v dislocated, dislocating [T] to put a bone out of its usual place: He dislocated his shoulder while playing rugby. | a dislocated ankle –dislocation /ˌdɪsləˈkeɪʃən ‖ -ləʊ-/ n [C;U]

dis·lodge /dɪsˈlɒdʒ ‖ -lɑːdʒ/ v dislodged, dislodging [T] to force or knock out of position: I managed to dislodge the fishbone from my throat by coughing.

dis·loy·al /dɪsˈlɔɪəl/ adj not loyal: You don't expect a diplomat ever to be disloyal to his country. –disloyally adv –disloyalty n [C;U]

dis·mal /ˈdɪzməl/ adj lacking hope or happiness: a dismal failure | dismal weather –dismally adv

dis·man·tle /dɪsˈmæntl/ v dismantled, dismantling [I;T] to come to pieces or to take something to pieces: This tent dismantles easily. | I'll have to dismantle the engine.

dis·may¹ /dɪsˈmeɪ/ n [U] a strong feeling of fear, anxiety, and hopelessness: They were filled with dismay by the news. | To their dismay the door was locked.

dismay² v [T] to make someone feel afraid, worried, or disappointed

dis·mem·ber /dɪsˈmembər/ v [T] to cut or tear the arms and legs from a body: The young man's dismembered body was found in the car boot.

dis·miss /dɪsˈmɪs/ v [T] 1 to refuse to consider something: He dismissed the idea as impossible. 2 fml to remove someone from a job: If you're late again you'll be dismissed. 3 to send someone away: The teacher dismissed the class early. –dismissal n [C;U]

dis·miss·ive /dɪsˈmɪsɪv/ adj considering something to be not worthy of attention or respect: He was too dismissive of the problems, in my opinion.

dis·mount /dɪsˈmaʊnt/ v [I] to get off a horse or bicycle –see TRANSPORT (USAGE)

dis·o·be·di·ent /ˌdɪsəˈbiːdiənt, ˌdɪsəʊ-/ adj not doing what you are told to do: a disobedient child –opposite **obedient** –disobediently adv –disobedience n [U]

dis·o·bey /ˌdɪsəˈbeɪ, ˌdɪsəʊ-/ v [I;T] to choose not to do what you are told to do: He disobeyed his mother and went to the party. | to disobey the rules

dis·or·der /dɪsˈɔːdər ‖ -ˈɔːr-/ n 1 [U] untidiness: The house was in a state of complete disorder. 2 [U] noisy and violent behaviour by the public, usually showing great political dissatisfaction: Increased taxation gave rise to widespread public disorder. 3 [C;U] a disease or illness that is not very serious: suffering from a stomach disorder

dis·or·der·ly /dɪsˈɔːdəli ‖ -ˈɔːrdər-/ adj 1 (also disordered) untidy: a disorderly room 2 noisy or violent in public: disorderly behaviour

dis·or·gan·ized /dɪsˈɔːɡənaɪzd ‖ -ˈɔːr-/ adj (also disorganised BrE) showing no order or planning: She's so disorganized I'll be surprised if she ever finds herself a job. –disorganization /dɪsˌɔːɡənaɪˈzeɪʃən ‖ -ˌɔːrɡənə-/ n [U]

dis·or·i·en·tate /dɪsˈɔːriənteɪt/ v disorientated, disorientating (also disorient /-riənt/) [T] 1 to make someone lose their sense of direction: I'm completely disorientated. Which direction are we heading in? 2 to make someone feel confused: When I retired I felt quite disorientated for a while. –disorientation /dɪsˌɔːriənˈteɪʃən/ n [U]

dis·own /dɪsˈəʊn/ v [T] to say that you have no connection with someone or something: Peter's father disowned him when he was caught taking drugs.

di·spar·age /dɪˈspærɪdʒ/ v disparaged, disparaging [T] to make someone or something sound of little value or importance: In spite of your disparaging remarks, I think he did well. –disparagingly adv –disparagement n [C;U]

di·spar·i·ty /dɪˈspærɪti/ n disparities [C;U] fml the state of being different or unequal: There is a great *disparity* in *age between him and his wife.* | *Disparity of pay* between *men and women is a serious concern.*

dis·pas·sion·ate /dɪs'pæʃənɨt/ *adj* calm, fair, and not easily influenced by personal feelings –**dispassionately** *adv*

di·spatch[1] /dɪ'spætʃ/ *v* (also **despatch**) [T] to send something away: *The parcels were dispatched yesterday.*

dispatch[2] *n* (also **despatch**) a message carried by a government official, or sent to a newspaper by one of its writers: *to send a dispatch from Rome to London*

di·spel /dɪ'spel/ *v* -ll- [T] to get rid of or drive away: *His calm words dispelled our fears.*

di·spen·sa·ble /dɪ'spensəbəl/ *adj* not necessary –opposite **indispensable**

di·spen·sa·ry /dɪ'spensəri/ *n* **dispensaries** a place where medicines are prepared and given out in a hospital

dis·pen·sa·tion /ˌdɪspən'seɪʃən, -pen-/ *n* [C;U] permission to do something not usually allowed: *We normally have to be in by 10.30, but we've got a special dispensation for Cup Final night.*

di·spense /dɪ'spens/ *v* **dispensed, dispensing** [T] **1** to give out to a number of people: *A judge dispenses justice.* | *This machine dispenses coffee.* **2** to mix and give out medicines
dispense with sbdy/sthg *phr v* [T] to get rid of and manage without: *I think we can safely dispense with his services now.* | *This new computer system dispenses with the need for keeping files.*

di·spens·er /dɪ'spensər/ *n* a machine from which you can get something, for example by pressing a button: *a cash dispenser*

di·sperse /dɪ'spɜːs ‖ -ɜːrs/ *v* **dispersed, dispersing** [I;T] to scatter in different directions: *The wind dispersed the smoke.* | *Slowly, the crowds began to disperse.*

di·spir·it·ed /dɪ'spɪrɨtɨd/ *adj lit* sad and without hope

dis·place /dɪs'pleɪs/ *v* **displaced, displacing** [T] **1** to force something out of its usual place: *He displaced a bone in his knee while playing rugby.* **2** to take the place of someone or something: *The indigenous population were displaced by the settlers.* **3 displaced person** someone who has been forced to leave their country –**displacement** *n* [U]

di·splay[1] /dɪ'spleɪ/ *v* [T] **1** to put things where they can be easily seen: *to display goods in a shop window* **2** to show something: *He displayed no emotion when he failed his exam.* | *The computer screen was displaying the figures for last year.*

display[2] *n* **1** the showing of something in public or in a clear way: *a fine display of fruit* | *a display of skill* **2 on display** being displayed: *The goods were on display in the shop window.*

dis·please /dɪs'pliːz/ *v* **displeased, displeasing** [T] *fml* to annoy someone or make them angry: *The headmaster and I are very displeased with your general behaviour.* –**displeasure** /dɪs'pleʒər/ *n* [U]

dis·po·sa·ble /dɪ'spəʊzəbəl/ *adj* intended to be thrown away after use: *disposable paper plates*

dis·pos·al /dɪ'spəʊzəl/ *n* [U] **1** the removal of something that is not wanted: *waste disposal* **2** *fml* the way that people or things are arranged: *the disposal of troops along the frontier* **3 at your disposal** free for you to use: *During his visit I put my car at his disposal.*

dis·pose /dɪ'spəʊz/ *v* **disposed, disposing dispose of something** to get rid of something: *Let's dispose of these old papers.* | *She disposed of my arguments quite easily.*

dis·posed /dɪ'spəʊzd/ *adj fml* **1 be disposed to** tending to have: *She's rather disposed to fits of temper.* **2 be disposed to do something** to be willing to do something: *I don't feel disposed to help you.*

dis·po·si·tion /ˌdɪspə'zɪʃən/ *n fml* **1** the way you usually behave: *He has a cheerful disposition.* | *a nervous disposition* **2 a disposition to do something** a willingness to do something: *He showed no disposition to help.*

dis·pos·sess /ˌdɪspə'zes/ *v* [T] *fml* to take someone's land and house away from them

dis·pro·por·tion·ate /ˌdɪsprə'pɔːʃənɨt ‖ -ɔːr-/ *adj* too much or too little relative to something else: *We spend a disproportionate amount of our money on rent.* –**disproportionately** *adv*

dis·prove /dɪs'pruːv/ *v* **disproved, disproving** [T] to show something to be false

di·spute[1] /dɪ'spjuːt/ *v* **disputed, disputing 1** [T] to argue about something angrily and for a long time: *The question was hotly disputed in the Senate.* **2** [T; + that] to question the correctness of something: *"It's a very common attitude among the upper classes." "I would dispute that."*

di·spute[2] /dɪ'spjuːt, 'dɪspjuːt/ *n* **1** an argument or quarrel, especially an official one: *a pay dispute* **2 in dispute** having an argument or quarrel: *The men are still in dispute with their employers.* **3 in dispute, under dispute** being talked or argued about: *The question is still under dispute.* **4 open to dispute** able to be questioned

dis·qual·i·fy /dɪs'kwɒlɨfaɪ ‖ -'kwɑː-/ *v* **disqualified, disqualifying** [T] to say that someone cannot take part in an activity usually because they have done something wrong: *She's been disqualified from driving.* | *The winner was disqualified for cheating, and the prize given to the runner-up.* –**disqualification** /dɪsˌkwɒlɨfɨ'keɪʃən ‖ -ˌkwɑː-/ *n* [C;U]

dis·quiet /dɪs'kwaɪət/ *v* [T] *fml* to make someone feel anxious: *disquieted by his long silences* | *a disquieting remark* –**disquiet** *n* [U]

dis·re·gard /ˌdɪsrɪ'gɑːd ‖ -ɑːrd/ *v* [T] to pay no attention to something: *The "No Smoking" sign was being completely disregarded.* –**disregard** *n* [U] : *She showed a total disregard for my feelings.* | *his reckless disregard for his passengers' safety.*

dis·re·pair /ˌdɪsrɪ'peər/ *n* [U] a bad condition, needing repair: *The old houses had fallen into disrepair.*

dis·rep·u·ta·ble /dɪs'repjɨtəbəl/ *adj* thought to have poor standards and probably not to be trusted: *his disreputable friends* | *a disreputable gambling club* –opposite **reputable** –**disreputably** *adv*

dis·re·pute /ˌdɪsrɪ'pjuːt/ *n* **bring something into disrepute** to cause something to lose people's respect: *These strikes only bring the nursing profession into disrepute.* [RELATED PHRASE: **fall into disrepute**]

dis·re·spect /ˌdɪsrɪ'spekt/ *n* [U] lack of respect or politeness –**disrespectful** *adj* –**disrespectfully** *adv*

dis·rupt /dɪs'rʌpt/ *v* [T] to stop something from continuing as expected: *A crowd of protesters disrupted the meeting.* –**disruption** /-'rʌpʃən/ *n* [C;U] : *The accident has caused widespread disruption to railway services in the south of the city.* –**disruptive** /-'rʌptɪv/ *adj* :*He has a disruptive influence on the other children.*

dis·sat·is·fac·tion /dɪˌsætɪsˈfækʃən, dɪsˌsæ-/ n [U] the state of not being pleased: *There is widespread dissatisfaction in the coal industry.*

dis·sat·is·fied /dɪˈsætɪsfaɪd, dɪsˈsæ-/ *adj* not pleased, especially because you expect more of something or a better standard: *I have been very dissatisfied with your work this year.* | *dissatisfied customers*

dis·sect /dɪˈsekt, daɪ-/ *v* [T] to cut up a plant or animal into small pieces for detailed study **2** to look very carefully at all the details of something: *to dissect the witnesses' accounts to find the truth* –**dissection** /-ˈsekʃən/ n [C;U]

dis·sem·i·nate /dɪˈsemɪneɪt/ *v* **disseminated, disseminating** [T] *fml* to spread news or ideas widely –**dissemination** /dɪˌsemɪˈneɪʃən/ n [U] : *the dissemination of their views*

dis·sen·sion /dɪˈsenʃən/ n [U] disagreement, often leading to argument: *His comments caused a great deal of dissension among his followers.*

dis·sent /dɪˈsent/ n [U] disagreement with the opinion that is held by most people: *Voices of dissent are not tolerated in some countries.* –**dissent** *v* [I] –**dissenter** n

dis·ser·ta·tion /ˌdɪsəˈteɪʃən ‖ ˌdɪsər-/ n a long piece of writing done after studying a subject, especially at university

dis·ser·vice /dɪˈsɜːvɪs, dɪsˈsɜː- ‖ -ɜːr-/ n [sing] harm or a harmful action: *You have done a serious disservice to your country by selling these papers to our enemies.*

dis·si·dent /ˈdɪsɪdənt/ n someone who openly and often strongly disagrees with an opinion, a group, or a government: *political dissidents* –**dissident** *adj* –**dissidence** n [U]

dis·sim·i·lar /dɪˈsɪmɪlər, dɪsˈsɪ-/ *adj* unlike: *The two girls are not dissimilar in appearance; they both take after their mother.*

dis·si·pate /ˈdɪsɪpeɪt/ *v* **dissipated, dissipating** *fml* **1** [I;T] to disappear or make something disappear: *The morning mist began to dissipate as the sun rose in the sky* | *Her encouragement gradually dissipated his fears.* **2** [T] to spend or waste something foolishly: *He dissipated his large fortune in a few years.*

dis·so·ci·ate /dɪˈsəʊʃieɪt, -sieɪt/ *v* **dissociated, dissociating** (also **disassociate**) [T] to believe or claim that one thing or person has no connection with another: *He dissociated himself from the decision to close the school.* –**dissociation** /dɪˌsəʊʃiˈeɪʃən, -siˈeɪʃən/ n [U]

dis·so·lute /ˈdɪsəluːt/ *adj fml* with bad or immoral habits: *He had led a dissolute life.* –**dissolutely** *adv*

dis·so·lu·tion /ˌdɪsəˈluːʃən/ n [U] *fml* the ending or breaking up of an association, group, or marriage: *the dissolution of Parliament before a general election*

dis·solve /dɪˈzɒlv ‖ dɪˈzɑːlv/ *v* **dissolved, dissolving** **1** [I;T] to make or become liquid when put into a liquid: *Sugar dissolves in water.* | *Dissolve the tablets in warm water.* **2** [T] to end or break up a group or a formal relationship: *The military government dissolved the parliament and suspended all political activity.* | *She left him, and their marriage was later dissolved.* **3** [I] to disappear: *His fears gradually dissolved.* **4 dissolve in to** start showing your feelings in some way because you are unable to control them any longer: *She suddenly dissolved in tears.* | *We all dissolved into laughter.*

dis·suade /dɪˈsweɪd/ *v* **dissuaded, dissuading** [T] to persuade someone not to do something: *I tried to dissuade her from joining the club.*

dis·tance¹ /ˈdɪstəns/ n **1** [C;U] the amount of space or time between two points: *What is the distance from London to Glasgow?* | *We were within easy walking distance of home.* | *You can't expect me to remember at this distance in time!* **2** [sing] a point or place that is far away: *The ruins look very impressive from a distance.* | *The pyramids are visible at a distance of several kilometres.* **3 in the distance** far away: *We could just see the spire of the cathedral in the distance.* **4 keep your distance** to stay away: *It's not a very friendly area. The neighbours keep their distance.*

distance² *v* [T] to cause someone to feel or want less connection with someone or something: *She tried to distance herself from the actions of her government.* | *a parental attitude which tends to distance young Indian girls from their culture*

dis·tant /ˈdɪstənt/ *adj* **1** far away in space or time: *distant lands* | *the distant sound of a bell* | *events in the distant past* **2** [only before a noun] not very closely connected: *Those two boys are distant relations.* **3** showing a lack of friendliness or attention –**distantly** *adv* : *Jeremy and Susan are distantly related.* | *"Very likely," he said distantly.*

dis·taste /dɪsˈteɪst/ n [sing;U] a feeling of dislike or disapproval: *She looked at him with distaste.* | *a distaste for town life*

dis·taste·ful /dɪsˈteɪstfəl/ *adj* unpleasant: *a rather distasteful duty*

dis·tend /dɪˈstend/ *v* [T] *fml* to make something swell because of pressure from inside: *The children's stomachs were distended because of lack of food.*

dis·til /dɪˈstɪl/ *v* **-ll- (distill** *AmE*) [T] **1** to turn a liquid into gas and then turn the gas into liquid to make it pure or to obtain alcoholic spirit from it: *distilled water* | *Brandy is distilled from wine.* **2** to express something clearly in a shorter form: *a distilled account of his travels* –**distillation** /ˌdɪstɪˈleɪʃən/ n [C;U]

dis·til·le·ry /dɪˈstɪləri/ n **distilleries** a factory where strong alcoholic drinks are distilled: *a whisky distillery*

dis·tinct /dɪˈstɪŋkt/ *adj* **1** clearly different or separate: *The party split into two distinct groups.* **2 as distinct from** a phrase used to make it very clear that two things or situations are different: *That rule only applies to locally recruited teachers, as distinct from those recruited elsewhere.* **3** clearly seen, heard, or understood: *a distinct smell of burning* | *There's a distinct possibility that we'll all lose our jobs.* –**distinctly** *adv* –**distinctness** n [U]

dis·tinc·tion /dɪˈstɪŋkʃən/ n **1** [C;U] a clear difference: *It's important to draw a distinction between those under 30 and those over 30.* | *Why are you making a distinction between men and women?* **2** [U] the quality of being unusually good: *a writer of distinction* **3** [C] a special mark of honour: *This is one of the highest distinctions awarded by the Queen.*

dis·tinc·tive /dɪˈstɪŋktɪv/ *adj* clearly marking a person or thing as different from others: *a distinctive way of walking* –**distinctively** *adv* –**distinctiveness** n [U]

dis·tin·guish /dɪˈstɪŋgwɪʃ/ *v* **1** [I;T] to recognize the differences between things: *to distinguish right from wrong* | *I think you have to distinguish between the women who want to have children and those that don't.* **2** [T] to hear, see, or recognize something, often with difficulty: *We could just distinguish the buildings on the horizon.* **3** [T] to mark something as different: *Elephants are distinguished by their long trunks.* **4 distinguish yourself** to behave or perform something so well that people praise you: *He distinguished himself in his final examination.*

dis·tin·gui·sha·ble /dɪ'stɪŋgwɪʃəbəl/ *adj* able to be clearly or easily distinguished: *The twins were not easily distinguishable from each other.* | *A black cat is not easily distinguishable on a dark night.* –opposite **indistinguishable**

dis·tin·guished /dɪ'stɪŋgwɪʃt/ *adj* **1** of excellent quality or deserving respect: *a distinguished performance* | *a distinguished writer* **2 look distinguished** to have a noble appearance which you admire or respect: *Grey hair can look very distinguished.*

dis·tort /dɪ'stɔːt ‖ -ɔːrt/ *v* [T] **1** to twist out of the usual shape, appearance, or sound: *trees distorted by the wind* | *Her voice sounded distorted on the phone.* **2** to twist the meaning of something so that it is untrue: *He gave a very distorted account of what happened.* –**distortion** /-'tɔːʃən ‖ -ɔːr-/ *n* [C;U]

dis·tract /dɪ'strækt/ *v* [T] **1** to take someone's mind away from what they are doing: *Don't distract me.* | *She was distracted from her work by the noise outside.* | *It's very distracting having children in the office.* **2** to take someone's mind off their troubles: *We took the children out for the day to distract them.*

dis·tract·ed /dɪ'stræktᵻd/ *adj* anxious or troubled about many things –**distractedly** *adv*

dis·trac·tion /dɪ'strækʃən/ *n* **1** something that takes your mind away from what you are doing: *There are too many distractions here for me to work properly.* **2** something that entertains you or takes your mind off your troubles: *games, concerts, television – all the usual distractions* **3 drive someone to distraction** to make someone almost mad by continually annoying them: *The child's crying drove him to distraction.*

dis·traught /dɪ'strɔːt/ *adj* very anxious and troubled: *She was clearly distraught.*

dis·tress¹ /dɪ'stres/ *n* [U] **1** great suffering, pain, or discomfort: *The sick man showed signs of distress.* | *people in distress because of lack of money* **2** a state of danger or great difficulty: *a ship in distress* | *a distress signal*

distress² *v* [T] to cause someone great pain, unhappiness, or anxiety: *He was very distressed about the situation.*

dis·tress·ing /dɪ'stresɪŋ/ *adj* causing great unhappiness or anxiety: *His parents' divorce was a distressing experience.*

dis·trib·ute /dɪ'strɪbjuːt/ *v* **distributed, distributing** [T] **1** to give out or divide things among several people: *He was asked to distribute the prizes.* | *Food is being distributed to the refugees.* **2** to spread things out: *This new machine distributes seed evenly and quickly over the whole field.* **3** to deliver goods to shops or businesses: *Newspapers are distributed by road, not rail.*

dis·tri·bu·tion /ˌdɪstrɪ'bjuːʃən/ *n* [C;U] an act of distributing things or the state of being distributed: *the distribution of prizes* | *food distribution centres* | *The distribution of wealth among the population is very unequal.*

dis·trict /'dɪstrɪkt/ *n* an area of a country or city, especially one made officially for a particular purpose: *a postal district* | *a district council* | *a poor district of the city*

dis·trust¹ /dɪs'trʌst/ *v* [T] to have no trust in someone: *He distrusts banks so he keeps his money at home.*

distrust² *n* [sing;U] lack of trust: *He regards banks with distrust.* | *his distrust of anyone in authority* –**distrustful** *adj*

dis·turb /dɪ'stɜːb ‖ -ɜːrb/ *v* [T] **1** to interrupt someone, especially a person who is working or sleeping: *I'm sorry to disturb you, but....* | *Did the storm disturb you in the night?* **2** to upset someone: *We were very disturbed by the government announcement.* | *This is very disturbing news.* **3** to change the usual or natural condition of something: *A light wind disturbed the surface of the water.*

dis·turb·ance /dɪ'stɜːbəns ‖ -ɜːr-/ *n* **1** [C] a situation in which there is public disorder: *They were charged by the police with causing a disturbance.* **2** [C;U] something that interrupts you or makes you unable to think clearly about what you are doing: *The noise of traffic is a continual disturbance.* **3** [C;U] a change in a usual condition: *signs of serious mental disturbance*

dis·turbed /dɪ'stɜːbd ‖ -ɜːr-/ *adj* having or showing signs of an illness of the mind or the feelings: *She is emotionally disturbed.*

dis·use /dɪs'juːs/ *n* **fall into disuse** to stop being used: *an old law that had fallen into disuse*

dis·used /ˌdɪs'juːzd◂/ *adj* no longer used: *a disused mine*

ditch¹ /dɪtʃ/ *n* a narrow passage cut into the ground for water to flow through: *The water drains into the ditch at the edge of the field.*

ditch² *v* [T] *infml* to get rid of someone or something: *She got bored with her boyfriend and ditched him.* | *He took the money and ditched the wallet in a rubbish bin.*

dith·er /'dɪðəʳ/ *v* [I] *infml* to act nervously because you are unable to decide

dit·to /'dɪtəʊ/ *n* a mark (··) meaning the same as the word above: *one black pencil at 27p*
    ·· *blue* ·· *at 32p*

di·van /dɪ'væn ‖ 'daɪvæn/ *n* a bed which has a base and the part you sleep on, but no frame

dive¹ /daɪv/ *v* **dived** (also **dove** /dəʊv/ *AmE*) **diving** [I] **1** to jump head first into water: *The boy dived into the swimming pool from the diving board.* **2** to go under the surface of the water: *They are diving for gold from the Spanish wreck.* **3** to go down quickly: *The plane dived towards the sea.* **4** to move quickly, especially downwards or out of sight: *The goalkeeper dived for the ball.*

dive² *n* **1** an act of jumping head first into water: *a graceful dive into the pool* **2** a sudden rapid movement, especially downwards or out of sight: *When the shots sounded, we made a dive for the nearest doorway.*

div·er /'daɪvəʳ/ *n* a person who dives, especially one who works at the bottom of the sea in a diving suit with a supply of air

di·verge /daɪ'vɜːdʒ, dᵻ- ‖ -ɜːr-/ *v* **diverged, diverging** [I] *fml* to separate and go on in different directions: *That's where the two systems diverged.* | *That's where the new system diverges from the old one.* –**divergence** *n* [C;U] : *a divergence of opinion* –**divergent** *adj*

di·verse /daɪ'vɜːs ‖ dᵻ'vɜːrs, daɪ-/ *adj fml* very different: *many diverse interests*

di·ver·si·fy /daɪ'vɜːsᵻfaɪ ‖ dᵻ'vɜːr-, daɪ-/ *v* **diversified, diversifying** [I;T] to start to make different sorts of product: *Some major tobacco companies diversified* **into** *food in the late sixties.* | *The company needs to diversify its products.* –**diversification** /daɪ‚vɜːsɪfɪ'keɪʃən ‖ -ɜːr-/ *n* [U]

i·ver·sion /daɪ'vɜːʃən, dɪ̱- ‖ -ɜːrʒən/ *n* **1** [C;U] a turning aside from a course, activity, or use: *the diversion of a river to supply water to the farms* | *The traffic had to follow a diversion because of an accident on the main road.* **2** [C] something that a person uses on purpose to turn your attention away from something they do not want you to notice: *All those statistics were just a diversion.* **3** [C] an entertaining thing to do: *Big cities have lots of cinemas and other diversions.*

i·ver·si·ty /daɪ'vɜːsɪti, dɪ̱- ‖ -ɜːr-/ *n* [U] variety: *The plants of Asia show great diversity of form.*

i·vert /daɪ'vɜːt, dɪ̱- ‖ -ɜːr-/ *v* [T] **1** to turn something aside or from one use or direction to another: *They diverted the river to supply water to the town.* | *diverted traffic* | *Money was diverted from scientific research into marketing.* **2** *fml* to amuse: *a game to divert the children* **3** **divert someone's attention** to turn someone's attention away from something: *A loud noise diverted my attention.*

i·vest /daɪ'vest, dɪ̱-/ *v fml* **1** **divest someone of something** to take away the position, rights, or property of someone: *The disgraced leader was divested of all his power.* **2** **divest yourself of** to get rid of something: *The brewing company Eastern Ales have divested themselves of their interest in Allied Whisky.*

i·vide¹ /dɪ̱'vaɪd/ *v* **divided, dividing** **1** [I;T] to separate into parts: *Divide the cake into twelve.* | *He divides his time between working and looking after the children.* | *This class is too large. We shall have to divide it.* | *The class divided into groups.* **2** [T] to give part of something to each of several people: *He divided the money equally between his children.* | *They divided the food among themselves.* **3** [T] to cause people to disagree or quarrel: *an issue which has divided the country* **4** [T] to calculate how many times a small number will go into a larger number: *120 divided by 3 is 40.* | *You can't divide 7 into 53.*

divide sth ↔ **up** *phr v* [T] to separate something into parts or share it between several people: *The land was divided up among the sons.*

ivide² *n* a difference between two systems or groups: *the North-South divide*

iv·i·ded high·way /dɪ̱'vaɪdɪd ‚haɪweɪ/ *n* the usual American word for DUAL CARRIAGEWAY

iv·i·dend /'dɪvɪ‚dənd, -dend/ *n* **1** the part of the money made by a business which is divided among the people who own shares in the business: *The company declared a large dividend at the end of the year.* **2** **pay dividends** to produce an advantage, especially as the result of earlier action: *Their decision five years ago to computerize the company is now paying handsome dividends.*

i·vid·ers /dɪ̱'vaɪdəz, -ərz/ *n* [pl] a V-shaped instrument for measuring distances on paper

i·vine¹ /dɪ̱'vaɪn/ *adj* **1** connected with a god: *divine inspiration* **2** *old-fash infml* extremely good: *That meal was simply divine!* –**divinely** *adv*

ivine² *v* **divined, divining** [T; + that] *fml* to discover or guess something correctly: *Although Churchill knew of their agreement, he was unable to divine its exact nature.*

i·ving·board /'daɪvɪŋbɔːd ‖ -bɔːrd/ *n* a board off which people jump head first into water

i·vin·i·ty /dɪ̱'vɪnɪti/ *n* **divinities** **1** [U] the quality

or state of being a god or connected with a god **2** [C] (also **Divinity**) a god or goddess **3** [U] *old-fash* the study of religion

di·vis·i·ble /dɪ̱'vɪzɪbəl/ *adj* able to be divided: *15 is divisible by 3.*

di·vi·sion /dɪ̱'vɪʒən/ *n* **1** [U] the act of separating things into parts: *the division of Germany* **2** [U] sharing things among a number of people: *the division of responsibility among the teachers* **3** [C] something that divides or separates: *The river forms the division between the old and new parts of the city.* **4** [C] a part of a large organization: *He works in the foreign division of the company.* **5** [C] a deep and painful disagreement between different groups in a society: *Now that the war is over, attempts must be made to heal the divisions in our society.* **6** [U] a MATHEMATICAL operation in which you decide how many times one number will go into another, for example $15 ÷ 3 = 5$

di·vi·sive /dɪ̱'vaɪsɪv/ *adj* tending to cause people to disagree or quarrel: *He is a divisive influence at meetings.*

di·vorce¹ /dɪ̱'vɔːs ‖ -ɔːrs/ *n* [C;U] the ending of a marriage as declared by a court of law: *Is divorce allowed in your country?* | *She got a divorce after years of unhappiness.*

divorce² *v* **divorced, divorcing** **1** [I;T] to end a marriage legally: *They divorced in 1989.* | *He divorced his first wife.* **2 get divorced** to end a marriage legally: *My parents got divorced last year.* **3** [T] *fml* to separate: *She finds it hard to divorce fact from fantasy.* –**divorced** *adj* : *Is he single, married, or divorced?*

di·vor·cée /dɪ̱‚vɔː'siː ‖ dɪ̱‚vɔːr'seɪ, -'siː/ *n* a divorced woman

di·vulge /daɪ'vʌldʒ, dɪ̱-/ *v* **divulged, divulging** [T; + that] *fml* to tell something that has been secret: *His doctor divulged that the President had been ill for some time before he died.*

DIY /‚diː aɪ 'waɪ/ *n* [U] building, repairing, or decorating your house yourself and not paying a workman to do it; an abbreviation for DO-IT-YOURSELF

diz·zy /'dɪzi/ *adj* **dizzier, dizziest** having an unpleasant feeling of losing your balance, as if things are going round and round: *The room was so hot that she felt dizzy.* –**dizziness** *n* [U]

DJ /‚diː 'dʒeɪ/ *n* a broadcaster who introduces records of popular music on a radio or television show; an abbreviation for DISC JOCKEY

DNA /‚diː en 'eɪ/ *n tech* [U] the acid which carries GENETIC information; an abbreviation for **deoxyribonucleic acid**

do¹ – see box on pages 210 and 211.

do·cile /'dəʊsaɪl ‖ 'dɑːsəl/ *adj* quiet and easily controlled: *a docile animal* –**docility** /dəʊ'sɪlɪti ‖ dɑː-/ *n* [U]

dock¹ /dɒk ‖ dɑːk/ *n* **1** a place where ships are loaded and unloaded, or repaired: *The ship moved away from the dock.* | *Liverpool docks* –see picture on page 735 **2 the dock** the place in a court of law where the prisoner stands

dock² *v* **1** [I;T] to sail into a dock: *The ship docked at Portsmouth.* | *We'll be docking in about half an hour.* **2 dock someone's wages** to reduce the amount of money that someone is paid: *They docked his wages by £5 last week because one day he was late.*

dock·er /'dɒkəʳ ‖ 'dɑː-/ *n* a person who works at a dock, loading and unloading ships

do¹ /duː/ *v*

present tense	past tense	*past participle*
I **do**	I **did**	**done**
You **do**	You **did**	
He / she / it **does**	He / she / it **did**	*present participle*
We **do**	We **did**	**doing**
You **do**	You **did**	*negative short forms*
They **do**	They **did**	**don't doesn't didn't**

For the pronunciation of these forms look up at their own place in the dictionary.

1 [auxiliary verb] used with other verbs to form negatives (NEGATIVE) and questions, and sometimes to replace the main verb:
Don't touch that. | She doesn't work here any more. | I didn't go to the party. | Do you like fish? What did he say? | They live in London, don't they? You saw Jane on Friday, didn't you? | She eats a lot more than I do. | Michael didn't enjoy the holiday, but I did. | "Her parents live in London." "No they don't, they live in Birmingham." | "Why didn't you tell me?" "I did tell you!"

2 [T] to perform an action or take action in some way:
I must do the ironing this afternoon. | What are you doing? | Have you done your homework? He did a little dance to celebrate. | He's doing some repairs to the car. | Don't forget to do your teeth. | He does the garden for us. | One drink won't do any harm. | I'm hoping to do biology at university. | Our old car can only do about 40 miles per hour.

3 **do as you're told** a phrase used to tell a child that they must do something that you are telling them to do:
Don't argue with me – just do as you're told!

4 **do something** to take action to solve a problem:
*The government must do something **about** the rising levels of unemployment. | Don't just stand there – do something!*

5 **do someone good** to improve someone's health or make them feel better:
A holiday would do her good.

6 **do well** to be successful:
He did very well in the exams. | You did very well to get all the work finished on time.

7 **do your best** to try as much as you can to do something:
We'll do our best to be there on time.

8 **how do you do** a polite greeting that you say to someone when you meet them for the first time

9 **what do you do?** = what is your job?
"What does your wife do?" "She's a designer".

10 **would do well to do something** a phrase used when you are advising someone to do something:
You'd do well to keep quiet about this.

do away with sthg *phr v*
[T]
to end something or get rid of it:
The government are planning to do away with this tax altogether.

do sbdy ↔ **down** *phr v*
[T]
to say unpleasant things about someone:
He's always doing her down.

do sbdy **in** *phr v*
[T]
infml to kill someone:
They've threatened to do him in if he tells the police anything.

do sbdy **out of** sthg *phr v*

[T]

infml to cause someone to lose something by cheating them:
old people being done out of their savings

do sthg ↔ **up** *phr v*

[T]

1 to fasten something:
Do your buttons up. | *I can't do up my shoelaces.*
2 to repair and improve an old building:
They've done their house up beautifully. | *old barns that have been done up and sold as houses*
3 to wrap something:
The present was done up in yellow wrapping paper.

do with *phr v*

[T]

1 **could do with** to need or want something:
I could do with a drink. | *That car could do with a good wash!*
2 **what have you done with...?** = where have you put...?
"What have you done with the scissors?" "I've put them in the drawer." | *What did Mark do with the shopping?*
3 **to do with** concerned with something or someone::
I don't know exactly what his job is, but it's something to do with computers. | *Keep out of this dispute. It's nothing to do with you.*

do without sthg *phr v*

[T]

to continue to live or do something without having a particular thing:
I couldn't do without my car. | *If there are no biscuits in the house, you'll just have to do without.*

do² *n*

dos or do's

infml

1 a big party
They're having a big do at a hotel in town.
2 **dos and dont's** things that you must do and things that you must not do:
Doctors are giving out lists of dos and don'ts for people wanting to lose weight.

doc·tor[1] /ˈdɒktəʳ ‖ ˈdɑːk-/ n **1** a person whose profession is to treat sick people: *If you feel so ill, you should go and see a doctor.* **2 the doctor's** the place where you go to be treated by a doctor: *I went to the doctor's this morning.* **3** a person holding one of the highest degrees given by a university, such as a PhD

doctor[2] v [T] *infml* **1** to change something, especially in a dishonest way: *The report had been doctored.* **2** to make an animal unable to breed by removing its sexual organs

doc·tor·ate /ˈdɒktərɪt ‖ ˈdɑːk-/ n the highest degree given by a university

doc·tri·naire /ˌdɒktrɪˈneəʳ ‖ ˌdɑːk-/ adj believing in or acting on a system of ideas without allowing it to be questioned or considering the practical difficulties

doc·trine /ˈdɒktrɪn ‖ ˈdɑːk-/ n [C;U] a religious or political belief, or set of beliefs: *the doctrines of the Catholic church* –**doctrinal** /dɒkˈtraɪnəl ‖ ˈdɑːktrɪnəl/ adj

doc·u·ment[1] /ˈdɒkjɨmənt ‖ ˈdɑːk-/ n a paper that gives information about something or proof of something: *Let me see all the official documents concerning the sale of this land.*

doc·u·ment[2] /ˈdɒkjɨment ‖ ˈdɑːk-/ v [T] to prove or support something with documents: *The history of this area is very well documented.* –**documentation** /ˌdɒkjɨmənˈteɪʃən, -men- ‖ ˌdɑːk-/ n [U]

doc·u·men·ta·ry[1] /ˌdɒkjɨˈmentəri ‖ ˌdɑːk-/ n documentaries a film, television, or radio broadcast that presents facts: *We saw a documentary about Yorkshire coal miners.* | *a documentary film* –compare FEATURE

documentary[2] adj consisting of or related to documents: *documentary evidence*

dod·der·ing /ˈdɒdərɪŋ ‖ ˈdɑː-/ adj *infml* (also **doddery** /dəri/) weak, shaky, and slow, usually from age: *a doddering old man*

dod·dle /ˈdɒdl ‖ ˈdɑːdl/ n *BrE infml* something that is very easy: *The last test was a real doddle!*

dodge /dɒdʒ ‖ dɑːdʒ/ v **dodged, dodging 1** [I;T] to avoid something by suddenly moving aside: *He dodged the falling rock and escaped unhurt.* | *He dodged past me.* **2** [T] *infml* to avoid something in a dishonest way: *He tried to dodge the tax.*

dodg·y /ˈdɒdʒi ‖ ˈdɑː-/ adj **dodgier, dodgiest** *BrE infml* **1** not safe: *Don't sit on that chair. The leg's a bit dodgy.* **2** dishonest and unable to be trusted: *a dodgy business*

does /dəz; *strong* dʌz/ the 3rd person singular present tense of DO

doesn't /ˈdʌzənt/ short for "does not": *He doesn't know why.* | *She likes it, doesn't she?* | *Doesn't he know the way?*

dog[1] /dɒg ‖ dɔːg/ n **1** an animal kept as a pet in some countries, and sometimes used for hunting or for guarding houses: *He's taken the dog for a walk.* **2** a male dog or fox **3 a dog in a manger** a person who does not want something but still stops others from having or enjoying it **4 a dog's life** a very unhappy life **5 go to the dogs** to become ruined: *"This country's going to the dogs!" said the old man.* **6 not have a dog's chance** *infml* to have no chance at all

dog[2] v **-gg-** [T] **1** to follow someone closely **2** to affect someone continuously: *We were dogged by bad luck.*

dog col·lar /ˈ· ·ˌ··/ n *infml* a priest's round white collar

dog-eared /ˈ· ·/ adj looking old and much used (used of books and papers)

dog·ged /ˈdɒgɨd ‖ ˈdɔː-/ adj refusing to give up in spite of difficulty or opposition –**doggedly** adv

dog·ge·rel /ˈdɒgərəl ‖ ˈdɔː-, ˈdɑː-/ n [U] poetry not usually intended to be serious

dog·gy /ˈdɒgi ‖ ˈdɔːgi/ n **doggies** (also **doggie**) a dog (used by and to small children)

dog·house /ˈdɒghaʊs ‖ ˈdɔːg-/ n **in the doghouse** *infml* being disapproved of because you have done something wrong

dog·ma /ˈdɒgmə ‖ ˈdɔːgmə, ˈdɑːgmə/ n [C;U] an important belief or set of beliefs that people are often expected to accept without questioning: *church dogma* | *Marxist dogma*

dog·mat·ic /dɒgˈmætɪk ‖ dɔːg-, dɑːg-/ adj holding or expressing your beliefs very strongly and expecting other people to accept them without question: *He had a very dogmatic manner.* –**dogmatically** /-kli/ adv

dogs·bod·y /ˈdɒgzˌbɒdi ‖ ˈdɔːgzˌbɑːdi/ n **dogsbodies** *BrE infml* a person in a low position who has to do the least interesting work: *I'm just the dogsbody in this office.*

do·ing[1] /ˈduːɪŋ/ the present participle of DO

doing[2] n **1** [U] something that a person has done: *This must be your doing.* **2 doings** [pl] *infml* activities: *It's a programme about the daily doings of a vet and his family.*

do-it-your·self /ˌ· · ·ˈ·/ n see DIY

dol·drums /ˈdɒldrəmz ‖ ˈdəʊl-, ˈdɑːl-, ˈdɔːl-/ n **in the doldrums** *infml:* **a** quiet, with not much happening (used of business) **b** in a sad state of mind

dole[1] /dəʊl/ n **1 the dole** *BrE infml* money that you receive from the government because you are unemployed **2 on the dole** receiving money from the government because you are unemployed: *I've been on the dole for six months.*

dole[2] v **doled, doling**

dole sthg ↔ **out** *phr v infml* [T] to give something out in small shares, especially money or food: *Shall I dole the soup out?*

dole·ful /ˈdəʊlfəl/ adj unhappy or in low spirits: *She gave me a doleful look.* –**dolefully** adv

doll[1] /dɒl ‖ dɑːl, dɔːl/ n a small figure of a person, for a child to play with

doll[2] v

doll sbdy ↔ **up** *phr v* [T] to make your own or someone else's appearance attractive, perhaps too much or in a way that is not honest: *She was all dolled up to go to a party.*

dol·lar /ˈdɒləʳ ‖ ˈdɑː-/ n **1** a standard of money, as used in the US, and some other countries; the sign for it is $ and it is worth 100 cents. **2** a piece of paper or a coin of this value

dol·lop /ˈdɒləp ‖ ˈdɑː-/ n *infml* a large spoonful of sticky food: *a dollop of mashed potato*

dol·ly /ˈdɒli ‖ ˈdɑːli, ˈdɔːli/ n **dollies** a DOLL (used by and to small children)

dol·phin /ˈdɒlfɨn ‖ ˈdɑːl-, ˈdɔːl-/ n an intelligent seaanimal two to three metres long, which swims about in a group with others

do·main /dəˈmeɪn, dəʊ-/ n **1** an area of activity, interest, or knowledge: *This problem lies outside the domain of medical science.* **2** *old fash* the land owned or controlled by one person or a government

dome /dəʊm/ n a rounded roof on a building or room

domed /dəʊmd/ adj having a rounded roof

do·mes·tic¹ /dəˈmestɪk/ adj **1** relating to the house, home, or family: *Don't neglect your domestic responsibilities.* **2** skilled at housework or taking pleasure in home life: *I'm afraid I'm not very domestic.* **3** not wild (used of animals): *The sheep is a domestic animal.* **4** relating to your own country or some particular country: *the government's domestic policies | the domestic news followed by the foreign news* –domestically /-kli/ adv

domestic² n a servant who works in a house

do·mes·ti·cate /dəˈmestɪkeɪt/ v **domesticated, domesticating** [T] **1** to make an animal able to live with people and serve them, especially on a farm **2** **be domesticated** to enjoy and be interested in home life and duties –**domestication** /dəˌmestɪˈkeɪʃən/ n [U]

do·mes·tic·i·ty /ˌdəʊmesˈtɪsəti/ n [U] home or family life

dom·i·cile /ˈdɒmɪsaɪl ‖ ˈdɑː-, ˈdəʊ-/ n fml the place where a person lives or is considered to live for official purposes

dom·i·nance /ˈdɒmɪnəns ‖ ˈdɑː-/ n [U] importance, power, or controlling influence: *Their dominance of the market is challenged by these new products.*

dom·i·nant /ˈdɒmɪnənt ‖ ˈdɑː-/ adj **1** most important: *The United States is the dominant partner in the alliance.* **2** very noticeable, often because of being high: *The castle was in a dominant position overlooking a bend in the river.* **3** liking to control other people: *My sister had a very dominant nature.*

dom·i·nate /ˈdɒmɪneɪt ‖ ˈdɑː-/ v **dominated, dominating** **1** [I;T] to have controlling power over someone or something: *The big banks dominate industry. | a dominating personality* **2** [T] to have the most important place or position in something: *The earthquake dominated the news for several days.* **3** [T] to look over something from a high position: *The castle dominated the whole town.* –**domination** /ˌdɒmɪˈneɪʃən ‖ ˌdɑː-/ n [U]

dom·i·neer·ing /ˌdɒmɪˈnɪərɪŋ ‖ ˌdɑː-/ adj showing a desire to control others, usually without any consideration of their feelings or wishes

do·min·ion /dəˈmɪnjən/ n **1** [U] fml the power or right to rule: *Alexander the Great held dominion over a large area.* **2** [C] the land held in complete control by one person, ruler, or government: *the King's dominions* **3** [C] a self-governing nation of the British COMMONWEALTH: *the dominion of Canada*

dom·i·no /ˈdɒmɪnəʊ ‖ ˈdɑː-/ n **dominoes** one of a set of small flat pieces of wood or plastic with a different number of spots on each, used for playing a game called **dominoes**

don¹ /dɒn ‖ dɑːn/ v **-nn-** old fash [T] to put on a piece of clothing

don² n a teacher at a university, especially at Oxford or Cambridge

do·nate /dəʊˈneɪt ‖ ˈdəʊneɪt/ v **donated, donating** [I;T] to make a gift of something to someone for a good purpose: *The school donated £500 to a local charity.*

do·na·tion /dəʊˈneɪʃən/ n [C;U] a gift made for a good purpose: *She made a generous donation of £1000 to the Children's Hospital.*

done¹ /dʌn/ the past participle of DO

done² adj **1** [never before a noun] finished: *The job's nearly done.* **2** **Done!** = I accept!: *"I'll give you £5 for it." "Done!"* **3** **done for** /ˈ··/ (also **done in** /ˌ·ˈ·/) infml very tired: *I feel completely done in!* **4**

done for dead or about to die: *The prisoner is done for.* **5** **not done** not socially acceptable: *It isn't done to call your teachers by their first names.*

don·key /ˈdɒŋki ‖ ˈdɑːŋki/ n **1** a grey or brown animal like a horse, but smaller and with longer ears **2** **donkey's years** a very long time: *I've known her for donkey's years.*

don·key·work /ˈdɒŋkiwɜːk ‖ ˈdɑːŋkiwɜːrk/ n [U] BrE infml the hard uninteresting part of a piece of work: *Why do I always have to do the donkeywork?*

do·nor /ˈdəʊnəʳ/ n **1** a person who makes a gift of something to someone for a good purpose **2** a person who allows some of their blood or a part of their body to be used for medical purposes: *a blood donor | a kidney donor*

don't /dəʊnt/ short for: "do not": *You know him, don't you?*

doo·dle /ˈduːdl/ v **doodled, doodling** [I] to draw things like lines or figures while you are thinking about something else –**doodle** n

doom /duːm/ n [C;U] a terrible fate which you cannot avoid: *A sense of doom overwhelmed me.*

doomed /duːmd/ adj unable to avoid a terrible fate: *The plan was doomed to failure. | the doomed ship*

door /dɔːʳ/ n **1** a movable flat surface that opens and closes the entrance to a building, room, piece of furniture, or vehicle: *the kitchen door | Close the door to the kitchen, will you? | There's someone at the front door; can you answer it please. | Have you locked the back door? | He slammed the car door angrily. | Thank you for coming, Mr Jackson. My secretary will show you to the door.* –see pictures on pages 49 and 441 **2** an opening for a door: *She stepped through the door.* **3** **be on the door** infml to have a duty at the entrance to a theatre or event such as collecting tickets **4** **door to door:** **a** from the starting point to the finishing point of a journey: *It's 110 kilometres door to door.* **b** from one building to the next building: *We went from door to door collecting money for charity. | a door-to-door salesman* **5** **next door to** in the building or room next to something: *His office is next door to my secretary's.*

door·bell /ˈdɔːbel ‖ ˈdɔːr-/ n a bell at the front door of a house which you ring when you go to visit someone

door·knob /ˈdɔːnɒb ‖ ˈdɔːrnɑːb/ n a round handle on a door to open it with

door·mat /ˈdɔːmæt ‖ ˈdɔːr-/ n a mat placed in front of or inside a door for cleaning your shoes on

door·step /ˈdɔːstep ‖ ˈdɔːr-/ n **1** a step in front of an outer door –see picture on page 441 **2** **on your doorstep** very close to where you live or are staying

door·way /ˈdɔːweɪ ‖ ˈdɔːr-/ n an opening at the door into a building or room: *She stood in the doorway, unable to decide whether or not to go in.*

dope¹ /dəʊp/ n infml **1** [U] an illegal drug, especially MARIJUANA **2** [C] a stupid person

dope² v **doped, doping** [T] infml to give a drug to a person or an animal to change their behaviour: *The horse won the race but it had been doped.*

dop·ey /ˈdəʊpi/ adj **dopier, dopiest** infml (also **dopy**) **1** slow, sleepy, and unable to think clearly: *I'm always a bit dopey before breakfast.* **2** rather stupid

dorm /dɔːm ‖ dɔːrm/ n see DORMITORY

dor·mant /ˈdɔːmənt ‖ ˈdɔːr-/ adj **1** not active or growing: *a dormant volcano | Most plants lie*

dormant in winter. **2** not producing any effects: *Opposition to the new motorway remained dormant because there was no organized campaign against it.*

dor·mi·to·ry /ˈdɔːmɪtəri ‖ ˈdɔːrmɪˌtɔːri/ n **dormitories** (also **dorm** *infml*) **1** a large room for sleeping in, containing a number of beds: *a school dormitory* **2** *AmE* a building in a college or university where students live and sleep

dor·mouse /ˈdɔːmaʊs ‖ ˈdɔːr-/ n **dormice** /-maɪs/ a small field mouse which sleeps through the winter

dor·sal /ˈdɔːsəl ‖ ˈdɔːr-/ adj [only before a noun] *tech* of the back part of a fish or animal: *That fish has a large dorsal fin.*

dos·age /ˈdəʊsɪdʒ/ n an amount of medicine to be taken over a period of time: *The required dosage is two tablets daily.*

dose¹ /dəʊs/ n **1** an amount of medicine to be taken at one time: *Take one dose, three times a day.* **2** a period of experiencing something unpleasant: *Your son needs a dose of hard work, if you ask me!*

dose² v **dosed, dosing** [T] (also **dose** sbdy ↔ **up**) to give an amount of medicine to someone

doss /dɒs ‖ dɑːs/
 doss down *phr* v [I] *BrE infml* to sleep in a place which is convenient but uncomfortable: *It was too late to go home so he dossed down on the floor.*

dos·si·er /ˈdɒsɪeɪ ‖ ˈdɒsjeɪ, ˈdɑː-/ n a set of papers containing detailed information: *The secret police keep dossiers on all foreign journalists.*

dot¹ /dɒt ‖ dɑːt/ n **1** a small round mark: *a dot on the letter i* **2 on the dot** *infml* at the exact point in time: *The three o'clock train arrived on the dot.*

dot² v -tt- [T] **1** to mark something with a dot **2** be **dotted with** to have things scattered over an area: *a lake dotted with boats*

do·tage /ˈdəʊtɪdʒ/ n **in your dotage** weak in your mind because of old age: *Don't keep on telling me the same thing – I'm not in my dotage yet, you know!*

dote /dəʊt/ v **doted, doting dote on someone** to love and care for someone very much, especially in a way that seems foolish to other people: *He absolutely dotes on his youngest son.*

dot·ing /ˈdəʊtɪŋ/ adj [only before a noun] showing great love and care for someone: *a doting husband* –**dotingly** adv

dot·ty /ˈdɒti ‖ ˈdɑːti/ adj **dottier, dottiest** *infml* behaving in a strange way

doub·le¹ /ˈdʌbəl/ adj **1** twice the usual size: *He asked for a double whisky.* **2** made up of two things or two parts: *We put a double lock on the door.* **3** made for two people: *a double bed* | *We booked a double room at the hotel.* **4 see double** to see two things instead of one

double² n **1** [U] something that is twice as large as something else: *Normally it only costs £3 to get in, but because it was a Sunday I had to pay double.* **2** [C] a drink of something such as WHISKY which is twice as large as a normal drink: *I'll have a brandy-a double, please.* **3** [C] someone who looks very much like another person: *I was sure it was Jane I saw in the pub last night, but perhaps it was her double.* **4 doubles** [pl] a game of something such as tennis in which two pairs of players play against each other **5 at the double, on the double** very fast: *Now go and tidy your room-at the double!*

double³ *predeterminer* twice as much: *The recipe said two cupfuls of milk, but I used double that amount.* | *His weight is double what it was.*

double⁴ v **doubled, doubling** **1** [I] to become twice as large as before: *The price of coal has doubled over the last ten years.* **2** [T] to make something twice as large as before: *The company has managed to double its profits this year.*

double as sthg *phr* v [T] to have something as a second job or a second use: *She's the secretary really, but she doubles as the receptionist.* | *The sofa doubles as a bed.*

double back *phr* v [I] to return along the path or road that you have just come along: *He must have set off along this path and then doubled back to confuse us.*

double up *phr* v **1** [I] to bend at the waist, usually because you are in pain or laughing a lot: *We all doubled up with laughter.* **2 be doubled up** to be bent at the waist, usually because you are in pain or laughing a lot: *He was doubled up with the pain.*

double-bar·relled /ˌ… ˈ…◂/ adj (**double-barreled** *AmE*) **1** having two barrels fixed side by side (used of a gun) **2** *BrE* having two parts which are joined by a HYPHEN (used of family names)

double-breast·ed /ˌ… ˈ…◂/ adj having two wide parts at the front that cross over each other, and a double row of buttons (used of a coat or JACKET)

double-check /ˌ… ˈ-/ v [I;T; + that] to examine something twice for exactness, safety, or quality: *She went back to the house to double-check that the front door had been locked.*

double-cross /ˌ… ˈ-/ v [T] *infml* to cheat a person even though you have encouraged them to trust you –**double cross** n

double-deck·er /ˌ… ˈ…◂/ n having two levels: *a double-decker bus* | *a double-decker sandwich*

double-dutch /ˌ… ˈ-/ n [U] *BrE* speech or writing that you cannot understand at all (a word which is often used in a humorous way): *All this jargon is double-dutch to me!*

double-glaze /ˌ… ˈ-/ v **double-glazed, double-glazing** [T] to fit a window with an additional sheet of glass in order to keep a building warmer or quieter –**double-glazing** n

double-joint·ed /ˌ… ˈ…◂/ adj having body joints which allow you to bend easily either backwards or forwards

double-quick /ˌ… ˈ-◂/ adj,adv *infml* very quick: *Get the doctor double-quick!*

doub·let /ˈdʌblɪt/ n a short tight-fitting piece of clothing that men used to wear in former times

doub·ly /ˈdʌbli/ adv **1** to twice the degree: *You've got to be doubly careful when you're driving in fog.* **2** in two ways

doubt¹ /daʊt/ v **1** [T; + (that) not in progressive forms] to consider something to be unlikely: *She may have remembered, but I rather doubt it.* | *I doubt that John will come.* **2** [T not in progressive forms] not to have confidence in: *I doubt his honesty.* | *How could you ever doubt me?* –**doubter** n

doubt² n **1** [C; U] a feeling of uncertainty of belief or opinion: *There is some doubt whether John will come.* | *I've no doubt at all who did it.* | *There's no doubt that the plan will succeed.* | *He says he can cure me, but I still have my doubts about it.* **2 be in doubt; be open to doubt** (used of a situation) to be in a condition of uncertainty: *The whole matter is still in doubt.* **3 no doubt** almost certainly: *No doubt he'll resign.* | *"I expect Sally will tell him." "No doubt."* **4 without doubt** certainly: *That was without doubt the worst movie I've ever seen!*

■ USAGE 1 Note that in the following positive sentences **doubt** is followed by **whether** or **as to whether**: *There is some* **doubt** *(as to) whether he'll come.* | *I have a small* **doubt** *as to whether he is suitable for the job.* But in the following negative sentences **no doubt** is followed by **that**: *There is no* **doubt** *that he'll come.* | *I have no* **doubt** *that he is the best person for the job.* 2 **No doubt** means only "I think" or "I expect": **No doubt** (= I expect) *we'll meet again some day.* **Undoubtedly** is a much stronger expression: **Undoubtedly** (= I'm certain) *the government has made a serious error of judgement.*

doubt·ful /ˈdautfəl/ *adj* 1 uncertain: *She's very keen on the idea, but I feel very doubtful about it.* | *I'm doubtful whether they'll agree to this.* 2 unlikely: *It's doubtful that we'll be home before midnight.* 3 probably worthless or dishonest: *a doubtful character* –**doubtfully** *adv*

doubt·less /ˈdautləs/ *adv* certainly: *John will doubtless say something to make everyone feel welcome.*

dough /dəu/ *n* [U] 1 flour mixed with water ready for baking 2 *infml AmE* money

dough·nut /ˈdəunʌt/ *n* a small round cake fried in fat and covered with sugar

dour /duər, ˈdauər ‖ daur, duər/ *adj* cold and unfriendly: *a dour look* –**dourly** *adv*

douse /daus/ *v* **doused, dousing** (also **dowse**) [T] to pour water over something

dove[1] /dʌv/ *n* a bird of the PIGEON family, often used as a sign of peace

dove[2] /dəuv/ *AmE* the past tense of DIVE

dow·dy /ˈdaudi/ *adj* **dowdier, dowdiest** 1 dull and unfashionable (used of clothes) 2 dull and uninteresting (used of people) –**dowdily** *adv* –**dowdiness** *n* [U]

down[1] /daun/ *adv, prep* 1 *adv, prep* in or towards a lower place or position, for example towards the floor or the ground. *She bent down to kiss the child.* | *She came running down the hill towards us.* | *Please sit down.* | *I put the parcel down on the table.* | *Several trees were blown down in the storm.* | *He's down in the cellar.* –see picture on page 540 2 *adv* in or towards the South: *We're driving down to London tomorrow.* | *She lives down in the South of France.* 3 *adv* written on paper: *Did you write down her name?* | *Make sure you get everything down in writing.* | *Your name's not down on the list.* 4 *adv* showing decrease: *Production has gone down this year.* | *Can you please turn the radio down a bit?* 5 *adv* from the past towards the present: *The title is passed down from father to son.* 6 **down the road, down the street** further along or at the far end of the road or street: *people walking down the street* | *He lives just down the road.* 7 **down a river** along a river in the same direction as the current 8 **down to something** even including something which seems small and unimportant: *The event had been very carefully planned, down to the last detail.* 9 **down to someone** someone's choice or responsibility: *It's down to you to do it yourself.* | *It's down to him to decide whether or not to accept the job.* 10 **down under** *infml* in or to Australia or New Zealand 11 **down with something** ill with something: *She's gone down with flu.* | *He's down with bronchitis at the moment.* 12 **Down with ...** a phrase used to show that you do not like a person or group of people in power: *Down with the Government!*

down[2] *adj* [never before a noun] 1 sad: *I'm feeling a bit down today.* 2 showing decrease: *Our profits are down by 20%.*

down[3] *v* [T] 1 to drink something quickly: *She downed her drink and left.* 2 **down tools** *infml* to stop working as a way of showing that you are angry about something: *After the pay negotiations had broken down, many workers simply downed tools and went home.*

down[4] *n* [U] fine soft feathers or hair –**downy** *adj*

down-and-out /ˌ·· ˈ·◄/ *n* a person who sleeps on the streets because they have no home or money

down·cast /ˈdaunkaːst ‖ -kæst/ *adj* sad and discouraged

down·fall /ˈdaunfɔːl/ *n* something that causes a successful person to be ruined: *Greed led to his downfall.*

down·grade /ˈdaungreid/ *v* **downgraded, downgrading** [T] to give a lower position to an employed person or a lower level to a job or plan: *He was downgraded from sergeant to private.*

down-heart·ed /ˌdaunˈhaːtɪd ‖ -aːr-/ *adj* sad and discouraged

down·hill /ˌdaunˈhil◄/ *adj, adv* 1 sloping or going towards the bottom of a hill: *The road runs downhill.* | *downhill skiing* 2 *infml* becoming easier: *We've done the hardest part of the job – it's all downhill from now on.* 3 **go downhill** to become less acceptable or pleasant: *His work has been going downhill recently.*

Dow·ning Street /ˈdaunɪŋ ˌstriːt/ *n* [U + sing/pl verb] the government of Great Britain: *talks between Dublin and Downing Street*

down·pour /ˈdaunpɔːr/ *n* a heavy fall of rain

down·right /ˈdaunrait/ *adv infml* thoroughly or completely (used of a bad quality): *She was worse than unfriendly – she was downright rude!*

down·stairs /ˌdaunˈsteəz ‖ -eərz/ *adj, adv* situated on or going towards the ground floor of a house: *She carried her suitcase downstairs.* | *a downstairs bedroom*

down·stream /ˌdaunˈstriːm◄/ *adv* moving with the current of a river or stream: *They travelled downstream.*

down-to-earth /ˌ·· ˈ·◄/ *adj* practical and honest: *a very down-to-earth person*

down·town /ˌdaunˈtaun◄/ *adj, adv* to or in the business centre of a town or city: *Let's go downtown.* | *downtown offices*

down·trod·den /ˈdaunˌtrɒdn ‖ -ˌtraː-/ *adj lit* treated badly or without respect by people in positions of power

down·turn /ˈdauntɜːn ‖ -ɜːrn/ *n* a lessening of business activity or production: *the recent unfortunate downturn in car production*

down·ward /ˈdaunwəd ‖ -wərd/ *adj* going down: *a downward movement of the head* | *the downward movement of prices*

down·wards /ˈdaunwədz ‖ -ər-/ *adv* (also **downward** *AmE*) going, looking, or facing down: *The plane moved gently downwards towards the runway.* | *He lay on the floor face downwards.* | *Inflation seems to be moving downwards.*

down·wind /ˌdaunˈwind/ *adj, adv* in the same direction as the wind is moving

down·y /ˈdauni/ *adj* **downier, downiest** covered in fine soft feathers or hair

dow·ry /ˈdauəri/ *n* **dowries** money or property that a woman brings to her future husband as a gift from her own family

dowse /daus/ *v* **dowsed, dowsing** see DOUSE

doze /dəuz/ *v* **dozed, dozing** [I] to sleep lightly or for a short period of time –**doze** *n* : *I'll just have a little doze.*

doze off *phr v* [I] to go to sleep unintentionally: *I just dozed off for a moment.*

doz·en /ˈdʌzən/ *det, n* **dozen** or **dozens** **1** a group of 12: *a dozen eggs* **2 dozens** *infml* very many: *I've been there dozens of times.*

doz·y /ˈdəʊzi/ *adj* **dozier, doziest** **1** sleepy: *The heat made me feel dozy.* **2** *BrE infml* stupid: *a dozy person* –**dozily** *adv*

Dr an abbreviation for DOCTOR

drab /dræb/ *adj* dull and uninteresting: *a drab colour* –**drabness** *n* [U]

draft¹ /drɑːft ‖ dræft/ *n* **1** the first rough written form of a plan, letter, speech, or book: *I've made a first draft of my speech for Friday.* | *a plan still in draft form* **2** a written order for money to be paid by a bank, especially from one bank to another **3 the draft** *AmE* the act of making people serve in one of the armed forces

draft² *v* [T] **1** to make the first rough written form of a plan, letter, speech, or book **2** *AmE* to make someone serve in one of the armed forces

drafts·man /ˈdrɑːftsmən ‖ ˈdræfts-/ *n* **draftsmen** /-mən/ –see DRAUGHTSMAN

draft·y /ˈdrɑːfti ‖ ˈdræfti/ *adj* **draftier, draftiest** –see DRAUGHTY

drag¹ /dræg/ *v* **-gg-** **1** [T] to pull a heavy object along a surface slowly and with difficulty: *He dragged his suitcase along the platform.* –see picture on page 736 **2** [T + adv/prep] to pull someone with force: *He dragged her to her feet.* **3** [I + adv/prep] to move along while touching the ground: *Her long dress dragged in the dust.* **4** [I + adv/prep] to move along more slowly than necessary: *He dragged behind the others.* **5** [T + adv/prep] *infml* to make someone go somewhere they do not want to: *Why must you drag me out to a concert on a cold night like this?*

drag on *phr v* [I] to continue for an unreasonably long time: *The meeting seemed to drag on for hours.*

drag out *phr v* **1** [drag sthg ↔ out] to make something last an unnecessarily long time **2 drag something out of someone** to force someone to say something: *The police finally dragged the truth out of her.*

drag sthg ↔ **up** *phr v* [T] *infml* to raise a subject unnecessarily: *The newspapers keep dragging up the mistakes he made ten years ago.*

drag² *n* **1** [C;U] a heavy, pulling action: *the drag of the waves* **2** [C] something or someone that makes it harder to do something: *He felt that his family was a drag on his career.* **3** [C] *infml* something dull and uninteresting: *The party was a drag, so we left early.* **4** [C] *infml* an act of breathing in cigarette smoke: *He took a quick drag on his cigarette.* **5** *infml* **in drag** wearing a woman's clothing (used of a man)

drag·on /ˈdrægən/ *n* **1** an imaginary fire-breathing animal with wings **2** *infml* a bad-tempered old woman

drag·on·fly /ˈdrægənflaɪ/ *n* **dragonflies** a long thin brightly-coloured flying insect

drain¹ /dreɪn/ *v* **1** [I;T] to make a liquid flow out until there is none left: *Drain the water off the vegetables.* | *The rainwater had all drained away.* **2** [I;T] to make something gradually become dry as the liquid in it or on it flows away: *They intend to drain the land to make their crops grow better.* **3** [I;T] to use up or remove all of something: *What strength she had left suddenly drained away.* | *The*

country *is being drained of its best doctors.* **4** [T] to finish drinking something completely: *She drained the very last drop of her wine.* | *He drained his glass and left.* **5 be drained** to be extremely tired or weak: *She felt completely drained of all emotion.* | *looking tired and drained*

drain² *n* **1** a pipe which carries water or waste away from a place: *Make sure the drains don't get blocked.* **2** a metal cover with openings, found in a street, which carries rainwater away –see picture on page 441 **3** something that empties or uses up something: *All this spending is a drain on the money I have saved.* **4 down the drain** *infml* wasted: *He's failed his driving test again – all that money down the drain!*

drain·age /ˈdreɪnɪdʒ/ *n* [U] a system of pipes or ditches used for draining water or other liquids: *The crops suffered damage as a result of poor drainage.*

drain·ing board /ˈ··· ·/ *n* a board next to a SINK in the kitchen where the wet dishes are left to dry

drainpipe /ˈdreɪnpaɪp/ *n* a pipe which carries waste, usually water, away from buildings, or from the roof of a building into a DRAIN² –see picture on page 441

drake /dreɪk/ *n* a male duck

dram /dræm/ *n* a small amount of alcohol

dra·ma /ˈdrɑːmə ‖ ˈdrɑːmə, ˈdræmə/ *n* **1** [C] a serious work of literature for the theatre, radio, or television that can be acted or read **2** [U] the study of plays: *Do you prefer music or drama?* **3** [U] a situation which is made up of exciting events: *the drama of international politics* | *Their holidays are always full of drama.*

dra·mat·ic /drəˈmætɪk/ *adj* **1** related to the theatre or to plays: *I'd like to read more of Ibsen's dramatic works.* **2** exciting and unusual, like something that could happen in a drama: *a dramatic moment* | *She made a dramatic entrance.* –**dramatically** /-kli/ *adv*

dra·mat·ics /drəˈmætɪks/ *n* **1** [U] activities connected with the theatre: *He's taken up amateur dramatics.* **2** [pl] behaviour that shows too much feeling: *All your dramatics aren't going to make me change my mind.*

dram·a·tist /ˈdræmətɪst/ *n* a writer of plays

dram·a·tize /ˈdræmətaɪz/ *v* **dramatized, dramatizing** (also **dramatise** *BrE*) **1** [T] to change a book into a play so that it can be acted: *His novel has been dramatized for television.* **2** [I;T] to present something in a dramatic manner: *Don't dramatize so much –just give us the facts!* –**dramatization** /ˌdræmətaɪˈzeɪʃən ‖ -mətə-/ *n* [C;U]

drank /dræŋk/ the past tense of DRINK

drape /dreɪp/ *v* **draped, draping** [T] **1** to cover or decorate something with cloth: *a picture of their leader draped with the national flag.* | *Drape the flag over the picture.* **2** to make something hang loosely or carelessly: *He draped his legs over the arm of the chair.*

drap·er·y /ˈdreɪpəri/ *n* **draperies** **1** [C;U] cloth or clothing arranged in folds **2** [U] *BrE* cloth sold in a shop: *the drapery department*

drapes /dreɪps/ *n* [pl] the usual American word for CURTAINS

dras·tic /ˈdræstɪk/ *adj* strong, sudden, and extreme: *Drastic changes are needed to improve our sales figures.* –**drastically** /-kli/ *adv* : *His work has changed drastically since his illness.*

draught /drɑːft ‖ dræft/ *n* (**draft** *AmE*) **1** [C] a current of air blowing through a room: *You may catch* _cold if you sit in a draught._ **2** [C] an amount of water or air swallowed or breathed in at one time **3 on draught** kept in a barrel (used of beer) **4 draughts** [U] _BrE_ a game played by two people, each with 12 round pieces, on a board of 64 squares

draughts·man /ˈdrɑːftsmən ‖ ˈdræfts-/ n **draughtsmen** /mən/ (**draftsman** _AmE_) **1** a person whose job is to make detailed drawings of all the parts of a new building or machine **2** _fml_ a person who draws well

draught·y /ˈdrɑːfti ‖ ˈdræfti/ _adj_ **draughtier, draughtiest** with cold air currents blowing: _a draughty room_

draw[1] /drɔː/ v **drew** /druː/, **drawn** /drɔːn/ **1** [I;T] to make pictures using a pencil or pen: _He drew a plan of the building._ | _Lines had been drawn all over the photograph._ | _I can't draw very well._ **2** [T] to pull something along: _a cart drawn by a horse_ **3** [T] to remove something from a place: _He drew a wallet from his pocket._ | _Suddenly she drew a knife out of her bag._ | _I drew some money out of the bank._ **4** [I] _fml_ to move slowly or gradually: _The train drew into the station._ | _The people drew nearer to watch._ | _She drew away from the fire._ | _Winter was drawing near._ **5** [T] to attract someone: _The match is expected to draw a very large crowd._ | _I was somehow drawn to her._ **6** [I;T] to end a game or match with neither side winning: _We drew the game three all._ **7 be drawn into something** to become concerned in something even though you did not want to be: _I was trying not to get drawn into the conflict._ **8 draw blood** to make someone bleed: _The dog bit me but didn't draw blood._ **9 draw a conclusion** to come to an idea after consideration: _We can all draw our own conclusions from these statistics._ **10 draw breath** _fml_ to breathe **11 draw lots** to decide who should do something by each choosing one from a group of objects; one object is marked in some way and the person who chooses this one will do the thing that is being decided on **12 draw someone's attention to someone** to show something to someone, or tell them about it, so that they notice it: _I'd like to draw your attention to the latest unemployment figures._ **13 draw the curtains** to move curtains so that they are open or shut: _It was getting dark so I drew the curtains._ **14 draw the line** to state that something is a limit for you: _I draw the line at stealing._
draw back _phr v_ [I] to move away from someone or something: _The crowd drew back in terror as the building crashed to the ground._
draw in _phr v_ [I] **1** to move to one side of the road and stop: _The bus drew in to let the cars pass._ **2 the evenings/nights are drawing in** = it is getting darker earlier in the evenings because winter is coming
draw on sthg _phr v_ [T] to use something: _Writers have to draw on their imagination and experience._
draw out _phr v_ **1** [T **draw** sthg ↔ **out**] to take money out of a bank account: _I need to draw out £50._ **2 the days are drawing out** = the days are becoming longer because spring is coming
draw up _phr v_ **1** [T **draw** sthg ↔ **up**] to form and write a plan or an agreement: _Your solicitor will draw up a contract for you to sign._ **2** [I] (of a vehicle) to stop: _A car drew up outside the bank and three men got out._ **3 draw yourself up** _lit_ to stand up straight
draw upon sthg _phr v_ [T] to use something: _We have a large pool of talent that we can draw upon._

draw[2] n **1** a game in which people buy tickets with numbers on; some numbers are then chosen by chance, and the people with those numbers win a

prize **2** a result in a game or match in which neither side has won: _The match ended in a draw._

draw·back /ˈdrɔːbæk/ n something which causes a difficulty: _The only drawback of the plan is its cost._

drawer /drɔːr/ n a part of a table or desk which slides out so you can put things in or take them out: _Put your things away in the drawer._

draw·ing /ˈdrɔːɪŋ/ n **1** [U] the skill of making pictures with a pen or pencil: _She's very good at drawing._ **2** [C] a picture made with a pen or pencil: _He made a detailed drawing of the scene._ **3 go back to the drawing board** _infml_ to try and think of another and better idea because something has been unsuccessful

drawing pin /ˈ·· ˌ·/ n a short pin with a broad flat head, used especially for putting notices on boards or walls

drawing room /ˈ·· ·/ n _fml_ a room where people sit or entertain other people

drawl /drɔːl/ v [I;T] to speak slowly and unclearly with the vowel sounds lengthened: –**drawl** : _a southern drawl_

drawn[1] /drɔːn/ the past participle of DRAW

drawn[2] _adj_ **1** pulled across: _All the curtains were drawn._ **2** tired and worried: _She looked tired and drawn._ **3** ended with neither side winning (used of games or competitions)

dread /dred/ v **1** [T; + that] to feel great fear or anxiety about something: _I'm dreading my driving test._ | _We all dreaded having to go to the headmaster's office._ | _He dreaded that she would find out._
□ USEFUL PATTERNS to dread something; to dread doing something; to dread that…
2 I dread to think… = it worries me very much when I think about…: _I dread to think what will happen if they ever meet each other again._ –**dread** n : _her dread of being caught_

dread·ful /ˈdredfəl/ _adj_ very bad or unpleasant: _What a dreadful noise!_ | _The play last night was absolutely dreadful!_ | _This is dreadful news!_

dread·ful·ly /ˈdredfəli/ _adv_ extremely: _I'm dreadfully sorry._

dream[1] /driːm/ n **1** a set of events and feelings that you experience when you are asleep: _She woke up in the middle of a frightening dream._ **2** something that you think about and hope for: _It was his dream to play football for his country._ | _The huge number of people at the concert was beyond their wildest dreams._ **3 in a dream** in a state of mind in which you do not pay much attention to the real world: _John lives in a dream._ **4 go like a dream** _infml_ to work well: _My new car goes like a dream._

dream[2] v **dreamed** /driːmd, dremt/ or **dreamt** /dremt/, **dreamed** or **dreamt** [I; + (that)] **1** to have a dream: _I dreamt that I was back at school._ | _What did you dream about last night?_ **2** to imagine something: _I never said that! You must have been dreaming._ | _I never dreamed I would get the job._ **3 wouldn't dream of** = would never do something because you think it is wrong: _I wouldn't dream of hurting the child._
■ USAGE For the past tense and the past participle, **dreamed** and **dreamt** are both used in British English, but Americans more often use **dreamed**.
dream sthg ↔ **up** _phr v_ [T] _infml_ to think of or imagine something surprising or which is not true: _My parents are always dreaming up some reason why I can't stay out late._

dream·er /ˈdriːmər/ n **1** a person who dreams **2** a person who has impractical ideas or plans

dreamt /dremt/ the past tense and past participle of DREAM.

dream·y /'dri:mi/ adj **dreamier, dreamiest 1** living more in the imagination than in the real world **2** gentle and beautiful: soft dreamy music –**dreamily** adv

drear·y /'drɪəri/ adj dull and uninteresting: Addressing envelopes all the time is dreary work. | this awful dreary weather –**drearily** adv –**dreariness** n [U]

dredge /dredʒ/ v **dredged, dredging** [I;T] to use a dredger: They dredged the lake in their search for the missing child.
   dredge sthg ↔ **up** phr v [T] **1** to find something by using a dredger **2** to talk about something unpleasant that has been forgotten: He dredged up all our old quarrels.

dredg·er /'dredʒər/ n (also **dredge**) a ship used for digging up mud from the bottom of a river

dregs /dregz/ n [pl] **1** little bits of solid in a liquid that sink to the bottom and are thrown away: coffee dregs **2** the worst and most useless parts of something: the dregs of society

drench /drentʃ/ v [T] to make something thoroughly wet: He went out in the storm and got drenched to the skin.

dress¹ /dres/ v **1** (also **get dressed**): to put on clothes: It only took me ten minutes to wash and dress. | I dressed quickly. | I'm just getting dressed. **2 be dressed** to be wearing clothes, often of a particular type: I'm not dressed yet. | She was dressed in black. | He arrived dressed in a suit and tie. **3** [I] to wear clothes of a particular type: He dresses to attract attention. | She dresses well. **4** [I] to put on formal clothes for the evening: We normally dress for dinner. **5** [T] to put clothes on someone else, especially a child: He was busy dressing the baby. **6** [T] to clean and put a protective covering on a wound **7** [T] to prepare meat or fish for cooking or eating by removing the parts that are not usually eaten **8** [T] to put a mixture of oil and other things over food to improve its taste: a salad dressed with oil and vinegar
   ■ USAGE Compare **dress, get dressed, put on, wear**. We can use **dress, get dressed,** or **put your clothes on** to talk about the action of getting into clothes. **Dress** is the most formal and **put your clothes on** the most informal: I got up and dressed. | I got up and got dressed. | I got up and put my clothes on. We use **wear** to talk about the state of having clothes on: You're wearing a nice tie today.
   dress up phr v **1** [I] (usually of children) to wear someone else's clothes for fun **2** [I] to put on formal clothes: Don't bother to dress up. **3** [T **dress** sthg ↔ **up**] to make something seem different or more attractive: The report was rather short so he dressed it up with some additional details.

dress² n **1** [C] a piece of clothing worn by a woman or girl; it covers her body from her shoulder to her knee –see picture on page 50 **2** [U] clothing of a certain type: Do we have to wear evening dress for this party?

dress³ adj [only before a noun] **1** used for a dress: dress material **2** suitable for a formal occasion (used of clothing): a dress shirt

dress cir·cle /'· ,··/ n the upper floor in a theatre

dress·er /'dresər/ n **1** BrE a piece of furniture for holding dishes, with open shelves above and cupboards below **2** AmE a chest of drawers, often with a mirror on top

dress·ing /'dresɪŋ/ n **1** [C;U] a mixture of oil and other things which can be added to food, often SALADS: salad dressing | French dressing **2** [C] a covering for a cut or wound **3** [U] the action of putting on your clothes: She finds dressing difficult since her accident.

dressing down /,·· '·/ n angry words spoken when someone has done something wrong: The children got a good dressing down.

dressing gown /'·· ·/ n a garment rather like a long loose coat, that you wear before you get dressed

dressing ta·ble /'·· ,··/ n a low table with a mirror, usually in a bedroom

dress·y /'dresi/ adj **dressier, dressiest** suitable for wearing on formal occasions (used of clothes)

drew /dru:/ the past tense of DRAW

drib·ble /'drɪbəl/ v **dribbled, dribbling 1** [I;T] to flow in drops or a thin stream, or to make a liquid flow in this way: The water dribbled from the tap. | She dribbled the oil into the mayonnaise. **2** [I] to let SALIVA flow slowly out of your mouth: The baby has just dribbled down my blouse. **3** [T] to move a ball forward by a number of short kicks or hits –**dribble** n [C;U]

dribs /drɪbz/ n **dribs and drabs** infml small and unimportant amounts: He's paying me back in dribs and drabs.

dried /draɪd/ the past tense and past participle of DRY

dri·er /'draɪər/ n –see DRYER

drift¹ /drɪft/ n **1** [C;U] a general tendency or movement: the drift of young people from the country to the city **2** [C] a lot of snow or sand blown into a pile by the wind: deep drifts of snow **3** a drifting movement: the drift of the tide | the drift of the current **4 the drift** the general meaning of something: "Did you understand what he was talking about?" "Well I got the general drift."

drift² v [I] **1** to float or be moved gently by wind, waves, or currents: They drifted out to sea. **2** to pile up under the force of the wind: The snow was drifting badly and several roads were closed. **3** to live without any real aim or purpose: She drifts through life taking one job after another.
   drift off phr v [I] infml to go to sleep

drift·er /'drɪftər/ n **1** a person who travels about without any purpose (a word used to express disapproval) **2** a fishing boat that uses a floating net

drill¹ /drɪl/ v **1** [I;T] to make a hole with a drill: to drill for oil | I drilled a hole in the wood. **2** [T] to train people by making them do the same thing many times: The soldiers were thoroughly drilled in how to respond to attack.

drill² n **1** [C] a tool or machine for making holes: a pneumatic drill | a dentist's drill –see picture on page 638 **2** [U] military training and exercises **3** [C;U] training and instruction in a subject **4** [C] practice in what to do in a particular situation: a fire drill

dri·ly /'draɪli/ adv **dryly** in a way that is amusing, but you do not notice this at first

drink¹ /drɪŋk/ v **drank** /dræŋk/, **drunk** /drʌŋk/, **drinking 1** [I;T] to take a liquid into your mouth and swallow it: She gave me some water and I drank. | She was drinking a cup of tea. **2** [I] to take in alcohol, either regularly or too much: He doesn't smoke or drink. **3 drink to someone, drink a toast to someone** to have an alcoholic drink to wish someone success or happiness: We drank a toast to the bride and groom.

drink sth ↔ **in** *phr v* [T] to listen, see, or smell something with great enjoyment: *They drank in the sights and sounds of the city.*

drink up *phr v* [I;T **drink** sth ↔ **up**] to finish a drink: *Drink up. It's time to go home.* | *Drink up your tea before it gets cold.*

drink[2] *n* **1** [C] a liquid suitable for swallowing: *Can I have a drink of water, please?* **2** [U;C] an alcoholic drink: *Would you like another drink?* | *There's no drink in the house.* **3** [C] a small quantity of a drink: *He took a drink of his beer and thought about what she had said.*

drink·er /ˈdrɪŋkəʳ/ *n* a person who drinks alcohol, especially too much: *Her father was a heavy drinker.*

drip /drɪp/ *v* [I] **-pp-** **1** (of a liquid) to fall in drops: *Water was dripping from the tap.* **2** to let liquid fall in drops: *The tap was still dripping.*

drip[2] *n* **1** the action or sound of falling in drops: *All night I heard the drip drip drip of the water.* **2** an apparatus for putting drops of a liquid directly through a tube into a blood vessel **3** *slang* a dull person

drip-dry /ˌ· ˈ·◂/ *adj* drying smooth and needing no ironing (used of clothing): *a drip-dry shirt*

drip·ping[1] /ˈdrɪpɪŋ/ *n* [U] fat and juices that have come from meat during cooking

dripping[2] *adj* (also **dripping wet**) very wet

drive[1] /draɪv/ *v* **drove** /drəʊv/, **driven** /ˈdrɪvən/, **driving** **1** [I;T] to guide and control a vehicle: *She drives well.* | *I never learnt to drive a car.* **2** [T + adv/prep] to take someone somewhere in a vehicle: *Can you drive me to the station?* **3** [T + adv/prep] to force animals to move in a particular direction: *The farmer was driving his cattle along the road.* **4** [T] to provide the power for something: *The engines drive the ship.* **5** [T + adv/prep] to force someone into a particular situation, usually unpleasant: *That noise is driving me out of my mind.* | *It was her pride that drove her to do it.* | *He's driving me mad.* **6** [T + adv/prep] to hit something very hard so that it moves in a particular direction: *He drove the nail into the wood.* | *She drove the ball 150 metres.* **7** **drive something home** to make something unmistakably clear: *He tried to drive it home to her that they had no money.* **8 what are you driving at?** = what do you mean? **9 drive someone up the wall/round the bend** to make someone lose their patience and become angry

drive off *phr v* **1** [T **drive** sbdy/sthg ↔ **off**] to force someone or something away or back: *He drove off his attackers.* **2** [I] to start moving away in a car: *He got into the car and drove off.*

drive[2] *n* **1** [C] a journey in a vehicle, especially for pleasure: *Let's go for a drive in the country.* **2** [C] (also **driveway**) a road from a private house to the street: *She parks her car in the drive.* –see picture on page 441 **3** [C] an act of hitting a ball forcefully in GOLF or tennis so that it covers a long distance **4** [C] a strong well-planned effort by a group for a particular purpose: *The club is having a membership drive.* **5** [C] an important natural need which must be fulfilled: *People of that age have a strong sex drive.* **6** [U] a forceful quality of mind that gets things done: *He lacks the drive to succeed.* **7** [C;U] the power from the engine of a vehicle to particular wheels to make it move: *This car has front-wheel drive.*

drive-in /ˈ· ·/ *n* a place that people can use while remaining in their cars –**drive-in** *adj* [only before a noun] : *a drive-in restaurant*

driv·el /ˈdrɪvəl/ *v* **-ll-** *BrE* (**-l-** *AmE*) [I] to talk nonsense: *What's he drivelling on about?* –**driveller** *n* [U]

driv·en /ˈdrɪvən/ the past participle of DRIVE

driv·er /ˈdraɪvəʳ/ *n* a person who drives: *a bus driver*

drive·way /ˈdraɪvweɪ/ *n* the usual American word for the DRIVE in front of a house

driv·ing[1] /ˈdraɪvɪŋ/ *n* [U] **1** the action of operating a vehicle: *He enjoys driving fast cars.* **2** the way a person drives: *She was warned about dangerous driving.*

driving[2] *adj* [only before a noun] **1** very strong and powerful: *driving rain* | *driving ambition* **2 in the driving seat** in charge

driving li·cence /ˈ·· ˌ·◂/ *n* (also **driver's licence/ driver's license** *AmE*) an official form that shows you are allowed to drive

driving school /ˈ·· ˌ·/ *n* a place where people learn how to drive

driz·zle /ˈdrɪzəl/ *v* **drizzled, drizzling** [I] to rain very lightly : *It started to drizzle.* –**drizzle** *n* [U]

droll /drəʊl/ *adj old-fash* odd and amusing: *a droll expression*

drom·e·da·ry /ˈdrɒmədəri ‖ ˈdrɑːmədəri/ *n* **dromedaries** a camel with one HUMP[1](2)

drone[1] /drəʊn/ *v* **droned, droning** [I] to make a continuous low sound like that of bees

drone on *phr v* [I] to talk for a long time in an uninteresting way: *The teacher droned on and on.*

drone[2] *n* **1** a continuous low dull sound like that of bees: *the distant drone of traffic* **2** a male bee

drool /druːl/ *v* [I] **1** to let liquid flow from your mouth, especially because you can see or smell something pleasant **2 drool over something** to admire something in a slightly silly way: *The boys were all drooling over a picture of a girl in a bikini.*

droop /druːp/ *v* [I] **1** to hang or bend downwards: *His shoulders drooped with tiredness.* | *The flowers drooped in the vase.* **2** to become sad or weakened: *Our spirits drooped.* –**droop** *n*

drop[1] /drɒp/ *n* **1** a small amount of liquid in the shape of a ball: *a drop of oil* | *a tear drop* | *Drops of rain fell on the window.* **2** *infml* a small amount of liquid: *"Would you like some more tea?" "Just a drop please."* **3** a small round sweet: *fruit drops* | *chocolate drops* **4** a distance or movement straight down: *a long drop to the bottom of the cliff* | *a drop in temperature* | *a drop of 10 metres* **5** something that is dropped, especially from a plane: *an air drop of medical supplies* **6 drops** [pl] a liquid medicine that is taken in very small amounts: *Add four drops to a glass of water and stir.* **7 a drop in the ocean** a small unimportant quantity **8 at the drop of a hat** suddenly

drop[2] *v* **-pp-** **1** [T] to let something fall unintentionally, unexpectedly, or suddenly: *He dropped the bag and ran.* –see picture on page 736 **2** [I] to fall: *The leaves were starting to drop from the trees.* **3** [I;T] to fall or let something fall to a lower level or amount: *The price of oil has dropped sharply.* | *He dropped his voice to a whisper.* | *The temperature has dropped.* **4** [T + adv/prep] *infml* to let someone travelling in your car, taxi, or bus get out at a particular place: *Could you drop me at the station please?* **5** [T] to stop doing or considering something: *Let's drop the subject.* | *When the baby cries her mother drops everything to go and attend to her.* **6** [T] to leave someone out: *George has been dropped from the football team.* **7** [I] *infml* to fall down because you are tired or ill: *We worked until we*

dropped. **8 drop a hint** to give a small piece of advice or warning **9 drop dead** to die suddenly **10 drop someone a line** to write a short letter to someone

drop in *phr v* [I] to visit someone unexpectedly or informally: *I'll drop in some time next week.*

drop off *phr v* **1** [I] to lessen: *Interest in the game has dropped off.* **2** [I] *infml* to go to sleep often without intending to **3** [T **drop** sbdy ↔ **off**] to let someone get out of your car at a particular place: *Can you drop me off in town?*

drop out *phr v* [I] to stop attending or taking part: *He dropped out of college after only two weeks.*

drop round *phr v* [I] to visit someone unexpectedly or informally

drop·out /'drɒp-aʊt || 'drɑːp-/ *n* **1** a person who leaves school or college without completing the course **2** someone who leaves ordinary society because they do not agree with the accepted ways of living

drop·per /'drɒpər || 'drɑː-/ *n* a short glass tube with a rubber part at one end used for measuring out liquids in drops

drop·pings /'drɒpɪŋz || 'drɑː-/ *n* [pl] waste matter from the bowels of animals and birds

dross /drɒs || drɑːs, drɔːs/ *n* [U] something that is useless or not needed

drought /draʊt/ *n* [C;U] a long period of dry weather, when there is not enough water: *The drought continued for two years.* | *in times of drought*

drove¹ /drəʊv/ *n* **1** a large group of animals being driven together **2 droves** [pl] large crowds of people: *The tourists came in droves.*

drove² past tense of DRIVE

drown /draʊn/ *v* **1** [I;T] to die or make someone die under water because it is impossible to breathe: *All the passengers drowned in the shipwreck.* | *He drowned her in the lake.* **2** [T] to cover something completely with water: *Villages were drowned when the reservoir was constructed.* **3** [T] (also **drown** sthg ↔ **out**) (of a noise) to be so loud that other sounds cannot be heard: *The music was drowned out by the noise of the traffic.* **4 drown your sorrows** to drink alcohol in an attempt to forget your troubles

drowse /draʊz/ *v* **drowsed, drowsing** [I] to be almost asleep or in a light sleep

drow·sy /'draʊzi/ *adj* **drowsier, drowsiest 1** sleepy: *These tablets may make you feel drowsy.* **2** peaceful, and making you feel sleepy: *a drowsy summer afternoon* –**drowsily** *adv* –**drowsiness** *n* [U]

drudge /drʌdʒ/ *n* a person who does hard, uninteresting work

drudg·e·ry /'drʌdʒəri/ *n* [U] hard, uninteresting work

drug¹ /drʌg/ *n* **1** a medicine or something used for making medicines: *a drug used to treat cancer* **2** a substance which some people take for pleasure or excitement; drugs are often illegal and can make you dependent on them: *Tobacco and alcohol can be dangerous drugs.* | *A growing number of young people are addicted to drugs.*

drug² *v* -**gg**- [T] **1** to add drugs to something to make someone unconscious: *The coffee was drugged.* **2** to give a person or animal a drug to hide pain or make them sleepy: *He had been heavily drugged.*

drug·gist /'drʌgɪst/ *n AmE* someone who prepares and sells medicines and drugs

drug·store /'drʌgstɔːr/ *n AmE* a shop which sells

medicine and beauty products and also simple meals

dru·id /'druːɪd/ *n* a member of the ancient CELTIC priesthood of Britain, Ireland, and France, before the Christian religion

drum¹ /drʌm/ *n* **1** a musical instrument consisting of a skin stretched tight over one or both sides of a hollow circular frame; you hit it with your hand or with a stick **2** a large, round container: *an oil drum* –see picture on page 148

drum² *v* -**mm**- **1** [I] to beat or play a drum **2** [I + adv/prep] to make drum-like noises by continuous beating or striking: *He drummed on the table with his fingers.* | *the sound of rain drumming against the window* **3 drum something into someone** to say something to someone so often that they will remember and learn it: *She drummed it into the children that they must not cross the road alone.*

drum up sthg *phr v* [T] to attract something through hard work and advertising: *Let's try to drum up some more business.* | *to drum up support*

drum·mer /'drʌmər/ *n* someone who plays a drum

drum·stick /'drʌm,stɪk/ *n* a stick for beating a drum **2** the lower part of the leg of a bird, eaten when cooked

drunk¹ /drʌŋk/ the past participle of DRINK

drunk² *adj* [never before a noun] suffering from the effects of too much alcohol: *He gets drunk on only two glasses of wine!*

drunk³ *n* (also **drunkard** /'drʌŋkəd || -ərd/) a person who is drunk, especially often or continually (a word used to show disapproval)

drunk·en /'drʌŋkən/ *adj* [only before a noun] **1** drunk: *a drunken sailor* **2** resulting from or connected with too much drinking of alcohol: *a drunken sleep* | *a drunken party* –**drunkenly** *adv* –**drunkenness** *n* [U]

dry¹ /draɪ/ *adj* **drier, driest 1** having no water or other liquid inside or on the surface: *The wood won't burn unless it's dry.* | *Be careful! The paint isn't dry yet.* **2** without rain or wetness: *dry weather* | *a dry month* | *dry heat* **3** feeling thirsty, or making you feel thirsty: *It's dry work digging in the sun.* **4** not sweet (used of wine) **5** amusing without appearing to be so at first: *I like his dry sense of humour.* **6 as dry as a bone** *infml* very dry **7 as dry as dust** very uninteresting **8 dry dock** a place in which a ship is held in position while the water around it is pumped out, leaving the ship dry for repairs **9 dry ice** CARBON DIOXIDE in a solid state, used mainly to keep food and other things cold **10 dry rot** a serious disease of wood that makes it decay: *They didn't buy the house because it had terrible dry rot.* –**dryness** *n* [U]

dry² *v* **dried, 1** [I] to become dry: *They laid the clothes out to dry in the sun.* **2** [T] to make something dry: *I need a towel to dry my hair.* | *Shall I dry the dishes?*

dry out *phr v* [I;T **dry** sbdy/sthg ↔ **out**] **1** to make or become completely dry: *Hang your clothes up and they'll soon dry out.* **2** to cure someone from depending on alcohol, or to be cured from this: *He's gone into hospital to dry out.*

dry up *phr v* **1** [I;T **dry** sthg ↔ **up**] to make or become completely dry: *The river dries up in the hot season.* **2** [I] to come to an end: *Sources of ivory have dried up following the international ban on the trade.*

dry-clean /ˌ·'·/ *v* [T] to clean clothes with chemicals instead of water

dry-clean·er's /ˌ·ˈ··/ n a place where clothes can be taken to be dry-cleaned

dry·er /ˈdraɪəʳ/ n (also **drier**) a machine that dries something: *a hair dryer*

dry·ly /ˈdraɪli/ adv see DRILY

du·al /ˈdjuːəl ‖ ˈduːəl/ adj [only before a noun] **1** having two parts: *He has a dual interest in the football team; he's the trainer and his son plays for them.* | *a dual-purpose instrument* **2 dual carriageway** *BrE* a main road on which the traffic travelling in opposite directions is kept apart by a bar or a narrow piece of land –see picture on page 735

dub /dʌb/ v **-bb-** [T] **1** to name someone or something humorously or descriptively: *They immediately dubbed him Fatty.* **2** to change the original language of a film or television broadcast so that it is spoken by actors using a foreign language: *an English film dubbed into Spanish* | *Is the film dubbed or does it have subtitles?*

du·bi·ous /ˈdjuːbiəs ‖ ˈduː-/ adj **1** feeling doubt: *I'm still rather dubious about that plan.* **2** of uncertain value: *a dubious suggestion* **3** probably not completely honest: *a rather dubious character* –**dubiously** adv –**dubiousness** n [U]

duch·ess /ˈdʌtʃɪs/ n (also **Duchess**) the title of a woman equal in rank to a DUKE

duck¹ /dʌk/ n **1** a common water bird with a wide beak, sometimes kept for its meat, eggs, and soft feathers –see MEAT (USAGE) **2 take to something like a duck to water** *infml* to learn or get used to something naturally and very easily

duck² v **1** [I] to lower your head or body quickly, especially to avoid being hit or seen: *She had to duck to get through the doorway.* | *He saw a policeman coming, and ducked behind a car.* **2** [T] *infml* to try to avoid a difficulty or unpleasant responsibility: *a speech that ducked all the real issues* **3 duck out of something** to escape your responsibility for something: *Don't try to duck out of cleaning up the kitchen!*

duck·ling /ˈdʌklɪŋ/ n a young duck

duct /dʌkt/ n **1** a thin, narrow tube in your body or in plants which carries liquids or air: *tearducts* **2** any kind of pipe or tube for carrying things like liquids, air, or electric power lines

dud /dʌd/ n *infml* a person or thing that is worthless or useless: *a dud cheque* | *This new battery is a complete dud.*

due¹ /djuː ‖ duː/ adj **1** [never before a noun] expected to happen at a particular time: *The next train to London is due at 4 o'clock.* | *The plane is due to arrive at 11.30.* **2 be due to do something** to be going to do something because it has been planned: *I'm due to meet him this afternoon.* **3 be due for something** to be expecting to receive something: *I'm due for a pay rise soon.* **4** [never before a noun] payable: *a bill due today* **5** [never before a noun] *fml* owed or owing as a debt or right: *We have discovered that a great deal of money is due to you.* | *Our grateful thanks are due to this young man for his prompt action.* **6** [only before a noun] *fml* suitable: *driving without due care and attention* **7 due to** because of: *Her success is entirely due to hard work.* | *The dollar is weak at the moment, due partly to distrust of the new government.* **8 in due course** in the future, before too long: *We will be writing to you in due course.*

■ USAGE Compare **due to** and **owing to**. 1 Both expressions are similar in meaning, but **due to** is used after the verb *to be*: *His absence was due to the storm.* (You should not use **owing to** in this sentence.) 2 Some people consider it wrong to use **due to** except after the verb *to be*, but many speakers use it after other verbs, in the same way as **owing to**: *He arrived late due to/owing to the storm.*

due² n **1 give someone their due** to admit the good things about someone: *I don't like the man, but to give him his due, he's good at his job.* **2 dues** [pl] official charges or payments: *union dues*

due³ adv exactly (used before **north, south, east,** and **west**): *It's due north.*

du·el¹ /ˈdjuːəl ‖ ˈduːəl/ n a fight between two people with guns or swords to settle a quarrel

duel² v **-ll-** *BrE* (**-l-** *AmE*) [I] to fight a duel

du·et /djuːˈet ‖ duːˈet/ n a piece of music for two performers

duf·fel coat /ˈdʌfəl ˌkəʊt/ n (also **duffle coat**) a coat made of heavy woollen cloth, fastened with long tubelike buttons and often with a covering for your head

dug /dʌg/ the past tense and past participle of DIG

dug·out /ˈdʌgaʊt/ n **1** a small light boat made by cutting out a deep hollow space in a log **2** a shelter dug in the ground with an earth roof

duke /djuːk ‖ duːk/ n (also **Duke**) the title of a nobleman of the highest rank: *the Duke of Norfolk* | *He became a duke on the death of his father.*

dul·cet /ˈdʌlsɪt/ adj *lit* sweet and pleasant (used of sounds)

dull¹ /dʌl/ adj **1** not bright: *a dull grey day* **2** not clear or sharp: *a dull banging sound somewhere in the house* | *a dull ache* **3** uninteresting: *The party was very dull.* **4** slow in thinking and understanding things –**dully** /ˈdʌli/ adv –**dullness** n [U]

dull² v [T] to make something dull: *eyes and ears dulled by age* | *Give me something to dull the pain.*

du·ly /ˈdjuːli ‖ ˈduːli/ adv *fml* at the correct time or in the correct way: *The taxi that we had ordered duly arrived, and we drove off.* | *Your suggestion has been duly noted.*

dumb /dʌm/ adj **1** unable to speak: *dumb animals* | *Children who are deaf and dumb go to a special school.* **2** *infml* stupid –**dumbly** adv –**dumbness** n [U]

dumb·bell /ˈdʌmbel/ n a weight consisting of two large metal balls connected by a short bar, often used for exercises

dumb·found·ed /dʌmˈfaʊndɪd/ adj so surprised that you cannot speak: *He just stood there, dumbfounded by the news.*

dum·my¹ /ˈdʌmi/ n **dummies 1** an object made to make people believe it is the real thing: *The guns the robbers carried were just dummies.* **2** something like a human figure made of wood or plastic and used to make or show clothes: *a dressmaker's dummy* **3** *BrE* a rubber object for sucking, put in a baby's mouth to keep it quiet **4** *infml AmE* a stupid fool **5 a dummy run** a test to see if a plan works properly before it is actually needed

dummy² adj something that is made to seem real but is not: *a dummy computer*

dump¹ /dʌmp/ v [T] **1** to drop or unload something, especially heavily or carelessly, in a rough pile: *Don't dump that sand in the middle of the path!* | *They dumped their bags on my floor and left!* **2** to throw something away irresponsibly: *They dumped their rubbish in the sea.* **3** to get rid of unwanted goods by selling them to another country at a very low price (a word used to show disapproval)

dump² *n* **1** a place for dumping something such as waste material: *a rubbish dump* **2** *infml* an uninteresting, dirty, or untidy place: *This town's a real dump.* **3 be down in the dumps** to be feeling sad

dump·ling /ˈdʌmplɪŋ/ *n* **1** a lump of boiled flour and water, often served with meat or with meat inside it **2** a sweet food made of pastry with fruit inside it: *apple dumplings*

dump·y /ˈdʌmpi/ *adj* **dumpier, dumpiest** *infml* short and fat: *a dumpy little man*

dunce /dʌns/ *n* a person who is slow at learning

dune /djuːn ‖ duːn/ *n* (also **sand dune**) a hill of sand made by the wind on the seashore or in a desert

dung /dʌŋ/ *n* [U] solid waste material from the bowels of large animals

dun·ga·rees /ˌdʌŋɡəˈriːz/ *n* [pl] trousers with an additional part covering the top of your body, usually made of heavy cotton cloth

dun·geon /ˈdʌndʒən/ *n* a dark underground prison, especially beneath a castle

dunk /dʌŋk/ *v* [T] *infml* to dip something into liquid: *He enjoyed dunking his biscuits in his tea.*

du·o /ˈdjuːəʊ ‖ ˈduːəʊ/ *n* **duos** two musicians who play or sing together

dupe /djuːp ‖ duːp/ *v* **duped, duping** [T] to trick or deceive someone: *The salesman duped me into buying a faulty washing machine.* –**dupe** *n*

du·pli·cate¹ /ˈdjuːplɪkət ‖ ˈduː-/ *n* something that is exactly like something else in its appearance, pattern, or contents: *If you've lost your key, I can give you a duplicate.* –**duplicate** *adj* [only before a noun] : *a duplicate key*

du·pli·cate² /ˈdjuːplɪkeɪt ‖ ˈduː-/ *v* **duplicated, duplicating** [T] to copy something exactly: *The information was duplicated.* | *I'll get these notes typed up and duplicated.* –**duplication** /ˌdjuːplɪˈkeɪʃən ‖ ˌduː-/ *n* [U]

du·plic·i·ty /djuːˈplɪsəti ‖ duː-/ *n* [U] *fml* trying by words or actions to make someone believe something that is not true

dur·a·ble /ˈdjʊərəbəl ‖ ˈduː-/ *adj* lasting for a long time: *durable clothing* –**durability** /ˌdjʊərəˈbɪləti ‖ ˌduː-/ *n* [U]

du·ra·tion /djʊˈreɪʃən ‖ dʊ-/ *n* [U] the time during which something exists or lasts: *He will be in hospital for the duration of the school year.*

du·ress /djʊˈres ‖ dʊ-/ *n* [U] **under duress** as a result of illegal or unfair pressure: *His promise was made under duress.*

during /ˈdjʊərɪŋ ‖ ˈdʊ-/ *prep* **1** all through a period of time: *We go swimming every day during the summer.* | *They lived abroad during the war.* **2** at one moment in a period of time: *He died during the night.*

dusk /dʌsk/ *n* [U] the time when daylight changes to darkness: *The street lights go on at dusk.*

dusk·y /ˈdʌski/ *adj* **duskier, duskiest** quite dark in colour: *her dusky complexion*

dust¹ /dʌst/ *n* [U] **1** dry powder made up of extremely small pieces of dirt or another substance which is stated: *There was a thick layer of dust on the books.* | *gold dust* | *coal dust* **2** finely powdered earth: *The car raised a cloud of dust as it went down the dirt road.*

dust² *v* **1** [I;T] to clean the dust from something: *Please dust all the books.* | *She just hates dusting.* **2** [T] to cover something with a fine powder: *The crops were dusted with insecticide.*

dust·bin /ˈdʌstbɪn/ *n* a container with a lid, for holding waste material such as empty tins and bottles until they can be taken away

dust·cart /ˈdʌstkɑːt ‖ -kɑːrt/ *n* a large motor vehicle which goes from house to house in a town to collect the contents of dustbins

dust·er /ˈdʌstər/ *n* a cloth for dusting furniture

dust jack·et /ˈ· ˌ··/ *n* (also **dust cover**) a paper cover put as a protection round the cover of a book, often with writing or pictures describing the book

dust·man /ˈdʌstmən/ *n* **dustmen** /-mən/ someone employed to remove waste material from DUSTBINS

dust·pan /ˈdʌstpæn/ *n* a flat container with a handle into which household dust and other waste materials can be brushed

dust·up /ˈdʌst·ʌp/ *n* BrE *infml* a quarrel or fight

dust·y /ˈdʌsti/ *adj* **dustier, dustiest** covered or filled with dust: *a dusty room*

Dutch¹ /dʌtʃ/ *adj* **1** of or connected with Holland

Dutch² *n* **1 the Dutch** the people of Holland **2** the language of Holland

Dutch cour·age /ˌ· ˈ··/ *n* [U] *infml* the courage that comes from drinking alcohol

du·ti·ful /ˈdjuːtɪfəl ‖ ˈduː-/ *adj* having or showing proper respect and obedience –**dutifully** *adv*

du·ty /ˈdjuːti ‖ ˈduːti/ *n* **duties** **1** [C;U] what you must do either because of your job or because you think it is right: *His duties include taking the letters to the post and arranging meetings.* | *I feel it's my duty to help you.* | *Please report for duty tomorrow morning.* **2 duties** [pl] taxes: *Customs duties are paid on goods entering the country.* **3 off duty** not working (used of people like policemen, soldiers, or nurses): *When I'm off duty I like to play tennis.* **4 on duty** working at that particular time (used of people like policemen, soldiers, or nurses): *When does he come on duty?*

duty-bound /ˌ·· ˈ·/ *adj* [never before a noun] having to do a particular thing because it is right: *As her parents we are duty-bound to help her.*

duty-free /ˌ·· ˈ·◂/ *adj,adv* allowed to come into the country without tax: *We bought some duty-free whisky at the airport.*

du·vet /ˈduːveɪ, ˈdjuː- ‖ duːˈveɪ/ *n* a large bag filled with feathers or man-made material, used on a bed instead of other coverings

dwarf¹ /dwɔːf ‖ dwɔːrf/ *n* **dwarfs** *or* **dwarves** /dwɔːvz ‖ dwɔːrvz/ **1** a person, animal, or plant of much less than the usual size: *Without the correct treatment, the child will remain a dwarf.* | *a dwarf apple tree* **2** a small imaginary manlike creature in fairy stories: *Snow White and the Seven Dwarfs*

dwarf² *v* [T] to make something appear small by comparison: *That new skyscraper dwarfs all the surrounding buildings.*

dwell /dwel/ *v* **dwelt** /dwelt/ *or* **dwelled 1** [I + adv/prep] *lit* to live in a particular place: *They dwelt in a forest.* **2 dwell on/upon something** to think, speak, or write too much about something: *You shouldn't dwell on the past.* **3 -dweller** a person or animal that lives in the stated place: *cave-dwellers* | *city-dwellers*

dwell·ing /ˈdwelɪŋ/ *n fml* the building where people live: *Welcome to my humble dwelling!*

dwelt /dwelt/ the past tense and past participle of DWELL

dwin·dle /ˈdwɪndl/ *v* **dwindled, dwindling** [I] to become gradually fewer or smaller: *The number of people who live on the island is dwindling.* | *Her money gradually dwindled away.*

dye¹ /daɪ/ n [C;U] a vegetable or chemical substance, usually liquid, used to change the colour of things

dye² v **dyes, dyed, dyeing** [T] to make something a particular colour by means of dye: *She dyes her hair.* | *She dyed the dress red.*

dyed-in-the-wool /ˌ· · · ˈ·◄/ adj [only before a noun] impossible to change (a word used to express disapproval): *Charles is a dyed-in-the-wool Republican.*

dy·ing /ˈdaɪ-ɪŋ/ the present participle of DIE

dyke /daɪk/ n (also **dike**) 1 a thick bank or wall built to control water and prevent flooding 2 a narrow passage dug to carry water away

dy·nam·ic /daɪˈnæmɪk/ adj 1 interesting, exciting, and full of activity: *a dynamic executive* | *a dynamic period in history* 2 tech relating to a force or power that causes movement or change: *dynamic energy* −**dynamically** /-kli/ adv

dy·nam·ics /daɪˈnæmɪks/ n [U] the science that deals with movement

dy·na·mis·m /ˈdaɪnəmɪzəm/ n [U] the quality of being dynamic: *The job requires someone with energy and dynamism.*

dy·na·mite¹ /ˈdaɪnəmaɪt/ n [U] 1 a powerful explosive used in MINING 2 infml something or someone that will cause great shock, surprise, admiration: *That news story is really dynamite!*

dynamite² v **dynamited, dynamiting** [T] to blow something up with dynamite

dy·na·mo /ˈdaɪnəməʊ/ n **dynamos** a machine which turns some other kind of power into electricity

dyn·a·sty /ˈdɪnəsti ‖ ˈdaɪ-/ n **dynasties** a line of rulers all of the same family: *a dynasty of Scottish kings* −**dynastic** /dɪˈnæstɪk ‖ daɪ-/ adj

dys·en·te·ry /ˈdɪsəntəri ‖ -teri/ n [U] a painful disease of the bowels that causes them to be emptied more often than usual and to produce blood and MUCUS

dys·lex·i·a /dɪsˈleksiə/ n [U] a problem in reading caused by difficulty in seeing letter shapes −**dyslexic** adj

E,e

E, e /iː/ **E's, e's** *or* **Es, es** the 5th letter of the English alphabet

E a written abbreviation for EAST or EASTERN

each¹ /iːtʃ/ *det, pron* every single one of two or more things or people: *Each speaker will talk for ten minutes.* | *She tried to spend a few minutes with each of her guests.* | *They each want to do something different.*

each² *adv* for or to every thing or every person: *The tickets are £1 each.* | *She picked up the books and gave the children one each.*

each oth·er /ˌ·ˈ·/ *pron* used to show that two or more people do something to the others: *Susan and Robert kissed each other.* | *We all cried and hugged each other.*

ea·ger /ˈiːgəʳ/ *adj* having a strong desire to do something or a strong interest in something: *I was very eager to meet him.* | *He's eager for success.* | *crowds of eager tourists*
□ USEFUL PATTERNS be eager to do something; be eager for something –**eagerly** *adv* –**eagerness** *n* [U]

ea·gle /ˈiːgəl/ *n* a large bird which eats small animals and birds

eagle-eyed /ˌ··ˈ·◂/ *adj* noticing every small detail or mistake

ear¹ /ɪəʳ/ *n* **1** part of your body used for hearing: *Rabbits have long ears.* | *an ear infection* **2** the head of a grain-producing plant, used for food: *an ear of wheat* **3 be all ears** to be listening eagerly to someone **4 be up to your ears in something** to be very busy with something: *I'm up to my ears in work.* **5 by ear** without needing written musical notes: *Peter can play almost anything by ear.* **6 go in one ear and out the other** (of information) to be listened to but not understood or remembered **7 have an ear for** to have good recognition of sounds in music or languages: *I've got no ear for music.*

ear·ache /ˈɪəreɪk/ *n* [U] a pain inside your ear

ear·drum /ˈɪədrʌm ‖ ˈɪər-/ *n* a tight thin skin inside your ear, which allows you to hear sound

earl /ɜːl ‖ ɜːrl/ *n* the title of a British nobleman of high rank: *the Earl of Warwick* –compare COUNTESS

ear·lobe /ˈɪələub ‖ ˈɪər-/ *n* the fleshy bottom part of your ear

ear·ly /ˈɜːli ‖ ˈɜːrli/ *adj, adv* **earlier, earliest 1** before the usual or expected time: *He always arrives early.* | *The train was 10 minutes early.* **2** near the beginning of the day or a period of time: *She returned in the early morning.* | *I've got to get up early tomorrow.* | *We always go on holiday early in the season.* | *a man in his early twenties* | *We didn't need to put the chairs out because Mary had done it earlier.* **3 at the earliest** but not before that time; a phrase used when you are saying that a particular date or time is the soonest that something can happen: *The letter will reach him on Monday at the earliest.* **4 it's early days** = it is too soon to know something for certain **5 have an early night** to go to bed before your usual bedtime: *I think I'll have an early night tonight.*

ear·mark /ˈɪəmɑːk ‖ ˈɪərmɑːrk/ *v* [T] to set something aside for a particular purpose: *This money has been earmarked for a new project.*

earn /ɜːn ‖ ɜːrn/ *v* [T] **1** to get money by working: *He earns a lot of money.* **2** to get something that you

deserve because of your qualities or actions: *She earned her place in the team by training hard.* –see WIN (USAGE)

ear·nest¹ /ˈɜːnɪst ‖ ˈɜːr-/ *adj* serious and sincere (a word often used to express disapproval): *a rather earnest young man* –**earnestly** *adv*

earnest² *n* **1 be in earnest** to be serious about something: *Is he in earnest about his intention to retire?* **2 begin in earnest, start in earnest** to begin happening seriously: *I began working in earnest.*

earn·ings /ˈɜːnɪŋz ‖ ˈɜːr-/ *n* [pl] money which is earned by working

ear·phones /ˈɪəfəunz ‖ ˈɪər-/ *n* [pl] two pieces of a WALKMAN that you fit over your ears so that you can listen to music in private

ear·plug /ˈɪəplʌg ‖ ˈɪər-/ *n* a piece of soft material which you put in your ear to keep out water or noise

ear·ring /ˈɪəˌrɪŋ/ *n* a piece of jewellery that you wear on your ear –see picture on page 50

ear·shot /ˈɪəʃɒt ‖ ˈɪərʃɑːt/ *n* **within earshot** within the distance at which a sound can be heard [RELATED PHRASE **out of earshot**]

earth¹ /ɜːθ ‖ ɜːrθ/ *n* **1** [U] (also **the earth**) the world in which we live: *They returned from the moon to the earth.* | *Earth is the third planet from the sun.* | *the most beautiful woman on earth* –see LAND (USAGE) **2** [U] soil in which plants grow: *He planted the seeds in damp earth.* –see LAND (USAGE) **3** [C] *BrE* an additional safety wire which makes a connection between an electrical apparatus and the ground **4 what on earth, how on earth, who on earth, etc.** phrases used to express surprise or disapproval: *What on earth have you done to your hair?*
■ USAGE If you are using **earth** with the meaning "the world", remember to use the preposition **on**: *It's the biggest lake **on** earth.* | *We all live **on** the same earth.* If you are using **world**, remember to use the preposition **in**: *It's the biggest lake **in** the world.* | *We all live **in** the same world.*

earth² *v* [T] to make an electrical apparatus safer by connecting it to the ground with a wire

earth·en·ware /ˈɜːθənweəʳ, -ðən- ‖ ˈɜːr-/ *adj* made of baked clay: *an earthenware pot* –**earthenware** *n* [U] : *bowls and plates made of earthenware*

earth·ly /ˈɜːθli ‖ ˈɜːrθli/ *adj* [only before a noun] **1** belonging to this world as opposed to heaven: *earthly possessions* **2** *infml* a word used in questions and negatives to give force to what you are saying: *There's no earthly reason for me to go.*

earth·quake /ˈɜːθkweɪk ‖ ˈɜːrθ-/ *n* (also **quake**) a sudden violent shaking of the earth's surface: *The town was destroyed by the earthquake.*

earth·worm /ˈɜːθwɜːm ‖ ˈɜːrθwɜːrm/ *n* a worm

earth·y /ˈɜːθi ‖ ˈɜːrθi/ *adj* **1** often talking about things such as sex, which other people consider rude: *Peter has an earthy sense of humour.* **2** of or like earth: *an earthy taste* –**earthiness** *n* [U]

ear·wig /ˈɪəˌwɪg ‖ ˈɪər-/ *n* a kind of insect

ease¹ /iːz/ *n* [U] **1** lack of difficulty: *He jumped the wall with ease.* **2 a life of ease** a life in which you have plenty of money and no worries **3 at ease** feeling comfortable and confident: *He seemed totally at ease in the new surroundings.* **4 ill at ease** worried and nervous

ease² *v* **eased, easing 1** [I;T] to make or become

less severe or difficult: *I gave him some medicine to ease the pain.* | *The pain has eased.* | *Tensions in the region have eased slightly.* **2** [T] to move something carefully, slowly, and gently: *He eased the window open.*

ease off *phr v* [I] to become less severe: *The rain was beginning to ease off.*

ease up *phr v* [I] *infml* to do less of something: *I think it's time you eased up on the cigarettes.*

ea·sel /ˈiːzəl/ *n* a wooden frame to hold a BLACK-BOARD or a picture that is being painted

eas·i·ly /ˈiːzˌli/ *adv* **1** without difficulty: *I can easily finish it today.* **2** without doubt: *She is easily the cleverest girl in the class.*

east¹ /iːst/ *n* **1** [sing;U] the direction in which the sun rises **2 the east** the eastern part of a country: *Rain will spread to the east later today.* **3 the East** the countries of Asia, especially China, India, and Japan: *the mysteries of the East* **4 the East** the USSR and other countries of eastern Europe: *relations between East and West*

east² *adj* **1** (also **East**) in the east or facing east: *the east coast* **2 east wind** a wind coming from the east

east³ *adv* (also **East**) **1** towards the east: *The room faces east.* | *We travelled East.* **2** from the east (used of wind)

east·bound /ˈiːstbaʊnd/ *adj* travelling towards the east: *eastbound traffic*

Eas·ter /ˈiːstər/ *n* [U] a special Sunday in March or April when Christians remember Christ's death and his return to life; and when people give chocolate eggs as presents

Easter egg /ˈ·· ·/ *n* a chocolate egg eaten at Easter

eas·ter·ly /ˈiːstəli ‖ -ərli/ *adj* **1** towards the east: *in an easterly direction* **2** coming from the east (used of a wind)

east·ern /ˈiːstən ‖ -ərn/ *adj* (also **Eastern**) **1** belonging to the east part of a country or area: *a village in Eastern England* **2** belonging to the countries of Asia, especially India, China, and Japan: *Eastern religions* **3** belonging to the USSR and other countries in the east of Europe

east·ward /ˈiːstwəd ‖ -ərd/ *adj* going towards the east: *We set off in an eastward direction* **–eastwards** (also **eastward** *AmE*) *adv* : *We sailed eastwards.*

eas·y¹ /ˈiːzi/ *adj* **easier, easiest 1** not difficult: *an easy book* | *It's easy for us to get to London.* | *This machine is very easy to use.*
□ USEFUL PATTERNS it is easy for someone to do something; something is easy to do **2** comfortable and without worry or anxiety: *He has stopped working now, and leads a very easy life.* | *with an easy mind* **3 I'm easy** *infml* = I don't mind at all **–easiness** *n* [U]

easy² *adv* **easier, easiest 1 easier said than done** easy to talk about doing, but difficult to actually do: *Passing exams is much easier said than done.* **2 go easy on someone** to be kinder and less severe to someone **3 go easy on something** to not use too much of something **4 take it easy, take things easy** not to work too hard

easy chair /ˈ·· ˌ·/ *n* a big comfortable chair with arms

eas·y·go·ing /ˌiːziˈgəʊɪŋ◂/ *adj* not easily worried or annoyed: *He's an easygoing sort of person.*

eat /iːt/ *v* **ate** /et, eɪt ‖ eɪt/, **eaten** /ˈiːtn/ **1** [T] to take food into your mouth and swallow it: *Eat your dinner!* | *Tigers eat meat.* **2** [I] to have a meal: *What*

time do we eat? **3 be eaten up with** to be completely and violently full of feeling such as jealousy or desire **4 eat into something** to damage something by chemical action: *The acid had eaten into the metal.* **5 have someone eating out of your hand** to have someone in your power so that they will always do what you tell them to

eat sthg ↔ **away** *phr v* [T] to destroy something by chemical action

eat up *phr v* [I;T,**eat** sthg ↔ **up**] to eat all your food: *She ate up what was left of the pie.*

ea·ta·ble /ˈiːtəbəl/ *adj* fresh enough and pleasant enough to eat

eat·en /ˈiːtn/ the past participle of EAT

eat·er /ˈiːtər/ *n* a person who eats in a certain way: *He's a fussy eater.*

eau de co·logne /ˌəʊ də kəˈləʊn/ *n* [U] a kind of perfume that does not have a very strong smell

eaves /iːvz/ *n* [pl] the edges of a roof which come out beyond the walls: *birds nesting under the eaves*

eaves·drop /ˈiːvzdrɒp ‖ -drɑːp/ *v* **-pp-** [I] to listen secretly to other people's conversation: *He had eavesdropped on our conversation.* **–eaves·dropper** *n*

ebb¹ /eb/ *n* [U] **1** the flow of the sea away from the shore: *The tide is on the ebb.* **2 at a low ebb** not very happy or successful at the moment: *Fred seems to be at rather a low ebb.*

ebb² *v* [I] **1** (of the sea) to flow away from the shore **2** *lit* to become gradually weaker: *His courage slowly ebbed away.*

eb·o·ny /ˈebəni/ *n* [U] a hard black wood

e·bul·li·ence /ɪˈbʌliəns, ɪˈbʊ-/ *n* [U] *fml or lit* the quality of being full of happiness and excitement **–ebullient** *adj* : *He arrived at the party in a happy, ebullient mood.*

EC /ˌiːˈsiː/ *n* –see EEC

ec·cen·tric¹ /ɪkˈsentrɪk/ *adj* unusual and rather strange (used of a person or their behaviour): *The old lady has some eccentric habits.* **–eccentrically** /-kli/ *adv* **–eccentricity** /ˌeksenˈtrɪsˌti, -sən-/, eccentricities [C;U] : *his little eccentricities*

eccentric² *n* an unusual and rather strange person

ec·cle·si·as·tio /ɪˌkliːziˈæstɪk/ *n* a Christian priest

ec·cle·si·as·ti·cal /ɪˌkliːziˈæstɪkəl/ *adj* (also **ecclesiastic**) connected with the Christian church: *ecclesiastical history*

ech·o¹ /ˈekəʊ/ *n* **echoes** a sound sent back or repeated, for example from a wall or inside a cave

echo² *v* **echoed, echoing 1** [I] to come back as an echo: *Their voices echoed round the cave.* **2** [T] to repeat what someone else has said: *His laughter was echoed by the others in the room.* **3 echo with** to be full of a sound: *The room echoed with the sound of music.*

é·clair /ɪˈkleər, eɪ-/ *n* a finger-shaped pastry with a cream filling inside

e·clipse¹ /ɪˈklɪps/ *n* **1** [C] the disappearance of the sun's light when the moon passes between it and the earth **2** [C;U] the loss of fame, power, or success

eclipse² *v* **eclipsed, eclipsing** [T] **1** to cause an eclipse of the sun or moon: *The moon is partly eclipsed.* **2** to be much better than someone else, with the result that they seem unimportant

e·col·o·gy /ɪˈkɒlədʒi ‖ ɪˈkɑː-/ *n* [U] **1** the pattern of the natural relations of plants, animals, and people to each other and to their surroundings: *the ecology of the rainforest* **2** the study of ecology **–ecologist** *n*

e·col·o·gi·cal /ˌiːkəˈlɒdʒɪkəl ‖ -ˈlɑː-/ adj relating to the ecology of a place and the protection of the plants and animals that are there: *the ecological balance of the rainforests* | *Experts have described the oil slick as an ecological disaster.* –**ecologically** /-kli/ adv

ec·o·nom·ic /ˌekəˈnɒmɪk◂, ˌiː- ‖ -ˈnɑː-/ adj 1 [only before a noun] connected with trade, industry, and wealth: *The country is heading for economic disaster.* 2 likely to bring a profit: *It's no longer economic to run trains to the village.*

ec·o·nom·i·cal /ˌekəˈnɒmɪkəl, ˌiː- ‖ -ˈnɑː-/ adj 1 not costing a lot of money to use: *A small car is more economical than a large one.* 2 using only the amount that is necessary, without waste: *an economical use of time*

ec·o·nom·i·cal·ly /ˌekəˈnɒmɪkli, ˌiː- ‖ -ˈnɑː-/ adv 1 not wastefully: *She cooks very economically.* 2 in a way which produces a profit: *Is the company economically viable?*

ec·o·nom·ics /ˌekəˈnɒmɪks, ˌiː- ‖ -ˈnɑː-/ n [pl;U] the science or principles of the way in which industry and trade produce and use wealth: *The economics of national growth are of great importance to all governments.* | *He has a degree in economics.* –**economist** /ɪˈkɒnəmɪst ‖ ɪˈkɑː-/ n

e·con·o·mize /ɪˈkɒnəmaɪz ‖ ɪˈkɑː-/ v (also **economise** BrE) [I] to save money, time, or goods by using them sensibly: *We could economize on petrol by all going in one car.*

e·con·o·my [1] /ɪˈkɒnəmi ‖ ɪˈkɑː-/ n **economies** 1 [C] the system by which a country's money supply, industry, and trade are organized: *A new government might improve the state of the economy.* 2 [C;U] the careful use of money, time, or goods: *economy of effort* | *We will have to make some economies.*

economy [2] adj [only before a noun] cheap or intended to save money: *an economy class air ticket*

ec·sta·sy /ˈekstəsi/ n **ecstasies** 1 [U] a feeling of very great happiness: *an expression of ecstasy* 2 **go into ecstasies** to show that you are very pleased about something

ec·stat·ic /ɪkˈstætɪk, ek-/ adj feeling very happy: *She was ecstatic when I told her the news.* –**ecstatically** /-kli/ adv

e·cu·men·i·cal /ˌiːkjʊˈmenɪkəl ‖ ˌek-/ adj favouring unity between the different branches of the Christian religion

ec·ze·ma /ˈeksᵻmə ‖ ˈeksᵻmə, ˈegzᵻmə, ɪgˈziːmə/ n [U] a medical condition in which your skin is red and swollen

ed·dy /ˈedi/ n **eddies** a circular movement of water, wind, smoke, dust, or air

edge [1] /edʒ/ n 1 the part along the outside of something: *the edge of a plate* | *the water's edge* 2 the point at which something begins to happen: *This brought us to the edge of disaster.* 3 the thin sharp cutting part of a blade or tool: 4 **have the edge on** to be better than someone or have an advantage over them: *He has the edge on the other students because he works harder.* 5 **on edge** nervous and worried 6 **-edged** having a certain kind or number of edges: *a two-edged sword*

edge [2] v **edged, edging** 1 [T] to place an edge or border on something: *a white handkerchief edged with blue* 2 [I + adv/prep;T + adv/prep] to move very slowly: *He edged away.* | *She edged her chair closer to mine.*

edge·ways /ˈedʒweɪz/ adv 1 sideways 2 I

couldn't get a word in edgeways = I couldn't say anything because someone else was talking all the time

edg·ing /ˈedʒɪŋ/ n something that forms an edge or border: *a white handkerchief with a blue edging*

edg·y /ˈedʒi/ adj infml nervous: *She's been a bit edgy lately, waiting for the examination results.*

ed·i·ble /ˈedᵻbəl/ adj able to be eaten safely: *Can you tell the difference between edible and poisonous berries?* –opposite **inedible**

e·dict /ˈiːdɪkt/ n fml an official public order made by a person in power

ed·i·fice /ˈedᵻfᵻs/ n fml a large fine building

ed·i·fy /ˈedᵻfaɪ/ v **edified, edifying** [T] fml to improve someone's mind or character: *He always reads edifying books.* –**edification** /ˌedᵻfᵻˈkeɪʃən/ n [U]

ed·it /ˈedᵻt/ v [T] to prepare a book, newspaper, or film for printing or showing by removing mistakes and deciding what parts should be included or left out

e·di·tion /ɪˈdɪʃən/ n one printing of a book, newspaper, or magazine: *a new edition of the dictionary*

ed·i·tor /ˈedᵻtəʳ/ n 1 a person who edits something such as a book, newspaper article, or film before it is printed or shown 2 a person in charge of a newspaper or magazine: *the editor of the Daily Mail*

ed·i·to·ri·al [1] /ˌedᵻˈtɔːriəl/ adj belonging to or done by an editor: *an editorial office* –**editorially** adv

editorial [2] n a part of a newspaper giving the editor's opinion on a problem or event

ed·u·cate /ˈedjʊkeɪt ‖ ˈedʒə-/ v **educated, educating** [T] to teach someone, especially in a school or college: *He was educated at a very good school.* | *We need to educate the public about the dangers of smoking.* –**educated** adj : *an educated man* | *educated tastes in art and literature*

ed·u·ca·tion /ˌedjʊˈkeɪʃən ‖ ˌedʒə-/ n [U] the process of teaching people, especially in a school or college: *She has had a good education.* | *This government believes in the importance of education.*

ed·u·ca·tion·al /ˌedjʊˈkeɪʃənəl ‖ ˌedʒə-/ adj 1 of or about education: *an educational establishment* 2 providing information or teaching you something: *an educational film* –**educationally** adv

ed·u·ca·tion·ist /ˌedjʊˈkeɪʃənɪst ‖ ˌedʒə-/ n (also **educationalist**) a specialist in education

EEC /ˌiː iː ˈsiː/ n (also **EC**) a European organization established to encourage trade and friendly relations between its members; an abbreviation for European Economic Community

eel /iːl/ n a long snake-like fish

ee·rie /ˈɪəri/ adj strange and frightening: *walking through the dark, eerie woods* –**eerily** adv –**eeriness** n [U]

ef·face /ɪˈfeɪs/ v **effaced, effacing** [T] fml to rub something out or remove it: *Someone has effaced part of the address on this letter.*

ef·fect [1] /ɪˈfekt/ n 1 [C;U] a result: *the effects of an illness* | *The advertising campaign didn't have much effect on sales.* 2 **effects** fml belongings: *No personal effects are to be left here overnight.* 3 **in effect:** **a** in operation: *The rules will remain in effect until October.* **b** in fact: *Although she's his assistant, she has, in effect, full control.* 4 **come into effect** to come into operation: *The rule will come into effect on Monday.* [RELATED PHRASES **be brought**

into effect; be put into effect; go into effect] **5 take effect** to come into operation or start to have results: *The new tax system will take effect next May.* | *The medicine quickly took effect.* **6 to this effect, to that effect, to the effect that…** with this meaning: *He called me a fool or words to that effect.*

effect² *v* [T] *fml* to cause something to happen: *I want to effect changes in the management structure of the company.* –see AFFECT (USAGE)

ef·fec·tive /ɪˈfektɪv/ *adj* **1** producing the desired result: *His efforts to improve the school have been very effective.* –opposite **ineffective** **2** actual or real: *Although there is a parliament, the army is in effective control of the country.* –**effectively** *adv* –**effectiveness** *n* [U]

ef·fec·tu·al /ɪˈfektʃuəl/ *adj fml* producing the results intended: *Measures to combat unemployment have not been very effectual.* –opposite **ineffectual**

ef·fem·i·nate /ɪˈfemɪnət/ *adj* looking or behaving like a woman (used of men, usually to express disapproval) –**effeminacy** *n* [U]

ef·fer·vesc·ent /ˌefəˈvesənt◄ ‖ ˌefər-/ *adj fml* **1** forming BUBBLES inside (used of liquids) **2** full of life and excitement (used of people) –**effervescence** *n* [U]

ef·fi·ca·cious /ˌefɪˈkeɪʃəs/ *adj fml* producing the desired effect (used especially of medicines) –**efficacy** /ˈefɪkəsi/ *n* [U]

ef·fi·cient /ɪˈfɪʃənt/ *adj* working well, quickly, and without waste: *She is a quick, efficient worker.* | *This new machine is more efficient than the old one.* –opposite **inefficient** –**efficiently** *adv* –**efficiency** *n* [U] : *attempts to improve efficiency*

ef·fi·gy /ˈefɪdʒi/ *n* **effigies** *fml* the face or head and body of someone, usually cut out of wood or stone: *an effigy of Christ*

ef·flu·ent /ˈefluənt/ *n* [C;U] *tech* chemical waste or SEWAGE that flows out from a factory or similar place; *Dangerous effluent is being poured into our rivers.* –see picture on page 246

ef·fort /ˈefət ‖ ˈefərt/ *n* **1** [U] the use of strength or determination: *It took a lot of effort to lift the boxes.* | *We managed to do it without much effort.* **2 an effort** something which needs strength or determination to do: *It was an effort to get up this morning.* **3** [C] an attempt to do something, especially one done with a lot of determination: *Despite all our efforts, we failed.* **4 make an effort to do something** to try very hard to do something: *He made an effort to arrive on time.*

ef·fort·less /ˈefətləs ‖ ˈefərt-/ *adj* seeming to need very little effort: *She skis with such effortless ease.* –**effortlessly** *adv*

ef·fron·te·ry /ɪˈfrʌntəri/ *n* [U] bold or rude behaviour

ef·fu·sive /ɪˈfjuːsɪv/ *adj* showing too much pleasure or thanks: *I was taken aback by her effusive welcome.*

EFL /ˌiː ef ˈel/ *n* relating to the teaching of English to people whose first language is not English; an abbreviation for **English as a foreign language**

e.g. /ˌiː ˈdʒiː/ for example; an abbreviation for the Latin words **exempli gratia**: *sweet foods, e.g. cake, chocolate, sugar, and ice cream*

e·gal·i·tar·i·an /ɪˌɡælɪˈteəriən/ *adj fml* having the belief that all people are equal and should have equal rights

egg¹ /eɡ/ *n* **1** [C;U] a rounded object with a hard shell, which can contain a baby bird, insect, or snake; eggs are often eaten as food: *Each female lays five or six eggs.* | *I never eat bacon and egg.* | *A dozen eggs, please.* –see picture on page 344 **2** [C] a cell produced inside a female that can develop into a baby if it joins with the male SPERM **3 put all your eggs in one basket** *infml* to risk everything you have on the success of one thing

egg² *v*

egg sbdy ↔ **on** *phr v* [T] to give someone encouragement to do something foolish or daring: *I didn't mean to do it. The others just egged me on.*

egg·beat·er /ˈeɡbiːtər/ *n* a kitchen tool with a turning handle, used for mixing –see picture on page 638

egg·cup /ˈeɡ-kʌp/ *n* a small container which you put a boiled egg in so that you can eat it easily

egg·head /ˈeɡhed/ *n* a person who is very highly educated but not very good at practical things

egg·shell /ˈeɡʃel/ *n* the thin hard part around the outside of an egg

egg·plant /ˈeɡplɑːnt ‖ ˈeɡplænt/ *n AmE* [C;U] a plant that has a large purple fruit which is eaten as a vegetable

e·go /ˈiːɡəʊ, ˈeɡəʊ/ *n* your opinion of your own importance: *It was quite a blow to her ego when she failed her driving test.*

e·go·cen·tric /ˌiːɡəʊˈsentrɪk, ˌe-/ *adj* thinking only about yourself and what you want (a word used to express disapproval)

e·go·is·m /ˈiːɡəʊɪzəm, ˈe-/ *n* [U] behaviour that shows that you are always thinking about yourself and not other people (a word used to express disapproval) –**egoist** *n* –**egoistic** /ˌiːɡəʊˈɪstɪk, ˌe-/ *adj*

eg·o·tis·m /ˈeɡətɪzəm, ˈiː- ‖ ˈiː-/ *n* [U] the tendency to talk too much about yourself and to believe that you are better and more important than other people (a word used to express disapproval) –**egotist** *n* –**egotistic** /ˌiːɡəʊˈtɪstɪk, ˌi- ‖ ˌiː-/ *adj*

ei·der·down /ˈaɪdədaʊn ‖ -dər-/ *n* a thick warm bed covering filled with feathers or soft material

eight /eɪt/ *det, n, pron* the number 8

eigh·teen /ˌeɪˈtiːn◄/ *det, n, pron* the number 18 –**eighteenth** *det, n, pron, adv*

eighth /eɪtθ/ **1** *det, pron, adv* 8th **2** *n* one of eight equal parts

eigh·ty /ˈeɪti/ *det, n, pron* **eighties 1** the number 80 **2 the Eighties, the eighties** the years 1980–1989 **3 in his eighties, in their eighties,** etc. aged between 80 and 89 –**eightieth** /ˈeɪtiɪθ/ *det, n, pron, adv*

ei·ther¹ /ˈaɪðər ‖ ˈiː-/ *det,pron* **1** one or the other of two people or things: *There's coffee or tea-you can have either.* | *Is either of the boys coming?* **2** both of two things: *He sat in the car with a policeman on either side of him.*

■ USAGE In the sentence *Is either of you ready?* the pronoun **either** is used with the singular verb *is*. This is the usual pattern in formal writing, but in speech and informal writing many people use a plural verb: *Are either of you ready?* (The same is true for **neither** and **none**.)

either² *conj* used at the beginning or a list of possibilities; the other possibilities are introduced by "or": *The baby will be born either at home or in the local hospital.* | *Either say you're sorry or get out!* | *It was either in 1964, 1965, or 1966 – I can't remember.*

■ USAGE **Either…or** and **neither…nor** are usually followed by a plural verb and a plural pronoun, except in formal English: *If either John or Mary are here, they will get the message.* In formal English this would be *If either John or Mary is here, he or she will get the message.* (The same is true for **neither…nor**.)

either³ /adv [used with negatives] also; you use "either" when you add another negative idea: *I haven't read this book, and none of the other students has either.* | *"I can't swim," "I can't either."*

e·jac·u·late /ı'dʒækjɣleıt/ v **ejaculated, ejaculating** [I;T] **1** *fml* to say or shout something suddenly **2** to let out SEMEN suddenly and with force through the PENIS –**ejaculation** /ı.dʒækjɣ'leıʃən/ n [C;U]

e·ject /ı'dʒekt/ v [T] *fml* to push or throw someone or something out with force: *Two boys were ejected from the cinema by the police last night.* –**ejection** /ı'dʒekʃən/ n [C;U]

eke /iːk/ v **eked, eking**
eke sthg ↔ **out** *phr* v [T] to make a small supply last as long as possible: *During the war we had to eke out our food rations.*

e·lab·o·rate¹ /ı'læbərət/ adj full of detail with a large number of parts or very carefully planned: *She wore an elaborate costume.* | *Elaborate precautions were taken to ensure her safety.* –**elaborately** adv

e·lab·o·rate² /ı'læbəreıt/ v **elaborated, elaborating** [I;T] *fml* to add more detail to something so that it is easier to understand: *Would you care to elaborate a little on what you have already said?*

e·lapse /ı'læps/ v **elapsed, elapsing** [I] *fml* (of time) to pass: *A month elapsed before they could make a final decision.*

e·las·tic¹ /ı'læstık/ n [U] a long thin piece of rubber material which springs back into shape after being stretched; elastic is often used in clothing, for example round the waist

elastic adj **1** able to spring back into shape after being stretched: *The skirt had an elastic waistband.* **2** able to change if the situation changes: *The rules are elastic.* –**elasticity** /ˌiːlæ'stısɣti/ n [U]

elastic band /·ˌ·· '·/ n a thin piece of elastic which is used to hold things together

e·lat·ed /ı'leıtɣd/ adj very happy and excited: *The crowds were elated by the appearance of the new president.* –**elation** /ı'leıʃən/ n [U]

el·bow¹ /'elbəʊ/ n **1** the joint in the middle of your arm where it bends **2** the part of a shirt, or coat which covers the middle part of your arm

elbow² v [T + adv/prep] to push someone away with the middle part of your arm bent in front of you: *He elbowed his way through the crowd.*

el·bow·room /'elbəʊrʊm, -ruːm/ n [U] freedom to move or do as you want to

el·der¹ /'eldəʳ/ adj [only before a noun] the older of two people in a family: *My elder brother is a nurse.* | *My elder daughter is married.*

■ USAGE Compare **elder** and **older**. We use **elder** only to talk about people in families and we do not use it in comparisons. We use **older** to make comparisons between all kinds of people and things: *Mary is Tom's* **elder** *sister.* | *Mary is* **older** *than Tom.*

elder² n **1** the older of two people: *Which is the elder of the two sisters?* **2** older people: *As children, we were taught to respect our elders.* **3** someone holding a respected official position: *a Church elder* **4** a small tree with white flowers and red or black berries

el·der·ly /'eldəli ‖ 'eldərli/ adj *euph* **1** old (a more polite word for **old**): *My father is getting rather elderly.* **2** **the elderly** old people in general (a more polite expression than "old people")

el·dest /'eldɣst/ n the person in a family who is the oldest of three or more: *She has three children, and her eldest has just started school.* –**eldest** adj

e·lect¹ /ı'lekt/ v [T] **1** to choose someone for an official position by voting: *She was elected treasurer.* | *John Major has been elected* as *leader of the Conservative Party.* | *They elected her to represent them on the committee.*
□ USEFUL PATTERNS to elect someone; to elect someone as something; to elect someone to do something
2 elect to do something *fml* to decide to do something: *She elected to return to work after her baby was born.*

elect² adj [only after a noun] *fml* chosen for a position, but not yet officially in it: *the president elect*

e·lec·tion /ı'lekʃən/ n [C;U] a process in which you choose someone to represent you, or for an official position by voting for them: *Have you heard the election results?* | *Representatives are chosen by election.* | *She's standing for election.* | *Labour did badly in the last election.*

elec·tor /ı'lektəʳ/ n someone who has the right to vote in an election –**electoral** adj : *Have you checked that your name is on the electoral roll?*

e·lec·to·rate /ı'lektərɣt/ n [+sing/pl verb] all the people in a country or in an area who have the right to vote in an election

e·lec·tric /ı'lektrık/ adj **1** worked by electricity: *an electric cooker* | *an electric razor* **2** producing, produced by, or carrying electricity: *an electric plug* | *an electric generator* **3** very exciting: *The atmosphere at the concert was electric.*

■ USAGE Compare **electric** and **electrical**. **Electric** has a more direct association with electricity. We use **electric** for things that produce electricity: *an* **electric** *generator*, things directly produced by electricity: *an* **electric** *shock* | *an* **electric** *spark* and particular types of machines worked by electricity: *an* **electric** *clock* | *an* **electric** *light*. We use **electrical** for people: *an* **electrical** *engineer* or things associated with electricity in a general way: **electrical** *apparatus* | *an* **electrical** *fault in the system.*

e·lec·tri·cal /ı'lektrıkəl/ adj concerned with or using electricity: *an electrical engineer* | *an electrical fault* –compare ELECTRIC –see ELECTRIC (USAGE) –**electrically** /-kli/ adv : *an electrically powered motor*

electric chair /·ˌ·· '·/ n (also **the chair** *infml*) a punishment of death, used in some states of the US, in which a person is tied to a chair and is killed by a powerful electric current

electric shock /·ˌ·· '·/ n a sudden feeling of pain caused by touching something which has electricity flowing through it

el·ec·tri·cian /ı.lek'trıʃən/ n someone whose job is to fit and repair electrical machinery

e·lec·tri·ci·ty /ı.lek'trısɣti/ n [U] the power which is used for heating, lighting, and making some machines work

e·lec·tri·fy /ı'lektrɣfaı/ v **electrified, electrifying** [T] **1** to change something to a system using electric power: *The national railways have now been electrified.* **2** to excite or surprise someone very much: *The band gave an electrifying performance.* –**electrification** /ı.lektrɣfɣ'keıʃən/ n [U]

e·lec·tro·cute /ı'lektrəkjuːt/ v **electrocuted, electrocuting** [T] to kill someone by passing an electric current through their body –**electrocution** /ı.lektrə'kjuːʃən/ n [C;U]

e·lec·trode /ɪ'lektrəʊd/ n tech a small piece of metal that carries an electric current to or from electrical apparatus

e·lec·tron /ɪ'lektrɒn ‖ -trɑːn/ n tech one of the parts of an atom that has a NEGATIVE electric charge

el·ec·tron·ic /ɪˌlek'trɒnɪk ‖ -'trɑː-/ adj relating to machinery such as radios, television, and computers, which work by means of an electric current passing through different parts of them –**electronically** /-klɪ/ adv

e·lec·tron·ics /ɪˌlek'trɒnɪks ‖ -'trɑː-/ n [U] the study or making of machinery that works electronically: the electronics industry

el·e·gant /'eləgənt/ adj with a pleasing and stylish appearance: an elegant woman | an elegant piece of furniture –opposite **inelegant** –**elegantly** adv –**elegance** n [U]

el·e·gy /'elədʒi/ n elegies a sad poem or song for someone who has died

el·e·ment /'eləmənt/ n 1 tech a substance that consists of only one type of atom 2 **an element of** a small amount of something: There is an element of truth in what you say. 3 a part of a whole: Publicizing the company is an important element of the job. 4 the metal part of a piece of electrical apparatus which changes the electric current into heat 5 **the elements** the weather, especially bad conditions: Shall we brave the elements and go for a walk? 6 a group of people with similar aims or beliefs: The rowdy element in the class spoils things for the rest. 7 **in your element** doing what you are happiest doing

el·e·men·tal /ˌelə'mentl◄/ adj like the powerful forces of nature

el·e·men·ta·ry /ˌelə'mentəri◄/ adj 1 simple and easy 2 concerned with the most simple rules and methods: some elementary exercises for the piano

el·e·phant /'eləfənt/ n a very large grey animal, with a long nose called a TRUNK

el·e·vate /'eləveɪt/ v elevated, elevating [T] 1 to make your mind or soul better or more educated: an elevating experience | Can't you read something more elevating than those silly romantic novels? 2 fml to raise something or someone to a higher position: He was elevated to the rank of captain

el·e·va·ted /'eləveɪtɪd/ adj in a high position

el·e·va·tion /ˌelə'veɪʃən/ n 1 [sing] a particular height above sea-level: The ski resort is at an elevation of 3000 metres. 2 [C] tech a drawing of the front, back, or side of a building: the front elevation of a house 3 [U] fml the act of raising someone to a higher position: His elevation to First Secretary was announced yesterday.

el·e·va·tor /'eləveɪtər/ n the usual American word for LIFT

e·lev·en /ɪ'levən/ det, n, pron the number 11 –**eleventh** det, n, pron, adv

eleventh hour /·ˌ··· '·-/ n the eleventh hour the very last moment: War, which had seemed certain, was averted at the eleventh hour.

elf /elf/ n elves /elvz/ a small fairy with pointed ears –**elfin** /'elfɪn/ adj

e·li·cit /ɪ'lɪsɪt/ v [T] fml to get information from someone by asking questions

el·i·gi·ble /'elədʒəbəl/ adj 1 [never before a noun] legally allowed to do or receive something: He will become eligible to vote on his next birthday. | She is eligible for sickness pay? 2 suitable as a marriage partner: The hostess introduced me to an extremely eligible bachelor. –**eligibility** /ˌelədʒə'bɪləti/ n [U]

e·lim·i·nate /ɪ'lɪmɪneɪt/ v eliminated, eliminating [T] 1 to get rid of something: Waste matter is regularly eliminated from the body. 2 to lose a round in a competition and stop taking part: He was eliminated in the quarter-finals. –**elimination** /ɪˌlɪmɪ'neɪʃən/ n [U]

e·lite /eɪ'liːt, ɪ-/ n [+sing/pl verb] a small group of people considered the most important because they are very rich, powerful, or clever: the aristocratic elite

e·lit·is·m /eɪ'liːtɪzəm, ɪ-/ n [U] belief in a system that gives advantages to an elite social group –**elitist** adj

e·lix·ir /ɪ'lɪksər/ n lit an imaginary liquid having the power to change ordinary metals into gold, or make a person live for ever

elk /elk/ n a very large deer, with big flat branching horns called ANTLERS

el·lip·tical /ɪ'lɪptɪkəl/ adj (also **elliptic**) 1 having the curved shape of a circle when you look at it sideways: The Earth's path round the sun is elliptical. 2 a style of writing or speaking that leaves out some words or meaning –**elliptically** /-klɪ/ adv

elm /elm/ n [C;U] a tall broad-leaved tree which produces hard heavy wood

el·o·cu·tion /ˌelə'kjuːʃən/ n [U] the art of speaking well and clearly in public

e·lon·gated /'iːlɒŋgeɪtɪd ‖ ɪ'lɔːŋ-/ adj long and thin

e·lope /ɪ'ləʊp/ v eloped, eloping [I] to run away secretly with a lover and get married: She eloped with her tutor. –**elopement** n [C;U]

el·o·quent /'eləkwənt/ adj fml able to express ideas and opinions well, so that the hearers are influenced: He's an eloquent speaker. –**eloquently** adv –**eloquence** n [U]

else /els/ adv 1 a word you use to refer to people or things besides the ones that have already been mentioned: Who else would like a drink? | If you don't like it here, you'd better go somewhere else. | Apart from John, there was nobody else there that I knew. | I'm afraid there's nothing else to eat. | She looked odd, as if she was wearing someone else's clothes. | **or else:** a a phrase you use when you are saying what might happen if someone does not do what you suggest: You'd better leave now, or else you'll miss your train. | Pay me now, or else there'll be trouble! b a phrase you use when you are giving a second possibility: Perhaps he's still at work, or else in a pub somewhere.

else·where /els'weər, 'elsweər ‖ 'elsweər/ adv in or to another place: The effects of the war will be felt in this country and elsewhere. | If you don't like my food, you can go elsewhere to eat!

ELT /ˌiː el 'tiː/ n the principles and practice of teaching English to speakers of other languages; an abbreviation for **English Language Teaching**

e·lu·ci·date /ɪ'luːsɪdeɪt/ v elucidated, elucidating [T] fml to make something clear by explaining it fully

e·lude /ɪ'luːd/ v eluded, eluding [T] 1 **it eludes me** = I cannot remember or understand it: The meaning of his speech eludes me. | His name eludes me for the moment. 2 to avoid or escape from someone, especially by means of a trick: The fox eluded the hunters.

e·lu·sive /ɪ'luːsɪv/ adj difficult to find or remember: I've been trying to get him on the phone, but he's very elusive. –**elusively** adv –**elusiveness** n [U]

elves /elvz/ the plural of ELF

'em /əm/ *pron infml* short for THEM

e·ma·ci·at·ed /ɪˈmeɪʃieɪtɪd/ *adj* very thin and weak because of illness or lack of food —see THIN¹ (USAGE) **–emaciation** /ɪˌmeɪsiˈeɪʃən/ *n* [U]

em·a·nate /ˈeməneɪt/ *v* emanated, emanating **emanate from** to come from: *Do you know where these rumours emanate from?*

e·man·ci·pate /ɪˈmænsɪpeɪt/ *v fml* emancipated, emancipating [T] to make someone free socially, politically, or legally **–emancipation** /ɪˌmænsɪˈpeɪʃən/ *n* [U] : *the emancipation of women | emancipation from slavery*

em·balm /ɪmˈbɑːm ‖ -ˈbɑːm, -ˈbɑːlm/ *v* [T] to put chemicals and oils on a dead body to prevent its decay

em·bank·ment /ɪmˈbæŋkmənt/ *n* a wide wall which is built to keep water back or to carry a road or railway over low ground: *The Thames Embankment*

em·bar·go¹ /ɪmˈbɑːɡəʊ ‖ -ɑːr-/ *n* embargoes an official order to stop trade with another country: *an oil embargo | They've decided to lift the embargo on meat imports from Europe.*

embargo² *v* embargoed, embargoing [T] to officially stop trade with another country

em·bark /ɪmˈbɑːk ‖ -ɑːrk/ *v* [I] **1** to get on a ship before the start of its voyage: *We embarked at Southampton, and disembarked in New York a week later.* **2 embark on something** to start something new, difficult, or exciting: *Haven't you left it rather late to embark on a new career?* **–embarkation** /ˌembɑːˈkeɪʃən ‖ -ɑːr-/ *n* [C;U] : *the port of embarkation*

em·bar·rass /ɪmˈbærəs/ *v* [T] to make someone feel ashamed or uncomfortable in front of other people **–embarrassment** *n* [C;U] : *He could not hide his embarrassment.*

em·bar·rassed /ɪmˈbærəst/ *adj* ashamed, nervous, or uncomfortable in front of other people: *I feel so embarrassed when I think of how I behaved. | He was too embarrassed to ask her to the cinema.*

em·bar·rass·ing /ɪmˈbærəsɪŋ/ *adj* making you feel ashamed: *It was a very embarrassing incident.*

em·bas·sy /ˈembəsi/ *n* embassies a group of officials living in a foreign country and led by an AMBASSADOR, who represent their government and try to keep good relations between the two countries; **embassy** can also be used for the building where these officials work

em·bat·tled /ɪmˈbætld/ *adj* continually troubled by problems: *He's leading an increasingly embattled Labour Party.*

em·bed·ded /ɪmˈbedɪd/ *adj* fixed firmly and deeply: *He found his bucket firmly embedded in the new concrete.*

em·bel·lish /ɪmˈbelɪʃ/ *v* [T] **1** to add decorations in order to make something more beautiful: *a white hat embellished with pink roses* **2** to add details which may not be true to a story to make it more interesting **–embellishment** *n* [C;U]

em·ber /ˈembər/ *n* embers red-hot pieces of wood or coal that remain in a fire when there are no more flames

em·bez·zle /ɪmˈbezəl/ *v* embezzled, embezzling [T] to steal money that has been put into your care when it really belongs to the company or organization that you work for **–embezzlement** *n* [U]

em·bit·tered /ɪmˈbɪtəd/ *adj* feeling angry, sad, or bitter about what has happened to you: *a lonely and embittered man*

em·bla·zon /ɪmˈbleɪzən/ *v* [T] to decorate a shield or flag with a COAT OF ARMS

em·blem /ˈembləm/ *n* an object which is the sign of something: *The national emblem of England is a rose.* **–emblematic** /ˌembləˈmætɪk◂/ *adj*

em·bod·y /ɪmˈbɒdi ‖ ɪmˈbɑːdi/ *v* embodied, embodying [T] **1** *fml* to contain or include something **2** to express an idea or quality in something physical: *The ideals of freedom and equality are embodied in the constitution.* **–embodiment** *n* : *He was regarded by his enemies as the embodiment of evil.*

em·boss /ɪmˈbɒs ‖ ɪmˈbɑːs, -ˈbɔːs/ *v* [T] to decorate something with a raised pattern: *The name and address of the firm are embossed on its paper.*

em·brace¹ /ɪmˈbreɪs/ *v* embraced, embracing **1** [I;T] to take and hold someone as a sign of love: *The two sisters embraced. | She embraced her son tenderly.* **2** [T] *fml* to include something: *This course of study embraces every aspect of the subject.* **3** [T] *fml* to become a believer in a religion or political system

embrace² *n* the holding of someone close to you as a sign of love

em·broi·der /ɪmˈbrɔɪdər/ *v* [T] **1** to do decorative work with a needle on cloth: *a dress embroidered with flowers* **2** to add imaginary details to a story to make it more exciting: *Don't embroider the truth!*

em·broi·der·y /ɪmˈbrɔɪdəri/ *n* [C;U] decorative work done with a needle on cloth or the action of doing this

em·broiled /ɪmˈbrɔɪld/ *adj* **get/become embroiled in something** to become part of a difficult situation: *I refused to get embroiled in their quarrel.*

em·bry·o /ˈembriəʊ/ *n* **1** the young of any creature in its first state before it is born **2 in embryo** still being developed **–embryonic** /ˌembriˈɒnɪk◂ ‖ -ˈɑːnɪk/ *adj*

em·e·rald /ˈemərəld/ *n* a bright green precious stone **–emerald** *adj*

e·merge /ɪˈmɜːdʒ ‖ -ɜːr-/ *v* emerged, emerging [I] **1** to come or appear from out of somewhere hidden: *The sun emerged from behind the clouds.* **2** to become known: *The facts began to emerge.* **3 it emerged that** = it became known as the result of an enquiry: *It emerged that the driver of the car had been drunk.* **4** to come out from a difficult situation: *The President has emerged from the incident with his reputation intact.* **–emergence** *n* [U] *fml*

e·mer·gen·cy /ɪˈmɜːdʒənsi ‖ -ɜːr-/ *n* emergencies an unexpected and dangerous situation which must be dealt with quickly: *Ring the bell in an emergency. | an emergency exit*

emergency brake /·ˈ··· ˌ·/ *n* the usual American word for the HANDBRAKE in a car

e·mer·gent /ɪˈmɜːdʒənt ‖ -ɜːr-/ *adj* [only before a noun] in the early stages of existence or development: *the emergent countries of Africa*

em·i·grate /ˈeməɡreɪt/ *v* emigrated, emigrating [I] to leave your own country in order to go and live in another country: *They emigrated to Australia in 1960.* **–emigrant** *n* **–emigration** /ˌeməˈɡreɪʃən/ *n*

■ USAGE Compare **emigrate** and **immigrate**. People **emigrate** if they leave their own country and go to live in another: *He couldn't find work in his own country so he decided to emigrate.* These people are **emigrants** and their action is **emigration**. People **immigrate** if they come to live in a country from another. The verb **immigrate** is rare, but the nouns **immigrant** and **immigration** are common: *an illegal* **immigrant** | *The government is trying to reduce* **immigration** *from countries outside Europe.*

ém·i·gré /'emɪɡreɪ/ *n* someone who leaves their own country for political reasons

em·i·nent /'emɪnənt/ *adj* famous and admired (used of people): *an eminent doctor* **–eminence** *n* [U]

em·i·nent·ly /'emɪnəntli/ *adv fml* very: *Your decision was eminently fair.*

em·is·sa·ry /'emɪsəri || -seri/ *n* **emissaries** *fml* a person who is sent from one government to another with an official message

e·mit /ɪ'mɪt/ *v* -tt- [T] *fml* to send out heat, light, smell, or sound: *The chimney emitted smoke.* **–emission** /ɪ'mɪʃən/ *n* [C;U]: *We must try to reduce emissions from power stations.*

e·mol·u·ments /ɪ'mɒljumənts || ɪ'mɑː-/ *n fml* [pl] money received for work

e·mo·tion /ɪ'məuʃən/ *n* [C;U] a strong feeling: *Love and hatred are basic emotions.* | *His voice was shaking with emotion.* **–emotionless** *adj*

e·mo·tion·al /ɪ'məuʃənəl/ *adj* **1** having strong feelings and showing them, often by crying: *He became very emotional when she said she would leave.* **–opposite unemotional 2** causing you to cry: *an emotional film* **3** relating to a person's emotions: *The child's bad behaviour is a result of emotional problems.* **–emotionally** *adv*

e·mo·tive /ɪ'məutɪv/ *adj* causing strong feeling: *Capital punishment is a very emotive issue.*

em·pa·thy /'empəθi/ *n* [U] the ability to imagine and experience someone else's feelings

em·pe·ror /'empərər/ *n* the ruler of an empire

em·pha·sis /'emfəsɪs/ *n* **emphases** /-siːz/ [C;U] special force given to something to show that it is particularly important: *The boss lays great emphasis on politeness and punctuality.* **–see EMPHASIZE (USAGE)**

em·pha·size /'emfəsaɪz/ *v* **emphasized, emphasizing** (also **emphasise** *BrE*) [T;+that] to put special force or importance on something: *I must emphasize the fact that they are only children.*
■ **USAGE** Remember that the verb **emphasize** is transitive and is NOT, therefore, followed by a preposition. (The noun **emphasis** is followed by the preposition **on** in the phrase **to put/place emphasis on** something.) Compare: *In her speech she* **emphasized** *the importance of hard work.* | *The company puts a lot of* **emphasis on** *hard work.*

em·phat·ic /ɪm'fætɪk/ *adj* speaking or spoken forcefully to show that something is very important: *He answered with an emphatic "No".* **–emphatically** /-kli/ *adv*

em·pire /'empaɪər/ *n* **1** a group of countries under one government: *the former British Empire* **2** a large group of business organisations: *the industrial empire of Standard Oil*

em·pir·i·cal /ɪm'pɪrɪkəl/ *adj* coming from practical experience of the world not from ideas out of books **–empirically** /-kli/ *adv* **–empiricism** /ɪm'pɪrɪsɪzəm/ *n* [U]

em·ploy /ɪm'plɔɪ/ *v* [T] **1** to give someone a job: *We employ her as an adviser.* | *He's now employed as a teacher.* **2** *fml* to use something: *This bird employs its beak as a weapon.*

em·ploy·ee /ɪm'plɔɪ-iː, ˌemplɔɪ'iː/ *n* a person who works for someone else: *a Government employee*

em·ploy·er /ɪm'plɔɪər/ *n* a person or group that pays people to work for them: *The car factory is a big employer in the area.*

em·ploy·ment /ɪm'plɔɪmənt/ *n* [U] **1** the state of having paid work: *The number of people in regular employment has fallen.* | *He's looking for employment.* **–opposite unemployment 2** the act of using something: *Do you think the employment of force was justified?*

em·pow·er /ɪm'pauər/ *v fml* **empower someone to do something** to give someone the power or legal right to do something: *The police are now empowered to search private houses.*

em·press /'emprɪs/ *n* a woman who is an EMPEROR or the wife of an EMPEROR

emp·ty¹ /'empti/ *adj* **1** containing nothing or nobody: *an empty cup* | *There are three empty houses in our street.* **2 empty of** without: *streets empty of traffic* **3** without sense, meaning, or importance: *empty promises* | *Her life seemed empty now.* **–emptiness** *n* [U]

empty² *v* **emptied, emptying 1** [T] to remove the contents of a container: *They emptied the bottle of wine.* **2** [T+adv/prep] to take the contents out of something and put them somewhere else: *He emptied the biscuits onto the plate.* **3** [I] to become empty: *The room emptied very quickly.*

empty-hand·ed /ˌ·· '··/ *adj* bringing nothing with you because you have not got what you hoped to get

e·mu /'iːmjuː/ *n* a large Australian bird with a long neck which cannot fly

em·u·late /'emj‿leɪt/ *v* **emulated, emulating** [T] *fml* to copy someone's good behaviour or success **–emulation** /ˌemj‿'leɪʃən/ *n* [U]

e·mul·sion /ɪ'mʌlʃən/ *n* [C;U] **1** *tech* a creamy mixture of liquids which do not mix together completely **2** a type of paint used especially for painting walls

en·a·ble /ɪ'neɪbəl/ *v* **enabled, enabling** *fml* enable someone to do something to make someone able to do something: *The fall in the value of the pound will enable us to export more goods.*

en·act /ɪ'nækt/ *v* [T] *fml* **1** to make something a law: *Several bills were enacted at the end of this session of Parliament.* **2** to perform a story as a play **–enactment** *n* [C;U]

e·nam·el /ɪ'næməl/ *n* [U] **1** a glassy substance used as decoration or protection on metal, glass, or clay objects **2** a very shiny kind of paint **3** the hard, smooth, white surface of your teeth **–enamel** *v* [-ll-] [T]

en·am·oured /ɪ'næməd || -ərd/ *adj fml* (**enamored** *AmE*) **be enamoured of something** to be very fond of something

en bloc /ˌɒn 'blɒk || ˌɑːn 'blɑːk/ *adv* all together as a single unit: *The whole department resigned en bloc.*

en·camp·ment /ɪn'kæmpmənt/ *n* a large military camp

en·case /ɪn'keɪs/ *v* **encased, encasing** [T] **be encased in something** to be completely covered by something: *His body was encased in armour.*

en·chant /ɪn'tʃɑːnt || ɪn'tʃænt/ *v* [T] to fill someone with a feeling of delight **–enchantment** *n* [C;U]

en·chant·ed /ɪn'tʃɑːntɪd || ɪn'tʃæn-/ *adj* **1** filled with delight: *He was enchanted by the idea.* **2** strange and magical: *an enchanted wood*

en·chant·ing /ɪn'tʃɑːntɪŋ || ɪn'tʃæn-/ *adj* delightful and attractive in appearance or behaviour: *an enchanting child*

en·cir·cle /ɪn'sɜːkəl ‖ -ɜːr-/ v encircled, encircling [T] to surround something: *The army encircled the airport.*

en·clave /'enkleɪv, 'eŋ-/ n a place or group of people which is completely surrounded by another place or a different group of people

en·close /ɪn'kləʊz/ v enclosed, enclosing [T] 1 to surround something completely: *a garden enclosed by a high wall* | *The key was enclosed in a small wooden box.* 2 to put something inside an envelope with a letter: *I enclose a cheque for £50.*

en·clo·sure /ɪn'kləʊʒəʳ/ n 1 a piece of land that is surrounded by a fence or wall: *There's a special enclosure for the horses.* 2 something that is put in with a letter

en·com·pass /ɪn'kʌmpəs/ v [T] 1 to include several things: *The company's activities encompass printing, publishing, and computing.* 2 fml to surround a place on all sides

en·core /'ɒŋkɔːʳ ‖ 'ɑːŋ-/ interj a call made by listeners at a concert or a theatre to show that they liked a performance and want part of it to be performed again –**encore** n

en·coun·ter /ɪn'kaʊntəʳ/ v [T] fml 1 to meet something difficult or dangerous: *He encountered a lot of opposition to his plan.* 2 to meet someone unexpectedly: *She encountered a friend on the plane.* –**encounter** n : *an unpleasant encounter with a dangerous snake*

en·cour·age /ɪn'kʌrɪdʒ ‖ ɪn'kɜːr-/ v encouraged, encouraging [T] 1 to try to persuade someone to do something: *We encouraged him to go to university.*
□ USEFUL PATTERN encourage someone to do something
2 to make it easier for something to happen: *It's in the company's interest to encourage union membership.* –**encouragement** n [C;U]

en·cour·ag·ing /ɪn'kʌrɪdʒɪŋ ‖ ɪn'kɜːr-/ adj making you feel hopeful and confident: *The latest trade figures are encouraging.*

en·croach /ɪn'krəʊtʃ/ v encroach on/upon something to take more of something than is right, usual, or acceptable: *His new farm buildings encroach on his neighbour's land.* –**encroachment** n [C;U]

en·cum·ber /ɪn'kʌmbəʳ/ v [T] fml to make it difficult for you to move or do something: *He is encumbered with debts.* –**encumbrance** n

en·cy·clo·pe·di·a /ɪnˌsaɪklə'piːdiə/ n (also ency·clopaedia) a book or set of books dealing with every branch of knowledge, usually in alphabetical order –**encyclopedic** /-'piːdɪk/ adj (also encyclo·paedic)

end¹ /end/ n 1 the point where something stops or finishes: *the ends of a rope* | *He walked to the end of the road.* | *I start work at the end of August.* | *He is killed right at the end of the film.* 2 a little piece of something that is left over: *cigarette ends* 3 fml an aim or purpose: *He does everything for his own political ends.* | *He is totally dedicated to this end.* 4 at a loose end having nothing to do 5 at an end finished: *The strike is finally at an end.* 6 at the end of the day when everything is considered: *At the end of the day it's the government's responsibility to stop this from happening.* 7 come to an end to finish: *The war has finally come to an end.* 8 end to end with the narrow sides of two objects touching each other: *Place the tables end to end.* 9 get hold of the wrong end of the stick to understand something wrongly 10 in the end at last: *He managed*

to pass his driving test in the end. | *Then he falls in love with a beautiful Spanish dancer and marries her. In the end, they go to Madrid and open a dancing school.* 11 make ends meet to get just enough money for your needs 12 infml no end of very much or very many: *You have caused me no end of worry.* 13 hours on end, days on end, weeks on end happening continuously for hours, days, or weeks: *We sat there for hours on end.* 14 put an end to something to stop something from happening any more
■ USAGE 1 Note the use of the preposition at in phrases such as: at the end of the lesson | at the end of the summer | at the end of the holiday | at the end of the dinner. (Do NOT use in the end to refer to the end of something particular.) 2 In the end often suggests that something happens after a lot of time or effort: *It was a difficult decision but in the end she decided to take the job.*

end² v [I;T] 1 to stop or finish: *The party ended at midnight.* | *The war ended in 1975.* | *He ended his letter with good wishes to the family.* 2 end in something to result in something: *Her efforts finally ended in success.*

end up phr v [I] to finish in a particular place or way: *He ended up in a cell for the night.* | *We ended up taking the train.*

en·dan·ger /ɪn'deɪndʒəʳ/ v [T] 1 to cause danger to someone or something 2 **endangered species** a type of animal that might soon no longer exist

en·dear /ɪn'dɪəʳ/ v [T] **endear yourself to someone** to make someone feel fond of you –**endearing** adj: *an endearing smile* –**endearingly** adv

en·dear·ment /ɪn'dɪəmənt ‖ ɪn'dɪər-/ n [C;U] an expression of love: *He whispered endearments to her.*

en·deav·our /ɪn'devəʳ/ v (**endeavor** AmE) fml **endeavour to do something** to try to do something: *You must endeavour to improve your work.* –**endeavour** n [C;U]

en·dem·ic /en'demɪk, ɪn-/ adj found regularly in a particular place (used of diseases): *This chest disease is endemic among miners in this area.*

end·ing /'endɪŋ/ n the end of a story, film, play, or word: *a happy ending*

en·dive / 'endɪv ‖ 'endaɪv/ n [C;U] 1 a plant with curly green leaves which are eaten raw 2 the usual American word for CHICORY(2)

end·less /'endləs/ adj unpleasant, and seeming never to end: *The journey seemed endless.* –**endlessly** adv

en·dorse /ɪn'dɔːs ‖ -ɔːrs/ v **endorsed, endorsing** [T] 1 to say that you support or approve of something or someone: *The President endorsed her candidacy.* 2 to write your name on the back of a cheque 3 BrE to show on a driving LICENCE that the driver has broken the law –**endorsement** n [C;U]

en·dow /ɪn'daʊ/ v [T] 1 to provide a school, hospital, or college with a large amount of money that gives a continuing income 2 **be endowed with something** to have a good quality or ability –**endowment** n [C;U]

en·dur·ance /ɪn'djʊərəns ‖ ɪn'dʊər-/ n [U] the ability to bear pain or suffering for a long time: *Marathon runners need tremendous endurance.*

en·dure /ɪn'djʊəʳ ‖ ɪn'dʊər-/ v **endured, enduring** fml 1 [T] to bear pain or suffering for a long time: *I can't endure that noise a moment longer.* –see BEAR² (USAGE) 2 [I] to continue to exist: *his enduring fame*

en·e·my /ˈenəmi/ *n* **enemies** **1** [C] a person who hates and opposes another person: *He's made a lot of enemies at work.* **2** [+ sing/pl verb] the army that you are fighting against in a war: *The enemy is advancing.*

en·er·get·ic /ˌenəˈdʒetɪk ‖ -ər-/ *adj* very active: *an energetic tennis player*

en·er·gy /ˈenədʒi ‖ -ər-/ *n* **1** [U] the ability to be active and do a lot of work or sport without feeling tired: *Young people usually have more energy than the old.* **2** [U] the power which can produce heat and drive machines: *atomic energy | a cheap source of energy* **3** **energies** [pl] the ability to spend a lot of time and effort doing something: *We'll now need to direct our energies into the election campaign.*

en·force /ɪnˈfɔːs ‖ -ɔːrs/ *v* **enforced, enforcing** [T] **1** to cause a rule or law to be obeyed: *The new law about safety belts in the back seats of cars will be difficult to enforce.* **2** to make something happen, especially by threats or force: *They tried to enforce agreement by torturing the prisoners.* **–enforceable** *adj* **–enforcement** *n* [U]

en·gage /ɪnˈɡeɪdʒ/ *v* **engaged, engaging** *fml* **1** [T] to arrange to employ someone: *I've engaged a new secretary.* | *I've engaged him as my assistant.* **2** [T] to attract someone and keep their interest or attention: *The new toy didn't engage the child for long.* **3** [I;T] to attack someone: *They engaged the enemy in battle.* **4 engage in something** *fml* to do or take part in something: *We are now engaged in a legal battle with our suppliers.* **5 engage someone in conversation** to talk to someone, especially because you do not want them to notice something that is happening

en·gaged /ɪnˈɡeɪdʒd/ *adj* [never before a noun] **1** having agreed to marry someone: *My daughter is engaged to a doctor.* | *They're engaged.* | *They got engaged in January.* **2** *fml* busy (used of people): "*Can Mr Jones come to the meeting on Monday?*" "*No, I'm afraid he's otherwise engaged.*" **3** in use (used of a telephone line): *Sorry! The number is engaged.* –see TELEPHONE (USAGE) **4** in use (used of a public TOILET)

en·gage·ment /ɪnˈɡeɪdʒmənt/ *n* **1** an agreement to marry or the period during which two people are engaged: *Have you heard that John has broken off his engagement to Mary?* **2** *fml* an arrangement to meet someone or to do something, especially at a particular time: *I am unable to attend the meeting because of a previous engagement.*

en·gag·ing /ɪnˈɡeɪdʒɪŋ/ *adj* charming: *an engaging smile* **–engagingly** *adv*

en·gen·der /ɪnˈdʒendər/ *v* [T] *fml* to produce a state or feeling

en·gine /ˈendʒɪn/ *n* **1** a machine with moving parts which produces power from steam, electricity, or oil and uses it to make something move: *the engine of a car | a jet engine* **2** a machine which pulls a railway train

en·gi·neer[1] /ˌendʒɪˈnɪər/ *n* **1** a person who is professionally trained to build and repair machines, roads, bridges, and harbours: *a telephone engineer | a civil engineer* **2** a skilled person who controls the engine on a ship

engineer[2] *v* [T] to arrange or cause something by clever secret planning: *He had powerful enemies who engineered his ruin.*

en·gi·neer·ing /ˌendʒɪˈnɪərɪŋ/ *n* [U] the science or profession of an engineer

En·glish[1] /ˈɪŋɡlɪʃ/ *adj* from or connected with England: *She's studying English literature.*

English[2] *n* **1 the English** the people of England **2** [U] the language of the UK, the USA, Australia and many other countries: *How long have you been learning English?*

Eng·lish·man /ˈɪŋɡlɪʃmən/ **-men** /-mən/ *n* a man who comes from England or who has English parents

Eng·lish·wom·an /ˈɪŋɡlɪʃˌwʊmən/ **-women** /-ˌwɪmɪn/ *n* a woman who comes from England or who has English parents

en·grave /ɪnˈɡreɪv/ *v* **engraved, engraving** [T] **1** to cut words or pictures on wood, stone, or metal: *His name was engraved on the tombstone.* **2 be engraved on your mind/memory** to be fixed deeply in your mind so that you are unable to forget anything: *The terrible scene was engraved on his memory for ever.* **–engraver** *n* **–engraving** *n* [C;U]

en·gross·ed /ɪnˈɡrəʊst/ *adj* [never before a noun] completely holding your attention so that you do not think of anything else: *He was so engrossed in his work that he forgot to eat.*

en·gulf /ɪnˈɡʌlf/ *v* [T] *lit* (of the earth, the sea, fire) to surround something and swallow it up: *The stormy sea engulfed the small boat.*

en·hance /ɪnˈhɑːns ‖ ɪnˈhæns/ *v* **enhanced, enhancing** [T] to increase the quality, value, or beauty of something: *Passing the examination should enhance your chances of getting a job.*

e·nig·ma /ɪˈnɪɡmə/ *n* a person, thing, or event that is mysterious and very hard to understand: *Her disappearance remains an enigma.* **–enigmatic** /ˌenɪɡˈmætɪk◂/ *adj* : *an enigmatic smile* **–enigmatically** /-kli/ *adv*

en·joy /ɪnˈdʒɔɪ/ *v* [T] **1** to get pleasure from things and experiences: *I enjoyed the film very much.* | *He thoroughly enjoyed his day out.* | *She enjoys listening to music.*
□ USEFUL PATTERNS to enjoy something; to enjoy doing something
2 *fml* to have something good: *He has always enjoyed very good health.* | *They enjoy a high standard of living.* **3 enjoy yourself** to have a good time: *Did you enjoy yourself at the party?* **–enjoyment** *n* [C;U]: *We hope the interruption didn't spoil your enjoyment of the programme.*

en·joy·a·ble /ɪnˈdʒɔɪəbəl/ *adj* providing pleasure or happiness (used of activities and experiences): *an enjoyable holiday | an enjoyable film* **–enjoyably** *adv*

en·large /ɪnˈlɑːdʒ ‖ -ɑːr-/ *v* **enlarged, enlarging** **1** [I;T] to make something get larger: *We're enlarging the vegetable garden to grow more food.* | *I'd like to have this photograph enlarged.* **2 enlarge on something** to add more length and detail to writing or speech **–enlargement** *n* [C;U]

en·light·en /ɪnˈlaɪtn/ *v* [T] to make someone understand something or free them from false beliefs: *I'm rather confused about what this is for; can you enlighten me?*

en·light·ened /ɪnˈlaɪtnd/ *adj* extremely sensible, especially because of being wiser and more modern: *the government's enlightened housing policy*

en·list /ɪnˈlɪst/ *v* **1** [I;T] to join or let someone join the army, navy, or airforce: *He enlisted when he was 18.* | *We must enlist more men.* **2** [T] to get someone's help or support **–enlistment** *n* [C;U]

en·liv·en /ɪnˈlaɪvən/ *v* [T] to make people or events more active, cheerful, or interesting

en masse /ˌɒn ˈmæs ‖ ˌɑːn-/ *adv* all together: *The senior management resigned en masse.*

en·mi·ty /'enmɪti/ n [U] a strong feeling of hatred towards another person or group of people

en·no·ble /ɪ'nəubəl/ v **ennobled, ennobling** [T] **1** to make someone better and more honourable: *His character has been ennobled by his sufferings.* **2** to make someone a nobleman

e·nor·mi·ty /ɪ'nɔːmɪti ‖ -ɔːr-/ n **the enormity** of the size or seriousness of something: *the enormity of the housing problem* | *He didn't seem to comprehend the enormity of his crime.*

e·nor·mous /ɪ'nɔːməs ‖ -ɔːr-/ adj extremely large: *an enormous house* | *an enormous meal* | *an enormous amount of money* | *The film was an enormous success.*

e·nor·mous·ly /ɪ'nɔːməsli ‖ -ɔːr-/ adv extremely: *an enormously rich woman* | *He's enormously popular.*

e·nough¹ /ɪ'nʌf/ det, pron as much or as many as is necessary: *We should have enough seats for everyone.* | *They didn't have enough money to buy a car.* | *Has everyone had enough to eat?* | *I've ordered five pints of milk – that should be enough.*

■ USAGE **1 Enough** comes after adjectives: *Is he old enough?* 2 When we use **enough** with a noun it usually comes before the noun: *I haven't got enough money.* Putting **enough** after the noun sounds rather formal or literary: *Ah! If only I had money enough to travel there!*

enough² adv **1** to the necessary extent or degree: *The water isn't warm enough to swim in.* | *She could have passed the exam, but she didn't work hard enough.* **2** not very, but to a certain degree: *He's nice enough, but I wouldn't want to see too much of him!* **3 strangely enough, oddly enough, interestingly enough,** etc a phrase you use to say that something is quite strange, odd, interesting, etc: *Strangely enough, I didn't see Jim at the party.*

en·quire /ɪn'kwaɪəʳ/ v **enquired, enquiring** [I;T] –see INQUIRE –see INQUIRY (USAGE)

en·qui·ry /ɪŋ'kwaɪəri ‖ 'ɪŋkwaɪəri, ɪŋ'kwaɪəri, 'ɪŋkwɜ:ri/ n –see INQUIRY

en·rage /ɪn'reɪdʒ/ v **enraged, enraging** [T] to make someone very angry: *Her behaviour enraged him.* | *He was enraged to find she didn't care.* –**enraged** adj : *her enraged parents*

en·rich /ɪn'rɪtʃ/ v [T] **1** to make someone rich: *The discovery of oil will enrich the nation.* **2** to improve the quality of something by adding something to it: *Music can enrich your whole life.* –**enrichment** n [U]

en·rol /ɪn'rəul/ v -ll- (also **enroll**) [I;T] to make yourself or another person officially a member of a course or school –**enrolment** n [C;U] : *Enrolment begins on Tuesday.*

en route /ˌɒn 'ruːt ‖ ˌɑːn-/ adv on the way: *I was en route to New York.*

en·sconced /ɪn'skɒnst ‖ ɪn'skɑːnst/ **be ensconced in** to be comfortably positioned somewhere: *He was ensconced in a big armchair in front of the fire.*

en·sem·ble /ɒn'sɒmbəl ‖ ɑːn'sɑːm-/ n **1** a set of things that combine with or match each other to make a whole: *Your coat, hat, and shoes make an attractive ensemble.* **2** a small group of musicians who regularly play together

en·sign /'ensaɪn, -sən ‖ 'ensən/ n **1** a flag on a ship, especially to show what nation the ship belongs to **2** an officer of the lowest rank in the US navy

en·slave /ɪn'sleɪv/ v **enslaved, enslaving** [T] **1** to make someone into a slave **2** to put someone in a very difficult situation from which they cannot escape: *He felt enslaved by his family's demands.* –**enslavement** n [U]

en·sue /ɪn'sjuː ‖ ɪn'suː/ v **ensued, ensuing** [I] *fml* to happen afterwards, often as a result: *Terrible fighting ensued.* | *Thousands were killed in the ensuing battle*

en·sure /ɪn'ʃuəʳ/ v **ensured, ensuring** [T;that] to make something certain to happen: *If you want to ensure that you catch the plane, take a taxi to the airport.* | *We need to change the law to ensure fair treatment for all people.*

en·tail /ɪn'teɪl/ v [T] to make something necessary; or have something as a necessary part: *Writing a history book entails a lot of work.*

en·tan·gle /ɪn'tæŋgəl/ v **entangled, entangling** [T] **1** to cause something to become caught up or twisted with something else: *The bird flapped about and entangled itself in the wire.* **2 be entangled** to be connected with someone or something bad that it is difficult to escape from: *He became entangled in dishonest business dealings.* | *She became entangled with a real drunkard.* –**entanglement** n [C;U]

en·ter /'entəʳ/ v **1** [I;T] *fml* to come or go into a particular place: *He entered the room cautiously.* | *Please knock before entering.* | *Enter Hamlet, stage left.* | *Further west, the river enters the forest.* **2** [T] to become a member of a profession or organization: *More and more people want to enter the medical profession.* | *He wants to enter Parliament.* **3** [I;T] to say that you want to take part in something: *Five Germans entered the race.* | *He entered himself for the exam.*

□ USEFUL PATTERNS to enter something; to enter for something; to enter someone for something

4 [T] to begin a new period of time: *The talks have now entered their third week.* **5** [T] to include in a store of information on a computer: *Have you entered the new data yet?* **6** [T] to write down names or amounts in a record book: *Please enter her name on the register.*

enter into sthg *phr v* [T] **1** to share in or take part in: *She entered into the children's game enthusiastically.* **2** to be an important part of or influence on something: *Money doesn't enter into it at all – it's the principle that matters to me.* **3** to start to take part in something formally: *They have entered into an agreement with their bankers.*

en·ter·prise /'entəpraɪz ‖ -ər-/ n **1** [C] a company or business: *This company's one of the largest enterprises of its kind.* **2** [U] a way of organizing business: *Do you believe in private enterprise, or in government ownership of industry?* **3** [C] a plan or action that is daring or difficult: *Have you heard about their latest enterprise?* **4** [U] the courage and ability that is needed to do something daring or difficult: *I admire their enterprise.*

en·ter·pris·ing /'entəpraɪzɪŋ ‖ -ər-/ adj having or showing the willingness to do things that are difficult, new, or daring

en·ter·tain /ˌentə'teɪn ‖ -ər-/ v **1** [T] to amuse and interest someone: *She entertained her friends with a description of herself learning to ski.* **2** [I;T] to treat someone as a guest by providing food and drink for them: *He does most of his entertaining in restaurants.* | *We're entertaining Harold's business partners this evening.* **3** [T] *fml* to be ready and willing to think about an idea, doubt, or suggestion

en·ter·tain·er /ˌentə'teɪnəʳ ‖ -tər-/ n a person who amuses and entertains people professionally, for example by singing or telling jokes: *a popular television entertainer*

en·ter·tain·ing /ˌentəˈteɪnɪŋ ‖ -ər-/ adj amusing and interesting: *an entertaining story* –**entertainingly** adv

en·ter·tain·ment /ˌentəˈteɪnmənt ‖ -tər-/ n 1 [U] activities which amuse or interest people: *Senior staff get an allowance for the entertainment of foreign visitors.* | *the entertainment industry* 2 [U] amusement or interest: *The little girl tried to put on her mother's shoes, much to our entertainment.* 3 [C] a public performance, for example at a cinema or theatre: *The tourist office will tell you about local entertainments.*

en·thral /ɪnˈθrɔːl/ v -ll- (also **enthrall**) [T] to completely hold someone's attention and interest: *The boy was enthralled by the soldier's stories.* –**enthralling** adj

en·throne /ɪnˈθrəʊn/ v **enthroned, enthroning** [T] to mark the official beginning of the period of rule of a king or queen by placing them on an official seat –**enthronement** n [C;U]

en·thuse /ɪnˈθjuːz ‖ ɪnˈθuːz/ v **enthused, enthusing** [I] to say how wonderful you think something is: *He was enthusing about his new radio.*

en·thu·si·as·m /ɪnˈθjuːziæzəm ‖ ɪnˈθuː-/ n [C;U] a strong feeling of interest, admiration, or eagerness: *The new teacher is full of enthusiasm for her work.*

en·thu·si·ast /ɪnˈθjuːziæst ‖ ɪnˈθuː-/ n someone who is very interested in and keen on something: *a cycling enthusiast*

en·thu·si·as·tic /ɪnˌθjuːziˈæstɪk ‖ -ˌθuː-/ adj very interested in something or keen on something: *She seemed enthusiastic about the idea.* | *We got an enthusiastic response from our customers.*

en·tice /ɪnˈtaɪs/ v **enticed, enticing** [T] to persuade someone to do something by offering something pleasant: *The good weather enticed me away from doing housework and into the garden.* –**enticement** n [C;U]

en·tire /ɪnˈtaɪəʳ/ adj [only before a noun] complete: *She spent the entire day in bed.* | *I am in entire agreement with you.* –**entirely** adv : *I'm afraid your work is not entirely satisfactory.*

en·tir·e·ty /ɪnˈtaɪərˌti/ n **in its entirety** as a complete whole: *He bought the collection of books in its entirety.*

en·ti·tle /ɪnˈtaɪtl/ v **entitled, entitling** [T] 1 to give someone the right to have or do something: *This ticket entitles you to a first class seat.* | *I think I'm entitled to know why I wasn't given the job.* □ USEFUL PATTERNS to entitle someone to something; to entitle someone to do something 2 to give a title to a book, play, film, or painting –**entitlement** n [U]: *You've used up all your holiday entitlement.*

en·ti·ty /ˈentˌti/ n **entities** something that has a single separate and independent existence: *After the war Germany was divided; it was no longer one political entity.*

en·to·mol·o·gy /ˌentəˈmɒlədʒi ‖ -ˈmɑː-/ n [U] the scientific study of insects –**entomologist** n

en·tou·rage /ˈɒntʊrɑːʒ ‖ ˈɑːn-/ n [+ sing/pl verb] all the people who look after and travel with an important person: *The president's entourage occupied six cars.*

en·trails /ˈentreɪlz/ n [pl] the inside parts of a person or animal, especially the bowels

en·trance¹ /ˈentrəns/ n 1 [C] a gate, door, or other opening by which you go into a place: *Excuse me – where is the entrance to the cinema?* 2 [C] someone's arrival in a particular place: *The minister's entrance was greeted with a loud cheer.* 3 [U] the right to enter a place: *Known football hooligans will be refused entrance to the match.* | *We will have to charge an entrance fee.* 4 **make an entrance** to come into a place, often in a way which makes people notice you: *She made a dramatic entrance leading her two pet lions.*
■ USAGE Compare **entrance** and **entry**. For the ordinary act of entering, the usual word is **entry**: *Britain's entry into the EEC* | *"No entry"* (road sign). **Entrance** is used especially to talk about a ceremony or performance: *to make an entrance onto the stage,* or to talk about the right to enter: *a university entrance exam* | *an entrance fee.*

en·trance² /ɪnˈtrɑːns ‖ ɪnˈtræns/ v **entranced, entrancing** [T] to fill someone with great wonder and delight: *The children watched entranced as the circus animals performed.*

en·trant /ˈentrənt/ n a person who enters a profession, race, or competition

en·treat /ɪnˈtriːt/ v [T] fml to beg someone humbly to do something: *She entreated him to forgive her.* –**entreaty** n **entreaties** [C;U]

en·trenched /ɪnˈtrentʃt/ adj firmly established and difficult to change (used of rights, customs, and beliefs; a word often used to express disapproval): *his entrenched political ideas*

en·tre·pre·neur /ˌɒntrəprəˈnɜːʳ ‖ ˌɑːn-/ n a person who starts a business or arranges for a piece of work to be done in the hope of making a profit –**entrepreneurial** adj

en·trust /ɪnˈtrʌst/ v [T] to give someone something to be responsible for: *The lawyers entrusted the child to his care.* | *She was entrusted with the responsibility for organizing the event.*
□ USEFUL PATTERNS to entrust something to someone; to entrust someone with something

en·try /ˈentri/ n **entries** 1 [C] a person or thing entered for a race or competition: *The winning entry was a portrait of an old man.* | *There were 800 entries for the marathon.* 2 [C] a piece of information listed in a book or on a computer: *The next entry in this dictionary is the word "entwine".* 3 [C;U] the act of joining a group or organization: *Britain's entry into the European Monetary System* 4 [U] the right to enter a building or country: *The refugees were refused entry to Britain.* 5 [C] someone's arrival in a room: *She pretended not to notice his entry.* 6 [C] a door, gate, or passage by which you enter a place –see ENTRANCE (USAGE) 7 **No Entry** words used on a sign to show you cannot go into a place

en·twine /ɪnˈtwaɪn/ v **entwined, entwining** [T] to twist something round something else: *They walked along with their fingers entwined.*

e·nu·me·rate /ɪˈnjuːməreɪt ‖ ɪˈnuː-/ v **enumerated, enumerating** [T] fml to name things on a list one after the other –**enumeration** /ɪˌnjuːməˈreɪʃən ‖ -ˌnuː-/ n [C;U]

e·nun·ci·ate /ɪˈnʌnsieɪt/ v **enunciated, enunciating** 1 [I;T] to pronounce words or sounds clearly: *An actor must learn to enunciate properly.* 2 [T] fml to express ideas or principles clearly and firmly –**enunciation** /ɪˌnʌnsiˈeɪʃən/ n [C;U]

en·vel·op /ɪnˈveləp/ v [T] to cover something completely: *The building was soon enveloped in flames.*

en·ve·lope /ˈenvələʊp/ n the paper container for a letter or a card

en·vi·a·ble /ˈenviəbəl/ adj making you wish you had something or could do something: *He has a very*

enviable position in society. | *It's not an enviable task, trying to get the two sides to agree.* –opposite **unenviable** –enviable *adv*

en·vi·ous /ˈenviəs/ *adj* wishing that you had someone else's qualities or possessions: *She was envious of her sister's new job.* –see JEALOUS (USAGE) –enviously *adv*

en·vi·ron·ment /ɪnˈvaɪərənmənt/ *n* **1** the physical and social conditions in which people live and which influence their lives: *Children need a happy home environment.* | *a pleasant working environment* **2 the environment** the natural world of land, sea, and air in which people, plants, and animals live: *the destruction of the environment by pollution*

■ USAGE Compare **environment** and **surroundings**. Your environment means all the things, people and ideas among which you live and which make you the person you are: *His political beliefs were influenced by the environment he grew up in.* Your **surroundings** are simply the physical things (such as buildings, hills and trees) that you can see around you: *My new house is in pleasant surroundings.*

en·vi·ron·men·tal /ɪnˌvaɪərənˈmentl◂/ *adj* **1** relating to the natural world of land, sea and air: *The accident could do a lot of environmental damage.* | *They are very interested in environmental issues.* **2** relating to the physical and social conditions in which people live –environmentally *adv* : *products which are environmentally friendly*

en·vi·ron·men·tal·ist /ɪnˌvaɪərənˈmentlɪst/ *n* a person who wants and tries to prevent the natural world from being spoilt

en·vi·rons /ˈenvɪrənz, ɪnˈvaɪərənz ‖ ɪnˈvaɪərənz/ *n* [pl] *fml* the area surrounding a town

en·vis·age /ɪnˈvɪzɪdʒ/ *v* envisaged, envisaging (also **envision** /ɪnˈvɪʒən/ *AmE*) [T;+that] to think that something is a future possibility: *When do you envisage being able to pay back the money?*

en·voy /ˈenvɔɪ/ *n* a messenger, especially one sent to a foreign government

en·vy[1] /ˈenvi/ *n* [U] **1** an unpleasant feeling you have towards someone when you wish that you had their qualities or possessions: *They were full of envy when they saw his new car.* **2 be the envy of** to have something which other people wish they had: *Their health service is the envy of the world.*

envy[2] *v* envied, envying [T] to wish that you had what someone else has got: *I envy your ability to work so fast.* | *I don't envy you your journey in this bad weather.*

☐ USEFUL PATTERNS to envy someone; to envy something; to envy someone something

ep·au·let /ˌepəˈlet/ *n* (also **epaulette**) a shoulder decoration, especially on a military or naval uniform

e·phem·e·ral /ɪˈfemərəl/ *adj* lasting only for a short time: *ephemeral pleasures* | *ephemeral fashions*

ep·ic[1] /ˈepɪk/ *adj* full of brave action and excitement (used of stories or events): *an epic journey to the South Pole*

epic[2] *n* a long poem, book, or film about the deeds of gods and great men, or the early history of a nation: *a Hollywood epic about the Roman Empire*

ep·i·dem·ic /ˌepɪˈdemɪk/ *n* **1** a large number of cases of the same infectious disease at the same time: *an epidemic of cholera* | *a flu epidemic* **2** something which develops and spreads quickly: *an epidemic of violent crime* –epidemic *adj*

ep·i·gram /ˈepɪɡræm/ *n* a short amusing poem or saying which expresses a clever idea –epigrammatic /ˌepɪɡrəˈmætɪk/ *adj*

ep·i·lep·sy /ˈepɪlepsi/ *n* [U] a disease of the brain which causes sudden attacks of uncontrolled violent movement and loss of consciousness

ep·i·lep·tic /ˌepɪˈleptɪk◂/ *n* someone who suffers from epilepsy –epileptic *adj* : *an epileptic fit*

ep·i·logue /ˈepɪlɒɡ ‖ -lɔːɡ, -lɑːɡ/ *n* (also **epilog** *AmE*) something at the end of a piece of literature which finishes it neatly

ep·i·sode /ˈepɪsəʊd/ *n* **1** one part of a book or play which appears on radio, on television, or in a magazine in separate parts which make a story: *The next episode will be broadcast next week.* **2** one separate event: *There was a rather amusing episode in the pub last night.*

e·pis·tle /ɪˈpɪsəl/ *n* **1** *fml* a letter, especially a long and important one (a word which is often used in a humorous way) **2 Epistle** one of the letters in the Bible written by the first followers of Christ

ep·i·taph /ˈepɪtɑːf ‖ -tæf/ *n* a description of or thought about a dead person, often written on a stone above their grave

ep·i·thet /ˈepɪθet/ *n* an adjective or descriptive phrase, especially of praise or blame, which is used about a person

e·pit·o·me /ɪˈpɪtəmi/ *n* be the epitome of to be the perfect or most typical example of something: *She's the epitome of good taste in her elegant new coat.*

e·pit·o·mize /ɪˈpɪtəmaɪz/ *v* epitomized, epitomizing (also **epitomise** *BrE*) [T] to be very typical of: *The conduct of this strike epitomizes what is wrong with industrial relations in this country.*

e·poch /ˈiːpɒk ‖ ˈepək/ *n* a period of time in history during which important events or developments happened

e·qual[1] /ˈiːkwəl/ *adj* **1** the same in size, number, amount, or value: *Cut the cake into six equal pieces.* | *The two squares are equal in size.* | *I owe him £100. That's equal to one week's salary.* **2** the same as something that another more fortunate group of people already has: *Men can't complain if women want equal pay for equal work.* | *Black citizens demanded equal rights.* **3 equal to something** *fml* having the necessary strength, ability, or courage for something: *Is Bill equal to the job of running the office?* **4 on equal terms** without one person or group having any advantage over another one: *The diplomats chose a neutral country so they could meet on equal terms.*

equal[2] *n* a person who has the same ability, position, or rights as someone else: *He's a popular teacher because he treats the children as equals.*

equal[3] *v* -ll- (-l- *AmE*) [T] **1** to be the same as something else in number or amount: *"x = y" means that x equals y.* **2** to be as good or the same standard as someone or something else: *Thompson has equalled the world record for the 400 metres.*

e·qual·i·ty /ɪˈkwɒləti ‖ ɪˈkwɑː-/ *n* [U] having the same conditions, possibilities, and rights as everyone else: *racial equality* –opposite **inequality**

e·qual·ize /ˈiːkwəlaɪz/ *v* equalized, equalizing (also **equalise** *BrE*) **1** [T] to make things equal in size, numbers, or amount: *Our party's policy is to try to equalize the tax burden.* **2** [I] to reach the same total of points as your opponent in sport: *Scotland equalized a few minutes before the end of the match.*

eq·ual·ly /'iːkwəli/ *adv* **1** to the same degree: *They are both equally qualified for the job.* **2** in parts which are the same size: *They shared the work equally between them.* **3** a word used to compare two ideas which have the same importance: *I think a new road should be built through the city centre, but equally, we shouldn't forget that this will be unpopular with local residents.*

eq·ua·nim·i·ty /ˌiːkwə'nɪmɨti, ˌekwə-/ *n* [U] *fml* calmness of mind in a difficult situation: *He received the bad news with surprising equanimity.*

e·quate /ɪ'kweɪt/ *v* **equated, equating** [T] to consider something to be the same as something else: *You can't equate passing examinations with being intelligent.*

e·qua·tion /ɪ'kweɪʒən/ *n tech* a statement that two amounts or values are the same: *In the equation x+2y=7 what is x?*

E·qua·tor /ɪ'kweɪtəʳ/ *n* **the Equator** an imaginary line drawn round the world at an equal distance between its most northern and southern points

e·qua·to·ri·al /ˌekwə'tɔːriəl◂/ *adj* on or near the Equator and therefore very hot: *equatorial rainforests*

e·ques·tri·an /ɪ'kwestriən/ *adj* connected with horse-riding: *equestrian sports*

e·qui·dis·tant /ˌiːkwɨ'dɪstənt◂/ *adj* the same distance from two places: *Rome is about equidistant from Cairo and Oslo.*

e·qui·lat·e·ral /ˌiːkwɨ'lætərəl◂/ *adj* having all three sides equal: *an equilateral triangle*

e·qui·lib·ri·um /ˌiːkwɨ'lɪbriəm/ *n* [U] *fml* a balance between different forces or influences so that everything stays calm or at the same level: *Inflation has been rising during the past few months, but now seems to be in a state of equilibrium.*

eq·uine /'ekwaɪn, 'iː-/ *adj* of or like horses

eq·ui·nox /'iːkwɨnɒks, 'e-‖ -nɑːks/ *n* one of the two times in the year when day and night are of equal length

e·quip /ɪ'kwɪp/ *v* **-pp-** [T] **1** to supply someone with what is needed for a particular purpose: *The council can't afford to equip the school properly.* | *They equipped themselves with ropes before beginning to climb.* **2** to prepare someone for a particular situation or experience: *His education hadn't equippped him for life's problems.* **-equipped** *adj* : *a well equipped kitchen* | *students ill equipped to pass an exam*

e·quip·ment /ɪ'kwɪpmənt/ *n* [U] the things which are used for a particular activity: *modern office equipment* | *photographic equipment*

eq·ui·ta·ble /'ekwɨtəbəl/ *adj* fair and just: *an equitable division of the money* **-equitably** *adv*

eq·ui·ty /'ekwɨti/ *n* **equities 1** [U] the quality of being fair and just: *the equity of the judgment* **2 equities** [pl] the equal parts into which ownership of a company is divided, on which no fixed interest is paid: *the equities market*

e·quiv·a·lent¹ /ɪ'kwɪvələnt/ *adj* having the same number, amount, or value as something else: *He changed his pounds for the equivalent amount in dollars.* **-equivalence** *n* [U]

equivalent² *n* something that has the same value, size, or meaning as something else: *Some American words have no British equivalents.*

e·quiv·o·cal /ɪ'kwɪvəkəl/ *adj* **1** having a double or doubtful meaning (used of words) **2** difficult to understand or explain **-opposite unequivocal** **-equivocally** /-kli/ *adv*

e·ra /'ɪərə/ *n* a long period of time begun or marked by an important event or discovery: *the post-war era* | *With the invention of the computer we moved into a new era.*

e·rad·i·cate /ɪ'rædɨkeɪt/ *v* **eradicated, eradicating** [T] to completely destroy something: *Many tropical diseases have still not been successfully eradicated.* **-eradication** /ɪˌrædɨ'keɪʃən/ *n* [U]

e·rase /ɪ'reɪz‖ ɪ'reɪs/ *v* **erased, erasing** [T] to rub out or remove something completely

e·ras·er /ɪ'reɪzəʳ‖ -sər/ *n* the usual American word for RUBBER

e·rect¹ /ɪ'rekt/ *adj* in an upright position: *With her head erect, she walked slowly down the aisle.*

erect² *v* [T] **1** *fml* to build something: *This monument was erected in honour of Queen Charlotte.* **2** to fit something together and put it in an upright position: *This garden furniture is easy to erect.*

e·rec·tion /ɪ'rekʃən/ *n* **1** [U] the building or placing of something in an upright position: *the erection of a new hospital* **2** [C;U] the hardening and swelling of a man's PENIS in sexual excitement

e·rode /ɪ'rəʊd/ *v* **eroded, eroding** [I;T] **1** to gradually destroy or be destroyed: *His authority has been eroded away.* | *Confidence in the new government is eroding.* **2** to wear or be worn away gradually by wind, rain, or acid: *The coast is slowly being eroded.* | *The cliffs are eroding.* **-erosion** /ɪ'rəʊʒən/ *n* [U]: *soil erosion*

e·rot·ic /ɪ'rɒtɪk‖ ɪ'rɑː-/ *adj* relating to sexual love and desire: *erotic feelings* | *an erotic picture* **-erotically** /-kli/ *adv* **-eroticism** /-tɪsɪzəm/ *n* [U]

err /ɜːʳ/ *v fml* [I] **1** *fml* to make a mistake: *I think the government has erred in its decision to abolish this tax.* **2 err on the side of** to show a tendency towards a particular way of behaving

er·rand /'erənd/ *n* a short journey to take a message or to buy something: *I've got a few errands to do in town.*

er·rant /'erənt/ *adj fml* [only before a noun] behaving in a bad and irresponsible way: *She went to London to bring back her errant daughter.*

er·rat·ic /ɪ'rætɪk/ *adj* changeable or irregular in movement or behaviour: *I'm rather an erratic tennis-player.* **-erratically** /-kli/ *adv*

er·ro·ne·ous /ɪ'rəʊniəs/ *adj fml* mistaken or incorrect: *erroneous opinions* | *erroneous ideas* **-erroneously** *adv*

er·ror /'erəʳ/ *n* [C;U] **1** a mistake: *an error of judgment* | *a computer error* | *The accident was caused by human error.* **2 in error** by mistake: *It was done in error.*

■ USAGE Compare **error** and **mistake. Error** is a more formal word than **mistake** and often suggests something more serious: *Your homework is full of mistakes* | *a serious political error* 2 **Error** sometimes suggests something which is morally wrong: *the errors of his youth* 3 Notice these fixed phrases: *an error of judgment/by mistake.*

er·u·dite /'erʊdaɪt‖ 'erə-/ *adj* showing deep knowledge and learning: *an erudite philosopher*

e·rupt /ɪ'rʌpt/ *v* [I] **1** (of a VOLCANO) to explode and throw out fire, ash, and smoke **2** to suddenly happen or begin in a frightening way: *Violence erupted after the match.* **3** to suddenly become angry or violent: *The crowd erupted.* **-eruption** /ɪ'rʌpʃən/ *n* [C;U]

es·ca·late /ˈeskəleɪt/ v escalated, escalating [I;T] to make or become more serious, bigger, or more widespread: *Government policies escalated unemployment.* | *The cost of property is escalating dramatically.* –**escalation** /ˌeskəˈleɪʃən/ n [U]

es·ca·la·tor /ˈeskəleɪtəʳ/ n a set of moving stairs carrying people up or down between different levels

es·ca·pade /ˈeskəpeɪd/ n a wild, exciting, and sometimes dangerous adventure that disobeys rules or causes trouble

escape¹ /ɪˈskeɪp/ v escaped, escaping **1** [I] to succeed in getting out of a place where you are kept by force: *They escaped* **from** *prison.* **2** [T] to avoid something difficult or dangerous: *She tried to escape her responsibilities.* | *He narrowly escaped being drowned.* **3** [T] to be forgotten or remain unnoticed: *I'm afraid your name escapes me.* | *Nothing escaped his attention.* **4** [I] to get out of a hole or crack in a container: *I think gas is escaping from the pipe.*

escape² n **1** [C;U] the getting out or away from somewhere free and alive: *The thief jumped into a car and made his escape.* | *She had a narrow escape when the wall nearly fell on her.* **2** [C;U] something that makes you free from something unpleasant or dull: *He reads thrillers as an escape* **from** *his boring routine.* **3** [C] an amount of something that gets out of a hole or crack in a container: *an escape of gas*

es·cap·is·m /ɪˈskeɪpɪzəm/ n [U] activity that provides something pleasant and imaginary to think about instead of unpleasant or dull reality: *Science-fiction stories are pure escapism!* –**escapist** adj,n

e·scarp·ment /ɪˈskɑːpmənt ‖ -ɑːr-/ n a long steep slope or cliff on a mountain-side

es·cort¹ /ˈeskɔːt ‖ -ɔːrt/ n **1** a person or vehicle that travels with someone as a guard or an honour **2 under escort** with an escort: *The prisoner travelled* **under** *police escort.* **3** fml a person of the opposite sex who goes with someone as a companion to a social event: *Mary's escort arrived to take her out for the evening.*

e·scort² /ɪˈskɔːt ‖ -ɔːrt/ v [T] to go with someone: *The politician was escorted by the directors as he toured the factory.*

e·soph·a·gus /ɪˈsɒfəgəs ‖ ɪˈsɑː-/ n –see OESOPHAGUS

es·o·ter·ic /ˌesəˈterɪk, ˌiːsə-/ adj understood by only a small number of people who have a specialist knowledge: *Some words are really too esoteric for this dictionary.*

ESP /ˌiː es ˈpiː/ **1** the teaching of English to students who need it for a particular job or purpose; an abbreviation for **English for Specific Purposes 2** knowledge which seems to have been gained without the use of sound, touch, taste or smell, or sight; an abbreviation for **extra-sensory perception**

es·pe·cial /ɪˈspeʃəl/ adj [only before a noun] fml not ordinary or usual

es·pe·cial·ly /ɪˈspeʃəli/ adv (also **specially**) **1** to a particularly great degree: *"Do you like chocolate?" "Not especially."* **2** in particular: *I love Italy, especially in summer.* **3** for a particular person or purpose: *This crown was made especially for the King.*

es·pi·o·nage /ˈespiənɑːʒ/ n [U] the activity of finding out the secret information of a country or company and sending it to enemies or competitors

es·pla·nade /ˈespləneɪd ‖ -nɑːd/ n a level open space where people walk for pleasure, often near the sea in seaside towns

Esq. /ɪˈskwaɪəʳ ‖ esk-, ɪˈskwaɪəʳ/ n [only after a noun] BrE a title of politeness after a man's full name; a written abbreviation for **esquire**; not used much now: *The envelope is addressed to Peter Jones, Esq.*

es·say /ˈeseɪ/ n a short piece of writing on a particular subject, written especially as part of a course of study: *We've got to write an essay on the war with Napoleon.*

es·sence /ˈesəns/ n **1** [U] the most important part of something which contains its most typical qualities: *The essence of his argument is that we should not destroy the ozone layer.* **2** [C;U] the best part of a substance that has been taken out and reduced to a liquid: *vanilla essence* **3 in essence** a phrase used when you are talking about the most important part of an idea, situation, or event

es·sen·tial /ɪˈsenʃəl/ adj **1** completely necessary: *Previous experience of this type of job is not essential.* **2** [only before a noun] central or most important: *What is the essential difference between these two political systems?* –**essential** n : *The room was furnished with the bare essentials: a bed, a chair, and a table.*

es·sen·tial·ly /ɪˈsenʃəli/ adv **1** most importantly: *She's essentially a very kind person.* | *The problem is essentially one of cost.* **2** a word used to show that something is generally true: *In spite of some silly mistakes, his work is essentially sound.*

es·tab·lish /ɪˈstæblɪʃ/ v **1** [T] to set up or begin something: *This company was established in 1850.* | *The club has established a new rule allowing women to join.* | *We're trying to establish contact with the crashed plane.* **2** [T] to make people recognize your or someone else's position, ability, or claim: *He quickly established himself as a powerful member of the new government.* | *His next film, "Taxi Driver", established his fame as an actor.* **3** [T;+ (that)] to find out or prove something: *His lawyer tried to establish that he had been abroad at the time.* | *They couldn't establish the cause of the accident.*

es·tab·lish·ment /ɪˈstæblɪʃmənt/ n **1** [U] the setting up of a system or organization: *the establishment of new laws protecting children* **2** [C] fml a place run as a business or for a special purpose: *This hotel is a very well-run establishment.* | *a research establishment* **3 the Establishment** the powerful organizations and people who control public life and usually do not like making great changes

es·tate /ɪˈsteɪt/ n **1** a piece of land on which buildings of a similar type have been built together: *an industrial estate* | *a housing estate* **2** an area of land in the country with a large house on it owned by one person or a family **3** law all the money and property a person leaves behind them when they die

estate a·gent /·ˈ· ˌ··/ n (**real estate agent** AmE) a person whose job is to buy and sell houses and land for people

estate car /·ˈ· ·/ n BrE a car with a door at the back and a lot of room to put bags and cases –see picture on page 49

es·teem¹ /ɪˈstiːm/ n [U] respect and admiration for another person: *She is held in high esteem by her male colleagues.*

esteem² v [T] fml **1** to respect and admire someone greatly: *The old teacher was much loved and esteemed.* **2** to consider someone to be a particular thing: *I did not esteem him to be trustworthy.*

es·ti·ma·ble /ˈestɪməbəl/ *adj fml* deserving admiration and respect

es·ti·mate¹ /ˈestɪmeɪt/ *v* **estimated, estimating 1** [I;T; +(that)] to judge or calculate the value, size or amount of something: *Can you estimate how far it is?* | *That film cost an estimated £25 million to make.* | *It has been estimated that more and more old people will live to be 100.*

es·ti·mate² /ˈestɪmɪt/ *n* **1** a statement of the probable cost of doing a job: *I got several estimates for having the roof repaired, and accepted the lowest.* **2** a calculation or judgment of the value, size, or amount of something: *an estimate of the painting's value.* | *At a rough estimate I'd say it was 300 years old.*

es·ti·ma·tion /ˌestɪˈmeɪʃən/ *n* [sing] judgment or opinion: *She's really gone down in my estimation since she used all my ideas in her book.*

es·tranged /ɪˈstreɪndʒd/ *adj* **1** no longer living with your husband or wife **2** no longer speaking to your family –**estrangement** *n* [C;U] *fml*

es·tu·a·ry /ˈestʃuəri, -tʃəri/ *n* **estuaries** the wide part of a river where it joins the sea: *the Thames estuary*

etc. /ˌet ˈsetərə/ *adv* a word used at the end of a list to show that there are other things which you could also include; an abbreviation for the Latin phrase *et cetera*: *They bought tea, coffee, sugar, etc.*

etch /etʃ/ *v* [I;T] to draw a picture by cutting lines on a metal plate with a needle and acid –**etching** *n*

e·ter·nal /ɪˈtɜːnl ‖ -ɜːr-/ *adj* going on for ever or for a very long time: *Do you believe in eternal life?* –**eternally** *adv*

e·ter·ni·ty /ɪˈtɜːnɪti ‖ -ɜːr-/ **1** [U] time without end, particularly time after death, which is said to last forever **2 an eternity** a period of time that seems very long because you are annoyed, anxious, or not interested: *Every moment seemed an eternity.*

e·ther /ˈiːθəʳ/ *n* [U] a light colourless liquid, easily changed into a gas, which was used in the past to put people to sleep before a medical operation

e·the·re·al /ɪˈθɪəriəl/ *adj* unnaturally light and delicate

eth·ic /ˈeθɪk/ *n* **1** an idea that influences people's behaviour and beliefs: *the Christian ethic* **2 ethics** [pl] moral rules or principles of behaviour which you believe in: *Whether you agree or disagree with the death penalty is a question of ethics.*

eth·i·cal /ˈeθɪkəl/ *adj* **1** relating to what you believe is right and wrong: *The use of animals in scientific tests raises some difficult ethical questions.* **2** morally good or correct: *The judge said that the doctor's behaviour had not been ethical.* –**opposite unethical** –**ethically** /-kli/ *adv*

eth·nic /ˈeθnɪk/ *adj* relating to a particular racial, national, or tribal group: *ethnic minorities* | *ethnic food*

eth·nol·o·gy /eθˈnɒlədʒi ‖ eθˈnɑː-/ *n* [U] the study and comparison of different races of people

e·thos /ˈiːθɒs ‖ ˈiːθɑːs/ *n* the typical values, ideas, and beliefs of a certain group of people

et·i·quette /ˈetɪket ‖ -ket/ *n* [U] the formal rules of polite and proper behaviour in society or in a particular profession

et·y·mol·o·gy /ˌetɪˈmɒlədʒi ‖ -ˈmɑː-/ *n* [U] the study of the origins, history, and changing meanings of words

eu·ca·lyp·tus /ˌjuːkəˈlɪptəs/ *n* [C;U] a tall tree that produces an oil used in medicine

eu·lo·gize /ˈjuːlədʒaɪz/ *v* **eulogized, eulogizing** (also **eulogise** *BrE*) [T] *fml* to praise someone or something very highly

eu·lo·gy /ˈjuːlədʒi/ *n* **eulogies** [C;U] *fml* a speech or a piece of writing that praises the qualities of a person

eu·nuch /ˈjuːnək/ *n* a man who has had part of his sex organs removed

eu·phe·mis·m /ˈjuːfɪmɪzəm/ *n* [C;U] a pleasanter or less direct word or phrase used to talk about something that is considered awkward or unpleasant –**euphemistic** /ˌjuːfɪˈmɪstɪk◂/ *adj*

eu·pho·ri·a /juːˈfɔːriə ‖ juː-/ *n* [U] a feeling of extreme happiness and excitement –**euphoric** *adj*

Eu·ro·pe·an¹ /ˌjuərəˈpiːən◂/ *adj* from or connected with a country in Europe: *the European Community* | *Eastern European wines*

European² *n* a person from a country in Europe

European Ec·o·nom·ic Com·mu·ni·ty (also **European Community** /ˌ···· ··,··· ·ˈ···/) *n* a European organization established to encourage trade and friendly relations between its member countries

eu·tha·na·si·a /ˌjuːθəˈneɪziə ‖ -ˈneɪʒə/ *n* [U] the practice of killing incurably ill or old people in a painless way

e·vac·u·ate /ɪˈvækjueɪt/ *v* **evacuated, evacuating** [T] to move people from a dangerous place to a safer place: *During the war, children living in cities were evacuated to the country.* –**evacuation** /ɪˌvækjuˈeɪʃən/ *n* [C;U]

e·vac·u·ee /ɪˌvækjuˈiː/ *n* a person who has been sent from a dangerous to a safe place

e·vade /ɪˈveɪd/ *v* **evaded, evading** [T] **1** to avoid doing something you should do: *If you try to evade paying your taxes you risk going to prison.* | *He evaded the question.* **2** to manage to avoid being caught: *After his escape he evaded capture for several days.*

e·val·u·ate /ɪˈvæljueɪt/ *v* **evaluated, evaluating** [T] *fml* to judge the importance or value of something after studying its good and bad points: *The students' work is evaluated regularly.* –**evaluation** /ɪˌvæljuˈeɪʃən/ *n* [C;U]

e·van·gel·i·cal /ˌiːvænˈdʒelɪkəl/ *adj* **1** believing in the importance of a personal Christian faith and of studying the Bible, rather than in religious ceremonies **2** being too eager to spread your own beliefs and ideas

e·van·ge·list /ɪˈvændʒɪlɪst/ *n* someone who travels from place to place in order to tell people about Christianity –**evangelism** *n* [U]

e·vap·o·rate /ɪˈvæpəreɪt/ *v* **evaporated, evaporating** [I;T] **1** to change into steam and disappear: *The puddle evaporated in the sun.* **2** to become less and less before disappearing completely: *My anger evaporated when I saw her.* –**evaporation** /ɪˌvæpəˈreɪʃən/ *n* [U]

e·va·sion /ɪˈveɪʒən/ *n* [C;U] the act of avoiding something by being clever or deceitful: *George is in prison for tax evasion.*

e·va·sive /ɪˈveɪsɪv/ *adj* trying not to talk about something: *an evasive answer* –**evasively** *adv* –**evasiveness** *n* [U]

eve /iːv/ *n* **1** the night or day before a religious holiday: *Christmas Eve* **2 the eve of** the time just before an important event: *on the eve of the election*

e·ven /ˈiːvən/ *adj* **1** level and smooth: *You need a*

nice even surface to work on. | *The roads were narrow and not very even.* **2** staying at the same level: *The seeds need an even temperature to germinate.* **3** equal: *It was quite an even competition.* | *I won three points in the last game, which means that I'm now even with the leader.* | *We think there should be a more even distribution of wealth in the world.* **4 get even with someone** to do something unpleasant to someone in return for something unpleasant that they did to you **5 even number** a number that can be divided by 2: *The answer should always be an even number.* **6 an even chance** an equal possibility that something will happen or not happen: *He's got an even chance of winning.*

even² *adv* **1** a word you use when you are saying that something is surprising or unusual: *We went down to the beach, and we even had a quick swim in the sea.* | *Even Mary seemed to enjoy herself, and she usually hates parties!* | *This is a sport that can be enjoyed by everyone, even old people.* **2** a word you use for making comparisons stronger: *It was cold yesterday, but it's even colder today.* | *The film was even more boring than I'd expected.* **3 even if** no matter if: *Even if we could afford it we wouldn't go abroad for our holidays.* | *We'll still have the garden party, even if it rains.* **4 even though** although: *He forgot to bring the book with him, even though I reminded him several times.* **5 even so** in spite of this: *I know she's not been very well and I know she's had a hard time recently. Even so, you'd think she could do a little bit to help.*

even³ *v*
even out *phr v* [I;T **even** sthg ↔ **out**] to make or become more equal: *The distribution of wealth within our society is gradually being evened out.*

eve·ning /ˈiːvnɪŋ/ *n* [C;U] the end of the day and early part of the night: *Are you planning to go out this evening?*

evening dress /ˈ··· / *n* **1** [U] special clothes worn for formal occasions in the evening **2** [C] a dress, usually long, worn by women for a formal occasion

e·vent /ɪˈvent/ *n* **1** something that happens which is important, interesting, or unusual: *a social event* | *The article discusses the course of events leading up to her death.* **2** a race or competition arranged as part of a day's sports: *The next event will be the 100 metres race.* **3 at all events** at least: *She lost nearly everything but at all events she's still alive.* **4 in any event** whatever happens: *I'll probably see you tomorrow, but in any event I'll phone.* **5 in the event** when something actually happened: *We thought he'd be nervous on stage, but in the event he was fine.* **6 in the event of** *fml* if something happens: *In the event of rain, the party will be held indoors.*

e·vent·ful /ɪˈventfəl/ *adj* full of exciting or interesting events: *an eventful life* | *We've had rather an eventful day.* –opposite **uneventful**

e·ven·tu·al /ɪˈventʃuəl/ *adj* [only before a noun] happening in the end as a result: *a research programme aimed at the eventual eradication of this disease*

e·ven·tu·al·i·ty /ɪˌventʃuˈælₔti/ *n* **eventualities** a possible event or result, especially an unpleasant one: *We must be prepared for all eventualities.*

e·ven·tu·al·ly /ɪˈventʃuəli, -tʃəli/ *adv* in the end: *She worked so hard that she eventually made herself ill.* –see Study Note on page 508

ev·er /ˈevəʳ/ *adv* **1** at any time: *Nothing ever makes him angry.* | *Have you ever met my wife?* | *If you ever come to Spain, we must meet.* | *It was the best holiday we've ever had.* | *I don't think I'll ever go back*

to live in London. **2 ever since** since a particular time, which is a long time ago: *We've been good friends ever since we were children.* | *This factory closed down two years ago, and it's been empty ever since.* **3** used in questions to give more force to what you are saying: *"He says he won't be coming to the meeting." "Why ever not?"* **4** continuing to happen all the time: *the ever-increasing population* | *our ever-expanding economy* **5 ever after** for all time in the future: *They got married and lived happily ever after.* **6 ever so, ever such** *infml* very; used to add force to what you are saying: *She's ever so upset about it.* | *It's ever such a good film.* | *They're ever such nice people.*

■ USAGE Compare **whatever** and **what ever**. We usually write **whatever** as one word. *Do whatever she tells you.* But we write **what ever** (two separate words) for questions expressing great surprise: *What ever gave you such a strange idea?* The same is true of **however** and **how ever**.

ev·er·green /ˈevəɡriːn ‖ -ər-/ *n* a tree or bush that does not lose its leaves in winter

ev·er·last·ing /ˌevəˈlɑːstɪŋ◂ ‖ ˌevərˈlæs-/ *adj fml* continuing for ever: *God has promised us everlasting life.* | *By winning so often she has won everlasting fame.*

ev·er·more /ˌevəˈmɔːʳ ‖ ˌevər-/ *adv lit* always: *He swore to love her for evermore.*

ev·ery /ˈevri/ *det* **1** all of more than two people or things: *I believe every word he says.* | *I enjoyed every minute of the party.* **2** once in each: *He comes to see us every day* | *We go to Scotland every three months or so.* | *Change the oil in the car every 5000 miles.* **3** as much as possible, or very much or very many: *We made every attempt to get there on time.* | *There is every chance that we will lose our jobs.* | *We have every reason to believe that we will be successful.* **4 every other day, week, year, etc** each second day, week, year, etc: *Take the medicine every other day.* | *We go to visit them every other week.*

■ USAGE Compare **every one** and **everyone**. **Every one** means "every person or thing already mentioned" and it is often followed by *of: There are 16 students in the class and* **every one** *of them passed.* **Everyone** (or **everybody**) means "every person" and it is not usually followed by *of:* **Everyone** *in the class passed the exam.*

ev·ery·bod·y /ˈevribɒdi ‖ -bɑːdi/ *pron* (also **everyone**) [used with a singular verb] every person: *I hope that everybody enjoys the party.* | *She gets on well with everyone.*

■ USAGE **Everybody, somebody, anybody** always take a singular verb: *Has* **everybody** *finished?* | *Does* **anybody** *want a drink?* But they are often followed by a plural pronoun, except in very formal language: **Everybody** *understands, don't they?* | **Anybody** *can do that if they try.* | **Somebody's** *left their gloves in my office.* (**Everyone, someone, anyone** behave in the same way.)

ev·ery·day /ˈevrideɪ/ *adj* [only before a noun] ordinary, common, and usual: *Accidents are an everyday occurrence in our house.*

ev·ery·one /ˈevriwʌn/ *pron* –see EVERYBODY

ev·ery·thing /ˈevriθɪŋ/ *pron* [used with a singular verb] all things: *Everything was going according to plan.* | *Is everything ready for the party?* | *I've forgotten everything I learnt at school.* | *I was fed up with my job, with my home life, with everything.*

ev·ery·where /ˈevriweəʳ/ *adv* in or to every place: *We looked everywhere for her.* | *This situation will affect people everywhere in Britain.* | *She follows me everywhere I go.*

e·vict /ɪˈvɪkt/ v [T] to make someone leave a house or land by law: *My cousin was evicted from his flat because he hadn't paid the rent all year.* –**eviction** /ɪˈvɪkʃən/ n [C;U]

ev·i·dence /ˈevɪdəns/ n 1 [U] words or objects which prove a statement, support a belief, or make something more clearly true: *There is some evidence to suggest that he was there on the night she was murdered.* | *An important piece of evidence has been found.* | *We saw no evidence of damage to crops.* | *He gave evidence for the accused.* 2 **in evidence** clearly and easily seen: *The police were much in evidence whenever the President made a public appearance.*

ev·i·dent /ˈevɪdənt/ adj plain or clear from signs you notice: *It's evident that you've been drinking.* | *her evident unhappiness* –**evidently** adv : *He is evidently unwilling to discuss it.*

e·vil[1] /ˈiːvəl/ adj 1 wicked and harmful, especially in thought or behaviour: *an evil influence* | *an evil regime* 2 infml very unpleasant: *What an evil smell!* –**evilly** /ˈiːvəl-li/ adv

evil[2] n [C;U] fml something that is very unpleasant and harmful: *He gave me a lecture on the evils of drink.* | *Taxation is a necessary evil.*

e·voc·a·tion /ˌevəˈkeɪʃən, ˌiːvəʊ-/ n [C;U] something that makes you remember or think about something else: *evocations of her childhood*

e·voc·a·tive /ɪˈvɒkətɪv ‖ ɪˈvɑː-/ adj producing memories and feelings: *The smell of those flowers is evocative of my childhood in India.*

e·voke /ɪˈvəʊk/ v evoked, evoking fml [T] to produce or call up a memory or feeling: *The old film evoked memories of my childhood.* | *His comments evoked great anger.*

ev·o·lu·tion /ˌiːvəˈluːʃən, ˌevə- ‖ ˌevə-/ n [U] 1 the gradual development of the various types of plants and animals from simpler forms over thousands of years: *Darwin's theory of evolution* | *In the course of evolution, some birds have lost the power of flight.* 2 gradual change and development: *the evolution of the motor car* –**evolutionary** adj

e·volve /ɪˈvɒlv ‖ ɪˈvɑːlv/ v evolved, evolving [I;T] to develop gradually by a long continuous process: *The British political system has evolved over several centuries.* | *Some people believe that we evolved from the apes.*

ewe /juː/ n a female sheep

ex·a·cer·bate /ɪɡˈzæsəbeɪt ‖ -ər-/ v exacerbated, exacerbating [T] fml to make something worse: *The drugs they gave her only exacerbated the pain.*

ex·act[1] /ɪɡˈzækt/ adj correct in every detail: *an exact amount* | *It is two minutes and five seconds past twelve, to be exact.* | *You have to be very exact to do this job.* –**exactness** n [U]

exact[2] v [T] fml to demand something, usually forcefully and get it: *I finally managed to exact a promise from them.*

ex·act·ing /ɪɡˈzæktɪŋ/ adj demanding a lot of care, effort, and attention: *an exacting boss* | *exacting standards of safety*

ex·act·ly /ɪɡˈzæktli/ adv 1 with complete correctness: *I don't know exactly where she lives, but it's in London somewhere.* | *What exactly were you doing here last night?* 2 a word used for adding force to what you are saying: *Our new house is exactly what we've always wanted.* 3 a word used to agree with someone or with what they are saying: *"So you believe, minister, that we must spend more on education?" "Exactly!"* 4 **not exactly**: a not really: *He's not exactly stupid, but he's no Einstein either!* b a

word used as a reply to show that something is not completely true: *"So you missed the meeting." "Not exactly. I got there ten minutes before it ended."*

ex·ag·ge·rate /ɪɡˈzædʒəreɪt/ v exaggerated, exaggerating [I;T] to make something seem larger or more important than it really is: *The seriousness of the situation has been exaggerated in the press.* –**exaggerated** adj : *walking with an exaggerated limp* –**exaggeration** /ɪɡˌzædʒəˈreɪʃən/ n [C;U] : *It's a bit of an exaggeration to call him a millionaire.*

ex·alt /ɪɡˈzɔːlt/ v [T] fml 1 to praise someone very highly 2 to raise someone to a high rank

ex·al·ta·tion /ˌeɡzɔːlˈteɪʃən, ˌeksɔːl-/ n [U] fml great joyfulness

ex·alt·ed /ɪɡˈzɔːltɪd/ adj of high rank

ex·am /ɪɡˈzæm/ n an official test of knowledge or ability in a particular subject: *When do we get the exam results?* | *I've failed my chemistry exam.*

ex·am·i·na·tion /ɪɡˌzæmɪˈneɪʃən/ n 1 [C;U] a detailed consideration of or check on something: *Before we can offer you the job, you will have to have a medical examination.* | *The proposal is still under examination.* 2 [C] fml an official test of knowledge or ability in a particular subject: *Did you pass your history examination?*

ex·am·ine /ɪɡˈzæmɪn/ v examined, examining [T] 1 to look at someone or something carefully and closely, in order to find out something: *My luggage was examined when I entered the country.* | *The doctor examined him thoroughly.* | *The police examined the room for fingerprints.* 2 to ask someone questions to get information, for example in a court of law: *The witness was examined on her relationship with the accused.* 3 to consider an idea in detail

ex·am·in·er /ɪɡˈzæmɪnər/ n someone who thinks of the questions for an examination, or marks them

ex·am·ple /ɪɡˈzɑːmpəl ‖ ɪɡˈzæm-/ n 1 one of a particular kind of thing which shows the typical qualities of those things: *This church is a wonderful example of medieval architecture.* 2 a person or behaviour that other people should be encouraged to copy: *Her courage is a shining example to us all.* | *Peter, you should try to set a good example to your younger brothers.* 3 **for example** you use this phrase when you are giving an example to support what you are saying and make your meaning clearer: *There has been a serious rise in food prices this year. The price of meat, for example, has doubled since March.* | *Seeds are naturally protected in various ways. For example, they are usually hard on the outside.* | *I'd really like to go somewhere interesting this summer – Tokyo or Hong Kong, for example.* –see Study Note on page 508 4 **make an example of someone** to punish someone so that others will be afraid to behave as they did

ex·as·pe·rate /ɪɡˈzɑːspəreɪt ‖ ɪɡˈzæ-/ v exasperated, exasperating [T] to annoy someone or make them extremely angry: *I was exasperated by all the delays.* –**exasperating** adj : *You are the most exasperating man I have ever known.* –**exasperation** /ɪɡˌzɑːspəˈreɪʃən ‖ ɪɡˌzæ-/ n [U] : *In sheer exasperation, she kicked the photocopying machine.*

ex·ca·vate /ˈekskəveɪt/ v [T] 1 to make a hole by digging: *They plan to excavate a large hole before putting in the foundations.* 2 to remove earth to find remains of the past: *We have been excavating a Roman house.* –**excavation** /ˌekskəˈveɪʃən/ n [C;U] : *archaeological excavations*

ex·ca·va·tor /ˈekskəveɪtər/ n a large machine that digs and moves earth

ex·ceed /ɪkˈsiːd/ v [T] *fml* **1** to be greater than a particular amount: *The cost will not exceed £50.* **2** to do more than what is lawful or acceptable: *He was fined for exceeding the speed limit.*

ex·ceed·ing·ly /ɪkˈsiːdɪŋli/ *adv old fash* extremely or to an unusual degree: *They were exceedingly kind to me.*

ex·cel /ɪkˈsel/ v -ll- *fml* **1** [I] to be extremely good at something: *I've never excelled at sports.* **2** excel yourself to do even better than usual: *What a wonderful meal: You've really excelled yourself, Jim.*

ex·cel·lence /ˈeksələns/ n [U] the quality of being excellent: *the excellence of his cooking*

Ex·cel·len·cy /ˈeksələnsi/ n Excellencies a title for certain people of very high rank: *The King will see you now, your Excellency.* | *His Excellency the Spanish ambassador*

ex·cel·lent /ˈeksələnt/ adj extremely good: *He's in excellent health.* | *Your examination results are excellent.* –excellently *adv*

ex·cept¹ /ɪkˈsept/ prep,conj (also except for) not including a particular person or thing: *I answered all the questions except the last one.* | *I know nothing about it except what I read in the paper.* | *We can do nothing except hope that they are all right.* | *The bus was empty except for one old lady.*

ex·cept·ed /ɪkˈseptɪd/ adj [only after a noun] not included: *He's not interested in anything, politics excepted.*

ex·cept·ing /ɪkˈseptɪŋ/ prep except

ex·cep·tion /ɪkˈsepʃən/ n **1** someone or something that is not included in a general statement: *It's been very cold, but today's an exception.* **2** make an exception to treat someone or something differently: *We don't normally accept credit cards, but we'll make an exception in your case.* **3** take exception to to be offended and made angry by something: *I took the greatest exception to his rudeness.* **4** without exception including everyone: *I see him every day, without exception.* **5** with the exception of apart from: *Everyone was tired, with the exception of John.*

ex·cep·tion·al /ɪkˈsepʃənəl/ adj of unusually high quality or ability: *All her children are clever, but the youngest boy is really exceptional.* –exceptionally *adv*

ex·cerpt /ˈeksɜːpt ‖ -ɜːr-/ n a small part of a book, speech, or musical work

ex·cess¹ /ɪkˈses, ˈekses/ n **1** [sing] a larger amount than is needed or usual: *There is an excess of violence in the film.* **2** in excess of more than: *This year's profits were in excess of a million pounds.* **3** to excess too much: *He drinks to excess.* **4** excesses [pl] unacceptable, immoral, or cruel actions: *Hitler's excesses in the last war*

ex·cess² /ˈekses/ adj [only before a noun] more than is usual or allowed: *She paid excess postal charges on the letter.*

ex·ces·sive /ɪkˈsesɪv/ adj too much or too great: *The charge for the room was excessive.* –excessively *adv*

ex·change¹ /ɪksˈtʃeɪndʒ/ n **1** the giving of something to someone who gives you something else: *an exchange of political prisoners between the two countries* **2** in exchange given to someone because they are giving something to you: *I gave him my bike in exchange for some records.* **3** a short period of fighting or talking between two people or groups: *Two soldiers were wounded in the exchange.* | *There were some bitter exchanges of views in Parliament*

yesterday. **4** a period in someone else's house or job while they come to your house or job: *She's going on an exchange to Munich.* **5** (also Exchange) a place where businessmen meet to buy and sell: *I worked at the Stock Exchange for two years, selling shares in companies.* **6** a TELEPHONE EXCHANGE

exchange² v exchanged, exchanging [T] to give something to someone who gives you something else: *The two armies exchanged prisoners.* | *They exchanged glances.* | *I exchanged the goods for cash.* | *This jumper is far too big. Perhaps the shop will exchange it.*

exchange rate /·ˈ··/ n (also rate of exchange) the value of the money of one country compared to that of another country

Ex·cheq·uer /ɪksˈtʃekər ‖ ˈekstʃekər/ n the Exchequer the department of the British government which collects taxes and pays out public money

ex·cise¹ /ˈeksaɪz/ n [U] the government tax on certain goods produced and used inside a country

ex·cise² /ɪkˈsaɪz/ v excised, excising [T] *fml* to remove something completely by cutting it out: *The tumour was excised.*

ex·ci·ta·ble /ɪkˈsaɪtəbəl/ adj easily excited –excitability /ɪkˌsaɪtəˈbɪlɪti/ n [U]

ex·cite /ɪkˈsaɪt/ v excited, exciting [T] **1** to make someone very happy, eager, or nervous about something: *The story excited the little boy very much.* | *Don't excite yourself please. Keep calm.* **2** *fml* to make people have strong feelings: *The court case has excited a lot of public interest.*

ex·cit·ed /ɪkˈsaɪtɪd/ adj full of strong feelings of expectation or happiness: *excited children opening their Christmas presents* | *She's very excited about getting the part in the film.* | *It's nothing to get excited about.* –excitedly *adv*

ex·cite·ment /ɪkˈsaɪtmənt/ n **1** [U] the condition of being excited: *As the end of the game grew near, the crowd's excitement increased.* **2** [C] something that makes you excited: *Life will seem very quiet after the excitements of the holiday.*

ex·cit·ing /ɪkˈsaɪtɪŋ/ adj causing excitement: *an exciting story* | *an exciting football match* –opposite unexciting

ex·claim /ɪkˈskleɪm/ v [I] to speak loudly and suddenly, because of pain, shock, or surprise: *"Good heavens!" he exclaimed.* *"It's six o'clock already."* | *She exclaimed in delight when she saw the presents.*

ex·cla·ma·tion /ˌekskləˈmeɪʃən/ n a word or words expressing a sudden strong feeling

exclamation mark /···ˈ·· ·/ n (also exclamation point *AmE*) a mark (!) which is written after an exclamation, as in the sentence "I'm hungry!"

ex·clude /ɪkˈskluːd/ v excluded, excluding [T] **1** to stop someone entering somewhere or doing something: *Women are excluded from the club.* | *I was excluded from taking part in the discussions.* **2** to not include something: *The policy definitely excludes damage by fire.* **3** to not accept a reason or possibility: *We can't exclude the possibility that his wife killed him.* –exclusion /-ˈkluːʒən/ n [U]

ex·clud·ing /ɪkˈskluːdɪŋ/ prep not including: *There were 30 people in the hotel, excluding the hotel staff.* –opposite including

ex·clu·sive¹ /ɪkˈskluːsɪv/ adj **1** for people who are wealthy and of a high social class: *one of London's most exclusive hotels* **2** [only before a noun] limited to use by one particular person or group: *This bathroom is for the President's exclusive use.* | "The

Times" got an exclusive interview with Mr Gorbachev. **3 mutually exclusive** unable to exist together (used of two things): *The two plans are mutually exclusive.* **4 exclusive of** not including: *The hotel charges £45 a day, exclusive of meals.* **–exclusiveness** *n* [U]

exclusive² *n* a newspaper story given to or printed by only one newspaper

ex·clu·sive·ly /ɪkˈskluːsɪvli/ *adv* only: *This room is exclusively for women.*

ex·com·mu·ni·cate /ˌekskəˈmjuːnɪˌkeɪt/ *v* **excommunicated, excommunicating** [T] to punish someone by taking away their membership of the church **–excommunication** /ˌekskəmjuːnɪˈkeɪʃən/ *n* [C;U]

ex·cre·ment /ˈekskrɪmənt/ *n* [U] *fml* the solid waste matter passed out from your body through your bowels

ex·crete /ɪkˈskriːt/ *v* **excreted, excreting** [I;T] *fml* to get rid of waste matter from your body, especially from your bowels **–excretion** /-ˈkriːʃən/ *n* [C;U]

ex·cru·ci·at·ing /ɪkˈskruːʃieɪtɪŋ/ *adj* extremely bad (used of pain): *an excruciating headache* **–excruciatingly** *adv*

ex·cur·sion /ɪkˈskɜːʃən ‖ ɪkˈskɜːrʒən/ *n* a short journey made for pleasure, usually by several people together: *We went on a day excursion to Blackpool.*

ex·cu·sa·ble /ɪkˈskjuːzəbəl/ *adj* that can be forgiven (used of behaviour) **–opposite inexcusable** **–excusably** *adv*

ex·cuse¹ /ɪkˈskjuːz/ *v* **excused, excusing** [T] **1** to forgive someone, often for something not very serious: *Please excuse my bad handwriting.* | *You must excuse my behaving so badly last night.* | *I can never excuse her for her rudeness.* | *She always excuses him for lying to her.*
□ USEFUL PATTERNS: to excuse something; to excuse your doing something; to excuse someone for something; to excuse someone for doing something
2 to provide a reason for bad behaviour so that it seems less serious: *He admitted that he hadn't punished her, excusing it as a moment of weakness.* | *I can't excuse myself: I shouldn't have done it.* | *Nothing can excuse lying to your parents.*
□ USEFUL PATTERNS: to excuse yourself; to excuse doing something; to excuse your doing something
3 excuse yourself to ask permission to be absent: *She excused herself from the meeting.* **4** to free someone from a duty or give them permission to leave: *He was excused piano practice.* | *She was excused from going to the school sports day.* | *Would you excuse me for a moment?*
□ USEFUL PATTERNS: to excuse someone (from) something; to excuse someone from doing something
5 excuse me a polite expression used when you want to get someone's attention, when you want to get past someone, when you want to leave a group of people who are talking, when you have done something slightly embarrassing or rude, or, in American English, when you want someone to repeat what they have said: *Excuse me, but have you got the time, please?* | *She stepped on my foot, and immediately said "Excuse me".* | *Excuse me for interrupting, but there's a phone call for you.* **–see** SORRY¹ (USAGE)

ex·cuse² /ɪkˈskjuːs/ *n* [C;U] **1** the reason given, whether true or not, to explain a mistake, bad behaviour, or absence: *Have you any excuse for*

coming so late? | *Stop making excuses!* **2** a reason for doing something or for not doing something: *She has a party whenever she can find an excuse.*
■ USAGE Compare **excuse, reason, pretext**: *His* **excuse** *for being absent was that he was ill.* (= he said he was ill and this may or may not have been true) | *His* **reason** *for being absent was that he was ill.* (= he really was ill) | *He took a week off work on the* **pretext** *that he was ill.* (= he said he was ill but this was not the real reason)

ex·e·cra·ble /ˈeksɪkrəbəl/ *adj fml* extremely bad: *execrable manners* **–execrably** *adv*

ex·e·cute /ˈeksɪkjuːt/ *v* **executed, executing** [T] **1** to kill someone as a lawful punishment: *She was executed for murder.* **2** *fml* to follow an order, plan, or instruction: *The lawyer duly executed the old lady's will.* **3** *fml* to perform a difficult movement or dance step: *The pilot successfully executed the manoeuvre.*

ex·e·cu·tion /ˌeksɪˈkjuːʃən/ *n* **1** [C;U] a lawful killing as a punishment: *Executions used to be held in public.* **2** [U] *fml* the performance or completion of an order, plan, or instructions: *It was a good idea but it was never put into execution.* | *The execution of a will can take a long time.* **3** [U] *fml* skill in performing something difficult: *The pianist's execution was brilliant but he played without feelings.*

ex·e·cu·tion·er /ˌeksɪˈkjuːʃənər/ *n* the official who executes someone

ex·ec·u·tive¹ /ɪgˈzekjʊtɪv/ *adj* [only before a noun] having the power to make and carry out decisions, especially in business: *He has been given full executive powers.* | *the executive branch of government*

executive² *n* **1** a person in a company with the power to make decisions: *a meeting with senior executives* **2 the executive** [+ sing/pl verb] the group in an organization who have the power to make decisions: *The union executive are opposed to a strike.*

ex·ec·u·tor /ɪgˈzekjʊtər/ *n* the person who carries out the orders in the will made by someone before they died

ex·em·pla·ry /ɪgˈzempləri/ *n* [only before a noun] suitable as an example or as a warning: *exemplary behaviour* | *an exemplary punishment*

ex·em·pli·fy /ɪgˈzemplɪfaɪ/ *v* **exemplified, exemplifying** [T] to be or give a typical example of something: *The recent oil price rises exemplify the difficulties which the motor industry is now facing.* **–exemplification** /ɪgˌzemplɪfɪˈkeɪʃən/ *n* [C;U]

ex·empt¹ /ɪgˈzempt/ *adj* [never before a noun] officially freed from a duty, service, or payment: *He is* **exempt from** *military service.*

exempt² *v* [T] to officially free someone from a duty, service, or payment: *His bad health exempted him* **from** *military service.* **–exemption** /-ˈzempʃən/ *n* [C;U]

ex·er·cise¹ /ˈeksəsaɪz ‖ -ər-/ *n* **1** [C;U] the use of any part of your body or mind so as to strengthen it or practise a skill: *If you don't take more exercise you'll get fat.* | *She does exercises to strengthen her voice.* | *piano exercises* **2** [C] a question or set of questions to be answered by a pupil for practice: *Look at Exercise 2 on page 3.* **3** [C] a set of actions carried out by soldiers in time of peace to practise fighting: *They're here for a NATO exercise.* **4** [U] *fml* the use of a stated power or right: *the exercise of one's right to vote*

exercise² *v* **exercised, exercising** **1** [I] to do physical exercises in order to be healthy: *You should exercise more.* **2** [T] *fml* to use a power, quality, or right: *The police urged the demonstrators to exercise restraint.*

ex·ert /ɪɡ'zɜːt ‖ -ɜːrt/ v [T] **1** to use strength or skill in a determined way for a particular purpose: *My wife's been exerting a lot of pressure on me to change my job.* | *Please exert all your influence on the Company directors.* **2 exert yourself** to make an effort: *He never exerts himself to help anyone.*

ex·er·tion /ɪɡ'zɜːʃən ‖ -ɜːr-/ n [C;U] great effort: *I was really tired after all my exertions.*

ex·hale /eks'heɪl/ v **exhaled, exhaling** [I;T] to breathe out air −opposite **inhale** −**exhalation** /ˌekshə'leɪʃən/ n [C;U]

ex·haust¹ /ɪɡ'zɔːst/ v [T] **1** to tire someone out: *What an exhausting day!* | *I'm absolutely exhausted!* | *That child exhausts me.* **2** to use something up: *The soldiers have nearly exhausted their food supplies.* **3** to say everything there is to say about something: *Well, we've exhausted the subject of work.*

exhaust² n **1** [C] (also **exhaust pipe** /·'· ·/) the pipe which allows unwanted gas or steam to escape from an engine or machine −see picture on page 49 **2** [U] the gas or steam which escapes through this pipe

ex·haus·tion /ɪɡ'zɔːstʃən/ n [U] extreme tiredness: *She's suffering from exhaustion.*

ex·haus·tive /ɪɡ'zɔːstɪv/ adj extremely thorough: *an exhaustive study of the problem* −**exhaustively** adv

ex·hib·it¹ /ɪɡ'zɪbɪt/ v [T] **1** to show something in public: *Her paintings were exhibited in France.* **2** fml to show a sign of a feeling or quality: *They exhibited no emotion when they heard of her death.*

exhibit² n **1** something that is exhibited, especially in a MUSEUM **2** AmE a public show of objects

ex·hi·bi·tion /ˌeksɪ'bɪʃən/ n **1** [C;U] a public show of objects: *an international trade exhibition* | *The children's paintings are on exhibition at the school.* **2** [C] the act of showing particular behaviour: *an exhibition of bad temper* **3 make an exhibition of yourself** to behave foolishly

ex·hi·bi·tion·is·m /ˌeksɪ'bɪʃənɪzəm/ n [U] the behaviour of a person who wants to get attention from other people all the time (a word used to express disapproval): *I was really embarrassed by his exhibitionism at the party.* −**exhibitionist** n

ex·hib·i·tor /ɪɡ'zɪbɪtər/ n someone whose work is shown at an exhibition

ex·hil·a·rate /ɪɡ'zɪləreɪt/ v **exhilarated, exhilarating** [T] to make someone feel very cheerful and excited: *We felt very exhilarated after our long walk in the fresh air.* | *an exhilarating ride in his sports car* −**exhilaration** /ɪɡˌzɪlə'reɪʃən/ n [U]

ex·hort /ɪɡ'zɔːt ‖ -ɔːrt/ v [T] fml to urge or advise someone strongly to do something: *The general exhorted his men to fight well.* −**exhortation** /ˌeksɔː'teɪʃən ‖ -ɔːr-/ [C;U]

ex·hume /ɪɡ'zjuːm, eks'hjuːm ‖ ɪɡ'zuːm, ɪk'sjuːm/ v **exhumed, exhuming** [T] fml to take a dead body out of the grave −**exhumation** /ˌeksjuː'meɪʃən/ n [C;U]

ex·ile¹ /'eksaɪl, 'egzaɪl/ n **1** [U] forced absence from your own country, often for political reasons: *Napoleon was sent into exile.* | *He died in exile.* **2** [C] someone who has been forced to leave their country, especially for political reasons

exile² v **exiled, exiling** [T] to send someone away from their own country

ex·ist /ɪɡ'zɪst/ v [I] **1** to be real or present, and not imagined: *The technology for performing these*

DESCRIBING PEOPLE

Exercise 1

How would you describe yourself? Using words you know and words from the illustration, complete the table below.

Can you fill in a similar table for someone you know well? It should be someone who you can't see at the moment. See how well you can describe the person.

Hairstyle
Colour of hair
Body shape (build)
Colour of eyes
Complexion
Other details (beard, glasses etc.)

Hairstyle
Colour of hair
Body shape (build)
Colour of eyes
Complexion
Other details (beard, glasses etc.)

Exercise 2

Read this description of Mr Sampson:

Mr Sampson is small and stout. He has short brown hair. He has bright blue eyes and a fair complexion. He has a brown moustache and he wears glasses.

Now write a description of the person you described in Exercise 1 in the same way. Would you prefer to be taller, shorter, thinner, fatter? Would you prefer to have curlier/ straighter hair? Write a description of the way you would like to look.

describing people

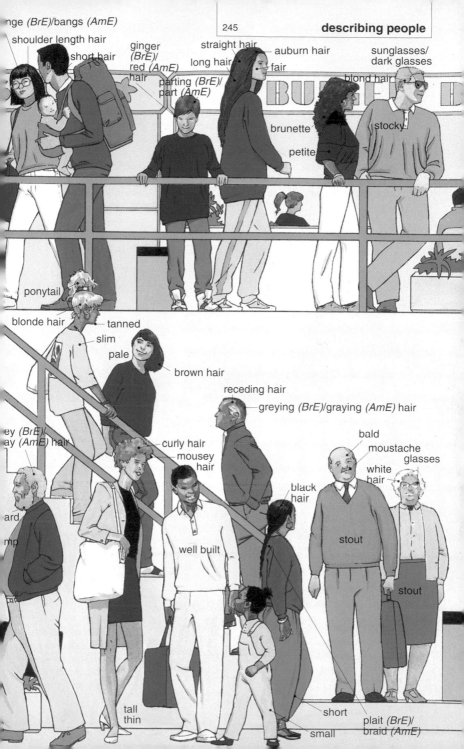

nge (BrE)/bangs (AmE)

shoulder length hair

short hair

ginger (BrE)/ red (AmE) hair

parting (BrE)/ part (AmE)

straight hair

long hair

auburn hair

fair

sunglasses/ dark glasses

blond hair

brunette

stocky

petite

ponytail

blonde hair

tanned

slim

pale

brown hair

receding hair

greying (BrE)/graying (AmE) hair

ey (BrE)/ ay (AmE) hair

curly hair

mousey hair

bald

moustache

glasses

white hair

black hair

beard

mp

well built

stout

stout

tall thin

short

small

plait (BrE)/ braid (AmE)

global warming
Heat from the sun reaches the earth, but pollution in the atmosphere prevents it escaping back into space, and the temperature of the atmosphere rises. This is also called the 'The Greenhouse Effect'.

air pollution
Cars, factories, power stations and rubbish dumps all emit gases which add to air pollution.

deforestation
Cutting down and burning trees destroys wildlife habitats and adds to air pollution.

ozone laye

acid rain

forest

power station

smog

rubbish dump

factory

effluent

pesticide

traffic jam

exhaust fumes

sewage

contamination
Pesticides used to spray crops can contaminate water supplies as well as soil.

litter

congestion
More and more cars appear on our roads each year, causing congestion and pollution.

oil slick

oil tanker

water pollution
Oil spills, effluent from factories and sewage all add to pollution in our rivers and seas.

operations already exists. | *Do you think fairies exist?* **2** (of a person) to live under difficult conditions, especially with very little money or food: *She exists on tea and bread.*

ex·ist·ence /ɪgˈzɪstəns/ *n* **1** [U] the state of being alive, real, or present: *This law came into existence in 1918.* | *She doesn't believe in the existence of God.* **2** [sing] a way of living: *Working as a writer can be a very lonely existence.*

ex·ist·ing /ɪgˈzɪstɪŋ/ *adj* [only before a noun] present or being used now: *We'll get new computers to replace the existing ones.*

ex·it¹ /ˈegzɪt, ˈeksɪt/ *n* **1** a door or other way out from a public place **2** a point where a road leaves a MOTORWAY **3 make an exit** *fml* to leave a place often in a way which makes people notice you: *She made a hasty exit.*

exit² *v* **1** [I] to leave: *She exited pretty quickly when she heard him arriving.* **2 exit** a word used as an instruction to an actor or actress to leave the stage: *Exit Hamlet, bearing the body of Polonius.* **3** [I;T] to leave a computer program

ex·o·dus /ˈeksədəs/ *n* [sing] the movement of a lot of people leaving a place at the same time: *an exodus of cars from the city every evening*

ex·on·e·rate /ɪgˈzɒnəreɪt ‖ ɪgˈzɑː-/ *v* **exonerated, exonerating** *fml* [T] to show that someone is not guilty: *The report on the accident exonerates the company from any responsibility.*

ex·or·bi·tant /ɪgˈzɔːbɪtənt ‖ -ɔːr-/ *adj* much greater than is reasonable (used of prices and demands): *That hotel charges exorbitant prices.* –**exorbitantly** *adv*

ex·or·cis·m /ˈeksɔːsɪzəm ‖ -ɔːr-/ *n* [C;U] a way of driving an evil spirit away by prayer or command –**exorcist** *n*

ex·or·cize /ˈeksɔːsaɪz ‖ -ɔːr-/ *v* **exorcized, exorcizing** (also **exorcise** *BrE*) [T] to free a person or place from an evil spirit in a religious ceremony

ex·ot·ic /ɪgˈzɒtɪk ‖ ɪgˈzɑː-/ *adj* **1** unusual and exciting: *exotic clothes* **2** from a distant and interesting country: *exotic food* | *exotic smells*

ex·pand /ɪkˈspænd/ *v* [I;T] **1** to increase in size or number: *Iron expands when it is heated.* | *The company has expanded its operations in Scotland.* **2 expand on something** to give more details about something you have said or written: *Could you expand on your last point, please?* –**expandable** *adj*

ex·panse /ɪkˈspæns/ *n* a large area of something: *a vast expanse of sand*

ex·pan·sion /ɪkˈspænʃən/ *n* [U] the process of increasing in size: *the expansion of metals when heated* | *economic expansion*

ex·pan·sive /ɪkˈspænsɪv/ *adj* friendly and willing to talk: *Later, after dinner, he became quite expansive.* –**expansively** *adv*

ex·pat·ri·ate /ekˈspætriət, -trieɪt ‖ ekˈspeɪ-/ *n* (also **expat** /eksˈpæt/ *infml*) someone living in a country which is not their own

ex·pect /ɪkˈspekt/ *v* **1** [T; + (that)] to believe that something will happen: *I expect she'll do well.* | *We fully expected it to be a complete disaster.* | *Do you expect to travel a lot this year?* | *The Prime Minister was re-elected, as expected.* | *I had no idea what to expect.*

☐ USEFUL PATTERNS to expect something; to expect (that) something will happen; to expect something to happen; to expect to do something –see WAIT¹ (USAGE)

2 half expect to believe that something is possible, although in fact it is very unlikely: *Your grandfather looked so much better last night that I half*

ENVIRONMENTAL PROBLEMS

Use the words in the box to complete these two newspaper articles about environmental problems. Write the number of the space beside each word.

pesticides	spray	chemicals
rain	mixture	smog
chimneys	power	clouds
forests	blood	

TALL CHIMNEYS CAUSE ACID RAIN

In December 1952, nearly four thousand people died in London. They died because they breathed a terrible ¹___ of smoke and fog which the Londoners called ²_____. Scientists discovered that most of the smoke came from factories and ³___ stations. The government told them to build tall ⁴___ so the smoke would blow away. This solved the problem in London but it caused more problems elsewhere. The smoke went high up into the ⁵___ where the chemicals in the smoke mixed with water to make acid ⁶___. These blew across the English Channel and caused acid rain to fall in Scandinavia and Northern Europe. This acid rain destroyed buildings, ⁷___ and lakes in those countries.

CHEMICALS MAKE BLOOD-RED SEA

The valley of the River Po in Northern Italy is an important agricultural area. The farmers in this region produce a lot of very good food but they use a lot of chemicals to help them. They ⁸___ the fields with fertilisers and ⁹___ to feed and protect the crops. Unfortunately, when it rains, a lot of these ¹⁰___ are washed away from the earth into streams and eventually into the River Po. This river carries the chemicals into the Adriatic sea. In 1989, parts of the Adriatic sea became as red as ¹¹___. An algae, a type of sea weed, was growing in the rich mixture of chemicals in the water. Tourists didn't want to swim in red sea water and they cancelled their holidays.

expected him to join in the dancing. **3 I expect**... a phrase used to say that you think something is probably true: "Is she coming?" "I expect so." | I expect you're hungry. Let's have dinner. **4 be expecting someone or something** to feel sure that someone or something will arrive, often because you have arranged it: We're expecting them for lunch. | Are you expecting a parcel? **5 be expecting a baby, be expecting** to be going to have a baby **6** [T] to hope for or demand certain behaviour because you think that this behaviour is desirable or necessary: Visitors to the hospital are expected not to smoke. | We expect the highest standards from all our employees. | Her teachers always expected too much of her.

□ USEFUL PATTERNS to expect something from/of someone; to expect someone to do something

7 what do you expect? a phrase used to show that you are not surprised by something: "I feel sick." "Well what do you expect after a six-course meal?"

ex·pec·tan·cy /ɪk'spektənsi/ n [U] a feeling of excitement about something that is going to happen

ex·pec·tant /ɪk'spektənt/ adj **1** waiting with excitement: the expectant crowds outside the palace **2 expectant mother**, a woman whose baby is soon going to be born **–expectantly** adv

ex·pec·ta·tion /ˌekspek'teɪʃən/ n **1** [U] strong belief that something will happen: She has little expectation of getting married now. | Contrary to expectation it was John who failed the exam. **2** [C] a feeling of hope or confidence that something will happen: the high expectations of young people today

ex·pe·di·en·cy /ɪk'spiːdiənsi/ n [U] convenience rather than what it is morally correct to do (a word used to express disapproval): All his actions are governed by expediency.

ex·pe·di·ent¹ /ɪk'spiːdiənt/ adj [never before a noun] useful or helpful but not necessarily morally correct: She thought it expedient not to tell her mother where she had been.

expedient² n a useful plan, idea, or action which provides an answer for an urgent problem: When she forgot her keys she got into the house by the simple expedient of climbing through a window.

ex·pe·dite /'ekspədaɪt/ v **expedited, expediting** fml [T] to make something happen more quickly

ex·pe·di·tion /ˌekspə'dɪʃən/ n a journey, usually long and carefully organized, which is made for a particular purpose: an expedition to the North Pole | a shopping expedition

ex·pel /ɪk'spel/ v **-ll-** [T] **1** to force someone to leave a country: Six American diplomats have already been expelled. **2** to send someone away officially from a school or club: I was expelled from school for smoking. **3** to force something out from your body or a container: The pressure causes air to be expelled from the lungs.

ex·pend /ɪk'spend/ v fml [T] to spend or use something: A great deal of time, money and energy have been expended unnecessarily.

ex·pen·da·ble /ɪk'spendəbəl/ adj no longer needed, and so able to be thrown away or destroyed

ex·pen·di·ture /ɪk'spendɪtʃəʳ/ n [U] **1** the amount of money that someone spends: promises to increase government expenditure on education **2** spending or using of time, money, or effort for a particular purpose

ex·pense /ɪk'spens/ n [C;U] **1** cost in money: It's quite an expense, having a car. | the expense of

private school fees **2 expenses** [pl] the money you use or need for a purpose: While she's abroad on business her company pay all her expenses. | travelling expenses **3 great expense, little expense, no expense** by paying a lot of money, a little money only, no money at all: They went to great expense to make the party a success. | She's had her flat redecorated at very little expense to herself. **4 at the expense of** causing loss or damage to something: He finished the job at the expense of his health. **5 at someone's expense: a** with someone paying the cost: He had his book printed at his own expense. **b** as a joke against someone so as to make them seem silly: We had a good laugh at Mike's expense.

ex·pen·sive /ɪk'spensɪv/ adj costing a lot of money: It's much too expensive! | an expensive new coat –opposite **inexpensive** –**expensively** adv

ex·pe·ri·ence¹ /ɪk'spɪəriəns/ n **1** [U] knowledge or skill which comes from doing or feeling something for a long time rather than from books: a teacher with five years' experience | I know from experience that it won't work. **2** [C] something that happens to you and has an effect on your mind and feelings: Our journey by camel was quite an experience.

experience² v **experienced, experiencing** [T] to feel, or to be influenced by something that happens: The country is experiencing a sharp economic decline. | She's experienced a few difficulties at work recently.

ex·pe·ri·enced /ɪk'spɪəriənst/ adj good at something because you have spent a lot of time doing it: an experienced doctor | experienced travellers –opposite **inexperienced**

ex·per·i·ment¹ /ɪk'sperɪmənt/ n [C;U] **1** a scientific test done in order to learn something or prove the truth of an idea: The architect wanted to carry out an experiment in town planning. | The theory has been proved conclusively by experiment. **2** the trying out of a new idea or process: The school is an experiment in bilingual education.

ex·per·i·ment² /ɪk'sperɪment/ v [I] **1** to do a scientific test to find out or prove something: Is it right to experiment on animals? **2** to try out a new idea or process to see what results it has: She likes experimenting with different recipes. –**experimentation** /ɪk,sperɪmen'teɪʃən/ n [U]

ex·per·i·men·tal /ɪk,sperɪ'mentl◂/ adj using or testing new ideas: an experimental farm –**experimentally** adv

ex·pert /'eksp3ːt ‖ -3ːrt/ n a person with special knowledge or skills as a result of experience or study: She's an expert in 19th century literature. –**expert** adj: He's expert at handling teenagers. | an expert cook –**expertly** adv

ex·per·tise /ˌeksp3ː'tiːz ‖ -3ːr-/ n [U] a skill or knowledge of something which comes from experience or training: Her technical expertise saved the company.

ex·pire /ɪk'spaɪəʳ/ v **expired, expiring** [I] **1** to come to the end of the time that something can be legally used: My visa expires next month. **2** lit to die

ex·pi·ry /ɪk'spaɪəri/ n [U] the end of a stated period of time for which a legal DOCUMENT or agreement can be used: What is the expiry date on your driving licence? | the expiry of our lease

ex·plain /ɪk'spleɪn/ v [I;T;+that] **1** to make something clear and easy to understand: I don't understand this but the lawyer will explain. | Can you explain the new policy to us? | Could you explain how to turn the heating on? | She explained that the farm belonged to her brother.

□ USEFUL PATTERNS to explain something; to explain something to someone; to explain that..., to explain how, why, etc.
2 to give a reason for something: *Can you explain your stupid behaviour?* | *That explains why he's not here.* | *I explained that I'd missed the bus.*
□ USEFUL PATTERNS to explain something; to explain something to someone; to explain that...; to explain how, why, etc.
3 explain yourself to make your meaning clear or give a reason for your behaviour: *Could you explain yourself please?*
explain sthg ↔ **away** *phr v* [T] to make something seem unimportant or not your fault: *Your department will have to explain away the poor sales figures.*

ex·pla·na·tion /ˌekspləˈneɪʃən/ *n* [C;U] **1** what you say or write to make something easily understood: *First, I'll give you a short explanation of how the machine works.* **2** something that gives a reason for something else: *Can you think of any explanation for his rudeness?*

ex·plan·a·to·ry /ɪkˈsplænətəri ‖ -tɔːri/ *adj* giving more information about something or a reason for something

ex·ple·tive /ɪkˈspliːtɪv ‖ ˈeksplətɪv/ *n* a word which is said loudly and suddenly to express anger or annoyance

ex·pli·ca·ble /ekˈsplɪkəbəl/ *adj* [never before a noun] *fml* understandable: *Her behaviour is explicable if you consider her age.* –opposite **inexplicable** –**explicably** *adv*

ex·pli·cit /ɪkˈsplɪsɪt/ *adj* clear and fully expressed: *Could you ask her for more explicit instructions?* –compare IMPLICIT –**explicitly** *adv*

ex·plode /ɪkˈspləʊd/ *v* **exploded, exploding 1** [I;T] to blow up or burst suddenly with a lot of noise and force: *A bomb has exploded in the centre of London.* **2** [I] to show very strong feeling suddenly: *He exploded with anger.* **3** [T] to prove a general idea or belief to be wrong: *These statistics explode the myth that women are worse drivers than men.* **4** [I] to increase quickly: *The population is exploding.*

ex·ploit¹ /ɪkˈsplɔɪt/ *v* [T] **1** to use someone unfairly, usually by paying them very little for their hard work: *Farm workers are being exploited by the big landowners.* **2** to use or develop something fully in order to make money from it: *We must exploit the country's mineral resources.* –**exploitation** /ˌeksplɔɪˈteɪʃən/ *n* [U]

ex·ploit² /ˈeksplɔɪt/ *n* an action which is brave, clever, or interesting in some way

ex·plore /ɪkˈsplɔːʳ/ *v* **explored, exploring** [T] **1** to travel into or through a place to find out about it: *We spent a week exploring the coast.* **2** to examine or think about something carefully: *We must explore all the possibilities.* –**exploration** /ˌeksplə ˈreɪʃən/ *n* [C;U] : *a journey of exploration into China* –**exploratory** /ɪkˈsplɒrətəri ‖ -ˈsplɔːrətɔːri/ *adj*

ex·plo·rer /ɪkˈsplɔːrəʳ/ *n* someone who travels to distant places to find out about them

ex·plo·sion /ɪkˈspləʊʒən/ *n* **1** a loud noise caused by something bursting: *When she lit the gas there was a loud explosion.* **2** a sudden increase: *the population explosion* **3** a sudden expression of very strong feeling: *an explosion of anger*

ex·plo·sive¹ /ɪkˈspləʊsɪv/ *adj* **1** which could blow up: *It's dangerous to smoke when handling explosive materials.* **2** able to cause very strong feelings or argument: *Race relations is an explosive issue.* –**explosively** *adv*

explosive² *n* [C;U] something in a bomb which makes it blow up

ex·po·nent /ɪkˈspəʊnənt/ *n* a person who expresses or supports a particular belief or idea: *She's an exponent of Marxism.*

ex·port¹ /ɪkˈspɔːt ‖ -ɔːrt/ *v* [I;T] to send things to another country, usually to sell them: *The country was exporting cigars and revolutionary ideas.* –compare IMPORT¹

ex·port² /ˈekspɔːt ‖ -ɔːrt/ *n* **1** [U] the business of sending goods to another country and selling them: *the export trade* | *The export of gold is forbidden.* **2** [C] something that is sold and sent to another country: *Wool is one of the chief exports of Australia.* –compare IMPORT²

ex·port·er /ɪkˈspɔːtəʳ ‖ -ɔːr-/ *n* a person, company, or country that sells goods to other countries: *Zambia is the world's largest exporter of copper.*

ex·pose /ɪkˈspəʊz/ *v* **exposed, exposing** [T] **1** to uncover something: *You mustn't expose your skin to the sun.* **2 be exposed** to be put in a situation where you might be harmed: *She was exposed to a lot of danger in the war.* **3** to tell people about something bad or someone who has done something bad and kept it secret: *He was exposed on television as a persistent liar.* **4** to uncover a film to the light, when taking a photograph **5 expose yourself** (of a man) to show your sexual parts on purpose in the hope of exciting or shocking people

ex·po·sé /ekˈspəʊzeɪ ‖ ˌekspəˈzeɪ/ *n* a public statement of the facts about something: *The film is an exposé of the President's connections with organized crime.*

ex·posed /ɪkˈspəʊzd/ *adj* not protected from attack or sheltered from bad weather

ex·po·si·tion /ˌekspəˈzɪʃən/ *n* **1** [C;U] *fml* a detailed explanation of something: *a full exposition of her political beliefs* **2** [C] an international show of industrial products

ex·po·sure /ɪkˈspəʊʒəʳ/ *n* **1** [U] a situation where you are influenced and affected by something: *They risked exposure to harmful radiation.* **2** [U] the harmful effect on someone's body of being out in cold weather for a long time: *We nearly died of exposure on the cold mountain.* **3** [C;U] a situation where the truth about something shocking is made known: *I threatened him with public exposure.* **4** [C] the amount of film that must be uncovered to the light to take one photograph: *I have three exposures left on this film.* **5** [U] treatment: *The situation received a lot of exposure on television.*

ex·pound /ɪkˈspaʊnd/ *v* [T] *fml* to give a reasoned and detailed explanation of something: *The priest expounded his beliefs to us.*

ex·press¹ /ɪkˈspres/ *v* [T] **1** to show a feeling or thought by saying or doing something: *I can't express how grateful I am.* | *She expressed surprise when I told her you were coming.* **2** to write a price or quantity in a particular way: *The figure is expressed as a percentage.* **3 express yourself** to write or say what you think or feel: *He expresses himself well in English.*

express² *n* **1** [C] (also **express train** /·ˈ· ·/) a fast train which stops at only a few stations **2** [U] a service given by the post office or railways for carrying things faster than usual: *Send the letter by express.*

express³ *adv* by a very quick service: *I sent the parcel express.*

express⁴ adj [only before a noun] **1** clearly stated or exact: *It was her express wish that you should have her jewels after her death.* | *I came here with the express purpose of seeing you.* **2** going or sent quickly: *an express train* | *express delivery*

ex·pres·sion /ɪkˈspreʃən/ n **1** [C;U] the act of saying or showing what you think or feel: *freedom of expression* | *the expression of strong beliefs* **2** [U] the ability to show feeling when you are acting or performing music: *She doesn't sing with much expression.* **3** [C] a word or group of words which has a particular meaning: *"Fly off the handle" is an expression which means "lose your temper".* **4** [C] a look on someone's face: *an angry expression*

ex·pres·sion·less /ɪkˈspreʃənləs/ adj showing no feeling (used of someone's voice or face)

ex·pres·sive /ɪkˈspresɪv/ adj showing feelings or meaning: *A baby's cry may be expressive of hunger or pain.* | *an expressive silence* –**expressively** adv

ex·press·ly /ɪkˈspresli/ adv fml clearly or specially: *I told you expressly to lock the door.* | *The lift has been put in expressly for the disabled.*

ex·press·way /ɪkˈspreswei/ n the usual American word for MOTORWAY

ex·pro·pri·ate /ɪkˈsprəʊprieɪt/ v expropriated, expropriating [T] fml to take away another person's property, often for public use: *The State expropriated all land owned by foreigners.*

ex·pul·sion /ɪkˈspʌlʃən/ n [C;U] the act of forcing someone to leave a place such as a country, a club, or a school as a result of an official decision: *the child's expulsion from school* | *the expulsion of three diplomats*

ex·pur·gate /ˈekspəgeit ‖ -ər-/ v expurgated, expurgating [T] fml to make something such as a book or a play acceptable by taking out anything which might shock or offend people

ex·qui·site /ɪkˈskwɪzt, ˈekskwɪ-/ adj **1** extremely beautiful, delicate, or sensitive: *exquisite manners* | *an exquisite piece of jewellery* | *He has exquisite taste in music.* **2** strongly felt or experienced: *exquisite pleasure* –**exquisitely** adv

ex·tem·po·rize /ɪkˈstempəraɪz/ v extemporized, extemporizing [I] to speak without time for thought or preparation: *The actress forgot her lines and had to extemporize.*

ex·tend /ɪkˈstend/ v **1** [I+adv/prep] to reach, stretch, or continue: *The hot weather extended into October.* | *His land extends all the way to the river.* **2** [T] to make something longer or bigger: *They are extending the railway to the next town.* **3** [T] to make something exist over a longer period: *I need to extend my visa.* **4** [T] to stretch out a part of your body: *She extended her hand and I took told of it.* **5** [T] fml to give or offer something to someone: *I'd like to extend a warm welcome to our guests.* | *The bank will extend more credit to you.*

ex·ten·sion /ɪkˈstenʃən/ n **1** [C;U] something which increases what is already there: *the extension of the copyright laws to cover recorded material* **2** [C] a part which is added to make something longer or bigger: *We plan to build an extension onto the house.* **3** [C] a telephone line which leads from one central point to various rooms or offices in a large building: *Could I have extension 45, please?*

ex·ten·sive /ɪkˈstensɪv/ adj large in amount or area: *an extensive garden* | *extensive damage* | *extensive knowledge* –**extensively** adv

ex·tent /ɪkˈstent/ n **1** [U] the size or limit of something: *The full extent of the Sahara desert is not*

known. | *I was surprised at the extent of his knowledge.* **2 to a certain extent, to some extent, to a large extent** partly but not completely: *I agree with what you say to a certain extent.* **3 to the extent that, to the extent of, to such an extent that** to a point where something else happens: *The temperature rose to such an extent that the firemen had to leave the burning building.*

ex·ten·u·ate /ɪkˈstenjueit/ v extenuated, extenuating [T] **1** fml to make bad behaviour less serious by finding excuses for it **2 extenuating circumstances** facts which help to excuse bad behaviour

ex·te·ri·or¹ /ɪkˈstɪəriər/ adj on the outside surface: *the exterior walls* –opposite **interior**

exterior² n the outer appearance or surface of something: *the exterior of the house* | *Deep unhappiness was hidden beneath his cheerful exterior.* –opposite **interior**

ex·ter·mi·nate /ɪkˈstɜːmɪneit ‖ -ɜːr-/ v exterminated, exterminating [T] to kill every member of a group of people or animals –**extermination** /ɪkˌstɜːmɪˈneiʃən ‖ -ɜːr-/ n [U]

ex·ter·nal /ɪkˈstɜːnəl ‖ -ɜːr-/ adj **1** outside a place, person, or thing: *external walls* | *There are a lot of external pressures on her.* **2** coming to do a job at your organization from another one: *an external examiner* **3** able to be seen, but not real or natural: *Despite external appearances, she's very shy.* **4 for external use only** not to be drunk or eaten –opposite **internal** –**externally** adv

ex·tinct /ɪkˈstɪŋkt/ adj **1** having no living example: *Every year several species of bird become extinct.* **2** no longer active (used of VOLCANOS)

ex·tinc·tion /ɪkˈstɪŋkʃən/ n [U] **1** the killing or death of the last remaining animals of a certain kind: *The human race is now threatened with complete extinction.* **2** the end or ending of something: *the extinction of his hopes*

ex·tin·guish /ɪkˈstɪŋgwɪʃ/ v [T] fml **1** to put out a light or fire: *Please extinguish all cigarettes.* **2** to destroy a feeling or an idea: *Nothing could extinguish his belief that she would get better.*

ex·tol /ɪkˈstəʊl/ v -ll- [T] fml to praise someone or something very highly: *He extols her virtues and sees none of her faults.*

ex·tort /ɪkˈstɔːt ‖ -ɔːrt/ v [T] to obtain something by force or threats: *He's been accused of extorting money* from *local shopkeepers.* –**extortion** /-ˈstɔːʃən ‖ -ɔːr-/ n [U] : *a promise obtained by extortion*

ex·tor·tion·ate /ɪkˈstɔːʃənt ‖ -ɔːr-/ adj unfairly high or great (used of demands and prices) –**extortionately** adv

ex·tra¹ /ˈekstrə/ adj,adv **1** [only before a noun] beyond what is usual or necessary: *an extra loaf of bread* | *I'll have to work extra hard.* **2** [never before a noun] as well as the regular charge: *Dinner costs £8, and wine is extra.* | *They charge extra for a cooked breakfast.*

extra² n **1** something that is added and for which you usually have to pay more: *It's £500 a term without any extras such as piano lessons.* **2** someone who has a very small part in a film, for example in a crowd scene

ex·tract¹ /ɪkˈstrækt/ v fml [T] **1** to pull or take something out, often with difficulty: *She extracted some papers* from *the file.* **2** to remove something from another substance using a machine or some other process: *They are extracting gold* from *those rocks.* |

Oil is extracted from the seeds of certain plants. **3** to obtain something from someone with difficulty: *See if you can extract any more information from him.* **4** to remove a tooth from someone's mouth: *I had a tooth extracted.*

ex·tract² /ˈekstrækt/ *n* **1** [C] a passage taken from a longer piece of speech or writing, for example to show the style: *She read me a few extracts from his letter.* **2** [C;U] a product obtained by removing it from some other substance: *meat extract*

ex·trac·tion /ɪkˈstrækʃən/ *n* **1** [C;U] the removal of something: *Her teeth are so bad that she needs five extractions.* | *the extraction of coal from a mine* **2** [U] the origin of a person's family: *an American of Russian extraction*

ex·tra·cur·ric·u·lar /ˌekstrəkəˈrɪkjʊlər/ *adj* outside the regular course of work in a school or college: *extracurricular activities*

ex·tra·dite /ˈekstrədaɪt/ *v* **extradited, extraditing** [T] to send someone, who may be guilty of a crime and who has escaped to another country back to their own country for trial −**extradition** /ˌekstrəˈdɪʃən/ *n* [C;U]

ex·tra·ne·ous /ɪkˈstreɪniəs/ *adj fml* not belonging to or directly connected with the subject: *His account of the evening includes a lot of extraneous details.*

extra·or·di·na·ry /ɪkˈstrɔːdənəri ‖ ɪkˈstrɔːrdn-eri, ˌekstrəˈɔːr-/ *adj* **1** very strange: *What an extraordinary idea!* **2** unusual or special: *a girl of extraordinary beauty* | *An act was passed giving the army extraordinary powers.* **3 extraordinary meeting** a meeting which is not a regular one but arranged to deal with a particular problem −**extraordinarily** *adv*

ex·trap·o·late /ɪkˈstræpəleɪt/ *v* **extrapolated, extrapolating** [I;T] *fml* to use the information you have to decide what might happen in the future

ex·trav·a·gant /ɪkˈstrævəgənt/ *adj* **1** spending or costing too much money: *the government's extravagant policies* | *When it comes to books, he's always been extravagant.* **2** beyond what is reasonable: *He makes the most extravagant claims about this new invention of his.* | *extravagant praise* −**extravagantly** *adv* −**extravagance** *n* [C;U] : *I was shocked at his extravagance.*

ex·treme¹ /ɪkˈstriːm/ *adj* **1** [only before a noun] at the far edge or end of something: *in the extreme north* **2** [only before a noun] very great: *extreme heat* | *extreme danger* **3** going beyond the usual limits and likely to be disapproved of by most people: *His political ideas are rather extreme.* | *an extreme right-wing party*

extreme² *n* **1** a point beyond what is usual or reasonable: *He used to be a Communist, but now he's gone to the other extreme and joined the Fascists.* | *Sometimes he eats enormous amounts and sometimes nothing. He goes from one extreme to the other.* **2 carry something to extremes** to behave in a way which is good in itself, but to do it to an unreasonable degree: *That's carrying efficiency to extremes.* [RELATED PHRASES **go to extremes, take something to extremes**] **3 in the extreme** to a very great degree: *She was uncooperative in the extreme.*

ex·treme·ly /ɪkˈstriːmli/ *adv* very: *I'm extremely sorry.*

ex·trem·ist /ɪkˈstriːmɪst/ *n* a person with strong political opinions which most people consider are beyond the limits of what is reasonable: *The laboratory was destroyed by extremists protesting about animal rights.* −**extremist** *adj* −**extremism** *n* [U]

ex·trem·i·ty /ɪkˈstremɪti/ *n* **extremities 1** [sing] the highest degree of suffering and sorrow: *an extremity of pain* **2 extremities** [pl] your hands and feet: *The fire will warm our extremities, at least.* **3** [C] *fml* the furthest point or edge of something: *The huts were situated at the extremity of the field.*

ex·tri·cate /ˈekstrɪkeɪt/ *v* **extricated, extricating** [T] to free someone or something from a place or a difficult situation: *Help me extricate this bird from the fence.* | *It was two hours before he managed to extricate himself from the meeting.*

ex·tro·vert, /ˈekstrəvɜːt ‖ -ɜːrt/ *n* a person who likes to be with other people and finds them easy to talk to

ex·u·be·rant /ɪgˈzjuːbərənt ‖ ɪgˈzuː-/ *adj* very happy, excited, and active: *an exuberant child* −**exuberantly** *adv* −**exuberance** *n* [U]

ex·ude /ɪgˈzjuːd ‖ ɪgˈzuːd/ *v* **exuded, exuding 1** [I;T] to flow out slowly or cause a liquid to flow out slowly: *Sweat exuded from every part of his body.* **2** [T] to show a feeling or quality strongly: *He exuded great charm to those around him.*

ex·ult /ɪgˈzʌlt/ *v* *lit* [I] to be very pleased about something that has been successful: *The people exulted in the victory.* | *They exulted at the enemy's defeat.* −**exultant** *adj* −**exultation** /ˌegzʌlˈteɪʃən/ [U] : *They heard a cry of exultation as the climber reached the mountain top.*

eye¹ /aɪ/ *n* **1** one of the two organs on your face with which you see: *He lost an eye in an accident.* | *She has beautiful blue eyes.* **2** the hole in a needle through which the thread passes **3** the dark spot on a potato from which a new plant can grow **4** the calm centre of a storm **5 an eye for** good judgment about something: *She's got a good eye for fashion.* **6 have an eye on** to watch and judge someone: *They've got their eyes on you for promotion.* **7 have eyes in the back of your head** *infml* to be able to see or notice everything: *You need eyes in the back of your head with small children.* **8 in the eyes of, in someone's eyes** in someone's opinion: *In her father's eyes, she can do nothing wrong.* | *In the eyes of the law, she's a dangerous criminal.* **9 keep an eye on** *infml* to watch someone or something to check that they are safe: *Our neighbours keep an eye on the house while we're away.* **10 keep an eye out for, keep your eyes open for** *infml* to try to notice and remember someone or something: *The police are keeping an eye out for trouble.* **11 keep your eyes peeled/skinned** *infml* to watch carefully: *The thieves kept their eyes peeled for the police.* **12 make eyes at someone** *infml* to show that you find someone sexually attractive by looking at them in an inviting way **13 see eye to eye** to agree with someone completely: *He and his brother don't always see eye to eye.* **14 under your very eyes, before your very eyes** in front of you, so that you can see it with no difficulty: *They must have stolen the papers under my very eyes.* **15 up to your eyes in, up to the eyes in** *infml* having a lot of something to deal with: *I'm up to my eyes in work.* **16 with your eyes open** knowing about the possible problems: *You married him with your eyes open, so don't complain now!* **17 -eyed** having eyes of a particular type or number: *blue-eyed* | *one-eyed* | *bright-eyed*

eye² *v* **eyed, eyeing** [T] to look at something carefully with interest or distrust

eye·ball /ˈaɪbɔːl/ *n* the whole of your eye, including the part hidden inside your head

eye·brow /ˈaɪbraʊ/ *n* **1** the line of hairs above each of your eyes **2 raise your eyebrows** to show surprise, doubt, or disapproval:" *A lot of eyebrows were raised at the news of the minister's dismissal.*

eye-catch·ing /ˈ· ˌ··/ *adj* so unusual or attractive that you cannot help looking at it: *an eye-catching advertisement | an eye-catching dress*

eye·lash /ˈaɪlæʃ/ *n* one of the small hairs which grow from the edge of each eyelid

eye·lid /ˈaɪˌlɪd/ *n* one of the two pieces of skin which can move down to cover your eyes

eye-o·pen·er /ˈ· ˌ···/ *n* [sing] something surprising, from which you learn something for the first time: *The film about China was a real eye-opener.*

eye·sight /ˈaɪsaɪt/ *n* [U] the ability to see: *He's got very poor eyesight.*

eye·sore /ˈaɪsɔːr/ *n* something ugly which many people have to look at: *That new shopping centre is a real eyesore.*

eye·strain /ˈaɪstreɪn/ *n* [U] a painful and tired condition of the eyes caused, for example, by reading in bad light

eye·wit·ness /ˈaɪˌwɪtnɪ̌s/ *n* a person who sees an event and is able to describe it, especially in a court of law: *Were there any eyewitnesses to the crime?*

F,f

F, f /ef/ **F's, f's** or **Fs, fs** the 6th letter of the English alphabet

F an abbreviation for FAHRENHEIT

fa·ble /ˈfeɪbəl/ n a short story, often about animals, that teaches a lesson or truth

fab·ric /ˈfæbrɪk/ n **1** [C;U] cloth: *a delicate silk fabric* **2** [U] the walls and roof of a building **3 the fabric of society** the way society is organized and the customs of society

fab·ri·cate /ˈfæbrɪkeɪt/ v **fabricated, fabricating** [T] to invent information in order to deceive people: *Later we realized that he'd fabricated the whole story.* –**fabrication** /ˌfæbrɪˈkeɪʃən/ n [C;U]

fab·u·lous /ˈfæbjḁləs/ adj **1** *infml* very good or pleasant: *You look fabulous!* | *We had a fabulous holiday.* **2** [only before a noun] extremely great (used especially of someone's beauty or wealth) **3** existing only in stories: *fabulous creatures*

fab·u·lous·ly /ˈfæbjḁləsli/ adv **fabulously rich, fabulously beautiful** extremely rich or beautiful

fa·cade /fəˈsɑːd, fæ-/ n (also **façade**) **1** the front of a building **2** a way of behaving which hides your real feelings or character

face¹ /feɪs/ n **1** the front part of your head, which has your eyes, nose, and mouth on it: *a happy face* | *She had a surprised expression on her face.* **2 a long face** an unhappy expression **3 a straight face** a serious expression: *I felt bad about laughing at him but I just couldn't keep a straight face.* **4 face to face** looking directly at someone: *I'd like to talk to him face to face.* **5** the surface of a clock or watch, which has numbers on it to show the time **6** the side of a mountain or wall of rock: *the north face of Everest* | *workers at the coal face* **7** *fml* the appearance or nature of something; *the changing face of capitalism* **8 on the face of it** judging by what you already know or can see **9 take something at face value** to accept or believe something without questioning it **10 come face to face with something** to be forced to deal with something unpleasant: *She came face to face with death.* **11 in the face of** in spite of: *She succeeded in the face of great difficulties.* **12 lose face** to lose the respect of other people **13 save face** to avoid losing the respect of other people

face² v **faced, facing** [T] **1** to be looking towards something: *She turned to face me.* **2** to have the front pointing towards something: *The house faces north.* **3** to have to deal with something unpleasant: *There are a lot of problems that we need to face.* **4 be faced with something** to have to deal with something difficult or unpleasant: *We were faced with a difficult choice.* **5 face the music** to accept punishment for something you have done **6 can't face** to be unwilling to do something because it is too difficult or unpleasant: *I can't face going to the dentist today.*

face up to sthg *phr* v [T] to accept something difficult or unpleasant: *You'll have to face up to your responsibilities now.*

face·cloth /ˈfeɪsklɒθ ‖ -klɔːθ/ n a small cloth that you use to wash your body

face·less /ˈfeɪsləs/ adj dull and without human feeling: *faceless bureaucrats*

face-lift /ˈ‑ ˌ‑/ n a medical operation to make your face look younger by tightening the skin

face-sav·ing /ˈ‑ ˌ‑/ adj allowing someone to appear worthy of respect even though they may not be: *The union quickly negotiated a face-saving agreement with the management.*

fac·et /ˈfæsɪt/ n **1** a part of something to be considered: *That is only one facet of his personality.* **2** a flat side of a cut jewel or precious stone

fa·ce·tious /fəˈsiːʃəs/ adj tending to use unsuitable jokes in a serious situation (a word used to express disapproval) –**facetiously** adv –**facetiousness** n [U]

fa·cial¹ /ˈfeɪʃəl/ adj relating to or concerning your face: *facial hair* –**facially** adv

facial² n a beauty treatment for your face

fa·cile /ˈfæsaɪl ‖ ˈfæsəl/ adj too simple, and therefore meaningless (a word used to express disapproval): *facile remarks* | *a facile explanation*

fa·cil·i·tate /fəˈsɪlɪteɪt/ v **facilitated, facilitating** [T] *fml* to make something easier: *The new railway line will facilitate north-south communications.*

fa·cil·i·ty /fəˈsɪlɪti/ n **1** [C] an additional useful service or ability: *The computerized phone has a call-back facility.* **2** [sing] *fml* an ability to do something easily: *She's got a real facility for languages.* **3 facilities** [pl] things which can be used for a particular purpose: *The college has excellent sports facilities.*

fac·ing /ˈfeɪsɪŋ/ n [U] **1** an outer surface put onto a wall to protect it or make it attractive **2** material sewn into parts of a garment to make those parts thicker

fac·sim·i·le /fækˈsɪmḁli/ n an exact copy of a picture or piece of writing

fact /fækt/ n **1** [C] something that is known for certain to be true or to have happened: *We must learn all the facts before we make any judgements.* | *The report contains a lot of theories but very few facts.* | *The fact that you haven't got these qualifications doesn't necessarily mean that you can't go to university.* | *The fact is that I don't have enough money to go on holiday this year.* **2** [U] the truth. *Often it is difficult to separate fact from fiction.* **3 in fact, in point of fact, in actual fact, as a matter of fact** phrases you use when you are stating that something is true, especially when it is surprising: *I don't mind if you can't give me a lift. In fact, I'd quite like to walk.* | *The government is claiming that inflation is coming down, but in actual fact it is higher than ever before.* **4 know something for a fact** to know that something is certainly true: *I know for a fact that he intends to hand in his resignation.*

fac·tion /ˈfækʃən/ n **1** [C] a group within a larger group, which has different aims or ideas from the larger group **2** [U] disagreement between members of a group

fac·tor /ˈfæktəʳ/ n **1** one of the conditions or influences which has an effect on a situation: *His friendly manner was an important factor in his success.* **2** *tech* a whole number which can be multiplied by another whole number to produce a given number: *2 and 3 are factors of 6*

fac·to·ry /ˈfæktəri/ n **factories** a building or group of buildings where goods are made in large quantities –see picture on page 246

facts of life /ˌ·· '·/ n the facts of life the details about sex and how babies are born

fac·tu·al /ˈfæktʃuəl/ adj containing facts or based on facts: a factual account of the war –**factually** adv

fac·ul·ty /ˈfækəlti/ n **faculties 1** a natural ability, for example the ability to see or think: The old man was still in command of all his faculties. **2** a group of university departments: the science faculty

fad /fæd/ n an interest or fashion that only lasts a short time: His interest in photography is just a passing fad.

fade /feɪd/ v **faded, fading 1** [I;T] to make or become paler in colour: My T-shirt faded in the sun. | The photographs have been faded by the light. **2** [I] to become weaker or not as strong: Hopes of a peace settlement are now fading.

fade away phr v [I] to become gradually weaker and then disappear: The sound of thunder faded away.

fae·ces /ˈfiːsiːz/ n (also **feces** AmE) [pl] tech the solid waste material that you pass from your bowels

fag /fæg/ n infml **1 a fag** an unpleasant and tiring thing to do: I find the housework a real fag. **2** BrE a CIGARETTE **3** AmE a HOMOSEXUAL (a word used to express disapproval, and which some people find offensive)

fagged /fægd/ adj BrE infml [never before a noun] (also **fagged out**) very tired

fag·got /ˈfægət/ n (also **fagot** AmE) **1** a ball of cut-up meat which is cooked and eaten **2** a bunch of small sticks for burning (a word no longer used in modern English)

Fah·ren·heit /ˈfærənhaɪt/ n a scale of temperature in which water freezes at 32° and boils at 212° –compare CENTIGRADE

fail¹ /feɪl/ v **1** [I] to be unsuccessful: She failed in her attempt to convince him. **2 fail to do something** to not do something which was expected or needed: He failed to turn up for the meeting. **3** [I;T] to be unsuccessful in an examination: I've failed my driving test three times. | Oh no, I've failed! **4** [I] to stop working properly: The engine failed just after the plane took off. **5** [T] fml to disappoint someone: I know you won't fail me. **6** [T] to be not enough: My courage failed me at the last minute.

fail² n **1** an unsuccessful result in an examination **2 without fail: a** certainly: I shall bring you that book without fail. **b** always: He's there every Friday without fail.

fail·ing¹ /ˈfeɪlɪŋ/ n a fault or weakness: His main failing is greed.

failing² prep in the absence of: Failing instructions, I did what I thought best.

fail·ure /ˈfeɪljər/ n **1** [U] lack of success: His plans ended in failure. **2** [C] a person or thing that has not succeeded: As a writer, he was a failure. | The party was a total failure. **3** [C;U] a situation in which something stops working or does not produce what people expect: He died of heart failure. | The country has suffered a series of crop failures. **4 failure to do something** the fact that someone has not done something: We were worried about his failure to contact us.

SPELLING NOTE
Words with the sound / f / may be spelt **ph-**, like **photograph**.

faint¹ /feɪnt/ adj **1** weak and about to lose consciousness: I began to feel a little bit faint. **2** not strong or clear: a faint sound | a faint smell of coffee | a faint possibility **3 not have the faintest idea** to have no idea at all: I didn't have the faintest idea what he was talking about. –**faintly** adv –**faintness** n [U]

faint² v [I] to lose consciousness for a short time: Several people fainted in the heat.

fair¹ /feər/ adj **1** just or reasonable: a fair decision | That's not fair! It's my turn. | We need to find a taxation system that is fair to everyone. –opposite **unfair 2 fair enough** a phrase used to say that something is reasonable, although you have or have had some doubts: I suppose it's fair enough to take time off work for a sick child. **3 fair play** just and honest treatment of everyone concerned **4** fairly good or large: She's got a fair command of the language. | a fair-sized garden **5** fine and without clouds (used of the weather) **6** light in colour (used of someone's hair or skin) –see picture on page 245 **7** with light-coloured hair or skin: She's very fair. –**fairness** n [U]

fair² adv **play fair** to play or behave honestly and fairly

fair³ n **1** BrE a FUNFAIR **2** a market for farm produce and animals: cattle fairs **3** a very large show of goods or advertising: a book fair

fair·ground /ˈfeəɡraʊnd/ ‖ ˈfeər-/ n an open space where a FUNFAIR is held

fair·ly /ˈfeəli ‖ ˈfeərli/ adv **1** in a just and reasonable way: I felt that I hadn't been treated fairly. **2** quite: She speaks English fairly well. –see RATHER (USAGE)

fai·ry /ˈfeəri/ n fairies an imaginary figure that looks like a very small human, often with wings, and has magical powers

fairy tale /ˈ·· ·/ n (also **fairy story** /ˈ·· ˌ··/) a story for children about fairies and other imaginary magical people

fait ac·com·pli /ˌfeɪt əˈkɒmpli ‖ -ˌækɑːmˈpliː/ n **faits accomplis** /ˌfeɪt əˈkɒmpliːz ‖ -ˌækɑːmˈpliːz/ something that has already happened and cannot be changed

faith /feɪθ/ n **1** [U] trust and confidence: I've got great faith in her ability to succeed. **2 break faith with someone** to fail to keep a promise that you had made to someone **3 keep faith with someone** to keep a promise that you had made to someone **4 in good faith** sincerely, believing that what you are doing is right: They had acted in good faith. **5** [C] a religion: the Christian faith **6** [U] religious belief: a man of great faith

faith·ful /ˈfeɪθfəl/ adj **1** loyal to someone, and continuing to support them: a faithful friend **2** true to the facts or to the original meaning: a faithful translation **3** loyal to your partner by not having a sexual relationship with anyone else: She was always faithful to him. –opposite **unfaithful** (for sense 3) **4 the faithful** the people who belong to a particular religion –**faithfulness** n [U]

faith·ful·ly /ˈfeɪθfəl-i/ adv **1** in a legal or sincere way: I promised you faithfully. **2** exactly: I copied the letter faithfully. **3 Yours faithfully** the usual way of ending a letter that begins "Dear Sir" or "Dear Madam" –compare SINCERELY

faith·less /ˈfeɪθləs/ adj disloyal or dishonest

fake¹ /feɪk/ v **faked, faking** [T] **1** to copy something in order to deceive people: She faked her mother's handwriting. **2** to pretend to experience something: He faked illness.

fake² /n/ **1** something that is not real, but only a copy **2** someone who pretends to be something that they are not really: *Do you think all astrologers are fakes?*

fake³ *adj* made to look like something real in order to deceive people: *fake money*

fal·con /ˈfɔːlkən ‖ ˈfæl-/ *n* a hunting bird that can be trained by people

fal·con·ry /ˈfɔːlkənri ‖ ˈfæl-/ *n* [U] the art of training falcons to hunt

fall¹ /fɔːl/ *v* **fell** /fel/, **fallen** /ˈfɔːlən/, **falling** [I] **1** to move downwards towards the ground: *A tile fell off the roof.* | *The glass fell to the floor and broke.* | *Snow was falling.* **2** to move from being in a standing position to lying on the ground, usually as the result of an accident: *She tripped and fell.* | *Several trees fell down in the gales.* –see picture on page 736 **3** to become lower in level or amount: *The temperature fell to freezing point.* | *Inflation is falling at last.* **4** (of hair) to hang loosely: *Her hair fell over her shoulders.* **5** to be killed in a battle: *soldiers who had fallen in the war* **6** to be defeated or lose power: *The government may well fall at the next election.* **7** to happen: *Night fell quickly.* | *Christmas falls on a Friday this year.* | *A silence fell as he entered the room.* **8** to pass into a new state: *She fell asleep in her chair.* | *She fell ill.* | *He's fallen in love again.* | *She fell silent.* **9 his face fell** = he started to look sad or disappointed **10 fall flat** to fail to produce the desired effect on people: *His jokes all fell flat.* **11 fall into place** to become understandable: *Suddenly everything fell into place and I realized what a fool I'd been.* **12 fall on your feet** to come out of a difficult situation without being harmed **13 fall short** to fail to reach a desired result or standard: *The council planned to build 100 houses this year, but they have fallen short of their target.* **14 fall to bits, fall to pieces** to break into pieces: *I picked the book up and it fell to bits.*

fall about *phr v* [I] *infml* to laugh a lot: *They all fell about laughing.*

fall apart *phr v* [I] to break into pieces: *That coat's falling apart!*

fall back *phr v* [I] to move away from something: *The crowd fell back to let the doctor through.*

fall back on sthg *phr v* [T] to use something because other things have failed: *You'll always have your training as a teacher to fall back on.*

fall behind *phr v* [I] to fail to make progress as quickly as you should: *I've fallen behind with my work.*

fall for *phr v* **1** [T **fall for** sthg] to be cheated or deceived by something: *I knew it was just a trick, and I wasn't going to fall for it.* **2** [T **fall for** sbdy] to start loving someone suddenly and strongly

fall in with sbdy/sthg *phr v* [T] to agree with someone or agree to something: *I'm quite prepared to fall in with this idea.*

fall off *phr v* [I] to decrease in quality or amount: *Membership has fallen off this year.*

fall out *phr v* [I] to quarrel: *I've fallen out with my mother.* | *We fell out over money.*

fall over *phr v* [I] to fall to the ground: *She tripped and fell over.*

fall through *phr v* [I] to fail to happen or fail to be completed: *We had planned to go on holiday, but it all fell through.*

fall² *n* **1** [C] an act of falling: *He had a nasty fall and broke his wrist.* | *a fall of 70 metres* **2** [C] something that has fallen to the ground: *A fall of rocks blocked the road.* | *We've had a heavy fall of snow.* **3** [C] a decrease: *a sudden fall in temperature* | *We're hoping for a fall in interest rates.* **4 the fall of** the defeat of a person or country: *This crisis could lead to the*

fall of the government. **5 the fall** the usual American word for AUTUMN

fal·la·cious /fəˈleɪʃəs/ *adj fml* based on false reasoning: *a fallacious argument*

fal·la·cy /ˈfæləsi/ *n* **fallacies** a false idea or argument: *It is a popular fallacy that success always brings happiness.*

fall·en /ˈfɔːlən/ the past participle of FALL

fal·li·ble /ˈfæləbəl/ *adj fml* able to make a mistake: *Everybody is fallible.* –opposite **infallible** –**fallibility** /ˌfæləˈbɪləti/ *n* [U]

falling-off /ˌ·· ˈ·/ *n* [sing] a decrease: *a falling-off in the numbers of men reporting for duty*

fall·out /ˈfɔːlaʊt/ *n* [U] the dangerous RADIOACTIVE dust left in the air after an atomic or NUCLEAR explosion

fal·low /ˈfæləʊ/ *adj* dug but left for a while with no crops planted (used of land)

false /fɔːls/ *adj* **1** not true or correct: *He gave the police false information.* | *We had given them the false impression that everything was under control.* **2** not real, but made to look like the real thing: *false teeth* | *She was using a false passport.* **3** not sincere in your behaviour: *Everything about her seemed false.* **4 false alarm** a warning of something dangerous, which does not happen **5 under false pretences** by deceiving people and hiding the truth: *He had got into the building under false pretences.* –**falsely** *adv* –**falseness** *n* [U]

false·hood /ˈfɔːlshʊd/ *n* **1** [C] a statement that is untrue **2** [U] the quality of being untrue: *We must establish the truth or falsehood of these claims.*

fal·set·to /fɔːlˈsetəʊ/ *adv* an extremely high male singing voice

fal·si·fy /ˈfɔːlsɪfaɪ/ *v* **falsified, falsifying** [T] to change information and make it untrue: *He was accused of falsifying the facts.* –**falsification** /ˌfɔːlsɪfɪˈkeɪʃən/ *n* [C;U]

fal·si·ty /ˈfɔːlsəti/ *n* [U] the quality of being false or untrue

fal·ter /ˈfɔːltəʳ/ *v* [I] **1** to become weaker and more unsteady: *Her voice faltered and she began to cry.* | *He faltered and almost fell.* **2** to lose confidence in what you are doing: *He never faltered in his resolve to prove his innocence.* –**falteringly** *adv*

fame /feɪm/ *n* [U] the condition of being well known and admired: *She hoped to find fame as a dancer.*

famed /feɪmd/ *adj* well known and admired: *The mountains are famed for their beauty.*

fa·mil·i·ar /fəˈmɪliəʳ/ *adj* **1** known, seen, or experienced before: *Your face seems familiar to me.* | *It was a familiar sight.* **2 familiar with something** already knowing something: *Are you familiar with Harrison's poetry?* –opposite **unfamiliar** (for senses 1 and 2) **3** too friendly and informal for a particular situation: *I didn't like his familiar way of talking to me.* –**familiarity** /fəˌmɪliˈærəti/ *n* [U]

fa·mil·i·ar·ize /fəˈmɪliəraɪz/ *v* **familiarized, familiarizing** (also **familiarise** BrE) **1** [T] to help someone understand something: *First of all, we'd like to familiarize you with the regulations.* **2 familiarize yourself with something** to inform yourself about something: *I need to familiarize myself with the dictionary codes.*

fa·mil·i·ar·ly /fəˈmɪliəli ‖ -liərˌ-/ *adv* in a way which is too friendly and informal for the situation: *He slapped me on the back familiarly.*

fam·i·ly¹ /ˈfæməli/ n **families** 1 [C+sing/pl verb] a group of people related by blood or marriage, especially a group of two parents and their children: *Our family has lived in this house for over a hundred years.* | *the Spanish family next door* | *a one-parent family* | *family photographs* | *Are your family coming?* 2 [U] part of someone's family: *He can come; he's family.* 3 [C] a number of children in one family: *They are both trying to bring up large families on very little money.* 4 [C] a group of things related by being similar in some way: *tigers and other members of the cat family*

family² adj suitable for children as well as older people: *The new Disney film is good family entertainment.*

family plan·ning /ˌ··· ˈ··/ n [U] the controlling of the number of children born in a family by the use of any of various CONTRACEPTIVE methods: *family planning clinics*

family tree /ˌ··· ˈ·/ n a plan of the relationships between the members of a family

fam·ine /ˈfæmɪn/ n [C;U] very serious lack of food: *widespread famine* | *The famine has already caused 300 deaths in rural areas.*

fam·ished /ˈfæmɪʃt/ adj infml **be famished** to be extremely hungry

fa·mous /ˈfeɪməs/ adj very well known: *a famous actor* | *France is famous for its fine food and wine.* ■ USAGE Compare **famous, well-known, notorious, infamous. Famous** is like **well-known** but is a stronger word and means "known over a wide area": *the doctor, the postman and other* **well-known** *people in our village* | *He's a* **famous** *actor – people everywhere in the world recognize his face.* **Notorious** means "famous for something bad": *He was* **notorious** *for his evil deeds.* **Infamous** (rather literary) can mean the same as **notorious** when used before a noun: *an* **infamous** *criminal,* but it can also mean simply wicked or evil (not necessarily **famous**): *Not many people knew about his infamous crimes.*

fa·mous·ly /ˈfeɪməsli/ adv infml very well: *I've always got on famously with my mother-in-law.*

fan¹ /fæn/ n 1 an instrument used to keep you cool by making a flow of air: *a paper fan* | *an electric fan* 2 something with the shape of a half circle: *a fan of papers* 3 a keen supporter: *football fans* | *I've always been a great fan of the Beatles.*

fan² v **-nn-** [T] 1 to cause air to move onto something: *She fanned her face with a newspaper.* | *Use this to fan the fire.* 2 to cause a feeling to become stronger: *His rudeness fanned her irritation into anger.*
fan out phr v [I;T **fan** sthg ↔ **out**] to spread out from a central point: *The soldiers fanned out across the hillside.* | *Watch the swans fanning out their wings.*

fa·nat·ic /fəˈnætɪk/ n a person whose beliefs and behaviour are extreme and often unquestioning, especially in religious or political matters: *a religious fanatic* | *health food fanatics* **–fanatic, fanatical** adj **–fanatically** /-kli/ adv **–fanaticism** /-ˌsɪzəm/ n [U]

SPELLING NOTE
Words with the sound / f /, may be spelt **ph-**, like **photograph.**

---

fan·ci·er /ˈfænsɪər/ n a person who has a strong interest in a certain type of animal or plant: *a pigeon-fancier*

fan·ci·ful /ˈfænsɪfəl/ adj 1 unrelated to reality: *fanciful ideas* 2 showing unusual imagination: *a fanciful poet* **–fancifully** adv

fan·cy¹ /ˈfænsi/ n **fancies** 1 **take a fancy to** to be attracted to a person or thing: *I've taken a sudden fancy to that pink hat.* 2 **take someone's fancy** to attract someone: *The idea of travelling alone took my fancy.* 3 an idea with little relation to reality: *her strange fancies* 4 a liking for something: *How do I know that your wanting a dog is not just a passing fancy?*

fancy² v **fancied, fancying** 1 [T] infml to have a desire for something: *I fancy a swim.* | *Do you fancy going for a walk?* 2 [T] infml to be attracted to someone: *I fancy the man with the beard.* 3 [+ (that)] old fash to believe: *He fancied he had met her before.* 4 a word used to express surprise or disapproval: *Fancy him being married to both of them!* | *Fancy that!* 5 **fancy yourself** to have too high an opinion of yourself: *He really fancies himself as a dancer!*

fancy³ adj not ordinary, but highly decorated, brightly coloured, or unusually expensive: *fancy cakes* | *fancy ideas* | *His furnishings are too fancy for my liking.*

fancy dress /ˌ·· ˈ·/ n [U] unusual or amusing clothes worn for a special occasion: *We've got to go in fancy dress, so I'm making a frog costume.* | *a fancy dress party*

fancy-free /ˌ·· ˈ·/ adj free to do anything you want, especially because you do not have the responsibilities of a close relationship with someone

fan·fare /ˈfænfeər/ n a short, loud piece of music played, especially on the TRUMPET, to introduce a person or event

fang /fæŋ/ n a long sharp tooth

fan·ta·size /ˈfæntəsaɪz/ v **fantasized, fantasizing** (also **fantasise** BrE) [I; +(that)] to have strange or wonderful ideas about something: *He fantasized about acting in Hollywood.* | *We were fantasizing that we would be rich one day.*

fan·tas·tic /fænˈtæstɪk/ adj 1 infml extremely good: *a fantastic meal* | *That's a fantastic idea!* 2 infml very large: *She's spent a fantastic amount of money on that house.* 3 very strange and unrelated to reality: *a fantastic dream* | *fantastic fears* **–fantastically** /-kli/ adv

fan·ta·sy /ˈfæntəsi/ n **fantasies** [C;U] something quite unreal which you imagine: *She's trying to live out one of her fantasies.* | *The story is pure fantasy.* | *He lives in a fantasy world.*

far¹ /fɑː/ adv **farther** /ˈfɑːðər/ ‖ /ˈfɑːr-/ or **further** /ˈfɜːðər/ ‖ /ˈfɜːr-/, **farthest** /ˈfɑːðəst/ ‖ /ˈfɑːr-/ or **furthest** /ˈfɜːðəst/ ‖ /ˈfɜːr-/ 1 a long way away: *Is it far to your house?* | *Shall we walk? It's not very far.* | *How far is the station from here?* | *We walked quite far into the woods.* | *We don't see him very often because he lives too far away.* | *Christmas is still quite far off.* 2 very much: *This essay is far better than your last one.* | *I'm afraid I'm far too busy to stop and chat.* 3 **as far as I know** = to the degree that I know something, although I do not know for certain: *As far as I know, she's still intending to come.* | *As far as we know, the deal was still on.* 4 **by far, far and away** by a large amount: *This is by far the best machine on the market at the moment.* | *This is far and away the most important medical achievement this century.* 5 **far from: a** not at all: *She* *looked far from happy!* **b** instead of: *Far from being angry, he was actually quite pleased.* **6 go so far as to do something** to do something surprising: *He even went so far as to say that all money should be abolished.* **7 go far** to be successful and reach a position of power: *She's very clever and will go far in this profession.* **8 not go very far** to not be enough: *It sounds a lot of money but it won't go very far these days.* **9 go too far** to do something too much, in a way that other people find unacceptable: *He's often slightly rude to people, but this time he just went too far!* **10 how far** to what degree: *I don't know how far to believe him.* | *I wasn't sure how far I could trust him.* **11 not far off, not far out** not wrong by a very large amount: *He predicted that inflation would rise to 10%, which was not far off.* **12 so far** until now: *I've been here for three weeks now, and so far I've enjoyed myself.* | *So far these reports have not been confirmed officially.* **13 so far so good** a phrase you use to say that until now things have been successful

■ USAGE You can use **far** to talk about distance in questions and negatives: *Did you walk far?* | *How far did you walk?* You can also use **far** in statements after *too*, *as* and *so*: *It's too far to reach in one day.* | *I went as far as I could.* | *The boy walked so far that he could not find his way back.* Note, however, that you should NOT use **far** in ordinary statements. Instead use **a long way** or **a long distance**: *He walked* **a long way.** | *It's* **a long way** *from the station to the school.* | *My house is* **a long way** *from the town centre.*

far² *adj* **1** distant (used especially of the more distant of two things): *A few people were fishing on the far bank of the river.* | *I could see Jane walking along on the far side of the road.* | *She was sitting at the far end of the room.* | *They live in the far South of the country.* **2 as/so far as... is concerned** you use this expression when you say what subject you are talking or writing about, that is, which particular part of a situation or which particular person's opinion: *As far as money is concerned, things are a bit difficult. But otherwise, I think they're fine.* | *As far as Beryl is concerned, there's no problem, but of course Alan always finds something to complain about.* **3 a far cry from something** very different from something: *It's a lovely house, and a far cry from that tiny flat they used to live in.*

far·a·way /ˈfɑːrəweɪ/ *adj* distant: *a faraway place* | *She's got that faraway look in her eyes. I think she's in love.*

farce /fɑːs ‖ fɑːrs/ *n* **1** [C;U] a light humorous play in which a lot of silly things happen **2** [C] an occasion or set of events that is silly and pointless: *The meeting was a complete farce.*

far·ci·cal /ˈfɑːsɪkḷ ‖ ˈfɑːr-/ *adj* silly and pointless: *a farcical attempt to reform the tax system* –**farcically** /-kli/ *adv*

fare¹ /feəʳ/ *n* **1** [C] the money that you pay to travel in a public vehicle: *Train fares have gone up again.* **2** [U] food, especially as provided at a meal: *simple country fare*

fare² *v* **fared, faring** *fml* **fare well** to do well: *The company did not fare very well under his leadership.* [RELATED PHRASE **fare badly**]

Far East /ˌ· ˈ·◂/ *n* **the Far East** the countries in Asia that are east of India, such as China and Japan

fare·well /feəˈwel ‖ feər-/ *n* GOODBYE: *a farewell party* | *Say your farewells, and we'll go.* –**farewell** *interj old fash* : *Farewell, my darling!*

far·fetched /ˌfɑːˈfetʃt◂ ‖ ˌfɑːr-/ *adj* difficult to believe: *a farfetched excuse*

far-flung /ˌ· ˈ·◂/ *adj* **1** spread over a wide area: *This map shows their far-flung trade connections.* **2** distant: *a far-flung corner of the Empire*

farm¹ /fɑːm ‖ fɑːrm/ *n* **1** an area of land and buildings, where crops are grown or animals raised: *a pig farm* | *We work on the farm.* | *Do you sell farm produce?* **2** a farmhouse

farm² *v* [I;T] to use land for growing crops or raising animals: *Our family has been farming for generations.* | *to farm the land*

farm sbdy/sthg ↔ **out** *phr v* [T] **1** to send work out to other people to do: *We must farm out some of these projects.* **2** to send a person into the care of someone else: *As children, we were often farmed out to friends and relatives.*

farm·er /ˈfɑːməʳ ‖ ˈfɑːrm-/ *n* the owner or manager of a farm

farm·hand /ˈfɑːmhænd ‖ ˈfɑːrm-/ *n* a person who is employed to work on a farm

farm·house /ˈfɑːmhaʊs ‖ ˈfɑːrm-/ *n* (*also* **farm**) the main house on a farm, where the farmer lives

farm·ing /ˈfɑːmɪŋ ‖ ˈfɑːrm-/ *n* [U] the activity or business of working on a farm

farm·yard /ˈfɑːmjɑːd ‖ ˈfɑːrmjɑːrd/ *n* a yard next to or among farm buildings

far-off /ˌ· ˈ·◂/ *adj* distant in space or time

far-reach·ing /ˌ· ˈ·◂/ *adj* having a wide influence: *They're demanding far-reaching political changes.*

far-sight·ed /ˌfɑːˈsaɪtɪd◂ ‖ ˌfɑːr-/ *adj* **1** able to see clearly the future effects of present actions **2** the usual American word for LONGSIGHTED –**farsightedness** *n* [U]

far·ther /ˈfɑːðəʳ ‖ ˈfɑːrr-/ *adv,adj* the COMPARATIVE form of FAR: *We walked a mile farther down the road.*

■ USAGE You can use either **farther** or **further** to talk about places and distances: **further/ farther** *down the road.* But when the meaning is "more" or "extra" use **further**: *For further information write to the above address.*

far·thest /ˈfɑːðɪst ‖ ˈfɑːr-/ *adv,adj* the SUPERLATIVE form of FAR: *We wanted to find out who could swim the farthest.*

far·thing /ˈfɑːðɪŋ ‖ ˈfɑːr-/ *n* an old British coin of little value

fas·ci·nate /ˈfæsɪneɪt/ *v* **fascinated, fascinating** [T] to be extremely interesting or attractive to someone: *Other people's beliefs fascinate me.* | *I've always been fascinated by astrology.* –**fascinating** *adj* : *I find his latest theory fascinating.* –**fascination** /ˌfæsɪˈneɪʃən/ [U] : *Old castles have a certain strange fascination for me.*

fas·cis·m /ˈfæʃɪzəm/ *n* (*also* **Fascism**) [U] an extreme political system which supports nationalism and very strong central government control

fas·cist /ˈfæʃɪst/ *n* **1** (*also* **Fascist**) a supporter of fascism: *the Fascist Party* **2** *infml* a person who acts in a cruel, hard way which allows no opposition –**fascist** *adj*

fash·ion /ˈfæʃən/ *n* **1** [C] a way of dressing or behaving that is usual or popular at a certain time: *Narrow trousers are the latest fashion.* | *It's not the fashion to send children away to school now.* **2 in fashion** popular now **3 out of fashion** no longer popular **4** [U] changing custom, especially in women's clothing: *the history of fashion* **5** [sing] *fml* a certain way of behaving or doing something:

He behaved in a very strange fashion all evening. | *She wore her hair schoolgirl-fashion.* **6 after a fashion** not very well: *Well, yes, I do speak Russian, after a fashion.*

fashion² *v* [T] *fml* to shape or make something, usually with your hands: *He fashioned the clay into an elegant pot.*

fash·ion·a·ble /ˈfæʃənəbəl/ *adj* usual or popular at a particular time: *a fashionable dress* | *a fashionable restaurant* | *Those ideas were fashionable in the '60s.* −opposite **unfashionable** −**fashionably** *adv*: *fashionably dressed*

fast¹ /fɑːst ‖ fæst/ *adj* **1** moving, happening, or acting quickly: *a fast car* | *fast music* | *a fast journey* **2** firmly fixed: *Are the colours in this shirt fast?* | *Make the boat fast with that rope.* **3** [never before a noun] showing a time that is later than the true time (used of a clock or watch): *My watch is fast.* | *The clock's five minutes fast.*

fast² *adv* **1** quickly: *You're learning very fast.* | *He ran faster and faster.* **2** firmly: *It's stuck fast in the mud.* | *Hold fast to that branch!* **3 fast asleep** sleeping deeply

fast³ *v* [I] to eat no food for a period, especially for religious or health reasons: *Muslims fast during Ramadan.*

fast⁴ *n* an act or period of eating no food: *He broke his fast by drinking a little milk.*

fas·ten /ˈfɑːsən ‖ ˈfæ-/ *v* **1** [I;T] to fix or close firmly: *He fastened his coat.* | *The door fastens with a hook.* | *Can you fasten that board to the wall?* −opposite **unfasten** **2 fasten on/upon something** to take something eagerly and use it: *The President fastened on the idea at once.*

fasten sthg ↔ **up** *phr v* [T] to close something: *Fasten that suitcase up.*

fas·ten·er /ˈfɑːsənə^r ‖ ˈfæ-/ *n* something that closes something or fixes things together: *a zip fastener*

fa·sten·ing /ˈfɑːsənɪŋ ‖ ˈfæ-/ *n* something that holds things shut, especially doors and windows

fast food /ˌ· ·/ *n* [U] food that is prepared quickly and sold by restaurants to be eaten at once or taken away: *a fast food restaurant selling pizzas and hamburgers*

fas·tid·i·ous /fæˈstɪdiəs/ *adj* **1** worried about quality or cleanliness, and very difficult to satisfy (a word used to express disapproval): *a fastidious eater* **2** careful and concerned with detail: *He was extremely fastidious about all aspects of his work.* −**fastidiously** *adv*

fast·ness /ˈfɑːstn̩s ‖ ˈfæst-/ *n* [U] the quality of being firm and fixed (used especially of colours in cloth)

■ USAGE The noun **fastness** has nothing to do with the adjective **fast**, meaning "quick". If we need a noun we have to use **speed** or **quickness**.

fat¹ /fæt/ *adj* **1** having a lot of fat, and especially too much fat, on your body: *He's got very fat recently.* | *a fat baby* **2** large, wide, or thick: *a fat salary* | *fat books* | *a fat cucumber* **3 a fat lot of** *infml* not any at all: *She's a fat lot of help.* −**fatness** *n* [U]

■ USAGE If you want to be polite about someone

do not say that they are **fat**. (**Rather**) **overweight** is a more polite way of saying that you think someone is too big and heavy. **Plump** means "slightly fat" and is often used to show that you think this is quite pleasant. **Chubby** has a similar meaning and is most commonly used of children and babies. If someone is extremely fat and unhealthy they can be described as **obese**.

fat² *n* **1** [U] the substance under the skins of animals and human beings which helps to keep them warm **2** [C;U] an oily substance from animals or vegetables, which is used in cooking: *animal fats* | *potatoes fried in deep fat*

fa·tal /ˈfeɪtl/ *adj* **1** causing or resulting in death: *a disease which is usually fatal to cows* | *a fatal accident* **2** very important and unfortunate: *She made the fatal decision to marry Henry.* | *a fatal mistake* −**fatally** *adv*: *He was shot and fatally wounded.*

fa·tal·is·m /ˈfeɪtl-ɪzəm/ *n* [U] the belief that events are decided by a power beyond human control −**fatalist** *n* −**fatalistic** /ˌfeɪtlˈɪstɪk/ *adj*

fa·tal·i·ty /fəˈtæləti/ *n* **fatalities** *fml* **1** [C] a death as a result of violence or an accident: *It was a terrible crash, but there were surprisingly few fatalities.* **2** [U] the belief that events are decided by a power beyond human control

fate /feɪt/ *n* **1** [U] (also **Fate**) a power beyond human control that is believed to decide events: *Fate has brought us together.* **2** [C] an end, especially death: *They met with a terrible fate.* **3** [sing] what will happen to someone or something: *I wonder whether the examiners have decided our fate yet.* | *Now that oil is scarce, the fate of the motor car is uncertain.* **4 a fate worse than death** *infml* a terrible experience: *Going out with him would be a fate worse than death!*

fat·ed /ˈfeɪtɪd/ *adj* [never before a noun] caused or decided by a power beyond human control: *It was fated that we should never reach Tokyo.* | *We were fated to meet.*

fate·ful /ˈfeɪtfəl/ *adj* important for the future, especially because of its unpleasant effects: *the fateful decision to start his own company*

fa·ther¹ /ˈfɑːðə^r/ *n* **1** a male parent: *That's my father.* | *their adoptive father* −see picture on page 343 **2** *fml* a word used to talk to or about a male parent: *Father says we can go.* **3** a man who is respected for having started something: *the father of modern scientific thought* **4** (also **Father**) a priest, especially in the Roman Catholic church: *Father Brown* | *Come in, father.* **5 Father** God, in the CHRISTIAN religion

father² *v* [T] to become a male parent (a formal word which is often used in a humorous way): *his desire to father a child*

Father Christ·mas /ˌ·· ˈ··/ *n* an old man dressed in red with a long white beard who, children believe, comes down the chimney to bring them presents at CHRISTMAS

father fig·ure /ˈ·· ˌ··/ *n* an older man who you depend on for advice and help

fa·ther·hood /ˈfɑːðəhʊd ‖ -ðər-/ *n* [U] the state of being a father: *the pleasures and responsibilities of fatherhood*

father-in-law /ˈ··· ·/ *n* **fathers-in-law** the father of your wife or husband −see picture on page 343

fa·ther·less /ˈfɑːðələs ‖ -ðər-/ *adj* without a father who is alive or who you see regularly

fa·ther·ly /ˈfɑːðəli ‖ -ðər-/ *adj* typical of a kind or concerned father: *Mr Smith was just trying to give you some fatherly advice.*

SPELLING NOTE
Words with the sound / f / may be spelt **ph-**, like **photograph**.

fath·om[1] /ˈfæðəm/ n a measure of the depth of water; a fathom is equal to 6 feet or 1·8 metres

fathom[2] v [T] (also **fathom** sbdy/sthg ↔ **out**) to understand the meaning of something or the reason for it: *I can't quite fathom your last remark.* | *Nobody could fathom out why he had been invited.*

fa·tigue[1] /fəˈtiːg/ n **1** [U] great tiredness: *He was pale with fatigue.* **2** [U] *tech* weakness in a substance such as metal which may cause it to break **3 fatigues** [pl] clothes worn by soldiers for certain duties

fatigue[2] v fatigued, fatiguing [T] *fml* to make someone very tired: *a fatiguing job*

fat·ten /ˈfætn/ v [T] (also **fatten** sbdy/sthg ↔ **up**) to make a person or animal fatter: *Those chickens are being fattened for market.* | *We must fatten you up a bit, now that you're feeling better.* –**fattening** adj : *Stop eating fattening foods like chocolate and cakes.*

fat·ty /ˈfæti/ adj fattier, fattiest containing or consisting of a lot of fat (used especially of food) –**fattiness** n [U]

fat·u·ous /ˈfætʃuəs/ adj without any sensible or intelligent meaning or purpose: *What a fatuous remark!* –**fatuously** adv

fau·cet /ˈfɔːsɪt/ n the usual American word for a TAP[1](1)

fault[1] /fɔːlt/ n **1** [C] a problem with something which stops it working properly: *a small electrical fault in the motor* **2** [C] a weakness in someone: *His only fault is that he has no sense of humour.* **3** [sing] responsibility for a bad situation: *"It's not our fault that we're late." "Whose fault is it, then?"* –see BLAME[2] (USAGE) **4 at fault** wrong or mistaken: *I admit that I was at fault.* **5** [C] tech a crack in the Earth's surface: *the San Andreas fault* **6** [C] a SERVICE[1] in tennis which is not allowed by the rules: *a double fault* **7 find fault** to complain about something, especially too much: *She's always finding fault with the way I dress.* **8 to a fault** to an extreme degree: *She's generous to a fault.*

fault[2] v [T usually used in negatives and questions] to find things that are wrong with someone or something: *We couldn't fault her performance.*

fault·less /ˈfɔːltləs/ adj perfect: *a faultless display of gymnastics* –**faultlessly** adv

fault·y /ˈfɔːlti/ adj **1** not working properly: *a faulty wire in the electrical system* **2** not correct: *faulty reasoning*

fau·na /ˈfɔːnə/ n [U] *tech* animals, especially all those living in a particular place at a particular time: *the fauna of the Brazilian rainforests* | *interesting flora and fauna*

faux pas /ˌfəʊ ˈpɑː, ˈfəʊ pɑː/ n faux pas /ˌfəʊ ˈpɑːz/ something you do or say which, unknown to you, is not socially acceptable

fa·vour[1] /ˈfeɪvəʳ/ n (**favor** AmE) **1** [C] something you do from kindness, and not because you have to: *As a special favour, I'll let you boys stay up late tonight.* | *Can I ask a favour of you? Will you lend me your car?* **2 do someone a favour** to help someone by doing something they ask you to do: *Can you do me a favour and look after the children for an hour?* **3** [U] active approval: *How do you think I can win her favour?* | *He has never looked on any of my ideas with favour.* **4 in favour** *fml* popular: *His political ideas seem to be very much in favour at the moment.* [RELATED PHRASE **out of favour**] **5 in favour of something: a** in support of something: *Are you in favour of making divorce more difficult?* **b** in

order to do something else: *He refused a job in industry in favour of a university appointment.* **6** [U] unfairly kind treatment of one person, to the disadvantage of others: *I try not to show favour to my own child above the others in the class.* **7 in someone's favour: a** to a person's advantage: *At least the bank's mistakes are always in our favour!* **b** deciding that someone is right: *The tribunal decided in his favour.*

favour[2] v (**favor** AmE) [T] **1** to like something more than the other possibilities: *The president is believed to favour further tax cuts.* **2** to treat someone with unfair kindness, to the disadvantage of other people: *It's clear she favours Jack more than her other children.* **3** to give someone an advantage: *The position of the sun favoured the visiting team.* **4 favour someone with something** *fml* to give someone something that you think they will like: *She favoured him with a charming smile.*

fa·vou·ra·ble /ˈfeɪvərəbəl/ adj *fml* (**favorable** AmE) **1** pleasing: *Try and make a favourable impression on my mother.* **2** approving: *I hear favourable accounts of your work.* **3** helpful or useful: *The company will lend you money on very favourable terms.* –opposite **unfavourable** –**favourably** adv

fa·vou·rite[1] /ˈfeɪvərɪt/ n (**favorite** AmE) **1** a person or thing that you like more than any other one of its kind: *This book is one of my favourites.* **2** someone who receives more attention and approval than is right and fair: *Teachers should not have favourites.* **3** the competitor in each race that is expected to win: *The favourite came in second.*

favourite[2] adj (**favorite** AmE) liked more than all other ones of its kind: *What's your favourite television programme?*

fa·vou·ri·tis·m /ˈfeɪvərɪtɪzəm/ n (**favoritism** AmE) [U] the giving of unfair approval or advantage to one person or group of people out of many

fawn[1] /fɔːn/ n **1** [C] a young deer **2** [U] a light yellowish-brown colour

fawn[2] v **fawn on someone** to try very hard to win someone's approval by paying them a lot of attention and praising them a lot, without being sincere: *They were fawning on their rich uncle.*

fax /fæks/ v [T] to send copies of writing or pictures along a telephone line using special machines: *Could you fax the information to me?* | *I'll fax you a copy of the letter.*

☐ USEFUL PATTERNS to fax something to someone; to fax someone something –**fax** n : *I'll send a fax.* –see picture on page 539

FBI /ˌef biː ˈaɪ/ n a US government department concerned with crime and the protection of national secrets; an abbreviation for **Federal Bureau of Investigation**: *an FBI agent*

fear[1] /fɪəʳ/ n **1** [C;U] the feeling that you have when danger is near or something unpleasant is likely to happen: *She has a great fear* **of** *fire.* | *The government's fear that the unemployment figures would rise again was today proved correct.* | *We live in fear of an enemy attack.* **2** [U] the possibility that something will happen, usually something undesirable: *There's not much fear of snow at this time of year.* | *Is there any fear of him arriving early?* **3 for fear of** because of anxiety about: *I couldn't move for fear of falling.* **4 no fear!** *infml* a phrase used in answer to a question or suggestion to say that you certainly will not do something

fear[2] v [not in progressive forms] *fml* **1** [T; +(that)] to be afraid of something or someone: *They feared*

being attacked on the road. | She has always feared old age. | Experts fear that there will be a new outbreak of the disease. **2 fear for** to be afraid for the safety of someone or something: She feared for the lost child. **3 I fear** fml a phrase used when the news you are telling someone is bad: "Is there enough money?" "I fear not." | I fear we've missed our chance.

fear·ful /'fɪəfəl ‖ 'fɪər-/ adj fml **1** afraid: He was fearful of her anger. **2** terrible: a fearful storm —**fearfully** adv

fear·less /'fɪələs ‖ 'fɪər-/ adj unafraid: a fearless climber —**fearlessly** adv —**fearlessness** n [U]

fear·some /'fɪəsəm ‖ 'fɪər-/ adj fml frightening: a fearsome sight

fea·si·ble /'fiːzǐbəl/ adj possible to do: Your plan sounds quite feasible. —**feasibly** adv —**feasibility** /ˌfiːzǐ'bɪlǐti/ n [U] : We're doing a feasibility study of the scheme.

feast[1] /fiːst/ n **1** an unusually large and often public meal for a special occasion: The king held a feast. | What a feast! **2** a day when a particular religious event is remembered: Christmas is an important feast for Christians.

feast[2] v **1** [I] to eat a large, special meal **2 feast your eyes on something** to look at something for a long time because you like it

feat /fiːt/ n a clever action, showing strength, skill, or courage: It was quite a feat to move that piano by yourself.

fea·ther[1] /'feðər/ n one of the light, soft things which cover a bird's body

feather[2] v **feather your nest** to make yourself rich, especially dishonestly

fea·ture[1] /'fiːtʃər/ n **1** a typical part of something, or a quality that something has: Wet weather is a feature of life in Scotland. | The car has a lot of new features. **2 features** [pl] a person's eyes, nose, and mouth **3** a special long newspaper article or a special treatment of a subject on radio or television: a feature on personal computers **4** (also **feature film**) a full-length cinema film which tells a story

feature[2] v **featured, featuring 1** [T] to include someone special as a performer: a new film featuring Jack Nicholson **2 feature in something** to be present as an important part of something: Art doesn't feature at all in their lives. **3** [T] to advertise something more than usual: We're featuring bedroom furniture this month.

Feb·ru·a·ry /'februari, 'febjuri ‖ 'febjueri/ n (also **Feb.**) the 2nd month of the year

fe·ces /'fiːsiːz/ n see FAECES

feck·less /'fekləs/ adj unable to plan and manage your life properly

fed /fed/ the past tense and past participle of FEED

fed·e·ral /'fedərəl/ adj [only before a noun] **1** formed of states which decide their own affairs, but are controlled by a central government: Switzerland is a federal republic. **2** relating to the central government of a country as opposed to the states that form it: Americans pay both federal taxes and state taxes.

SPELLING NOTE

Words with the sound / f / may be spelt **ph-**, like **photograph**.

---

fed·e·ra·tion /ˌfedə'reɪʃən/ n **1** a group of states which each decide their own affairs, but are controlled by a central government **2** a group of societies or organizations that have come together to form a larger organization: the Federation of British Industry

fed up /ˌ· '·/ adj [never before a noun] infml unhappy, tired, and uninterested: I'm really fed up with my job!

fee /fiː/ n a sum of money that you pay for professional services, for example to a doctor, lawyer, or private school –see PAY[2] (USAGE)

fee·ble /'fiːbəl/ adj extremely weak: He became very feeble after the operation. | a feeble joke –**feebly** adv –**feebleness** n [U]

feed[1] /fiːd/ v fed /fed/, fed **1** [T] to give food to someone: He doesn't even earn enough to feed his family. | Have you fed the dog? **2** [I] (of animals and babies) to eat: Birds feed on seeds and berries. **3** [T + adv/prep] to put something slowly and continuously into something else: The information is fed into the computer. | Keep feeding the wire through the hole. **4** [T] to make something grow bigger or stronger: This kind of book only serves to feed people's prejudices. | The lake is fed by several streams.

feed[2] n **1** [C] a meal taken by an animal or baby **2** [U] food for animals

feed·back /'fiːdbæk/ n [U] **1** information about how good or how successful something is, which is given to the person who did or made the thing: The company welcomes feedback from customers. **2** uncontrolled noise from an AMPLIFIER

feel[1] /fiːl/ v felt /felt/, felt **1** [+complement] to experience a sensation: I felt very happy. | She felt ill. | We were all feeling tired and hungry. | How do you feel today? | She felt as if she was going to faint. | He felt a sudden desire to laugh. | I have never felt pain like that before. **2** [+complement] to make you experience a sensation: It feels strange being back here after all these years. | I have often wondered what it would feel like to be rich and famous. **3** [T] to touch something with your fingers in order to find out what it is like: He felt my arm to see if it was broken. **4** [T] to experience something touching you: I felt something crawling up my leg. | I could feel the warm sun on my arms and legs. **5** [+complement] to seem to have a particular quality which you experience by touching: Your feet feel cold. | The sheet feels wet. | It looked and felt like glue. **6** [T; + complement] to believe something, or have it as an idea or opinion: I feel that something must be done to help these people. | I felt certain that something terrible was going to happen. | You know how I feel about violence on television. | What do you feel about this idea? | I felt that I had to talk to him. | I felt it necessary to apologize. | She felt tempted to shut the door in his face. **7 feel for something** to try to find something by searching with your fingers: She felt in her bag for a pencil. **8 feel for someone** to be sorry because someone is suffering: Poor child! I really feel for her! **9 feel like** to want to do or have something: Do you feel like a drink? | I don't feel like dancing today. **10 feel your way** to move slowly and carefully because it is dark and you have to use your hands to find out where you are going

feel[2] n [sing] **1** the sensation that you experience when you touch and feel something: The skin has a rough feel. **2 have a feel** to feel something: Can I have a feel of it? **3 get the feel of something** to become used to something: The car seemed strange at first, but I soon got the feel of it.

feel·ers /ˈfiːləz ‖ -ərz/ n [pl] **1** the thread-like parts on the front of an insect's head, with which it touches things **2 put out feelers** to make informal suggestions in order to find out what other people will think of them

feel·ing /ˈfiːlɪŋ/ n **1** [C] a sensation that you experience, either in your body or in your mind: *The fever was accompanied by feelings of tiredness and nausea.* | *feelings of shame* | *You shouldn't try to hide your feelings.* **2** [C] a belief or opinion: *I have a feeling we're being followed.* | *My feeling is that we should go ahead and publish the book.* **3** [U] the ability to notice physical sensations: *He lost all feeling in his legs.* **4** [U] sympathy and understanding: *She plays the piano with great feeling.* **5 bad feelings** feelings of anger between people: *The new working hours caused a lot of bad feeling at the factory.* **6 hurt someone's feelings** to make someone feel upset **7 no hard feelings** no feelings of anger between people who have quarrelled: *He apologized, and there are no hard feelings.*

feet /fiːt/ the plural of FOOT

feign /feɪn/ v [T] *lit* to pretend: *She feigned death.*

feint /feɪnt/ n *fml* a false attack or blow made to deceive your opponent

fe·line /ˈfiːlaɪn/ adj like a cat, or relating to a cat or a member of the cat family

fell¹ /fel/ the past tense of FALL¹

fell² v [T] **1** to cut down a tree **2** *lit* to knock someone down

fell³ n BrE high, wild, rocky country

fel·low¹ /ˈfeləʊ/ n **1** *infml old fash* a man **2** (also **Fellow**) a member of a society connected with a branch of learning or of some universities: *She's now a Fellow of the Royal Society.*

fellow² adj [only before a noun] being in the same situation as you are: *You'll soon get to know your fellow students.* **2 fellow feeling** a feeling of sympathy and understanding for other people

fel·low·ship /ˈfeləʊʃɪp/ n **1** [C] a group of people who have come together because they have a shared interest **2** [C] the job of a FELLOW¹ (2) at a university **3** [U] the condition of being friends through sharing or doing something together: *There was a strong feeling of fellowship among the team members.*

fel·o·ny /ˈfeləni/ n **felonies** *law* a serious crime such as murder

felt¹ /felt/ the past tense and past participle of FEEL

felt² n [U] firm thick cloth made of wool or other material pressed flat: *a felt hat*

felt-tip /ˈ· ˌ·/ n (also **felt-tip pen**) a coloured pen with a small piece of felt for a NIB

fe·male¹ /ˈfiːmeɪl/ n **1** any animal of the sex that can give birth to young **2** a woman (a word which is usually used by men to express disapproval, and which is considered offensive in this use)

female² adj **1** relating to or belonging to the sex that gives birth to young: *a female elephant* **2** *tech* producing fruit (used of plants or parts of plants) **3** concerning or relating to women: *We only employ female workers.*

■ USAGE **Female** and **male** are used to show what sex a creature is: *a female gorilla.* They are also used when talking about things which relate to one sex or the other: *The male body is usually heavier than the female body.* **Feminine** and **masculine** are used to describe qualities that are supposed to be typical of one sex or the other: *delicate feminine hands* | *She wears rather masculine clothes.*

fem·i·nine /ˈfemɪnɪn/ adj **1** having qualities that are considered typical of women: *She always wears very feminine clothes.* –see FEMALE (USAGE) **2** *tech* relating to a certain class of words in some languages

fem·i·nin·i·ty /ˌfemɪˈnɪnɪti/ n [U] the quality of being feminine

fem·i·nis·m /ˈfemɪnɪzəm/ n [U] the belief that women should have the same rights and chances as men –**feminist** n,adj

fe·mur /ˈfiːmər/ n *tech* the long bone in the upper part of your leg

fen /fen/ n an area of low, wet land, especially in the east of England

fence¹ /fens/ n **1** something upright like a wall, but made of wood or wire, dividing two areas of land –see picture on page 441 **2** *infml* someone who buys and sells stolen goods **3 sit on the fence** to avoid taking sides in an argument (a phrase which is usually used to express disapproval)

fence² v **fenced, fencing 1** [I] to fight with a long thin pointed sword as a sport **2** [T] to put a fence round something

fence sth **in** phr v [T] to keep something in a place by putting a fence round it

fence sth **off** phr v [T] to separate an area by putting a fence round it: *We've fenced off part of the garden.*

fenc·ing /ˈfensɪŋ/ n [U] **1** the sport of fencing **2** material for making fences

fend /fend/ v **fend for yourself** to look after yourself: *I've had to fend for myself since I was 14.*

fend sbdy/sthg **off** phr v [T] **1** to defend yourself against attack: *He struggled to fend her off.* **2** to avoid a person or thing: *He spent the meeting trying to fend off difficult questions.*

fend·er /ˈfendər/ n **1** a low metal wall round an open fireplace, to stop the coal from falling out **2** *AmE* the WING of a car

fer·ment¹ /fəˈment ‖ fər-/ v [I;T] to change chemically by the action of a living substance such as YEAST: *The wine is beginning to ferment.* –**fermentation** /ˌfɜːmenˈteɪʃən ‖ ˌfɜr-/ n [U]

ferment² /ˈfɜːment ‖ ˈfɜːr-/ n [U] political trouble and excitement caused by change: *Eastern Europe was in ferment.*

fern /fɜːn ‖ fɜːrn/ n a green plant with leaves shaped like feathers, and no flowers

fe·ro·cious /fəˈrəʊʃəs/ adj fierce and violent: *a ferocious animal* | *ferocious punishments* –**ferociously** adv –**ferocity** /fəˈrɒsɪti ‖ fəˈrɑː-/ n (also **ferociousness** /fəˈrəʊʃəsnɪs/) [U]

ferret /ˈferɪt/ v
ferret sthg **out** phr v *infml* [T] to discover information by searching for it carefully: *She managed to ferret out the truth.*

fer·ry¹ /ˈferi/ n **ferries** (also **ferryboat** /ˈferibəʊt/) **1** a boat that carries people and things across a narrow stretch of water: *cross-Channel ferries* **2** by ferry travelling in a ferry: *You can cross the river by ferry.*

ferry² v **ferried, ferrying** [T + adv/prep] to carry people or goods from one place to another, usually regularly: *I spend the day ferrying the children to and from their various activities.*

fer·tile /ˈfɜːtaɪl ‖ ˈfɜːrtl/ adj **1** able to produce or grow many fruits or seeds: *The agricultural land is very fertile round here.* **2** able to have babies or young **3 fertile imagination** a mind that can easily imagine things, or think of new and original ideas –opposite **infertile** –**fertility** /fɜː'tɪləti ‖ fɜːr-/ n [U]

fer·ti·lize /'fɜːtɪlaɪz ‖ 'fɜːrtl-aɪz/ v **fertilized, fertilizing** (also **fertilise** BrE) [T] **1** to start the development of young in a female creature or plant; in animals, the male's SPERM fertilizes the female's egg **2** to put fertilizer on land –**fertilization** /ˌfɜːtɪlaɪ'zeɪʃən ‖ ˌfɜːrtələ-/ n [U]

fer·ti·liz·er /'fɜːtɪlaɪzəᵣ ‖ 'fɜːrtl-aɪzər/ n [C;U] a chemical or natural substance that you put on the land to make crops grow better

fer·vent /'fɜːvənt ‖ 'fɜːr-/ adj feeling or showing strong and sincere feelings: a fervent desire to win | He's a fervent believer in free speech. –**fervently** adv

fer·vour /'fɜːvəᵣ ‖ 'fɜːr-/ n (**fervor** AmE) [U] strong and sincere feeling

fes·ter /'festəᵣ/ v [I] **1** (of a wound) to become infected **2** to become increasingly unpleasant: Don't let these feelings of resentment fester!

fes·ti·val /'festɪvəl/ n **1** an occasion when people come together to enjoy themselves, especially to mark a special religious event: Christmas is one of the festivals of the Christian church. **2** an event consisting of many artistic, musical, or theatrical performances: the Edinburgh Festival | the Cannes Film Festival

fes·tive /'festɪv/ adj full of happiness because people have come together to enjoy themselves: We were all in a festive mood.

fes·tiv·i·ty /fe'stɪvəti/ n **festivities 1 festivities** [pl] a happy event when people come together to enjoy themselves: the wedding festivities **2** [U] happiness because people have come together to enjoy themselves: There was a feeling of festivity in the town.

fes·toon /fe'stuːn/ v fml **festooned with** decorated with attractive things

fe·tal /'fiːtl/ adj see FOETAL

fetch /fetʃ/ v [T] **1** to go and get a person or thing and bring them back: Run and fetch the doctor! | Quick! Fetch me a cloth!
□ USEFUL PATTERNS to fetch something; to fetch something for someone; to fetch someone something
2 infml to be sold for a particular amount: The house should fetch at least £80,000.

fetch·ing /'fetʃɪŋ/ adj attractive: That's a very fetching blouse.

fete[1] /feɪt/ n an outdoor event with games, competitions, and things for sale, to collect money for a special purpose

fete[2] v feted, feting fml [T] to welcome someone and do honour to them with public parties and ceremonies: The Queen was feted everywhere she went.

fet·id /'fiːtɪd ‖ 'fetɪd/ adj smelling very unpleasant: fetid air

fet·ish /'fetɪʃ ‖ 'fiː-/ n **1** an object that is worshipped and thought to have magic power **2** something to which a person pays an unreasonable amount of attention –**fetishism** n [U]

fet·ter /'fetəᵣ/ v [T] fml **1** to tie someone up with chains around their ankles **2** to prevent someone from behaving freely

SPELLING NOTE
Words with the sound / f / may be spelt **ph-**, like **photograph.**

fet·ters /'fetəz ‖ -tərz/ n [pl] **1** chains fixed around a prisoner's ankles **2** things that prevent you from behaving freely

fet·tle /'fetl/ n **in fine fettle** infml in good health

fe·tus /'fiːtəs/ n see FOETUS

feud /fjuːd/ n a strong and long-lasting quarrel between two people or groups of people: The two families were engaged in a bitter feud.

feud·al /'fjuːdl/ adj relating to the system common in the past by which people held land and received protection from land owners in return for doing work for them –**feudalism** n [U]

fe·ver /'fiːvəᵣ/ n **1** [C;U] an illness in which you develop a very high temperature: Has she got a fever? | a yellow fever epidemic **2** [sing] a very excited state: She was in a fever of impatience.

fe·ver·ish /'fiːvərɪʃ/ adj **1** suffering from a very high temperature: She looked hot and feverish. **2** extremely active or excited –**feverishly** adv : They were working feverishly.

few /fjuː/ det, pron, n [used with a plural verb] **1** not very many: She has very few friends. | The few people who came were all members of the family. | The pilots are all highly trained, and they make few mistakes. **2** a small number: Let's stay a few days longer. | I need to buy a few things. | Why not invite a few of your friends? | We printed 200 leaflets, but there are only a few left now. **3 few and far between** not happening or found very often: Our holidays are few and far between. **4 quite a few, a good few** quite a lot: Quite a few people came out to watch. | Quite a few of us were beginning to get worried.

fez /fez/ n **fezzes** a kind of round red hat with a flat top, worn by some Muslim men

fi·an·cé /fi'ɒnseɪ ‖ ˌfiːɑːn'seɪ/ n a man to whom a woman is ENGAGED to be married; a woman who is ENGAGED to a man is called his **fiancée**: This is my fiancé, George.

fi·as·co /fi'æskəʊ/ n **fiascos** (also **fiascoes** AmE) an event which is a complete failure: The meeting was a total fiasco.

fib[1] /fɪb/ n infml a small unimportant lie: Don't tell fibs!

fib[2] v **-bb-** [I] to tell fibs –**fibber** n : You fibber!

fi·bre /'faɪbəᵣ/ n (**fiber** AmE) **1** [C] one of the thin thread-like parts that form many natural substances such as wool, wood, or muscle and some substances made by humans **2** [C;U] a thread used for making things such as cloth or rope: natural cotton fibre | man-made fibres such as nylon **3** [U] strength of character: He lacks moral fibre. **4** [U] a part of plants that can be eaten but is passed through the body; fibre is supposed to be good for your health: Some breakfast cereals are high in fibre.

fi·bre·glass /'faɪbəɡlɑːs ‖ -bərɡlæs/ n (**fiberglass** AmE) [U] a material made from glass fibres and plastic, used for making things such as small boats

fi·brous /'faɪbrəs/ adj like or made of fibres

fick·le /'fɪkəl/ adj changing your mind often about what you want or what you like –**fickleness** n [U]

fic·tion /'fɪkʃən/ n **1** [U] stories or books about imaginary things and events: a writer of popular fiction **2** [C;U] something that you pretend is true although it is not: The newspaper report was a complete fiction.

fic·tion·al /'fɪkʃənəl/ adj happening or told in a story: a fictional account of a journey to the moon

fic·ti·tious /fɪkˈtɪʃəs/ adj **1** false or untrue: *His account of what happened was completely fictitious.* **2** existing only in a story: *The characters in this film are purely fictitious.*

fid·dle¹ /ˈfɪdl/ n infml **1** a VIOLIN **2** a dishonest action in which someone gets money for themselves: *He was involved in an insurance fiddle.*

fiddle² v fiddled, fiddling infml **1** fiddle with something, fiddle about/around with something to move something around or play with it with no particular purpose: *Stop fiddling with your pencil and pay attention!* **2** [T] BrE to prepare something dishonestly for your own advantage: *He had been fiddling his income tax for years.*

fid·dler /ˈfɪdlər/ n infml someone who plays the VIOLIN

fid·dly /ˈfɪdli/ adj infml needing delicate movements of your fingers: *a very fiddly job*

fi·del·i·ty /fɪˈdeləti/ n [U] **1** fml faithfulness: *He spoke on the theme of fidelity in marriage.* –opposite **infidelity**(2) **2** the exactness of something that has been copied or recorded

fid·get¹ /ˈfɪdʒət/ v [I] to move your body around in a restless, impatient way: *Stop fidgeting, children, and listen!* –fidgety adj

fidget² n infml a person who fidgets

field¹ /fiːld/ n **1** an enclosed area of land on a farm, used for animals or crops: *fields of corn* **2** an open area where sport is played: *a football field* **3** an area where there are mines: *coal and oil fields* **4** a branch of knowledge or activity: *There have been exciting new developments in the field of cancer research.* | *a man famous in his own field* **5 the field:** **a** the place where battles take place in a war **b** tech all the horses in a race **6 in the field** in the place or conditions in which events really happen: *We haven't yet tested the new equipment in the field.* **7** the area in which a certain force is felt: *the moon's gravitational field* | *a magnetic field* **8 field of vision** the area that you can see: *I looked through the hole in the fence, but he was outside my field of vision.* **9 have a field day** to enjoy yourself very much by doing something which you do not often get the chance to do: *If the newspapers hear about this, they'll have a field day!*

field² v [I;T] to try to catch or stop the ball in a game of cricket or BASEBALL, so that the other team does not get any points –fielder n

field e·vent /ˈ· ·,·/ n a sports event in ATHLETICS which does not take place on the running track; the high jump is one field event

field hock·ey /ˈ· ,··/ n the usual American expression for HOCKEY

field mar·shal /ˈ· ,··/ n (also **Field Marshal**) the officer of highest rank in the British army: *Field Marshal Montgomery*

field trip /ˈ· ·/ n a trip to a place in order to study something which is found or happens in that place

field·work /ˈfiːldwɜːk ‖ -ɜːrk/ n [U] scientific or social study done in the place where things are found or happen naturally: *Most of the anthropologists I know have done fieldwork in West Africa.*

fiend /fiːnd/ n **1** a very cruel and wicked person **2** infml a person who is very keen on a particular thing: *a fresh air fiend*

fiend·ish /ˈfiːndɪʃ/ adj **1** fierce and cruel: *a fiendish temper* **2** infml very clever and full of imagination: *a fiendish plan* –fiendishly adv : *a fiendishly difficult question*

fierce /fɪəs ‖ fɪərs/ adj **1** angry, violent, and likely to attack: *a fierce guard dog* | *He had a fierce look on his face.* **2** very great or strong: *the fierce heat of the sun* | *Competition for jobs is very fierce.* –fiercely adv –fierceness n [U]

fi·er·y /ˈfaɪəri/ adj **1** the colour of fire: *fiery red hair* | *a fiery sunset* **2** full of violent feeling: *He has a fiery temper.*

fi·es·ta /fiˈestə/ n a religious holiday in Spain or Latin America, at which people come together to enjoy themselves

fif·teen /ˌfɪfˈtiːn◄/ det,n,pron the number 15 –fifteenth det,n,pron,adv

fifth /fɪfθ, fɪθ/ det,n,pron,adv **1** 5th **2** one of five equal parts

fif·ty /ˈfɪfti/ det,n,pron **fifties 1** the number 50 **2 the Fifties, the fifties** the years 1950–1959 **3 in her fifties, in their fifties, etc.** aged between 50 and 59 –fiftieth det,n,pron,adv

fifty-fifty /ˌ·· ˈ··◄/ adj,adv **1** divided equally between two people: *Let's split the bill fifty-fifty.* **2 a fifty-fifty chance** an equal chance that something will happen or not happen: *He's got a fifty-fifty chance of survival.*

fig /fɪg/ n a soft sweet fruit with many small seeds, often eaten dried

fig. a written abbreviation for FIGURE¹(6)

fight¹ /faɪt/ v fought /fɔːt/, fought **1** [I;T] to use violence against other people in an attempt to hurt or kill them: *Did your father fight in the war?* | *They fought to the death.* | *The two boys fought each other.* | *Many battles have been fought here.* **2** [I] to quarrel: *Let's try not to fight about money.* **3** [I;T] to try very hard to prevent or stop something: *This government is determined to fight crime.* | *We must fight against injustice.* **4** [I] to try very hard to do or obtain something: *We've been fighting for equal rights for nearly 100 years.* | *Car workers are fighting to keep their jobs.*

☐ USEFUL PATTERNS to fight for something; to fight to do something

5 fight an election to try to win an election and be elected **6 fight your way** to move along by pushing past other people: *He had to fight his way through the crowd.* **7 be fighting a losing battle** to be trying to do or prevent something without being successful: *She's fighting a losing battle against cancer.*

fight back phr v **1** [I] to protect yourself by fighting someone who is attacking you **2** [T fight back sthg] to try not to show a particular feeling: *He was fighting back tears.*

fight off phr v **1** [T fight sthg ↔ off] to succeed in making something unpleasant go away: *A good diet should help you to fight off infections.* **2** [T fight sbdy ↔ off] to make someone who is attacking you go away by fighting them: *They managed to fight off their attackers.*

fight out phr v **fight it out** to settle a disagreement by fighting or arguing

fight² n **1** [C] an attempt by two or more people to hurt or kill each other: *The police were called to stop a fight outside the pub.* **2** [C] a determined attempt to prevent something or obtain something: *the fight against inflation* | *our fight for equality* **3** [U] the desire or strength to fight: *There's not much fight left in the old man now.* **4 put up a good fight** to fight well against someone stronger than yourself

fight·er /ˈfaɪtər/ n **1** someone who fights **2** someone who continues trying to do something although it is very difficult **3** (also **fighter plane**) an aircraft used for fighting battles

fig·ment /ˈfɪgmənt/ n a figment of someone's imagination something imagined and not real

fig·u·ra·tive /ˈfɪgjʊrətɪv, -gə-/ adj using a word in a way which develops its main or usual meaning in an imaginative way: a figurative use of the word –compare LITERAL (3) –**figuratively** adv : I was using the word figuratively.

fig·ure¹ /ˈfɪgəʳ ‖ ˈfɪgjər/ n 1 a written sign used to represent a number: Write the amount in words and in figures. | a four-figure number 2 an amount of something expressed as a number: The Government has not yet published this year's export figures. | Recent figures indicate that inflation is rising. 3 a person, seen in a picture or from a distance: a group of figures on the left of the picture | I could see a figure in the distance. 4 your shape, considered from the point of view of how attractive it is: She's got a lovely figure. 5 an important person: He is one of the senior figures in the government. | leading literary figures 6 a numbered drawing used in a book to explain something

figure² v figured, figuring 1 [I] to be included in something: He figured prominently in a recent magazine story. | Both men figure in the list. 2 [+ (that)] AmE to believe that something is the case or that something should be done: We figured we'd better get a new car. 3 that figures infml that is what I would expect
figure sthg/sbdy ↔ **out** phr v [T] to understand someone or something: I was trying to figure out what was happening.

fig·ure·head /ˈfɪgəhed ‖ ˈfɪgjər-/ n 1 a leader who has no real power 2 an ornament on the front of a sailing ship, often in the shape of a person

figure of eight /ˌ··· ˈ·/ n anything of the shape of the number 8, such as a knot or pattern

figure of speech /ˌ··· ˈ·/ n a word or phrase used with a FIGURATIVE meaning: I didn't really mean you're wicked; it was just a figure of speech.

fil·a·ment /ˈfɪləmənt/ n a thin thread, such as the wire producing light inside an electric light BULB

filch /fɪltʃ/ v [T] infml to steal something of small value secretly

file¹ /faɪl/ n 1 a box or other container for storing important papers –see picture on page 539 2 a collection of papers stored together: Here's our file on the Middle East. | We keep a file on each student's progress. 3 a collection of information stored in a computer under one name: a data file | Open a new file for this project. 4 a tool used for making hard or rough surfaces smooth: Use a file for these rough edges. | a nail file –see picture on page 638 5 in single file one behind the other in a line: We walked along in single file.

file² v filed, filing 1 [T] to put something in a file with other papers: File this under "Accounts". 2 [I;T] law to make an official request or complaint: He has filed an application for planning permission.| She is filing for divorce. 3 [I;T] to make something smoother by using a file: She was filing her nails. 4 [I+adv/prep] to walk one behind the other: They filed slowly past the president's grave.

fil·et /ˈfɪlɪt ‖ ˈfɪlɪt, -leɪ, fɪˈleɪ/ n see FILLET

SPELLING NOTE
Words with the sound / f / may be spelt ph-, like **photograph**.

---

fi·li·al /ˈfɪliəl/ adj fml expected of a son or daughter: filial respect

fil·i·gree /ˈfɪlɪgriː/ n [U] delicate decorative work in gold or silver wire

fil·ing cab·i·net /ˈ··· ˌ···/ n a set of drawers in an office, used for storing important papers –see picture on page 539

fil·ings /ˈfaɪlɪŋz/ n [pl] very small sharp bits of metal: iron filings

fill¹ /fɪl/ v 1 [I] to become full: The room soon filled with people. | His eyes filled with tears. 2 [T] to make something full: Fill the bucket with water. | Crowds of people filled the streets. 3 [T] to cause strong feelings in someone: The news has filled my colleagues with anxiety. | She was filled with anger. 4 [T] to have or perform a particular job or position: The White House didn't have anyone who could fill the role of negotiator. | There are not enough young people available to fill the job vacancies. 5 [T] to satisfy a need or demand: This larger vehicle more closely fills their needs.
fill in phr v 1 [T fill sthg ↔ in] to put something into a space so that the space is filled: I filled in all the cracks. 2 [T fill sthg ↔ in] to complete a form by writing information on it: I haven't filled in my application form yet. 3 [T fill sbdy in] to give someone information about something 4 [I] to do someone's job or take their place: Can you fill in for Steve tonight as he's ill? | If Jane can't come, I'll fill in.
fill out phr v 1 [T fill sthg ↔ out] to complete a form by writing information on it 2 [I] to get fatter: Her face is beginning to fill out.
fill up phr v [I;T fill sbdy/sthg ↔ up] to become or make something completely full: Could you fill the kettle up with water, please? | The room soon filled up with people.

fill² n 1 your fill as much as you need or want: He had drunk his fill. 2 have had your fill of something to have had enough of something and not want any more of it: I've had my fill of arguments.

fil·let¹ /ˈfɪlɪt ‖ ˈfɪlɪt, -leɪ, fɪˈleɪ/ n (also filet AmE) a piece of fish or meat with no bones in it: a fillet steak | fillets of sole –see picture on page 344

fillet² v (also filet AmE) [T] to prepare a piece of fish or meat by taking out the bones

fill·ing¹ /ˈfɪlɪŋ/ n 1 [C] a small amount of a special substance put into a hole in a tooth to preserve the tooth: You've got a lot of fillings. 2 [C;U] something put inside a cake or chocolate, or between two pieces of bread: a delicious chocolate cream filling

filling² adj making you feel full quickly (used of food): This pudding is very filling.

filling sta·tion /ˈ··· ˌ··/ n a place that sells petrol and oil for cars and other vehicles

fil·ly /ˈfɪli/ n fillies a young female horse

film¹ /fɪlm/ n 1 [C;U] a roll of a plastic substance which you put inside a camera and on which photographs are taken: I used three whole films while I was on holiday. | My camera's run out of film. 2 [C] a story or play recorded on film and shown in a cinema or on television: Have you seen any good films lately? 3 [C] a small amount of a substance spread over a surface: Everything was covered with a thin film of dust. 4 [U] a very thin sheet of plastic used for covering or wrapping things

film² v [I;T] to make a film of something for the cinema or television: We'll be filming all day tomorrow. | They filmed the Queen's arrival in Paris.

film star /ˈ· ·/ n a well-known actor or actress who acts in films

film·strip /ˈfɪlmˌstrɪp/ n [C;U] a length of photographic film used to show photographs or drawings one after the other as still pictures

film·y /ˈfɪlmi/ adj fine and almost transparent: a filmy silk dress

fil·ter¹ /ˈfɪltəʳ/ n 1 an apparatus used to keep a substance clean; filters work by allowing only the substance itself to pass through, but not unwanted substances such as dirt or chemicals: a water filter 2 a coloured glass that changes the light which passes through it into a camera

filter² v [I;T] 1 to pass a substance through a filter: We always filter our drinking water. 2 [I+adv/prep] to reach people or a place gradually: The visitors are filtering into the dining-room. | The news slowly filtered through to everyone in the office.
filter sbdy/sthg ↔ **out** phr v [T] to remove by means of a filter or a system for choosing between people: We managed to filter out the dirt. | Try and filter out unsuitable applicants before the interviews.

filth /fɪlθ/ n [U] 1 very nasty dirt: Go and wash that filth off your hands. 2 language or pictures which people find rude or offensive, especially because they are connected with sex: I don't know how you can read such filth.

filth·y /ˈfɪlθi/ adj filthier, filthiest 1 very dirty: Your hands are filthy! 2 rude or offensive, especially concerning sex: filthy language –**filthiness** n [U]

fin /fɪn/ n a part of a fish's body shaped like a small wing, which helps it to swim

fi·nal¹ /ˈfaɪnl/ adj 1 [only before a noun] coming last or at the end of something: the final episode of the TV series | the final stages of the game | We had a final cup of coffee before we left. 2 unable to be changed or questioned (=used of a decision or an offer): I won't go, and that's final! | Is that your final offer?

final² n 1 [C] the last and most important game in a competition: the World Cup Final | She got through to the finals. 2 **finals** [pl] the last and most important set of examinations in a college course: How did you get on in your finals?

fi·na·le /fɪˈnɑːli || fɪˈnæli/ n the last part of a piece of music or a musical show: a spectacular grand finale

fi·nal·ist /ˈfaɪnəl-ʒst/ n one of the people or teams who have reached the final in a competition

fi·nal·i·ty /faɪˈnælʒti, fɪ-/ n [U] the quality of being certain and unchangeable: "No!" he said with finality.

fi·nal·ize /ˈfaɪnəl-aɪz/ v **finalized, finalizing** (also **finalise** BrE) [T] to complete an arrangement: It's time to finalize our plans for the concert.

fi·nal·ly /ˈfaɪnəl-i/ adv 1 after a long delay: We finally set off after lunch. 2 a word used when you have several points to make and you come to the last one: We've seen how different soils suit different plants, and how rainfall affects their growth. Finally, I'd like to look at the significance of light. | And finally, I'd like to thank you all for coming tonight. 3 a word used when you are describing a number of events that happen one after the other, and you come to the last one: We had a week at the seaside in Holland. Then we spent a couple of days in Antwerp. Finally, we went to Bruges. 4 a word used when you come to the last of a number of instructions: Make a cheese sauce. Boil the pasta in

salted water until it is just soft. Mix the pasta with the sauce. Finally, put the dish into a hot oven for 20 minutes to brown it. 5 in a way that does not allow further change: It's not finally settled yet.

fi·nance¹ /ˈfaɪnæns, fʒˈnæns || fʒˈnæns, ˈfaɪnæns/ n 1 [U] the management of money, especially for a company or a government: He's an accountant in the Finance Department. 2 [U] money provided by a bank or other organization to help run a business: Unless we get more finance, we'll have to close the school down. 3 **finances** [pl] the amount of money that a person or an organization has: We'd better review our finances before we buy a new car.

finance² v **financed, financing** [T] to provide money for something: The repairs will be financed by the local council.

fi·nan·cial /fʒˈnænʃəl, faɪ-/ adj connected with money: The City of London is a great financial centre. | He works as a financial adviser. | The project was a financial success. –**financially** adv

fi·nan·cier /fʒˈnænsɪəʳ, faɪˈnæn- || ˌfaɪnænˈsɪər/ n someone who controls or lends large sums of money

finch /fɪntʃ/ n a small bird

find¹ /faɪnd/ v **found** /faʊnd/, **found** 1 [T] to discover or obtain something, usually when you have been looking for it or when you need it: I can't find my boots! | Did you find what you were looking for? | Oil has been found in the North Sea. | I found a Roman coin in the garden. | We need to find a solution to this problem. | There are many people who cannot find a place to live. 2 [+that] to learn or discover a fact: Scientists have found that this disease will respond to treatment by drugs. | We went to her house, but found that she was out. | I'm finding that the job is not as easy as I thought it would be. 3 [T] to have a particular feeling about something or someone: I find him boring! | I found the film very interesting. 4 [T] to have enough of something to be able to do something that you want to do: I can never find the time to read novels. | We couldn't find enough money to pay for the holiday. | I couldn't find the courage to tell him the bad news. 5 **find fault with** someone/something to complain about someone or something: She's always finding fault with my work! 6 **find someone guilty** to declare that someone is guilty of a crime: The jury found him guilty. [RELATED PHRASE **find someone not guilty**] 7 **find yourself somewhere** to become conscious that you are in a particular place or doing a particular thing, but without having planned it: When I woke up I found myself in hospital. | I found myself shouting and swearing at him. 8 **find your feet** to become used to new or strange surroundings 9 **find your way** to reach a place by discovering the right way to get there: I managed to find my way back to the station.
find out phr v 1 [I;T find sthg ↔ **out**] to learn or discover a fact: Did you ever find out who got the job? | I found out that he'd been stealing things from the company. | We never found out his name. 2 [T **find** sbdy **out**] to discover that someone has been doing something dishonest: He'd been fiddling the books for years before he was found out.

find² n something good that you find: That Greek restaurant is a real find!

find·ing /ˈfaɪndɪŋ/ n something learnt or decided as the result of an official enquiry: The committee on child care will publish its findings next week.

fine¹ /faɪn/ n an amount of money paid as a punishment: a parking fine

fine² v **fined, fining** [T] to make someone pay a sum of money as a punishment: *He was fined £200.*

fine³ adj **1** of very good quality: *She's a fine musician.* | *one of the finest buildings in Europe* **2** [not used in questions or negatives] acceptable: *"I'll be there at two o'clock." "Yes, that's fine."* | *"What's your new flat like?" "It's fine."* **3** very thin: *a pencil with a fine point* | *I've got very fine hair.* –see THIN¹ (USAGE) **4** in very small grains or bits: *a fine powdery dust* **5** bright and sunny: *a fine summer morning* **6** [not used in questions or negatives] reasonably healthy and happy: *"How are you?" "I'm fine."* **7** delicate and careful: *He made a few fine adjustments to the engine.* | *I missed some of the finer points in the argument.* **8 fine art** beautiful paintings and other works of art: *She's doing a course in fine art.* **9 the fine arts** activities such as painting and music, which are concerned with producing beautiful things

fine⁴ adv well: *That suits me fine.* | *We get on fine.*

fine·ly /ˈfaɪnli/ adv **1** carefully and delicately: *These instruments are very finely tuned.* **2** until very thin or in very small bits: *finely cut vegetables*

fi·ne·ry /ˈfaɪnəri/ n [U] beautiful clothes and jewellery worn on special occasions: *the guests in all their wedding finery*

fi·nesse /fɪˈnes/ n [U] a clever way of dealing with people and situations: *Paul handled the meeting with great finesse.*

fin·ger¹ /ˈfɪŋgəʳ/ n **1** one of the movable parts, with joints, at the end of each of your hands **2** the part of a GLOVE that covers a finger **3 cross your fingers, keep your fingers crossed** *infml* to hope for the best: *I hope the weather stays fine for tomorrow's game. We must just keep our fingers crossed.* **4 have a finger in every pie** *infml* to be connected with everything that is happening **5 lift a finger, raise a finger** to make any effort to help: *No one lifted a finger to save the prisoners.* **6 pull your finger out, get your finger out** *infml* to start working hard **7 put your finger on something** to recognize the truth of something: *I can't quite put my finger on what's wrong.*

finger² v [T] to feel or touch something with your fingers: *She fingered the fine silk.*

fin·ger·nail /ˈfɪŋgəneɪl ‖ -ər-/ n one of the hard flat pieces at the end of each finger: *The baby's fingernails need cutting.*

fin·ger·print /ˈfɪŋgəˌprɪnt ‖ -ər-/ n a mark made of the lines on the end of your finger: *The police interviewed him and took his fingerprints.* | *The burglars left their fingerprints all over the house.*

fin·ger·tip /ˈfɪŋgəˌtɪp ‖ -ər-/ n **1** the end of a finger **2 have something at your fingertips** to know something well and be able to find or remember it easily: *You'd better ask David – he has all the information at his fingertips.*

fin·i·cky /ˈfɪnɪki/ adj *infml* **1** disliking many things: *Eat up your fish and don't be so finicky.* **2** needing great attention to detail: *It's a very finicky job being a typesetter.*

fin·ish¹ /ˈfɪnɪʃ/ v [I;T] to come to an end or complete something: *What time does the concert finish?* |

When do you finish your college course? | *I haven't finished reading that book yet.*
□ **USEFUL PATTERNS** to finish something; to finish doing something
2 [I;T] to stop work: *What time do you finish on Friday?* **3** [T] to eat, drink, or use the rest of something: *The cat will finish the fish.* | *Let's finish the wine.* | *Have you finished the blue paint?* **4** [T] *infml* to make someone extremely tired: *Climbing all those stairs has really finished me.*

finish off phr v **1** [T **finish** sbdy/sthg ↔ **off**] to kill a person or animal that is hurt **2** [I;T **finish** sthg ↔ **off**] to complete something: *I'm just finishing off the report.* | *I'm just finishing off here.* **3** [T **finish** sthg ↔ **off**] to eat, drink, or use the rest of something

finish up phr v **1** [I] to be in a particular situation or do something at the end of something: *We finished up with a brandy.* | *They finished up at a disco.* **2** [T **finish** sthg ↔ **up**] to eat, drink, or use the rest of something

finish with sbdy/sthg phr v [T] **1** to have no more use for a person or thing: *I'll borrow the scissors if you've finished with them.* | *Have you finished with the typist?* **2** to end a relationship: *He's finished with Mary at last!*

finish² n **1** end **2** [sing;U] the appearance at the end: *the beautiful finish of old French furniture* | *a metallic finish* **3** [sing] the end of a race **4 a close finish** an end of a race, at which point the leading competitors are very close together –compare START²

fin·ished /ˈfɪnɪʃt/ adj **1** at the end of an activity or relationship: *I'll be finished in about an hour.* **2** [never before a noun] without hope of continuing: *If the bank refuses to lend us the money, we're finished.* **3** [only before a noun] completed: *the finished product* | *a beautifully finished old table*

finishing school /ˈ··· ·/ n a private school where rich girls learn social behaviour and other useful skills

fi·nite /ˈfaɪnaɪt/ adj limited: *a finite number of possibilities* –opposite **infinite**

fi·ord /ˈfiːɔːd, fjɔːd ‖ fiːˈɔːrd, fjɔːrd/ n see FJORD

fir /fɜːʳ/ n (also **firtree** /ˈfɜːtriː ‖ ˈfɜːr-/) a tree that keeps its thin sharp leaves in winter, forms seeds in a CONE, and grows mainly in cold countries

fire¹ /faɪəʳ/ n **1** [U] flames, light, and great heat: *People discovered fire thousands of years ago.* **2** [C;U] flames which are out of control and destroying things: *a forest fire* | *The hotel was seriously damaged by fire.* | *Is the cottage insured against fire?* **3** [C] a pile of burning coal or wood used to heat a room or to cook food over: *We sat in front of the roaring fire and chatted.* | *The campers lit a fire to boil some water.* **4** [C] a gas or electrical apparatus with red-hot wires or flames, used to heat a room: *Could you switch the fire on?* **5 on fire** burning and being damaged by fire: *The house is on fire!* **6 under fire** being shot at: *The regiment was under fire from all sides.* **7 -fired** operated by a particular substance which is burnt: *oil-fired central heating* | *a coal-fired power station*

fire² v **fired, firing 1** [I;T] to shoot with a gun: *He's firing at us!* | *The German guns were firing all night.* | *He ran into the bank and fired his gun into the air.* | *Gunmen fired five shots at the President.* **2** [T] *infml* to dismiss someone from a job: *Get out! You're fired!* **3** [T] to say things very quickly one after the other: *The journalists fired questions at the Prime Minister.* **4** [T] to produce strong feelings in

someone: *The speech fired the crowd's imagination.*
5 [I] (of an engine) to make the petrol burn and the engine work: *The engine is only firing on three cylinders.* **6** [T] to bake clay objects

fire away *phr v* [I] to begin to speak or ask questions: *If anyone has any questions, fire away!*

fire a·larm /'· ·ˌ·/ *n* a signal, such as a ringing bell, to warn people of fire

fire·arm /'faɪərɑːm ‖ -ɑːrm/ *n* a gun: *Do I need a licence to carry firearms?*

fire bri·gade /'· ·ˌ·/ *n* (**fire department** /'· ·ˌ·/ *AmE*) [+ sing/pl verb] an organization of people who are trained to put out fires: *Phone for the fire brigade!*

fire en·gine /'·ˌ··/ *n* a special vehicle that carries firemen and apparatus to put out fires

fire es·cape /'· ·ˌ·/ *n* a set of metal stairs leading down outside a building to the ground, by which people can escape from a fire –see picture on page 441

fire ex·tin·guish·er /'· ·ˌ···/ *n* a metal container with water or chemicals inside for putting out a fire

fire-guard /'faɪəgɑːd ‖ 'faɪərgɑːrd/ *n* a protective metal framework put round a fireplace

fire·man /'faɪəmən ‖ 'faɪər-/ *n* **firemen** /-mən/ a person whose job is to put out fires

fire·place /'faɪəpleɪs ‖ -ər-/ *n* an opening for a fire in the wall of a room –see picture on page 442

fire·proof /'faɪəpruːf ‖ -ər-/ *adj* protected so that it cannot be changed by fire –**fireproof** *v* [T]

fire-rais·ing /'·ˌ··/ *n* [U] the crime of starting fires on purpose

fire·side /'faɪəsaɪd ‖ -ər-/ *n* the area around the fireplace: *Let's sit and read by the fireside.*

fire sta·tion /'·ˌ··/ *n* a building for firemen (FIRE-MAN) and their apparatus and vehicles

fire·wood /'faɪəwʊd ‖ -ər-/ *n* [U] wood that has been cut for use on fires

fire·work /'faɪəwɜːk ‖ 'faɪərwɜːrk/ *n* a small container filled with an explosive powder that is burnt to produce a show of light, noise, and smoke: *a firework display* | *Shall we let off some fireworks?*

fir·ing squad /'·· ˌ·/ *n* a group of soldiers ordered to shoot and kill a prisoner

firm¹ /fɜːm ‖ fɜːrm/ *adj* **1** not soft and not moving much when pressed: *a firm bed* | *Choose firm tomatoes.* **2** with no uncertainty: *a firm belief in God* | *a firm date for the wedding* | *firm evidence* **3** solidly fixed: *I don't think that chair is firm enough to stand on.* | *firm foundations* **4** strong: *a firm handshake* **5** using strong control: *If parents were firmer with their children, there would be fewer discipline problems.* **6** not decreasing in value: *The pound remained firm against the dollar yesterday.*

firm² *n* a business company

fir·ma·ment /'fɜːməmənt ‖ 'fɜːr-/ *n* **the firmament** *lit* the sky

first¹ /fɜːst ‖ fɜːrst/ *n,pron* **1 the first** the person or thing that does something before all others: *Jim was the first to arrive.* **2** [C] the highest class of degree that you can get from a British university **3** **a first** something that has never happened before **4 at first** in the beginning: *At first I didn't believe him but then I realized that he was telling the truth.* –see BEGINNING (USAGE) **5 from the first, from the very first** from the beginning: *I knew from the first that I wasn't going to like the job.*

first² *det, adv* **1** before anything or anyone else:

George arrived first. | *I want to go into town, but first I must finish writing this letter.* | *She came first in the competition.* **2** for the first time: *Is this your first visit to London?* | *We first met back in 1967.* **3** when you have several points you want to make, you can order them and number them "First,...", "Second,...", etc: *There are several reasons why the plan will not work. First, there has not been enough preparation. Second, there is not enough money.* **4** you can use "first" when you are going to mention the first of several events: *We had soup first. Then we had a lovely piece of beef. And then for pudding we had lemon mousse.* | *First we cleared the ground. Then we built a low platform.* **5** you can use "first" when you are going to give the first of a number of instructions: *First, put one spoonful of coffee per person into the righthand compartment. Then put one cup of water per person into the lefthand compartment.* **6 first of all: a** before anything else **b** firstly and most importantly; when you have several points you want to make, you can use this expression to introduce the first: *First of all, let me say how glad I am to be here.* **c** you can use this expression when you are talking about the first of several events: *First of all, we had something to eat. Then we went to see one of the famous temples.* | *Let's, first of all, try and decide about holiday dates.* | *"Have you fixed the holiday dates?" "Yes, we did that first of all."* **d** you can use this expression when you are giving the first of a number of instructions: *First of all, make sure that the two pieces of wood are thoroughly clean. Then put a thin layer of glue on each piece.* **7 at first** at the beginning of a period, as opposed to later on in the same period: *At first I didn't like him, but now I do.* **8 in the first place: a** when you have several points you want to make, you can use this expression to introduce the first one: *They won't be interested in that house. In the first place, it's too far from where they work. And in the second place, it's more than they are prepared to pay.* **b** to start with; you use this expression when you are finding fault with someone and saying that you have no sympathy with them: *It's no use complaining about getting hurt. You shouldn't have been riding on the roof in the first place.* **9 first thing** at the beginning of the day: *I'll phone you first thing tomorrow morning.*

first aid /ˌ· '·/ *n* [U] treatment you could give someone hurt in an accident or suddenly taken ill before the doctor arrives: *Get me the first-aid box, quickly!*

first class /ˌ· '·◂/ *adv* **1** in the most comfortable and most expensive part of the train, plane, or ship: *There's a lot more space if you travel first class.* **2** by a class of mail delivered as quickly as possible and costing more money: *You'll have to send it first class to get it there on Saturday.*

first-class /ˌ· '·◂/ *adj* **1** of the highest or best quality: *a first-class piece of work* | *Her cooking is absolutely first-class.* **2** for travel in the most comfortable and most expensive part of a train, plane, or ship: *a first-class ticket* | *a first-class compartment*

first floor /ˌ· '·◂/ *n* **1** *BrE* the first floor of a building above ground level **2** *AmE* the floor of a building at ground level –compare GROUND FLOOR (1)

first-hand /ˌfɜːst'hænd◂ ‖ -ɜːr-/ *adj, adv* learnt directly and not from other people: *It's not firsthand information, so I don't know if we should believe it.*

first la·dy /ˌ· '··/ *n* **the First Lady** the wife of the President of the USA

first·ly /'fɜːstli ‖ -ɜːr-/ *adv* when you have several

points you want to make, you can order them and number them "Firstly,…", "Secondly,…", etc.: *There are several reasons why the plan will not work. Firstly, there has not been enough preparation. Secondly, there is not enough money.*

first name /ˈ· ·/ *n* the name or names that come before your family name: *Mr Smith's first name is Peter.* | *His first names are Peter George.* –compare SURNAME

■ USAGE In English-speaking countries your **first name** usually means the first of the names which your parents give you at birth, but it can also mean *all* the names your parents give you. In Christian countries people sometimes use **Christian name** in the same way. People also use **given name** and (less commonly) **forename** in the same way, especially on official forms.

first per·son /ˌ· ˈ··◂/ *n* [sing] **1** a form of verb which you use with "I" or "we" **2** a way of telling a story in which the teller uses the first person: *The story was written in the first person. It began "I was born in…"*

first-rate /ˌ· ˈ·◂/ *adj* of the highest quality: *to use first-rate materials* | *This beer is first-rate!*

fis·cal /ˈfɪskəl/ *adj* of or related to public money, taxes, or debts

fish[1] /fɪʃ/ *n* **fish** *or* **fishes** **1** [C] a creature which lives in water and uses its fins (FIN) and tail to swim: *We only caught three fish all day.* **2** [U] the flesh of a fish when used as food: *We had fish and chips for dinner.* –see picture on page 344

fish[2] *v* **1** [I] to try to catch fish: *He's fishing for trout.* | *Dad's taken John fishing.* **2 go fishing** to go to a suitable place and fish: *"Where are Sandy and Les?" "They've gone fishing."* **3** [T + adv/prep] to search: *She fished around in her handbag for her purse.* **4 fish for** to try to get something in an indirect way: *She's always fishing for compliments.* **fish** sthg ↔ **out** *phr v* [T] to bring something out after searching for it: *She fished out a small red box from the bottom of her handbag.*

fish·er·man /ˈfɪʃəmən ‖ -ʃər-/ *n* **fishermen** /-mən/ someone who catches fish, for sport or as a job

fish·ing /ˈfɪʃɪŋ/ *n* [U] the sport or job of catching fish: *Fishing is a very popular pastime in Ireland.* | *Can we do some fishing on holiday?*

fishing rod /ˈ·· ˌ·/ *n* a long thin stick with a string with a hook, used for catching fish

fish·mon·ger /ˈfɪʃmʌŋgəʳ ‖ -maːŋ-, -mʌn-/ *n* **1** someone who works in a shop that sells fish **2 fishmonger's** a shop where you buy fish: *I'm going to the fishmonger's.* | *I got it at the fishmonger's.*

fish slice /ˈ· ·/ *n BrE* a kitchen tool used for lifting and turning foods –see picture on page 639

fish·y /ˈfɪʃi/ *adj* **fishier, fishiest** **1** tasting or smelling of fish **2** seeming false: *That story sounds very fishy to me.*

fis·sion /ˈfɪʃən/ *n* [U] *tech* the splitting into parts of certain atoms to produce a powerful force

fis·sure /ˈfɪʃəʳ/ *n fml* a deep crack in rock or earth

fist /fɪst/ *n* a hand with the fingers tightly curled: *She shook her fist angrily.*

fit[1] /fɪt/ *v* **-tt-** **1** [I;T] to be the right size or shape: *This door fits very badly.* | *This dress doesn't fit me.* **2** [T

+ adv/prep] to find enough space for something: *I can't fit any more books onto this shelf.* | *We should be able to fit some more desks into this room.* **3** [T] to put something correctly into place: *We're having new locks fitted on all the doors.* **4** [T] to be suitable for something: *to make the punishment fit the crime* **5 fit the bill** to be just what is needed: *We needed a journalist who spoke French and Arabic, and she fitted the bill.* **6 fit like a glove** to fit very well and closely

■ USAGE The usual past form of **fit** is **fitted.** But when talking about size and shape, Americans sometimes use **fit** as a past form: *He said that the suit fit him perfectly.*

fit in *phr v* **1** [I] to have a friendly, easy relationship with other people in a group because you are similar to them: *He fitted in very well with the group.* **2** [I] to happen or do things at a time that is suitable and does not affect other arrangements: *The trouble with this job is that the hours don't fit in with the school day.* | *Don't change your arrangements. I'll fit in with you.* **3** [T **fit** sbdy/sthg ↔ **in**] to find a time to see someone or do something: *Doctor Jones can fit you in on Thursday afternoon.* **fit** sthg ↔ **out** *phr v* [T] to fit something with all the things necessary for a particular purpose: *The old warehouse has been fitted out as a car showroom.*

fit[2] *n* **1** the way in which something fits: *This coat's a beautiful fit.* | *I'll try to climb through, but it's a tight fit.* **2** a loss of consciousness, with strange uncontrolled movements of the body: *He suffers from epileptic fits.* **3** a short attack of a slight illness or violent feeling: *a fit of coughing* | *I hit her in a fit of anger.* **4 have a fit** *infml* to get very angry: *Mum will have a fit when she sees what you've done.* **5** a sudden need to laugh or do something particular: *The children burst into fits of laughter.* | *I had a fit of letter writing yesterday.* **6 in fits and starts** continually starting and stopping

fit[3] *adj* **1** [never before a noun] right and suitable: *She's not fit to be in charge of small children.* | *a meal fit for a king*
☐ USEFUL PATTERNS be fit for something; be fit to do something
2 physically healthy and strong, often as a result of regular exercise: *He runs three miles every morning. That's why he's so fit.* | *She goes to keep-fit classes and does exercises every day.* –opposite **unfit** **3 fit to do something** almost ready to do something: *He looked fit to burst.* | *We worked until we were fit to drop.* **4 as fit as a fiddle** very healthy **5 see fit to, think fit** to consider it right to do something: *He saw fit to phone me up in the middle of the night!* | *You must do as you see fit.*

fit·ful /ˈfɪtfəl/ *adj* happening in many short periods and not continuous –**fitfully** *adv* : *She slept fitfully.*

fit·ment /ˈfɪtmənt/ *n* a piece of fitted furniture: *bathroom fitments*

fit·ness /ˈfɪtnəs/ *n* [U] **1** the condition of being physically fit: *doing exercises to improve their fitness* **2** the quality of being suitable: *his fitness to command the army* | *her fitness for the job*

fit·ted /ˈfɪtɪd/ *adj* **1** [never before a noun] having a part or piece of apparatus: *Is the car fitted with a C.D. player?* | *It's got a CD player fitted.* **2** fixed in place: *a fitted carpet*

fit·ter /ˈfɪtəʳ/ *n* someone who puts together machines or electrical parts

fit·ting[1] /ˈfɪtɪŋ/ *adj fml* right or suitable: *It is fitting that we should remember those who have given their lives for freedom.* –opposite **unfitting**

When you are writing in English it is helpful to know if a word is usually followed by a particular kind of grammatical pattern. This dictionary helps you in various ways.

1 Grammar codes

The following codes tell you which grammatical patterns can follow a word:

+ *that*

In this entry the code [**+ that**] tells you that **contend** can be followed by a clause introduced by **that**. The example gives you more help with how to use the word.

> **con·tend** /kən'tend/ v **1** [T; + that] to claim that something is true: *The lawyer contended that she had not returned home until 11.00.*

+ *adv/prep*

In this entry the code [**I + adv/prep**] tells you that, when it means "to come or go to a place in large numbers," the verb **flood** is intransitive. It also tells you that it must be followed by an adverb or a preposition. So you can say, *The letters came flooding in*, or *The spectators flooded onto the pitch.* But you should NOT say, *The spectators flooded.* ✗

> **flood²** v .... **2** [I + adv/prep] to come or go to a place in large numbers: *Requests for information flooded in after the advertisement.* | *Settlers flooded from Europe to America in the 19th century.*

+ *complement*

This entry tells you that the verb **become** is not usually used alone but should be followed by a complement. The examples show you what kind of complements you can use.

> **be·come** /bɪ'kʌm/ v became /bɪ'keɪm/, become, becoming **1** [+ complement] to begin to be something: *He became king in 1958.* | *The weather became warmer.*

2 Patterns shown in dark print

Some words are nearly always used with the same grammatical pattern. And some words are always used with a particular pattern when they have a particular meaning. The dictionary shows you these patterns in special dark print before giving you the definition.

This entry shows you that, when it means "to

> **seek** /siːk/ v sought /sɔːt/, sought [T] *fml or lit*
> **2 seek to do something** to try to do something: *The company is seeking to improve its profitability.*

try to do something", the verb **seek** is always followed by the infinitive with 'to'. The examples give you more help with how to use it.

3 Useful patterns

When you are writing in English it can sometimes be difficult to know which pattern to use after a particular word. There are some words which you will need to use quite frequently in your writing but which might give you problems because of their grammatical patterns. This dictionary gives you **extra** help with these words by suggesting some patterns for you to use.

The USEFUL PATTERNS note at the first meaning of **consider** gives you some patterns to use with this verb when it means "to think about something carefully".

> **con·sid·er** /kən'sɪdəʳ/ v **1** [I;T] to think about something carefully: *I'm considering changing my job.* | *We need some time to consider.*
> ☐ USEFUL PATTERNS to consider; to consider something; to consider doing something

This tells you that you can say:
– Consider carefully before making up your mind. ✓
– I'm considering your offer. ✓
– She's considering going abroad. ✓

You should, therefore, avoid mistakes such as:
– I'm considering to change my job. ✗

The USEFUL PATTERNS note at the first meaning of **confess** gives you some patterns to use with this verb when it means "to admit to a fault or crime".

> **con·fess** /kən'fes/ v **1** [I;T;+(that)] to admit to a fault or crime: *It's time to confess.* | *He has confessed to the murder.* | *She confessed all her crimes.* | *Jean confessed that she'd eaten all the cakes.*
> ☐ USEFUL PATTERNS to confess; to confess something; to confess to something; to confess to doing something; to confess that...

This tells you that you can say:
– They made him confess. ✓
– He's already confessed his part in the crime. ✓
– She confessed to the theft. ✓
– She confessed to opening/to having opened the letter. ✓
– They confessed that they had lost the money. ✓

You should, therefore, avoid mistakes such as:
– She confessed to have opened the letter. ✗

Examples

Remember that, in addition to looking at codes and patterns, you should always read the example sentences. These will give you a lot of help with finding out how to use the word you are looking up.

fitting² n **1** an occasion when you put on clothes that are being made for you, to see if they fit: *I'm going for a fitting on Tuesday.* **2 fittings** [pl] things that are fixed into a building but can be moved if necessary: *electric light fittings*

five /faɪv/ det, n, pron the number 5

fiv·er /ˈfaɪvəʳ/ n infml £5 or a five-pound note: *It costs a fiver.* | *I've only got fivers.*

fix¹ /fɪks/ v **1** [T + adv/prep] to fasten something firmly: *She fixed the mirror onto the wall.* **2** [T] to arrange and establish an exact time, price, or place: *Let's fix a time for the meeting.* | *The rent was fixed at £100.* | *If you want to meet them I can fix it.* **3** [T] to arrange the result of something unfairly: *The election was fixed.* **4** [T] to repair something or make small changes to it: *I must get the car fixed.* | *She's in the Ladies fixing her make up.* **5** [T] to remember something because it is important or unusual: *Let me fix the address in my mind.* **6** [T + adv/prep] to direct your attention steadily at something: *She fixed her eyes on the clock.* | *He fixed me with his intense gaze.* **7** [T] AmE to prepare food or drink for someone: *Let me fix you a drink.* **8** [T] infml to punish someone: *I'll fix him for calling me a liar!* **9 fix the blame on someone** to decide that someone is guilty

fix on sbdy/sthg phr v [I] to decide on someone or something: *We've fixed on 14th April for the wedding.*

fix up phr v **1** [I;T **fix** sthg ↔ **up**] to arrange something: *I've fixed up another meeting.* | *We'd already fixed up to go to Majorca.* | *I've fixed up for you to see the doctor.* **2** [T **fix** sthg ↔ **up**] to put something in place, often something that is only wanted for a short period: *Doug's going to fix up some lights for the party.* | *Daisy fixed me up some shelves above the worktop.* **3 fix someone up with something** to provide someone with something they need: *Can you fix me up with a bed for the night?* | *He fixed him up with a holiday job.* **4** [T **fix** sthg ↔ **up**] to repair something or make it suitable for new needs: *We'll have to fix up the attic as a bedroom.* **5 get fixed up: a** to find somewhere to live **b** to succeed in making suitable arrangements: *He was hoping to go to university, but I don't know whether he's got fixed up yet.*

fix² n infml **1** an awkward or difficult position: *We're in a real fix. We can't get any spare parts for the car before Monday.* **2** infml something that has been dishonestly arranged: *It was a fix, that election!* **3** an INJECTION of a drug like HEROIN: *They looked as if they needed a fix of something.*

fix·a·tion /fɪkˈseɪʃ ən/ n a strong unhealthy feeling about or love for: *He has a fixation about cleanliness.* | *a mother fixation*

fixed /fɪkst/ adj **1** not movable or changeable: *The tables are firmly fixed to the floor.* | *The date is fixed now.* **2** held firmly and unchangingly: *He has very fixed ideas on this subject.* **3 how are you fixed…?** = are you free…?: *I think we need another meeting. How are you fixed for Thursday morning?*

fix·ed·ly /ˈfɪksɪdli/ adv unchangingly: *Harry stared fixedly at the ground and looked embarrassed.*

fix·ture /ˈfɪkstʃəʳ/ n **1** something that is fixed into

SPELLING NOTE

Words with the sound /f/ may be spelt **ph-**, like **photograph**.

---

a building and sold with it: *bathroom fixtures* **2** a match or sports competition taking place on an agreed date

fizz¹ /fɪz/ v [I] (of a liquid) to produce bubbles (BUBBLE), or make the sound of very small bubbles bursting

fizz² n **1** the bubbles (BUBBLE) of gas in a liquid: *This champagne has lost all its fizz!* **2** the sound of fizzing –**fizzy** adj fizzier, fizziest: *fizzy drinks like Coca-cola*

fiz·zle /ˈfɪzəl/ v
fizzle out phr v [I] to end in nothing after a good start: *The party fizzled out before midnight.*

fjord /ˈfiːɔːd, fjɔːd || fiːˈɔːrd, fjɔːrd/ n (also **fiord**) a narrow bit of the sea between cliffs or steep slopes, especially in Norway

flab·ber·gast·ed /ˈflæbəgɑːstꜰd || -ərgæst-/ adj infml extremely surprised: *I was flabbergasted when he told me how much it had cost.*

flab·by /ˈflæbi/ adj flabbier, flabbiest having soft, loose flesh and muscles: *I'm getting very flabby. I suppose I ought to take more exercise.* –**flabbiness** n [U]

flag¹ /flæg/ n **1** a square or OBLONG piece of cloth with a pattern in certain colours, used as a sign of a country or organization, or as a signal: *The Egyptian flag was fluttering in the breeze.* | *The ship was flying the national flag of Japan.* **2** a small piece of paper joined to a pin given out by people collecting money for the poor or sick **3** a big square piece of stone for a floor or path

flag² v -gg- [I] to become tired or less interested: *After walking for three hours, we began to flag.* | *I tried to revive his flagging interest in the subject.*
flag sbdy/sthg ↔ **down** phr v [T] to signal to a vehicle to stop by waving at the driver: *They flagged down a lorry, which took them to a garage.*

flag·pole /ˈflæɡpəʊl/ n a tall pole for a flag

fla·grant /ˈfleɪɡrənt/ adj open and showing no sign of guilt: *a flagrant abuse of taxpayers' money* | *a flagrant liar* –**flagrantly** adv

flag·stone /ˈflæɡstəʊn/ n a hard, smooth, flat piece of stone for a floor or path

flail /fleɪl/ v [I;T] to wave violently but aimlessly about: *Her legs flailed in the water.*

flair /fleəʳ/ n [sing;U] the natural ability to do something well: *She's got a real flair for making people feel at home.*

flake¹ /fleɪk/ n a small, thin piece of something: *soap flakes* | *snowflakes* | *Flakes of plaster had fallen from the ceiling.* –**flaky** adj : *flaky pastry*

flake² v flaked, flaking [I] to fall off in flakes: *The paint's beginning to flake off.*
flake out phr v [I] infml to fall asleep or become unconscious because of great tiredness

flaked out /ˌ · ˈ · / adj infml extremely tired because of what you have been doing: *After one game of tennis I was absolutely flaked out.*

flam·boy·ant /flæmˈbɔɪənt/ adj **1** showy and confident: *With a flamboyant gesture he threw off the cover to reveal the statue.* **2** brightly coloured and noticeable: *a flamboyant orange shirt* –**flamboyantly** adv –**flamboyance** n [U]

flame¹ /fleɪm/ n **1** [C;U] red or yellow burning gas seen when something is on fire: *The dry sticks burst into flames.* | *Suddenly the car disappeared in a sheet of flame.* **2 in flames** burning **3 naked flame** a flame which is not covered or protected

flame² *v* **flamed, flaming** to become red or bright by or as if by burning: *The evening sky flamed red and gold.*

fla·men·co /fləˈmeŋkəʊ/ *n* a form of very fast and exciting Spanish dancing and music

flam·ing /ˈfleɪmɪŋ/ *adj* **flaming row** a very angry quarrel: *I've just had a flaming row with my mother.*

fla·min·go /fləˈmɪŋgəʊ/ *n* **flamingos** *or* **flamingoes** a tall tropical water bird with long thin legs and pink and red feathers

flam·ma·ble /ˈflæməbəl/ *adj* easily set on fire –opposite **non-flammable**

■ USAGE **Flammable** is not the opposite of **inflammable**. The two words have the same meaning, but **flammable** is the usual form in American English and is also the technical word in British English.

flan /flæn/ *n* a round open case made of pastry or cake, with a filling such as fruit or cheese

flange /flændʒ/ *n* the flat edge that stands out from the main surface of an object such as a railway wheel, to keep it in position

flank¹ /flæŋk/ *n* **1** the fleshy side of an animal between its RIBS and its HIP **2** the side of an army in battle: *The enemy attacked on the left flank.*

flank² *v* [T] **be flanked with** to have things on one or both sides: *a road flanked with tall buildings*

flan·nel /ˈflænl/ *n* **1** [U] soft light woollen cloth: *flannel trousers* **2** [C] a piece of cloth used for washing yourself

flan·nels /ˈflænlz/ *n* [pl] men's flannel trousers, often worn for games like cricket

flap¹ /flæp/ **1** [C] a wide flat part of anything that hangs down often to cover an opening: *a cap with flaps to cover my ears* | *They crept under the flap of the tent.* | *the flap on an envelope* **2** [sing] the sound of flapping: *the slow flap of the sails* **3** **in a flap** *infml* in a state of excited anxiety: *Don't get in a flap – we'll soon find it.*

flap² *v* **-pp-** **1** [I;T] to move something flat and large up and down or backwards and forwards making a noise: *The large bird flapped its wings.* | *The sails flapped in the wind.* **2** [I] *infml* to become very excited and anxious

flap·jack /ˈflæpdʒæk/ *n* a small flat cake

flare¹ /fleə²/ *v* **flared, flaring** (also **flare up**) **1** [I] to burn suddenly with a bright flame: *The fire suddenly flared up.* (also **flare up**) to become suddenly very bad after being quiet for a period: *Fighting in the area has flared up again.*

flare² *n* **1** an object which sends out a bright light; it is shot into the air as a signal that someone needs help **2** a sudden bright flame: *There was a sudden flare as she lit the gas.* **3 flares** [pl] trousers which become wider from the knee down

flared /fleəd ‖ fleərd/ *adj* shaped so as to get wider towards the bottom (used of trousers or skirts)

flare-up /ˈ· ·/ *n* a sudden burst of activity in the opposition between two groups: *a sudden flare-up of the fighting*

flash¹ /flæʃ/ *v* **1** [I] (of a light) to appear or shine for a moment: *The lightning flashed.* | *the flashing light on top of the police car* **2** [T] to make a light shine for a moment: *Why is that driver flashing his lights at me?* | *Stop flashing that light in my eyes.*

flash back *phr v* [I] to return suddenly to an earlier time: *My mind flashed back to last Christmas.*

flash² *n* **1** [C] a sudden quick bright light: *flashes of lightning* **2 flash of inspiration** a sudden good idea **3** [C;U] the method or apparatus for taking photographs in the dark: *Did you use a flash?* **4 flash in the pan** a sudden success that will not be repeated: *This book was just a flash in the pan. I don't think he'll ever write another one as good.* **5 in a flash**, **like a flash** very quickly

flash·back /ˈflæʃbæk/ *n* part of a film or book that goes back in time to show what happened earlier in the story: *Then there's a flashback to his childhood.*

flash·light /ˈflæʃlaɪt/ *n* the usual American word for TORCH

flash·y /ˈflæʃi/ *adj* **flashier, flashiest** bright and expensive-looking in a way which you find unpleasant: *a large flashy car* | *cheap flashy clothes* –**flashily** *adv* : *flashily dressed*

flask /flɑːsk ‖ flæsk/ *n* **1** a bottle which is specially made for keeping liquids either hot or cold –see picture on page 148 **2** a narrow-necked glass bottle used by scientists **3** a flat bottle for carrying alcohol or other drinks in your pocket

flat¹ /flæt/ *adj* **flatter, flattest** **1** smooth and level without any raised parts, and not curved, pointed, or sloping: *I need a flat surface to write on.* | *He's got quite a flat nose.* | *a flat roof* **2** not hilly or mountainous: *Western Holland is very flat.* **3** without enough air inside (used of tyres): *I've got a flat tyre.* **4** no longer fresh because the gas has been lost (used of beer and other gassy drinks) **5** having no more electric current left inside (used of batteries (BATTERY)): *The car won't start. I left my lights on, so I expect the battery's flat.* **6** dull and uninteresting: *Life seems very flat since you left.* **7** [only after a noun] *tech* lower than the main note (used of musical notes): *a piano concerto in E flat* **8** slightly too low (used of musical notes) **9** not having a high heel (used of shoes) **10 flat rate, flat fee** a fixed amount paid for something **11 flat refusal** a complete and firm refusal **12 and that's flat** *infml* = that is my decision and I won't change it: *I won't go, and that's flat!*

flat² *n* **1** a set of rooms on one floor which are a home in a building or block: *The house is divided into flats.* | *the people in the top flat* –see picture on page 441 –see HOUSE (USAGE) **2 flats** [pl] low level plains especially near water: *mud flats* **3** the flat part or side of something: *I hit him with the flat of my hand.* **4** a flat note in music **5** the sign for a flat note in music **6** *infml* a flat tyre

flat³ *adv* **1** lower than the note you are trying to sing or play **2** exactly, and not more than a certain period of time: *I got dressed in three minutes flat!* **3 flat broke** completely without money **4 flat out** at full speed: *I've been working flat out for two weeks now.*

flat·ly /ˈflætli/ *adv* **1** spoken in a dull way with no feeling: *"It's hopeless," he said flatly.* **2 flatly refuse, flatly deny** to say very strongly that you will not do something or did not do something

flat rac·ing /ˈ· ˌ··/ *n* [U] the sport of horseracing on flat ground

flat·ten /ˈflætn/ *v* [T] to make something flat: *Their crops had been flattened by the rain.* | *I flattened myself against the wall.*

flat·ter /ˈflætə²/ *v* **1** [T] to praise someone too much or insincerely in order to please them: *He flattered her on her cooking.* **2 be flattered** to feel pleased that someone has shown that they think well of you: *She was flattered at the invitation.* **3 flatter yourself: a** to claim reasonably that something good is the case: *I flatter myself that I know a good wine when I taste one.* **b** to believe unreasonably that something good is the case: *He is flattering himself if he thinks he can cook better than Sandy.*

flat·ter·ing /ˈflætərɪŋ/ *adj* making someone look attractive: *That dress is very flattering.*

flat·ter·y /ˈflætəri/ *n* [U] praising someone too much or insincerely in order to please them

flat·u·lence /ˈflætjʊləns ‖ ˈflætʃə-/ *n* [U] *fml* the condition of having too much gas in your stomach

flaunt /flɔːnt ‖ flɔːnt, flɑːnt/ *v* [T] to show something to people so that they will admire it (a word used showing disapproval): *She came into school flaunting her new gold watch.*

flau·tist /ˈflɔːtɨst/ *n* (**flutist** *AmE*) someone who plays the FLUTE

fla·vour[1] /ˈfleɪvəʳ/ *n* (**flavor** *AmE*) [C;U] **1** a taste that you experience when you eat or drink something: *a strong flavour of cheese* | *Choose from six popular flavours of ice cream!* | *This bread has plenty of flavour.* **2 -flavoured** having a particular flavour: *strawberry-flavoured ice cream* –**flavourless** *adj*

flavour[2] *v* (**flavor** *AmE*) [T] to give food a particular taste: *I flavoured the cake with chocolate.*

fla·vour·ing /ˈfleɪvərɪŋ/ *n* (**flavoring** *AmE*) [U] something added to food to improve the taste: *Add a spoonful of banana flavouring.*

flaw /flɔː/ *n* a small mistake or weakness that makes something not perfect: *a flaw in the material* | *the flaws in a contract*

flawed /flɔːd/ *adj* [T] not perfect: *a flawed argument*

flaw·less /ˈflɔːləs/ *adj* without any mistake or weakness: *flawless beauty* | *a flawless performance*

flax /flæks/ *n* [U] the thread made from the stem of a plant with blue flowers, used for making LINEN

flax·en /ˈflæksən/ *adj esp. lit* pale yellow (used of hair)

flea /fliː/ *n* a small jumping insect without wings, that feeds on human or animal blood

flea mar·ket /ˈ· ˌ··/ *n* a street market where you can buy old or used goods

fleck /flek/ *n* a small coloured mark or spot on something: *brown cloth with flecks of red*

flecked /flekt/ *adj* **flecked with** marked or covered with small marks or spots

flee /fliː/ *v* **fled** /fled/, **fled** [I;T] to escape by hurrying away: *They all fled from the burning building.* | *thousands of refugees fleeing from the civil war* | *Once the police were on their trail, they fled the country.*

fleece[1] /fliːs/ *n* a sheep's woolly coat

fleece[2] *v* **fleeced, fleecing** [T] *infml* to rob someone by tricking them or by charging too much money: *They really fleeced us at that hotel!*

fleec·y /ˈfliːsi/ *adj* soft and woolly

fleet /fliːt/ *n* **1** a group of ships, especially warships in the navy working together **2** a group of vehicles belonging to one company

fleet·ing /ˈfliːtɪŋ/ *adj* short and passing or happening quickly: *a fleeting smile*

flesh /fleʃ/ *n* [U] **1** the soft substance including fat and muscle, that covers bones and lies under your skin **2** your skin: *her soft, white flesh* **3** the soft part of a fruit or vegetable, which can be eaten **4 the pleasures of the flesh** sexual pleasures **5 your own flesh and blood** your own family or relations **6 in the flesh** in real life, as opposed to on television or in a picture: *He's more handsome in the flesh than in his photographs.*

flesh·y /ˈfleʃi/ *adj* **fleshier, fleshiest 1** like flesh **2** fat: *his round, fleshy face*

flew /fluː/ the past tense of FLY

flex[1] /fleks/ *v* [T] to bend and move your limbs or muscles so as to stretch and loosen them: *The runners flexed their muscles as they waited for the race to begin.*

flex[2] *n BrE* [C;U] electric wire in a protective covering, which connects an electrical machine to a supply of electricity –see picture on page 638

flex·i·ble /ˈfleksɨbəl/ *adj* **1** easily bent **2** able to change to suit different needs or situations: *flexible working hours* –opposite **inflexible** –**flexibility** /ˌfleksɨˈbɪlɨti/ *n* [U]

flick /flɪk/ *v* **1** [I;T] to move or hit something quickly and lightly: *He flicked ash into the ashtray.* | *The snake's tongue flicked in and out of its mouth.* **2** [T] to move something such as a piece of string quickly at one end so that the other end moves quickly and suddenly: *Taking a tea towel, he flicked the crumbs off the table.* **3 flick a switch** to move a button or control on a machine so that it is on or off: *Could you just flick that switch off?* **4 flick through** something to turn the pages of something such as a book or a newspaper quickly in order to find a particular thing or to get an idea of what is in it: *She flicked through the paper until she found the TV times.* –**flick** *n*: *Isn't it marvellous to have the house warm at the flick of a switch?*

flick·er[1] /ˈflɪkəʳ/ *v* [I] to burn or move unsteadily: *The wind blew the flickering candle out.* | *Shadows flickered on the wall.*

flicker[2] *n* [sing] **1** an unsteady movement from a light or a fire **2** a slight feeling that lasts only a very short time: *a flicker of interest*

flick knife /ˈ· ·/ *n* a knife with a blade that springs out from inside the handle when a button is pressed

flight /flaɪt/ *n* **1** [C;U] the act of flying: *a bird in flight* | *a bird's first flight from the nest* **2** [C] a trip by plane: *"Did you have a good flight?" "No, it was the worst flight I've ever been on."* | *Flight 705 to Paris* **3** [C] a set of stairs between different floors: *She fell down a flight of stairs.* **4** [sing] the act of running away or escaping: *the flight of refugees from the war zone* **5 take flight** to run away from something in a hurry: *When the police arrived the thieves took flight.*

flight·less /ˈflaɪtləs/ *adj* unable to fly: *The penguin is a flightless bird.*

flight·y /ˈflaɪti/ *adj* **flightier, flightiest** not serious enough and often changing from one man to another, or from one idea to another (used of women and their behaviour) –**flightiness** *n* [U]

flim·sy /ˈflɪmzi/ *adj* **flimsier, flimsiest** light, thin and not strong: *flimsy cloth* | *a flimsy argument* –**flimsiness** *n* [U]

flinch /flɪntʃ/ *v* [I] **1** to move back in fear when shocked or in pain: *He didn't flinch once when the*

SPELLING NOTE
Words with the sound / f /, may be spelt **ph-**, like **photograph**.

doctor was cleaning the wound. **2 flinch from something** to feel unwilling to do something unpleasant: She's not the sort to flinch from an argument, however fierce.

fling[1] /flɪŋ/ v flung /flʌŋ/, flung [T] to throw something violently or with force: She always flings her coat on the floor when she comes home. | The military government flung its opponents into prison. | She flung her arms around him.

fling[2] n **1** a short time when you really enjoy yourself, especially if it is your last chance to do it **2** a short love affair

flint /flɪnt/ n **1** [C;U] a type of very hard grey stone that makes very small flames when struck with steel **2** [C] a small piece of metal used in cigarette lighters to light the petrol or gas

flip /flɪp/ v -pp- **1 flip through something** to turn the pages of something such as a book or a newspaper quickly in order to find a particular thing or to get an idea of what is in it: Hang on. I just want to flip through Radio Times. **2** [T + adv/prep] to change the position of something by a quick light movement: Could you just flip up the lid of the bin for me? | She flipped the eggs over and cooked the other side. **3 flip a coin** to use your finger and thumb to send a coin spinning into the air in order to make a decision according to which way up it lands **4** [I] infml to become suddenly very angry or upset –**flip** n

flip·pant /ˈflɪpənt/ adj disrespectful about serious subjects: flippant remarks –**flippantly** adv –**flippancy** n [U]

flip·per /ˈflɪpər/ n a limb of certain larger sea animals which has a flat edge and is used for swimming

flirt[1] /flɜːt/ v [I] to behave with a member of the opposite sex in a way that attracts his or her attention: He's always flirting with the women in the office. –**flirtation** /flɜːˈteɪʃən/ n [C;U]

flirt[2] n a person who often flirts with members of the opposite sex

flir·ta·tious /flɜːˈteɪʃəs/ adj behaving in a way which attracts the attention of someone of the opposite sex

flit /flɪt/ v -tt- [I + adv/prep] to fly or move from one place to another with quick light movements: The birds flitted from branch to branch.

float[1] /fləʊt/ v **1** [I] to stay at the top of liquid: Wood floats on water. **2** [T] to make something float **3** [I + adv/prep] to travel on the surface of water as it travels along, or with a current of air: The logs float down the river. **4** [I + adv/prep] to move easily and lightly **5** [T] to allow the exchange value of money to vary freely in value against other countries' money from day to day: After the pound was floated, its value went down. **6** [T] to start to sell shares in a company to the public

float[2] n **1** a light flat object that helps someone or something float **2** a small object that floats on a fishing line or net **3** a large vehicle which is specially decorated for processions **4** a small amount of coins which a salesperson has before they start to sell so that they will be able to give change

float·ing /ˈfləʊtɪŋ/ adj **1** not fixed or settled: London has a large floating population. **2 floating voter** a person who does not always vote for the same political party

flock[1] /flɒk ‖ flɑːk/ n **1** a group of sheep, goats, or birds **2** a large crowd of people

flock[2] v [I + adv/prep] to go somewhere in large crowds: People flocked to the cinema to see the new film.

flog /flɒg ‖ flɑːg/ v -gg- [T] **1** to beat someone severely with a whip or stick, as a punishment **2** infml to sell something **3 flog a dead horse** infml to waste your time with useless efforts

flog·ging /ˈflɒgɪŋ ‖ ˈflɑːgɪŋ/ n [C;U] a severe beating with a whip or stick, as punishment

flood[1] /flʌd/ n **1** a great overflow of water on to a place that is usually dry: The town was destroyed by the floods. | The river rose to flood level. **2** a large number of things that arrive together: There was a flood of complaints about the bad language used in the show.

flood[2] v **1** [I;T] to fill or cover with water: Every spring the river floods the valley. | Our street floods whenever we have rain. **2** [I + adv/prep] to come or go to a place in large numbers: Requests for information flooded in after the advertisement. | Settlers flooded from Europe to America in the 19th century. **3** [T] to fill a place with things: The market has been flooded with cheap imitations. –**flooding** n [U] : When the snow melted, there was widescale flooding.

flood·gate /ˈflʌdgeɪt/ n **1** a gate used for controlling the flow from a large body of water **2 open the floodgates** to make it possible for a lot of people to do something: The new freedom of the press has opened the floodgates to the democracy movement.

flood·light[1] /ˈflʌdlaɪt/ n a large electric light used for lighting sports grounds, or the outside of buildings at night

floodlight[2] v -lighted or -lit /lɪt/, -lighted or -lit [T] to light a place by using floodlights: Buckingham Palace is floodlit at night.

floor[1] /flɔːr/ n **1** the surface on which you stand indoors: He threw the book onto the floor. **2** a level of a building: I live on the ground floor of a block of flats. | Our office is on the sixth floor. –see picture on page 441 **3 the floor** the part of a parliament or council building where members sit and speak ■ USAGE In British English the bottom floor of a building (at ground level) is called the **ground floor**. In American English this is called the **first floor**. In British English the next level up is called the **first floor**. In American English it is called the **second floor**.

floor[2] v [T] **1** to knock someone down: He floored his attacker with one heavy blow. **2** to ask someone a question or put them in a situation to which they have no answer: The teacher seemed completely floored by my question.

floor·board /ˈflɔːbɔːd ‖ ˈflɔːrbɔːrd/ n a board in a wooden floor

flop[1] /flɒp ‖ flɑːp/ v -pp- **1** [I + adv/prep] to move or fall heavily or awkwardly: He can't swim much. He just flops about in the water. | She flopped into an armchair. **2** [I] infml to be very unsuccessful: The new play flopped after only two weeks.

flop[2] n **1** a heavy, falling movement **2** an event that is very unsuccessful

flop·py /ˈflɒpi ‖ ˈflɑːpi/ adj floppier, floppiest soft and not at all stiff: a floppy hat

floppy disk /ˌ··· ˈ·/ n a specially treated piece of plastic on which information for a computer is stored –see picture on page 539

flo·ra /ˈflɔːrə/ n [U] tech all the plants growing wild in a particular place

flo·ral /ˈflɔːrəl/ adj made of flowers or containing flowers: floral patterns –see picture on page 147

flor·id /ˈflɒrɪd ‖ ˈflɔː-, ˈflɑː-/ *adj fml* **1** having too much decoration: *florid language* **2** having a red face

flor·ist /ˈflɒrɪst ‖ ˈflɔː-/ *n* **1** a person who sells flowers **2** florist's a shop which sells flowers: *Did you get the daffodils at the florist's?*

flo·til·la /fləˈtɪlə ‖ fləʊ-/ *n* a group of small ships, especially warships

flounce /flaʊns/ *v* **flounced, flouncing** [I + adv/prep] to walk showing you are angry: *She refused my advice and flounced out of the house.*

floun·der /ˈflaʊndəʳ/ *v* [I] **1** to move wildly about in the water when you are trying to save yourself from drowning **2** to continue to act but without producing good results because you do not really know what to do

flour /flaʊəʳ/ *n* [U] powder made from wheat and used for making bread, pastry, or cakes

flour·ish¹ /ˈflʌrɪʃ ‖ ˈflɜːrɪʃ/ *v* **1** [I] to grow healthily or successfully: *Plants like that will not flourish in the shade.* | *The company has really flourished since we moved our factory to Scotland.* **2** [T] to wave something in your hand and so draw attention to it: *"I've passed my examination!" shouted Jane, flourishing a letter.*

flourish² *n* a special showy movement to do honour to someone or to draw attention to yourself: *He opened the door with a flourish.*

flour·ish·ing /ˈflʌrɪʃɪŋ ‖ ˈflɜː-/ *adj* happy and successful: *a flourishing market town of about 12,000 people* | *"How's David?" "Oh, he's flourishing. Everything's going very well."*

flout /flaʊt/ *v* [T] to disobey a rule or law: *He had flouted all the rules.*

flow¹ /fləʊ/ *v* [I] **1** (of liquid) to move or pour smoothly: *The river's flowing quite fast here.* | *Her tears flowed fast.* **2** to move forward steadily or smoothly: *The traffic never flows freely in the town centre.* **3** (of hair and clothes) to hang loosely: *Her hair flowed over her shoulders.* | *long flowing robes*

flow² *n* [U] a smooth steady movement: *the gentle flow of the river* | *the flow of electricity to our homes*

flow·er¹ /ˈflaʊəʳ/ *n* **1** the part of a plant, often beautiful and coloured, that produces seeds or fruit **2** a plant that is grown for the beauty of its flowers: *I think I'll plant some flowers under the windows.* **3** in flower having flowers on: *The roses are in flower.*

flower² *v* [I] (of a plant) to produce flowers: *This bush flowers in the spring.*

flow·er·bed /ˈflaʊəbed ‖ -ər-/ *n* a piece of ground in a garden or park, in which flowers are grown –see picture on page 441

flow·ered /ˈflaʊəd ‖ -ərd/ *adj* decorated with flower patterns: *flowered dress material* –see picture on page 147

flow·er·pot /ˈflaʊəpɒt ‖ -ərpɑːt/ *n* a pot in which a plant can be grown

flow·er·y /ˈflaʊəri/ *adj* **1** decorated with flowers: *a flowery pattern* –see picture on page 147 **2** containing fancy language (used of speech or writing)

SPELLING NOTE
Words with the sound /f/ may be spelt ph-, like **photograph**.

---

flown /fləʊn/ the past participle of FLY

flu /fluː/ *n* [U] a disease which is like a bad cold but more serious

fluc·tu·ate /ˈflʌktʃueɪt/ *v* **fluctuated, fluctuating** [I] to change often: *The price of vegetables fluctuates according to the season.* | *His feelings fluctuated between excitement and fear.* –**fluctuation** /ˌflʌktʃuˈeɪʃən/ *n* [C;U]

flue /fluː/ *n* a pipe in a chimney up which smoke or heat passes

flu·en·cy /ˈfluːənsi/ *n* [U] the ability to speak a language easily and without thinking

flu·ent /ˈfluːənt/ *adj* **1** able to speak or write a language easily and well: *She is fluent in English.* **2** very good (used of languages): *Her English is fluent.* | *She speaks fluent English.* –**fluently** *adv*

fluff¹ /flʌf/ *n* [U] **1** soft loose waste from woollen or other materials: *The carpet needs cleaning – it's covered in fluff.* **2** very soft fur or hair on a young animal or bird

fluff² *v*
fluff sthg ↔ out *phr v* [T] (also **fluff** sthg ↔ up) to make something soft appear larger by getting lots of air into it: *The bird fluffed out its feathers in the sun.* | *She fluffed up the pillows.*

fluff·y /ˈflʌfi/ *adj* **fluffier, fluffiest** soft and light, like hair or fur: *a fluffy jumper* –**fluffiness** *n* [U]

flu·id¹ /ˈfluːɪd/ *adj* **1** having a moving, flowing quality, like liquids, air, or gas **2** not fixed or settled: *Our ideas on the subject are still fluid.* –**fluidity** /fluːˈɪdɪti/ *n* [U]

fluid² *n* [C;U] a liquid

fluid ounce /ˌ··ˈ·/ *n* a measure of liquid equal to one 20th of a PINT or 0·0284 of a litre

fluke /fluːk/ *n infml* something lucky that happens by chance: *She isn't usually good at tennis. That winning stroke was a fluke.*

flum·mox /ˈflʌməks/ *v* [T] *infml* to confuse someone and make them uncertain what to say or do

flung /flʌŋ/ the past tense and past participle of FLING

flu·o·res·cent /fluəˈresənt ‖ fluə-, flɔː-/ *adj* **1** fluorescent light a very bright light in the form of a tube **2** seeming to shine very brightly when lit up

flu·o·ride /ˈfluəraɪd/ *n* [U] a chemical substance that helps protect teeth against decay

flur·ry /ˈflʌri ‖ ˈflɜːri/ *n* **flurries 1** a sudden sharp rush of wind, rain, or snow **2** a sudden short and very active period: *His arrival produced a flurry of excitement.*

flush¹ /flʌʃ/ *v* **1** [T] to clean a TOILET or pipe with a sudden flow of water: *Remember to flush the toilet.* **2** [I] to be cleaned by means of a flow of water: *The lavatory won't flush.* **3** [I] to become red in the face because you feel ashamed: *She flushed when she couldn't answer the question.*
flush out *phr v* **1** [T flush sthg ↔ out] to clean something or to remove something blocking a pipe by running water through it **2** [T flush sbdy ↔ out] to force someone to leave a hiding place

flush² *n* **1** a sudden flow of water that cleans a TOILET or pipe **2** redness of your face caused by being hot, ill, or ashamed **3** in the first flush of in the first part of something pleasant: *In the first flush of success he ordered drinks for everybody.*

flush³ *adj* **1** flat and level with a surface: *These cupboards aren't flush with the wall.* **2** [never before a noun] *infml* having plenty of money: *I've just been paid, so I'm feeling quite flush.*

flushed /flʌʃt/ adj **1** red in the face: *Louisa's looking rather flushed. I hope she isn't sickening for anything.* **2** very excited or pleased about something: *He arrived late, flushed with excitement.*

flus·ter /ˈflʌstər/ n **in a fluster** feeling hot, nervous, and confused

flus·tered /ˈflʌstəd ‖ -ərd/ adj made to feel nervous and confused, and perhaps hot and uncomfortable

flute /fluːt/ n a musical instrument like a pipe, which you play by blowing across a hole in the side

flut·ist /ˈfluːtɪst/ n see FLAUTIST

flut·ter¹ /ˈflʌtər/ v **1** [I] to fly or move through the air with light quick movements in different directions: *There were moths fluttering round the light.* | *The dead leaves fluttered to the ground.* **2** [I;T] to wave or move quickly up and down or backwards and forwards: *The flag fluttered in the wind.* | *The geese stood up and fluttered their wings.* **3 her heart fluttered** = she felt excited and nervous

flutter² n [sing] **1** a light, quick movement in different directions: *There was a flutter of wings among the trees.* **2 in a flutter** feeling nervous and excited

flux /flʌks/ n [U] fml a state of continual change: *Our future plans are unsettled. Everything is in a state of flux.*

fly¹ /flaɪ/ v **flew** /fluː/, **flown** /fləʊn/ **1** [I] to move through the air: *A small bird flew up into the tree.* | *This plane is due to fly to New York this evening.* **2** [I;T] to travel by plane, or take a person or thing somewhere by plane: *She flew to London yesterday.* | *I hate flying.* | *Our goods are flown all over the world.* **3** [T] to be the pilot of a plane: *I've always wanted to fly an aeroplane.* **4** [I;T] to move about in the wind, or hold or fix something so that it moves about in the wind: *A flag was flying on top of the building.* | *We're going off to fly our kite.* **5** [I + adv/prep] to move quickly or suddenly: *The train flew past the station.* | *She flew up the stairs.* **6** [I] to pass quickly: *Our holiday has just flown!* | *Doesn't time fly?* **7 fly at someone**, let fly at someone to attack someone, physically or with words **8 fly into a temper, fly into a rage** to become very angry **9 fly off the handle** to become very angry **10 I must fly** = I must leave quickly

fly² n **flies** /flaɪz/ **1** a small flying insect with two wings **2 flies** [pl] the front opening of a pair of trousers: *Your flies are open!* **3 fly in the ointment** a small unwanted thing that spoils the pleasure of something

fly·ing /ˈflaɪ-ɪŋ/ adj **1** [only before a noun] able to fly **2 flying jump, flying leap** a long or high jump: *He took a flying leap and jumped across the stream.* **3 flying visit** a very short visit **4 get off to a flying start** to make a very good beginning **5 pass with flying colours** to succeed very well in an examination or a test **6 send/knock something flying** to knock something over by pushing or hitting it violently

flying sau·cer /ˌ·· ˈ··/ n a plate-shaped space vehicle which is believed to come from another world

fly·o·ver /ˈflaɪ-əʊvər/ n a kind of bridge where one road crosses another

FM /ˌef ˈem◂/ a system of broadcasting by radio in which the signal comes at a varying number of times per second; an abbreviation for **frequency modulation**

foal /fəʊl/ n a young horse

foam¹ /fəʊm/ n [U] **1** a mass of small bubbles (BUBBLE) formed when air is mixed with a liquid: *The breaking waves had edges of foam.* **2** soft rubber or a man-made material full of small bubbles (BUBBLE) of air –**foamy** adj

foam² v [I] **1** to be full of small bubbles (BUBBLE): *a glass of foaming beer* | *He looked as if he was foaming at the mouth.* **2** to have foam coming out: *It was foaming at the mouth.*

fob /fɒb ‖ faːb/ v

fob sbdy ↔ **off** phr v [T] to give someone something unsatisfactory as a way of making them go away or keep quiet: *She just fobbed me off with a stupid excuse.*

fo·cal point /ˈfəʊkl̩ ˌpɔɪnt/ n [sing] the centre of interest: *Television is now the focal point of family life in many British homes.*

fo·cus¹ /ˈfəʊkəs/ n **1** the point at which beams of light or heat, or waves of sound meet after their direction has been changed **2** a centre of attention, activity, or interest: *He immediately became the focus of attention.* **3 in focus** giving a clear picture: *That photograph's not quite in focus.* | *Those trees aren't in focus.* [RELATED PHRASE **out of focus**]

focus² v -s- or -ss- [I;T] **1** to bring something into focus, or to come into focus: *I think I must have forgotten to focus the camera.* | *I'll focus on the main group of people over there.* | *The beams of light moved across the sky and focused on the aircraft.* **2** to make something or someone the central point of interest: *All eyes were focused on him.* | *Attention focused on the new Prime Minister.*

fod·der /ˈfɒdər ‖ ˈfaː-/ n [U] food for horses and farm animals

foe /fəʊ/ n lit an enemy

foe·tus /ˈfiːtəs/ n (also **fetus**) a young human or animal that is still developing inside its mother –**foetal** adj

fog /fɒg ‖ faːg, fɔːg/ n [C;U] very thick mist which makes it difficult to see

fog·bound /ˈfɒgbaʊnd ‖ ˈfaːg-, ˈfɔːg-/ adj unable to travel or operate because of fog: *Heathrow Airport is fogbound.*

fog·gy /ˈfɒgi ‖ ˈfaːgi, ˈfɔːgi/ adj **foggier, foggiest** **1** very misty: *Foggy weather has made driving conditions very dangerous.* **2 not have the foggiest idea** infml to not know at all: *"What time is it?" "I haven't the foggiest idea."*

foi·ble /ˈfɔɪbəl/ n fml a rather strange or foolish personal habit

foil¹ /fɔɪl/ v [T] fml to prevent someone from doing something successfully: *The attempted robbery was foiled by security guards.*

foil² n **1** [U] metal beaten into very thin sheets like paper and used to wrap food: *Our food is wrapped in foil to keep it fresh.* **2** [C] a person or thing that makes the good qualities of another person or thing more noticeable

foist /fɔɪst/ v **foist something on someone** to force someone to accept something that they do not want: *I wish he wouldn't try to foist his political ideas on other people.*

fold¹ /fəʊld/ v **1** [T] to bend or press back one part of something onto the remaining part: *She folded the letter in half.* | *Her clothes had all been neatly folded and put in a drawer.* **2** [I] to be able to be folded: *a folding chair* | *Does this bed fold?* **3** [T + adv/prep] to wrap something: *He folded the seeds in a piece of paper.* **4 fold your arms** to cross your arms in two places over your chest **5** [I] (of a business) to fail: *The company folded and she lost her job.*

fold up phr v 1 [T **fold** sthg ↔ **up**] to fold something several times so that it becomes smaller: *Could you fold your clothes up, please?* 2 [I] (of a business) to fail

fold² n a folded part or place: *The curtain hung in heavy folds.*

fold·er /ˈfəʊldəʳ/ n a folded piece of cardboard used for holding loose papers

fo·li·age /ˈfəʊli-ɪdʒ/ n [U] fml leaves

folk¹ /fəʊk/ n infml [pl] people: *He's gone into an old folk's home.*

folk² adj [always before a noun] belonging to or typical of the people of a particular country or area or of ordinary people who have no special knowledge: *folk music | folk songs | folk art*

folk·lore /ˈfəʊklɔːʳ/ n [U] all the ancient knowledge, beliefs, and stories of a racial or national group

fol·low /ˈfɒləʊ ‖ ˈfɑː-/ v 1 [I;T] to go after someone: *She followed me into the kitchen. | You go first and I'll follow later. | I think we're being followed!* 2 [I;T] to come after something: *Disease often follows war. | We expect even greater successes to follow. | The lightning was followed by a loud crash of thunder.* 3 [T] to go in the same direction as a road, path, or river: *Follow the road until you come to the hotel.* 4 [T] to pay attention to something and take an interest in it as it develops: *I followed her speech with great attention. | This particular murder case was followed with interest by hundreds of people.* 5 [I;T] to understand something clearly: *I didn't quite follow what you said.* 6 [T] to accept someone's instructions, advice, or example, and act according to it: *Did you follow the instructions on the packet? | If you follow my advice, you'll sell the house immediately.* 7 [I; + that] to be true because something else is true: *Just because you are rich, it doesn't follow that you are happy.* 8 **as follows** as comes after this 9 **follow in someone's footsteps** to do the same as someone else did in the past 10 **follow suit** to do what someone else has just done: *Mr Higgs stood up to leave. Mr and Mrs White followed suit.* 11 **follow your nose** to do what you naturally feel you should do, as opposed to following rules

follow sthg ↔ **through** phr v [T] to complete something or carry it out to the end: *We intend to follow through this line of enquiry.*

follow sthg ↔ **up** phr v [T] 1 to act further on something or find out more about it: *That's an interesting suggestion, and I'll certainly follow it up.* 2 to do something else after you have done a first thing: *I wrote to them, and then followed up my letter with a visit.*

fol·low·er /ˈfɒləʊəʳ/ n an admirer or supporter of a person, belief, or cause: *the followers of Marx | a follower of fashion*

fol·low·ing¹ /ˈfɒləʊɪŋ ‖ ˈfɑː-/ adj 1 **the following** day, week, year, etc. the next day, week, year, etc.: *I arranged to meet her on the following day. | We went to Spain again the following year.* 2 **the following** going to be mentioned next: *Please bring with you the following things: a change of clothes, shoes, a towel, and some food.*

following² n 1 **the following** the people or things that are going to be mentioned next: *The following*

have been chosen to play in tomorrow's match: Duncan Ferguson, Hugh Williams, Robin Sinclair... 2 [sing] a group of supporters or admirers: *She has quite a large following in the North.*

following³ prep after: *Following the speech, there will be a few minutes for questions.*

follow-up /ˈ··· ·/ adj done as the continuation of something started earlier: *a follow-up visit from the doctor* –**follow-up** n : *This meeting was a follow-up to the one held last year.*

fol·ly /ˈfɒli ‖ ˈfɑːli/ n **follies** [C;U] fml a very foolish action: *He remembered the follies of his own youth. | To reduce public spending on health would be an act of the greatest folly.*

fond /fɒnd ‖ fɑːnd/ adj 1 **fond of** liking someone or something: *I'm very fond of her. | I'm not particularly fond of spicy food. | We're all quite fond of sightseeing.*
□ USEFUL PATTERNS be fond of someone/something; be fond of doing something
2 [only before a noun] having or showing loving feelings: *Her fond parents were there to watch her perform. | I got on the boat after a fond farewell from friends.* 3 [only before a noun] foolishly hopeful: *He's still waiting, in the fond belief that she'll come back to him.* –**fondness** n [U]

fon·dle /ˈfɒndl ‖ ˈfɑːndl/ v **fondled, fondling** [T] to touch or stroke someone or something gently and lovingly: *A cat sat on her knee, and she was fondling it gently.*

fond·ly /ˈfɒndli ‖ ˈfɑːndli/ adv 1 in a loving way: *He was smiling at me fondly.* 2 in a foolishly hopeful way: *She fondly imagined that she could pass her examination without working.*

font /fɒnt ‖ fɑːnt/ n a large vessel in a church, that contains water for baptizing (BAPTIZE) people

food /fuːd/ n [C;U] 1 anything that people or animals eat: *Milk is the natural food for young babies. | They gave us plenty of food and drink.* 2 **food for thought** something which makes you think carefully

food pro·ces·sor /ˈ· ˌ···/ n an electric apparatus used for mixing and cutting up food –see picture on page 638

fool¹ /fuːl/ n 1 a silly person: *You silly fool! What did you leave the bag there for? | I felt such a fool when I realized I'd got on the wrong bus.* 2 **make a fool of yourself** to do something silly 3 **make a fool of someone** to make someone seem silly 4 **fool's paradise** a happy situation which is not going to last, but the people in the situation do not know that

fool² v [T] to deceive or trick someone: *You can't fool him. He's much too clever for that.*

fool about/around phr v [I] to behave in a silly way: *You shouldn't fool around with dangerous chemicals.*

fool·har·dy /ˈfuːlhɑːdi ‖ -ɑːr-/ adj taking unwise risks: *It would be foolhardy to borrow any more money.* –**foolhardiness** n [U]

fool·ish /ˈfuːlɪʃ/ adj 1 not sensible: *It was very foolish of you to park the car in the middle of the road.* 2 stupid and silly: *I felt very foolish when I realized what I'd done.* –**foolishly** adv –**foolishness** n [U]

fool·proof /ˈfuːlpruːf/ adj 1 that cannot go wrong: *I've found a foolproof way of doing it. | Our plan is completely foolproof.* 2 infml very simple to understand or use: *The new machines are foolproof.*

fools·cap /ˈfuːlskæp/ n [U] a large size of writing paper

SPELLING NOTE
Words with the sound /f/ may be spelt **ph-**, like **photograph**.

foot¹ /fʊt/ n feet /fiːt/ **1** [C] the part of your body at the end of your leg, on which you stand: *My feet hurt!* **2** [sing] the bottom or lower part of something: *He stood at the foot of the stairs.* | *She sat at the foot of the bed.* **3** [C] [plural is **foot** or **feet**] a measure of length equal to 12 inches or about ·305 metres: *"How tall are you?" "Five foot six inches."* | *He's at least six feet tall.* **4 leap to your feet** to stand up: *He leapt to his feet as I walked in.* **5 not put a foot wrong** to not say or do anything wrong **6 on foot** walking: *We'll have to go on foot.* **7 on your feet: a** standing up: *I've been on my feet all day!* **b** in good health: *I should be back on my feet again by next week.* | *We must get the economy back on its feet.* **8 put your feet up** to rest by lying or sitting with your feet supported on something: *I think I'll put my feet up for half an hour.* **9 put your foot down** to forbid something by saying very firmly that it must not happen **10 put your foot in it** to say something unsuitable and so cause an awkward situation **11 set foot in a place** to go into a place: *I hope he never sets foot in this house again!* **12 -footed** having a particular number of feet or a particular type of feet: *four-footed animals* | *Ducks are web-footed.*

foot² v **foot the bill** *infml* to pay for something: *Hopefully, the insurance company will foot the bill for the damage.*

foot·ball /ˈfʊtbɔːl/ n **1** [U] a game for two teams in which a ball is kicked about a field and the players try to get goals (GOAL): *They play football at school.* | *Where are my football boots?* **2** [C] a large ball filled with air, used for playing football **3** see AMERICAN FOOTBALL **–footballer** n

football pools /ˈ··/ n **the football pools** a game in which people risk small amounts of money on the results of football matches

foot·bridge /ˈfʊtˌbrɪdʒ/ n a narrow bridge for people who are walking –see picture on page 735

foot·hills /ˈfʊtˌhɪlz/ n [pl] low hills at the bottom of a mountain or chain of mountains: *the foothills of the Himalayas*

foot·hold /ˈfʊthəʊld/ n **1** a space where you can put your foot to help you to climb up or down a rock or mountain **2** a job or position from which you can advance: *I need to get a foothold in the profession.*

foot·ing /ˈfʊtɪŋ/ n [sing] **1** a firm hold with your feet on a surface: *She lost her footing and fell.* **2** a particular way of working or operating: *The army was put on a war footing.* **3** a relationship: *I was on a very good footing with the director.*

foot·lights /ˈfʊtlaɪts/ n [pl] a row of lights along the front edge of the stage in a theatre

foot·loose /ˈfʊtluːs/ adj not liking to settle down in one place and accept the usual responsibilities of work or family

foot·man /ˈfʊtmən/ n footmen /-mən/ a male servant in the past

foot·note /ˈfʊtnəʊt/ n a note at the bottom of a page in a book, to explain something or add more information

foot·path /ˈfʊtpɑːθ ‖ -pæθ/ n a narrow path or track for people to walk on

foot·print /ˈfʊtˌprɪnt/ n a mark shaped like a foot, which you make when you walk on a surface: *Who left these muddy footprints on the kitchen floor?*

foot·sore /ˈfʊtsɔːʳ/ adj having painful or swollen feet because you have been walking a lot

foot·step /ˈfʊtstep/ n a mark or sound of a person's step: *Her footsteps were clearly marked in the snow.* | *He heard soft footsteps coming up the stairs.*

foot·wear /ˈfʊtweəʳ/ n [U] *fml* shoes and boots

for¹ /fəʳ; *strong* fɔːʳ/ prep **1** meant to be given to someone or used by someone or something: *I've got a present for you.* | *He offered to buy a drink for me.* | *I've bought some new chairs for the office.* **2** used to show who is helped or supported by something: *Shall I carry your case for you?* | *Is there anything I can do for you?* | *She works for a local manufacturing company.* | *I'd love to play football for England.* **3** used to show who a feeling is directed towards: *I feel very happy for you.* | *She felt nothing but contempt for him.* **4** used to show the purpose of something: *These scissors are very good for cutting carpet.* | *It's very nice, but what's it for?* **5** used to show the reason for something or the cause of something: *They were punished for talking in class.* | *He got twenty years in prison for robbery with violence.* **6** towards a particular place: *We set off for France.* | *Is that the boat for Ireland?* **7** with a particular meaning: *What's the French word for "dog"?* **8** used to show how much you have to pay in order to get something: *You can get a room in a hotel for £40 a night.* **9** used to show a length of time or distance: *We've lived here for ten years.* | *They walked for twenty miles before they found a village.* **10** by or at a particular time: *They asked us to be there for six o'clock.* | *Are you coming home for Christmas?* | *We must get there for the start of the play.* | *What did you get for your birthday?* **11** in favour of someone or something: *24 people voted for the proposal and 16 voted against.* **12** when considering a particular fact: *She's very tall for her age.*

for² *conj fml* because: *He was surprised that she was late, for she was usually very punctual.*

for·age /ˈfɒrɪdʒ ‖ ˈfɑː-, ˈfɔː-/ v foraged, foraging **1** [I] (of animals) to wander about looking for food **2 forage for something, forage around for something** to look for something busily

foray /ˈfɒreɪ ‖ ˈfɔː-, ˈfɑː-/ n **1** a sudden rush into enemy country by a small number of soldiers **2** a short attempt at doing something: *his unsuccessful foray into politics*

for·bade /fəˈbeɪd ‖ fərˈbæd/ forbad /-ˈbæd/ the past tense of FORBID

for·bear /fɔːˈbeəʳ, fə- ‖ fɔːr-, fər-/ v forbore /-ˈbɔːʳ/, forborne /-ˈbɔːn ‖ -ˈbɔːrn/ [I] *fml* not to do something that you could do because you think that it is wiser not to do it

for·bear·ance /fɔːˈbeərəns ‖ fɔːr-/ n [U] *fml* patience and forgiveness

for·bear·ing /fɔːˈbeərɪŋ ‖ fɔːr-/ adj *fml* gentle, patient, and forgiving

for·bid /fəˈbɪd ‖ fər-/ v forbade /-ˈbeɪd ‖ -ˈbæd/, forbidden /-ˈbɪdn/, forbidding [T] to order someone not to do something: *Smoking is strictly forbidden.* | *The law forbids the use of chemical fertilizers.* | *He forbade her to tell anyone about it.*
□ USEFUL PATTERNS to forbid something; to forbid someone to do something

for·bid·ding /fəˈbɪdɪŋ ‖ fər-/ adj looking fierce, unfriendly, or dangerous: *The mountains looked dark and forbidding.* **–forbiddingly** adv

force¹ /fɔːs ‖ fɔːrs/ n **1** [U] power or strength: *The force of the explosion destroyed the building completely.* **2** [U] physical strength: *She had lost her key, so we had to open the door by force.* **3** [U] violence: *The regime was removed by force.* | *The police have said that they will use force if necessary to*

remove the demonstrators. **4** [C] someone or something that has a strong influence or a lot of power: *She is a powerful force in world politics.* | *the forces of evil* **5** [C;U] a natural power that has a strong physical effect on things: *the force of gravity* | *a magnetic force* **6** [C] a group of people who are trained to fight together: *Both land and sea forces were used in the attack.* | *the police force* **7 force of habit** the fact that you have done something many times before, which makes you do it again without thinking about it: *I locked the door from force of habit.* **8 in force: a** in effect or in operation (used of a law or a system): *The law has been in force for six months now.* | *The new arrangements will come into force from next week.* **b** in large numbers: *The police were out in force to prevent any trouble.* **9 join forces** to work together to do something: *Scientists have joined forces with environmentalists to find a solution to the problem.*

force² *v* **forced, forcing** [T] **1** to make someone do something that they do not want to do: *He forced her to give him the key.* | *They may agree to help me, but I can't force them to.*
□ USEFUL PATTERN to force someone to do something
2 to use physical effort to make an object do what you want it to do: *She tried to force her suitcase through the tiny hole in the fence.* | *The burglars had forced the window open.* **3** to produce something with difficulty or by unwilling effort: *She managed to force a smile.* **4 force something on someone** to make someone accept something that they do not want: *He didn't want any reward, and we had to force the money on him.* **5 force a lock** to break a lock open **6 force your way** to go into or through somewhere by using physical strength: *He forced his way through the crowd.*

forced /fɔːst ‖ fɔːrst/ *adj* [only before a noun] **1** done or made because it is necessary to act without delay: *The aircraft had to make a forced landing.* **2** done with unwilling and unnatural effort: *forced laughter*

force·ful /ˈfɔːsfəl ‖ ˈfɔːrs-/ *adj* powerful and confident: *a forceful speech* | *She made a forceful impression on the girls.* – **forcefully** *adv* – **forcefulness** *n* [U]

for·ceps /ˈfɔːseps, -sⱥps ‖ ˈfɔːr-/ *n* [pl] a medical instrument used for holding objects firmly

for·ci·ble /ˈfɔːsⱥbəl ‖ ˈfɔːr-/ *adj* [only before a noun] **1** using physical force: *The police had to make a forcible entry.* **2** having power to influence the minds of others: *His death was a forcible reminder of the dangers around us.* – **forcibly** *adv*

ford¹ /fɔːd ‖ fɔːrd/ *n* a place in a river where the water is not very deep and it is possible to cross without using a bridge

ford² *v* [T] to cross a river or stream on foot or in a vehicle

fore /fɔːʳ/ *n* **come to the fore** to become popular and well-known: *He came to the fore in the early '80s.*

fore·arm /ˈfɔːrɑːm ‖ -ɑːrm/ *n* the lower part of your arm, between your hand and elbow

fore·bear /ˈfɔːbeəʳ ‖ ˈfɔːr-/ *n* your forebears people who were members of your family, usually a long time ago

SPELLING NOTE
Words with the sound /f/ may be spelt **ph-**, like **photograph**.

fore·bod·ing /fɔːˈbəʊdɪŋ ‖ fɔːr-/ *n* [U] *fml* a feeling that something bad or evil is going to happen: *I waited for the phone call with foreboding.*

fore·cast¹ /ˈfɔːkɑːst ‖ ˈfɔːrkæst/ *v* **forecast, forecast** [T] to say what will probably happen in the future: *Heavy rain has been forecast for tomorrow.* | *Their political opponents are forecasting a huge rise in unemployment.*

forecast² *n* a statement of what is expected to happen in the future: *The weather forecast said it would rain.* | *forecasts of impending financial disaster*

fore·court /ˈfɔːkɔːt ‖ ˈfɔːrkɔːrt/ *n* an open space in front of a large building: *the car park in the station forecourt*

fore·fa·ther /ˈfɔːˌfɑːðəʳ ‖ ˈfɔːr-/ *n* your forefathers people who were members of your family a long time ago: *their custom since the days of their forefathers*

fore·fin·ger /ˈfɔːˌfɪŋɡəʳ ‖ ˈfɔːr-/ *n* the finger next to your thumb

fore·front /ˈfɔːfrʌnt ‖ ˈfɔːr-/ *n* **the forefront** the leading position: *She's been at the forefront of the struggle for equal rights.*

fore·go /fɔːˈɡəʊ ‖ fɔːr-/ *v* **forewent** /-went/, **foregone** /-ˈɡɒn ‖ -ˈɡɔːn/ (also **forgo**) [T] *fml* to choose not to have something pleasant: *You shouldn't forego this opportunity to visit New York.*

fore·gone /ˈfɔːɡɒn ‖ ˈfɔːrɡɔːn/ *adj* **foregone conclusion** a result that is certain

fore·ground /ˈfɔːɡraʊnd ‖ ˈfɔːr-/ *n* **the foreground** the nearest part of a scene: *This is a photograph of our new house, with my parents in the foreground.*

fore·hand /ˈfɔːhænd ‖ ˈfɔːr-/ *n* a tennis stroke played with the inner part of your hand and arm facing forward – compare BACKHAND – **forehand** *adj*

fore·head /ˈfɒrⱥd, ˈfɔːhed ‖ ˈfɔːrⱥd, ˈfɑːrⱥd, ˈfɔːrhed/ *n* the part of your face above your eyes and below your hair

for·eign /ˈfɒrⱥn ‖ ˈfɔː-, ˈfɑː-/ *adj* **1** coming from a country or nation that is not your own: *Do you speak any foreign languages?* | *I collect foreign coins.* **2 foreign to** unfamiliar to someone: *He's a very good person. Unkindness is foreign to his nature.* **3 foreign body** something that is in the wrong place and likely to cause harm **4 foreign affairs** matters concerning relationships with other countries: *the Ministry of Foreign Affairs* **5 foreign exchange** the practice of buying and selling foreign money

for·eign·er /ˈfɒrⱥnəʳ ‖ ˈfɔː-, ˈfɑː-/ *n* a person belonging to a race or country other than your own

fore·leg /ˈfɔːleɡ ‖ ˈfɔːr-/ *n* either of the two front legs of an animal

fore·man /ˈfɔːmən ‖ ˈfɔːr-/ *n* **foremen** /-mən/ an experienced worker who is put in charge of a group of workers

fore·most¹ /ˈfɔːməʊst ‖ ˈfɔːr-/ *adj* [only before a noun] **the foremost** the most important or best of a group of things: *Shakespeare is said to be the foremost writer in the English language.*

foremost² *adv* **first and foremost** you use this phrase when you have several points you want to make and you are going to talk about the most important one first

fore·name /ˈfɔːneɪm ‖ ˈfɔːr-/ *n* *fml* the name that your parents give you, in addition to your family name – see FIRST NAME (USAGE)

fo·ren·sic /fə'rensɪk, -zɪk/ *adj* [only before a noun] *tech* related to the scientific examination of a crime: *A specialist in forensic medicine was called as a witness.*

fore·run·ner /'fɔː,rʌnər/ *n* a person or thing that prepares the way for someone or something that follows: *Mrs Pankhurst, who fought for votes for women, was a forerunner of modern feminists.*

fore·see /fɔː'siː ‖ fɔːr-/ *v* **foresaw** /-'sɔː/, **foreseen** /-'siːn/ [T] to form an idea or judgment about what is going to happen in the future: *Who could have foreseen such problems in 1938?*

fore·see·a·ble /fɔː'siːəbəl ‖ fɔːr-/ *adj* **1** which can be expected to happen: *a foreseeable accident* **2 in the foreseeable future** as far ahead in time as we can see

fore·shad·ow /fɔː'ʃædəʊ ‖ fɔːr-/ *v* [T] *lit* to be a sign of what is to come

fore·sight /'fɔːsaɪt ‖ 'fɔːr-/ *n* [U] the ability to imagine what will probably happen in the future: *He had the foresight to invest his money outside the oil industry.*

fore·skin /'fɔː,skɪn ‖ 'fɔːr-/ *n* a loose fold of skin covering the end of a man's PENIS

for·est /'fɒrɪst ‖ 'fɔː-, 'fɑː-/ *n* [C;U] a large area of land with many trees growing close together: *A large part of Africa is made up of thick forest.* | *Most of the ancient forests of England have been cut down.*

fore·stall /fɔː'stɔːl ‖ fɔːr-/ *v* [T] *fml* to defeat someone, or someone's plan, by acting first: *We forestalled his attempt to steal the map back by handing it over to the police first.*

for·est·ry /'fɒrɪstri ‖ 'fɔː-, 'fɑː-/ *n* [U] the science of planting and caring for large areas of trees —**forester** *n*

fore·taste /'fɔːteɪst ‖ 'fɔːr-/ *n* [sing] a small early experience of something that will come later

fore·tell /fɔː'tel ‖ fɔːr-/ *v* **foretold** /-'təʊld/, **foretold** [T; + that] to say what will happen in the future: *Who can foretell what will happen in the year 2030?*

fore·thought /'fɔːθɔːt ‖ 'fɔːr-/ *n* [U] wise planning for the future: *With a little forethought, you wouldn't have got yourself into such a mess.*

fore·told /fɔː'təʊld ‖ fɔːr-/ the past tense and past participle of FORETELL

for·ev·er /fər'evər/ *adv* **1** for all future time: *I want to stay here forever.* | *This way of life has now gone forever.* **2 be forever doing something** to do something very often in an annoying way: *He's forever asking silly questions.*

fore·warn /fɔː'wɔːn ‖ fɔːr'wɔːrn/ *v* [T; + that] to warn someone of something dangerous or unpleasant which will happen: *We had been forewarned about his terrible temper.*

fore·word /'fɔːwɜːd ‖ 'fɔːrwɜːrd/ *n* a short introduction at the beginning of a book: *a book on architecture with a foreword by Prince Charles*

for·feit¹ /'fɔːfɪt ‖ 'fɔːr-/ *v* [T] to have something taken away from you, for example as a punishment: *Because he's complained about the goods so late, he's forfeited his right to exchange them.*

forfeit² *n* something that you have taken away from you: *If you guess wrongly, you have to pay a forfeit.*

for·gave /fə'geɪv ‖ fər-/ the past tense of FORGIVE

forge¹ /fɔːdʒ ‖ fɔːrdʒ/ *v* **forged**, **forging** **1** [T] to make a copy of something in order to deceive people: *He got the money by forging his brother's signature on a cheque.* | *She was sent to prison for forging*

a passport. **2** [T] to form objects by heating metal and beating it with a hammer **3** [T] to succeed in making a good relationship with someone: *They have forged an alliance with the French Socialists.* **4** [I + adv/prep] to move with a sudden increase of speed and power: *She forged into the lead just before the end of the race.* | *He didn't do very well at school, but he's forged ahead in the last two years.*

forge² *n* **1** a place with a fire used for heating and shaping metal objects: *a working village forge* **2** a large apparatus that produces great heat inside itself, used for melting metal and making iron

forg·er /'fɔːdʒər ‖ 'fɔːr-/ *n* a person who makes copies of things in order to deceive people

for·ge·ry /'fɔːdʒəri ‖ 'fɔːr-/ *n* **forgeries** **1** [U] the act of making a copy of something in order to deceive people: *He was sent to prison for forgery.* **2** [C] something that has been copied in order to deceive people: *The bank manager told me the notes were all forgeries.*

for·get /fə'get ‖ fər-/ *v* **forgot** /-'gɒt ‖ -'gɑːt/, **forgotten** /-'gɒtn ‖ -'gɑː-/, **forgetting** **1** [I;T; + (that)] to fail to remember something: *She asked me to post some letters, but I forgot.* | *I've forgotten his name.* | *Don't forget to bring something to drink.* | *I forget who said it.* | *They'd forgotten that we were coming.* □ USEFUL PATTERNS to forget something; to forget to do something; to forget that... **2** [I;T] to stop thinking about someone or something: *Let's forget about all the arguments and be friends again.* | *"I'm sorry I broke your teapot." "Forget it."* **3** [T] to fail to give attention to someone: *Don't forget your friends when you are rich!* **4 forget yourself** to lose your temper or self-control and act in an unacceptable way

■ USAGE If you want to mention the place where something has been left, do NOT use forget. Use the verb leave instead. Compare: *I'm sorry, I've forgotten my book.* | *I'm sorry, I've left my book at home.* | *I parked the car and forgot to take my keys with me.* | *I parked the car and left my keys inside.* | *She's forgotten her passport!* | *She's left her passport behind.*

for·get·ful /fə'getfəl ‖ fər-/ *adj* **1** having the habit of forgetting things: *My old aunt has become rather forgetful.* **2 forgetful of** not thinking about something –**forgetfully** *adv* –**forgetfulness** *n* [U]

for·give /fə'gɪv ‖ fər-/ *v* **forgave** /-'geɪv/, **forgiven** /-'gɪvən/, **forgiving** [I;T] to say or feel that you are no longer angry with someone about something: *I'll never forgive you for what you said to me last night.* | *He forgave her the awful things she said about him.* | *Do you think he'll forgive me for scratching his car?* □ USEFUL PATTERNS to forgive someone for something; to forgive someone for doing something

for·give·ness /fə'gɪvnəs ‖ fər-/ *n* [U] the act of forgiving someone: *He begged his victim for forgiveness.*

for·giv·ing /fə'gɪvɪŋ ‖ fər-/ *adj* willing to forgive people: *She has a gentle, forgiving nature.*

for·go /fɔː'gəʊ ‖ fɔːr-/ *v* see FOREGO

for·got /fə'gɒt ‖ fər'gɑːt/ the past tense of FORGET

for·got·ten /fə'gɒtn ‖ fər'gɑːtn/ the past participle of FORGET

fork¹ /fɔːk ‖ fɔːrk/ *n* **1** an instrument for eating food which has a handle at one end with two or more points at the other end **2** a farm or gardening tool which has a wooden handle with two or more metal points at the other end –see picture on page 638 **3** a place where something such as a road or a river divides: *We came to a fork in the road.*

fork² v **1** [I] to divide like the shape of the letter Y: *You'll see our house on the left, just before the road forks.* **2 fork left, fork right** to take either the left or the right road at a place where the road divides: *Fork left at the bus station.*

fork out phr v [I;T **fork** sth ↔ **out**] infml to pay money unwillingly: *I had to fork out another £10 for the school fund.*

forked /fɔːkt ‖ fɔːrkt/ adj dividing into two or more parts at a point: *a forked road | a snake's forked tongue*

fork-lift truck /ˌfɔːklɪft ˈtrʌk ‖ ˌfɔːrk-/ n a small vehicle for lifting and carrying heavy goods, for example inside a factory; it has a fork on the front which goes underneath the goods

for·lorn /fəˈlɔːn ‖ fərˈlɔːrn/ adj **1** left alone and unhappy **2 forlorn hope** a plan or attempt that is very unlikely to succeed –**forlornly** adv

form¹ /fɔːm ‖ fɔːrm/ n **1** [C;U] a shape: *The tall graceful form of a woman appeared at the top of the stairs.| a church built in the form of a cross* **2** [C] a kind or sort: *different forms of government | I dislike any form of exercise.* **3** [C] an official printed paper with spaces in which to answer questions and give other information: *Please fill in this form, giving your name, age, and address. | an application form* **4 on form** performing well, either at your job or at a sport [RELATED PHRASE **off form**] **5 in fine form, on good form, on great form** in good spirits, and especially good at entertaining other people **6** [C] a class in a school: *Her older brother is in the sixth form.* **7** [C] a long low wooden seat without a back

form² v **1** [I] to come gradually into existence: *A cloud of smoke formed over the burning city. | A plan began to form in his mind.* **2** [T] to gradually get an idea: *I formed the impression that she was not being completely honest.* **3** [T] to make or produce something: *The past tense of "help" is formed by adding "-ed". | We need to form a new committee.* **4** [T] to make a particular shape: *She tied the two sticks together to form a cross. | The men formed a chain to pass the goods from the carts to the boats.* **5** [+ complement] to be: *Flour, eggs, fat, and sugar form the main contents of a cake.*

form·al /ˈfɔːməl ‖ ˈfɔːr-/ adj **1** based or done according to accepted rules or customs: *a formal dinner party | Formal dress must be worn.* **2** suitable for official occasions or serious writing, but not usually used in ordinary conversation: *The letter was very formal.* –**formally** adv

for·mal·i·ty /fɔːˈmælɪti ‖ fɔːr-/ n **formalities 1** [C] something done according to laws or customs: *There are a few formalities to settle before you become the legal owner of the car.* **2** [C] an act which has lost its real meaning: *The written part of the examination is just a formality – no one ever fails it.* **3** [U] careful attention to rules and behaviour: *There's no time for formality in everyday life.*

for·mal·ize /ˈfɔːməlaɪz ‖ ˈfɔːr-/ v **formalized, formalizing** (also **formalise** BrE) [T] to put an agreement or plan into a clear form and make it official: *The agreement must be formalized before it can have the force of law.*

SPELLING NOTE
Words with the sound /f/ may be spelt **ph-**, like **photograph.**

for·mat /ˈfɔːmæt ‖ ˈfɔːr-/ n the way in which something is arranged or produced: *We're trying a new format for our television show this year. | Official reports are usually written to a set format.*

for·ma·tion /fɔːˈmeɪʃən ‖ fɔːr-/ n **1** [U] the shaping or developing of something: *the formation of a child's character* **2** [C;U] an arrangement of people, ships, or aircraft: *drawn up in battle formation | formation dancing* **3** [C] the shape of something which is formed by a natural process: *There are several kinds of cloud formation. | volcanic rock formations*

for·ma·tive /ˈfɔːmətɪv ‖ ˈfɔːr-/ adj **1** having an influence on your development **2 the formative years** the time when a child's character is formed and developed

for·mer¹ /ˈfɔːməʳ ‖ ˈfɔːr-/ adj [only before a noun] fml of an earlier time: *a former President of the United States | In former times the building was a prison, but it is currently in use as a government office.*

for·mer² n [plural is **former**] fml the first of two people or things just mentioned: *Germany and the United States are Britain's two most important trading partners, the former being the major supplier of goods, the latter being Britain's main export market. | Will they negotiate or will they go to war? At present the former seems more likely.* –compare LATTER

for·mer·ly /ˈfɔːməli ‖ ˈfɔːrmərli/ adv in the past: *Peru was formerly ruled by the Spanish.*

for·mi·da·ble /ˈfɔːmɪdəbəl, fəˈmɪd- ‖ ˈfɔːr-/ adj fml **1** very great or powerful so that you feel respect or fear: *a formidable voice | a formidable old lady* **2** hard to defeat or deal with: *They faced formidable difficulties in their attempt to reach the South Pole. | formidable weather conditions* –**formidably** adv

form·less /ˈfɔːmləs ‖ ˈfɔːrm-/ adj without shape: *a formless old woolly jumper*

for·mu·la /ˈfɔːmjələ ‖ ˈfɔːr-/ n **formulas** or **formulae** /-liː/ **1** a group of letters, signs, or numbers expressing a general scientific law or rule: *The chemical formula for water is H_2O.* **2** a list of instructions for making something: *Someone has stolen the secret formula for the new drink.* **3** a plan for dealing with a difficult problem: *to draw up a formula for a lasting peace*

for·mu·late /ˈfɔːmjəleɪt ‖ ˈfɔːr-/ v **formulated, formulating** [T] **1** to express something in a short clear form: *He took care to formulate his reply very clearly.* **2** to invent and prepare a plan or suggestion: *They are currently formulating a new policy on Northern Ireland.* –**formulation** /ˌfɔːmjəˈleɪʃən ‖ ˌfɔːr-/ n [C;U]

for·ni·cate /ˈfɔːnɪkeɪt ‖ ˈfɔːr-/ v **fornicated, fornicating** [I] biblical to have sexual relations with someone without being married to them –**fornication** /ˌfɔːnɪˈkeɪʃən ‖ fɔːr-/ n [U]

for·sake /fəˈseɪk ‖ fər-/ v **forsook** /-ˈsʊk/, **forsaken** /-ˈseɪkən/ **forsaking** [T] fml to leave someone or something completely: *They felt that their leader had forsaken them in their hour of need.*

fort /fɔːt ‖ fɔːrt/ n **1** a strongly made building used for defence **2 hold the fort** infml to manage affairs for someone while they are away: *I have to make a phone call. Can you hold the fort for ten minutes please?*

for·te /ˈfɔːteɪ ‖ fɔːrt/ n [sing] a strong point in a person's character or abilities: *Games are not my forte.*

forth /fɔːθ ‖ fɔːrθ/ adv **1** lit out from a place: He went forth into the desert to pray. **2 and so forth** used to say that there are lots of other things that you could add to a list: The place was full of junk – old furniture, paintings, and so forth. **3 back and forth** first in one direction and then in the other

forth·com·ing /ˌfɔːθˈkʌmɪŋ◄ ‖ ˌfɔːrθ-/ adj fml **1** happening or appearing very soon: a list of forthcoming events **2** [never before a noun] given or offered: Funds will soon be forthcoming. **3** [never before a noun] ready to be helpful and give information: I asked several villagers, but none of them was very forthcoming.

forth·right /ˈfɔːθraɪt ‖ ˈfɔːrθ-/ adj very direct and honest in manner and speech: She made the point in her usual forthright manner. –**forthrightness** n [U]

forth·with /fɔːθˈwɪð, -ˈwɪθ ‖ fɔːrθ-/ adv fml without delay

for·ti·fi·ca·tion /ˌfɔːtɪfɪˈkeɪʃən ‖ ˌfɔːr-/ n **1** fortifications [pl] towers and walls set up as a means of defence **2** [U] the act of making something stronger or more effective

for·ti·fy /ˈfɔːtɪfaɪ ‖ ˈfɔːr-/ v fortified [T] **1** to strengthen something against attack: a fortified city | They had only two weeks in which to fortify the coastal areas against the enemy. **2** to make something stronger or more effective: a breakfast cereal fortified with vitamins

for·ti·tude /ˈfɔːtɪtjuːd ‖ ˈfɔːrtɪtuːd/ n [U] fml firm and lasting courage in bearing trouble or pain, without complaining

fort·night /ˈfɔːtnaɪt ‖ ˈfɔːrt-/ n a period of two weeks: I'm going away for a fortnight. | He's coming in a fortnight's time.

fort·night·ly /ˈfɔːtnaɪtli ‖ ˈfɔːrt-/ adv happening or appearing every two weeks –**fortnightly** adj : a fortnightly visit

for·tress /ˈfɔːtrɪs ‖ ˈfɔːr-/ n a castle or other very large strongly made building used for defence

for·tu·i·tous /fɔːˈtjuːɪtəs ‖ fɔːrˈtuː-/ adj fml lucky and happening by chance: a fortuitous meeting –**fortuitously** adv

for·tu·nate /ˈfɔːtʃənət ‖ ˈfɔːr-/ adj lucky: He's fortunate in having a good job. | She's fortunate to have very good health. | It was fortunate for her that she had enough money to get the car repaired. –opposite **unfortunate**

for·tu·nate·ly /ˈfɔːtʃənətli ‖ ˈfɔːr-/ adv luckily: I was late in getting to the station, but fortunately for me, the train was late too. | Fortunately, the wind dropped and the fire died down. –opposite **unfortunately**

for·tune /ˈfɔːtʃən ‖ ˈfɔːr-/ n **1** [C] a large amount of money: His house must be worth a fortune by now. | He made a fortune on the stock exchange. **2** [U] luck: She had the good fortune to be free from illness all her life. **3** [C] whatever happens by chance to a person, good or bad: Through all his changing fortunes, he never lost courage. **4 tell someone's fortune** to tell someone what will happen to them in the future **5 make your fortune** to become very rich: He made his fortune by getting into the market at the right time. **6 a small fortune** infml a large amount of money: That new car must have cost you a small fortune.

fortune-tell·er /ˈ··ˌ··/ n a person who tells you what is going to happen in the future

for·ty /ˈfɔːti ‖ ˈfɔːrti/ det, n, pron **forties** **1** the number 40 **2 the Forties, the forties** the years

1940–1949: He went to school in the Forties, just after the war. **3 in her forties, in their forties,** etc. aged between 40 and 49: I first got reading glasses when I was in my forties. **4 forty winks** a short sleep –**fortieth** det, n, pron, adv

for·um /ˈfɔːrəm/ n a place or meeting where people talk about public matters: The letters page of this newspaper is a forum for public argument.

for·ward¹ /ˈfɔːwəd ‖ ˈfɔːrwərd/ adj **1** in the direction that is in front of you: a forward movement **2** quick to learn things (used of babies) **3** too bold and too sure of yourself

forward² v [T] **1** to send letters and parcels to someone's new address: Could you forward our mail to us? **2 forwarding address** someone's new address, to which letters and parcels should be sent

for·wards /ˈfɔːwədz ‖ ˈfɔːrwərdz/ adv (also **forward**) **1** in the direction that is in front of you: They crept forwards. **2** towards the future: We must look forwards, not backwards. | He described the change in the law as a big step forwards.

fos·sil /ˈfɒsəl ‖ ˈfɑː-/ n the hardened remains of an animal or plant of long ago, or the print in the rock that shows where it has been

fossil fuel /ˈ·· ˌ·/ n [U] a substance such as coal or oil which has been formed from things that were living a long time ago; fossil fuels are burnt to produce heat

fos·sil·ize /ˈfɒsɪlaɪz ‖ ˈfɑː-/ v fossilized, fossilizing (also **fossilise** BrE) [I;T] to make or become a fossil: the fossilized remains of a prehistoric bird

fos·ter /ˈfɒstər ‖ ˈfɔː-, ˈfɑː-/ v [T] **1** to care for someone else's child for a period of time in return for payment; the child lives with you, but you do not have the legal rights or responsibilities of the parent –compare ADOPT (1) **2** fml to encourage something to grow or develop: We hope these meetings will foster friendly relations between our two countries.

foster child /ˈ·· ˌ·/ n foster children a child who is fostered

foster par·ent /ˈ·· ˌ··/ n an adult who fosters a child

fought /fɔːt/ the past tense and past participle of FIGHT

foul¹ /faʊl/ adj **1** very dirty, or with a very unpleasant smell: The air in the cellar was damp and foul. **2** very unpleasant: What foul weather! | She's got a foul temper. **3 foul language** rude and unpleasant language **4 foul play: a** play which is against the rules in a sport **b** tech criminal violence which causes death: He is thought to have died of natural causes, and foul play is not suspected.

foul² n an act that is against the rules in a sport

foul³ v **1** [T] fml to make something dirty in a very unpleasant way: Dogs must not foul the pavement. **2** [I] to do something which is against the rules of a sport, especially football

foul sthg ↔ **up** phr v [T] infml to spoil something

found¹ /faʊnd/ the past tense and past participle of FIND

found² v [T] **1** to start to build a town or a building, or establish an organization: The Romans founded a great city here. | The company was founded in 1724. **2 be founded on** to be based on: The story is not founded on facts.

foun·da·tion /faʊnˈdeɪʃən/ n **1** [sing] the act of starting to build a town or building, or establishing an organization **2** [C] an organization that gives out money for certain special purposes: The Gulbenkian Foundation gives money to help artists. **3**

[C] the belief or idea on which a belief or way of life is based: *built on the foundation of Christian beliefs* **4** [U] facts that prove that something is true: *The allegations are completely without foundation.* **5 foundations** [pl] a solid base deep in the earth on which something is supported or built

found·er[1] /ˈfaʊndəʳ/ *n* **1** a person who founds something: *Mohammed was the founder of the Muslim religion.* **2 a founder member** a member of a club or an organization from its beginning

founder[2] *v* [I] **1** (of a ship) to fill with water and sink **2** to fail: *The plan foundered for lack of support.*

foun·dry /ˈfaʊndri/ *n* **foundries** a place where metal or glass is melted down and formed into shapes or parts of machinery

foun·tain /ˈfaʊntʂn/ *n* **1** a decorative structure that pumps a stream of water up into the air **2** a strong flow of liquid that goes straight up into the air: *A fountain of water was shooting up from the burst pipe.*

fountain pen /ˈ··· ·/ *n* a pen which you fill with ink and which has a metal point for writing with

four /fɔːʳ/ *det, n, pron* **1** the number 4 **2 on all fours** on your hands and knees: *He was crawling about on all fours.*

four·teen /ˌfɔːˈtiːn◂ ‖ ˌfɔːr-/ *det, n, pron* the number 14 –**fourteenth** *det, n, pron, adv*

fourth /fɔːθ ‖ fɔːrθ/ *det, pron, adv, n* **1** 4th **2** one of four equal parts

fowl /faʊl/ *n* **fowl** or **fowls** a bird such as a hen which is kept and eaten

fox[1] /fɒks ‖ fɑːks/ *n* a doglike wild animal with reddish fur

fox[2] *v* [T] to tell or ask someone something they cannot understand or find an answer to

fox·trot /ˈfɒkstrɒt ‖ ˈfɑːkstrɑːt/ *n* a formal dance with short quick steps

foy·er /ˈfɔɪeɪ ‖ ˈfɔɪər/ *n* an entrance hall of a theatre or hotel

frac·as /ˈfrækɑː ‖ ˈfreɪkəs/ *n* [sing] a noisy quarrel or fight in which a lot of people take part

frac·tion /ˈfrækʃən/ *n* **1** a division or part of a whole number; ⅓ and ½ are fractions **2** a very small piece or amount: *We're selling it at a fraction of the original price.*

frac·tion·al /ˈfrækʃənəl/ *adj* very small or to a very small degree –**fractionally** *adv*

frac·tious /ˈfrækʃəs/ *adj fml* bad-tempered about small things and ready to quarrel (used especially of a child)

frac·ture[1] /ˈfræktʃəʳ/ *n tech* a break or crack in something, especially a bone: *a fracture of the hip*

fracture[2] *v* **fractured, fracturing** [I;T] to break or crack: *He fell and fractured his leg.* | *a fractured rib*

fra·gile /ˈfrædʒaɪl ‖ -dʒəl/ *adj* **1** easily broken or damaged: *Things made of glass are always fragile.* | *a fragile relationship* **2** weak in health: *a fragile old lady* –**fragility** /frəˈdʒɪl̩ti/ *n* [U]

frag·ment[1] /ˈfrægmənt/ *n* a small piece or part of something: *I overheard a fragment of their conversation.* | *tiny fragments of glass*

SPELLING NOTE

Words with the sound / f / may be spelt **ph-**, like **photograph**.

---

frag·ment[2] /fræɡˈment ‖ ˈfræɡment/ *v* [I] to break into small pieces –**fragmentation** /ˌfræɡmən-ˈteɪʃən, -men-/ *n* [U]

frag·ment·ary /ˈfræɡməntəri ‖ -teri/ *adj* made up of only a few pieces of information, which do not seem to be connected: *There was only fragmentary evidence linking him to the bombings.*

frag·ment·ed /fræɡˈmentɪd/ *adj* made up of different pieces of information which are not connected very well: *We received only a fragmented account of the incident.*

fra·grance /ˈfreɪɡrəns/ *n* [C;U] a sweet or pleasant smell: *a light, flowery fragrance* | *The fragrance of the roses filled the room.*

fra·grant /ˈfreɪɡrənt/ *adj* having a sweet or pleasant smell: *The air in the garden was warm and fragrant.*

frail /freɪl/ *adj* weak and in poor health: *a frail old woman*

frail·ty /ˈfreɪlti/ *n* **frailties** **1** [U] the state of being weak: *an old man of increasing age and frailty* **2** [C] a weakness: *We all have our little frailties.*

frame[1] /freɪm/ *v* **framed, framing** [T] **1** to fix a firm border or case round a picture or photograph: *I'm having her photo professionally framed.* **2** *fml* to express something in a particular way: *An examiner must frame his questions clearly.* **3** *infml* to make someone appear guilty of a crime by giving false statements or producing false proofs

frame[2] *n* **1** the main supports over and around which something is built: *Their boats are made of skins stretched over a wooden frame.* | *a bicycle frame* **2** *lit* the body of a person or an animal: *a man with a powerful frame* **3** a firm border or case into which something is fixed: *a window frame* | *sunglasses with pink plastic frames* **4** one of the many separate photographs which make a cinema film **5 frame of mind** the state of your mind or feelings at a particular time: *I'm in the wrong frame of mind to make a decision now.*

frame·work /ˈfreɪmwɜːk ‖ -ɜːrk/ *n* **1** a supporting frame or structure: *This building has a steel framework.* **2** a general set of rules or beliefs within which a society or an organization works

franc /fræŋk/ *n* the standard coin of France, Switzerland, Belgium, and some other countries

fran·chise /ˈfræntʃaɪz/ *n* **1** [sing] the right to vote in a public election **2** [C] a right given by a company to someone, allowing them to sell the company's goods or services

frank /fræŋk/ *adj* direct and honest in the way that you speak to someone (a word usually used to show approval): *To be perfectly frank, I don't like her.* | *He was quite frank with me about my chances of getting the job.* –**frankness** *n* [U]

frank·ly /ˈfræŋkli/ *adv* **1** you say this when you are going to give an honest opinion which is not favourable: *Frankly, I think he's useless.* **2** in an honest and open way: *She spoke frankly about her fears for the future.*

fran·tic /ˈfræntɪk/ *adj* **1** very worried and frightened: *We were frantic with worry about you.* **2** very hurried: *It was a frantic rush to get everything ready.* –**frantically** /-kli/ *adv*

fra·ter·nal /frəˈtɜːnl ‖ -ɜːr-/ *adj fml* **1** relating to brothers **2** friendly –**fraternally** *adv*

fra·ter·ni·ty /frəˈtɜːnɪti ‖ -ɜːr-/ *n* **fraternities** **1** [C] people who do the same job or have the same interests: *members of the medical fraternity* **2** [U] *fml* the state of showing friendship or support to other people

frat·er·nize /'frætənaɪz ‖ -ər-/ v **fraternized, fraternizing** (also **fraternise** BrE) [I] fml to meet people and talk to them in a friendly way: *The university lecturers tend not to fraternize with their students.*

fraud /frɔːd/ n **1** [C;U] dishonest behaviour which is intended to deceive people, often in order to gain money: *He was found guilty of fraud.* | *The whole thing had been an elaborate fraud.* **2** [C] a person who is not what they claim to be

fraud·u·lent /'frɔːdjʊlənt ‖ -dʒə-/ adj fml deceitful or dishonest, often in order to gain money: *He obtained the money by fraudulent means.* –**fraudulently** adv

fraught /frɔːt/ adj **1 fraught with danger, fraught with problems, etc.** full of danger, full of problems, etc.: *The long journey was fraught with danger.* **2** infml very worried and anxious

fray¹ /freɪ/ v **1** [I] to develop loose threads round the edges, sometimes when thin and worn: *This material frays when you cut it. It's a real nuisance.* **2 my temper frayed** = I started to feel very angry

fray² n **the fray** busy and tiring action or a fight or argument (a word which is often used in a humorous way): *Are you ready for the fray?*

frayed /freɪd/ adj thin and worn with loose threads round the edges

freak¹ /friːk/ n **1** a person or an animal that is unnatural or unusual in some way **2** a strange, unexpected happening: *By some strange freak, a little snow fell in Egypt a few years ago.* **3** infml a person who takes a special interest in something: *a film freak*

freak² adj [only before a noun] very unusual and unlikely to happen: *a freak storm*

freak³ v

freak out phr v [I] infml to become very excited, upset, or angry

freak·ish /'friːkɪʃ/ adj very unusual and strange: *rather mad, freakish behaviour*

freck·le /'frekəl/ n a small brown spot on a person's skin, especially on their face –**freckled** adj : *a freckled face*

free¹ /friː/ adj **1** able to act as you wish, and not limited or controlled: *People are demanding the right to free speech and a free press.* | *You are free to come and go as you want.* **2** not a prisoner: *He walked from the police station a free man.* | *All political prisoners will be set free next week.* **3** costing nothing: *All the drinks are free.* | *I've got a couple of free tickets for tonight's concert.* **4 do/get something for free** to do or get something without paying for it **5 free of charge** without asking for any payment: *Meals will be provided free of charge.* **6** without work or duty: *I'm free all afternoon.* | *She doesn't get much free time.* **7** not being used: *Is this seat free?* **8 free from something, free of something** not having or suffering from something unpleasant: *She is never free from pain.* | *Keep all parts of the machine free of dust and dirt.* **9 free with something** very willing to give something: *She's very free with her money.* **10 free and easy** not taking things too seriously **11 a free kick** in football, the chance for a player on one side to kick the ball freely from the place where a player on the other side has broken the rules **12 a free agent** someone who can act as they choose

free² adv **1** in an uncontrolled manner: *Don't let the dog run free on the main road.* **2** without payment: *Babies are allowed to travel free on buses.* **3** so as to become loose or disconnected: *I pushed the gate hard and at last it swung free.*

free³ v **freed** /friːd/, **freeing** [T] **1** to let someone leave a place so that they are free: *All the political prisoners have now been freed.* **2** to move or loosen someone or something that is stuck or trapped: *He managed to free his hands.* **3** to take away something unpleasant from someone: *We must try to free the world from hunger.* | *He had been freed of all his responsibilities.* **4** to make it possible for someone or something to be used: *The Government is being asked to free money for new housing.*

free·dom /'friːdəm/ n **1** [C;U] the power to do, say, think, or write what you want: *They are calling for freedom of speech and freedom of religion.* | *We must defend our fundamental freedoms.* | *Women are demanding the freedom to choose when they have children.* **2** [U] the state of being free, and not a prisoner or under anyone's control: *He just stood there, enjoying his first moments of freedom.* **3 freedom from something** the state of not being hurt by something unpleasant: *freedom from hunger* **4 freedom fighters** people who use violence to try and get rid of the government of their country (a word used showing approval)

free en·ter·prise /ˌ· '···/ n [U] a social system in which trade and business are carried on without much government control

free-for-all /ˌ··· ·'·/ n infml a fight or noisy argument in which a lot of people take part

free·hand /'friːhænd/ adj, adv drawn by hand, without the use of a ruler or other instrument

free·lance /'friːlɑːns ‖ -læns/ adj, adv not employed by anyone else, but selling your work to an organization or organizations: *a freelance journalist* | *He works freelance.* –**freelance, freelancer** n : *Most of the work is done by freelances.*

free·ly /'friːli/ adv **1** of your own will, without being forced: *I freely admit that what I said was wrong.* **2** in an open and honest way, without being limited by fear of what will happen as a result: *You can speak freely in front of us.* **3** without any difficulty or any limitation on movement: *Oil the wheel. Then it will turn more freely.* **4 freely available** easily obtainable **5** in large amounts: *He gives his time freely to help the party.* | *The wound bled freely.*

free·ma·son /'friːˌmeɪsən/ n (also **Freemason, Mason**) a man belonging to an ancient and widespread secret society whose members treat each other as brothers and have certain special signs and words by which they recognize each other

free·ma·son·ry /'friːˌmeɪsənri, ˌfriːˈmeɪ-/ n [U] **1** (also **Freemasonry, Masonry**) the organization and practices of the freemasons **2** a natural feeling of friendliness between people who are alike

free·think·er /ˌfriːˈθɪŋkəʳ/ n someone who forms their opinions according to reason and does not accept official teachings, especially about religion

free·way /'friːweɪ/ n the usual American word for a MOTORWAY

free·wheel /ˌfriːˈwiːl/ v [I] to move forward on a bicycle or in a vehicle without using any power

free will /ˌ· '·/ n [U] **1** the belief that people are able to choose what they will do, and are not controlled by God or NECESSITY **2 of your own free will** by choice: *She left of her own free will.*

freeze¹ /friːz/ v **froze** /frəʊz/, **frozen** /'frəʊzən/, **freezing** **1** [I;T] to make or become hard because of extreme cold: *The milk has frozen solid.* | *The cold*

weather might freeze the water in the pipes. **2** [I] (of the weather) to be at or below the temperature at which water becomes ice: *It's freezing tonight.* **3** [I] *infml* to feel very cold: *I'm freezing!* **4** [T] **a** to preserve food by means of very low temperatures: *I'll freeze the rest of these beans.* [I] **b** (of food) to be preserved in this way: *Not all fruit freezes well.* **5** [I] to stop suddenly and become still, usually with fear: *He froze at the sight of the snake.* **6** to officially fix something such as prices or wages at a certain level for a period of time

freeze² *n* **1** a fixing of something such as prices or wages at a certain level: *a wage freeze* **2** a period of very cold icy weather

freez·er /ˈfriːzəʳ/ *n* a large container like a cupboard in which food can be stored for a long time because the temperature is below zero

freezing point /ˈ·· ˌ·/ *n* **1** [U] (also **freezing**) the temperature at which water becomes ice (0 degrees CENTIGRADE): *The temperature has dropped to below freezing.* **2** [C] the temperature at which a liquid freezes: *The freezing point of alcohol is much lower than that of water.*

freight /freɪt/ *n* [U] goods carried by ship, train, or plane: *This aircraft company deals with freight only. It has no passenger service.*

freight·er /ˈfreɪtəʳ/ *n* a ship or aircraft for carrying goods

French¹ /frentʃ/ *adj* from or connected with France: *French wine* | *Her husband's French.*

French² *n* **1** the French the people of France **2** [U] the language of France: *She speaks fluent French.*

French fries /ˌ· ˈ·/ *n* [pl] thin pieces of potato fried in oil

French loaf /ˌ· ˈ·/ *n* a long thin loaf of white bread

French·man /ˈfrentʃmən/ *n* **Frenchmen** /ˈ·-mən/ a man who is a French citizen

French stick /ˌ· ˈ·/ *n* a long thin loaf of white bread

French win·dows /ˌ·ˈ··/ *n* [pl] glass doors opening out onto the garden of a house

French·wo·man /ˈfrentʃˌwumən/ *n* **Frenchwomen** /-ˌwɪmɪn/ a woman who is a French citizen

fre·net·ic /frəˈnetɪk/ *adj* very fast, excited, and wild (used of actions) **–frenetically** /-kli/ *adv*

fren·zied /ˈfrenzid/ *adj* too excited and wild or very busy (used of actions): *The place was full of frenzied activity.* **–frenziedly** *adv*

fren·zy /ˈfrenzi/ *n* [sing;U] a state of mind in which you are very excited, worried, or angry: *He worked himself up into a frenzy before his exams.* | *The atmosphere was one of panic and frenzy.*

fre·quen·cy /ˈfriːkwənsi/ *n* **frequencies** **1** [U] the number of times that something happens: *This type of accident appears to be happening with increasing frequency.* **2** [C] the number of radio waves per second at which a radio signal is broadcast: *We broadcast on three different frequencies.*

fre·quent¹ /ˈfriːkwənt/ *adj* happening often: *Sudden rainstorms are frequent on this coast.* | *He's a frequent visitor.* **–opposite infrequent –frequently** *adv*

fre·quent² /frɪˈkwent ‖ frɪˈkwent, ˈfriːkwənt/ *v* [T] *fml* to go to a place often: *He frequents the best clubs in town.*

fresh /freʃ/ *adj* **1** [only before a noun] new and different: *There has been no fresh news since yesterday.* | *It's time to take a fresh look at this problem.* | *I'll make a fresh pot of tea.* **2** recently picked, caught, or produced and therefore in good condition (used of food): *fresh bread* | *This milk doesn't smell very fresh.* **3** clean, cool, and pleasant: *I must go outside for a breath of fresh air.* | *The sheets smelled clean and fresh.* **4** clear and healthy (used of someone's skin): *a young man with a fresh complexion* **5** fresh water water that is not salty and can be drunk **6** cool and windy (used of the weather) **7** fresh from, fresh out of having recently left a place: *a new teacher fresh from university* **–freshness** *n* [U]

fresh·en /ˈfreʃən/ *v* **1** [T] to make something cleaner, fresher, and more pleasant **2** [I] (of the wind) to become stronger
  freshen up *phr v* **1** [I] to wash yourself: *I'll just go and freshen up.* **2** [T **freshen** sbdy/sthg ↔ **up**] to make someone or something cleaner, fresher, and more pleasant

fresh·er /ˈfreʃəʳ/ *n infml* a first year student at university

fresh·ly /ˈfreʃli/ *adv* [only before a past participle] recently: *a wonderful smell of freshly baked bread* | *a freshly mown lawn*

fresh·wa·ter /ˈfreʃˌwɔːtəʳ ‖ -ˌwɔː-, -ˌwɑː-/ *adj* [only before a noun] living in or belonging to rivers or lakes, not the sea: *freshwater fish*

fret /fret/ *v* **-tt-** to be worried: *Don't fret. Everything will be all right.* | *She's still fretting about getting there late.*

fret·ful /ˈfretfəl/ *adj* tending to complain a lot because of unhappiness: *The child was tired and fretful.* **–fretfully** *adv*

fri·ar /fraɪəʳ/ *n* a man belonging to a Christian religious group; in the Middle Ages friars travelled around teaching people about the Christian religion

fri·ar·y /ˈfraɪəri/ *n* **friaries** a building in which friars live

fric·tion /ˈfrɪkʃən/ *n* [U] **1** the natural force which prevents one surface from sliding easily over another **2** the repeated rubbing of two surfaces together **3** unfriendliness and disagreement between people: *There's been a lot of friction in the office recently.*

Fri·day /ˈfraɪdi/ *n* [C;U] the last day of the working week, the day before the weekend

fridge /frɪdʒ/ *n* a large metal container in which food or drink can be stored to keep it cold for a short time

friend /frend/ *n* **1** a person you know well and like: *She's a close friend of mine.* | *my best friend* | *He's an old friend of the family.* **2** be friends with someone to have a close relationship with someone: *I've been friends with her for years.* **3** make friends to form a close relationship with people: *He has a pleasant manner, and makes friends very easily.* | *Have you made friends with your new neighbours yet?* **4** a helper or supporter of something: *the friends of Norwich Cathedral*
  ■ USAGE Remember to use a possessive noun or pronoun in phrases such as: *He's a friend of mine.* | *A friend of ours told us…* | *some friends of Peter's* | *a great friend of hers/his*

friend·ly[1] /'frendli/ *adj* **friendlier, friendliest** 1 acting in a kind and pleasant way, like a friend: *He's not very friendly* to newcomers. | *a friendly nation* –opposite **unfriendly** 2 **be friendly with someone** to have someone as your friend: *She's quite friendly with the manager.* 3 not causing unpleasant feelings: *We've been having a friendly argument on politics.* 4 done just for pleasure, and not part of a competition: *It's only a friendly game.* –**friendliness** *n* [U]

friendly[2] *n* **friendlies** a game played for pleasure or practice and not as part of a competition

friend·ship /'frendʃɪp/ *n* [C;U] a relationship between friends: *True friendship is worth more than money.* | *His friendships never last very long.*

frieze /friːz/ *n* a decorative border along the top of a wall

frig·ate /'frɪɡət/ *n* a small fast warship

fright /fraɪt/ *n* 1 [U] a feeling of fear: *I was shaking with fright.* 2 **get a fright** to feel suddenly frightened by something: *I got a terrible fright when I saw your face at the window.* 3 **give someone a fright** to make someone feel frightened suddenly 4 **take fright** to become frightened suddenly

fright·en /'fraɪtn/ *v* [T] 1 to make someone feel afraid: *The thought of losing my job frightened me.* | *The horse was frightened by the sudden noise.* 2 **frighten someone into doing something** to make someone do something by frightening them 3 **frighten someone out of their wits** to frighten someone very much
frighten sbdy ↔ **away** *phr v* [T] to make someone go away by frightening them
frighten sbdy ↔ **off** *phr v* [T] to make someone stop doing something by frightening them: *He managed to frighten off his attackers.*

fright·ened /'fraɪtnd/ *adj* afraid or worried: *a crowd of frightened children* | *A lot of people are frightened of snakes.* | *I was frightened to look at him.* | *I was frightened that I'd upset you.* | *It had grown dark and he felt very frightened.*
□ USEFUL PATTERNS be frightened of something; be frightened to do something; be frightened that...

fright·en·ing /'fraɪtnɪŋ/ *adj* making you feel afraid or worried: *It was a very frightening experience.* | *It's frightening how quickly a child can drown.* –**frighteningly** *adv*

fright·ful /'fraɪtfəl/ *adj* terrible: *The battlefield was a frightful scene.* | *The place was in a frightful mess.*

fright·ful·ly /'fraɪtfəli/ *adv old fash infml* extremely: *I'm afraid I'm frightfully late.*

fri·gid /'frɪdʒɪd/ *adj* 1 having an unnatural dislike of sexual activity (used of a woman) 2 formal and unfriendly: *a frigid smile* 3 *tech* very cold: *a frigid zone* –**frigidly** *adv* –**frigidity** /frɪ'dʒɪdəti/ *n* [U]

frill /frɪl/ *n* 1 a decorative edge on a piece of material made of a band of cloth 2 **frills** [pl] attractive but unnecessary additions: *I just want an ordinary car, without the frills.*

frill·y /'frɪli/ *adj* **frillier, frilliest** decorated with frills: *The little girl wore a frilly party dress.*

fringe[1] /frɪndʒ/ *n* 1 a short border of hair hanging over a person's forehead: *Her fringe isn't straight because she tried to cut it herself.* –see picture on page 245 2 a decorative edge of hanging threads on a curtain, tablecloth, or piece of clothing 3 the edge, or the part farthest from the centre: *It was easier to move about on the fringe of the crowd.* 4 the

most extreme part of an organization: *a policy supported only by a fringe element in the party* | *fringe theatre*

fringe[2] *v* **fringed, fringing** [T] to act as a border to something: *A line of trees fringed the river.* | *a pool fringed with trees*

fringe ben·e·fit /'·,···/ *n* something received from an employer in addition to wages, for example a car or house: *The pay's awful but there are a lot of fringe benefits.*

frisk /frɪsk/ *v* 1 [I] (of an animal or child) to run and jump about playfully: *new lambs frisking in the fields* 2 [T] *infml* to search someone for hidden weapons or goods by passing your hands over their body: *All the passengers were frisked before being allowed onto the plane.*

frisk·y /'frɪski/ *adj* **friskier, friskiest** full of life and joyful activity: *frisky lambs* –**friskily** *adv*

frit·ter[1] /'frɪtər/ *v*
fritter sth ↔ **away** *phr v* [T] to waste your time or money on small unimportant things: *He fritters away his time doing crossword puzzles.*

fri·vol·i·ty /frɪ'vɒləti ‖ -'vɑː-/ *n* **frivolities** 1 [U] failure to be properly serious about things: *We feel that his frivolity makes him unsuited to a position of trust.* 2 [C] an act or remark which is silly, when it should be serious: *A political speech should not be full of frivolities.*

friv·o·lous /'frɪvələs/ *adj* 1 silly or not giving serious attention to important matters: *When he tried to make a little joke, the judge warned him not to give frivolous replies to the lawyer's questions.* | *a frivolous empty-headed young man who thought about nothing except clothes and parties* 2 amusing and light and not at all useful: *I feel like doing something frivolous. Let's go and have an ice cream in Harrod's.* –**frivolously** *adv* –**frivolousness** *n* [U]

frizz /frɪz/ *v* [T] *infml* to force hair into short tight curls

frizz·y /'frɪzi/ *adj* **frizzier, frizziest** *infml* with a lot of small, tight curls (used of hair): *Some people have naturally frizzy hair.*

fro /frəʊ/ *adv* **to and fro** from one place to another and back again: *While she waited, she paced anxiously to and fro.*

frock /frɒk ‖ frɑːk/ *n old fash* a dress worn by a woman or girl

frog /frɒɡ ‖ frɑːɡ, frɔːɡ/ *n* 1 a small hairless animal with long legs, usually brownish-green in colour, that lives in water and on land, and makes a deep rough sound 2 **a frog in your throat** *infml* difficulty in speaking because of roughness in your throat

frog·man /'frɒɡmən ‖ 'frɑːɡ-, 'frɔːɡ-/ *n* **frogmen** /-mən/ a skilled underwater swimmer who wears a rubber suit with large flat shoes and a special apparatus for breathing

frog·march /'frɒɡmɑːtʃ ‖ 'frɑːɡmɑːrtʃ, 'frɔːɡ-/ *v* [T + adv/prep] to force a person to move forward with their arms held together firmly from behind

frol·ic /'frɒlɪk ‖ 'frɑː-/ *v* **frolicked, frolicked, frolicking** [I] to play and jump about gaily: *The young lambs were frolicking about in the field.* –**frolic** *n* : *The children are having a frolic before bedtime.*

from /frəm; *strong* frɒm ‖ frəm; *strong* frʌm, frɑːm/ *prep* 1 used to show where or when something started, or where someone or something used to be: *Is this the train from London?* | *They stayed from*

Monday till Friday. | *I'm from Leeds originally.* | *I'll get a book from the library.* | *The new motorway will go from London to Plymouth.* **2** sent or given by a particular person: *I've had a letter from my mother.* | *I didn't get a present from John.* | *I didn't expect to get any sympathy from her.* **3** out of: *Bread is made from flour and water.* | *Can you translate this from German into English for me?* **4** used to show distance or separation: *The village is five miles from the coast.* **5** used to show removal: *Everything valuable had been taken from the house.* **6** used to show subtraction: *Take 24 from the total.* **7** because of: *He's suffering from depression.*

frond /frond ‖ frɑːnd/ n a leaf of a FERN or of a PALM

front¹ /frʌnt/ n **1** the most forward part of something, or the part that you usually see: *The teacher called him out to the front of the class.* | *There were roses growing up the front of the house.* | *He was sitting in the front of the car.* | *It's a blue jacket with gold buttons down the front.* **2 a front** a way of behaving which is intended to give people a particular idea about you: *She was very upset but she put on a brave front.* | *We must show a united front.* **3 the front** the line along which fighting takes place in a war **4** *tech* a line of separation between two masses of air of different temperatures: *A cold front is moving across the country.* **5** a person or place used for hiding an illegal activity: *The drug dealers used a travel company as a front for their operations.* **6 in front: a** ahead: *John walked in front and the others followed behind.* **b** winning in a game or competition: *We were in front at half time.* **7 in front of: a** at the front of something or someone: *There was a car parked in front of the house.* | *She was standing right in front of me.* –see picture on page 540 **b** with a particular person present: *Don't swear in front of the children.*

■ USAGE Use **in front of** when one thing is separate from the other: *A child ran into the road **in front of** the bus, so the driver had to stop.* | *We had our photo taken on the lawn **in front of** the school.* Use **at/in the front of** when one thing is inside or part of the other: *The no-smoking seats are **at/in the front** of the plane.* | *We were right **at the front** of the theatre so we had a good view of the stage.*

front² v [T] (of a building) to have something at the front: *The hotel fronts the beach.*

front³ adj [only before a noun] at the front of something: *His name was written on the front cover of the book.* | *She was sitting in the front seat of the car.* | *The house has no front garden.*

front·age /ˈfrʌntɪdʒ/ n a part of a building or of a piece of land that stretches along a road or river: *The shop has frontages on two busy streets.* | *a restaurant with a river frontage*

front·al /ˈfrʌntl/ adj [always before a noun] **1** direct: *The Opposition have launched a frontal attack on the Government's economic policies.* **2** of, at, or to the front

front door /ˌ·ˈ·/ n the main entrance door to a house, usually at the front –see picture on page 441

fron·tier /ˈfrʌntɪəʳ ‖ frʌnˈtɪər/ n **1** a border, especially where the land of two countries meets: *They were shot trying to cross the frontier.* | *Sweden has*

frontiers with *Norway and Finland.* **2 the frontiers of something** the limits of knowledge about something: *to advance the frontiers of science* | *the frontiers of medical knowledge*

frost¹ /frost ‖ frɔːst/ n **1** [U] a white powdery substance formed on outside surfaces from very small drops of water when the temperature of the air is below freezing point: *The car windows were covered with frost.* **2** [C;U] the weather condition when frost forms: *Frost has killed several of our new young plants.* | *There was a hard frost last night.*

frost² v **1 be frosted, get frosted** (of plants) to be damaged or killed by frost **2** [T] to make something become covered with frost: *The cold has frosted the windows.*

frost over phr v [I] to become covered with frost: *The fields have frosted over.*

frost up phr v [I] to become covered in frost and unable to be used: *My windscreen's frosted up.*

frost·bite /ˈfrostbaɪt ‖ ˈfrɔːst-/ n [U] swelling and discoloration of a person's body, especially of their fingers, toes, or ears, caused by great cold: *The climbers were suffering from frostbite.* –**frostbitten** adj

fros·ted glass /ˌ·· ˈ·/ n glass which has a pattern in it, so that it is not possible to see through it: *a frosted glass door*

frost·y /ˈfrosti ‖ ˈfrɔːsti/ adj frostier, frostiest **1** very cold: *It was a frosty morning.* **2** covered with frost **3** not friendly: *a frosty greeting* –**frostily** adv: *"Good morning," he said frostily.* –**frostiness** n [U]

froth¹ /froθ ‖ frɔːθ/ n [sing;U] a white mass of bubbles (BUBBLE) formed on top of or in a liquid, or in your mouth

froth² v [I] to make or produce froth: *The beer frothed as it was poured out.* | *The sick animal was frothing at the mouth.*

froth·y /ˈfroθi ‖ ˈfrɔːθi/ adj frothier, frothiest full of or covered with froth: *frothy beer* –**frothily** adv –**frothiness** n [U]

frown /fraʊn/ v [I] to bring your eyebrows (EYEBROW) together, especially in anger or effort, or to show disapproval, so that lines appear on your forehead: *The teacher frowned angrily at them.* –**frown** n: *She looked at her examination paper with a worried frown.*

frown on sthg phr v [T] to disapprove of something: *She wanted to go to France by herself, but her parents frowned on the idea.*

froze /frəʊz/ the past tense of FREEZE

fro·zen¹ /ˈfrəʊzən/ the past participle of FREEZE

frozen² adj **1** infml very cold: *I'm absolutely frozen. Do you mind if I put the heating on?* **2** turned to ice because of the cold: *the frozen river* **3** preserved by being kept at a temperature below zero: *frozen food* | *frozen peas* | *You can use fresh or frozen raspberries.* **4 frozen with fear** unable to move because you are frightened

fru·gal /ˈfruːɡəl/ adj **1** careful in your use of money or food: *Although he's become rich, he's kept his frugal habits.* **2** small in quantity and cost: *a frugal supper of bread and cheese* –**frugally** adv –**frugality** /fruːˈɡælɪti/ n [U]

fruit /fruːt/ n **1** [C;U] the part of a tree or bush that contains seeds and is often eaten as food: *We need some more fruit. We haven't got any bananas or oranges.* | *fruit and vegetables* | *There was a bowl of fruit on the table.* | *a fruit bowl* **2 the fruits of** the result of something, especially when gained through hard work: *The old man was enjoying the fruits of his life's work.*

SPELLING NOTE

Words with the sound / f / may be spelt **ph-**, like **photograph.**

fruit·ful /ˈfruːtfəl/ adj successful and producing good results: a fruitful meeting –**fruitfully** adv –**fruitfulness** n [U]

fru·i·tion /fruˈɪʃən/ n [U] fml fulfilment of plans or aims: After much delay, the plan to build the new hospital came to fruition.

fruit·less /ˈfruːtləs/ adj unsuccessful or not bringing the desired result (used of an effort): So far the search for the missing boy has been fruitless. –**fruitlessly** adv –**fruitlessness** n [U]

fruit ma·chine /ˈ·· ·ˌ·/ n a machine which you put money in for amusement; if certain combinations of pictures of fruit appear, you win money back

fruit·y /ˈfruːti/ adj **fruitier, fruitiest 1** tasting or smelling of fruit: This red wine is lovely and fruity. **2** infml rich and deep (used of a person's voice): a fruity laugh

frus·trate /frʌˈstreɪt ‖ ˈfrʌstreɪt/ v **frustrated, frustrating** [T] to prevent something that someone planned or intended to happen from happening: The prisoner's attempt at escape was frustrated by a watchful guard. –**frustration** /frʌˈstreɪʃən/ n [U]

frus·trat·ed /frʌˈstreɪtɪd ‖ ˈfrʌstreɪtɪd/ adj dissatisfied because you are unable to do something: She feels very frustrated now that she can't see well enough to read.

frus·trat·ing /frʌˈstreɪtɪŋ ‖ ˈfrʌstreɪtɪŋ/ adj making you feel dissatisfied because you are unable to do something: It's very frustrating not being able to read.

fry /fraɪ/ v **fried, fried** [I;T] to cook in hot fat or oil: Shall I fry the fish for dinner? | The eggs were frying in the pan. | fried rice –see COOK¹ (USAGE)

fry·ing pan /ˈ·· ˌ·/ n **1** a flat pan with a long handle, used for cooking food in oil or fat –see picture on page 148 **2 out of the frying pan into the fire** out of a bad situation and into a worse one

ft a written abbreviation for FOOT or FEET, in measurements

fudge /fʌdʒ/ n [U] a soft creamy sugary sweet: chocolate fudge | Do you want a piece of fudge?

fuel¹ /fjuəl ‖ ˈfjuːəl/ n [C;U] **1** material which is burned to produce heat or power, for example wood, coal, oil, and gas: Of course, all public buildings use more fuel in the winter. | fuel bills | a car with high fuel consumption **2 add fuel to something** to make a situation worse

fuel² v -ll- (-l- AmE) **1 be fuelled by** to work using a particular fuel: cars fuelled by electricity **2** [T] to make a feeling or situation worse

fu·gi·tive /ˈfjuːdʒɪtɪv/ n fml a person escaping from danger or punishment: a **fugitive** from justice

ful·crum /ˈfʊlkrəm, ˈfʌl-/ n the point on which a bar that is being used for lifting something turns or is supported: the fulcrum of a pair of scales

ful·fil /fʊlˈfɪl/ v -ll- (also **fulfill** AmE) [T] **1** to perform or carry out an order, duty, or promise: He always fulfils his obligations. | You have not fulfilled the conditions of the contract. **2** to supply or satisfy a need, demand, or purpose: Do you know anyone who can fulfil our requirements? **3** to make something true or cause something to happen: If he's lazy, he'll never fulfil his ambition to be a doctor. | to fulfil a prophecy **4 fulfil yourself** to develop your character and abilities fully: She fulfilled herself both as a mother and as a writer. –**fulfilling** adj : a very fulfilling job

ful·fil·ment /fʊlˈfɪlmənt/ n (also **fulfillment** AmE) [U] **1** the act of fulfilling or state of being fulfilled:

After many years, his plans have come to fulfilment. **2** satisfaction after successful effort: a sense of fulfilment

full¹ /fʊl/ adj **1** holding or containing as much or as many as possible (used of a space or container): This car park's full. You'll have to find somewhere else to park. | a full glass of wine | This bottle's only half full. | Your bag's too full. Take out some of the fruit or it'll fall out. | The lecture hall is full to overflowing. **2 be full up: a** to be completely full: The bus is full up. We'll have to wait for the next one. **b** infml (also **be full**) to have had enough to eat: "Do you want any more?" "No, thanks. I'm full up." **3 be full of: a** to contain or have a lot of: The field was full of sheep. | This work's full of mistakes. | He was full of enthusiasm. **b** to think and talk about only one subject which you are very interested in: She's full of this trip to America. **4** complete or whole: Please write down your full name and address. | I want a full account of what happened. | The roses are in full bloom. | The course lasts a full year. | A full moon shone brightly. **5** [only before a noun] the highest or greatest possible: He drove the car at full speed through the town. | She got full marks in all the tests. **6** very busy, often in a satisfying way: He has led a full life. | The doctor has a very full day today. **7** fitting loosely and made with plenty of material (used of clothes): a full skirt | full sleeves **8** fleshy (used of someone's body or of a part of it): She's rather full in the face. | a full figure | full lips **9** deep, strong, and powerful (a word used of colour, smell, sound, or taste which expresses approval): This cheese has a good full flavour. **10 full frontal** showing people with no clothes on from the front: two full frontal shots in the film **11 full of beans** infml feeling cheerful and ready for action **12 on a full stomach** as soon as you have eaten: You shouldn't go swimming on a full stomach. **13 in full swing** at the most active part: By the time we arrived, the party was in full swing. **14 be full of yourself** to think you are better than other people (an expression used to express disapproval)

full² adv **1** straight or directly: The sun shone full on her face. **2 full on** working at the greatest speed or power possible (used of a machine): The fire was full on. **3 full well** with complete certainty: They knew full well that he wouldn't keep his promise.

full³ n **1 in full** completely: The debt must be paid in full. **2 to the full** as much as it is possible to: We enjoyed our holiday to the full.

full-blown /ˌ·ˈ·◂/ adj **1** [only before a noun] fully developed: We're afraid that the fighting may develop into a full-blown war. **2** lit completely open (used of a flower)

full board /ˌ· ˈ·/ adj with all meals provided: Is your holiday full or half board?

full-grown /ˌ·ˈ·◂/ adj (also **fully-grown**) completely developed (used of an animal, plant, or person): A full-grown elephant can weigh over 6000 kilograms.

full-length /ˌ·ˈ·◂/ adj, adv **1** showing all of a person, from their head to their feet (used of a painting, photograph, or mirror) **2** reaching to the ground (used of a piece of clothing): a full-length evening dress **3** of the usual length (used of a play or book): a full-length feature **4** completely flat on the ground (used of a person): She fell full-length.

full·ness /ˈfʊlnɪs/ n (also **fulness**) [U] **1** the condition of being full or busy **2 in the fullness of time** fml at last, though probably after a long time

full-scale /ˌ·ˈ·◂/ adj **1** [only before a noun] using all possible powers or forces: a full-scale attack on an enemy position **2** of the same size as the object represented (of a model, drawing, or copy): *a full-scale model of an elephant at the museum*

full stop /ˌ· ·⎮/ *n* a written point (.) marking the end of a sentence or a shortened form of a word: *Put in a full stop after "now".*

full-time /ˌ·'·⎮/ *adj, adv* working for the usual number of hours or days in a job or course of study: *a full-time student* | *full-time employment* | *He used to work full-time, but now he only works three days a week.* —compare PART-TIME

ful·ly /ˈfʊli/ *adv* completely or thoroughly: *I don't fully understand his reasons for leaving.* | *a fully trained nurse*

fully-fledged /ˌ··'·⎮/ *adj* completely trained: *a fully-fledged doctor*

fully-grown /ˌ··'·⎮/ *adj* see FULL-GROWN

fum·ble /ˈfʌmbəl/ *v* **fumbled, fumbling 1** [I] to move your fingers or hands awkwardly when you are looking for something or trying to do something: *She fumbled about in her handbag for a pen.* | *He fumbled for the light switch in the dark.* **2** [I] to search with some difficulty for a word or expression: *He's not a very good speaker. He often has to fumble for the right word.* **3** [I;T] to handle something, usually a ball, without skill

fume /fjuːm/ *v* **fumed, fuming** [I] to show signs of great anger and impatience: *"Was he angry?" "Yes, he was really fuming."*

fumes /fjuːmz/ *n* [pl] heavy strong-smelling air given off from things such as smoke, gas, or fresh paint: *The air was thick with tobacco fumes.* | *petrol fumes*

fu·mi·gate /ˈfjuːmɪɡeɪt/ *v* **fumigated, fumigating** [T] to clear something of disease, bacteria, or harmful insects by means of chemical smoke or gas: *The man was found to have an infectious disease, so all his clothes had to be fumigated.* —**fumigation** /ˌfjuːmɪˈɡeɪʃən/ *n* [U]

fun /fʌn/ *n* [U] **1** amusement, enjoyment, or pleasure, or something that causes these: *Have fun at the party tonight.* | *It's no fun playing football in the rain.* | *Going to the fair is good fun.* **2 have fun** enjoy yourself: *We had some good fun when we all worked together.* **3 for fun, for the fun of it** just for pleasure, and not for a serious purpose: *He's learning French just for fun.* **4** playfulness: *She's very cheerful and full of fun.* **5 in fun** as a joke, without any serious or harmful intention: *I only threw it at you in fun. I didn't mean to hurt you.* **6 make fun of someone, poke fun at someone** to laugh, or cause other people to laugh, unkindly at someone: *People make fun of her because she wears such strange clothes.* —see FUNNY (USAGE)

func·tion¹ /ˈfʌŋkʃən/ *n* **1** the natural or usual purpose of a thing or duty of a person: *The function of an adjective is to describe a noun.* | *The function of a chairman is to lead and control meetings.* **2** a large or important gathering of people for pleasure or on some special occasion: *This room may be hired for weddings and other functions.* | *The minister has to attend all kinds of official functions.*

function² *v* [I] (especially of a thing) to work or be in action: *The machine won't function properly if you don't oil it.*

SPELLING NOTE

Words with the sound / f / may be spelt **ph-**, like **photograph**.

---

func·tion·al /ˈfʌŋkʃənəl/ *adj* **1** made for or concerned with practical use only, without decoration: *functional furniture* **2** working properly —**functionally** *adv*

fund¹ /fʌnd/ *n* **1** [C] a supply or sum of money set apart for a special purpose: *the school sports fund* **2 funds** [pl] money for a special purpose: *We're having a dance to raise funds for the new swimming-pool.*

fund² *v* [T] to provide money for an activity or organization: *The search for a cure for this disease is being funded by the government.*

fun·da·men·tal /ˌfʌndəˈmentl⎮/ *adj* relating to the most important parts of something, which other parts depend on: *Our sales campaign is failing badly and we will have to make some fundamental changes to it.* | *a fundamental difference of opinion* | *This agreement is of fundamental importance for world trade.* —**fundamentally** *adv* : *She is fundamentally unsuited to office work.*

fun·da·men·tal·is·m /ˌfʌndəˈmentəlɪzəm/ *n* [U] the practice of following the rules of a religion, such as Christianity or Islam, very exactly: *the rise of Islamic fundamentalism* —**fundamentalist** *n, adj*

fun·da·men·tals /ˌfʌndəˈmentlz/ *n* [pl] the most important or necessary parts or rules: *If the boys are going to camp for ten days, they'll need to know the fundamentals of cooking.*

fu·ne·ral /ˈfjuːnərəl/ *n* a ceremony, usually religious, in which a dead person is buried or burned: *a funeral service* | *a funeral procession*

fu·ne·re·al /fjuːˈnɪəriəl/ *adj* heavy and sad and suitable for a funeral: *There was a funereal silence.*

fun·fair /ˈfʌnfeər/ *n* (also **fair**) a noisy brightly-lit show at which you can ride on machines and play games for small prizes

fun·gus /ˈfʌŋɡəs/ *n* **fungi** /-dʒaɪ, -ɡaɪ/ *or* **funguses** a plant without flowers, leaves, or green colouring matter; it is usually a fleshy stem supporting a broad rounded top, or in a very small form that looks like powder: *Mushrooms and mould are both types of fungi.*

funk /fʌŋk/ *n* [U] a type of modern popular music with a heavy regular beat used for dancing

funk·y /ˈfʌŋki/ *adj* **funkier, funkiest** *infml* **1** having a simple direct style and feeling (used of JAZZ or similar music) **2** good, attractive, or fashionable: *a funky party*

fun·nel¹ /ˈfʌnl/ *n* **1** an object used for pouring liquids or powders into a container; it has a wide, round top and a narrow tube coming out at the bottom –see picture on page 638 **2** a metal chimney for letting out smoke from a steam engine or steamship

funnel² *v* **-ll-** (**-l-** *AmE*) **1** [I;T] to pass through a funnel or a narrow space like a funnel: *The wind is funnelled between the skyscrapers.* **2** [T] to send things which have come from different places to a single place: *We will funnel the money collected to the famine areas.*

fun·ni·ly /ˈfʌnli/ *adv* **1** in a strange or unusual way: *She's been acting rather funnily just recently.* **2** in an amusing way **3 funnily enough** strangely: *There were black clouds and loud thunder, but funnily enough it didn't rain.*

fun·ny /ˈfʌni/ *adj* **funnier, funniest 1** amusing and causing laughter: *a funny story* | *a funny joke* | *I don't think that's at all funny.* **2** strange, unexpected, or hard to explain: *What's that funny noise?* | *That's funny! I'm sure I parked the car here, but now it's gone!* | *A funny thing happened to me at work* *today.* **3** [never before a noun] *infml* slightly ill: *She always feels a bit funny if she looks down from a high place.*

■ USAGE If you want to say that you enjoy something use **fun** but NOT **funny**: *Skiing is fun.* | *We all went to the coast on Sunday. It was fun.* | *It's great fun trying out new recipes.*

funny-look·ing /ˈ··ˌ··/ *adj* having a strange appearance: *He's a funny-looking boy. He's got a very long neck.*

fur /fɜːʳ/ *n* **1** [U] the soft thin hair that grows thickly over the bodies of some types of animal, for example bears, rabbits, and cats **2** [C] a hair-covered skin of certain animals, such as foxes or rabbits: *Several valuable furs were stolen from the shop.* **3** [C] a coat made of fur, or a piece of fur that a woman wears round her shoulders **4** [U] a hard covering on the inside of pots, or hot-water pipes, which comes out of the water

fu·ri·ous /ˈfjʊəriəs/ *adj* **1** very angry: *He'll be furious with us if we're late.* | *He'll be absolutely furious at being kept waiting.* **2** [always before a noun] wild or uncontrolled: *a furious temper* | *There was a furious knocking at the door.* **–furiously** *adv*

fur·long /ˈfɜːlɒŋ ‖ ˈfɜːrlɔːŋ/ *n* a unit for measuring length, equal to 220 yards or 201 metres, used mainly in horseracing

fur·nace /ˈfɜːnɪs ‖ ˈfɜːr-/ *n* an enclosed space where metals or other materials are heated to very high temperatures, or where certain materials are burned to produce steam

fur·nish /ˈfɜːnɪʃ ‖ ˈfɜːr-/ *v* [T] **1** to put furniture in a room or building: *They furnished the house in traditional style.* **2** *fml* to supply what is necessary for a special purpose

fur·nished /ˈfɜːnɪʃt ‖ ˈfɜːr-/ *adj* containing furniture: *We're renting a furnished flat.*

fur·nish·ings /ˈfɜːnɪʃɪŋz ‖ ˈfɜːr-/ *n* [pl] articles of furniture or other articles fixed in a room, such as a bath, curtains, etc.

fur·ni·ture /ˈfɜːnɪtʃəʳ ‖ ˈfɜːr-/ *n* [U] large objects that are used in houses, like beds, tables, or chairs: *The house was full of heavy, old-fashioned furniture.* | *garden furniture*

fu·ro·re /fjʊˈrɔːri, ˈfjʊərɔːʳ ‖ ˈfjʊəror/ *n* (also **furor**) [sing] a sudden burst of angry or excited interest among a large group of people: *His news caused quite a furore.*

fur·row /ˈfʌrəʊ ‖ ˈfɜːr-/ *n* **1** one of the long deep lines made across a field when a farmer turns the earth over: *The deep furrows made it difficult to walk across the field.* **2** any long deep cut or fold

fur·rowed /ˈfʌrəʊd ‖ ˈfɜːr-/ *adj* **1** having furrows **2 a furrowed brow** a forehead with lines in it because of worry or deep thought

fur·ry /ˈfɜːri/ *adj* **furrier, furriest** of, like, or covered with fur: *furry material* | *a furry little rabbit*

fur·ther¹ /ˈfɜːðəʳ ‖ ˈfɜːr-/ *adv* **1** the COMPARATIVE form of FAR: *She can swim much further than I can.* | *I can't remember any further back than 1980.* **2** more: *I have nothing further to say.* –see FARTHER (USAGE)

further² *adj* [only before a noun] additional: *I have one further question for you.*

further³ *v fml* [T] to help something to advance or succeed: *They hope that the strike will further the cause of women's rights.*

fur·ther·ance /ˈfɜːðərəns ‖ ˈfɜːr-/ *n fml* [U] action to help something succeed

further ed·u·ca·tion /ˌ··· ···ˈ··/ *n* [U] education after leaving school, but not at a university

fur·ther·more /ˌfɜːðəˈmɔːʳ ‖ ˈfɜːrðərmɔːr/ *adv fml* in addition to what has been said; you use "furthermore" to say that you are going to make an additional point: *The development of this land as an industrial estate will destroy an area of outstanding natural beauty. Furthermore, it will make quite unreasonable demands on the scarce local water supply.*

fur·ther·most /ˈfɜːðəməʊst ‖ ˈfɜːrðər-/ *adj lit* most distant: *the furthermost station on the railway line*

fur·thest /ˈfɜːðɪst ‖ ˈfɜːr-/ *adj, adv* the SUPERLATIVE of FAR: *Let's see who can swim the furthest.* | *He walked off into the furthest field.*

fur·tive /ˈfɜːtɪv ‖ ˈfɜːr-/ *adj* acting as if you want to keep something secret: *The man's furtive manner made the policeman suspicious.* **–furtively** *adv* **–furtiveness** *n* [U]

fu·ry /ˈfjʊəri/ *n* **furies 1** [C;U] very great anger: *She was filled with fury.* | *He stormed out of the meeting in a fury.* **2** [sing] wild force or activity: *At last the fury of the storm lessened.*

fuse¹ /fjuːz/ *n* **1** a thin piece of wire in a PLUG or electric system that prevents damage by melting if there is too much power **2** this wire and its container: *She had to change the fuse before the hairdryer would work.* **3** a string or narrow pipe connected to a bomb or FIREWORK which allows you to light it and move away before it explodes

fuse² *v* **fused, fusing** [I;T] **1** to stop working, or make something stop working, because a fuse has melted: *All the lights fused.* | *You'll fuse the system if you aren't careful.* **2** to melt together because of heat and become or make into one thing: *The old coins had fused together in the fire.* **3** to join together and become one thing: *In this work, the writer successfully fuses past and present.*

fu·se·lage /ˈfjuːzəlɑːʒ ‖ -sə-/ *n* the main body of an aircraft, in which travellers and goods are carried

fu·sion /ˈfjuːʒən/ *n* [C;U] melting, or joining together by melting: *This metal is formed by the fusion of two other types of metal.* | *nuclear fusion*

fuss¹ /fʌs/ *n* [sing;U] **1** unnecessary or unwelcome excitement, anger, or impatience: *What a fuss about nothing!* | *You can't believe anyone would make so much fuss over losing a penny.* | *There's sure to be a fuss when they find the window's broken.* **2 kick up a fuss, make a fuss** to cause trouble, especially by complaining loudly or angrily **3 make a fuss of someone** to pay a lot of attention to someone

fuss² *v* [I] to act or behave in a nervous, restless, and anxious way over small matters: *Don't fuss. We're sure to catch our train.* | *She fusses too much about her health. She's always going to the doctor.* | *You fuss over me as if I were a child.*

fuss·y /ˈfʌsi/ *adj* **fussier, fussiest 1** too concerned about details: *He's fussy about his food. If it isn't cooked just right, he won't eat it.* **2** nervous and excitable (used especially of a person's actions): *small fussy movements of her hands* **3** having too much detailed decoration: *a fussy hat* **–fussily** *adv* **–fussiness** *n* [U]

fus·ty /ˈfʌsti/ *adj* **fustier, fustiest** having an unpleasant smell as a result of having been shut up for a long time, especially when not quite dry (used of a room, a box, or clothes) **–fustiness** *n* [U]

fu·tile /ˈfjuːtaɪl ‖ -tl/ *adj* useless or unsuccessful: *She threw away her purse, in a futile attempt to shake off*

her pursuers. | Don't waste my time with such futile questions! | It's futile to complain. -**futility** /fjuː'tɪlᵻti/ n [U] : the futility of war

fu·ture /'fjuːtʃəʳ/ n **1 the future** the time that has not yet come: You should start saving money for the future. | At some time in the future, we will all eat pills instead of food. | What will the future bring? **2 in future** from now on: In future, you'll have to be more careful. **3** [sing] what will happen to a person or thing: It is impossible to predict the future of the company. | I'm thinking about your future. **4** [C;U] likelihood of success, especially in your job: There's no future in teaching these days. | There's quite a future in computing. **5 the future** tech in grammar, the tense of the verb that expresses what will happen at a later time: In the sentence, "I will leave tomorrow", the verb is in the future. -**future** adj : future generations | the future tense

fu·tur·is·tic /ˌfjuːtʃə'rɪstɪk◂/ adj of strange modern appearance: a futuristic building -**futuristically** /-kli/ adv

fuzz /fʌz/ n [U] **1** infml soft light loose waste that rubs off a woollen article **2** infml short hairs on your face or arms, or other parts of your body **3 the fuzz** slang the police

fuzz·y /'fʌzi/ adj **fuzzier, fuzziest** infml **1** standing up in a light short mass (used of hair) **2** not clear in shape or sound: The television picture is rather fuzzy tonight. **3** having a raised soft hairy surface (used of clothes or material) -**fuzzily** adv -**fuzziness** n [U]

G, g

G, g /dʒiː/ **G's, g's** *or* **Gs, gs** the 7th letter of the English alphabet

g *tech* a written abbreviation for GRAM(s) or GRAVITY

gab·ble /ˈgæbəl/ *v* **gabbled, gabbling** [I;T] to say words so quickly that they cannot be heard clearly: *Stop gabbling!* | *What on earth are you gabbling about?*

ga·ble /ˈgeɪbəl/ *n* the three-cornered upper end of the wall of a building where it meets the roof

gad /gæd/ *v* **-dd-**
gad about *phr v* [I;T **gad about** sthg] *infml* to travel round a place to enjoy yourself: *He's always gadding about.* | *She's away, gadding about Europe.*

gad·get /ˈgædʒɪt/ *n* a small machine or useful apparatus: *a clever little gadget for opening tins* –see MACHINE¹ (USAGE)

gag¹ /gæg/ *n* a piece of cloth put over or into someone's mouth to prevent them from talking or shouting

gag² *v* **-gg-** **1** [T] to prevent someone from speaking by using a gag **2** [I] to nearly throw food up after you have taken it into your mouth and it has gone down your throat

ga·ga /ˈgɑːgɑː/ *adj infml* **1** having a weak mind, especially in old age **2** **go gaga** to lose your powers of mind, especially in old age **3** **be gaga about someone, be gaga over someone** to love someone so much that you seem silly

gage /geɪdʒ/ *n,v* **gaged, gaging** see GAUGE

gag·gle /ˈgægəl/ *n* [sing] a group, usually of geese (GOOSE) or of people who make a lot of noise

gai·e·ty /ˈgeɪəti/ *n* [U] a feeling of fun and enjoyment

gai·ly /ˈgeɪli/ *adv* in a cheerful way

gain¹ /geɪn/ *v* [I;T] **1** to have an increase in something: *I'm sure he's gaining weight.* | *The train gained speed.* | *Surprisingly, the government gained in popularity.* **2** to get something useful or wanted: *It's not an interesting job but at least I'm gaining experience.* | *Who stands to gain from the contract?* –see WIN¹ (USAGE) **3** (of a watch or clock) to work too fast: *My watch is gaining five minutes a week.* **4** **gain ground** to become stronger or more popular **gain on** sbdy/sthg *phr v* [T] to reduce the distance between yourself and someone else you are following and trying to catch up with

gain² *n* **1** an increase, often in weight or wealth: *The baby showed a considerable gain in weight.* **2** an advantage or improvement: *The workforce secured considerable gains in their conditions of employment.* **3** **do something for gain** to do something for your own advantage and especially for money

gait /geɪt/ *n fml* someone's way of walking

ga·la /ˈgɑːlə ‖ ˈgeɪlə, ˈgælə/ *n* an occasion or performance for public enjoyment: *a swimming gala*

gal·ax·y /ˈgæləksi/ *n* **galaxies** any of the large groups of stars which make up the universe –**galactic** /gəˈlæktɪk/ *adj*

gale /geɪl/ *n* a strong wind: *The old tree was blown down in the gale.* –see WIND¹ (USAGE)

gall /gɔːl/ *n* **have the gall to do something** to have the boldness and rudeness to do something without being at all ashamed: *They had the gall to call me lazy, after all the work I'd done!*

gal·lant /ˈgælənt/ *adj* **1** courageous: *a gallant soldier* **2** *lit* attentive and polite to women (used of men) –**gallantly** *adv* –**gallantry** *n* [U]

gal·le·on /ˈgæliən/ *n* a large sailing ship, used in the past

gal·le·ry /ˈgæləri/ *n* **galleries** **1** a room, hall, or building where paintings or other works of art are shown, and sometimes offered for sale **2** an upper floor built out from an inner wall of a hall, from which activities in the hall may be watched **3** a long narrow room, such as one used for shooting practice **4** a level underground passage in a mine **5** the highest upper floor in a theatre

gal·ley /ˈgæli/ *n* **1** a ship which was rowed by slaves, especially an ancient Greek or Roman warship **2** a ship's kitchen

gal·lon /ˈgælən/ *n* a unit for measuring liquids equal to 8 pints (PINT); a British gallon equals 4.54 litres (LITRE) and an American gallon equals 3.78 litres

gal·lop¹ /ˈgæləp/ *v* **1** [I] (of a horse, or a person riding a horse) to go at the fastest speed: *The horse galloped down the hill.* | *The riders galloped off.* **2** [I + adv/prep] *infml* (of a person) to run very fast

gallop² *n* **1** [sing] the movement of a horse at its fastest speed **2** [C] a ride at this speed: *a long gallop before breakfast* **3** **at a gallop** very fast

gal·lop·ing /ˈgæləpɪŋ/ *adj* [always before a noun] increasing very quickly: *galloping inflation*

gal·lows /ˈgæləʊz/ *n* [plural is **gallows**] the wooden frame on which murderers used to be killed by being hanged with a rope

ga·lore /gəˈlɔːʳ/ *adj* [only after a noun] in large amounts or numbers: *He's got money galore.* | *friends galore*

ga·losh·es /gəˈlɒʃɪz ‖ gəˈlɑːʃɪz/ *n* [pl] rubber shoes worn over ordinary shoes when it rains or snows

gal·va·nize /ˈgælvənaɪz/ *v* **galvanized, galvanizing** (also **galvanise** *BrE*) [T] **1** to put a covering of metal over a sheet of another metal using electricity: *galvanized iron* **2** to shock someone so much that they take action without delay: *The fear of losing his life galvanized him into action.*

gam·bit /ˈgæmbɪt/ *n* **1** a set of opening moves in the game of CHESS in which a piece is risked to gain an advantage later **2** an action made to produce a future effect, especially an opening move in an argument or conversation

gam·ble¹ /ˈgæmbəl/ *v* **gambled, gambling** [I] **1** to risk your money or property on horse races, in card games, or in business: *He lost a fortune gambling at the casino.* **2** to take a risk in the hope of gaining something: *We're having the party outside. Of course, we're gambling on the weather.* –**gambler** *n* **gamble** sthg ↔ **away** *phr v* [T] to lose money by gambling: *He's gambled away all his money.*

gamble² *n* [sing] an act in which you take a risk in the hope of success: *The operation may not succeed. It's a bit of a gamble.*

gam·bol /ˈgæmbəl/ *v* **-ll-** (**-l-** *AmE*) *lit* [I] to jump about playfully, like lambs or children

game¹ /geɪm/ *n* **1** [C] a form of play or sport: *Football is a game which doesn't interest me.* | *He's very good at ball games.* **2** [C] a particular occasion when you play a game: *Let's have another game of cards.* | *a game of football* **3** [C] a part of a competition with a fixed number of points, as in tennis: *She won the first three games but lost the set 3–6.* **4 games: a** [pl] a particular set of sports competitions: *The Olympic Games are held every four years.* **b** [U] the playing of team games and other forms of physical exercise out of doors at school –see SPORT (USAGE) **5** [U] wild animals, birds, and fish which are hunted for food and as a sport: *Pheasants are the commonest game birds in Britain.| big game hunting in Africa* **6** [C] *infml* a secret intention or plan, usually dishonest: *What's your little game, then?* **7 give the game away** *infml* to tell people something which is intended to be kept secret **8 the game is up** = you've been caught

game² *adj* **1** willing to try something: *"Shall we try and climb up to the ridge?" "Yes, I'm game."* **2** brave and determined: *The little boy fell and hurt himself, but he was game enough to get up and try again.* –**gamely** *adv*

game·keep·er /ˈɡeɪmˌkiːpəʳ/ *n* a man employed to raise and protect the wild animals and birds kept for hunting on private land

gam·mon /ˈɡæmən/ *n* [U] meat from a pig, when it has been preserved by smoke or salt

gam·ut /ˈɡæmət/ *n* **1 the gamut of something** the complete range of a subject **2 run the whole gamut of** to experience everything connected with a subject

gan·der /ˈɡændəʳ/ *n* a male GOOSE

gang¹ /ɡæŋ/ *n* [+ sing/pl verb] **1** a group of people working together, especially criminals, prisoners, or building workers: *The gang was planning a robbery.* **2** a group of young people, mostly young men, who cause trouble or fill other people with fear: *a gang fight in downtown New York* **3 the gang, our gang** *infml* our group of friends: *Have you seen any of the gang lately?*

gang² *v*
gang up *phr v* [I] to work together as a close group against someone: *She feels that everyone's ganging up on her.*

gang·ling /ˈɡæŋɡlɪŋ/ *adj* unusually tall and thin, and so appearing awkward in movement

gan·grene /ˈɡæŋɡriːn/ *n* [U] the decay of the flesh of part of a person's body, caused when blood has stopped flowing there –**gangrenous** /-ɡrɪnəs/ *adj*

gang·ster /ˈɡæŋstəʳ/ *n* a member of a group of armed criminals

gang·way /ˈɡæŋweɪ/ *n* **1** *BrE* a clear space between two rows of seats in a cinema, theatre, bus, or train **2** a bridge by which people get onto or off a ship

gan·try /ˈɡæntri/ *n* **gantries** a structure like a bridge used to support things such as railway signals and signs on large roads

gaol /dʒeɪl/ *n,v* see JAIL

gaol·er /ˈdʒeɪləʳ/ *n* see JAILER

gap /ɡæp/ *n* **1** an empty space between two objects or two parts of an object: *The gate was locked but we went through a gap in the fence.* **2** a time which is not filled by the usual or wanted activity: *uncomfortable gaps in the conversation* **3** an absence of something which prevents something from being complete: *There are wide gaps in my knowledge of history.| a gap in the market* **4** a difference between two things or groups of people: *the gap between management and unions*

gape /ɡeɪp/ *v* **gaped, gaping** [I] **1** to look hard in surprise, with your mouth open: *"What are you gaping at?" "Look, over there, it's the President!"* **2** to come apart or open widely: *a gaping hole*

gar·age /ˈɡærɑːʒ, -ɪdʒ ‖ ɡəˈrɑːʒ/ *n* **1** a building in which cars and other vehicles can be kept –see picture on page 441 **2** a place where petrol can be bought and cars can be repaired

garb /ɡɑːb ‖ ɡɑːrb/ *n* [U] *lit* clothing of a particular style

gar·bage /ˈɡɑːbɪdʒ ‖ ˈɡɑːr-/ *n* [U] **1** *AmE* things that have been thrown away because they are no longer needed **2** stupid and worthless ideas or words

garbage can /ˈ··· ·/ *n* the usual American word for a DUSTBIN

garbage col·lec·tor /ˈ··· ·,··/ *n* the usual American word for a DUSTMAN

garbage truck /ˈ··· ·/ *n* the usual American word for a DUSTCART

gar·bled /ˈɡɑːbəld ‖ ˈɡɑːr-/ *adj* confused and giving a false idea of the facts: *The newspaper gave a garbled account of the meeting.*

gar·den¹ /ˈɡɑːdn ‖ ˈɡɑːr-/ *n* **1** a piece of land, usually near a house, on which grass, flowers, and vegetables can be grown: *She's in the front garden.* –see picture on page 441 **2** (also **gardens**) a public park with flowers, grass, paths, and seats

garden² *v* [I] to work in a garden, making plants grow –**gardener** *n* –**gardening** *n* [U] : *My mother's very keen on gardening.*

gar·gan·tu·an /ɡɑːˈɡæntʃuən ‖ ɡɑːr-/ *adj* extremely big: *a gargantuan meal*

gar·gle /ˈɡɑːɡəl ‖ ˈɡɑːr-/ *v* **gargled, gargling** [I] to treat a bad throat medically by blowing air through a special liquid held at the back of your mouth –**gargle** *n*

gar·goyle /ˈɡɑːɡɔɪl ‖ ˈɡɑːr-/ *n* a hollow figure of a person or animal, especially on the roof of a church, through whose mouth rainwater is carried away

gar·ish /ˈɡeərɪʃ/ *adj* unpleasantly bright: *garish colours* –**garishly** *adv* –**garishness** *n* [U]

gar·land /ˈɡɑːlənd ‖ ˈɡɑːr-/ *n* **1** a circle of flowers or leaves placed round your neck for decoration or as a sign of victory **2** a long line of decorations used to decorate a house at special times such as Christmas

gar·lic /ˈɡɑːlɪk ‖ ˈɡɑːr-/ *n* [U] a plant rather like an onion, which is used in cooking to give a strong taste: *a clove of garlic*

gar·ment /ˈɡɑːmənt ‖ ˈɡɑːr-/ *n* *fml or tech* a piece of clothing: *This garment should be hand-washed.*

gar·ner /ˈɡɑːnəʳ ‖ ˈɡɑːr-/ *v* [T] *fml* to collect something, for example information, usually with difficulty

gar·nish /ˈɡɑːnɪʃ ‖ ˈɡɑːr-/ *n* something that is used to improve the appearance of food, such as small pieces of fruit or vegetable –**garnish** *v* [T]

gar·ret /ˈɡærɪt/ *n* a small usually unpleasant room at the top of a house

gar·ri·son /ˈɡærɪsən/ *n* a group of soldiers living in a town and defending it

gar·ru·lous /ˈɡærələs/ *adj* habitually talking too much, especially about unimportant things –**garrulously** *adv*

gar·ter /ˈɡɑːtəʳ ‖ ˈɡɑːr-/ *n* a band of elastic material worn round your leg to keep a sock or STOCKING up

gas¹ /ɡæs/ *n* **gases** (also **gasses** *AmE*) **1** [C;U] a substance like air, which is not solid or liquid: *Three of the main greenhouse gases are carbon dioxide, methane, and nitrous oxide.* **2** [U] a substance of this type which is burnt in the home for heating and cooking **3** [U] *AmE infml* PETROL

gas² *v* -ss- [T] to poison or kill a person or animal with gas

gas cham·ber /ˈ· ˌ··/ *n* a room which can be filled with gas so that people or animals can be killed

gas·e·ous /ˈgæsɪəs/ *adj* of or like gas

gash /gæʃ/ *v* [T] to make a deep cut in something –**gash** *n*

gas·ket /ˈgæskɪt/ *n* a flat piece of soft material which is placed between two surfaces so that steam, oil, or gas cannot escape

gas mask /ˈ· ·/ *n* a breathing apparatus worn over your face to protect you against poisonous gases

gas·o·line /ˈgæsəliːn/ *n* (also **gasolene, gas** *infml*) [U] the usual American word for PETROL

gas·o·me·ter /gæˈsɒmɪtəʳ ‖ -ˈsɑː-/ *n* a round metal container, bigger than most buildings, in which gas is stored

gasp /gɑːsp ‖ gæsp/ *v* [I] **1** to take a quick short breath or breaths, making a sudden noise: *As her head came above the water she gasped for breath.* **2** to take in your breath suddenly, especially because of surprise, or shock: *The audience gasped in amazement as she put her head in the lion's mouth.* –**gasp** *n* : *He gave a gasp of surprise.*

gasp·ing /ˈgɑːspɪŋ/ *adj* [never before a noun] *infml* very thirsty: *Is there any orange juice? I'm absolutely gasping.* | *gasping* **for** *a drink*

gas sta·tion /ˈ· ˌ··/ *n* the usual American word for a FILLING STATION

gas·sy /ˈgæsi/ *adj* **gassier, gassiest** full of gas: *a gassy drink*

gas·tric /ˈgæstrɪk/ *adj* [only before a noun] *tech* relating to or belonging to your stomach: *the gastric juices*

gas·tro·en·te·ri·tis /ˌgæstrəʊ-entəˈraɪtɪs/ *n* [U] an illness in which your food passages, including your stomach and intestines (INTESTINE), are swollen

gas·tron·o·my /gæˈstrɒnəmi ‖ gæˈstrɑː-/ *n* [U] the art and science of cooking and eating good food **gastronomic** /ˌgæstrəˈnɒmɪk+/ *adj* : *The dinner was a great gastronomic success.* –**gastronomically** /-kli/ *adv*

gas·works /ˈgæswɜːks ‖ -ɜːr-/ *n* [plural is **gasworks**] a place where gas for use in the home and industry is made from coal

gate /geɪt/ *n* **1** an object like a low or wide door that is used outside to close an opening in a fence or wall: *chatting over the garden gate* | *park gates* –see picture on page 441 **2** an entrance or way out, especially in an airport

ga·teau /ˈgætəʊ ‖ gɑːˈtəʊ/ *n* **gateaux** /təʊz/ [C;U] a special large cake that looks very decorative and has cream and often fruit in it

gate·crash /ˈgeɪtkræʃ/ *v* [I;T] to go to a party or official occasion without having been invited –**gatecrasher** *n*

gate·post /ˈgeɪtpəʊst/ *n* a post from which a gate is hung or to which it fastens –see picture on page 441

gate·way /ˈgeɪt-weɪ/ *n* **1** an opening in a fence or wall across which a gate may be put **2** a way of reaching something desirable: *Higher education can be the gateway* **to** *a worthwhile career.* **3** a place which leads you somewhere else: *Come to Singapore – gateway to the East.*

gath·er /ˈgæðəʳ/ *v* **1** [I;T] to come together in a group: *A crowd soon gathered to see what had happened.* | *If you can just gather round, I'll explain what I want you to do.* | *The sheep had gathered together in a corner of the field.* **2** [T] to collect flowers, crops, or several objects: *I gathered a few roses.* **3** [T] to obtain something gradually from different places: *Scientists have been gathering information about the disease.* **4** [T] to slowly increase force or speed: *As the bus came onto the open road it gathered speed.* **5** [T; +(that)] to understand from something said or done: *I gather she's ill, and that's why she hasn't come.* | *"She's ill." "So I gather."* **6** [T] to pull material into small folds by using a long thread: *a skirt gathered at the waist*

gath·er·ing /ˈgæðərɪŋ/ *n* a meeting or coming together of a group of people: *It was not a happy gathering.*

gauche /gəʊʃ/ *adj* awkward in social behaviour

gau·dy /ˈgɔːdi/ *adj* **gaudier, gaudiest** too bright in colour –**gaudily** *adv*

gauge¹ /geɪdʒ/ *n* (also **gage** *AmE*) **1** an instrument for measuring the quantity or amount of something: *the fuel gauge* **2** a fact you can use to judge a person or situation: *Is the number of people passing exams a reliable gauge* **of** *educational success?*

gauge² *v* **gauged, gauging** (also **gage** *AmE*) [T] **1** to measure something by using a gauge **2** to judge the value or meaning of something or of someone's actions: *It's difficult to gauge his reaction.*

gaunt /gɔːnt/ *adj* **1** very thin, as if ill **2** bare or severe in appearance

gaunt·let /ˈgɔːntlɪt/ *n* **gauntlets** [pl] long thick gloves (GLOVE) which protect your hand; people on motorbicycles wear gauntlets

gauze /gɔːz/ *n* [U] soft net-like material: *cotton gauze* | *gauze curtains* | *Dress the wound with gauze.*

gave /geɪv/ the past tense of GIVE

gaw·ky /ˈgɔːki/ *adj* **gawkier, gawkiest** awkward in movement, especially because of having long thin limbs

gawp /gɔːp/ *v* [I] to look at something in a rude and foolish way

gay¹ /geɪ/ *adj* **1** *infml* HOMOSEXUAL: *gay rights* **2** bright or attractive: *gay colours* **3** *old fash* cheerful and happy

gay² *n* a HOMOSEXUAL person, especially a man: *a more liberal attitude to gays and lesbians*

gaze¹ /geɪz/ *v* **gazed, gazing** [I; + adv/prep] to look steadily at someone or something for a long time: *He gazed fondly at his children.* | *She sat gazing into the distance.* –**gaze** *n* [sing] a steady fixed look: *her worried gaze*

ga·zelle /gəˈzel/ *n* a graceful animal like a small deer

ga·zumped /gəˈzʌmpt/ *v* **be gazumped** *infml* to be unable to buy a house that the owner agreed to sell you because they have decided to sell it instead to someone who has offered more money

GB /ˌdʒiː ˈbiː/ an abbreviation for **Great Britain**

GCSE /ˌdʒiː siː es ˈiː/ an examination in any of a range of subjects, taken in British schools by pupils aged 15 or 16; an abbreviation for **General Certificate of Secondary Education**

gear¹ /gɪəʳ/ *n* **1** [C;U] an apparatus, especially one consisting of a set of toothed wheels, that allows power to be passed from one part of a machine to another so as to control its power, speed, and direction of movement: *Most cars have four forward gears.* | *The hill was so steep I had to go into second gear.* | *She changed gear as she approached the bend.* **2 in gear** having the engine directly connected to the wheels (used of a car or other vehicle): *Don't leave it in gear. Put it into neutral.* **3** [U] the special clothes or objects you need for a particular activity, especially a sport: *climbing gear*

gear² *v* **1 gear something to something** to make one thing be in accordance with another thing: *Education should be geared to the children's needs and abilities.* **2 be geared up to do something** to be prepared to do something, and, often, nervous about doing it

gear·box /ˈgɪəbɒks ‖ ˈgɪərbɑːks/ *n* a metal case containing the gears of a vehicle

gear le·ver /ˈ· ˌ··/ *n* (also **gearshift** /ˈgɪəʃɪft/ *AmE*) a metal rod which controls the gears of a vehicle –see picture on page 49

gee /dʒiː/ *interj AmE infml* people sometimes say this when they are surprised or they are enjoying themselves: *Gee, honey. That sure is a nice dress.*

geese /giːs/ the plural of GOOSE

gel¹ /dʒel/ *n* [C;U] a substance in a state between solid and liquid: *hair gel*

gel² *v* **-ll-** [I] **1** (of a liquid) to become firmer and like a jelly **2** (of ideas) to take a clear shape **3** (of a group of people) to become united

gel·a·tine /ˈdʒelətiːn ‖ -tn/ *n* (also **gelatin** /ˈdʒelətɪn/ *AmE*) [U] a clear substance used for making jellies

ge·lat·i·nous /dʒɪˈlætɪnəs/ *adj tech* in a state between solid and liquid like jelly

gel·ig·nite /ˈdʒelɪgnaɪt/ *n* [U] a very powerful explosive

gem /dʒem/ *n* **1** a precious stone, especially when cut into a regular shape **2** a thing or person of special value

Gem·i·ni /ˈdʒemɪnaɪ ‖ -niː/ *n* one of the signs of the ZODIAC

gen /dʒen/ *n* [U] *infml* the correct or complete information: *He gave me all the gen on the new office arrangements.*

gen·der /ˈdʒendəʳ/ *n* [C;U] *tech* **1** the sexual division into male and female: *There must be no discrimination according to race or gender.* **2** in grammar, the division of nouns, adjectives, etc., into MASCULINE, FEMININE, or NEUTER: *German has three genders.* | *Differences of gender in French are shown in the different endings of adjectives.*

gene /dʒiːn/ *n* the part of a cell which controls the development of all the qualities in a living thing which have been passed on from its parents

ge·ne·al·o·gy /ˌdʒiːniˈælədʒi/ *n* **genealogies 1** [U] the study of the history of the members of a family **2** [C] an account of the history of a particular family –**genealogist** *n* –**genealogical** /ˌdʒiːniəˈlɒdʒɪkəl ‖ -ˈlɑː-/ *adj*

gen·e·ra /ˈdʒenərə/ the plural of GENUS

gen·e·ral¹ /ˈdʒenərəl/ *adj* **1** concerning most people or places: *The general feeling is that it's wrong.* | *Concern about pollution is now very general.* **2** concerning the whole of something, rather than its parts: *a general increase in prices* | *The general condition of the car is good, although the battery needs replacing.* | *the general manager* **3** not limited to one subject only: *a general university degree* | *general education* **4** not limited to providing only one service or product: *a general hospital* | *the general store* **5** describing the main points, but not the details: *Give me a general idea of what the job involves.* **6** true or usual in most cases: *As a general rule, patients must make an appointment to see the doctor.* **7 in general** mainly or in most cases: *In general, my colleagues are very hardworking.* | *People in general are fed up with the present government.*

general² *n* (also **General**) an officer of very high rank in the armed forces, especially the army: *General De Gaulle* | *Yes, General.*

general an·aes·thet·ic /ˌ··· ····/ *n* [C;U] a substance used in hospitals to make someone unconscious while an operation is performed on them

general e·lec·tion /ˌ··· ·ˈ··/ *n* an election in which all the voters in a country choose the members of the government

gen·er·al·i·ty /ˌdʒenəˈrælɪti/ *n* **generalities** a general statement which is not at all detailed: *The President's speech was full of vague generalities.*

gen·er·al·i·za·tion /ˌdʒenərəlaɪˈzeɪʃən ‖ -lə-/ *n* **1** [C] a statement made about a group as a whole; it may not be true in every case **2** [U] the act of generalizing

gen·er·al·ize /ˈdʒenərəlaɪz/ *v* **generalized, generalizing** (also **generalise** *BrE*) to make a general statement or form a general principle by looking at particular examples: *I don't think it's fair to generalize from only two examples.*

gen·er·al·ized /ˈdʒenərəlaɪzd/ *adj* concerning or having an effect on a large number of people or things: *Use of this equipment in hospitals is now fairly generalized.*

general know·ledge /ˌ··· ˈ··/ *n* [U] **1** knowledge about many different subjects: *For a child, his general knowledge is excellent.* **2** knowledge shared by most people, such as the names of important cities

gen·er·al·ly /ˈdʒenərəli/ *adv* **1** usually: *We generally go to the seaside for our holidays.* **2** by most people: *It was generally agreed that the plan was a good one.* **3** considering something as a whole: *Her work is generally of a high standard.*

general prac·ti·tion·er /ˌ··· ·ˈ···/ *n* see GP

general pub·lic /ˌ··· ˈ··/ *n* [+sing/pl verb] ordinary people, who have no special part in an event or organization: *The general public were not allowed in the courtroom.*

general strike /ˌ··· ˈ·/ *n* the stopping of work by most of the workers in a country at the same time: *The unions have called for a general strike next Friday.*

gen·e·rate /ˈdʒenəreɪt/ *v* **generated, generating** [T] **1** *tech* to produce heat, power, or electricity: *Our electricity comes from the new generating station.* **2** to cause something to exist: *Our discussion generated a lot of new ideas.*

gen·e·ra·tion /ˌdʒenəˈreɪʃən/ *n* **1** [C] the group of people in a family at the same stage in its development; for example you and your aunt's children belong to the same generation **2** [C] all people of about the same age: *the younger generation* | *Most people of my father's generation can remember the hardship of war.* **3 generation gap** the difference in ideas between one generation and another **4** [C] the average period of time that it takes for children to become adults, about 25 to 30 years: *It will take at least another generation to solve this country's problems.* **5** [C] all the members of a particular class of things at a stage of their development: *the new generation of word processors* **6** [U] the production of heat, power, or electricity: *Solar energy may soon be used for the generation of all our electricity.*

gen·e·ra·tor /ˈdʒenəreɪtəʳ/ *n* a machine which produces electricity

ge·ner·ic /dʒɪˈnerɪk/ *adj* shared by or typical of a whole class of things

gen·e·rous /ˈdʒenərəs/ *adj* **1** willing to give money, help, and kindness: *It was very generous of you to lend them your new car to go on holiday.* **2** larger in amount than usual: *a generous meal* | *a generous*

gift –generously adv –generosity /₁dʒenə'rɒsɨti ‖ -'rɑ:-/ n [U]: a letter thanking her for her generosity

gen·e·sis /'dʒenɨsɨs/ n fml the beginning of something

ge·net·ic /dʒɨ'netɨk/ adj 1 of or concerning genes (GENE) or genetics 2 the genetic code tech the arrangement of genes which gives a living thing the qualities of its parents 3 genetic engineering tech the changing of the nature of a living thing by changing its genes –genetically /-kli/ adv

ge·net·ics /dʒɨ'netɨks/ n [U] the study of how living things develop particular qualities according to the influence of those substances in their cells which are passed on from their parents

ge·ni·al /'dʒi:nɨəl/ adj cheerful, friendly, and good-tempered: "See you," he said with a genial wave. –genially adv –geniality /₁dʒi:ni'ælɨti/ n [U]

gen·i·tals /'dʒenɨtlz/ n (also genitalia /₁dʒenɨ'teɪliə/ fml) [pl] the outer sex organs –genital adj

gen·i·tive /'dʒenɨtɪv/ n tech the special form of a noun or adjective which is used in some languages to show possession –genitive adj

ge·ni·us /'dʒi:nɨəs/ n 1 [U] great and rare powers of thought and imagination: Her latest book is a work of sheer genius. 2 [C] a person of very great ability: Einstein was a true genius. | That's it! You're an absolute genius! 3 [sing] a special ability: She has a genius for making people feel at home.

gen·o·cide /'dʒenəsaɪd/ n [U] the killing of a whole race or nation

gen·re /'ʒɒnrə ‖ 'ʒɑːnrə/ n a class of literature, music, paintings, or SCULPTURE that shares a particular style or subject: the genre of horror fiction

gen·teel /dʒen'tiːl/ adj trying to be unnaturally polite or respected: a genteel suburb | a genteel old lady –genteelly /-'tiːl-li/ adv –gentility /-'tɪlɨti/ n [U]

gen·tile /'dʒentaɪl/ n (also Gentile) a person who is not Jewish –gentile, Gentile adj

gen·tle /'dʒentl/ adj 1 not rough or violent in manner or movement: Be gentle when you brush the baby's hair. | a gentle wind 2 kind and calm: a gentle voice | gentle brown eyes 3 not steep or sharp: a gentle slope –gentleness n [U] –gently adv: "Don't cry," he said gently. | She rocked the baby gently in her arms.

gen·tle·man /'dʒentlmən/ n gentlemen /-mən/ 1 a man who behaves well towards other people and who can always be trusted to act honourably 2 fml a man

■ USAGE We often use gentleman and lady as a respectful way of speaking about a man or woman, especially when the person is present: It isn't my turn – this gentleman/lady was here before me. We also use the phrase ladies and gentlemen at the beginning of a speech: Ladies and gentlemen, I'd like to introduce our speaker for this evening. In other cases man and woman are the usual words.

gen·tri·fy /'dʒentrɨfaɪ/ v gentrified, gentrified: be gentrified (of an area) to become more typical of an area where rich people live by the process of richer people gradually moving there –gentrification /₁dʒentrɨfɨ'keɪʃən/ n [U]

gen·try /'dʒentri/ n [pl] the gentry formerly, people born of high, but not the highest, social class

gents /dʒents/ n [plural is gents] BrE infml a public TOILET for men

gen·u·ine /'dʒenjuɨn/ adj 1 real: a genuine leather handbag | There's no doubt this Picasso is genuine. 2 sincere and honest: a very genuine person –genuinely adv –genuineness n [U]

ge·nus /'dʒiːnəs, 'dʒen-/ n genera /'dʒenərə/ tech a group of closely related kinds of animal or plant

ge·og·ra·phy /dʒi'ɒgrəfi, 'dʒɒgrəfi ‖ dʒi'ɑːg-/ n [U] 1 the study of the countries of the world, including such things as seas, rivers, mountains, population, and weather 2 infml the arrangement of the parts of a particular place: I can't show you the way, because I don't know the geography of the neighbourhood. –geographer n –geographic /₁dʒiə'græfɨk/, geographical /-fɨkəl/ adj –geographically /-kli/ adv

ge·ol·o·gy /dʒi'ɒlədʒi ‖ -'ɑːlə-/ n [U] the study of the structure of materials like rocks and soil and their changes during the history of the Earth –geologist n –geological /₁dʒiə'lɒdʒɨkəl ‖ -'lɑː-/ adj –geologically /-kli/ adv

ge·o·met·ric /₁dʒiə'metrɨk/ adj (also geometrical /-trɨkəl/) 1 concerning geometry 2 involving repeated angles and shapes formed by lines: the abstract geometric patterns of Islamic art –geometrically /-kli/ adv

ge·om·e·try /dʒi'ɒmɨtri ‖ -'ɑːm-/ n [U] the study in MATHEMATICS of shape and form, using angles and lines

Geor·gian /'dʒɔːdʒən, -dʒiən ‖ 'dʒɔːrdʒən/ adj of the period of rule of the first four British kings named George (1711–1830): Georgian architecture | a beautiful Georgian house

ge·ra·ni·um /dʒə'reɪniəm/ n a plant with red, pink, or white flowers

ge·ri·at·rics /₁dʒeri'ætrɨks/ n [U] the branch of medicine concerning the illnesses, treatment, and care of old people –geriatric adj: a geriatric hospital

germ /dʒɜːm ‖ dʒɜːrm/ n 1 a very small living thing which causes illness 2 the germ of an idea the beginning of an idea which may develop further

Ger·man[1] /'dʒɜːmən ‖ 'dʒɜːr-/ adj from or connected with Germany

German[2] n 1 [C] a person from Germany 2 [U] the language of Germany, Switzerland, and Austria: In this part of the country we speak a dialect of German.

German mea·sles /₁·· '··/ n [U] an infectious illness in which red spots appear on your body

ger·mi·nate /'dʒɜːmɨneɪt ‖ 'dʒɜːr-/ v germinated, germinating 1 [I] (of a seed) to start growing 2 [T] to make a seed start growing –germination /₁dʒɜːmɨ'neɪʃən ‖ ₁dʒɜːr-/ n [U]

ger·und /'dʒerənd/ n in grammar, a noun made from a verb; in the sentence "I like swimming", "swimming" is a gerund; in English gerunds end in -ing

ges·ta·tion /dʒe'steɪʃən/ n tech [U] 1 the carrying of a child or young animal inside its mother's body before birth 2 the beginning and development of an idea or plan

ges·tic·u·late /dʒe'stɪkjᵿleɪt/ v gesticulated, gesticulating [I] to move your hands and arms, often while you are speaking, to express something like urgency or excitement –gesticulation /dʒe₁stɪkjᵿ'leɪʃən/ n [C;U]

ges·ture[1] /'dʒestʃəʳ/ n 1 [C;U] movement, usually with your hands or head, to express a certain meaning: He made an angry gesture. | He didn't speak a word of English, so we communicated entirely by gesture. 2 [C] an action which is done to show your feelings or intentions: "We've invited our new neighbours to dinner." "That's a nice gesture." | a gesture of friendship

gesture[2] v gestured, gesturing [I;+that] to tell someone something by moving your hands or head: She gestured that it was time to leave. | They gestured *to us to go away.* | *He gestured in the direction of the station.*

get – see box on pages 297 to 302.

get·a·way /ˈgetəweɪ/ n **1** [sing] an escape: *the getaway car* **2 make a getaway** to leave a place quickly, especially after doing something criminal: *The thieves made a quick getaway.*

get-to-geth·er /ˈ··ˌ··/ n a friendly informal meeting or party: *a get-together of old school friends*

get·up /ˈgetʌp/ n *infml* an unusual set of clothes

gey·ser /ˈgiːzəʳ ‖ ˈgaɪzər/ n **1** a natural spring of hot water and steam which can rise suddenly into the air from the earth **2** an apparatus for heating water by gas, used in a kitchen or bathroom

ghast·ly /ˈgɑːstli ‖ ˈgæstli/ adj **ghastlier, ghastliest 1** *infml* extremely bad or unpleasant: *a really ghastly man* | *ghastly food* | *I felt ghastly after drinking that wine.* | *ghastly news* | *the most ghastly crime* **2** very pale and ill-looking (used of a person)

gher·kin /ˈgɜːkɪn ‖ ˈgɜːr-/ n a small green vegetable usually eaten after being kept in VINEGAR

ghet·to /ˈgetəʊ/ n **ghettos** or **ghettoes** a part of a city in which a group of people of similar race or nationality live, usually because they are poor or not accepted as full citizens

ghetto blast·er /ˈ·· ˌ··/ n *infml* a large CASSETTE RECORDER that can be carried around

ghost /gəʊst/ n **1** the spirit of a dead person who appears again: *Do you believe in ghosts?* | *The ghost of Lady Margaret is said to haunt the castle.* **2 give up the ghost: a** *infml* to die **b** to stop working because something has gone wrong that cannot be repaired (used especially of machines) **3 the ghost of a** *infml* the slightest: *You haven't got the ghost of a chance of getting the job.*

ghost·ly /ˈgəʊstli/ adj having the unnatural and frightening qualities of a ghost: *I saw a ghostly light ahead of me in the darkness.*

ghost town /ˈ· ·/ n a town which is now empty because all the people have left

ghoul /guːl/ n **1** a spirit in stories which takes bodies from graves to eat them **2** a person who is unnaturally interested in death and dead bodies **–ghoulish** adj

GI /ˌdʒiː ˈaɪ/ n **GI's** or **GIs** a soldier in the US army, especially during World War Two

gi·ant¹ /ˈdʒaɪənt/ n **1** an extremely big strong man in fairy stories, who is often unfriendly or cruel **2** a large business organization: *The company he works for is one of the giants of the pharmaceutical industry.* **3** something which is a much larger size than usual

giant² adj [only before a noun] extremely large: *a giant cucumber* | *It's better value to get the giant-size packet.*

gib·ber·ish /ˈdʒɪbərɪʃ/ n [U] meaningless sounds, talk, or ideas

gib·bet /ˈdʒɪbɪt/ n the wooden post from which criminals were hanged

gib·bon /ˈgɪbən/ n an animal like a monkey with long arms and no tail

gibe /dʒaɪb/ n (also **jibe**) a remark which makes someone look foolish

gib·lets /ˈdʒɪbləts/ n [pl] the parts of a bird, such as the heart and LIVER, which are taken out before it is cooked

gid·dy /ˈgɪdi/ adj **giddier, giddiest 1** feeling as though everything is moving round you and that

you are going to fall: *I felt giddy just watching the children jumping up and down.* **2** [only before a noun] causing a feeling of unsteady movement or falling: *We looked down from a giddy height.* **–giddily** adv **–giddiness** n [U]

gift /gɪft/ n **1** something which you give or receive as a present: *a free gift* | *a gift shop* **2** a natural ability to do something: *He has a gift for music.* | *a gift for learning languages* **3** *infml* something very easy or very cheap: *That last exam question was a gift!* | *At that price it's a gift!*

gift·ed /ˈgɪftɪd/ adj **1** naturally very good at something: *a gifted painter* **2** unusually clever: *Their daughter is very gifted.*

gig /gɪg/ n *infml* a performance of popular music or JAZZ: *They're doing a gig in Glasgow next month.*

gi·gan·tic /dʒaɪˈgæntɪk/ adj unusually large in amount or size: *a gigantic appetite* | *a gigantic waste of money* **–gigantically** /-kli/ adv

gig·gle /ˈgɪgəl/ v **giggled, giggling** [I] to laugh in a silly childish way **–giggle** n

gild /gɪld/ v [T] to cover something with a thin coat of gold or gold paint

gill¹ /gɪl/ n an opening through which a fish breathes

gill² /dʒɪl/ n a unit for measuring liquids equal to ¼ PINT or 0·142 of a LITRE

gilt /gɪlt/ n [U] a thin covering of gold or gold paint: *All the paintings had elaborate gilt frames.*

gim·mick /ˈgɪmɪk/ n *infml* something unusual or clever, used to attract people: *The picture of the pretty girl on the cover of the book is just a sales gimmick.* **–gimmicky** adj

gin /dʒɪn/ n [C;U] a strong colourless alcoholic drink made from grain and certain berries

gin·ger¹ /ˈdʒɪndʒəʳ/ n [U] **1** a plant with a root which can be used in cooking to give a hot strong taste **2** an orange brown colour: *ginger hair* | *a ginger cat* –see picture on page 245

ginger² v

ginger sthg ↔ **up** phr v [T] to make something more exciting or active: *We need some more youngsters to ginger up the group.*

ginger ale /ˌ·· ˈ·/ n [U] a gassy non-alcoholic drink made with ginger and often mixed with other drinks

ginger beer /ˌ·· ˈ·/ n [U] a gassy non-alcoholic drink with a strong taste, made with ginger

gin·ger·ly /ˈdʒɪndʒəli ‖ -ər-/ adv carefully, slowly, and gently: *I reached out gingerly to touch the snake.*

ging·ham /ˈgɪŋəm/ n [U] white and coloured cotton cloth which has a pattern of small squares

gip·sy /ˈdʒɪpsi/ n **gipsies** (also **gypsy**) a member of a race of people who travel about in covered carts, and who earn money by telling the future, selling flowers, singing, etc.

gi·raffe /dʒəˈrɑːf ‖ -ˈræf/ n an African animal with a very long neck and legs, and yellow skin with brown spots

gir·der /ˈgɜːdəʳ ‖ ˈgɜːr-/ n a long strong thick piece of iron or steel, which supports a floor, roof, or part of a bridge

gir·dle /ˈgɜːdl ‖ ˈgɜːr-/ n a tight undergarment for women, worn to make them look thinner

girl /gɜːl ‖ gɜːrl/ n **1** a female child: *There are more girls than boys in this school.* **2** a daughter: *I've got two boys and a girl.* **3** a woman: *I'm going out with the girls from work.* | *We girls must stick together.* | *the girls in the office* **4** *old fash* girlfriend: *He's got a new girl.*

get¹ /get/ *v*

got /gɒt || gɑːt/ (also **gotten** /'gɒtn || 'gɑːtn/ *AmE*), **getting**

1 [T] to obtain something:
I must get a new car. | *Where did you get those shoes?* | *I must get a birthday present for my mother.* | *Shall I get you a drink?*
USEFUL PATTERNS to get something for someone; to get someone something
2 [T] to receive or have something:
Did you get my letter? | *I got loads of presents for my birthday.* | *I don't get much time for reading.* | *I can't remember when I first got the idea for the story.* | *I don't want her to get the wrong impression.*
3 [+ complement] to become:
The food's getting cold. | *She must have got lost.* | *The economic situation seems to be getting worse.* | *I started to get angry with him.*
4 [I; + adv/prep] to move somewhere or arrive somewhere:
She got onto the train. | *Hundreds of people were trying to get into the building.* | *We finally got to London at eleven o'clock.* | *I'll have to leave early in the morning, and I won't get back until late at night.* | *He was looking forward to getting home.*
5 [T; + adv/prep] to move something somewhere:
We couldn't get the table through the door.
6 [T] to cause something to happen or be done:
She couldn't get the car started. | *We must get this job finished.* | *I must get hair cut.* | *Why don't you get those shoes mended?*
7 [T] to suffer something unpleasant that happens to you:
She got her fingers caught in the door.
8 [+ complement] to be the person that something happens to:
He got run over by a car. | *She was hoping she might get promoted.* | *Let's hope that nobody gets killed.*
9 [T] to prepare a meal:
Dad's just getting the dinner.
10 [T] to catch an illness:
I think I'm getting flu. | *She got some rare tropical disease.*
11 [T] to go on a bus, train, or plane:
Shall we walk or get the bus? | *I got a taxi to the station.*
12 [T] to catch a person:
The police haven't managed to get the man who committed these murders.
13 [T] *infml* to understand something:
Nobody got the joke.
14 [T] *infml* to annoy you:
What gets me is the fact that he's so incompetent!
15 **get to do something** to succeed in doing something, or be allowed to do something:
I hope I'll get to know him better in time. | *I never got to see the original documents.*
16 **get someone to do something** to ask or tell someone to do something:
If I can't manage to move it on my own, I'll get Sam to help me.
17 **get doing something** to start doing something:
We'd better get walking if we want to make it by lunch time. | *Let's get going with the cleaning.*
18 **be getting somewhere** to be making progress:
I think we're finally getting somewhere with this project. | *I've spent a lot of time on this essay, but I don't seem to be getting anywhere.*
19 **it's getting to me** = it is making me tired or annoyed:
At first all the teasing was a joke, but now it's really getting to me.

get about *phr v*

[I]

1 to move or travel around:
I don't get about much these days.

2 (of news) to spread:
News of the affair soon got about.

get sthg ↔ **across** *phr v*

[T]

to explain something in a way that people can understand:
He's not very good at getting his ideas across to people.

get ahead *phr v*

[I]

to be successful in your job and so reach a high position:
She's clever and ambitious, and determined to get ahead.

get along *phr v*

[I]

1 to advance or make progress with a job that you are doing:
How are you getting along with the decorating?

2 to have a friendly relationship with someone:
I get along quite well with my family. | We don't get along very well.

3 I must be getting along = I must leave now

get around *phr v*

1 [I] to move or travel around:
I don't get around much these days.

2 [I] (of news) to spread:
News of the affair soon got around.

3 [T **get around** sthg] to avoid or manage to deal with a difficulty:
I'm sure we can get around this problem somehow.

get around to sthg *phr v*

[T]

to find the time to do something:
I finally got around to writing to her.

get at *phr v*

1 [T **get at** sthg] to manage to reach something:
Put the tools up on that shelf where the children can't get at them.

2 [T **get at** sbdy] to say unkind things to someone:
Stop getting at me!

3 what are getting at? = what do you mean?

get away *phr v*

[I]

to escape from a place or manage to leave it:
In the confusion one of the prisoners managed to get away. | I'm sorry I'm late. I was in a meeting and couldn't get away. | We're hoping to get away on holiday this year. | I didn't get away from the office until eight o'clock..

get away from sthg *phr v*

[T]

you can't get away from this fact = you must admit that this fact is true:
The government can't get away from the fact that the Health Service needs more money.

get away with sthg *phr v*
[T]
to do something bad and escape being punished for it:
He stole thousands of pounds from the company – and got away with it!

get back *phr v*
1 [I] to return, usually to your home:
I heard you were on holiday. When did you get back?
2 [I] to return to a state or a situation that you were in before:
Labour are hoping to get back into power at the next election. | *I hope that things will soon get back to normal.*
3 [I] to move away from something:
The police shouted to the crowd to get back.
4 [T **get** sthg ↔ **back**] to have or be given something that you used to have:
I lent Jane one of my records and I haven't got it back yet.
5 **get back to someone** to speak or write to someone later, especially in order to give them some information or tell them your decision about something:
I'll think about the offer and get back to you this afternoon.

get behind *phr v*
[I]
to fail to do your work on time:
I've got a bit behind with my work.

get by *phr v*
[I]
to manage to continue your way of life:
We don't have much money but we get by.

get down *phr v*
1 [T **get** sthg ↔ **down**] to manage to swallow something:
Try to get a bit of food down if you can.
2 [T **get** sthg ↔ **down**] to record something in writing:
It's no use just coming to an informal agreement – you've got to get it down in writing.
3 [T **get** sbdy ↔ **down**] to make you feel sad:
This dreadful weather's really getting me down.

get down to sthg *phr v*
[T]
to begin doing something seriously:
Right, let's get down to work.

get in *phr v*
1 [T] (of a bus, train, or plane) to arrive at a place:
The plane got in late.
2 [I] to arrive home:
What time did you get in last night?
3 [I] to be elected:
I hope the Conservatives don't get in again at the next election.
4 [T **get** sbdy ↔ **in**] to ask someone to come and help you do something in your home:
I'll have to get a plumber in to look at that tap.
5 [T **get** sthg ↔ **in**] to manage to say something during a discussion:
I couldn't get a single word in at the meeting.

get in on sthg *phr v*
[T]
to take part in something:
It sounds like a very interesting project; I'd like to get in on it.

get into *phr v*

1 [T **get into** sthg] to start doing something or experiencing something:
She wants to get into teaching. | *I don't want to get into trouble with the police.* | *We got into a conversation about gardening.*

2 [T **get** sbdy **into** sthg] to cause someone else to start doing something or experiencing something:
I hope I didn't make you late and get you into trouble.

3 **what has got into you?** = why are you behaving in such a strange way?:
He used to be very friendly, but I don't know what's got into him recently.

get off *phr v*

1 [I;T **get off** sthg] to climb down from something that you were on, such as a bus, train, bicycle, or horse:
The bus stopped and several people got off. | *I got off the train at Leeds.*

2 [I;T **get off** sthg] *infml* to leave work:
I should be able to get off by five o'clock. | *When do you get off work today?*

3 [T **get** sthg ↔ **off**] to remove a piece of clothing:
Give me time to get my coat off!

4 [I] to escape punishment for something bad that you have done:
The boys got off with just a warning.

5 [T **get** sbdy **off**] to help someone to escape punishment for something bad that they have done:
I had a good lawyer who managed to get me off with just a fine.

6 **get off!** a phrase you use when you are telling someone not to touch something

get off with sbdy *phr v*

[T]

to start a sexual relationship with someone:
She got off with him at Julie's party.

get on *phr v*

1 [I;T **get on** sthg] to climb onto something such as a bus, train, bicycle or horse:
The bus stopped and I got on. | *She got on the bus.*

2 [I] to have a friendly relationship with someone:
Do you get on well with your parents? | *We've always got on very well.*

3 [I] to continue doing something seriously:
We'll have a quick break for lunch, then we'll get on. | *I must get on with the cooking.*

4 [I] to succeed and reach a high position in your job:
You'll have to work harder than this if you want to get on.

5 [T **get** sthg **on**] to put on a piece of clothing:
Ask the children to get their shoes on.

6 **be getting on: a** to be getting quite old:
She's getting on a bit now – she must be nearly seventy.
b to be getting quite late:
Time's getting on, so we'd better hurry up.

get on for *phr v*

getting on for nearly a particular age, time, or amount:
She must be getting on for fifty now. | *It was getting on for lunch time.* | *There were getting on for two hundred people there.*

get onto *phr v*

1 [T **get onto** sbdy] to speak or write to someone:
I'll get onto our solicitor as soon as possible.

2 [T **get onto** sthg] to begin to talk about something:
I'll talk about the theory first, and then get onto the practical details.

3 [T **get onto** sthg] to climb onto something such as a bus, train, bicycle, or horse:
I got onto the train and sat down.

get out *phr v*
1 [T **get** sthg ↔ **out**] to take something from the container that it was in:
She opened her bag and got out a handkerchief.
2 [I;T **get** sbdy ↔ **out**] to leave a place or make someone else leave a place:
She told me to get out. | Hundreds of people are still stranded in the country, and we must get them out.
3 [T **get** sthg ↔ **out**] to produce something:
We've got to get that report out by next week.
4 [I] (of news) to become known:
This story mustn't get out.

get out of *phr v*
1 [T **get out of** sthg] to avoid doing something:
I'm supposed to be going to a meeting later, but I'm hoping to get out of it.
2 [T **get out of** sthg] to be able to leave something or stop doing something:
I hope we'll be able to get out of this mess. | You must get out of the habit of calling me "darling" at work.
3 [T **get** sthg **out of** sbdy] force someone to tell you something:
I couldn't get the man's name out of her.
4 **get a lot out of something** to learn a lot from something, or enjoy it a lot.
I got a lot out of the course.

get over *phr v*
1 [T **get over** sthg] to recover from something unpleasant such as an illness or a disappointment:
She still hasn't got over the shock of her mother's death.
2 **can't get over something** to find something very surprising:
I can't get over how rude he was to you.

get sthg **over with** *phr v*
[T]
to do something that is unpleasant because you want it to be done and finished:
I want to get the operation over with as soon as possible.

get round *phr v*
1 [T **get around** sthg] to avoid or manage to deal with a difficulty:
We should be able to get around this problem.
2 [T **get around** sbdy] to persuade someone to do what you want them to do:
My father doesn't want to let us go but I'm sure I can get round him.
3 [I] (of news) to spread:
News of the affair soon got around.

get round to sthg *phr v*
[T]
to find the time to do something:
I must get round to writing some letters.

get through *phr v*
1 [I] to reach someone by telephone:
I can't get through to my office.
2 **get through to someone** to make someone understand what you are saying:
Whatever I say, I can't seem to get through to him.
3 [T **get through** sthg] to do or finish something successfully:
Of course you'll get through the exam!
4 [T **get** sbdy **through** sthg] to help someone to do or finish something successfully:
good friends who got me through a difficult time
5 [T **get through** sthg] to use a large amount of something:
We got through loads of money on holiday.

get together *phr v*
[I] to meet with people in order to discuss something for a social event:
Let's get together for a drink one evening. | *I got together* **with** *a few friends to plan the trip.*

get up *phr v*
1 [I] to rise from a sitting or lying position, especially to rise from your bed after sleeping:
What time do you usually get up in the morning? | *He got up from his chair and walked to the window.*
2 [T **get** sbdy **up**] to make someone rise from their bed:
Can you go and get the children up?
3 [I] (of the wind) to become stronger

get up to sthg *phr v*
1 to reach a particular place in a story or a piece of writing:
Have you got up to chapter five yet?
2 to do something bad:
She'd be furious if she knew what her children got up to.

■ USAGE Although the word **girl** is sometimes used to refer to an adult woman, some people find this offensive, especially if the speaker is a man.

girl·friend /ˈgɜːlfrend ‖ ˈgɜːrl-/ *n* **1** a special female friend of a boy or man: *He seems to have a new girlfriend every week.* **2** a woman's female friend: *She's going out with some girlfriends tonight.*

girl guide /ˌ· ˈ·/ *n* (also **girl scout** /ˈ· ·/ *AmE*) a member of an association for girls, the **Girl Guides**, who take part in activities like camping, and learn to be practical and helpful —compare SCOUT[1] (2)

girl·hood /ˈgɜːlhʊd ‖ ˈgɜːrl-/ *n* [C;U] the state or time of being a young girl

girl·ish /ˈgɜːlɪʃ ‖ ˈgɜːr-/ *adj* like a young girl: *sounds of girlish laughter* –**girlishly** *adv* –**girlishness** *n* [U]

gi·ro /ˈdʒaɪərəʊ/ *n* [U] a system of banking run by a bank or post office, where payments can be made from one account to another: *I'll pay by giro.*

girth /gɜːθ ‖ gɜːrθ/ *n fml* **1** [C;U] the distance around something round: *the girth of a tree* **2** [C] a long piece of leather which is fastened tightly round a horse to keep the SADDLE on

gist /dʒɪst/ *n* **the gist** the main points or general meaning: *I didn't understand everything, but I got the gist.*

give[1] /gɪv/ *v* **gave** /geɪv/, **given** /ˈgɪvən/, **giving** **1** [T] to hand or pass something to someone, either for them to look at or use, or as a present: *He picked up the book and gave it to me.* | *She gave me a gold bracelet for my birthday.*
□ USEFUL PATTERNS to give something to someone; to give someone something
2 [T] to allow or cause someone to have something: *Give me a chance to try the job.* | *This is a great*

opportunity that has been given to me. | *The news gave us a terrible shock.* | *That child has given us a lot of trouble.* | *The noise gave me a headache.* | *Give me a few more days, and I'll get the work finished.* | *Can you give me some more information?* | *Don't forget to give the message to John.* | *Let me give you a piece of advice.*
□ USEFUL PATTERNS to give someone something; to give something to someone

3 [T] to perform an action: *She gave a sudden cry of delight.* | *She gave the child a smack.* | *He gave me a long disapproving look.* | *He gave the door a push.* | *They gave an excellent performance.* | *He's giving us a talk about bee-keeping.* | *She's giving a lecture to first-year students this evening.*
□ USEFUL PATTERNS to give something; to give someone something; to give something to someone

4 [I] to bend, stretch, or break under the weight or pressure of something: *The branch he was sitting on began to give.* | *The leather will give a little bit as you wear the shoes.* **5 give something some thought, give something your attention** to think about something or pay attention to it: *I'd like to give the matter a bit more thought.* | *I haven't been able to give my attention to the problem yet.* **6 give a party** to have a party: *We're giving a big party on Saturday – would you like to come?* **7 be given to understand/believe** to think that something is true because someone has told you that it is true: *I was given to understand that the job would involve a lot of travelling.* **8 give or take a certain amount** perhaps a certain amount more or less than the amount you have mentioned: *The test takes an hour, give or take a few minutes.* | *She must be sixty, give or take a few years.* **9 I give you that, I'll give you that** = I admit what you say: *The hotel's* *not cheap, I give you that, but it's really good.* **10 give way: a** to yield in an argument: *In the end my mother gave way and said that I could go to the concert.* | *He refused to give way and admit that he was wrong.* **b** to break: *The floor gave way under the weight.* **c** to allow other vehicles to go before you when you are driving: *You have to give way to traffic coming from the left.* **d** to become less important or less useful than something else: *Steam trains gave way to electric ones.* **e** to allow yourself to show a feeling: *He gave way to his grief.*

give away *phr v* **1** [T **give** sthg ↔ **away**] to give something to someone as a present, usually because you do not want it any more: *I've given away most of the children's toys, now that they've grown up.* **2** [T **give** sbdy ↔ **away**] to hand a woman to her husband at a wedding: *She was given away by her father.* **3** [T **give** sthg ↔ **away**] to make known something that was secret: *They were determined not to give their names away.* **4 give the game away** to make known something that was secret: *It was the fact that you laughed that gave the game away.*

give sthg ↔ **back** *phr v* [T] to return something to its owner: *I'll give you your book back next week.* | *Give me my pen back.* | *I gave the records back to Julie.*

☐ USEFUL PATTERNS to give something back to someone; to give someone something back; to give someone back something

give in *phr v* **1** [I] to yield in an argument or fight: *We will not give in to threats or intimidation.* **2** [T **give** sthg ↔ **in**] to hand something in to someone who has authority: *Give your examination papers in to the teacher at the front of the class.*

give sthg ↔ **off** *phr v* [T] to send out a liquid, gas, or smell: *The dustbin was giving off a horrible smell.*

give out *phr v* **1** [T **give** sthg ↔ **out**] to give something to each of several people: *She gave the books out to the children.* **2** [I] to no longer work properly: *The power's given out.* | *His strength gave out.*

give over *phr v* [I;T **give over** doing sthg] *infml* to stop doing something: *Will you give over nagging me!*

give up *phr v* **1** [T **give up** sthg] to stop having something or doing something: *I'm trying to give up smoking.* | *I gave up that idea a long time ago.* | *They refused to give up hope.* | *He'll probably have to give up his job.* **2** [T **give** sthg ↔ **up**] to allow someone else to have or use something: *Very few people will give their seat up to an elderly person.* **3** [I] to admit that you cannot do something and so stop trying to do it: *She was determined to finish the task, and refused to give up.* **4** [T **give** sbdy **up**] to tell the police where someone is: *His brother gave him up to the police.* **5 give someone up for dead** to start believing that someone is dead: *The search has been abandoned and the children have been given up for dead.*

give² *n* [U] the quality that something has of moving, bending, or stretching: *Make sure that the shoes have enough give to allow your feet to move about comfortably.*

give-and-take /ˌ··'·/ *n* [U] willingness of people involved in an argument to listen to each other and accept some of the other person's wishes: *We can only settle this argument if there is a bit of give-and-take on both sides.*

give-a-way /'gɪvəweɪ/ *n* [sing] a remark, look, or object that tells people what was being hidden from them: *She tried to hide her feelings, but the tears in*

her eyes were a give-away. | *The packet of cigarettes on the table was a dead give-away.*

giv-en¹ /'gɪvən/ the past participle of GIVE

given² *adj* **1** [only before a noun] decided on and stated: *The work must be done within the given time.* **2** particular: *The problems of any given society are unique.* **3 be given to** to be in the habit of: *He's given to heavy drinking.*

given³ *prep* if you consider: *Given that they're inexperienced, they've done a good job.*

given name /'··· ·/ *n* the usual American word for FIRST NAME

giz-zard /'gɪzəd ‖ -əd/ *n* the second stomach of a bird

gla-cial /'gleɪʃəl/ *adj* **1** of ice or glaciers: *glacial deposits* **2** relating to an ICE AGE **3** very unfriendly: *He gave me a glacial smile.*

gla-ci-er /'glæsɪəʳ ‖ 'gleɪʃər/ *n* a mass of ice which moves very slowly down a mountain valley

glad /glæd/ *adj* **gladder, gladdest** **1** [never before a noun] pleased and happy: *I'm glad he's got the job.* | *I'm glad about her promotion.* | *We were so glad to hear that your daughter's recovering from her illness.* **2 glad of** grateful for: *I'd be glad of some help with the luggage.* **3 be glad to do something** to be very willing to do something **4** [only before a noun] *old fash* bringing happiness: *Have you heard the glad tidings?* –**gladness** *n* [U]

glad-den /'glædn/ *v* [T] to make someone happy: *The sight of his son running about after his long illness gladdened his father's heart.*

glade /gleɪd/ *n lit* an open space without trees in a wood or forest

glad-i-a-tor /'glædieɪtəʳ/ *n* an armed man who fought against men or wild animals in a public place to entertain people

glad-ly /'glædli/ *adv* very willingly or eagerly: *I'll gladly come and help you.*

glam-o-rize /'glæm*əraɪz/ *v* **glamorized, glamorizing** (*also* **glamorise** *BrE*) [T] to make something appear more attractive than it really is

glam-o-rous /'glæmərəs/ *adj* (*also* **glamourous**) having glamour: *a glamorous job* | *a glamorous girl* –**glamorously** *adv*

glam-our /'glæmər/ *n* (**glamor** *AmE*) [U] a special quality of charm, beauty, and excitement, *the glamour of foreign countries* | *the glamour of a job in pop music*

glance¹ /glɑːns ‖ glæns/ *v* **glanced, glancing** [I; + adv/prep] to look for a very short time: *He glanced at his watch.* | *I glanced round the room before I left.* | *She glanced down the list of names.*

glance off *phr v* [I;T **glance off** sthg] to hit lightly and move quickly off at an angle: *The ball glanced off his racket into the corner.*

■ USAGE Compare **glance** and **glimpse**. The verb **glance** means "to look at something quickly": *As he spoke he glanced at his watch.* **Glimpse** (or more commonly **catch a glimpse of**) means "to see by chance just for a moment": *I glimpsed /caught a glimpse of his face as he disappeared round the corner.*

glance² *n* **1** a quick short look: *One glance at his face told me he was ill.* | *She cast a quick glance at her notes and began to speak.* | *At first glance the essay looked quite good, but actually it was full of mistakes.* **2 at a glance** at once: *She saw at a glance that he'd been crying.*

glanc-ing /'glɑːnsɪŋ ‖ 'glæn-/ *adj* [only before a noun] **glancing blow** a hit which slips to one side: *He caught me with a glancing blow on the chin.*

gland /glænd/ n an organ of your body which produces a liquid substance, either to be passed out of your body or into your blood: *a sweat gland* –**glandular** /ˈglændjʊləʳ/ ‖ -dʒə-/ *adj* : *glandular fever*

glare[1] /gleəʳ/ v **glared, glaring** [I] **1** to look at someone in an angry way: *They didn't fight, but stood there glaring at one another*. **2** to shine with a strong light, usually in a way that hurts your eyes: *The sun glared down on them out of a cloudless sky*. | *The headlights glared through the darkness*.

glare[2] n **1** an angry unfriendly look: *I started to offer help, but he gave me a fierce glare so I stopped.* **2 the glare** a hard unpleasant effect given by a strong light: *She put on her dark glasses to reduce the glare of the sun.* **3 the glare of publicity** continuous attention from newspapers and television

glar·ing /ˈgleərɪŋ/ *adj* **1** too bright: *glaring stage lights* | *a glaring red* **2** very noticeable (used of something bad): *The report is full of glaring errors.* | *a glaring omission* –**glaringly** *adv*

glass /glɑːs ‖ glæs/ n **1** [U] a hard easily-broken substance that lets light through and is used for windows and bottles: *We'll have to get a new pane of glass for the window.* | *I've cut my hand on some broken glass.* **2** [U] (also **glassware**) a collection of objects made of this: *She collects china and glass.* **3** [C] a small glass container with no handle which you drink from: *a whisky glass* | *He asked the waiter for a clean glass.* –see picture on page 148 **4** [C] the drink in a glass container: *I'd like a glass of wine, please.* | *Have one more glass before you go.* **5 the glass** *BrE* the measurement shown on a BAROMETER, an apparatus with a pointer which moves downwards when bad weather is coming: *The glass is falling; it's going to rain.* **6 glasses** [pl] two pieces of specially cut glass in a frame worn in front of your eyes to help you to see better: *I have to wear glasses for reading.* | *I need a new pair of glasses.* | *That man in the dark glasses is a film star.* –see picture on page 245

glass fi·bre /ˌ· ˈ·· ◂/ n (also **fibre glass**) [U] a substance made from very thin pieces of glass, used to keep out the cold or for making things like boats

glass·house /ˈglɑːshaʊs ‖ ˈglæs-/ n *BrE* a glass building used for growing plants in

glass·ware /ˈglɑːsweəʳ ‖ ˈglæs-/ n (also **glass**) [U] glass objects such as dishes and drinking glasses

glass·y /ˈglɑːsi ‖ ˈglæsi/ *adj* **glassier, glassiest** **1** smooth and shining, like glass **2** with no expression or sign of life in the eyes: *a glassy stare*

glaze[1] /gleɪz/ v **glazed, glazing** [T] **1** to fit glass into a frame: *a glazed door* **2** to put a shiny surface on pots and bricks **3** to put a little beaten egg or milk onto food to make it shine

glaze over *phr* v [I] (of eyes) to become dull and lifeless: *His eyes glazed over and he fell back unconscious.*

glaze[2] n a shiny surface on pots and food

gla·zi·er /ˈgleɪziəʳ ‖ -ʒər/ n someone whose job it is to fit glass into window frames

gleam[1] /gliːm/ n **1** a small amount of gentle light: *The gleam of the camp fire was a welcome sight.* **2** an expression on someone's face which you see only for a short time: *a gleam of interest* | *a gleam of hope*

gleam[2] v [I] **1** to shine: *The river gleamed softly in the moonlight.* | *I polished the furniture until it gleamed.* **2** to show an expression or feeling: *Her eyes gleamed with excitement.*

glean /gliːn/ v [T] *fml* to get information in small amounts and with difficulty: *She wasn't giving much away, but I managed to glean a few interesting facts.*

glee /gliː/ n [U] joy and delight: *The children laughed with glee.* –**gleeful** *adj* –**gleefully** *adv*

glen /glen/ n a narrow mountain valley in Scotland

glib /glɪb/ *adj* **glibber, glibbest** **1** good at speaking quickly so that you persuade other people, whether speaking the truth or not: *a glib salesman* **2** spoken too easily to be true: *He's always ready with a glib excuse.* –**glibly** *adv*

glide /glaɪd/ v **glided, gliding** [I + adv/prep] **1** to move forward noiselessly in a smooth, effortless way: *The boat glided over the river.* | *The dancers glided across the floor.* **2** to fly smoothly following air currents –**glide** n

glid·er /ˈglaɪdəʳ/ n a plane without an engine

glid·ing /ˈglaɪdɪŋ/ n [U] the sport of flying gliders –**gliding** v [only in progressive forms] : *Have you ever been gliding?*

glim·mer[1] /ˈglɪməʳ/ v [I] to give a very faint unsteady light: *The lights glimmered in the valley below.*

glimmer[2] n **1** a faint unsteady light **2** a small uncertain sign: *a glimmer of hope*

glimpse[1] /glɪmps/ v **glimpsed, glimpsing** [T] to get a quick incomplete look at something or someone: *I just glimpsed her in the crowd and then she was gone.*

glimpse[2] n a quick look at or incomplete view of something: *I only caught a fleeting glimpse of the thief, so I can't describe him very well, I'm afraid.* –see GLANCE (USAGE)

glint[1] /glɪnt/ v [I] **1** to give out small flashes of light, like those from a metal surface: *The car park was full of shiny new cars glinting in the sun.* **2** (of eyes) to show a particular feeling: *His bright blue eyes glinted with fury.*

glint[2] n **1** a flash of light, like that from a hard shiny surface: *I could see the glint of coins in her hand.* **2** a feeling clearly seen in someone's eyes: *There was a wicked glint in his eye.*

glis·ten /ˈglɪsən/ v [I] to shine with a lot of very small flashes as if from a wet surface: *Her eyes were glistening with tears.* | *The grass glistened with dew in the early morning sun.*

glit·ter[1] /ˈglɪtəʳ/ v [I] to shine brightly with flashes of light: *Her diamond earrings glittered in the candlelight.*

glitter[2] n **1** [sing] a bright light, which seems to flash: *the glitter of the sun on the waves* **2** [U] attractiveness and excitement: *Beneath all the glitter, the fashion industry is a tough place to work in.*

glit·ter·ing /ˈglɪtərɪŋ/ *adj* [only before a noun] **1** splendid or excellent: *a glittering performance* | *a glittering career* **2** shining: *a glittering diamond*

gloat /gləʊt/ v [I] to be extremely pleased with your own success or someone else's bad luck: *He gloated over the failure of his competitors.* –**gloatingly** *adv*

glo·bal /ˈgləʊbəl/ *adj* **1** of or concerning the whole world: *global warming* | *events of global importance* **2** taking account of all possible considerations: *The report takes a global view of the company's problems.* –**globally** *adv*

globe /gləʊb/ n **1** the Earth: *She has travelled all over the globe.* **2** an object in the shape of a round ball **3** a round object with a map of the world on it which can be turned around on its base

globe·trot·ter /ˈgləʊbtrɒtəʳ ‖ -trɑː-/ n someone who travels to a lot of different countries

glob·u·lar /ˈglɒbjələʳ ‖ ˈglɑːb-/ adj round like a ball

glob·ule /ˈglɒbjuːl ‖ ˈglɑː-/ n a small drop of a liquid or something that has melted: *Wax fell from the candle in small globules.*

gloom /gluːm/ n 1 a feeling of deep sadness or hopelessness: *The Stock Market crash filled them all with gloom.* | *She goes around spreading gloom and doom wherever she goes.* 2 darkness that is not quite complete: *We peered through the gloom, trying to see the road ahead.*

gloom·y /ˈgluːmi/ adj gloomier, gloomiest 1 rather dark and unpleasant: *a gloomy day* | *a gloomy house* 2 having or giving little hope or cheerfulness: *Our future seems gloomy.* | *Cheer up – there's no need to look so gloomy.* **–gloomily** adv

glo·ri·fy /ˈglɔːrɪfaɪ/ v glorified, glorifying [T] 1 to give glory or fame to something 2 to make something appear more important than it really is: *She was glorified in the press for her work with the poor.* **–glorification** /ˌglɔːrɪfɪˈkeɪʃən/ n [U]

glo·ri·ous /ˈglɔːriəs/ adj 1 having, or deserving, great fame and honour: *a glorious victory* 2 beautiful and splendid: *glorious colours* | *a glorious day* 3 infml very enjoyable: *We had a glorious time at the beach.* **–gloriously** adv

glo·ry¹ /ˈglɔːri/ n glories 1 [U] great fame, honour, and admiration: *The soldiers died bravely on the battlefield, earning themselves everlasting glory.* 2 [U] beautiful and splendid appearance: *The bright moonlight lit up the castle in all its glory.* 3 the glory of, the glories of the thing or things that are especially beautiful or give cause for pride: *Receiving a knighthood from the Queen was the crowning glory of his career.* | *the glories of Paris* 4 [U] fml praise, honour, and thanks: *Glory be to God!*

glory² v gloried, glorying
glory in sthg phr v [T] to enjoy something very much: *They gloried in their new freedom.*

gloss¹ /glɒs ‖ glɔːs, glɑːs/ n 1 [sing; U] a bright shine on a smooth surface: *gloss paint* | *the gloss on her hair* 2 [sing; U] a pleasant appearance which hides the truth: *What is there beneath the gloss?* 3 [C] an explanation of a written word or idea

gloss² v [T] to provide an explanation of a difficult word or idea: *Textbooks sometimes gloss difficult expressions.*
gloss over sthg phr v [T] to write or talk of something favourably or quickly to hide its faults: *The company has tried to gloss over its recent losses in its annual report.*

glos·sa·ry /ˈglɒsəri ‖ ˈglɔː-, ˈglɑː-/ n glossaries a list of explanations of words, especially unusual ones, at the end of a book

gloss·y /ˈglɒsi ‖ ˈglɔːsi, ˈglɑːsi/ adj glossier, glossiest 1 bright and smooth: *Our cat has glossy black fur.* 2 glossy magazine a magazine printed on good quality shiny paper with coloured pictures

glove /glʌv/ n a piece of clothing worn on your hand, with separate parts for the thumb and each finger –see picture on page 50

glove compartment /ˈ· ·ˌ··/ n (also **glove box** /ˈ· ˌ·/ AmE) a hollow area in front of the passenger seat of a car, used for storing small objects –see picture on page 49

glow¹ /gləʊ/ v [I] 1 to shine with a dull steady light: *The blacksmith heated the iron bar till it glowed.* | *Their cigarettes glowed in the darkness.* 2 to look warm or red in the face, because of hard work or strong feelings: *She was glowing with embarrassment.* | *Her cheeks glowed.* 3 to look bright and colourful: *The hills glowed in the evening sunlight.*

glow² n [sing] 1 a soft warm light: *There was a dull red glow in the night sky showing us where the city lay.* 2 a red colour on someone's face after exercise or because of good health: *the rosy glow of health* 3 a strong good feeling: *a glow of satisfaction* | *I felt a glow of happiness at the news.*

glow·er /ˈglaʊəʳ/ v [I] to look at someone with an angry expression: *He just glowered at me and went on eating.*

glow·ing /ˈgləʊɪŋ/ adj very favourable: *We have always received glowing reports from his teachers.*

glow-worm /ˈ· ·/ n an insect which gives out a greenish light from the end of its tail

glu·cose /ˈgluːkəʊs, -kəʊz/ n [U] a natural form of sugar found in fruit

glue¹ /gluː/ n [U] a sticky substance used for joining things together **–gluey** adj

glue² v glued, gluing or glueing [T] 1 to join things together with glue: *She glued the two pieces together.* 2 glued to something watching something with such interest and attention that you are unwilling to stop: *He sat glued to the television all afternoon.*

glue-snif·fing /ˈ· ˌ··/ n [U] the harmful breathing in of fumes (FUME) of glue to produce a state of changed consciousness

glum /glʌm/ adj -mm- sad: *Why are you looking so glum?* **–glumly** adv

glut /glʌt/ n [sing] a larger supply than is necessary: *a glut of eggs on the market*

glu·ti·nous /ˈgluːtɪnəs/ adj sticky: *a bowl of glutinous rice*

glut·ton /ˈglʌtn/ n 1 a person who frequently eats too much 2 a glutton for punishment infml a person who is always ready to do or accept more of something hard or unpleasant

glut·ton·y /ˈglʌtəni/ n [U] the habit of eating too much **–gluttonous** adj

gly·ce·rine /ˈglɪsərɪn/ n (also **glycerin** AmE) [U] a sticky colourless liquid used in making soap, medicines, and explosives

gm n an abbreviation for GRAMS

GMT /ˌdʒiː em ˈtiː/ n [U] an abbreviation for Greenwich Mean Time

gnarled /nɑːld ‖ nɑːrld/ adj rough and twisted, with hard lumps, especially as a result of old age or hard work: *a gnarled tree trunk* | *the old man's gnarled hands*

gnash /næʃ/ v [T] gnash your teeth to make a noise with your teeth by biting hard, especially because you are angry or in pain

gnat /næt/ n a small flying insect that bites

gnaw /nɔː/ v 1 [I;T] to keep biting on something, often until you make a hole: *The bones are for the dog to gnaw on.* | *Rats have gnawed their way through the wall.* 2 gnaw (away) at someone to worry someone over a period of time

gnaw·ing /ˈnɔːɪŋ/ adj [only before a noun] worrying you over a period of time: *gnawing hunger*

gnome /nəʊm/ n 1 a little old man in children's stories who lives under the ground and often guards stores of gold 2 a decorative figure of one of these: *a garden gnome*

go¹ /gəʊ/ v went /went/, gone /gɒn ‖ gɔːn/, going 1 [I + adv/prep] to move towards a place, usually away from the place where the speaker is: *We went to France for our holidays.* | *She went into the kitchen.* | *We went by bus.* | *This car's going too fast.* | *His hand went to his pocket.* 2 [I] to leave a place:

It's late; I must be going. | *The train goes in 15 minutes.* **3** [I] to travel somewhere in order to do something: *They've gone shopping.* | *Let's go fishing.* | *He had gone to buy a newspaper.* | *She's gone for a walk.* **4** [I + adv/prep] to reach as far as a particular place, or lead to a particular place: *Does this road go to the station?* | *The valley goes from east to west.* | *Some trees have roots that go very deep.* | *Where does this path go?* **5** [I + adv/prep] to be placed somewhere, or fit there: *"Where do the knives go?" "In this drawer."* | *The bottles won't all go in the box.* **6** [+complement] to become: *Her hair's going grey.* | *She went red in the face and ran out of the room.* | *He's gone blind.* | *I think I'm going mad.* –see BECOME (USAGE) **7** [+complement] to be or remain in a particular state: *When the crops fail, the people go hungry.* | *Her complaints went unnoticed.* | *The murderer went unpunished.* **8** [I] (of a machine) to work properly: *The car won't go.* | *The clock's stopped and I can't get it to go again.* **9** [I] to be sold: *In the end, the painting went for £2000.* **10** [I] to become weakened and not work properly any more: *I had a bad cold and my voice went.* | *These shoes are very old and the soles are going.* | *Her sight is going.* **11** [T] to make a particular sound or have particular words: *Ducks go "quack".* | *How does that song go?* **12** [I] to look or taste nice together: *Those colours don't go together very well.* | *Do you think this hat will go with my red dress?* | *Does red wine go with chicken?* **13 be going to** a phrase you use to say that something will happen in the future: *I think it's going to rain.* | *She's going to have a baby.* | *I'm going to apply for a new job.* | *I'm not going to let her bully me!* **14 get going** to start doing something: *Come on, let's get going.* **15 keep going** to keep doing something although it is difficult: *I was determined to keep going and finish the race.* **16 be gone** to have left or disappeared: *When I turned round she was gone.* | *Those days are gone now.* **17 go and** to go somewhere in order to do something: *Go and see if there's anyone at the door.* **18 go to someone** to be given to someone: *The first prize went to the team from Manchester.* | *The job went to a local woman.* **19 go well** to be successful: *Business is going very well at the moment.* | *My talk went very well.* [RELATED PHRASE **go badly**] **20 to go** remaining: *There are just three weeks to go until Christmas.*

go about *phr v* **1** [I] to spend a lot of time with someone, often going to a lot of different places with them: *She goes about with a group of school friends.* **2** [I] (of a disease) to spread: *Chicken pox seems to be going about at the moment.* **3 go about doing something** to begin working at something: *I'm not quite sure how to go about mending a clock.*

go after sthg *phr v* [T] to try to get something: *He's gone after a job in the civil service.*

go against *phr v* **1** [T **go against** sthg] to be in opposition to something, or do something that is in opposition to something: *I couldn't work for that company – it would go against all my principles.* | *She went against her mother's wishes and became a dancer.* **2** [T **go against** sbdy] to be unfavourable to someone: *Public opinion is going against us.* | *The case may go against you.*

go ahead *phr v* [I] **1** to do something that you had planned to do: *We decided to go ahead with our building plans.* **2** to take place as planned: *We all hope that the carnival will go ahead.*

go along with sbdy/sthg *phr v* [T] to agree with someone or something: *They were quite happy to go along with our suggestion.* | *I'll go along with you.*

go around *phr v* **1** [I;T **go around** sthg] to spread or be told to a lot of people: *There are a lot of colds going around at the moment.* | *There's a really funny joke going around the office.* **2** [I] to spend a lot of time with someone, often going to a lot of different places with them: *Why do you go around with such strange people?* | *Those two always go around together.* **3** [I] to be enough for everyone: *Are there enough chairs to go around?*

go back *phr v* [I] **1** to return: *I left Scotland fifty years ago and I don't think I'll ever go back.* | *I'd like to go back to what the chairman said earlier.* **2 go back to something** to start doing something again: *She went back to her work.* | *He went back to cleaning the window.* **3** to reach backwards in time: *My family goes back to the 18th century.*

go back on sthg *phr v* [T] to fail to keep a promise or an agreement: *I won't go back on my promise.*

go by *phr v* **1** [I] to move past someone or something: *A car went by.* **2** [I] (of time) to pass: *Two years went by before he got another letter from her.* **3** [T **go by** sthg] to act or make a judgement according to a particular thing: *He always goes by the rules.* | *You can't go by what he says.*

go down *phr v* [T] **1** to decrease: *The standard of work has gone down.* | *Inflation seems to be going down.* **2** to become less swollen: *That tyre's going down.* **3 a ship/boat goes down** = a ship or boat sinks: *Three boats went down in the Channel last night.* **4 the sun goes down** = the sun disappears from the sky at the end of the day **5 go down well** to be accepted: *His speech went down very well.* [RELATED PHRASE **go down badly**] **6 go down in history** to be recorded as being very important: *This day will go down in history.*

go down with sthg *phr v* [T] to catch an illness: *He's gone down with flu.*

go for *phr v* **1** [T **go for** sbdy] to attack someone: *She went for him with a knife.* **2** [T **go for** sthg] to try to get something: *I've decided to go for the job at the BBC.* **3** [T **go for** sbdy/sthg] to like or be attracted to someone or something: *I don't really go for modern music.* | *I don't go for men like him.* **4** [T **go for** sthg] to choose something: *She always tends to go for brightly-coloured clothes.* **5** [T **go for** sbdy/sthg] to be true for a particular person or thing as well as for other people or things: *I think this report is very badly done, and that goes for all the other work done in this office.*

go in for sthg *phr v* [T] **1** to take part in something: *I didn't go in for the crossword competition this year.* **2** to make a habit of doing something: *I don't go in for sport very much.* | *I've never really gone in for dancing.*

go into sthg *phr v* [T] **1** to start doing something as your job: *She decided to go into politics.* | *I'd like to go into journalism.* **2** to examine or describe something in detail: *I don't want to go into all the details of this case.* | *The book goes into all the complexities of English grammar.*

go off *phr v* **1** [I] to explode: *A bomb went off in central London this morning.* **2** [I] to ring or sound loudly: *The fire alarm went off.* **3** [I] (of food) to go bad: *The milk's gone off.* **4** [I] to stop operating: *The heating goes off at night.* **5** [T **go off** sbdy/sthg] to stop liking someone or something: *I've gone off coffee.* | *I've gone off the idea of sharing a house with friends.* **6 go off well** (of an event) to be successful: *The conference went off very well.* [RELATED PHRASE **go off badly**]

go off with sthg *phr v* [T] to take away something that belongs to someone else: *Someone's gone off with my pen.*

go on phr v **1** [I] to take place or happen: *What's going on here?* | *There was a party going on next door.* **2 go on with something, go on doing something** to continue doing something: *He went on talking even though no one was listening.* | *She went on with her work.* **3 go on to do something** to do something later: *She did her degree and went on to become a university lecturer.* **4** [I] (of time) to pass: *As the day went on, it became hotter.* **5** [I] to come into operation and start working: *The lights went on at six o'clock.* **6** [I] to keep talking or complaining about the same thing: *He keeps going on about his diet.* | *She's been going on at me all morning!* **7** [T **go on** sthg] to use a piece of information in order to understand something or prove something: *As yet, the police have very little to go on.* **8 Go on!** a phrase you use when you want to encourage someone to do something: *Go on, try it.* **9 to be going on with, to go on with** for the moment: *Here's £10. That should be enough to be going on with.*

go out phr v [I] **1** to leave a house or other building: *She's gone out for a walk.* | *We don't go out very much in the evenings.* **2** to spend time regularly with someone of the opposite sex: *Are you still going out with Graham?* | *They've been going out together for years.* **3** (of a fire) to stop burning: *The fire's gone out again.* **4** (of a light) to stop shining: *Suddenly the kitchen light went out.* **5** to be no longer fashionable or popular: *Clogs went out years ago!*

go over sthg phr v [T] **1** to look at something or examine it in detail: *I need to go over the accounts again to see if they're accurate.* **2** to explain something in detail: *I'll go over this point again later.*

go over to sthg phr v [T] to change your mind and join a new religion or political party: *She went over to the Republicans after their election victory.*

go round phr v **1** [I;T **go round** sthg] to spread or be told to a lot of people: *There are a lot of colds going round at the moment.* | *There's a really funny joke going round the office.* **2** [I] to spend a lot of time with someone, often going to a lot of different places with them: *Who does she usually go round with?* | *Those two always go round together.* **3** [I] to be enough for everyone: *There wasn't enough wine to go round.*

go through phr v **1** [T **go through** sthg] to suffer or experience something unpleasant: *I couldn't go through another experience like that.* | *Let's hope we never have to go through another war.* **2** [I;T **go through** sthg] to be accepted and approved: *The government proposed a change to the tax law, but it never went through.* | *The Bill has now gone through Parliament.* **3** [T **go through** sthg] to read, look at, or explain something carefully: *I went through the article again.* | *I went through the whole house looking for my purse.* | *Could you go through that last point again?*

go through with sthg phr v [T] to complete something that you had planned or agreed to do: *At the last minute she realized that she couldn't go through with the murder.*

go towards sthg phr v [T] to help with the cost of something: *This money will go towards a deposit for a house.*

go under phr v [I] **1** (of a ship or boat) to sink **2** (of a business) to fail: *The firm finally went under last year.*

go up phr v [I] **1** to increase: *Prices have gone up sharply this year.* **2** to be built: *A lot of new houses are going up round here.* **3 go up in flames** to burn: *The whole house went up in flames.*

go with sthg phr v [T] to be found or given with something: *the responsibilities that go with owning your own home* | *There are quite a lot of perks that go with the job.*

go without phr v **1** [I;T **go without** sthg] to manage without something: *We had to go without a lot of things when I was a child.* | *If there's no coffee, you'll just have to go without.* **2 it goes without saying** = it is clear, without needing to be stated: *It goes without saying that water is critical to our survival.*

go² n goes infml **1** [U] the quality of being full of life and very active: *The children are full of go.* **2** [C] an attempt to do something: *I'd like to have a go at mending the roof myself.* | *He's had three goes at his driving test now.* **3 your go** your turn in a game: *It's my go now!* **4 on the go** busy all the time: *Those children are always on the go!*

goad /gəʊd/ v [T] to annoy or encourage someone continually, causing them to do something: *The journalists goaded him until he lost his temper completely.* | *She was goaded into action by the fear of losing her job.*

go-a·head¹ /ˈ· ·ˌ·/ n **the go-ahead** permission to act: *We can't start building until we get the go-ahead from the council.*

go-ahead² adj [only before a noun] active in using new methods for better results (used especially of people and companies)

goal /gəʊl/ n **1** the space, usually between two posts, where you must put the ball in games such as football in order to win a point: *Jones will be in goal for tomorrow's match.* **2** the point which you win when you do this: *We won by three goals to one.* | *He scored two goals in the first half of the game.* **3 an own goal** a point which you give to the other team when you accidentally put the ball into your own goal **4** your aim or purpose: *Set yourself new goals, and try to achieve them!*

goal·keep·er /ˈgəʊlˌkiːpəʳ/ n (also **goalie** /ˈgəʊli/ infml) the player who is responsible for stopping the ball before it goes into the goal, in games such as football

goat /gəʊt/ n an animal with a beard and horns which gives milk and a rough wool

gob·ble /ˈgɒbəl/ ‖ /ˈgɑː-/ v **gobbled, gobbling 1** [I;T] to eat very quickly, and sometimes noisily: *The children gobbled up their food and rushed out to play.* | *They gobbled it down.* **2** [I] to make the sound a TURKEY makes

gob·ble·dy·gook /ˈgɒbəldiguːk/ ‖ /ˈgɑːbəldiguk, -guːk/ n (also **gobbledegook**) [U] important-sounding but meaningless official language: *This form is a load of gobbledygook!*

go-be·tween /ˈ· ·ˌ·/ n a person who takes messages from one person or side to another, because they are unwilling or unable to meet each other

gob·let /ˈgɒblɪt/ ‖ /ˈgɑːb-/ n a special cup, usually made of glass or metal, used for drinking wine

gob·lin /ˈgɒblɪn/ ‖ /ˈgɑːb-/ n a small ugly fairy in children's stories that enjoys playing tricks on people

god /gɒd/ ‖ /gɑːd/ n **1** one of the beings or spirits which are worshipped because of the power they are believed to have over nature and the lives of human beings **2** the being who, especially in the Christian, Jewish, and Muslim religions, is worshipped as maker and ruler of the world: *to ask God for forgiveness* **3 for God's sake** an expression which is used to show that you are annoyed or impatient about something **4 God forbid** = I hope it does not happen: *God forbid that my parents should find out about this!* **5 God knows, God alone**

knows *infml* I really do not know: *God knows where he's gone!* **6 God willing** *old fash* if God allows it to happen, or if all goes well: *She'll be married soon, God willing.* **7 Oh God, My God, Good God** phrases which are used to express strong feelings such as surprise or fear: *Oh God, I'm in real trouble now!* **8 Thank God** a phrase which you use to express your happiness that trouble has passed: *Thank God you're safe!*
■ USAGE Many expressions with the word **God** are commonly used in a non-religious way to show surprise, anger, fear, etc. Note, however, that some people might find these offensive.

god·child /ˈgɒdtʃaɪld ‖ ˈgɑːd-/ *n* a person, usually a child, whose religious education you have promised at a Christian ceremony to be responsible for

god·daugh·ter /ˈgɒdˌdɔːtər ‖ ˈgɑːd-/ *n* a female godchild

god·dess /ˈgɒdɪs ‖ ˈgɑː-/ *n* a female being or spirit worshipped because of the power she is believed to have over nature and the lives of human beings

god·fa·ther /ˈgɒdˌfɑːðər ‖ ˈgɑːd-/ *n* a man who has promised to be responsible for someone's religious education

god·fear·ing /ˈ· ˌ··/ *adj fml* good and well-behaved according to the rules of religion

god·for·sak·en /ˈgɒdfəseɪkən ‖ ˈgɑːdfər-/ *adj* having no pleasant or desirable qualities (used of a place)

god·less /ˈgɒdləs ‖ ˈgɑːd-/ *adj fml* showing no respect towards or belief in God

god·ly /ˈgɒdli ‖ ˈgɑːdli/ *adj* godlier, godliest *fml* showing obedience to God by behaving according to the rules and standards of your religion

god·moth·er /ˈgɒdˌmʌðər ‖ ˈgɑːd-/ *n* a woman who has promised to be responsible for someone's religious education

god·pa·rent /ˈgɒdˌpeərənt ‖ ˈgɑːd-/ *n* the person who promises at a Christian ceremony to help a person with their religious education

god·send /ˈgɒdsend ‖ ˈgɑːd-/ *n* something which is unexpected and very fortunate

god·son /ˈgɒdˌsʌn ‖ ˈgɑːd-/ *n* a male GODCHILD

goes /gəʊz/ **1** the 3rd person singular present of GO¹ **2** the plural of GO²

gog·gle /ˈgɒgəl ‖ ˈgɑː-/ *v* goggled, goggling [I] to look hard at something with your eyes wide open, especially because you are surprised: *They all goggled in astonishment* at *my uniform.*

gog·gles /ˈgɒgəlz ‖ ˈgɑː-/ *n* [pl] large round glasses with an edge which fits against your skin, used to protect your eyes: *skiing goggles*

going¹ /ˈgəʊɪŋ/ *adj* **1** [never before a noun] *infml* able to be obtained: *There's plenty of work going in the shipyard.* **2** [only before a noun] as paid at present: *The going rate for the job is £4 per hour.* **3 a going concern** an active profitable business **4 have a lot going for it, have a lot going for you** to have a lot of advantages or good qualities

going² *n* [U] **1** the act of someone's leaving: *Her going will be a great loss to the company.* **2** the rate of travel or progress: *We climbed the mountain in three hours, which was pretty good going.* **3** the condition or possibility of travel or progress: *The mud made it heavy going for the car.* **4 while the going is good** while it is still easy or possible to leave

going-o·ver /ˌ·· ˈ··/ *n* [sing] *infml* **1** an examination of something, and treatment of problems that are found: *The car needs a good going-over before we take it on a long journey.* **2** a beating

goings-on /ˌ··· ˈ·/ *n* [pl] activities, usually of an unusual or undesirable kind: *You wouldn't believe the goings-on at the party last night!*

gold¹ /gəʊld/ *adj* **1** made of gold: *a gold coin* **2 gold medal** a piece of gold that you win when you come first in a race or competition **3** the colour of gold: *gold paint*

gold² *n* **1** [U] a valuable yellow metal: *a gold mine* | *gold dust* **2** [C] a gold medal

gold·en /ˈgəʊldən/ *adj* **1** made of gold or looking like gold: *a golden crown* | *golden hair* **2** [only before a noun] wonderful: *a golden opportunity* **3 golden handshake** a large amount of money given to someone when they leave a job **4 golden rule** a very important way of behaving, that you must remember **5 golden wedding** the date that is exactly 50 years after the date of a wedding

gold·fish /ˈgəʊldˌfɪʃ/ *n* [plural is **goldfish**] a small orange fish which is usually kept in glass bowls or in garden pools

gold·mine /ˈgəʊldmaɪn/ *n* **1** a place where gold is taken out of the ground **2** a successful business or activity which makes large profits **3 be sitting on a goldmine** to possess something extremely valuable

golf /gɒlf ‖ gɑːlf, gɔːlf/ *n* [U] a game in which people hit small hard balls into holes, using a special set of sticks: *golf balls* | *a golf course* | *Let's play a round of golf before tea.* –see picture on page 637 –**golfer** *n* : *He's a professional golfer.*

golf club /ˈ· ·/ *n* **1** an association of people who play golf **2** the buildings and land they use **3** (also **club**) a wooden or metal stick used for hitting the ball in a game of golf

gone¹ /gɒn ‖ gɔːn/ the past participle of GO

gone² *prep* later or older than: *It's gone midnight.* | *He's gone seventy.*

gong /gɒŋ ‖ gɑːŋ, gɔːŋ/ *n* a round piece of metal hanging from a frame, which makes a deep ringing sound when it is hit

gon·na /ˈgɒnə, ˈgənə ‖ ˈgɑːnə,/ going to
■ USAGE People sometimes write **gonna** to suggest an American or nonstandard British English pronunciation of **going to**. But before a verb, to show the future: *"I'm gonna find her,"* he said. They do not write or say **gonna** to talk about movement, as in *I'm going to Canada.*

gon·or·rhe·a /ˌgɒnəˈrɪə ‖ ˌgɑː-/ *n* (also **gonorrhoea**) [U] a disease of the sex organs, passed on during sexual activity

good¹ /gʊd/ *adj* better, best **1** of a high standard: *a good book* | *a very good memory* | *good reading skills* **2** skilful or successful at something: *a good cook* | *She's good at languages.* | *He's always been good with children.* **3** useful or suitable for a particular purpose: *It's a good day for painting the windows.* | *That's a good idea.* | *good advice* **4 it's a good thing, it's a good job** it is fortunate: *He would have been furious – it's a good job you didn't tell him!* **5 no good, not much good, not any good** useless or bad: *It's no good trying to explain it to her; she's too young.* | *Is that book any good?* | *A car's not much good to me, since I can't drive!* **6** pleasant or favourable: *good weather* | *Have a good time!* | *You stand a good chance of getting the job.* | *That's very good news.* **7** useful to your health or character:

Milk is good for *you.* | *It's actually good for a child to eat chips occasionally.* **8** healthy: *Sit here so that you can talk into her good ear.* **9** morally right: *St Francis led a good life and did many good deeds.* **10** kind: *She's always been very good* to *me.* | *It's good* of *you to help.* **11** well-behaved (used especially of children): *Be good when we visit your aunt.* **12** [only before a noun] a word used to show that something is great in degree, amount, or size: *Have a good look.* | *Their team gave us a good beating.* | *We waited a good long while.* | *It's a good five kilometres away.* **13 a good deal** quite a lot : *We're expecting a good deal of support for our new movement.* **14 a good many, a good few** quite a large number of **15 as good as** almost: *He as good as refused.* | *We're as good as ruined.* **16 as good as gold** very well behaved **17** a word you use to show that you are pleased about something; or that you agree with someone: *"I've finished." "Good."* **18 Good for you!** a phrase used to express approval and pleasure at someone's success: *"I've passed all my exams." "Good for you!"* **19 good gracious, good grief, good heavens, good Lord, good God** phrases used as an expression of surprise, shock, anger, or another strong feeling: *Good heavens! Is that the time? I must be going.* **20 in good time** early, or early enough for something: *We got to the airport in good time.* **21 make good** to become successful and wealthy **22 make good something** to pay for something that has been lost or damaged: *The loss to the company was made good by the other directors.*

good² n **1** [U] advantage: *It's no good crying now!* | *What's the good of having a car if you can't drive?* **2 do you good** to help you in some way: *A holiday would do you good.* **3 for the good of something** or **someone** to be helpful to someone or something: *We must do it, for the good of the company.* | *I'm punishing you for your own good.* **4** [U] action or behaviour which is morally right, worthy of praise, and in accordance with religious beliefs and principles: *the battle between good and evil* **5 be up to no good** to be doing, or intending to do, something wrong or bad **6 for good** for ever: *They've decided to move up north for good now.* **7 goods** [pl] **a** things such as clothes, food, or kitchen materials that can be owned, bought, or sold: *The shop sells a variety of goods.* | *all my worldly goods* **b** BrE heavy articles to be moved from one place to another: *a goods train* **8 deliver the goods, come up with the goods** infml to do what is needed or expected

good af·ter·noon /ˌ·ˌ··ˈ·/ interj a phrase used to greet someone in the afternoon: *"Good afternoon, Mr Davis." "Hello, Jack."*

good-bye /ɡʊdˈbaɪ/ interj (also **bye** infml) a word that you use when you leave someone or someone leaves you: *"Goodbye, Mrs Jackson." "Goodbye."* —**goodbye** n : *They said their goodbyes and left.*

good eve·ning /ˌ· ˈ··/ interj a phrase used to greet someone in the evening

good-for-noth·ing /ˈ·· ˌ··/ n a useless and worthless person —**good-for-nothing** adj [only before a noun]

Good Fri·day /ˌ· ˈ··/ n the Friday before EASTER, a Christian religious holiday

good-hu·moured /ˌ· ˈ··◁/ n (**good-humored** AmE) cheerful and pleasant in a difficult situation: *He was good-humoured about the mess the children made in his kitchen.* —**good-humouredly** adv

good·ies /ˈɡʊdiz/ n [pl] infml something particularly attractive or pleasant, especially something good to eat: *a bag full of all sorts of goodies*

good-look·ing /ˌ·ˈ··◁/ adj attractive (used of a person): *He's very good-looking.* —see BEAUTIFUL (USAGE)

good mor·ning /ˌ· ˈ··/ interj a greeting used in the morning: *Good morning, Mrs Brown. How are you today?*

good-na·tured /ˌ·ˈ··◁/ adj friendly, pleasant, and rarely angry —**good-naturedly** adv

good·ness /ˈɡʊdnɪs/ n [U] **1** a word used in expressions of surprise and annoyance: *Goodness me!* | *For goodness' sake, stop making such a noise!* **2** the quality of being kind **3** the part of food which is good for your health: *All the goodness has been boiled out of the vegetables.*

good·night /ɡʊdˈnaɪt/ interj an expression used when you are going home at night or before you go to bed or to sleep: *"Goodnight, Jimmy." "Goodnight, Mum."*

good·will /ˌɡʊdˈwɪl/ n [U] kind feelings towards people: *The agreement will need a certain amount of goodwill on both sides if it is to succeed.*

good·y /ˈɡʊdi/ interj an expression of pleasure, used especially by children: *Oh goody! We're going to have ice cream.*

goody-good·y /ˌ·· ˌ··/ n **goody-goodies** a person who tries too hard to be good and please others (a word which shows disapproval, used especially by children): *Why did you tell the teacher, you goody-goody?*

goo·ey /ˈɡuːi/ adj **gooier, gooiest** infml **1** sticky and usually sweet: *gooey cream cakes* **2** showing too much tenderness: *I hate gooey romantic films!*

goof /ɡuːf/ v [I] infml to make a silly mistake —**goof** n

goof·y /ˈɡuːfi/ adj **goofier, goofiest** silly and slightly mad

goon /ɡuːn/ n infml a foolish person

goose /ɡuːs/ n **geese** /ɡiːs/ a large white bird similar to a duck, kept for its meat and eggs

goose·ber·ry /ˈɡʊzbəri, ˈɡuːz- ǁ ˈɡuːsberi/ n **gooseberries** **1** a small, round green fruit used in cooking: *a gooseberry bush* | *a gooseberry pie* **2 play gooseberry** BrE to be present as a third person in the company of two lovers who want to be alone

goose-flesh /ˈɡuːsfleʃ/ n [U] (also **goose pimples** /ˈ· ˌ··/ [pl]) a condition in which the hair on your skin is raised because you are cold or frightened

gore¹ /ɡɔːʳ/ v **gored, goring** [T] (of an animal) to wound with the horns: *He was attacked by the bull and severely gored.*

gore² n [U] thick blood from a wound

gorge¹ /ɡɔːdʒ/ n a deep narrow valley

gorge² v **gorged, gorging: gorge yourself on something** to fill yourself with food: *She gorged herself all day on cream cakes.*

gor·geous /ˈɡɔːdʒəs ǁ ˈɡɔːr-/ adj infml very beautiful and nice: *What a gorgeous, sunny day!* | *She was wearing an absolutely gorgeous dress.*

go·ril·la /ɡəˈrɪlə/ n a very large strong animal similar to a monkey, with dark fur

gorse /ɡɔːs ǁ ɡɔːrs/ n [U] a wild bush with prickles and bright yellow flowers

gor·y /ˈɡɔːri/ adj **gorier, goriest** full of violence and blood: *a gory film* | *There had been a murder. He told them all the gory details.*

gosh /ɡɒʃ ǁ ɡɑːʃ/ interj an expression of surprise: *Gosh! What a coincidence!*

gos·ling /ˈgɒzlɪŋ ‖ ˈgɑːz-, ˈgɔːz-/ n a young GOOSE

go-slow /ˌ·ˈ·◂/ n BrE a period of working as slowly as possible because of a disagreement with your employer

gos·pel /ˈgɒspəl ‖ ˈgɑːs-/ n 1 the Gospels the four books in the Bible about the life and teachings of Christ 2 [U] (also gospel truth) something which is completely true: What I'm telling you is gospel. | No, honestly, it's the gospel truth. 3 [C] infml a set of ideas that someone believes in strongly: spreading the feminist gospel 4 [U] (also gospel music) a style of music popular in America with black Christians

gos·sa·mer /ˈgɒsəməʳ ‖ ˈgɑː-/ n [U] 1 light silky thread made by spiders (SPIDER) 2 a very light thin material

gos·sip¹ /ˈgɒsᵻp ‖ ˈgɑː-/ n 1 [C;U] informal talk or writing about other people's actions and private lives: I don't approve of gossip. | two neighbours having a gossip in the street 2 [C] a person who likes talking about other people's private lives (a word used to show disapproval): a nosey old gossip

gossip² v [I] to talk or write gossip about someone or something

gossip col·umn /ˈ·· ˌ··/ n part of a newspaper where the private lives of famous people are written about

got /gɒt ‖ gɑːt/ 1 the past tense and past participle of GET 2 have got, have got to – see HAVE

Goth·ic /ˈgɒθɪk ‖ ˈgɑː-/ adj 1 of a style of building common in Western Europe between the 12th and 16th centuries, with pointed arches: a Gothic cathedral 2 with a lot of detailed decoration (used of printing): Gothic script 3 happening in dark strange places (used of stories)

got·ta /ˈgɒtə ‖ ˈgɑːtə/ 1 have/has got to 2 have/has a
■ USAGE People only write gotta when they want to suggest a very informal or nonstandard pronunciation of have got to and have got a: I gotta go. (= I must go) | Gotta match? (= Have you got a match?). But this pronunciation is quite common in ordinary speech.

got·ten /ˈgɒtn ‖ ˈgɑːtn/ the usual American past participle of GET

gouge /gaʊdʒ/ v gouged, gouging
gouge sthg ↔ out phr v [T] to dig a hole in something or get something out, with a pointed tool

gourd /gʊəd ‖ gɔːrd, gʊərd/ n a fruit with a hard shell which is often used as a drinking vessel or dish

gour·met /ˈgʊəmeɪ ‖ ˈgʊər-, gʊərˈmeɪ/ n a person who knows a lot about food and drink and enjoys eating good food

gout /gaʊt/ n [U] a disease which makes your toes, knees, and fingers hurt and swell

gov·ern /ˈgʌvən ‖ -ərn/ 1 [I;T] to control and direct the affairs of a country and its people: a state governed by the top army officers | Is this man fit to govern? 2 [T] to control or fix something: The price of coffee is governed by the quantity which has been produced.

gov·ern·ess /ˈgʌvənᵻs ‖ -ər-/ n a woman who lives with a family and teaches the children at home

gov·ern·ment /ˈgʌvəmənt, ˈgʌvənmənt ‖ ˈgʌvərn-/ n 1 [C + sing/pl verb] (also the Government) the people who rule a country: The Government is planning new tax increases. | the French government 2 [U] the action, form, or method of ruling: a government of the people by the people | The country has not always had fair government.

gov·er·nor /ˈgʌvənəʳ ‖ -vər-/ n (also Governor) a person who controls an organization or place: the Governor of the prison | the Governor of California | She's one of the school governors. –governorship n [U]

gown /gaʊn/ n 1 a woman's dress, especially one worn on formal occasions: a beautiful evening gown 2 a special long loose piece of clothing worn by a judge, lawyer, teacher, or doctor

GP /ˌdʒiː ˈpiː/ n a doctor who is trained in ordinary medicine and works in a particular area of a town; an abbreviation for GENERAL PRACTITIONER: Who's your GP?

grab¹ /græb/ v -bb- [T] 1 to seize something with a sudden rough movement, especially for a selfish reason: He grabbed the money and ran off. 2 grab at something to try to take something or pick something up: She grabbed at the key, but he drew his hand back. 3 to eat some food or get some sleep quickly: I have to work through lunch; I'll just pop out and grab a sandwich. 4 grab at a chance/opportunity to take a chance eagerly: She grabbed at the opportunity to travel. 5 how does it grab you? infml = what do you feel about it?: How does the idea of a trip to Zambia grab you?

grab² n a sudden attempt to seize something: The thief made a grab at my bag.

grace¹ /greɪs/ n [U] 1 the quality of being effortless and attractive in movement: She dances with tremendous grace. 2 have the grace to do something to say or do something that shows you know you have been wrong or deserve blame: She had the grace to admit that he had been right after all. 3 with good grace, with a good grace willingly: He admitted defeat with a good grace. [RELATED PHRASE with bad grace] 4 the grace of God the favour or mercy of God: By the grace of God the ship came safely home through the storm. 5 fall from grace to fall from a position of favour 6 a delay allowed as a favour: I can't pay by Friday, but luckily they're giving me a week's grace. 7 a prayer said before a meal 8 Your Grace a way of speaking to a DUKE, DUCHESS, or ARCHBISHOP: Yes, Your Grace.

grace² v graced, gracing [T] fml (of important people) to agree to be present at an event (a word which is often used in a humorous way): The chairman graced us with his presence.

grace·ful /ˈgreɪsfəl/ adj 1 attractively and effortlessly smooth in movement: a graceful dancer 2 showing fair and honourable behaviour: a graceful apology –gracefully adv
■ USAGE Compare graceful and gracious. Graceful means attractive or pleasant. We use it especially to describe the shape or movements of a person or animal: a graceful dancer | the graceful movement of a deer. But we can also use it to describe people when they are sorry for something or are accepting defeat: He made a graceful apology. | The defeated candidate accepted the result of the election gracefully. We use gracious to describe people's manners. It suggests an important person being polite to someone less important: The Queen thanked them graciously.

grace·less /ˈgreɪsləs/ adj 1 awkward and unattractive in movement or form 2 lacking in good manners –gracelessly adv

gra·cious /ˈgreɪʃəs/ adj fml 1 polite, kind, and pleasant, especially in a generous way: Lord Watchet was gracious enough to show us around his beautiful home. –see GRACEFUL (USAGE) 2 [only before a noun] having qualities such as comfort and beauty made possible by wealth: gracious living 3

Gracious, Good gracious! *old fash* an expression of surprise **–graciously** *adv*

gra·da·tion /grə'deɪʃən/ *n* a stage in a set of changes or degrees of development: *expressing every gradation of feeling from joy to grief* | *gradations of colour*

grade¹ /greɪd/ *n* **1** a particular level of rank or quality: *This grade of wool can be sold at a lower price.* | *These teachers are only on the second grade of the pay scale.* **2** *AmE* a class of a particular year group at school: *She's in the fifth grade.* **3** a mark for an examination or a piece of schoolwork: *Did you get a good grade for your essay?* **4** **make the grade** to reach the necessary standard

grade² *v* **graded, grading** [T] to separate things into levels of rank or quality: *These potatoes have been graded according to size.*

grade cross·ing /'· ˌ··/ *n* the usual American word for LEVEL CROSSING

gra·di·ent /'greɪdiənt/ *n* the degree of steepness of a slope: *a steep hill with a gradient of 1 in 8*

grad·u·al /'grædʒuəl/ *adj* happening slowly and by degrees: *a gradual increase in the number of home owners* **–gradually** *adv* : *He gradually began to understand.*

grad·u·ate¹ /'grædʒuɪt/ *n* **1** a person who has completed a university first degree course: *a graduate of Oxford University* **2** *AmE* a person who has completed a course at a college, school, etc.: *a high school graduate* **3** the usual American word for POSTGRADUATE: *graduate school* | *a graduate student*

grad·u·ate² /'grædʒueɪt/ *v* **graduated, graduating** **1** [I] to obtain a degree at a university **2** [I] *AmE* to complete an educational course **3** [T] to divide something into levels: *a graduated pay scale* **4** **graduate to something** to move on to something that is more important or more difficult

grad·u·a·tion /ˌgrædʒu'eɪʃən/ *n* **1** [U] the act of graduating with a university degree or American high school DIPLOMA: *graduation with honours* **2** [C] the ceremony at which you receive a degree or diploma: *Are your parents coming to your graduation?*

graf·fi·ti /grə'fiːti/ *n* [U] drawings or writing on a wall, often of a humorous, rude, or political nature: *The walls of the subway are covered in graffiti.*

graft¹ /grɑːft ‖ græft/ *v* [T] **1** to add something to part of a damaged human body: *The doctors grafted some skin from her thigh onto her face.* **2** to add something to something else: *The last part of the report had just been grafted on as an afterthought.* **3** to join one plant to another in order to make a new one: *The rose had been grafted onto strong root stock.*

graft² *n* **1** [C] a piece cut from one plant and joined to another one so that it grows there **2** [C] a piece of healthy living skin or bone put onto or into a part of your body which has been damaged: *She's badly burnt and will need a lot of skin grafts.* **3** [U] *AmE* the practice of gaining money dishonestly by the use of political influence **4** [U] *infml* hard work

grain /greɪn/ *n* **1** [C] a single seed of rice, wheat, or other food plants: *He lived on a few grains of rice a day.* **2** [U] crops from plants which produce such seeds, especially wheat: *a cargo of grain* **3** [C] a single very small piece of a hard substance: *a grain of sand* | *grains of salt* **4** **there's not a grain of truth in it** = there is no truth at all in it **5** **the grain** the natural arrangement of the threads or FIBRES in wood, rock, and cloth: *Cut the wood in the direction of the grain.* **6** **it goes against the grain** = I am not used to doing this and I do not approve of it

gram /græm/ *n* (also **gramme**) a unit for measuring weight equal to 1/1000 of a kilogram

gram·mar /'græməʳ/ *n* **1** [U] the rules of a language by which words change their forms and are combined into sentences: *I find German grammar very difficult.* | *She keeps correcting my grammar.* **2** [C] a book which teaches these rules: *This is the best Italian grammar I've seen.*

grammar school /'··· ·/ *n* a school in Britain, especially in the past, for children over the age of 11 who are considered to be of high ability **–compare** COMPREHENSIVE²

gram·mat·i·cal /grə'mætɪkəl/ *adj* **1** [only before a noun] concerning grammar: *grammatical rules* **2** correct according to the rules of grammar: *That is not a grammatical sentence.* **–grammatically** /-kli/ *adv* : *Is this grammatically correct?*

gramme /græm/ *n* see GRAM

gram·o·phone /'græməfəʊn/ *n* *old fash* a RECORD PLAYER

gran /græn/ *n* *BrE* *infml* grandmother

gra·na·ry /'grænəri ‖ 'greɪ-, 'græ-/ *n* **granaries** a building in which grain, especially wheat, is stored

grand¹ /grænd/ *adj* **1** splendid in appearance: *a grand occasion* | *a millionaire who entertained his guests on a grand scale* **2** important but perhaps too proud (used of a person): *He's too grand to associate with people from the village.* **3** *old fash infml* very pleasant: *That was a grand party.* **4** **the grand total** the amount in the end **–grandly** *adv* **–grandness** *n* [U]

grand² *n* **1** [plural is **grand**] *infml* 1000 dollars or pounds: *He paid fifteen grand for that car.* **2** (also **grand piano**) a large flat piano, usually played at concerts

gran·dad /'grændæd/ *n* (also **granddad**) *infml* a grandfather

grand·child /'græntʃaɪld/ *n* **grandchildren** /-ˌtʃɪldrən/ the child of your son or daughter **–see** picture on page 343

grand·daugh·ter /'grænˌdɔːtəʳ/ *n* the daughter of your son or daughter **–see picture on page 343**

gran·deur /'grændʒəʳ/ *n* [U] *fml* **1** great beauty, power, and size: *the grandeur of nature* **2** great personal importance

grand·fa·ther /'grænˌfɑːðəʳ/ *n* the father of your father or mother **–see picture on page 343**

grandfather clock /'··· ·, ˌ··· '·/ *n* a tall clock in a wooden case which stands on the floor

gran·di·ose /'grændiəʊs/ *adj* intended to be important and splendid but seeming useless: *He's always producing grandiose schemes for making money.*

grand·ma /'grænmɑː/ *n* *infml* grandmother

grand·moth·er /'grænˌmʌðəʳ/ *n* the mother of your father or mother **–see picture on page 343**

grand·pa /'grænpɑː/ *n* *infml* grandfather

grand·par·ent /'grænˌpeərənt/ *n* the parent of your father or mother **–see picture on page 343**

grand·son /'grænsʌn/ *n* the son of your son or daughter **–see picture on page 343**

grand·stand /'grændstænd/ *n* a structure, with a roof and seats, from which people watch sports matches and races

grange /greɪndʒ/ *n* a large country house with farm buildings

gran·ite /'grænɪt/ *n* [U] a very hard rock often used for building

gran·ny /'græni/ *n* **grannies** *infml* grandmother

grant[1] /grɑːnt ‖ grænt/ n money given by the state or local council for a particular purpose: *student grants* | *a house improvement grant*

grant[2] v [T] **1** *fml* to give someone something that they want or ask for, especially officially: *They granted her request.* | *The country was granted its independence in 1968.* | *They have been granted permission to build a garage.*
□ USEFUL PATTERNS to grant something; to grant someone something; to grant something to someone
2 I grant you that a phrase you use to say that another person's statement is true in an exact sense, but you think that the main idea that you are expressing is still correct: *"The Prime Minister doesn't support the strikers." "I grant you that, but it's obvious they have his sympathy."* **3 granted** that is true: *"We've been very successful this year." "Granted. But can we do it again next year?"* **4 take something for granted** to believe a fact or action, without questioning: *I just took it for granted that you were married.* **5 take someone for granted** to treat someone with no thought and not be conscious of their true value: *He's so busy with his job that he takes his family completely for granted.*

gran·u·lated /ˈgrænjʊleɪtɪd/ adj **granulated sugar** sugar consisting of very small bits

gran·ule /ˈgrænjuːl/ n a small round piece: *instant coffee granules* –**granular** /-njʊləʳ/ adj

grape /greɪp/ n a small green or dark purple juicy fruit which grows on a VINE, used to make wine: *a bunch of seedless grapes* –see picture on page 344

grape·fruit /ˈgreɪpfruːt/ n **grapefruit** or **grapefruits** a large round yellow fruit with a thick skin, similar to an orange but with a more acid taste –see picture on page 344

grape·vine /ˈgreɪpvaɪn/ n **on the grapevine, through the grapevine** because of people talking informally: *News of how she felt about it finally reached him through the office grapevine.*

graph /græf, grɑːf ‖ græf/ n a drawing showing how two different values are related to each other: *Plot a graph showing the average temperature for each month.* | *a piece of graph paper*

graph·ic /ˈgræfɪk/ adj **1** giving a clear and detailed description in words: *a graphic account of the operation on his stomach* **2** concerned with drawing, letters, or signs: *the graphic arts*

graph·ics /ˈgræfɪks/ n [pl] drawings or representations of an object: *Computer graphics are used in many areas of industrial design.*

graph·i·cal·ly /ˈgræfɪkli/ adv in a very clear and detailed manner: *She described the events so graphically that I could almost see them.*

grap·ple /ˈgræpəl/ v **grappled, grappling grapple with** phr v **1** [T **grapple with** sbdy] to seize someone and struggle with them: *He grappled with the thief.* **2** [T **grapple with** sthg] to try hard to deal with a difficult problem: *grappling with my physics homework*

grasp[1] /grɑːsp ‖ græsp/ v [T] **1** to take or keep a firm hold of something with one or both of your hands: *She suddenly grasped my arm.* | *He grasped the rope with both hands.* **2** to succeed in understanding: *The speech was in French, but I managed to grasp the main ideas.* **3 grasp at something** to try to take, hold, or use: *He grasped at the first excuse that came to mind.* **4 grasp the nettle** to deal firmly with an unpleasant job or subject

grasp[2] n [sing] **1** a firm hold: *The kitten wriggled out of my grasp.* **2** the ability to reach something: *The prize was suddenly within her grasp.* **3** understanding: *This work is beyond my grasp.* | *She has a good grasp of the English language.*

grasp·ing /ˈgrɑːspɪŋ ‖ ˈgræs-/ adj eager for more money (a word used to express disapproval): *Most landlords are mean and grasping.*

grass /grɑːs ‖ græs/ n **1** [U] a common low-growing green plant that covers wide areas of ground on hills and in fields, gardens, parks, etc.: *Sheep were grazing on the rich green grass.* | *The sign said 'Keep off the grass'.* **2** [C;U] a green or brown plant with tall straight stems and flat blades: *He hid behind some tall grasses.* **3** [U] MARIJUANA

grass·hop·per /ˈgrɑːsˌhɒpəʳ ‖ ˈgræsˌhɑː-/ n an insect which makes a loud noise and can jump high in the air

grass·land /ˈgrɑːslænd ‖ ˈgræs-/ n [C;U] land covered mainly with grass, used especially for cattle to feed on

grass roots /ˌ·ˈ·/ n [pl] the ordinary people in an organization or political party, not the leaders: *the views of the grass roots* | *at the grass roots level*

gras·sy /ˈgrɑːsi ‖ ˈgræsi/ adj **grassier, grassiest** covered with growing grass

grate[1] /greɪt/ n the metal bars and frame which hold the coal and wood in a fireplace

grate[2] v **grated, grating 1** [T] to rub food against a hard rough surface so as to break it into small pieces: *grated cheese* **2** [I] to make a sharp unpleasant sound: *The chalk grated on the blackboard.* **3 grate on someone's nerves** (of a noise or behaviour) to make someone annoyed: *His whistling grated on her nerves.*

grate·ful /ˈgreɪtfəl/ adj feeling or showing thanks to another person: *I'd be grateful if you could let me know by Friday.* | *I'll always be grateful to Joe for not telling my father about it.* –**gratefully** adv: *She gratefully accepted their offer of help.* –**gratefulness** n [U]

grat·er /ˈgreɪtəʳ/ n an instrument for grating things into small pieces –see picture on page 638

grat·i·fy /ˈgrætɪfaɪ/ v **gratified, gratifying** [T] *fml* **1** to give pleasure and satisfaction to someone: *I was gratified to hear that he had taken my advice.* **2** to fulfil a need or desire: *Just gratify our curiosity and tell us how he reacted.* –**gratifying** adj : *an immensely gratifying response to our appeal* –**gratification** /ˌgrætɪfɪˈkeɪʃən/ n [C;U]

grat·ing[1] /ˈgreɪtɪŋ/ n a frame or network of metal bars, often used to protect a hole or window: *The coin fell through a grating at the side of the road.*

grat·ing[2] adj sharp, hard, and unpleasant (used of a sound): *a grating voice* –**gratingly** adv

grat·i·tude /ˈgrætɪtjuːd ‖ -tuːd/ n [U] the feeling of being grateful: *I'd like to express my gratitude to everyone involved.*

gra·tu·i·tous /grəˈtjuːɪtəs ‖ -ˈtuː-/ adj unnecessary or undeserved: *films full of gratuitous violence* | *a gratuitous insult* –**gratuitously** adv

gra·tu·i·ty /grəˈtjuːɪti ‖ -ˈtuː-/ n **gratuities** *fml* a gift of money for a service: *Gratuities are not accepted in the hotel.*

grave[1] /greɪv/ n the place where a dead person is buried: *a simple grave with a wooden cross*

grave[2] adj **graver, gravest 1** giving cause for worry, and often needing urgent attention: *The growth in the world's population is a matter of grave* concern to us all. | "I'm afraid his condition is grave," said the doctor. **2** serious or solemn: His face was grave as he told them about the accident. –**gravely** adv

grav·el /ˈgrævəl/ n [U] a mixture of small stones with sand, used on the surface of roads or paths: footsteps crunching on the gravel

grav·el·ly /ˈgrævəli/ adj **1** (also **gravelled** /ˈgrævəld/) made of or covered with gravel **2** having a low rough sound: a gravelly voice

grave·stone /ˈgreɪvstəʊn/ n a stone put up over a grave with the name and dates of birth and death of the dead person on it: a white marble gravestone

grave·yard /ˈgreɪvjɑːd ‖ -ɑːrd/ n a piece of ground, often near a church, where people are buried

grav·i·tate /ˈgrævɨteɪt/ v **gravitated, gravitating gravitate towards** to be attracted by and move gradually towards a place, an idea, etc.: She gravitated towards her boss's point of view.

grav·i·ta·tion /ˌgrævɨˈteɪʃən/ n [U] **1** the act of moving gradually towards something **2** see GRAVITY (1) –**gravitational** adj

grav·i·ty /ˈgrævɨti/ n [U] **1** (also **gravitation**) the natural force which makes objects fall when they are dropped **2** seriousness: You must understand the gravity of the situation.

gra·vy /ˈgreɪvi/ n [U] liquid made with the juice which comes out of meat as it cooks, and served with the meat

gray /greɪ/ adj,n,v AmE see GREY

graze[1] /greɪz/ v **grazed, grazing 1** [I;T] (of animals) to feed on grass: There were cattle grazing in the field. **2** [T] to break the surface of your skin by rubbing it against something: She fell down and grazed her knee. **3** [T] to touch something lightly while passing it: The bullet just grazed his hand.

graze[2] n a small wound on your skin: It's nothing serious – just a graze.

grease[1] /griːs/ n [U] **1** melted animal fat: Strain the grease off the gravy. **2** a thick oily substance: The valves need a bit more grease on them.

grease[2] /griːs, griːz/ v **greased, greasing** [T] to put grease on something: If you grease the lock it will turn more easily. | Grease the tin with butter before baking the cake.

grease-proof pa·per /ˌgriːs-pruːf ˈpeɪpər/ n [U] paper which does not let grease pass through it

greas·y /ˈgriːsi, -zi/ adj **greasier, greasiest** slippery and covered with grease: I can't bear greasy food. –**greasily** adv –**greasiness** n [U]

great /greɪt/ adj **1** large in size, amount, or degree: The great ship sailed away. | a great big fish | It was a great loss to us all. | These peace talks are of the greatest importance. | The great majority of people are in favour of this change. | She's a great friend of mine. **2** very important: the great civilizations of the past | one of our greatest living poets | great works of art | This is a great occasion. **3** infml very good: What a great idea! | I feel great today. | I think she's great! **4** [only before a noun] a word used to say that someone does something a lot: He's a great talker. | She's a great one for saying what she thinks. –**greatness** n [U]

great·ly /ˈgreɪtli/ adv fml [used before past participles] very much: I was greatly moved by his kindness. | He was greatly influenced by his father.

greed /griːd/ n [U] a strong desire to obtain too much food, money, or power: He asked for more out of sheer greed. | their greed for gold

greed·y /ˈgriːdi/ adj **greedier, greediest** wanting too much of something, especially food or power: It's greedy to take so many biscuits. | greedy for power –**greedily** adv –**greediness** n [U]

Greek[1] /griːk/ adj from or connected with Greece

Greek[2] n **1** [C] a person from Greece **2** [U] the language of Greece

green[1] /griːn/ adj **1** the colour of leaves and grass: She was wearing a green dress. –see picture on page 147 **2** covered with grass and trees rather than buildings: We must preserve the green areas in our cities. **3** connected with the protection of the natural world: More and more people are becoming interested in green issues. | the Green party | We should look for green alternatives to harmful chemicals. **4 a green salad** a salad made with green vegetables such as LETTUCE **5 have green fingers** BrE, **have a green thumb** AmE to have natural skill in making plants grow well **6** young and inexperienced: He's still a bit green. **7 be green with envy** to be very jealous because you want something that someone else has **8 the green light** permission to begin doing something –**greenness** n [U]

green[2] n **1** [U] the colour of leaves and grass: She was dressed in green. **2** [C] an area of grass for the general use of the people of a town: playing cricket on the village green **3** [C] a smooth flat area of grass used for playing a game: a bowling green **4 greens** [pl] green vegetables whose leaves are cooked and eaten **5 the Greens** [pl] members of political parties concerned with the protection of the natural world

green belt /ˈ· ·/ n [C;U] a stretch of land round a town, where building is not allowed and fields and woods remain

green·e·ry /ˈgriːnəri/ n [U] attractive green leaves and plants

green-gage /ˈgriːngeɪdʒ/ n a soft juicy greenish-yellow fruit like a PLUM

green·gro·cer /ˈgriːnˌgrəʊsər/ n BrE **1** a person who has a shop selling vegetables and fruit: I bought some oranges from the greengrocer. **2 greengrocer's** a shop selling vegetables and fruit: The greengrocer's didn't have any carrots this morning. | I got the onions at the greengrocer's on the corner.

green·house /ˈgriːnhaʊs/ n a glass building used for growing plants which need heat, light, and protection from winds

greenhouse ef·fect /ˈ··· ·ˌ·/ n the **greenhouse effect** the gradual warming of the air around the Earth, thought to be caused by the increased level of gases such as CARBON DIOXIDE in the air; the gases which are thought to cause the greenhouse effect are called **greenhouse gases**

Green·wich Mean Time /ˌgrenɪtʃ ˈmiːn taɪm, ˌgrɪnɪdʒ-/ n (also **GMT**) the time at Greenwich, in London, which is on an imaginary line dividing east from west; times in the rest of the world are fixed in relation to this

greet /griːt/ v [T] **1** to welcome someone when you meet them: She greeted us by shouting a friendly "Hello!" **2** to receive something in a particular way: His ideas were greeted with scorn.

greet·ing /ˈgriːtɪŋ/ n [C;U] words produced when you meet someone or send them good wishes: "Good morning," I said, but she didn't return the greeting. | Christmas greetings

gre·gar·i·ous /grɪˈgeəriəs/ adj fml enjoying being with other people

gre·nade /grɪˈneɪd/ n a small bomb which can be thrown by hand or fired from a gun

grew /gruː/ the past tense of GROW

grey¹ /greɪ/ adj **greyer, greyest** (also **gray** AmE) **1** the colour like black mixed with white: heavy, grey rain clouds –see picture on page 147 **2 go grey** to start to have grey hair: She's starting to go grey. –see picture on page 245 **3** dull and cloudy (used of the weather) **4** pale in colour because of fear or worry (used of someone's face) –**greyness** n [U]

grey² n (also **gray** AmE) [C;U] a grey colour: She was dressed in grey. | dull greys and browns

grey³ v (also **gray** AmE) [I] **be greying** to be turning grey; you say that a person's hair is greying or that a person is greying: He's greying a bit on top. –see picture on page 245

grey ar·e·a /ˈ· ˌ···/ n an area of knowledge that is not clear or fully understood

grey·hound /ˈgreɪhaʊnd/ n a thin dog with long legs that can run very fast

grid /grɪd/ n **1** a set of straight lines that cross each other to form a lot of small squares **2** a network of wires supplying electricity: the national grid **3** a system of numbered squares printed on a map so that you can describe the exact position of something

grid·dle /ˈgrɪdl/ n an iron plate used for baking flat cakes over a fire

grief /griːf/ n [U] **1** great sorrow, caused especially by the death of someone you love: She went nearly mad with grief. **2 come to grief** to fail or be hurt: All my schemes came to grief. **3 good grief!** an expression of surprise

griev·ance /ˈgriːvəns/ n a reason for complaint: We have called a meeting with the unions to discuss their grievances.

grieve /griːv/ v **grieved, grieving 1** [I] to feel very sad, especially because someone you love has died: She is still grieving for her dead husband. **2** [T] fml to make you very unhappy

griev·ous /ˈgriːvəs/ adj fml very harmful: a grievous mistake –**grievously** adv

grill¹ /grɪl/ v [T] **1** to cook food under direct heat: We grilled the sausages and tomatoes. –see COOK² (USAGE) **2** infml to question someone severely and continuously: He was grilled for two hours before the police let him go.

grill² n **1** an open metal shelf under direct heat in a cooker, where food can be cooked quickly: Put the meat under the grill. **2** a set of bars which can be put over a fire to cook food on

grille /grɪl/ n a metal framework of bars over a door or window used for protection

grim /grɪm/ adj **1** very unpleasant or sad: the grim news of his death | The future looks grim. **2** determined and serious: He gave a grim smile. –**grimly** adv

gri·mace /grɪˈmeɪs, ˈgrɪmɪs/ v **grimaced, grimacing** [I] to make an expression of pain or anger which makes your face look twisted and unattractive: He grimaced with pain. –**grimace** n: She gave a grimace at the mention of his name.

grime /graɪm/ n [U] thick black dirt: His face and hands were covered with grime.

grim·y /ˈgraɪmi/ adj **grimier, grimiest** covered with thick dirt

grin¹ /grɪn/ v -nn- [I] **1** to give a very wide smile: He grinned at me. **2 grin and bear it** infml to suffer an unpleasant situation without complaining

grin² n a very wide smile: She had a big grin on her face.

grind¹ /graɪnd/ v **ground** /graʊnd/, **ground** [T] **1** (also **grind sthg ↔ up**) to crush something into small pieces or a powder: new machines to grind wheat | freshly-ground coffee **2** to sharpen something such as a knife by rubbing it on a hard surface **3** to press something with a lot of force against something else: The dirt was deeply ground into the carpet. **4 grind to a halt** to come slowly to a stop **grind sbdy ↔ down** phr v [T] to keep someone in a state of suffering and hopelessness

grind² n [sing] hard, uninteresting work: He finds any kind of study a real grind.

grind·er /ˈgraɪndəʳ/ n a machine that grinds something: a coffee grinder

grind·ing /ˈgraɪndɪŋ/ adj **grinding poverty** extreme POVERTY

grip¹ /grɪp/ v -pp- [T] **1** to hold something very tightly: He gripped my hand in fear. **2** to hold your attention completely: The audience was gripped by the young actor's performance.

grip² n **1** a very tight forceful hold: He kept a tight grip on the handle. **2 be losing your grip** infml to be becoming less able to do or understand something **3** AmE a bag for carrying your belongings when you are travelling **4 come/get to grips with something** to start dealing seriously with something difficult

gripe¹ /graɪp/ v **griped, griping** [I] infml to complain continually: He's always griping.

gripe² n infml a complaint: My main gripe is that there's no hot water.

grip·ping /ˈgrɪpɪŋ/ adj holding your attention completely: I found the film really gripping.

gris·ly /ˈgrɪzli/ adj **grislier, grisliest** very unpleasant and nasty: the grisly remains of the bodies | the grisly details of the murder

gris·tle /ˈgrɪsəl/ n [U] the part of meat which is not soft enough to eat

grit¹ /grɪt/ n [U] **1** very small pieces of stone: There was a piece of grit in the rice. **2** infml determination and courage –**gritty** adj

grit² v -tt- [T] **1** to put grit on top of ice or snow on the surface of a road in order to stop cars slipping **2 grit your teeth** to become determined and continue when you are in a difficult situation: She just had to grit her teeth and carry on.

groan¹ /grəʊn/ v [I] to make a loud, low sound of pain, worry, or disapproval: She groaned in agony. | "Not another test!" groaned the students.

groan² n a loud, low sound of pain, worry, or disapproval: There were loud groans when he asked them to work late.

gro·cer /ˈgrəʊsəʳ/ n a shopkeeper who sells many kinds of food and goods for the house

gro·cer·ies /ˈgrəʊsəriz/ n [pl] foods such as flour, coffee, and rice which you buy from a grocer's shop

grog·gy /ˈgrɒgi ‖ ˈgrɑːgi/ adj **groggier, groggiest** infml feeling weak and ill: I always feel a bit groggy in the mornings.

groin /grɔɪn/ n the part of your body where your legs meet

groom¹ /gruːm, grʊm/ n **1** a person who looks after horses **2** (also **bridegroom** fml) a man who is getting married

groom² v [T] **1** to clean horses by rubbing and brushing them **2** to prepare someone for a special position or occasion: *He's being groomed for the star role.*

groomed /gru:md, grumd/ adj **well groomed** having a neat, tidy appearance

groove /gru:v/ n a narrow track cut in a surface of something: *The needle moves along the groove on a record.* | *The cupboard door slides open along a groove.*

grope /grəup/ v **groped, groping** [I +adv/prep] **1** to search for something that you cannot see, using your hands: *He groped in his pocket for his ticket.* **2 grope your way somewhere** to move towards a place by feeling with your hands because you cannot see: *I groped my way back to my seat.* **3 grope for something** to try to find or discover something such as the answer to a problem

gross¹ /grəus/ adj **1** unpleasantly fat **2** very rude and offensive: *We were all shocked by his gross behaviour.* **3** [only before a noun] very bad and unacceptable: *the gross inequalities in our society* **4** total: *The gross weight of the product is 250g.* **5** calculated before you have paid any taxes: *What's your gross annual income?* –compare NET³ –**grossly** adv –**grossness** n [U]

gross² v [T] to earn as a total amount: *The company grossed £2,000,000 last year.*

gross³ n [plural is **gross**] a group of 144 things: *three gross of eggs*

gro·tesque /grəu'tesk/ adj very ugly or nasty: *people wearing grotesque masks* | *The very idea is grotesque!* –**grotesquely** adv

grot·to /'grɒtəu ‖ 'grɑː-/ n **grottoes** or **grottos** a small attractive cave

grot·ty /'grɒti ‖ 'grɑːti/ adj **grottier, grottiest** slang unpleasant and of bad quality: *She lives in a grotty little room with nowhere to cook.* –**grottiness** n [U]

grouch¹ /grautʃ/ n infml **1** a small complaint **2** a person who keeps complaining

grouch² v [I] infml to complain in a bad-tempered way

grouchy /'grautʃi/ adj **grouchier, grouchiest** infml often complaining in a bad-tempered way

ground¹ /graund/ n **1 the ground** the surface of the earth: *The branch broke and fell to the ground.* **2 below ground** below the surface of the earth **3 above ground** on or above the surface of the earth **4** [U] land: *The ground is too dry for planting seeds.* **5** [C] a piece of land used for a particular purpose: *a football ground* | *a burial ground* **6 grounds** [pl] land belonging to a large building: *Let's take a walk through the grounds.* **7** [U] a subject or an area of knowledge: *I think that the book tries to cover too much ground.* | *We spent hours going over the same old ground.* **8 grounds** [pl] a reason why you do something: *We have good grounds for thinking that she was involved in the affair.* | *You have no grounds for complaint.* **9 on grounds of…, on the grounds of…, because of:** *She divorced him on the grounds of his adultery.* **10 on the grounds that…** because: *He resigned on the grounds that he needed to spend more time with his family.* **11 gain ground** to become more popular: *These ideas seem to be gaining ground.* [RELATED PHRASE **lose ground:** *The government have lost a lot of ground over this issue.*] **12 get something off the ground** to start something successfully

■ USAGE Compare **ground** and **floor**. Both words can mean "the surface that we walk on", but **floor** is most commonly used when the surface is indoors: *The branch fell to the ground.* | *The cup fell to the floor.* | *The ground was covered with dead leaves.* | *The floor was covered with thick carpet.* –see LAND (USAGE)

ground² v **1** [I] (of a boat) to hit the bottom of a sea or lake and be unable to move **2** [T] to cause a boat to hit the bottom of a sea or lake **3** [T] to prevent a person or plane from flying: *All planes have been grounded because of thick fog.* **4 be grounded on/in something** to be based on something: *an argument grounded on personal experience*

ground³ the past tense and past participle of GRIND

ground floor /ˌ· '·◂/ n (**first floor** AmE) the part of a building at ground level: *I live on the ground floor.*

ground·ing /'graundɪŋ/ n [sing] a complete training in the main points of a skill or subject: *a good grounding in the basic skills of reading and writing*

ground·less /'graundləs/ adj not based on reason or on facts (used of feelings or ideas): *groundless fears* | *Fortunately, my suspicions proved groundless.*

grounds·man /'graundzmən/ n **groundsmen** /-mən/ a man employed to look after a sports field or park

ground·swell /'graundswel/ n [sing] a sudden increase in the number of people who think or feel something: *a groundswell of opinion*

ground·work /'graundwɜːk ‖ -ɜːrk/ n [U] the work which forms the base for some kind of study or skill: *We'll have to do most of the groundwork early in 1993.*

group¹ /gru:p/ n [+sing/pl verb] **1** a number of people or things that are together, or that are connected in some way: *a family group* | *a group of tall trees* | *Schoolchildren are taught according to age groups.* **2** a small number of people who sing and play popular music together: *My favourite group are playing here tonight.*

group² v [I;T] to form into one or more groups: *People can be grouped into several types.* | *We must group together to fight this proposal.*

group·ie /'gru:pi/ n infml a young girl who follows the members of a POP group, especially to have sex with them

group·ing /'gru:pɪŋ/ n a number of people or things that form a group: *We are now seeing several new political groupings in Parliament.*

grouse¹ /graus/ n [plural is **grouse**] [C;U] a smallish fat bird which is shot for food and sport, or its flesh as food

grouse² v **groused, grousing** [I] infml to complain: *You're always grousing and grumbling about something!*

grove /grəuv/ n **1** lit a small group of trees **2** an area planted with certain types of trees: *an orange grove* | *olive groves* **3 Grove** part of the name of a road

grov·el /'grɒvəl ‖ 'grɑː-, 'grʌ-/ v **-ll-** (-l- AmE) [I] **1** to show extreme respect for someone because they are important or powerful and you are frightened of them **2** to lie or move flat on the ground, especially because you are afraid of someone –**groveller** n

grow /grəu/ v **grew** /gru:/, **grown** /grəun/, **growing 1** [I] to get bigger by natural development: *A lot of weeds grow very quickly.* | *A lamb grows into a*

sheep. | *The population is growing too quickly.* **2** [I] (of plants) to be alive in a particular place: *Cotton grows wild here.* | *trees growing beside the river* **3** [T] to care for plants and help them to grow: *We're not growing potatoes this year.* **4** [T] to allow your hair to grow: *He's grown a beard.* **5** [+ complement] to gradually become: *She's growing old.* | *The noise grew louder.* | *It's growing dark; we must go home soon.* **6 grow to do something** to start gradually to do something: *After a while I grew to like him.* **7** [I] to become larger or more important: *The problem of homelessness is growing all the time.*

grow away from sbdy *phr v* [T] to have a less close relationship with someone: *Since she went to university she's grown away from the family.*

grow into sthg *phr v* [T] **1** to become something: *She's grown into a fine young woman.* **2** to become big enough for clothes or shoes: *The coat is too long, but she'll grow into it.*

grow on sbdy *phr v* [T] **1** to become gradually more pleasant or enjoyable to you: *I didn't like this house at first, but it's grown on me.*

grow out of sthg *phr v* [T] **1** to become too big or too old for something: *She's grown out of all her clothes.* | *Most children grow out of wetting the bed.* **2** to develop as a result of something: *Her political beliefs grew out of her hatred of injustice.*

grow up *phr v* [I] **1** (of people) to develop from a child into a man or woman **2** to begin or develop: *The custom grew up of dividing the father's land between the sons.*

grow·er /ˈɡrəʊər/ *n* a person who grows plants or fruit for sale

growl /ɡraʊl/ *v* [I] **1** (of a dog) to make a deep, unfriendly sound: *The dog looked up and growled at me.* **2** to say something in a rough, angry voice −**growl** *n*

grown¹ /ɡrəʊn/ the past participle of GROW

grown² *adj* [only before a noun] adult: *A grown man like you shouldn't act like that.*

grown-up¹ /ˌ·ˈ·◂/ *adj* adult: *She has a grown-up daughter who lives abroad.* | *He's very grown-up for his age.*

grown-up² /ˈ·· ·/ *n* an adult (a word used by children): *Quick! The grown-ups are coming!*

growth /ɡrəʊθ/ *n* **1** [U] the act or rate of growing and developing: *the slow growth of world literacy* | *The animals are fed on hormones to stimulate growth.* **2** [sing] increase in numbers or amount: *a sudden growth in the membership of the club* **3** [C] an unnatural lump that has grown in a part of someone's body

grub¹ /ɡrʌb/ *n* **1** [C] a young insect that has just come out of the egg and looks like a small worm **2** [U] *infml* food

grub² *v* -**bb**-
grub about/around *phr v* [I] to dig with your hands, often in order to find something

grub·by /ˈɡrʌbi/ *adj* **grubbier, grubbiest** *infml* dirty

grudge¹ /ɡrʌdʒ/ *v* **grudged, grudging** [T] to allow someone to have something unwillingly, or feel annoyed that they have it: *I don't grudge him his success.*
□ USEFUL PATTERNS to grudge something to someone; to grudge someone something

grudge² *n* **1** a cause for disliking or hating another person: *I always feel he has a grudge against me* **2 bear a grudge** to continue to have feelings of anger about someone's past actions: *Don't worry − I'm not the sort to bear grudges.*

grudg·ing /ˈɡrʌdʒɪŋ/ *adj* given unwillingly: *her grudging praise* −**grudgingly** *adv*

gru·el /ˈɡruːəl/ *n* [U] a thin liquid food used especially for sick people

gru·el·ling /ˈɡruːəlɪŋ/ *adj* (**grueling** *AmE*) very difficult and tiring

grue·some /ˈɡruːsəm/ *adj* connected with death in a way which is shocking and which makes you feel sick: *a gruesome murder*

gruff /ɡrʌf/ *adj* rough and unfriendly: *In spite of his gruff manner, he is really very kind.* −**gruffly** *adv* −**gruffness** *n* [U]

grum·ble¹ /ˈɡrʌmbəl/ *v* **grumbled, grumbling** [I] to complain in a quiet but bad-tempered way: *He keeps grumbling about his neighbours.*

grumble² *n* a complaint or expression of dissatisfaction

grump·y /ˈɡrʌmpi/ *adj* **grumpier, grumpiest** bad-tempered: *You're very grumpy today − what's the matter?*

grunt /ɡrʌnt/ *v* [I] **1** to make the low rough sound that pigs make **2** to make a short deep rough sound in the throat, often when dissatisfied or unwilling to talk: *He didn't say anything, just grunted from behind his newspaper.* −**grunt** *n*

guar·an·tee¹ /ˌɡærənˈtiː/ *n* **1** an agreement by the maker of an article to repair it or give you another one if it goes wrong within a certain period of time: *The radio has a two-year guarantee.* **2** a formal declaration that something will happen or be done: *There's no guarantee she will accept the offer.* | *Can you give me a guarantee that the goods will be delivered this week?* **3** an agreement to be responsible for the fulfilment of someone else's promise, for example paying a debt **4 under guarantee** (of an article) covered by a maker's guarantee

guarantee² *v* **guaranteed, guaranteeing 1** [T; + that] to give a promise of quality, or that faults will be repaired: *All our food is guaranteed free of artificial preservatives.* | *The manufacturers guarantee the watch for three years.* | *They have guaranteed that any faulty parts will be replaced free of charge.* | *Our products are guaranteed to last for years.* **2** [+ (that)] to promise or make sure that something will certainly happen: *I guarantee that you'll enjoy yourself.* | *I can't guarantee this will work.*

guar·an·tor /ˌɡærənˈtɔːr/ *n* a person who agrees to be responsible for the fulfilment of someone else's promise, for example paying a debt

guard¹ /ɡɑːd ‖ ɡɑːrd/ *n* **1** someone like a soldier, policeman, or prison officer, who watches over someone or something to prevent escape, danger, or attack: *security guards* **2** a group of people, especially soldiers, whose duty it is to guard someone or something: *They all went to watch the changing of the guard.* **3** a railway official in charge of a train **4** something which covers and protects: *Football players sometimes wear shin guards.* **5 be on guard, stand guard** to be in a state of watchful readiness to protect or defend something: *There's a policeman on guard at the entrance.* | *They are standing guard over the house.* **6 on your guard** ready to deal with a sudden trick or attack: *Be on your guard against pickpockets.* [RELATED PHRASE **off your guard**] **7 under guard** being guarded: *The prisoner was brought in under guard.*

guard² *v* [T] **1** to keep something safe by watching for danger: *The dog guarded the house.* | *The soldiers were guarding the bridge against attack.* **2** to watch a prisoner so that they do not escape

guard against sthg *phr v* [T] to try to prevent something by taking special care: *You should wash your hands when preparing food, to guard against spreading infection.*

guard·ed /ˈgɑːdʒd ‖ ˈgɑːr-/ *adj* careful not to say too much (used of speech) –**guardedly** *adv*

guard·i·an /ˈgɑːdiən ‖ ˈgɑːr-/ *n* 1 a person or place that guards or protects: *The Bank of England is the guardian of our wealth.* 2 someone who is legally responsible for looking after a child whose parents have died 3 **guardian angel** a good spirit believed by some people to protect them

guard of hon·our /ˌ· ·ˈ··/ *n* a group of people, usually soldiers, who act as a ceremonial guard to an important person on a special occasion

gua·va /ˈgwɑːvə/ *n* the round fruit of a small tropical tree with pink or white flesh and seeds in the centre

guer·ril·la /gəˈrɪlə/ *n* (also **guerilla**) a member of an independent military group, often fighting for political reasons, which fights larger forces by making surprise attacks or by planting explosives: *guerrilla warfare*

guess¹ /ges/ *v* 1 [I;T; +(that)] to give an opinion without knowing or considering all the facts: *Can you guess my age?* | *I guessed I'd find you in here.* | *Guess where I've been.* | *I guessed it to be about £300.* | *I had no idea so I guessed.*
□ USEFUL PATTERNS to guess something; to guess (that); to guess something to be…; to guess who/where/what/how…
2 [T + (that)] to know or learn something by using all the facts that you know: *I guessed from the look on her face that he had died.* 3 [+(that)] *infml AmE* to think that something is true or likely: *I guess you don't have time to go out now you have young children.* 4 **keep someone guessing** to keep someone uninformed and uncertain about what will happen next

guess² *n* 1 an attempt at working out the correct answer: *She made a wild guess but it was completely wrong.* 2 a judgment made without knowing all the facts: *My guess is that he didn't come because his parents wouldn't let him.* | *At a guess, I'd say she was 35.*

guess·work /ˈgeswɜːk ‖ -ɜːrk/ *n* [U] the process of trying to work out the answer without knowing all the facts

guest /gest/ *n* 1 a person who is in someone's home by invitation to stay for a short time or for a meal: *I'll phone you when our guests have left.* 2 a person who is invited and paid for at a theatre or restaurant: *They are coming to the concert as my guests.* 3 a person who is staying in a hotel or guesthouse: *Guests are requested not to remove the coathangers.* –see CUSTOMER (USAGE) 4 **be my guest!** *infml* = please feel free to do so: *"May I borrow your pen?" "Be my guest!"*

guest·house /ˈgesthaʊs/ *n* **guesthouses** /haʊzɪz/ a private house where visitors may stay and have meals for payment

guest of hon·our /ˌ· · ˈ··/ *n* the most important person who has been invited to a party or meal

guest·room /ˈgest-ruːm, -rʊm/ *n* a bedroom in a private house which is kept for visitors to sleep in

guf·faw /gəˈfɔː/ *n* a loud and perhaps rude laugh –**guffaw** *v* [I]

guid·ance /ˈgaɪdəns/ *n* [U] helpful advice

guide¹ /gaɪd/ *n* 1 someone who takes you round a place of interest explaining things to you, or someone who helps you travel in a dangerous area: *You need a guide to show you the city.* | *a mountain guide*

2 something which provides a model on which opinions or behaviour can be based: *As a rough guide you should cover one question an hour.* 3 a book which teaches the way to do something or provides information about something: *a parents' guide to chilhood diseases* 4 see GIRL GUIDE

guide² *v* **guided, guiding** [T+adv/prep] 1 to show someone where to go: *She guides people around the city.* | *The light guided them back to harbour.* 2 to control the movement of something: *The pilot guided the plane onto the runway.* | *The government will guide the country through the difficulties ahead.* –see LEAD¹ (USAGE)

guide book /ˈ· ·/ *n* (also **guide**) a book which gives tourists information about a place

guide·lines /ˈgaɪdlaɪnz/ *n* [pl] rules or instructions about how something should be done

guild /gɪld/ *n* an association of people who share the same interests or the same skills or profession: *the guild of tailors*

guile /gaɪl/ *n* [U] deceit of a clever, indirect kind

guile·less /ˈgaɪl-ləs/ *adj* simple and sincere

guil·lo·tine¹ /ˈgɪlətiːn/ *n* 1 a machine used in France for cutting off the heads of criminals, which worked by means of a heavy blade sliding down between two posts 2 a machine for cutting paper

guillotine² *v* **guillotined, guillotining** [T] to cut off someone's head with a guillotine

guilt /gɪlt/ *n* [U] 1 the fact of having broken a law: *The jury acquitted him because his guilt could not be proved.* 2 responsibility for something wrong: *When children behave badly the guilt sometimes lies with the parents.* 3 the unhappy feelings produced by knowledge or belief that you have done something wrong: *She was tortured by guilt.* –**guiltless** *adj*

guilt·y /ˈgɪlti/ *adj* **guiltier, guiltiest** 1 having broken a law or disobeyed a moral or social rule: *He was guilty of murder.* | *He was found guilty.* 2 showing or feeling unhappiness because you have done something wrong: *a guilty look* | *a guilty conscience* –**guiltily** *adv*

guinea pig /ˈgɪni pɪg/ *n* 1 a small furry animal rather like a rat without a tail, which is often kept by children as a pet 2 a person or animal used in some kind of test: *They want us to be their guinea pigs and try out their new soap.*

guise /gaɪz/ *n fml* the outward appearance of something, which hides the truth: *In his new film he appears in various guises: as a lawyer, a soldier, and a window cleaner.*

gui·tar /gɪˈtɑːr/ *n* a musical instrument with six strings which are plucked (PLUCK), a long neck, and a wooden or plastic body

gulf /gʌlf/ *n* 1 a large deep stretch of sea partly enclosed by land: *the Gulf of Mexico* 2 a serious difference or separation between people and their understanding of each other: *a huge gulf between the bosses and their employees* 3 a deep hollow place in the earth's surface

gull /gʌl/ *n* see SEAGULL

gul·let /ˈgʌlət/ *n infml* the foodpipe from your mouth to your stomach

gul·li·ble /ˈgʌləbəl/ *adj* easily tricked or persuaded to believe something: *He's so gullible you could sell him anything.*

gul·ly /ˈgʌli/ *n* **gullies** also **gulley** 1 a small narrow valley cut into a hillside by heavy rain 2 a deep ditch made to take water away

gulp[1] /gʌlp/ v 1 [T] to swallow food or drink quickly: *She gulped down her coffee and rushed out.* 2 [I] to make a sudden swallowing movement as if you are surprised or nervous
gulp sthg ↔ **back** *phr v* [T] to prevent the expression of feeling by swallowing: *She gulped back her tears.*

gulp[2] *n* 1 a large mouthful: *He took a few gulps of water and felt much better.* 2 an act of swallowing quickly: *He gave a nervous gulp.*

gum[1] /gʌm/ *n* 1 see CHEWING GUM 2 [U] a sticky substance used for sticking things together 3 **gums** the areas in your mouth where your teeth are fixed 4 [C] a hard jelly-like sweet: *a fruit gum*

gum[2] *v* -**mm**- [T] to stick something in position with glue: *He gummed the labels onto the parcels.*
gum sthg ↔ **up** *phr v* [T] *infml* to prevent something from working or moving properly because a sticky substance has been produced and dried up: *The baby's eyes were all gummed up.*

gum·boot /ˈgʌmbuːt/ *n* a long rubber boot that you wear to keep your feet dry

gump·tion /ˈgʌmpʃən/ *n* [U] *infml* the ability to think or act in a sensible or courageous way

gun[1] /gʌn/ *n* a weapon from which bullets or larger metal objects are fired through a metal tube

gun[2] *v*
gun sbdy ↔ **down** *phr v* [T] to shoot someone and kill or wound them without pity

gun·boat /ˈgʌnbəʊt/ *n* a small but heavily armed warship

gun·fire /ˈgʌnfaɪəʳ/ *n* [U] the repeated firing of guns

gunge /gʌndʒ/ *n BrE infml* [U] an unpleasant, dirty, and sticky substance: *What's this horrible gunge in the bottom of the bucket?*

gun·man /ˈgʌnmən/ *n* **gunmen** /-mən/ a criminal armed with a gun

gun·ner /ˈgʌnəʳ/ *n* a soldier in a part of the British Army which uses heavy guns

gun·point /ˈgʌnpɔɪnt/ *n* **at gunpoint** while pointing a gun or having a gun pointed at you: *They were forced at gunpoint to hand over the money.*

gun·pow·der /ˈgʌnˌpaʊdəʳ/ *n* [U] an explosive material in the form of a powder

gun·run·ner /ˈgʌnˌrʌnəʳ/ *n* a person who illegally and secretly brings guns into a country, especially for the use of those who wish to fight against the government –**gunrunning** *n* [U]

gun·shot /ˈgʌnʃɒt ‖ -ʃɑːt/ *n* the act or sound of firing a gun

gur·gle /ˈgɜːgəl ‖ ˈgɜːr-/ *v* **gurgled, gurgling** [I] 1 to make a sound like water flowing unevenly, for example out of a bottle or over stones 2 (of a baby) to make sounds of delight in the throat: *The baby gurgled contentedly.* –**gurgle** *n*

gu·ru /ˈguruː/ *n* 1 an Indian priest or teacher of religion 2 a greatly respected person whose ideas are followed: *He has become the great guru of modern technology.*

gush[1] /gʌʃ/ *v* 1 [I +adv/prep] to flow or pour out quickly in large quantities: *Oil gushed out of the broken pipe. | Blood gushed from his wound.* 2 [I] to express admiration or pleasure too strongly and perhaps without true feeling –**gushing** *adj* : *gushing praise*

gush[2] *n* a sudden flow of something: *There was a gush of blood as the wound re-opened. | a gush of enthusiasm*

gust /gʌst/ *n* a sudden strong rush of wind: *A gust of wind blew the door shut.* –see WIND (USAGE) –**gust** *v* [I]

gus·to /ˈgʌstəʊ/ *n* **with gusto** with eager enjoyment: *He started painting with great gusto.*

gust·y /ˈgʌsti/ *adj* with strong gusts of wind: *a gusty day*

gut[1] /gʌt/ *n* 1 [C] the foodpipe which passes through your body 2 [U] strong thread made from this part of animals: *The fishing line is made of gut.* 3 **guts** [pl] the inner organs of your stomach 4 **guts** [U] courage: *We all knew the boss was making a terrible mistake, but no one had the guts to tell him.*

gut[2] *v* -**tt**- [T] 1 to take out the inner organs of a dead animal 2 to destroy the inside of a building completely: *The huge factory was gutted by the fire in minutes.*

gut[3] *adj infml* [only before a noun] coming from natural feelings rather than from careful thought: *I had a gut feeling that something terrible would happen. | a gut reaction*

gut·ter /ˈgʌtəʳ/ *n* 1 a narrow ditch at the side of a road, or an open pipe fixed to a roof, to collect and carry away rainwater –see picture on page 441 2 **the gutter** the extremely poor social conditions of a big dirty city

gutter press /ˈ·· ˌ·/ *n* **the gutter press** newspapers which are full of shocking stories about people's private lives

gut·tur·al /ˈgʌtərəl/ *adj* sounding as though it is produced deep in the throat: *a guttural voice*

guy /gaɪ/ *n infml* a man: *a nice guy*

guz·zle /ˈgʌzəl/ *v* **guzzled, guzzling** [I;T] to eat or drink eagerly, quickly, and often continuously: *He's been guzzling beer all evening.*

gym /dʒɪm/ *n* 1 [C] see GYMNASIUM 2 [U] for the teaching of GYMNASTICS: *a gym class*

gym·kha·na /dʒɪmˈkɑːnə/ *n BrE* an event with competitions for horses and their riders

gym·na·si·um /dʒɪmˈneɪziəm/ *n* (also **gym**) a hall with apparatus for physical exercise

gym·nast /ˈdʒɪmnæst, -nəst/ *n* a person who trains and is skilled in particular physical exercises

gym·nas·tics /dʒɪmˈnæstɪks/ *n* [U] exercises to develop your physical strength and ability to move quickly and easily –**gymnastic** *adj* [only before a noun]

gy·nae·col·o·gy /ˌgaɪnɪˈkɒlədʒi ‖ -ˈkɑː-/ *n* (**gynecology** *AmE*) [U] the branch of medicine which deals with women's illnesses and the female sex organs –**gynaecological** /-kəˈlɒdʒɪkəl ‖ -ˈlɑː-/ *adj* (**gynecological** *AmE*) –**gynaecologist** /ˌgaɪnɪˈkɒlədʒɪst ‖ -ˈkɑː-/ *n* (**gynecologist** *AmE*)

gyp·sy /ˈdʒɪpsi/ *n* **gypsies** see GIPSY

gy·rate /dʒaɪˈreɪt ‖ ˈdʒaɪəreɪt/ *v* **gyrated, gyrating** [I] to swing round and round a fixed point, in one direction or with changes of direction: *The dancers gyrated wildly to the strong beat of the music.* –**gyration** /dʒaɪˈreɪʃən/ *n* [C;U]

gy·ro·scope /ˈdʒaɪərəskəʊp/ *n* (also **gyro** /ˈdʒaɪərəʊ/ *infml*) a heavy wheel which spins inside a frame, used for keeping ships and aircraft steady, and also as a children's toy –**gyroscopic** /ˌdʒaɪərəˈskɒpɪk ‖ -ˈskɑː-/ *adj*

H,h

H, h /eɪtʃ/ H's, h's *or* Hs, hs the 8th letter of the English alphabet

ha /hɑː/ *interj* a shout of surprise

hab·er·dash·er /ˈhæbədæʃəʳ ‖ -bər-/ *n* **1** *BrE* a shopkeeper who sells pins, sewing thread, and other small things used in dressmaking **2** *AmE* a shopkeeper who sells men's clothing

hab·er·dash·er·y /ˈhæbədæʃəri ‖ -bər-/ *n* [U] pins, thread, and other things used in dressmaking

hab·it /ˈhæbɪt/ *n* **1** [C;U] something you do regularly, often without thinking: *She has the annoying habit of biting her fingernails.* | *He smokes only out of habit.* | *I can't get him to break the habit.* **2** [C] a special set of clothes worn by members of some religious groups **3 be in the habit of doing something** to do something regularly: *We're in the habit of meeting for lunch on Fridays.* [RELATED PHRASES **get into the habit of; make a habit of:** *Make a habit of cleaning your teeth after meals.*]
■ USAGE Compare **habit, custom, practice, convention.** A **habit** is something which one person does regularly: *He has an annoying* **habit** *of biting his nails.* A **custom** usually means something a whole society has done for a long time: *The* **custom** *of giving presents at Christmas.* **Practice** can mean the same as **custom,** but it often has a derogatory meaning: *Many people condemn the* **practice** *of shooting animals for sport.* It can also mean the usual way of doing things in a business or organization: *The normal* **practice** *in this company is to send the bill as soon as the job is done.* The **conventions** of a society are the rules of behaviour that it expects people to follow: *It is a* **convention** *in Britain that people attending funerals should wear dark clothes.*

hab·i·ta·ble /ˈhæbɪtəbəl/ *adj* good enough to live in –opposite **uninhabitable**

hab·i·tat /ˈhæbɪtæt/ *n* the place where a plant or animal usually lives: *plants in their natural habitat*

hab·i·ta·tion /ˌhæbɪˈteɪʃən/ *n fml* **1** [U] the activity of people living in a place: *a house unfit for human habitation* **2** [C] a place to live in

ha·bit·u·al /həˈbɪtʃuəl/ *adj* [only before a noun] **1** usual: *her habitual rudeness* **2** done as a habit, or doing something as a habit: *He's a habitual cigar smoker.* –**habitually** *adv* : *She's habitually late.*

hack¹ /hæk/ *v* [I + adv/prep;T] to cut roughly, violently, or in uneven pieces: *They hacked a path through the forest.* | *They hacked away at the brambles.* | *The victim was hacked to death.*

hack² *n* **1** a horse kept for riding **2** a ride on a horse, often in the countryside **3** a writer who does a lot of poor quality work

hack·er /ˈhækəʳ/ *n* a person who spends a lot of time using a computer, especially one who secretly tries to use or change the information in someone else's computer

hack·ing cough /ˌ·· ˈ·/ *n* a cough with a rough unpleasant sound

hack·neyed /ˈhæknid/ *adj* meaningless because used and repeated too often

hack·saw /ˈhæksɔː/ *n* a tool that has a fine-toothed blade and is used for cutting metal

had /d, əd, həd; *strong* hæd/ the past tense and past participle of HAVE

had·dock /ˈhædək/ *n* [plural is **haddock**] [C;U] a common fish found in northern seas, or its flesh as food

had·n't /ˈhædnt/ *v* short for "had not": *They'd arrived, hadn't they?*

hae·mo·glo·bin /ˌhiːməˈɡləʊbɪn/ *n* (**hemoglobin** *AmE*) [U] a red colouring matter in the blood which contains iron and carries oxygen

hae·mo·phil·i·a /ˌhiːməˈfɪliə/ *n* (**hemophilia** *AmE*) [U] an illness in which the sufferer bleeds for a long time after they are cut or injured; the mother or the father may pass it to the children, but only males show the effects of it

hae·mo·phil·i·ac /ˌhiːməˈfɪliæk/ *n* (**hemophiliac** *AmE*) a person who suffers from haemophilia

haem·or·rhage¹ /ˈhemərɪdʒ/ *n tech* (**hemorrhage** *AmE*) [C;U] a flow of blood, especially a long, large, or unexpected one

haemorrhage² *v tech* (**hemorrhage** *AmE*) [I] to have a haemorrhage

haem·or·rhoid /ˈhemərɔɪd/ *n* (**hemorrhoid** *AmE*) **haemorrhoids** blocked and swollen blood-carrying tubes at the opening of the lower end of a person's bowel

hag /hæɡ/ *n* an ugly old woman, who might also be evil

hag·gard /ˈhæɡəd ‖ -ərd/ *adj* showing tiredness or anxiety in the lines on your face and around your eyes

hag·gle /ˈhæɡəl/ *v* **haggled, haggling** [I] to argue over the price of something: *He haggled over the price of the horse with the dealer.* | *The British are not used to haggling.*

ha-ha /ˌ· ˈ·/ *interj* a shout of laughter

hail¹ /heɪl/ *n* **1** [U] small drops of ice which fall from the sky **2** [C] a lot of things which strike suddenly and violently: *a hail of bullets*

hail² *v* **1** [I] to fall as very small drops of ice: *It's hailing.* **2** [T] to call out to someone in greeting or to gain attention: *I hailed a taxi.*
hail sbdy/sthg ↔ as sthg *phr v* [T] to praise something publicly as being a particular thing: *They hailed the statue as an important work of art.*
hail from somewhere *phr v* [T] to come from a place: *She hails from Liverpool.*

hail·stone /ˈheɪlstəʊn/ *n* a small ball of ice

hail·storm /ˈheɪlstɔːm ‖ -ɔːrm/ *n* a storm when small balls of ice fall heavily

hair /heəʳ/ *n* **1** [C] a fine threadlike thing which grows from the skin of a person or animal: *The cat has left her loose hairs all over my clothes.* **2** [U] a lot of these threadlike things together, for example on your head: *I must get my hair cut.* **3 let your hair down** *infml* to behave freely and perhaps wildly, especially after acting formally **4 make someone's hair stand on end** to make someone feel very afraid **5 not turn a hair** *infml* to show no fear or worry **6 -haired** *adj* having a certain kind of hair: *long-haired* | *fair-haired*

hair·brush /ˈheəbrʌʃ ‖ ˈheər-/ *n* a brush you use on your hair

hair·cut /ˈheəkʌt ‖ ˈheər-/ *n* **1** having your hair cut: *I need a haircut.* **2** the style your hair is cut in: *soldiers with short haircuts*

hair·do /ˈheəduː ‖ ˈheər-/ *n infml* the style a woman's hair is shaped into

hair·dress·er /ˈheəˌdresəʳ ‖ ˈheər-/ *n* **1** a person who cuts, washes, and arranges people's hair **2 hairdresser's** a shop where you go to get your hair cut and washed: *I'm going to the hairdresser's on*

Monday | *The hairdresser's is next to the Post Office.* –**hairdressing** *n* [U]

hair·dry·er /ˈheəˌdraɪəʳ ‖ ˈheər-/ *n* a machine that dries your hair by blowing hot air onto it

hair·grip /ˈheəgrɪp ‖ ˈheər-/ *n* a flat pin with two sides used to hold women's hair in place

hair·line /ˈheəlaɪn ‖ ˈheər-/ *n* **1** the place above your forehead where your hair starts growing **2** [only before another line] a very thin line or crack: *a hairline fracture of the arm*

hair·net /ˈheənet ‖ ˈheər-/ *n* a net worn by women over their hair to keep it in place

hair·piece /ˈheəpiːs ‖ ˈheər-/ *n* a piece of false hair used to make your own hair seem thicker

hair·pin /ˈheəˌpɪn ‖ ˈheər-/ *n* a pin made of wire bent into a U-shape to hold your hair in position

hairpin bend /ˌ··ˈ·/ *n* a narrow U-shaped curve on a road

hair·rais·ing /ˈ·ˌ··/ *adj* that makes one very afraid: *a hair-raising experience*

hair's breadth /ˈ··/ *n* [sing] a very short distance: *We missed the other car by a hair's breadth.*

hair slide /ˈ··/ *n* a small decorative fastener to keep your hair in place

hair·split·ting /ˈ·ˌ··/ *n* [U] too much interest in unimportant differences and points of detail

hair·style /ˈheəstaɪl ‖ ˈheər-/ *n* the style your hair is shaped into

hair·y /ˈheəri/ *adj* **1** having a lot of hair on your body or limbs: *hairy legs* | *a hairy chest* **2** *infml* exciting and rather dangerous: *It was rather hairy driving down through the mountains in the dark.* –**hairiness** *n* [U]

hal·cy·on days /ˌhælsiən ˈdeɪz/ *n* [pl] *lit* a time of peace and happiness

hale /heɪl/ *adj* **hale and hearty** /ˌ·· ·ˈ··/ very healthy

half¹ /hɑːf ‖ hæf/ *n* **halves** /hɑːvz ‖ hævz/ **1** one of two equal parts of something: *the first half of the football match* **2 in half** into two equal parts: *Cut it in half.* | *We split the profits in half.* **3** half a pint of beer: *Two halves please.* **4** a ticket that costs only half the amount of an ordinary ticket, for example because it is for a child: *One and two halves to Oxford Circus, please.* **5 by half** by half of the full amount: *We've had to reduce our workforce by half.* **6 go halves** to share the cost of something: *Why don't you buy it, and I'll go halves with you?*

half² *predeterminer, pron* half in amount: *Half of the guests are already here.* | *Of the people who work here, about half are women.* | *She lives about half a mile from here.* | *Three and a half months have passed since he died.* | *Half the people here are strangers to me.*

half³ *adj* not complete, but only a half of something: *I've ordered a half portion because I'm not very hungry.* | *a half mile* | *She gave me a half smile.*

half⁴ *adv* **1** only partly, but not completely: *She's half French and half English.* | *I half thought that you might come and join us.* **2 half and half** made or done with two equal parts of two things: *"Do you use milk or water?" "Half and half."*

half·back /ˈhɑːfbæk ‖ ˈhæf-/ *n* a football player who plays in the middle of the field

half-baked /ˌ·· ·ˈ·◂/ *adj infml* not properly planned or thought about

half board /ˌ·· ·ˈ·/ *adj* with bed, breakfast, and an evening meal provided: *Half-board accommodation is enough for us – we don't eat lunch.*

half-broth·er /ˈ·· ˌ··/ *n* a brother related to you through only one of your parents

half-caste /ˈ·· ·/ *n* a person whose parents are of different races (a word which some people consider to be offensive) –**half-caste** *adj*

half-heart·ed /ˌ·· ·ˈ··◂ ‖ ˈ· ˌ··/ *adj* showing little effort and no real interest: *a half-hearted attempt* –**half-heartedly** *adv*

half-life /ˈ·· ·/ *n* the time it takes for half the atoms in a RADIOACTIVE substance to decay

half-mast /ˌ·· ·ˈ·/ *n* **at half-mast** a phrase used to describe a flag placed half-way down the flagpole as a sign of sorrow

half·penny /ˈheɪpni/ *n* a very small old British coin, two of which were equal to a penny

half-sis·ter /ˈ·· ˌ··/ *n* a sister related to you through only one of your parents

half term /ˌ·· ·ˈ·◂/ *n* a short holiday in the middle of a school TERM

half-tim·bered /ˌ·· ·ˈ··◂/ *adj* having the wooden frame of an old building showing in the outer walls

half time /ˌ·· ·ˈ· ◂ ‖ ·ˈ··/ *n* [U] the period of rest between two parts of a sports match

half·way /ˌhɑːfˈweɪ◂ ‖ ˌhæf-/ *adj,adv* at the middle point between two things: *We live half-way between London and Oxford.* | *the halfway mark in a race*

half-wit /ˈ·· ·/ *n* a stupid person –**half-witted** /ˌ·· ·ˈ··◂/ *adj*

half year·ly /ˌ·· ·ˈ··◂/ *adj* happening twice a year

hal·i·but /ˈhælɪbət/ *n* [C;U] a very large flat sea fish used as food

hall /hɔːl/ *n* **1** the passage just inside the front door of a house, from which the other rooms are reached **2** a large room in which meetings, dances, dinners, or concerts can be held **3** see HALL OF RESIDENCE

hal·le·lu·ja /ˌhælɪˈluːjə/ *interj,n* (also **alleluia**) an expression of praise, joy, and thanks to God

hall·mark /ˈhɔːlmɑːk ‖ -ɑːrk/ *n* **1** the mark made on objects of precious metal to prove that they are silver or gold **2** a particular quality or way of behaving that is very typical of a certain person or thing: *Clear expression is the hallmark of a good writer.* –**hallmark** *v* : *hallmarked silver*

hal·lo /həˈləʊ, he-, hæ-/ *interj, n* see HELLO

hall of res·i·dence /ˌ·· ·ˈ···/ *n* (also **hall**) a building belonging to a college or university where students live

hal·lowed /ˈhæləʊd/ *adj lit* honoured and respected: *the hallowed memories of great people*

Hal·low·e'en /ˌhæləʊˈiːn/ *n* the night of October 31, when children play tricks and dress up in strange clothes

hal·lu·ci·nate /həˈluːsɪˌneɪt/ *v* **hallucinated, hallucinating** [I] to see things which are not there: *Some drugs cause people to hallucinate.*

hal·lu·ci·na·tion /həˌluːsɪˈneɪʃən/ *n* [C;U] seeing something that is imagined, often as the result of a drug or an illness of the mind

hall·way /ˈhɔːlweɪ/ *n* the passage just inside the front door of a house

ha·lo /ˈheɪləʊ/ *n* a golden circle representing light around the heads of holy people in religious paintings

halt¹ /hɔːlt/ *v* [I;T] *fml* to stop or make something stop: *The train was halted by work on the line ahead.*

halt² *n* a stop or pause: *The train came to a sudden halt just before the station.*

hal·ter /ˈhɔːltəʳ/ n a rope or leather band fastened round a horse's head to lead it

halt·ing /ˈhɔːltɪŋ/ adj stopping and starting as if uncertain –**haltingly** adv

halve /hɑːv ‖ hæv/ v **halved, halving** [T] **1** to divide something into two equal parts **2** to reduce something to half the amount that it was before: By introducing computers we should be able to halve the time we spend in administration.

halves /hɑːvz ‖ hævz/ the plural of HALF

ham /hæm/ n **1** [C;U] preserved meat from the upper part of a pig's leg: a ham sandwich –see MEAT (USAGE) **2** [C] an actor whose acting is unnatural with too much movement and expression: a ham actor

ham v **-mm- ham it up** to act in an unnatural, artificial way with too much movement and expression: Stop hamming it up!

ham·burg·er /ˈhæmbɜːgəʳ ‖ -ɜːr-/ n small pieces of meat made into a flat circular shape, cooked and eaten between pieces of bread

ham-fist·ed /ˌ· ˈ··◂/ adj (also **ham-handed**) awkward when using your hands, so that you knock things over easily

ham·let /ˈhæmlɪt/ n a small village

ham·mer[1] /ˈhæməʳ/ **1** a tool with a heavy metal head on a wooden handle used for hitting nails or breaking things –see picture on page 638 **2** something made to hit something else, for example in a piano, or part of a gun **3 be/go at it hammer and tongs** to fight or argue violently

hammer[2] v **1** [I;T] to hit something with a hammer: Hammer the nails to the wall. | They've been hammering away all day next door. **2** [I;T] to hit something repeatedly: The police hammered at the door. **3** [T] infml to defeat someone beyond any doubt by fighting, or in a game: We hammered the other team. **hammer away at** sthg phr v [T] to keep working hard on something: We've been hammering away at the problem for ages.
hammer sthg ↔ **in** phr v [T] to force someone to understand something by repeating it often: I've been trying to hammer into them the importance of writing clearly.
hammer sthg ↔ **out** phr v [T] to talk about something in detail and come to a decision about it: We've got to get together and try to hammer out a solution.

ham·mock /ˈhæmək/ n a long piece of cloth or net which can be hung up by its ends and used for sleeping in

ham·per[1] /ˈhæmpəʳ/ v [T] to make someone's movement or activity difficult: The snow hampered our efforts. | Business is often hampered by bureaucracy.

hamper[2] n a large basket with a lid, often used for carrying food

ham·ster /ˈhæmstəʳ/ n a small mouse-like animal which is kept as a pet and which stores food in its cheeks

ham·string[1] /ˈhæmˌstrɪŋ/ n one of the strong cords in the back of your leg, which join the muscles to the bones

hamstring[2] v **hamstring** /strʌŋ/, **hamstrung** [T] to make it difficult for someone to do something: The social services are hamstrung by lack of funds.

hand[1] /hænd/ n **1** one of the parts of your body that are at the ends of your arms and that you use for picking things up: She had a book in her hand. **2** a pointer on a clock that shows you what the time is: The minute hand's broken on my watch. **3** a set of playing cards that one person holds in a game: I've got a really good hand. **4** a worker who works using his or her hands: The farm hands were coming in from the fields. | All hands on deck! **5 a hand** some help: Could you give me a hand with this suitcase? | I could do with a hand in the garden. **6 a big hand** a lot of clapping (CLAP) to show support or enjoyment: Let's have a big hand for our next guest singer! **7 an old hand** someone who has a lot of experience at something: She's an old hand at this sort of work. **8 at first hand** by your own direct experience: I found out about it at first hand. **9 at hand** fml near in time or place: The great day is at hand. **10 by hand: a** made by someone using their hands rather than a machine: All the stitching has been done by hand. **b** written, not printed: Our essays all had to be written by hand. **11 have your hands full** to be very busy: With three young children I should think you've got your hands full! **12 get/lay your hands on something** to get or obtain something: If only I could get my hands on a bit of extra money! **13 get out of hand** to become difficult to control: The party seemed to be getting out of hand. **14 hand in hand: a** holding each other's hand: They walked down the road hand in hand. **b** always happening together: Dirt and disease go hand in hand. **15 Hands off!** a phrase you use when you are telling someone not to touch something **16 have a hand in something** to be partly responsible for something: I had no hand in organizing the trip. **17 in hand** being dealt with: I have the matter well in hand. **18 in good hands** being well cared for: At least I know that the children are in good hands. **19 in your hands** in your possession: The painting is no longer in my hands. | An interesting book has come into my hands. **20 off your hands** no longer your responsibility: I shall be glad when the children are finally off my hands. **21 on hand** ready to help or ready to be used: The emergency services were on hand in case there was any trouble. **22 on the one hand, on the other hand** phrases that you use when you are comparing different ideas: On the one hand the job isn't very well paid, but on the other hand I enjoy it. –see CONTRARY[2] (USAGE) **23 to hand** near to you and ready to be used: I haven't got a pen to hand.

hand[2] v [T] **1** to pass something to someone: She handed the letter to John. | He handed the book back to me. | Could you hand me that cup please?
□ USEFUL PATTERNS to hand something to someone; to hand someone something
2 have to hand it to someone to have to admit that someone is very good at something or has done something very well: You have to hand it to her, she gives very good speeches.
hand sthg ↔ **down** phr v [T] to give or leave something to people who are younger than you or come after you: This ring was handed down from my aunt.
hand sthg ↔ **in** phr v [T] to give something to someone in a position of authority: Please hand in your books at the end of the lesson.
hand sthg ↔ **on** phr v [T] to give something to someone else after you have used it: Please read this notice and hand it on.
hand sthg ↔ **out** phr v [T] to give things to each member of a group of people: Hand out the pencils.
hand over phr v **1** [T **hand** sbdy/sthg ↔ **over**] to give someone or something to a person: Come on, hand over the money. | He was handed over to the police. **2** [I;T **hand** sthg ↔ **over**] to give power or responsibility to someone else: The old government will hand over to the new one next week. | The

captain refused to hand over command of his ship to anyone else.

hand·bag /ˈhændbæg/ n a small bag for a person, usually a woman, to carry money and personal things in

hand baggage /ˈ· ˌ··/ n see HAND LUGGAGE

hand·book /ˈhændbʊk/ n a short book giving instructions and information about something

hand·brake /ˈhændbreɪk/ n BrE an apparatus in a vehicle which you work with your hand and which prevents the vehicle from moving –see picture on page 49

hand·cuff /ˈhændkʌf/ v [T] to put handcuffs around someone's wrists

hand·cuffs /ˈhændkʌfs/ n [pl] two metal rings joined together which can be locked around the wrists of a prisoner

hand·ful /ˈhændfʊl/ n 1 the quantity of something which can easily be held in the hand: *She picked up a handful of pebbles and threw them into the sea.* 2 a small number of people: *We invited thirty people, but only a handful of them came.* 3 a child or animal which is difficult to control: *That child is quite a handful.*

hand·i·cap¹ /ˈhændikæp/ n 1 a disability or disadvantage: *Blindness is a great handicap.* | *Being small is a handicap in a crowd like this.* 2 a disadvantage given to the stronger competitors in a race or other sport, such as making them carry more weight or run further than others

handicap² v -pp- [T] to disadvantage someone or make it difficult for them to do something: *We were handicapped by lack of money.*

hand·i·capped /ˈhændikæpt/ adj suffering from a disability of your mind or body, which prevents you from living a normal life: *He's both mentally and physically handicapped.*

hand·i·craft /ˈhændikrɑːft ‖ -kræft/ n 1 a skill such as sewing or weaving in which you use your hands carefully to make something 2 **handicrafts** [pl] objects which you make by careful use of your hands

hand·i·work /ˈhændiwɜːk ‖ -ɜːrk/ n [U] 1 work which demands skilful use of your hands 2 something which is done or made by someone: *The extension to the house is his handiwork.*

hand·ker·chief /ˈhæŋkətʃɪf ‖ -kər-/ n a piece of cloth or thin soft paper used for wiping your nose

han·dle¹ /ˈhændl/ n a part of an object which is specially made for holding it or for moving it

handle² v **handled, handling** [T] 1 to hold or move something with your hands: *She handled the pieces of glass carefully.* 2 to deal with someone or something: *He handled a difficult argument skilfully.* | *Ms Brown handles the company's accounts.* | *He has no idea how to handle children.*

han·dle·bars /ˈhændlbɑːz ‖ -ɑːrz/ n [pl] a long piece of metal above the front wheel of a bicycle or motorcycle, which you move with your hands to control the direction it goes in

han·dler /ˈhændlər/ n 1 a person who is responsible for the control of an animal 2 a person whose job is to deal with a particular type of object: *baggage handler*

hand lug·gage /ˈ· ˌ··/ n (also **hand baggage** AmE) [U] the small bags of a traveller, which can easily be carried by hand

hand·made /ˌhændˈmeɪd◄/ adj made by hand, not by machine

hand·out /ˈhændaʊt/ n 1 something, such as food or clothes, which is given free to someone who is poor 2 information which is given out, especially on a printed sheet: *Handouts will be distributed at the end of the lecture.*

hand·picked /ˌhændˈpɪkt◄/ adj chosen with great care

hand·shake /ˈhændʃeɪk/ n an act in which two people take each other's right hand when they meet or leave each other

hand·some /ˈhænsəm/ adj 1 physically attractive (used especially of men) –see BEAUTIFUL (USAGE) 2 generous: *a handsome reward* | *a handsome offer* –**handsomely** adv

hand·stand /ˈhændstænd/ n a movement in which you kick your legs into the air so that your body is upside down and supported on your hands

hand-to-mouth /ˌ· · ˈ·◄/ adj **hand-to-mouth existence** a way of life in which you have very little money –**hand-to-mouth** adv

hand·writ·ing /ˈhændˌraɪtɪŋ/ n [U] writing done by hand with a pen or pencil, or a particular person's style of writing: *She has very clear handwriting.*

hand·y /ˈhændi/ adj **handier, handiest** 1 useful and simple to use: *This is a handy little box.* | *An answer-phone to take calls while I'm out would be very handy.* 2 **handy with something** clever at using something with your hands: *He's very handy with a needle.* 3 infml conveniently near: *The shops are quite handy.* | *Keep the pills handy!* 4 **come in handy** to be useful: *A few more traveller's cheques may come in handy on holiday.* –**handily** adv

hand·y·man /ˈhændimæn/ n **handymen** /-men/ a person who is good at doing repairs and practical jobs in the house

hang¹ /hæŋ/ v **hung** /hʌŋ/, **hung** 1 [T] to fix something somewhere by its top part, so that the lower part is free: *You can hang your coat on the hook over there.* 2 [I] to be fixed somewhere by the top part, with the lower part free: *Her coat was hanging on the door.* 3 [T] to fix wallpaper onto a wall 4 [T] [past tense is **hanged**] to kill someone, usually as a punishment, by putting a rope around their neck and dropping them so that all their weight is taken by it: *He was hanged for murder.*

hang about/around phr v [I;T **hang about** sthg] to wait near a place without any clear purpose: *There were a lot of people hanging about near the entrance.* | *I hung around the station for nearly an hour.*

hang back phr v [I] to be unwilling to do something

hang on phr v infml 1 [I] to keep hold of something 2 [I] to wait: *Hang on a minute: I'm just coming.* 3 [T **hang on** sthg] to depend on something: *A lot hangs on his success tomorrow.*

hang onto sthg phr v [T] 1 to keep hold of something: *We had to hang onto the sides of the boat.* 2 to keep something: *We decided to hang onto the house until prices were higher.*

hang up phr v 1 [I] to finish a telephone conversation by putting the telephone down: *I said goodbye and hung up.* –see TELEPHONE¹ (USAGE) 2 [I;T **hang up** sthg ↔ **up**] to fix something or be fixed by the top part, with the lower part free: *Hang your coat up.* | *Your dress is hanging up in the wardrobe.*

hang up on sbdy phr v [T] to finish a telephone conversation with someone by putting the telephone down before they have finished speaking: *I was trying to explain, but he hung up on me.*

hang² n **get the hang of something** infml to develop the skill of doing something, or an understanding of how something works: *Typing is difficult at first, but you'll soon get the hang of it.*

han·gar /ˈhæŋəʳ/ n a big building where aircraft are kept –see picture on page 735

hang·er /ˈhæŋəʳ/ n (also **coat hanger**) a piece of wood, metal, or plastic with a hook on top, which you use to hang up a piece of clothing

hanger-on /ˌ··ˈ·/ n **hangers-on** a person who tries to be friendly with another person or group, for their own advantage

hang-glid·er /ˈhæŋˌglaɪdəʳ/ n a type of large KITE which you hang from and use to fly through the air

hang-glid·ing /ˈ·ˌ··/ n [U] a sport of flying using a hang-glider: *Hang-gliding is very popular.* –**hang-gliding** v [only in progressive forms] : *They've gone hang-gliding.*

hang·ing /ˈhæŋɪŋ/ n [C;U] death caused by putting a rope around someone's neck and dropping them so that all their weight is taken by it: *Are you in favour of hanging?*

hang·man /ˈhæŋmən/ n **hangmen** /-mən/ a person whose work is hanging criminals

hang·o·ver /ˈhæŋˌəʊvəʳ/ n 1 the feeling of sickness and headache which you have the day after drinking too much alcohol 2 something that results or remains from an earlier event or state: *That rule is a hangover from the days when all doctors were men.*

hang-up /ˈhæŋʌp/ n infml something which a person gets unusually worried about: *He's got a real hang-up about his appearance.*

han·ker /ˈhæŋkəʳ/ v **hanker after something, hanker for something** to have a great desire for something –**hankering** n : *a hankering after fame and wealth*

han·kie /ˈhæŋki/ n **hankies** (also **hanky**) infml a handkerchief

hap·haz·ard /ˌhæpˈhæzəd◄ ‖ -əd/ adj unplanned or disorderly: *It's a very haphazard system.* –**haphazardly** adv

hap·pen /ˈhæpən/ v 1 [I] to take place: *A funny thing happened yesterday.* | *What will happen if your parents find out?* 2 **happen to**: a to do or to be something by chance: *I happened to see him yesterday.* | *She happened to be at the gate when I went by.* b a phrase used to give force to what you are saying, when you are angry: *That happens to be my bike you just knocked over!* 3 **happen to someone/something** to take place and have an effect on somebody or something: *She's very late – I hope nothing's happened to her.* 4 **as it happens, it so happens** that a phrase used when what you are saying is slightly surprising, or when the thing mentioned is so by chance: *As it happens, I still have the money.* | *It so happened that we moved away from that area.* 5 **happen on something** to find something by chance

■ USAGE 1 Compare **happen, occur, take place**. Events usually **happen** or (more formal) **occur** by accident: *When did the explosion happen/occur?* Events usually **take place** by arrangement: *When will the wedding take place?* 2 If you want to ask about a problem which someone has at the present moment, it is usually better not to use the word **happen**. Instead, ask: **What's the matter?** | **What's wrong?** | **Is anything the matter?**

hap·pen·ing /ˈhæpənɪŋ/ n an event, especially a strange one

hap·pi·ly /ˈhæpɪli/ adv 1 in a happy manner: *laughing happily* | *happily married* 2 willingly: *I'll happily go to the shops for you.* 3 fortunately: *Happily, the accident was prevented.*

hap·pi·ness /ˈhæpinəs/ n [U] the state of being pleased or satisfied

hap·py /ˈhæpi/ adj **happier, happiest** 1 feeling, expressing, or giving pleasure and satisfaction: *a happy child* | *You look very happy.* | *a happy marriage* | *I'm not very happy about their decision.* –opposite **unhappy** 2 **be happy to do something** to be willing to do something: *I'll be happy to meet him when I have time.* 3 a word which you use in greetings to express your good wishes for a particular occasion: *Happy New Year!* | *Happy Birthday!*

happy-go-luck·y /ˌ··· ˈ··◄/ adj showing a cheerful lack of concern for the need to think or plan carefully

ha·rangue /həˈræŋ/ v **harangued, haranguing** [T] to try to persuade someone that you are right with a long, loud angry speech –**harangue** n

har·ass /ˈhærəs, həˈræs ‖ həˈræs, ˈhærəs/ v [T] to annoy or worry someone by causing trouble for them on repeated occasions: *Please stop harassing me!* –**harassment** n [U]

har·bour[1] /ˈhɑːbəʳ ‖ ˈhɑːr-/ n (also **harbor** AmE) [C;U] an area of water where ships can shelter from the rough waters of the open sea –see picture on page 735

harbour[2] v (also **harbor** AmE) [T] 1 to give protection and shelter to someone who is hiding from the police: *He was arrested on suspicion of harbouring terrorists.* 2 to keep a thought or feeling in your mind for a long time: *She harbours a secret desire to be a film star.*

hard[1] /hɑːd ‖ hɑːrd/ adj 1 firm and stiff: *This cheese is as hard as rock!* 2 difficult to do or understand: *That's a very hard question.* | *It's hard to know what he's really thinking.*

□ USEFUL PATTERNS **be hard to do something; be hard for someone to do something**

3 needing a lot of force or effort: *It was hard work moving those logs.* | *Give it a good hard push.* 4 unpleasant and full of difficulties: *The police gave him a hard time.* | *Their life had always been hard.* 5 showing no kindness: *He's a very hard man,* 6 **be hard on someone** to treat someone severely and unkindly: *Don't be too hard on him; he didn't mean to do it.* 7 containing a lot of LIME, that prevents soap from mixing properly (used of water) 8 certain (used of facts): *We need some hard evidence.* | *These are the hard facts of the situation.* 9 pronounced as /k/ rather than /s/ (used of the letter c) or pronounced as /g/ rather than /dʒ/ (used of the letter g) 10 **hard as nails**: a physically strong and very fit b showing no tenderness 11 **hard drugs** strong illegal drugs 12 **a hard winter** a very cold winter –**hardness** n [U]

hard[2] adv 1 making a great effort: *Push hard!* | *She's working hard.* | *I had to think long and hard before I could find the answer.* | *However hard he listened, he could hear nothing.* 2 strongly or heavily: *It's raining harder than ever.* | *She laughed so hard that she fell off her chair.* 3 **be hard hit** to suffer because of something that has happened: *Farmers have been hard hit by the bad weather.* 4 **be hard pushed, be hard put** to have great difficulty doing something: *I was hard pushed to hand in my essay on time.* 5 **hard done by** unfairly treated: *She's beginning to feel very hard done by.* 6 **hard at it** infml working with great effort: *She's been hard at it since six this morning.*

hard-and-fast /ˌ·· ˈ·◄/ adj **hard-and-fast rules** rules which are fixed and unchangeable

hard·back /ˈhɑːdbæk ‖ ˈhɑːrd-/ n a book with a strong stiff cover

hard·board /'hɑːdbɔːd ‖ 'hɑːrdbɔːrd/ n [U] a kind of wood made out of small pieces of wood which have been pressed into sheets

hard-boiled /ˌ·'·◂/ adj boiled until the yellow part is hard (used of eggs)

hard cash /ˌ·'·/ n [U] coins and notes, not a cheque: He will only accept hard cash.

hard core /ˌ·'·/ n the people most concerned at the centre of a group or activity, or the most determined in following its aims: The hard core in the party make all the decisions. | Now only the hard core remains. –**hard-core** adj [only before a noun] : hard-core opposition to the government's plans

hard currency /ˌ·'·◦·/ n money from particular countries which can be exchanged freely

hard disk /ˌ·'·/ n a part of a computer on which you can store information, and which you cannot remove from the computer – see picture on page 539

hard·en /'hɑːdn ‖ 'hɑːrdn/ v 1 [I;T] to make or become firm and stiff: The cement was beginning to harden. | The pottery is then baked to harden it. 2 [I;T] to make or become stronger and more determined: Opposition to the government hardened after the crisis. | The government has hardened its attitude to trade unions. 3 [T] to make someone more severe, and less kind and sensitive: I'm becoming hardened to criticism. | a hardened criminal

hard·head·ed /ˌhɑːd'hedʒd◂ ‖ ˌhɑːrd-/ adj able to make decisions based only on reason and not feelings: a hardheaded businesswoman

hard-heart·ed /ˌ·'·◦·◂/ adj having no kind feelings or sympathy for people –**hard-heartedness** n [U]

hard·line /ˌhɑːd'laɪn◂ ‖ ˌhɑːrd-/ adj infml unwilling to change your strong and fixed beliefs: hardline supporters of the government's policies –**hardliner** n

hard luck /ˌ·'·◂/ interj, n infml [U] 1 bad luck: Failing the test was really hard luck. 2 **hard luck!** a phrase used to show that you are sorry about something unpleasant that has happened to someone

hard·ly /'hɑːdli ‖ 'hɑːrdli/ adv 1 **can hardly, could hardly** able to do something only with difficulty: I can hardly see. | She could hardly speak. 2 **hardly ever, hardly any** almost never or almost none: We hardly ever go out. | I've got hardly any money. | You've eaten hardly anything. 3 only just: I hardly know the people I work with. | We had hardly started our journey when the car broke down. 4 not at all: It's hardly surprising that he got annoyed! | This is hardly the time for making jokes!

■ USAGE Compare **hardly, scarcely, barely, no sooner.** 1 **Hardly, scarcely,** and **barely** are followed by when, but **no sooner** are followed by than in sentences like these: The game had hardly/ scarcely/barely begun when it started raining. | The game had no sooner begun than it started raining. 2 All of these expressions change the usual word order of the sentence when they come at the beginning: **Hardly/scarcely/barely** had the game begun when it started raining. | **No sooner** had the game begun than it started raining. 3 **Hardly** and **scarcely** can come before any, ever and at all to mean "almost no", "almost never", "almost not". We've **hardly/scarcely** any money left. | He's **hardly/scarcely** ever late. | We **hardly/scarcely** got wet at all. (**Barely** can also take this pattern but is less common.)

hard of hear·ing /ˌ· · '·◦·/ adj unable to hear properly

hard·ship /'hɑːdʃɪp ‖ 'hɑːrd-/ n [C;U] a difficult situation, such as lack of money or food, which causes great suffering: The new tax laws are causing the poor a lot of hardship. | They suffered many hardships.

hard up /ˌ·'·◂/ adj not having enough money: We were very hard up after I lost my job.

hard·ware /'hɑːdweəʳ ‖ 'hɑːrd-/ n [U] 1 metal tools and other goods for use in the home and garden 2 machinery which makes up a computer system 3 military machinery and weapons

hard·wear·ing /ˌhɑːd'weərɪŋ◂ ‖ ˌhɑːrd-/ adj strong, and lasting for a long time (used especially of clothes and shoes)

hard·wood /'hɑːdwʊd ‖ 'hɑːrd-/ n [C;U] strong heavy wood from certain types of tree, used to make good furniture

har·dy /'hɑːdi ‖ 'hɑːrdi/ adj **hardier, hardiest** 1 strong and able to bear difficult conditions: You have to be really hardy to live in such a cold climate. 2 able to live through the winter above ground (used of plants) –**hardiness** n [U]

hare¹ /heəʳ/ n an animal like a rabbit, but larger, with long ears, a short tail, and long back legs which allow it to run fast

hare² v **hared, haring** [I + adv/prep] infml to run very fast: He hared off down the road.

hare·brained /'heəbreɪnd ‖ 'heər-/ adj impractical and foolish (used of people or ideas): a harebrained scheme

hare·lip /ˌheə'lɪp ‖ ˌheər-/ n a top lip which is divided into two parts because it did not develop properly before birth

har·em /'hɑːriːm, hɑː'riːm ‖ 'hærəm, 'heər-/ n 1 the place in a Muslim house where the women live 2 the group of women who live in this place

hark /hɑːk ‖ hɑːrk/ v
hark back to sthg phr v [T] to mention things which happened in the past: You're always harking back to how things were when you were young.

harm¹ /hɑːm ‖ hɑːrm/ n [U] 1 damage: The whole incident did his reputation a lot of harm. | Speeches like this do more harm than good. 2 **come to no harm** to not be hurt or damaged: We got caught in the storm, but luckily the ship came to no harm. 3 **out of harm's way:** a safe from danger: At last he was home, and out of harm's way. b unable to cause hurt or damage: Put the knife in the drawer, out of harm's way. 4 **there's no harm** there is nothing to lose by doing something: There's no harm in finding out how much it would cost. 5 **do no harm, not do any harm** to not do any damage, and probably do some good: She might refuse, but it would do no harm to ask her. | It wouldn't do you any harm to go to bed early.

harm² v [T] to hurt or damage someone or something: Our house wasn't harmed at all in the storms.

harm·ful /'hɑːmfəl ‖ 'hɑːrm-/ adj causing someone to be hurt or causing something to be damaged: the harmful effects of smoking

harm·less /'hɑːmləs ‖ 'hɑːrm-/ adj not likely to hurt or offend people, or damage things: The dog is completely harmless. | a harmless question –**harmlessly** adv

har·mon·i·ca /hɑː'mɒnɪkə ‖ hɑːr'mɑː-/ n a musical instrument that you play by holding it to your mouth, moving it from side to side, and blowing or sucking

har·mo·nize /'hɑːmənaɪz ‖ 'hɑːr-/ v **harmonized, harmonizing** (also **harmonise** BrE) [I] 1 to sing or play a piece of music so that the notes combine with the main tune in a pleasant way 2 to go together well: *The design for the house harmonized well with the surrounding buildings.*

har·mo·ny /ˈhɑːməni ‖ ˈhɑːr-/ *n* harmonies 1 [C;U] notes of music combined together in a way which sounds pleasant 2 [U] a state of peaceful agreement: *We lived together in perfect harmony until the baby was born.* –**harmonious** /hɑːˈməʊniəs ‖ hɑːr-/ *adj*

har·ness¹ /ˈhɑːnɪs ‖ ˈhɑːr-/ *n* 1 the bands which are used to control a horse or small child 2 in harness wearing a harness (used of a horse)

harness² *v* [T] 1 to put a harness on a working animal such as a horse 2 to use a natural force to produce useful power: *River water is harnessed to produce electricity.*

harp¹ /hɑːp ‖ hɑːrp/ *n* a large musical instrument with strings running from top to bottom of an open three-cornered frame; you play the harp by stroking (STROKE¹) or pulling the strings with your fingers –**harpist** *n*

harp² *v* harp on something, harp on about something to talk a lot about something even when other people are not interested in it

har·poon /hɑːˈpuːn ‖ hɑːr-/ *n* a spear at the end of a long rope, which is used for hunting large sea animals –**harpoon** *v* [T]

harp·si·chord /ˈhɑːpsɪkɔːd ‖ ˈhɑːrpsɪkɔːrd/ *n* a musical instrument like a small piano, used especially in former times

har·row·ing /ˈhærəʊɪŋ/ *adj* very upsetting: *a harrowing experience*

harsh /hɑːʃ ‖ hɑːrʃ/ *adj* 1 unpleasantly bright, loud, or rough: *The colours are too harsh.* | *a harsh voice* 2 very severe, cruel, or unkind: *a harsh punishment* | *harsh words* | *It was a very harsh winter.* –**harshly** *adv* –**harshness** *n* [U]

har·vest¹ /ˈhɑːvɪst ‖ ˈhɑːr-/ *n* 1 the act or period of gathering the crops: *We all helped with the harvest.* | *It's harvest time again.* 2 the crops that are gathered: *We've got a good harvest this year.*

harvest² *v* [T] to gather a crop

has /s, z, əz, həz; *strong* hæz/ *v* the 3rd person singular present tense of HAVE –see ʼs (USAGE)

has-been /ˈ··-/ *n infml* a person who is no longer important or successful

hash /hæʃ/ *n* 1 [C;U] a meal containing meat which has been cut up in small pieces and re-cooked: 2 make a hash of something to do something badly: *She made a complete hash of her report.* 3 [U] see HASHISH

hash·ish /ˈhæʃɪʃ, -iːʃ/ *n* (also hash *infml*) [U] a drug which is made from the dried leaves or hardened juice of the CANNABIS plant and which is often rolled into cigarettes for smoking

has·n't /ˈhæzənt/ *v* short for "has not": *Hasn't he finished yet?*

has·sle¹ /ˈhæsəl/ *n infml* [C;U] 1 an annoying difficulty: *It's a real hassle to get this child to eat.* | *the hassle of using public transport* 2 an annoying argument: *It's bad enough at work – I don't need any hassle from you too!*

hassle² *v* hassled, hassling [T] *infml* to cause someone continuing annoyance: *Don't keep hassling me about the washing-up!* | *He was hassling her for money.*

haste /heɪst/ *n* [U] the act of doing things too quickly: *In his haste, he forgot to put on his coat.*

has·ten /ˈheɪsən/ *v* 1 [I] to hurry, or be quick to do something: *She hastened home.* | *She hastened to add that she had never taken drugs herself.* 2 [T] to make something happen more quickly: *His progress to high office was hastened by his family connections.*

hast·y /ˈheɪsti/ *adj* hastier, hastiest 1 hurried: *a hasty meal* 2 acting or deciding something too quickly, without thinking about it carefully: *Let's not be hasty.* | *We don't want to make a hasty decision.* –**hastily** *adv*

hat /hæt/ *n* a piece of clothing which you wear on top of your head to cover it, often for protection against the weather –see picture on page 50

hatch¹ /hætʃ/ *v* 1 [I;T] to break open, or to cause an egg to break open, letting a young bird out of an egg: *Three eggs have already hatched.* | *We hatch the eggs by keeping them in a warm place.* 2 [I] (of a young bird or animal) to break through an eggshell and be born 3 hatch a plot, hatch a plan to plan something secretly, usually something bad: *They hatched a plan to murder the king.*

hatch² *n* 1 the cover or door of an opening on a ship or plane through which people and things can pass 2 an opening in a wall, for passing food from a kitchen to the room where people eat

hatch·back /ˈhætʃbæk/ *n* a car with a door at the back which opens upwards –see picture on page 49

hatch·et /ˈhætʃət/ *n* a small axe with a short handle

hate¹ /heɪt/ *n* [U] a strong feeling of dislike: *She looked at me with hate in her eyes.*

hate² *v* hated, hating [T] 1 to have a great dislike of someone or something: *I hate violence.* | *They really hate each other.* 2 *infml* to dislike something or not enjoy it: *I hate tomatoes.* | *I hate using the telephone.*
◻ USEFUL PATTERNS to hate something; to hate doing something
3 I would hate to = I would not enjoy: *I would hate to live in London.* 4 I hate to tell you a phrase used when you are telling someone some bad news

hate·ful /ˈheɪtfəl/ *adj* very unpleasant and unkind: *That was a hateful thing to say.* –**hatefully** *adv*

ha·tred /ˈheɪtrəd/ *n* [U] a very strong feeling of dislike: *She is full of hatred for the driver who killed her dog.* | *a hatred of computers*

hat·ter /ˈhætə/ *n* a person who makes or sells hats

hat trick /ˈ·-/ *n* three successes coming one after the other especially in sports such as football or cricket: *He scored a brilliant hat trick!*

haugh·ty /ˈhɔːti/ *adj* haughtier, haughtiest *fml* appearing proud and showing that you think other people are less important than yourself (a word used to express disapproval) –**haughtily** *adv* –**haughtiness** *n* [U]

haul¹ /hɔːl/ *v* 1 [I;T] to pull hard using a lot of effort: *The logs had to be hauled along the ground.* | *They hauled away on the ropes.*
haul up *phr v* be hauled up in court to be made to appear before a court

haul² *n* 1 an act of pulling hard 2 a long haul a long and difficult journey or job: *It was a long haul home.* 3 the amount of fish caught at one time with a net 4 an amount of stolen or forbidden goods: *The thieves got away with a valuable haul of jewellery.*

haul·age /ˈhɔːlɪdʒ/ *n* [U] 1 the business of carrying goods by road 2 the amount of money charged for carrying goods by road

haunch /hɔːntʃ/ *n* part of your body which includes

your bottom and the tops of your legs: *They were squatting on their haunches.*

haunt[1] /hɔːnt/ v [T] **1** (of the spirit of a dead person) to visit someone or appear in a place: *A headless man haunts the castle.* **2** (of something unpleasant) to keep coming into someone's thoughts: *His words will haunt me for the rest of my life.*

haunt[2] n *infml* a place where someone goes regularly: *This pub is one of my favourite haunts*

haunt·ed /ˈhɔːntɪd/ adj **1** lived in or visited by the spirits of dead people: *a haunted house | That castle is thought to be haunted.* **2** looking very worried: *She had a haunted look on her face.*

haunt·ing /ˈhɔːntɪŋ/ adj strange in a sad or pleasant way and remaining in your thoughts for a long time: *a haunting memory | a haunting melody* –**hauntingly** adv

have – see box on pages 327 and 328.

ha·ven /ˈheɪvən/ n *lit* a place of calm and safety

have·n't /ˈhævənt/ v short for "have not": *You've been here before, haven't you? | I haven't got any money.*

hav·oc /ˈhævək/ n [U] **1** widespread damage or confusion: *The storm last night caused havoc everywhere.* **2 play havoc with something, wreak havoc on something** to confuse something or cause serious damage to it: *The delay played havoc with our plans. | The floods wreaked havoc on the city.*

hawk[1] /hɔːk/ n a large bird with very good eyesight which catches other birds and small animals for food

hawk[2] v [T] **1** to sell goods on the street or at the doors of houses, especially while travelling from place to place: *He's hawking his paintings from door to door.* **2** to try to sell your ideas by taking them from place to place: *He's been hawking his ideas around from publisher to publisher.* –**hawker** n

haw·thorn /ˈhɔːθɔːn ‖ -ɔːrn/ n a tree which has white or red flowers, and red berries in autumn

hay /heɪ/ n [U] grass which has been cut and dried, especially for cattle food

hay fe·ver /ˈ· ˌ··/ n [U] an illness like a bad cold, caused by breathing in POLLEN dust from plants

hay·stack /ˈheɪstæk/ n a large pile of dried grass built for storing

hay·wire /ˈheɪwaɪər/ adj **go haywire** to become confused and out of control: *My plans have all gone haywire since they changed the times of our holidays. | The computer's gone haywire after the power cut.*

haz·ard[1] /ˈhæzəd ‖ -ərd/ n a danger: *Drinking too much alcohol can be a real health hazard. | hazard warning lights*

hazard[2] v [T] *fml* **1** to risk something or put it in danger: *He hazarded all his money in the attempt to save the business.* **2 hazard a guess** to make a guess which may be wrong

haz·ard·ous /ˈhæzədəs ‖ -zər-/ adj likely to harm people: *hazardous chemicals*

haze /heɪz/ n [U] a light mist or smoke: *a haze of cigarette smoke | a heat haze*

ha·zel[1] /ˈheɪzəl/ n a tree which bears nuts that can be eaten

hazel[2] adj having a light greenish brown colour: *She has hazel eyes.*

haz·y /ˈheɪzi/ adj **hazier, haziest 1** misty or rather cloudy: *The mountains were hazy in the distance.* **2** uncertain or confused: *I'm rather hazy about the details of their plans.*

H-bomb /ˈeɪtʃ bɒm ‖ -bɑːm/ n see HYDROGEN BOMB

he /i, hi; *strong* hiː/ pron [used as the subject of a verb] **1** the male person or animal who has already been mentioned: *"Where's John?" "He's gone to the cinema."* **2** the person who has already been mentioned, when it has not been stated whether they are male or female: *Every doctor should do what he thinks best.*

head[1] /hed/ n **1** the part of your body which contains your brain, and where your eyes, ears, nose, and mouth are: *He nodded his head.* **2** your mind: *His head's full of silly ideas!* **3** the part at the top or front of something: *He sat at the head of the table. | Move to the head of the queue.* **4** a person who is in charge of a group or an organization: *She's the head of a large computer firm.* **5** (also **head teacher**) the teacher in charge of a school **6 heads** the front side of a coin, which often has a picture of a person's head on it: *Let's toss a coin; you call, heads or tails?* **7** a word used for counting farm animals: *They've got 40 head of cattle.* **8 a head, per head** for each person: *They do set meals at £8 a head.* **9 above your head** too difficult for you to understand **10 bang your head against a brick wall** to waste your efforts by trying to do something impossible **11 bite someone's head off, snap someone's head off** to speak very angrily to someone **12 bring something to a head** to make a situation reach a point where something must be done or decided [RELATED PHRASE: **come to a head**] **13 go to your head: a** to make you drunk: *The wine's gone straight to my head.* **b** to make you too proud: *His success has gone to his head.* **14 head over heels** turning right over in the air: *She tripped and fell head over heels.* **15 head over heels in love** completely in love **16 keep your head** to remain calm **17 keep your head above water** to keep out of difficulties, especially out of debt **18 lose your head** to act wildly or without reason because you are afraid or angry **19 I can't make head nor tail of this** = I can't understand this **20 off your head** *infml* mad **21 off the top of your head** without thinking very carefully about something: *I can't give you any more details off the top of my head.* **22 on your own head be it** = you will be responsible for any bad results of your actions **23 put your heads together** to talk about something together: *We'll have to put our heads together to find an answer.* **24 shout your head off, scream your head off** to shout very loudly **25 take it into your head to do something** to suddenly decide to do something: *He took it into his head to learn Russian.*

head[2] v **1** [T] to be at the front or top of something: *The car headed the procession.* **2** [T] to be in charge of a group or an organization: *Who heads the government?* **4** [T] to hit a ball with your head: *He headed it into the goal* **3** [I + adv/prep; T + adv/prep] to move or make something move in a certain direction: *We're heading home. | We were heading for the coast. | We headed him towards the house. | You're heading for trouble.* **4 be headed** to have a particular title: *The letter was headed 'Confidential'.*

head sbdy ↔ **off** *phr* v [T] to make somebody move in a different direction by moving in front of them: *They were running towards the house, but we headed them off at the gate.*

head·ache /ˈhedeɪk/ n **1** a pain in your head: *I've got a headache again.* –see ACHE[2] (USAGE) **2** something that causes problems or worry: *The problem of unemployment is a big headache for the government.*

head·band /ˈhedbænd/ n a band that you wear on your head usually to keep hair back from your face

have /v,əv, həv; *strong* hæv/ *v*

present tense	past tense	past participle
I **have**, I'**ve**	I **had**, I'**d**	**had**
You **have**	You **had**, you'**d**	
He / she / it **has**, he'**s**, she'**s**, it'**s**	He / she / it **had**, he'**d**, she'**d**, it'**d**	present participle **having**
We **have**, we'**ve**	We **had**, we'**d**	negative short forms
You **have**, you'**ve**	You **had**, you'**d**	**haven't hasn't hadn't**
They **have**, they'**ve**	They **had**, they'**d**	

For the pronunciation of these forms look them up at their own place in the dictionary.

1 [auxiliary verb] used to form the perfect tenses of verbs:
I've written a letter to him. | *He's gone home.* | *Have you finished?* | *She had already spent the money.* | *I've lived here for ten years.* | *Have you ever been to Spain?*

2 have to, have got to an expression you use to say that someone must do something or something must happen:
You have to press that switch to turn the machine on. | *I'm sorry I've got to go now.* | *Have we got to show our passports on the boat?* | *Did you have to queue for long?* | *I'll have to phone him later.* | *We signed the agreement, but we didn't have to pay any money immediately.*

3 [T] (also **have got** *BrE*) to own or possess something:
Most people have a washing machine now. | *Have you got a pencil?* | *I haven't got any money.* | *Do you have many friends?* | *They've got three children.* | *She has a very good job.*

4 [T] to receive something:
I had a letter from Jane today. | *Have you had any news from Steve yet?*

5 [T] to experience, enjoy, or do something:
Let's have a swim. | *I had breakfast at eight o'clock.* | *Have a look at this.* | *We're having a meeting this afternoon.* | *This policy will have a serious effect on young people.* | *I had my watch stolen yesterday.*

6 have something done to cause something to be done:
I need to have my hair cut. | *I must have this tap mended.*

7 have a baby to give birth to a baby:
She had her first baby last year.

8 have done with something to finish something:
I decided to tell him immediately and have done with it.

9 have had it to be too old and no longer useful:
That old car's had it.

10 have it in for someone *infml* to behave in an unpleasant way towards someone because you do not like them

11 have it off, have it away *BrE infml* to have sex

12 have to do with to have a connection with something:
Her job has something to do with banking. | *This problem has nothing to do with you!*

13 I won't have = I will not allow:
I won't have behaviour like this in my house!

have on *phr v*

1 [T **have** sthg ↔ **on, have got** sthg ↔ **on**]
to be wearing something:
What did she have on? | *He had nothing on except a pair of shorts.* | *It was cold, so I'd got my coat on.*

2 [T **have** sthg on, **have got** sthg on] to have arranged to do something:
Do you have anything on tonight? | *I've got nothing on all this week.*

3 be having someone on *infml* to be tricking someone, by telling them something that is not true

have out *phr v*

1 [T **have** sthg ↔ **out**]
to get something removed from inside your body:
I had three teeth out last week. | *She had her appendix out.*

2 have it out with someone
to settle an argument with someone by talking freely and angrily to them.

have up *phr v*

be had up to be taken to court for doing something illegal:
He was had up for dangerous driving.

---

head·dress /ˈhed-dres/ *n* an ornamental covering for the head

head·first /ˌhedˈfɜːst◂ ‖ -ɜːrst/ *adv* with your head first and the rest of your body following: *He fell headfirst into the lake.*

head·gear /ˈhedgɪəʳ/ *n* [U] hats or anything that you wear on your head

head·ing /ˈhedɪŋ/ *n* the words written as a title at the top of a piece of writing

head·lamp /ˈhedlæmp/ *n* a HEADLIGHT

head·land /ˈhedlənd/ *n* a narrow piece of land running out into the sea

head·light /ˈhedlaɪt/ *n* a powerful light at the front of a vehicle: *Switch your headlights on!* –see picture on page 49

head·line /ˈhedlaɪn/ *n* **1** the title printed in large letters above a story in a newspaper **2 the headlines** the main points of the news read on radio or television

head·long /ˈhedlɒŋ ‖ -lɔːŋ/ *adv,adj* **1** done very quickly: *a headlong descent into anarchy and disorder* **2 rush headlong into something** to do something without stopping to think about it carefully: *They rushed headlong into marriage.*

head·mas·ter /ˌhedˈmɑːstəʳ ‖ ˈhedˌmæstər/ *n* the male teacher in charge of a school

head·mis·tress /ˌhedˈmɪstrɪ̱s ‖ ˈhedˌmɪstrɪ̱s/ *n* the female teacher in charge of a school

head·on /ˌ·ˈ◂/ *adv,adj* with the heads or front parts hitting each other: *a head-on collision* | *We hit the bus head-on.*

head·phones /ˈhedfəʊnz/ *n* [pl] an apparatus which fits over your ears and is used to receive radio messages or listen to records or tapes

head·quar·ters /ˈhedˌkwɔːtəz, ˌhedˈkwɔːtəz ‖ -ɔːrtərz/ *n* (also **HQ**) [+ sing/pl verb] the office or place where the people work, controlling a large organization, such as the police or army: *Our firm's headquarters are in Geneva.*

head·room /ˈhed-rʊm, -ruːm/ *n* [U] space above a vehicle passing under a bridge or through a TUNNEL

head·set /ˈhedset/ *n* a set of headphones

head·stand /ˈhedstænd/ *n* a position with your head and hands on the ground and your legs in the air: *Can you do a headstand?*

head start /ˌ·ˈ·/ *n* **have a head start** to have an advantage over other people: *He had a head start over the other players as he was so much stronger.*

head·stone /ˈhedstəʊn/ *n* a stone which marks the top end of a grave, and which usually has the dead person's name on it

head·strong /ˈhedstrɒŋ ‖ -strɔːŋ/ *adj* determined to do what you want against all other advice

head·way /ˈhedweɪ/ *n* **make headway** to get good results when dealing with a difficulty

head·wind /ˈhedˌwɪnd/ *n* a wind blowing directly against you

head·y /ˈhedi/ *adj* **headier, headiest 1** making you feel drunk: *a heady wine* **2** with a feeling of lightness and excitement: *We were all heady with success.*

heal /hiːl/ *v* [I;T] to make or become healthy again: *His wounds are healing nicely.* | *This cream should help to heal the cuts.*

heal up *phr v* [I] to become healthy again –**healer** *n*

health /helθ/ n [U] **1** the state of being well and without illness or disease: *Health is more important to me than money.* **2** the general condition of your body: *She's in very good health.* | *Smoking is very bad for your health.*

health food /'· ·/ n food that is natural and without added chemicals, and believed to be better for your health

health·y /'helθi/ adj **healthier, healthiest 1** strong and usually in good health: *healthy children* | *a healthy plant* **2** likely to improve your health: *healthy seaside air* | *healthy food* **3** showing that your health is good: *a clear healthy skin* | *a healthy appetite* –**healthily** adv –**healthiness** n [U]

heap[1] /hiːp/ n a pile or mass of things one on top of the other: *The books lay in a heap on the floor.* –**heaped** adj : *a heaped teaspoon of sugar*

heap[2] v [T] **1** to pile something up in large amounts: *He heaped the plate with food.* | *He heaped food on the plate.* **2** heap praise/criticism on someone to give a lot of praise or criticism to someone

hear /hɪər/ v heard /hɜːd ‖ hɜːrd/, **hearing 1** [I;T not in progressive forms] to be conscious of a sound through your ears: *I can't hear very well.* | *I can hear someone knocking.* **2** [T; + (that) not in progressive forms] to be told or informed about something: *I heard that he was ill.* | *I've heard a lot about him, but I've never met him.* **3** [T] to listen with attention especially to a case in court: *The judge heard the case.* | *She heard what he had to say.* **4** won't hear of something = refuse to allow something: *I won't hear of you walking home; I'll pick you up at the station.* **5** hear from someone to receive news from someone, usually by letter: *I heard from her last week.* **6** have heard of someone/something to know about someone or something: *Who's he? – I've never heard of him.* **7** Hear! Hear! a shout of agreement

■ USAGE Compare **hear** and **listen to**. If you **hear** something you take in sound with your ears, whether you want to or not. If you **listen to** something you pay attention in order to hear: *I wasn't listening to the conversation, but I heard my name mentioned.*

hear sbdy ↔ **out** phr v [T] to listen until that person has finished: *Don't interrupt, just hear me out before you start talking.*

hear·ing /'hɪərɪŋ/ n **1** [U] the sense by which you hear sound: *Her hearing is getting worse.* **2** [C] law a trial of a case before a judge **3** get a hearing to be given the chance to explain something: *It's a good idea, so try to get a hearing for it.* [RELATED PHRASE **give someone a hearing**] **4** hard of hearing not able to hear very well **5** hearing aid a small machine which makes sounds louder, used by people who cannot hear well **6** in someone's hearing, within someone's hearing within the distance at which someone can hear what is being said: *Don't talk about it in his hearing.*

hear·say /'hɪəseɪ ‖ 'hɪər-/ n [U] things which are said rather than proved : *I don't know if he's really leaving his job; it may only be hearsay.*

hearse /hɜːs ‖ hɜːrs/ n a car which is used to carry a dead body to the funeral

heart /hɑːt ‖ hɑːrt/ n **1** the organ inside your chest which controls the flow of blood by pushing it round your body **2** this organ when thought of as the centre of your feelings, especially love: *He seems rather fierce, but has a kind heart.* **3** the centre of something or the most important part of it: *the heart of a cabbage* | *the heart of the city* | *Let's get to the*

heart of the matter. **4** a shape which is supposed to be like the shape of a heart **5** hearts a set of playing-cards with one or more heart-shaped figures printed on it in red **6 a person after your own heart** a person who is like you in some way and who you like: *He's a man after my own heart.* **7** at heart a phrase used when saying what someone is really like: *He's very kind at heart.* **8** break someone's heart to make someone very unhappy **9** from the heart, from the bottom of your heart said sincerely or with deep feeling **10** my heart leapt = I felt very happy **11** my heart sank = I felt very unhappy or disappointed **12** know/learn something by heart to know or learn something so that you can remember it perfectly: *We had to learn the speech by heart for homework.* **13** lose heart to no longer have the courage or will to do something **14** not have the heart to do something to be unable to do something because it seems too unkind: *I didn't have the heart to tell her the bad news.* **15** set your heart on something to want something very much: *She has set her heart on going to university.* **16** take heart to feel encouraged and so able to do something difficult **17** take something to heart to feel very sad or upset by something: *Don't take it to heart! I was only joking.* **18** with all your heart said sincerely or with deep feeling **19** -hearted having a certain type of character: *She's very kind-hearted.* | *a cold-hearted business man*

heart·ache /'hɑːteɪk ‖ 'hɑːrt-/ n lit [U] deep feelings of sorrow and pain

heart at·tack /'· ·,·/ n a very dangerous medical condition in which a person's heart suddenly stops working properly: *He died of a heart attack.*

heart·beat /'hɑːtbiːt ‖ 'hɑːrt-/ n [C;U] the regular movement of someone's heart: *The doctor listened to the rapid heartbeat of the sick child.*

heart·break /'hɑːtbreɪk ‖ 'hɑːrt-/ n [C;U] lit deep sorrow and disappointment

heart·break·ing /'hɑːt,breɪkɪŋ ‖ 'hɑːrt-/ adj making you feel very sad: *heartbreaking photos of the refugees*

heart·brok·en /'hɑːt,brəʊkən ‖ 'hɑːrt-/ adj (also **broken-hearted**) feeling very upset

heart·burn /'hɑːtbɜːn ‖ 'hɑːrtbɜːrn/ n [U] a condition in which you feel an unpleasant burning in your chest, caused by INDIGESTION

heart·en /'hɑːtn ‖ 'hɑːr-/ v [T] to encourage someone and make them more cheerful: *He was heartened by her kindness.*

heart·felt /'hɑːtfelt ‖ 'hɑːrt-/ adj deeply felt and sincere: *She gave him her heartfelt thanks.*

hearth /hɑːθ ‖ hɑːrθ/ n the floor of a fireplace in a house –see picture on page 442

heart·i·ly /'hɑːtɪli ‖ 'hɑːrt-/ adv **1** done strongly and cheerfully: *She laughed heartily.* | *They ate heartily.* **2** very or completely: *I'm heartily sick of your questions.*

heart·less /'hɑːtləs ‖ 'hɑːrt-/ adj cruel and showing no pity

heart·rend·ing /'hɑːt,rendɪŋ ‖ 'hɑːrt-/ adj causing a feeling of deep sorrow or pity: *the heartrending cries of the wounded*

heart·strings /'hɑːt,strɪŋz ‖ 'hɑːrt-/ n [pl] play on someone's heartstrings to cause someone to feel deep love or pity

heart-to-heart /,· · '·◄/ n an open and honest talk, usually in private, and mentioning personal details

heart·y /ˈhɑːti ‖ ˈhɑːrti/ adj **heartier, heartiest 1** very friendly: a hearty greeting | a hearty welcome **2 hale and hearty** strong and healthy **3** large (used of meals): a hearty breakfast –**heartiness** n [U]

heat¹ /hiːt/ n **1** [U] the temperature of something, especially when it is warm or being made hot: Test the heat of the water before you get in the bath. **2** [U] a feeling of warmth: This radiator doesn't give off much heat. | Can you feel the heat of the sun's rays? | Does this metal react to heat? **3** [sing] hot weather or the hottest part of the day: I can't stand this heat. | I really suffer from the heat. | He went out in the heat and got sunstroke. **4** [U] **the heat of** a time of great anger or excitement: In the heat of the argument I called him an idiot. | In the heat of the moment I forgot to thank them properly. **5 be on heat** (of certain female animals, usually dogs) to be in a state of sexual excitement during the breeding season **6** [C] a part of a race or competition where the winners compete against other winners to decide the end result: She was knocked out in the qualifying heats.

heat² v [T] to make something warm or hot: I'll heat some milk for the coffee. | It's expensive to heat these big rooms.
heat up phr v [I;T **heat** sthg ↔ **up**] to make or become warm or hot: I'll heat up the soup.

heat·ed /ˈhiːtɪd/ adj angry and excited: a heated argument | She got very heated about it. –**heatedly** adv

heat·er /ˈhiːtər/ n a machine for heating air or water: a fan heater | Please would you switch off the heater?

heath /hiːθ/ n an open piece of wild land without any farms

hea·then /ˈhiːðən/ n old fash a person who does not belong to one of the large established religions –**heathen** adj

heath·er /ˈheðər/ n [U] a plant with small pink or purple flowers which grows wild on open windy land

heat·ing /ˈhiːtɪŋ/ n [U] a system for keeping rooms and buildings warm

heat-stroke /ˈhiːtstrəʊk/ n [U] a condition of fever and weakness caused by too much heat

heat wave /ˈ· ·/ n a period of unusually hot weather

heave¹ /hiːv/ v **heaved, heaving 1** [I;T] to pull and lift something with effort: We heaved him to his feet. | They all heaved on the rope, and at last the rock moved. **2** [I] to move up and down regularly: Her chest heaved as she breathed with difficulty. **3** [I] to feel sick or VOMIT: The sight of so much blood made my stomach heave. **4 heave a sigh** to let out a deep breath with a sound expressing emotion: We all heaved a sigh of relief when we heard the plane had landed safely.

heave² n a pull or throw: Just one more heave, and the stone will be in the right place.

heav·en /ˈhevən/ n **1** [U] a place of complete happiness, where God or the gods are supposed to live and where the souls of good people go after they die –compare HELL **2 the heavens** lit the sky **3 for heaven's sake** a phrase used to show anger or impatience: For heaven's sake hurry up! **4 good heavens, heavens** a phrase used to show surprise: Good heavens! Have you finished already? | Heavens, no! **5 heaven knows** a phrase used to say that you do not know something: Heaven knows why he's taking so long!

heav·en·ly /ˈhevənli/ adj **1** [only before a noun] of or from heaven: a heavenly vision | a heavenly angel **2** infml wonderful: What heavenly weather!

heav·en·wards /ˈhevənwədz ‖ -ərdz/ adv (also **heavenward** /ˈhevənwəd ‖ -ərd/ AmE) towards the sky or heaven

heav·y /ˈhevi/ adj **heavier, heaviest 1** weighing a lot: The bag is too heavy for me to carry. **2** used when asking the weight of something: How heavy are you? **3** great in amount: heavy rain | heavy traffic | There were heavy casualties. **4** using a lot of force: a heavy blow to the head **5** slow and ungraceful: his heavy movements **6** difficult and full of hard work (used of a period of time): I've had a heavy day at the office. **7** serious and difficult to understand (used of a piece of writing) **8** solid and difficult for your stomach to deal with (used of food) **9** hot and without wind (used of the weather) **10 heavy breathing** loud, deep breathing **11 heavy drinker** someone who drinks a lot of alcohol **12 heavy industry** organizations that produce goods such as coal, steel, and chemicals that are used in the production of other goods **13 heavy metal** a style of rock music played loudly on electric musical instruments and drums **14 heavy sleeper** someone who sleeps deeply and is not easily woken **15 heavy smoker** someone who smokes a lot **16 heavy work** work which needs a lot of physical strength **17 make heavy weather of something** to make something more difficult than it really is –**heavily** adv –**heaviness** n [U]

heavy-du·ty /ˌ·· ˈ··◂/ adj made to be used a lot or for rough treatment (used of clothes and machines)

heavy-hand·ed /ˌ·· ˈ··◂/ adj unkind or unfair in the way you treat other people

heav·y·weight /ˈheviweɪt/ n **1** a BOXER in the heaviest class **2** a person of great importance or influence

He·brew /ˈhiːbruː/ n [U] the language used by the Jews, in ancient times and at present –**Hebrew** adj

heck·le /ˈhekəl/ v **heckled, heckling** [I;T] to interrupt a speaker or speech with confusing or unfriendly remarks, especially at a political meeting –**heckler** n : a crowd of hecklers –**heckling** n [U]

hec·tare /ˈhektɑːr, -teər ‖ -teər/ n a unit for measuring areas of land, which equals 10,000 square metres

hec·tic /ˈhektɪk/ adj very busy or full of excitement: a hectic day –**hectically** /-kli/ adv

he'd /id, hid; strong hiːd/ **1** short for "he would": He'd go there now if he could afford it. **2** short for "he had": He'd gone. | He'd got a few minutes to spend with her.

hedge¹ /hedʒ/ n **1** a row of bushes round the edge of a garden or field –see picture on page 441 **2 hedge against inflation** protection against money losing its value

hedge² v **hedged, hedging 1** [T] to make a hedge round something **2** [I] to avoid answering a question directly: You're hedging again – have you or haven't you got the money? **3 hedge your bets** to protect yourself by supporting more than one side in a competition or struggle

hedge·hog /ˈhedʒhɒg ‖ -hɔːg/ n a small animal which has a prickly back

hedge·row /ˈhedʒrəʊ/ n a row of bushes along a country road or separating fields

he·don·is·m /ˈhiːdən-ɪzəm/ n [U] the idea that pleasure is the most important thing in life –**hedonist** n –**hedonistic** /ˌhiːdənˈɪstɪk/ adj

heed¹ /hiːd/ v [T] fml to take notice of a warning or piece of advice: The Government did not heed earlier warnings about hijacking.

heed² n [U] fml **take heed of, pay heed to** to take notice of something: *The Minister must take heed of public demand for better food safety.*

heed·less /'hi:dləs/ adj fml **heedless of** without taking any notice of something or someone

heel¹ /hi:l/ n **1** the back part of your foot **2** the part of a shoe or sock under your heel: *I've got a hole in the heel of my sock | boots with high heels* –see picture on page 50 **3 on your heels, at your heels** very closely behind you: *He was right on my heels.*

heel² v [T] to put a heel on a shoe or boot

hef·ty /'hefti/ adj **heftier, heftiest** big or strong: *a hefty blow to the jaw | a hefty price increase*

height /hait/ n **1** [C;U] the measurement from the bottom to the top of something: *a woman of medium height | the height of the building* **2** [C] a particular distance above the ground: *The plane reached a height of 60,000 feet. | The river rose to the height of the road. | The shelf needs fixing at waist height.* –compare DEPTH **3** [C;U] the quality of being tall or high: *His height makes him stand out in a crowd.* **4** [C] a high position or place: *We looked down from a great height to the town below.* **5 the height of: a** the most powerful part of: *at the height of the storm* **b** the greatest possible kind of: *It's the height of stupidity to go sailing when you can't swim.*

height·en /'haitn/ v [I;T] to make or become greater in degree: *As she waited, her excitement heightened. | Tension heightened in the run-up to the election.*

hei·nous /'heinəs/ adj fml very evil: *heinous crimes*

heir /eəʳ/ n the person who will have the money, property, or title of someone who dies: *The Prince of Wales is the heir to the throne.*

heir·ess /'eərɪs, 'eəres/ n a woman or girl who will receive great wealth when someone dies

heir·loom /'eəlu:m ‖ 'eər-/ n a valuable object given by older members of a family to younger ones over many years: *a family heirloom*

held /held/ the past tense and past participle of HOLD

hel·i·cop·ter /'helɪkɒptəʳ ‖ -kɑ:p-/ n an aircraft which is made to fly by a set of large fast-turning metal blades fixed on top of it –see picture on page 735

hel·i·port /'helɪpɔ:t ‖ -pɔ:rt/ n a helicopter airport

he·li·um /'hi:liəm/ n [U] a gas that is lighter than air, will not burn, and is used in hot air balloons (BALLOON¹)

hell¹ /hel/ n **1** [U] in the Christian and Muslim religions, a place where the souls of bad people are said to be punished after death –compare HEAVEN **2** [U] a very unpleasant situation: *Driving a car in a snowstorm is real hell!* **3 what the hell, who the hell, etc.** infml expressions used in anger or to give strength to what you are saying: *What the hell's that thing on your head?* **4 a hell of a lot** infml a lot: *He must earn a hell of a lot of money.* **5 for the hell of it** infml for fun: *Then we decided to go swimming at midnight just for the hell of it.* **6 give someone hell** infml: **a** to make life very unhappy for someone **b** to speak very angrily to someone who has done something wrong: *My father was in bed when I got in, but he gave me hell the next morning.* **7 go to hell** infml an expression which some people use to tell someone very rudely to go away **8 like hell** infml very much: *We had to run like hell to catch the bus.* **9 play hell** with infml to really spoil something: *The snow played hell with the weekend sports programme.* **10 to hell with** infml an expression some people use when they decide to forget about something they should do: *To hell with the washing up! Let's watch the film.*

hell² interj infml a swear word which some people use to express annoyance: *Oh, hell! I've missed the last train.*

■ USAGE The word **hell** is commonly used in spoken English to show anger or to add strength to an expression. Although it is not generally considered to be very strong, some people might find this use offensive.

he'll /il, hil; strong hi:l/ **1** short for "he will" **2** short for "he shall"

hell·ish /'helɪʃ/ adj infml very unpleasant: *The weather's been hellish recently.* –compare HEAVENLY –hellishly adv

hel·lo /hə'ləu, he-/ interj,n hellos (also **hallo, hullo** BrE) **1** the usual word of greeting: *Hello, John! How are you?* **2** the word used for starting a telephone conversation: *Hello, who's speaking, please?* **3** BrE an expression of surprise: *Hello! Somebody's left their hat behind.* **4** a word used to attract someone's attention: *Hello! Is anybody there?*

■ USAGE When you are speaking on the telephone use the phrase **this is**...to say who you are: *Hello, this is Jane Jones. May I speak to Jim? | Hello Jim. This is Jane.* If you know the other person quite well then you may use the less formal phrase **it's**: *Hello Penny. It's Sue.*

helm /helm/ n **at the helm** in control of a group or organization

hel·met /'helmɪt/ n a hard hat that you wear to protect your head; motorcyclists, policemen, and miners wear helmets

help¹ /help/ v **1** [I;T] to make things easier for someone, especially by doing part of their work: *Could you help me move this cupboard? | We helped him to decorate the sitting-room. | Is there anything I can do to help? | "Can I help you?" "Yes, I'd like some information, please." | He helped his mother into the car. | Can you help me with my homework?*

☐ USEFUL PATTERNS to help someone; to help someone with something; to help someone (to) do something

2 [I;T] to make something better: *Crying won't help. | Have you got anything to help a cold? | The fall in the dollar will help the pound.* **3** [I;T] to share in producing a result: *The cold winter has helped to keep oil prices high.* **4** [T] to give food to someone during a meal: *Can I help you to some potatoes?* **5 can't help** infml can't avoid, prevent, or have control over: *I couldn't help laughing when I saw his haircut. | She can't help her big feet.* **6 I can't help it** infml = it's not my fault: *I can't help it if all the trains are cancelled.* **7 help yourself** infml: **a** to take something for yourself: *"Can I have a drink?" "Help yourself!" | Help yourself to a drink.* **b** to take something without permission: *He just helped himself to the money when no one was looking.*

help out phr v [I;T **help** sbdy ↔ **out**] to help when there is a special need: *The cook's ill, so I'm helping out this week. | Can I help you out?* –**helper** n

■ USAGE Compare **help, assist, aid**. 1 **Assist** is more formal than **help**, and **aid** is even more formal. 2 Notice the forms which can come after **help**: *He helped me to improve. | He helped me improve.* Notice the forms which come after **assist** and **aid**: *These loans will assist/aid our country in improving its economy.* 3 **Assist** always suggests that the person being assisted is doing part of the work. Compare: *The police are asking the public to assist them. | If you are ill, this medicine will help you.*

help² n **1** [U] the act of helping someone: *If you want any help, just ask me.* **2 a help** something or someone that helps you: *This machine is a great help in* *making cakes more quickly.* **3 be of help** to help someone: *Can I be of any help?* **4 Help!** a word that you shout if you need help, especially if you are in danger

help·ful /'helpfəl/ *adj* **1** providing help or willing to help: *She's so kind and helpful.* **2** useful: *Thanks for your helpful suggestions.* **-helpfully** *adv* **-helpfulness** *n* [U]

help·ing /'helpɪŋ/ *n* a serving of food: *I'd like a second helping, I'm still hungry!*

help·less /'helpləs/ *adj* unable to look after yourself or to do things without help: *a helpless child* | *They were helpless against another enemy attack.* **-helplessly** *adv* **-helplessness** *n* [U]

he-man /'· ·/ *n* **he-men** *infml* a strong man, proud of his powerful muscles

hem[1] /hem/ *n* the lower edge of a piece of cloth when turned under and sewn down, for example on a skirt or dress

hem[2] *v* **-mm-** [T] to put a hem on a piece of clothing **hem sbdy** ↔ **in** *phr v* [T] to surround someone tightly, with the result that they cannot move or escape: *The whole army was hemmed in by the enemy, and there was no hope of escape.*

hem·i·sphere /'hemɪsfɪəʳ/ *n* **1** half of a SPHERE, an object like a ball **2** a half of the earth, especially the northern or southern half, or the eastern or western half

hem-line /'hemlaɪn/ *n* length of a dress or skirt

hem-lock /'hemlɒk/ -lɑːk/ *n* [U] a poisonous drug

he·mo·glo·bin /ˌhiːmə'gləʊbɪn || 'hiːməˌgləʊbɪn/ *n* see HAEMOGLOBIN

he·mo·phil·i·a /ˌhiːmə'fɪliə/ *n* see HAEMOPHILIA

he·mo·phil·i·ac /ˌhiːmə'fɪliæk/ *n* see HAEMOPHILIAC

hem·or·rhage /'hemərɪdʒ/ *n,v* see HAEMORRHAGE

hem·or·rhoid /'hemərɔɪd/ *n* see HAEMORRHOID

hemp /hemp/ *n* [U] a plant used for making strong rope, a rough cloth, and the drug CANNABIS

hen /hen/ *n* **1** a female chicken **2** a female bird: *a hen pheasant*

hence /hens/ *adv fml* **1** for this reason: *The town was built near a bridge on the River Cam: hence the name Cambridge.* **2** from this time: *three days hence*

hence·forth /ˌhens'fɔːθ, 'hensfɔːθ || -ɔːrθ/ *adv fml* (also **henceforward** /ˌhens'fɔːwəd || -'fɔːrwərd/) from now on: *The company will henceforth be known as Johnson and Brown Inc.*

hench·man /'hentʃmən/ *n* **henchmen** /-mən/ a faithful supporter, especially of a political leader, who obeys without question and does violent or dishonest acts

hen·na /'henə/ *n* [U] a reddish-brown substance used to colour people's hair

hen·pecked /'henpekt/ *adj* **henpecked husband** a husband whose wife continually finds fault with him and tells him what to do

hep·a·ti·tis /ˌhepə'taɪtɪs/ *n* [U] a LIVER disease which causes your skin to go yellow and which makes you feel very weak

her[1] /əʳ, hɜːʳ; *strong* hɜːʳ/ *det* relating to or belonging to the female person or animal who has already been mentioned: *My mother came in and sat down in her chair.* | *She was sitting drinking her coffee.*

her[2] *pron* [used as the object of a verb] the female person or animal who has already been mentioned: *"Do you like Mary?" "No, I can't stand her!"* –see ME (USAGE)

her·ald[1] /'herəld/ *n* **1** a person who carried messages for a ruler in the past **2** *lit* a sign that something is going to come soon: *a herald of a new age*

herald[2] *v* [T] **1** to be a sign that something is going to come soon: *This reform heralds the birth of a new era.* **2** to say publicly that something is going to happen so that people are expecting it to happen: *the much heralded education reforms*

her·ald·ry /'herəldri/ *n* [U] the study and use of COATS OF ARMS **-heraldic** /he'rældɪk/ *adj*

herb /hɜːb || ɜːrb, hɜːrb/ *n* a plant used to improve the taste of food, or as a medicine –compare SPICE **-herbal** *adj* : *a herbal remedy*

her·ba·ceous /hə'beɪʃəs || ɜːr'beɪ-, hɜːr'beɪ-/ *adj* having a stem that is soft and not woody (used of plants)

herb·al·ist /'hɜːbəlɪst || 'ɜːr-, 'hɜːr-/ *n* a person who treats diseases with herbs

her·bi·vore /'hɜːbɪvɔːʳ || 'ɜːr-, 'hɜːr-/ *n* an animal which only eats grass and plants **-herbivorous** /hɜː'bɪvərəs || ɜːr-, hɜːr-/ *adj*

herd[1] /hɜːd || hɜːrd/ *n* **1** a group of animals of one kind which live and feed together: *a herd of elephants* **2 the herd** people generally thought of as acting or thinking all alike: *Don't just follow the herd – do what you really want to!*

herd[2] *v* [T + adv/prep] to make people or animals move together in a herd or like a herd: *The farmer herded the cows into the field.* | *We were herded into the room.*

herds·man /'hɜːdzmən || -ɜːr-/ *n* **herdsmen** /-mən/ a man who looks after a herd of animals

here /hɪəʳ/ *adv* **1** in or to this place: *I've lived here for ten years.* | *Come over here.* | *It's two miles from here.* | *Could you sign here, please?* | *My friend here will help you.* **2** at this point: *I think I agree with you here.* **3 here is, here are** a phrase used for drawing attention to someone or something: *Here's the money.* | *Here they are.* **4 here and there** in several places: *The landscape was empty except for odd houses here and there.* **5 here's to** a phrase you use when you are having a drink and wishing someone good luck: *Here's to your new job.* **6 here you are** a phrase you use when you are giving someone something that they want

here·af·ter /ˌhɪər'ɑːftəʳ || -'æf-/ *adv fml* after this time

here·by /ˌhɪə'baɪ, 'hɪəbaɪ || -ər-/ *adv fml* or *law* by doing or saying this: *I hereby declare her elected.*

he·red·i·ta·ry /hɪ'redɪtəri || -teri/ *adj* able to be passed down from parent to child: *a hereditary disease*

he·red·i·ty /hɪ'redɪti/ *n* [U] the passing on of qualities from parent to child in the cells of the body: *According to the laws of heredity, tall parents tend to have tall children.*

here·in /ˌhɪər'ɪn/ *adv fml* or *law* in this piece of writing

her·e·sy /'herəsi/ *n* **heresies** [C;U] belief, especially religious or political, opposed to the official or generally accepted one

her·e·tic /'herətɪk/ *n* a person who holds a religious or political belief opposed to the official or generally accepted one **-heretical** /hɪ'retɪkəl/ *adj*

here·with /ˌhɪə'wɪð || ˌhɪər-/ *adv fml* or *law* with this piece of writing: *I send you herewith two copies of the contract.*

her·i·tage /'herɪtɪdʒ/ *n* [sing] objects and customs which are passed down over many years within a family or nation: *Much of our country's artistic heritage was destroyed during the war.*

her·met·ic /hɜːˈmetɪk ‖ hɜːr-/ *adj* very tightly closed so that no air can get in or out **–hermetically** /-klɪ/ *adv*

her·mit /ˈhɜːmɪt ‖ ˈhɜːr-/ *n* a person who lives away from other people in order to think and pray

her·mit·age /ˈhɜːmɪtɪdʒ ‖ ˈhɜːr-/ *n* a place where a hermit lives

her·ni·a /ˈhɜːniə ‖ ˈhɜːr-/ *n* [C;U] the medical condition in which an organ pushes through its covering wall, usually the bowel through the stomach wall

he·ro /ˈhɪərəʊ/ *n* **heroes** **1** a person remembered or admired for bravery or goodness **2** the most important male character in a play, film, or story

he·ro·ic /hɪˈrəʊɪk/ *adj* **1** showing bravery, strength, and goodness: *heroic deeds* **2** needing great effort and determination: *her heroic attempt to succeed* **–heroically** /-klɪ/ *adv*

he·ro·ics /hɪˈrəʊɪks/ *n* [pl] speech or actions which are meant to appear grand, though they mean nothing

her·o·in /ˈherəʊɪn/ *n* [U] a drug which some people take illegally for pleasure, and which the user can become dependent on; doctors sometimes give heroin to lessen pain

her·o·ine /ˈherəʊɪn/ *n* **1** a woman remembered or admired for bravery or goodness **2** the most important female character in a play, film, or story

her·o·is·m /ˈherəʊɪzəm/ *n* [U] very great courage: *an act of great heroism*

her·on /ˈherən/ *n* a bird with long legs which lives near water

her·ring /ˈherɪŋ/ *n* a silver-coloured fish which lives in the sea

hers /hɜːz ‖ hɜːrz/ *pron* something relating to or belonging to the female person or animal who has already been mentioned: *When we went to collect our coats, my mother realized that she had left hers in the car.* | *My hand touched hers.*

herself /əˈself, hə-; *strong* hɜː- ‖ ər-, hər-; *strong* hɜːr-/ *pron* **1** used as the object of a verb or a PREPOSITION when the subject of a verb is female and the action is done to the same person: *She washed herself and got dressed.* | *Mary looked at herself in the mirror.* | *She had scratched herself on a rusty nail.* | *Sarah decided to buy herself some new clothes.* **2** used to add force to the word "she", or to the name of a female person or animal: *She herself admitted that it wasn't her best painting.* | *I'd like to speak to the doctor herself, please.* | *She had done all the decorating herself.* **3 by herself** alone, with no one with her or helping her: *Mary had spent the day by herself.* | *She had managed to mend the roof by herself.*

he's /iz, hiz; *strong* hiːz/ **1** short for "he is": *He's a writer.* | *He's coming.* **2** short for "he has": *He's got two cars.* | *He's had a cold.*

hes·i·tant /ˈhezɪtənt/ *adj* unwilling or being slow to do something because you are worried or uncertain about it: *She's hesitant about making new friends.* **–hesitantly** *adv*

hes·i·tate /ˈhezɪteɪt/ *v* **hesitated, hesitating 1** [I] to pause or wait for a while before you do something because you are worried or uncertain about it: *He hesitated before entering the room.* | *I'm hesitating about this new job after I've had.* **2 hesitate to do something** to be unwilling to do something because you think that it might not be the right thing to do: *I hesitate to ask him to lend me some money* **3 don't hesitate** a phrase used when you are saying that someone should do something which they

might feel worried or uncertain about: *Don't hesitate to ask me if you need any help.*

hes·i·ta·tion /ˌhezɪˈteɪʃən/ *n* **1** [C;U] a pause or wait before you do something because you feel worried or uncertain about it: *Without a moment's hesitation she jumped into the river.* | *After some hesitation he agreed to do what we asked.* **2 have no hesitation** to feel certain that what you are saying or doing is right: *I have no hesitation in saying that the government is doing everything possible to solve our economic problems.*

het·e·ro·ge·ne·ous /ˌhetərəʊˈdʒiːniəs/ *adj fml* of many different kinds: *a heterogeneous mix of nationalities*

het·e·ro·sex·u·al /ˌhetərəˈsekʃuəl/ *adj* attracted by people of the opposite sex **–compare** HOMOSEXUAL, BISEXUAL **–heterosexual** *n*

het up /ˌhet ˈʌp/ *adj* [never before a noun] *infml* anxious and worried: *He's all het up about tomorrow's examination.*

hew /hjuː/ *v* **hewed, hewed** *or* **hewn** /hjuːn/ [T] *fml* *or lit* to cut something heavy or hard with an axe or other tool

hex·a·gon /ˈheksəgən ‖ -gɑːn/ *n* a figure with six sides **–hexagonal** /hekˈsægənəl/ *adj*

hey /heɪ/ *interj infml* a shout used to call attention or to express surprise or interest: *Hey! Where are you going?*

hey·day /ˈheɪdeɪ/ *n* [sing] the period of greatest power or success: *In the heyday of their empire, the Romans controlled most of the western world.* | *In his heyday, he was one of the best footballers in the world.*

hi /haɪ/ *interj infml* HELLO

hi·a·tus /haɪˈeɪtəs/ *n* [sing] *fml* a pause when nothing happens

hi·ber·nate /ˈhaɪbəneɪt ‖ -ər-/ *v* hibernated, hibernating [I] (of animals) to be in or go into a sleep-like state during the winter **–hibernation** /ˌhaɪbəˈneɪʃən ‖ -bər-/ *n* [U]

hic·cup /ˈhɪkʌp, -kəp/ *n* (also **hiccough**) **1 hiccups** [pl] repeated sharp sounds in your throat which you sometimes get after eating or drinking: *"I've got hiccups again." "You shouldn't eat so fast."* **2** a small problem: *"How's the new system working?" "Well, we had a few hiccups at the beginning, but nothing major."* **–hiccup** *v* **-pp-** [I]

hid·den /ˈhɪdn/ *adj* difficult to see, find, or notice: *a hidden danger* | *a hidden meaning*

hide¹ /haɪd/ *v* **hid** /hɪd/, **hidden** /ˈhɪdn/ **hiding 1** [T] to put something in a place where no one can see it or find it: *He hid the letter inside his jacket.* | *Where have you hidden the presents?* **2** [T] to keep something secret: *She seems to be hiding information from them.* | *Don't hide your feelings. Say what you think.* **3** [I] to go to a place where no one can see you or find you: *I'll hide behind the door.*

hide² *n* [C;U] the skin of a large animal used for leather

hide·bound /ˈhaɪdbaʊnd/ *adj* having fixed, unchangeable opinions (a word used to express disapproval)

hid·e·ous /ˈhɪdiəs/ *adj* extremely ugly or shocking to see, hear, or experience: *a hideous wound* | *a hideous scream* **–hideously** *adv* : *the hideously mutilated body of a young woman*

hid·ing /ˈhaɪdɪŋ/ *n* **1 give someone a good hiding** *infml* to beat someone as a punishment: *I'll give you a good hiding when we get home!* **2 go into hiding**

to hide yourself: *The escaped prisoner went into hiding in the mountains.* [RELATED PHRASE **be in hiding**]

hi·er·ar·chy /ˈhaɪərɑːki ‖ -ɑːr-/ *n* **hierarchies 1** [C;U] a system of organization in which the members are arranged into higher and lower ranks: *There's a very rigid hierarchy in the civil service.* **2** [C + sing/pl verb] the most powerful members of an organization: *The party hierarchy will never accept him as leader.* –**hierarchical** /haɪəˈrɑːkɪkəl ‖ -ɑːr-/ *adj*

hi·e·ro·glyph /ˈhaɪərəglɪf/ *n* a picture-like sign which represents a word in ancient Egyptian writing

hi·e·ro·glyph·ics /ˌhaɪərəˈglɪfɪks/ *n* [pl] the ancient Egyptian system of writing which uses picture-like signs to represent words

hi-fi /ˈhaɪ faɪ, ˌhaɪ ˈfaɪ/ *n* [C;U] high quality apparatus for reproducing recorded sound: *Modern hi-fi is so good that it's just like sitting in the concert hall!* | *a hi-fi shop* –see picture on page 442

hig·gle·dy-pig·gle·dy /ˌhɪgəldi ˈpɪgəldi/ *adj, adv infml* in disorder

high¹ /haɪ/ *adj* **1** having a top that is a large distance above the ground or above the bottom (not usually used of living things): *It's a very high building.* | *a high mountain* –compare TALL **2** used in giving measurements: *How high is it?* | *four metres high* **3** at a point a large distance above the ground: *That shelf's too high for me. I can't reach it.* | *the highest town in England* **4** above or greater than what is usual: *the high cost of food* | *travelling at high speed* **5** near the top in rank: *She held high office in the last government.* | *high social status* **6** very good: *I have a very high opinion of his work.* | *a very high standard* | *high principles* **7** excited by alcohol or drugs: *She was high on drugs.* **8** near the top of the set of sounds which the ear can hear: *a high voice* | *a high note* **9** **the High Court** the most important court for non-criminal cases **10** **higher education** education at university or college **11** **high explosive** a very powerful explosive **12** **high fidelity** very good quality (used of apparatus for playing COMPACT DISCS, tapes (TAPE¹), and records) **13** **high heels** women's shoes with high heels **14** **high jump** a sport in which people jump over a bar which is gradually raised higher and higher **15** **be for the high jump** *BrE infml* to be about to be told by a person in a position of responsibility that you should not have done something **16** **the high life** the enjoyable life of rich and fashionable people **17** **high profile** the state of attracting a lot of attention to yourself or your actions: *The company has a high profile in the area of personal computers.* **18** **high school** a school for children aged 11–18 **19** **the high season** the time when the largest number of people are on holiday **20** **high spirits** great cheerfulness or readiness to have rather wild fun: *He was in great high spirits after the match.* **21** **the High Street** the main street of a town: *I bought it in the High Street.* | *Camden High Street* **22** **high tea** *BrE* a large early-evening meal **23** **high tide** the point at which the sea is highest up the shore or river: *It's a dangerous place at high tide.* **24** **It's high time** a phrase you use when you think someone should do something that has been delayed too long: *It's high time you bought a new car.*

■ USAGE **1** Note that we use **high** to describe measurements even if these measurements are not very big: *The wall was only three feet* **high**. **2** Compare **high** and **tall**. We use **high** (opposite **low**) for most things, but **tall** (opposite **short**) for people: *The*

building was more than 30 storeys **high**. | *She was well over six feet* **tall**. | *a* **high** *mountain* | *a* **high** *shelf* | *a* **tall** *man|woman*. We can also use **tall** for things when the height is very much greater than the width: *a* **tall** *pine tree* | *the* **tall** *skyscrapers of Hong Kong*

high² *adv* **1** to or at a high level or position: *They climbed high.* | *The plane flew high above.* | *He's high up in the civil service now.* | *He's risen high in the world.* **2** **high and low** everywhere: *I searched high and low for it.*

high³ *n* **1** the highest level: *The price of food reached a new high this week.* **2** *infml* a state of great excitement and happiness, sometimes produced by a drug

high-brow /ˈhaɪbraʊ/ *adj* connected with art, music, or books and often difficult to understand: *highbrow classical music*

high-class /ˌ· ˈ·◂/ *adj* **1** of good quality **2** of high social position

high-flown /ˌ· ˈ·◂/ *adj* sounding very grand but having very little meaning (used of language)

high-hand·ed /ˌ· ˈ·◂/ *adj* making decisions or acting without talking to other people first (a word used to express disapproval): *a high-handed decision* –**high-handedness** *n* [U]

high·land /ˈhaɪlənd/ *adj* coming from or relating to a mountainous area: *highland cattle*

Highland fling /ˌ· ˈ·/ *n* a fast Scottish country dance

High·lands /ˈhaɪləndz/ *n* [pl] **the Highlands** mountainous areas: *the Scottish Highlands*

high-lev·el /ˌ· ˈ·◂/ *adj* [only before a noun] concerning people at the top of an organization: *high-level peace talks*

high·light¹ /ˈhaɪlaɪt/ *n* **1** an important detail which stands out from the rest because it is the best or most interesting part: *a film of the highlights of the competition* **2** **highlights** [pl] small light-coloured areas in someone's hair, produced by colouring the hair artificially

highlight² *v* [T] to pick out something as an important part: *The report highlights the problems of the unemployed.*

high·ly /ˈhaɪli/ *adv* **1** to a high or great degree: *highly skilled* | *highly enjoyable* | *He's very highly paid.* **2** **speak highly of someone** to praise someone's qualities or abilities

highly-strung /ˌ·· ˈ·◂/ *adj* nervous and excitable

high-mind·ed /ˌ· ˈ·◂/ *adj* having high principles or moral standards (sometimes used to express disapproval) –**high-mindedness** *n* [U]

High·ness /ˈhaɪnəs/ *n* a title used of or to certain royal people: *Your Highness* | *His Highness Prince Leopold*

high-pow·ered /ˌ· ˈ·◂/ *adj* **1** very powerful: *a high-powered car* **2** very successful: *high-powered businessmen*

high-pres·sure /ˌ· ˈ·◂/ *adj* [only before a noun] **1** having or using high pressure (used of a machine or substance): *a high-pressure hosepipe* **2** carried out or working with great speed and force (used of an action, job, or person): *A high-pressure salesman may make you buy something you don't want.*

high-rise /ˈ· ·/ *adj* [only before a noun] very tall, with many floors (used of buildings): *She lives in a high-rise flat.*

high-spir·it·ed /ˌ· ˈ···◂/ *adj* full of fun

high-tech /ˌ· ˈ·◂/ n [U] the use of the most modern and advanced machines, processes, and methods in business and industry –**high-tech** adj : a new high-tech washing machine

high tech·no·l·ogy /ˌ· ·ˈ··◂/ n [U] the use of the most modern and advanced machines, processes, and methods in business and industry: the age of high technology

high·way /ˈhaɪweɪ/ n AmE or law 1 a broad main road, especially one going from one town to another 2 **the Highway Code** the official list of rules for vehicle drivers in Britain

high·way·man /ˈhaɪweɪmən/ n **highwaymen** /mən/ a man who used to stop travellers on the roads and rob them of their money in the past

hi·jack /ˈhaɪdʒæk/ v [T] to take control of a vehicle or aircraft illegally, often for political aims –**hijacker** n –**hijacking** n [C;U]

hike[1] /haɪk/ n a long walk in the country

hike[2] v **hiked, hiking** [I] to go on a long walk in the country –**hiker** n –**hiking** n [U]

hi·lar·i·ous /hɪˈleəriəs/ adj very funny and making you laugh a lot: The party got quite hilarious after they'd had a few glasses. | a hilarious film –**hilariously** adv

hi·lar·i·ty /hɪˈlærˌti/ n [U] cheerfulness and laughter

hill /hɪl/ n a raised area of land not as high as a mountain

hill·ock /ˈhɪlək/ n a little hill

hill·side /ˈhɪlsaɪd/ n the side of a hill

hil·ly /ˈhɪli/ adj having many hills: hilly countryside

hilt /hɪlt/ n 1 the handle of a sword, or of a knife which is used as a weapon 2 **to the hilt** completely: I'll support you to the hilt. | We're up to the hilt in debt.

him /ɪm; strong hɪm/ pron [used as the object of a verb] the male person or animal who has already been mentioned: "Where's John?" "I think I saw him in town." –see ME (USAGE)

himself /ɪmˈself; strong hɪm-/ pron 1 used as the object of a verb or a PREPOSITION when the subject of a verb is male and the action is done to the same person: He washed himself and got dressed. | John looked at himself in the mirror. | He had scratched himself on a rusty nail. | Peter decided to buy himself some new clothes. 2 used to add force to the word "he", or to the name of a male person or animal: He himself admitted that it wasn't his best painting. | I'd like to speak to the doctor himself, please. | He had done all the decorating himself. 3 **by himself** alone, with no one with him or helping him: John had spent the day by himself. | He had managed to mend the roof by himself.

hind /haɪnd/ adj **hind legs** the back legs of an animal

hin·der /ˈhɪndər/ v [T] to prevent from doing something: The bomb attack may hinder the progress of the peace talks.

hind·quar·ters /ˈhaɪndˌkwɔːtəz ‖ -ˌkwɔːrtərz/ n [pl] the back part of an animal including its legs

hin·drance /ˈhɪndrəns/ n something or somebody that prevents you from doing something: He said he'd help me do the job, but he was more of a hindrance than a help.

hind·sight /ˈhaɪndsaɪt/ n [U] understanding why and how something happened, but only after it has happened: With the benefit of hindsight I can see it was a mistake to buy that car.

Hin·du /ˈhɪnduː, hɪnˈduː/ n a person whose religion is Hinduism –**Hindu** adj

Hin·du·is·m /ˈhɪnduː-ɪzəm/ n [U] the chief religion of India, notable especially for its belief in many gods and that people return after death in another form

hinge[1] /hɪndʒ/ n a metal part which joins two things together so that one of them can swing freely; a hinge joins a door to a frame, or a lid to a box: I must oil the hinges to stop the gate creaking.

hinge[2] v **hinged, hinging** [T] to join things together with a hinge: The fridge door is hinged on the right. **hinge on/upon** sthg phr v [T] to depend on something: The success of the plan hinges on local support.

hint[1] /hɪnt/ n 1 an indirect suggestion: I wish you would give us a hint about the winner. 2 **a hint of** a small sign or amount of something: There's a hint of summer in the air, although it's only April. | a sauce with a hint of garlic 3 useful advice: helpful hints for removing stains 4 **drop a hint** to suggest something to someone in an indirect way 5 **take a hint** to understand someone's indirect suggestion: They took the hint and left immediately.

hint[2] v [I;T; + (that)] to suggest or mention something indirectly: I hinted to him that I was dissatisfied with his work. | The minister hinted at an early election.

☐ USEFUL PATTERNS to hint at something; to hint that...; to hint to someone that...

hin·ter·land /ˈhɪntəlænd ‖ -ər-/ n **the hinterland** the inner part of a country, beyond the coast or the banks of an important river

hip /hɪp/ n the fleshy part on either side of your body above your legs and below your waist: He stood with his hands on his hips.

hip·pie /ˈhɪpi/ n **hippies** (also **hippy**) a person who is against the standards of ordinary society, believes in love and peace and dresses in a colourful way; hippies were common in the 1960s

hip·po·pot·a·mus /ˌhɪpəˈpɒtəməs ‖ -ˈpɑː-/ n **hippopotamuses** or **hippopotami** /-maɪ/ (also **hippo** /ˈhɪpəʊ/ infml) a large African animal with short legs and thick hairless skin, which lives near rivers

hire[1] /haɪər/ v **hired, hiring** [T] 1 BrE to get the use of something for a short time by paying a certain amount of money: I'm going to hire an evening dress for the dance. 2 to employ someone to work for you for a short time: The fruit is picked by hired labourers.

■ USAGE Compare **hire** and **rent**. In British English you **hire** things for just a short time: Let's **hire** a car for the weekend. | I'll have to **hire** a suit for the wedding. If you are talking about a longer period, use the word **rent**: Is that your own television or do you **rent** it? Always use the word **rent** when talking about houses or flats: They live in a **rented** flat in the city centre. (In American English the word **rent** is used for all these things.)

hire sbdy/sthg ↔ **out** phr v [T] to give your services or the use of something for payment: Why don't you hire out your car to your neighbours while you're away? | Farm labourers used to hire themselves out for the summer.

hire[2] n [U] the use of something on payment of some money: Boats for hire. | We'll have to pay for the hire of a room.

hire pur·chase /ˌ· ˈ··/ n [U] (also **HP**) a system of payment for goods by which you pay small regular sums of money until you have paid the full price: I bought the stereo system on hire purchase.

his¹ /ɪz; *strong* hɪz/ *det* **1** relating to or belonging to the male person or animal who has already been mentioned: *My father came in and sat down in his chair.* | *He was sitting drinking his coffee.* **2** relating to or belonging to the person who has already been mentioned, when it has not been stated whether they are male or female: *Everyone should do his best.*

his² *pron* something relating to or belonging to the male person or animal who has already been mentioned: *When we went to collect our coats, my father realized that he had left his in the car.* | *My hand touched his.*

hiss /hɪs/ *v* **1** [I] to make a sound like a continuous "s": *Gas escaped with a hissing noise from the broken pipe.* **2** [I;T] to say in a sharp whisper: *The boy hissed a warning to be quiet.* **3** to make this sound in order to show anger or disapproval: *She was hissed off the stage.* –**hiss** *n* : *The snake gave an angry hiss.*

his·to·ri·an /hɪˈstɔːriən/ *n* a person who studies or writes about history

his·tor·ic /hɪˈstɒrɪk ‖ -ˈstɔː-, -ˈstɑː-/ *adj* important in history : *a historic occasion* | *historic buildings*

his·tor·i·cal /hɪˈstɒrɪkəl ‖ ˈstɔː-, -ˈstɑː-/ *adj* **1** concerning events that really happened or people that really existed in the past: *We cannot be sure whether King Arthur was a historical figure.* | *a historical novel* **2** connected with the study of history: *an institute for historical research* –**historically** /-kli/ *adv*

his·to·ry /ˈhɪstəri/ *n* **histories** **1** [U] events in the past, especially when seen as a whole: *a significant moment in South African history* **2** [U] the study of events in the past, especially those concerned with politics or social conditions: *History is my favourite subject at school.* **3** [C] a description of the development of something during the period in which it has existed: *the history of the computer* **4** [C] a set of facts relating to the past of a person: *the patient's medical history* **5** **have a history of** to have a record of illness, social difficulties, or criminal activities in the past: *She has a history of back trouble* | *The accused has a history of shoplifting.* **6** **make history, go down in history** to do something important which will be remembered

his·tri·on·ic /ˌhɪstriˈɒnɪk ‖ -ˈɑːnɪk/ *adj* showing strong feelings which are too theatrical to be sincere (a word used to express disapproval) –**histrionically** /-kli/ *adv*

his·tri·on·ics /ˌhɪstriˈɒnɪks, ‖ -ˈɑːn-/ *n* [pl] behaviour which is insincere and like a theatrical performance (a word used to express disapproval)

hit /hɪt/ *v* **hit, hit, hitting** [T] **1** to bring your hand, or something held in your hand, forcefully against someone or something: *She hit the burglar on the head.* | *He hit the ball over the net.* | *The demonstrator was hit by a rubber bullet.* –see picture on page 736 **2** to come up against something forcefully and suddenly: *She hit her head on the low ceiling.* | *The dog was hit by a truck.* **3** to have a bad effect on someone: *Inflation has hit poor people the hardest.* **4** to arrive at a place or position: *We hit the main road two miles further on.* | *The dollar hit an all time low today on the money markets.* **5** **hit it off with** *infml* to have a good relationship with: *I'm glad to see the two girls hitting it off so well.* **6** **hit the jackpot** *infml* to have a big success **7** **hit the nail on the head** to be exactly correct in what you have said **8** **hit the road** *infml* to start on a journey **9** **hit the roof** (also **hit the ceiling** *AmE*) *infml* to show great anger **10** **hit the sack** *infml* to go to bed

hit back *phr v* [I] to reply forcefully to an attack on yourself: *The Prime Minister has hit back angrily at these criticisms.*

hit on/upon sthg *phr v* [T] to have a good idea about something by chance: *Peter has hit upon an idea that will get us out of our difficulty.*

hit out at sbdy/sthg (also **hit out against** sbdy/sthg) *phr v* [T] to disagree violently with someone or something: *The newspapers are hitting out at the government's latest decision.*

hit² *n* **1** a blow with your hand or something held in your hand: *He aimed a wild hit at his attacker.* | *That was a good hit. It almost saved the game.* **2** the act of successfully striking something aimed at: *I scored a direct hit with my first shot.* **3** something, especially a film, song, or play, that is very successful: *Her first record was a big hit.* **4** **make a hit with someone** to make someone have a good opinion of you: *You've made a real hit with my parents!*

hit-and-miss /ˌ·· ˈ·-/ *adj* unplanned and depending on chance

hit-and-run /ˌ·· ˈ·◄/ *adj* **1** **hit-and-run accident** a road accident in which the person who causes the accident drives away quickly **2** **hit-and-run driver** a driver who causes an accident but does not stop to help

hitch¹ /hɪtʃ/ *v* **1** [T] to fasten by hooking something over something else: *Another railway carriage has been hitched on.* | *Hitch your horse to the gate.* **2** [I;T] *infml* to travel by getting free rides in other people's cars: *He hitched across Europe.* | *Let's hitch a ride.* **hitch** sthg ↔ **up** *phr v* [T] to pull a piece of clothing upwards into the proper position: *John hitched up his trousers.*

hitch² *n* a slight difficulty which delays something for a while: *a technical hitch* | *The first performance went off without a hitch.*

hitch-hike /ˈhɪtʃhaɪk/ *v* **hitchhiked, hitchhiking** [I] to travel by getting free rides in other people's cars by standing at the side of the road and signalling to drivers –**hitch-hiker** *n*

hith·er /ˈhɪðər/ *adv* **1** *old fash* to this place: *Come hither!* **2** **hither and thither** *lit* in all directions

hith·er·to /ˌhɪðəˈtuː◄ ‖ -ər-/ *adv fml* up until now: *Hitherto we have always paid the rent on Mondays.*

hit-list /ˈhɪtlɪst/ *n* a list of people against whom something bad is planned

hive /haɪv/ *n* **1** (also **beehive**) a small container or hut in which bees are kept **2** a very busy place: *The classroom was a hive of activity.*

h'm /m, hm/ *interj* (also **hm**) a sound made with your lips closed to express doubt or disagreement; or to give yourself time to think before speaking

HMS /ˌeɪtʃ em es/ title for a ship in the British Royal Navy; an abbreviation for **His/Her Majesty's Ship**: *HMS Belfast*

hoard¹ /hɔːd ‖ hɔːrd/ *n* a store of things which someone has collected very carefully and often secretly

hoard² *v* [T] to store things secretly in large amounts –**hoarder** *n*

hoard·ing /ˈhɔːdɪŋ ‖ ˈhɔːr-/ *n BrE* **1** a fence put round a piece of land when building is going on **2** a high fence or board on which large advertisements are stuck

hoar·frost /ˈhɔːfrɒst ‖ ˈhɔːrfrɔːst/ *n* [U] white frozen drops of water, seen on grass and plants after a cold night

hoarse /hɔːs ‖ hɔːrs/ *adj* sounding rough and hard, for example when you have a cold (used of a person or voice): *We shouted ourselves hoarse at the football match.* –**hoarsely** *adv* –**hoarseness** *n* [U]

hoar·y /ˈhɔːri/ adj lit grey or white with age (used of hair)

hoax /həʊks/ n a trick which makes someone believe something which is not true: We all left the building after a telephone caller said there was a bomb, but it was just a hoax. –**hoax** v (T)

hob /hɒb ‖ hɑːb/ n the flat top of a gas or electric cooker on which pans are placed

hob·ble /ˈhɒbəl ‖ ˈhɑː-/ v **1** [I] to walk with difficulty, taking small steps: She hobbled home, clutching her stick. **2** [T] to tie two legs of an animal together so that it cannot run away

hob·by /ˈhɒbi ‖ ˈhɑː-/ n **hobbies** an activity which you enjoy doing in your free time: Do you have a hobby? –see RECREATION (USAGE)

hob·by·horse /ˈhɒbihɔːs ‖ ˈhɑːbihɔːrs/ n **1** a child's toy like a horse's head on a stick **2** a subject which someone has strong opinions about and likes to talk about

hob·nob /ˈhɒbnɒb ‖ ˈhɑːbnɑːb/ v **-bb-** [I] to have a social relationship, often with someone in a higher position: I've been hobnobbing with the directors at the office party.

ho·bo /ˈhəʊbəʊ/ n **hoboes** or **hobos** AmE infml a person with no home or regular work

hock /hɒk ‖ hɑːk/ n [C;U] a type of German white wine

hock·ey /ˈhɒki ‖ ˈhɑːki/ n (**field hockey** AmE) a game for two teams of 11 players, who use special sticks to hit a ball around a field

hod /hɒd ‖ hɑːd/ n a container with a long handle, used by builders' workmen for carrying bricks

hodge·podge /ˈhɒdʒpɒdʒ ‖ ˈhɑːdʒpɑːdʒ/ n –see HOTCHPOTCH

hoe¹ /həʊ/ n a long-handled garden tool used for removing wild plants and making the soil loose –see picture on page 638

hoe² v **hoed, hoeing** [I;T] to use a hoe

hog¹ /hɒg ‖ hɑːg, hɔːg/ n **1** AmE a pig, especially a fat male one for eating **2** infml a rude person who eats too much **3 go the whole hog** infml to do something thoroughly or completely **4 road hog** a person who drives in a rude manner

hog² v **-gg-** [T] infml to take or use all of something so that no one else can use it: I can't overtake because the car in front is hogging the middle of the road.

hoist¹ /hɔɪst/ v [T] **1** to lift up something heavy: He hoisted the bag over his shoulder. **2** to raise something using ropes or a special machine: The sailors hoisted the flag. | The cargo was hoisted onto the ship.

hoist² n a machine for lifting heavy goods

hold¹ /həʊld/ v **held** /held/, **held, holding 1** [T] to keep something in your hands, arms, or mouth: She was holding a book. | He held her in his arms. | The dog was holding a newspaper in its mouth. –see picture on page 736 **2** [T] to move a part of your body into a particular position, or keep it there: She held her hand up. | They held their heads up. **3** [T] to keep someone somewhere as a prisoner: He is being held in police custody. **4** [T] to keep something in a particular position: The roof is held up by four enormous pillars. | The picture is held in place by a hook. **5** [T] to be able to contain a particular amount: The pan holds about one litre. | The cinema holds 500 people. **6** [T] to have something: Who holds the keys to the church? | He held the office of prime minister for four years. | Do you hold a current driving licence? **7** [T+that] to have a particular opinion: A lot of people hold the view that criminals are not punished severely enough. | She holds that the government's policy is mistaken. | I hold you

personally responsible for this tragedy. **8** [T] to cause an event to take place: We're holding a party next week. | The meeting was held at the company's headquarters. **9** [I] to remain good or true: The invitation still holds. | Let's hope the good weather holds. | What I said before still holds. **10 hold a conversation** to have a conversation: It was impossible to hold a conversation with all that noise going on. **11 hold your breath** to stop breathing for a short while: Don't forget to hold your breath when you dive into the water! **12 Hold it!** a phrase you use when you are telling someone to stop doing something **13 hold still** to remain still and not move: Hold still while I take a photo. **14 hold the line** to wait for a short time when you are talking on the telephone, for example so that someone can find the person that you want to talk to: If you'll just hold the line for a minute I'll put you through to Mr Atkins. **15 hold your own** to do as well as other people: Although he was by far the youngest competitor he certainly held his own.

hold sthg **against** sbdy phr v [T] to continue to feel angry with someone or dislike them because of something bad that they did in the past: The fact that someone has been in prison should not be held against them.

hold back phr v **1** [T **hold** sbdy/sthg ↔ **back**] to prevent someone or something from moving forwards: Police held the crowd back. | People built banks of earth to hold back the flood waters. **2** [I] to be unwilling to do something because you are not sure that it is the right thing to do: She held back for a long time before she finally went to the police. **3** [T **hold** sbdy ↔ **back**] to prevent someone from developing properly: Illness can hold a child back quite significantly. **4** [T **hold** sthg ↔ **back**] to keep something secret: I knew that he was holding something back.

hold sthg ↔ **down** phr v [T] **1** to keep a job: He seems to be unable to hold down a job for more than a few weeks. **2** to keep something at a low level: the government's determination to hold down prices

hold forth phr v [T] fml to talk for a long time about something

hold sbdy/sthg ↔ **off** phr v [T] to cause someone or something to remain at a distance: They managed to hold off the enemy's attack.

hold on phr v [I] infml to wait for a short time: Could you hold on? I'll just see if he's in.

hold onto sthg phr v [T] **1** to hold something with your hand: She held onto the side of the boat. **2** to manage to keep something: He held onto his job.

hold out phr v **1** [T **hold** sthg ↔ **out**] to offer something to someone by moving it towards them: He held out his hand to her. **2** [I] to manage to last in spite of difficulties: The people held out until help arrived. **3 hold out hope** to remain hopeful: I don't hold out much hope that the weather will improve.

hold out for sthg phr v [T] to demand something firmly and wait until you get it: The men are still holding out for more pay.

hold sthg **over** phr v [T] to move something to a later date: We may have to hold the meeting over until next week.

hold sbdy **to** sthg phr v [T] to make someone do what they said that they would do: I shall hold him to his promise.

hold up phr v **1** [T **hold** sbdy/sthg ↔ **up**] to delay someone or something: The building work was held up by the bad weather. **2** [T **hold** sbdy ↔ **up**] to stop someone in order to rob them: He was held up at gunpoint and robbed. **3** [**hold** sbdy/sthg ↔

up] to give someone or something as an example of something: *He always held up his youngest son as a model of hard work.*

hold with sthg *phr v* [T] **not hold with something** to not agree with something: *I don't hold with these modern teaching methods.*

hold² *n* **1** the part of a ship where goods are stored **2** the act of holding something: *I seemed to be losing my hold of the rope.* **3** something that you can hold when you are climbing: *I couldn't find a hold for my hands.* **4 a hold over someone** power or control over someone: *Religion has a strong hold over these people.* | *His hold over her seemed to be weakening.* **5 get hold of something: a** to take something in your hand and hold it: *I got hold of the sack and lifted it up.* **b** to find someone or obtain something: *I need to get hold of some money quickly.* **6 take hold of something** to take something in your hand and hold it: *He took hold of the rope and pulled.*

hold·all /ˈhəʊldɔːl/ *n* a large bag or small case used when travelling

hold·er /ˈhəʊldəʳ/ *n* **1** a person who has control of or owns a place, a position, or a thing: *the holder of the office of chairman* | *Only ticket-holders will be admitted to the show.* **2** something which contains or supports something else: *a cigarette holder* | *a candle holder*

hold·ing /ˈhəʊldɪŋ/ *n* **1** a piece of land which you own or rent **2** shares in a company

hold·up /ˈhəʊld-ʌp/ *n* **1** a delay, for example one caused by traffic: *Sorry I'm late, there was a holdup down by the bridge.* **2** a robbery in which people are threatened with a gun: *a masked holdup at the bank*

hole¹ /həʊl/ *n* **1** an empty space or opening in or through something solid: *The men have dug a hole in the road.* | *There's a hole in my sock.* **2** the home of a small animal: *a rabbit hole* **3** a hollow place into which the ball must be hit in the game of GOLF: *an 18-hole golf course* **4** *infml* a small unpleasant place: *His flat's a bit of a hole.* **5 pick holes in something** to find the weak points in something such as an argument or idea

hole² *v* **holed, holing** [T] **1** to make a hole in something: *Our ship was holed and began to sink.* **2** to hit a ball into a hole when playing GOLF

hol·i·day /ˈhɒlɪdi ‖ ˈhɑːlɪdeɪ/ *n* **1** a day of rest from work; often religious or political importance: *The Fourth of July is a national holiday in the United States.* | *Next Friday is a holiday.* **2** a period of time when you do not go to work, school, or university, but have a rest or go away somewhere: *the school holidays* | *We spent the Easter holidays in Crete.* | *a skiing holiday* | *According to the contract you get 25 days paid holiday a year.* | *a holiday resort* | *Where did Mary go for her holiday?* **3 on holiday, on your holidays** having a holiday: *I'm afraid Mr Jones is away on holiday.* | *When you go on holiday don't forget to write to me!* –**holiday** *v* [I]

hol·i·day·mak·er /ˈhɒlɪdiˌmeɪkəʳ ‖ ˈhɑːlɪdeɪ-/ *n* a person on holiday

hol·i·ness /ˈhəʊlinɪs/ *n* **1** [U] the state or quality of being holy **2 Holiness** a title of the POPE: *Your Holiness* | *His Holiness Pope John Paul*

hol·ler /ˈhɒləʳ ‖ ˈhɑː-/ *v* [I;T] *infml AmE* to shout out: *"Let go," she hollered.* –**holler** *n*

hol·low¹ /ˈhɒləʊ ‖ ˈhɑː-/ *adj* **1** having an empty space or hole inside: *The pillars look solid, but in fact they're hollow.* **2** sunken inwards (used of parts of a person's face): *hollow cheeks* **3** having a ringing sound which goes on for some time: *the hollow sound of a large bell* **4** not sincere, or

without real value: *the hollow promises of politicians* –**hollowness** *n* [U]

hollow² *n* a space or hole in the surface of something, often the ground

hollow³ *v*

hollow sthg ↔ **out** *phr v* [T] to remove the inside of something: *He hollowed out a log.*

hol·ly /ˈhɒli ‖ ˈhɑːli/ *n* **hollies** [C;U] a small tree with dark green prickly leaves and red berries

hol·o·caust /ˈhɒləkɔːst ‖ ˈhɑː-/ *n* great destruction and the loss of many lives by fire or war: *fear of a nuclear holocaust*

hol·o·gram /ˈhɒləgræm ‖ ˈhəʊlə-, ˈhɑː-/ *n* a picture of something made with LASER beams which makes it look solid, not flat

hol·ster /ˈhəʊlstəʳ/ *n* a leather holder for a gun, usually worn on a belt around the waist

ho·ly /ˈhəʊli/ *adj* **holier, holiest 1** connected with God and religion: *the Holy Bible* | *the holy city of Mecca* **2** morally pure and giving yourself to God: *a holy man* | *She led a holy life.* **3 take holy orders** to become a priest

hom·age /ˈhɒmɪdʒ ‖ ˈhɑː-/ *n* [U] things said or done as signs of great respect: *They paid homage to the king.*

home¹ /həʊm/ *n* **1** [C;U] the place where you usually live especially with your family: *"Where do you live?" "Well, Nigeria is my home, but I'm living in London just now."* | *Buckingham Palace is the home of the Queen and her family.* | *He's not at home now; he should be back at seven.* **2** [sing] a place where a thing usually lives or comes from: *India is the home of elephants and tigers.* | *America is the home of baseball.* **3** [C] a place for the care of a group of people or animals of the same type, who do not live with a family: *a children's home* | *an old people's home* | *Battersea Dogs' Home* **4 be/feel at home** not to feel worried, and especially about your skills or experience: *He's completely at home working with children.* **5 make yourself at home** a phrase used to invite someone to behave as they like in your home

■ USAGE 1 There is no **to** in these sentences: *I'm coming* home. 2 British people use **at home** in sentences like these: *Let's stay* **at home** *tonight.* | *Is John* **at home**? Americans often miss out **at**: *Let's stay* **home** *tonight.* | *Is John* **home**?

home² *adv* **1** to or at your home: *Is she home yet?* | *I must be getting home.* | *We're home at last.* **2** to the right place: *He struck the nail home.* **3 come home to someone** to be fully understood by someone: *At last it's come home to me how much I owe to my parents.* [RELATED PHRASE **bring something home to someone**]

home³ *v*

home in on sthg *phr v* [T] to aim or move exactly towards something

home⁴ *adj* [only before a noun] **1** related to or being a home, place of origin, or base: *the home office of an international firm* | *Birmingham is my home town.* **2** not foreign: *the home country* | *home affairs* **3** playing on your own sports field rather than that of an opponent: *We've watched all the home matches.* | *the home team*

home-brew /ˈ· ·/ *n* [U] beer made at home

home·com·ing /ˈhəʊmˌkʌmɪŋ/ *n* an arrival home, especially after a long absence

home ec·o·nom·ics /ˌ· ··ˈ···/ *n* a school subject dealing with cooking and learning to manage a home

home help /ˌ· ·ˈ·/ *n BrE* a person who is sent in by the local council to help clean and cook for someone who is ill or very old

home·land /ˈhəʊmlænd, -lənd/ n the country where you were born

home·ly /ˈhəʊmli/ adj **1** simple and ordinary: a homely meal of bread and cheese **2** AmE ordinary and not good-looking (used of a person) –**homeliness** n [U]

Home Of·fice /ˈ· ˌ··/ n [+ sing/pl verb] **the Home Office** the British government department which deals with keeping order inside the country and controlling who comes into it: The Home Office is considering your request. –compare FOREIGN OFFICE

home·less /ˈhəʊmləs/ adj **1** having nowhere to live: So now he's unemployed and homeless. **2** the homeless people who have nowhere to live –**homelessness** n [U]

home-made /ˌ· ˈ· ◄/ adj made in someone's home rather than in a factory or a shop: delicious home-made cakes

ho·me·op·athy /ˌhəʊmiˈɒpəθi ‖ -ˈɑːp-/ n see HOMOEOPATHY

home·sick /ˈhəʊmˌsɪk/ adj sad because you are away from home: I was homesick for the old farm and for my friends. | He says he never feels homesick. –**homesickness** n [U]

home·spun /ˈhəʊmspʌn/ adj containing only a few simple ideas: a homespun philosophy

home·stead /ˈhəʊmsted, -stɪd/ n a farm with its buildings and land

home truth /ˌ· ˈ·/ n something unpleasant but true about yourself which you learn from someone else

home·ward /ˈhəʊmwəd ‖ -ərd/ adj [always before a noun] going towards home: the homeward journey –**homewards** adv (also **homeward** AmE): hurrying homewards after work

home·work /ˈhəʊmwɜːk ‖ -ɜːrk/ n [U] **1** work which teachers give students to do at home: We've got loads of homework tonight. **2** preparation for a meeting or speech: The politicians had obviously done their homework well and knew the problems.

hom·i·cid·al /ˌhɒmɪˈsaɪdl ◄ ‖ ˌhɑː-/ adj likely to murder someone: a homicidal maniac

hom·i·cide /ˈhɒmɪsaɪd ‖ ˈhɑː-/ n fml or law **1** [C;U] the crime of murder **2** [C] a murderer

hom·i·ly /ˈhɒmɪli ‖ ˈhɑː-/ n homilies fml a long and dull talk giving advice on how to behave

hom·ing /ˈhəʊmɪŋ/ adj [only before a noun] **1** having the ability, which is found in certain birds and animals, to find the way home: a homing pigeon **2** able to guide itself to something it is aimed at (of a modern weapon of war)

ho·moe·op·athy /ˌhəʊmiˈɒpəθi ‖ -ˈɑːp-/ n (also **homeopathy**) [U] a way of treating a disease by giving small amounts of a drug which, in larger amounts, would produce an illness like the disease –**homoeopath** /ˈhəʊmiəpæθ/ n –**homoeopathic** /ˌhəʊmiəˈpæθɪk◄/ adj

ho·mo·ge·ne·ous /ˌhəʊməˈdʒiːniəs/ adj (also **ho·mog·enous**) formed of parts which are all the same –**homogeneity** /ˌhəʊmədʒɪˈniːəti/ n [U]

ho·mo·ge·nized /həˈmɒdʒənaɪzd ‖ -ˈmɑː-/ adj (also **homogenised** BrE) **homogenized milk** milk without any cream on top because the fat is broken up and mixed with the milk

ho·mo·sex·u·al /ˌhəʊməˈsekʃuəl/ n someone who is sexually attracted to members of the same sex –**homosexual** adj : a homosexual relationship –compare BISEXUAL, HETEROSEXUAL, LESBIAN

hone /həʊn/ v honed, honing [T] fml to sharpen a tool

hon·est /ˈɒnɪst ‖ ˈɑːn-/ adj **1** open and direct: To be quite honest with you, I don't think you'll pass. **2** not likely to lie, steal, or cheat: An honest employee is a rare thing. **3** truthful and sincere: an honest face | an honest opinion –opposite **dishonest**

hon·est·ly /ˈɒnɪstli ‖ ˈɑːn-/ adv **1** without lying, stealing, or cheating: And if I can't get the money honestly, I'll have to think of something else. **2** speaking truthfully: I honestly don't mind working late tonight. **3 Honestly!** a word used to express annoyance: Honestly! What a stupid thing to do!

hon·es·ty /ˈɒnɪsti ‖ ˈɑːn-/ n [U] **1** the quality of being honest: We've never doubted your honesty. **2 in all honesty** being open and truthful: In all honesty, the chances of getting the money back are slim.

hon·ey /ˈhʌni/ n **1** [U] the sweet sticky golden-brown substance produced by bees, which can be eaten on bread **2** [C] AmE a word used when speaking to someone you love: Hurry up, honey, we're going to be late.

hon·ey·comb /ˈhʌnikəʊm/ n a wax container made by bees and consisting of six-sided cells in which honey is stored

hon·ey·moon /ˈhʌnimuːn/ n **1** the holiday taken by a man and woman who have just got married: Where are they going for their honeymoon? **2** a short period at the beginning of a new job or government when everyone is happy with the people concerned: The honeymoon's over for the new President. –**honeymoon** v [I]

hon·ey·suck·le /ˈhʌniˌsʌkəl/ n [C;U] a climbing plant with sweet-smelling flowers

honk /hɒŋk ‖ hɑːŋk, hɔːŋk/ n [I;T] to make the sound like a GOOSE or a car horn: As she drove past, she honked the horn. –**honk** n

hon·or·ar·y /ˈɒnərəri ‖ ˈɑːnəreri/ adj **1** given as an honour without the usual work necessary: an honorary degree | an honorary title **2** without payment: the honorary chairman | the honorary treasurer

hon·our¹ /ˈɒnə ‖ ˈɑːnər/ n (**honor** AmE) **1** [U] great respect and admiration: They fought for the honour of their country. | We award you this trophy as a mark of honour. **2** [sing] something that brings great respect and pride: It is a great honour to have the Duke here today. | She's an honour to the profession. | Will you do me the honour of accepting my invitation? **3** [U] high principles and standards of behaviour: a man of honour | It's a matter of honour. **4 in honour of someone, in someone's honour** to show respect for someone: A rose bush was planted in honour of the Queen Mother's birthday. **5 Honour** a respectful title for a judge: Good morning, your Honour. | His Honour Judge Thompson

hon·our² v (**honor** AmE) [T] **1** to show respect to someone or to praise them publicly: Today the Queen is honouring us with her presence. | The villagers came to honour their chief. **2** to keep an agreement: The bank has refused to honour his cheque. | You must honour your commitments to the firm.

hon·our·a·ble /ˈɒnərəbəl ‖ ˈɑːn-/ adj (**honorable** AmE) **1** showing or deserving respect and admiration: an honourable settlement to the strike **2** showing high principles: The honourable thing to do would be to marry her. **3** [only before a noun] a title given to the children of certain British noblemen, and various official people, including Members of Parliament: Will the Honourable member *please answer the question?* | *the Honourable Miss Fortescue* –**honourably** *adv*

hon·ours /ˈɒnəz ‖ ˈɑːnərz/ *n* (**honors** *AmE*) [pl] **1** (also **Hons**) a university UNDERGRADUATE degree of a higher standard than an Ordinary degree: *James Brown BA (Hons)* | *a first class honours degree in History* **2 do the honours** *infml* to act as the host or hostess by offering drinks or food

hood /hʊd/ *n* **1** part of a coat which can be pulled up to cover your head in bad weather **2** a movable cover over a car or PRAM **3** *AmE* the BONNET covering the engine of a car

hood·ed /ˈhʊdəd/ *adj* **1** a garment with a hood: *a hooded raincoat* **2** half closed (used of eyelids)

hood·wink /ˈhʊdˌwɪŋk/ *v* [T] to trick or deceive someone

hoof /huːf ‖ hʊf/ *n* **hoofs** or **hooves** /huːvz, hʊvz/ the hard foot of certain animals like the horse

hook¹ /hʊk/ *n* **1** a curved piece of metal, plastic, or wood for hanging things on: *She hung up her coat on the hook behind the door.* | *curtain hooks* **2** a curved piece of metal: *a fish hook* | *a crochet hook* | *a picture hook* **3 hook and eye** a small metal hook and bar used for fastening clothes **4** a hit given in BOXING with the elbow bent **5 get off the hook** to get out of a difficult situation **6 off the hook** having the telephone receiver lifted off so that the telephone will not ring

hook² *v* [T] **1** to catch or fasten something with a hook: *Those two bits hook together.* | *We've hooked a fish!* **2** to place something in a position like a hook: *He hung his leg over the arm of the chair.* | *Hook the rope over that nail.* **3** to hit a ball in GOLF or cricket so that it does not go in a straight line: *Oh no! I've hooked it!*

hook sthg ↔ **up** [T] *infml* to connect something: *Can you hook up this computer to the mainframe?*

hooked /hʊkt/ *adj* **1** shaped like a hook: *a hooked nose* **2** [never before a noun] *infml* dependent on drugs: *She's hooked on crack.* **3** having a great liking for: *I'm absolutely hooked on that new television soap opera.* | *She's really hooked on him.*

hoo·li·gan /ˈhuːlɪɡən/ *n* a noisy, violent, young person who causes trouble by fighting and breaking things –**hooliganism** *n* [U]

hoop /huːp ‖ hʊp, huːp/ *n* a circular band of wood or metal round a barrel or used as a child's toy –**hooped** *adj*

hoo·ray /hʊˈreɪ/ *interj* a shout of joy or approval: *Hooray! We've won!*

hoot¹ /huːt/ *v* **1** [I;T] to make a loud noise: *I hooted my horn at the children playing in the road.* | *Did you hear the owl hooting last night?* **2** [I] to laugh loudly, often unkindly: *The children hooted with delight.*

hoot² *n* **1** the sound made by an OWL or by a car or ship's horn **2** a shout of laughter, often unkind: *His speech was greeted with hoots of laughter.* **3** *infml* something very amusing: *That play was a real hoot!* **4 I don't give two hoots, I don't care a hoot** *infml* I don't care at all: *He doesn't care two hoots whether he passes his examination or not.*

hoot·er /ˈhuːtəʳ/ *n* **1** a car horn **2** a whistle which signals the beginning or end of work **3** *slang* a nose

hoo·ver /ˈhuːvəʳ/ *n tdmk* (also **Hoover**) a machine you use to clean a carpet –**hoover** *v* [I;T] : *Jim hoovered the flat before the guests arrived.*

hooves /huːvz/ the plural of HOOF

hop¹ /hɒp ‖ hɑːp/ *v* **-pp-** **1** [I] (of people) to jump on one leg –see picture on page 736 **2** [I] (of small creatures) to jump with the legs together: *The bird hopped onto my finger.* **3** [I + adv/prep] *infml* to get quickly onto, into, or out of something: *She hopped on her bicycle and rushed off.* | *Hop in and I'll give you a lift to the station.* **4 Hop it!** *infml* Go away! **5 hopping mad** very angry

hop² *n* **1** a small jump **2** *infml* a short aircraft flight: *We'll do the final hop from Cairo to Luxor the following day.* **3 on the hop** *infml* unprepared or very busy: *Their sudden arrival caught me on the hop.* **4** a tall climbing plant with flowers **5 hops** the dried seed-cases of a plant, used for giving taste to beer

hope¹ /həʊp/ *v* **hoped, hoping** **1** [I; +(that)] to want something to happen and have some confidence that it probably will happen: *I hope he comes tomorrow.* | *She hopes to go to college next year.* | *We're hoping for a big order from the Middle East.* | *"Is she coming?" "I hope so."* | *I hope not.*
□ USEFUL PATTERNS to hope that…; to hope to do something; to hope for something
2 hope for the best to hope that everything will work out satisfactorily

■ USAGE **Hope** and **wish** can both be used to give people good wishes for the future. **I hope (that)** is commonly used in this way: **I hope that** *you have a good journey.* | **I hope** *you get better soon.* | **I hope** *your exam goes well.* **I wish you + noun** is a much more formal expression: *May* **I wish you** *a very pleasant journey, Sir?* | **We wish you a speedy recovery.**

hope² *n* **1** [C;U] the expectation of something happening as you want it to: *Hopes of reaching a peace settlement are now fading.* | *Don't give up hope. He may still come.* | *I have high hopes of passing the exam.* | *The doctors don't hold out much hope for her.* **2** [C] someone or something that could bring success: *Please help me – you're my last hope.* | *The only hope we have of a settlement is for both sides to compromise.*

hope·ful /ˈhəʊpfəl/ *adj* **1** feeling quite confident: *I'm hopeful that he'll arrive early.* **2** giving reason to think success is possible: *hopeful signs of economic recovery* –**hopefulness** *n* [U]

hope·ful·ly /ˈhəʊpfəli/ *adv* **1** in a hopeful way **2** if everything goes well: *Hopefully we'll be there by dinnertime.*

■ USAGE This second meaning of **hopefully** is now very common, especially in speech, but some people still consider that it is incorrect.

hope·less /ˈhəʊpləs/ *adj* **1** having or giving no signs of hope: *tears of hopeless despair* | *a hopeless situation* **2** *infml* very bad or unskilled: *I'm hopeless at maths.* –**hopelessly** *adv* –**hopelessness** *n* [U]

hop·scotch /ˈhɒpskɒtʃ ‖ ˈhɑːpskɑːtʃ/ *n* [U] a children's game in which a stone is thrown onto numbered squares and each child hops (HOP) from one to another

horde /hɔːd ‖ hɔːrd/ *n* a large crowd of people: *There were hordes of tourists at the castle.*

ho·ri·zon /həˈraɪzən/ *n* **1** the horizon the line in the distance where the sky seems to meet the earth or sea **2 horizons** [pl] the limit of your ideas, knowledge, or experience: *Reading is said to broaden your horizons.*

hor·i·zon·tal /ˌhɒrɪˈzɒntl◂ ‖ ˌhɑːrɪˈzɑːntl/ *adj* in a flat position, along or parallel to the ground: *Stand the table on its legs, so that the top is horizontal.* –compare VERTICAL –**horizontally** *adv*

hor·mone /ˈhɔːməʊn ‖ ˈhɔːr-/ n a substance produced by your body and passed into your blood to encourage growth

horn /hɔːn ‖ hɔːrn/ n 1 [C] a hard pointed growth on the heads of some cattle, sheep, and wild animals 2 [U] the substance that horns are made of: *The knife has a horn handle.* 3 [C] something which gives a short loud sound as a warning: *a car horn* | *He sounded his horn as he approached the bend in the road.* 4 [C] a musical instrument consisting of a long metal tube, usually bent several times and played by blowing: *the French horn* | *a hunting horn*

hor·net /ˈhɔːnɪt ‖ ˈhɔːr-/ n a large insect which can sting, related to the WASP

horn·pipe /ˈhɔːnpaɪp ‖ ˈhɔːrn-/ n a dance performed by sailors, or the music for a hornpipe

horn·y /ˈhɔːni ‖ ˈhɔːrni/ adj hornier, horniest hard and rough: *The old gardener had horny hands.*

hor·o·scope /ˈhɒrəskəʊp ‖ ˈhɑː-, ˈhɔː-/ n a statement about someone's character, life, and future, based on the positions of the stars or planets (PLANET) at the time of their birth

hor·ren·dous /həˈrendəs ‖ hɑː-, hɔː-/ adj extremely unpleasant: *What horrendous weather!* –**horrendously** adv

hor·ri·ble /ˈhɒrɪbəl ‖ ˈhɔː-, ˈhɑː-/ adj 1 causing shock and dislike: *a horrible accident* 2 infml very unpleasant: *What a horrible dress!* | *I have a horrible feeling we're going to miss the train.* –**horribly** adv

hor·rid /ˈhɒrɪd ‖ ˈhɔː-, ˈhɑː-/ adj very unpleasant or unkind: *Don't be so horrid to your little sister.* –**horridly** adv

hor·rif·ic /həˈrɪfɪk ‖ hɔː-, hɑː-/ adj very shocking and unpleasant: *The film showed the most horrific murder scenes.* –**horrifically** /-kli/ adv

hor·ri·fy /ˈhɒrɪfaɪ ‖ ˈhɔː-, ˈhɑː-/ v horrified, horrifying [T] to shock someone greatly: *I was horrified by the news of her murder.* | *a horrifying story* –**horrifyingly** adv

hor·ror /ˈhɒrəʳ ‖ ˈhɔː-, ˈhɑː-/ n 1 [U] a feeling of great shock, anxiety, and fear: *Seeing the children playing on the cliff filled me with horror.* | *I watched in horror as the cars crashed into each other.* 2 **the horror of, the horrors of** the unpleasantness of something that is shocking and frightening: *the horrors of war* | *The full horror of the accident only hit me later.* 3 **have a horror of** to hate something and be afraid of it: *I have a horror of snakes.* 4 [C] infml an unpleasant child: *The little horror never stops playing tricks on his parents.*

horror film /ˈ·· ˌ·/ n a film in which strange and frightening things happen

hors d'oeu·vre /ˌɔːˈdɜːv ‖ ˌɔːr ˈdɜːrv/ n hors d'oeuvres- small amounts of cold meat and vegetables served at the beginning of a meal

horse /hɔːs ‖ hɔːrs/ n 1 a large four-legged animal which people ride on and use for pulling heavy things –see TRANSPORT (USAGE) 2 an exercise apparatus for jumping over 3 **straight from the horse's mouth** infml told to you directly from the person concerned: *"Who told you she was leaving?" "I heard it straight from the horse's mouth."*

horse·back /ˈhɔːsbæk ‖ ˈhɔːrs-/ n **on horseback** riding on a horse

horse·box /ˈhɔːsbɒks ‖ ˈhɔːrsbɑːks/ n a large enclosed container pulled by another vehicle and used for carrying horses

horse chest·nut /ˌ· ˈ·· ‖ ˈ· ˌ·-/ n 1 a large tree with white or pink flowers 2 a shiny brown nut from this tree

horse·play /ˈhɔːspleɪ ‖ ˈhɔːrs-/ n [U] rough noisy behaviour by young people for fun

horse·pow·er /ˈhɔːsˌpaʊəʳ ‖ ˈhɔːrs-/ n [U] (also **HP**) a measure of the power of an engine

horse·rac·ing /ˈhɔːsˌreɪsɪŋ ‖ ˈhɔːrs-/ n [U] the sport of racing horses –see picture on page 637

horse·rad·ish /ˈhɔːsˌrædɪʃ ‖ ˈhɔːrs-/ n a plant whose root is used to make a strong-tasting SAUCE usually eaten with meat

horse·shoe /ˈhɔːʃ-ʃuː, ˈhɔːs- ‖ ˈhɔːr-/ n 1 a curved piece of iron nailed to the bottom of a horse's foot 2 something with this shape, often believed to bring good luck

hors·y /ˈhɔːsi ‖ ˈhɔːrsi/ adj (also **horsey**) 1 very interested in horses and riding 2 looking like a horse –**horsiness** n [U]

hor·ti·cul·ture /ˈhɔːtɪˌkʌltʃəʳ ‖ ˈhɔːr-/ n [U] the practice of growing fruit, flowers, and vegetables –**horticultural** /ˌhɔːtɪˈkʌltʃərəl◂ ‖ ˌhɔːr-/ adj –**horticulturalist** n

hose¹ /həʊz/ n 1 [C;U] (also **hosepipe**) a piece of rubber or plastic tube used to direct water onto fires, a garden, or a car –see picture on page 638 2 [U] old fash TIGHTS, STOCKINGS, or socks

hose² v hosed, hosing [T] (also **hose sthg ↔ down**) to water or wash something using a hose: *I'll just hose the car down.* | *We'll have to hose the garden soon.*

ho·sie·ry /ˈhəʊzjəri ‖ ˈhəʊʒəri/ n [U] fml the word used in a shop for socks, STOCKINGS, and TIGHTS

hos·pice /ˈhɒspɪs ‖ ˈhɑː-/ n a hospital where people who are dying of incurable illnesses are cared for

hos·pi·ta·ble /ˈhɒspɪtəbəl, hɒˈspɪ- ‖ hɑːˈspɪ-/ adj being welcoming to guests or visitors, asking them into your home and feeding them –opposite **inhospitable** –**hospitably** adv

hos·pi·tal /ˈhɒspɪtl ‖ ˈhɑː-/ n [C;U] a place where people who are hurt or ill have medical treatment: *Did you know that Jane's in hospital?*

hos·pi·tal·ity /ˌhɒspɪˈtælɪti ‖ ˌhɑː-/ n [U] 1 welcoming behaviour towards guests 2 food and a place to sleep given to guests

hos·pi·tal·ize /ˈhɒspɪtl-aɪz ‖ ˈhɑː-/ v (also **hospitalise** BrE) hospitalized, hospitalizing [T] to send someone into hospital: *He broke a leg and was hospitalized for a month.* –**hospitalization** /ˌhɒspɪtl-aɪˈzeɪʃən ‖ ˌhɑːspɪtl-əˈzeɪ-/ n [U]

host¹ /həʊst/ n 1 someone who invites guests: *We thanked our host and left the party.* 2 a country or organization which provides the space and equipment for a special event: *the host nation for the next Olympics* 3 [+ sing/pl verb] a large number: *A whole host of difficulties have arisen.* 4 someone who introduces other performers, such as those on a TV show

host² v [T] to act as a host for a special event: *Which country is hosting the next Commonwealth Games?*

hos·tage /ˈhɒstɪdʒ ‖ ˈhɑː-/ n 1 someone kept as a prisoner by a group of people who threaten to hurt them if certain things are not done: *He has been held hostage now for three years.* 2 **take/hold someone hostage** to keep someone as a hostage: *Three children have been taken hostage.*

hos·tel /ˈhɒstl ‖ ˈhɑː-/ n a building in which students, or young people working or travelling away from home, can eat and sleep cheaply: *a youth hostel*

hos·tel·ry /ˈhɒstəlri ‖ ˈhɑː-/ n old fash a place where alcoholic drinks may be bought and drunk

host·ess /ˈhəʊstɪ̯s/ n 1 a woman who invites guests 2 (also **airhostess**) a woman who looks after the passengers on an aeroplane 3 a woman who is paid by a man to be his companion for the evening

hos·tile /ˈhɒstaɪl ‖ ˈhɑːstl, ˈhɑːstaɪl/ adj 1 unfriendly: The Prime Minister was greeted by a hostile crowd. 2 belonging to an enemy: hostile territory

hos·til·i·ties /hɒˈstɪlɪ̯tiz ‖ hɑː-/ n [pl] fml war-like fighting: Hostilities have broken out between the two countries.

hos·til·i·ty /hɒˈstɪlɪ̯ti ‖ hɑː-/ n [U] strong dislike or disapproval

hot¹ /hɒt ‖ hɑːt/ adj **hotter, hottest** 1 having a high temperature: It's very hot in here – can I open a window? | The water isn't hot yet. | Bake the pie in a hot oven for half an hour. | If you're hot, take your pullover off. 2 causing a burning taste in the mouth: a hot curry 3 very excitable or exciting: a hot temper | The battle for the presidency is likely to grow hotter in the next few weeks. 4 very recent and interesting (used of news) 5 **hot air** meaningless talk or ideas 6 **hot and bothered** so worried about something that you do not think clearly 7 **hot on someone's trail/track** chasing and ready to catch someone 8 **hot on something** skilled in and knowledgeable about something: I'm not very hot on mental arithmetic. 9 **hot on the heels of** following or happening just after someone or something 10 **hot under the collar** angry or excited and ready to argue

hot² v -tt-
hot up phr v [I] infml to become more exciting or active: The election campaign is hotting up.

hot·bed /ˈhɒtbed ‖ ˈhɑːt-/ n a place where a lot of something undesirable develops: The city is a hotbed of crime.

hot-blood·ed /ˌ· ˈ···◀/ adj showing strong feelings of anger or love

hotch·potch /ˈhɒtʃpɒtʃ ‖ ˈhɑːtʃpɑːtʃ/ n (also **hodgepodge** AmE) [sing] a number of things mixed up without any sensible order or arrangement

hot dog /ˌ· ˈ· ‖ ˈ· ·/ n a special sort of long red SAUSAGE in a bread ROLL

ho·tel /həʊˈtel/ n a building where people can stay by paying for their rooms and meals

ho·tel·i·er /həʊˈteliəɪ, -liəʳ/ n a person who owns or manages a hotel

hot·foot¹ /ˌ·ˈhɒtˈfʊt ‖ ˈhɑːtfʊt/ adv moving quickly and eagerly

hotfoot² v **hotfoot it** infml to move fast: We hotfooted it down the street.

hot·head /ˈhɒthed ‖ ˈhɑːt-/ n someone who does things too quickly, without thinking – **hotheaded** /ˌhɒtˈhedɪ̯d◀ ‖ ˌhɑːt-/ adj

hot·house /ˈhɒthaʊs ‖ ˈhɑːt-/ n a warm glass building where flowers and delicate plants can grow

hot·line /ˈhɒtlaɪn ‖ ˈhɑːt-/ n a direct telephone line between heads of government

hot·ly /ˈhɒtli ‖ ˈhɑːtli/ adv 1 in anger and with force: The rumour was hotly denied. 2 closely and eagerly: He was hotly pursued by his dog.

hot·plate /ˈhɒtpleɪt ‖ ˈhɑːt-/ n a flat metal surface, usually on an electric cooker, which is used to heat food in pans or keep food warm

hot-water bot·tle /ˌ· ˈ··· ˌ··/ n a rubber container which is filled with hot water and is placed inside a bed to warm it

---

FAMILY TREE

Exercise 1 Complete these sentences about the illustration

1 Ted is Bill's _____.
2 Ted is Pat's _____.
3 Ruth is Geoff's _____.
4 Joe is Cathy's _____.
5 Dawn is Eric's _____.
6 Karen is Anne's _____.
7 Jean is Jane's _____.
8 Helen and John are Eric's _____.

Puzzle
A man is standing in front of a picture of a boy. He says:

Brothers and sisters have I none
But this boy's father
Is my father's son.

Who can the man see in the picture?

Exercise 2 Match the two parts of these sentences.

1 My father's mother
2 My mother's sister's daughter
3 My son's wife
4 My father's brother
5 My mother's father
6 My uncle's wife
7 My husband's father
8 My daughter's husband
9 My husband's mother
10 My sister's husband

A is my brother in law.
B is my uncle.
C is my son in law.
D is my grandfather.
E is my father in law.
F is my aunt.
G is my mother in law.
H is my grandmother.
I is my cousin.
J is my daughter in law.

Can you make a family tree of your family, or a family you know well, like the one in the illustration?

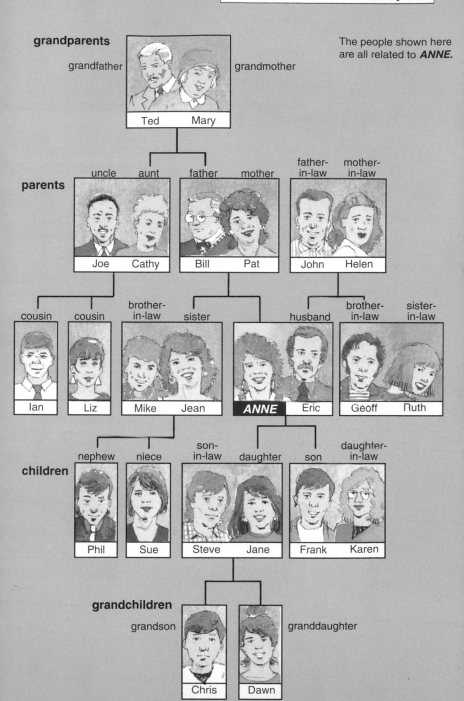

grandparents

grandfather   grandmother

The people shown here are all related to *ANNE*.

Ted   Mary

parents

uncle   aunt   father   mother   father-in-law   mother-in-law

Joe   Cathy   Bill   Pat   John   Helen

cousin   cousin   brother-in-law   sister   husband   brother-in-law   sister-in-law

Ian   Liz   Mike   Jean   *ANNE*   Eric   Geoff   Ruth

children

nephew   niece   son-in-law   daughter   son   daughter-in-law

Phil   Sue   Steve   Jane   Frank   Karen

grandchildren

grandson   granddaughter

Chris   Dawn

bread

milk

cheese

eggs

butter

bananas

apples

grapefruit

oranges

peaches

lemons

plums

pears

turnips

strawberries

cabbage

potatoes

beans

cauliflower

carrots

onions

Brussels sprouts

leeks

beetroot (BrE) /beets (AmE)

sweetcorn (BrE)/corn (AmE)

peas

mushrooms

radishes

celery

peppers

cucumbers

tomatoes

lettuce

sausage

chicken

bacon

chop

minced (BrE)/ ground (AmE) beef

Steak

fillet

Fi

lobster

crab

mussels

raspberries

blackberries

cherries

grapes

hound[1] /haʊnd/ n a dog used for hunting or racing

hound[2] v [T] to follow someone continually usually trying to get them to do or say something: *I'm fed up being hounded by the press.*

hour /aʊər/ n 1 a period of 60 minutes: *There are 24 hours in a day.* | *It takes five hours to get to Glasgow by train.* | *a two-hour journey* 2 a time when a new hour starts: *The clock struck the hour.* | *The attack began at 1600 hours.* 3 (also **hours**) a period of time set aside for a particular purpose or activity: *I'll meet you in my lunch hour.* | *During office hours I can be contacted at this number.* | *the hospital's visiting hours* 4 a particular time of day or night: *The trains don't run at this hour of the night.* | *She arrived at the appointed hour.* 5 an important moment or period: *He supported me in my hour of need.* | *It was our country's finest hour.* 6 **after hours** after work has normally finished 7 **for hours** for a long time: *I've been waiting here for hours.* 8 **in an hour** after one hour has passed: *I'll be back in an hour.* 9 **on the hour** at one o'clock, two o'clock, etc: *The trains leave on the hour and twenty five minutes past the hour.* 10 **at all hours** at any time during the whole day or night 11 **keep late/regular hours** to go to bed late or at regular hours 12 **out of hours** before or after the usual times of work 13 **by the hour** for each hour that passes: *We're paid by the hour.*

hour hand /'· ·/ n the small pointer on a clock which shows the time in hours

hour·ly /'aʊəli ‖ 'aʊərli/ adj,adv 1 every hour or once an hour: *Take one tablet hourly.* | *There's an hourly train to Oxford.* 2 at any time soon: *We're expecting him hourly.* 3 for each hour: *hourly-paid workers*

house[1] /haʊs/ n **houses** /'haʊzɪz/ 1 a building of one or more levels where people, often one family, live: *Do you live in a house or a flat?* 2 [+ sing/pl verb] the people living in this type of building: *Be quiet or you'll wake the whole house!* 3 a building used for a particular thing: *a hen-house* | *the opera-house* 4 a business firm: *a publishing house* | *He works for a Paris fashion house.* 5 one of several divisions of a school, each with its own name, whose pupils compete against each other 6 **House** a group of people who can make laws: *the House of Commons* | *the House of Representatives* 7 an important noble or royal family: *The House of Windsor is the British royal family.* 8 the people watching a performance in a theatre or concert hall: *They played to a packed house.* 9 the people at a DEBATE: *The motion to be debated today is "This house believes that nuclear power has a future."* 10 **bring the house down** to make the people watching a play laugh or CLAP very loudly in admiration 11 **get on like a house on fire** to be or become very good friends with someone very quickly 12 **on the house** paid for by the management, not by you 13 **put/set your house in order** to sort out your affairs and problems

■ USAGE A **house** is a building for people to live in, and usually has more than one level (storey). A **cottage** is usually a small, old house, especially in the country. A **bungalow** is a fairly modern house built on only one level. A set of rooms (including a kitchen and a bathroom) inside a larger building is called a **flat** in British English and an **apartment** in American English. A small one-room flat is sometimes called a **bedsitter** or **bedsit** in British English.

house[2] /haʊz/ v **housed, housing** [T] 1 to provide someone with a place to live: *The refugees have been housed in an old warehouse.* 2 to provide space for

---

FOOD

Exercise 1

Look at this list of different kinds of fruit. Which ones grow in your country? Do you know where the other fruits grow?

apples	bananas	blackberries
cherries	grapefruit	grapes
lemons	oranges	peaches
pears	plums	raspberries
strawberries		

Exercise 2

Do you like these vegetables? Mark the list like this:–

✔✔ = *I like this vegetable very much*
✔ = *I like this vegetable*
✗ = *I don't like this vegetable*
? = *I don't know this vegetable*

beans	beetroot	cabbage
carrots	cauliflower	celery
cucumber	leeks	lettuce
mushrooms	onions	peas
peppers	potatoes	radishes
sprouts	sweetcorn	tomatoes
turnips		

Exercise 3

Use the words in the box to complete this passage.

bananas	mushrooms	ham
butter	milk	eggs
cheese	onions	

It is quite easy to make an omelette. First, break three [1]e_____ into a bowl. Add some [2]m_____, season the mixture with salt and pepper and use a whisk to beat. Melt some [3]b_____ in a frying pan and pour in the mixture. Cook for a few minutes until it begins to set. You can then add [4]m_____ or other savoury fillings such as [5]c_____, [6]h_____ or [7]o_____. Omelettes can sometimes also be made with sweet foods like [8]b_____.

something: *That new building will house the Smith collection of painting.*

house ar·rest /ˈ· ·ˌ·/ *n* **under house arrest** forbidden to leave your house because the government thinks you are dangerous

house·boat /ˈhaʊsbəʊt/ *n* a boat which people live in, and which is not usually moved

house·bound /ˈhaʊsbaʊnd/ *adj* not able to move out of the house, because of illness or old age

house·break·er /ˈhaʊsˌbreɪkəʳ/ *n* a thief who enters a house by force in order to steal things

house·hold¹ /ˈhaʊshəʊld/ *n* [+ sing/pl verb] all the people living together in a house: *The whole household was up early.*

household² *adj* [only before a noun] **1** concerned with the management of a house: *household expenses* | *household chores* **2** (also **Household**) concerned with the protection of the royal family: *the household cavalry*

house·hold·er /ˈhaʊsˌhəʊldəʳ/ *n* someone who owns or is in charge of a house

household name /ˌ·· ˈ·/ *n* (also **household word**) someone or something very well-known and talked about a lot

house·keep·er /ˈhaʊsˌkiːpəʳ/ *n* someone who is paid to clean and organize your house and to cook for you

house·keep·ing /ˈhaʊsˌkiːpɪŋ/ *n* [U] **1** the cleaning and management of a house, and the cooking for the people who live in it **2** (also **housekeeping money**) the money provided for food and other things needed in the home

house-to-house /ˌ· · ˈ· ◂/ *adj* going to every house in an area: *a house-to-house search*

house·man /ˈhaʊsmən/ *n* **housemen** /-mən/ a JUNIOR doctor who is completing hospital training and often living in the hospital

house·mas·ter /ˈhaʊsˌmɑːstəʳ ‖ -ˌmæ-/ *n* a teacher who is in charge of one of the houses in a school; a woman housemaster is called a **housemistress**

house-proud /ˈ· ·/ *adj* spending a lot of time keeping your house clean and in perfect order

house-trained /ˈ· ·/ *adj* (**housebroken** /ˈhaʊsˌbrəʊkən/ *AmE*) trained to go out of the house to empty the bowels or BLADDER (used of house pets)

house-warm·ing /ˈhaʊsˌwɔːmɪŋ ‖ -ˌwɔːr-/ *n* a party given when you have moved into a new house

house·wife /ˈhaʊs-waɪf/ *n* **housewives** /-waɪvz/ a married woman who does not usually work outside the home

house·work /ˈhaʊswɜːk ‖ -ɜːrk/ *n* [U] work done in a house, such as cooking, washing, and cleaning

hous·ing /ˈhaʊzɪŋ/ *n* **1** [U] buildings to live in: *The number of people in poor housing is increasing.* | *Housing conditions in inner London must be improved.* **2** [C] protective covering for machinery: *the engine housing*

housing es·tate /ˈ·· ·ˌ·/ *n* a group of houses or flats built in one place at the same time

hove /həʊv/ the past tense and past participle of HEAVE

hov·el /ˈhɒvəl ‖ ˈhʌ-, ˈhɑː-/ *n* a small dirty house

hov·er /ˈhɒvəʳ ‖ ˈhʌ-, ˈhɑː-/ *v* [I] **1** to stay in the air in one place: *A helicopter was hovering above the crowd.* **2** to wait around one place: *He was hovering by the door, waiting to talk to me.*

hov·er·craft /ˈhɒvəkrɑːft ‖ ˈhʌvərkræft, ˈhɑː-/ *n* a boat which flies over the water, lifted up on a bed of air –see picture on page 735

how¹ /haʊ/ *adv* **1** used in questions when you are asking in what way something is done: *How do you spell it?* | *How did you find out about this?* **2** used in questions about amount or number: *How old are you?* | *How many people were there?* | *How tall is he?* **3 how is, how are** used to ask about a person's health: *How is your mother?* | *How are you?* **4** *lit* used to make a statement stronger: *How kind she is!* | *How I hate that man!*

how² *conj* used when you are stating the way in which something happens: *I can't remember how I did it now.*

how·ev·er /haʊˈevəʳ/ *adv* **1** in spite of this; used when you are adding a fact or statement that is surprising or is not what people expect from the last thing you said: *The company's profits have fallen slightly this year. However, a spokesman for the company said that he expected the situation to improve very soon.* | *She failed to win the gold in the European Championships last week. This does not, however, mean that she has no chance in the Olympics.* | *The room was very small. It was very comfortable, however.* –see Study Note on page 508 –see EVER (USAGE) **2** no matter how: *She always goes swimming, however cold it is.* **3** (also **how ever**) used when you are surprised and are asking how something happened: *However did you get here?*

howl¹ /haʊl/ *v* [I] **1** to make a long loud crying sound: *The dogs howled all night.* | *The wind howled in the trees.* **2** to cry loudly: *The baby's howling.* **3 howl with laughter** to laugh loudly

howl sbdy ↔ **down** *phr v* [T] to make a loud noise so that someone who is speaking cannot be heard by other people

howl² *n* a long loud cry

HP /ˌeɪtʃ ˈpiː/ **1** an abbreviation for HIRE PURCHASE **2** an abbreviation for HORSEPOWER

HQ /ˌeɪtʃ ˈkjuː/ an abbreviation for HEADQUARTERS: *See you back at HQ.*

hr, hrs a written abbreviation for HOUR or HOURS

HRH part of the title of a prince or princess; an abbreviation for **His Royal Highness** or **Her Royal Highness**

hub /hʌb/ *n* **1** the central part of a wheel **2** the place which is most important, or where most things happen

hub·bub /ˈhʌbʌb/ *n* [sing] a loud noise made by lots of people talking at the same time

hud·dle¹ /ˈhʌdl/ *v* **huddled, huddling** [I + adv/ prep] to crowd closely together in a group: *We huddled round the fire to keep warm.*

huddle² *n* a group of people or things very close together

hue /hjuː/ *n fml* a colour or shade of a colour

huff¹ /hʌf/ *n* **in a huff** in a bad temper: *He left the party in a huff.*

huff² *v* [I] **huff and puff** to breathe noisily because you are doing something difficult and tiring

hug /hʌg/ *v* **-gg-** [T] **1** to hold someone tightly in your arms because you love them **2** to stay close to something: *The boat hugged the coast.* –**hug** *n*: *He gave me a quick hug.*

huge /hjuːdʒ/ *adj* very big: *a huge house* | *The film was a huge success.* –**hugely** *adv*: *a hugely successful film*

huh /hʌ, hʌh/ *interj* a word used for asking a question or for expressing surprise or disapproval

hulk /hʌlk/ n 1 the body of an old broken ship 2 a person or thing that looks very large and heavy

hulk·ing /'hʌlkɪŋ/ adj [always before a noun] very large and heavy: *a hulking great man*

hull¹ /hʌl/ n the main body of a ship

hull² v [T] to take the outer covering off some grains, seeds, or vegetables, or to take the group of leaves off the top of some fruits such as strawberries (STRAWBERRY)

hul·la·ba·loo /ˌhʌləbə'luː/ , 'hʌləbəluː/ n [sing] a lot of noise made by people shouting

hul·lo /hʌ'ləʊ/ interj,n see HELLO

hum /hʌm/ v -mm- 1 [I] to make a continuous low noise like the noise that bees make 2 [I;T] to sing a piece of music by making a continuous sound with your lips closed: *Hum the tune if you don't know the words.* 3 [I] (of a place) to be full of activity: *The office was humming.* –**hum** n : *the hum of traffic outside*

hu·man¹ /'hjuːmən/ adj 1 of or concerning people: *the human voice* 2 typical of people, especially when showing feelings or weaknesses: *You can never eliminate the possibility of human error. | Of course I make mistakes – I'm only human.* –opposite **inhuman**

human² n (also **human being**) a man, woman, or child, not an animal: *Human beings have only been on the Earth for a relatively short time.*

hu·mane /hjuː'meɪn/ adj showing kindness and sympathy –opposite **inhumane** –**humanely** adv : *Animals should be killed as humanely as possible.*

hu·man·is·m /'hjuːmənɪzəm/ n [U] a system of beliefs concerned with the needs of people, and with finding answers to human problems by people themselves rather than by a God or a religion –**humanist** n

hu·man·i·tar·i·an /hjuːˌmænɪ'teəriən/ n a person who works to improve people's lives and reduce people's suffering –**humanitarian** adj

hu·man·i·ty /hjuː'mænɪti/ n **humanities** 1 [U] sympathy and kindness: *a man of great humanity* 2 [U] people of the world in general: *The regime stands accused of crimes against humanity.* 3 [U] fml the state or fact of being a human being 4 **humanities** [pl] studies such as literature, languages, and history, which are concerned with people rather than with science

hu·man·ize /'hjuːmənaɪz/ v **humanized, humanizing** (also **humanise** BrE) [T] to make something more pleasant for people

hu·man·ly /'hjuːmənli/ adv **humanly possible** possible for any person: *It's not humanly possible to complete all the work in such a short time.*

human na·ture /ˌ·· '··/ n [U] the behaviour, qualities, and desires of a typical ordinary person: *It's only human nature to want a comfortable life.*

human race /ˌ·· '·/ n **the human race** all people in the world thought of as a group

human rights /ˌ·· '·/ n [pl] the rights such as freedom, equality, and justice which every person should have

hum·ble¹ /'hʌmbəl/ adj 1 believing that you are not any better or more important than other people 2 unimportant, and having a low social position: *He was only a humble bank clerk.* 3 **in my humble opinion** a phrase used when you are giving your opinion quite strongly, but do not want to offend other people

humble² v **humbled, humbling** [T] to make someone feel less proud and less important: *I felt humbled by the experience.*

hum·bug /'hʌmbʌg/ n 1 [U] old fash nonsense 2 [C] a hard sweet which tastes of MINT

hum·drum /'hʌmdrʌm/ adj ordinary and dull, without any variety: *We lead a humdrum life.*

hu·mer·us /'hjuːmərəs/ n the bone in the top half of your arm

hu·mid /'hjuːmɪd/ adj having a lot of wetness in the air, and usually very hot (used of the weather): *The afternoon was hot and humid.*

hu·mid·i·fy /hjuː'mɪdɪfaɪ/ v **humidified, humidifying** [T] to make the air less dry

hu·mid·i·ty /hjuː'mɪdɪti/ n [U] the wetness that is in the air: *It's uncomfortable working outside in this humidity.*

hu·mil·i·ate /hjuː'mɪlieɪt/ v **humiliated, humiliating** [T] to make someone feel ashamed and lose other people's respect: *She could not forgive him for humiliating her in front of her friend.* –**humiliation** /hjuːˌmɪli'eɪʃən/ n [C;U]

hu·mil·i·ty /hjuː'mɪlɪti/ n [U] the quality of being humble

hu·mor·ist /'hjuːmərɪst ‖ 'hjuː-, 'juː-/ n a person who makes jokes or writes amusing things

hu·mor·ous /'hjuːmərəs ‖ 'hjuː-, 'juː-/ adj funny and amusing in a clever way: *She kept making humorous remarks.* –**humorously** adv

hu·mour¹ /'hjuːməʳ ‖ 'hjuː-, 'juː-/ n (**humor** AmE) [U] 1 the ability to laugh and find things funny: *She doesn't have a sense of humour.* 2 the quality of being funny and making people laugh: *I'm afraid I couldn't see the humour in the situation.* 3 **in a good humour** happy and behaving pleasantly: *She seems to be in a good humour today.* [RELATED PHRASE **in a bad humour**]

humour² v (also **humor** AmE) [T] to accept someone's unreasonable behaviour or wishes to keep them happy: *Don't argue, just humour him and he'll stop.*

hump¹ /hʌmp/ n 1 a large lump on the back of a person or camel 2 a small hill or raised part in a road

hump² v [T + adv/prep] infml to carry something heavy: *I humped the case upstairs.*

hu·mus /'hjuːməs/ n [U] rich soil made of decayed plants and leaves

hunch¹ /hʌntʃ/ n an idea based on feeling rather than on facts or proof: *I had a hunch we would find him at the airport.*

hunch² v [T] to pull your back or shoulders into a rounded shape: *He was sitting hunched in a corner.*

hunch·back /'hʌntʃbæk/ n a person with a large lump on their back

hun·dred /'hʌndrɪd/ det, n, pron **hundred** or **hundreds** 1 the number 100 2 **hundreds** a very large number of people or things: *We received hundreds of letters.* –**hundredth** det, n, pron, adv

■ USAGE 1 British people say **hundred and** in numbers, like this: *326 = three* **hundred and** *twenty six.* Americans usually miss out **and**: *326 = three* **hundred** *twenty six* 2 We can use plural forms like **hundreds** and **thousands** when they are not part of another number: **Hundreds** *of people attended the concert.* | **Thousands** *of pounds have been spent on the new hospital.*

hun·dred·weight /'hʌndrɪ̩dweɪt/ [plural is **hundred weight**] a measure of weight equal to 112 pounds in Britain, and 100 pounds in America

hung /hʌŋ/ the past tense and past participle of HANG

Hung·ar·i·an[1] /hʌŋ'geəriən/ adj from or connected with Hungary

Hungarian[2] n. **1** [C] a person from Hungary **2** [U] the language of Hungary

hun·ger[1] /'hʌŋgəʳ/ n [U] **1** the feeling that you want or need to eat: *He could feel pangs of hunger in his stomach.* **2** lack of food: *people dying of hunger*

hunger[2] v **hunger for something, hunger after something** to want something very much

hunger strike /'··· ·/ n a refusal to eat, especially by prisoners, as a sign of strong dissatisfaction

hun·gry /'hʌŋgri/ adj **hungrier, hungriest 1** wanting or needing food **2 go hungry** to have no food or not enough food: *We often went hungry.* **3 hungry work** hard work that makes you feel hungry **4 hungry for something** wanting or needing something very much **–hungrily** adv

hunk /hʌŋk/ n a thick piece of something, for example bread or meat

hunt[1] /hʌnt/ v **1** [I;T] to chase animals in order to catch and kill them, either for food or for sport: *Owls prefer to hunt at night.* | *They hunt small birds and animals.* | *The men were out hunting.* **2** [T] to try to find and catch someone: *Police hunting the murderer have appealed for help from the public.* **3 hunt for something** to search carefully for something: *I spent the morning hunting for my passport.* **hunt** sbdy/sthg ↔ **down** phr v [T] to succeed in finding someone or something after a lot of effort

hunt[2] n **1** the chasing and sometimes killing of animals: *an elephant hunt* **2** a careful search for someone or something: *The police hunt for the missing child continued today.* **3** a group of people who regularly hunt foxes together or the place where they do this

hunt·er /'hʌntəʳ/ n **1** a person or animal that hunts wild animals **2** a person who searches for something with a lot of interest: *The auction was full of bargain hunters.*

hur·dle[1] /'hɜːdl ‖ 'hɜːr-/ n **1** a frame for jumping over in a race **2** a difficulty which must be dealt with before you can do something else

hurdle[2] v **hurdled, hurdling** [T] to jump over something

hurl /hɜːl ‖ hɜːrl/ v [T] **1** to throw something with force: *He hurled a brick through the window.* **2 hurl abuse, hurl insults** to shout unpleasant things at someone

hur·ly-bur·ly /'hɜːli ˌbɜːli ‖ ˌhɜːrli 'bɜːrli/ n [sing] noisy activity: *the hurly-burly of city life*

hur·ray /huˈreɪ/ interj (also hooray /huˈreɪ/, **hurrah** /huˈrɑː/) a shout of joy, excitement, or approval: *We've done it! Hurray!*

hur·ri·cane /'hʌrɪ̩kən ‖ 'hɜːrɪ̩keɪn/ n a storm with a very strong fast wind

hurricane lamp /'··· ·/ n a lamp which has a strong cover to protect the flame inside from wind

hur·ried /'hʌrid ‖ 'hɜːrid/ adj done very quickly because there is not much time: *a hurried meeting* – **hurriedly** adv

hur·ry[1] /'hʌri ‖ 'hɜːri/ v **hurried, hurrying 1** [I] to go somewhere quickly: *He hurried across the road.* | *We hurried home.* | *We're late. We'd better hurry.* **2** [T] to send or bring someone somewhere quickly or make them do something quickly: *She hurried us to the airport.* | *Don't hurry me. I'm working as fast as I can.*

hurry up phr v [I;T **hurry** sbdy/sthg ↔ **up**] to do something more quickly, or make something happen more quickly: *I wish you'd hurry up!* | *I tried to hurry them up.* | *Can you hurry the work up a bit?*

hurry[2] n [U] **1 be in a hurry** to be trying to do something quickly, or eager to do something quickly: *I can't stop and talk. I'm in a hurry.* | *She seems in a hurry to leave.* | *I'm in no hurry to change my job.* | *There's no need to rush. I'm not in any hurry.* **2 do something in a hurry** to do something quickly because you do not have much time: *I always make mistakes if I try to do things in a hurry.* **3 there's no hurry** = there is no need to do things quickly because there is plenty of time **4 what's the hurry?** = why are you doing things so quickly? **5 I won't do this again in a hurry** = I won't be very eager to do this again because it was unpleasant in some way

hurt[1] /hɜːt ‖ hɜːrt/ v **hurt, hurting 1** [T] to cause pain or damage to your own body or someone else's body: *I fell over and hurt myself.* | *She hurt her leg when she fell.* | *Sorry. Did I hurt you?* | *The light was hurting my eyes.* **2** [I] to cause you pain: *My feet are hurting.* | *My back hurts.* | *Does this hurt?* **3** [T] to upset someone and make them unhappy: *She knew that she had hurt him very badly. I tried not to hurt her feelings.* **4 it won't hurt** = it will do no harm: *It won't hurt her to do a bit of hard work for a change!* | *It won't hurt if we're a few minutes late.* **–hurt** n [U]

■ USAGE When **hurt** is used in the sense of bodily damage, you may be *slightly/badly/seriously* **hurt** but do not use these adverbs when speaking of unhappiness caused by someone's behaviour. Compare: *She was badly/slightly* **hurt** *when she fell off the ladder,* and *She was very deeply/rather* **hurt** *by his unkind words.* –see WOUND (USAGE)

hurt[2] adj **1** [never before a noun] suffering pain, for example after an accident: *He was obviously badly hurt.* **2** unhappy and offended: *I was very hurt when they didn't turn up.*

hurt·ful /'hɜːtfəl ‖ 'hɜːrt-/ adj making you feel offended and unhappy: *What he said was very hurtful.*

hur·tle /'hɜːtl ‖ 'hɜːr-/ v **hurtled, hurtling** [I + adv/prep] to move very fast: *A car came hurtling round the corner.*

hus·band /'hʌzbənd/ n the man a woman is married to –see picture on page 343

hus·band·ry /'hʌzbəndri/ n fml [U] farming

hush[1] /hʌʃ/ v **Hush!** a word used to ask someone to be quiet **hush** sthg ↔ **up** phr v [T] to keep something secret that should be public knowledge: *The whole affair had been hushed up.*

hush[2] n [sing] a peaceful silence: *A hush fell over the room.*

hushed /hʌʃt/ adj quiet: *talking in hushed voices*

hush-hush /ˌ·· '·◂ ‖ '·· ·/ adj infml secret (used especially of official plans)

husk /hʌsk/ n the outer covering of some grains and seeds

hus·ky[1] /'hʌski/ adj **huskier, huskiest** having a pleasant rough sound (used of someone's voice) **–huskily** adv **–huskiness** n [U]

husky² /ˈhʌski/ *n* **huskies** a working dog with thick hair, used to pull SLEDGES over the snow

hus·sy /ˈhʌsi, ˈhʌzi/ *n* **hussies** *old fash* a young woman who behaves in a sexually improper way

hus·tings /ˈhʌstɪŋz/ *n* **the hustings** [pl] speeches and other political activities which go on just before an election, when the political parties are trying to win votes

hus·tle¹ /ˈhʌsəl/ *v* **hustled, hustling** [T + adv/prep] to make someone move fast by pushing them: *He was hustled into the car.*

hustle² *n* **hustle and bustle** activity in which a lot of people are busy doing things and moving about: *the hustle and bustle of city life*

hus·tler /ˈhʌslər/ *n AmE* someone who tries to earn money in any way that they can, often in an illegal or deceitful way

hut /hʌt/ *n* a small house or shelter, often made of wood

hutch /hʌtʃ/ *n* a small cage for keeping rabbits in

hy·a·cinth /ˈhaɪəsɪnθ/ *n* a plant with bell-shaped flowers, which grows in winter and spring

hy·ae·na /haɪˈiːnə/ *n* see HYENA

hy·brid /ˈhaɪbrɪd/ *n* an animal or plant that is produced from parents of different breeds: *A mule is a hybrid of a donkey and a horse.*

hy·drant /ˈhaɪdrənt/ *n* a water pipe in the street from which water can be taken to put out fires

hy·draul·ic /haɪˈdrɒlɪk, -ˈdrɔː- ‖ -ˈdrɑː-, -ˈdrɔː-/ *adj* concerning or moved by the pressure of water or other liquids: *hydraulic power*

hy·draul·ics /haɪˈdrɒlɪks, -ˈdrɔː- ‖ -ˈdrɑː-, -ˈdrɔː-/ *n* [U] the science which studies the use of water to produce power

hy·dro·e·lec·tric /ˌhaɪdrəʊ-ɪˈlektrɪk◀/ *adj* related to producing electricity by the power of moving water, for example the water in a river

hy·dro·foil /ˈhaɪdrəfɔɪl/ *n* a large motorboat with special parts fitted on the bottom, on which it moves along the surface of the water

hy·dro·gen /ˈhaɪdrədʒən/ *n* [U] a gas that has no colour or smell, that is lighter than air, and that burns very easily

hydrogen bomb /ˈ··· ·/ *n* (also **H-bomb**) a very powerful type of ATOM BOMB

hy·e·na /haɪˈiːnə/ *n* (also **hyaena**) a wild dog-like animal of Africa and Asia, which has a cry like a laugh

hy·giene /ˈhaɪdʒiːn/ *n* [U] the practice of keeping yourself and the things around you clean in order to prevent illnesses from spreading

hy·gien·ic /haɪˈdʒiːnɪk ‖ -ˈdʒe-, -ˈdʒiː-/ *adj* clean and not likely to spread illness –opposite **unhygienic** –**hygienically** /-kli/ *adv*

hymn /hɪm/ *n* a religious song of the Christian church which people sing together during a religious service

hy·per·bo·le /haɪˈpɜːbəli ‖ -ɜːr-/ *n* [C;U] the use of language which makes something sound bigger, smaller, better, or worse than it really is

hy·per·mar·ket /ˈhaɪpəˌmɑːkɪt ‖ -pərˌmɑːr-/ *n* a very large SUPERMARKET

hy·phen /ˈhaɪfən/ *n* a short line (-) which is used to join words or parts of words

hy·phen·ate /ˈhaɪfəneɪt/ *v* **hyphenated, hyphenating** [T] to join words with a hyphen

hyp·no·sis /hɪpˈnəʊsɪs/ *n* [U] the production of a sleep-like state in someone's mind: *She told him all her secrets when she was under hypnosis.* –**hypnotic** /hɪpˈnɒtɪk ‖ -ˈnɑː-/ *adj* –**hypnotically** /-kli/ *adv*

hyp·no·tis·m /ˈhɪpnətɪzəm/ *n* [U] the practice of hypnotizing someone –**hypnotist** *n*

hyp·no·tize /ˈhɪpnətaɪz/ *v* **hypnotized, hypnotizing** (also **hypnotise** *BrE*) [T] to put someone into a sleep-like state in order to control them or find out information

hy·po·chon·dri·ac /ˌhaɪpəˈkɒndriæk ‖ -ˈkɑːn-/ *n* a person who worries about their health all the time, although they are usually perfectly healthy –**hypochondria** /-driə/ *n* [U]

hy·poc·ri·sy /hɪˈpɒkrəsi ‖ -ˈpɑː-/ *n* [U] pretending to be or believe something different from, and usually better than, what you really are or really believe: *The government's claim to be concerned about poverty is sheer hypocrisy.*

hyp·o·crite /ˈhɪpəkrɪt/ *n* a person who says one thing and does another, usually something worse: *What a hypocrite! He should practise what he preaches.* –**hypocritical** /ˌhɪpəˈkrɪtɪkəl/ *adj* –**hypocritically** /-kli/ *adv*

hy·po·der·mic /ˌhaɪpəˈdɜːmɪk ‖ -ɜːr-/ *n* an instrument for putting drugs directly into a person's body through their skin –**hypodermic** *adj*: *a hypodermic syringe*

hy·po·ther·mi·a /ˌhaɪpəˈθɜːmiə ‖ -ɜːr-/ *n* [U] *tech* a condition in which your body temperature falls below the usual level and you are very ill: *Every winter some old people die from hypothermia.*

hy·poth·e·sis /haɪˈpɒθəsɪs ‖ -ˈpɑː-/ *n* **hypotheses** /-siːz/ an explanation which has not yet been proved to be true: *If we accept this hypothesis, it could explain why our weather is changing so rapidly.*

hy·po·thet·i·cal /ˌhaɪpəˈθetɪkəl/ *adj* based on a situation which is either not known to have happened, or has not yet been proved to be true: *Let's imagine a hypothetical situation in which Britain begins to suffer from major earthquakes...* –**hypothetically** /-kli/ *adv*

hys·ter·ec·to·my /ˌhɪstəˈrektəmi/ *n* [C;U] the medical operation for removing a woman's WOMB

hys·te·ri·a /hɪˈstɪəriə ‖ -ˈsteriə/ *n* [U] **1** a condition of uncontrollable nervous excitement or anger **2** **mass hysteria** wild excitement in a crowd of people: *News of the victory produced mass hysteria in the streets of the capital.*

hys·ter·i·cal /hɪˈsterɪkəl/ *adj* **1** in a state of hysteria or as a result of hysteria: *a hysterical woman* | *hysterical crying* **2** *infml* extremely funny: *You should go and see the film – it's absolutely hysterical.* –**hysterically** /-kli/ *adv*

hys·ter·ics /hɪˈsterɪks/ *n* [pl] **1** an attack of uncontrollable nervous excitement or anger: *He always has hysterics at the sight of blood.* **2** **in hysterics** laughing uncontrollably

I,i

SPELLING NOTE

Words with the sound / aɪ / may be spelt **e-**, like **eye**, or **ai-** like **aisle**.

I, i /aɪ/ **I's, i's** or **Is, is** is the 9th letter of the English alphabet

I /aɪ/ *pron* [used as the subject of a verb] the person who is speaking: *I don't like coffee.* | *My brother and I waited outside.*

ice¹ /aɪs/ *n* **1** [U] water which has frozen so that it is solid: *We get ice on the lake in winter.* | *Would you like ice in your whisky?* | *Her hands were as cold as ice.* **2** [C] *old fash* a serving of ICE CREAM: *Two ices, please.* **3 keep something on ice** to keep something for later use: *Let's keep that idea on ice for now.*

ice² *v* **iced, icing** [T] **1** to make something very cold by using ice: *iced drinks* **2** to cover a cake with ICING
ice over, ice up *phr v* [I] to become covered with ice: *The lake iced over during the night.*

Ice Age /'· ·/ *n* a time in the past when ice covered many parts of the earth

ice·berg /'aɪsbɜːg ‖ -ɜːrg/ *n* a very large piece of ice floating in the sea

ice·box /'aɪsbɒks ‖ -baːks/ *n* a box where food is kept cool with blocks of ice

ice cream /ˌ· '·◄ ‖ '·· / *n* [C;U] a frozen sweet food: *Two ice creams, please.* | *a bowl of chocolate ice cream*

ice cube /'· ·/ *n* a small block of ice that you put in a drink to make it cold

ice hock·ey /'· ˌ··/ *n* [U] a game played between two teams on ice; each team tries to hit a small object into a GOAL with a long stick

ice lol·ly /'· ˌ··/ *n* a piece of sweet-tasting ice on a stick

ice skate /'· ·/ *n* a boot with a metal blade on the bottom which you wear to move over ice **–ice-skate** *v* **ice-skated, ice-skating** [I]

i·ci·cle /'aɪsɪkəl/ *n* a pointed stick of ice that hangs down from a surface: *icicles hanging from the roof*

ic·ing /'aɪsɪŋ/ *n* [U] a mixture of fine powdery sugar and water or butter, used to decorate cakes

i·con /'aɪkɒn ‖ -kaːn/ *n* (also **ikon**) a picture or figure of a holy person, used in the Eastern branches of Christianity

ic·y /'aɪsi/ *adj* **icier, iciest 1** extremely cold: *an icy wind* **2** covered with ice: *Drive carefully. The roads are icy.* **3** showing annoyance in a quiet, controlled manner: *She gave me an icy look.* **–icily** *adv* **–iciness** *n* [U]

I'd /aɪd/ **1** short for "I had": *I'd already left by the time you arrived.* **2** short for "I would": *I'd love to go but I can't afford it.*

i·dea /aɪ'dɪə/ *n* **1** [C] a plan or suggestion: *What a brilliant idea! Let's do it.* | *She's full of good ideas.* | *It was Bill's idea to have the race.* **2** [C] an opinion or belief: *He's got some weird religious ideas.* | *I've an idea that he's on holiday this week.* **3** [C;U] a picture in your mind: *I've got a good idea of what he wants.* | *Have you any idea of the problems involved?*

4 get the idea to begin to believe something, often mistakenly: *He's somehow got the idea that I don't like him.* **5 have no idea** not to know about something at all: *You've no idea how worried I was!* **6 put ideas in someone's head** to make someone hope for things they cannot have

i·deal¹ /aɪ'dɪəl/ *adj* **1** perfect: *an ideal place for a holiday with young children* **2** expressing perfection which is unlikely to exist in the real world: *Plato's ideal system of government*

ideal² *n* **1** a perfect example: *That's my ideal of what a house should be like.* **2** a belief in high or perfect standards: *a woman with high ideals* | *democratic ideals*

i·deal·is·m /aɪ'dɪəlɪzəm/ *n* [U] the belief that you should live according to your ideals: *youthful idealism* **–idealist** *n* **–idealistic** /ˌaɪdɪə'lɪstɪk/ *adj* **–idealistically** /-kli/ *adv*

i·deal·ize /aɪ'dɪəlaɪz/ *v* **idealized, idealizing** (also **idealise** *BrE*) [T] to imagine something as perfect or better than it really is **–idealization** /aɪˌdɪəlaɪ'zeɪʃən ‖ -lə-/ *n* [C;U]

i·deal·ly /aɪ'dɪəli/ *adv* **1** perfectly: *She's ideally suited to the job.* **2** if conditions were perfect, which they aren't: *Ideally, I would like to be a teacher, but there are so few jobs now.*

i·den·ti·cal /aɪ'dentɪkəl/ *adj* **1** exactly alike: *We were wearing identical dresses.* | *Your voice is identical to your sister's.* **2** the same: *This is the identical hotel that we stayed in last year.* **–identically** /-kli/ *adv*

i·den·ti·fi·ca·tion /aɪˌdentɪfɪ'keɪʃən/ *n* **1** [C;U] the recognizing and naming of someone or something: *identification of the dead body by the brother* **2** [U] an official paper which proves who you are: *Let me see your identification.* | *His only means of identification was his passport.* **3** [U] the feeling that you share the ideas, feelings, and problems of another person: *He felt a strong sense of identification with the hero of the book.*

i·den·ti·fy /aɪ'dentɪfaɪ/ *v* **identified, identifying** [T] to recognize and name someone or something: *I identified the coat at once – it was my brother's.* | *He identified the criminal.*
identify with *phr v* **1** [T **identify with** sbdy/sthg] to feel sympathy for someone or feel that you share something with someone: *Reading this book, we can identify with the main character's struggle.* **2 be identified with something** to be considered to be connected with something: *We can't use him in our advertisements – he's too closely identified with our competitor's products.*

i·den·ti·ty /aɪ'dentɪti/ *n* **identities** [C;U] **1** who someone is: *The identity of the murdered woman has not yet been established.* **2** something that makes you feel that you belong to a certain group of people: *our own cultural identity*

i·de·ol·o·gy /ˌaɪdi'ɒlədʒi ‖ -'aːlə-/ *n* **ideologies** [C;U] a set of ideas typical of a social or political group: *Marxist ideology* **–ideological** /ˌaɪdɪə'lɒdʒɪkəl ‖ -'laː-/ *adj* **–ideologically** *adv*

id·i·o·cy /'ɪdiəsi/ *n* **idiocies** [C;U] great stupidity

id·i·om /'ɪdiəm/ *n* **1** a phrase which means something different from the meanings of the separate words: *To "kick the bucket" is an English idiom meaning "to die".* **2** a person's typical style of expression in language: *the idiom of the young*

id·i·o·mat·ic /ˌɪdiə'mætɪk/ *adj* natural and informal (used of language): *idiomatic English* –**idiomatically** /-kli/ *adv*

id·i·o·syn·cra·sy /ˌɪdiə'sɪŋkrəsi/ *n* **idiosyncrasies** a strange or unusual habit or way of behaving that a person has: *Keeping pet snakes is an idiosyncrasy of his.* –**idiosyncratic** /ˌɪdiəsɪn'krætɪk/ *adj*

id·i·ot /'ɪdiət/ *n* a foolish person: *Idiot! You've dropped my watch!* | *He's a complete idiot.* –**idiotic** /ˌɪdi'ɒtɪk || -'ɑː-/ *adj* –**idiotically** /-kli/ *adv*

i·dle¹ /'aɪdl/ *adj* **1** lazy **2** not working: *We can't afford to have all this expensive machinery lying idle.* **3** having no useful result: *idle gossip* | *His words were just idle threats; he can't harm us.* –**idleness** *n* [U] –**idly** *adv*

idle² *v* **idled, idling** [I] **1** to waste time doing nothing **2** to run slowly (used of an engine) –**idler** *n* **idle away** sth *phr v* [T] to waste time doing nothing: *We idled away a few hours talking.*

i·dol /'aɪdl/ *n* **1** an image worshipped as a god **2** a famous person who is loved and admired

i·dol·a·try /aɪ'dɒlətri || -'dɑː-/ *n* [U] the worship of idols –**idolatrous** *adj*

i·dol·ize /'aɪdəl-aɪz/ *v* **idolized, idolizing** (also **idolise** *BrE*) [T] to love or admire someone greatly, perhaps too much: *He idolizes his father.*

i·dyll /'ɪdəl, 'ɪdɪl || 'aɪdl/ *n* (also **idyl**) a peaceful happy scene or period of life –**idyllic** /ɪ'dɪlɪk, aɪ || aɪ-/ *adj* : *an idyllic scene* –**idyllically** /-kli/ *adv*

i.e. /ˌaɪ 'iː/ a phrase used when you want to give more information about something you have just said; an abbreviation for the Latin words **id est**: *The cinema is only open to adults, i.e. people over 18.*

if /ɪf/ *conj* **1** supposing that something happens or is true: *If we don't get much rain this summer there could be serious water shortages.* | *Give me a ring if you need any help.* | *If I had enough money I would retire tomorrow.* | *I think I'll be free on Friday night. If not, I can manage Saturday morning.* **2** used after verbs like "ask", "know", and "wonder": *Do you know if Jane's coming?* | *I wonder if he's all right.* **3** although: *It was a good film, if a little long.* **4** do you **mind if?** a polite way of asking someone if you can do something: *Do you mind if I smoke?* **5** if **anything** a phrase you use when you are saying something that is the opposite of what you have just said: *She didn't seem upset about losing her job. If anything she seemed very happy.* **6** if I **were you** a phrase you use when you are giving advice to someone: *If I were you I'd sell that house and buy a smaller one.* **7** if **only** a phrase you use to express a strong wish: *If only we had a bit more money.*

■ USAGE Do not use **if** with *will/won't* unless you mean "be willing": **If** *you'll* (=if you are willing to) *give me a lift I'll be extremely grateful.* | **If** *you won't* (=if you are unwilling to) *help me I'll do it myself.* Compare: **If** *this car gives me any more trouble I'll be really angry.*

ig·loo /'ɪgluː/ *n* **igloos** a rounded house made of hard icy blocks of snow

ig·ne·ous /'ɪgniəs/ *adj tech* formed from hot liquid rock which has become cool and gone hard

ig·nite /ɪg'naɪt/ *v* **ignited, igniting** [I;T] *fml* to start burning, or make something start burning: *The petrol suddenly ignited and there was a terrific explosion.*

ig·ni·tion /ɪg'nɪʃən/ *n* **1** [C] the electrical CIRCUIT which starts a car engine: *Turn on the ignition.* –see picture on page 49 **2** [U] *fml* the process of making something start burning

ig·no·ble /ɪg'nəʊbəl/ *adj lit* not showing high principles or honour

ig·no·min·i·ous /ˌɪgnə'mɪniəs/ *adj* bringing shame or strong public disapproval: *an ignominious defeat* –**ignominiously** *adv*

ig·no·ra·mus /ˌɪgnə'reɪməs/ *n* someone who does not know about something they should know

ig·no·rance /'ɪgnərəns/ *n* [U] lack of knowledge: *We were kept in complete ignorance of the company takeover.*

ig·no·rant /'ɪgnərənt/ *adj* **1** lacking knowledge or education (a word often used to show disapproval): *How can he be so ignorant?* **2** having no information about something: *Many people are totally ignorant of their rights.* –see IGNORE (USAGE)

ig·nore /ɪg'nɔːʳ/ *v* **ignored, ignoring** [T] to take no notice of someone or something: *Ignore those boys and they'll soon stop misbehaving.*

■ USAGE Compare **ignore** and **be ignorant of**. If you **ignore** something you know about it but pay no attention: *He knew there was a speed limit but he* **ignored** *it and drove very fast.* If you **are ignorant** of something you don't know about it: *Most passengers were totally* **ignorant** *of the safety procedures.*

i·kon /'aɪkɒn || -kɑːn/ *n* see ICON

ill¹ /ɪl/ *adj* **worse** /wɜːs || wɜːrs/, **worst** /wɜːst || wɜːrst/ **1** [never before a noun] hurt or not in good health: *critically ill in hospital with gunshot wounds* | *mentally ill* **2** [only before a noun] bad or harmful: *ill luck* | *I'm suffering from the ill effects of having eaten too much over Christmas.* | *There's a lot of ill feeling about her being promoted.*

ill² *adv* [no comparative] **1** unpleasantly or badly: *You shouldn't speak ill of your neighbours.* | *She seems ill-suited to this job.* **2** can **ill afford** cannot very easily afford: *I can ill afford the time.*

ill³ *n* a bad thing, especially a problem or cause of worry: *the social ills of unemployment and poverty*

I'll /aɪl/ **1** short for "I will" **2** short for "I shall"

ill-ad·vised /ˌ· ·'·◂/ *adj* not wise

il·le·gal /ɪ'liːgəl/ *adj* against the law: *It's illegal for people under 17 to drive a car in Britain.* –**illegally** *adv* : *illegally parked* –**illegality** /ˌɪlɪ'gælɪti/ *n* [C;U]

il·le·gi·ble /ɪ'ledʒəbəl/ *adj* impossible to read: *illegible handwriting* –**illegibly** *adv* –**illegibility** /ɪˌledʒə'bɪlɪti/ *n* [U]

il·le·git·i·mate /ˌɪlɪ'dʒɪtɪmɪt/ *adj* **1** born to parents who are not married: *an illegitimate child* **2** not allowed by the rules –**illegitimately** *adv* –**illegitimacy** *n* [U]

ill-e·quipped /ˌ· ·'·◂/ *adj* not having something needed for a particular activity

ill-fat·ed /ˌ· '··◂/ *adj* unlucky: *an ill-fated attempt to climb Everest*

il·li·cit /ɪ'lɪsɪt/ *adj* not allowed by law or approved of by society: *illicit trade in drugs* | *an illicit love affair* –**illicitly** *adv*

ill-in·formed /ˌ· ·'·◂/ *adj* having incorrect or not enough information about something

il·lit·e·rate /ɪ'lɪtərɪt/ *adj* unable to read and write: *About half the population is still illiterate.* –**illiteracy** *n* [U] : *the battle against illiteracy*

ill·ness /'ɪlnɪs/ *n* **1** [C] a disease: *It could be one of several illnesses going around at present.* **2** [C;U] a period of being ill: *We haven't seen her since her illness. How is she now?* –see DISEASE (USAGE)

il·log·i·cal /ɪ'lɒdʒɪkəl || ɪ'lɑː-/ *adj* not reasonable or sensible: *That statement is totally illogical!* –**illogically** /-kli/ *adv*

ill-treat /ˌ·ˈ·/ v [T] to be cruel to someone: *an ill-treated child*

il·lu·mi·nate /ɪˈluːmɪ̱neɪt, ɪˈljuː- ‖ ɪˈluː-/ v **illuminated, illuminating** [T] **1** to shine light on something: *The room was illuminated by candles.* **2** to make something clearer: *His article illuminates a much misunderstood area of study.*

il·lu·mi·nat·ing /ɪˈluːmɪ̱neɪtɪŋ, ɪˈljuː- ‖ ɪˈluː-/ *adj* helping to understand something: *an illuminating remark that showed her real character*

il·lu·mi·na·tion /ɪˌluːmɪ̱ˈneɪʃən, ɪˌljuː- ‖ ɪˌluː-/ n [U] **1** lighting: *The illumination is too weak to show the detail of the painting.* **2 illuminations** [pl] the show of coloured lights used to make a town bright and colourful for a special occasion

il·lu·sion /ɪˈluːʒən/ n **1** something seen wrongly, not as it really is: *The lake in the desert was just an optical illusion.* **2** a false belief or idea: *He liked having two secretaries; it gave him an illusion of power.* | *I have no illusions about him; I know he's a liar.*

il·lus·trate /ˈɪləstreɪt/ v **illustrated, illustrating** [T] **1** to add pictures to a book or magazine: *a beautifully illustrated history of science* **2** to explain something by giving examples: *"I can illustrate the point with these graphs."*

il·lus·tra·tion /ˌɪləˈstreɪʃən/ n **1** [C] a picture in a book or magazine: *It's not a very good story, but I like the illustrations.* **2** [C] an example which explains something: *That's a typical illustration of his meanness.* **3** [U] the drawing of pictures for books or the giving of examples to explain something **4 by way of illustration** as an example

il·lus·tra·tive /ˈɪləstreɪtɪv, -strət- ‖ ɪˈlʌstrətɪv/ *adj fml* helping to show or explain something: *an illustrative example* | *Such situations are illustrative of the need for immediate action.*

il·lus·tra·tor /ˈɪləstreɪtər/ n a person who draws pictures for books or magazines

il·lus·tri·ous /ɪˈlʌstriəs/ *adj* extremely famous and widely admired: *the illustrious name of Shakespeare*

I'm /aɪm/ short for "I am"

im·age /ˈɪmɪdʒ/ n **1** a picture of someone or something in your mind: *As she spoke, an image of a country garden came into my mind.* **2** the opinion which people have of someone or of an organization: *The government will have to improve its image if it wants to win the election.* **3 be the image of** to look very like someone else: *He's the image of his father.* **4** something in a poem or painting that suggests a particular quality: *The image of the butterfly creates a strong sense of beauty and powerlessness.* **5** an object representing a god or person to be worshipped

im·ag·e·ry /ˈɪmɪ̱dʒəri/ n [U] the use of phrases in literature which suggest feelings and ideas

i·ma·gi·na·ble /ɪˈmædʒɪ̱nəbəl/ *adj* able to be thought of: *every imaginable possibility*

i·ma·gi·na·ry /ɪˈmædʒɪ̱nəri ‖ -dʒəneri/ *adj* not real, but produced from someone's mind: *All the characters in this book are imaginary.*

i·ma·gi·na·tion /ɪˌmædʒɪ̱ˈneɪʃən/ n **1** [C;U] the ability to form pictures or ideas in your mind: *Your*

---

story shows plenty of imagination. | *a vivid imagination* **2** [C] your mind: *The difficulties are all in your imagination.*

i·ma·gi·na·tive /ɪˈmædʒɪ̱nətɪv/ *adj* using or having imagination: *imaginative writing* | *She is a highly imaginative child.* –opposite **unimaginative** –**imaginatively** *adv*

i·ma·gine /ɪˈmædʒɪ̱n/ v **imagined, imagining 1** [T; + (that)] to form a picture or idea in your mind: *Try to imagine life in a hundred years time.* | *You can imagine how amazed I was!* | *Imagine that you've won a million pounds.* | *It's hard to imagine living in a palace.* | *I simply can't imagine George helping with the baby!*
□ USEFUL PATTERNS to imagine something; to imagine what, how, etc....; to imagine that...; to imagine doing something; to imagine someone doing something
2 [T; + (that)] to believe or have an idea about something, especially mistakenly or without proof: *No one's listening to your phone calls – you're just imagining the whole thing!* | *She imagined that everyone was talking about her.* **3** [+ (that)] [not in progressive forms] to consider something to be probable: *I imagine she's exhausted after her journey.*

im·bal·ance /ɪmˈbæləns/ n a lack of balance or equality: *When more males are born than females, there is a population imbalance.* | *a serious trade imbalance* **between** *the two countries*

im·be·cile /ˈɪmbəsiːl ‖ -səl/ n an extremely stupid person –**imbecility** /ˌɪmbɪ̱ˈsɪlɪ̱ti/ n [U]

im·bibe /ɪmˈbaɪb/ v **imbibed, imbibing** [I;T] *fml* to drink, especially alcohol

im·bue /ɪmˈbjuː/ v **imbued, imbuing**
imbue sbdy **with** sthg *phr v* [T] *fml* to fill someone with a particular quality: *A President should be imbued with a sense of responsibility for the nation.*

im·i·tate /ˈɪmɪ̱teɪt/ v **imitated, imitating** [T] to copy someone's behaviour, appearance, or speech: *James can imitate his father perfectly.* | *imitating American dress and culture* –**imitator** n –**imitative** *adj* : *imitative behaviour*

im·i·ta·tion /ˌɪmɪ̱ˈteɪʃən/ n **1** [C] a copy in appearance or behaviour: *He does a good imitation of the President.* | *They're not real diamonds, just imitations.* **2** [U] the act of copying something: *They say that imitation is the sincerest form of flattery.*

im·mac·u·late /ɪˈmækjʊ̱lɪ̱t/ *adj* **1** completely clean and unspoilt: *immaculate white shoes* **2** without fault: *immaculate behaviour* –**immaculately** *adv* : *immaculately dressed*

im·ma·te·ri·al /ˌɪməˈtɪ̱əriəl/ *adj* unimportant: *The time is immaterial – it's the place the accident happened that we need to know.*

im·ma·ture /ˌɪməˈtʃʊəʳ ‖ -ˈtʊər/ *adj* **1** not behaving in an adult manner: *I think he's rather immature for a man of 30.* **2** not fully formed or developed: *an immature salmon* –**immaturely** *adv* –**immaturity** n [U]

im·mea·su·ra·ble /ɪˈmeʒərəbəl/ *adj* too large to be measured: *the immeasurable depths of the ocean* | *The storm has done immeasurable damage.*

im·me·di·a·cy /ɪˈmiːdiəsi/ n [U] *fml* the closeness of something, which causes it to be noticed or means that it must be dealt with immediately: *He did not realize the immediacy of the danger.*

im·me·di·ate /ɪˈmiːdiət/ *adj* **1** done or needed at once and without delay: *an immediate reply* | *We must take immediate action.* **2** nearest: *in the*

immediate future | *My immediate family consists of my son and my wife.*

im·me·di·ate·ly[1] /ɪˈmiːdiətli/ *adv* **1** without delay: *Stop that immediately!* | *I went immediately after I'd eaten.* **2** directly: *Everyone who is immediately involved will be informed of developments.* | *I'd parked immediately in front of the theatre.*

■ USAGE **Immediately** is usually too direct to use in polite requests. It is better to use the phrase **as soon as possible**: *I would be grateful if you could send me the information* **as soon as possible.** | *Could you let me know* **as soon as possible?**

immediately[2] *conj* as soon as: *I came immediately I heard the news.*

im·me·mo·ri·al /ˌɪmɪˈmɔːriəl/ *adj* going back longer than people can remember

im·mense /ɪˈmens/ *adj* very large: *an immense palace* | *That's an immense improvement on your first attempt!* –**immensity** *n* [U] : *the immensity of space*

im·mense·ly /ɪˈmensli/ *adv* very much: *I enjoyed it immensely.* | *an immensely complex situation*

im·merse /ɪˈmɜːs ‖ -ɜːrs/ *v* **immersed, immersing 1** [T] to cover something completely in a liquid: *Immerse the cloth in the dye.* **2 immerse yourself in something** to direct all your thoughts and attention to something: *I immersed myself in my work to try to forget her.* –**immersion** /ɪˈmɜːʃən, -ʒən ‖ -ɜːr-/ *n* [U]

im·mer·sion heat·er /ˈ·· ˌ··/ *n* an electric water heater in a TANK

im·mi·grant /ˈɪmɪɡrənt/ *n* a person coming into a country from abroad to make their home there –compare EMIGRANT –see EMIGRATE (USAGE)

im·mi·gra·tion /ˌɪmɪˈɡreɪʃən/ *n* [U] the process of entering another country to make your life and home there: *the immigration office at the airport* | *There are strict controls on immigration into this country.* –see EMIGRATE (USAGE)

im·mi·nence /ˈɪmɪnəns/ *n* [U] the nearness of something which is going to happen, especially something unpleasant: *The imminence of the exams made them work harder.*

im·mi·nent /ˈɪmɪnənt/ *adj* going to happen very soon: *A general election is now imminent.* | *in imminent danger of death*

im·mo·bile /ɪˈməʊbaɪl ‖ -bəl/ *adj* **1** completely still: *Keep the broken leg immobile.* **2** not able to move –**immobility** /ˌɪməʊˈbɪləti/ *n* [U]

im·mo·bi·lize /ɪˈməʊbəlaɪz/ *v* **immobilized, immobilizing** (also **immobilise** BrE) [T] to make something unable to move: *The fishing boats have been immobilized by the storms.*

im·mod·e·rate /ɪˈmɒdərət ‖ ɪˈmɑː-/ *adj* not kept within sensible limits: *immoderate wage demands*

im·mod·est /ɪˈmɒdəst ‖ ɪˈmɑː-/ *adj* **1** telling the good things about yourself instead of hiding them: *He was most immodest about his promotion.* **2** improper and likely to shock other people: *an immodest dress* –**immodestly** *adv* –**immodesty** *n* [U]

im·mor·al /ɪˈmɒrəl ‖ ɪˈmɔː-/ *adj* **1** not considered good or right: *Using other people for your own profit is immoral.* **2** going against accepted standards of sexual behaviour: *A pimp lives off the immoral earnings of a prostitute.* –**immorally** *adv* –**immorality** /ˌɪməˈræləti/ *n* [U]

im·mor·tal /ɪˈmɔːtl ‖ -ɔːr-/ *adj* **1** that will not die: *Nobody is immortal.* **2** remembered for ever: *Shakespeare's immortal plays* –**immortality** /ˌɪmɔːˈtæləti ‖ -ɔːr-/ *n* [U]

im·mor·tal·ize /ɪˈmɔːtəl-aɪz ‖ -ɔːr-/ *v* **immortalized, immortalizing** (also **immortalise** BrE) [T] to cause someone or something to be remembered for ever: *Dickens' father was immortalized as Mr Micawber in "David Copperfield".*

im·mo·va·ble /ɪˈmuːvəbəl/ *adj* impossible to move –**immovably** *adv*

im·mune /ɪˈmjuːn/ *adj* **1** not harmed by something: *Most of them are immune to hepatitis.* | *The president seems to be immune to criticism.* **2 immune from something** specially protected from something: *You will probably be immune from punishment if you help the police.* –**immunity** *n* [U] : *diplomatic immunity*

immune sys·tem /·'· ˌ··/ *n* the immune system a system in your body which produces special substances to fight against disease-causing substances that have entered your body

im·mu·nize /ˈɪmjɵnaɪz/ *v* **immunized, immunizing** (also **immunise** BrE) [T] to protect someone from disease, usually by putting certain substances into their body with a special needle –**immunization** /ˌɪmjɵnaɪˈzeɪʃən ‖ -nə-/ *n* [C;U]

im·mu·ta·ble /ɪˈmjuːtəbəl/ *adj fml* never changing: *the immutable laws of nature*

imp /ɪmp/ *n* a playful, troublesome little character in fairy stories

im·pact /ˈɪmpækt/ *n* **1** [C] the strong effect that something has on something else: *That new computer has made quite an impact on our office.* **2** [U] the force of one object hitting another **3 on impact** at the moment when one object hits another

im·pair /ɪmˈpeə/ *v* [T] to damage or weaken something: *His hearing was impaired after the explosion.* –**impairment** *n* [U]

im·pale /ɪmˈpeɪl/ *v* **impaled, impaling** [T] **be impaled on something** to have something sharp and pointed going through your body: *He fell out of the window and was impaled on the iron railings.*

im·part /ɪmˈpaːt ‖ -aːrt/ *v* [T] *fml* **1** to pass on qualities or feelings: *The herbs imparted a delicious flavour to the stew.* **2** to tell or pass on information: *I've no news to impart.*

im·par·tial /ɪmˈpaːʃəl ‖ -aːr-/ *adj* fair and not giving special support to one side: *an impartial judge* | *an impartial news report* –**impartially** *adv* –**impartiality** /ɪmˌpaːʃiˈæləti ‖ -aːr-/ *n* [U]

im·pass·a·ble /ɪmˈpaːsəbəl ‖ ɪmˈpæ-/ *adj* not able to be travelled over: *The snow has made the road impassable.*

im·passe /æmˈpaːs ‖ ˈɪmpæs/ *n* [sing] a difficult situation in which neither side will give way: *Negotiations have reached an impasse.*

im·pas·sioned /ɪmˈpæʃənd/ *adj* filled with deep feelings (used of speech): *an impassioned plea for the prisoners to be freed*

im·pas·sive /ɪmˈpæsɪv/ *adj* showing no feelings –**impassively** *adv* : *He watched impassively as his house burned down.*

im·pa·tient /ɪmˈpeɪʃənt/ *adj* **1** easily annoyed by delays, or other people's weaknesses: *The teacher was too impatient with slow learners.* **2** annoyed and bad-tempered: *an impatient reply* **3 impatient for something** eager for something: *impatient for his dinner* **4 impatient to do something** wanting to do something very much: *I was impatient to leave.* –**impatience** *n* [U] : *He could barely conceal his impatience.* –**impatiently** *adv*

im·peach /ɪmˈpiːtʃ/ *v* [T] *law* to say a public official is guilty of a serious crime against the state –**impeachment** *n* [U]

im·pec·ca·ble /ɪmˈpekəbəl/ *adj* without any faults: *impeccable manners* –**impeccably** *adv*

im·pe·cu·ni·ous /ˌɪmpɪˈkjuːniəs/ *adj fml* having little or no money, especially continually

im·pede /ɪmˈpiːd/ *v* **impeded, impeding** [T] to slow down the process of doing something by making it difficult: *The attempt to rescue the climbers was impeded by bad weather.*

im·ped·i·ment /ɪmˈpedɪmənt/ *n* **1** a fact or event which makes action difficult or impossible: *The country's huge foreign debt will be a major impediment to its development.* **2 a speech impediment** a physical or nervous difficulty which prevents someone from speaking clearly

im·pel /ɪmˈpel/ *v* **-ll-** [T] *fml* (of an idea or feeling) to drive someone to take action: *He felt impelled to write to the paper about it.*
□ USEFUL PATTERN to impel someone to do something

im·pend·ing /ɪmˈpendɪŋ/ *adj* going to happen soon (used of something unpleasant): *We had no warning of the impending disaster.*

im·pen·e·tra·ble /ɪmˈpenɪtrəbəl/ *adj* **1** impossible to get through: *the impenetrable forest* | *impenetrable darkness* **2** impossible to understand: *an impenetrable mystery*

im·per·a·tive[1] /ɪmˈperətɪv/ *adj fml* very urgent and important: *It's imperative that you go at once.*

imperative[2] *n* the form of a verb which expresses a command: *In "Come here!" the verb "come" is in the imperative.*

im·per·cep·ti·ble /ˌɪmpəˈseptɪbəl ‖ -pər-/ *adj* not noticed because of being very small or slight: *an almost imperceptible movement of her eyelid* –**imperceptibly** *adv* –**imperceptibility** /ˌɪmpəˌseptəˈbɪlɪti ‖ -pər-/ *n* [U]

im·per·fect[1] /ɪmˈpɜːfɪkt ‖ -ɜːr-/ *adj* with some fault or problem: *I have only an imperfect knowledge of French.* –**imperfectly** *adv* –**imperfection** /ˌɪmpəˈfekʃən ‖ -pər-/ *n* [C;U]

imperfect[2] *n* **the imperfect, the imperfect tense** the tense of a verb which shows an incomplete or repeated action in the past: *In "we were walking down the road" the verb "were walking" is in the imperfect.*

im·pe·ri·al /ɪmˈpɪəriəl/ *adj* (also **Imperial**) **1** relating to an empire or its ruler: *the Imperial Palace* **2** relating to the British system of measurement: *The Imperial gallon is not the same size as the American one.*

im·pe·ri·al·is·m /ɪmˈpɪəriəlɪzəm/ *n* [U] the gaining of political and trade advantages over poorer nations by a powerful country which rules them or helps them –**imperialist** *n, adj* –**imperialistic** /ɪmˌpɪəriəˈlɪstɪk◂/ *adj*

im·per·il /ɪmˈperɪl/ *v* **-ll-** (also **-l-** *AmE*) [T] *fml* to put someone in danger

im·pe·ri·ous /ɪmˈpɪəriəs/ *adj fml* proud, and expecting other people to obey you *an imperious voice* –**imperiously** *adv* –**imperiousness** *n* [U]

im·per·son·al /ɪmˈpɜːsənəl ‖ -ɜːr-/ *adj* not showing or including personal feelings: *an impersonal letter* | *a large impersonal organization* –**impersonally** *adv*

im·per·so·nate /ɪmˈpɜːsəneɪt ‖ -ɜːr-/ *v* **impersonated, impersonating** [T] to pretend to be another person by copying their appearance and behaviour: *He impersonates all the well-known politicians.* –**impersonator** *n* –**impersonation** /ɪmˌpɜːsəˈneɪʃən ‖ -ɜːr-/ *n* [C;U]

im·per·ti·nent /ɪmˈpɜːtɪnənt ‖ -ɜːr-/ *adj* rude or not respectful, especially to an older or more important person: *I will not tolerate such impertinent remarks.* –**impertinence** *n* [U] –**impertinently** *adv*

im·per·tur·ba·ble /ˌɪmpəˈtɜːbəbəl ‖ -pərˈtɜːr-/ *adj* remaining calm in spite of difficulties –**imperturbably** *adv* –**imperturbability** /ˌɪmpətɜːbəˈbɪlɪti ‖ -pərtɜːr-/ *n* [U]

im·per·vi·ous /ɪmˈpɜːviəs ‖ -ɜːr-/ *adj* **1 impervious** to not influenced or changed by something: *He seemed totally impervious to reason.* **2** not allowing anything to pass through: *an impervious rock such as granite*

im·pet·u·ous /ɪmˈpetʃuəs/ *adj* **1** tending to be quick to act, but without thinking carefully: *an impetuous young man* **2** done or made too quickly: *an impetuous decision which she soon regretted* –**impetuously** *adv*

im·pe·tus /ˈɪmpɪtəs/ *n* **1** [C;U] encouragement: *The government's plan gave fresh impetus to our industry.* **2** [U] the force of something moving: *The car ran down the hill under its own impetus.*

im·pi·e·ty /ɪmˈpaɪɪti/ *n* [U] lack of respect for religion –**impious** /ˈɪmpiəs/ *adj*

im·pinge /ɪmˈpɪndʒ/ *v* **impinged, impinging impinge on/upon** to have an effect on someone or something: *The economic crisis is impinging on every aspect of our lives.*

imp·ish /ˈɪmpɪʃ/ *adj* like a little devil: *an impish smile* –**impishly** *adv*

im·plac·a·ble /ɪmˈplækəbəl/ *adj* impossible to make less angry: *an implacable enemy*

im·plant /ɪmˈplɑːnt ‖ ɪmˈplænt/ *v* [T] **1** to fix something into someone's body by means of an operation **2** to make an idea become completely accepted: *They were accused of trying to implant their own political values into the students.* –**implant** /ˈɪmplɑːnt ‖ -plænt/ *n* : *hormone implants*

im·plau·si·ble /ɪmˈplɔːzɪbəl/ *adj* unlikely to be true: *an implausible explanation*

im·ple·ment[1] /ˈɪmplɪmənt/ *n* a tool: *gardening implements*

im·ple·ment[2] /ˈɪmplɪment/ *v* [T] to carry out or put into practice: *The committee's suggestions will be implemented immediately.* –**implementation** /ˌɪmplɪmenˈteɪʃən, -mən-/ *n* [U]

im·pli·cate /ˈɪmplɪkeɪt/ *v* **implicated, implicating** [T] *fml* to show that someone is connected with something, especially a crime: *The police found a letter which implicated him in the robbery.*

im·pli·ca·tion /ˌɪmplɪˈkeɪʃən/ *n* **1** something that is suggested but not expressed directly: *He smiled, but the implication was that he didn't believe me.* **2 by implication** by expressing something indirectly: *She said very little directly, but a great deal by implication.* **3** a possible later effect of an action or decision: *The article assesses the wider implications of the nuclear accident.*

im·pli·cit /ɪmˈplɪsɪt/ *adj* **1** suggested or understood though not directly expressed: *an implicit threat* | *Her opposition was implicit in her failure to support the plan.* –compare EXPLICIT **2** [only before a noun] complete and unquestioning: *She has implicit trust in her doctor.* –**implicitly** *adv*

SPELLING NOTE

Words with the sound /aɪ/ may be spelt **e-**, like **eye**, or **ai-**, like **aisle**.

im·plore /ɪmˈplɔːʳ/ v **implored, imploring** [T] fml to ask someone for something or to do something with great eagerness and anxiety: *She implored his forgiveness.* | *I implore you to go now.* **–imploring** adj

im·ply /ɪmˈplaɪ/ v **implied, implying** [T; + (that)] **1** to suggest something in an indirect way: *He didn't actually say he'd been invited, but he certainly implied that he had.* | *Are you implying that we're not telling the truth?* – see INFER (USAGE) **2** to suggest that something is necessary or true: *Taking responsibility for organizing the event implies real commitment.* | *The fact that no one answered the phone implies that they're not at home.*

im·po·lite /ˌɪmpəˈlaɪt/ adj slightly rude: *It was impolite of her not to say goodbye.* **–impolitely** adv **–impoliteness** n [U]

im·pol·i·tic /ɪmˈpɒlɪtɪk ‖ ɪmˈpɑː-/ adj fml not wise or well-judged for your purpose: *It's unlike him to make such an impolitic decision.*

im·pon·de·ra·ble /ɪmˈpɒndərəbəl ‖ -ˈpɑːn-/ adj impossible to calculate or measure exactly **–imponderables** n [pl]: *You cannot anticipate the effect of imponderables such as power and influence.*

im·port¹ /ɪmˈpɔːt ‖ -ɔːrt/ v [T] to bring goods in from another country: *We import thousands of cars from Japan.* –compare EXPORT **–importer** n

im·port² /ˈɪmpɔːt ‖ -ɔːrt/ n **1** [C] something brought in from another country: *Imports rose last month.* | *flooding the market with cheap imports* **2** [U] the bringing of something in from another country: *the import of food from abroad* **3** [U] fml importance: *a matter of no great import*

im·por·tance /ɪmˈpɔːtəns ‖ -ɔːr-/ n [U] **1** the quality or state of being important: *It is a matter of national importance.* –opposite **unimportance 2** the reason why something or someone is important: *Explain the importance of North Sea oil to the British economy.*

im·por·tant /ɪmˈpɔːtənt ‖ -ɔːr-/ adj **1** special or particularly useful or valuable: *Don't worry about it; it's not important.* | *a very important meeting* | *It's important to get the right qualifications.* | *It's important that you get well again quickly.* | *Privacy is important to her.* □ USEFUL PATTERNS be important to do something; be important that...; be important to someone **2** having influence or power: *an important new writer* –opposite **unimportant –importantly** adv

im·por·ta·tion /ˌɪmpɔːˈteɪʃən ‖ -ɔːr-/ n [U] bringing something in from another place

im·pose /ɪmˈpəʊz/ v **imposed, imposing 1** [T] to force someone to accept something they do not want: *Economic sanctions have been imposed on South Africa.* | *The judge imposed a fine of £10,000.* **2** [T] to establish an additional payment officially: *A new tax has been imposed on cigarettes.* **3** [I] to expect someone to help you by doing something that they may not really want to do: *Thank you for the offer, but I don't want to impose on you.* **–imposition** /ˌɪmpəˈzɪʃən/ n [C;U] : *protesting against the imposition of a sales tax on books*

im·pos·ing /ɪmˈpəʊzɪŋ/ adj large or powerful in appearance: *an imposing building* **–imposingly** adv

im·pos·si·ble /ɪmˈpɒsəbəl ‖ ɪmˈpɑː-/ adj **1** that cannot happen or exist, or that cannot be done: *I'm afraid that's quite impossible.* | *It's impossible to explain how angry I felt.* | *an impossible task* | *It's impossible for me to get there before eight o'clock.*

□ USEFUL PATTERNS be impossible to do something; be impossible for someone to do something **2** very unpleasant or difficult to deal with: *You're putting me in an impossible position.* **–impossibly** adv : *impossibly difficult* **–impossibility** /ɪmˌpɒsəˈbɪlɪti ‖ ɪmˌpɑː-/ n [U]

im·pos·tor /ɪmˈpɒstəʳ ‖ ɪmˈpɑːs-/ n **(imposter** AmE) someone who pretends to be someone else in order to get something they want: *You're not a doctor! You're an impostor!*

im·po·tent /ˈɪmpətənt/ adj **1** lacking power to influence people or events: *a government which seemed impotent in its last years of office* **2** unable to perform the sex act (used of a man) **–impotence** n [U] **–impotently** adv

im·pound /ɪmˈpaʊnd/ v [T] fml to take official possession of something: *If you park your car there, it will be impounded by the police.*

im·pov·e·rished /ɪmˈpɒvərɪʃt ‖ ɪmˈpɑː-/ adj made poor: *an impoverished African country* | *the spiritually impoverished Western lifestyle*

im·prac·ti·ca·ble /ɪmˈpræktɪkəbəl/ adj impossible to do or use: *It would be impracticable to stop using insecticides completely.* **–impracticably** adv **–impracticability** /ɪˌpræktɪkəˈbɪlɪti/ n [U]

im·prac·ti·cal /ɪmˈpræktɪkəl/ adj not good at dealing with ordinary situations and problems in a sensible way: *an impractical person who can't even boil an egg* | *I need helpful ideas – his are completely impractical.* **–impractically** adv

im·pre·cise /ˌɪmprɪˈsaɪs/ adj not exact or clear: *Her directions were very imprecise.*

im·preg·na·ble /ɪmˈpregnəbəl/ adj very strong and unable to be entered or conquered: *an impregnable castle*

im·preg·nate /ˈɪmpregneɪt ‖ ɪmˈpreg-/ v **impregnated, impregnating** [T] **1** to cause a substance to enter and spread completely through another substance: *a cleaning cloth impregnated with polish* **2** fml to make a female PREGNANT

im·pre·sa·ri·o /ˌɪmprɪˈsɑːriəʊ/ n a person who arranges theatrical or musical performances

im·press /ɪmˈpres/ v **1** [T] to fill someone with admiration or respect: *I was very impressed* **with** *their new house.* | *The teacher told me he was impressed* **by** *your essay.* **2 impress something on someone** to make someone understand the importance of something: *My father impressed on me the value of hard work.*

im·pres·sion /ɪmˈpreʃən/ n **1** the way something looks or appears to you: *If the shop is untidy, it makes a bad impression on the customers.* | *She said she was happy, but I got the impression that something was wrong.* **2 make an impression** to cause people to remember you, usually favourably **3 be under the impression that** to believe that something is true: *Oh, is he only the form master? I was under the impression that he was the headmaster.* **4** a mark left by pressure: *He took an impression of the key to make a copy.* **5** a copy of a person's appearance or behaviour as a funny theatrical performance: *He did his impression of the president.*

im·pres·sio·na·ble /ɪmˈpreʃənəbəl/ adj easy to influence: *My son's at an impressionable age.*

im·pres·sion·is·m /ɪmˈpreʃənɪzəm/ n [U] a style of painting which produces effects by light and colour rather than by details of form; it was popular in France between 1870 and 1900 **–Impressionist** n

im·pres·sion·is·tic /ɪmˌpreʃəˈnɪstɪk◂/ adj based on the way something appears to someone, rather than on knowledge or facts: *We need facts, not an impressionistic account of what happened.* –**impressionistically** /-kli/ *adv*

im·pres·sive /ɪmˈpresɪv/ *adj* causing admiration: *We've succeeded in collecting an impressive amount of money.* | *an impressive stamp collection* –**impressively** *adv* –**impressiveness** *n* [U]

im·print[1] /ɪmˈprɪnt/ *v* [T] **1** to print or press a mark on something **2** **be imprinted on your mind/memory** to leave a clear picture in your mind that you will never forget: *Every detail is imprinted on my mind.*

im·print[2] /ˈɪmprɪnt/ *n* **1** a mark left on or in something: *An imprint of his thumb was left in the concrete.* **2** the clear picture or effect of something in your mind

im·pris·on /ɪmˈprɪzən/ *v* [T] to keep someone in a place from which they cannot escape, especially in a prison: *He's been imprisoned for over 27 years.* –**imprisonment** *n* [U]

im·prob·a·ble /ɪmˈprɒbəbəl ‖ -ˈprɑː-/ *adj* not likely to happen or to be true: *It's possible that no one saw him leave, but it seems highly improbable.*

im·promp·tu /ɪmˈprɒmptjuː ‖ ɪmˈprɑːmptuː/ *adj fml* done without preparation: *an impromptu speech*

im·prop·er /ɪmˈprɒpəʳ ‖ -ˈprɑː-/ *adj* **1** not suitable or correct: *The director of the charity was accused of improper use of funds.* **2** rude or socially unacceptable: *an improper suggestion* –**improperly** *adv* –**impropriety** /ˌɪmprəˈpraɪɪti/ *n* **improprieties** [C;U]

im·prove /ɪmˈpruːv/ *v* **improved, improving** **1** [I] to become better: *I think your English is improving.* **2** [T] to make something better: *Security precautions have now been improved.* **3** **improve yourself** to rise higher in society, especially through education **4** **improve on/upon something** to produce something better than something else: *I don't think anyone can improve on her score.*

im·prove·ment /ɪmˈpruːvmənt/ *n* [C;U] a change which makes something better or shows that something is getting better: *His health is showing signs of improvement.* | *a considerable improvement in our exam results* | *This year's exam results are a vast improvement on last year's.* | *He's talking of making more improvements to the house.*
■ USAGE We speak about an **improvement** in something if it has got better: *There has been an* **improvement** in *the weather.* | *There has been a definite* **improvement** in *your work recently.* We speak about an **improvement on** something if we are comparing two things, and one of them is better than the other: *Today's weather is an* **improvement** **on** *yesterday's.* | *Your results this term are a great* **improvement** **on** *last term's performance.*

im·prov·i·dent /ɪmˈprɒvɪdənt ‖ -ˈprɑː-/ *adj fml* wasting money and not preparing for the future –**improvidence** *n* [U]

im·pro·vise /ˈɪmprəvaɪz/ *v* **improvised, improvising** [I;T] to do or make something without planning in advance: *I forgot the words of my speech, so I had to improvise.* –**improvisation** /ˌɪmprəvaɪˈzeɪʃən ‖ ɪmˌprɑːvə-/ *n* [C;U]

im·pru·dent /ɪmˈpruːdənt/ *adj* not wise or thoughtful –**imprudence** *n* [U] –**imprudently** *adv*

im·pu·dent /ˈɪmpjʊ̆dənt/ *adj* rude and not showing any respect –**impudence** *n* [U] –**impudently** *adv*

im·pulse /ˈɪmpʌls/ *n* **1** a sudden strong wish to do something: *She had a sudden impulse to hit him.* **2** **on impulse** because of a sudden strong wish: *He bought the bicycle on impulse.* **3** *tech* a short electrical signal sent in one direction along a wire or a nerve, or through the air: *an electrical impulse*

im·pul·sive /ɪmˈpʌlsɪv/ *adj* tending to do things suddenly without thinking about the results: *Don't be so impulsive, or you'll regret it later!* –**impulsively** *adv* –**impulsiveness** *n* [U]

im·pu·ni·ty /ɪmˈpjuːnɪ̆ti/ *n* **with impunity** without any danger of being punished: *Students ignored the new regulations with impunity.*

im·pure /ɪmˈpjʊəʳ/ *adj* **1** *old fash* concerned with sex and regarded as bad: *impure thoughts* **2** not pure, but mixed with other substances: *The heroin was found to be impure.* –**impurity** *n* **impurities** [C;U] : *impurities in the water supply*

im·pute /ɪmˈpjuːt/ *v* **imputed, imputing impute** something to someone *fml* to claim that someone has something or has done something: *How can they impute such disgraceful motives to the teachers?* –**imputation** /ˌɪmpjʊˈteɪʃən/ *n* [C;U]

in[1] /ɪn/ *adv,prep* **1** *adv,prep* surrounded by something or contained by it: *The cups are in the cupboard.* | *There was nobody in the house.* | *Put the butter in the fridge.* | *people swimming in the sea* | *There were sheep in the field.* | *She lives in London.* | *By tomorrow we'll be in France.* | *She's in hospital.* | *She opened her bag and put the packet in.* | *I knocked on the door and she shouted "come in."* –see picture on page 540 **2** *adv* given or sent to someone who has a position of power: *Applications must be in by next Thursday.* | *Letters of support have been flooding in this week.* **3** *adv* present at your home or your place of work: *I'm afraid Mr Jones isn't in at the moment.* **4** *prep* wearing something: *men in dark suits* | *a woman dressed in a red coat* **5** *prep* during a period of time: *I hope we'll see you in the Spring.* | *We had a lot of snow in January.* | *I haven't seen much of John in the last few weeks.* **6** *prep* after a period of time: *I'll be back in an hour.* | *The train leaves in a few minutes.* | *We're going on holiday in two weeks.* **7** *prep* as a result of a feeling that you have: *In my excitement, I knocked the flowers off the table.* | *She looked round in surprise.* **8** *prep* having a particular job: *She's in politics* | *a job in insurance* **9** *prep* using something in order to write or say something: *They were talking in French.* | *a note written in pencil* **10** *prep* used in expressions showing the relation between two amounts: *a slope of 1 in 3* | *a tax of 40p in the pound* **11** *adv* batting (BAT) in a game of cricket: *England are in at the moment.* **12 the tide is in** = the sea is at the point when it is highest and closest to the land **13 day in day out, week in week out, etc** every day, week etc for a long time without any change **14 in and out of somewhere** sometimes in a place, sometimes out of it over a long period of time: *He's been in and out of prison for years.* **15 in all** in total: *There were 20 people there in all.* **16 in for something** going to have something bad or unpleasant: *She's in for a nasty surprise!* | *I think we're in for trouble.* **17 in on something** concerned with something or sharing in it: *I wanted to be in on the deal.* **18 in with someone** friendly with someone **19 the ins and outs of something** the various parts of something such as a job, some of which are good and some bad

in² adj fashionable: *Bright colours are in at the moment.* | *the in place to go*

in³ a written abbreviation for INCH(es)

in·a·bil·i·ty /ˌɪnəˈbɪlɪti/ n [sing] lack of ability, power, or skill: *an inability to work alone* | *inability to stop smoking*

in·ac·ces·si·ble /ˌɪnəkˈsesɪbəl/ adj very difficult or impossible to reach: *Heavy snow made the village inaccessible to traffic.* | *inaccessible mountain villages* –**inaccessibility** /ˌɪnəksesɪˈbɪlɪti/ n [U]

in·ac·cu·rate /ɪnˈækjʊrɪt/ adj not correct –**inaccurately** adv –**inaccuracy** n **inaccuracies** [C;U]

in·ac·tion /ɪnˈækʃən/ n [U] lack of action

in·ac·tive /ɪnˈæktɪv/ adj not active –**inactivity** /ˌɪnækˈtɪvɪti/ n [U]

in·ad·e·qua·cy /ɪnˈædɪkwəsi/ n **inadequacies** [C;U] an example of the state of being inadequate

in·ad·e·quate /ɪnˈædɪkwɪt/ adj not good enough in quality, ability, or amount: *I felt inadequate in my new job, so I left.* | *The food was inadequate for 14 people.* –**inadequately** adv

in·ad·ver·tent /ˌɪnədˈvɜːtənt || -ɜːr-/ adj done without thinking or by accident –**inadvertently** adv: *He inadvertently knocked over his cup of coffee.*

in·a·li·en·a·ble /ɪnˈeɪliənəbəl/ adj/fml inalienable right a right which cannot be taken away: *Freedom of speech should be an inalienable right.*

i·nane /ɪˈneɪn/ adj stupid and without meaning: *an inane remark* | *inane behaviour* –**inanely** adv

in·an·i·mate /ɪnˈænɪmɪt/ adj not living: *an inanimate object*

in·ap·pli·ca·ble /ˌɪnəˈplɪkəbəl, ɪnˈæplɪkəbl || ɪnˈæplɪk-/ adj unrelated to the subject –**inapplicability** /ˌɪnəplɪkəˈbɪlɪti, ɪnˌæplɪk- || ɪnˌæplɪk-/ n [U]

in·ap·pro·pri·ate /ˌɪnəˈprəʊprɪɪt/ adj not suitable for a particular event or purpose: *Your short dress is inappropriate for a formal party.* –**inappropriately** adv –**inappropriateness** n [U]

in·ar·tic·u·late /ˌɪnɑːˈtɪkjʊlɪt || -ɑːr-/ adj **1** unable to express yourself clearly when speaking: *He's very intelligent, but completely inarticulate.* **2** not well-formed or not clearly expressed: *an inarticulate speech* –**inarticulately** adv

in·as·much as /ˌɪnəzˈmʌtʃ əz/ conj fml owing to the fact that: *Their father is also guilty, inasmuch as he knew what they were going to do.*

in·at·ten·tion /ˌɪnəˈtenʃən/ n [U] lack of attention

in·at·ten·tive /ˌɪnəˈtentɪv/ adj not giving attention: *an inattentive pupil* –**inattentively** adv –**inattentiveness** n [U]

in·au·di·ble /ɪnˈɔːdɪbəl/ adj too quiet to be heard –**inaudibly** adv –**inaudibility** /ɪnˌɔːdɪˈbɪlɪti/ n [U]

in·au·gu·rate /ɪˈnɔːgjʊreɪt/ v **inaugurated, inaugurating** [T] **1** to introduce a new leader or official into an important job in an organization by holding a special ceremony: *The president was inaugurated last week.* **2** to open a new building or start a public event with a special ceremony: *The new school was inaugurated last week.* –**inaugural** adj [only before a noun]: *an inaugural ceremony to open the new hospital* –**inauguration** /ɪˌnɔːgjʊˈreɪʃən || -ɔːr-/ n [C;U]

in·aus·pi·cious /ˌɪnɔːˈspɪʃəs/ adj showing signs that the future will be unlucky: *an inauspicious start to the term* –**inauspiciously** adv –**inauspiciousness** n [U]

in·born /ˌɪnˈbɔːn◂ || -ɔːrn◂/ adj present from birth as part of a person or animal's nature or behaviour: *Birds have an inborn ability to fly.*

in·bred /ˌɪnˈbred◂/ adj **1** having become part of your nature as a result of early training **2** bred from closely related members of a family

in·breed·ing /ˈɪnbriːdɪŋ/ n [U] breeding from closely related members of a family

Inc /ɪŋk/ an abbreviation for INCORPORATED

in·cal·cu·la·ble /ɪnˈkælkjʊləbəl/ adj too great to be counted or measured: *an incalculable risk* –**incalculably** adv

in·can·des·cent /ˌɪnkænˈdesənt || -kən-/ adj giving a bright light when heated –**incandescence** n [U]

in·can·ta·tion /ˌɪnkænˈteɪʃən/ n the saying or singing of words used in magic

in·ca·pa·ble /ɪnˈkeɪpəbəl/ adj not able to do something: *He's incapable of deceiving anyone.* | *He seems completely incapable.*
□ USEFUL PATTERNS be incapable of something; be incapable of doing something

in·ca·pa·ci·tate /ˌɪnkəˈpæsɪteɪt/ v **incapacitated, incapacitating** [T] to weaken or harm someone physically so they are not able to do something: *He was incapacitated as a result of the accident.*

in·ca·pa·ci·ty /ˌɪnkəˈpæsɪti/ n [U] lack of ability, strength, or power to do something: *an incapacity to lie* | *the country's incapacity to solve its economic problems*

in·car·ce·rate /ɪnˈkɑːsəreɪt || -ɑːr-/ v **incarcerated, incarcerating** [T] fml to imprison someone –**incarceration** /ɪnˌkɑːsəˈreɪʃən || -ɑːr-/ n [U]

in·car·nate /ɪnˈkɑːnɪt || -ɑːr-/ adj [only after a noun] **1** in the form of a physical body: *the devil incarnate* **2** a word used to show strongly that something or someone has a particular quality: *She was happiness incarnate.*

in·car·na·tion /ˌɪnkɑːˈneɪʃən || -ɑːr-/ n **1** the act of putting a spirit into physical form: *Local people believe this god has many incarnations.* **2** a person or thing that is the perfect example of a quality: *She's the very incarnation of generosity.*

in·cen·di·a·ry /ɪnˈsendiəri || -dieri/ adj [only before a noun] causing fires: *an incendiary bomb*

in·cense¹ /ˈɪnsens/ n [U] a substance that gives off a sweet smell when burnt, often used in religious services

in·cense² /ɪnˈsens/ v **incensed, incensing** [T] to make someone very angry: *I was incensed at his rudeness.*

in·cen·tive /ɪnˈsentɪv/ n [C;U] an encouragement to do something: *The prospect of being chosen for the team gave me an incentive and I trained twice as hard.* | *He's got no incentive to study further.*

in·cep·tion /ɪnˈsepʃən/ n [U] fml the beginning of an activity or organization: *He's worked for that company since its inception.*

in·ces·sant /ɪnˈsesənt/ adj never stopping: *incessant noise* –**incessantly** adv

in·cest /ˈɪnsest/ n [U] a sexual relationship between close relatives in a family, for example between a brother and sister –**incestuous** /ɪnˈsestʃuəs/ adj –**incestuously** adv

inch¹ /ɪntʃ/ n **1** a unit for measuring length, equal to 1/12 of a foot or about 0·025 metres **2 inch by inch** very slowly and by a small amount at a time

inch² v [I + adv/prep] (also **inch your way**) to move

slowly with care or difficulty: *I inched through the narrow space.*

in·ci·dence /ˈɪnsɪdəns/ *n* [sing] how often something happens: *There's a high incidence of disease there.*

in·ci·dent /ˈɪnsɪdənt/ *n* a single event which is usually not very important

in·ci·den·tal /ˌɪnsɪˈdentl◂/ *adj* happening or existing in connection with something else: *incidental details* | *an event incidental to the main action*

in·ci·den·tal·ly /ˌɪnsɪˈdentəli/ *adv* you say "incidentally" when you say something you have just thought of; it may be unconnected with the last subject or it may be about another part of it: *I must go now. Incidentally, if you want that book I'll bring it next time.* | *I think that's Joan's bag. Incidentally, did you know she was expecting a baby?*

in·cin·e·rate /ɪnˈsɪnəreɪt/ *v* **incinerated, incinerating** [T] *fml* to destroy unwanted things by burning them –**incineration** /ɪnˌsɪnəˈreɪʃən/ *n* [U]

in·cin·e·ra·tor /ɪnˈsɪnəreɪtər/ *n* a machine for burning unwanted things

in·cip·i·ent /ɪnˈsɪpiənt/ *adj fml* starting to happen or exist: *incipient disease*

in·ci·sion /ɪnˈsɪʒən/ *n fml* a sharp cut into something made with a special tool, often by a doctor during an operation: *An incision was made into the patient's stomach.*

in·ci·sive /ɪnˈsaɪsɪv/ *adj* going clearly and directly to the main point of a subject: *incisive statements* | *an incisive mind* –**incisively** *adv*

in·ci·sor /ɪnˈsaɪzər/ *n* any of your eight front teeth which have a cutting edge

in·cite /ɪnˈsaɪt/ *v* **incited, inciting** [T] **1** to cause or encourage someone to do something by making them feel angry or excited: *a violent speech inciting the army to rebel*
□ USEFUL PATTERN to incite someone to do something
2 to cause a strong feeling or action: *He was charged with inciting a riot.* –**incitement** *n* [C;U]

in·clem·ent /ɪnˈklemənt/ *adj fml* cold or stormy (used of weather)

in·cli·na·tion /ˌɪnklɪˈneɪʃən/ *n* **1** [C;U] a liking or wish to do something: *You always follow your own inclinations instead of thinking of our feelings.* | *I've no inclination to be a doctor.* **2** [C] a bending movement of your head or hand: *He gave an inclination of the head.* **3** [sing] a slope

in·cline[1] /ɪnˈklaɪn/ *v* **inclined, inclining 1** [T] to encourage or influence someone to have certain feelings or opinions: *The strangeness of her story inclines me to believe she is telling the truth.* –compare INCLINED **2** [T] *fml* to make a part of your body bend downward: *She inclined her head in greeting.* **3** [I] to slope: *The garden inclines towards the street.*

incline[2] /ˈɪnklaɪn/ *n* a slope: *a steep incline*

in·clined /ɪnˈklaɪnd/ *adj* [never before a noun] **1** feeling you want to do something or are going to do it: *The news makes me inclined to change my mind.*
□ USEFUL PATTERN be inclined to do something
–see also DISINCLINED
2 likely or tending to do something: *He's inclined to lose his temper.*

SPELLING NOTE
Words with the sound / aɪ / may be spelt **e-**, like **eye**, or **ai-**, like **aisle**.

□ USEFUL PATTERN be inclined to do something
3 be inclined to think/believe/agree etc used to show you hold an opinion, but not very strongly: *I'm inclined to agree with Jim.*

in·clude /ɪnˈkluːd/ *v* **included, including** [T] **1** to have or contain something as a part of a whole: *The price includes postage charges.* | *Is service included in the bill?* | *This fitness programme includes swimming regularly.* **2** to make something part of a whole or larger set: *I included eggs on the list of things to buy.*

in·clud·ed /ɪnˈkluːdɪd/ *adj* [only after a noun] including: *all of us, me included*

in·clud·ing /ɪnˈkluːdɪŋ/ *prep* a word used to show that some people or things form part of the larger set or whole that you are talking about: *There are six people, including three women.* | *Your total expenses, including these bills, are £200.* –opposite **excluding**

in·clu·sion /ɪnˈkluːʒən/ *n* [U] the act of including or state of being included

in·clu·sive /ɪnˈkluːsɪv/ *adj* **1** containing or including everything: *an inclusive charge* **2** [only after a noun] including other costs that are often paid separately (used of a price or charge): *The rent is £10 inclusive of heating.* **3** [only after a noun] including all the numbers or dates: *Wednesday to Friday inclusive* –**inclusively** *adv*

in·cog·ni·to /ˌɪnkɒgˈniːtəʊ ‖ ˌɪnkɑːg-/ *adj,adv* [never before a noun] hiding who you really are, especially by taking another name when your own is well-known: *She was travelling incognito.*

in·co·her·ent /ˌɪnkəʊˈhɪərənt/ *adj* unclear and without connections between ideas or words: *When he got her letter, he became incoherent with rage.* –**incoherence** *n* [U] –**incoherently** *adv*

in·come /ˈɪŋkʌm, ˈɪn-/ *n* [C;U] money which you receive, usually payment for work: *Half our income goes on rent.* | *Low-income families need government help.* –see PAY[2] (USAGE)

in·com·ing /ˈɪnkʌmɪŋ/ *adj* [only before a noun] **1** coming towards you: *an incoming tide* **2** moving towards a particular place and about to arrive there: *incoming passengers* | *incoming traffic* **3** appointed or elected to a new job: *the incoming director* **4 incoming calls** telephone calls you receive

in·com·mu·ni·ca·do /ˌɪnkəmjuːnɪˈkɑːdəʊ/ *adv,adj* [never before a noun] kept away from people so that you cannot give or receive messages

in·com·pa·ra·ble /ɪnˈkɒmpərəbl ‖ -ˈkɑːm-/ *adj* too good or great to be compared with other examples of the same thing: *incomparable wealth* | *incomparable beauty* –**incomparably** *adv*: *This model is incomparably better than the other.* –**incomparability** /ɪnˌkɒmpərəˈbɪlɪti ‖ -ˌkɑːm-/ *n* [U]

in·com·pat·i·ble /ˌɪnkəmˈpætəbl/ *adj* too different from another person or thing to be able to live or exist with them: *Their marriage broke up because they were basically incompatible.* | *His plan is incompatible with the company's intentions.* –**incompatibility** /ˌɪnkəmpætəˈbɪlɪti/ *n* **incompatibilities** [C;U]

in·com·pe·tence /ɪnˈkɒmpɪtəns ‖ -ˈkɑːm-/ *n* [U] lack of ability and skill resulting in useless work

in·com·pe·tent /ɪnˈkɒmpɪtənt ‖ -ˈkɑːm-/ *adj* lacking the skill or ability to do something properly: *an incompetent lawyer* –**incompetent** *n* : *He is a total incompetent.* –**incompetently** *adv*

in·com·plete /ˌɪnkəmˈpliːt/ *adj* without all its parts or not complete

in·com·pre·hen·si·ble /ɪnˌkɒmprɪˈhensɪbəl ‖ -ˌkɑːm-/ *adj* unable to be understood **–incomprehensibility** /ɪnˌkɒmprɪhensɪˈbɪlɪti ‖ -ˌkɑːm-/ *n* [U] *adv*

in·com·pre·hen·sion /ɪnˌkɒmprɪˈhenʃən ‖ -ˌkɑːm-/ *n* [U] the state of not understanding

in·con·cei·va·ble /ˌɪnkənˈsiːvəbəl/ *adj* difficult or impossible to believe: *It once seemed inconceivable that men should travel to the moon.* | *He can't go on holiday alone; it's inconceivable.* **–inconceivably** *adv*

in·con·clu·sive /ˌɪnkənˈkluːsɪv/ *adj* **1** not leading to a firm decision or result: *an inconclusive discussion* **2** which has not proved anything: *inconclusive evidence* **–inconclusively** *adv*

in·con·gru·ous /ɪnˈkɒŋɡruəs ‖ -ˈkɑːŋ-/ *adj* strange or surprising in relation to the surroundings: *A modern church would look incongruous in that village.* **–incongruously** *adv* **–incongruity** /ˌɪnkənˈɡruːɪti/ *n* [U]

in·con·se·quen·tial /ɪnˌkɒnsɪˈkwenʃəl ‖ -ˌkɑːn-/ *adj* unimportant: *an inconsequential idea* **–inconsequentially** *adv*

in·con·sid·e·ra·ble /ˌɪnkənˈsɪdərəbəl/ *adj* not inconsiderable large in size or value: *The actress paid a not inconsiderable sum of money for the house.*

in·con·sid·er·ate /ˌɪnkənˈsɪdərɪt/ *adj* not thinking of other people's feelings or the effect of your behaviour on them: *It was rather inconsiderate of her to keep us waiting.* **–inconsiderately** *adv*

in·con·sis·tent /ˌɪnkənˈsɪstənt/ *adj* **1** having different parts that do not agree (used of ideas and opinions): *Those remarks are inconsistent with what you said yesterday.* | *The two statements are inconsistent.* **2** tending to change: *This weather is so inconsistent – one moment it's raining and the next it's sunny.* | *inconsistent behaviour* **–inconsistency** *n* **inconsistencies** [C;U]

in·con·so·la·ble /ˌɪnkənˈsəʊləbəl/ *adj* feeling too full of sorrow to be comforted: *She is inconsolable over the loss of her dog.* | *inconsolable grief* **–inconsolably** *adv: inconsolably sad*

in·con·spic·u·ous /ˌɪnkənˈspɪkjuəs/ *adj* **1** too small or hidden to be easily noticed: *an inconspicuous doorway* **2** not attracting attention: *He was a quiet, inconspicuous figure.* **–inconspicuously** *adv*

in·con·ti·nent /ɪnˈkɒntɪnənt ‖ -ˈkɑːn-/ *adj* unable to control your BLADDER or bowels: *With old age, he became increasingly incontinent.* **–incontinence** *n* [U]

in·con·tro·ver·ti·ble /ɪnˌkɒntrəˈvɜːtɪbəl ‖ ɪnˌkɑːntrəˈvɜːr-/ *adj* which cannot be disproved: *incontrovertible evidence* **–incontrovertibly** *adv*

in·con·ve·ni·ence /ˌɪnkənˈviːniəns/ *n* [C;U] difficulty or discomfort: *Commuters suffered great inconvenience because the trains were always late.* | *It's really no inconvenience for you to stay here.*

inconvenience² *v* inconvenienced, inconveniencing [T] to make things difficult or inconvenient for someone: *I hope it won't inconvenience you to drive me to the station.*

in·con·ve·ni·ent /ˌɪnkənˈviːniənt/ *adj* causing difficulty because something does not suit you: *an inconvenient time* **–inconveniently** *adv*

in·cor·po·rate /ɪnˈkɔːpəreɪt ‖ -ɔːr-/ *v* incorporated, incorporating [T] to include something or make it part of a whole: *They incorporated his suggestions into their plans.* | *The design for the shopping centre incorporates parking facilities.* **–incorporation** /ɪnˌkɔːˈreɪʃən ‖ -ɔːr-/ *n* [U]

in·cor·po·rat·ed /ɪnˈkɔːpəreɪtɪd ‖ -ɔːr-/ *adj AmE* (also **Inc**) [only after a noun] formed into a CORPORATION according to law – compare LIMITED

in·cor·rect /ˌɪnkəˈrekt/ *adj* not correct **–incorrectly** *adv* **–incorrectness** *n* [U]

in·cor·ri·gi·ble /ɪnˈkɒrɪdʒəbəl ‖ -ˈkɔː-/ *adj* having faults which will never be changed (used of people or behaviour): *She's an incorrigible liar.* **–incorrigibly** *adv*

in·cor·rup·ti·ble /ˌɪnkəˈrʌptɪbəl/ *adj* too honest to be improperly influenced, particularly by being offered money to do something illegal

in·crease¹ /ɪnˈkriːs/ *v* increased, increasing **1** [I] to become larger in amount, number, or degree: *The population of this town has increased dramatically.* **2** [T] to make something larger in amount, number, or degree: *They have increased the price of petrol by 3%.* | *His speech has increased speculation that he will resign soon.* –opposite **decrease**

increase² /ˈɪnkriːs/ *n* [C;U] **1** a rise in amount, number, or degree: *a sharp increase in spending* | *an increase of 10%* –opposite **decrease 2 on the increase** becoming more frequent than in the past: *Smoking seems to be on the increase among teenagers.*

in·creas·ing·ly /ɪnˈkriːsɪŋli/ *adv* more and more: *I'm finding it increasingly difficult to live on my wages.*

in·cred·i·ble /ɪnˈkredɪbəl/ *adj* **1** difficult or impossible to believe: *His story sounded pretty incredible to me.* | *an incredible excuse* **2** *infml* extremely good or wonderful: *What an incredible house!* **3** very large in amount: *They pay some incredible amount for his school fees.* **–incredibly** *adv*

in·cred·u·lous /ɪnˈkredjʊləs ‖ -dʒə-/ *adj* unable to believe something, or showing disbelief: *He sounded incredulous when I told him what had happened.* | *an incredulous look* **–incredulously** *adv* **–incredulity** /ˌɪnkrɪˈdjuːlɪti ‖ -ˈduː-/ *n* [U]

in·cre·ment /ˈɪŋkrɪmənt/ *n* a regular increase in the amount of money you earn in your job: *They get annual increments of £400.* **–incremental** /ˌɪŋkrɪˈmentl◂/ *adj*

in·crim·i·nate /ɪnˈkrɪmɪneɪt/ *v* incriminated, incriminating [T] to make someone seem guilty of a crime: *incriminating evidence* | *She incriminated herself by refusing to answer the police's questions.* **–incrimination** /ɪnˌkrɪmɪˈneɪʃən/ *n* [U]

in·cu·bate /ˈɪŋkjʊbeɪt/ *v* incubated, incubating **1** [T] to sit on eggs and keep them warm until the young birds come out **2** [I] (of eggs) to be kept warm until the young birds come out **–incubation** /ˌɪŋkjʊˈbeɪʃən/ *n* [U]

in·cu·ba·tor /ˈɪŋkjʊbeɪtə⁄/ *n* **1** a machine for keeping eggs warm until the young birds come out **2** a place where small weak babies are given help to live

in·cul·cate /ˈɪnkʌlkeɪt ‖ ɪnˈkʌl-/ *v* inculcated, inculcating [T] *fml* to fix beliefs or principles in someone's mind by repeating them frequently: *He inculcated his religious beliefs into his children.*

in·cum·bent /ɪnˈkʌmbənt/ *adj* **1 be incumbent on/upon someone** *fml* to have a duty or responsibility to do something: *It's incumbent on the purchaser to check the contract before buying.* **2** [only before a noun] holding a particular office: *the incumbent president* **–incumbent** *n : the present incumbent*

in·cur /ɪnˈkɜːʳ/ v -rr- [T] to receive something unpleasant as a result of certain behaviour or actions: *I incurred his dislike from that day on.* | *to incur a debt*

in·cur·a·ble /ɪnˈkjʊərəbəl/ adj 1 impossible to cure: *an incurable disease* 2 impossible to change: *incurable optimism* –**incurably** adv –**incurability** /ɪnˌkjʊərəˈbɪlɪti/ n [U]

in·cur·sion /ɪnˈkɜːʃən, -ʒən ‖ ɪnˈkɜːrʒən/ n fml a sudden attack on or entrance into a place by a person or thing that should not be there

in·debt·ed /ɪnˈdetɪd/ adj indebted to someone very grateful to someone for help that they have given you: *I'm indebted to all the people who have contributed to the success of this party.* –**indebtedness** n [U]

in·de·cent /ɪnˈdiːsənt/ adj offensive to general standards of behaviour: *an indecent remark* | *That dress is indecent!* –**indecently** adv : *indecently dressed* –**indecency** n indecencies [C;U]

in·de·ci·sion /ˌɪndɪˈsɪʒən/ n [U] the inability to decide about what to do: *His indecision lost him the chance of a new job.*

in·de·ci·sive /ˌɪndɪˈsaɪsɪv/ adj 1 unable to make decisions 2 giving an uncertain or unsatisfactory result: *an indecisive answer* | *an indecisive victory* –**indecisively** adv –**indecisiveness** n [U]

in·deed /ɪnˈdiːd/ adv 1 used in answers when you want to say "yes" or "no" very strongly: *"Did you hear the explosion?" "I did indeed."* 2 used with the word "very" when you want to make your meaning stronger: *It was very successful indeed.* | *Thank you very much indeed.* 3 used when you are adding something that gives force to what you have already said: *These changes will benefit very few people. Indeed, a lot of people will be much worse off.* –see Study Note on page 508 4 used to show surprise or anger: *"He left without finishing the job." "Did he indeed!"*

in·de·fen·si·ble /ˌɪndɪˈfensəbəl/ adj impossible to excuse or defend: *indefensible behaviour*

in·de·fi·na·ble /ˌɪndɪˈfaɪnəbəl/ adj which cannot easily be described or explained: *There's an indefinable air of tension in this town.* –**indefinably** adv

in·def·i·nite /ɪnˈdefənɪt/ adj not clear or fixed: *indefinite opinions* | *He's gone away for an indefinite period.*

in·def·i·nite·ly /ɪnˈdefənɪtli/ adv for a period of time without a fixed limit: *Books can be borrowed indefinitely unless requested by another reader.*

in·del·i·ble /ɪnˈdeləbəl/ adj unable to be rubbed out: *indelible ink* –**indelibly** adv : *an experience indelibly printed on my memory*

in·del·i·cate /ɪnˈdeləkɪt/ adj slightly impolite or offensive: *an indelicate remark* –**indelicately** adv –**indelicacy** n indelicacies [C;U]

in·dem·ni·fy /ɪnˈdemnɪfaɪ/ v indemnified, indemnifying [T] to promise to pay someone in case of loss or damage –**indemnification** /ɪnˌdemnɪfɪˈkeɪʃən/ n [C;U]

in·dem·ni·ty /ɪnˈdemnɪti/ n indemnities 1 [U] protection against loss or damage, especially in the form of a promise to pay 2 [C] payment for loss or damage

in·dent /ɪnˈdent/ v [T] to start one line of writing further from the left of the page than the others: *Don't forget to indent the first line of a new paragraph.*

in·de·pen·dence /ˌɪndɪˈpendəns/ n [U] the quality or state of being independent or free: *This money gives me independence from my family.* | *India gained independence from Britain in 1947.*

in·de·pen·dent /ˌɪndɪˈpendənt◂/ adj 1 free from government by another country: *Zimbabwe became independent in 1980.* 2 not dependent on other people or things for help, money, or support: *She's a very independent person.* | *an independent inquiry* | *an independent school* –**independently** adv

in·de·scri·ba·ble /ˌɪndɪˈskraɪbəbəl/ adj too extreme to be described: *My feelings were indescribable.* –**indescribably** adv : *indescribably awful*

in·de·struc·ti·ble /ˌɪndɪˈstrʌktəbəl/ adj too strong to be destroyed –**indestructibility** /ˌɪndɪstʌktɪˈbɪlɪti/ n [U]

in·de·ter·mi·nate /ˌɪndɪˈtɜːmɪnət ‖ -ɜːr-/ adj not clear or fixed: *a trip of indeterminate length* | *an indeterminate colour*

in·dex¹ /ˈɪndeks/ n indexes or indices /-dɪsiːz/ 1 an alphabetical list at the back of a book which gives the names and subjects mentioned in it and the pages where these can be found –compare CONTENTS 2 a system of figures by which prices and costs can be compared with a former level: *the cost of living index* 3 a sign of something that is changing: *The steady fall in share prices is an index of the uncertainty about the government's future.*

index² v [T] 1 to provide something with an index or include something in an index 2 to connect two things so that they change together: *Pensions should be indexed to inflation.*

index fin·ger /ˈ·· ˌ··/ n the finger next to your thumb

In·di·an¹ /ˈɪndiən/ adj from or connected with India or Indians: *Do you like Indian food?*

Indian² n 1 a person from India 2 (also American Indian) a person descended from any of the original peoples of America

in·di·cate /ˈɪndɪkeɪt/ v indicated, indicating 1 [T] to point at or show someone something: *She indicated the room where he might be.* 2 [T; + that] to show something in a way that may not be quite clear: *I indicated that his help was not welcome.* | *All the signs indicate that people will want to buy our product.* 3 [I;T] to show which way you are turning in a vehicle by the use of lights or hand signals: *He's indicating left.* | *Don't forget to indicate.*

in·di·ca·tion /ˌɪndɪˈkeɪʃən/ n [C;U] something which tells you what may be true or may happen: *He has given us no indication of his intentions.*

in·dic·a·tive /ɪnˈdɪkətɪv/ adj [never before a noun] a sign of something: *Surely his presence is indicative of his desire to help?* –**indicatively** adv

in·di·ca·tor /ˈɪndɪkeɪtəʳ/ n 1 BrE a light on certain vehicles like a car which flashes to show which way it is turning –see picture on page 49 2 a needle or pointer on a machine showing the measure of something, such as speed

in·di·ces /ˈɪndɪsiːz/ the plural of INDEX

in·dict /ɪnˈdaɪt/ v [T] fml to charge someone formally with a legal offence –**indictment** n [C;U] –**indictable** adj : *an indictable offence*

in·dif·fer·ent /ɪnˈdɪfərənt/ adj 1 not caring about or noticing something: *I was so excited to see snow* *that I was indifferent* **to** *the cold.* **2** not very good: *I must warn you I'm an indifferent cook.* −**indifferently** *adv* −**indifference** *n* [U] : *He treats me with indifference.*

in·di·ge·nous /ɪn'dɪdʒənəs/ *adj* belonging to a place originally: *the indigenous population* | *Rubber is not indigenous to Malaysia.* −**indigenously** *adv*

in·di·gest·ti·ble /ˌɪndɪ'dʒestɪbəl/ *adj* **1** not easily broken down in your stomach into substances to be used by your body (used of food) **2** difficult to understand: *Such a mass of facts and figures made the report indigestible.* −**indigestibility** /ˌɪndɪd-ʒestɪ'bɪlɪti / *n* [U]

in·di·ges·tion /ˌɪndɪ'dʒestʃən/ *n* [U] illness or pain which is caused by your stomach being unable to deal with the food that you have eaten

in·dig·nant /ɪn'dɪgnənt/ *adj* feeling or expressing surprised anger at something which you think is not right: *He was indignant at her lack of cooperation.* −**indignantly** *adv*

in·dig·na·tion /ˌɪndɪg'neɪʃən/ *n* [U] feelings of surprised anger about something which you think is not right: *I expressed my indignation at such rudeness.*

in·dig·ni·ty /ɪn'dɪgnɪti/ *n* **indignities** [C;U] something that offends your sense of self-respect: *I suffered the indignity of having to apologise in front of all those people.*

in·di·go /'ɪndɪgəʊ/ *adj* dark purplish blue −**indigo** *n* [U]

in·di·rect /ˌɪndɪ'rekt/ *adj* not directly connected to or with something: *This is a very indirect route to the station!* | *The accident was an indirect result of her carelessness.* | *an indirect answer* −**indirectly** *adv*

in·dis·ci·pline /ɪn'dɪsɪplɪn/ *n* [U] state of disorder resulting from lack of control

in·dis·creet /ˌɪndɪ'skriːt/ *adj* saying or doing things which you should not say or do −**indiscreetly** *adv* **indiscretion** /-'skreʃən/ *n* [C;U]: *Her indiscretion caused a major scandal.*

in·dis·crim·i·nate /ˌɪndɪ'skrɪmɪnɪt/ *adj* not choosing or chosen carefully: *the indiscriminate murder of ordinary people by terrorists* −**indiscriminately** *adv*

in·di·spen·sa·ble /ˌɪndɪ'spensəbəl/ *adj* too important to be without: *She's become quite indispensable to the company.* −**indispensability** /ˌɪndɪspensə'bɪlɪti / *n* [U]

in·dis·posed /ˌɪndɪ'spəʊzd/ *adj* [never before a noun] *fml* ill: *Mrs Blythe is indisposed and therefore unable to attend the meeting.*

in·dis·pu·ta·ble /ˌɪndɪ'spjuːtəbəl/ *adj* too certain to be questioned −**indisputably** *adv* : *That is indisputably true.*

in·dis·tinct /ˌɪndɪ'stɪŋkt/ *adj* not easily seen, heard, or remembered: *I have only an indistinct memory of my father.* −**indistinctly** *adv*

in·dis·tin·guish·a·ble /ˌɪndɪ'stɪŋgwɪʃəbəl/ *adj* which cannot be recognized as different from something else: *The material is indistinguishable from real silk, but much cheaper.* | *The twins are indistinguishable.* −**indistinguishably** *adv*

in·di·vid·u·al¹ /ˌɪndɪ'vɪdʒuəl/ *adj* **1** single or separate: *Each individual leaf on the tree is different.* | *Individual attention must be given to every student.* **2** personal and different: *She wears very individual clothes.*

individual² *n* **1** a single person or member of a group, treated separately: *the rights of the individual* | *People want to be treated as individuals.* **2** *infml* a person, especially one who is different in some way: *What a bad-tempered individual you are!*

in·di·vid·u·al·i·ty /ˌɪndɪˌvɪdʒu'ælɪti/ *n* [U] the quality which makes someone or something different from all others: *Her work shows great individuality.*

in·di·vid·u·al·ly /ˌɪndɪ'vɪdʒuəli/ *adv* separately: *Individually I find children easy to deal with.*

in·di·vis·i·ble /ˌɪndɪ'vɪzɪbəl/ *adj* impossible to divide or to separate into parts

in·doc·tri·nate /ɪn'dɒktrɪneɪt ‖ ɪn'dɑːk-/ *v* **indoctrinated, indoctrinating** [T] to put ideas into someone's mind in such a way that they will not accept other different ideas: *They've been indoctrinated from childhood to believe only what the government tells them.* −**indoctrination** /ɪnˌdɒktrɪ'neɪʃən ‖ -ˌdɑːk-/ *n* [U]

in·do·lent /'ɪndələnt/ *adj* *fml* lazy: *an indolent student* −**indolently** *adv* −**indolence** *n* [U]

in·dom·i·ta·ble /ɪn'dɒmɪtəbəl ‖ ɪn'dɑː-/ *adj* *fml* too strong to be discouraged: *a man of indomitable spirit* −**indomitably** *adv*

in·door /'ɪndɔːʳ/ *adj* [only before a noun] which is done, used, or belongs inside a building: *indoor sports* | *indoor clothes* −opposite **outdoor**

in·doors /ˌɪn'dɔːz ‖ -ɔːrz/ *adv* inside a building: *We went indoors.* | *We spent the afternoon indoors.* −opposite **outdoors**

in·du·bi·ta·ble /ɪn'djuːbɪtəbəl ‖ ɪn'duː-/ *adj* *fml* certain and unquestionable −**indubitably** *adv*

in·duce /ɪn'djuːs ‖ ɪn'duːs/ *v* **induced, inducing** [T] *fml* **1** to persuade someone to do something, or to make them do it: *What induced you to spend so much money on a pair of shoes?* **2** to cause something: *Too much food induces sleepiness.* **3** to make a woman start giving birth by the use of drugs or other medical treatment

in·duce·ment /ɪn'djuːsmənt ‖ ɪn'duːs-/ *n* [C;U] encouragement to do something: *I gave him money as an inducement to leave.*

in·duc·tion /ɪn'dʌkʃən/ *n* **1** [C;U] introduction to something like a new job or organization: *an induction course* **2** [U] the process of making a woman begin to give birth by the use of drugs or other medical treatment **3** [U] a way of reasoning in which you arrive at general ideas by considering particular examples

in·dulge /ɪn'dʌldʒ/ *v* **indulged, indulging 1** [T] to allow someone to do or have what they want: *He indulges his children terribly.* **2** *infml* [I;T] to let yourself have what you want, especially too much of something that is bad for you: *I'm not a big chocolate eater, but I do indulge occasionally.* | *I sometimes indulge in a cigarette.*

in·dul·gence /ɪn'dʌldʒəns/ *n* **1** [U] the habit of allowing someone to do or have what they want **2** [C] something which you want and let yourself have, especially too much of something that is bad for you: *Sweets are my only indulgence.* −**indulgent** *adj*: *indulgent parents* −**indulgently** *adv*

in·dus·tri·al /ɪn'dʌstriəl/ *adj* **1** relating to industry and the people who work in it: *industrial processes* **2** having highly developed industries: *Japan is an industrial nation.* −**industrially** *adv*

in·dus·tri·al·ist /ɪn'dʌstriəlɪst/ *n* a person who is closely concerned in the system of earning profits in industry, especially a factory owner

in·dus·tri·al·ize /ɪn'dʌstriəlaɪz/ *v* **industrialized, industrializing** (also **industrialise** *BrE*) [I;T] to make or become industrially developed –**industrialization** /ɪnˌdʌstriəlaɪˈzeɪʃən ‖ -lə-/ n [U]

in·dus·tri·ous /ɪnˈdʌstriəs/ adj hard-working: an industrious student | an industrious nation –**industriously** adv –**industriousness** n [U]

in·dus·try /ˈɪndəstri/ n **industries 1** [C;U] work, or a particular kind of work, which uses people and machinery to produce goods: the clothing industry | the development of heavy industry **2** [U] fml continual hard work

i·ne·bri·at·ed /ɪˈniːbrieɪtɪd/ adj fml drunk

in·ed·i·ble /ɪnˈedəbəl/ adj not suitable for eating

in·ef·fa·ble /ɪnˈefəbəl/ adj fml too great to be described in words

in·ef·fec·tive /ˌɪnɪˈfektɪv/ adj (also **ineffectual** /ˌɪnɪˈfektʃuəl/) unable to produce the intended result or to do anything well: He's too ineffective to be chairman. | ineffectual measures –**ineffectively** adv

in·ef·fi·cient /ˌɪnɪˈfɪʃənt/ adj not working as well as possible and so not producing good results quickly: inefficient management | an inefficient secretary –**inefficiently** adv –**inefficiency** n [U]

in·el·e·gant /ɪnˈeligənt/ adj without grace or style –**inelegantly** adv –**inelegance** n [U]

in·el·i·gi·ble /ɪnˈelədʒəbəl/ adj not permitted to do or have something: As a foreign national, he is ineligible to vote. | She is ineligible for legal aid. –**ineligibility** /ɪnˌelədʒəˈbɪləti/ n [U]

in·ept /ɪˈnept/ adj **1** foolishly unsuitable: an inept remark **2** totally unable to do something: He's inept at tennis. –**ineptly** adv –**ineptitude** n [U]

in·e·qual·i·ty /ˌɪnɪˈkwɒləti ‖ -ˈkwɑː-/ n **inequalities** [C;U] lack of equality: social inequality | There are many inequalities in our legal system.

in·ert /ɪˈnɜːt ‖ -ɜːrt/ adj **1** without the power or will to move or act **2** tech not acting chemically with other substances

in·er·tia /ɪˈnɜːʃə ‖ -ɜːr-/ n [U] **1** unwillingness to move or to do anything active: a feeling of inertia **2** tech a quality in something which causes it to stay where it is or to continue moving in the same direction

in·es·ca·pa·ble /ˌɪnɪsˈkeɪpəbəl/ adj impossible to avoid

in·es·sen·tial /ˌɪnɪˈsenʃəl/ adj not necessary

in·es·ti·ma·ble /ɪnˈestɪməbəl/ adj too great to be calculated: a jewel of inestimable value –**inestimably** adv

in·ev·i·ta·ble /ɪˈnevɪtəbəl/ adj **1** impossible to prevent: She could see that conflict was inevitable. **2** [only before a noun] infml so usual that you expect it: We were served the inevitable cucumber sandwiches and tiny cakes. **3** the inevitable something that is sure to happen: He was forced to accept the inevitable and resign. –**inevitably** adv –**inevitability** /ɪˌnevɪtəˈbɪləti/ n [U]

in·ex·act /ˌɪnɪɡˈzækt/ adj not exact –**inexactitude** n

in·ex·cu·sa·ble /ˌɪnɪkˈskjuːzəbəl/ adj too bad to be excused: inexcusable behaviour –**inexcusably** adv

in·ex·haus·ti·ble /ˌɪnɪɡˈzɔːstəbəl/ adj so much that it can never all be used: an inexhaustible supply of energy –**inexhaustibly** adv

in·ex·o·ra·ble /ɪnˈeksərəbəl/ adj fml impossible to change or stop –**inexorably** adv –**inexorability** /ɪnˌeksərəˈbɪləti/ n [U]

in·ex·pe·di·ent /ˌɪnɪkˈspiːdiənt/ adj not useful or advisable

in·ex·pen·sive /ˌɪnɪkˈspensɪv/ adj fml cheap –**inexpensively** adv

in·ex·pe·ri·ence /ˌɪnɪkˈspɪəriəns/ n [U] lack of experience

in·ex·pe·ri·enced /ˌɪnɪkˈspɪəriənst/ adj without the necessary experience of something: an inexperienced driver

in·ex·plic·a·ble /ˌɪnɪkˈsplɪkəbəl/ adj impossible to explain or understand: the inexplicable disappearance of the documents –**inexplicably** adv

in·ex·pres·si·ble /ˌɪnɪkˈspresəbəl/ adj too great to be expressed in words (used of feelings) –**inexpressibly** adv

in·ex·tri·ca·ble /ɪnˈekstrɪkəbəl, ˌɪnɪkˈstrɪ-/ adj fml impossible to separate or to escape from: an inextricable connection between smoking and illness –**inextricably** adv

in·fal·li·ble /ɪnˈfæləbəl/ adj **1** never wrong (used of people) **2** unable to fail: an infallible plan **3** always having the intended effect: an infallible cure –**infallibility** /ɪnˌfæləˈbɪləti/ n [U]

in·fa·mous /ˈɪnfəməs/ adj well known for something bad: an infamous criminal –see FAMOUS (USAGE)

in·fa·my /ˈɪnfəmi/ n **infamies** [C;U] the state of being well known for bad behaviour

in·fan·cy /ˈɪnfənsi/ n **1** [U] early childhood **2** in its infancy, in their infancy at an early stage: The project is still in its infancy.

in·fant /ˈɪnfənt/ n a very young child: He's still an infant. | an infant school –see CHILD (USAGE)

in·fan·tile /ˈɪnfəntaɪl/ adj **1** relating to small children: infantile illnesses **2** like that of a small child: infantile behaviour

in·fan·try /ˈɪnfəntri/ n [U] soldiers who fight on foot

in·fat·u·at·ed /ɪnˈfætʃueɪtɪd/ adj filled with a strong unreasonable feeling of love for someone –**infatuation** /ɪnˌfætʃuˈeɪʃən/ n [C;U]

in·fect /ɪnˈfekt/ v [T] **1** to give someone or something a disease: She was infected by a dirty needle. | 10% of the town's population was infected at the height of the epidemic. | He was infected with cholera. **2** to make a place or a thing dangerous: infected food | an infected area **3** to influence people and make them feel or behave in the same way as you: We were all infected by her enthusiasm.

in·fec·tious /ɪnˈfekʃəs/ adj **1** able to be spread and caught, especially through the air (used of diseases): I know it's serious, but is it infectious? **2** likely to influence others: infectious laughter –**infectiously** adv –**infectiousness** n [U]

in·fer /ɪnˈfɜː/ v -rr- [T; + that] to understand a meaning that is not clearly stated: I infer from your letter that you do not wish to see us. –**inference** /ˈɪnfərəns/ n [C;U]

■ USAGE Compare **infer** and **imply**. As a listener you **infer** something (= take a certain meaning from) the words of the speaker: I inferred from his remarks that he hadn't enjoyed his holiday. As a speaker, your words **imply** something (= suggest a certain meaning indirectly): His remarks implied that he hadn't enjoyed his holiday.

SPELLING NOTE

Words with the sound / aɪ / may be spelt **e-**, like **eye**, or **ai-**, like **aisle**.

in·fe·ri·or¹ /ɪn'fɪəriəʳ/ *adj* not as good or as important as another person or thing: *His work is inferior to mine.* | *He's so clever, he makes me feel inferior.* –opposite **superior** –**inferiority** /ɪn,fɪəri'ɒrɨti ‖ -'ɔːr-/ *n* [U]

inferior² *n* a person in a lower position, especially at work (a word used to show disapproval)

in·fer·nal /ɪn'fɜːnl ‖ -ɜːr-/ *adj* 1 *infml* terrible and often very annoying: *Stop that infernal noise!* 2 relating to HELL: *the infernal powers*

in·fer·no /ɪn'fɜːnəʊ ‖ -ɜːr-/ *n* **infernos** a very large fire: *The burning building became an inferno.*

in·fer·tile /ɪn'fɜːtaɪl ‖ -ɜːrtl/ *adj* 1 unable to have babies 2 unable to grow plants: *infertile soil* –**infertility** /,ɪnfɜː'tɪlɨti ‖ -fər-/ *n* [U]

in·fest /ɪn'fest/ *v* [T] to cause trouble to a person or thing by being present in large numbers: *The fields are infested with snakes.* –**infestation** /,ɪnfe'steɪʃən/ *n* [C;U]

in·fi·del /'ɪnfɨdəl/ *n* a person with a different religion from your own or with no religion at all (a word no longer used in modern English)

in·fi·del·i·ty /,ɪnfɨ'delɨti/ *n* **infidelities** [C;U] disloyalty or an act of disloyalty to your marriage partner or the person you live with, which usually includes having sex with someone else

in·fight·ing /'ɪnfaɪtɪŋ/ *n* [U] competition and disagreement between close members of a group, which can become very unpleasant

in·fil·trate /'ɪnfɪltreɪt ‖ ɪn'fɪltreɪt, 'ɪnfɪl-/ *v* **infiltrated, infiltrating** [T] to go into something, often secretly and with an unfriendly purpose: *The terrorist organization was infiltrated by police informers.* | *That smell infiltrated every corner of the house.* –**infiltrator** *n* –**infiltration** /,ɪnfɪl'treɪʃən/ *n* [U]

in·fi·nite /'ɪnfɨnɨt/ *adj* very great or without limits: *infinite kindness* | *infinite possibilities* –**infinitely** *adv*

in·fin·i·tes·i·mal /,ɪnfɪnɨ'tesɨməl◂/ *adj* very, very small –**infinitesimally** *adv*

in·fin·i·tive /ɪn'fɪnɨtɪv/ *n tech* the form of the verb that can be used after other verbs and with *to* before it, such as *go* in *I can go, I want to go,* and *It is important to go* –**infinitive** *adj*

in·fin·i·ty /ɪn'fɪnɨti/ *n* [U] 1 limitless time or space 2 an infinity of a number of something which is too great to count: *an infinity of tasks to do* 3 a number which is greater than any other

in·firm /ɪn'fɜːm ‖ -ɜːrm/ *adj fml* weak in body or mind, especially because of old age –**infirmity** *n* [C;U]

in·fir·ma·ry /ɪn'fɜːməri/ *n* **infirmaries** a hospital or other place where the sick are given care and treatment

in·flame /ɪn'fleɪm/ *v* **inflamed, inflaming** [T] to fill someone with strong feelings: *The speech inflamed his enemies.* | *inflamed* **with** *desire*

in·flamed /ɪn'fleɪmd/ *adj* red and swollen as a result of infection: *The cut has become inflamed.*

in·flam·ma·ble /ɪn'flæməbəl/ *adj* (also **flammable** *AmE* or *tech*) which catches fire and burns easily: *Be careful! Those gases are highly inflammable.* –opposite **nonflammable** –see FLAMMABLE (USAGE)

in·flam·ma·tion /,ɪnflə'meɪʃən/ *n* [C;U] swelling and soreness as a result of infection

in·flam·ma·to·ry /ɪn'flæmətəri ‖ -tɔːri/ *adj* likely to cause strong feelings or violence: *an inflammatory speech*

in·fla·ta·ble /ɪn'fleɪtəbəl/ *adj* which you fill with air before use: *an inflatable mattress*

in·flate /ɪn'fleɪt/ *v* **inflated, inflating** [I;T] *fml* to fill with air or gas and so make or become bigger –opposite **deflate**

in·flat·ed /ɪn'fleɪtɨd/ *adj* 1 filled with air or gas: *an inflated tyre* 2 *fml* greater than is reasonable: *He has an inflated opinion of his own importance.*

in·fla·tion /ɪn'fleɪʃən/ *n* [U] general rise in prices: *The government is introducing new measures to control inflation.* –**inflationary** *adj* : *the government's inflationary policies*

in·flect /ɪn'flekt/ *v tech* 1 [I] (of a word) to change the form of its ending according to its use 2 [T] to change the sound of your speech

in·flex·i·ble /ɪn'fleksɨbəl/ *adj* 1 hard and impossible to bend 2 impossible to influence or change: *He's being completely inflexible about this.* | *inflexible rules* –**inflexibly** *adv* –**inflexibility** /ɪn,fleksɨ'bɪlɨti/ *n* [U]

in·flict /ɪn'flɪkt/ *v* **inflict something on/upon someone** to force something unwanted or unpleasant on someone: *Don't inflict your own problems on me.* –**infliction** /-'flɪkʃən/ *n* [U]

in·flu·ence¹ /'ɪnfluəns/ *n* 1 [C;U] an effect that someone or something has on events, behaviour, or opinions: *He used his influence to get his son a job.* | *My parents have no influence* **over** *what I do.* 2 a person with the power to have an effect on people or events: *She's a good influence* **on** *her friends.* 3 **under the influence of** experiencing the effects of a person or thing: *driving under the influence of alcohol*

influence² *v* **influenced, influencing** [T] to have an effect on someone or something: *Don't let me influence your decision.*

in·flu·en·tial /,ɪnflu'enʃəl/ *adj* having or able to have an effect on others: *an influential person* | *an influential decision* –**influentially** *adv*

in·flu·en·za /,ɪnflu'enzə/ *n* [U] (also **flu**) an illness where you have a cold and a temperature

in·flux /'ɪnflʌks/ *n* the arrival of large numbers of people or things: *There was a sudden influx of goods from Japan.*

in·form /ɪn'fɔːm ‖ -ɔːrm/ *v* [T] *fml* 1 to tell someone something: *I informed him of my decision.* | *She informed me that she was leaving.*

□ USEFUL PATTERNS to inform someone **of** something; to inform someone **that**…

2 **inform against someone, inform on someone** to tell the police, or someone in charge, about a person who has done something wrong

in·for·mal /ɪn'fɔːməl ‖ -ɔːr-/ *adj* 1 not following official rules or methods, and therefore friendly and easy in manner: *The new director held an informal party to celebrate his promotion.* | *informal talks between the two presidents* 2 suitable for ordinary situations but not for official occasions (used of clothes or behaviour): *The invitation said "Dress: informal".* | *an informal wave of his hand* 3 used in ordinary conversation or writing, for example between friends, but not when writing or speaking on official occasions (used of speech or words): *'Kid' is an informal word for 'child'.* –**informally** *adv* –**informality** /,ɪnfɔː'mælɨti ‖ -ɔːr-/ *n* [U]

in·for·mant /ɪn'fɔːmənt ‖ -ɔːr-/ *n* a person who gives information, especially secretly: *The journalist would not reveal the identity of his informant.*

in·for·ma·tion /,ɪnfə'meɪʃən ‖ -fər-/ *n* [U] knowledge about something or someone in the form of facts: *Have you got any information* **about** *local events, please?* | *I need some information* **on** *changes in weather patterns.* | *an interesting piece of information* | *According to my information, he is now safely in Morocco.*

in·for·ma·tive /ɪn'fɔːmətɪv ‖ -ɔːr-/ *adj* giving useful or interesting facts: *an informative television programme* –opposite **uninformative** –**informatively** *adv*

in·formed /ɪn'fɔːmd ‖ -ɔːr-/ *adj* **1** having or showing knowledge: *well-informed* | *badly informed* | *Please keep me informed* **of** *the latest developments in the situation.* **2** using your knowledge of a situation: *an informed opinion*

in·form·er /ɪn'fɔːmə^r ‖ -ɔːr-/ *n* a person who gives information about someone else to the police, often in return for money: *The police informer was found murdered soon after the trial.*

in·fra·red /ˌɪnfrə'red◂/ *adj* using beams of light that cannot be seen: *an infrared lamp*

in·fra·struc·ture /'ɪnfrəˌstrʌktʃə^r/ *n* the system which is necessary to support the operation of a country or an organization: *More money is needed for roads and railways if the country's transport infrastructure is to be maintained.*

in·fre·quent /ɪn'friːkwənt/ *adj* not coming or happening very often: *infrequent visits* | *infrequent buses* –**infrequently** *adv*

in·fringe /ɪn'frɪndʒ/ *v* **infringed, infringing 1** [T] to go against a law: *He infringed the regulations.* **2** [I;T] to take away someone's rights: *He felt that his liberty had been infringed.* | *This law infringes* **on** *our basic right to freedom of speech.* –**infringement** *n* [C;U] : *an infringement of copyright*

in·fu·ri·ate /ɪn'fjʊərieɪt/ *v* **infuriated, infuriating** [T] to make someone very angry: *Her attitude really infuriates me!* –**infuriating** *adj*: *His silence on the subject is absolutely infuriating.*

in·fuse /ɪn'fjuːz/ *v* **infused, infusing 1** [T] to give hot water a certain taste by putting in a substance such as tea leaves **2 infuse someone with something** to fill someone with a quality: *He was infused with enthusiasm for the project.* –**infusion** /-'fjuːʒən/ *n* [C;U]: *an infusion of herbs* | *an infusion of new ideas*

in·ge·ni·ous /ɪn'dʒiːniəs/ *adj* having or showing cleverness at making or inventing things: *What an ingenious gadget!* | *an ingenious solution to the problem* –**ingeniously** *adv*

in·ge·nu·i·ty /ˌɪndʒɪ'njuːɪti ‖ -'nuː-/ *n* [U] skill and cleverness in making, inventing, or arranging things

in·gen·u·ous /ɪn'dʒenjuəs/ *adj* honest, trusting, and inexperienced –**ingenuously** *adv*

in·got /'ɪŋɡət/ *n* a lump of metal in a regular shape

in·grained /ɪn'ɡreɪnd/ *adj* fixed firmly and deeply, and so difficult to remove or destroy: *ingrained dirt* | *ingrained habits*

in·gra·ti·ate /ɪn'ɡreɪʃieɪt/ *v* **ingratiated, ingratiating ingratiate yourself with someone** to gain favour with someone by making yourself pleasant to them and saying things that will please them (used to show disapproval): *I hate the way he tries*

to ingratiate himself with the boss. –**ingratiating** *adj* : *an ingratiating smile* –**ingratiatingly** *adv*

in·grat·i·tude /ɪn'ɡrætɪtjuːd ‖ -tuːd/ *n* [U] lack of gratefulness: *Everyone was shocked by her ingratitude.*

in·gre·di·ent /ɪn'ɡriːdiənt/ *n* one of the things that goes into a mixture when something is made, especially in cooking: *Flour and eggs are the most important ingredients.* | *Let me check the ingredients* for *this recipe.*

in·hab·it /ɪn'hæbɪt/ *v* [T not in progressive forms] *fml* to live in a place: *That island is inhabited by dangerous tribes.*

in·hab·i·tant /ɪn'hæbɪtənt/ *n* a person who lives in a particular place: *inhabitants* **of** *large cities*

in·hale /ɪn'heɪl/ *v* **inhaled, inhaling** [I;T] to breathe air or something else into your body: *Once outside in the fresh air, he inhaled deeply.* | *These days none of us can avoid inhaling car exhaust fumes.*

in·her·ent /ɪn'hɪərənt, -'he-/ *adj* naturally present in a person or thing, and not able to be thought of as separate: *I'm afraid there's an inherent weakness in the design.* | *the problems inherent* **in** *this system*

in·her·ent·ly /ɪn'hɪərəntli, -'he-/ *adv* having a certain quality naturally present: *He was misguided on this occasion, but he's not inherently evil.*

in·her·it /ɪn'herɪt/ *v* [T] **1** to receive something from someone who has died or moved on: *He's inherited a fortune* **from** *his rich uncle.* | *We have inherited these housing problems from the last government.* **2** to have the same qualities as your parents: *She inherited her mother's beauty and her father's weak character.* –**inheritance** *n* [C;U] : *the laws of inheritance* | *leaving his successors an appalling inheritance of corruption and poverty*

in·hib·it /ɪn'hɪbɪt/ *v* [T] **1** to stop something from happening or developing in the usual or expected way: *Recent regulations have inhibited the growth of new businesses.* **2** to make someone feel unable to express themselves freely: *His presence inhibits me* **from** *saying what I want to.* | *I find him inhibiting.*

in·hib·it·ed /ɪn'hɪbɪtɪd/ *adj* unable to feel easy and express yourself freely and naturally: *She's far too inhibited to talk frankly about sex.*

in·hi·bi·tion /ˌɪnhɪ'bɪʃən/ *n* [C;U] a feeling of being inhibited: *She soon loses her inhibitions when she's had two or three glasses of wine.*

in·hos·pi·ta·ble /ˌɪnhɒ'spɪtəbəl ‖ -hɑː-/ *adj* **1** not welcoming guests, especially into your home **2** not suitable to stay in (used of a place): *inhospitable desert areas* –**inhospitably** *adv*

in·hu·man /ɪn'hjuːmən/ *adj* **1** too cruel and lacking in feelings to be considered as human: *an inhuman act* **2** not human: *an inhuman scream*

in·hu·mane /ˌɪnhjuː'meɪn/ *adj* not showing ordinary human kindness to living creatures: *inhumane treatment of animals* –**inhumanely** *adv*

in·hu·man·i·ty /ˌɪnhjuː'mænɪti/ *n* **inhumanities** [C;U] the quality of being cruel and harming other human beings: *an example of man's inhumanity to man* | *the inhumanities of war*

in·im·i·ta·ble /ɪ'nɪmɪtəbəl/ *adj* impossible for anyone else to copy with the same quality

in·iq·ui·tous /ɪ'nɪkwɪtəs/ *adj fml* extremely unjust or wicked –**iniquity** *n* **iniquities** [C;U]

i·ni·tial¹ /ɪ'nɪʃəl/ *adj* [only before a noun] at the beginning: *The initial talks formed the basis of the later agreement.* | *She calmed down after the initial shock.* | *the initial stages of an illness*

initial² *n* the letter at the beginning of a name: *The briefcase had the initials S.L. on it.*

initial³ *v* -ll- (also -l- *AmE*) [T] to sign a piece of writing with the initials of your name to show approval or agreement: *Could you initial these memos, sir?*

i·ni·tial·ly /ɪˈnɪʃəli/ *adv* in the early stages but not the later stages: *The project was set up in 1990. Initially, we didn't have a great deal of success, but later on, after J. F. Danby took over as head, a lot of valuable work was done.*

i·ni·ti·ate /ɪˈnɪʃieɪt/ *v* **initiated, initiating** **1** [T] to be responsible for starting something: *The government has recently initiated a massive new house-building programme.* **2 initiate someone into something** to introduce someone to some secret knowledge or into a club or group, especially with a special ceremony –**initiation** /ɪˌnɪʃiˈeɪʃən/ *n* [C;U] : *initiation into a secret society*

i·ni·tia·tive /ɪˈnɪʃətɪv/ *n* **1** [C] the first movement or action which starts something happening: *The government is making some fresh initiatives to try to resolve the dispute.* **2 take the initiative** to be the first to do something: *I think you should take the initiative and ask your boss if she'll send you to Paris.* **3** [U] the ability to make decisions and take action without the help of other people: *I wish you'd show some initiative instead of always asking me what to do.* **4 on your own initiative** according to your own plan and without help: *Did he do it on his own initiative?*

in·ject /ɪnˈdʒekt/ *v* [T] **1** to force liquid into someone's body with a special needle: *The drug can't be swallowed; it has to be injected.* | *She injected the rat with a new drug.* **2** to introduce new ideas or feelings: *I hope the new teacher can inject some life into that class!*

in·jec·tion /ɪnˈdʒekʃən/ *n* **1** [C;U] the act of forcing a liquid into something with a needle: *The nurse gave him an injection against typhoid.* **2** [C] putting more money into a business or government organization or plan: *The business was in need of an injection of new capital.*

in·ju·di·cious /ˌɪndʒuːˈdɪʃəs/ *adj fml* showing poor judgment of a situation (used of an action or statement) –**injudiciously** *adv*

in·junc·tion /ɪnˈdʒʌŋkʃən/ *n law* a command or official order that tells you to do or not to do something: *The actress took out an injunction against the magazine to prevent it from publishing the article about her.*

in·jure /ˈɪndʒər/ *v* **injured, injuring** [T] to hurt a living thing: *She was badly injured in the accident.* | *He injured his knee during training.* | *The injured people were taken to hospital.* –see WOUND² (USAGE) –**injurious** /ɪnˈdʒʊəriəs/ *adj* : *Smoking is injurious to health.*

in·ju·ry /ˈɪndʒəri/ *n* **injuries** [C;U] harm or damage to a living thing: *insurance against injury at work* | *He suffered serious injuries to the head and neck.*

in·jus·tice /ɪnˈdʒʌstɪs/ *n* **1** [U] unfairness: *the injustice of the charge* **2** [C] an unfair act: *life's little injustices* **3 do someone an injustice** to judge someone in an unfair way and believe something bad about them

ink /ɪŋk/ *n* [U] coloured liquid used for writing or printing

ink·ling /ˈɪŋklɪŋ/ *n* [sing] a slight idea: *I had an inkling something like this was going to happen.*

ink·y /ˈɪŋki/ *adj* **1** marked with ink **2** very dark

in·laid /ˌɪnˈleɪd◂/ *adj* with another material set in

the surface to form a pattern: *wood inlaid with gold* | *inlaid wood*

in·land /ˈɪnlənd/ *adj* [only before a noun] in or towards the centre of the country, not near the coast or near other countries: *an inland sea* | *inland trade* –**inland** /ɪnˈlænd/ *adv: travelling inland*

in·laws /ˈ- -/ *n* [pl] relatives because of marriage, especially the mother and father of the person you have married

in·let /ˈɪnlet, ˈɪnlɪt/ *n* **1** a narrow stretch of water going from the sea or a lake into the land **2** a way in for water or another liquid

in·mate /ˈɪnmeɪt/ *n* a person who is kept in a place, usually with a lot of other people: *The prison governor talked the inmates into coming down from the roof.* | *She's an inmate of the local mental hospital.*

in·most /ˈɪnməʊst/ *adj* farthest inside

inn /ɪn/ *n* a small hotel, usually an old one, which also serves food and drink

in·nate /ˌɪˈneɪt◂/ *adj* which someone was born with (used of a quality): *She has an innate sense of fun.* –**innately** *adv*

in·ner /ˈɪnər/ *adj* [only before a noun] **1** on the inside: *the inner ear* | *an inner room* **2** not expressed (of feelings): *inner doubts* | *words with an inner meaning* **3** closest to the centre: *the inner circle of power* **4 inner city** the central part of a city, especially an area with a lot of poor people and bad conditions of life: *the problem of inner city decay*

in·ner·most /ˈɪnəməʊst ‖ -nər-/ *adj* farthest inside

in·nings /ˈɪnɪŋz/ *n* (plural is **innings**) the period of time during which a team or player has their turn to hit the ball in a sport

inn·keep·er /ˈɪnˌkiːpər/ *n* a person in the past who owned and ran an inn

in·no·cent /ˈɪnəsənt/ *adj* **1** not guilty of a crime: *"But I'm innocent!" he protested.* | *He was innocent of the crime.* | *The bomb exploded, injuring dozens of innocent people.* **2** harmless in effect or intention (used of a thing): *innocent pleasures* | *an innocent remark* **3** not able to recognize evil or unpleasant intentions: *a trusting and innocent young child* –**innocently** *adv: "Who, me?" she said innocently.* –**innocence** *n* [U]: *determined to prove his innocence*

in·noc·u·ous /ɪˈnɒkjuəs ‖ ɪˈnɑːk-/ *adj* not likely or intended to harm or offend people: *It seemed a perfectly innocuous remark to me, but he was very annoyed by it.*

in·no·va·tion /ˌɪnəˈveɪʃən/ *n* [C;U] the introduction of something new: *recent innovations in printing methods* | *an attempt at innovation* –**innovative** /ˈɪnəˌveɪtɪv/ *adj: innovative ideas*

in·nu·en·do /ˌɪnjuˈendəʊ/ *n* **innuendoes** *or* **innuendos** [C;U] the suggestion of something unpleasant in words, without saying it directly: *her neighbour's innuendoes about her behaviour*

in·nu·me·ra·ble /ɪˈnjuːmərəbəl ‖ ɪˈnuː-/ *adj* too many to be counted

i·noc·u·late /ɪˈnɒkjəleɪt ‖ ɪˈnɑː-/ *v* **inoculated, inoculating** [I;T] to introduce a weak form of a disease into a living body as a protection against catching the disease –**inoculation** /ɪˌnɒkj̩ˈleɪʃən ‖ ɪˌnɑː-/ *n* [C;U] : *a government programme of inoculation*

in·of·fen·sive /ˌɪnəˈfensɪv/ *adj* not causing any harm, or not causing dislike in other people: *an inoffensive manner* | *Anne is a quiet, inoffensive sort of woman.* –**inoffensively** *adv*

in·op·por·tune /ɪnˈɒpətjuːn ‖ ˌɪnɑːpərˈtuːn/ *adj fml* not suitable at the time: *an inopportune remark* | *He*

called at rather an inopportune moment. **-inopportunely** *adv*

in·or·di·nate /ɪnˈnɔːdənɪt ‖ -ɔːr-/ *adj fml* beyond reasonable limits: *an inordinate amount of work to do* **-inordinately** *adv*

in·or·gan·ic /ˌɪnɔːˈgænɪk ‖ -ɔːr-/ *adj* not made of living material **-inorganically** /-kli/ *adv*

in·put /ˈɪnpʊt/ *n* **1** [C;U] something put in or given for use by someone or something **2** [U] information that is put into a computer **-input** *v* : *to input information*

in·quest /ˈɪŋkwest/ *n* an official inquiry to find out the cause of a sudden or unexpected death, especially when there is a possibility of crime

in·quire /ɪnˈkwaɪəʳ/ *v* **inquired, inquiring** *fml* (also **enquire**) **1** [I;T] to ask for information: *I'll inquire about the trains.* | *I inquired what he wanted.* | *They inquired whether he would attend.* **2 inquire after** someone to ask about someone's health: *She inquired after my mother.* **3 inquire into** to search for the facts about something: *The police are inquiring into the matter.* **-see** ASK (USAGE)

in·quir·ing /ɪnˈkwaɪərɪŋ/ *adj* (also **enquiring**) showing an interest in learning about things: *a child with an inquiring mind*

in·quir·y /ɪnˈkwaɪəri ‖ ɪnˈkwaɪəri, ˈɪŋkwəri/ *n* **inquiries** (also **enquiry**) **1** [C;U] a question that tries to find out information: *We've had several hundred inquiries about the new plans.* **2** [C] a search for facts: *Two people are helping the police with their inquiries.* | *The papers are calling for a government inquiry into the incident.* **3 make inquiries** to ask for information: *I'm going to make some inquiries about his previous employers.*

■ USAGE **Enquiry** and **inquiry** are almost the same, but **enquiry** is more often used for a simple request for information, and **inquiry** for a long serious study: *Thank you for your enquiries about my health.* | *a government inquiry into the dangers of smoking*

in·qui·si·tion /ˌɪŋkwɪˈzɪʃən/ *n* an attempt to find out the facts about something, especially one that is carried out using violent methods

in·quis·i·tive /ɪnˈkwɪzɪtɪv/ *adj* trying to find out too many details about things and people: *Don't be so inquisitive!* | *an inquisitive face at the window* **-inquisitively** *adv* **-inquisitiveness** *n* [U]

in·roads /ˈɪnrəʊdz/ **make inroads into: a** to take away or use up large amounts of something: *My holiday made terrible inroads into my savings.* **b** to advance into a new area: *Their new soft drink is already making inroads into the market.*

in·sane /ɪnˈseɪn/ *adj* mad or senseless: *He suggested what? The man must be totally insane!* | *an insane idea* **-insanely** *adv* : *insanely jealous*

in·san·i·ta·ry /ɪnˈsænɪtəri ‖ -teri/ *adj* likely to harm people's health by causing disease: *living in appallingly insanitary conditions*

in·san·i·ty /ɪnˈsænɪti/ *n* [U] madness: *There is a family history of insanity.*

in·sa·tia·ble /ɪnˈseɪʃəbəl/ *adj* that cannot be satisfied: *an insatiable appetite* **-insatiably** *adv*

SPELLING NOTE

Words with the sound / aɪ / may be spelt **e-**, like **eye**, or **ai-**, like **aisle**.

---

in·scribe /ɪnˈskraɪb/ *v* **inscribed, inscribing** [T] *fml* to write words on or cut words into the surface of something, especially as a lasting record: *The president was presented with a specially inscribed copy of the book.* **-inscription** /ɪnˈskrɪpʃən/ *n*

in·scru·ta·ble /ɪnˈskruːtəbəl/ *adj* mysterious and not easy to understand: *"We'll see," he said with an inscrutable smile.* **-inscrutably** *adv* **-inscrutability** /ɪnˌskruːtəˈbɪlɪti/ *n* [U]

in·sect /ˈɪnsekt/ *n* a small creature with no bones and a hard outer covering, six legs, and a body divided into three parts; ants and flies are insects

in·sec·ti·cide /ɪnˈsektɪsaɪd/ *n* [C;U] a chemical substance used to kill insects

in·se·cure /ˌɪnsɪˈkjʊəʳ/ *adj* **1** afraid or unsure of yourself: *She shouts at her staff a lot; I think she's rather insecure.* **2** not safe, and likely to fall: *I feel very insecure up this ladder.* **3** likely to fail or be lost: *an insecure investment* **-insecurely** *adv* **-insecurity** *n* [U]

in·sen·si·tive /ɪnˈsensɪtɪv/ *adj* **1** not kind or helpful to others because you do not understand how they feel: *an insensitive remark* **2** not having the feeling which is usual when you have a particular experience: *insensitive to pain* **-insensitively** *adv* **-insensitivity** /ɪnˌsensɪˈtɪvɪti/ *n* [U]

in·sep·a·ra·ble /ɪnˈsepərəbəl/ *adj* impossible to separate from something else or from one another: *The government's energy policy is surely inseparable from its policy on environmental issues.* **-inseparably** *adv*

in·sert /ɪnˈsɜːt/ *v* [T] to put something inside something else: *He inserted the key in the lock.* **-insertion** /ɪnˈsɜːʃən ‖ -ɜːr-/ *n* [U]

in·shore /ˌɪnˈʃɔː◄/ *adv, adj* near, towards, or to the shore: *He rowed inshore.* | *an inshore lifeboat*

in·side¹ /ˌɪnˈsaɪd◄/ *n* **1** the part of something that is in the middle of it or within it: *The inside of the house needs painting.* **-see** picture on page 540 **2 your insides** [pl] your stomach: *My insides were hurting.*

inside² *adv, prep* **1** in or into something: *I opened the box to see what was inside.* | *There was nobody inside the house.* **2** *prep* within a particular amount of time: *They should be here inside an hour.* **3 inside out** with the usual inside parts on the outside: *You've got your jumper on inside out.*

inside³ *adj* [only before a noun] **1** situated on the inside of something: *the inside pages of the book* **2 inside lane** the part of a MOTORWAY or large road where vehicles drive more slowly **3 inside information** information that is given by someone who knows about something because they are part of it

in·sid·er /ɪnˈsaɪdəʳ/ *n* someone in a group who has special knowledge or power: *Police are investigating recent insider trading on the stock market.*

in·sid·i·ous /ɪnˈsɪdiəs/ *adj* unnoticed while developing but causing a bad result: *an insidious trend towards a police state* **-insidiously** *adv* **-insidiousness** *n* [U]

in·sight /ˈɪnsaɪt/ *n* [C;U] the power of using your mind to understand something deeply: *Visiting the hospital gave me an insight into the problems of the people who live there.* | *a writer who shows great insight into human nature*

in·sig·ni·a /ɪnˈsɪgniə/ *n* [plural is **insignia**] a BADGE or other object which shows the power of an official or important person: *the insignia of office* | *I could tell he was an officer by the insignia on his uniform.*

in·sig·nif·i·cant /ˌɪnsɪgˈnɪfɪkənt/ adj of little or no value or importance: *The cost will be insignificant compared to the benefits it will bring us.* –**insignificance** n [U]

in·sin·cere /ˌɪnsɪnˈsɪər/ adj not sincere: *an insincere smile* –**insincerity** /-ˈserˌti/ n [U]

in·sin·u·ate /ɪnˈsɪnjueɪt/ v **insinuated, insinuating** **1** [+ (that)] to suggest something unpleasant indirectly, by behaviour or remarks: *Are you insinuating that I'm not telling the truth?* **2 insinuate yourself into something** to succeed in becoming part of something or accepted by someone, by using rather unpleasant indirect methods: *He gradually insinuated himself into the boss's favour.*

in·sin·u·a·tion /ɪnˌsɪnjuˈeɪʃən/ n words or actions which suggest something unpleasant: *I object to these malicious insinuations about my father's honesty!*

in·sip·id /ɪnˈsɪpɪd/ adj lacking a strong character, taste, or effect: *This food is quite insipid.* | *an insipid smile*

in·sist /ɪnˈsɪst/ v **1** [I; + (that)] to declare firmly and repeatedly, especially when someone else doubts you or opposes you: *I insisted that he was mistaken.* | *She insisted on her innocence.*
□ USEFUL PATTERNS to insist on something; to insist that…
2 [I; + (that)] to order or demand that something must happen or be done: *They are insisting on immediate repayment.* | *I insisted that he should go.* | *You must come to dinner with us – I insist!*
□ USEFUL PATTERNS to insist on something; to insist that…
3 if you insist a phrase used when you are agreeing to do something you don't really want to do: *OK, OK, I'll ask my father about it, if you insist.*

in·sis·tence /ɪnˈsɪstəns/ n [U] the act of stating or demanding something very strongly: *I did it, but only at your insistence.* | *His insistence on a vegetarian diet makes socializing very difficult.*

in·sis·tent /ɪnˈsɪstənt/ adj **1** repeatedly stating or demanding something: *The government is insistent that industry should be more competitive.* **2** needing or demanding urgent attention: *the insistent ringing of the telephone* | *The calls for tax reform are becoming more insistent.* –**insistently** adv

in si·tu /ˌɪn ˈsɪtjuː ‖ ˌɪn ˈsaɪtuː/ adv in its original place

insofar as /ˌɪnsəˈfɑːr əz/ conj (also **in as far as, in so far as**) to the degree that: *I'll help you insofar as I can.*

in·so·lent /ˈɪnsələnt/ adj rude or disrespectful: *an insolent child* | *an insolent remark* | *insolent behaviour* –**insolently** adv –**insolence** n [U]

in·sol·u·ble /ɪnˈsɒljʊbəl ‖ ɪnˈsɑːl-/ adj (also **insolvable** /ɪnˈsɒlvəbəl ‖ -ˈsɑːl-/ AmE) **1** impossible to explain or to find an answer to: *an insoluble problem* **2** which cannot be DISSOLVED in a liquid –opposite **soluble**

in·sol·vent /ɪnˈsɒlvənt ‖ ɪnˈsɑːl-, ɪnˈsɔːl-/ adj without enough money to pay what you owe –**insolvency** n [U]

in·som·ni·a /ɪnˈsɒmniə ‖ -ˈsɑːm-/ n [U] an inability to sleep over a period of time –**insomniac** /-niæk/ n : *all-night television for insomniacs*

in·spect /ɪnˈspekt/ v [T] **1** to examine something carefully: *The college will need to inspect all previous academic records.* **2** to make an official visit to judge the quality of something such as an organization: *Most schools are inspected at least once a year.* –**inspection** /-ˈspekʃən/ n [C;U] : *We must arrange a thorough inspection of all our equipment.* | *Officials came to carry out a safety inspection.* | *On closer inspection, the painting was found to be genuine.*

in·spec·tor /ɪnˈspektər/ n **1** an official whose job is to establish the quality or legality of something: *a ticket inspector* | *a school inspector* **2** a police officer of middle rank: *a police inspector* | *Inspector Grant*

in·spi·ra·tion /ˌɪnspɨˈreɪʃən/ n **1** [C;U] something or someone that encourages you to do or produce something good, especially a work of art: *Dante was the inspiration for my book on Italy.* | *Her hard work and imagination are an inspiration to everyone in the company.* **2** [C] a good idea: *I've had an inspiration – let's paint the doors black!* –**inspirational** adj

in·spire /ɪnˈspaɪər/ v **inspired, inspiring** [T] **1** to encourage someone to do something, especially by your own confidence or excitement: *The trainer inspired the team to even greater efforts.* | *I was inspired to work harder.* | *an inspiring speech*
□ USEFUL PATTERNS to inspire someone to something; to inspire someone to do something **2** cause someone to feel something: *He inspires confidence in everyone he works with.*

in·spired /ɪnˈspaɪəd ‖ -ərd/ adj caused by or filled with inspiration: *an inspired guess* | *She sang as if inspired.*

in·sta·bil·i·ty /ˌɪnstəˈbɪlɨti/ n [U] lack of STABILITY

in·stall /ɪnˈstɔːl/ v (also **instal**) **1** [T] to put something in place ready for use: *We're installing a new heating system.* **2** [T] to give someone an official position, especially with ceremony: *The new head of the university is being installed today.* **3 install yourself** to settle yourself in a particular place: *I installed myself in front of the fire.* –**installation** /ˌɪnstəˈleɪʃən/ n [C;U]

in·stal·ment /ɪnˈstɔːlmənt/ n (also **installment** AmE) **1** a single payment of a number of payments which will, in time, complete the full payment: *I'm paying for the car in instalments.* **2** a single part of a book, play, or television broadcast which appears in regular parts until the story is completed: *The final instalment will appear in next month's edition of the magazine.*

in·stance /ˈɪnstəns/ n **1** a single example or case of something: *I have noted several instances of disrespectful behaviour.* **2 for instance** for example; you use this phrase when you are giving an example to support what you are saying, and make your meaning clearer: *Roman civilization was very advanced technologically. They had underfloor central heating, for instance.* | *Bees are very strong for their size. For instance, they can carry up to a quarter of their own body weight.* | *Have you considered, for instance, the damage it would do to staff relations?* –see Study Note on page 508 **3 in the first instance** first of all

in·stant¹ /ˈɪnstənt/ n **1** a moment: *Not for an instant did I believe he had lied.* | *The instant I saw him I knew he was angry.* **2 this instant** now, without delay: *Do as I say this instant!*

instant² adj **1** happening at once: *The new diet was an instant success.* **2** very quick to prepare for use: *instant coffee* | *instant mashed potatoes*

in·stan·ta·ne·ous /ˌɪnstənˈteɪniəs/ adj happening at once –**instantaneously** adv

in·stant·ly /ˈɪnstəntli/ adv at once: *The car hit a tree and the driver was killed instantly.*

in·stead /ɪn'sted/ adv **1** in place of something else: *There was no chicken left so we had fish instead.* | *He didn't go to the play as he had planned. Instead, he met up with some friends and went for a drink.* **2** **instead of** in place of something else: *Can we change our meeting to Tuesday instead of Thursday?* | Instead of just complaining all the time, why don't you do something about it!

in·step /'ɪnstep/ n the middle part of your foot between your toes and your ankle, or the part of a shoe which covers this

in·sti·gate /'ɪnstɪgeɪt/ v **instigated, instigating** [T] fml to make something begin to happen: *He has instigated legal proceedings against the company.* –**instigator** n –**instigation** /ˌɪnstɪ'geɪʃən/ n [U]

in·stil /ɪn'stɪl/ v (also **instill** AmE)-ll- [T] fml to put something, especially ideas or feelings, into someone's mind, usually by a continuing effort: *I instilled the need for good manners into all my children.*

in·stinct /'ɪnstɪŋkt/ n [C;U] **1** the natural force in people and animals which causes certain behaviour patterns, such as nest-building, and which seems not to be based on learning or thinking: *Some animals hunt by instinct.* **2** a feeling about how to act or what is true: *Trust your instincts and do what you think is right.* | *Instinct tells me he'll be back!* –**instinctive** /ɪn'stɪŋktɪv/ adj : *an instinctive fear of snakes* –**instinctively** adv : *Instinctively, I knew she was ill.*

in·sti·tute¹ /'ɪnstɪtjuːt/ || -tuːt/ n an organization formed for a special purpose, or the building in which it carries out its affairs: *a research institute*

institute² v **instituted, instituting** [T] fml to introduce or start something: *The president agreed to institute reforms.*

in·sti·tu·tion /ˌɪnstɪ'tjuːʃən/ || -'tuː-/ n **1** an established organization which provides people with help, work, medical treatment, or protection, such as a school or hospital: *a mental institution* **2** something, such as a custom, which has been in existence for a long time and which is considered important: *the institution of marriage* **3** the act of introducing or starting something: *the institution of a new law* –**institutional** adj

in·struct /ɪn'strʌkt/ v [T] **1** to give someone knowledge or information: *They instructed me in the best ways of doing the job.* **2** to order someone to do something: *I've been instructed to wait here until the teacher arrives.* | *He's instructed his lawyer to proceed with the sale of his house.*
□ USEFUL PATTERN to instruct someone to do something

in·struc·tion /ɪn'strʌkʃən/ n **1** [U] teaching: *He's still under instruction, but should finish his training next year.* **2** [C] an order or some advice on how to do something: *a book of instructions for operating the new washing machine* | *an instruction manual* –**instructional** adj

in·struc·tive /ɪn'strʌktɪv/ adj giving useful information –**instructively** adv

in·struc·tor /ɪn'strʌktər/ a person who teaches an activity: *a driving instructor*

SPELLING NOTE
Words with the sound / aɪ / may be spelt **e-**, like **eye**, or **ai-**, like **aisle**.

in·stru·ment /'ɪnstrʊmənt/ n **1** an object which you use to help you in your work: *medical instruments* **2** (also **musical instrument**) an object, such as a piano, which you play to make musical sounds **3** an object which you use to measure something **4** the means of something happening or being done –see MACHINE (USAGE)

in·stru·men·tal /ˌɪnstrʊ'mentl◂/ adj **1** the cause or means of something happening or being done: *I was instrumental in getting the company to change its policy.* **2** played by musical instruments, not voices: *an instrumental piece*

in·sub·or·di·nate /ˌɪnsə'bɔːdɪnət || -ɔːr-/ adj disobedient (used of a person of lower rank or their behaviour) –**insubordination** /ˌɪnsəbɔːdɪ'neɪʃən || -ɔːr-/ n [U]

in·sub·stan·tial /ˌɪnsəb'stænʃəl/ adj not solid, strong, or satisfying: *insubstantial evidence* | *an insubstantial meal*

in·suf·fe·ra·ble /ɪn'sʌfərəbəl/ adj unpleasant and too proud in manner or behaviour: *insufferable rudeness* | *He's insufferable.* –**insufferably** adv

in·suf·fi·cient /ˌɪnsə'fɪʃənt◂/ adj fml not enough: *insufficient evidence* | *The food was insufficient for our needs.* –**insufficiently** adv –**insufficiency** n [U]: *an insufficiency of medical facilities*

in·su·lar /'ɪnsjʊlər || 'ɪnsələr, 'ɪnfə-/ adj **1** not interested in new ideas or experiences, or having no knowledge of them **2** of or like an island –**insularity** /ˌɪnsjʊ'lærɪti || ˌɪnsə-, ˌɪnfə-/ n [U]

in·su·late /'ɪnsjʊleɪt || 'ɪnsə-, 'ɪnfə-/ v **insulated, insulating** [T] **1** to cover something in order to prevent electricity, heat, or sound from passing through it: *We should insulate the loft.* | *insulated against heat loss* **2** to protect someone from ordinary experiences or outside influences: *The royal family is insulated from many of the difficulties faced by ordinary people.*

in·su·la·tion /ˌɪnsjʊ'leɪʃən || ˌɪnsə-, ˌɪnfə-/ n [U] **1** the action of insulating or the state of being insulated: *Insulation will cut your heating bills.* **2** material which insulates

in·sult¹ /ɪn'sʌlt/ v [T] to offend someone by your speech or behaviour: *He felt insulted by her lack of interest in his achievements.* | *an insulting remark*

insult² /'ɪnsʌlt/ n something which someone says or does that offends you: *He shouted insults at the other driver.*

in·su·pe·ra·ble /ɪn'sjuːpərəbəl || ɪn'suː-/ adj fml too difficult to deal with: *insuperable difficulties* | *an insuperable obstacle* –**insuperably** adv

in·sur·ance /ɪn'ʃʊərəns/ n **1** [U] an agreement by contract to pay money in case of a misfortune such as damage, loss, or accident: *life insurance* | *car insurance* | *an insurance policy* | *to claim on your insurance* **2** [U] the business of making and selling such agreements: *He works in insurance.* **3** [U] money which you pay to an insurance company or which the company pays to you in order to make or keep such a contract: *The insurance on my house has gone up again.* **4** [sing] protection against something: *I bought another lock as an additional insurance against thieves.*

in·sure /ɪn'ʃʊər/ v **insured, insuring 1** to protect someone or something from the costs of damage, loss, or an accident by making an agreement with a company that will pay those costs: *My house is insured against fire.* | *Are you insured?* **2** the usual American word for ENSURE

in·sur·gent /ɪnˈsɜːdʒənt ‖ -ɜːr-/ n a person who is trying to take power by force from the people who have power in a country –**insurgent** adj –**insurgency** n [C;U]

in·sur·moun·ta·ble /ˌɪnsəˈmaʊntəbəl ‖ -sər-/ adj too large or difficult to deal with

in·sur·rec·tion /ˌɪnsəˈrekʃən/ n [C;U] action taken to try and remove the people who have power, such as the government

in·tact /ɪnˈtækt/ adj [never before a noun] whole because no part has been touched or spoilt: *the last vase of a set that remained intact*

in·take /ˈɪnteɪk/ n [sing] **1** the process of taking something in: *fuel intake* **2** the amount or number of something which is taken in somewhere: *the yearly intake of students*

in·tan·gi·ble /ɪnˈtændʒəbəl/ adj which cannot be clearly understood or known: *an intangible quality* | *We felt an intangible presence in the room.* –**intangibly** adv –**intangibility** /ɪnˌtændʒəˈbɪləti/ n [U]

in·te·gral /ˈɪntɪɡrəl/ adj necessary to complete something: *an integral part of the argument*

in·te·grate /ˈɪntɪɡreɪt/ v **integrated, integrating 1** [I;T]to become or to make a person part of a social group: *Some immigrants integrate into the community surprisingly quickly.* | *We need to integrate deaf children with hearing children of a similar age.* **2** [T] to put two or more things together: *We need to integrate these findings with the results of previous research.* –**integration** /ˌɪntɪˈɡreɪʃən/ n [U]

in·te·grat·ed /ˈɪntɪɡreɪtɪd/ adj with a good mixture of qualities and groups: *This is an integrated school which children of many different races and social classes attend.* | *an integrated system*

in·teg·ri·ty /ɪnˈteɡrəti/ n [U] **1** strength and honesty of character or moral principle: *a man of complete integrity* **2** fml a state of being whole or complete: *Our national integrity is being threatened.*

in·tel·lect /ˈɪntəlekt/ n **1** [C;U] the ability to use the power of reason, rather than to feel or act **2** [U] the quality of being very intelligent: *His father was also noted for his intellect.*

in·tel·lec·tual¹ /ˌɪntəˈlektʃuəl◂/ adj needing, using, or concerning the ability to reason: *intellectual subjects* | *an intellectual argument* | *intellectual stimulation* –see INTELLIGENT (USAGE) –**intellectually** adv

intellectual² n a person who is well educated and interested in activities which demand a lot of thought and understanding: *university lecturers and other intellectuals*

in·tel·li·gence /ɪnˈtelɪdʒəns/ n [U] **1** the ability to learn and understand: *an intelligence test* | *a boy of low intelligence*. **2** information gathered about a country's enemies, or the group of people who gather it: *military intelligence* | *the Central Intelligence Agency of the US*

in·tel·li·gent /ɪnˈtelɪdʒənt/ adj having or showing powers of reasoning and understanding: *a highly intelligent woman* | *an intelligent suggestion* –opposite **unintelligent** –**intelligently** adv

■ USAGE Compare **intelligent** and **intellectual**. **Intelligent** is an adjective. An **intelligent** person is someone with a quick and clever mind. **Intellectual** can be an adjective or a noun. An **intellectual** (person) is someone who is well educated and interested in subjects which need long periods of study. A small child, or even a dog, can be **intelligent** but cannot be called an **intellectual**.

in·tel·li·gi·ble /ɪnˈtelɪdʒəbəl/ adj that can be understood (used especially of speech or writing) –**intelligibly** adv –**intelligibility** /ɪnˌtelɪdʒəˈbɪləti/ n [U]

in·tend /ɪnˈtend/ v **1** [I] to have the intention of doing something: *I had to leave sooner than I had intended.* | *I intended to catch the early train, but I didn't get up in time.* | *He didn't intend to cause so much unhappiness.*

□ USEFUL PATTERN to intend to do something **2** [T] to mean someone or something to be or do something: *The flowers were intended for you.* | *It was intended as a joke.* | *It was intended to be cooked slowly.* | *He didn't intend them to wait for him.*

□ USEFUL PATTERNS to intend someone to do something; to intend something to happen; to be intended for someone or something; to be intended as something

in·tense /ɪnˈtens/ adj **1** great or strong (used especially of feelings and sensations): *intense cold* | *intense sorrow* **2** having very strong feelings about things (used of people): *I find her a little too intense.* –**intensely** adv –**intensity** n : *He was surprised by the intensity of her feelings.*

in·ten·si·fy /ɪnˈtensɪfaɪ/ v **intensified, intensifying** [I;T] to become or to make something stronger: *Police have intensified their search for the criminal.* –**intensified** adj

in·ten·sive /ɪnˈtensɪv/ adj **1** giving a lot of attention or action to something, often only for a short time: *intensive farming* | *a short intensive English course* **2 intensive care** very special hospital care for people who are dangerously ill or very badly hurt: *the intensive care unit* | *He's been transferred to intensive care.* –**intensively** adv

in·tent¹ /ɪnˈtent/ n fml [U] **1** intention: *a declaration of intent* | *He entered the building with intent to steal.* | *with good intent* **2 to all intents and purposes** in every important way: *His proposal is, to all intents and purposes, exactly what we had in mind.*

intent² adj **1** showing or doing something with fixed attention: *an intent look* | *She's intent on her studies.* **2 intent on doing something** determined to do something: *He's intent on going to France next year.* –**intently** adv –**intentness** n [U]

in·ten·tion /ɪnˈtenʃən/ n [C;U] a plan or purpose: *I've got no intention of changing my mind.* | *It wasn't my intention to make you miss your train.* | *He is full of good intentions, but can do nothing to help.*

in·ten·tion·al /ɪnˈtenʃənəl/ adj intended or done on purpose –opposite **unintentional** –**intentionally** adv : *I'm sorry if I upset you – I didn't do it intentionally.*

in·ter /ɪnˈtɜː/ v -rr- [T] fml to bury a dead person

in·ter·act /ˌɪntərˈækt/ v [I] **1** to have an effect on each other or something else: *The two chemicals interact, causing a violent explosion.* **2** to talk to other people and form relationships with them: *When honest discussion is possible, couples interact more effectively.* –**interaction** /ˌɪntərˈækʃən/ n [U]: *There should be more interaction between doctors and the social services.*

in·ter·cede /ˌɪntəˈsiːd ‖ -ər-/ v **interceded, interceding** [I] to speak in favour of someone else in order to help them: *He interceded with the governor on my behalf.* –**intercession** /-ˈseʃən/ n [C;U]

in·ter·cept /ˌɪntəˈsept ‖ -ər-/ v [T] to stop and often seize a person or thing that is moving from one place to another: *The parcel of drugs was intercepted by the police* | *I think someone in the Ministry is*

intercepting confidential memos. | *He was intercepted before he reached the border.* –**interception** /-'sepʃən/ *n* [U]

in·ter·change /'ıntətʃeındʒ ‖ -ər-/ *n* **1** [C;U] exchange: *an interchange of ideas* **2** [C] a system of smaller roads by which two main roads are connected: *You leave the motorway at the next interchange.*

in·ter·chan·gea·ble /ˌıntə'tʃeındʒəbəl ‖ -tər-/ *adj* which can be used in place of each other or something else –**interchangeably** *adv*: *The two words are used interchangeably.*

in·ter·com /'ıntəkɒm ‖ 'ıntərkɑːm/ *n* a system by which you can talk through a machine to people who are in a different room or in different parts of a building: *There was an announcement on the intercom.*

in·ter·con·ti·nen·tal /ˌıntəkɒntɪˈnentl ◂ ‖ -tərkɑːn-/ *adj* between different land masses: *intercontinental trade* | *Intercontinental flights leave from Terminal 4.*

in·ter·course /'ıntəkɔːs ‖ 'ıntərkɔːrs/ *n* [U] **1** see SEXUAL INTERCOURSE **2** a sharing of feelings, ideas, activities, and so on allowing people to know each other better: *social intercourse*

in·ter·de·pen·dent /ˌıntədɪ'pendənt ‖ -tər-/ *adj* depending on each other –**interdependence** *n* [U]

in·terest¹ /'ıntrɪst/ *n* **1** [C;U] a desire to give your attention to something: *I have no interest in politics.* | *He's showing an interest in music.* **2** of interest able to hold your attention *Is there anything of interest on the news?* [RELATED PHRASE of no interest] **3** [C] an activity or subject to which you give time and attention: *Eating seems to be his only interest in life.* **4** [C;U] an advantage: *The child's interests must come first.* | *We have an interest in selling quickly before prices fall.* **5 in someone's interest** to someone's advantage: *It is not in your interest to sell now.* | *I have agreed to this only in the interests of better working relations.* **6 have someone's interests at heart** to care about someone being treated fairly **7** [U] money paid for borrowing money: *Interest rates on property loans are now at 15%.* | *an interest-free loan* **8** [C] a share in a company: *She sold her interest in the company.* | *business interests*

interest² *v* [T] **1** to make you want to know more about something: *Football doesn't interest me at all.* **2** to persuade someone to buy or do something: *Can I interest you in a cup of coffee?*

in·terest·ed /'ıntrɪstɪd/ *adj* **1** concerned to know more about something, or wanting to take part in something: *He was interested in my suggestion for increasing productivity.* | *an interested look on his face* | *I would be very interested in being involved in the scheme.*
□ USEFUL PATTERNS be interested in something; be interested in doing something –opposite **uninterested**
2 [only before a noun] personally concerned and therefore possibly unable to make a fair judgment: *We shall be calling a meeting of all interested parties.* –opposite **disinterested** –**interestedly** *adv*

in·terest·ing /'ıntrɪstıŋ/ *adj* catching and keeping

SPELLING NOTE
Words with the sound / aı / may be spelt **e-**, like **eye**, or **ai-**, like **aisle**.

---

your attention: *an interesting idea* | *That's very interesting!* –opposite **uninteresting** –**interestingly** *adv*

in·ter·fere /ˌıntə'fıər ‖ -tər-/ *v* interfered, interfering [I] **1** to concern yourself with other people's affairs: *Don't interfere!* | *You're always interfering in my private life.* **2** to get in the way or make something difficult: *Having to work late interferes with my social life.* | *Don't interfere with our affairs and we won't interfere with yours.*

in·ter·fer·ence /ˌıntə'fıərəns ‖ -tər-/ *n* [U] **1** the act or action of interfering: *I resent Ruth's mother's interference in our relationship.* **2** the confused noises which, for example, make a radio station difficult to listen to: *"We apologize for the interference, which is due to bad weather conditions."*

in·ter·im¹ /'ıntərım/ *n* **in the interim** in the time between two events

interim² *adj* useful for a limited time: *an interim report* | *interim measures to control football hooligans*

in·te·ri·or¹ /ın'tıərıər/ *n* **1** the inside part of something: *the palace's restored interior* **2** the interior the part of a country away from the coast: *journeys into the interior* **3** affairs within a particular country: *the Ministry of the Interior*

interior² *adj* indoors: *interior design* | *an interior decorator* – opposite **exterior**

in·ter·ject /ˌıntə'dʒekt ‖ -ər-/ *v* [I;T] *fml* to interrupt, or to put in a sudden remark when someone is speaking

in·ter·jec·tion /ˌıntə'dʒekʃən ‖ -ər-/ *n fml* **1** [C] a phrase, word, or set of sounds used as a sudden remark: *interjections such as "Oh!" or "Well done!"* **2** [U] the act of interrupting someone with a sudden remark

in·ter·lock /ˌıntə'lɒk ‖ ˌıntər'lɑːk/ *v* [I;T] to fasten or be fastened together so as to be firmly joined together: *to interlock the fingers of two hands* | *The gear wheels interlock.*

in·ter·lop·er /'ıntələupər ‖ -tər-/ *n fml* a person who enters a place without any right to be there

in·ter·lude /'ıntəluːd ‖ -ər-/ *n* **1** a period of time between activities or events **2** the time between parts of a play, film, or concert

in·ter·mar·ry /ˌıntə'mæri ‖ -ər-/ *v* intermarried, intermarrying [I] (of different groups of people) to marry each other: *The two families have been intermarrying for hundreds of years.* –**intermarriage** *n* [U]

in·ter·me·di·a·ry /ˌıntə'miːdiəri ‖ ˌıntər'miːdieri/ *n* intermediaries a person who comes between two other groups or people so as to bring them into agreement

in·ter·me·di·ate /ˌıntə'miːdiət ‖ -tər-/ *adj* between two levels or stages: *an intermediate student of English* | *an intermediate step towards the final design*

in·ter·ment /ın'tɜːmənt ‖ -ɜːr-/ *n* [C;U] *fml* burial

in·ter·mi·na·ble /ın'tɜːmɪnəbəl ‖ -ɜːr-/ *adj* not interesting and seeming endless: *an interminable speech* | *interminable delays* –**interminably** *adv*

in·ter·mis·sion /ˌıntə'mıʃən ‖ -tər-/ *n* the usual American word for INTERVAL

in·ter·mit·tent /ˌıntə'mıtənt ‖ -tər-/ *adj* happening at some times and not at other times: *an intermittent fault* | *an intermittent noise* –**intermittently** *adv*

in·tern /ın'tɜːn ‖ -ɜːrn/ *v* [T] to put someone in prison or limit their freedom of movement for political reasons

in·ter·nal /ɪnˈtɜːnl ‖ -ɜːr-/ adj **1** of or in the inside of something such as your body or an organization: *internal damage* | *an internal report* **2** inside a particular country, or concerning the affairs of that country: *internal trade* | *internal flights* –opposite **external** –**internally** adv

internal-com·bus·tion en·gine /·ˌ··· ·ˈ·· ˌ··/ n an engine which produces power inside itself by burning a substance such as petrol

in·ter·na·tion·al¹ /ˌɪntəˈnæʃənəl ‖ -tər-/ adj between nations or concerning more than one nation: *international relations* | *an international organization* | *an international star* –**internationally** adv

international² n **1** an international sports match **2** a player who performs in such a match: *an England international*

in·ter·plan·e·ta·ry /ˌɪntəˈplænʒtəri◄ ‖ ˌɪntərˈplænʒteri/ adj [only before a noun] happening or done between the PLANETS: *interplanetary travel*

in·ter·play /ˈɪntəpleɪ ‖ -ər-/ n [U] the action or effect of two or more things on each other: *the interplay of light and sound* | *the interplay between the forces of good and evil*

in·ter·pose /ˌɪntəˈpəʊz ‖ -ər-/ v **interposed, interposing** *fml* **1** [T] to put something between two people or things **2** [I;T] to interrupt, or to introduce something into a conversation: *"But we've tried that," she interposed.*

in·ter·pret /ɪnˈtɜːprʒt ‖ -ɜːr-/ v [T] **1** to put language into the words of another language, usually by talking: *We need somebody to interpret* **from** *Russian* **into** *English.* **2** to understand the meaning of something: *Her silence is being interpreted* **as** *cowardice.* | *He can interpret your dreams.* **3** to perform a work of art in a particular way that shows your own understanding of it: *He interpreted Hamlet* **as** *a man lost between two social orders.*

in·ter·pre·ta·tion /ɪnˌtɜːprʒˈteɪʃən ‖ -ɜːr-/ n [C;U] **1** your own particular understanding: *What's your interpretation* **of** *recent political events?* **2** explanation: *I would put a different interpretation on the murder myself.* **3** a particular understanding of a work of art, especially as shown in performance: *Schnabel's interpretation of Beethoven*

in·ter·pret·er /ɪnˈtɜːprʒtər ‖ -ɜːr-/ n a person who interprets from one language into another: *The Russian ambassador answered* **through** *an interpreter.*

in·ter·ro·gate /ɪnˈterəgeɪt/ v **interrogated, interrogating** [T] to question someone formally for a special purpose especially for a long time and perhaps with threats or violence: *She was interrogated for several hours by two officers.* –**interrogator** n –**interrogation** /ɪnˌterəˈgeɪʃən/ n [C;U]

in·ter·rog·a·tive /ˌɪntəˈrɒgətɪv ‖ -ˈrɑː-/ n a sentence, phrase, or word which asks a question –**interrogative** adj –**interrogatively** adv

in·ter·rupt /ˌɪntəˈrʌpt/ v [I;T] **1** to break someone's flow of speech or action by saying or doing something: *I'm sorry to interrupt, but I'd just like to make a point.* | *Don't interrupt him now.* **2** to break the flow of something continuous: *During the strike milk supplies were interrupted.* –**interruption** /-ˈrʌpʃən/ n [C;U]

in·ter·sect /ˌɪntəˈsekt ‖ -ər-/ v [I;T] (of lines and roads) to cross

in·ter·sec·tion /ˌɪntəˈsekʃən ‖ -ər-/ n a place where roads or lines cross: *a busy intersection*

in·ter·spersed /ˌɪntəˈspɜːs ‖ ˌɪntərˈspɜːrs/ adj **interspersed with** having things mixed in here and there: *a field of grass, interspersed with a few flowers*

in·ter·val /ˈɪntəvəl ‖ -tər-/ n **1** a period of time between the parts of a play, concert, or other public performance: *We had an ice cream in the interval.* **2** a period of time between events: *There was a long interval before he replied.* | *the interval* **between** *the arrest and the trial* **3 at intervals:** **a** happening regularly after periods of time: *The bell rang at 20-minute intervals.* **b** at equal distances: *The seeds are planted at intervals of six inches.*

in·ter·vene /ˌɪntəˈviːn ‖ -ər-/ v **intervened, intervening** [I] **1** to interrupt something, especially to prevent a bad result: *The government refused to intervene in the dispute between British Coal and the miners.* **2** to happen between events –**intervention** /-ˈvenʃən/ n [C;U]

in·ter·ven·ing /ˌɪntəˈviːnɪŋ ‖ -ər-/ adj **in the intervening years** in the time between two events: *I hadn't seen him since 1986 and he'd aged a lot in the intervening years.*

in·ter·view¹ /ˈɪntəvjuː ‖ -ər-/ n **1** a meeting where a person is asked questions to decide whether they should be given a job or a place on an educational course: *I didn't even get an interview.* | *She's got an interview for a place at Warwick University.* **2** a meeting where a person is asked questions to find out about their actions or opinions, sometimes broadcast on radio or television or printed in a newspaper or magazine: *The film star agreed to give an interview after the wedding.*

interview² v [T] to ask somebody questions in an interview: *She's being interviewed* **for** *the job.* | *A Dutch reporter interviewed the prime minister.* –**interviewer** n

in·ter·view·ee /ˌɪntəvjuːˈiː ‖ -ər-/ n someone who is interviewed

in·ter·weave /ˌɪntəˈwiːv ‖ -ər-/ v **interwove** /-ˈwəʊv/, **interwoven** /-ˈwəʊvən/, **interweaving** [T] to weave things together: *curtains made of red cloth interwoven* **with** *gold*

in·ter·wo·ven /ˌɪntəˈwəʊvən ‖ -ər-/ adj mixed together: *The two ideas are so interwoven you can't really separate them.*

in·tes·tate /ɪnˈtesteɪt, -stʒt/ adj law not having made a will giving the names of the people who should have your property after your death: *He died intestate.*

in·tes·tine /ɪnˈtestʒn/ n the tube carrying food from your stomach out of your body –**intestinal** adj

in·ti·ma·cy /ˈɪntʒməsi/ n **1** a close, often sexual, relationship: **2** pleasant and close familiarity: *in the intimacy of your own home* **3** physical nearness

in·ti·mate¹ /ˈɪntʒmʒt/ adj **1** having an extremely close relationship: *intimate friends* | *They had been intimate* **with** *the president for some time.* **2** most personal and private: *her intimate beliefs* **3** detailed: *an intimate knowledge of the city* **4** pleasantly close and informal: *an intimate atmosphere* | *an intimate candlelit dinner for two* **5** [never before a noun] *fml* having sex with someone **6 on intimate terms with** having a close relationship with –**intimately** adv

in·ti·mate² /ˈɪntʒmeɪt/ v [T; + that] **intimated, intimating** *fml* to make something known indirectly: *He intimated that we should leave.* | *She intimated her feelings with a look.* –**intimation** /ɪntʒˈmeɪʃən/ n [C;U]

in·tim·i·date /ɪnˈtɪmʒdeɪt/ v **intimidated, intimidating** [T] to make someone frightened, especially by threatening violence, because you want them to do something: *They tried to intimidate me*

into *getting them the key.* –**intimidation** /ɪn‚tɪmɪ‚deɪʃən/ [U]

in·to /ˈɪntə; *before vowels* ˈɪntʊ; *strong* ˈɪntuː/ *prep* **1** so as to be inside or in something: *He got into the car and drove off.* | *She dived into the water.* –see picture on page 540 **2** so as to be in a particular state: *This government has got the economy into a terrible mess.* | *He had worked himself up into a temper.* **3** so as to be wearing something: *She changed into her jeans.* **4** so as to hit something: *The car crashed into a tree.* **5** used when dividing one number by another: *Three into six goes twice.* **6** *infml* very interested in something or keen on it: *He's really into music at the moment.*

in·tol·e·ra·ble /ɪnˈtɒlərəbəl ‖ -ˈtɑː-/ *adj* **1** completely unacceptable: *intolerable behaviour* | *It's an intolerable situation.* **2** so bad that you cannot bear it: *intolerable pain* –**intolerably** *adv*

in·tol·e·rant /ɪnˈtɒlərənt ‖ -ˈtɑː-/ *adj* not willing to accept ways of thinking and behaving which are different from your own: *intolerant* of *any opposition* –**intolerantly** *adv* –**intolerance** *n* [U] : *racial intolerance*

in·to·na·tion /‚ɪntəˈneɪʃən/ *n* [U] the rise and fall in the level of someone's voice

in·tox·i·cate /ɪnˈtɒksɪ‚keɪt ‖ ɪnˈtɑːk-/ *v* **intoxicated, intoxicating** *fml* [T] **1** to make someone drunk **2** to cause strong feelings of wild excitement –**intoxication** /ɪn‚tɒksɪˈkeɪʃən ‖ ɪn‚tɑːk-/ *n* [U]

in·tox·i·ca·ted /ɪnˈtɒksɪ‚keɪtɪd ‖ ɪnˈtɑːk-/ *adj* **1** *fml* drunk **2** wildly excited: *intoxicated by success*

in·tox·i·ca·ting /ɪnˈtɒksɪ‚keɪtɪŋ ‖ ɪnˈtɑːk-/ *adj* **1** containing alcohol and likely to make you drunk **2** causing strong feelings of wild excitement: *the first intoxicating taste of freedom*

in·trac·ta·ble /ɪnˈtræktəbəl/ *adj fml* **1** difficult to do anything about or change: *an intractable problem* **2** difficult to control or influence: *She's such an intractable child!* –**intractability** /ɪn‚træktəˈbɪlɨti/ *n* [U]

in·tran·si·gent /ɪnˈtrænsɨdʒənt/ *adj fml* unwilling to change your ideas when other people want you to (a word used to express disapproval) –**intransigence** *n* [U]

in·tran·si·tive /ɪnˈtrænsɨtɪv/ *adj* having no object (used of verbs) : *In this dictionary the mark* [I] *shows that a verb is intransitive.* –see Study Note on page 589

in·tra·u·te·rine de·vice /‚ɪntrəˈjuːtəraɪn dɪˈvaɪs ‖ -tərən-/ *n* (also **IUD**) a metal or plastic object in the shape of a spring or ring, which is put into the child-bearing organ of a woman to prevent her from having children.

in·tra·ve·nous /‚ɪntrəˈviːnəs◂/ *adj* put directly into a VEIN which takes blood back to the heart: *an intravenous injection* –**intravenously** *adv*

in·trep·id /ɪnˈtrepɨd/ *adj lit* showing no fear: *intrepid explorers* –**intrepidly** *adv*

in·tri·ca·cy /ˈɪntrɪkəsi/ *n* **intricacies** **1** [U] the quality of containing many small detailed parts and often being difficult: *I don't think you appreciate the intricacy of the problem.* **2** **intricacies** [pl] many small details which are not at all simple: *the intricacies of political behaviour*

SPELLING NOTE

Words with the sound / aɪ / may be spelt **e-**, like **eye**, or **ai-**, like **aisle**.

---

in·tri·cate /ˈɪntrɪkɨt/ *adj* containing many detailed parts and being difficult to understand or follow: *an intricate pattern* –**intricately** *adv*

in·trigue[1] /ɪnˈtriːg/ *v* **intrigued, intriguing** **1** [T] to interest someone greatly: *Your story intrigues me.* | *an intriguing idea* | *I'm very intrigued by this new idea for saving paper.* **2** [I] to make secret plans or to get an advantage for yourself by indirect and dishonest means

in·trigue[2] /ˈɪntriːg, ɪnˈtriːg/ *n* [C;U] the act or practice of making secret plans to get an advantage for yourself by indirect and dishonest means: *There was talk of political intrigue.* | *He told me of various financial intrigues in the City.*

in·trin·sic /ɪnˈtrɪnsɪk, -zɪk/ *adj* being part of the nature of the stated thing: *The dirt doesn't affect its intrinsic value.* –**intrinsically** /-kli/ *adv*

in·tro·duce /‚ɪntrəˈdjuːs ‖ -ˈduːs/ *v* **introduced, introducing** [T] **1** to make one person known for the first time to another: *John, may I introduce you to Debbie Jones?* | *Let me introduce myself: my name is Simpson.* | *He introduced himself as the parish clerk.* **2** to bring in or use something for the first time: *Potatoes were introduced into Europe from South America.* | *A new examination will be introduced next year.* **3** to produce the first part of something, especially to suggest or explain the main part: *This song introduces the most important part of the play.* **4** to cause someone to experience or know about something for the first time: *They introduced me to the latest methods.*

in·tro·duc·tion /‚ɪntrəˈdʌkʃən/ *n* **1** [U] the act of introducing or the state of being introduced: *the introduction of a new product* **2** [C] the first part of something such as a book, which tells you about the rest: *The Active Study Dictionary has a useful introduction.* **3** [C] a first experience: *It was my first real introduction to flying.* **4** **make the introductions** to introduce people to each other

in·tro·duc·to·ry /‚ɪntrəˈdʌktəri◂/ *adj* which introduces: *a few introductory remarks before the main points*

in·tro·spec·tion /‚ɪntrəˈspekʃən/ *n* [U] *fml* the habit of looking into your own thoughts and feelings

in·tro·vert /ˈɪntrəvɜːt ‖ -ɜːrt/ *n* a person who is inward-looking and does not find it easy to be in other people's company –compare EXTROVERT

in·tro·vert·ed /ˈɪntrəvɜːtɨd ‖ -ɜːr-/ *adj* concerned with your own thoughts, acts, and personal life, rather than wanting to spend time with others –**introversion** /‚ɪntrəˈvɜːʃən ‖ -ˈvɜːrʒən/ *n* [U]

in·trude /ɪnˈtruːd/ *v* **intruded, intruding** [I] to go into a place where you are not wanted: *I don't want to intrude on them if they're busy.* | *I really don't think we should intrude.*

in·trud·er /ɪnˈtruːdəʳ/ *n* a person who has come in secretly and without permission

in·tru·sion /ɪnˈtruːʒən/ *n* [C;U] the act of intruding: *This advertising by phone is a real intrusion into your private life.* | *intrusions on my time* –**intrusive** /-sɪv/ *adj*

in·tu·i·tion /‚ɪntjuˈɪʃən ‖ -tu-, -tju-/ *n* [C;U] the power of understanding something without reasoning or proof: *You have no evidence, only intuition!* | *She had an intuition that her daughter was in trouble.* –**intuitive** /ɪnˈtjuːɨtɪv ‖ -ˈtuː-, -ˈtjuː-/ *adj* –**intuitively** *adv*

in·un·date /ˈɪnəndeɪt/ *v* **inundated, inundating** **1** **be inundated with** to receive so many of something that it is difficult to manage: *We were absolutely inundated with requests for advice.* **2** [T] *fml* to flood a place badly –**inundation** /ˌɪnʌn'deɪʃən/ n [C;U]

in·vade /ɪn'veɪd/ v **invaded, invading** 1 [I;T] to attack a country with an army and go into it and take control: *Poland was invaded in 1939.* | *He had secret plans to invade France.* 2 [I;T] to enter a place in large numbers: *Tourists invaded the seaside town in summer months.* 3 [T] to enter and spoil something: *Don't invade someone's privacy.* –**invader** n

in·va·lid¹ /'ɪnvəliːd, -lɪd || -lɪd/ n a person made weak by illness: *After the accident, my mother spent the rest of her life as an invalid.*

invalid² /ɪn'vælɪd/ adj no longer correct or fit for use: *an invalid ticket*

in·val·i·date /ɪn'vælɪˌdeɪt/ v **invalidated, invalidating** [T] fml 1 to make something invalid 2 to show that an argument or position is not good –**invalidity** /ˌɪnvə'lɪdɪʃən/ n [U]

in·val·u·a·ble /ɪn'væljuəbəl, -j‌bəl || -'vælj‌bəl/ adj so useful that you could not easily manage without it: *Thank you for your invaluable help* –see VALUABLE (USAGE)

in·var·i·a·ble /ɪn'veəriəbəl/ adj happening regularly or never changing: *an invariable routine*

in·var·i·a·bly /ɪn'veəriəbli/ adv fml always: *The bosses are invariably middle-aged men.*

in·va·sion /ɪn'veɪʒən/ n 1 [C;U] an action in which an army attacks a country and takes control: *the invasion of Italy* 2 [U] the arrival or spread of something harmful

in·vec·tive /ɪn'vektɪv/ n [U] fml rude, forceful, attacking speech, used for blaming someone for something

in·vent /ɪn'vent/ v [T] 1 to make up, think of, or produce something for the first time: *Alexander Graham Bell invented the telephone in 1876.* 2 to make up something unreal or untrue: *The whole story was invented.* | *I tried to invent an excuse.*

■ USAGE You **discover** something that existed before, such as a place or a fact: *They discovered oil in the North Sea.* | *Fleming discovered penicillin.* You **invent** something that did not exist before, such as a machine or a method: *Who first invented the computer?*

in·ven·tion /ɪn'venʃən/ n 1 [U] the act of inventing something: *The invention of the telephone was the start of modern telecommunications systems.* 2 [C] something that has been invented: *The telephone is a wonderful invention.* 3 [U] the ability to invent things: *a wonderful story, full of invention*

in·ven·tive /ɪn'ventɪv/ adj able to think of good, new ideas: *an inventive person* –**inventiveness** n [U]

in·ven·tor /ɪn'ventəʳ/ n a person who invents something new

in·ven·to·ry /'ɪnvəntri || -tɔːri/ n **inventories** a list of all the goods in a place: *an inventory of all the office furniture*

in·verse /ˌɪn'vɜːs◂ || -ɜːrs/ n the inverse of the opposite of –**inverse** adj –**inversely** adv

in·vert /ɪn'vɜːt || -ɜːrt/ v [T] to put something upside down or back to front: *She caught the insect by inverting her cup over it.* –**inversion** /-'vɜːʃən || -'vɜːrʒən/ n [C;U]

in·ver·te·brate /ɪn'vɜːtɪbrɪt, -breɪt || -ɜːr-/ n tech a creature which has no BACKBONE

inverted com·mas /·,·· '··/ n [pl] 1 marks used in writing to show that somebody's real words are being given 2 **in inverted commas** used by the speaker to suggest the opposite of what has just been said: *Her friends, in inverted commas, all disappeared when she was in trouble.*

in·vest /ɪn'vest/ v [I;T] 1 to use money to make a profit out of something that will increase in value: *She decided to invest £10,000 in the gas industry.* 2 to put time, effort, or money into something in the hope that later it will be worth it: *I've invested a lot of time and effort in this plan.*

in·ves·ti·gate /ɪn'vestɪɡeɪt/ v **investigated, investigating** [I;T] to examine carefully, or inquire about the reasons for something, or the character of someone: *The police are investigating the incident.* –**investigator** n –**investigation** /ɪnˌvestɪ'ɡeɪʃən/ n [C;U]: *an investigation into corruption in the Civil Service*

in·ves·ti·ture /ɪn'vestɪtʃəʳ || -tʃʊəʳ/ n a ceremony giving someone a position of high rank

in·vest·ment /ɪn'vestmənt/ n 1 [C;U] the act of putting money into a business in order to get a profit: *He regards the house as an investment.* 2 [C] an amount of money put into a business so that you get a profit: *an investment of £1000 in a growing business* | *I believe he's sold all his South African investments now.*

in·vet·e·rate /ɪn'vetərɪt/ adj [only before a noun] fixed in a bad habit or way of thinking: *an inveterate liar*

in·vid·i·ous /ɪn'vɪdiəs/ adj 1 which will make people unjustly offended or jealous: *They all sing equally well, so I don't want to make invidious distinctions between them.* 2 unfair: *an invidious comparison*

in·vi·gi·late /ɪn'vɪdʒɪleɪt/ v **invigilated, invigilating** [I;T] BrE to be in charge of an examination and watch over the people taking it in order to prevent dishonesty –**invigilator** n –**invigilation** /ɪnˌvɪdʒɪ'leɪʃən/ n [C;U]

in·vig·o·rating /ɪn'vɪɡəreɪtɪŋ/ adj making you feel strong and healthy: *an invigorating swim in the lake*

in·vin·ci·ble /ɪn'vɪnsɪbəl/ adj too strong to be defeated

in·vis·i·ble /ɪn'vɪzɪbəl/ adj 1 that cannot be seen: *Germs are invisible to the naked eye.* | *The magic had made her invisible.* 2 that is not recorded (used of profit and loss): *invisible earnings* –**invisibly** adv –**invisibility** /ɪnˌvɪzɪ'bɪlɪti/ n [U]

in·vi·ta·tion /ˌɪnvɪ'teɪʃən/ n a spoken or written offer of a chance to go to something such as a meal or party or to do something: *an invitation to a party* | *an invitation to visit our factory in Birmingham* | *Did you receive my invitation?*

in·vite /ɪn'vaɪt/ v **invited, inviting** [T] 1 to ask someone to something such as a meal or a party: *She invited me to her party.* | *They've invited us to stay for the weekend.*
□ USEFUL PATTERNS to invite someone to something, to invite someone to do something
2 to request something formally: *The television interviewer invited the minister to comment on the recent events.* | *Questions were invited after the lecture.*
□ USEFUL PATTERNS to invite something; to invite someone to do something
3 to make it too easy for something to happen: *Some shops invite crime by making it easy to take things.*

■ USAGE It is not necessary to use the word **invite** when you are actually inviting someone to do something. In fact, it often sounds more natural in informal English to use a different expression: **Will you come to my party?** | **Would you like to come to the cinema?** | **We were wondering if you'd like to come to dinner.** The verb **invite** is more common, however, in formal invitations: *Mr and Mrs Jones*

invite you *to the wedding of their daughter*.... | **We would like to invite you** *to a celebration lunch to launch our new product*.

invite sbdy in *phr v* [T] to ask someone who comes to your door to come inside: *When I called at the house, she invited me in for a coffee*.

invite sbdy out *phr v* [T] to ask someone to go to a show, play, or social event with you: *After my husband died, I wasn't invited out for months*.

invite sbdy over *phr v* [T] to ask someone to come and visit you in your home: *I've invited four people over for dinner tonight*.

in·vit·ing /ɪnˈvaɪtɪŋ/ *adj* attractive: *an inviting prospect* –**invitingly** *adv*

in·voice /ˈɪnvɔɪs/ *n* a bill for goods sent or work done

invoice *v* invoiced, invoicing [T] to send someone a bill for work done or goods sent to them

in·voke /ɪnˈvəʊk/ *v* invoked, invoking [T] *fml* **1** to mention something such as a law because it supports your position **2** to call out to a power, especially God, for help **3** to request or beg for something: *She invoked their forgiveness*.

in·vol·un·ta·ry /ɪnˈvɒləntəri ‖ ɪnˈvɑːləntəri/ *adj* not done from choice or intention: *He gave an involuntary smile* –**involuntarily** *adv*

in·volve /ɪnˈvɒlv ‖ ɪnˈvɑːlv/ *v* **involved, involving** [T] **1** to cause someone to become connected with or concerned: *It shouldn't be necessary to involve the other departments*. | *Please don't involve me* **in** *your domestic problems*. | *I wouldn't get involved* **with** *him if I were you*. **2** to have something as a necessary part or result: *Taking the job involves living abroad*.

☐ USEFUL PATTERNS to involve something; to involve doing something –**involvement** *n* [U]

in·volved /ɪnˈvɒlvd ‖ ɪnˈvɑːlvd/ *adj* **1** concerned with an activity: *He got involved* **in** *smuggling*. | *She's involved in Red Cross work*. | *He's involved* **with** *the drama society*. **2** closely connected in a relationship, especially a sexual one: *He was involved* **with** *another woman*. **3** not simple: *a long and involved explanation*

in·ward /ˈɪnwəd ‖ -ərd/ *adj* [only before a noun] **1** on or towards the inside of something **2** felt by a person but not shown to other people: *a feeling of inward contentment*

in·wards /ˈɪnwədz ‖ -ɔːr-/ *adv* (also **inward** *AmE*) towards the inside of something

i·o·dine /ˈaɪədiːn ‖ -daɪn/ *n* [U] a substance used in photography, and on wounds to prevent infection

i·on /ˈaɪən ‖ ˈaɪən, ˈaɪɑːn/ *n* an electrically charged atom

i·o·ta /aɪˈəʊtə/ *n* **not an iota of** not any at all: *There's not an iota of truth in that*.

IOU /ˌaɪ əʊ ˈjuː/ *n* a piece of paper saying that you owe a certain amount of money to someone else, with your signature at the bottom; an abbreviation for **I owe you**: *I can't give you the money now. Can I give you an IOU?*

IPA /ˌaɪ piː ˈeɪ/ *n* a system of signs used for representing speech sounds; an abbreviation for **International Phonetic Alphabet**: *This dictionary uses the IPA*.

SPELLING NOTE

Words with the sound / aɪ / may be spelt **e-**, like **eye**, or **ai-**, like **aisle**.

IQ /ˌaɪ ˈkjuː/ a measure of how clever someone is; an abbreviation for **Intelligence Quotient**: *a very high IQ* | *She has an IQ of 127*.

IRA /ˌaɪ ɑːr ˈeɪ/ an illegal organization whose aim is to unite Northern and Southern Ireland by force; an abbreviation for **Irish Republican Army**

i·ras·ci·ble /ɪˈræsəbəl/ *adj fml* tending to get angry easily –**irascibly** *adv* –**irascibility** /ɪˌræsəˈbɪləti/ *n* [U]

i·rate /ˌaɪˈreɪt◁/ *adj fml* angry: *an irate letter to the editor* –**irately** *adv*

ir·i·des·cent /ˌɪrɪˈdesənt/ *adj lit* showing changing colours as light falls on it: *iridescent soap bubbles* –**iridescence** *n* [U]

I·rish¹ /ˈaɪrɪʃ/ *adj* from or connected with Ireland: *Irish whiskey* | *the Irish President* | *an Irish accent*

Irish² *n* the Irish the people of Ireland

i·ris /ˈaɪərɪs/ *n* **1** a tall flower, typically yellow or purple, with long thin leaves **2** the round, coloured part of your eye

irk /ɜːk ‖ ɜːrk/ *v* [T] to annoy someone: *It really irks me to have to do his work as well as mine*.

irk·some /ˈɜːksəm ‖ ˈɜːrk-/ *adj* annoying: *irksome duties*

i·ron¹ /ˈaɪən ‖ ˈaɪərn/ *n* **1** [U] a very common and useful MAGNETIC metal that is used in the making of steel, and is found in very small quantities in certain foods, and in your blood: *an iron foundry* | *iron pills* **2** [C] a flat-bottomed object with a handle on top, which is heated and used for making clothing smooth: *an electric iron* | *Use a hot iron on your jeans*. –see picture on page 638

iron² *v* [T] to make clothes smooth with an iron: *I've been doing the ironing all day*. | *Would you like me to iron your shirt for you?*

iron sth ↔ out *phr v* [T] to remove difficulties or find an answer to problems: *We need to iron out a few problems*.

iron³ *adj* **1** made of iron: *iron gates* **2** firm and unchanging (used of people and their way of thinking): *the Iron Lady* | *iron discipline*

Iron Cur·tain /ˌ··· ˈ··/ *n* the western border between the COMMUNIST countries of Eastern Europe and the rest of the world which in the period after the Second World War could not easily be crossed for purposes of trade, the exchange of information, or travel: *behind the Iron Curtain*

i·ron·ic /aɪˈrɒnɪk ‖ aɪˈrɑː-/ *adj* (also **ironical**) **1** using words in a humorous way to mean the opposite of what they usually mean **2** amusing, often in a bitter way, because not what is expected or suitable –**ironically** /-kli/ *adv*

ironing board /ˈ··· ·/ *n* a long narrow table on which clothes are spread to be ironed –see picture on page 638

i·ron·mon·ger /ˈaɪənˌmʌŋɡər ‖ ˈaɪərnˌmʌŋ-, -ˌmɑːŋ-/ *n BrE* **1** a shopkeeper who sells things which you need in your house and garden such as pans and tools **2** **ironmonger's** a shop selling equipment for the house and garden

i·ron·mon·ger·y /ˈaɪənˌmʌŋɡəri ‖ ˈaɪərnˌmʌŋ-, -ˌmɑːŋ-/ *n* [U] *BrE* things which you need in your house and garden such as pots and pans, especially those made of metal

i·ron·y /ˈaɪərəni/ *n* ironies **1** [U] the amusing use of words which are clearly opposite to your meaning: *"Oh, well done!" she said with irony*. **2** [C;U] a course of events or a condition which has the opposite result from what is expected, usually a bad result: *life's little ironies* | *The irony of it all was that he turned out to be right*.

ir·ra·tion·al /ɪˈræʃənəl/ *adj* **1** without reasonable behaviour: *The drugs made her quite irrational.* **2** not supported by reason: *irrational fears* **–irrationally** *adv*

ir·rec·on·ci·la·ble /ɪˌrekənˈsaɪləbəl/ *adj* which cannot be brought into agreement: *irreconcilable differences of opinion | a hobby irreconcilable with his job* **–irreconcilably** *adv*

ir·re·fu·ta·ble /ˌɪrɪˈfjuːtəbəl/ *adj* too strong to be disproved: *an irrefutable argument* **–irrefutably** *adv*

ir·reg·u·lar /ɪˈregjˈlər/ *adj* **1** not evenly shaped: *an irregular coastline | She has irregular features.* **2** happening again and again, but with different lengths of time between the occasions: *an irregular heartbeat | I hate working irregular hours.* **3** not according to the usual rules or habits: *"No permit? This is most irregular, Sir."* **4** not following the usual pattern in grammar: *an irregular verb* **–irregularly** *adv* **–irregularity** /ɪˌregjˈlærˈti/ *n* **irregularities** [C;U]

ir·rel·e·vance /ɪˈreləvəns/ *n* [U] the state of not having any real connection or importance

ir·rel·e·van·cy /ɪˈreləvənsi/ *n* **irrelevancies** something which has no importance: *Don't waste time with irrelevancies like that.*

ir·rel·e·vant /ɪˈreləvənt/ *adj* not having any real connection or importance: *If he can do the job well, his age is irrelevant. | His age is irrelevant to the situation.* **–irrelevantly** *adv*

ir·rep·a·ra·ble /ɪˈrepərəbəl/ *adj* too bad to be repaired or put right: *The assassination did irreparable damage to relations between the two countries.* **–irreparably** *adv*

ir·re·place·a·ble /ˌɪrɪˈpleɪsəbəl/ *adj* too special or unusual for another one to take its place: *Be careful! That antique vase is irreplaceable. | No one's irreplaceable.*

ir·re·pres·si·ble /ˌɪrɪˈpresˈbəl/ *adj* too strong or forceful to be held back: *irrepressible high spirits* **–irrepressibly** *adv*

ir·re·proa·cha·ble /ˌɪrɪˈprəʊtʃəbəl/ *adj fml* without blame **–irreproachably** *adv*

ir·re·sis·ti·ble /ˌɪrɪˈzɪstˈbəl/ *adj* too powerful or pleasant to leave or fight against: *an irresistible argument | Those chocolates look quite irresistible!* **–irresistibly** *adv*

ir·re·spec·tive /ˌɪrɪˈspektɪv əv/ *adv* **irrespective** without being connected to: *a film that can be enjoyed by anyone, irrespective of age*

ir·re·spon·si·ble /ˌɪrɪˈspɒnsˈbəl ‖ -ˈspɑːn-/ *adj* showing no ability to think of the effect of your actions: *His behaviour was very irresponsible – he might have hurt somebody.* **–irresponsibly** *adv* **–irresponsibility** /ˌɪrɪspɒnsˈbɪlˈti ‖ -spɑː-/ *n* [U]

ir·rev·e·rent /ɪˈrevərənt/ *adj* showing lack of respect, especially for religion **–irreverently** *adv* **–irreverence** *n* [U]

ir·rev·o·ca·ble /ɪˈrevəkəbəl/ *adj* that cannot be changed: *an irrevocable decision* **–irrevocably** *adv*

ir·ri·gate /ˈɪrˈgeɪt/ *v* **irrigated, irrigating** [T] to supply water to dry land to help crops grow **–irrigated** *adj* **–irrigation** /ˌɪrˈgeɪʃən/ *n* [U]

ir·ri·ta·ble /ˈɪrˈtəbəl/ *adj* easily made angry: *Don't take any notice, he's always irritable in the mornings.* **–irritably** *adv* **–irritability** /ˌɪrɪtəˈbɪlˈti/ *n* [U]

ir·ri·tant /ˈɪrˈtənt/ *n* a substance which makes a part of your body painful and sore: *Wash the irritant out of your eyes immediately.*

ir·ri·tate /ˈɪrˈteɪt/ *v* **irritated, irritating** [T] **1** to make angry or excite in an unpleasant way: *The way she bites her nails really irritates me.* **2** to make a part of your body painful and sore: *Wool irritates my skin.* **–irritation** /ˌɪrˈteɪʃən/ [C;U]

is /s, z, əz; *strong* ɪz/ *v* the third person singular of the present tense of BE **–see 's** (USAGE)

Is·lam /ˈɪslɑːm, ˈɪz-, ɪsˈlɑːm/ *n* **1** the MUSLIM religion, started by MOHAMMED **2** the people and countries that practise the Muslim religion **–Islamic** /ɪzˈlæmɪk, ɪs-/ *adj*

is·land /ˈaɪlənd/ *n* **1** a piece of land surrounded by water: *Britain is an island* **2** (also **traffic island**) – a raised place in the middle of the road where people crossing can wait for traffic to pass

isle /aɪl/ *n lit* an island

is·n't /ˈɪzənt/ *short for:* "is not": *It's Monday, isn't it? | Isn't she pretty? | That's strange, isn't it? | Dinner isn't ready yet.*

i·so·late /ˈaɪsəleɪt/ *v* **isolated, isolating** [T] to separate one person or thing from others: *Several villages have been isolated by the floods. | When you isolate someone from their friends, they soon become depressed.*

i·so·lat·ed /ˈaɪsəleɪtˈd/ *adj* **1** a long way from other houses: *an isolated farmhouse* **2** lonely and without friends: *At first, she felt very isolated.* **3** single, and not part of a general pattern: *an isolated incident*

i·so·la·tion /ˌaɪsəˈleɪʃən/ *n* **1** in isolation existing or happening separately from other things: *You can't consider one sentence in isolation.* **2** [U] loneliness: *the isolation and poverty of the homeless*

is·sue¹ /ˈɪʃuː, ˈɪsjuː ‖ ˈɪʃuː/ *n* **1** [C] a subject which people are talking and arguing about: *The economy is no longer the main issue in this election. | key issues | a side issue* **2** [C] something printed in large numbers and sold or given out at one time: *the new issue of Radio Times, on sale today | a new issue of stamps* **3** [U] the act of coming out or being produced **4** make an issue of something to make something appear more important than it really is, by talking about it a lot: *She makes such an issue of her divorce.* **5** at issue under consideration: *Her ability is not at issue; it's her health we're worried about.* **6** take issue with someone to disagree with someone

issue² *v* **issued, issuing** [T] **1** to bring out something printed or official for the notice of the public: *"Greek Cookery" was later issued in paperback.* **2** to supply someone with something officially: *They issued the soldiers with guns.*

issue from sthg *phr v* [T] to come out of or result from something

isth·mus /ˈɪsməs/ *n* a narrow area of land which joins two larger land masses

it /ɪt/ *pron* [used as the subject or the object of a verb] **1** the thing that has already been mentioned: *"Where's my coat?" "It's in the cupboard." | I picked up the letter and put it in my cupboard. | The government has become very unpopular since it introduced the new tax.* **2** the baby or animal that has already been mentioned: *What a beautiful baby – is it a boy?* **3** a situation or fact generally: *It's lovely here. | It's a pity that you can't come. | Sometimes I find it difficult to concentrate on my work.* **4** used when making statements about the weather, time, or date: *It's two o'clock. | Is it raining? | It's the 23rd June.* **5** used as the subject of a sentence when you want to make one part of the sentence more important: *It was John who told me, not Helen. | It's the*

money that I'm worried about. **6 that's it: a** a phrase used to say that something is finished: *We've just got one more wall to paint and then that's it.* | *That's it! I'm not working for that company any more!* **b** a phrase used to agree with someone or say that something is correct: *Hold the ladder for me – that's it.*

■ USAGE 1 Do not confuse **it's** and **its. It's** (with an apostrophe) is the short form of "it is": **It's** *very hot today.* | *Whose coat is this?* **It's** *mine.* **It's** is also the short form of "it has" when this is used as part of the present perfect tense: **It's** *been raining for hours.* | *"Where's the cat?"* *"* **It's** *gone next door."* **Its** (with no apostrophe) is the possessive form of "it": *The cat licked* **its** *paws.* | *The baby's playing with* **its** *toys.*

i·tal·ics /ɪˈtælɪks/ *n* [pl] the style of printing with small letters sloping to the right: *This example is printed in italics.* **–italic** *adj*

I·tal·i·an[1] /ɪˈtæliən/ *adj* from or connected with Italy: *His wife is Italian.*

Italian[2] *n* **1** [C] a person from Italy **2** [U] the language of Italy: *an opera sung in Italian*

itch[1] /ɪtʃ/ *v* [I] **1** to have a feeling on your skin that makes you want to rub that part with something rough or sharp: *This mosquito bite itches all the time.* | *I itch all over.* **2 be itching to do something** *infml* to have a desire to do something soon: *I'm itching to go.* **3 be itching for something** to have an urgent desire for something: *He seems to be itching for a fight.*

itch[2] *n* **1** a feeling on your skin which makes you want to rub that part with something rough or sharp **2** a strong desire –**itchy** *adj* –**itchiness** *n* [U]

it'd /ˈɪtəd/ **1** short for "it would": *It'd be all right if I had enough money.* **2** short for "it had": *It'd been raining earlier that morning.*

■ USAGE Although **it'd** is frequently used as a short form in spoken English, it is not often used in writing. It is more usual to use the full forms, **it would** or **it had.**

i·tem /ˈaɪtɪm/ *n* **1** a single thing among a set or on a list: *The police examined several items of clothing.* **2 news item** a piece of news on television or in a newspaper

i·tem·ize /ˈaɪtɪmaɪz/ *v* itemized, itemizing (also **itemise** *BrE*) [T] to write down all the separate parts of something in a list: *an itemized bill*

i·tin·e·rant /aɪˈtɪnərənt/ *adj* [only before a noun] *fml* travelling from place to place: *an itinerant worker*

i·tin·e·ra·ry /aɪˈtɪnərəri ‖ -nəreri/ *n* **itineraries** a plan of a journey

it'll /ˈɪtl/ short for "it will"

its /ɪts/ *det* connected with or belonging to the thing that has already been mentioned: *The cat was sitting drinking its milk.* | *The committee had its final meeting last night.*

it's /ɪts/ **1** short for "it is": *It's a lovely day today.* **2** short for "it has": *It's been a long time since we last met.*

■ USAGE Note that "it has" does NOT have a short form if "has" is being used as a full verb: *I've lost my cat.* **It has** *a green collar.*

it·self /ɪtˈself/ *pron* **1** used as the object of a verb or a PREPOSITION when the subject of a verb is an animal or a thing and the action is done to the same animal or thing: *The cat washed itself in front of the fire.* | *The government has made itself unpopular.* **2** used to add force to the word "it", or to the name of a thing or an animal: *There's no point in putting new tyres on, when the car itself is so old.* **3 in itself** by its own nature, without considering anything else: *Do you think that art is important in itself?*

ITV /ˌaɪ tiː ˈviː/ a group of British broadcasting companies supported by private money an abbreviation for **Independent Television**: *It was on ITV last Saturday.*

IUD /ˌaɪ juː ˈdiː/ an abbreviation for INTRAUTERINE DEVICE

I've /aɪv/ short for "I have": *I've been here before.* | *I've got lots of time.* | *I've no doubt she's forgotten.*

i·vo·ry /ˈaɪvəri/ *n* [U] **1** hard white bone from which an elephant's *tusks* are made: *ivory beads* | *piano keys made of ivory* **2** creamy white *a wedding dress of ivory silk*

i·vy /ˈaɪvi/ *n* [U] a climbing plant with shiny three- or five-pointed leaves

J, j

J, j /dʒeɪ/ **J's, j's** or **Js, js** the 10th letter of the English alphabet

jab¹ /dʒæb/ v **-bb-** [T] to push or hit something with quick, forceful movements: *He jabbed the stick into the ground.*

jab² n **1** a sudden forceful push or blow **2** *infml* an INJECTION: *Have you had your cholera jabs yet?*

jab·ber /ˈdʒæbəʳ/ v [I] *infml* to talk quickly but not clearly: *I can't understand you if you keep jabbering away like that.*

jack¹ /dʒæk/ n **1** an apparatus for lifting a heavy weight, such as a car, off the ground **2** a playing card with a picture of a young man on it: *the Jack of Hearts*

jack² v
jack sthg ↔ **up** *phr* v [T] to lift up a heavy object with a jack: *You jack the car up and I'll change the wheel.*

jack·al /ˈdʒækɔːl, -kəl ‖ -kəl/ n a wild animal of the dog family

jack·daw /ˈdʒækdɔː/ n a kind of bird which is believed to steal small bright objects

jack·et /ˈdʒækɪt/ n **1** a short coat –see picture on page 50 **2** the skin of a baked potato: *potatoes cooked in their jackets* **3** an outer cover for certain machines or engines that get very hot **4** (also **dust jacket**) a loose paper cover put as protection round the hard cover of a book **5** *AmE* a stiff envelope for keeping a record in

jack-in-the-box /ˈ· · · ˌ·/ n a children's toy which is a box from which an amusing figure jumps when the top is opened

jack knife /ˈ· ·/ n **jack knives** a pocket knife with a blade that folds into the handle

jack-knife v **jack-knifed, jack-knifing** [I] (of a large vehicle) to bend suddenly in the middle in an uncontrolled way: *An articulated lorry has jack-knifed on the bend up the hill.*

jack-of-all-trades /ˌ· · ˈ· ·/ n a person who can do many different kinds of work

jack·pot /ˈdʒækpɒt ‖ -pɑːt/ n **1** the biggest amount of money to be won in a game of cards or chance **2** **hit the jackpot** *infml* to win a large amount of money or have a big success

jade /dʒeɪd/ n [U] a precious green stone which is used to make jewellery

ja·ded /ˈdʒeɪdɪd/ adj tired and uninterested because you have had too much of something: *She seemed jaded and in need of a break.*

jag·ged /ˈdʒægɪd/ adj having a rough uneven edge with many sharp points

jag·u·ar /ˈdʒægjuəʳ ‖ -ˈdʒægwɑːr/ n a large spotted wild cat of Central and South America

jail¹ /dʒeɪl/ n (also **gaol** *BrE*) [C;U] a prison: *He had spent 20 years in jail.*

jail² v (also **gaol** *BrE*) [T] to put someone in jail

jail·er /ˈdʒeɪləʳ/ n old fash (also **jailor; gaoler** *BrE*) a person who is in charge of a prison or prisoners

jam¹ /dʒæm/ n [U] **1** a sweet food made by boiling and preserving fruit in sugar; jam is usually spread on bread: *a little pot of strawberry jam* | *jam tarts* **2** a mass of people, vehicles, or things pressed so close together that movement is difficult or impossible: *a traffic jam* **3** **be in a jam** *infml* to be in trouble or difficulty: *Could you lend me £5? I'm in a bit of a jam.*

jam² v **-mm-** **1** [T + adv/prep] to pack or press things tightly together in a place: *I jammed everything into my bag.* **2** [I;T] to make or become stuck: *The wheels have jammed.* | *She tried to open the window, but it was jammed.* **3** [T] to block a road so that no vehicles can move in it: *The roads were all jammed with cars.* **4** [T] to block radio messages by broadcasting noise **5** **jam on the brakes** to stop a vehicle by using the BRAKES forcefully and suddenly

jamb /dʒæm/ n a side post of a door or window

jam·bo·ree /ˌdʒæmbəˈriː/ n old fash a happy party or gathering

jam-packed /ˌ·ˈ·◄/ adj *infml* very full of people or things: *The town is always jam-packed for the carnival.*

jan·gle /ˈdʒæŋgəl/ v **jangled, jangling** [I;T] to make a sharp sound like metal striking against metal or move something so that it makes such a sound: *The fire bell jangled.* | *She jangled her keys.*

jan·i·tor /ˈdʒænɪtəʳ/ n a person who looks after a large public building

Jan·u·a·ry /ˈdʒænjuəri, -njuri ‖ -jueri/ n (also **Jan.**) the 1st month of the year

Jap·an·ese¹ /ˌdʒæpəˈniːz◄/ adj of or connected with Japan: *My car is Japanese.*

Japanese² n **1** the **Japanese** the people of Japan **2** [U] the language of Japan

jar¹ /dʒɑːʳ/ n **1** a wide-mouthed container, usually made of glass, and used for storing food: *a jar of cherry jam* –see picture on page 148 **2** the food or other contents in a jar: *He was so hungry he ate two jars of fish paste.* **3** an unpleasant shock to the body: *Sudden jars can cause injuries to joggers.*

jar² v **-rr-** **1** [I] to make an unpleasant or annoying sound: *His voice really jarred on me.* **2** [T] to give you an unpleasant shock: *The fall jarred every bone in my body.* | *He seemed jarred by the news.*

jar·gon /ˈdʒɑːgən ‖ ˈdʒɑːrgən, -gɑːn/ n [U] special words that most people find hard to understand, because they are used only by a particular group of people: *computer jargon*

jaun·dice /ˈdʒɔːndɪs ‖ ˈdʒɔːn-, ˈdʒɑːn-/ n [U] a disease that makes your eyes and skin turn yellow

jaun·diced /ˈdʒɔːndɪst ‖ ˈdʒɔːn-, ˈdʒɑːn-/ adj **1** suffering from jaundice **2** tending to judge other people unfavourably: *a jaundiced view of life*

jaunt /dʒɔːnt ‖ dʒɔːnt, dʒɑːnt/ n a short journey, usually for pleasure

jaun·ty /ˈdʒɔːnti ‖ ˈdʒɔːnti, ˈdʒɑːnti/ adj **jauntier, jauntiest** showing that you feel cheerful and confident: *a jaunty wave of the hand* –**jauntily** adv

jav·e·lin /ˈdʒævəlɪn/ n a light spear which is thrown as a sport

jaw /dʒɔː/ n one of the two bony parts of your face in which your teeth are set

jay /dʒeɪ/ n a noisy brightly-coloured bird

jay·walk /'dʒeɪwɔːk/ v [I] to cross streets in a careless and dangerous way –**jaywalker** n

jazz[1] /dʒæz/ n [U] music with a strong beat and some free playing by each musician in the band

jazz[2] v
jazz sthg ↔ up phr v [T] infml to make something more interesting, bright, or enjoyable: We need to jazz this room up a bit.

jazz·y /'dʒæzi/ adj **jazzier, jazziest** infml attracting attention, for example by using bright loud colours: a very jazzy dress

jeal·ous /'dʒeləs/ adj **1** feeling bitter, unhappy, and angry towards someone because they have something that you want: He's jealous of their success. | She was a jealous child who never got on with her sisters. | He's just jealous of you! **2** feeling fearful and protective because you think someone may try to take something that belongs to you: Pat is very jealous of her possessions. | He's insanely jealous of his wife's love. –**jealously** adv : a dog jealously guarding its bone

■ USAGE Compare **jealous** and **envious**. **Jealous** suggests a stronger and more unpleasant feeling than **envious**. If you are **jealous** you are angry because of a person's good luck or because a person shows love to someone else. If you are **envious** you would simply like to have what another person has: Tom was so **jealous** when Ann got the job that he could hardly speak to her. | The little boy is **jealous** of the new baby. | Congratulations on your new job – I'm really **envious**!

jeal·ous·y /'dʒeləsi/ n jealousies [C;U] a jealous feeling: I was trying to hide my jealousy. | petty rivalries and jealousies

jeans /dʒiːnz/ n [pl] trousers made of strong cotton cloth, which are worn informally: a pair of blue denim jeans –see picture on page 50

jeep /dʒiːp/ n a small vehicle suitable for travelling over rough ground

jeer /dʒɪər/ v [I;T] to laugh rudely at someone: The crowd jeered at us. | He was jeered by the audience. –**jeers** n [pl]

jell /dʒel/ v [I] **1** (also **gel**) to become a thicker, firmer substance **2** (of ideas and thoughts) to become clearer and more certain

jel·ly /'dʒeli/ n **jellies 1** [C;U] a soft sweet food made with fruit and eaten as part of a meal: jelly and ice cream **2** [U] a sweet food made with fruit and sugar and used for spreading on bread: apple jelly **3** [sing] any material that is between a liquid and a solid state: The juices had solidified into a jelly. **4** my legs felt like jelly = I felt very nervous

jel·ly·fish /'dʒelifɪʃ/ n jellyfishes or jellyfish a sea creature with a body that looks like jelly

jem·my /'dʒemi/ n jemmies (**jimmy** AmE) an iron bar used by thieves to break open locked doors and windows

jeop·ar·dize /'dʒepədaɪz ‖ -ər-/ v jeopardized, jeopardizing (also **jeopardise** BrE) [T] fml to put something in danger of being destroyed or harmed:

SPELLING NOTE
Words with the sound /dʒ/ may be spelt **g-**, like **general**.

If you are rude to the boss it may jeopardize your chances of success.

jeop·ar·dy /'dʒepədi ‖ -ər-/ n [U] fml in jeopardy in danger of being destroyed or harmed: He has put his whole future in jeopardy.

jerk[1] /dʒɜːk ‖ dʒɜːrk/ v **1** [T] to pull suddenly and quickly: She jerked the string of the puppet. | He jerked his head forward. **2** [I] to move with a sudden quick movement: The bus jerked to a stop.

jerk[2] n a short quick pull or movement: The bus stopped with a jerk. –**jerky** adj

jer·kin /'dʒɜːkɪn ‖ -ɜːr-/ n a short coat with no covering for your arms

jer·ry-built /'dʒeri bɪlt/ adj built quickly, cheaply, and badly (used of buildings)

jer·sey /'dʒɜːzi ‖ -ɜːr-/ n **1** [C] a piece of woollen clothing, usually worn over a shirt **2** [U] a fine, soft woollen cloth used for women's dresses

jest /dʒest/ n old fash **1** a joke **2** in jest in fun: He only said it in jest! –**jest** v [I]

jest·er /'dʒestər/ n a man kept in the past by a king or queen to amuse them and tell jokes

jet[1] /dʒet/ n **1** [C] a narrow stream of liquid, gas, or steam which comes forcefully out of a small hole: A jet of water shot up into the air. **2** [C] a hole in a machine through which gas or a flame comes: She put a match to the gas jet to light the gas. **3** [C] a powerful, modern aircraft: a jet fighter **4** [U] a hard black substance used for making jewellery

jet[2] v -tt- [I + adv/prep] infml to travel by aircraft: She jetted in from Hollywood last week. | jetting around the world

jet-black /ˌ· '·◂/ adj very dark shiny black

jet en·gine /ˌ· '··/ n an engine that pushes out a stream of hot air and gases behind it, and is used for making aircraft fly

jet-lag /'· ·/ n [U] a tired and confused feeling that you have after a long journey in an aircraft –**jet-lagged** adj

jet-pro·pelled /ˌ· ·'·◂/ adj made to fly or given power by a jet engine –**jet propulsion** n [U]

jet set /'· ·/ n the jet set a group of rich, successful, and fashionable people: a member of the international jet set

jet·ti·son /'dʒetɪsən, -zən/ v [T] fml **1** to decide not to use an idea, chance, or plan: The company decided to jettison the project. **2** to throw something away, especially from a moving vehicle: We had to jettison the cargo to make the ship lighter.

jet·ty /'dʒeti/ n jetties a wall built out into the sea or a river, used for getting on and off ships –see picture on page 735

Jew /dʒuː/ n a person whose religion is JUDAISM or who is descended from Jews –**Jewish** adj : the Jewish religion | My husband is Jewish.

jew·el /'dʒuːəl/ n **1** a precious stone that is worn or used to decorate ornaments: the Crown Jewels **2** a person or thing of great value: This painting is the jewel of my collection.

jew·elled /'dʒuːəld/ adj (**jeweled** AmE) decorated with jewels

jew·el·ler /'dʒuːələr/ n (**jeweler** AmE) **1** a person who buys, sells, and repairs watches and jewellery **2** jeweller's a shop selling watches and jewellery: I got my watch repaired at the jeweller's in the High Street.

jew·el·lery /'dʒuːəlri/ n (**jewelry** AmE) [U] things such as rings which people wear to make themselves look attractive: I've never worn a lot of *jewellery.* | *I keep brooches, necklaces, and rings in my jewellery box.*

jibe /dʒaɪb/ *n* (also **gibe**) a remark which makes someone else look foolish

jif·fy /'dʒɪfi/ *n infml* a **jiffy** a moment: *I'll be ready in a jiffy.* | *I won't be a jiffy.*

jig¹ /dʒɪg/ *n* a quick merry dance, popular in the past

jig² *v* **-gg-**
 jig about/around *phr v* [I] to dance or move up and down with quick short movements

jig·gle /'dʒɪgəl/ *v* **jiggled, jiggling** [T] *infml* to move something from side to side with short quick movements: *Jiggle the key in the lock – maybe the door will open.*

jig·saw /'dʒɪgsɔ:/ *n* (also **jigsaw puzzle** /'·· ‚··/) a game consisting of a wooden or cardboard picture cut up into many small irregular shaped pieces which you have to fit together again

jilt /dʒɪlt/ *v* [T] to refuse to see a lover any more or refuse to marry someone after you have promised to do so (a word used to express disapproval)

jim·my /'dʒɪmi/ *n* **jimmies** *AmE* – see JEMMY

jin·gle¹ /'dʒɪŋgəl/ *v* **jingled, jingling** 1 [T] to move something so that it makes a sound like metal striking gently against metal: *He jingled the money in his pocket.* 2 [I] to make a soft sound like small bells ringing: *We could hear their bracelets jingling.*

jingle² *n* 1 a soft ringing sound like the sound of small bells or keys being knocked together 2 a simple poem or song which is easy to remember and is used in a radio or TV advertisement

jinx /dʒɪŋks/ *n infml* a person or thing that brings bad luck: *There seems to be a jinx* **on** *our team.*

jinxed /dʒɪŋkst/ *adj infml* causing or bringing bad luck

jit·ters /'dʒɪtəz ‖ -ərz/ *n infml* **the jitters** feelings of great nervousness: *I always get the jitters before an exam.*

jit·ter·y /'dʒɪtəri/ *adj nervous: I get jittery waiting for the results.*

jive¹ /dʒaɪv/ *n* [sing] a fast dance done to popular music with a strong regular beat

jive² *v* **jived, jiving** [I] to dance a jive

job /dʒɒb ‖ dʒɑːb/ *n* 1 regular work you do to earn money: *He has a good job in a bank.* | *Many jobs will be lost if the factory closes down.* | *a part-time job* 2 a piece of work: *The plumber's done a really good job.* | *Here's a nice little job for you – washing up!* | *The nurses have now completed the job of weighing all the children.* 3 responsibility, duty, or purpose: *It's not my job to interfere.* | *It's the job of this computer to calculate prices.* 4 **do the job** *infml* to succeed in doing what is needed or wanted: *For peeling potatoes this knife does the job nicely.* 5 **a good job** an informal phrase you use when you want to say that it was a good thing that something happened: *She's lost a lot of weight – and a good job too!* 6 **have a job doing something** to find it difficult to do something: *I had a real job finding somewhere to park the car.* 7 **just the job** *infml* exactly the thing that is wanted or needed: *Thanks for that book; it was just the job.* 8 **give something up as a bad job** to decide that you will not be concerned with someone or something any more, because they cannot change or improve: *I'm afraid his teachers have just given him up as a bad job.* 9 **make a good job of something, make a bad job of something** to do something well or badly 10 **make the best of a bad job** to do as much or as well as possible in a difficult or unsatisfactory situation 11 **a nine-to-five job** a job with regular hours: *Like*

most actors, Pete would hate a nine-to-five job.* 12 **on the job** while working or at work: *Junior doctors are sometimes so tired they fall asleep on the job.* 13 **out of a job** unemployed

■ USAGE Compare **job**, **work**, **occupation**, **post**, **position**, **trade**, **profession**. Your **job** is what you do to earn a living. **Job** is a countable word. **Work** has the same meaning but is uncountable. **Occupation** has the same meaning but is more formal: *Please state your* **occupation** *on this form.* **Post** and **position** are formal words for a particular job: *the* **post/position** *of lecturer in English at Newcastle University* A **trade** is a skilled job in which you use your hands: *She's an electrician by* **trade**. A **profession** is a job such as that of a doctor or lawyer, for which you need special training and a long education.

job lot /'·· ‚·'·/ *n* a group of different things which are cheap, of poor quality, and bought or sold together

jock·ey /'dʒɒki ‖ 'dʒɑːki/ *n* a person who rides in horse races, especially as a job

joc·u·lar /'dʒɒkjʊlər ‖ 'dʒɑː-/ *adj fml* cheerful and amusing: *He was in a jocular mood.* | *a jocular remark* –**jocularly** *adv*

jodh·purs /'dʒɒdpəz ‖ 'dʒɑːdpərz/ *n* [pl] special trousers that you wear for horse riding

jog¹ /dʒɒg ‖ dʒɑːg/ *v* **-gg-** 1 [I] to run slowly, usually for exercise: *I go jogging in the park before breakfast.* | *She jogged off down the road.* –see picture on page 736 2 [T] to knock or push something slightly: *He jogged my elbow and spoiled what I was drawing.* 3 **jog someone's memory** to make someone remember something

jog² *n* 1 a slight shake, push, or knock 2 a slow steady run, usually done for exercise: *Let's go for a jog.*

jog·ging /'dʒɒgɪŋ ‖ 'dʒɑː-/ *n* [U] the activity of running slowly and steadily as a form of exercise: *Jogging's the in thing at the moment.*

joie de viv·re /‚ʒwɑː də 'viːvrə/ *n* [U] great enjoyment of life

join¹ /dʒɔɪn/ *v* 1 [T] to fix or connect two things to each other. *The plumber joined this pipe to a new one.* | *Join the two ends of the rope* **together**. | *The two villages are joined* **by** *a country path.* 2 [I;T] to come together or be united with someone or something else: *Won't you join us for a drink?* | *I'll be joining my family next week in Paris.* | *Where do the roads join?* 3 [I;T] to become a member of an organization or start work in an organization: *He joined the Labour Party.* | *I joined the company in 1986.* | *I went along to the club, but they wouldn't let me join.* 4 [T] to take part in an activity: *Come on in and join the fun!* 5 **join a queue** to take your place at the end of a line of people: *We joined the queue for tickets.* 6 **join hands** to hold each other's hands: *We all joined hands and danced around in a circle.*

 join in *phr v* [I;T **join in** sthg] to take part in an activity: *Sarah never joins in, but prefers to play on her own.* | *We all joined in the singing.*

 join up *phr v* 1 [I] *BrE* to become a member of the army, navy, or air force 2 [I;T **join** sthg ↔ **up**] to come together to form one group or thing: *Both classes are joining up for their history lessons.* | *He was trying to join up the pieces of a jigsaw puzzle.* | *I've been trying to join the bits up.*

join² *n* a place where two things are joined together: *It's so well made that you can't see the join.*

join·er /ˈdʒɔɪnəʳ/ n BrE a person who makes doors, window frames, and door frames

join·er·y /ˈdʒɔɪnəri/ n [U] BrE the trade and work of a joiner

joint¹ /dʒɔɪnt/ n 1 a part of your body where two bones meet, for example at your knee: My hip joints feel very stiff. 2 the place where two things are fixed together: The pipe was leaking at one of the joints. 3 BrE a large piece of meat for cooking, usually with a bone in it: a roast Sunday joint 4 infml a public place like a club or bar where people go for fun 5 infml a cigarette containing the drug CANNABIS

joint² adj [only before a noun] shared by or belonging to two or more people: to take joint action | We are joint owners. | It was a joint effort. –**jointly** adv: The project will be financed jointly by the government and the company.

joint³ v [T] to separate meat into fairly large pieces for cooking

joint·ed /ˈdʒɔɪntɪd/ adj having joints which can move: a jointed doll

joist /dʒɔɪst/ n a beam of wood or metal which supports the floor or roof of a building

joke¹ /dʒəʊk/ n 1 something such as a funny story which you tell people to make them laugh: Have you heard the joke about the doctor and the taxi-driver? | He made a joke about politicians. | They chatted and cracked jokes until late that night. 2 a joke someone or something which you cannot respect or take seriously: The exam was a complete joke – far too easy! 3 beyond a joke serious and worrying: The noise made by our neighbour is really getting beyond a joke now. 4 the joke's on him = he looks foolish, instead of the person he tried to play a joke on 5 make a joke of something to be funny or amusing about something serious 6 no joke infml very difficult or serious: Looking after four children is no joke! 7 play a joke to do something funny, such as an amusing trick, to make people laugh: He played a joke on us by pretending to lose the tickets. 8 take a joke to be amused by a joke against yourself: Can't you take a joke?

joke² v **joked, joking** [I] 1 to tell an amusing story or make a funny remark: You mustn't joke with him about religion. 2 to tell someone something which you do not mean seriously: She smiled when she realized I was only joking. 3 you must be joking, you're joking infml a phrase you use when you don't believe something: "Sue passed the exam!" "You must be joking – she didn't do any work for it." –**jokingly** adv: I'm sure his remarks were meant jokingly.

jok·er /ˈdʒəʊkəʳ/ n 1 a person who likes to make jokes 2 an additional playing card, which may have any value in certain games

jol·lit·y /ˈdʒɒlɪti || ˈdʒɑː-/ n [U] fml cheerfulness

jol·ly¹ /ˈdʒɒli || ˈdʒɑːli/ adj **jollier, jolliest** happy and cheerful: She's a very jolly person. | a jolly laugh

jolly² adv old fash, infml 1 very: You were jolly lucky! 2 jolly well really: No, I jolly well won't apologize!

jolly³ v **jollied, jollying**
  jolly sbdy **along** phr v [T] to encourage someone in a friendly or joking way

jolt /dʒəʊlt/ v 1 [I;T] to make something shake or move suddenly: The cart jolted along over the rough road. 2 [T] to give someone a shock: Her angry words jolted him out of the belief that she loved him. –**jolt** n

jos·tle /ˈdʒɒsəl || ˈdʒɑː-/ v [I;T] 1 to knock or push against another person: The players were jostled by an angry crowd as they left the field. | Don't jostle! 2 to compete for attention or money: film stars jostling for fame and fortune

jot¹ /dʒɒt || dʒɑːt/ n **not a jot** not at all or none at all: not a jot of truth in it

jot² v -tt- [T] to write something down quickly and without thinking about it very carefully: He jotted her address down in his newspaper.

jot·ter /ˈdʒɒtəʳ || ˈdʒɑː-/ n a number of pieces of paper joined together, used for writing notes on

jour·nal /ˈdʒɜːnl || -ɜːr-/ n 1 a serious newspaper or magazine connected with a particular subject or profession: She's reading the British Medical Journal. | a trade journal 2 lit a daily record of events or your activities

jour·nal·is·m /ˈdʒɜːnəl-ɪzəm || -ɜːr-/ n [U] the job of collecting information and writing things for newspapers and magazines, radio, and television

jour·nal·ist /ˈdʒɜːnəl-ɪst || -ɜːr-/ n a person whose profession is journalism –**journalistic** adj

jour·ney¹ /ˈdʒɜːni || -ɜːr-/ n 1 a trip from one place to another, usually by land: He made the long journey to Scotland by train. | a car journey | a three-day journey | They're going on a journey. –see TRAVEL (USAGE) 2 **break a journey** to interrupt a journey for a short time: We decided to break our journey in London, and spend the night there.

journey² v **journeyed, journeying** [I+ adv/prep] lit to travel somewhere: She's journeyed all over the world. | journeying south

joust /dʒaʊst/ v [I] to fight on horseback with long spears, especially as a sport; men used to joust in the Middle Ages

jo·vi·al /ˈdʒəʊviəl/ adj cheerful and friendly: a jovial old man | a jovial greeting –**joviality** /ˌdʒəʊviˈælɪti/ n [U]

jowl /dʒaʊl/ n the lower part of the side of your face, especially the skin covering your lower jaw

joy /dʒɔɪ/ n 1 [U] a feeling of great happiness: He was filled with joy. | To our joy, she won first prize. 2 [C] a person or thing that makes you feel happy or gives you pleasure: That dancer's a joy to watch. | the joy of skiing

joy·ful /ˈdʒɔɪfəl/ adj extremely happy: It was a joyful occasion. –**joyfully** adv –**joyfulness** n [U]

joy·less /ˈdʒɔɪləs/ adj unhappy and without pleasure

joy·ous /ˈdʒɔɪəs/ adj lit extremely happy –**joyously** adv

joy·ride /ˈdʒɔɪraɪd/ n infml a ride taken for fun in a stolen vehicle

joy·stick /ˈdʒɔɪˌstɪk/ n an upright handle moved to control the operation of something such as an aircraft or a computer game

JP /ˌdʒeɪ ˈpiː/ n a person who gives judgments in a local court of law in Britain; an abbreviation for JUSTICE OF THE PEACE

jub·i·lant /ˈdʒuːbɪlənt/ adj very happy because you have been successful: crowds of jubilant football supporters –**jubilation** /ˌdʒuːbɪˈleɪʃən/ [U]

ju·bi·lee /ˈdʒuːbɪliː, ˌdʒuːbɪˈliː/ n a period of great rejoicing to remember an important event, usually after 25 or 50 years: the Club's silver jubilee party

---

SPELLING NOTE
Words with the sound /dʒ/ may be spelt **g-**, like **general.**

Ju·da·is·m /ˈdʒuːdeɪ-ɪzəm, ˈdʒuːdə- ‖ ˈdʒuːdə-, ˈdʒuːdiː-/ n [U] the religion and civilization of the JEWS, which is based on the OLD TESTAMENT of the Bible and JEWISH books of law

jud·der /ˈdʒʌdər/ v [I] BrE (of a machine or a vehicle) to shake violently

judge[1] /dʒʌdʒ/ v judged, judging 1 [I;T] to decide who or what is the winner in a competition: She had been asked to judge an essay-writing competition. 2 [T; + that] to form or give an opinion about someone or something after careful thought: The directors judged that the project was too expensive. | Schools tend to be judged by their exam results. | Try to judge the distance from here to the car. | It's difficult to judge who is responsible for the accident. 3 [T] to form an opinion of someone after thinking about their behaviour and character: I could never relax with her, because I felt she was always judging me. | The new model was judged a failure. | We judged it better to cancel the match. 4 [T] to make decisions in a law court: Who will judge the next case? 5 judging by, judging from a phrase used when you are giving a reason for saying or thinking something: Judging by the look on his face, I'd say he passed!

judge[2] n 1 a public official who has the power to decide questions brought before a court of law: a high court judge | Judge Anderson 2 a person who is appointed to make a decision in a competition: The panel of judges included several well-known writers. 3 a person who has the knowledge and experience to give an opinion about the value of something: She's a good judge of wine. | a poor judge of character

judg·ment /ˈdʒʌdʒmənt/ n (also judgement) 1 [C] an official decision given by a judge or a court of law: The judgment was given yesterday. 2 [C] an opinion formed after careful thought: In my judgment, the plan is unlikely to succeed. 3 [U] the ability to make sensible, wise decisions: a man of sound judgment | Her decision shows a lack of political judgment. 4 pass judgment: a to give a decision in a court of law b to form an opinion of someone or something, often a bad one

Judgment Day /ˈ··· ·/ n (also Judgement Day) the day when Christians believe God will judge everybody

ju·di·cial /dʒuːˈdɪʃəl/ adj belonging to or concerned with a court of law, a judge, or a judge's decisions

ju·di·cia·ry /dʒuːˈdɪʃəri ‖ -ʃieri, -ʃəri/ n [+ sing/pl verb] fml the judiciary all the judges in a court of law considered as one group, and forming a branch of government

ju·di·cious /dʒuːˈdɪʃəs/ adj having or showing good judgment or good sense –judiciously adv

ju·do /ˈdʒuːdəʊ/ n [U] a type of self-defence, often practised as a sport, in which you try to throw your opponent to the ground: He's got a black belt in judo.

jug /dʒʌg/ BrE n a container for liquids with a handle and a lip for pouring –see picture on page 148

jug·ger·naut /ˈdʒʌgənɔːt ‖ -ər-/ n BrE a very large LORRY

jug·gle /ˈdʒʌgəl/ v juggled, juggling 1 [I;T] to keep several objects in the air at the same time by throwing them up quickly and catching them again: He can juggle with plates. | Can you juggle? 2 [T] to change numbers or ideas cleverly: I'm just juggling the figures to see if we can afford to buy the house.

jug·gler /ˈdʒʌglər/ n someone who juggles to entertain people

juice /dʒuːs/ n [C;U] 1 the liquid part of fruit or vegetable, often made into a drink: orange juice 2 the liquid in your stomach, that helps you to DIGEST food 3 the liquid from meat that is cooking: Spoon the juices over the meat.

juic·y /ˈdʒuːsi/ adj juicier, juiciest 1 having a lot of juice: a juicy orange 2 interesting, especially because of providing information about bad or improper behaviour: I want all the juicy details. 3 infml desirable: a fat juicy contract to end all our problems

juke·box /ˈdʒuːkbɒks ‖ -bɑːks/ n jukeboxes a music machine, often found in bars, which plays records when you put a coin into it

Ju·ly /dʒʊˈlaɪ/ n (also Jul.) the 7th month of the year

jum·ble /ˈdʒʌmbəl/ (also jumble sth ↔ up) v jumbled, jumbling [T] to mix things in a disordered way: My thoughts were all jumbled up. | The clothes lay jumbled on the floor. –jumble n [sing]: a chaotic jumble of toys and books

jumble sale /ˈ·· ·/ BrE n a sale of used things to collect money for a good purpose: The Brownies are holding a jumble sale for the orphans.

jum·bo[1] /ˈdʒʌmbəʊ/ adj (also jumbo-sized /ˈ··· ·/) [only before a noun] extremely large (a word often used in advertisements): a jumbo pack of washing powder

jumbo[2] n (also jumbo jet /ˈ·· ·/) a very large passenger aircraft

jump[1] /dʒʌmp/ v 1 [I] to push yourself into the air by using the strength of your legs and feet: The children were jumping up and down. | She jumped out of the window. | He jumped over the fence. –see picture on page 736 2 jump up, jump to your feet to stand up quickly and suddenly: I jumped up and ran to the door. 3 [T] to cross something by jumping over it: He jumped the stream. | None of the horses managed to jump the fence. 4 [I] to make a quick sudden movement because something has frightened you or surprised you: The noise made me jump. | Oh, you frightened me! I nearly jumped out of my skin! 5 [I] to increase suddenly and by a large amount: The price of oil jumped sharply in 1973. 6 jump on the bandwagon to do or say something just because most people are doing it or saying it 7 jump to a conclusion to decide that something is true before you have all the information you need. Wait a minute! Don't start jumping to conclusions. 8 jump the gun to do something before it is the proper time 9 jump a queue to move to the front of a line of people who are all waiting for something (a phrase used to express disapproval): I'm really fed up with people jumping the queue.

jump at sth phr v [T] to accept something eagerly: I'd jump at the chance of going abroad.

jump on sbdy phr v [T] to speak sharply to someone, often unfairly: She jumps on me every time I make the slightest mistake.

jump[2] n 1 an act of jumping: a parachute jump 2 a sudden large increase in amount: a huge jump in population. 3 a thing to be jumped over: The horse cleared all the jumps. 4 be/stay one jump ahead infml to manage to have an advantage over your competitors by knowing what they are doing

jump·er /ˈdʒʌmpər/ n 1 BrE a piece of woollen clothing for the upper half of your body, which you put on by pulling it over your head –see picture on page 50 2 AmE a dress that does not cover your arms and is usually worn over a shirt or woollen garment

jump·y /ˈdʒʌmpi/ adj jumpier, jumpiest infml nervous: I was very jumpy about flying.

junc·tion /ˈdʒʌŋkʃən/ n a place where roads or railway lines join

junc·ture /ˈdʒʌŋktʃəʳ/ n fml **at this juncture** at this important moment

June /dʒuːn/ n (also **Jun.**) the 6th month of the year

jun·gle /ˈdʒʌŋgəl/ n **1** [C,U] a thick tropical forest: *the jungles of South America* **2** [C] a difficult situation in which you have to struggle very hard: *This city is a real jungle.* | *the jungle of tax laws*

ju·ni·or¹ /ˈdʒuːniəʳ/ adj **1** of lower rank or position: *a junior officer* | *a junior minister* | *He's still very junior within the company.* **2** [never before a noun] younger than somebody else: *She is junior to me.* | *Bill is three years my junior.*

junior² n **1** [C] someone who has a low rank or position: *the office junior* **2** [only after a name] the younger one of two men in the same family who have exactly the same name: *John B. Heathcote Junior*

junk /dʒʌŋk/ n **1** [U] infml old useless things: *This is just a load of old junk.* **2** [C] a flat-bottomed Chinese sailing ship

junk food /ˈ· ·/ n [C;U] bad quality food which is not good for you, especially because it contains a lot of chemicals

junk·ie /ˈdʒʌŋki/ n infml (also **junky**) a person who takes drugs and is dependent on them, especially HEROIN

jun·ta /ˈdʒʌntə, ˈhʊntə/ n a military government that has come to power by force, not through elections

Ju·pi·ter /ˈdʒuːpɪtəʳ/ n the largest PLANET of the group that includes the Earth

jur·is·dic·tion /ˌdʒʊərɪsˈdɪkʃən/ n [U] the right of an official person or court of law to carry out the law or make decisions about it: *This matter is outside the jurisdiction of the health department.*

ju·ris·pru·dence /ˌdʒʊərɪsˈpruːdəns/ n [U] fml the science or study of the law

ju·rist /ˈdʒʊərɪst/ n fml a person with a thorough knowledge of law

ju·ror /ˈdʒʊərəʳ/ n a member of a jury

ju·ry /ˈdʒʊəri/ n **juries** [+ sing/pl verb] **1** a group of people chosen to hear all the details of a case in a court of law and give their decision on it: *The jury found him guilty of murder.* **2** a group of people chosen to decide the winners in a competition: *And the jury has voted number two a hit!*

just¹ /dʒʌst/ adj fair and morally right: *This is a just punishment.* | *a just war*

just² /dʒəst; strong dʒʌst/ adv **1** exactly at a particular time or place: *He was sitting just here.* | *He arrived just as I was leaving.* | *I was just about to phone you.* **2** exactly: *Thank you-it's just what I wanted.* **3** not by a very great amount: *They've been away for just over two weeks.* | *The skirt came to just below her knees.* **4** (also **only just**) not very easily: *I could just see her in the distance.* | *I can only just lift it.* **5** very recently: *We've just moved in.* | *I've just spoken to him on the telephone.* **6** only: *I don't want anything to eat. Just a coffee, please.* | *He just stood there laughing at us.* **7** used to make a command stronger: *Just do as you are told!* | *Just imagine what it would be like.* **8** **just about** almost: *The*

house is just about ready. **9** **just now: a** at this moment: *We're having dinner just now-can I phone you back later?* **b** a moment ago: *I was talking to her just now so she can't be far away.* **10** **just the same** in spite of that: *I know she's probably fast asleep, but I think I'll pop up and make sure just the same.*

■ USAGE British people usually use **just, already** and **yet** with the present perfect tense: *The bell has just rung.* | *I've already seen him.* | *Have you eaten yet?* Americans often use the simple past tense in informal speech and this is becoming more common in British English also: *The bell just rang.* | *I already saw him.* | *Did you eat yet?* But many people still consider this form incorrect.

jus·tice /ˈdʒʌstɪs/ n **1** [U] treatment of other people which is fair and morally right: *the struggle for justice* | *a strong sense of justice* **2** [U] the system in a country which makes laws and punishes people who break them: *a court of justice* **3** [C] AmE a judge in a law court **4** **bring someone to justice** to catch a criminal and bring them before a court **5** **do justice to someone or something** to treat someone or something in a fair and proper way: *She's a boring teacher, but to do her justice, fairly thorough.* **6** **do yourself justice** to behave in a way which is worthy of your qualities or abilities: *She was so nervous that she really didn't do herself justice in the exam.*

Justice of the Peace /ˌ· ·· · ˈ·/ n fml (also **JP**) a person who gives judgments in a local court of law in Britain

jus·ti·fi·a·ble /ˈdʒʌstɪfaɪəbəl/ adj reasonable, and able to be justified –opposite **unjustifiable** –**justifiably** adv: *He was justifiably angry.*

jus·ti·fied /ˈdʒʌstɪfaɪd/ adj **1** having a good and acceptable reason for doing something: *I don't think you were justified in being so angry with him.* **2** reasonable and acceptable: *I don't think that military intervention is justified.*

jus·ti·fy /ˈdʒʌstɪfaɪ/ v **justified, justifying** [T] to show or give a good reason for something: *How can you justify your rude behaviour?* | *We can't justify spending any more money on this project.* □ USEFUL PATTERNS to justify something; to justify doing something –**justification** /ˌdʒʌstɪfɪˈkeɪʃən/ [U]

jute /dʒuːt/ n [U] a substance from a plant used for making rope and rough cloth

jut /dʒʌt/ v **-tt-** **jut out** phr v [I] to stick out or up further than other things around it: *The wall juts out here to allow room for the chimney.*

ju·ve·nile¹ /ˈdʒuːvənaɪl ‖ -nəl, -naɪl/ adj **1** concerned with young people who are not yet adults: *a juvenile court* **2** childish or foolish: *a juvenile sense of humour*

juvenile² n fml or tech **1** a young person **2** **juvenile delinquent** a young person who has been found guilty of a crime: *Juvenile delinquents vandalized the children's playground.*

jux·ta·pose /ˌdʒʌkstəˈpəʊz ‖ ˈdʒʌkstəpəʊz/ v **juxtaposed, juxtaposing** [T] fml to put two things close together, often to show how different they are –**juxtaposition** n /ˌdʒʌkstəpəˈzɪʃən/ [U]

SPELLING NOTE
Words with the sound /dʒ/ may be spelt **g-**, like **general.**

K, k

K, k /keɪ/ **K's, k's** or **Ks, ks** the 11th letter of the English alphabet

kaf·tan /ˈkæftæn ‖ kæfˈtæn/ n a long, loose piece of clothing with long sleeves

ka·lei·do·scope /kəˈlaɪdəskəʊp/ n **1** a tube fitted at one end with mirrors and pieces of coloured glass which shows many coloured patterns when you turn it **2** a pattern of changing colours continuously: *The sky became a kaleidoscope of colours.*

kan·ga·roo /ˌkæŋgəˈruː◂/ n an Australian animal which jumps along on its large back legs and carries its young in a special pocket

kar·at /ˈkærət/ n see CARAT

ka·ra·te /kəˈrɑːti/ n [U] an Asian sport in which people fight using their hands and feet as weapons

K.C. /ˌkeɪ ˈsiː/ a British lawyer of high rank; an abbreviation for KING'S COUNSEL –compare Q.C.

ke·bab /kɪˈbæb ‖ kɪˈbɑːb/ n small pieces of meat cooked on a stick

keel¹ /kiːl/ n **1** a bar along the bottom of a ship from which the whole frame of the boat is built up **2** a piece going down into the water from the bottom of a ship to keep it upright **3 keep on an even keel** to keep going steadily without any sudden changes

keel² v
keel over v [I] to fall over sideways: *The ship keeled over in the storm.*

keen /kiːn/ adj **1** having a strong and active interest in something: *She was very keen to talk to him.* | *I'm not very keen on football.* | *She's a very keen gardener.*
□ USEFUL PATTERNS be keen on something, be keen to do something
2 strong and deep (used of feelings): *a keen sense of failure* | *a keen desire* **3** clever and quick at understanding: *a keen mind* | *a keen sense of humour* **4** very sensitive (used of the senses): *a keen sense of smell* **5** very hard (used of competitions): *a keen contest* | *There has been keen competition for the job.*
–**keenly** adv –**keenness** n [U]

keep¹ /kiːp/ v **kept** /kept/, **kept, keeping 1** [T] to continue to have something and not need to return it to anyone else: *You can keep it; I don't need it any more.* | *He gave me £5 and told me to keep the change.* | *There's no point in keeping all those old clothes.* **2** [T] to have something in a particular place: *Where do you keep the coffee?* | *I always keep a spare key in my bag.* **3** [T] to look after something for a short time: *Could you keep this for me until I get back?* **4** [+complement] to remain: *It's difficult to keep warm in this cold weather.* | *Keep still for a minute while I take a photo.* **5** [T] to make someone or something remain in a place or state: *They kept her in hospital for three weeks.* | *The noise kept me awake.* | *She put on her sunglasses to keep the sun out of her eyes.* **6** [T] to make regular written records of things: *Keep an account of what you spend.* | *I've kept a diary for years.* **7** [T] to provide food, clothes, and other

necessary things for someone: *What he earns isn't enough to keep him and his family.* **8** [T] to have animals and look after them, often for food: *I'd love to keep chickens.* **9** [I] (of food) to remain fresh and fit to eat: *Milk only keeps for a few days.* **10** [T] to delay someone: *What kept you?* | *I know you're busy so I won't keep you for long.* **11** [T] to fulfil a promise or an agreement: *I always keep my promises.* | *He failed to keep his appointment.* **12 keep doing something** to continue doing something: *Don't keep interrupting me!* | *Just keep walking in the same direction and you'll get to the village.* **13 keep someone from doing something** to prevent someone from doing something: *She tried to keep me from seeing the letter.* **14 keep something from someone** to fail to tell someone something: *She knew his name but she kept it from me.* | *Details of the plan were kept from the public.* **15 keep a secret** to not tell people a secret: *Can you keep a secret?* **16 keep someone company** to remain with someone so that they are not alone: *I stayed with her in the afternoon to keep her company.* **17 keep your head** to remain calm

keep at sthg phr v [T] to continue doing something: *I found the work difficult but I kept at it and passed the exam.*

keep sthg ↔ **back** phr v [T] to fail to give someone a piece of information: *She told us what happened, but I'm sure she's keeping something back.*

keep down phr v **1** [T **keep** sthg ↔ **down**] to prevent something from increasing: *The government is determined to keep down inflation.* **2** [T **keep** sbdy ↔ **down**] to keep people in a state where they are not free

keep off phr v **1** [I] to remain off or away from a place: *Notices warned us to keep off the grass.* **2** [T **keep** sthg ↔ **off** (sthg)] to prevent someone or something from going onto something: *I put my umbrella up to keep the rain off.*

keep on phr v **1 keep on doing something** to continue doing something: *Prices keep on increasing.* | *She keeps on asking me what the time is!* **2** [T **keep** sthg ↔ **on**] to continue to have a house or flat: *I think I'll keep the flat on during the summer.*

keep on about sthg phr v [T] to keep talking about something: *He kept on about the good old days when he was in the army.*

keep on at sbdy phr v [T] to keep complaining to someone

keep out phr v **1** [I] to remain outside a place: *Notices on the fence warned us to keep out.* **2** [T **keep** sbdy/sthg ↔ **out**] to cause someone or something to remain outside a place: *They had put up barriers to keep people out.*

keep to phr v **1** [T **keep to** sthg] to stay in a place or position: *Traffic must keep to the left.* | *He kept to the footpaths.* **2** [T **keep to** sthg] to limit yourself to something: *Please keep to the subject.* | *You must keep to your budget.* **3 keep something to yourself** to not tell other people about something: *He kept the news to himself.* **4 keep yourself to yourself** to spend a lot of time by yourself, and not talk to other people very much

keep up phr v **1** [T **keep** sthg ↔ **up**] to cause something to remain high: *She kept her spirits up by singing.* **2** [T **keep** sbdy **up**] to cause someone to remain awake and out of bed: *I hope I'm not keeping you up.* **3** [**keep** sthg ↔ **up**] to continue to do something: *She started screaming with rage, but I knew she wouldn't keep it up for long.* **4** [I] to remain level with someone: *I ran as fast as I could, but I couldn't keep up* **with** *the others.* **5 keep up with something** to know about things that are happening: *I like to try and keep up with what's happening in the world.* **6 keep up with the Joneses** to compete with your neighbours socially, for example by trying to have a nicer house or a better car

keep² *n* **1** [U] the cost of necessary things such as food and lodgings: *He gave them £50 a week to pay for his keep.* **2** [C] a main tower in a castle

keep·er /'ki:pəʳ/ *n* **1** a person who looks after the animals in a zoo **2** a person who is responsible for the objects in a MUSEUM

keep·ing /'ki:pɪŋ/ *n* **1 in someone's keeping** in someone's care or charge: *The money will remain in my keeping.* **2 in keeping with something** suitable for something: *a silly joke not quite in keeping with the occasion* [RELATED PHRASE **out of keeping with something**]

keep·sake /'ki:pseɪk/ *n* a small present that someone gives you so that you will remember them

keg /keg/ *n* a small barrel

ken·nel /'kenl/ *n* **1** a small hut for a dog to sleep in **2 kennels** [pl] a place where dogs are bred or where they are cared for when their owners are away

kept /kept/ the past tense and past participle of KEEP

kerb /kɜ:b ‖ kɜ:rb/ *n* (**curb** *AmE*) a line of raised stones separating the footpath from the road – see picture on page 441

ker·nel /'kɜ:nl ‖ 'kɜ:r-/ *n* **1** the part of a nut, fruit stone, or seed inside its shell **2** the most important part of something: *The kernel of his argument is that we need more teachers.*

ker·o·sene /'kerəsi:n/ *n* (also **kerosine**) [U] the usual American word for PARAFFIN(1)

kes·trel /'kestrəl/ *n* a type of bird that kills and eats animals

ketch·up /'ketʃəp/ *n* [U] a thick liquid made from tomatoes (TOMATO), used for giving a pleasant taste to food

ket·tle /'ketl/ *n* a covered container for boiling water in; it has a handle and a narrow mouth for pouring – see picture on page 148

ket·tle·drum /'ketldrʌm/ *n* a large drum with a curved bottom

key¹ /ki:/ *n* **1** a specially shaped piece of metal that you put in a lock to open or close something, to wind a clock, or stop or start an engine: *I've lost the car keys.* | *the key to the cupboard* **2 keys** the buttons on a computer or TYPEWRITER which you press when you use it **3 keys** the narrow black and white bars on a musical instrument which you press to make a particular sound: *the keys of an organ* **4** a list of the answers to problems or exercises: *the key to the grammar exercises* **5** the explanation for, or way to get, a particular result: *Her unhappy childhood is the key to her character.* | *Diet is the key to good health.* **6** a set of musical notes based on a particular note: *a song in the key of C*

key² *v*

key sthg ↔ **in** *phr v* [T] to put information into a computer by pressing the keys

SPELLING NOTE
Words with the sound / k /, may be spelt **c-**, like **cool**, or **qu-**, like **queen**.

key³ *adj* [only before a noun] very important or necessary: *a key witness*

key·board¹ /'ki:bɔ:d ‖ -bɔ:rd/ *n* **1** the set of keys on a machine such as a computer which you press when you use it: *a typewriter keyboard* – see picture on page 539 **2** a row of keys on a musical instrument: *the keyboard of a piano*

keyboard² *v* [I;T] to make a piece of writing ready to print or to put information into a computer by operating a keyboard: *Applicants for this post should have good keyboarding skills.* – **keyboarder** *n*

keyed up /ˌki:d 'ʌp/ *adj infml* excited or nervous: *We're all very keyed up about the examination.*

key·hole /'ki:həʊl/ *n* a hole in a lock, where you put a key

key·note /'ki:nəʊt/ *n* **1** the particular note on which a musical KEY is based **2** the central or most important idea in something: *The keynote of their election campaign has been educational reforms.*

key ring /'· ·/ *n* a ring on which keys are kept

kg a written abbreviation for KILOGRAM(S)

kha·ki /'ka:ki ‖ 'kæki/ *n* [U] **1** a yellow-brown colour – see picture on page 147 **2** strong cloth of this colour, often worn by soldiers – **khaki** *adj*

kib·butz /kɪ'bʊts/ *n* **kibbutzim** /-sɪm/ *or* **kibbutzes** a farm or factory in Israel where many people live together and share their work and income

kick¹ /kɪk/ *v* **1** [T] to hit something forcefully with your foot: *She kicked the pile of books over.* | *Stop kicking the dog!* – see picture on page 736 **2** [I;T] to move your legs or feet strongly and forcefully: *The baby kicked happily.* | *He was lying in the water, kicking his legs.* **3** [T] to hit a ball or other object with your foot so that it moves: *He kicked the ball over the fence.* **4 kick a habit** *infml* to stop doing something which you used to do as a habit **5 I could kick myself, I kicked myself** a phrase used when you are cross with yourself for not doing something better or differently: *I could have kicked myself for making such a stupid mistake.*

kick about/around *phr v* [I] **be kicking about** to be somewhere in a place, although you do not know exactly where: *There are a couple of old buckets kicking about in the shed.*

kick off *phr v* **1** [I] to start a football match **2** [I;T **kick** sthg ↔ **off**] *infml* to start a conversation or a meeting

kick sbdy ↔ **out** *phr v* [T] to force someone to leave a place or a job

kick up *phr v* **kick up a fuss, kick up a row** *infml* to cause trouble about something, sometimes something unimportant: *If they don't empty the dustbin this week, I'm going to kick up a real fuss.*

kick² *n* **1** a strong, sometimes violent, movement of your leg or foot: *Give the door a kick to open it.* **2** *infml* a strong feeling of excitement or pleasure: *She drives fast just for kicks.* | *He gets a real kick out of skiing.*

kick·off /'kɪk-ɒf ‖ -ɔ:f/ *n* the kick which begins a game of football: *The kickoff is at three o'clock today.*

kid¹ /kɪd/ *n* **1** [C] *infml* a child or young person: *My kids are two and six.* | *college kids* | *It's immoral putting kids in uniform and sending them to fight a war.* – see CHILD (USAGE) **2 kid sister, kid brother** *AmE infml* a younger sister or brother **3** [C] a young goat **4** [U] leather made from the skin of a young goat

kid² *v* **-dd-** *infml* **1** [I;T] to pretend as a joke that something is true: *He's not really hurt. He's only* *kidding.* | *You can't kid me. I know you're not telling the truth.* **2** [T] to joke playfully with someone: *We kidded him about his new haircut.* **3 kid yourself** to deceive yourself: *He's been kidding himself that he'll win.* **4 you're kidding, you must be kidding** a phrase used when you don't believe something that someone is telling you

kid·nap /ˈkɪdnæp/ *v* -**pp**- (also -**p**- *AmE*) [T] to take someone away by force in order to demand money or something else for their safe return –**kidnapper** *n*

kid·ney /ˈkɪdni/ *n* **1** either of the pair of organs in your body which separate waste from your blood and produce URINE **2** an animal's kidney used as food

kidney ma·chine /ˈ··· ·,·/ *n* a machine that can do the work of diseased human kidneys

kill¹ /kɪl/ *v* **1** [I;T] to make a plant, an animal, or a person die: *These chemicals can kill.* | *First she killed her husband, then she killed herself.* | *Some of the plants were killed by the frost.* **2 be killing you** *infml* to be causing you great pain: *My feet are killing me!* **3 kill time** to make time pass by finding something unimportant to do: *I read a book to kill time.* **4 kill two birds with one stone** to get two good results from one action

■ USAGE Compare **kill**, **murder**, **slaughter**, **butcher**, **assassinate**, **massacre**. **Kill** is a general word meaning "to cause (anything) to die". **Murder** means "to kill a person on purpose": *He murdered his wife by putting poison in her food.* **Slaughter** means "to kill animals for food", but it can also describe the cruel, or unnecessary killing of humans: *Thousands of people were needlessly slaughtered in a senseless war.* **Butcher** is even stronger: *Our small army was butchered by the much larger enemy forces.* To **assassinate** means "to kill an important political figure": *an attempt to assassinate the president.* To **massacre** means "to kill large numbers of defenceless people": *The army entered the town and massacred all the women and children.*

kill sbdy/sthg ↔ **off** *phr v* [T] to kill or destroy people or things one at a time: *The trees were killed off by the severe winter.*

kill² *n* **1** [sing] the bird or animal killed in hunting: *They drag their kill to a safe place before eating it.* **2 the kill** the act or moment of killing a hunted bird or animal

kill·er /ˈkɪlər/ *n* a person, animal, or thing that kills: *This disease is a killer.* | *Police are still looking for the killer.* | *a killer shark*

kill·ing¹ /ˈkɪlɪŋ/ *n* **1** a murder: *a series of brutal killings* **2 make a killing** to make a large amount of money quickly and easily

killing² *adj infml* extremely tiring: *This work is really killing.*

kill·joy /ˈkɪldʒɔɪ/ *n infml* a person who intentionally spoils other people's enjoyment

kil·o·gram /ˈkɪləgræm/ *n* (also **kilogramme**) a unit for measuring weight, equal to 1,000 grams or 2.205 pounds

kil·o·me·tre /ˈkɪləˌmiːtə, kɪˈlɒmɪtə‖ kɪˈlɑːmɪtər/ *n* (kilometer *AmE*) a unit for measuring length, equal to 1,000 metres or 0.6214 miles

kiln /kɪln/ *n* a machine for baking pots or bricks or drying wood: *a brick kiln*

kil·o·watt /ˈkɪləwɒt‖ -wɑːt/ *n* 1,000 WATTS: *a three-kilowatt electric fire*

kilt /kɪlt/ *n* a short woollen skirt with many pressed folds, worn by women, or by men from Scotland as their national dress

ki·mo·no /kɪˈməʊnəʊ/ *n* a long loose Japanese garment

kin /kɪn/ *n* [pl] **1** members of your family (a word no longer used in modern English) **2 your next of kin** *fml* your closest relatives

kind¹ /kaɪnd/ *n* **1** [C] a group with its own character, different from other groups: *"She likes to read these big fat books about rich people in America – that kind of thing." "Oh, I don't like that kind of book." | different kinds of biscuits – plain ones, chocolate ones, nut ones, spicy ones... | "What kind of car has she got?" "Some sort of small hatchback, I think." | all kinds of people | People of that kind really annoy me. | I don't like this one much. Have you got any other kinds? | They are different in size, but not in kind.* **2 kind of: a** a phrase used when you are describing something not very exactly: *It's a kind of reddish-brown colour.* **b** a phrase used in very informal conversation which does not have any exact meaning: *She kind of hoped to be invited.* **3 in kind** with the same treatment: *He spoke to her very angrily, and she replied in kind.* **4 pay someone in kind** to pay someone using goods or services, not money **5 of a kind: a** *old fash* of the same sort: *They're all of a kind, politicans. It doesn't matter which party they belong to.* **b** of a sort which is not very good: *She gave us coffee of a kind.*

■ USAGE If you use **kind** or **sort** in the singular, they should be followed by a singular noun: *I don't like that* **kind/sort** *of book.* | *This* **kind/sort** *or question is never easy.* | *I've never understood that* **kind/sort** *of thing.* If you use the plural **kinds** or **sorts**, follow them with a noun in the plural: *We sell all* **kinds/sorts** *of shoes.* | *I meet many different* **kinds/sorts** *of people in my work.* Unless, of course, the noun is uncountable: *three* **kinds/sorts** *of cheese* | *new* **kinds/sorts** *of pollution* (You will sometimes hear sentences such as "I hate those kind/sort of questions", but this is considered incorrect.)

kind² *adj* **1** helpful, caring, and friendly towards other people: *a kind person* | *a kind voice* | *She's very kind to animals.* | *It was so kind of you to write to me.* **2 would you be so kind as to...?, would you be kind enough to...?** phrases used when you are asking someone politely to do something: *Would you be so kind as to help me with my suitcase?* –opposite **unkind**

kin·der·gar·ten /ˈkɪndəgɑːtn‖ -dərgɑːrtn/ *n* a school for children under five years old

kind-heart·ed /ˌ·ˈ··· ‖ ˌ·ˈ··/ *adj* caring and sympathetic: *a kind-hearted person* –**kind-heartedly** *adv*

kin·dle /ˈkɪndl/ *v* **kindled, kindling** [T] **1** to make something start to burn: *We managed to kindle a fire.* **2** to make someone begin to have a particular feeling: *The news kindled hopes that he might still be alive.*

kin·dling /ˈkɪndlɪŋ/ *n* [U] things such as dry wood, leaves, and grass which are used for lighting a fire

kind·ly¹ /ˈkaɪndli/ *adj* **kindlier, kindliest** having a gentle and caring nature: *She's the kindliest person I've ever met.* | *He gave me a kindly smile.* –**kindliness** *n* [U]

kind·ly² *adv* **1** in a kind manner: *She spoke kindly to him.* –opposite **unkindly** **2** a word you use to show you are cross when you want someone to do something: *Would you kindly put that book back?*

3 a word you use when you ask someone very politely to do something: *Would you kindly pass me my bag?* **4 not take kindly to something** to not like: *He didn't take kindly to what I said.*

■ USAGE 1 Remember that **kindly** is not always used in polite requests. On the contrary, it often expresses anger or annoyance: *Would you* **kindly** *remove your feet from that seat!* | **Kindly** *shut up at the back!* 2 If you want to make a request very polite, one way is to use the phrase **Could you possibly**…?: *Could you* **possibly** *give me a hand with this? | Could you* **possibly** *spare me a minute?*

kind·ness /ˈkaɪndnǝs/ *n* **1** [U] the quality of being kind: *kindness to animals* **2** [C] a kind action: *It would be a kindness to tell him the bad news immediately.* | *their many small kindnesses to us*

kin·dred[1] /ˈkɪndrɪd/ *n* [pl] your relatives or family (a word no longer used in modern English)

kindred[2] *adj* **kindred spirit** a person whose interests, taste, and views are similar to your own: *We soon realised that we were kindred spirits.*

ki·net·ic /kɪˈnetɪk, kaɪ-/ *adj tech* relating to movement

ki·net·ics /kɪˈnetɪks, kaɪ-/ *n* [U] the science that studies movement

king /kɪŋ/ *n* **1** (also **King**) the male ruler of a country who is not elected but is usually the son of a former ruler; King is also used as a title: *the King of Spain* | *King Edward* **2** the most important or famous male member of a group: *The lion is the king* **of** *the jungle.* | *Ladies and gentlemen – the king of comedy!* **3** one of the pieces in the game of CHESS **4** a playing card with a picture of a king on it: *the king of diamonds*

king·dom /ˈkɪŋdǝm/ *n* **1** a country governed by a king or queen **2** any of the three great divisions of the natural world: *the animal kingdom* | *the plant kingdom*

king·fish·er /ˈkɪŋˌfɪʃǝʳ/ *n* a small brightly-coloured bird that feeds on fish in rivers and lakes

king·ly /ˈkɪŋli/ *adj* belonging to or suitable for a king

king·pin /ˈkɪŋˌpɪn/ *n* the most important person in a group, upon whom the success of the group depends

King's Coun·sel /ˌ· ˈ··/ *n fml* see K.C.

kink /kɪŋk/ *n* a curve or twist in something such as wire that is usually straight **2** *infml* a strangeness of someone's mind or character, especially with regard to sex –**kinky** *adj*

kins·man /ˈkɪnzmǝn/ *n* **kinsmen** /-mǝn/ a relative; a female kinsman is called a **kinswoman** (a word no longer used in modern English)

ki·osk /ˈkiːɒsk ‖ -ɑːsk/ *n* **1** a small shop on the street with an open window through which you buy things such as newspapers and sweets **2** a public telephone box

kip /kɪp/ *v* **-pp-** *infml* [I] to sleep –**kip** *n* [sing;U]: *He's going to have a kip*

kip·per /ˈkɪpǝʳ/ *n* a salted and smoked fish

kiss[1] /kɪs/ *v* [I;T] to touch someone with your lips as a sign of love or fondness or as a greeting: *She kissed him lightly on the forehead.* | *They kissed under the stars.* | *He kissed the children goodnight.* | *The returning exiles kneeled and kissed the ground.*

SPELLING NOTE
Words with the sound / k /, may be spelt **c-**, like **cool**, or **qu-**, like **queen**.

---

kiss[2] *n* **1** a touch with your lips: *She gave him a kiss.* **2 kiss of life** a method of preventing the death of a person by breathing into their mouth

kissagram /ˈkɪsǝgræm/ *n* a person who is paid to visit someone on a special occasion and give them a kiss

kit[1] /kɪt/ *n* **1** [U] the special clothes and other articles needed by a soldier or sailor, or used in a particular sport: *I've forgotten my tennis kit.* | *There will be a kit inspection at 0800 hrs.* **2** [C] a set of articles or tools needed for a particular purpose and usually kept together: *my shaving kit* | *a make-up kit* | *a repair kit* **3** [C] a set of separate pieces sold ready to be put together: *a model aircraft kit*

kit[2] *v* **-tt-**
kit sbdy ↔ **out** *phr v* [T] to supply someone with everything that they need for a particular purpose: *She was well kitted out for the trip.*

kit bag /ˈ· ·/ *n* a long narrow bag used by soldiers and sailors for carrying their kit

kitch·en /ˈkɪtʃǝn/ *n* a room used for preparing and cooking food

kitch·en·ette /ˌkɪtʃɪˈnet/ *n* a very small kitchen, or a part of a room used for cooking

kitchen gar·den /ˌ·· ˈ··/ *n* a garden where fruit and vegetables are grown

kite /kaɪt/ *n* **1** a light frame, usually made of wood or metal and covered with paper, cloth, or plastic; you hold the kite by a long string and make it fly in the air **2** a large bird that eats small birds and animals

kith and kin /ˌkɪθ ǝn ˈkɪn/ *n old fash* [pl] **1** friends and relatives: *We may not agree with their politics, but we must remember that they are our kith and kin.* **2** people who share your country's way of life and values because of a shared past: *British people's kith and kin in New Zealand*

kit·ten /ˈkɪtn/ *n* a young cat

kit·ten·ish /ˈkɪtn-ɪʃ/ *adj* playful like a kitten

kit·ty /ˈkɪti/ *n* **kitties 1** an amount of money collected by all the players at the beginning of a card game, and taken by the winner **2** *infml* a sum of money collected by a group of people, and used for an agreed purpose **3** a child's word for a cat: *"Here, kitty kitty," called the little girl.*

kiwi fruit /ˈkiːwiː fruːt/ *n* **kiwi fruit** or **kiwi fruits** a fruit with brown skin and green flesh

klep·to·ma·ni·a /ˌkleptǝˈmeɪniǝ/ *n* [U] a disease of the mind that causes a strong and uncontrollable desire to steal –**kleptomaniac** /-niæk/ *n*

km a written abbreviation for KILOMETRE(s)

knack /næk/ *n infml* a special skill or clever way of doing something difficult: *He has the knack of making friends wherever he goes.*

knave /neɪv/ *n* **1** a dishonest man (a word no longer used in modern English) **2** the JACK in a game of cards –**knavish** *adj*

knead /niːd/ *v* [T] **1** to press something firmly and repeatedly with your hands to make a smooth paste: *Flour and water are kneaded to make bread.* **2** to press a muscle or other part of someone's body with your fingers to cure pain or stiffness

knee[1] /niː/ *n* **1** the middle joint of your leg, where it bends: *He had fallen and hurt his knee.* **2** the part of a garment that covers your knee: *He had big holes in the knees of his trousers.* **3 on your knee** on the top part of your legs when you are sitting down: *Come and sit on my knee.* **4 bring/force someone to their knees** to force someone to admit defeat **5 bring/force something to its knees** to nearly destroy something

knee² *v* **kneed, kneeing** [T] to hit someone or something with your knee

knee-cap /ˈniːkæp/ *n* the bone in front of your knee

knee-deep /ˌ· ˈ·◄/ *adj* [never before a noun] **1** deep enough to reach your knees: *The water is knee-deep.* **2 knee-deep in something: a** standing in something that comes up as far as your knees: *We were knee-deep in mud.* **b** very busy with something: *I'm knee-deep in work.*

kneel /niːl/ *v* **knelt** /nelt/, **knelt** [I] (also **kneel down**) to go down or remain on one or both of your knees: *She knelt down to pray.* | *He was kneeling by the fire.* –see picture on page 736

knell /nel/ *n lit* **1** the sound of a bell rung for a death or funeral **2** the sign that something has ended

knelt /nelt/ the past tense and past participle of KNEEL

knew /njuː ‖ nuː/ the past tense of KNOW

knick-ers /ˈnɪkəz ‖ -ərz/ *n BrE* [pl] a woman's undergarment worn below the waist –see picture on page 50

knick-knack /ˈnɪk næk/ *n infml* (also **nick-nack**) a small ornament for the house

knife¹ /naɪf/ *n* **knives** /naɪvz/ **1** a sharp blade fixed in a handle and used for cutting or as a weapon: *a table knife* | *sharpen the knife* **2 have/get one's knife in someone** *infml* to treat someone as an enemy and always try to harm them
■ USAGE Note the word order in this fixed phrase: **knife and fork**

knife² *v* **knifed, knifing** [T] to push a knife into someone so that they are hurt: *He had been attacked and knifed.*

knight¹ /naɪt/ *n* **1** a man of noble rank trained to fight on horseback during the Middle Ages **2** a man who has the title SIR given to him by the king or queen for his service to the country **3** a piece with a horse's head used in the game of CHESS

knight² *v* [T] to make someone a knight: *He was knighted by the Queen in 1981.*

knight-hood /ˈnaɪthʊd/ *n* [C;U] the rank or title of a knight

knit /nɪt/ *v* -tt- **1** [I;T] to make clothes by using wool or other threads and long needles or a special machine: *I'm knitting a pair of socks.* | *She knitted the baby a jumper.* | *He likes to watch TV and knit.* | *She does a lot of knitting.* **2** [I] (of broken bones) to grow together properly **3 knit your brows** to show that you are angry or worried by making lines appear on your forehead

knit-ting /ˈnɪtɪŋ/ *n* [U] something which is being knitted: *She keeps her knitting in a bag.*

knitting nee-dle /ˈ·· ˌ··/ *n* a long thin stick that you use when you are knitting

knit-wear /ˈnɪtweəʳ/ *n* [U] knitted clothing: *I'm afraid we don't sell knitwear.*

knives /naɪvz/ the plural of KNIFE

knob /nɒb ‖ nɑːb/ *n* **1** a round lump at the end of a stick **2** a round handle on a door or drawer **3** a round control button on a machine **4 a knob of butter** a small amount of butter

knob-bly /ˈnɒbli ‖ ˈnɑːbli/ *adj* **knobblier, knobbliest** having round hard lumps: *knobbly knees*

knock¹ /nɒk ‖ nɑːk/ *v* **1** [I] to make a noise by hitting something several times with your closed hand in order to attract attention: *I knocked at the door.* | *He knocked on the window.* **2** [T] to hit something hard or roughly, often so that it moves or falls: *She*

knocked the cup off the table. | *The doorway was so low that he knocked his head against it.* | *He knocked the nails into the wall.* **3** [T] to make someone fall in a particular position or become unconscious by hitting them hard: *He was knocked unconscious with a hammer.* | *His opponent knocked him flat on his back.* **4** [T] *infml* to say unfavourable things about someone or something: *Stop knocking him – he's a good singer really.* **5 knock something out of someone** to force someone to stop behaving in a particular way: *We'll soon knock that arrogance out of her!*

knock about/around *phr v infml* **1** [I] to get a lot of experience in different situations or places: *He's been knocking about in different countries for years.* **2** [I] to spend your free time with someone because they are your friend or lover: *Sally's been knocking about with Jim for years.* **3** [T knock sbdy **about**] to hit someone roughly: *She had been quite badly knocked about.*

knock sthg ↔ **back** *phr v infml* [T] to drink something quickly or in large quantities: *She knocked back ten glasses of wine.*

knock down *phr v* **1** [T knock sthg ↔ **down**] to intentionally destroy and remove a building: *Our house is being knocked down to make way for a new road.* **2** [T knock sbdy ↔ **down**] to hit someone with the vehicle you are driving so that they fall to the ground: *She was knocked down by a bus.* **3** [T knock sthg ↔ **down**] to reduce in price: *The price was knocked down to £3.* **4** [T knock sbdy ↔ **down**] to persuade someone to reduce a price: *I knocked him down to £3.*

knock off *phr v* **1** [I] *infml* to stop doing something, especially work: *Let's knock off early today.* **2** [T knock sthg ↔ **off**] to lower a price by a particular amount: *I'll knock $2 off.* **3** [T knock sthg ↔ **off**] *infml* to steal something

knock out *phr v* **1** [T knock sbdy ↔ **out**] to make someone go to sleep or become unconscious **2 be knocked out** *infml* to be very surprised or shocked by something **3** [T knock sbdy ↔ **out**] to defeat a person or team so that they do not continue in a competition: *Our team was knocked out in the first round.*

knock sbdy ↔ **over** *phr v* to hit someone with the vehicle you are driving so that they fall to the ground

knock sthg ↔ **up** *phr v infml* to make something in a hurry: *Can you knock up a meal for us now?*

knock² *n* **1** the sound made by hitting a surface with your closed hand in order to attract attention: *a knock at the door* **2** a rough blow: *Suddenly he felt a knock on the back of his head.* **3** a piece of bad luck or trouble: *He's taken a few knocks recently.*

knock-er /ˈnɒkəʳ ‖ ˈnɑː-/ *n* a piece of metal fixed to a door and used by visitors for knocking at the door

knock-kneed /ˌ· ˈ·◄/ *adj* having legs that turn inwards so that your knees touch when you are walking

knock-on ef-fect /ˌ· ·ˌ·/ *n* have a **knock-on effect** to cause something which causes something else, which causes something else, etc: *A rise in the price of petrol will have a knock-on effect right through the economy.*

knock-out /ˈnɒk-aʊt ‖ ˈnɑːk-/ *n* **1** a situation in a fighting match in which one fighter makes the other unconscious: *He won the fight by a knockout.* **2** *infml* someone or something that is very good or very attractive **3 knockout competition** a competition in which only the people or teams that win one match continue in the competition and play other matches

knoll /nəʊl/ n a small round hill

knot[1] /nɒt ‖ nɑːt/ n 1 a fastening formed by tying together the ends of pieces of string, rope, or wire: *She tied her belt with a knot.* 2 a small hard spot in wood where a branch joined a tree 3 a small group of people gathered close together 4 a measure of the speed of a ship, about 1,853 metres per hour 5 **a knot in your stomach** an uncomfortable feeling in your stomach caused by fear or anxiety

knot[2] v -tt- [T] to fasten something by tying its ends together: *Knot the ends of the rope together.* | *I knotted the rope round the branch.*

knot·ty /ˈnɒti ‖ ˈnɑːti/ adj **knottier, knottiest** full of difficulties: *a knotty problem*

know[1] /nəʊ/ v **knew** /njuː ‖ nuː/, **known** /nəʊn/ 1 [I; T + (that)] not in progressive forms] to have information in your mind which you are sure is true: *I know that Bill left yesterday.* | *They don't know your telephone number.* | *Do you know where she lives?* | *"He's very ill." "Yes, I know."* □ USEFUL PATTERNS to know something; to know that...; to know who, why, where, etc. 2 **know about something, know of something** to have heard about someone or something, although you do not have a lot of information: *Did you know about the meeting yesterday?* | *I know of only one factory which has closed down.* 3 **know something backwards** to know or understand something perfectly: *She knows her subject backwards.* 4 **know one thing from another** to understand the difference between two things: *She doesn't know her left from her right.* 5 [T] to have learnt and be able to use a language or skill: *Do you know any Spanish?* | *I don't know how to ski.* □ USEFUL PATTERNS to know something; to know how to do something 6 [T] to have learnt and understood about a subject from studying or personal experience: *The professor knows a lot about architecture.* | *She doesn't know anything about teaching – she's never taught.* 7 [T] to be familiar with a person or place: *He's known Jack for years.* | *Do you know London?* 8 [T] to be able to recognize someone or something: *She knows a good wine when she tastes it.* | *You'll know him by his pink jacket!* 9 [T] *fml* to experience something deeply and fully: *She has known both grief and happiness.* 10 **I know** a phrase used to show that you agree with what someone says: *"He's a most unpleasant person." "I know."* 11 **you know: a** a phrase used in informal conversation when you are explaining something: *She's an easy child, you know, never seems to get upset.* **b** an informal phrase used when you are trying to explain what you mean more clearly: *...the building on the left. You know, the black one.* 12 **you know something? do you know something? you know what? do you know what?** informal phrases used when you are going to tell someone something you have just understood; you expect that they will agree with you: *"Do you know something? We've got this upside down." "I thought it didn't seem right."* 13 **do you know what?** a phrase used in informal conversation when you want to get attention for a new idea or a surprising piece of information: *"Do you know what? Fred's bought a dog." "Has he! I thought he said he'd never buy another one."* 14 get

---

SPELLING NOTE

Words with the sound / k /, may be spelt **c-**, like **cool**, or **qu-**, like **queen**.

---

to know to become familiar with a person or a place: *I got to know Harry when we worked together.* | *The best way to get to know the city is to visit it on foot.* 15 **let someone know** to tell or inform someone about something: *Let me know when you're arriving.* 16 **know best** a phrase used about someone when you think they will make the right decision about something because of their experience: *Let the teachers decide – they know best.* 17 **know better** to be sensible or wise enough not to do something: *She's old enough to know better than to talk to strangers.* 18 **know your own mind** to have firm ideas about what you want or like 19 **you never know** a phrase used to say that it is not certain what is going to happen: *You never know, you might get the job.* 20 **there's no knowing** it is impossible to know: *There's no knowing what he'll do next.*

■ USAGE Compare **know** and **learn**. We use **know** especially when a person is conscious of something: *I know you're lying*, has skill in something: *I know how to drive*, or has met someone before: *I know your brother.* To **learn** means "to get to know something": *I was shocked to learn of his death.* | *I'm learning to drive.*

know[2] n **in the know** knowing about something that other people do not know about, especially something secret

know-all /ˈ· ·/ n a person who behaves as if he or she knows everything (a word used to express disapproval)

know-how /ˈ· ·/ n [U] *infml* special knowledge in a scientific or industrial field: *These countries rely on Western technology and know-how.*

know·ing /ˈnəʊɪŋ/ adj showing that you understand something secret about someone even though you do not express this directly: *a knowing smile*

know·ing·ly /ˈnəʊɪŋli/ adv 1 in a way that shows you understand about something even though you do not express this directly 2 intentionally: *She would never knowingly hurt anyone.* –opposite **unknowingly**

knowl·edge /ˈnɒlɪdʒ ‖ ˈnɑː-/ n [U] 1 information and understanding about something, gained through learning and experience: *She has a detailed knowledge of this period.* | *all branches of scientific knowledge* | *His knowledge of Russian is excellent.* 2 **to your knowledge** as far as you know: *To my knowledge, he now lives in Manchester.* 3 **without someone's knowledge** without informing someone about something: *He called a meeting without the Minister's knowledge.* [RELATED PHRASE **with someone's knowledge**]

knowl·edge·a·ble /ˈnɒlɪdʒəbəl ‖ ˈnɑː-/ adj well-informed and showing a good understanding of a subject: *He's very knowledgeable about plants.* –**knowledgeably** adv

known[1] /nəʊn/ adj 1 generally recognized as being something or having particular qualities: *He's a known criminal.* | *a plant known for it's healing properties* 2 **known as: a** popular or famous as: *She's known as a singer.* **b** called publicly: *Samuel Clemens, known as Mark Twain, became a famous American writer.* 3 **make it known** *fml* to tell people about something openly and publicly: *He made it known to his friends that he did not wish to enter politics.*

known[2] the past participle of KNOW

knuck·le[1] /ˈnʌkəl/ n a joint in your fingers, especially where they join the wide part of your hand

knuckle² *v* **knuckled, knuckling**
  knuckle down *phr v* [I] *infml* to start working hard:
  I think I'd better knuckle down to work now.
  knuckle under *phr v* [I] to be forced to accept that
  you have to do what someone powerful tells you
  to do

knuckle-dust·er /ˈ··ˌ··/ *n* a metal covering for your
knuckles, that people wear for fighting

ko·a·la /kəʊˈɑːlə/ *n* (also **koala bear** /·ˌ··ˈ·/) an Australian animal like a small bear

Ko·ran /kɔːˈrɑːn, kəˈrɑːn ‖ kəˈrɑːn/ *n* **the Koran** the
holy book of the Muslims

ko·sher /ˈkəʊʃəʳ/ *adj* prepared according to Jewish
law (used of food): *kosher meat*

kow·tow /ˌkaʊˈtaʊ/ *v* [I] *infml* to behave towards
someone in a way which is too humble and too
respectful

Krem·lin /ˈkremlɪn/ *n* [+ sing/pl verb] **the Kremlin**
the central government of the Soviet Union or the
group of buildings which are the central offices of
the government: *As yet there has been no response
from the Kremlin.*

ku·dos /ˈkjuːdɒs ‖ ˈkuːdɑɪs/ *n* [U] honour, praise, or
fame for doing something: *He got a great deal of
kudos for his work at the university.*

kung fu /ˌkʊŋ ˈfuː/ *n* [U] a Chinese style of fighting
using your hands and feet

kw a written abbreviation for KILOWATT(s)

L,l

L, l /el/ **L's, l's** or **Ls, ls** the 12th letter of the English alphabet

L a sign used on a car to show that the driver is a learner and has not passed the official driving test –see picture on page 49

l a written abbreviation for litre(s)

lab /læb/ *n infml* see LABORATORY

la·bel¹ /ˈleɪbəl/ *n* a piece of paper or cloth which is fixed to something and gives information about what it is

label² *v* **-ll- (-l-** *AmE*) [T] **1** to fix or tie a label on something: *The bottle was labelled "poisonous".* **2** to describe someone as belonging to a particular type or group: *He had been labelled a thief.* | *I don't want to be labelled* **as** *a fool.*

la·bor·a·tory /ləˈbɒrətri ‖ ˈlæbrətɔːri/ *n* **laboratories** (also **lab** *infml*) a building or room which contains scientific apparatus and in which a scientist works

la·bo·ri·ous /ləˈbɔːriəs/ *adj* needing great effort: *a laborious task* –**laboriously** *adv*

la·bour¹ /ˈleɪbəʳ/ *n* (**labor** *AmE*) **1** [C;U] hard work, especially tiring physical work: *The job involves a lot of manual labour.* **2** [U] the workers of an industry or country considered as a group or class: *unskilled labour* | *organized labour* **3** [C;U] the act of giving birth to a baby: *She was in labour for three hours.* | *a difficult labour* **4 labour of love** work that you do because you want to do it or enjoy doing it **5 Labour** [U + sing/pl verb] the British Labour Party: *Do you think Labour will win the next election?* | *Labour intend to renationalize electricity.*

labour² *v* (**labor** *AmE*) **1** [I] to work hard using your hands: *They saw peasants labouring in the fields.* **2** [I] to do something with great effort or difficulty: *She laboured up the hill with her bags.* | *Jack laboured over the report for hours.* –see WORK (USAGE) **3** [T] **labour the point** to talk about something in too great detail or at unnecessary length: *I understand – there's no need to labour the point!* **4 labour under a delusion/misapprehension** to believe something that is not true: *He laboured under the delusion that she loved him.*

la·bour·er /ˈleɪbərəʳ/ *n* (**laborer** *AmE*) a worker whose job needs physical strength rather than skill

Labour Par·ty /ˌ·· ˌ··/ *n* [+ sing/pl verb] **the Labour Party** the political party in Britain and some other countries which represents workers and the less wealthy: *The Labour Party is hoping to win the election.* | *I first joined the Labour Party ten years ago.*

labour-sav·ing /ˈ·· ˌ··/ *adj* saving you a lot of hard work, especially physical work: *I don't know how our grandmothers managed without all our labour-saving devices.*

Lab·ra·dor /ˈlæbrədɔːʳ/ *n* a type of large dog

la·bur·num /ləˈbɜːnəm ‖ -ɜːr-/ *n* [C;U] an ornamental tree with yellow flowers

lab·y·rinth /ˈlæbərɪnθ/ *n* a network of narrow twisting passages or paths, through which it is difficult to find your way: *We made our way through the labyrinth of narrow, twisting alleyways in the old city.*

lace¹ /leɪs/ *n* **1** [U] a very fine cloth with a lot of holes in it, which is used to decorate clothes and other things: *lace curtains* **2** [C] a string or cord which goes through two holes on the edges of clothes or shoes in order to fasten them together –see picture on page 50

lace² *v* **laced, lacing** [T] **1** (also **lace** sthg ↔ **up**) to fasten something with a lace or laces: *He laced up his shoes.* –opposite **unlace 2** to add a small amount of something strong to a drink: *coffee laced* **with** *brandy* | *to lace a drink with poison*

la·ce·rate /ˈlæsəreɪt/ *v* **lacerated, lacerating** [T] *fml* to cut skin very badly: *Her face was badly lacerated by the broken glass.* –**laceration** /ˌlæsəˈreɪʃən/ [C;U]

lace-up /ˈ· ·/ *n* **lace-ups** (also **lace-up shoes**) shoes which have pairs of holes on the top that are used for fastening them with a cord

lack¹ /læk/ *v* [T not in progressive forms] to be without or not have enough of something you need or want: *He's talented, but he lacks confidence.* | *The company lacks the capital to invest in new projects.*

lack² *n* [sing;U] the state of not having something or not having enough of it: *The plants died through lack of water.* | *There's a certain lack of enthusiasm for the project.*

lack·ey /ˈlæki/ *n* a person who behaves too much like a servant and obeys other people without question (a word used to express disapproval)

lack·ing /ˈlækɪŋ/ *adj* [never before a noun] *fml* **1** not present when needed: *Accurate information about the accident is lacking so that we do not know what really happened.* **2 be lacking in something** to be without the needed amount of a particular quality: *She's certainly not lacking in courage.*

la·con·ic /ləˈkɒnɪk ‖ -ˈkɑː-/ *adj* using few words –**laconically** /-kli/ *adv*

lac·quer /ˈlækəʳ/ *n* [U] a transparent or coloured substance used for forming a hard shiny surface on metal or wood, or for making hair stay in place –**lacquer** *v* [T] : *a lacquered table*

la·crosse /ləˈkrɒs ‖ ləˈkrɔːs/ *n* [U] an outdoor game played by two teams; each player has a long stick with a net at the end to throw and catch the ball

lac·tic /ˈlæktɪk/ *adj tech* relating to or obtained from milk

lac·y /ˈleɪsi/ *adj* **lacier, laciest 1** made from lace or decorated with lace **2** looking like LACE

lad /læd/ *n infml* a boy or young man

lad·der¹ /ˈlædəʳ/ *n* **1** a wooden, metal, or rope frame with steps on it, which is used for climbing up and down things –see picture on page 638 **2** the different stages and levels of an organization: *the promotion ladder* **3** the torn part of a woman's STOCKING or TIGHTS

ladder² *v* **1** [T] to tear a pair of STOCKINGS or TIGHTS: *Damn! I've laddered my tights.* **2** [I] (of STOCKINGS or TIGHTS) to become torn

la·den /ˈleɪdn/ *adj* heavily loaded: *The bushes were laden* **with** *fruit.* | *lorries fully laden with vegetables*

la·dle¹ /ˈleɪdl/ *n* a large, round, deep spoon with a long handle, used especially for putting soup into bowls –see picture on page 638

ladle² *v* **ladled, ladling** [T] to serve food with a ladle

la·dy /ˈleɪdi/ *n* **ladies 1** a polite word for a woman: *Ask the lady in the shop to get them.* | *Good morning, ladies.* | *a lady doctor* **2** a woman of good manners and behaviour: *She's a real lady – never criticizes anyone.* **3** a woman from a good family and of high social rank: *The lords and ladies danced at the ball.* **4** *AmE slang* a word used for talking to a woman, or attracting her attention: *You dropped your glove,*

lady. −see GENTLEMAN (USAGE) **5 Lady** a title put before the name of a woman of high social rank or position: *Lady Henrietta Woods* **6 Ladies** [plural is **Ladies**] a public TOILET for women: *Can you tell me where the Ladies is?*

la·dy·bird /ˈleɪdibɜːd ‖ -ɜːrd/ *n BrE* a small round flying insect which is usually red with black dots

lady-in-wait·ing /ˌ¦ ··· ˈ··/ *n* **ladies-in-waiting** a woman who is the servant of a queen or princess

lag /læg/ *v* **-gg-** [T] to cover water pipes and containers with a special material to prevent loss of heat
  lag behind *phr v* [I] to move or develop more slowly than others: *I walked in front with the children lagging behind.* | *Our car industry is starting to lag behind that in other countries.*

la·ger /ˈlɑːgəʳ/ *n* **1** [U] a kind of light beer **2** [C] a glass, bottle, or can of light beer: *Two lagers, please.*

la·ger lout /ˈ·· ˌ·/ *n* a young man who drinks a lot of lager and behaves in a rough and violent way

la·goon /ləˈguːn/ *n* a lake of sea water, separated from the sea by banks of sand

laid /leɪd/ the past tense and past participle of LAY

lain /leɪn/ the past participle of LIE

lair /leəʳ/ *n* **1** a hidden place where a wild animal rests and sleeps: *a wolf in its lair* **2** a place where someone hides: *The robbers were too scared to leave their lair.*

lake /leɪk/ *n* a large mass of fresh water surrounded by land: *We took a boat across the lake.*

lamb¹ /læm/ *n* **1** [C] a young sheep **2** [U] the meat of a young sheep

lamb² *v* [I] (of sheep) to give birth to lambs

lame¹ /leɪm/ *adj* **1** not able to walk properly because one or both your legs are hurt or damaged **2** weak or not easily believed (used of an excuse or argument) *He came up with a pretty lame excuse.* **3 lame duck** a person or business that does not produce good results or get things done −**lamely** *adv* −**lameness** *n* [U]

lame² *v* **lamed, laming** [T] to make someone lame

la·ment¹ /ləˈment/ *v fml* [I;T] to feel or express deep sorrow or disappointment

lament² *n fml* **1** a strong expression of disappointment or sorrow **2** a song or piece of music expressing grief at the death of somebody

lam·en·ta·ble /ˈlæməntəbəl, ləˈmentəbəl/ *adj* very bad and disappointing: *Many of our schools are in a lamentable state.* −**lamentably** *adv*

lam·i·nated /ˈlæmɪneɪt/ *adj* covered with a thin sheet of plastic for protection: *a laminated wall chart*

lamp /læmp/ *n* an apparatus, usually one that you can move, for giving light; lamps use electricity, gas, or oil −see picture on page 442

lam·poon¹ /læmˈpuːn/ *n* a piece of humorous writing strongly attacking a person or government

lampoon² *v* [T] to attack a person or government by means of a lampoon

lamp·post /ˈlæmp-pəʊst/ *n* a tall pole with a lamp on top which lights a street or other public area −see picture on page 441

lamp·shade /ˈlæmpʃeɪd/ *n* a cover placed over a lamp to soften its light or decorate it

lance /lɑːns ‖ læns/ *n* a long spear used by soldiers on horseback in the past

land¹ /lænd/ *n* **1** [U] ground owned as property: *Who owns this land?* | *Our garden is very small so we're buying some land from the council.* | *a shortage of building land* **2** [U] the solid dry part of the earth's surface, compared with the sea or air: *We decided to travel by land.* **3** [U] ground used for farming: *This is excellent land for wheat.* **4 the land:** **a** the country as opposed to towns and cities: *People in cities often dream of returning to the land.* **b** the solid dry part of the earth's surface, compared with the sea or air: *The ship was about two miles from the land.* **c** farming **5** [C] *lit* a country or nation: *the special feeling you have for your native land* | *a land of opportunities* **6 lands** [pl]: **a** large areas of the earth's surface which are of the same natural type: *the forest lands of Norway* **b** large areas of ground owned as property: *the lands of the Duke of Burgundy*

■ USAGE Compare **land** and **earth** as surfaces where people live and work. If we own an area that we can build things on we call it a piece of **land**: *the high price of land in London.* We also use **land** when we compare the dry surface of the world with the sea: *After a week at sea, the sailors saw land.* But when we compare it with the sky or space we call it **earth** or **the Earth**: *After a week in space, the spacecraft returned to earth.* **2** Compare **land, ground, soil, earth** as places where plants grow. We use **land** when we talk about areas used for farming: *good land for growing corn.* For smaller areas we can use **ground**: *a small piece of ground where I can grow a few potatoes.* The substance in which plants grow is **soil** or **earth**: *a tub filled with soil/earth*

land² *v* **1** [I] to arrive somewhere after a journey by air: *We landed at Heathrow at three o'clock in the morning.* **2** [I] to fall or come down to the ground after moving through the air: *The bird landed on a branch.* | *The ball landed in the water.* **3** [T] to bring goods or people onto land after a journey: *The ship landed its cargo at Dover.* **4** [T] to get something that is very difficult to get: *She's just landed a great new job.* **5 land someone in something** to put someone in a difficult situation or an unpleasant place: *She landed us in a real mess!* **6 land someone with something** to cause someone to have something difficult or unpleasant to deal with: *We were landed with a huge bill at the end of the day.* **7 land on your feet** to come successfully out of a difficulty
  land up *phr v* [I] to find yourself after a long journey or a number of events in a place or situation that you did not expect: *They landed up in Rio de Janeiro.* | *She landed up married to a widower with three children.*

land·ed /ˈlændɪd/ *adj* [only before a noun] owning large amounts of land: *a landed family* | *the landed gentry*

land·ing /ˈlændɪŋ/ *n* **1** the space at the top of a set of stairs in a building: *His bedroom leads off the landing.* **2** the act of arriving on land or bringing something onto land: *The plane's landing was delayed because of fog.* **3** (also **landing stage**) a flat surface where boats stop to let people get on or off

land·la·dy /ˈlænd‚leɪdi/ *n* **landladies** **1** a woman from whom you rent a room, building, or piece of land: *My landlady keeps complaining about the noise.* **2** a woman who owns or is in charge of a PUB

land·locked /ˈlændlɒkt ‖ -lɑːkt/ *adj* surrounded by land, with no coast: *Switzerland is a landlocked country.*

land·lord /ˈlændlɔːd ‖ -ɔːrd/ *n* **1** a man from whom

Modal verbs are a small group of verbs that are used with other verbs to change their meaning in the sentence in various ways. The English modal verbs are: **can, could, may, might, shall, should, will, would, must, ought to,** and **used to. Need** and **dare** also behave like modals in some cases. Table 1 explains the grammar of modal verbs – how they are used in forming sentences. Table 2 describes the various meanings that modal verbs are used to express.

Table 1: grammar

In their grammar, modal verbs are different from most other verbs in the following ways:

1 they are followed by an infinitive verb without **to**: *I **can** swim. You **must** go.*	but **ought** and used are followed by **to** + infinitive: *You **ought** to go. They **used** to live in London*
2 they have no **-s** in the 3rd person singular: *She **can**. He **must** go.*	
3 they form questions without using **do**, with the subject coming after the modal verb: ***Can** I go now? **Dare** you ask her? **Ought** we to tell the police? **Will** the train be late?*	the question form of **used to** is either *Did they **use** to live there* or *Did they **used** to live there?*
4 they form negatives by adding **not** or **n't**, but without using **do** or **did**. *I **couldn't / could not** lift it. It **won't / will not** rain. You **oughtn't / ought not** to do that.*	the negative form of **used to** is either *They **didn't use to / used to** live here* or (less common) *They **usedn't to / used not to** live here.*
5 in indirect speech (when you are describing what someone else said) these modals change their form: **can**: "*I **can** speak French.*" She said that she **could** speak French. **may**: "*We **may** not be able to come.*" They said they **might** not be able to come. **shall**: "*Shall I post the letter?*" She asked if she **should** post the letter. **will**: "*We **will** probably be late.*" They said they **would** probably be late.	the other modals do not usually change their form. For example: "*I **would** like some coffee*" She said she **would** like some coffee. "*You **ought** to work harder.*" He told me I **ought** to work harder.

Table 2: meaning

Modal verbs are use for many different purposes. The most common ones are:

1	talking about ability	*She **can** speak French. I **could** swim when I was five. I **couldn't** lift it – it was too heavy.*	**could** describes ability in the past, but expressions like **was able to** or **managed to** are often used instead: *With John's help I **was able to** lift it/ **managed to** lift it*
2	asking for and giving permission	*You **can** go now if you like. Students **may** borrow up to six books. **Could** we go now, please? **Might** I open the window?*	**can** is the usual word for asking for and giving permission. **May** is more formal. **Could** and **might** are polite ways of asking for (but not giving) permission.
3	making requests	***Will** you / **would** you / **could** you close the door, please? **Can** you help me to lift this?*	**will, would** and **could** are more polite than **can** for making requests

4	making offers and suggestions	*Shall* I open it for you? *Shall* we go to the cinema? *Can* I help you with your bags? *I'll* carry your bags if you like.	**shall** is used only with **I** and **we** in offers and suggestions
5	showing something is necessary	You *must* finish this work today. I *have* to go / *I've* to go now. I *must* phone my mother. (= I feel a strong duty to do this)	**had to** is used to describe what was necessary in the past: I *had to* leave early yesterday.
6	showing that something is not necessary	You *needn't* finish it today. (= but you can if you want to). You *don't have* to finish it today. I *needn't have* / *didn't need* to put on my thick coat.	
7	giving advice	You *should* / *ought* to see the doctor. He *shouldn't have* / *oughtn't to* have said that. You *could* have told me you were going to be late! (= I wish you had told me) You *might* knock before you come in! (=I am annoyed because you did not knock)	
8	talking about future events or what you intend to do in the future	It *will* probably rain tomorrow We *shall* be away next week.	**shall** is usually used only with **I** and **we**, and is less common than **will** for talking about the future
9	talking about the past	We *used to* work in the same office. We *would* often go to the cinema together.	**would** is used to describe an action in the past only if it is a repeated action
10	talking about what is possible but not certain	It *may* / *might* snow tonight. Don't touch that wire– it *could* be dangerous. Learning English *can* be fun (= is sometimes fun)	**might** and **could** make something sound less likely than **may**
11	talking about what is probable	They *should have* / *ought to have* arrived by now. (= I expect they have, but I am not certain)	
12	talking about what you believe to be certain	You've been working all day – you *must* be tired. (= I'm sure you are) Her office is empty – she *must* have gone home (= I'm sure she has)	**can't** is the opposite of **must** in this meaning, showing that something is certainly not true: You haven't done any work – you *can't* be tired. (= I'm sure you're not) Her car is still here – she *can't* have gone home yet.

you rent a room, building, or piece of land 2 a man who owns or is in charge of a PUB

land·mark /ˈlændmɑːk ‖ -ɑːrk/ n 1 an easily recognizable object, such as a tall tree or building, by which you can tell where you are 2 an event, idea, or discovery which marks a very important stage in a process: *The discovery of penicillin was a landmark in the history of medicine.*

land·scape¹ /ˈlændskeɪp/ n 1 a view across an area of land: *a gentle landscape of rolling hills* | *an ugly urban landscape* 2 a picture of country scenery –see VIEW¹ (USAGE)

landscape² v **landscaped, landscaping** [T] to make a piece of land look attractive by planting trees and flowers in a pleasant arrangement: *beautiful landscaped gardens*

land·slide /ˈlændslaɪd/ n 1 a sudden large fall of earth or rocks down a mountain, hill, or cliff: *The road was blocked by a landslide.* 2 the winning of an election by a person or political party when they get many more votes than their opponents: *a landslide victory*

land·slip /ˈlændslɪp/ n a small landslide

lane /leɪn/ n 1 a narrow country road or a narrow street in a town 2 part of the name of a street: *205 Cedar Lane* 3 one of the parts of a main road which are separated by white lines so that fast and slow cars travelling in the same direction can stay apart –see picture on page 735 4 a fixed path across the sea or through the air used regularly by ships or aircraft

lan·guage /ˈlæŋgwɪdʒ/ n 1 [U] the ability of human beings to express themselves through a system of sounds, words, and grammar: *Some children acquire language faster than others.* 2 [C] a system of sounds, words, and grammar used by the people of a particular area or country to express themselves in speech or writing: *People from this region often speak three languages.* | *foreign languages* | *the Zulu language* 3 [U] words or phrases used by a particular group of people, in a particular subject, or in a particular piece of writing: *the language of anthropology* | *the language of teenagers* | *The language in the novel is beautiful.* 4 [C;U] any system of signs or movements used to express meanings or feelings: *the language of music* | *a computer language*

language la·bor·a·tory /ˈ· · ·‚· · · ‖ ˈ· · ‚· · · ·/ n a special room in a school or college in which people can learn other languages using TAPE RECORDERS

lan·guid /ˈlæŋgwɪd/ adj lacking strength and moving slowly but attractively –**languidly** adv : *She sipped her wine languidly.*

lan·guish /ˈlæŋgwɪʃ/ v [I] lit 1 to be forced to suffer an unpleasant experience for a long time: *The hostages are still languishing in prison.* 2 to be or become weak: *The flowers were languishing in the heat.*

lan·guor /ˈlæŋgəʳ/ n [U] lit pleasant tiredness or lack of strength: *the languor of a summer afternoon* –**languorous** adj

lank /læŋk/ adj unattractive, long, and dull (used of hair)

lank·y /ˈlæŋki/ adj **lankier, lankiest** very thin, tall, and ungraceful (used of people)

lan·tern /ˈlæntən ‖ -ərn/ n a lamp used in the past, consisting of a container made of glass and metal, enclosing a candle

lap¹ /læp/ n 1 the part of your body between your waist and your knees when you are sitting down:

She was sitting on her mother's lap. 2 a single journey round the track in a race 3 **the lap of luxury** conditions of very great comfort

lap² v -pp- 1 [T] (of an animal) to drink by using short, quick movements of the tongue: *The cat was lapping the milk off the floor.* 2 [I] (of water) to touch something gently while making soft, gentle sounds: *The sea lapped against the rocks.* 3 [I] to run completely round the track in a race: *Alan Jones lapped in under two minutes.* 4 [T] to pass another competitor in a race so that you are one full lap ahead of them

lap sth ↔ up phr v [T] 1 (of an animal) to drink liquid by using short, quick movements of the tongue: *The dog lapped the water up.* 2 to accept something eagerly, although it may be false or insincere: *He lapped up all their praise.*

la·pel /ləˈpel/ n the part of the front of a coat or JACKET that is joined to the collar and folded back on each side of the front opening –see picture on page 50

lapse¹ /læps/ n 1 [C] a small example of bad behaviour, especially by someone who usually behaves well: *After that little lapse, he was his usual charming self.* 2 [C] a moment when you do not pay attention, or when you forget something: *a lapse of memory* 3 [sing] the passing away of a period of time: *After a lapse of several years he came back to see us.*

lapse² v **lapsed, lapsing** [I] 1 **lapse into something** to gradually pass into a less desirable or less active state: *After a year of fame, the group lapsed back into obscurity.* | *She lapsed into silence.* 2 (of a legal right or an agreement) to end: *Their agreement lapsed last year, and neither company renewed it.* 3 to no longer believe in or practise your religion: *a lapsed Catholic*

lar·ce·ny /ˈlɑːsəni ‖ ˈlɑːr-/ n **larcenies** [C;U] law the act of stealing something

larch /lɑːtʃ ‖ lɑːrtʃ/ n a tall tree with bright green needles

lard /lɑːd ‖ lɑːrd/ n [U] pig fat used in cooking

lar·der /ˈlɑːdəʳ ‖ ˈlɑːr-/ n a cupboard or small room in a house where food is stored

large /lɑːdʒ ‖ lɑːrdʒ/ adj 1 greater or bigger than usual in size, number, or amount: *a large sum of money* | *a large house* | *a large family* –opposite **small** 2 **at large: a** as a whole: *The country at large is hoping for great changes.* **b** free after escaping, and not caught yet: *Two of the prisoners are still at large.* 3 **as large as life** a phrase used of someone whose presence you find surprising: *And suddenly there he was, as large as life.* –**largeness** n [U]

large·ly /ˈlɑːdʒli ‖ ˈlɑːr-/ adv mostly or mainly: *This country is largely desert.* | *He left his job largely because he was bored.*

large-scale /ˈ· ·/ adj 1 happening over a large area or with large numbers or quantities: *Supplying the troops with food is a very large-scale operation.* | *large-scale migrations of birds* 2 showing a small area in great detail (used of maps): *Large-scale maps, on a scale of 1:1250, are only available for large towns.*

lar·gesse /lɑːˈʒes ‖ lɑːrˈdʒes/ n (also **largess** AmE) [U] the generous giving of money or gifts to people of a lower social position than yourself

lark¹ /lɑːk ‖ lɑːrk/ n infml 1 something daring done for a bit of fun: *He did it for a lark, he didn't mean any harm.* 2 a small brown singing bird

lark² v
  lark about/around phr v [I] to do silly things for fun or amusement

lar·va /ˈlɑːvə ‖ ˈlɑːrvə/ n **larvae** /viː/ the wormlike young of an insect –**larval** adj

lar·yn·gi·tis /ˌlærɪnˈdʒaɪtɪs/ n [U] a painful infection of the larynx, which makes it difficult to speak

lar·ynx /ˈlærɪŋks/ n **larynxes or larynges** /ləˈrɪndʒiːz/ the hollow boxlike part in your throat, in which the sounds of your voice are produced

las·civ·i·ous /ləˈsɪviəs/ adj feeling or showing very strong sexual desire in a way that you do not like –**lasciviously** adv

la·ser /ˈleɪzəʳ/ n a very powerful narrow beam of light which is used to cut hard substances and in medical operations; the machine which produces these beams is also called a **laser**

lash¹ /læʃ/ v **1** [T] to hit someone violently with a whip **2** [I;T] to beat against something violently: waves lashing against the shore **3** [I;T] to move violently or suddenly: The cat lashed its tail angrily. **4** [T] to tie things firmly together with rope: During the storm all the boxes had to be lashed down. | They lashed the crates together.
  lash out phr v [I] **1** to hit someone suddenly and violently with your hands, feet, or a weapon: He suddenly lashed out at me. **2** to speak very angrily to someone: An opposition spokesman lashed out against government policy.

lash² n **1** the thin leather part of a whip **2** a blow with a whip **3** **lashes** the hairs that grow round the edges of your eyes

lass /læs/ n dialect a young girl or woman

las·so¹ /ləˈsuː, ˈlæsəʊ/ n **lassos or lassoes** a rope with one end that can be tightened in a circle, used for catching horses and cattle

lasso² v [T] to catch an animal with a lasso

last¹ /lɑːst ‖ læst/ n, pron **1** the person or thing after all the others: He was the last to arrive. **2** **at last, at long last** in the end, after a long time: At last I've found a job that I enjoy. **3** **to the last** until the end

last² det, adv **1** after everything or everyone else: George arrived last. | He came last in the competition. | This was the last thing that he did before he died. **2** used when talking about the most recent occasion or the most recent period of time mentioned: When did you last see him? | I didn't go to the class last week. **3** **last but not least** used when you are making your last point and want to say that it is just as important as the others **4** **last thing** at the end of the day: I always try and tidy up the house last thing at night. **5** **last of all** a phrase you can use when you come to your last point: Last of all, don't forget to check your spelling.
  ■ USAGE 1 When your point of view is in the present, looking back to the past, say **last** night, last week, etc.: I went to bed late last night. | I spoke to Sue last Monday. But when your point of view is in the past, looking even further back into the past, use expressions like the **previous** night/the night **before**, the **previous** week/the week **before**: I told her I had spoken to Sue the **previous** Monday. Compare **latest** and **last**. Use **latest** when you mean "new and most recent": Have you heard the **latest** news? Use **last** when you mean "coming at the end" or "coming before the latest one": 'The Magic Flute' was Mozart's **last** opera. | Have you read Bigg's **latest** novel? It's better than her **last** one.

last³ v [I] **1** to continue to happen for a period of time: The hot weather lasted until September. | Each class lasts for one hour. **2** to remain in good condition: A cheap watch won't last as long as a more expensive one.

last·ing /ˈlɑːstɪŋ ‖ ˈlæs-/ adj continuing for a long time: a lasting sorrow

last·ly /ˈlɑːstli ‖ ˈlæst-/ adv **1** a word used when you come to the last of several points you are making: We've seen how different soils suit different plants, and how rainfall affects their growth. Lastly, I'd like to look at the significance of light. | I'd like, lastly, to thank my parents for their help. **2** a word used when you are describing a number of events that happen one after the other and you come to the last one, or when you come to the last in a list of instructions: She closed the windows and turned off the lights. Lastly, she locked the door. | Leave the cake to cool. Lastly, decorate the top with cherries.
  ■ USAGE Do not confuse **lastly** and **at last**. 1 Use **lastly** when you are talking about several things in order and you want to show that you have reached the final thing on the list: ...And lastly I would like to thank everyone for making this such a memorable occasion. | I'll start by asking you about your previous experience, then we can talk about your present employment, and lastly I'll tell you a bit about the job here. (Note that you can also use **finally** in the same way.) 2 Use **at last** when you want to show that something has happened after a long time or after a lot of waiting: She tried again and again until at last she succeeded. | When at last the rescuers found them, two people had already died. | "At last!" she exclaimed as she managed to catch the waiter's eye. (Note that you can also use **finally** in this way.)

latch¹ /lætʃ/ n **1** a fastening for a door, gate, or window, which works by putting a metal bar in a space **2** a lock for a house door that can be opened from the inside with a handle but from the outside only with a key **3** **on the latch** fastened only with a latch, but not locked

latch² v [T] to fasten a door, gate, or window with a latch: She forgot to latch the door. –opposite **unlatch**
  latch on phr v [I] infml to understand something
  latch onto phr v infml **1** [T **latch onto** sthg] to gain an understanding of something: He soon latched onto how to do it. **2** [T **latch onto** sbdy/sthg] to become very interested in a person or idea, so that you do not let them go: She had latched onto me at the conference.

late /leɪt/ adj,adv **1** arriving or happening after the usual, arranged, or expected time: The train was 10 minutes late. | She was late for the meeting. | We had a late breakfast. | We arrived a few minutes late. **2** towards the end of a period of time: She returned in the late afternoon. | She's in her late thirties. | We always go on holiday late in the summer. | I'll see you later on this evening. –compare EARLY² **3** **late night** a night when you stay up late and do not go to bed at your usual time **4** **too late for something** no longer possible to do something: It's too late to apply for this job. | It was too late for the doctors to save him. **5** [always before a noun] who has died: her late husband **6** **of late** fml recently: He's been behaving very strangely of late. –**lateness** n [U]

late·ly /ˈleɪtli/ adv in the recent past: I haven't seen her much lately. | He's been doing a lot of gardening lately.

la·tent /ˈleɪtənt/ adj present but not yet noticeable, active, or fully developed: the latent tensions between the two countries

lat·er /ˈleɪtəʳ/ adv **1** after some time: *I can't do it now, but I'll do it later.* | *At first they said 32 people had died, but later they said it was 15.* | *She had a cup of coffee and read for a while. Later that afternoon she took a walk down to the beach.* **2 later on** after some time: *I can't do it now, but I'll do it later on.*

lat·er·al /ˈlætərəl/ adj [only before a noun] tech **1** connected with the side of something: *a lateral movement* **2 lateral thinking** a way of thinking about problems in which you use your imagination in order to find new answers

lat·est /ˈleɪtᵻst/ adj infml **1** the most recent: *Here's our reporter in New York with the latest news on the crisis.* | *the latest fashions from Paris* **2 at the latest** a phrase used to give the latest time by which something will happen: *I'll ring you on Friday at the latest.*

la·tex /ˈleɪteks/ n [U] a whitish substance produced by certain kinds of tree and used to make rubber

lathe /leɪð/ n a machine for shaping metal or wood by turning it round against a sharp tool

la·ther¹ /ˈlɑːðəʳ ‖ ˈlæ-/ n [sing;U] a white mass produced by mixing soap and water together: *His chin was covered with a thick lather.*

lather² v **1** [I] of soap to produce a lather: *This washing powder doesn't lather very well.* **2** [T] to cover something with lather

Lat·in¹ /ˈlætɪn ‖ ˈlætn/ n [U] the language of the ancient Romans

Latin² adj **1** written in Latin: *a Latin inscription* **2** relating to a nation that speaks a language developed from Latin, such as Spanish, Portuguese, Italian, or French

Latin A·mer·i·can /ˌ… ·ˈ…·/ adj relating to the Spanish or Portuguese speaking countries of South and Central America

lat·i·tude /ˈlætᵻtjuːd ‖ -tuːd/ n **1** [C;U] the distance north or south of the EQUATOR measured in degrees: *The latitude of the ship is 20 degrees south.* –compare LONGITUDE **2 latitudes** [pl] an area of the world which is at a certain distance from the EQUATOR: *At these latitudes you often get strong winds.* **3** [U] freedom to do or say what you like: *That school allows its students a great deal of latitude in deciding which subjects to study.*

la·trine /ləˈtriːn/ n a hole in the ground used as a TOILET, for example in a military camp

lat·ter¹ /ˈlætəʳ/ adj fml [only before a noun] **1** nearer to the end; later: *the latter years of her life* **2** the second of two people or things just mentioned: *Of the pig and the cow, the latter animal is more valuable.* | *Of pigs and cows, the latter animals are more valuable.*

latter² n **the latter** the second of two people or things just mentioned: *Cotton-manufacturing and steel-making are in decline, the former because of cheap imports from the East, the latter because of over-production.*

lat·ter·ly /ˈlætəli ‖ -ər-/ adv fml recently or lately

lat·tice /ˈlætᵻs/ n a wooden or metal framework consisting of thin pieces of wood or metal crossed over each other; a lattice is often used as a fence or as a support for climbing flowers

lau·da·ble /ˈlɔːdəbəl/ adj fml deserving praise (used of behaviour or actions) –**laudably** adv

laugh¹ /lɑːf ‖ læf/ v **1** [I] to make a sound with your voice, usually while smiling, because you find something funny: *It was so funny we couldn't stop laughing.* | *Nobody laughs at his jokes.* | *Ben laughed nervously.* **2 laugh your head off** to laugh for a long time very loudly

laugh at sbdy/sthg phr v [T] to treat a person or thing as very foolish, or make jokes about them: *They'll just laugh at you for listening to him.*

laugh sthg ↔ off phr v [T] to pretend, by laughing or joking, that something is less serious than it is: *She tried to laugh it off, but I could see that she was upset.*

laugh² n **1** the sound you make when you find something funny: *a hearty laugh* | *When I mentioned Jim, he let out a loud laugh.* **2 do something for a laugh/for laughs** to do something for fun: *We all dressed up in silly hats just for a laugh.*

laugh·a·ble /ˈlɑːfəbəl ‖ ˈlæ-/ adj extremely foolish, and not worth taking seriously –**laughably** adv

laugh·ter /ˈlɑːftəʳ ‖ ˈlæf-/ n [U] the act or sound of laughing

launch¹ /lɔːntʃ/ v [T] **1** to make a newly-built boat move into the water for the first time **2** to send a modern weapon or spacecraft into the sky: *to launch a missile* | *The rocket is due to be launched this afternoon.* **3** to start an important activity or plan: *They might be planning to launch an attack very soon.* | *A new campaign has just been launched by the government.* **4** to let people know about a new product: *The new chocolate was launched last week.*

launch² n **1** the act of launching something **2** a large motor boat used for carrying people on rivers and lakes

laun·der /ˈlɔːndəʳ/ v [T] to wash and iron clothes and sheets

laun·derette /lɔːnˈdret/ n a shop where you pay to wash and dry your clothes and sheets in machines

laun·dry /ˈlɔːndri/ n **laundries 1** [C] a place where clothes and sheets are washed and ironed **2** [U] clothes and sheets that need washing or that have just been washed

lau·rel /ˈlɒrəl ‖ ˈlɔː-, ˈlɑː-/ n **1** a small tree with shiny leaves that do not fall in winter **2 laurels** [pl] fml honour that you receive for something that you have done

la·va /ˈlɑːvə/ n [U] rock in a very hot liquid state which flows from a VOLCANO; when this rock becomes cool and solid it is still called lava

lav·a·to·ry /ˈlævətəri ‖ -tɔːri/ n lavatories a TOILET: *I need to go to the lavatory.* | *a public lavatory*

lav·en·der /ˈlævᵻndəʳ/ n [U] a plant with sweet-smelling pale purple flowers

lav·ish¹ /ˈlævɪʃ/ adj **1** very generous: *She's very lavish with presents for the children.* **2** given in great quantity: *lavish praise* –**lavishly** adv : *We were entertained lavishly by various Hollywood directors.*

lavish² v **lavish something on someone** to give someone a lot of something in a very generous way: *He lavished gifts on us.*

law /lɔː/ n **1** [C] a rule developed by a society, and supported by the power of the government, to control social and business relationships: *a law against drinking and driving* | *There should be a law against that kind of behaviour.* | *Parliament has passed a new law aimed at reducing the amount of fraud in businesses.* | *Under the new law, shops will be able to open all day on Sundays.* **2** [U] (also **the law**) the system of rules developed by a government or society to control social and business relationships: *If you break the law, you will be punished.* | *tribal law* | *You are obliged by law to pay taxes.* **3 against the law** not legal: *Driving without a seat belt is against the law.* **4** [U] the system of law, and the way particular laws work, studied as a subject: *She's studying law at university.* | *a law degree*

5 [U] a particular group of rules in a system of law: *He's been charged under military law.* **6** [C] a statement describing a natural process which, in certain conditions, always has the same effect: *Boyle's law is a scientific principle.* | *the law of gravity* **7 the law** *infml* the police, or a policeman or policewoman: *The law was there in force.* **8 law and order** a situation in which people respect and obey the law: *a breakdown in law and order* | *Finally, the army was used to maintain law and order.*

law·a·bid·ing /ˈ·ˌ·ˌ··/ *adj* obeying the law

law court /ˈ· ·/ *n* a room or building in which law cases are heard and judged

law·ful /ˈlɔːfəl/ *adj fml* allowed by law: *a lawful marriage* | *I was going about my lawful business.:* –see LEGAL (USAGE) –opposite **unlawful** –**lawfully** *adv*

law·less /ˈlɔːləs/ *adj fml* **1** breaking the law in a wild and violent way: *a lawless mob* **2** not governed by law (used of a country or place): *a lawless frontier town*

lawn /lɔːn/ *n* a stretch of ground covered with closely cut grass in a garden or park – see picture on page 441

lawn·mow·er /ˈ· ˌ··/ *n* a machine that you use to cut the grass in a garden –see picture on page 638

law·suit /ˈlɔːsjuːt, -suɪt || -suːt/ *n* a case in a court of law concerning a disagreement between two people or companies, rather than a criminal and the police

law·yer /ˈlɔːjəʳ/ *n* a person whose business it is to advise people about laws and to represent them in court; lawyers in Britain are either SOLICITORS or BARRISTERS

lax /læks/ *adj* not obeying the rules, following correct standards, or behaving properly: *lax morals* | *Lax security allowed the thieves to enter.* | *Discipline at this school is lax.*

lax·a·tive /ˈlæksətɪv/ *n* a medicine or something you eat that causes your bowels to empty easily

lay¹ /leɪ/ *v* **laid** /leɪd/, **laid 1** [T+adv/prep] to put someone or something in a particular position or on a flat surface: *They laid the injured woman down on the grass.* | *He laid his coat over a chair.* **2** [T] to put something in the proper position on the ground or in the ground: *He was learning how to lay bricks so he could build his own house.* | *to lay pipes* | *to lay a new carpet* **3 lay the table** to arrange knives, forks, plates, and other things on a table ready for a meal **4 lay an egg** (of a bird or an insect) to produce an egg **5** [T] *fml* to make a statement, charge, or complaint in an official or public way: *The proposal was laid before the committee.* | *The police have laid a serious charge against you.* **6 lay the blame on someone** to blame someone **7 lay the blame for something at someone's door** to blame someone for something **8 lay emphasis on something** to say that something is very important: *We must lay more emphasis on the protection of the environment.* **9 lay claim to something** *fml* to state that something belongs to you **10 lay your hands on something** to find something: *It's here somewhere, but I can't lay my hands on it at the moment.* **11 lay hold of someone/something** to take hold of someone or something very firmly **12 be laid low** to be weak with an illness: *I was laid low with flu all last week.* **13 lay something to rest: a** to bring a feeling such as fear or grief to an end: *Her fears were soon laid to rest.* **b** to show that something is false or not true: *The report should lay to rest recent allegations of police brutality.* **14 lay a trap** to prepare a trap to catch a person or an animal

■ USAGE Do not confuse the transitive verb **lay** (**laid, laid**) with the intransitive verb **lie** (**lay, lain**): *He* **laid** *his trousers on the bed.* | *He* **lay** *on the bed.* A third verb **lie** (**lied, lied**) is intransitive and means "to tell a lie".

lay sthg ↔ **down** *phr v* [T] **1** to put something down when you have finished using it **2** to make a firm statement or give a rule: *It's laid down in the regulations.* **3 lay down the law** to give other people orders in an unpleasant commanding manner: *I can't stand the way she lays down the law.*

lay sthg ↔ **in** *phr v* [T] to obtain and store a supply of something: *We've laid in enough food for the winter.*

lay into sbdy *phr v infml* [T] to attack someone physically or with words

lay off *phr v* **1** [T **lay** sbdy ↔ **off**] to stop employing a worker, because there is not enough work: *They laid us off for three months.* **2** [I;T **lay off** sthg] *infml* to stop doing something annoying or harmful: *You'd better lay off smoking!*

lay sthg ↔ **on** *phr v* [T] to provide food, entertainment or a service, especially in a generous way: *They laid on a party for all the old people in the village.*

lay sthg ↔ **out** *phr v* [T] **1** to spread out or arrange things: *She laid out her new clothes on the bed.* **2 be laid out** to be planned and arranged in a particular way: *The garden is laid out rather formally.*

lay up *phr v* **be laid up** to be kept indoors or in bed with an illness: *I was laid up with a cold.*

lay² *adj* [only before a noun] **1** of or done by people who are not in official positions within a religion: *a lay preacher* **2** not trained in or having knowledge of a particular profession or subject, such as law or medicine: *No lay person can understand all these technical terms.*

lay³ the past tense of LIE¹

lay·a·bout /ˈleɪəbaʊt/ *n infml* a lazy person who avoids work

lay-by /ˈ· ·/ *n* a space next to a road where vehicles may stop for a short while

lay·er¹ /ˈleɪəʳ/ *n* a piece of some material or a quantity of a substance which is laid flat on a surface or placed between two things: *These seeds must be covered with a layer of earth.* | *She's wearing several layers of clothing to try to stay warm.*

layer² *v* [T] to put things down in layers: *Layer cheese and potatoes in the dish.*

lay·man /ˈleɪmən/ *n* **laymen** /-mən/ **1** a person who is not trained in a particular profession or subject **2** a person who is a member of a religion, but does not have an official position

lay-off /ˈ· ·/ *n* the stopping of a worker's job at a time when there is little work

lay·out /ˈleɪaʊt/ *n* **1** the way in which the parts of something are arranged, especially on a drawing or plan: *the layout of the new shopping centre* **2** the way in which printed matter is set out on a page

laze /leɪz/ *v* **lazed, lazing** [I] (also **laze around**) to spend time enjoyably resting and doing nothing: *I spent the morning just lazing around.*

la·zy /ˈleɪzi/ *adj* **lazier, laziest 1** disliking and avoiding activity, effort, or work: *He won't work – he's just too lazy!* **2** slow and without much effort (used of an action or movement): *a lazy smile* **3** spent doing nothing (used of periods of time): *a lazy afternoon* –**lazily** *adv* –**laziness** *n* [U]

lb **lbs** a written abbreviation for POUND, when it is a measure of weight

lead¹ /li:d/ *v* **led** /led/, **led** 1 [T + adv/prep] to show someone the way somewhere, or take them there by going in front of them: *The stewardess led them onto the plane.* | *She led me to her office.* | *The horses were led into the yard.* 2 [I + adv/prep; T +adv/prep] to go towards a place or be the means of reaching a place: *a small path leading to the top of the hill* | *This road leads you to the town centre.* 3 [T] to be responsible for directing a group of people: *He's been chosen to lead the new team.* 4 [I] to be winning in a game or race: *England were leading 1-0 at half time.* 5 **lead to something** to cause something or result in something: *The strike could lead to a loss of jobs.* 6 **lead someone to do something** to persuade someone to do something, or influence them so that they do something: *What led you to resign?* | *I was led to believe that you were ill.* 7 **lead the way:** **a** to show other people where to go by going in front of them **b** to be more advanced than other people: *This university leads the way in cancer research.* 8 **lead a … life** to experience a particular kind of life: *He led a very lonely life.*

■ USAGE Compare **lead**, **guide**, **direct**. To **lead** is to show the way by going first: *You lead and we'll follow.* To **guide** is to go with someone who needs help, in order to show the way and explain things: *He guided the tourists round the castle.* To **direct** is to explain to someone how to get to a place: *Could you direct me to the station, please?*

lead sbdy ↔ **on** *phr v infml* [T] to persuade somebody to believe something that is not true: *I don't believe you – you're just leading me on!*

lead up to sthg *phr v* [T] 1 to come before and result in something: *the events leading up to his arrest* 2 to guide a conversation to the point where you can talk about a particular subject or ask for something: *His flattering remarks were leading up to a request for money.*

lead² *n* 1 a more advanced position: *Japan has a lead in the industrial use of robots.* 2 [C] a good example for other people to follow: *The Prime Minister always provides a strong lead.* | *the company's lead in helping the community* 3 **take the lead** to be more advanced or more successful than others: *Japan took the lead in car production.* 4 **be in the lead** to be winning in a game or competition: *England were in the lead at half time.* 5 [sing] the number of points by which one competitor is ahead of another: *England has a lead of ten points to three.* 6 [C] the most important part in a play or film: *A French actress plays the lead in this film.* 7 [C] a rope, chain, or narrow piece of leather tied to a dog to control it 8 *BrE* [C] an electric wire which carries power to a machine –see picture on page 638 9 [C] a piece of information which may lead to a discovery of something not known: *The police have several leads to follow in this case.*

lead³ /led/ *n* 1 [U] a soft heavy grey metal, used for waterpipes and for covering roofs 2 [C;U] a thin stick of a black substance used in the centre of pencils: *a soft lead pencil.*

lead·en /ˈledn/ *adj lit* 1 dull grey: *a leaden sky* 2 without cheerfulness or excitement

lead·er /ˈliːdəʳ/ *n* 1 a person who guides or directs a group, team, or organization: *the leader of a political party.* | *union leaders* 2 a person or thing who is winning a race or competition at a particular moment 3 the main article in a newspaper, which gives the newspaper's opinion about something that is happening

lead·er·ship /ˈliːdəʃɪp ‖ -ərˈ/ *n* [U] 1 the position of leader: *the battle for the leadership of the Labour Party* 2 the qualities necessary in a leader

lead·ing /ˈliːdɪŋ/ *adj* [always before a noun] 1 most important or main: *the leading role in the film* | *one of Greece's leading modern composers* 2 **leading question** a question formed in such a way that it suggests one particular answer

leaf¹ /liːf/ *n* **leaves** /liːvz/ 1 [C] one of the flat green parts of a plant that are joined to its stem or branch 2 **be in leaf** to be covered with leaves: *The poplar trees are in leaf again.* 3 [C] a thin sheet of paper, especially a page in a book 4 [U] metal, especially gold or silver, in a very thin sheet: *a book decorated with gold leaf* 5 **take a leaf out of someone's book** to behave like someone else because their behaviour has had very good results 6 **turn over a new leaf** to begin to behave in a better, more responsible way

leaf² *v*

leaf through sthg *phr v* [I;T] to turn the pages of a book or magazine to see if there is anything you are interested in or to find particular information

leaf·let /ˈliːflɪt/ *n* a printed sheet of paper, given free to the public, which provides information about a particular subject or advertises something

leaf·y /ˈliːfi/ *adj* **leafier**, **leafiest** 1 having a lot of leaves: *leafy vegetables* 2 having a lot of trees (used of a place)

league /liːg/ *n* [sing/pl verb] 1 a group of sports clubs or players that play matches between themselves: *the Football League* | *a league match* 2 a group of people or countries who have joined together to work for a common aim 3 **in league** working together, often secretly or for a bad purpose: *He was accused of being in league with the terrorists.*

leak¹ /liːk/ *n* 1 a small hole or crack, for example in a container or pipe, through which a gas or liquid escapes or passes: *There's a leak in the flat roof.* | *a leak in the tank* | *a petrol leak* 2 the telling of news or other information to the public that is supposed to be secret

leak² *v* 1 [I;T] to let a liquid or gas in or out of a hole or crack: *The bottle leaks.* | *The tank is leaking petrol.* 2 [I + adv/prep] (of a liquid or gas) to pass through a hole or crack: *Oil was leaking out of the tank.* 3 [T] to make information known to the public when it is supposed to be secret: *Someone in the ministry leaked the story to the newspapers.*

leak out *phr v* [I] (of information that is supposed to be secret) to become known to the public

leak·age /ˈliːkɪdʒ/ *n* [C;U] 1 an act of leaking 2 an amount of liquid or gas which escapes through a hole or crack

leak·y /ˈliːki/ *adj* **leakier**, **leakiest** letting liquid leak in or out: *a leaky bucket*

lean¹ /liːn/ *v* **leant** /lent/ *or* **leaned**, **leant** *or* **leaned** 1 [I] to slope or bend from an upright position: *That wall leans so much it might fall over.* | *He leaned forward to hear what she said.* 2 [I + adv/prep] to rest or bend against something so that your weight is supported: *He leaned on the back of the chair.* –see picture on page 736 3 [T + adv/prep] to place something so that its weight is supported on or against something else: *Lean it against the wall.* 4 **lean on someone** to need someone's help or depend on them: *She leans on her family a lot.*

lean² *adj* 1 without much fat (used of meat) 2 thin but strong and healthy (used of people) –see THIN¹ (USAGE) 3 producing little of value: *This has been a lean year for business.* | *a lean harvest* –**leanness** *n* [U]

lean·ing /ˈliːnɪŋ/ n a tendency to have a particular belief or opinion: *At one time, Jack had a strong leaning* **towards** *socialism.*

leant /lent/ the past tense and past participle of LEAN

leap¹ /liːp/ v **leapt** /lept/ or **leaped** /lept‖liːpt/, **leapt** or **leaped** 1 [I;T] to jump through the air very high or over a distance: *The horse leapt over the stream.* | *The prisoner leapt the wall and ran away.* –see picture on page 736 2 [I + adv/prep] to move or act quickly: *When she heard the knock at the door, she leapt to her feet.* | *She leapt to my defence.* 3 [I + adv/prep] to increase suddenly: *Unemployment has leapt up to 10%.* 4 **leap at something** to accept something eagerly: *I leapt at the chance to go to Paris.*

leap² n 1 a sudden jump which is high or over a distance: *With a leap she crossed the stream.* 2 a large increase in number or amount: *There has been a sudden leap* **in** *oil prices.*

leapt /lept/ the past tense and past participle of LEAP

leap year /ˈ· ·/ n [C] a year in which February has 29 days instead of 28 days: *There is a leap year every four years.*

learn /lɜːn ‖ lɜːrn/ v **learned** or **learnt** /lɜːnt‖lɜːrnt/, **learned** or **learnt** 1 [I;T] to gain knowledge of something or skill in doing something: *The child is learning quickly.* | *I'm trying to learn French.* | *He is learning to write.* | *She is learning how to dance.* □ USEFUL PATTERNS to learn something; to learn to do something; to learn how to do something 2 [T] to put and hold something in your memory: *Learn this list of words.* 3 [I; T + (that)] to become informed of something: *She learnt* **of** *her son's success in the newspapers.* □ USEFUL PATTERNS to learn something; to learn that...; to learn of/about something 4 [I] to come to understand something, especially that you should behave in a certain way: *You must learn not to spend all your money on records.* –see KNOW (USAGE) □ USEFUL PATTERNS to learn something; to learn to do something 5 **learn your lesson**, **learn the hard way**, **learn from your mistakes** to suffer so much from doing something that you will not do something again 6 **learn parrot-fashion**, **learn by rote** to learn something by repeating it over and over again, without trying to understand it 7 **learn the ropes** to find out how things are done [RELATED PHRASE **show someone the ropes**]

learn·ed /ˈlɜːnɪd ‖ ˈlɜːr-/ adj respected for having or expressing a lot of knowledge: *a learned man* | *a learned book* –**learnedly** adv

learn·er /ˈlɜːnəʳ ‖ ˈlɜːr-/ n a person who is learning: *She's a slow learner.* | *a learner driver*

learn·ing /ˈlɜːnɪŋ ‖ ˈlɜːr-/ n [U] great knowledge that you have got by studying

learnt /lɜːnt ‖ lɜːrnt/ the past tense and past participle of LEARN

lease /liːs/ n a written agreement by which property is given to someone to use for a certain time in return for rent or a sum of money: *a five-year lease* –**lease** v **leased**, **leasing** [T] : *They've leased the house out while they're abroad.* | *I've leased a small shop.*

leash /liːʃ/ n fml a length of leather, chain, or rope tied to a dog to control it: *Dogs must be kept on a leash.*

least¹ /liːst/ adv [superlative of LITTLE] 1 to the smallest degree: *The attack happened just when we least expected it.* | *This is the least friendly place I've*

ever been to! 2 **least of all** especially not: *Nobody was pleased to see him, least of all me.* 3 **not least** a phrase used when you are giving an important reason for something, or an important example of something: *Trade has been bad, not least because of the increased cost of raw materials.*

least² det, pron [superlative of LITTLE] 1 the smallest amount: *In the end I chose the one that cost the least.* | *I chose the meat that had the least fat on it.* 2 **at least**: a used when you are giving the smallest amount of something: *There must have been at least 500 people there.* | *Shoes like that cost £50 at least!* b used when you are giving the smallest thing that someone should do: *She should at least apologize!* | *They could at least have answered my letter!* c used when you are giving one advantage that exists among a lot of disadvantages: *The hotel was noisy and dirty, but at least it was cheap.* d used when you have made a statement which you are correcting because it was too strong: *She's coming with us. At least, I think she is.* 3 **not in the least** not at all: *She's not in the least worried.*

leath·er /ˈleðəʳ/ n [U] treated animal skin used for making things like shoes and bags: *a leather coat*

leath·er·y /ˈleðəri/ adj hard and stiff like leather: *leathery meat*

leave¹ /liːv/ v **left** /left/, **leaving** 1 [I;T] to go away from a person or place: *They're just leaving.* | *His brother has left home.* | *The ship is leaving* **for** *New York soon.* | *She's left her husband.* 2 [T] to allow something to remain, especially after you have gone away: *She's left your dinner in the oven.* | *Someone has left the window open.* | *Is there any coffee left?* | *Why have you left your vegetables?* | *I'll leave the rest of the work until tomorrow.* | *2 from 8 leaves 6.* 3 [T + adv/prep] to forget to take or bring something: *Don't leave your coat behind!* | *I've done my homework, but I've left it at home.* –see FORGET (USAGE) 4 [T] to pass on property after your death: *My father left everything to my sister.* 5 **leave something to someone** to make someone responsible for something: *I don't mind where we go. I'll leave that to you.* | *He left the accounts to me.* 6 **leave someone alone** to allow someone to be by themselves 7 **leave someone/something alone** not to touch, move, worry, or annoy them: *Don't tease the dog – leave him alone!* | *Leave those cakes alone or there won't be enough for tea.* 8 **leave go** to stop holding a person or thing: *Don't leave go* **of** *the handle.* 9 **leave no stone unturned** to try everything possible in order to do something or to find something: *We will leave no stone unturned in our efforts to find an answer.*

leave off phr v [I;T **leave off** sthg] to stop or give up doing something: *I wish the rain would leave off.* | *I didn't leave off work until ten o'clock last night.*

leave sbdy/sthg ↔ **out** phr v [T] to fail to include a person or thing: *I left out the important point.* | *They left me out of the team.*

leave² n [U] 1 a period of time away from work or duty: *Those soldiers are on leave.* | *I'm spending my next leave in Greece.* | *She's taking three months maternity leave.* 2 fml permission: *Have you been given leave to swim here?*

leaves /liːvz/ the plural of LEAF

lech·er·ous /ˈletʃərəs/ adj having or showing openly a desire for continual sexual pleasure (a word used to express disapproval) –**lecherously** adv [U] –**lecher** n

lech·er·y /ˈletʃəri/ n [U] strong and continual interest in sexual pleasure (a word used to express disapproval)

lec·ture /ˈlektʃəʳ/ v lectured, lecturing 1 [I] to give a formal talk or a number of talks to a group of people, especially as a method of teaching in a college: *She lectures on English history.* 2 [T] to give someone a long solemn scolding or warning: *He lectured us on the evils of drink.* –lecture n : *a history lecture* | *He gave a very good lecture on computer programming.* | *a lecture on good manners*

lec·tur·er /ˈlektʃərəʳ/ n a person who teaches at a university or college or who gives formal talks to people interested in a particular subject: *a lecturer in economics* | *a biology lecturer* –lectureship n : *She's got a lectureship at Oxford.*

led /led/ v the past tense and past participle of LEAD¹

ledge /ledʒ/ n 1 a flat, narrow shelf: *There's a bird on the window ledge.* 2 a flat shelf on the side of a cliff or rock

led·ger /ˈledʒəʳ/ n an account book in which the money going in and out of a company is recorded

leech /liːtʃ/ n a small wormlike creature that lives by drinking the blood of living animals

leek /liːk/ n a green and white vegetable with a long stem and a taste similar to that of an onion –see picture on page 344

leer /lɪəʳ/ n an unpleasant smile expressing cruel enjoyment or thoughts of sex –leer v [I] : *He leered at the young girl.* –leeringly adv

lee·way /ˈliːweɪ/ n [C;U] the additional time, space, money and so on that allows you to do or change something if necessary: *We should allow a bit of leeway in case the traffic is bad.*

left¹ /left/ adj [only before a noun] 1 on the side of the body that contains a person's heart: *her left arm* 2 on your left side: *the left bank of the stream* –opposite right

left² n 1 the left the left side or direction: *Keep to the left.* | *The shop is on the left, past the traffic lights.* | *The window is to the left of the door.* 2 [C] a blow with the left hand 3 the Left, the left political parties or groups that generally support the workers and work for social change: *supporters of the left* | *The extreme left are calling for a wealth tax.* –opposite right

left³ adv towards the left: *Go down to the crossroads and turn left.* –opposite right

left⁴ the past tense and past participle of LEAVE

left-hand /ˌ· ˈ·◁/ adj [only before a noun] 1 on or going to the left: *the left-hand page* | *a left-hand bend in the road* | *on the left-hand side* 2 of, for, with, or done by the left hand

left-hand·ed /ˌ· ˈ···◁/ adj 1 using the left hand more easily than the right for certain actions 2 made for a left-handed person to use: *left-handed scissors* 3 done with the left hand –opposite right-handed –left-handedness n [U]

left lug·gage of·fice /ˌ· ˈ··· ˌ··/ n a place, especially in a station, where you can leave your bags for a certain period

left·o·ver /ˈleft‚əʊvəʳ/ adj remaining after you have used what you need: *I made the curtains, and there was enough leftover material for some cushion covers.*

left·o·vers /ˈleft‚əʊvəz ‖ -ərz/ n [pl] food which remains uneaten after a meal

left·wards /ˈleftwədz ‖ -ərdz/ adv (also leftward AmE) towards the left –opposite rightwards –leftward adj

left wing /ˌ· ˈ·◁/ adj having certain political ideas which include support for greater social change: *a left-wing politician* | *She's very left wing.* –left wing n : *the left wing of the party* –opposite right wing –left-winger /ˌ· ˈ·· / n

leg /leg/ n 1 one of the limbs on which a person or an animal walks –see PAIR (USAGE) 2 the part of a pair of trousers that covers your leg 3 one of the long thin supports on which a piece of furniture stands 4 one stage of a journey or competition: *The last leg of the journey always seems the longest.* 5 -legged with legs of a certain number or kind: *a four-legged animal* | *sitting cross-legged*

leg·a·cy /ˈlegəsi/ n legacies 1 money or property that passes to you on the death of the owner, following their official written wishes: *I got a small legacy from my aunt.* 2 a situation which is passed on or left behind by someone or something that came before: *The legacies of the war were disease and hunger.*

le·gal /ˈliːgəl/ adj 1 allowed by law: *Are her business dealings really legal?* –opposite ILLEGAL 2 [only before a noun] relating to or using the law: *the legal system* | *The Council is taking legal action against its accountant.* –legally adv –legality /lɪˈgælɪti/ [U]

■ USAGE Compare legal, lawful, legitimate. Legal is the ordinary word for actions allowed by the law, and the general word for things connected with the law: *It is legal for people over 18 to buy alcohol.* | *the legal profession.* Lawful suggests that the law has moral or religious force: *a lawful marriage* | *your lawful king.* Legitimate means "accepted by law, custom or common belief": *the legitimate government* | *He claimed that bombing the town was a legitimate act of war.* | *Her illness was a legitimate reason for being absent from work.*

le·gal·ize /ˈliːgəlaɪz/ v legalized, legalizing (also legalise BrE) [T] to make something legal: *The use of certain drugs may be legalized.* –legalization /ˌliːgəlaɪˈzeɪʃ ən ‖ -gələ- / n [U]

legal ten·der /ˌ·· ˈ··/ n any form of money which, by law, must be accepted if it is offered in payment

le·ga·tion /lɪˈgeɪʃ ən/ n a group of people who are employed to represent their government in a foreign country

le·gend /ˈledʒənd/ n 1 [C] an old story, usually about ancient times, which is probably not true: *the legend of King Arthur* 2 [U] stories of this kind considered together: *a character in Chinese legend* 3 [C] a person who has become famous in a particular area of activity: *Dylan has become a legend in his own lifetime.* 4 [C] words written on something like a map to describe its contents

le·gen·da·ry /ˈledʒəndəri ‖ -deri/ adj 1 told of in a legend: *the legendary kings of Ireland* 2 very famous but perhaps hard to believe: *His drinking was legendary.*

leg·gings /ˈlegɪŋz/ n [pl] an outer covering which you wear to protect your legs –see picture on page 50

leg·gy /ˈlegi/ adj leggier, leggiest with particularly long legs (used especially of women, children, and young animals) –legginess n [U]

le·gi·ble /ˈledʒəbəl/ adj clear enough to be read, or to be read easily (used of writing or print) –opposite illegible –legibly adv : *Please write legibly.* –legibility /ˌledʒəˈbɪlɪti/ n [U]

le·gion /ˈliːdʒən/ n 1 a group of soldiers or other armed men 2 a large group of people: *A legion of admirers had gathered outside to see the star leave.*

le·gis·late /ˈledʒɪsleɪt/ v **legislated, legislating** [I] to make laws: *Parliament may legislate against the selling of human organs.* **–legislator** n

le·gis·la·tion /ˌledʒɪsˈleɪʃən/ n [U] **1** the act of making laws **2** a body of laws: *new legislation concerning the employment of children*

le·gis·la·tive /ˈledʒɪslətɪv ‖ -leɪtɪv/ adj [only before a noun] **1** concerning the making of laws **2** having the power and duty to make laws: *a legislative assembly*

le·gis·la·ture /ˈledʒɪsleɪtʃəʳ, -lətʃəʳ/ n the group of people who have the power to make and change laws

le·git·i·mate /lɪˈdʒɪtɪmɪt/ adj **1** legal or correct: *Her demand for compensation is perfectly legitimate.* –opposite **illegitimate 2** born of parents who are legally married to each other –opposite **illegitimate 3** reasonable: *They had a legitimate reason for being late.* –see LEGAL (USAGE) **–legitimately** adv **–legitimacy** n [U]

lei·sure /ˈleʒəʳ ‖ ˈliːr-/ n **1** [U] free time: *A wide variety of leisure activities is available to students outside class time.* **2 at leisure, at your leisure:** a not working or busy b without hurrying: *You can finish that at your leisure, it's not urgent.*

lei·sured /ˈleʒəd ‖ ˈliːʒərd/ adj having plenty of free time: *the leisured classes*

lei·sure·ly /ˈleʒəli ‖ ˈliːʒərli/ adj [only before a noun] done without hurrying: *a leisurely walk*

lem·on /ˈlemən/ n [C;U] a fruit with a thick yellow skin and a sour taste: *a lemon drink | mineral water with a slice of lemon* –see picture on page 344

lem·on·ade /ˌleməˈneɪd◂/ n [U] **1** a sweet, gassy drink **2** a drink made from the juice of fresh lemons with sugar and water

lend /lend/ v **lent** /lent/, **lent** [T] **1** to give someone the use of something for a limited time: *Can you lend me £10? | I've lent my notes to Bob.* □ USEFUL PATTERNS to lend something to someone; to lend someone something **2** fml to add something to a person, thing or situation: *The flags lent colour to the streets. | The new evidence lends support to claims that she is innocent.* **3 lend a hand** to help someone do something: *Could you come and lend a hand in the kitchen?* **4 lend an ear** to listen sympathetically **5 lend yourself to** to be easily used or thought of in a certain way: *This hall lends itself to large meetings.*

length /leŋθ/ n **1** [C;U] the measurement or distance from one end of something to the other along its longest side: *The length of the room is 10 metres. | The garden is 40 metres in length. | We walked the length of the street.* –compare BREADTH **2** [C] a piece of something, especially of a certain length or for a particular purpose: *a length of rope* **3** [C] the amount of something: *He judges a book by its length!* **4** [C;U] the amount of time something takes: *We are all worried about the length of her visit.* **5 at length:** a after a long time: *At length he came back.* b in detail: *They spoke at length about the situation.* **6 go to any lengths, go to considerable lengths, go to great lengths** to be prepared to do anything, or more than is usual, to succeed: *He would go to any lengths to keep his government in power.*

length·en /ˈleŋθən/ v [I;T] to become or to make something longer –opposite **shorten**

length·ways /ˈleŋθweɪz/ adv (also **lengthwise** /-waɪz/, **longways**) in the direction of the length: *Fold the cloth lengthways.*

length·y /ˈleŋθi/ adj **lengthier, lengthiest** very long, and sometimes too long: *a lengthy speech* **–lengthily** adv

le·ni·ent /ˈliːniənt/ adj not severe: *a lenient teacher | a lenient view of his behaviour | a lenient punishment* **–lenience** (also **leniency**) n [U]

lens /lenz/ n **1** a special piece of glass or plastic, curved on one or both sides, which you use to see things more clearly: *He has changed his glasses for contact lenses. | A simple telescope has two lenses.* **2** the part of your eye which collects the light

lent /lent/ the past tense and past participle of LEND

Lent n [U] the 40 days before EASTER, during which many Christians give up certain foods or other pleasures

len·til /ˈlentl, -tɪl/ n a small round seed which is dried and used for food

Le·o /ˈliːəʊ/ n one of the signs of the ZODIAC

leop·ard /ˈlepəd ‖ -ərd/ n a large, fierce animal belonging to the cat family, which has a yellow coat with black spots; a female leopard is called a **leopardess**

le·o·tard /ˈliːətɑːd ‖ -tɑːrd/ n a tight-fitting garment which covers a person's body from their neck to the top of their legs; it is worn by dancers and by people doing exercises

lep·er /ˈlepəʳ/ n **1** a person who has leprosy: *a leper hospital* **2** a person who is avoided by other people, perhaps because of something bad they have done

lep·ro·sy /ˈleprəsi/ n [U] a serious illness in which your skin becomes hard and thick and loses its feeling, and your flesh is badly damaged **–leprous** /ˈleprəs/ adj

les·bi·an /ˈlezbiən/ n a woman who is sexually attracted to other women **–lesbian** adj **–lesbianism** n [U]

less¹ /les/ det, pron, adv [comparative of LITTLE] **1** not as much: *The next train should be less crowded than this. | I go to London less frequently than before. | He works less than he used to. | People in this country spend less money on food than people in other European countries. | Could you try to make less noise? | Let's have less of that shouting!* **2 less and less** continuing to become smaller in amount or degree: *I seem to be spending less and less of my time working. | People are becoming less and less interested in politics.* **3 no less than** a phrase used to show that you are surprised that a number or amount is so large: *There were no less than 2000 people at the rally.*

■ USAGE In informal English many people now use **less** and **least** with plural nouns, but this is still considered to be incorrect. **Fewer** and **fewest** are the generally accepted correct forms: *There were fewer people than I expected. | Who has made the fewest mistakes?*

less² prep subtracting a particular number or amount: *You will be paid £200 a week, less tax.*

less·en /ˈlesən/ v [I;T] to become or to make something smaller in size, amount, or importance

less·er /ˈlesəʳ/ adj, adv [only before a noun] not so great or not so much: *the lesser of two evils | one of the lesser-known African writers*

les·son /ˈlesən/ n **1** something which is taught to or learned by a pupil: *a physics lesson | piano lessons* **2** the period of time in which a subject is studied: *The school day is divided into eight forty-minute lessons.* **3** an experience from which you should learn: *His car accident was a lesson to him.* **4** a passage from the BIBLE which is read to people in church

lest /lest/ *prep* in case something unwanted should happen: *I wrote down the date lest I should forget it.*

let /let/ *v* **let, let, letting** [T] **1** to allow someone to do something, or allow something to happen: *My dad wouldn't let me smoke.* | *They let the prisoners go.* | *I knocked on the door but he didn't let me in.* | *Please let the doctor through.* | *Don't let the paper get wet.*

☐ USEFUL PATTERNS to let someone do something; to let something happen; to let someone in, out, through, past, etc

2 a word you use to say that someone can do something or should do something: *Let him do what he likes; I don't care.* | *Let there be no mistake about it.* **3** to allow someone to use a room, building, or piece of land in return for regular payments: *We decided to let the house rather than sell it.* **4 let alone** not to mention something which is even less possible: *The baby can't even walk, let alone run.* **5 let someone alone, leave someone alone** to not touch or trouble someone: *Let your sister alone!* | *I wish the press would just let me alone.* **6 let go of someone/something, let someone/something go** to stop holding someone or something: *Let go of my arm.* | *Don't let go of the handle.* | *Let me go!* | *The police held him for 24 hours before letting him go.* **7 let yourself go** to behave more freely and more naturally than you would usually: *She had a few drinks and let herself go a bit.* **8 let someone know** to tell someone about something: *Let me know what day you'll be arriving.* **9 let me** a phrase you use when you are going to do something: *Let me just get my coat and we can go.* | *Let me start by talking about pollution in general.* **10 let us, let's** a phrase you use when you are suggesting to someone that you should both do something or all do something: *Let's meet in town.* | *Come on, let's get going.*

■ USAGE **1 Let us** is usually shortened to **let's** when it is used in conversation to make a suggestion which includes the person you are speaking to: *Come on, Jim,* **let's** *go and have lunch!* | **Let's** *have a party at the end of term.* **2 Let's** can be used by itself to show that you agree with someone else's suggestion: *"Shall we go to the cinema tonight?" "Oh, yes,* **Let's.***"* **3** The negative of **let's** is **let's not:** *let's not waste time on this.* (In British English **don't let's** is also possible)

let down *phr v* **1** [T let sbdy ↔ **down**] to cause someone to be disappointed: *I'm sorry to let you down, but I really can't come this evening.* | *She felt that the education system had let her down.* **2** [T let sthg ↔ **down**] to make a piece of clothing longer

let in for *phr v* **let yourself in for something** to cause yourself to experience something unpleasant or unwanted: *I don't think he realizes what he's letting himself in for.*

let sbdy **in on** sthg *phr v* [T] to allow someone to know something that was secret: *They refused to let me in on the joke.*

let off *phr v* **1** [T let sbdy ↔ **off** (sthg)] to allow someone not to do something that it is their duty to do: *They let him off his homework because he was ill.* **2** [T let sbdy ↔ **off**] to not give someone a punishment when they have done something wrong: *The police let him off with a caution.* **3** [T let sthg ↔ **off**] to cause something to explode: *people letting off fireworks*

let on *phr v* [I] to tell a secret: *He asked me where John was, but I didn't let on.*

let sthg ↔ **out** *phr v* [T] **1** to express a sound: *She let out a sharp cry of pain.* **2** to make clothes bigger: *I had to let my skirt out.*

let up *phr v* [I] to become less or stop: *Will this rain ever let up?*

let·down /ˈletdaʊn/ *n infml* a disappointment: *Rain on our wedding day; what a letdown!*

le·thal /ˈliːθəl/ *adj* able to kill people or destroy things: *a lethal dose of a poison* | *His business tactics can be lethal to small companies.*

leth·ar·gy /ˈleθədʒi ‖ -ər-/ *n* [U] the state of being unwilling or physically unable to make the effort to do anything because you feel lazy, tired, or ill –**lethargic** /lɪˈθɑːdʒɪk ‖ -ɑːr-/ *adj*

let·ter /ˈletər/ *n* **1** a written or printed message which is usually sent to someone in an envelope: *Would you post my letter when you go out?* | *I must write them a letter.* **2** one of the signs in writing or printing that represents a speech sound: *Start the sentence with a capital letter.* | *How many letters are there in your name?* **3 the letter of** the exact words of an agreement or law, rather than its real or intended meaning **4 to the letter** exactly as something is written or told to you: *Follow the instructions to the letter.*

let·ter·box /ˈletəbɒks ‖ ˈletərbɑːks/ *n* **1** a box in a place such as a post office or the street in which letters can be posted **2** *BrE* a hole in the front door or wall of a building into which letters are delivered –see picture on page 441

let·ter·head /ˈletəhed ‖ -ər-/ *n* the name and address of a person or business printed at the top of their writing paper

let·ter·ing /ˈletərɪŋ/ *n* [U] letters or words that are written or drawn in a particular style

let·tuce /ˈletɪs/ *n* [C;U] a plant with large pale green leaves, which are eaten raw –see picture on page 344

let·up /ˈletʌp/ *n* [C;U] an end to or decrease in activity

leu·kae·mia /luːˈkiːmiə/ *n* (also **leukemia**) [U] a very serious illness in which the blood has too many white cells

lev·el¹ /ˈlevəl/ *n* **1** [C;U] a position of height in relation to a flat surface: *We are now at 5,000 metres above sea level.* | *The garden is arranged on two levels.* | *an eye-level grill* **2** [C;U] a position in a system of ranks: *pay increases for lower-level managers* | *talks at ministerial level* **3** [C] a smooth flat surface, especially a wide area of flat ground: *You should build on the level, not on the slope.* **4** [C] the amount, degree, or number of something: *Workers have been told to increase production levels.* | *The general level of achievement is satisfactory.* **5** the usual American word for SPIRIT LEVEL **6 on the level** *infml* honest, or honestly

lev·el² *v* **-ll-** (**-l-** *AmE*) [T] **1** to make something flat and even: *Level the ground before you plant the seeds.* **2** to knock something down to the ground: *They levelled all the old trees to make way for the road.* **3 level something at** to aim a weapon at a person or thing **4 level something at someone, level something against someone** to make a complaint about someone: *A serious charge was levelled at the minister.* **5 level with someone** *infml* to be honest with someone

level off *phr v* [I] (also **level out**) to become steady or equal: *Prices have begun to level off now.*

lev·el³ *adj* **1** flat, with no part higher than the rest: *If the table top isn't level, things will roll off.* | *a level teaspoonful of salt* **2** at the same height, position, or standard: *The child's head is level with his father's knee.* | *The horses are level now, but Blue Magic is looking tired.* **3** steady and calm (used of a person's voice or the way they look at something) **4 do your level best** *infml* to do all that you can

level⁴ *adv* so as to be level with or parallel to a flat surface: *missiles flying level with the ground*

level cross·ing /ˌ·· ˈ··/ *n BrE* a place where a road and a railway cross each other –see picture on page 735

level-head·ed /ˌ·· ˈ···◂/ *adj* calm and sensible in making judgments

le·ver¹ /ˈliːvəʳ ‖ ˈle-, ˈliː-/ *n* **1** a bar which you place under something heavy or stiff and push down on to move the object **2** a handle on a machine which you push or pull to operate it: *a gear lever* **3** something which you can use to influence someone: *They used the threat of strike action as a lever.*

lever² *v* [T + adv/prep] to move a person or thing, using a lever or similar movement: *They levered the rocks into position.* | *He had to lever open the window.* | *She managed to lever herself up from the sofa.*

le·ver·age /ˈliːvərɪdʒ ‖ ˈle-, ˈliː-/ *n* [U] **1** the action, use, or power of a lever **2** power, influence, or other means of obtaining a result

lev·e·ret /ˈlevərɪt/ *n* a young HARE

lev·i·tate /ˈlevɪteɪt/ *v* levitated, levitating [I;T] to rise and float in the air as if by magic, or to make a person or thing do this –**levitation** /ˌlevɪˈteɪʃən/ *n* [U]

lev·i·ty /ˈlevɪti/ *n* [U] *fml* lack of seriousness or respect for serious matters

lev·y /ˈlevi/ *n* levies an official demand for a tax or for people to become soldiers –**levy** *v* levied, levying [T] : *to levy a tax on tobacco*

lewd /luːd/ *adj* dealing with sex, or showing an interest in it, in a way that is not socially acceptable: *a lewd gesture* –**lewdly** *adv* –**lewdness** *n* [U]

lex·i·cal /ˈleksɪkəl/ *adj* tech about or relating to words –**lexically** /-kli/ *adv*

lex·i·con /ˈleksɪkən ‖ -kɑːn, -kən/ *n* a list of the words of a language or subject, often recorded in a dictionary

li·a·bil·i·ty /ˌlaɪəˈbɪlɪti/ *n* liabilities **1** [C;U] some thing for which you are legally responsible, or the condition of being responsible for it: *The firm does not accept liability for the accident.* **2** [C] a debt: *Our liabilities exceed our assets.* **3** [C] a person or thing that makes what you want to do more difficult: *A small child is a real liability in a restaurant.*

li·a·ble /ˈlaɪəbəl/ *adj* [never before a noun] **1** likely to do something or to happen, especially from habit or a certain tendency: *He is liable to lose his temper in situations like this.* **2** legally responsible for something: *I am not liable for my son's debts.*

li·aise /liˈeɪz/ *v* liaised, liaising [I] **1** to work together so that the different people concerned are informed about what is being done: *We must liaise closely with the government on this.* **2** to keep different groups or people informed about what the others are doing: *My main job is to liaise between management and the unions.*

li·ai·son /liˈeɪzən ‖ ˈliəzɑːn, liˈeɪ-/ *n* **1** [sing; U] a working association or connection: *There was close liaison between the school and the parents.* **2** [C] a short sexual relationship between a man and a woman who are not married to each other

li·ar /ˈlaɪəʳ/ *n* a person who tells lies

li·bel /ˈlaɪbəl/ *n* [C;U] *law* something which is written about someone which is not true or not fair and which makes other people lose respect for them –**libel** *v* -ll- (-l- *AmE*) [T]

li·bel·lous /ˈlaɪbələs/ *adj* (**libelous** *AmE*) **1** containing a libel against someone: *a libellous article in a newspaper* **2** in the habit of writing libels –**libellously** *adv*

lib·e·ral¹ /ˈlɪbərəl/ *adj* **1** willing to respect the ideas of others: *a liberal attitude to drugs* **2** favouring a wide general knowledge and possibilities for self-expression: *a liberal education* **3** giving or given freely and generously: *a liberal supporter of the hospital* | *a liberal supply of food* **4** (also **Liberal**) supporting gradual social and political change –**liberalism** *n* [U]

liberal² *n* **1** a person who is willing to respect the ideas of others **2** a person who is in favour of gradual social change **3 Liberal** a person who supports the Liberal Democrats in Britain, or a similar political party in other countries

Liberal Dem·o·crats /ˌ··· ˈ···/ *n* the Liberal Democrats [pl] a British political party which works for gradual social and political change

lib·e·ral·i·ty /ˌlɪbəˈrælɪti/ *n* [U] (also **liberalness** /ˈlɪbərəlnəs/) **1** generosity **2** willingness to respect other ideas

lib·e·ral·ly /ˈlɪbərəli/ *adv* generously, or in large quantities

lib·e·rate /ˈlɪbəreɪt/ *v* liberated, liberating [T] *fml* to free a person, animal, or a country: *The government has promised to liberate all political prisoners.* | *The country was liberated after five years of enemy occupation.* –**liberator** *n* –**liberation** /ˌlɪbəˈreɪʃən/ *n* [U]

lib·e·rat·ed /ˈlɪbəreɪtɪd/ *adj* acting according to modern ideas of what is acceptable in social and sexual matters: *a liberated woman*

lib·er·ty /ˈlɪbəti ‖ -ər-/ *n* liberties **1** [U] personal or political freedom from outside control: *the ideals of liberty and democracy* **2** liberties [pl] personal or political freedoms: *the need to protect our civil liberties* **3** [U] the right or permission to do something **4 at liberty: a** free from prison or other control **b** allowed to do something **5 take the liberty** to do something without asking permission, because you think you would be allowed to do so: *I took the liberty of helping myself to a drink. Is that all right?*

li·bi·do /lɪˈbiːdəʊ/ *n* libidos tech sexual desire

Li·bra /ˈliːbrə/ *n* one of the signs of the ZODIAC

li·brar·i·an /laɪˈbreəriən/ *n* a person who is in charge of a library or who helps to run one –**librarianship** *n* [U]

li·bra·ry /ˈlaɪbrəri, -bri ‖ -breri/ *n* libraries **1** a building or room containing books and magazines which the public or members of a special group can look at or borrow: *the school library* **2** a collection usually of books, but sometimes of other objects, which may be looked at or borrowed: *a record library* | *a toy library*

lice /laɪs/ *n* the plural of LOUSE

li·cence /ˈlaɪsəns/ – *n* (**license** *AmE*) **1** [U] permission to do something **2** [C] an official paper showing that you have permission to do something: *a driving licence* | *a licence to sell alcohol* **3** [U] freedom, or too much freedom, of action or expression

li·cense /ˈlaɪsəns/ *v* (also **licence**) licensed, licensing [T] to give official permission for someone to do something

li·censed /ˈlaɪsənst/ *adj* having a licence, especially to sell alcohol or to practise a certain profession: *a licensed restaurant* | *a licensed debt-collector*

license plate /ˈ··· ·/ *n* the usual American word for NUMBERPLATE

li·cen·tious /laɪˈsenʃəs/ *fml* behaving in a sexually uncontrolled manner –**licentiously** *adv* –**licentiousness** *n* [U]

li·chen /ˈlaɪkən, ˈlɪtʃən/ *n* [C;U] a flat spreading plant that covers the surfaces of stones and trees

lick¹ /lɪk/ *v* [T] **1** to move your tongue across a surface: *She licked the stamps and stuck them on.* | *The dog always licks his dish clean.* **2** *infml* to defeat a person or group of people: *Our team was well and truly licked.* **3 lick your lips** to move your tongue across your lips, showing that you are looking forward to something, or you have enjoyed something **4 lick your wounds** to feel sorry for yourself after a defeat

lick² *n* **1** a movement of your tongue across a surface **2** *infml* a small amount of something: *This door needs a lick of paint.*

lic·o·rice /ˈlɪkərɪs, -rɪʃ/ *n* [U] see LIQUORICE

lid /lɪd/ *n* **1** the piece that covers the open top of a pot, box, or other container and that you can lift up or remove **2** see EYELID

lie¹ /laɪ/ *v* **lay** /leɪ/, **lain** /leɪn/, **lying** /ˈlaɪ-ɪŋ/ [I + adv/prep] **1** to be in a flat position on a surface: *The book is lying on the table.* | *He lay on the floor, reading a book.* **2** to be in a certain place or position: *The town lies to the east of us.* **3** to be found: *The truth lies somewhere between the statements of the two men.* **4** to remain or be kept in a certain place or condition: *Don't leave your money lying in the bank.* | *The town lay in ruins.* **5 lie ahead, lie in store** to happen in the future: *The situation is fine now, but who knows what lies ahead?* **6 lie behind something** to be the hidden reason for something: *It's not clear what lies behind her decision to leave.* **7 lie in wait** to wait for someone who is not expecting you and usually does not want to see you **8 lie low** to stay hidden so that people, especially the police, cannot find you

lie about/around *phr v* [I] to spend your time doing nothing because you are lazy

lie down *phr v* [I] to put yourself into a flat position on a surface: *Lie down and sleep for a while.* –see LAY¹ (USAGE)

lie in *phr v* [I] to stay in bed later than usual in the morning

lie² *v* **lied, lied, lying** [I] to say something that you know is not true: *Don't lie to me! I know where you've been.* | *She lied about her age to get the job.*

lie³ *n* a statement which you know is not true: *That child tells lies all the time.* | *She said she loved me, but it was all a lie.*

lie-down /ˈ· ·, ˌ· ˈ·/ *n infml* a short rest, usually on a bed

lie-in *n* /ˈ· ·, ˌ· ˈ·/ *n infml* a longer rest in bed than usual, so that you get up later in the morning: *I really enjoy a lie-in at the weekend.*

lieu /ljuː, luː ‖ luː/ *n fml* **in lieu** instead of something: *I'll take your watch in lieu of payment.*

lieu·ten·ant /lefˈtenənt ‖ luː-/ *n* an officer of low rank in the armed forces

life /laɪf/ *n* **lives** /laɪvz/ **1** [U] the quality that allows animals and plants to continue existing: *He lost his life in an accident.* | *Is there life after death?* **2** [U] living things: *There is no life on the moon.* | *plant life* **3** [U] human existence: *Life isn't all fun.* **4** [C] the period during which you are alive, or from your birth until now: *a long and happy life* | *I have lived in England all my life.* **5** [C;U] the way in which you live: *They lead very busy lives.* | *How do you like married life?* **6** [C] the period during which something continues to work or to exist: *Many new magazines*

have a very short life. **7** [U] activity: *There were signs of life in the forest as the sun rose.* | *The children are full of life this morning.* **8 be the life and soul of something** to amuse and entertain other people in a group: *He was the life and soul of the party.* **9** [U] (also **life imprisonment** /ˌ· ·ˈ···/) the punishment of being put in prison for the rest of your life, or for a very long time: *sentenced to life for the murder* **10** [C] (also **life story** /ˈ· ··/) a written, filmed, or other account of a person's existence: *a short life of Shakespeare* **11 Not on your life!** *infml* certainly not!

■ USAGE Notice that some fixed phrases use **life**, but others use **living**. For example **life** is used in **quality of life**, **way of life**, and **lifestyle**: *They claim that* **quality of life** *is more important than a big salary.* | *We soon got used to the American* **way of life**. | *modern diseases caused by poor diet and a* **hectic lifestyle**. But **living** is used in **cost of living**, **standard of living**, and **earn/make a living**: *The* **cost of living** *has more than doubled in the last two years.* | *industrialized countries enjoying a high* **standard of living** | *It's hard to* **earn your living** *as a poet.*

life belt /ˈ· ·/ *n* a belt or ring that will float, and that you hold or wear if you fall into water to stop you sinking

life-blood /ˈlaɪfblʌd/ *n* [U] something that gives continuing strength and force to a person or thing: *Trade is the lifeblood of most modern states.*

life-boat /ˈlaɪfbəʊt/ *n* a boat used for saving people who are in danger at sea

life ex·pec·tan·cy /ˌ· ·ˈ···/ *n* [C;U] the average number of years that a person can expect to live: *The life expectancy of people in Britain has increased in this century.*

life·guard /ˈlaɪfɡɑːd ‖ -ɑːrd/ *n* a person whose job is to help swimmers if they are in danger

life jack·et /ˈ· ˌ··/ *n* a garment filled with air that you wear round your chest to support you in water

life·less /ˈlaɪfləs/ *adj* **1** dead or seeming to be dead: *the lifeless body of the victim* **2** without strength, interest, or activity: *a lifeless performance* –**lifelessly** *adv* –**lifelessness** *n* [U]

life·like /ˈlaɪflaɪk/ *adj* very much like real life or a real person: *a lifelike statue*

life·line /ˈlaɪflaɪn/ *n* **1** a rope which is used for saving people who are in danger in the water **2** something which is very necessary to someone: *The telephone is my lifeline to the outside world.*

life·long /ˈlaɪflɒŋ ‖ -lɔːŋ/ *adj* [only before a noun] continuing all your life: *a lifelong friendship*

life sci·ence /ˈ· ˌ··/ *n* **the life sciences** [pl] the sciences that study plant, animal, and human life

life-size /ˌ· ˈ·◂/ *adj* (also **life-sized** /ˌ· ˈ·◂/) of the same size as what it represents (used of a work of art): *a life-size portrait*

life-style /ˈlaɪfstaɪl/ *n* the way you live, including the conditions you live in, the things you own, and the things you do: *a healthy lifestyle with a sensible diet and plenty of exercise*

life·time /ˈlaɪftaɪm/ *n* the period of time during which a person is alive or something continues

lift¹ /lɪft/ *v* **1** [T] to move something to a higher level: *I can't lift this suitcase.* | *Can you lift the carpet while I sweep under it.* | *He lifted his head as she entered the room.* –see picture on page 736 **2** [I] to move upwards and often disappear: *As the mist lifted, the farmhouse became visible.* **3** [T] to remove a limit or rule: *Restrictions on journalists have been lifted* *by the new government.* **4** [I;T] to make or become happier: *My heart lifted at the news.* **5** [T] *infml* to steal something **6** [T] *infml* to use other people's ideas without saying that they are not your own **7** [T + adv/prep] to carry something into or out of a place by plane **8 not lift a finger** to do nothing to help someone: *None of my children lifts a finger at home.*

lift off *phr v* [I] (of a space vehicle) to rise up into the air *The rocket lifts off at 12.00.*

lift² *n* **1** [C] an apparatus in a building that carries people or goods up and down between floors **2** [C] a free ride in a vehicle: *Can you give me a lift into town?* **3** [sing] *infml* a feeling of new confidence or cheerfulness: *The exam results gave me a real lift.* **4** [C;U] upward pressure of air on the wings of an aircraft

lift-off /'·‿·/ *n* the moment when a space vehicle rises up into the air

lig·a·ment /'lɪgəmənt/ *n* one of the strong bands that join bones or hold some part of your body in position: *He tore a ligament playing football.*

light¹ /laɪt/ *n* **1** [U] the natural force that allows us to see things: *This light is not good enough to read by.* | *She worked by candlelight.* **2** [U] the light of the sun or the time it lasts: *I must finish this painting before the light goes.* **3** [C] something that produces light: *Turn off the lights when you go to bed.* | *a neon light* **4** [C] something that is used to start a cigarette burning: *Have you got a light, please?* **5** [sing;U] brightness in your eyes which shows your feelings **6** [C] the way something or someone appears: *Workers and employers see the problem in quite a different light.* **7 come to light, be brought to light** to become known: *New information has come to light.* **8 go out like a light** to fall asleep as soon as you get into bed or to become unconscious **9 in the light of** taking something into account: *In the light of your recent behaviour, I'm afraid I must ask you to leave the company.* **10 see the light** to understand or accept something, especially a religious belief **11 throw light on, shed light on, cast light on** to make something clearer: *The report sheds light on the real cause of the problem.*

light² *v* **lit** /lɪt/, **lit 1** [I;T] to start burning, or to start something burning: *He lit a cigarette.* | *The fire won't light.* **2** [T] to give light to something: *The room is lit by several large lamps.*
■ USAGE The usual past participle of **light** is **lit**: *He's lit a match.* | *The match is lit.* But if the past participle stands as an adjective before the noun we use **lighted**: *a lighted match.*

light up *phr v* **1** [I;T stg sthg ↔ up] to become or to make something bright: *Her face lit up with joy.* | *The factory fire lit up the surrounding area.* **2** [I] to begin to smoke a cigarette: *He borrowed some matches and lit up.*

light³ *adj* **1** weighing little: *It's so light a child could lift it.* **2** not heavy, strong, or serious: *You need a light touch to play the piano quietly.* | *a light wind* | *These stories are just light bedtime reading.* **3** bright: *a light room* **4** pale: *light blue* –see picture on page 147 **5 a light meal** a small meal **6 a light sleeper** someone who wakes easily from sleep **7 make light of something** to treat something as if it were not important **8 make light work of something** to do something as if it were easy

light⁴ *adv* **travel light** to travel without many possessions: *I always travel light.*

light bulb /'·‿·/ *n* the glass part of an electric lamp that gives out light

light·en /'laɪtn/ *v* **1** [T] to make something less heavy **2** [I;T] to become or to make something less dark **3** [I] (of someone's face, voice, or mood) to become more cheerful

light·er /'laɪtər/ *n* an instrument which produces a flame for lighting things like fires or cigarettes: *a cigarette lighter*

light-fin·gered /ˌ·ˈ·‿·◂/ *adj infml* in the habit of stealing small things

light-head·ed /ˌ·ˈ·‿·◂/ *adj* **1** feeling slightly ill in your head **2** foolish or irresponsible

light-heart·ed /ˌ·ˈ·‿·◂/ *adj* cheerful

light·house /'laɪthaʊs/ *n* a tall building with a powerful flashing light that guides ships or warns them of dangerous rocks –see picture on page 735

light·ing /'laɪtɪŋ/ *n* [U] **1** the system or apparatus that gives light to a place: *We need more lighting in this office.* **2** the kind of light that this system produces: *I want stronger lighting above the desks.*

light·ly /'laɪtli/ *adv* **1** with little weight or force: *He pressed lightly on the handle.* **2** to a small degree: *lightly cooked* | *lightly armed* **3** without thinking carefully about something or knowing its importance: *I didn't start this court action lightly, you know!*

light·ning¹ /'laɪtnɪŋ/ *n* [U] a flash of bright light in the sky, usually followed by thunder: *The tower has been struck by lightning.*

lightning² *adj* [only before a noun] very quick, short, or sudden: *a lightning visit*

lightning con·duc·tor /'·· ·ˌ··/ *n* (**lightning rod** /'·· ˌ·/ *AmE*) a piece of metal fixed to the top of a building and leading down to the ground, which prevents the building being damaged if it is struck by lightning

light·weight /'laɪt-weɪt/ *adj* **1** of less than average weight or importance: *a lightweight camera* | *His books are lightweight, but quite amusing.* **2** *tech* weighing between 59 and 61 kilos (used of people who fight as a sport): *a lightweight boxer* –**lightweight** *n*

light year /'·‿·/ *n* the distance that light travels in one year

like¹ /laɪk/ *v* **liked, liking** [T] **1** to find someone or something pleasant: *Do you like bananas?* | *I've never liked her brother.* | *I didn't like the film very much.* | *I don't like the way this crisis is being handled.* | *Do you like reading?*
□ USEFUL PATTERNS to like someone/something; to like doing something
2 like to do something to do something if it is possible because you think that it is a good idea: *I like to go to the dentist every six months.* **3 not like to do something** to be unwilling to do something: *I don't like to interrupt them again.* **4 would like something, would like to do something** to choose something or choose to do something: *Would you like tea or coffee?* | *Would you like a biscuit?* | *I'd like to meet him.* **5 if you like** if you want this: *We can go out if you like.* | *I'll carry that for you, if you like.*
■ USAGE **Like** used on its own means "to be fond of or enjoy": *I like coffee.* (= I'm fond of it). **2** When asking for something **I would like/I'd like** is more common and more polite than **I want**: *I'd like a cup of coffee.* | *I'd like to go to the cinema.* **3** When offering something to someone use **Would you like…?**: *Would you like a cup of coffee?*

like² *adj fml* similar: *running, swimming, and other like sports*

like³ *prep* **1** similar to something or someone in some way: *She looks like her mother.* | *It tastes like chicken.* | *He was like a son to me.* | *Once the car has been painted it 'll look like new.* | *Like you, I was very disappointed by the announcement.* **2** used when you are asking someone to describe a person or thing or give their opinion: *What's she like?* | *What was the film like?* **3** typical of someone or something: *It was just like Mary to be late.* | *You're acting like a child!* **4** for example: *I enjoy outdoor sports like tennis and football.* | *A lot of people are still fit and healthy when they retire, like my parents for example.*
■ USAGE Note the difference between these uses of **like** and **as**: *He plays tennis like a professional.* (= He plays as well as a professional) | *He plays tennis as a professional.* (= He is a professional)

like⁴ *n* **1 the like** things that are similar: *running, swimming, and the like* **2 likes and dislikes** things that you do or do not like

like·a·ble /ˈlaɪkəbəl/ *adj* (also **likable**) easy to like (used of a person)

like·ly¹ /ˈlaɪkli/ *adj* **likelier, likeliest 1** probable or expected: *It seems likely that she'll pass her exams.* | *The likeliest result of the match is a draw.* –opposite **unlikely 2 be likely to do something** to be probably going to do something: *Inflation is likely to increase again this month.* | *Are we likely to arrive on time?* **3** suitable to give results: *a likely plan* | *a likely candidate for promotion*

likely² *adv* **1 very likely, most likely** probably: *They'll very likely come by car.* **2 as likely as not** probably **3 not likely!** *infml* certainly not!

like·ness /ˈlaɪknəs/ *n* [C;U] similarity to something or someone else: *Have you noticed the strong family likeness among the girls?*

lik·en /ˈlaɪkən/ *v* [T] *fml* **liken something to** to compare a person or thing with something which is similar: *Our little company can be likened to a big, happy family.*

like·wise /ˈlaɪk-waɪz/ *adv* **1** the same or in the same way: *John took off his shoes, so Peter did likewise.* **2** also: *For this job you need a lot of patience; likewise a sense of humour.*

lik·ing /ˈlaɪkɪŋ/ *n* [sing] **1** fondness for something: *I have only recently developed a liking for cigars.* **2 to your liking** as you like it: *Is the food to your liking, sir?* **3 for your liking** for your taste: *The wallpaper is too bright for my liking.*

li·lac /ˈlaɪlək/ *n* **1** [C] a tree with pink, purple, or white flowers which smell nice **2** [U] a pale purple colour –see picture on page 147

li·lo /ˈlaɪləʊ/ *n* **lilos** a plastic bed filled with air which you can lie on by the sea or floating on the water

lilt /lɪlt/ *n* [sing] the pleasant rise and fall of a voice or tune –**lilt** *v*

lil·y /ˈlɪli/ *n* **lilies** a plant, usually with large white flowers

limb /lɪm/ *n* **1** a leg, arm, or wing of an animal **2** a large branch of a tree **3 out on a limb** alone, without support

lim·ber /ˈlɪmbəʳ/ *v*
limber up *phr v* [I] to prepare for serious exercise by stretching your muscles

lim·bo /ˈlɪmbəʊ/ *n* **limbos 1** a state of uncertainty or waiting: *I'm in limbo until I start my new job.* **2** a dance from the West Indies in which a dancer leans back and passes under a rope or bar near the floor

lime /laɪm/ *n* **1** [U] a white substance used in making cement or to improve the soil **2** [C] a tree with yellow flowers and heart-shaped leaves **3** [C] a small green fruit which is juicy and tastes sour

lime·light /ˈlaɪmlaɪt/ *n* **the limelight** attention from the public: *The rich and famous have to get used to being in the limelight.*

lim·e·rick /ˈlɪmərɪk/ *n* a short, usually funny poem with five lines

lim·it¹ /ˈlɪmɪt/ *n* **1** the outside of something: *the limits* of *his kingdom* **2** the greatest quantity of something that is possible or acceptable: *My patience has reached its limit.* | *Don't break the speed limit.* **3 the limit** something or someone which is very annoying or upsetting: *This bus service is the limit. It's never on time.* **4 off limits** *AmE* where you are not allowed to go: *The air base is off limits to civilians.* **5 within limits** to a reasonable point

limit² *v* [T] to keep something below a certain point or amount: *We must limit our spending.* | *We must limit him to an hour's television a night.*

lim·i·ta·tion /ˌlɪmɪˈteɪʃən/ *n* **1** [C;U] a limit or the fact or condition of limiting or being limited, or the limit imposed: *There are limitations on what we can spend in this tax year.* **2 limitations** the limits to what you are able to do: *I know my limitations, so I'll get someone else to put the new roof on.*

lim·it·ed /ˈlɪmɪtɪd/ *adj* **1** small in amount or degree: *He has a limited understanding of the facts.* –opposite **unlimited 2** (also **Ltd.** after the name of the company) having a reduced duty to pay back debts: *a limited company* | *Longman Group Ltd*

lim·it·ing /ˈlɪmɪtɪŋ/ *adj* preventing improvement or increase in something: *One limiting factor in the improvement of health care is the shortage of doctors.*

lim·ou·sine /ˈlɪməziːn, ˌlɪməˈziːn/ *n* a large expensive car, usually with the driver's seat separated from the back by a sheet of glass

limp¹ /lɪmp/ *v* [I] to walk in an uneven way because one leg moves less easily than the other –**limp** *n* : *He walks with a limp.*

limp² *adj* without strength or firmness: *She suddenly went limp and fell to the ground.* | *a limp handshake* –**limply** *adv* –**limpness** *n* [U]

lim·pet /ˈlɪmpɪt/ *n* a small sea animal with a shell, which holds on tightly to rocks

lim·pid /ˈlɪmpɪd/ *adj* *lit* clear (used especially of liquid)

linc·tus /ˈlɪŋktəs/ *n* [U] liquid medicine to cure coughing

line¹ /laɪn/ *n* **1** a long, thin mark on a surface: *Can you draw a straight line?* | *a line drawing* | *Deep lines covered my grandfather's face.* **2** something that acts as a limit or border: *Jones crossed the finishing line two seconds ahead of the next runner.* | *There's a very fine line* **between** *punishment and cruelty.* **3** a row of people or things: *A line of people queued outside the cinema* | *My word-processor gives me 54 lines of text to each page.* **4** a piece of string, wire, or cord: *a clothes line* | *a washing line* | *a fishing line* **5** a telephone connection or wire: *The lines to Indonesia are terrible.* | *Hold the line, please!* **6** a railway track: *Passengers may not cross the lines.* **7** a company that provides a system for travelling or for moving goods, especially by sea or air: *an airline* | *a shipping line* **8** an opinion or way of behaving: *What is the government's line on overcrowding in prisons?* | *The police will take a tough line* **with** *hooligans.* **9** a job or other activity that you do or that interests you: *Her line is selling* *children's clothes.* | *Fishing isn't really my line.* **10** a type of goods: *Brooks are advertising a new line in hats.* **11** a number of people who are descended from each other: *He comes from a long line of actors.* **12 lines** [pl] the positions or defences of an army: *He disappeared behind enemy lines.* **13 lines** [pl] the words an actor learns and says in a play **14 along the line** at some point: *Somewhere along the line I stopped loving him.* **15 along the lines of** meaning more or less this: *He said something along the lines of, "I have no respect for them".* **16 be in line for** being seriously considered for a job: *She's in line for promotion at work.* **17 be in line with:** a to form a straight line with something: *Plant the trees in line with the hedge.* b to fit in with something: *That isn't in line with my ideas at all.* **18 be in the firing line** to be where you could be attacked or blamed **19 be on the right lines** to be working towards a good result **20 be out of line** to be different, or to behave in a way which is not acceptable: *Your comments on the president's decision are out of line.*

line² *v* **lined, lining** [T] **1** to draw or mark lines on something: *lined paper* | *Worry lined his forehead.* **2** to form rows along something: *Crowds lined the streets.* **3** to put some kind of material closely around the inside of something: *a coat lined with fur* **4 line your own pocket, line your pockets** to make money for yourself, perhaps dishonestly **line up** *phr v* **1** [I;T **line** sbdy/sthg ↔ **up**] to move into a row: *He lined up behind the others.* | *Line the glasses up and I'll fill them.* **2** [T **line** sbdy/sthg ↔ **up**] to arrange something, or to arrange for someone to be present: *I've lined up a famous singer for the school concert.*

lin·e·ar /ˈlɪniəʳ/ *adj* **1** of or in lines: *a linear diagram* **2** relating to length: *linear measurements* **3** in one direction: *linear change*

lin·en /ˈlɪnɪn/ *n* [U] **1** a kind of heavy cloth **2** things like sheets and tablecloths that are made of cloth: *Is there any clean bed linen?*

lin·er /ˈlaɪnəʳ/ *n* **1** a large passenger ship **2** a piece of material used inside something to protect it: *a dustbin liner*

lines·man /ˈlaɪnzmən/ *n* **linesmen** /-mən/ **1** a sports official who stays near the edge of the playing area and decides when the ball has gone outside it **2** a person whose job is to take care of electrical or telephone lines

line-up /ˈlaɪn-ʌp/ *n* **line-ups** **1** a row of people, especially one organized by the police so that someone might recognize a person they had seen doing a crime **2** a collection of people or things for a reason: *Tonight's line-up on BBC1 includes this week's episode of "Dallas".*

lin·ger /ˈlɪŋgəʳ/ *v* [I] to continue or wait for a time before going: *The pain lingered on for weeks.* | *He lingered outside the school after everybody else had gone home.* | *She was left with the lingering fear that he would not return.* **–lingerer** *n*

lin·ge·rie /ˈlænʒəriː/ ‖ ˌlɑːnʒəˈreɪ, ˌlænʒəˈriː/ *n* [U] *fml* underclothes and night-clothes for women

lin·guist /ˈlɪŋgwɪst/ *n* **1** a person who studies and is good at foreign languages **2** a person who studies human language

lin·guis·tics /lɪŋˈgwɪstɪks/ *n* [U] the study of language in general and of particular languages **–linguistic** *adj* **–linguistically** /-kli/ *adv*

lin·i·ment /ˈlɪnɪmənt/ *n* [C;U] an oily liquid that you rub on to your skin, especially to treat pain and stiffness in your joints

lin·ing /ˈlaɪnɪŋ/ *n* a piece of material covering the inner surface of something like a drawer or an article of clothing

link¹ /lɪŋk/ *n* **1** something which connects two other things: *There's a new rail link* **between** *the two towns.* **2** a connection between two things: *a link* **between** *smoking and lung diseases* **3** one ring of a chain

link² *v* [I;T] (also **link up; link** sthg ↔ **up**) to connect: *The road links all the new towns.* | *They walked with linked arms.* | *She was able to link up all the different pieces of information.*

link·age /ˈlɪŋkɪdʒ/ *n* [U] the fact or process in which things are connected, or the way in which they are connected

links /lɪŋks/ *n* [plural is **links**] a piece of ground on which GOLF is played

link-up /ˈlɪŋk-ʌp/ *n* a connection

li·no·le·um /lɪˈnəʊliəm/ *n* (also **lino** /ˈlaɪnəʊ/ *infml*) [U] a floor covering which is made of strong cloth under a hard surface

lin·seed oil /ˌlɪnsiːd ˈɔɪl/ *n* [U] an oil which is used in some paints and inks

lint /lɪnt/ *n* [U] **1** soft material which is used for protecting wounds **2** small pieces or threads that come off a piece of cloth: *This tea towel leaves lint on the glasses.*

lin·tel /ˈlɪntl/ *n* a piece of stone or wood across the top of a window or door

li·on /ˈlaɪən/ *n* **1** a large yellow animal which belongs to the cat family and lives mainly in Africa; a female lion is called a **lioness 2 the lion's share** the largest part of something

lip /lɪp/ *n* **1** one of the two edges of your mouth: *He kissed her on the lips.* **2** the edge of a container or opening: *the lip of the cup* **3 a stiff upper lip** a lack of expression of feeling **4 -lipped** with lips of a certain kind: *red-lipped* | *thin-lipped with anger*

lip-read /ˈlɪp riːd/ *v* [I] to watch people's lip movements to understand what they are saying because you cannot hear them **–lipreading** *n* [U]

lip·stick /ˈlɪpˌstɪk/ *n* [C;U] colour which women put on their lips to make them brighter: *I'll just put on some lipstick.* | *I bought a new lipstick today.*

liq·ue·fy /ˈlɪkwɪfaɪ/ *v* **liquefied, liquefying** [I;T] to become or make something liquid: *Butter liquefies in heat.*

li·queur /lɪˈkjʊəʳ/ ‖ lɪˈkɜːr/ *n* a strong, usually sweet alcoholic drink which is often drunk after a meal

liq·uid¹ /ˈlɪkwɪd/ *n* [C;U] a substance which flows and is not solid or gas: *It is important to drink a lot of liquid in hot climates.*

liquid² *adj* **1** in the form of a liquid (used especially of something which is usually solid or gas): *liquid gold* | *liquid oxygen* **2** clear and flowing, with pure notes (used of sounds)

liq·ui·date /ˈlɪkwɪdeɪt/ *v* **liquidated, liquidating** [T] **1** to kill or destroy someone: *The government is suspected of liquidating its political opponents.* **2** to close a business, usually because it has too many debts **–liquidation** /ˌlɪkwɪˈdeɪʃən/ *n* [U] : *The company has gone into liquidation.*

liq·uid·ize /ˈlɪkwɪdaɪz/ *v* **liquidized, liquidizing** [T] to crush food into a liquid **–liquidizer** *n:* *making soup in the liquidizer*

liq·uor /ˈlɪkəʳ/ *n* [U] **1** *BrE tech* alcoholic drink **2** *AmE* strong alcoholic drink, such as WHISKY

liq·uo·rice /ˈlɪkərɪs, -rɪʃ/ *n* (also **licorice**) [U] a sweet black substance used especially in sweets

lisp /lɪsp/ v [I;T] to speak in such a way that you pronounce /s/ sounds as /θ/ –**lisp** n [sing] : *She speaks with a lisp.*

lis·som /ˈlɪsəm/ adj (also **lissome**) *lit* graceful in shape and movement (used of a person or their body) –**lissomly** adv –**lissomness** n [U]

list¹ /lɪst/ n **1** [C] a set of names of things that you write one below the other to remember them or keep them in order: *He checked their names against his list.* | *We'd better make a shopping list before we go out.* **2** [sing] a position leaning to one side: *The ship had a list of 30 degrees.*

list² v **1** [T] to write things down or mention them one after the other: *He listed all the things he had to do.* **2** [I] (of a ship) to lean to one side

lis·ten /ˈlɪsən/ v [I] **1** to give attention to a person or sound that you can hear: *She's listening to the radio.* | *Listen to me.* –see HEAR (USAGE) **2** to pay attention to what someone says: *Listen to people who have experience of these problems.* | *Listen, I'll tell you a story.* **3 listen for, listen out for** to be prepared to hear a certain sound: *Can you listen out for the baby crying while I'm upstairs?*
listen in *phr v* [I] **1** to pay attention to the private conversation of others **2** to listen to a radio broadcast –**listen** n [sing] *infml* : *Have a listen to this!*

list·less /ˈlɪstləs/ adj without the strength or the interest to do anything –**listlessly** adv

lit /lɪt/ the past tense and past participle of LIGHT

li·ter /ˈliːtər/ n see LITRE

lit·e·ra·cy /ˈlɪtərəsi/ n [U] the ability to read and write: *The government is funding a new adult literacy campaign.* –opposite **illiteracy**

lit·e·ral /ˈlɪtərəl/ adj **1** according to the usual meaning of the words –compare FIGURATIVE **2** exact: *a literal account of a conversation* **3** word by word: *a literal translation* **4** showing little imagination: *a literal approach to a subject* –**literalness** n [U]

lit·e·ral·ly /ˈlɪtərəli/ adv **1** really (a word used to give force to what you say): *The house is literally 10 metres from the sea.* | *She's done literally nothing to help.* | *He was literally blue with cold.* **2** word by word: *Can you translate that literally?* **3** according to the words and not the intention: *I took what he said literally, which may have been a mistake.*
■ USAGE Although **literally** means "really", it is often used simply to give force to expressions which are not at all "real": *He literally exploded with anger.* | *She'll literally kill me if she finds out.* Note, however that some people consider this use to be incorrect.

lit·e·ra·ry /ˈlɪtərəri ‖ ˈlɪtəreri/ adj concerned with or related to literature: *a literary magazine* | *a literary prize*

lit·e·rate /ˈlɪtərət/ adj **1** able to read and write **2** well-educated –opposite **illiterate**

lit·e·ra·ture /ˈlɪtərətʃər ‖ -tʃʊər/ n [U] **1** written works which are of artistic value: *English literature* | *modern literature* **2** *infml* printed material on a certain subject or to help sell a product: *I've read all the literature on plant care.* | *He's sent off for literature on different makes of car.*

lit·i·gate /ˈlɪtɪgeɪt/ v litigated, litigating [I;T] *tech* to bring or defend a case in a court of law –**litigant** n –**litigation** /ˌlɪtɪˈgeɪʃən/ n

lit·mus /ˈlɪtməs/ n [U] a material which turns red when it is touched by an acid substance and blue when touched by an ALKALI: *litmus paper*

li·tre /ˈliːtər/ n (also **liter** AmE) a unit for measuring liquid, equal to about 1¾ PINTS: *a litre of oil*

lit·ter¹ /ˈlɪtər/ n **1** [U] small things which have been thrown away: *Please place litter in the bin provided.* –see picture on page 246 **2** [C] a group of young animals born at the same time to one mother: *a litter of puppies* **3** [U] something that farm animals sleep on or that cats use in a box as a TOILET

litter² v [T] to cover a surface with things untidily: *The floor was littered with old newspapers.*

lit·tle¹ /ˈlɪtl/ adj **1** [only before a noun] small: *It's only a little house.* | *a little wooden box* **2** [only before a noun] short: *I had to wait a little while before my name was called.* **3** young: *a group of little children* **4** not important: *These are all little problems.*
■ USAGE **Little** and **small** can both mean "of less than average size", but **little** is often used to suggest the speaker's feelings or opinion as well. It is frequently used to show approval of something which you think is pleasantly small: *a sweet little kitten* | *We're looking for a little cottage in the country.* But it can also be used, together with another adjective, to show dislike or disapproval: *a silly little man* | *a classroom full of horrible little boys* | *Keep your nasty little hands to yourself!*

little² adv less /les/, least /liːst/ not much: *a little known fact* | *She goes out very little.*

little³ det, pron less, least **1** not very much: *I have very little money left.* | *We had little to talk about.* | *I understood little of his speech.* **2 a little:** a a small amount: *Add two eggs and a little milk.* | *May I have a little of that cake?* **b** quite: *I was a little annoyed.* **3 little by little** gradually: *Little by little the people came to accept us.*

little fin·ger /ˌ… ˈ…/ n the smallest finger on your hand

live¹ /lɪv/ v lived, living **1** [I] to be or to continue to be alive: *The rich live while the poor die.* | *He is unlikely to live much longer.* **2** [I + adv/prep] to have your home in a certain place: *Where do you live?* | *I live in a flat in Liverpool.* –see STAY¹ (USAGE) **3** [I;T] to lead a certain kind of life: *We can't earn enough to live comfortably.* | *She lived a quiet, country life.* **4** [I] to exist: *He still lives in my imagination.* **5 live and let live** to accept other people's behaviour **6 live a lie** to lead a life that hides who you really are, or what you are like **7 live by doing something** to make an income from a certain activity: *He lives by stealing.* **8 live by something** to behave according to the rules of something: *I live by my own moral code.* **9 live in sin** *old fash* to live with a person of the opposite sex who is not married to you **10 live it up** to have a very good and active social life: *Shall we live it up at the disco tonight?*
live sthg ↔ **down** *phr v* [T] to make people forget something shameful or strange that you have done: *He arrived as the meeting ended, and he'll never live that down.*
live in *phr v* [I] to sleep and eat in the building where you work or study: *I've decided to live in for my first term at college.*
live off sbdy/sthg *phr v* [T] to obtain your food or income from a person or thing: *She's still living off her parents.* | *I live off the money from my first book.*
live on *phr v* **1** [I] to continue living: *She lived on for 20 years after her husband's death.* **2** [T **live on** sthg] a to eat only a certain kind of food: *She lives on fruit and vegetables.* **3** [T **live on** sthg] to get your money from a person or thing: *He lives on the rent from his tenants.*
live out *phr v* [I] to eat and sleep in a place away from your place of work or study
live up to sthg *phr v* [T] to reach someone's high standards: *Did the film live up to your expectations?*

live with sbdy *phr v* [T] **1** to share your home with someone you love but that you are not married to: *She's living with her boyfriend.* **2** to accept something unpleasant: *You learn to live with the pain.*

live² /laɪv/ *adj* **1** alive: *The cat was playing with a live mouse.* –opposite **dead 2** broadcast as it happens: *The programme was live.* **3** connected to the electricity supply and able to shock anyone who touches it: *a live wire* **4** slowly burning: *live coals* **5** ready to explode or fire: *a live bomb*

live·li·hood /ˈlaɪvlihʊd/ *n* the way in which you earn your money: *The oil spill has taken away fishermen's livelihood.*

live·ly /ˈlaɪvli/ *adj* **livelier, liveliest** active or full of life: *Both children have very lively minds.* | *It was a lively debate.* | *She takes a lively interest in our affairs.* –**liveliness** *n* [U]

liv·en /ˈlaɪvən/ **liven up** *phr v* [I;T] **liven** sbdy/sthg ↔ **up**] to become or to make a person or thing more active or full of life: *How can we liven this party up?*

liv·er /ˈlɪvəʳ/ *n* **1** [C] a large organ in your body which cleans your blood **2** [U] this organ from an animal's body, used as food

lives /laɪvz/ the plural of LIFE

live·stock /ˈlaɪvstɒk ‖ -staːk/ *n* [U] animals kept on a farm

liv·id /ˈlɪvɪd/ *adj* **1** *infml* very angry **2** blue-grey (used of discoloured skin): *His legs were covered with livid bruises.* –**lividly** *adv*

liv·ing¹ /ˈlɪvɪŋ/ *adj* **1** alive now: *She has no living relatives.* **2** having life: *plants, animals, and other living things* **3** used now: *a living language*

living² *n* **1** [C] the way in which you earn money: *What does she do for a living?* | *I'm trying to make a living out of painting.* **2** [U] way of life: *Our standard of living has dropped because the cost of living is increasing faster than my salary.*

living room /ˈ··· ·/ *n* the main room in a house where people usually sit and do things together

liz·ard /ˈlɪzəd ‖ -əʳd/ *n* an animal with a rough skin, four legs, and a long tail

-'ll /əl, l/ short for WILL or SHALL: *He'll soon be here.* –see 's (USAGE)

lla·ma /ˈlaːmə/ *n* a South American animal with thick woolly hair, often used for carrying goods

load¹ /ləʊd/ *n* **1** a quantity of something, especially something heavy, that is being carried or to be carried: *The lorry is transporting a load of furniture.* **2** the amount which a certain vehicle or apparatus can carry: *a car load of people* | *two loads of washing* **3** the work that must be done by a person or apparatus: *Increased business has increased the load on our staff.* **4** the power of an electricity supply **5** something difficult or unpleasant that you have to bear: *Knowledge of his crime is a heavy load for her to carry.* **6 a load of, loads of** *infml* a lot of something: *She's got loads of money.* | *That book is a load of rubbish.*

load² *v* **1** [I;T] to put a quantity of things on or into something: *Load the suitcases into the car.* **2** [T] to give someone a lot of things: *They loaded me* **with** *gifts.* **3** [T] to put a bullet into a gun or a film into a camera **4** [T] to move information into the memory of a computer

load sbdy/sthg ↔ **down** *phr v* [T] to make a person or thing carry a lot of heavy things: *I was loaded down* **with** *shopping.*

load up *phr v* [I;T **load** sthg ↔ **up**] to put a quantity of things into or onto something: *Have you loaded the car up yet?*

load·ed /ˈləʊdɪd/ *adj* **1** giving an unfair advantage: *The argument was loaded in his favour.* | *He's playing with loaded dice.* **2** containing more meanings than that which appears at first: *a loaded question* **3** [never before a noun] *infml* having lots of money: *Let him pay; he's loaded.*

loaf¹ /ləʊf/ *n* **loaves** /ləʊvz/ bread that has been shaped and baked in one large piece: *a loaf of bread*

loaf² *v*
loaf about/around *phr v* [I] *infml* to waste time, especially by not working when you should –**loafer** *n*

loan¹ /ləʊn/ *n* **1** something which is lent, especially money: *We've applied for a £10,000 bank loan.* **2** the act of lending or the condition of being lent: *She asked for the loan of my car.* | *The book you want is on loan at the moment.*

loan² *v* [T] to lend something to someone: *She loaned her pictures to the gallery for a year.*
☐ USEFUL PATTERNS to loan something to someone; to loan someone something

loath /ləʊθ/ *adj* (also **loth**) **be loath to do something** to be unwilling to do something: *I am loath to lend you any more money.*

loathe /ləʊð/ *v* **loathed, loathing** [T] to feel great dislike for a person or thing: *I loathed all my teachers.* | *He loathes getting up so early.* –**loathing** *n* [C;U]

loath·some /ˈləʊðsəm/ *adj* very unpleasant

loaves /ləʊvz/ the plural of LOAF

lob /lɒb ‖ laːb/ *v* **-bb-** [T + adv/prep] to throw or hit a ball high in the air in a gentle curve –**lob** *n*: *a lob into the back corner of the court*

lob·by¹ /ˈlɒbi ‖ ˈlaːbi/ *n* **lobbies 1** an entrance hall just inside the main door to a building: *I'll meet you in the hotel lobby.* **2** a group of people who try to influence the decisions of those in power in relation to a particular matter: *The clean air lobby is fighting plans for a new chemical factory.*

lobby² *v* [I;T] to meet or try to influence a person in power in relation to a particular matter: *We're going to lobby our MP to ask him to vote against the proposal.*

lobe /ləʊb/ *n* **1** (also **earlobe**) the round fleshy part at the bottom of your ear **2** *tech* any rounded division of a body organ, especially your brain and lungs

lob·ster /ˈlɒbstəʳ ‖ ˈlaːb-/ *n* [C;U] a sea animal with a shell, a long body, and eight legs, or its flesh as a food –see picture on page 344

lo·cal¹ /ˈləʊkəl/ *adj* **1** belonging to or in a certain place, especially the place where you live: *There are two local newspapers.* | *The local council is improving public services.* **2** *tech* having an effect on a particular part of something, especially a part of your body: *local anaesthetic*

local² *n* **1** *infml* a bar near your home, especially one which you often drink at **2** a person who lives in a certain place: *Let's ask one of the locals for directions.*

lo·cal·i·ty /ləʊˈkæləti/ *n* **localities** a place or position

lo·cal·ize /ˈləʊkəlaɪz/ *v* **localized, localizing** (also **localise** *BrE*) [T] to keep something within a small area –**localization** /ˌləʊkəlaɪˈzeɪʃən ‖ -kələ-/ *n* [U]

lo·cal·ly /ˈləʊkəli/ *adv* in the area that you are in or you have mentioned: *Do you live locally?*

lo·cate /ləʊˈkeɪt ‖ ˈləʊkeɪt/ *v* **located, locating** [T] **1** to find the position of something: *We located the nearest schools before we decided to move to this part*

of town. **2 be located** to be placed in a certain position: *The house is located next to the river.* | *The offices are conveniently located in the town centre.*

lo-ca-tion /ləʊˈkeɪʃən/ n **1** a place or position: *This is a suitable location for a camp.* **2** in a suitable place, outside the buildings owned by the film company, where part of a film is made: *The desert scenes were shot on location in the Sahara.*

lock¹ /lɒk || lɑːk/ n **1** an apparatus for fastening something, usually with a key: *He put new locks on the doors.* | *I need a lock and chain for my bike.* **2** a stretch of water closed off by gates so that the water level can be raised or lowered to move boats up or down: *The canal climbs the hill by means of a series of locks.* **3** a small number of hairs that grow together **4 lock, stock, and barrel** completely: *We sold everything, lock, stock and barrel.* **5 under lock and key** safely locked away

lock² v **1** [I;T] to fasten something, usually with a key: *Lock the door.* | *The door won't lock.* **2** [T + adv/prep] to put something in a place and close it with a key: *I've locked the medicines in the cupboard.* **3** [I] to become fixed in a certain position: *I can't move the car; the wheels have locked.*

lock sthg/sbdy ↔ away *phr v* [T] to put a thing or person in a safe place which you close with a key: *Lock your money away.* | *The beautiful princess was locked away in a high tower.*

lock in *phr v* **1** [T **lock sbdy ↔ in**] to keep someone in a place by closing the door with a key: *She heard the key turn; she was locked in.* **2 be locked in something** to be unable to get out of a situation: *locked in a struggle which neither side can win*

lock sbdy ↔ out *phr v* [T] to keep someone out of a place by closing the door with a key: *Somehow I managed to lock myself out of the house.*

lock up *phr v* **1** [I;T **lock sthg ↔ up**] to make a building safe by closing the doors with keys: *Don't forget to lock up when you go out.* | *Have you locked up the garage?* **2** [T **lock sbdy/sthg ↔ up**] to put someone or something in a safe place which you close with a key: *Lock your bike up in the shed.* | *People like him should be locked up!* **–lockable** adj

lock-er /ˈlɒkəʳ || ˈlɑː-/ n a small cupboard for keeping things in, for example at a school or in a station, which is closed with a key

lock-et /ˈlɒkɪt || ˈlɑː-/ n a small metal case which you wear on a chain around your neck, and in which you can keep a small picture of someone you love, or a lock of their hair

lock-out /ˈlɒk-aʊt || ˈlɑːk-/ n the employers' action of not allowing people to go back to work until they accept an agreement

lo-co-mo-tive¹ /ˌləʊkəˈməʊtɪv◂/ adj tech concerning or causing movement: *locomotive powers* **–locomotion** /-ˈməʊʃən/ [U]

locomotive² n fml a railway engine

lo-cum /ˈləʊkəm/ n a doctor or priest who is doing the work of another doctor or priest who is away for a period

lo-cust /ˈləʊkəst/ n an insect which flies in large groups, often destroying crops

lodge¹ /lɒdʒ || lɑːdʒ/ v **lodged, lodging** **1** [I + adv/prep] to stay in someone's house for payment: *She's lodging with friends at the moment.* **2** [T + adv/prep] to arrange a place for someone to stay in: *They have been lodged in a guesthouse.* **3** [I + adv/prep; T + adv/prep] to stick firmly in a certain position: *He got a chicken bone lodged in his throat.* **4** [T] to make a statement officially: *You must lodge a complaint with the authorities.* **5** [T + adv/prep]

fml to put something in a safe place: *You had better lodge those papers with your lawyer.*

lodge² n **1** a small house on the land of a great house and usually at the entrance to its park **2** a small house for people to stay in while doing certain activities such as skiing (SKI)

lodg-er /ˈlɒdʒəʳ || ˈlɑː-/ n a person who pays rent to live in someone's house

lodg-ing /ˈlɒdʒɪŋ || ˈlɑː-/ n **1** [U] a place to stay for payment: *a night's lodging* | *board and lodging* **2 lodgings** [pl] a room or rooms in someone's house where you may live for payment: *I'm staying in lodgings until I find a flat.*

loft /lɒft || lɔːft/ n a room or space under the roof of a building

loft-y /ˈlɒfti || ˈlɔːfti/ adj **loftier, loftiest** **1** showing an unusually high standard of thought or feeling: *lofty aims* **2** showing that you believe you are better than other people: *a lofty smile* **3** lit very high **–loftily** adv **–loftiness** n [U]

log¹ /lɒg || lɔːg, lɑːg/ n **1** a thick piece of wood from a tree **2** an official written record of the journey of a ship or plane **3** see LOGARITHM

log² v **-gg-** [T] to record something officially

log in *phr v* [I] (also **log on**) to enter a computer system

log out *phr v* [I] (also **log off**) to leave a computer system

lo-gan-ber-ry /ˈləʊgənbəri || -beri/ n **loganberries** a small red fruit

log-a-rith-m /ˈlɒgərɪðəm || ˈlɔː-, ˈlɑː-/ n (also **log** *infml*) a number which represents a value of another number, and which can be added to another logarithm instead of multiplying the original number **–logarithmic** /ˌlɒgəˈrɪðmɪk◂ || ˌlɔː-, ˌlɑː-/

log-ger-heads /ˈlɒgəhedz || ˈlɔːgər-, ˈlɑː-/ n **at loggerheads** in strong disagreement with someone

lo-gic /ˈlɒdʒɪk || ˈlɑː-/ n [U] **1** the science of reasoning by formal methods **2** a way of reasoning **3** *infml* good sense

lo-gic-al /ˈlɒdʒɪkəl || ˈlɑː-/ adj **1** in accordance with the rules of logic: *a logical argument* **2** sensible: *It seems a logical decision.* **–opposite illogical;** **–logically** /-kli/ adv

lo-gis-tics /ləˈdʒɪstɪks || ləʊ-/ n [pl] the organization of a lot of people or things in a difficult operation: *The logistics of distributing so many food parcels are extremely complex.* **–logistic** adj **–logistically** /-kli/ adv

loins /lɔɪnz/ n [pl] the part of your body below your waist and above your legs

loi-ter /ˈlɔɪtəʳ/ v [I] **1** to stay in or near a place for no clear reason: *He was caught loitering near the security entrance to the bank.* **2** to move slowly, with frequent stops: *Don't loiter on your way home!* **–loiterer** n

loll /lɒl || lɑːl/ v [I] **1** (also **loll about/around**) to sit or lie in a way that looks lazy **2** (of your head or tongue) to hang down loosely

lol-li-pop /ˈlɒlipɒp || ˈlɑːlipɑːp/ n **1** a hard sweet made of boiled sugar on the end of a stick **2** (also **lolly** BrE) ice cream or frozen juice on the end of a stick

lollipop man /ˈ··· ˌ··/ n BrE a person whose job is to stop traffic with a stick shaped like a lollipop so that school children can cross; a woman who does this is called a **lollipop lady**

lol-ly /ˈlɒli || ˈlɑːli/ n **lollies** see LOLLIPOP

lone /ləʊn/ adj [only before a noun] without companions: *A lone rider was coming towards me.*

lone·ly /ˈləʊnli/ adj **lonelier, loneliest 1** alone and unhappy: *He was lonely without his wife.* **2** far from where people live, and not often visited: *a lonely country road* –see ALONE (USAGE) **–loneliness** n [U]

lon·er /ˈləʊnəʳ/ n a person who seems to like being alone

lone·some /ˈləʊnsəm/ adj AmE infml lonely –see ALONE (USAGE)

long¹ /lɒŋ ‖ lɔːŋ/ adj **1** measuring a large amount in length, distance, or time: *long hair | a long journey | He took a long time to get here.* –opposite **short 2** covering a certain distance or time: *How long was her speech? | It was an hour long. | The garden is 20 metres long and 15 metres wide.* **3** lasting or seeming to last more time than usual or than you want it to: *It's been a long day. | long hours of waiting* **4 in the long run** in the end: *Everything should be all right in the long run.* **5 in the long term** in the distant future: *The company's position in the long term looks very good.* **6 long in the tooth** old (used of a person or animal) **7 not by a long chalk, not by a long shot** infml not at all: *"Is he ready yet?" "No, not by a long chalk."*

long² adv **1** a long time or for a long time: *Will you be long? | I can't wait much longer.* **2 as long as, so long as** on condition that: *We'll go out as long as the weather is fine.* **3 long ago** at a distant time in the past **4 no longer, not any longer** not any more: *He no longer lives here. | He doesn't work here any longer.* **5 so long** infml you say this when you leave or someone leaves you

long³ n **1** a long time: *Were you there for long?* **2 before long** soon: *I'll be back before long.* **3 the long and the short of it** the general result

long⁴ v [I;T] to want something very much: *I'm longing to go. | I'm longing for him to come home. | He longed for the end of term.*
□ USEFUL PATTERNS to long for something; to long to do something; to long for something to happen

long-dis·tance /ˌ· ˈ··◄/ adj [only before a noun] from one point to a far point: *He's a long-distance runner. | I want to make a long-distance telephone call.* **–long-distance** adv: *to telephone long-distance*

long drink /ˈ· ·/ n a drink which usually contains a little alcohol in a large amount of liquid

lon·gev·i·ty /lɒnˈdʒevⱥti ‖ lɑːn-, lɔːn-/ n [U] fml long life

long face /ˌ· ˈ·/ n a face with a sad expression: *Don't pull such a long face, it's not that bad!*

long·hand /ˈlɒŋhænd ‖ ˈlɔːŋ-/ n [U] ordinary writing by hand: *Can you write those notes out in longhand?*

long·ing /ˈlɒŋɪŋ ‖ ˈlɔːŋɪŋ/ n [C;U] a strong feeling of wanting something: *He had a secret longing for the lifestyle of the rich and famous. | gazing at her with longing.* **–longingly** adv

lon·gi·tude /ˈlɒndʒⱥtjuːd ‖ ˈlɑːndʒⱥtuːd/ n [C;U] a position on the Earth measured in degrees east or west of an imaginary line which runs through London

lon·gi·tu·di·nal /ˌlɒndʒⱥˈtjuːdⱥnəl ‖ ˌlɑːndʒəˈtuː-/ adj from one end of a line or an object to the other **–longitudinally** adv

long jump /ˈ· ·/ n [sing] a sport in which people jump as far as possible along the ground

long-range /ˌ· ˈ··◄/ adj [only before a noun] covering a long distance or time: *long-range weapons | long-range forecasts*

long·sight·ed /ˌlɒŋˈsaɪtⱥd◄ ‖ ˌlɔːŋ-/ adj not able to see things clearly when they are very close to your eyes –opposite **shortsighted**

long·stand·ing /ˌlɒŋˈstændɪŋ◄ ‖ ˌlɔːŋ-/ adj which has existed for a long time: *There is a longstanding trade agreement between the two countries.*

long-term /ˌ· ˈ·◄/ adj for or in the distant future: *a long-term plan | No one knows what the long-term effects of these drugs will be.* –opposite **short-term**

long wave /ˌ· ˈ·◄/ n [U] radio broadcasting on waves of 1,000 metres or more

long·ways /ˈlɒŋweɪz ‖ ˈlɔːŋ-/ adv see LENGTHWAYS

long-wind·ed /ˌlɒŋˈwɪndⱥd◄ ‖ ˌlɔːŋ-/ adj saying or writing too much in a dull way: *He made a long-winded speech about social reform.*

loo /luː/ n BrE infml a TOILET

look¹ /lʊk/ v **1** [I] to turn your eyes towards something so that you can see it: *She looked at me angrily. | He was sitting looking out of the window. | The scene was so horrible I couldn't bear to look. | I called to him but he looked away.* **2** [+ complement] to have a particular appearance: *You look tired. | He looks like my brother.* **3** [I+adv/prep] to face in a particular direction: *The house looks out onto the river.* **4 Look!, Look here!** a word or phrase you use when you want someone to notice something or pay attention to something: *Look where you're going! | Look at the time – we're late.* **5 look as if, look like** to seem probable: *It looks as if we're going to miss the plane. | It looks like it's going to rain.* **6 look on the bright side** to think about the good parts of a situation, not the bad ones **7 look someone in the eye** to look directly and boldly at someone: *He was too ashamed of himself to look me in the eye.* **8 not much to look at** not very attractive

look after sbdy/sthg phr v [T] to take care of someone or something: *Who will look after the baby? | Are you being well looked after? | She will look after the business for me while I'm away.*

look ahead phr v [I] to plan for the future: *We must look ahead and invest for the future.*

look around phr v [I] to search: *I'm looking around for a new job.*

look at sbdy/sthg phr v [T] **1** to watch someone or something: *looking at the children playing in the street* **2** to regard or judge someone or something in a particular way: *I look at life differently now, since the accident.* **3** to read something: *Could you look at this report for me?* **4** to consider or examine something: *A committee has been set up to look at the problem of homelessness.*

look back phr v [I] **1** to think about or remember things that happened in the past: *When I look back I realize how happy my childhood was.* **2 he never looked back** = he became very successful: *He won his first game at the age of 18 and then never looked back.*

look down on sbdy/sthg phr v [T] to have a low opinion of someone or something or think that they are socially inferior: *She looks down on me because I'm only a secretary.*

look for sbdy/sthg phr v [T] to try to find someone or something: *I'm looking for Mr Baker. | She's gone to look for a public telephone.*

look forward to sthg phr v [T] to feel happy because you are going to do something that you will enjoy: *We're looking forward to the party. | I'm looking forward to meeting you.*

look into sthg *phr v* [T] to examine the facts about something: *Police are looking into the allegations of corruption.* | *There's a fault in the machine and we're looking into it.*

look on *phr v* **1** [I] to watch something while other people take part: *I looked on in dismay as the fight started.* **2** [T **look on** sbdy/sthg] to consider someone or something in a particular way: *I look on him as a friend.*

look out *phr v* **1 Look out!** a phrase you use to tell someone to be careful: *Look out! There's a car coming!* **2** [T **look** sthg ↔ **out**] to find something from among your possessions: *I'll look out some old clothes for the jumble sale.*

look out for sbdy/sthg *phr v* [T] to make sure that you notice someone or something: *Look out for Jane at the conference.*

look sthg ↔ **over** *phr v* [T] to examine something quickly: *Could you look the car over for me before I buy it?*

look round *phr v* **1** [I;T **look round** sthg] to look at a lot of things, especially before you buy something: *It's a good idea to look round for a while before buying a car.* | *Let's go and look round the shops.* **2** [I] to search: *She looked round for a piece of paper.*

look through sthg *phr v* [T] to examine something carefully: *Could you look through this article for me?* | *I looked through the pile of papers.*

look up *phr v* **1** [I] to get better: *Things are looking up at last!* **2** [T **look** sthg ↔ **up**] to find a piece of information in a book: *Can you look up the word "instigate" for me?* **3** [T **look** sbdy ↔ **up**] to visit someone when you are in the place where they live: *Look me up if you're ever in this part of the country.*

look upon sbdy/sthg *phr v* [T] to consider someone or something in a particular way: *I look upon him as a friend.*

look up to sbdy *phr v* [T] to respect and admire someone: *All his pupils look up to him.*

look² *n* **1** an act of looking at something: *She gave me an angry look.* | *Did you have a look at the new computer?* | *Take a look at this huge spider!* | *Have you had a look at that newspaper article yet?* | *We need to have another look at the whole question of teachers' pay.* **2** a person's appearance, or an expression on their face: *I knew she didn't like it by the look on her face.* | *He had a frightened look in his eyes.* | *She had the look of someone who would succeed in life.* **3 looks** [pl] someone's appearance, especially when it is attractive: *Good looks aren't everything.* | *He kept his looks even in old age.* **4 by the look of it, by the looks of it** judging by the appearance of something: *That car's ready for the scrap heap by the look of it.* | *We're in for some rain by the looks of it.* **5 not like the look of something** to feel worried by something: *The whole deal sounds dishonest to me – I don't like the look of it.*

look-out /'lʊk-aʊt/ *n* **1** [C] a person whose duty is to watch, usually for danger: *The general posted a lookout on each hill.* **2** [C] a place to watch from **3** [sing] *infml* a future possibility that may be unpleasant for you: *It's a bad lookout for us if he gets ill now.* | *It's your lookout if you're caught.* **4 be on the lookout for, keep a lookout for** to be watching or searching for a person or thing: *He's on the lookout for a job.*

loom¹ /luːm/ *n* a frame or machine for weaving cloth

loom² *v* [I] **1** to come into sight in a way that seems unfriendly: *A figure loomed out of the mist.* **2** to cause fear or worry as the time comes closer: *The exams are looming.*

loon·y /'luːni/ *adj infml* **loonier, looniest** mad or strange (used of a person) **–loony** *n*

loop¹ /luːp/ *n* the circular shape made by something like a piece of string when it is bent into a curve

loop² *v* **1** [I;T] to form a curve with something like a piece of string **2** [T + adv/prep] to fasten with a circular piece of something like a piece of string: *Loop the rope round the gate.*

loop·hole /'luːphəʊl/ *n* a way of avoiding something, especially one provided by faults in a law or agreement: *The company has found a loophole in the tax laws.*

loose¹ /luːs/ *adj* **1** not fixed or held together by or in anything: *They sell chocolates loose or in boxes.* **2** not firmly fixed: *That screw is loose – you'd better tighten it.* **3** free from control: *Dogs are not allowed to wander loose in the park.* **4** not fitting tightly (used of clothes): *He lost so much weight his trousers were quite loose.* **5** not exact: *a loose translation* **6** without morals (used of people or their behaviour) **7 at a loose end** having nothing to do **–loosely** *adv* **–looseness** *n* [U]

loose² *v* **loosed, loosing** [T] *fml* or *lit* to free a person or animal from control **–compare** LOOSEN

loose³ *n* **on the loose** free from control, especially of the law: *a dangerous criminal on the loose*

loos·en /'luːsən/ *v* [I;T] to become or to make something less firm, fixed, or tight: *He loosened his collar.* **–opposite tighten**
loosen up *phr v* [I] **1** to exercise your muscles in preparation for physical activity: *I need time to loosen up before the race.* **2** to become less tense: *A drink will help you to loosen up.*

loot¹ /luːt/ *n* [U] money or goods stolen by soldiers in war time, or by thieves, especially during periods of violence in society

loot² *v* [I;T] to steal things from a place, especially in war time or during periods of social unrest: *After the riots, crowds of people looted the shops.* | *Food and farm animals were looted.* **–looter** *n*

lop /lɒp ‖ laːp/ *v* **-pp-** [T] to cut something off, especially a branch from a tree

lope /ləʊp/ *v* **loped, loping** [I + adv/prep] (especially of animals) to move quite fast with long, easy steps

lop-sid·ed /ˌ· '·-◄/ *adj infml* uneven because the two sides are different

loq·ua·cious /ləʊ'kweɪʃəs/ *adj fml* tending to talk a lot **–loquacity** /ləʊ'kwæsɪti/ *n* [U]

lord¹ /lɔːd ‖ lɔːrd/ *n* **1** a ruler or master **2** a nobleman **3 Lord** a title that you use when you are talking to or about certain official people or noblemen: *the Lord Mayor of London* | *Lord Grade* | *Not guilty, my Lord.* **4 the Lord** God **5 Our Lord** the son of God **6 Lord, Good Lord** words used to express surprise or worry: *Good Lord!* | *Oh Lord, I forgot!*

lord² *v* **lord it over someone** to behave towards someone as if you are better and more important than they are

lord·ly /'lɔːdli ‖ -ɔːr-/ *adj* showing people that you think you are better and more important than they are

lord·ship /'lɔːdʃɪp ‖ -ɔːr-/ *n* (also **Lordship**) a title that you use when you are talking to or about certain official people or noblemen: *Good morning, your Lordship.* | *I've written to their Lordships.*

lore /lɔːʳ/ *n* [U] knowledge or old beliefs about a certain subject, or held by a particular group

lor·ry /'lɒri ‖ 'lɔːri, 'laːri/ *n BrE* **lorries** a large motor vehicle for carrying heavy goods **–see picture on page 735**

lose /luːz/ v lost /lɒst‖lɔːst/, **losing** 1 [T] to be without something because you cannot find it: *I've lost my notes.* 2 **lose your way** not to know where you are any longer 3 [T] not to have something any longer, or to cause it to be taken away from you: *I've lost all interest in football.* | *She lost her parents while she was very young.* | *He lost an eye in the accident.* | *His foolish behaviour lost him his job.* 4 **lose touch with someone** not to have contact with a person any longer 5 **lose track of** not to have knowledge of a person or thing any longer: *Dinner already? I'd lost track of the time.* 6 **lose face** not to have the respect of other people any longer 7 [I;T] to fail to win something: *He lost the argument.* | *England lost to Australia by 2 goals to 3.* 8 [T] to have less money than before, or to cause you to have less money: *We lost £200 on that job.* | *His accident lost him a week's wages.* 9 [T] to have less of something than before: *He's lost a lot of weight recently.* 9 **be lost on someone** to have no effect on someone: *His charm is completely lost on me.* 10 [T] to waste time or a chance to do something: *The doctor lost no time in calling an ambulance.* 11 [I;T] (of a watch or clock) to move too slowly: *This watch loses 5 minutes a day.* –opposite **gain** 12 **lose your cool, lose your temper** to become angry
lose out phr v [I] infml to make a loss: *The firm lost out on the deal.*

los·er /ˈluːzəʳ/ n 1 a person who has been defeated: *Nobody will play with him because he is such a bad loser.* –compare WINNER 2 a person who is always unsuccessful: *I sometimes think I'm a born loser!*

loss /lɒs ‖ lɔːs/ n 1 [U] the act or fact of losing something: *Have you reported the loss of your car?* 2 [C] the sadness or disadvantage that you feel when you lose a person or thing: *His death was a great loss to his friends.* 3 [C] income which is less than what you have spent: *The company has made a big loss this year.* 4 [C;U] death: *The enemy suffered heavy losses.* | *There's a danger of loss of life.* 5 **at a loss** uncertain about what to do or say: *I'm at a loss for words.* 6 **be a dead loss** infml to be useless: *He's a dead loss as a manager.*

lost¹ the past tense and past participle of LOSE

lost² /lɒst ‖ lɔːst/ adj 1 unable to be found: *Our keys* 2 no longer possessed by you: *I regret the lost opportunity.* 3 **be lost, get lost** to be unable to find your way: *I always get lost in London.* 4 killed or destroyed: *The fund is for the families of fishermen lost at sea.*

lot /lɒt ‖ lɑːt/ n 1 **a lot, lots** a great number or amount: *A lot of people have applied for the job.* | *She's got lots of money.* 2 **a lot: a** very much: *I like him a lot.* | *She looks a lot older now.* **b** often: *I see John quite a lot.* 3 **the lot** the whole number or amount: *I'll give you £10 for the lot.* 4 [C] a group of people or things: *Another lot of students will be arriving soon.* 5 [C] an article or group of articles sold together at an AUCTION sale 6 *AmE* an area of land used for parking cars on 7 **someone's lot** someone's way of life: *Generally I'm quite happy with my lot.*

lo·tion /ˈləʊʃən/ n [C;U] a liquid mixture that you use to make your skin clean or healthy

lot·te·ry /ˈlɒtəri ‖ ˈlɑː-/ n **lotteries** 1 a competition in which prizes are given to people who have bought the winning numbered tickets which are picked by chance 2 something which is decided by chance

lo·tus /ˈləʊtəs/ n a white or pink flower that grows on the surface of lakes, especially in Asia

loud¹ /laʊd/ adj 1 making a lot of noise: *loud music* | *a loud voice* 2 unpleasantly noisy or colourful: *Don't you think that wallpaper is rather loud?* –**loudly** adv –**loudness** n [U]

loud² adv 1 in a way that makes a lot of noise: *Shout louder and someone might hear.* 2 **out loud** see ALOUD

loud·speak·er /ˌlaʊdˈspiːkəʳ, ˈlaʊdˌspiːkəʳ/ n something which makes what you say seem louder

lounge¹ /laʊndʒ/ n 1 a comfortable room for sitting in, in a house or a hotel 2 a waiting room at an airport: *the departure lounge*

lounge² v **lounged, lounging** [I + adv/prep] (also **lounge about, lounge around**) to stand, sit or lie somewhere in a lazy way: *He just lounges around all day doing nothing.*

lounge bar /ˈ· ·/ n a comfortably furnished room in a PUB or hotel, where drinks cost a little more than in other bars

louse¹ /laʊs/ n **lice** /laɪs/ 1 a small insect that lives on the skin and in the hair of people and animals 2 infml an unpleasant, worthless person

louse² v **loused, lousing**
louse sthg ↔ **up** phr v [T] AmE infml to deal unsuccessfully with something

lou·sy /ˈlaʊzi/ adj **lousier, lousiest** 1 infml terrible: *What lousy weather!* | *I feel lousy.* 2 [never before a noun] covered with lice

lout /laʊt/ n an unpleasant and often threatening young man with bad manners –**loutish** adj

lov·a·ble /ˈlʌvəbəl/ adj producing feelings of love and liking: *a lovable child*

love¹ /lʌv/ n 1 [C;U] a strong feeling of warmth for another person or thing: *He has a great love of children.* | *Her love for her husband is strong and constant.* | *He died for the love of his country.* –opposites **hate, hatred** 2 **be in love, fall in love with** someone to feel or to begin to feel great warmth for a person, usually of the opposite sex: *He fell in love with her at their first meeting.* 3 [C] a person who you love: *I'll do it, my love.* 4 [C] something that you like doing very much: *Music was the love of his life.* 5 [U] warm interest and enjoyment of something: *Her love of sport leaves little time for meeting friends.* 6 [U] no points (used in tennis); *McEnroe leads 15-love.* 7 **be little love lost between people, be no love lost between people** bad relations between two or more people: *There's been no love lost between the sisters since their mother's death.* 8 **not for love nor money** not by any means

love² v **loved, loving** 1 [T] to feel love, desire, or strong friendship for someone: *I love my mother very much.* 2 [I;T] to like or enjoy something very much: *He loves singing.* | *I'd love a drink.* | *She'd love to see you again.*
□ USEFUL PATTERNS to love something, to love doing something; to love to do something –opposite **hate**

love af·fair /ˈ· ·ˌ·/ n an experience of love, and often sexual love, between two people who are not married to each other

love·ly /ˈlʌvli/ adj **lovelier, loveliest** 1 beautiful: *We had a lovely view of the mountains.* 2 infml very pleasant: *That was a lovely meal.* –**loveliness** n [U]

lov·er /ˈlʌvəʳ/ n 1 a person who you have sex with outside marriage: *They were lovers first and then became friends.* 2 a person who enjoys something: *an art lover*

lov·ing /ˈlʌvɪŋ/ adj showing or feeling love: *He gave her a loving look.* | *a loving father* –**lovingly** adv

low¹ /ləʊ/ **1** not high above the ground or from the bottom of something to the top: *a low wall* | *We need two low shelves, and then one higher up the wall.* **2** small in size, degree, amount, or value: *Prices in that shop are very low.* | *Temperatures are low for June.* | *I have a low opinion of his work.* | *low-fat milk* | *a low-paid job* **3** weak or unhappy: *She's still feeling a bit low after her operation.* | *He's been in low spirits since his girlfriend left.* **4** not loud: *a low voice* **5** deep (used of a musical note) **6** near the bottom in position or rank: *a man of low birth* **7** not morally acceptable: *Lying to get the job was a very low trick.* **8** have a low opinion of someone or something not to respect a person or like a thing –opposite **high** (for 1, 2, 4, 5, 6, 7, 8) –lowness *n* [U]

low² *adv* **1** in or to a low position, standard or level: *He was bent low over a book.* **2** quietly **3** (in music) with deep notes –opposite **high**

low³ *n* a level that is low: *Profits have reached a new low this month.* –opposite **high**

low-down /ˈləʊdaʊn/ *n* **the lowdown on** *infml* information about a person or thing

low-down /ˈ· ·/ *adj* [only before a noun] unfair and not worthy of respect

low·er¹ /ˈləʊəʳ/ *adj* [only before a noun] being the bottom part of something, or the bottom one of two or more things: *The bottle is on the lower shelf.* –opposite **upper**

lower² *v* [T] **1** to make something smaller in amount or quality: *Please lower your voice.* **2** to move something down: *Lower the flags!* –opposite **raise** (for 1,2) **3 lower yourself** to lose your own or others' respect for you by doing something **4 lower your voice** speak more quietly

lower case /ˌ· ·◂/ *adj* printed as small letters such as a and b, rather than in capital letters such as A and B –**lower case** *n* [U]

low-key /ˌ· ·◂/ *adj* (also **low-keyed**) quiet and controlled

low·land /ˈləʊlənd/ *adj* at about sea level (used of land) –**lowlands** *n* [pl]

low·ly /ˈləʊli/ *adj* **lowlier, lowliest** low in rank or position –**lowly** *adv* –**lowliness** *n* [U]

low-ly-ing /ˌ· ˈ· ·◂/ *adj* at about sea level (used of land)

loy·al /ˈlɔɪəl/ *adj* faithful to people, places, or things: *He's a loyal supporter of the local football club.* –**loyally** *adv*

loy·al·ty /ˈlɔɪəlti/ *n* **loyalties 1** [U] behaviour in which you remain faithful to someone or something: *his loyalty to his friends* **2 loyalties** [pl] feelings of friendship and faithfulness: *Work or home – you've got to decide where your loyalties lie.*

loy·al·ist /ˈlɔɪəlɪst/ *n* a person who remains faithful to an existing ruler or government

loz·enge /ˈlɒzɪndʒ ‖ ˈlɑ:-/ *n* a small sweet, especially one that you suck to make a sore throat feel better

LP /ˌel ˈpi:/ *n* a record which plays for about 20 minutes on each side –compare SINGLE

L-plate /ˈel pleɪt/ *n* the letter L, put on a vehicle in Britain to show that the driver is a learner

LSD /ˌel es ˈdi:/ *n* [U] a strong drug that makes you see things in a strange and different way

Ltd a written abbreviation for LIMITED: *M.Y. Dixon and Son, Ltd, Booksellers*

lu·bri·cant /ˈlu:brɪkənt/ *n* [C;U] a substance which helps the parts of something like a machine to move easily

lu·bri·cate /ˈlu:brɪkeɪt/ *v* **lubricated, lubricating** [T] to make something move easily by adding a substance such as oil –**lubrication** /ˌlu:brɪˈkeɪʃən/ *n* [U]

lu·cid /ˈlu:sɪd/ *adj* **1** easy to understand: *a lucid explanation* **2** able to express yourself clearly: *There are lucid moments in her madness.* –**lucidly** *adv* –**lucidity** /lu:ˈsɪdəti/ *n* [U]

luck /lʌk/ *n* [U] **1** something that brings you good or bad fortune, as if by chance: *Luck was with us and we won easily.* | *I've had bad luck all week.* **2** good fortune: *She phoned to wish me luck.* **3 Any luck?** = Were you successful? **4 be in luck** to have good fortune [RELATED PHRASE **be out of luck**] **5 Bad luck!, Hard luck!** phrases that you use to express sympathy with someone **6 be down on your luck** to be in a period when nothing is going well for you **7 the luck of the draw** the result of chance

luck·y /ˈlʌki/ *adj* **luckier, luckiest** having, resulting from, or bringing good luck: *He's a lucky man.* | *That was a lucky find!* | *I carry a lucky charm to protect me when I travel.* –opposite **unlucky** –**luckily** *adv* : *Luckily, she was in when I called.*

lu·cra·tive /ˈlu:krətɪv/ *adj fml* making a lot of money: *I am working on a very lucrative business deal.* –**lucratively** *adv*

lu·di·crous /ˈlu:dɪkrəs/ *adj* very foolish: *What a ludicrous suggestion!*

lug /lʌg/ *v* **-gg-** [T + adv/prep] *infml* to pull or carry something with great effort and difficulty

lug·gage /ˈlʌgɪdʒ/ *n* [U] the bags and cases of a traveller: *I don't want to take too much luggage on this trip.*

lu·gu·bri·ous /lu:ˈgu:briəs/ *adj fml* sad, especially sadder than necessary –**lugubriously** *adv*

luke·warm /ˌlu:kˈwɔ:m◂ ‖ -ɔ:rm◂/ *adj* **1** not very hot (used of liquid) **2** showing little interest or pleasure

lull¹ /lʌl/ *v* [T] to make someone feel sleepy, less active, or safe: *The movement of the train soon lulled me to sleep.* | *We were lulled into a false sense of security.*

lull² *n* a period in which there is less activity: *During a lull in the fighting he managed to sleep for a while.*

lul·la·by /ˈlʌləbaɪ/ *n* **lullabies** a pleasant song that you sing to help a child fall asleep

lum·ba·go /lʌmˈbeɪgəʊ/ *n* [U] pain in the lower part of your back

lum·ber¹ /ˈlʌmbəʳ/ *v* [I + adv/prep] to move in a slow, awkward manner **2 lumber someone with something** *BrE infml* to give someone something that they do not want: *I was lumbered with the cooking and cleaning.*

lumber² *n* [U] *AmE* TIMBER

lum·ber·jack /ˈlʌmbədʒæk ‖ -ər-/ *n* a person whose job it is to cut down trees for wood

lu·mi·na·ry /ˈlu:mɪnəri ‖ -neri/ *n* **luminaries** *fml* a person whose mind, knowledge, or actions are famous and respected

lu·mi·nous /ˈlu:mɪnəs/ *adj* shining in the dark: *luminous paint* –**luminously** *adv*

lump¹ /lʌmp/ *n* **1** a mass of something solid: *He took a simple lump of clay and made a beautiful pot.* **2** a hard swelling on or in your body: *She found a lump in her left breast.* **3** a small block of sugar: *How much sugar – one lump or two?* **4 a lump in your throat** a tight sensation in the throat caused by strong feelings such as pity

lump² *adj* **lump sum** a single undivided amount of money: *I can give you a lump sum or weekly payments.*

lump³ *v* **1 lump it** *infml* to accept a bad situation without complaining: *That's my decision, and you'll just have to lump it.* **2 lump people or things together** to put two or more people or things together or treat them in the same way: *All these costs can be lumped together as "expenses".*

lump·y /'lʌmpi/ *adj* **lumpier, lumpiest** having lumps: *The sauce was lumpy.*

lu·na·cy /'luːnəsi/ *n* [U] **1** madness **2** strange or foolish behaviour

lu·nar /'luːnəʳ/ *adj* concerning or going to the moon: *a lunar voyage*

lunar month /ˌ·· '·/ *n* a period of about 29 days, which is the time the moon takes to circle the earth

lu·na·tic /'luːnətɪk/ *n* a person who is mad, foolish, or strange: *You can't just go round insulting people, you lunatic!* **–lunatic** *adj*

lunch¹ /lʌntʃ/ *n* (also **luncheon** /'lʌntʃən/ *fml*) [C;U] a meal that you eat in the middle of the day: *Shall we meet for lunch? | The lunch hour is from 1 to 2 pm.* –see DINNER (USAGE)

lunch² *v* [I] to eat lunch, especially when it is a formal meal: *I'm lunching* **with** *the directors today.*

lunch·time /'lʌntʃtaɪm/ *n* [U] the time at which you have lunch

lung /lʌŋ/ *n* one of the two organs which you use to breathe

lunge /lʌndʒ/ *v* **lunged, lunging** [I + adv/prep] to make a sudden forceful movement, especially to attack someone: *He lunged* **at** *me with a knife.* **–lunge** *n*

lurch¹ /lɜːtʃ ‖ lɜːrtʃ/ *n* a sudden, uncontrolled movement: *The boat gave a lurch sideways towards the rocks.*

lurch² *v* [I + adv/prep] to move with irregular, sudden steps: *The drunken man lurched across the road.*

lure¹ /lʊəʳ, ljʊəʳ ‖ lʊər/ *n* [C] **1** something that attracts you: *It is the lure of money that brings them to the city.* **2** something used to attract animals so that they can be caught

lure² *v* **lured, luring** [T] to attract a person or animal: *She's been lured here by the promise of a high salary.*

lu·rid /'lʊərɪd, 'ljʊərɪd ‖ 'lʊərɪd/ *adj* **1** very brightly coloured (a word used to show disapproval): *It was a lurid picture of a sunset.* **2** very unpleasant (a word used to show disapproval): *The papers gave the lurid details of the murder.* **–luridly** *adv*

lurk /lɜːk ‖ lɜːrk/ *v* **1** [I + adv/prep] to wait in hiding, especially for an evil purpose: *A man was seen lurking near the scene of the crime.* **2** [I] to remain, especially in your mind: *He had the lurking suspicion that she might be guilty.*

lus·cious /'lʌʃəs/ *adj* pleasant or sweet in taste, smell, or appearance: *luscious fruit* **–lusciousness** *n* [U]

lush /lʌʃ/ *adj* thick, healthy and growing well (used especially of plants)

lust¹ /lʌst/ *n* [C;U] strong desire for a person or thing, especially sexual desire: *His feelings for her were little more than lust. | She was driven by a lust* **for** *power.*

lust² *v* **lust after, lust for** to have a strong desire for someone or something: *He lusted after wealth. | She lusts for her tenant.* –see DESIRE (USAGE)

lust·ful /'lʌstfəl/ *adj* feeling or showing strong sexual desire **–lustfully** *adv*

lus·tre /'lʌstəʳ/ *n* (also **luster** *AmE*) [U] the brightness of a polished surface **–lustrous** /'lʌstrəs/ *adj* **–lustrously** *adv*

lust·y /'lʌsti/ *adj* **lustier, lustiest** strong and healthy **–lustiness** *n* [U]

lute /luːt/ *n* an old musical instrument with strings

lux·u·ri·ant /lʌg'zjʊəriənt, ləg'ʒʊəriənt ‖ ləg'ʒʊəriənt/ *adj* thick, healthy and growing well (used especially of plants): *The plant was covered in luxuriant foliage.* –compare LUXURIOUS **–luxuriantly** *adv* **–luxuriance** *n* [U]

lux·u·ri·ate /lʌg'zjʊərieɪt, ləg'ʒʊəri- ‖ ləg'ʒʊəri-/ *v* **luxuriated, luxuriating, luxuriate in** something to enjoy doing something pleasurable in a lazy way

lux·u·ri·ous /lʌg'zjʊəriəs, ləg'ʒʊəriəs ‖ ləg'ʒʊəriəs/ *adj* very comfortable and expensive: *Life in prison will be difficult for someone used to such luxurious surroundings.* **–luxuriously** *adv*

lux·u·ry /'lʌkʃəri/ *n* **luxuries 1** [U] great comfort, which is provided by wealth: *He leads a life of luxury. | We're moving to a luxury flat in central London.* **2** [C] something pleasant that you do not need and cannot often afford: *Foreign holidays are a real luxury.*

ly·chee /'laɪtʃiː/ *n* an Asian fruit with sweet white flesh

ly·ing /'laɪ-ɪŋ/ the present participle of LIE

lynch /lɪntʃ/ *v* [T] to attack and kill someone thought to be guilty of a crime, without a legal trial and usually by hanging them: *He was lynched by the angry townspeople.*

lynx /lɪŋks/ *n* **lynxes** a wild animal with a short tail that belongs to the cat family

lyre /laɪəʳ/ *n* an ancient Greek musical instrument with strings stretched on a U-shaped frame

lyr·ic /'lɪrɪk/ *n* **1** [C] a poem that expresses strong personal feeling **2 lyrics** [pl] the words of a song

lyr·i·cal /'lɪrɪkəl/ *adj* **1** full of pleasure about something **2** POETIC **–lyrically** /-kli/ *adv*

lyr·i·cist /'lɪrɪsɪst/ *n* a person who writes the words for songs

M,m

M, m /em/ **M's, m's** or **Ms, ms** the 13th letter of the English alphabet

m a written abbreviation for metre

MA /ˌem ˈeɪ/ **1** a higher university degree; an abbreviation for **Master of Arts**: *He has an MA in English Literature*. **2** a person who has an MA

ma'am /mæm, mɑːm, məm ‖ mæm/ *n old fash* or *AmE* a polite way of addressing a woman: *Can I help you, ma'am?*

mac /mæk/ *n* see MACKINTOSH

ma·ca·bre /məˈkɑːbrə, -bəʳ/ *adj* strange, frightening, and often connected with death: *macabre tales of violent murders*

mac·a·ro·ni /ˌmækəˈrəʊni◂/ *n* [U] a food made of short thin tubes of PASTA

mace /meɪs/ *n* a decorative rod carried by an official in certain ceremonies as a sign of power

Mach /mæk ‖ mɑːk/ *n* [sing] a unit of measurement for very high speeds: *If a plane is flying at Mach 1, it is flying at the speed of sound.*

ma·chet·e /məˈʃeti, məˈtʃeɪti/ *n* a knife with a broad heavy blade

ma·chine¹ /məˈʃiːn/ *n* **1** a man-made apparatus which uses electricity or other power to perform work: *a sewing machine* | *a washing machine* **2 by machine** using a machine: *The books are all packed by machine.*

■ USAGE Compare **machine, appliance, tool, instrument, device,** and **gadget.** A **machine** usually uses power, and you do not work it directly with your hands: *the machines in the factory* | *Tickets are available from the machine on the platform.* | *a knitting machine.* Electrical machines used in the home (such as washing machines) can also be called **appliances**: *a shop selling household appliances.* A **tool** is an object which you hold in your hand and which you use for making things from wood, metal, or other materials: *carpenter's tools such as hammers, drills and saws.* An **instrument** is an object which you use to do very exact or careful work, usually by hand: *medical/surgical instruments* | *A thermometer is an instrument for measuring temperature.* **Device** is a general word for any object which has been produced for doing work, and is usually used when there is no suitable particular word: *an electronic device which controlled the opening of the doors* | *I have no idea how this device works.* **Gadget** is an informal word for a small and perhaps unusual device for doing a particular job: *a clever little gadget for opening bottles*

machine² *v* **machined, machining** [T] to make something by machine, usually in a factory –**machinist** *n*

ma·chine-gun /məˈʃiːngʌn/ *n* a gun which fires bullets very quickly one after another

ma·chin·e·ry /məˈʃiːnəri/ *n* [U] **1** machines in general: *The machinery must be kept in good working order.* **2** the operation of a system or process: *The machinery of the law works slowly.*

ma·cho /ˈmætʃəʊ ‖ ˈmɑː-/ *adj infml* showing very male qualities (a word used to show disapproval)

mack·e·rel /ˈmækərəl/ *n* [C;U] a sea fish with a blue and silver skin

mack·in·tosh /ˈmækɪntɒʃ ‖ -tɑːʃ/ *n* (also **mac**) a coat which keeps out water

mac·ro·bi·ot·ic /ˌmækrəʊbaɪˈɒtɪk◂ ‖ -ˈɑːtɪk/ *adj* concerning food such as vegetables and whole grains which are thought to produce good health

mad /mæd/ *adj* **1** ill in the mind: *He's gone quite mad in his old age.* **2** extremely foolish: *You're mad to drive so fast!* | *What a mad idea!* **3 mad about** *infml* filled with strong feeling, interest, or admiration: *He's mad about football.* | *She's mad about him.* **4** *infml* angry: *I got mad with him for being late.* **5 drive someone mad** to annoy someone very much **6 like mad** *infml* very hard or fast: *If you run like mad you might just catch the train.*

mad·am /ˈmædəm/ *n* **1 Madam** a formal way of addressing a woman in a business letter: *Dear Madam...* –compare SIR **2** a formal way of addressing a female customer: *Would Madam like to try another size?*

mad·den /ˈmædn/ *v* [T] to make someone very angry or annoyed

mad·den·ing /ˈmædənɪŋ/ *adj infml* very annoying *maddening traffic delays*

made¹ /meɪd/ the past tense and past participle of MAKE¹

made² *adj* [never before a noun] **1** formed of something: *The frame is made of silver.* | *Pancakes are made from eggs, flour, and milk.* **2** completely suited for someone: *Those two are made for each other.* **3** sure of success: *If you find gold you're made for life.*

■ USAGE **Made of** and **made from** have very similar meanings, but they are often used in slightly different ways. If the original material has been completely changed, use **made from**: *Bread is made from flour and water.* | *luxury soap made from the finest ingredients* | *some jam made from the fruit in our garden* If the original materials can still be recognized, use **made of**: *a statue made of the finest marble* | *handbags made of cheap black plastic*

mad·ly /ˈmædli/ *adv* **1** in a mad, wild way: *He rushed madly out of the room.* **2 love someone madly** to love someone very much

mad·man /ˈmædmən/ *n* **madmen** /-mən/ a man who is mad: *He drives like a madman.*

mad·ness /ˈmædnəs/ *n* [U] **1** the state of being mad **2** extremely foolish behaviour: *It would be sheer madness to try to cross the desert on your own.*

mad·wom·an /ˈmæd.wʊmən/ *n* **madwomen** /ˌwɪmɪn/ a woman who is mad

mael·strom /ˈmeɪlstrəm/ *n* the uncontrollable violent force of events which may lead to destruction: *She got sucked into the maelstrom of political controversy.*

maes·tro /ˈmaɪstrəʊ/ *n* a great or famous musician

Maf·i·a /ˈmæfiə ‖ ˈmɑː-, ˈmæ-/ *n* [+sing/pl verb] **the Mafia** an organization of criminals who control many activities by violent means

mag·a·zine /ˌmæɡəˈziːn ‖ ˈmæɡəziːn/ *n* **1** (also **mag** /mæɡ/ *infml*) a sort of book with large pages and a paper cover, containing writing, photographs, and advertisements, printed every week or month: *a photography magazine* | *a woman's weekly magazine* –see picture on page 442 **2** the part of a gun in which bullets are placed before firing **3** a place in which weapons and bullets are kept

ma·gen·ta /mə'dʒɛntə/ *n, adj* [U] a dark purplish pink colour –see picture on page 147

mag·got /'mægət/ *n* a creature like a small worm; maggots are the young of flies or other insects

ma·gic /'mædʒɪk/ *n* [U] **1** a special power sometimes believed to control events by calling on spirits, or saying special words *They say the old witch practises black magic.* **2** the art of a CONJURER who entertains by producing unexpected objects and results by tricks *He pulled the rabbit out of the hat by magic.* –**magic** *adj* [only before a noun] : *a magic trick*

ma·gic·al /'mædʒɪkəl/ *adj* mysterious, strange, and exciting: *a magical evening beneath the stars* –**magically** /-kli/ *adv*

ma·gi·cian /mə'dʒɪʃən/ *n* a person who performs tricks or magic

ma·gis·te·ri·al /ˌmædʒɨ'stɪəriəl/ *adj* **1** *fml* having the power of a master or ruler *a proud magisterial manner* **2** [only before a noun] relating to a magistrate

ma·gis·trate /'mædʒɨstreɪt, -strɨt/ *n* an official who judges cases in the lowest law courts

mag·nan·i·mous /mæg'nænɨməs/ *adj* very generous and forgiving towards other people –**magnanimity** /ˌmægnə'nɪmɨti/ *n* [U]

mag·nate /'mægneɪt, -nɨt/ *n* a wealthy and powerful person in business

mag·ne·si·um /mæg'niːziəm/ *n* [U] a silver-white metal that burns with a bright light

mag·net /'mægnɨt/ *n* a piece of iron which can make other metal objects come towards it (either naturally or by passing an electric current through it)

mag·net·ic /mæg'nɛtɪk/ *adj* **1** having the power of a magnet: *a powerful magnetic force* **2** attracting people easily: *a magnetic personality* – **magnetically** /-kli/ *adv*

magnetic field /·ˌ·· ·ˈ·/ *n* the space in which the force of a magnet is effective: *the Earth's magnetic field*

magnetic pole /·ˌ·· ·ˈ·/ *n* either of two points near the NORTH POLE and the SOUTH POLE of the Earth towards which the compass needle points

magnetic tape /·ˌ·· ·ˈ·/ *n* [C;U] a TAPE on which sound or other information can be recorded

mag·net·is·m /'mægnɨtɪzəm/ *n* [U] **1** the qualities of a MAGNET **2** strong personal charm: *We were overwhelmed by the sheer magnetism of his personality.*

mag·net·ize /'mægnɨtaɪz/ *v* (also **magnetise** *BrE*) [T] to make a piece of iron into a MAGNET

mag·nif·i·cent /mæg'nɪfɨsənt/ *adj* extremely good or beautiful: *There were magnificent gold decorations inside the ballroom.* –**magnificence** *n* [U] –**magnificently** *adv*

mag·ni·fy /'mægnɨfaɪ/ *v* **magnified, magnifying** [T] **1** to make something appear larger than it is: *If you look through the microscope you will see the specimen magnified clearly.* **2** to make something seem more important than it really is: *You really mustn't magnify these little problems.* –**magnification** /ˌmægnɨfɨ'keɪʃən/ *n* [C;U]

mag·ni·fy·ing glass /'···· ·/ *n* a curved piece of glass with a handle which makes objects appear larger than they really are

mag·ni·tude /'mægnɨtjuːd ‖ -tuːd/ *n* [U] *fml* great size or importance

mag·no·li·a /mæg'nəʊliə/ *n* a tree with large white or pink flowers

mag·pie /'mægpaɪ/ *n* a fairly large black and white bird which has a noisy cry

ma·hog·a·ny /mə'hɒgəni ‖ mə'hɑː-/ *n* [U] **1** a hard dark wood often used for making furniture **2** a dark reddish brown colour

maid /meɪd/ *n* **1** a female servant **2** *lit* a young unmarried woman

maid·en[1] /'meɪdn/ *n lit* a young unmarried woman

maiden[2] *adj* [only before a noun] **1** first: *The ship made its maiden voyage last year.* **2 maiden aunt** an old, unmarried aunt

maid·en·ly /'meɪdnli/ *adj lit* gentle and modest

maiden name /'·· ·/ *n* a woman's family name before marriage

mail[1] /meɪl/ *n* [U] **1** the system for sending things by post: *The bad weather caused a disruption to the mail.* **2** letters and anything else sent by post: *She was sitting in the garden opening her mail.*

mail[2] *v* [T] *AmE* to send something to someone by the mail: *Can you mail these cards for me, please?* | *I'll mail the book to you.*

mail·bag /'meɪlbæg/ *n* a strong bag for carrying letters and parcels

mail·box /'meɪlbɒks ‖ -bɑːks/ *n AmE* **1** a place outside the house where letters are delivered **2** an outdoor POSTBOX

maim /meɪm/ *v* [T] to harm someone very badly, so that they are damaged for life

main[1] /meɪn/ *adj* [only before a noun] most important: *the main meal of the day* | *Here are the main points of the news again.* –**mainly** *adv* : *We sell mainly children's clothes.* | *I like all music, but I'm mainly interested in jazz.*

main[2] *n* **1 in the main** usually **2 the mains** large pipes or wires supplying water, gas, or electricity

main·land /'meɪnlənd, -lænd/ *n* **the mainland** the main part of a country, without its islands

main·spring /'meɪnˌsprɪŋ/ *n* [sing] *fml* the most important reason for an action: *His belief in freedom was the mainspring of his fight against slavery.*

main·stay /'meɪnsteɪ/ *n* [sing] the most important part of something: *Farming is still the mainstay of this country's economy.*

main·stream /'meɪnstriːm/ *n* **the mainstream** the group of people who are considered to behave in a usual way: *Her views are very much those of the mainstream.* –**mainstream** *adj* : *mainstream education*

main·tain /meɪn'teɪn, mən-/ *v* **1** [T] to continue to have or do something as before: *He maintained his interest in football all his life.* | *We need to maintain good relations with the suppliers.* **2** [T] to support someone with money: *He is too poor to maintain a wife and children.* **3** [T] to keep something in good condition or look after it: *It costs a lot of money to maintain an old house.* **4** [T (+that)] to argue that something is the case: *Throughout the trial he maintained his innocence.*
□ USEFUL PATTERNS to maintain something; to maintain that...

main·te·nance /'meɪntənəns/ *n* [U] **1** the act of keeping something in good condition: *I'm going to classes in car maintenance.* **2** money that a person sends regularly to someone to provide for things they need: *He has to pay maintenance to his ex-wife.*

mai·son·ette /ˌmeɪzəˈnet/ n a flat on two floors, that is part of a larger house

maize /meɪz/ n [U] a tall plant which bears SWEETCORN

ma·jes·ty /ˈmædʒɪsti/ n 1 [U] greatness or power: *We admired the majesty of the snow-topped mountains.* 2 **your Majesty, his Majesty, their Majesties** a title for a king or queen: *Her Majesty the Queen* | *Thank you, your Majesty.* –**majestic** /məˈdʒestɪk/ adj –**majestically** /-kli/ adv

ma·jor¹ /ˈmeɪdʒəʳ/ adj [only before a noun] more important or serious than other things: *The car needs major repairs.* | *a major operation*

major² n 1 **Major** an officer of middle rank in an army or air force 2 *tech* a person who has, in law, reached the age of being an adult

major³ v **major in something** to study something as your main subject at university: *He's majoring in physics.*

ma·jor·i·ty¹ /məˈdʒɒrɪti ‖ məˈdʒɔː-, məˈdʒɑː-/ n **majorities** 1 [U+sing/pl verb] more than half of a group of people: *The majority of primary school teachers are women.* | *At the meeting, young people were in the majority.* 2 [C] the difference between the number of votes gained by the winner and the loser: *She won by a large majority.* | *He had a majority of 900 votes.* 3 [C] the age when you become an adult in law

majority² adj [only before a noun] reached by the agreement of most members of a group: *a majority decision*

make – see box on pages 419 and 420

make-be·lieve /ˈ···ˌ·/ n [U] a state of pretending or imagining things which are not real: *She lives in a world of make-believe.*

mak·er /ˈmeɪkəʳ/ n a person or company that makes something: *If your watch doesn't work properly, it's best to send it back to the makers.*

make·shift /ˈmeɪkˌʃɪft/ adj [only before a noun] used only for a short time because there is nothing better to use: *They made a makeshift table from some old pieces of wood.*

make-up /ˈ· ·/ n 1 [C;U] powder or paint worn on the face: *Too much make-up looks unnatural.* | *eye make-up* 2 [C] the combination of qualities (in a person's character)

mak·ing /ˈmeɪkɪŋ/ n 1 [U] the act or business of making something with your hands: *She's really good at dressmaking.* 2 **the making of someone** the reason for someone's success: *Hard work will be the making of him.* 3 **in the making** in the process of becoming something: *He's a company chairman in the making.* 4 **the makings of** everything necessary for developing into something: *He has the makings of a good doctor.*

mal·ad·just·ed /ˌmæləˈdʒʌstɪd◂/ adj having problems in your mind which prevent a happy or normal life

mal·a·dy /ˈmælədi/ n **maladies** *fml* something that is wrong with a system or an organization

ma·laise /məˈleɪz, mæ-/ n [C;U] a general feeling of dissatisfaction because something is wrong: *the underlying social malaise in this country*

ma·lar·i·a /məˈleəriə/ n [U] a common tropical disease caused by the bite of a certain MOSQUITO –**malarial** adj [only before a noun]

mal·con·tent /ˈmælkəntent ‖ ˌmælkənˈtent/ n a dissatisfied person who is likely to make trouble

male /meɪl/ adj belonging to the sex that does not give birth to young: *The male bird is very brightly coloured.* | *a male voice* –see FEMALE (USAGE) –**male** n

male chau·vin·ist /ˌ· ˈ···◂/ n a man who believes men are better than women –**male chauvinism** n [U]

ma·lev·o·lent /məˈlevələnt/ adj *lit* wishing to do evil to others –**malevolence** n [U] –**malevolently** adv

mal·for·ma·tion /ˌmælfɔːˈmeɪʃən ‖ -ɔːr-/ n [C;U] *tech* the condition of being formed or shaped wrongly –**malformed** /ˌmælˈfɔːmd◂ ‖ -ɔːr-/ adj

mal·func·tion /mælˈfʌŋkʃən/ n a fault in the way a machine works: *delays owing to malfunctions of the computer* –**malfunction** v [I]

mal·ice /ˈmælɪs/ n [U] the wish to hurt other people: *He assured us that he bore us no malice, but I still didn't trust him.*

ma·li·cious /məˈlɪʃəs/ adj intended to hurt people: *malicious gossip* –**maliciously** adv

ma·lign /məˈlaɪn/ v [T] to say unpleasant and untrue things about someone: *a politician who has been much maligned by the newspapers*

ma·lig·nant /məˈlɪgnənt/ adj 1 full of hate and a strong wish to hurt people 2 serious enough to cause death if not stopped: *a malignant tumour*

ma·lin·ger /məˈlɪŋgəʳ/ v [I] to avoid work by pretending to be ill: *He says he's got flu, but I think he's malingering.* –**malingerer** n

mal·lard /ˈmælɑːd ‖ -ərd/ n a wild duck

mal·le·a·ble /ˈmæliəbəl/ adj 1 able to be beaten or made into a new shape (used of metals) 2 easily influenced (used of people)

mal·let /ˈmælɪt/ n a wooden hammer –see picture on page 638

mal·nu·tri·tion /ˌmælnjuˈtrɪʃən ‖ -nu-/ n [U] bad health resulting from lack of food or from the wrong sorts of food

mal·prac·tice /ˌmælˈpræktɪs/ n [U] a failure to carry out your professional duty properly, often resulting in loss or physical harm to someone: *He sued his doctor for malpractice.*

malt /mɔːlt/ n [U] grain such as BARLEY, which has been specially treated and is used for making alcoholic drinks: *a bottle of malt whisky*

mal·treat /mælˈtriːt/ v [T] *fml* to treat someone cruelly and roughly: *The children had been physically maltreated too.* –**maltreatment** n [U]

mam·mal /ˈmæməl/ n a type of animal born live, not in an egg, which is fed on its mother's milk

mam·moth¹ /ˈmæməθ/ n a very large hairy elephant which used to live on earth

mammoth² adj [only before a noun] extremely large: *a mammoth task*

man /mæn/ n **men** /men/ 1 [C] an adult human male: *men, women, and children* | *a Polish man and his German wife* 2 [C] a human being, male or female: *No man could have survived that.* 3 [U] the human race: *Man cannot live by bread alone.* 4 [C] a male employed by someone: *The men are threatening to go on strike.* 5 [C] a soldier of low rank 6 [C] a male member of a team 7 [C] any of the objects moved by each player in a board game: *chess men* 8 **as one man** everyone together: *The audience stood up as one man and cheered.* 9 **man and wife** husband and wife 10 **the man in the street** the average person, who represents general opinion: *This kind of film doesn't appeal to the man in the street.* 11 **a man of the world** a man with a lot of experience of life

make¹ /meɪk/ *v*

made /meɪd/, **making**

1 [T] to do something:
We need to make a decision. | *They were making a dreadful noise.* | *She made a brilliant speech.* | *I need to make a phone call.* | *He made several mistakes.* | *Try not to make a mess.*
2 [T] to produce something:
I'm just going to make a cup of coffee. | *She made herself a dress.* | *We make 2,000 cars a week in this factory.* | *The film was made on location in Africa.*
USEFUL PATTERNS: to make something; to make something for someone; to make someone something
3 [T] to earn;
I don't make enough money to go on expensive holidays! | *The company made a huge profit this year.* | *She makes her living writing children's books.*
4 [T; + complement] to cause someone to do something, or cause something to happen:
His behaviour made me angry. | *We want to make the kitchen bigger.* | *We're going to make the spare bedroom into a study.* | *I feel that my experiences have made me a better person.* | *She was made a director of the company.* | *The army will make a man of you!*
5 [T] to cause someone to do something, or cause something to happen:
How do you make this machine work? | *The smell made me feel ill.* | *You made me jump!* | *These people should be made to work!* | *That hairstyle makes you look very young.*
USEFUL PATTERNS: to make someone do something; to be made to do something
6 [T] to calculate an answer or result:
"Have you got the answer yet?" "Yes, I make it 425."
7 [T] to add up to:
Two and two make four.
8 [T] to have the right qualities for something:
This will make a good present for my mother. | *I think she'll make an excellent doctor.*
9 [T] to manage to get to a place or an event:
I'm afraid I won't be able to make the party on Friday.
10 [T] *infml* to cause something to be good or attractive:
That wallpaper really makes the room. | *The trip round the islands really made our holiday.*
11 **make a bed** to tidy a bed that someone has slept in by straightening the sheet and pulling up the covers
12 **he made her his wife** *lit* = he married her
13 **make a friend, make friends** to become become friendly with someone:
I see you've made a friend already. | *I've made friends **with** quite a number of people since we moved here.*
[RELATED PHRASE: **make an enemy:** *He's made quite a few enemies.*]
14 **make someone's day** to make someone feel very happy:
It made my day when he told me I was going to get a pay rise.
15 **make it: a** to arrive in time:
If we set off now, we should make it to the station before the train goes.
b to be able to attend an event:
I wanted to go to her lecture, but I couldn't make it.
c to succeed:
She feels she's finally made it as a singer.
16 **What time do you make it?** = What time does your watch say?
"What time do you make it?" "I make it four o'clock."
17 **make do** to use something even though it is not very good or is not enough:
*I haven't got any cream, so we'll have to make do **with** milk.*
18 **be made of** to be formed of a particular substance:
cups made of plastic | *a table made of old wooden crates*

19 what do you make of this? a phrase used to ask someone's opinion about something that you think is strange
20 make as if to do something to show that you are about to do something:
She made as if to leave.
21 make your way somewhere to go somewhere:
We slowly made our way home.
22 make way to move so that someone else can go where you were

make for sthg *phr v*
[T]
1 to move towards something:
He made for the door.
2 to result in something:
The large print makes for easy reading.

make off *phr v*
to leave a place quickly:
The thieves made off **with** *a considerable amount of money and jewellery.*

make out *phr v*
1 [T **make** sthg ↔ **out**] to see, hear, or understand something with difficulty:
I could just make out the shape of the building. | I could hear voices, but I couldn't make out what they were saying.
2 [T **make** sthg ↔ **out**] to write the necessary information on a cheque:
The cheque was made out to me.
3 **make out that...** to pretend:
He makes out that he's a qualified doctor.
4 **make yourself out to be** to pretend that you are something:
He makes himself out to be the most important person in the whole company.

make sthg ↔ **over** *phr v*
[T] *fml*
to pass over money or goods to someone:
The house was made over to his children.

make up *phr v*
1 [T **make** sthg ↔ **up**] to invent a story or a piece of information in order to deceive people:
We later found out that he'd made the whole thing up.
2 [T **make** sthg ↔ **up**] to form something:
the members who make up the committee | Society is made up of lots of different groups of people.
3 [I;T **make** sbdy **up**] to put special powder and paints on your face in order to make yourself more attractive:
She made herself up carefully.
4 [T **make** sthg ↔ **up**] to form or prepare something by putting the different parts together:
I made up a bed on the floor.
5 [T **make** sthg ↔ **up**] to make an amount complete:
The rest of the money will be made up by the government.
6 [I] to become friends again after a quarrel

make up for sthg *phr v*
[T] to reduce the bad effect of something:
The long hot summer made up for the miserable spring.

make ² *n*
1 a product produced by a particular maker:
"What make is your car?" "It's a Ford."
2 **on the make** trying to gain money and power

■ USAGE Many people do not like the use of **man** to mean human beings (men and women) in general. If you want to avoid this use, you can use other words such as: **humans, human beings, the human race, people.**

man² v **-nn-** [T] to operate or be in charge of equipment: *Man the guns!* | *the first manned spacecraft*

man³ interj AmE infml used when speaking to a person, expressing anger or impatience with them: *For goodness' sake, man, think of others for a change!*

man·a·cles /ˈmænəkəlz/ n [pl] rings or chains on the hands or feet of a prisoner

man·age /ˈmænɪdʒ/ v **managed, managing** 1 [T] to control or be in charge of a business or activity: *He managed the company while his father was away.* | *She manages the money very well.* 2 [I;T] to succeed in dealing with something such as a problem: *We don't have much money, but we manage.* | *Do you think we'll manage to finish the work by Friday?*
□ USEFUL PATTERNS to manage something; to manage to do something

man·age·a·ble /ˈmænɪdʒəbəl/ adj easy or possible to control or deal with: *a manageable hair style* | *Our new garden is quite small, and much more manageable than our last one.*

man·age·ment /ˈmænɪdʒmənt/ n 1 [U] the control of something such as a business or money 2 [C;U] the people in charge of a firm or organization: *a breakdown in communication between management and the workforce* | *The management is having talks with the workers.*

man·ag·er /ˈmænɪdʒəʳ/ n a person who directs the affairs of a business or team of workers: *the manager of a football team* | *My bank manager is extremely helpful.* | *Why don't you complain to the manager?*

man·ag·er·ess /ˌmænɪdʒəˈres ‖ ˈmænɪdʒərɨs/ n a woman who controls a shop or restaurant: *I'd like to see the manageress, please.*

man·a·ge·ri·al /ˌmænɨˈdʒɪəriəl/ adj [only before a noun] concerned with or belonging to the work of a manager: *She has excellent managerial skills.*

man·date /ˈmændeɪt/ n fml 1 the power given to a government to act according to the wishes of the people of a country: *It is ridiculous for the government to claim it has a mandate from the people for these measures.* 2 a formal command given by a high official

man·da·to·ry /ˈmændətəri ‖ -tɔːri/ adj fml which must be done

mane /meɪn/ n the long thick hair growing from the neck of a horse or a lion

ma·neu·ver /məˈnuːvəʳ/ n –see MANOEUVRE

man·ger /ˈmeɪndʒəʳ/ n a long open container used for feeding horses and cattle

man·gled /ˈmæŋgəld/ adj crushed or cut to pieces: *The mangled wreckage was towed away from the scene of the crash.*

man·go /ˈmæŋgəʊ/ n **mangoes** or **mangos** a sweet yellow fruit

man·grove /ˈmæŋgrəʊv/ n a tropical tree which grows in water or on muddy land

mang·y /ˈmeɪndʒi/ adj **mangier, mangiest** of bad appearance because of loss of hair: *a mangy old dog*

man·han·dle /ˈmænhændl/ v **manhandled, manhandling** [T] to move someone roughly, using force: *She complained that she had been manhandled by the police.*

man·hole /ˈmænhəʊl/ n a covered opening in a road leading to underground pipes

man·hood /ˈmænhʊd/ n [U] the state of being a man rather than a boy

ma·ni·a /ˈmeɪniə/ n 1 a strong desire or liking for something: *a mania for driving fast cars* 2 tech an illness of the mind

ma·ni·ac /ˈmeɪniæk/ n 1 a person who suffers from a certain illness of the mind: *a sex maniac* 2 a wild thoughtless person: *You're driving like a maniac.*

man·ic /ˈmænɪk/ adj very excited and wild: *a manic outburst*

man·i·cure /ˈmænɨkjʊəʳ/ n a beauty treatment for your hands and fingernails –**manicure** v **manicured, manicuring** [T] –**manicurist** n

man·i·fest¹ /ˈmænɨfest/ adj fml very easy and clear to see –**manifestly** adv: *It was manifestly obvious that they were in love.*

manifest² v [T] fml 1 to show something plainly: *Such rash actions manifest a total disregard for personal safety.* 2 **manifest itself** to become clear and easy to see: *Her creativity manifests itself in many ways.*

man·i·fes·ta·tion /ˌmænɨfeˈsteɪʃən ‖ -fə-/ n [C;U] fml a sign showing that something exists or is happening: *Riots are a clear manifestation of growing discontent with the government.*

man·i·fes·to /ˌmænɨˈfestəʊ/ n **manifestos** or **manifestoes** a written declaration which states the aims and opinions of a political party

man·i·fold /ˈmænɨfəʊld/ adj fml many in number or kind: *The problems facing the government are manifold.*

ma·nil·a /məˈnɪlə/ adj (also **manilla**) [only before a noun] made of strong brown paper

ma·nip·u·late /məˈnɪpjɨleɪt/ v **manipulated, manipulating** [T] 1 to control and influence someone or something for a particular purpose: *He accused the government of manipulating public opinion.* 2 to work with skilful use of your hands: *He manipulated the control buttons and achieved the required result.* –**manipulative** adj –**manipulation** n [C;U]

man·kind /ˌmænˈkaɪnd/ n [U] the human race, both men and women: *the worst war in the history of mankind*

man·ly /ˈmænli/ adj **manlier, manliest** having qualities typical of a man, especially strength and courage: *a manly voice* –**manliness** n [U]

man-made /ˌ ˈ ◂/ adj 1 produced by people and not found in nature: *a man-made lake* 2 made from chemical substances: *Nylon is a man-made material.*

manned /mænd/ adj controlled by the people inside it (used of a vehicle): *a manned spacecraft* –opposite **unmanned**

man·ner /ˈmænəʳ/ n 1 [sing] the way of doing something: *Let's discuss things in a calm manner.* 2 [sing] the way in which someone talks and behaves towards other people: *I don't like his rude manner.* 3 **manners** [pl] ways of behaving and speaking which are considered to be socially acceptable or socially unacceptable: *It's bad manners to eat like that!* | *Her manners were perfect.* 4 **all manner of** many different kinds of 5 **in a manner of speaking** a phrase used when you want to say that something is generally true, but not exactly true

man·nered /ˈmænəd ‖ -nərd/ adj fml having an unnatural way of behaving: *a mannered way of speaking*

man·ner·is·m /ˈmænərɪzəm/ n a personal habit of behaviour or speech

ma·noeu·vra·ble /məˈnuːvərəbəl/ adj (**man·euverable** AmE) easily moved or turned: a very light and manoeuvrable car –**manoeuvrability** /maˌnuːvərəˈbɪlţi/ n [U]

ma·noeu·vre¹ /məˈnuːvəʳ/ n (**maneuver** AmE) 1 a set of planned moves for an army or navy for training purposes: naval manoeuvres | The regiment is abroad on manoeuvres. 2 a skilful move or clever trick

manoeuvre² v **manoeuvred, manoeuvring** (**maneuver** AmE) [T] to move or turn something skilfully: It was difficult to manoeuvre the furniture through the door.

man·or /ˈmænəʳ/ n a large country house with land

man·pow·er /ˈmænˌpaʊəʳ/ n [U] the number of people needed for a certain type of work: a need for skilled manpower

man·sion /ˈmænʃən/ n a large house

man·slaugh·ter /ˈmænˌslɔːtəʳ/ n [U] law the crime of killing a person unlawfully but not intentionally

man·tel·piece /ˈmæntlpiːs/ n the shelf above a fireplace –see picture on page 442

man·u·al¹ /ˈmænjuəl/ adj using your hands: craftwork requiring great manual dexterity –**manually** adv

manual² n a book of information telling you how to do something, or use a machine

man·u·fac·ture¹ /ˌmænjʊˈfæktʃəʳ/ v **manufactured, manufacturing** [T] to make or produce something by machinery in a factory: We manufacture door knobs. –**manufacturer** n

manufacture² n [U] the act of manufacturing something: the manufacture of computer parts

ma·nure /məˈnjʊəʳ ‖ məˈnʊər/ n [U] waste matter from animals, which is put on the land to improve the soil

man·u·script /ˈmænjʊskrɪpt/ n 1 the first copy of a book or piece of writing before it is printed 2 an old book written by hand before printing was invented: a medieval manuscript

man·y /ˈmeni/ det, pron **more** /mɔːʳ/, **most** /məʊst/ 1 a large number: Many people are afraid to go out after dark. | Not many of the children can read. | There are simply too many cars on the roads. 2 used in questions about the number of people or things that there are: How many people were there? 3 **a good many**, **a great many** a very large number: A good many MPs have signed the petition. 4 **many a** a lot of: I've been to Paris many a time.

map¹ /mæp/ n a detailed plan of a place or area as it would appear if you saw it from above: a map of Europe | a street map of Brighton

map² v **-pp-** [T] to make a map of a place **map** sthg ↔ **out** phr v [T] to plan something in detail: She felt that her whole life had been mapped out for her.

ma·ple /ˈmeɪpəl/ n a tree which has leaves with five points

mar /mɑːʳ/ v **-rr-** [T] to spoil: motorways which mar the beauty of the countryside

mar·a·thon¹ /ˈmærəθən ‖ -θɑːn/ n a 26-mile running race

marathon² adj lasting a long time: a marathon speech

ma·raud·ing /məˈrɔːdɪŋ/ adj [only before a noun] searching for something to steal, burn, or destroy: They were attacked by marauding soldiers.

mar·ble /ˈmɑːbəl ‖ ˈmɑːr-/ n 1 [U] a hard cold stone used for building, which is often polished to show the irregular pattern of colour in it: a marble fireplace | a gravestone made of marble 2 **marbles** small coloured glass balls which children roll along the ground as a game

march¹ /mɑːtʃ ‖ mɑːrtʃ/ v 1 [I;T] to walk with firm regular steps like a soldier: The soldiers marched along the road. | protesters marching through the streets | We've marched twenty miles today. –see picture on page 736 2 [I + adv/prep] to walk to a place in a determined manner: She slammed the door and marched out of the house. –see WALK¹ (USAGE) 3 [T + adv/prep] to take someone roughly to a place, by holding them: I was marched out of the building.

march² n 1 [C;U] the act of marching: The soldiers had a long march ahead of them. 2 [C] the distance covered while marching for a certain period of time: Our destination is four days' march away. 3 [C] a piece of music with a regular beat 4 [C] a large number of people who march from one place to another to show their opinions or dissatisfaction: Many bystanders joined in the student march. 5 [sing] the steady development of something: the march of time | the slow march to equality

March n (also **Mar**) the 3rd month of the year

mar·chio·ness /ˌmɑːʃəˈnes ‖ ˈmɑːrʃənǎs/ n the wife of a MARQUIS, or her title

mare /meəʳ/ n an adult female horse

mar·ga·rine /ˌmɑːdʒəˈriːn, ˌmɑːgə- ‖ ˈmɑːrdʒərǎn/ n [U] a yellow substance similar to butter made from animal or vegetable fat

mar·gin /ˈmɑːdʒɪn ‖ ˈmɑːr-/ n 1 a space near the edge of a page: Make notes in the margin of your book. 2 an amount greater than what is necessary: In the end, we won by a decisive margin. | Our profit margin is very low this year.

mar·gin·al /ˈmɑːdʒɪnəl ‖ ˈmɑːr-/ adj 1 not very important or large: The new law will cause only a marginal increase in the cost of living. 2 **marginal seat** a place in parliament which can be lost or won by a small number of votes, and so pass from one party's control to that of another –**marginally** adv

mar·i·gold /ˈmærɪɡəʊld/ n a garden plant with yellow or orange flowers

mar·i·jua·na /ˌmærɪˈwɑːnə, -ˈhwɑːnə/ n (also **marihuana**) [U] a form of the illegal drug CANNABIS smoked in cigarettes for pleasure

ma·ri·na /məˈriːnə/ n a harbour for pleasure boats

mar·i·nate /ˈmærɪneɪt/ v **marinated, marinating** (also **marinade** /ˈmærɪneɪd/) [T] to leave meat or fish in a mixture of wine, oil, and SPICES, to give it a special taste before cooking

ma·rine¹ /məˈriːn/ adj [only before a noun] related to or concerning the sea: Marine life was badly affected by oil pollution. | a marine biologist

marine² n a soldier who serves in the navy

mar·i·o·nette /ˌmærɪəˈnet/ n a PUPPET worked by strings or wires

mar·i·tal /ˈmærɪtl/ adj 1 concerning marriage: marital bliss 2 **marital status** your state with regard to marriage, for example whether you are single or married

mar·i·time /ˈmærɪtaɪm/ adj [only before a noun] 1 concerning ships or the sea: maritime law | a great maritime power 2 living or existing near the sea: the maritime provinces

mar·jo·ram /ˈmɑːdʒərəm ‖ ˈmɑːr-/ n [U] a plant with small dark green leaves which are used in cooking

mark¹ /mɑːk ‖ mɑːrk/ n **1** a spot or cut that spoils the natural colour or appearance of something: *His feet left dirty marks all over the floor.* | *The table was covered in scratch marks.* **2** something printed or written which has a meaning: *She picked up her pen and made a couple of marks on the page.* **3** a figure or letter given by a teacher to represent how good someone's work is: *The highest mark in the test was nine out of ten.* | *Did you get a good mark?* **4** a number or point on a scale: *We must get unemployment down below the two million mark.* **5 as a mark of** in order to show a particular feeling or quality: *We stood up as a mark of respect when he came in.* **6** a particular type of a machine: *The Mark 4 model is the best we've ever produced.* **7** a German coin **8 have the marks of,** bear the marks of to be typical of something: *He bore all the marks of a politician.* **9 make a mark, leave a mark** to have a lasting effect: *His years in prison have left their mark on him.* **10 on your marks, get set, go!** an expression used to tell runners to get ready for a race and then to start

mark² v [T] **1** to make a mark on something in a way that spoils its appearance: *Water can easily mark a polished wooden surface.* **2** to write or print words or signs onto something in order to give information about it: *The letter was marked "confidential".* **3** to show where something is: *A heap of stones marked his grave.* **4** to be a sign of something: *This new legislation marks the end of the National Health Service as we know it.* | *a concert to mark the 50th anniversary of the composer's death* **5** to give a mark to a piece of work to show how good it is: *I've got a pile of exam papers to mark.* **6 mark my words =** you will see later that I am right **7 mark time** to spend time working but not advancing at all **mark** sthg ↔ **down** phr v [T] to lower the price of goods: *These winter coats have been marked down from £45 to £25.* **mark out** phr v **1** [T **mark** sthg ↔ **out**] to draw lines round an area: *They marked out the tennis court with white paint.* **2 mark someone out for something** to show that someone is suitable for something: *Her powerful speeches marked her out for political success*

marked /mɑːkt ‖ mɑːrkt/ adj **1** noticeable: *He showed a marked lack of interest.* **2 a marked man** a man who is in danger and being watched by an enemy –**markedly** /ˈmɑːkɪdli ‖ ˈmɑːr-/ adv: *They have markedly different approaches to the problem.*

mark·er /ˈmɑːkər ‖ ˈmɑːr-/ n **1** a large pen: *a felt-tip marker* **2** an object which shows where something is: *a boundary marker*

mar·ket¹ /ˈmɑːkɪt ‖ ˈmɑːr-/ n **1** a building or open place where people meet to buy and sell goods: *a cattle market* | *an antiques market* **2** an area or country where there is a demand for goods: *They sell to new markets in the Far East.* | *the home market* **3** demand for goods: *There's not much of a market for ice cream in the winter.* **4 on the market** able to be bought: *Their house is now on the market.*

market² v [T] to offer something for sale and try to encourage people to buy it: *The firm markets many types of goods.* –**marketable** adj

market gar·den /ˌ·· ˈ·-/ n BrE an area for growing vegetables and fruit for sale

mar·ket·ing /ˈmɑːkɪtɪŋ ‖ ˈmɑːr-/ n [U] the business activities concerned with advertising and selling

mar·ket·place /ˈmɑːkɪtpleɪs ‖ ˈmɑːr-/ n **1** an open area where a market is held **2 the marketplace** the business of buying and selling in competition with others: *The marketplace is the real test for a new product.*

mark·ings /ˈmɑːkɪŋz ‖ ˈmɑːr-/ n [pl] coloured marks on an animal or bird: *The leopard has beautiful markings.*

marks·man /ˈmɑːksmən ‖ ˈmɑːrks-/ n **marksmen** a person who can shoot well with a gun

mark·up /ˈmɑːk·ʌp ‖ ˈmɑːrk-/ n the amount by which a price is raised by the seller to allow him to make a profit: *a markup of 20% on cigarettes*

mar·ma·lade /ˈmɑːməleɪd ‖ ˈmɑːr-/ n [U] a kind of JAM, made from oranges or similar fruit

ma·roon¹ /məˈruːn/ v [T] to leave someone alone in a place where no one lives, with no way of escaping: *The boat sank and we were marooned on a little island.*

maroon² n, adj [U] dark red-brown colour –see picture on page 147

mar·quee /mɑːˈkiː ‖ mɑːr-/ n a large tent used for outdoor public events

mar·quis /ˈmɑːkwɪs ‖ ˈmɑːr-/ n (also **marquess**) the title of a nobleman of high rank

mar·riage /ˈmærɪdʒ/ n **1** [C] the act of making a man and woman husband and wife by a legal ceremony: *The marriage took place in church.* **2** [C;U] the relationship between a man and wife: *They have had twenty years of happy marriage together.* | *This is his second marriage.* **3** [U] the state of being married: *I've never seen the advantage of marriage, myself.*

mar·ried /ˈmærɪd/ adj **1** having a husband or wife: *a married man* | *She's much happier single than married.* **2 married to** having someone as a husband or wife: *She's married to my cousin.* **3 get married** to take a person as your husband or wife: *I'm getting married next week.*

mar·row /ˈmærəʊ/ n **1** [U] the soft fatty substance in the hollow centre of bones **2** [C] a long dark green vegetable

mar·ry /ˈmæri/ v **married, marrying 1** [I;T] to take a person as your husband or wife in a legal ceremony: *Will you marry me?* **2** [T] to perform the ceremony of marriage: *An old priest married them.* | *We were married by the ship's captain.*

Mars /mɑːz ‖ mɑːrz/ n the PLANET nearest to the Earth and fourth away from the sun

marsh /mɑːʃ ‖ mɑːrʃ/ n [C;U] an area of soft and wet low land –**marshy** adj

mar·shal¹ /ˈmɑːʃəl ‖ ˈmɑːr-/ n **1** an officer of the highest rank in certain armed forces **2** an official who helps with the organization of a public ceremony or event **3** AmE a chief officer of a police or fire-fighting force

marshal² v -ll- (-l- AmE) [T] **1** to arrange facts in good order: *He gave a good speech, and he marshalled the arguments very clearly.* **2** to lead or show the way to the correct place: *Police were on duty to marshall the crowds.*

marsh·mal·low /ˌmɑːʃˈmæləʊ ‖ ˈmɑːrʃmeləʊ/ n a light round soft sweet

mar·su·pi·al /mɑːˈsiuːpiəl, -ˈsjuː- ‖ mɑːrˈsuː-/ n tech a type of animal which carries its young in a pocket of skin on the mother's body

mar·tial /ˈmɑːʃəl ‖ ˈmɑːr-/ adj [only before a noun] concerning war or soldiers: *martial music* | *The country is now under martial law.*

martial arts /ˌ·· ˈ·/ n [pl] sports concerned with fighting skills that come from China or Japan, for example JUDO

Mar·tian /ˈmɑːʃən ‖ ˈmɑːr-/ adj,n an imaginary creature from MARS

mar·tyr¹ /ˈmɑːtəʳ ‖ ˈmɑːr-/ n 1 a person who is killed or made to suffer for their beliefs: *the early Christian martyrs* 2 someone who suffers in the hope of receiving sympathy (a word used to express disapproval): *I think she actually enjoys being a martyr.*

martyr² v [T] to kill someone or make them suffer for their beliefs

mar·tyr·dom /ˈmɑːtədəm ‖ ˈmɑːrtər-/ n [U] the death or suffering of a martyr

mar·vel¹ /ˈmɑːvəl ‖ ˈmɑːr-/ n a wonderful thing or example: *The operation was a marvel of medical skill.*

marvel² v -ll- (-l- AmE) [I;T;+that] to wonder or be surprised at something: *We marvelled at their skill.* | *They marvelled that he was unharmed.*

mar·vel·lous /ˈmɑːvələs ‖ ˈmɑːr-/ adj (**marvelous** AmE) wonderful or surprisingly good: *What marvellous weather!* | *That's a marvellous idea!* –**marvellously** adv

Marx·is·m /ˈmɑːksɪzəm ‖ ˈmɑːr-/ n [U] the teachings of Karl Marx on which COMMUNISM is based –**Marxist** n,adj

mar·zi·pan /ˈmɑːzɪˌpæn ‖ ˈmɑːrts‿-, ˌmɑːrz‿-/ n [U] a sweet paste made of almonds (ALMOND), sugar, and egg, used for making sweets and covering cakes

mas·ca·ra /mæˈskɑːrə ‖ mæˈskærə/ n [U] a substance used for colouring a person's eyelashes (EYELASH) and making them look longer

mas·cot /ˈmæskət ‖ ˈmæskɑːt/ n something that is thought to bring good luck to a particular person: *I always carry this keyring; it's my lucky mascot.*

mas·cu·line /ˈmæskjˌlˌn/ adj 1 having the qualities of a man –see FEMALE (USAGE) 2 belonging to the class in grammar that includes words for males: *"Drake" is the masculine word for "duck".* –**masculinity** /ˌmæskjˌˈlɪnˌti/ n [U]

mash /mæʃ/ v [T] to crush food into a soft substance after cooking: *Mash the potatoes with a fork.*

mask¹ /mɑːsk ‖ mæsk/ n a covering over all or part of someone's face: *bank robbers wearing masks* | *a surgeon's mask* –**masked** adj

mask² v [T] to keep something from being noticed: *His smile masked his anger.* | *The sugar masked the bitter taste of the medicine.*

mas·o·chis·m /ˈmæsəkɪzəm/ n [U] the wish to be hurt in order to gain pleasure, especially sexual pleasure –**masochist** n –**masochistic** /-ˈkɪstɪk/ adj: *masochistic tendencies*

ma·son /ˈmeɪsən/ n 1 someone who is skilled at making things with stone 2 **Mason** a FREEMASON

Ma·son·ic /məˈsɒnɪk ‖ məˈsɑː-/ adj connected with Freemasons (FREEMASON)

ma·son·ry /ˈmeɪsənri/ n [U] brick or stone from which a building is made: *She was hit by a piece of falling masonry.*

mas·que·rade /ˌmæskəˈreɪd/ v **masqueraded**, **masquerading** [I] to pretend to be: *He masqueraded as her brother.*

mass¹ /mæs/ n 1 [C] a solid lump: *a solid mass of rock* 2 **masses** [pl] *infml* a large number: *Help yourself; I've got masses of spare copies.* 3 [U] *tech* the amount of physical material in something: *A litre of gas has less mass than a litre of water.* 4 **Mass** a religious service in some Christian churches in which people share bread and wine 5 **the masses** ordinary people considered as a group: *entertainment for the masses*

mass² v [I;T] to gather together in large numbers: *Crowds massed at the airport to greet the President.*

mass³ adj [only before a noun] of or for a large number of people: *a mass murderer* | *mass unemployment*

mas·sa·cre /ˈmæsəkəʳ/ v **massacred, massacring** [T] to kill a large number of people in a violent and cruel manner –see KILL¹ (USAGE) –**massacre** n

mas·sage /ˈmæsɑːʒ ‖ məˈsɑːʒ/ v **massaged, massaging** [T] to press and rub someone's body with your hands to take away pain or stiffness –**massage** n [C;U] : *His trainer gave him a massage.*

mas·seur /mæˈsɜːʳ, mə-/ n a person who gives massages; a woman masseur can be called a **masseuse**

mas·sive /ˈmæsɪv/ adj extremely large, strong, or powerful: *a massive increase in the cost of living* | *massive castle walls* –**massively** adv

mass me·di·a /ˌ· ˈ·‿·/ n [+sing/pl verb] **the mass media** the means of giving information to the general public, through radio, television, and the newspapers

mass-pro·duce /ˌ· ·ˈ·/ v **mass-produced, mass-producing** [U] to make large quantities of an object in a factory: *cheap mass-produced furniture* –**mass-production** n [U]

mast /mɑːst ‖ mæst/ n 1 a long upright pole for carrying sails on a ship 2 a pole for radio or television aerials (AERIAL) or for a flag

mas·ter¹ /ˈmɑːstəʳ ‖ ˈmæ-/ n 1 a man in control of people, animals, or things: *The slaves rebelled against their masters.* | *The dog has been trained to carry its master's newspaper.* 2 a male teacher: *the history master* 3 a man of great skill in art or in working with his hands: *The painting is the work of a master.*

master² adj [only before a noun] 1 most important: *the master bedroom* 2 having a lot of skill and experience: *a master plumber* | *a master chef*

master³ v [T] 1 to learn something thoroughly, or gain a lot of skill in managing something: *It takes years to master a new language.* | *Master the art of public speaking in six easy lessons!* 2 to learn to control a bad feeling: *I've never been able to master my fear of spiders.*

mas·ter·ful /ˈmɑːstəfəl ‖ ˈmæstər-/ adj showing full control and understanding of people and situations –**masterfully** adv

master key /ˈ·· ·/ n a key that will open several different locks

mas·ter·ly /ˈmɑːstəli ‖ ˈmæstərli/ adj extremely clever and skilful: *a masterly move*

mas·ter·mind /ˈmɑːstəmaɪnd ‖ ˈmæstər-/ n a very clever person who is responsible for a plan: *the mastermind behind the robbery* –**mastermind** v [T]

Master of Arts /ˌ··· · ˈ·/ n –see MA

Master of Science /ˌ··· · ˈ·‿·/ n –see MSc

mas·ter·piece /ˈmɑːstəpiːs ‖ ˈmæstər-/ n an extremely good painting, book, or other work of art which is the best a person has done

mas·ter·y /ˈmɑːstəri ‖ ˈmæ-/ n 1 [U] excellence in skill or art: *He shows complete mastery of the dance routine.* 2 full control over something: *He finally achieved mastery over his fear.*

mas·tiff /ˈmæstˌf/ n a large powerful guard dog

mat /mæt/ n **1** a small piece of rough strong material used for covering part of a floor **2** a small piece of material placed on a table to protect its surface when something hot or wet is put on it

match¹ /mætʃ/ n **1** [C] a short thin stick of wood that produces a flame when it is struck against a rough surface: *a box of matches* **2** [C] a game or sports event: *a football match | a chess match* **3** [sing] a thing that is like another thing or is suitable to be put together with another thing: *The hat and shoes are a perfect match.* **4 no match for someone** not as good as someone in some way: *He's good, but he's no match for a real professional.*

match² v **1** [I;T] to be like something or suitable for use with something: *The curtains don't match the paint. | The curtains and paint don't match. | a brown skirt with a jacket to match* **2** [T] to find something like something or suitable for use with something: *I'm trying to match this yellow wool.* **3** [T] to be equal to something or find an equal to something: *a book which doesn't match the standard of his earlier ones | This hotel can't be matched for service and food.* **4 well-matched** suitable for each other or to compete with each other: *John and his wife are well-matched. | The two fighters aren't very well-matched.*

match-box /ˈmætʃbɒks ‖ -bɑːks/ n a small box in which matches are sold

match-ing /ˈmætʃɪŋ/ adj [only before a noun] the same or suited: *The twins wore matching T-shirts.*

match-less /ˈmætʃləs/ adj so good that nothing can equal it: *her matchless beauty*

match-mak-er /ˈmætʃˌmeɪkəʳ/ n a person who tries to arrange marriages or relationships

mate¹ /meɪt/ n **1** a friend, or a person you work with: *He's a mate of mine. | my old schoolmates* **2** *BrE infml* a friendly way of addressing a man (used mainly by men): *What time is it, mate?* **3** the rank below a ship's captain: *the first mate* **4** an animal's sexual partner: *the search for a mate*

mate² v mated, mating [I] to come together sexually for the production of young: *Birds mate in the spring.*

ma-te-ri-al¹ /məˈtɪərɪəl/ n **1** [C;U] a substance from which something is or can be made: *Building materials are expensive. | material for floor coverings* **2** [C;U] cloth: *a few metres of dress material* **3** [U] information for use in a book, film, or play: *research material* **4 materials** [pl] the things you use for an activity: *writing materials*

material² adj of or concerning possessions and money, not things of the mind or soul: *material comforts | Our material needs are food and clothing.* **–materially** adv

ma-te-ri-al-is-m /məˈtɪərɪəlɪzəm/ n [U] a great interest in and desire for possessions and money (a word used to express disapproval) **–materialistic** /-ˈlɪstɪk/ adj **–materialist** adj,n

ma-te-ri-al-ize /məˈtɪərɪəlaɪz/ v **materialized**, **materializing** (also **materialise** *BrE*) [I] (of something planned or expected) to become real or actual: *His hopes never materialized.*

ma-ter-nal /məˈtɜːnl ‖ -ɜːr-/ adj **1** like a mother or received from a mother: *maternal feelings* **2** [only before a noun] related through the mother's part of the family: *my maternal grandfather* **–maternally** adv

ma-ter-ni-ty /məˈtɜːnəti ‖ -ɜːr-/ adj [only before a noun] concerning or belonging to the mother before the baby is born, and to giving birth: *a maternity dress | a maternity hospital* **–maternity** n [U]

math-e-ma-ti-cian /ˌmæθəmməˈtɪʃən/ n a person who studies or who is skilled in mathematics

math-e-mat-ics /ˌmæθəˈmætɪks/ n [U] (also **maths** /mæθs/, **math** /mæθ/ *AmE*) the science of numbers and of the structure and measurement of shapes **–mathematical** adj **–mathematically** /-kli/ adv

mat-i-née /ˈmætɪneɪ ‖ ˌmætəˈneɪ/ n a performance of a play or film given in the afternoon

ma-tric-u-late /məˈtrɪkjəleɪt/ v **matriculated**, **matriculating** *fml* [I] to pass an examination and gain entrance to a university **–matriculation** /məˌtrɪkjəˈleɪʃən/ n [U]

mat-ri-mo-ny /ˈmætrɪməni ‖ -məuni/ n [U] *fml* the state of being married **–matrimonial** /ˌmætrɪˈməunɪəl◁/ adj

ma-trix /ˈmeɪtrɪks/ n **matrices** /-trəsiːz/ or **matrixes** *tech* a set of numbers, figures, or signs shown in rows in table form

ma-tron /ˈmeɪtrən/ n **1** a female nursing officer who has control over the nurses in a hospital **2** a woman in a boarding school who looks after the health of the children **3** *lit* an older married woman

matt /mæt/ adj having a surface which is dull rather than shiny: *Do you want a gloss or matt finish on these photos?*

mat-ted /ˈmætɪd/ adj twisted in a thick untidy mass: *matted hair*

mat-ter¹ /ˈmætəʳ/ n **1** [C] something you have to deal with or give attention to: *There are several important matters we should discuss. | a business matter* **2 make matters worse** to make a bad situation even more serious: *I lost my purse and, to make matters worse, my doorkey was in it.* **3 the matter** a trouble or a cause of trouble or illness: *Is something the matter? Are you all right? | What's the matter with the radio?* **4** [U] the physical material which makes up the world and everything which can be seen or touched **5** [U] things of a particular kind for a particular purpose: *reading matter | waste matter* **6 as a matter of fact** a *infml*: *"I don't suppose you've got a key." "No, as a matter of fact, I haven't."* **b** you use this expression when you are saying something unexpected after the last thing: *"Would you like a chocolate?" "As a matter of fact, I don't eat chocolates."* **7 a matter of:** **a** a little more or less than: *We only had to wait a matter of ten minutes.* **b** a question of: *Answering this question is just a matter of using your intelligence. | a matter of opinion* **8 a matter of course** a usual event: *When I go out of the house I lock the door as a matter of course.* **9 a matter of life or death** something very serious and urgent **10 for that matter** a phrase to show that what you have said about one thing can also be said about another: *I've never approved of divorce and nor, for that matter, does your father.* **11 no matter** it makes no difference: *We'll finish the job, no matter how long it takes.*

matter² v [I] to be important: *It doesn't matter if I miss the train, because there's another one in ten minutes. | I don't think anybody matters to her apart from herself.*

matter-of-fact /ˌ··· ˈ·◁/ adj concerned with facts, not imagination or feelings: *She described the attack in a very matter-of-fact manner.*

mat-ting /ˈmætɪŋ/ n [U] a thick woven material used for floor covering

mat-tress /ˈmætrɪs/ n a thick mat filled with feathers or springs, for sleeping on

ma-ture /məˈtʃuəʳ ‖ məˈtjuər/ adj **1** fully grown and developed **2** sensible and typical of an adult: *a*

mature approach to life **3** ready to be eaten or drunk (used of cheese or wine) –opposite **immature** –mature *v* **matured, maturing** [I;T] : *After six years the wine will have matured.* –**maturity** *n* [U]

mature stu·dent /·ᵢ· ˈ··/ *n BrE* a student at a university or college who begins their course at the age of 25 or over

maud·lin /ˈmɔːdlɪn/ *adj* stupidly sad, probably because of drinking too much alcohol

maul /mɔːl/ *v* [T] **1** (of animals) to hurt someone badly by tearing their flesh: *The hunter was mauled by a lion.* **2** to handle something roughly or in an unwelcome way

mau·so·le·um /ˌmɔːsəˈliːəm/ *n* a large and decorative stone building built over a grave or graves

mauve /məʊv/ *adj, n* [U] pale purple

mav·e·rick /ˈmævərɪk/ *n* someone, especially a politician, who is determined to be different to the rest of the group (a word used to express disapproval)

max. *adj* a written abbreviation for MAXIMUM: *max headroom 4 metres*

max·im /ˈmæksᵻm/ *n* a short saying that expresses a general truth: *"Waste not, want not" is her favourite maxim.*

max·i·mize /ˈmæksᵻmaɪz/ *v* **maximized, maximizing** (also **maximise** *BrE*) [T] to increase something to the greatest possible size: *We must maximize our chances of success.*

max·i·mum /ˈmæksᵻməm/ *adj* [only before a noun] the largest, or most that is possible: *Today's maximum temperature will be 17 degrees.* | *driving at maximum speed* –opposite **minimum** –**maximum** *n* : *This lamp will give you the maximum of light.* | *I smoke a maximum of 15 cigarettes a day.*

may /meɪ/ *v* [modal verb] **1** used to show that something is possible: *He may come or he may not.* | *What he says may be true.* | *There may be a link between this drug and various forms of cancer.* | *I don't know where John is. He may have missed his train.* **2** *fml* to be allowed to do something: –see Study Note on page 392 *You may come in now.* **3 may I, may we,** etc a very polite way of asking someone if they will let you do something: *May I use your telephone?* | *May we go home now?* **4** *fml* used when you are expressing a wish that something will happen: *May you always be happy together.* **5 may as well** a phrase you use to say that you are going to do something because there is nothing else that you really want to do: *If we're not going out we may as well go to bed.*

May *n* the 5th month of the year

may·be /ˈmeɪbi/ *adv* perhaps: *"Are you coming tonight?" "Maybe."* | *Maybe I ought to phone her.* | *There were a lot of people there – maybe a couple of hundred.*

■ USAGE **Maybe** and **perhaps** are commonly used in suggestions, requests, and orders to make them sound less forceful and, therefore, more polite: **Maybe/Perhaps** *we ought to go now.* | **Maybe/Perhaps** *you should phone your mother.* | *Could you* **maybe/perhaps** *help me carry these boxes to the car?* | **Maybe/perhaps** *you'd like to phone me this evening.* They can also be used to "soften" criticism: *He's not exactly fat, but he's* **maybe/perhaps** *a bit overweight.*

may·day /ˈmeɪdeɪ/ *n* **1** a radio signal used as a call for help from a ship or plane **2 May Day** 1st May, when public events and processions are held to mark the coming of spring, or by workers' organizations

mayn't /meɪnt/ *v* short for "may not"

may·on·naise /ˌmeɪəˈneɪz ‖ ˈmeɪəneɪz/ *n* [U] a thick yellow SAUCE eaten with salads SALAD and other cold food

mayor /meə^r ‖ ˈmeɪər/ *n* a person elected each year to be the head of a city or town council; a woman mayor or the wife of a mayor is called a **mayoress**

may·pole /ˈmeɪpəʊl/ *n* a tall decorated pole round which people dance on MAY DAY

maze /meɪz/ *n* a system of twisting passages which it is difficult to find your way through: *lost in the maze* | *a maze* of *narrow winding streets*

me /mi; *strong* miː/ *pron* [used as the object of a verb] the person who is speaking: *Can you see me?* | *That's me on the left of the photograph.* | *He handed the book to me.* | *She bought me a drink.*

■ USAGE In conversation we usually use **me** after *as, than,* and *be: He isn't as thin as* **me**. | *He's fatter than* **me**. | *It's* **me**. In formal language we usually try to express the idea in a different way: *He isn't as thin as* **I** am. | *He's fatter than* **I** am. | *I am the one/the person/etc.* The same is true of **her, him, us, them.**

mead·ow /ˈmedəʊ/ *n* [C;U] a field with grass and flowers growing on it

mea·gre /ˈmiːgə^r/ *adj* very small in amount: *He cannot exist on his meagre income.* | *a meagre diet*

meal /miːl/ *n* **1** [C] an amount of food eaten at one time: *She cooks a hot meal in the evenings.* | *Breakfast is my favourite meal.* **2** [C] (also **mealtime**) the time when you eat a meal: *The whole family meets at meals.* | *When the meal was over, the men went outside.* **3 make a meal of something** to give something more effort, consideration, or time than it deserves **4** [U] grain which has been crushed into a powder

meal·y-mouthed /ˌmiːli ˈmaʊðd◂/ *adj* expressing things indirectly, not plainly, especially when something unpleasant must be said (used of people and speech; a word that expresses disapproval): *mealy-mouthed politicians*

mean¹ /miːn/ *v* **meant** /ment/ **1** [T;+(that) not in progressive forms] to represent or express a meaning: *What does this French word mean?* | *The red light means "Stop".* | *The sign means that vehicles are not allowed in this area.* **2** [I;T] to plan or intend something: *Sorry, I didn't mean to interrupt.* | *I've been meaning to ask you – how did you get on at the interview?* | *The flowers were meant for you, not her.* | *She said Tuesday, but she meant Thursday.*

□ USEFUL PATTERNS to mean something; to mean something for someone; to mean to do something

3 [T;+(that) not in progressive forms] to be a sign of: *Those clouds mean rain.* | *A red rose means "I love you".* **4 I mean** you use "I mean" when you want to explain more clearly or in detail something that you have just said: *I don't think he can really afford it. I mean, it's not as if he's a rich man.* **5 you mean, do you mean...?** you use these expressions when you are making sure that you have understood what someone else has just said: *"He's got a new job in the City." "You mean he isn't going to go back to Ireland?"* **6 mean everything to, mean a lot to** to be very important to: *Her children mean everything to her.* | *His work means a lot to him.* [RELATED PHRASES **mean nothing to, mean very little to**] **7 be meant to do something** to be supposed to do something: *He's meant to be the best plumber in town.* | *Boys are meant to be tough.* | *You're not meant to eat the orange peel!* **8 mean business, mean it** to act with serious intentions:

I'm leaving you – and I really mean it! | *Watch out! Your competitors mean business.* **9 mean well** to intend to be helpful: *She can be rather tactless, but I know she means well.*

mean² *adj* **1** not generous, and unwilling to share: *He's so mean, he didn't even get his son a birthday present.* **2** unkind and nasty: *Don't be mean to your little sister!* **3** *AmE* bad-tempered: *That's a mean dog; be careful!* **4** *lit* of low social position: *a man of mean birth* **5** [only before a noun] average (used of measurements): *The mean yearly rainfall is 20 inches.* **6** *infml* very good: *She plays a mean game of tennis.* **7 no mean** a phrase you use to say that something is very good: *She's no mean tennis player.* | *It's no mean achievement, winning the contest at your age.* –**meanly** *adv* –**meanness** *n* [U]

mean³ *n* **1** an average of a set of numbers: *The mean of 7, 9, and 14 is 10.* **2** a course of action which is the middle way of doing something and is not extreme

me·an·der /mi'ændər/ *v* [I] **1** (of rivers and roads) to have a lot of bends **2** (of people or talk) to wander slowly without any particular purpose

mean·ing /'miːnɪŋ/ *n* [C;U] **1** what you are intended to understand from something spoken or written, from a sign or mark: *One word can have several meanings.* **2 What's the meaning of this?** a phrase used when you are angry and want someone to explain what they are doing, or have done **3** importance or value: *He says his life has lost its meaning since his wife died.*

mean·ing·ful /'miːnɪŋfəl/ *adj* containing an important meaning: *He gave her a meaningful look.* –**meaningfully** *adv*

mean·ing·less /'miːnɪŋləs/ *adj* without meaning or purpose: *meaningless scribble*

means /miːnz/ *n* [plural is **means**] **1** [C] a method: *We now have the means to save most of these children.* | *Use whatever means you think best.* **2** *fml* a **means to an end** a way of getting the result that you want **3** [U] money or wealth: *Have you the means to support a family?* | *a man of means* **4 by all means** *fml* a phrase used when you are saying politely that someone may do something: *"May I borrow your paper?" "By all means".* **5 by means of** by using something: *The deaf often communicate by means of signs.* **6 by no means** *fml* not at all: *It is by no means certain that you will be acquitted.*

meant /ment/ the past tense and past participle of MEAN

mean·time /'miːntaɪm/ *n* **in the meantime** in the time between two events: *I'll phone for a taxi. In the meantime you must get packed.*

mean·while /'miːnwaɪl/ *adv* (also **meantime** *infml*) during the same period of time when something else is happening: *All my friends have been getting on well in their jobs and meanwhile I've been unemployed.* | *Add all the ingredients except the spaghetti and cook slowly for half an hour. Meanwhile, cook the spaghetti in boiling salted water until it is just beginning to soften.* | *The photocopies won't be ready until half past three, so shall we sort these files out meanwhile?*

mea·sles /'miːzəlz/ *n* [the U] an infectious illness that gives you a fever and small red spots on your skin

mea·sly /'miːzli/ *adj infml* small and not enough: *She gave me a measly little piece of cheese.*

mea·su·ra·ble /'meʒərəbəl/ *adj* large enough to be reasonably measured or noticed: *There was a measurable improvement in productivity this year.* –**measurably** *adv*

mea·sure¹ /'meʒər/ *v* measured, measuring **1** [T] to find out the size, length, amount, or degree of something: *He measured the height of the cupboard.* | *His tailor is measuring him for a new suit.* **2** [T] to show or record the amount or size of something: *A clock measures time.* **3** [+ complement] to have the stated size: *He measures more round the waist than he used to.* | *It measures six feet from edge to edge.*

measure sthg ↔ **out** *phr v* [T] to take a measured quantity from a larger amount: *To make the cake, first measure out 250 grams of flour.*

measure up *phr v* [I] to show good enough qualities: *I'm afraid he just didn't measure up to the job.*

mea·sure² *n* **1** an action taken to bring about a certain result: *The government has promised to take measures to help the unemployed.* **2** an amount or unit in a measuring system: *An hour is a measure of time.* | *He poured himself a large measure of brandy.* **3 a measure of, a certain measure of, some measure of** *fml* some amount of: *I think we can claim some measure of success in persuading young people not to smoke.* **4 be a measure of something** to show how good something is: *It's a measure of his skill in business that the firm is doing so well.* **5** an instrument used for calculating amount, length, or weight: *This glass is a litre measure.* **6 for good measure** in addition, to make everything more satisfactory: *After I'd weighed out the apples, I put in another one for good measure.*

mea·sure·ment /'meʒəmənt ‖ -ʒər-/ *n* **2** [U] the act of measuring **1** [C] a length or height found by measuring: *What's your measurement? | I'll just take your measurements, sir.*

meat /miːt/ *n* [U] **1** the flesh of animals that is cooked and eaten: *There's not much meat on that bone.* **2** valuable ideas or material: *It was a clever speech, but there was no real meat in it.* –**meaty** *adj*
■ USAGE The meat from some animals has a different name from the name of the animal it comes from. For example, the meat from a **cow** is called **beef**, the meat from a **pig** is **pork** or **ham** or **bacon**, the meat from a **deer** is **venison**, and the meat from a **sheep** is **mutton**. But the meat from a **lamb** is **lamb**, and for birds the same word is used for both the meat and the bird it comes from: *Shall we have **chicken** or **duck** for dinner?*

mec·ca /'mekə/ *n* a place that many people wish to go to

me·chan·ic /mɪ'kænɪk/ *n* a person who is skilled in using and repairing machinery: *a car mechanic*

me·chan·i·cal /mɪ'kænɪkəl/ *adj* **1** moved, worked, or produced by machinery: *a mechanical digger* **2** done without thought or feeling: *She seemed distracted and nodded with a mechanical smile.* –**mechanically** /-kli/ *adv*

me·chan·ics /mɪ'kænɪks/ *n* [U] **1** the science of the action of forces on objects **2 the mechanics of something** the ways in which something works or is carried out: *Now we'll have to work out the mechanics of setting up the scheme.*

mech·a·nis·m /'mekənɪzəm/ *n* **1** the arrangement and action of the parts of a machine: *The clock doesn't go; there's something wrong with the mechanism.* **2** something which makes it possible to carry out actions: *the mechanism of the brain* | *the mechanism of local government*

mech·a·nize /'mekənaɪz/ *v* **mechanized, mechanizing** (also **mechanise** *BrE*) [T] to use machines for doing work: *Most of the men lost their jobs when the process was mechanized.* –**mechanization** /ˌmekənaɪ'zeɪʃən ‖ -nə-/ *n* [U]

med·al /ˈmedl/ n a flat piece of metal, usually round or cross-shaped, given as an honour for an act of bravery or skill: *She won a gold medal at the Olympic Games.* | *The old soldier wore his war medals on his jacket.*

me·dal·li·on /mɪˈdæliən/ n a round medal piece of jewellery worn round the neck, usually by men

med·al·list /ˈmedəlɪst/ n (**medalist** AmE) a person who has won a medal, especially in sport: *He was the silver medallist in the 800 metres.*

med·dle /ˈmedl/ v **meddled, meddling** [I] to interest yourself in something which is not your business: *I dared not meddle* with *the papers on his desk.* | *Don't meddle* in *his affairs.*

me·di·a /ˈmiːdiə/ n **1** the plural of MEDIUM **2** the **media** [+ sing/pl verb] the newspapers, television, and radio: *The media have a lot of power these days.* | *Media coverage of the event was very limited.*

med·i·ae·val /ˌmediˈiːvəl || ˌmiː-/ adj – see MEDIEVAL

me·di·ate /ˈmiːdieɪt/ v **mediated, mediating** fml **1** [I] to act as a peacemaker: *The government mediated* between *the workers and the employers.* **2** [T] to produce an agreement by mediating: *The army leaders have mediated a settlement.* –**mediation** /ˌmiːdiˈeɪʃən/ n [U] –**mediator** n

med·i·cal¹ /ˈmedɪkəl/ adj **1** concerning medicine and treating the sick: *a medical student* | *It is extremely difficult to get to the top of the medical profession.* | *medical care for the elderly* **2** concerning the treatment of disease by medicine rather than by operation: *the hospital's new medical ward* –**medically** /-kli/ adv

medical² n infml a thorough examination of your body: *I have to have a medical before I can start my new job.*

med·i·cat·ed /ˈmedɪkeɪtɪd/ adj mixed with a medical substance: *medicated shampoo*

med·i·ca·tion /ˌmedɪˈkeɪʃən/ n [C;U] a drug used to treat an illness: *It is better to sleep naturally, without taking medication.* | *She's on medication for her heart.*

me·di·ci·nal /mɪˈdɪsɪnəl/ adj **1** used as medicine: *medicinal alcohol* **2** connected with curing illness: *for medicinal purposes*

medi·cine /ˈmedsən || ˈmedɪsən/ n **1** [C;U] a substance that you drink or swallow to treat illness: *a bottle of medicine* | *Keep all medicines away from children.* **2** [U] the science of treating illness and damage to the body

med·i·e·val /ˌmediˈiːvəl || ˌmiː-/ adj (also **mediaeval**) of the period in European history between about AD 1100 and AD 1500, the Middle Ages

me·di·o·cre /ˌmiːdiˈəʊkəʳ/ adj neither very good nor very bad, but not really good enough: *He reads a lot of mediocre detective stories.* –**mediocrity** /ˌmiːdiˈɒkrəti || -ˈɑːk-/ n [U]

med·i·tate /ˈmedɪteɪt/ v **meditated, meditating** [I] **1** to fix your mind on one idea or activity, especially for religious reasons or to gain a calm peaceful mind **2** to think seriously or deeply: *He meditated* on *the matter for two days before giving his answer.* –**meditation** /ˌmedɪˈteɪʃən/ n [U] : *He was interested in yoga and meditation.*

med·i·ta·tive /ˈmedɪtətɪv || -teɪtɪv/ adj showing deep and careful thought –**meditatively** adv

me·di·um¹ /ˈmiːdiəm/ adj [only before a noun] of middle size, amount, or quality: *a medium-sized apple* | *He's of medium height.*

medium² n **media** /-diə/ or **mediums 1** a method for giving information or expressing yourself in art: *He writes books, but the theatre is his favourite medium.* **2** a substance in which objects or living things exist, or through which a force travels: *A fish in water is in its natural medium.* | *Sound travels through the medium of air.* **3** [plural is **mediums**] a person who claims to have power to receive messages from the spirits of the dead **4** a middle position: *There's a happy medium between eating all the time and not eating at all.*

medium wave /ˈ··· ˌ·/ n [U] radio receiving or broadcasting on waves of between about 180 and 600 metres in length

meek /miːk/ adj gentle and uncomplaining –**meekly** adv –**meekness** n [U]

meet /miːt/ v **met** /met/, **met, meeting 1** [I;T] to come together with another person or thing: *Let's meet for dinner.* | *I met him in the street.* | *I'll drive to the station and meet her off the train.* **2** [I;T] to be introduced to someone: *Come to the party and meet some interesting people.* | *Haven't we met before?* **3** [I;T] to touch or come together: *Their lips met.* | *The two cars met head-on.* | *His eyes met mine and I knew that he understood.* **4** [I] to join: *My trousers won't meet round my waist.* | *The two roads meet just north of Birmingham.* **5** to experience something unpleasant: *She met her death in a plane crash.* **6** [T] to answer or greet something in a particular way: *His speech was met* with *cries of anger.* **7** [T] to satisfy a need, desire, or demand: *Does the hotel meet your expectations?* | *Can you meet your debts?* **8 meet someone halfway** to come to an agreement by giving the other person some of what they want **9 there's more to something than meets the eye** there are hidden facts, difficulties, or reasons in something: *The job seems easy, but there's more to it than meets the eye.*

meet up phr v [I] to meet, by arrangement, to do something together: *Let's meet up after the play.* | *I met up* with *Pete the other day.*

meet with sbdy/sthg phr v [T] **1** to find someone or something by chance: *I met with some difficulties when I tried to enter the country.* | *They met with an accident on their way back.* **2** to have a meeting with: *The Prince met with several heads of state.*

meet·ing /ˈmiːtɪŋ/ n **1** a gathering of people for a purpose: *The Chairman declared the meeting open.* | *There's a council meeting in the Church Hall tonight.* **2** the people in such a gathering: *The meeting voted in favour of the proposal.* **3** the coming together of two or more people, by chance or arrangement: *Our meeting at the station was quite by chance.*

meg·a·lo·ma·ni·a /ˌmegələʊˈmeɪniə/ n [U] the belief that you are more important or powerful than you really are –**megalomaniac** /-ˈmeɪniæk/ n

meg·a·phone /ˈmegəfəʊn/ n an instrument shaped like a horn which makes your voice louder when you speak into it

meg·a·ton /ˈmegətʌn/ a measure of the explosive power of bombs: *A one megaton bomb has the same power as a million tons of TNT.*

mel·an·chol·y /ˈmelənkəli || -kɑːli/ n [U] lit a feeling of great sadness –**melancholy** adj lit : *We found her alone and feeling melancholy.*

mel·ee /ˈmeleɪ || ˈmeɪleɪ, meɪˈleɪ/ n a struggling or disorderly crowd

mel·low /ˈmeləʊ/ adj **1** sweet and ripe or fully developed, especially after being kept for a long time (used of fruit and wine) **2** soft, warm, and smooth (used of colours, light, and sound): *the mellow notes of the saxophone* **3** gentle and friendly, because you are quite old or in a pleasant state of mind (used of people) –**mellow** *v* [I;T] : *The years have mellowed him.*

me·lo·di·ous /mɪˈləʊdiəs/ *adj* sweet-sounding and tuneful

mel·o·dra·ma /ˈmelədrɑːmə ‖ -drɑːmə, -dræmə/ *n* [C;U] a type of story or play that is full of sudden events and unusually strong feelings

mel·o·dra·mat·ic /ˌmelədrəˈmætɪk◂/ *adj* showing unreasonably strong and excited feelings: *He says he's going to kill her, but he's just being melodramatic.*

mel·o·dy /ˈmelədi/ *n* **melodies 1** a song or tune **2** a clearly recognizable tune in a larger musical arrangement of notes

mel·on /ˈmelən/ *n* [C;U] a large juicy fruit with a thick green or yellow skin

melt /melt/ *v* **1** [I;T] to become liquid or to cause a substance to become a liquid by heating it: *The ice is melting in the sun.* | *Melt the chocolate in a saucepan.* **2** [I;T] to become or cause someone to become gentle or sympathetic: *His anger quickly melted.* | *My heart melted when I heard her crying.*

■ USAGE The adjective **molten** means **melted**, but is used only of things that melt at a very high temperature: *molten rock/metal* but *melted chocolate/ice*

melt away *phr v* [I] to disappear easily: *I don't know where my money goes – it just seems to melt away.*

melt sthg ↔ **down** *phr v* [T] to make a metal object liquid by heating it, in order to use the metal again: *They melted down the silver sixpences to make jewellery.*

mem·ber /ˈmembəʳ/ *n* **1** a person belonging to a club, group, or organization: *a member of the family* | *a Member of Parliament* | *She became a member of the Labour party.* **2 a member country, a member state** a country which has joined an international organization

mem·ber·ship /ˈmembəʃɪp ‖ -ər-/ *n* **1** [U] the state of being a member of a club, group, or organization: *Have you applied for membership yet?* **2** [C + sing/pl verb] all the members of a club, group, or organization: *We're trying to increase our membership.* | *The membership disagree about the proposed change in the rules.*

mem·brane /ˈmembreɪn/ *n tech* a soft thin skin which covers or connects part of your body: *A delicate, vibrating membrane in the ear helps to convey sounds to the brain.*

me·men·to /mɪˈmentəʊ/ *n* **mementos** a small object which reminds you of a special occasion or person

mem·o /ˈmeməʊ/ *n* **memos** (also **memorandum**) a note from one person or office to another within the same organization

mem·oirs /ˈmemwɑːz ‖ -ɑːrz/ *n* [pl] a book written by an important person telling about their experiences

mem·o·ra·ble /ˈmemərəbəl/ *adj* special and worth remembering: *The film was memorable for its wonderful photography.* | *a memorable trip abroad*

mem·o·ran·dum /ˌmeməˈrændəm/ *n* **memoranda** /-də/ *or* **memorandums** *fml* a memo

me·mo·ri·al /mɪˈmɔːriəl/ *n* **1** a stone structure built in a public place in memory of a person or an important event: *a war memorial* **2** something which exists or is done in memory of someone: *a*

memorial service at the parish church for those killed in the explosion | *the Winston Churchill Memorial Award for young musicians*

mem·o·rize /ˈmeməraɪz/ *v* **memorized, memorizing** (also **memorise** *BrE*) [T] to learn and remember something exactly: *He memorized the list of phone numbers.*

mem·o·ry /ˈmeməri/ *n* **memories 1** [C;U] your ability to remember events and experience: *She's got a good memory for faces.* | *After the accident, he completely lost his memory.* **2** [C] something that you remember from the past: *One of my earliest memories is of playing at my grandmother's house.* | *The music brought back vivid memories of happier days.* **3** [C] the part of a computer in which information is stored: *The system can't cope if you overload the memory.* **4 within living memory** during the time which people now alive can remember: *The great storm is well within living memory.* **5 in memory of someone** as a way of remembering or reminding others of someone: *The gravestone read "In loving memory of a dear husband and father".*

men /men/ *the plural of* MAN

men·ace¹ /ˈmenɪs/ *n* **1** someone or something which brings danger or threatens you: *a busy road which is a menace to the children's safety* **2** [U] the quality of appearing threatening: *He spoke with menace in his voice.* **3** [C] a troublesome person or thing: *That child's an absolute menace.*

menace² *v* **menaced, menacing** [T] to be likely to harm someone or something

men·ac·ing /ˈmenɪsɪŋ/ *adj* threatening: *a menacing look* | *Dark menacing clouds brought a sudden end to the picnic.* –**menacingly** *adv*

me·na·ge·rie /mɪˈnædʒəri/ *n* a collection of wild animals in a private zoo

mend¹ /mend/ *v* **1** [T] to repair something: *We ought to mend that hole in the fence.* | *I hate mending socks.* **2** [I] to become well or healthy again: *That leg's mending nicely now.* **3 mend your ways** to improve your behaviour: *If you don't mend your ways, you'll end up in prison.*

mend² *n* **be on the mend** to get better after illness

me·ni·al /ˈmiːniəl/ *adj* not interesting or skilled and not regarded as important (used of work): *She was furious at being given such a menial job.*

men·o·pause /ˈmenəpɔːz/ *n* **the menopause** the time when a woman's periods (PERIOD¹) stop, usually when she is middle-aged

men·stru·al /ˈmenstruəl/ *adj* concerning a woman's monthly PERIOD¹

men·stru·ate /ˈmenstrueɪt/ *v* **menstruated, menstruating** [I] to have a monthly PERIOD¹ –**menstruation** /ˌmenstruˈeɪʃən/ *n* [U]

men·tal /ˈmentl/ *adj* **1** concerned with the brain or thinking: *her declining mental powers* **2** [only before a noun] done or made only in the mind: *mental arithmetic* | *He made a mental note to remember to get the lock fixed.* **3** [only before a noun] concerning illness of the mind: *a mental hospital* | *a mental patient* –**mentally** *adv* : *He's mentally ill.*

men·tal·i·ty /menˈtæləti/ *n* **mentalities** someone's character and ways of thinking: *I can't understand the mentality of anyone who would hurt a child deliberately.*

men·tion¹ /ˈmenʃən/ *v* [T; + (that)] to say or write about something in a few words: *"We had another meeting last week." "Yes. Jill mentioned it."* | *We mentioned that we would like to see the match and he arranged it for us immediately.*

□ USEFUL PATTERNS to mention something; to mention something to someone; to mention that... **2** [T] to say the name of someone or something: *He mentioned a useful contact in London.* **3 Don't mention it** a phrase used as a polite reply when someone thanks you **4 not to mention** = and in addition there is...: *They have three dogs to look after, not to mention the cat and the parrot.*

mention² *n* [sing] a short remark about something or naming of a person: *I got a mention in the list of helpers.*

men·tor /ˈmentɔːʳ/ *n* someone who regularly gives advice to another person, especially to someone a lot younger older than them

men·u /ˈmenjuː/ *n* **1** a list of the foods available in a restaurant **2** a list of different choices shown on a computer SCREEN

mer·ce·na·ry¹ /ˈmɜːsənəri ‖ ˈmɜːrsəneri/ *n* **mercenaries** a soldier who fights for a foreign country for money

mercenary² *adj* having too great an interest in gaining money

mer·chan·dise /ˈmɜːtʃəndaɪz, -daɪs ‖ ˈmɜːr-/ *n* [U] things for sale

mer·chant /ˈmɜːtʃənt ‖ ˈmɜːr-/ *n* a person who buys and sells goods, usually in large amounts, especially from and to foreign countries

merchant na·vy /ˌ·· ˈ··/ *n* a nation's ships which are used in trade, not war

mer·ci·ful /ˈmɜːsɪfəl ‖ ˈmɜːr-/ *adj fml* **1** willing to forgive people instead of punishing them: *a merciful king* **2** fortunate and preventing suffering: *Death came as a merciful release from all his pain.* **–mercifully** *adv*

mer·ci·less /ˈmɜːsɪləs ‖ ˈmɜːr-/ *adj* showing no mercy to others: *The king was totally merciless and had all the villagers put to death.* **–mercilessly** *adv*

mer·cu·ry /ˈmɜːkjʊri ‖ ˈmɜːr-/ *n* [U] a silver-coloured metal that is liquid at ordinary temperatures and is used in thermometers (THERMOMETER)

mer·cy /ˈmɜːsi ‖ ˈmɜːrsi/ *n* **1** [U] kindness, pity, and willingness to forgive people: *The prisoner begged the judge for mercy.* **2 a mercy** a fortunate thing: *It was a mercy the fire didn't reach the house.* **3 at the mercy of** powerless against someone or something: *They were lost at sea, at the mercy of wind and weather.*

mere /mɪəʳ/ *adj* **1** [only before a noun] nothing more than: *He lost the election by a mere 20 votes.* | *She's not ready for marriage; she's a mere child.* **2 the merest** the smallest possible: *The merest little criticism makes him angry.*

mere·ly /ˈmɪəli ‖ -ər/ *adv* only: *Don't blame me for the bad news; I'm merely the messenger.*

merge /mɜːdʒ ‖ mɜːrdʒ/ *v* **merged, merging** **1** [I] to disappear into the background or the darkness: *One colour merged into the darkness.* | *My friends merged into the darkness and were soon out of sight.* **2** [I] to combine, especially gradually: *The two roads merge a mile ahead.* | *The company has recently been merged with Apex Electronics.*

merg·er /ˈmɜːdʒəʳ ‖ ˈmɜːr-/ *n* a joining together of two or more companies or organizations

me·rid·i·an /məˈrɪdiən/ *n* one of the imaginary lines drawn on a map from the North Pole to the South Pole over the surface of the Earth

me·ringue /məˈræŋ/ *n* [U] a light sweet white cake made of sugar and egg whites

mer·it¹ /ˈmerɪt/ *n* **1** [U] the quality of deserving praise or reward: *This controversial novel is undoubtedly of great literary merit.* **2** [C] a good quality: *One of his many merits is absolute honesty.* **3 judge something on its merits** to decide about something purely because of its qualities, without letting your feelings affect your decision

merit² *v* [T] *fml* to deserve something: *Your suggestion merits serious consideration.*

mer·i·to·ri·ous /ˌmerɪˈtɔːriəs/ *adj fml* deserving reward or praise

mer·maid /ˈmɜːmeɪd ‖ ˈmɜːr-/ *n* an imaginary creature with a woman's body and a fish's tail instead of legs

mer·ri·ly /ˈmerɪli/ *adv* **1** in a happy way: *She laughed merrily.* **2** without proper thought: *You can't just go on merrily ignoring your debts, you know.*

mer·ri·ment /ˈmerɪmənt/ *n* [U] *fml* laughter and enjoyment

mer·ry /ˈmeri/ *adj* **merrier, merriest** **1** happy and cheerful: *a merry laugh* **2** *infml* slightly drunk: *We got a bit merry at the party.* **3 Merry Christmas!** = Have a happy time at Christmas

mer·ry·mak·ing /ˈmeriˌmeɪkɪŋ/ *n* [U] *lit* fun and enjoyment

mesh¹ /meʃ/ *n* **1** [U] material like a net, made from plastic, wire, or thread: *We made a fence from some wire mesh.* **2** [C] the spaces of a certain size in such a network: *Use a net with a large mesh so that smaller fish can escape.*

mesh² *v* [I] to fit together closely

mes·mer·ize /ˈmezməraɪz/ *v* **mesmerized, mesmerizing** (also **mesmerise** *BrE*) **be mesmerized** to be so attracted by something that you cannot think about anything else: *We stood quite still, mesmerized by the falling snowflakes.*

mess¹ /mes/ *n* **1** [U] a dirty or untidy state: *Your bedroom's in a terrible mess.* | *Someone's dropped a plate of cakes. Please would you clean up the mess?* **2 a mess** a person who looks untidy or dirty: *Sorry I look such a mess. I've been working in the garden.* **3** [C] a place in which members of the armed forces eat: *the officers' mess* **4** [C] a situation full of problems and trouble: *I've made such a mess of my life.* | *That's another fine mess you've got me into!*

mess² *v*

mess about/around *phr v* **1** [I] to spend time doing things slowly and with no particular purpose: *We usually spend Sundays messing about in the garden.* **2** [I] to behave stupidly: *Oh, stop messing about and be serious for a minute!* **3** [T **mess about/around**] to treat a person badly by not being honest or fair to them

mess sthg ↔ **up** *phr v* **1** [T] to spoil something or make it untidy: *Who messed up all the papers on my desk?* | *The rain has messed up all our plans.*

mess with sbdy/sthg *phr v* [T] *infml* to become connected with a person or thing that is dangerous in some way: *He told us not to start messing with drugs.*

mes·sage /ˈmesɪdʒ/ *n* **1** a spoken or written piece of information passed from one person to another: *There's an important message for you.* | *I'm afraid he's out. Can I take a message?* | *We left a message telling her to meet us at the station.* **2** an important or central idea: *a film with a clear message* **3 get the message** *infml* to understand what someone is trying to tell you

mes·sen·ger /ˈmesɪndʒəʳ, -sən-/ n a person who brings a message

mes·si·ah /mɪˈsaɪə/ n **1** a great religious leader who will save the world **2 the Messiah** Christ, in the Christian religion

Mes·srs /ˈmesəz ‖ -ərz/ a written abbreviation for the plural of MR, especially in the names of firms: *Messrs Ford and Dobson, solicitors*

mess·y /ˈmesi/ adj **messier, messiest 1** untidy or dirty: *What a messy bedroom!* **2** unpleasant and causing a lot of trouble (used of a situation): *She's trying to settle down after a messy divorce.* –**messily** adv

met /met/ the past tense and past participle of MEET

me·tab·o·lis·m /mɪˈtæbəlɪzəm/ n the chemical processes in your body that use food for growing and for the power you need to do things

met·al /ˈmetl/ n [C;U] any of the hard shiny substances which can usually be used for passing an electric current: *common metals such as lead, copper, and tin | a metal pipe | pouring the molten metal*

me·tal·lic /mɪˈtælɪk/ adj made of or like metal: *shiny metallic colours | a metallic sound*

met·a·mor·pho·sis /ˌmetəˈmɔːfəsɪs ‖ -ɔːr-/ n metamorphoses /-siːz/ [C;U] complete change from one form to another: *the metamorphosis of a rather ugly caterpillar into a beautiful butterfly*

met·a·phor /ˈmetəfəʳ, -fɔːʳ/ n [C;U] a way of describing something by saying it has the qualities of something else; it compares things without using the words "as" or "like"; examples are *the sunshine of her smile* and *What a toad that man is!* –compare SIMILE –**metaphorical** /ˌmetəˈfɒrɪkəl ‖ -ˈfɔː-, -ˈfɑː-/ adj –**metaphorically** /-kli/ adv : *When I say he's got green fingers I am, of course, speaking metaphorically.*

mete /miːt/ v

  mete sthg ↔ **out** phr v [T] to officially give someone a punishment, or bad treatment of some kind

me·te·or /ˈmiːtiəʳ/ n a small piece of rock or metal that burns brightly when it falls from space into the air around the Earth

me·te·or·ic /ˌmiːtiˈɒrɪk ‖ -ˈɔːrɪk, -ˈɑːrɪk/ adj very fast and lasting only a short time: *a meteoric rise to fame*

me·te·o·rite /ˈmiːtiəraɪt/ n a small meteor that has landed on the Earth

me·te·o·rol·og·i·cal /ˌmiːtiərəˈlɒdʒɪkəl ‖ -ˈlɑː-/ n [U] relating to the scientific study of weather conditions

me·ter /ˈmiːtəʳ/ n **1** a machine which measures the amount of something used: *a gas meter* **2** the American spelling of METRE

meth·od /ˈmeθəd/ n **1** [C] a way of doing something: *They've developed a new method of testing for the virus. | old-fashioned teaching methods* **2** [C;U] an orderly arrangement or plan: *There's not much method in the way they do their accounts.*

me·thod·i·cal /mɪˈθɒdɪkəl ‖ mɪˈθɑː-/ adj doing things carefully using an ordered system: *He's rather slapdash, but she's very methodical.* –**methodically** /-kli/ adv

Meth·o·dist /ˈmeθədɪst/ n a person from a branch of the Christian Church begun by John Wesley in the 18th century –**Methodist** adj –**Methodism** n [U]

meth·o·dol·o·gy /ˌmeθəˈdɒlədʒi ‖ -ˈdɑː-/ n methodologies [C;U] tech a set of methods or principles for doing something

meth·yl·at·ed spir·its /ˌmeθɪleɪtɪd ˈspɪrɪts/ n [U] (also **meths** /meθs/ BrE infml) alcohol used for cleaning purposes or for burning in lamps or heaters

me·tic·u·lous /mɪˈtɪkjɪləs/ adj with very careful attention to detail: *meticulous drawings | She dusted the room with meticulous care.* –**meticulously** adv

me·tre /ˈmiːtəʳ/ n (**meter** AmE) **1** a unit for measuring length, equal to 39.37 INCHES: *It's ten metres long.* **2** an arrangement of words in poetry into strong and weak beats

met·ric /ˈmetrɪk/ adj concerning the system of measurement based on the metre and kilogram

Met·ro /ˈmetrəʊ/ n **the Metro** an underground railway system in some cities: *Did you go on the Metro in Paris?*

me·trop·o·lis /mɪˈtrɒpəlɪs ‖ mɪˈtrɑː-/ n fml a very large city, or the capital city of a country –**metropolitan** /ˌmetrəˈpɒlɪtən ‖ -ˈpɑː-/ adj

mew /mjuː/ v [I] to make the sound a cat makes –**mew** n

mg the written abbreviation for MILLIGRAM

mi·aow /miˈaʊ/ v [I] to make the crying sound a cat makes –**miaow** n

mice /maɪs/ the plural of MOUSE

mick·ey /ˈmɪki/ n **take the mickey out of someone** infml to make someone feel or look foolish by copying them or laughing at them

mi·cro /ˈmaɪkrəʊ/ n **micros** infml a microcomputer

mi·crobe /ˈmaɪkrəʊb/ n a very small living creature that can only be seen with a microscope

mi·cro·chip /ˈmaɪkrəˌtʃɪp/ n –see CHIP¹

mi·cro·com·put·er /ˌmaɪkrəʊkəmˈpjuːtəʳ/ n (also **micro** infml) a small computer, for use at home or in schools or offices

mi·cro·cos·m /ˈmaɪkrəkɒzəm ‖ -kɑː-/ n a little world that contains all the qualities and activities of a larger world

mi·cro·fiche /ˈmaɪkrəʊfiːʃ/ n [C;U] a sheet of microfilm with information printed in very small type: *The entire catalogue is now on microfiche.*

mi·cro·film /ˈmaɪkrəʊˌfɪlm/ n [C;U] a film for photographing a printed page reduced to a very small size

mi·cro·phone /ˈmaɪkrəfəʊn/ n (also **mike** infml) an instrument for making sounds louder or recording them: *Speak into the microphone, or the people at the back won't be able to hear you.*

mi·cro·pro·ces·sor /ˌmaɪkrəʊˈprəʊsesəʳ ‖ -ˈprɑː-/ n tech the central CHIP in a small computer which controls most of its operations

mi·cro·scope /ˈmaɪkrəskəʊp/ n a scientific instrument that makes extremely small objects look larger, and is used for examining them

mi·cro·scop·ic /ˌmaɪkrəˈskɒpɪk ‖ -ˈskɑː-/ adj **1** by means of a microscope: *The police scientist made a microscopic examination of the dust from the prisoner's clothes.* **2** very detailed: *a microscopic examination of the house and grounds* **3** infml very small: *microscopic organisms | microscopic handwriting*

mi·cro·wave /ˈmaɪkrəweɪv/ n (also **microwave oven** /ˌ··· ˈ··/) a machine which cooks food very quickly by short wave RADIATION rather than by heat

mid·day /ˌmɪdˈdeɪ ◂ ‖ ˈmɪd-deɪ/ n [U] at 12 o'clock in the middle of the day: *We had lunch around midday.*

mid·dle¹ /ˈmɪdl/ adj [only before a noun] in or nearly in the centre: *He was the middle child of the five.*

middle² n [sing] **1** the central part, point, or position: *Here's a photo of them – he's the one in the middle.* | *Draw a line down the middle of the page.* **2** *infml* your waist: *He's getting fatter round the middle.* **3 in the middle of doing something** busy doing something

■ USAGE **Centre** has a similar meaning to **middle** when used to talk about physical position. **Centre** usually suggests a more exact physical point: *the centre of the circle.* Use **middle** when you cannot be so exact: *the middle of the forest.* **Middle** is more usual when you are thinking of things as lines rather than areas: *He was driving down the middle of the road.* and when talking about rows of objects or people: *Eve was on the left, Tom on the right, and Ted in the middle.*

middle age /ˌ‥ ˈ‥◂/ n [U] **1** the time in your life when you are between about 40 and 60 years old **2 the Middle Ages** the period in European history between about AD 1100 and AD 1500

middle-aged /ˌ‥ ˈ‥◂/ adj between about 40 and 60 years old (used of people)

middle class /ˌ‥ ˈ‥◂/ **the middle class, the middle classes** [pl] the social class which is made up of people who are not noble or wealthy, and do not work with their hands, but work in offices or do professional jobs such as teaching –**middle-class** adj

Middle East /ˌ‥ ˈ‥◂/ n the Middle East part of Asia, between the eastern Mediterranean and India –**Middle Eastern** adj

mid·dle·man /ˈmɪdlmæn/ n **middlemen** /-mən/ a person who buys goods and sells them again

middle-of-the-road /ˌ‥ ‥ ‥ ˈ‥◂/ adj not extreme (used of ideas, especially political ideas)

mid·dling /ˈmɪdlɪŋ/ adj infml of average quality

midge /mɪdʒ/ n a very small flying insect that can bite

midg·et /ˈmɪdʒ‿t/ n a very small person –**midget** adj

Mid·lands /ˈmɪdləndz/ n the Midlands the central parts of England

mid·night /ˈmɪdnaɪt/ n [U] 12 o'clock at night: *The party finished at midnight.*

mid·riff /ˈmɪdrɪf/ n the part of your body between your chest and your waist

midst /mɪdst/ n [U] *lit* **1 in the midst of** in the middle of **2 in their midst** = among them

mid·way /ˌmɪdˈweɪ◂ ‖ ˈmɪdweɪ/ adv halfway: *There's a small village midway between these two towns.* | *I arrived midway through the concert.*

mid·week /ˌmɪdˈwiːk◂ ‖ ˈmɪdwiːk/ n [U] the middle days of the week, Tuesday, Wednesday, and Thursday –**midweek** adj: *a midweek match*

mid·wife /ˈmɪdwaɪf/ n **midwives** /-waɪvz/ someone who advises and helps women when they give birth to children

mien /miːn/ n *lit* a person's appearance or expression

might¹ /maɪt/ v *negative short form* **mightn't** [modal verb] **1** used to show that something is possible: *I might come and see you this evening.* | *We might not have enough money to go on holiday.* | *I don't know where Jane is – she might have gone into town.* | *I think that might be an eagle over there.* | *We were afraid that it might rain.* –see Study Note on page 392 **2 might I, might we, etc** *fml* a very polite way of asking someone if they will let you do something:

Might I borrow your newspaper? | *Might we park our car here for a few minutes?* **3 you might, you might at least** = you should: *You might tell me when you're going to be late home!* | *You might have phoned to let us know where you were!* **4 might well** a phrase you use to say that something is very likely: *He might well lose his job.* | *I haven't seen my aunt for thirty years. She might well be dead now.* **5 might as well** a phrase you use to say that you are going to do something because there is nothing else that you really want to do: *If there's nothing else to do here, we might as well go home.* **6 I might have known** a phrase you use to say that you do not find something surprising: *I might have known she'd refuse.*

might² n [U] great power or strength: *the might of the American army* | *I pushed with all my might but the rock wouldn't move.*

might·n't /ˈmaɪtənt/ v short for "might not": *They mightn't come.*

might·y /ˈmaɪti/ adj **mightier, mightiest 1** strong and powerful: *He struck the rock a mighty blow.* | *Even the mightiest of empires come to an end.* **2 high and mighty** too proud of your own importance –**mightily** adv

mi·graine /ˈmiːgreɪn, ˈmaɪ- ‖ ˈmaɪ-/ n [C;U] a severe headache

mi·grant /ˈmaɪgrənt/ n a person, animal, or bird that moves from one place to another: *Migrant workers move from country to country in search of work.*

mi·grate /maɪˈgreɪt ‖ ˈmaɪgreɪt/ v **migrated, migrating** [I] **1** (of birds and fish) to travel regularly from one part of the world to another, according to the seasons of the year **2** to move from one place to another to live or work, often for a limited period: *Some tribes migrate with their cattle in search of fresh grass.* –**migratory** /ˈmaɪgrətəri ‖ -tɔːri/ adj

mi·gra·tion /maɪˈgreɪʃən/ n [C;U] moving to another place: *Scientists have studied the migration of fish over long distances.* | *Wars always cause great migrations of people.*

mike /maɪk/ n *infml* –see MICROPHONE

mild /maɪld/ adj **1** gentle (used of people): *He has too mild a nature to get angry, even if he has good reason.* **2** not severe: *The thief was given a milder punishment than he deserved.* | *It's been a mild winter this year.* **3** not strong, rough, or bitter: *mild cheese* | *mild soap* –**mildness** n [U]

mil·dew /ˈmɪldjuː ‖ -duː/ n [U] a growth that forms on food, leather or plants, that have been kept for a long time in warm and wet conditions

mild·ly /ˈmaɪldli/ adv **1** in a mild way: *She complained loudly to the shopkeeper, who answered her mildly.* **2** slightly: *I was only mildly interested in the story I read in the newspaper.* **3 to put it mildly** using gentle words to describe something you think is bad: *The government's policy has not been a great success, to put it mildly.*

mile /maɪl/ n a unit for measuring length, equal to 1,609 metres or 1,760 yards: *He has a 10-mile drive each day to and from his work.* | *He walked for miles without getting tired.*

mile·age /ˈmaɪlɪdʒ/ n **1** [C;U] the distance that is travelled, measured in miles: *What mileage has your car done?* | *What mileage does your car do per gallon?* **2** [U] *infml* an amount of use: *The newspapers are getting a lot of mileage out of the royal wedding – there's a new story about it every day.*

mile·om·e·ter /maɪˈlɒmɪtəʳ ‖ -ˈlɑː-/ *n BrE* (also **milometer**) an instrument fitted in a vehicle to record the number of miles it travels –see picture on page 49

mile·stone /ˈmaɪlstəʊn/ *n* **1** a stone at the side of a road, on which the number of miles to the next town is marked **2** an important event in a person's life or in history: *The invention of the wheel was a milestone in the history of the world.*

mi·lieu /ˈmiːljɜː ‖ miːˈljɜː, -ˈjuː/ *n* **milieus** *or* **milieux** /-ljɜːz, -ljɜː ‖ -ˈljɜːz, -ˈljuːz, ˈljɜː, ˈjuː/ surroundings, especially a person's social surroundings

mil·i·tant /ˈmɪlɪtənt/ *adj* being ready to fight or use force, or saying that you are: *A few militant members of the crowd started throwing stones at the police.* | *a militant speech* –**militant** *n* : *The student disorders were blamed on a few militants.* –**militancy** *n* [U] **militantly** *adv*

mil·i·ta·ry[1] /ˈmɪlɪtəri ‖ -teri/ *adj* [only before a noun] connected with soldiers, armies, or war: *In some countries all the young men do a year's military service.* | *combined naval and military operations* | *a military hospital*

military[2] *n* [pl] **the military** the army: *The military were called in to restore order in the city.*

mil·i·tate /ˈmɪlɪteɪt/ *v* **militated, militating militate against** sthg *phr v* [T] to act as a reason against something: *The fact that he'd been in prison militated against his chances of getting a job in a bank.*

mi·li·tia /mᵻˈlɪʃə/ *n* men trained as soldiers who are not members of the regular army but used only in special situations: *The militia are sometimes used for dealing with riots.*

milk[1] /mɪlk/ *n* [U] **1** a white liquid produced by female animals to feed their young; the milk of some animals is drunk by human beings or made into butter or cheese: *a bottle of milk* –see picture on page 344 **2** a whitish liquid or juice obtained from certain plants and trees: *coconut milk*

milk[2] *v* **1** [I;T] to take milk from a cow, goat, or other animal: *The farmer milks the cows twice a day.* **2** [T] to get money from someone or something by clever or dishonest means: *He lives by milking his parents for all they are worth.*

milk float /ˈ· ·/ *n BrE* a vehicle driven by electricity which is used by a milkman for delivering milk

milk·man /ˈmɪlkmən/ *n* **milkmen** /-mən/ a man who sells milk, especially one who goes from house to house each day to deliver it

milk shake /ˌ· ˈ· ‖ ˈ· ·/ *n* a drink of milk and ICE CREAM shaken up together and given the taste of fruit, chocolate or other things

milk·y /ˈmɪlki/ *adj* **milkier, milkiest** **1** containing a lot of milk: *I like my coffee milky.* **2** not clear (used of liquids) –**milkiness** *n* [U]

mill[1] /mɪl/ *n* **1** a large machine for crushing corn or grain into flour **2** a building where certain goods are produced: *Cotton cloth is made in a cotton mill.* | *The valley was full of disused mills.* **3** a small machine, used in a kitchen, for crushing certain things into powder: *a coffee mill* | *a pepper mill*

mill[2] *v* [T] to crush something in a mill and produce it in the form of a powder: *The flour was milled only two miles from where the corn had grown.*

mill about/around *phr v* [I] to move without purpose in large numbers: *There were a lot of people milling about in the streets.*

mil·len·ni·um /mᵻˈleniəm/ *n* **millennia** /-nɪə/ **1** a period of 1,000 years **2 the millennium** a future age in which all people will be happy and contented

mil·le·pede /ˈmɪlᵻpiːd/ *n* –see MILLIPEDE

mill·er /ˈmɪləʳ/ *n* a man who owns or works a mill that produces flour

mil·let /ˈmɪlᵻt/ *n* [U] the small seeds of certain grain plants used as food: *millet cakes* | *a bag of millet*

mil·li·gram /ˈmɪlᵻgræm/ *n* (also **milligramme**) a unit for measuring weight, equal to 1,000th of a gram

mil·li·li·tre /ˈmɪlᵻ liːtəʳ/ *n* (**milliliter** *AmE*) a liquid measure equal to 1,000th of a litre

mil·li·me·tre (**millimeter** *AmE*) /ˈmɪlᵻmiːtəʳ/ *n* a unit for measuring length, equal to 1,000th of a metre

mil·li·ner /ˈmɪlᵻnəʳ/ *n* a person who makes or sells women's hats

mil·li·ne·ry /ˈmɪlᵻnəri ‖ -neri/ *n* [U] the goods made or sold by a milliner: *the millinery department in a large shop*

mil·lion /ˈmɪljən/ *det, n, pron* **million** *or* **millions** the number 1,000,000 –**millionth** *det, n, pron*

mil·lion·aire /ˌmɪljəˈneəʳ◂/ *n* a very wealthy person person who has at least 1,000,000 pounds or dollars; a woman millionaire is called a **millionairess**

mil·li·pede /ˈmɪlᵻpiːd/ *n* (also **millepede**) a small creature rather like a worm, but with a lot of legs

mill·stone /ˈmɪlstəʊn/ *n* **1** a circular stone used to make flour **2 a millstone round your neck** a person or thing that gives you trouble or worries

mil·om·e·ter /maɪˈlɒmᵻtəʳ ‖ -ˈlɑː-/ *n* –see MILEOMETER

mime[1] /maɪm/ *n* **1** [U] the practice of using actions without language to show meaning: *I couldn't speak Chinese, but I showed in mime that I wanted a drink.* | *the art of mime* **2** [C] an actor who performs without using words

mime[2] *v* **mimed, miming** [I;T] to act something in mime: *The actor was miming the movements of a bird.*

mim·ic /ˈmɪmɪk/ *n* a person who is good at copying someone else's manners or speech especially in a way that causes laughter –**mimic** *v* **mimicked, mimicking** [T] : *She made us all laugh by mimicking the teacher.*

min.[1] *n* a written abbreviation for MINUTES: *Boil for 10 min., drain, and serve.*

min.[2] *adj* a written abbreviation for MINIMUM: *min. length 30 metres*

min·a·ret /ˌmɪnəˈret, ˈmɪnəret/ *n* a tall thin tower on a MOSQUE, from which Muslims are called to prayer

mince[1] /mɪns/ *v* **minced, mincing** **1** [T] to cut meat into very small pieces **2** [I+adv/prep] to walk in an unnatural way, taking short little steps **3 not mince matters, not mince your words** to speak of something bad or unpleasant using plain direct language

mince[2] *n* [U] **1** *BrE* meat that has been minced **2** *AmE* mincemeat

mince·meat /ˈmɪns-miːt/ *n* [U] **1** a mixture of dried fruit, used as a sweet filling inside pastry **2 make mincemeat of** *infml* to defeat or destroy a person or thing: *She makes mincemeat of the people she interviews.*

mind[1] /maɪnd/ *n* **1** [C;U] your way of thinking or the thoughts that you have: *She has a very quick mind.* | *I can't get that picture out of my mind.* | *I'm sorry, I wasn't listening – my mind was on other things.* **2** [C] a person who is able to think well and has good ideas: *She's among the best scientific minds in the country.* **3 be in two minds about something** to be unable to make a decision about something: *I'm still in two minds about whether to accept the job.* **4 change your mind** to change your opinion: *I was going to leave tomorrow, but I've changed my mind.* **5 come to mind, spring to mind** to come into your mind suddenly: *One or two ideas sprang to mind.* **6 in your mind's eye** in a picture that you have in your mind: *In my mind's eye I could see him sitting at a desk in a dingy office.* **7 it went out of my mind** = I forgot about it **8 have a good mind to do something** to feel that you would like to do something: *I've got a good mind to leave home!* **9 have something on your mind** to be thinking or worrying about something: *I've had a lot on my mind recently.* **10 keep your mind on something** to continue thinking about something: *Try to keep your mind on your work.* **11 keep something in mind** to remember something: *You must keep in mind the fact that most of these women have never worked before.* **12 make up your mind** to decide: *I can't make up my mind whether to accept his offer or not.* **13 no one in their right mind** no one who is sensible: *No one in their right mind would buy that house!* **14 of one mind, of the same mind** having the same opinion about something: *We are of the same mind on this matter.* **15 out of your mind** *infml* mad **16 put your mind to something** to give your attention to something: *She could easily pass the exam if she put her mind to it.* **17 state of mind** the way that you are feeling, for example how happy or sad you are feeling: *At the moment he's in a very unconfident state of mind.* **18 take your mind off something** to make you stop thinking about something: *I need a holiday to take my mind off all my problems.* **19 to my mind** in my opinion: *To my mind it's the government's responsibility to help these people.* **20 turn your mind to something** to begin to think about something seriously: *Now let's turn our minds to tomorrow's meeting.*

mind² *v* **1** [I;T] used in commands to tell someone to be careful: *Mind the step.* | *Mind you don't drop that glass.* | *Mind! You nearly knocked me over!* **2 Mind out!** a phrase you use when you are warning someone that there is danger: *Mind out! There's a car coming!* **3** [T] to take care of a child or an animal: *I need someone to mind the baby while I'm out.* **4** [I;T] to be annoyed about something or be opposed to it: *I borrowed your car yesterday – I hope you don't mind.* | *Would you mind if I opened the window?* | *Do you mind if I use your telephone?* **5 I don't mind** I would be happy with either thing: *"Would you like red or white wine?" "I don't mind."* **6 I wouldn't mind** *infml* a phrase you use to say that you would like something: *I wouldn't mind a little rest!* **7 mind your own business** a phrase you use to tell someone not to be too interested in things that do not concern them **8 mind you** a phrase you use when you are adding more information to what you have just said: *He spends a lot of his time in bed now. Mind you, he is 93.* **9 never mind** it doesn't matter: *"I'm afraid I've broken your dish." "Never mind, it was only a cheap one."*

mind·er /ˈmaɪndəʳ/ *n* a person whose job is to look after someone, especially a young child

mind·less /ˈmaɪndləs/ *adj* **1** stupid, and done without thought: *mindless cruelty* **2** so simple that no thought is needed: *a mindless task* **–mindlessly** *adv*

mine¹ /maɪn/ *pron* something relating to or belonging to the person who is speaking: *His house is very similar to mine.* | *Put that book down – it's mine!*

mine² *n* **1** a deep hole or network of holes under the ground from which coal, gold, tin, and other mineral substances are dug: *a coal mine* | *There's been an accident at the mine!* –compare QUARRY **2** a kind of bomb that is placed just below the ground or in the sea and is exploded electrically from far away or when touched **3 a mine of information** a person who knows a lot about a particular subject

mine³ *v* **mined, mining 1** [I;T] to dig substances out of the ground: *Coal was mined here for centuries.* | *He's interested in a career in mining.* | *They are mining for diamonds.* **2** [T] to put bombs in the ground or the sea: *All the roads leading to the city had been mined.*

mine·field /ˈmaɪnfiːld/ *n* a piece of land or water in which mines have been placed

min·er /ˈmaɪnəʳ/ *n* a person who works underground digging out mineral substances

min·e·ral /ˈmɪnərəl/ *n* any solid substance like salt or coal formed naturally in the earth

mineral wa·ter /ˈ··· ˌ··/ *n* [C;U] water that comes from a natural spring and contains minerals which are thought to be good for you: *a bottle of mineral water* | *I'll have a mineral water, please.*

min·gle /ˈmɪŋgəl/ *v* **mingled, mingling** [I;T] to mix with another thing or with other people: *The king often left his palace at night and mingled with the people in the streets.* | *mingled joy and sorrow*

min·i·a·ture /ˈmɪniətʃəʳ, ˈmɪnɪtʃəʳ ‖ ˈmɪniətʃuəʳ/ *n* **1** a very small copy of something that is usually bigger: *The child was playing with his miniature railway.* **2 in miniature** in a much smaller form **3** a very small painting of a person

min·i·bus /ˈmɪnibʌs/ *n* **1** a small bus with seats for between six and twelve people: *The children go to school in a minibus.* **2 by minibus** travelling in a small bus: *We're travelling by minibus.*

min·i·mal /ˈmɪnɪməl/ *adj* the smallest possible amount or size: *Fortunately, the storm only did minimal damage to the crops.* **–minimally** *adv*

min·i·mize /ˈmɪnɪmaɪz/ *v* **minimized, minimizing** (also **minimise** *BrE*) [T] to reduce something to the smallest possible amount or degree: *You can minimize the danger of driving at night by driving slowly and with great care.* –compare MAXIMIZE

min·i·mum /ˈmɪnɪməm/ *adj* smallest in amount or lowest in price of what is possible or needed: *He does the minimum amount of work and then expects promotion!* –compare MAXIMUM **–minimum** *n:* *Let's try and keep the cost to a minimum.*

min·ing /ˈmaɪnɪŋ/ *n* [U] the action or industry of getting minerals out of the earth by digging: *coalmining* | *a mining company*

min·is·ter¹ /ˈmɪnɪstəʳ/ *n* **1** a politician who is a member of the government and is in charge of a particular government department: *the Minister of Transport* | *the Foreign Minister* **2** a priest in some branches of the Christian church –see PRIEST (USAGE)

minister² *v* [I] *fml* **minister to someone** to help someone and provide what is needed: *We minister to the sick.*

min·is·ter·i·al /ˌmɪnɪˈstɪəriəl/ *adj* connected with a government minister or ministry: *As part of her ministerial duties, she often had to travel abroad.*

min·is·try /ˈmɪnɪstri/ *n* **ministries 1** (also **Ministry**) a government department led by a minister: *The army, navy, and airforce are all controlled by the Ministry of Defence.* **2 the ministry** the profession or work of a priest: *Our son wants to enter the ministry.*

mink /mɪŋk/ n [C;U] a small brown animal which produces valuable fur: *a mink coat*

mi·nor¹ /ˈmaɪnəʳ/ adj small in degree, size, or importance, especially in comparison with something else: *She has been given a minor part in the new play.* | *a very minor illness* –opposite **major**

minor² n *law* a person below the age at which they are fully responsible in law for their actions; in Britain a minor is a person who is not yet 18 years old

mi·nor·i·ty /maɪˈnɒrˌti || mˌ¹ˈnɔː-, mˌ¹ˈnɑː-/ n **minorities** [+ sing/pl verb] **1** the smaller number or part of something: *Only a minority of people want the war to continue.* –compare MAJORITY **2** a small part of a population which is different from the rest in race or religion: *a law to protect religious minorities* **3** [only before a noun] supported by a small number of people: *Cricket is a minority sport in the US.*

min·ster /ˈmɪnstəʳ/ n a large or important church

min·strel /ˈmɪnstrəl/ n a musician in the Middle Ages who travelled around the country playing and singing songs

mint¹ /mɪnt/ n **1** [U] a small plant whose leaves have a strong fresh smell and taste and are used in preparing drinks or food **2** [C] a sweet with the taste of PEPPERMINT: *Have one of these mints!* **3** [C] a place in which coins and banknotes are officially made by the government: *the Royal Mint* **4 in mint condition** new or like new and so in perfect condition

mint² v [T] to produce money officially

min·u·et /ˌmɪnjuˈet/ n a type of slow graceful dance or the music for it

mi·nus¹ /ˈmaɪnəs/ prep **1** less: *17 minus 5 leaves 12.* **2** below the freezing point of water by the stated number of degrees: *The temperature was minus 10 degrees.* **3** without a person or thing that is missing: *Now the team is minus a goalkeeper.*

minus² n (also **minus sign**) a sign (–) used to show that the stated number is less than zero or that the second number is to be taken away from the first

minus³ adj [only before a noun] less than zero –compare PLUS³

min·us·cule /ˈmɪnˌskjuːl/ adj very, very small

min·ute¹ /ˈmɪnˌt/ n **1** [C] one of the sixty parts into which an hour is divided: *The train arrived at exactly four minutes past eight.* | *It's only a few minutes' walk from here to the station.* **2** [sing] *infml* a very short space of time: *I'll be ready in a minute* | *"Are you ready yet?" "No, but I won't be a minute."* | *It'll just take a minute.* **3 at any minute** very soon: *We're expecting him at any minute.* **4 the minute** as soon as: *I recognized him the minute I saw him.* **5 this minute** immediately: *Come here this minute!* **6** [C] a unit of measurement equal to a 60th of a degree: *The exact measurement of this angle is 80 degrees 30 minutes (80° 30').* **7 minutes** [pl] a written record of business done, suggestions made, and decisions taken at a meeting: *The minutes of the last meeting were read out to the committee.*

mi·nute² /maɪˈnjuːt || -ˈnuːt/ adj very small indeed: *I've never seen such minute writing.* | *minute details* –minutely adv

mir·a·cle /ˈmɪrəkəl/ n **1** a wonderful happening that cannot be explained by the laws of nature and is said to be the work of God or a holy person: *Christ is supposed to have performed miracles such as turning water into wine.* **2** a surprising and wonderful happening: *It will be a miracle if I pass the examination.* | *a miracle cure*

mi·rac·u·lous /mɪˈrækjˌləs/ adj surprising and wonderful: *He made a miraculous recovery from his illness.* | *miraculous beauty* –miraculously adv : *It was a terrible explosion, but miraculously no one was killed.*

mi·rage /ˈmɪrɑːʒ || mˌ¹ˈrɑːʒ/ n a strange effect of hot air conditions in a desert, in which objects can be seen which are not really there

mir·ror¹ /ˈmɪrəʳ/ n a piece of glass, or other shiny or polished surface, which shows images that fall on it: *He examined himself carefully in the bathroom mirror.*

mirror² v [T] to represent or to be similar to something else

mirth /mɜːθ || mɜːrθ/ n [U] *fml* joy and laughter –mirthless adj

mis·ad·ven·ture /ˌmɪsədˈventʃəʳ/ n [C;U] *law* or *lit* bad luck, like an accident: *A verdict was recorded of death by misadventure.*

mis·an·throp·ic /ˌmɪsənˈθrɒpɪk || -ˈθrɑː-/ adj a word used to describe someone who hates everybody, trusts no one, and avoids being in the company of others

mis·ap·ply /ˌmɪsəˈplaɪ/ v **misapplied, misapplying** [T] *fml* to use something for the wrong purpose –misapplication /ˌmɪsæplˌ¹ˈkeɪʃən/ n [C;U]

mis·ap·pre·hend /ˌmɪsæprɪˈhend/ v [T] *fml* to understand something wrongly: *The accident was caused by one motorist completely misapprehending the intentions of the other.* –misapprehension n [C;U]

mis·ap·pro·pri·ate /ˌmɪsəˈprəʊprieɪt/ v **misappropriated, misappropriating** [T] *fml* or *law* to take something and use it dishonestly: *He was sent to prison for misappropriating company money.* –misappropriation /ˌmɪsəprəʊpriˈeɪʃən/ n [C;U]

mis·be·have /ˌmɪsbɪˈheɪv/ v **misbehaved, misbehaving** [T] to behave badly: *She was punished for misbehaving in class.*

mis·be·ha·viour /ˌmɪsbɪˈheɪvjəʳ/ n *BrE* (**misbehavior** *AmE*) [U] bad behaviour

mis·cal·cu·late /ˌmɪsˈkælkjˌleɪt/ v **miscalculated, miscalculating** [I;T] to calculate wrongly: *I miscalculated the time it would take me to reach the station.* –miscalculation /ˌmɪsˌkælkjˌ¹ˈleɪʃən/ n [C;U]

mis·car·riage /ˌmɪsˈkærɪdʒ, ˈmɪskærɪdʒ/ n **1** an act of giving birth too early for the baby to live: *She's had another miscarriage.* –compare ABORTION, STILLBIRTH **2 miscarriage of justice** a wrong decision by the law courts, which results in the punishment of a person who is not guilty

mis·car·ry /mɪsˈkæri/ v **miscarried, miscarrying** [I] **1** (of a woman) to give birth to a baby too early for it to live **2** (of an intention or plan) to be unsuccessful

mis·cel·la·ne·ous /ˌmɪsəˈleɪniəs/ adj of different kinds

mis·chief /ˈmɪstʃˌf/ n [U] **1** enjoyable behaviour, often by children, which others do not approve of: *She's always getting into mischief.* | *It's very quiet, so I expect they're up to some mischief.* **2** behaviour which is intended to cause harm: *Be careful who you tell. There's always someone ready to make mischief.*

mis·chie·vous /ˈmɪstʃˌvəs/ adj **1** showing enjoyment of things that others do not approve of: *a mischievous smile* | *a mischievous child* **2** intended to cause trouble: *a mischievous remark* –mischievously adv

mis·con·ceived /ˌmɪskən'siːvd/ adj unsuitable and badly thought out: *The government's plan for the railways is wholly misconceived.*

mis·con·cep·tion /ˌmɪskən'sepʃən/ n a wrong understanding of something: *Public attitudes to doctors are based on the misconception that they are well-paid.*

mis·con·duct /ˌmɪs'kɒndʌkt ‖ -'kɑːn-/ n [U] fml bad behaviour, especially by a professional person: *Both lawyers have been accused of misconduct.*

mis·con·struc·tion /ˌmɪskən'strʌkʃən/ n [C;U] fml mistaken understanding: *A law must be stated in the clearest language, so that there is no danger of misconstruction.*

mis·con·strue /ˌmɪskən'struː/ v **misconstrued, misconstruing** [T] fml to understand something in a way that was not intended: *Do you think my behaviour could have been misconstrued?*

mis·deeds /ˌmɪs'diːdz/ n [pl] fml or lit wrong or wicked acts: *He was punished at last for his many misdeeds.*

mis·de·mea·nour /ˌmɪsdɪ'miːnər/ n BrE (**misdemeanor** AmE) **1** fml an action that is wrong but not very serious **2** law a crime that is less serious than, for example, stealing or murder –compare FELONY

mis·di·rect /ˌmɪsdɪ'rekt/ v [T] to direct a person wrongly: *I asked a boy the way to the station, but he misdirected me.*

mi·ser /'maɪzər/ n derog a person who hates spending money, and who saves it instead (a word used to express disapproval) –**miserly** adj

mis·e·ra·ble /'mɪzərəbəl/ adj **1** very unhappy: *The child is cold, hungry, and tired, so of course he's feeling miserable.* **2** very poor in quality or amount: *What miserable weather!* | *Who can live on such a miserable salary?* –**miserably** adv : *a miserably cold day* | *She failed miserably.*

mis·e·ry /'mɪzəri/ n [U] great unhappiness or suffering: *Her baby died and, to add to her misery, she lost her job.*

mis·fire /ˌmɪs'faɪər/ v **misfired, misfiring** [I] **1** (of a gun) to fail to send out the bullet when fired **2** (of a plan or joke) to fail to have the desired result

mis·fit /'mɪsˌfɪt/ n a person who does not fit well and happily into their social or work situation

mis·for·tune /mɪs'fɔːtʃən ‖ -ɔːr-/ n [C;U] bad luck, often of a serious nature: *His failure in business was due to misfortune, not his own mistakes.*

mis·giv·ing /ˌmɪs'gɪvɪŋ/ n [C;U] a feeling of doubt: *He looked with misgiving at the strange food on his plate.* | *I could see he had some misgivings about lending me his car.*

mis·guid·ed /mɪs'gaɪdəd/ adj wrong, as a result of ideas that are not correct (used of opinions or actions): *She has a misguided view of human nature.*

mis·han·dle /mɪs'hændl/ v **mishandled, mishandling** [T] to deal with something in the wrong way: *The sale of the house was mishandled by the estate agents.*

mis·hap /'mɪshæp/ n something that happens to you which is unpleasant but not very serious: *A mishap like losing his coat won't make him less cheerful.*

mis·in·form /ˌmɪsɪn'fɔːm ‖ -ɔːrm/ v [T] to give someone the wrong information: *I believe that we have been misinformed about the cost of the new building.*

mis·in·ter·pret /ˌmɪsɪn'tɜːprɪt ‖ -ɜːr-/ v [T] to understand something wrongly: *The driver misinterpreted the sign and took the wrong road.* –**misinterpretation** /ˌmɪsɪntɜːprɪ'teɪʃən ‖ -ɜːr-/ n [C;U]

mis·judge /ˌmɪs'dʒʌdʒ/ v **misjudged, misjudging** [T] to form a wrong opinion of someone: *He's honest, and you misjudge him if you think he isn't.*

mis·lay /mɪs'leɪ/ v **mislaid** /-'leɪd/, **mislaid** [T] to put something somewhere and then forget where you put it: *She's mislaid her glasses again.*

mis·lead /mɪs'liːd/ v **misled** /-'led/, **misled** [T] to cause someone to have the wrong idea: *Don't let his friendly manner mislead you into trusting him.* | *a misleading description*

mis·man·age /ˌmɪs'mænɪdʒ/ v **mismanaged, mismanaging** [T] to handle private or public affairs so badly that they are not successful: *The company has been mismanaged for years.* –**mismanagement** n [U]

mis·no·mer /mɪs'nəʊmər/ n a wrong or unsuitable name: *To call it a hotel is a misnomer – it was more like a prison!*

mi·so·gy·nist /mɪˈsɒdʒən‍ɪst ‖ mɪˈsɑː-/ n a person who hates women

mis·place /ˌmɪs'pleɪs/ v **misplaced, misplacing** [T] to have good feelings for a person or thing that does not deserve them: *Your trust in that man is misplaced.*

mis·print /'mɪs-prɪnt/ n a mistake in printing: *This newspaper is full of misprints.*

mis·pro·nounce /ˌmɪs-prə'naʊns/ v **mispronounced, mispronouncing** [T] to pronounce a word incorrectly –**mispronunciation** /ˌmɪsprənʌnsi'eɪʃən/ n [C;U]

mis·quote /ˌmɪs'kwəʊt/ v **misquoted, misquoting** [T] to make a mistake in reporting words spoken or written by a person: *The politician complained that the newspapers had misquoted him.* –**misquotation** /-kwəʊ'teɪʃən/ n [C;U]

mis·read /ˌmɪs'riːd/ v **misread** /-'red/, **misread** /-'red/ [T] to read or understand something wrongly: *Did you misread the date on the letter?* | *The general misread the enemy's intentions.*

mis·rep·re·sent /ˌmɪsreprɪ'zent/ v [T] to give an untrue explanation or description of someone, or someone's words or actions, in such a way that unfavourable ideas may be spread: *Our decision to reduce taxes has been misrepresented as an attempt to gain popularity.*

miss¹ /mɪs/ v **1** [I;T] to fail to do something that was intended or possible, such as hitting or finding a person or thing: *The falling rock just missed my head.* | *He arrived too late and missed the train.* | *He shot at me but missed.* | *I don't want to miss seeing that play on television tonight.* **2** [T] to feel unhappy because you are not with a certain person, in a certain place, or in possession of something: *Her children have gone to Australia and she misses them very much.* | *I miss living in the country.* | *Give the beggar a coin; you won't miss it.* **3** [T] to discover that you do not have something: *I didn't miss the key until I reached the front door.* **4 miss the boat** infml to lose a good chance, especially because you are too slow **5 miss the point** to fail to understand something that has been said

miss out phr v **1** [T **miss** sbdy/sthg ↔ **out**] to fail to include a person or thing: *You have missed out two important points in your report.* **2** [I] to lose a chance of advantage or enjoyment: *You're the one who'll miss out if you don't come.* | *I missed out on the Christmas party.*

miss² n **1 Miss** [only before a noun] a title used before the name of a girl or an unmarried woman: *Miss Brown* | *Miss Edna Smith* –compare MRS, MS **2** (also **Miss**) a form of address used to women in certain situations, for example by pupils to a female teacher: *Can I go home now, Miss?* **3 a near miss** something which is almost what is intended, but just fails: *There were several near misses before a goal was scored.* **4 give something a miss** BrE *infml* to decide not to do something: *I think I'll give the film a miss, if you don't mind.*

mis·shap·en /ˌmɪsˈʃeɪpən, mɪˈʃeɪ-/ *adj* shaped in a way that is not natural, normal, or intended

mis·sile /ˈmɪsaɪl ‖ ˈmɪsəl/ *n* **1** an explosive weapon which can fly under its own power and which can be aimed at a distant object **2** an object or a weapon thrown by hand or shot from a gun: *Bottles and other missiles were thrown at the police.*

miss·ing /ˈmɪsɪŋ/ *adj* **1** not in the expected or proper place and so needing to be found: *Will the police have a list of missing persons?* | *There are papers missing from the file.* **2** not included: *One important point was missing from his account.* **3** not in the expected place: *Two people were missing, but we started the meeting without them.* | *I noticed he had a finger missing from his left hand.*

mis·sion /ˈmɪʃən/ *n* **1** a group of people who are sent abroad for a special reason: *a British trade mission to Russia* **2** the duty or purpose for which these people are sent: *The soldiers' mission was to blow up the enemy's radio station.* **3** a place where a particular form of religion is taught and medical services are often given: *A hospital and a school are being built at the mission.* **4** the particular work which you believe you should do: *Her mission in life seems to be helping lonely old people.*

mis·sion·a·ry /ˈmɪʃənəri ‖ -neri/ *n* **missionaries** a person who is sent to a foreign country to teach and spread religion

mis·spell /ˌmɪsˈspel/ *v* **misspelt** /ˈspelt/ *or* **misspelled, misspelt** *or* **misspelled** [T] to spell a word wrongly –**misspelling** *n* [C;U]

mis·spend /ˌmɪsˈspend/ *v* **misspent** /-ˈspent-/ **misspent** [T] to spend things like time or money wrongly or unwisely: *I regret my misspent youth.*

mist¹ /mɪst/ *n* [C;U] very small drops of water floating in the air making it difficult to see: *The mountain top was covered in mist.*

mist² *v*

　　mist over *phr v* [I] to become covered with mist: *The window misted over.*

　　mist sthg ↔ up *phr v* [I;T] to cover or become covered with mist: *The hot air misted up the windows.*

mis·take¹ /mɪˈsteɪk/ *v* **mistook** /mɪˈstʊk/, **mistaken** /mɪˈsteɪkən/, **mistaking** [T] **1** to have the wrong idea about something: *He'd mistaken the address, and gone to the wrong house.* **2** to confuse one person or thing with another: *She was a complete stranger who I mistook for my friend's sister.*

mistake² *n* **1** something which is not correct: *There were several spelling mistakes in your written work.* | *There must be some mistake in this bill.* | *Tom made a mistake in his calculations.* –see ERROR (USAGE) **2 by mistake** without intending to do something: *I paid the bill twice by mistake.*

mis·tak·en /mɪˈsteɪkən/ *adj* wrong: *If you thought she intended to be rude, you were mistaken.* | *I had the mistaken idea that it would be quicker to take the train.* –**mistakenly** *adv*

Mis·ter /ˈmɪstər/ *n* [only before a noun] see MR

mis·time /ˌmɪsˈtaɪm/ *v* **mistimed, mistiming** [T] to do or say something at a wrong or unsuitable time: *The general mistimed his attack.*

mis·tle·toe /ˈmɪsəltəʊ/ *n* [U] a plant with small white berries that is often hung in rooms at Christmas time

mis·tress /ˈmɪstrəs/ *n* **1** a woman who is in control: *She felt she was no longer mistress in her own house when her husband's mother came to stay.* **2** BrE a teacher in a secondary school: *Do you like the new English mistress?* –compare MASTER¹ **3** a woman with whom a man has a sexual relationship but to whom he is not married: *His wife left him when she discovered he had a mistress.*

mis·trust /mɪsˈtrʌst/ *v* [T] to be unable to trust someone or their reasons for behaving in a certain way: *I mistrust his motives.* –**mistrust** *n* [U] : *We both have a great mistrust of politicians.* –**mistrustful** *adj*

mist·y /ˈmɪsti/ *adj* **mistier, mistiest** covered with mist: *a misty morning* | *eyes misty with tears*

mis·un·der·stand /ˌmɪsʌndəˈstænd ‖ -ər-/ *v* **misunderstood** /-ˈstʊd/, **misunderstanding** **1** [I;T] to understand something wrongly: *I think you misunderstand me.* | *Have I misunderstood?* **2** [T] to fail to recognize the true character or qualities of someone: *Why am I always misunderstood by people who work for me?*

mis·un·der·stand·ing /ˌmɪsʌndəˈstændɪŋ ‖ -ər-/ *n* **1** [C;U] confusion: *I think there's been a misunderstanding about the arrangements.* **2** [C] a disagreement less serious than a quarrel: *We've had our misunderstandings in the past, but we're the best of friends now.*

mis·use¹ /ˌmɪsˈjuːz/ *v* **misused, misusing** [T] to use something in the wrong way or for the wrong purpose

mis·use² /ˌmɪsˈjuːs/ *n* [C;U] a bad, wrong, or unsuitable use: *It was an unforgivable misuse of his power.*

mite /maɪt/ *n* **1** a very small creature that lives, for example, in the fur of animals **2** a small child, especially one you feel sorry for: *The poor little mite looked ill and hungry.*

mit·i·gate /ˈmɪtɪɡeɪt/ *v* **mitigated, mitigating** [T] *fml* to make a wrong or harmful action less serious: *Only increased foreign aid can mitigate the terrible effects of the war.* | *Are there any mitigating circumstances in this case?* –**mitigation** /ˌmɪtɪˈɡeɪʃən/ *n* [U]

mi·tre /ˈmaɪtər/ *n* (**miter** AmE) a tall pointed hat worn by priests of high rank

mit·ten /ˈmɪtn/ *n* a garment for your hand; one part covers your thumb, and a larger part covers all four fingers –see PAIR (USAGE) –see picture on page 50

mix¹ /mɪks/ *v* **1** [I;T] to combine into a single substance or thing: *You can't mix oil and water.* | *Oil and water don't mix.* | *Oil doesn't mix with water.* | *Put the flour, eggs, and milk into a bowl and mix them together.* | *You can mix blue and yellow to produce green.* **2** [I] to talk to other people, usually with enjoyment, at social events: *He's such a friendly person that he mixes well in any company.*

　　mix sbdy/sthg ↔ **up** *phr v* [T] **1** to confuse one person or thing with another: *It's easy to mix him up with his brother.* | *Do you mix the twins up?* **2** to put into disorder: *If you mix up those papers, I'll be angry.*

mix² *n* **1** [C;U] a combination of different substances, ready to use: *cake mix* **2** [sing] a group of different things or people: *There was rather a strange mix of people at the party.*

mixed /mɪkst/ *adj* **1** of different kinds: *I have mixed feelings about the book.* **2** of or for both sexes: *a mixed school | mixed bathing*

mixed up /ˌ·ˈ·◂/ *adj* **1** confused: *I've had so much conflicting advice that I'm a bit mixed up. | a mixed up kid* **2 mixed up in something, mixed up with someone** connected with something or someone bad: *I'm afraid he's mixed up in some dishonest business. | Are you mixed up with those troublemakers?*

mix·er /ˈmɪksəʳ/ *n* **1** a machine in which substances are mixed: *a food mixer* **2** a person who gets on well or badly with other people: *To do this job well, you need to be a good mixer.*

mix·ture /ˈmɪkstʃəʳ/ *n* **1** [C;U] a number of substances mixed together: *This tobacco is a mixture of three different sorts. | You need some cough mixture.* **2** [sing] a combination of things or people of different types or qualities: *I listened to his excuse with a mixture of amusement and disbelief.* **3** [U] *fml* the action of mixing or state of being mixed

mix-up /ˈ··/ *n infml* a state of disorder caused by bad planning or confusion: *There was a mix-up at the station and some of our group got on the wrong train.*

mm a written abbreviation for MILLIMETRES

moan[1] /məʊn/ *n* **1** a low sound expressing pain or suffering: *The moans of the patient in the next bed kept me awake.* **2** a complaint (a word used to express disapproval): *He always has some moan or another about his job.*

moan[2] *v* [I] **1** to make a low sound expressing pain or suffering: *The sick child moaned a little, and then fell asleep.* **2** to complain (a word used to express disapproval): *Stop moaning and think about how lucky you are.*

moat /məʊt/ *n* a deep ditch that in former times was dug for defence round a castle and was usually filled with water

mob[1] /mɒb/ *n* a large noisy crowd, especially one which is violent (a word often used to express disapproval): *An angry mob gathered outside the town hall. | mob violence*

mob[2] *v* -bb- [T] to crowd around someone because of interest or admiration: *The party leader was mobbed by his supporters.*

mo·bile[1] /ˈməʊbaɪl ‖ -bəl, -biːl/ *adj* able to move, or be moved, quickly and easily: *She's much more mobile now that she's bought a car. | Out here in the country, we buy all our food from the mobile shop.* –opposite **immobile** –**mobility** /məʊˈbɪlˌti/ *n* [U]

mo·bile[2] /ˈməʊbaɪl ‖ -biːl/ *n* an ornament made of small objects tied to wires or string and hung up so that they are moved by currents of air

mo·bil·ize /ˈməʊbˌlaɪz/ *v* **mobilized, mobilizing** (also **mobilise** *BrE*) [I;T] to gather together for a particular service or purpose, especially for war: *Our country's in great danger; we must mobilize. | He's trying to mobilize all the support he can get for his new political party.* –**mobilization** /ˌməʊbˌlaɪˈzeɪʃən ‖ -bələ-/ *n* (also **mobilisation** *BrE*) [C;U]

moc·ca·sin /ˈmɒkəsɪn ‖ ˈmɑː-/ *n* a low shoe made of soft leather

mock[1] /mɒk ‖ mɑːk/ *v* **1** [I;T] to make fun of a person or thing in an unkind way: *The pupil did his best, and the teacher was wrong to mock his efforts. | Don't mock – it could happen to anyone!* **2** [T] to make fun of someone by copying their behaviour: *He made them laugh by mocking the way the teacher walked.* –**mocking** *adj* –**mockingly** *adv*

mock[2] *adj* [only before a noun] like something real but not actually the real thing: *The army training exercises ended with a mock battle. | a mock exam*

mock·er·y /ˈmɒkəri ‖ ˈmɑː-/ *n* **1** [U] the act of making fun of someone or something **2** [sing] something that is not what it should be: *The medical examination was a mockery; the doctor hardly looked at the child.* **3 make a mockery of** to make something seem stupid: *If everyone is accepted, it makes a mockery of the entrance exam.*

mod·al verb /ˌməʊdl ˈvɜːb ‖ -ɜːrb/ *n* a verb such as "can", "might", or "must", which is used with other verbs –see Study Note on page 392

mod cons /ˌmɒd ˈkɒnz ‖ ˌmɑːd ˈkɑːnz/ *n BrE infml* [pl] all modern conveniences in a building such as hot water and central heating

mode /məʊd/ *n fml* a way of doing something: *There is no single mode of transport which you can rely on.*

mod·el[1] /ˈmɒdl ‖ ˈmɑːdl/ *n* **1** a small copy of something: *a model of the Eiffel Tower | model aircraft* **2** a person employed to wear clothes and show them to possible buyers in a shop or in photographs: *He's a male model.* **3** a person employed to be painted, drawn, or photographed by an artist **4** a person or thing that can serve as a perfect example of something, for others to copy: *This pupil's written work is a model of care and neatness. | She's a model student.* **5** a particular type of object, especially a vehicle or machine, made by a particular company: *Rolls-Royce have produced two new models this year.*

model[2] *v* -ll- (-l- *AmE*) **1** [T] to make a small copy of something: *He modelled a ship out of bits of wood.* **2** [I;T] to shape a soft substance, such as clay, into an object: *I model in clay. | She was modelling pots out of clay.* **3** [I] to work as a model, showing clothes or sitting for artists **4** [T] to wear and show a garment to possible buyers: *Angela is modelling an attractive blue silk dress.* **5 model yourself on someone** to copy another person or the way that they do something: *She has always modelled herself on her mother.*

mod·e·rate[1] /ˈmɒdərˌt ‖ ˈmɑː-/ *adj* **1** not extreme: *At the time of the accident, the train was travelling at a moderate speed. | a child of only moderate ability | moderate wage demands* **2** supporting political ideas that are not extreme: *moderate political opinions*

mod·e·rate[2] /ˈmɒdəreɪt ‖ ˈmɑː-/ *v* **moderated, moderating** [I;T] to make or become less strong: *He should moderate his language when children are present. | The wind was strong all day, but it moderated in the evening.*

mod·e·rate[3] /ˈmɒdərˌt ‖ ˈmɑː-/ *n* a person whose political opinions are not extreme –compare EXTREMIST

mod·e·rate·ly /ˈmɒdərˌtli ‖ ˈmɑː-/ *adv* quite: *a moderately successful film*

mod·e·ra·tion /ˌmɒdəˈreɪʃən ‖ ˌmɑː-/ *n* [U] **1** control of your behaviour or remarks to within reasonable limits: *He showed great moderation in his response to his attackers.* **2 in moderation** within sensible limits: *I only drink in moderation.*

mod·ern /ˈmɒdn ‖ ˈmɑːdərn/ *adj* belonging to the present time: *In this part of the city, you can see ancient and modern buildings next to each other. | modern languages | modern ideas* –**modernity** /mɒˈdɜːnˌti ‖ mɑˈdɜːr-/ *n* [U]

mod·ern·ize /ˈmɒdənaɪz ‖ ˈmɑːdər-/ *v* **modernized, modernizing** (also **modernise** *BrE*) [T] to make something suitable for the needs of the present time: *We're modernizing the house, starting with a* *new bathroom.* −**modernization** /ˌmɒdənaɪˈzeɪʃən ‖ ˌmɑːdərnə-/ *n* [C;U]

mod·est /ˈmɒdɪst ‖ ˈmɑː-/ *adj* **1** having or expressing a lower opinion of your own abilities than you deserve (a word used to express approval): *She's very modest* **about** *her success.* | *a modest child* **2** small in quantity, size, or value: *There has been a modest rise in house prices this year.* **3** avoiding or not showing anything that might offend (used of people, their behaviour, and their clothing) −**modestly** *adv*

mod·es·ty /ˈmɒdɪsti ‖ ˈmɑː-/ *n* [U] the quality, state, or fact of being modest (a word usually used to express approval): *His natural modesty saved him from being spoilt by fame and success.*

mod·i·cum /ˈmɒdɪkəm ‖ ˈmɑː-/ *n* **a modicum of** something a small amount of something: *If he had a modicum of sense, he would go to college.*

mod·i·fi·ca·tion /ˌmɒdɪfɪˈkeɪʃən ‖ ˌmɑː-/ *n* [C;U] a slight change made to something: *A few simple modifications to this design would greatly improve it.* | *Modification of the plans may be necessary later.*

mod·i·fy /ˈmɒdɪfaɪ ‖ ˈmɑː-/ *v* **modified, modifying** [T] to change something slightly: *The car has been modified so that it can be used in the desert.*

mod·ish /ˈməʊdɪʃ/ *adj fml* fashionable

mod·u·late /ˈmɒdjʊleɪt ‖ ˈmɑːdʒə-/ *v* **modulated, modulating** *tech* [T] to vary the strength or nature of a sound

mod·ule /ˈmɒdjuːl ‖ ˈmɑːdʒuːl/ *n* **1** one of a number of standard parts used to make a building or piece of furniture **2** a part of a space vehicle that can be used independently of the other parts **3** one of a number of parts that combine to make a full course at some colleges

Mo·ham·me·dan /məʊˈhæmɪdən, mə-/ *adj, n old fash* (also **Muhammadan**) see MUSLIM

moist /mɔɪst/ *adj* slightly wet: *Water the plants just enough to keep the earth moist.* | *eyes moist with tears*

moist·en /ˈmɔɪsən/ *v* [I;T] to make or become slightly wet

mois·ture /ˈmɔɪstʃər/ *n* [U] water in small quantities or in the form of steam or mist: *There is little moisture in the desert air.*

mo·lar /ˈməʊlər/ *n* one of the large teeth at the side of your mouth used for breaking up food

mo·las·ses /məˈlæsɪz/ *n* [U] **1** a thick, dark, sweet liquid produced from sugar plants **2** the usual American word for TREACLE

mold /məʊld/ *n,v* −see MOULD

mole /məʊl/ *n* **1** a small furry animal that digs passages underground to live in **2** *BrE infml* a person who provides secret information to an enemy or competitor about the organization they work for **3** a small dark brown mark on your skin

mol·e·cule /ˈmɒlɪkjuːl/ *n tech* the smallest part of any substance that can exist without losing its own chemical nature, consisting of one or more atoms −**molecular** /məˈlekjʊlər/ *adj*

mole·hill /ˈməʊlˌhɪl/ *n* **1** a small heap of earth made by a mole digging underground **2** **make a mountain out of a molehill** to make an unimportant matter seem more important than it is

mo·lest /məˈlest/ *v* [T] **1** to annoy or attack someone or something: *A dog that molests sheep has to be killed.* **2** to annoy or attack a person sexually

mol·li·fy /ˈmɒlɪfaɪ ‖ ˈmɑː-/ *v* **mollified, mollifying** [T] to make someone calmer: *She refused to be mollified by a bunch of flowers.*

mol·lusc /ˈmɒləsk ‖ ˈmɑː-/ *n* (also **mollusk** *AmE*) any of a class of animals with soft bodies and no backbone or limbs, usually covered with a shell

molt /məʊlt/ *v* −see MOULT

mol·ten /ˈməʊltən/ *adj* turned to liquid by very great heat (used of metal or rock)

mom /mɒm ‖ mɑːm/ *n* the usual American word for MUM

mo·ment /ˈməʊmənt/ *n* **1** [C] a very short period of time: *It will only take a moment.* | *I'll be back in a moment* | *Just a moment! I want to speak to you.* **2** [C] a particular point in time: *At that moment, the door opened and the teacher walked in.* **3** [C] the right time for doing something: *That is the moment to attack.* **4** [U] *fml* importance: *a matter of the greatest moment* **5** **at any moment** at an unknown time but very soon: *He might come back at any moment.* **6** **at the moment** at the present time: *We have no car at the moment.* **7** **the moment** at exactly the time when: *I recognized him the moment I saw him.*

mo·men·ta·ry /ˈməʊməntəri ‖ -teri/ *adj* lasting for a very short time: *She experienced a momentary feeling of fear.* −**momentarily** *adv*: *He was so surprised that he was momentarily unable to speak.*

mo·men·tous /məʊˈmentəs, mə-/ *adj* very important: *It was a momentous decision that we have never regretted.*

mo·men·tum /məʊˈmentəm, mə-/ *n* [U] **1** *tech* the quantity of movement of an object: *The rock gained momentum as it rolled down the mountainside.* **2** the development of a powerful force: *The struggle for political independence is gathering momentum.*

mon·arch /ˈmɒnək ‖ ˈmɑːnərk, -ɑːrk/ *n* a ruler of a state, such as a king or queen, who has the right to rule by birth

mon·arch·ist /ˈmɒnəkɪst ‖ ˈmɑːnər-/ *n* a person in favour of the idea that members of a royal family should rule rather than elected leaders

mon·ar·chy /ˈmɒnəki ‖ ˈmɑːnərki/ *n* **monarchies 1** [U] rule by a king or queen **2** [C] a state ruled by a king or queen

mon·as·tery /ˈmɒnəstri ‖ ˈmɑːnəsteri/ *n* **monasteries** a building in which religious men called monks (MONK) live

mo·nas·tic /məˈnæstɪk/ *adj* **1** connected with monasteries **2** **a monastic life** a simple life for which you need little money

mo·nas·ti·cis·m /məˈnæstɪsɪzəm/ *n* [U] the way of life of monks (MONK) in a monastery

Mon·day /ˈmʌndi/ *n* the day of the week after Sunday and before Tuesday

mon·e·ta·ry /ˈmʌntəri ‖ ˈmʌnɪteri/ *adj* connected with money: *the international monetary system*

mon·ey /ˈmʌni/ *n* [U] **1** coins or paper notes with their value printed on them, which you use when you buy and sell things: *He doesn't usually carry much money on him.* | *The repairs will cost a lot of money.* | *He earns a lot of money as a TV presenter.* **2** wealth: *Money doesn't always bring happiness.* | *She comes from a family with money.* | *Money makes the world go around.* | *He made his money in property.* **3** **be in the money** to be rich **4** **have money to burn** to have more money than you need **5** **your money's worth** full value for the money you have spent: *Theatre tickets were expensive, but we felt we got our money's worth.*

mon·grel /ˈmʌŋɡrəl ‖ ˈmɑːŋ-, ˈmʌŋ-/ *n* a dog with parents of different breeds

mon·i·tor[1] /'mɒnɪtəʳ ‖ 'mɑː-/ *n* **1** a person or machine that examines or shows what is happening **2** a pupil chosen to help the teacher in various ways

monitor[2] *v* [T] to watch, listen to, or examine what is happening: *We have been monitoring the enemy's radio broadcasts.* | *Monitor the child's progress and let me know of any problems.*

monk /mʌŋk/ *n* a member of an all-male religious group that lives together in a MONASTERY

mon·key /'mʌŋki/ *n* **monkeys 1** an active tree-climbing animal with a long tail, belonging to the class of animals most like man **2** *infml* a very active child who enjoys playing: *He's a little monkey.*

monkey wrench /'·· ·/ *n* a tool used for holding or turning things of different widths

mon·o /'mɒnəʊ ‖ 'mɑː-/ *adj* using a system of sound recording, broadcasting, or receiving in which the sound appears to come from one direction only when played back: *a mono record* –compare STEREO

mon·o·chrome /'mɒnəkrəʊm ‖ 'mɑː-/ *adj* **1** one colour only: *a monochrome painting* **2** showing black, white, and grey only: *a monochrome film*

mon·o·cle /'mɒnəkəl ‖ 'mɑː-/ *n* a special piece of glass worn over one eye only, to help you see better with that eye

mo·nog·a·my /mə'nɒgəmi ‖ mə'nɑː-/ *n* [U] the custom or practice of having only one wife or husband at a time –**monogamous** *adj*

mon·o·gram /'mɒnəgræm ‖ 'mɑː-/ *n* a sign, usually formed of the first letters of your names, printed on writing paper or marked on other possessions –**monogrammed** *adj*

mon·o·lith /'mɒnəlɪθ ‖ 'mɑː-/ *n* a large piece of stone placed so that it stands by itself

mon·o·lith·ic /ˌmɒnə'lɪθɪk◄ ‖ ˌmɑː-/ *adj* **1** very large: *a monolithic building* **2** forming a system that seems unlikely to change (a word often used to express disapproval): *a monolithic system of government*

mon·o·logue /'mɒnəlɒg ‖ 'mɑːnəlɔːg,-lɑːg/ *n* (also **monolog** *AmE*) **1** a long speech in a play or film spoken by one person **2** a rather long speech by one person, which prevents others from taking part in the conversation (a word often used to express disapproval)

mon·o·plane /'mɒnəupleɪn ‖ 'mɑː-/ *n* an aircraft with a single wing on each side

mo·nop·o·lize /mə'nɒpəlaɪz ‖ mə'nɑː-/ *v* **monopolized,** **monopolizing** (also **monopolise** *BrE*) [T] to have complete control of something: *The cigarette industry is monopolized by a few large companies.* | *She monopolizes the teacher's attention.*

mo·nop·o·ly /mə'nɒpəli ‖ mə'nɑː-/ *n* **monopolies 1** [C] the right or power, shared with no one else, to provide a service or to produce something: *The postal services are a government monopoly.* **2** [sing] possession of something or control over something, which others do not share: *He seems to think he has a monopoly* **of** *brains.*

mon·o·rail /'mɒnəʊreɪl ‖ 'mɑː-/ *n* a railway system using a single rail

mon·o·syl·lab·ic /ˌmɒnəsɪ'læbɪk ‖ ˌmɑː-/ *adj* **1** having one SYLLABLE (used of a word) **2** short and rather rude (used of remarks): *He gave monosyllabic answers to my questions.*

mon·o·syl·la·ble /'mɒnəˌsɪləbəl ‖ 'mɑː-/ *n* a word with only one SYLLABLE

HOUSE

Try to draw a picture of Colin Taylor's house.

Colin Taylor lives in a small detached house. There is a small garden in front of the house. On the left there is a low brick wall and on the right there is a wooden fence. A hedge separates the garden from the pavement. On the left, there is a small gate and a path which leads to the front door. On both sides of the path, there are narrow flowerbeds containing plants and small bushes. On the right, there is a small square lawn.

Just outside the gate, close to the hedge, there are a pillar box and a telephone box.

Colin Taylor's house has two storeys. There is one large window on the ground floor on the right hand side. On the left there is a small porch over the front door.

There are two smaller windows on the first floor. Colin has put his satellite dish between the two windows. A gutter runs around the house at the bottom of the roof. This collects the water which falls on the roof. A drainpipe on the left carries the water down to the ground. The chimney is on the right hand side of the roof. There is a TV aerial attached to the chimney.

house

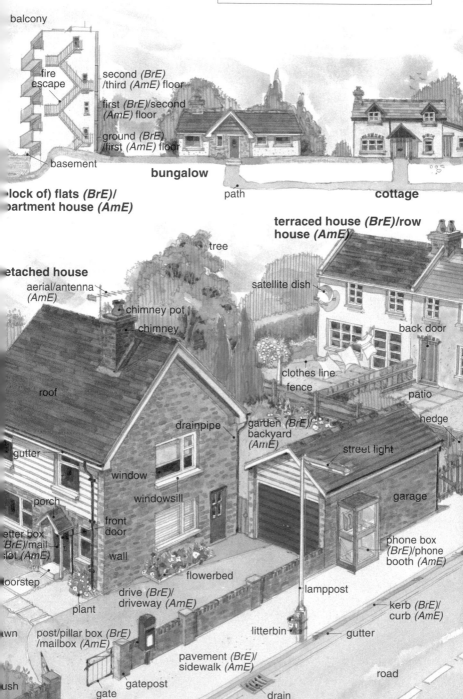

balcony

fire escape

second *(BrE)* /third *(AmE)* floor

first *(BrE)*/second *(AmE)* floor

ground *(BrE)* /first *(AmE)* floor

basement

bungalow

(block of) flats *(BrE)*/ apartment house *(AmE)*

path

cottage

terraced house *(BrE)*/row house *(AmE)*

detached house

tree

aerial/antenna *(AmE)*

satellite dish

chimney pot

chimney

back door

roof

clothes line

fence

patio

hedge

gutter

drainpipe

garden *(BrE)*/ backyard *(AmE)*

street light

window

windowsill

porch

front door

garage

letter box *(BrE)*/mail slot *(AmE)*

wall

phone box *(BrE)*/phone booth *(AmE)*

doorstep

flowerbed

plant

drive *(BrE)*/ driveway *(AmE)*

lamppost

kerb *(BrE)*/ curb *(AmE)*

lawn

post/pillar box *(BrE)* /mailbox *(AmE)*

litterbin

gutter

pavement *(BrE)*/ sidewalk *(AmE)*

road

bush

gate

gatepost

drain

picture

frame

lampshade

lamp

curtains

record player

speaker

TV

video/VCR

bookcase

CDs

ornament

radio

amplifier

tape deck

CD (player)

hi-fi unit/stereo system

video tapes

mantelpiece

cushion

sofa/settee/couch

carpet

fireplace

coffee table

TV remote control

rug

hearth

magazines

armchair

mon·o·tone /ˈmɒnətəʊn ‖ ˈmɑː-/ n [sing] a manner of speaking or singing in which the voice continues on the same note: *He spoke in a monotone.*

mo·not·o·nous /məˈnɒtənəs ‖ məˈnɑː-/ adj always the same: *I'm beginning to find my job rather monotonous.* –**monotonously** adv –**monotony** n [U]

mon·soon /mɒnˈsuːn ‖ mɑːn-/ n [C] **1** the heavy rains which fall in parts of Asia at a particular time of the year **2** the wind that brings these rains

mon·ster /ˈmɒnstəʳ ‖ ˈmɑːn-/ n **1** a creature, imaginary or real, that causes fear because of its unnatural shape, size, or qualities: *a sea monster* | *I'll tell you a story about a terrible monster who lived in the woods.* **2** a very evil person: *The judge told the murderer that he was a monster.* **3** a very large or strange animal, plant or thing: *That dog's a real monster!* | *a monster potato*

mon·stros·i·ty /mɒnˈstrɒsɪti ‖ mɑːnˈstrɑː-/ n **monstrosities** something made or built in such a way that it is very ugly: *Have you seen that new office building in the town centre? It's a monstrosity!*

mon·strous /ˈmɒnstrəs ‖ ˈmɑːn-/ adj **1** very ugly **2** shocking: *monstrous cruelty* | *Your behaviour in class is monstrous!* –**monstrously** adv: *monstrously expensive*

month /mʌnθ/ n **1** any one of the 12 parts into which the year is divided **2** a period of about four weeks: *The baby will be exactly six months old tomorrow.*

month·ly /ˈmʌnθli/ adj, adv every month or once a month: *a monthly meeting* | *We meet monthly.*

mon·u·ment /ˈmɒnjÿmənt ‖ ˈmɑːn-/ n **1** a structure that preserves the memory of a person or event: *This pillar is a monument to all those who died in*

the war. | *That big empty office building is a monument to bad planning.* **2** an old building, or what remains of it, considered worthy of preservation for its historic interest or beauty: *an ancient monument*

mon·u·ment·al /ˌmɒnjÿˈmentl◂ ‖ ˌmɑːn-/ adj **1** very large, and of great and lasting worth: *The artist spent years on one monumental painting.* **2** very great in degree: *monumental stupidity*

moo /muː/ n the noise that a cow makes –**moo** v [I]

mood /muːd/ n **1** the state of your feelings at a particular time: *The beautiful sunny morning put him in a happy mood.* | *His moods change very quickly.* | *She's in a bad mood today.* **2** a state of mind which makes you bad-tempered: *Ignore him when he's in one of his moods.* **3** the right state of mind for a particular activity: *She was very tired, and in no mood for dancing.* **4** tech any of three groups of forms of a verb; the INDICATIVE expresses a fact, the IMPERATIVE a command or request, and the SUBJUNCTIVE a condition

mood·y /ˈmuːdi/ adj **moodier, moodiest 1** bad-tempered, angry, displeased, or unhappy **2** having feelings that change often and quickly (a word often used to express disapproval) –**moodily** adv –**moodiness** n [U]

moon /muːn/ n **1 the moon** the object which moves round the earth once every 28 days, and can be seen shining in the sky at night **2** the shape of this object as it appears at a particular time: *Last night there was a full moon.* **3** a body that turns round a PLANET other than the earth: *Saturn has several moons.* **4 over the moon** very happy: *She's over the moon about her new job.* **5 once in a blue moon** very rarely: *I see him once in a blue moon.*

LIVING ROOM

Exercise 1
Here is a list of household items whose names have got mixed up. Unscramble the words and decide where you would expect to find them. Complete the table by putting the words in the appropriate columns.

rachairm	pleenamteci	pat
lektet	palm	habt
basna wish	etlow	recaus
dwarboer	sichoun	plowil

Living room	Kitchen	Bathroom	Bedroom

Exercise 2
How does your living room differ from the one pictured opposite? Write a short paragraph describing your living room.

moon v
moon about/around phr v [I] to wander about or behave in an unhappy way, often because you are in love

moon·beam /'mu:nbi:m/ n a beam of light from the moon

moon·light /'mu:nlaɪt/ n [U] the light of the moon: *The moonlight on the calm sea added to the beauty of the scene.*

moon·lit /'mu:n‚lɪt/ adj [only before a noun] given light by the moon: *a beautiful moonlit night*

moor¹ /mʊəʳ/ n a wide, open area of land, covered with rough grass or low bushes, not farmed because of its poor soil: *Shall we go for a walk on the moors?*

moor² v [T] to fasten a boat to land, or to an object in the water, by means of ropes or chains

moor·ings /'mʊərɪŋz/ n [pl] a place where a boat is moored: *Several ships broke away from their moorings in the storm.*

moose /mu:s/ n [plural is **moose**] a type of large deer that lives in north America

moot point /‚mu:t 'pɔɪnt/ n a point about which there is disagreement or doubt

mop¹ /mɒp/ ‖ /mɑːp/ n 1 a tool for washing floors or dishes, made of a stick with soft material fastened to one end 2 *infml* a thick untidy mass of hair: *a dark mop of curls*

mop² v -pp- [T] 1 to clean something with a mop: *I mopped the kitchen floor an hour ago, and look at it now!* 2 to dry something by rubbing it with a cloth: *He mopped his sweaty face with a handkerchief.*
mop sthg ↔ **up** phr v [T] to remove unwanted liquid or dirt with a mop: *Can you mop up the milk you spilt?*

mope /məʊp/ v **moped, moping** [I] to be unhappy, often without trying to become more cheerful
mope about/around phr v [I] to sit or wander around without taking an interest in anything because you are unhappy

mo·ped /'məʊped/ n a bicycle which has a small engine

mor·al¹ /'mɒrəl ‖ 'mɔː-/ adj 1 [only before a noun] concerning or based on what is considered right or wrong: *a man of high moral standards* | *She refused to join the army for moral reasons.* | *What right have you to make moral judgments about my behaviour?* 2 behaving only in a way that is considered by society to be good or acceptable: *My grandfather was a very moral man who never told a lie in his life.* −opposite **immoral** 3 **moral support** support in the form of encouragement rather than practical help 4 **moral victory** the result of a contest or argument in which the losing side feels it has proved itself to be right

moral² n 1 a lesson that can be learnt from a story or event, which shows you the right way to behave: *The moral of this story is that crime does not pay.* 2 **morals** [pl] principles which you live by, based on what is considered right and wrong: *He has no morals.*

mo·rale /mə'rɑːl ‖ mə'ræl/ n [U] a confident state of mind, especially in a bad situation: *The team's morale is high despite their recent defeat.*

mor·al·ist /'mɒrəlɪst ‖ 'mɔː-/ n a person who tries to make others behave in the way that person strongly believes to be right (a word usually used to express disapproval) −**moralistic** /‚mɒrə'lɪstɪk◂ ‖ ‚mɔː-/ adj

mo·ral·i·ty /mə'rælɪti/ n [U] an idea of what is good or acceptable behaviour: *One sometimes wonders if there's any morality in politics.*

mor·al·ize /'mɒrəlaɪz ‖ 'mɔː-/ v **moralized, moralizing** (also **moralise** BrE) [I] to express your ideas about what is correct behaviour (a word usually used to express disapproval) −**moralizer** n

mor·al·ly /'mɒrəli ‖ 'mɔː-/ adv 1 in a way which is considered right and proper (a word used to express approval) −opposite **immorally** 2 with regard to right or good behaviour: *What you did wasn't actually against the law, but it was morally wrong.*

mo·rass /mə'ræs/ n 1 a confusion which is difficult to make sense of: *The report took a long time to read because of the morass of details.* 2 an area of very wet ground

mor·a·to·ri·um /‚mɒrə'tɔːriəm ‖ ‚mɔː-/ n **moratoria** /-riə/ 1 a declaration that a particular activity will be stopped or delayed for a time: *a moratorium on the building of new houses* 2 the length of such a delay

mor·bid /'mɔːbɪd ‖ 'mɔːr-/ adj having an unhealthy, unnatural interest in unpleasant subjects, especially death (a word used to express disapproval): *a morbid interest in fatal diseases* −**morbidly** adv −**morbidity** /mɔː'bɪdɪti ‖ mɔːr-/ n [U]

more /mɔːʳ/ det, pron, adv [comparative of MANY, MUCH] 1 a greater amount, or to a greater degree: *People tend to sleep more in winter.* | *I wanted to discuss the matter more.* | *This book is much more interesting than his last one.* | *There were more people at this meeting than there were at the last one.* | *I wish I could spend more time gardening.* | *We seem to spend more of our money on food these days.* 2 **once more, twice more, etc** happening once again, twice again, etc: *I wanted to see her once more before she left.* 3 an additional number or amount: *Have some more tea.* | *I've got to write two more letters this morning.* 4 **not any more** no longer: *They don't live here any more.* | *After this trip, I won't be going abroad any more.* 5 **more and more** an increasing amount: *Our task was becoming more and more difficult.* | *We seem to spend more and more each month.* | *The children were trampling more and more mud into the house.* 6 **more or less** about or almost: *The building work will cost £300, more or less.* | *"Have you finished your work yet?" "More or less."* 7 **more than** more important than: *She was much more than a friend to me.* 8 **what's more** a phrase used to introduce an additional point that you are making: *The country is in a terrible state. Inflation is high, unemployment is high, and what's more the government doesn't seem able to do anything about it.*

more·o·ver /mɔːr'əʊvəʳ/ adv fml used when you are saying something which adds to what you have already said or supports it: *The Government should have acted long ago. Moreover, they should not have discouraged private companies from taking action.*

morgue /mɔːg ‖ mɔːrg/ n a building in which the dead bodies of unknown people are kept until they are buried or burned

Mor·mon /'mɔːmən ‖ 'mɔːr-/ n a member of a religious body originally formed in the US

morn /mɔːn ‖ mɔːrn/ n a morning

morn·ing /'mɔːnɪŋ ‖ 'mɔːr-/ n [C;U] the first part of the day, usually until the time when the midday meal is eaten: *I must go to the shops some time during the morning.* | *Can't the decision wait until morning?* | *I'll see you in the morning.* | *She met him in town this morning.* | *He didn't get home until two o'clock in the morning.*

mo·ron /ˈmɔːrɒn ‖ ˈmɔːrɑːn/ n a very stupid person (a word used to express disapproval) –**moronic** /məˈrɒnɪk ‖ məˈrɑː-/ adj

mo·rose /məˈrəʊs/ adj bad-tempered –**morosely** adv

mor·phine /ˈmɔːfiːn ‖ ˈmɔːr-/ n [U] a powerful drug used for stopping pain

mor·sel /ˈmɔːsəl ‖ ˈmɔːr-/ n a very small piece of food

mor·tal[1] /ˈmɔːtl ‖ ˈmɔːrtl/ adj **1** unable to live for ever –opposite **immortal 2** causing death: *a mortal wound* **3** [only before a noun] very serious: *in mortal danger*

mortal[2] n a human being (a literary word; it is also often used in a humorous way): *We mortals can only do our best.*

mor·tal·i·ty /mɔːˈtælₔti ‖ mɔːr-/ n [U] **1** the number of deaths, often from a particular cause or among a certain type of people: *Infant mortality has declined with the rise in the standard of living.* **2** the fact that people die –opposite **immortality** (for sense 2)

mor·tal·ly /ˈmɔːtəl-i ‖ ˈmɔːr-/ adv in a manner that causes death: *He was mortally wounded in the fight.*

mor·tar /ˈmɔːtəʳ ‖ ˈmɔːr-/ n **1** [C] a heavy gun with a short barrel, which fires explosives that fall from a great height **2** [C] a bowl made from a hard material, in which substances are crushed into very small pieces or powder **3** [U] a mixture of lime, sand, and water, used in building

mort·gage[1] /ˈmɔːgɪdʒ ‖ ˈmɔːr-/ n a sum of money borrowed, especially to buy a house: *We took out a £30,000 mortgage on our new house.*

mortgage[2] v [T] to borrow money, especially from a bank; if you do not pay back the money, you lose your house or land

mor·ti·fy /ˈmɔːtₔfaɪ ‖ ˈmɔːr-/ v **mortified, mortifying be mortified** to feel very ashamed: *The teacher was mortified by his own inability to answer such a simple question.* –**mortification** /ˌmɔːtₔfₔˈkeɪʃən ‖ ˌmɔːr-/ n [U]

mor·tu·a·ry /ˈmɔːtʃuəri ‖ ˈmɔːrtʃueri/ n **mortuaries** a place, especially in a hospital, where a dead body is kept until it is buried or burned

mo·sa·ic /məʊˈzeɪ-ɪk/ n [C;U] a piece of ornamental work produced by the fitting together of small pieces of coloured stone or glass to form a pattern or picture

Mos·lem /ˈmɒzlₔm ‖ ˈmɑːz-/ n, adj see MUSLIM

mosque /mɒsk ‖ mɑːsk/ n a building in which Muslims worship

mos·qui·to /məˈskiːtəʊ/ n **mosquitoes** a small flying insect that pricks the skin of people or animals and then drinks blood; some mosquitoes carry the disease of MALARIA

moss /mɒs ‖ mɔːs/ n [U] a small green or yellow plant that grows in a thick mass on wet soil or on a wet surface –**mossy** adj

most[1] /məʊst/ adv [superlative of MUCH] **1** to the greatest degree: *the most comfortable hotel in the town* | *What annoyed me most was the way he laughed at me!* **2** very: *It was a most enjoyable evening.*

most[2] det, pron [superlative of MANY,MUCH] **1** the greatest number or amount: *Most people go on holiday in July and August.* | *I spend most of my time at home now.* | *As usual, John was the one who ate the most food and drank the most wine.* | *Of course, the one that I liked best cost the most.* **2 at most, at the most** a phrase used when you are giving the largest

number or amount that is possible: *I would guess that at most she's thirty.* | *It'll take a couple of hours at the most.* **3 for the most part** usually: *Summers in this area are for the most part dry and sunny.* **4 make the most of something** to enjoy something as much as possible, or get the best advantage from it: *We've only got two more days here, so let's make the most of them.*

■ USAGE With nouns which already have a determiner (**the, this, these, that, those, his, her,** etc.) use **most of**: *I know* **most** *of the students who live in London.* | *I've read* **most** *of his novels.* | **most** *of the population of France.* With pronouns you should also use **most of**: *Most of us agree on this point.* | *I've already spoken to* **most** *of them.* However, with nouns that do not already have a determiner remember to use **most** (WITHOUT **of**): *Most people hate violence.* | *Most Americans seem friendly.* | *I like* **most** *French food.*

most·ly /ˈməʊstli/ adv mainly or usually: *The people in the room were mostly quite young.* | *When I go to London, it's mostly on business.*

MOT /ˌem əʊ ˈtiː/ n BrE a regular official examination of cars more than three years old, carried out to make sure that they are fit to be driven; an abbreviation for **Ministry of Transport**: *My car failed its MOT.*

mo·tel /məʊˈtel/ n a hotel specially built for travelling motorists

moth /mɒθ ‖ mɔːθ/ n a winged insect which flies mainly at night; the young of some types of moth eat and make holes in clothes

moth·ball /ˈmɒθbɔːl ‖ ˈmɔːθ-/ n a small ball made of a strong-smelling substance, used for keeping moths away from clothes

moth-eat·en /ˈ· ˌ··/ adj destroyed, or appearing to have been destroyed, by moths (used of clothing): *Isn't it time you threw some of those moth-eaten garments away?*

moth·er[1] /ˈmʌðəʳ/ n **1** a female parent: *His mother and father are both doctors.* | *a mother hen and her young chicks* –see picture on page 343 **2 Mother** a word used to address or talk about your female parent: *Can I borrow your car please, Mother?* **3 mother tongue** a person's first language **4 the mother country** the country where you were born –**motherless** adj

mother[2] v [T] **1** to care for someone like a mother **2** to treat someone with too much protectiveness and care

moth·er·hood /ˈmʌðəhʊd ‖ -ər-/ n [U] the state of being a mother: *I'm still trying to adjust to motherhood.* –compare FATHERHOOD

mother-in-law /ˈ·· · ·/ n **mothers-in-law** the mother of your husband or wife –see picture on page 343

moth·er·ly /ˈmʌðəli ‖ -ər-/ adj having or showing the loving feelings that you expect of a mother: *She's a motherly sort of person.* –**motherliness** n [U]

mother-of-pearl /ˌ··· ·ˈ·/ n [U] a hard smooth substance on the inside of certain shells, used for making ornamental articles

mo·tif /məʊˈtiːf/ n a subject, pattern, or idea which is repeated many times or is the most important, especially in a work of music, art, or theatre

mo·tion[1] /ˈməʊʃən/ n **1** [U] the action or way of moving: *The gentle rolling motion of the ship made me feel sleepy.* | *The train was already in motion when he jumped on.* **2** [C] a single movement: *He made a motion with his hand, as if to tell me to keep back.* **3** [C] a suggestion formally put before a meeting: *The motion to increase the club's membership charges was defeated by 15 votes to 10.* **4** [C] *fml* an act of emptying your bowels **5 go through the motions** to do something without much interest or belief that it worth doing **6 in slow motion** making the movements slower than in real life, especially in a film **7 set things in motion** to start things working

motion² *v* [I;T] to direct by means of a movement, usually with your hand: *She motioned me into the room.*

mo·tion·less /ˈməʊʃənləs/ *adj* not moving: *The cat remained motionless, waiting for the mouse to move.* –**motionlessly** *adv*

mo·ti·vate /ˈməʊt̬ɪveɪt/ *v* **motivated, motivating** [T] to provide someone with a reason for doing something: *His attempt to get elected to parliament was motivated only by a desire for power.*

mo·ti·va·tion /ˌməʊt̬ɪˈveɪʃən/ *n* [C;U] a reason or the knowledge of a reason for doing something: *How can we provide them with the motivation to learn?*

mo·tive /ˈməʊt̬ɪv/ *n* a reason for action: *The police are questioning everyone who might have a motive to kill the man.* | *What do you think his motives were in buying the director a drink?*

mot·ley /ˈmɒtli ‖ ˈmɑːtli/ *adj* of many different kinds (a word used to express disapproval or used in a humorous way): *a motley crowd of people*

mo·tor¹ /ˈməʊtər/ *n* a machine that changes power, especially electrical power, into movement: *This grass-cutting machine is driven by a small electric motor.*

motor² *adj* [only before a noun] **1** driven by an engine: *a motorboat* | *a motor scooter* | *a motor mower* **2** related to vehicles driven by an engine, especially those used on roads: *the motor industry* | *motor racing*

motor³ *v* [I+adv/prep] *BrE old fash* to travel by car: *We motored over to Cambridge to see some friends.*

mo·tor·car /ˈməʊtəkɑːr ‖ -tər-/ *n BrE old fash* a car

mo·tor·cy·cle /ˈməʊtəˌsaɪkəl ‖ -tər-/ *n* (also **motorbike** *BrE infml*) a large heavy bicycle driven by an engine –**motorcyclist** *n*

mo·tor·ist /ˈməʊtərɪst/ *n* a person who drives a car

mo·tor·ized /ˈməʊtəraɪzd/ *adj* having an engine (used of vehicles)

mo·tor·way /ˈməʊtəweɪ ‖ -tər-/ *n BrE* a very wide road built for fast long-distance travel

mot·tled /ˈmɒtld ‖ ˈmɑː-/ *adj* marked irregularly with different coloured spots or parts: *The underside of this snake is yellow, but its back is mottled.*

mot·to /ˈmɒtəʊ ‖ ˈmɑː-/ *n* **mottos** *or* **mottoes** a short sentence or a few words taken as the guiding principle of a person, a school, or an organization: *The school motto is "Never lose hope".*

mould¹ /məʊld/ *n* (also **mold** *AmE*) [U] **1** a soft greenish growth on bread or cheese that has been kept too long, or on objects which have been left for a long time in warm wet air **2** loose soft soil that is rich in decayed vegetable substances: *He planted the seeds in a box filled with leaf mould.* **3** a hollow container with a particular shape, into which some soft or liquid substance is poured; when the substance hardens, it takes this shape: *a jelly mould shaped like a rabbit*

mould² *v* (also **mold** *AmE*) [T] to give shape or form to something especially by using a mould: *The car body is moulded in the factory.* | *a figure of a man*

moulded out of clay | *His character has been moulded more by his experiences in life than by his education.*

mould·y /ˈməʊldi/ *adj* **mouldier, mouldiest** (also **moldy** *AmE*) old, and covered with mould: *mouldy cheese* | *The house has been empty for years, and smells rather mouldy.*

moult /məʊlt/ *v* (also **molt** *AmE*) [I] (of birds or animals) to lose feathers, fur, or hair as part of a natural process of loss and regrowth

mound /maʊnd/ *n* **1** a pile of earth or stones, sometimes making a small hill **2** a large pile of objects: *a mound of newspapers*

mount¹ /maʊnt/ *n* **1** an animal on which you can ride: *This pony is a good quiet mount for a child.* **2 Mount** a word used as part of the name of a mountain: *Mount Everest*

mount² *v* **1** [I;T] to get on a horse or a bicycle: *He mounted his horse and rode away.* | *Shall I hold it while you mount?* **2** [T] *fml* to go up: *My grandmother can hardly mount the stairs.* **3** [I] to increase: *mounting debts* | *The government faced mounting opposition.* **4** [T] to fix something on a support or in a frame: *She mounted the photograph on stiff paper.* **5** [T] to prepare and carry out an action: *The unions are getting ready to mount a powerful attack on the government.*

mount up *phr v* [I] to increase: *Our debts are mounting up at an alarming rate.*

moun·tain /ˈmaʊntɪn/ *n* a very high hill: *I have no wish to climb any mountains.* | *mountain goats*

moun·tain bike /ˈ·· ˌ·/ *n* a special strong bicycle for riding over rough ground

moun·tain·eer /ˌmaʊntɪˈnɪər/ *n* a person who climbs mountains as a sport or profession

moun·tain·eer·ing /ˌmaʊntɪˈnɪərɪŋ/ *n* [U] the sport of climbing mountains: *Mountaineering is very popular.* –**mountaineering** *v* [only in progressive forms]

moun·tain·ous /ˈmaʊntɪnəs/ *adj* full of mountains: *mountainous country*

mourn /mɔːn ‖ mɔːrn/ *v* [I;T] to feel or show grief, especially when someone has died: *The old woman still mourns for her son.* | *The whole nation mourned his death.*

mourn·er /ˈmɔːnər ‖ ˈmɔːr-/ *n* a person who attends a funeral, especially a relative or friend of the one who is dead

mourn·ful /ˈmɔːnfəl ‖ ˈmɔːrn-/ *adj* sad –**mournfully** *adv*

mourn·ing /ˈmɔːnɪŋ ‖ ˈmɔːr-/ *n* [U] **1** the expression of grief, especially when someone has died: *All the theatres and cinemas closed as a sign of mourning for the dead president.* **2 in mourning** behaving or dressed in a way that expresses your grief at someone's death

mouse /maʊs/ *n* **1** [plural is **mice** /maɪs/] a small furry animal with a long tail that lives in houses and in fields: *a field mouse* | *I think we've got mice in the kitchen.* **2** [plural is **mouses**] a small box connected to a computer by a wire which you move around on a surface in order to work the computer –see picture on page 539

mousse /muːs/ *n* [C;U] a dish made from cream, eggs, and other substances mixed together and then served cold: *chocolate mousse*

mous·tache /məˈstɑːʃ ‖ ˈmʌstæʃ/ *n* (also **mustache** *AmE*) hair growing on a man's upper lip –see picture on page 245

mous·y /ˈmaʊsi/ adj **1** a dull brown colour (used of hair) –see picture on page 245 **2** unattractively plain or quiet and uninteresting (used of a person)

mouth¹ /maʊθ/ n **1** the opening in your face through which you speak and take food into your body **2** an opening, entrance, or way out: *the mouth of a cave* | *the mouth of a river* **3** down in the mouth unhappy **4** keep your mouth shut: a to remain silent b to not reveal a secret **5** make someone's mouth water to make someone eager to eat: *The smells from the kitchen are making my mouth water.* **6** put words into someone's mouth to tell someone what to say **7** take the words out of someone's mouth to say something that someone else was going to say, before they have had time to speak **8** -mouthed having the stated way of speaking (usually part of a word expressing disapproval): *loud-mouthed* | *foul-mouthed*

mouth² /maʊð/ v [T] **1** to speak or say something without understanding or sincerity **2** to move your lips as if you are speaking but without making any sound

mouth·ful /ˈmaʊθful/ n **1** as much food or drink as you usually put into your mouth at one time: *I'm too full to eat another mouthful.* **2** infml a long word or phrase that you find difficult to say: *Her name is quite a mouthful!*

mouth·or·gan /ˈmaʊθˌɔːɡən ‖ -ˌɔːr-/ n a small musical instrument; you play it by blowing into it as you move it from side to side

mouth·piece /ˈmaʊθpiːs/ n **1** part of something like a musical instrument or a telephone, that you hold in or near the mouth **2** a person or newspaper that expresses the opinions of others: *This newspaper is just the mouthpiece of the government.*

mouth-wa·ter·ing /ˈ·ˌ···/ adj so good that you feel a desire to eat the food which is smelt, seen or described: *He gave me a mouth-watering account of the dinner I missed*

mo·va·ble /ˈmuːvəbəl/ adj (also **moveable**) able to be moved: *toy soldiers with movable arms and legs*

move¹ /muːv/ v **moved, moving 1** [I] to change position or go to a new place: *Sit still and don't move!* | *I could hear someone moving around downstairs.* | *That bird hasn't moved for half an hour.* **2** [T] to change something's position or take it to a new place: *I can't move my legs.* | *Could you move your car, please?* **3** [I] (also **move house**) to go to a new home: *We're moving to a bigger house.* | *I moved house three times last year.* **4** [I + adv/prep] to advance: *Events in Europe are moving very quickly now.* | *We seem to be moving towards a peace agreement.* **5** [T] to make you feel a strong emotion such as anger or sadness: *I was very moved by her story.* **6** move someone to do something fml to cause someone to do something: *What finally moved the prime minister to resign?* **7** [T;+that] to put forward a suggestion at a meeting: *I move that we reject this application.* | *I wish to move an amendment to this law.*

move in phr v [I] to go and live in a new home: *We've bought a house now, and should be able to move in next month.*

move off phr v [I] to move away from a place: *The guard blew his whistle and the train moved off.*

move on phr v **1** [I] to change to something new: *Can we move on to the next item on our agenda?* **2** [I] to go away to a new place: *He stopped to look in a shop window, then moved on.* **3** [T **move** sbdy ↔ **on**] to make someone move away from where they are: *He was moved on by the police.*

move over phr v [I] to change your position so that there is room for someone else: *Move over a bit so that I can sit down.*

move² n **1** a movement or an act of moving: *He was watching my every move.* | *Don't make a move, or I'll shoot.* **2** an act of going to a new home or a new job: *The move went very smoothly.* | *I couldn't face another job move.* **3** an act of moving a piece in a game such as CHESS: *Come on, it's your move.* **4** an action that you take in order to gain a particular result: *The latest moves towards peace seem to have ended in failure.* **5** get a move on infml to hurry up: *We'd better get a move on or we'll be late.*

move·ment /ˈmuːvmənt/ n **1** [C;U] change in position or from one place to another: *Any movement can be painful when you've hurt your back.* | *the movement of goods by road* | *I noticed a sudden movement behind the curtain.* | *The police are watching this man's movements very carefully.* **2** [C] a group of people who make united efforts for a particular purpose: *The trade union movement works to obtain higher wages and better conditions.* **3** [C] a general development in something, often not directed by any particular person or group: *The movement towards complete equality for women still has a long way to go.* **4** [C] one of the main parts into which many longer pieces of music are divided **5** [C] the moving parts of a piece of machinery, especially a clock or watch

mov·ie /ˈmuːvi/ n the usual American word for a FILM

mov·ies /ˈmuːviz/ n [pl] **the movies** the usual American word for the CINEMA: *Let's go to the movies!*

mov·ing /ˈmuːvɪŋ/ adj **1** causing strong feelings, especially of pity: *The film was so moving that we were all in tears.* **2** [only before a noun] able to move: *Oil the moving parts of this machine regularly.*

mow /məʊ/ v **mowed, mown** /məʊn/ or **mowed** [I;T] to cut grass or crops with a machine

mow sbdy ↔ **down** phr v [T] to kill people or knock them down, especially in large numbers: *Protesters were mown down by army guns.*

mow·er /ˈməʊəʳ/ n a machine for cutting grass or crops

MP /ˌem ˈpiː/ n a person who has been elected to represent people from a particular area in parliament; an abbreviation for **Member of Parliament**: *Michael Foot, MP* | *our local MP* | *the MP for Witney*

mpg an abbreviation for **miles per gallon**: *a car that does 35 mpg*

mph an abbreviation for **miles per hour**: *driving along at 60 mph*

Mr /ˈmɪstəʳ/ n [only before a noun] (also **mister**) **1** a title used to address or talk about a man who has no other title: *Mr Smith* | *Mr John Smith* **2** a title used to address men in certain official positions: *Mr Chairman* | *Mr President*

Mrs /ˈmɪsɪz/ n [only before a noun] a title used to address or talk about a married woman: *Mrs Jones* | *Mrs Sarah Jones* –compare MISS, MS

Ms /mɪz, məz/ n [only before a noun] a title for a woman who does not wish to call herself either "Mrs" or "Miss"

MS n **MSS** a written abbreviation for MANUSCRIPT

MSc /ˌem es ˈsiː/ (also **MS** AmE) **1** a higher university degree; an abbreviation for **Master of Science**: *Jill Smith, MSc* | *an MSc from Cambridge University* **2** a person who has an MSc

Mt a written abbreviation for MOUNT¹ (2): *Mt Everest*

much¹ /mʌtʃ/ *adv* more /mɔːʳ/, most /məʊst/ **1** by a great amount or degree: *She's much cleverer than I am.* | *We're looking forward very much to seeing you.* **2 not much** not very often: *We don't go out very much.* | *I don't see him much these days.* **3** in most ways: *Jane was much the same as usual.*
■ USAGE We use **much** instead of **very** before expressions like admired, improved, commented on, talked about (expressions containing the passive form of verbs). Compare *This picture is* **much** admired. and *This picture is* **very** famous.

much² *det, pron, n* more, most **1** used in questions asking about the amount of something that there is: *How much cheese have we got left?* | *How much does it cost.* **2** *fml* a large amount: *I have much pleasure in welcoming you today.* | *Much of what he says is true.* **3 not much** not a great amount: *She doesn't earn very much money.* | "*Did you enjoy the party?*" "*Not much.*" **4 too much** too great an amount: *I've got far too much work to do.* **5 much as** although: *Much as I'd love to come, I'm afraid I won't be able to.* **6 not much of a** a phrase you use to say that someone or something is not very good: *I'm not much of a sportsman.* **7 not up to much** *infml* not very good: *The film's not up to much.* **8 so much for** a phrase you use to say that something is not possible or not helpful **9 too much for someone** too difficult for someone
■ USAGE **Much** is not usually used in simple statements. Instead use **a great deal of** or **a lot of**: *She's got* **a lot of** *money.* | *We've already collected* **a great deal of** *information.* | **a lot of** *trouble* | **a great deal of** *discomfort*

muck¹ /mʌk/ *n* [U] *infml* **1** dirt: *What's that muck on the carpet?* **2** waste matter from animals, especially as used for spreading on the land –**mucky** *adj* muckier, muckiest

muck² *v*
muck about/around *phr v* [I] *BrE infml* to behave in a silly way: *Stop mucking about and listen to what I'm saying.*
muck in *phr v* [I] *infml* to join in work or activity with others: *If we all muck in we'll soon be finished.*
muck sthg ↔ up *phr v* [T] *BrE infml* **1** to spoil something: *The change in the weather has mucked up our plans.* **2** to make something dirty: *I've mucked up my shirt, working in the garden.*

mu·cus /ˈmjuːkəs/ *n* [U] a liquid produced in certain parts of your body, especially your nose

mud /mʌd/ *n* [U] **1** very wet earth in a sticky mass, or the same substance when it has dried on something: *The garden became a sea of mud.* | *You've got mud on your trousers.* **2 your name is mud** = people speak badly of you after you have caused trouble

mud·dle¹ /ˈmʌdl/ *n* a state of confusion and disorder: *I was in such a muddle that I couldn't find anything.*

muddle² *v* muddled, muddling [T] **1** (also **muddle sthg ↔ up**) to put things into disorder: *You're muddling up my papers.* **2** (also **muddle** sbdy/sthg ↔ **up**) to confuse people or things, or to make someone confused: *Don't muddle me up with all these different instructions.* | *I keep muddling up James with his brother.*
muddle along *phr v* [I] to continue in a confused manner, without a plan
muddle through *phr v* [I;T] to manage to do something although you do not have the necessary plans or means: *I expect the country will muddle through this crisis too.* | *We had no idea what was expected, but we muddled through.*

mud·dled /ˈmʌdld/ *adj* confused

mud·dy¹ /ˈmʌdi/ *adj* muddier, muddiest covered with or containing mud: *the muddy waters of the river* | *Take off those muddy boots.*

muddy² *v* n.uddied, muddying [T] to make something dirty with mud: *Your dog's muddying the kitchen floor.*

mud·guard /ˈmʌdgɑːd ‖ -ɑːrd/ *n* a metal cover over the wheel of a vehicle to keep the mud from flying up

muf·fle /ˈmʌfəl/ *v* muffled, muffling [T] to make a sound less easy to hear: *I heard muffled voices through the wall.*

mug¹ /mʌg/ *n* **1** a kind of large cup with a flat bottom, straight sides, and a handle: *a mug of coffee* –see picture on page 148 **2** *BrE infml* a foolish person who is easily deceived

mug² *v* -gg- [T] to rob someone with violence, especially in a dark street –**mugger** *n* –**mugging** *n* [C;U]

mug·gy /ˈmʌgi/ *adj* unpleasantly warm but not dry (used of weather) –**mugginess** *n* [U]

Mu·ham·ma·dan /mʊˈhæm‿dən, mə-/ *adj,n* see MUSLIM

mul·ber·ry /ˈmʌlbəri ‖ -beri/ *n* mulberries a small dark purple fruit which can be eaten

mulch /mʌltʃ/ *n* a covering of material, often made from decaying plants, which is put over the soil and over the roots of plants to help plants grow

mule /mjuːl/ *n* an animal whose parents are a donkey and a horse

mull /mʌl/ *v* [T] to heat alcohol with sugar and other things to make a special drink: *mulled wine*
mull sthg ↔ over *phr v* [T] to consider something for a time: *I'm mulling over what she said.*

mul·lah /ˈmʌlə, ˈmʊlə/ *n* a Muslim teacher of law and religion

mul·ti·far·i·ous /ˌmʌltɪˈfeəriəs/ *adj fml* of many different types: *multifarious interests* –**multifariously** *adv*

mul·ti·lat·e·ral /ˌmʌltɪˈlætərəl/ *adj* concerning more than two groups of people, often with different opinions: *a multilateral agreement on world oil prices*

mul·ti·ple¹ /ˈmʌltɪpəl/ *adj* including many different parts, things, or people: *The driver of the crashed car received multiple injuries.*

multiple² *n* a number which contains a smaller number an exact number of times: 3 × 4 = 12, so 12 is a multiple of 3.

mul·ti·pli·ca·tion /ˌmʌltɪplɪˈkeɪʃən/ *n* [U] the method of combining two numbers by adding one of them to itself as many times as the other number states: 2 × 4 = 8 is an example of multiplication.

mul·ti·plic·i·ty /ˌmʌltɪˈplɪsɪti/ *n* [sing] a large variety of things: *a multiplicity of ideas*

mul·ti·ply /ˈmʌltɪplaɪ/ *v* [I;T] **1** to combine numbers by MULTIPLICATION: *to multiply 2* **by** *3* | *2 multiplied by 3 (2 × 3) = 2 + 2 + 2.* | *You added when you should have multiplied.* –compare DIVIDE² (6) **2** to increase in number or make something increase in number: *We can multiply our chances of success.* | *Our problems seem to be multiplying.*

mul·ti·ra·cial /ˌmʌltɪˈreɪʃəl‿/ *adj* consisting of or involving several races of people

mul·ti·sto·rey /ˌmʌltɪˈstɔːri‿/ *adj* [only before a noun] with several levels or floors (used of a building): *a multistorey car park*

mul·ti·tude /ˈmʌltɪtjuːd ‖ -tuːd/ *n fml* a large number: *A multitude of thoughts filled her mind.*

mum /mʌm/ n BrE infml (also **Mum; mom** AmE) mother: Can I go to the cinema please, Mum? | My mum's gone to work. | Have you seen Mum?

mum·ble /ˈmʌmbəl/ v **mumbled, mumbling** [I;T] to speak unclearly: She mumbled a reply. | I wish you wouldn't mumble when you speak to me.

mum·mi·fy /ˈmʌmɪfaɪ/ v **mummified, mummifying** [T] to preserve a dead body as a mummy (2)

mum·my /ˈmʌmi/ n **mummies** BrE (also **Mummy**) **1** a word for mother used especially by or to children: I want my mummy! | Ask your mummy if she will help you. **2** a dead body preserved from decay by treatment with special substances, especially in ancient Egypt

mumps /mʌmps/ n [U] an infectious illness common in children which causes swelling in the neck

munch /mʌntʃ/ v [I;T] to eat something noisily: He was munching an apple. | We sat there munching on biscuits.

mun·dane /mʌnˈdeɪn/ adj ordinary, with nothing exciting or unusual in it (a word usually used to express disapproval): a mundane life

mu·ni·ci·pal /mjuːˈnɪsɪpəl ‖ mjʊ-/ adj relating or belonging to a town with its own local government: municipal buildings | the municipal council

mu·ni·ci·pal·i·ty /mjuː,nɪsɪ'pælɪti ‖ mjʊ-/ n **municipalities** a town, city, or other small area, which has its own government for local affairs

mu·nif·i·cence /mjuːˈnɪfɪsəns ‖ mjʊ-/ n [U] fml generous action or thought –**munificent** adj

mu·ni·tions /mjuːˈnɪʃənz ‖ mjʊ-/ n [pl] large weapons for war, such as bombs

mu·ral /ˈmjʊərəl/ n a picture which is painted on a wall

mur·der¹ /ˈmɜːdəʳ ‖ ˈmɜːr-/ n **1** [C;U] the crime of killing a human being illegally: Police investigating the two murders believed they were committed by the same person. | She was found guilty of murder. | Police are still looking for the murder weapon. **2** [U] infml a very difficult or tiring experience: It was murder putting the clock together. | The traffic was murder.

murder² v [I;T] to kill someone illegally and on purpose: She was murdered in the most brutal way. | We suspect that he has murdered before. –see KILL (USAGE) –**murderer** n

mur·der·ous /ˈmɜːdərəs ‖ ˈmɜːr-/ adj likely to kill someone, or expressing that possibility: murderous intentions | a murderous expression on his face | murderous road conditions

murk·y /ˈmɜːki ‖ ˈmɜːr-/ adj **murkier, murkiest** dark and unpleasant: a murky night

mur·mur¹ /ˈmɜːməʳ ‖ ˈmɜːr-/ n **1** a soft low sound: the murmur of the stream **2** without a murmur without complaint: The children went to bed without a murmur.

murmur² v [I;T] to make a soft sound, especially when speaking in a quiet voice: a child murmuring in her sleep | As she delivered her speech, the crowd murmured their approval.

mus·cle /ˈmʌsəl/ n **1** [C;U] pieces of flesh in your body joining the bones: I'm playing tennis to develop my arm muscles. | He's all muscle! **2** [U] strength: the military muscle of the world's great powers **3** not move a muscle to stay quite still

muscle v
muscle in phr v [I] infml to force your way into a situation where you have no right to be: He's trying to muscle in on the contracts that I have been responsible for winning.

mus·cu·lar /ˈmʌskjʊ̇ləʳ/ adj **1** connected with muscles: a muscular disease **2** having big strong muscles: a muscular body

muse /mjuːz/ v **mused, musing** [I] to think deeply, forgetting about the world around you: She sat musing for hours.

mu·se·um /mjuːˈziːəm ‖ mjʊ-/ n a building where objects are kept and shown to the public because of their scientific, historical, or artistic interest: the Museum of Modern Art

mush /mʌʃ/ n [U] infml a soft mass of half-liquid, half-solid material, especially food (a word often used to express disapproval): I can't eat this mush! –**mushy** adj **mushier, mushiest** : mushy potatoes | mushy peas

mush·room¹ /ˈmʌʃruːm, -rʊm/ n a plant with a short stem and round top, often eaten and sometimes poisonous –see picture on page 344

mushroom² v [I] to develop or spread fast: Since the opening of the first shop, new branches have mushroomed all over the country.

mu·sic /ˈmjuːzɪk/ n [U] **1** the arrangement of sounds in pleasant patterns and tunes: That's a beautiful piece of music. | What's your favourite kind of music? **2** the art of arranging sounds and tunes: to study music | a music student **3** a written or printed set of notes: a sheet of music | I've lost my music. **4** face the music to admit to blame and accept the results

mu·sic·al¹ /ˈmjuːzɪkəl/ adj **1** [only before a noun] sounding like music or producing music: musical instruments | a rather musical way of speaking **2** skilled in and fond of music: a very musical child

musical² n a play or film with songs and often dances

music cen·tre /ˈ·· ,··/ n a piece of electrical apparatus which can play records and cassettes (CASSETTE), and also contains a radio

mu·si·cian /mjuːˈzɪʃən ‖ mjʊ-/ n a person who performs on a musical instrument

musk /mʌsk/ n [U] a strong smelling substance used in making PERFUME –**musky** adj : a musky smell

Mus·lim /ˈmʊzlɪm, ˈmʌz-, ˈmʊs-/ n (also **Moslem, Mohammedan, Muhammadan**) a person who believes in ISLAM **Muslim** adj : a Muslim country

mus·lin /ˈmʌzlɪn/ n [U] a very fine thin cotton material, used for light dresses especially in the past

mus·sel /ˈmʌsəl/ n a small sea animal that lives inside a dark shell, and whose soft body can be eaten as food –see picture on page 344

must¹ /məst; strong mʌst/ v negative short form **mustn't** [modal verb] **1** used to show that something is necessary or should be done: I must go or I'll be late. | You mustn't tell anyone about this. | Dogs must be kept on a lead. | The government must do something about this problem. **2** used to show that you think something is very likely or certain: You must be tired after your walk. | You must be the new English teacher. | There's nobody here – they must have all gone home. –see Study Note on page 392 **3** you must a phrase you use when you are inviting someone to do something or suggesting that they do something nice: You must come round for dinner one evening. | You must go and see that new film. **4** I must admit, I must say phrases you use when you are giving your opinion about something: I must admit I don't know very much about classical music. | I must say I don't like the design of that new shopping centre. **5** if you must know a phrase you use when you are telling someone something but you do not think that they really need to know it: *I live in London, if you must know.*

must² *n* **a must** *infml* something that is necessary or very important: *Warm clothes are a must in the mountains.*

mus·tache /mə'stɑːʃ ‖ 'mʌstæʃ/ *n* see MOUSTACHE

mus·tard /'mʌstəd ‖ -ərd/ *n* [U] a yellow-flowered plant; mustard seeds produce a hot-tasting powder which is eaten with some kinds of meat

mus·ter /'mʌstər/ *v* **1** [I;T] to gather in one place: *The troops mustered on the hill.* | *Will you muster the troops?* **2** [T] (also **muster** sthg ↔ **up**) to find as much of something as possible: *I'm trying to muster up the courage to speak to her.*

must·n't /'mʌsənt/ *v* short for 'must not': *You mustn't talk in class.*

must·y /'mʌsti/ *adj* **mustier, mustiest** smelling unpleasant, often because of age or lack of fresh air: *musty old books* | *a musty room* –**mustiness** *n* [U]

mu·ta·tion /mju:'teɪʃən/ *n* [C;U] the action of change in the cells of a living thing

mute¹ /mju:t/ *adj* silent, often because you are unable to speak –**mutely** *adv*

mute² *n* a person who cannot speak

mut·ed /'mju:tɪd/ *adj* made softer than is usual (used of a sound or a colour)

mu·ti·late /'mju:tɪ̩leɪt/ *v* **mutilated, mutilating** [T] to damage something, usually by removing a part of it: *The police found a badly mutilated body.* –**mutilation** /ˌmju:tɪ'leɪʃən/ *n* [C;U]

mu·ti·neer /ˌmju:tɪ'nɪər, -tən'ɪər/ *n* a person who takes part in a mutiny

mu·ti·nous /'mju:tɪnəs, -tən-/ *adj* dissatisfied and refusing to obey orders: *A number of crew members are becoming mutinous.* –**mutinously** *adv*

mu·ti·ny¹ /'mju:tɪni, -təni/ *n* **mutinies** [C;U] the act of taking power away from the person in charge, especially from a captain on a ship

mutiny² *v* **mutinied, mutinying** [I] to take part in a mutiny: *The crew has mutinied and taken over the ship.*

mut·ter /'mʌtər/ *v* [I;T] to speak in a low voice, often expressing anger or dissatisfaction: *He muttered a threat.* | *She was muttering to herself.* –**mutter** *n* [sing]

mut·ton /'mʌtn/ *n* [U] the meat from a sheep –see MEAT (USAGE)

mu·tu·al /'mju:tʃuəl/ *adj* **1** shared by two people and directed towards each other (used of feelings): *Stalin and Trotsky were mutual enemies.* | *their mutual dislike* –**mutually** *adv* **2** shared by two or more people: *We have a number of mutual interests.* | *our mutual friend*

muz·zle¹ /'mʌzəl/ *n* **1** the front part of an animal's face, including its nose and mouth **2** a covering

round an animal's mouth, to prevent it from biting people **3** the front end of a gun

muzzle² *v* **muzzled, muzzling** [T] **1** to put a muzzle on an animal **2** to stop someone talking about something: *It is a worrying attempt to muzzle the press.*

my /maɪ/ *det* relating to or belonging to the person who is speaking: *I went in and sat down in my chair.* | *I was sitting drinking my coffee.*

my·o·pic /maɪ'ɒpɪk, -'əʊpɪk ‖ -'ɑːpɪk/ *adj* unable to see distant objects clearly

myr·i·ad /'mɪriəd/ *n lit* a great number and variety of things –**myriad** *adj*

my·self /maɪ'self/ *pron* **1** used as the object of a verb or a PREPOSITION when the subject of a verb is the person who is speaking and the action is done to the same person: *I washed myself and got dressed.* | *I looked at myself in the mirror.* | *I decided to buy myself some new clothes.* **2** used to add force to the word "I": *I myself admit that it's not my best painting.* | *I did all the decorating myself.* **3 by myself** alone, with no-one with me or helping me: *I had spent the day by myself.* | *I had managed to mend the roof by myself.*

mys·te·ri·ous /mɪ'stɪəriəs/ *adj* not easily understood: *the mysterious disappearance of my brother* | *They're being very mysterious about their holiday plans.* –**mysteriously** *adv* –**mysteriousness** *n* [U]

mys·te·ry /'mɪstəri/ *n* **mysteries** **1** [C] something which cannot be explained or understood: *Her death is a mystery.* **2** [U] a strange secret quality: *stories full of mystery*

mys·tic /'mɪstɪk/ *n* a person who practises mysticism

mys·tic·al /'mɪstɪkəl/ *adj* (also **mystic**) **1** concerning mysticism **2** concerning hidden religious power and importance –**mystically** /-kli/ *adv*

mys·ti·cis·m /'mɪstɪ̩sɪzəm/ *n* [U] a search for God or religious knowledge through prayer

mys·ti·fy /'mɪstɪ̩faɪ/ *v* **mystified, mystifying** [T] to make someone confused and unable to understand things: *I'm completely mystified about what happened.* | *Physics mystifies me.* –**mystification** /ˌmɪstɪfɪ'keɪʃən/ *n* [C;U]

mys·tique /mɪ'stiːk/ *n* [U] a sense of mystery which surrounds certain things, people, or professions: *the mystique of the film industry*

myth /mɪθ/ *n* **1** [C] an old story, often containing religious or magical ideas, which may explain natural or historical events **2** [U] such stories generally: *an idea common in myth* **3** [C] a false story or idea, which may be widely believed: *It's a myth that men are better drivers than women!*

myth·i·cal /'mɪθɪkəl/ *adj* **1** concerning myths or coming from a myth **2** not real

my·thol·o·gy /mɪ'θɒlədʒi ‖ -'θɑː-/ *n* **mythologies** [C;U] stories made up in the past to explain events –**mythological** /ˌmɪθə'lɒdʒɪkəl ‖ -'lɑː-/ *adj*

N,n

N, n /en/ **N's, n's** or **Ns, ns** the 14th letter of the English alphabet

N a written abbreviation for NORTH(ERN)

'n' /ən/ short for AND: *rock 'n' roll*

nab /næb/ v **-bb-** [T] *infml* to catch someone or take something quickly: *The thief was nabbed as he rushed out of the bank.* | *Nab that table over there and I'll get the drinks.*

nag¹ /næg/ v **-gg-** [I;T] to try to make someone do something by continuously complaining: *I wish you'd stop nagging – I'm doing my best.* | *She's been nagging me for ages to take her to the theatre.* | *They finally nagged me into taking them to the zoo.*

nag² n a horse that is old or in bad condition

nag·ging /'nægɪŋ/ adj [only before a noun] worrying or annoying you continuously: *a nagging headache* | *a nagging doubt*

nail¹ /neɪl/ n **1** a thin pointed piece of metal which you hammer into a wall or two pieces of wood to fasten them together **2** (also **fingernail** or **toenail**) the hard flat substance that covers the top of the end of each finger and toe **3 a nail in someone's coffin** something bad which, with other bad things, might gradually bring failure to someone

nail² v [T] **1** (+ adv/prep) to fasten with a nail or nails: *She nailed a sign to the tree.* | *We must nail up the windows of the old house.* **2** *infml* to catch or trap: *They've finally nailed the thief.*
nail down phr v **1** [T] **nail** sthg ↔ **down** to fasten down, with a nail or nails: *Will you nail down the carpet?* | *Shall I nail the lid down?* **2** [T **nail** sbdy ↔ **down**] *infml* to force someone to agree to something or to tell you what they are thinking: *Before they repair the car, nail them down to a price.* | *I can never nail her down.*

nail·brush /'neɪlbrʌʃ/ n a small stiff brush for your fingernails

nail file /'· ·/ n a small flat piece of metal with a rough surface for shaping your fingernails

nail pol·ish /'· ˌ··/ n see NAIL VARNISH

nail var·nish /'· ˌ··/ BrE (**nail polish** AmE) n [U] coloured or transparent liquid which can be painted on fingernails

na·ive /naɪ'iːv ‖ nɑː'iːv/ adj (also **naïve**) showing a lack of worldly experience in what you believe and say: *They laughed at his naive remarks.* | *He told her he was a millionaire and she was naive enough to believe him.* **–naively, naively** adv **–naivety, naivety, naiveté** n [U]

na·ked /'neɪkɪd/ adj **1** without any clothes on: *a naked body* **2** without any covering: *a naked lightbulb* | *a naked flame* **3** not hidden or covered up: *the naked truth* | *naked fear* **4 with the naked eye** without any instrument to help you see: *Bacteria are too small to see with the naked eye.*

name¹ /neɪm/ n **1** [C] the word or words that someone or something is known by: *What's your name?* | *I've forgotten the name of the company.* | *Please print your full name and address at the top of your exam paper.* **2** [sing] the opinion other people have of something: *That firm's got a good name for reliability.* | *The slow service gave the restaurant a bad name.* **3** [C] *infml* a well known person: *He's a big name around here.* **4 by name** using or saying the name of someone: *It's a big firm but she knows everyone by name.* **5 make a name for yourself** to become well known: *She's made a name for herself as a designer.* **6 have something to your name** *infml* to own something: *He hasn't a penny to his name.*

name² v **named, naming** [T] **1** to give a name to someone: *They named their baby son Philip.* **2** to say what the name of someone or something is: *Can you name this plant?* **3** to choose or appoint: *"When are you going to take me out to dinner?" "Just name the day!"* | *She's just been named as the new manager.* **4 name someone after someone else** to give someone the same name as someone else: *They named him after his grandfather.*

name-drop /'neɪmdrɒp ‖ -drɑːp/ v **-pp-** [I] to talk about famous or important people as if you know them so that other people will admire you (a word used to express disapproval) **–namedropping** n [U]

name·less /'neɪmləs/ adj **1** having no name or no known name: *the work of a nameless 13th century poet* | *a nameless tomb* **2** whose name you decide not to mention: *I was told by a certain politician who will remain nameless.* **3** too terrible to describe: *guilty of nameless crimes*

name·ly /'neɪmli/ adv that is to say: *Only one person can do the job, namely you.*

name·sake /'neɪmseɪk/ n someone who has the same name as someone else: *I often get letters that are addressed to my namesake down the street.*

nan·ny /'næni/ n **nannies** a woman employed to take care of children in a family

nanny goat /'·· ·/ n a female GOAT

nap /næp/ n **1** a short sleep during the day: *Grannie likes to have a short nap after lunch.* **2** the short fine threads or hairs on the surface of some cloth, which are brushed in one direction

na·palm /'neɪpɑːm ‖ -pɑːm, -pɑːlm/ n [U] a jelly made from petrol, which burns fiercely and is used in bombs

nape /neɪp/ n [sing] the back of your neck

nap·kin /'næpkɪn/ n a square piece of cloth or paper used for protecting your clothes and for cleaning your hands and lips during a meal

nap·py /'næpi/ BrE n **nappies** a piece of soft cloth or paper worn between a baby's legs and around its bottom to hold its URINE and FAECES

nar·cis·sus /nɑː'sɪsəs ‖ nɑːr-/ n **narcissuses** or **narcissi** a family of white or yellow spring flowers, including the DAFFODIL

nar·cot·ic¹ /nɑː'kɒtɪk ‖ nɑːr'kɑː-/ n narcotics drugs which in small amounts cause sleep or take away pain, and in large amounts are harmful and habit-forming: *The illegal trade in narcotics is growing.*

narcotic² adj **1** taking away pain or causing sleep **2** [only before a noun] concerning or related to drugs

nar·rate /nəˈreɪt ‖ ˈnæreɪt, næˈreɪt, nə-/ v **narrated, narrating** [T] *fml* to tell a story –**narration** /nəˈreɪʃən ‖ næ-, nə-/ n

nar·ra·tive /ˈnærətɪv/ n **1** [C;U] a story or account of events **2** [U] the art of telling a story: *She's very good at narrative.* –**narrative** *adj* : *a narrative poem*

nar·ra·tor /nəˈreɪtəʳ ‖ ˈnæreɪ-, næˈreɪtər, nə-/ n someone in some books, television shows, or plays who tells the story or explains what is happening

nar·row¹ /ˈnærəʊ/ *adj* **1** small in distance from one side to the other, in comparison with length or with what is usual: *a narrow street* | *The gate is too narrow for a car to get through.* –see THIN¹ (USAGE) **2** not including many people, ideas, or other important facts, which is usually regarded as a bad thing: *a narrow group of friends* | *She has a very narrow view of religion.* **3** only just successful: *to win by a narrow majority* | *a narrow escape* –**narrowness** n [U]

narrow² v [I] **1** to become narrower: *The river narrows at this point.* **2** [I;T] to make a difference smaller: *The tax aims to narrow the gap between rich and poor.*

narrow sthg/sbdy ↔ **down** *phr v* [T] to reduce the number of things that you have to consider or deal with: *The police have now narrowed down their list of suspects.* | *I've narrowed the potential candidates down to three.*

nar·row·ly /ˈnærəʊli/ *adv* only just: *We narrowly missed hitting that car!*

narrow-mind·ed /ˌ··ˈ··◂ ‖ ˈ·· ˌ··/ *adj* unwilling to accept or try to understand ideas that are new or different from your own (a word used to express disapproval): *His views are very narrow-minded.* –opposite **broadminded** –**narrowmindedness** n [U]

na·sal¹ /ˈneɪzəl/ *adj* **1** related to the nose: *We breathe through our nasal passages.* –**nasally** *adv*

nasal² n *tech* a speech sound such as /m/, /n/, or /ŋ/ made through the nose –**nasal** *adj*

nas·ty /ˈnɑːsti ‖ ˈnæsti/ *adj* **nastier, nastiest 1** unpleasant to see, taste, smell, touch, or experience: *nasty weather* | *a nasty smell* **2** unkind or unpleasant in manner: *a nasty temper* | *He turned nasty when I said I couldn't pay him.* **3** serious, and causing people to be hurt or killed: *a nasty accident with one person killed* | *a nasty cut on the head* | *It gave me a nasty shock.* **4** in bad taste: *cheap and nasty furniture* –**nastily** *adv* –**nastiness** n [U]

na·tion /ˈneɪʃən/ n a large group of people living in one country usually with an independent government, and sharing the same history: *the African nations* | *The Queen spoke to the nation.*

na·tion·al¹ /ˈnæʃənəl/ *adj* **1** of or for the whole of one country: *a national holiday* **2** owned or controlled by the central government of a country: *a national bank* **3** typical of the people of a nation: *national dress* | *the national characteristics of the Welsh* **4 national anthem** the official song of a nation, which is sung or played on certain formal occasions **5 national service** the system of making young people in some countries serve in the armed forces for a limited period **6 National Health Service** see NHS **7 National Insurance** a system

of insurance in Britain which is run by the government, into which workers and employers make regular payments, and which provides money for people who are unemployed, old, or ill **8 national park** a large area of attractive country, beautiful plants, and wild animals which are protected by the government so that people can visit them –**nationally** *adv*

national² n someone living abroad who belongs to another country: *American nationals in England* | *foreign nationals*

na·tion·al·is·m /ˈnæʃənəlɪzəm/ n [U] **1** love of and pride in your country which sometimes makes people believe unfairly that their country is better than others **2** desire by a racial group to form an independent country: *Scottish nationalism*

na·tion·al·ist /ˈnæʃənəlɪst/ n someone who believes their racial group or part of the country should form an independent country: *a Basque nationalist* –**nationalist** *adj* : *the nationalist party in Wales*

na·tion·al·is·tic /ˌnæʃənəˈlɪstɪk◂/ *adj* showing a great love of your country because you think it is better than others (a word used to express disapproval): *a nationalistic election speech* –**nationalistically** /-kli/ *adv*

na·tion·al·i·ty /ˌnæʃəˈnælɪti/ n **nationalities** [C;U] the fact of belonging to a particular country: *She lives in France but has British nationality.* | *people of many different nationalities*

na·tion·al·ize /ˈnæʃənəlaɪz/ v **nationalized, nationalizing** (also **nationalise** *BrE*) [T] (of a central government) to buy or take control of a business or industry for the state: *The British government nationalized the railways in 1948.* –**nationalization** /ˌnæʃənəlaɪˈzeɪʃən ‖ -nələ-/ n [U]

na·tion·wide /ˌneɪʃənˈwaɪd◂/ *adj,adv* happening over a whole country: *a nationwide search* | *The speech will be broadcast nationwide.*

na·tive¹ /ˈneɪtɪv/ *adj* **1** [only before a noun] connected with where you were born: *her native language* | *He was never popular in his native Australia.* **2** first found in a particular place and not brought there by anyone: *a plant native to the eastern USA* | *Pandas are native to China.* **3** belonging to someone's character from birth and therefore not learned: *native ability* | *native intelligence* **4** [only before a noun] *old fash* belonging to the people of poor non-European countries when considered by people who think Western customs are better: *a native village* **5 native speaker** someone who has learnt a particular language from birth: *a native speaker of English*

native² n **1** someone who was born in a place: *a native of New York City* **3** *old fash* a poor non-European person living in their own country where Europeans consider themselves to be better in some way: *The government of the island treated the natives badly.* **2** a plant or animal living naturally in a place: *The bear was once a native of Britain.*

Na·tiv·i·ty /nəˈtɪvɪti/ n **the Nativity** the birth of Christ

NATO /ˈneɪtəʊ/ n a group of countries including the USA and Britain which give military help to each other; an abbreviation for **North Atlantic Treaty Organization**

nat·ter /ˈnætəʳ/ v [I] *infml* to talk for a long time about unimportant things: *She nattered on about her holiday.* –**natter** n [sing] : *We had a good natter.*

nat·ty /ˈnæti/ *adj* **nattier, nattiest** *infml* neat in appearance: *He's a very natty dresser.* –**nattily** *adv*

nat·u·ral¹ /ˈnætʃərəl/ adj **1** not caused, made, or controlled by people: *the natural mineral wealth of a country* | *death from natural causes* **2** usual or expected: *It's natural to feel nervous when you have an exam.* | *It's natural for her to feel upset.* | *She's the natural choice for the job.*
□ USEFUL PATTERNS it is natural to do something; it is natural for someone to do something **3** [only before a noun] having a skill or ability from birth without being taught: *a man with a lot of natural charm* | *a natural musician* **4** not looking or sounding different from usual: *Try to look natural for your photograph.* **5 natural gas** gas which is taken from under the earth or sea and mainly burnt for cooking and heating **6 natural history** the study of plants, animals, and rocks **7 natural resources** the land, forests, and mineral wealth that a country possesses **8 natural science** one of the sciences which deal with the natural world, BIOLOGY, chemistry, and PHYSICS **9 natural selection** the process by which only the plants and animals best suited to the conditions around them continue to live **–naturalness** n [U]

natural² n infml someone who can do something very well without studying or learning: *As an actor, he's a natural.*

nat·u·ral·ist /ˈnætʃərəlɪst/ n a person who studies plants, birds, or animals

nat·u·ral·ize /ˈnætʃərəlaɪz/ v **naturalized, naturalizing** (also **naturalise** BrE) [T] to make someone born in one country a citizen of a different country: *He was naturalized after living in Britain for ten years.* **–naturalization** /ˌnætʃərəlaɪˈzeɪʃən ‖ -lə-/ n [U]

nat·u·ral·ly /ˈnætʃərəli ‖ -tʃərəli, -tʃərli/ adv **1** not made or caused by anyone: *Her cheeks are naturally red.* | *Mould occurs naturally in damp places.* **2** having a quality with which you were born *She's just naturally clever.* **3** without trying to look or sound different from usual: *Try to speak naturally while I'm taping you.* **4** of course: *"Did you win the game?" "Naturally."* | *Naturally you will want to discuss the proposal with your wife.* **5** as an expected development: *That will lead naturally into the subject of money.* **6 come naturally to someone** to be easy for someone: *Swimming seems to come naturally to him.*

na·ture /ˈneɪtʃəʳ/ n **1** [U] everything that exists in the world which is not made or controlled by people, such as earth, rocks, the weather, plants, and animals: *Farming on such bad land is a struggle against nature.* **2** [C;U] the particular qualities or character of someone: *She is generous by nature.* | *It's not in her nature to be rude.* | *What is the nature of the new chemical?* | *It's only human nature to want more money.* **3** [sing] a kind: *ceremonies of a solemn nature* | *He's an engineer or something of that nature.* **4 in the nature of** things as may be expected: *In the nature of things there's bound to be the occasional accident.*

naugh·ty /ˈnɔːti ‖ ˈnɔːti, ˈnɑːti/ adj **naughtier, naughtiest 1** behaving badly, or not obeying a parent, teacher, or set of rules (used of children): *You naughty boy! I told you not to play in the road.* **2** slightly rude or morally offensive: *a naughty joke* **–naughtily** adv **–naughtiness** n [U]

nau·se·a /ˈnɔːziə, -siə ‖ -ziə, -ʃə/ n [U] a feeling of sickness and desire to throw up the contents of your stomach through your mouth

nau·se·ate /ˈnɔːzieɪt, -si- ‖ -zi, -ʒi-/ v **nauseated, nauseating** [T] **1** to make you feel sick: *That smell nauseates me.* **2** to make you feel strong dislike: *The way he treats his wife nauseates me.* **–nauseating** adj : *a nauseating meal* | *nauseating stupidity*

nau·se·ous /ˈnɔːziəs, -siəs ‖ -ziəs, -ʃəs/ adj sick with a desire to throw up the contents of your stomach: *I felt nauseous in the cabin of the boat.*

nau·ti·cal /ˈnɔːtɪkəl/ adj relating to ships, or sailing

nautical mile /ˌ··· ˈ·/ n a measure of distance, used at sea, equal to 1,852 metres

na·val /ˈneɪvəl/ adj relating to the navy or ships of war: *a naval officer* | *naval battles*

nave /neɪv/ n the long central part of a church where the people sit

na·vel /ˈneɪvəl/ n a small sunken place in the middle of your stomach, left when the connection to your mother was cut at birth

nav·i·ga·ble /ˈnævɪɡəbəl/ adj deep and wide enough to allow ships to travel (used of water): *The St Lawrence River is navigable from the Great Lakes to the sea.*

nav·i·gate /ˈnævɪɡeɪt/ v **navigated, navigating** [I;T] to calculate your position and the direction you should travel in, for example by using a map

nav·i·ga·tion /ˌnævɪˈɡeɪʃən/ n [U] the planning and directing of the movements of ships or planes: *Navigation is difficult on this river because of the rocks.*

nav·i·ga·tor /ˈnævɪɡeɪtəʳ/ n the officer on a ship or aircraft who plans and directs its movements

na·vy /ˈneɪvi/ n **1 the Navy** [+ sing/pl verb] the part of a country's military forces that fights at sea: *The Navy want to recruit more officers.* **2** the ships of war belonging to a country: *a small navy of ten ships*

navy blue /ˌ·· ˈ·◂/ adj, n [U] (also **navy**) a colour which is very dark blue –see picture on page 50

NB read what follows carefully (used in writing to begin a note); an abbreviation for the Latin phrase **nota bene**

NCO /ˌen siː ˈəʊ/ n an abbreviation for NON-COMMISSIONED OFFICER

NE a written abbreviation for NORTHEAST(ERN)

near¹ /nɪəʳ/ adj **1** not far away from something: *She walked to the nearest tree and picked an apple.* | *My office is quite near.* | *We're hoping this will happen in the near future.* –see picture on page 540 **2** close in relationship: *He's one of my nearest relatives.* **3** [only before a noun] closer: *the near bank of the river* ■ USAGE **Near** and **close** have almost the same meaning, but in some phrases you must use one word and not the other. We say *the near future* | *a near miss* (not **close**). But we say *a close friend* | *close behind* (not **near**).

near² adv, prep not far away in place or time: *people who live near London* | *We live quite near to the church.* | *Don't go too near the edge.* | *Remind me again nearer the time.* | *The day of the interview was getting nearer.*

near³ v **1** [T] to move closer to something: *I started to feel quite nervous as we neared the town.* **2** [I] to come closer in time: *The time was nearing for me to leave.*

near·by /ˌnɪəˈbaɪ◂ ‖ ˌnɪər-/ adj, adv near to a place: *He lives in a nearby town.* | *Are there any shops nearby?*

near·ly /ˈnɪəli ‖ ˈnɪərli/ adv **1** almost: *I was nearly asleep.* | *She was ill for nearly a year.* | *He very nearly died.* **2 not nearly** not at all: *We haven't got nearly enough money.*

near·side /ˈnɪəsaɪd ‖ ˈnɪər-/ adj [only before a noun] on the side of a vehicle nearest to the edge of the road: *the nearside back light of a car*

near·sight·ed /ˌnɪəˈsaɪtᵻd◂ ‖ ˈnɪərsaɪtᵻd/ adj the usual American word for SHORTSIGHTED –**nearsightedness** n [U]

neat /niːt/ adj 1 arranged carefully or tidy: *neat handwriting* | *He keeps his office very neat and tidy.* | *What a neat child!* 2 simple and effective: *a neat trick* | *There are no neat solutions to this problem.* 3 without ice or any added liquid (used of alcoholic drinks): *I like my whisky neat.* 4 AmE infml very good or pleasant: *That was a neat party.* –**neatly** adv –**neatness** n [U]

neb·u·lous /ˈnebjᵿləs/ adj not clear (used of a plan or idea) *nebulous political beliefs*

ne·ces·sar·i·ly /ˈnesᵻsərᵻli, ˌnesᵻˈserᵻli ‖ ˌnesᵻ ˈserᵻli/ adv 1 **not necessarily** not always: *Food that looks good doesn't necessarily taste good.* 2 unavoidably: *New laws are necessarily difficult to make.*

ne·ces·sa·ry /ˈnesᵻsəri ‖ -seri/ adj 1 needed: *Food is necessary for life.* | *It's not necessary to wear a tie.* | *I'll leave you to make the necessary arrangements.* | *Is it necessary for me to be at the meeting?*
□ USEFUL PATTERNS it is necessary to do something; it is necessary for someone to do something 2 unavoidable: *the necessary conclusion* | *a necessary evil*

ne·ces·si·tate /nᵻˈsesᵻteɪt/ v necessitated, necessitating [T] fml to make something necessary: *Lack of money necessitated a change of plan.* | *This idea would necessitate starting all over again.*

ne·ces·si·ty /nᵻˈsesᵻti/ n necessities 1 [U] a need or condition which makes you do something: *Is there any necessity for another election?* | *We won't buy a car until the necessity arises.* | *There's no necessity to buy tickets in advance.* | *He was forced by necessity to steal a loaf of bread for his starving son.* 2 [C] something that you must have: *Food and clothing are the bare necessities of life.* 3 **of necessity** in a way that is unavoidable: *These examples are, of necessity, very short.*

neck /nek/ n 1 the part of your body which joins your head to your shoulders –see PAIN (USAGE) 2 the part of a garment, for example a dress or a shirt, that fits round your neck 3 a narrow part at one end of something broader: *the neck of a bottle* | *the neck of a violin* 4 **by a neck** infml winning or losing by a very short distance 5 **neck and neck** infml with an equal chance of winning (used of two people or animals in a race): *The horses were neck and neck to the finish.* | *The two candidates are neck and neck in the opinion polls.* 6 **up to your neck in** infml in or deeply concerned with a difficult situation: *I'm up to my neck in debt.* 7 **-necked** having a certain shape or style of neck: *a V-necked dress* | *an open-necked shirt*

neck·lace /ˈnek-lᵻs/ n a string of jewels or beads (BEAD), or a chain of gold or silver that a person wears around their neck –see picture on page 50

neck·line /ˈnek-laɪn/ n the position of the top of a dress or garment at or below your neck: *a low neckline*

SPELLING NOTE
Words with the sound /n/, may be spelt **kn-**, like **know**, or **pn-**, like **pneumonia.**

---

neck·tie /ˈnektaɪ/ n the usual American word for TIE

nec·tar /ˈnektəʳ/ n [U] 1 the sweet liquid collected by bees from flowers 2 the drink of the gods in ancient Greek and Roman literature

née /neɪ/ adv a word used to show what a woman's family name was before she got married: *Mrs Carol Cook née Williams*

need¹ /niːd/ n 1 [U] the situation in which something necessary or very useful is missing or wanted: *There's a growing need for new housing in this area.* | *This accident shows the need for stricter safety regulations.* 2 [C] something that you want or must have: *She didn't earn enough money to satisfy all her needs.* | *The hotel staff are here to attend to your every need.* 3 **in need** without enough food and money: *We are collecting money for children in need.* 4 **in need of something** wanting or needing something: *The doctor told me I was in need of a holiday.* | *Please come to me if ever you're in need of help.* 5 **if need be** if it is necessary 6 **no need for something** a phrase you use to say that something is not necessary or not wanted: *There's no need for you to be at the meeting.* | *There's no need for all that noise!*

need² v [not in progressive forms] negative short form **needn't** 1 [T] to want something that is necessary: *Children need milk.* | *The soup needs more salt.* | *I need a holiday.* | *That jumper needs a wash.* –see Study Note on page 392 2 **need to do something** to have to do something because it is necessary: *I need to talk to you.* | *We need to borrow some money.* | *You don't need to come if you don't want to.* 3 **need not do something, needn't do something** used when you are saying that something is not necessary or not wanted: *You needn't be afraid.* | *The government needn't become involved in this dispute at all.* | *Holidays abroad needn't be expensive.* | *You needn't shout at me like that!* | *If he had been given proper treatment he need not have died.*

nee·dle¹ /ˈniːdl/ n 1 a long pointed metal pin with a hole in one end for the thread, used in sewing 2 a thin pointed object: *a pine needle* 3 a long, thin pointed piece of plastic or metal used to make woollen garments: *knitting needles* 4 the very small pointed jewel in a RECORD PLAYER which picks up the sound from a record 5 a very thin hollow pointed tube, at the end of a SYRINGE, which is pushed into someone's skin to put medicine into their body 6 a long thin pointer that shows the reading on a measuring instrument: *the needle of a compass*

needle² v needled, needling [T] infml to annoy someone with repeated unkind remarks: *The boys always needled Jim about being fat.* | *They needled me into losing my temper.*

need·less /ˈniːdləs/ adj 1 unnecessary: *What a lot of needless trouble preparing for guests who don't turn up!* 2 **needless to say** of course: *Needless to say, it rained when I left my window open.* –**needlessly** adv

nee·dle·work /ˈniːdlwɜːk ‖ -wɜːrk/ n [U] decorative sewing: *two beautiful needlework cushion covers*

need·n't /ˈniːdnt/ short for "need not" *You needn't go if you don't want to.*

need·y /ˈniːdi/ adj needier, neediest 1 without good food, clothing, or housing: *a needy family* 2 **the needy** poor people: *I'm collecting money to help the needy.*

ne·far·i·ous /nɪˈfeəriəs/ adj fml immoral and wicked: *nefarious activities* –**nefariously** adv

neg·ate /nɪˈgeɪt/ v **negated, negating 1** [T] *fml* to take away the value or effect of something: *The new evidence negates all previous theories.* **2** to say that something does not exist –**negation** /nɪˈgeɪʃən/ n [C;U]

neg·a·tive¹ /ˈnegətɪv/ adj **1** saying or meaning "no": *a negative answer to my request | negative expressions like "not at all"* –opposite **affirmative 2** considering only the bad side of something: *Don't be so negative – I think we could still win. | a negative attitude* **3** showing no signs of what was looked for or expected: *Her pregnancy test was negative.* **4** less than zero (used of a number): *If x is positive then* –x *is negative.* **5** *tech* having the same type of electric charge as an ELECTRON –**negatively** adv

negative² n **1** a word, expression, or statement saying or meaning "no": *The answer to my request was a strong negative. | "Never" and "not at all" are negatives.* –opposite **affirmative 2** a photograph or film showing dark areas as light and light areas as dark and from which the pictures will be developed **3 in the negative** *fml* meaning "no": *He answered in the negative.*

ne·glect¹ /nɪˈglekt/ v **1** [T] to give too little attention or care to someone or something: *You've been neglecting your work recently.* **2** [I;T] to fail to do something because of carelessness or forgetfulness: *Don't neglect to lock the door when you leave. | They have neglected their duties.*
□ USEFUL PATTERNS to neglect something; to neglect to do something

neglect² n [U] **1** failure to take care of something properly: *The tenants complained about the landlord's neglect of the building.* **2** the condition something is in when it is not cared for: *The garden is in a state of neglect.*

ne·glec·ted /nɪˈglektɪd/ adj showing a lack of care or attention: *The children looked sad and neglected.*

ne·glect·ful /nɪˈglektfəl/ adj not giving enough attention to something: *a mother who is neglectful of her children | neglectful of your responsibilities*

neg·li·gee /ˈneglɪʒeɪ || ˌneglɪˈʒeɪ/ n a woman's light, fancy garment worn over a NIGHTDRESS

neg·li·gent /ˈneglɪdʒənt/ adj careless or irresponsible: *The doctor was negligent in not giving the woman a full examination.* –**negligently** adv –**negligence** n [U]: *The driver's negligence was the cause of the accident.*

neg·li·gi·ble /ˈneglɪdʒəbəl/ adj so small or unimportant that it need not be considered: *The damage to my car is negligible.*

ne·go·ti·a·ble /nɪˈgəʊʃiəbəl, -ʃə-/ adj **1** able to be settled or changed by talking: *The price is not negotiable.* **2** able to be exchanged for money (used of a cheque or order to pay money) **3** able to be travelled through or along: *The road is only negotiable in the dry season.*

ne·go·ti·ate /nɪˈgəʊʃieɪt/ v **negotiated, negotiating 1** [I] to try to come to an agreement through talking: *The government says it will not negotiate with the terrorists.* **2** [T] to produce an agreement or settle a piece of business through talking: *The trade union negotiated a new contract with the management.* **3** [T] to go safely over, through, or along something: *Will this small car negotiate that steep hill?*

ne·go·ti·a·tion /nɪˌgəʊʃiˈeɪʃən/ n [C;U] (also **negotiations**) talks in which people with different views try to agree: *Negotiations are still in progress. | the negotiation of new wage levels | The contract is under negotiation.*

ne·go·ti·a·tor /nɪˈgəʊʃieɪtər/ n someone who tries to get people with different views in business or politics to agree

Ne·gro /ˈniːgrəʊ/ n Negroes someone with dark or black skin (a word that is considered offensive)

neigh /neɪ/ v [I] to make the loud long cry of a horse –**neigh** n

neigh·bour /ˈneɪbər/ n (**neighbor** AmE) **1** someone who lives next to or near someone else: *my next-door neighbour | We're neighbours now.* **2** someone sitting next to you

neigh·bour·hood /ˈneɪbəhʊd || -ər-/ n (**neighborhood** AmE) **1** [C] a small area in a town and the people living there: *a quiet neighbourhood with good shops | a neighbourhood advice centre* **2 in the neighbourhood of** near or about: *a price in the neighbourhood of £500*

neigh·bour·ing /ˈneɪbərɪŋ/ adj (**neighboring** AmE) [only before a noun] situated near: *a bus service between the town and the neighbouring villages*

neigh·bour·ly /ˈneɪbəli || -ər-/ adj (**neighborly** AmE) friendly and helpful like a good neighbour –**neighbourliness** n [U]

nei·ther¹ /ˈnaɪðər || ˈniː-/ det, pron [used with a singular verb] not one and not the other of two people or things: *Neither solution is ideal. | Neither of the roads is very good. | "Will you have tea or coffee?" "Neither." | Neither of us wanted to go.*

neither² conj **1** used in negative expressions when you are saying that two or more things are not true: *He neither smokes nor drinks. | I was neither shocked nor upset. | I spoke to neither my father nor my mother. | I didn't want things to end like this, and neither did anyone else. | "I can't swim." "Neither can I."* **2 neither here nor there** not important: *The fact that he owns the building is neither here nor there.*

■ USAGE The word order after **neither** and **nor** is the same as the word order in a question: *Neither/Nor can I. | Neither/Nor does he.* –see EITHER (USAGE)

ne·o·lith·ic /ˌniːəˈlɪθɪk◂/ adj of a period of history about 10,000 years ago, when people began to settle in villages, grow crops, and keep animals

ne·on /ˈniːɒn || -ɑːn/ n [U] a chemically inactive gas that is present in small amounts in the air

neon light /ˈ·· ·/ n a glass tube filled with neon which lights when an electric current goes through it, often shaped to form a sign advertising something

neph·ew /ˈnevjuː, ˈnef- || ˈnef-/ n the son of your brother or sister or your brother-in-law or sister-in-law –see picture on page 343 –compare NIECE

nep·o·tis·m /ˈnepətɪzəm/ n [U] the practice of favouring your relatives when you have power by getting them good jobs

Nep·tune /ˈneptjuːn || -tuːn/ n the PLANET 8th in order from the sun

nerve¹ /nɜːv || nɜːrv/ n **1** [C] a very thin part inside your body which carries feelings and messages between your brain and different parts of your body **2 nerves** [pl] *infml* great excitement or nervousness: *She is in a state of nerves before every examination. | I must try and steady my nerves. | He's a bundle of nerves.* **3** [U] determination and courage: *I wanted to tell her what I thought of her but I lost my nerve. | You need a lot of nerve to be a rock climber.* **4** [sing;U] rudeness: *He's the dirtiest man I know, and he has the nerve to tell me my shoes need* *cleaning!* | *She's got a nerve asking to borrow money from my father.* **5 get on someone's nerves** to make someone annoyed or bad-tempered: *That loud music is getting on my nerves.*

nerve² *v* **nerved, nerving, nerve yourself** *fml* to give yourself courage: *The parachutist nerved himself to jump.* | *She nerved herself for the speech.*

nerve-rack·ing /'·ˌ··/ *adj infml* very worrying or frightening: *a nerve-racking journey through the high mountains*

ner·vous /'nɜːvəs ‖ 'nɜːr-/ *adj* **1** frightened or worried: *She's nervous of being left alone in that big house at night.* **2** tense and easily excited: *I'm always nervous before an interview.* | *a child full of nervous energy* **3** related to the nerves in your body: *a nervous disorder* **4 nervous breakdown** serious medical condition in which a person suffers from great anxiety, tiredness, and uncontrollable crying **5 nervous system** the system in people and animals made up of the brain, SPINAL CORD, and nerves, which receives and passes on feelings and messages from inside and outside the body **6 nervous wreck** someone who is very worried and anxious –**nervously** *adv* –**nervousness** *n* [U]

■ USAGE Compare **nervous, concerned, anxious.** You can be **nervous** (= rather afraid) before or during an event: *I'm always nervous when I have to go to the dentist.* You can be **concerned** (= worried) about something that is happening now, and often about another person: *We're rather concerned about your father's health.* **Anxious** usually means "worried about something which might happen": *I'm always anxious when the children go cycling on busy roads.*

nerv·y /'nɜːvi ‖ 'nɜːr-/ *adj* **nervier, nerviest** *infml* **1** *BrE* nervous and anxious **2** *AmE* disrespectfully rude

nest¹ /nest/ *n* **1** a hollow place or a structure built of branches, feathers, and leaves where a bird places its eggs and brings up its young **2** the home of certain other animals or insects: *an ants' nest* | *a wasps' nest* **3** a comfortable place: *They made the cottage into a cosy nest.* **4** a place where bad people or activities are safe: *a nest of intrigue* **5** a group of similar objects which fit closely inside one another: *a nest of tables*

nest² *v* [I] to build or use a nest: *Most birds nest in trees.*

nest egg /'· ·/ *n* an amount of money saved for future use

nes·tle /'nesəl/ *v* **nestled, nestling 1** [I + adv/prep; T + adv/prep] to settle warmly or comfortably often by pressing against something: *I'd love to nestle down in a big chair with a book.* | *She nestled her head on his shoulder.* **2** [I + adv/prep] to lie in a sheltered position: *The village nestled among the hills.*

net¹ /net/ *n* **1** [U] a material of strings, wires, or threads twisted, tied, or woven together with regular spaces between them: *net curtains* **2** [C] a piece of this woven material which is used for a particular purpose: *The fishermen put out their nets.* | *a butterfly net* | *The footballer kicked the ball into the net.* | *I'm hopeless at tennis – I'm always hitting the ball into the net.* | *a hair net* | *a mosquito net*

SPELLING NOTE

Words with the sound /n/, may be spelt **kn-**, like **know**, or **pn-**, like **pneumonia.**

---

net² *v* **-tt-** [T] **1** to catch something in a net: *We netted three fish.* **2** to cover something with a net: *You'll have to net those strawberries or the birds will get them.* **3** to get something by using skill: *She managed to net herself a rich husband.* **4** to gain as a profit when everything else has been paid: *The sale netted a fat profit for the company.* –compare GROSS³

net³ *adj* [only before or after a noun] (also **nett** *BrE*) **1** after all the things like tax, rent, and electricity have been paid: *net profit* **2** without the container or packet: *net weight* | *This jar of coffee weighs 350 grams net.* **3 net result** the result when everything has been considered: *The net result of this policy was even worse inflation.*

net·ball /'netbɔːl/ *n* [U] a game usually played by women in which teams of seven players win points by throwing a ball so that it falls through one of the two high rings at the opposite ends of a court

net·ting /'netɪŋ/ *n* [U] string, wire, or thread made into a net: *a fence of wire netting*

net·tle¹ /'netl/ *n* a wild plant with hairs on its leaves which may sting and make red marks on the skin

nettle² *v* **nettled, nettling** [T] *infml* to make someone annoyed: *I was rather nettled by his rudeness.*

net·work¹ /'netwɜːk ‖ -wɜːrk/ *n* **1** a large system of roads, wires, or lines of things that cross or meet one another: *Britain's railway network* | *the network of blood vessels in the body* **2** a group of people, companies, or organizations that are connected and work together: *a network of restaurants in different parts of the country* | *a spy network* **3** a group of radio or television stations in different places using many of the same broadcasts **4** a set of computers that are connected to each other and can be used as a means of sending and sharing information

network² *v* [T] to connect computers together to share information

neu·ro·sis /njʊ'rəʊsɪs ‖ nʊ-/ *n* **neuroses** /-siːz/ [C;U] *tech* an illness of the mind marked by strong unreasonable fears and ideas about the outside world

neu·rot·ic /njʊ'rɒtɪk ‖ nʊ'rɑː-/ *adj* unreasonably anxious or sensitive: *She's neurotic about her children's hygiene.* –**neurotic** *n*

neu·ter¹ /'njuːtər ‖ 'nuː-/ *adj* **1** related to a class of words which are neither MASCULINE nor FEMININE: *a neuter noun* **2** with no sexual organs, or undeveloped sexual organs (used of plants or animals): *Worker bees are neuter.*

neuter² *v* [T] to remove part of the sex organs of an animal by an operation

neu·tral¹ /'njuːtrəl ‖ 'nuː-/ *adj* **1** without strong feelings or opinions for or against something: *"Who do you want to win?" "Oh, I'm neutral."* | *neutral reporting of a political issue* **2** belonging to a country which is not fighting or helping either side in a war: *neutral waters* **3** of a very pale colour such as grey or cream: *The carpet is a neutral colour.* **4** containing no colour: *neutral shoe polish* **5** neither acid nor ALKALINE in chemistry **6** having no electrical charge (used of a wire) –**neutrally** *adv*

neutral² *n* **1** [U] the position of the gears (GEAR) in a car in which no power is carried from the engine to the wheels: *When you start the engine, be sure the car is in neutral.* **2** [C] a neutral person or country

neu·tral·i·ty /njuː'trælɪti ‖ nuː-/ *n* [U] the supporting of neither side in a disagreement or war

neu·tral·ize /'njuːtrəlaɪz ‖ 'nuː-/ *v* **neutralized, neutralizing** (also **neutralise** *BrE*) [T] **1** to stop something having an effect: *The acid was neutralized* with a base. | *High taxes will neutralize increased wages.* **2** to make a country or area neutral by international agreement –**neutralization** /ˌnjuːtrəlaɪˈzeɪʃən ‖ ˌnuːtrələ-/ n [U]

neu·tron /ˈnjuːtrɒn ‖ ˈnuːtraːn/ n a very small piece of matter that carries no electricity and that together with the PROTON forms the central part of an atom

nev·er /ˈnevəʳ/ adv **1** not at any time: *I've never been to Paris.* | *Never give your name and address to someone you don't know.* | *I shall never leave you.* | *She never finished the book she was writing.* **2 never ever** a stronger way of saying "never": *You must never ever tell anyone about this.*

nev·er·more /ˌnevəˈmɔːʳ◂ ‖ -vər-/ adv lit never again

nev·er·the·less /ˌnevəðəˈles ‖ -vər-/ adv in spite of what someone has just said: *The politicians admit that the tax is unpopular. Nevertheless they seem determined not to get rid of it.* | *Seat belts undoubtedly save lives. Many people, nevertheless, do not wear them.*

new /njuː ‖ nuː/ adj **1** recently produced, made, or built: *They're going to put 150 new houses in that field.* | *This idea isn't new.* | *Have you seen their new baby?* | *the newest fashions* | *a new system of drainage* **2** recently bought: *We're moving to our new house in May.* **3** not used or owned by anyone before: *They sell new and used cars.* | *a brand new bicycle* **4** only recently discovered: *new reserves of coal* | *important new evidence* **5 new to something** unfamiliar with something: *a young clerk new to the job* **6 new to someone** not known by someone: *The experience was new to me.* | *Her name is new to me.* **7** recently begun or joined: *He's just started at a new school.* | *new members of the club* **8** different or another: *I've got a new teacher.* | *They've gone to Australia to start a new life.* | *He wants to learn a new language.* **9** picked or dug up when small and young (used of a crop): *new potatoes* | *fresh new garden peas* **10 new blood, young blood** young members taken into an organization to give it fresh ideas: *We need new blood in this company.* **11 new moon** the bright thin edge of the moon seen at the beginning of its four-week cycle **12 new wave** a group of people who make a conscious effort to change the styles of art, music, photography, or film making **13 New Year, new year** the beginning of January: *Business should improve in the new year.* | *Happy New Year!* **14 New Year's Day** in Western countries, January 1st **15 New Year's Eve** in Western countries, December 31st **16 the New Testament** the second half of the Bible, which tells us about the teachings of Jesus Christ and his followers –compare OLD TESTAMENT **17 the New World** North, Central, and South America **18 new-** recently: *a newborn baby* | *a new-found friend* –**newness** n [U]

■ USAGE Compare **new**, **recent**, **modern**, **current**, **contemporary**. **New** is the general word for something that has only been in existence for a short time: *a new road*. **Recent** describes events that happened a short time ago: *our recent holiday*. **Modern** means "belonging to the present time or the not-too-distant past": *an examination in modern history, from 1789 to the present*. **Contemporary** means "belonging to the present": *contemporary art/music*. **Current** describes something that exists now, but was different before and may be different again: *The current fashion is for men to have short hair.*

new·com·er /ˈnjuːkʌməʳ ‖ ˈnuː-/ n someone who has recently come to a place or has started an activity:

a newcomer to the city | *I'm a newcomer to teaching.*

new·fan·gled /ˌnjuːˈfæŋɡəld◂ ‖ ˌnuː-/ adj (only before a noun) new and disapproved of by the person speaking (used of ideas or machines): *We need better teachers, not newfangled ideas of education!*

new-found /ˈ· ·/ adj recently made or discovered: *new-found friends* | *a new-found ability*

new·ly /ˈnjuːli ‖ ˈnuːli/ adv recently: *a newly built house* | *a newly qualified teacher*

new·ly·wed /ˈnjuːliwed ‖ ˈnuː-/ n a man or woman recently married: *You can tell they're newlyweds.* | *a newlywed couple*

news /njuːz ‖ nuːz/ n [U] **1** new information about a recent event: *I've got some news of the election results.* | *Have you heard the news about Mary? She's going to have a baby.* | *I'm afraid the news isn't very good.* **2 the news** a regular report of recent events broadcast on radio and television: *I'd like to see the news at 9 o'clock.* | *It'll be on the news this evening.* **3 that's news to me** infml a phrase used about something that you did not know which surprises you

news·a·gent /ˈnjuːzˌeɪdʒənt ‖ ˈnuːz-/ n **1** a person in charge of a shop selling newspapers and magazines: *The newsagent was shot by the thieves.* **2 newsagent's** a shop selling newspapers, magazines and sometimes sweets and cigarettes: *The newsagent's has got that new magazine.*

news·cast·er /ˈnjuːzkɑːstəʳ ‖ ˈnuːzkæ-/ n (also **newsreader** /-ˌriːdəʳ/) someone who reads the news on radio or television

news con·fer·ence /ˈ· ˌ···/ n a meeting during which an important person gives a statement to news reporters or answers questions

news-flash /ˈ· ·/ n a short news report on radio or television: *The programme was interrupted with a news-flash about the war.*

news·let·ter /ˈnjuːzˌletəʳ ‖ ˈnuːz-/ n a short report of news about a club or organization sent weekly or monthly to its members: *the company newsletter*

news·pa·per /ˈnjuːsˌpeɪpəʳ ‖ ˈnuːz-/ n **1** [C] (also **paper**) a set of large folded sheets of paper containing news, articles, and advertisements, printed and sold daily or weekly: *an evening newspaper* | *the Sunday newspapers* | *an interesting article in the newspaper* **2** [U] the paper on which newspapers are printed: *Wrap it up in newspaper.* **3** [C] a company which produces a newspaper: *He works for a national newspaper.*

■ USAGE Remember to use the preposition **in** for expressions such as: *I read it* **in the newspaper**. | *an advertisement* **in the Evening Standard**

news·print /ˈnjuːzˌprɪnt ‖ ˈnuːz-/ n [U] tech a cheap paper used mostly for printing newspapers on

news·reel /ˈnjuːzriːl ‖ ˈnuːz-/ n a short film of news made for showing in the cinema

news·stand /ˈnjuːzstænd ‖ ˈnuːz-/ n a table, often in a street or in a station, from which newspapers, and magazines are sold

news·wor·thy /ˈnjuːzˌwɜːði ‖ ˈnuːzˌwɜːrði/ adj important and interesting enough to be reported as news

newt /njuːt ‖ nuːt/ n a small four-legged animal with a long tail which can live on land and in water

next¹ /nekst/ adj **1** nearest: *They live in the next house.* | *I could hear music coming from the next room.* **2** coming straight after the present one: *If I miss this train I'll catch the next one.* | *Are you coming to our next meeting?* | *I'll see you next week.* **3 next best** the thing that is the best one except for one other

next² *adv* **1** just after something: *What will you do next?* **2** on the first occasion after this one: *I'll tell you the rest when I next see you.* **3** you use "next" when you move on to the following stage in a story that you are telling: *He took the scissors from the drawer and cut a small article from the newspaper. Next, he took a large file down from a shelf behind him.* **4** you use "next" when you move on to the next stage of a process you are describing: *The letters are taken to the sorting offices and sorted. Next, they are sent out to the main postal towns, where they are sorted again.* **5** you use "next" when you go on to the following instruction in a set of instructions: *You select the water temperature. Next, you put the detergent in.* **6** you use "next" when you move on to make another point in an argument: *So now we've got an idea of some of the social problems in the towns. Next, I'd like to have a look at some of the social problems in the villages.* **7 next to** close beside: *She was sitting next to Lucy.* –see picture on page 540 **8 next to nothing** almost nothing: *He earns next to nothing.*

next-door /ˌ·ˈ·◄/ *adj, adv* in the next building or room: *next-door neighbours* | *The director's office is next-door.* | *We live next-door to a cinema.*

next of kin /ˌ·ˈ·/ *n* [plural is **next of kin**] *law* [+ sing/pl verb] your closest relative or relatives: *Her next of kin have now been informed.*

NHS /ˌen eɪtʃ ˈes/ a system of medical treatment for everyone in Britain, paid for by taxes; an abbreviation for **National Health Service**: *Can I get my glasses on the NHS?*

nib /nɪb/ *n* the pointed piece on the end of a pen through which the ink flows

nib·ble /ˈnɪbəl/ *v* **nibbled, nibbling** [I;T] to eat slowly with small repeated bites: *Aren't you hungry? You're only nibbling at your food.* –**nibble** *n*

nice /naɪs/ *adj* **1** *infml* pleasant or pleasing: *Have a nice time at the party* | *a nice piece of work* | *a nice sunny day* | *This soup tastes very nice.* | *How nice to see you!* **2** kind or friendly: *She's the nicest person I know.* **3** *fml* showing or needing careful understanding: *a nice point of law* **4** *old fash* having high standards of moral and social behaviour: *Nice girls don't do that!* **5** **nice and** *infml* pleasantly: *The soup is nice and hot.* | *The speech was nice and short.* –**niceness** *n* [U]

■ USAGE In informal English **nice** is often used to add strength to another adjective which describes a pleasant quality. When the adjectives follow the verb "to be" (or a similar linking verb) they are joined by **and**: *The room was nice and cosy.* | *I know a restaurant where the food is nice and cheap.* | *You look nice and warm in that coat.* But when they come before the noun they should NOT be joined by **and**: *a nice cosy room* | *a nice warm coat* | *a nice big tip for the waiter*

nice·ly /ˈnaɪsli/ *adv* in a good, pleasant, kind, or skilful way: *smile nicely at the camera!* | *She always dresses nicely.* **2** in an exact, or delicate way: *a nicely calculated distance* **3 do nicely** be satisfactory: *"Here's £10." "Thank you. That will do nicely."* **4 doing nicely** doing well: *The injured man is doing nicely in hospital.* | *James in now financial director and doing very nicely for himself.*

SPELLING NOTE

Words with the sound /n/, may be spelt **kn-**, like **know**, or **pn-**, like **pneumonia**.

---

ni·ce·ty /ˈnaɪsəti/ *n* **niceties** a fine or delicate point: *We haven't time to consider all the niceties of the situation.* | *I wish she would try to observe the social niceties.*

niche /niːʃ, nɪtʃ ‖ nɪtʃ/ *n* **1** a hollow place in a wall, usually made to hold a piece of art **2** a suitable place, job, or position: *He's found a niche for himself in the book trade.*

nick¹ /nɪk/ *n* **1** a small accidental cut in a surface or edge **2 in good nick** *infml* in good condition [RELATED PHRASE **in bad nick**] **3 in the nick** *slang* in prison **4 in the nick of time** at the last possible moment: *I caught the baby in the nick of time before he fell down the stairs.*

nick² *v* [T] **1** to make or cut a nick in something: *I nicked my chin when I was shaving this morning.* **2** *infml* to steal something: *Someone's nicked my bicycle.* **3** *infml* to ARREST someone: *He was nicked as he ran out of the bank.*

nick·el /ˈnɪkəl/ *n* **1** [U] a hard silver-white metal that is used in the production of other metals **2** [C] a coin of the US and Canada worth five cents

nick·nack /ˈnɪknæk/ *n* see KNICK-KNACK

nick·name¹ /ˈnɪkneɪm/ *n* a name used informally instead of someone's own name, usually given because of their character or as a short form of the actual name: *"Mac" is just my nickname – my real name is MacDonald.*

nickname² *v* **nicknamed, nicknaming** [T] to give someone a nickname: *They nicknamed him "Fats" because of his weight.*

nic·o·tine /ˈnɪkətiːn/ *n* [U] a poisonous chemical contained in tobacco

niece /niːs/ *n* the daughter of your brother or sister or your wife's or husband's brother or sister –see picture on page 343 –compare NEPHEW

nif·ty /ˈnɪfti/ *adj* **niftier, niftiest** *infml* very attractive, or clever and useful: *That's a very nifty outfit you're wearing!* | *a nifty little gadget for squeezing oranges*

nig·gard·ly /ˈnɪɡədli ‖ -ər-/ *adj* **1** not generous, and unwilling to spend money or time (a word used to express disapproval): *a niggardly offer for such a good bicycle* | *a niggardly old man* –**niggardliness** *n* [U]

nig·ger /ˈnɪɡər/ *n* a black person (a word that is considered very offensive)

nig·gle¹ /ˈnɪɡəl/ *v* **niggled, niggling** **1** [I] to give too much attention to finding faults in small details: *She niggled over every detail of the bill.* **2** [T] to annoy or worry someone slightly but continually: *Her laziness constantly niggled him.*

niggle² *n* a small worry that you think about continually: *There's a niggle at the back of my mind about something but I can't remember what.*

nig·gling /ˈnɪɡəlɪŋ/ *adj* [only before a noun] **1** worrying or annoying you slightly but continually: *a niggling doubt* **2** needing too much attention to detail: *a niggling job*

nigh /naɪ/ *adv, prep* *old fash* **1** near **2 well nigh, nigh on** almost: *It's well nigh impossible to see any difference between the twins.*

night /naɪt/ *n* **1** [C;U] the dark part of each day, when the sun cannot be seen: *The nights are longer in winter.* | *Nurses have to work at night.* | *Night began to fall and we could no longer see what we were doing.* | *a few nights ago* | *Where were you on the night of 16th January?* | *The hotel charges £50 a night.* **2** [C;U] the evening: *We'll be out tomorrow night.* | *Let's go to the cinema on Saturday night.* **3** [C;U] the period when most people are sleeping: *I slept well last night.* | *She lay awake all night long.* **4** [C] a particular occasion or performance of something in the evening: *We're going to a Scottish Burns Night tonight.* | *the first night of a play* **5** [C] the evening of a holiday: *Christmas night* **6 by night** during the night: *I hate travelling by night.* **7 night after night** *infml* regularly every night: *He goes out drinking night after night.* **8 night and day, day and night** *infml* all the time **9 the other night** a few nights ago: *I saw David the other night.*

night·cap /ˈnaɪtkæp/ *n* **1** a drink taken before going to bed, usually alcoholic **2** a soft cloth cap that people used to wear in bed

night·club /ˈnaɪtklʌb/ *n* a club open late at night where people can eat, drink, dance, and often see a show

night·dress /ˈnaɪtdres/ *n* (also **nightgown** /ˈnaɪtɡaʊn/) a type of loose dress, which women and girls wear in bed –see picture on page 50

night·fall /ˈnaɪtfɔːl/ *n* [U] the time when it begins to get dark

night·ie /ˈnaɪti/ *n infml* a nightdress

nigh·tin·gale /ˈnaɪtɪŋɡeɪl/ *n* a brown European bird known for its beautiful song

night·life /ˈnaɪtlaɪf/ *n* [U] evening entertainment such as bars and nightclubs (NIGHTCLUB) in towns and cities

night·ly /ˈnaɪtli/ *adj,adv* happening every night: *a play performed nightly* | *a nightly news broadcast*

night·mare /ˈnaɪtmeəʳ/ *n* **1** a terrible dream **2** a terrible experience or event: *Driving through that snowstorm was a nightmare.* –**nightmarish** *adj*

night school /ˈ· ·/ *n* [C;U] a school or set of classes meeting in the evening, especially for people who have jobs during the day: *You can learn French at night school.*

night shift /ˈ· ·/ *n* **1** a period of time during the night, when people regularly work somewhere like a hospital or a factory: *I'm on the night shift this week.* **2 the night shift** [+ sing/pl verb] the group of workers who do the night shift: *The night shift is just coming off duty.*

night·time /ˈnaɪt-taɪm/ *n* [U] the time each day when it is dark –opposite **daytime**

night watch·man /ˌ· ˈ··/ *n* a man with the job of guarding a building at night

nil /nɪl/ *n* nothing or zero: *The new machine reduced labour costs to almost nil.* | *Our football team won by four goals to nil.*

nim·ble /ˈnɪmbəl/ *adj* **1** quick, light, and neat in movement: *a nimble climber* **2** able to think quickly: *a nimble mind* –**nimbleness** *n* [U] –**nimbly** *adv*

nin·com·poop /ˈnɪŋkəmpuːp/ *n infml* a stupid person

nine /naɪn/ *det, n, pron* **1** the number 9 **2 nine times out of ten** *infml* almost always

nine·teen /ˌnaɪnˈtiːn◂/ *det, n, pron* **1** the number 19 **2 talk nineteen to the dozen** *infml* to talk quickly and continuously –**nineteenth** *det, n, adv, pron*

nine·ty /ˈnaɪnti/ *det, n, pron* **nineties 1** the number 90 **2 the Nineties, the nineties** the years 1990–1999 **3** in her nineties, in their nineties, etc. aged between 90 and 99 –**ninetieth** /ˈnaɪntiˌθ/ *det, n, adv, pron*

nin·ny /ˈnɪni/ *n* **ninnies** *infml* a silly foolish person

ninth /naɪnθ/ *det, n, adv, pron* **1** 9th **2** one of nine equal parts

nip¹ /nɪp/ *v* **-pp- 1** [T] to catch in a tight sharp hold between two points or surfaces: *I nipped my finger in the door.* **2** [I;T] to take a small bite: *The dog has nipped the postman on the leg.* **3** [I + adv/prep] *BrE infml* to move or go quickly or for a short time: *I'll nip out and buy a newspaper.* | *Let's nip in there for a quick cup of tea.* **4 nip something in the bud** to stop something before it develops very much: *Her plans to go out were nipped in the bud when her mother arrived for the evening.*

nip² *n* [sing] **1** a coldness: *There's a nip in the air today: winter's coming.* **2** a small bite or PINCH: *I gave my fingers a nasty nip when I caught them in the door.* **3** *infml* a small amount of a strong alcoholic drink, usually spirits: *a nip of whisky*

nip·per /ˈnɪpəʳ/ *n infml* a small child

nip·ple /ˈnɪpəl/ *n* **1** the dark area in the middle of each of your breasts **2** *AmE* the piece of rubber on the end of a baby's bottle **3** something shaped like a nipple with a small opening for oil to come out of

nip·py /ˈnɪpi/ *adj* **nippier, nippiest** *infml* **1** rather cold (used of weather): *It's nippy this morning. I wish I had a coat.* **2** quick in movement: *My new car is really nippy.*

nit /nɪt/ *n* **1** an egg of an insect that is sometimes found in people's hair **2** *infml* a stupid person

nit-pick·ing /ˈnɪtˌpɪkɪŋ/ *n* [U] the paying of too much attention to small and unimportant details –**nit-pick·ing** *adj*

ni·trate /ˈnaɪtreɪt, -trˌt/ *n* [C;U] a chemical used to improve soil in order to grow crops

ni·tric ac·id /ˌnaɪtrɪk ˈæsˌd/ *n* [U] a powerful acid which eats away other substances and is used in explosives and other chemical products

ni·tro·gen /ˈnaɪtrədʒən/ *n* [U] a gas that has no colour or smell, and which forms most of the earth's air

ni·tro·gly·ce·rine /ˌnaɪtrəʊˈɡlɪsərˌn, -trə-, -riːn ‖ -rˌn/ *n* [U] (also **nitroglycerin**) a powerful liquid explosive

nit·wit /ˈnɪt-ˌwɪt/ *n infml* a silly foolish person

no¹ /nəʊ/ *det, adv* **1** used to show that you disagree with someone or something, or refuse to do something: *"Is it raining?" "No, but it's quite cold."* | *"She's got a new job, I think." "No she hasn't.* | *"Would you like a cup of tea?" "No thanks."* | *"Can I have a word with you?" "No, not at the moment."* **2** used to show that something is not allowed: *No Smoking.* **3** not any: *There's no sugar in the bowl.* | *There's no reason for you to worry.* –see SOME (USAGE) **4 oh no** a phrase used to show disappointment

■ USAGE Compare **no** and **not**. You can use **no** where the meaning is "not any": **no** *smoking* | **no** *children* | **no** *good.* For other meanings use **not**: *I'm* **not** *coming.* | **not** *a chance* | *She's* **not** *stupid.*

no² *n* a decision or an answer that says "no": *The answer was a definite no.*

no. nos. an abbreviation for NUMBER

no·bil·i·ty /nəʊˈbɪlˌti, nə-/ *n* **1 the nobility** the group of people in certain countries of the highest social class who have titles such as DUKE and EARL **2** [U] grandness and high moral qualities

no·ble¹ /ˈnəʊbəl/ *adj* **1** deserving praise and admiration because of unselfishness, honesty, and high morals: *noble and generous feelings* **2** admirable in appearance: *a noble monument* **3** of or belonging to a high social rank which has a title: *a woman of noble birth*

noble² *n old fash* a person of the highest social class

no·ble·man /'nəʊbəlmən/ *n* **noblemen** /-mən/ a titled man born into the highest social class; a woman in this social class or the wife of a nobleman is called a **noblewoman**

no·bly /'nəʊbli/ *adv* generously and unselfishly: *She nobly did my work as well as hers while I was ill.*

no·bod·y¹ /'nəʊbədi ‖ -,bɑːdi, -bədi/ *pron* (also **no one**) no person at all: *There's nobody here at the moment.* | *No one knew anything about it.* | *I spoke to Jane, but to nobody else.*

nobody² *n* **nobodies** someone who is not at all important: *I don't want to be a nobody all my life.*

noc·tur·nal /nɒk'tɜːnl ‖ nɑːk'tɜːr-/ *adj* **1** happening at night: *a nocturnal visit* **2** active at night: *a nocturnal bird* –**nocturnally** *adv*

nod /nɒd ‖ nɑːd/ *v* -**dd-** **1** [I;T] to move your head forward and down and then up again to show agreement or give a greeting: *She nodded her head when she passed me in the street.* | *I asked her if she was ready to go and she nodded.* | *They all nodded in agreement.* **2** [I;T] to show something or give a signal by nodding: *"Give it to him," she said, nodding towards the boy.* **3** [I] to move gently up and down: *The flowers nodded in the wind.*

nod off *phr v* [I] to fall asleep, often unintentionally: *The meeting was so boring I nodded off.* –**nod** *n* : *He greeted us with a nod.*

nod·ule /'nɒdjuːl ‖ 'nɑːdʒuːl/ *n* a small hard lump or swelling

No·el /nəʊ'el/ *n lit* Christmas

no-go ar·e·a /ˌ· '· ·,···/ *n infml* an area controlled by a group of people who make it dangerous for anyone else to enter

noise /nɔɪz/ *n* **1** [C;U] a sound, often unwanted, unpleasant, or confused: *Try not to make a noise when you go upstairs – the baby's asleep.* | *There's so much noise in this restaurant I can hardly hear you talking.* | *Seals make a very unusual noise.* | *The washing machine's been making funny noises lately.* **2** **make a noise about something** to complain about something: *She was making a lot of noise about the lack of child care facilities.* **3** **make all the right noises** to say things which suggest that you are interested, although sometimes you are not: *She made all the right noises about helping us, but I know she's too lazy to do anything.* **4** **make noises** *infml* to say something which indirectly shows your ideas or feelings: *My teacher made encouraging noises when I said I wanted to go to university.* ■ USAGE Compare **sound, noise, voice**. **Sound** is the general word for anything you hear: *the sound of voices|of music|of breaking glass.* A **noise** is usually a loud, unpleasant sound: *Stop making so much noise!* A **voice** is the sound of a person speaking or singing: *He spoke in a loud voice.*

noise·less /'nɔɪzləs/ *adj* making no sound: *The car was smooth and noiseless.* –**noiselessly** *adv*

nois·y /'nɔɪzi/ *adj* **noisier, noisiest** making a lot of noise: *a noisy car* | *It's very noisy in this office.* | *This is a very noisy pub.* | *a noisy group of tourists* –**noisily** *adv* –**noisiness** *n* [U]

no·mad /'nəʊmæd/ *n* a member of a tribe which does not live in one place but travels about, usually to find grass for its animals

no·mad·ic /nəʊ'mædɪk/ *adj* not living in one fixed place, but moving from place to place: *nomadic tribes* | *a nomadic way of life* –**nomadically** *adv*

no-man's-land /'· · ,·/ *n* [sing; U] the area of land which no one owns or controls between two borders or two opposing armies

nom de plume /ˌnɒm də 'pluːm ‖ ˌnɑːm-/ *n* **noms de plume** (*same pronunciation*) a name a writer uses instead of their real name

no·men·cla·ture /nəʊ'menklətʃəʳ ‖ 'nəʊmənkleɪ-/ *n* [C;U] *fml* a system of naming things, especially in science: *the nomenclature of chemical compounds*

nom·i·nal /'nɒmɪnəl ‖ 'nɑː-/ *adj* **1** in name or position but usually not in reality: *The old man is only the nominal head of the business; his daughter makes all the decisions.* **2** very small (used of an amount of money): *The rent for the cottage is nominal.* –**nominally** *adv*

nom·i·nate /'nɒmɪneɪt ‖ 'nɑː-/ *v* **nominated, nominating** [T] **1** to suggest or name someone formally for election to a position, office, or honour: *I wish to nominate Jane Morrison for president of the club.* | *I nominate Susan to represent us.* □ USEFUL PATTERNS to nominate someone for something; to nominate someone to do something **2** to appoint someone to a position, office, or duty: *The director nominated me as his representative at the conference.*

nom·i·na·tion /ˌnɒmɪ'neɪʃən ‖ ˌnɑː-/ *n* [C;U] **1** the formal suggestion that someone is appointed to a position: *His nomination as chief executive was approved by the board.* **2** someone's official appointment to a position: *He was delighted by his nomination to the committee.*

nom·i·na·tive /'nɒmɪnətɪv, 'nɒmnə- ‖ 'nɑː-/ *n tech* a particular form of a noun in certain languages, such as Latin, Greek, and German, which shows that a noun is the subject of a verb –**nominative** *adj*

nom·i·nee /ˌnɒmɪ'niː ‖ ˌnɑː-/ *n* a person who has been formally suggested for a position or honour

non-ag·gres·sion /ˌnɒn-ə'greʃən ‖ ˌnɑːn-/ *n* [U] the idea that countries should not attack or fight each other: *a non-aggression pact*

non-al·co·hol·ic /ˌ· ·· '···/ *adj* containing no alcohol: *non-alcoholic beer*

non-a·ligned /ˌ· ·'· ·/ *adj* not dependent on or supporting any particular powerful country or group of countries –**non-alignment** *n* [U]

non·cha·lant /'nɒnʃələnt ‖ ˌnɑːnʃə'lɑːnt/ *adj* showing calmness, lack of anxiety, and often lack of interest: *He showed a nonchalant attitude to his debts.* –**nonchalance** *n* [U] : *She showed a surprising nonchalance when she was awarded the trophy.* –**nonchalantly** *adv*

non-com·ba·tant /ˌnɒn'kɒmbətənt ‖ ˌnɑːnkəm'bætənt/ *n* someone in the armed forces who does not take part in actual fighting, for example a doctor

non-com·mis·sioned of·fi·cer /ˌnɒnkə,mɪʃənd 'ɒfɪsəʳ ‖ ˌnɑːn-, 'ɔːf-, 'ɑːf-/ *n* (also **NCO**) a member of the armed forces who has some responsibility to command others

non-com·mit·tal /ˌnɒnkə'mɪtl◄ ‖ ˌnɑːn-/ *adj* not expressing a clear opinion or intention: *I asked him if he approved of our plan, but he was noncommittal.* –**noncommittally** *adv*

non·con·form·ist /ˌnɒnkən'fɔːmɪst◂ ‖ ˌnɑːnkən'fɔːr-/ n **1** someone who does not follow generally accepted ways of living, acting, or thinking: *a political nonconformist | nonconformist views* **2** **Nonconformist** a member of one of the Christian religious groups which have separated from the CHURCH OF ENGLAND: *a Nonconformist minister* –**nonconformist** *adj* –**nonconformity, nonconformism** *n* [U]

non·de·script /'nɒndɪ̣ˌskrɪpt ‖ ˌnɑːndɪ̣'skrɪpt/ *adj* without any noticeable or interesting qualities: *Her clothes were so nondescript that I can't remember what she was wearing.*

none /nʌn/ *pron; adv* **1** not any: *None of the money is mine. | None of these subjects interests me. | None of my friends are going to university. | Even an old car is better than none at all.* **2 none but** *fml* only **3 none other than** a phrase used to show that you are surprised that it is the person mentioned: *I opened the door, and it was none other than Tom Robinson!* **4 none the** not at all: *He's got plenty of money now, but he seems none the happier for it.* **5 none too** not very: *She came out of the meeting looking none too pleased.*

■ USAGE When **none of** is followed by a plural noun it usually takes a plural verb in informal spoken English: **None of** *us* **are** *ready yet.* Some people, however, consider this to be incorrect and so in formal writing it is safer to use a singular verb: **None of** *our factories* **is** *in operation yet.*

non·en·ti·ty /nɒ'nentɪ̣ti ‖ nɑː-/ n **nonentities** someone without much ability, character, or importance: *a weak government, full of politicians who are nonentities*

nonetheless /ˌnʌnðə'les◂/ *adv* in spite of what someone has just said: *The government has introduced strict economic controls, but inflation has continued to rise nonetheless. | Profits have not been as good lately. Nonetheless, Regis are hoping to expand.*

non-e·vent /ˌ·'··/ n *infml* something that is much less important, interesting, or exciting than expected: *The party was a real non-event; only three people came.*

non-ex·ist·ent /ˌnɒng'zɪstənt◂ ‖ ˌnɑːn-/ *adj* not existing: *This year's profits were very small; in fact, almost non-existent.*

non-fic·tion /ˌnɒn'fɪkʃən ‖ ˌnɑːn-/ n [U] writing that is about real facts or events, rather than the imagined things in poetry, plays, and stories

non-flam·ma·ble /ˌnɒn'flæməbəl ‖ ˌnɑːn-/ *adj* difficult or impossible to burn

non-in·ter·ven·tion /ˌnɒnɪntə'venʃən ‖ ˌnɑːnɪntər-/ n [U] the practice, especially by a government, of taking no part in the affairs or arguments of another person or country

non-nu·cle·ar /ˌ·'····◂/ *adj* not using NUCLEAR power or ENERGY: *non-nuclear weapons*

no-non·sense /ˌ·'···◂/ *adj* practical and direct: *a no-nonsense approach to the problem*

non-pay·ment /ˌnɒn'peɪmənt ‖ ˌnɑːn-/ n [U] failure to pay bills, tax, or a debt: *They were taken to court for non-payment of rent.*

non-plussed /ˌnɒn'plʌst ‖ ˌnɑːn-/ *adj* surprised and uncertain what to think or do: *The speaker seemed completely nonplussed by my question.*

non-pro·lif·e·ra·tion /ˌnɒnprəˌlɪfə'reɪʃən ‖ ˌnɑːn-/ n [U] the limitation of the number and spread of NUCLEAR and chemical weapons: *a nonproliferation agreement*

non·sense /'nɒnsəns ‖ 'nɑːnsens/ n [U] **1** speech and writing with no meaning: *If you leave out this paragraph, the report is nonsense. | You're talking utter nonsense.* **2** a word you use when you think that someone is saying something silly and untrue: *"I can't go out dressed like this." "Nonsense, you look fine."* **3** foolish behaviour: *Stop that nonsense, children. | A strict teacher stands no nonsense from the pupils.* **4 make nonsense of, make a nonsense of** to make something seem pointless and useless: *Remarks like that make nonsense of his claim that he is unbiased.*

non·sen·si·cal /nɒn'sensɪ̣kəl ‖ nɑːn-/ *adj* stupid or full of nonsense: *nonsensical opinions* –**nonsensically** /-kli/ *adv*

non seq·ui·tur /ˌnɒn 'sekwɪ̣təʳ ‖ ˌnɑːn-/ n *fml* a statement which does not follow from the facts or arguments which have gone before

non-smok·er /ˌ·'··/ n someone who does not smoke –**non-smoking** *adj* : *the non-smoking section on the plane*

non-stan·dard /ˌnɒn'stændəd◂ ‖ ˌnɑːn'stændərd◂/ *adj* not usually regarded as correct by educated native speakers of a language (used of words, expressions, pronunciations)

non-start·er /ˌnɒn'stɑːtəʳ ‖ ˌnɑːn'stɑːrtər/ n *infml* a plan or idea without any chance of success: *The idea of buying a house was a non-starter, as we didn't have enough money.*

non-stick /ˌnɒn'stɪk◂ ‖ ˌnɑːn-/ *adj* having a specially treated smooth inside surface that food will not stick to: *a non-stick frying pan*

non-stop /ˌnɒn'stɒp◂ ‖ ˌnɑːn'stɑːp◂/ *adj, adv* without a pause or interruption: *The flight from London to Singapore is non-stop. | We worked nonstop for three days.*

non-vi·o·lence /ˌnɒn'vaɪələns ‖ ˌnɑːn-/ n [U] attempts to make political changes without using violence or hurting anyone –**non-violent** *adj* : *non-violent protest* –**non-violently** *adv*

noo·dle /'nuːdl/ n **noodles** long thin pieces of a paste made from flour, water, and eggs; the pieces are boiled until soft and eaten in soups, or with meat

nook /nʊk/ n **1** *lit* a sheltered and private place: *a shady nook in the garden* **2 every nook and cranny** every part of a place

noon /nuːn/ n 12 o'clock in the middle of the day: *We left home at noon. | I can't come before noon.*

noon·day /'nuːndeɪ/ n *old fash* in the middle of the day: *the noonday sun*

no one /ˈ· ·/ *pron* see NOBODY

noose /nuːs/ n a circle formed by the end of a cord or rope which closes more tightly as it is pulled

nor /nɔːʳ/ *conj* used in negative expressions when you are giving the second thing that is not true: *He neither smokes nor drinks. | I was neither shocked nor upset. | I spoke to neither my father nor my mother. | I wasn't pleased about what had happened, and nor was anyone else. | "I can't swim." "Nor can I."*

norm /nɔːm ‖ nɔːrm/ n **1 norms** [pl] ways of behaving that are regarded as usual or generally acceptable: *social norms | the norms of civilised society* **2 the norm** a situation that is regarded as average or usual: *Large families are no longer the norm in Western Europe. | a pay increase well below the national norm*

nor·mal /'nɔːməl ‖ 'nɔːr-/ *adj* expected, usual, or average: *normal working hours from nine to five | Rainfall has been above normal this July. | She is a normal child in every way.*

nor·mal·i·ty /nɔːˈmælɨti ‖ nɔːr-/ (also **normalcy** /ˈnɔːmælsi ‖ ˈnɔːr-/ AmE) n [U] a situation where everything is usual and as expected

nor·mal·ize /ˈnɔːmɘlaɪz ‖ ˈnɔːr-/ v **normalized, normalizing** (also **normalise** BrE) [I;T] to return something to a good or friendly state: Relations between the two countries were slow to normalize after the war. | You can normalize the situation by remaining calm. –**normalization** /ˌnɔːmɘlaɪˈzeɪʃən ‖ ˌnɔːrmɘlɘ-/ n [U]

nor·mal·ly /ˈnɔːmɘli ‖ ˈnɔːr-/ adv **1** in the usual or expected way: The factory is running normally again. **2** usually: I normally go to bed early, but I stayed up late last night.

north¹ /nɔːθ ‖ nɔːrθ/ n **1** [U] the direction to the left of someone facing the rising sun: I'm lost: which direction is north? | Cheshunt is a few kilometres to the north of London. **2 the North** the northern part of a country: The problem of unemployment is much worse in the North than in the South.

north² adj **1** (also **North**) in the north or facing the north: The north side of the house doesn't get much sun. | He lives in North Korea. **2 north wind** a wind coming from the north

north³ adv (also **North**) **1** towards the north: The room faces North, so it's always rather cold. | Edinburgh is a long way north of London. | Birds fly north in summer. **2** from the north (used of a wind)

north·bound /ˈnɔːθbaʊnd ‖ ˈnɔːrθ-/ adj travelling towards the north: northbound traffic

north·east¹ /ˌnɔːθˈiːst◂ ‖ ˌnɔːrθ-/ (also **Northeast**) n **1** [sing;U] the direction which is half-way between north and east **2 the northeast** the northeastern part of a country: Houses are cheaper in the northeast.

northeast² adj [only before a noun] **1** in the northeastern part of something: the northeast gate of the park **2 northeast wind** a wind coming from the northeast –**northeasterly** adj

northeast³ adv towards the northeast: The ship sailed northeast.

north·east·ern /ˌnɔːθˈiːstən◂ ‖ ˌnɔːrθˈiːstərn◂/ adj in or from the northeast part, especially of a country

nor·ther·ly /ˈnɔːðɘli ‖ ˈnɔːrðɘrli/ adj **1** towards the north: in a northerly direction **2** from the north (used of a wind)

nor·thern /ˈnɔːðən ‖ ˈnɔːrðərn/ adj (also **Northern**) of or in the north part of an area: The northern half of the Earth is called the Northern hemisphere.

nor·thern·most /ˈnɔːðənməʊst ‖ ˈnɔːrðərn-/ adj furthest north: the northernmost parts of Scotland

North Pole /ˌ· ˈ·/ n **the north pole** the most northern point on the surface of the earth

north·ward /ˈnɔːθwɘd ‖ ˈnɔːrθwɘrd/ adj going towards the north: a northward journey –**northwards** (also **northward** AmE) adv : We sailed northwards.

north·west¹ /ˌnɔːθˈwest◂ ‖ ˌnɔːrθ-/ (also **Northwest**) n **1** [sing;U] the direction which is halfway between north and west **2 the northwest** the northwestern part of a country –**northwesterly** adj

northwest² adj [only before a noun] **1** in the northwestern part of something: the northwest tower of the castle **2 northwest wind** a wind coming from the northwest

northwest³ adv towards the northwest: Birmingham is northwest of London.

north·west·ern /ˌnɔːθˈwestən◂ ‖ ˌnɔːrθˈwestərn◂/ adj in or from the northwest part, especially of a country

nose¹ /nəʊz/ n **1** the part of your face above your mouth through which you smell and breathe: He's got a broken nose. | She punched him on the nose. **2** the front part of something that sticks out, for example a car or plane **3 a nose for something** a special ability to find or recognize something: A newspaper reporter must have a nose for a good story. **4 stick/poke your nose into** to show too great an interest in things which do not concern you: Stop poking your nose into other people's affairs. **5 get up someone's nose** BrE infml to annoy someone very much **6 keep your nose to the grindstone** infml to continue with hard and dull work **7 turn up your nose at something** infml to consider something not good, interesting, or important enough for you **8 under someone's nose** infml right in front of someone: He passed me the note under the very nose of the examiner! **9 -nosed** having a certain shape of nose: red-nosed | broken-nosed | snub-nosed

nose² v **nosed, nosing** [I+adv/prep;T+adv/prep] to move or push ahead slowly or carefully: I nosed the car out into the traffic. | The ship nosed along the narrow channel. | The plane nosed its way down the runway.

nose about/around phr v [I] infml to look at things which do not belong to you for something of interest: I found her nosing about among my private papers.

nose·bag /ˈnəʊzbæg/ n a bag hung around a horse's head to hold its food

nose·bleed /ˈnəʊzbliːd/ n bleeding from the nose: James had a nosebleed earlier today after Simon hit him.

nose-dive /ˈnəʊzdaɪv/ v **nosedived, nosediving** [I] **1** (of an aircraft) to drop suddenly with the nose pointing straight down **2** (of prices and money) to go down a lot suddenly: Profits have nosedived in the last year. –**nosedive** n

nosh /nɒʃ ‖ nɑːʃ/ n BrE infml [U] food: Let's have some nosh before the film starts.

nos·tal·gia /nɒˈstældʒɘ ‖ nɑː-/ n [U] a feeling of fondness and sadness for the past: The old song filled me with nostalgia. –**nostalgic** adj –**nostalgically** /-kli/ adv

nos·tril /ˈnɒstrɘl ‖ nɑː-/ n one of two openings at the end of your nose, through which you breathe

nos·y /ˈnəʊzi/ adj **nosier, nosiest** (also **nosey**) interested in things that do not concern you (a word used to express disapproval): Don't be so nosy. –**nosiness** n [U]

not /nɒt ‖ nɑːt/ adv (also **n't** after verbs such as "be" and "have") **1** used for changing a word or expression to one with an opposite meaning: I'm not thirsty. | It's a fox, not a dog. | She said she wasn't frightened. | I'm afraid I'm not coming to the party. | I don't think that's very funny! | Not everyone likes this book. | "Is it going to rain?" "I hope not." **2 not a** not even one: Not a drop of rain has fallen this month. **3 not that** a phrase used when you are adding something which means that what you said before is less important: Where were you last night? Not that I care, of course. –see NO (USAGE)

no·ta·ble¹ /ˈnəʊtəbəl/ adj interesting, important, or excellent: *an area notable for its excellent climate* | *Most of the directors are men. Miss Parker is a notable exception.* –**notability** /ˌnəʊtəˈbɪləti/ n [U]

notable² n a famous or important person

no·ta·bly /ˈnəʊtəbli/ adv **1** especially or particularly: *A lot of people were absent:, notably the vice-chairman.* **2** noticeably: *Prices are notably higher this year.*

no·ta·tion /nəʊˈteɪʃən/ n [C;U] a system of showing numbers or musical notes in writing by using signs

notch¹ /nɒtʃ/ ‖ nɑːtʃ/ n **1** a V-shaped cut in a surface or edge: *He cut a notch in the stick with a sharp knife.* **2** infml a degree or level on a scale: *He went up a notch or two in my estimation when he helped my father.*

notch² v [T] to make a notch in something
notch sthg ↔ up phr v [T] infml to reach a total of: *The team notched up their third victory in a row.*

note¹ /nəʊt/ v noted:, noting [T; + that] fml to call attention to a particular fact: *Please note that this bill must be paid within ten days.* | *Note the way the writer uses the present tense for dramatic effect.* | *The report notes with approval the government's efforts to resolve this problem.*
note sthg ↔ down phr v [T] to write something down as a record or reminder: *He noted down my new address.*

note² n **1** [C] a written reminder of something: *Make a note of how much money you spend.* | *You don't need to take notes. I'll give you a handout at the end.* **2** [C] additional information about something in a book given at the bottom of a page or at the end **3** [C] a short informal letter: *I'll write her a note to thank her for dinner.* **4** [C] a single musical sound of a particular length and degree of highness or lowness or the written sign for it: *I can't sing the high notes.* **5** [sing] the suggestion of a particular feeling: *There was a note of anger in what he said.* | *The report ended on an optimistic note.* **6** [C] a piece of paper money: *a £5 note* **7** of note fml of fame or importance: *She's a musician of great note.* **8** take note of something to pay careful attention to something: *The committee took note of his objections.*

note·book /ˈnəʊtbʊk/ n a book in which you can make notes

not·ed /ˈnəʊtɪd/ adj well-known because of a special quality or ability: *a noted violinist* | *a town noted for its cheeses*

note·pa·per /ˈnəʊtˌpeɪpər/ n [U] paper for writing letters and notes on

note·wor·thy /ˈnəʊtˌwɜːði ‖ -ɜːr-/ adj interesting or worth paying attention to

noth·ing /ˈnʌθɪŋ/ pron **1** no thing or things: *There's nothing in this box.* | *She told me nothing about her plans.* | *By three o'clock I'd finished my work and had nothing to do.* **2** something that is not at all important: *£50 is nothing these days.* | *She means nothing to me.* **3** for nothing: a for no money: *When we bought the house we got all the furniture as well, for nothing.* b with no satisfactory result: *I realized that I had spent three years studying for nothing.* **4** nothing but only: *We could see nothing but trees and open fields.* **5** nothing like not at all: *It's nothing like as cold today as it was yesterday.* **6** nothing of the sort a phrase used to say that something is completely untrue: *They claim that these weapons are purely defensive, but they're nothing of the sort.* **7** nothing to do with having no connection with someone or something: *Keep out of this argument – it's nothing to do with you!* **8** there's nothing for it = there is nothing else that we can do: *There was nothing for it but to swim across the river.* **9** there's nothing in it = it is completely untrue **10** there's nothing to it = it is very easy

noth·ing·ness /ˈnʌθɪŋnəs/ n [U] the state of emptiness where nothing exists: *Is there only nothingness after death?*

no·tice¹ /ˈnəʊtɪs/ n **1** [C] a written or printed statement which gives information to the public: *The notice on the wall says "No Smoking".* **2** [U] a warning that something is going to happen: *These rules may be changed without notice.* | *The factory is closed until further notice.* **3** at a moment's notice, at short notice without having much time or advance warning to get ready: *I can leave at a moment's notice.* **4** [U] a formal warning to end an agreement: *I'm fed up with this job. I'm going to give in my notice.* | *Our landlady has given us notice to quit.* | *If the company wants to dismiss me, they have to give me three months' notice.* **5** take no notice of to pay no attention to someone or something: *Don't take any notice of what he says.* [RELATED PHRASE **take notice of:** *Managers need to take notice of the report.*] **6** come to your notice fml to become known to you: *It has come to my notice that you have been missing school.* [RELATED PHRASE **bring something to someone's notice**]

notice² v noticed, noticing [I; T; + (that); not in progressive forms] to see or pay attention to: *She was wearing a new dress, but he didn't even notice.* | *I noticed that he was looking rather nervous.* | *Did you notice whether I locked the door?* | *I noticed her leaving.*
☐ USEFUL PATTERNS to notice something; to notice that...; to notice when, how, why, where, etc.; to notice someone doing something

no·tice·a·ble /ˈnəʊtɪsəbəl/ adj easily seen or clearly recognized: *The damage to my car is hardly noticeable.* | *a noticeable drop in the amount of crime* –**noticeably** adv : *Noticeably fewer people came this year.*

notice board /ˈ·· ˌ·/ n BrE a board on a wall, which notices may be fixed to –see picture on page 539

no·ti·fy /ˈnəʊtɪfaɪ/ v notified, notifying [T] to tell someone something formally: *Have you notified the police?* | *Please notify all staff that the inspectors will be here on Monday.* –**notification** /ˌnəʊtɪfɪˈkeɪʃən/ n [C;U]

no·tion /ˈnəʊʃən/ n an idea or belief: *I haven't the faintest notion what you're talking about.* | *He is full of silly notions.* | *the old notion that the sun moved round the Earth* | *notions of equality*

no·to·ri·e·ty /ˌnəʊtəˈraɪəti/ n [U] fame for something bad

no·to·ri·ous /nəʊˈtɔːriəs, nə-/ adj widely known for something bad: *a notorious thief* | *This airport is notorious for its bad security.* –*see* FAMOUS (USAGE) –**notoriously** adv

not·with·stand·ing /ˌnɒtwɪθˈstændɪŋ, -wɪð- ‖ ˌnɑːt-/ prep fml in spite of something: *They are determined to go ahead with the plan, notwithstanding public opposition.* | *They bought the building, cost notwithstanding.*

nought /nɔːt/ n BrE the number 0: *0·6 is usually read "nought point six".*

noun /naʊn/ n a word that describes a person, place, thing, quality, or action, and can be used as the subject or object of a verb; nouns are marked n in this dictionary –see Study Note on page 687

nour·ish /ˈnʌrɪʃ ‖ ˈnɜːrɪʃ, ˈnʌ-/ v [T] **1** to give some-one the food that they need to live, grow, and stay healthy: *Milk is a nourishing drink.* | *a well-nourished baby* **2** to encourage a feeling or idea

nour·ish·ment /ˈnʌrɪʃmənt ‖ ˈnɜːrɪʃ-, ˈnʌ-/ n [U] food needed to live, grow and stay healthy: *Plants get nourishment from the soil.*

nov·el[1] /ˈnɒvəl ‖ ˈnɑː-/ n a book which tells a long story about people and events that are not real: *"War and Peace" is a great novel by Leo Tolstoy.*

novel[2] *adj* new, different, and interesting: *a novel suggestion* | *a novel idea*

nov·el·ist /ˈnɒvəlɪst ‖ ˈnɑː-/ n someone who writes novels

nov·el·ty /ˈnɒvəlti ‖ ˈnɑː-/ n **novelties 1** [U] the quality of being new, different, and interesting: *After ten weeks of camping, the novelty had worn off.* **2** [sing] something new and unusual: *I go out so rarely that it was quite a novelty for me to go to the cinema last night.* **3** [C] an unusual, cheap object often given as a small present: *The shops are full of Christmas novelties.*

No·vem·ber /nəʊˈvembər, nə-/ (also **Nov.**) n the 11th month of the year

nov·ice /ˈnɒvɪs ‖ ˈnɑː-/ n **1** someone with no ex-perience in a skill or job: *When it comes to sailing, I'm a complete novice.* **2** someone who has recently joined a religious group to become a MONK or NUN

now[1] /naʊ/ *adv* **1** at the present time: *We're living in London now.* | *Most women work now.* | *It's two years now since I left Birmingham.* **2** at the time mentioned in a story: *He was feeling happier now.* **3** used when you are starting to talk about a new subject: *I think that's enough on Question 5. Now, let's move on to the next question.* **4 now and then, every now and then, now and again** sometimes **5 now, now** a phrase you use to calm someone or to express amused disapproval of what someone says: *Now, now, stop crying.*

now[2] *conj* (also **now that**) because something has happened: *Now that everyone's here we can start the meeting.*

now·a·days /ˈnaʊədeɪz/ *adv* at the present time: *Most women work nowadays.*

no·where /ˈnəʊweər/ *adv* **1** in or to no place: *He now had nowhere to live.* | *I've been to Paris, but nowhere else in France.* **2 nowhere near** not at all: *£100 will be nowhere near enough.*

nox·ious /ˈnɒkʃəs ‖ ˈnɑːk-/ *adj fml* harmful or poisonous: *They pour noxious chemicals into that river.*

noz·zle /ˈnɒzəl ‖ ˈnɑː-/ n a short tube fitted to the end of a HOSE or pipe to direct and control the stream of liquid or gas coming out

n't /ənt/ short for NOT: *hadn't* | *didn't* | *wouldn't* | *isn't*

nu·ance /ˈnjuːɑːns ‖ ˈnuː-/ n a slight delicate differ-ence in colour, appearance, meaning, or feeling: *You have to be fluent at a language to understand the nuances of what people are saying.*

nu·bile /ˈnjuːbaɪl ‖ ˈnuːbəl/ *adj* young and sexually attractive (used of a girl or young woman)

SPELLING NOTE
Words with the sound /n/, may be spelt **kn-**, like **know**, or **pn-**, like **pneumonia**.

---

nu·cle·ar /ˈnjuːkliər ‖ ˈnuː-/ *adj* **1** concerned with the nucleus of an atom and the way it behaves: *nuclear fission* | *nuclear physics* **2** concerned with the powerful force produced by breaking atoms up: *a nuclear power station* | *nuclear energy* **3 nuclear reactor** a large machine that produces nuclear ENERGY as a means of producing electricity **4** related to or using weapons that explode because of the force of atoms breaking up inside them: *nuclear war* | *a nuclear missile* **5 nuclear-free** without any nuclear ENERGY or nuclear weapons: *Lambeth is a nuclear-free zone.*

nu·cle·us /ˈnjuːkliəs ‖ ˈnuː-/ n **nuclei** /-kliaɪ/ **1** the small group of people or things which form the central part of something larger: *These 100 books will form the nucleus of the new school library.* **2** the central part of an atom, made up of neutrons (NEU-TRON) and protons (PROTON) **3** the central part of almost all cells of living matter

nude[1] /njuːd ‖ nuːd/ *adj* not wearing clothes

nude[2] n **1** a picture of someone not wearing any clothes **2 in the nude** without any clothes on: *They went swimming in the nude.*

nudge /nʌdʒ/ v **nudged, nudging** [T] to touch or push someone gently, usually with your elbow: *She nudged me when he came into the room.* −**nudge** n : *Give me a nudge when it's time to leave.*

nud·is·m /ˈnjuːdɪzəm ‖ ˈnuː-/ n [U] the practice of not wearing clothes because you think it is good for you −**nudist** *adj* : *a nudist camp* −**nudist** n

nu·di·ty /ˈnjuːdɪti ‖ ˈnuː-/ n [U] the state of not wear-ing any clothes: *Many people regard nudity in films as wrong.*

nug·get /ˈnʌgɪt/ n **1** a small rough lump of a precious metal, found in the earth: *a gold nugget* **2** an interesting or useful piece of information

nui·sance /ˈnjuːsəns ‖ ˈnuː-/ n a person, thing, or sit-uation that causes annoyance: *Sit down and stop making a nuisance of yourself.* | *It's a real nuisance having to go back for her.*

nul·li·fy /ˈnʌlɪfaɪ/ v **nullified, nullifying** [T] *fml* to cause or declare something to have no legal force: *a claim nullified by the court* −**nullification** /ˌnʌlɪfɪˈkeɪʃən/ n [U]

numb[1] /nʌm/ *adj* unable to feel or express anything: *My hands are numb with cold.* | *The anaesthetic made my arm go numb.* | *numb with shock* −**numb-ness** n [U]

numb[2] v [T] to stop you feeling anything or behav-ing normally: *The cold numbed my fingers.* | *He was numbed by his wife's death.*

num·ber[1] /ˈnʌmbər/ n **1** [C] a word such as three, eight, or sixteen, or a sign such as 1, 14, or 23 which is part of the system we use to count or measure: *Choose any number between one and ten.* | *Six is my lucky number.* **2** [C] a telephone number: *What's your number?* | *Do you know Jane's number?* **3** [C] a figure used to explain what you are talking about from things in an ordered list: *Who lives at number 10?* | *Please look at question number four.* **4** [C;U] [always with a plural verb] a quantity or amount: *Large numbers of tourists visit London every year.* | *They were twelve in number.* | *A small number of women are now holding key jobs.* **5 a number of** several: *A number of people have complained re-cently.* **6 any number of** a lot of: *Any number of people might apply for the job.* **7** [C] a copy of a magazine printed at a particular time: *the latest number of "Vogue" magazine* **8** [C] a piece of popu-lar music

number² *v* **1** [T] to give a number to something: *Number the questions from 1 to 10.* | *All the seats are numbered.* **2** [+ complement] to reach as a total: *The children who were affected numbered several hundred.* **3 be numbered among** to be included as one of a group or set: *He is numbered among the best of modern writers.*

num·ber·plate /ˈnʌmbəpleɪt ‖ -ər-/ *BrE n* (**license plate** *AmE*) one of two signs at the front and back of a vehicle showing its official number –see picture on page 49

Number Ten /ˌ·· ˈ·/ *n* (**No. 10**) 10 Downing Street; the place where the British PRIME MINISTER lives

nu·me·ral /ˈnjuːmərəl ‖ ˈnuː-/ *n* a sign that represents a number

nu·me·rate /ˈnjuːmərɪt ‖ ˈnuː-/ *adj* able to do calculations with numbers –**numeracy** *n* [U]

nu·mer·i·cal /njuːˈmerɪkəl ‖ nuː-/ *adj* expressed in numbers: *The files are kept in numerical order.* –**numerically** /-kli/ *adv*: *Their army is numerically greater than ours but less well trained.*

nu·me·rous /ˈnjuːmərəs ‖ ˈnuː-/ *adj* many: *one of my numerous relatives* | *for numerous reasons*

nun /nʌn/ *n* a member of an all-female religious group who live together in a CONVENT

nun·ne·ry /ˈnʌnəri/ *n* **nunneries** *old fash* a building in which nuns live

nup·tial /ˈnʌpʃəl/ *adj* [only before a noun] *fml* concerning marriage or the marriage ceremony: *a nuptial mass* –**nuptials** *n* [pl] : *The nuptials were performed by the local priest.*

nurse¹ /nɜːs ‖ nɜːrs/ *n* **1** someone, often a woman, who is trained to help a doctor or to take care of sick, hurt, or old people in a hospital: *a student nurse* | *Nurse Jones* | *Our daughter is a nurse.* | *Thank you, nurse.* **2** a woman employed to take care of a young child –compare NANNY

nurse² *v* **nursed, nursing 1** [T] to take care of someone who is ill: *He nursed her back to health.* | *She spends all her time nursing her old father.* **2** [T] to try to cure an illness: *She's in bed nursing a cold.* **3** [I] to be a professional nurse: *She spent some time nursing in a military hospital.* **4** [I;T] to give a baby milk from the breast: *a nursing mother* **5** [T] to think a lot about something: *She still nursed a grudge against her old boss.* | *I've always nursed a desire to be a politician.* **6** to hold someone or something lovingly: *The child nursed the kitten in her arms.*

nurse·maid /ˈnɜːsmeɪd ‖ ˈnɜːrs-/ *n* a woman employed to look after young children

nur·se·ry /ˈnɜːsəri ‖ ˈnɜːr-/ *n* **nurseries 1** a place where small children are taken care of while their parents are at work or shopping **2** an area where young plants and trees are grown to be sold or planted in other places **3** a small child's bedroom or playroom in a house

nur·se·ry·man /ˈnɜːsərimən ‖ ˈnɜːr-/ *n* **nurserymen** /-mən/ someone who grows plants in a nursery

nursery rhyme /ˈ··· ·/ *n* a short, well-known song or poem for small children

nursery school /ˈ··· ·/ *n* [C;U] a school for young children between three and five years of age

nurs·ing /ˈnɜːsɪŋ ‖ ˈnɜːr-/ *n* [U] the job of looking after people who are sick, hurt, or old: *the nursing profession* | *Have you thought of going into nursing?*

nursing home /ˈ·· ·/ *n* **1** a usually private establishment where old or sick people can live and be looked after **2** *BrE* a small private hospital

nur·ture /ˈnɜːtʃəʳ ‖ ˈnɜːr-/ *v* **nurtured, nurturing** [T] *lit* to care for and encourage the development of something or someone: *children nurtured by loving parents* | *I looked at the plants I had nurtured through the winter.* | *He nurtured a desire to be completely independent.*

nut /nʌt/ *n* **1** a dry fruit which consists of a seed surrounded by a hard shell; the seed is also called a nut: *a cashew nut* **2** a small piece of metal with a hole through it for screwing onto a BOLT to fasten things together **3** (also **nutter**) *infml* someone who seems to be mad: *He's a bit of a nut.* **4** someone who likes a particular thing much more than most people can understand: *She's a health nut.* **5 off your nut** *slang* mad: *You must be off your nut!* **6 a hard nut to crack, a tough nut to crack** *infml* a difficult person or situation to deal with **7 do your nut** *slang* to suddenly become very angry or worried: *Dad will do his nut if he finds out where you've been.*

nut·case /ˈnʌtkeɪs/ *n* *infml* a mad person

nut-crack·ers /ˈnʌtˌkrækəz ‖ kərz/ *n* [pl] a tool for cracking the shell of a nut: *Have we got any nutcrackers?*

nut·meg /ˈnʌtmeg/ *n* [C;U] a small hard seed of a tropical tree which is made into powder and used to give a particular taste to food

nu·tri·ent /ˈnjuːtriənt ‖ ˈnuː-/ *n* *tech* a chemical or food which helps plants and animals to grow

nu·tri·tion /njuːˈtrɪʃən ‖ nuː-/ *n* [U] the process of giving and getting food to remain healthy

nu·tri·tious /njuːˈtrɪʃəs ‖ nuː-/ *adj* valuable to the body as food: *a nutritious diet*

nuts /nʌts/ *adj* [never before a noun] *infml* **1** mad: *I'll go nuts if I have to wait much longer.* | *He's nuts.* **2 nuts about** very keen on someone or something: *She's nuts about Jason Donovan.*

nut·ty /ˈnʌti/ *adj* **nuttier, nuttiest 1** filled with nuts or tasting like them: *wine with a nutty taste* | *a nutty cake* **2** *infml* mad –**nuttiness** *n* [U]

nuz·zle /ˈnʌzəl/ *v* **nuzzled, nuzzling** [I;T] to rub or push something gently often with the nose: *The horse nuzzled me, looking for food.* | *He nuzzled up against her on the sofa.*

NW a written abbreviation for NORTHWESTERN

ny·lon /ˈnaɪlɒn ‖ -lɑːn/ *n* [U] a strong man-made material made into clothes, cords, and plastics: *nylon thread* | *a nylon shirt*

ny·lons /ˈnaɪlɒnz ‖ -lɑːnz/ *n* [pl] *old fash* women's nylon stockings: *a pair of nylons*

nymph /nɪmf/ *n* one of the less important goddesses of nature in Greek and Roman literature, represented as young girls

nym·pho·ma·ni·ac /ˌnɪmfəˈmeɪniæk/ *n* a woman who has unusually strong sexual desires –**nymphomaniac** *adj*

O, o

O, o /əʊ/ **O's, o's** or **Os, os** **1** the 15th letter of the English alphabet **2** (used in speech when referring to numbers) zero: *His phone number is 071-283-9462.* –see ZERO (USAGE)

oaf /əʊf/ n a stupid awkward person: *You clumsy oaf!*

oak /əʊk/ n [C;U] a large tree common in Britain or the wood of this tree: *an oak table*

OAP /ˌəʊ eɪ 'piː/ n someone who is over 60 or 65 years old, and who no longer works; an abbreviation for **old age pensioner**

oar /ɔːr/ n a long pole with a wide flat blade at one end, used to move a boat through the water: *He pulled hard on the oars.*

o·a·sis /əʊ'eɪsᵻs/ n **oases** /-siːz/ **1** a place in a desert where there is water and where trees can grow **2** a pleasant place in the middle of unpleasant places

oath /əʊθ/ n **oaths** /əʊðz/ **1** a solemn promise: *The soldiers swore an oath of allegiance.* **2** *old fash* an expression of strong feeling using the name of God in a disrespectful way **3** **be on oath, be under oath** *law* to have made a solemn promise to tell the truth in a court of law

oat·meal /'əʊtmiːl/ n [U] crushed oats used for making dry flat cakes and PORRIDGE

oats /əʊts/ n [pl] a grain that is used in PORRIDGE and fed to animals

ob·du·rate /'ɒbdjʊrᵻt ‖ 'aːbdə-/ adj *fml* refusing to change your beliefs or feelings about something –**obduracy** n [U]

o·be·di·ent /ə'biːdiənt/ adj willing to do what you are told to do by someone, for example a parent or teacher: *an obedient child | an obedient dog* –opposite **disobedient** –**obediently** adv –**obedience** n [U]

o·bese /əʊ'biːs/ adj very fat –**obesity** n [U]

o·bey /əʊ'beɪ, ə-/ v **obeyed, obeying** [I;T] to do what you are told to do: *Soldiers are expected to obey. | Everyone has to obey the law.* –opposite **disobey**

o·bit·u·ary /ə'bɪtʃʊəri ‖ -tʃueri/ n **obituaries** a formal notice in a newspaper of someone's death, with a short account of their life

ob·ject¹ /'ɒbdʒɪkt ‖ 'aːb-/ n **1** a thing that can be seen or touched and is not alive **2** someone or something towards which interest or another feeling is directed: *The vase was an object of admiration. | She had become an object of pity.* **3** purpose or aim: *The object of his visit was to meet as many people as possible.* **4** *tech* a term used in grammar to describe words in a certain situation; in the sentences "John gave Mary a book" and "John gave a book to Mary", "Mary" is the **indirect object** of the verb, and "book" is the **direct object** **5** **no object** not a difficulty: *I want the best seats in the theatre; money is no object.*

ob·ject² /əb'dʒekt/ v **1** [I] to feel or say that you dislike and disapprove of something: *I'll go ahead if no one objects. | What I object to is the way he orders everyone around. | They objected to the adoption of children from abroad.* **2** [+(that)] to give as a reason for not doing something: *I wanted to climb the hill, but Bill objected that he was too tired.* –**objector** n

ob·jec·tion /əb'dʒekʃən/ n **1** a statement or feeling of dislike, disapproval, or opposition: *She voiced her objection to travelling by bus.* **2** a reason or argument against something: *The only objection is that she can't drive.*

ob·jec·tio·na·ble /əb'dʒekʃənəbəl/ adj unpleasant and offensive: *I find his behaviour quite objectionable.* –**objectionably** adv

ob·jec·tive¹ /əb'dʒektɪv/ adj **1** not influenced by personal feelings: *The reporter gave an objective analysis of the political situation.* **2** based on things which can be seen and touched: *We need objective evidence before we can convict him.* –**objectively** adv : *Try to look at the problem objectively.* –**objectivity** /ˌɒbdʒek'tɪvᵻti ‖ ˌaːb-/ n [U]

objective² n an aim towards which you have to work: *We've achieved our main objective – to produce a first class engine.*

ob·jet d'art /ˌɒbʒeɪ 'daːr ‖ ˌaːb-/ n **objets d'art** (*same pronunciation*) a small object considered to have some artistic value

ob·li·ga·tion /ˌɒblᵻ'geɪʃən ‖ ˌaːb-/ n something which must be done because of a duty or promise: *Have a look round the shop – you're under no obligation to buy anything. | I said I would help her and I have to fulfil that obligation.*

ob·lig·a·to·ry /ə'blɪgətəri ‖ -tɔːri/ adj which must be done because of a law, or rule: *The wearing of uniform is obligatory.*

o·blige /ə'blaɪdʒ/ v **obliged, obliging** **1** [T] to make it necessary for someone to do something: *He felt obliged to leave after such an unpleasant quarrel. | Falling profits obliged them to close the factory.* ☐ USEFUL PATTERNS to oblige someone to do something; to be obliged to do something **2** [I;T] to be helpful to someone: *I asked Oliver to lend us his car and he was only too happy to oblige.* **3** **much obliged** *fml* very grateful: *I'm much obliged to you.* **4** **I should/would be obliged if** a formal phrase meaning that you want someone to do something: *I'd be obliged if you could make less noise.*

o·blig·ing /ə'blaɪdʒɪŋ/ adj willing and eager to help –**obligingly** adv

o·blique /ə'bliːk/ adj **1** indirect: *I think what he said was an oblique reference to my driving.* **2** sloping: *an oblique line*

o·blit·er·ate /ə'blɪtəreɪt/ v **obliterated, obliterating** [T] to destroy something completely –**obliteration** /əˌblɪtə'reɪʃən/ n [U]

o·bliv·i·on /ə'blɪviən/ n [U] **1** the state of being unconscious or not noticing your surroundings **2** the state of being forgotten: *Her fame soon sank into oblivion.*

o·bliv·i·ous /ə'blɪviəs/ adj not noticing: *He was quite oblivious to the danger he was in. | She was oblivious of the effect she had on him.* –**obliviously** adv –**obliviousness** n [U]

ob·long /'ɒblɒŋ ‖ 'aːblɔːŋ/ n a shape with four straight sides, two long and two short, which form four right angles

ob·nox·ious /əb'nɒkʃəs ‖ -'naːk-/ adj very unpleasant or offensive: *He's an obnoxious little man.* –**obnoxiously** adv

o·boe /'əʊbəʊ/ n a musical instrument of the woodwind family; it is a long tube with a double REED at the top which you blow through

ob·scene /əb'siːn/ adj shocking and offensive, usually in a sexual way –**obscenely** adv –**obscenity** /əb'senᵻti/ n **obscenities** [C;U]

ob·scure¹ /əb'skjʊər/ adj **1** unclear or hard to understand: *a speech full of obscure political jokes*

2 not well known: *an obscure poet* –**obscurely** *adv* –**obscurity** *n* **obscurities** [C;U]

obscure² *v* **obscured, obscuring** [T] to make something difficult to see or understand: *The clouds obscured the moon.* | *The report obscures the fact that prices have risen.*

ob·se·qui·ous /əb'siːkwiəs/ *adj fml* too eager to agree with someone and do what they want (a word used to express disapproval)

ob·ser·vance /əb'zɜːvəns ‖ -ɜːr-/ *n fml* **1** [U] the obeying or following of a law, ceremony, or custom: *strict observance* **of** *the school rules* | *the observance of Christmas* **2** [C] a part of a religious ceremony: *religious observances*

ob·ser·vant /əb'zɜːvənt ‖ -ɜːr-/ *adj* quick at noticing things –opposite **unobservant**

ob·ser·va·tion /ˌɒbzə'veɪʃən ‖ ˌɑːbzər-/ *n* **1** [U] the action of noticing or watching something in order to learn about it: *During our observation of the rats, we made several new discoveries.* | *He left by the back door to escape observation.* **2** [C] something that you have learned by watching: *The scientific observations of Professor Jones are extremely interesting.* **3** [C] a remark: *She made a few general observations before a more detailed analysis.* **4** [U] the ability to notice things: *poor powers of observation* **5 under observation** carefully watched: *The police are keeping him under observation.* | *She has been put under observation at the local hospital.*

ob·ser·va·to·ry /əb'zɜːvətəri ‖ əb'zɜːrvətɔːri/ *n* **observatories** a place from which scientists can watch the moon, stars, and the weather

ob·serve /əb'zɜːv ‖ -ɜːrv/ *v* **observed, observing** **1** [T] to watch carefully, often to learn or understand something: *They observed the stars.* **2** [T; + that] *fml* to see and notice: *The police observed them entering the bank.* | *Did you observe where they went?* | *I observed that they were late.*
☐ **USEFUL PATTERNS** to observe something; to observe someone doing/do something; to observe where, how, who, etc.; to observe that...
3 [T] to obey or follow a law or custom **4** [I; + that] to make a remark about something you have noticed: *"It's going to rain," he observed.* | *He observed that she looked rather upset.*

ob·serv·er /əb'zɜːvəʳ ‖ -ɜːr-/ *n* **1** someone who sees or watches something **2** someone who attends meetings or classes to see what happens without taking part

ob·sess /əb'ses/ *v* [T] to fill your thoughts completely so that you think of nothing else

ob·sessed /əb,sest/ *adj* thinking about only one thing: *She's obsessed* **by** *the thought of another war.* | *He's obsessed* **with** *getting fit.*

ob·ses·sion /əb'seʃən/ *n* something that you cannot stop thinking about –**obsessional** / *adj*

ob·ses·sive /əb'sesɪv/ *adj* continually filling your thoughts so that you can think of nothing else: *He has an obsessive interest in death.*

ob·so·les·cent /ˌɒbsə'lesənt◂ ‖ ˌɑːb-/ *adj* being used less and less –**obsolescence** *n* [U]

ob·so·lete /'ɒbsəliːt ‖ ˌɑːbsə'liːt/ *adj* no longer used: *obsolete machinery*

ob·sta·cle /'ɒbstəkəl ‖ 'ɑːb-/ *n* something which gets in the way and prevents action, movement, or success: *Their different religions were an obstacle* **to** *their marriage.*

ob·stet·rics /əb'stetrɪks/ *n* [U] the branch of medicine concerned with the birth of children –**obstetric** *adj* –**obstetrician** /ˌɒbstə'trɪʃən ‖ ˌɑːb-/ *n*

ob·sti·nate /'ɒbstɪnət ‖ 'ɑːb-/ *adj* **1** determined not to change your opinions or behaviour: *He's a very obstinate child.* **2** difficult to get rid of: *an obstinate pain* –**obstinately** *adv* –**obstinacy** *n* [U]

ob·struct /əb'strʌkt/ *v* [T] **1** to block: *The accident obstructed the road.* **2** to prevent something from advancing: *obstructing the course of justice by withholding information* –**obstruction** /əb'strʌkʃən/ *n* [C;U] : *an obstruction in the road* –**obstructive** /-tɪv/ *adj*

ob·tain /əb'teɪn/ *v* [T] to get something: *Further information can be obtained* **from** *our head office.* –**obtainable** *adj* : *I'm afraid that the record you asked for is no longer obtainable.*

ob·tru·sive /əb'truːsɪv/ *adj* unpleasantly noticeable –**obtrusively** *adv*

ob·tuse /əb'tjuːs ‖ -'tuːs/ *adj* **1** *fml* stupid or slow to understand **2 obtuse angle** *tech* an angle between 90° and 180° –**obtusely** *adv* –**obtuseness** *n*

ob·vi·ous /'ɒbviəs ‖ 'ɑːb-/ *adj* easy to see and understand: *It's quite obvious that he's lying.* –**obviousness** *n* [U]

ob·vi·ous·ly /'ɒbviəsli ‖ 'ɑːb-/ *adv* it can be easily seen that: *Obviously, you didn't read it.*

oc·ca·sion /ə'keɪʒən/ *n* **1** [C] a time when something happens: *On that occasion I was not at home.* –see CHANCE (USAGE) **2** [sing] a suitable time: *This is hardly the occasion* **for** *an argument.* **3** [sing] reason: *There was no occasion to be so rude to your uncle.* **4** [C] a special event or ceremony: *The royal visit was quite an occasion.* **5 on occasion** from time to time

oc·ca·sion·al /ə'keɪʒənəl/ *adj* [only before a noun] happening from time to time: *I get the occasional business trip abroad.* –**occasionally** *adv*

oc·cult /'ɒkʌlt, ə'kʌlt ‖ ə'kʌlt, 'ɑːkʌlt/ *adj* secret, magical, and mysterious –**the occult** *n*

oc·cu·pant /'ɒkjəpənt ‖ 'ɑːk-/ *n fml* someone who lives, works, or is in a certain place: *The letter was addressed to the occupant* **of** *the house.*

oc·cu·pa·tion /ˌɒkjʊ'peɪʃən ‖ ˌɑːk-/ *n* **1** [C] a job –see JOB (USAGE) **2** [C] something you like doing in your free time: *Gardening is a peaceful occupation.* **3** [U] the act of taking control of a place or the period when that place is under your control: *She was born in France during the German occupation.*

oc·cu·pa·tion·al /ˌɒkjʊ'peɪʃənəl ‖ ˌɑːk-/ *adj* caused by or connected with your job: *For professional footballers, broken bones are an occupational hazard.*

oc·cu·pi·er /'ɒkjʊpaɪəʳ ‖ 'ɑːk-/ *n* the person who lives or works in a place

oc·cu·py /'ɒkjʊpaɪ ‖ 'ɑːk-/ *v* **occupied, occupying** [T] **1** to live in a building or place: *Is that house occupied at present?* | *His family has occupied that land for years.* **2** to fill a certain position, space, or time: *His father occupies a senior position in the company.* | *His books occupy a lot of space.* | *Voluntary work occupies most of his spare time.* **3 be occupied** to spend time doing something: *For most of the day I was occupied* **in** *writing letters.* **4 occupy yourself** to fill your time by keeping yourself busy doing something: *What do you do to occupy yourself now that you're retired?* | *The old woman occupied herself playing cards with her neighbour.* **5** to move into and hold possession of an enemy's country or town

oc·cur /əˈkɜːʳ/ v occurred, occurring [I] 1 to happen: *Many accidents occur in the home.* –see HAPPEN (USAGE) 2 to exist: *That sound doesn't occur in his language.* 3 occur to someone (of an idea) to come into someone's mind: *Just as I was leaving the house, it occurred to me that I had forgotten my keys.* ■ USAGE If you say that something "occurred" you mean that it happened: *The accident occurred while passengers were waiting to board the plane.* But if you say that something "occurred to you" you mean that an idea came into your mind: *Something suddenly occurred to me while I was waiting for the plane.* (= I had an idea) Be careful, therefore, NOT to use this expression if you mean that something happened which concerned you. Instead you can say: *Something suddenly happened to me while I was waiting for the plane.*

oc·cur·rence /əˈkʌrəns ‖ əˈkɜː-/ n an event or happening: *What a strange occurrence!* | *an everyday occurrence*

o·cean /ˈəʊʃən/ n 1 [U] the great mass of salt water that covers most of the earth: *Have you ever seen the ocean?* 2 [C] (also Ocean) any of the great seas into which this mass is divided: *the Pacific Ocean* –oceanic /ˌəʊʃiˈænɪk◂/ adj

o·clock /əˈklɒk ‖ əˈklɑːk/ adv used when you are saying what time it is: *"What time is it?" "It's 9 o'clock".*

oc·ta·gon /ˈɒktəgən ‖ ˈɑːktəgɑːn/ n tech a flat figure with eight sides and eight angles –octagonal /ɒkˈtægənəl ‖ ɑːk-/ adj

oc·tave /ˈɒktɪv, -teɪv ‖ ˈɑːk-/ n a space of eight degrees between musical notes

Oc·to·ber /ɒkˈtəʊbəʳ ‖ ɑːk-/ (also Oct.) n the 10th month of the year

oc·to·pus /ˈɒktəpəs ‖ ˈɑːk-/ n a sea creature with eight arms

oc·u·list /ˈɒkjəlist ‖ ˈɑːk-/ n fml an eye-doctor

odd /ɒd ‖ ɑːd/ adj 1 strange and unusual: *He's such an odd man!* | *It was a really odd thing to do.* 2 [only before a noun] separated from a part or set to which it belongs: *After sorting out all the washing, I was left with two odd socks.* 3 that cannot be divided exactly by 2 (used of numbers) 4 not happening regularly: *He likes the odd drink.* 5 [only after a noun] near in number: *They lived abroad for some thirty odd years.* 6 odd jobs small practical jobs that you do in your home, for example mending things

odd·i·ty /ˈɒdɪti ‖ ˈɑː-/ n oddities a strange person or thing

odd·ly /ˈɒdli ‖ ˈɑːdli/ adv 1 strangely: *He spoke oddly.* 2 oddly enough a phrase used to introduce something that is strange: *Oddly enough, he didn't remember his own birthday.*

odd·ments /ˈɒdmənt ‖ ˈɑːd-/ n [pl] pieces left over, usually from a roll of material: *I'm going to make a quilt out of all these oddments.*

odds /ɒdz ‖ ɑːdz/ n [pl] 1 the probability that something will or will not happen: *The odds are that he will fail his exam.* 2 this probability expressed in numbers when making a BET: *If you bet £1 on a horse with the odds at 10 to 1 and the horse wins, you get £11 back.* 3 at odds with in disagreement with 4 it makes no odds BrE it makes no difference or has no importance

odds and ends /ˌ· ·ˈ·/ n [pl] small articles without much value

odds-on /ˌ· ˈ·◂/ adj very likely to win: *It's odds-on that he'll win.* | *the odds-on favourite to win*

ode /əʊd/ n a poem addressed to a person or thing

o·di·ous /ˈəʊdiəs/ adj fml very unpleasant

o·dom·e·ter /əʊˈdɒmɪtəʳ ‖ -ˈdɑː-/ n the usual American word for MILEOMETER

o·dour /ˈəʊdəʳ/ n (odor AmE) a smell, especially an unpleasant one –see SMELL (USAGE) –odourless adj

oe·soph·a·gus /ɪˈsɒfəgəs ‖ ɪˈsɑː-/ n (also esophagus) tech the food tube leading down into the stomach

of /əv, ə; strong ɒv ‖ əv, ə; strong ɑːv/ prep 1 forming part of something, relating to something, or belonging to something: *One of the legs of the table was broken.* | *the colour of her hair* | *the size of the room* | *the King of England* | *a friend of mine* | *the University of London* | *the economic boom of the 1980s* 2 made from something: *a crown of gold* 3 containing something: *a bag of potatoes* | *a cup of tea* 4 showing something: *a picture of a lion* | *a map of England* 5 used in expressions showing amounts: *two pounds of sugar* | *a group of students* | *a piece of cake* 6 used when giving a detailed amount: *a pay rise of 9%* | *a child of eight years old* | *a man of fifty* 7 by: *the plays of Shakespeare* 8 used when you are giving the name of a place: *the city of New York* | *the town of Stamford* 9 used in dates: *the 27th of February* 10 of a, of an during a period of time: *I like to go to the park of an afternoon.*

off¹ /ɒf ‖ ɔːf/ adv, prep 1 adv, prep away from a place, or no longer on or in a place: *Keep off the grass.* | *She cut a piece off the loaf.* | *The door handle's fallen off.* | *The car drove off.* | *My parents have gone off to America for the summer.* | *She got off the train.* | *The bus stopped and I got off.* | *He took his shoes off.* | *A picture had fallen off the wall.* –see picture on page 540 2 adv not switched on (used of a light or a machine): *Switch the light off, please.* | *Can you check that the cooker's off?* 3 adv not going to happen: *I'm afraid the party's off.* | *The deal's off.* 4 adv, prep away from work, either because you are ill or on holiday: *I've just had two weeks off.* | *It's his day off today.* | *I'm off work today.* 5 prep leading from a road: *a narrow street off the High Street* 6 prep in the sea near a place: *an island off the West coast of Africa* 7 adv no longer good to eat (used of food): *The milk's gone off.* 8 off your food not wanting to eat because you are ill 9 prep no longer taking a drug or a medicine regularly: *She finally managed to come off tranquillizers.* 10 a bit off infml not acceptable: *I thought it was a bit off that she didn't bother to thank me.* 11 they're off = the people or animals in a race have started running 12 off and on sometimes, but not continuously: *It's been raining off and on all morning.*

off² adj 1 [never before a noun] no longer good to eat (used of food): *I think this meat is off.* 2 an off day a day when you are not able to do things as well as you usually do, for example because you are not feeling very well 3 the off season the winter, when people do not go on holiday

off-col·our /ˌ· ˈ···/ adj infml not well: *I didn't go to work that day because I felt a bit off-colour.*

off-day /ˈ· ˌ·/ n infml a day when you don't do things well: *He's having a bit of an off-day.*

of·fence /əˈfens/ n (offense AmE) 1 [C] a crime: *Driving while drunk is a serious offence.* 2 [C;U] cause for hurt feelings or displeasure: *He's always causing offence to his colleagues.* | *He takes offence at everything I say.*

of·fend /əˈfend/ v 1 [T] to hurt someone's feelings: *She was very offended that I forgot her birthday.* 2 [T] to cause someone displeasure: *That new office block offends the eye.* 3 [I] to do wrong: *His behaviour offends against the religious laws of this country.*

of·fend·er /ə'fendə^r/ n law a criminal

of·fen·sive[1] /ə'fensɪv/ adj **1** unpleasant or causing offence: *offensive behaviour* | *an offensive remark* **2** offensive weapon an object used to attack someone: *He was charged with carrying an offensive weapon.* **–offensively** adv

offensive[2] n **1** a continued attack **2 on the offensive** making a continued attack

of·fer[1] /'ɒfə^r ‖ 'ɔː-, 'ɑː-/ v **1** [T] to hold out something to a person for acceptance or refusal: *Offer the guests some coffee.* | *They've offered us £85,000 for the house. Shall we take it?* | *I've been offered a job in Canada.*
□ USEFUL PATTERNS to offer something to someone; to offer someone something
2 [I;T] to express willingness to do something: *She offered, and I didn't say no.* | *She offered to help.* | *He's always willing to offer advice.*
□ USEFUL PATTERNS to offer something; to offer to do something
3 [T] to give something to God

offer[2] n **1** a statement offering to do something: *Thanks for your offer of help.* **2** something which is offered: *He made me an offer of £5.*

of·fer·ing /'ɒfərɪŋ ‖ 'ɔː-, 'ɑː-/ n something offered, especially to God

off·hand /ˌɒf'hænd◂ ‖ ˌɔːf-/ adv,adj **1** careless and disrespectful: *an offhand manner* **2** at once and without time to think: *I can't give you an answer offhand.*

of·fice /'ɒfɪs ‖ 'ɔː-, 'ɑː-/ n **1** [C] a place where business is done: *I work in an office.* | *a ticket office* **2** [C] (also **Office**) a government department: *the Foreign Office* **3** [C;U] a position of responsibility or power, especially in government: *That politician has been in office for 20 years.* | *That party has held office for over a decade.*

of·fi·cer /'ɒfɪsə^r ‖ 'ɔː-, 'ɑː-/ n **1** a person in a position of command in the armed forces **2** a person who holds a position of some importance, especially in government or a business: *a local government officer* **3** a policeman
■ USAGE **Civil servants** are people in general who work for the government, and **officials** are people who work for a government or other large organization in a position of responsibility: *A strike by* **civil servants** *could damage the government.* | **officials** *from the Department of Trade and Industry* | *British Rail* **officials** *are to hold high level meetings tomorrow.* An **officer** is often a member of the armed forces in a position of command, or a member of the police force, but the word is also used in a similar way to **official**: *a customs* **officer** *at the airport* | *the university Careers* **Officer** | *the Public Health* **Officer**

of·fi·cial[1] /ə'fɪʃəl/ n a person who holds a position of responsibility: *a union official* –see OFFICER (USAGE)

official[2] adj approved by or connected with those in power: *an official investigation* | *The Prince is engaged – and that's official.* | *He was accused of using his official car for private business.* | *This uniform is to be worn on official occasions.*

of·fi·cial·ly /ə'fɪʃəli/ adv **1** formally or publicly: *They have officially announced their engagement.* **2** according to what is said by an official but which may not be true: *Officially he's on holiday but actually he's in hospital.* –opposite **unofficially**

of·fi·ci·ate /ə'fɪʃieɪt/ v officiated, officiating [I] to perform official duties: *Who's going to officiate at your wedding?*

of·fi·cious /ə'fɪʃəs/ adj too eager to give orders or to offer advice (a word used to show disapproval): *an officious manner* **–officiously** adv **–officiousness** n

off·ing /'ɒfɪŋ ‖ 'ɔː-, 'ɑː-/ n **in the offing** about to happen

off-li·cence /'· ‚··/ n a shop where alcohol is sold to be taken away

off-peak /ˌ· '·◂/ adj **1** less busy: *Telephone charges are lower during off-peak periods.* **2** used during less busy periods: *off-peak electricity*

off·set /'ɒfset, ˌɒf'set ‖ 'ɔːfset, ˌɔːf'set/ v off-set, offset, offsetting [T] to make up for something or act as a balance to it: *The cost of getting there was offset by the fact that it's a very cheap place to live.*

off·shoot /'ɒfʃuːt ‖ 'ɔːf-/ n something which grows out of something else, for example a new stem or branch

off·shore /ˌɒf 'ʃɔː^r◂ ‖ ˌɔːf-/ adv, adj at a distance from the coast: *Britain's offshore oil* | *two miles offshore*

off·side /ˌɒf'saɪd◂ ‖ ˌɔːf-/ adj,adv **1** in a position in which play is not allowed (used of certain sports) **2** the side of a vehicle farthest from the edge of the road

off·spring /'ɒf‚sprɪŋ ‖ 'ɔːf-/ n [U] child or children: *All his offspring were musicians.*

off-white /ˌ· '·◂/ adj having a colour that is not a pure white but with some grey or yellow in it

of·ten /'ɒfən, 'ɒftən ‖ 'ɔːfən/ adv **1** many times: *I often spend the afternoon reading.* | *I don't often see my parents.* **2 how often?** how many times, or how frequently?: *How often do you go to France?* **3** in many cases: *It's often very difficult to understand what he's saying.* **4 as often as not** at least half of the time: *As often as not he forgets his homework.* **5 every so often** sometimes **6 more often than not** more than half of the time: *More often than not she's late for school.*

o·gle /'əʊgəl/ v ogled, ogling [I;T] to look at someone with great interest, especially sexual interest: *Most women hate being ogled.*

o·gre /'əʊgə^r/ n **1** (in fairy stories) a frightening creature like a very large man, who is thought to eat children **2** a person who makes others afraid

oh /əʊ/ interj an expression of surprise, fear, or pleasure

ohm /əʊm/ n tech a measure of electrical RESISTANCE

oil[1] /ɔɪl/ n [U] **1** a fatty liquid used for burning, for making machines run easily, or for cooking: *an oil burner* | *engine oil* | *olive oil* **2 oils** [pl] paints containing oil

oil[2] v [T] to put oil onto something or rub oil onto someone

oil·field /'ɔɪlfiːld/ n an area under which there is oil

oil paint·ing /'· ‚··/ n **1** [U] the art of painting in oils **2** [C] a picture painted in oils

oil·rig /'ɔɪl‚rɪg/ n a large piece of apparatus for getting oil from underground, especially from under the sea

oil·skin /'ɔɪl‚skɪn/ n [C] a piece of clothing treated with oil so that water will not pass through it

oil slick /'· ·/ n a thin sheet of oil floating on water, especially as a result of an accident to an oil-carrying ship –see picture on page 246

oil-well /'· ·/ n a hole made in the ground in order to get oil

oil·y /'ɔɪli/ adj oilier, oiliest **1** like oil: *an oily liquid* **2** covered with or containing oil: *dirty oily clothes* |

oily food **3** too polite (a word used to show disapproval): *I don't like his oily manner.*

oint·ment /ˈɔɪntmənt/ *n* [C;U] a substance to be rubbed on the skin for medical purposes

o·kay[1] /əʊˈkeɪ/ *adj,adv* (also **OK**) *infml* **1** all right: *That car goes okay now.* | *She's OK now.* **2** an expression used when asking for or expressing agreement, or giving permission: *Let's go there, okay?* | *"Shall we go there?" "Okay."* | *"Can I use your car?" "Okay".*

okay[2] *v* **okayed, okaying** [T] *infml* to approve something: *Has the bank okayed your request for a loan?*

okay[3] *n* **okays** *infml* (also **OK**) approval or permission: *I got the OK to leave early.*

old /əʊld/ *adj* **1** having a particular age: *How old are you?* | *The baby is 8 months old.* | *a thirty-year-old man* | *This castle is centuries old.* **2** having lived for a long time: *an old man* | *old and young people* **3** **the old** old people: *The old and the young often don't agree.* **4** having existed or lasted for a long time: *old and new books* | *old friends* | *an old building* **5** having been in use for a long time and often no longer useful: *an old pair of shoes* | *rather old ideas* | *I'm going to throw away these old clothes.* **6** belonging to past times: *old customs* | *an old civilization* | *the good old days* **7** former: *He's got his old job back.* | *my old school* **8** **of old**: a long ago: *days of old* **b** since a long time ago: *I know him of old.*

■ USAGE 1 Compare **old, ancient, antique**. **Old** is the general word for people or things that have existed for a long time: *an old man* | *an old house.* **Ancient** means "belonging to times long ago": *the ancient Romans* | *ancient history.* **Antique** describes something that is old and usually valuable: *an antique piece of furniture made by a famous craftsman* | *a collector of antiques.* **2** When you speak about a person, **elderly** is a polite way of saying **old**: Compare *an old church* and *an old/elderly lady.*

old age pen·sion /ˌ· ˈ··/ *n* [U] money paid regularly by the state to old people –**old age pensioner** *n* (also **OAP**)

old boy /ˈ· ˌ·/ *n BrE* a former pupil of a school; a woman who is a former pupil of a school is called an **old girl**

old·en /ˈəʊldən/ *adj* [only before a noun] *lit* long ago: *in olden days* | *olden times*

old-fash·ioned /ˌ· ˈ···◁/ *adj* of a type that is no longer common or popular: *old-fashioned ideas* | *old-fashioned clothes*

old mas·ter /ˌ· ˈ··/ *n* a picture by an important painter of an earlier period

Old Tes·ta·ment /ˌ· ˈ···◁/ *n* the first half of the Bible, containing events before the birth of Christ

old-tim·er /ˌ· ˈ··/ *n* **1** a person who has lived somewhere or done something for a long time **2** *AmE* an old man

O lev·el /ˈ· ˌ··/ *n* the lower of the two standards of examination formerly taken at most British schools; an abbreviation for **Ordinary Level**

ol·i·gar·chy /ˈɒlɪɡɑːki ‖ ˈɑːlɪɡɑːrki, ˈəʊ-/ *n* **oligarchies** **1** [C;U] a type of government in which a few people have all the power **2** [C] the group who govern such a state

ol·ive /ˈɒlɪv ‖ ˈɑː-/ *n* a small green or black bitter-tasting fruit which produces oil used in cooking and which can be used as food

olive branch /ˈ·· ·/ *n* a sign of peace

O·lym·pic Games /əˌlɪmpɪk ˈɡeɪmz/ *n* [plural is **Olympic Games**] (also **Olympics**) an international sports event held once every four years in different countries –**Olympic** *adj* [only before a noun]

o·me·ga /ˈəʊmɪɡə ‖ əʊˈmegə, -ˈmiː-, -ˈmeɪ-/ *n* the last letter of the Greek alphabet

ome·let /ˈɒmlɪt ‖ ˈɑːm-/ *n* (also **omelette**) eggs beaten together and cooked in hot fat in a pan: *a cheese omelet*

o·men /ˈəʊmən/ *n* a sign that something is going to happen in the future: *a good omen* | *a bad omen*

om·i·nous /ˈɒmɪnəs ‖ ˈɑː-/ *adj* being a sign of something bad: *ominous black clouds* –**ominously** *adv*

o·mis·sion /əʊˈmɪʃən, ə-/ *n* **1** [U] the act of leaving something out: *He's annoyed about his omission from the team.* **2** [C] something or someone that has been left out

o·mit /əʊˈmɪt, ə-/ *v* **omitted** [T] **1** to leave something out by mistake or on purpose **2** to not do something: *He omitted to tell me when he was leaving.*

□ USEFUL PATTERNS: to omit something, to omit to do something; to omit doing something

om·ni·bus /ˈɒmnɪbəs, -ˌbʌs ‖ ˈɑːm-/ *n* a book containing several works, especially by one writer, which have already been printed separately: *a Dickens omnibus*

om·nip·o·tent /ɒmˈnɪpətənt ‖ ɑːm-/ *adj* having complete power –**omnipotence** *n* [U]

om·nis·ci·ent /ɒmˈnɪʃənt, -ˈnɪsiənt ‖ ɑːmˈnɪʃənt/ *adj* knowing everything: *an omniscient god* –**omniscience** *n* [U]

on /ɒn ‖ ɔːn, ɑːn/ *adv,prep* **1** *adv, prep* touching something and supported or held by it: *There was a lamp on the table.* | *Put the cup on the shelf.* | *shelves with books on* | *the pictures on the walls* | *There were a lot of cars on the road.* | *a blue hat with a ribbon on it* | *Write your name on a piece of paper.* **2** *adv, prep* inside a bus, train, or plane: *I've never been on an aeroplane.* | *The bus stopped and several people got on.* –see picture on page 540 **3** *prep* during the day mentioned: *I'll see you on Tuesday.* | *We're going out on Monday evening.* | *I always go to town on Fridays.* | *He's leaving on July 1st.* **4** *adv* used to show that someone continues to do something: *We worked on all night.* | *We walked on, and came to a village.* | *Please read on.* **5** **have something on** to be wearing something: *He had no coat on.* | *men with smart suits on* **6** *adv* working (used of a light or a machine): *Put the light on, please.* | *Is the cooker still on?* **7** *adv* happening: *There's a new film on at the cinema in town.* | *There's a dance on in the village hall tonight.* | *We had very little money when the war was on.* **8** *prep* about something: *a lecture on medieval history* | *They sell books on all subjects.* **9** *prep* taking a drug or a medicine regularly: *She's on five or six different drugs.* **10** *prep* receiving an amount of money as your wage: *She's on about £20,000 a year.* **11** *prep* used when you are saying that one thing happens as soon as another one has happened: *On hearing of our success, she poured herself a large drink.* | *He was greeted with cheers on his arrival.* | *On thinking about it, I decided not to go.* **12** **on the left**, **on the right** at the left or right: *The school is just down the road on the left.* | *You'll see the cinema on your right.* **13** **on someone** *infml* paid for by someone: *The drinks are all on me tonight!* **14** **from now on**, **from then on**, etc starting now, then, etc and continuing from that time: *From now on I'll always drive within the speed limit.* **15** **on about something** talking about something for a long time and in a dull way: *What's he on about now?* **16 on at someone** complaining to someone or asking them to do something for a long time: *She's always on at me to tidy my room.* **17 on and off** sometimes, but not continuously: *It's been raining on and off all morning.* **18 on and on** continuing to do something for a very long time, in a way that is dull or annoying: *His talk just went on and on for ages!* **19 not on** *infml* not acceptable: *That kind of behaviour's just not on!*

once[1] /wʌns/ *adv* **1** one time and no more: *I've only met him once.* | *We go to the cinema once a week.* | *I'll help you just this once.* **2** some time ago: *He once lived in Rome.* **3 all at once** suddenly: *All at once I heard a noise.* **4 at once: a** now, without delay: *We set to work at once.* **b** all together, at the same time: *Everyone was talking at once.* **5 for once** for this one time only: *For once he was telling the truth.* **6 once and for all** completely and for the last time **7 once in a while** sometimes: *We go to London once in a while.* **8 once more, once again: a** one more time: *I'll write to her once more.* **b** now again, like before: *Once again unemployment is rising.* **9 once or twice** only a few times **10 once upon a time** at some time in the past; used as the beginning of a children's story

once[2] *conj* from the moment that something happens: *Once he arrives we can start.*

once-o-ver /ˈ· ˌ··/ *n infml* **the once-over** a quick look or examination: *He gave the car the once-over and decided not to buy it.*

on-com-ing /ˈɒnˌkʌmɪŋ ‖ ˈɔːn-, ˈɑːn-/ *adj* [only before a noun] coming towards you: *oncoming traffic*

one[1] /wʌn/ *det, n* **1** the number 1: *Only one person came.* | *I'll see you at one o'clock.* | *one of your friends* **2** only: *She's the one person who can do it.* **3** a particular or person: *I saw her one day in June.* | *You must come round for a drink one evening.* | *He can't tell one tree from another.* **4** the same: *They all ran in one direction.*

one[2] *pron* **ones 1** a particular thing or person: *New houses aren't generally as well built as old ones.* | *Is that record the one that I lent you?* **2** *fml* used when you are talking about people in general: *One should never leave one's keys lying around.*

■ USAGE The use of **one** to mean "any person" is now considered to be very formal: **One** *should attempt to understand* **one's** *own culture to the best of* **one's** *ability.* In conversation and in informal writing **you** is commonly used instead: *It is important to understand* **your** *own culture.* | **You** *can spend the day enjoying* **yourself** *on the beach.*

one an-oth-er /ˌ·· ·ˈ··/ *pron* see EACH OTHER: *They hit one another.* | *We often stay in one another's houses.*

one-armed ban-dit /ˌ·· ·ˈ··/ *n infml* a machine with one long handle, into which you put money to try to win more money

one-off /ˌ·ˈ·/ *n infml* something done or made once only: *Do you often go abroad on business, or is this trip just a one-off?*

o-ner-ous /ˈɒnərəs, ˈəʊ- ‖ ˈɑː-, ˈəʊ-/ *adj fml* difficult or troublesome: *an onerous duty*

one-self /wʌnˈself/ *pron fml* used as the object of a verb or PREPOSITION when the subject of a verb is "one"

one-sid-ed /ˌ·ˈ··◄/ *adj* **1** unfair because it takes into account only one side: *a one-sided view of the problem* **2** with one side or team much stronger than the other: *a one-sided football match*

one-time /ˈwʌntaɪm/ *adj* former

one-up-man-ship /wʌnˈʌpmənʃɪp/ *n* [U] the art of getting an advantage over others

one-way /ˌ·ˈ·◄/ *adj* **1** moving or allowing movement in only one direction: *one-way traffic* | *a one-way street* **2** allowing travel to a place but not the return: *a one-way ticket*

on-go-ing /ˈɒnˌgəʊɪŋ ‖ ˈɑːn-/ *adj* continuing: *an ongoing situation* | *ongoing discussions*

on-ion /ˈʌnjən/ *n* [C;U] a strong-smelling round white vegetable with a dry skin, used in cooking –see picture on page 344

on-look-er /ˈɒnˌlʊkəʳ ‖ ˈɔːn-, ˈɑːn-/ *n* a person who sees something happening without taking part in it

only[1] /ˈəʊnli/ *adj* [only before a noun] **1** with no others: *Jane was the only one who came.* **2 only child** a child with no brothers or sisters

only[2] *adv* **1** not more than: *It took only five minutes.* | *Only three people came.* **2** used to show that something happened very recently: *This law was introduced only last year.* **3** used to show that something is sure to happen: *Don't eat all that cake-it will only make you feel sick.* **4 not only** a phrase you use when you are giving the first of two surprising facts: *The cuts will affect not only this school but also other schools in the area.* **5 only just** hardly: *I could only just lift it.* **6 only too** very: *What you say is only too true.*

■ USAGE In writing, put **only** in front of the part of the sentence which it concerns: **Only** *Jill saw the lion.* (= nobody else saw it) | *Jill* **only** *saw the lion.* (= she didn't shoot it) | *Jill saw* **only** *the lion.* (= she didn't see the tiger). Note, however, that in conversation **only** is usually put before the verb, and the meaning is made clear by the way the sentence is said.

only[3] *conj* except that; but: *He wants to go, only he can't.*

o.n.o. a written abbreviation for "or near offer": *Car for sale £850 o.n.o.*

on-rush /ˈɒnrʌʃ ‖ ˈɔːn-, ˈɑːn-/ *n* a strong movement forward: *an onrush of water* | *an onrush of people* –**onrushing** *adj*

on-set /ˈɒnset ‖ ˈɔːn-, ˈɑːn-/ *n* **the onset** the first attack or beginning of something: *the onset of a nasty cold* | *the onset of winter*

on-shore /ˌɒnˈʃɔːʳ◄ ‖ ˌɔːnˈʃɔːrˌ, ˌɑːn-/ *adv, adj* **1** happening on or near the shore: *the search for onshore oil* **2** moving towards the shore: *an onshore breeze*

on-side /ˌɒnˈsaɪd◄ ‖ ˌɔːn-, ˌɑːn-/ *adj,adv* in a position in certain sports in which play is allowed

on-slaught /ˈɒnslɔːt ‖ ˈɔːn-, ˈɑːn-/ *n* a fierce attack on something or someone: *In his speech, the politician made a strong onslaught* **on** *the unions.*

on-to /ˈɒntə; *before vowels* ˈɒntu ‖ ˈɔːn-, ˈɑːn-/ *prep* to a position or point on something or someone: *He jumped onto the horse.* –see picture on page 540

o-nus /ˈəʊnəs/ *n* responsibility: *The onus of proof lies with you.*

on-ward /ˈɒnwəd ‖ ˈɔːnwərd, ˈɑːn-/ *adj* [only before a noun] forward in space or time: *the onward march of events* –**onwards** (also **onward** *AmE*) *adv* :*We decided to travel onwards.* | *from 1984 onwards*

oops /ʊps/ *interj infml* an expression used when someone has made a mistake: *Oops! I nearly dropped my cup of tea!*

ooze[1] /uːz/ *n* [U] mud or thick liquid, especially at the bottom of a river

ooze² v oozed, oozing 1 [I + adv/prep] (of a liquid) to pass or flow slowly: *Blood was oozing from his wound.* 2 [T] to allow liquid to pass slowly out: *The wound was oozing blood.*

o·pal /ˈəʊpəl/ n [C;U] a precious stone which looks like milky water with colours in it

o·paque /əʊˈpeɪk/ adj 1 not allowing light to pass through: *opaque glass* 2 hard to understand: *an opaque argument* –opaquely adv –opaqueness, opacity /əʊˈpæsˌti/ n [U]

OPEC /ˈəʊpek/ a group of countries who produce oil, and plan together how to sell it; an abbreviation for **Organization of Petroleum Exporting Countries**

o·pen¹ /ˈəʊpən/ adj 1 not shut: *Come in! The door's open.* | *with open eyes* 2 **an open mind** not closed to new ideas 3 [only before a noun] not enclosed: *the open country* | *open fields* 4 not covered: *an open boat* | *Let's eat in the open air.* | *The courtyard is open to the skies.* 5 not fastened: *an open shirt* 6 spread out or unfolded: *an open book* 7 not certainly decided: *an open question* | *The job is still open.* 8 not hiding anything: *Let's be open with each other.* 9 ready for business: *The bank isn't open yet.* 10 that anyone can enter: *an open competition* 11 **open to something**: a not safe from something: *This book is open to misunderstanding.* b willing to receive something: *I'm always open to suggestions*

open² v 1 [I;T] to make open or become open: *He opened the door.* | *The door opened.* | *Open your eyes.* 2 [I;T] to start: *The story opens in a country house.* | *He opened the meeting with a welcoming speech.* | *When was the new hospital opened?* 3 [I;T] to begin business: *The bank opens every morning at 9 am.* | *They open their shop 7 days a week.* 4 [I;T] to unfold or spread out: *He opened his umbrella.* | *The flowers open in the sunshine.* 5 [T] to make it possible to use a passage by removing the things that are blocking it: *They cleared away the rocks to open the tunnel.* **open fire** to start shooting at someone or something

open out phr v [I] to become wider

open up phr v 1 [T **open** sthg ↔ **up**] to open something: *They opened the country up to trade.* 2 [I] infml to open a door: *Open up or we'll break the door down.*

open³ n [U] 1 **in the open** outdoors: *We love eating in the open.* 2 **be out in the open** to become generally known (of opinions, secrets): *I'm glad the news of their divorce is finally out in the open; it's so difficult to keep secrets.*

open-air /ˌ·ˈ··◄/ adj [only before a noun] outdoor: *an open-air theatre*

open-end·ed /ˌ·ˈ··◄/ adj without stating any clear aim in advance: *an open-ended discussion*

o·pen·er /ˈəʊpənəʳ/ n a tool used for opening something: *a tin opener*

open-hand·ed /ˌ·ˈ··◄/ adj generous

o·pen·ing¹ /ˈəʊpənɪŋ/ n 1 the act of becoming open or of opening: *the opening of a new supermarket* 2 a hole or space: *We squeezed through an opening in the fence.* 3 a favourable set of conditions which will allow you to do something: *She's looking for an opening in advertising.*

opening² adj [only before a noun] 1 coming first or at the beginning: *The opening night of the new play went very well.* 2 **opening hours** the hours when a shop or business is open: *What are your opening hours?*

o·pen·ly /ˈəʊpənli/ adv without trying to hide anything: *They talked openly about their plans.*

open-mind·ed /ˌ·ˈ··◄/ adj willing to consider new ideas and opinions

open-plan /ˌ·ˈ·◄/ adj open, not divided into closed rooms (used of offices and buildings)

op·e·ra /ˈɒpərə ‖ ˈɑː-/ n [C;U] a musical play in which most of the words are sung –operatic /ˌɒpəˈrætɪk◄ ‖ ˌɑː-/ adj

op·e·rate /ˈɒpəreɪt ‖ ˈɑː-/ v operated, operating 1 [I;T] to work or make something work: *He operates the loading machine.* | *I'm not sure exactly how computers operate.* 2 [I] (of a business) to be in action: *We operate mainly in Europe.* 3 [I] to cut someone's body in order to remove or repair a diseased or damaged part: *I'm afraid we'll have to operate.* | *They're operating on her left eye.*

operating thea·tre /ˈ···· ‖ ˈ···/ n (also **theatre**) a special room in a hospital where medical operations are done

op·e·ra·tion /ˌɒpəˈreɪʃən ‖ ˌɑː-/ n 1 [U] in operation working or having an effect: *The new system is now in operation.* | *When does the new law come into operation?* 2 [C] a planned activity: *We've been asked to finance a mining operation.* | *a famine relief operation* 3 [C] a hospital treatment to repair or remove a diseased part of someone's body: *a hip replacement operation*

op·e·ra·tion·al /ˌɒpəˈreɪʃənəl◄ ‖ ˌɑː-/ adj 1 working and ready for use: *The new machines are not yet operational.* 2 [only before a noun] happening while a plan is in operation: *We've had a few operational difficulties.*

op·e·ra·tive¹ /ˈɒpərətɪv ‖ ˈɑːpərə-, ˈɑːpəreɪ-/ adj 1 working or having an effect: *The school should be fully operative by the new year.* 2 **the operative word** the most suitable word

operative² n a worker

op·e·ra·tor /ˈɒpəreɪtəʳ ‖ ˈɑː-/ n 1 a person who works a machine or a business: *a lathe operator* | *tour operators* 2 someone who works a telephone SWITCHBOARD: *I'll have to dial the operator.* –see TELEPHONE¹ (USAGE)

oph·thal·mic /ɒfˈθælmɪk, ɒp- ‖ ɑːf-/ adj tech concerning the medical treatment of people's eyes

o·pin·ion /əˈpɪnjən/ n 1 [C;U] what a person thinks about something: *His opinions are always interesting.* | *There has been a shift in public opinion.* –see ACCORDING TO (USAGE) 2 **in my opinion** a phrase used when you are giving your opinion 3 **have a good/high opinion of** to think that someone or something has good qualities [RELATED PHRASE: **have a low opinion of**]

opinion poll /·ˈ·· ˌ·/ n a way of finding out what people think about particular events or subjects by asking them questions: *An opinion poll of over a thousand people showed 80% in support of the government.*

o·pin·ion·at·ed /əˈpɪnjəneɪtˌd/ adj too sure that your own opinions are always right (a word used to show disapproval)

o·pi·um /ˈəʊpiəm/ n [U] a drug made from the seeds of the POPPY; it is used in medicines and as an illegal drug

op·po·nent /əˈpəʊnənt/ n 1 a person who takes the opposite side in a game or competition 2 a person who opposes something: *He is one of the government's strongest opponents.*

op·por·tune /ˈɒpətjuːn ‖ ˌɑːpərˈtuːn/ adj fml coming at the right time: *an opportune remark* | *They called at an opportune moment.* –opposite **inopportune**

op·por·tun·ist /ˌɒpə'tjuːnᵻst ‖ ˌɑːpər'tuː-/ n a person who takes advantage of every chance for success without considering other people's needs –**opportunism** n [U] –**opportunistic** /ˌɒpətjuː'nɪstɪk◂ ‖ ˌɑːpərtuː-/ adj

op·por·tu·ni·ty /ˌɒpə'tjuːnᵻti ‖ ˌɑːpər'tuː-/ n opportunities [C;U] a favourable moment or occasion which allows you to do something: *This job offers the opportunity to work abroad.* | *equality of opportunity* | *She had no opportunity to develop her talents.* –see CHANCE (USAGE)

□ USEFUL PATTERNS an opportunity to do something; an opportunity for someone to do something

op·pose /ə'pəʊz/ v **opposed, opposing** [T] to try to prevent something because you do not agree with it: *Local residents opposed the building of a new road.*

op·posed /ə'pəʊzd/ adj **1** not in agreement with someone or something: *She is opposed* **to** *the death penalty.* **2** opposite or completely different from something: *Their opinions are diametrically opposed.* **3 as opposed to** rather than: *We're talking about business practice as opposed to theory.*

op·po·site¹ /'ɒpəzᵻt ‖ 'ɑː-/ n a person or thing that is completely different to another: *Black and white are opposites.* | *She is very generous, but her sister is just the opposite.*

opposite² adj **1** completely different: *They set off in opposite directions.* **2** facing: *There were illustrations on the opposite page.* | *We live on the opposite side of the street.* | *There were lights on in the houses opposite.* | *I was watching the man sitting opposite.* **3 opposite number** a person who does the same job as you but in a different department or organization

opposite³ prep facing: *We live opposite the village green.* –see picture on page 540

op·po·si·tion /ˌɒpə'zɪʃ*ə*n ‖ ˌɑː-/ n **1** [U] the act of being opposed to something or fighting against it: *The changes met with a lot of opposition* **from** *the workforce.* **2 the opposition** [+ sing/pl verb] the political parties who are not in power: *The opposition are going to vote against the government.* | *The opposition is united on this issue.* | *opposition groups* **3** the sports team or person you are playing against: *Two players managed to break through the opposition's defence.*

op·press /ə'pres/ v [T] **1** to treat people in a hard and cruel way **2** to make you feel worried or sad: *The threat of war oppressed us all.*

op·pres·sion /ə'preʃ*ə*n/ n [U] **1** the act of treating people in a hard and cruel way **2** a feeling of worry or sadness

op·pres·sive /ə'presɪv/ adj **1** cruel and unjust: *an oppressive government* **2** unpleasantly hot (used of the weather) **3** making you feel worried or sad: *an oppressive silence* –**oppressively** adv –**oppressiveness** n [U]

op·pres·sor /ə'presəʳ/ n a person who rules in a cruel way

opt /ɒpt ‖ ɑːpt/ v **1 opt for something** to choose something **2 opt to do something** to choose to do something
opt out phr v [I] to choose not to take part in something

op·tic /'ɒptɪk ‖ 'ɑːp-/ adj [only before a noun] related to the eyes

op·ti·cal /'ɒptɪk*ə*l ‖ 'ɑːp-/ adj [only before a noun] **1** related to your sense of sight: *an optical illusion* **2** using light for recording and storing information: *an optical disk* –**optically** adv

op·ti·cian /ɒp'tɪʃ*ə*n ‖ ɑːp-/ n a person who makes and sells glasses and CONTACT LENSES

op·tics /'ɒptɪks ‖ 'ɑːp-/ n [U] the scientific study of light

op·ti·mis·m /'ɒptᵻmɪzəm ‖ 'ɑːp-/ n [U] the belief that the future will be good, and that things will end well –**optimist** n

op·ti·mis·tic /ˌɒptᵻ'mɪstɪk◂ ‖ ˌɑːp-/ adj feeling hopeful about the future –**optimistically** /-kli/ adv

op·ti·mum /'ɒptᵻməm ‖ 'ɑːp-/ adj [only before a noun] the best possible: *optimum conditions for growing rice*

op·tion /'ɒpʃ*ə*n ‖ 'ɑːp-/ n **1** [sing] the freedom to choose whether you will do something or not: *You must do it; you have no option.* **2** [C] a choice: *As I see it, there are two options open to us.*

op·tion·al /'ɒpʃ*ə*nəl ‖ 'ɑːp-/ adj which may be chosen or not chosen: *All students have to take Maths and English, but other subjects are optional.*

op·u·lent /'ɒpjᵻlənt ‖ 'ɑːp-/ adj very wealthy and expensive-looking –**opulence** n [U]

or /əʳ; strong ɔːʳ/ conj **1** used when you are giving a list of possibilities: *Would you like coffee or tea?* | *I'll see you either on Monday or Tuesday.* | *They cost two or three hundred pounds.* | *"Bank" may mean the edge of a river. Or, it may mean a place where you can leave your money safely.* **2** otherwise: *Put your coat on or you'll be cold.* | *He can't be that ill or he wouldn't have gone out.* **3 or so** about: *I'll be there in an hour or so.* **4 or else** used when you mention a second possibility: *We could do it now or else we could leave it till the morning.*

o·ral /'ɔːrəl/ adj **1** spoken, not written: *an oral examination* **2** concerning your mouth or using your mouth: *oral hygiene* –**orally** adv

or·ange¹ /'ɒrᵻndʒ ‖ 'ɔː-, 'ɑː-/ n a very common reddish-yellow round fruit which is sweet and juicy and has a thick skin –see picture on page 344

orange² adj, n [U] reddish-yellow –see picture on page 147

o·rang·u·tang /ɔː,ræŋuː'tæŋ, -'tæŋ ‖ ə'ræŋətæŋ/ n (also **orang-utan**) a large monkey with reddish-brown hair and no tail

o·ra·tion /ə'reɪʃ*ə*n, ɔː-/ n fml a formal and solemn public speech

or·a·tor /'ɒrətəʳ ‖ 'ɔː-, 'ɑː-/ n a person who is good at making formal speeches in public –**oratory** n [U]

or·bit¹ /'ɔːbᵻt ‖ 'ɔːr-/ n the curved path of an object moving round a PLANET or the sun –**orbital** adj

orbit² v [I;T] to move round something in an orbit

or·chard /'ɔːtʃəd ‖ 'ɔːrtʃərd/ n a field where fruit trees grow

or·ches·tra /'ɔːkᵻstrə ‖ 'ɔːr-/ n a large group of people who play musical instruments together: *The orchestra meets for rehearsal every Tuesday evening.* –**orchestral** /ɔː'kestrəl ‖ ɔːr-/ adj [only before a noun]

or·chid /'ɔːkᵻd ‖ 'ɔːr-/ n a plant with unusual and beautiful flowers

or·dain /ɔː'deɪn ‖ ɔːr-/ v **1 be ordained** become a priest in a special ceremony: *She was ordained the first woman priest of her church.* **2** [T; + that] fml to order something to happen

or·deal /ɔː'diːl, 'ɔːdiːl ‖ ɔːr'diːl, 'ɔːrdiːl/ n a difficult or painful experience

order¹ /'ɔːdəʳ ‖ 'ɔːr-/ n **1** [U] the way in which things are arranged in relation to each other: *The names are filed in alphabetical order.* | *The items are listed in order of importance.* | *We must work*

towards a new social order. **2** [U] the state in which things are neatly arranged in their proper place: *She longed for stability and order in her life.* | *It only took me a few minutes to put the room in order.* **3** [U] the state in which people are behaving well and laws or rules are being obeyed: *He couldn't keep order in the classroom.* | *The police were called in to help restore order.* **4** [C] a command: *You must obey my orders.* | *I give the orders round here!* **5** [C] a request to supply goods: *You can either write to us or place your order by telephone.* **6** [C] the goods that are supplied in accordance with your request: *Your order will be sent off today and should reach you tomorrow.* **7** [C] a group of people who live according to a particular set of religious rules **8 in order: a** arranged in the correct way: *Are those invoices in order?* **b** *fml* acceptable: *It would be quite in order for you to ask for a refund of your money.* **9 in order to, in order that** with a particular purpose: *We went by car in order to save time.* | *I walked quietly in order not to wake the children.* | *The government has to continue with these policies in order that inflation can be brought down as quickly as possible.* **10 in the order of, of the order of** about: *We spent something in the order of £50,000.* **11 on order** (of goods) asked for but not yet supplied: *The book you want is still on order and should be here next week.* **12 out of order: a** not arranged in the correct way: *These papers are all out of order.* **b** not working: *The telephone's out of order.* **c** not in accordance with the rules of a formal meeting, and so not acceptable: *His interruption was ruled to be out of order.* **13 under orders** obeying someone's orders: *They claimed that they were simply acting under orders.*

order² *v* [T;+that] to give a command to someone: *The minister has ordered an inquiry into the accident.* | *She ordered me to leave the room.* | *The commander has ordered that the troops should withdraw from the area.*
□ USEFUL PATTERNS to order something; to order someone to do something; to order that... **2** [I;T] to ask for something to be brought or sent to you: *Shall I order a taxi?* | *I've ordered a new carpet for the sitting room.* | *The waiter came over and asked if we were ready to order.* **3** [T] to arrange things in a particular way: *the way in which we order our lives*
■ USAGE Compare **order, command, tell**. People can **order** or **give orders** if they have the right to be obeyed: *The doctor* **ordered** *me to rest for a week.* **Command** has the same meaning, but is most often used in a military sense: *The general* **ordered/commanded** *his men to advance.* **Tell** is similar to **order** but less strong: *She* **told** *me to come as early as possible.*

or·dered /'ɔːdəd ‖ 'ɔːrdərd/ *adj* done or arranged in a regular, tidy way: *In the hospital, everything was well ordered.*

or·der·ly¹ /'ɔːdəli ‖ 'ɔːrdərli/ *adj* **1** arranged in a regular, tidy way: *He did everything in an orderly manner.* **2** peaceful and well-behaved: *orderly behaviour* –**orderliness** *n* [U]

orderly² *n* **1** a soldier who looks after an officer **2** an untrained attendant in a hospital

or·din·al /'ɔːdɪnəl ‖ 'ɔːr-/ *n* (also **ordinal number** /ˌ··· '··/) a number which shows the order of a set of things; 1st, 2nd, and 3rd are all ordinals

or·di·na·ri·ly /'ɔːdənərɪli ‖ ˌɔːrdən'erəli/ *adv* usually: *Ordinarily, of course, we would telephone first.*

or·di·nary /'ɔːdənri ‖ 'ɔːrdəneri/ *adj* **1** not unusual or special in any way: *I've got an ordinary sort of car, nothing special.* **2 out of the ordinary**

unusual **3 ordinary degree** a first degree that is lower than an honours degree

or·di·na·tion /ˌɔːdɪ'neɪʃən ‖ ˌɔːr-/ *n* [C;U] the act of making someone a priest in a special ceremony

ore /ɔːr/ *n* [U] rock or earth from which metal can be obtained

or·gan /'ɔːgən ‖ 'ɔːr-/ *n* **1** a part of your body that has a particular purpose: *Vital organs such as the liver and the heart are now being used in transplant operations.* **2** an official organization that has a special purpose: *The newspaper was seen as the organ of the government.* **3** a musical instrument with pipes of different lengths through which air is forced; organs are often found in churches and are played like a piano

or·gan·ic /ɔː'gænɪk ‖ ɔːr-/ *adj* **1** [only before a noun] produced by or found in animals or plants –opposite **inorganic 2** [only before a noun] made of many parts with specialized purposes: *an organic system* **3** using only natural products and no chemicals, or produced in this way: *organic vegetables* | *organic farming methods* –opposite **nonorganic** –**organically** /-kli/ *adv*

or·gan·is·m /'ɔːgənɪzəm ‖ 'ɔːr-/ *n* a very small living being, especially one that can only be seen using a microscope

or·gan·ist /'ɔːgənɪst ‖ 'ɔːr-/ *n* a musician who plays an organ

or·gan·i·za·tion /ˌɔːgənaɪ'zeɪʃən ‖ ˌɔːrgənə-/ *n* (also **organisation** *BrE*) **1** [C] a group, club, or business: *a charity organization* **2** [U] the way in which something is arranged or planned: *The merger will bring about major changes in organization.* **3** [U] the act of planning an event and making the arrangements for it –**organizational** *adj*

or·gan·ize /'ɔːgənaɪz ‖ 'ɔːr-/ *v* **organized, organizing** (also **organise** *BrE*) **1** [T] to plan and arrange an event: *Who's organizing the party?* **2** [T] to arrange things in a sensible order: *You need to organize your ideas better in this essay.* **3** [I] to form into a group in order to ask for better pay and working conditions –**organizer** *n*

or·gan·i·zed /'ɔːgənaɪzd ‖ 'ɔːr-/ *adj* (also **organised** *BrE*) **1** well arranged and so working well **2** able to arrange things well

or·gas·m /'ɔːgæzəm ‖ 'ɔːr-/ *n* [C;U] the moment of greatest pleasure in sexual activity –**orgasmic** /ɔː'gæzmɪk ‖ ɔːr-/ *adj*

or·gy /'ɔːdʒi ‖ 'ɔːr-/ *n* **orgies 1** a wild party with a lot of alcohol and sexual activity **2** a period of a lot of activity of a particular kind: *They embarked on an orgy of spending.*

o·ri·ent¹ /'ɔːriənt, 'pri- ‖ 'ɔː-/ *v* (also **orientate**) **orient yourself, orientate yourself: a** to discover where you are by looking at a map **b** to become familiar with a new situation

o·ri·ent² /'ɔːrient, 'pri- ‖ 'ɔːr-/ *n lit* **the Orient** the Eastern part of the world, including India, China, and Japan –**Oriental** /ˌɔːri'entl◂, ˌɒ- ‖ ˌɔː-/ *adj*

o·ri·en·ta·tion /ˌɔːriən'teɪʃən, ˌɒ- ‖ ˌɔː-/ *n* [U] aims or direction

o·ri·en·ted /'ɔːrientɪd, 'pri- ‖ 'ɔːr-/ *adj* (also **oriented**) interested in something: *an export-oriented company*

or·i·fice /'ɒrɪfɪs ‖ 'ɔː-, 'ɑː-/ *n fml* an opening or hole

or·i·gin /'ɒrɪdʒɪn ‖ 'ɔː-, 'ɑː-/ *n* [C;U] **1** the beginning or cause of something: *The riot had its origins in unemployment.* | *a word of unknown origin* **2** the race or social class of your parents: *a young man of West Indian origin* | *He was proud of his working class origins.*

In this dictionary a verb is called a phrasal verb if it consists of two or more words. One of these words is always a verb; the other may be an adverb or a preposition (or sometimes both together). The meaning of a phrasal verb is often quite different from the meaning of the verb on its own. For example, **look into** (= investigate) and **look after** (= take care of) have quite separate meanings from **look**.

How are phrasal verbs listed?

Phrasal verbs are listed in alphabetical order underneath the entry for the main verb. They are marked *phr v*.

In this entry **cry off** and **cry out for** are phrasal verbs listed under the entry for **cry**.

---

cry[1] /kraɪ/ *v* **cried, cried, crying** **1** [I] to produce tears from your eyes usually, as a sign of sadness: *She cried when she heard of her friend's death.* | *The children cried for their father.* **2** [I] to speak loudly or shout, usually with fear or excitement: *"Run, run!" he cried.* | *"That's wonderful!" she cried.*

cry off *phr v* [I] *infml* to fail to fulfil a promise or agreement: *He said he'd help, but then he cried off.*

cry out *phr v* [I] to shout loudly, usually with fear or pain: *He cried out in pain.*

Sometimes the main verb of a phrasal verb is not used alone.

This entry shows you that **gad** is not used as a verb by itself, but only as part of the phrasal verb **gad about**.

---

gad /gæd/ *v* **-dd-**

gad about *phr v* [I;T **gad about** sthg] *infml* to travel round a place to enjoy yourself: *He's always gadding about.* | *She's away, gadding about Europe.*

Transitive or intransitive?

Phrasal verbs, like all verbs, may be transitive or intransitive and are marked [T] or [I] accordingly.

These sample entries show that **grow out of** is a transitive verb and **grow up** is an intransitive verb.

---

grow out of sthg *phr v* [T] **1** to become too big or too old for something: *She's grown out of all her clothes.* | *Most children grow out of wetting the bed.*

---

grow up *phr v* [I] **1** (of people) to develop from a child into a man or woman

---

Some phrasal verbs can be used both transitively and intransitively

– sometimes with similar meanings like **join in**.

---

join in *phr v* [I;T **join in** sthg] to take part in an activity: *Sarah never joins in, but prefers to play on her own.* | *We all joined in the singing.*

– sometimes with different meanings like **wrap up**

---

wrap up *phr v* **1** [T **wrap** sthg ↔ **up**] to put paper around a parcel or present **2** [I] to wear warm clothes: *It's cold outside. Wrap up well.*

Position of the direct object.

When a phrasal verb is transitive [T], the dictionary shows you where to put the direct object. You should look at the beginning of the entry to see how the verb is written.

This entry tells you the the direct object of **pick on** always comes at the end of the phrasal verb.

---

pick on sbdy *phr v* [T] to punish or blame someone unfairly because you do not like them: *He's always picking on me!*

In a few cases, such as **get up**, the direct object must always come between the two parts of the phrasal verb.

---

get up *phr v*

2 [T **get** sbdy **up**] to make someone rise from their bed: *Can you go and get the children up?*

For very many phrasal verbs, however, the direct object can appear in either position. This is shown in the dictionary by the symbol ↔ .

---

hand sthg ↔ **in** *phr v* [T] to give something to someone in a position of authority: *Please hand in your books at the end of the lesson.*

This entry shows you that you can say <u>either</u> **Hand in** *your papers* <u>or</u> **Hand** *your papers* **in**. Note, however, that with the verbs of this type, when the direct object is a pronoun it MUST be put between the two parts of the phrasal verb. **Hand in** *your papers.* **Hand** *them* **in.**
They **knocked down** *the building.*
They **knocked** *it* **down.**

More than one object

Some transitive phrasal verbs can have more than one object. The dictionary will show you where to put these.

This entry tells you that **put down to** has two objects; the first comes after **put** and the second after **to**.

---

put sthg **down to** sbdy/sthg *phr v* [T] to say or think that something was caused by a particular person or thing: *He didn't look well but I just put it down to the fact that he was tired.*

o·rig·i·nal¹ /ə'rɪdʒɪnəl, -dʒənəl/ adj **1** [only before a noun] first or earliest: *The original owner of the house was the Duke of Wellington.* **2** new, different, and interesting: *a very original idea* –opposite **unoriginal 3** not copied: *We have a few original paintings.* –**originally** adv: *My family originally came from Ireland.*

original² n a painting or piece of writing which was the first one made, and is not a copy

o·rig·i·nal·i·ty /ə,rɪdʒɪ'nælɪti/ n [U] the quality of being new, different, and interesting: *Her book shows great originality.*

o·rig·i·nate /ə'rɪdʒəneɪt/ v originated, originating [I] to begin to happen or exist: *This TV series originated from a short story.* –**originator** n

or·na·ment¹ /'ɔːnəmənt ‖ 'ɔːr-/ n **1** [C] a small attractive object for show in the home: *Their house is full of little ornaments.* –see picture on page 442 **2** [U] something which is added to make something else more beautiful

or·na·ment² /'ɔːnəmənt ‖ 'ɔːr-/ v [T] to add attractive things to something

or·na·men·tal /,ɔːnə'mentl◂ ‖ ,ɔːr-/ adj intended to look attractive rather than to be useful: *an ornamental garden pond* –**ornamentally** adv

or·nate /ɔː'neɪt ‖ ɔːr-/ adj having a lot of decoration

or·ni·thol·o·gy /,ɔːnɪ'θɒlədʒi ‖ ,ɔːrnɪ'θɑː-/ n [U] the scientific study of birds –**ornithologist** n –**ornithological** /,ɔːnɪθə'lɒdʒɪkəl ‖ ,ɔːrnɪθɑ'lɑː-/ adj

or·phan¹ /'ɔːfən ‖ 'ɔːr-/ n a child whose parents are dead

orphan² v be orphaned to become an orphan

or·phan·age /'ɔːfənɪdʒ ‖ 'ɔːr-/ n a place where orphans are cared for

or·tho·dox /'ɔːθədɒks ‖ 'ɔːrθədɑːks/ adj **1** generally or officially accepted (used of ideas and beliefs) **2** holding accepted religious or political opinions –**orthodoxy** n [U]

Orthodox Church /,··· '·/ n the Orthodox Church part of the Christian church in eastern Europe

or·tho·pae·dic /,ɔːθ'piːdɪk◂ ‖ ,ɔːr-/ adj (also **orthopedic**) [only before a noun] related to the branch of medicine that deals with bones: *I had to see the orthopaedic specialist.*

Os·car /'ɒskər ‖ 'ɑː-/ n an American cinema prize

os·cil·late /'ɒsɪleɪt ‖ 'ɑː-/ v oscillated, oscillating **1** [I] *tech* to keep moving backwards and forwards between two positions **2** to keep changing from one opinion or state of mind to another –**oscillation** /,ɒsɪ'leɪʃən ‖ ,ɑː-/ n [C;U]

os·prey /'ɒspri, -preɪ ‖ 'ɑː-/ n a large bird which catches and eats fish

os·ten·si·ble /ɒ'stensɪbəl ‖ ɑː-/ adj [only before a noun] seeming to be true, but perhaps not really true: *the ostensible reason* –**ostensibly** adv

os·ten·ta·tion /,ɒstən'teɪʃən, -ten- ‖ ,ɑː-/ n [U] fml unnecessary show of wealth or knowledge: *Having four cars and parking them outside the house is pure ostentation.*

os·ten·ta·tious /,ɒstən'teɪʃəs, -ten- ‖ ,ɑː-/ adj showing your wealth and knowledge in such a way that everybody sees it –**ostentatiously** adv

os·tra·cize /'ɒstrəsaɪz ‖ 'ɑː-/ v ostracized, ostracizing (also **ostracise**) [T] to stop accepting someone as a member of a group: *Conscientious objectors were ostracized during the war.* –**ostracism** n [U]

os·trich /'ɒstrɪtʃ ‖ 'ɔː-, 'ɑː-/ n a large African bird which runs quickly but cannot fly

oth·er /'ʌðər/ det, pron **1** the remaining one or ones that you have not already mentioned: *He was holding the wheel with one hand and waving with the other one.* | *One of their children is 15 years old, and the other is 12.* | *Put that box over there with the other boxes.* | *Mary's here. Where are the others?* **2** an additional or different person or thing: *There were two other boys with him.* | *I'd love to travel to other countries.* | *Some people adapt to change more quickly than others.* **3** other people people in general, not including yourself: *She gets on well with other people.* | *He's always keen to spend other people's money.* **4** other than except: *There's no one here other than me.* **5** the other day, the other night, etc on a recent day, night, etc: *I saw Jane the other day.* | *Your letter arrived the other morning.*

oth·er·wise /'ʌðəwaɪz ‖ 'ʌðər-/ adv **1** used when you are saying what the result would be if something did not happen or was not true: *Let's go now otherwise we'll be late.* **2** in a different way: *She was determined to go ahead with it although I tried to persuade her otherwise.* **3** in every other way: *It was a bit long, but otherwise it was a good film.* –see Study Note on page 508

ot·ter /'ɒtər ‖ 'ɑː-/ n a small animal which can swim well, and catches and eats fish

ouch /aʊtʃ/ interj a cry expressing sudden pain

ought /ɔːt/ v negative short form oughtn't [modal verb] **1** used to show that you think someone has a moral duty to do something: *She ought to look after her children a bit better.* | *You ought to be ashamed of yourself.* | *She ought not to talk to you like that.* | *You ought to have helped her.* | *He ought to be punished for what he did.* **2** used when you are suggesting what someone should do, or saying that something would be a good idea: *You ought to see a doctor.* | *He ought to give up that job and find something better.* | *We really ought to buy a new car.* | *I ought to have bought some bread.* | *Ought I to phone her?* **3** used to show that you expect something to happen or be true: *They ought to win easily.* | *She ought to be home by now.* | *The weather ought to start improving soon.* | *They ought to have set out by now.* –see Study Note on page 392

ounce /aʊns/ n (also oz) **1** a unit for measuring weight, equal to 28.35 grams **2** an ounce of a small amount: *Haven't you got an ounce of sense?*

our /aʊər/ det connected with or belonging to the people who are speaking: *We went in and took off our coats.* | *We must look after our planet for the sake of future generations.*

ours /aʊəz ‖ aʊərz/ pron something connected with or belonging to the people who are speaking: *This is your room, and that one over there is ours.* | *Their house is very similar to ours.*

ourselves /aʊə'selvz ‖ aʊər-/ pron **1** used as the object of a verb or a preposition when the subject of a verb is the people who are speaking and the action is done to the same people: *We were thrilled to see ourselves on television.* | *We bought a few things for ourselves.* | *We've bought ourselves a new car.* **2** used to add force to the word "we": *We did all the decorating ourselves.* **3** by ourselves alone, with no-one with us or helping us: *We spent the evening by ourselves.* | *We had managed to mend the roof by ourselves.*

oust /aʊst/ v [T] to force someone to leave a place or job: *The government has been ousted by the army.*

out /aʊt/ adv,adj **1** adv not in a place, or so as to be no longer in a place: *She opened her bag, and took* some money out. | *The gate was open and several animals had got out.* **2** *adv* away from your home or your place of work: *I'm afraid Miss Hall is out at the moment.* | *He's gone out for the afternoon.* **3** *adj* not correct: *Our calculations were out by quite a lot.* **4** *adv* no longer batting (BAT) in a game of cricket: *England were all out for 347.* **5** *adv, adj* no longer fashionable: *Long skirts are definitely out now.* **6** *adv* no longer burning (used of a fire): *The fire's gone out.* **7** *adv* no longer shining (used of a light): *Could you turn the light out, please?* **8** *adv* open (used of flowers): *The roses are out early this year.* **9** *adv* not acceptable: *I'm afraid that idea's out.* **10** *adv infml* not working because of a STRIKE: *The men have been out for two months now.* **11 the tide is out** = the sea is at the point when it is lowest and furthest from the land **12 out and about** able to get out of bed and go outside again after an illness **13 out for something** trying to get something: *They're only out for profit.* **14 out to do something** trying to do something: *She's out to make as much money as she can from the deal.*

out of *prep* **1** towards the outside of something, or away from something: *He took a small packet out of his pocket.* | *She got up and walked out of the room.* | *He fell out of the window.* | *It's time you got out of bed!* –see picture on page 540 **2** used when stating the relation between two numbers: *Four out of five people agree with the government's economic policies.* **3** having no more of something: *We're nearly out of petrol.* | *I'm afraid we're right out of coffee.* **4** because of a feeling that you have: *I went to see her out of curiosity.* | *He only did it out of spite.* **5** used when stating what something is made from: *I thought I'd make the frame out of wood.* **6 out of it** feeling sad because you are not included in something: *All the others were enjoying themselves and I felt rather out of it.*

out-and-out /ˌ· · ·/ *adj* [only before a noun] complete: *He's an out-and-out liar.*

out·back /ˈaʊtbæk/ *n* **the outback** the part of Australia far away from cities, where few people live

out·bid /aʊtˈbɪd/ *v* **outbid, outbid, outbidding** [T] to offer more money than someone else for something that you both want to buy

out·board mo·tor /ˌaʊtbɔːd ˈməʊtəʳ ‖ -bɔːrd-/ *n* a motor fixed to the back end of a small boat

out·break /ˈaʊtbreɪk/ *n* a sudden start or appearance: *After the hurricane, there was an outbreak of cholera.* | *the outbreak of war*

out·burst /ˈaʊtbɜːst ‖ -ɜːr-/ *n* a sudden powerful period of activity or expression of feeling: *There was an unexpected outburst of gunfire.* | *an outburst of anger*

out·cast /ˈaʊtkɑːst ‖ -kæst/ *n* a person who is forced to live away from other people or is not accepted by other people

out·class /aʊtˈklɑːs ‖ -ˈklæs/ *v* [T] to be much better than someone else

out·come /ˈaʊtkʌm/ *n* an effect or result: *What was the outcome of the election?*

out·crop /ˈaʊtkrɒp ‖ -krɑːp/ *n* a large area of rock which stands up out of the ground

out·cry /ˈaʊtkraɪ/ *n* **outcries** a public expression of anger: *If they try to close the railway, there'll be an outcry.*

out·dat·ed /ˌaʊtˈdeɪtɪd◂/ *adj* no longer in fashion

out·dis·tance /aʊtˈdɪstəns/ *v* **outdistanced, outdistancing** [T] to go a lot faster than someone else in a race

out·do /aʊtˈduː/ *v* **outdid** /aʊtˈdɪd/, **outdone** /aʊtˈdʌn/, **outdoing** [T] to be better or more successful than someone else

out·door /ˌaʊtˈdɔːʳ◂/ *adj* [only before a noun] happening or used in the open air: *the outdoor life* | *outdoor shoes* –opposite **indoor**

out·doors /ˌaʊtˈdɔːz ‖ -ɔːrz/ *adv* (also **out of doors**) outside in the open air: *Go and play outdoors.* –opposite **indoors**

out·er /ˈaʊtəʳ/ *adj* [only before a noun] on the outside or at a greater distance from the middle: *outer London* | *The outer walls seem sound.* –opposite **inner**

out·er·most /ˈaʊtəməʊst ‖ -tər-/ *adj* [only before a noun] furthest from the middle –opposites **inmost**, **innermost**

outer space /ˌ·· ˈ·/ *n* [U] the area beyond the Earth's ATMOSPHERE

out·fit /ˈaʊtˌfɪt/ *n* **1** a set of clothes **2** *infml* a group of people working together: *I joined this outfit last year.*

out·flank /aʊtˈflæŋk/ *v* [T] to go round the side and attack an enemy from behind

out·go·ing /ˌaʊtˈgəʊɪŋ◂/ *adj* **1** [only before a noun] leaving an important job: *The outgoing president was praised for his commitment to the Party.* **2** friendly and eager to make friends

out·go·ings /ˈaʊtˌgəʊɪŋz/ *n* [pl] amounts of money that are spent: *You will have to reduce your outgoings if you want to pay off your debts.*

out·grow /aʊtˈgrəʊ/ *v* **outgrew** /-ˈgruː/, **outgrown** /-ˈgrəʊn/ [T] to grow too big or too old for something: *Children outgrow their shoes every few months.*

out·house /ˈaʊthaʊs/ *n* a small building connected to or near a house

out·ing /ˈaʊtɪŋ/ *n* a short pleasure trip

out·land·ish /aʊtˈlændɪʃ/ *adj* strange and not very pleasant: *outlandish behaviour*

out·last /aʊtˈlɑːst ‖ -ˈlæst/ *v* [T] to last longer than something else

out·law¹ /ˈaʊtlɔː/ *n old fash* a criminal who has not been caught and is hiding from the police

outlaw² *v* [T] to declare that something is against the law

out·lay /ˈaʊtleɪ/ *n* an amount of money that is spent for a particular purpose

out·let /ˈaʊtlet, -lɪt/ *n* **1** a pipe through which a liquid or gas may go out **2** an activity that lets you express your ideas or feelings **3** an American word for an electrical SOCKET

out·line¹ /ˈaʊtlaɪn/ *n* **1** a line showing the shape of something: *the outline of her face* **2** the main ideas or facts of something, with no details: *an outline of the main points of the talk*

outline² *v* **outlined, outlining** [T] to explain a plan or idea in a general way: *The director outlined his plans for the company's future.*

out·live /aʊtˈlɪv/ *v* **outlived, outliving** [T] to live longer than someone

out·look /ˈaʊtlʊk/ *n* **1** a general point of view about life: *We are now much more European in our outlook.* **2** the way a situation is likely to develop: *The weather outlook for the weekend is bad.*

out·ly·ing /ˈaʊtˌlaɪ·ɪŋ/ *adj* [only before a noun] far from cities: *Outlying villages were cut off by the heavy snow.*

out·ma·noeu·vre /ˌaʊtməˈnuːvəʳ/ *v* **outmanoeuvred, outmanoeuvring (outmaneuver** *AmE*) [T] to do something clever which results in you having an advantage over your opponent

out·mod·ed /aʊtˈməʊdɪd/ *adj* no longer in fashion

out·num·ber /aʊtˈnʌmbər/ *v* [T] to be larger in number than something: *Women in this age-group outnumber men* **by** *three to one.*

out-of-date /ˌ··ˈ·◂/ *adj* no longer in fashion

out-of-the-way /ˌ···ˈ·◂/ *adj* far away from cities, and so not often visited

out of work /ˌ·ˈ·◂/ *adj* without a job: *The number of people out of work is expected to reach 3 million by the end of the year.* | *an out of work actor*

out·pa·tient /ˈaʊtˌpeɪʃənt/ *n* a person who receives hospital treatment without staying there at night

out·post /ˈaʊtpəʊst/ *n* a small village at some distance from a main centre

out·pour·ing /ˈaʊtˌpɔːrɪŋ/ *n* a strong expression of your feelings or ideas, especially in an uncontrolled way: *hysterical outpourings of grief*

out·put /ˈaʊtpʊt/ *n* [C;U] **1** the amount of something that is produced by a person or business: *The company hopes to increase its output by 30% next year.* **2** the information printed or shown on a computer: *Run the program, then we'll have a look at the output.*

out·rage¹ /ˈaʊtreɪdʒ/ *n* **1** [U] a strong feeling of anger and shock: *There was a general sense of outrage at the killing.* **2** [C] an event which people find very shocking: *Another bomb outrage has shocked the city.*

outrage² *v* **outraged, outraging** [T] *fml* to offend and shock someone greatly

out·ra·geous /aʊtˈreɪdʒəs/ *adj* very shocking and offensive: *outrageous remarks* –**outrageously** *adv*

out·right¹ /aʊtˈraɪt/ *adv* **1** completely: *The government have banned the drug outright.* **2** openly and in a direct manner: *I asked him outright what he thought.*

out·right² /ˈaʊtraɪt/ *adj* [only before a noun] complete: *an outright victory* | *an outright refusal*

out·set /ˈaʊtset/ *n* **1 at the outset** at the very beginning of an event: *You must tell the builders what you want at the outset.* [RELATED PHRASE: **from the outset**: *I've been involved with the project from the outset.*]

out·shine /aʊtˈʃaɪn/ *v* **outshone** /-ˈʃɒn/ -ˈʃəʊn/, **outshining** [T] to do something much better than someone else

out·side¹ /aʊtˈsaɪd, ˈaʊtsaɪd/ *n* **1** the outer part of something, or the part that is furthest from the middle: *We need to paint the outside of the house.* **2 at the outside** at the most: *The job will take three weeks at the outside.*

out·side² /aʊtˈsaɪd/ *adv, prep* **1** out of something, towards the open air: *She opened the door and went outside.* | *He was standing outside the door.* –see picture on page 540 **2** not within a group of people: *We had to bring in extra help from outside.*

outside³ *adj* [only before a noun] **1** on the outside of something: *the outside walls of the house* **2** connected with people who are not within a particular group: *We need some outside help.* **3 outside chance** a very small chance: *There's an outside chance that she'll win.* **4 outside lane** the part of a MOTORWAY or large road where cars drive more quickly

out·sid·er /aʊtˈsaɪdər/ *n* a person who is not a member of a particular group, or is not accepted by a group: *I've lived here for five years but I still feel an outsider.*

out·size /ˈaʊtsaɪz/ *adj* larger than the usual size: *outsize clothes* | *"What sizes do you have?" "Small, medium, large and outsize."*

out·skirts /ˈaʊtskɜːts ǁ -ɜːr-/ *n* **the outskirts** the outer area of a town: *They live on the outskirts of Paris.*

out·smart /aʊtˈsmɑːt ǁ -ɑːr-/ *v* [T] *infml* to cleverly defeat someone and gain an advantage over them

out·spo·ken /aʊtˈspəʊkən/ *adj* expressing your opinions openly, even if they offend people

out·spread /ˌaʊtˈspred◂/ *adj* spread out flat or stretched out to full width

out·stand·ing /aʊtˈstændɪŋ/ *adj* **1** extremely good **2** not yet done or paid: *I've got two essays outstanding this term.* | *outstanding debts* –**outstandingly** *adv*

out·stretched /ˌaʊtˈstretʃt◂/ *adj* stretched out as far as possible (used of your arms or hands)

out·strip /aʊtˈstrɪp/ *v* -**pp-** [T] to be larger or more successful than someone else

out·ward /ˈaʊtwəd ǁ -ərd/ *adj* [only before a noun] **1** away from a place: *the outward journey* **2** shown to other people (used of feelings): *I knew he was unhappy despite his outward cheerfulness.*

out·ward·ly /ˈaʊtwədli ǁ -ər-/ *adv* in a way that is shown to other people: *She seemed happy, at least outwardly.*

out·wards /ˈaʊtwədz ǁ -ər-/ *adv* (also **outward** *AmE*) towards the outside: *The door opens outwards.*

out·weigh /aʊtˈweɪ/ *v* [T] to be more important than something, or have more advantages than something

out·wit /aʊtˈwɪt/ *v* -**tt-** [T] to cleverly defeat someone and gain an advantage over them

out·worn /ˌaʊtˈwɔːn ǁ -ˈwɔːrn-/ *adj* old-fashioned and no longer useful (used of ideas, beliefs and customs)

o·val /ˈəʊvəl/ *n* a shape like that of an egg –**oval** *adj*

o·va·ry /ˈəʊvəri/ *n* **ovaries** the female organ that produces eggs

o·va·tion /əʊˈveɪʃən/ *n fml* **1** a loud burst of AP-PLAUSE: *The soloist received a thunderous ovation.* **2 standing ovation** a burst of APPLAUSE in which people stand up to show their great approval of someone

ov·en /ˈʌvən/ *n* the part of a COOKER that is like a small box, in which you put food to bake it

o·ver¹ /ˈəʊvər/ *adv, prep* **1** *prep* directly above something, on the top of something, or covering something: *There was a picture hanging over the fireplace.* | *Put a cloth over the table.* | *She put a coat on over her jumper.* –see picture on page 540 **2** *adv, prep* going across from side of something to the other side, or on the other side: *He jumped over the hedge.* | *She looked at me over the wall.* | *He walked quickly over the road.* | *The shops are just over the road.* | *We'll have to cross over to the other side of the river.* **3** *adv* used when you are saying where someone or something is, and are pointing to the place: *The telephone is over by the door.* | *Jane is over there by the window.* **4 over** to towards a place: *She walked over to the radio and switched it on.* | *They're flying over to America.* **5** *adv, prep* downwards from an upright position: *I fell over.* | *She leaned over to look at the map.* | *He was sitting bending over his work.* **6** *adv, prep* more than a particular amount: *We've had over two thousand letters.* | *It all happened over five years ago.* | *children aged seven and over* **7** *prep* about: *a disagreement over rates of pay* **8** *prep* during a period of time: *She gradually got better over the summer.* | *We'll talk over dinner.* **9**

adv remaining: *Was there any money over after you'd paid the bills?* **10** *adv* too: *Don't be over anxious about it.* **11 all over** everywhere in a place: *We've been looking all over for you.* | *They've travelled all over Europe.* **12 all over again** starting from the beginning again: *I'm afraid you'll have to do the test all over again.* **13 over and done with** completely finished: *At least we've got our exams over and done with.* **14 over and over again** again and again, many times

over² *adj* [never before a noun] finished: *I'll talk to you once the meeting's over.*

over³ *n* a set of six balls that are bowled (BOWL) in a game of cricket

o·ver·all¹ /ˌəʊvərˈɔːl◂/ *adj* including everything or the whole of something: *The fish measured 5 feet 3 inches overall.* | *The overall cost of the repairs is more than we anticipated.*

overall² *adv* generally: *Overall, the future looks bright.* | *This was a good attempt overall.*

o·ver·all³ /ˈəʊvərɔːl/ *n* **1** a loose coat that you wear when you are working, to protect your other clothes **2 overalls** [pl] loose trousers and a top that you wear when you are working, to protect your other clothes

o·ver·arm /ˈəʊvəraːm ‖ -aːr-/ *adj,adv* thrown with your arm moving above your shoulder: *He bowled overarm.*

o·ver·awe /ˌəʊvərˈɔː/ *v* **overawed, overawing be overawed** to be filled with respect and fear

o·ver·bal·ance /ˌəʊvəˈbæləns ‖ -vər-/ *v* **overbalanced, overbalancing** [I] to become unbalanced and fall over

o·ver·bear·ing /ˌəʊvəˈbeərɪŋ ‖ -vər-/ *adj* always trying to make other people obey you or do what you want −**overbearingly** *adv*

o·ver·board /ˈəʊvəbɔːd ‖ ˈəʊvərbɔːrd/ *adv* **1** over the side of a boat into the water: *He fell overboard and drowned.* **2 go overboard** *infml* to do something too much **3 throw something overboard** to get rid of something or not to accept an idea or plan

o·ver·bur·dened /ˌəʊvəˈbɜːdnd ‖ ˌəʊvərˈbɜːrdnd/ *adj* carrying or doing too much: *I felt overburdened with work.*

o·ver·cast /ˌəʊvəˈkaːst ‖ ˌəʊvərˈkæst◂/ *adj* dark with clouds: *There was a grey, overcast sky.*

o·ver·charge /ˌəʊvəˈtʃaːdʒ ‖ ˌəʊvərˈtʃaːrdʒ/ *v* **overcharged, overcharging** [T] to charge someone too much: *The waiter overcharged us for the wine.*

o·ver·coat /ˈəʊvəkəʊt ‖ -vər-/ *n* a thick warm coat

o·ver·come /ˌəʊvəˈkʌm ‖ -vər-/ *v* **overcame** /-ˈkeɪm/, **overcome, overcoming** [T] **1** to fight successfully against something such as a feeling or a problem: *I managed to overcome my fear of the dark.* **2 be overcome** to be made helpless, especially by a strong feeling: *overcome by smoke* | *overcome with emotion*

o·ver·com·pen·sate /ˌəʊvəˈkɒmpənseɪt, -pen- ‖ -vərˈkaːm-/ *v* **overcompensated, overcompensating** [I] to try too hard to correct a weakness

o·ver·crowd·ed /ˌəʊvəˈkraʊdɪd ‖ -vər-/ *adj* having too many people or things inside: *an overcrowded classroom*

o·ver·do /ˌəʊvəˈduː ‖ -vər-/ *v* **overdid** /-ˈdɪd/, **overdone** /-ˈdʌn/, **overdoing** [T] **1** to do something in a way which is more than is expected or more than you can manage: *The love scenes in the play were a bit overdone.* | *When you first start jogging, you have to be careful not to overdo it.* **2** to use too much of something: *Don't overdo the salt.*

o·ver·done /ˌəʊvəˈdʌn ‖ -vər-/ *adj* cooked too much

o·ver·dose /ˈəʊvədəʊs ‖ -vər-/ *n* a dangerous amount of a drug: *He died from an overdose of heroin.*

o·ver·draft /ˈəʊvədraːft ‖ ˈəʊvərdræft/ *n* permission from a bank to spend more money than you have in your bank account, or the amount by which you are overdrawn

o·ver·drawn /ˌəʊvəˈdrɔːn ‖ -vər-/ *adj* **1** having taken out more money than you had in your bank account: *I'm often overdrawn at the end of the month.* **2** in a state where you have taken out an amount of money lent to you by the bank: *My account is £300 overdrawn.*

o·ver·due /ˌəʊvəˈdjuː◂ ‖ ˌəʊvərˈduː◂/ *adj* late, or later than expected: *My library books are overdue; I should have returned them last week.* | *Changes in the law are long overdue.*

o·ver·es·ti·mate /ˌəʊvərˈestɬmeɪt/ *v* [T] **overestimated, overestimating** to think that something is bigger or more important than it really is: *We overestimated the cost, so we still have some money left.* | *I think you're overestimating his abilities.*

o·ver·flow /ˌəʊvəˈfləʊ ‖ -vər-/ *v* **1** [I;T] to flow over the edges: *The river overflowed and flooded the fields.* **2** [I + adv/prep] to move out of a place because there are too many people inside: *The crowd overflowed into the street.* **3 be overflowing** to be full of: *His heart was overflowing with pride.* **4 full to overflowing** extremely full

o·ver·flow² /ˈəʊvəfləʊ ‖ -vər-/ *n* **1** something that overflows: *We used a bucket to catch the overflow from the gutter.* **2** a pipe through which water can flow out of a container when it gets too full

o·ver·grown /ˌəʊvəˈgrəʊn◂ ‖ -vər-/ *adj* thickly covered with plants that are not growing in a controlled way

o·ver·hang /ˌəʊvəˈhæŋ ‖ -vər-/ *v* **overhung** /-ˈhʌŋ/, **overhung** [I;T] to hang over something or stick out above it: *A large tree overhangs the wall.* −**overhang** /ˈəʊvəhæŋ ‖ -vər-/ *n*

o·ver·haul /ˌəʊvəˈhɔːl ‖ -vər-/ *v* [T] to examine something thoroughly and repair or change anything that is not working properly −**overhaul** /ˈəʊvəhɔːl ‖ -vər-/ *n*

o·ver·head /ˌəʊvəˈhed◂ ‖ -vər-/ *adv, adj* above you: *electricity carried by overhead wires*

o·ver·heads /ˈəʊvəhedz ‖ -vər-/ *n* [pl] the regular costs involved in running a business

o·ver·hear /ˌəʊvəˈhɪər ‖ -vər-/ *v* **overheard** /-ˈɜːd ‖ -ˈhɜːrd/, **overheard** [T] to hear what other people are saying by accident, when they do not know that you are listening: *I overheard them talking about me.*

o·ver·heat /ˌəʊvəˈhiːt ‖ -vər-/ *v* [I] to become too hot because of a fault: *The kettle overheated and burnt out.*

o·ver·joyed /ˌəʊvəˈdʒɔɪd ‖ -vər-/ *adj* [never before a noun] extremely pleased: *We were overjoyed when our baby was born.*

o·ver·land /ˌəʊvəˈlænd◂ ‖ -vər-/ *adv,adj* travelling across land, rather than by sea or air

o·ver·lap¹ /ˌəʊvəˈlæp ‖ -vər-/ *v* **-pp-** **1** [I;T] to cover part of something else: *a pattern of overlapping circles* **2** [I] to be concerned with some of the same subjects: *History and politics overlap quite a bit.*

o·ver·lap² /ˈəʊvəlæp ‖ -vər-/ *n* [C;U] the amount by which two or more things overlap each other

o·ver·leaf /ˌəʊvəˈliːf ‖ ˈəʊvərliːf/ *adv* on the next page

o·ver·load /ˌəʊvəˈləʊd ‖ -vər-/ v [T] **1** to give some-one or something too much to do or carry **2** to damage an electrical system by connecting too many machines together

o·ver·look /ˌəʊvəˈlʊk ‖ -vər-/ v [T] **1** to have a view of something from above: *Our room overlooked the sea.* **2** to not notice the importance of something: *I overlooked the dangers involved when I planned this trip.* **3** to forgive a fault or a mistake: *I'll over-look it this time, but don't do it again!*

o·ver·much /ˌəʊvəˈmʌtʃ◂ ‖ -vər-/ adv fml too much

o·ver·night /ˌəʊvəˈnaɪt◂ ‖ -vər-/ adv, adj **1** for or during the night: *We'll stay in Paris overnight.* **2** happening very suddenly: *Byron became famous overnight.*

o·ver·pass /ˈəʊvəpɑːs ‖ ˈəʊvərpæs/ n the usual American word for FLYOVER

o·ver·pop·u·lat·ed /ˌəʊvəˈpɒpjˌleɪtˌd ˌəʊvərˈpɑːp-/ adj having too many people living there (used of places)

o·ver·pop·u·la·tion /ˌəʊvəpɒpjˌˈleɪʃən ‖ ˌəʊvərpɑː-/ n [U] the situation in which there are too many people living in a place

o·ver·pow·er /ˌəʊvəˈpaʊər ‖ -vər-/ v [T] **1** to defeat someone by being stronger than they are **2** to give you a particular feeling very strongly

o·ver·rate /ˌəʊvəˈreɪt/ v overrated, overrating [T] to think that something is greater or better than it really is: *I think that film is overrated.*

o·ver·ride /ˌəʊvəˈraɪd/ v overrode /-ˈrəʊd/, over-ridden /-ˈrɪdn/, overriding [T] **1** to become more important than other things: *The fight for freedom overrode all other issues.* **2** to change someone's decisions because you have the power to do so

o·ver·rid·ing /ˌəʊvəˈraɪdɪŋ◂/ adj [only before a noun] more important than anything else

o·ver·rule /ˌəʊvəˈruːl/ v overruled, overruling [T to officially decide that someone else's decision was wrong: *The local council has been overruled by the government.*

o·ver·run /ˌəʊvəˈrʌn/ v overran /-ˈræn/, overrun, overrunning **1** [T] to take over a place very quickly: *Troops overran the country.* | *The house is overrun with mice.* **2** [I;T] to continue beyond a time limit: *Sorry I'm late – the meeting overran.*

o·ver·seas /ˌəʊvəˈsiːz◂ ‖ -vər-/ adv, adj across the sea: *They've gone to live overseas.* | *overseas students*

o·ver·see /ˌəʊvəˈsiː ‖ -vər-/ v oversaw /-ˈsɔː/, overseen /-ˈsiːn/ [T] to watch a piece of work to see that it is done properly: *I'll oversee this job myself.*

o·ver·shad·ow /ˌəʊvəˈʃædəʊ ‖ -vər-/ v [T] **1** to be taller than something and throw a shadow over it **2** to make something appear less important, less successful, or less happy: *He always felt over-shadowed by his brothers.*

o·ver·shoot /ˌəʊvəˈʃuːt ‖ -vər-/ v overshot /-ˈʃɒt ‖ -ˈʃɑːt/, overshot [I;T] to go too far past a place: *We overshot the entrance and had to come back.*

o·ver·sight /ˈəʊvəsaɪt ‖ -vər-/ n [C;U] something which you forgot to do or fail to notice: *I'm sorry there was no one to meet you; it was an oversight on my part.*

o·ver·sim·pli·fy /ˌəʊvəˈsɪmplˌfaɪ ‖ -vər-/ v over-simplified, oversimplified [I;T] to make some-thing seem simpler than it really is –**oversim-plification** /ˌəʊvəˌsɪmplˌfˌˈkeɪʃən- ‖ -vər-/ n [C;U]

o·ver·sized /ˌəʊvəˈsaɪzd◂ ‖ -vər-/ adj (also over-size) too big, or bigger than usual

o·ver·sleep /ˌəʊvəˈsliːp ‖ -vər-/ v overslept /-ˈslept/, overslept [I] to sleep for too long, or for longer than you intended

o·ver·state /ˌəʊvəˈsteɪt ‖ -vər-/ v overstated, over-stating [T] to state something too strongly, making things seem greater or more important than they really are –**overstatement** n [C;U]

o·ver·step /ˌəʊvəˈstep ‖ -vər-/ v overstep the mark to go beyond acceptable limits in the way that you behave

o·vert /ˈəʊvɜːt, əʊˈvɜːt ‖ -ɜːrt/ adj fml shown in an open, public way: *There have been overt moves to undermine his authority.* –**overtly** adv

o·ver·take /ˌəʊvəˈteɪk ‖ -vər-/ v overtook /-ˈtʊk/, overtaken /-ˈteɪkən/, overtaking **1** [I;T] to go past something because you are travelling faster than it is: *A car overtook me just before the bend.* | *All clear, you can overtake now.* **2** [T] to have an effect on you suddenly: *I was overtaken by exhaustion.*

o·ver·throw /ˌəʊvəˈθrəʊ ‖ -vər-/ v overthrew /-ˈθruː/, overthrown /-ˈθrəʊn/ [T] to defeat a government or ruler and remove them from power –**overthrow** /ˈ····/ n [sing]

o·ver·time /ˈəʊvətaɪm ‖ -vər-/ n [U] time that some-one works beyond the usual working hours: *I've done six hours' overtime this week.* –**overtime** adv : *We're working overtime to finish the job.*

o·ver·tone /ˈəʊvətəʊn ‖ -vər-/ n something, such as an idea or feeling, that is suggested, without being shown or stated openly: *The poems have clear polit-ical overtones.*

o·ver·ture /ˈəʊvətjʊər, -tʃər ‖ -vər-/ n **1** a musical introduction to a play or an OPERA **2 make over-tures to someone** to behave in a friendly manner to someone because you want to have a more friendly relationship with them

o·ver·turn /ˌəʊvəˈtɜːn ‖ ˌəʊvərˈtɜːrn/ v **1** [I] to turn something over so that it is upside down: *She was in the boat when it overturned.* **2** [T] to make some-thing turn over: *The intruders had overturned all the furniture.* **3** [T] to officially change a decision that someone else had made: *The verdict was overturned by the Court of Appeal.*

o·ver·weight /ˌəʊvəˈweɪt ‖ -vər-/ adj **1** too fat: *Fat parents tend to have children who are overweight too.* **2** too heavy: *This parcel is half a kilo overweight.*

o·ver·whelm /ˌəʊvəˈwelm ‖ -vər-/ v [T] **1** to gain complete control or victory over a group of people **2** to give someone a particular feeling very strongly: *I was overwhelmed by grief.*

o·ver·whelm·ing /ˌəʊvəˈwelmɪŋ ‖ -vər-/ adj very large or very great: *an overwhelming majority of voters* | *an overwhelming feeling of guilt* –**overwhelmingly** adv

o·ver·work¹ /ˌəʊvəˈwɜːk ‖ ˌəʊvərˈwɜːrk/ v **1** [I;T] to work too hard, or make someone work too hard **2** [T] to use something too much: *This soil has been overworked.*

overwork² n [U] too much hard work

o·ver·wrought /ˌəʊvəˈrɔːt◂/ adj feeling very ner-vous and excited.

ow /aʊ/ interj an expression used to show sudden pain: *Ow! You stepped on my toe!*

owe /əʊ/ v owed, owing [T] **1** to have to pay money to someone because they lent it to you: *He owes me £20.* | *I'll pay what I owe you but no more.*

☐ [USEFUL PATTERNS: to owe something; to owe something to someone; to owe someone something] –see DUE¹ (USAGE)
2 to feel grateful to someone for a quality or an ability that they have given you: *We owe our parents a lot.* | *I owe most of my technique to a very good music teacher.*

ow·ing /ˈəʊɪŋ/ *adj* [never before a noun] still to be paid: *How much is owing to you?* | *There is still £5 owing.*

owing to /ˈ··· ·/ *prep* because of: *We were late, owing to the snow.*

owl /aʊl/ *n* a bird that flies at night, and hunts small animals

own¹ /əʊn/ *det, pron* **1** belonging to or for a particular person: *I'd love to have my own house.* | *The country has its own oil so it doesn't need to import any.* | *I need a room of my own.* **2 get your own back** to do something to punish someone who harmed you in some way **3 on your own** alone, with no one with you or helping you: *I spent the afternoon on my own.* | *Did you manage to do it on your own?*
■ USAGE **Own** is used only after possessive words like *my, our, John's, the school's: He has his own room/a room of his own.* | *The company has its own canteen.* | *Was that your own idea?* | *Does Sue have a car of her own?* | *Is that Sue's own car?*

own² *v* **1** [T] to possess something: *We only rent the house, we don't own it.* **2** [+that] *fml* to admit something

own·er /ˈəʊnər/ *n* a person who owns something –**ownership** *n* [U]

ox /ɒks ‖ ɑːks/ *n* **oxen** /ˈɒksən‖ˈɑːk-/ a large animal like a cow, sometimes used for pulling carts or carrying things

ox·ide /ˈɒksaɪd ‖ ˈɑːk-/ *n* [C;U] a compound of oxygen and another chemical substance: *iron oxide*

ox·i·dize /ˈɒksɪdaɪz ‖ ˈɑːk-/ *v* **oxidized, oxidizing** (also **oxidise** *BrE*) [I;T] to change chemically by combining with oxygen; when metal oxidizes, it becomes RUSTY

ox·y·gen /ˈɒksɪdʒən ‖ ˈɑːk-/ *n* [U] a gas present in the air, without colour, taste, or smell; oxygen is necessary for all forms of life on earth

oy·ster /ˈɔɪstər/ *n* a flat shellfish which is often eaten raw, and which can produce pearls (PEARL)

oy·ster·catch·er /ˈɔɪstəˌkætʃər ‖ -tər-/ *n* a seabird that eats shellfish

oz a written abbreviation for OUNCE

o·zone /ˈəʊzəʊn/ *n* [U] **1** a poisonous form of oxygen **2** the air near the sea, which is thought to be healthy

ozone-friend·ly /ˌ·· ˈ···◄/ *adj* not harmful to the ozone round the earth

ozone lay·er /ˈ·· ˌ··/ *n* **the ozone layer** a layer of ozone high above the Earth's surface which protects the Earth from harmful rays (RAY) from the sun –see picture on page 246

P,p

P, p /piː/ **P's, p's** or **Ps, ps** the 16th letter of the English alphabet

p n **1** [plural is **p**] the smallest unit of money in Britain; 100p = £1: *It cost 49p.* | *a 10p piece* –see PENNY (USAGE) **2** [plural is **pp**] a written abbreviation for PAGE

PA /ˌpiːˈeɪ/ n BrE a secretary employed to look after the affairs of one person; an abbreviation for **personal assistant**

pace¹ /peɪs/ n **1** [sing;U] the rate at which you move forward in many activities, especially walking and running: *He set off at a very fast pace.* | *The pace of reform has been rather slow.* **2** [C] a single step in running or walking, or the distance moved in it: *The fence is ten paces from the house.* **3 keep pace with** to go at the same speed as someone or something **4 put someone through their paces** to make someone do something as a test or proof of their abilities **5 set the pace** to set a speed for others to try to equal

pace² v **paced, pacing** [I; + adv/prep; T] to walk backwards and forwards when you are waiting or worried: *She paced up and down, waiting for him to appear.* | *restlessly pacing the floor*

pace-mak-er /ˈpeɪsˌmeɪkəʳ/ n **1** a machine fitted under someone's skin near the heart to make it beat regularly **2** a person who sets a speed that others in a race try to equal

pac-i-fis-m /ˈpæsɪfɪzəm/ n [U] the belief that all wars are wrong

pac-i-fist /ˈpæsɪfɪst/ n a believer in pacifism, especially one who refuses to fight in a war because of their belief

pac-i-fy /ˈpæsɪfaɪ/ v **pacified, pacifying** [T] to make someone stop being angry or upset and become calm, quiet, and satisfied: *to pacify a crying baby* –**pacification** /ˌpæsɪfɪˈkeɪʃən/ n [U]

pack¹ /pæk/ v **1** [I;T] to put things into a case or other container: *She packed her bags and left.* | *I'm leaving in an hour and I haven't packed yet!* | *Could you pack me a few sandwiches?* | *a packed meal* –opposite **unpack 2** [T] to put goods into containers ready for transport or sale: *The eggs are packed and sent off the following day.* **3** [T] to cover, fill, or surround closely with a protective material: *Pack some paper round the dishes so that they won't break.* **4** [T; + adv/prep] to fit, crush, or push things into a space: *If you pack those things down we can get some more clothes into the box.* | *The hotel manager wanted to pack all of us into one small room.*

pack sthg ↔ **in** phr v [T] BrE infml **1** to stop doing a job or piece of work, often because you are dissatisfied or tired: *He used to work for Smith's, but he packed his job in.* | *It's ten o'clock. I think I'll pack it in and go to bed.* **2 pack it in** a phrase used to tell someone fairly rudely to stop doing something that is annoying you; used especially by parents to children: *Pack it in, you two!*

pack sbdy ↔ **off** phr v [T] infml to send someone away quickly, especially without spending time being nice to them: *They packed their children off to boarding school at the earliest possible age.*

pack up phr v [I] infml **1** to finish work **2** to put all your things in boxes because you are leaving **3** BrE (used of machines) to stop working

pack² n **1** a quantity of things packed together for sale or for giving out: *a pack of bacon* | *You can't buy just one lightbulb. You have to buy a pack.* | *an information pack* **2** (also **backpack**) a large bag which goes on your back and in which you can carry things **3** a number of things wrapped or tied together which a homeless person carries on their back as they travel from place to place **4** a group of wild animals that hunt together, or a group of dogs trained together for hunting: *a pack of hounds* | *a wolf pack* **5** a set of cards used in playing a game

pack-age¹ /ˈpækɪdʒ/ n **1** a small parcel or a large envelope with things inside it **2** a set of related things sold or offered all together: *a new software package for home computers* | *The union has won a new package of benefits.*

package² v **packaged, packaging** [T] **1** to put a number of things all together into a parcel **2** to put a product in a box, bag, or other wrapping for protection, easy handling, and attractive appearance: *attractively packaged chocolates*

package deal /ˈ··· ·/ n infml (also **package**) an agreement that includes a number of things all of which must be accepted together

package hol-i-day /ˈ··· ˈ···/ n a completely planned holiday arranged by a company at a fixed price

pack-ag-ing /ˈpækɪdʒɪŋ/ n [U] material used for packing goods: *These days the packaging often costs more than the goods.*

packed /pækt/ adj infml (also **packed out** /ˌ· ˈ·/) full of people

pack-er /ˈpækəʳ/ n a person whose job is to pack goods for travelling or selling

pack-et /ˈpækɪt/ n **1** a small box, envelope, bag, or wrapper in which goods are packed: *a packet of envelopes* | *an empty cigarette packet* –see picture on page 148 **2** infml a large amount of money: *That car cost me a packet.*

pack-ing /ˈpækɪŋ/ n [U] **1** the act of putting things into cases or boxes: *I'll do my packing the night before we leave.* **2** material used in packing

packing case /ˈ··· ·/ n a strong wooden box in which things are packed to be stored or sent to another place

pact /pækt/ n an important formal agreement, often between countries: *They signed a non-aggression pact.*

pad¹ /pæd/ n **1** a thick piece of soft material, such as plastic FOAM or cotton, used to clean or protect something, shape it, or make it more comfortable: *American footballers wear shoulder-pads for protection.* | *Put a clean pad of cotton over the wound.* **2** a number of sheets of paper fastened together: *a writing pad* **3** the ground where a HELICOPTER lands and takes off or where a ROCKET takes off **4** the thick-skinned underpart of the foot of some animals, such as cats

pad² v **padded, padding 1** [T] to fill with soft material in order to protect, shape, or make more comfortable: *a coat with padded shoulders* **2** [I; + adv/prep] to walk steadily and softly: *John rode his bicycle slowly, and his dog padded along beside him.*

pad sthg ↔ **out** phr v [T] to fill up space in a written article by adding unnecessary or unconnected material

pad-ding /ˈpædɪŋ/ n [U] material used to pad something

pad-dle¹ /ˈpædl/ n **1** a short pole with a wide flat blade at one or both ends, used for moving a small boat, especially a CANOE **2** a walk in the sea, a river, or a stream where the water is only a few centimetres deep: *The children went for a paddle.*

paddle² *v* **paddled, paddling** **1** [I;T] to move a small light boat through water, using one or more paddles **2** [I] *BrE* to walk about in water only a few centimetres deep

paddle steam·er /'·· ‚··/ *n* a steam ship which is pushed forward by large wheels

padd·ling pool /'·· ·/ *n* a container for water only a few centimetres deep for children to play in

pad·dock /'pædək/ *n* a small field where horses are kept and exercised, or where horses are brought together before a race so that people can see them

pad·dy /'pædi/ *n* **paddies** (also **paddy field** /'·· ·/) a field where rice is grown in water

pad·lock /'pædlɒk ‖ -laːk/ *n* a movable lock with a U-shaped metal bar, which can be used to lock things such as gates and bicycles –**padlock** *v* [T] : *Did you remember to padlock the gate?*

pae·di·a·tri·cian /‚piːdiə'trɪʃən/ *n* (**pediatrician** *AmE*) a doctor concerned with children's medicine

pae·di·at·rics /‚piːdi'ætrɪks/ *n* (**pediatrics** *AmE*) [U] the branch of medicine concerned with children and their diseases

pae·do·phile /'piːdəʊfaɪl ‖ 'ped-/ *n* (**pedophile** *AmE*) a person whose sexual desires are directed towards children

pa·el·la /paɪ'elə ‖ paː-/ *n* [U] a Spanish dish of rice cooked with pieces of meat, fish, and vegetables

pa·gan /'peɪɡən/ *n* a person who is not a believer in any of the chief religions of the world

page¹ /peɪdʒ/ *n* **1** one or both sides of a sheet of paper in, for example, a book or newspaper: *There is a picture of a ship on page 44.* | *Someone's torn a page out of this book.* **2** (also **page boy** /'· ·/) a uniformed boy servant in a hotel or club **3** a boy attendant on a woman when she is getting married, or, in the past, on a king or queen

page² *v* **paged, paging** [T] to call aloud in a public place for someone who is wanted, especially through a LOUDSPEAKER: *The hotel manager had my boss paged for me.*

pag·eant /'pædʒənt/ *n* a public show or ceremony, usually out of doors, especially one in which there is a procession of people in rich dress or in which historical scenes are acted

pag·eant·ry /'pædʒəntri/ *n* [U] a splendid show of ceremonial grandness with people in fine dress: *the pageantry of a royal wedding*

pa·go·da /pə'ɡəʊdə/ *n* a temple, especially a Buddhist or Hindu one built on several floors with a decorative roof at each level

paid¹ /peɪd/ the past tense and past participle of PAY¹

paid² *adj* which you receive wages for: *a paid job* –opposite **unpaid**

paid-up /‚· '·◂/ *adj* having paid in full, especially in order to continue being a member of an organization

pail /peɪl/ *n* a bucket: *a milk pail*

pain¹ /peɪn/ *n* **1** [U] suffering of body or mind: *She was crying with pain.* | *He's in constant pain.* | *His behaviour caused his parents a great deal of pain.* **2** [C] a feeling of suffering or discomfort in a particular part of your body: *I've got a terrible pain in my chest.* | *slight stomach pains* **3 a pain, a pain in the neck** *infml* a really annoying person, thing,

or happening: *He can be a real pain at times.* **4 pains** [pl] effort: *All I got for my pains was the door slammed in my face!* **5 take great pains** to make a very big effort to do something well

■ USAGE Remember to use the preposition **in** for expressions such as: *I've got a pain in my leg/in my neck/in my shoulder.* | *She felt a sudden pain in her back/in her chest/in her stomach.*

pain² *v* [T] *fml* to cause someone to feel very unhappy

pained /peɪnd/ *adj* showing that your feelings have been hurt: *There was a pained silence before she replied.*

pain·ful /'peɪnfəl/ *adj* causing pain or hurting: *My wrist is really painful today.* | *a painful cut on his thumb* | *painful memories* –**painfully** *adv*

pain·kill·er /'peɪn‚kɪləʳ/ *n* a medicine which lessens or removes pain

pain·less /'peɪnləs/ *adj* **1** causing no pain: *X-rays are quite painless.* **2** needing no effort or hard work: *a painless way of learning a foreign language* –**painlessly** *adv*

pains·tak·ing /'peɪnz‚teɪkɪŋ/ *adj* very careful and thorough: *a painstaking examination of the whole area* –**painstakingly** *adv*

paint¹ /peɪnt/ *n* **1** [U] liquid colouring matter which is put on a surface to protect it or make it look attractive: *a tin of green paint* | *The sign said "Wet Paint".* **2** [C;U] colouring matter which you use for painting pictures: *a box of paints*

paint² *v* [I;T] **1** to put paint on a surface: *I wear my old clothes when I'm painting.* | *She painted the door blue.* | *They painted it a bright colour.* **2** to make a picture of someone or something using paint: *Who painted this picture?* | *I wish I could paint as well as you.* | *Paint the view from your window.*

paint·brush /'peɪntbrʌʃ/ *n* a brush for spreading paint on a surface –see picture on page 638

paint·er /'peɪntəʳ/ *n* **1** a person whose job is painting the inside or outside of houses **2** a person who paints pictures: *a portrait painter*

paint·ing /'peɪntɪŋ/ *n* **1** [U] the act of painting, or the skill of painting pictures **2** [C] a picture made by painting

paint·work /'peɪntwɜːk ‖ -wɜːrk/ *n* [U] a painted surface: *The paintwork on my car needs a bit of attention.*

pair¹ /peəʳ/ *n* **1** something made up of two parts that are alike and are joined and used together: *a pair of trousers* | *a pair of scissors* **2** two things that are alike or of the same kind, and are usually used together: *a pair of shoes* | *a pair of vases* **3** two people who are closely connected, especially a man and woman or husband and wife: *They're a nice pair.* | *Let's ask them to dinner with the Harrisons.* | *The pair of them are going.*

■ USAGE Some words like **trousers** are in the plural form, but we do not usually think of them as "more than one". If we say *Those* **trousers** *are old*, it is not clear whether we are talking about one or more than one item of clothing. To make it clear we can use **pair** or **pairs**: *a pair of trousers* | *three* **pairs** *of trousers.* We can use *a pair of* with any word in this dictionary which has "–see PAIR (USAGE)" after it.

pair² *v* [I;T] to form into pairs:

pair up *phr v* [I] to form into a pair for a particular purpose: *They paired up on holiday.*

pair sbdy ↔ **off** *phr v* [T] to encourage people to start a relationship: *My parents are always trying to pair me off with people.*

pa·ja·mas /pə'dʒɑːməz ‖ -'dʒɑː-, -'dʒæ-/ n [pl] see PYJAMAS

pal /pæl/ n infml a close friend: an old pal of mine

pal·ace /'pæləs/ n a large and splendid house, especially one where a king or queen officially lives

pal·ae·o·lith·ic /ˌpæliəʊ'lɪθɪk, ˌpeɪ- ‖ ˌpeɪ-/ adj (also **paleolithic**) of the earliest known period of human existence, the Old Stone Age, when people made weapons and tools of stone

pal·a·ta·ble /'pælətəbəl/ adj 1 pleasant to taste 2 agreeable to the mind

pal·ate /'pælət/ n 1 the top part of the inside of your mouth 2 the ability to judge food or wine

pa·la·tial /pə'leɪʃəl/ adj large and splendid like a palace (usually used of buildings): a palatial hotel

pale¹ /peɪl/ adj 1 having little colour (used of your face or skin): a pale complexion | still pale and tired after her illness –see picture on page 245 2 not bright: pale blue | the pale light of the moon –**paleness** n [U] –see picture on page 147

pale² v **paled, paling** [I] to become unimportant: All our other worries paled into insignificance beside the possibility that the country would go to war.

pal·ette /'pælət/ n a board with a curved edge and a hole for the thumb, on which an artist mixes colours

pal·ings /'peɪlɪŋz/ n [pl] a fence made of pointed pieces of wood

pall¹ /pɔːl/ n 1 a low dark cloud: A pall of smoke hung over the city. 2 a covering of dark cloth spread over the box in which a dead body is carried

pall² v [I] to become less interesting or enjoyable: His new job began to pall after a while.

pall·bear·er /'pɔːlˌbeərər/ n a person who walks beside or helps to carry the box in which the body is carried at a funeral

pal·let /'pælət/ n a large metal plate or flat wooden frame for lifting and moving goods, used with a special small vehicle

pal·li·a·tive /'pæliətɪv/ n something that lessens pain or a problem without removing the cause of it –**palliative** adj : palliative measures

pal·lid /'pælɪd/ adj unusually or unhealthily pale (used of your face or skin) –**pallor** n [sing;U] : the unusual pallor of her skin

pal·ly /'pæli/ adj having a friendly relationship: I didn't know you were pally with her.

palm /pɑːm ‖ pɑːm, pɑːlm/ n 1 (also **palm tree** /'·· ·/) a tall tropical tree with no branches, but with a mass of large leaves at the top: a date palm | a coconut palm 2 the inner surface of your hand between the base of your fingers and your wrist

palm·ist /'pɑːmɪst ‖ 'pɑːm-, 'pɑːlm-/ n a person who claims to be able to tell someone's future by examining the lines on their palm –**palmistry** n [U]

pal·pa·ble /'pælpəbəl/ adj fml easily and clearly known by your senses or your mind: a palpable atmosphere of mistrust –**palpably** adv: What you say is palpably untrue.

pal·pi·ta·tions /ˌpælpɪ'teɪʃənz/ n [pl] irregular or unusually fast beating of your heart, caused by illness or too much effort

pal·try /'pɔːltri/ adj so small that it is almost worthless: The management offered us a paltry 3% increase.

pam·pas /'pæmpəs, -pəs/ n **the pampas** the large grass-covered plains in parts of South America

pam·per /'pæmpər/ v [T] to treat too kindly: a pampered cat | Pamper your skin with our rich creamy soap.

pam·phlet /'pæmflət/ n a small thin book with paper covers which deals usually with some matter of public interest or gives information on a product or service

pan /pæn/ n 1 metal container used in cooking, usually with one long handle, and sometimes with a lid 2 the bowl of a LAVATORY

pan·a·ce·a /ˌpænə'siə/ n something that is supposed to cure any illness, or put any trouble right

pa·nache /pə'næʃ, pæ-/ n [U] a manner of doing things that is showy and splendid

pan·cake /'pænkeɪk/ n a thin soft flat cake made of flour, milk, and eggs, cooked in a flat pan and eaten hot with a filling, often sweet

pan·da /'pændə/ n (also **giant panda**) a large animal like a bear, with black and white fur, originally from China

pan·de·mo·ni·um /ˌpændɪ'məʊniəm/ n [U] a state of wild and noisy disorder

pan·der /'pændər/ v **pander to** to provide something that satisfies unreasonable wishes: a newspaper that panders to people's interest in sex

pane /peɪn/ n a single sheet of glass for use in a frame, especially a window frame

pan·el /'pænl/ n 1 [+ sing/pl verb] a group of speakers who answer questions to inform or amuse the public, usually on a radio or television show: a panel game | What do the panel think? 2 [+ sing/pl verb] a committee chosen to find out about something or make a decision 3 one of a number of sheets of wood, glass, or metal which fit into a frame to form a door, wall, or CEILING 4 a board on which controls or instruments of various kinds are fastened

pan·elled /'pænld/ adj (**paneled** AmE) decorated or fitted with panels

pan·el·ling /'pænəl-ɪŋ/ n (**paneling** AmE) [U] a set of panels used to decorate an inside wall

pan·el·list /'pænəl-ɪst/ n (**panelist** AmE) a member of a panel of people

pang /pæŋ/ n a sudden sharp feeling of pain: pangs of hunger | a pang of sadness

pan·ic¹ /'pænɪk/ n [C;U] great anxiety or fear which makes it difficult to act reasonably: There was panic when the fire started. | She's getting into a panic now because it's only two weeks to the exams.

panic² v **panicked, panicked, panicking** [I;T] to lose control of yourself because you suddenly feel very frightened or worried: The crowd panicked at the sound of the guns. | Don't panic. It's only some fireworks going off!

panic-strick·en /'·· ˌ··/ adj extremely frightened and anxious

pan·ni·er /'pæniər/ n a basket or bag, especially one of a pair, carried on a bicycle or by a horse or donkey

pan·o·ra·ma /ˌpænə'rɑːmə ‖ -'ræmə/ n a complete view over a wide area –**panoramic** /-'ræmɪk/ adj : a panoramic view of the city from the tenth floor of the building

pant /pænt/ v [I] to take quick short breaths, especially after great effort or in great heat: The dog panted in the heat. | "Stop, stop," he panted.

pan·ties /'pæntiz/ n (also **pants**) [pl] a short piece of underclothing worn by women and girls

pan·to·mime /ˈpæntəmaɪm/ n BrE (also **panto** /ˈpæntəʊ/ infml) [C;U] a funny play for children, based on a fairy story, and usually produced at Christmas

pants /pænts/ n [pl] 1 BrE a piece of underclothing which men wear under trousers and women under skirts or trousers 2 the usual American word for TROUSERS

pa·pa /ˈpɑːpə/ n AmE infml a father

pa·pa·cy /ˈpeɪpəsi/ n the papacy the power and office of the POPE

pa·pal /ˈpeɪpəl/ adj of or about the POPE

pa·pa·ya /pəˈpaɪə/ n (also **pawpaw**) [C;U] a large yellow-green tropical fruit

pa·per¹ /ˈpeɪpər/ n 1 [U] a substance used to make the pages of books, for writing on, or for wrapping parcels with: a piece of paper | a paper bag | Have you got any writing paper? 2 [C] a newspaper: Have you seen today's paper? 3 [C] a set of printed questions used as an examination: We're doing both the biology papers today. 4 [C] a piece of writing for specialists, often read aloud 5 papers [pl] pieces of paper with writing on them 6 papers [pl] official pieces of paper, for example your passport, which give information about who you are and what you have the right to do 7 on paper as written down or printed, but not yet tested by experience: This idea seems all right on paper, but I'm not sure how it would work out in practice.

paper² v [T] to cover a wall with decorative paper: She papered the main bedroom green.

paper over sthg phr v [T] to try to hide the difficulties of something and make it look as though everything is all right

pa·per·back /ˈpeɪpəbæk ‖ -ər-/ n a book with a thin cardboard cover: This shop only sells paperbacks. | a paperback edition | Is it out in paperback yet?

paper clip /ˈ·· ·/ n a small piece of curved wire used for holding sheets of paper together – see picture on page 539

paper shop /ˈ·· ,·/ n a shop which sells newspapers and magazines

pa·per·weight /ˈpeɪpəweɪt ‖ -ər-/ n a heavy object placed on top of loose papers to keep them from being scattered

pa·per·work /ˈpeɪpəwɜːk ‖ -pərwɜːrk/ n [U] 1 regular work of writing reports, letters, keeping records, etc. 2 the paperwork the papers connected with one piece of business: I'll have to go through all the paperwork again.

pa·pi·er-mâ·ché /ˌpæpieɪ ˈmæʃeɪ, ˌpeɪpə- ‖ ˌpeɪpər məˈʃeɪ/ n [U] paper mixed with a sticky substance to form a soft mass, and used for making objects such as boxes; it is quite hard when dry

pap·ri·ka /ˈpæprɪkə ‖ pəˈpriːkə/ n [U] red pepper with a sweet taste

pa·py·rus /pəˈpaɪ ə rəs/ n [U] paper made in ancient Egypt from a plant similar to grass, or the plant itself

par /pɑːr/ n [sing] 1 in the game of GOLF, the number of strokes the average player should take to hit the ball into a hole 2 below par infml not in the usual or average condition of health or activity 3 on a par equal or almost the same: Our results this year are on a par with those of our rivals.

par·a·ble /ˈpærəbəl/ n a short simple story which teaches a moral or religious lesson

par·a·chute¹ /ˈpærəʃuːt/ n an apparatus which is made of cloth and is fastened to a person or an object dropped from an aircraft in order to make them fall slowly: a parachute jump

parachute² v parachuted, parachuting [I;T] to drop from an aircraft using a parachute

pa·rade¹ /pəˈreɪd/ n 1 a public procession: The Olympic Games begin with a parade of all the competing nations. 2 an ordered procession of soldiers in front of a higher officer 3 a wide street, often beside the seashore 4 on parade taking part in a parade (used of soldiers)

parade² v paraded, parading 1 [I;T] to march in a public procession: soldiers parading in front of the Queen | The prisoners were paraded around the town. 2 [I; + adv/prep] to walk around an area in order to attract attention: Groups of lads were parading along the main street, showing off to the girls. 3 [T] to show something unnecessarily, just in order to gain admiration: He is always parading his knowledge.

par·a·dise /ˈpærədaɪs/ n 1 **Paradise** Heaven 2 a place of perfect happiness: This hotel is a sportsman's paradise.

par·a·dox /ˈpærədɒks ‖ -dɑːks/ n 1 a statement which seems to be impossible, because it says two opposite things, but which has some truth in it: "More haste, less speed" is a paradox. 2 an improbable combination of opposing qualities or ideas: It is a paradox that in such a rich country there should be so many poor people. –**paradoxical** /ˌpærəˈdɒksɪkəl ‖ -ˈdɑːk-/ adj –**paradoxically** adv

par·af·fin /ˈpærəfɪn/ n [U] an oil made from PETROLEUM or coal, burnt for heat and in lamps for light

par·a·gon /ˈpærəgən ‖ -gɑːn/ n a person or thing that is a perfect model to copy: She's an absolute paragon of virtue.

par·a·graph /ˈpærəgrɑːf ‖ -græf/ n a part of a longer piece of writing which deals with one particular idea; each new paragraph starts on a new line: Look at the third paragraph on page 23.

par·al·lel¹ /ˈpærəlel/ adj 1 running side by side but never getting nearer to or further away from each other (used of lines and rows): parallel lines | The railway line runs parallel with the road. | The line is parallel to the road. 2 of the same type and done at the same time: Parallel experiments were carried out in London and Paris.

parallel² n 1 [C] a parallel line or surface 2 [C;U] a person or thing that is similar to another person or thing: There are few parallels between American football and European football. | an actor without parallel in the modern cinema

parallel³ v -l- (also -ll- BrE) [T] to equal: No one has paralleled her success in business.

par·a·lyse /ˈpærəlaɪz/ v paralysed, paralysing (**paralyze** AmE) [T] 1 to make your muscles unable to move: paralysed from the neck down | paralysed with fear 2 to cause something to stop working: The electricity failure paralysed the train service.

pa·ral·y·sis /pəˈrælɪ̵sɪ̵s/ n [U] loss of feeling in and control of your muscles: suffering from partial paralysis of the arm

par·a·lyt·ic /ˌpærəˈlɪtɪk◂/ adj 1 suffering from paralysis 2 causing paralysis: a paralytic stroke 3 infml very drunk

par·a·med·ic /ˌpærəˈmedɪk/ n a person who is trained to help with the care of sick people, but who is not a doctor or a nurse

pa·ram·e·ter /pəˈræmɪtəʳ/ n any of the established limits within which something must operate

par·a·mil·i·tary /ˌpærəˈmɪlɪtəri ‖ -teri/ adj like or used as a regular military force: *In some countries the police have paramilitary duties.* | *the paramilitary organizations of Northern Ireland*

par·a·mount /ˈpærəmaʊnt/ adj great above all others: *of paramount importance*

par·a·noi·a /ˌpærəˈnɔɪə/ n [U] a disease of the mind in which the sufferers believe that others hate them and are purposely mistreating them, or that they are a person of great importance

par·a·noid /ˈpærənɔɪd/ adj 1 full of unreasonable distrust of other people: *My father locks every door in the house when he goes out. He's absolutely paranoid about being burgled.* 2 suffering from paranoia

par·a·pet /ˈpærəpɪt, -pet/ n a low wall at the edge of a roof or bridge

par·a·pher·na·li·a /ˌpærəfəˈneɪliə ‖ -fər-/ n [U] a number of articles of various kinds, especially personal belongings or those needed for some skill or work: *I keep all my photographic paraphernalia in that cupboard.*

par·a·phrase /ˈpærəfreɪz/ v **paraphrased, paraphrasing** [T] to re-express something in words that are easier to understand –**paraphrase** n

par·a·ple·gic /ˌpærəˈpliːdʒɪk/ n a person suffering from a condition in which they are unable to control the muscles of the lower part of their body

par·a·site /ˈpærəsaɪt/ n 1 a plant or animal that lives on or in another and gets food from it 2 a useless person who is supported by the wealth or efforts of other people –**parasitic** /ˌpærəˈsɪtɪk◄/ adj : *a parasitic plant* –**parasitically** /-kli/ adv

par·a·sol /ˈpærəsɒl ‖ -sɔːl, -sɑːl/ n a light UMBRELLA used for protection from the sun

par·a·troops /ˈpærətruːps/ n [pl] soldiers trained to drop from an aircraft using a PARACHUTE

par·boil /ˈpɑːbɔɪl ‖ ˈpɑːr-/ v [T] to boil food until it is partly cooked

par·cel¹ /ˈpɑːsəl ‖ ˈpɑːr-/ n 1 a thing or things wrapped in paper and tied or fastened for easy carrying, or posting: *I'm taking this parcel to the post office.* | *a parcel of clothes* 2 **part and parcel of** a most important part that cannot be separated from the whole of something

parcel² v -ll- (-l- AmE)
parcel sthg ↔ **out** phr v [T] to divide something into parts or shares and give it to several people
parcel sthg ↔ **up** phr v [T] to make something into a parcel

parched /pɑːtʃt ‖ pɑːrtʃt/ adj 1 infml very thirsty 2 dried up by the hot sun and in need of water (used of land)

parch·ment /ˈpɑːtʃmənt ‖ ˈpɑːr-/ n [U] 1 a writing material used especially in ancient times, made from the skin of a sheep or goat 2 a paper of good quality that looks like this material

par·don¹ /ˈpɑːdn ‖ ˈpɑːrdn/ n 1 official forgiveness for an illegal act, or the action of a court in forgiving someone and freeing them from punishment 2 a word you use to ask someone to repeat something they have just said, because you did not hear it properly –see SORRY ¹ (USAGE) 3 **I beg your pardon** a very polite phrase that you use when you want someone to repeat what they have just said, or when you have done something that might

offend them; you might also use it if someone said something that made you angry: *I beg your pardon, I didn't quite hear you.* | *I beg your pardon, I didn't mean to push in front of you.* | *I beg your pardon, that's not true at all!*

pardon² v [T] 1 fml to forgive or excuse someone: *You'll have to pardon me while I just make a quick phone call.* 2 to give an official pardon to someone for an unlawful act 3 **pardon me** AmE excuse me: *Pardon me, could you tell me the way to the station?*

par·don·a·ble /ˈpɑːdənəbəl ‖ ˈpɑːr-/ adj possible to forgive or excuse: *a pardonable mistake*

pare /peəʳ/ v **pared, paring** [T] to cut away the thin outer covering, edge, or skin of something: *to pare an apple*
pare sthg ↔ **down** phr v [T] to reduce something, especially a cost

par·ent /ˈpeərənt/ n the father or mother of a person: *His parents are both teachers.* –**parental** /pəˈrentl/ adj

par·ent·age /ˈpeərəntɪdʒ/ n [U] the fact of who your parents are, including their social class: *a child of unknown parentage*

pa·ren·the·sis /pəˈrenθɪsɪs/ n 1 **parentheses** [pl] the usual American word for BRACKETS 2 **in parenthesis** as an interruption to the main idea that you are talking or writing about –**parenthetic** /ˌpærənˈθetɪk◄/, **parenthetical** adj

par·ent·hood /ˈpeərənthʊd/ n [U] the state of being a parent

par ex·cel·lence /ˌpɑːr ˈeksəlɑːns ‖ -eksəˈlɑːns/ adj [only after a noun] lit without equal, as the best or most typical of its kind

pa·ri·ah /pəˈraɪə, ˈpæriə/ n a person not accepted by society

par·ish /ˈpærɪʃ/ n 1 an area with a single priest in charge, and served by one main church: *a parish church* | *a parish priest* 2 the smallest area of local government in the countryside, usually a village

pa·rish·io·ner /pəˈrɪʃənəʳ/ n a person living in a parish

par·i·ty /ˈpærɪti/ n [U] the state or quality of being equal, especially in pay and working conditions: *They want parity with the car workers.*

park¹ /pɑːk ‖ pɑːrk/ n 1 a large, usually grassy, enclosed piece of land in a town, used by the public for pleasure and rest 2 a large enclosed stretch of land with grass and trees round a large country house

park² v [I;T] 1 to put a car or other vehicle somewhere for a time: *Don't park the car in the main road.* | *a parked car* 2 **be parked** to have parked your car: *I'm parked outside the paper shop.*

par·ka /ˈpɑːkə ‖ ˈpɑːrkə/ n 1 a short coat with a part that covers your head and is decorated with fur 2 the usual American word for ANORAK

park·ing /ˈpɑːkɪŋ ‖ ˈpɑːr-/ n [U] the leaving of a car or other vehicle in a particular place for a time
■ USAGE 1 The special open space where people can park their cars is called a **car park**. If you park your car in the street in a place which you find yourself (often between other cars) you can talk about a **parking place** or a **parking space**: *I can never find a parking place outside your house!* 2 The sign **"No Parking"** means that you are not allowed to park in a particular place.

parking lights /ˈ·· ˌ·/ n [pl] the usual American word for SIDELIGHTS

parking lot /ˈ·· ·/ n the usual American word for CAR PARK

parking me·ter /ˈ·· ˌ··/ *n* an apparatus at the side of a street, into which you put money to pay for parking a car beside it for a certain time

parking tick·et /ˈ·· ˌ··/ *n* a piece of paper which is put on your car if you have parked it where it is against the law to do so; it tells you to pay some money as a punishment

park·land /ˈpɑːk-lænd ‖ ˈpɑːrk-/ *n* [U] *BrE* a large enclosed stretch of land with grass and trees round a large country house

par·lance /ˈpɑːləns ‖ ˈpɑːr-/ *n* [U] *fml* a particular kind of language: *In naval parlance, the left side of a ship is the "port" side.*

par·lia·ment /ˈpɑːləmənt ‖ ˈpɑːr-/ *n* **1** a large group of people elected by the people of a country to make laws **2 Parliament** in the United Kingdom, the main law-making body, made up of the King or Queen, the Lords, and the elected representatives of the people: *Parliament has been debating industrial relations.* –**parliamentary** /ˌpɑːləˈmentəri◂ ‖ ˌpɑːr-/ *adj* : *during this parliamentary session*

pa·ro·chi·al /pəˈrəukiəl/ *adj* **1** too concerned with local affairs and not taking enough interest in the wider world **2** related to a PARISH

par·o·dy¹ /ˈpærədi/ *n* **parodies** **1** [C;U] a piece of writing or music intended to amuse by copying the style of another writer or musician **2** [C] a weak and unsuccessful copy: *The trial was a parody of justice.*

parody² *v* **parodied, parodying** [T] to make a parody of something

pa·role /pəˈrəul/ *n* [U] letting someone out of prison early, on the condition that they promise to behave well: *He was released on parole to attend his daughter's wedding.* –**parole** *v* [T] : *Prisoners may be paroled after serving half their sentence.*

par·ox·ys·m /ˈpærəksɪzəm/ *n* a sudden uncontrollable burst of strong feeling: *paroxysms of laughter*

par·quet /ˈpɑːkeɪ, ˈpɑːki ‖ pɑːrˈkeɪ/ *n* [U] small flat blocks of wood fitted together in a pattern on to the floor of a room: *a parquet floor*

par·rot¹ /ˈpærət/ *n* a tropical bird with a curved beak; sometimes people teach parrots to speak

parrot² *v* [T] to repeat words without understanding what they mean

par·ry /ˈpæri/ *v* **parried, parrying** [T] **1** to cleverly avoid answering a question **2** to turn aside an attack

par·si·mo·ni·ous /ˌpɑːsɪˈməuniəs ‖ ˌpɑːr-/ *adj fml* very unwilling to spend money –**parsimoniously** *adv* –**parsimony** /ˈpɑːsɪməni ‖ ˈpɑːrsɪməuni/ *n* [U]

pars·ley /ˈpɑːsli ‖ ˈpɑːr-/ *n* [U] a small plant with strong-tasting leaves, used in cooking

pars·nip /ˈpɑːsnɪp ‖ ˈpɑːr-/ *n* a cream-coloured vegetable which grows under the ground

part¹ /pɑːt ‖ pɑːrt/ *n* **1** [C;U] a piece of something, not all of it: *Which part of the town do you live in? | Part of the house was damaged in the fire. | The hard part of the scheme was raising the money. | Wales is part of the United Kingdom.* **2** [C] any of the pieces into which something is divided: *Cut the cake into eight parts. | You can see the second part of our new drama series at the same time next week.* **3** [C] (also **spare part**) a piece of a machine which you use in place of a broken one: *That big garage up the top of the hill stocks parts for Renaults.* **4** [C] a character acted by an actor in a play or film: *She plays the part of an old woman who has lost her whole family.* **5** [C] an

equal quantity: *Mix two parts sand to one of cement.* **6** [C] a share or responsibility in some activity: *For his part in the burglary, Matthews was given two years' imprisonment.* **7** the usual American word for a PARTING in the hair **8 play a part in, take a part in, have a part in** to be responsible for a result to some degree, but not completely: *Cheap accommodation played a part in my decision to stay in the north.* **9 take part** to do an activity with other people: *He took part in the International Student Games.* **10 take someone's part** to be on someone's side in an argument **11 for my part** *fml* speaking for myself **12 for the most part** *fml* generally **13 in part** partly **14 on someone's part** by someone: *This was a serious mistake on the Government's part.* **15 part and parcel** an important piece which cannot be separated from the rest: *Getting hot is part and parcel of being a cook!* **16 the best part, the better part** most: *Registering at the university took the best part of the day.*

part² *v* **1** [I;T] to separate: *She tried to part the two fighting dogs. | If we must part, I hope we can part friends. | The clouds parted, and the sun shone down. | Young children don't like to be parted from their mothers.* **2 part your hair** to separate your hair along a line with a comb **3 part company: a** to end a relationship **b** no longer to be together **c** to disagree

part with *sth phr v* [T] to get rid of something that you are fond of: *He hates parting with his old toys.*

part³ *adv* **part** ..., **part** ... consisting partly of one thing and partly of another: *The medical exams are part written, part practical.*

part⁴ *adj* not complete: *We're part owners of the land; we share with our neighbours.*

par·tial /ˈpɑːʃəl ‖ ˈpɑːr-/ *adj* **1** not complete: *The attempt was only a partial success.* **2** unfairly favouring one person or side more than another –opposite **impartial 3 partial to** *infml* having a strong liking for: *I'm very partial to sweet foods.*

par·ti·al·i·ty /ˌpɑːʃiˈæləti ‖ ˌpɑːr-/ *n* **1** [U] the favouring of one person or side more than another –opposite **impartiality 2** [sing] a special liking for something

par·tial·ly /ˈpɑːʃəli ‖ ˈpɑːr-/ *adv* **1** not completely: *I'm partially to blame for the accident.* **2** in a way that favours one person or side more than another

par·tic·i·pant /pɑːˈtɪsɪpənt ‖ pɑːr-/ *n* a person who takes part in an activity or event

par·tic·i·pate /pɑːˈtɪsɪpeɪt ‖ pɑːr-/ *v* **participated, participating** [I] *fml* to take part in an activity: *We were invited to participate in the discussion.* –**participation** /pɑːˌtɪsɪˈpeɪʃən ‖ pɑːr-/ *n* [U]

par·ti·ci·ple /ˈpɑːtɪsɪpəl ‖ ˈpɑːr-/ *n* a part of a verb which is used to make compound forms of the verb or as an adjective; with the verb **take** the present participle is *taking* and the past participle is *taken* –**participial** /ˌpɑːtɪˈsɪpiəl ‖ ˌpɑːr-/ *adj*

par·ti·cle /ˈpɑːtɪkəl ‖ ˈpɑːr-/ *n* a very small piece or amount: *dust particles floating in the sunlight | There wasn't a particle of truth in what he said.*

par·tic·u·lar /pəˈtɪkjᵘlər ‖ pər-/ *adj* **1** [only before a noun] special: *There was nothing of particular importance in the letter.* **2** [only before a noun] this one and not others: *On this particular day we had got up very early.* **3** demanding that everything is exactly right, including the smallest details: *She's very particular about hygiene.* **4 in particular** especially: *I'm interested in insects, and beetles in particular.*

par·tic·u·lar·ly /pəˈtɪkjᵘləli ‖ pərˈtɪkjᵘlərli/ *adv* especially: *He isn't particularly clever.*

par·tic·u·lars /pəˈtɪkjỵləz ‖ pərˈtɪkjỵlərz/ n [pl] the detailed facts about something

part·ing /ˈpɑːtɪŋ ‖ ˈpɑːr-/ n 1 [C;U] separation 2 BrE [C] the line in a person's hair where they have divided it with a comb – see picture on page 245 3 **the parting of the ways** the point at which two people must separate, or a choice must be made

par·ti·san¹ /ˌpɑːtɪˈzæn ‖ ˈpɑːrtɪzən, -sən/ adj looking at things from one particular point of view, and not trying to see things fairly

partisan² n 1 a strong supporter of someone or something 2 a member of an armed group that fights in secret against an enemy that has conquered its country

par·ti·tion /pɑːˈtɪʃən ‖ pər-, pɑːr-/ n 1 [C] a thin wall that separates one part of a room from another 2 [U] division of a country into two or more independent countries – **partition** v [T]: The kitchen area was partitioned off.

part·ly /ˈpɑːtli ‖ ˈpɑːr-/ adv to some degree, but not completely: It was partly my fault. | The problem is partly money and partly time. | We didn't go, partly because the public transport was so poor.

part·ner¹ /ˈpɑːtnəʳ ‖ ˈpɑːr-/ n 1 a person or group that you share an activity with: Britain's partners in NATO 2 a person that you dance with or who makes a pair with you to play a game such as tennis: I can't find a partner. 3 any of the owners of a business, who share the profits and losses: She's a partner in a law firm. 4 a person who you are married to or who you live with, go out with, or have sex with

partner² v [T] to be someone's partner in a game or dance

part·ner·ship /ˈpɑːtnəʃɪp ‖ ˈpɑːrtnər-/ n 1 [U] the state of being a partner, especially in business: We've been in partnership for five years. 2 [C] a business owned by two or more people who share the profits and losses

part of speech /ˌ · · ˈ · / n a class of words in grammar, for example nouns, verbs, and adjectives: What part of speech is "do" in this sentence?

par·took /pɑːˈtʊk ‖ pɑːr-/ the past tense of PARTAKE

par·tridge /ˈpɑːtrɪdʒ ‖ ˈpɑːr-/ n a middle-size bird shot for sport and food

part-time /ˌ · ˈ · ◂/ adj working during only a part of the regular working time: a part-time job | a part-time secretary – **part time** adv: She works part time.

par·ty /ˈpɑːti ‖ ˈpɑːrti/ n parties 1 a social event at which people eat, drink, and enjoy themselves: We went to a party at Nicky's. | We had a party to celebrate the end of the exams. | a birthday party | They gave a party for their parents' fiftieth wedding anniversary. 2 [+ sing/pl verb] a group of people doing something together: a party of schoolchildren on their way to France 3 [+ sing/pl verb] an organization of people with the same political aims who try to win elections: the Green Party | Three parties are contesting the election. 4 **party politics** political activity for the advantage of your party and not your country: This is not a time to play party politics. 5 **the party line: a** the official view of a political party **b** a view which the more powerful members of an organization try to force on the rest 6 law one of the people or sides in an agreement or argument

pass¹ /pɑːs ‖ pæs/ v 1 [T] to go past a person or thing: We passed the school and then saw the library in front of us. | She waved at me as she passed. – see

PAST² (USAGE) 2 [I+adv/prep] to move in a particular direction: We passed through Germany on our way to Austria. | A cloud passed across the sun. 3 [T; +adv/prep] to move something in a particular direction: She passed the rope around the tree. 4 [T] to give something to someone by putting it into their hand: I looked at the photograph then passed it to Jane. | Could you pass the salt, please? | He passed me a glass of wine.

☐ USEFUL PATTERNS to pass something to someone; to pass someone something

5 [I;T] to kick, throw, or hit a ball to someone in your own team during a game such as football 6 [I] (of time) to go by: The time seemed to pass very slowly. | He gradually grew stronger as the summer passed. 7 [T] to spend time in a particular way: We passed an enjoyable evening together. 8 [I] to go from one person's control or possession to another's: When she died the house passed to her son. 9 [T] to officially accept a new law or a suggestion: The new law will be passed next month. 10 [I;T] to succeed in a test or an examination: I've finally passed my driving test! | Most of the students passed the exam. 11 **pass judgement** to give your opinion about something, especially when it is unfavourable: My job is just to collect the facts – not to pass judgement. 12 **pass sentence** to say what someone's punishment will be for a crime that they have done 13 **pass the buck** infml to refuse to accept responsibility for something and say that it is someone else's responsibility 14 **pass the time** to do something so that you do not feel BORED: We played cards to pass the time. 15 **pass the time of day** to have a short conversation with someone that you meet 16 **pass unnoticed** to not be noticed by people: His odd behaviour passed unnoticed. 17 **pass water** tech to URINATE

pass away phr v [I] euph to die (a less direct word than die): She passed away peacefully in her sleep.

pass by phr v [I] to go past a person or thing: She waved as she passed by.

pass sthg ↔ **down** phr v [T] to give or leave something to people who are younger than you or come after you: The knowledge was passed down from father to son.

pass off phr v 1 [I] to stop: The feelings of depression gradually passed off. 2 **pass off well** to take place successfully: The meeting passed off very well. 3 [T **pass** sbdy/sthg **off**] to present a person or thing as something false: They tried to pass the painting off as a genuine Piccasso. | He passed himself off as a doctor.

pass on phr v 1 [I] euph to die (a less direct word than die): My mother passed on last year. 2 [T **pass** sthg ↔ **on**] to give something to someone else after you have used it: Please read this notice and pass it on.

pass out phr v [I] to faint: I always pass out at the sight of blood.

pass over sthg phr v [T] to not talk about something because you do not want to pay attention to it: He passed over the subject of salaries very quickly!

pass sthg ↔ **up** phr v [T] to fail to take advantage of a chance to do something: I'd never pass up a chance to travel.

pass² n 1 a successful result in an examination 2 a piece of paper which shows that you are allowed to do something, for example enter a building 3 an act of passing a ball to a member of your own team in a game such as football 4 a narrow way which you can go through in a mountain range 5 **make a pass at someone** to try to begin a sexual relationship with someone

pass·a·ble /ˈpɑːsəbəl ‖ ˈpæ-/ adj **1** satisfactory **2** just good enough to be accepted **3** possible to use or cross (used of roads and rivers)

pas·sage /ˈpæsɪdʒ/ n **1** [C] (also **passageway**) a narrow way, especially inside a building, connecting rooms or places together: *It's along this passage on the left.* **2** [C] a narrow way through: *He forced a passage through the crowd.* **3** [C] a natural tube which is part of your body and which air or waste matter may pass along: *Clear the air passages.* **4** [U] movement from one place to another: *The bridge is not strong enough to allow the passage of heavy vehicles.* **5** the passage of time the passing of time **6** [sing] a long journey by ship **7** [C] a short part of a piece of writing or music: *an interesting passage on page 32*

pas·sage·way /ˈpæsɪdʒweɪ/ n a passage in a building or between buildings

pas·sen·ger /ˈpæsɪndʒər, -sən-/ n a person, not the driver or a member of the crew, travelling in a public or private vehicle

pass·er·by /ˌpɑːsəˈbaɪ ‖ ˌpæsər-/ n **passersby** /-səz-‖-sərz-/ a person who, by chance, is going past: *Several passersby saw the accident.*

pas·sing¹ /ˈpɑːsɪŋ ‖ ˈpæ-/ adj [only before a noun] **1** moving or going by: *She watched the passing cars.* **2** not lasting very long: *She did not give the matter even a passing thought.*

passing² n **in passing** in the course of talking about something else: *He was talking about Spain, and he mentioned in passing that you went there last year.*

pas·sion /ˈpæʃən/ n [C;U] a strong, deep, often uncontrollable feeling, especially of love, hatred, or anger: *The poet was expressing his burning passion for the woman he loved.* | *He has a passion for cream cakes.*

pas·sion·ate /ˈpæʃənɪt/ adj showing or filled with passion: *a passionate speech* | *a passionate woman* | *a passionate interest in politics* –**passionately** adv

pas·sive¹ /ˈpæsɪv/ adj **1** not active, but allowing things to happen to you (a word often used to express disapproval): *his passive acceptance of his fate* **2** a verb relating to or containing as its subject the person or thing to which an action is done; in "The boy was thrown from his horse", "was thrown" is a passive verb –**passively** adv

passive² n **the passive** the passive part or form of a verb

Pass·o·ver /ˈpɑːsəʊvər ‖ ˈpæs-/ n [U; sing] a holiday in the Jewish religion in memory of the freeing of the Jews from Egypt

pass·port /ˈpɑːspɔːt ‖ ˈpæspɔːrt/ n **1** a small official book that proves which country you belong to; you use it when you enter a foreign country **2** a passport to something a way to get something: *Money isn't a passport to happiness.*

pass·word /ˈpɑːswɜːd ‖ ˈpæswɜːrd/ n **1** a secret word which you have to know in order to get into a place, such as a military area **2** a word you put into a computer in order to use it

past¹ /pɑːst ‖ pæst/ adj **1** [only before a noun] having happened or existed before the present time: *He blamed past governments for creating these problems.* | *Things have got much worse in the past few years.* **2** finished and no longer happening or existing: *The time for talking is past – we must act now.* **3** past tense the form of a verb that expresses an action or an event that happened before the present time

past² adv,prep **1** adv,prep used to show that someone moves up to and beyond something: *We drove past the house.* | *He didn't stop – he just walked straight past.* –see picture on page 540 **2** prep farther on than something: *The hospital is about a mile past the school.* **3** past beyond a particular time: *It's just past ten o'clock.* **4** past caring no longer caring what happens

past³ n **1** [sing] the time that existed before the present time: *Housework is much easier now than it was in the past.* | *He never talks about his past.* **2** the past the past tense of a verb

■ USAGE The past participle of **pass** is **passed**: *The week has passed quickly.* But the adjective from **pass** is **past**: *The past week has been very busy.*

pas·ta /ˈpæstə ‖ ˈpɑː-/ n [U] an Italian food made, in various different shapes, from flour paste, and often covered with SAUCE or cheese; SPAGHETTI is a kind of pasta

paste¹ /peɪst/ n [C;U] **1** a wet substance used for sticking paper together, or onto other surfaces **2** any soft wet mixture of powder and liquid that is easily shaped or spread: *Mix it all up into a paste.* **3** a food made by crushing solid foods into a smooth soft mass, used for spreading on bread: *meat paste* | *fish paste* **4** a shining glassy substance, used to copy the appearance of real jewels

paste² v **pasted, pasting** [T] to stick paper with paste

pas·tel /ˈpæstl ‖ pæˈstel/ n **1** [C;U] a kind of dry colour in sticks used by artists **2** [C] a picture drawn with pastels

pas·teur·ize /ˈpɑːstʃəraɪz, -stə- ‖ ˈpæs-/ v **pasteurized, pasteurizing** (also **pasteurise** BrE) [T] to heat a liquid, especially milk, in a certain way in order to destroy bacteria –**pasteurization** /ˌpɑːstʃəraɪˈzeɪʃən, -stə- ‖ ˌpæstərə-/ n [U]

pas·time /ˈpɑːstaɪm ‖ ˈpæs-/ n something you do to pass your time in a pleasant way

past mas·ter /ˌ· ˈ··/ n a person who is very skilled in a particular subject or action

pas·tor·al /ˈpɑːstərəl ‖ ˈpæ-/ adj **1** concerning simple peaceful country life: *a pastoral scene of cows in a meadow* | *pastoral poetry* **2** connected with looking after people's happiness, especially their religious happiness: *The priest makes pastoral visits every Tuesday.*

past par·ti·ci·ple /ˌ· ·ˈ····/ n a part of a verb which is used in compound forms of the verb to express an action done or happening in the past; it is sometimes used as an adjective: *"Done" and "walked" are the past participles of "do" and "walk".* –see IRREGULAR VERB FORMS TABLE

past per·fect /ˌ· ·ˈ···/ n the past perfect a verb form used to show that one thing had happened before another in the past: *"Had done" is the past perfect of "do".*

pas·try /ˈpeɪstri/ n **pastries** **1** [U] a mixture of flour, fat, and milk or water, eaten when baked and often used to enclose other food **2** [C] a small sweet cake made with pastry

pas·ture /ˈpɑːstʃər ‖ ˈpæs-/ n [C;U] grassy land where cattle feed

pas·ty /ˈpæsti/ n **pasties** a folded piece of pastry baked with meat and potatoes in it

past·y² /ˈpeɪsti/ adj white and unhealthy-looking (used to describe someone's face)

pat¹ /pæt/ v -tt- [T] to touch something gently and repeatedly with your hand flat, often to show kindness or pity: *She patted her hair into place.* | *He patted her hand sympathetically.*

pat² *n* **1** a light friendly touch with your hand flat: *He gave the dog a pat as he walked past.* **2 a pat on the back** *infml* an expression of praise or satisfaction for something done **3 a pat of butter** a small lump of butter

patch¹ /pætʃ/ *n* **1** a piece of material used to cover a hole or a damaged place **2** a small area that looks different from the rest: *wet patches on the wall* | *There will be a few patches of mist near the coast.* **3** a small piece of ground: *a potato patch* **4 a bad patch** *BrE* a time of trouble or misfortune **5 not a patch on** *infml* not nearly as good as

patch² *v* [T] **1** to put a patch on a hole or worn place: *patched trousers* **2 patch something together** to quickly put together something which is of low quality but better than nothing

patch sthg ↔ **up** *phr v* [T] **1** to mend something with patches so that it can be used, even though it is not as good as new: *They patched the car up well enough to get us home.* **2 patch up a quarrel** to become friendly with someone again after a disagreement

patch·work /ˈpætʃwɜːk ‖ -ɜːrk/ *n* [C;U] **1** material made by sewing together a lot of small pieces of cloth, of regular shape but different colours and patterns: *a patchwork bedcover* **2** something that has a surface made up of lots of little pieces and looks like patchwork: *From the aircraft we could see a marvellous patchwork of fields.*

patch·y /ˈpætʃi/ *adj* **patchier, patchiest** **1** made up of patches, or appearing in patches: *patchy mist* **2** incomplete or uneven: *My knowledge of science is rather patchy.* –**patchily** *adv* –**patchiness** *n* [U]

pât·é /ˈpæteɪ ‖ paːˈteɪ, pæˈ/ *n* [U] a meat paste made by cutting PORK and other meat very finely and cooking it

pa·tent¹ /ˈpeɪtnt, ˈpæ- ‖ ˈpæ-/ *adj* **1** easy and plain to see (mostly used to describe feelings or qualities): *her patent discomfort at this odd situation* **2** protected, by a patent, from being copied or sold by those who do not have a right to do so: *a patent lock*

patent² *n* a piece of paper from a government office called the Patent Office giving someone the right to make or sell a new invention for a certain number of years

patent³ *v* [T] to obtain a patent for something

patent leath·er /ˌpeɪtnt ˈleðə⁻◂ ‖ ˌpæ-/ *n* [U] fine very shiny leather: *patent-leather shoes*

pa·tent·ly /ˈpeɪtntli ‖ ˈpæ-/ *adv* clearly and plainly: *a patently false statement*

pa·ter·nal /pəˈtɜːnl ‖ -ɜːr-/ *adj* **1** like a father or received from a father: *paternal love* **2** related to a person through their father's side of the family: *my paternal grandmother* –**paternally** *adv*

pa·ter·nal·is·m /pəˈtɜːnəl-ɪzəm ‖ -ɜːr-/ *n* [U] a way of ruling a country or controlling a company, which treats people like children –**paternalistic** /pəˌtɜːnəlˈɪstɪk◂ ‖ -ɜːr-/ *adj*

pa·ter·ni·ty /pəˈtɜːnɪti ‖ -ɜːr-/ *n* [U] *law* the fact of being the father of a child

path /paːθ ‖ pæθ/ *n* **1** (also **pathway**) a track for people on foot: *a path through the woods* | *We went down the garden path.* –see WAY1 (USAGE) –see picture on page 441 **2** the hard raised part at the side of the street which people on foot use: *Stay on the path. Don't go out into the road.* **3** a way through: *The police cleared a path through the crowd.* **4** a line along which something moves: *the path of an arrow* | *He stepped into the path of an oncoming car.*

5 a course of action with an expected result: *Development of the railways is the path to a successful transport structure.*

pa·thet·ic /pəˈθetɪk/ *adj* **1** very bad or weak when there is no good reason for it: *The Government's treatment of the disabled is quite pathetic.* **2** very bad: *He's a pathetic actor.* **3** making you feel sorry for someone: *the child's pathetic cries of pain* –**pathetically** /-kli/ *adv* : *a dog whimpering pathetically*

path·o·log·i·cal /ˌpæθəˈlɒdʒɪkəl ‖ -ˈlɑː-/ *adj* **1** behaving again and again in an unreasonable way, but unable to stop yourself: *a pathological liar* **2** *infml* unreasonable and caused by the imagination only: *a pathological fear of the dark* **3** *tech* caused by disease, or connected with the study of disease **4** –**pathologically** *adv* : *pathologically jealous*

pa·thol·o·gist /pəˈθɒlədʒɪst ‖ -ˈθɑː-/ *n* a specialist in pathology, especially a doctor who examines a dead body to find out how the person died

pa·thol·o·gy /pəˈθɒlədʒi ‖ -ˈθɑː-/ *n* [U] the study of disease

pa·thos /ˈpeɪθɒs ‖ -θɑːs/ *n* [U] *lit* something in a sad situation which makes you feel very sorry for the people in it

path·way /ˈpaːθweɪ ‖ ˈpæθ-/ *n* a path

pa·tience /ˈpeɪʃəns/ *n* [U] **1** the ability to wait, or to deal with difficulties, for a long time without getting annoyed: *You need a lot of patience if you want to get served in this shop.* | *She showed great patience with them all.* –opposite **impatience** **2** a card game for one player

pa·tient¹ /ˈpeɪʃənt/ *adj* having or showing patience: *Try to be patient.* –opposite **impatient** –**patiently** *adv*

patient² *n* a person receiving medical treatment: *clinics for private patients* –see CUSTOMER (USAGE)

pat·i·o /ˈpætiəʊ/ *n* **patios** an area of the garden with a hard surface; it is near the house, and people use it for sitting outside –see picture on page 441

pat·ri·ot /ˈpætriət, -triɒt, ˈpeɪ- ‖ ˈpeɪtriət, -triɑːt/ *n* a person who loves their country

pat·ri·ot·is·m /ˈpætriətɪzəm, ˈpeɪ- ‖ ˈpeɪ-/ *n* [U] love for your country –**patriotic** /ˌpætriˈɒtɪk◂ ‖ ˌpeɪtriˈɒtɪk◂/ *adj* : *patriotic songs* –**patriotically** /-kli/ *adv*

pa·trol¹ /pəˈtrəʊl/ *n* **1** [+ sing/pl verb] a small group of soldiers who move round the outside of a military camp to make sure that the enemy do not enter it **2 on patrol** working in a patrol

patrol² *v* **-ll-** [I;T] to go round an area or building at regular times to see that there is no trouble, and that no one is trying to get in or out illegally: *Armed guards patrol the grounds.*

pa·trol·man /pəˈtrəʊlmən/ *n* **patrolmen** /-mən/ *AmE* a policeman who regularly patrols a particular area

pa·tron /ˈpeɪtrən/ *n* **1** a well-known person who officially supports an organization which helps people **2** a person who supports artists, musicians, and writers by buying their works or giving them money **3** a person who uses a particular shop or hotel, especially regularly

pat·ron·age /ˈpætrənɪdʒ/ *n* [U] **1** the support given by a patron **2** the right to appoint people to important positions (a word which is often used to express disapproval)

pat·ron·ize /ˈpætrənaɪz ‖ ˈpeɪ-, ˈpæ-/ *v* **patronized, patronizing** (also **patronise** *BrE*) [T] **1** to behave to someone as if you think that you are better or more important than they are: *He cannot speak to women without patronizing them.* | *a patronizing smile* **2** *fml* to be a patron of a shop or hotel

patron saint /ˌ··ˈ·/ *n* a Christian holy man or woman in the past, regarded as giving special protection to a particular place or activity: *Saint Christopher is the patron saint of travellers.*

pat·ter[1] /ˈpætə^r/ *n* **1** [sing] the sound of something hitting a hard surface lightly, quickly, and repeatedly: *the patter of rain on the window* **2** [U] the quick talk of a salesperson or a performer

patter[2] *v* [I;+adv/prep] to make the sound of something hitting a hard surface lightly, quickly, and repeatedly: *The dog pattered down the stairs.*

pat·tern /ˈpætn ‖ ˈpætərn/ *n* **1** a regularly repeated arrangement especially of lines or shapes on a surface or of sounds or words: *The cloth has a pattern of red and white squares.* **2** the way in which something usually happens or develops: *The illness is not following its usual pattern.* **3** a shape used as a guide for making something, especially a piece of paper used to show the shape of the parts of a piece of clothing: *a dress pattern*

pat·terned /ˈpætnd ‖ ˈpætərnd/ *adj* having a pattern: *a patterned carpet* –see picture on page 147

paunch /pɔːntʃ/ *n* a fat stomach, especially a man's

pau·per /ˈpɔːpə^r/ *n* a person who is very poor

pause[1] /pɔːz/ *n* a short but noticeable break in activity or speech: *a pause in the conversation*

pause[2] *v* **paused, pausing** [I] to stop for a short time: *She paused to light a cigarette, then continued reading.*

pave /peɪv/ *v* **paved, paving** [T] **1** to cover a path or area with a surface of flat stones: *a paved courtyard* **2 pave the way for** to do something now which will make something else possible in the future

pave·ment /ˈpeɪvmənt/ *n* **1** *BrE* a paved surface at the side of a street for people to walk on **2** *AmE* the hard black part of a road that vehicles drive on –see picture on page 441

pa·vil·ion /pəˈvɪljən/ *n* **1** *BrE* a building at the side of a sports field where players can change their clothes and wash **2** a large decorative building used for public amusements or exhibitions, (EXHIBITION) especially one intended to be used only for a short time

pav·ing /ˈpeɪvɪŋ/ *n* [U] material used to pave a surface: *a paving stone*

paw[1] /pɔː/ *n* an animal's foot that has nails called claws (CLAW) and a soft part to walk on, called a PAD *a dog with an injured paw*

paw[2] *v* [I;T] (of animals) to keep moving or rubbing something with a front foot: *an angry bull pawing the ground* | *The dog was pawing at the door, trying to get out.*

pawn[1] /pɔːn/ *v* [T] to take something to a pawnbroker, who then lends you money

pawn[2] *n* **1** a piece in the game of CHESS **2** an unimportant person used by someone else for their own advantage

pawn·bro·ker /ˈpɔːnˌbrəʊkə^r/ *n* a person who lends you money if you give him something of yours; if you don't pay the money back, he sells it

paw·paw /ˈpɔːpɔː/ *n* see PAPAYA

pay[1] /peɪ/ *v* **paid** /peɪd/, paid **1** [I;T] to give money for something you buy: *How do you want to pay? Cash or cheque?* | *You must pay in dollars.* | *She paid*

over the money. | *She paid the girl £5.* | *She paid the money to the girl.* | *Who's going to pay* for *the drinks?* | *You can't take them until they've been paid for.* | *He paid extra to have a reserved seat.*
☐ [USEFUL PATTERNS: to pay someone money; to pay money to someone]
2 pay through the nose *infml* to pay far too much for something **3 pay your way** to pay for what you need yourself and not have to ask for help **4** [I] to be profitable: *If we can't make our farm pay, we'll sell it.* | *It's a paying concern.* **5** [I;T] to give an advantage, even though it costs more or takes more effort at the beginning: *It pays to get up early.* | *It really pays you to buy a large quantity.* | *Crime doesn't pay.* **6** [I;T] to give someone wages: *How much do they pay?* | *They pay £7.50 an hour.* | *We got paid weekly.* | *They pay someone to cut the grass.* **7** [T] to give money which you owe: *Have you paid the electricity bill yet?* | *She'll have to pay her debts first.* **8 pay for something** to suffer because you have done something bad: *I'll make you pay for this!* | *You'll pay for your late night tomorrow.* **9 pay attention: a** to listen or watch carefully: *Now, pay attention or you won't know what to do.* **b** to take care: *Pay particular attention to the backs of your teeth.* **c** to think only about what you are supposed to be doing: *You've got to pay attention when you're driving. It's no good day-dreaming.* **10 pay a call on someone** to make a short social visit to someone **11 pay a compliment to someone** to praise someone directly to their face **12 pay for itself** to save as much money as it cost: *Insulating the roof pays for itself within five years.* **13 pay lip service to** to say that you support something, but not to act as though you do: *The government pays lip service to better education, but it won't provide the money.* **14 pay no attention** to take no notice **15 pay a visit to** to make a visit to **16 pay your respects** to visit someone as a way of showing your respect for them **17 pay your last respects** to go and see someone after they have died as a way of showing your respect for them

pay back *phr v* **1** [T **pay** sbdy/sthg ↔ **back**] to return money you have borrowed: *Have I paid back the £10 you lent me?* | *You must pay me back by Friday.* **2** [T **pay** sbdy ↔ **back**] to treat someone badly because they have treated you badly: *I'll pay you back for what you did to me!*

pay sthg ↔ **in** *phr v* [T] to put money into the bank: *I've got to call at the bank and pay this cheque in.* | *I paid it into my current account.*

pay off *phr v* **1** [T **pay** sthg ↔ **off**] to finish paying money that you owe **2** [I] to be worth the trouble: *His careful preparation really paid off.*

pay sthg ↔ **out** *phr v* [T] to spend large amounts of money: *We paid out a lot of money to get the roof mended.*

pay up *phr v* [I] to give someone all the money you owe them, especially unwillingly

pay[2] *n* [U] **1** money received for work: *He gets his pay every Friday.* | *a pay rise* | *Very few office cleaners get good pay.* **2 in the pay of** employed by someone: *He is in the pay of the enemy.*

■ USAGE Compare **pay**, **salary**, **wages**, **fee**, **income**. **Pay** is a general word for the money you receive for work. A **salary** is paid monthly into a bank (especially to professional people) and **wages** are paid weekly in cash (especially to people who work with their hands). A **fee** is money paid to a professional person (e.g. a lawyer) for a particular service. Your **income** is all the money you receive over a longer period of time, whether from work, rents, etc.: *My total income last year was £15,000.*

pay·a·ble /ˈpeɪəbəl/ adj [never before a noun] showing that something may or must be paid: This bill is payable within seven days. | Your cheque should be made payable to "The London Electricity Board".

pay·day /ˈpeɪdeɪ/ n the day on which wages are paid

PAYE /ˌpiː eɪ waɪ ˈiː/ BrE a system by which income tax is taken away from wages before the wages are paid; an abbreviation for **pay as you earn**

pay·ee /peɪˈiː/ n tech a person to whom money is or should be paid

pay en·ve·lope /ˈ.ˌ.../ n the usual American word for PAY PACKET

pay·ing guest /ˌ.·ˈ.·/ n a person who stays in someone else's house and pays money to have a room and meals

pay·ing-in slip /ˌ.·· ˈ.ˌ.·/ a small form which you fill in when you pay money into your bank account

pay·ment /ˈpeɪmənt/ n 1 [U] the act of paying: I enclose a cheque in payment of my account. 2 [C] an amount of money that is paid: monthly payments for rent

pay·off /ˈpeɪɒf ‖ -ɔːf/ n **the payoff: a** the end of a story when everything is explained **b** the end of a number of connected acts when there is some good result

pay pack·et /ˈ.·ˌ.·/ n BrE an envelope containing wages, given to an employed person each week

pay phone /ˈ.·/ n a public telephone that you put coins into when you use it

pay·roll /ˈpeɪrəʊl/ n **1** [C] a list of workers employed by a company and the amount of wages each person is to be paid **2** [sing] the total amount of wages paid in a particular company

PC /ˌpiː ˈsiː/ n **1** an abbreviation for PERSONAL COMPUTER **2** a male member of the British police force having the lowest rank; an abbreviation for **Police Constable**: PC Johnson | Two PCs were attacked.

PE /ˌpiː ˈiː/ n sport and exercise done as a subject in school; an abbreviation for **physical education**

pea /piː/ n a very small round green vegetable –see picture on page 344

peace /piːs/ n **1** [U] quiet and restful conditions with nothing to worry you: She'd just like to get on with her work in peace. **2** [sing;U] a condition or period in which there is no war: a dangerous situation that threatens world peace | a lasting peace **3** [U] a state of freedom from disorder within a country, with the citizens living according to the law: Peace has returned to the streets of Wigham after last Saturday night's disturbances. **4 peace and quiet** freedom from noise, interruption, and worry **5 peace of mind** freedom from worry **6 keep the peace: a** not to cause violent disorder **b** to stop people quarrelling **7 make your peace with someone** to bring your quarrel with someone to an end

peace·a·ble /ˈpiːsəbəl/ adj disliking argument or quarrelling –**peaceably** adv

peace·ful /ˈpiːsfəl/ adj **1** quiet and untroubled: to spend a peaceful day in the garden **2** liking peace: peaceful nations **3** not violent: a peaceful demonstration –**peacefully** adv –**peacefulness** n [U]

peace·time /ˈpiːstaɪm/ n [U] a time when a nation is not at war

peach¹ /piːtʃ/ n a round fruit with soft yellowish-red skin and sweet juicy flesh, and a large seed in its centre –see picture on page 344

peach² adj pale orange-pink, the colour of a peach

pea·cock /ˈpiːkɒk ‖ -kɑːk/ n a large bird with beautiful long tail feathers which have large blue-green spots like eyes; a female peacock is called a **peahen**

peak¹ /piːk/ n **1** a sharply pointed mountain top: The mountain peaks are covered with snow all the year round. **2** the point when activity is greatest or performance is best: Sales have reached a new peak. | The roads are full of traffic at peak hours. | The Kenyan runner was at his peak in the 1989 Games. **3** the part of a cap which sticks out in front above your eyes to keep the sun out of them

peak² v [I] to reach and pass the highest point: Sales have now peaked, and we expect them to decrease soon.

peal¹ /piːl/ n **1** the sound of the loud ringing of bells **2** a long, loud sound or number of sounds one after the other: a peal of thunder | a peal of laughter

peal² v [I;T] to ring out or sound loudly: All the church bells are pealed on Christmas morning.

pea·nut /ˈpiːnʌt/ n a small nut which grows in a shell under the ground, and can be eaten

peanut but·ter /ˌ.·· ˈ.·/ n [U] a soft food which looks like brown butter, but is made of crushed peanuts; you eat it on bread

pear /peəʳ/ n a sweet yellow-green juicy fruit which grows on a tree; it is about the size of an apple, but narrow at the stem end and wide at the other end –see picture on page 344

pearl /pɜːl ‖ pɜːrl/ n a small round hard silvery-white object found inside a shellfish called an OYSTER; pearls are used for making expensive jewellery

pearl·y /ˈpɜːli ‖ ˈpɜːrli/ adj pearlier, pearliest like pearls: a pale pearly grey

peas·ant /ˈpezənt/ n **1** a person who works on the land, especially one who owns and lives on a small piece of land **2** a person without education or manners

peas·ant·ry /ˈpezəntri/ n [+ sing/pl verb] **the peasantry** all the peasants of a particular country

peat /piːt/ n [U] dark brown decaying plant material which takes the place of ordinary soil in certain areas; it is used for improving garden soil and for burning instead of coal –**peaty** adj

peb·ble /ˈpebəl/ n a small roundish smooth stone found especially beside the sea or in a river

peck¹ /pek/ v **1** [I;T] (used of birds) to take a small quick bite of something: chickens pecking in the dust | The parrot tried to peck me. **2 peck at your food** to eat a few small bites of your food, when you do not really want it **3** [T] infml to kiss someone in a hurry or without much feeling

peck² n **1** an act of pecking **2** infml a hurried kiss: He gave her a quick peck on the cheek.

peck·ish /ˈpekɪʃ/ adj BrE infml slightly hungry

pe·cu·li·ar /pɪˈkjuːliəʳ/ adj **1** strange, especially in a troubling or displeasing way: This food has got a peculiar taste. Do you think it's all right? **2 peculiar to** belonging only to a particular person, place, or thing: This style of cooking is peculiar to the south-west of the country.

pe·cu·li·ar·i·ty /pɪˌkjuːliˈærɪti/ n peculiarities **1** [U] the quality of being peculiar **2** [C] something which belongs only to a particular person, place, etc.: One of the peculiarities of her behaviour is that she shouts instead of talking.

pe·cu·li·ar·ly /pɪˈkjuːliəli ‖ -ər-/ adv **1** especially: This question is peculiarly difficult. **2** strangely

pe·cu·ni·a·ry /pɪˈkjuːniəri ‖ -nieri/ adj fml connected with or consisting of money

ped·al[1] /'pedl/ *n* a part of a machine which you press with your foot: *One of the pedals has come off my bicycle.* | *When you want to stop the car, press the brake pedal.*

pedal[2] *v* -ll- (-l- *AmE*) [I;T] to ride a bicycle: *She pedalled the bicycle up the hill.* | *I was just pedalling along.*

pe·dan·tic /pɪ'dæntɪk/ *adj* paying too much attention to small details, and wanting everything to be done exactly according to the rules –**pedant** /'pednt/ *n* : *Our teacher's a bit of a pedant about punctuation.*

ped·dle /'pedl/ *v* **peddled, peddling** [I; T] **1** to go from place to place trying to sell small goods **2** to sell illegal drugs **3** to keep trying to get other people to accept your poor ideas

ped·dler /'pedlə*r*/ *n* **1** a person who sells illegal drugs **2** see PEDLAR

ped·es·tal /'pedɨstəl/ *n* **1** the base on which a pillar or STATUE stands **2 put someone on a pedestal** to admire someone very much although they may not really be so wonderful

pe·des·tri·an[1] /pɨ'destriən/ *n* a person walking in a street, and not travelling in a vehicle

pedestrian[2] *adj* not interesting or unusual or having much imagination: *He was rather a pedestrian student.*

pedestrian cross·ing /·,··· '··/ *n* a special place for pedestrians to cross the road

pe·di·a·tri·cian /ˌpiːdiə'trɪʃən/ *n* see PAEDIATRICIAN

pe·di·at·rics /ˌpiːdi'ætrɪks/ *n* [U] see PAEDIATRICS

ped·i·gree[1] /'pedɨgriː/ *n* [C;U] the record of the specially chosen animals that a particular animal has been bred from

pedigree[2] *adj* [only before a noun] descended from a recorded and specially chosen family, and therefore of high quality (used of animals, especially dogs): *a pedigree spaniel*

ped·lar /'pedlə*r*/ *n* (also **peddler** *AmE*) a person who goes from place to place trying to sell small articles

pe·do·phile /'piːdəʊfaɪl ‖ 'ped-/ *n* see PAEDOPHILE

peek[1] /piːk/ *v* [I] *infml* to look at something quickly, especially when you should not: *He just had time to peek into the room before the door closed.*

peek[2] *n infml* a quick look: *Just have a peek and see what the children are doing.*

peel[1] /piːl/ *v* **1** [T] to remove the skin from fruit or vegetables: *a machine that peels potatoes* **2** [I] to come off in small pieces: *My skin always peels when I've been in the sun.*

peel off *phr v* **1** [T **peel** sthg ↔ **off**] to remove an outer covering from something: *Can you peel the label off?* **2** [I] to come off in small pieces: *The paint was beginning to peel off.*

peel[2] *n* [U] the skin of those fruits and vegetables which you usually peel before you eat them: *orange peel* | *apple peel*

peel·ings /'piːlɪŋz/ *n* [pl] pieces of skin peeled from fruit and vegetables, especially potatoes

peep[1] /piːp/ *v* **1** [I] to look quickly and secretly: *His hands were covering his face, but I could see him peeping through his fingers.* **2** [I; + adv/prep] to come partly into view: *strands of hair peeping out from under her hat*

peep[2] *n* **1** a quick, incomplete, and perhaps secret look: *He took a peep at the back of the book to find the answers.* **2** a short high sound like that made by a

young bird or a mouse **3 a peep** *infml* words spoken, or small sound made: *I don't want to hear a peep out of you until dinnertime.*

peer[1] /pɪə*r*/ *v* [I; +adv/prep] to look very carefully or hard: *She peered through the window.* | *He peered at me over the top of his glasses.*

peer[2] *n* **1 peers** [pl] (also **peer group** /'· ·/) people that you know who are the same age as you or who have the same social position: *The opinion of his peers is more important to him than his parents' ideas.* | *There's a lot of peer group pressure on teenagers.* **2** a member of the noble ranks such as Lord in Britain

peer·age /'pɪərɪdʒ/ *n* [C;U] **1 the peerage** all the peers as a group **2** the noble rank of a peer: *After twenty years as a member of parliament she was given a peerage.*

peer·ess /'pɪərɨs/ *n* a female member of the nobility

peer·less /'pɪələs ‖ 'pɪər-/ *adj fml* better than any other

peeved /piːvd/ *adj* annoyed

peev·ish /'piːvɪʃ/ *adj* easily annoyed by unimportant things –**peevishly** *adv* –**peevishness** *n* [U]

peg[1] /peg/ *n* **1** a short piece of wood or other material which is fixed on a wall or door so that you can hang clothes or other things on it: *Hang your coat on the peg in the hall.* **2** a small piece of wood which goes into a hole; pegs are used for joining things together, and also in games **3** a small wooden or plastic thing you use to fasten clothes to a washing line to dry **4 off the peg** not specially made to fit you (used of clothes) **5 square peg in a round hole** a person who is not suited to the position or group in which they are placed **6 take somebody down a peg** *infml* to show somebody that they are not as important as they thought they were

peg[2] *v* -gg- [T] **1** to fasten with pegs: *Peg the clothes on the line.* **2** to fix prices or wages and not allow them to rise: *Wages have been pegged for 12 months.*

pe·jo·ra·tive /pɨ'dʒɒrətɪv ‖ -'dʒɔː-, -'dʒɑː-/ *adj fml* expressing disapproval or suggesting that someone or something is of little value (used of a word or phrase): *Many women now think the word "housewife" is pejorative, because it makes them seem unimportant.*

pe·kin·ese /ˌpiːkɨ'niːz◂/ *n* a small dog with long silky hair

pel·i·can /'pelɪkən/ *n* a large water bird which catches fish and stores them under its beak in part of its body that is like a long bag

pelican cross·ing /ˌ··· '··/ *n* a place where people can cross the road by pressing a button at traffic lights to stop the traffic

pel·let /'pelɨt/ *n* **1** a small ball of paper, animal food, or other material **2** a small metal ball that can be fired from a gun

pel·met /'pelmɨt/ *n* a narrow piece of wood or cloth across the top of a window that hides the curtain rod

pelt[1] /pelt/ *n* **1** the skin of a dead animal, especially one with the fur still on it **2 at full pelt** as fast as possible

pelt[2] *v* **1** [T] to attack someone by throwing things at them: *They pelted the police with stones.* **2** [I] (also **pelt down**) (of rain) to fall heavily and continuously: *I'm not going out there – it's really pelting down!* **3** [I] to run very fast: *They came pelting down the hill.*

pel·vis /'pelvɪs/ n the bowl-shaped frame of bones at the base of the backbone that joins your leg bones to your pelvis –**pelvic** adj

pen¹ /pen/ n **1** a narrow metal or plastic object which contains ink, and is used to write or draw with –see picture on page 539 **2** a small piece of land enclosed by a fence, used for keeping animals in

pen² v -nn- [T] lit **1** to write **2** (also **pen up/in**) to shut animals in a pen

pe·nal /'piːnl/ adj **1** about the punishment of criminals: the penal system | the need for penal reform **2** for which you can be punished by law: a penal offence

pe·nal·ize (also **penalise** BrE) /'piːnəl-aɪz ‖ 'piːnəl-, 'penəl-/ v **penalized, penalizing** [T] **1** to put someone in an unfair position: She felt penalized for having children and going to work as well. **2** in sports, to punish a player's action by giving an advantage to the other team: Their team was penalized for intentionally wasting time.

pen·al·ty /'penlti/ n **penalties 1** the punishment for breaking a law or rule: Fishing in this river is forbidden – penalty £5. **2** in football and other games, an advantage given to a team when the other team has broken the rules: We were given a penalty after one of our players was hit.

pen·ance /'penəns/ n [C;U] something which you do as a punishment to show that you are sorry about something you have done wrong, according to your religion

pence /pens/ BrE (also **p**) the unit of money in Britain that is smaller than a pound: There are a hundred pence to the pound. | It only cost a few pence. –see PENNY (USAGE)

pen·chant /'pɒnʃɒn, 'pentʃɒnt ‖ 'pentʃənt/ n a strong liking: a penchant for Indian food

pen·cil¹ /'pensəl/ n a narrow wooden object which contains a thin stick of a black or coloured substance, and is used to write or draw with –see picture on page 539

pencil² v -ll- (-l- AmE) [T] to write something or mark something with a pencil

pen·dant (also **pendent**) /'pendənt/ n a small piece of jewellery on a chain that you wear round your neck

pend·ing¹ /'pendɪŋ/ prep fml while waiting for or until: This decision must wait pending her return from Europe.

pending² adj fml **1** waiting to be decided or settled: She put the file into a box marked "pending". **2** going to happen soon

pen·du·lum /'pendjʊləm ‖ -dʒə-/ n a rod with a weight at the bottom which swings from side to side and works a clock

pen·e·trate /'penɪtreɪt/ v **penetrated, penetrating 1** [I;T] to get through or force a way into something that is difficult to enter: The sun penetrated through the thick clouds and started to shine. | The car lights penetrated the darkness. | Japanese car manufacturers have penetrated the European market. **2** to get inside an organization in order to get information or make it difficult for them

pen·e·trat·ing /'penɪtreɪtɪŋ/ adj **1** sharp and searching (used of a person's eyes, or the way they look at you) **2** able to understand clearly and deeply (used of a person's mind) **3** sharp and loud (used of sounds): a penetrating voice –**penetratingly** adv

pen·e·tra·tion /ˌpenɪ'treɪʃən/ n [U] **1** the act or action of penetrating: The army's penetration of the enemy territory has been successful. **2** the ability to understand quickly and clearly

pen friend /'· ·/ n a person in a foreign country who you make friends with by exchanging letters, even though you may never meet

pen·guin /'peŋgwɪn/ n large black and white bird found mainly in the Antarctic

pen·i·cil·lin /ˌpenɪ'sɪlɪn/ n [U] a substance called an ANTIBIOTIC which is used as a medicine to kill harmful bacteria in your body

pe·nin·su·la /pɪ'nɪnsjʊlə ‖ -sələ/ n a piece of land almost completely surrounded by water but joined to a larger mass of land: Italy is a peninsula. –**peninsular** adj

pe·nis /'piːnɪs/ n the outer sex organ of males

pen·i·tent /'penɪtənt/ adj fml feeling or showing that you are sorry for having done wrong, and that you intend not to do so again –**penitently** adv –**penitence** n [U]

pen·i·ten·tia·ry /ˌpenɪ'tenʃəri/ n penitentiaries a prison, especially in the US

pen·knife /'pen-naɪf/ n penknives /-naɪvz/ a small knife with a blade that folds into the handle

pen name /'· ·/ n a name used by a writer instead of their real name

pen·ni·less /'penɪləs/ adj having no money

pen·ny /'peni/ n **1** [plural is **pence**] (also **p**) the smallest unit of money in Britain; there are 100 pence in one pound **2** [plural is **pennies**] a small brown coin, the British coin of lowest value **3** in the US and Canada, a coin worth a cent **4** not a penny [usually used in negatives] no money at all: It won't cost you a penny. **5** in for a penny, in for a pound if something has been begun it should be finished whatever the cost may be **6** spend a penny a less direct expression for "go to the TOILET" **7** the penny dropped BrE infml the meaning of something said has finally been understood

■ USAGE In British English the words **penny** and **pennies** are no longer used very much to talk about money or prices. When speaking or writing about an amount of money use **pence** or **p**: It costs twenty pence/twenty p/20 p a packet. | You owe me ten pence/ten p/10 p. | a ten pence piece/a 10 p piece | one pence/one p/1 p

pen pal /'· ·/ n AmE the usual American word for PEN FRIEND

pen·sion¹ /'penʃən/ n money paid to you regularly by your employer or the government when you no longer work because you are old or ill

pension² v

pension sbdy ↔ off phr v [T] to dismiss someone from a job and give them a pension

pen·sion·a·ble /'penʃənəbəl/ adj giving you the right to receive a pension: a pensionable job

pen·sion·er /'penʃənəʳ/ n a person who has stopped working and is receiving a pension

pen·sive /'pensɪv/ adj thinking about something: a pensive smile

pen·ta·gon /'pentəgən ‖ -gɑːn/ n **1** a flat shape with five sides and five angles **2** the Pentagon the leaders of the US army and the building they work from –**pentagonal** /pen'tægənəl/ adj

pen·tath·lon /pen'tæθlən/ n a sports event in which people have to compete in five different sports

pent·house /'penthaʊs/ n a desirable set of rooms built at the top of a tall building

pent-up /ˌpent ˈʌp◂/ adj shut up inside you instead of being expressed: *pent-up anger*

pe·nul·ti·mate /peˈnʌltᵻmᵻt, pə-/ adj next to the last: *the penultimate scene in the play*

pen·u·ry /ˈpenjᵿri/ n [U] fml the state of being very poor

peo·ple¹ /ˈpiːpəl/ n 1 [pl] men, women, and children; "people" is the usual plural of PERSON: *Were there many people at the party?* | *young people* | *It's hard to meet people in a foreign country.* 2 **the people** [pl] all the ordinary people in a society 3 [C] a race or nation: *The Chinese are a hard-working people.* | *the peoples of Africa*

people² v peopled, peopling [T] fml (of people) to live in a place: *The desert is peopled by wandering tribes.*

pep·per¹ /ˈpepəʳ/ n 1 [U] a hot-tasting powder made from crushed seeds that you add to food: *salt and pepper* 2 [C] (also **green pepper, red pepper**) a red or green hollow vegetable –see picture on page 344 –**peppery** adj

pepper² v [T] 1 to put pepper on food 2 to hit with a lot of small bullets or other things

pep·pered /ˈpepəd ‖ -ərd/ adj full of: *Her essay was absolutely peppered with mistakes.*

pep·per·mint /ˈpepəˌmɪnt ‖ -ər-/ (also **mint**) n 1 [U] a plant with a special strong taste, used in sweets and to make toothpaste taste nice 2 [C] a sweet with this taste

pep pill /ˈ· ·/ n slang a PILL containing a drug which makes you think or act more quickly

pep talk /ˈ· ·/ n infml a talk which you give to people you are in charge of to encourage them to do better: *Our new teacher gave us a pep talk.*

per /pəʳ; strong pɜːʳ/ prep for each: *We're paid £10 per hour.* | *Allow half a pound of meat per person.*

per·ceive /pəˈsiːv ‖ pər-/ v perceived, perceiving fml 1 [T; + that] to see, hear or notice something which it is not easy to notice: *He perceived that he was unwelcome and left.* | *I couldn't perceive any difference between the two sounds.* 2 [T] to understand something in a particular way: *The new tax is perceived as an attack on the poor.* –**perceivable** adj

per cent /· ˈ·/ adv 1 parts for each 100: *The restaurant has a service charge of ten per cent (10%).* | *The bank has increased its interest rate by one per cent.* 2 **a hundred per cent** a phrase used to show you agree with something completely: *I agree with you 100 per cent.*

per·cen·tage /pəˈsentɪdʒ ‖ pər-/ n an amount stated as if it is part of a whole which is 100: *What percentage of babies die of this disease every year?* | *A high percentage of people still smoke.*

per·cep·ti·ble /pəˈseptᵻbəl ‖ pər-/ adj fml noticeable: *A barely perceptible smile crossed his face.* –opposite **imperceptible** –**perceptibly** adv

per·cep·tion /pəˈsepʃən ‖ pər-/ n 1 [U] (also **perceptiveness**) natural ability to notice and understand things: *a woman of great perception* 2 [C] understanding of something: *Her perceptions and insight into the book were fascinating.* 3 [U] noticing things with your senses and understanding them with your mind: *He's studying the psychology of perception.*

per·cep·tive /pəˈseptɪv ‖ pər-/ adj quick to notice and understand –**perceptively** adv –**perceptiveness** n [U]

perch¹ /pɜːtʃ ‖ pɜːrtʃ/ v 1 [I] (of a bird) to come to rest from flying: *The birds perched on the telephone wires.* 2 [I;T] to sit or to put something on the edge of something: *She perched herself on a tall chair.* | *The house was perched on the edge of the cliffs.*

perch² n 1 a branch, or rod where a bird rests 2 a high position in which a person or building is placed: *From our perch up there on top of the hill we can see the whole town.* 3 **perch** [pl] a lake and river fish that is caught and eaten

per·co·late /ˈpɜːkəleɪt ‖ ˈpɜːr-/ v **percolated, percolating** 1 [I] (of liquid) to pass slowly down through a material which has small holes in it: *It takes several days for the rain to percolate through the rock and into the rivers.* 2 to pass slowly from one person to another in a group: *Opposition to the Prime Minister began to percolate through all sections of the government.* 3 [T] (also **perk**) infml to make coffee in a special pot by passing hot water slowly through crushed coffee beans –**percolation** /ˌpɜːkəˈleɪʃən ‖ ˌpɜːr-/ n [U]

per·co·la·tor /ˈpɜːkəleɪtəʳ ‖ ˈpɜːr-/ n a pot in which coffee is percolated

per·cus·sion /pəˈkʌʃən ‖ pər-/ n 1 **the percussion** [+sing/pl verb] the group of musical instruments in a band or ORCHESTRA which you play by hitting them, for example drums: *The percussion is too loud.* 2 **percussion instrument** a musical instrument which you play by hitting it 3 [U] the forceful striking together of two hard objects

pe·remp·to·ry /pəˈrɛmptəri/ adj fml showing an expectation of being obeyed at once –**peremptorily** adv

pe·ren·ni·al¹ /pəˈreniəl/ adj 1 happening repeatedly or lasting forever: *Politics provides a perennial subject of argument.* 2 living for more than two years (used of plants) –**perennially** adv

perennial² n a perennial plant

per·fect¹ /ˈpɜːfɪkt ‖ ˈpɜːr-/ adj 1 the very best possible kind: *The weather was absolutely perfect.* | *The optician said he had perfect vision.* 2 having no mistakes or faults: *a perfect set of teeth* | *Her English is perfect.* 3 complete: *perfect strangers* 4 suitable and satisfying in every way: *The house was perfect for a big family.* 5 tech (of the form of a verb) concerning a period of time up to and including the present (**present perfect**), past (**past perfect**), or future (**future perfect**) (as in "*She has gone*", "*She had gone*", "*She will have gone*"): *the Present Perfect tense*

per·fect² /pəˈfekt ‖ pər-/ v [T] to make perfect: *She practised hard to perfect her singing voice.*

per·fec·tion /pəˈfekʃən ‖ pər-/ n [U] 1 the quality of being perfect: *We don't need perfection – just a good general standard.* 2 the process of developing completely or making perfect: *The perfection of this new medical treatment may take several years.* 3 **to perfection** perfectly: *The meat was done to perfection.*

per·fec·tion·ist /pəˈfekʃənᵻst ‖ pər-/ n a person who is not satisfied with anything that is not perfect: *It takes him hours to cook a simple meal because he's such a perfectionist.*

per·fect·ly /ˈpɜːfɪktli ‖ ˈpɜːr-/ adv 1 so well that it would be impossible to do it better: *She understood perfectly.* 2 completely or very: *The walls must be perfectly clean before you paint them.* | *You know perfectly well that you're not supposed to go in there.*

per·fo·rated /ˈpɜːfəreɪtᵻd ‖ ˈpɜːr-/ adj having a lot of small holes through the surface: *You can separate the stamps along the perforated line.*

per·fo·ra·tion /ˌpɜːfəˈreɪʃən ‖ ˌpɜːr-/ n **1** [U] the action of perforating **2** [C] a small hole made in the surface of something: *tear along the perforations*

per·form /pəˈfɔːm ‖ pərˈfɔːrm/ v **1** [T] to do a piece of work: *This operation can now safely be performed by a junior doctor.* **2** [I;T] to do something to amuse people: *They're performing a Shakespeare play.* | *She's performing at the National Theatre.* | *a performing elephant* **3** [I] to work or operate: *This car performs well in busy traffic.*

per·form·ance /pəˈfɔːməns ‖ pərˈfɔːr-/ n **1** [C] an act of performing: *The singer's performance was terrible.* | *There are two performances a day.* **2** [U] the action of doing a piece of work: *Her performance in the exam was disappointing.* **3** [U] the ability of a person or machine to do something well: *Our team's performance needs to improve if we're going to win.* | *a high performance car*

per·form·er /pəˈfɔːməʳ ‖ pərˈfɔːr-/ n a person who performs, for example an actor or musician

per·fume /ˈpɜːfjuːm ‖ pərˈfjuːm/ (also **scent**) n [C;U] **1** a sweet or pleasant smell –see SMELL (USAGE) **2** sweet-smelling liquid, often made from flowers, which women put on their skin – compare AFTER-SHAVE

per·fumed /ˈpɜːfjuːmd ‖ pərˈfjuːmd/ adj **1** fml filled with a sweet or pleasant smell: *a garden perfumed with flowers* **2** having perfume on it: *a perfumed handkerchief*

per·func·to·ry /pəˈfʌŋktəri ‖ pər-/ adj fml done in a hurry and without thinking or caring –**perfunctorily** adv

per·haps /pəˈhæps ‖ pər-/ adv **1** possibly: *Perhaps their train has been delayed.* | *This is perhaps her best novel.* **2** used when you are asking for something politely: *Perhaps you could phone me later to let me know what has been decided?*

per·il /ˈperəl/ n fml **1** [U] danger of being harmed or killed **2** [C] something that causes danger **3 at your peril** a phrase used to warn someone that they are very unwise to do something because they are taking a serious risk

per·il·ous /ˈperələs/ adj fml very dangerous or risky –**perilously** adv

pe·rim·e·ter /pəˈrɪmɪtəʳ/ n the edge all round a closed flat area: *The perimeter of the airfield is protected by guard-dogs.* | *a perimeter fence* | *the perimeter of a circle*

pe·ri·od /ˈpɪəriəd/ n **1** a length of time: *There were long periods when we had no news of him.* | *Tomorrow's weather will be dry with sunny periods.* **2** a particular length of time in history, or in a person's life: *the Victorian period* | *She went through a difficult period after her divorce.* **3** a lesson at school: *a history period* **4** (also **menstrual period** fml) a monthly flow of blood from the body of a woman

period² adj belonging to an earlier period in history: *period costumes*

pe·ri·od·ic /ˌpɪəriˈɒdɪk◄ ‖ -ˈɑː-/ (also **periodical**) adj happening occasionally, usually at regular times: *He suffered from periodic attacks of depression.* –**periodically** /-kli/ adv

pe·ri·od·i·cal /ˌpɪəriˈɒdɪkəl ‖ -ˈɑː-/ n a magazine which appears at regular times, for example every month

pe·riph·e·ral /pəˈrɪfərəl/ adj **1** of relatively little importance: *This is a subject of only peripheral interest to many men.* **2** on the edge of an area –**peripherally** adv

pe·riph·e·ry /pəˈrɪfəri/ n **peripheries** fml the **periphery** the outside area or edge: *the periphery of the town*

per·i·scope /ˈperɪskəʊp/ n a long tube with mirrors fitted in it so that people in a SUBMARINE can see what is above them

per·ish /ˈperɪʃ/ v fml **1** [I] to die, because of something terrible that happens: *Almost a hundred people perished in the hotel fire last night.* **2** [I;T] to decay or cause to decay: *The rubber in this tyre has perished.*

per·ish·a·ble /ˈperɪʃəbəl/ adj that goes bad quickly (used of food) –opposite **nonperishable**

per·ish·ing /ˈperɪʃɪŋ/ adj very cold (used of weather): *the perishing winter*

per·jure /ˈpɜːdʒəʳ ‖ ˈpɜːr-/ v **perjured**, **perjuring perjure yourself** to tell lies in court even though you have promised solemnly to tell the truth

per·jur·er /ˈpɜːdʒərəʳ ‖ ˈpɜːr-/ n a person who tells lies in court, even though they have promised solemnly to tell the truth

per·ju·ry /ˈpɜːdʒəri ‖ ˈpɜːr-/ n [U] the act of telling lies in court, even though you have promised solemnly to tell the truth

perk¹ /pɜːk ‖ pɜːrk/ n (also **perquisite** /ˈpɜːkwɪzɪt ‖ ˈpɜːr-/ fml) infml money, goods, or other advantages that you get regularly from your work in addition to your pay: *The perks include a company car.* | *One of the perks of this job is free meals.*

perk² v

perk up phr v [I;T **perk** sbdy/sthg ↔ **up**] infml to become more cheerful and begin to show interest, or make someone become more cheerful and begin to show interest: *I had a cup of coffee to perk me up.* | *He perked up when the party started.*

perk·y /ˈpɜːki ‖ ˈpɜːrki/ adj cheerful and full of life and interest –**perkily** adv –**perkiness** n [U]

perm¹ /pɜːm ‖ pɜːrm/ n infml waves or curls put into someone's hair by chemical treatment so that they will last for several months

perm² v [T] infml to put waves or curls into someone's hair by chemical treatment so that they will last for several months: *I'm going to have my hair permed tomorrow.*

per·ma·nence /ˈpɜːmənəns ‖ ˈpɜːr-/ n [U] the state of being permanent

per·ma·nent /ˈpɜːmənənt ‖ ˈpɜːr-/ adj lasting for a very long time or for ever: *a permanent job* | *Pollution is causing permanent damage to the environment.* –**permanently** adv

per·me·ate /ˈpɜːmieɪt ‖ ˈpɜːr-/ v **permeated**, **permeating** [I;T] to pass through or into every part of something: *Water permeated* **through** *the cracks in the wall.* | *A strong desire for political change permeated the country.*

per·mis·si·ble /pəˈmɪsɪbəl ‖ pər-/ adj fml allowed by the rules: *What is the maximum permissible level of nitrates in water?*

per·mis·sion /pəˈmɪʃən ‖ pər-/ n [U] the right to do something which somebody else allows you: *We asked his permission to use the computer.* | *Did she give you permission to take that?* | *He took the car without permission.*

per·mis·sive /pəˈmɪsɪv ‖ pər-/ adj allowing people a great deal of or too much freedom, especially in sexual matters (a word often used to express disapproval): *The permissive society developed during the 1960s.* –**permissively** adv –**permissiveness** n [U]

per·mit¹ /pə'mɪt ‖ pər-/ v -tt- **1** [T] to allow someone to do or have something: *I cannot permit this to
happen.* | *The rules of the club do not permit alcohol.*|
She wasn't permitted to drive. | *permitted food colour-
ing* | *the maximum permitted dose*
☐ USEFUL PATTERNS to permit something; to
permit someone to do something; to permit someone something
2 [I;T] to make it possible to happen: *I will come i*
June if my health permits. | *weather permitting* | *The
facts permit no other explanation.*

per·mit² /'pɜːmɪt ‖ 'pɜːr-/ n an official written statement giving you the right to do something: *You are
not allowed to enter the building without a permit.*

per·mu·ta·tion /ˌpɜːmjʊ'teɪʃən ‖ ˌpɜːr-/ n **1** any
of the ways in which a group of things can be
arranged in order **2** [U] the act of changing the
order of a group of things in MATHEMATICS

per·ni·cious /pə'nɪʃəs ‖ pər-/ adj fml very harmful
–**perniciously** adv –**perniciousness** n [U]

per·nick·e·ty /pə'nɪkɪti ‖ pər-/ adj infml too concerned that every small detail should be exactly
right

per·ox·ide /pə'rɒksaɪd ‖ -'rɑːk-/ n [U] (also **hydrogen peroxide** fml) infml a chemical liquid used to
take the colour out of dark hair and to kill bacteria

per·pen·dic·u·lar /ˌpɜːpən'dɪkjʊlər ‖ ˌpɜːr-/ adj **1**
exactly upright and not leaning to one side or the
other **2** at an angle of 90 degrees to a line or surface
–**perpendicularly** adv

per·pe·trate /'pɜːpɪtreɪt ‖ 'pɜːr-/ v perpetrated,
perpetrating [T] fml to do something wrong or
criminal –**perpetrator** n –**perpetration** /ˌpɜːpɪ
'treɪʃən ‖ ˌpɜːr-/ n [U]

per·pet·u·al /pə'petʃuəl ‖ pər-/ adj **1** lasting for
ever or for a long time: *the perpetual snow on the
mountains* **2** happening often or all the time (a
word used to express disapproval): *I'm tired of your
perpetual complaints.* –**perpetually** adv: *He's perpetually losing things.*

per·pet·u·ate /pə'petʃueɪt ‖ pər-/ v perpetuated,
perpetuating [T] to cause something to continue:
*The tax laws perpetuate inequality between men and
women.* –**perpetuation** /pəˌpetʃu'eɪʃən ‖ pər-/ n
[U]

per·pe·tu·i·ty /ˌpɜːpɪ'tjuːɪti ‖ ˌpɜːrpɪ'tuː-/ n [U]
fml in perpetuity for ever

per·plexed /pə'plekst ‖ pər-/ adj confused by something difficult to understand: *She looked perplexed
and asked me to repeat what I had said.*

per·plex·i·ty /pə'pleksɪti ‖ pər-/ n [U] the feeling of
being confused and worried because you do not
understand something

per se /ˌpɜː 'seɪ ‖ ˌpɜːr 'siː, ˌpɜːr 'seɪ, ˌpeər 'seɪ/
adv fml considered alone and not in connection
with other things

per·se·cute /'pɜːsɪkjuːt ‖ 'pɜːr-/ v persecuted,
persecuting [T] to treat someone cruelly and make
them suffer, especially because of their religious or
political beliefs –**persecutor** n –**persecution**
/ˌpɜːsɪ'kjuːʃən ‖ ˌpɜːr-/ n [C;U]: *the persecution of
the Jewish people*

per·se·ver·ance /ˌpɜːsɪ'vɪərəns ‖ ˌpɜːr-/ n [U]
steady and continued effort

per·se·vere /ˌpɜːsɪ'vɪər ‖ ˌpɜːr-/ v persevered,
persevering [I] to keep trying to do something
although it is difficult: *Learning to drive was
difficult but I persevered with it.* –**persevering** adj

per·sist /pə'sɪst ‖ pər-/ v [I] **1** to continue doing
something with determination in spite of opposition: *If you persist in breaking the law you will go*

to prison. | *Why must the government persist with
this unpopular plan?* **2** to continue to exist: *The cold
weather will persist for the rest of the week.*

per·sis·tent /pə'sɪstənt ‖ pər-/ adj **1** continuing to
do something with determination in spite of oppo-
sition: *a persistent thief* | *His persistent questions
really started to annoy me.* **2** continuing to exist for
a long time and not going away: *a persistent cough*
–**persistence** n [U]: *He showed such persistence that
they finally had to give him a job.* –**persistently** adv

per·son /'pɜːsən ‖ 'pɜːr-/ n **1** [C] [plural is **people**]
a man or woman: *You're just the person I wanted to
see.* **2** [C;U] in grammar, any of the three special
forms of verbs that show who is speaking (the first
person), who is spoken to (the second person) or the
human being or thing being spoken about (the third
person) **3 in person** being physically present in a
place: *The minister could not come in person so she
sent her secretary instead.* | *After speaking so often
on the telephone, I finally met her in person.*

■ USAGE 1 The usual plural of **person** is **people**.
The doctor sees one **person** *at a time.* | *Five* **people**
sat in the waiting room. (**Persons** is very formal and
is used in official writing or notices: *He was murdered by a* **person** *or* **persons** *unknown.*) 2 Many
people do not like the use of words such as **chairman** or **spokesman** to refer to women or to both
sexes. If you want to avoid this use, you can often
use words formed with **person**: *She/he is our new*
chairperson. | *She/he agreed to act as*
spokesperson.

-person n a man or woman who does a particular
job: *She's an excellent chairperson.* | *a spokesperson
for the organization.*

per·so·na /pə'səʊnə ‖ pər-/ n personas or perso-
nae /-niː, -naɪ-/ the sides of your character you show
to other people

per·son·a·ble /'pɜːsənəbəl ‖ 'pɜːr-/ adj attractive
in appearance or character

per·son·age /'pɜːsənɪdʒ ‖ 'pɜːr-/ n fml a famous
or important person

per·son·al /'pɜːsənəl ‖ 'pɜːr-/ adj **1** relating to the
feelings of a particular person rather than a group:
My personal opinion was that she should not go. | *a
question of personal choice* **2** concerning, or belonging to a particular person: *The letter was marked
"Personal".* | *his personal possessions* **3** concerning
your body: *personal cleanliness* **4** directed against
a person's character or appearance in an unpleasant way: *I was upset by his personal remarks
about my family.* **5** done by a particular person, not
a representative: *The minister made a personal appearance on television.* **6** concerning private feelings or actions: *The problem is too personal to be dis-
cussed.* | *I try and keep my personal life separate from
my professional life.* **7** in grammar, showing the
person concerned: *a personal pronoun*

personal as·sis·tant /ˌ··· ·'··/ n see PA

personal col·umn /'··· ˌ··/ n a part of a newspaper
that provides information or private messages for
particular people

personal com·put·er /ˌ··· ·'··/ n a small computer
for business or personal use

personal or·gan·iz·er /ˌ··· '···/ n a book with loose
pages you can add to in which to keep a record of
things you plan to do in the current year, appointments, names and addresses, notes, and other information you need to carry with you

per·son·al·i·ty /ˌpɜːsə'nælɪti ‖ ˌpɜːr-/ n personalities **1** [C;U] the whole nature and character of a

particular person: *She has a lovely personality.* | *They don't get on well because of differences of personality.* **2** [U] interesting or exciting qualities of character: *He has no personality.* **3** [C] a person who is well known to the public: *a television personality*

per·son·al·ize /ˈpɜːsənəlaɪz ‖ ˈpɜːr-/ v [T] **personalized, personalizing** (also **personalise** *BrE*) **1** to consider something not from the facts but from the characters or relationships of the people concerned: *Let's not personalize this argument.* **2** to make or do something so that it is for a particular person, often by adding their name or address: *personalized handkerchiefs*

per·son·al·ly /ˈpɜːsənəli ‖ ˈpɜːr-/ adv **1** directly and not through a representative: *He is personally in charge of all the arrangements.* **2** a word you use when you are giving your own opinion about something: *Personally, I thought the film was very good.* **3** as a person: *Personally she may be very charming, but is she a good doctor?* **4** directed against a particular person's character or appearance: *You must not take my remarks about your work personally.*

personal pro·noun /ˌ··· ˈ··/ n a word standing for a noun and used for showing the speaker, the person spoken to, or the person spoken about; "I", "you", and "they" are personal pronouns

per·son·i·fy /pəˈsɒnɪfaɪ ‖ pərˈsɑː-/ v personified, personifying [T] to be a perfect example of something –**personification** /pəˌsɒnɪfɪˈkeɪʃən ‖ pərˌsɑː-/ n [C;U]

per·son·nel /ˌpɜːsəˈnel ‖ ˌpɜːr-/ n [pl] all the people employed by an organization: *army personnel* | *New personnel are needed for our operations in the Middle East.*

per·spec·tive /pəˈspektɪv ‖ pər-/ n **1** [C] a way of thinking about something, related to your background, experience, or beliefs: *He views everything from a political perspective.* | *an historical perspective* **2** [U] the ability to think clearly, considering all the facts: *She was under such stress that she lost all sense of perspective.* **3 keep things in perspective** to keep a sense of what is really important and what is not important. [RELATED PHRASE: **get things into perspective**] **4** [U] the rules of drawing used by artists to give a feeling of distance and solidity to objects painted on a flat surface: *The streets in the background are out of perspective.*

per·spex /ˈpɜːspeks ‖ ˈpɜːr-/ n (also **Perspex**) [U] *tdmk* a strong plastic material that can be used instead of glass

per·spi·ca·cious /ˌpɜːspɪˈkeɪʃəs ‖ ˌpɜːr-/ adj *fml* having or showing good judgment and understanding –**perspicacity** /-ˈkæsɪti/ n [U]

per·spi·ra·tion /ˌpɜːspəˈreɪʃən ‖ ˌpɜːr-/ n [U] *fml* liquid that comes out through your skin when you are very hot

per·spire /pəˈspaɪər ‖ pər-/ v **perspired, perspiring** [I] *fml* to lose liquid through your skin when you are very hot

per·suade /pəˈsweɪd ‖ pər-/ v **persuaded, persuading** [T] **1** to cause someone to do something they had been unwilling to do by giving good reasons: *She didn't want to come, but I persuaded her.* | *My mother persuaded me to buy this dress.*
□ USEFUL PATTERN to persuade someone to do something
2 to make someone feel certain that something is true: *He persuaded himself that things were best left as they were.* –see CONVINCE (USAGE)

per·sua·sion /pəˈsweɪʒən ‖ pər-/ n **1** [U] the act of persuading someone: *I'm sure she'll agree – it just needs a little persuasion.* **2** [U] the ability to influence others: *He has great powers of persuasion.* **3** [C] a person or group holding a particular belief: *People of many different political persuasions attended the meeting.*

per·sua·sive /pəˈsweɪsɪv ‖ pər-/ adj having the power to influence other people into believing or doing something: *He can be very persuasive when he wants something.* –**persuasively** adv

pert /pɜːt ‖ pɜːrt/ adj slightly disrespectful in an amusing way

per·tain /pəˈteɪn ‖ pər-/ v *fml* **pertain to** to belong to something or have a connection with it

per·ti·na·cious /ˌpɜːtɪˈneɪʃəs ‖ ˌpɜːr-/ adj *fml* determined –**pertinacity** /-ˈnæsɪti/ n [U]

per·ti·nent /ˈpɜːtɪnənt ‖ ˈpɜːr-/ adj *fml* directly connected with something being considered: *She asked several pertinent questions.*

per·turbed /pəˈtɜːbd ‖ pərˈtɜːrbd/ adj [T] *fml* worried

pe·ruse /pəˈruːz/ v **perused, perusing** [T] *fml* to read through something carefully –**perusal** n [C;U]

per·vade /pəˈveɪd ‖ pər-/ v **pervaded, pervading** [T] *fml* to be present strongly in a place: *The smell of cooking pervaded the whole house.*

per·va·sive /pəˈveɪsɪv ‖ pər-/ adj present strongly in a place (a word often used to express disapproval): *the pervasive influence of television* –**pervasively** adv

per·verse /pəˈvɜːs ‖ pərˈvɜːrs/ adj continuing to do something you know is wrong or unreasonable and that other people do not want you to do: *He gets a perverse pleasure from arguing with people.* –**perversely** adv –**perversity** n [C;U]

per·ver·sion /pəˈvɜːʃən, -ʒən ‖ pərˈvɜːrʒən/ n **1** [C;U] something that has been changed or the action of changing something so that it is no longer reasonable, right or true: *perversion of the truth* **2** [C] an unnatural form of sexual behaviour

per·vert¹ /pəˈvɜːt ‖ pərˈvɜːrt/ v [T] **1** to cause someone to behave in ways that are considered wrong or unnatural **2** to change something and use it for a bad purpose: *Scientific knowledge has been perverted to help cause destruction and war.* **3 pervert the course of justice** to prevent justice being done

per·vert² /ˈpɜːvɜːt ‖ ˈpɜːrvɜːrt/ n a person whose sexual behaviour is not considered natural

pe·se·ta /pəˈseɪtə/ n a Spanish coin, on which the Spanish money system is based

pes·si·mis·m /ˈpesɪmɪzəm/ n [U] the habit of thinking that whatever happens will be bad –**pessimist** n : *Don't be such a pessimist!* –**pessimistic** /ˌpesɪˈmɪstɪk◂/ adj –**pessimistically** /-kli/ adv

pest /pest/ n **1** a small animal or insect that harms or destroys food supplies **2** *infml* an annoying person or thing

pes·ter /ˈpestər/ v [T] to annoy somebody by continually asking for something: *He keeps pestering me for money.*

pes·ti·cide /ˈpestɪsaɪd/ n [C;U] a chemical substance used to kill harmful animals and insects –see picture on page 246

pes·ti·lence /ˈpestɪləns/ n [C;U] *old fash* a disease that kills large numbers of people

pes·tle /ˈpesəl, ˈpestl/ n an instrument with a heavy rounded end, used for crushing things in a special bowl called a MORTAR

pet[1] /pet/ n 1 an animal you keep in your home as a companion: *a pet dog* | *She keeps a monkey as a pet.* 2 a person who is specially liked by someone in power: *She is the teacher's pet.* 3 [only before another noun] something that you feel very strongly about or that you like very much: *He's talking about his pet theories again.* 4 pet hate the thing you hate most: *Teabags are my pet hate.*

pet[2] v -tt- 1 [T] to touch gently and treat lovingly 2 [I;T] *infml* to kiss and touch someone in sexual play

pet·al /'petl/ n one of the coloured parts of a flower

pe·ter /'piːtəʳ/ v
peter out *phr* v [I] to gradually come to an end

pe·tite /pə'tiːt/ *adj* small in an attractive way (used of women) –see picture on page 245

pe·ti·tion[1] /pɪ'tɪʃən/ n a request signed by a lot of people made to a government or other official group: *Will you sign a petition against the closure of the local railway line?*

petition[2] v [I;T] to make a request in the form of a petition: *They have petitioned the government to improve bus services.*

pet·ri·fy /'petrɪfaɪ/ v petrified, petrifying 1 [T] *infml* to make someone feel very afraid: *I was so petrified by the face at the window that I couldn't move.* 2 [I;T] to turn into stone: *the Petrified Forest in Arizona*

pet·ro·chem·i·cal /ˌpetrə'kemɪkəl/ n a chemical substance obtained from petroleum or natural gas: *the petrochemical industry*

pet·rol /'petrəl/ n *BrE* [U] a liquid obtained from petroleum, used especially for producing power in engines: *I need to fill the car up with petrol.* | *a petrol station*

pe·tro·le·um /pə'trəʊliəm/ n [U] a mineral oil obtained from below the surface of the Earth, and used to produce petrol and various other chemical substances

petrol sta·tion /'·· ˌ··/ n *BrE* a place where you can buy petrol for vehicles

pet·ti·coat /'petikəʊt/ n a thin skirt worn by women under a dress or skirt

pet·ty /'peti/ *adj* pettier, pettiest 1 small and not important: *our petty problems* 2 unkind, and too concerned with small, unimportant things (a word used to express disapproval): *John can be very petty about money.*

petty cash /ˌ·· '·/ n [U] an amount of money kept in an office ready for making small payments

petty of·fi·cer /ˌ·· '····◂/ n an officer in the navy

pet·u·lant /'petʃʊlənt/ *adj* showing childish anger over unimportant things –petulantly *adv* –petulance n [U]

pew /pjuː/ n 1 a long seat for people to sit on in church 2 take a pew to sit down (a phrase which is often used in a humorous way)

pew·ter /'pjuːtəʳ/ n [U] a grey metal made by mixing lead and tin

pha·lanx /'fælæŋks ‖ 'feɪ-/ n phalanxes *or* phalanges /fə'lændʒiːz/ any group of people or soldiers who are packed closely together for attack or defence

phal·lus /'fæləs/ n an image of the male sex organ –phallic *adj*

phan·tom /'fæntəm/ n 1 an image of a dead person that appears like a shadow 2 something which exists only in someone's imagination

pha·raoh /'feərəʊ/ n (also **Pharaoh**) the title of the ruler of ancient Egypt

phar·ma·ceu·ti·cal /ˌfɑːmə'sjuːtɪkəl ‖ ˌfɑːrmə'suː-/ *adj* [only before a noun] connected with the production of medicines: *a pharmaceutical company*

phar·ma·cist /'fɑːməsˌɪst ‖ 'fɑːr-/ n *fml* a person who prepares and sells medicines

phar·ma·col·o·gy /ˌfɑːmə'kɒlədʒi ‖ ˌfɑːrmə'kɑː-/ n [U] the scientific study of medicines and drugs –pharmacologist n

phar·ma·cy /'fɑːməsi ‖ 'fɑːr-/ n pharmacies 1 [U] the making or giving out of medicines 2 [C] a shop where medicines are given out or sold

phase[1] /feɪz/ n 1 a stage of change or development: *East-West relations are entering a new phase.* | *the most dangerous phase of the illness* 2 go through a phase to experience a particular period of change or development: *The band's music is going through a boring phase at the moment.* 3 one of the changes in the appearance of the moon as seen from the Earth at different times

phase[2] v phased, phasing [T] to do something gradually, in stages: *a phased withdrawal of nuclear weapons*
phase sth ↔ in *phr* v [T] to introduce something gradually: *The new exam system is being phased in over two years.*
phase sth ↔ out *phr* v [T] to remove something gradually: *They are phasing out the old coins.*

PhD /ˌpiː eɪtʃ 'diː/ n 1 an advanced university degree; an abbreviation for Doctor of Philosophy 2 a person who has gained a PhD

pheas·ant /'fezənt/ n [C;U] a large long-tailed bird hunted for food

phe·nom·e·nal /fɪ'nɒmˌnəl ‖ -'nɑː-/ *adj* very unusual and great: *She has a phenomenal memory.* –phenomenally *adv*

phe·nom·e·non /fɪ'nɒmˌnən ‖ fɪ'nɑːmˌnɑːn, -nən/ n phenomena /-nə/ 1 something that happens in nature, science, or society, and can be seen: *natural phenomena* | *Unemployment is not a new phenomenon.* 2 a very unusual person, thing, or event

phew /fjuː/ *interj* (also **whew**) a word used to represent a whistling sound that you make when you are tired, shocked, or pleased

phi·al /'faɪəl/ n a small bottle for medicine

phi·lan·thro·pist /fɪ'lænθrəpˌɪst/ n a person who makes generous gifts of money to people who need it

phi·lan·thro·py /fɪ'lænθrəpi/ n [U] giving money and help to those who need it –philanthropic /ˌfɪlən'θrɒpɪk◂ ‖ -'θrɑː-/ *adj*

phi·lat·e·ly /fɪ'lætəli/ n [U] *tech* stamp collecting –philatelist n

phil·is·tine /'fɪlˌstaɪn ‖ -stiːn/ n a person who has no understanding of, or interest in, art, music, or beautiful things (a word used to express disapproval)

phi·lol·o·gy /fɪ'lɒlədʒi ‖ -'lɑː-/ n [U] *tech* the study of the nature and development of words and language –philologist n

phi·los·o·pher /fɪ'lɒsəfəʳ ‖ -'lɑː-/ n 1 a person who studies or develops systems of thought about reality and the meaning of life: *the Greek philosophers* 2 someone who thinks deeply about life

phil·o·soph·i·cal /ˌfɪlə'sɒfɪkəl ‖ -'sɑː-/ *adj* 1 accepting difficulty or unhappiness calmly 2 of or concerning systems of thought: *the philosophical writings of Sartre* –philosophically /-kli/ *adv*

phi·los·o·phize /fɪˈlɒsəfaɪz ‖ -ˈlɑː-/ v **philosophized, philosophizing** (also **philosophise**) [I] to think, talk, or write about important subjects and ideas in a very serious way

phi·los·o·phy /fɪˈlɒsəfi ‖ -ˈlɑː-/ n **philosophies 1** [U] the study of the meaning of existence, reality, and knowledge **2** [C] a set of ideas about the meaning of existence, reality, and knowledge: *the philosophy of Aristotle* **3** a set of personal beliefs about how life should be lived

phlegm /flem/ n [U] **1** the thick yellow substance produced in your nose and throat when you have a cold **2** calmness

phleg·mat·ic /fleg'mætɪk/ adj fml calm and not easily upset or worried –**phlegmatically** /-kli/ adv

pho·bi·a /ˈfəʊbiə/ n a strong and unreasonable fear: *I've got a phobia about insects.*

phoe·nix /ˈfiːnɪks/ n an imaginary bird believed to burn itself and be born again from the ashes

phone¹ /fəʊn/ n **1** a telephone: *What's your phone number? | Could I make a phone call please? | a car phone* **2** **be on the phone: a** to be talking on the telephone: *We were on the phone for an hour.* **b** to have a telephone in your house: *I'm afraid we're not on the phone.*

phone² v **phoned, phoning** [I;T] (also **phone up**; **phone** sbdy ↔ **up**) to telephone someone: *Phone me when you arrive at the station. | He phoned to say he couldn't come.* –see TELEPHONE 1 (USAGE)

phone book /ˈ··/ n a book containing an alphabetical list of the names, addresses and telephone numbers of all the people who own a telephone in a certain area

phone box /ˈ··/ n (also **phone booth** AmE) a small enclosure containing a public telephone –see picture on page 441

phone-in /ˈ··/ n a radio or television broadcast during which telephoned questions or opinions from the public are heard

pho·net·ic /fəˈnetɪk/ adj **1** of or concerning the sounds of human speech **2** using special letters and signs to represent the actual sounds of speech: *This dictionary uses a phonetic alphabet as a guide to pronunciation.* –**phonetically** /-kli/ adv

pho·net·ics /fəˈnetɪks/ n [U] tech the study and science of speech sounds

pho·ney /ˈfəʊni/ adj (also **phony**) infml false

phos·pho·res·cence /ˌfɒsfəˈresəns ‖ ˌfɑːs-/ n [U] the giving out of light with little or no heat –**phosphorescent** adj

phos·pho·rus /ˈfɒsfərəs ‖ ˈfɑːs-/ n [U] a poisonous yellowish substance that shines in the dark and starts to burn when brought into the air

pho·to /ˈfəʊtəʊ/ n **photos** infml a photograph: *holiday photos | I took a photo of the baby.*

pho·to·cop·i·er /ˈfəʊtəʊˌkɒpiəʳ ‖ -təˌkɑː-/ n a machine that makes photocopies –see picture on page 539

pho·to·cop·y /ˈfəʊtəʊˌkɒpi ‖ -təˌkɑːpi/ v **photocopied, photocopying, photocopies** [C;T] to make a photographic copy of a letter or piece of writing –**photocopy** n : *I'll send you a photocopy of the letter.*

photo fin·ish /ˌ·· ˈ··/ n the end of a race in which the leaders finish so close together that a photograph has to be taken to show which is the winner

pho·to·gen·ic /ˌfəʊtəʊˈdʒenɪk◂, ˌfəʊtə-/ adj having an appearance that looks attractive when photographed (used of people)

pho·to·graph¹ /ˈfəʊtəgrɑːf ‖ -græf/ n (also **photo** infml) a picture of someone or something obtained by using a camera and film sensitive to light: *Visitors to the castle are not allowed to take photographs. | a black and white photograph | I saw your photograph in the newspaper.*

photograph² v [T] to take a photograph of someone or something: *She has photographed hundreds of famous people.*

pho·tog·ra·pher /fəˈtɒgrəfəʳ ‖ -ˈtɑː-/ n a person who takes photographs as their job or for pleasure

pho·to·graph·ic /ˌfəʊtəˈgræfɪk◂/ adj [only before a noun] **1** used in producing photographs: *photographic equipment* **2** **photographic memory** an ability to remember exactly things that you have seen –**photographically** /-kli/ adv

pho·tog·ra·phy /fəˈtɒgrəfi ‖ -ˈtɑː-/ n [U] the art or process of producing photographs

pho·to·stat /ˈfəʊtəstæt/ v -tt- [T] tdmk to make a photographic copy of a letter or piece of writing –**photostat** n

phras·al verb /ˌfreɪzəl ˈvɜːb ‖ -ˈvɜːrb/ n a small group of words that act like a verb and consist of a verb with an adverb or a PREPOSITION; "run out" and "use up" are phrasal verbs –see Study Note on page 475

phrase¹ /freɪz/ n **1** a small group of words that form part of a sentence or which have particular meaning: *I learned a few Greek phrases on holiday.* **2** a short expression, especially one that is clever

phrase² v **phrased, phrasing** [T] to express something in a particular way or using a particular kind of word: *Her letter was phrased very carefully.*

phrase·book /ˈfreɪzbʊk/ n a book giving and explaining phrases of a foreign language, for people to use when they go abroad

phra·se·ol·o·gy /ˌfreɪziˈɒlədʒi ‖ -ˈɑː-/ n [U] fml the way in which words are chosen, arranged, or used

phys·i·cal /ˈfɪzɪkəl/ adj **1** concerning the body rather than the mind: *physical exercise | The doctor will give you a complete physical examination.* **2** concerning material things that you can see and touch: *Babies need to explore physical objects with their mouths as well as their hands.* **3** according to the laws of nature: *the physical world* **4** [always before a noun] concerning the natural formation of the Earth's surface: *physical geography*

phys·i·cally /ˈfɪzɪkli/ adv **1** concerning the body: *My elderly uncle is still physically fit, but mentally rather confused.* **2** according to the laws of nature: *It's physically impossible to travel faster than the speed of light.*

physical train·ing /ˌ··· ˈ··/ n (also **physical education** /ˌ··· ···/, **PT, PE**) [U] development of your body by games or exercises

phy·si·cian /fɪˈzɪʃən/ n a doctor, especially one who treats diseases with medicines

phys·i·cist /ˈfɪzɪsɪst/ n a person who studies physics

phys·ics /ˈfɪzɪks/ n [U] the science concerned with the study of matter and natural forces such as light, heat, and movement

phys·i·ol·o·gy /ˌfɪziˈɒlədʒi ‖ -ˈɑː-/ n [U] the science concerned with the study of the bodies of living things, and how they work –**physiologist** n –**physiological** /ˌfɪziəˈlɒdʒɪkəl ‖ -ˈlɑː-/ adj

phys·i·o·ther·a·py /ˌfɪziəʊˈθerəpi/ n [U] the use of exercises, rubbing, or heat in the treatment of illness –**physiotherapist** n

phy·sique /fɪ'ziːk/ n the shape and size of someone's body

pi /paɪ/ n a Greek letter (Π, π) used for representing the fixed relationship between the distance round the edge of a circle and the distance across its middle; pi is almost equal to ²¹⁄₇ or 3·142

pi·a·nist /'piːənɪst, 'pjɑː- ‖ pi'ænɪst, 'piːə-/ n a person who plays the piano

pi·an·o /pi'ænəʊ/ n (also **pianoforte** /piˌænəʊ'fɔːti ‖ -'fɔːrteɪ/ fml) a large musical instrument, played by pressing narrow black or white bars which make small hammers hit wire strings

pic·co·lo /'pɪkələʊ/ n a small musical instrument that looks like a FLUTE but plays higher notes

pick¹ /pɪk/ v [T] **1** to choose someone or something: He looked at all the cakes, then picked the biggest one. | She has been picked to play a leading role in a new film. **2** to pull a flower or fruit from a plant: She was picking flowers in the garden. | They've gone strawberry-picking. **3** to remove something from a place using your hands or fingers: He was picking crumbs off the floor. | Pick all the meat off the bone. **4 pick your nose** to remove unwanted bits of MUCUS from your nose using your finger **5 pick your teeth** to remove small bits of food from your teeth **6 pick a fight/quarrel** to be unpleasant to someone so that you cause a fight or quarrel **7 pick a lock** to unlock a lock with an instrument that is not the proper key, especially so that you can steal something **8 pick someone's brains** to try to find out information from someone in order to help you with a problem **9 pick someone's pocket** to steal things from someone's pocket **10 pick your way** to walk carefully so that you do not fall or stand on things: Firemen were picking their way over the rubble. **11 pick a hole in something** to make a hole in something with a pointed instrument **12 pick holes in something** to find lots of faults in something **13 pick and choose** to choose very carefully, considering each choice for a long time

pick at sthg phr v [T] to eat only small amounts of something, as if you are not really hungry

pick sbdy ↔ **off** phr v [T] to shoot people or animals by aiming at them carefully and shooting them one by one

pick on sbdy phr v [T] to punish or blame someone unfairly because you do not like them: He's always picking on me!

pick sbdy/sthg ↔ **out** phr v [T] **1** to choose someone or something: She picked out a red scarf to go with her dress. **2** to see someone or something clearly: She managed to pick out her sister in the crowd.

pick up phr v **1** [T **pick** sbdy/sthg ↔ **up**] to take hold of something and lift it up: He picked up his suitcase and walked out. | Come and pick all your toys up. -see picture on page 736 **2** [T **pick** sthg ↔ **up**] to gain or obtain something: I picked up quite a lot of French when I lived in France. | I picked up quite a few tips about painting and decorating. **3** [T **pick** sbdy/sthg ↔ **up**] to collect someone or something from a place: I'll pick you up at your hotel. | I've got to go and pick up my coat from the cleaner's. **4** [T **pick** sbdy ↔ **up**] to catch a criminal: The thieves were picked up by the police later that day. **5** [T **pick** sbdy ↔ **up**] to become friendly with someone because you want to have a sexual relationship with them: I could see that he was trying to pick me up. **6** [T **pick** sbdy **up**] to make someone feel better and stronger: You need a tonic to pick you up. **7** [T **pick** sthg ↔ **up**] to be able to hear or receive something on a radio: We picked up distress signals from another ship. **8**

pick up speed to start to travel more quickly: We picked up speed when we got onto the motorway. **9** [I] to improve: Trade is picking up again. | The economy is starting to pick up now.

pick² n **1 take your pick** to choose something: I've been offered three jobs so I can take my pick. | Here are the prints that we've got – take your pick. **2 the pick of the bunch** the best one in a group **3** a pickaxe

pick·axe /'pɪk-æks/ n (**pickax** AmE) a large tool which has a curved iron bar with two sharp points, used for breaking up rock

pick·er /'pɪkəʳ/ n a person or machine that gathers crops: potato pickers

pick·et¹ /'pɪkɪt/ n someone placed outside a factory or shop during an argument with employers to prevent anyone going to work

picket² v [I;T] to stand outside a factory or shop during an argument with employers to prevent anyone going to work: No coal could be delivered to the factory, because the workers were picketing the gates. –**picketing** n [U]

pick·le¹ /'pɪkəl/ n **1** [U] a liquid, for example salt water, used to preserve meat or vegetables **2 pickles** vegetables preserved in liquid such as salt water **3 in a pickle** infml in a difficult situation

pickle² v **pickled, pickling** [T] to preserve food in liquid such as salt water –**pickled** adj : pickled cucumbers

pick-me-up /'·· ˌ·/ n infml a drink or a medicine that makes you feel stronger and more cheerful

pick·pock·et /'pɪkˌpɒkɪt ‖ -ˌpɑːk-/ n a person who steals things from people's pockets, especially in a crowd –see THIEF (USAGE)

pick-up /'·· /n **1** the part of a record-player which receives and plays the sound from a record **2** a vehicle with an open body with low sides

pic·nic¹ /'pɪknɪk/ n **1** an occasion when you take food somewhere outdoors and eat it there: We went for a picnic in the country. **2** food taken to eat outdoors: Let's take a picnic. | a picnic lunch

picnic² v **picnicked, picnicking** [I] to have a picnic

pic·to·ri·al /pɪk'tɔːriəl/ adj connected with or using pictures

pic·ture¹ /'pɪktʃəʳ/ n **1** [C] a painting or drawing: Draw a picture of that tree. –see picture on page 442 **2** [C] a photograph: This is a lovely picture of the princess. **3** [sing] a person or thing that is beautiful to look at: This garden is a picture in the summer. **4 the picture of** the perfect example: That baby is the picture of health. **5** [sing] what is seen on a television set or at the cinema: You can't get a clear picture on this set. **6** [C] an image or idea in your mind: This book gives a good picture of life in England 200 years ago. **7** BrE **the pictures** the cinema: We went to the pictures last night. **8** [sing] a situation: The political picture seems to be changing. **9 get the picture** to understand something **10 put someone in the picture** to tell someone about something that has been happening

picture² v **pictured, picturing** [T] **1** to imagine: I can't quite picture myself as a mother. **2** to paint or draw someone or something to give a particular idea: The artist has pictured him as a clown.

pic·tur·esque /ˌpɪktʃəˈresk◄/ adj **1** charming or interesting enough to be made into a picture **2** very clear, strong, and descriptive (used to describe language)

pid·dling /'pɪdlɪŋ/ adj small and unimportant (a word used to express disapproval)

pid·gin /ˈpɪdʒɪn/ n [C;U] a language which is a mixture of two or more other languages

pie /paɪ/ n [C;U] **1** a pastry case filled with meat or fruit, often baked in a deep dish: *an apple pie | meat pies | Have some more pie.* **2 pie in the sky** *infml* a hopeful plan or suggestion that is unlikely to happen

piece¹ /piːs/ n **1** a part of something solid which is separated from the whole or larger thing: *a piece of meat | a piece of cake | pieces of wood* **2** part of something that has broken or come off: *The glass broke into pieces.* **3** a single object that is an example of a certain type: *Have you got a piece of paper? | a piece of furniture | a beautiful piece of music* **4** a single example of something that is part of a set: *a piece of cutlery | This tea set has a piece missing.* **5** the separate parts which make a whole object: *a 50 piece jigsaw puzzle | He cleaned all the pieces of the saxophone and put them back in the case.* **6** an example or amount of something someone has made, thought, or done: *She offered me a piece of advice.| a good piece of work* **7** a particular coin: *a 10p piece* **8 go to pieces** to be so nervous that you can't do what you want to: *He usually plays the piano beautifully but he went to pieces in the exam.* **9 in one piece** not hurt or damaged **10 a piece of cake** something that is very easy and takes no effort **11 take something to pieces** to take something apart: *Jo took her bike to pieces to try and fix it.*

piece² v **pieced, piecing piece something together** to make something complete by putting different parts together: *She tried to piece the information together so she could write about what had happened.*

pi·èce de ré·sis·tance /piːˌes də rezɪˈstɑːns/ n **pièces de résistance** *(same pronunciation)* the best or most important thing or event, among a number of things or events

piece·meal /ˈpiːsmiːl/ adj,adv bit by bit: *We used to do the work piecemeal, but now we do everything in one operation.*

piece·work /ˈpiːswɜːk ‖ -wɜːrk/ n [U] work paid for by the amount that you do rather than by the hours that you work

pied /paɪd/ adj [only before a noun] coloured with two or more colours (used of certain types of birds)

pier /pɪəʳ/ n **1** a structure built out into the sea at which boats can stop to take on or land passengers or goods –see picture on page 735 **2** a structure like this at places where people go for holidays, where people can walk and enjoy themselves

pierce /pɪəs ‖ pɪərs/ v **pierced, piercing** [T] **1** to make a hole in or through something with a point: *The needle pierced her skin.* **2** to be suddenly heard, seen, or felt through something else: *A loud scream pierced the silence.* **3 pierced ears** small holes in your ears for jewellery

pierc·ing /ˈpɪəsɪŋ ‖ ˈpɪər-/ adj **1** loud and unpleasant (used of sounds): *a piercing cry* **2** looking very hard, or going straight to the centre of something: *He gave me a piercing look.* **3** very strong and cold (used of wind) **–piercingly** adv

pi·e·ty /ˈpaɪəti/ n [U] deep respect for God and religion

pig /pɪg/ n **1** a fat, pink, short-legged animal kept on farms for food –see MEAT (USAGE) **2** an ill-mannered person who eats too much (a word used to express disapproval)

pi·geon /ˈpɪdʒɪn/ n a common, grey short-legged bird that can be eaten

pi·geon·hole /ˈpɪdʒɪnhəʊl/ n one of a set of small boxes in a frame on a wall in an office or on a desk for putting papers in

pigeon-toed /ˌ·· ˈ·◂/ adj having feet that point inwards

pig·gy·back /ˈpɪgibæk/ n a ride given to a child who is carried in a sitting position on your back –**piggyback** adj, adv

pig·gy·bank /ˈpɪgibæŋk/ n a small container, often in the shape of a pig, used by children for saving coins

pig·head·ed /ˌpɪgˈhedɪd◂/ adj being determined to continue thinking or doing something in spite of good reasons not to

pig·let /ˈpɪglɪt/ n a young pig

pig·ment /ˈpɪgmənt/ n **1** [C;U] a dry coloured powder that is mixed with oil or water to make paint **2** [U] natural colouring matter of plants and animals, for example in leaves, hair or skin

pig·men·ta·tion /ˌpɪgmənˈteɪʃən/ n [U] the colouring of living things

pig·my /ˈpɪgmi/ n see PYGMY

pig·sty /ˈpɪgstaɪ/ n **pigsties 1** an enclosure with a small building in it, where pigs are kept **2** *infml* a very dirty room or house

pig·tail /ˈpɪgteɪl/ n a length of hair that has been twisted together and hangs down the back of the neck and worn by girls

pike /paɪk/ n **1** a large fish that lives in rivers and lakes and eats other fish **2** a long-handled spear used in the past by soldiers fighting on foot

pil·chard /ˈpɪltʃəd ‖ -ərd/ n a small sea fish, often preserved in tins as food

pile¹ /paɪl/ n **1** [C] a number of things of the same kind placed on top of each other: *There's a pile of dirty washing to do. | We arranged the books in piles on the floor.* **2** [C] *infml* (also **piles**) a lot: *I've got a pile of work to do today. | They've got piles of money!* **3** [sing] the soft surface of short threads on floor coverings or cloth **4 piles** [pl] painful swellings on a person's bottom

pile² v **piled, piling 1** [T] to put a number of things of the same kind on top of each other: *He piled the boxes one on top of the other.* **2** [T] to load, fill, or cover: *The bowl was piled high with fruit.*

pile in phr v [I] to get into a vehicle in a disorderly way: *The driver opened the door of the bus and they all piled in.*

pile out phr v [I] to get out of a vehicle in a disorderly way: *I stopped the car and the kids piled out.*

pile up phr v **1** [T **pile** sthg ↔ **up**] to put things one on top of another: *He piled up the letters on the table.* **2** [I] to increase: *His debts piled up and finally he had to sell his house.*

pile-up /ˈpaɪlʌp/ n *infml* a traffic accident in which a number of vehicles crash into each other

pil·fer /ˈpɪlfəʳ/ v [I;T] to steal something small and not particularly valuable:

pil·grim /ˈpɪlgrɪm/ n a person who travels to a holy place as a religious act of respect

pil·grim·age /ˈpɪlgrɪmɪdʒ/ n [C;U] a journey made by a pilgrim: *Aziz is planning to go on/make a pilgrimage to Mecca.*

pill /pɪl/ n **1** [C] a small ball of solid medicine, made to be swallowed whole: *a bottle of vitamin pills* **2 the pill** a pill taken regularly by women as a means of birth control **3 be on the pill** to take the pill as a means of birth control: *"Are you on the pill?"*

pil·lage¹ /'pɪlɪdʒ/ n [U] old fash violent stealing of property

pillage² v pillaged, pillaging [T] old fash to steal things violently

pil·lar /'pɪlər/ n 1 a tall round post made of stone used as a support or decoration 2 something in this shape: a pillar of smoke 3 an important member and active supporter: She has been a pillar of the church all her life.

pillar-box /'···/ n BrE a tall, round box in the street, into which letters are posted

pil·lion /'pɪljən/ n a seat for a second person on a motorcycle, placed behind the driver

pil·low /'pɪləʊ/ n a cloth bag filled with soft material, used to support your head while you are sleeping

pil·low·case /'pɪləʊkeɪs/ n (also pillow slip /'·· ·/) a washable cloth covering for a pillow

pi·lot¹ /'paɪlət/ n 1 a person who flies an aircraft 2 a person with a special knowledge of a particular stretch of water, who is employed to go on board and guide ships that use it

pilot² v [T] 1 to act as pilot of an aircraft or ship 2 to try out something new before it is introduced: The scheme is being piloted in several large cities.

pilot³ adj [only before a noun] done to find out if or how something works: We're doing a pilot study to see if this product will sell well.

pilot light /'··· ·/ n a small gas flame kept burning all the time, used for lighting larger gas burners

pimp /pɪmp/ n a man who controls and makes a profit from a woman who sells sex for money

pim·ple /'pɪmpəl/ n a small raised spot on your skin –pimply adj : pimply skin

pin¹ /pɪn/ n 1 a short thin piece of metal, pointed at one end and used for fastening together pieces of cloth or paper 2 a thin piece of metal, pointed at one end and with a decoration at the other, used to position clothing, or a hat 3 a short piece of wood or metal used as a support, for fastening things together

pin² v -nn- [T; + adv/prep] 1 to fasten or join with a pin or pins: She pinned the pieces of the dress together before sewing it. | You can pin your notice up on the noticeboard. | She pinned the brooch on her coat. –opposite unpin 2 to keep in one position: In the accident, he was pinned under the car. 3 pin something on someone to fix the responsibility for something bad: Don't try to pin the blame on me. 4 pin your hopes on someone/something to hope that someone or something will be successful: Paul has pinned his hopes on passing the exams.
　pin down phr v [T pin sbdy/sthg ↔ down] 1 to fasten down and so prevent from moving: He pinned my arms down and I couldn't move. 2 to make firm arrangements or decisions: I won't pin you down to a particular time; come any day next week.

pin·a·fore /'pɪnəfɔːr/ n 1 a loose piece of clothing that does not cover your arms or back, worn over a dress to keep it clean 2 (also pinafore dress /'··· ·/) a dress that does not cover your arms, under which other clothes are usually worn

pin·cers /'pɪnsəz ‖ -ərz/ n [pl] 1 a tool made of two crossed pieces of metal which is used for holding small things tightly and pulling them 2 the sharp pointed nails of certain shellfish

pinch¹ /pɪntʃ/ v 1 [T] to press tightly between the thumb and a finger: He pinched her arm. | Don't pinch me! 2 [I] to cause pain by being too tight:

Don't buy the shoes if they pinch. 3 [T] infml to steal: Somebody's pinched my car!

pinch² n 1 an act of pressing tightly between the thumb and a finger 2 an amount that can be picked up between the thumb and a finger: a pinch of salt 3 at a pinch only just and if necessary: I can afford to buy the books at a pinch. 4 feel the pinch to be in difficulties because of lack of money

pinched /pɪntʃt/ adj thin or tired-looking (used to describe a face)

pin·cush·ion /'pɪnˌkuʃən/ n a filled bag into which PINS are stuck until they are needed

pine¹ /paɪn/ v pined, pining [I] 1 to feel very sad and lonely, and lose interest in life so that you become ill: Uncle pined away after his wife died. 2 to have a strong desire for something you can no longer have: They pined for the country they had left behind.

pine² n 1 [C] (also pinetree /'paɪntriː/) a tall tree with woody fruits and thin sharp leaves that do not drop off in winter, found especially in colder parts of the world 2 [U] the white or yellowish soft wood of this tree

pine·ap·ple /'paɪnæpəl/ n [C;U] a large yellow tropical fruit with a thick skin and stiff leaves on top

ping /pɪŋ/ v [I] to make a short sharp ringing sound: The bell pinged. –ping n

ping-pong /'· ·/ n [U] infml see TABLE TENNIS

pin·ion /'pɪnjən/ v [T] fml to prevent someone moving by holding or tying up the arms or legs: Two of them pinioned me against the wall, while a third searched my pockets.

pink¹ /pɪŋk/ adj 1 pale red: a pink dress –see picture on page 147 2 in the pink in good health

pink² v [I] (of a car engine) to make high knocking sounds because it is not working properly

pink·ish /'pɪŋkɪʃ/ adj slightly pink

pin·na·cle /'pɪnəkəl/ n 1 a thin tall pointed rock or rocky mountain top 2 the highest point: She reached the pinnacle of success when she moved to America.

pin·point /'pɪnpɔɪnt/ v [T] 1 to find or describe the exact nature or cause of something: The police are trying to pinpoint the cause of the accident. 2 to show the exact position of something: He pinpointed the village on the map.

pin·prick /'pɪnprɪk/ n a small mark made by a pin

pins and nee·dles /ˌ· '··/ n [pl] infml slight continuous pricking feelings in a part of the body to which the supply of blood is returning: I've got pins and needles in my legs.

pin·stripe /'pɪnstraɪp/ n a pattern of thin lines repeated at regular spaces along cloth –pinstriped adj

pint /paɪnt/ n 1 a unit for measuring liquids, equal to about 0·57 of a litre: a pint of milk 2 infml a drink of beer or other liquid of this amount: Two pints please.

pin-up /'pɪnʌp/ n a picture of an attractive person, usually a woman wearing no clothes which is often fixed to a wall

pi·o·neer¹ /ˌpaɪə'nɪər/ n 1 one of the first settlers in a new or unknown country 2 a person who does something first, often in science or medicine: He was a pioneer of heart surgery.

pioneer² v [T] to begin or help in the early development of something

pi·ous /ˈpaɪəs/ adj showing and feeling deep respect for God and religion **–piously** adv

pip¹ /pɪp/ n a small seed from a fruit

pip² n a short high-sounding note, heard on the radio to show the exact time, or as used in the operation of telephones: *Don't put any money into the telephone until you hear the pips.*

pip³ v **-pp-** *BrE infml* **pipped at the post** just beaten at the end of some struggle

pipe¹ /paɪp/ n **1** a tube used for carrying liquids, air, and gas: *a metal pipe* | *a hot-water pipe* **2** a small tube with a little bowl at one end, used for smoking tobacco: *Grandfather lit his pipe.* **3** a simple musical instrument, played by blowing **4 pipes** [pl] see BAGPIPES

pipe² v **piped, piping** [T] to carry things like liquid or gas through pipes
   pipe down phr v [I] infml to stop talking: *"Pipe down, will you!"*
   pipe up phr v [I] infml to begin to speak or sing, especially in a high voice

piped mu·sic /ˌ· ˈ··/ n [U] recorded music played continuously in a public place, such as a shop or restaurant

pipe dream /ˈ· ·/ n an impossible hope, plan, or idea

pipe·line /ˈpaɪp-laɪn/ n **1** a long line of pipes, often underground, for carrying liquids or gas **2 in the pipeline** on the way

pip·er /ˈpaɪpəʳ/ n a musician who plays on a pipe

pip·ing¹ /ˈpaɪpɪŋ/ n [U] **1** a number or system of tubes used for carrying liquids or gas **2** the act or art of playing music on a pipe

piping² adv **piping hot** very hot (used of liquids and foods): *piping hot soup*

pi·quant /ˈpiːkənt/ adj fml **1** having a pleasant sharp taste **2** pleasantly interesting and exciting to the mind **–piquancy** n [U] **–piquantly** adv

pique /piːk/ n [U] a feeling of displeasure, especially when your pride is hurt: *He left in a fit of pique.*

piqued /piːkt/ adj angry because your pride is hurt

pi·ra·cy /ˈpaɪərəsi/ n [U] **1** robbery carried out by pirates **2** the act of stealing ideas or copying the work of others without permission

pi·ra·nha /pəˈrɑːnjə, -nə/ n a fierce South American river fish, that will eat meat

pi·rate¹ /ˈpaɪərət/ n **1** a person who sails the seas attacking and robbing ships **2** a person who copies the work of other people without official permission; for example, a person who prints and sells a book without the writer's permission

pirate² v **pirated, pirating** [T] to copy and sell the work of other people without permission

pir·ou·ette¹ /ˌpɪruˈet/ n a very fast turn made by a dancer on the front part of one foot

pirouette² v **pirouetted, pirouetting** [I] to dance one or more pirouettes

Pis·ces /ˈpaɪsiːz/ n one of the signs of the ZODIAC

pis·ta·chi·o /pəˈstɑːʃiəʊ ‖ pəˈstæ-/ n a small green nut

pis·tol /ˈpɪstl/ n a small gun that you hold and fire with one hand

pis·ton /ˈpɪstn/ n a solid pipe-shaped piece of metal in pumps and engines that fits tightly into a tube; it moves up and down by pressure or explosion and causes other parts of the machine to move

pit¹ /pɪt/ n **1** a large natural or man-made hole in the ground: *The children were playing in the sandpit.* **2** a deep hole dug in the ground to get coal out: *He worked down the pit all his life.* **3** a small hollow mark or place in the surface of something **4 the pit of your stomach** your stomach, when you are describing a physical feeling of fear **5** (also **orchestra pit**) the low space in front of a theatre stage where musicians sit and play during a performance **6 the pit** the seats at the back of the ground floor of a theatre **7 the pits** a place in motor racing beside a track where cars can come during a race to be examined and repaired quickly **8** infml **the pits** a person or thing that you feel a strong dislike for: *Exams are the pits, aren't they!* | *My little brother is the pits.*

pit² **-tt-** [T] **1** to cover something in hollow marks: *The walls had been pitted by gunfire.* **2 pit your wits against** to compete against in a test of knowledge

pit-a-pat /ˈ· · · ,·/ n infml (also **pitter-patter**) the sound or movement of a number of quick light beats on a surface

pitch¹ /pɪtʃ/ v **1** [T] to throw: *He pitched the ball at the batsman.* **2** to fall suddenly and heavily: *She pitched heavily into the mud.* **3** [T] to force someone into a situation: *He was pitched into the debate by the publication of his controversial new novel.* **4** [I] (of a ship) to move violently up and down **5** [T] to fix a sound at a particular level **6** [T] to arrange or deliver something at a particular level that is suitable for a particular group of people: *His speech was pitched at a level that even children could understand.* **7** [T] to set up something like a tent or camp **8 pitch into someone** to attack someone, using words or physical violence
   pitch in phr v [I] infml to start to work or to help other people do a particular job: *If we all pitch in, it shouldn't take long.*

pitch² n **pitches 1** [C] an area of ground with markings on it where certain sports are played: *a football pitch* **2** [C] the level, high or low of a particular sound **3** [sing] a high level: *Their excitement rose to fever pitch.* **4** [C] the amount of slope of part of a building: *the pitch of the roof* **5** [U] a black substance used as a protective covering for ships and houses, to prevent water coming in

pitch-black /ˌ· ˈ··/ adj (also **pitch-dark**) very dark indeed

pitched bat·tle /ˌ· ˈ··/ n a violent fight between armies or groups of people who are determined to win

pitch·er /ˈpɪtʃəʳ/ n **1** a large container for holding and pouring liquids, usually made of clay **2** the usual American word for JUG

pitch·fork /ˈpɪtʃfɔːk ‖ -fɔːrk/ n a farm tool with a long handle and two curved metal points at one end, used for lifting cut grass or HAY

pit·e·ous /ˈpɪtiəs/ adj causing or intended to cause pity: *the piteous cries of the abandoned kittens* **–piteously** adv

pit·fall /ˈpɪtfɔːl/ n a mistake that may easily be made: *The English spelling system provides many pitfalls for foreign students.*

pith /pɪθ/ n [U] **1** a soft white substance that fills the stems of certain plants and trees **2** a white substance just under the skin of oranges and certain other fruits

pit·head /ˈpɪt-hed/ n the entrance to a coal mine

pith·y /ˈpɪθi/ adj **1** having a lot of pith (used of fruit) **2** spoken or written in strong, direct language without wasting words

pit·i·a·ble /ˈpɪtiəbəl/ adj worthy of pity **–pitiably** adv

pit·i·ful /'pɪtɪfəl/ adj causing or deserving pity: *The poor old man was a pitiful sight.* | *His performance on the piano was pitiful.* –**pitifully** adv : *She's pitifully thin these days.*

pit·i·less /'pɪtɪləs/ adj showing no pity: *a pitiless ruler*

pit·tance /'pɪtəns/ n a pittance a very small amount of pay: *They pay me a pittance and then expect me to work long hours.*

pit·ted /'pɪtɪd/ adj **1** covered in hollow marks: *pitted skin* **2** with the stone removed: *pitted olives*

pit·ter-pat·ter /'pɪtə ˌpætər || 'pɪtər-/ n see PIT-A-PAT

pit·y¹ /'pɪti/ n **1** [U] a feeling of sadness and sorrow for the suffering of others: *I invited you here out of pity, but you're taking advantage of my generosity.* **2** [sing] a sad or unfortunate situation: *What a pity you won't be back before I leave!* | *It's a great pity you can't come to the party.* **3 take pity on someone** to help someone because you feel sorry for them

pity² v **pitied, pitying** [T] to feel sorry for the suffering of another person: *I pity anyone who has to live on £40 a week.* | *I pity his poor wife!*

piv·ot¹ /'pɪvət/ n a fixed central point or pin on which something turns or balances

pivot² v **1** [I] to move around or balance on a central point **2 pivot on** to depend on something: *The success of the venture pivots on the signing of this contract.*

pix·ie /'pɪksi/ n **pixies** a small fairy said to enjoy playing tricks on people

piz·za /'piːtsə/ n [C;U] a round flat piece of DOUGH covered with a mixture of cheese, tomatoes (TOMATO), and other kinds of food and then baked

pl. an abbreviation for "plural"

plac·ard /'plækɑːd || -ərd/ n a large printed or written notice or advertisement

pla·cate /plə'keɪt || 'pleɪkeɪt/ v **placated, placating** [T] to calm someone and stop them feeling angry –**placatory** /plə'keɪtəri, 'plækə- || 'pleɪkətɔːri/ adj

place¹ /pleɪs/ n **1** a particular area or position in space: *This is the place where the accident happened.* | *He travelled to places all over the world.* | *Moscow is a very cold place in winter.* | *Let's find a place where we can eat.* | *cinemas and other places of entertainment* **2** the spot or position where something usually goes: *She put the clock back in its place.* **3** *infml* your house or home: *How long have you lived in this place?* | *We all went over to John's place for coffee.* **4** a seat: *There were no empty places on the bus.* | *Is this place taken?* **5** the position that you have reached when you are reading something or talking about something: *I've lost my place.* | *This would be a good place for me to stop and answer some of your questions.* **6** a position in an order: *She finished the race in second place.* **7** a position as a member of a team or a student at a college: *She's been offered a place at Cardiff University.* | *He'll take up his place on the committee next month.* **8** a position in society: *Will this weaken Britain's place within the European Community?* | *I felt that it wasn't my place to criticize his work.* **9 all over the place** in many different parts or places: *She travels all over the place.* | *There were books and magazines all over the place.* **10 in high places** among people who have power and high social positions: *There was much talk of corruption in high places.* **11 in place** in the proper place: *All the technical equipment was now in place.* **12 in place of** instead of: *And now, in place of advertised programmes, there*

will be a special news broadcast. **13 in the first place** in the beginning: *We weren't even sure how this situation had arisen in the first place.* **14 in the first place, in the second place, etc** phrases you use when you are listing reasons or ideas **15 out of place: a** not in the proper place: *Everything was untidy and out of place.* **b** unsuitable: *The modern paintings looked out of place in such an old building.* **16 put someone in their place** to remind someone that they are not as important as they would like to be **17 take place** to happen: *When did the accident take place exactly?* **18 take the place of** to do something or be used instead of someone or something else: *Robots have now taken the place of workers in some factories.*

■ USAGE Compare **place** and **room.** Both words can mean "space that we can use". But **place** is a countable noun and we use it for a single particular piece of space: *This is the place where we keep our coal.* | *There's a place for you in the corner.* **Room** is uncountable and we use it for free space in general: *There's no room for any more coal in here.* | *Is there (any) room for me to sit down?*

place² v **placed, placing** [T] **1** to put something somewhere: *He placed the book carefully on the shelf.* **2 place an order** to order goods: *We placed an order with them for 500 pairs of shoes.* **3** to state that someone has a particular position in a race or competition: *She was placed second.* **4 can't place** to be unable to remember fully what someone's name is or when you last saw them: *I recognize his face, but I can't quite place him.* **5 be well placed to do something** to have the information or other things that are necessary in order to do something: *As we have offices all over the country, we are very well placed to carry out a national survey.*

plac·id /'plæsɪd/ adj calm and peaceful: *A placid expression hid her real feelings.* | *the placid surface of the lake* –**placidly** adv

pla·gia·ris·m /'pleɪdʒərɪzəm/ n [U] the action of taking someone's words, ideas or work and using them as if they are your own: *He was accused of plagiarism in his doctoral thesis.* –**plagiarist** n

pla·gia·rize /'pleɪdʒəraɪz/ v **plagiarized, plagiarizing** (also **plagiarise** BrE) [I;T] to take words or ideas from someone else's work and use them as if they are your own

plague¹ /pleɪg/ n **1** [C;U] a very serious disease that spreads quickly, especially a particular one that produces high fever and swellings on your body **2** [C] a very large number of things of a type that is unpleasant, possibly harmful, and certainly very difficult to control: *a plague of rats*

plague² v **plagued, plaguing** [T] to annoy someone by doing some repeated action: *You've been plaguing me with silly questions all day!*

plaice /pleɪs/ n [plural is **plaice**] [C;U] a flat European fish eaten as food

plaid /plæd/ n [C;U] woollen cloth, often with a special coloured pattern, which is typical of Scotland

plain¹ /pleɪn/ n **1** [C] a large stretch of flat land: *In winter they move down from the mountains to the plains below.* **2** [U] a simple stitch in knitting (KNIT)

plain² adj **1** easy to see, hear, or understand: *It's plain that you don't agree.* | *Explain it in plain language.* **2** simple, without decoration or pattern: *plain food* | *plain paper* –see picture on page 147 **3** *euph* not pretty or good-looking (a less direct word than ugly) **4** direct and honest (used of speech or writing) –**plainness** n [U]

plain choc·o·late /ₜˈ·ˈ··/ n [U] dark chocolate made without milk and with little sugar

plain-clothes /ₜˈ·ˈ·◂/ adj wearing ordinary clothes, not uniform, while on duty, (used of policemen)

plain·ly /ˈpleɪnli/ adv clearly: The child is plainly cold and hungry.

plain sail·ing /ₜˈ·ˈ··/ n [U] a course of action that is simple and without problems: If we can persuade the bank to lend us money, the rest should be plain sailing.

plain-spo·ken /ₜpleɪnˈspəʊkən◂/ adj direct and so often rude in the way you speak

plain-tiff /ˈpleɪntɜf/ n law a person who brings a charge against somebody in a court of law

plain-tive /ˈpleɪntɪv/ adj sad: the plaintive cries of the hungry child

plait¹ /plæt ‖ pleɪt/ n (also **braid** AmE) three or more lengths of something, especially hair, twisted over and under each other into one piece –see picture on page 245

plait² v (also **braid** AmE) to twist three or more lengths of something over and under each other into one piece

plan¹ /plæn/ n 1 an arrangement for some future activity: Have you made any plans for tomorrow night? | a government plan to change the education system 2 a list or line drawing showing how something is or will be arranged: a street-plan of London | Have you seen the plans for the new library? | an essay plan 3 **go according to plan** to happen as planned, without any difficulties

plan² v -nn- 1 to decide what to do and how to do it: We planned our holiday trip in great detail. | What do you plan to do after you leave school? □ USEFUL PATTERNS to plan something; to plan to do something 2 to decide how things will be arranged: They planned the layout of the kitchen with great care. 3 **plan for something** to take into account something that you expect to happen when you make an arrangement: We were planning for rain but it looks fine enough to eat outside. 4 **plan on something** to intend to do something: How long do you plan on staying in Spain? **plan sth ↔ out** phr v [T] to decide something in great detail: We planned everything out in advance.

plane¹ /pleɪn/ n 1 a vehicle that flies: The plane will be landing on time. 2 a tool with a blade that takes thin pieces off wooden surfaces to make them smooth –see picture on page 638 3 a flat or level surface in GEOMETRY 4 a particular level: Let's try to keep the conversation on a friendly plane.

plane² v **planed, planing** [T] to make a wooden surface smooth by taking off small pieces with a special tool

plan·et /ˈplænɜt/ n a large body in space that moves round a star, especially round the sun: the Earth and other planets –**planetary** /ˈplænɜtəri ‖ -teri/ adj [only before a noun] : planetary movements

plan·e·tar·i·um /ₜplænɜˈteəriəm/ n a building inside which lights are directed onto the CEILING to represent the stars and planets and to show how they move

plane tree /ˈ· ·/ n (also **plane**) a tree with wide-spreading branches and broad leaves that grows in towns

plank /plæŋk/ n 1 a long flat piece of wood 2 a main principle of a political party's intentions

plank·ton /ˈplæŋktən/ n [U] the very small forms of plant and animal life that live in water and form the food of many fish

plan·ner /ˈplænəʳ/ n a person who plans, especially one who plans the development of towns: city planners

plant¹ /plɑːnt ‖ plænt/ v 1 [I;T] to put plants or seeds in the ground to grow: April is the time to plant. | Where are you going to plant those roses? 2 [T] to supply an area of land with seeds or growing plants: We're planting a small herb garden. | The sides of the motorway were planted with trees. 3 [T] to place a person or thing firmly in a certain place: He planted himself between Jones and the door. 4 [T] to hide something among another person's possessions so that they will appear guilty if caught: The drugs must have been planted on me at the airport! 5 to send someone somewhere secretly to collect information: Spies were planted in key ministries. **plant sth ↔ out** phr v [T] to move plants outside to grow

plant² n 1 [C] a living thing that has leaves and roots, and usually grows in earth: Those plants need more water. | the plant life of the area | a potato plant –see picture on page 441 2 [C] a place where something, often power, is produced: a car plant | a power plant 3 [U] heavy machinery: We've ordered new plant for the factory.

plan·ta·tion /plænˈteɪʃən, plɑːn- ‖ plæn-/ n 1 a large piece of land, especially in hot countries, on which crops such as tea, sugar, and rubber are grown: a rubber plantation 2 a large group of trees planted to produce wood

plant·er /ˈplɑːntəʳ ‖ ˈplæn-/ n a person who owns or is in charge of a large area of land on which tropical crops are grown: a tea planter

plaque /plɑːk, plæk ‖ plæk/ n 1 [C] a flat metal or stone plate with writing on it, usually fixed to a wall in memory of a person or event 2 [U] tech a substance that forms on your teeth, and in which bacteria live and breed

plas·ma /ˈplæzmə/ n [U] the liquid part of blood

plas·ter¹ /ˈplɑːstəʳ ‖ ˈplæ-/ n 1 [U] a paste of lime, water, and sand, which hardens as it dries and is used to give a smooth surface, especially on walls and ceilings (CEILING) 2 **in plaster** covered with a special plaster mixture which dries and hardens to protect a broken bone: His arm has been in plaster for a month now. 3 [C;U] (also **sticking plaster**) a thin band of sticky material put on the skin to protect small wounds

plaster² v [T] 1 to cover a surface with plaster: Shall we plaster the ceiling next? 2 to cover a surface with something, perhaps too thickly: The wall was plastered with signs. | She plastered cream on her face.

plaster cast /ₜ·· ˈ·, ˈ··-/ n 1 a hollow copy of a stone or metal figure made out of plaster 2 a case made of a special plaster, which covers a part of your body to protect or support a broken bone

plas·tered /ˈplɑːstəd ‖ ˈplæstəd/ adj [never before a noun] infml very drunk (a word which is often used in a humorous way): By midnight everyone was plastered!

plas·ter·er /ˈplɑːstərəʳ ‖ ˈplæ-/ n a person whose job is to plaster the inside of houses

plaster of Par·is /ₜplɑːstər əv ˈpærɜs ‖ ₜplæ-/ n [U] a quick-drying white paste made of a mixture of powder and water, used for plaster casts or in decorative building work

plas·tic¹ /'plæstɪk/ n [C;U] a light man-made material produced chemically from oil or coal, which can be made into different shapes when soft and keeps its shape when hard: *The chairs are made of plastic.* | *manufacturers of plastics*

plastic² adj **1** made of plastic: *a plastic spoon* **2** easily formed into different shapes by pressing **3** [only before a noun] *fml* connected with the art of shaping forms in clay, stone, or wood: *the plastic arts*

plas·ti·cine /'plæstɨsiːn/ n [U] *tdmk* (also **Plasticine**) a soft substance like clay, which is produced in many different colours and used by young children for making small models

plas·tic·i·ty /plæ'stɪsɨti/ n [U] the state or quality of being easy to form into different shapes

plastic sur·ge·ry /ˌ·· '···/ n [U] the repairing of damaged parts of the body, or the improvement of parts that a person is unhappy about: *She is planning plastic surgery to change the shape of her nose.*

plate¹ /pleɪt/ n **1** [C] a flat, usually round dish used to put food on: *a dinner plate* | *a paper plate* **2 have a lot on your plate** have a lot of things to do **3** [C] a flat sheet of metal or glass used in building: *There was a metal plate covering the hole.* | *a plate glass window* **4** [C] a piece of metal outside an office with a name on it: **5** [U] metal covered with gold or silver: *Those forks are silver plate; I couldn't afford silver.* **6** [U] dishes made of PRECIOUS metals like silver and gold **7** [C] a picture or photograph in a book **8** [C] a piece of plastic into which false teeth have been fixed

plate² v **plated, plating** [T] to cover a metal article thinly with another metal, especially gold, silver, or tin: *a silver-plated spoon*

plat·eau /'plætəʊ ‖ plæ'təʊ/ n plateaus *or* plateaux /-təʊz/ **1** a large area of high level land **2** a state in which an activity has stopped developing: *Business has now reached a plateau.*

plate glass /ˌ· '·◁/ n [U] clear glass made in large sheets for use in windows and doors **–plate-glass** adj [only before a noun] : *plate-glass windows*

plat·form /'plætfɔːm ‖ -fɔːrm/ n **1** a raised structure on which people or things may stand: *We had a good view of the speakers on the platform.* | *There was a fire on an oil platform in the North Sea.* **2** an area beside the track at a railway station where passengers wait or get on and off trains: *The train now standing at Platform 1 is the 12.15 to Birmingham.* | *I'll meet you on the platform.* –see picture on page 735 **3** a chance for someone to tell people something: *He used the interview as a platform for his views on ecology.* **4** what a political party says it will do if it wins an election

plat·ing /'pleɪtɪŋ/ n [U] a thin covering of metal

plat·i·num /'plætɨnəm/ n [U] an expensive grey metal often used to make very valuable jewellery: *a platinum ring*

plat·i·tude /'plætɨtjuːd ‖ -tuːd/ n a statement that is not new, interesting, or clever: *He speaks in platitudes.*

pla·ton·ic /plə'tɒnɪk ‖ -'tɑː-/ adj a word used to describe relationships between friends that are not sexual: *platonic love* **–platonically** /-kli/ adv

pla·toon /plə'tuːn/ n a small group of soldiers

plat·ter /'plætər/ n a large flat plate used for serving food

plau·dits /'plɔːdɨts/ n [pl] *fml* a show of pleased approval

plau·si·ble /'plɔːzɨbəl/ adj **1** seeming to be true or reasonable: *His explanation sounds plausible. I*

think we'd better accept it. –opposite **implausible** **2** skilled in producing reasonable statements which may not be true (used of a person)

play¹ /pleɪ/ v **1** [I] (of children) to do things that are enjoyable and interesting, for example running and jumping and using toys: *The children were playing in the garden.* | *She was playing with her toys.* **2** [I;T] to take part in a game: *Let's go and play football.* | *Shall we play cards?* **3** [T] to compete against someone in a game: *England are playing France in the final.* **4** [T] to hit or kick a ball in a particular way during a game: *She played that ball very well.* **5** [I] to be switched on and producing sounds: *A radio was playing in the background.* | *I could hear a record playing somewhere.* **6** [T] to make something produce musical sounds: *Can you play the piano?* | *The orchestra was playing beautifully.* | *Let me play you a tune.* | *I'd like to play this tune to you.* **7** [T] to perform a part on the stage or on television: *The part of Hamlet was played by Laurence Olivier.* **8** [T] to put a particular card down onto the table during a game of cards: *She played the Queen of Hearts.* **9** [+complement] to pretend to be: *The children are playing doctors and nurses.* | *Don't play the innocent with me!* **10** [I+adv/prep] *lit* to move lightly and irregularly: *The sunlight played on the water.* **11 play a hose** to direct a HOSE so that the water goes in a particular direction **12 play a joke/trick on someone** to deceive someone in some way for amusement **13 play a part, play a role** to be important and have an effect: *The family plays a significant part in any child's development.* **14 play for time** to cause a delay in order to gain time **15 play hard to get** to pretend not to be interested in someone sexually in order to make them more interested in you **16 play into someone's hands** to do something which gives another person an advantage over you **17 play it by ear** to let things develop in their own way, rather than making plans in advance **18 play it safe, play safe** to not take risks in order to avoid danger or difficulties **19 play with fire** to take great risks **20 play your cards right** to use the chances and advantages that you have: *If I play my cards right I might get a promotion out of this deal.*

play along with sbdy *phr v* [T] to accept what someone says or wants, even though you do not really agree with them

play at sthg *phr v* [T] **1** to pretend to be something: *She loves playing at being the teacher.* **2 what are you playing at?** a phrase you use when you think that someone is doing something foolish or wrong

play sthg ↔ **back** *phr v* [T] to go through and listen to or watch something that you have just recorded

play sthg ↔ **down** *phr v* [T] to say that something is less important than it really is: *The government's mistakes have been played down by the media.*

play sbdy **off against** sbdy *phr v* [T] to set one person against another in order to gain advantage for yourself: *Children love to play one parent off against the other.*

play on/upon sthg *phr v* [T] to use a feeling or a weakness that someone has for your own advantage: *The government has strengthened its position by playing on people's fears about a possible war.*

play up *phr v* [I;T **play** sbdy **up**] to cause difficulties for someone: *The coffee machine's playing up again.* | *My back has been playing me up recently.* | *Have the children been playing up?*

play² n **1** [U] activity that is done for amusement, especially by children: *Children learn a lot through play.* **2** [C] a piece of writing that is acted in a

When you are writing it is important that your reader understands **the connection** between the things that you are saying.
What is the connection between these two sentences?

There has been a serious rise in food prices this year.
The price of meat has doubled since March.

The second sentence gives an example of the idea in the first sentence.

You can help people to understand what you are saying by showing how one idea is connected to another. To show connections, you can use words and phrases such as **for example, however** and **on the other hand.**
By using **for example,** the connection between the two sentences can be shown:

*There has been a serious rise in food prices this year. **For example,** the price of meat has doubled since March.*

Position

These connecting words can go in various places. For example, they can go:

–at the beginning of a sentence
*We see that you have an income of less than £2000 a year. **Accordingly**, we have decided to offer you free tuition.*

– after the subject
*Seat belts undoubtedly save lives. Many people, **however,** do not wear them.*

– at the end
*Tim's not coming to the concert. He says he's too busy. He hasn't got any money, **in any case.***

What sort of connections are there?

You use sentence connectors to show connections like these:

– you are making an argument stronger by adding another idea:
*I don't think I'm going to Scotland for Christmas. It's such a long way. **Besides,** I haven't much money left.*

– you are listing a group of things:
*There are several reasons why the plan will not work. **First**, there has not been enough preparation. **Second**, there is not enough money.*

– the next idea is unexpected after the idea before:
*The room was very small. It was very comfortable, **however.***

– you are talking about the result of the situation described in the first sentence.
*You have repeatedly failed to deliver the goods on time. We **therefore** feel that we have no alternative but to find another supplier.*

– you are saying in what order events happened:
*The letters are collected from postboxes. They are **then** taken to the sorting office.*

– you are giving an example of the idea in the sentence before:
*Roman civilization was very advanced technologically. They had underfloor central heating, **for instance.***

– you are giving an example of the idea in the sentence before:
*This examination tests both spoken and written English. It demands the ability to communicate, as well as a knowledge of grammar and vocabulary. Candidates are required to do extensive reading. **In short,** this is a very good examination.*

– you are explaining the idea before:
*The company has to reduce labour costs. **In other words**, some of us are going to lose our jobs.*

How does the dictionary help you with sentence connectors?

This dictionary gives you a lot of help with sentence connectors.
It explains when you use them:

in other words
you use this phrase when you are repeating an idea in other words because you think that people may not have understood the real meaning behind the words and you need to explain it.

It gives you examples which are long enough for you to see how they connect sentences:

In the second place
*They won't be interested in that house. In the first place, it's too far from where they work. And **in the second place**, it's more than they are prepared to pay.*

It shows you in the examples where you can put sentence connectors:

for example
*There has been a serious rise in food prices this year. The price of meat, **for example**, has doubled since March.*
*Seeds are naturally protected in various ways. **For example**, they are usually hard on the outside.*
*He seems to have been rather an unpleasant man. He used to throw his rubbish into the garden next door, **for example**.*

The dictionary helps you not only with the sentence connectors you use when you are writing, but also with those you use when you are speaking:

Well
You say "well" when you are changing or correcting the idea before: *There's no problem at all. **Well**, maybe there's a small problem.*

The following passage shows how some important sentence connectors work.

Most scientists nowadays accept the idea of the greenhouse effect, that is, the dangerous increase in temperature of the earth's atmosphere as a result of human activities. There are those, **however,** who think that the danger has been greatly exaggerated. **Indeed**, there are a few who think that the present increase is simply part of the normal cycle of climate variation.

The rise in temperature began with the Industrial Revolution. **At first**, it was very slow, but now it is gathering speed. **As a result**, the Government are beginning to introduce laws to control the causes of the greenhouse effect. They are **also** trying to find ways in which to lessen the effect of human activities ·on the atmosphere. **For example,** they are investigating the use of wind power as a source of electricity. **Eventually,** the people of the world will be forced to consume less. **Otherwise,** the earth will be destroyed.

theatre or on television: *You must go and see the new play on in town.* | *I've just read a wonderful play.* **3** [U] the action in a sport game: *We've seen some excellent play here this afternoon.* **4** [U] freedom of movement caused by something not being fixed firmly in place: *There's a bit too much play in that handle.* **5** [U] *lit* quick movement: *the play of sunlight on the water* **6 at play** playing: *watching the children at play* **7 bring something into play** to use something and make it have an effect: *He has an awful lot of experience that he can bring into play to help solve these problems.* [RELATED PHRASE **come into play**: *Several new factors have now come into play.*] **8 in play** (of a ball) in a position where the rules allow it to be played. [RELATED PHRASE **out of play**]

play·boy /'pleɪbɔɪ/ *n* a rich man who spends his time enjoying himself

play·er /'pleɪəʳ/ *n* **1** a person taking part in a game or sport **2** *old fash* an actor **3** a person who plays a musical instrument: *a piano player*

play·ful /'pleɪfəl/ *adj* **1** full of fun: *a playful little dog* **2** not intended seriously: *a playful kiss on the cheek*

play·ground /'pleɪgraʊnd/ *n* a special piece of land for children to play on

play·group /'pleɪgruːp/ *n* an informal school where very young children play together

play·house /'pleɪhaʊs/ *n* **playhouses** /-ˌhaʊzɪz/ a theatre: *the Provincetown Playhouse*

playing card /'··· ·/ *n fml* see CARD³(1)

play·mate /'pleɪmeɪt/ *n fml* (also **playfellow** /'pleɪˌfeləʊ/) a particular child who often plays with another one: *A lot of Mary's playmates live nearby.*

play·off /'· ·/ *n* a second match played to decide a winner, when the first has not done so

play on words /ˌ· · '·/ *n* **plays on words** see PUN

play·pen /'pleɪpen/ *n* a frame enclosed by bars or a net in which a small child can play safely

play·room /'pleɪrʊm, -ruːm/ *n* a room for children to play in

play·thing /'pleɪˌθɪŋ/ *n* **1** a toy **2** a person who is treated without respect by another

play·time /'pleɪtaɪm/ *n* a short period of time, especially at a school, when children can play

play·wright /'pleɪraɪt/ *n* a writer of plays

plc /ˌpiː el 'siː/ *n* an abbreviation for **'public limited company'**

plea /pliː/ *n* **1** *fml* a request based on strong feelings: *his plea for forgiveness* **2** *law* a statement by a person in a court of law, saying whether or not they are guilty of a charge: *She has entered a plea of guilty.*

plead /pliːd/ *v* **pleaded** *or* **plead** (also **pled** /pled/ *AmE*) **1** [I] to make continual and deeply felt requests: *He pleaded with her until she agreed to do as he wished.* **2** [T] to give an excuse for your behaviour: *The player tried to explain his poor performance by pleading injury.* **3** [I] *law* to state whether or not you are guilty of a charge in a court of law: *The man pleaded not guilty.* **4** [I;T] to speak in support of someone or something: *He has promised to plead our case.* | *We need someone to plead for us.*

pleas·ant /'plezənt/ *adj* **1** nice or enjoyable: *What a pleasant surprise!* | *a flower with a pleasant smell* | *pleasant weather* **2** friendly: *She seems a pleasant woman.* | *Make an effort to be pleasant to our guests, will you!* –opposite **unpleasant**

pleas·ant·ry /'plezəntri/ *n* **pleasantries** a friendly remark made in conversation

please¹ /pliːz/ *v* **pleases, pleasing 1** [I;T] to give pleasure to someone: *You can't please everybody.* | *He did it to please me.* | *He's always eager to please.* **2** [I] **as you please, whatever you please, whenever you please,** etc used when you are saying that someone can do whatever they want: *You can come and go as you please.* | *She can stay as long as she pleases.* **3 if you please** *fml* a polite way of asking someone to do something: *Come this way, if you please.* **4 please yourself** a phrase you use when you are angry to say that someone can do whatever they want and you do not care what they do

please² *interj* **1** used when you are politely asking for something: *Could I have a drink, please?* | *"More coffee?" "Please."* **2** used when you are politely asking someone to do something: *Can you close the window, please?* | *Please be quiet!*

pleased /pliːzd/ *adj* happy or satisfied: *I'm very pleased you decided to come.* | *We're pleased* with *your work.* | *He was looking very pleased with himself, so I knew he had passed his test.* –opposite **displeased**

pleas·ing /'pliːzɪŋ/ *adj* giving someone pleasure or satisfaction: *The results are very pleasing.*

plea·sur·a·ble /'pleʒərəbəl/ *adj fml* enjoyable

plea·sure /'pleʒəʳ/ *n* **1** [U] the feeling of happiness or satisfaction resulting from an experience that you enjoy: *He listened with pleasure to the beautiful music.* | *It gives me no pleasure to have to tell you this.* | *He took great pleasure in telling me that my team had lost.* –opposite **displeasure 2** [C] a cause of happiness, enjoyment, or satisfaction: *It's been a pleasure talking to you.* | *My grandmother has very few pleasures in life.* **3** [U] enjoyment: *Are you here on business or just for pleasure?* | *a pleasure trip* **4 it's a pleasure** a phrase used as a polite reply to someone who thanks you. [RELATED PHRASES **my pleasure, pleasure**]

pleat¹ /pliːt/ *v* to make folds in cloth: *a pleated skirt*

pleat² *n* a specially pressed narrow fold in cloth

pleb·is·cite /'plebɪsɪt ‖ -saɪt/ *n* a direct vote of the people of a nation on a matter of national importance: *The government plans to hold a plebiscite.* | *It was decided by plebiscite.* –compare REFERENDUM

plec·trum /'plektrəm/ *n* a small thin piece of wood or plastic used for playing certain stringed instruments such as the GUITAR

pled /pled/ *v AmE* the past tense and past participle of PLEAD

pledge¹ /pledʒ/ *n fml* **1** a solemn promise or agreement: *He gave a pledge to make the company a success.* **2** something valuable left with someone else as proof that you will fulfil an agreement **3** something given or received as a sign of faithful love or friendship: *Take this ring as a pledge of our friendship.*

pledge² *v* **pledged, pledging** *fml* **1** [I;T;+that] to make a solemn promise or agreement: *They have pledged that they will stay together.* | *The director pledged to reduce working hours.* | *Hundreds of people have pledged time and money to the campaign.* **2 pledge yourself to something** to promise that you will do something: *They pledged themselves to the fight against corruption.*

ple·na·ry /'pliːnəri/ *adj fml* **1** attended by everyone who has the right to do so (used of a meeting) **2** complete (used to describe the power of government)

plume

plen·i·po·ten·tia·ry /ˌplenʌpə'tenʃərɪ ‖ -ʃierɪ/ n plenipotentiaries a person who has complete power to act for a government or organization

plen·ti·ful /'plentɪfəl/ adj existing in quantities or numbers that are more than enough: *The camp is a plentiful supply of food.*

plen·ty /'plentɪ/ n [U] as much or as many as you need: *They've got plenty of money.* | *£200 is plenty.* | *There are plenty more chairs in here.*

pleth·o·ra /'pleθərə/ n fml an amount or supply much greater than is necessary

pli·a·ble /'plaɪəbəl/ adj (also **pliant** /'plaɪənt/) 1 easily bent without breaking 2 easy to persuade or to use for your own purposes (used of a person) –**pliability** /ˌplaɪə'bɪlʌtɪ/ n [U]

pli·ers /'plaɪəz ‖ -ərz/ n [pl] a small tool used to remove things like nails or to bend and cut wire –see picture on page 638

plight /plaɪt/ n a bad situation: *The poor girl was in a terrible plight.* | *the plight of homeless children*

plim·soll /'plɪmsəl, -səʊl/ n BrE one of a pair of light shoes with a top made of heavy cloth and a flat rubber bottom, used especially for games and sports –see picture on page 50 –see PAIR (USAGE)

plinth /plɪnθ/ n a square block, usually made of stone, serving as the base of a pillar or STATUE

plod /plɒd ‖ plɑːd/ v -dd- [I;T] to walk slowly and without pleasure: *The old man plodded wearily home.* | *We plodded the streets in search of a place to stay.*

plod away phr v [I] (also **plod on**) to work steadily, especially at something uninteresting: *I'm plodding away* at *my work while she's out shopping.* | *We'd better plod on* with *our revision.*

plod·der /'plɒdə^r ‖ 'plɑː-/ n a slow, steady, but not very clever worker who often succeeds in the end

plonk¹ /plɒŋk ‖ plɑːŋk, plɔːŋk/ n 1 [C] the sound of something quite heavy falling or being dropped 2 [U] infml cheap wine: *How about a glass of plonk?*

plonk² v infml 1 [T; + adv/prep] to put something down heavily and without care: *Just plonk the bags on the table.* 2 **plonk yourself** to sit down in this way: *She plonked herself in the only armchair.*

plop /plɒp ‖ plɑːp/ v [I] infml to fall with a sound like something dropping smoothly into liquid: *The stone plopped into the stream.* –**plop** n

plot¹ /plɒt ‖ plɑːt/ n 1 a small marked or measured piece of ground for building or growing things: *a building plot* | *I grow potatoes on the little plot of land beside the house.* 2 the set of connected events on which a story, play, or film is based: *Don't tell me the plot! I might want to read it.* 3 a secret plan by a group of people to do something, usually against those in power: *a plot to kill the President*

plot² v -tt- 1 [I;T] to plan something secretly: *They're plotting against him.* | *They're plotting his downfall.* 2 [T] to mark the position of a moving aircraft or ship on a map 3 [T] to mark points on a piece of paper in the form of a GRAPH: *I'm plotting the monthly sales figures for each region last year.* –**plotter** n

plough¹ /plaʊ/ n (also **plow** AmE) 1 a farming tool with a heavy cutting blade which is used to break up and turn over the earth, especially before seeds are planted 2 any tool or machine that works like this: *a snowplough*

plough² v (also **plow** AmE) 1 [I;T] to break up or turn over land with a special tool: *The farmers are out ploughing their fields.* 2 [I] to force a way or

make a track through something: *The car ploughed through the bushes and stopped in the next field.* 3 **plough into something** to crash into something: *The car ploughed into the back of the bus.* 4 **plough money into something** to put a lot of money into a business

plough sthg ↔ **back** phr v [T] to put money that has been earned back into a business to build it up

plough on phr v [I] 1 to continue moving with difficulty 2 to continue doing something difficult or unpleasant: *I'm finding the book boring, but I'll plough on for a few more chapters.*

ploy /plɔɪ/ n ploys infml a carefully planned way of behaving to get something you want: *His usual ploy is to pretend to be ill.* | *It was a ploy to avoid working.*

pluck¹ /plʌk/ v 1 [T] to pull the feathers off a bird before cooking it: *Will you pluck the chicken?* 2 [T] to take something, often with a quick movement: *He plucked the bill from my hand.* 3 **pluck your eyebrows** to pull out hairs from above your eyes 4 **pluck up courage, pluck up the courage to do something** to act bravely although you are afraid: *He couldn't pluck up the courage to complain.* 5 [I;T] to play a stringed instrument by pulling at the strings with your fingers

pluck² n [U] infml courage: *Mountain climbers need a lot of pluck.*

pluck·y /'plʌkɪ/ adj **pluckier, pluckiest** infml brave and determined –**pluckily** adv

plug¹ /plʌɡ/ n 1 a small plastic object with two or three metal pins which are pushed into an electric power point to obtain power for an electrical apparatus –see picture on page 638 2 a small piece of rubber or plastic used to block a hole, especially in a pipe: *She finished her bath and pulled the plug out.* 3 infml a favourable opinion of something like a book or record expressed in order to encourage people to buy it

plug² v -gg- [T] 1 to block or close a hole with something: *Use this to plug the hole in your boat.* 2 infml to talk about or praise something in order to encourage people to buy or see it: *He's been plugging his new book on the radio.*

plug sthg ↔ **in** phr v [T] to connect an electrical apparatus to a supply of electricity –opposite **unplug**

plum /plʌm/ n 1 [C] a sweet smooth-skinned fruit, usually red or yellow, with a single hard stone in the middle –see picture on page 344 2 [U] a dark reddish-blue colour 3 **a plum job** a very desirable job

plum·age /'pluːmɪdʒ/ n [U] all the feathers on a bird

plumb¹ /plʌm/ n a mass of lead tied to the end of a string, used to find out the depth of water or whether a wall is straight from top to bottom: *Have you got a plumb line I could use?*

plumb² v [T] fml 1 to try to find out the meaning of something: *plumbing the deep mysteries of man's mind* 2 **plumb the depths** to reach the lowest point of an unpleasant feeling or way of behaving: *The hero plumbs the depths of unhappiness.*

plumb·er /'plʌmə^r/ n a person whose job is to fit and repair water pipes

plumb·ing /'plʌmɪŋ/ n [U] 1 all the pipes and containers for storing water in a building: *We'll need to put in new plumbing.* 2 the work of looking after the water system in buildings: *He specializes in plumbing and electrical repairs.*

plume /pluːm/ n 1 a large bright feather 2 **a plume of smoke** smoke rising high into the air

plum·met /ˈplʌmɪt/ v [I] to fall steeply or suddenly: *The damaged aircraft plummeted to earth.* | *Prices have plummeted.*

plump¹ /plʌmp/ adj slightly fat (a word often used to express approval): *a baby with plump little arms and legs* –see picture on page 245 –**plumpness** n [U]

plump² v infml **plump for** to decide in favour of something or someone: *We finally plumped for the second house we looked at.*
plump sthg ↔ **up** phr v [T] to make cushions (CUSHION¹) rounded and soft by shaking or knocking them into the right shape

plun·der¹ /ˈplʌndəʳ/ v [I;T] to steal goods from people or a place, often by force and during a war: *Rebels plundered the farms and villages for food.*

plunder² n [U] goods stolen, often by force and during a war

plunge¹ /plʌndʒ/ v **plunged, plunging 1** [I] to move suddenly in a particular direction, often downwards: *Prices on the stock market plunged following the poor trade figures.* | *The divers plunged into the river.* **2** [T] to push something suddenly into a person or thing: *He plunged the knife into her heart.* **3** [I;T] to experience or cause a sudden change in state: *The room was plunged into darkness.* **4 plunge into something** to start an activity eagerly, suddenly, or giving it your complete attention: *She plunged into her studies with terrific enthusiasm.*

plunge² n **1** a sudden move downwards **2 take the plunge** to make a difficult decision to do something

plung·er /ˈplʌndʒəʳ/ n a rubber cup on the end of a handle, used for unblocking pipes

plung·ing /ˈplʌndʒɪŋ/ adj showing a large area of chest: *a dress with a plunging neckline*

plu·per·fect /pluːˈpɜːfɪkt ‖ -ɜːr-/ n a tense that expresses an action completed before a particular time in the past, formed in English with "had" and a past participle

plu·ral /ˈplʊərəl/ n a word form that expresses more than one of a person or thing: *"Dogs" is a plural noun.* | *"Dogs" is the plural of "dog".*

plus¹ /plʌs/ prep and, in addition: *3 plus 6 is 9 (3+6=9).* | *It costs a pound, plus ten pence for postage.*

plus² n (also **plus sign** /ˈ· ·/) **1** a sign (+) showing that two or more numbers are to be added together, or that a number is greater than zero **2** infml something that is good about a situation

plus³ adj **1** [only before a noun] greater than zero: *a plus quantity* **2** [never before a noun] more than the stated number: *All the children here are 12 plus.*

plush /plʌʃ/ adj comfortable and expensive: *the town's plush new cinema*

Plu·to /ˈpluːtəʊ/ n the PLANET 9th in order from the sun, the most distant of the group that includes the Earth

plu·to·crat /ˈpluːtəkræt/ n a person who has power because of their wealth (a word used to express disapproval) –**plutocracy** n –**plutocratic** /ˌpluːtəˈkrætɪk/ adj

plu·to·ni·um /pluːˈtəʊniəm/ n [U] a substance used in the production of NUCLEAR power and weapons

ply¹ /plaɪ/ v **plied 1 ply someone with something** to keep supplying someone with things, especially food, drink, or questions **2** [I;T] old fash (of taxis, buses, and especially boats) to travel regularly: *This ship plies between London and Australia.* **3** lit **ply your trade** to work at a particular job

ply² n [U] a measure of the thickness of wool or rope, according to the number of threads it is made from: *This is four-ply wool.*

ply·wood /ˈplaɪwʊd/ n [U] strong board made of several thin sheets of wood stuck together

p.m. /ˌpiː ˈem/ letters which follow numbers to show that a time is after midday: *He caught the 5 p.m. train from Manchester.* –compare **a.m.**

P M see PRIME MINISTER

pneu·mat·ic /njuːˈmætɪk ‖ nʊ-/ adj **1** worked by air pressure: *a pneumatic drill* **2** containing air: *a pneumatic tyre*

pneu·mo·ni·a /njuːˈməʊniə ‖ nʊ-/ n [U] a serious disease of the lungs causing difficulty in breathing

poach /pəʊtʃ/ v **1** [T] to cook food in gently boiling liquid: *poached eggs* **2** [I;T] to catch animals or birds on private land without permission: *One of the villagers was caught poaching.* | *They were charged with poaching salmon.* **3** [T] to use someone else's work or idea without permission: *All his best ideas were poached from someone else.* **4** [T] to persuade someone to leave another group and join your own, either secretly or dishonestly: *They are poaching all our best managers.* –**poacher** n

P O Box /ˌpiː əʊ ˈbɒks ‖ -ˌbɑːks/ n (also **Post Office Box** fml) a numbered box at a post office, to which a person's letters can be sent: *For further details, write to PO Box 179.*

pock·et¹ /ˈpɒkɪt ‖ ˈpɑːkɪt/ n **1** a small flat cloth bag sewn into or onto a garment, for keeping small articles in: *Do you know what's in your child's pockets?* –see picture on page 50 **2** a container made by fitting a piece of cloth or other material into the inside of a case or a car door, or onto the back of an aircraft seat, for putting things in: *You will find a list of duty-free items in the pocket in front of you.* **3** a small area or group that is separated from others like it: *pockets of mist* | *There are pockets of unemployment in the industrial areas.* **4 out of pocket** having less money than you should after spending some: *She paid for everyone and ended up badly out of pocket.* –**pocket** adj : *a pocket dictionary*

pocket² v [T] **1** to put something into your pocket **2** to take something for your own use dishonestly: *We shared the bill, but John pocketed the change.*

pock·et·book /ˈpɒkɪtbʊk ‖ ˈpɑː-/ n **1** a small book or notebook **2** AmE a small container for carrying papers or money

pock·et·ful /ˈpɒkɪtfʊl ‖ ˈpɑː-/ n the amount of something that can fit into a pocket: *a pocketful of coins*

pocket mon·ey /ˈ·· ˌ··/ n BrE (**allowance** AmE) [U] money given to a child by its parents every week: *How much pocket money do you get?*

pock·mark /ˈpɒkmɑːk ‖ ˈpɑːkmɑːrk/ n a hollow mark left on your skin where a raised spot has been –**pockmarked** adj

pod¹ /pɒd ‖ pɑːd/ n a long narrow seed container of various plants such as beans

pod² v **-dd-** [T] to take beans and other vegetables out of their pods before cooking them

podg·y /ˈpɒdʒi ‖ ˈpɑː-/ adj infml short and fat

po·di·um /ˈpəʊdiəm/ n **podiums** or **podia** /-diə/ a raised part of a floor, or a large movable block, for a performer to stand on

po·em /ˈpəʊɪm/ n a piece of writing, carefully arranged in patterns of lines and sounds

po·et /ˈpəʊɪt/ n a person who writes poems

po·et·ic /pəʊˈetɪk/ *adj* (also **poetical**) **1** of poets or poetry: *poetic language* | *Some plays are written in poetic form.* **2** beautiful or pleasing in a way which is similar to poetry **3 poetic justice** perfect justice, by which people who do wrong are punished in a suitable way **4 poetic licence** freedom to change facts or not obey the usual rules

po·et·ry /ˈpəʊ‚ʌtri/ *n* [U] **1** poems in general: *a book of poetry* –compare PROSE (1) **2** a quality of beauty, grace, or deep feeling (a word used to express approval)

poi·gnant /ˈpɔɪnjənt/ *adj* producing a strong feeling of sadness or pity: *poignant memories of my childhood* –**poignancy** *n* [U]

point¹ /pɔɪnt/ *n* **1** [C] a sharp end of something: *Mind those scissors–they've got sharp points.* **2** [C] an exact position or place: *I showed him the point in the road where the accident had happened.* **3** [C] an exact moment in time: *It was at that point that I realized what had happened.* **4** [C] a stage in a process when something begins to happen: *Heat the water until it reaches boiling point.* | *This government has brought the economy to the point of collapse.* | *He finally reached the point where he could no longer continue working.* **5** [C] a unit used for recording the SCORE in a game or competition: *We won by 12 points to 3.* **6** [C] a sign (.) used for separating a whole number from the decimals that follow it **7** [C] a single fact or idea: *There are two or three points in your speech that I didn't understand.* | *I'd like to make a couple of points.* | *He quoted a whole series of figures and statistics to prove his point.* **8 the point** the most important idea or argument: *Stop messing around and get to the point!* | *The point is that we don't have enough money to move house.* | *I know he's nice, but that's not the point.* **9** [C] a noticeable quality or ability that someone or something has: *You should wear clothes that show off your good points.* | *Work isn't her strong point.* **10** [U] purpose or use: *If your car's that old, there isn't much point in repairing it.* | *He couldn't see any point in learning foreign languages.* **11** [C] a set of holes in a wall into which you can put an electric PLUG **12** [C] one of the 32 marks on a compass that show direction **13 points** [pl] a pair of rails (RAIL) that can be moved to allow a train to change onto another track **14 at the point of** just before something happens: *Even at the point of death he would not reveal his secret.* **15 at the point of a gun, at gun point** turning the dangerous end of a gun towards someone: *They were held up and robbed at gun point.* **16 beside the point** not important to the subject being talked about: *The fact that he's your brother is beside the point.* **17 have a point** a phrase you use to show that you agree with something that someone has said: *You have a point, I suppose.* **18 in point of fact** in fact: *In point of fact, she's only worked for the company for two months.* **19 make a point of doing something** to make sure that you do something: *She made a point of introducing herself to all the new recruits.* **20 on the point of doing something** just about to do something: *I was just on the point of phoning you.* **21 point of no return** a point at which it becomes clear that you cannot change your mind and stop doing something **22 point of order** a question or statement concerned with the proper running of an official meeting **23 point of view** a way of considering or judging someone or something: *Look at it from my point of view.* | *I find it difficult to understand his point of view.* **24 take someone's point** to accept what someone has said: *I take your point about the place needing decorating.* **25 to the point** covering the most important facts or ideas about a subject: *His speech was short and to the point.* **26 to the point of** so as to be almost: *Her way of speaking is direct to the point of rudeness.* **27 up to a point** partly, but not completely; you sometimes say "up to a point" when you do not really agree with what someone says, but you do not want to be rude: *"Do you think it's a good idea for mothers to go out to work?" "Up to a point, but I don't think it's a good idea for a young child to be in a nursery all day."*

point² *v* **1** [I] to hold your finger out towards someone or something: *She pointed at him and said, "He's the one.* | *"He pointed to the house on the corner and said, "That's where I live."* **2** [T] to aim or direct something towards a person or thing: *He pointed the gun at her.* **3 point the finger at someone** to say that someone has done something wrong

point out *phr v* **1** [T **point** sbdy/sthg ↔ **out**] to indicate a person or thing by pointing: *I pointed out the house where I was born.* | *He pointed her out to me.* **2** [T **point** sthg ↔ **out**; +that] to state a fact so that you draw attention to it: *He pointed out a few contradictions in my argument.* | *I pointed out that I had lived in the town for a lot longer than she had.*

point to/towards sthg *phr v* [T] to suggest that something is the case: *All the evidence points towards Briggs as the murderer.* | *These latest figures seem to point to the fact that the country is entering a recession.*

point-blank /ˌ·ˈ·◄/ *adj,adv* **1** from very close to the person or thing being shot at: *He was shot at point-blank range.* | *He fired at the animal point-blank.* **2** forceful and direct: *a point-blank refusal* | *He refused point-blank.*

point·ed /ˈpɔɪnt‚d/ *adj* **1** shaped to a point at one end: *long, pointed fingernails* **2** expressing a clear and often unfriendly message to a particular person or group: *She looked in a pointed manner at the clock and I stood up to leave.* –**pointedly** *adv*

point·er /ˈpɔɪntəʳ/ *n* **1** a long stick used to point at things on a board **2** a thin piece of metal that points to numbers on a measuring apparatus **3** a useful suggestion or piece of advice: *He gave me some useful pointers about how to approach the boss.* **4** a type of hunting dog

point·less /ˈpɔɪntləs/ *adj* without sense or purpose: *a pointless activity* –**pointlessly** *adv* –**pointlessness** *n* [U]

poise /pɔɪz/ *n* [U] **1** calm self-control: *I admire his poise in these difficult negotiations.* **2** a graceful way of holding your head or body upright: *She had the poise of a ballet dancer.*

poised /pɔɪzd/ *adj* **1** [never before a noun] in a delicate state of balance: *The sick man is poised between life and death.* **2** [never before a noun] ready to act or move: *The army was poised for action.* **3** possessing calm self-control

poi·son¹ /ˈpɔɪzən/ *n* [C;U] a substance that can harm or kill people, animals, or plants: *He tried to kill himself by taking poison.* | *A number of these are poisons.*

poison² *v* [T] **1** to give poison to people or animals: *We managed to poison the rats.* **2** to put poison into or onto something: *Someone tried to poison the water supply.* | *a poisoned arrow* **3** to spoil or ruin something: *Her remarks poisoned the atmosphere.* **4 poison someone's mind** to make someone believe bad or false things about another person: *She tried to poison her husband's mind against his sister.* –**poisoner** *n* –**poisoning** *n* [U] : *This paint has caused severe cases of lead poisoning.*

poi·son·ous /ˈpɔɪzənəs/ adj 1 containing or producing poison: *poisonous snakes* | *Don't touch these flowers; they're poisonous.* 2 intended to hurt or harm someone: *poisonous remarks* –**poisonously** adv

poke¹ /pəʊk/ v poked, poking 1 [T] to push a pointed thing into someone or something: *You nearly poked me in the eye with your pencil.* | *Stop poking me!* 2 [I;T] to appear or to show part of something through an opening or out of something else: *She poked her head round the door.* | *His handkerchief was poking out of his sleeve.* 3 **poke fun at** to make jokes against someone or something: *They were poking fun at my hair.* 4 **poke your nose into something** infml to show interest in something that does not concern you

poke about/around phr v infml [I] to search: *She poked about in her bag for her ticket.*

poke at sbdy/sthg phr v [T] to make lots of small movements as you push something with something pointed

poke² n a quick push with something pointed

pok·er /ˈpəʊkər/ n 1 [C] a thin metal rod used to move the wood or coal in a fire in order to make it burn better 2 [U] a card game usually played for money

pok·y /ˈpəʊki/ adj pokier, pokiest infml uncomfortably small (used to describe buildings): *a poky little house*

po·lar /ˈpəʊlər/ adj [only before a noun] of or from the area around the North or South Pole

polar bear /ˌ··ˈ·/ ‖ /ˈ···/ n a large white bear that lives near the North Pole

po·lar·i·ty /pəˈlærəti/ n polarities [C;U] great difference: *We have observed a growing polarity between the opinions of the government and those of the trade unions.*

po·lar·ize /ˈpəʊləraɪz/ v polarized, polarizing (also **polarise** BrE) [I;T] to move into two opposing groups: *The government's policy seems to have polarized society into two classes.* | *Society has polarized into two classes.* –**polarization** /-raɪˈzeɪʃən ‖ -rə-/ n (also **polarisation** BrE) [C;U]

Po·lar·oid /ˈpəʊlərɔɪd/ n tdmk 1 [U] a substance used in glass to make light shine less brightly through it 2 [C] a camera that produces a finished photograph only seconds after the picture has been taken

pole /pəʊl/ n 1 a long thin round stick or post: *a flagpole* | *telegraph poles* 2 either of the two ends of the AXIS on which the Earth turns 3 one of the two points at which wires may be fixed onto an electricity-storing apparatus 4 **poles apart** having very different views

Pole n see POLISH 2

pole star /ˈ· ·/ n the pole star (also **the Pole Star, the North Star**) the bright star that is nearest to the centre of the sky in the northern part of the world

pole vault /ˈ· ·/ n 1 a sport in which a person uses a pole to jump over a high raised bar 2 a jump in this sport –**pole-vault** v [I]

po·lice¹ /pəˈliːs/ n [pl] 1 **the police** an official body of men and women whose duty is to protect people and property, and to make sure that everyone obeys the law: *The police are searching for him now.* | *the police force* | *a police car* 2 members of this official body: *There were police everywhere.*

police² v policed, policing [T] to keep order in a place, usually by using police: *This area has to be carefully policed on Saturday nights.*

po·lice·man /pəˈliːsmən/ n policemen /-mən/ (also **police officer** /·ˈ· ˌ···/) a male member of a police force

police state /·ˈ· ·/ n a country in which most activities of the citizens are controlled by secret political police (a phrase used to express disapproval)

police sta·tion /·ˈ· ˌ··/ n the local office of a police force

po·lice·wom·an /pəˈliːsˌwʊmən/ n policewomen /-ˌwɪmɪn/ (also **police officer** /·ˈ· ˌ···/) a female member of a police force

pol·i·cy /ˈpɒləsi/ n policies [C;U] 1 a plan or course of action that is agreed by a political party, government, or business: *One of the party's policies is to control public spending.* | *It's against government policy to sell weapons to that country.* 2 a written agreement by a company to insure health, lives or property for a stated sum of money: *an insurance policy*

po·li·o /ˈpəʊliəʊ/ n (also **poliomyelitis** /ˌpəʊliəʊmaɪəˈlaɪtɪs/ tech) [U] a serious infectious disease of the nerves in your backbone, which often causes you to lose the power to move certain muscles

pol·ish¹ /ˈpɒlɪʃ ‖ ˈpɑː-/ v 1 [I;T] to make or become smooth and shiny by rubbing: *Polish your shoes with that brush.* | *Silver polishes easily with this special cloth.* 2 [T] to make something as perfect as possible: *The musicians gave a very polished performance.* | *This essay needs polishing.*

polish sthg ↔ off phr v [T] infml to finish food or work quickly: *I must polish this report off before I leave.*

polish² n 1 [U] a liquid, powder, or paste used to make a surface smooth and shiny: *a tin of shoe/furniture polish* 2 [sing] a rub to make a surface smooth and shiny: *Could you give the table a polish?* 3 [sing] the smooth shine of a surface: *That hot plate will spoil the polish on this table.* 4 [U] the fine quality of something, especially manners or writing

Po·lish¹ /ˈpəʊlɪʃ/ adj from or connected with Poland

Polish² n 1 **the Polish** (also **the Poles**) the people of Poland 2 [U] the language of Poland

po·lite /pəˈlaɪt/ adj having good manners, and showing respect and consideration for others: *What polite children!* | *I wish you'd be more polite to my parents.* –opposite **impolite** –**politely** adv –**politeness** n [U]

pol·i·tic /ˈpɒlɪtɪk ‖ ˈpɑː-/ adj fml sensible because you will gain some advantage: *It would be politic to agree with him.*

po·lit·i·cal /pəˈlɪtɪkəl/ adj 1 concerning politics: *a political party* | *the loss of political freedoms* | *political beliefs* 2 interested in politics: *Our students used to be more political.* –**politically** /-kli/ adv

po·lit·i·cal prisoner /·ˌ···ˈ···/ n someone who is in prison because of their political beliefs

pol·i·ti·cian /ˌpɒlɪˈtɪʃən ‖ ˌpɑː-/ n a person who works in politics, especially a member of a parliament

pol·i·tics /ˈpɒlətɪks ‖ ˈpɑː-/ n 1 [pl;U] activities concerned with power relationships or government: *Are you interested in politics?* | *She takes an active part in local politics.* | *I try to avoid company politics.* 2 [U] the study of political affairs: *Politics is my main subject.* | *the politics department* 3 [pl] political opinions: *What are your politics?*

pol·ka /ˈpɒlkə, ˈpəʊlkə ‖ ˈpəʊlkə/ n a quick simple dance for people in pairs, or the music it is danced to

polka dot /ˈ··· ·/ adj esp. AmE (of cloth) having a pattern of round spots **polka dot** n

poll¹ /pəʊl/ n **1 the polls** an election: *Voters go to the polls next Thursday.* **2** (also **opinion poll**) a set of questions given to a number of people chosen by chance, to find out the general opinion about something or someone: *The latest poll gives the opposition a 10% lead over the Government.* **3 poll tax** money collected by the local council from people living in the area; the money is used to help pay for local services: *Have you paid your poll tax?*

poll² v [T] **1** to receive a certain number of votes in an election: *She polled 10,542 votes.* **2** to ask people for their opinions on a particular subject: *The majority of people polled supported the Prime Minister's decision.*

pol·len /'pɒlən ‖ 'pɑː-/ n [U] fine yellow dust on a flower that causes other flowers to produce seeds

pollen count /'·· ·/ n a measure of the amount of pollen floating in the air

pol·li·nate /'pɒlɪneɪt ‖ 'pɑː-/ v **pollinated, pollinating** [T] to make a plant able to produce seeds by bringing pollen to it –**pollination** /ˌpɒlɪ'neɪʃən ‖ ˌpɑː-/ n [U]

poll·ing /'pəʊlɪŋ/ n [U] voting at an election

pol·lut·ant /pə'luːtənt/ n [C] a substance that pollutes the air, water, or soil

pol·lute /pə'luːt/ v **polluted, polluting** [T] to make the air, water, or soil dirty or dangerous by adding harmful substances: *The river has been polluted by chemicals.*

pol·lu·tion /pə'luːʃən/ n [U] **1** the process of polluting the air, water, or soil: *water pollution | the pollution of the environment* **2** a substance that pollutes the air, water, or soil: *There's so much pollution in the air here that it's becoming dangerous to breathe!*

po·lo /'pəʊləʊ/ n [U] a game played between two teams on horses, who hit the ball with long wooden hammers

polo neck /'·· ·/ n a high rolled collar –**polo-neck** adj : *a polo-neck sweater*

pol·ter·geist /'pɒltəgaɪst ‖ 'pəʊltər-/ n a spirit that is said to make noises and move objects around

pol·y /'pɒli ‖ 'pɑːli/ n **polys** BrE infml see POLYTECHNIC

pol·y·es·ter /'pɒliestər, ˌpɒli'estər ‖ 'pɑːliestər/ n [U] a man-made material used to make cloth: *a polyester shirt*

pol·y·eth·y·lene /ˌpɒli'eθəliːn ‖ ˌpɑː-/ n [U] the usual American word for POLYTHENE

po·lyg·a·my /pə'lɪgəmi/ n [U] the practice of having more than one wife at the same time –**polygamist** n –**polygamous** adj : *a polygamous society*

pol·y·gon /'pɒlɪgən ‖ 'pɑːlɪgɑːn/ n tech a shape that has three or more straight sides

pol·y·sty·rene /ˌpɒlɪ'staɪəriːn ‖ ˌpɑː-/ n [U] a light plastic, used especially for making containers

pol·y·tech·nic /ˌpɒlɪ'teknɪk ‖ ˌpɑː-/ n (also **poly** infml) a college of higher education where you can train in practical skills as well as study a wide range of subjects

pol·y·thene /'pɒlɪθiːn ‖ 'pɑː-/ n (also **polyethylene** AmE) [U] a strong, thin plastic used to cover and protect things: *a polythene bag*

pom·e·gran·ate /'pɒmɪɡrænɪt ‖ 'pɑːm-/ n a round fruit containing a lot of small seeds in a red juicy flesh

pomp /pɒmp ‖ pɑːmp/ n [U] grand and solemn ceremony shown on public or official occasions

pom·pous /'pɒmpəs ‖ 'pɑːm-/ adj behaving or speaking in a very serious way, as if you are trying to appear more important than you are (a word used to express disapproval): *pompous language | a pompous official* –**pomposity** /pɒm'pɒsɪti ‖ pɑːm'pɑː-/ n (also **pompousness**) [U] –**pompously** adv

pond /pɒnd ‖ pɑːnd/ n an area of still water, smaller than a lake: *a duck pond*

pon·der /'pɒndər ‖ 'pɑːn-/ v [I;T] fml to spend time thinking carefully about something: *She pondered the problem for a while. | I need time to ponder over the best thing to do.*

pon·der·ous /'pɒndərəs ‖ 'pɑːn-/ adj fml **1** slow and awkward in moving **2** slow and dull (used especially of speech) –**ponderously** adv –**ponderousness** n [U]

pong /pɒŋ ‖ pɑːŋ/ v [I] BrE infml to make an unpleasant smell –**pong** n : *What a terrible pong!* –**pongy** adj

the pon·tiff /'pɒntɪf ‖ 'pɑːn-/ n fml see POPE

pon·tif·i·cate /pɒn'tɪfɪkeɪt ‖ pɑːn-/ v **pontificated, pontificating** [I] to speak or write as if your own judgment is the only correct one (a word used to express disapproval)

pon·toon /pɒn'tuːn ‖ pɑːn-/ n **1** [C] a flat-bottomed boat fastened to others side by side to support a floating bridge across a river: *a pontoon bridge* **2** (also **twenty-one** AmE) [U] a card game played for money

po·ny /'pəʊni/ n **ponies** a small horse

po·ny·tail /'pəʊniteɪl/ n a bunch of hair tied high at the back of the head –see picture on page 245

poo·dle /'puːdl/ n a dog with thick curling hair

pooh /puː/ interj **1** a word you use to express your feelings when you smell something unpleasant **2** a word used to express disbelief or disapproval

pooh-pooh /ˌ· '·/ v [T] infml to show that you consider something foolish: *They pooh-poohed the idea of health food in those days.*

pool¹ /puːl/ n **1** [C] a small area of still water, usually formed naturally: *There were little pools of rainwater in the street. | a rock pool on the beach* **2** [C] a small amount of any liquid on a surface: *She was lying in a pool of blood.* **3** a SWIMMING POOL **4** [C] a collection of money, goods, or people that may be used or shared by a number of people: *I can borrow a car from the company car pool. | Give the report to someone in the typing pool.* **5** [U] a game played with hard coloured balls on a flat green table with pockets at the corners: *They were in the bar shooting pool all evening.*

pool² v [T] to put things together and share them: *If we pool our ideas it'll be much easier. | They pooled their resources to buy a house.*

pools /puːlz/ n BrE **the pools**, **the football pools** a competition in which people risk money on the results of certain football matches

poop /puːp/ n tech the back end of a ship

poor /pʊər/ adj **1** having very little money and therefore a low standard of living: *They were too poor to afford shoes for their children. | It's a very poor country.* **2 the poor** the people in society who are poor: *The government must do more to help the poor and the sick.* **3** low in quality, or below the usual standard: *a poor crop of beans | The light was too poor to see his face. | He has very poor eyesight. | It was a poor performance.* **4** [only before a noun] deserving sympathy: *The poor old man had lost both his sons in the war.* **5 in poor health** ill

poor·ly¹ /ˈpʊəli ‖ ˈpʊərli/ adv badly: a poorly paid job

poorly² adj [never before a noun] BrE ill: I'm feeling rather poorly today.

pop¹ /pɒp ‖ pɑːp/ v -pp- **1** [I;T] to burst with a short sharp sound: She popped the balloon with a pin. | The balloon popped. **2** [I] to make a short sharp sound: The champagne cork popped when he pulled it out. **3** [I] infml to do something or go somewhere quickly or for a short time: I've just popped in to return your book. | I'm afraid she's just popped out to the shops. **4** [T] infml to put something somewhere quickly: Will you pop the bread in the oven? | He popped his head round the door. **5** [I] infml (of eyes) to show great surprise by opening wide: Her eyes almost popped out of her head when she saw me. **6 pop the question** infml to ask someone to marry you

pop² n **1** [C] a sound like that of a slight explosion: There was a loud pop and the lights went out. **2** [U] modern music that has a strong beat and is popular with young people: Do you like pop music? | a pop star **3 pop group** a group of people who sing and play pop music **4** [C] AmE infml father: Can I borrow the car, pop? **5** [U] infml a sweet drink containing a harmless gas

pop·corn /ˈpɒpkɔːn ‖ ˈpɑːpkɔːrn/ n [U] grains of corn that are heated until they burst and are eaten with salt or sugar

pope /pəʊp/ n **the Pope** the head of the ROMAN CATHOLIC Church: the election of a new pope | Pope John Paul | a message from the Pope

pop·lar /ˈpɒplər ‖ ˈpɑːp-/ n [C;U] a very tall straight thin tree, or the wood from this tree

pop·py /ˈpɒpi ‖ ˈpɑːpi/ n poppies a plant with large, round, red flowers

pop·u·lace /ˈpɒpjʊləs ‖ ˈpɑːp-/ n fml [U; + sing/pl verb] all the people of a country, especially the people who do not govern it: The populace no longer supports this policy.

pop·u·lar /ˈpɒpjʊlər ‖ ˈpɑːp-/ adj **1** liked by a lot of people: a popular TV programme | She's very popular with her students. –opposite **unpopular 2** [only before a noun] aimed at the understanding and interests of ordinary people (a word often used to express disapproval): An article like this could only appear in the popular press. **3** [only before a noun] fml of the general public: popular opinion | the popular vote

pop·u·lar·i·ty /ˌpɒpjʊˈlærɨti ‖ ˌpɑːp-/ n [U] the quality or state of being liked by a lot of people: His popularity comes from his genuine concern for others. –opposite **unpopularity**

pop·u·lar·ize /ˈpɒpjʊləraɪz ‖ ˈpɑːp-/ v **popularized**, **popularizing** (also **popularise**) [T] **1** to make something known to and liked by a lot of people **2** to make something difficult easier for ordinary people to understand –**popularization** /ˌpɒpjʊlər-aɪˈzeɪʃən ‖ ˌpɑːpjʊlərə-/ n [C;U]

pop·u·lar·ly /ˈpɒpjʊləli ‖ ˈpɑːpjʊlərli/ adv by most people: The London Underground is popularly known as the Tube.

pop·u·late /ˈpɒpjʊleɪt ‖ ˈpɑːp-/ v **populated**, **populating** [T] to fill an area with people who move or live there: a densely-populated area | North America was mainly populated by immigrants from Europe.

pop·u·la·tion /ˌpɒpjʊˈleɪʃən ‖ ˌpɑːp-/ n **1** [C;U] the number of people living in a particular area, or country: What was the population of Europe in 1900? | a population of 8 million | population levels **2** [C] the people, or sometimes animals, living in an area: Most of Australia's population lives near the coast.

pop·u·lous /ˈpɒpjʊləs ‖ ˈpɑːp-/ adj fml full of people (used of an area)

porce·lain /ˈpɔːslɨn ‖ ˈpɔːrsəlɨn/ n [U] a thin shiny substance made of baked clay which is used to make fine quality cups and dishes

porch /pɔːtʃ ‖ pɔːrtʃ/ n **1** an entrance to a house or church which has sides and a roof –see picture on page 441 **2** the usual American word for VERANDA

por·cu·pine /ˈpɔːkjʊpaɪn ‖ ˈpɔːr-/ n a short-legged animal that has very long stiff sharp points all over its back and sides

pore¹ /pɔːr/ n a very small hole in your skin or a leaf which allows liquid to come out

pore² v **pored**, **poring**
pore over sthg phr v [T] to study something closely: She's always poring over a book.

pork /pɔːk ‖ pɔːrk/ n [U] meat from a pig –see MEAT (USAGE) –compare BACON, HAM

porn /pɔːn ‖ pɔːrn/ n [U] infml see PORNOGRAPHY

por·nog·ra·phy /pɔːˈnɒɡrəfi ‖ pɔːrˈnɑːɡ-/ n [U] books, photographs or films showing sexual acts in a way that is meant to excite people (a word often used to express disapproval) –**pornographer** n –**pornographic** /ˌpɔːnəˈɡræfɪk◄ ‖ ˌpɔːr-/ adj : a pornographic film

po·rous /ˈpɔːrəs/ adj allowing liquid to pass through: porous soil

por·poise /ˈpɔːpəs ‖ ˈpɔːr-/ n a large sea animal that swims about in groups

por·ridge /ˈpɒrɪdʒ ‖ ˈpɑː-, ˈpɔː-/ n [U] a breakfast food made by boiling grain, especially oats (OAT), in milk or water

port /pɔːt ‖ pɔːrt/ n **1** [C] a town or an area by the water which ships arrive at and leave from: a fishing port | It is one of the world's busiest ports. | Port Said **2 port of call** a place where a ship will stop: Singapore is our next port of call. **3** [U] the left side of a ship or aircraft as you face the front: The ship was leaning to port. **4** [U] strong sweet Portuguese wine

por·ta·ble /ˈpɔːtəbəl ‖ ˈpɔːr-/ adj quite small, light, and easy to move or carry: a portable television

por·tal /ˈpɔːtl ‖ ˈpɔːrtl/ n fml or lit a very grand door or entrance to a building

port·cul·lis /pɔːtˈkʌlɨs ‖ pɔːrt-/ n a strong gate above an entrance to an old castle or fort, which was lowered as a protection against attack

por·ter /ˈpɔːtər ‖ ˈpɔːr-/ n **1** a person who looks after a building, such as a school or a block of flats, and who often sits near the entrance **2** a person employed to carry travellers' bags at railway stations, airports, or hotels

port·fo·li·o /pɔːtˈfəʊliəʊ ‖ pɔːrt-/ n **portfolios 1** a large flat case for carrying drawings and papers in **2** a set of examples of a person's work: an artist's portfolio **3** the office and duties of a government minister

port·hole /ˈpɔːthəʊl ‖ ˈpɔːrt-/ n a small circular window along the side of a ship or aircraft

por·ti·co /ˈpɔːtɪkəʊ ‖ ˈpɔːr-/ n **porticoes** or **porticos** a grand entrance to a building, consisting of a roof supported by pillars

por·tion¹ /ˈpɔːʃən ‖ ˈpɔːr-/ n **1** a part that can be separated from the rest, or is different from it: Keep this portion of your ticket. **2** an amount or share of something: *The driver must bear a portion of the blame for the accident.* **3** a quantity of food for one person: *How many portions of meat are there?*

portion² v

portion sthg ↔ **out** *phr* v [T] to share something among a group of people

port·ly /ˈpɔːtli ‖ ˈpɔr-/ *adj* **portlier, portliest** *old fash* fat (a word which is sometimes used instead of 'fat' in order to be more polite or humorous): *Men in our family tend to be rather portly.* –**portliness** *n* [U]

port·man·teau /pɔːtˈmæntəu ‖ pɔːrt-/ *n* **portmanteaus** *or* **portmanteaux** /-təuz/ a large travelling case that opens out into two equal parts

por·trait /ˈpɔːtr₁t ‖ ˈpɔːr-/ *n* **1** a painting, drawing, or photograph of a real person, especially of their face: *She's just painted a portrait* **of** *her mother.* | *a self-portrait* **2** a written description of a person, place or thing: *The book is a portrait* **of** *a country at war.*

por·tray /pɔːˈtreɪ ‖ pɔːr-/ v **portrayed, portraying** [T] **1** to show a person or thing in a particular way, using words or pictures: *Her book portrays women as domestic slaves.* **2** to act the part of a particular character in a play or film: *He portrays a young doctor.* –**portrayal** *n* [C;U] : *I particularly enjoyed his portrayal of King Arthur.*

Por·tu·guese¹ /ˌpɔːtʃʊˈgiːz◄ ‖ ˌpɔːr-/ *adj* from or connected with Portugal.

Portuguese² *n* **1 the Portuguese** the people of Portugal **2** [U] the language of Portugal

pose¹ /pəuz/ v **posed, posing 1** [I] to sit or stand in a particular manner so that you can be drawn, painted, or photographed: *How would you like me to pose?* | *I've never posed for a painting before.* **2** [I] to behave unnaturally in order to attract interest or attention (a word used to express disapproval) **3 pose as someone** to pretend to be someone else: *The prisoner escaped by posing as a prison officer.* **4** [T] to be the cause of a difficulty or problem: *This new law poses several problems for the farmers.* **5** [T] to ask or suggest something: *That poses the question of where the party should be held.*

pose² *n* **1** a position in which someone sits or stands while they are being drawn, painted, or photographed: *This pose is more flattering, I think.* **2** an unnatural way of behaving which is intended to attract interest or attention (a word used to express disapproval)

posh /pɒʃ ‖ pɑːʃ/ *adj infml* **1** typical of people from a high social class (a word used to express disapproval): *She has a rather posh accent.* **2** grand and expensive-looking: *a posh hotel*

po·si·tion¹ /pəˈzɪʃ ən/ *n* **1** [C;U] the place where someone or something is: *Can you find our position on this map?* | *Our seats were in a very good position.* | *Shall we change position?* **2** [U] the place where something is supposed to be: *The screws will hold the shelves in position.* **3** [C] a situation someone is in: *I'm in a difficult financial position at the moment.* | *You're putting me in an impossible position.* **4 not be in a position to do something** to be unable to do something: *I'm afraid I'm not in a position to lend you any money.* **5** [C] the way in which someone stands, sits or lies: *She slept in an uncomfortable position.* **6** [C] the way in which something has been placed: *The switch was in the off position.* **7** [C;U] a particular place or rank in relation to others: *She finished the race in second position.* **8** [C] a job that is professional, or in an office: *I have a position of responsibility at the bank.*

–see JOB (USAGE) **9** [C] an opinion about something: *The government's position* **on** *this matter is clear.*

position² v [T] **1** to move a person or thing to a particular place, or so that they sit, stand, or lie in a particular way: *Most of the soldiers will be positioned near the border.* **2 position yourself** to move to a particular place: *She positioned herself beside the fire exit.*

pos·i·tive /ˈpɒz₁tɪv ‖ ˈpɑː-/ *adj* **1** [never before a noun] sure that something is true (used of a person): *"Are you sure this is the right number?" "Positive."* | *He was positive that he had seen the man before.* **2** certain: *The police have positive proof that it was murder.* **3** hopeful or confident: *a positive attitude to life* | *He's being very positive about the future.* **4** helpful, decisive, or encouraging: *She offered me some very positive advice.* | *At least you're taking some positive steps towards solving the problem.* **5** showing signs that a substance is present (used of a medical test) **6** greater than zero (used of a number, in MATHEMATICS) **7** having the charge carried by PROTONS (used of a flow of electricity): *The red is positive and the black is negative.* **8** a word used to give force to a noun, to say that something is really true: *It's a positive pleasure to work with her.*

pos·i·tive·ly /ˈpɒz₁tɪvli ‖ ˈpɑː-/ *adv* **1** with certainty: *He said quite positively that he would come.* **2** *infml* a word used to show that you feel strongly when you say that something is true: *This food is positively delicious!*

pos·sess /pəˈzes/ v [T not in progressive forms] **1** *fml* to own or have something: *They asked me if I possessed a gun.* **2** to influence or take control of someone's mind or actions: *He was possessed by jealousy.* | *What possessed you to behave like that?*

pos·sessed /pəˈzest/ *adj fml or lit* controlled by an evil spirit (used of people or animals)

pos·ses·sion /pəˈzeʃ ən/ *n* **1** [U] the state of owning or having something: *Possession of a large fortune does not always bring happiness.* | *The papers are in my possession now.* **2 in possession of something** having something, especially something surprising or illegal: *He was found in possession of stolen goods.* **3 take possession of something** to get control or become the owner of something: *The rebels took possession of the airport.* | *We take possession of our new house next week.* **4** [C] a piece of personal property: *They lost most of their possessions in the fire.*

pos·ses·sive /pəˈzesɪv/ *adj* **1** wanting to have all of a person's love or attention (a word used to express disapproval): *Don't be so possessive! He's just a friend.* **2** unwilling to share your things (a word used to express disapproval): *Children can be very possessive about their toys.* **3** showing ownership or connection (used in grammar); "my" and "their" are possessive adjectives

possessive² *n* a word or grammatical form showing ownership or connection; "hers" is a possessive

pos·ses·sor /pəˈzesəʳ/ *n fml* a person who owns something (a word that is often used in a humorous way): *I was now the proud possessor of a university degree.*

pos·si·bil·i·ty /ˌpɒs₁ˈbɪl₁ti ‖ ˌpɑː-/ *n* **possibilities 1** [sing;U] the chance that something is likely to happen or to be true: *Is there any possibility that you'll be able to come tomorrow?* | *There's a slight possibility of rain.* **2** [C] something that might happen or that might be true: *War is now a strong possibility.* | *"He might have left already." "Yes:, it's a possibility."*

pos·si·ble /ˈpɒsᵻbəl ‖ ˈpɑː-/ *adj* **1** that can exist, happen, or be done: *It's no longer possible to find a cheap flat in London.* | *It's possible that we might be a bit late.* | *Everything is possible.*
□ USEFUL PATTERNS it is possible to do something; it is possible that…
2 if possible if it is possible –opposite **impossible 3** that may or may not be, happen, or be expected **4** acceptable or suitable: *one of many possible answers*

pos·si·bly /ˈpɒsᵻbli ‖ ˈpɑː-/ *adv* **1** in accordance with what is POSSIBLE1): *I'll do all I possibly can.* | *You can't possibly walk 20 miles in an hour.* **2** perhaps: *"Will you come with us tomorrow?" "Possibly."*
■ USAGE **Possibly** is commonly used in requests to make them sound less direct and, therefore, more polite: **Could you possibly** *give me a hand with the washing up?* | **Could I possibly** *borrow your bike this afternoon?* | **I wonder if I could possibly** *borrow £10.*

post¹ /pəʊst/ *n* **1** [C] an upright wooden or metal pole fixed into the ground: *a gate post* | *a signpost* **2** the place where a race begins or ends **3** *BrE* (also **mail** *AmE*) [C;U] the official system for sending and receiving letters: *He sent it by post.* | *I'll put it in the post today.* **4** [U] a single official collection or delivery of letters: *Has the afternoon post gone yet?* | *Is there any post for me?* **5** [C] a job: *I saw an advertisement for the post.* | *the post* **of** *head teacher* –see JOB (USAGE) **6** [C] a place where someone, especially a soldier, does their job: *I want all soldiers at their posts by 6 a.m.*

post² *v* [T] **1** to show something publicly, on a wall or board: *Examination results will be posted outside the staffroom.* **2** *BrE* (also **mail** *AmE*) to take a letter or parcel to a post office or put one into a collection box for sending: *Did you remember to post the letters?* **3 keep someone posted** to continue to give someone all the latest news about something **4** to send someone, especially a soldier, to a particular place to work: *John has been posted to Hong Kong.*

post·age /ˈpəʊstɪdʒ/ *n* [U] the charge for sending or delivering something by post: *The books will cost £9, including postage.*

postage stamp /ˈ··· ·/ *n fml* see STAMP²(1)

post·al /ˈpəʊstl/ *adj* [only before a noun] connected with the post service: *The postal workers are on strike again.*

postal or·der /ˈ··· ,··/ *n* a small piece of paper that can be bought from a post office and sent to someone, who can exchange it at a post office for a stated amount of money

post·box /ˈpəʊstbɒks ‖ -baːks/ *n* **1** *BrE* (also **letter-box**) an official box which you put letters into if you want to send them by post **2** *AmE* a small numbered box in a post office for receiving mail –see picture on page 441

post·card /ˈpəʊstkɑːd ‖ -kɑːrd/ *n* a card, often with a picture on one side, on which a message can be sent by post

post·code /ˈpəʊstkəʊd/ *n BrE* a group of letters and numbers written at the end of an address so that letters will be delivered more quickly

post·date /ˌpəʊstˈdeɪt/ *v* postdated, postdating [T] to write a date later than the actual date of writing on a letter or cheque: *I'll give you a postdated cheque*

post·er /ˈpəʊstəʳ/ *n* a large printed notice or picture put up in a public place: *gazing at the posters in the travel agent's window*

pos·te·ri·or /pɒˈstɪərɪəʳ ‖ pɑː-/ *n* the part of your body that you sit on (a word which is often used in a humorous way)

pos·ter·i·ty /pɒˈsterᵻti ‖ pɑː-/ *n* [U] *fml* people who will be born and live after your own time

post·grad·u·ate /ˌpəʊstˈgrædjuᵻt ‖ -ˈgrædʒuᵻt/ *n* (also **graduate** *AmE*) a person doing advanced studies at a university, done after a first degree –**postgraduate** *adj* : *postgraduate studies*

post·hu·mous /ˈpɒstjᵿməs ‖ ˈpɑːstʃə-/ *adj* coming after a person's death –**posthumously** *adv* : *His last book was published posthumously.*

post·ing /ˈpəʊstɪŋ/ *n* being sent to a job in another town or country

post·man /ˈpəʊstmən/ *n* postmen /-mən/ a person employed to collect and deliver letters and parcels

post·mark /ˈpəʊstmɑːk ‖ -mɑːrk/ *n* an official mark made on letters or parcels, over the stamp, showing when and from where they are sent –**postmark** *v* [T] : *The parcel was postmarked London.*

post·mas·ter /ˈpəʊst,mɑːstəʳ ‖ -,mæ-/ *n* a person officially in charge of a post office; a female postmaster is usually called a **postmistress**

post·mor·tem /ˌpəʊstˈmɔːtəm ‖ -ˈmɔːr-/ *n* an examination of a dead body by doctors to discover the cause of death

post·natal /ˌpəʊstˈneɪtl/ *adj tech* concerning the time after a birth: *postnatal depression*

post of·fice /ˈ· ,··/ *n* **1** a building where you can buy stamps, send parcels, collect money paid to you by the government, and make certain payments **2 the Post Office** the national organization which provides these services

post·pone /pəʊsˈpəʊn/ *v* postponed, postponing [T] to move to a later time: *We're postponing our holiday* until *August.* –**postponement** *n* [C;U]

post·script /ˈpəʊst,skrɪpt/ *n* (also **P.S.** *infml*) a short addition to a letter, below the place where you have signed your name

pos·tu·late /ˈpɒstjᵿleɪt ‖ ˈpɑːstʃə-/ *v* postulated, postulating [T; + that] *fml* to suggest that something is true, often so that you can continue talking about a subject

pos·ture¹ /ˈpɒstʃəʳ ‖ ˈpɑːs-/ *n* **1** [U] the way a person holds their body when they are walking or sitting: *She's got very good posture.* **2** [C] a particular position of the body: *She photographed me in a relaxed posture.*

posture² *v* postured, posturing [I] to behave unnaturally in order to attract attention or deceive people

post·vi·ral syn·drome /ˌ··· ·· ˈ··/ *n* [U] an illness which makes you very tired and unable to work for many months

post·war /ˌpəʊstˈwɔːʳ ◂/ *adj* [only before a noun] in the time after a war

po·sy /ˈpəʊzi/ *n* posies a small bunch of flowers

pot¹ /pɒt ‖ pɑːt/ *n* **1** [C] a round container, used especially for cooking: *I've made a big pot of soup.* | *pots and pans* | *a cast-iron pot* –see picture on page 148 **2** [C] (also **potful** /ˈpɒtfʊl ‖ ˈpɑːt-/) the amount that a pot will hold: *A pot of tea for two, please.* **3 pots of money** *infml* a large amount of money **4** [U] *infml* MARIJUANA **5 go to pot** *infml* to become ruined from lack of care **6 take pot luck** *infml* to take what is offered, without having any choice:

*Come to dinner tonight – though I'm afraid you'll
have to take pot luck!*

pot² *v* -tt- [T] to put a plant in a pot filled with earth

po·ta·to /pə'teɪtəʊ/ *n* **potatoes** [C;U] a round white
vegetable with a thin brown or yellow skin, that is
cooked and served in many different ways: *I've
peeled the potatoes.* | *baked potatoes* | *Is there any
mashed potato left?* –see picture on page 344

potato chip /·'·· ·/ *n* (also **chip**) the usual American
and Australian word for a CRISP³

pot·bel·ly /'pɒt,beli ‖ 'pɑːt-/ *n* **potbellies** a large
round stomach (a word used to express disap-
proval, but usually used in a humorous way)

po·tent /'pəʊtənt/ *adj fml* **1** very effective: *a potent
argument* **2** having a strong effect on your body or
mind (used of medicines, drugs, or drinks) **3** able
to have sex (used of a man) –**potency** *n* [U]

po·ten·tate /'pəʊtənteɪt/ *n fml* a ruler with direct
power over his or her people

po·ten·tial¹ /pə'tenʃəl/ *adj* possibly going to happen
or develop, although not existing at present: *Every
seed is a potential plant.* | *She is seen as a potential
Prime Minister.* –**potentially** *adv*

potential² *n* [sing; U] the possibility for developing
or being developed: *a new product with a big sales
potential* | *She has great potential as a writer.*

pot·hole /'pɒthəʊl ‖ 'pɑːt-/ *n* **1** a deep hole in a rocky
area which often leads to caves underground **2** a
large hole in the surface of a road

pot·hol·ing /'pɒt,həʊlɪŋ ‖ 'pɑːt-/ *n* [U] the sport of
climbing down inside potholes –**potholer** *n*

po·tion /'pəʊʃən/ *n lit* a liquid mixture, given as
medicine, poison, or a magic charm: *a love potion*

pot·shot /'pɒt-ʃɒt ‖ 'pɑːt-ʃɑːt/ *n infml* a carelessly
aimed shot

pot·ted /'pɒtɪd ‖ 'pɑː-/ *adj* [only before a noun] **1**
cooked and preserved in a small pot (used of meat
or fish) **2** grown in a pot (used of a plant): *potted
palms* **3** produced in a short, simple form (a word
used of a book, often to express disapproval): *pot
ted biographies of world leaders*

pot·ter¹ /'pɒtəʳ ‖ 'pɑː-/ *n* a person who makes pots,
dishes, etc., out of baked clay using their hands

potter² *v*

potter about *phr v* [I] *infml* to spend time doing
unimportant things in an unhurried way: *I spent
the afternoon pottering about in the garden.*

pot·ter·y /'pɒtəri ‖ 'pɑː-/ *n* **1** [U] the work of a potter **2** [U] objects made out of baked clay: *Modern
pottery is usually decorated.* | *a pottery dish* **3** [C] a
place where pottery is made

pot·ty¹ /'pɒti ‖ 'pɑːti/ *adj* **pottier, pottiest** *BrE infml*
1 slightly mad: *That noise is driving me potty.* **2 to
be potty about** to like very much: *He's just potty
about her!*

potty² *n* **potties** a plastic pot for children to use as
a TOILET

pouch /paʊtʃ/ *n* **1** a small leather bag to hold
tobacco or other things **2** a pocket of skin in which
kangaroos (KANGAROO) and other animals carry
their young

pouf /puːf/ *n* (also **pouffe**) a drum-shaped low soft
seat

poul·tice /'pəʊltɪs/ *n* a soft heated mixture, spread
on a cloth and laid against your skin to reduce pain
or swelling

poul·try /'pəʊltri/ *n* **1** [pl] chickens and other farmyard birds kept for supplying eggs and meat **2** [U]

meat from chickens and other farmyard birds:
Poultry is quite cheap nowadays.

pounce /paʊns/ *v* **pounced, pouncing** [I] **1** to jump
on something in order to catch and eat it: *The lio-
ness suddenly pounced.* | *The cat pounced* **on** *the
bird.* **2** to jump out and catch: *Policemen were hiding in the bank, ready to pounce* **on** *the thieves.*

pound¹ /paʊnd/ *n* **1** the British unit of money,
divided into 100 pence: *Five pounds is usually writ-
ten £5.* | *a five-pound note* | *An eye test now costs ten
pounds.* **2 the pound** the value of British money
compared with the money of other countries:
*What's the current exchange rate of the pound
against the dollar?* **3** a unit for measuring weight,
equal to 0·454 kilograms: *Sugar is sold by the
pound.* | *Two pounds of apples, please.* | *a baby
weighing eight pounds three ounces (8lb 3oz)* **4** a
place where lost animals, or illegally parked cars,
are kept by the police **5** **-pounder** something
weighing a certain number of pounds: *I caught a
five-pounder the last time I went fishing.*

pound² *v* **1** [T] to crush something by hitting it
repeatedly with a heavy object: *This machine
pounds the stones into a powder.* **2** [I; + adv/prep; T]
to hit repeatedly, heavily, and noisily: *The stormy
waves pounded* **against** *the rocks.* | *He pounded the
table angrily.* **3 my heart pounded** a phrase used
when you have a very strong feeling, such as fear
or excitement: *My heart pounded* **with** *excitement.*
–**pounding** *n* [sing; U] : *the pounding of my heart*

pour /pɔːʳ/ *v* **1** [T] to cause a liquid or a loose substance to flow into or out of a container: *She poured
some sugar into a bowl.* | *Pour the dirty water away
outside.* **2** [T] (also **pour out**) to fill a glass or cup
with a drink: *Could you pour the tea?* | *I poured out
two cups of coffee.* **3 pour yourself/someone a
drink** to fill a glass or cup with a drink for yourself
or someone else: *He poured himself a stiff whisky.*
4 [I; + adv/prep] to flow steadily and rapidly: *Smoke
was pouring from the engine.* | *Water poured into the
boat.* | *At four o'clock children poured out of the
school.* **5** [I] to rain hard and steadily: *The rain
poured* **down** *all day.* | *We waited in the pouring
rain.* **6 it's pouring with rain** = it's raining very
hard

pour sthg ↔ out *v* [T] **1** to POUR (2) **2** to tell someone your thoughts or experiences, freely and
quickly: *He suddenly poured out all his troubles.*

pout /paʊt/ *v* [I] to push forward your lips in order
to show that you are annoyed or to attract sexual
interest –**pout** *n*

pov·er·ty /'pɒvəti ‖ 'pɑːvərti/ *n* [U] the state of being
poor: *families living in poverty*

poverty-strick·en /'··· ,··/ *adj* very poor

POW /,piː əʊ 'dʌbəljuː/ see PRISONER OF WAR:

pow·der¹ /'paʊdəʳ/ *n* **1** [C;U] a substance in the
form of very small grains: *That packet of white
powder the police found in his room turned out to be
cocaine.* | *These soap powders are all the same.* **2** [U]
a pleasant-smelling substance in this form which
you use on your skin: *baby powder* | *The only make-
up she uses is powder and lipstick.*

powder² *v* [T] to put face powder or TALCUM POWDER
on your skin: *John powdered the baby after her
bath.*

pow·dered /'paʊdəd ‖ -ərd/ *adj* **1** produced or dried
in the form of powder: *powdered milk* **2** covered
with powder: *powdered hair*

powder room /'·· ·/ *n AmE* a women's public
TOILET in a theatre, hotel, restaurant, or large shop

pow·der·y /ˈpaʊdəri/ *adj* like powder, or easily broken into powder

pow·er¹ /ˈpaʊər/ *n* **1** [sing; U] control over people, a place, or a situation: *Now I've got him in my power!* | *The British Queen doesn't have any real power.* **2 be in power** to govern or control a country: *This government has been in power for two years.* **3 come to power** to begin to be in control of the government: *She came to power in 1990.* **4 return someone to power** to give someone control of the government as the result of an election: *I'm hoping the Democratic Party will be returned to power.* **5 seize power** to take control of the government: *The army seized power in a coup d'état.* **6** [C] legal rights to act or official permission to do something: *He doesn't have the power to make a final decision.* | *The police now have greater powers than they used to.* **7** [U] (also **powers** [pl]) a physical ability or a skill: *the power of speech* | *I don't have the power to see into the future, you know.* **8 be in/ within someone's power** to be possible for someone to do: *I did everything in my power to help them.* **9** [C] a strong and important country or group: *a meeting of world powers* **10 the powers that be** *infml* the people in official positions who make decisions that change our lives (a word which is often used in a humorous way) **11** [U] a force that can be used to produce electricity or make a machine work: **b** electricity: *solar power* | *nuclear power* | *Switch on the power.* | *in darkness because of a power cut* **12** [U] force or strength: *the power of words* | *Japan's industrial power* **13 to the power of** multiplied by itself a particular number of times (used of a number, in MATHEMATICS): *2 to the power of 3, or 2³, means 2 × 2 × 2.* **14 -powered** using a certain type of ENERGY: *a nuclear-powered submarine*

power² *v* [T] to supply power to a vehicle or machine: *This train is powered by electricity.*

pow·er·ful /ˈpaʊəfəl‖ˈpaʊər-/ *adj* **1** very strong, or having great power: *a powerful swimmer* | *a meeting of the world's most powerful nations* | *The ship is driven by two powerful motors.* **2** having a strong effect: *The minister made a powerful speech.* | *a powerful drug* **–powerfully** *adv*

pow·er·less /ˈpaʊələs‖ˈpaʊər-/ *adj* **1** not having any power or influence **2 powerless to do something** completely unable to do something: *He was powerless to stop the accident.* **–powerlessly** *adv* **–powerlessness** *n* [U]

power sta·tion /ˈ··ˌ··/ *n* (also **power plant** /ˈ·· ·/) a large building in which electricity is made –see picture on page 246

pp a written abbreviation for **pages**: *see pp 15-37*

PR /piː ˈɑːr/ *n* [U] see PUBLIC RELATIONS

prac·ti·ca·ble /ˈpræktɪkəbəl/ *adj* that can be done successfully: *Is it practicable to try to grow crops in deserts?* –opposite **impracticable** **–practicably** *adv* **–practicability** /ˌpræktɪkəˈbɪlɪti/ *n* [U]

■ USAGE People are beginning to use **practical** with the same meaning as **practicable**; a **practical/practicable** plan or suggestion is one that will work. **Practicable** is not used of people.

prac·ti·cal¹ /ˈpræktɪkəl/ *adj* **1** concerned with real situations and actions, rather than with ideas: *She has finished her training but hasn't had any practical experience yet.* –see PRACTICABLE (USAGE) **2** sensible and good at dealing with real situations: *We've got to be practical and buy only what we can afford.* **3** good at doing or making things with your

hands: *My father is very clever, but he's not very practical.* **4** useful and suitable for a particular purpose: *a very practical little table that folds up out of the way when it is not needed* | *Their new carpet is beautiful, but I don't think white is a very practical colour.* **–practicality** /ˌpræktɪˈkælɪti/ *n* **practicalities** [C;U] : *Please stick to practicalities.*

practical² *n infml* a lesson or test in which you have to do or make something, instead of writing about it: *a chemistry practical*

practical joke /ˌ··· ˈ·/ *n* a trick played on someone to make them look silly and to amuse other people

prac·ti·cal·ly /ˈpræktɪkli/ *adv* **1** almost: *The holidays are practically over; there's only one day left.* **2** in a practical way

prac·tice¹ /ˈpræktɪs/ *v* **practiced, practicing** [I;T] the usual American spelling of PRACTISE¹

practice² *n* (also **practise** *AmE*) **1** [U] regularly repeated performance of an activity in order to improve your ability or skill: *It takes a lot of practice to become a good swimmer.* | *He's going to football practice after school.* | *The trainees now have six weeks teaching practice.* –see HABIT (USAGE) **2 out of practice** unable to do something well because of lack of practice **3 in practice** when something is actually done, rather than just talked about: *It sounded a good idea, but in practice it simply didn't work.* **4 put something into practice** to take action regarding something: *We've made our plans, and now we must put them into practice.* **5** [U] *fml* the usual way of doing something: *Tipping is common practice in most restaurants.* **6** [C] an activity or habit that is regularly repeated: *religious practices* **7** [C] the business of a doctor or lawyer

prac·tise¹ /ˈpræktɪs/ *n* the usual American spelling of PRACTISE²

practise² *v* **practised, practising** (also **practice** *AmE*) **1** [I;T] to regularly repeat an activity in order to improve your ability or skill: *She practises the piano for two hours every day.* | *I'm not very good at parking the car; I'll have to practise.* | *He's practising doing handstands.* **2** [T] *fml* to do: *an old custom still practised in the smaller communities* **3 practise what you preach** to do yourself what you are always telling other people to do **4** [I;T] to do the work of a doctor or lawyer: *She practises medicine.* | *He practises as a doctor.* | *a practising lawyer* **5** [T] to act according to the ideas and customs of your religion: *She's a practising Muslim.*

prac·tised /ˈpræktɪst/ *adj* (also **practiced** *AmE*) skilled because of having had a lot of practice: *a practised liar* | *Our mother was practised in the art of storytelling.*

prac·ti·tion·er /prækˈtɪʃənər/ *n* a person who works in a profession, especially a doctor or a lawyer: *medical practitioners*

prag·mat·ic /prægˈmætɪk/ *adj* dealing with matters in the way that seems best in the real situation, rather than following a principle or rule **–pragmatically** /-kli/ *adv*

prag·ma·tis·m /ˈprægmətɪzəm/ *n* [U] pragmatic ways of considering things **–pragmatist** *n*

prai·rie /ˈpreəri/ *n* a wide treeless grassy plain, especially in North America

praise¹ /preɪz/ *v* **praised, praising** [T] **1** to speak of someone or something with admiration and approval: *She was praised for her achievements as a sportswoman.* **2** *fml* or *lit* to offer thanks and honour to God, especially in song

praise² n **1** [U] expression of admiration: *His new film has received high praise from the critics.* **2** [U] *fml or lit* worship: *Let us give praise to God.* **3** *sing* the praises of to praise very strongly: *He's always singing your praises.*

praise·wor·thy /ˈpreɪzwɜːði ‖ -ɜːr-/ *adj fml* deserving praise −**praiseworthiness** n [U]

pram /præm/ n a four-wheeled carriage, pushed by hand, for a baby

prance /prɑːns ‖ præns/ v pranced, prancing [I] **1** (of a horse) to move making quick high steps **2** to move or walk in a proud or excited way that attracts attention: *Jane pranced about in front of the mirror trying on the clothes.*

prank /præŋk/ n a playful trick, not intended to harm anyone

prat·tle /ˈprætl/ v prattled, prattling [I] to talk continually about unimportant or meaningless things: *He prattled on about his job.* −**prattle** n [U]

prawn /prɔːn/ n a small pink sea animal that you can eat, larger than a SHRIMP

pray /preɪ/ v [I;T;+(that)] **1** to speak to God giving thanks, or asking for help: *They went to the mosque to pray.* | *I will pray to God for your safety.* | *They prayed that their enemies might be defeated.* **2** *infml* to hope very strongly: *We're praying for good weather on our wedding day.* | *He prayed that she wouldn't turn around.*

prayer /preəʳ/ n **1** [U] the act of praying to God: *They believe that prayer can bring peace to the world.* **2** [C] a solemn request made to God: *Her prayer was answered, and her parents came home safely.* **3** [C] a fixed form of words said to God: *The children said their prayers at bedtime.* | *a prayer book* **4** prayers [pl] a religious service for a particular group of people: *school prayers*

preach /priːtʃ/ v **1** [I;T] to give a religious talk as part of a service in church: *Christ preached to large crowds.* | *The priest preached a sermon on the importance of caring for the old and sick.* **2** [T] to advise or urge other people to accept something that you believe in: *She's always preaching socialism.* **3** [I] to give unwanted advice on matters of right and wrong: *The teacher preached at us about being lazy.* −**preacher** n

pre·am·ble /ˈpriːæmbəl/ n an introduction to a speech or piece of writing, stating its purpose, and often using too many words

pre·ar·range /ˌpriːəˈreɪndʒ/ v prearranged, prearranging [T] to arrange in advance: *The car arrived at a prearranged time.*

pre·car·i·ous /prɪˈkeəriəs/ *adj* unsafe and likely to fall: *John was in a precarious position at the top of the ladder.* −**precariously** *adv* −**precariousness** n [U]

pre·cau·tion /prɪˈkɔːʃən/ n an action done to avoid something dangerous or unpleasant happening: *You should make a copy of the disk, as a precaution.* | *They've taken every precaution against theft.* −**precautionary** *adj* : *a precautionary X-ray*

pre·cede /prɪˈsiːd/ v preceded, preceding [I;T] *fml* to come or go before someone or something else: *The wedding was preceded by weeks of preparation.* | *Several bodyguards preceded the President into the palace.* −**preceding** *adj* [always before a noun] : *This is described in detail in the preceding chapter.*

pre·ce·dence /ˈpresɪdəns/ n [U] **1** the right of something to be put first because it is more important than something else: *The needs of the community must take precedence over the wishes of*

individuals. **2** in order of precedence in order of importance

pre·ce·dent /ˈpresɪdənt/ n [C;U] an action or decision that is used as an example for a similar action or decision at a later time: *The judge's decision has set a precedent for women seeking equal pay.*

pre·cept /ˈpriːsept/ n a rule which guides behaviour

pre·cinct /ˈpriːsɪŋkt/ n **1** [C] *BrE* a shopping area in a town, where no cars are allowed: *a new shopping precinct* **2** [C] *AmE* a division of a town or city for election or police purposes **3** precincts [pl] the enclosed space that surrounds important buildings: *It's quiet within the precincts of the old college.*

pre·cious¹ /ˈpreʃəs/ *adj* **1** of great value because of being rare or expensive: *Water is a very precious resource.* **2** very special to you: *I have some precious memories of our time together.* **3** delicate and rather unnatural in manner: *a rather precious young man* **4** a word you use when you want to show your annoyance concerning something that someone else thinks is important: *I wish you'd shut up about your precious car!*

precious² *adv* precious few, precious little very few or very little: *We have precious little time left.*

precious met·al /ˌ·· ˈ·-/ n [C;U] a valuable metal, such as gold or silver

precious stone /ˌ·· ˈ·/ n a valuable jewel, such as a diamond or EMERALD

pre·ci·pice /ˈpresɪpəs/ n a steep side of a high mountain or cliff

pre·cip·i·tate¹ /prɪˈsɪpɪteɪt/ v precipitated, precipitating [T] *fml* to make something happen quickly and suddenly: *the fears of the public which precipitated the great economic crash of 1929*

pre·cip·i·tate² /prɪˈsɪpɪtət/ *adj fml* done in a hurry, without thinking −**precipitately** *adv*

pre·cip·i·tous /prɪˈsɪpɪtəs/ *adj* dangerously steep

pré·cis /ˈpreɪsiː ‖ preɪˈsiː/ n [plural is précis /ˈpreɪsiːz ‖ preɪˈsiːz/] a short piece of writing which gives only the main points of a longer piece

pre·cise /prɪˈsaɪs/ *adj* **1** exact and correct: *The measurements need to be very precise.* **2** to be precise a phrase you use when you are adding slightly more exact information to something you have just said: *It's a little after three o'clock. Five past three, to be precise.* **3** careful about small details: *She was very precise in her calculations.*

pre·cise·ly /prɪˈsaɪsli/ *adv* **1** exactly: *She didn't know precisely how he made his money.* **2** a word used to show you agree with what has been said: *"So you think it was a mistake?" "Precisely."*

pre·ci·sion¹ /prɪˈsɪʒən/ n (also preciseness /prɪˈsaɪsnəs/) [U] exactness: *The distance to the moon has been measured with great precision.*

precision² *adj* [only before another noun] **1** made or done with great exactness: *precision bombing* **2** used for producing exact results: *precision engineering*

pre·clude /prɪˈkluːd/ v precluded, precluding [T] *fml* to make impossible: *These terrorist attacks preclude any prospect of a peaceful settlement.*

pre·co·cious /prɪˈkəʊʃəs/ *adj* showing unusually early development or behaviour in a way that is too grown up (used of a child) −**precociousness, precocity** /prɪˈkɒsəti‖-ˈkɑː-/ n [U]

pre·con·ceived /ˌpriːkənˈsiːvd◂/ *adj* formed in advance, without enough knowledge or experience to be true or fair (used of an idea) −**preconception** /-kənˈsepʃən/ n : *I had a lot of preconceptions about America, but when I actually went there, I loved it!*

pre·con·di·tion /ˌpriːkənˈdɪʃən/ n something that must be agreed to in advance if something else is to happen: *The management have laid down certain preconditions to talks.*

pre·cur·sor /priˈkɜːsər ‖ -ˈkɜːr-/ n fml something that exists before something else and leads to it or develops into it: *Here it is. The precursor of the modern car!*

pred·a·tor /ˈpredətər/ n an animal that kills and eats other animals

pred·a·to·ry /ˈpredətəri ‖ -tɔːri/ adj 1 living by killing and eating other animals 2 trying to take advantage of other people in order to gain something: *Tourists should watch out for predatory shopkeepers.*

pre·de·ces·sor /ˈpriːdɪˌsesər ‖ ˈpre-/ n 1 a person who held a position before someone else: *Our new doctor is much younger than his predecessor.* 2 something which has now been followed by something else: *This latest plan to save the company seems to me no better than any of its predecessors.*

pre·des·ti·na·tion /priˌdestɪˈneɪʃən, ˌpriːdes-/ n [U] the belief that God or fate has decided everything that will happen, and that no human effort can change things

pre·des·tined /priˈdestɪnd/ adj fml decided in advance by God or fate: *I felt we were predestined to meet.*

pre·de·ter·mine /ˌpriːdɪˈtɜːmɪn ‖ -ɜːr-/ v predetermined, predetermining [T] to fix in advance: *The colour of a person's eyes is predetermined by those of his parents.*

pre·dic·a·ment /prɪˈdɪkəmənt/ n a difficult or unpleasant situation in which you must decide what to do

pred·i·cate /ˈpredɪkət/ n the part of a sentence which tells you about the subject: *In "She is an artist", "is an artist" is the predicate.*

pre·dic·a·tive /prɪˈdɪkətɪv ‖ ˈpredɪkeɪ-/ adj coming after a verb (used of an adjective or phrase): *In "She is happy", "happy" is a predicative adjective.* –compare ATTRIBUTIVE

pre·dict /prɪˈdɪkt/ v [T;+(that)] to say in advance that something will happen: *A fortune-teller predicted that she would become famous.* | *Weather forecasters are predicting storms over the weekend.* | *They can't predict when it must occur.*

pre·dic·ta·ble /prɪˈdɪktəbəl/ adj not being or doing anything unexpected (a word sometimes used to show disapproval): *I'd say his reaction was entirely predictable!* | *Honestly, George, you're so predictable!* –opposite **unpredictable** –**predictably** adv –**predictability** /prɪˌdɪktəˈbɪlɪti/ n [U]

pre·dic·tion /prɪˈdɪkʃən/ n 1 [C] a statement that something is likely to happen in the future: *He made several wildly inaccurate predictions.* 2 [U] the act of saying in advance what will happen

pre·di·lec·tion /ˌpriːdɪˈlekʃən ‖ ˌpredlˈek-/ n fml a special liking: *Charles has always had a predilection for expensive clothes.*

pre·dis·pose /ˌpriːdɪˈspəʊz/ v predisposed, predisposing [T] fml to influence someone in advance, in a particular way

pre·dis·po·si·tion /ˌpriːdɪspəˈzɪʃən/ n fml a predisposition to/towards something a tendency to act in a particular way, or to feel or suffer a particular thing

pre·dom·i·nance /prɪˈdɒmɪnəns ‖ -ˈdɑː-/ n [U] fml 1 a greater number of something than of other similar things: *the recent predominance of women in the*

movement 2 the most influence or power: *The Japanese have long had predominance in the world's electronics markets.*

pre·dom·i·nant /prɪˈdɒmɪnənt ‖ -ˈdɑː-/ adj most powerful, noticeable, or important: *I'd say death is the predominant theme of her paintings.*

pre·dom·i·nant·ly /prɪˈdɒmɪnəntli ‖ -ˈdɑː-/ adv mostly or mainly: *The votes were predominantly in support of the government.*

pre·dom·i·nate /prɪˈdɒmɪneɪt ‖ -ˈdɑː-/ v predominated, predominating [I] to be the most noticeable or influential, or exist in the greatest numbers

pre·em·i·nent /priːˈemɪnənt/ adj fml above all others in importance or in having a particular quality or ability: *a lawyer who is preeminent in his field* –**preeminently** adv –**preeminence** n [U]

pre·empt /priːˈempt/ v [T] to prevent something by taking action in advance which makes it ineffective or impossible

preen /priːn/ v 1 **preen itself** (of a bird) to clean or smooth itself or its feathers with its beak 2 **preen yourself** to spend a long time making yourself look neat and tidy (a word usually used to express disapproval)

pre·fab /ˈpriːfæb ‖ ˌpriːˈfæb/ n infml a small house made from parts prepared in a factory

pre·fab·ri·ca·ted /priːˈfæbrɪkeɪtɪd/ adj made of parts prepared in a factory ready for fitting together later (used of a building)

pref·ace[1] /ˈprefɪs/ n an introduction to a book

preface[2] v prefaced, prefacing [T] to provide a book or speech with an introduction

pre·fect /ˈpriːfekt/ n an older pupil who helps control other pupils, in some British schools

pre·fer /prɪˈfɜːr/ v -rr- [T] 1 to choose one thing rather than another because you like it better: *Some coffee? Or would you prefer tea?* | *I'd prefer to live abroad if I could.* | *Richard prefers riding a bike to driving.* | *I think she'd prefer you not to ask that question.* | *We'd prefer that you didn't say anything about it just yet.*
□ USEFUL PATTERNS to prefer something to something else; to prefer to do something; to prefer doing something; to prefer someone to do something; to prefer that…
2 **prefer charges** fml to officially charge someone with a crime

pref·e·ra·ble /ˈprefərəbəl/ adj more suitable, or that you like better than something else: *We accept credit cards, but cash or a cheque would be preferable.* | *Anything is preferable to having her stay for the whole week!* –**preferably** adv : *Can we meet for lunch tomorrow? Preferably an early one.*

pref·e·rence /ˈprefərəns/ n 1 [C;U] a liking for one thing rather than another: *"Would you like to sit on the left or the right?" "It doesn't matter; I have no great preference."* 2 [U] special favour or consideration shown to someone: *In considering people for this job, we have to give preference to those with some experience.*

pref·e·ren·tial /ˌprefəˈrenʃəl/ adj [always before a noun] giving, receiving, or showing special consideration: *The minister admitted that he gave preferential treatment to people from his own party.*

pre·fix /ˈpriːfɪks/ n a letter or group of letters that is put at the beginning of a word to change its meaning or its use: *The prefix in "refill" is "re-", meaning "again". So "refill" means "to fill again".* –compare SUFFIX

preg·nan·cy /ˈpregnənsi/ n pregnancies [C;U] the condition of being pregnant: *It is unwise to smoke during pregnancy.* | *She had a difficult pregnancy.*

preg·nant /ˈpregnənt/ adj 1 having a baby developing in your body (used of a woman or female animal): *She is five months pregnant.* | *She was pregnant with her second child at the time.* 2 [always before a noun] full of important but unexpressed meaning: *His words were followed by a pregnant pause.*

pre·his·tor·ic /ˌpriːhɪˈstɒrɪk ‖ -ˈstɔː-, -ˈstɑː-/ adj of a time before history was written down: *prehistoric art* –**prehistory** /priːˈhɪstəri/ n [U]

pre·judge /ˌpriːˈdʒʌdʒ/ v prejudged, prejudging [T] to form an opinion about someone or something before knowing or examining all the facts –**prejudgment, prejudgement** n [C;U]

prej·u·dice¹ /ˈpredʒ꜕dʒ꜕s/ n [C;U] unfair feeling or opinion, formed without enough thought or knowledge, or as the result of fear or distrust: *A judge must be completely free from prejudice.* | *He admits that he has a prejudice against women drivers.*

prejudice² v prejudiced, prejudicing [T] 1 to influence someone to have an unfair opinion about something: *The stories I had heard about his father prejudiced me against him.* 2 to harm someone's case, or expectations: *Your bad spelling may prejudice your chances of getting this job.*

prej·u·diced /ˈpredʒ꜕dʒ꜕st/ adj having an unfair feeling or opinion: *She doesn't think Italian wine is very good, but then, as she's French, she's prejudiced!*

prel·ate /ˈprel꜕t/ n a priest of very high rank

pre·lim·i·na·ry¹ /prɪˈlɪm꜕nəri ‖ -neri/ n preliminaries something done first, to prepare for a later thing: *There are a lot of preliminaries to be gone through before you can visit the prison.*

preliminary² adj [always before a noun] coming first, to prepare for something more important later: *The team must pass the preliminary competition before they can enter the final.*

prel·ude /ˈprelju:d/ n [sing] 1 something that comes before and acts as an introduction to something more important: *The political crisis may be a prelude to civil war.* 2 a short piece of music that introduces a large musical work

pre·mar·i·tal /priːˈmær꜕təl/ adj happening before marriage

pre·ma·ture /ˈpremətʃər, -tʃuər, ˌpreməˈtʃuər ‖ ˌpriːməˈtʊər/ adj 1 happening before the natural or expected time: *His premature death at the age of 32 is a great loss.* 2 born before expected (used of a baby): *She was a tiny baby, six weeks premature.* 3 done too early or too soon: *I think the decision was a bit premature.* –**prematurely** adv

pre·med·i·tat·ed /priːˈmed꜕teɪt꜕d ‖ prɪ-/ adj planned in advance: *premeditated murder*

prem·i·er¹ /ˈpremiər ‖ prɪˈmɪər/ adj [always before a noun] fml most important: *Britain's premier industry*

premier² n the head of the government of a country (used especially in newspapers): *the Irish Premier* –**premiership** n [U]

prem·i·ere /ˈpremiər ‖ prɪˈmɪər/ n (also première) the first public performance of a play or a film

prem·ise /ˈprem꜕s/ n fml a statement or idea that you consider is true and on which you base your reasoning: *The law is based on the premise that people are innocent until they are proved to be guilty.*

prem·is·es /ˈprem꜕s꜕z/ n [pl] 1 the buildings and land that a property or business consist of: *I have warned you before to keep off my premises!* | *The company is moving to new premises.* 2 **on the premises** in the building: *No smoking on the premises, please.*

pre·mi·um /ˈpriːmiəm/ n 1 a payment made to buy insurance 2 **at a premium: a** at a higher price than usual **b** difficult to get, because of being wanted by many people: *During the summer, hotel rooms are at a premium.* 3 **put a premium on something** to regard a quality or action as very important

pre·mo·ni·tion /ˌpreməˈnɪʃən, ˌpriː-/ n a feeling that something bad is going to happen: *The day before her accident, she had a premonition of danger.*

pre·na·tal /ˌpriːˈneɪtl/ adj the usual American word for ANTENATAL

pre·oc·cu·pa·tion /priːˌɒkj꜕ˈpeɪʃən ‖ -,ɑːk-/ n 1 [sing;U] the state of mind in which you think about something so much that you forget about other things: *his total preoccupation with his health* 2 [C] something which you think about a lot

pre·oc·cu·pied /priːˈɒkj꜕paɪd ‖ -ˈɑːk-/ adj thinking or worrying about something so that you forget about other things

pre·oc·cu·py /priːˈɒkj꜕paɪ ‖ -ˈɑːk-/ v preoccupied, preoccupying [T] to fill your thoughts so much that you forget about other things

prep /prep/ n [U] BrE infml school work that is done at home

prep·a·ra·tion /ˌprepəˈreɪʃən/ n 1 [U] the act of making something ready: *Teachers have a lot of preparation to do.* | *Today we're studying food preparation and handling.* 2 **in preparation: a** being made ready: *Plans for the new school are now in preparation.* **b** getting ready: *Paul is studying hard in preparation for his exams.* 3 **preparations** [pl] arrangements for a future event: *They've started making preparations for the wedding.* 4 [C] a mixture of substances made for use as a medicine, COSMETIC, etc.: *beauty preparations*

pre·par·a·to·ry /prɪˈpærətəri ‖ -tɔːri/ adj [only before a noun] done first, in order to prepare for something else: *some preparatory talks before drawing up the contract*

preparatory school /·ˈ····· ·/ n (also **prep school** infml) [C;U] a private school in Britain for young pupils

pre·pare /prɪˈpeər/ v prepared, preparing 1 [T] to make something ready for a future action or action: *She prepared the room for the guests.* | *The training will prepare you to work with computers.* 2 [I] to get ready to do something: *They are busy preparing to go on holiday.* | *Will you help me prepare for the party?* 3 [T] to get food ready to eat: *My job was to help prepare the vegetables.* | *Grandma prepared us a delicious meal.* 4 [T] to get someone ready to accept a new idea or situation: *Prepare yourself for some bad news.*

pre·pared /prɪˈpeəd ‖ -ˈpeərd/ adj 1 got ready in advance: *The chairman read out a prepared statement.* 2 **be prepared to do something** to be willing to: *I'm not prepared to accept less than £500 for the car.*

pre·pon·de·rance /prɪˈpɒndərəns ‖ -ˈpɑːn-/ n [sing] fml more of one type of person or thing than of another: *There is now a preponderance of women students at the college.* –**preponderantly** adv

prep·o·si·tion /ˌprepəˈzɪʃən/ n a word used with a noun or PRONOUN to show its connection with another word: *In "He walked into the house" and*

"She succeeded by working hard", "into" and "by" are prepositions. –see Study Note on page 687 –**prepositional** adj : *"In bed" and "on top" are prepositional phrases.*

pre·pos·ter·ous /prɪ'pɒstərəs ‖ -'pɑːs-/ adj completely unreasonable and improbable: *That's the most preposterous idea I've ever heard!* –**preposterously** adv

prep school /'· ·/ n [C;U] infml see PREPARATORY SCHOOL

pre·req·ui·site /priː'rekwɪzɪt/ n fml something that is necessary before something else can happen or be done: *A good education is not a prerequisite for success in business.* | *working in every part of the store as a prerequisite to her management training*

pre·rog·a·tive /prɪ'rɒgətɪv ‖ -'rɑː-/ n fml a special right that a particular person has: *It is the President's prerogative to pardon a criminal.*

pres·age /'presɪdʒ, prɪ'seɪdʒ/ v presaged, presaging [T not in progressive forms] fml to be a warning of something that will happen

Pres·by·te·ri·an /ˌprezbɪ'tɪəriən/ n a member of a PROTESTANT Church governed by a body of official people all of equal rank, as in Scotland

pre·scribe /prɪ'skraɪb/ v prescribed, prescribing [T] 1 to say what medicine or treatment someone needs when they are ill: *The doctor prescribed some medicine for the baby's cough.* | *Take one tablet a day, or as prescribed by your doctor.* 2 fml to order something to be done: *What punishment does the law prescribe for such a crime?*

pre·scrip·tion /prɪ'skrɪpʃən/ n 1 a special written order from a doctor which allows you to get medicine: *Take your prescription to the hospital pharmacist's and they'll make it up for you.* | *Children under 16 can get free prescriptions.* 2 **on prescription** on the order of a doctor: *This drug is only available on prescription.*

pres·ence /'prezəns/ n 1 [U] the state of being present at a particular place: *She was so quiet that her presence was hardly noticed.* | *Your presence is requested at the meeting on Thursday.* –opposite **absence** 2 **in the presence of someone, in someone's presence** seen or heard by someone: *The performance is to be in the presence of the Queen.* 3 [C] a spirit or influence that cannot be seen but is felt to be near: *I could sense a strange presence in the room.* 4 [sing;U] personal qualities that have a strong effect on other people (a word used to express approval): *a man of great presence* 5 [sing] soldiers or police at a particular place: *There is a strong military presence on the frontier.*

pres·ence of mind /ˌ··· · '·/ n [U] the ability to act calmly and quickly in a dangerous situation: *A fire started in the kitchen, and John had the presence of mind to turn off the gas immediately.*

pre·sent¹ /prɪ'zent/ v [T] 1 to give something to someone, especially at an official ceremony: *He presented a silver cup to the winner.* | *When she left the company, the director presented her with a set of golf clubs.* 2 to be the cause of a problem or difficulty: *His resignation presented us with rather a tricky situation.* 3 to give or show to people in a formal way: *The committee is presenting its report next week.* 4 to show to the public in a theatre, cinema, etc.: *The local theatre company is presenting "Hamlet" next week.* 5 to introduce a television or radio show 6 fml to introduce someone in an official way, especially to someone important: *May I present Mr Jobbings?* 7 **present itself** (of something possible) to happen: *The opportunity I had been waiting for suddenly presented itself.*

pres·ent² /'prezənt/ n 1 something that you give to someone as a gift, often on a special occasion: *They unwrapped their Christmas presents.* 2 **the present** the time that is happening now: *You should live in the present – don't worry about the future.* 3 **the present, the present tense** the tense of a verb which expresses the time that is now or the time of speaking 4 **at present** at this time 5 **for the present** now but not necessarily in the future: *Let's leave it as it is for the present.*

pres·ent³ /'prezənt/ adj 1 [never before a noun] in a particular place at a particular time: *How many people were present at the meeting?* | *Small amounts of the gas are present in the atmosphere.* –opposite **absent** 2 [only before a noun] existing now: *It is very difficult to sell a house in the present economic climate.*

pre·sen·ta·ble /prɪ'zentəbəl/ adj in a good enough state to be seen, shown, or judged: *He looked very presentable in his new suit.* –**presentably** adv

pre·sen·ta·tion /ˌprezən'teɪʃən ‖ ˌprizzən-, -zən-/ n 1 [C;U] the act or action of giving something to someone at a ceremony or an official occasion: *The presentation of prizes will begin at three o'clock.* 2 [U] the way something looks: *Your essays are good, but you should pay more attention to presentation.* 3 [C] the act of giving or showing something to people in a formal way: *She will give a presentation on her company at the sales conference.*

pres·ent-day /ˌprezənt 'deɪ ◂/ adj [only before a noun] of the period of time that is happening now: *the architecture of present-day Egypt*

pre·sent·er /prɪ'zentəʳ/ n a person who introduces a television or radio show

pre·sen·ti·ment /prɪ'zentɪmənt/ n fml an unexplained uncomfortable feeling that something bad is going to happen

pres·ent·ly /'prezəntli/ adv 1 soon: *The doctor will be here presently.* 2 after some time: *They sat talking through the long, hot afternoon. Presently, an old man approached them.* 3 now: *The doctor is presently writing a book.*

present par·ti·ci·ple /ˌ·· '····/ n tech a form of a verb which ends in -ing and can be used in compound forms of the verb to show PROGRESSIVE tenses (such as barking in *The dog is barking*) or sometimes as an adjective (such as barking in *a barking dog*)

pres·er·va·tion /ˌprezə'veɪʃən ‖ -zər-/ n [U] 1 the act or action of keeping something unharmed or unchanged: *The police are responsible for the preservation of law and order.* 2 the state of being or remaining in a particular condition after a long time: *The old building is in a good state of preservation, except for the wooden floors.*

pre·ser·va·tive /prɪ'zɜːvətɪv ‖ -ɜːr-/ n [C;U] a chemical substance used to keep something, especially food, in good condition for a long time

pre·serve¹ /prɪ'zɜːv ‖ -ɜːrv/ v preserved, preserving [T] 1 to keep someone or something alive or safe from destruction: *The Town Council has spent a lot of money to preserve this remarkable old building.* 2 to cause a condition to remain unchanged: *It is the duty of the police to preserve public order.* 3 to keep something, especially food, in good condition for a long time by some special treatment: *preserved fruit* | *The Ancient Egyptians knew how to preserve dead bodies from decay.*

preserve² n 1 [C;U] old fash (also **jam**) a sweet food made from fruit that is often spread on bread 2 [C] an activity considered to be limited to a certain person or group of people: *Politics is still very much a male preserve.*

pre·side /prɪˈzaɪd/ v **presided, presiding** [I] to be in charge and lead: *The presiding officer reads out the result of an election.*

preside over sthg *phr v* [T] to be in charge of a group of people gathered for a formal purpose: *The meeting was presided over by Mr Jarrett, the chairman.*

pres·i·den·cy /ˈprezɪdənsi/ n **presidencies 1** the position of president: *Roosevelt was elected four times to the presidency of the US.* **2** the length of time a person is president: *two wars during his presidency*

pres·i·dent /ˈprezɪdənt/ n (also **President**) **1** the head of government in many modern states that do not have a king or queen: *the President of France* | *President Bush* **2** the head of a club or important organization: *the President of the Board of Trade* **3** *AmE* the head of a business, bank, or company –**presidential** /ˌprezɪˈdenʃəl◂/ *adj* [only before a noun] : *presidential advisers*

press¹ /pres/ v **1** [T] to push firmly and steadily: *Press this button to start the engine.* | *She pressed her face up against the window.* **2** [T] to put weight onto something in order to flatten it: *She pressed the flowers between the pages of a book.* **3** [T] to crush fruit in order to get juice out: *The olives are pressed in this machine.* **4** [T] to give clothes a smooth surface and a sharp fold by using a hot iron **5** [T] to hold firmly as a sign of friendship or love: *He pressed my hand warmly when we met.* **6** [I;T] to strongly try to persuade or demand: *She pressed her guest to stay a little longer.* | *The company is pressing* **for** *a decision.*

press on with sthg *phr v* (also **press ahead** with sthg *fml*) [T] to continue doing something without delay: *Let's press on with our work.*

press² n **1 the press** [U; + sing/pl verb] newspapers and magazines, and the reporters who write for them: *the local press* | *a press photographer* | *The press have been invited to listen to the minister's statement.* **2** [sing] a good or bad opinion of an event or person, given by newspapers, radio, or television: *The play had a good press.* **3** [C] see PRINTING PRESS **4** [C] (also **Press**) a business for printing books and magazines: *the Cambridge University Press* **5 go to press** to start being printed **6** [C] an act of smoothing an item of clothing with a hot iron **7** [C] a machine used for pressing clothes

press con·fer·ence /ˈ· ˌ···/ n (also **news conference**) a meeting during which an important person gives a statement or answers questions

press cut·ting /ˈ· ˌ···/ n a picture or piece of writing cut out of a newspaper or magazine

pressed /prest/ *adj* **pressed for** not having very much: *I'm rather pressed for time this morning, so I'll get back to you later.*

press-gang¹ /ˈpresgæŋ/ n a band of sailors who in former times seized men for service in the navy

pressgang² v [T] *infml* to force someone to do something unwillingly

pres·sing /ˈpresɪŋ/ *adj* demanding or needing urgent attention: *Pressing business matters prevented her from taking a holiday.*

press·man /ˈpresmæn/ n **pressmen** /-mən/ *BrE infml* a newspaper reporter

press-stud /ˈ· ·/ n a small round metal fastener for clothing

press-up /ˈ· ·/ n a form of exercise in which you lie face down and push your body up with your arms

pres·sure¹ /ˈpreʃəʳ/ n **1** [U] the force that is produced by the weight of one thing pressing against another: *The pressure of the water caused the banks of the river to burst.* **2** [C;U] the strength of the force produced by a gas or liquid pressing against something: *I'd better check the pressure in the tyres.* | *Low atmospheric pressure means it may rain.* **3 put pressure on, bring pressure to bear on** to use strong influence or force on someone to make something happen: *We must put pressure on the government to change this law.* **4** [C;U] the demands of your work, family, or style of life which cause worry and problems: *the pressures of modern life* **5 under pressure** having a lot of demands made on you at the same time: *He definitely works better under a certain amount of pressure.*

pressure² v **pressured, pressuring** [T] see PRESSURIZE

pressure cook·er /ˈ··· ˌ··/ n a tightly covered metal cooking pot in which food cooks very quickly by the pressure of hot steam

pressure group /ˈ··· ·/ n [+ sing/pl verb] a group of people that actively tries to influence public opinion and government action

pres·sur·ize /ˈpreʃəraɪz/ v **pressurized, pressurizing** (also **pressurise** *BrE*) [T] **1** (also **pressure**) to try to make someone do something by means of forceful demands or influence: *These government measures have pressurized the farmers into producing more milk.* **2** to control the air pressure inside an aircraft so that the pressure does not become much lower than that on Earth: *a pressurized cabin*

pres·tige /preˈstiːʒ/ n [U] general respect or admiration felt for someone or something because of their position, history, or quality: *The old universities of Oxford and Cambridge still have a lot of prestige.*

pres·ti·gious /preˈstɪdʒəs ‖ -ˈstiː-, -ˈstɪ-/ *adj* having or bringing prestige

pre·su·ma·bly /prɪˈzjuːməbli ‖ -ˈzuː-/ *adv* it is reasonable to suppose that: *Presumably there's a good reason for her absence, as she doesn't usually stay away from work.*

pre·sume /prɪˈzjuːm ‖ -ˈzuːm/ v **presumed, presuming 1** [I;T;+(that)] to suppose that something is true, without having direct proof or certainty: *From the way they talked I presumed they were married.* | *He went missing in the war and is presumed dead.* | *This course presumes you already know something about computers.* **2 presume to do something** *fml* to dare to do something which you have no right to do: *Do not presume to tell me how to do my job!*

pre·sump·tion /prɪˈzʌmpʃən/ n **1** [C] an act of supposing that something is true: *The book is full of false presumptions.* **2** [U] self-confident behaviour in doing something you have no right to do: *I was furious at his presumption in telling me we were engaged.*

pre·sump·tu·ous /prɪˈzʌmptʃuəs/ *adj* having no right to do something, but supposing you can do it because you are very self-confident (a word used to express disapproval) –**presumptuously** *adv*

pre·sup·pose /ˌpriːsəˈpəʊz/ v **presupposed, presupposing** [T;+that] to suppose or consider one thing to be true before another thing can also be true: *All these plans presuppose that the bank will be willing to lend us the money.* –**presupposition** /-sʌpəˈzɪʃən/ n [C;U]

pre·tence /prɪˈtens ‖ ˈpriːtens/ n (also **pretense** *AmE*) [sing;U] an action that is intended to deceive people or make them believe something that is not true: *He made a pretence of enjoying the food.* | *How much longer are you going to keep up this pretence that you're ill?*

pre·tend /prɪ'tend/ v [I; +(that)] **1** to make something appear true, or real, when it is not: *She pretended she didn't know me when I passed her in the street.* | *He pretended to be asleep.* | *She wasn't really crying; she was only pretending.*
□ USEFUL PATTERNS to pretend to do something; to pretend that...
2 to imagine as a game when you are a child: *Let's pretend we're on the moon!*

pre·tend·er /prɪ'tendə^r/ n a person who makes a claim to some high position, such as to be the rightful king

pre·ten·sion /prɪ'tenʃən/ n **1** [C] a claim to possess certain skills, qualities, or importance: *I have no pretensions as an artist, but I enjoy painting.* **2** [U] *fml* the quality of being pretentious

pre·ten·tious /prɪ'tenʃəs/ adj trying or claiming to be more important or clever than is really the case: *His style of writing is really pretentious.* –**pretentiously** adv –**pretentiousness** n [U]

pre·text /'priːtekst/ n a reason given for doing something which hides the real reason: *I went to see Richard, under the pretext of wanting to borrow a book.* | *She called round on some pretext or other.* –see EXCUSE² (USAGE)

pret·ty /'prɪti/ adj prettier, prettiest **1** attractive and nice to look at (used of a woman, a child, or something small): *She looks much prettier with long hair than with short hair.* | *What a pretty little garden!* | *That's a pretty colour.* | *a pretty girl* –see BEAUTIFUL (USAGE) **2** sitting pretty *infml* in a favourable situation (used of a person) –**prettily** adv –**prettiness** n [U]

pretty² adv infml **1** to quite a large degree: *It's pretty cold today.* **2** pretty much, pretty well almost: *The work is pretty much finished.*

pre·vail /prɪ'veɪl/ v [I] *fml* **1** to exist or be widespread: *A belief in magic still prevails among some tribes.* **2** to succeed after a struggle: *Justice prevailed when they found him guilty and he was sent to prison.*
prevail upon sbdy *phr v* (also **prevail on** sbdy) [T] *fml* to succeed in persuading someone to do something

pre·vail·ing /prɪ'veɪlɪŋ/ adj [always before a noun] **1** the most common or general in a particular place or time: *prevailing attitudes among young people* **2 a prevailing wind** a wind that blows over an area most of the time

prev·a·lent /'prevələnt/ adj fml existing commonly, generally, or widely: *Eye diseases are prevalent in some tropical countries.* –**prevalence** n [U]

pre·var·i·cate /prɪ'værɪkeɪt/ v prevaricated, **prevaricating** [I] *fml* to try to hide the truth by not answering questions clearly or completely truthfully –**prevarication** /prɪ,værɪ'keɪʃən/ n [C;U]

pre·vent /prɪ'vent/ v [T] **1** to stop something from happening: *I couldn't prevent the accident.* | *What can we do to prevent this disease spreading?*
□ USEFUL PATTERNS to prevent something; to prevent something from happening
2 to stop someone from doing something: *The police prevented them from leaving the country.* –**preventable** adj: *Most of these cancers are entirely preventable.*

pre·ven·tion /prɪ'venʃən/ n [U] the action of stopping something happening: *crime prevention* | *a society for the prevention of cruelty to children*

pre·ven·tive /prɪ'ventɪv/ adj (also **preventative** /-tətɪv/) intended to prevent something, such as crime or illness: *preventive medicine*

pre·view /'priːvjuː/ n **1** a private showing of paintings or a film before they are shown to the general public **2** a short written description of a book or film that is about to come out

pre·vi·ous /'priːviəs/ adj [always before a noun] **1** happening or existing at an earlier time: *They gave me the job, even though I had no previous experience.* | *We had a previous engagement and so we couldn't go to the party.* **2** coming just before the time or place you are talking about: *She had telephoned him the previous day.* **3 previous to** *fml* before

pre·vi·ous·ly /'priːviəsli/ adv before that: *Pym, of no fixed address, was found guilty of driving without due care and attention. He had previously been convicted of drunken driving.* –see AGO (USAGE)

pre·war /,priː'wɔː^r◂/ adj belonging to the time before a war, especially the First or Second World Wars: *pre-war Europe*

prey¹ /preɪ/ n [U] **1** an animal that is hunted and eaten by another animal **2 a bird of prey** a bird which lives by killing and eating other animals **3** someone or something that is used or deceived by someone else: *People like her are easy prey for a clever salesman.* **4 fall prey to** to become used or controlled by

prey² v
prey on sbdy/sthg *phr v* (also **prey upon** sbdy/sthg) [T] **1** (of an animal) to hunt and eat: *Cats prey on birds and mice.* **2** (of a person) to live by using or controlling other people unfairly: *antiques dealers who prey on old people* **3 prey on your mind** to make you worry a lot

price¹ /praɪs/ n **1** the amount of money that you must pay in order to buy something: *The price is £50.* | *Prices are rising fast.* | *Our shops give you good value at a low price.* | *Prices have gone up again.* –see COST² (USAGE) **2** something you have to do or suffer in order to have what you want: *I'm afraid the price you pay for smoking is bad health.* **3 at a price:** a for a lot of money: *You can buy excellent wine here – at a price.* b with an unwanted result **4 at any price** by doing or suffering anything at all to get something: *He wanted fame at any price.*

price² v **priced, pricing** [T] **1** to fix the price of something in order to sell it: *The chairs were very reasonably priced.* **2 price yourself out of the market** to make your prices so high that people are unwilling to pay

price·less /'praɪsləs/ adj **1** very valuable: *a priceless collection of paintings* –see WORTHLESS (USAGE) **2** old fash infml very amusing

pric·ey /'praɪsi/ adj pricier, priciest infml expensive: *Houses in this area are getting rather pricey.*

prick¹ /prɪk/ n a small sharp pain: *She felt a sharp prick as a needle went into her finger.*

prick² v **1** [T] to make a very small hole in something with a sharp-pointed object: *She pricked the potatoes with a fork before putting them in the oven.* **2** [I] to cause a light sharp pain on your skin: *Careful, Johnny! The thorns on that bush will prick you.* **3 prick up its ears** (of an animal) to raise its ears **4 prick up your ears** to listen very carefully: *He pricked up his ears when they started to talk about him.*

prick·le /'prɪkəl/ n a small sharp point that grows on the skin of some plants or animals: *The cactus was covered with tiny prickles.*

prickle² *v* **prickled, prickling** [I] to give or feel a sensation of small sharp points sticking into your skin: *I can't wear this woollen shirt – it prickles.*

prick·ly /ˈprɪkli/ *adj* **pricklier, prickliest** **1** covered with prickles: *prickly bushes* **2** giving a sensation of small sharp points sticking into your skin

pride¹ /praɪd/ *n* [U] **1** a feeling of satisfaction and pleasure in something you or someone else has done, or in something you own: *He looked at the new baby with pride and happiness.* **2 take pride/a pride in something** to feel pleased or proud about something: *They take a great pride in their daughter's success.* | *He takes no pride in his appearance.* **3** self-respect: *I think you hurt his pride by laughing at the way he speaks English.* **4** too high an opinion of yourself or what you have done: *His pride made him an arrogant and cold person.* **5 be someone's pride and joy** to be the most valuable and important thing or person in someone's life: *His roses are his pride and joy.* **6 be the pride of** to be the most valuable thing in: *This is the pride of my collection.* **7 have pride of place in** to have the best or most important position in

pride² *v* **prided, priding pride yourself on something** to be pleased and satisfied with yourself about something: *She prided herself on her ability to speak eight languages.*

priest /priːst/ *n* **1** a specially trained person in the Christian Church, who performs various religious duties: *the argument over having women priests* **2** a specially-trained person with religious duties, in many non-Christian religions

■ USAGE **Priest** is a general word for someone who is in charge of the religious worship of a group of Christian people, but the word is used especially in the Roman Catholic Church. A priest in the Church of England is called a **clergyman**, and a clergyman in charge of a particular area is the **vicar** of that area. In the Nonconformist churches the usual word is **minister**.

priest·ess /ˈpriːstes/ *n* a specially-trained woman with religious duties, in many non-Christian religions

priest·hood /ˈpriːsthʊd/ *n* **the priesthood** the position of being a priest: *He entered the priesthood.*

prig /prɪg/ *n* a person who is very careful about rules of moral behaviour, and so thinks they behave better than other people (a word used to express disapproval). *Come on, Margaret, join in – don't be such a prig!* –**priggish** *adj* –**priggishness** *n* [U]

prim /prɪm/ *adj* **-mm-** very formal and correct in behaviour and easily shocked by anything rude (a word that is usually used to express disapproval) –**primly** *adv* –**primness** *n* [U]

pri·ma don·na /ˌpriːmə ˈdɒnə ‖ -ˈdɑːnə/ *n* **1** the leading woman singer in an OPERA **2** a person who changes their mind easily and expects everyone to do as they wish (a word used to express disapproval): *Their marketing director is a bit of a prima donna.*

pri·mae·val /praɪˈmiːvəl/ *adj* see PRIMEVAL

pri·ma·ri·ly /ˈpraɪmərəli ‖ praɪˈmerəli/ *adv* mainly or most importantly: *The village is primarily a fishing community, but a lot of tourists come here.*

pri·ma·ry¹ /ˈpraɪməri ‖ -meri/ *adj* **1** main or most important: *The primary cause of Tom's failure was simply his laziness.* **2 primary education, primary schools** education or schools for children between 5 and 11 years old, in Britain: *There's Billy's primary school teacher.*

primary² *n* **primaries** an election in the US at which people vote for someone to be their party's choice for a political office

primary col·our /ˌ··· ˈ··/ *n* one of the three colours red, yellow, and blue; all other colours can be made by mixing these together in different ways

pri·mate¹ /ˈpraɪmeɪt/ *n* a member of the most highly developed group of animals, which includes humans and monkeys

pri·mate² /ˈpraɪmət/ *n* (also **Primate**) a priest of the highest rank

prime¹ /praɪm/ *adj* [always before a noun] **1** the first or greatest: *This is a matter of prime importance.* **2** of the very best quality: *a prime piece of beef* **3** that is completely typical: *Look, over there. That's a prime example of what I was saying about office workers.*

prime² *n* [sing] **your prime** the time when you are strongest, most active, or in the best condition: *As a tennis player she is now in her prime, at 23.*

prime³ *v* **primed, priming** [T] **1** to prepare someone for an event by giving them information: *The lawyer has been carefully primed about the case.* **2** to prepare wood for painting by covering it with a special liquid or paint

prime min·is·ter /ˌ· ˈ···/ (also **Prime Minister**; also **PM** *infml*) *n* the leader of the government in certain countries: *talks with the British Prime Minister*

prim·er /ˈpraɪmər/ *n* [C;U] a paint spread over the bare surface of wood before the main painting

prime time /ˈ· ˌ·/ *n* [U] the time when most people are thought to watch television

pri·me·val /praɪˈmiːvəl/ *adj* (also **primaeval**) of the earliest period of the Earth's existence: *primeval forests*

prim·i·tive /ˈprɪmətɪv/ *adj* **1** [always before a noun] of an early stage of human development or human society: *In primitive societies tools were made from sharp stones and animal bones.* **2** in a simple style and without having anything more than is necessary: *Their living conditions are somewhat primitive – there's no running water, for a start.* –**primitively** *adv* –**primitiveness** *n* [U]

prim·rose /ˈprɪmrəʊz/ *n* a common wild plant with pale yellow flowers

prince /prɪns/ *n* (also **Prince**) **1** a son or other near male relation of a king or queen: *He bowed to the prince.* | *Prince Charles* **2** a ruler of a small country or state: *Prince Rainier of Monaco*

prince·ly /ˈprɪnsli/ *adj* **1** of or belonging to a prince **2** splendid and generous: *a princely gift*

prin·cess /ˌprɪnˈses◂ ‖ ˈprɪnsəs/ *n* (also **Princess**) **1** a daughter or other near female relation of a king or queen **2** the wife of a prince: *Princess Diana*

prin·ci·pal¹ /ˈprɪnsəpəl/ *adj* [always before a noun] first in importance: *The principal character in the book is a young woman called Scarlett O'Hara.*

principal² *n* **1** (also **Principal**) the head of some colleges, and schools **2** a leading performer in a play or in a group of musicians

prin·ci·pal·i·ty /ˌprɪnsəˈpæləti/ *n* **principalities** a country that a prince rules

prin·ci·pally /ˈprɪnsəpli/ *adv* mostly: *The money is principally invested in the oil industry.*

prin·ci·ple /ˈprɪnsəpəl/ *n* **1** [C] a general truth or rule that ideas or beliefs are based on: *One of the principles of this dictionary is that it is written in simple language.* | *Socialism is based on the principle that everyone is equal.* **2 in principle** as far as the general idea is concerned: *I agree with your plan in principle, but I'm not sure if it will work in practice.* **3** [C] a law of nature or science which controls how something works: *Einstein's theories form the basic principles of modern physics.* **4** [C;U] a moral belief or rule that you follow when you do something or that guides your behaviour: *She is a woman of great principle.* | *He has no principles; he just wants to make money in any way he can.* | *I couldn't have a servant; it goes against my principles.* **5 on principle** because of a moral belief that you have: *We don't eat meat, on principle.*

print¹ /prɪnt/ n **1** [U] words printed on a page: *I can't read small print without my glasses.* **2** [C] a photograph or picture printed on paper **3 in print**: **a** printed in a book or newspaper: *I was very excited to see my name in print.* **b** that you can still buy (used of a book) **4 out of print** that you can no longer buy (used of a book) **5** [C] a mark made on a surface showing the shape of the thing pressed into it, especially a FINGERPRINT: *the thief's prints on the door handle* | *footprints in the snow*

print² v **1** [I;T] to press letters or pictures onto paper using ink in a machine: *They've printed the leaflet on the wrong paper.* | *The books are printed in Spain.* **2** [I;T] to produce books, newspapers, or magazines in large numbers: *We are printing 10,000 copies of his new book.* **3** [T] to include in a book or newspaper: *All today's newspapers have printed the minister's speech in full.* **4** [T] to make or copy a photograph on paper sensitive to light **5** [I;T] to write without joining the letters: *Please print the address clearly in capital letters.*
  print sthg ↔ out *phr v* [T] (of a computer) to produce a printed record of information

print·er /ˈprɪntər/ n **1** a person who owns or works in a printing business **2** a machine which is connected to a computer and makes a printed record of its information –see picture on page 539

print·ing /ˈprɪntɪŋ/ n [U] the act or art of producing books or newspapers using a machine: *The invention of printing made it possible for many more people to learn to read.*

printing press /ˈ·· ·/ n (also **press**) a machine that prints books or newspapers

print·out /ˈprɪnt.aʊt/ n [C;U] a printed record produced by a computer –see picture on page 539

pri·or¹ /ˈpraɪər/ adj [always before a noun] **1** that is done or exists already: *I was unable to attend the wedding because of a prior engagement.* **2** coming first in importance: *He felt his family had a prior claim on his time.* **3 prior to** fml before: *The contract will be signed prior to the ceremony.*

prior² n the head of a priory; a female prior is called a **prioress**

pri·or·i·ty /praɪˈɒrəti ‖ -ˈɔːr-/ n **priorities 1 have priority, be given priority** to be treated as more important than someone or something else: *We are treating the children first – they have absolute priority over everyone else.* **2** [C] something that needs attention immediately or first, before other things: *The government should make education a priority.* | *It's simply a matter of priorities.* **3 get your priorities right** to deal with the most important things first

pri·o·ry /ˈpraɪəri/ n **priories** a Christian religious house where monks (MONK) live and work together

prise /praɪz/ v **prised, prising** (also **prize**) [T; + adv/prep] to move, lift, or force with a tool: *We finally managed to prise the box open.*

pris·m /ˈprɪzəm/ n a transparent three-sided block of glass, that breaks up white light into different colours

pris·on /ˈprɪzən/ n **1** [C;U] a large building where criminals are kept locked up as a punishment: *The thief was sent to prison for a year.* | locked up in a **prison cell 2** [sing] a place or situation which you feel you cannot escape from: *Tom hates school; he thinks it's a prison.*

pris·on·er /ˈprɪzənər/ n **1** a person kept in a prison for a crime: *Three prisoners were caught trying to escape.* **2 take someone prisoner** to seize someone in a war: *He was taken prisoner by enemy soldiers.* **3** a person taken by force and kept somewhere against their will **4 keep/hold someone prisoner** to keep someone somewhere by force: *The kidnappers held him prisoner for five months.*

prisoner of war /ˌ··· · ·/ n (also **POW** infml) a soldier caught by the enemy during a war and kept as a prisoner

pris·tine /ˈprɪstiːn/ adj fml fresh, clean, and undamaged: *an old book still in pristine condition*

priv·a·cy /ˈprɪvəsi, ˈpraɪ- ‖ ˈpraɪ-/ n [U] the state of being able to be alone, and not seen or heard by other people: *There's not much privacy in these flats: the walls are so thin you can hear everything your neighbour is saying.*

pri·vate¹ /ˈpraɪvɪt/ adj **1** only for use by one person, and not people in general: *a room with a private bathroom* | *She has a private plane.* **2** not connected with or paid for by the government, or a public service: *a private hospital* | *a private bus company* | *pay increases in the private sector* **3** not connected with your work or business: *The Queen is on a private visit to Scotland.* | *I don't discuss my private life at the office.* **4** secret and personal and not for sharing with others: *private papers* | *I was lost in my own private thoughts.* **5** quiet and without lots of people: *Is there a private corner where we can sit and talk by ourselves?* **6 in private** without other people listening or watching **7 a private person** someone who likes to be on their own – compare PUBLIC¹ **–privately** adv: *May I speak to you privately?*

private² n (also **Private**) a soldier of the lowest rank

private en·ter·prise /ˌ·· ·ˈ···/ n [U] see CAPITALISM

private school /ˌ·· ·ˈ·/ n a school paid for by parents, not supported with government money –compare PUBLIC SCHOOL

pri·va·tion /praɪˈveɪʃən/ n [C;U] fml lack of the necessary things of life: *Everyone suffered privations during the war, when there wasn't enough food in the country.*

pri·vat·ize /ˈpraɪvətaɪz/ v **privatized, privatizing** (also **privatise** BrE) [T] to sell a government-owned industry or organization: *Their rail services have recently been privatized.*

priv·i·lege /ˈprɪvəlɪdʒ/ n **1** [C] a special right or advantage given only to one person or group of people: *You may be rich, but no one gets any special privileges in this prison.* **2** [U] advantage possessed by one person or group because of their wealth, social rank, etc. (a word often used to express disapproval): *Their oldest universities are criticized for being bastions of privilege.* **3** [sing] a special chance to do something that gives you great pleasure: *It was a privilege to meet such a talented musician.* **–privileged** adj: *We are privileged tonight to have as our main speaker the Foreign Minister of France.*

priv·y /ˈprɪvi/ adj **privy to** fml sharing secret knowledge of: *I was not privy to the discussions.*

prize[1] /praiz/ n something of value given to someone who is successful in a game, race, or competition, or given for some action that is admired: *Her roses won first prize at the flower show.*

prize[2] adj [only before a noun] **1** that has gained a prize: *prize cattle* | *a prize rose* **2** given as a prize: *prize money* **3** infml worthy of a prize for quality, size, etc. (a word often used in a humorous way): *The new hen has produced a prize egg!*

prize[3] v **prized, prizing 1** [T] to value highly: *His new bicycle was his most prized possession.* **2** [T; + adv/prep] (also **prise**) to move, lift, or force with a tool: *With a long iron bar we prized the top off the box.*

pro /prəu/ n **pros 1** see PROFESSIONAL[2] (3) **2 the pros and cons** the arguments or reasons for and against something: *We discussed all the pros and cons thoroughly.*

prob·a·bil·i·ty /ˌprɒbəˈbɪlɪti ‖ ˌprɑː-/ n **probabilities 1** [sing;U] likelihood that something will happen: *I don't think there's much probability of an agreement being reached.* | *There's a high probability that oil prices will fall next year.* **2 in all probability** almost certainly **3** [C] an event or result that will probably happen: *War is a real probability in the present crisis.*

prob·a·ble /ˈprɒbəbəl ‖ ˈprɑː-/ adj that has a good chance of happening or being true: *He may just get the job, but judging from his account of the interview it doesn't seem very probable.* | *It is probable that they will win the election.* –**probably** adv : *We'll probably go to Greece later in the year.*

pro·ba·tion /prəˈbeɪʃən ‖ prəu-/ n [U] **1** a period of time during which someone's abilities are tested: *I will be on probation for the first three months of my new job.* **2** law the system of allowing someone who has broken the law to go free if they promise to behave well and report to the court –**probationary** adj

probation of·fi·cer /·ˈ··· ˌ···/ n a person whose job is to watch, advise, and help law-breakers who are put on probation

probe[1] /prəub/ n **1** a long thin metal instrument used by doctors and dentists to examine a part of the body carefully **2** (also **space probe**) a machine sent into the sky to examine conditions in outer space **3** a careful and thorough inquiry into a situation

probe[2] v **probed, probing** [I;T] **1** to search or examine something very carefully with a long thin instrument **2** to make a careful and thorough inquiry into a situation

prob·lem /ˈprɒbləm ‖ ˈprɑː-/ n **1** a difficult situation that has to be dealt with or thought about: *I've got a problem with the gears on my bike.* | *The problem is, I just don't have enough time.* | *The unemployment problem is getting worse.* **2** a question connected with numbers, or facts for which an answer is needed: *He's only three, but he can already do simple problems in addition and subtraction.*

prob·lem·at·ic /ˌprɒbləˈmætɪk◂ ‖ ˌprɑː-/ adj (also **problematical**) having difficulties and problems: *The situation is somewhat problematic.*

pro·ce·dure /prəˈsiːdʒər/ n [C;U] a particular formal way of doing something: *Writing a cheque is quite a simple procedure.* | *a review of government procedure* –**procedural** adj

pro·ceed /prəˈsiːd/ v [I] **1** fml to continue with something you have already started: *Now that*

everyone has arrived we can proceed with *the meeting.* | *The work is proceeding according to plan.* **2** to do something, especially something rather unexpected, after someone has just said or done something: *We asked if anything was wrong, and he proceeded to tell us all his troubles.* **3** fml to move in a forward direction: *Do not proceed across a main road without first checking your mirror.*

pro·ceed·ings /prəˈsiːdɪŋz/ n [pl] **1** an action taken in law: *They're taking legal proceedings against the manufacturer.* **2** events that happen in a formal way: *We had a bird's eye view of the proceedings.*

pro·ceeds /ˈprəusiːdz/ n [pl] money gained from selling something or from an event or activity

pro·cess[1] /ˈprəuses ‖ ˈprɑː-/ n **1** a set of actions or changes that develop or happen naturally: *the process of breathing* | *Coal was formed out of dead forests by chemical processes.* **2** a continued set of actions performed in order to make or do something: *She's learning to walk again, but it's a slow process.* | *the electoral process* **3 in the process** while something is or was being done **4 be in the process of** to have started something and still be doing it: *We are now in the process of moving the machines to a new factory.* **5** a method of treating raw materials in order to produce goods: *an advanced process for rubber production*

process[2] v [T] **1** to treat something by a particular method: *processed cheese* | *They will process a film in 24 hours.* **2** to deal with information in a formal way: *Your mortgage application is still being processed.* **3** to put information into a computer for examination: *new techniques of data processing*

pro·ces·sion /prəˈseʃən/ n **1** [C] a line of people or vehicles moving forward in a ceremonial way: *a carnival procession* **2** [C;U] a continuous onward movement of people or things: *The workers marched in procession to the minister's office.* | *to hold a procession*

pro·ces·sor /ˈprəusesər/ n see WORD PROCESSOR

pro·claim /prəˈkleɪm ‖ prəu-/ v [T; + that] **1** fml to declare officially and publicly: *Our country proclaimed its independence after the war.* | *A national holiday was proclaimed.* **2** lit to show clearly: *His pronunciation proclaimed that he was an American.*

proc·la·ma·tion /ˌprɒkləˈmeɪʃən ‖ ˌprɑː-/ n an official public statement: *a royal proclamation*

pro·cras·ti·nate /prəˈkræstɪneɪt/ v **procrastinated, procrastinating** [I] fml to repeatedly delay doing something that is necessary –**procrastination** /prəˌkræstɪˈneɪʃən/ n [U]

pro·cre·ate /ˈprəukrieɪt/ v **procreated, procreating** [I;T] fml or tech to produce babies or young animals –**procreation** /ˌprəukriˈeɪʃən/ n [U]

pro·cure /prəˈkjuər ‖ prəu-/ v **procured, procuring 1** [T] fml to obtain something that may be difficult to find **2** [I;T] to provide a woman for someone else's sexual satisfaction

prod /prɒd ‖ prɑːd/ v **-dd-** [I;T] **1** to push or press something or someone with a pointed object: *She prodded the spider cautiously to make sure it was really dead.* **2** to urge someone to do something which they might forget –**prod** n : *He gave the snake a prod with a stick.*

prod·i·gal[1] /ˈprɒdɪgəl ‖ ˈprɑː-/ adj fml careless and wasteful with money

prodigal[2] n **the prodigal returns** a person who has left to live a wasteful or immoral life is now returning (a phrase often used in a humorous way)

pro·di·gious /prə'dɪdʒəs/ adj great in size or amount and causing admiration: *He is one of the country's most prodigious writers.* –**prodigiously** adv

prod·i·gy /'prɒdɪdʒi ‖ 'prɑː-/ n **prodigies** a person who shows unusual and very noticeable abilities at an early age: *a child prodigy*

pro·duce¹ /prə'djuːs ‖ -'duːs/ v **produced, producing** [T] **1** to have as a result or effect: *Gordon's jokes produced a great deal of laughter.* | *The two lasers combine to produce a powerful cutting tool.* **2** to make something, especially in large quantities: *Gas can be produced from coal.* | *The factory produces 500 cars a week.* | *to produce a work of art* –see PRODUCTION (USAGE) **3** to grow or supply: *Canada produces good wheat.* **4** to give birth to young or make as a natural process: *Bees produce honey.* **5** to show, or bring out for examination: *We had to produce our passports on the train.* | *He suddenly produced a gun.* **6** to control, prepare, and present to the public: *The play was badly produced.*

prod·uce² /'prɒdjuːs ‖ 'prɑːduːs/ n [U] something that has been grown in large quantities: *The wine bottle was marked "Produce of Spain".*

pro·duc·er /prə'djuːsəʳ ‖ -'duː-/ n **1** a person or company that produces goods, foods, or materials: *one of the world's leading oil producers* **2** a person who has general control of the money for and preparation of a play, film, or broadcast

prod·uct /'prɒdʌkt ‖ 'prɑː-/ n **1** something that is produced or made somewhere: *a new range of kitchen products* –see PRODUCTION (USAGE) **2** the result of experiences or certain situations: *Criminals are sometimes the product of bad homes.*

pro·duc·tion /prə'dʌkʃən/ n **1** [U] the act of producing something, especially for sale: *This factory specializes in the production of larger cars.* | *There are problems with the production process.* **2** [U] the amount of something which is produced: *Oil production is falling world-wide.* **3** [C;U] a play, film, or broadcast, or the act of producing it: *There are two productions of 'Hamlet' playing in London now.* **4** [U] the act of showing something to someone: *Entry is permitted only on production of a ticket.*

■ USAGE Compare **production**, **product**, **produce**. **Production** is the process in which things are made: *a good rate of production.* A **production** is a play, film, etc. made for the theatre, television, etc.: *a new production of 'Hamlet'.* A **product** is something made by industry: *various industrial products.* **Produce** is the general word for things from a farm, such as milk, potatoes, or wool: *a large quantity of agricultural produce.*

production line /·'··· ·/ n a set of machines that are used to make something in a factory

pro·duc·tive /prə'dʌktɪv/ adj **1** useful because of having results: *It was a productive meeting, at which some important decisions were made.* **2** producing a lot: *They form a productive team of workers.* –opposite **unproductive** –**productively** adv

pro·duc·tiv·i·ty /ˌprɒdʌk'tɪvɪti, -dək- ‖ ˌprɑː-/ n [U] the success of a company or area in making goods or growing things for sale: *Industrial productivity continues to increase in Japan.* | *to get a productivity bonus*

Prof a written abbreviation for PROFESSOR

pro·fane¹ /prə'feɪn/ adj fml showing lack of respect for religion or religious things: *Smoking in a church is a profane act.*

profane² v **profaned, profaning** [T] fml to show a lack of respect for something religious or holy

pro·fan·i·ty /prə'fænɪti/ n **profanities** [C;U] fml words or actions that show a lack of respect for religion or religious things

pro·fess /prə'fes/ v [T] **1** to claim something which may not be true: *We professed ignorance.* | *He professes to be an expert in management skills, but I have my doubts.* **2** fml to express a feeling, opinion, or belief: *She professed her surprise at the decision.* –**professed** adj [only before a noun] : *a professed Catholic*

pro·fes·sion /prə'feʃən/ n **1** [C] a job that is socially respected because you need a high standard of education and also special training to do it: *She wants to go into one of the professions; medicine, perhaps.* –see JOB (USAGE) **2** [sing + sing/pl verb] all the people who are trained to do a particular job: *There is a lot of pressure from the teaching profession for higher salaries.* | *The legal profession is extremely upset about this case.* **3** [C] fml a declaration of your belief, opinion, or feeling: *professions of regret*

pro·fes·sion·al /prə'feʃənəl/ adj **1** [only before a noun] working in or concerning a job that is socially respected because it needs a high standard of education and special training: *You should ask a lawyer for professional advice.* **2** showing that you have great experience and high standards in what you do (a word used to express approval): *It's a very professional report.* –opposite **unprofessional** **3** doing something for money rather than for interest or enjoyment: *a professional painter* | *professional football* –**professionally** adv : *She was professionally trained.*

professional² n **1** a person who is working in a job that is socially respected because it needs a high standard of education and special training **2** a person who has great experience and high standards (a word used to express approval): *She's a real professional.* **3** (also **pro** infml) a person who earns money for doing something which other people do for interest or enjoyment, for example, sport: *Large prizes are encouraging tennis-players to become professionals.*

pro·fes·sion·al·is·m /prə'feʃənəlɪzəm/ n [U] behaviour or skill which shows that a person has the experience and high standards that would be expected of a member of a PROFESSION (1): *I admire her professionalism.*

pro·fes·sor /prə'fesəʳ/ n (also **Professor**) **1** BrE a teacher of the highest rank in a university department: *A new history professor will be appointed next term.* | *Certainly, Professor Ingham.* **2** AmE a teacher at a university or college

prof·fer /'prɒfəʳ ‖ 'prɑː-/ v [T] fml **1** to hold something out towards someone: *She refused the proffered drink.* **2** to offer: *to proffer a suggestion*

pro·fi·cient /prə'fɪʃənt/ adj very good at something: *She's a highly proficient swimmer.* –**proficiency** n [U] : *He's taking his cycling proficiency test.*

pro·file /'prəʊfaɪl/ n **1** a view of a person's face from one side: *He had an attractive profile.* **2** in profile seen from the side: *He drew her in profile.* **3** a short description of a person's life and character, that is written or broadcast **4** keep a low profile to avoid drawing attention to yourself or your actions

prof·it¹ /'prɒfɪt ‖ 'prɑː-/ n **1** [C;U] money which is earned by doing business, after all the costs are taken from it: *He made a profit of £50,000 on the sale of his house.* | *Company profits have fallen this year.* | *There's not much profit in selling hats these days.* –opposite **loss** **2** sell something at a profit to sell something for more than it cost you: *She sold the car* *again later at a profit.* **3** [U] *fml* advantage which you get from something you do

profit² *v* [T] *fml* **profit by/from something** to learn or gain from something: *You must profit by my mistakes.*

prof·it·a·ble /ˈprɒfɪtəbəl ‖ ˈprɑː-/ *adj* **1** successful because of the money that is earned: *The company has had a profitable year.* | *Farming in this country is rarely profitable.* **2** *fml* useful: *I hope you found the seminar profitable.* **–profitably** *adv*

pro·fi·teer /ˌprɒfɪˈtɪər ‖ ˌprɑː-/ *n* a person who makes large profits from people who need goods or services but cannot get them anywhere else (a word used to express disapproval) **–profiteer** *v* [I]

profit mar·gin /ˈ·· ˌ··/ *n* the difference between the cost of producing something and the price at which it is sold

prof·li·gate /ˈprɒflɪɡət ‖ ˈprɑː-/ *adj fml* **1** wasting money or other things: *profligate spending* **2** without morals or shame

pro·found /prəˈfaʊnd/ *adj* **1** very great or strong: *Her death was a profound shock to all of us.* **2** having, showing, or using great knowledge and understanding: *a very profound remark* **–profoundly** *adv fml* : *I am profoundly grateful.*

pro·fuse /prəˈfjuːs/ *adj* large in quantity: *She offered her profuse thanks.* **–profusely** *adv* **–profusion** /prəˈfjuːʒən/ *n* [sing;U] : *The room was covered in a profusion of flowers.* | *Weeds grow in profusion.*

prog·e·ny /ˈprɒdʒəni ‖ ˈprɑː-/ *n* [U; + sing/pl verb] *lit* someone's children (a word often used in a humorous way): *Her numerous progeny were all asleep.*

prog·no·sis /prɒɡˈnəʊsɪs ‖ prɑːɡ-/ *n* **prognoses** /-siːz/ **1** *tech* a doctor's judgment of how a particular disease will develop **–compare** DIAGNOSIS **2** a judgment of how something will develop

pro·gram¹ /ˈprəʊɡræm/ *n* **1** the instructions which a computer follows to perform an operation **2** the usual American spelling for PROGRAMME¹

program² *v* **-mm-** *or* **-m-** [T] **1** to give a computer the instructions it needs to perform an operation: *The computer can be programmed to list all the people who are over 35.* **2** the usual American spelling for PROGRAMME²

pro·gram·er /ˈprəʊɡræmər/ *n* the usual American spelling for PROGRAMMER

pro·gramme¹ /ˈprəʊɡræm/ *n* (**program** *AmE*) **1** a show or performance which is broadcast on television or radio: *What is your favourite television programme?* **2** a plan of what you are going to do: *They're discussing a new research programme.* | *We must include shopping in the programme for tomorrow.* **3** printed information about performers, or things to be performed, at an event such as a concert or sports competition

programme² *v* **-mm-** (**program** *AmE*) [T] to make a person or thing operate in a particular way: *The central heating system is programmed to switch itself on in the mornings.* | *Society programmes us to think like this.*

pro·gram·mer /ˈprəʊɡræmər/ *n* (**programer** *AmE*) a person who prepares instructions for computers: *She's training to be a computer programmer.*

pro·gress¹ /ˈprəʊɡres ‖ ˈprɑː-/ *n* [U] **1** movement in a particular direction: *The ship made slow progress through the rough sea.* **2** continual improvement or development: *Jane is making progress in her research.* | *We've been following the progress of the*

case with interest. **3** the idea of advancing generally in science, the organization of human society, etc.: *These ridiculous changes in the education system are being made in the name of progress.* **4 in progress** happening now: *Repairs to the building are in progress.*

pro·gress² /prəˈɡres/ *v* [I] **1** to move on: *As the journey progressed he became increasingly tired.* **2** to improve or develop: *We progressed from being total beginners to a high level of competence.* | *As the conversation progressed, her feelings became clear.*

pro·gres·sion /prəˈɡreʃən/ *n* [sing;U] **1** development or improvement over time **2** a number of things which follow each other: *It was due to an unfortunate progression of events.*

pro·gres·sive /prəˈɡresɪv/ *adj* **1** developing or changing continuously over a period of time: *progressive loss of sight in old age* **2** supporting or using new ideas: *The company is very progressive in the benefits and facilities it offers its employees.* **–progressively** *adv* : *The situation got progressively worse.* | *thinking very progressively*

pro·hib·it /prəˈhɪbɪt ‖ prəʊ-/ *v* [T] *fml* **1** to forbid something by law or by a rule: *Smoking is strictly prohibited.* **2** to make something impossible: *His height prohibits him from becoming a policeman.*

pro·hi·bi·tion /ˌprəʊhɪˈbɪʃən/ *n* **1** [U] the act of forbidding something **2** [C] *fml* an order which forbids something

pro·hib·i·tive /prəˈhɪbɪtɪv ‖ prəʊ-/ *adj* costing so much that people cannot afford to do or buy something: *We wanted to buy a video recorder, but the cost was prohibitive.* **–prohibitively** *adv* : *Meat has become prohibitively expensive.*

proj·ect¹ /ˈprɒdʒekt ‖ ˈprɑː-/ *n* **1** a plan to do something: *Our current project is to build a garage.* **2** an educational activity in which students collect and present information about a subject: *We're doing a project on the history of London.*

pro·ject² /prəˈdʒekt/ *v* **1** [I] to stand out beyond an edge or surface: *The roof projects a metre beyond the walls.* **2** [T] to make something move through the air with force **3** [T] to direct light, sound, or heat into space or onto a surface: *He's learning to project his voice so that he can be heard by a large audience.* | *Pictures of the earthquake were projected on a screen.*

pro·ject·ed /prəˈdʒektɪd/ *adj* **1** planned: *our projected trip* **2** calculated in advance: *projected unemployment figures*

pro·jec·tile /prəˈdʒektaɪl ‖ -tl/ *n fml* an object that is shot from a gun or other weapon

pro·jec·tion /prəˈdʒekʃən/ *n* **1** [C] a part of something that stands out beyond an edge or surface **2** [C] an amount calculated in advance: *Sales projections for next year look encouraging.* **3** [U] the act of projecting something

pro·jec·tion·ist /prəˈdʒekʃənɪst/ *n* a person who works a projector, especially in a cinema

pro·jec·tor /prəˈdʒektər/ *n* an apparatus for showing images like films on a surface

pro·le·tar·i·an /ˌprəʊlɪˈteəriən/ *adj* of the proletariat (a word used to express disapproval): *the proletarian masses* **–proletarian** *n*

pro·le·tar·i·at /ˌprəʊlɪˈteəriət/ *n* the proletariat [+ sing/pl verb] the class of workers who have to work for wages and do not own property **–compare** BOURGEOISIE

pro·lif·e·rate /prəˈlɪfəreɪt/ *v* **proliferated, proliferating** [I] *fml* to increase in number rapidly **–proliferation** /prəˌlɪfəˈreɪʃən/ *n* [U]

pro·lif·ic /prə'lɪfɪk/ adj producing a lot of something: *Agatha Christie was a prolific writer.* –**prolifically** /-kli/ adv

pro·logue /'prəʊlɒg ‖ -lɔːg, -laːg/ n (also **prolog** AmE) **1** an introduction to a play or a long poem –compare EPILOGUE **2** an event which comes before another one and often causes it to happen: *The border incident proved to be just the prologue to a full-scale invasion.*

pro·long /prə'lɒŋ ‖ -'lɔːŋ/ v [T] to make something continue for a longer time: *They're prolonging their visit because they've fallen in love with the city.*

pro·longed /prə'lɒŋd ‖ -'lɔːŋd/ adj continuing for a long time, or longer than expected: *I am worried about his prolonged absence from school.*

prom·e·nade¹ /ˌprɒmə'naːd◂, ˌprɒmə'naːd ‖ ˌpraː-mə'neɪd/ n (also **prom** infml) **1** a wide path along the coast in a holiday town **2** fml a slow walk or drive for pleasure or exercise

promenade² v promenaded, promenading [I] fml to walk slowly for pleasure or exercise

prom·i·nent /'prɒmɪnənt ‖ 'praː-/ adj **1** standing out beyond a surface: *His teeth are rather prominent.* **2** famous or important: *A number of prominent politicians will be present.* **3** easily seen: *She left a note for him in a prominent position.* –**prominence** n [U] –**prominently** adv

pro·mis·cu·ous /prə'mɪskjuəs/ adj having sex with more than one sexual partner (a word used to show disapproval): *a promiscuous girl | a promiscuous life-style* –**promiscuously** adv –**promiscuity** /ˌprɒmɪˈskjuːəti ‖ ˌpraː-/ (also **promiscuousness** /prə'mɪskjuəsnəs/) n [U]

prom·ise¹ /'prɒmɪs ‖ 'praː-/ n **1** [C] a statement that you certainly will or will not do something: *I trust him to keep his promise. | She made a promise and then broke it. | a promise of support* **2** [U] signs or hope of success or improvement: *His son is showing great promise as a footballer.*

promise² v promised, promising **1** [I;T] to state that you will certainly do something: *She promised to phone me later. | "I'm afraid I can't come this evening." "But you promised!" | He promised that he would do his best. | I promised her that I would never reveal her secret.*
☐ USEFUL PATTERNS to promise to do something; to promise that...; to promise someone that... **2** [T] to state that you will certainly give something to someone: *I've promised this book to Susan. | We've promised her a puppy for her birthday.*
☐ USEFUL PATTERNS to promise something to someone; to promise someone something
3 [T] fml to show signs that something good will happen: *It promises to be a fine day.*

prom·is·ing /'prɒmɪsɪŋ ‖ 'praː-/ adj showing signs that something good will happen or that something will succeed: *That was a promising performance.* –**promisingly** adv

prom·on·to·ry /'prɒməntəri ‖ 'praːməntɔːri/ n promontories a long, narrow piece of land stretching out into the sea

pro·mote /prə'məʊt/ v promoted, promoting [T] **1** to give someone a higher position at work: *She's been promoted to senior editor.* **2** to advertise a product or event: *We are spending millions of pounds on promoting our new cat food.* **3** to help something to develop or succeed: *The society's aim is to promote peace and understanding between nations.*

pro·mot·er /prə'məʊtəʳ/ n a person who arranges an event or works for the success of something: *The*

concert promoters warn us that there will be a rush for tickets.

pro·mo·tion /prə'məʊʃən/ n **1** [C;U] a move to a higher position at work: *Congratulations on your promotion! | good chances of promotion.* **2** [C;U] advertising, or a particular set of activities for advertising something: *the promotion of our products on national television. | We're mounting a new promotion.* **3** [U] fml action to help something develop or succeed: *The promotion of social values among teenagers has been neglected.*

prompt¹ /prɒmpt ‖ praːmpt/ v [T] **1** to cause something to happen: *Hunger prompted him to steal. | News of the scandal prompted an inquiry into the conduct of local councillors.* **2** to remind someone, especially an actor of the next words in a speech

prompt² adj arriving at the correct time: *Please be prompt. | We request prompt payment of bills.* –**promptly** adv : *I arrived promptly at 6 o'clock.* –**promptness** n [U]

prompt³ adv at a certain time exactly: *The performance will start at seven o'clock prompt.*

prompt·er /'prɒmptəʳ ‖ 'praːmp-/ n (also **prompt**) a person who reminds actors of the words they forget during a performance

prone /prəʊn/ adj **1** prone to something, prone to do something likely to do something or to suffer from something: *He's prone to colds in winter. | People are more prone to make mistakes when they are tired.* **2** fml lying flat, with your face and the front of your body downwards

prong /prɒŋ ‖ prɔːŋ/ n **1** a thin sharp-pointed part of something, especially of a fork **2** -**pronged** /prɒŋd ‖ prɔːŋd/ a having a certain number of prongs: *a four-pronged fork* **b** coming from a certain number of directions at the same time: *a two-pronged attack*

pro·noun /'prəʊnaʊn/ n a word like 'she' or 'we' that is used in place of a noun or a noun phrase –see Study Note on page 687

pro·nounce /prə'naʊns/ v pronounced, pronouncing [T] **1** to make the sound of letters or words: *In the word "knew", the "k" is not pronounced. | How do you pronounce his name?* **2** fml to state something formally or officially: *The priest said: "I now pronounce you man and wife," and they were married. | The jury pronounced their verdict.*

pro·nounced /prə'naʊnst/ adj very strong or noticeable: *He has very pronounced ideas about politics. | She walks with a pronounced limp.*

pro·nounce·ment /prə'naʊnsmənt/ n fml an official statement

pro·nun·ci·a·tion /prəˌnʌnsi'eɪʃən/ n **1** [C;U] the way in which something is spoken: *the normal Australian pronunciation | There are several different pronunciations of this word.* **2** [sing;U] a particular person's way of speaking a language or the words of a language: *She's always correcting my pronunciation.*

proof¹ /pruːf/ n **1** [C;U] a sign that something is certainly true: *There's no proof of his guilt.* **2** [C] a first copy of something printed, on which mistakes can be corrected before the printing process continues **3** [U; after a noun] the standard of strength of some kinds of alcoholic drink: *This whisky is 40 per cent proof.*

proof² adj not influenced by something unpleasant: *His honesty is proof against temptation.*

prop¹ /prɒp ‖ praːp/ n **1** a support which is placed to hold something up: *a clothes prop for the washing line* **2** a person or thing that gives support to others **3** an object used on the stage during the acting of a play or film: *The costumes and props should be ready by Friday.*

prop² *v* **-pp-** [T; + adv/prep] to support something in a particular position: *Prop the gate open with a brick!* | *She propped it against the shed.*

prop sthg ↔ **up** *phr v* [T] **1** to support something: *Prop it up against the wall.* **2** to help something to continue: *We just can't afford to prop up so many needy causes.*

prop·a·gan·da /ˌprɒpəˈgændə ‖ ˌprɑː-/ *n* [U] ideas and information which are spread about officially, especially by a government for its own purposes: *Those aren't facts; it's just propaganda.* **–propagandist** *n* : *political activists and propagandists*

prop·a·gate /ˈprɒpəgeɪt ‖ ˈprɑː-/ *v* **propagated, propagating** **1** [I] *tech* to grow young plants from an original plant: *Cuttings propagate easily.* **2** [T] *fml* to spread ideas and information to a great number of people: *The government is able to use national newspapers and television to propagate its ideas.* **–propagation** /ˌprɒpəˈgeɪʃən ‖ ˌprɑː-/ *n* [U]

pro·pel /prəˈpel/ *v* **-ll-** [T] to move a person or thing in a certain direction, usually forwards

pro·pel·ler /prəˈpeləʳ/ *n* two or more blades fixed to a central bar that is turned at high speed by an engine; propellers are used for moving a ship or aircraft forwards

pro·pen·si·ty /prəˈpensɨti/ *n* **propensities** *fml* a tendency to behave in a particular and usually undesirable way: *She has a propensity to sudden anger.* | *He has a propensity for getting into trouble.*

prop·er /ˈprɒpəʳ ‖ ˈprɑː-/ *adj* **1** [only before a noun] suitable and correct: *She needs proper medical attention.* | *These pages aren't in their proper order.* | *What do you think is the proper role of the press in our society?* **2** socially acceptable: *That is not proper conduct for a girl of your age.* | *the proper thing to do* **3** [after a noun] itself: *We don't live in London proper.*

prop·er·ly /ˈprɒpəli ‖ ˈprɑːpərli/ *adv* in a correct or acceptable way: *I've been learning German for years but I still can't speak it properly.* | *I believe in doing a job properly.*

proper noun /ˌ··ˈ·/ *n* a name used for a particular person or thing and spelt with a capital letter; "James", "London", and "China" are all proper nouns –compare COMMON NOUN

prop·er·ty /ˈprɒpəti ‖ ˈprɑːpərti/ *n* **properties** **1** [U] something which you own: *Always lock your car to protect your property.* **2** [C;U] land, buildings, or both together: *Property in the town centre is now very valuable.* | *There are a number of properties for sale in this street.* **3** [C;] a natural quality of something: *The leaves of this plant have medicinal properties.*

proph·e·cy /ˈprɒfɨsi ‖ ˈprɑː-/ *n* **prophecies** **1** [U] the telling of future events: *the art of prophecy* **2** [C] a statement saying that something will happen in the future: *his prophecies of war* | *The prophecy that he would live to be king was fulfilled.*

proph·e·sy /ˈprɒfɨsaɪ ‖ ˈprɑː-/ *v* **prophesied, prophesied** [I;T; + that] to say that something will happen in the future: *They prophesied disaster.* | *I wouldn't like to prophesy who will win the election.* | *They prophesied that there would be a bad winter.*

proph·et /ˈprɒfɨt ‖ ˈprɑː-/ *n* **1** a person who says what will happen in the future **2 a prophet of doom** a person who is always talking about the

terrible things that they think will happen **3** a person who believes that they are directed by God to teach people religion and acceptable behaviour **4 the Prophet** Mohammed, who formed the Muslim religion **5** an important thinker who introduces and teaches a new idea

pro·phet·ic /prəˈfetɪk/ *adj* (also **prophetical**) correctly telling of things that will happen in the future: *He made a number of prophetic remarks before he died.* **–prophetically** /-kli/ *adv*

pro·pi·ti·ate /prəˈpɪʃieɪt/ *v* **propitiated, propitiating** [T] *fml* to do something to please someone who is angry or unfriendly

pro·pi·tious /prəˈpɪʃəs/ *adj fml* favourable or likely to bring good results: *It is not a propitious time to invest in oil.* **–propitiously** *adv*

pro·po·nent /prəˈpəʊnənt/ *n* a person who argues in favour of something: *an enthusiastic proponent of yoga*

pro·por·tion /prəˈpɔːʃən ‖ -ˈpɔːr-/ *n* **1** [U] the correct relationship between the size and shape of the different parts of something: *The painting lacks proportion.* **2 in proportion** having everything of the correct size or amount compared to other things: *The drawing wasn't in proportion.* [RELATED PHRASE **out of proportion**] **3 keep/see things in proportion** to remember what is important and what is not important: *Try to keep things in proportion.* [RELATED PHRASE **get things out of proportion**] **4** [C] the amount of one thing compared to the amount of something else: *What's the proportion of men to women in your office?* **5** [C] a part or share of something: *Londoners have to spend a large proportion of their salary on rent.* **6 in proportion to:** a compared with the size of something else: *The garage is big in proportion to the house.* **b** happening at the same rate as something else: *The tax increases in proportion to the amount you earn.* **7 out of all proportion to something** much too great compared to something: *The suffering caused by the law is out of all proportion to the benefits it brings.* **8 proportions** [pl] the size and shape of something: *a building of fine proportions*

pro·por·tion·al /prəˈpɔːʃənəl ‖ -ˈpɔːr-/ *adj* in the correct relationship to something else: *His pay is proportional to the amount of work he does.* **–proportionally** *adv*

pro·por·tion·ate /prəˈpɔːʃənɨt ‖ -ˈpɔːr-/ *adj* correct in relation to something else **–proportionately** *adv*

pro·pos·al /prəˈpəʊzəl/ *n* **1** a plan or suggestion: *There's a proposal to build a new supermarket.* | *They are discussing peace proposals.* | *She's made a proposal for new childcare facilities.* **2** an offer of marriage

pro·pose /prəˈpəʊz/ *v* **proposed, proposing** **1** [T; +(that)] *fml* to suggest something: *He proposed delaying our decision for a few days.* | *I propose that we all speak to the manager.* | *He has been proposed for membership of the club.* **2 propose to do something** to intend to do something: *"I'm very upset about their decision."* | *"And what do you propose to do about it?"* **3** [I;T] to ask someone to marry you: *He proposed to her after dinner.* | *He proposed marriage.* **4 propose a motion** to suggest the subject for DEBATE, and speak about why you believe in it **5 propose a toast** *fml* to invite people at a social gathering to raise their glasses and drink as a sign of wishing someone good luck or success: *I would like to propose a toast to the bride and groom.*

prop·o·si·tion¹ /ˌprɒpə'zɪʃən ‖ ˌprɑː-/ n **1** fml a statement in which an opinion or judgment is expressed **2** a suggestion or offer, especially in business: *I've got a proposition to put to you.*

proposition² v [T] infml to offer to have sex with someone: *I was propositioned in the hotel bar.*

pro·pound /prə'paʊnd/ v [T] fml to suggest something such as a problem or a THEORY for people to consider

pro·pri·e·ta·ry /prə'praɪətəri ‖ -teri/ adj sold under the name of a person or company: *proprietary medicines*

pro·pri·e·tor /prə'praɪətəʳ/ n fml the owner of a business; a female owner of a business is sometimes called a **proprietress**

pro·pri·e·ty /prə'praɪəti/ n [U] fml correctness of social or moral behaviour: *You can trust John to behave with perfect propriety.*

pro·pul·sion /prə'pʌlʃən/ n [U] tech the force that moves something forward

pro·sa·ic /prəʊ'zeɪ-ɪk, prə-/ adj dull and uninteresting: *a prosaic job* **–prosaically** /-kli/ adv

pro·scribe /prəʊ'skraɪb/ v proscribed, proscribing [T] fml to forbid something officially **–proscription** /prəʊ'skrɪpʃən, prə-/ n [C;U]

prose /prəʊz/ n [U] language written in its usual form and not as poetry: *He usually writes in prose.*

pros·e·cute /'prɒsɪkjuːt ‖ 'prɑː-/ v prosecuted, prosecuting [I;T] to bring a criminal charge against someone in a court of law: *He was prosecuted for stealing.* | *Shop-lifters warned – we always prosecute!*

pros·e·cu·tion /ˌprɒsɪ'kjuːʃən ‖ ˌprɑː-/ n **1** [C;U] the bringing of a criminal charge against someone: *The sale of alcohol to children can lead to prosecution.* | *The police brought a successful prosecution against him.* **2 the prosecution** [U; + sing/pl verb] the lawyers who try to prove someone's guilt in a court of law: *The prosecution is calling its final witness.* | *Mr Jones is acting for the prosecution.* –compare DEFENCE

pros·e·cu·tor /'prɒsɪkjuːtəʳ ‖ 'prɑː-/ n the lawyer who tries to prove someone's guilt in a court of law

pros·pect¹ /'prɒspekt ‖ 'prɑː-/ n **1** [C;U] a possibility that something will happen: *There's not much prospect of my being able to see you soon.* | *The prospects for a peaceful solution to the crisis are quite good.* **2** [sing] something which you expect to happen: *She hates the prospect of having to live alone.* | *That's not a very cheerful prospect.* **3** someone's prospects someone's chances of being successful in their job: *His prospects are very good.* **4** [sing] fml a wide or distant view

pros·pect² /prə'spekt ‖ 'prɑːspekt/ v [I] to look for things like gold, oil, or minerals in a particular area **–prospector** n

pro·spec·tive /prə'spektɪv/ adj probable or expected: *We've found a prospective buyer for the house.*

pro·spec·tus /prə'spektəs/ n a printed statement giving information about a university, a school, or a company

pros·per /'prɒspəʳ ‖ 'prɑː-/ v [I] **1** to become successful and rich: *Our business has just started to prosper.* **2** to develop favourably

pro·sper·i·ty /prɒ'sperɪti ‖ prɑː-/ n [U] success and wealth: *We live in a period of great prosperity.*

pros·per·ous /'prɒspərəs ‖ 'prɑː-/ adj rich and successful **–prosperously** adv

pros·ti·tute¹ /'prɒstɪtjuːt ‖ 'prɑːstɪtuːt/ n a person, especially a woman, who has sex with people for money

prostitute² v prostituted, prostituting [T] fml **1 prostitute yourself** to have sex with people for money **2** to use an ability for doing things which are not important and do not deserve respect, and that usually you do not have to do, especially in order to make money: *He prostituted his talent by acting in such terrible films.*

pros·ti·tu·tion /ˌprɒstɪ'tjuːʃən ‖ ˌprɑːstɪ'tuː-/ n [U] the act or work of having sex with people for money

pros·trate¹ /'prɒstreɪt ‖ 'prɑː-/ adj **1** lying flat, with your face and the front of your body downwards **2** so upset or weak that you are unable to act: *She was prostrate with grief.* **–prostration** /prɒ'streɪʃən ‖ prɑː-/ n [C;U]

pros·trate² /prɒ'streɪt ‖ 'prɑːstreɪt/ v prostrated, prostrating **1 prostrate yourself** to lie face down on the ground, usually as a sign of worship **2 be prostrated by something** to be made so weak by something that you are unable to do anything: *She was prostrated by illness.*

pro·tag·o·nist /prəʊ'tægənɪst/ n **1** a leader or supporter of an idea or purpose: *Mrs Pankhurst was one of the chief protagonists of women's rights.* **2** one of the most important characters in a play, story, or actual event

pro·tect /prə'tekt/ v [T] to keep a person or thing safe from something unpleasant: *He raised his arm to protect his face from the blow.* | *We must protect ourselves against further attack.* **–protector** n

pro·tec·tion /prə'tekʃən/ n **1** [U] the act of keeping a person or thing safe, or the state of being kept safe: *That coat's too thin to give you any protection against the cold.* | *I've hired a bodyguard for the children's protection.* **2** [sing] a person or thing that keeps someone or something safe: *He bought a hat as a protection against the sun.*

pro·tec·tive /prə'tektɪv/ adj **1** [only before a noun] giving protection against harm: *All workers must wear protective clothing.* **2** having a desire to protect and look after someone: *He is very protective towards his younger sister.* **–protectiveness** n [U]

pro·tec·tor·ate /prə'tektərɪt/ n a country which is controlled and protected by a more powerful nation

prot·é·gé /'prɒtɪʒeɪ ‖ 'prəʊ-/ n a person who is guided and helped by someone of influence or power; a woman who is guided and helped in this way is called a **protégée**

pro·tein /'prəʊtiːn/ n [C;U] a substance which is found in foods like meat and eggs, and which helps your body to grow and stay healthy

pro·test¹ /'prəʊtest/ n **1** [C;U] a complaint about something: *I would like to register a protest about local services.* | *They are demonstrating in protest against the new law.* | *You should write a letter of protest to your M.P.* **2 under protest** unwillingly and complaining that something is not fair: *They led him away under protest.*

pro·test² /prə'test/ v **1** [I] to express your disagreement or annoyance about something: *They protested about the bad food at the hotel.* | *We protested to the manager.* | *a crowd protesting against the war* **2** [T; + that] to state firmly that something is true when other people do not believe you: *She protested that she was too tired to continue dancing.* | *He has always protested his innocence.* **–protester** n

Prot·es·tant /'prɒtɪstənt ‖ 'prɑː-/ adj belonging to a part of the Christian church that separated from the ROMAN CATHOLIC Church in the 16th century –**Protestant** n –**Protestantism** n [U]

prot·es·ta·tion /ˌprotɬ'steɪʃən ˌprəʊ-‖ ˌprɑː-, prəʊ-/ n fml a strong declaration that what you say is true

pro·to·col /'prəʊtəkɒl ‖ -kɔːl/ n [U] the system of rules about acceptable behaviour on official occasions, which is used especially by representatives of governments

pro·ton /'prəʊtɒn ‖ -tɑːn/ n a very small piece of matter present in the central part of an atom

pro·to·type /'prəʊtətaɪp/ n the first form of something, from which all later forms develop: *They are working on the prototype* of *a new car.*

pro·trac·ted /prə'træktɬd ‖ prəʊ-/ adj lasting a long time: *a protracted argument | a protracted stay in hospital*

pro·trac·tor /prə'træktəʳ ‖ prəʊ-/ n an instrument, usually in the form of a half-circle, which is used for measuring and drawing angles

pro·trude /prə'truːd ‖ prəʊ-/ v **protruded, protruding** [I] fml to stick out from a place or through a surface: *She saw a gun protruding* from *the man's pocket. | protruding teeth* –**protrusion** /-'truːʒən/ n [C;U]

pro·tu·ber·ance /prə'tjuːbərəns ‖ prəʊ'tuː-/ n fml something curved that stands out from a surface

proud /praʊd/ adj **1** having or showing self-respect (a word used to express approval): *They are proud people despite their poverty.* **2** having too high an opinion of yourself (a word used to express disapproval): *She's too proud to mix with people like us.* **3** feeling satisfaction and pleasure about something that you have done or something that someone close to you has done: *You should be proud* of *your achievements. | We're all very proud of you. | I'm very proud to be invited to give this speech. | It was a proud day for her parents.*
□ USEFUL PATTERNS be proud of something or someone; be proud to do something; be proud that... **4 do someone proud** infml to treat a guest very well –**proudly** adv

prove /pruːv/ v **proved, proved** or **proven** /'pruːvən/, **proving 1** [T] to show that something is certainly real or true: *He has proved his courage in battle. | There is enough evidence to prove that she is guilty.* **2** [T + complement] to show over time that something has, or you have, a certain quality: *It proved to be a terrible mistake. | He proved more talented than anyone had imagined.*

prov·en /'pruːvən; Scot 'prəʊvən/ adj shown to be real or true: *I can recommend Mr. Jones as a manager of proven ability.*

prov·erb /'prɒvɜːb ‖ 'prɑːvɜːrb/ n a short well-known saying about a general truth: *My favourite proverb is "Don't put all your eggs in one basket".*

pro·ver·bi·al /prə'vɜːbiəl ‖ -ɜːr-/ adj **1** of or from a proverb **2** very widely known and talked about: *his proverbial generosity*

pro·vide /prə'vaɪd/ v **provided, providing** [T] **1** to give or supply something to someone: *The hotel provides very good meals. | The school does not provide paper for students. | These letters should provide us with all the information we need.*
□ USEFUL PATTERNS to provide something for someone; to provide someone with something **2 provide for someone** to supply someone with all the things that they need: *He has to provide for his elderly parents.* **3 provide for something** to make the necessary arrangements for a possible future event: *The budget must provide for a possible increase in unemployment levels.* **4 provide that** fml

to state that something should happen or will happen: *The law provides that ancient buildings must be preserved.*

pro·vid·ed /prə'vaɪdɬd/ conj (also **provided that, providing, providing that**) on condition that: *I will go, provided you go too. | I'll dry the dishes, providing that you do the washing-up.*

prov·i·dence /'prɒvɬdəns ‖ 'prɑː-/ n [U] good fortune which is said to be brought by God or fate

prov·i·dent /'prɒvɬdənt ‖ 'prɑː-/ adj careful about providing for future needs

prov·i·den·tial /ˌprɒvɬ'denʃəl◄ ‖ ˌprɑː-/ adj fml fortunate –**providentially** adv

prov·ince /'prɒvɬns ‖ 'prɑː-/ n **1** [C] one of the main divisions of a country, that has its own local government: *Eastern Province in Zambia is the most densely populated.* **2** [U] an area of thought, knowledge, or responsibility: *Persian art is outside my province, I'm afraid.* **3 the provinces** [pl] the parts of a country outside its main city: *The film is new, so it is not yet being shown in the provinces.*

pro·vin·cial /prə'vɪnʃəl/ adj **1** [only before a noun] of or from a province or the provinces: *a provincial newspaper* **2** having old-fashioned ideas and habits which are believed to be typical of people from the provinces: *I found him rather narrow-minded and provincial.* –**provincialism** n [U]

pro·vi·sion¹ /prə'vɪʒən/ n **1** [U] the act of supplying something: *Local councils are responsible for the provision* of *books to schools.* **2 make provision** for to prepare for future needs: *We must make some provision for our retirement.* **3** [C] a condition in an agreement or law: *According to the provisions of the agreement the money must be paid back quickly.* **4 provisions** [pl] supplies of food and drink

provision² v [T] fml to supply someone with food and other necessary things

pro·vi·sion·al /prə'vɪʒənəl/ adj existing for the present time only and likely to be changed later: *It's just a provisional arrangement.* –**provisionally** adv

pro·vi·so /prə'vaɪzəʊ/ n a condition that must be fulfilled before an agreement is accepted: *I've agreed to do the work, with the proviso that I'm paid in advance.*

prov·o·ca·tion /ˌprɒvə'keɪʃən ‖ ˌprɑː-/ n [C;U] the act of trying to make someone angry or the state of being made angry: *Bringing her here was a deliberate provocation. | She hit me, without the least provocation.*

pro·voc·a·tive /prə'vɒkətɪv ‖ -'vɑː-/ adj intending to cause anger, or sexual desire: *a provocative speech | provocative behaviour* –**provocatively** adv

pro·voke /prə'vəʊk/ v **provoked, provoking** [T] **1** to make someone very angry, especially by continually annoying them: *I don't want to fight, so don't provoke me.*
□ USEFUL PATTERNS to provoke someone; to provoke someone into doing something; to provoke someone to do something **2** to cause an unpleasant feeling or action: *The article provoked many letters of complaint.*

pro·vok·ing /prə'vəʊkɪŋ/ adj annoying

prow /praʊ/ n the pointed front part of a ship or boat

prow·ess /'praʊɬs/ n [U] fml great skill: *I admire his prowess* as *a footballer.*

prowl¹ /praʊl/ v (also **prowl about**) [I] to move about quietly, trying not to be seen or heard: *I thought I heard someone prowling about in the garden last night.* –**prowler** n

prowl² n [sing] **on the prowl** moving about quietly trying not to be seen or heard

prox·im·i·ty /prɒkˈsɪmɪti ‖ praːk-/ n [U] fml **1** nearness: *We chose the house because of its proximity to the school.* **2 in the proximity of** near to a place

prox·y /ˈprɒksi ‖ ˈpraːksi/ n **proxies 1** someone who has the right to represent another person, especially as a voter at an election **2 by proxy** by sending another person to represent you: *You can vote by proxy.*

prude /pruːd/ n a person who is easily shocked by things which they consider improper, especially sexual things (a word used to express disapproval) –**prudish** adj –**prudishly** adv

pru·dent /ˈpruːdənt/ adj sensible and careful: *We were taught to be prudent with money.* –opposite **imprudent** –**prudence** n [U]

prud·er·y /ˈpruːdəri/ n (also **prudishness** /ˈpruːdɪʃn‿ɪs/) [U] the behaviour or opinions of someone who is easily shocked by improper things, especially sexual things (a word used to express disapproval)

prune¹ /pruːn/ n a dried PLUM

prune² v **pruned, pruning** [T] to cut off some of the branches of a tree or bush to improve its shape and help it grow better

pry /praɪ/ v **pried, pried 1** [I] to try to find out about someone else's private affairs (a word used to express disapproval): *Those journalists are paid to pry into the affairs of the royal family.* | *I'm sorry, I didn't mean to pry.* **2** [T; + adv/prep] to force something open, or to force two things apart, using a tool or metal bar: *I can't pry the lid off this box without breaking it.*

P.S. /ˌpiː ˈes/ n infml a short addition to the end of a letter or message; an abbreviation for POSTSCRIPT: *Look. There's a P.S. at the bottom.* | *Yours sincerely, J. Smith. P.S. I shan't be able to come before Thursday.*

psalm /sɑːm ‖ sɑːm, sɑːlm/ n (also **Psalm**) a song or poem in praise of God

pseud /sjuːd ‖ suːd/ n infml a person who tries to appear better than others in their knowledge, experience, and social position (a word used to express disapproval)

pseu·do·nym /ˈsjuːdənɪm ‖ ˈsuːdənɪm/ n a name which a writer uses instead of his or her real name: *Eric Blair wrote under the pseudonym of George Orwell.*

psy·che /ˈsaɪki/ n tech or fml the human mind, soul, or spirit

psy·che·del·ic /ˌsaɪk‿ɪˈdelɪk‿/ adj **1** concerning certain drugs which cause changes in your mind and in the way your senses experience reality **2** concerning art forms which have an effect on your brain because they use strong or strange patterns and colours

psy·chi·a·trist /saɪˈkaɪətr‿ɪst ‖ sə-/ n a doctor who is trained to study and treat illnesses of the mind

psy·chi·a·try /saɪˈkaɪətri ‖ sə-/ n [U] the study and treatment of illnesses of the mind –**psychiatric** /ˌsaɪkiˈætrɪk/ adj

psy·chic /ˈsaɪkɪk/ adj (also **psychical** /-kɪkəl/) **1** concerning strange powers or events which cannot be explained by scientists: *They claim that his psychic powers enabled him to predict his mother's death.* **2** fml concerning the mind rather than the body: *We are studying psychic disorders caused by great unhappiness in childhood.* –**psychic** n : *Psychics were used to try and find the kidnapped girl.*

psy·cho·an·a·lyse /ˌsaɪkəʊˈænəlaɪz/ v **psychoanalysed, psychoanalysing** (also **psychoanalyze** AmE) [T] to treat disorders of the mind by using psychoanalysis

psy·cho·a·nal·y·sis /ˌsaɪkəʊ-əˈnæl‿ɪs‿ɪs/ n [U] a way of treating certain disorders of the mind by examining the sufferer's past life, feelings, and dreams in an effort to find the hidden causes of their illness

psy·cho·an·a·lyst /ˌsaɪkəʊˈænəl-‿ɪst/ n (also **analyst**) a person who is trained to treat disorders of the mind by using psychoanalysis

psy·cho·log·i·cal /ˌsaɪkəˈlɒdʒɪkəl‿ ‖ -ˈlɑː-/ adj **1** concerning your mind and thoughts: *Your problems are psychological and can be solved if you change your attitude.* **2** [only before a noun] using psychology: *Psychological tests are being used to analyse the personalities of job applicants.* –**psychologically** /-kli/ adv

psy·chol·o·gist /saɪˈkɒlədʒ‿ɪst ‖ -ˈkɑː-/ n a person who is trained to study and explain how the human mind works

psy·chol·o·gy /saɪˈkɒlədʒi ‖ -ˈkɑː-/ n [U] **1** the scientific study of the mind and how it works **2 the psychology of someone** the way in which the mind of a particular person or group works: *We must take into account the psychology of both teachers and pupils.*

psy·cho·path /ˈsaɪkəpæθ/ n a person who has a serious disorder of the mind that may cause violent or criminal behaviour –**psychopathic** /ˌsaɪkəˈpæθɪk‿/ adj

psy·cho·sis /saɪˈkəʊs‿ɪs/ n **psychoses** /-siːz/ [C;U] tech a serious disorder of the mind that may produce character changes

psy·cho·so·mat·ic /ˌsaɪkəʊsəˈmætɪk‿ ‖ -kəsə-/ n caused by fear or anxiety rather than by a disease or physical disorder: *Her illness appears to be psychosomatic.*

psy·cho·ther·a·py /ˌsaɪkəʊˈθerəpi/ n [U] tech treatment of disorders of the mind using PSYCHOLOGY rather than drugs –**psychotherapist** n

psy·chot·ic /saɪˈkɒtɪk ‖ -ˈkɑː-/ n tech a person suffering from a serious disorder of the mind which may produce character changes –**psychotic** adj : *psychotic behaviour*

pt a written abbreviation for PINT(S)

PTO /ˌpiː tiː ˈəʊ/ a request to the reader to look at the next page; it is an abbreviation for "please turn over", and is written at the bottom of a page

pub /pʌb/ n a building which is not a club or hotel, where alcohol may be bought and drunk during fixed hours and where people meet and talk: *We all went down to the pub last night.*

pu·ber·ty /ˈpjuːbəti ‖ -ər-/ n [U] the stage in the development of your body when you are becoming an adult and you become able to have children

pu·bic /ˈpjuːbɪk/ adj [only before a noun] concerning the area around your sexual organs: *pubic hair*

pub·lic¹ /ˈpʌblɪk/ adj [only before a noun] **1** concerning people in general: *There has been a change in public opinion.* | *the increasing public awareness of environmental issues* **2** for everyone to use, see, or attend: *a public library* | *public telephones* | *We're calling a public meeting next week.* | *They want smoking to be banned in all public places.* **3** connected with the government and the services it provides: *The government is increasing public spending on health.* **4** well-known to people in general: *the prime minister and other public figures* **5 make something public** to make something known to people, so that it is no longer secret: *The figures have not yet been made public.*

public² *n* [+ sing/pl verb] **1 the public, the general public** people in general: *The park is only open to the public at weekends. | The public are requested to remain silent during parliamentary debates.* **2** a group of people who share an interest in a particular person or activity: *He writes songs that he knows will please his public.* **3 in public** in the presence of other people

pub·li·can /ˈpʌblɪkən/ *n* a person who owns or manages a PUB

pub·li·ca·tion /ˌpʌblɪˈkeɪʃən/ *n* **1** [U] the act of making something known to the public: *We are waiting for the publication of the election results.* **2** [U] the process of printing something and offering it for sale to the public: *The publication of his diaries caused embarrassment to other politicians.* **3** [C] something, such as a book or magazine, which is printed and sold to the public: *His latest publication is by far the best.*

public bar /ˌ·· ˈ·/ *n* a room in a PUB or a hotel which is plainly furnished, and where the cheapest prices are charged for drinks –compare SALOON BAR

public con·ve·ni·ence /ˌ·· ·ˈ····/ *n* BrE euph a TOILET which is provided for the public to use, often in the centre of a town (a less direct word than "toilet")

public house /ˌ·· ˈ·/ *n fml* a PUB

pub·li·cist /ˈpʌblɪsɪst/ *n* a person who brings something to the attention of the public, especially someone who works in advertising

pub·lic·i·ty /pʌˈblɪsɪti/ *n* [U] **1** public attention: *The prime minister's recent speech on the environment got a lot of publicity.* **2** the business of bringing someone or something to the attention of the public: *The recent publicity campaign has changed people's attitudes to unleaded petrol.*

pub·li·cize /ˈpʌblɪsaɪz/ *v* **publicized, publicizing** (also **publicise** *BrE*) [T] to bring something to the attention of the public: *We're using posters to publicize the contest.*

public pros·e·cu·tor /ˌ·· ·ˈ····/ *n* a government lawyer who acts for the state in bringing charges against criminals in a court of law

public re·la·tions /ˌ·· ·ˈ··/ *n* (also **PR**) **1** [pl] the relations between an organization and the general public: *Inviting people to visit the factory would be good for public relations.* **2** [U] the job of encouraging good relations between an organization and the general public: *He works in public relations.*

public school /ˌ·· ˈ·/ *n* **1** BrE a private school for 13 to 18-year-old children who usually also live there; it is paid for by their parents **2** AmE a free local state school –compare PRIVATE SCHOOL

public spir·it·ed /ˌ·· ˈ····/ *adj* showing a desire to serve people and do what is helpful for society

pub·lish /ˈpʌblɪʃ/ *v* [T] **1** to have a book, magazine, or piece of writing printed, and offer it for sale to the public: *The book was first published in 1982. | He refused to publish my poem.* **2** to make something known to the public: *News of his death wasn't published for several days.*

pub·lish·er /ˈpʌblɪʃər/ *n* a person or firm whose business is to publish books, newspapers, or magazines

pub·lish·ing /ˈpʌblɪʃɪŋ/ *n* [U] the business or job of preparing books, newspapers, or magazines and offering them for sale: *She works in publishing.*

puce /pjuːs/ *adj,n* [U] a dark pinkish purple colour

puck·er /ˈpʌkər/ *v* (also **pucker up**) [I;T] to form into folds: *She puckered her lips in disapproval.*

pud·ding /ˈpʊdɪŋ/ *n* [C;U] **1** BrE infml the sweet dish of a meal, served after the main dish: *What's for pudding, John?* **2** a dish based on flour or rice which is usually solid and served hot: *We're having rice pudding. | There's a steak and kidney pudding in the oven.*

pud·dle /ˈpʌdl/ *n* a small amount of rain water lying in a hollow place in the ground: *Don't step in the puddles!*

pu·er·ile /ˈpjʊəraɪl ‖ -rəl/ *adj fml* silly and suitable only for children

puff¹ /pʌf/ *v* **1** [I] to breathe rapidly and with effort, usually because you have been running or doing something tiring: *He jumped onto the bus, puffing with exhaustion.* **2** [I;T] to blow out smoke repeatedly, in small amounts: *Don't puff cigarette smoke in my face. | Smoke was puffing from the engine of the train.* **3** [I;T] to breathe smoke into your mouth and then blow it out: *She was puffing away on small cigars all evening!* **4** [I] to move while sending out small clouds of smoke: *The train finally puffed into the station.*

puff out *phr v* [I;T **puff** sthg ↔ **out**] to become or to make something larger, especially with air: *The bird puffed out its feathers.*

puff up *phr v* [I] to swell: *My leg puffed up so that I could hardly walk.*

puff² *n* **1** an act of breathing smoke into your mouth and blowing it out again: *He took a puff of his cigarette.* **2** a sudden short rush of air or smoke: *The paper was blown away by a puff of wind.*

puffed /pʌft/ *adj* (also **puffed out**) *infml* tired and finding it difficult to breathe

puf·fin /ˈpʌfɪn/ *n* a seabird with a very large brightly coloured beak

puff·y /ˈpʌfi/ *adj* **puffier, puffiest** swollen –**puffiness** *n* [U]

pug /pʌg/ *n* a small dog with a wide face and a flat nose

pug·na·cious /pʌɡˈneɪʃəs/ *adj fml* fond of quarrelling and fighting –**pugnaciously** *adv*

puke /pjuːk/ *v* **puked, puking** (also **puke** sthg ↔ **up**) [I;T] *slang* to be sick: *The worst moment was when someone puked all over my dress.* –**puke** *n* [U]

pull¹ /pʊl/ *v* **1** [I;T] to move something or someone towards yourself: *She pulled the door open. | He pulled his chair up to the table. | I got hold of the rope and pulled as hard as I could. | He pulled her into the kitchen.* –see picture on page 736 **2** [T] to move something along: *carts pulled by horses and ponies | The train is pulled by a powerful engine.* **3** [T] to attract people: *She managed to pull a number of new voters. | The match pulled a crowd of 20,000.* **4 pull a gun** to bring out a small gun that you had kept hidden: *Suddenly she pulled a gun on me.* **5 pull a face** to make an expression with your face to show that you disagree with something or do not like it **6 pull a fast one** *infml* to gain an advantage over someone by deceiving them in some way **7 pull a muscle** to hurt a muscle in your body by stretching it too much **8 pull the trigger** to press the TRIGGER of a gun so that it fires: *He pointed her at her and pulled the trigger.* **9 pull someone's leg** to tell someone things that are not true for amusement: *He said that I'd failed, but I think he was only pulling my leg.* **10 pull something to pieces** to say that something is worthless by pointing out all its faults **11 pull strings** to use influence in order to get something: *I think he pulled a few strings to get that job.* **12 pull your socks up** to start making a greater effort **13 pull your weight** to do your full share of work

pull at sthg *phr v* [T] to try to pull something towards you: *The children pulled at her coat.*

pull away *phr v* [I] (of a vehicle) to start moving away: *I arrived just as the bus was pulling away.*

pull sthg ↔ **down** *phr v* [T] to destroy a building: *A lot of the old houses have been pulled down.*

pull in *phr v* [I] **1** (of a train) to arrive at a station: *We arrived just as the train was pulling in.* **2** (of a vehicle) to move to one side of the road and stop

pull sthg ↔ **off** *phr v* [T] **1** to take off clothes quickly and roughly: *She ran in and pulled off her coat.* **2 pull it off** *infml* to succeed in doing something difficult

pull sthg ↔ **on** *phr v* [T] to put on clothes quickly and roughly: *She pulled on her socks and shoes.*

pull out *phr v* **1** [I] (of a train) to leave a station: *The guard blew his whistle and the train pulled out.* **2** [I;T **pull** sbdy ↔ **out**] to leave a place or cause people to leave a place: *The army has started to pull out of the area.* | *Troops will be pulled out as soon as possible.* **3** [I] to say that you do not want to go ahead with something that you had agreed to do: *I decided to pull out of the agreement.*

pull over *phr v* [I] (of a vehicle) to move to one side of the road and stop

pull through *phr v* **1** [I;T **pull through** sthg] to continue to live in spite of an illness or accident: *Will she pull through, doctor?* | *It's not certain that he'll pull through the operation.* **2** [T **pull** sbdy **through** (sthg)] to help someone to continue to live in spite of an illness or accident

pull together *phr v* **1** [I] to all work together for a common aim **2 pull yourself together** to control your feelings and behave in a calm way

pull up *phr v* [I] (of a vehicle) to stop: *A car pulled up outside the house.*

pull² *n* **1** an act of pulling something: *I took hold of the rope and gave it a pull.* **2** *fml* a force which attracts you to something or makes you want to do something: *I still felt the pull of the sea.*

pul·let /ˈpʊlət/ *n* a young hen

pul·ley /ˈpʊli/ *n* an apparatus which consists of a wheel over which a rope or chain can be moved, and which is used for lifting heavy things: *We managed to hoist up the trunk using a system of pulleys.*

pull·o·ver /ˈpʊlˌəʊvəʳ/ *n* a woollen piece of clothing for the top half of your body, which you pull on over your head

pul·mo·na·ry /ˈpʌlmənəri, pʊl- ‖ ˈpʊlməneri, ˈpʌl-/ *adj* [only before a noun] *tech* concerning your lungs

pulp¹ /pʌlp/ *n* **1** [sing;U] a soft almost liquid mass, such as the soft inside part of many fruits or vegetables: *The vegetables were boiled to a pulp.* **2** [U] wood or other vegetable materials which have been softened and are used for making paper **3** [U] poor quality books or magazines

pulp² *v* [T] to crush something so that it becomes a pulp

pul·pit /ˈpʊlpɪt/ *n* a small raised enclosure in a church, from which the priest talks to the worshippers

pul·sate /pʌlˈseɪt ‖ ˈpʌlseɪt/ *v* **pulsated, pulsating** [I] to move or shake very regularly, like the beating of your heart: *The room pulsated with the rhythm of deafening music.*

pulse¹ /pʌls/ *n* **1** [C] the regular beating of blood in the main blood tubes carrying blood from your

---

THE OFFICE

Exercise 1

Match the words in the box to the descriptions. Write the number of the description beside the correct word.

calculator		waste paper basket	
disk drive		V. D. U.	
fax machine		answering machine	
photocopier		pencil sharpener	
printer		stapler	

1 A machine which records telephone messages.

2 A machine which sends copies of documents along telephone lines.

3 A container for paper which you don't need.

4 A machine which copies documents.

5 A machine for passing information to and from a computer.

6 A small machine which can perform calculations.

7 A small machine which uses short pieces of metal wire to join papers together.

8 A machine which prints information from a computer onto paper.

9 A machine which cuts away the wooden part of a pencil.

10 A machine with a screen which shows information from a computer.

Exercise 2

Can you explain the difference between these things? Look up the words in the dictionary if you don't know.

1 calendar / diary

2 floppy disk / hard disk

3 paper clips / staples

539

office

calendar

noticeboard *(BrE)*/bulletin board *(AmE)*

pencil

filing trays

lamp

pencil sharpener
diary *(BrE)*/desk calendar *(AmE)*

window

rsonal mputer

printer

desk

rd disk

printout

mouse

typewriter

keyboard
disk drive

calculator

index cards

loppy disk

(ring) binder

photocopier

word processor

screen

v.d.u.

fax machine

telephone

answering machine

secretary

shorthand pad

fax

pen

stapler

(typist's) chair

staples
paper clips

waste-paper basket/bin *(BrE)*

filing cabinet

file(s)

PREPOSITIONS

In the picture opposite the following prepositions are shown by the numbers

1 ... (going) **down** the steps
2 ... climbing) **up** the ladder
3 ... **beside/next to** the ladder
4 ... **outside** the supermarket
5 ... **over/above** the doorway
6 ... (going) **into** the supermarket
7 ... (coming) **out of** the supermarket
8 ... (going) **through** the doorway
9 ... **between** the bank and the supermarket
10 ... (walking) **past** the newsagent's
11 ... (leaning) **against** the wall, **below/**

under the sign
12 ... (standing) **by/near** the bank
13 ... **on** the motorbike
14 ... **behind** the car
15 ... **at** the crossing
16 ... (walking) **across** the road, **in front of** the car, **towards/in the direction of** the bank
17 ... (pointing) **to/at** the car
18 ... **inside/on** the bus, (looking) **through** the window
19 ... (getting) **off** the bus
20 ... (getting) **on/onto** the bus
21 ... **opposite** the bank
22 ... (walking) **away from** the bus stop
23 ... (dancing) **round** the flowerbed
24 ... (walking) **along** the pavement, **to** the bus stop
25 ... **in** the car

Choose the correct preposition or phrase in this passage.

Mrs Macdonald walked [1] towards / into the railway station and went [2] near / to the ticket office, where she bought a ticket to Brighton. [3]Under / outside her arm she carried a box, [4]inside / into which was her cat, Cleopatra. She walked [5] out of / towards the ticket office [6] to / through the newsagent where she bought a newspaper to read [7] on / on to the train. Mrs Macdonald showed her tickets to the inspector at the barrier and then she walked [8] along / beside the platform looking for a first class non-smoking compartment. She found one which was nearly empty. There was a man sitting [9] in / at the corner. Mrs Macdonald opened the door and got [10] in / into the compartment. She bent down and tried to put the box [11] under / down the seat but it was too big so she put it on the seat [12]between / beside her. Then she notice

that the man had a box on the seat [13] next to / behind him.

When the train arrived in Brighton station, Mrs Macdonald opened the box to make sure that her cat was safe. At the same moment, the man opened his box. A small dog jumped [14] out of / out the box! Mrs Macdonald's cat jumped [15] against / through the open window. The small dog tried to follow the cat but the man caught caught it before it got [16] out / outside the compartment. Mrs Macdonald opened the door and called to her cat. Slowly the cat came [17] towards / in the direction of her. "Come here, Cleopatra," she said "Don't be frightened." When the cat was [18] near / at her, Mrs Macdonald put her hand [19]under / down the cat's body and picked it up.

heart, especially as it can be felt by a finger on your wrist: *The doctor frowned as he took my pulse.* | *a weak pulse* **2** (C) a regular beat or VIBRATION, for example of music or sound **3 pulses** [pl] seeds from particular plants, such as beans, which can be eaten

pulse² *v* **pulsed, pulsing** [I] to move or shake very regularly, like the beating of your heart: *He could feel the blood pulsing through his body as he waited for the next explosion.*

pul·ver·ize /ˈpʌlvəraɪz/ *v* **pulverized, pulverizing** (also **pulverise** *BrE*) [T] **1** to reduce something to a fine powder or dust through crushing **2** *infml* to defeat someone or destroy something completely

pu·ma /ˈpjuːmə/ *n* a large member of the cat family which lives in the Americas

pum·ice /ˈpʌmɪs/ *n* (also **pumice stone** /ˈ··· ·/) [U] a light, silver-grey rock, used for rubbing surfaces smooth

pum·mel /ˈpʌməl/ *v* **-ll-** (**-l-** *AmE*) [T] to hit a person or thing repeatedly, usually with your closed hand

pump¹ /pʌmp/ *n* a machine which is used to force liquids, air, or gas into or out of something: *Pumps are used to irrigate the fields in the dry season.* | *a petrol pump*

pump² *v* **1** [I;T] to empty or fill with a liquid or gas by means of a pump, or something like a pump: *They had pumped all the water out of the well.* | *His heart was pumping fast.* **2 pump money into something** *infml* to spend a lot of money on something: *She has pumped money into the business.* **3 pump someone** *infml* to ask someone a lot of questions in the hope of finding out something that you want to know **4 pump someone's hand** to shake someone's hand with force
pump sthg ↔ up *phr v* [T] to fill something with air: *My front tyre needs to be pumped up.*

pump·kin /ˈpʌmpkɪn/ *n* [C;U] a very large, round, dark yellow fruit that grows on the ground

pun¹ /pʌn/ *n* an amusing use of a word or phrase that has two meanings, or of two words which have the same sound; an example of a pun is 'Seven days without water make one weak'

pun² *v* **-nn-** [I] to make puns

punch¹ /pʌntʃ/ *v* **1** [I;T] to hit a person or thing hard with your closed hand: *I was very tempted to punch him on the nose.* –see picture on page 736 **2** [T] to make a hole in something using a special machine: *He's coming to punch our tickets.*

punch² *n* **1** [C] a quick strong blow made with your closed hand: *She gave him a tremendous punch on the nose.* **2** [U] forcefulness (a word used to express approval): *His speech lacked punch.* **3** [C] a tool or machine for cutting holes in things **4** [U] a hot or cold drink made mainly from fruit juice and alcohol

punch line /ˈ·· ·/ *n* the last few words of a joke or story, that cause amusement or surprise

punch-up /ˈ·· ·/ *n infml* a fight

punc·til·i·ous /pʌŋkˈtɪliəs/ *adj fml* very exact and particular about details, especially of behaviour, (a word that is usually used to express approval) –**punctiliously** *adv*

punc·tu·al /ˈpʌŋktʃuəl/ *adj* arriving or doing things at exactly the right time: *She's always punctual for appointments.* –**punctually** *adv*: *He arrived punctually at eight o'clock.* –**punctuality** /ˌpʌŋktʃu·ˈælɪti/ *n* [U]

punc·tu·ate /ˈpʌŋktʃueɪt/ *v* **punctuated, punctuating** [T] **1** to divide a piece of writing into sentences, phrases, and other units by means of special marks, such as full stops (FULL STOP) **2 be punctuated with/by** to be interrupted repeatedly by something: *The match was punctuated by the cheers of supporters.*

punc·tu·a·tion /ˌpʌŋktʃuˈeɪʃən/ *n* [U] the marks used to divide a piece of writing into sentences, phrases, and other units, for example commas (COMMA) or colons (COLON)

punctuation mark /ˌ···ˈ··· ·/ *n* a sign such as a COMMA (,) or FULL STOP (.) that is used to divide up a piece of writing and make it easier to read

punc·ture¹ /ˈpʌŋktʃəʳ/ *n* a small hole in a tyre: *I'm afraid we've got a puncture, so we'll have to change the wheel.*

puncture² *v* **punctured, puncturing** [I;T] to make or get a small hole in something, with the result that air or liquid can get out: *The ball punctured when it fell on a broken bottle.* | *He is in hospital, suffering from a punctured lung.*

pun·dit /ˈpʌndɪt/ *n infml* a person with a lot of knowledge of a particular subject

pun·gent /ˈpʌndʒənt/ *adj* **1** having a strong, sharp taste or smell **2** clever and effective (used of speech or writing) –**pungently** *adv* –**pungency** *n* [U]

pun·ish /ˈpʌnɪʃ/ *v* [T] to make someone suffer for a fault or crime: *She was punished for talking during the lesson.* | *Dangerous driving should be severely punished.*

pun·ish·a·ble /ˈpʌnɪʃəbəl/ *adj* that can be punished by law: *In many countries murder is punishable by death.*

pun·ish·ing /ˈpʌnɪʃɪŋ/ *adj infml* making you very tired and weak: *It was a long and punishing climb to the top.*

pun·ish·ment /ˈpʌnɪʃmənt/ *n* **1** [U] the act of making someone suffer for a fault or crime: *They won't escape punishment again.* **2** [C] a way in which a person is made to suffer for a fault or crime: *In his case the punishment certainly fits the crime.* | *She accepted her punishment without complaint.*

pu·ni·tive /ˈpjuːnɪtɪv/ *adj* intended as punishment and therefore very severe –**punitively** *adv*

punk /pʌŋk/ *n* **1** [U] loud, often violent music which was played in the 1970s and 1980s by and for people opposed to current social values **2** [C] a person who dresses and cuts their hair in a way which is intended to shock people, and who enjoys punk music –**punk** *adj*

pun·net /ˈpʌnɪt/ *n* a small square basket in which soft fruits are sold

punt /pʌnt/ *n* a long narrow boat with a flat bottom, which is moved by someone pushing a long pole against the bottom of the river –**punt** *v* [I;T]

punt·er /ˈpʌntəʳ/ *n BrE infml* **1** a person who risks money on the result of a horse race **2 the punters** your customers: *It looks good, but will the punters buy it?*

pu·ny /ˈpjuːni/ *adj* **punier, puniest** small and weak (a word used to express disapproval): *He's a puny little child.*

pup /pʌp/ *n* **1** see PUPPY **2** a young SEAL¹ or OTTER

pu·pa /ˈpjuːpə/ *n* **pupas** or **pupae** /-piː/ an insect in the middle stage of its development, protected by a hard covering

pu·pil /ˈpjuːpəl/ *n* **1** a person, usually a child, who is being taught **2** the small round black opening in the middle of the coloured part of your eye, through which light passes

pup·pet /'pʌpɪt/ n **1** a figure of a person or animal that can be made to move by someone who pulls the wires or strings that are fixed to different parts of its body **2** a cloth figure of a person or animal that can be made to move by someone who puts their hand inside it **3** a person or government that is controlled by others who are more powerful: *They invaded the country and set up a puppet government.*

pup·pe·teer /ˌpʌpɪ'tɪə^r/ n a person who performs with puppets

pup·py /'pʌpi/ n **puppies** (also **pup**) a young dog

pur·chase[1] /'pɜːtʃɪs ‖ 'pɜːr-/ v **purchased, purchasing** [T] *fml* to buy: *We intend to purchase a house in the country.*

purchase[2] n *fml* **1** [U] the act of buying something: *The purchase of the house should be completed by the end of June.* **2** [C] something that you have bought: *Can I look at your purchases, then?* **3** **make a purchase** to buy something

pur·chas·er /'pɜːtʃəsə^r ‖ 'pɜːr-/ n *fml* a person who buys something from someone else

pure /pjʊə^r/ adj **1** not mixed with anything else, and especially with dirt or harmful substances: *It's made of pure silver.* | *The sea air is so pure and healthy.* **2** free from bad thoughts or actions: *a pure young girl* **3** clear: *a cloudless sky of the purest blue* | *The voices of the young boys were high and pure.* **4** [only before a noun] considered only as a subject for study and not for doing or gaining anything practical: *He's studying pure science.* –compare APPLIED **5** [only before a noun] *infml* complete: *By pure chance she met him again 20 years later.* **6** **pure and simple** [never before a noun] only: *He is motivated by a desire for power, pure and simple.*

pu·ree /'pjʊəreɪ ‖ pjʊ'reɪ/ n [C;U] food boiled to a soft half-liquid mass, with all lumps removed: *apple puree* –**puree** v [T]

pure·ly /'pjʊəli ‖ 'pjʊərli/ adv **1** only: *a decision taken for purely political reasons* **2** **purely and simply** a phrase you use when you want to make it very clear that there is no other reason for something: *I helped him out of friendship, purely and simply.*

pur·ga·tive /'pɜːgətɪv ‖ 'pɜːr-/ n a medicine that causes you to empty your bowels –**purgative** adj

pur·ga·to·ry /'pɜːgətəri ‖ 'pɜːrgətɔːri/ n [U] **1** (also **Purgatory**) a state or place in which, Roman Catholics believe, the soul of a dead person suffers for wrong-doing on earth until it is pure enough to enter Heaven **2** a place or time when you are suffering a lot

purge[1] /pɜːdʒ ‖ pɜːrdʒ/ v **purged, purging** [T] **1** to make yourself or another person clean and free from bad thoughts or actions: *I felt the need to purge myself of my sins.* **2** to remove unwanted people from a group or organization, usually by forceful means

purge[2] n a set of actions intended to remove unwanted members of a group or organization suddenly and often, by force: *The president carried out a purge of disloyal army officers.*

pu·ri·fy /'pjʊərɪfaɪ/ v **purified, purifying** [T] to make a person or thing pure: *Has the water been purified?* –**purification** /ˌpjʊərɪfɪ'keɪʃən/ n [U]

pur·ist /'pjʊərɪst/ n a person who is very careful to do things in the correct way and to try to make sure that others do too: *She's a terrible purist about language.*

pu·ri·tan /'pjʊərɪtən/ n a person who has fixed standards of behaviour and self-control, and thinks that pleasure is unnecessary or wrong (a word usually used to express disapproval) –**puritanical** /ˌpjʊərɪ'tænɪkəl/ adj : *a puritanical attitude toward sex* –**puritanically** /-kli/ adv

pu·ri·ty /'pjʊərɪti/ n [U] the quality or state of being pure

purl /pɜːl ‖ pɜːrl/ n [U] *tech* a simple stitch in knitting (KNIT) –**purl** v [I;T]

pur·loin /pɜː'lɔɪn, 'pɜːlɔɪn ‖ -ɜːr-/ v [T] to steal something or take it without permission (a formal word which is also often used in a humorous way)

pur·ple /'pɜːpəl ‖ 'pɜːr-/ adj,n [U] a dark colour which is a mixture of red and blue –see picture on page 147

pur·port[1] /pɜː'pɔːt ‖ pɜːr'pɔːrt/ v [T] **purport to do/be something** to claim to do something or be something: *His plans are not what they purport to be.*

pur·port[2] /'pɜːpɔːt, -pət ‖ 'pɜːrpɔːrt/ n [U] *fml* the general meaning of someone's words: *The purport of the message seemed to be that she would deal with the situation.*

pur·pose /'pɜːpəs ‖ 'pɜːr-/ n **1** [C] your reason for doing something: *What was the purpose of her visit?* | *Have you come to London to see your family, or for business purposes?* **2** **on purpose** intentionally: *You broke that on purpose!* **3** [C] a use: *Don't waste your money; put it to some good purpose.* | *I haven't got a pen, but a pencil will serve the same purpose.* **4** **to little purpose, to no purpose** without much, or any, effect: *Are you saying that I worked all night to no purpose?* **5** [U] determination to succeed in what you want to do: *Getting a job has given him a new sense of purpose.*

purpose-built /ˌ·· '··◁/ adj specially made for a particular use: *a purpose-built flat*

pur·pose·ful /'pɜːpəsfəl ‖ 'pɜːr-/ adj determined and having a clear purposeful stride: *a purposeful stride* –**purposefully** adv

pur·pose·less /'pɜːpəsləs ‖ 'pɜːr-/ adj without any clear aim or purpose

pur·pose·ly /'pɜːpəsli ‖ 'pɜːr-/ adv intentionally: *He purposely left the letter lying around.*

purr /pɜː^r/ v **1** [I] to make the low continuous sound which a happy cat produces in its throat, or some similar sound **2** [T] to say something in a low pleasant voice –**purr** n

purse[1] /pɜːs ‖ pɜːrs/ n **1** a small leather or plastic bag that people, especially women, use to carry money in –compare WALLET **2** *AmE* a bag in which a woman carries the things she needs when she goes out

purse[2] v **pursed, pursing** [T] **purse your lips** to bring your lips together into a round shape: *She pursed her lips to show her displeasure.*

purs·er /'pɜːsə^r ‖ 'pɜːr-/ n an officer on a ship who keeps the ship's accounts and is also in charge of the travellers' comfort

pur·sue /pə'sjuː ‖ pər'suː/ v **pursued, pursuing** [T] *fml* **1** to follow someone, especially in order to catch or hurt them: *The police realized that they were pursuing the wrong man.* **2** *fml* to be busy with an activity or interest, or continue to develop it: *He is pursuing his studies at the university.* | *She was keen to pursue her interest in painting.*

pur·su·er /pə'sjuːə^r ‖ pər'suːər/ n a person or animal that is following another one in order to catch or hurt them: *She managed to escape her pursuers.*

pur·suit /pə'sjuːt ‖ pər'suːt/ n **1** [U] the act of following a person or thing in order to catch or hurt them:

The police car raced through the streets in pursuit of the stolen motorbike. **2** [U] the search for something that you want: *They emigrated to Australia in pursuit of a better life.* **3** [C] any activity which you spend time doing, usually for pleasure: *One of his favourite pursuits was stamp collecting.*

pur·vey /pɜː'veɪ ‖ pɜːr-/ *v* **purveyed, purveying** [T] *fml or tech* to supply food or other needed goods to people as a trade – **purveyor** *n*

pus /pʌs/ *n* [U] a thick yellowish liquid that is produced in an infected wound

push¹ /pʊʃ/ *v* **1** [I;T] to use sudden or steady pressure to move someone or something: *He pushed me into the water.* | *Don't push; there's room for all of us.* | *I pushed the door open and went in.* | *Inflation is pushing prices up.* –see picture on page 736 **2** [I; + adv/prep] (also **push your way**) to move somewhere by roughly moving other people or things out of your way: *She pushed past me.* **3** [T] to force someone to do something, or urge them strongly to do it: *My friends are all pushing me to enter politics.* | *I was pushed into signing the contract.* **4 push for something** to try very hard to get something, or to have something accepted: *Workers are pushing for higher wages.* **5** [T] *infml* to try to make something more popular or attractive to people: *The company are pushing their new range of furniture.* | *She is pushing the idea of free childcare for everyone.* **6** [T] *infml* to sell illegal drugs **7 push your luck** to take an increasing risk in the hope of success

push ahead *phr v* [I] to move forward with a plan or activity: *The government is pushing ahead with changes to the tax laws.*

push sbdy **around** *phr v* [T] *infml* to treat someone in a rough and unfair way

push sbdy/sthg ↔ **aside** *phr v* [T] to pay no attention to a person or thing that you feel is not important

push in *phr v* [I] *infml* to move in front of other people who have been waiting for something longer than you have

push off *phr v* [I] *infml* to go away: *Push off before I call the police.*

push on *phr v* [I] *infml* to continue a journey: *We must push on or we'll be late.*

push sbdy/sthg ↔ **over** *phr v* [T] to make a person or thing fall over

push sthg ↔ **through** *phr v* [T] to persuade people to accept something: *Our M.P. has pushed through new legislation about drinking and driving.*

push² *n* **1** an act of pushing someone or something: *They gave the car a push to start it.* **2** a planned attack and advance of great strength by an army **3 a push for something** *infml* a determined attempt to achieve something **4 give someone the push** *infml* to dismiss someone from a job: *I was given the push after 30 years.* [RELATED PHRASE **get the push**] **5 at a push** *infml* with difficulty, if it is necessary: *I could do the work by Tuesday at a push.*

push·bike /'pʊʃbaɪk/ *n BrE infml* a bicycle

push·chair /'pʊʃ-tʃeər/ *n* a small folding chair on wheels for pushing a small child around

pushed /pʊʃt/ *adj* **be pushed** *infml* to have difficulty in finding enough money or time to do something: *I'm always rather pushed for money at the end of the month.*

push·er /'pʊʃər/ *n infml* a person who sells illegal drugs

push·ing /'pʊʃɪŋ/ *prep infml* nearly a particular age: *She must be pushing forty by now.*

push·o·ver /'pʊʃ,əʊvər/ *n* [sing] *infml* **1** something that is very easy to do or win: *The examination was a pushover.* **2** a person who can easily be persuaded: *He was a pushover; he'll lend us whatever we need.*

push-up /'· ·/ *n* the usual American word for a PRESS-UP

push·y /'pʊʃi/ *adj* **pushier, pushiest** *infml* too forceful in getting things done or in getting other people's attention: *Don't be so pushy – your turn will come.*

pus·sy /'pʊsi/ *n* **pussies** *infml* (also **puss, pussycat**) a cat, or a word for calling one to you

put /pʊt/ *v* **put, put, putting** **1** [T; + adv/prep] to place or lay something in a particular place or position: *He put the letter on the table.* | *She put her bags down on the floor.* | *You've put too much salt in this soup.* | *Where did I put my keys?* –see picture on page 736 **2** [T; + adv/prep] to cause someone or something to be in a particular state or condition: *She put me in a bad mood by being late.* | *You have put me in a very awkward position.* **3** [T; + adv/prep] to express something in words in a particular way: *Her ideas were cleverly put.* | *To put it bluntly, the whole event was a total disaster.* **4 put a question to someone** to ask someone a question: *I'd like to put this same question to the other members of the group.* **5 put a shot** to throw a heavy metal ball called a SHOT in a sporting competition **6 put an end to something** to cause something to end: *We must put an end to these ridiculous rumours.* **7 put it to someone** to suggest to someone that something is true: *I put it to him that the police had known all along that these men were innocent.* **8 put paid to something** to ruin something or end it completely: *This accident has put paid to his chances of becoming a professional athlete.* **9 put someone to death** to kill someone

put sthg ↔ **about** *phr v* [T] *infml* to spread news about by telling it to people: *Rumours have been put about that he is working for the security forces.*

put sthg ↔ **across** *phr v* [T] to explain something so that people can understand it: *She didn't succeed in putting her ideas across very well.*

put sthg ↔ **aside** *phr v* [T] to save something so that you can use it or deal with it later: *I've got a bit of money put aside for a new car.*

put away *phr v* **1** [T **put** sthg ↔ **away**] to put something into a safe place or into the place where it is kept: *Put your toys away, please.* | *We've put a bit of money away in the building society.* **2** [T **put** sbdy ↔ **away**] *infml* to send someone to prison

put back *phr v* **1** [T **put** sthg ↔ **back**] to delay something: *Publication has been put back by three months.* **2 put the clocks back** to change the time on all clocks so that they show an earlier time

put sthg ↔ **by** *phr v* [T] to save money so that you can use it later: *I've got a bit of money put by for my old age.*

put down *phr v* **1** [T **put** sthg ↔ **down**] to defeat a protest, usually by using force: *Troops were called in to help put down the rebellion.* **2** [T **put** sbdy ↔ **down**] *infml* to make someone feel ashamed or foolish **3** [T **put** sthg ↔ **down**] to kill an animal, usually because it is old or ill: *Two horses had to be put down after the race.*

put sbdy **down for** sthg *phr v* [T] to put someone's name on a list of people who are going to do something

put sthg **down to** sbdy/sthg *phr v* [T] to say or think that something was caused by a particular person or thing: *He didn't look well but I just put it down to the fact that he was tired.*

put forward *phr v* **1** [T **put** sbdy/sthg ↔ **forward**] to suggest or offer someone or something: *I've put your name forward for the job of chairman of the committee.* **2 put the clocks forward** to change the time on all clocks so that they show a later time

put in *phr v* **1** [T **put** sthg ↔ **in**] to send a request or claim: *I've put in a claim for compensation.* **2** [T **put** sthg ↔ **in**] to spend time doing something: *I've only put in ten hours of work this week.* **3** [I] (of a ship) to enter a port

put in for sthg *phr v* [T] to make a formal request for something: *Unions have put in for a pay rise of 15%.*

put into sthg *phr v* [T] (of a ship) to enter a port: *The ship had to put into Sydney for supplies.*

put off *phr v* **1** [T **put** sthg ↔ **off**] to delay something until a later date: *The meeting's been put off until next month.* **2** [T **put** sbdy ↔ **off**] to tell someone that you cannot do something that you had agreed to do: *We're expecting them for dinner, but we'll have to put them off because the children aren't well.* **3** [T **put** sbdy **off**(sbdy/sthg)] to make someone feel that they no longer like a person or thing, or that they no longer want to do something: *My first week at university put me off university life completely.* | *Don't tell him all the unpleasant aspects of the work – you'll put him off.*

put on *phr v* **1** [T **put** sthg ↔ **on**] to put clothes onto your body: *She got up and put her coat on.* –see DRESS[1] (USAGE) **2** [T **put** sthg ↔ **on**] to cause a light or a machine to work by pressing a button or turning a SWITCH: *Could you put the light on, please?* **3** [T **put** sthg ↔ **on**] to gain weight and become fatter: *He's put on a lot of weight recently.* **4** [T **put** sthg ↔ **on**] to perform a play or show on a stage **5** [T **put** sthg ↔ **on**] to pretend to have a quality or feeling: *I don't believe she's really ill – I think she's just putting it on to get sympathy.* **6** [T **put** sthg **on** sthg] to add an amount to a cost or price: *a tax increase that will put another 10p on the price of petrol* **7** [T **put** sthg **on** sthg] risk money on the result of something: *I've put £10 on Liverpool to win the cup.*

put sbdy **onto** sthg *phr v* [T] to tell someone information that will be useful: *I phoned my solicitor and he put me onto a good lawyer.*

put out *phr v* **1** [T **put** sthg ↔ **out**] to broadcast or print official information: *The government will put out a new statement on the economy tomorrow.* **2** [T **put** sthg ↔ **out**] to stop a fire from burning **3** [T **put** sthg ↔ **out**] to stop a light from shining: *Don't forget to put the lights out when you leave.* **4** [T **put** sbdy **out**] to trouble or annoy someone: *I felt somewhat put out by his behaviour.* **5 put yourself out** to take trouble and make an effort to do something: *He'll never put himself out to help anyone.*

put sthg ↔ **over** *phr v* [T] to explain something so that people can understand it: *She didn't succeed in putting her ideas over very well.*

put through *phr v* **1** [T **put** sbdy **through**] to connect someone by telephone to the person that they want to talk to: *If you'll just hold the line for a minute I'll put you through to Mr Brown.* **2** [T **put** sbdy **through** sthg] to make someone suffer something unpleasant: *I don't want to put you through all that distress and anguish again.*

put sthg **to** sbdy *phr v* [T] to suggest something to someone: *I put my ideas to him but he didn't seem very enthusiastic.*

put together *phr v* **1** [T **put** sthg ↔ **together**] to make something into a single unit or group by joining or bringing together different parts: *We managed to put together a football team.* **2 put your heads together** to all think about a problem in order to find an answer **3 put together** combined: *He earns more than the rest of us put together.*

put up *phr v* **1** [T **put** sthg ↔ **up**] to build or raise something: *They're going to put up 20 new houses here.* | *I've never put up a tent on my own.* | *She put up her umbrella.* **2** [T **put** sthg ↔ **up**] to put a notice in a public place: *The exam results will be put up on the main notice board.* | *They put up posters advertising the meeting.* **3** [T **put** sthg ↔ **up**] to increase a cost or price: *Most companies are expected to put their prices up by about 10% this year.* **4** [T **put** sbdy ↔ **up**] to give someone food and lodging: *Will you be able to put me up tonight?* **5 put up a fight, put up resistance** to struggle to avoid something happening to you: *Local groups are putting up a lot of resistance to the scheme.* | *In the end he was arrested without putting up much of a fight.* **6 put something up for sale** to offer something for sale: *She's decided to put her house up for sale.*

put sbdy **up to** sthg *phr v* [T] give someone the idea of doing something bad: *I think it was Michael who put them up to it.*

put up with sbdy/sthg *phr v* [T] to suffer someone or something unpleasant without complaining: *I won't put up with her rudeness any longer!* | *I don't know why she puts up with him!*

pu·ta·tive /ˈpjuːtətɪv/ *adj* [only before a noun] *fml* generally accepted as being something: *his putative parents*

pu·tre·fy /ˈpjuːtrɪˌfaɪ/ *v* putrefied, putrefied [I] to decay

pu·trid /ˈpjuːtrɪd/ *adj* very decayed and bad-smelling (used especially of a dead animal or a plant substance)

putt /pʌt/ *v* [I;T] to hit a GOLF ball gently along the ground towards the hole –**putt** *n*

put·ty /ˈpʌti/ *n* [U] a soft paste, used to fix glass to window frames

put-up·on /ˈ· ·ˌ·/ *adj* [never before a noun] *infml* badly treated by someone for their own advantage: *Everyone thinks I'll lend them money; I'm beginning to feel put-upon.*

puz·zle[1] /ˈpʌzəl/ *v* puzzled, puzzling **1** [T] to make someone feel confused and unable to understand something: *Her illness puzzled the doctor for months.* | *I was puzzled by his response.* **2 puzzle over something** to think about something a lot in order to understand it: *He was puzzling over the map, unwilling to ask for directions.* | *I've been puzzling as to why she'd said that, too.* –**puzzled** *adj* : *He had a puzzled expression on his face.*

puzzle sthg ↔ **out** *phr v* [T] to find the answer to something after a lot of thought

puzzle[2] *n* **1** a person or thing that you cannot understand or explain **2** a game or toy which is made in a way that forces you to think carefully in order to SOLVE it or put it together: *I do the Times crossword puzzle every day.* | *Can you help me finish this jigsaw puzzle?*

PVC /ˌpiː viː ˈsiː/ *n* [U] a type of plastic

pyg·my /ˈpɪgmi/ *n* pygmies (also **pigmy**) **1** a very small person, especially one belonging to certain African groups **2** a particularly small type of animal

py·ja·mas /pəˈdʒɑːməz ‖ -ˈdʒæ-, -ˈdʒɑː-/ *n* (also **pajamas** *AmE*) [pl] a loose-fitting pair of trousers and short coat worn in bed, especially by men –see picture on page 50 –see PAIR (USAGE)

py·lon /ˈpaɪlən ‖ -lɑːn, -lən/ n a tall framework of steel bars used for supporting wires that carry electricity over land

pyr·a·mid /ˈpɪrəmɪd/ n 1 a solid shape with a flat square base and three-angled sides that slope upwards to meet at a point 2 (also **Pyramid**) a very large ancient stone building in this shape, used formerly in Egypt as the burial place of a king 3 the structure of an organization, in which there are fewer people at the top than lower down

pyre /paɪəʳ/ n lit a high pile of wood for the ceremonial burning of a dead body

py·thon /ˈpaɪθən ‖ -θɑːn, -θən/ n a large tropical snake that kills animals for food by winding itself round them and crushing them

Q,q

Q,q /kjuː/ **Q's, q's** or **Qs, qs** the 17th letter of the English alphabet

Q.C. /ˌkjuː ˈsiː/ n a British lawyer of high rank; an abbreviation for QUEEN'S COUNSEL: Sir John Smithers, Q.C.

quack[1] /kwæk/ v [I] to make the sound that ducks make

quack[2] n 1 a person dishonestly claiming to have medical knowledge or skills 2 the sound that ducks make

quad /kwɒd ‖ kwɑːd/ n 1 a square open area with buildings around it, especially in a college 2 see QUADRUPLET

quad·rant /ˈkwɒdrənt ‖ ˈkwɑː-/ n 1 a quarter of a circle 2 an instrument for measuring angles

quad·ri·lat·er·al /ˌkwɒdrɪˈlætərəl◂ ‖ ˌkwɑː-/ n a shape with four straight sides –**quadrilateral** adj

quad·ru·ped /ˈkwɒdrʊped ‖ ˈkwɑːd-/ n an animal with four legs

quad·ru·ple[1] /ˈkwɒdrʊpəl, kwɒˈdruː- ‖ kwɑːˈdruː-/ v **quadrupled, quadrupling** 1 [T] to multiply a number or an amount by four 2 [I] to become four times as great: Our profits have quadrupled this year.

quadruple[2] adj fml four times as big as something mentioned, or four times as big as usual

quad·ru·plet /ˈkwɒdrʊplɪt ‖ kwɑːˈdruːp-/ n (also **quad** infml) one of four children born to the same mother at the same time

quag·mire /ˈkwægmaɪəʳ, ˈkwɒg- ‖ ˈkwæg-/ n 1 a large area of soft wet ground 2 a very difficult situation

quail[1] /kweɪl/ n [C;U] a type of small bird which is often eaten

quail[2] v [I] lit to feel afraid: He quailed at the thought of telling her about the accident.

quaint /kweɪnt/ adj unusual or old-fashioned in an attractive way: We visited a quaint little village in the hills. –**quaintly** adv

quake[1] /kweɪk/ v **quaked, quaking** [I] to tremble because you are very afraid: She was quaking with fear.

quake[2] n infml see EARTHQUAKE

Quak·er /ˈkweɪkəʳ/ n a member of a Christian religious group which opposes violence

qual·i·fi·ca·tion /ˌkwɒlɪfɪˈkeɪʃən ‖ ˌkwɑː-/ n 1 [C] a proof that you have passed an examination: She has the right qualifications for the job. 2 [C] a skill or quality that you need to do a particular job: Previous experience is not an essential qualification for the job. 3 [U] the act of completing the necessary training for a particular job 4 [C] something which limits what has just been said: We support their policy statement, but with certain qualifications. Points 5 and 7 will have to be changed.

qual·i·fied /ˈkwɒlɪfaɪd ‖ ˈkwɑː-/ adj 1 having the right training, knowledge, or skills to do something: He's not qualified to teach young children. | You're certainly well qualified for the job. | a qualified doctor
□ USEFUL PATTERNS be qualified to do something; be qualified for something
2 limited: Her response to the idea was one of qualified agreement.

qual·i·fy /ˈkwɒlɪfaɪ ‖ ˈkwɑː-/ v **qualified, qualified** 1 [I] to pass an examination or gain the knowledge or experience necessary for a particular job: I came to this school immediately after I had qualified as a teacher. 2 **qualify for something** to have the right to do or have something: I'm afraid you don't qualify for a pension. | We're hoping to qualify for the next round of the competition. 3 **qualify someone to do something** to allow someone to do something or give them the right to do it: This test will qualify you to fly an aircraft. 4 [T] to limit what you are saying in some way: I'd like to qualify my last remark.

qual·i·ta·tive /ˈkwɒlɪtətɪv ‖ ˈkwɑːlɪteɪ-/ adj concerning the quality of something –**qualitatively** adv

qual·i·ty /ˈkwɒlɪti ‖ ˈkwɑː-/ n **qualities** 1 [U] the degree to which something is good or bad: The report criticized the poor quality of many TV programmes. 2 [U] a very high standard: He's an actor of real quality. 3 [C] something that is typical of a person or thing: Her writing has a rather sinister quality. 4 [C] a good part of someone's character, such as kindness or honesty: She showed all the qualities of a great leader.

qualm /kwɑːm ‖ kwɑːm, kwɑːlm/ n a feeling of nervousness or uncertainty about an action or situation:W He seems to have no qualms **about** going to work abroad.

quan·da·ry /ˈkwɒndəri ‖ ˈkwɑːn-/ n **quandaries** a feeling of not knowing what to do: I was in a quandary **about** whether or not to go.

quan·ti·fy /ˈkwɒntɪfaɪ ‖ ˈkwɑːn-/ v **quantified, quantified** [T] fml to measure an amount or quantity of something: It is difficult to quantify the value of a good education. –**quantifiable** adj

quan·ti·ta·tive /ˈkwɒntɪtətɪv ‖ ˈkwɑːntɪteɪ-/ adj concerning the number or amount of something –**quantitatively** adv

quan·ti·ty /ˈkwɒntɪti ‖ ˈkwɑːn-/ n **quantities** 1 [C] a number or amount of something: Police found a large quantity **of** illegal drugs. | expensive cars that *are manufactured in small quantities* **2** [U] amount: *manufacturers who are more concerned with quantity than quality* **3 in quantity** in a large numbers or amounts: *We buy in quantity, and then resell most of it.*

quan·tum /ˈkwɒntəm ‖ ˈkwɑːn-/ n **quanta** /-tə/ **1** tech a very small amount **2 quantum jump, quantum leap** a very important advance or improvement

quar·an·tine[1] /ˈkwɒrəntiːn ‖ ˈkwɑː-/ n [U] a period of time when a person or animal that may be carrying disease is kept separate from others so that the disease cannot spread: *The dogs were put in quarantine for six months.*

quarantine[2] v **quarantined, quarantining** [T] to put a person or an animal in quarantine

quar·rel[1] /ˈkwɒrəl ‖ ˈkwɔː-, ˈkwɑː-/ n **1** an angry argument **2 have no quarrel with something** to have no reason to disagree with something: *I have no quarrel with what the minister says.*

quarrel[2] v **-ll-** (**-l-** *AmE*) [I] to have an angry argument: *They used to quarrel all the time.* | *I don't want to quarrel with you.* | *What are you two quarrelling about?* | *quarrelling over whose pen it was*

quar·rel·some /ˈkwɒrəlsəm ‖ ˈkwɔː-, ˈkwɑː-/ adj frequently starting arguments

quar·ry[1] /ˈkwɒri ‖ ˈkwɔː-, ˈkwɑː-/ n **quarries 1** [C] a place on the surface of the earth from which stone or sand are dug out **2** [sing] a person or animal that is being hunted

quarry[2] v **quarried, quarried** [I;T] to dig out stone or sand from the surface of the earth

quart /kwɔːt ‖ kwɔːrt/ n a unit for measuring liquids, equal to two pints (PINT)

quar·ter[1] /ˈkwɔːtəʳ ‖ ˈkwɔːrtər/ n **1** one of four equal parts which make up a whole, ¼: *It's a quarter of a mile to the bus stop.* **2** 15 minutes before or after the hour: *We started at a quarter to 10 and didn't finish until quarter past.* –see TIME¹ (USAGE) **3** a period of three months of the year, used especially for making payments: *I pay my bills each quarter.* **4** a coin in the US and Canada worth 25 cents, or ¼ of a dollar, **5** ¼ of a pound in weight: *I'd like a quarter of those chocolates, please.* **6** a part of a town, often one where a certain type of person lives: *the student quarter* **7** a place or person from which something comes: *Help came from several quarters.* **8 quarters** [pl] lodgings, especially for soldiers and their families

quarter[2] v [T] **1** to divide something into four parts **2** to provide lodgings for people, especially soldiers

quar·ter·fi·nal /ˌkwɔːtəˈfaɪnl ‖ ˌkwɔːrtər-/ n any of the four matches in a competition; the winners of them will play in the two semifinals (SEMIFINAL)

quar·ter·ly[1] /ˈkwɔːtəli ‖ ˈkwɔːrtər-/ n a magazine which is produced four times a year

quarterly[2] adv,adj every three months: *We pay the phone bill quarterly.* | *the company's quarterly accounts*

quar·ter·mas·ter /ˈkwɔːtəˌmɑːstəʳ ‖ ˈkwɔːrtərˌmæ-/ n a military officer who is in charge of food and supplies

quar·tet /kwɔːˈtet ‖ kwɔːr-/ n **1** four people playing instruments or singing together **2** a piece of music written for such a group

quartz /kwɔːts ‖ kwɔːrts/ n [U] a hard mineral substance which is used in making very exact watches and clocks

quash /kwɒʃ ‖ kwɑːʃ, kwɔːʃ/ v [T] **1** to change a legal decision or dismiss a suggestion officially: *The*

high court judge quashed the decision of the lower court. **2** to bring something to an end by force: *The army quashed the rebellion.*

qua·ver /ˈkweɪvəʳ/ v **1** [I] (of a voice or a sound) to shake slightly **2** [T] to say something in a shaky voice –**quaver** n

quay /kiː/ n a place, usually built of stone, where ships can land and be loaded

quea·sy /ˈkwiːzi/ adj **queasier, queasiest** feeling slightly sick: *I felt a little queasy when the sea got rough.* –**queasiness** n [U]

queen /kwiːn/ n **1** (also **Queen**) a female ruler of a country who is not elected but is usually the daughter of a former king; **Queen** is also used as a title: *She became queen at an early age.* | *Queen Elizabeth II* **2** (also **Queen**) the wife of a king **3** a woman who is considered to be, or is voted, the best of her kind: *a beauty queen* | *the queen of opera* **4** the large female that leads a group of certain insects: *the queen bee* **5** a playing card with a picture of a queen on it: *the queen of hearts* **6** one of the pieces in a game of CHESS

queen·ly /ˈkwiːnli/ adj like a queen or suitable for a queen

queen moth·er /ˌ·ˈ···/ n (also **Queen Mother**) the mother of a ruler

Queen's Coun·sel /ˌ·ˈ···/ n fml see Q.C.

queer[1] /kwɪəʳ/ adj **1** strange: *It was a queer situation.* **2** infml rather ill: *I've been feeling a little queer since dinner.* **3** infml HOMOSEXUAL (a word which is considered offensive)

queer[2] n infml a male HOMOSEXUAL (a word which is considered offensive)

quell /kwel/ v [T] to stop opposition, violent behaviour, or unpleasant feelings: *The prime minister quelled disagreement among her ministers.*

quench /kwentʃ/ v [T] **1 quench your thirst** to drink enough so that you are no longer thirsty **2** to put out a fire using water: *Firemen quenched the flames.*

quer·u·lous /ˈkwerʊləs/ adj fml often complaining, especially in a rather weak and unnecessary way

que·ry[1] /ˈkwɪəri/ n **queries** a question: *I've got a few queries about the salary and conditions.*

query[2] v **queried, queried** [T] to express doubt about something: *The directors have queried our findings.*

quest /kwest/ n fml or lit **1** a search for something: *The quest for a cure is nearly over.* **2 in quest of** searching for something

ques·tion[1] /ˈkwestʃən/ n **1** [C] a sentence or phrase which asks for information: *I asked you a question and you didn't answer.* | *The question is: how was he killed?* | *Turn over your exam papers now. You must answer three questions on each subject.* –see ASK (USAGE) **2** [C] a problem to be dealt with: *It's a question of finding enough time.* **3** [C;U] doubt: *There was some question as to his honesty.* | *They did it. There's no question about it.* **4 beyond question** not to be doubted: *Her good intentions were beyond question.* **5 call something into question** to express doubts about something **6 in question** being considered: *Let's return to the subject in question.* **7 out of the question** impossible or not allowed **8 there's no question of** a phrase you use when you want to stop someone worrying and tell them that there is no possibility of something happening: *It's just a rumour. There's no question of my leaving the company.*

question[2] v [T] **1** to ask someone questions about something: *She questioned him about his past.* **2**

to express doubts about something: *I would never question her honesty.* –**questioning** *n* [U] : *They were taken to the police station for questioning.*

ques·tion·a·ble /'kwestʃənəbəl/ *adj* **1** not certain: *It's questionable whether this type of research is useful.* **2** perhaps not right or honest: *highly questionable goings-on at the bank* –**questionably** *adv*

ques·tion·ing /'kwestʃənɪŋ/ *adj* showing that you want an answer to something: *She gave him a questioning look.* –**questioningly** *adv*

question mark /'··· ·/ *n* a sign (?) used to show that something you have written is a question

ques·tion·naire /ˌkwestʃə'neər, ˌkes-/ *n* a set of questions to be answered by a number of people in order to provide information: *We all had to fill in a questionnaire about our working habits.*

queue¹ /kjuː/ *n BrE* a line of people or vehicles waiting to do something: *There was a long queue outside the cinema.*

queue² *v* queued, queuing [I] *BrE* (also **queue up**) to wait for something in a line of people or vehicles: *Have you been queuing for long?* | *She had to queue up to pay for the books.*

quib·ble /'kwɪbəl/ *v* quibbled, quibbling [I] to argue about small, unimportant points: *He quibbles over every penny we spend.* –**quibble** *n*

quick¹ /kwɪk/ *adj* **1** performing an action in an unusually short time: *a quick worker* | *She's very quick to learn.* | *You're quick at knitting!* **2** done in a short time: *a quick journey* | *Have you got time for a quick drink?* **3** a **quick temper** a tendency to get angry very easily **4** **quick as a flash** very quickly **5** **quick off the mark** wasting no time before beginning to do something **6** **quick on the uptake** able to understand things very fast –**quickly** *adv*: *Come quickly!* –**quickness** –see FASTNESS (USAGE) *n* [U]

quick² *adv* quickly: *Quick! She's coming!* | *Come quick!* | *I need a quick-acting painkiller.*

quick·en /'kwɪkən/ *v* [I;T] to become faster, or to make something faster: *The music quickened, and the dancing began.*

quick·sand /'kwɪksænd/ *n* [U] wet sand which sucks down anyone or anything that tries to cross it

quick·step /'kwɪkstep/ *n* a dance with small, quick steps

quick-wit·ted /ˌ·'···/ *adj* quick to understand things and to act quickly: *A quick-witted neighbour heard the screams and called the police.*

quid /kwɪd/ *n* [plural is **quid**] *infml* a pound in British money: *This dress cost me 40 quid.*

qui·et¹ /'kwaɪət/ *adj* **1** making little noise: *quiet music* | *a quiet voice* | *Be quiet! I'm trying to make a phone call!* **2** without very much activity or excitement: *I just want a quiet life.* | *They're having a quiet wedding.* **3** calm and often silent (used of people) **4** not bright (used of colours) **5** not attracting attention from other people: *Can I have a quiet word with you?* –**quietly** *adv*: *He crept quietly down the hall.* –**quietness** *n* [U]

quiet² *n* [U] **1** the state of being quiet: *We drove to the mountains for some peace and quiet.* **2** **on the quiet** *infml* secretly

qui·et·en /'kwaɪətn/ *v* (also **quiet** *AmE*) [T] to make someone less noisy: *Can't you quieten those children?*

quieten down *phr v* [I;T **quieten** sbdy ↔ **down**] to become less noisy, or to make someone less noisy: *She soon quietened down.* | *I was trying to quieten the children down.*

quill /kwɪl/ *n* **1** a bird's long stiff feather, or a pen made from this **2** one of the many sharp points sticking out from the body of some animals, such as the PORCUPINE

quilt /kwɪlt/ *n* a cover for a bed which is filled with soft, warm material

quilt·ed /'kwɪltɪd/ *adj* made with cloth which contains soft material that is kept in place by lines of stitching

quin /kwɪn/ *n* (**quint** /kwɪnt/ *AmE*) see QUINTUPLET

quince /kwɪns/ *n* a hard fruit used for making jelly

quin·ine /'kwɪniːn ‖ 'kwaɪnaɪn/ *n* [U] a drug used for treating fevers, especially MALARIA

quin·tes·sence /kwɪn'tesəns/ *n fml* **1** the quintessence of the perfect example of something: *John is the quintessence of good manners.* **2** the central character of something –**quintessential** /ˌkwɪntɪ'senʃəl/ *adj* –**quintessentially** *adv*

quin·tet /kwɪn'tet/ *n* **1** five people playing instruments or singing together **2** a piece of music written for such a group

quin·tu·plet /'kwɪntjʊplɪt, kwɪn'tjuːp- ‖ kwɪn'tʌp-/ *n* (also **quin** *infml*, **quint** *AmE infml*) one of five children born to the same mother at the same time

quip /kwɪp/ *v* -pp- [I] to make a clever or amusing remark –**quip** *n*

quirk /kwɜːk ‖ kwɜːrk/ *n* **1** a strange happening that is difficult to explain: *By some quirk of fate the two of us were on the same train.* **2** a strange type of behaviour or part of someone's character: *He has some unusual quirks in his character.*

quis·ling /'kwɪzlɪŋ/ *n* a person who helps an enemy power that has taken control of their country

quit /kwɪt/ *v* quit, quit, quitting [I;T] *infml* **1** to stop doing something: *She quit smoking when she got pregnant.* **2** to leave your job: *I had an argument with my boss and quit.*

quite /kwaɪt/ *predeterminer,adv* **1** to some degree: *He must be quite old now.* | *It was quite expensive.* | *Quite a lot of people came.* **2** completely: *Their second child is quite different.* | *Are you quite sure?* | *I'm not quite ready.* **3** **quite a** a phrase used to say that something is important or unusual in some way: *Bullying is quite a problem in some schools.* **4** **quite something** *infml* unusual and good: *It's quite something to get a degree at the age of 82.*

■ USAGE 1 If you want to use **quite** with an adjective which comes in front of a noun, remember to put **quite** before the indefinite article (**a** or **an**): *The book is quite long.* | *It's quite a long book.* | *Her mouth is quite small.* | *She's got quite a small mouth.* 2 If you want to say something nice to somebody, it is often better to avoid the word **quite**. In sentences such as: *Your shirt is quite nice.* | *This wine is quite good.* | *"Do you like my hair?" "Yes, it's quite nice"* **quite** usually means "fairly but not very". It is safer to use **very** or **really** instead: *Your shirt is really nice.* | *This wine is very/extremely good.* | *Your hair looks really nice.*

quits /kwɪts/ *adj infml* **be quits** to have returned to a situation in which neither of two people is at a disadvantage *Now we're quits.*

quiv·er¹ /'kwɪvər/ *v* [I] to tremble slightly –**quiver** *n* : *A quiver of excitement ran down her spine.*

quiver² *n* a container for arrows which you carry on your back

quix·ot·ic /kwɪk'sɒtɪk ‖ -'sɑː-/ *adj* trying to do something impossible, often to help other people

quiz¹ /kwɪz/ n **quizzes** a competition or game in which people try to answer questions: *a general knowledge quiz*

quiz² v *-zz-* [T] to ask someone questions: *He quizzed me* **about** *where I'd spent the evening.*

quiz·zi·cal /ˈkwɪzɪkəl/ adj a **quizzical smile/look** a smile or look that seems to suggest that you are asking a question or showing amusement, though you are not doing it openly – **quizzically** /-kli/ adv

quoit /kwɔɪt, kɔɪt/ n a ring that you try to throw over a small upright post in a game called **quoits**

quo·rum /ˈkwɔːrəm/ n fml a particular number of people, without which a meeting cannot begin: *No decisions were made because we didn't have a quorum.*

quo·ta /ˈkwəʊtə/ n a limited number or share of something: *Quotas have been imposed for most imports.* | *I've done my quota of work, so I'm leaving now.*

quo·ta·ble /ˈkwəʊtəbəl/ adj worth quoting

quo·ta·tion /kwəʊˈteɪʃən/ n **1** [C] (also **quote** *infml*) words taken from speech or writing and repeated exactly by someone else: *Support your ideas with quotations from the play.* **2** [U] the act of quoting someone or something **3** [C] (also **quote** *infml*) the calculated cost of a piece of work, given before the work is started: *He gave me a quotation for installing the central heating.*

quotation marks /·ˈ·· ·/ n a pair of marks (" ") or (' ') showing the beginning and end of words which are being quoted: *Phrases from someone else's work must always be written in quotation marks.*

quote¹ /kwəʊt/ v **quoted, quoting 1** [I;T] to repeat in speech or writing someone else's exact words: *He quotes* **from** *the Bible at every opportunity.* | *That's my honest opinion, but don't quote me!* | *"When a man is tired of London, he is tired of life," she quoted.* **2** [T] to mention an example to support your argument: *She quoted several cases in which such mistakes had occurred.* **3** [T] to give someone a price for your goods or services: *We've asked two builders to quote for replacing the roof.*

quote² n infml **1** see QUOTATION 1, 3 **2 in quotes** in QUOTATION MARKS.

R,r

R, r /ɑːʳ/ **R's, r's** *or* **Rs, rs** **1** the 18th letter of the English alphabet **2** the three R's reading, writing, and ARITHMETIC, thought to be the very important base of a child's education

rab·bi /ˈræbaɪ/ *n* a person who is a Jewish religious leader and teacher of Jewish law

rab·bit¹ /ˈræbɪt/ *n* **1** [C] a small long-eared animal that lives in a hole in the ground **2** [U] the fur or meat obtained from a rabbit

rabbit² *v* -tt- (also -t- *AmE*)
  rabbit on *phr v* [I] to talk continuously in an uninteresting way: *He keeps rabbitting on* about *his health.*

rab·ble /ˈræbəl/ *n* a noisy disorderly crowd of people

rab·ble-rous·ing /ˈ··ˌ···/ *adj* encouraging a group of people to feel or do things which are uncontrolled and violent: *a rabble-rousing speech*

rab·id /ˈræbɪd/ *adj* **1** infected with rabies: *a rabid dog* **2** [only before a noun] unreasonably violent or strong in your opinions, particularly about politics: *a rabid conservative*

ra·bies /ˈreɪbiːz/ *n* [U] a disease of humans and certain animals, particularly dogs, which causes madness and death

race¹ /reɪs/ *n* **1** [C] a competition to see which person, vehicle, or animal is the fastest: *Who won the race?* | *Let's have a race!* | *a boat race* **2** a **race against time** an attempt to do or finish something in a limited amount of time: *We had to get her to hospital before the baby was born.! It was a race against time.* **3** the **races** [pl] an occasion when people go to a racecourse to watch horses racing: *She won a lot of money at the races.* **4** [C] a struggle for power or control between people or countries: *the arms race* **5** [C;U] any of the groups into which human beings can be divided according to physical type: *the black races* | *the Mongolian race* | *The law forbids discrimination on grounds of race or religion.* **6** [C] a group of people with the same history, language, and customs: *the German race*

race² *v* **raced, racing** **1** [I;T] to compete in a race: *She's a very good swimmer and often races.* | *I'll race you to the end of the road.* **2** [T] to make an animal or vehicle run a race: *My horse has hurt his leg so I can't race him.* **3** [I+adv/prep;T+adv/prep] to go very fast or take someone somewhere very fast: *She raced off to get milk before the shop closed.* | *We raced the sick woman to hospital.* | *The holidays raced by.* **4** [I] (of your heart) to beat very fast

race·course /ˈreɪs-kɔːs ‖ -kɔːrs/ *n* a track which horses race around

race·horse /ˈreɪshɔːs ‖ -hɔːrs/ *n* a horse specially bred and trained for racing

race re·la·tions /ˌ· ·ˈ··/ *n* [pl] the behaviour of different groups of people in a society towards each other

race·track /ˈreɪs-træk/ *n* a course which runners, vehicles, or horses race around

ra·cial /ˈreɪʃəl/ *adj* **1** connected with the group of people to which someone belongs: *racial pride* | *racial origins* **2** existing or happening between different races of people: *racial discrimination* | *racial harmony* **3 racial prejudice** unreasonable dislike of people of other races

ra·cial·is·m /ˈreɪʃəlɪzəm/ *n* see RACISM

ra·cial·ly /ˈreɪʃəli/ *adv* concerning the group of people to which someone belongs: *Racially, there is no difference between the two nations.* | *a racially mixed population*

rac·ing /ˈreɪsɪŋ/ *adj* [only before a noun] used for racing in competitions: *a racing car* | *a racing pigeon*

rac·ism /ˈreɪsɪzəm/ *n* (also **racialism**) [U] **1** the belief that some races of people are better than others **2** dislike of people or unfair treatment of people because they belong to a particular race –**racist** *adj, n*: *a racist attack*

rack¹ /ræk/ *n* **1** a frame or shelf with bars or hooks for holding or hanging things: *He washed the dishes and put them in the plate rack to dry.* | *a luggage rack* | *shops full of racks of clothes* **2 the rack** an instrument used in the past to cause great pain to people by stretching them on a frame **3 rack and ruin** the ruined state of a building caused by lack of care: *The house went to rack and ruin after they moved out.*

rack² *v* **1 be racked by/with** *lit* to suffer great pain or anxiety because of: *He was racked by doubts.* **2 rack your brains** *infml* to think very hard about something

rack·et /ˈrækɪt/ *n* **1** [C] (also **racquet**) a light frame with a handle across which strings are stretched; it is used for hitting the ball in various games such as tennis **2** [sing] *infml* a loud noise: *Stop making such a racket! I can't sleep.* **3** [C] a dishonest way of getting money

rack·e·teer /ˌrækɪˈtɪəʳ/ *n* someone who gets money in a dishonest or illegal way

rac·on·teur /ˌrækɒnˈtɜːʳ ‖ ˌrækɑːn-/ *n* someone who is good at telling stories in an amusing and interesting way

rac·quet /ˈrækɪt/ *n* see RACKET

rac·y /ˈreɪsi/ *adj* **racier, raciest** amusing, full of life, and often dealing with sex (used of speech and writing): *Paul shocked the priest with his racy stories.*

ra·dar /ˈreɪdɑːʳ/ *n* [U] a method of finding the position and speed of ships and aircraft by using radio waves

ra·di·ance /ˈreɪdiəns/ *n* [U] the quality of being radiant

ra·di·ant /ˈreɪdiənt/ *adj* **1** [only before a noun] shining brightly: *the radiant sun* **2** showing love, hope, or happiness in your face so that you look very attractive: *The bride was radiant with joy.* –**radiantly** *adv*

ra·di·ate /ˈreɪdieɪt/ *v* **radiated, radiating** [T] **1** to send out light or heat: *a fire radiating warmth* **2** to express a good quality or feeling in your appearance or behaviour: *Jenny absolutely radiates confidence.*
  radiate from sthg *phr v* [T] to come out in all directions from a central point: *a system of roads radiating from the town centre*

ra·di·a·tion /ˌreɪdiˈeɪʃən/ *n* [U] **1** the giving or sending out of heat or light **2** amounts of RADIOACTIVITY which can seriously harm you if you are not protected against them: *the effects of nuclear radiation*

ra·di·a·tor /ˈreɪdieɪtəʳ/ n **1** an apparatus, consisting of pipes with steam or hot water passing through them, which is used for heating buildings **2** an apparatus which keeps the engine of a motor vehicle cool

rad·i·cal¹ /ˈrædɪkəl/ adj **1** thorough, complete, and at the most basic level: *The government made radical improvements to the tax system.* **2** in favour of rapid and great political change: *a radical priest | radical views* –**radically** /-kli/ adv

radical² n a person who believes in rapid and great social and political changes –**radicalism** n [U]

rad·i·i /ˈreɪdiaɪ/ n the plural of RADIUS

ra·di·o¹ /ˈreɪdiəʊ/ n **1** [U] the sending or receiving of sounds through the air by electrical waves: *Air traffic controllers were in radio contact with the ship. | radio signals* **2** [C] an apparatus to receive sounds broadcast in this way: *Turn on the radio.* –see picture on page 442 **3 on the radio** broadcast by radio: *I heard it on the radio. | Jean was on the radio again today.* **4** [U] the radio broadcasting industry: *Her first job was in radio. | a radio play*

radio² v [I;T] to send a message by radio: *The ship radioed for help.*

ra·di·o·ac·tiv·i·ty /ˌreɪdiəʊækˈtɪvᵻti/ n [U] **1** the quality that some substances have of giving out a powerful and sometimes harmful force by breaking up atoms **2** the force given out in this way –**radioactive** /-ˈæktɪv◂/ adj: *The train was carrying dangerous radioactive waste.*

ra·di·og·ra·phy /ˌreɪdiˈɒɡrəfi ‖ -ˈɑːɡ-/ n [U] the taking of photographs using x-rays (X-RAY), usually for medical reasons –**radiographer** n

ra·di·o·ther·a·py /ˌreɪdiəʊˈθerəpi/ n [U] the treatment of diseases by RADIOACTIVITY (2)

rad·ish /ˈrædɪʃ/ n a small strong-tasting red and white vegetable which is eaten raw –see picture on page 344

ra·di·um /ˈreɪdiəm/ n [U] a rare white metal that has a high level of RADIOACTIVITY, and is used in the treatment of certain diseases

ra·di·us /ˈreɪdiəs/ n radii /-diaɪ/ **1** the distance of a straight line from the centre of a circle to its edge **2** a circular area which measures the same distance from a central point to its edges in all directions: *The tax affects everyone within a ten-mile radius of the town.*

R.A.F. /ˌɑːr eɪ ˈef, ˌinfml ræf/ n the Royal Air Force, the British airforce: *Join the R.A.F.*

raf·fi·a /ˈræfiə/ n [U] the soft substance from a PALM tree, used for making hats, baskets, and mats

raf·fle¹ /ˈræfəl/ n a way of making money, especially for a good public purpose, by selling numbered tickets, some of which win prizes: *He won a car in the raffle. | a raffle ticket*

raffle² v raffled, raffling [T] to offer something as a prize in a raffle

raft /rɑːft ‖ ræft/ n **1** a flat floating structure, usually made of pieces of wood or of barrels and used as a boat **2** (also **life raft**) a flat rubber boat that can be filled with air, for the use of passengers if a plane crashes or a ship sinks

raf·ter /ˈrɑːftəʳ ‖ ˈræf-/ n one of the large sloping beams that hold up a roof

rag /ræɡ/ n **1** [C;U] an old cloth: *He cleaned the machine with an oily rag. | a piece of rag* **2 rags** [pl] torn old clothes: *The beggar was dressed in rags.* **3** [C] infml a badly written newspaper: *Why are you*

reading that rag? **4 from rags to riches** from being very poor to being rich and successful: *Her exceptional musical talent took her from rags to riches.* **5 like a red rag to a bull** BrE likely to make someone very angry: *Asking him to drive more carefully is like a red rag to a bull.* **6** [C] BrE a procession of college students through the streets on some particular day in the year, collecting money for a good public purpose

rag·a·muf·fin /ˈræɡəˌmʌfᵻn/ n lit a dirty young child in torn clothes

rag·bag /ˈræɡbæɡ/ n infml a confused mixture of things which are different from each other: *His argument is a ragbag of disconnected facts.*

rage¹ /reɪdʒ/ n **1** [C;U] strong uncontrollable anger: *The director's in a terrible rage. | The child wept with rage.* **2 all the rage** infml fashionable and popular: *Short hair is all the rage again.*

rage² v raged, raging [I] **1** to feel extremely angry and to show this in your behaviour: *He raged at their stupidity.* **2** to spread or continue with great force or violence: *The disease raged through the city. | The argument over the new road is still raging.*

rag·ged /ˈræɡᵻd/ adj **1** old and torn: *a ragged shirt* **2** dressed in old torn clothes: *a ragged little boy* **3** with uneven, rough edges: *a ragged beard* **4** imperfect and disorganized: *The musicians gave rather a ragged performance.* –**raggedly** adv –**raggedness** n [U]

ra·ging /ˈreɪdʒɪŋ/ adj very strong and severe: *a raging thirst*

rag·time /ˈræɡtaɪm/ n [U] a type of music popular in the 1920's, of black US origin: *a ragtime band*

raid¹ /reɪd/ n **1** a sudden military attack in order to cause damage to the enemy: *The fighter jets made a raid on the enemy camp.* **2** an unexpected visit by the police, in search of criminals or illegal goods: *Two million pounds' worth of drugs were discovered during a raid on a house in South London this morning.* **3** a secret or violent entering of a place to steal something: *a bank raid*

raid² v [T] to visit or attack a place on a raid: *Soldiers raided the village at dawn.* –**raider** n

rail¹ /reɪl/ n **1** [C] a fixed bar, used to hang things on or to support someone or something: *Keep your hand on the rail as you climb the steps. | a towel rail* **2** [C] one of the pair of metal bars fixed to the ground, along which a train runs: *Passengers must not cross the rails.* **3** [U] the railway: *rail travel | the rail strike* **4 by rail** by train: *The goods were sent by rail.* **5 go off the rails** to start to behave in a strange, confused way: *Since she lost her job, she seems to have gone off the rails.*

rail² v [I] fml to complain angrily and noisily: *Doctors railed against the increased costs of medicines.*

rail·card /ˈreɪlkɑːd ‖ -kɑːrd/ n a card which allows you to travel on trains more cheaply

rail·ing /ˈreɪlɪŋ/ n one of a set of rails making up a fence: *The dog got its head stuck between the railings.*

rail·road /ˈreɪlrəʊd/ v [T] **1** to hurry someone into doing something unwillingly: *The workers were railroaded into signing the agreement.* **2** to pass a law or carry out a plan quickly in spite of opposition: *The chairman railroaded the plan through the committee.*

rail·way /ˈreɪlweɪ/ n (also **railroad** AmE) **1** (also **railway line** /ˈ··· ·/) a track for trains to run on: *They're building a new railway to the south.* **2** (also **railways** [pl]) the organization that runs trains and stations: *I'm a ticket collector on the railway.*

rain¹ /reɪn/ n **1** [U] water falling in separate drops from the clouds: *The rain fell throughout the night.* | *She went out in the rain without a coat.* | *Heavy rain destroyed the plants.* **2** [sing] a thick fall of large quantities of something: *The car was stopped by a rain of bullets.* **3 the rains** [pl] the season in tropical countries when rain falls continuously: *The rains came early that year.*

rain² v **1 it is raining** = rain is falling: *It's raining.* | *It began to rain hard.* **2 rain cats and dogs** *infml* to rain very heavily **3 be rained off** to be stopped or prevented because of rain: *Last week's football match was rained off.*

rain down *phr* v **1** [I] to be directed at someone: *Insults rained down* on him. **2** [I;T **rain** sthg ↔ **down**] to fall rapidly and in large amounts: *The army rained bullets down* on the village.

■ USAGE With the verb **to rain** you can use the adverbs **heavily** or **hard**: *It rained heavily all day.* | *It's raining really hard now.* With the noun **rain** use the adjective **heavy**: *The bridge was washed away by heavy rain.* If there is not very much rain, you can say: *It's not raining very hard; heavily.* | *A light rain was falling.*

rain·bow /'reɪnbəʊ/ n an arch of different colours that sometimes appears in the sky immediately after rain

rain·coat /'reɪnkəʊt/ n a light coat worn to protect yourself from rain –see picture on page 50

rain·drop /'reɪndrɒp ‖ -draɪp/ n a single drop of rain

rain·fall /'reɪnfɔːl/ n [C;U] the total amount of rain or snow that falls in an area in a particular period of time

rain for·est /'·‚···/ n a wet tropical forest with tall trees growing thickly together

rain·storm /'reɪnstɔːm ‖ -ɔːrm/ n a sudden heavy fall of rain

rain·y /'reɪni/ adj **1** having a lot of rain: *a very rainy day* | *Vancouver is a rainy city.* **2 for a rainy day** for a future time when something may be needed: *Save your money for a rainy day.*

raise¹ /reɪz/ v **raised, raising** [T] **1** to lift or move something to a higher position: *He raised the lid of the box.* | *She raised her finger to her lips as a sign for silence.* –see RISE¹ (USAGE) **2** to increase in amount, degree, or size: *Our rent's just been raised again.* | *This radiator automatically raises the temperature.* **3 raise someone's hopes** to make someone feel hopeful that something will happen, when often it will not **4 raise your voice** to speak loudly and angrily **5 raise yourself to your full height** to stretch your body so that you are standing very tall **6** to manage to get or collect an amount of money: *They're raising money for charity.* | *I raised £500 by selling my car.* **7** to look after a child until it is an adult: *They finally got married and raised six children.* **8** to breed animals or grow crops: *They raise chickens on this farm.* **9** to mention something to be talked about or given attention: *There's an important point I want to raise.* **10** to cause people to do or feel something: *His joke raised a laugh.* | *His long absence raised fears about his safety.* | *That smell raises memories of hot summer days.* **11** to make something appear: *The car raised a cloud of dust as it rushed by.*

SPELLING NOTE

Words with the sound / r /, may be spelt **wr-**, like **wrong.**

■ USAGE **Raise** and **bring up** can both be used to mean "look after and be responsible for children until they become adults". *My grandmother raised/brought up a family of ten single-handed.* Note, however, that in British English **bring up** is more commonly used if you want to talk about *the process* of looking after children and *the way* in which this happens: **Bringing up** *children is never easy.* | *She's devoted the last ten years to* **bringing up** *her daughters.* | *We were* **brought up** *to respect our elders.* | *a very well* **brought-up** *little boy*

raise² n AmE an increase in wages: *He asked his boss for a raise.*

rai·sin /'reɪzən/ n a dried GRAPE used in cooking or eaten raw

rake¹ /reɪk/ n **1** a garden tool consisting of a row of metal points at the end of a long handle; it is used for making the soil level or gathering up dead leaves –see picture on page 638 **2** *old fash* a man, especially a rich one, who has had many sexual relations with women and drinks too much

rake² v **raked, raking 1** [I;T] to use a rake to make the ground smooth, loosen the soil, or collect leaves: *He raked the garden paths.* | *They raked up the dead leaves.* **2** [I+adv/prep] to search quite carefully, but rather quickly through a pile of things: *She raked through her papers to see if she could find it.*

rake sthg ↔ **in** *phr* v [T] *infml* to earn a lot of money: *He must be raking in at least £500 a week!* | *They're absolutely raking it in!*

rake sthg ↔ **up** *phr* v [T] *infml* to talk about something and remind people of something unpleasant that happened in the past: *Please don't rake up that old quarrel again.*

rake-off /'·‚·/ n *infml* a dishonest share of profits: *The taxi-driver gets a rake-off from the hotel if he takes travellers there.*

ral·ly¹ /'ræli/ v **rallied, rallied 1** [I;T] to come or bring together to give support for a shared purpose: *The general his tired soldiers and they drove the enemy back.* | *Her colleagues rallied to her defence when she was fired.* **2** [I] to become stronger after illness or other difficulties: *Prices on the stockmarket rallied after yesterday's falls.*

rally round *phr* v [I;T **rally round** sbdy] *infml* to come together as a group to support someone: *Her friends all rallied round when she was ill.* | *The teachers all rallied round the headmaster.*

rally² n **rallies 1** a large public meeting to support a cause or political party **2** a motor race over public roads **3** a long struggle in tennis and similar games, with each player trying to win a point by hitting the ball again and again

ram¹ /ræm/ n **1** [C] a fully grown male sheep **2** [C] any machine that uses a weight to push or force things into a particular position **3 RAM** [U] a computer memory holding information that is needed by the computer for a limited period, and that can be searched in any order you like; an abbreviation for Random-Access Memory

ram² v **-mm- 1** [I + adv/prep; T] to crash into something very forcefully: *His car rammed into a large tree.* **2** [T+adv/prep] to force into place with heavy pressure: *He rammed the stick into the hole.* **3 ram something home** to force people to recognize or accept something: *The attack on the military base rammed home the need for tighter security.*

Ram·a·dan /'ræmədæn, -dɑːn, ‚ræmə'dɑːn, -'dæn/ n the 9th month of the Muslim year, during which no food or drink may be taken between sunrise and sunset

ram·ble[1] /ˈræmbəl/ v **rambled, rambling** 1 [I;+adv/prep] to go on a long walk in the country for pleasure: *They rambled through the woods.* 2 [I] to talk in a disordered way without keeping to the subject: *Since her operation she seems to ramble a lot.* 3 **ramble on** to talk or write for a long time in a disordered way: *He's always rambling on about his life in India.*

ramble[2] *n* a long country walk taken for enjoyment: *We went for a ramble along the river.*

ram·bler /ˈræmbləʳ/ *n* someone who goes on long walks in the country

ram·bling /ˈræmblɪŋ/ *adj* 1 disordered and confused (used of speech or writing): *a long and rambling letter* 2 of irregular shape and spreading over a large area: *a rambling old house*

ram·i·fi·ca·tion /ˌræmɪfɪˈkeɪʃən/ *n fml* a result or effect of an action or decision which is not always clear at first: *I think we should consider the ramifications of this decision very carefully.*

ramp /ræmp/ *n* an artificial slope that connects two levels: *Drive the car up the ramp.*

ram·page[1] /ræmˈpeɪdʒ, ˈræmpeɪdʒ/ v **rampaged, rampaging** [I +adv/prep] to rush about wildly and violently: *The elephants rampaged through the forest.*

ram·page[2] /ˈræmpeɪdʒ, ræmˈpeɪdʒ/ *n* **on the rampage** rushing about behaving wildly and violently: *During the match, some supporters went on the rampage.*

ram·pant /ˈræmpənt/ *adj* widespread and impossible to control (used of crime, disease, and false beliefs): *Malaria was rampant in that area.* -**rampantly** *adv*

ram·part /ˈræmpɑːt ‖ -ɑːrt/ *n* (also **ramparts** pl)) a wide bank of earth or a stone wall built to protect a fort or city

ram·rod /ˈræmrɒd ‖ -rɑːd/ *n* **stiff/straight as a ramrod** extremely stiff or straight in the way you walk or stand: *The soldier stood as stiff as a ramrod while waiting for his orders.*

ram·shack·le /ˈræmʃækəl/ *adj* almost falling to pieces (used of a building or vehicle): *a ramshackle old house*

ran /ræn/ the past tense of RUN

ranch /rɑːntʃ ‖ ræntʃ/ *n* a very large farm in the US and Canada where sheep, cattle, or horses are bred

ranch·er /ˈrɑːntʃəʳ ‖ ˈræn-/ *n* a person who owns or works on a ranch

ran·cid /ˈrænsɪd/ *adj* not fresh and with an unpleasant taste or smell (used of fatty food): *rancid butter* | *a rancid taste*

ran·cour /ˈræŋkəʳ/ *n* (**rancor** *AmE*) [U] *fml* a feeling of bitter, unforgiving hatred towards someone -**rancorous** *adj* -**rancorously** *adv*

rand /rænd/ *n* [plural is **rand**] the standard money unit of South Africa, divided into 100 cents

ran·dom[1] /ˈrændəm/ *adj* done or chosen without any plan, aim, or pattern: *He fired a few random shots.* | *They need a random sample of people for the experiment.* -**randomly** *adv*

random[2] *n* **at random** without any plan, aim, or pattern: *He chose a few people at random.*

rand·y /ˈrændi/ *adj slang* full of sexual desire -**randiness** *n* [U]

rang /ræŋ/ the past tense of RING

range[1] /reɪndʒ/ *n* 1 [sing;U] the distance that a gun or other weapon can fire or within which an apparatus can operate effectively: *He shot the rabbit at close range.* | *medium-range nuclear weapons* | *This radio transmitter only has a range of a few miles.* 2 **within range** near enough to see, hear, or hit: *Shout as soon as she comes within range.* [RELATED PHRASE **out of range**] 3 [sing] the measurable limits within which something varies: *Several cars are available within the price range.* | *I'm afraid that high note is beyond my range.* | *an age range of between 25 and 35 years old* 4 [sing] the limits of what something includes: *This decision lies outside the range of my responsibility.* 5 [sing] a group of different things which are of the same general type: *The talks will consider a range of topics important to both countries.* | *She uses a range of techniques to help her patients to relax.* 6 [C] a set of different products of the same kind sold by a shop or made by a company: *We sell a wide range of gardening tools.* 7 [C] a connected line of mountains or hills: *The lake is to the north of a high mountain range.* 8 [C] an area where shooting is practised: *a rifle range* 9 **the range** a wide stretch of grassy land in North America where cattle feed

range[2] *v* **ranged, ranging** 1 [I not in progressive forms] to vary between particular limits: *The children's ages range from 5 to 15.* | *The pay ranges from £5 to £7 an hour.* | *Her hobbies range from cooking to cycling.* 2 [I] (of writing or speech) to be concerned with or include: *Our conversation ranged over many subjects.* 3 [I +adv/prep] *lit* to wander freely without a fixed purpose: *We ranged through deserted countryside.* 4 [T+adv/prep] to arrange in rows: *She ranged the goods neatly in the shop window.* | *Soldiers were ranged along the walls.*

rang·er /ˈreɪndʒəʳ/ *n* 1 a person who is responsible for looking after a forest or park 2 a policeman in North America who works in a country area on horseback

rank[1] /ræŋk/ *n* 1 [C;U] an official position in an organization, especially the armed forces: *He reached the rank of general before he was 40.* | *officers of high rank* 2 [C] a line of people or things: *Rank upon rank of ancient trees stretched to the horizon.* 3 **join the ranks of** to become a member of a particular group of people: *She's joined the ranks of the unemployed.* 4 **the ranks** [pl] the ordinary people in the armed forces and other organizations as opposed to those in high positions: *He rose from the ranks to become a colonel.* 5 [C;U] *old fash* social class: *People of all ranks attended the ceremony.*

rank[2] *v* [I;T] to have, or to regard as having, a particular position on a scale: *The city ranks as one of the most polluted in the country.* | *a tennis-player ranked third in the world*

rank[3] *adj* 1 too thick and widespread (used of a plant): *rank grass* 2 very strong and unpleasant in taste or smell: *rank tobacco* 3 [only before a noun] complete or extreme (used especially of bad qualities): *rank bad luck* | *rank stupidity* | *The race was won by a rank outsider.*

rank and file /ˌ·· ·ˈ·/ *n* **the rank and file** [+ sing/pl verb] the ordinary members of an organization as opposed to the leaders: *The rank and file refused to accept the committee's decision.*

ran·kle /ˈræŋkəl/ *v* **rankled, rankling** [I] to continue to be remembered with bitterness and anger: *His rudeness to me still rankles.*

ran·sack /ˈrænsæk/ *v* [T] 1 to search a place or building thoroughly and roughly: *The police ransacked the house looking for drugs.* 2 to go through a place stealing and causing damage: *The town was ransacked by enemy soldiers.*

ran·som /ˈrænsəm/ n 1 a sum of money paid to free someone who is held illegally as a prisoner: *The boy's family paid a large ransom to the kidnappers.* 2 **hold someone to ransom** to keep someone prisoner and demand to be given money before you will let them go: *The terrorists kidnapped a priest and held him to ransom.* –ransom v [T]

rant /rænt/ v [I] to talk in a loud, excited, and angry way: *The priest ranted on about the devil and all his works.* | *He's ranting and raving about the way they treated him.* –ranting n

rap¹ /ræp/ n 1 a quick light hit or knock: *I heard a rap on the door.* 2 **take the rap** infml to be punished for something even if you did not do it

rap² v -pp- [I+adv/prep;T+adv/prep] to hit quickly and lightly: *She rapped her pen on the table and called for silence.*

rap out sthg phr v [T] to say sharply and suddenly: *The officer rapped out an order.*

ra·pa·cious /rəˈpeɪʃəs/ adj fml having an extremely strong desire to have a lot of something, especially money: *a rapacious businessman* –rapaciously adv –rapacity /rəˈpæsˌti/ n [U]

rape¹ /reɪp/ v **raped, raping** [T] (of a man) to violently force a woman to have sex when she does not want to

rape² n 1 [C;U] the act or crime of raping someone: *He was sent to prison for rape.* | *a rape victim* 2 [sing] fml spoiling or destruction: *the rape of our beautiful forests* 3 [U] a plant grown as animal food and for oil

rap·id /ˈræpˌd/ adj with great speed: *The patient's recovery was rapid.* | *The school promised rapid results in the learning of languages.* | *a rapid growth in population* –rapidly adv : *the rapidly changing world of computer technology* –rapidity /rəˈpɪdˌti/ n [U]

rap·ids /ˈræpˌds/ n [pl] a part of a river where the water moves very fast over rocks

ra·pi·er /ˈreɪpɪəʳ/ n a long thin sharp sword

rap·ist /ˈreɪpˌst/ n a man guilty of forcing a woman to have sex with him

rap·port /ræˈpɔː/ n [U] close and sympathetic understanding of someone's feelings or opinions: *a teacher who has an excellent rapport with her class*

rap·proche·ment /ræˈprɒʃmɒn, ræˈprəʊʃ- ‖ ˌræprəʊʃˈmɑːŋ/ n fml an increase in friendship between countries, groups, or people who were enemies: *At last there are signs of a rapprochement between our two countries.*

rapt /ræpt/ adj so interested in something that you do not notice anything else: *We listened to the song with rapt attention.*

rap·ture /ˈræptʃəʳ/ n fml 1 [U] great joy and delight: *He stared with rapture at his baby son.* 2 **go into raptures** to feel or express great delight about something: *They went into raptures about their new house.* –rapturous adj : *a rapturous welcome* –rapturously adv

rare /reəʳ/ adj rarer, rarest 1 very unusual or uncommon: *a rare disease* | *It's very rare for him to be late.* 2 unusually good in quality: *his rare talent for*

learning languages 3 thin, with less oxygen than usual (used of air): *the rare air of the mountains* 4 lightly cooked so that it is still red (used of meat) –compare WELL-DONE

■ USAGE Compare **rare** and **scarce**. We use **rare** for things that are uncommon, and perhaps valuable: *a rare bird/a rare coin.* We use **scarce** for ordinary useful things when we have not got enough of them: *Potatoes were scarce last winter.* We can use **rare**, but not **scarce**, about time: *one of my rare* (= not happening often) *visits to Paris.*

rar·e·fied /ˈreərˌfaɪd/ adj 1 thin and with less oxygen than usual (used of air) 2 separate from ordinary people because of wealth, high social position, or cleverness: *He moves in very rarefied circles; his friends are all lords.*

rare·ly /ˈreəli ‖ ˈreərli/ adv not at all often: *Rarely has so much been achieved in such a short time.* | *She very rarely complains.*

rar·ing /ˈreərɪŋ/ adj infml 1 **raring to do something** very eager to do something: *The children were raring to get out in the snow.* 2 **raring to go** very keen to start: *Hurry up! We're raring to go.*

rar·i·ty /ˈreərˌti/ n rarities 1 [C] an uncommon or unusual thing: *This type of flower is becoming something of a rarity.* 2 [U] the quality of being very uncommon or unusual: *rarity value*

ras·cal /ˈrɑːskəl ‖ ˈræs-/ n 1 old fash a dishonest person 2 a child who misbehaves but with whom you are not really angry: *You little rascal! Where have you hidden my shoes?*

rash¹ /ræʃ/ adj acting foolishly because of not thinking enough of the possible results: *a rash decision* | *I promised in a rash moment to take the children swimming.* –rashly adv –rashness n [U]

rash² n 1 [C] a lot of small red spots on your skin: *a heat rash* 2 **come out in a rash** to become covered in a rash: *When she eats strawberries, she comes out in a rash.* 3 [sing] a number of events that happen suddenly in a short time: *We've had a rash of complaints at the office.*

rash·er /ˈræʃəʳ/ n a thin piece of BACON

rasp /rɑːsp ‖ ræsp/ v [I] to make a rough unpleasant sound: *The noise of their sawing rasped loudly in his ears.* | *a rasping voice*

rasp·ber·ry /ˈrɑːzbəri ‖ ˈræzberi/ n raspberries 1 a soft sweet red berry: *a bowl of raspberries and cream* –see picture on page 344 2 the bush this grows on 3 infml a sound made by putting your tongue out and blowing; this expresses your low opinion of someone: *He blew a raspberry at the general.*

rat¹ /ræt/ n 1 a long-tailed animal related to but larger than a mouse 2 infml a disloyal and deceiving person (a word which is often used in a humorous way): *But you promised to help us, you rat!*

rat² v -tt- [I] infml to act in a disloyal way or break a promise: *They said they'd help but they've ratted on us.*

ratch·et /ˈrætʃˌt/ n a toothed wheel or bar fitted with a piece of metal that allows it to turn in one direction but not the other

rate¹ /reɪt/ n 1 [C] a quantity, such as a value, cost, or speed, measured by its relation to some other amount: *a drug with a high success rate in curing people* | *We drove at a steady rate.* | *a fall in the rate of inflation* 2 [C] a charge or payment fixed according to a standard scale: *They're demanding higher rates of pay.* | *The interest rate has gone down.* 3 **the**

rates [pl] a local tax which was formerly paid by owners of buildings in Britain for locally provided services **4 at any rate: a** at least; used when you are giving one advantage that exists among a lot of disadvantages: *"The house is far too small." "Oh well, not so much to keep clean, at any rate."* **b** used when you have said something which you are correcting because you are not really certain about it: *She's coming with us. At any rate, I think she is.* **5 at this rate, at that rate** if events continue in the same way: *At this rate we won't be able to afford a holiday.*

rate² *v* **rated, rating 1** [T + adv/prep] to have a particular opinion about the value or worth of someone or something: *She was generally rated highly as a poet.* **2** [T] to deserve: *It was an item of local interest, and didn't really rate a mention in the national newspapers.*

ra·tea·ble val·ue /ˌreɪtəbəl ˈvæljuː/ *adj* (also **ratable value**) a value given to a building for the purpose of calculating the rates (RATE) to be charged on it

rate of ex·change /ˌ···ˈ·/ *n* see EXCHANGE RATE

rate-pay·er /ˈreɪtpeɪəʳ/ *n* someone in Britain who has to pay the rates (RATE)

ra·ther /ˈrɑːðəʳ ‖ ˈræðəʳ/ *predeterminer,adv* **1** to some degree: *It's rather cold today.* | *It was rather an unsuccessful day.* | *His behaviour rather surprised me.* **2 would rather** would prefer to: *"Shall we go and see that film?" "I'd rather stay in."* | *I'd rather not talk about it.* **3 rather than** instead of: *I prefer to live near to my work rather than spend a lot of time travelling every day.* **4** used when you are stating something that is opposite to what you have just said or makes what you have just said correct: *He came home very late last night, or rather very early this morning.*

■ USAGE Compare **rather** and **fairly**. **Rather** often suggests a quality that is bad or unsuitable: *I was driving rather fast.* (= too fast for the conditions on the road). But British speakers sometimes use **rather** about things they like very much: *I was rather pleased when I won the prize.* We use **fairly** for qualities that are neither good nor bad: *I was driving fairly fast.* (= fast, but not very fast)

rat·i·fy /ˈrætɪfaɪ/ *v* **ratified, ratified** [T] *fml* to officially approve a written agreement by signing it: *The heads of the two governments met to ratify the treaty.* –**ratification** /ˌrætɪfɪˈkeɪʃən/ *n* [U]

rat·ing /ˈreɪtɪŋ/ *n* **1** [C] the position that someone or something has on a scale of values or amounts: *The president has a favourable rating in the opinion polls.* **2 ratings** [pl] lists showing the position of popularity of a particular song, or radio or television show: *"Newsnight" has been getting excellent ratings.* | the **ratings war**

ra·ti·o /ˈreɪʃiəu ‖ ˈreɪʃəu/ *n* a figure showing the number of times one quantity contains another; it is used to show the relationship between two amounts: *The ratio of 10 to 5 is 2 to 1.* | *The ratio of nursing staff to doctors at this hospital is 3 to 1.*

ra·tion¹ /ˈræʃən ‖ ˈræ-, ˈreɪ-/ *n* **1** [C] a limited quantity of food, petrol, etc., allowed to each person for a period, especially during a war **2 rations** [pl] the amount of food given to a soldier each day

ration² *v* [T] **1** to limit someone to a fixed amount of something: *On this diet, you are rationed to two eggs a week.* **2** to control supplies of something: *The government had to ration petrol during the war.*

ration sthg ↔ **out** *phr v* [T] to give out supplies in limited amounts: *He rationed out the water to the sailors.*

ra·tion·al /ˈræʃənəl/ *adj* **1** having the ability to think and understand things clearly, and make decisions based on reason **2** based on reason (used of ideas and behaviour): *There must be a rational explanation.* –opposite **irrational** –**rationally** *adv*: *We must try to think rationally.* –**rationality** /ˌræʃəˈnælɪti/ *n* [U]

ra·tio·nale /ˌræʃəˈnɑːl ‖ -ˈnæl/ *n* [C;U] *fml* the reasons and principles on which a system, practice, or belief is based: *What do you think is the rationale behind his decision?*

ra·tion·al·ize, ration·alize /ˈræʃənəlaɪz/ *v* **rationalized, rationalizing** (also **rationalise** *BrE*) **1** [I;T] to think of reasons to explain unreasonable behaviour or opinions: *He tried to rationalize his behaviour by blaming his son.* **2** [T] to make an organization or industry more modern and less wasteful: *Production was rationalized by buying new machinery.* –**rationalization** /ˌræʃənəlaɪˈzeɪʃən ‖ -lə-/ *n* [C;U]

rat race /ˈ· ·/ *n* **the rat race** *infml* the endless competition for success, especially at work: *Paul got so tired of the rat race that he went to live in the country.*

rat·tle¹ /ˈrætl/ *v* **rattled, rattling 1** [I;T] to make a number of short sharp sounds like small objects knocking repeatedly against each other: *The beggar rattled the coins in his tin cup* | *The windows rattled in the wind.* **2** [I + adv/prep] to move quickly while making these noises: *The cart rattled along the stony road.* **3** [T] *infml* to make someone lose confidence and become anxious: *Keep calm – don't get rattled.*

rattle sthg ↔ **off** *phr v* [T] to say something quickly and easily from memory: *He rattled off the poem.*

rattle on *phr v* [I] to talk quickly and for a long time about something unimportant: *He rattled on about his holidays, although nobody was listening.*

rattle through sthg *phr v* [T] to do something quickly: *He rattled through his speech.*

rattle² *n* **1** [C] a baby's toy with loose pieces inside, that make a rattling noise when it is shaken **2** [sing] the noise of small objects being knocked against each other: *the rattle of milk bottles*

rat·tle·snake /ˈrætlsneɪk/ *n* (also **rattler** /ˈrætləʳ/ *AmE*) a poisonous American snake that makes a rattling noise with its tail

rat·ty /ˈræti/ *adj* *infml* bad-tempered: *She always gets a bit ratty when she hasn't had enough sleep.*

rau·cous /ˈrɔːkəs/ *adj* rough, loud, and unpleasant (used of sounds): *raucous shouts* –**raucously** *adv* –**raucousness** *n* [U]

raunch·y /ˈrɔːntʃi/ *adj* **raunchier, raunchiest** *infml* having or suggesting a strong desire for sex: *a raunchy dance* | *a raunchy voice*

rav·age /ˈrævɪdʒ/ *v* **ravaged, ravaging** [T] to damage something so that it is nearly destroyed: *The whole area was ravaged by forest fires.*

rav·ag·es /ˈrævɪdʒɪz/ *n* [pl] **the ravages of** the harmful effects of something: *the ravages of war*

rave¹ /reɪv/ *v* **raved, raving 1** [I] to talk wildly and with strong feeling: *He was very feverish, and raved all night.* **2 rave about something** *infml* to speak about something with great admiration and praise: *Everybody raved about her new book.* **3 rave it up** *infml* to enjoy yourself in a very unworried and happy way

rave² *adj* **a rave review** a judgment about a book, film, or play that praises it very highly

ra·ven /ˈreɪvən/ *n* a large shiny black bird with a deep unpleasant voice

rav·e·nous /ˈrævənəs/ *adj* *infml* extremely hungry –**ravenously** *adv*

rave-up /'··/ n infml a very wild exciting party

ra·vine /rə'viːn/ n a deep narrow valley with steep sides

rav·ing /'reɪvɪŋ/ adj,adv infml **1** talking and behaving wildly: a raving madman | He's stark raving mad. **2** very great: She's hardly a raving beauty. | The party was not a raving success.

rav·ings /'reɪvɪŋz/ n [pl] wild, uncontrolled talking or writing: the ravings of a madman

rav·i·o·li /ˌrævi'əʊli/ n [U] small squares of PASTA filled with meat and cooked by boiling

rav·ish /'rævɪʃ/ v [T] lit **1** to force a woman to have sex when she does not want to **2 be ravished by** to get great pleasure and delight from the beauty of something

rav·ish·ing /'rævɪʃɪŋ/ adj very beautiful and so causing great delight: a ravishing sight –ravishingly adv

raw /rɔː/ adj **1** not cooked: raw vegetables | Don't cook it. I'll eat it raw. **2** in a natural state: raw silk | raw cotton **3 raw material** a natural substance from which industrial products are made: Coal and oil are important raw materials for the manufacture of plastic. **4** not yet trained or experienced (used of a person): intensive army courses for raw recruits **5** painful because part of the skin has come off or is sore: a raw patch where his shoe had rubbed **6** unpleasantly cold and wet (used of weather): a raw winter day **7 get a raw deal, be given a raw deal** infml to be treated unfairly –rawness n [U]

ray /reɪ/ n **1** a narrow beam of heat, light, or ENERGY the sun's rays | a ray of light | gamma rays **2** a very small amount of a good feeling which might help to improve a bad situation: There's just one ray of hope left. Debbie may talk him into joining us.

ray·on /'reɪɒn ‖ -ɑːn/ n [U] a smooth material which looks like silk and is used for making clothes

raze /reɪz/ v razed, razing [T] fml to completely destroy a town or building so that no part is left standing: An earthquake razed the city to the ground.

ra·zor /'reɪzəʳ/ n a sharp instrument for removing hair from your skin: his electric razor

razor blade /'·· ·/ n a thin very sharp piece of metal that is put inside a razor

RC /ˌɑː 'siː ‖ ˌɑːr-/ n an abbreviation for ROMAN CATHOLIC

Rd a written abbreviation for ROAD: 17, Nelson Rd, Oxford

re /riː/ prep a word used when you are writing something formal, like a business letter, to show that you are going to talk about a particular subject: re your enquiry of the 19th October

-'re /əʳ/ short for ARE: We're ready, but they're not. –see 'S (USAGE)

reach¹ /riːtʃ/ v **1** [T] to arrive at or get to a place or person: They reached London on Thursday. | The news only reached me yesterday. **2** [I+adv/prep] to stretch out your hand or arm for some purpose: He reached across the table and picked up the book. | The shopkeeper reached for a packet of tea. | She reached out to hug him. **3** [I; T; not in progressive

---

SPELLING NOTE

Words with the sound / r /, may be spelt **wr-**, like **wrong**.

---

forms] to be able to touch or get something by stretching out your arm or hand: Are you tall enough to reach that light switch? | It's no good. I can't reach. **4** [I+adv/prep;T; not in progressive forms] to stretch as far as a particular place: The ladder won't quite reach the roof. | fields reaching down to the sea **5** [T] to get as far as a particular point or level: Haven't you reached the end of that book yet? | She's now reached the age of 50. | Our sales to Japan have reached record levels. **6 reach an agreement, reach a decision** to succeed in making an agreement or decision after a lot of thought or effort: After weeks of talks, the two sides reached an agreement. **7** [T] to get in touch with someone by telephone: She can be reached on 72894.

reach sthg ↔ **out** phr v [T] to stretch out your hand or arm: The little girl reached out a hand to touch the doll.

reach² n **1 within reach**: **a** near enough to touch by stretching out your arm or hand: He lay in bed with all his books within reach. **b** a phrase used to describe a place you can travel to easily: We live within easy reach of the shops. [RELATED PHRASES: **out of reach**; **beyond reach**] **2 the reaches of** large stretches of a river or of land: the upper reaches of the Nile

re·act /ri'ækt/ v [I] **1** to behave in a particular way as a result of a particular action or situation: The firm reacted to the workers' complaints by dismissing the director. | How did he react when you told him? **2 react against** to behave differently to what is expected because you do not agree with something: He reacted against his father's influence by running away. **3** tech (of a substance) to change when mixed with another substance: An acid can react with a base to form a salt.

re·ac·tion /ri'ækʃən/ n **1** [C] something that you say or do as an answer to a particular situation: What was his reaction to the news? | I made myself stand there, though my instinctive reaction was to turn and run. **2 a reaction against something** a change back to a previous belief or a change because of opposition to something: Their old-fashioned views are a reaction against the permissive age. | His wild behaviour was simply a reaction against his strict schooling. **3 your reactions** how quickly your body can act: Now I'm going to test your reactions. **4** [C;U] tech change caused in a chemical substance when it combines with another **5** [U] fml the quality of being strongly opposed to social or political change: The revolution was defeated by the forces of reaction.

re·ac·tion·a·ry /ri'ækʃənəri ‖ -ʃəneri/ n reactionaries a person strongly opposed to social or political change (a word used to express disapproval) –reactionary adj

re·ac·tiv·ate /ri'æktɪˌveɪt/ v reactivated, reactivating [T] to make something become active or work again

read¹ /riːd/ v read /red/, read, reading **1** [I;T] to look at and understand printed or written signs: The child is learning to read. | She reads well for a six-year-old. | I often read a book at night. | Can you read music? | He can't read a map. **2** [I;T; +that] to learn particular information from print or writing: I read about the murder in the paper. | I read that the new director was Spanish. **3** [I not in progressive forms] to be written in a particular form or style: Her letters always read as if she copied them from books. | The name reads "Benson" not "Fenton". **4** [T] to say printed or written words aloud to others:

He read the children a story. | *The teacher read a poem to the class.* | *The nurse read aloud to the old man.*
☐ USEFUL PATTERNS to read something to someone; to read someone something
5 [T] to show a particular amount or piece of information: *The thermometer reads 33 degrees.* | *The name on the door read Finnegan.* **6** [T] to understand someone's thoughts or feelings even if they are not directly expressed: *He can always read my mood.* **7** [T] to understand the meaning of a statement or situation in a particular way: *How do you read the latest trade figures?* | *This could be read as an attack on the government.* **8** [T] to study a subject at university: *Helen's reading History at Oxford.* **9 read between the lines** to understand something that is not directly expressed: *If you read between the lines, this letter is really a request for money.* **10 -read: a** having a certain amount of knowledge gained from books (used of a person): *a well-read woman* **b** read by a certain number of people (used of a book or newspaper): *a little-read novel*
read sthg **into** sthg *phr v* [T] to believe something means something more than what it really does: *Don't read more into her reply than she intended.*
read sthg ↔ **out** *phr v* [T] to read aloud for others to hear: *Can you read out the list of names?*
read up *phr v* [I; T **read** sthg ↔ **up**] *infml* to become informed about a subject by reading thoroughly: *I'll need to to read up on the tax laws to answer your question.*

read² *n infml* [sing] **1** an act of reading: *Can I have a read of your paper?* **2 a good read, an excellent read** something which is enjoyable and interesting to read: *Her latest novel is a very good read.*

rea·da·ble /ˈriːdəbəl/ *adj* **1** interesting or easy to read **2** written or printed in a way that is clear to read **–readability** /ˌriːdəˈbɪlɪti/ *n* [U]

re·ad·dress /ˌriːəˈdres/ *v* [T] to write a different address on a letter that has already been delivered to your house: *Could you readdress my letters to the new house please?*

read·er /ˈriːdəʳ/ *n* **1** a person who reads: *Are you a fast reader?* | *My brother is a keen reader.* **2** a person who reads a particular book, magazine, or newspaper: *We got a lot of letters about this from our readers.*

read·er·ship /ˈriːdəʃɪp ‖ -ər-/ *n* [sing] the number or type of people who read a particular newspaper or magazine: *The paper has a readership of 500,000.* | *a very well-educated readership.*

read·i·ly /ˈredɪli/ *adv* **1** willingly: *He readily agreed to their suggestion.* **2** with no difficulty: *This type of plug is readily available.*

read·i·ness /ˈredɪnɪs/ *n* **1** [sing;U] willingness or eagerness: *She showed a great readiness to learn.* **2 in readiness for** ready or prepared for something: *The soldiers were lined up in readiness for the parade.*

read·ing /ˈriːdɪŋ/ *n* **1** [U] the activity or practice of reading: *Children learn reading and writing at school.* | *She loves reading.* **2** [C] an opinion about the meaning of something: *My reading of the law is that we needn't pay.* **3** [C] a figure shown by a measuring instrument: *What are the temperature readings for this machine?* **4** [C] a gathering of people at which something is read aloud: *a poetry reading* **5** [only before a noun] for reading: *the reading room at the library*

re·ad·just /ˌriːəˈdʒʌst/ *v* **1** [T] to move or put something back into a particular position: *You'll have to*

readjust the driving mirror. **2** [I;T] to change in order to fit into a situation: *It's hard readjusting to work after a holiday.* **–readjustment** *n* [C;U] : *a period of readjustment*

read·y¹ /ˈredi/ *adj* **readier, readiest 1** [never before a noun] prepared fully for use or having the right qualities: *Is breakfast ready?* | *Come on – aren't you ready yet?* | *Is everything ready for the party?* | *These apples are nearly ready to eat.*
☐ USEFUL PATTERNS be ready for something; be ready to do something
2 [never before a noun] willing and eager to do or give something: *She's always ready to help.* | *He's always ready with an excuse.*
☐ USEFUL PATTERNS be ready to do something; be ready with something
3 [never before a noun] likely or about to do something: *I felt ready to cry with frustration.* **4** quick and easy: *a ready solution to the problem*

read·y² *interj* **Ready, steady, go!** a phrase used when telling people to begin a race

read·y³ *adv* [used before a past participle] in advance: *a ready-cooked dinner* | *You can buy the bread ready-cut.*

read·y⁴ *v fml* [T] to prepare something or someone for a particular event or purpose: *The government is readying itself for the elections.*

read·y-made /ˌ··ˈ·◄/ *adj* able to be used at once: *a ready-made suit* | *Many shops now have ready-made curtains.*

re·af·firm /ˌriːəˈfɜːm ‖ -ɜːrm/ *v* [T] to state or declare something again

real /rɪəl/ *adj* **1** not imaginary but actually existing: *a story of real life* **2** true or actual: *What was the real reason for your absence?* **3** not false: *Is this ring real gold?* | *real leather* **4** [only before a noun] made in the proper old way rather than a modern way: *real ale* **5** [only before a noun] a word used when you want to add force to a statement or to show that something actually exists: *You're a real idiot! It's been a real pleasure to meet you.* **6 for real** *infml* a phrase used to show that something actually exists or happens, and is not pretended or imagined: *I suddenly realized that the gun was for real.* **7 in real terms** a phrase used to talk about the real cost or value of something; for example, if your wages increase by a certain amount but prices also increase by the same amount, in real terms you are not earning any more money

real es·tate /ˈ···ˌ·/ *n* [U] *law* property in the form of land and houses

re·a·lis·m /ˈrɪəlɪzəm/ *n* [U] **1** accepting a situation as it actually is and dealing with it practically, without being influenced by your feelings **2** the showing of things in art and literature as they really are **–compare** ROMANTICISM, CLASSICISM **–realist** *n*

re·a·lis·tic /rɪəˈlɪstɪk/ *adj* **1** sensible and reasonable: *Our income has got smaller, so we must be realistic and give up our car.* **–opposite unrealistic 2** life-like (used of art or literature): *a realistic drawing of a horse* **–realistically** /-kli/ *adv*

re·al·i·ty /riˈælɪti/ *n* **realities 1** [U] the quality or state of existing or being real rather than imagined: *She believes in the reality of God.* **2** [C;U] everything that is real or true about a situation, especially when these things are unpleasant: *You'll have to face up to reality.* | *He liked to escape from reality by going to the cinema.* | *the harsh realities of life in the desert* **3** [C] a situation which actually exists: *His*

dream of marrying Jean became a reality. **4 in reality** a phrase used to show that something is different from what you believed or imagined: *We thought they had come to repair the phone, but in reality, they were burglars.*

re·a·li·za·tion /ˌrɪəlaɪˈzeɪʃən ‖ -lə-/ n (also **realisation**) **1** [sing;U] understanding or becoming conscious of something you did not know before: *I was struck by the full realization that he was guilty.* **2 the realization of** the becoming real of a hope, plan, or fear: *Travelling there was the the realization of all my dreams.*

re·a·lize /ˈrɪəlaɪz/ v **realized, realizing** (also **realise**) **1** [T;+(that)] to understand or become conscious of something: *He didn't realize his mistake.* | *Do you realize how late it is?* | *She spoke such good English that I didn't realize she was German.* □ USEFUL PATTERNS to realize something; to realize how, where, why, etc.; to realize that **2** [T] to make a hope, fear, or purpose real: *She realized her ambition of becoming an actress.* | *My worst fears were realized when I saw the exam questions.* **3** [T] *tech* to get money by selling something: *The company realized a considerable profit by selling the land.*

really /ˈrɪəli/ adv **1** truly or in fact: *Did she really say that?* | *Tell us what really happened.* | *I've just put a sheet of plastic over the hole for now. Really, it needs mending properly.* **2** to a great degree: *It's really cold today.* | *I was really pleased when they offered me the job.* | *I really hate him.* **3** used to show that you are interested in something or surprised by it: *"Have you heard, Jane's going to have a baby?" "Really?"*

realm /relm/ n **1** (also **Realm**) *lit* a country which has a king or queen as its official ruler: *the defence of the Realm* **2** a particular area of activity, interest, or thought: *This theory belongs more to the the realm of science than art.*

reams /riːmz/ n *infml* [pl] a large quantity of something written: *She wrote reams of notes.*

reap /riːp/ v **1** [I;T] to cut and gather a crop of grain: *The men are all out reaping.* | *Machines are used to reap the corn.* **2** [T] to get something because of your hard work or thorough planning: *The company is now reaping the benefits of its investments.*

reap·er /ˈriːpər/ n a person or machine that reaps

re·ap·pear /ˌriːəˈpɪər/ v [I] to appear again after an absence –**reappearance** n [U]

re·ap·prais·al /ˌriːəˈpreɪzəl/ n *fml* [C;U] careful thought about something to decide whether you should change your opinion of it: *There needs to be a reappraisal* of *our trade policy.*

rear¹ /rɪər/ v **1** [T] to care for children, animals, or plants until they are fully grown: *They reared a large family.* **2** [I] (also **rear up**) (of a horse) to lift the front part of the body and stand on the back legs: *The horse reared and threw me off.* **3 rear its ugly head** (of a problem or something unpleasant) to appear: *Disagreement again reared its ugly head among the staff.*

rear² n the **rear** *fml* the back: *a garden at the rear of the house* –**rear** adj : *a rear window*

SPELLING NOTE
Words with the sound / r /, may be spelt **wr-**, like **wrong.**

re·arm /riːˈɑːm ‖ -ˈɑːrm/ v [I;T] to supply a country or army again with new or better weapons: *They rearmed with modern missiles.* –**rearmament** n [U]

re·ar·range /ˌriːəˈreɪndʒ/ v **rearranged, rearranging** [T] to organize or arrange differently: *She rearranged the furniture in her room.* –**rearrangement** n [C;U]

rea·son¹ /ˈriːzən/ n **1** [C;U] the fact or cause which explains why something happens or exists: *She suddenly left without giving any reason.* | *There is reason to believe she was murdered.* | *What were his reasons for leaving his last job?* | *The reason for the flood was all that heavy rain.* | *Can you tell me the reason why you didn't come that night?* | *The animal hunts at night. For this reason, it has large ears.* –see EXCUSE² (USAGE) **2** [U] the ability to think, understand, and form opinions or judgments based on facts: *His writings appeal to emotion rather than reason.* **3** [U] good sense: *He won't listen to reason.* **4 by reason of** *fml* because of: *He escaped punishment by reason of his youth.* **5 for some reason** a phrase used to describe something that happens or exists although you do not know why: *For some reason, she felt terribly tired.* **6 with reason** correctly: *He thinks, with reason, that I don't like him.* **7 within reason** within sensible and fair limits: *The bank will lend you as much as you need, within reason.*

■ USAGE **1** Remember to use the preposition **for** in phrases such as: *the* **reason** *for my absence* | *the* **reason** *for his success* | *one of the* **reasons** *for doing this.* **2** Compare **cause** and **reason**. A **cause** is something which produces a result: *Bad driving is the* **cause** *of many accidents.* A **reason** is something which explains an action: *The* **reason** *he gave for his bad driving was that he was late for work.*

reason² v **1** [I] to think about or understand facts clearly: *Animals do not have the power to reason.* **2** [+that] to give an opinion or make a judgment based on careful thought: *I reasoned that since she had not answered my letter she must be angry with me.*

reason with sbdy *phr* v [T] to try to persuade someone to be more sensible: *There's no point in trying to reason with him – he'll never change.*

rea·so·na·ble /ˈriːzənəbəl/ adj **1** sensible and fair (used of people or behaviour): *Be reasonable, Mary! It wasn't my fault.* –opposite **unreasonable 2** correct or based on good reasons: *Scientists agree there is no reasonable explanation for these results.* **3** fair and not too expensive (used of prices): *The price of bananas is quite reasonable this month.* **4** not small, but not too great either: *We live a reasonable distance away from my parents.* –**reasonableness** n [U]

rea·son·a·bly /ˈriːzənəbli/ adv **1** fairly and sensibly: *He said quite reasonably that he didn't agree.* **2** quite: *The car is in reasonably good order.* | *They live reasonably close.*

rea·soned /ˈriːzənd/ adj [only before a noun] clearly thought out and sensible (used of an argument or explanation): *In a reasoned statement, the minister explained the new economic policy.*

rea·son·ing /ˈriːzənɪŋ/ n [U] the process of thinking carefully about particular facts in order to form an opinion or judgment: *Your reasoning on this point was quite correct.*

re·as·sure /ˌriːəˈʃʊər/ v **reassured, reassuring** [T] to comfort someone and stop them feeling anxious: *His boss reassured him that his work was satisfactory.* –**reassurance** n [C;U] : *She won't believe it in spite of all our reassurances.* –**reassuringly** adv

re·bate /ˈriːbeɪt/ n an amount of money that is paid back to you because you have paid too much tax or rent: *a tax rebate*

reb·el[1] /ˈrebəl/ n a person who rebels: *She joined the rebels when her father was killed.* | *Even at school Joe was a rebel who dressed differently to the others.*

re·bel[2] /rɪˈbel/ v -ll- [I] to oppose or fight against someone in a position of control: *The people have rebelled against their foreign rulers.* | *Teenagers always rebel against authority.*

re·bel·lion /rɪˈbeljən/ n [C;U] opposition to someone in a position of control

re·bel·lious /rɪˈbeljəs/ adj disobedient and hard to control: *rebellious behaviour* –**rebelliously** adv –**rebelliousness** n [U]

re·birth /ˌriːˈbɜːθ ‖ -ɜːrθ/ n [sing]fml a change leading to a new development: *the rebirth of learning in the Western world*

re·bound[1] /rɪˈbaʊnd/ v 1 [I] to fly or spring back after hitting something solid: *The ball rebounded from the wall and I caught it.* 2 **rebound on/upon** someone to have a bad effect on a person who has done something harmful: *His lies rebounded on himself because nobody trusted him any more.*

re·bound[2] /ˈriːbaʊnd/ n **on the rebound** to quickly start a new relationship because you are unhappy or disappointed that another relationship has just ended: *He married Mary on the rebound after Sue left him.*

re·buff /rɪˈbʌf/ n fml an unkind or unfriendly answer given to someone who is trying to be helpful or is asking for help: *Her tactful advice met only with a cruel rebuff.* –**rebuff** v [T] : *She rebuffed all my offers of friendship.*

re·build /ˌriːˈbɪld/ v **rebuilt** /-bɪlt/, **rebuilt** [T] to build again or add new parts to a building or town, usually after it has been damaged: *The church was rebuilt after the fire.*

re·buke /rɪˈbjuːk/ v **rebuked, rebuking** fml [T] to speak severely to someone because you do not like something they have said or done: *The judge rebuked the police for their behaviour.* –**rebuke** n

re·cal·ci·trant /rɪˈkælsɪ̩trənt/ adj fml refusing to obey or be controlled, even after being punished: *recalcitrant children* –**recalcitrance** n [U]

re·call[1] /rɪˈkɔːl/ v 1 [T; + that; not in progressive forms]fml to remember something: *I can't recall the exact details of the report.* | *I don't recall meeting her.* | *Do you recall where he lives?* | *She recalled that there was no supermarket then.*
□ USEFUL PATTERNS to recall something; to recall doing something; to recall where, how, why, etc.; to recall that…
2 to order someone to return to a particular place: *The government recalled its ambassador when war was declared.*

re·call[2] /rɪˈkɔːl ‖ rɪˈkɔːl, ˈriːkɔːl/ n 1 [U] the ability to remember something learned or experienced in the past: *She has amazing recall of her early childhood.* 2 **beyond recall** impossible to remember or change 3 [sing;U] the act of ordering someone to return: *The recall of the general from abroad caused a scandal.*

re·cant /rɪˈkænt/ v [I;T] fml to say publicly that you no longer hold a former political or religious belief: *She recanted and became a Christian.*

re·ca·pit·u·late /ˌriːkəˈpɪtʃʊleɪt/ v **recapitulated, recapitulating** (also **recap** /ˈriːkæp/ infml) [I;T] to repeat the main points of a statement or argument:

He recapitulated the main reasons for accepting the employers' offer. –**recapitulation** /ˌriːkəpɪtʃʊˈleɪʃən/ n [C;U]

re·cap·ture /riːˈkæptʃəʳ/ v **recapturing** [T] 1 to take control of or take as prisoner again: *The police recaptured the escaped criminal.* 2 lit to make someone experience or feel something again: *a book that recaptures the happiness of youth*

re·cede /rɪˈsiːd/ v **receded, receding** [I] 1 to move back or away into the distance: *She could see the lights of the ship receding on the horizon.* 2 to become less strong or less likely: *Hopes for their safety are receding fast.* 3 **be receding** to be losing hair at the front of your head –see picture on page 245

re·ceipt /rɪˈsiːt/ n 1 [C] a piece of paper showing you have received money: *Ask him to give you a receipt when you pay the bill.* 2 [U] the getting of something: *Did you write to acknowledge receipt of the goods?* 3 **receipts** [pl] the amount of money received by a business during a particular period

re·ceive /rɪˈsiːv/ v **received, receiving** [T] 1 fml to get something: *Did you receive my letter?* | *The children received a lot of attention.* | *We've just received some good news.* 2 to experience: *During the fight, he received a blow on the head.* 3 to welcome a visitor, often formally: *The director received her in the library.* 4 **be at/on the receiving end** of infml to be suffering something unpleasant done by someone else: *We were on the receiving end of several complaints.*

re·ceiv·er /rɪˈsiːvəʳ/ n 1 the part of a telephone that you hold to your ear –see TELEPHONE[1] (USAGE) 2 a radio or television set 3 a person who deals in stolen property

re·cent /ˈriːsənt/ adj having happened or appeared a short time ago: *recent history* | *her recent trip to China* | *one of the most exciting developments in medicine in recent years*

re·cent·ly /ˈriːsəntli/ adv not long ago: *I lived in London until quite recently.* | *Mike's only recently started learning French.*

re·cep·ta·cle /rɪˈseptəkəl/ n tech fml a container

re·cep·tion /rɪˈsepʃən/ n 1 [U] the office or department in a hotel or large organization which helps visitors and gives information: *Leave your key at reception.* 2 [C] a large formal party: *a wedding reception* 3 [C] a particular way of behaving which shows your opinion about someone or something: *The ambassador got a cool reception from the president.* 4 [U] the receiving of radio or television signals: *Radio reception isn't very good here.*

re·cep·tion·ist /rɪˈsepʃənɪ̩st/ n a person working in an office or hotel who deals with people when they first arrive and makes appointments for people

re·cep·tive /rɪˈseptɪv/ adj willing to consider new ideas: *He's not very receptive to my suggestions.* | *a receptive mind* –**receptively** adv –**receptiveness** n [U]

re·cess /rɪˈses ‖ ˈriːses/ n 1 [C;U] a period of holiday during the working year: *Parliament is in recess now.* | *the summer recess* 2 [C] a space in the wall of a room for shelves or cupboards 3 **the recesses** [pl] lit the secret inner parts of something

re·ces·sion /rɪˈseʃən/ n a period of reduced trade and business activity

re·ci·pe /ˈresɪpi/ n 1 a set of instructions for cooking a particular type of food: *a recipe for making chocolate cake* | *He didn't follow the recipe but it still*

tasted great. | a recipe book 2 a recipe for something a way of making something likely to happen: These proposals look like a recipe for disaster.

re·cip·i·ent /rɪˈsɪpiənt/ n fml a person who receives something

re·cip·ro·cal /rɪˈsɪprəkəl/ adj fml exchanged between two people or two groups of people: a reciprocal trade agreement between two nations −**reciprocally** /-kli/ adv

re·cip·ro·cate /rɪˈsɪprəkeɪt/ v **reciprocated, reciprocating** fml (I;T) to give or do something in return: They invited us to their party, and we reciprocated by inviting them to ours.

re·cit·al /rɪˈsaɪtl/ n **1** a performance of poetry or music, usually given by one performer: a piano recital **2** fml an account or report: He gave us a long recital of his experiences.

re·cite /rɪˈsaɪt/ v [T] **recited, reciting 1** to say a poem or other piece of writing aloud from memory: I don't like reciting poetry in public. **2** to say a list of something aloud: He recited a list of his complaints. −**recitation** /ˌresɪˈteɪʃən/ n [C;U]

reck·less /ˈrekləs/ adj not caring about danger or the possible bad results of your behaviour: Wasn't it a bit reckless of you to leave the job before you had another one? | reckless driving −**recklessly** adv −**recklessness** n [U]

reck·on /ˈrekən/ v **1** [+(that)] infml to think or suppose: I reckon that he'll come soon. **2** [+(that)] to guess or believe as a result of calculating roughly: How much do you reckon she earns? | The experts reckon about 10,000 tons of grain are needed. **3** [T] to calculate an amount or cost: My pay is reckoned from the 1st of the month.

reckon on sthg phr v [T] to expect or depend on something happening: We're reckoning on a large profit. | You can't always reckon on seeing him.

reckon with phr v **1** [T **reckon with** sbdy/sthg] to have to deal with someone or something: If they try to dismiss you, they'll have the union to reckon with. **2** [T **reckon with** sthg] to make your plans because you expect something: We hadn't reckoned with the possibility that it might rain. **3 to be reckoned with** to be treated seriously as a possible competitor or problem: The new team is already a force to be reckoned with.

reckon without sthg phr v [T] to fail to expect a possible problem when making a plan: When he decided to change his job, he reckoned without the difficulty of selling his house.

reck·on·ing /ˈrekənɪŋ/ n [U] **1** a rough calculation: By my reckoning, it must be 60 kilometres from here to the coast. **2 day of reckoning** the time when you must be punished for a mistake or bad behaviour

re·claim /rɪˈkleɪm/ v [T] **1** to get something back: I want to reclaim some of the tax I paid last year. **2** to make land fit for use: This land was reclaimed from the sea. −**reclamation** /ˌrekləˈmeɪʃən/ n [U]

re·cline /rɪˈklaɪn/ v **reclined, reclining** [I;T] to lean or lie back so that part of your body is supported: in a reclining position | She reclined her head against my shoulder.

re·cluse /rɪˈkluːs ‖ ˈrekluːs/ n a person who purposely lives alone and avoids other people

---

SPELLING NOTE

Words with the sound / r /, may be spelt **wr-**, like **wrong**.

---

rec·og·ni·tion /ˌrekəgˈnɪʃən/ n [U] **1** the act of being seen and known as someone or something: She hoped to avoid recognition by wearing dark glasses and a hat. **2** acceptance as legal or true: The new government has not yet received recognition from other countries. **3 change beyond recognition, change out of all recognition** to change so as to be impossible to recognize: Illness and age had changed her out of all recognition. **4 in recognition of** in order to show official gratefulness for: He received a large cheque in recognition of his years of service.

rec·og·nize /ˈrekəgnaɪz/ v **recognized, recognizing** (also **recognise**) **1** [T] to know someone or something you have seen or heard before: I recognized Mary in the photograph. | The town has changed so much you wouldn't recognize it! **2** [T] to officially accept something as being lawful: They refused to recognize the new government. | a recognized qualification in medicine **3** [+(that)] to accept or agree that something is true or real: I recognize that this is an unpleasant choice to make. **4** [T] to show official gratefulness for something: The government recognized his services by making him a lord. −**recognizable** adj −**recognizably** adv

re·coil /rɪˈkɔɪl/ v [I] **1** to suddenly experience a strong feeling of fear or dislike: She recoiled at their cruel behaviour. **2** to move back suddenly from someone or something because you fear or dislike it: She recoiled from her attacker. −**recoil** n [U]

rec·ol·lect /ˌrekəˈlekt/ v [T; not in progressive forms] to remember: Do you recollect her name? | I don't recollect meeting her.

□ USEFUL PATTERNS to recollect something; to recollect doing something

rec·ol·lec·tion /ˌrekəˈlekʃən/ n **1** [U] the power or action of remembering the past **2** [C] a memory of the past: I have a vivid recollection of that evening.

rec·om·mend /ˌrekəˈmend/ v **1** [T] to praise someone or something as being good for a particular purpose: Can you recommend a good dictionary? | He recommended a very good book to me. | They recommended him for the job. **2** [T; +(that)] to advise or suggest something as a correct or suitable course of action: I recommend caution in dealing with this matter. | He recommends wearing safety equipment. | The committee has recommended that the training programme be improved.

□ USEFUL PATTERNS to recommend something; to recommend doing something; to recommend that…

3 [T] (of a particular quality) to make something or somebody attractive: The hotel has nothing to recommend it except cheapness.

rec·om·men·da·tion /ˌrekəmenˈdeɪʃən/ n **1** [C;U] the suggestion that someone or something is good for a particular purpose: I wrote him an excellent recommendation. | They bought the car on Paul's recommendation. **2** [C] the suggestion that a particular action should be done: The committee's recommendations will be discussed tomorrow.

rec·om·pense¹ /ˈrekəmpens/ v **recompensed, recompensing** fml [T] to give a reward or payment for trouble or loss

recompense² n [sing;U] fml reward or payment given for causing trouble or loss, or to thank someone: They received £500 as a recompense for the damage to their house.

rec·on·cile /ˈrekənsaɪl/ v **reconciled, reconciling** [T] **1** to find agreement between ideas or situations which seem to be in opposition: How do you reconcile your political principles with your religious *beliefs?* **2** to have friendly relations again after a quarrel: *Her parents were completely reconciled.* **3** **reconcile yourself to something** to accept something difficult or unpleasant without trying to change it: *I can't reconcile myself to living in such a boring place.* | *He never became reconciled to the death of his wife.*

rec·on·cil·i·a·tion /ˌrekənsɪliˈeɪʃən/ *n* [sing;U] the bringing back of friendly relations after a quarrel: *There was no hope of a reconciliation* **between** *the two families.* | *There is now a spirit of reconciliation between the two nations.*

re·con·di·tion /ˌriːkənˈdɪʃən/ *v* [T] to repair something so that it works well again: *A reconditioned engine is cheaper than a new one.*

re·con·nais·sance /rɪˈkɒnɪsəns ‖ rɪˈkɑː-/ *n* [C;U] the sending out of soldiers to get information about the enemy

re·con·noi·tre /ˌrekəˈnɔɪtəʳ ‖ ˌriː-/ *v* **reconnoitred, reconnoitring** (also **reconnoiter** *AmE*) [I;T] to send aircraft or a small group of soldiers near the place where an enemy is in order to get information about the enemy

re·con·sid·er /ˌriːkənˈsɪdəʳ/ *v* [I;T] to think again about something and decide whether you need to change your opinion about it: *Won't you reconsider your decision to leave the club?* **–reconsideration** /ˌriːkənsɪdəˈreɪʃən/ *n* [U]

re·con·sti·tute /riːˈkɒnstɪtjuːt ‖ rɪˈkɑːnstɪtuːt/ *v* [T] **1** to bring an organization back into existence in a changed form: *We decided to reconstitute the committee under a new chairman.* **2** to change dried food into its original state by adding water: *reconstituted potato*

re·con·struct /ˌriːkənˈstrʌkt/ *v* [T] **1** to rebuild a town or building after destruction or damage **2** to get a complete description of something by putting together different pieces of information: *The police are trying to reconstruct the crime from the few clues they have.* **–reconstruction** /-ˈstrʌkʃən/ *n* [C;U] : *a reconstruction of the events leading up to the accident*

re·cord¹ /rɪˈkɔːd ‖ -ɔːrd/ *v* **1** [T] to write down something or put it on a computer so that it can be looked at later: *All the statistics are recorded on this disc.* | *How he died is not recorded.* | *Please record the score in this book.* **2** [I;T] to preserve sound or events so that they can be heard and seen again: *The broadcast was recorded, not live.* | *She has recorded several songs.* | *The wedding ceremony was recorded on video.* **3** [T] (of an instrument) to show an amount by measuring: *The thermometer recorded a temperature of 28 degrees.*

rec·ord² /ˈrekɔːd ‖ -ərd/ *n* [C] **1** information kept as a written statement or on a computer so that it can be looked at later: *Keep a record* **of** *how much you spend.* **2** the known facts about the past behaviour or performance of a person or organization: *She has a long criminal record.* | *The company has an outstanding record in industrial relations.* **3** the best figure ever reached: *He broke the record* **for** *long distance swimming.* | *She holds the world record for discus throwing.* **4** a circular piece of plastic on which sound is stored so that it can be played back again: *Have you heard my new record?* | *He put a record on.* **5 off the record** *infml* unofficial and intended to be known only in private: *He told us off the record that the firm was doing badly this year.* **6 on record: a** having said something publicly: *She is on record as having said that she opposed high taxation.* **b** ever recorded: *It was the coldest winter on*

record. **7 put/set the record straight** to correct someone's information about or understanding of something by giving them the correct facts: *This article really sets the record straight.*

rec·ord³ /ˈrekɔːd ‖ -ərd/ *adj* [only before a noun] more, faster, better, etc., than ever before: *a record crop of corn* | *We finished the work in record time.*

record-break·ing /ˈ·· ˌ··/ *adj* better than the former record, especially in sport: *a record-breaking speed*

recorded de·liv·er·y /·ˌ·· ·ˈ···/ *n* [U] a method of sending mail through the Post Office, by which you can get proof that it has been posted and delivered

re·cord·er /rɪˈkɔːdəʳ ‖ -ɔːr-/ *n* **1** a musical instrument that you play by blowing through a hollow tube and putting your fingers over different holes **2** a machine used for listening to or recording TAPES or CASSETTES, or watching or recording VIDEOS

re·cord·ing /rɪˈkɔːdɪŋ ‖ -ɔːr-/ *n* **1** a performance, speech, or piece of music that has been recorded: *the latest recording* **of** *the London Symphony Orchestra* **2** the process of preserving sound or events so that they can be heard again: *recording equipment*

record play·er /ˈ·· ˌ··/ *n* a machine which is used to play records –see picture on page 442

re·count¹ /rɪˈkaʊnt/ *v* [T] **1** *fml* to tell a story or describe something that happened: *She recounted her adventures.* **2** to count again: *They had to recount the votes.*

re·count² /ˈriːkaʊnt/ *n* a second count of votes in an election

re·course /rɪˈkɔːs ‖ ˈriːkɔːrs/ *n* **1 have recourse to** to use something as a means of help: *Patients have recourse to drugs to ease their pain.* **2 without recourse to** without making use of something: *We hope to solve the problem without recourse to further borrowing.*

re·cov·er /rɪˈkʌvəʳ/ *v* **1** [I] to be well again after an illness: *I'm still recovering* **from** *a bad cold.* | *He never fully recovered from the heart attack.* **2** [I] to return to a former state of body or mind: *She recovered consciousness soon after the accident.* | *The country had not yet recovered* **from** *the effects of the war.* | *They never recovered from the shock.* **3** [T] to get back or bring back something lost or stolen: *The police managed to recover the stolen goods.* | *The bodies were recovered* **from** *the wreck.* **4** [T] to get back the amount of money you spent: *The company recovered its investment in two years.* **5** [T] to put a new cover on something: *The chairs were re-covered in green silk.* **–recoverable** *adj*

re·cov·er·y /rɪˈkʌvəri/ *n* **1** [U] the getting back of something lost or stolen: *the recovery* **of** *the stolen jewels* **2** [sing] a return to good health or a strong condition: *She made a quick recovery* **from** *her fever.* | *The government's policies led to an economic recovery.*

re·cre·ate /ˌriːkriˈeɪt/ *v* **recreated, recreating** [T] to make something exist or be experienced again: *You can't recreate the past.*

rec·re·a·tion /ˌrekriˈeɪʃən/ *n* [C;U] a way of amusing and enjoying yourself when you are not working: *His only recreations are drinking beer and reading.* | *What do you do for recreation?*

■ USAGE We use **recreation** as a general word for the things people do in their spare time. Forms of recreation include **sports** such as tennis and football. They also include **hobbies**, which people do on their own, not in order to compete: *Her hobbies*

are gardening, stamp-collecting and playing the piano. **–recreational** *adj*

re·crim·i·nate /rɪˈkrɪmɪneɪt/ *v* **recriminated, recriminating** *fml* [I] to blame someone for bad behaviour after they have already blamed you **–recriminatory** /-nətəri ‖ -tɔːri / *adj* **–recrimination** /riːˌkrɪmɪˈneɪʃən/ *n* [C;U] : *Let's make friends, instead of wasting our time on recriminations.*

re·cruit[1] /rɪˈkruːt/ *n* **1** a new member of an organization: *New recruits to our music club are always welcome.* **2** someone who has recently joined the armed services

recruit[2] *v* **1** [I;T] attract new members to join the armed forces or other organization: *His job is recruiting for the Conservative Party.* **2** [T] to find someone to employ for a particular job: *We're having a lot of difficulty recruiting well-qualified staff.* **–recruitment** *n* [U]

rec·tan·gle /ˈrektæŋgəl/ *n* a shape with four straight sides; the sides opposite each other are of equal length

rec·tan·gu·lar /rekˈtæŋgjᵿləʳ/ *adj* in the shape of a rectangle

rec·ti·fy /ˈrektɪfaɪ/ *v* **rectified, rectifying** *fml* [T] to correct something or change it to something better: *Would you rectify the mistakes in my bill? | A good manager could rectify the situation.* **–rectification** /ˌrektɪfᵻˈkeɪʃən/ [C;U]

rec·tor /ˈrektəʳ/ *n* **1** the priest in the CHURCH OF ENGLAND who is in charge of a PARISH **2** the head of certain colleges and schools

rec·to·ry /ˈrektəri/ *n* the house where a rector lives

rec·tum /ˈrektəm/ *n* tech the lowest end of your bowel, through which solid waste matter passes out of your body

re·cu·pe·rate /rɪˈkjuːpəreɪt, -ˈkuː-/ *v* **recuperated, recuperating** [I] to get well or strong again after an illness: *He went to the mountains to recuperate.* **–recuperation** /rɪˌkjuːpəˈreɪʃən, -ˌkuː-/ *n* [U]

re·cur /rɪˈkɜːʳ/ *v* **-rr-** [I] to happen or appear again or many times: *If the pain recurs, take this medicine.* **–recurrence** /rɪˈkʌrəns ‖ -ˈkɜːr-/ *n* [U] : *the frequent recurrence of this problem* **–recurrent** *adj*

re·cy·cle /ˌriːˈsaɪkəl/ *v* **recycled, recycling** [T] to treat something which has already been used so that it is fit to use again: *These bottles can be recycled. | a bag made of recycled paper*

red[1] /red/ *adj* **1** of the colour of blood: *Let's paint the door red. | a red dress* –see picture on page 147 **2** of a copper colour (used of hair) **3** stronger in colour than usual because of a feeling of anger or shame (used of someone's face): *She turned red with embarrassment.* **4** (also **Red**) COMMUNIST (a word used to show disapproval) **–redness** *n* [U]

red[2] *n* **1** [C;U] a red colour: *the pinks and reds of the sunset* **2** [U] red clothes: *dressed in red* **3 in the red** in debt: *Your account is in the red.* **4** (also **Red**) a COMMUNIST

red car·pet /ˌ· ˈ··/ *n* **the red carpet** a special ceremonial welcome to a guest: *We'll roll out the red carpet for the president.*

SPELLING NOTE

Words with the sound / r /, may be spelt **wr-**, like **wrong**.

Red Cross /ˌ· ˈ·/ *n* **the Red Cross** [+sing/pl verb] an international Christian organization that looks after sick and wounded people: *The Red Cross is active in a lot of different countries.*

red·cur·rant /ˌredˈkʌrənt ‖ -ˈkɜːr-/ *n* a small red berry or the bush on which it grows

red·den /ˈredn/ *v* **1** [I;T] to turn red from anger or another strong feeling: *Her face reddened when I mentioned Jack.* **2** [T] to make something red: *The sunset reddened the clouds.*

red·dish /ˈredɪʃ/ *adj* slightly red

re·deem /rɪˈdiːm/ *v* [T] **1** to make a bad thing or situation slightly less bad: *Oliver's performance redeems an otherwise awful production.* **2 redeem yourself** to do something to improve people's opinion of you after you have behaved badly: *He'll never redeem himself for hitting her.* **3** to buy back something you have given to someone in return for money **4 redeeming feature** a single good point in a person or thing that is bad in all other ways: *His only redeeming feature is his honesty.*

re·demp·tion /rɪˈdempʃən/ *n* [U] **1** the state of being saved from evil which CHRISTIANS believe was made possible by the death of JESUS CHRIST **2 beyond/past redemption** too bad to be saved or improved

re·de·ploy /ˌriːdɪˈplɔɪ/ *v* to rearrange soldiers, workers, or apparatus in a more effective way **–redeployment** *n* [U]

re·de·vel·op·ment /ˌriːdɪˈveləpmənt/ *n* the knocking down and rebuilding of part of a town

red·head /ˈredhed/ *n* infml a woman with red hair: *He married a beautiful redhead.*

red her·ring /ˌ· ˈ··/ *n* a fact or subject which is introduced to draw people's attention away from the main point

red-hot /ˌ· ˈ· ◄/ *adj* so hot that it shines red (used of metal)

re·di·rect /ˌriːdaɪˈrekt, -dᵻ-/ *v* [T] to send post in a different direction or to a new address

re·do /riːˈduː/ *v* **redid** /-ˈdɪd/, **redone** /-ˈdʌn/ [T] to do something again so that you can change it or make it better: *You'll have to redo your homework.*

red·o·lent /ˈredələnt/ *adj* fml [never before a noun] making you think of something: *an old house redolent of mystery*

re·dou·ble /riːˈdʌbəl/ *v* **redoubled, redoubling** **redouble your efforts** to greatly increase your efforts: *The police redoubled their efforts to find the missing child.*

re·doub·ta·ble /rɪˈdaʊtəbəl/ *adj* lit greatly respected and feared (used of people): *a redoubtable opponent*

re·dress[1] /rɪˈdres/ *v* fml [T] **1** to correct an injustice or improve the situation for someone who has been treated unfairly **2 redress the balance** to make things equal or fair again

re·dress[2] /rɪˈdres ‖ ˈriːdres/ *n* fml [U] satisfaction or payment for something wrong that has been done: *You must seek redress in the law courts for the damage to your car.*

red tape /ˌ· ˈ·/ *n* [U] unnecessary official rules that delay action

re·duce /rɪˈdjuːs ‖ rɪˈduːs/ *v* **reduced, reducing** **1** [T] to make less in size, amount, or degree: *I bought this shirt because it was reduced from £10 to £5. | He won't reduce the rent of our house. | a defence policy that reduces the risk of war* **2 be reduced to doing**

something to be forced to behave in a particular way: *She was reduced to begging for her living.* **3 reduce someone to tears** to make someone cry
reduce sbdy/sthg **to** sthg *phr v* [T] **1** to change something into a simpler form: *We can reduce his argument to three simple facts.* **2** to cause someone or something to be in an unfortunate or bad state: *The bomb reduced the city to ashes.* | *His bad behaviour reduces me to despair.*

re·duc·tion /rɪˈdʌkʃən/ *n* **1** [C;U] the act of making something less in size, amount, or degree: *price reductions* **2** [C] the amount by which something is made less: *a 2% reduction in the rate of inflation*

re·dun·dan·cy /rɪˈdʌndənsi/ *n* **redundancies** [C;U] **1** a case of losing your job because there is not enough work: *The government action will cause a lot of redundancy among coalminers.* | *There have been 200 redundancies at the factory.* **2 redundancy payment** an amount of money paid to someone employed by a company when they become redundant

re·dun·dant /rɪˈdʌndənt/ *adj* **1** no longer employed by a company or organization because there is not enough work: *Seventy men at the factory were made redundant when the machines were installed.* **2** no longer needed for a particular purpose: *The new road has made rail travel almost redundant.*

reed /riːd/ *n* **1** a plant with tall, hollow stems; reeds grow in wet places **2** a thin piece of wood or metal in a musical instrument that produces sound when air is blown over it

reef /riːf/ *n* a line of sharp rocks or a bank of sand above or near the surface of the sea: *The ship was wrecked on a reef.*

reek /riːk/ *n* [sing] a strong unpleasant smell: *a reek of tobacco and beer*

reek *v* [I] to smell strongly and unpleasantly of: *His clothes reek of cigarettes.*

reel¹ /riːl/ *n* **1** a round object around which you wind things such as thread for sewing or film **2** a Scottish dance

reel² *v* **1** [I] to move unsteadily as if drunk: *He was reeling when he left the pub.* **2** [I] to be in a state of confusion or shock: *All these figures make my head reel.* | *The party is still reeling from its defeat in the election.*
reel sthg ↔ **off** *phr v* [T] to repeat information quickly and easily from memory: *He could reel off the names of all the kings of England.*

re·en·try /riːˈentri/ *n* [C;U] an act of entering again: *The spacecraft made a successful re-entry into the earth's atmosphere.*

re·fec·to·ry /rɪˈfektəri/ *n* refectories a large hall, for example in a college, in which meals are served

re·fer /rɪˈfɜːr/ **-rr-** *v*
refer to *phr v* **1** [T **refer to** sbdy/sthg] to mention or speak about someone or something: *Which companies did the prime minister refer to in his speech?* | *He didn't refer to Jack in his letter.* | *He referred to her simply as "my friend".* **2** [T **refer to** sthg] to look at something in order to get information: *Refer to a dictionary if you don't know what this word means.* **3** [T **refer** sbdy **to** sbdy/sthg] to tell a particular person or organization about something or someone so they can do what is needed: *Her doctor referred her to a specialist.* | *The proposal was referred to the Finance Committee.* **4** [T **refer** sbdy **to** sthg] to suggest that someone looks at a particular piece of writing to get information they need: *The professor referred him to an article in the latest journal.*

ref·er·ee¹ /ˌrefəˈriː/ *n* **1** (also **ref** *infml*) an official in charge of judging certain games **2** a person who provides a statement about your character and abilities
■ **USAGE Referee** is used in connection with **basketball, boxing, football, hockey, lacrosse, rugby, snooker, squash,** and **wrestling. Umpire** is used in connection with **badminton, baseball, cricket, tennis,** and **volleyball.**

referee² *v* [I;T] to act as referee for a game or match: *Who's going to referee Monday's game?*

ref·er·ence /ˈrefərəns/ *n* **1** [C;U] an example of mentioning or talking about something or someone: *In the letter, he made no reference to his illness.* | *Her remark was a nasty reference to her previous boss.* **2** [U] an act of looking at something for information: *Keep this dictionary on your desk for easy reference.* **3 for future reference** for use in the future: *He kept the article for future reference.* **4** [C] a letter written by someone about your character and ability which you use when looking for a job: *She had excellent references so we hired her.* **5** [C] something that tells a reader where a piece of information came from: *There's a list of references at the back of the book.* **6 in/with reference to** *fml* a phrase used to show what subject you are talking or writing about: *Dear Sir, with reference to your letter of the 15th May...*

reference book /ˈ···· ·/ *n* a book, for example a dictionary, which you look at to get particular information about a subject

ref·e·ren·dum /ˌrefəˈrendəm/ *n* a direct vote by all the people of a country or area to decide on a political matter about which there is strong disagreement

re·fill¹ /ˌriːˈfɪl/ *v* [T] to fill something again: *I'll refill my cigarette lighter.*

re·fill² /ˈriːfɪl/ *n* a container holding a quantity of a particular substance which is used to refill something: *I bought two refills for this pen.*

re·fine /rɪˈfaɪn/ *v* **refined, refining** [T] **1** to make something pure: *Oil must be refined before it can be used.* **2** to improve an idea, method, or plan by changing some of its details

re·fined /rɪˈfaɪnd/ *adj* **1** made pure: *refined oil* **2** having good education, manners, and often an interest in art, music, and literature: *She's so refined she eats cake with a little fork!* –opposite **unrefined**

re·fine·ment /rɪˈfaɪnmənt/ *n* **1** [C] a small, but useful addition or improvement to a product or system: *The new car has many new refinements such as a compact disc player.* **2** [U] the process of making a substance pure: *the refinement of sugar* **3** [U] the quality of being polite and well-educated: *a woman of great refinement*

re·fin·e·ry /rɪˈfaɪnəri/ *n* **refineries** a factory for refining metals, oil, or sugar: *a sugar refinery*

re·flect /rɪˈflekt/ *v* **1** be reflected to be shown as an image, for example in water or a mirror: *Clouds were reflected in the lake.* **2** [T] to throw back heat, light, or sound: *The material is designed to reflect the heat.* **3** [T] to express or show a feeling or belief: *Does the letter reflect your real opinions?* **4** [T] to be the result of a particular situation or feeling: *The increase in crime reflects rising unemployment.* **5** [I] to think carefully: *After reflecting for a time he decided not to go.*
reflect on sbdy/sthg *phr v* [T] to make something considered in a particular way: *These exam results reflect badly on your school.*

re·flec·tion /rɪˈflekʃən/ n 1 [C] an image reflected in a mirror or water: *We looked at our reflections in the lake.* 2 [U] the process by which heat, light, or sound, is reflected 3 [C;U] deep and careful thought: *his reflections on Indian politics* | *After a moment's reflection, she agreed to go.* 4 **on reflection** after thinking carefully: *She admitted, on reflection, that it was foolish.* 5 [C] something that is a result or sign of a particular situation: *The results of the election are an accurate reflection of the public mood.*

re·flec·tor /rɪˈflektəʳ/ n a surface that reflects light

re·flex /ˈriːfleks/ n a movement which you cannot control made by a part of the body in reply to something: *The doctor hit my knee with a hammer to test my reflexes.*

re·flex·ive /rɪˈfleksɪv/ 1 **reflexive verb** a verb in which the object is always the same as the subject; for example in the sentence "He studied himself in the mirror." "He" and "himself" mean the same person 2 **reflexive pronoun** a word which points back to the subject of the verb; for example in the sentence "She washed herself." "herself" is a reflexive pronoun which tells us about the subject "she"

re·form¹ /rɪˈfɔːm ‖ -ɔːrm/ v [T] to improve an organization or system by making changes to it: *This law will help to reform the prisons.* 2 [I;T] to improve or change unacceptable behaviour: *You can't reform criminals by punishing them.* | *Harry has completely reformed since he stopped taking drugs.*

reform² n [C;U] a change that improves an organization or social system: *The minister announced the reform of the tax system.* | *Reform of unfair laws will take many years.*

Ref·or·ma·tion /ˌrefəˈmeɪʃən ‖ -fər-/ n **the Reformation** the religious movement in Europe in the 16th century leading to the establishment of the PROTESTANT churches

re·for·mer /rɪˈfɔːməʳ ‖ -ˈfɔːr-/ n a person who tries to change and improve conditions in society

re·fract /rɪˈfrækt/ v [I;T] to make light or sound change direction when passing through a substance like glass or water at an angle **–refraction** /-ˈfrækʃən/ n

re·frain¹ /rɪˈfreɪn/ v [I] **refrain from doing something** to intentionally stop yourself from doing something: *Please refrain from smoking.*

refrain² n a part of a song that you repeat a number of times when you sing the song

re·fresh /rɪˈfreʃ/ v [T] 1 to make someone less hot or tired: *A hot bath will refresh you.* | *He refreshed himself with a glass of beer.* 2 **refresh your memory** to remind you about something: *Please refresh my memory – what was your last job?*

refresher course /ˈ·ˈ··/ n a training course given to a group of members of the same profession so that they know about recent changes in their field: *She attended a refresher course on modern teaching methods.*

re·fresh·ing /rɪˈfreʃɪŋ/ adj 1 making you feel cool and strong again after being unpleasantly hot or tired: *a refreshing drink* | *a refreshing sleep* 2

SPELLING NOTE
Words with the sound / r /, may be spelt **wr-**, like **wrong.**

---

pleasantly new and interesting: *It's refreshing to see a film with so little violence.* **–refreshingly** adv

re·fresh·ment /rɪˈfreʃmənt/ n 1 [U] fml food and drink: *We worked all day without refreshment.* 2 **refreshments** small quantities of food and drink, usually served at a social gathering: *Refreshments will be served after the performance.*

re·fri·ge·rate /rɪˈfrɪdʒəreɪt/ v **refrigerated, refrigerating** [T] to make food or liquid cold as a way of preserving it: *refrigerated meat* **–refrigeration** /rɪˌfrɪdʒəˈreɪʃən/ n [U]

re·fri·ge·ra·tor /rɪˈfrɪdʒəreɪtəʳ/ n (also **fridge** infml) a large box, usually working by electricity, in which food and drink can be kept cool in order to preserve them

re·fu·el /ˌriːˈfjuːəl/ v -ll- (also -l- AmE) [I;T] to fill up or be filled up again with FUEL: *The aircraft stopped in Cairo to refuel.*

ref·uge /ˈrefjuːdʒ/ n 1 [U] protection or shelter from unhappiness or physical danger: *The prisoners sought refuge in telling stories.* | *We found refuge from the storm under a tree.* 2 [C] a place which provides protection or shelter: *She's been living in a refuge for battered wives.* 3 **take refuge** to find shelter or protection

ref·u·gee /ˌrefjuˈdʒiː/ n a person who has been forced to leave their country for political or religious reasons, or because they have no food

re·fund¹ /rɪˈfʌnd/ v [T] to give back money which has been paid to you: *They refunded our money when the play was cancelled.*

re·fund² /ˈriːfʌnd/ n an amount of money which is paid back to you, for example when you return unsatisfactory goods to a shop: *Can I get a refund on these tickets?*

re·fus·al /rɪˈfjuːzəl/ n [C;U] a case of refusing to do, accept, or allow something: *Their refusal to negotiate with us made progress difficult.*

re·fuse¹ /rɪˈfjuːz/ v **refused, refusing** 1 [I;T] to say firmly that you are not willing to accept or do something: *He asked her to marry him but she refused.* | *She refused his offer.* | *He refuses to do any extra work.*
□ USEFUL PATTERNS to refuse; to refuse something; to refuse to do something
2 **refuse someone something** to say firmly that you will not give or allow something: *They refused me an extension of my visa.* | *We were refused permission to enter the country.*
■ USAGE Compare **refuse, decline, reject, turn down.** 1 You can **refuse** an invitation, a suggestion, an offer, or permission. You can **decline** an invitation, a suggestion, or an offer. You can **reject** or **turn down** a suggestion, an offer, or a plan. 2 **Decline** is more polite than **refuse**, and not so strong: *I'm afraid I must decline your invitation.*

ref·use² /ˈrefjuːs/ n [U] fml waste material: *When is the refuse collected?* | *a refuse dump*

re·fute /rɪˈfjuːt/ v **refuted, refuting** fml [T] to prove that a person or an argument is wrong: *This argument cannot be easily refuted.* **–refutation** /ˌrefjuˈteɪʃən/ n [C;U]

re·gain /rɪˈgeɪn/ v [T] to get something back: *She is slowly regaining her health.* | *The army has regained control of the town.*

re·gal /ˈriːgəl/ adj splendid enough to be fit for a king or queen: *regal manners* **–regally** adv

re·gale /rɪˈgeɪl/ v **regaled, regaling** [T] **regale someone with something** to entertain someone with jokes and stories: *He regaled us with tales of his foreign adventures.*

re·ga·li·a /rɪˈgeɪliə/ n [U] ceremonial clothes and decorations, used especially on official occasions: *The mayor was dressed in full regalia.*

re·gard¹ /rɪˈɡɑːd ‖ -ɑːrd/ n 1 [U] respect for someone or something: **2 have high regard for** to have great respect for someone or something: *I have a high regard for his abilities.* 3 **hold someone/something in high regard** to have great respect for a person or thing: *She has always held her son-in-law in high regard.* [RELATED PHRASE **hold someone/something in low regard**] 4 [U] attention or consideration: *You have no regard for my feelings!* | *The report pays little regard to the facts.* 5 **regards** a word used to express your good wishes to someone: *Please give my best regards to your wife.* | *With kind regards, John.* 6 **with regard to, as regards** a phrase used to show which subject is being talked or written about: *With regard to your recent application, I am afraid we cannot offer you a job.*

regard² v [T] 1 to consider someone or something in a particular way: *I have always regarded him highly.* | *I regard him as my friend.* | *She regards this painting as her best ever.* 2 *fml* to look at someone in a particular way: *She regarded him thoughtfully.*

re·gard·ing /rɪˈɡɑːdɪŋ ‖ -ɑːr-/ prep fml a word used, especially in letters, to show what subject you are writing or talking about: *Regarding your recent enquiry, I enclose a college prospectus.*

re·gard·less /rɪˈɡɑːdləs ‖ -ɑːr-/ adv 1 **regardless of** in spite of: *They signed the contract regardless of their lawyer's advice.* 2 without worrying about a problem: *The baby was crying, but she carried on painting regardless.*

re·gat·ta /rɪˈɡætə/ n an event in which races between rowing or sailing boats take place

re·gen·cy /ˈriːdʒənsi/ n [U] the period of government by a regent

re·gent /ˈriːdʒənt/ n (also **Regent**) a person who governs in place of a king or queen who is ill, absent, or still a child

reg·gae /ˈreɡeɪ/ n [U] a type of popular music from the West Indies with a strong regular beat

re·gime /reɪˈʒiːm/ n (also **régime**) 1 a particular type of government (a word often used to express disapproval): *The country is under a military regime.* 2 a particular government that rules a country (a word often used to express disapproval): *The old regime killed hundreds of people.* 3 a way of life intended to improve your health: *Giving up smoking is part of my new regime.*

re·gi·ment¹ /ˈredʒɪmənt/ n [+sing/pl verb] a large group of soldiers, commanded by a COLONEL –**regimental** /ˈmentl/ adj [only before a noun]: *the regimental band*

re·gi·ment² /ˈredʒɪment/ v [T] to control people tightly: *Children today don't like being regimented.* –**regimented** adj : *a regimented society* –**regimentation** /ˌredʒɪmenˈteɪʃən ‖ -mən-/ n [U]

re·gion /ˈriːdʒən/ n 1 a large area of land, usually with clear borders or particular qualities: *Snow is expected in southern regions.* 2 an area around a particular part of your body: *He experienced pains in the region of his heart.* 3 **in the region of** about: *It will cost in the region of £200.* –**regional** adj : *strange regional customs* –**regionally** adv

re·gis·ter¹ /ˈredʒɪstər/ n 1 [C] an official record: *We could consult the register of births and deaths.* | *a*

school attendance register 2 [C;U] tech a way of speaking or writing which depends on the situation you are in and whether it is formal or informal

register² v 1 [I;T] to record a name or event on an official list: *Have you registered the birth of the baby yet?* | *The car is registered in my name.* | *They registered at my hotel last night.* 2 [T] (of a machine or instrument) to show an amount or a measurement: *The thermometer registered 35°C.* 3 [I] to show as a measurement on an instrument: *The speed is not registering.* 4 [T] to express your feelings or opinions about something: *Her face registered surprise.* | *I want to register my opposition to this project.* 5 [T] to pay more to send a letter in order to insure it against loss: *You'd better register this letter.*

registered post /ˌ··· ˈ·/ n (also **registered mail** *AmE*) [U] a postal service which, for an additional charge, insures the sender of a valuable letter or parcel against loss: *I'll send it by registered post.*

re·gis·trar /ˌredʒɪˈstrɑːʳ◀ ‖ ˈredʒɪstrɑːr/ n (also **Registrar**) 1 a person whose job is to keep official records, for example of births and deaths 2 a person whose job is to admit students and organize examinations at a college or university 3 a high-level hospital doctor

re·gis·tra·tion /ˌredʒɪˈstreɪʃən/ n [U] the act of recording something on an official list: *Registration of new students takes place on Monday.*

registration num·ber /··ˈ·· ˌ···/ n the official set of numbers and letters that must be shown on the front and back of a car or other motor vehicle

re·gis·try /ˈredʒɪstri/ n **registries** (also **Registry**) a place where official records are kept: *the Land Registry*

re·gress /rɪˈɡres/ v fml [I] to return to a worse or less developed state: *The boy's behaviour regressed after his parents' divorce.* –**regression** /-ˈɡreʃən/ n [U]

re·gret¹ /rɪˈɡret/ v -tt- [T; +(that)] 1 to feel sorry about something you did and wish you had not done it: *Later, I regretted that I hadn't taken the job.* | *Mary deeply regrets her decision not to have children.* | *Do you regret selling the farm?* □ USEFUL PATTERNS to regret something; to regret doing something; to regret that… 2 [T; + that] *fml* a word used to show you are sorry about certain bad news: *I regret that I will be unable to attend.* | *We regret to inform you that your application has been rejected.*

regret² n 1 [U] a feeling of sadness or disappointment about something: *The prime minister expressed his regret at the failure of the talks.* 2 **have no regrets** not to feel sorry about something that has happened or that you have done: *He has no regrets about leaving college.* –**regretful** adj : *She said goodbye with a regretful smile.* –**regretfully** adv

re·gret·ta·ble /rɪˈɡretəbəl/ adj unfortunate: *a regrettable mistake* –**regrettably** adv : *Regrettably, teaching methods have not improved.*

re·group /ˌriːˈɡruːp/ v [I;T] to form into new groups, or into the same groups as before

reg·u·lar¹ /ˈreɡjʊləʳ/ adj 1 repeated, with the same amount of time or space between one thing and the next: *His heartbeat is not very regular.* | *the regular tick of the clock* | *Plant the seeds at regular intervals.* 2 planned for the same time every day, week, or month: *We hold regular meetings.* | *They give regular performances throughout the summer.* 3 arranged or shaped evenly: *He had an attractive face, with regular features.* 4 frequent enough to be expected: *James was one of my regular visitors.* | *his regular failure to finish the work on time* **5** usual: *Who's your regular doctor?* | *Our regular customers always pay cash.* **6** following a common pattern (used in grammar): *The verb "to walk" is regular, while the verb "to be" is not.*

regular² *n infml* a person who often goes to a particular shop or place: *Mr Bennett is one of the regulars at the village pub.*

reg·u·lar·i·ty /ˌregjʊ'lærˌti/ *n* [U] the situation or state of happening repeatedly: *The building is cleaned with great regularity.*

reg·u·lar·ly /'regjʊləli ‖ -lər-/ *adv* **1** at regular times: *Take the medicine regularly three times a day.* | *They met regularly to discuss business.* **2** often: *Sue regularly leaves work early.*

reg·u·late /'regjʊleɪt/ *v* **regulated, regulating** [T] **1** to control something, usually by having rules: *Gun sales are strictly regulated by the government.* **2** to control the way a machine works: *Use this button to regulate the sound.*

reg·u·la·tion /ˌregjʊ'leɪʃən/ *n* **1** [C] an official rule to control a particular activity: *safety regulations* | *Don't do anything that's against the regulations.* **2** [U] control of a process or activity: *the regulation of public spending*

re·gur·gi·tate /rɪ'gɜːdʒɪteɪt ‖ -ɜːr-/ *v* **regurgitated, regurgitating** [T] *fml* **1** *fml* to bring back into your mouth food that you have already swallowed **2** to repeat facts or ideas without understanding them clearly –**regurgitation** /rɪˌgɜːdʒɪ'teɪʃən ‖ -ɜːr-/ *n* [U]

re·ha·bil·i·tate /ˌriːhə'bɪlɪteɪt/ *v* **rehabilitated, rehabilitating** [T] to help someone live a healthy or useful life again after they have been ill or in prison: *The organization helps to rehabilitate young offenders.* –**rehabilitation** /ˌriːhəbɪlɪ'teɪʃən/ *n* [U]

re·hash /riː'hæʃ/ *v* [T] *infml* to use the same ideas again in a new form which is not really different or better: *He keeps rehashing the same old speech* –**rehash** /'riːhæʃ/ *n*

re·hears·al /rɪ'hɜːsəl ‖ -ɜːr-/ *n* [C;U] practice as preparation for a public performance: *This play will need a lot of rehearsal.* | *Rehearsals will take place every Saturday.*

re·hearse /rɪ'hɜːs ‖ -ɜːrs/ *v* **rehearsed, rehearsing** [I; T] **1** to practise a play, dance, or music in order to prepare for a public performance: *The actors were rehearsing until late last night.* | *She's only rehearsed the song a couple of times.* **2** to think about the words you are going to use later

re·house /ˌriː'haʊz/ *v* **rehoused, rehousing** [T] to move someone into a different or better house: *Many families were rehoused after the war.*

reign¹ /reɪn/ *n* **1** a period of time during which someone rules a country: *It happened in the reign of King George IV.* **2** a period of time during which a particular situation or state exists: *a reign of terror*

reign² *v* [I] **1** (of a king or queen) to rule a country: *Queen Victoria reigned for over 60 years.* **2** *lit* to exist for a period of time in a very noticeable or influential way: *The thunder died away and silence*

reigned once more. | *Anarchy reigned during the revolution.*

re·im·burse /ˌriːɪm'bɜːs ‖ -ɜːrs/ *v* **reimbursed, reimbursing** *fml* to pay money back to someone: *We will reimburse you for the loss of the painting.* | *The cost will be reimbursed.* –**reimbursement** *n* [U]

rein /reɪn/ *n* **1** a long narrow band of leather, by which a horse is controlled **2 give (a) free rein to someone** to give someone the freedom to do what they like: *We've given the architects free rein in designing the building.* **3 keep a tight rein on** to control a person or thing firmly: *We intend to keep a tight rein on public spending.*

re·in·car·nate /ˌriːɪn'kɑːneɪt, ‖ -ɑːr-/ *v* **reincarnated, reincarnating be reincarnated** to return to life in a new body after dying

re·in·car·na·tion /ˌriːɪnkɑː'neɪʃən ‖ -ɑːr-/ *n* **1** [U] return to life in a new body after dying: *Do you believe in reincarnation?* **2** [C] the person or animal in whose body a dead person is thought to live again: *He claims to be a reincarnation of Napoleon.*

rein·deer /'reɪndɪər/ *n* **reindeer** a type of large deer with long branching horns, found in northern parts of the world

re·in·force /ˌriːɪn'fɔːs ‖ -'fɔːrs/ *v* **reinforced, reinforcing** [T] **1** to strengthen something by adding to it: *The knees on Tim's trousers need reinforcing before he rubs a hole in them.* **2** to support or strengthen a situation, feeling, or idea: *This argument is strongly reinforced by the latest trade figures.* –**reinforcement** *n* [U] : *This roof needs some reinforcement.*

re·in·force·ments /ˌriːɪn'fɔːsmənts ‖ -'fɔːrs-/ *n* [pl] more soldiers sent to strengthen an army: *We've sent for reinforcements.*

re·in·state /ˌriːɪn'steɪt/ *v* **reinstated, reinstating** [T] to put someone back into a position or job they held before: *He was reinstated after the real thief was caught.* –**reinstatement** *n* [C;U]

re·it·e·rate /riː'ɪtəreɪt/ *v* **reiterated, reiterating** [T; + that] to say something more than once: *The miners reiterated their demands for an inquiry into the accident.* –**reiteration** /riːˌɪtə'reɪʃən/ *n* [C;U]

re·ject¹ /rɪ'dʒekt/ *v* [T] **1** to refuse to accept or agree with something: *She rejected my suggestion.* | *The teachers voted to reject the government's pay offer.* –see REFUSE (USAGE) **2** to throw away something because it is useless or imperfect **3** to refuse someone, especially for a job: *He was rejected by the army because of his poor eyesight.* **4** to behave in a cruel way to someone who expects love or kindness from you: *He was rejected by his father.*

re·ject² /'riːdʒekt/ *n* a product which is not accepted for use because it is damaged or imperfect

re·jec·tion /rɪ'dʒekʃən/ *n* **1** [C;U] refusal to accept or agree with something: *Rejection of the proposal could lead to disaster.* **2** [C] refusal to accept a person, especially for a job: *I'm trying to get a job, but have so far received only rejections.* **3** [U] cruel behaviour to someone who expects love or kindness from you: *Total rejection of a child by the mother is fortunately rare.*

re·joice /rɪ'dʒɔɪs/ *v* **rejoiced, rejoicing** [I] *fml lit* to feel or show great joy: *The people rejoiced at the happy news.* | *He rejoiced over the birth of his son.*

re·joic·ing /rɪ'dʒɔɪsɪŋ/ *n* [U] *fml* great joy, shown by a large number of people

re·join·der /rɪ'dʒɔɪndər/ *n* a quick or rude reply: *He answered me with a sharp rejoinder.*

SPELLING NOTE

Words with the sound / r /, may be spelt **wr-**, like **wrong.**

re·ju·ve·nate /rɪˈdʒuːvəneɪt/ v **rejuvenated, rejuvenating** [T] to make someone look or feel young and strong again: *They were completely rejuvenated by their holiday.* –**rejuvenation** /rɪˌdʒuːvəˈneɪʃən/ n [U]

re·lapse /rɪˈlæps/ v **relapsed, relapsing** [I] to return to poor health or bad behaviour after an improvement: *He soon relapsed into his bad habits.* –**relapse** /ˈriːlæps, rɪˈlæps/ n : *Jack had a relapse a few weeks after the operation.*

re·late /rɪˈleɪt/ v **related, relating** [T] **1** to make a connection between two things: *The police are trying to relate the girl's disappearance to an attack which took place last week.* **2** fml to tell a story: *He related to us the events which led to his escape.* **3 relate to something: a** to concern or be connected with something: *secret documents relating to war crimes* **b** to feel that something has meaning for you personally: *I can't relate to those kind of religious beliefs.* **4 relate to someone** to understand someone and have a comfortable relationship with them: *She doesn't relate very well to other women.*

re·lat·ed /rɪˈleɪtɪd/ adj **1** connected by a family relationship: *She is related to me by marriage.* **2** connected in some way: *The book deals with drug addiction and related problems.* –opposite **unrelated**

re·la·tion /rɪˈleɪʃən/ n **1** [C] a member of your family: *I saw a lot of my relations at the wedding.* **2** [U] the connection between one thing and another: *His argument bears no relation to the facts.* **3 relations** [pl] the way that two people or groups feel and behave towards each other: *Relations with neighbouring countries are excellent.* **4 in relation to** a phrase used to talk about the size or position of something compared with something else: *Her salary is high in relation to that of state school teachers.* | *Where is the village in relation to the lake?*

re·la·tion·ship /rɪˈleɪʃənʃɪp/ n **1** a connection between two things: *What's the relationship between art and revolution?* **2** the way two people or groups feel and behave towards each other: *The police have a good relationship with local people.* **3** a close friendship between two people which is often sexual: *My relationship with my boyfriend has lasted six months.* | *He isn't in a relationship at the moment.*

rel·a·tive¹ /ˈrelətɪv/ n a member of your family: *My uncle is my nearest relative.*

relative² adj compared to each other or to something else: *the relative costs of building in stone and brick* | *After his money troubles, he's now living in relative comfort.*

rel·a·tive·ly /ˈrelətɪvli/ adv to quite a large degree when compared to something similar or what you might expect: *She walks relatively fast for a small child.* | *The baby's been relatively quiet.*

relative pro·noun /ˌ··· ˈ···/ n tech a word that connects a relative CLAUSE to the rest of a sentence; 'who' and 'which' can be relative pronouns: *In the sentence "The man who lives next door is a doctor.", "who" is a relative pronoun.*

rel·a·tiv·i·ty /ˌreləˈtɪvɪti/ n [U] the relationship between time, size, and mass, which is said to change with increased speed: *Einstein's theory of relativity*

re·lax /rɪˈlæks/ v **1** [I;T] to calm someone, or to become calmer and less worried: *Sit down and relax!* | *The music will help to relax you.* **2** [I;T] to make a part of your body become less stiff or tight: *His muscles relaxed.* | *Try to relax your shoulders.* **3** [T] to make a form of control over something less severe: *The police sometimes relax the rules in special cases.*

re·lax·a·tion /ˌriːlækˈseɪʃən/ n **1** [C;U] rest and amusement, or an activity that gives you this: *Playing the piano is one of his favourite relaxations.* | *I desperately need some relaxation.* **2** [U] the act of making some form of control less severe: *the relaxation of exchange controls*

re·lay¹ /ˈriːleɪ/ n [C;U] **1** (also **relay race**) a race in which each member of each team runs or swims part of the distance **2 in relays** using a fresh group of people or animals in the place of a tired one: *The men worked in relays to repair the railway.* **3** an apparatus that receives and passes on messages by telephone, radio, or television: *This broadcast is coming from America by relay.*

relay² v [T] **1** to send out a radio or television signal: *The broadcast was relayed to Europe.* **2** to pass on a message to someone else: *Please relay the news to the other teachers.*

re·lease¹ /rɪˈliːs/ v **released, releasing** [T] **1** to set free a person or animal: *The hijackers released three of the hostages.* **2** to free someone from a difficult feeling or duty: *Her awful behaviour released him from any sense of obligation.* **3** to stop holding something: *He released his grip on her hand.* **4** to make something move by freeing a handle: *He released the handbrake.* **5** to allow a new film or record to be shown or bought publicly: *The record was released recently.*

release² n **1** [U] the act of setting someone free or of being set free: *After his release from prison he went abroad.* **2** [U] the act of freeing someone from a difficult feeling or duty: *After the exam, I had such a feeling of release.* **3** [C] a new film or record that has been released: *I'd like to see some of the latest releases.* **4 on release, on general release** able to be seen at public cinemas

rel·e·gate /ˈrelɪɡeɪt/ v **relegated, relegating** [T] to move someone or something to a less important position: *Jack was relegated to the role of assistant.* | *Everyone was surprised when the football team was relegated to a lower division.*

re·lent /rɪˈlent/ v [I] to let someone do something that you would not let them do before, or to decide not to carry out a threat: *She threatened to make me pay for the damage, but then she relented.*

re·lent·less /rɪˈlentləs/ adj continuous and strong: *the relentless desert heat* | *relentless ambition* –**relentlessly** adv : *He beat the dog relentlessly.*

rel·e·vant /ˈrelɪvənt/ adj **1** directly connected with a particular subject, especially one being talked or written about: *This book isn't really relevant to my research.* **2** valuable or important to someone or something: *This type of course is no longer relevant to nurses.* –opposite **irrelevant** –**relevance** n [U] : *What you say has no relevance to what we're talking about.*

re·li·a·ble /rɪˈlaɪəbəl/ adj **1** that you can trust to perform well at all times: *My memory is not very reliable.* | *a reliable car* **2** that you can trust to be true or to provide correct information: *reliable evidence* | *A reliable source told journalists the hospital would close.* –opposite **unreliable** –**reliably** adv : *I am reliably informed that he takes drugs.* –**reliability** /rɪˌlaɪəˈbɪlɪti/ n [U]

re·li·ant /rɪˈlaɪənt/ adj **reliant on** dependent on: *We should not be so reliant on imported food.* –**reliance** n [U]

rel·ic /ˈrelɪk/ n **1** a part of a holy person's body, or something that belonged to a holy person, which is kept and respected after their death **2** an old custom, idea, or thing which still exists: *This stone*

axe is a relic of ancient times. | *These beliefs are relics from the last century.*

re·lief /rɪˈliːf/ *n* **1** [sing;U] a feeling of comfort and happiness after a period of anxiety or some other unpleasant feeling: *This medicine will give you some relief.* | *To my relief, they arrived safely.* | *She heaved a sigh of relief when she got the contract.* **2** [U] money, food, or clothing provided for people in trouble: *The government sent relief to people who lost their homes in the flood.*

re·lieve /rɪˈliːv/ *v* **relieved, relieving** [T] **1** to lessen pain or some other unpleasant feeling: *This pill will relieve your headache.* | *I went for a walk to relieve my boredom.* **2 relieve someone of** to free someone of something heavy or difficult: *Let me relieve you of those parcels.* | *Her letter relieved him of his anxieties.* **3** to take someone's place in a job: *Will you relieve me at 5.00?* **4 relieve someone of their duties** to dismiss someone from their position at work

re·lieved /rɪˈliːvd/ *adj* happy after a period of anxiety: *Your mother will be very relieved to hear that you are safe.* | *You look relieved!*

re·li·gion /rɪˈlɪdʒən/ *n* **1** [U] belief in one or more gods, and the behaviour and worship connected with this: *a book on religion* **2** [C] a particular system of belief in one or more gods and the behaviour and worship connected with this: *the Muslim religion*

re·li·gious /rɪˈlɪdʒəs/ *adj* **1** connected with religion: *religious beliefs* **2** showing a strong belief in a particular religion and careful obedience to its rules (used of a person or behaviour): *a very religious man*

re·li·gious·ly /rɪˈlɪdʒəsli/ *adv* thoroughly and regularly from a sense of duty: *He visits his mother religiously every morning.*

re·lin·quish /rɪˈlɪŋkwɪʃ/ *v* [T] *fml* to give up a position or right: *He relinquished his claim to the land.*

rel·ish¹ /ˈrelɪʃ/ *n* **1 with relish** with great enjoyment and satisfaction: *He ate the cake with relish.* **2** [C;U] a substance eaten with a meal to add taste

relish² *v* [T] to look forward to something with great enjoyment: *John won't relish having to wash all those dishes!* | *She didn't relish the prospect of explaining her decision.*

re·live /ˌriːˈlɪv/ *v* **relived, reliving** [T] to remember something from the past in such detail that it is as if you experience it again: *We spent the whole morning reliving our schooldays.*

re·lo·cate /ˌriːləʊˈkeɪt ‖ riːˈləʊkeɪt/ *v* **relocated, relocating** [I;T] to move to a new place: *We're relocating to the Bristol area.* | *The factory was relocated outside London.* –**relocation** /ˌriːləʊˈkeɪʃən/ *n* [U]

re·luc·tant /rɪˈlʌktənt/ *adj* unwilling, and therefore perhaps slow to act: *He gave a reluctant promise.* | *He was very reluctant to help.*
☐ USEFUL PATTERN be reluctant to do something –**reluctance** *n* [U] –**reluctantly** *adv*

re·ly /rɪˈlaɪ/ *v* **relied, relying** [I] rely on to depend on someone or something: *We're relying on your support.* | *Don't rely on his taking the job.* | *They rely on the river for water.*

SPELLING NOTE
Words with the sound / r /, may be spelt **wr-**, like **wrong**.

---

re·main /rɪˈmeɪn/ *v* **1** [I] to stay or be left behind after others have gone: *She remained at home with the children.* **2** [+complement] to continue unchanged in a particular state or condition: *Peter became a judge but John remained a fisherman.* | *The situation remained the same.* | *Please remain calm!* **3** [I] to continue to exist: *Little of the original building remains.* **4 it remains to be seen** it is still unclear and will only be known in the future: *It remains to be seen what the results of the tests will be.*

re·main·der /rɪˈmeɪndəʳ/ *n* **the remainder** [+sing/pl verb] the rest: *We'll eat the remainder of the food tomorrow.*

re·mains /rɪˈmeɪnz/ *n* [pl] **1** parts which are left after the larger whole has gone or been destroyed: *the remains of dinner* | *the remains of an old castle* **2** *fml* the parts of a body that are left after a person's death: *His remains lie in the churchyard.*

re·make /ˌriːˈmeɪk/ *v* **remade, remade, remaking** [T] to make something again, usually a film which has the same story as an earlier film –**remake** /ˈriːmeɪk/ *n* : *It's supposed to be a remake of "Gone with the Wind".*

re·mand /rɪˈmɑːnd ‖ rɪˈmænd/ *v* **1 be remanded to** be ordered to return later to a court of law to be tried for a crime: *She was remanded for trial two weeks later.* **2 be remanded in custody** to be held in prison until a trial in a court of law

remand *n* **on remand** waiting to be tried after already appearing in court

re·mark¹ /rɪˈmɑːk ‖ -ɑːrk/ *v* **1** [+ that] to say something: *He remarked that it was getting late.* | *"She was very kind to me", Ben remarked.* **2 remark on/upon** to notice something and talk or write about it: *Everyone remarked loudly on his absence.*

remark² *n* something said or written: *Hilda made some rude remarks about his appearance.*

re·mark·a·ble /rɪˈmɑːkəbəl ‖ -ɑːr-/ *adj* extremely unusual or noticeable: *a most remarkable sunset* | *Finland is remarkable for its large number of lakes.* –**remarkably** *adv* : *a remarkably fine day* | *He sings remarkably well.*

re·me·di·al /rɪˈmiːdiəl/ *adj* **1** intended to provide a cure or some improvement: *He has to do remedial exercises for his weak back.* **2** intended to help someone learn something that they find difficult or did not learn at the usual age: *a remedial reading class* –**remedially** *adv*

rem·e·dy¹ /ˈremədi/ *n* **remedies 1** something that cures pain or illness: *herbal remedies* | *a new remedy for indigestion* **2** a means of dealing properly with a difficulty: *A holiday may be the best remedy for his unhappiness.*

remedy² *v* **remedied, remedying** [T] to correct a bad situation: *How can we remedy this mistake?*

re·mem·ber /rɪˈmembəʳ/ *v* **1** [I;T; + (that)] to keep in your memory people or events from the past: *I definitely remember posting the letter.* | *I'll always remember that wonderful day.* | *Do you remember me phoning you that afternoon?* | *He remembered that she worked in a pub.*
☐ USEFUL PATTERNS to remember something; to remember doing something; to remember someone doing something; to remember that…
2 [I;T] to come back or bring back into your mind: *She suddenly remembered that she hadn't locked the door.* | *Can you remember where they live?* **3** [I; +(that)] to take care not to forget: *Remember to post my letter!* | *Remember I need the car by 10.00.*
☐ USEFUL PATTERNS to remember to do something; to remember that…

4 [T] to think about someone or something with honour and respect: *On this day, we remember those who died in the war.* **5 remember someone to someone** to carry greetings from one person to another: *Please remember me to your mother.*
■ USAGE Note the difference between "remember doing something" and "remember to do something". *I remember locking the door* means "I locked the door, and this event is still in my mind". *I remembered to lock the door* means "It was in my mind then that I must lock the door, and I locked it".

re·mem·brance /rɪˈmembrəns/ *n* **1** [C;U] memory of someone or something: *A church service was held in remembrance of those killed in the earthquake.* **2** [C] something kept or given to remind you of someone or something: *He gave me his photograph as a remembrance.*

re·mind /rɪˈmaɪnd/ *v* [T; + (that)] **1** to make someone remember something: *Remind me to write to Dave.* | *She reminded me that Sue was in Paris.*
□ USEFUL PATTERNS to remind someone about something; to remind someone to do something; to remind someone that…
2 remind someone of to appear very similar to another person or thing: *This hotel reminds me of the one we stayed in last year.* | *He reminds me of Mick Jagger.*

re·mind·er /rɪˈmaɪndəʳ/ *n* **1** something that makes you remember something else: *The photographs are a lasting reminder of life in the 1920s.* **2** a letter telling you to do something you have not done: *He hasn't paid his bill. We'd better send him a reminder.*

rem·i·nisce /ˌremɪˈnɪs/ *v* **reminisced, reminiscing** [I] to talk with enjoyment about the past: *We meet to reminisce about our schooldays.* –**reminiscence** *n* [C;U]

rem·i·nis·cent /ˌremɪˈnɪsənt/ *adj* **reminiscent of** that reminds you of: *a taste reminiscent of strawberries*

re·miss /rɪˈmɪs/ *adj* [never before a noun] *fml* careless about a duty: *It was remiss of me not to answer your letter.*

re·mis·sion /rɪˈmɪʃən/ *n* [U] a decrease in the time a person has to stay in prison: *The prisoner was given six months' remission for good behaviour.*

re·mit·tance /rɪˈmɪtəns/ *n* an amount of money sent by post as payment for something

rem·nant /ˈremnənt/ *n* **1** a small part that is left of something larger: *We fed the dogs the remnants of our meal.* **2** a small piece of cloth left over from a larger piece and sold cheaply

re·mod·el /ˌriːˈmɒdl || ˌriːˈmɑːdl/ *v* **-ll-** (also **-l-** *AmE*) [T] to change the shape of something, especially a room: *Pat had her kitchen remodelled.*

rem·on·strate /ˈremənstreɪt || rɪˈmɑːn-/ *v* **remonstrated, remonstrating** [I] *fml* to complain about something you do not approve of: *She remonstrated with the driver about the poor bus service.*

re·morse /rɪˈmɔːs || -ɔːrs/ *n* a feeling of guilt and sorrow for something you have done which was wrong: *He was filled with remorse after hitting the child.* –**remorseful** *adj* –**remorseless** *adj*

re·mote /rɪˈməʊt/ *adj* **1** distant in space or time: *remote stars* | *the remote future* | *a remote village* **2** not closely connected: *What is studied on the course seems rather remote from ordinary life.* **3** unlikely (used of a chance or possibility): *Your chances of success are rather remote.* **4** not friendly or interested: *Her behaviour was polite but remote.* –**remoteness** *n* [U]

remote con·trol /ˌ·ˌ···ˈ·/ *n* [C;U] a system or a small apparatus for controlling a machine from a distance by radio signals

re·mote·ly /rɪˈməʊtli/ *adv* **not remotely** not even to a very small degree: *She isn't remotely interested in what you're saying.*

re·mov·al /rɪˈmuːvəl/ *n* [U] an act of taking something away or moving it: *The teacher agreed to the removal of maps from the walls.*

removal van /·ˈ··· ·/ *n BrE* a large covered vehicle used for moving furniture

re·move /rɪˈmuːv/ *v* **removed, removing** [T] **1** to take a person or thing away: *The parents removed their child from the school.* | *Could you remove your suitcase from the hall?* **2** to get rid of something: *Please remove the mud from your shoes.* | *an operation to remove a tumour* **3** to take off clothing: *She removed her jacket.* **4** to dismiss someone from a job or position: *We voted to remove her from the committee.* **5 far removed from** very different from: *What you now say is far removed from what you said before.*

re·mu·ne·rate /rɪˈmjuːnəreɪt/ *v* **remunerated, remunerating** [T] *fml* to pay someone for work done –**remuneration** /rɪˌmjuːnəˈreɪʃən/ *n* [sing; U] *You'll receive a small remuneration.*

re·mu·ne·ra·tive /rɪˈmjuːnərətɪv || -nəreɪtɪv/ *adj fml* well-paid (used of work)

renaissance /rɪˈneɪsəns || ˌrenəˈsɑːns/ *n* **1 the Renaissance** the period in Europe between the 14th and 17th centuries, when the art, literature, and ideas of ancient Greece were discovered again and widely studied: *the poetry of the early Renaissance* **2** a period in which something becomes popular again, especially a style of art, music, or literature

ren·der /ˈrendəʳ/ *v* [T] *fml* **1** to give someone something, especially help: *You have rendered me a great service.* **2** to cause a person or thing to be in a particular state: *He was rendered helpless by the accident.*

ren·der·ing /ˈrendərɪŋ/ *n* (also **rendition**) a performance of a poem, play, or piece of music: *a splendid rendering of the song*

ren·dez·vous /ˈrɒndɪvuː, -deɪ- || ˈrɑːn-/ *n* **rendezvous** /-vuːz/ **1** an arrangement to meet at a certain time and place: *John arrived late for their rendezvous.* **2** a place where you have arranged to meet someone **3** a popular place for people to meet: *This club is a rendezvous for writers.* –**rendezvous** *v* [I]

ren·di·tion /renˈdɪʃən/ *n* see RENDERING

ren·e·gade /ˈrenɪgeɪd/ *n* a person who gives up their old beliefs and accepts new ones (a word used to express disapproval)

re·new /rɪˈnjuː || rɪˈnuː/ *v* [T] **1** to begin something again: *In the morning the enemy renewed their attack.* **2** to give someone or something new life and freshness: *I came back from my holiday with renewed strength.* **3** to put something new in the place of something of the same kind: *to renew your library ticket* –**renewal** *n* [C;U]

re·new·a·ble /rɪˈnjuːəbəl || rɪˈnuː-/ *adj* **1** that can or must have a new one in its place after a certain period of time: *All contracts are renewable.* **2** that gets some more in its place as it is used or lost: *renewable energy sources*

re·nounce /rɪˈnaʊns/ *v* **renounced, renouncing** [T] *fml* **1** to give up a claim or a right to something in a formal or official way: *He renounced his claim to the property.* **2** to say formally that you will have no more connection with someone or something: *He has renounced his entire family.*

ren·o·vate /ˈrenəveɪt/ v **renovated, renovating** [T] to repair something and put it back into good condition: *I renovate old houses.* **–renovation** /ˌrenəˈveɪʃən/ n [C;U]

re·nown /rɪˈnaʊn/ n [U] *fml* fame: *a painter of world renown* **–renowned** *adj* : *renowned as an inventor* | *renowned for his inventions*

rent¹ /rent/ n [C;U] money paid regularly for the use of something, especially a room, building, or piece of land: *Are you paying rent?* | *They are charging a high rent for the flat.*

rent² v [T] **1** to pay rent for the use of something: *I rent a room from Mrs Jones.* **2** to pay money for the use of something for a short time: *Shall we rent a car?*

rent sthg ↔ **out** *phr* v [T] to allow something to be used for a certain time in return for payment: *They've rented out their house for the summer.*

rent·al /ˈrentl/ n **1** the amount of money that you pay to rent something: *The television rental is going up again.* **2** the process of renting something out or something connected with this process: *a rental agreement*

rent-free /ˌ· ˈ·◂/ *adv,adj* without payment of rent: *a rent-free flat* | *He lives there rent-free!*

re·nun·ci·a·tion /rɪˌnʌnsiˈeɪʃən/ n [C;U] *fml* an act of giving up a claim or a connection with something

re·or·gan·ize /riːˈɔːɡənaɪz/ ‖ -ˈɔːr-/ v **reorganized, reorganizing** (also **reorganise** *BrE*) [I;T] to organize something in a different and usually better way: *We're reorganizing the filing system.* **–reorganization** /riːˌɔːɡənaɪˈzeɪʃən ‖ -ˌɔːrɡənə-/ n [C;U]

rep /rep/ n *infml* **1** an elected representative of a group of people: *Take your complaints to the union rep.* **2** (also **sales rep**) a salesman: *Our rep will call on Monday.* **3** (also **repertory**) a theatre company: *the local rep* | *He's in rep at Bristol.*

re·paid /rɪˈpeɪd/ the past tense and past participle of REPAY

re·pair¹ /rɪˈpeəʳ/ v [T] **1** to mend something: *The TV has just been repaired.* **2** *fml* to put right something wrong: *The company is trying to repair the damage done to its reputation.* **–repairable** *adj* **–repairer** n

repair² n **1** what is done to mend something or make it work: *Who is responsible for carrying out repairs to the road?* **2 beyond repair** in such terrible condition that mending is no longer possible **3 in good repair** in good condition [RELATED PHRASE **in bad repair**]

rep·a·ra·tion /ˌrepəˈreɪʃən/ n [U] *fml* money or help given for loss or suffering by those who caused it: *I expect you to make reparation for any damage.* | *We will demand reparations after the war is over.*

rep·ar·tee /ˌrepɑːˈtiː ‖ ˌrepərˈtiː/ n [U] quick amusing remarks and replies in conversation: *I enjoy listening to their witty repartee.*

re·past /rɪˈpɑːst ‖ rɪˈpæst/ n *lit* a meal

re·pat·ri·ate /riːˈpætrieɪt ‖ riːˈpeɪ-/ v **repatriated, repatriating** [T] to send someone back to their own country: *He's being repatriated.* **–repatriation** /ˌriːpætriˈeɪʃən ‖ -peɪ-/ n [U]

SPELLING NOTE

Words with the sound / r /, may be spelt **wr-**, like **wrong.**

---

re·pay /rɪˈpeɪ/ v **repaid** /-ˈpeɪd/, **repaid, repaying** [T] **1** to pay back what you owe: *When can you repay the £5 I lent you?* | *He'll never repay me.* **2** to give something in return for something given or done to you: *How can I ever repay your kindness?*

re·pay·a·ble /rɪˈpeɪəbəl/ *adj* that can or must be paid back: *The money is repayable at the end of the month.*

re·pay·ment /rɪˈpeɪmənt/ n [C;U] the act of paying back money that you owe: *I'm making monthly repayments on my bank loan.*

re·peal /rɪˈpiːl/ v [T] to put an official end to a law **–repeal** n [U]

re·peat¹ /rɪˈpiːt/ v **1** [T; + (that)] to say, write, or do something again: *Repeat the word after me!* | *'It wasn't her,' he repeated.* | *She repeated that she had not been there.* **2** [T] to say something that you have heard or learnt: *Don't repeat what I told you.* **3 repeat yourself** to say or do the same thing again and again: *History seems to be repeating itself.*

repeat² n a broadcast on TV or radio that has been sent out before: *All these programmes are repeats!*

re·peat·ed /rɪˈpiːtɪd/ *adj* [only before a noun] done again and again: *I've made repeated attempts to contact him.* **–repeatedly** *adv*

re·pel /rɪˈpel/ v -ll- [T] **1** to drive someone or something back by force: *They managed to repel the attack.* **2** to consider something to be very unpleasant: *The smell repels me.*

re·pel·lent¹ /rɪˈpelənt/ *adj* very unpleasant: *She found his behaviour repellent.*

repellent² n [C;U] a substance that drives something, especially insects, away: *insect repellent* | *a mosquito repellent*

re·pent /rɪˈpent/ v [I;T] *fml* to be sorry for something that you have done which was wrong **–repentance** n [U] **–repentant** *adj*

re·per·cus·sion /ˌriːpəˈkʌʃən ‖ -pər-/ n an unplanned effect of some action or event, which may only be known much later: *The president's death had unexpected repercussions.*

rep·er·toire /ˈrepətwɑːʳ ‖ -ər-/ n all the things like plays or pieces of music that a performer or theatre company can perform: *Their repertoire includes a number of foreign plays.*

rep·er·to·ry /ˈrepətəri ‖ ˈrepərtɔːri/ n **repertories** [U] the practice of performing several plays, with the same actors and in the same theatre, one after the other on different days: *a repertory company* | *The play is in repertory at the National Theatre.*

rep·e·ti·tion /ˌrepɪˈtɪʃən/ n **1** [U] the act of saying or doing something again **2** [C] something said or done again: *This accident is a repetition of one that happened here three weeks ago.*

rep·e·ti·tious /ˌrepɪˈtɪʃəs◂/ *adj* containing parts that are said or done too many times (a word used to express disapproval): *a repetitious speech*

re·pet·i·tive /rɪˈpetɪtɪv/ *adj* said or done too many times

re·place /rɪˈpleɪs/ v **replaced, replacing** [T] **1** to put something back where it was: *He replaced the book on the shelf.* **2** to take the place of someone or something: *George has replaced Edward as captain of the team.* **3** to change one thing for another that is newer or better: *We've replaced the old adding machine with a computer.* | *You'll have to replace those tyres.* **–replaceable** *adj*

re·place·ment /rɪˈpleɪsmənt/ n **1** [U] the action of replacing a person or thing **2** [C] a person or thing that takes the place of another one: *We need a replacement for the secretary who's leaving.* | *I'm Mr. Smith's replacement.*

re·play /ˌriːˈpleɪ/ *v* **replayed, replaying** [T] to play something, especially a match, again: *Let's replay the tape from the beginning.* –**replay** /ˈriːpleɪ/ *n* : *The score was 2-2, so there'll be a replay next Saturday.*

re·plen·ish /rɪˈplenɪʃ/ *v* [T] to fill something up again: *I must replenish the food cupboard.*

re·plete /rɪˈpliːt/ *adj* [never before a noun] *fml* full, especially of food and drink

rep·li·ca /ˈreplɪkə/ *n* a close copy of a painting or other work of art

re·ply[1] /rɪˈplaɪ/ *v* **replied, replying** [I;T; + that] to give an answer: *'Did you forget?' I asked. 'Of course not,' she replied.* | *I replied that I would do it later.* | *Have you replied to his letter?* –see ANSWER (USAGE)

reply[2] *n* **replies** [C;U] **1** something said or written as an answer: *I had twelve replies to my advertisement.* | *She's free to criticize me, but I demand the right of reply.* **2 in reply** as an answer to what someone has said or done

re·port[1] /rɪˈpɔːt ‖ -ɔːrt/ *n* **1** a spoken or written account of a situation or event: *We read a report of the accident.* | *a newspaper report* **2** the noise of an explosion or shot: *a loud report*

report[2] *v* **1** [T; + that] to tell people about something, often because it is your job or duty: *He reported the accident to his insurance company.* | *She reported that sixteen students had been taken ill on the trip.* | *'He's disappeared,' she reported on her return.* **2 report on something** to provide information and often ideas about something: *He reported on the conference he had attended.* | *The committee is reporting on ways of improving the Health Service.* **3** [T] to make a complaint about someone: *The clerk was so rude that I reported him to his superior.* **4** [I] to go to a person or place and say that you have arrived or that you are ready for work: *I have to report for duty at 5 o'clock.* | *Report to the main desk on arrival.*

reported speech /ˌ·ˈ·ˌ· ˈ·/ *n* [U] writing which shows what someone said, without using their exact words

re·port·er /rɪˈpɔːtər ‖ -ˈpɔːr-/ *n* a person who writes about news for a newspaper, or for radio and television

re·pose /rɪˈpəʊz/ *n* [U] *fml* rest –**repose** *v* **reposed, reposing** [I;T]

rep·re·hen·si·ble /ˌreprɪˈhensɪbəl/ *adj* very bad: *reprehensible behaviour* –**reprehensibly** *adv*

rep·re·sent /ˌreprɪˈzent/ *v* [T] **1** to act officially for another person or group of people: *The workers were represented in the negotiations by the union secretary.* | *Prince Charles is representing the Queen at today's ceremony.* **2** to be typical of something, or of a group of people: *She represents the typical teenager.* **3** to be a sign for another thing: *This line is supposed to represent her head.* **4** to express the true nature of something: *Nothing represents home more than my mother's cooking.* **5** to be the result of something: *His final book represented twenty years of hard work.* **6** to describe or show a person or thing in a particular way: *The former dictator was represented as a tyrant.*

rep·re·sen·ta·tion /ˌreprɪzenˈteɪʃən/ *n* **1** [U] the situation of being represented by someone: *They demanded political representation.* **2** [C] something that is shown in a particular way: *This painting is*

a representation of a storm at sea. **3 representations** [pl] formal statements, complaints, or requests: *We made representations on behalf of the political prisoners.*

rep·re·sen·ta·tive[1] /ˌreprɪˈzentətɪv/ *adj* **1** typical of a particular group: *Are your opinions representative of those of the other students?* **2** [only before a noun] related to a system of government in which people and their opinions are represented by people who speak for them: *a representative council*

representative[2] *n* a person acting in place of one or more others: *They sent a representative to the meeting.*

re·press /rɪˈpres/ *v* [T] **1** to control or hold back natural feelings: *I could hardly repress my laughter.* | *She tends to repress her emotions.* **2** to control people by force –**repressed** *adj* : *a repressed desire to steal* | *He's very repressed.* –**repression** /-ˈpreʃən/ *n* [U] : *the repression of political opposition*

re·pres·sive /rɪˈpresɪv/ *adj* hard and cruel: *The country has an extremely repressive political system.*

re·prieve[1] /rɪˈpriːv/ *v* **reprieved, reprieving** [T] to change a sentence of death so that a person is not killed: *Both men have been reprieved.*

reprieve[2] *n* **1** an official order delaying or ending a sentence, especially a death sentence: *There is little hope of a reprieve.* **2** a delay before something unpleasant happens or continues

rep·ri·mand /ˈreprɪmɑːnd ‖ -mænd/ *v* [T] to give someone a serious official warning about unacceptable behaviour –**reprimand** *n* [U]

re·print[1] /ˌriːˈprɪnt/ *v* [T] to print a book again when supplies have run out

re·print[2] /ˈriːˌprɪnt/ *n* a reprinted book

re·pri·sal /rɪˈpraɪzəl/ *n* [C;U] violent action taken as punishment for harm done: *Bombs were dropped on an enemy village as a reprisal* | *In an act of reprisal seventy men were taken prisoner.*

re·proach[1] /rɪˈprəʊtʃ/ *n* **1** [U] quiet blame: *She gave me a look of reproach.* **2** [C] a word or words of blame: *He can't live with his wife's constant reproaches.* **3 beyond reproach** perfect –**reproachful** *adj* –**reproachfully** *adv*

reproach[2] *v* [T] **1** to blame someone, usually in a sad and quiet way **2 reproach yourself** to blame yourself for something that you wish you had not done: *She reproached herself for not having made enough effort.*

rep·ro·bate /ˈreprəbeɪt/ *n* a person of bad character: *He's an old reprobate, who spends all his money on beer.* –**reprobate** *adj*

re·pro·duce /ˌriːprəˈdjuːs ‖ -ˈduːs/ *v* **reproduced, reproducing 1** [I] to produce young: *Some tropical fish reproduce by laying eggs.* **2** [T] to produce a copy: *a painting that reproduces every detail of the scene*

re·pro·duc·tion /ˌriːprəˈdʌkʃən/ *n* **1** [U] the act or method of producing young: *a book on insect reproduction* **2** [U] the copying of things like sound and printed materials: *The quality of reproduction isn't very good on this recording.* **3** [C] a copy, especially of a work of art: *a cheap reproduction of a great painting* –**reproductive** *adj* [only before a noun] : *the female reproductive organs*

re·prove /rɪˈpruːv/ *v* **reproved, reproving** [T] *fml* to tell someone they have done something wrong –**reproof** /rɪˈpruːf/ *n* [C;U]

rep·tile /ˈreptaɪl ‖ ˈreptl/ *n* a creature with a rough skin whose blood changes temperature according to the temperature around it: *Snakes and lizards are reptiles.* –**reptilian** /rep'tɪlɪən/ *adj*

re·pub·lic /rɪ'pʌblɪk/ *n* a nation which is usually governed by elected representatives; the head of state is a president

re·pub·li·can[1] /rɪ'pʌblɪkən/ *adj* belonging to or favouring a republic: *a republican system of government* | *republican ideas*

republican[2] *n* **1** a person who believes in a republican system of government **2 Republican** a member or supporter of the Republican Party, one of the two largest political parties of the US

re·pu·di·ate /rɪ'pjuːdɪeɪt/ *v* **repudiated, repudiating** [T] *fml* to refuse to accept or recognize someone or something: *He repudiated the charge of having shot his sister.* –**repudiation** /rɪ,pjuːdi'eɪʃən/ *n* [U]

re·pug·nance /rɪ'pʌgnəns/ *n* [sing;U] a feeling of strong dislike: *She turned away from him in repugnance.* –**repugnant** *adj*

re·pulse /rɪ'pʌls/ *v* **repulsed, repulsing** [T] **1** to cause someone to feel a strong dislike: *He repulses me.* **2** to drive back an enemy attack

re·pul·sion /rɪ'pʌlʃən/ *n* **1** [sing;U] a feeling of strong dislike: *He looked with repulsion at the dead body.* **2** [U] a force that pushes something away from something else

re·pul·sive /rɪ'pʌlsɪv/ *adj* extremely unpleasant: *a repulsive smell* | *repulsive behaviour*

rep·u·ta·ble /'repjʊtəbəl/ *adj* known to be good: *a reputable firm of builders* –opposite **disreputable** –**reputably** *adv*

rep·u·ta·tion /,repjʊ'teɪʃən/ *n* [C;U] **1** the opinion people have of a person or thing: *This will ruin my reputation!* | *The restaurant has a good reputation.* | *He has a reputation for finishing work on time.* **2 live up to your reputation** to behave in the way that people have come to expect of you: *He's living up to his reputation as a troublemaker.*

re·pute /rɪ'pjuːt/ *n* [U] *fml* the opinion people have of someone or something: *a hotel of high repute*

re·put·ed /rɪ'pjuːtɪd/ *adj* generally considered to be: *the reputed father of her baby* | *She is reputed to be the richest woman in Europe.* –**reputedly** *adv*

re·quest[1] /rɪ'kwest/ *n* **1** a polite demand: *He made a request for help.* **2** something that is asked for, especially music to be played on the radio **3 at someone's request** because someone asked: *I bought it at the request of my father.* **4 on request** if you ask: *Further details are available on request.*

request[2] *v fml* [T; + that] to ask politely: *The judge requested silence.* | *Staff have requested that we discuss this matter at the next meeting.* | *Guests are requested not to use the pool after 9pm.*

□ USEFUL PATTERNS to request something; to request that..., to be requested (not) to do something

■ USAGE Remember that the verb **request** is transitive and is NOT, therefore, followed by a preposition. (The noun **request**, however, may be followed by the preposition **for**.) Compare: *They have requested more information on this issue.* | *We have received a request for more information on this issue.*

SPELLING NOTE
Words with the sound /r/, may be spelt **wr-**, like **wrong**.

req·ui·em /'rekwiəm, 'rekwiem/ *n* a piece of music usually played or sung at a Christian ceremony (MASS) for the soul of a dead person

re·quire /rɪ'kwaɪəʳ/ *v* **required, requiring** [T] **1** to need something: *This suggestion requires careful thought.* **2** *fml* to make someone do something that is necessary: *All passengers are required to show their tickets.* | *to pass the required examinations to become a doctor*

re·quire·ment /rɪ'kwaɪəmənt || -aɪər-/ *n* **1** something needed or demanded: *This shop can supply all your requirements.* **2 meet someone's requirements** to be what someone needs or demands: *We can't find an office that meets our requirements.*

req·ui·site /'rekwɪzɪt/ *n fml* something that is necessary for a certain purpose: *sports requisites* –**requisite** *adj*: *Have you got the requisite stamp on your passport?*

req·ui·si·tion /,rekwɪ'zɪʃən/ *n* a formal demand for the use of something, especially by the army: *The soldiers made a requisition for horses.* –**requisition** *v* [T]: *The army has requisitioned the local hotel.*

res·cue[1] /'reskjuː/ *v* **rescued, rescuing** [T] to save someone or something from harm or danger: *The boys were rescued after hours at sea.* –**rescuer** *n*

rescue[2] *n* [C;U] **1** an act of saving a person or thing from harm or danger: *A rescue team is trying to reach the trapped miners.* **2 come/go to someone's rescue** to help someone who is in a difficult or dangerous situation

re·search[1] /rɪ'sɜːtʃ, 'riːsɜːtʃ || -ɜːr-/ *n* [C;U] advanced and detailed study of a subject, in order to find out something new : *research students* | *He's doing research into the causes of cancer.*

research[2] *v* [I;T] to try and get information in order to find out something new: *They are researching attitudes to health food.* | *We've been researching for three years without result.* –**researcher** *n*

re·sem·ble /rɪ'zembəl/ *v* **resembled, resembling** [T] to look or be like another person or thing: *She resembles her sister in many ways.* –**resemblance** *n* [C;U] : *There's a strong resemblance between the two sisters.* | *Can you see a family resemblance?*

re·sent /rɪ'zent/ *v* [T] to feel angry or bitter about something: *He resents being treated as a child.* –**resentful** *adj* : *a resentful look*

re·sent·ment /rɪ'zentmənt/ *n* [C;U] the feeling of being angry and bitter: *I don't bear you any resentment.*

res·er·va·tion /,rezə'veɪʃən || -zər-/ *n* [C] **1** a doubt in your mind: *I have some reservations about the truth of his story.* **2 without reservation** with no uncertainty: *I accepted his explanation without reservation.* **3** a piece of land set apart for North American Indians to live on **4** an arrangement to make sure that something is kept for your use: *Have you made the flight reservations yet?*

re·serve[1] /rɪ'zɜːv || -ɜːrv/ *v* **reserved, reserving** [T] **1** to keep something for a special purpose: *These seats are reserved for old people.* **2** to arrange for something to be kept for your use: *I need to reserve a seat on the plane.*

reserve[2] *n* **1** [C] a supply of something which is kept for possible future use: *Our water reserves are low at the moment.* **2** [C] a piece of land kept for a particular purpose: *a nature reserve* **3** [U] the quality of not showing your thoughts or feelings: *the well-known reserve of the English* **4** [C] a player whose job is to play in a team game in place of any member who cannot play: *I'm a reserve for the school football team.* **5 in reserve** ready for use if needed

re·served /rɪ'zɜːvd ‖ -ɜːr-/ *adj* **1** unwilling to talk about your thoughts or feelings **2** kept for someone's use: *reserved seats*

res·er·voir /'rezəvwɑːr ‖ -ərvwɑːr, -vɔːr/ *n* **1** a place where liquid is stored, especially a man-made lake that supplies water to places in the area **2** a supply of something that may be used if necessary

re·shuf·fle /riːˈʃʌfəl, ˈriːˌʃʌfəl/ *n* a change in the positions of a number of people employed in an organization **–reshuffle** /riːˈʃʌfəl/ *v* **reshuffled, reshuffling** [I; T]

re·side /rɪ'zaɪd/ *v* **resided, residing** [I] *fml* to have your home in a particular place: *They reside overseas.*

res·i·dence /'rezɪdəns/ *n* **1** [C] *fml* the place where you live: *the Prime Minister's official residence* **2** [U] the situation of living in a place: *Payment of the tax depends on residence, not house ownership.* **3 in residence** actually living in a place: *The students are not in residence during the holidays.* **4 take up residence** *fml* to move to a place where you are going to live

res·i·dent¹ /'rezɪdənt/ *adj* **1** living in a place: *He's resident in Britain.* **2** living in the place where you work: *Boarding schools have resident nurses.* –opposite **non-resident 3** working in a place all the time: *Is there a resident painter at the arts centre?*

resident² *n* a person who lives in a place: *residents of Oxford* | *This hotel serves meals to residents only.* –opposite **non-resident**

res·i·den·tial /ˌrezɪ'denʃəl/ *adj* **1** consisting of private houses, without offices or factories (used to describe an area of a town) **2** where people live in the building: *residential accommodation* | *a residential course*

re·sid·u·al /rɪ'zɪdʒuəl/ *adj* left over

res·i·due /'rezɪdjuː ‖ -duː/ *n tech* what is left, especially after chemical treatment

re·sign /rɪ'zaɪn/ *v* [I;T] **1** to leave a job or position: *I'm considering resigning.* | *Has he resigned his post?* **2 resign yourself to something** to accept something unpleasant without complaint: *You must resign yourselves to waiting a bit longer.*

res·ig·na·tion /ˌrezɪg'neɪʃən/ *n* **1** [C;U] a statement that you intend to leave a job or position: *You have the choice between resignation and dismissal.* | *He handed in his resignation.* **2** [U] acceptance of something unpleasant: *She accepted her fate with resignation.*

re·signed /rɪ'zaɪnd/ *adj* prepared to accept something unpleasant without complaint: *He seems quite resigned to living alone.* **–resignedly** /-nɪdli/ *adv*

re·sil·i·ent /rɪ'zɪliənt/ *adj* **1** able to spring back to its former shape when pressure is removed (used to describe substances) *Rubber is more resilient than wood.* **2** strong enough to recover from a bad situation or event: *He'll cope with the situation. He's very resilient.* **–resilience** *n* [U]

res·in /'rezɪn/ *n* **1** [U] a thick sticky liquid obtained from certain trees **2** [C] any of various man-made plastic substances, used in industry **–resinous** *adj*

re·sist /rɪ'zɪst/ *v* [T] **1** to fight back against attack: *They tried to resist the enemy attack.* **2** to fight against something: *He resists any kind of change.* **3** to stop yourself accepting or doing something: *I can't resist chocolate cake.* | *She couldn't resist laughing.* **–resistible** *adj*

re·sist·ance /rɪ'zɪstəns/ *n* [U] **1** refusal to accept something: *There was a lot of resistance to the plan.* **2** fighting back against attack: *resistance fighters* **3** the ability of a living body not to be harmed by disease: *This vaccine improves resistance to certain diseases.*

re·sis·tant /rɪ'zɪstənt/ *adj* **1** unwilling to accept something: *Many teachers are resistant to new ideas.* **2** not harmed by something: *rats that are resistant to poison*

res·o·lute /'rezəluːt/ *adj* firm and determined –compare IRRESOLUTE **–resolutely** *adv*

res·o·lu·tion /ˌrezə'luːʃən/ *n* **1** [U] strength of purpose: *You might be taken seriously if you showed more resolution.* **2** [C;U] the settling of a problem: *The lawyer's advice led to the resolution of all our difficulties.* **3** [C] a formal decision made by a group of people at a meeting: *A resolution to build a new road was passed easily.* **4** [C] a decision: *She made a resolution to eat more healthy food.*

re·solve¹ /rɪ'zɒlv ‖ rɪ'zɑːlv, rɪ'zɔːlv/ *v* **resolved, resolving 1** [T] to deal with a problem: *We must find a way of resolving these difficulties.* **2** [I; +(that)] to make a decision about something: *They resolved to work harder.* | *She resolved that in future she would not lose her temper.*
□ USEFUL PATTERNS to resolve to do something; to resolve that…

resolve² *n fml* **1** [C] a decision: *He made a firm resolve to be more considerate.* **2** [U] strength of purpose: *He showed great resolve.*

res·o·nant /'rezənənt/ *adj* strong and continuing (used of a sound) *the resonant note of a bell* **–resonance** *n* [U]

re·sort /rɪ'zɔːt ‖ -ɔːrt/ *n* **1** [C] a place to which a lot of people go on holiday: *a tourist resort* | *a beach resort* **2** [U] making use of something, often something bad: *You can all pass the examination without resort to cheating!* **3 in the last resort, as a last resort** if everything else fails: *In the last resort we can always spend the night in the car.*

resort *v* **resort to something** to turn to something bad or unpleasant because you know no other way: *When her money ran out, she resorted to stealing.*

re·sound /rɪ'zaʊnd/ *v* [I] **1** to be heard loudly and clearly: *Their laughter resounded through the hall.* **2** (of a place) to be filled with sound: *The hall resounded with laughter.*

re·sound·ing /rɪ'zaʊndɪŋ/ *adj* [only before a noun] **1** loud and clear: *a resounding crash* **2** very great: *a resounding success*

re·source /rɪ'zɔːs, -'sɔːs ‖ -ɔːrs/ *n* **1** something that a place possesses and that can be used: *The country is rich in natural resources.* **2** something that you can use to help you: *Are there many resources available to teachers here?* | *Religion is her only resource now.* **3 leave someone to their own resources** to let someone pass the time as they wish

re·source·ful /rɪ'zɔːsfəl, -'sɔːs- ‖ -ɔːrs-/ *adj* good at dealing with difficulties: *Someone as resourceful as you will be able to find a way of making money!* **–resourcefulness** *n* [U]

re·spect¹ /rɪ'spekt/ *n* **1** [U] admiration of someone's position or personal qualities: *Of course I feel respect for my father.* | *He expects to be treated with respect.* –opposite **disrespect 2** [U] attention to something: *Drivers have no respect for speed limits.* **3** [C] a detail or way of judging something: *The new job is better paid, but in some respects less interesting.* | *In this respect, the service we provide is better now.* **4 with**

respect to fml concerning: *With respect to your recent enquiry, I enclose a form for your insurance claim.* **5 pay your last respects** to show honour to a person who has recently died

respect² v [T] **1** to treat someone in a way that shows you accept their position or admire their personal qualities: *Her students don't respect her any more.* **2** to agree that something has value, even if your view is different: *They respect my judgment, but they are in a difficult situation.* **3** to act in accordance with something: *I promise to respect your wishes.*

re·spec·ta·ble /rɪˈspektəbəl/ adj **1** showing or having standards that society approves of: *Please try to look respectable this evening! | She's a very respectable woman.* **2** enough in amount or quality: *I earn a respectable income.* –**respectability** /rɪˌspektəˈbɪlɪti/ n [U]

re·spect·ful /rɪˈspektfəl/ adj feeling or showing respect –opposite **disrespectful**

re·spec·tive /rɪˈspektɪv/ adj [only before a noun] particular and separate: *They went home to their respective houses.*

re·spec·tive·ly /rɪˈspektɪvli/ adv each separately in the order mentioned: *The nurses and the miners received pay rises of 8% and 12% respectively.*

re·spects /rɪˈspekts/ n [pl] polite formal greetings: *Give my respects to your wife.*

res·pi·ra·tion /ˌrespəˈreɪʃən/ n [U] tech breathing

res·pi·ra·tor /ˈrespəreɪtəʳ/ n an apparatus that helps people to breathe

re·spi·ra·to·ry /rɪˈspɪrətəri, ˈrespɪreɪtəri, rɪˈspaɪərə- ‖ ˈrespərətɔːri, rɪˈspaɪərə-/ adj [only before a noun] connected with breathing: *respiratory diseases*

res·pite /ˈrespɪt, -paɪt ‖ -pɪt/ n [C;U] pause or rest, during a time of effort, pain, or trouble: *The noise went on all night without a moment's respite. | There was no respite from the bombing.*

re·splen·dent /rɪˈsplendənt/ adj fml or lit bright and striking (used of appearance) –**resplendence** n [U] –**resplendently** adv

re·spond /rɪˈspɒnd ‖ rɪˈspɑːnd/ v fml **1** [I; + that] to answer someone or something: *They still haven't responded to my letter. | He responded that he had not been in the building at the time.* –see ANSWER (USAGE) **2** [I] to act in answer to something: *He responded to my suggestion with a laugh.* **3** to improve as a result of something: *The disease failed to respond to drugs. | He doesn't respond to discipline.*

re·sponse /rɪˈspɒns ‖ rɪˈspɑːns/ n [C;U] **1** answer: *He gave no response. | I'm waiting for a response from the airline. | I am writing in response to your recent letter.* **2** action or feelings caused by something: *There has been little response to our appeal.*

re·spon·si·bil·i·ty /rɪˌspɒnsɪˈbɪlɪti ‖ rɪˌspɑːn-/ n **responsibilities 1** [U] the ability or need to deal with important matters in a correct and useful way: *He's not ready for such responsibility. | She's in a position of great responsibility.* **2** [U] control over someone or something in your charge, which means you must take the blame if anything goes wrong: *Who has responsibility for the work of this*

SPELLING NOTE
Words with the sound / r /, may be spelt **wr-**, like **wrong.**

department? **3** [C] something which you have the duty to do or to look after: *Parents have many responsibilities. | The children are our responsibility.* **4 responsibility for something** the blame for something: *I accept full responsibility for the disaster.*

re·spon·si·ble /rɪˈspɒnsɪbəl ‖ rɪˈspɑːn-/ adj **1** worthy of trust: *We're looking for a responsible adult to look after the child.* –opposite **irresponsible 2** needing a person who can be trusted with important matters: *a responsible job* **3** [never before a noun] in charge of people or things, and prepared to accept blame if anything goes wrong: *I am responsible for making sure that the company is profitable. | Who's responsible here?* **4 be responsible to someone** to have the duty to keep someone in a higher position informed about your actions, and to accept their power over you: *I'm responsible to the Board of Governors.* **5 be responsible for something** to be the cause of something: *Who is responsible for breaking the mirror?*

re·spon·si·bly /rɪˈspɒnsɪbli ‖ rɪˈspɑːn-/ adv in a way that shows you can be trusted: *Can I trust you to behave responsibly while I'm out?* –opposite **irresponsibly**

re·spon·sive /rɪˈspɒnsɪv ‖ rɪˈspɑːn-/ adj quick to answer or return actions, words, or feelings: *The child is very responsive to kindness. | To what extent are politicians responsive to public opinion?* –opposite **unresponsive** –**responsiveness** n [U]

rest¹ /rest/ n **1** [C;U] a period of freedom from any tiring activity: *We all need a rest! | Shall we have a rest? | Will they be able to get any rest later?* **2 the rest** the remaining part or parts of something: *He's out for the rest of the evening. | Let's keep the rest of the soup for tomorrow. | While Tim and Anna went to get help, the rest of us stayed in the car.* **3** [C] a support for something: *an armrest* **4 be at rest** to be still, without moving **5 come to rest** to stop: *The rocks crashed down the mountainside and came to rest by the river.* **6 give something a rest** infml to stop doing something for a period of time **7 put/set someone's mind at rest** to give someone information that makes them stop worrying

rest² v **1** [I] to spend time free of any tiring activity: *It's good to rest after lunch.* **2** [T] to keep a part of your body still for a period of time, because it is tired or painful: *I need to rest my poor feet!* **3 rest on** lit to stop at the sight or thought of something: *His eyes rested on the picture.* **4** [I;T] to provide or be given support: *Rest your bicycle against the wall. | She rested her head on his shoulder.* **5 rest assured** fml a phrase used to stop someone worrying: *Rest assured, I'll be there if you need me.* **6 rest your case** to stop putting an argument when you are confident that you have proved your case, and leave it for other people to consider **7 rest with someone** to be the responsibility of someone: *The decision rests with you.* **8 rest on something** (of an argument) to be based on something: *His case rested on the fragile alibi of the accused man.*

res·tau·rant /ˈrestərɒnt ‖ -rənt, -rɑːnt/ n a place where meals are sold and eaten

res·tau·ra·teur /ˌrestərəˈtɜːʳ/ n the owner of a restaurant, especially a person who also runs it

rest·ful /ˈrestfəl/ adj pleasantly peaceful: *We spent a restful evening watching television.* –**restfully** adv –**restfulness** n [U]

res·ti·tu·tion /ˌrestɪˈtjuːʃən ‖ -ˈtuː-/ n [U] fml the act of returning something lost or stolen to its owner, or of paying for damage

res·tive /'restɪv/ adj 1 unable to keep still 2 dissatisfied and wanting change

rest·less /'restləs/ adj 1 unable to keep still: You were very restless last night! 2 dissatisfied and in need of a change After a year in the job, she's feeling restless. **–restlessness** n [U]

re·sto·ra·tive /rɪ'stɔːrətɪv/ n fml a drink, food, or medicine that brings back health and strength **–restorative** adj : the drink's restorative qualities

re·store /rɪ'stɔːʳ/ v restored, restoring [T] 1 to give back something lost or stolen: The goods were restored to their original owners. 2 to make something exist again: The army was called in to restore law and order. 3 to make a person or thing return to its original or former condition: A long stay in the country restored her health. | He makes his living restoring old buildings. **–restoration** /ˌrestə'reɪʃən/ n [U] : the restoration of public order | the restoration of a painting

re·strain /rɪ'streɪn/ v [T] 1 to prevent someone or something from doing something: If you can't restrain your dog, you should lock him up. 2 to control something: The government tried to restrain demand for foreign goods.

re·strained /rɪ'streɪnd/ adj calm and controlled, especially when it is difficult to behave in this way

re·straint /rɪ'streɪnt/ n 1 [U] controlled behaviour (a word usually used to express approval): I think you show great restraint in ignoring his insults. 2 [C;U] something that limits what you can do (a word often used to express disapproval): He hates the restraints of life in a small town. 3 [C;U] control over something

re·strict /rɪ'strɪkt/ v [T] to keep something within limits: The speaker restricted his comments to the situation in Europe. | New laws have been introduced to restrict the sale of alcohol. **–restriction** /-'strɪkʃən/ n [C; U]

re·strict·ed /rɪ'strɪktɪd/ adj 1 limited: The space in this house is quite restricted. 2 for the use of a particular group only: a restricted document | a restricted area

re·stric·tive /rɪ'strɪktɪv/ adj limiting because you are not free to behave as you want: He finds the job too restrictive.

rest room /'· ·/ n the usual American word for a public TOILET

re·sult¹ /rɪ'zʌlt/ v [I] 1 to be caused by something: His tiredness resulted from lack of sleep. **result in** to cause something: The accident resulted in the death of two passengers.

result² n 1 something that happens because of something else: His illness is the result of eating bad food. 2 the situation at the end of a competition or examination: I heard the football results on the radio. | When will you know your examination results? 3 the answer to a calculation **as a result** because of something: He didn't practise, and as a result he lost. | As a result of the warning, nobody was hurt.

re·sul·tant /rɪ'zʌltənt/ adj [only before a noun] caused by something: The drivers all sounded their horns and the resultant noise was unbearable.

re·sume /rɪ'zjuːm ‖ rɪ'zuːm/ v resumed, resuming fml 1 [I;T] to begin something again after a pause: We'll stop now and resume at two o'clock. | The negotiators resumed their discussion. 2 [T] to return to a place: Could we ask you, please, to resume your seats. **–resumption** /rɪ'zʌmpʃən/ n [U]

ré·su·mé /'rezjumeɪ, 'reɪ- ‖ ˌrezʊ'meɪ/ n 1 a short account of something giving only the main points 2 the usual American word for cv

re·sur·gence /rɪ'sɜːdʒəns ‖ -ɜːr-/ n fml [C;U] return to power, life, or activity: a resurgence of nationalist feeling **–resurgent** adj [only before a noun]

res·ur·rect /ˌrezə'rekt/ v [T] to bring something back into use or fashion, or to someone's attention: Old customs are being resurrected.

res·ur·rec·tion /ˌrezə'rekʃən/ n [C;U] 1 the return of something or giving something new life 2 **the Resurrection** the return to life of Christ, according to Christian belief

re·sus·ci·tate /rɪ'sʌsɪteɪt/ v resuscitated, resuscitating [T] to bring someone back to life: They tried to resuscitate the dying man. **–resuscitation** /rɪˌsʌsɪ'teɪʃən/ n [U]

re·tail·er /'riːteɪl/ n [U] the sale of goods to people for their own use, usually in shops: the retail of goods | retail prices **–retail** adj : We bought it retail.

re·tail·er /'riːteɪləʳ/ n a person who sells goods to the public

re·tain /rɪ'teɪn/ v [T] to keep or keep possession of something: I can't retain all that information. | She sold everything, retaining only a few pieces of furniture.

re·take /ˌriː'teɪk/ v retook /-'tʊk/, retaken /-'teɪkən/, retaking [T] to take something again: He's retaking his physics exam. | The city has been retaken by enemy forces. | Can we retake the last scene, please? **–retake** /'riːteɪk/ n

re·tal·i·ate /rɪ'tælieɪt/ v retaliated, retaliating [I] to return the harm that someone has done to you: Two diplomats have been expelled, and their country is expected to retaliate. **–retaliation** /rɪˌtæli'eɪʃən/ n [U] **–retaliatory** /rɪ'tæliətʳi/ adj [only before a noun]

re·tard·ed /rɪ'tɑːdɪd ‖ -ɑːr-/ adj slower in development than other people

retch /retʃ/ v [I] to try to be sick

re·ten·tion /rɪ'tenʃən/ n [U] the state or action of keeping something: Retention of the territory will cause problems with neighbouring countries. **–retentive** adj : He has a very retentive memory.

re·think /ˌriː'θɪŋk/ v rethought /-θɔːt/, rethinking [I; T] to reconsider: We'd better rethink the whole plan. **–rethink** /'riːθɪŋk/ n [sing]

ret·i·cent /'retɪsənt/ adj not saying as much as you know or feel: She was reticent about the reasons for the quarrel. **–reticence** n [U]

ret·i·na /'retɪnə/ n retinas or retinae /-niː/ the area at the back of your eye that sends images to your brain

ret·i·nue /'retɪnjuː ‖ -nuː/ n [+ sing/pl verb] a group of servants and followers travelling with an important person: The president's retinue is arriving tomorrow.

re·tire /rɪ'taɪəʳ/ v retired, retiring 1 [I; T] to stop working, usually because of your age: My father has retired now. | He was retired early because of bad health. 2 [I] fml leave a place or group of people: The ministers retired to the committee-room to make their decision. 3 [I] fml to go to bed: shall we retire?

re·tired /rɪ'taɪəd ‖ -ərd/ adj no longer working: My parents are both retired. | a retired doctor

re·tire·ment /rɪ'taɪəmənt ‖ -'taɪər-/ n [U] 1 the time at which a person stops working: He was given a gold watch on his retirement. 2 the period after a person has stopped working: He intends to spend his retirement in France. | Is she in retirement?

re·tir·ing /rɪ'taɪərɪŋ/ adj 1 too quiet in the company of others: a retiring man 2 [only before a noun]

when a person stops working: *What's the retiring age for miners?* **3** soon to stop working: *The retiring president wished his successor well.*

re·tort /rɪˈtɔːt ‖ -ɔːrt/ *v* [I; + that] to make a quick angry or amusing answer: *He retorted that it was all my fault.* | *'You, of course, are perfect!' she retorted.*

re·trace /rɪˈtreɪs, riː-/ *v* **retraced, retracing** [T] to follow the same way again: *She retraced her steps along the path to the beach.*

re·tract /rɪˈtrækt/ *v* [I;T] **1** to admit that something you said earlier should not have been said: *I would like to retract my previous remark.* **2** to move back or in again: *The cat retracted its claws when I screamed.*

re·treat¹ /rɪˈtriːt/ *v* [I] **1** to move away, especially because you are uncomfortable or you are forced to move: *The entire army is retreating.* **2** to give up something like a plan or an idea: *The government seems to be retreating* **from** *its position on local taxation.*

retreat² *n* **1** [C;U] movement away from someone or something: *Napoleon's retreat from Moscow* | *The army is in retreat.* **2** [C;U] a place to which you can go for peace and safety: *a country retreat* | *He's joined the monks in retreat.* **3** [C;U] removal of support for something like a plan or an idea: *It's a retreat from his original position on staff relations.*

re·tri·al /ˈriːtraɪəl/ *n* a second trial of a legal case: *Her lawyer has demanded a retrial.*

ret·ri·bu·tion /ˌretrɪˈbjuːʃən/ *n* [U] *fml* deserved punishment, sometimes believed to come from a god: *Retribution was quick and decisive.* | *divine retribution*

re·trieve /rɪˈtriːv/ *v* **retrieved, retrieving** [T] to find something and bring it back: *I managed to retrieve the bag I had left in the train* | *How do you retrieve information from this computer system?* **2 retrieve a situation** to improve a situation that looked very bad **–retrieval** *n* [U]

ret·ro·grade /ˈretrəgreɪd/ *adj* returning to something that is no longer considered good or useful: *Limiting the power of the unions is a retrograde step.*

ret·ro·gress /ˌretrəˈgres/ *v* [I] *fml* to return to a state that is no longer satisfactory **–retrogression** /-ˈgreʃən/ *n* [U]

ret·ro·spect /ˈretrəspekt/ *n* **in retrospect** looking back on the past: *In retrospect my childhood was a relatively happy one.*

re·tro·spec·tive /ˌretrəˈspektɪv◄/ *adj* **1** concerned with the past: *retrospective thoughts* **2** effective from before the time they were decided on (used of laws): *retrospective legislation*

re·turn¹ /rɪˈtɜːn ‖ -ɜːrn/ *v* **1** [I] to come or go back: *He returned home after years of travel.* | *She has just returned* **to** *work.* | *Let's return to that subject later.* | *The government returned to power with an increased majority.* | *I hope the good weather returns soon.* **2** [T] to give, put, send, or hit something back: *Library books must be returned at the end of term.* | *Please return the keys to the housekeeper.* | *She returned the vase to its place on the shelf.* | *Complete and return the enclosed form.* | *I couldn't even return the ball today!* **3** [T] to do or feel the same as another person: *She doesn't return his feelings.* | *I hope they'll*

SPELLING NOTE

Words with the sound / r /, may be spelt **wr-**, like **wrong.**

---

return the favour. **4 return a Member of Parliament** to elect someone as a Member of Parliament **5 return a verdict** *law* to say in a law court if someone is guilty or not: *The jury returned a verdict of not guilty.*

return² *n* **1** [C;U] a journey back to a place you have left, or your arrival in that place: *I expect to meet him on his return.* | *Since her return she has felt unsettled.* | *The workers agreed on a return to work.* **2** [U] taking, giving, sending, or putting something back: *The library books are due for return on Friday.* **3 by return, by return of post** by the next post **4** [C] (also **return ticket**) a ticket you use on a plane, bus, or train to go somewhere and come back again: *Is it cheaper to buy a return than two singles?* **5 in return** in exchange: *She helps everyone and expects nothing in return.* | *He sold his invention in return* **for** *a share of the profits.* **6** [C;U] the profit you make when you put money into, for example, a business: *He expects a good return on his capital.* **7** [U] something which happens again: *the return of spring* **8 returns** [pl] results in an election **9 many happy returns** what you say to wish someone a happy birthday

re·tur·na·ble /rɪˈtɜːnəbəl ‖ -ɜːr-/ *adj* intended to be given or sent back after use: *returnable bottles*

re·u·nion /riːˈjuːnjən/ *n* [C;U] a meeting between people who have not seen each other recently: *an emotional reunion* | *There was no hope of reunion.* | *a college reunion*

re·u·nite /ˌriːjuːˈnaɪt/ *v* **reunited, reuniting** **1** [I;T] to meet, or help people meet, after a period of separation: *Returning soldiers have been reunited with their families.* | *It's time for all members of the party to reunite.* **2** [T] to bring things together again

rev¹ /rev/ *n* *infml* **1 Rev** an abbreviation for REVEREND **2** *infml* see REVOLUTION(4)

rev² *v* **-vv-** [I;T] *infml* (also **rev up**) to increase the speed of an engine: *Don't rev your engine so loudly.* | *The engine is revving.*

re·val·ue /riːˈvæljuː/ *v* **revalued, revaluing** [T] **1** to increase the exchange value of a country's money: **2** to make a new judgment about the value of something: *We're having our paintings revalued.* **–revaluation** /riːˌvæljuˈeɪʃən/ *n* [C;U]

re·veal /rɪˈviːl/ *v* **1** [T] to allow someone or something to be seen: *The front door opened to reveal a magnificent entrance hall.* **2** [T; + (that)] to make something known to people: *She suddenly revealed that she was married.* | *His expression reveals his true feelings.* **3 reveal yourself** to show yourself in a particular way, especially one that is unexpected: *She revealed herself to be a member of the royal family.* | *He revealed himself as a fraud.*

re·veal·ing /rɪˈviːlɪŋ/ *adj* allowing something private or personal to be seen or known: *a very revealing dress* | *Her remarks were very revealing.*

rev·el /ˈrevəl/ *v* **-ll-** (also **-l-** *AmE*) [I] **1** to pass the time eating, drinking, and dancing in a noisy and sometimes wild way (an old-fashioned word which is often used in a humorous way) *They were drinking and revelling all night.* **2 revel in something** to enjoy something greatly: *She revels in hearing about my problems.* **–reveller** *n* (also **reveler** *AmE*)

rev·e·la·tion /ˌrevəˈleɪʃən/ *n* **1** [U] the making known of something secret **2** [C] a surprising fact that is made known: *We listened to her strange revelations about her past.* **3** something surprising: *His exposure of corruption in the government was a revelation*

rev·el·ry /ˈrevəlri/ n revelries [pl;U] wild, noisy, active entertainment: *Shall we join in the revelries?*

re·venge¹ /rɪˈvendʒ/ v revenged, revenging **1 revenge yourself on someone** to take action in return for harm done to you: **2** [T] to take action in return for harm done to someone or something

revenge² n [U] action taken against someone who has done something to harm you: *a revenge attack* | *He took his revenge by humiliating me in public.* | *Her house was burnt down in revenge for her statement to the police.*

rev·e·nue /ˈrevɪnjuː ‖ -nuː/ n [U] income that a government receives as tax or that is earned by a company

re·ver·be·rate /rɪˈvɜːbəreɪt ‖ -ɜːr-/ v reverberated, reverberating [I] **1** to sound again and again: *The thunder reverberated across the valley.* **2** to shake as a result of loud noises: *The hall reverberated with the applause.* **3** to have a strong and lasting effect: *The consequences reverberated throughout the political world.* –**reverberation** /rɪˌvɜːbəˈreɪʃən ‖ -ɜːr-/ n [C;U]

re·vere /rɪˈvɪər/ v revered, revering [T] *fml* to feel great respect and admiration for someone: *You revered your father, didn't you?*

Rev·e·rend /ˈrevərənd/ n adv (also **Rev** in written English) a title used to address or talk about a person holding a religious position: *The Reverend Donald Jones* | *Good morning, Reverend!*

rev·e·rent /ˈrevərənt/ adj having or showing a feeling of great respect or admiration: –opposite **irreverent** –**reverence** n [U]

rev·e·rie /ˈrevəri/ n [C;U] a kind of dream that you have while you are awake: *She fell into a reverie about the past.*

re·vers·al /rɪˈvɜːsəl ‖ -ɜːr-/ n [C; U] a complete change: *That's a reversal of your usual position on relations with the US*

re·verse¹ /rɪˈvɜːs ‖ -ɜːrs/ adj [only before a noun] **1** opposite or back: *the reverse side of the coin* **2 in reverse order** from the last to the first: *Why are these names in reverse order?*

reverse² v reversed, reversing **1** [I;T] to move backwards: *He reversed the car through the gate.* | *The car reversed and drove off.* **2** [T] to change a process, decision, or judgment completely: *The judgment was reversed in a higher law court.* | *I'm trying to reverse the company's fortunes.* **3** [T] to change round the usual order or position of things: *Today we'll reverse the usual order of the lesson, and start with a written exercise.* **4 reverse the charges** to make a telephone call which the person receiving it will pay for –**reversible** adj : *a reversible coat*

reverse³ n **1 in reverse: a** with the controls of a vehicle in such a position that you will move backwards: *Put the car in reverse!* **b** in reverse in the opposite way: *His career went into reverse.* **2 the reverse** the opposite: *He did the reverse of what we expected and bought us all a drink.*

re·vert /rɪˈvɜːt ‖ -ɜːrt/ **1 revert to something** to return to an earlier state, habit, or subject: *He's stopped taking drugs now, but he may revert to taking them again.* **2 revert to someone** law (of property) to return to a previous owner –**reversion** /rɪˈvɜːʃən ‖ -ˈvɜːrʒən/ n [C; U] : *reversion to bad habits*

re·view¹ /rɪˈvjuː/ n **1** [C;U] a study of something: *After a careful review of the situation, he decided on a few changes.* | *The matter is open to review.* **2** [C] a magazine, newspaper, or article giving judgments

on things like new books or plays: *a page of book reviews* **3** a show of the armed forces, in the presence of a ruler or an important general: *a naval review* **4 under review** being considered carefully to see if changes are necessary: *The company's wage system is currently under review.*

review² v [T] **1** to consider something carefully, especially to decide whether changes are necessary: *The government is reviewing its education policy.* | *Your salary will be reviewed annually.* **2** to give publicly a written or spoken opinion of something like a new book or play: *The play was well reviewed in all the newspapers.*

re·view·er /rɪˈvjuːər/ n a person who gives opinions publicly on new plays, books, and other things

re·vile /rɪˈvaɪl/ v reviled, reviling [T] *fml* to express strong and angry feelings about or to someone or something

re·vise /rɪˈvaɪz/ v revised, revising **1** [T] to read through something carefully, making improvements to it **2** [T] to change your opinions or behaviour because of new information or more thought **3** to change something, especially a figure, to make it more correct: *We are revising our estimates as news of further deaths reaches us.* **4** [I;T] to prepare for a test by studying: *I must revise for my exam.* | *Have you revised these notes yet?*

re·vi·sion /rɪˈvɪʒən/ n **1** [C;U] a change made to improve something **2** [U] study in preparation for a test: *Have you done any revision for the English exam?*

re·vi·tal·ize /riːˈvaɪtəl-aɪz/ v revitalized, revitalizing (also **revitalise** *BrE*) [T] to put new strength or power into something: *attempts to revitalize the economy* –**revitalization** /riːˌvaɪtəl-aɪˈzeɪʃən ‖ -tələ-/ n [U]

re·vi·val /rɪˈvaɪvəl/ n **1** [C;U] a process in which something becomes active or popular again: *There has been a revival of interest in the fashions of the 1930's.* **2** [C] a new performance of an old play after many years

re·vive /rɪˈvaɪv/ v revived, reviving [I;T] **1** to return to consciousness or health: *A drink might revive him.* | *That rose will revive if you water it.* **2** to start a custom or habit again: *We're trying to revive old customs.* | *Her interest in sport is reviving.*

re·voke /rɪˈvəʊk/ v revoked, revoking [T] to put an end to an official agreement: *His driving licence has been revoked.*

re·volt¹ /rɪˈvəʊlt/ v **1** [I] to act violently against those in power in an attempt to change the system of government: *The people revolted against the military government.* **2** [T] to make someone feel violent dislike and sickness: *Such cruelty revolted him.*

revolt² n [C;U] a violent attempt to change the way a country is governed: *The whole nation is in a state of revolt.* | *The revolt is over.*

re·volt·ing /rɪˈvəʊltɪŋ/ adj very unpleasant indeed: *What a revolting smell!* | *I've never had a more revolting meal.* –**revoltingly** adv : *a revoltingly dirty room*

rev·o·lu·tion /ˌrevəˈluːʃən/ n **1** [C;U] great social change, especially the changing of a ruler or political system by force: *the Russian revolution* **2** [C] a complete change in ways of thinking or acting: *The invention of the aeroplane caused a revolution in travel and communications.* | *the computer revolution* **3** [C;U] circular movement round a fixed point: *The earth makes one revolution round the sun each year.* **4** [C] (also **rev** *infml*) one complete circular movement on a central point in a machine: *a speed of 100 revolutions per minute*

rev·o·lu·tion·a·ry[1] /ˌrevəˈluːʃənəri ‖ -ʃəneri/ adj 1 connected with revolution(1): a revolutionary leader | revolutionary ideas 2 completely new and different: a revolutionary new way of growing rice

revolutionary[2] n revolutionaries a person who supports or takes part in a revolution(1)

rev·o·lu·tion·ize /ˌrevəˈluːʃənaɪz/ (also revolutionise BrE) v revolutionized, revolutionizing [T] to cause a complete change: The discovery of the new drug has revolutionized the treatment of many diseases.

re·volve /rɪˈvɒlv ‖ rɪˈvɑːlv/ v revolved, revolving [I] to spin round on a central point: The wheels began to revolve slowly. | revolving doors
revolve around sbdy/sthg phr v [T] to have something as a centre or main subject: Her life revolves around her work.

re·volv·er /rɪˈvɒlvəʳ ‖ rɪˈvɑːl-/ n a type of small gun

re·vue /rɪˈvjuː/ n a light theatrical show with songs, dances, and jokes

re·vul·sion /rɪˈvʌlʃən/ n [U] the feeling of finding something shocking and very unpleasant: We looked away in revulsion from the scene of the accident. | a feeling of utter revulsion

re·ward[1] /rɪˈwɔːd ‖ -ɔːrd/ v [T] to give someone something because they have done something useful for you: He rewarded the boy for bringing back the lost dog. | How can I reward you for all your help? | He rewarded me with a £5 note.

reward[2] n [C;U] something given or gained as return for work or service: She got nothing as a reward for her kindness. | The police are offering a reward for information about the robbery.

re·ward·ing /rɪˈwɔːdɪŋ ‖ -ɔːr-/ adj giving a feeling of satisfaction: Nursing can be a very rewarding job.

re·wind /ˌriːˈwaɪnd/ v rewound /-ˈwaʊnd/, rewound [I;T] to make a TAPE on a TAPE-RECORDER or VIDEO-RECORDER go back to the beginning: He rewound the tape. | I had to rewind to the beginning.

re·wire /ˌriːˈwaɪəʳ/ v rewired, rewiring [T] to put new electric wires into a building

re·write /ˌriːˈraɪt/ v rewrote /ˈrəʊt/, rewritten /-ˈrɪtn/, rewriting [T] to write again in a different, more suitable, way –rewrite /ˈriːraɪt/ n

rhap·so·dy /ˈræpsədi/ n rhapsodies an expression of great praise and wild excitement

rhet·o·ric /ˈretərɪk/ n [U] 1 the art of speaking or writing so as to persuade people effectively 2 speech or writing that sounds important, but is not really sincere or is without meaning –rhetorical /rɪˈtɒrɪkəl ‖ -ˈtɔː-, -ˈtɑː-/ adj –rhetorically /-kli/ adv

rhetorical ques·tion /-ˌ⋯ ˈ⋯/ n a question asked only for effect, and not expecting any answer

rheu·mat·ic /ruːˈmætɪk/ adj connected with or having rheumatism: a rheumatic condition of the joints | stiff rheumatic hands

rheu·ma·tis·m /ˈruːmətɪzəm/ n [U] a disease causing pain and stiffness in the joints or muscles

rhi·no·ce·ros /raɪˈnɒsərəs ‖ -ˈnɑː-/ n rhinoceros or rhinoceroses (also rhino /ˈraɪnəʊ/ infml) a large, heavy animal of Africa or Asia, with either one or two horns on its nose and a thick skin

---

SPELLING NOTE

Words with the sound /r/, may be spelt **wr-**, like **wrong**.

---

rho·do·den·dron /ˌrəʊdəˈdendrən/ n a bush that is grown for its large bright flowers

rhu·barb /ˈruːbɑːb ‖ -ɑːrb/ n [U] a broad-leaved garden plant whose thick red juicy stems are boiled with sugar and eaten

rhyme[1] /raɪm/ n 1 a word that ends with the same sound as another word: "Bold" and "cold" are rhymes. | I can't find a rhyme for "donkey". 2 [U] the use of words that rhyme in poetry: Shakespeare sometimes wrote in rhyme. 3 [C] a short piece of writing, using words that rhyme: a nursery rhyme | He made up funny rhymes to make us laugh.

rhyme[2] v rhymed, rhyming [I] (of words or lines of poetry) to end with the same sound: "House" rhymes with "mouse". | The last two lines of this poem don't rhyme properly.

rhyth·m /ˈrɪðəm/ n [C;U] a regular, repeated pattern of sounds or movements in speech, dancing, music, or nature: the exciting rhythms of African drum music | the rhythm of the seasons

rhyth·mic /ˈrɪðmɪk/ adj (also rhythmical) having rhythm: the rhythmic beating of one's heart –rhythmically /-kli/ adv

rib[1] /rɪb/ n one of the 12 pairs of bones running round your chest from your SPINE to where they join at the front

rib[2] v -bb- [T] old fash to make fun of someone in a friendly way: All the boys ribbed him for keeping a pet pig.

rib·ald /ˈrɪbəld/ adj fml humorously rude in a disrespectful way: ribald jokes –ribaldry n [U]

rib·bon /ˈrɪbən/ n [C;U] 1 a long, narrow piece of silk or other cloth used for tying your hair or for decoration: red ribbons in her hair 2 the piece of cloth that provides ink when you write with a machine

rib cage /ˈ⋅ ⋅/ n the wall of ribs that encloses and protects your lungs

rice /raɪs/ n [U] a food of white or brown grains grown in wet tropical places, especially in India and China: Would you like rice with your meat?

rich /rɪtʃ/ adj 1 possessing a lot of money or property: a very rich industrialist 2 [never before a noun] containing a lot of a certain desirable thing: This country is rich in oil. | rich in vitamins 3 costly, valuable, and beautiful (used of objects): The walls were hung with rich silk. 4 containing a lot of cream, sugar, or eggs: a very rich Christmas cake | The pudding was too rich for me. 5 good for growing plants (used of land): rich soil 6 deep and strong (used of sounds and colours): a rich dark red –richness n [U]

rich·es /ˈrɪtʃɪz/ n [pl] lit wealth: Riches are worth nothing without health. | the earth's riches

rich·ly /ˈrɪtʃli/ adv 1 in a large quantity: richly rewarded | richly decorated 2 fully: They got the punishment they so richly deserved.

rick·et·y /ˈrɪkɨti/ adj weak and likely to break: a rickety old cart

rick·shaw /ˈrɪkʃɔː/ n a small vehicle used in East Asia for carrying passengers; they are pulled by a man either running or cycling in front

ric·o·chet /ˈrɪkəʃeɪ/ v ricocheted /-ʃeɪd/, ricocheting /-ʃeɪɪŋ/ [I] (of a stone, or bullet) to change direction when it hits a surface at an angle: The bullet ricocheted off the bridge. –ricochet n

rid /rɪd/ v rid, rid [T] 1 fml to remove something unpleasant from a place: The new ruler rid the city of its corrupt officials. 2 fml to remove something so that it no longer has any effect on you: You must rid yourself of these unfortunate friends. 3 be rid of to be free from something unpleasant: *She was glad to be rid of her financial worries.* **4 get rid of** to remove something or someone you no longer want: *At the end of his studies he got rid of his coursebooks.* | *The company quickly gets rid of poor salesmen.* | *I'll be glad to get rid of this cold.*

rid-dance /ˈrɪdəns/ *n* **Good riddance!** an expression used to show you are glad that someone or something has gone

ridden /ˈrɪdn/ the past participle of RIDE

rid-dle /ˈrɪdl/ *n* **1** a difficult and amusing question to which you must guess the answer **2** something you cannot understand: *Where the woman disappeared to was a complete riddle.*

rid-dled /ˈrɪdld/ *adj* [only before a noun] **riddled with** full of holes: *The man's body was riddled with bullets.* | *The beam was riddled with woodworm.*

ride¹ /raɪd/ *v* **rode** [rəʊd], **ridden** /ˈrɪdn/, **riding 1** [I;T] to sit on a horse and control it: *She rides every day.* | *He rode the new horse.* **2** [I;T] to travel in or on a vehicle: *She rode a bicycle to work.* | *He rode to work on a bus.* | *We rode to town in a Land Rover.* | *Can you ride a motorbike?*
 ride sthg ↔ out *phr v* [T] to come safely through a difficulty: *The prime minister rode out the crisis.*
 ride up *phr v* [I] (of a dress or skirt) to move up away from its proper position

ride² *n* **1** a journey on an animal or in a vehicle especially for pleasure: *Shall we go for a ride in the car?* | *a ride in the country* | *a ride on a donkey* **2 take someone for a ride** *infml* to deceive someone

rid-er /ˈraɪdər/ *n* a person who rides, especially someone who rides a horse: *The rider was thrown off into a hedge.*

ridge /rɪdʒ/ *n* a long narrow raised part of any surface: *He walked along the mountain ridge.* | *He looked at the ridges in the ploughed field.*

rid-i-cule¹ /ˈrɪdɪkjuːl/ *n* [U] being made fun of: *His behaviour deserves ridicule rather than blame.* | *He didn't want to risk being exposed to ridicule.*

ridicule² *v* **ridiculed, ridiculing** [T] to laugh unkindly at someone or something: *They all ridiculed the idea.*

ri-dic-u-lous /rɪˈdɪkjʊləs/ *adj* silly and deserving to be laughed at: *She looks ridiculous in those tight trousers.* | *What a ridiculous suggestion!* **–ridiculously** *adv*: *The examination was ridiculously easy.* **–ridiculousness** *n* [U]

rid-ing /ˈraɪdɪŋ/ *n* [U] the skill or exercise of travelling on a horse: *a riding lesson*

rife /raɪf/ *adj* [never before a noun] *lit* **1** common (used of bad things): *Disease and violence were rife in the city.* **2** full of bad things: *The city was rife with disease and violence.*

ri-fle¹ /ˈraɪfəl/ *n* a gun with a long barrel, fired from the shoulder

rifle² *v* **rifled, rifling** [I;T] to search through and steal everything worth taking from a place: *Somebody has been rifling through my files.* | *He rifled the biscuit tin.*

rift /rɪft/ *n fml* **1** a narrow opening in something solid, especially in the ground: *The Great Rift Valley* **2** a serious disagreement: *The argument caused a rift* **between** *mother and daughter.*

rig¹ /rɪg/ *v* **-gg-** [T] to arrange an event dishonestly for your own advantage: *The election had been rigged.*
 rig sthg ↔ up *phr v* [T] to make something out of materials that you can find quickly: *The climbers rigged up a shelter to protect them from the rain.*

rig² *n* a large structure used when digging to find oil or gas: *an oil rig*

rig-ging /ˈrɪgɪŋ/ *n* [U] all the ropes which hold up the sails on a ship: *The ship lost most of her rigging in the storm.*

right¹ /raɪt/ *n* **1** [U] the side of your body that does not contain your heart, or the direction that is on this side of your body: *You'll see the library on your right.* | *Take the first turning on the right.* **2 the Right** political parties or groups such as the Conservatives in Britain that are in favour of fewer social and political changes: *Politicians on the Right are very unhappy about these reforms.* **3** [U] things that are morally good: *Children must learn the difference between right and wrong.* **4** [C] something that you can claim because it is morally or legally just: *Everyone over 18 has the right to vote.* | *She has a right to half your money.* | *people campaigning for women's rights* **5 be within your rights to do something** a phrase you use when you are saying that someone is allowed to do something because it is morally or legally just: *You'd be quite within your rights to refuse to work on a Sunday.* **6 by rights** a phrase you use when you are saying that something should be true, although it is not: *He should by rights be going to university this year, but he failed his exams and will have to retake them.* **7 in your own right** because of a personal claim that you have rather than because of someone else: *After the death of her husband she became the country's leader in her own right.* **8 in the right** having moral or legal justice on your side: *I was convinced that I was in the right.* **9 put/set something to rights** *fml* to make something correct or just

right² *adj* **1** [only before a noun] on or belonging to the side of your body that does not contain your heart, or the direction that is on this side of your body: *Most people write with their right hand.* | *Take a right turn just after the supermarket.* **2** [never before a noun] morally good or just: *I don't think it's right to let children have a lot of sweets.* | *She thinks it's not right for women to work when they have small children.* | *You were right to report it to the police.* **3** correct or true: *Is that the right time?* | *Nobody got the right answer.* | *She said that the party would be no good, and she was absolutely right.* | *I think it's the right job for you.* | *"Is this Piccadilly Circus?" "Yes, that's right."* **4** **put/set something right** to change a situation that is bad to one that is good: *I'm sorry about all the trouble I've caused – I'll do my best to put things right.* **5 That's right** a phrase you use when you agree with someone else's opinion: *"Some people really don't look after their children properly." "That's right."* **6 right you are, right oh** phrases that you use to show that you agree to do something that someone has asked you to do: *"We'll see you on Saturday, then." "Right you are."*

right³ *adv* **1** towards the right side: *Go to the bottom of the road and turn right.* **2** exactly in a particular place: *He was standing right in the middle of the lawn.* | *It's right in front of you!* **3** as far as a particular place: *Did you go right to the top of the tower?* | *Go right back to the beginning.* **4** *infml* without delay at or after a particular time: *We'll set off right after breakfast.* **5** properly or correctly: *She had guessed right.* | *Did I do it right?* **6** used to show that you agree with someone or agree to do something: *"Come tomorrow." "Right, what time?"* **7 right away** immediately: *I phoned the doctor and he said that he'd come right away.* **8 right now** at this exact moment: *He should be getting on the train right now.*

right⁴ v [T] **1** to put something back into its correct position: *The boat nearly capsized, but then righted itself.* **2 right a wrong** to do something to take away the harmful or bad effects of something else

right an·gle /¹· ,·¹/ n an angle of 90 degrees, like any of the four corners of a square: *The fence was at right angles to the path.* –**right-angled** *adj*

right·eous /¹raɪtʃəs/ *adj fml* lawful and morally good: *a righteous man | righteous indignation* –**righteousness** n [U]

right·ful /¹raɪtfəl/ *adj* [only before a noun] *fml* according to a just and legal claim: *The land was restored to its rightful owner after the war.* –**rightfully** *adv*

right-hand /¸·¹·◄/ *adj* [only before a noun] **1** on or to the right side: *Take a right-hand turn.* | *on the right-hand side* **2 your right-hand, your right-hand man** your most useful and valuable helper

right-hand·ed /¸·¹···◄/ *adj* using the right hand rather than the left for most actions: *Most people are right-handed.* –**opposite left-handed**

right·ly /¹raɪtli/ *adv* correctly: *He believed, rightly or wrongly, that she was guilty.* | *I don't rightly know whether she phoned on Tuesday or Wednesday.*

right of way /¸·· ·¹·/ n **rights of way 1** [C] a legal right to follow a path across someone else's land: *We have a right of way across his field to our house.* **2** [U] the right of traffic to drive, or pass in front of other vehicles: *We have right of way at this road junction.*

right wing /¸· ¹··◄/ n [U; + sing/pl verb] the members of a political party or group, favouring fewer political changes, and CAPITALISM: *The right wing of the party is opposed to this plan.* –**opposite left wing** –**right-wing** *adj* : *a right-wing politician* –**right-winger** n

ri·gid /¹rɪdʒɪd/ *adj* **1** hard and not able to be changed, used of rules and laws: *a rigid system of control* **2** refusing to change: *The headmaster is very rigid in his approach.* **3** stiff, and not bending easily: *a tent supported on a rigid framework* –**rigidly** *adv* –**rigidity** /rɪ¹dʒɪdʒti/ n [U]

ri·gid·ly /¹rɪdʒɪdli/ *adv* **1** not moving: *The soldier stood rigidly to attention.* **2** in a very severe way: *The laws were rigidly enforced.*

rig·ma·role /¹rɪgmərəʊl/ n [sing;U] *infml* a long, confusing story or set of actions that seem to lack meaning or importance: *She told me some rigmarole or other about having lost her keys.*

rig·or mor·tis /¸rɪgə ¹mɔːtɨs, ¸raɪgɔː-‖ ¸rɪgər ¹mɔːr-/ n [U] the stiffening of the muscles after death: *Rigor mortis set in a few hours ago.*

rig·or·ous /¹rɪgərəs/ *adj* **1** careful and thorough: *The new cars are given rigorous safety checks.* **2** severe and painful: *the rigorous hardships of the journey* –**rigorously** *adv*

rig·our /¹rɪgəʳ/ n (**rigor**, *AmE*) [U] **1** hardness: *He deserves to be punished with the full rigour of the law.* **2 the rigours** severe conditions: *the rigours of a Canadian winter* **3** thoroughness in a subject of study: *the rigour of scientific proof*

rile /raɪl/ v **riled, riling** [T] *infml* to make someone angry: *I was really riled by the way he treated me.*

SPELLING NOTE

Words with the sound /r/, may be spelt **wr-**, like **wrong**.

---

rim /rɪm/ n the outside edge or border, usually of a round or circular object: *the rim of a cup* | *the rim of a wheel* –**rimless** *adj* : *She wore rimless glasses.*

rind /raɪnd/ n [U] the thick, outer covering of certain foods or fruits: *a piece of lemon rind* | *cheese rind* | *bacon rinds*

ring¹ /rɪŋ/ n **1** a circular metal band, usually worn on a finger: *a wedding ring* | *a key ring* –see picture on page 50 **2** something in the shape of a circle: *a ring of oil around the wrecked ship* | *children dancing in a ring* **3** a group of people acting together in a dishonest way: *The police were searching for the head of the drugs ring.* **4** an enclosed space with seats around it in which an activity takes place: *a boxing ring* | *a circus ring* **5** the sound of a bell: *I thought I heard a ring at the door.* **6 give someone a ring** *infml* to telephone someone: *Give me a ring when you get home.* **7 run rings round someone** to do things much better than someone *I tried my best, but he ran rings round me.*

ring² v **ringed, ringed** [T] to put a ring around something: *The teacher ringed every mistake in red.* | *Police ringed the building.*

ring³ v **rang** /ræŋ/, **rung** /rʌŋ/ **1** [T] to make a bell sound: *He rang the doorbell.* **2** [I] to sound: *The phone rang.* | *I could hear the church bells ringing.* **3** [I;T] to telephone: *I rang twice but got no reply.* | *I'll ring you tonight.* **4** [I;T] to ring a bell because you want something: *He rang for his secretary.* | *He rang for some sandwiches.* **5** [I] to be filled with a continuous sound: *The theatre rang with applause.* | *My ears were ringing.* **6 ring a bell** *infml* to make you remember something: *His name doesn't ring a bell.* **7 ring false** to sound untrue: *Her explanation rang false.* [RELATED PHRASE **ring true**] **8 ring the changes** to introduce variety

ring sbdy ↔ back *phr v* [I;T] to telephone later: *I'll ring you back when I've got more news.* | *I forgot to ring back.*

ring off *phr v* [I] to end a telephone conversation: *I'd better ring off now, there's someone at the door.*

ring out *phr v* [I] to sound loudly and clearly: *The climber's shouts rang out across the valley.*

ring up *phr v* [I;T **ring sbdy ↔ up**] to telephone: *She rang me up to say she'd be home late.* –see TELEPHONE¹ (USAGE)

ring·lead·er /¹rɪŋ,liːdəʳ/ n a person who leads others to do wrong or make trouble

ring·let /¹rɪŋlɨt/ n a long hanging curl of hair

ring·mas·ter /¹rɪŋ,mɑːstəʳ ‖ -,mæ-/ n a person whose job is directing performances in the CIRCUS ring

ring road /¹· ·/ n a road that goes round the edge of a large town so that traffic need not pass through the centre

ring·side /¹rɪŋsaɪd/ n **the ringside** at the edge of a ring such as in a CIRCUS –**ringside** *adj* : *We had ringside seats for the big fight, and saw it all.*

rink /rɪŋk/ n a specially prepared indoor surface, on which people SKATE, or ROLLER-SKATE: *They met at the ice rink.*

rinse¹ /rɪns/ v **rinsed, rinsing** [T] to wash something in clean water: *I'll just rinse these shirts.* | *Rinse your mouth out.*

rinse² n **1** [C] washing in clean water: *Give the shirts at least three rinses.* **2** [C;U] a liquid for colouring the hair: *blue rinse for grey hair*

ri·ot¹ /¹raɪət/ n **1** [C] a lot of violent actions by a number of people in a public place: *The army was called* *in to put down a riot.* **2 a riot** *infml* a very funny and successful occasion or person: *I hear the new show is a riot – let's go and see it!* **3 run riot** to become violent and uncontrollable: *The football supporters ran riot through the town after their team lost.*

riot² *v* [I] to behave violently in a public place: *The crowds are rioting in the city centre.* **–rioter** *n*

ri·ot·ous /ˈraɪətəs/ *adj* **1** wild and disorderly: *a riotous crowd* | *riotous laughter* **2** noisy and exciting (a word used to express approval): *They spent a riotous night drinking and singing.* **–riotously** *adv*

rip¹ /rɪp/ *v* **-pp-** [I;T] **1** to tear or be torn quickly and violently: *The sail ripped under the force of the wind.* | *He ripped the cloth with his knife.* | *I ripped the letter open.* | *The curtains were ripped to pieces.* **2** to remove something quickly and often violently: *He ripped the letter from my hand.* | *He ripped off his clothes and jumped into the pool.*

rip sbdy ↔ **off** *phr v* [T] *infml* to charge someone far too much money: *They really ripped us off at that hotel.*

rip sthg ↔ **up** *phr v* [T] to tear violently into pieces: *Angrily, she ripped the letter up.*

rip² *n* a long tear or cut: *a rip in the tyre caused by a sharp stone*

rip·cord /ˈrɪpkɔːd ‖ -kɔːrd/ *n* the cord that one pulls to open a PARACHUTE after jumping from an aircraft

ripe /raɪp/ *adj* **1** fully grown and ready to be eaten (used of food and crops): *a field of ripe corn* | *These apples aren't ripe yet.* **2** [never before a noun] ready for something: *land ripe for industrial development* **3 the time is ripe** a suitable time has arrived for a particular action: *The time is ripe* **for** *a change of attitude.* **4 live to a ripe old age** to live until you are very old: *His grandmother lived to a ripe old age.* **–ripeness** *n* [U]

rip·en /ˈraɪpən/ *v* [I;T] to make or become ripe: *The sun ripens the corn.* | *The corn ripens in the sun.*

rip-off /ˈ· ·/ *n* *infml* an act of charging too much: *"What a rip-off!"*

rip·ple¹ /ˈrɪpəl/ *v* **rippled, rippling 1** [I;T] to move or be made to move in gentle waves: *The wind rippled the surface of the cornfield.* **2** [I] to make a sound like gently running water: *The water rippled over the stones.*

ripple² *n* **1** [C] a very small wave: *ripples on a pool when the wind blows* **2** [sing] a sound of gently running water: *I heard the ripple of the stream.* **3** a sound heard for a short time: *a ripple of laughter* | *a ripple of applause*

rise¹ /raɪz/ *v* **rose** /rəʊz/, **risen** /ˈrɪzən/, **rising** [I] **1** to go up or move to a higher position: *The river is rising after the rains.* | *Smoke rose from the factory chimney.* | *Her voice rose higher and higher as she got more excited.* | *The price of bread has risen by 10% in the last year.* | *The road rises steeply when you leave the village.* | *He rose to an important position in the firm.* | *My spirits rose when I heard the wonderful news.* **–opposite fall 2** to appear above the horizon: *The sun rises in the east.* | *The trees rose above the roof-tops.* **3** to stand up: *She used always to rise at daybreak.* **4** to stand up: *She rose to greet her guests.* **5** to begin to be active in opposition: *The people rose* **against** *their cruel oppressors.* **6** (of wind and storms) to become stronger: *The storm rose without warning.* **7** to begin: *The Rhine rises in Switzerland.* **8 rise to the occasion** to show that you can deal with a difficult situation when it happens

■ USAGE Compare **rise** and **raise**. **Rise** is intransitive. If you **rise**, you yourself move to a higher position: *I rose from my seat.* **Raise** is transitive. If you **raise** something you lift it to a higher position: *We raised the ship from the seabed.*

rise above sthg *phr v* [T] not to allow something to have a bad effect on you: *She was able to rise above the disadvantages of her family background.*

rise² *n* **1** [C] an increase: *a rise in the cost of living* **2** [U] the act of growing greater or more powerful: *the rise and fall of the Roman Empire* **3** [C] a small hill: *a house on top of a small rise* **4** [C] *BrE* an increase in wages: *We all got a £6-a-week rise last month.* **5 give rise to** to be the cause of: *The minister's comments gave rise to rumours he would soon resign.*

risk¹ /rɪsk/ *n* **1** [C;U] a possibility something bad may happen: *He was taking a risk by overtaking on a bend.* | *There was no risk of infection.* **2** [C] a danger: *The house is a fire risk.* | *We took out an all risks insurance policy.* **3 at risk** in danger: *Babies and old people are at greatest risk in this influenza epidemic.* | *You really are at risk if you do not wear a seat-belt.* **4 at the risk of** knowing something unpleasant might happen: *He went ahead with the plan at the risk of infuriating his colleagues.* | *At the risk of seeming rude, I must refuse your request I'm afraid.* **5 at your own risk** taking responsibility for what happens: *People bathing here do so at their own risk.* **6 run the risk of** to do something knowing that a particular unpleasant thing might happen: *He ran the risk of losing his job by criticizing his boss.* | *They're unlikely to run the risk of holding an election before the summer.*

risk² *v* [T] **1** to place something in danger: *Don't risk your health.* **2** to take a chance, knowing something may happen: *He risked his parents' anger by marrying me.*

risk·y /ˈrɪski/ *adj* **riskier, riskiest** rather dangerous: *You drove too fast round that corner – it was a risky thing to do.* **–riskily** *adv*

ri·sot·to /rɪˈzɒtəʊ ‖ -ˈsɔː-/ *n* **risottos** [C;U] a dish made from rice cooked with vegetables or meat.

ris·qué /ˈrɪskeɪ ‖ rɪˈskeɪ/ *adj* slightly rude because it is concerned with sex (used of jokes and stories)

ris·sole /ˈrɪsəʊl/ *n* a small flat or round cake made from cut up meat or fish and cooked in hot fat

rite /raɪt/ *n* a ceremony with a serious, often religious, purpose: *funeral rites*

rit·u·al /ˈrɪtʃuəl/ *n* [C;U] one or more ceremonies or customary acts often repeated in the same form: *the ritual of morning prayers in school* **–ritual** *adj* : *ritual dancing* **–ritually** *adv*

ri·val¹ /ˈraɪvəl/ *n* a person with whom one competes: *Who will be his main rival in the presidential election?*

rival² *adj* [only before a noun] competing: *Michael has left and joined a rival company.*

rival³ *v* **-ll-** (-l- *AmE*) [T] to be as good as something else: *Ships can't rival aircraft for speed.*

ri·val·ry /ˈraɪvəlri/ *n* **rivalries** [C;U] competition: *Should we encourage international rivalry in sport?* | *fierce rivalry* **between** *the two companies*

riv·er /ˈrɪvəʳ/ *n* a wide natural stream of water flowing between banks into a lake, into another wider stream, or into the sea: *the river Amazon* | *The river meanders down to the sea.*

riv·et¹ /ˈrɪvɪt/ *n* a metal pin for fastening flat pieces of metal together

rivet² v [T] **1** to fasten something with rivets **2** to attract and hold someone's attention: *All the people in the theatre were riveted by his performance.*

riv·et·ing /ˈrɪvɨtɪŋ/ adj extremely interesting: *a riveting book*

RN /ˌɑːr ˈen/ an abbreviation for **Royal Navy**, used in titles: *Captain Brown, RN*

road /rəʊd/ n **1** a prepared track of hard ground along which vehicles can travel: *Snow blocked the road.* | *The rain ran out into the road and nearly caused an accident.* | *3, St. Mary's Road* –see STREET (USAGE) –see picture on pages 735 and 441 **2 by road** travelling on a road: *The journey takes longer by road than by rail.* **3 on the road** travelling: *We'd been on the road for forty-eight hours and were quite exhausted.* **4 on the road to something** on the way to something: *on the road to disaster* –see WAY (USAGE)

road·block /ˈrəʊdblɒk ǁ -blɑːk/ n something which prevents traffic passing through: *The police set up roadblocks to try to catch the terrorists.*

road·side /ˈrəʊdsaɪd/ n the roadside at or near the edge of the road: *We ate our meal by the roadside.* –**roadside** adj : *a roadside café*

road·way /ˈrəʊdweɪ/ n the part of a road where vehicles drive: *Don't stop in the roadway.*

road works /ˈ· ·/ n [pl] a sign which means road repairs are being carried out

road·wor·thy /ˈrəʊd,wɜːði ǁ -ɜɪr / adj in a fit condition to be driven on the road (used of a vehicle) –**roadworthiness** n [U]

roam /rəʊm/ v [I; + adv/prep;T] to wander with no very clear purpose: *roaming from place to place*

roar¹ /rɔːʳ/ v **1** [I] to make a loud noise: *The lion roared.* **2** [I; + adv/prep] to travel along very fast, making a loud noise: *The traffic roared past.* **3** [I;T] to say or express with a deep loud continuing sound: *The crowd roared their approval.* | *He roared with laughter.*

roar² n a deep loud continuing sound: *the roar of an angry lion* | *roars of laughter*

roar·ing /ˈrɔːrɪŋ/ adj **1** making a loud noise: *roaring laughter* | *a roaring fire* **2** very great: *The play was a roaring success.* **3 do a roaring trade** to do very good business: *The new restaurant is doing a roaring trade.*

roast¹ /rəʊst/ v [I;T] to cook or be cooked by dry heat, either in front of an open fire or in an OVEN: *roasted coffee beans* | *Roast the chicken for two hours.* –see COOK¹ (USAGE)

roast² n a large piece of meat for roasting: *Let's have a nice roast for Sunday dinner.* –**roast** adj : *a roast chicken* | *roast potatoes*

rob /rɒb ǁ rɑːb/ v **-bb-** [T] to take something which belongs to someone else: *They planned to rob a bank.* | *I've been robbed!* | *They robbed him of everything he possessed.*

◾ USAGE Compare **rob** and **steal**. Things are **stolen**; people or organizations are **robbed** (of things): *He stole my pen.* | *Two video recorders were stolen.* | *We've been robbed!* | *He was robbed of his wallet and £10 in cash.*

rob·ber /ˈrɒbəʳ ǁ ˈrɑː-/ n a person who steals: *a band of robbers* –see THIEF (USAGE)

SPELLING NOTE

Words with the sound / r /, may be spelt **wr-**, like **wrong**.

---

rob·ber·y /ˈrɒbəri ǁ ˈrɑː-/ n **robberies** [C;U] **1** the crime of taking someone else's property: *He was charged with robbery.* | *The robbery took place during the hours of darkness.* **2 daylight robbery** *infml* charging too much money: *£2 for a beer? It's daylight robbery!*

robe /rəʊb/ n a long flowing garment: *a bath robe* | *a judge's black robes*

rob·in /ˈrɒbɨn ǁ ˈrɑː-/ n a small brown bird with a red breast

ro·bot /ˈrəʊbɒt ǁ -baːt, -bət/ n a machine that can move and do some of the work of a person: *Some of the work in the car factory is now done by robots.*

ro·bust /rəˈbʌst, ˈrəʊbʌst/ adj having or showing very good health or strength

rock¹ /rɒk ǁ rɑːk/ v [I;T] to move regularly backwards and forwards or from side to side: *She rocked the child in her arms.* | *The boat rocked on the water.* **2** [T] to cause great shock and surprise: *The news of the president's murder rocked the nation.* **3 rock the boat** to spoil a good or comfortable situation

rock² n **1** [U] a type of stone forming part of the earth's surface: *a passage cut through solid rock* **2** [C] a large piece or mass of stone: *danger from falling rocks* | *ships driven onto the rocks by a storm* **3** [U] *BrE* a hard sticky kind of sweet made in long round bars: *a stick of Brighton rock* **4 on the rocks** with ice: *whisky on the rocks* **5 their marriage is on the rocks** = their marriage is in difficulties and about to end

rock bot·tom /ˌ· ˈ···◂/ n [U] the lowest point: *Prices have reached rock bottom.*

rock·er /ˈrɒkəʳ ǁ ˈrɑː-/ n **1** one of the curved pieces of wood which certain types of furniture have at the bottom so that they can be rocked backwards and forwards **2** the usual American word for ROCKING CHAIR **3 off your rocker** *infml* mad

rock·e·ry /ˈrɒkəri ǁ ˈrɑː-/ n **rockeries** (also **rock garden**) a part of a garden laid out with rocks and low-growing plants

rock·et¹ /ˈrɒkɨt ǁ ˈrɑː-/ n **1** a tube-shaped machine used for space travel, and to power bombs: *an anti-tank rocket* | *the launch of the new American space rocket* **2** a FIREWORK that goes high in the air and then explodes with many bright colours

rock·et² v [I] to rise quickly and suddenly: *The price of sugar has rocketed.*

rocking chair /ˈ··· ·/ n (also **rocker** *AmE*) a chair with special curved pieces at the bottom so that you can ROCK in it

rocking horse /ˈ··· ·/ n a toy horse for a child to ride on; it has curved pieces at the bottom so that the child can ROCK on it

rock 'n' roll /ˌrɒk ən ˈrəʊl ǁ ˌrɑːk-/ n (also **rock, rock and roll**) [U] popular modern dance music with a strong beat, which is played on electric instruments

rock·y /ˈrɒki ǁ ˈrɑːki/ adj **rockier, rockiest 1** covered with rocks: *a rocky path up the mountain* **2** unsteady: *She felt a bit rocky after the accident.* –**rockiness** n [U]

rod /rɒd ǁ rɑːd/ n a long thin pole or bar of wood, metal, or plastic: *to go fishing with rod and line* | *curtain rods* | *a rod of iron*

rode /rəʊd/ the past tense of RIDE

ro·dent /ˈrəʊdənt/ n a member of the family of small plant-eating animals with strong sharp teeth, that includes rats, mice, and rabbits

roe /rəʊ/ n [C;U] a mass of eggs or male seed in a fish, often eaten as food

rogue /rəʊg/ n old fash 1 a very dishonest person: *Don't buy a used car from that rogue.* 2 infml a boy who likes playing tricks: *You little rogue – where are my shoes?*

role /rəʊl/ n the part taken by someone in life or in any activity, especially the part of some particular actor in a play: *Olivier played the role of Hamlet.* | *She needed to fulfil her role as a mother.*

roll¹ /rəʊl/ n 1 a piece of a particular material that has been rolled into or around a tube: *a roll of film* | *a roll of cloth* 2 a small round or long loaf of bread for one person: *little bread rolls* | *a cheese roll* 3 an official list of names: *The teacher called the roll.* 4 [sing] a long deep sound: *a roll of thunder* | *the roll of drums* 5 a rolling movement from side to side: *the slow roll of a ship on a rough sea*

roll² v 1 [I;T] to move by turning over and over, or from side to side: *The golfer hit the ball and it rolled straight into the hole.* | *The dog rolled in the grass.* | *We rolled the barrels of wine into their correct position in the cellar.* | *The ship rolled with the waves.* 2 [I] to move steadily and smoothly: *The train rolled slowly into the station.* | *Tears rolled down her cheek.* 3 [T] to form into a particular shape by moving round and round: *He rolled himself a cigarette.* | *She rolled the clay into a ball.* | *She rolled the paper instead of folding it.* 4 [T] to make something flat by pressing it down: *The grass needs rolling.* | *He rolled the pastry as thin as he could.* 5 [I] to make a long deep sound: *The drums rolled.* 6 [I;T] (of your eyes) to move round: *His eyes rolled with fear.*

roll about phr v [I] to move around in an uncontrolled way: *During the storm, the cargo got loose and rolled about on the deck of the ship.*

roll by phr v [I] to go steadily past: *The years rolled by.* | *The girl watched the heavy trucks roll by.*

roll in phr v [I] to be received in large quantities: *The money came rolling in.*

roll over phr v [I;T] to move to a different position: *The baby rolled over.*

roll up phr v 1 [I;T roll sthg ↔ up] to shape something like a tube or ball: *The paper kept rolling up.* | *They rolled up the carpet.* | *He rolled up his sleeves and started work.* 2 [I] infml to arrive: *John rolled up when everyone else had left.*

roll call /'· ·/ n [U] the time for an act of reading out a list of names to see who is there: *I arrived just before roll call.*

roll·er /'rəʊləʳ/ n 1 a hard tube-shaped object that rolls over and over: *The rollers under the armchair made it easy to move.* 2 tubes around which women wind their hair to make it curl: *She sleeps with her hair in rollers.* 3 a big, long wave on the coast: *The Atlantic rollers surged in.*

roller blind /'·· ·/ n BrE a kind of curtain that rolls up and down over a window

roller coast·er /'·· ͵··/ n a kind of small railway with sharp slopes and curves, popular in amusement parks

roller skate /'·· ·/ n a frame with wheels for fitting under a shoe, or a shoe with wheels fixed on, allowing you to move quickly on any smooth surface: *a boy on roller skates* –**roller-skate** v [I]

roll·ing /'rəʊlɪŋ/ adj [only before a noun] 1 rising and falling in long gentle slopes: *the rolling hills of England* 2 moving from side to side (used to describe the way someone walks): *the rolling walk of a very fat man* 3 **rolling in it** infml very rich: *Dave can pay. He's rolling in it.*

rolling pin /'·· ·/ n a tube-shaped piece of wood or other material, used for spreading pastry out flat and thin before cooking –see picture on page 638

rolling stock /'·· ·/ n [U] everything on wheels that belongs to a railway, such as engines and carriages

Ro·man /'rəʊmən/ n a citizen of the ancient empire or the city of Rome

Roman Cath·o·lic /͵·· '···/ adj someone belonging to the **Roman Catholic Church** whose leader rules from Rome: *a Roman Catholic nun* –**Roman Catholicism** /͵·· ·'····/ n [U]

ro·mance /rəʊ'mæns, rə-/ n 1 [C] a story about a love affair: *She spends her time reading silly romances.* 2 [U] the enjoyment of something new and exciting: *the romance of life in the Wild West* 3 [C] a love affair: *a holiday romance*

Ro·ma·ni·an¹ /ruː'meɪniən ‖ rəʊ-/ adj of or connected with Romania

Romanian² n 1 [C] a person from Romania 2 [U] the language of Romania

Roman nu·me·ral /͵·· '···/ n any of a set of signs, originally used in ancient Rome for numbers, such as I, II, III, IV, V, etc. –compare ARABIC NUMERAL

ro·man·tic¹ /rəʊ'mæntɪk, rə-/ adj 1 showing strong feelings of love: *a very romantic love story* 2 not practical; sometimes used to express disapproval: *She has romantic ideas about becoming a famous actress.* –**romantically** /-kli/ adv

romantic² n a person with wild impractical ideas: *He was a romantic who went off to the South Seas to paint pictures.*

ro·man·ti·cize /rəʊ'mæntɪ͵saɪz, rə-/ v **romanticized, romanticizing** (also **romanticise** BrE) [I;T] to talk about things in a way which makes them seem more romantic or attractive than they really are: *This novel romanticizes life in the country.*

romp /rɒmp ‖ rɑːmp/ v [I] to play noisily and roughly with a lot of running and jumping: *The children were romping about in the garden.* –**romp** n

romp·ers /'rɒmpəz ‖ 'rɑːmpərz/ n [pl] a one-piece garment for babies combining a top and short trousers: *a pair of rompers* –see PAIR (USAGE)

roof¹ /ruːf/ n 1 the outside covering on top of a building or vehicle: *A tile has fallen off the roof.* | *the roof of the car* –see pictures on pages 49 and 441 2 the highest part of something: *the roof of his mouth* | *like the roof of the world* 3 **under someone's roof** in someone's home: *It's impossible for her and her mother to live under the same roof.* 4 **have a roof over your head** to have a place to live 5 **hit the roof** infml to get extremely angry 6 **go through the roof** infml (of a price) to increase greatly

roof² v [T] to put a roof on a building: *a house roofed with slates* –**roofed** adj

roof·ing /'ruːfɪŋ/ n [U] material for making or covering roofs

roof rack /'·· ·/ n BrE a metal frame fixed on top of a car roof, for carrying things

rook /rʊk/ n 1 a large black European bird like a CROW 2 a piece in the game of CHESS

room /ruːm, rʊm/ n 1 [C] a division of a building, with its own walls and floor: *The house has six rooms.* 2 [U] enough space for a particular purpose: *There's no room to move.* | *Move along and make room for me!* | *A piano takes up a lot of room.* □ USEFUL PATTERNS there is room for something; there is room to do something 3 [U] a need for: *There's plenty of room for improvement in his work.* 4 a reason for: *There's no room for doubt.*

room·mate /ˈruːmˌmeɪt, ˈrʊm-/ n a person you share a room with: *Bill and I are roommates.*

room ser·vice /ˈ· ˌ·-/ n [U] a service provided by a hotel, by which food and drink are sent to a person's room: *Let's call room service and have tea sent up.*

room·y /ˈruːmi/ adj **roomier, roomiest** with plenty of space inside: *a roomy cupboard*

roost /ruːst/ v [I] (of a bird) to sit and sleep for the night

roost·er /ˈruːstəʳ/ n the usual American word for a male chicken

root¹ /ruːt/ n **1** roots the part of a plant that grows down into the soil in search of food and water: *Pull the plant up by the roots.* **2** the part of a tooth, hair, or organ that holds it to the rest of the body **3** the central part or cause of something: *Let's get to the root of this matter.* **4 your roots** the place where you grew up **5 put down roots** to settle in a place and feel you belong there **6 take root** (of plants and ideas) to become established and grow

root² v [I;T] to make or get roots: *Try to root this plant in the garden.* | *Do roses root easily?*

root about/around *phr* v [I] to search for something: *Someone's been rooting about in my papers.*

root sthg ↔ **out** *phr* v [T] to get rid of something bad: *Scientists doubt whether malaria can ever be totally rooted out.*

root crop /ˈ· ·/ n a crop that is grown for its roots

root·ed /ˈruːtɪd/ adj [never before a noun] unable to move or be moved: *He stood rooted to the spot.* | *a deeply rooted dislike of cats*

root·less /ˈruːtləs/ adj without a home or any sense of belonging somewhere **–rootlessness** n [U]

rope¹ /rəʊp/ n **1** [C;U] a strong thick cord made by twisting thinner pieces of string together **2 know the ropes** to know from experience the rules and customs in a place or activity: *I've done this before so I know the ropes; shall I show you how to do it?*

rope² v **roped, roping** [T] to tie up with a rope: *The prisoners were roped together.*

rope sbdy ↔ **in** *phr* v [T] *infml* to persuade someone to help: *I've been roped in to help sell the tickets.*

rope sthg ↔ **off** *phr* v [T] to separate an area from the rest with ropes: *They've roped off one end of the pool.*

rope lad·der /ˈ· ˌ··/ n a ladder made of two long ropes connected by cross pieces of wood, rope, or metal

ro·sa·ry /ˈrəʊzəri/ n **rosaries** a set of prayers or the string of small decorative balls used to count them in the ROMAN CATHOLIC religion

rose¹ /rəʊz/ **1** the sweet-smelling flower of a bush with prickly stems **2** a colour from pink to deep red **3 not a bed of roses** a phrase used to warn someone that something is not as pleasant or as easy as they think it will be: *University life won't be a bed of roses, I can tell you!*

rose² the past tense of RISE

ro·sé /ˈrəʊzeɪ ‖ rəʊˈzeɪ/ n [U] light pink wine: *a glass of rosé*

rose·ma·ry /ˈrəʊzməri ‖ -meri/ n [U] a bush with sweet-smelling leaves which are used in cooking

---

SPELLING NOTE

Words with the sound / r /, may be spelt **wr-**, like **wrong**.

---

ro·sette /rəʊˈzet/ n a BADGE made from narrow silk bands made up in the form of a rose: *The winner was given a red rosette in the riding competition.*

ros·ter /ˈrɒstəʳ ‖ ˈrɑː-/ n a list of people who each take it in turn to do a certain job: *the duty roster*

ros·trum /ˈrɒstrəm ‖ ˈrɑː-/ n **rostrums** or **rostra** /-trə/ a raised place for a public speaker or a music CONDUCTOR

ros·y /ˈrəʊzi/ adj **rosier, rosiest 1** pink and healthy (used of skin colour): *rosy cheeks* **2** giving hope for the future: *Things don't look very rosy at my firm;* *I'm looking for another job.* | *painting a rosy picture of the situation*

rot¹ /rɒt ‖ rɑːt/ v -tt- [I;T] to decay: *The rain has rotted away the roof beams.* | *The vegetables were left to rot.*

rot² n [U] **1** decay: *an old hollow tree full of rot* | *dry rot* **2** *BrE infml* foolish remarks or ideas: *Don't talk such rot!* **3 the rot is setting in** a situation is becoming bad

ro·ta /ˈrəʊtə/ n *BrE* a list of people who take turns to do a job: *a rota for parents to drive children to school* | *We can draw up a washing-up rota.*

ro·ta·ry /ˈrəʊtəri/ adj turning round a fixed point, like a wheel: *the rotary movement of the blades* | *a rotary lawn-mower*

ro·tate /rəʊˈteɪt ‖ ˈrəʊteɪt/ v **rotated, rotating** [I;T] **1** to turn round a fixed point: *The earth rotates once every 24 hours.* | *You can rotate the wheel with your hand.* **2** to use in regular order: *We try to rotate the crops, wheat following beans and so on.*

ro·ta·tion /rəʊˈteɪʃən/ n **1** [U] the action of rotating: *the rotation of the earth* | *The seasons follow each other in rotation.* **2** [C] one complete turn round a fixed point: *The wheel made ten rotations a second.*

ro·tis·ser·ie /rəʊˈtɪsəri/ n an apparatus for cooking meat by turning it over and over on a bar under direct heat

ro·tor /ˈrəʊtəʳ/ n a part of a machine that rotates: *helicopter rotor blades*

rot·ten /ˈrɒtn ‖ ˈrɑːtn/ adj **1** gone bad: *rotten eggs* | *a rotten apple* **2** *infml* bad or unpleasant: *I feel rotten today.* | *a rotten film* | *What a rotten thing to do to her!*

ro·tund /rəʊˈtʌnd/ adj *fml* fat and round

rou·ble /ˈruːbəl/ n a standard unit of money, or a note worth that amount, in the USSR

rouge /ruːʒ/ n [U] a red substance used for colouring your cheeks

rough¹ /rʌf/ adj **1** not even or smooth (used of a surface): *You need a car that will travel over rough ground.* | *My skin feels rough and dry.* **2** rather violent or rude: *He is rough with his sister and hurts her.* | *She spoke in a rough voice.* **3** difficult and unpleasant: *Life has always been rough in this part of town.* | *She's had a rough time since she lost her job.* **4** not yet finished or exact: *This is the rough version of her speech.* | *I've only got a rough idea where it is.* **5** having a lot of crime or violence (used of a place): *one of the roughest parts of town* | *a rough school* **6** stormy and violent (used of weather, the sea, or a sea journey): *a rough Channel crossing* **7 be rough on someone** to be unfair on someone: *It's a bit rough on him, having to do two people's work.* **8 rough and ready** simple and without comfort: *rough and ready accommodation* **–roughness** n [U]

rough² n [U] **1** uneven ground with long grass on a GOLF course: *He lost his ball in the rough.* **2 in rough** in an incomplete or inexact form: *Draw it in* *rough first.* **3 rough-and-tumble** noisy fighting: *the rough-and-tumble of politics*

rough³ *v* **rough it** *infml* to live in a simple way without any comforts

rough sthg ↔ **out** *phr v* [T] to write or draw your first ideas about something: *I've roughed out the conclusion for my article.*

rough sbdy ↔ **up** *phr v* [T] to attack and hurt someone: *They roughed him up as a warning.*

rough⁴ *adv* **1** in a rather violent way: *Keep away from anyone who plays rough!* **2 sleep rough** to sleep out of doors, without a bed: *He's been sleeping rough under the pier.*

rough·age /ˈrʌfɪdʒ/ *n* [U] a substance contained in food substances that help your bowels to work: *Brown bread provides valuable roughage.*

rough·en /ˈrʌfən/ *v* [I;T] to make a surface uneven or rough

rough·ly /ˈrʌfli/ *adv* **1** in a rather violent or rude manner: *He pushed her roughly away.* **2** about: *There were roughly 200 people there.* | *Roughly speaking, I'd say 200.* **3** in a way which is not complete or exact: *Just do the calculations roughly.*

rou·lette /ruːˈlet/ *n* [U] a game of chance in which a small ball is spun round a moving wheel and falls into a hole marked with a number

round¹ /raʊnd/ *adj* **1** curved in shape, like the shape of a circle, a ball, or the letter "c": *a large round plate* | *small round pebbles* | *her round face* | *The earth is round, not flat* **2 round number, round figure** a complete number, usually one such as 10, 20, 30, etc: *Let's make it 50 - that's a nice round number.*

round² *adv,prep* **1** *adv,prep* moving or positioned in a circle: *The wheel was still spinning round.* | *The earth goes round the sun.* | *He put his belt round his waist.* | *We sat round the table.* | *People were standing round the fire.* | *The children gathered round to listen to the story.* | *a large tree measuring three metres round the trunk* –see picture on page 540 **2 round and round** spinning many times in a circle: *The wheels were spinning round and round.* **3** *adv* so as to face the other way: *Turn the clock round so that I can see it.* | *He swung round to look at me.* **4** *adv,prep* visiting all the parts of a place, or a lot of different places: *They spent a year just travelling round.* | *We're driving round France this summer.* | *A guide showed us round the castle.* **5** *prep* near a place: *A lot of the people who live round here work in London.* **6** *adv* to someone's house: *He invited us round to his house for a meal.* | *Would you like to come round for a cup of tea?* **7 round a corner** turning a corner or past a corner: *He disappeared round the corner.* | *The post office is just round that corner.* **8 this way round, the other way round, the right way round, etc** a phrase used to say which way something is facing or in which order things are placed: *You've got that hat on the wrong way round.* | *Those two numbers should be the other way round.* **9 round about: a** about: *We've sold round about 200 cars this month.* | *It was round about five o'clock by the time we arrived.* **b** near a place: *Most of the people who live round about here have their own cars.* | *We've met quite a few people from this village and from the villages round about.*

round³ *n* **1** a set of events: *We're hoping for a new round of talks with the government.* | *Life seems to be a continual round of parties!* **2** a set of matches in a sports competition: *They were knocked out in the first round of the competition.* **3** a regular journey that someone makes to a number of houses or offices: *The milkman starts his round at five o'clock in the morning.* | *The doctor's out on his rounds at the moment.* **4 round of drinks** a drink for each person in a group: *Let me buy a round of drinks.* | *The next round's on me!* **5** a complete game of GOLF **6** one of the periods of fighting in a BOXING match **7** a bullet or something else fired from a weapon: *He fired a single round.* | *I had only two rounds of ammunition left.*

round⁴ *v* **round a corner** to go round a corner: *She rounded the corner at 95 miles per hour.*

round sthg ↔ **off** *phr v* [T] to end something in a suitable or satisfactory way: *Do you fancy a drink to round off the evening?*

round up *phr v* **1** [T **round** sthg ↔ **up**] to change a figure to the next highest whole number: *It's £2.99, so we'll round it up to £3.* **2** [T **round** sbdy ↔ **up**] to gather people together: *We should be able to round up a few friends to help.*

round·a·bout¹ /ˈraʊndəbaʊt/ *n BrE* **1** a central space at a road crossing, which cars must go round in a circle: *Turn left at the next roundabout.* –see picture on page 735 **2** a machine on which children can ride round and round sitting on wooden animals, cars, etc

roundabout² *adj* [only before a noun] not direct, and therefore taking longer: *We arrived in Birmingham by a rather roundabout route.* | *She told me in a very roundabout way.*

roun·ders /ˈraʊndəz ‖ -ərz/ *n* [U] a British ball game, usually played by children, in which a member of one team hits the ball and then runs round the edge of a square area

round-eyed /ˌ· ˈ·◂/ *adj* with your eyes wide open, usually because you are surprised or excited

round-shoul·dered /ˌ· ˈ··◂/ *adj* with bent shoulders and a curved back

round trip /ˌ· ˈ·◂/ *n* a journey to a place and back again

rouse /raʊz/ *v* **roused, rousing** **1** [I;T] to wake up, or to wake someone up: *He's very hard to rouse in the morning.* | *The noise roused me out of a deep sleep.* **2** [T] to make someone active and concerned: *John has roused the workers, and they are ready to strike.* | *roused from apathy* | *roused to action*

rous·ing /ˈraʊzɪŋ/ *adj* exciting, and encouraging people to act: *He made a rousing speech to his supporters.*

rout /raʊt/ *v* [T] to defeat your enemies or opponents completely: *The invading army was soon routed.*

rout sbdy ↔ **out** *phr v* [T] to find a person or thing, and often to make them move from where they are –**rout** *n* [C;U]

route¹ /ruːt ‖ ruːt, raʊt/ *n* a way which you plan or follow from one place to another: *What's the shortest route from London to Edinburgh?* | *It's not on the bus route.*

route² *v* **routed, routing** [T] to send people or things by a particular route: *All flights are being routed to Manchester.*

rou·tine¹ /ruːˈtiːn/ *n* **1** [C;U] a person's regular way of doing things: *I enjoy my daily routine.* | *Babies have different routines.* **2** [C] the performance of fixed steps, words, or actions in dance or theatre: *a dance routine*

rou·tine² /ˌruːˈtiːn◂/ *adj* **1** regular and usual: *a routine medical examination* **2** not unusual or exciting: *a dull, routine job* –**routinely** *adv*

row¹ /rəʊ/ *v* **1** [I;T] to move a boat through the water using OARS: *Shall we row to the island?* **2** [T] to carry people or things in this way: *He rowed his friends home.* –**row** *n* : *They've gone for a row round the lake.*

row² /rəʊ/ *n* **1** a neat line of people or things side by side: *I live in the row of houses beside the river.* | *The only seats left were in the back row.* **2 in a row** closely following each other: *She's failed three exams in a row.*

row³ /raʊ/ *n* **1** [C] a noisy quarrel: *My parents have had another row.* **2** [sing] a noise: *Will you stop making such a row!*

row⁴ /raʊ/ *v* [I] to quarrel noisily: *They always row about money.* | *He never rowed with his colleagues.*

row·dy /ˈraʊdi/ *adj* **rowdier, rowdiest** noisy and rough: *Their rowdy behaviour frightened me.* –**rowdily** *adv* –**rowdiness** *n* [U]

row house /ˈrəʊ haʊs/ *n* the usual American word for TERRACED HOUSE

row·ing boat /ˈrəʊɪŋ ˌbəʊt/ *n* (also **rowboat** /ˈrəʊbəʊt/ *AmE*) a small boat that is moved through the water using OARS –see picture on page 735

roy·al /ˈrɔɪəl/ *adj* **1** connected with a king or queen or their family: *Some of the royal palaces are open to the public.* | *the Royal Navy* **2 royal blue** a bright purplish-blue colour –see picture on page 147 –**royally** *adv*

Royal High·ness /ˌ·· ˈ··/ *n* a title used when you are speaking to or about a prince or princess: *Thank you, Your Royal Highness.* | *We hope that His Royal Highness, Prince Charles, will attend.*

roy·al·ist /ˈrɔɪəlɪst/ *n* someone who supports a king or queen, or believes that a country should be ruled by one –**royalist** *adj* : *He holds royalist views.*

roy·al·ty /ˈrɔɪəlti/ *n* **royalties 1** [U] royal power and rank **2** [+sing/pl verb] people of the royal family: *The flag is only raised when royalty is present.* **3 royalties** [pl] a payment made to people like writers and inventors as part of the profit from sales: *All the royalties from his books were given to charity.*

rpm /ˌɑː piː ˈem ‖ ˌɑːr-/ a measure of engine speed; an abbreviation for **revolutions per minute**

RSVP /ˌɑːr es viː ˈpiː/ *please reply*; an abbreviation for the French phrase **répondez s'il vous plaît**, which is written on invitations

rub¹ /rʌb/ *v* -**bb**- **1** [T] to press on a surface while you move something like your hand backwards and forwards: *Can you rub my back?* | *He rubbed his hands together with delight.* **2** [I] to press against another surface while moving backwards and forwards: *This tyre must be rubbing* **against** *something.* | *My new shoes have been rubbing* **on** *my heel.* **3 rub salt into the wound** to make someone's suffering or annoyance even worse **4 rub someone's nose in something** to make someone remember a mistake they have made **5 rub shoulders with someone** to meet someone, especially a well-known person **6 rub someone up the wrong way** to annoy someone by the way you talk or act with them

rub sbdy/sthg ↔ **down** *phr v* [T] **1** to dry a person or thing: *Rub yourself down with this towel.* **2** to make something smooth by rubbing it: *Rub the door down before you paint it.*

rub sthg ↔ **in** *phr v* [T] **1** to make a liquid go into a surface by rubbing: *Rub the polish well in.* **2** *infml* **rub it in** to keep talking about something

---

SPELLING NOTE

Words with the sound / r /, may be spelt **wr-**, like **wrong**.

---

that another person wants to forget: *"It was you who made the mistake." "I know; don't rub it in!"*

rub off *phr v* **1** [I;T] to come off a surface or to remove something from a surface by rubbing: *The paint marks will rub off quite easily.* **2** [I] *infml* to influence someone: *I hope that some of her good humour rubs off on him.*

rub sthg ↔ **on** *phr v* [T] to spread a liquid over a surface by rubbing

rub sthg ↔ **out** *phr v* [I;T] *BrE* to disappear or to remove something, especially writing, often with a piece of rubber: *Rub the first sentence out and start again.* | *Will it rub out?*

rub sthg ↔ **up** *phr v* [T] to polish something by rubbing it

rub² *n* [sing] an act of rubbing: *Give the table a good rub with this polish.*

rub·ber /ˈrʌbəʳ/ *n* **1** [U] a strong elastic substance, made either from the juice of a tropical tree or chemically, which can keep out water: *a rubber ball* | *Tyres are made of rubber.* | *rubber gloves* **2** [C] a piece of this substance, which is used to remove pencil marks **3** a match in the card game of bridge

rubber band /ˌ·· ˈ·/ *n* a thin circular piece of rubber which is used to keep things together: *Have you got a rubber band to put round these documents?*

rub·ber·y /ˈrʌbəri/ *adj* elastic like rubber and rather hard: *This meat's a bit rubbery!*

rub·bish /ˈrʌbɪʃ/ *n* [U] **1** waste material to be thrown away: *We can burn most of this rubbish.* | *a rubbish bin* **2** nonsense: *He's talking rubbish.* | *Rubbish! He's never even been as far as France!*

rub·bish·y /ˈrʌbɪʃi/ *adj infml* silly and worthless: *a rubbishy love story*

rub·ble /ˈrʌbəl/ *n* [U] broken stones, bricks or other materials: *The bomb reduced her house to a heap of rubble.*

ru·bel·la /ruːˈbelə/ *n* [U] *tech* the medical word for GERMAN MEASLES

ru·by /ˈruːbi/ *n* **rubies 1** [C] a dark red precious stone **2** [U] the colour of this stone –**ruby** *adj*

ruck·sack /ˈrʌksæk/ *n* a bag that you carry on your back, especially when you are climbing or walking

rud·der /ˈrʌdəʳ/ *n* a wooden or metal blade at the back of a ship or aircraft that moves from side to side to control the direction

rud·dy /ˈrʌdi/ *adj* **ruddier, ruddiest 1** pink and healthy-looking (used of a person's face) **2** red –**ruddiness** *n* [U]

rude /ruːd/ *adj* **1** not at all polite (of a person or behaviour): *It's rude to say you don't like the food.* | *Don't be so rude to your father.* **2** improper and usually concerned with sex: *a rude story* **3** [only before a noun] sudden and violent: *a rude shock* | *a rude awakening* **5 rude health** excellent health –**rudeness** *n* [U] –**rudely** *adv*

ru·di·men·ta·ry /ˌruːdɪˈmentəri◄/ *adj* at the simplest level and often not good enough: *I have only the most rudimentary knowledge of chemistry.* | *That's a rudimentary mistake.*

ru·di·ments /ˈruːdɪmənts/ *n* [pl] **the rudiments of** the simplest parts of (used of a subject): *We're just trying to learn the rudiments of Italian grammar.*

rue·ful /ˈruːfəl/ *adj* feeling or showing that you are sorry about something but that you accept it: *a rueful smile* –**ruefully** *adv*

ruff /rʌf/ *n* **1** a kind of stiff white collar with folds in it which was worn in Europe in the 16th century

2 a ring of fur or feathers round the neck of an animal or bird

ruf·fi·an /ˈrʌfiən/ n *old fash* a bad man who is often criminal and violent: *He was attacked by a gang of ruffians.*

ruf·fle¹ /ˈrʌfəl/ v **ruffled, ruffling 1** [T] to make uneven and untidy something that was neat and smooth: *She ruffled his hair affectionately.* | *The bird ruffled up its feathers.* **2** to annoy someone: *Don't get so ruffled.*

ruffle² n a band of cloth sewn in folds round the neck or wrists of a garment as decoration

rug /rʌg/ n **1** a thick floor mat, often made of wool – see picture on page 442 **2** a thick woollen covering which people use to keep themselves warm when travelling: *a tartan travel rug*

rug·by /ˈrʌgbi/ n (also **rugby football** /ˌ·· ˈ··/) *infml* **rugger** /ˈrʌgəʳ/) a type of ball game played by two teams; players win points by carrying or kicking an OVAL shaped ball to the opponents' end of the field –see picture on page 637

rug·ged /ˈrʌgɪd/ adj **1** rough and rocky: *rugged hills* **2** strongly built: *his rugged good looks* | *a rugged vehicle* –**ruggedly** adv –**ruggedness** n [U]

ru·in¹ /ˈruːɪn/ n **1** [U] the cause or state of destruction and decay: *The temple has fallen into ruin.* | *Drink was your father's ruin.* **2** [C] a building that has been badly damaged or destroyed: *We walked round the castle ruins.* **3 in ruins** badly damaged or destroyed: *Invaders left the city in ruins.* | *By the end of her speech, her career was in ruins.*

ruin² v [T] **1** to spoil or completely destroy a person or thing: *His complaints ruined the evening for everyone.* **2** to cause someone to lose all their money: *If I lose my law case, the costs will ruin me.* –**ruined** adj : *a ruined city*

ru·in·ous /ˈruːɪnəs/ adj causing destruction or total loss of money: *The cost of rebuilding will be ruinous.* –**ruinously** adv : *ruinously expensive*

rule¹ /ruːl/ n **1** [C] an instruction or principle which tells you what you must or must not do: *It's against the rules to pick up the ball.* | *Anyone caught breaking the rules will be punished.* **2** [C] a statement of the usual way of doing something: *the rules of grammar* **3 as a rule, as a general rule** usually: *He works hard as a rule.* **4 the rule** the way things usually are: *Companies providing childcare facilities are still the exception rather than the rule.* **5 rule of thumb** a rough guide to behaviour: *As a rule of thumb, you should expect to pay one third of your salary on rent.* **6** [U] government or control: *The country is now under foreign rule.* | *the days of British rule* **7** [C] a ruler for measuring lengths: *a two foot rule*

rule² v **ruled, ruling 1** [I;T] to govern or have power over an area or people: *The first king ruled for 30 years.* **2 rule the roost** to control a group of people: *It's my mother who rules the roost at home.* **3** [T; + that] to make an official and often legal decision: *The judge ruled that he should be allowed to see his children.* | *The committee ruled her actions unacceptable.* **4** to influence or control a person, their feelings or actions: *Don't let yourself be ruled by your personal feelings towards him.* **5** [T] to draw a straight line with the help of something like a ruler
rule sbdy/sthg ↔ **out** phr v [T] to dismiss something without considering it carefully: *We can't rule out the possibility that he'll come.*

rul·er /ˈruːləʳ/ n **1** a person who rules an area or people **2** a long, flat, narrow piece of a hard material

such as plastic, which has straight edges and is marked with inches or centimetres. It is used for measuring things or for drawing straight lines: *a 12-inch ruler*

rul·ing¹ /ˈruːlɪŋ/ n an official and usually legal decision: *The latest EEC ruling will be unpopular with British farmers.* | *the court's ruling on the matter* –compare RULE

ruling² adj [only before a noun] most powerful: *It was a popular revolt against the ruling classes.* | *His garden is his ruling passion.*

rum /rʌm/ n [U] a strong alcoholic drink

rum·ble /ˈrʌmbəl/ v **rumbled, rumbling 1** [I] to make a deep continuous rolling sound, often while moving: *The thunder rumbled in the distance.* | *The heavy cart rumbled through the village streets.* **2** *infml* to discover the truth about someone or something which was being hidden: *We've been rumbled; someone must have told the police.* –**rumble** n

ru·mi·nate /ˈruːmɪneɪt/ v **ruminated, ruminating** [I] to think carefully about something: *Let me ruminate over this plan of yours.* –**rumination** /ˌruːmɪˈneɪʃən/ n [U]

rum·mage /ˈrʌmɪdʒ/ v **rummaged, rummaging** (also **rummage around**) [I] to move things around while you are trying to find something: *Who's been rummaging through my papers?* | *Take one, don't just rummage about!* –**rummage** n

rum·my /ˈrʌmi/ n [U] a type of simple card game

ru·mour /ˈruːməʳ/ n (**rumor** AmE) [C;U] something that is talked about but may not be true: *Rumour has it that he's found a new job at last.* | *I heard a strange rumour about Jean at the club last night.* | *You mustn't spread rumours.* | *There are rumours of a spring election.*

ru·moured /ˈruːməd ‖ -əʳd/ v (**rumored** AmE) be rumoured to be talked about, although it may not be true: *It's rumoured that Jean's getting married.* | *The company is rumoured to be in serious difficulties.*

rump /rʌmp/ n the back part of an animal above the legs: *rump steak*

rum·ple /ˈrʌmpəl/ v **rumpled, rumpling** [T] to make something like hair or clothes untidy: *rumpled bedsheets*

rum·pus /ˈrʌmpəs/ n *infml* **kick up a rumpus** to make a lot of noise, or a noisy disagreement

run¹ /rʌn/ v **ran** /ræn/, **run, running 1** [I;T] to move along on your legs at a speed that is faster than walking: *The people ran to meet him.* | *She came running downstairs.* | *The dog ran after a rabbit.* | *He always runs three or four miles before breakfast.* –see picture on page 736 **2** [T;+adv/prep] to make something move quickly over or through something: *He ran his hand over the polished wood.* | *She ran her fingers through her hair.* **3** [I;+adv/prep] to pass or go somewhere: *The road runs along the river bank.* | *The stream runs along the bottom of that field.* | *There were tears running down her face.* **4** [I] (of a bus or train) to travel somewhere at an arranged time: *That train doesn't run on a Sunday.* **5** [T;+adv/prep] to take someone somewhere in a car: *I'll run you home if you like.* **6** [I] (of a machine) to work or be in operation: *Don't touch the engine while it's running.* | *Most cars run on petrol.* **7** [T] to operate something or make it work: *Can you just run the projector to check that it's working?* | *We don't have enough money to run the hospital properly.* | *I've got to run a couple of computer programs this afternoon.* **8** [T] to fill a bath with water: *I'm just running my bath.* | *Shall I run some water*

into the bath for you? **9 the tap is running** = water is coming out of the TAP **10 your nose is running** = liquid is coming out of your nose **11 a colour runs** = a colour on a piece of clothing spreads when it becomes wet: *Wash that shirt in cold water otherwise the colours will run.* **12** [I] to be one of the people trying to be elected in an election: *He has decided not to run* for *president again.* **13** [I] to last or continue happening for a particular period of time: *The play ran for 18 months.* | *My car insurance still has two months to run.* **14** [T] to control or be in charge of something: *They run a small export business.* | *We run all sorts of courses at the college.* **15** [T] to print a story or an article: *The magazine is running a series of features on European life.* **16 be running at** to be at a particular level: *Inflation is now running at 11%.* **17 be running late** to be taking longer than you had planned to do a number of things: *We were due to finish at lunch time, but we're running a bit late.* **18 run dry** (of a well) to no longer contain any water **19 run in the family** to be present in several members of a family: *Musical ability runs in the family.* **20 run low on something** to no longer have very much of something: *We're running a bit low on coffee.* **21 run short** to become less than enough: *Time is running short.* **22 run short of something** to no longer have enough of something: *We're running short of oil.*

run along *phr v* [I] used when you are telling a child to go away and leave you alone: *Run along and play now.*

run away *phr v* [I] **1** to escape from someone or something: *He was sent to boarding school but he ran away.* | *children who run away from home* | *He ran away with all my savings.* **2** to go away with someone of the opposite sex: *She ran away* with *her music teacher.*

run away with sbdy *phr v* [T] to make someone lose control of themselves: *Don't let your temper run away with you.*

run down *phr v* **1** [T **run** sbdy ↔ **down**] to knock down and hurt a person with a car or other vehicle: *Don't run into the road – you'll get run down.* **2** [T **run** sbdy/sthg ↔ **down**] to talk about someone or something in a way that shows that you do not like or respect them: *He shouldn't run me down in public like that.* **3** [T **run** sthg ↔ **down**] to reduce the size or importance of something: *The coal industry is gradually being run down.*

run in *phr v* **1** [T **run** sthg ↔ **in**] to use an engine gently for a while before you use it fully **2** [T **run** sbdy ↔ **in**] *infml* to catch someone who has done something against the law: *He was run in for possessing illegal drugs.*

run into *phr v* **1** [T **run into** sbdy/sthg] to hit someone or something with the car or other vehicle that you are driving: *I nearly ran into a lamp-post.* **2** [T **run into** sthg] to add up to a particular amount: *Her debts now ran into thousands of pounds.* **3** [T **run into** sbdy] to meet someone by chance **4** [T **run into** sthg] to meet a problem or difficulty: *We ran into problems with the authorities.*

run off *phr v* **1** [I] to go away with someone of the opposite sex: *She's run off* with *the man next door.* **2** [T **run** sthg ↔ **off**] to make a copy of a piece of

writing on a special copying machine: *I'll run off a few copies for you.*

run out *phr v* [I] **1** to come to an end or no longer be useful or acceptable: *Time is running out.* | *My car insurance runs out tomorrow – I must renew it.* **2** to no longer have enough of something: *I've run out of petrol.*

run sbdy ↔ **over** *phr v* [T] to hit someone and hurt them with the car or other vehicle that you are driving: *Mind you don't run that child over.*

run through sthg *phr v* [T] **1** to repeat something for practice: *Let's run through the first scene again.* **2** to read something quickly: *I'll just run through this list of figures.* **3** to be present in all the parts of something: *the prejudices that run through our society*

run sthg ↔ **up** *phr v* [T] **1** to cause bills or debts to grow: *I've run up debts of over £5,000.* **2** to raise a flag

run² *n* **1** an act of running: *I always go for a run before breakfast.* | *a five-mile run* **2** a journey by car or train: *Let's go for a run in the car.* | *We had quite a good run – it only took us 50 minutes.* **3** a period of time during which a play or film is shown every day: *The play had a run of three months.* **4 a run of** a group of similar events coming one after another: *I've had a run of bad luck recently.* **5 a run on** a lot of buying of something: *There's always a run on swimwear as soon as the weather warms up.* **6** an enclosed area where animals are kept: *a chicken run* **7** a point in a game of cricket or BASEBALL **8 a good run for your money** *infml* good results for the amount of effort that you have made or the amount of money that you have spent **9 in the long run** in the end, over a longer period of time: *Stone is more expensive, but in the long run it's better value.* **10 make a run for it** to try to escape by running away suddenly **11 on the run** trying to escape or hide from the police: *He's been on the run for nearly two months.* **12 the run of** the freedom to use a place and go anywhere in a place: *The children had the run of the house and garden.*

run·a·way /ˈrʌnəweɪ/ *adj* [only before a noun] **1** out of control: *a runaway horse* | *runaway inflation* **2** who has left the place where they are supposed to be: *a runaway child* **–runaway** *n*

run-down¹ /ˈ·· ·/ *n* a detailed report of events: *He gave me a run-down on everything that had happened while I was away.*

run-down² /ˌ·ˈ·◂/ *adj* **1** tired and rather ill: *When you feel run-down, it's time for a holiday!* **2** in bad condition: *We stayed in an old run-down hotel.*

rung¹ /rʌŋ/ *n* **1** one of the cross-bars that form the steps of a ladder **2** a level, especially of people at work: *I started on the bottom rung and now I run the company.*

rung² the past participle of RING

run·ner /ˈrʌnəʳ/ *n* **1** a person who runs, especially for sport or exercise: *She's a long-distance runner.* **2** a person who carries something illegal, such as guns or drugs, from one country to another **3** thin pieces of a material like wood which are fixed to the bottom of something and help it move easily: *sledge runners*

runner bean /ˌ·· ˈ·/ *n* a long green bean from a climbing plant

runner-up /ˌ·· ˈ·/ *n* **runners-up** the person or team that wins second place in a race or competition

run·ning¹ /ˈrʌnɪŋ/ *n* **1** [U] the act or sport of running **2 in the running** with some hope of succeeding in something: *Charles is in the running for the job of director.* [RELATED PHRASE **out of the running**]

SPELLING NOTE

Words with the sound / r /, may be spelt **wr-**, like **wrong**.

Transitive verbs

Ann   loves   apples

love, hit, thank and **enjoy** are all transitive verbs. This means that they must be followed by a noun or noun phrase as a direct object. If you take away the direct object, the sentence no longer makes sense.

subject	verb	object
Ann	loves	apples.
Sue	enjoys	playing tennis.
She	hit	the ball.
We	thanked	our teacher.

Note that you can add other nouns after the verb, but these are NOT direct objects:

We enjoy playing tennis <u>after work</u>.
She hit the ball <u>hard</u>.
We thanked our teacher <u>for her help</u>.

In the dictionary transitive verbs are shown like this: [T]

> **thank** /θæŋk/ v [T] **1** to show or tell someone that you are pleased that they helped you or gave you something: *I thanked him* **for** *his advice.* | *How can I ever thank you? You've been so helpful.*

Intransitive verbs

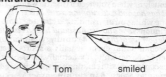

Tom   smiled

smile, sneeze, arrive and **rise** are all intransitive verbs. This means that their meaning is complete without a direct object.

subject	verb
Tom	smiled.
Ann	sneezed.
The train	has arrived.
The sun	is rising.

Note that you can add other nouns after the verb, but these are NOT direct objects:

Tom smiled <u>happily</u>.
The train has arrived <u>at platform 12</u>.
The sun is rising <u>over the mountains</u>.

In the dictionary intransitive verbs are shown like this: [I]

> **rise**[1] /raɪz/ v **rose** /rəʊz/, **risen** /ˈrɪzən/, **rising** [I] **1** to go up or move to a higher position: *The river is rising after the rains.* | *Smoke rose from the factory chimney.*

Verbs which can be both transitive and intransitive

Many English verbs can be used either transitively or intransitively

– sometimes with different meanings as in **study**:

> **study**[2] **1** [I;T] to spend time learning a subject: *She studies French.* | *She's studying to be a doctor.*

– sometimes with different meanings as in **fence**:

> **fence**[2] v **fenced, fencing** **1** [I] to fight with a long thin pointed sword as a sport **2** [T] to put a fence round something

The dictionary shows you when a verb can be both [I] and [T]. Read the examples carefully to find out how it is used in the two different ways.

Verbs which are followed by complements

Some verbs, like **become, seem** and **appear**, do not have [I] or [T] in their dictionary entry. Instead they are followed by the code [+ complement]. This means that they must be followed by another word for their meaning to be complete. These words can be nouns, adjectives, or adverbs, and they always tell us something about the subject of the sentence. Read the examples carefully to find out what kind of word is normally used.

> **be·come** /bɪˈkʌm/ v **became** /bɪˈkeɪm/, **become, becoming** **1** [+ complement] to begin to be something: *He became king in 1938.* | *The weather became warmer.*

running² *adj* [only before a noun] **1** flowing continuously or when you need it (used of water): *This hotel has hot and cold running water in every room.* **2** done while you are running: *a running jump* **3** continuous: *She and her husband have a running battle over use of the car.* **4 running commentary** an account of an event, usually a sports event, which is spoken while it is actually happening **5** for or concerned with running as a sport: *Where are my running shoes?* **6 in running order** working properly (used of a machine) **7 running costs** the money that you need to spend to keep something working

running³ *adv* one after the other; a word used after a number and a noun: *She won the prize three times running.* | *This is the tenth day running that it's snowed.*

running shoe /ˈ··· / *n* the usual American word for TRAINER²

run·ny /ˈrʌni/ *adj* **runnier, runniest** *infml* **1** more liquid than usual or than it should be: *This paint is too runny to use on the ceiling.* **2** producing liquid, often because you have a cold (used of your nose or eyes)

run-of-the-mill /ˌ··· ˈ·◄/ *adj* ordinary and unexciting (used to express disapproval): *He has a run-of-the-mill office job.*

run-up /ˈ·· / *n* **the run-up** the period of time leading up to an event, and the activities during that period: *There are more political broadcasts during the run-up to* an election.

run·way /ˈrʌnweɪ/ *n* a specially prepared hard, flat surface like a road, on which aircraft take off and land – see picture on page 735

ru·pee /ruːˈpiː/ *n* a unit of money in certain countries, such as India and Pakistan, or a note or coin worth that amount

rup·ture¹ /ˈrʌptʃəʳ/ *n* [C;U] **1** damage, especially to your body, which is caused by something breaking or bursting: *the rupture of a blood vessel* **2** *fml* the ending of relations between people

rupture² *v* **ruptured, rupturing 1** [I;T] *fml* to break or burst **2 rupture yourself** to give yourself a HERNIA: *She ruptured herself trying to move the sofa.* **3** [I;T] (of relations between people) to end

ru·ral /ˈrʊərəl/ *adj* concerning country areas and village life: *the peace and beauty of rural Britain*

ruse /ruːz ‖ ruːs, ruːz/ *n* a trick to deceive someone: *The plan was just a ruse to conceal his true intentions.*

rush¹ /rʌʃ/ *v* **1** [I;T] to move or to do something quickly: *There's plenty of time; we needn't rush.* | *The passengers rushed to get seats on the train.* | *Don't rush your breakfast!* **2** [T] to make someone hurry: *If you rush me, I'll do it badly.* **3** [T] to attack a person or thing suddenly: *Perhaps if we all rush him at once he'll drop his gun.* **4** [T;+adv/prep] to take a person or thing somewhere quickly: *He was rushed to hospital.* **5 rush someone off their feet** to make someone hurry too much or work too hard: *I've been rushed off my feet all day at the office and I'm exhausted.* **6 rush in, rush into something** to enter a situation too quickly and without thinking: *You're too young to rush into marriage.*

SPELLING NOTE
Words with the sound / r /, may be spelt **wr-**, like **wrong.**

rush sthg ↔ **out** *phr v* [T] to produce something very quickly: *Publishers are rushing out biographies of the new prime minister.*

rush sthg ↔ **through** *phr v* [T] to get something like a new law approved quickly

rush² *n* **1 a rush** a sudden rapid movement: *We made a rush for the best seats.* **2** [sing] hurry or great demand: *We needn't leave yet; what's the rush?* | *There will be a rush for tickets.* **3 the rush** a period of great activity: *I try and buy presents before the Christmas rush.* | *the morning rush* **4 rushes** tall, thin water plants whose stems are often dried and made into things like mats and baskets

rush hour /ˈ·· / *n* one of the periods in the day when people are travelling to and from work in a city and the streets are crowded: *Try not to travel in the rush hour.* | *rush-hour traffic*

rusk /rʌsk/ *n* a hard dry BISCUIT which is given to babies

rus·set /ˈrʌsɪt/ *adj lit* reddish brown

Rus·sian¹ /ˈrʌʃən/ *adj* from or connected with Russia or the USSR: *Russian ballet*

Russian² *n* **1** [C] a person from Russia or the USSR **2** [U] the main language of the USSR

rust¹ /rʌst/ *n* [U] a reddish brown substance that forms on iron and steel when they are attacked by water or air

rust² *v* [I;T] to cover something or become covered with rust: *I can't open the door because the lock has rusted.* – **rusted** *adj*

rus·tic /ˈrʌstɪk/ *adj* **1** concerning or typical of the country: *The village has a certain rustic charm.* **2** simple (used to express approval): *a rustic garden seat*

rus·tle¹ /ˈrʌsəl/ *v* **rustled, rustling 1** [I;T] to make or to cause something to make soft sounds when it moves gently: *Her long silk skirt rustled as she walked.* | *Stop rustling that newspaper and listen!* **2** [T] *AmE* to steal cattle or horses that are left loose in open country
rustle sthg ↔ **up** *phr v* [T] to find or prepare something quickly: *I'll rustle up something to eat while you unpack.*

rustle² *n* [sing] a soft sound caused by gentle movement: *a rustle of leaves* – **rustling** *n* [C;U] : *the rustling of papers in the library*

rus·tler /ˈrʌsləʳ/ *n AmE* a person who steals cattle or horses from open country – **rustling** *n* [U] : *They're suspected of cattle rustling.*

rust·y /ˈrʌsti/ *adj* **rustier, rustiest 1** covered with a reddish brown substance that forms on iron and steel when attacked by water or air: *a rusty nail* **2** mostly forgotten (used of a person's knowledge or ability in a particular area): *My French is rather rusty nowadays.* – **rustiness** *n* [U]

rut /rʌt/ *n* **1** a deep narrow track which a wheel leaves in soft ground **2** a fixed and uninteresting way of life or of doing things: *I've got into a rut at work, but I haven't got the courage to leave.*

ruth·less /ˈruːθləs/ *adj* cruel and without pity: *He has always been a ruthless manager.* – **ruthlessly** *adv* – **ruthlessness** *n* [U]

rye /raɪ/ *n* [U] a plant grown in cold countries for its grain and for flour: *rye bread*

S,s

S, s /es/ **S's, s's** or **Ss, ss** the 19th letter of the English alphabet

S a written abbreviation for SOUTH(ERN)

-'s /z, s/ v **1** a short form of "is": *What's that?* **2** a short form of "has": *He's gone.* **3** a short form of "us" (only in the phrase **let's**) **4** used to show who owns something: *Is that Jane's coat?*

■ USAGE Do not use **'s** as the short form for **is** at the end of a sentence. Compare *John's here* and *I don't know where John is.* The same is true of **'m** (short for **am**), **'re** (short for **are**), **'ll** (short for **will** or **shall**), **'d** (short for **would** or **had**), **'s** (short for **has**).

Sab·bath /ˈsæbəθ/ n **the Sabbath** a day of rest and prayer each week for followers of certain religions; Jews, for example, should not work on Saturdays

sab·bat·i·cal /səˈbætɪkəl/ n a period in which a person who works in education can leave their job to travel and study while still being paid: *Two of the history lecturers are away on sabbatical this term.*

sa·ble /ˈseɪbəl/ n **1** [C] a small animal that lives in northern Europe and Asia **2** [U] the fur of this animal, which is used to make expensive coats

sab·o·tage¹ /ˈsæbətɑːʒ/ n [U] intentional damage to an object or a plan, in order to weaken an enemy: *The telephones were not working and the police suspected sabotage.*

sabotage² v **sabotaged, sabotaging** [T] to cause intentional damage to an object or a plan in order to weaken an enemy: *a deliberate attempt to sabotage the country's economy*

sab·o·teur /ˌsæbəˈtɜːr/ n a person who intentionally damages an object or a plan, to weaken an enemy

sa·bre /ˈseɪbər/ n (**saber** AmE) a heavy military sword, or a light sword used in FENCING

sac·cha·rin /ˈsækərɪn/ n [U] a very sweet-tasting chemical which is used instead of sugar

sac·cha·rine /ˈsækəriːn/ adj **1** too sweet **2** too friendly, nice, or happy: *a saccharine love story*

sach·et /ˈsæʃeɪ ‖ sæˈʃeɪ/ n a small paper or plastic bag containing a quantity of something, for example SHAMPOO, all of which is used at the same time –see picture on page 148

sack¹ /sæk/ n **1** a large bag, usually made of strong plastic cloth, which is used for carrying things like coal and grain: *a sack of potatoes* **2 get the sack** *infml* to be dismissed from a job: *If you're late again, you'll get the sack.* [RELATED PHRASE **give someone the sack**]

sack² v [T] **1** to dismiss someone from their job: *She was caught stealing and sacked immediately.* **2** to destroy and steal from buildings in a conquered city

sack·ing /ˈsækɪŋ/ n [U] rough cloth for making sacks

sac·ra·ment /ˈsækrəmənt/ n an important Christian ceremony, such as marriage

sa·cred /ˈseɪkrɪd/ adj **1** holy because of a connection with God or religion: *sacred writings* | *sacred animals* **2** [only before a noun] connected with religion: *sacred music* **3** serious and important in the same way that religious things are: *a sacred oath* –**sacredness** n [U]

sac·ri·fice¹ /ˈsækrɪfaɪs/ n [C;U] **1** the act of offering something to a god or gods in a ceremony, often by

killing it: *The idea that anyone practises human sacrifice is ridiculous.* **2** something that is offered in this way **3** the act of giving up something important or useful for a particular purpose: *She made a lot of sacrifices to help her children go to university.* –**sacrificial** adj : *a sacrificial victim*

sacrifice² v [T] **sacrificed, sacrificing 1** to offer something as a sacrifice **2** to give up something important or useful for a particular purpose

sac·ri·lege /ˈsækrɪlɪdʒ/ n [U] treatment of a holy or widely admired thing which shows a lack of respect: *It would be sacrilege to destroy this beautiful old building.* –**sacrilegious** /-ˈlɪdʒəs/ adj

sac·ro·sanct /ˈsækrəsæŋkt/ adj too important to be changed in any way (a word that is often used in a humorous way): *I never take any work home at the weekend. My weekends are sacrosanct.*

sad /sæd/ adj **1** unhappy: *He looked sad and lonely.* | *It was a sad day for our team.* **2** undesirable and often deserving blame: *It's a sad state of affairs when our children aren't taught to read properly.*

sad·den /ˈsædn/ v [T] to make someone feel unhappy: *We were saddened by the news of his death.*

sad·dle¹ /ˈsædl/ n **1** a seat, usually made of leather, that you fit over the back of an animal such as a horse or camel **2** a seat on a bicycle or motorcycle **3** a piece of meat from the back of a sheep

saddle² v **saddled, saddling** [T] **1** to put a saddle on a horse **2** to give someone an unpleasant duty or responsibility: *He's saddled with a large house which he can't sell.*

saddle up phr v [I;T] **saddle** sthg ↔ **up**] to put a saddle on a horse

sad·dle·bag /ˈsædlbæg/ n a bag or a pair of bags fixed to the saddle on a horse, bicycle, or motorcycle

sa·dis·m /ˈseɪdɪzəm/ n [U] pleasure, which is sometimes sexual, from cruelty to other people –**sadist** n –**sadistic** /səˈdɪstɪk/ adj : *He took a sadistic delight in humiliating her.*

sad·ly /ˈsædli/ adv **1** with feelings of unhappiness: *I watched sadly as the old man was buried.* **2** unfortunately: *Sadly, she could not attend my wedding.*

sad·ness /ˈsædnəs/ n [U] a feeling of unhappiness

s.a.e. /ˌes eɪ ˈiː/ n an envelope which you put a stamp on and write your own address on; you send it to someone so that they can send something back to you: an abbreviation for **stamped addressed envelope**

sa·fa·ri /səˈfɑːri/ n a trip through wild country, especially in Africa, to hunt or watch large animals: *They're going on safari in Kenya.*

safe¹ /seɪf/ adj **1** in no danger: *I won't feel safe until the plane has landed.* | *For the moment we are safe from attack.* | *Your secret is safe with me.* **2 safe and sound** completely unharmed: *The child was found safe and sound at her grandparents'.* **3** not dangerous: *Is this a safe place to swim?* | *Keep these papers in a safe place.* | *a campaign for safe driving* | *a safe investment* **4** unlikely to be proved wrong: *It's safe to say that crime will continue at a high rate this year.* **5 in safe hands** with someone who can be trusted: *When the children are with my brother, I know they're in safe hands.* **6 to be on the safe side** to be sure that you are not taking a risk: *Carry a little more money with you, to be on the safe side.* –**safely** adv : *Did the parcel arrive safely?* | *I think I can safely say that he won't show his face in here again.* –**safeness** n [U]

safe² *n* a strong box or cupboard with thick metal sides and a lock, used for protecting valuable things from thieves

safe·de·pos·it box /ˌ· ·ˌ·· ˌ·/ *n* (also **safety-deposit box** /ˈ·· ·ˌ·· ˌ·/) a small box where you can store valuable objects, usually in a special room in a bank

safe·guard /ˈseɪfɡɑːd ‖ -ɡɑːrd/ *v* [T] to protect something from possible harm: *The new laws are designed to safeguard the rights of the individual.* –**safeguard** *n* : *safeguards against the misuse of government power*

safe·keep·ing /ˌseɪfˈkiːpɪŋ/ *n* [U] protection from harm or loss: *Put your important papers in the bank for safekeeping.*

safe sex /ˌ· ˈ·/ *n* [U] sexual activities in which people use contraceptives (CONTRACEPTIVE) to prevent the spread of disease

safe·ty /ˈseɪfti/ *n* [U] freedom from danger, harm, or risk: *My main concern is for the safety of my family.* | *She led the children to a place of safety.*

safety belt /ˈ·· ·/ *n* see SEAT BELT

safety cur·tain /ˈ·· ˌ·/ *n* a theatre curtain which will not burn if there is a fire; it is lowered at the front of the stage

safety pin /ˈ·· ·/ *n* a wire pin which is bent so that its sharp point is covered when the pin is being used to fasten two things together

safety ra·zor /ˈ·· ˌ·/ *n* a RAZOR with a cover above its blade to protect your skin from being cut

safety valve /ˈ·· ·/ *n* **1** a part of a machine which allows liquids or gas to escape when the pressure inside becomes too great **2** a way of expressing strong feelings, for example anger, without harming yourself or others: *Sport can be a safety valve for people under stress.*

sag /sæɡ/ *v* -**gg**- [I] to sink, bend, or hang downwards under pressure or because of lack of support: *The branch sagged under the weight of the apples.*

sa·ga /ˈsɑːɡə/ *n* a long story about a group of actions and events, often ones that are said to have happened a very long time ago

sa·ga·cious /səˈɡeɪʃəs/ *adj lit* wise

sage¹ /seɪdʒ/ *n* **1** [C] a person, especially an old man, who is wise as a result of long thinking and experience **2** [U] leaves from a plant, used in cooking

sage² *adj* wise as a result of experience and thinking for a long time: *his sage advice* –**sagely** *adv*

Sa·git·tar·i·us /ˌsædʒɪˈteəriəs/ *n* one of the signs of the ZODIAC

sa·go /ˈseɪɡəʊ/ *n* [U] a white food substance which is used for cooking sweet dishes with milk

said¹ /sed/ the past tense and past participle of SAY

said² *adj fml* **the said** [only before a noun] the one mentioned before: *Our first task was to find the murder weapon. The said weapon was discovered in Mr Law's garage.*

sail¹ /seɪl/ *n* **1** [C;U] a piece of strong cloth which moves a ship through the water when it is filled with wind: *Lower the sails!* **2** [C] **a sail** a short trip, usually for pleasure, in a boat with a sail: *Let's go for a sail this afternoon.* **3 set sail** to leave the shore

and begin a trip at sea: *On Thursday we set sail for New York.* **4** [C] any of the broad blades of a WIND-MILL, which move by the force of the wind

sail² *v* **1** [I+adv/prep; T] to travel on water or across an area of water in a ship or boat: *These boats sail between the islands.* | *We sailed the Pacific in eight days.* **2** [T] to direct or command a ship or boat on water *He sailed the ship while the captain slept.* **3** [I] to begin a journey across water: *We sail tomorrow at 10 o'clock.* **4** [I+adv/prep] to move smoothly and without pausing: *A flock of birds sailed across the sky.* | *She sailed past me without a word.* **5 sail through** to pass some kind of test easily: *All my children seem to sail through exams.*

sail·ing /ˈseɪlɪŋ/ *n* **1** [U] the skill of directing the course of a ship **2** [U] the sport of travelling in or directing a small boat with sails **3** [C] journey by ship: *When is the next sailing to France?*

sail·or /ˈseɪləʳ/ *n* **1** a person with a job on a ship, especially one who is not a ship's officer **2 a good sailor** a person who does not become sick on boats [RELATED PHRASE **a bad sailor**]

saint *n* **1** /seɪnt/ a person who is officially recognized after death as specially holy and worthy of formal honour in the Christian church **2** /seɪnt/ *infml* a person who is unusually unselfish or patient: *My mother was a real saint.* **3 Saint** /sənt; *strong* seɪnt/ (also written as **St**) a title which is used before a saint's name: *Saint Joan of Arc* | *St Francis*

saint·ly /ˈseɪntli/ *adj* like a saint: *a saintly man* | *She led a saintly life.* –**saintliness** *n* [U]

sake /seɪk/ *n* **1 for someone's sake** in order to help or please someone: *Do it for my sake.* **2 for the sake of** for a particular purpose: *He's just talking for the sake of hearing his own voice.* **3 for God's sake, for goodness sake, for pity's sake** phrases used to add force to what you are saying when you are annoyed: *For goodness sake, don't tell him!* | *For God's sake, can't you keep quiet for a minute!*

sa·la·cious /səˈleɪʃəs/ *adj fml* treating sexual matters in an improper or shocking way: *a salacious film* –**salaciously** *adv*

sal·ad /ˈsæləd/ *n* [C;U] a mixture of vegetables served cold and usually raw, sometimes with other foods added: *We'll have a green salad with the steak, so I need to get some lettuce.* | *Do you like chicken salad?*

sa·la·mi /səˈlɑːmi/ *n* [U] a large dark SAUSAGE with a strong taste

sal·a·ried /ˈsælərid/ *adj* earning a salary, as opposed to wages: *salaried workers* | *a salaried job*

sal·a·ry /ˈsæləri/ *n* salaries [C;U] money that you receive every month as payment for your job, especially if you are an office worker or a professional person, such as a teacher or lawyer: *I get a good salary.* | *He's on a salary of about £20,000 a year.* –see PAY² (USAGE)

sale /seɪl/ *n* **1** [C;U] an act or occasion of selling something: *The sale of my house hasn't been easy.* | *There's a second-hand clothes sale in the church hall today.* **2 for sale** offered to anyone who wants to buy it: *There are three houses for sale near us.* | *The sign said "For sale".* **3 on sale** in the shops for people to buy: *The latest model of this video recorder is now on sale in your high street.* **4** [C] a special offering of goods in a shop at lower prices than usual: *I got this hat cheap in the Harrods sale.* | *The sales are on so the streets are very crowded.* **5 sales** [pl] the total amount of something that is sold: *The company is hoping for improved sales this month.*

sales /seɪlz/ adj [only before a noun] concerned with selling something: *this year's sales figures* | *the sales department*

sales·clerk /'seɪlzklɑːk ‖ -klɔːrk/ n the usual American word for a SHOP ASSISTANT

sales·man /'seɪlzmən/ n **salesmen** /-mən/ a person, usually a man, whose job is to sell goods, either in a shop or directly to homes or businesses

sales·man·ship /'seɪlzmənʃɪp/ n [U] skill in selling or in persuading people to accept something

sales·wo·man /'seɪlz,wʊmən/ n **saleswomen** /-,wɪmɪn/ a woman whose job is to sell goods, either in a shop or directly to homes or businesses

sa·li·ent /'seɪliənt/ adj fml most noticeable or important: *Just tell me the salient points of her speech.*

sa·line /'seɪlaɪn/ adj containing salt: *a saline solution*

sa·li·va /sə'laɪvə/ n [U] the watery liquid produced naturally in your mouth

sal·i·vate /'sælɪveɪt/ v **salivated, salivating** [I] to produce more saliva than usual in your mouth, especially at the sight or thought of food

sal·low /'sæləʊ/ adj yellow and unhealthy-looking (used of a person's skin)

salm·on /'sæmən/ n [plural is **salmon**] [C;U] a large fish with silvery skin and pink flesh that is eaten as food: *I like salmon, but it's expensive.* | *smoked salmon*

sal·on /'sælɒn ‖ sə'lɑːn/ n a place of business, especially for beauty treatment or the sale of expensive clothes: *a hairdressing salon*

sa·loon /sə'luːn/ n 1 BrE (also **saloon car** /·'··/) a car for four to six passengers with a firm roof and a separate enclosed space for cases, bags, and boxes, etc. –see picture on page 49 2 a large room on a ship for the passengers to sit in 3 (also **saloon bar**, **lounge bar**) a comfortably furnished room in a PUB, where drinks cost a little more than in the other bars 4 a large public drinking place typical of the western US in former times

salt[1] /sɔːlt/ n 1 [U] a very common white substance found in the earth and in seawater which has many uses, including giving food more taste: *The vegetables need more salt.* | *Please pass the salt.* 2 [C] tech a chemical substance which may form when an acid and a metal combine 3 **salts** [pl] a mineral substance like salt which is used as a medicine or to make your bath smell sweet 4 **the salt of the earth** a person who is admired by other people

salt[2] v [T] to add salt to something: *Have you salted the vegetables?*

salt sthg ↔ **away** phr v [T] infml to hide something, usually money, away for the future

salt[3] adj containing or tasting of salt: *salt water* | *a salt lake*

salt·cel·lar /'sɔːlt,selər/ n a container for salt, used at meals

salt·wa·ter /'sɔːlt,wɔːtər ‖ -,wɔːr-, -,wɑːr-/ adj [only before a noun] living in or containing sea water: *saltwater fish*

salt·y /'sɔːlti/ adj **saltier, saltiest** containing or tasting of salt –**saltiness** n [U]

sa·lu·bri·ous /sə'luːbriəs/ adj fml or lit healthy or attractive: *This is not a very salubrious part of town.* –**salubriousness** n [U]

sal·u·ta·ry /'sæljʊtəri ‖ -teri/ adj fml useful because the effect is helpful: *The accident was a salutary experience; I'll never drink and drive again.*

sal·u·ta·tion /,sæljʊ'teɪʃən/ n [C;U] fml an expression of greeting through words or action: *He bowed in salutation.*

sa·lute[1] /sə'luːt/ v **saluted, saluting** 1 [I;T] to show someone respect with a special sign, such as the raising of your right hand to your forehead: *to salute your commanding officer* 2 [T] fml to honour and praise: *He saluted the splendid work of the local police.* 3 [T] lit to greet someone with words or a sign: *He saluted his friend with a wave.*

salute[2] n 1 [C] a military sign of respect for a person or an occasion, such as a raising of your right hand to your forehead or a ceremonial firing of guns 2 [C;U] lit a greeting 3 **take the salute** (of a person of high rank) to stand while soldiers march past and salute you

sal·vage[1] /'sælvɪdʒ/ n [U] 1 the act of saving things from destruction, especially of saving a wrecked ship or its contents from the sea 2 property which is saved from something that has been destroyed: *Salvage from the wreck will go to the maritime museum.*

salvage[2] v **salvaged, salvaging** [T] to save something from further damage: *We were unable to salvage anything when the factory burnt down.* | *Is there anything I can do now to salvage my reputation?*

sal·va·tion /sæl'veɪʃən/ n [U] 1 the means or state of being saved from the power and effect of evil, especially in the Christian religion: *praying for his salvation* 2 fml the means of saving a person or thing from loss, ruin, or destruction: *Business was terrible, but the new tax laws were our salvation.* 3 **the Salvation Army** a Christian organization which works to help poor people and whose members wear military uniforms

salve[1] /sælv, sɑːv/ n [C;U] an oily paste which you put on sore, cut, or burnt skin

salve[2] v **salved, salving** [T] lit **salve your conscience** to make yourself feel less guilty: *He rarely visited his mother, but he sent her expensive presents to salve his conscience.*

sal·ver /'sælvər/ n a fine metal plate, often made of silver, for serving food or drink

sal·vo /'sælvəʊ/ n **salvos** or **salvoes** a firing of several guns at once, in a ceremony or battle

Sa·mar·i·tan /sə'mærɪtən/ n 1 **a good Samaritan** a person who gives help to someone in need 2 **the Samaritans** an organization which gives help to people who are extremely unhappy and need someone to talk to

same[1] /seɪm/ adj 1 not changed or different: *He sits in the same chair every evening.* | *I don't want to make the same mistakes again.* 2 alike in every way: *Women and men should get the same pay for doing the same jobs.* 3 **one and the same** exactly the same 4 **same here** infml a phrase you use when you are agreeing with someone or saying that you have had a similar experience to them

same[2] pron the same thing: *John ordered a beer, and I asked for the same.* | *All the newspapers say the same.* | *Jane looks the same as ever.*

same·ness /'seɪmnəs/ n [U] the quality of being nearly or exactly the same: *We soon got bored with the sameness of the hotel meals.*

sam·ple[1] /'sɑːmpəl ‖ 'sæm-/ n a small part, quantity, or number which gives you information about something or a general idea of the whole of something: *The nurse took a blood sample for analysis.* | *These samples of a new washing powder came through the door today.* –**sample** adj

sample² *v* **sampled, sampling** [T] **1** to try or test a small part, quantity, or number of a whole thing or set of things: *She sampled the wine before filling the other glasses.* **2** to find out about something through a short experience of it: *I want to sample the pleasures of country life.*

san·a·to·ri·um /ˌsænəˈtɔːriəm/ *n* **sanatoriums** or **sanatoria** /-riə/ (also **sanitorium, sanitarium** *AmE*) a kind of hospital for sick people who need treatment or rest, often for long periods

sanc·ti·fy /ˈsæŋktɨfaɪ/ *v* **sanctified, sanctifying** [T] *fml* **1** to make something holy: *The priest sanctified the church with a special ceremony.* **2** to give something official approval or great importance: *These customs are sanctified by royal tradition.* –**sanctification** /ˌsæŋktɨfɨˈkeɪʃən/ *n* [U]

sanc·ti·mo·ni·ous /ˌsæŋktɨˈməʊniəs/ *adj* making a show of being extremely religious or moral (a word used to show disapproval): *sanctimonious behaviour* –**sanctimoniously** *adv* : *"I'd never do that," she said sanctimoniously.* –**sanctimoniousness** *n* [U]

sanc·tion¹ /ˈsæŋkʃən/ *n* **1** [C] an action, such as the stopping of trade, which is taken against a country that has behaved in an unacceptable way: *We will establish economic sanctions against any country that threatens to harm British citizens.* **2** [C] something that is intended to force people to obey a rule or moral standard: *"What about expelling these students from the university?" "Well, of course, that is the ultimate sanction."* **3** [U] *fml* official permission or approval: *The minister is acting with the sanction of Parliament.*

sanction² *v* [T] *fml* to accept, approve, or permit something: *The church would not sanction his second marriage.*

sanc·ti·ty /ˈsæŋktɨti/ *n* [U] the quality of being holy or so important that it should not be questioned: *These men have no respect for the sanctity of human life.*

sanc·tu·a·ry /ˈsæŋktʃuəri ‖ -tʃueri/ *n* **sanctuaries 1** [C;U] a place of protection or safety from harm: *He found sanctuary in his uncle's home.* **2** [C] an area where birds or animals are protected **3** [C] a building which is considered holy

sanc·tum /ˈsæŋktəm/ *n* **1** a holy place **2** your **inner sanctum** *infml* a private place or room where can be quiet and alone

sand¹ /sænd/ *n* **1** [U] loose material of many fine small grains which many beaches (BEACH) and deserts are made of and which is used for making things like cement and glass: *a heap of sand* | *children playing in the sand* **2** **sands** [pl] a large area of sand: *desert sands*

sand² *v* [T] **1** (also **sand** sth ↔ **down**) to make a surface smoother by rubbing it, usually with special rough paper: *Sand down the door-frames before painting them!* **2** to put sand on a surface

san·dal /ˈsændl/ *n* a light open shoe that is worn in warm weather –see picture on page 50

sand·bank /ˈsændbæŋk/ *n* a large raised mass of sand in a river or sea

sand·cas·tle /ˈsændˌkɑːsəl ‖ -ˌkæ-/ *n* a castle made by children out of sand

SPELLING NOTE
Words with the sound / s /, may be spelt **c-**, like **city**, or **ps-**, like **psychology**.

sand·pa·per /ˈsændˌpeɪpər/ *n* [U] special rough paper which you rub on surfaces to make them smoother –**sandpaper** *v* [T]

sand·pit /ˈsændˌpɪt/ *n* an enclosed hole or area which contains sand for children to play in

sand·stone /ˈsændstəʊn/ *n* [U] soft rock formed mainly from sand

sand·storm /ˈsændstɔːm ‖ -ɔːrm/ *n* a storm in which a strong wind blows large amounts of sand about, especially in a desert

sand·wich¹ /ˈsænwɪdʒ ‖ ˈsændwɪtʃ, ˈsænwɪtʃ/ *n* two pieces of bread with another food between them: *She made herself a chicken sandwich.*

sandwich² *v* [T] to put something between two other things, often so that it cannot move: *I found myself sandwiched between a group of teenagers and a brick wall.*

sandwich board /ˈ··· ·/ *n* a pair of advertising signs which hang over the front and back of a person who then walks about in public

sandwich course /ˈ··· ·/ *n* a course of study in which some periods are spent working for a company

sand·y /ˈsændi/ *adj* **sandier, sandiest 1** consisting of sand: *a sandy beach* **2** covered in sand: *My towel's all sandy.* **3** yellowish-brown (used especially of hair) –**sandiness** *n* [U]

sane /seɪn/ *adj* **1** having a healthy mind –opposite **insane 2** sensible: *The country needs a sane education policy.*

sang /sæŋ/ the past tense of SING

san·guine /ˈsæŋgwɨn/ *adj* *fml* quietly confident that there is no need to worry

san·i·ta·ry /ˈsænɨtəri ‖ -teri/ *adj* **1** of or concerned with health, especially the treatment or removal of human waste substances, dirt, or infection: *Sanitary inspectors will be visiting all local restaurants.* **2** clean and no threat to health: *The kitchen can't be very sanitary with all those flies about.*

sanitary tow·el /ˈ···· ·,··/ *n* (also **sanitary napkin** *AmE*) a small mass of soft paper which a woman may wear during her PERIOD to catch the blood

san·i·ta·tion /ˌsænɨˈteɪʃən/ *n* [U] means for protecting public health, especially by removing and treating waste

san·i·to·ri·um /ˌsænɨˈtɔːriəm/ *n* (also **sanitarium** /-ˈteəriəm/) the usual American spelling of SANATORIUM

san·i·ty /ˈsænɨti/ *n* [U] **1** the state of having a healthy mind: *She suffered temporary loss of sanity after her son's death.* **2** good sense and judgment: *We need someone to bring sanity to our meetings.*

sank /sæŋk/ the past tense of SINK

San·ta Claus /ˈsæntə klɔːz ‖ ˈsænti klɔːz, ˈsæntə-/ *n* see FATHER CHRISTMAS

sap¹ /sæp/ *v* **-pp-** [T] to weaken or destroy something, especially over a long period: *Her long illness gradually sapped her strength.*

sap² *n* [U] the watery liquid that carries food through a plant

sap·ling /ˈsæplɪŋ/ *n* a young tree

sap·phire /ˈsæfaɪər/ *n* [C;U] a bright blue precious stone

sar·cas·m /ˈsɑːkæzəm ‖ ˈsɑːr-/ *n* [U] speech or writing which clearly means the opposite to what is actually said and which is often intended to hurt someone: *"It was a great idea to leave the dog and the cat in the same room," she pointed out with heavy sarcasm.* –**sarcastic** *adj* : *a sarcastic remark* | *Do you have to be so sarcastic?* –**sarcastically** *adv*

sar·dine /ˌsɑːˈdiːn◂ ‖ ˌsɑːr-/ n 1 a small fish sold as food in tins and often preserved in oil 2 **like sardines** *infml* so close together that little movement is possible

sar·don·ic /sɑːˈdɒnɪk ‖ sɑːrˈdɑːnɪk/ adj showing complete lack of respect for people or matters that you consider unimportant or foolish: *a sardonic smile* –**sardonically** /-kli/ adv

sa·ri /ˈsɑːri/ n a length of light cloth that is wrapped around your body, worn especially by Hindu women –see picture on page 50

sa·rong /səˈrɒŋ ‖ səˈrɔːŋ, səˈrɑːŋ/ n a piece of cloth which is wrapped around the lower part of your body and tied at the waist, worn especially by Indonesian and Malaysian women and men

sar·to·ri·al /sɑːˈtɔːriəl ‖ sɑːr-/ adj fml concerning men's clothes or the way they are made

sash /sæʃ/ n a length of cloth which is worn round your waist or, usually as a mark of honour, over one shoulder

sash win·dow /ˈ· ˌ··/ n a window consisting of two frames with glass in them, which opens by sliding one of the frames up or down

sat /sæt/ the past tense and past participle of SIT

Sa·tan /ˈseɪtn/ n the Devil

sa·tan·ic /səˈtænɪk/ adj 1 evil or wicked 2 concerning the Devil

sat·an·ism /ˈsætənɪzəm/ n (also **Satanism**) [U] the worship of the Devil

satch·el /ˈsætʃəl/ n a small bag with a band for carrying over your shoulder, used by a child to carry things to and from school

sat·ed /ˈseɪtɪd/ adj **be sated with** fml to have reached the point when you do not want any more of something

sat·el·lite /ˈsætlˌaɪt/ n 1 a natural or man-made object which moves around a larger one in space: *The moon is a satellite of the Earth.* | *The broadcast came from America by satellite.* 2 a country or some form of organization that is dependent on a more powerful one

satellite dish /ˈ··· ˌ·/ (also DISH) n 1 the large round surface of a radio TELESCOPE 2 a small platelike object which people fix to their houses so that they can receive television pictures broadcast by satellites –see picture on page 441

sa·ti·ate /ˈseɪʃieɪt/ v **satiated, satiating** [T] to satisfy someone with enough, or even too much, of something: *We ate until everyone was completely satiated.*

sat·in /ˈsætn/ n [U] a kind of smooth and shiny silk cloth –**satin** adj: *satin pyjamas* –**satiny** adj: *satiny skin*

sat·ire /ˈsætaɪər/ n [C;U] a style, especially of writing, which attempts to show the foolishness of something by making you laugh at it: *The play is a satire on the government's defence policy.*

sa·tir·i·cal /səˈtɪrɪkəl/ adj (also **satiric**) using satire –**satirically** adv

sat·ir·ize /ˈsætɪˌraɪz/ v **satirized, satirizing** (also **satirise** BrE) [T] to try to make people laugh at a person or thing by showing their foolishness in an amusing way, especially in a work of literature: *She was arrested for writing a book which satirized the president and his family.*

sat·is·fac·tion /ˌsætɪsˈfækʃən/ n [U] 1 a feeling of pleasure which is the result of success: *We get great satisfaction from improving the house ourselves.*

–opposite **dissatisfaction** 2 fml the giving of something which is wanted or needed: *Take your complaint to the manager and demand satisfaction!* 3 **to someone's satisfaction** so that someone is pleased or believes that something is true: *The work was done to her satisfaction.* | *My version of events was proved to the satisfaction of the court.*

sat·is·fac·to·ry /ˌsætɪsˈfæktəri/ adj 1 good enough: *Jim's examination results are not satisfactory.* 2 pleasing: *This year's profits are very satisfactory.* –opposite **unsatisfactory** –**satisfactorily** adv

sat·is·fied /ˈsætɪsfaɪd/ adj 1 pleased or contented: *There goes another satisfied customer!* 2 certain: *I am satisfied that he is telling the truth.*

sat·is·fy /ˈsætɪsfaɪ/ v **satisfied, satisfied** [T] 1 to please someone: *Nothing I do ever satisfies my mother.* | *Some people are very hard to satisfy.* –opposite **dissatisfy** 2 to have or give what is wanted or needed: *First you must satisfy the college entry requirements.* | *Just satisfy my curiosity and tell me what happened next.* 3 fml to persuade someone that something is true: *Can you satisfy me that you were not involved in the fight?*

sat·is·fy·ing /ˈsætɪsfaɪ-ɪŋ/ adj giving pleasure: *a satisfying meal* | *a satisfying job* –**satisfyingly** adv

sat·su·ma /sætˈsuːmə/ n a fruit like a small orange, with skin that comes off easily

sat·u·rate /ˈsætʃəreɪt/ v **saturated, saturating** [T] 1 to make something extremely wet: *His shirt was completely saturated in blood.* | *a towel saturated with seawater* 2 to fill something completely: *The market is saturated with new products at the moment.* –**saturation** /ˌsætʃəˈreɪʃən/ n [U]

Sat·ur·day /ˈsætədi ‖ -ər-/ n (also **Sat.**) the day after Friday and before Sunday

Sat·urn /ˈsætən ‖ -ərn/ n the PLANET which is sixth in order from the sun and is surrounded by large rings

sat·ur·nine /ˈsætənaɪn ‖ -ər-/ adj lit solemn and unfriendly

sat·yr /ˈsætər/ n a god who is usually represented in ancient stories as half human and half goat

sauce /sɔːs/ n 1 [C;U] a thick liquid that is poured over or eaten with food: *ice cream with chocolate sauce* | *vegetables in a cheese sauce* 2 [U] infml disrespectful but usually harmless remarks, such as those a disobedient child might make to an adult: *I've had enough of your sauce; just do as you're told!*

sauce·pan /ˈsɔːspən/ n a deep metal cooking pot which has a handle and usually a lid –see picture on page 148

sau·cer /ˈsɔːsər/ n a small plate with curved edges which you put a cup on

sauc·y /ˈsɔːsi/ adj **saucier, sauciest** infml disrespectful in a way that is usually harmless and often amusing: *a saucy grin* –**saucily** adv –**sauciness** n [U]

sau·na /ˈsɔːnə ‖ ˈsaʊnə/ n 1 a period of sitting or lying in a room filled with hot steam, often followed by a cold bath 2 the room where you sit

saun·ter /ˈsɔːntər/ v [I + adv/prep] to walk in an unhurried way, and usually in a confident manner: *He sauntered off, looking as if he hadn't a care in the world.* –**saunter** n [sing]

saus·age /ˈsɒsɪdʒ ‖ ˈsɔː-/ n [C;U] a thin tube of animal skin filled mainly with meat and bread, which is eaten hot or cold: *Sausages and chips, please.* –see picture on page 344

sausage roll /ˌ··· ˈ·/ n a small quantity of sausage meat covered in pastry

sau·té /ˈsəʊteɪ ‖ səʊˈteɪ/ v **sautéed** or **sautéd, sautéeing** or **sautéing** [T] to cook something quickly in a little hot oil or fat: *Sauté the onions for five minutes.* –**sauté** adj : *sauté potatoes*

sav·age[1] /ˈsævɪdʒ/ adj **1** extremely cruel or violent: *a savage dog* | *a savage attack on her reputation* **2** [only before a noun] uncivilized: *savage customs* –**savagely** adv –**savageness** n [U]

savage[2] n an uncivilized person

savage[3] v **savaged, savaging** [T] to attack a person or animal and cause them serious harm: *I was savaged by a mad dog.*

sav·ag·e·ry /ˈsævɪdʒəri/ n [U] extreme violence or cruelty: *The judge was appalled by the savagery of his attack on his wife.*

sa·van·nah /səˈvænə/ n (also **savanna**) [C;U] a flat area of grassy land without trees, in a warm country

save[1] /seɪv/ v **1** [T] to prevent a person or thing being harmed or destroyed: *Help! Save me!* | *He saved his friend from falling.* | *I managed to save some of the furniture from the fire.* | *She saved his life.* **2 to save your life** infml however hard you try: *I couldn't pass an exam now to save my life!* **3 save face** to try to keep other people's respect: *She was late because she overslept, but she invented a car accident to save face.* **4** [I;T] to put something, especially money, aside for later use: *The children must learn to save.* | *I'm saving this pie for lunch tomorrow.* | *She saved her strength for the last minutes of the race.* **5** [T] to avoid unnecessary waste: *The council will save a lot of money by closing the leisure centre.* | *We'll save time if we go by car.* | *If you buy the family-size box it will save you £1.* **6 save your breath** to keep silent since there is no point in speaking: *I've already made a decision, so you can save your breath.* **7** [T] to make it unnecessary for someone to do something: *If we go out to eat, it'll save me cooking tonight.* | *Save yourself a lot of trouble and pay someone to do the work.* **8** [T] to stop the ball going into the net in some sports, such as football: *He saved three goals in the first half of the match.*

save on sthg *phr v* [T] to avoid wasting something: *We can all go in one car, to save on petrol.*

save up *phr v* [I] to put money aside for later use: *We're saving up to buy a new car.*

save[2] n a quick action by the GOALKEEPER in a game such as football, which prevents the opponents scoring a goal

save[3] prep (also **saving**) *lit* except (a word rarely used in modern English): *Save for one old lady, the bus was empty.*

sav·er /ˈseɪvər/ n **1** a person who puts money aside for future use, especially in a bank or BUILDING SOCIETY account **2 saver** something that prevents loss or waste: *The new motorway is a great time-saver for us.*

sav·ing[1] /ˈseɪvɪŋ/ n **1** the amount of something that is not lost or wasted: *We are hoping for a 30% saving in work time lost through illness.* **2 savings** [pl] money which is put aside for future use, especially in a bank or BUILDING SOCIETY account: *She won't need to touch her savings until she retires.*

SPELLING NOTE

Words with the sound / s /, may be spelt **c-**, like **city**, or **ps-**, like **psychology.**

---

saving[2] adj **1 a saving grace** a quality that makes something acceptable in spite of its weaknesses or faults: *The film's saving grace is its beautiful photography.* **2 saving** that prevents loss or waste: *labour-saving devices such as microwave ovens*

sa·viour /ˈseɪvjər/ n (**savior** AmE) **1** a person who saves someone else from danger: *She was her country's saviour during the war.* **2 the Saviour, our Saviour** Jesus Christ, in the Christian religion

sa·vour[1] /ˈseɪvər/ n (**savor** AmE) [sing;U] **1** a taste or smell **2** the power to interest someone

savour[2] v (**savor** AmE) [T] **1** to enjoy something, especially by tasting it slowly and purposefully: *She drank the wine slowly, savouring every drop.* | *He savoured every minute he spent with her.* **2 savour of** (of a situation or activity) to suggest something unpleasant: *His financial dealings savour of dishonesty to me.*

sa·vour·y /ˈseɪvəri/ adj (**savory** AmE) **1** salty rather than sweet (used of food) **2** pleasant or acceptable: *Her behaviour in this affair has not been very savoury.*

saw[1] /sɔː/ the past tense of SEE

saw[2] n a hand tool or power-driven tool for cutting hard substances such as wood or metal – see picture on page 638

saw[3] v **sawed, sawed** or **sawn** [I;T] **1** to cut something with a saw: *She sawed through a power cable by accident.* | *He sawed the logs into firewood.* **2** (also **saw at, saw away at**) to move something such as a knife backwards and forwards as if you are using a saw: *He sawed at the loaf of bread with the blunt knife.*

saw sthg ↔ **off** *phr v* [T] to separate something from something larger using a saw: *Will you saw off the dead branches?*

saw sthg ↔ **up** *phr v* [T] to cut something into pieces with a saw: *Saw this old table up so that it will fit in the dustbin.*

saw·dust /ˈsɔːdʌst/ n [U] a powder which is produced when wood is cut up: *The floor was covered in sawdust.*

sawn /sɔːn/ the past participle of SAW[3]

sax·o·phone /ˈsæksəfəʊn/ n (also **sax** infml) a metal musical instrument which you blow into, especially to play JAZZ –**saxophonist** /sækˈsɒfənɪst ‖ ˈsæksəfəʊnɪst/ n

say[1] /seɪ/ v **said** /sed/, **said**, 3rd person singular present tense **says** /sez/ **1** [I;T;+(that)] to express something in speech: *"I'd like another drink," he said.* | *She said she would come.* | *Don't believe anything he says.* | *I said no and I mean it!* | *Don't be afraid to say what you think.* | *Nobody would say you were lazy.* | *"What's he going to do now?" "I'd rather not say."* **2** [I;T; +(that)] to express something in words or by some other sign: *What does that notice say?* | *My watch says 5.30.* | *She didn't speak, but her expression said everything.* **3** [T] to repeat words that you have learned: *Say your prayers before you go to bed!* **4 say something to yourself** to think something: *"She's lying," John said to himself.* **5 I say** a phrase used to express surprise or to get someone's attention (it is not often used in modern English) **6 say, let's say**: a suppose; you can use these expressions when you want someone to consider a situation: *Say he refuses to help us. What are we going to do then?* | *Say he refused to help us. What would we do then?* **b** suppose; you can use these expressions when you are suggesting something: *"Say we meet at 5 o'clock. How would that be?" "Well, I think that's leaving it a bit* *late. Let's say 4.30."* **c** for example: *Let's go somewhere hot – Italy, say.* | *at an angle of, say, 60°* **7 that is to say** in other words **8 they say** the general feeling of most people is: *They say that too much sugar is bad for you, but it's never done me any harm.* **9 to say nothing of** a phrase used to add that something else should be considered: *Three people were hurt, to say nothing of the damage to the building.* **10 to say the least** a phrase used to suggest that you could express your feelings even more strongly: *I was upset by her attitude, to say the least.* **11 You can say that again!** *infml* a phrase used when someone has just said something which you strongly agree with: *"He hasn't been very easy to work with recently." "You can say that again!"* **12 You don't say, You don't say so!** *infml* phrases used to express surprise or, when spoken in a certain way, a lack of surprise

■ USAGE Compare **say** and **tell** in these sentences: *He said me he was tired.* | *He told me he was tired.* | *She said something.* | *She told me something.* **Say** cannot have a person as its object: *Please say something.* **Tell** often has a person as its object: *What's the problem? Please tell me.* If it has two objects, one of them must be a person: *Please tell me your secret.*

say² *n* [sing;U] the right to express an opinion which is then seriously considered: *The unions had very little say in the new pay agreement.* | *I want a say in any changes to the management structure.*

say·ing /ˈseɪ-ɪŋ/ *n* a well-known wise statement: *"There's no smoke without fire," as the saying goes.*

scab /skæb/ *n* **1** a hard mass of dried blood which forms over a cut or wound **2** *infml* a person who works in a place where other people are refusing to work because of a STRIKE²(2) (a word used to express disapproval)

scab·bard /ˈskæbəd ‖ -ərd/ *n* a leather or metal tube which holds the blade of a sword

scab·by /ˈskæbi/ *adj* covered with areas of dried blood which have formed over cuts or wounds

scaf·fold /ˈskæfəld, -fəʊld/ *n* a raised surface on which criminals were killed in the past: *He was led to the scaffold and executed.*

scaf·fold·ing /ˈskæfəldɪŋ/ *n* [U] poles and boards which are used to make a frame around a building for workmen to stand on

scald¹ /skɔːld/ *v* [T] **1** to burn with hot liquid: *The coffee was so hot that he scalded himself.* | *They were scalded to death by steam from a burst pipe.* **2** *tech* to heat a liquid like milk until it is nearly boiling

scald² *n* a skin burn caused by hot liquid or steam

scald·ing /ˈskɔːldɪŋ/ *adj* so hot that it can burn you: *scalding water* –**scalding** *adv* : *a scalding hot bath*

scale¹ /skeɪl/ *n* **1** [C] a set of numbers or standards for measuring or comparing things: *I am still at the bottom of the company's pay scale.* **2** [C] a set of marks, especially numbers, on an instrument which is used for measuring: *I need a ruler with a metric scale.* **3** [C] a set of numbers comparing measurements on a map or on a model with actual measurements: *This map uses a scale of 1 inch to the mile.* | *a scale of 1:25 000* **4** [C;U] the size of something, especially in relation to other things or to what is usual: *He has gone into business on a large scale.* **5 to scale** according to a fixed rule for reducing the size of something so that the measurements remain the same in relation to each other: *The plan of the building was carefully drawn to scale.* [RELATED PHRASE **out of scale**] **6 scales** [pl] a machine for weighing things: *He weighed himself*

on the bathroom scales. **7** [C] (also **scales** [pl]) a pair of pans for weighing an object by comparing it with a known weight: *a laboratory scale* **8** [C] a set of musical notes in upward or downward order from and to a particular note: *Start by playing the scale of A.* **9** [C] one of the small stiff pieces of skin which cover the body of animals like fish and snakes **10** [U] a substance which forms inside pipes and pots containing boiling water

scale² *v* **scaled, scaling** [T] to climb up something steep: *The burglar scaled the back wall and escaped.*
scale sthg ↔ **down** *phr v* [T] to reduce the size of something in a controlled way: *The company has begun to scale down its operations in Africa.*

scal·lop /ˈskɒləp ‖ ˈskɑː-/ *n* (also **scollop**) **1** a sea creature which can be eaten **2** one of a row of small curves forming an edge or pattern: *a dress with scallops around the neck*

scal·ly·wag /ˈskæliwæg/ *n* a person, especially a child, who behaves badly but without doing serious harm (a word which is often used in a humorous way)

scalp¹ /skælp/ *n* the skin on the top of your head, where your hair grows

scalp² *v* [T] (especially of North American Indians in the past) to cut the scalp off a dead enemy as a sign of victory

scal·pel /ˈskælpəl/ *n* a small sharp knife used by doctors during operations

scal·y /ˈskeɪli/ *adj* **scalier, scaliest** covered with scales (SCALE¹(9,10)) –**scaliness** *n* [U]

scamp /skæmp/ *n* a child who behaves badly but who you remain fond of

scam·per /ˈskæmpəʳ/ *v* [I + adv/prep] to run taking short quick steps, often playfully: *The children scampered off.* | *The mouse scampered into its hole.*

scam·pi /ˈskæmpi/ *n* [U] a dish of large prawns (PRAWN) covered in bread or flour and cooked in oil

scan /skæn/ *v* **-nn-** [T] **1** to look quickly at something written, without reading it carefully, often looking for a particular thing: *He scanned the list of names for someone he knew.* **2** to examine something closely, especially because you are looking for something: *The soldiers were scanning the sky for planes.* –**scan** *n* [sing] : *a quick scan of the paper* | *a brain scan*

scan·dal /ˈskændl/ *n* **1** [C;U] something which public feeling considers to be immoral and shocking: *The affair caused a scandal which led to the minister's resignation.* **2** [U] talk about someone's immoral and shocking behaviour: *All that newspaper prints is scandal!* **3 be a scandal** to be something that you strongly disapprove of: *It's a scandal that the streets aren't cleaned more often!*

scan·dal·ize /ˈskændəl-aɪz/ *v* **scandalized, scandalizing** (also **scandalise** *BrE*) to shock someone by doing something they consider morally wrong: *The clothes she wore to church scandalized the older people.*

scan·dal·ous /ˈskændələs/ *adj* morally offensive and shocking: *scandalous behaviour* –**scandalously** *adv*

Scan·di·na·vi·an¹ /ˌskændɪˈneɪviən/ *adj* of or connected with the peoples or languages of Denmark, Norway, Sweden, Finland, and Iceland

Scandinavian² *n* a person from one of the countries in Scandinavia

scan·ner /ˈskænəʳ/ *n* an ELECTRONIC instrument used for following or examining something closely:

The plane suddenly disappeared off their scanners. | *a brain scanner*

scant /skænt/ *adj* little, and often not enough: *He paid scant attention to what was said.*

scant·y /ˈskænti/ *adj* **scantier, scantiest** small in size or amount, and often not enough: *a scanty breakfast* | *scanty information* –**scantily** *adv* –**scantiness** *n* [U]

scape·goat /ˈskeɪpɡəʊt/ *n* a person who is blamed for something that others have done or have also done: *I was made the scapegoat for anything that went wrong.*

scar /skɑːʳ/ *n* **1** a mark on your skin from an old cut or wound: *The operation left a terrible scar.* **2** the effect of a very unpleasant experience: *Both countries bear the scars of last year's war.* –**scar** *v* -**rr**- [T]: *She was scarred by the accident, both physically and emotionally.*

scarce /skeəs ‖ skeərs/ *adj* **1** hard to find, and often not enough: *Food is becoming scarce in the cities.* –see RARE (USAGE) –compare COMMON **2** **make yourself scarce** *infml* to go away or keep away, especially in order to avoid trouble: *He told the children to make themselves scarce.*

scarce·ly /ˈskeəsli ‖ ˈskeər-/ *adv* **1** hardly: *She spoke scarcely a word of English.* | *"I didn't get hurt." "That's scarcely the point, is it?"* –see HARDLY (USAGE) **2** certainly not; a word you use to express strong opposition to an idea: *We can scarcely expect the child to travel alone!*

scar·ci·ty /ˈskeəsɪti ‖ ˈskeər-/ *n* **scarcities** [C;U] a situation in which there is not enough of something: *The floods caused a scarcity of food and drinking water.*

scare[1] /skeəʳ/ *v* **scared, scaring 1** [T] to frighten a person or animal: *Don't let the noise scare you: it's only the wind.* **2** **scare someone stiff** to make someone very frightened or nervous indeed: *Exams scare me stiff!* **3** [I] to become frightened: *She's a woman who doesn't scare easily.* **4** **scare someone into doing something** to frighten someone enough to make them do something

scare sbdy/sthg ↔ **away** *phr v* [T] (also **scare** sbdy/sthg ↔ **off**) to make a person or animal go or stay away by frightening them: *We've installed a burglar alarm to scare thieves off.*

scare[2] *n* **1** [sing] a sudden feeling of fear: *What a scare you gave me, disappearing like that!* **2** [C] a usually mistaken or unreasonable public fear: *a recent series of bomb scares*

scare·crow /ˈskeəkrəʊ ‖ ˈskeər-/ *n* an object in the shape of person which is put in a field to frighten birds away from crops

scared /skeəd ‖ skeərd/ *adj* **1** frightened or worried: *He was scared of the dog.* | *I'm scared of flying.* | *We're all scared that we might lose our jobs.* | *She's scared to leave the house.*

□ USEFUL PATTERNS be scared of something; be scared to do something; be scared that…

2 **scared stiff, scared to death** extremely frightened: *I was scared to death that he would return unexpectedly.*

scarf /skɑːf ‖ skɑːrf/ *n* **scarfs** *or* **scarves** /skɑːvz ‖ skɑːrvz/ a piece of cloth that you wear round your

---

SPELLING NOTE

Words with the sound / s /, may be spelt **c-**, like **city**, or **ps-**, like **psychology**.

---

neck, head, or shoulders to keep warm or to look attractive –see picture on page 50

scar·let /ˈskɑːlɪt ‖ -ɑːr-/ *adj* bright red: *She went scarlet with embarrassment.* –see picture on page 147 –**scarlet** *n* [U]

scarlet fe·ver /ˌ·· ˈ··/ *n* [U] a serious disease which gives you a very sore throat and red marks on your skin

scar·y /ˈskeəri/ *adj* **scarier, scariest** *infml* rather frightening: *a scary story*

scath·ing /ˈskeɪðɪŋ/ *adj* cruel in telling people what you think about a person or thing: *She was very scathing about my work.* | *He makes scathing remarks about my clothes.* –**scathingly** *adv*

scat·ter /ˈskætəʳ/ *v* **1** [T] to spread people or things over a wide area by moving or putting them there: *The loud noise scattered the birds.* | *His desk was scattered with papers.* **2** [I] to move quickly in different directions: *The crowd scattered when it began to rain.*

scat·ter·brain /ˈskætəbreɪn ‖ -ər-/ *n infml* a careless or forgetful person –**scatterbrained** *adj*

scat·ty /ˈskæti/ *adj* **scattier, scattiest** *infml* **1** careless or forgetful **2** mad: *Living with her would drive anyone scatty!*

scav·enge /ˈskævɪndʒ/ *v* **scavenged, scavenging** [I;T] to search for things to eat or use among used or unwanted food or objects: *At night you see homeless dogs scavenging for food.* | *We scavenged a few useful bits and pieces from the wreck of the car.*

scav·eng·er /ˈskævɪndʒəʳ/ *n* **1** a creature which feeds on decaying flesh or looks for food in waste matter **2** a person who scavenges

sce·na·ri·o /sɪˈnɑːriəʊ ‖ -ˈnæ-, -ˈne-/ *n* **scenarios 1** a brief description of the story of a film **2** a possible set of events: *She outlined several convincing scenarios for the outbreak of a nuclear war.*

scene /siːn/ *n* **1** [C] a part of a play, film, or book which describes the events happening in one place over a short period of time: *Is that the scene in which he kills his sister?* | *That speech comes in Act 2, Scene 3.* **2** [C] a view of a place, sometimes in a picture: *a peaceful country scene* | *He paints street scenes.* –see VIEW1 (USAGE) **3** [C;U] a place where something happens: *The murder weapon was found at the scene of the crime.* | *We're moving to the country for a change of scene.* **4** **on the scene: a** in or into the place where something has happened: *There had been an accident of some kind, and policemen started arriving on the scene.* **b** into public knowledge or use: *When did the video recorder really come on the scene?* **5 behind the scenes: a** out of sight of the people watching in a theatre **b** secretly: *Decisions are being made behind the scenes, and it's time we were told about them.* **6** [sing] *infml* an area of activity: *What do you think of the music scene in Britain?* | *the political scene* **7 not someone's scene** *infml* not something someone finds interesting: *Discos are just not my scene.* **8** [C] a show of anger or strong feelings, in public: *Don't make a scene here; people are watching.* | *The news caused angry scenes in Parliament.*

sce·ne·ry /ˈsiːnəri/ *n* [U] **1** natural surroundings, especially in beautiful and open country –see VIEW1 (USAGE) **2** the set of painted backgrounds and furniture used on a theatre stage to give an idea of the place where the action happens: *a piece of scenery*

sce·nic /ˈsiːnɪk/ *adj* having or showing attractive natural scenery: *We took the scenic route along the coast.* –**scenically** /-kli/ *adv*

scent¹ /sent/ n 1 [C] a pleasant smell: *the scent of roses* –see SMELL (USAGE) 2 [C;U] *BrE* a sweet-smelling liquid that women put on their skin: *a bottle of scent* 3 [C] the smell left behind by an animal 4 **on the scent of** making progress towards finding a person or thing: *We're on the scent of the killer.*

scent² v [T] 1 to feel the presence of something: *She scented danger.* 2 (especially of animals) to smell something, usually another animal

scent·ed /'sentɪd/ adj having a pleasant smell: *scented soap | rose-scented*

scep·tic /'skeptɪk/ n (**skeptic** *AmE*) a person who has doubts about the truth of other people's beliefs or claims

scep·ti·cal /'skeptɪkəl/ adj doubtful about one or many things that other people claim or believe: *I'm rather sceptical about the team's chances of winning.* –**sceptically** adv: *"It seems unlikely," he said sceptically.*

scep·ti·cis·m /'skeptɪsɪzəm/ n [U] doubt: *a claim which is being treated with some scepticism in Washington*

scep·tre /'septə‍ʳ/ n (**scepter** *AmE*) a rod carried by a ruler during ceremonies as a sign of power

sched·ule¹ /'ʃedjuːl ‖ 'skedʒul, -dʒəl/ n 1 a timetable: *Has the new train schedule been published? | This is my work schedule for the rest of the month.* 2 according to schedule in the way it was planned: *Is everything going according to schedule?* 3 **ahead of schedule, on schedule, behind schedule** before, at, or after the planned time: *We're about a week behind schedule.*

schedule² v **scheduled, scheduling** [T] 1 to arrange something for a certain time: *The meeting is scheduled to take place next week. | We've scheduled that trip for Friday.* 2 a **scheduled flight** a flight which appears on the regular airline timetable

scheme¹ /skiːm/ n 1 a plan or system for something: *He's got some new scheme to make money. | a health insurance scheme* 2 someone's **scheme of things** the way someone wants everything around them to be: *His sister getting married just didn't fit into his scheme of things.*

scheme² v **schemed, scheming** [I] to make plans in a way that is usually secret, clever, and morally unacceptable: *They're scheming to get the manager sacked.* –**schemer** n –**scheming** adj

schis·m /'sɪzəm, 'skɪzəm/ n [C;U] *fml* the separation of a group into two parts as a result of disagreement

schiz·oid /'skɪtsɔɪd/ adj tech like or suffering from schizophrenia

schiz·o·phre·ni·a /ˌskɪtsəʊ'friːniə, -sə-/ n [U] tech an illness of the mind which causes a person to live in their imagination and behave in strange and unexpected ways –**schizophrenic** /-'frenɪk/ adj, n tech

schol·ar /'skɒlə‍ʳ ‖ 'skɑː-/ n 1 a person with great knowledge of one or more ACADEMIC subjects 2 a person who has been given money by an organization to help pay for a course of study 3 **a good scholar, a bad scholar** a person who is or is not good at learning things they are being taught

schol·ar·ly /'skɒləli ‖ 'skɑːlərli/ adj concerned with serious detailed ACADEMIC study: *His new book is a scholarly work.*

schol·ar·ship /'skɒləʃɪp ‖ 'skɑːlər-/ n 1 [C] a sum of money given to a student by an organization to help pay for a course of study: *He won a scholarship to Oxford.* 2 [U] the method or result of serious detailed ACADEMIC study: *Her book is a fine piece of scholarship.*

scho·las·tic /skə'læstɪk/ adj concerning schools or teaching

school¹ /skuːl/ n 1 [C;U] a place of education for children: *That's the new secondary school. | I go to school by bus. | school uniform* 2 [U] the time spent at school: *What are you doing after school?* 3 [C + sing/pl verb] the students and teachers at a school: *The whole school was sorry when she left.* 4 [C;U] an establishment where a particular subject or skill is taught: *She goes to art school in London. | a school of dance* 5 [C] (also **School**) a department or college of certain universities in which a particular subject is taught: *the School of Law* 6 [C;U] the usual American word for university 7 [C] a group of people with the same style of painting, ideas, or opinions: *the Dutch school of painting* 8 a **school of thought** a group of people who have a shared opinion: *One school of thought says that hitting a child is the best form of discipline.* 9 [C] a large group of fish or other sea creatures swimming together

school² v [T] to teach or train a person or animal: *The children were schooled in obedience from a very early age.*

school·boy /'skuːlbɔɪ/ n a boy who attends school

school·child /'skuːltʃaɪld/ n **schoolchildren** /-tʃɪldrən/ a child who attends school

school·girl /'skuːlgɜːl ‖ -gɜːrl/ n a girl who attends school

school·ing /'skuːlɪŋ/ n [U] education at school: *He had only five years of schooling.*

school·mas·ter /'skuːlˌmɑːstə‍ʳ ‖ -ˌmæ-/ n a male teacher at a school (a word no longer used in modern English)

school·mis·tress /'skuːlˌmɪstrɪs/ n a female teacher at a school (a word no longer used in modern English)

school·teacher /'skuːlˌtiːtʃə‍ʳ/ n a teacher at a school

schoo·ner /'skuːnə‍ʳ/ n a fast sailing ship

sci·ence /'saɪəns/ n 1 [U] knowledge which depends on testing facts and stating general natural laws, or the study which produces this knowledge: *the marvels of modern science* 2 [C;U] a branch of such knowledge, such as chemistry: *She's taking exams in three science subjects.* –compare ARTS 3 [C;U] something that needs exact skill: *the science of cooking | military science*

science fic·tion /ˌ·· '··/ n (also **sci-fi** *infml*) [U] stories about imaginary worlds or imaginary scientific developments

science park /'·· ·/ n an area where there are a lot of companies that are concerned with new TECHNOLOGY and scientific study

sci·en·tif·ic /ˌsaɪən'tɪfɪk◂/ adj 1 [only before a noun] relating to science: *The microscope is a scientific instrument. | She has a scientific background.* 2 needing or showing exact skill or use of a system: *She has a very scientific approach to any problem.* –opposite **unscientific** (for 2) –**scientifically** /-kli/ adv

sci·en·tist /'saɪəntɪst/ n a person who works or studies in an area of science, especially chemistry, PHYSICS, or BIOLOGY: *nuclear scientists*

sci-fi /'saɪ-faɪ/ n [U] see SCIENCE FICTION

scim·i·tar /'sɪmɪtə‍ʳ/ n a curved sword, formerly used in the Middle East

scin·til·lat·ing /'sɪntɪleɪtɪŋ/ adj quick, clever, and interesting (used especially of speech): *scintillating conversation*

scis·sors /ˈsɪzəz ‖ -ərz/ n [pl] two sharp blades, fastened at the centre and with handles at one end, for cutting paper or cloth: *Have you got any scissors?* | *There's a pair of scissors in the drawer.* | *These scissors aren't very sharp.* –see PAIR (USAGE) –see picture on page 638

scoff /skɒf ‖ skɔːf, skɑːf/ v **1** [I] to laugh at a person or idea by making remarks that show you have a low opinion of them: *They just scoffed at my suggestion.* **2** [T] *infml* to eat something very fast and eagerly: *Don't scoff all those cakes!*

scold /skəʊld/ v [I;T] to express anger to someone about their behaviour (a word which is not used much in modern English): *Your father will scold you if he sees this mess.* –**scolding** n [C;U] : *She gave me a terrible scolding!*

scol·lop /ˈskɒləp ‖ ˈskɑː-/ n see SCALLOP

scone /skɒn, skəʊn ‖ skəʊn, skɑːn/ n a small soft round cake which is eaten with butter or JAM

scoop¹ /skuːp/ n **1** a container, or a special tool in the shape of a deep spoon, for picking up and moving liquids or loose materials: *a measuring scoop* **2** (also **scoopful** /-fʊl/) the amount held by this: *Two scoops of ice-cream, please.* **3** an exciting report that one particular newspaper manages to print before the public hears about it anywhere else

scoop² v **1** [T + adv/prep] to pick something up with a scoop or with your hand curved in the shape of a scoop: *He scooped up a handful of sand.* | *Can you scoop some sugar out of that bag?* **2** [T + adv/prep] to move something up with one quick, smooth movement: *She scooped the books into the rubbish bin.* **3** (of a newspaper) to print an exciting news report before any other newspaper
scoop sthg ↔ up phr v [T] to pick something up with a quick smooth movement

scoot /skuːt/ v [I] *infml* to go or go away quickly: *Scoot, before you do any more damage!*

scoot·er /ˈskuːtər/ n **1** (also **motor scooter** fml) a small motorcycle that does not move very fast **2** a child's vehicle with two small wheels which you move by pushing on the ground with one foot while the other foot rests on a narrow board between the wheels

scope /skəʊp/ n [U] **1** chance for action or thought: *There's a lot of scope for improvement in your homework, Jenny.* **2** the limits of a subject or activity: *I'm afraid that is outside the scope of our research.*

scorch¹ /skɔːtʃ ‖ -skɔːrtʃ/ v **1** [I;T] to burn slightly so that it has a mark or marks on it: *I've scorched my best shirt!* | *Heat it gently so that it doesn't scorch.* **2** [T] very dry indeed as a result of heat and no rain: *The garden is absolutely scorched!* **3** [I + adv/prep] *infml* to travel very fast

scorch² n (also **scorch mark** /ˈ· ˌ·/) a mark caused by a slight burn

scorch·er /ˈskɔːtʃər ‖ -ɔːr-/ n a **scorcher** *infml* a very hot day

scorch·ing /ˈskɔːtʃɪŋ ‖ -ɔːr-/ adj so hot that it can burn you: *It's scorching outside.* –**scorching** adv : *a scorching hot day*

score¹ /skɔːr/ n **1** [C] the number of points gained in a game, competition, or test: *The final score was*

SPELLING NOTE

Words with the sound / s /, may be spelt **c-**, like **city**, or **ps-**, like **psychology**.

---

two goals to nil. | *"What's the score so far?" "2–1."* | *He always gets high scores in IQ tests.* **2** [C] **a** a written copy of a piece of music **b** the music for a film or play **3 a score** 20 (a word which is no longer used in modern English) **4 scores** [pl] a large number: *There were scores of people waiting.* **5** [C] a cut in a hard surface **6** [C] harm that someone did to you in the past: *I've got some old scores to settle with him.* **7 know the score** *infml* to know the true, often unfavourable, facts of the situation **8 on that score** concerning the matter that has just been mentioned: *I've got enough money, so don't worry about me on that score.*

score² v scored, scoring **1** [I;T] to gain points in a game, competition, or test: *"He's got the ball... And he's scored!"* | *How many did the England team score?* | *He scored three goals.* **2** [I] to record the points won in a game while it is being played: *Will you score for us?* **3** [I;T] to succeed in something: *a well-known writer who has scored again with another popular book* | *The bomb scored a hit on the bridge.* **4** [I;T] to gain an advantage, especially in an argument: *I hate conversations where people try to score over each other.* | *I hate discussing things with him; he's only interested in scoring points off his opponent.* **5** [T] to cut or mark the top of a surface with a sharp instrument: *Score the paper before folding it.*
score sthg ↔ out phr v [T] fml (also **score sthg ↔ through**) to draw a line firmly through written words to show that they should not be read

score·board /ˈskɔːbɔːd ‖ ˈskɔːrbɔːrd/ n a board on which the points won in a game are recorded while the game is being played

scor·er /ˈskɔːrər/ n **1** a person who records the points won in a game while the game is being played **2** a player who wins points in a game

scorn¹ /skɔːn ‖ skɔːrn/ n **1** [U] strong and often angry feelings expressed when a person feels that something has no value: *He treats all my ideas with scorn.* **2 heap scorn on, pour scorn on** to show that you think something has no value at all –**scornful** adj –**scornfully** adv

scorn² v [T] **1** to refuse to accept something because you are proud or because it is not good enough: *She scorned our offers of help.* | *In those days unmarried women of her age were scorned by polite society.* **2** to feel or show strongly that a person or thing has no value

Scor·pi·o /ˈskɔːpiəʊ ‖ -ɔːr-/ n one of the signs of the ZODIAC

scor·pi·on /ˈskɔːpiən ‖ -ɔːr-/ n a small animal with a poisonous sting in its curving tail

Scot /skɒt ‖ skɑt/ n a person from Scotland

scotch /skɒtʃ ‖ skɑːtʃ/ v [T] fml to put an end to something: *How can we scotch these rumours?*

Scotch n (also **Scotch, Scotch whisky**) [C;U] a strong alcoholic drink (WHISKY) made in Scotland: *a bottle of Scotch* | *Two Scotches, please.*

scotch tape /ˌ· ˈ·, ˈ· ·/ n see SELLOTAPE

scot-free /ˌ· ˈ·/ adj [never before a noun] *infml* without harm or punishment: *Some of the children were punished, but the others escaped scot-free.*

Scot·land Yard /ˌskɒtlənd ˈjɑːd ‖ ˌskɑːtlənd ˈjɑːrd/ n [U + sing/pl verb] **1** the main office of the London police **2** the police who work there

Scot·tish /ˈskɒtɪʃ ‖ ˈskɑːtɪʃ/ adj (also **Scots** /skɒts‖skɑːts/) of or connected with Scotland

scoun·drel /ˈskaʊndrəl/ n a man whose behaviour is bad, selfish, and often criminal (a word which is only used in a formal or humorous way in modern English)

scour /skaʊəʳ/ v [T] 1 to search an area thoroughly for a person or thing: *scouring the horizon for a ship* 2 to clean something by rubbing its surface hard with something rough: *Can you scour those dirty pans?*

scour·er /ˈskaʊərəʳ/ n a piece of rough material which is used for cleaning cooking pots

scourge /skɜːdʒ ‖ skɜːrdʒ/ n something that causes great suffering to someone or something else: *Jack Evans, the self-appointed scourge of the political left*

scout¹ /skaʊt/ n 1 a soldier who is sent ahead to get information about the enemy 2 (also **boy scout**) a member of an association (**the Scouts**) which trains boys to have good characters and teaches them various useful skills 3 someone who tries to find suitable people for particular jobs 4 **a scout around** *infml* a search of an area: *Have a scout around for something to eat.*

scout² v

scout around for sthg *phr v* (also **scout for** sthg) [T] to look for something in different places: *He scouted around for a shop that sold guitars.*

scowl /skaʊl/ n an expression on a person's face which shows that they are not at all pleased – **scowl** v [I]: *She scowled at the pile of dirty plates.*

scrab·ble /ˈskræbəl/ v **scrabbled, scrabbling** [I] *infml* to move your fingers wildly and quickly, especially if you are looking for something: *She scrabbled about on the floor trying to pick up all the coins.*

scrag·gy /ˈskrægi/ adj **scraggier, scraggiest** thin and bony: *a scraggy dog*

scram /skræm/ v **-mm-** [I] *infml* to go away quickly: *You're not wanted here, so scram!*

scram·ble¹ /ˈskræmbəl/ v **scrambled, scrambling** 1 [I + adv/prep] to move quickly, especially over a rough surface or because you are in a hurry, often using your hands to help you: *I scrambled up the rock.* | *She scrambled to her feet.* 2 [I + adv/prep] to move quickly in competition with other people: *Customers scrambled for the few remaining loaves of bread.* 3 [T] to mix things so that they are not in their usual order: *The message has been scrambled for security reasons.* 4 [T] to mix the white and yellow parts of eggs together while cooking them: *scrambled eggs*

scramble² n [sing] 1 hurried and often difficult movement over a rough surface: *It's quite a scramble to get to the top of the hill.* 2 a disorderly struggle for something: *There was an undignified scramble for the best seats.*

scrap¹ /skræp/ n 1 [C] a small piece: *a scrap of paper* | *There isn't a scrap of evidence that she was involved.* 2 **scraps** [pl] bits of eatable food which are left after a meal and usually thrown away: *Give the dog those scraps.* 3 [U] material which has been used, and often thrown away, but which may still have some value: *scrap metal* | *scrap paper* 4 [C] *infml* a fight or quarrel which is not very serious: *He got into another scrap at school.*

scrap² v **-pp-** 1 [T] to get rid of something which is no longer useful or wanted: *Shall we scrap these plans and start again?* 2 [I] *infml* to fight or quarrel, but not very seriously

scrap·book /ˈskræpbʊk/ n a book of empty pages into which you can put things like newspaper articles or pictures that you want to keep safely

scrape¹ /skreɪp/ v **scraped, scraping** 1 [T] to remove something from a surface with a hard object: *Use a knife to scrape that dry paint off the washbasin.* 2 [T] to remove the surface of something with or on a hard object: *Could you scrape the carrots?* | *I scraped my leg when I fell.* 3 [I + adv/prep;T] to rub roughly against something: *He scraped his chair against the wall.* | *I hate the sound of fingernails scraping on the blackboard!* 4 **scrape a living** to manage to get just enough food or money to stay alive *We may have to scrape by on his salary alone.* 5 **scrape the bottom of the barrel** to use a person or thing that would be your last choice of all the possibilities

scrape along *phr v* (also **scrape by**) [I] to live with difficulty or with a small amount of money which is only just enough

scrape sthg ↔ **together** *phr v* (also **scrape** sthg ↔ **up**) [T] to collect an amount of something, especially money, from different places and with difficulty: *We should be able to scrape together enough money for a holiday this year.*

scrape through *phr v* [I;T] **scrape through** sthg] to succeed by performing in a way which is just acceptable: *She scraped through the exam by one mark.*

scrape² n 1 an act or sound of scraping 2 a sore area from which your skin has been scraped: *He suffered a few cuts and scrapes, nothing serious.* 3 *infml* a difficult situation you get into which is your own fault, but is not very serious: *As a child I kept getting into scrapes.*

scrap heap /ˈ··/ n 1 a pile of waste material, especially metal 2 **on the scrapheap** *infml* treated as useless

scrap·py /ˈskræpi/ adj **scrappier, scrappiest** untidy or badly organized, and often not complete: *a scrappy report*

scratch¹ /skrætʃ/ v [I; T] 1 to tear or mark a surface with something sharp or rough: *Did the cat scratch you?* | *The table top has been scratched.* | *Your dog was scratching at the door.* | *People scratch their names on the walls.* 2 to rub a part of your body lightly, usually with your fingernails (FINGERNAIL): *Stop scratching those mosquito bites!* | *The cat likes to be scratched behind its ears.* 3 **scratch your head** to think very hard about an answer or about what you should do, often rubbing your head lightly as you do so 4 to remove yourself or an animal from a race or competition before it starts: *I was scratched the day before the match.* | *This horse has been scratched.* 5 **scratch the surface** to begin to deal with something, but without getting to what is really important

scratch² n 1 [C] a mark or slight cut caused by something sharp or rough: *The cupboard looks new, except for a few scratches.* | *I got these scratches on my arm from picking roses.* 2 **without a scratch** *infml* without any hurt or damage at all: *The driver was seriously injured but his passenger escaped without a scratch.* 3 [sing] an act of rubbing a part of your body lightly: *The dog's having a good scratch.* 4 **from scratch** *infml* from nothing: *Instead of converting the garage, let's pull it down and start again from scratch.* 5 **up to scratch** *infml* at or to a good enough standard: *The team's performance just wasn't up to scratch.*

scratch·y /ˈskrætʃi/ adj 1 rough and uncomfortable (used of clothes) 2 making unpleasant sounds because of scratches on its surface (used of a record) 3 noisy to write with because it is damaged (used of a pen) – **scratchiness** n [U]

scrawl /skrɔːl/ v [T] to write something in a careless or untidy way –**scrawl** n : *Can you read her scrawl?*

scraw·ny /ˈskrɔːni/ adj so thin that the bones show through the skin (a word which is used of people or animals, and expresses disapproval)

scream[1] /skriːm/ v **1** [I] to cry out loudly on a high note, in fear, pain, or excitement: *The man was screaming with pain.* | *I screamed for help.* | *He screamed out a warning.* **2** [T; + that] to say something in this way: *He screamed a warning.* | *She was screaming that her finger was trapped.* | *"Get out!" he screamed.* **3** **scream with laughter** to laugh loudly and in an uncontrolled way

scream[2] n **1** [C] a sudden loud cry or a high note expressing pain, fear, or excitement: *We heard a terrible scream.* **2** [C] a noise that sounds like this: *screams of laughter* | *the scream of the electric saw* **3** [sing] infml a very funny person, thing, or event: *It was an absolute scream when she fell off her chair.*

scree /skriː/ n [U] a mass of small loose stones on the side of a mountain

screech /skriːtʃ/ v **1** [I] to make a high, sharp, and unpleasant sound: *He screeched in terror.* **2** [T; + that] to say something in this way: *"Leave me alone!" she screeched.* | *Birds were screeching above us.* | *The car screeched to a halt.* –**screech** n : *a screech of brakes*

screed /skriːd/ n a long and usually dull speech or piece of writing

screen[1] /skriːn/ n **1** a flat surface in a cinema on which a film is shown **2** **the screen, the big screen** films or the film industry: *This was written for the screen.* **3** the front surface of an electrical instrument, on which pictures and words are shown: *the television screen* | *a computer screen* –see picture on page 539 **4** an upright frame used as a small movable wall for dividing a room, for protecting people from cold air, or for hiding things from view: *The nurse will put some screens around your bed.* **5** something that protects, shelters, or hides things: *We're planting a screen of trees between the two houses.* | *She runs a travel company as a screen for her drug-smuggling operation.*

screen[2] v [T] **1** to shelter or protect a person or thing: *He screened his eyes with his hand as he looked into the sun.* | *I tried to screen her from their anger.* **2** to show a film or television PROGRAMME: *His new film is being screened on BBC1 tonight.* **3** to carry out medical tests on people to make sure they do not have a particular disease: *All older women are now being screened for breast cancer.* **4** to find out about people to see whether they are suitable for something: *A hundred carefully screened people were invited to have dinner with the President.*

screen sthg ↔ **off** phr v [T] to separate a part of a room from the rest: *We'll screen off this area here.*

screen·ing /ˈskriːnɪŋ/ n **1** [C;U] a showing of a film **2** [U] the process of finding out **a** whether people are ill, or **b** whether people are suitable for something

screen·play /ˈskriːnpleɪ/ n the written conversation, description, and instructions which are used in the production of a film

screw[1] /skruː/ n **1** a metal pin which is turned to push it into a surface where it is then fixed: *We need*

SPELLING NOTE

Words with the sound / s /, may be spelt **c-**, like **city**, or **ps-**, like **psychology**.

---

four large screws to hang that cupboard on the wall. **2** **have a screw loose** infml to be slightly mad

screw[2] v **1** [T +adv/prep] to fasten with one or more screws: *It won't move; it's screwed to the floor.* **2** [I; + adv/prep T; + adv/prep] to tighten something or fasten things together by turning: *Screw the two pipes together end to end.* | *Screw the lid on tightly.* | *The pieces screw together easily.* **3** **screw something out of someone** infml to get something from someone by force or by dishonest means: *See what you can screw out of him.* **4** **have your head screwed on** infml to be very sensible

screw sthg ↔ **up** phr v [T] infml **1** to twist something or change its shape from the usual one: *He screwed up the letter and threw it away.* | *She screwed up her eyes in the bright light.* **2** to ruin something or do it very badly: *You've really managed to screw everything up this time!* **3** **screw up your courage** to make yourself do something that you are afraid of doing: *He screwed up his courage and asked her to go out with him*

screw·driv·er /ˈskruːˌdraɪvəʳ/ n a tool with a narrow blade at one end, which is used to put screws into something or to remove them –see picture on page 638

scrib·ble /ˈskrɪbəl/ v **scribbled, scribbling** **1** [T] to write something carelessly or in a hurry, often so that it is hard to read: *He scribbled her a note.* **2** [I] to make meaningless marks with a pen or pencil: *The children will scribble on anything if you don't watch them.* –**scribble** n

scribe /skraɪb/ n a person employed to copy or record things in writing, especially before the invention of printing

scrimp /skrɪmp/ v **scrimp and save** to save money slowly and with difficulty by spending as little as possible: *She has to scrimp and save to buy clothes for the children.*

script /skrɪpt/ n **1** [C;U] the system of writing a language: *I'm learning to write the Arabic script.* **2** [U] writing done by hand, especially with the letters joined **3** [C] a written form of a speech, play, film, or broadcast: *Have the actors got their scripts yet?*

scrip·ture /ˈskrɪptʃəʳ/ n [C;U] holy writings, especially the Bible –**scriptural** adj

script·writ·er /ˈskrɪptˌraɪtəʳ/ n a person who writes the script for a film or broadcast

scroll /skrəʊl/ n **1** a long piece of paper or animal skin for writing on **2** an ancient book written on one of these

scrooge /skruːdʒ/ n (also **Scrooge**) infml a person who is not at all generous towards other people: *Oh, go on, give something towards his leaving present – don't be such an old Scrooge!*

scrounge /skraʊndʒ/ v **scrounged, scrounging** [I;T] to get something without paying for it (a word which is used to express disapproval): *He's always scrounging drinks and cigarettes off us.* –**scrounger** n

scrub[1] /skrʌb/ v **-bb-** **1** [I;T] to clean by rubbing hard, especially with a stiff wet brush: *Go on – scrub harder!* | *He's scrubbing the floor.* **2** [T] infml to stop something that was decided earlier: *We've had to scrub our holiday plans this year.*

scrub[2] n **1** a scrub an act of cleaning by scrubbing: *Give that floor a good hard scrub.* | *It needs a scrub.* **2** [U] low trees and bushes growing in poor soil

scruff /skrʌf/ n **1** **the scruff of the neck, the scruff of someone's neck** the flesh at the back of your neck, or your shirt collar: *He grabbed me by the scruff of the neck and shook me hard.* **2** *infml* a dirty and untidy person

scruf·fy /ˈskrʌfi/ *adj* **scruffier, scruffiest** dirty and untidy: *He always looks so scruffy.* −**scruffily** *adv* −**scruffiness** *n*

scrum /skrʌm/ *n* (also **scrummage** /ˈskrʌmɪdʒ/ *fml*) **1** an organized group of players from each team pushing against each other at particular times in a game of RUGBY **2** a disorderly struggling crowd

scrump·tious /ˈskrʌmpʃəs/ *adj infml* very good indeed (used especially of food): *What a scrumptious meal!*

scru·ple /ˈskruːpəl/ *n* **1** [C] a moral principle which stops you from doing something that is wrong: *I can't work for a man who has absolutely no scruples.* **2** [U] the feeling that what you do might be morally wrong: *He acted completely without scruple.*

scru·pu·lous /ˈskruːpjələs/ *adj* **1** careful about even the smallest detail: *He is known for his scrupulous research.* **2** careful to do only what is right: *She is scrupulous in her business activities.* −opposite **unscrupulous** (for 2) −**scrupulously** *adv* : *The room was scrupulously clean.* −**scrupulousness** *n* [U]

scru·ti·nize /ˈskruːtɪnaɪz/ *v* **scrutinized, scrutinizing** (also **scrutinise** *BrE*) [T] to examine something very carefully: *She scrutinized his work before allowing him to send it to clients.*

scru·ti·ny /ˈskruːtɪni/ *n* [U] careful and thorough examination: *Close scrutiny revealed a lot of errors.*

scu·ba-di·ving /ˈskuːbə ˌdaɪvɪŋ/ *n* [U] a sport in which you swim under water with a container of air on your back, breathing through a tube

scuff /skʌf/ *v* **scuff your feet** to walk along without picking up your feet properly, damaging the surface of your shoes

sculp·tor /ˈskʌlptər/ *n* an artist who makes sculptures

sculp·ture¹ /ˈskʌlptʃər/ *n* **1** [U] the art of shaping solid figures out of materials like stone or wood: *He's gone to art school to study sculpture.* **2** [C;U] work produced by this art: *There are some interesting sculptures in this church.*

sculpture² *v* **sculptured, sculpturing** (also **sculpt** /skʌlpt/) [T] to shape a solid work of art out of a material such as stone: *figures sculptured out of marble*

scum /skʌm/ *n* **1** [sing;U] an unpleasant sticky material on the surface of a liquid **2** [pl] very unpleasant people of the lowest kind: *The police treated the protesters like scum.* | *These hooligans are the scum of the earth.* −**scummy** *adj*

scur·ri·lous /ˈskʌrɪləs/ *adj fml* saying extremely offensive and unfair things about someone: *a scurrilous attack in the newspapers* −**scurrilously** *adv* −**scurrilousness,** −**scurrility** /skəˈrɪlɪti, skʌ-/ *n* [U]

scur·ry¹ /ˈskʌri/ *v* **scurried, scurried** [I +adv/prep] to move quickly with short steps: *The mouse scurried away.*

scurry² *n* [sing] a movement or sound of scurrying: *I heard the scurry of feet in the hall.*

scut·tle /ˈskʌtl/ *v* **scuttled, scuttling** [I +adv/prep] to run with short quick steps in order to escape: *The children scuttled away when they saw the policeman.*

scythe¹ /saɪð/ *n* a long-handled tool with a curved blade, used for cutting long grass

scythe² *v* **scythed, scything** [I;T] to cut grass with a scythe

a written abbreviation for SOUTHEAST(ERN)

sea /siː/ *n* **1** [C;U] the salty water that covers much of the Earth's surface: *boats sailing on the sea* | *sea water* | *sea travel* | *We sailed into quieter seas.* | *We went by sea, not by air.* | *We spent a week by the sea.* **2** [C] a large area of salty water smaller than an ocean, partly surrounded by land: *the Red Sea* | *the Mediterranean Sea* **3** [C] a strong movement of waves on the sea: *The ship ran into strong winds and heavy seas.* **4 at sea: a** working or travelling on the sea **b** *infml* not able to understand: *I'm all at sea with these new regulations.* **5 out to sea** away from the shore **6 a sea of** a large quantity of something spread out in front of you: *He looked out from the stage onto a sea of faces.*

sea·bed /ˈsiːbed/ *n* **the seabed** the land at the bottom of the sea

sea·far·ing /ˈsiːfeərɪŋ/ *adj* [only before a noun] having strong connections with the sea and sailing: *a seafaring man*

sea·food /ˈsiːfuːd/ *n* [U] sea creatures that you eat

sea·front /ˈsiːfrʌnt/ *n* the wide road next to the sea in a seaside town

sea·gull /ˈsiːgʌl/ *n* a rather large seabird with a loud cry

sea·horse /ˈsiːhɔːs ‖ -hɔːrs/ *n* a very small fish with a neck and head that look like those of a horse

seal¹ /siːl/ *n* **1** an official mark put on a paper that gives information or proof to show that it is really what it seems to be: *This letter carries the royal seal.* **2 someone's seal of approval** an official mark or statement to show that someone approves of something: *The headmaster has given their plan his seal of approval.* **3 put/set the seal on something** to be a sign that something **a** has officially ended or **b** will continue in the same way in the future **4** something fixed to a letter or container so that you can see whether anyone has opened it: *The seal on this bottle of pills is broken.* **5** a tight connection in a machine, for keeping a gas or liquid in or out: *The seal has worn and the machine is losing oil.* **6** a large sea animal with a tail and broad flat limbs for swimming; seals live mostly on cool sea-coasts

seal² *v* [T] **1** to close firmly: *She sealed the envelope.* | *a sealed envelope* **2** to close tightly or cover so that it is not possible for anything to get through: *The police sealed all the exits.* | *We've sealed all the holes.* | *The meat is sealed in polythene.* **3** to put an official mark on something **4** to make something certain or formal: *They sealed their agreement by shaking hands.*

seal sthg ↔ **in** *phr v* [T] to enclose something so that it cannot get out: *Brown the meat to seal in the juices.*

seal sthg ↔ **off** *phr v* [T] to close something so that it is impossible to go into it or get out of it: *After the explosion, the area was sealed off by the police.*

sea lev·el /ˈ· ˌ·· / *n* [U] the level of the sea, used as a standard for measuring the height of land: *500 metres above sea level*

sea li·on /ˈ· ˌ·· / *n* a sea animal of the Pacific Ocean which has broad flat limbs for swimming

seam /siːm/ *n* **1** a line of stitches joining two pieces of cloth **2** a narrow band of one kind of rock between large areas of other rocks: *a rich seam of coal*

sea·man /ˈsiːmən/ *n* **seamen** /-mən/ a sailor

sea·man·ship /ˈsiːmənʃɪp/ *n* [U] the skill of handling a ship and directing its course

seamed /siːmd/ *adj* deeply lined

seam·y /ˈsiːmi/ adj **seamier, seamiest** rough and immoral (not used of a person): *the seamy side of city life*

sé·ance /ˈseɪɑːns, -ɒns ‖ ˈseɪɑːns/ n a meeting where people try to talk to dead people, or receive messages from them

sea·port /ˈsiːpɔːt ‖ -pɔːrt/ n a large town on or near the coast to which large ships come

sear /sɪəʳ/ v **be seared on/into your memory** to be impossible to forget, usually because of being a very powerful experience

search[1] /sɜːtʃ ‖ sɜːrtʃ/ v **1** [I;T] to look carefully and thoroughly at or in a place when you are trying to find something: *We've searched the house from top to bottom.* | *The police searched the woods for the little girl.* | *She searched through her pockets for a cigarette.* **2 search for something** to try to find something: *They are searching for the missing child.* | *Scientists are still searching for a cure for the common cold.* **3** [T] to examine a person's body and clothing to try to find something: *The police searched the thief but found nothing.* **4 search your conscience** to think hard about whether you have acted correctly

search sthg ↔ out phr v [T] to find by searching

search[2] n **1** an act of searching: *a long search* for the lost treasure **2 in search of** looking for: *in search of happiness* | *He went in search of his long-lost brother.*

search·ing /ˈsɜːtʃɪŋ ‖ ˈsɜːr-/ adj determined to discover the truth: *She gave me a searching look.* | *a searching enquiry* **–searchingly** adv

search·light /ˈsɜːtʃlaɪt ‖ ˈsɜːr-/ n a powerful light used to find planes in the sky or people who have escaped

search par·ty /ˈ· ˌ··/ n **search parties** [C + sing/pl verb] a group of people looking for something or someone that is lost: *We sent out a search party.*

sear·ing /ˈsɪərɪŋ/ adj very painful and causing a burning feeling: *a searing pain*

sea·shell /ˈsiːʃel/ n a shell of a small sea animal

sea·shore /ˈsiːʃɔːʳ/ n [U] land along the edge of the sea, usually sand or rocks

sea·sick /ˈsiːˌsɪk/ adj feeling sick because of the movement of a ship on water **–seasickness** n [U]

sea·side /ˈsiːsaɪd/ n BrE **the seaside** a place by the sea where people go on holiday: *a holiday at the seaside* | *a seaside town* –see SHORE[1] (USAGE)

sea·son[1] /ˈsiːzən/ n **1** one of the four parts of the year, spring, summer, autumn, and winter: *Autumn is my favourite season.* **2** a period of time each year when something regularly happens: *the rainy season* | *the football season* | *the holiday season* **3 in season** easy to buy because it is the right time of year (used of fresh foods): *It's cheaper to buy fruit and vegetables that are in season.* **4 out of season:** **a** not easy to buy (used of fresh foods) **b** not at the busiest time of the year **5** a group of similar events, such as plays and concerts, given within a certain period: *a season of Shakespeare plays*

season[2] v [T] to give a special taste to food by adding salt, pepper, or a SPICE: *Season with a little paprika.*

SPELLING NOTE

Words with the sound / s /, may be spelt **c-**, like **city**, or **ps-**, like **psychology.**

---

sea·so·na·ble /ˈsiːzənəbəl/ adj fml suitable or typical for the time of year: *seasonable weather* **–seasonably** adv

sea·son·al /ˈsiːzənəl/ adj happening at a particular time of the year: *seasonal employment in the travel industry*

sea·soned /ˈsiːzənd/ adj with a great deal of experience: *a seasoned traveller*

sea·son·ing /ˈsiːzənɪŋ/ n [U] salt and pepper or similar things that you add to food to make it taste good

season tick·et /ˈ·· ˌ·· ‖ ˌ·· ˈ··/ n a special travel ticket which allows you to make as many journeys as you like within a certain period without having to pay each time

seat[1] /siːt/ n **1** something that you sit on, for example a chair: *What can we use for seats?* | *the back seat of a car* | *We sat in the best seats at the theatre.* **2 take a seat, have a seat** to sit down **3** the part on which you sit: *grass stains on the seat of his trousers* | *The seat of the chair is broken.* **4** a place as a member of an official body: *At the last election, the Labour Party won 252 seats.*

seat[2] v [T] **1** to have enough seats for a particular number of people: *a large hall which seats 950* **2 seated** sitting **3 Please be seated** a formal phrase used to ask someone to sit down

seat belt /ˈ· ·/ n (also **safety belt**) a fixed belt fastened around a person in a car or plane to protect them from sudden movement, especially in an accident –see picture on page 49

seat·ing /ˈsiːtɪŋ/ n [U] seats: *The hall has seating for three hundred.* | *the seating plan for the Football Club's annual dinner*

sea ur·chin /ˈ· ˌ··/ n a small ball-shaped sea animal that has a hard shell with many sharp points

sea·weed /ˈsiːwiːd/ n [U] a plant that grows in the sea

sea·wor·thy /ˈsiːwɜːði ‖ -ɜːr-/ adj in good condition and fit for a sea voyage (used of ships) **–seaworthiness** n [U]: *a certificate of seaworthiness*

sec /sek/ n infml a very short time: *Wait a sec.*

sec·a·teurs /ˈsekətɜːz ‖ ˌsekəˈtɜːrz/ n [pl] BrE strong scissors for cutting parts off garden plants

se·cede /sɪˈsiːd/ v **seceded, seceding** [I] fml to officially leave a larger country, group, or organization, especially because of disagreement **–secession** /sɪˈseʃən/ n [C;U]

se·clud·ed /sɪˈkluːdɪd/ adj very quiet and private: *a secluded country house*

se·clu·sion /sɪˈkluːʒən/ n [U] a state in which you are very quiet and private: *The famous actor now lives in seclusion.*

sec·ond[1] /ˈsekənd/ det, adv, pron **1** 2nd: *their second child* | *The second and third volumes are missing from the set.* | *"Did you win?" "No, I came second."* | *Maria's just had a baby. That's her second, isn't it?* **2** when you are speaking or writing and have several points you want to make, you can order them and number them **First...**, **Second...**, **Third...**, etc.: *There are several reasons why the plan will not work. First, there has not been enough preparation. Second, there is not enough money.* **3 in the second place** when you have several points you want to make, you can use this expression to introduce the second one: *They won't be interested in that house. In the first place, it's too far from where they work. And in the second place, it's more than* *they are prepared to pay.* **4 at second hand** from other people **5 second to none** *infml* the best: *As a tennis player, Ann is second to none.* **6 second only to something** not quite as good as something, but still very good

second² *n* **1** [C] a length of time equal to 1/60 of a minute: *The seconds ticked by.* **2** [C] a very short time: *Hang on just a second.* **3 seconds** [pl] goods sold cheaply because there is something slightly wrong with them

second³ *v* [T] to support a formal suggestion at a meeting so that argument or voting can follow: *"Will anyone second this motion?" "I second it, Mr Chairman."*

se·cond⁴ /sɪˈkɒnd ‖ sɪˈkɑːnd/ *v* **be seconded somewhere** *BrE fml* to be moved to a special duty for a limited time: *The finance officer was ill, so someone was seconded from another department to do his work.*

sec·ond·a·ry /ˈsekəndəri ‖ -deri/ *adj* **1** not as important as something else: *The question of public transport is secondary. We must spend more on developing our road networks.* **2 secondary education, secondary schools** education or schools for children over 11 years old, in Britain: *Are there many good secondary schools round here?* –compare PRIMARY **3** developing from something that happened earlier: *a secondary infection brought on by a cold*

secondary mod·ern /ˌ···· ˈ···/ *n* a school in Britain which does not prepare students for university or further study, common in the middle of the 20th century

second-best /ˌ··· ˈ·◦/ *adj* not quite as good as the best: *my second-best jacket*

second-class /ˌ··· ˈ·◦/ *adj,adv* **1** relating to the sending of letters by a system that is slightly cheaper and slower than the fastest one: *second-class letters | Ten second-class stamps, please. | How much is second-class postage these days? | I'm going to send that parcel second-class.* **2** relating to the ordinary class of travel by train or boat: *a second-class ticket | Two second-class returns to Birmingham, please.* **3** not as good or important as others: *He regards women as second-class citizens.* –compare FIRST-CLASS

second-hand /ˌ··· ˈ·◦/ *adj,adv* **1** used by an earlier owner, and not new: *a second-hand car | I got this book second-hand.* **2** [only before a noun] dealing in goods that are not new: *a second-hand shop* **3** passed on from someone else: *It was a second-hand report, based on what others had told him.*

sec·ond·ly /ˈsekəndli/ *adv* (also **second**) when you are speaking or writing and you have several points to make, you can order them using **Firstly**, **Secondly**, etc.: *There are several reasons why the plan will not work. Firstly, there has not been enough preparation. Secondly, there is not enough money.*

second na·ture /ˌ··· ˈ··/ *n* [U] a very firmly fixed habit: *It's second nature for me to lock the doors at night.*

second per·son /ˌ··· ˈ··/ *n* [sing] a form of the verb that you use with "you"

second-rate /ˌ··· ˈ·◦/ *adj* not very good: *a second-rate actor*

second thoughts /ˌ··· ˈ·/ *n* [pl] **1** doubts that a past decision or action was the correct one: *We had decided to sell our house, but then we began to have second thoughts.* **2 on second thoughts** a phrase

you use when you have suddenly changed your mind about something: *Let's go and see "Fury"… No, on second thoughts, there's a new French film at the Arts Centre.*

se·cre·cy /ˈsiːkrᵻsi/ *n* [U] **1** the keeping of secrets: *Secrecy is important to our plans.* **2** the state of being secret: *The secrecy of the plan was closely guarded.*

se·cret¹ /ˈsiːkrᵻt/ *adj* **1** kept from the view or knowledge of others: *secret plans | These plans must be kept secret* **from** *the enemy.* **2** [only before a noun] doing a particular thing only when other people will not find you (used of a person): *She became a secret drinker.* –**secretly** *adv*

secret² *n* **1** something kept hidden or known only to a few people: *Don't tell Mary about the party. It's a secret. | Can you keep a secret? | It's no secret that the two men dislike each other intensely.* **2** the unknown explanation of something: *the secret of how life on Earth began | What is the secret of your success?* **3 in secret** unknown to other people: *The two leaders met in secret.*

secret a·gent /ˌ·· ˈ··/ *n* a person gathering information secretly for a foreign government

sec·re·tar·i·al /ˌsekrəˈteəriəl/ *adj* of or concerning the work of a secretary: *secretarial college*

sec·re·tar·i·at /ˌsekrəˈteəriət/ *n* a department that manages the affairs of a government organization: *the United Nations Secretariat in New York*

sec·re·ta·ry /ˈsekrətəri ‖ -teri/ *n* **secretaries 1** a person with the job of preparing letters, arranging meetings, and so on, for someone else: *a job as private secretary* **to** *the company chairman* –see picture on page 539 **2** (also **Secretary**) a government minister at the head of a large government department: *the Foreign Secretary* **3** an officer of an organization who keeps records, writes official letters, and so on: *a union secretary*

se·crete /sɪˈkriːt/ *v* **secreted, secreting** [T] **1** (of an animal or plant) to produce a liquid **2** to hide

se·cre·tion /sɪˈkriːʃən/ *n* **1** [U] the production of a liquid by part of a plant or animal **2** [C] the liquid produced **3** [U] the act of hiding something

se·cre·tive /ˈsiːkrᵻtɪv, sɪˈkriːtɪv/ *adj* fond of keeping things secret (a word usually used to express disapproval) –**secretively** *adv* –**secretiveness** *n* [U]

secret ser·vice /ˌ··· ˈ··/ *n* the secret government department which tries to find out the secrets of enemy countries

sect /sekt/ *n* **1** a group of people with special beliefs, usually religious, which separate it from a larger group **2** an organized group of extreme people who think, unreasonably, that their ideas are the only correct ones

sec·tar·i·an /sekˈteəriən/ *adj* divided into sects or connected with the differences between sects: *sectarian differences | sectarian killings*

sec·tion /ˈsekʃən/ *n* **1** [C] a separate part of something: *a bookcase which comes apart into sections | signals controlling each section of railway track | She plays in the orchestra's woodwind section. | in the sports section of the paper* **2** [C;U] a representation of something as if it were cut from top to bottom and looked at from the side: *The architect drew the house in section.*

sec·tor /ˈsektər/ *n* **1** a part of a country's ECONOMY: *employment in the public and private sectors | the banking sector* **2** a part of a larger group

sec·u·lar /ˈsekjʊlər/ *adj* not connected with a church and not religious: *secular music*

se·cure¹ /sɪˈkjʊəʳ/ adj **1** safe: *Make sure your money is in a secure place.* | *a secure job* | *a secure investment* **2** tightly fastened or well protected so that no one can get in or out: *a secure door* | *a castle secure from attack* **3** feeling safe and not frightened or worried: *The little boy felt secure near his parents.* **4** firmly fixed: *Are you sure that shelf is secure?* | *a secure foundation* | *a secure belief in life after death* –opposite **insecure** (for **1,3**) –**securely** adv : *securely fastened*

secure² v **secured, securing** [T] **1** fml to get something after a lot of effort: *He's secured himself a good job.* **2** to fasten tightly: *They secured the windows when the storm began.* **3** to make safe: *The soldiers secured the camp against attack.*

se·cu·ri·ty /sɪˈkjʊərₐti/ n **securities 1** [U] the state of being secure: *Once the jewels were safely locked up in the bank, he had no more worries about their security.* | *A job in the Civil Service offers security.* | *the security of a good home and a loving family* **2** [U] something which protects: *The money is my security against hardship.* **3** [U] valuable property which you promise to give to a money-lender if you do not repay money you have borrowed: *What did you offer as security for the loan?* **4** [U] arrangements to keep people safe from attack, or to keep them in or out of a building: *For security reasons passengers have to be searched.* | *Tight security was in force during the President's visit.* | *the security forces* **5** [C] property in the form of shares

se·dan /sɪˈdæn/ n the usual American word for a SALOON car

se·date /sɪˈdeɪt/ adj not easily excited, and formal and unhurried in movement: *a calm, rather sedate manner* –**sedately** adv –**sedateness** n [U]

se·da·ted /sɪˈdeɪtₐd/ adj made sleepy or calm with a special drug –**sedation** /-ˈdeɪʃən/ n [U] : *He's under sedation and resting quietly in bed.*

sed·a·tive /ˈsedₐtɪv/ n a drug which causes sleep: *The doctor gave him a sedative to help him sleep.* –**sedative** adj

sed·en·ta·ry /ˈsedₐntₐri ‖ -teri/ adj fml sitting down, or done sitting down: *a sedentary job*

sed·i·ment /ˈsedₔmₐnt/ n [sing;U] solid material that settles at the bottom of a liquid

se·di·tion /sɪˈdɪʃən/ n [U] fml speaking, writing, or action intended to make people disobey a government –**seditious** ‖ -ˈdʊː∫əs/ : *a seditious speech*

se·duce /sɪˈdjuːs ‖ -ˈduːs/ v **seduced, seducing 1** [T] to persuade someone young and without sexual experience to have sex with you **2** [T + adv/prep] to encourage someone to do something wrong by making it seem attractive: *The warm weather seduced me away from my studies.* –**seducer** n –**seduction** /sɪˈdʌkʃən/ n [C;U]

se·duc·tive /sɪˈdʌktɪv/ adj having qualities likely to seduce: *a seductive voice* | *a seductive offer of higher pay* –**seductively** adv –**seductiveness** n [U]

see /siː/ v **saw** /sɔː/, **seen** /siːn/ **1** [I;T] to notice something with your eyes, or look at something: *Can you see the screen?* | *It was so dark that he could hardly see.* | *I can't see anything without my glasses.* | *Did you see that programme on television last night?* | *Shall we go and see a film?* | *You must go and see the Tower of London!* | *You ought to see how she*

SPELLING NOTE

Words with the sound / s /, may be spelt **c-**, like **city**, or **ps-**, like **psychology**.

---

dances! | *I saw him snatch the handbag and run.* | *I saw you talking to them.*

☐ USEFUL PATTERNS: to see something/someone; to see someone do something; to see someone doing something

2 [I;T] to understand something: *I don't see the logic of your argument.* | *He can't see why I want the day off work.* | *Do you see what I mean?*

☐ USEFUL PATTERN: to see how/why/what...

3 you see you use this expression when you are explaining something with information which will help another person to understand: *He's very worried about driving in London. You see, he's never driven in the city before.* **4** [T] to imagine something: *I can't see her lending me any money.* | *I don't see him changing his mind.* | *Nobody could see him as a married man.* | *I see no great advantage in expanding the company.* **5** [T] to believe that someone or something has a particular quality: *My mother still sees herself as a teenager.* | *I see his behaviour as unreasonable.* **6** [T] to meet or visit someone: *I'm going to see my Aunt.* | *She's too ill to see you.* | *We'll see you in the cafeteria.* | *You ought to see a doctor.* **7** [T] to find out something: *Let's see what time the train is.* | *I'll go and see if the postman's been.* **8** [T] to be present when something happens or to be the time when something happens: *In recent weeks we have seen a political crisis developing.* | *This century has seen huge social changes.* **9 see someone somewhere** to take someone somewhere: *I'll see you to the door.* **10 see that** to make sure that something is done: *See that you're home by eleven o'clock.* | *Will you see that all the doors are locked?* **11 what does she see in him?** = what does she find attractive about him? **12 see if you can** = try to do something: *See if you can get the report finished by next week.* **13 seeing that, seeing as** because: *Seeing as you're still here, you might as well help us to tidy up.* **14 see fit to do something** = to decide to do something, usually something which you think is wrong: *The government has seen fit to abolish this benefit.* **15 see red** to suddenly become very angry **16 have seen better days** to be old and in bad condition: *This coat's seen better days.* **17 see a lot of someone, not see much of someone, etc** to see someone often, not very often, etc: *We don't see very much of Philip these days.* **18 see the back of, see the last of** to finish doing something or finish dealing with someone: *I'll be glad to see the back of him!* **19 see the light: a** to understand something in the end: *He's finally seen the light and decided to scrap the project.* **b** to have a religious experience which makes you start believing in a particular religion **20 be seeing things** to be imagining that you can see things which are not really there **21 I see** a phrase you use to show that you understand something: *"You put the soap in here." "I see."* **22 you see** a phrase you use to show that you are explaining something or giving a reason: *"He's had an accident, you see."* **23 as I see it** = as I understand it: *As I see it, we need to recruit a few more people.* **24 I'll see, we'll see** a phrase you use when you do not want to decide something at once: *"Will you lend me the money?" "I'll see."* **25 let me see, let's see** a phrase you use when you are pausing to think about something: *Now, let me see, where did I put that list?* **26 see you, see you later** infml a phrase used to say goodbye to someone

■ USAGE Compare **see, look at, watch**. To see is to experience with the eyes, and it does not depend on what you want to do: *I wish I could forget the terrible things I saw during the war.* You **look at** something if you direct your eyes to it and try to see it: *Sometimes you have to* **look** *at a person to understand what they mean.* To **watch** is to look for some time at something that may move: *to* **watch** *television/a football match.* Compare *I* **saw** *him cross the road* (= I saw the whole journey from one side to the other) *and I* **saw** *him crossing the road* (= I saw him when he was halfway across). We can also **watch, feel,** and **hear** in these two ways.

see about sthg *phr v* [T] to make arrangements for something or deal with something: *I've got to go to the personnel department to see about my salary.*

see sbdy ↔ **off** *phr v* [T] to go with someone to the station or airport where they are leaving from, so that you can say GOODBYE to them: *We saw her off at the airport.*

see sbdy **out** *phr v* [T] to go to the door with someone when they are leaving a room or building: *I'll see you out.*

see through *phr v* **1** [T **see through** sbdy/sthg] to recognize that someone or something is false or not sincere: *I saw through him immediately.* **2** [T **see** sbdy **through** (sthg)] to help someone until the end of a difficult time: *I've only got a few pounds to see me through until I get paid.* | *We should have enough coal to see us through the winter.*

see to sthg *phr v* [T] to deal with something or make the arrangements for it: *Will you see to the holiday arrangements?* | *I must go and see to the dinner.*

seed¹ /siːd/ *n* **1** [C;U] a small thing produced by a flower from which another plant may grow: *grass seed* | *Sow the seeds in moist compost.* **2** [C] the beginning of something which develops later: *the seeds of future trouble* –**seedless** *adj* : *a seedless orange*

seed² *v* **1** [I] (of a plant) to produce seed **2** [T] to plant seeds in a piece of ground: *a newly-seeded lawn* **3** [T] to remove seeds from fruit **4** [T] (of tennis officials) to place tennis players in the order that they are likely to come in a tennis competition: *Navratilova has been seeded second.*

seed·ling /ˈsiːdlɪŋ/ *n* a young plant grown from a seed

seed·y /ˈsiːdi/ *adj* **seedier, seediest 1** having a poor, worn-out appearance: *a rather seedy and unpleasant part of the town* **2** *infml* slightly unwell: *feeling seedy* –**seedily** *adv* –**seediness** *n* [U]

see·ing /ˈsiːɪŋ/ *conj* (also **seeing that** /ˈ··· ·/, **seeing as**) *infml* as it is true that: *Seeing she's old enough to get married, I don't think you can stop her.*

seek /siːk/ *v* **sought** /sɔːt/, **sought** [T] *fml or lit* **1** to try to find or get something: *They sought shelter from the rain.* | *to seek the truth* | *We shall continue to seek* **for** *a solution to this problem.* | *Witnesses are being sought by the police.* **2 seek to do something** to try to do something: *The company is seeking to improve its profitability.* **3** to ask for: *You should seek advice from your lawyer.* –**seeker** *n* : *job seekers*

seek sbdy/sthg ↔ **out** *phr v* [T] to look for someone or something until you find them

seem /siːm/ *v* [not in progressive forms] **1** [I + complement] to appear or appear to be: *She always seems sad.* | *That seems a good idea.* | *That seems like a good idea to me.* | *There seems to be a problem of some kind.* | *There seems every hope that business will get better.* | *He seems to have forgotten the key.* **2 it seems that, it seems as if** it appears to be true that: *It seems as if there will be an election soon.* | *It seems that he has forgotten the key.* | *It seems to me that it's a waste of time.*

seem·ing /ˈsiːmɪŋ/ *adj* [only before a noun] *fml* that seems to be, but perhaps is not: *a seeming piece of good luck which later led to all kinds of trouble*

seem·ing·ly /ˈsiːmɪŋli/ *adv* as far as you can know: *Seemingly, there is nothing we can do.*

seen /siːn/ the past participle of SEE

seep /siːp/ *v* [I] to flow slowly through very small holes: *Water had seeped through the bathroom ceiling.*

see-saw¹ /ˈsiːsɔː/ *n* a board balanced in the middle for children to sit on at opposite ends so that when one end goes up the other goes down, used for fun

seesaw² *v* [I] to move strongly and suddenly up and down: *seesawing prices*

seethe /siːð/ *v* **seethed, seething** [I] **1 be seething with** to be full of people or things moving in a confused or excited way: *St Peter's Square was absolutely seething with tourists.* **2** to be extremely angry, although often not showing it openly: *By this time he was absolutely seething.* | *I silently seethed with rage* **at** *his thoughtlessness.*

see-through /ˈ· ·/ *adj* that you can see through or partly see through (used of material)

seg·ment¹ /ˈsegmənt/ *n* any of the parts into which something may be divided: *a large segment of the population* | *a dish of orange segments*

seg·ment² /segˈment/ *v* [I;T] to divide into segments –**segmentation** /ˌsegmənˈteɪʃən/ *n* [sing;U]

seg·re·gate /ˈsegrɪgeɪt/ *v* **segregated, segregating** [T] to separate different groups: *He went to a school where boys and girls were segregated.* | *Special cycle paths segregate bicycles* **from** *the rest of the traffic.* –compare INTEGRATE

seg·re·ga·tion /ˌsegrɪˈgeɪʃən/ *n* [U] **1** the separation of groups **2** the separation of a social or racial group from others, for example, by laws against using the same schools, hotels, or buses: *racial segregation*

seis·mic /ˈsaɪzmɪk/ *adj* *tech* relating to or caused by an EARTHQUAKE

seize /siːz/ *v* **seized, seizing** [T] **1** to take hold of something quickly and forcefully: *He seized my hand.* | *She seized hold of the child and pulled it away from the road.* **2** to take control of something by official order or by force: *Large quantities of drugs were seized by the police.* | *Anti-government forces seized the television station.* **3 seize on something, seize upon something** to accept something eagerly as soon as you get the chance: *She seized on the chance of a trip abroad.* **4 be seized by** to have a sudden urgent feeling: *He was seized by a sudden desire to see his native land again.*

seize up *phr v* [I] *BrE* (of part of a machine or your body) to become stuck and stop working

sei·zure /ˈsiːʒəʳ/ *n* **1** [U] the act of seizing: *The courts ordered the seizure of all her property.* **2** [C] a sudden attack of an illness, especially one in which your heart suddenly stops working: *Her father suffered a heart seizure.*

sel·dom /ˈseldəm/ *adv* not very often: *I seldom get up before nine o'clock.*

se·lect¹ /sɪˈlekt/ *v* [T] to choose someone or something: *He selected a shirt to match his suit.* | *He was selected to play for England.*

□ USEFUL PATTERNS to select someone for something; to select someone to do something

select² *adj* **1** carefully chosen **2** limited to the best people: *a select club*

se·lec·tion /sɪˈlekʃən/ *n* **1** [U] the act of choosing: *the selection of the England team for the World Cup*

2 [U] the fact of being chosen: *His selection as the new bishop was very unexpected.* **3** [C] a thing or person that is chosen from a larger group of things or people: *The orchestra played selections from Gilbert and Sullivan.* **4** [C] a collection of things that have been chosen, or of goods for sale: *The shop has a fine selection of cheeses.*

se·lec·tive /sɪˈlektɪv/ *adj* **1** not dealing with all, but choosing only a few for a special purpose: *selective controls on goods brought into the country for sale* | *They accused her of being highly selective in her reporting of the war.* **2** careful in choosing: *He is always very selective when he chooses his suits.* –**selectively** *adv*

se·lec·tor /sɪˈlektəʳ/ *n* a member of a committee choosing a sports team

self /self/ *n* **selves** /selvz/ **1** [C;U] a person's whole nature including their character and abilities: *I'm feeling better, but I'm still not quite my old self.* **2** [C] a part of your nature: *his better self*

self-ad·dressed /ˌ· · ·ˈ·◂/ *adj* a self-addressed envelope an envelope addressed for return to the sender: *Please enclose a self-addressed envelope with your order.*

self-as·sur·ance /ˌ· · ·ˈ·◂/ *n* [U] a sure belief in your own abilities –**self-assured** *adj*

self-ca·ter·ing /ˌ· ˈ···/ *adj* in which you cook your own meals (used of a place where you stay)

self-cen·tred /ˌ· ˈ···◂/ *adj* interested only in yourself, and not in other people

self-con·fessed /ˌ· · ·ˈ·◂/ *adj* [only before a noun] admitted by yourself to be a particular kind of person: *She is a self-confessed liar.*

self-con·fi·dence /ˌ· ˈ···/ *n* [U] belief in your own power to do things successfully –**self-confident** *adj*

self-con·scious /ˌ· ˈ···◂/ *adj* nervous and uncomfortable about yourself, wondering what other people are thinking about you –**self-consciously** *adv* –**self-consciousness** *n* [U]

self-con·tained /ˌ· ·ˈ·◂/ *adj* **1** not depending on help from outside **2 a self-contained flat/apartment** a set of rooms in a building to which you have your own entrance and which has its own bathroom and kitchen; they do not have to be shared with other people

self-con·trol /ˌ· ·ˈ·/ *n* [U] the ability to control your strong feelings: *I felt like hitting him, but I managed to keep my self-control.* –**self-controlled** *adj*

self-de·feat·ing /ˌ· · ·ˈ·◂/ *adj* having the effect of preventing its own success: *a self-defeating plan*

self-de·fence /ˌ· · ·ˈ·/ *n* [U] the act or skill of defending yourself from physical attack: *He shot the man in self-defence.*

self-de·ni·al /ˌ· · ·ˈ·/ *n* [U] the habit of not allowing yourself pleasures

self-de·ter·min·a·tion /ˌ· · ···ˈ··/ *n* [U] the right of the people of a place to make a free decision about the form of their government, especially whether or not to be independent of another country

self-dis·ci·pline /ˌ· ˈ···/ *n* [U] the ability to make yourself do the things that you must do

---

SPELLING NOTE

Words with the sound /s/, may be spelt **c-**, like **city**, or **ps-**, like **psychology**.

---

self-em·ployed /ˌ· ·ˈ·◂/ *adj* earning money from your own business and not being paid by an employer

self-ev·i·dent /ˌ· ˈ···◂/ *adj* clearly true, without need of proof

self-ex·plan·a·to·ry /ˌ· ·ˈ·····/ *adj* easy to understand and not needing any explanation (used especially of things like written instructions)

self-gov·ern·ment /ˌ· ˈ···/ *n* [U] government of a country or organization by its own people –**self-governing** *adj*

self-im·port·ance /ˌ· ·ˈ··/ *n* [U] thinking that you are more important than you really are –**self-important** *adj*

self-im·posed /ˌ· ·ˈ·◂/ *adj* that you have forced yourself to accept (used, for example, of a duty): *a self-imposed limit of three cigarettes a day*

self-in·dul·gent /ˌ· ·ˈ··/ *adj* [U] allowing yourself more pleasures and comfort than you should –**self-indulgence** *n* [U]

self-in·terest /ˌ· ˈ··/ *n* [U] concern for what is best for yourself, often hidden behind an appearance of caring for others: *It's sheer self-interest that makes her so kind to her elderly relatives.*

self·ish /ˈselfɪʃ/ *adj* caring only about your own advantage and not caring about other people: *He offered to help for purely selfish reasons.* | *Don't be so selfish!* –**selfishly** *adv* –**selfishness** *n* [U]

self·less /ˈselfləs/ *adj* always thinking about other people and not yourself –**selflessly** *adv* –**selflessness** *n* [U]

self-made /ˌ· ˈ·◂/ *adj* becoming successful and wealthy by your own efforts alone: *a self-made man*

self-pit·y /ˌ· ˈ··/ *n* [U] too much pity for yourself

self-pos·sessed /ˌ· ·ˈ·◂/ *adj* confident and having control over your own feelings and actions, especially in difficult or unexpected conditions –**self-possession** *n* [U]

self-pres·er·va·tion /ˌ· ···ˈ··/ *n* [U] the natural feeling that makes you keep yourself alive or free from trouble when you are in danger

self-re·li·ant /ˌ· ·ˈ·◂/ *adj* able to act without depending on help from other people –**self-reliance** *n* [U]

self-re·spect /ˌ· ·ˈ·/ *n* [U] the feeling that you need not be ashamed of yourself: *I refuse to ask him again. I value my self-respect.*

self-right·eous /ˌ· ˈ··◂/ *adj* too proud of your own rightness or goodness –**self-righteously** *adv* –**self-righteousness** *n* [U]

self-sac·ri·fice /ˌ· ˈ···/ *n* [U] the giving up of your own pleasure or interests for some good or important purpose or to help others –**self-sacrificing** *adj*

self-sat·is·fied /ˌ· ˈ···/ *adj* too pleased with yourself (a word used to show disapproval) –**self-satisfaction** /ˌ· ··ˈ··/ *n* [U]

self-seek·ing /ˌ· ˈ··◂/ *adj* doing things only to get an advantage for yourself: *a self-seeking politician* –**self-seeking** *n* [U]

self-serv·ice /ˌ· ˈ··◂/ *adj* working on the system where you serve yourself: *a self-service petrol station* | *Many restaurants are self-service these days.*

self-suf·fi·cient /ˌ· ·ˈ··◂/ *adj* able to provide for your own needs without outside help: *Britain is now self-sufficient in oil.*

self-suf·fi·cien·cy /ˌ· ·ˈ···/ *n* [U] **1** the ability to provide for your own needs without outside help **2** a system of farming in which the farm grows everything

sell /sel/ v **sold** /səuld/, **sold** 1 [I;T] to provide goods in exchange for money: *Do you sell matches?* | *He sold his house and bought a boat.* | *These days they sell bread at petrol stations.* | *She sold us her car for £4000.* | *She sold it to us for £4000.* | *It was sold before we arrived.* | *We sold fifty at £5 each.*
□ USEFUL PATTERNS to sell something to someone; to sell someone something
2 [I] to be bought: *Canned drinks sell well in a hot summer.* | *The tickets cost too much and did not sell.* | *They sell for about £1.* 3 [T] to make people want to buy things: *Bad news sells newspapers.* 4 **sell someone something** *infml* to make people think that something is a good idea: *He sold us the idea that we needed to replace our windows.* 5 **be sold on something** *infml* to think that something is a really good idea: *I'm really sold on this idea of taking a winter holiday.* 6 **sell yourself** *infml* to make your good qualities clear to people such as employers

sell sthg ↔ **off** *phr v* [T] 1 to sell all of one thing you own because you want the money for something else: *They have had to sell off the land to pay for the repairs to the house.* 2 to sell remaining or unprofitable goods or property, usually cheaply: *The garden centres are selling off the garden furniture now that summer is nearly over.*

sell out *phr v* [I] to sell all of what was for sale, so that there is nothing left: *"Is there any bread left?" "Sorry, we've completely sold out."* | *We've sold out of bread.* | *The tickets are sold out.*

sell up *phr v* [I;T **sell up** sthg] to sell a business: *They sold up and went to live in Spain.*

sell·er /ˈselər/ n a person who sells things

Sel·lo·tape /ˈseləteɪp, ˈseləu-/ n (also **sellotape**; **scotch tape** *AmE*) [U] *tdmk* sticky thin clear material sold in narrow rolls, and used for sticking things such as paper or cardboard together –**sellotape** v [T]

sell-out /ˈ··/ n 1 an event such as a concert or sports match for which all the tickets are sold 2 a failure to keep to your principles or promises, especially in politics

selves /selvz/ n the plural of SELF

se·man·tics /sɪˈmæntɪks/ n [U] the study of the meanings of words –**semantic** *adj*

sem·blance /ˈsembləns/ n a/some **semblance** of an outward appearance of something that usually does not really exist: *People were still shouting, but the chairman had managed to restore some semblance of order.*

se·men /ˈsiːmən/ n [U] the liquid produced by the male sex organs

se·mes·ter /sɪˈmestər/ n either of the two periods into which a year at universities in the US is divided

sem·i /ˈsemiː/ n *AmE* a large lorry

sem·i·cir·cle /ˈsemiˌsɜːkəl/ ‖ -ɜːr-/ n half a circle –**semicircular** /ˌsemiˈsɜːkjələr/ ‖ -ˈsɜːr-/ *adj*

sem·i·co·lon /ˌsemiˈkəʊlən ‖ ˈsemiˌkəʊlən/ n the mark (;) used to separate different members of lists and independent parts of a sentence

sem·i·de·tached /ˌsemidɪˈtætʃt◂/ *adj* that is one of a pair of houses joined to each other –**semidetached** n

sem·i·fi·nal /ˌsemiˈfaɪnl◂ ‖ ˈsemiˌfaɪnl/ n one of a pair or set of matches whose winners then compete against one another to decide the winner of the whole competition

sem·i·nar /ˈsemɪnɑːr/ n 1 a study meeting for university students with a teacher 2 a meeting organized by a business in which managers, other people who work in business, or the general public can learn about a particular business subject

sem·i·na·ry /ˈsemɪnəri ‖ -neri/ n **seminaries** a college for training priests

sem·i·pre·cious /ˌsemiˈpreʃəs◂/ *adj* of lower value than a PRECIOUS STONE (used of a jewel or stone): *Set with opals and other semi-precious stones*

sem·o·li·na /ˌseməˈliːnə◂/ n [U] a powder made from wheat, used in producing PASTA

Sen·ate /ˈsenɪt/ n [+ sing/pl verb] the upper house of parliament in the US and some other countries: *The Senate has voted to support the President's plans for the economy.* –compare CONGRESS

sen·a·tor /ˈsenətər/ n (also **Senator**) a member of a Senate: *Senator John Dole*

send /send/ v **sent** /sent/, **sent** 1 [T] to cause something to go to another place, often by post: *They sent a letter to her brother.* | *My parents send you their love.* | *A letter was sent to him.* | *They sent their children to London.* | *She sent us to wait in her office.* | *He was sent to buy some milk.* | *The explosion sent glass flying everywhere.* | *Bad news sent market prices down.*
□ USEFUL PATTERNS: to send something to someone; to send someone something; to send someone somewhere
2 [T + complement] to cause someone to have a particular feeling or to be in a particular state: *This noise is sending me mad!* | *His boring speeches always send me to sleep.*

send away for sthg *phr v* [T] to order goods to be sent by post: *I couldn't get a lamp like this in town, so I sent away for one.*

send for sbdy/sthg *phr v* [T] 1 to ask someone to come by sending them a message: *I think we'd better send for the doctor.* | *Did you send for the police?* 2 to ask in a message for someone or something to be brought or sent to you: *I'm going to send for the entry form for that competition.* | *The chief of police sent for reinforcements.*

send sthg ↔ **off** *phr v* [T] 1 to post something: *Have you sent the cheque off?* 2 to send a footballer off the field because of bad behaviour or a serious breaking of the rules

send sthg ↔ **on** *phr v* [T] to send something from someone's old address to their new address: *The landlady sent on all my mail.*

send sthg ↔ **out** *phr v* [T] 1 to broadcast: *The ship sent out an SOS.* 2 to send from one particular point: *We haven't sent the invitations out yet.* | *The sun sends out light.*

send-off /ˈ· ·/ n *infml* an occasion when a lot of people gather together to say GOODBYE to someone who is leaving: *The team were given a great send-off at the airport.*

se·nile /ˈsiːnaɪl/ *adj* weak in mind or body because of old age –**senility** /sɪˈnɪlɪti/ n [U]

se·ni·or¹ /ˈsiːniər/ n a person who is older or higher in rank than another person: *He's my senior.*

senior² *adj* 1 older or of higher rank: *He is senior to me.* 2 of high rank: *a meeting of the most senior army officers*

Senior n [after n] especially *AmE* the older: *John Smith Senior*

senior cit·i·zen /ˌ··· ˈ···/ n *euph* an old person, especially one over the age of 60 or 65 (a less direct expression than "old person" or "pensioner", though sometimes not liked by older people)

se·ni·or·i·ty /ˌsiːniˈɒrɪti ‖ -ˈɔːr-, -ˈɑːr-/ n [U] the quality of being senior in rank or age

sen·sa·tion /senˈseɪʃən/ n **1** [C;U] a physical feeling: *Since the accident he's had no sensation in the left side of his face.* | *It gave me a strange tingling sensation.* **2** [C] a general feeling in your mind or body that you cannot describe exactly: *I had the sensation that I was being watched.* **3** [C] a state of excited interest or the unexpected event that leads to it: *The discovery caused a great sensation.* | *The victory of the newcomer Perry over the champion Potter was a sensation.*

sen·sa·tion·al /senˈseɪʃənəl/ adj **1** causing or intended to cause excited interest: *a sensational murder* | *a sensational news report* **2** *infml* wonderful: *You won? That's sensational!* **-sensationally** adv

sen·sa·tion·al·is·m /senˈseɪʃənəlɪzəm/ n [U] the intentional producing of excitement or shock, for example, by books or magazines of low quality

sense[1] /sens/ n **1** [C] a way in which a person can know about the physical world, for example, through sight or hearing: *When you have a cold, you sometimes lose your sense of smell.* **2** [C;U] good practical understanding and judgment: *Haven't you got enough sense to come in out of the rain?* | *a successful man with good business sense* **3** there's **no sense in** *infml* there's no good reason for: *There's no sense in going by boat when the plane is just as cheap and much quicker.* **4** a sense of direction the ability to know where you are or where you are going: *Tom has absolutely no sense of direction – he's always getting lost.* **5** a sense of humour an ability to see what is funny in a situation: *I like John. He's got a good sense of humour.* | *Don't look so cross! Where's your sense of humour?* **6** [sing] a feeling: *a sense of fear* | *a sense that someone was standing behind him* **7** [sing] a belief in the importance of something: *a strong sense of justice* **8** [C] a meaning: *I'm using the word "man" in its broadest sense, meaning both men and women.* **9** make sense: **a** to have a clear meaning: *No matter how you read it, this sentence doesn't make sense.* **b** to be a wise course of action: *It makes sense to take care of your health.* **10** make sense of/out of something to understand something **11** in a sense, in one sense if something is looked at from only one point of view: *Yes, in a sense I agree with you, but the issue goes much deeper than that.*

sense[2] v sensed, sensing [T; +(that)] to have a feeling about something without being told directly: *The horse sensed danger and stopped.* | *She sensed that her husband was worried.*

sense·less /ˈsensləs/ adj **1** foolish or without a purpose: *senseless violence* **2** unconscious **-senselessly** adv **-senselessness** n [U]

sen·si·bil·i·ty /ˌsensɪˈbɪlɪti/ n sensibilities [C;U] *fml* tender or delicate feeling: *She plays the piano with great sensibility.*

sen·si·ble /ˈsensəbəl/ adj reasonable and practical: *a sensible child* | *a sensible plan* **-sensibly** adv: *You acted very sensibly*

■ USAGE Do not confuse **sensible** and **sensitive**. A **sensible** person is one who is reasonable and

practical, and who has good judgment. *She was very sensible in the way she dealt with a dangerous situation.* A **sensitive** person is one who is very conscious of other people's feelings and opinions: *She was sensitive enough not to ask too many questions about his unhappy childhood.* | *You shouldn't be so sensitive – I didn't mean anything bad in what I said.*

sen·si·tive /ˈsensɪtɪv/ adj **1** quick to show or feel the effect of something: *sensitive to cold* | *light-sensitive photographic paper* | *a sensitive pair of scales* **2** showing delicate feelings or judgment: *a sensitive performance* | *a sensitive actor* –opposite **insensitive** –see SENSIBLE (USAGE) **3** easily offended (a word often used to express disapproval): *For goodness sake, don't be so sensitive!* **4** needing to be dealt with very carefully: *This is rather a sensitive issue.* | *sensitive official papers* **-sensitively** adv **-sensitivity** /ˌsensɪˈtɪvɪti/ n (also **sensitiveness** /ˈsensɪtɪvnəs/) [U]

sen·so·ry /ˈsensəri/ adj of the physical senses: *sensory perception*

sen·su·al /ˈsenʃuəl/ adj **1** interested in the pleasure of the body, especially in sex: *her sensual curves* **2** of the senses: *sensual experiences* **-sensuality** /ˌsenʃuˈælɪti/ n [U]

sen·su·ous /ˈsenʃuəs/ adj causing pleasant feelings of the senses: *The cat stretched itself with sensuous pleasure.* **-sensuously** adv **-sensuousness** n [U]

sent /sent/ the past tense and past participle of SEND

sen·tence[1] /ˈsentəns/ n **1** a group of words that, in writing, begins with a capital letter and ends with a FULL STOP: *It was a fantastic story. It was absolutely gripping from the very first sentence.* | *Where's the verb in this sentence?* **2** a punishment for a criminal who has been found guilty in court: *The sentence was ten years in prison.* | *the death sentence*

sentence[2] v sentenced, sentencing [T] (of a judge or court) to give a punishment to someone: *He was sentenced to three years in prison.*

sen·ti·ment /ˈsentɪmənt/ n [C;U] **1** tender feelings: *There's no place for sentiment in this business!* **2** an opinion which comes from feeling: *strong public sentiment on the question of unemployment*

sen·ti·men·tal /ˌsentɪˈmentl◂/ adj **1** having or coming from tender feelings rather than reasonable or practical ones: *The clock doesn't work very well, but we keep it for sentimental reasons.* **2** showing too much of such feelings, especially of a weak or silly kind: *sentimental love stories* **-sentimentally** adv **-sentimentality** /-menˈtælɪti/ n [U]

sen·ti·nel /ˈsentɪnəl/ n old fash a guard

sen·try /ˈsentri/ n sentries a soldier standing as a guard outside a building or entrance

sep·a·ra·ble /ˈsepərəbəl/ adj able to be separated from something else

sep·a·rate[1] /ˈsepəreɪt/ v separated, separating **1** [I;T] to set or move apart: *They tried to separate the two men who were fighting.* | *He separated the boys from the girls.* | *The crowd pressed round us, and I got separated from my friends.* | *In discussing teachers' pay, the issues of their hours of work and types of work must be clearly separated.* **2** [I;T] to break or divide up into parts: *War separated the family.* | *The children separated into four groups.* **3** [T] to keep apart: *two communities separated by religious differences* **4** [I] (of a husband and wife) to decide to live apart, especially by a formal agreement

sep·a·rate² /ˈsepərɪt/ adj **1** [never before a noun] apart: *Keep the onions separate from the bread, or they'll make it smell.* **2** different: *This word has three separate meanings.* **3** not shared with another person: *We have separate rooms.* –**separateness** n [U] –**separately** adv: *They left separately.*

sep·a·rat·ed /ˈsepəreɪtɪd/ adj living apart, especially by a formal agreement (used of a husband and wife)

sep·a·ra·tion /ˌsepəˈreɪʃən/ n **1** [U] movement apart: *the separation of the rocket* **2** [C;U] the state of being separate or living apart: *the separation of government and administration* | *He was unhappy because of his separation from his mother.* **3** [C] law a formal agreement by a husband and wife to live apart –compare DIVORCE

sep·a·rat·ist /ˈsepərɵtɪst/ n a member of a group that wants to become separate from a larger political or religious organization

se·pi·a /ˈsiːpiə/ n [U] the brown colour of early photographs

Sep·tem·ber /sepˈtembəʳ/ n (also **Sept.**) the 9th month of the year

sep·tic /ˈseptɪk/ adj infected by disease bacteria

sep·ul·chre /ˈsepəlkəʳ/ n biblical a large TOMB where a person was buried –**sepulchral** /sɵˈpʌlkrəl/ adj

se·quel /ˈsiːkwəl/ n **1** a book or film which continues the action of an earlier one **2** something that follows something else, especially as a result

se·quence /ˈsiːkwəns/ n **1** [C] a group of things arranged in an order, especially following one another in time: *a strange sequence of events* **2** [U] the order in which things or events follow one another: *Please keep the cards in the correct sequence.* | *The slides were all in order, except for two that were slightly out of sequence.*

se·quin /ˈsiːkwɪn/ n a small shiny piece of metal or plastic sewn onto a piece of clothing for decoration

ser·e·nade¹ /ˌserɵˈneɪd/ n a song or other music sung or played in the open air at night, especially to a woman by a lover

serenade² v serenaded, serenading [T] to sing or play a serenade to someone

se·rene /sɵˈriːn/ adj completely calm and peaceful: *a serene summer night* –**serenely** adv –**serenity** /sɵˈrenəti/ n [U]

serf /sɜːf || sɜːrf/ n a person forced to stay and work on their master's land, in the Middle Ages in Europe and until the 19th century in Russia

ser·geant /ˈsɑːdʒənt || ˈsɑːr-/ n **1** a NONCOMMISSIONED OFFICER of middle rank in the army or air force **2** a police officer with next to the lowest rank

sergeant ma·jor /ˌ·· ˈ··◂/ n a NONCOMMISSIONED OFFICER of the highest rank in an army

se·ri·al /ˈsɪəriəl/ n a written or broadcast story appearing in parts at fixed times: *He's the star of a popular TV serial.*

se·ri·al·ize /ˈsɪəriəlaɪz/ v serialized, serializing (also **serialise** BrE) [T] to print or broadcast something in a number of parts, not all at once –**serialization** /ˌsɪəriəlaɪˈzeɪʃən || -lə-/ n [C;U]

serial num·ber /ˈ··· ˌ··/ n a number printed on a large number of similar things, so that you can tell them apart: *The police know the serial numbers of the stolen bank-notes.*

se·ries /ˈsɪəriːz/ n [plural is **series**] a group of things of the same kind, coming one after another: *a television series about modern art* | *After a series of*
unsuccessful attempts, he has at last passed his driving test.* | *The British team will be playing a series of matches in Australia this winter.*

se·ri·ous /ˈsɪəriəs/ adj **1** very bad and worrying: *serious damage* | *serious crime* | *A serious situation is developing in Fleetwood, where floods have devastated the town.* | *a serious illness* **2** solemn and not joking or cheerful: *a serious expression on his face* | *Are you serious about looking for a new job?* **3** concerned with important things: *a serious artist* | *a serious newspaper article* –**seriousness** n [U]

se·ri·ous·ly /ˈsɪəriəsli/ adv **1** in a serious way: *She likes art but has never studied it seriously.* | *seriously ill in hospital* **2** a word you use when you are surprised at something someone has just said, and are asking them if they really mean it: *"I'm going to emigrate." "Seriously?"* **3 take something seriously** to treat something as important and needing thought and attention

ser·mon /ˈsɜːmən || ˈsɜːr-/ n a talk given as part of a church service

ser·pent /ˈsɜːpənt || ˈsɜːr-/ n lit a snake

ser·rat·ed /sɵˈreɪtɪd, se-/ adj having a row of connected V-shapes like teeth: *a serrated edge* | *a serrated knife*

ser·vant /ˈsɜːvənt || ˈsɜːr-/ n a person who is paid to work for another person in their house: *They have two servants, a cook and a gardener.*

serve¹ /sɜːv || sɜːrv/ v served, serving. **1** [I;T] to work in the army or another organization or for an important person: *He served under Mrs Thatcher in the Department of Education and Science.* | *They served on the committee.* | *He served in the Korean War.* **2** [T] to provide something useful for people: *Travellers from Essex to Kent are served by the M25 motorway.* | *a single pipeline serving all the houses with water* **3** [I;T] to put food ready for people to eat: *Shall I serve the meat?* | *fish served with potatoes and beans* | *Breakfast is served from 8.15 until 10 a.m.* | *All the recipes serve six people.* | *She served us a lemon pudding.* **4** [I;T] to provide a customer in a shop with attention and help: *Are you being served?* **5** [T] to spend time in prison: *He served ten years for murder.* **6** [I;T] to do a job, often a job which is usually done by something else: *The entrance hall also serves as a dining-room.* | *This polythene sheet should serve to keep out the rain.* **7** [I;T] to hit the ball first to start a game such as tennis **8 it serves you right** = you deserve the trouble you've got

serve sthg ↔ out phr v [T] to put food on people's plates

serve up phr v [I;T **serve** sthg ↔ **up**] to put food on people's plates, especially when you have cooked it yourself

serve² n (also **service**) the ability to hit, or the act of hitting, the ball to start a game such as tennis: *She has a strong serve.*

serv·er /ˈsɜːvəʳ || ˈsɜːr-/ n a specially shaped tool for putting a particular kind of food onto a plate: *a pair of salad servers*

ser·vice¹ /ˈsɜːvɵs || ˈsɜːr-/ n **1** [U] attention to customers in a shop, or to business customers, or to guests in a hotel or restaurant: *The food was excellent, but the service was rather slow.* **2** [U] work done for someone else: *He was given an award for his service to the blind.* | *He died in the service of his country.* **3** [U] employment in an organization, or by a person: *He resigned after twenty years' service.* **4** [C] a particular job or kind of work offered to the public: *The centralized hotel booking system is a useful service for overseas visitors.* | *a free information*

service **5 services: a** work done for someone else: *You may need the services of a lawyer.* **b** useful work done by businesses for their customers but which does not produce goods: *service occupations such as hairdressing* **6 services** [C plural is **services**] a place on a very big road where people can stop to use the restaurant and the toilets (TOILET) and buy petrol: *On the way up to Scotland we stopped at the Scratchwood Services.* **7** [C] an organization or system which does something useful for the public: *the National Health Service | the Fire Service | a delivery service* **8 the services: a** the army, navy, and air force **b** the supply of water, electricity, and gas **9** [U] work done in the army, navy, or air force: *He's on service in the Far East.* **10** [C] *BrE* a particular area of government responsibility: *the foreign service* **11** [C] the regular examination and repair of a machine, for example a car or washing-machine: *I've got to take the car in for a service on Monday.* **12** [C] regular public buses, trains, planes, or boats between one place and another: *an hourly service between Manchester and London* **13** [C] a fixed form of public worship: *She attended the evening service at St Stephen's.* **14** [C] a set of plates and dishes, or a set of tea plates, cups, and saucers (SAUCER): *a dinner service* **15** [C] (also **serve**) the ability to hit the ball, or the act of hitting it, at the beginning of a game such as tennis **16 in service** in use or able to be used **17 out of service** not in use or able to be used: *We regret that the photocopier is out of service.*

service² *v* **serviced, servicing** [T] to examine a machine and repair it or put in good condition: *We have the car serviced once a year.*

ser·vi·cea·ble /ˈsɜːvɪsəbəl ‖ ˈsɜːr-/ *adj* fit to use and suitable for a purpose: *a serviceable pair of shoes*

service charge /ˈ··· ·/ *n* money added to a restaurant bill in order to pay for the waiter or waitress who serves you: *a 10% service charge*

ser·vice·man /ˈsɜːvɪˌsmən ‖ ˈsɜːr-/ *n* **servicemen** /-mən, -men/ a man in the army, navy, or AIRFORCE

service sta·tion /ˈ·· ˌ··/ *n* (also **garage** *BrE*) a place that sells petrol

ser·vi·ette /ˌsɜːviˈet ‖ ˌsɜːr-/ *n BrE* a small square of cloth or paper which you use at meals to keep your clothes, fingers, and lips clean

ser·vile /ˈsɜːvaɪl ‖ ˈsɜːrvəl, -vaɪl/ *adj* too eager to do what someone else wants, and giving them too much respect –**servility** /sɜːˈvɪlɪti ‖ sɜːr-/ *n* [U]

ser·vi·tude /ˈsɜːvɪˌtjuːd ‖ ˈsɜːrvɪˌtuːd/ *n* [U] *lit* the condition of a slave or of someone who is forced to obey another person all the time: *a life of servitude*

ses·sion /ˈseʃən/ *n* **1** a meeting of an organization or court: *a session of the United Nations Security Council* **2** a period in the year when a parliament or court meets **3** a period of time used for a particular activity: *a dancing session*

set¹ /set/ *v* **set, set, setting 1** [T+adv/prep] to put something somewhere carefully: *The waiter set a plate of food down in front of me. | She picked up the ornament and set it on the table.* **2** [T] to fix or establish a rule, time, or level: *The price has been set at £1000. | I always try to set a good example to the*

> **SPELLING NOTE**
> Words with the sound / s /, may be spelt **c-**, like **city**, or **ps-**, like **psychology.**

children. **3 set someone/something doing something** to cause someone or something to start doing something: *Your remarks have set me thinking. | He pushed the switch to set the wheel turning.* **4** [T] to give a piece of work to someone: *Who's setting the exam this year? | She forgot to set us any homework.* □ USEFUL PATTERNS to set something for someone; to set someone something **5** [T] to show the action of a story or play as happening in a particular place: *The story is set in 17th-century Spain.* **6** [T] to fix something into a surface: *a gold ring with three diamonds set into it.* **7** [T] to put a broken bone into a fixed position so that it will mend **8** [I] (of a broken bone) to become mended in a fixed position **9** [I] to become solid: *It will take two or three days for the concrete to set.* **10** [T] to arrange your hair while it is wet so that it has a particular style when it dries **11 set a table** to put plates, glasses, and other things onto a table ready for people to have a meal **12 set a trap** to prepare a trap **13 the sun sets** = the sun disappears from the sky at the end of the day **14 set eyes on** to see someone or something: *I'd never set eyes on him before.* **15 set fire to something, set something on fire** to cause something to burn: *Vandals had broken in and set fire to the building.* **16 set foot** to go into or onto a place: *You will never set foot in this house again!* **17 set free** to allow someone or something to go free: *Hundreds of political prisoners have been set free.* **18 set sail** to start sailing: *The boat is due to set sail tomorrow evening.* **19 set store by something** a phrase you use when you are saying how important you think something is: *We don't set much store by paper qualifications.* **20 set the pace** to fix the speed for other people to follow **21 set the scene for something** to make it possible for something to happen: *This agreement set the scene for future arguments and disagreements.* **22 set to music** to write music for a piece of writing: *The poems have been set to music.* **23 set to rights** to make something right or correct **24 set to work** to start working: *I think we should set to work as soon as possible.* **25 set your heart on something** to decide that you want something very strongly: *I've really set my heart on a holiday this summer.* **26 set your teeth on edge** (of a very unpleasant taste or sound) to give you an unpleasant feeling

set about sthg *phr v* [T] to start doing something: *We set about tidying the room.*

set against *phr v* **1** [T set sthg **against** sthg] to consider one thing along with something else that is different or opposite: *This defeat has to be set against a whole series of recent successes.* **2** [T set sbdy **against** sbdy] to make someone dislike or oppose another person: *a war which set family against family*

set sthg ↔ **aside** *phr v* [T] **1** to save something for a special purpose: *I'm trying to set aside a bit of money to pay for a holiday.* **2** to pay no attention to a particular idea or belief: *We must try to set aside our individual ambitions and work for the common good.*

set sbdy/sthg ↔ **apart** *phr v* [T] to make someone or something clearly different from others: *His deprived background set him apart from other children.*

set back *phr v* **1** [T set sbdy/sthg ↔ **back**] to cause someone or something to not make as much progress as they should: *The bad weather has set back the building work. | That illness really set him back.* **2** [T set sbdy **back**] *infml* to cost someone a particular amount of money: *The new car set me back £6000.* **3 be set back** to be at a distance from a road, not right next to a road: *The house is well set back from the road.*

set down *phr v* **1** [T **set** sbdy ↔ **down**] to stop a car and let someone get out: *Could you set me down just by the library?* **2** [T **set** sthg ↔ **down**] *fml* to write something down: *I felt the need to set my feelings down in writing.*

set in *phr v* [I] (of something unpleasant) to begin and seem likely to continue for a long time: *In the afternoon the rain really set in.*

set off *phr v* **1** [I] to begin a journey: *We set off early the next morning.* **2** [T **set** sthg ↔ **off**] to cause something to explode or make a loud noise: *The bomb could be set off at any time.* | *Children had set off the fire alarm.* **3** [T **set** sthg ↔ **off**] to cause something to start happening: *The relaxation of the licensing laws set off a sudden boom in the drinks industry.*

set on *phr v* **1** [T **set on** sbdy] to attack someone **2** [T **set** sthg **on** sbdy] to cause an animal to attack someone: *They set the dogs on him.*

set out *phr v* **1** [I] to begin a journey: *We set out for London.* **2 set out to do something** to start with the purpose of doing something: *It seems that he set out to destroy the company.* **3** [T **set** sthg ↔ **out**] to explain facts or ideas clearly: *The reasons for my decision are set out in my report.* **4** [T **set** sthg ↔ **out**] to arrange or spread things out in order: *The meal was set out on a long table.*

set up *phr v* **1** [T **set** sthg ↔ **up**] to put or build something somewhere: *Roadblocks have been set up by the police.* **2** [T **set** sthg ↔ **up**] to make the preparations for something and start it working: *The council set up a committee to look into ways of creating more jobs in the area.* **3** [I;T **set** sbdy **up**] to establish yourself or someone else in a new business: *She left the company where she had been working and set up on her own.* | *He set himself up as a painter and decorator.* **4** [T **set** sbdy **up**] *infml* to make someone seem guilty of something that they did not do: *He claims that the police set him up.*

set² *adj* **1** fixed and not able to be changed: *The meals are all a set price.* | *I have to study at set hours every day.* | *He has very set ideas about what a marriage should be like.* **2 set book** a book that students must study for an examination **3 be set to do something** to be ready to do something: *We were all set to leave when the phone rang.* **4 be set on doing something** to be determined to have or do something: *Everyone has told him how dangerous it is, but he still seems set on going.*

set³ *n* **1** a group of things that belong together: *I need a new set of gardening tools.* | *We are now facing a whole new set of problems.* **2** a machine on which you can watch television broadcasts: *a television set* | *We can't watch television at the moment – our set's broken.* **3** the scenery for a play or film **4** a group of games in a tennis match

set·back /ˈsetbæk/ *n* a return to a less good position: *She seemed better after her illness but then she had a sudden setback.* | *Hopes of an early end to the dispute have suffered a severe setback.*

set·square /ˈsetskweəʳ/ *n BrE* a flat three-sided plate used for drawing straight lines and angles exactly

set·tee /seˈtiː/ *n BrE* (also **sofa**) a comfortable seat for more than one person, with a back and arms – see picture on page 442

set·ting /ˈsetɪŋ/ *n* **1** the surroundings of a place: *high mountains forming a beautiful setting for a holiday* | *Our story has its setting in ancient Rome.* | *a diamond in a gold setting* **2** one of the positions

at which you can set the controls of something: *Turn the fridge to the coldest setting.*

set·tle /ˈsetl/ *v* settled, settling **1** [I;T] to put an end to an argument or a problem: *They agreed to settle their differences and work together.* **2** [T] to decide: *I'm going to settle this question once and for all.* | *That's the holiday settled, then.* **3 settle a bill** to pay a bill **4** [I] to go and live somewhere: *They got married and settled in Manchester.* | *They left Pakistan and settled in Canada.* **5** [I] to land: *The large bee settled briefly on the flower.* **6** [I] to sink slowly to the bottom: *The sand settled on the bottom of the pond.* **7** [I;T] to make or become quiet and calm: *I think I need to take something to settle my stomach.* **8 settle someone somewhere** to sit someone down and make them comfortable: *She settled the little boy on the sofa.* | *She settled herself in her chair.*

settle down *phr v* [I] **1** to become calmer and less active and noisy: *Settle down now, children, and go to sleep.* **2** to start to lead a quieter life in one place: *At the age of thirty he decided it was time to marry and settle down.* **3** to become used to a new way of life or something such as a new job or a new school: *How are you settling down in your new school?* **4** to get comfortable somewhere where you intend to stay for a time: *After tea she settled down in the armchair with her book.* | *He settled down for a sleep.* **5** to stop thinking about other things and attend to one particular thing: *Settle down to your homework.* | *He settled down to do his accounts.*

settle for sthg *phr v* [T] to accept something less than you hoped for: *The miners are asking for a 10% pay rise, but they'd probably settle for 8%.*

settle in *phr v* [I] to get used to something such as a new place to live or a new job: *How are you settling in?*

settle on sbdy/sthg *phr v* [T] to decide on one of the things you have been considering: *We liked all the colours, but in the end we settled on green.*

settle up *phr v* [I] **1** to pay your debts: *You pay for now and I'll settle up later.* **2** (of two or more people) to pay and receive what is owed: *We settled up at the end of the evening.*

set·tled /ˈsetld/ *adj* unlikely to change: *settled weather* | *settled habits*

set·tle·ment /ˈsetlmənt/ *n* **1** [C] a formal agreement or decision ending an argument or question: *the settlement of the miners' dispute* | *We've reached a settlement with the defence lawyers.* **2** [C] a place where people live: *a settlement on the edge of the desert* **3** [U] the movement of a new population into a place to live there: *the settlement of the American West* **4** [C] a payment of money claimed

set·tler /ˈsetləʳ/ *n* one of a large number of people who go to live in a new area: *early settlers in Australia*

set-up /ˈ· ·/ *n* [sing] the way something is organized: *He's new to the office and doesn't know the set-up yet.*

sev·en /ˈsevən/ *det, n, pron* the number 7

sev·enth /ˈsevənθ/ *det, n, pron, adv* **1** 7th **2** one of seven equal parts

sev·en·teen /ˌsevənˈtiːn◂/ *det, n, pron* the number 17 –**seventeenth** *det, n, pron, adv*

sev·en·ty /ˈsevənti/ *det, n, pron* **seventies 1** the number 70 **2 the seventies** (also **the 70's**) the years from 1970 to 1979: *He first became famous in the seventies.* **3 in your seventies** aged between 70 and 79: *She's in her seventies now.* –**seventieth** *det, n, pron, adv*

sev·er /ˈsevəʳ/ *v* [T] *fml* **1** to cut through something completely: *His arm was severed from his body in*

the accident. | a severed artery **2** to bring something completely to an end: Britain has severed diplomatic relations with Ruritania.

sev·er·al /ˈsevərəl/ det, pron some, or a few: Several people came to congratulate me after the performance. | I've made several visits to London this month. | There were several hundred people there. | Several of us had travelled down from Scotland.

se·vere /səˈvɪəʳ/ adj **1** not kind or gentle: a severe look on her face | severe military rules **2** very bad: severe pain | the severest winter for ten years | severe traffic congestion **–severely** adv : severely disabled **–severity** /səˈverɪti/ n [U] : the severity of winter in Norway

sew /səʊ/ v sewed, sewn /səʊn/ [I; T; + adv/prep] to join pieces of cloth together using a needle and thread: I used to hate sewing before I got a sewing machine.| She sewed a row of sequins along the pocket.

sew sthg ↔ **on** phr v [T] to fix something on to a piece of cloth using a needle and thread: Would you sew on this button for me?

sew sthg ↔ **up** phr v [T] **1** to close or repair something by sewing **2** sewn up infml decided and arranged in detail (used of a business deal, etc.): The People's Party have got the election sewn up: they're sure to win.

sew·age /ˈsjuːɪdʒ, ˈsuː- ‖ ˈsuː-/ n [U] the waste material and water from people's houses and from industry carried away in large pipes under the ground

sew·er /ˈsjuːəʳ, ˈsuːəʳ ‖ ˈsuːəʳ/ n a man-made passage or large pipe under the ground for carrying away water and waste material

sew·ing /ˈsəʊɪŋ/ n [U] **1** work that you are doing with a needle and thread **2** the activity of making or mending something with a needle and thread

sewing ma·chine /ˈ···ˌ·/ n a machine which you use to sew pieces of cloth together

sewn /səʊn/ the past participle of SEW

sex /seks/ n **1** [U] the condition of being either male or female: In the space marked "sex", put an "M" for male or an "F" for female. **2** [C] the set of all male or all female creatures: a member of the opposite sex **3** [U] the physical act between two people in which the sex organs are brought together: Do you think sex outside marriage is wrong? **4 have sex** (of two people) to perform the physical act in which the sex organs are brought together **5** [U] all the activity connected with the sex act: There's a lot of sex and violence in this film.

sex·is·m /ˈseksɪzəm/ n [U] the idea or belief that members of one sex (usually men) are more able and clever than those of the other sex; it is often used to suggest that certain jobs should only be done by members of one particular sex (a word used to show disapproval)

sex·ist /ˈseksɪst/ adj showing sexism: I'm tired of his sexist jokes about women drivers! **–sexist** n

sex·less /ˈseksləs/ adj **1** not showing any interest in sex **2** not exciting to someone of the opposite sex

sex·u·al /ˈsekʃuəl/ adj connected with sex: sexual reproduction | sexual excitement | the fight against

sexual discrimination **–sexually** adv : sexually attractive

sexual in·ter·course /ˌ··· ˈ···/ n (also **intercourse**) [U] the physical act in which a male and a female bring their sex organs together

sex·u·al·i·ty /ˌsekʃuˈælɪti/ n [U] fondness for or interest in sexual activity

sex·y /ˈseksi/ adj sexier, sexiest exciting in a sexual way: sexy girls | sexy pictures | sexy clothes **–sexily** adv

SF /ˌes ˈef/ n an abbreviation for SCIENCE FICTION

Sgt n a written abbreviation for SERGEANT

sh /ʃ/ interj (also **shh**) you say this when you want people to be quiet: Sh! You'll wake the baby!

shab·by /ˈʃæbi/ adj shabbier, shabbiest **1** in poor condition because of being old and worn: a shabby old coat **2** wearing old worn clothes **3** ungenerous: What a shabby trick, making me walk home! **–shabbily** adv : shabbily dressed | The company she worked for treated her very shabbily. **–shabbiness** n [U]

shack /ʃæk/ n a small roughly built building

shack·le /ˈʃækəl/ v shackled, shackling [T] **1** to put into shackles **2 to be shackled** to have your freedom limited: shackled by old customs

shack·les /ˈʃækəlz/ n [pl] **1** two joined metal rings for fastening around the wrist or ankle of a person such as a prisoner to prevent movement **2** lit something that prevents freedom of action or expression

shade¹ /ʃeɪd/ n **1** [U] shelter from direct light, especially from sunlight outdoors, made by something blocking it: sitting in the shade of a tree – see USAGE **2** [C] something that keeps out light or its full brightness: a lampshade | a green eyeshade **3** [C] a degree of colour: a lighter shade of blue **4** [C] a slight difference: a word with several shades of meaning **5** [sing] a little bit: That music is just a shade too loud. **6** [C] lit a GHOST

■ USAGE Compare **shade** and **shadow**. We can use **shade** for any place sheltered from the sun. In this meaning **shade** is uncountable: Let's find some shade. We can use **shadow** for the dark shape made by blocking a strong light. In this meaning **shadow** is countable: Under the floodlights, each player in the football match had four **shadows**.

shade² v shaded, shading **1** [T] to shelter from direct light or heat: She shaded her eyes from the sun. **2 shade into something** not to have a clear difference from something else

shad·ow¹ /ˈʃædəʊ/ n **1** [C] the clear dark shape of an object made on a surface behind it when the sun or a strong light falls on it: As the sun set, the shadows became longer. | The tree cast its shadow on the wall. – see SHADE¹ (USAGE) **2 a shadow of your former self** very much weaker or less powerful than you used to be: After his illness he was only a shadow of his former self. **3 There's not a shadow of doubt that**… There isn't the slightest doubt that…

shadow² v [T] to follow and watch someone closely and secretly: She was shadowed everywhere by the secret police.

shadow cab·i·net /ˌ··· ˈ···/ n the shadow cabinet a group of the leading politicians of the main opposition party in Parliament, who each study the work of a particular government minister

shad·ow·y /ˈʃædəʊi/ adj **1** not very clear in people's minds because little is known about it: a shadowy

---

SPELLING NOTE

Words with the sound /s/, may be spelt **c-**, like **city**, or **ps-**, like **psychology**.

and little-known historical figure **2** dark and full of shadows: *the shadowy depths of the forest* **3** hard to see

shad·y /ˈʃeɪdi/ *adj* **shadier, shadiest** **1** sheltered from sunlight: *a shady spot under the trees* **2** producing shade: *shady trees* **3** *infml* illegal or not very honest: *a shady politician | a shady deal*

shaft /ʃɑːft ‖ ʃæft/ *n* **1** the deep and narrow hole in the ground by which you enter a mine: *a mine shaft* **2** the tall narrow space in which a lift goes up and down: *a lift shaft* **3** a bar which turns, or around which a belt or wheel turns, to pass power through a machine: *a propeller shaft* **4** a narrow line of light: *a shaft of sunlight* **5** the long handle of a spear, hammer, axe, etc.

shag·gy /ˈʃægi/ *adj* **shaggier, shaggiest** **1** long and very untidy (used of hair or material): *a shaggy beard* **2** covered with long untidy hair: *a shaggy dog*

shake¹ /ʃeɪk/ *v* **shook** /ʃʊk/, **shaken** /ˈʃeɪkən/, **shaking** **1** [I;T] to move quickly up and down and backwards and forwards: *The explosion shook the house.* | *The house shook.* | *She was shaking with anger.* | *Shake the bottle before use.* | *She shook the sand from her shoes.* **2** **shake hands** to take someone's right hand in your own and shake it when you are introduced to them, greet them, say GOODBYE to them, or reach a formal agreement with them: *They shook hands with each other.* **3** [T] to upset: *She was badly shaken by the news.* **4** **shake your head** to move your head from side to side to say "no"
shake sbdy/sthg ↔ **off** *phr v* [T] to get rid of or escape from something or someone: *I've had a bad cold for weeks – I just can't shake it off.* | *The crooks managed to shake off the police car.*
shake sthg ↔ **out** *phr v* [T] to open or spread something with a shaking movement: *He shook out the dirty mat.*
shake sthg ↔ **up** *phr v* [T] **1** to make big changes in an organization: *The new chairman is really going to shake up the company.* **2** to mix by shaking

shake² *n* an action of shaking: *She answered "no" with a shake of the head.* | *Give the duvet a good shake.*

shak·en /ˈʃeɪkən/ the past participle of SHAKE

shake-up /ˈ· ·/ *n* a set of big changes in an organization: *a government shake-up with three ministers losing their jobs*

shak·y /ˈʃeɪki/ *adj* **shakier, shakiest** **1** shaking or unsteady, for example because of nervousness or weakness **2** not solid or firm: *a shaky ladder | shaky in her beliefs* **–shakily** *adv*

shale /ʃeɪl/ *n* [U] soft rock which naturally divides into thin sheets

shall /ʃəl; *strong* ʃæl/ *v negative short form* **shan't** [modal verb] **1** used with "I" and "we" to show that you are going to do something or intend to do something: *We shall see you on Saturday.* | *I shall have to go soon.* | *I shall be furious if they're late! | I shan't be at work tomorrow.* | *When I see him, I shall tell him about it.* **2** *fml* used with "you", "he", "she", "it", and "they" to show that something will certainly happen or you promise to make it happen: *The murderer shall be caught and punished.* | *The work shall be completed by the 15th July.* | *You shall not get away with this!* –see 's (USAGE) **3** **shall I** a polite way of asking someone if they would like you to do something: *Shall I answer the phone for you?* | *Shall I open the window?* **4** **shall we** a way of suggesting to someone that you should both do something or all do something: *Shall we go out tonight?*
■ USAGE In ordinary modern speech **will**, or the short form **'ll**, is used more often than **shall** in the first meaning.

shal·lot /ʃəˈlɒt ‖ ʃəˈlɑːt/ *n* a vegetable like a small onion

shal·low /ˈʃæləʊ/ *adj* **1** not deep: *the shallow end of the swimming pool* | *Her breathing was very shallow.* **2** lacking deep or serious thinking: *a shallow thinker whose opinions aren't worth much* **–shallowness** *n* [U]

sham¹ /ʃæm/ *n* something false pretending to be the real thing: *He seemed to be very concerned about her but it was all a sham.* –**sham** *adj*

sham² *v* **-mm-** [T] to pretend that you have got an illness or other condition which you have not really got: *He isn't really ill. He's shamming.*

sham·ble /ˈʃæmbəl/ *v* **shambled, shambling** [I; + adv/prep] to walk awkwardly, dragging your feet: *an old man shambling along the street*

sham·bles /ˈʃæmbəlz/ *n* [sing] *infml* something very disorderly or which should have been much better organized: *After the party the house was a shambles.* | *The whole event was a total shambles.*

shame¹ /ʃeɪm/ *n* **1** [U] the painful feeling you have when you have done something wrong or silly, or when a relative or close friend has: *I feel no shame for my action: I did what was right.* | *I was filled with shame when I realized how badly I'd behaved at the party.* **2** **bring shame on someone** to make people think that someone deserves blame: *Your bad behaviour brings shame on the whole school.* **3** **What a shame!, What a shame that**... an expression you use when you are disappointed or sorry: *What a shame that it rained on the day of your wedding!* **4** **put someone or something to shame** to show someone or something to be less good by comparison: *Your beautiful garden puts my few little flowers to shame.*

shame² *v* **shamed, shaming** [T] **1** to make someone feel ashamed: *He shamed his family by being sent to prison.* **2** **shame someone into doing something** to make someone feel so bad about not having done something that they then do it

shame·faced /ˌʃeɪmˈfeɪst◂/ *adj* showing suitable shame: *Looking suitably shamefaced, he apologized for being so rude.* **–shamefacedly** /-ˈfeɪsɪdli/ *adv*

shame·ful /ˈʃeɪmfəl/ *adj* very bad and which you ought to be ashamed of: *the most shameful disregard for other people's safety* **–shamefully** *adv*

shame·less /ˈʃeɪmləs/ *adj* **1** feeling no shame: *an immodest and shameless person* **2** done without shame: *shameless disloyalty* **–shamelessly** *adv*: *quite shamelessly asking for more money*

sham·poo¹ /ʃæmˈpuː/ *n* **shampoos** **1** [C;U] a soapy liquid which you use for washing something, especially your hair: *creamy shampoo for dry hair* **2** [C] an act of shampooing: *an appointment at the hairdresser's for a cut and shampoo*

shampoo² *v* **shampooed, shampooing** [T] to wash with shampoo

sham·rock /ˈʃæmrɒk ‖ -rɑːk/ *n* [C;U] a type of small plant with three round leaves on each stem, used as the national sign of Ireland

shan·dy /ˈʃændi/ *n* **shandies** [C;U] *BrE* a drink made from a mixture of beer and LEMONADE or GINGER ALE

shan't /ʃɑːnt ‖ ʃænt/ a short form of "shall not": *Shall I go, or shan't I?*

shan·ty town /ˈʃænti ˌtaʊn/ *n* a town or part of a town made up of small houses roughly built out of things such as old packing cases; poor people live there

shape¹ /ʃeɪp/ *n* **1** [C;U] the appearance or form of something; circles, squares, and triangles (TRIANGLE) are shapes: *The sign was triangular in shape.* | *a cake in the shape* of *a heart* | *We saw a shape through the mist but we couldn't see who it was.* **2** [U] *infml* a good state or condition: *He's taking lots of exercise to get into shape.* | *What do you do to keep in shape?* | *Our garden is in good shape after the rain.* **3 take shape** to begin to be like the finished form: *ideas taking shape in his mind* –**shapeless** *adj*

shape² *v* **shaped, shaping** [T] **1** to make something into a particular form: *The bird shaped its nest from mud and sticks.* | *We watched in amazement as she shaped the clay* into *a pot.* **2** to influence strongly: *His experience of the war shaped his whole outlook.*

shape up *phr v* [I] to develop well: *Our holiday plans are shaping up well.*

shaped /ʃeɪpt/ *adj* having a certain shape: *a cloud shaped like a camel* | *a heart-shaped cake*

shape·ly /ˈʃeɪpli/ *adj* **shapelier, shapeliest** having a good-looking shape (used especially of a woman) –**shapeliness** *n* [U]

share¹ /ʃeəʳ/ *v* **shared, sharing** **1** [I;T] to join with other people in owning, using, or doing something: *We haven't got enough books for everyone. Some of you will have to share.* | *Everyone in the house shares the same bathroom.* | *He's sure we'll win the match, but I don't share his faith in the team.* | *I share the house* with *my brother.* **2** [T] (also **share out**) to divide and give out in shares: *His property was shared* between *his children.* **3 share something with someone** to tell someone about or some news

share² *n* **1** [sing] a part in something which you have, do, or use with other people: *If you want a share* of *the pay, you'll have to do your share of the work.* | *Children should have a share in deciding which subjects they study.* **2** [C] any of the equal parts into which the ownership of a company may be divided: *She owns 5000 shares in the company.* | *a dividend of ten pence per share* | *Share prices rose yesterday.*

share·hold·er /ˈʃeəˌhəʊldəʳ ‖ ˈʃeər-/ *n* a person who owns shares in a company

shark /ʃɑːk ‖ ʃɑːrk/ *n* a very large fish with sharp teeth that is dangerous to people

sharp¹ /ʃɑːp ‖ ʃɑːrp/ *adj* **1** having a thin cutting edge or a fine point: *a sharp knife* | *a sharp needle* –opposite **blunt** **2** quick and sensitive: *a sharp mind* | *sharp eyes* **3** causing a sensation like that of cutting or biting: *a sharp wind* **4** very sour: *a sharp taste* **5** pointed, not gently rounded: *a sharp nose* | *a sharp bend* **6** sudden and big: *a sharp rise in prices* **7** clear: *a sharp photographic image* | *a sharp distinction between first and second class degrees* **8** severe and sudden (used of a pain)

–opposite **dull** **9** quick and strong: *a sharp blow on the head* **10** intended to hurt (used of words): *a sharp scolding* **11** [only after a noun] *tech* higher than the main note (used of musical notes): *Rachmaninov's Piano Concerto No 1 in F sharp minor* **12** slightly too high (used of a note in music) –**sharply** *adv* : *Prices have risen sharply.* | *"I don't care," he replied sharply.* **sharpness** *n* [U]

sharp² *n* a sharp note in music

sharp³ *adv* [after a noun] **1** exactly at the stated time: *The meeting starts at three o'clock sharp.* **2** slightly higher than the note you are trying to sing or play

sharp·en /ˈʃɑːpən ‖ ˈʃɑːr-/ *v* [I;T] to make or become sharp or sharper: *to sharpen a knife* | *His voice sharpened.*

sharp·en·er /ˈʃɑːpənəʳ, ˈʃɑːpnəʳ ‖ ˈʃɑːr-/ *n* something that you use to sharpen things: *a pencil sharpener*

shat·ter /ˈʃætəʳ/ *v* **1** [I;T] to break suddenly into small pieces: *A stone shattered the window.* | *The glass shattered.* **2** [T] to destroy something totally: *Hopes of reaching an agreement were shattered.* **3 be shattered by something** to begin to feel extremely upset and unhappy because of something that has happened

shat·tered /ˈʃætəd ‖ -tərd/ *adj* **1** very unhappy because you have had a sudden shock **2** *infml* very tired: *I felt completely shattered.*

shat·ter·ing /ˈʃætərɪŋ/ *adj* **1** very upsetting: *Failing the entrance exam was a shattering blow to his hopes of a career in the Civil Service.* **2** *infml* very tiring: *a shattering day at work*

shave¹ /ʃeɪv/ *v* **shaved, shaving** **1** [I;T] to cut hair from your face or another part of your body: *I've shaved off my beard.* | *I cut myself while I was shaving.* | *Do you shave your legs?* **2** [T] to cut off very thin pieces from a surface: *She shaved the bottom off the door to make it close properly.* **3** –**shaven** /ˈʃeɪvən/ having been shaved: *a shaven head* | *No, he hasn't got a beard. He's clean-shaven.*

shave² *n* an act or result of shaving: *He had a quick shave.*

shav·er /ˈʃeɪvəʳ/ *n* an electric tool for shaving

shav·ings /ˈʃeɪvɪŋz/ *n* [pl] very thin curly pieces of wood cut from a larger piece

shawl /ʃɔːl/ *n* a piece of cloth which a woman wears over her head or shoulders or which is wrapped round a baby

she¹ /ʃi; *strong* ʃiː/ *pron* [used as the subject of a verb] the female person or animal who has already been mentioned: *"Where's Mary?" "She's gone to the cinema."*

she² *n* a female animal: *Is your dog a he or a she?* | *a she-goat*

sheaf /ʃiːf/ *n* **sheaves** /ʃiːvz/ **1** a handful of papers: *She had a sheaf of notes in front of her.* **2** a bunch of grain plants cut and tied together and left to dry in the field

shear /ʃɪəʳ/ *v* **sheared, sheared** *or* **shorn** /ʃɔːn ‖ ʃɔːrn/ [T] to cut wool off a sheep

shear off *phr v* [I] *tech* (especially of thin rods, pins, etc.) to break in two under a sideways force

shears /ʃɪəz ‖ ʃɪərz/ *n* [pl] large heavy scissors, used for example for cutting grass –see picture on page 638

sheath /ʃiːθ/ *n* **sheaths** /ʃiːðz/ **1** a close-fitting case for a knife or sword blade **2** a covering worn over a man's sex organ when he is having sex, used as a means of birth control or as a protection against disease

sheathe /ʃiːð/ v **sheathed, sheathing** [T] to put into a sheath

sheaves /ʃiːvz/ n the plural of SHEAF

shed¹ /ʃed/ n a simple building usually used for storing things: *We keep our old newspapers in the shed.* | *a toolshed* | *a cattle shed* | *a woodshed* | *a garden shed*

shed² v **shed, shed, shedding** [T] **1** (of a plant or animal) to throw off something naturally: *trees shedding their leaves in autumn* | *Some snakes shed their skin each year.* **2** to get rid of something: *With costs rising, many firms are shedding labour.* | *I need to shed a few pounds before I can get into my new trousers.* **3 shed a load** (of a LORRY) to drop the goods being carried by accident: *There are long tailbacks on the A21 near Tonbridge where a lorry has shed its load.* **4 shed blood** to kill or hurt people: *It is hoped that the crisis can be solved without any blood being shed.* **5 shed light on something** to help to explain something **6 shed tears** to cry: *His mother shed a few tears when he left for Australia.*

she'd /ʃid; *strong* ʃiːd/ **1** a short form of "she would": *She said she'd try.* **2** a short form of "she had": *She'd been there before.*

sheen /ʃiːn/ n [sing;U] brightness on a surface: *hair with a beautiful sheen*

sheep /ʃiːp/ n [plural is **sheep**] **1** an animal that eats grass and is kept for its wool and its meat: *a flock of sheep* –see MEAT (USAGE) **2 the sheep and the goats** those who are good, clever, and successful, and those who are not: *a difficult examination, intended to separate the sheep from the goats*

sheep-dog /ˈʃiːpdɒg ‖ -dɔːg/ n a type of dog that can be trained to control sheep

sheep-ish /ˈʃiːpɪʃ/ adj slightly uncomfortable because you have done something foolish: *a sheepish smile* –**sheepishly** adv –**sheepishness** n [U]

sheep-skin /ˈʃiːpˌskɪn/ n the skin and wool of a sheep: *a sheepskin coat* | *a sheepskin rug*

sheer¹ /ʃɪəʳ/ adj **1** [only before a noun] pure and not mixed with anything else: *He won by sheer determination.* | *It was sheer luck.* **2** very steep: *a sheer cliff* **3** very thin and almost transparent: *ladies' sheer stockings*

sheer² adv straight up or down: *The mountain rises sheer from the plain.*

sheet /ʃiːt/ n **1** a large piece of cloth used under you or on top of you in a bed; the sheets are next to you: *We change the sheets every week.* **2 a sheet of paper** a single flat piece of paper: *a sheet of headed notepaper* | *wrapped in a sheet of newspaper* **3** a broad area or piece of something thin: *a sheet of ice over the lake* | *sheet metal*

sheikh /ʃeɪk ‖ ʃiːk/ n (also **sheik**) an Arab chief or prince: *Sheikh Yamani of Saudi Arabia*

shelf /ʃelf/ n **shelves** /ʃelvz/ a long board fixed against a wall or in a cupboard so that things can be kept on it: *a book-shelf* | *some new shelves for the kitchen*

shell¹ /ʃel/ n **1** [C;U] the hard covering of an egg, or nut, or of some sea animals: *The sea shore was covered with shells.* | *a nutshell* | *some pieces of eggshell* **2** [C] the frame of a building **3** [C] an explosive for firing from a large gun: *shells bursting all around*

shell² v **1** [T] to remove from a natural shell or POD: *to shell peas* **2** [I;T] to fire shells at a place or at the enemy: *The enemy lines were weakened by shelling before the attack.*

shell out phr v [I;T **shell out** sthg] *infml* to pay money unwillingly: *I'm going to have to shell out for some new tyres soon.*

she'll /ʃil; *strong* ʃiːl/ a short form of "she will": *She'll come if she can.*

shell-fish /ˈʃel,fɪʃ/ n [plural is **shellfish**] **1** any small animal that lives in the sea and has a shell **2** such animals as food: *I don't like any shellfish except lobsters.*

shel-ter¹ /ˈʃeltəʳ/ n **1** [U] protection, especially from bad weather or danger: *In the storm I took shelter under a tree.* | *The refugees are in urgent need of food and shelter.* **2** [C] a building that protects you from weather or danger: *a bus shelter*

shelter² v **1** [T] to protect someone or something from bad weather or danger: *This blind shelters the plants from the sun.* **2** [I] to stay in a place in order to be protected from bad weather or danger: *In the rain people were sheltering in the doorways of shops.* **3** [T] to give a homeless person a place to stay in **4** [T] to look after someone while they hide in your house

shel-tered /ˈʃeltəd ‖ -əʳd/ adj **1** protected from bad weather, especially wind: *a sheltered spot in the garden* **2** kept away from the hard facts of life: *She had led a sheltered life and was quite unprepared for city living.*

shelve /ʃelv/ v **shelved, shelving 1** [T] to put a plan on one side and do nothing about it at the present time: *We've had to shelve our holiday plans because Tom's mother is ill.* **2** [I] (of the seashore) to slope

shelves /ʃelvz/ n the plural of SHELF

shelv-ing /ˈʃelvɪŋ/ n [U] shelves

shep-herd¹ /ˈʃepəd ‖ -əʳd/ n someone whose job it is to look after sheep

shepherd² v [T] to look after a group of people by going with them and making sure they get to the right place: *We shepherded the children into the bus.*

sher-iff /ˈʃerɪf/ n (also **Sheriff**) an elected officer in the US responsible for making sure that people do not break the law: *Sheriff Wyatt appointed four deputies.*

sher-ry /ˈʃeri/ n **sherries 1** [U] strong wine from Spain, often drunk in Britain before a meal **2** [C] a small glass of this

she's /ʃiz; *strong* ʃiːz/ **1** short for "she is": *She's working in an office.* **2** short for "she has": *She's got a new job.*

shh /ʃ/ interj see SH

shield¹ /ʃiːld/ n **1** a large flat piece of metal or wood which, in the past, soldiers held in front of them to protect them from weapons **2** a protective cover, especially on a machine to protect the person operating it from moving parts: *an eye shield over his bad eye* **3** a formal and colourful sign for a family, town, team, or other group; the sign has the shape of a shield **4** a prize in the shape of a shield which you might win in a competition for something such as sport or public speaking

shield² v [T] to protect someone or something: *She lied to the police to shield her friend.* | *That wall will shield us from the wind.*

shift¹ /ʃɪft/ v **1** [I;T] to move: *The wind shifted from the south to the west.* | *I want to try and shift this sand before lunch.* | *It's stuck fast and we can't shift it.* | *Don't try to shift the blame onto me!* **2** [I] to change slightly: *Public opinion has shifted on this issue.* **3 shift for yourself** to do your best to look after yourself even if you do not do it very well

shift² *n* **1** a change in position or direction: *a shift in the wind* | *a shift in public opinion* **2** one of the work periods, usually eight hours, in a place such as a factory which is open many hours a day: *He's on the night shift this week.* **3** [+ sing/pl verb] a group of workers working together for one of these periods: *The early shift came on at six a.m.*

shift·less /ˈʃɪftləs/ *adj* without any sense of responsibility or the ability to organize anything

shift·y /ˈʃɪfti/ *adj* **shiftier, shiftiest** looking dishonest

shil·ling /ˈʃɪlɪŋ/ *n* **1** a unit of money in use in Britain until 1971; it was equal to 5 new pence; there were 12 old pennies in a shilling and 20 shillings in a pound **2** an amount of money in some African countries equal to 100 cents

shim·mer¹ /ˈʃɪmər/ *v* [I] to shine with a soft trembling light: *water shimmering in the moonlight*

shimmer² *n* [sing] a soft trembling shining effect: *the shimmer of candlelight in the old church*

shin¹ /ʃɪn/ *n* the bony front part of your leg between your knee and your ankle

shin² *v* **-nn- shin up something** to climb something such as a tree or pole quickly and easily, using your hands and legs: *She shinned up a tree to get a better view.*

shine¹ /ʃaɪn/ *v* **shone** /ʃɒn‖ʃəʊn/, **shone, shining 1** [I] to give out light: *It's a lovely day. The sun is shining.* **2** [I] to look bright: *The polished surface shone in the sun.* | *eyes shining with happiness* **3** [T] to point a lamp at something: *Shine your torch over here.* **4** [T] to make something bright by rubbing: *Shine your shoes before you go out.* **5** [I] to show special ability: *She's a good student generally, but chemistry is where she really shines.*

shine² *n* [sing] **1** brightness: *The wooden surface had a beautiful shine.* **2** an act of polishing: *These shoes need a shine.*

shin·gle /ˈʃɪŋɡəl/ *n* [U] small rough rounded pieces of stone found on a shore

shin·y /ˈʃaɪni/ *adj* **shinier, shiniest** bright with light which is thrown back from the surface: *a shiny new coin*

ship¹ /ʃɪp/ *n* a large boat for carrying people or goods on the sea: *The ship sailed at 9.30a.m. She was called the Princess Elizabeth.* | *We went by plane, but sent all our furniture by ship.* | *Life on board ship was enormous fun.* –see BOAT (USAGE) –see picture on page 735

ship² *v* **-pp-** [T] to send large articles by ship or by another vehicle: *I'm flying to America but my car is being shipped over.*

ship·ment /ˈʃɪpmənt/ *n* **1** [C] a load of goods sent together, usually by ship and usually from one country to another: *A large shipment of grain has just arrived.* **2** [U] the action of sending goods: *articles lost in shipment*

ship·per /ˈʃɪpər/ *n* a person or company who sends goods, usually by ship and usually from one country to another: *wine shippers*

ship·ping /ˈʃɪpɪŋ/ *n* [U] **1** ship traffic **2** ships as a group **3** the sending and delivery of something, usually by ship and usually from one country to another: *a shipping charge of £15*

ship·wreck¹ /ˈʃɪp-rek/ *n* [C;U] the destruction of a ship when it hits something at sea or sinks

shipwreck² *v* **be shipwrecked** to be on a ship when it is destroyed because it hits something at sea or sinks: *They were shipwrecked off the Irish coast.* | *a shipwrecked sailor*

ship·yard /ˈʃɪp-jɑːd ‖ -jɑːrd/ *n* a place where ships are built or repaired

shirk /ʃɜːk ‖ ʃɜːrk/ *v* [I;T] to avoid something or do something badly because you are lazy: *We mustn't shirk on the cleaning.* | *You mustn't shirk your responsibilities.* **–shirker** *n*

shirt /ʃɜːt ‖ ʃɜːrt/ *n* a piece of clothing which you wear on the upper part of your body, usually made of light cloth, with a collar, coverings for your arms, and buttons down the front opening –see picture on page 50

shirt·sleeves /ˈʃɜːtsliːvz ‖ ˈʃɜːrt-/ *n* [pl] **in your shirtsleeves** wearing nothing over your shirt: *On hot days the men in the office work in their shirtsleeves.*

shirt·y /ˈʃɜːti ‖ ˈʃɜːrt-/ *adj infml* bad-tempered and rude

shiv·er¹ /ˈʃɪvər/ *v* [I] to shake because you are cold or frightened: *It was so cold that we were all shivering.* **–shivery** *adj*

shiver² *n* **1** a shaking movement caused by cold or fear: *The strange noise sent a shiver down my spine.* **2 give someone the shivers** *infml* to make someone feel afraid

shoal /ʃəʊl/ *n* **1** a large group of fish swimming together **2 in shoals** in large numbers: *People arrived in shoals.*

shock¹ /ʃɒk ‖ ʃɑːk/ *n* **1** [C;U] the feeling you get after something unexpected and usually very unpleasant has suddenly happened, or you have received an unexpected piece of bad news: *His death came as a great shock to us all.* | *The survivors of the earthquake are still in a state of deep shock.* | *I had a shock when I saw how thin she had grown.* | *Oh, it's only you! You gave me a shock.* | *Her granddaughter's new clothes were a bit of a shock.* **2** [C;U] a violent force from something such as an explosion, a crash, or a hard blow: *The shock of the explosion was felt far away.* **3** [C;U] the sudden violent effect of electricity passing through someone's body: *Don't touch that wire! You'll get a shock.* **4** [U] *tech* the poor medical condition of someone who has had an accident and whose heart and lungs are not working properly: *suffering from minor injuries and shock*

shock² *v* [I;T] to make someone feel very upset, angry, or unpleasantly surprised: *I was shocked by his sudden death.* | *We were all shocked by her rudeness.* | *Take no notice. She's only doing it to shock.*

shock·ing /ˈʃɒkɪŋ ‖ ˈʃɑː-/ *adj* **1** very upsetting, wrong, or immoral: *a shocking accident* | *shocking and scandalous behaviour* **2** *infml* very bad: *What a shocking waste of time!* **–shockingly** *adv*: *shockingly underpaid*

■ USAGE Remember that **shocked** and **shocking** usually give the idea that you disapprove of something very strongly or that you find it offensive. If you do not want to give this meaning, you should use another expression. For example: *My first day at school in England was rather* **strange**/

disturbing. | *When I arrived in New York I felt completely* **disorientated**. | *I found the British education system very* **strange/confusing**.

shod /ʃɒd ‖ ʃɑːd/ *adj lit* provided with shoes: *poor badly-shod children*

shod·dy /ˈʃɒdi ‖ ˈʃɑːdi/ *adj* **shoddier, shoddiest 1** made or done badly or carelessly: *shoddy goods | shoddy workmanship* **2** ungenerous or dishonourable: *a shoddy trick* –**shoddily** *adv* –**shoddiness** *n* [U]

shoe /ʃuː/ *n* **1** the thing you wear on each of your feet to protect them from the hard ground; shoes are sometimes made of leather: *He took off his shoes.* | *a new pair of shoes to match her dress* –see PAIR (USAGE) –see picture on page 50 **2 in someone's shoes** in someone else's position, experiencing what they have to experience: *I'm glad I'm not in his shoes!*

shoe·lace /ˈʃuːleɪs/ *n* a thin cord that you use to tie the front parts of your shoe together –see PAIR (USAGE)

shoe·string /ˈʃuːˌstrɪŋ/ *n* **on a shoestring** on a very small amount of money: *He started his business on a shoestring and built it up.*

shone /ʃɒn ‖ ʃəʊn/ the past tense and past participle of SHINE

shoo¹ /ʃuː/ *interj* a word said, usually not angrily, to animals or small children when you want them to go away

shoo² *v* [T] **shooed, shooing** to make children or animals go somewhere by repeatedly waving your arms at them and telling them to go: *He shooed the children out of the kitchen.*

shook /ʃʊk/ the past tense of SHAKE

shoot¹ /ʃuːt/ *v* **shot** /ʃɒt‖ʃɑt/, **shooting 1** [T] to hit, wound, or kill with a gun: *He shot a bird.* | *He was shot three times in the arm.* | *She shot him dead.* **2** [I;T] to fire a gun: *I'm coming out with my hands up. Don't shoot.* **3 shoot at** to aim a gun at someone or something and fire it: *He shot at the bird, but missed.* **4** [I;T] to aim the ball at the place which gets you a point in games such as football and BASKETBALL: *Murano shot the winning goal just 30 seconds from the end. | Go on! Shoot!* **5** [I+adv/prep;T + adv/prep] to move or send something suddenly or quickly: *Blood shot out of the wound.* | *He shot past me without speaking.* | *She shot him an angry look.* | *They shot questions at us for over an hour.* | *The force of the gas in a bottle of champagne can shoot the cork across the room.* **6** [I;T] to use a camera to make a film: *"Room Downstairs" was shot in Italy.* **7** [I;T] to shoot birds or animals for sport: *He shoots most weekends.* | *duck shooting* | *We go shooting in Scotland every autumn.*

shoot sbdy/sthg ↔ **down** *phr v* [T] **1** to bring down and destroy a plane by shooting it when it is in the air **2** to say, sometimes without cause and without showing any respect for the person who had it, that an idea is no good at all: *another good idea shot down by the chairman*

shoot out *phr v* [I;T **shoot** sthg ↔ **out**] to move fast out of somewhere: *The snake shot out its tongue.* | *Its tongue shot out.*

shoot up *phr v* [I] to go upwards, increase, or grow quickly: *Flames shot up into the air.* | *Prices have shot up lately.*

shoot² *n* **1** the first part of a plant to appear above ground, or a new growth from a plant **2** an occasion for shooting birds or animals: *a weekend shoot*

shoot·ing /ˈʃuːtɪŋ/ *n* **1** [C] an act of wounding someone with a gun: *politically-motivated shootings* **2** [U] the sport of shooting birds or animals

shooting star /ˌ·· ˈ·/ *n* (also **falling star**) a piece of matter from space which burns brightly as it passes through the Earth's air

shop¹ /ʃɒp ‖ ʃɑrp/ *n* **1** (**store** *AmE*) a room or building where goods are regularly kept and sold: *the local village shop* | *The shops in town close at 5.30.* | *a bookshop* | *a sweetshop* **2** a place where things are made or repaired: *the body shop in a car factory* | *a repair shop*

shop² *v* **-pp-** [I] to go to the shops and buy things or try to find things you want to buy: *I was shopping for some new clothes, but I couldn't find anything.* | *I hate shopping.* | *People's shopping habits are changing now that we have the big out-of-town superstores.* | *He's gone shopping for a present for his mother.* –**shopper** *n* –see CUSTOMER (USAGE)

shop around *phr v* [I] to compare prices in different shops: *It pays to shop around for the lowest price.*

shop as·sis·tant /ˈ· ·ˌ··/ *n* (**salesclerk** *AmE*) a person who serves buyers in a shop

shop floor /ˌ· ˈ·◄/ *n* **1 the shop floor** the ordinary workers, as opposed to the managers: *They need to take more notice of shop floor opinion.* **2 on the shop floor** with or by the ordinary workers: *The decision was very popular on the shop floor.*

shop·keep·er /ˈʃɒpˌkiːpəʳ ‖ ˈʃɑrp-/ *n* (**storekeeper** *AmE*) a person who owns and runs a small shop

shop·lifting /ˈʃɒpˌlɪftɪŋ ‖ ˈʃɑrp-/ *v* [I only in progressive forms] taking things from a shop without paying for them: *She was caught shoplifting.* | *Shoplifting is on the increase.* –**shoplifter** *n* –see THIEF (USAGE)

shop·ping /ˈʃɒpɪŋ ‖ ˈʃɑr-/ *n* [U] **1** all the things that you need to buy or that you have bought on one trip to the shops: *Put the shopping on the table.* | *Can I carry some of your shopping for you?* | *Put it on the shopping list.* | *It's in my shopping bag.* **2 do the shopping** to go to the shops and buy things, especially the everyday things you need such as food: *My husband always does the shopping.*

shopping cen·tre /ˈ·· ˌ··/ *n* a group of shops of different kinds planned and built together in one area

shop-soiled /ˈʃɒpsɔɪld ‖ ˈʃɑrp-/ *adj BrE* slightly damaged or dirty from being in a shop for a long time

shop stew·ard /ˌ· ˈ··/ *n* an officer elected by trade union members in a particular place of work

shore¹ /ʃɔːʳ/ *n* [C;U] **1** the land along the edge of the sea or other large area of water: *walking along the shore* | *a boat about a mile from the shore* **2 on shore** on land, as opposed to at sea: *The sailors got into trouble while they were on shore.*

■ USAGE Compare **coast, shore, beach,** and **seaside.** The **coast** is the edge of an area of land where it meets the sea. Use it particularly when thinking about the position of a place on the map: *the French* **coast** | *the north* **coast** *of Spain* | *a house on the Suffolk* **coast. Shore** is the usual word for the land on the edge of a sea or lake: *We walked along the rocky* **shore.** | *The waves broke on the opposite* **shore.** A **beach** is part of the shore that is smooth, without cliffs or rocks: *The children are building sandcastles on the* **beach.** | *Rows of bodies lay sunbathing on the* **beach. The seaside** is used to talk about the area near the sea when we think of it as a place for a holiday or enjoyment: *We always take the children to the* **seaside** *in August.*

shore² *v* **shored, shoring**

shore sthg ↔ **up** *phr v* [T] to strengthen or give support to something weak or in danger of failing:

government action to shore up farm prices | *They shored up the damaged buildings.*

shorn /ʃɔːn ‖ ʃɔːrn/ **1** the past participle of SHEAR **2 be shorn** to have too much hair cut off

short¹ /ʃɔːt ‖ ʃɔːrt/ *adj* **1** not long: *a short break in the middle of the lesson* | *a short pencil* | *a short article on the front page* | *She has her hair short these days.* –see picture on page 245 **2** not as tall as usual: *the shortest boy in the class* | *a rather short tower* –see picture on page 245 –opposite **tall 3** not enough: *short measure* | *short rations* | *The team is one man short.* **4 short of:** a lacking something or not having enough of something: *short of money* | *short of breath* | *We've got most of the equipment we need, but we're still short of a thermometer.* **b** if something does not happen or is not done: *Short of a miracle, the harvest is going to fail.* **5 be short for something** to be a short way of saying a longer word or expression: *"Rep" is short for "representative".* | *"What's 'Cindy' short for?" "Lucinda."* **6 for short** as a shorter way of saying the same name: *My name is Alexander, Al for short.* | *the Association of South-East Asian Nations, or Asian for short* **7 be short with someone** to be a little rude to someone, not speaking to them much because you are in a hurry or they annoy you **8 have a short temper, be short-tempered** to be the sort of person who gets angry very quickly **9 in short** you use this expression when you have talked or written in detail about something and you want to make sure that people understand exactly what you mean by giving them the main idea or ideas again in few words and clearly; you use **in short** to tell them that you are going to SUMMARIZE your ideas: *It tests both spoken and written English. It demands the ability to communicate as well as a knowledge of grammar and vocabulary. Candidates are required to do extensive reading. In short, this is a very well-designed examination.* **10 go short** to have less than you really need: *The mother will sometimes go short in order to make sure that the children have enough.* | *We went short of food for a few days.* **11 at short notice** without being given much time to prepare: *When John Raven had an accident another actor took over his part at short notice.* **12 be in short supply** to be able to be obtained only in small quantities or with difficulty because there is not enough: *Water was in short supply.* | *Skilled engineers are in short supply now that business is booming again.* **13 in the short term** looked at over only a short period of time: *In the short term inflation will continue to rise, but we should begin to see a fall by mid-summer.* **14 make short work of** *infml* to deal with quickly and easily **15 be short on something** *infml* not to have enough of a desirable quality: *The trouble with her is that she's long on talk, but short on action.* **16 short and sweet** not lasting very long and saying only what is necessary – **shortness** *n* [U]

short² *adv* **1** just before reaching a certain point **2** suddenly

short³ *n* **1 shorts** [pl] **a** trousers ending at or above your knees **b** the usual American word for UNDER-PANTS **2** [C] a drink of strong alcohol, such as WHISKY or RUM, that has nothing added to it to make it weaker **3** [C] *infml* –see SHORT CIRCUIT

short·age /ˈʃɔːtɪdʒ ‖ ˈʃɔːrt-/ *n* a situation in which you do not have enough of something: *food shortages during the war* | *an acute shortage of skilled workers*

short·bread /ˈʃɔːtbred ‖ ˈʃɔːrt-/ *n* (also **shortcake**) [U] a thick hard sweet BISCUIT made with a lot of butter

short-change /ˌ·ˈ·/ *v* **short-changed, short-changing** [T] **1** to give back too little money to someone who has paid you for something **2** to treat someone badly by not giving them as much as you should: *There's a general feeling that the children of single-parent families have been short-changed by the new system.*

short cir·cuit¹ /ˌ· ˈ··/ *n* the touching of two electrical wires that should not touch; a short circuit usually makes the electricity go off

short-circuit² *v* [I;T] to have a short circuit or to cause one in something

short·com·ing /ˈʃɔːtˌkʌmɪŋ ‖ ˈʃɔːrt-/ *n* a fault: *In spite of all his shortcomings I still like him.*

short cut /ˌ· ˈ·, ˈ· ·/ /ˈ·-/ *n* **1** a quicker and more direct way of getting somewhere than the usual way: *They took a short cut through the fields.* **2** a quicker way of doing something; sometimes it is not as good as the usual way and people choose it because they are lazy or dishonest

short·en /ˈʃɔːtn ‖ ˈʃɔːrtn/ *v* [I;T] to make or become shorter: *Shorten this report to 2000 words.*

short·fall /ˈʃɔːtfɔːl ‖ ˈʃɔːrt-/ *n* less than is needed or expected: *Owing to the drought, there will be a shortfall in wheat supplies this year.*

short·hand /ˈʃɔːthænd ‖ ˈʃɔːrt-/ *n* [U] a system of rapid writing using signs for letters and words: *Her secretary made some notes in shorthand.*

short-hand·ed /ˌ· ˈ··/ *adj* see SHORT-STAFFED

short list /ˈ· ·/ *n BrE* a list of a small group of people from which the person who will get a job or prize is chosen: *I think I'm on their short list.* –**short-list** *v* [T] : *He's been short-listed for the director's job.*

short-lived /ˌ· ˈ·◄/ *adj* lasting only a short time

short·ly /ˈʃɔːtli ‖ ˈʃɔːrt-/ *adv* **1** soon: *He will be back shortly.* | *We received your message shortly after landing.* **2** in an impatient way: *She answered me rather shortly.*

short·sight·ed /ˌʃɔːtˈsaɪtɪd◄ ‖ ˈʃɔːrt-/ *adj* **1** unable to see things clearly if they are not close to your eyes **2** not considering the likely future effects of something: *You need to think of the future; don't make a short-sighted decision.* –**shortsightedly** *adv* –**shortsightedness** *n* [U]

short-staffed /ˌ· ˈ·/ *adj* (also **short-handed**) with too few workers

short-term /ˌ· ˈ·◄/ *adj* having an effect within or for a short time: *This is only a short-term solution to our problems.* –**short term** *n* [sing] : *Profits will fall in the short term*

short wave /ˌ· ˈ·◄/ *n* [U] radio broadcasting or receiving using waves of less than 120 metres in length: *Our only means of sending a message was by short-wave radio.*

shot¹ /ʃɒt ‖ ʃɑːt/ the past tense and past participle of SHOOT

shot² *n* **1** [C] an act of firing a gun: *He fired three shots.* | *I heard a shot outside.* **2** [C] an act of kicking or hitting a ball to make a point in a game: *His shot went wide of the goal.* | *Well done! That was a* *good shot!* **3 a good shot, a crack shot** a person who shoots very skilfully [RELATED PHRASE **a poor shot**] **4** [U] non-explosive metal balls for shooting from some kinds of guns: *We couldn't eat the rabbit, as it was full of lead shot.* **5** [C] a photograph, or a picture seen in a film: *He got some wonderful action shots.* **6** [C] an INJECTION of a drug: *The doctor gave me a shot of penicillin.* **7** [C] *infml* an attempt to do something: *I'm not much good at sewing, but I'll have a shot at mending it.* **8 a shot in the dark** *infml* a guess, without having any knowledge of something: *I was surprised that I got the answer right: it was a complete shot in the dark.* **9 like a shot** *infml* quickly and eagerly: *He offered me the job, and I accepted like a shot.*

shot·gun /ˈʃɒtɡʌn ‖ ˈʃɑːt-/ *n* a gun which fires shot, used for shooting birds and animals

should /ʃəd; *strong* ʃʊd/ *v negative short form* **shouldn't** [modal verb] **1** used to show that you think someone has a moral duty to do something: *The government should do something to help these people.* | *You should be ashamed of yourself.* | *You shouldn't tell lies.* | *He should have gone to prison for what he did.* **2** used when you are saying that something would be a good idea: *You should see a doctor.* | *He should go to college and get himself some qualifications.* | *We should sell this house and buy a bigger one.* | *I really should be going soon.* | *We should have booked in advance.* | *Should I phone her to check that she's there?* **3** used when you are saying that you expect something to happen or to be true: *They should be here soon.* | *It should be easy.* | *He should have got my letter by now.* | *We shouldn't have to wait long.* **4** *fml* used with "I" and "we" in sentences with "if", when you are saying what you would do: *I should be very surprised if he came now.* **5** used in some sentences after "that": *It's odd that he should say that.* | *We arranged that she should meet us in London.* **6** *fml* used when you are talking about things that might happen in the future: *If we should miss the train, we'll come by car.* | *Should you remember his name, please let me know.* –see Study Note on page 392 **7 I should** a phrase you use when you are giving advice to someone: *I should get that roof mended if I were you.* | *"What shall I do about the car?" "I should take it to a garage."* **8 I should like** a polite way of saying that you want something: *I should like to ask a question.* **9 I should think** I believe: *I should think he's about fifty.* | *"Will you be able to come tonight?" "I should think so."* **10 I should have thought** a phrase you use when you are giving your opinion and saying that you expected something to be true: *I should have thought that was obvious!*

shoul·der¹ /ˈʃəʊldəʳ/ *n* **1** [C] the part of your body between your neck and the tops of your arms: *Put my jacket round your shoulders.* | *She glanced over her shoulder nervously.* **2 shoulders** [pl] the parts of a piece of clothing that cover this part of your body: *a jacket with padded shoulders* **3 a shoulder to cry on** someone from whom you get sympathy

shoulder² *v* [T] **1** to put something heavy across your shoulders **2** to accept something such as responsibility or blame: *Local residents are being asked to shoulder the cost of the damage.*

shoulder blade /ˈ··· / *n* either of the two flat bones on each side of your back

should·n't /ˈʃʊdnt/ a short form of "should not": *You shouldn't laugh at him.*

should·'ve /ˈʃʊdəv/ a short form of "should have": *You should've come earlier – it's too late now.*

shout¹ /ʃaʊt/ *v* [I;T] to say something very loudly or speak very loudly: *"Help!" he shouted.* | *There's no need to shout; I can hear you.* | *He's always shouting at his children.* | *We shouted to him to look where he was going.*

shout sbdy ↔ down *phr v* [T] to prevent someone from being heard by shouting at them: *The speaker tried to reply but he was shouted down by the opposition.*

shout sthg ↔ out *phr v* [T] to suddenly shout loudly: *She shouted out a warning and I managed to jump clear.*

shout² *n* a loud cry or call: *a warning shout* | *shouts of delight from the crowd*

shove /ʃʌv/ *v* **shoved, shoving** [I;T] **1** to push in a quick, rough way: *I shoved the papers into my bag.* | *People always push and shove to squeeze into the trains.* **2 Shove off!** *infml* a phrase used when you are telling someone rudely to go away –**shove** *n*: *It's stuck. Give it a shove.*

shov·el¹ /ˈʃʌvəl/ *n* a long-handled tool with a flat broad surface at the bottom, used for lifting and moving earth, snow, sand, or coal

shovel² *v* **-ll-** (**-l-** *AmE*) **1** [I;T] to use a shovel to move and lift something: *shovelling snow* | *He shovelled the snow away.* **2** [T] to push quickly into a place: *She shovelled the papers into a drawer.* | *Don't shovel the chips into your mouth! Eat properly.*

show¹ /ʃəʊ/ *v* **showed, shown** /ʃəʊn/ *or* **showed** **1** [T] to allow or cause something to be seen: *He was showing them his holiday photographs.* | *She never shows her feelings.* | *I had to show my ticket to the inspector.* | *Show me that cut.* | *This picture shows us all practising.* □ USEFUL PATTERNS to show something; to show something to someone; to show someone something **2 show someone how to do something** to do something so that someone can watch and learn: *He showed us how to catch rabbits.* **3 show your face** to make an appearance: *I don't think he'd dare show his face here after his behaviour last week.* **4** [T] to make something clear: *The figures show a 9% increase in inflation.* | *His comments showed that he didn't understand.* | *Her behaviour shows you how bitter she feels.* | *This report shows the accident to have been the driver's fault.* **5 it goes to show** it proves the point: *Running away from the police, he fell under a bus ... which just goes to show that crime doesn't pay!* **6** [I] to appear or be noticeable: *Don't worry about that bit of dirt; it won't show.* | *The lights showed faintly through the mist.* **7 have nothing/not much to show for something** to have no or not much gain or profit from something: *We worked hard all night, but didn't have much to show for it when dawn came.* **8** [T] to behave with a particular feeling towards someone: *They showed their enemies no mercy.* | *You should show more respect to your parents!* **9 show someone somewhere** to go with someone and guide them: *I'll show you to your seat.* | *Could you show the gentleman in, please, Wendy?* **10 show someone the door** to make it clear to someone that they are not welcome and must leave **11** [I;T] to offer a film for people to watch: *They're showing six hours of cartoons on children's TV today.*

show off *phr v* **1** [I] to try to get other people's attention and admiration: *He came first in that exam, and he's been showing off ever since.* **2** [T **show sbdy/sthg ↔ off**] to show someone or something that you are proud of to as many people as possible: *showing off her new car*

show sbdy ↔ **round/around** *phr v* [T] to act as a guide to someone on their first visit to a place: *Before you start work, I'll show you round the office.*

show up *phr v* **1** [T **show** sthg ↔ **up**] to cause something to be easily seen: *The bright light really shows up the cracks in the wall.* **2** [T **show** sbdy ↔ **up**] to behave in a way that makes someone feel ashamed of you: *Now, don't show me up when we have dinner with my boss!* **3** [I] *infml* to arrive at a place where you are expected: *He didn't show up at the party until after midnight.*

show² *n* **1** a performance in a theatre or on radio or television, especially one that is not very serious in its contents: *tickets for a variety show* **2** a collection of things for the public to look at: *the village flower show* **3** **on show** being shown to the public: *All the items will be on show until Wednesday.* **4 a show of something: a** a showing of a particular quality: *The army put on a show of strength.* **b** an outward appearance, as opposed to what is really happening: *I made a show of interest, but I really didn't care about their problems.* **5 a show of hands** a vote taken by counting the raised hands of the voters **6 for show** for appearance only: *It's all done for show – it doesn't mean a thing.*

show busi·ness /'· ,··/ *n* (also **showbiz** /'ʃəʊbɪz/ *infml*) [U] the business of entertaining in television, films, or the theatre: *She's in show business.*

show·down /'ʃəʊdaʊn/ *n infml* the settlement of a disagreement through an argument

show·er¹ /'ʃaʊəʳ/ *n* **1 a** an act of washing yourself by standing under running water: *I'll just have a quick shower.* **b** a place where you wash yourself like this: *He's in the shower.* **c** the apparatus under which you wash yourself: *The plumber is putting in a new shower.* **2** a short period of light rain: *Scattered showers are expected this afternoon.* **3** a fall of many small things or drops of liquid: *a shower of confetti*

shower² *v* **1** [I] to pour down in a shower: *Nuts showered down from the tree.* **2** [T] to scatter something heavily on someone or something: *The pipe burst, showering us with oil.*

show·er·y /'ʃaʊəri/ *adj* raining sometimes, but not for long

show·ing /'ʃəʊɪŋ/ *n* **1** [C] an act of letting the public see something: *There's a showing of his latest paintings at the art gallery.* **2** [sing] performance: *On their current showing, the party should do well in the election.*

show-jump·ing /'· ,··/ *n* [U] a sport in which riders, one at a time, jump their horses over a course of fences **–showjumper** *n*

show·man /'ʃəʊmən/ *n* **showmen** /-mən/ **1** a person whose business is producing entertainment for the public: *a fairground showman* **2** a person who likes to gain public attention: *Our local doctor is a bit of a showman.*

shown /ʃəʊn/ the past participle of SHOW

show-off /'· ·/ *n infml* a person who behaves in a way intended to make others admire them: *I know he's a good player, but I don't like him because he's such a show-off.*

SPELLING NOTE

Words with the sound /ʃ/ may be spelt **ch-**, like **chauffeur.**

---

show·room /'ʃəʊrʊm, -ruːm/ *n* a shop where goods for sale can be looked at: *a car showroom*

show·y /'ʃəʊi/ *adj* **showier, showiest** too colourful or bright, but without much real value or beauty

shrank /ʃræŋk/ the past tense of SHRINK

shrap·nel /'ʃræpnəl/ *n* [U] small pieces of metal scattered from an exploding bomb

shred¹ /ʃred/ *n* **1** a small narrow piece of paper or material torn or roughly cut off: *His coat was torn to shreds.* **2 not a shred** not even a small bit: *He doesn't have a shred of evidence.*

shred² *v* **-dd-** [T] to cut or tear into small pieces: *shredded cabbage*

shrew /ʃruː/ *n* **1** a small animal like a mouse with a long pointed nose **2** *old fash* a bad-tempered woman

shrewd /ʃruːd/ *adj* **1** quick to understand and judge a situation: *He's shrewd enough to turn things to his own advantage.* **2** well-reasoned and likely to be right: *a shrewd guess* **–shrewdly** *adv*

shriek /ʃriːk/ *v* [I;T] to cry out in a high voice: *"Help!" she shrieked.* | *They were all shrieking with laughter.* **–shriek** *n* : *She gave a shriek of terror.*

shrill /ʃrɪl/ *adj* high and sharp (used of sound): *a shrill whistle* **–shrilly** /'ʃrɪl-li, 'ʃrɪli/ *adv*

shrimp /ʃrɪmp/ *n* a small sea creature with many legs and a long tail, used as food

shrine /ʃraɪn/ *n* a holy or respected place: *the shrine of St Augustine*

shrink¹ /ʃrɪŋk/ *v* **shrank** /ʃræŋk/, **shrunk** /ʃrʌŋk/ **1** [I;T] to become smaller or make something become smaller: *You shouldn't wash that jumper in the washing machine – it will shrink.* | *Oh no! I've shrunk my best cardigan in the wash.* | *shrinking profits* **2 shrink from something** to avoid or move away from something because you are afraid of it: *He shrank from the thought of having to kill anyone.*

shrink² *n infml* a PSYCHIATRIST (a word which is often used in a humorous way)

shrink·age /'ʃrɪŋkɪdʒ/ *n* [U;sing] a decrease in the size or amount of something: *There has been further shrinkage in the size of the workforce.*

shriv·el /'ʃrɪvəl/ *v* **-ll- (-l-** *AmE*) [I;T] to dry out, or make something dry out, and twist into small folds: *The plants shrivelled up in the heat.*

shroud¹ /ʃraʊd/ *n* **1** the cloth used for wrapping a dead body **2** something that covers and hides: *A shroud of secrecy surrounds the plan.*

shroud² *v* **be shrouded in** to be hidden by something: *Everything was shrouded in fog.* | *The case was shrouded in mystery.*

shrub /ʃrʌb/ *n* a low bush

shrub·be·ry /'ʃrʌbəri/ *n* **shrubberies** [C;U] part of a garden with a lot of shrubs

shrug /ʃrʌg/ *v* **-gg-** [I;T] (also **shrug your shoulders**) to raise your shoulders as an expression of doubt or lack of interest: *She just shrugged and said, "I don't care."* | *He shrugged his shoulders and wouldn't reply.* **–shrug** *n* : *She just gave a shrug.*
shrug sthg ↔ **off** *phr v* [T] to treat something as if it is not really serious or important: *You can't just shrug off something like this as if it didn't exist!*

shrunk /ʃrʌŋk/ the past tense and past participle of SHRINK

shrunk·en /'ʃrʌŋkən/ *adj* that has been shrunk: *shrunken heads*

shud·der /ˈʃʌdər/ v [I] **1** to shake uncontrollably for a moment with fear or strong dislike: *He saw the body on the floor, and shuddered.* **2 I shudder to think of something** I don't like to think about something at all: *I shudder to think of how often I told her I hated the boss.* | *"What will you have to pay?" "I shudder to think!"* **3 shudder to a halt** (of a vehicle) to stop, shaking at the same time: *The bus shuddered to a halt.* –**shudder** n : *She gave a shudder of repulsion.*

shuf·fle /ˈʃʌfəl/ v **shuffled, shuffling 1** [I] to walk slowly, without lifting your feet off the ground properly: *The old woman shuffled home.* **2** [I;T] to move your feet around impatiently or nervously, or move around in your chair like this: *Stop shuffling your feet!* **3** [I;T] to mix up the order of playing cards: *Your turn to shuffle.* –**shuffle** n : *Give the cards a shuffle.*

shun /ʃʌn/ v **-nn-** [T] to avoid on purpose: *He was shunned by the other prisoners.* | *Few politicians shun publicity.*

shunt /ʃʌnt/ v [T] to move objects or people, especially to a less important place: *The trains were shunted to a railway siding.* | *I've been shunted off to the branch office.*

shush /ʃʊʃ/ interj a word used when telling someone to be quiet: *Shush! Don't cry!*

shut /ʃʌt/ v **shut, shut, shutting 1** [I;T] to close something: *Please shut the gate.* | *He shut his eyes and tried to sleep.* | *She shut the book.* | *The doors shut, and the train moved off.* **2** [T + adv/prep] to lock or catch something inside or outside something: *He shut himself in his room to think.* | *She shut her skirt in the door and tore it.* **3** [I;T] to close: *The shops shut at 5.30.* | *He lost his job when they shut the factory.*

shut sbdy ↔ **away** phr v [T] to keep someone locked up away from other people: *He shut himself away in an attic and nobody knew he was there.*

shut down phr v [I;T **shut** sthg ↔ **down**] (of a business) to close and stop working: *He was made redundant when the pit shut down.*

shut sthg ↔ **off** phr v [T] to disconnect: *Don't forget to shut off the gas when you go on holiday.*

shut up phr v **1** [I] infml to stop talking: *Now shut up for a minute and listen!* | *"So I said…" "Shut up!"* **2** [T **shut** sbdy ↔ **up**] infml to prevent someone from talking: *He was going to tell the newspapers, so we gave him £1000 to shut him up.* **3** [T **shut** sbdy/sthg ↔ **up**] to keep enclosed: *They shut him up in a cupboard until he confessed.*

shut·down /ˈʃʌtdaʊn/ n a stopping of work or operation

shut·ter /ˈʃʌtər/ n **1** [C] a part of a camera which opens when a photograph is taken, to let light onto the film **2 shutters** [pl] wooden or metal covers that can be unfolded in front of a window

shut·tle[1] /ˈʃʌtl/ n an air, bus, or train service which makes frequent journeys between two places: *There is a shuttle between the station and the university.*

shuttle[2] v **shuttled, shuttling** [I;T] to move between two places often or regularly: *The new trains shuttle passengers across the town.*

shut·tle·cock /ˈʃʌtlkɒk ‖ -kɑːk/ n a small light feathered object hit across a net in the game of BADMINTON

shy[1] /ʃaɪ/ adj **shyer, shyest** (also **shier, shiest**) **1** nervous and uncomfortable in the company of other people: *When the children met the Queen, they* were too shy to speak. | *a shy smile* **2** unwilling to come near people (used of animals) **3 shy** afraid of or hating: *She's camera-shy and hates being photographed.* | *He's not ill – he's just work-shy.* –**shyly** adv –**shyness** n [U]

shy[2] v **shied, shying** (of a horse) to make a sudden movement through fear: *My horse shied at the dog, and I fell off.*

shy away from sthg phr v [T] to avoid doing something unpleasant: *She tends to shy away from accepting responsibility.*

sib·ling /ˈsɪblɪŋ/ n fml a brother or sister

sick[1] /sɪk/ adj **1** suffering from an illness: *My uncle is sick in hospital.* **2** (only before a noun) for illness: *sick pay* | *He's got two weeks' sick leave.* **3 be off sick** not to be at work because of illness: *Sarah's off sick this week.* **4 be sick** to throw up what is in your stomach **5 feel sick** to feel as if you are going to throw up what is in your stomach: *He began to feel rather sick when the ship started to move.* **6 make someone sick** infml to give someone feelings of annoyance or strong dislike: *Your complaining makes me sick!* **7 sick of, sick to death of, sick and tired of** infml annoyed with and tired of: *I'm sick of sitting around waiting for him.* **8** not treating death or cruelty in a properly serious way: *That's a really sick joke. I don't find it funny at all.*

sick[2] n [pl] the sick people who are ill

sick·en /ˈsɪkən/ v **1** [T] to cause strong feelings of dislike, anger, or shock: *Their hypocrisy sickens me.* | *His head hit the floor with a sickening thud.* **2** [I] to become ill: *The animal began to sicken and soon died.* **3 sicken for something** to be about to become ill: *She's got a high temperature; maybe she's sickening for something.*

sick·ly /ˈsɪkli/ adj **sicklier, sickliest 1** weak and unhealthy: *a sickly child* | *a sickly-looking plant* **2** looking or smelling unpleasant or unhealthy: *His face was a sickly yellow.* | *a foul sickly smell*

sick·ness /ˈsɪknəs/ n **1** [U] the condition of being ill or unhealthy: *Put up a notice: Closed due to staff sickness.* **2** [U] the condition of feeling or being sick: *Morning sickness is one of the first indications of pregnancy.* **3** [C;U] a particular form of illness: *sleeping sickness*

side[1] /saɪd/ n **1** a surface of something that is not its top, bottom, front, or back: *The front door is locked: we'll have to go around to the side of the house.* | *Standing on either side of her were her sons.* | *I sat down by his side.* **2** any of the flat surfaces of something: *A cube has six sides.* | *Which side of the box do you put the label on?* **3** either of the two surfaces of a thin flat object: *Write on only one side of the paper.* | *The queen's head is on one side of a pound coin.* **4** the right or left part of your body between the shoulder and the top of the leg: *I've got a pain all down my left side.* **5 side by side** next to one another: *We sat side by side on a long wooden bench.* **6** an edge or border: *A square has four equal sides.* | *We had a picnic by the side of the road.* **7** a slope: *a beautiful spot halfway up the side of the hill* **8** a place or division according to a real or imaginary central line: *She lives on the other side of town.* | *Cars drive on the left side of the road in England.* **9** one of the different points of view in an argument: *Don't just listen to my side of things – ask him too!* | *Try to look at all sides of the question before deciding.* **10** one of the two people or groups in a quarrel or war: *In most wars neither side wins.* | *Whose side are you on?* **11 on someone's side: a** agreeing with someone and ready to support them in an argument: *I'm*

on your side – I think you've been treated very badly. **b** relating to someone's relatives or family history: *He's Scottish on his mother's side.* **12** [+ sing/pl verb] a sports team: *Our side are winning.* | *My brother's side is always losing.* **13 take sides** to support one person against another in an argument: *Don't ask me to decide – I'm not taking sides!* **14 on the side** as an additional activity, often a dishonest one: *He runs a little business on the side.* **15 on the high side, on the low side, etc.** *infml* a phrase you use to show that you think something is a little high, low, etc.: *I like the house but I think the price is on the high side.* | *She's on the small side for her age.* | *I ought to lose some weight – I'm a bit on the plump side at the moment.* **16 put on/to one side** to keep for possible use later **17 -sided** having a particular number or type of sides: *an eight-sided coin* | *a steep-sided valley*

side² *adj* [only before a noun] **1** at, from, or towards the side: *a side door* **2** besides the main or regular thing: *Certain drugs have harmful side effects.* | *We serve curry with a selection of side dishes.* **3** a side street, a side road a narrow, less important street

side³ *v* **sided, siding**
side with sbdy *phr v* [T] to support one person or group in a quarrel or fight: *She always sides with her son against the teachers.*

side·board /ˈsaɪdbɔːd ‖ -bɔːrd/ *n* **1** [C] a long low cupboard, used to hold dishes and glasses **2 sideboards** [pl] (also **sideburns** /-bɜːnz‖-bɜːrnz/ *AmE*) hair grown on the sides of a man's face

side·car /ˈsaɪdkɑːʳ/ *n* a small vehicle fastened to the side of a motorcycle for carrying passengers

side ef·fect /ˈ·ˌ·ˌ·/ *n* **1** an effect that a drug has on you in addition to curing illness or pain: *Sleeping pills often have harmful side effects.* **2** an event that is not planned and happens in addition to the main result: *One side effect of inflation is unemployment.*

side·lights /ˈsaɪdlaɪts/ *n* [pl] the small lights at the front of a vehicle –see picture on page 49

side·line /ˈsaɪdlaɪn/ *n* **1** an activity done in addition to your regular job **2 sidelines** [pl] the lines marking the length of a football field or tennis court

side·long /ˈsaɪdlɒŋ ‖ -lɔːŋ/ *adj* directed sideways: *a sidelong glance*

side·show /ˈsaɪdʃəʊ/ *n* **1** a small show at a fair or CIRCUS with amusements or games **2** an unimportant activity compared to a more serious main one

side·step /ˈsaɪdstep/ *v* **-pp-** [T] to avoid something dangerous or unpleasant: *The minister neatly sidestepped the reporter's questions.*

side·tracked /ˈsaɪdtrækt/ *v* **get sidetracked** to leave an important activity and start an unimportant one: *I started to cook dinner but got sidetracked reading the recipe book.*

side·walk /ˈsaɪdwɔːk/ *n* the usual American word for a PAVEMENT

side·ways /ˈsaɪdweɪz/ *adv, adj* to or towards one side: *to step sideways* | *a sideways jump*

sid·ing /ˈsaɪdɪŋ/ *n* a short railway track connected to the main track, used to park carriages when they are not being used –see picture on page 735

SPELLING NOTE
Words with the sound / s /, may be spelt **c-**, like **city**, or **ps-**, like **psychology**.

---

si·dle /ˈsaɪdl/ *v* **sidled, sidling** [I] to walk in a nervous or uncertain way as if you do not want to be noticed: *He sidled up to the stranger and tried to sell him the stolen ring.*

siege /siːdʒ/ *n* **1** [C;U] a military operation in which an army surrounds a place and blocks supplies and help, in order to force the people inside to come out and admit they are defeated **2** [C] a situation in which an armed criminal keeps people as prisoners in a building

si·es·ta /siˈestə/ *n* a short sleep after the midday meal which people have in hot countries

sieve /sɪv/ *n* **1** a tool made of wire or plastic net on a frame, used for separating large and small solid bits, or solid things from liquid: *Use a sieve to get out the lumps.* –see picture on page 638 **2 a head/memory like a sieve** *infml* a very poor memory

sieve² *v* **sieved, sieving** [T] to put a liquid or a dry substance through a sieve: *Sieve the flour first.* | *Sieve out the stones from the soil.*

sift /sɪft/ *v* **1** [T] to put a dry substance through a sieve **2** [I;T] to examine things in a mass or group: *sifting through her papers to find his letter*

sigh¹ /saɪ/ *v* [I] to let out a deep breath slowly as a way of expressing tiredness, sadness, or pleasure: *She sighed heavily.*

sigh² *n* an act or sound of sighing: *We all breathed a sigh of relief when she left.* | *She gave a little sigh of contentment.*

sight¹ /saɪt/ *n* **1** [U] the ability to see: *He lost his sight in a road accident.* **2** [sing;U] an act of seeing something, or an occasion when you see: *I always faint at the sight of blood.* | *The house is hidden from sight by a row of trees.* | *I had my first sight of land for three weeks.* | *Do you believe in love at first sight?* **3** [C] something that is seen: *the familiar sight of the postman going along the street* **4** [U] the range of what can be seen: *The boat was within sight of land.* | *Keep out of sight until the police have gone.* | *There's no end in sight.* **5 a sight** something which looks very bad or so foolish that it cannot be taken seriously: *What a sight you are, with paint all over your clothes!* **6 a sight** *infml* a lot: *This hotel's a sight better than the place I usually stay at.* **7 the sights** the places that are interesting to see: *We'll take you to see the sights of London.* **8 sights** [pl] a part of an instrument or weapon which helps you to aim correctly **9 set your sights on something** to try very hard to obtain or become something: *She'd set her sights on going to college.* **10 catch sight of** to see something suddenly: *I caught sight of her hurrying away.* [RELATED PHRASE **lose sight of**: *I lost sight of her in the crowd.*]

sight² *v* [T] to get a sudden or quick view of someone or something after looking for them for a long time: *The missing child has been sighted in London.* | *We sighted a falcon and some other rare birds.* **–sighting** *n*

sight·ed /ˈsaɪtɪd/ *adj* (of a person) not blind: *Both blind and sighted learners will benefit from the new library system.*

sight·see·ing /ˈsaɪtˌsiːɪŋ/ *n* [U] going about as a tourist on holiday, visiting places of interest: *Allow three days for sightseeing in Paris.* **–sightseer** *n*

sign¹ /saɪn/ *n* **1** a mark that always has a particular meaning: *signs of military rank* | *the minus sign* **2** a movement of your body giving a particular meaning: *She put her finger to her lips as a sign to be quiet.* **3** a board or notice giving information or a warning: *Pay attention to the road signs.* | *There* *was a "No Smoking" sign on her door.* **4** something that shows the presence or likely future existence of something else: *Swollen ankles can be a sign of heart disease.* | *There are signs that the economy is improving.* **5 a sign of the zodiac** any of the 12 divisions of the year represented by groups of stars

sign² *v* **1** [I;T] to write your name on a paper or letter for official purposes: *The papers are ready to be signed.* | *She signed the cheque.* | *Can you sign here please?* **2 sign on the dotted line** to agree to something, especially by signing a contract

sign on *phr v* **1** [I] to officially agree to work or study by signing a contract: *He signed on with the Army.* | *You could sign on for a computer course.* **2** [T **sign** sbdy ↔ **on**] to officially give someone a job: *The foreman has signed on several new men this week.* **3** [I] to say officially that you are unemployed so that you can receive money from the state

sign sthg ↔ **away** *phr v* [T] to give something up formally by signing a paper: *He signed away his share in the property.*

sign for sthg *phr v* [T] to sign your name to show that you have received something

sign in *phr v* [I] to write your name when arriving at a hotel or club [RELATED PHRASE **sign out**]

sign up *phr v* **1** [I] to sign an agreement to do something: *I've signed up to take a course at the local college.* **2** [T **sign** sbdy ↔ **up**] to get someone to sign an agreement to do something: *Our manager's just signed up two new players.*

sig·nal¹ /ˈsɪɡnəl/ *n* **1** a sound or action intended to give a message: *A red lamp is often used as a danger signal.* | *smoke signals* **2** a piece of railway apparatus like traffic lights to tell train drivers whether to stop – see picture on page 735 **3** a sound, image, or message sent by waves: *We live too far from the city to get a strong television signal.* | *radar signals*

signal² *v* **-ll-** (**-l-** *AmE*) **1** [I] to give a signal: *The general signalled for the attack to begin.* **2** [T] to express, warn, or tell by a signal: *The policeman signalled the traffic to move forward.* | *Both sides have signalled their willingness to start negotiations.* **3** [T] to be a sign or proof of: *This defeat signalled the end of the war.*

signal³ *adj* [only before a noun] *fml* very noticeable and important: *a signal achievement* –**signally** *adv*

sig·na·to·ry /ˈsɪɡnətərɪ ‖ -tɔːrɪ/ *n* **signatories** *fml* any of the people or countries that sign an agreement

sig·na·ture /ˈsɪɡnətʃəʳ/ *n* a person's name written in their own handwriting, at the end of a letter, cheque, or official paper: *a petition with four thousand signatures* | *I couldn't decipher his signature.*

sig·nif·i·cance /sɪɡˈnɪfɪkəns/ *n* [U] importance and meaning: *The discovery of oil is of great significance to the country's economy.* | *It doesn't matter; it's of no significance.*

sig·nif·i·cant /sɪɡˈnɪfɪkənt/ *adj* **1** large or noticeable: *a significant increase in crime* **2** having a special meaning: *a significant discovery* –**significantly** *adv*

sig·ni·fy /ˈsɪɡnɪfaɪ/ *v* **signified, signified** [T] *fml* to have a particular meaning: *This latest shift signifies a real change in foreign policy.*

sign lan·guage /ˈ· ˌ··/ *n* [U] a language expressed by a system of hand movements, as used by people who cannot speak or hear properly

sign·post /ˈsaɪnpəʊst/ *n* a road sign showing directions and distances

Sikh /siːk/ *n* a member of a religious group that began in Northern India; the religion developed from HINDUISM but believes that there is only one god –**Sikhism** *n*

si·lage /ˈsaɪlɪdʒ/ *n* [U] grass or other green plants cut and stored for cattle food

si·lence¹ /ˈsaɪləns/ *n* [C;U] **1** total quietness: *The silence was broken by a loud cry.* **2 in silence** without speaking or making a noise: *She received the bad news in silence.* | *We walked downstairs in silence.* **3** failure or refusal to mention something: *I can't understand the government's silence on European issues.*

silence² *v* **silenced, silencing** [T] to make someone stop making a noise or expressing their opinions: *The enemy's guns were silenced by repeated bombings.* | *He silenced us with a menacing look.*

si·lenc·er /ˈsaɪlənsəʳ/ *n* an apparatus on a gun or on a car EXHAUST PIPE to reduce noise

si·lent /ˈsaɪlənt/ *adj* **1** not saying anything: *He looked thoughtful and was silent for a moment.* | *a silent film* | *She was silent on her plans for the company.* **2** without any noise: *the silent hours of the night* **3** not pronounced (of a letter in a word): *The "k" in "know" is silent.* –**silently** *adv*

sil·hou·ette¹ /ˌsɪluˈet/ *n* a shadow-like solid shape against a light background: *His silhouette appeared on the curtain.*

silhouette² *v* **be silhouetted** to appear as a silhouette: *The hills were silhouetted against a wonderful pink sunset.*

sil·i·con /ˈsɪlɪkən/ *n* [U] a non-metallic substance that is found in clay, sand, and stone

silicon chip /ˌ··· ˈ·/ *n* a small ELECTRONIC part used in a computer

silk /sɪlk/ *n* [U] fine smooth thread which is made into cloth: *a black silk dress*

silk·en /ˈsɪlkən/ *adj lit* soft, smooth, and shiny: *silken hair*

silk·worm /ˈsɪlkwɜːm ‖ -wɜːrm/ *n* an insect which produces a substance used to make silk

silk·y /ˈsɪlkɪ/ *adj* **silkier, silkiest** soft, smooth, or shiny: *the cat's silky fur* –**silkiness** *n* [U]

sill /sɪl/ *n* the shelf at the base of a window, either inside or outside a building

sil·ly /ˈsɪlɪ/ *adj* **sillier, silliest** foolish or not sensible: *Don't be silly!* | *It was pretty silly of you to forget your keys.*

si·lo /ˈsaɪləʊ/ *n* **1** a tall tower on a farm for storing SILAGE **2** an underground base from which a NUCLEAR weapon may be fired

silt¹ /sɪlt/ *n* [U] loose sand or mud carried along in a river

silt² *v* **silt up** *phr v* [I;T **silt** sthg ↔ **up**] to fill up or become filled with silt

sil·ver¹ /ˈsɪlvəʳ/ *n* [U] **1** a soft precious metal, greyish-white in colour, that can be brightly polished, and is used in jewellery and for making coins **2** coins made from this metal, or having that colour: *Could you give me £1 in silver, please?* **3** knives, forks, spoons, or dishes for the table, made from this metal: *The silver sparkled on the banquet table.* **4** a silver medal

silver² *adj* **1** made of silver: *silver earrings* **2 silver medal** a piece of silver that you win when you come second in a race or competition **3** greyish-white or silver in colour: *a silver-haired old man*

silver birch /ˌ·· ˈ·/ n a tree with a greyish-white trunk

silver ju·bi·lee /ˌ·· ˈ···/ n the 25th ANNIVERSARY of an important event

sil·ver·smith /ˈsɪlvəˌsmɪθ ‖ -ər-/ n a person who makes things out of silver

silver wed·ding /ˌ·· ˈ··/ (also **silver wedding anniversary** /ˌ·· ·· ··ˌ···/) n the 25th ANNIVERSARY of a wedding

sil·ver·y /ˈsɪlvəri/ adj 1 like silver in shine and colour 2 lit having a pleasant musical sound: silvery bells

sim·i·lar /ˈsɪmələr, ˈsɪmɪlər/ adj like or of the same kind: bread, cake, and other similar foods | We appear to have similar problems.

sim·i·lar·ly /ˈsɪmələli ‖ -lərli/ adv in a similar way; you can use this word when the point you are making is like the one before: Art students will be charged extra for materials. Similarly, catering students will have to pay for their ingredients.

sim·i·lar·i·ty /ˌsɪməˈlærəti/ n similarities [C;U] the quality of being alike: Despite the age difference, there are many similarities between the two brothers. | There's a certain similarity with the earlier version.

sim·i·le /ˈsɪməli/ n an expression in which someone or something is described as being similar to someone or something else: "As white as snow" is a simile.

sim·mer /ˈsɪmər/ v [I;T] to cook food gently in liquid at just below boiling point: Let the soup simmer. | Simmer the beans for two hours. –see COOK¹ (USAGE) –simmer n [sing] : Bring the potatoes to a simmer.

simmer down phr v [I] infml to become calmer after being angry: I was so furious that I went for a walk to simmer down.

sim·per /ˈsɪmpər/ v [I] to smile in a silly way –simper n

sim·ple /ˈsɪmpəl/ adj simpler, simplest 1 plain, and not decorated or fancy: The meal was simple but well-prepared. 2 easy to understand or do: There's quite a simple explanation. | It's a simple job, nothing complicated to worry about. 3 consisting of only one thing or part: A knife is one of the simplest of tools. | Bacteria are simple forms of life. 4 without anything added or mixed (of something nonphysical): She did it for the simple reason that she had no choice. 5 (also **simple-minded**) foolish or weak-minded: I'm afraid old Jack is a bit simple.

sim·ple·ton /ˈsɪmpəltən/ n old fash a weak-minded trusting person

sim·plic·i·ty /sɪmˈplɪsəti/ n [U] the quality of being simple: He believes everything you tell him, with childlike simplicity. | The main advantage of the new scheme is its simplicity.

sim·pli·fy /ˈsɪmpləˌfaɪ/ v simplified, simplifying [T] to make something easier to understand or do: Try to simplify your explanation for the children. –simplified adj –simplification /ˌsɪmpləfəˈkeɪʃən/ n [U]

sim·ply /ˈsɪmpli/ adv 1 in a simple way: On her small income they live very simply. 2 just or only:

I'd like to help. It's simply a question of money. 3 really: It was simply wonderful. | I simply couldn't believe him.

sim·u·late /ˈsɪmjɐleɪt/ v simulated, simulating [T] fml to give the effect or appearance of: The wood is carved to simulate rock. | Reality can now be simulated on screen. –simulation /ˌsɪmjɐˈleɪʃən/ n [C;U]: computer simulations

sim·u·lat·ed /ˈsɪmjɐleɪtɪd/ adj made to look or feel like the real thing: a simulated fur coat

sim·ul·ta·ne·ous /ˌsɪməlˈteɪniəs ‖ ˌsaɪ-/ adj happening at the same time: There was a flash of lightning and a simultaneous crash of thunder. –simultaneously adv

sin¹ /sɪn/ n [C;U] an offence against God or a religious law: guilty of the sin of pride | You must ask God for forgiveness for your sins.

sin² v -nn- [I] to do something wicked: You have sinned against God.

since /sɪns/ adv,prep,conj 1 adv,prep,conj starting at a time in the past and continuing until the present: It's a long time since our last holiday. | I've lived here since 1982. | I've worked abroad since leaving university. | We've been friends ever since we left school. 2 conj as a particular fact is true: Since you can't answer my question, I'll have to ask someone else.

sin·cere /sɪnˈsɪər/ adj real, true, or honest: a sincere apology | I don't think she was completely sincere in what she said.

sin·cere·ly /sɪnˈsɪəli ‖ -ˈsɪər-/ adv 1 in a sincere way: a sincerely held belief 2 Yours sincerely the usual way of ending a letter that begins "Dear Mr ...", "Dear Ms ...", etc. –compare FAITHFULLY(3)

sin·cer·i·ty /sɪnˈserəti/ n [U] the quality of being sincere

si·ne·cure /ˈsaɪnɪkjʊər, ˈsɪn-/ n a well-paid job with few duties (a word used to express disapproval)

sin·ew /ˈsɪnjuː/ n [C;U] a strong cord in your body which connects a muscle to a bone

sin·ew·y /ˈsɪnjuːi/ adj thin, with strong muscles

sin·ful /ˈsɪnfəl/ adj wicked or seriously wrong –sinfully adv –sinfulness n [U]

sing /sɪŋ/ v sang /sæŋ/, sung /sʌŋ/ 1 [I;T] to make musical sounds with your voice: I can hear the birds singing. | The children were singing Christmas carols. | Would you like me to sing you a song? 2 **sing someone's praises** to praise someone highly –singer n : an opera singer | She's a good singer.

sing. an abbreviation for SINGULAR

singe /sɪndʒ/ v singed, singeing [T] to burn slightly on the surface or edge: I'm afraid the iron was too hot – I've singed your shirt. –singe n

sing·ing /ˈsɪŋɪŋ/ n [U] the art or sound of singing: I'm taking singing lessons. | He could hear the singing down in the valley.

sin·gle¹ /ˈsɪŋgəl/ adj 1 [only before a noun] only one: A single tree gave shade from the sun. | Not a single one of my friends offered to help me. 2 [only before a noun] separate: There's no need to write down every single word I say. | You do that every single time. 3 having only one part: For strong sewing use double, not single, thread. | Inflation is now down to single figures. 4 unmarried: I intend to stay single for a while yet. 5 **a single bed, a single room** a bed or room for only one person 6 **a single ticket** BrE a ticket for a trip from one place to another but not for the return journey

single² n 1 BrE a ticket for a one-way journey: Two singles to Borchester, please. 2 a small record with only one song on each side **3 singles** a game of tennis, BADMINTON, or SQUASH between two players: *I prefer to play doubles; singles is too exhausting.*

single³ *v* **singled, singling**
    single sbdy/sthg ↔ **out** *phr v* [T] to choose one person or thing from a group for special treatment: *He was singled out for special praise.*

single file /₁·· '·/ *adv* in single file in a line one behind another: *We walked in single file down the corridor.*

single-hand·ed /₁·· '···◄/ *adv* on your own, without help from other people: *He rebuilt his house single-handed.* −**single-handed** *adj* : *a single-handed voyage across the Atlantic*

single-mind·ed /₁·· '···◄/ *adj* having one clear purpose: *He's quite single-minded about his work.* −**single-mindedly** *adv* −**single-mindedness** *n* [U] : *I admire his single-mindedness.*

sin·gly /'sɪŋgli/ *adv* separately: *Some guests came singly, others in groups.*

sing-song¹ /'sɪŋsɒŋ ‖ -sɔːŋ/ *adj* repeatedly rising and falling (used of the voice): *She has a lovely sing-song intonation.*

sing-song² *n* an occasion when a group of people sing songs together for pleasure: *We had a bit of a sing-song after the game.*

sin·gu·lar /'sɪŋgjələr/ *n* a word in the form which represents only one: *The singular of "mice" is "mouse".*

sin·gu·lar·ly /'sɪŋgjələli ‖ -lərli/ *adv fml* particularly: *a singularly unsuccessful attempt to gain publicity*

sin·is·ter /'sɪnɪstər/ *adj* seeming to be frightening and evil: *a sinister look on his face* | *a rather sinister figure dressed in black*

sink¹ /sɪŋk/ *v* **sank** /sæŋk/, **sunk** /sʌŋk/ **1** [I;T] to go down or make something go down below a surface, especially below the surface of water or to the bottom of the water: *The ship slowly sank* **beneath** *the waves.* | *The sun sank below the horizon.* | *They sank the ship with bombs.* **2** [I] to go down in number, strength, or value: *The population of the village has sunk from 100 to 27.* | *His voice sank to a whisper.* | *The value of money sank as inflation increased.* **3** [I] to fall or sit down, especially because of tiredness or lack of strength: *He fainted and suddenly sank to the ground.* | *She sank gracefully into the armchair.* **4 my heart sank, my spirits sank** = I lost confidence or hope: *My heart sank when I realized how much work I still had to do.* **5** [T] to put money into: *I've sunk all my money into buying this house.* **6 sink a well** to dig a well −**sinkable** *adj*
    sink in *phr v* [I] **1** to become fully understood: *The news was a terrible shock to her. I don't think it's really sunk in yet.* **2** to enter a solid through the surface: *Quick! If the ink sinks in it'll be harder to remove it.*
    sink into *phr v* [T] **1** [**sink** sthg **into** sthg] to put, force, or go into: *The dog sank its teeth into the meat.* **2** [**sink into** sthg] to pass gradually into a less active or worse state: *I sank back into a dreamless sleep.* | *He sank further into debt.*

sink² *n* **1** a large basin in a kitchen, used especially for washing pans, dishes, etc. **2** the usual American word for WASHBASIN

sin·ner /'sɪnər/ *n* biblical a person who has disobeyed God

sin·u·ous /'sɪnjuəs/ *adj lit* **1** twisting like a snake: *a sinuous belly dance* **2** having many bends or curves: *a sinuous mountain track*

si·nuses /'saɪnəsɪz/ *n* [pl] the air passages just behind your nose −**sinus** *adj* : *a sinus infection*

sip¹ /sɪp/ *v* **-pp-** [T] to drink, taking only a little at a time: *She sipped politely at her drink.*

sip² *n* a very small amount of a drink: *She took another sip of her tea.*

si·phon /'saɪfən/ *v* (also **syphon**) [T] **1** to draw out a liquid from one place through a tube by sucking it up the tube and letting it out in another place: *Siphon the liquid into a clean container.* | *Someone's siphoned* **off** *all our petrol!* **2** to cause something to change from one use or direction to another: *We need a new road to siphon* **off** *some of the traffic from the town centre.* −**siphon** *n*

sir /sər; *strong* sɜːr/ *n* **1** a respectful way of addressing a man: *Thank you, sir.* | *"Excuse me, sir," "Yes?" said his teacher absently.* **2 Sir** a title used before the name of a KNIGHT or BARONET: *We've got Sir Harold Wilson on the programme today.* | *Good morning, Sir Harold.* **3 Dear Sir** a formal way of beginning a letter to a man: *Dear Sir, I would like to apply for the position advertised in "The Times" this week.*

sire¹ /saɪər/ *n* **1** the father of an animal, especially of a dog or a horse **2 Sire** a way of addressing a king (no longer used in modern English)

sire² *v* [T] **sired, siring** to be the father of a dog or a horse: *This horse has sired several race winners.*

si·ren /'saɪərən/ *n* **1** an apparatus on ships, police cars, and other vehicles used to make a loud warning sound: *the wail of the sirens in the distance* **2** *lit* a beautiful woman who is dangerous to men

sir·loin /'sɜːlɔɪn ‖ 'sɜːr-/ *n* (also **sirloin steak** /₁·· '·/) [C;U] a piece of good quality BEEF cut from the lower back

sis·sy /'sɪsi/ *n* **sissies** (also **cissy**) *infml* a weak cowardly boy

sis·ter¹ /'sɪstər/ *n* **1** a female relative with the same parents: *Joan and Mary are sisters.* | *Joan is Mary's sister.* −see picture on page 343 **2 a** a nurse in charge of a hospital WARD: *the night sister* **b** the title for this job: *Sister Brown | Can you help me, Sister?* **3 a** a NUN or a woman member of a religious group: *a Christian sister* **b** the title for this: *Sister Mary Grace | the Sisters of Mercy*

sister² *adj* closely related or in the same group as: *a sister ship* | *We have a sister school in Tokyo.*

sis·ter·hood /'sɪstəhʊd ‖ -ər-/ *n* **1** [U] a strong sisterly friendship between women **2** [C + sing/pl verb] a society of women leading a religious life

sister-in-law /'··· ₁·/ *n* **sisters-in-law 1** the sister of your husband or wife −see picture on page 343 **2** the wife of your brother

sis·ter·ly /'sɪstəli ‖ -ər-/ *adj* typical of a loving sister

sit /sɪt/ *v* **sat** /sæt/, **sat, sitting 1** [I] to rest in a position in which your weight is on your bottom, usually on a chair: *She was sitting* **on** *a large sofa.* | *He was sitting* **at** *his desk working.* | *a group of people sitting in the corner of the room* −see picture on page 736 **2** [I] to lower yourself so that you are sitting on something: *She walked in and sat* **on** *the floor.* **3** [T] to make someone sit somewhere: *She sat the child on her knee.* | *He sat me in a corner and told me all about his problems.* **4** [I] (of an object) to be in a particular place or position: *The building sits in 10 acres of grounds.* | *The village sits on the top of a small hill.* | *The books just sit on the shelves without ever being read.* **5** [I] (of an official group) to have a meeting: *The court sits every morning.* **6** [T] to take an examination: *He decided to sit the*

exam despite the fact that he hadn't done much work. | *I'm sitting my finals next month.* **7 sit tight** to stay in the same place and do nothing: *If your car breaks down, sit tight and wait for the police.*

■ USAGE 1 **Sit** can be followed by various prepositions depending on the noun which comes next: *You sit on a sofa/a settee/a stool/a bench/the floor/a wall.* | *You sit in an armchair/a seat in a theatre/a seat in a car/the back or front row.* | *You sit at a table/a desk.* It can also depend on the meaning you want to give. Compare: *He sat at his desk working.* (= at a chair in front of his desk) | *He sat on his desk swinging his legs.* (= on top of his desk) 2 With the word **chair** you can use either **on** or **in**. If the chair is hard and has no arms use **on**; if it is soft or has arms use **in**.

sit about/around *phr v* [I] to spend time just resting and doing nothing: *We spent the days sitting around talking.*

sit back *phr v* [I] to not take an active part in something: *Just sit back and enjoy yourselves.*

sit down *phr v* **1** [I] to move to a sitting position after you have been standing: *Come in and sit down.* **2 sit yourself down** to move to a sitting position after you have been standing: *He walked in and sat himself down by the fire.* **3** [T **sit** sbdy **down**] to make someone sit somewhere: *She sat me down and gave me a cup of tea.*

sit in on sthg *phr v* [T] to be present during a meeting but not take part in it: *I asked if I could sit in on the board meeting.*

sit on sthg *phr v* [T] **1** to be a member of an official group that has regular meetings: *He sits on several committees.* **2** *infml* to keep something but not take action on it: *He's been sitting on my letter for weeks!*

sit sthg ↔ **out** *phr v* [T] to remain sitting or do nothing until something has finished

sit through sthg *phr v* [T] to remain sitting until something has finished: *We had to sit through three hours of speeches.*

sit up *phr v* **1** [I] to rise to a sitting position after you have been lying down: *He heard a noise and sat up in bed.* **2** [T **sit** sbdy **up**] to help someone into a sitting position after they have been lying down: *We managed to sit him up and give him a drink.* **3** [I] to stay up and not go to bed: *We sat up waiting for her to come home.*

sit·com /ˈsɪtkɒm ‖ -kɑːm/ *n infml* (also **situation comedy**) a form of humorous show on radio or television, in which the same characters appear in different situations each week

site¹ /saɪt/ *n* a place where something happens or is positioned: *the site of the Battle of Waterloo* | *a caravan site* | *the site for a new business centre*

site² *v* **sited, siting** [T] to build or position in a particular place: *We refused to have a factory sited so near to the school.*

sit-in /ˈ· ·/ *n* a public act of dissatisfaction and anger by a group of people who go into a place and stay sitting there for a long time: *There's a sit-in at the local hospital because of government cut-backs.*

sit·ting¹ /ˈsɪtɪŋ/ *n* **1** a period of time spent seated: *I read the book in a single sitting.* **2** one of the times for serving a meal: *The first sitting for school*

---

dinners is at 12.30. **3** a meeting of an official body such as a law court or government: *It was the first sitting of the House since the Prime Minister's return.*

sitting² *adj* [only before a noun] **1** currently having a seat on an official body: *The sitting member will be hard to defeat in the election.* **2 a sitting tenant** *BrE* a person currently renting a particular flat or house as their home: *We can't sell the flat unless the sitting tenant leaves.*

sitting room /ˈ··· ·/ *n BrE* a room in a home where people sit and rest

sit·u·at·ed /ˈsɪtʃueɪtʲd/ *adj* [never before a noun] in a particular place: *His office was very conveniently situated.*

■ USAGE **Situated** is a rather formal word. If you are speaking, or writing, in ordinary informal English it often sounds more natural NOT to use it. Compare: *The Royal Hotel is conveniently situated in the centre of the town* (in an advertisement) | *The emergency exits are situated at the rear of the plane* (in an official notice) and: *My house is in the centre of the town* (in a personal letter) | *The toilets are at the back of the plane* (in a conversation).

sit·u·a·tion /ˌsɪtʃuˈeɪʃən/ *n* **1** a position or condition at the moment: *the economic situation* | *Well, that's the situation as I see it.* **2** the place and surroundings of a building or town: *The cottage is in a beautiful situation.* **3** *old fash* a job: *the "Situations Vacant" advertisements in the newspaper*

situation com·e·dy /ˌ···· ˈ···/ see SITCOM

six /sɪks/ *det,n,pron* **1** the number 6 **2 at sixes and sevens** *infml* confused and not organized

six·pence /ˈsɪkspəns/ *n* an old silver coin in Britain

six·teen /ˌsɪkˈstiːn◂/ *det,n,pron* the number 16 **−sixteenth** *det,n,pron,adv*

sixth /sɪks/ *det, pron, adv, n* **1** 6th **2** one of six equal parts

sixth form /ˈ· ·/ *n* [+ sing/pl verb] the top class with the oldest pupils, in a British school: *She got her GCSEs last year and is now in the sixth form.*

sixth sense /ˌ· ˈ·/ *n* [sing] an ability to see or know things by INSTINCT

six·ty /ˈsɪksti/ *det,n,pron* **sixties 1** the number 60 **2 the Sixties, the sixties** the years 1960−1969 **3 in his sixties, in their sixties** aged between 60 and 69 **−sixtieth** *det, n, pron, adv*

siz·a·ble /ˈsaɪzəbəl/ *adj* (also **sizeable**) rather large: *He has a sizeable income.*

size¹ /saɪz/ *n* **1** [C;U] how big or small something is: *What's the size of your back garden?* | *Their army is about half the size of ours.* | *hailstones the size of golf balls* **2** [U] the fact of being big: *We're the only company of any size outside London.* | *The sheer size of the building amazed me.* **3** [C] a standard measure for clothes, shoes, and other things you buy: *There's a special offer on the giant-size pack.* | *What size shoe do you take?* | *I need a larger size.* **4 -sized** (also **-size**) of a certain size or number: *medium-sized* | *a good-sized crowd*

size² *v* **sized, sizing**

size sbdy/sthg ↔ **up** *phr v* [T] to form an opinion about: *He sized up the new boy critically.*

size·a·ble /ˈsaɪzəbəl/ *adj* see SIZABLE

siz·zle /ˈsɪzəl/ *v* **sizzled, sizzling** [I] to make a sound like food cooking in hot fat: *There were sausages sizzling in the pan.*

skate¹ /skeɪt/ *n* **1** (also **ice skate**) a special boot for moving on ice, with a metal blade beneath it **2** (also **roller skate**) a special boot with four wheels beneath it, for moving quickly on a smooth surface **3 get/put your skates on** *infml* to hurry **4** a large flat sea fish

skate² *v* **skated, skating** [I] to move about on ice skates: *We skated around the edge of the lake.* **–skater** *n*

skate over sthg (also **skate round** sthg) *phr v* [T] to avoid talking about something in detail: *He always skates round the subject.*

skate·board /'skeɪtbɔːd ‖ -bɔːrd/ *n* a short board with two wheels at each end for standing on and riding, for fun

skein /skeɪn/ *n* a loosely wound length of thread or wool: *a couple of skeins of pink tapestry wool*

skel·e·ton¹ /'skelɪtən/ *n* **1** the framework of bones in a human or animal body **2** something forming a framework: *the steel skeleton of a tall building* **3 have a skeleton in the cupboard** to keep a secret from the past which makes you feel anxious and uncomfortable

skeleton² *adj* [only before a noun] just enough to keep going: *British Rail managed to keep a skeleton service running during the strike.*

skep·tic /'skeptɪk/ *n* see SCEPTIC

sketch¹ /sketʃ/ *n* **1** a quick rough drawing: *He made a quick sketch of the house.* | *a charcoal sketch* **2** a short description in words: *a brief biographical sketch of the author* **3** a short humorous scene on stage or television that is part of a larger show: *I enjoyed the show. My favourite sketch was the one about the dead parrot.*

sketch² *v* [I;T] to draw quickly or roughly
sketch sthg ↔ **in** *phr v* [T] to give the details about something: *Can you sketch in the events that led to their decision?*
sketch sthg ↔ **out** *phr v* [T] to give a short description of something: *The Minister sketched out his plans for the next two years.*

sketch·y /'sketʃi/ *adj* **sketchier, sketchiest** not thorough or complete: *a sketchy knowledge of history* **–sketchily** *adv* **–sketchiness** *n* [U]

skew·er¹ /'skjuːəʳ/ *n* a long wooden or metal pin for holding pieces of food together while cooking

skewer² *v* [T] to push a skewer through food

ski¹ /skiː/ *n* one of a pair of long narrow pieces of wood, plastic, or metal which you fasten to your boots when travelling on snow –see SKI (USAGE)

ski² *v* **skied, skiing** [I] to go on skis: *We're going skiing at Christmas.* | *I learnt to ski in the Alps.* **–skier** *n* –see picture on page 637

skid /skɪd/ *v* **-dd-** [I] to slip sideways out of control (used of a vehicle): *Be careful not to skid on that icy surface.* | *The car skidded off the road.* **–skid** *n* : *The car went into a skid.*

skil·ful /'skɪlfəl/ *adj* (**skilfull** *AmE*) **1** having skill: *a very skilful driver* **2** showing skill: *her skilful handling of the situation* **–skilfully** *adv*

skill /skɪl/ *n* **1** [U] an ability to do something very well: *a pilot of great skill* | *He handled the negotiations with both skill and tact.* **2** [C] the ability to do a particular thing: *Reading and writing are related skills.* | *basic computer skills* | *management skills*

skilled /skɪld/ *adj* **1** having skill: *skilled workers* **2** needing skill: *a highly skilled job*

skil·let /'skɪlɪt/ an American word for FRYING PAN

skill·ful /'skɪlfəl/ *adj* see **skilful**

skim /skɪm/ *v* **-mm-** **1** [T] to remove something from the surface of a liquid: *skim the cream off the milk* **2** [I;T] to read quickly to get the main ideas: *Just skim the first chapter.* | *I skimmed through a few of*

the replies. **3** [I;T + adv/prep] to move or to make something move swiftly over a surface: *The children were skimming stones across the pond.* | *A seagull skimmed the waves.*

skimp /skɪmp/ *v* [I;T] to use less money, time, or material than is really needed: *The old lady had been skimping on food to save money.* | *Don't skimp the essays or you'll fail the exam.*

skimp·y /'skɪmpi/ *adj* **skimpier, skimpiest** too small in size or quantity: *a skimpy meal* | *shivering with cold in a skimpy little dress*

skin¹ /skɪn/ *n* **1** [U] the natural outer covering of your body: *a skin disease* | *Babies have soft skin.* **2** [C;U] the part of an animal body used for leather, fur, etc.: *a sheepskin coat* | *The skins are sent to the tannery.* **3** [C] **a** a natural outer covering of some fruits and vegetables: *banana skins* | *onion skins* **b** the outer covering of a SAUSAGE **4** [C;U] the solid surface that forms over some liquids when they get cool: *Paint forms a skin if you don't seal the tin properly.* | *the skin on the custard* **5 by the skin of your teeth** *infml* with very little time or space remaining: *We caught the train by the skin of our teeth.* **6 no skin off my nose** *infml* not something that will annoy or harm me: *If she won't accept my help that's her problem – it's no skin off my nose.* **7 skin and bone/bones** *infml* very thin: *The cattle were all skin and bone after the drought.* **8 skinned** having a certain type or colour of skin: *pale-skinned* | *smooth-skinned*

skin² *v* **-nn-** [T] to remove the skin from: *She skinned the rabbit for me.* | *I skinned my elbow.*

skin-deep /ˌ· ˈ·◂/ *adj* only on the surface: *Their differences of opinion are only skin-deep.*

skin·flint /'skɪnˌflɪnt/ *n* a person who is very mean

skin·ny /'skɪni/ *adj* **skinnier, skinniest** too thin (a word used to express disapproval) –see THIN (USAGE)

skint /skɪnt/ *adj* [never before a noun] *BrE slang* completely without money

skin-tight /ˌ· ˈ·◂/ *adj* fitting extremely tightly (used of clothes)

skip¹ /skɪp/ *v* **-pp-** **1** [I] to move in a light dancing way, jumping from one foot to the other: *The little boy skipped along at his mother's side.* **2** [I] to jump up and down over a rope as a game or as exercise: *Boxers skip to keep fit.* –see picture on page 736 **3** [I] to move in no fixed order: *The speaker kept skipping from one subject to another.* **4** [T] to leave out on purpose: *You can skip Chapter 3; it's not relevant.* | *Never skip a meal.*

skip² *n* **1** a light quick jumping movement **2** a large metal container for holding old bricks or other heavy things to be taken away

skip·per /'skɪpəʳ/ *n infml* a captain of a ship or sports team

skir·mish¹ /'skɜːmɪʃ ‖ -ɜːr-/ *n* **1** a short rough fight **2** a short sharp argument

skirmish² *v* [I] to fight in a skirmish

skirt¹ /skɜːt ‖ skɜːrt/ *n* a piece of clothing worn by women and girls which fits around the waist and hangs down: *a knee-length skirt* | *a straight skirt* –see picture on page 50

skirt² *v* [T] **1** (also **skirt round/around**) to go around the edge of: *The bus skirted the roadworks.* **2** to be around the edge of an area: *The motorway skirts the city centre.* **3** (also **skirt round/around**) to avoid dealing with a difficult question or problem: *Don't keep skirting round the main issue – get to the point!*

skirting board /'··· / n [C;U] *BrE* a board fixed along the base of a wall in a room

skit·tle /'skɪtl/ n 1 [C] a bottle-shaped object used in the game of skittles 2 **skittles** [U] the game in which a player tries to knock down these objects with a ball

skive /skaɪv/ v **skived, skiving** [I] *BrE infml* to avoid work, often by staying away from a place: *She's always skiving off. | Were you really at the dentist's?* –**skiver** n

skulk /skʌlk/ v [I] to stay quietly in a place because you do not want to be noticed: *robbers skulking behind the bushes, ready to jump out*

skull /skʌl/ n 1 the bone of your head which encloses your brain 2 **the skull and crossbones** a sign for death or danger, used on PIRATE flags in former times

skull·cap /'skʌlkæp/ n a simple close-fitting cap for the top of the head

skunk /skʌŋk/ n a small black and white North American animal which gives off a very bad smell when attacked

sky /skaɪ/ n **skies** 1 [C;U] the space above the Earth where you can see the clouds, sun, moon, and stars: *There's a bit of blue sky between the clouds. | The rocket shot up into the sky.* 2 **the sky's the limit** *infml* there is no upper limit

sky-high /ˌ· '··/ adj *infml* to a very high level: *Prices have gone sky-high.* –**sky-high** adj : *sky-high mortgage rates*

sky·light /'skaɪlaɪt/ n a window in a roof

sky·line /'skaɪlaɪn/ n a shape or view made by scenery, especially tall buildings, against the background of the sky

sky·scrap·er /'skaɪˌskreɪpəʳ/ n a very tall modern city building

slab /slæb/ n a thick flat piece of something: *The patio was made of stone slabs. | a thick slab of fruit cake*

slack¹ /slæk/ adj 1 not stretched tight: *a slack rope* 2 not firm: *slack discipline* 3 careless or without firmness: *You're getting very slack in your work! | Discipline in the class-room is too slack.* 4 not busy: *Business is slack just now.* –**slackly** adv –**slackness** n [U]

slack² v [I] not to work well or quickly enough: *Stop slacking!* –**slacker** n

slack³ n 1 **the slack** the part of a rope or wire that hangs loose 2 **slacks** [pl] *old fash* trousers for wearing informally

slack·en /'slækən/ v [I;T] 1 to make or become slower or less active: *We slackened our pace as we reached town.* 2 to make or become looser: *She was too frightened to slacken her grip on my arm.*

slacken off phr v [I] to become slower or less active: *Business has slackened off recently.*

slag heap /'slæg ˌhiːp/ n a hill made of waste material from mines and factories

slain /sleɪn/ the past participle of SLAY

slake /sleɪk/ v **slaked, slaking** lit **slake your thirst** to satisfy your thirst by having a drink

slam¹ /slæm/ v **-mm-** 1 [I;T] to shut loudly and with great force: *Please don't slam the door. | The door*

slammed shut behind him. 2 [T + adv/prep] to throw down quickly and violently: *He slammed the papers down on the desk. | I slammed the receiver down.* 3 [T] (used in newspapers) to attack with words: *"What's today's headline?" "Teachers slam education cuts."*

slam² n the act or the noise of a door closing violently: *He shut the door with a slam.*

slan·der¹ /'slɑːndəʳ ‖ 'slæn-/ n [C;U] a spoken report about someone that is intentionally false and harms them

slander² v [T] to say false things about someone in order to harm them –**slanderous** adj

slang /slæŋ/ n [U] very informal words and expressions often used only by a particular social group: *Slang often goes in and out of fashion quickly. | American slang | "I'm skint" is a slang expression meaning "I haven't got any money".* –**slangy** adj

slant¹ /slɑːnt ‖ slænt/ v 1 [I;T] to put or be at an angle: *The sitting room floor slants towards the window.* 2 **be slanted** to be reported in a way which favours one particular opinion: *His account was obviously slanted towards the government's view.*

slant² n 1 [sing] a slanting direction or position: *a steep upward slant | That shelf is on a slant. | a line drawn at a slant* 2 [C] a particular way of looking at or expressing news or facts: *an interesting new slant on the presidential elections*

slap¹ /slæp/ n 1 a quick blow with the flat part of your hand: *She gave him a slap on the cheek.* 2 **a slap in the face for someone** an action that seems to be intended to harm or upset someone

slap² v -pp- [T] 1 to hit quickly with the flat part of your hand: *She slapped his wrist playfully. | He slapped his friend on the back.* 2 to place roughly or carelessly: *He was slapping paint onto the wall. | She slapped the meal down on the table.*

slap³ adv *infml* (also **slap-bang**) directly, suddenly and forcefully: *The car ran slap into a tree. | I ran slap-bang into my boss. | I dropped a whole tin of paint slap-bang in the middle of the carpet.*

slap·dash /'slæpdæʃ/ adj hasty and careless: *a slapdash piece of work*

slap·stick /'slæpˌstɪk/ n [U] humorous acting with fast violent action and simple jokes: *slapstick comedy*

slap-up /'··/ adj **a slap-up meal** *BrE infml* a large and excellent meal

slash¹ /slæʃ/ v 1 [T] to make a long deep cut: *We slashed a path through the bushes. | The cinema seats had been slashed.* 2 **slash at something** to make wild long sweeping strokes in the direction of something 3 to reduce an amount of time or money greatly: *It's the last day of the sale and prices have really been slashed.*

slash² n 1 a long sweeping cut 2 a DIAGONAL line that separates letters, words, or numbers: *"2/4 can be read as "two slash four".*

slat /slæt/ n a thin flat piece of wood or plastic: *It's difficult to clean the slats of Venetian blinds.* –**slatted** adj

slate¹ /sleɪt/ n 1 [U] a dark grey rock that is easily split into flat thin pieces 2 [C] a thin flat piece of this rock used for covering a roof

slate² v **slated, slating** [T] 1 to cover a roof with slates 2 to judge a book, play, or film severely: *The critics really slated his latest production.*

slaugh·ter¹ /'slɔːtəʳ/ n [U] 1 the killing of many people or animals in a cruel way –see KILL¹ (USAGE) 2 the killing of animals for meat

slaughter² v [T] **1** to kill many people cruelly or wrongly: *They slaughtered thousands of innocent people.* **2** to kill an animal, especially for food

slaugh·ter·house /'slɔːtəhaʊs ‖ -ər-/ n (also **abattoir**) a building where farm animals are killed for meat

slave¹ /sleɪv/ n **1** a person who is owned by another person and must work for them **2 a slave to something, a slave of something** a person completely under the control of a particular thing: *He's a slave to drink.* | *We're all slaves of habit.*

slave² v **slaved, slaving** [I] to work hard: *She slaved for him all her life.* | *I've been slaving away all weekend in the garden.*

slave driv·er /'·· ‚··/ n *infml* a person who makes other people work very hard

slav·er /'slævər/ v [I] to let SALIVA come out of your mouth

sla·ve·ry /'sleɪvəri/ n [U] **1** the system of having slaves: *When was slavery abolished?* **2** the condition of being a slave: *sold into slavery*

slav·ish /'sleɪvɪʃ/ adj **1** copied very closely or exactly from something else: *a slavish translation* **2** showing complete obedience to the idea of serving someone or dependence on them: *slavish devotion to duty* **–slavishly** adv

slay /sleɪ/ v **slew** /sluː/, **slain** /sleɪn/ [T] *lit* to kill violently

slea·zy /'sliːzi/ adj **sleazier, sleaziest** cheap, dirty, and not respectable: *a sleazy hotel in a poor part of town* **–sleaziness** n [U]

sledge¹ /sledʒ/ n (also **sled** /sled/) a vehicle for sliding along on snow or ice, used in play and sport or for carrying heavy loads

sledge² v **sledged, sledging** [I] *BrE* to go down slopes on a sledge for fun

sledge·ham·mer /'sledʒ‚hæmər/ n a large heavy hammer

sleek /sliːk/ adj **1** smooth and shining (used of hair) **2** looking rich or expensive and stylish: *a sleek sports car*

sleep¹ /sliːp/ n **1** [U] the natural state of rest in which your eyes are shut and your mind and body are unconscious for a period of time: *I haven't had enough sleep lately.* **2** [sing] a period of sleeping: *I need a short sleep after lunch.* **3 go to sleep, get to sleep** to begin to sleep: *I couldn't get to sleep last night.* **4 go to sleep** (of a part of your body) to lose all sense of feeling: *I've been sitting here so long that my foot's gone to sleep.* **5 put to sleep**: *euph* to kill a sick or hurt animal painlessly: *The dog had been so badly injured that the vet had to put him to sleep.*

sleep² v **slept** /slept/, **slept 1** [I] to rest in sleep: *I didn't sleep very well last night.* | *I usually sleep for at least seven hours a night.* | *We like to sleep late on Sundays.* **2** [T] to provide sleeping-places for a number of people: *The sofa folds down to sleep two.* **3 sleep like a log** *infml* to sleep deeply without moving **4 sleep on something** to spend a night considering a problem: *I'm not sure. Can I sleep on it and let you know my decision in the morning?* **5 sleep rough** to sleep outdoors because you have nowhere to go

sleep in *phr v* [I] to sleep late in the morning: *We slept in after the party.*

sleep sthg ↔ **off** *phr v* [T] to get rid of the effects of drink, food, or drugs by sleeping: *He drank too much wine and went home early to sleep it off.*

sleep together *phr v* [I] (used of two people who are not married to each other) to have sex

sleep with sbdy *phr v* [T] to have sex with someone

sleep·er /'sliːpər/ n **1** a person sleeping: *He's a heavy sleeper, very difficult to wake.* **2** a train with beds for sleeping through a journey at night **3** a heavy piece of wood used to support a railway track

sleeping bag /'·· ‚·/ n a large warm bag for sleeping in, especially when camping

sleeping pill /'·· ‚·/ n (also **sleeping tablet** /'·· ‚··/) a PILL containing a medicine which helps a person to sleep

sleep·less /'sliːpləs/ adj **1 a sleepless night** a night during which you do not sleep: *We spent a sleepless night waiting for news.* **2** not able to sleep: *He lay sleepless on his bed.* **–sleeplessness** n [U]

sleep·walk /'sliːpˌwɔːk/ v [I] to walk around while you are asleep: *Do you know that you've been sleepwalking?* **–sleepwalker** n

sleep·y /'sliːpi/ adj **sleepier, sleepiest 1** tired and ready for sleep **2** without much activity or noise: *a sleepy country town* **–sleepily** adv **–sleepiness** n [U]

sleet /sliːt/ n [U] a mixture of rain and snow

sleeve /sliːv/ n **1** a part of a piece of clothing that covers your arm: *a dress with long sleeves* –see picture on page 50 **2** a stiff envelope in which a record is kept **3 have something up your sleeve** to keep an idea or plan secret for use at the right time in the future **4 -sleeved** having sleeves of a certain length or shape: *a short-sleeved shirt* **–sleeveless** adj

sleigh /sleɪ/ n a vehicle which slides along over snow, pulled by a horse

sleight of hand /‚slaɪt əv 'hænd/ n [U] a quick skilful movement of your hands, which other people cannot see: *He made a coin disappear by sleight of hand.*

slen·der /'slendər/ n **1** attractively thin and graceful: *a slender woman* –see THIN (USAGE) **2** small and hardly enough: *You have only the slenderest chance of success.* **–slenderness** n [U]

slept /slept/ the past tense and past participle of SLEEP

sleuth /sluːθ/ n *old fash* a person whose job is to find out information about criminals

slew¹ /sluː/ v (also **slue** *AmE*) [I;T] to turn or swing violently or make something turn or swing violently: *He lost control of the car and it slewed round.*

slew² the past tense of SLAY

slice¹ /slaɪs/ n **1** a thin flat piece cut from something: *a slice of bread* | *Cut the cake into slices.* **2** a kitchen tool for lifting and serving pieces of food **3** a shot in sports like GOLF and tennis, which makes the ball go to one side rather than straight ahead

slice² v **sliced, slicing 1** [T] to cut into slices: *a sliced loaf* | *She sliced up the meat.* **2** [I;T] to cut with something sharp: *I sliced into my finger with a vegetable knife.* **3** [I;T] to hit a ball to one side in various sports

slick¹ /slɪk/ adj **1** clever or attractive, but often not honest: *a slick salesman* **2** spoken too easily to be right or true: *slick excuses* **–slickly** adv **–slickness** n [U]

slick² n (also **oil slick**) a quantity of oil floating on the sea or a lake

slick³ v

slick sthg ↔ **down** *phr v* [T] to make your hair flat and shiny with water or oil

slid /slɪd/ the past tense and past participle of SLIDE

slide¹ /slaɪd/ v **slid** /slɪd/ **slid, sliding** 1 [I;T] to go or make something go smoothly over a surface: *He slid his glass across the table.* | *The children like sliding down the stairs.* 2 [I + adv/prep] to go silently and unnoticed: *She slid out of the room when no one was looking.* 3 **let something slide** *infml* to pay no attention to something, often because of laziness

slide² n 1 a slipping movement over a surface 2 an apparatus for sliding down: *a children's playground slide* 3 a fall: *How can we stop the slide in living standards?* | *a landslide* | *a rock slide* 4 a piece of photographic film through which you shine light to show a picture: *They showed us the slides of their holiday.* | *a slide show* 5 a small glass plate on which you put something that you want to examine under a microscope 6 a decorative fastener worn in your hair

sliding scale /ˌ·· '·/ n a system of pay or taxes calculated by rates which may vary according to changing conditions

slight¹ /slaɪt/ adj 1 small in amount: *There's a slight improvement in his condition.* 2 thin and delicate: *a rather slight old lady* 3 **not in the slightest** not at all: *"Do you mind if I open the window?" "Not in the slightest: please do."*

slight² v [T] to treat someone without respect ‒**slightingly** adv

slight³ n rude behaviour, not showing respect: *I'm afraid he took your remark as a slight on his work.*

slight·ly /ˈslaɪtli/ adv 1 a little bit: *"Do you know her?" "Only slightly".* | *He was slightly drunk.* 2 in a slight way: *a small, slightly-built man*

slim¹ /slɪm/ adj **slimmer, slimmest** 1 attractively thin and well-shaped (used of people): *She's pretty, with a lovely slim figure.* ‒see THIN¹ (USAGE) ‒see picture on page 245 2 slight or unlikely (used of a hope or probability): *Our chances of winning are slim.* 3 thinner than usual: *a slim paperback book*

slim² v -mm- [I] to try to lose weight: *I don't want any cake: I'm slimming.* ‒**slimmer** n ‒**slimming** n [U] : *a slimming club*

slime /slaɪm/ n [U] a thick slippery liquid: *a snail's trail of slime*

slim·y /ˈslaɪmi/ adj **slimier, slimiest** 1 unpleasantly slippery 2 *infml* friendly and pleasant in an insincere way: *He's such a slimy do-gooder.*

sling¹ /slɪŋ/ v **slung** /slʌŋ/, **slung, slinging** 1 [T] *infml* to throw something roughly: *Sling the empty boxes in the corner.* 2 [T + adv/prep] to put something in a position quickly and carelessly so that it hangs down: *He slung his coat over his shoulder.* 3 [T; + adv/prep] to hang with a rope: *The line of flags was slung up between two trees.*

sling² n 1 a piece of cloth for supporting a damaged arm or hand 2 an apparatus of ropes or cloth for carrying things: *a babysling* 3 a length of string with a piece of leather in the middle, used in former times for throwing stones

slink /slɪŋk/ v **slunk** /slʌŋk/, **slunk** [I] in a slow, quiet, and secretive way: *The leopard slunk back into the darkness.*

slip¹ /slɪp/ v -pp- 1 [I] to slide a short distance out of place by accident, or to fall by sliding: *My foot* slipped and I nearly fell. | *The hammer slipped and hit my fingers.* 2 [I] to get worse or lower: *Standards are slipping in this hotel.* | *Output has slipped by 15% this year.* 3 [I + adv/prep] to move smoothly, secretly, or unnoticed: *She slipped into the room when no one was looking.* | *As the years slipped by, I thought less about her.* 4 [T] to put or give smoothly, secretly, or unnoticed: *He slipped the waiter a five pound note to get a good table.* | *He slipped the papers quietly into his briefcase.* 5 **let something slip** to say something without intending to: *He carelessly let slip the date of the election to a reporter.* 6 **slip your mind** to be forgotten or unnoticed: *I'm sorry I forgot your birthday: it completely slipped my mind.*

slip into sthg *phr v* [T] to put a piece of clothing on
slip sthg ↔ **off** *phr v* [T] to take off a piece of clothing
slip sthg ↔ **on** *phr v* [T] to put on a piece of clothing: *I slipped my coat on and went out.*
slip out of sthg *phr v* [T] to take off a piece of clothing
slip up *phr v* [I] to make a slight mistake: *The secretary slipped up and forgot to post the letter.*

slip² n 1 a small mistake: *"Oh no! That's not right; I've made a slip somewhere."* | *a slip of the tongue* 2 a small piece of paper: *He scribbled his phone number on a slip of paper.* 3 a woman's undergarment worn under a dress or skirt 4 **slip of a boy/girl** a small thin young person: *She's just a slip of a girl.* 5 **give someone the slip** *infml* to escape from someone who is chasing you

slipped disc /ˌ· '·/ n a painful displacement of one of the connecting parts between the bones of your back

slip·per /ˈslɪpər/ n a loose soft shoe worn indoors: *a comfortable old pair of slippers* ‒see PAIR (USAGE) ‒see picture on page 50

slip·per·y /ˈslɪpəri/ adj 1 wet or smooth and difficult to hold or to stand on: *Drive carefully: the roads are wet and slippery.* 2 *infml* not to be trusted: *He looks a slippery character.* 3 **be on a slippery slope** to become worse and find it difficult to stop: *Once you've given in to temptation you're on the slippery slope.*

slip road /'· ·/ n BrE a road for driving onto or off a MOTORWAY

slip·shod /ˈslɪpʃɒd ‖ -ʃɑːd/ adj done in a careless or untidy way: *a slipshod piece of work*

slip-up /'· ·/ n a slight mistake

slip·way /ˈslɪpweɪ/ n a track sloping down into the water for moving ships into or out of the water

slit¹ /slɪt/ v **slit, slit, slitting** [T] to make a long narrow cut in something carefully or intentionally: *She slit the envelope open with a knife.* | *His throat had been slit.*

slit² n a long narrow cut or opening: *I could see a light through the slit under the door.*

slith·er /ˈslɪðər/ v [I + adv/prep] 1 to move in a slipping or twisting way like a snake 2 to slide unsteadily while trying to walk: *She slithered across the ice.*

sliv·er /ˈslɪvər/ n a small thin sharp piece cut or torn off something: *a sliver of glass from the broken window*

slob /slɒb ‖ slɑːb/ n *infml* a lazy or carelessly-dressed person

slob·ber /ˈslɒbər ‖ ˈslɑː-/ v [I] to have SALIVA running from your mouth, like a baby

slog¹ /slɒg ‖ slɑːg/ v -gg- [I] *infml* to work hard at something difficult or dull: *I don't want to slog away for years in a factory.*

slog² *n* [sing] *BrE infml* tiring work which requires a lot of effort: *It's a hard slog up to the top of the hill.*

slo·gan /ˈsləʊgən/ *n* a short easily-remembered phrase with a political or advertising message

sloop /sluːp/ *n* a small sailing ship with one MAST

slop /slɒp ‖ slɑːp/ *v* -**pp**- **1** [I] (used of a liquid) to go over the side of a container: *Some of the soup sloppped over the edge of the bowl.* **2** [T] to cause a liquid to do this: *I've slopped some coffee on the floor.*

slope¹ /sləʊp/ *v* **sloped, sloping** [I] to be at an angle: *a sloping roof* | *The road slopes up slightly at this point.*

slope off *phr v* [I] *BrE infml* to go away quietly, often in order to avoid work

slope² *n* **1** a surface that slopes: *a ski slope* | *a steep slope* **2** **a slope of 30 degrees** = the angle at which something slopes is 30 degrees

slop·py /ˈslɒpi ‖ ˈslɑːpi/ *adj* **sloppier, sloppiest 1** loose and very informal (used of clothes): *He wore jeans and a sloppy old jumper.* **2** not careful or thorough enough: *a sloppy piece of writing* **3** foolish in showing feelings: *sloppy romantic love songs* –**sloppily** *adv* –**sloppiness** *n* [U]

slops /slɒps ‖ slɑːps/ *n* [pl] **1** food waste for feeding to animals **2** liquid waste from food or drinks

slosh /slɒʃ ‖ slɑːʃ/ *v* [I] **1** to go through water or mud: *We sloshed along through the puddles.* **2** (of liquid) to move about against the sides of a container

sloshed /slɒʃt ‖ slɑːʃt/ *adj infml* drunk: *He was completely sloshed at the party.*

slot¹ /slɒt ‖ slɑːt/ *n* **1** a narrow opening in a machine or container: *to put a coin in the slot* **2** *infml* a position in a list or system: *the 7 o'clock slot on the radio*

slot² *v* -**tt**- [I;T] to go or to put something into a space where it fits: *The lid slots into the grooves, like this.*

sloth /sləʊθ/ *n* **1** [U] *fml* laziness **2** [C] a slow-moving animal of Central and South America

sloth·ful /ˈsləʊθfəl/ *adj fml* lazy –**slothfully** *adv*

slot ma·chine /ˈ· ·ˌ·/ *n* a machine which you operate by putting in coins

slouch /slaʊtʃ/ *v* [I] to sit, stand, or walk in a tired round-shouldered way: *Sit up properly – don't slouch!* –**slouch** *n* [sing]

slough /slʌf/ *v*

slough sthg ↔ **off** *phr v* [T] to get rid of something: *The snake sloughs off its skin every few months.*

slov·en·ly /ˈslʌvənli/ *adj* untidy and careless: *a slovenly piece of work* –**slovenliness** *n* [U]

slow¹ /sləʊ/ *adj* **1** moving or happening without much speed: *a slow train* | *slow music* | *the slow erosion of rock by wind and rain* **2** not very clever: *some of the slower pupils* **3** showing a time that is earlier than the correct time (used of clocks and watches): *The station clock is two minutes slow.* –**slowly** *adv* –**slowness** *n* [U]

slow² *adv* slowly: *You're going too slow.* | *slow-moving traffic*

slow³ *v*

slow sbdy/sthg ↔ **down** *phr v* (also **slow** sbdy/sthg ↔ **up**) [I;T] to start to move or happen more slowly, or to make someone or something do this: *Slow down, there's a bend ahead.* | *His bad leg slows him down a lot.* | *Business slows up in summer.*

slow-coach /ˈsləʊkəʊtʃ/ *n BrE infml* a person who does something too slowly

slow mo·tion /ˌ· ˈ··/ *n* [U] movement which takes place at a much slower speed than in real life,

especially in a film: *They showed the goal again in slow motion.*

sludge /slʌdʒ/ *n* [U] **1** thick mud **2** dirty waste oil in an engine

slue /sluː/ *v* **slued, sluing** [I;T] the usual American spelling of SLEW¹

slug¹ /slʌg/ *n* **1** a small soft limbless creature, like a SNAIL but with no shell **2** a lump or piece of metal **3** *AmE* a bullet **4** *AmE* a small quantity of an alcoholic drink drunk in one swallow: *a slug of whisky*

slug² *v* -**gg**- [T] to strike with a heavy blow

slug·gish /ˈslʌgɪʃ/ *adj* slow-moving and without strength: *a sluggish stream* | *I was feeling rather sluggish.* –**sluggishly** *adv*

sluice¹ /sluːs/ *n* a passage for water with a gate through which the flow can be controlled

sluice² *v* **sluiced, sluicing** [T] to wash with floods of water: *We sluiced out the cowshed.*

slum /slʌm/ *n* **1** (also **the slums**) a city area of poor living conditions and old unrepaired buildings: *They've moved out of the slums to a much better area.* | *I grew up in a slum.* **2** *infml* a very untidy place: *Your room is an absolute slum!*

slum·ber /ˈslʌmbəʳ/ *n lit* sleep: *waking from her slumbers* | *in a deep slumber* –**slumber** *v* [I]

slump¹ /slʌmp/ *v* [I] **1** (of a person) to fall heavily or in a heap: *He slumped into his chair.* **2** to fall suddenly by a large amount: *Sales have slumped in the last month.*

slump² *n* **1** a time of seriously bad business conditions and unemployment **2** a sudden fall in an amount or value: *There's been a slump in demand for electrical goods.*

slung /slʌŋ/ the past tense and past participle of SLING

slunk /slʌŋk/ the past tense and past participle of SLINK

slur¹ /slɜːʳ/ *v* -**rr**- [T] to pronounce words unclearly, often because you are ill or drunk: *I find him hard to understand because he slurs his speech.*

slur² *n* an unfair damaging remark: *He has cast a slur on the company's good name.*

slurp /slɜːp ‖ slɜːrp/ *v* [I;T] *infml* to drink noisily: *The children slurped their milkshakes greedily.*

slush /slʌʃ/ *n* [U] **1** wet, melted snow **2** *infml* literature, films, concerned with silly love stories –**slushy** *adj* **slushier, slushiest**

slut /slʌt/ *n* **1** a woman who is considered to be immoral **2** an untidy lazy woman –**sluttish** *adj*

sly /slaɪ/ *adj* **slier** *or* **slyer, sliest** *or* **slyest 1** clever in deceiving: *My granddad was a sly old fox.* **2** showing that you know something that others do not know: *She gave a sly smile.* **3** **on the sly** *infml* secretly –**slyly, slily** *adv* –**slyness** *n* [U]

smack¹ /smæk/ *v* [T] **1** to hit with your open hand: *She smacked his leg.* | *Don't smack me!* **2** **smack your lips** to open and close your lips noisily **3** **smack of something** to remind you of something: *His plan smacks of disloyalty to me.*

smack² *n* **1** [C] a quick forceful blow with an open hand: *If you don't stop making that noise, you'll get a smack!* **2** [sing] a loud sharp noise: *The book landed on the floor with a loud smack.* **3** [C] a small sailing boat

smack³ *adv infml* **1** with force: *The car ran smack into a wall.* **2** exactly in a place: *She lives right smack in the middle of the town.*

small /smɔːl/ *adj* **1** not large in size, weight, or amount: *a book written for small children* | *The*

Indian elephant is smaller than the African elephant.| She's rather small for her age. –see picture on page 245 –see LITTLE (USAGE) **2** not important: *We'll have to make a few small changes, that's all. | He's a small businessman.* **3 the small ads** short advertisements in a newspaper which people can use to buy or sell things, or to find or offer a job or a place to live **4 the small hours** the early morning hours just after midnight **5 small wonder** it's not surprising: *Small wonder you're fed up – you should go out more!* –**small** *adv* : *He writes so small I can hardly read it.* –**smallness** *n* [U]

small change /ˌ· ˈ·/ *n* [U] money in coins of small value

small·hold·ing /ˈsmɔːlˌhəʊldɪŋ/ *n* a small piece of land used for farming –**smallholder** *n*

small-mind·ed /ˌ· ˈ··◄/ *adj* having mean and selfish interests –**small-mindedness** *n* [U]

small-scale /ˌ· ˈ·◄/ *adj* **1** happening within a small area or with small numbers or quantities: *a small-scale operation involving only a few local people* **2** showing a large area, without much detail (used of maps)

small talk /ˈ·· ·/ *n* [U] conversation about unimportant subjects

small-time /ˌ· ˈ·◄/ *adj* unimportant: *a small-time criminal*

smarm·y /ˈsmɑːmi ‖ -ɑːr-/ *adj* **smarmier, smarmiest** *BrE infml* unpleasantly and falsely polite

smart¹ /smɑːt ‖ smɑːrt/ *adj* **1** neat and stylish in appearance: *You look very smart in that new shirt.* **2** clever: *He's a very smart young man.* **3** quick and sharp: *a smart blow on the head* **4** connected with wealthy or fashionable people: *a smart restaurant | He took me to a very smart party.* –**smartly** *adv* –**smartness** *n* [U]

smart² *v* [I] **1** to sting for a short time: *His knee was smarting.* **2** to feel hurt or upset about an unkindness: *She was still smarting over his criticism.*

smart·en /ˈsmɑːtn ‖ -ɑːr-/ *v*
smarten up *phr v* [I;T **smarten** sbdy/sthg ↔ **up**] to become or make something look neat or stylish: *We smartened the office up with a new coat of paint. | Try to smarten yourself up for the interview.*

smash¹ /smæʃ/ *v* **1** [I;T] to break something into pieces violently: *I nearly smashed the window. | The plate smashed on the floor.* –see BREAK (USAGE) **2** [I;T] to crash into something solid: *They smashed their way out of the building. | The waves smashed on to the beach.* **3** [T] to hit a ball with a hard downward attacking shot

smash² *n* **1** the sound of a violent breaking: *the smash of glass breaking* **2** a powerful blow **3** (also **smash-up**) a violent car accident: *There was a terrible smash-up on the motorway last night.* **4** a hard downward attacking shot in games such as tennis **5** (also **smash hit**) a very successful new play, film, book, or song: *a new smash musical*

smashed /smæʃt/ *adj* [never before a noun] *slang* drunk or under the influence of drugs

smash·ing /ˈsmæʃɪŋ/ *adj BrE infml* excellent: *We had a smashing holiday.*

smat·ter·ing /ˈsmætərɪŋ/ *n* a **smattering of** a little knowledge about: *I have a smattering of Italian.*

SPELLING NOTE

Words with the sound / s /, may be spelt **c-**, like **city**, or **ps-**, like **psychology**.

---

smear¹ /smɪəʳ/ *n* **1** a dirty oily mark: *There's a smear of grease on your forehead.* **2** an untrue charge made against someone to try to turn public feelings against them: *The newspapers ran a smear campaign against him. | a right-wing smear* **3** a **smear test** a medical test for CANCER of the CERVIX

smear² *v* **1** [T] to spread a thin covering of a sticky or greasy substance over the surface of something: *She smeared suntan lotion all over herself. | Smear the dish with butter.* **2** [I] to spread across a surface, leaving a dirty mark: *Be careful, the paint may smear.*

smell¹ /smel/ *v* **smelled or smelt** /smelt/, **smelled or smelt** **1** [I] to have or use the sense of the nose: *I've got a cold and I can't smell very well.* **2** [T; + (that)] to notice or recognize the smell of something: *Come and smell these roses. They're wonderful. | I can smell burning. | I could smell that the milk wasn't fresh.* **3** [I; + adv/prep; + complement] to have a particular smell: *This wine smells like honey. | The room smelt of stale beer. | This book smells old.* **4** [I] to have an unpleasant smell: *The meat had started to smell.* **5** [T] to feel that something, especially danger or trouble, is about to happen **6 smell a rat** *infml* to become conscious that something is wrong

smell sthg ↔ **out** *phr v* [T] **1** to discover something by smelling: *The hounds smelt out a fox.* **2** to work hard so that you find out something that someone is trying to keep hidden

smell² *n* **1** [U] the ability to use your nose: *I've got an excellent sense of smell.* **2** [C] the effect that something has on your nose: *There's a nice smell of coffee in the restaurant. | I love the smell of baking. | What's that awful smell?* **3 have a smell** to smell something: *Have a smell of this wine: is it all right?*

■ USAGE A **smell** can be either good or bad: *a wonderful* **smell** *of cooking | a strong* **smell** *of rotten eggs.* If you do not say whether it is good or bad, you usually mean that it is bad: *What's that* **smell** *in the bathroom?* (= it smells bad). **Odour** is a rather formal word usually meaning a bad smell: *A new disinfectant which destroys household* **odours** *instantly!* **Stink** is an informal word meaning a very strong, bad smell: *Phew! What a* **stink!** **Scent** and **perfume** can both be used for pleasant, sweet smells: *the sweet* **scents** *of a garden in springtime | The* **perfume** *of roses filled the room.*

smell·y /ˈsmeli/ *adj* **smellier, smelliest** unpleasant-smelling: *smelly old socks*

smelt /smelt/ *v* **1** the past tense and participle of SMELL **2** [T] to melt metal-containing earth in order to separate and remove the metal

smile¹ /smaɪl/ *n* an expression on your face in which your mouth moves upwards at the corners to show happiness: *She gave a shy smile. | He welcomed me with a smile.*

smile² *v* **smiled, smiling** **1** [I] to have or give a smile: *He smiled at me. | She smiled with satisfaction.* **2** [T] to express with a smile: *She smiled her approval.* –**smilingly** *adv*

smirk /smɜːk ‖ smɜːrk/ *v* [I] to smile in a silly satisfied way

smith /smɪθ/ *n* a person who makes things out of metals such as gold, silver, or iron: *a blacksmith | a goldsmith | a gunsmith*

smith·e·reens /ˌsmɪðəˈriːnz/ *n* into/to **smithereens** *infml* into very small bits: *The glass was smashed to smithereens.*

smit·ten /ˈsmɪtn/ *adj* **be smitten** to have a sudden

strong feeling, especially of approval, for something or someone: *He only spoke to her for a moment, but he was absolutely smitten.*

smock /smɒk ‖ smɑːk/ n a loose piece of clothing like a long shirt

smog /smɒg ‖ smɑːg, smɔːg/ n [U] an unhealthy mixture of FOG and smoke which is found in the air in some industrial cities –see picture on page 246

smoke¹ /sməʊk/ n **1** [U] the white, grey, or black gas produced when something burns: *There's a lot of smoke coming from that bonfire.* | *a puff of smoke* | *the smell of tobacco smoke* **2** [C] an act of smoking tobacco: *There's just time for a cup of coffee and a smoke.* **3 go up in smoke** to end without results, especially suddenly

smoke² v smoked, smoking **1** [I;T] to light something containing tobacco and breathe in the smoke from it: *Do you mind if I smoke?* | *He smokes a pipe.* **2** [I] to send out smoke: *The chimneys were smoking on the industrial estate.*

smoke sbdy/sthg ↔ **out** phr v [T] to fill a place with smoke to force a person or animal to come out from hiding

smoked /sməʊkt/ adj **1** preserved by hanging in smoke: *smoked mackerel* | *smoked meats* **2** darkened by the colour of smoke: *smoked glass* | *smoked quartz*

smok·er /ˈsməʊkəʳ/ n **1** a person who smokes **2** a railway carriage where smoking is allowed –opposite **non-smoker**

smoke-screen /ˈsməʊkskriːn/ n **1** a cloud of smoke produced in order to hide a place or an activity from your enemy **2** something which hides your real intentions: *It wasn't easy to find out as they had thrown up a bit of a smokescreen.*

smok·ing /ˈsməʊkɪŋ/ n [U] the practice or habit of breathing in tobacco smoke from cigarettes or a pipe: *I'm trying to give up smoking.* | *The sign says "No smoking".*

smok·y /ˈsməʊki/ adj smokier, smokiest **1** full of smoke: *a smoky bar* | *I hate this smoky atmosphere.* **2** with the taste or appearance of smoke: *smoky-tasting fish* | *a smoky-blue uniform* –smokiness n [U]

smol·der /ˈsməʊldəʳ/ v the usual American spelling of SMOULDER

smooth¹ /smuːð/ adj **1** without any holes or lumps in its surface: *a baby's smooth skin* | *a smooth road* | *The tyres were worn smooth.* **2** without lumps (of a liquid mixture): *Beat the mixture until smooth.* **3** even in movement, without sudden changes: *He brought the car to a smooth stop.* **4** free from problems or difficulties: *a smooth journey* | *progress in this matter has not been smooth* **5** too pleasant or polite in manner (used of a man): *I don't trust that man; he's far too smooth.* –**smoothly** adv –**smoothness** n [U]

smooth² v [T] to make something smooth: *He smoothed down his hair.* | *This face cream is good at smoothing* **away** *wrinkles.*

smooth sthg ↔ **out** phr v [T] to move your hands over something to make it smooth

smooth sthg ↔ **over** phr v [T] to make something less important or less of a problem: *We managed to smooth over the bad feeling in the office.*

smoth·er /ˈsmʌðəʳ/ v [T] **1** to cover completely: *I threw a blanket down to smother the flames.* | *The cake was smothered* **with** *chocolate icing.* **2** to control your feelings so that other people do not notice them: *I tried to smother my anger.* **3** to cover someone's face with something so that they cannot

breathe: *She'd been smothered with a pillow.* **4** to give too much love and protection: *Don't smother the child; let him make his own mistakes.*

smoul·der /ˈsməʊldəʳ/ v (**smolder** AmE) [I] **1** to burn slowly without a flame **2** lit to have violent feelings inside you that you do not show: *Inside, I was smouldering* **with** *anger.*

smudge¹ /smʌdʒ/ v smudged, smudging **1** [T] to make something look dirty and unclear because you have touched it: *I'm afraid I've smudged your signature.* **2** [I] to become dirty and unclear because of being touched: *The ink has smudged.*

smudge² n a dirty mark

smug /smʌg/ adj smugger, smuggest too pleased with yourself because you think you are good or clever: *a smug expression on her face* | *He's unbearably smug about getting into university.* –**smugly** adv –**smugness** n [U]

smug·gle /ˈsmʌgəl/ v smuggled, smuggling [T] to take goods or people from one country to another illegally: *The drugs had been smuggled in by a gang.* | *smuggling refugees into Europe* –**smuggler** n –**smuggling** n [U]

smut /smʌt/ n **1** [C;U] a small piece of dirt that makes dark marks **2** [U] morally offensive books, stories, pictures, or remarks

smut·ty /ˈsmʌti/ adj smuttier, smuttiest rather rude and morally improper: *a smutty joke* –**smuttily** adv –**smuttiness** n [U]

snack /snæk/ n a quick light meal: *I haven't got time for lunch, I'll just have a snack.*

snack bar /ˈ· ·/ n a place where you can buy snacks and drinks

snag¹ /snæg/ n a small unexpected difficulty: *It's a good idea. The only snag is, we haven't any money.*

snag² v [T] to pull a thread in clothing by catching it on something sharp: *Oh no! I've snagged my jumper on your rose bush.*

snail /sneɪl/ n **1** a small slow-moving creature with a soft body and a hard shell on its back **2** at a **snail's pace** at a very slow speed

snake¹ /sneɪk/ n a long thin REPTILE with no legs, often having a poisonous bite

snake² v snaked, snaking [I] (also **snake its way**) to move in a twisting way: *The train snaked its way through the mountains.*

snake charm·er /ˈ· ˌ··/ n a person who entertains people by controlling snakes, for example by playing music

snap¹ /snæp/ v -pp- **1** [I;T] to break suddenly with a sharp cracking noise: *The branch snapped under all the snow.* | *I snapped the stick in half.* **2** [I;T] to move into a particular position with a sharp noise: *The lid snapped shut.* **3 snap your fingers** to make a noise by moving your second finger quickly across your thumb, usually to attract attention **4** [I] (used of animals) to try to bite: *The dog snapped at my ankles.* **5** [I] to speak quickly in a sharp, unfriendly way: *"You're late!," she snapped.* | *I'm sorry I snapped at you.* **6** [T] infml to photograph **7 snap out of it** infml a phrase used when you are telling someone to stop feeling unhappy and be cheerful again

snap sthg ↔ **up** phr v [T] to buy quickly and eagerly: *We snapped up lots of bargains in the sales.*

snap² n **1** [C] a sudden sharp sound **2** [C] infml an informal photograph: *holiday snaps* **3** [U] a children's card game in which players shout "Snap!" when they see two cards which are the same

snap³ *adj* [only before a noun] done in haste and without careful thought: *a snap decision*

snap·py /'snæpi/ *adj* **1** speaking in a sharp, unfriendly way **2 a snappy dresser** a person who wears stylish, fashionable clothes **3 Make it snappy!** Look snappy *infml* Hurry up!

snap·shot /'snæpʃɒt/ -ʃɑːt/ *n* an informal photograph: *holiday snapshots*

snare¹ /sneəʳ/ *n* **1** a trap for catching birds or small animals **2** something which attracts you, but is really a trap for you

snare² *v* snared, snaring [T] to catch in a snare: *We snared a couple of rabbits.*

snarl¹ /snɑːl ‖ snɑːrl/ *v* [I] **1** (of an animal) to make a fierce angry sound and show its teeth: *a snarling dog* **2** to say something in a fierce angry way

snarl² *n* the expression an animal has or the sound it makes when it snarls

snarled /snɑːld ‖ snɑːrld/ *adj* snarled up blocked or confused: *Traffic was badly snarled up near the accident.*

snarl-up /'· ·/ *n infml* a confused situation

snatch¹ /snætʃ/ *v* [T] **1** to get hold of something quickly and forcefully: *The thief snatched her handbag and ran off.* **2** to make use of time or a chance quickly: *I snatched a moment at lunchtime to read your letter.* **3 snatch at something** to try to get something or to take it eagerly: *You must snatch at any opportunity to go abroad.* –**snatcher** *n*

snatch² *n* **1 make a snatch at** to try to get something by snatching: *He made a snatch at the ball but just missed.* **2** a short and incomplete period of something: *We slept fitfully, in snatches.* | *I heard a snatch of their conversation.*

sneak¹ /sniːk/ *v* **1** [I + adv/prep] to go quietly and secretly: *He sneaked past the guard.* **2** [T] to take secretly or cleverly: *We sneaked the food up to our rooms.* | *I sneaked a look at his diary.*

sneak up *phr v* [I] to come quietly and secretly near: *Don't sneak up behind me like that!* | *Our teacher has a nasty habit of sneaking up on you when you're not working.*

sneak² *n infml* a person who informs officials that you have done something wrong (a word used to express disapproval)

sneak·er /'sniːkəʳ/ *n* the usual American word for PLIMSOLL or TRAINER

sneak·ing /'sniːkɪŋ/ *adj* [only before a noun] secret and not openly expressed: *I have a sneaking suspicion that he knows about us.*

sneak·y /'sniːki/ *adj* sneakier, sneakiest *infml* acting or done secretly and deceitfully –**sneakiness** *n* [U]

sneer¹ /snɪəʳ/ *v* [I] **1** to have an unpleasant expression on your face, with a one-sided smile **2** to speak or to behave as if something is not worthy of serious attention: *Don't sneer at their religion.* –**sneeringly** *adv*

sneer² *n* the expression on someone's face when they sneer, or a sneering remark

sneeze /sniːz/ *v* sneezed, sneezing [I] to suddenly blow down your nose noisily in an uncontrolled way, for example when you have a cold: *The dust made him sneeze.* –**sneeze** *n* : *He gave a sudden sneeze.*

snick·er /'snɪkəʳ/ *v* [I] to laugh quietly to yourself, in a disrespectful way

snide /snaɪd/ *adj* amusing but unfair and hurtful: *a snide remark*

SPORTS

Exercise 1

Some sports are played by individuals, others are played in teams. Can you unscramble the names of the sports to complete the table?

	Individual		Team	
ceathletis	athletics		gyrbu	rugby
xingob			cineramA	
			boollfat	
yingccl			bleatblask	
flog			treckic	
kingsi			cresco	
roseh caring				
miwsming				
nestin				

Exercise 2

Can you answer these questions about the sports in the picture?

1 Which two sports are played with an egg-shaped ball?

2 In which three sports do you hit the ball with something?

3 Which sport involves water?

4 Which sport involves an animal?

5 Which three sports involve kicking a ball?

Exercise 3

Which sports are played in these places? Write the names of the sports. The number in brackets shows the number of sports.

pitch (4)
track (2)
court (2)
course (2)
pool (1)
slope (1)
ring (1)

cricket, American football, soccer, rugby
....
....
....
....
....
....

xkboard
football
American football
helmet

bowler
batsman
bails
bat
pad

cricket
stumps
(tennis) ball

xket
basketball
basketball

cyclist
tennis
racket
bicycle
track
cycling

club
golfer
net
golfbag
court
(rugby) ball
player
rugby

flag
bunker
golf
riding hat
jockey/rider
saddle
reins

swimming
cap
swimmer
goggles

runner
tape
boxing gloves
referee

ck
athletics (BrE)/track and field (AmE)
goal
defender
goalkeeper
player
(foot)ball
soccer
horse racing
helmet
skiing
ski
pole
ski boot
ring
boxing

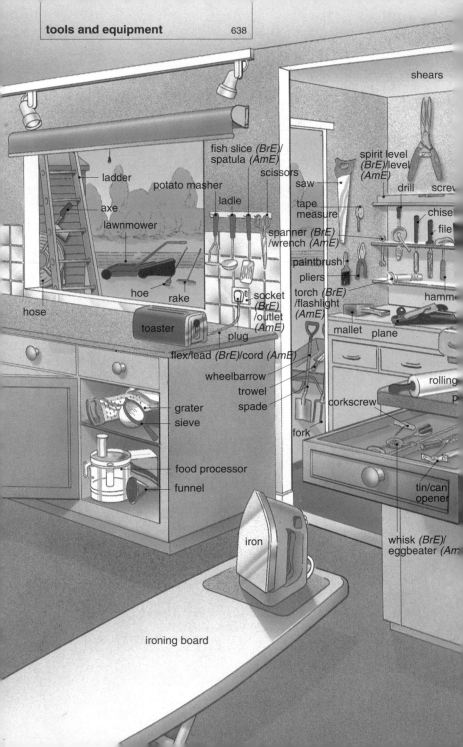

shears

ladder

potato masher

fish slice *(BrE)/*
spatula *(AmE)*

scissors

saw

spirit level
*(BrE)/*level
(AmE)

drill   screw

axe

ladle

tape
measure

chisel

lawnmower

spanner *(BrE)*
/wrench *(AmE)*

file

paintbrush

pliers

hammer

hoe   rake

socket
(BrE)
/outlet
(AmE)

torch *(BrE)*
/flashlight
(AmE)

hose

toaster

plug

mallet   plane

flex/lead *(BrE)*/cord *(AmE)*

wheelbarrow

trowel

rolling

spade

corkscrew

p

grater

fork

sieve

food processor

funnel

tin/can
opener

iron

whisk *(BrE)/*
eggbeater *(Am*

ironing board

sniff¹ /snɪf/ v **1** [I] to breathe air up into the nose with a sound: *She sniffed, trying hard not to cry.* **2** [I;T] to smell something by breathing air up into the nose: *The dogs sniffed at my shopping bag.* | *"That's a nice perfume," she said, sniffing the air.* | *I'm afraid your son's been sniffing glue.* **3 not to be sniffed at** not to be refused without careful thought, or because of pride: *A good offer like that is not to be sniffed at.*
sniff sth ↔ out *phr v* [T] *infml* to discover after searching: *The police dogs finally sniffed out the drugs.*

sniff² *n* **1** the sound you make when you sniff **2 have a sniff** *infml* to smell: *Have a sniff of this perfume.*

snif·fle /ˈsnɪfəl/ v **sniffled, sniffling** (also **snuffle**) [I] to sniff repeatedly, as if you are crying or have a cold –**sniffle** *n*

snig·ger /ˈsnɪɡəʳ/ v [I] to laugh quietly to yourself in a disrespectful way –**snigger** *n*

snip¹ /snɪp/ *n* **1** a short quick cut made with scissors **2** *BrE infml* a surprisingly cheap article for sale

snip² *v* **-pp-** [I;T] to cut something with scissors, especially in short quick strokes: *Just snip a hole in the paper here.* | *Keep still while I snip around your ears!*

snipe /snaɪp/ v **sniped, sniping** [I] **1** to shoot at people from a hidden position: *People were sniping at us from above.* **2** to attack someone with unpleasant remarks: *He should learn to work with his colleagues instead of sniping at them.* –**sniper** *n*

snip·pet /ˈsnɪpɪt/ *n* a small bit of something: *a snippet of information* | *snippets of conversation*

sniv·el /ˈsnɪvəl/ v **-ll-** (also **-l-** *AmE*) [I] to cry, act, or speak in a weak complaining way: *If you fail, don't come snivelling back to me.* –**sniveller** *n*

snob /snɒb ‖ snɑːb/ *n* **1** a person who dislikes those considered to be of a lower social class, and admires people of a higher social class (a word used to express disapproval) **2** a person who is proud of having greater knowledge or better taste than others (a word used to express disapproval): *She's a musical snob who despises all pop music.* –**snobbish** *adj* –**snobbishly** *adv*

snob·be·ry /ˈsnɒbəri ‖ ˈsnɑːb-/ *n* [U] the feelings, behaviour, or language of a snob

snoo·ker /ˈsnuːkəʳ ‖ ˈsnu-/ *n* [U] a game played on a table covered with green cloth; players must knock coloured balls into pockets at the edge of the table, using long sticks

snooker² *v* [T] *infml* to trap or trick someone so that they cannot act as they wish

snoop /snuːp/ v [I] to look into other people's property or activities without permission: *I caught him snooping around in my office.* –**snooper** *n*

snoot·y /ˈsnuːti/ *adj* **snootier, snootiest** *infml* showing that you feel more important than others (a word used to express disapproval): *Now that he's rich, he's too snooty to be interested in his old friends.* –**snootily** *adv*

snooze /snuːz/ v **snoozed, snoozing** [I] *infml* to have a short, light sleep –**snooze** *n* : *I'm going to have a snooze after lunch.*

snore¹ /snɔːʳ/ v **snored, snoring** [I] to breathe noisily through your nose and mouth while you are asleep: *How can I stop him snoring?* –**snorer** *n*

snore² *n* a noisy way of breathing while you are asleep

snor·kel /ˈsnɔːkəl ‖ -ɔːr-/ *n* an air tube that allows a swimmer to breathe under water –**snorkel** *v* [I]: *Do you want to go snorkelling?*

TOOLS AND EQUIPMENT

Exercise 1
Can you explain the connection between these things?

1 bottle opener, corkscrew, tin opener
2 scissors, secateurs, shears
3 trowel, spade, fork, hoe

Exercise 2
Mr Sampson always makes mistakes. He always uses the wrong tools. Read these sentences and say which tool Mr Sampson should use in each case.

1 He uses a **ladle** to water the lawn.
2 He uses a **pair of scissors** to cut the grass.
3 He uses a **spade** to cut down trees.
4 He uses a **plane** to peel potatoes.
5 He uses a **mallet** to mash the potatoes.
6 He uses a **rolling pin** to press his trousers.
7 He uses a **screwdriver** to take the cork out of a wine bottle.
8 He uses an **iron** to make toast.
9 He uses a **chisel** to drive in a nail.
10 He uses a **saw** to open a tin of peas.

Exercise 3
Complete this passage with words from the illustration. Put in one letter for each dash.
If you want to join two pieces of wood together, you can use a ¹h _ _ _ _ _ and a nail. Another way is to use a ²d _ _ _ _ to make a small hole in the pieces of wood and then use a ³s _ _ _ _ _ _ _ _ _ and a screw to join them. Alternatively, you can make a hole through both pieces of wood and slide a bolt through the hole. You should then twist a nut on the other end and tighten it with a ⁴s _ _ _ _ _ _.

The most professional way of joining two pieces of wood is to cut a joint. First, you should use a ⁵t _ _ _ _ _ _ _ _ _ to measure the pieces carefully. Then use the ⁶s _ _ to cut the end of one piece of wood into a tongue shape. After that, use your ⁷c _ _ _ _ _ and ⁸m _ _ _ _ _ to cut a hole of the same size in the other piece of wood. Put some glue on the tongue and in the hole and stick the two pieces of wood together.

snort /snɔːt ‖ snɔːrt/ v [I] to make a noise by blowing air through your nose, to express feelings like anger or impatience –**snort** n

snout /snaʊt/ n the long nose of animals like pigs

snow¹ /snəʊ/ n 1 [U] water frozen into soft white pieces that fall like rain in cold weather and cover the ground 2 **the snows** [pl] *lit* falls of snow

snow² v [I] (of snow) to fall: *Look! It's snowing.*

snow·ball¹ /'snəʊbɔːl/ n a ball made of snow pressed together, which children throw at each other

snowball² v [I] to grow at a faster and faster rate: *The effect of rising prices has snowballed.*

snow·bound /'snəʊbaʊnd/ adj blocked or kept indoors by heavy snow

snow·drift /'snəʊˌdrɪft/ n a deep bank of snow formed by the wind

snow·drop /'snəʊdrɒp ‖ -drɑːp/ n a small white European flower which appears in the early spring

snowed in /ˌ· '·/ adj unable to go anywhere because of deep snow: *We were snowed in for three days last winter.*

snowed un·der /ˌ· '··/ adj having more work to do than you can easily deal with: *I'm completely snowed under at the moment.*

snow·fall /'snəʊfɔːl/ n 1 [C] a fall of snow 2 [sing;U] the amount of snow that falls: *an average snowfall of five inches per year*

snow·flake /'snəʊfleɪk/ n one of the soft white pieces of frozen water which fall as snow

snow·man /'snəʊmæn/ n **snowmen** /-men/ a figure of a person made out of snow

snow·plough /'snəʊplaʊ/ n BrE (**snowplow** AmE) a vehicle for pushing snow off roads or railways

snow·storm /'snəʊstɔːrm ‖ -ɔːrm/ n a very heavy fall of snow, especially when blown by strong winds

snow-white /ˌ· '·◂/ adj as white as snow

snow·y /'snəʊi/ adj **snowier, snowiest** 1 covered in or full of snow: *snowy mountains | snowy weather* 2 pure white: *snowy white hair*

Snr n an abbreviation for SENIOR

snub¹ /snʌb/ v -bb- [T] to treat someone rudely, usually by paying them no attention or by making an unkind remark: *I said hello, but she just snubbed me and walked on.* –**snub** n

snub² adj **snub nose** a short, flat nose

snuff /snʌf/ n [U] tobacco made into a powder which you breathe up through your nose: *a snuff box | a pinch of snuff*

snuf·fle /'snʌfəl/ v,n [I] to make a noise inside your nose, often because you have a cold

snug /snʌg/ adj 1 warm and comfortable: *a snug little room with a warm fire* 2 fitting closely (used to describe clothes)

snug·gle /'snʌgəl/ v **snuggled, snuggling** [I] to settle into a warm comfortable position: *Snuggle up to me and I'll keep you warm.*

SPELLING NOTE

Words with the sound /s/, may be spelt **c-,** like **city,** or **ps-,** like **psychology.**

---

so¹ /səʊ/ adv 1 used when you are talking again about something that has already been mentioned: *"Will you be coming to the party tonight?" "I think so." | He hopes he'll get the job and I hope so too. | Are you married? If so, please give your wife's name.* 2 used when you are making sure that you have understood something that you have been told: *So he didn't go to America after all. | So she didn't get the job?* 3 used when you are going to tell someone something again, but more briefly, to make sure that they have understood: *The Birmingham factory produces sweets. The other section of the business, the one in Derby, is concerned with soft drinks. So we've got sweets in Birmingham and soft drinks in Derby.* 4 used when you are describing something by showing it with your hands: *Then you have to fold the paper so. | It was about so big.* 5 to such a degree, or to a very great degree: *He was so fat that he couldn't get through the door. | He's a lovely child, and so clever.* –see SUCH (USAGE) 6 also: *"I need a drink." "So do I." | "Ann can play the piano." "So can Sally."* 7 **and so on, and so forth** used to say that there are lots of other things that you could add to a list: *The place was full of junk – old furniture, paintings, and so on.* 8 **so as to** in order to do something: *She put her arms up so as to protect herself.* 9 **so long** infml GOODBYE 10 **so much for**... you use this phrase when you are disappointed that something has not happened: *I see they've appointed another man as Head of Department. So much for equality!*

so² conj 1 therefore: *It was dark so I couldn't see very well. | It was quite late so I went to bed.* 2 (also **so that**) with the purpose that: *I put the heating on so that the house would warm up. | Put your umbrella up so you don't get wet.* 3 **so what?** infml a phrase you use to show that you think that something is not at all important

so³ adj [never before a noun] true: *Is that really so? | You know very well that just isn't so.*

soak¹ /səʊk/ v [I;T] 1 to put something in liquid and leave it there: *Leave the dirty clothes to soak. | Soak the bread in milk. | I'm going to soak in the bath for a while.* 2 (of a liquid) to get into something and make it very wet: *The ink had soaked through the thin paper.*

soak sthg ↔ **up** phr v [T] 1 to take in liquid: *Use a cloth to soak up the water.* 2 infml to take in the sun through your skin: *He's at the beach soaking up some sunshine.*

soak² n 1 an act of leaving something in liquid: *Give the clothes a good soak before you wash them.* 2 infml a person who is frequently drunk

soaked /səʊkt/ adj [never before a noun] thoroughly wet: *You're soaked! Take off those wet clothes!*

soak·ing /'səʊkɪŋ/ adj very wet indeed: *My coat's soaking wet. | I'm soaking!*

so-and-so /'·· ˌ·/ n 1 [U] a person or thing that has not been named and is usually one of a group of similar people: *When Mrs So-and-so comes into the shop, make her feel welcome.* 2 [C] a person who has done something bad (a word used to express disapproval): *The so-and-so charged me £20 for ten minutes' work!*

soap¹ /səʊp/ n [U] a product made from fat and used for washing: *a bar of soap | soap powder* –**soapy** adj **soapier, soapiest** : *soapy water*

soap² v [T] (also **soap yourself**) to rub soap on or over yourself: *I was just soaping myself in the bath when the telephone rang.*

soap op·e·ra /ˈ· ˌ···/ n a continuing television or radio story about the lives and problems of imaginary characters

soar /sɔːʳ/ v [I] *lit* **1** to fly: *birds soaring over the hills* **2** to rise far or fast: *The temperature soared to 35°C.* | *soaring prices* | *The cliffs soar 500 ft into the air.*

sob /sɒb ‖ sɑːb/ v -bb- [I] to cry while breathing in sudden short bursts: *The little boy was sobbing in the corner.* | *She sobbed herself to sleep.* -sob n : *"Don't be so nasty to me!" she said with a sob.*

so·ber¹ /ˈsəubəʳ/ adj **1** not drunk **2** thoughtful, serious, or solemn **3** plain and dull: *a sober dress* -soberly adv -sobriety /səˈbraɪəti/ n [U]

sober² v
sober up phr v [I; T sober sbdy up] to lose or take away the effects of alcohol: *I hope this coffee sobers him up.* | *You'd better sober up before your wife sees you!*

so·ber·ing /ˈsəubərɪŋ/ adj making you become serious or thoughtful: *Her illness had a sobering effect on her.*

so-called /ˌ· ˈ·◄/ adj [only before a noun] **1** wrongly named: *so-called Christians who show no love to anyone* **2** known by a particular name: *Do you mean the so-called 'Gang of Five'?*

soc·cer /ˈsɒkəʳ ‖ ˈsɑː-/ n [U] *BrE* football: *a soccer match* | *Do you play soccer at school?* -see picture on page 637

so·cia·ble /ˈsəuʃəbəl/ fond of being with other people -sociability /ˌ-ʃəˈbrɪləti/ n [U]

so·cial /ˈsəuʃəl/ adj **1** concerning human society or its organization: *social change* | *social, political, and economic systems* **2** based on rank in society: *people of different social classes* **3** relating to activities that you do with other people in your free time: *We have an active social life.* **4** forming groups or living together by nature: *social insects such as ants* -socially adv

so·cial·is·m /ˈsəuʃəlɪzəm/ n [U] a set of beliefs which aims for the establishment of a society in which every person is equal

so·cial·ist¹ /ˈsəuʃəlɪst/ n **1** a believer in socialism **2** a member of a socialist political party

socialist² adj of, concerning, or following socialism: *socialist principles* | *a socialist government*

so·cial·ize /ˈsəuʃəl-aɪz/ v socialized, socializing (also **socialise** *BrE*) [I] to spend time with other people in a friendly way: *There will be no socializing during business hours!*

social sci·ence /ˌ·· ˈ·· ‖ ˈ·· ˌ··/ n [C;U] the study of people in society: *I intend to study social science.* | *the importance of social sciences such as economics or politics*

social sci·en·tist /ˌ·· ˈ···/ n a person who studies or teaches social science

social se·cu·ri·ty /ˌ·· ·ˈ···/ n *BrE* (welfare *AmE*) [U] a system that allows money to be paid to people who have no job or little money

social serv·ic·es /ˌ·· ˈ··· ‖ ˈ·· ˌ··/ n [pl] *BrE* the services provided by the government for people in need

social work /ˈ·· ·/ n [U] work done to improve bad social conditions and help people in need -social worker n

so·ci·e·ty /səˈsaɪəti/ n societies **1** [C;U] a large group of people with shared customs and laws: *That is unacceptable in our society.* | *Far Eastern societies* | *in Western society* **2** [U] people living

together, considered as a whole: *Society has a right to expect obedience to the law.* **3** [C] an organization of people with similar aims and interests: *a film society* **4** [U] *fml* the company of others: *I prefer to spend time in the society of my friends.* **5** (also **Society**) [U] the fashionable people in an area: *Her marriage to a road-sweeper shocked London Society.*

so·ci·ol·o·gy /ˌsəusiˈɒlədʒi, ˌsəuʃi- ‖ -ˈɑːlə-/ n [U] the study of societies and human behaviour in groups -sociologist n -sociological /ˌsəusiəˈlɒdʒɪkəl, ˌsəuʃiə- ‖ -ˈlɑː-/ adj

sock /sɒk ‖ sɑːk/ n **1** a garment which covers your foot and is usually worn inside a shoe -see PAIR (USAGE) -see picture on page 50 **2 pull your socks up** *BrE infml* to stop being lazy and start working hard

sock·et /ˈsɒkɪt ‖ ˈsɑː-/ n an opening into which something fits: *eye sockets* | *Could you fit an electric light bulb into that socket?* -see picture on page 638

sod /sɒd ‖ sɑːd/ n [C;U] earth with grass and roots growing in it

so·da /ˈsəudə/ n [U] **1** see SODA WATER **2** the usual American word for POP² (2): *a bottle of orange soda*

soda wa·ter /ˈ·· ˌ··/ n [U] water filled with gas: *Whisky and soda, please.*

sod·den /ˈsɒdn ‖ ˈsɑːdn/ adj extremely wet: *sodden clothes*

so·di·um /ˈsəudiəm/ n [U] a silver-white metal that is found only in combination with other substances

so·fa /ˈsəufə/ n a comfortable seat long enough for two or three people to sit on -see picture on page 442

soft /sɒft ‖ sɔːft/ adj **1** easily pressed into a different shape: *a soft cushion* | *His foot sank into the soft snow.* **2** smooth and delicate to the touch: *soft skin* **3** restful and pleasant to the senses, especially to your eyes: *soft lights* | *soft colours* **4** quiet: *soft music* | *a soft voice* **5** *infml* not severe enough: *Don't let him do that; you're too soft with him.* **6** soft drink a drink containing no alcohol **7** allowing soap to spread easily (used of water): *We're lucky that the local water here is quite soft.* **8** not of the strongest, most harmful kind: *soft pornography* | *soft drugs like cannabis* **9** *infml* foolish or mad: *Have you gone soft in the head?* **10** easy: *a soft job* | *Selling the company would be the soft option, but I want to try and make a success of it.* -softly adv -softness n [U]

soft-boiled /ˌ· ˈ·◄/ adj boiled for a short time so that the inside is still soft (used of an egg)

soft·en /ˈsɒfən ‖ ˈsɔː-/ v **1** [I;T] to make something or to become softer, more gentle, less hard, or less severe: *This cream softens dry skin.* | *His attitude towards children softened when he had a son of his own.* **2 soften the blow** to make unpleasant news easier to accept
soften sbdy ↔ up phr v [T] to make someone feel good so that they will do something for you

soft-heart·ed /ˌsɒftˈhɑːtɪd◄ ‖ ˌsɔːftˈhɑːr-/ adj kind and sympathetic -softheartedness n [U]

soft-spok·en /ˌ· ˈ··◄/ adj having a gentle voice

soft·ware /ˈsɒftweəʳ ‖ ˈsɔːft-/ n [U] lists of instructions that must be given to a computer in order to make it perform operations; these lists are called programs (PROGRAM): *Is there any new software for this machine?*

soft·wood /ˈsɒftwud ‖ ˈsɔːft-/ n [U] wood that comes from particular trees and is easy to cut

sog·gy /ˈsɒgi ‖ ˈsɑːgi/ adj soggier, soggiest unpleasantly wet: *The ground is still soggy from yesterday's rain.* | *If you boil the vegetables for too long, they'll go soggy.*

soil¹ /sɔɪl/ n [U] **1** the top covering of the earth, in which plants grow: *fertile soil | poor soil* **2** the land that forms part of a country: *It was his first experience of being on foreign soil.* –see LAND¹ (USAGE)

soil² v [T] to make something dirty: *Your shirt collar is badly soiled.*

sol·ace /ˈsɒlɪs ‖ ˈsɑː-/ n [C;U] something that provides comfort when you are unhappy or worried

so·lar /ˈsəʊləʳ/ adj of, from, or using the sun or its light: *solar power | a solar heating system* –compare LUNAR

solar sys·tem /ˈ··· ˌ··/ n **1 the solar system** the sun together with the bodies that move around it **2** [C] a system like this around another star

sold /səʊld/ v the past tense and past participle of SELL

solder¹ /ˈsɒldəʳ, ˈsəʊl- ‖ ˈsɑːdər/ n [U] soft metal which is used to join together other metal surfaces

solder² v [T] to join or repair metal with solder: *I'll solder those pipes together.*

sol·dier¹ /ˈsəʊldʒəʳ/ n a member of an army

soldier² v

soldier on phr v [I] BrE to continue doing something in spite of difficulties

sole¹ /səʊl/ n **1** [C] the bottom surface of your foot **2** [C] the part of a sock, shoe, or boot that covers the bottom of your foot **3** [C;U] a flat white fish eaten as food

sole² v **soled, soling** [T] to put a new surface on the bottom of a shoe: *I'd better get my shoes soled.*

sole³ adj [only before a noun] **1** only: *The sole survivor of the crash was a baby.* **2** not shared with another person: *You have sole responsibility for this department.*

sole·ly /ˈsəʊl-li/ adv only: *I did it solely for your own good.*

sol·emn /ˈsɒləm ‖ ˈsɑː-/ adj **1** serious: *His expression was unusually solemn.* **2** formal: *a solemn promise* –**solemnly** adv –**solemnity** /səˈlemnɪti/ n [U]

so·li·cit /səˈlɪsɪt/ v **1** [I;T] fml to ask for something such as help or support: *Beggars are not allowed to solicit in public places.* | *We intend to solicit the views of all our members.* **2** [I] to offer to have sex for money: *The police charged her with soliciting.*

so·lic·i·tor /səˈlɪsɪtəʳ/ n a lawyer who gives advice, prepares legal cases, and appears in lower law courts

so·lic·i·tous /səˈlɪsɪtəs/ adj fml concerned or anxious to help –**solicitously** adv –**solicitousness** n [U]

sol·id¹ /ˈsɒlɪd ‖ ˈsɑː-/ adj **1** hard, so that it keeps its shape: *The milk had frozen solid.* | *a solid lump of fat* **2** tightly packed together, with no empty space inside: *solid rubber tyres | solid rock* **3** without spaces or breaks: *She overtook another car on a solid white line.* | *I waited for three solid hours.* **4** [only before a noun] completely of one material: *a solid gold watch* **5** strong and dependable: *solid furniture | solid evidence* **6** continuous and useful: *I need*

> **SPELLING NOTE**
> Words with the sound / s /, may be spelt **c-**, like **city**, or **ps-**, like **psychology**.

to get a few years' solid work experience. **7** tech having length, width, and height: *A sphere is a solid figure.* –**solidly** adv –**solidity** /ˈlɪdɪti/ n [U]

solid² n **1** something that is firm and keeps its shape: *Water becomes a solid when it freezes.* **2 solids** non-liquid food: *He is still too ill to take solids.* **3** tech a figure with length, width, and height

sol·i·dar·i·ty /ˌsɒlɪˈdærɪti ‖ ˌsɑː-/ n [U] agreement among a group of people about their common interests, aims, or standards

so·lid·i·fy /səˈlɪdɪfaɪ/ v **solidified, solidifying** [I;T] to make something or to become hard or firm –**solidification** /səˌlɪdɪfɪˈkeɪʃən/ n [U]

so·lil·o·quy /səˈlɪləkwi/ n **soliloquies** a speech especially in a play where you speak your thoughts aloud to yourself

sol·i·ta·ry /ˈsɒlɪtəri ‖ ˈsɑːlɪteri/ adj **1** spending a lot of time alone: *He's a rather solitary young man.* **2** done alone: *Reading is usually a solitary activity.* **3** standing alone, away from others: *a solitary building* **4** single: *Can you give me one solitary piece of proof for what you say?* **5 in solitary confinement** alone in a prison cell without seeing the other prisoners [RELATED PHRASE **in solitary**]

sol·i·tude /ˈsɒlɪtjuːd ‖ ˈsɑːlɪtuːd/ n [U] the state of being alone and away from other people

so·lo¹ /ˈsəʊləʊ/ n **solos** a piece of music played or sung by one person –compare DUET

solo² adj done by one person alone: *my first solo flight* –**solo** adv : *Have you ever flown solo?*

so·lo·ist /ˈsəʊləʊɪst/ n a person who performs a piece of music written for one person to play or sing alone

sol·stice /ˈsɒlstɪs ‖ ˈsɑːl-/ n either the shortest or the longest day in the year; in the northern half of the world the **winter solstice** is December 21 or 22 and the **summer solstice** is June 21 or 22

sol·u·ble /ˈsɒljʊbəl ‖ ˈsɑːl-/ adj **1** that will become part of a liquid when mixed with it: *Salt is soluble in water.* **2** to which an answer can be found: *a soluble problem* –opposite **insoluble**

so·lu·tion /səˈluːʃən/ n **1** [C] an answer to a difficulty or problem: *It's difficult to find a solution that we can all agree on.* | *the solution to yesterday's crossword* **2** [U] ways of dealing with a difficulty or problem: *We're investigating approaches to the solution of domestic problems.* **3** [C;U] a liquid containing a solid or gas mixed into it: *chemical solution*

solve /sɒlv ‖ sɑːlv, sɔːlv/ v **solved, solving** [T] to find an answer to something or way of dealing with it: *I'm trying to solve the problem.* –**solvable** adj

sol·vent¹ /ˈsɒlvənt ‖ ˈsɑːl-, ˈsɔːl-/ adj having enough money to pay all that you owe –opposite **insolvent** –**solvency** n [U]

solvent² n [C;U] a liquid that can DISSOLVE(2) a substance: *Alcohol and petrol are useful solvents.*

som·bre /ˈsɒmbəʳ ‖ ˈsɑːm-/ adj BrE (also **somber** AmE) **1** sad and serious: *a sombre speech* **2** dark and dull: *a sombre business suit* –**sombrely** adv

some /səm; strong sʌm/ det, pron **1** a certain amount or number: *Some parts of the country are very cold in winter.* | *He asked for money and I gave him some.* | *Some of the stories are very good.* **2** used when you mention an unknown person or thing: *There must be some reason for it.* | *She met some man while she was living in Italy.* **3 some … or other** a phrase used when you mention an unknown person or thing: *I read it in some book or other.*

■ USAGE In negative sentences we use **any** and **no** instead of **some**: *I haven't* **any** *socks.* | *I have* **no** *socks.* In questions we usually use **any**: *Is there* **any** *chance that he'll pass the exam?* But we use **some** in offers, suggestions, and requests: *Would you like* **some** *tea?* | *Shall we have* **some** *tea?* | *Can I have* **some** *tea, please?* The same is true of compounds of **some**, **any**, and **no** such as **something**, **anyone**, **nobody**.

some·bod·y /ˈsʌmbɒdi, -bədi ‖ -bɑːdi/ *pron* (also **someone**) a person, but not a particular one and not one who is known: *There's somebody on the telephone for you.* | *You'd better ask someone to help you.* | *I thought the parcel was for me, but it was for somebody else.* –see EVERYBODY (USAGE)

some·day /ˈsʌmdeɪ/ *adv* (also **some day**) at some future time: *Perhaps someday I'll be rich.*

some·how /ˈsʌmhaʊ/ *adv* **1** in some way that is not known: *We'll get the money somehow.* | *Somehow the thieves had managed to get in through a tiny bathroom window.* **2** for some reason that is not clear: *Somehow I don't trust him completely.*

some·one /ˈsʌmwʌn/ *pron* see SOMEBODY

som·er·sault /ˈsʌməsɔːlt ‖ -ər-/ *v* to do a rolling backward or forward movement in which your feet go over your head while your body stays close to the ground –**somersault** *n*

some·thing /ˈsʌmθɪŋ/ *pron* **1** a thing that is not known or not described in detail: *I could see something moving in the bushes.* | *I think I've dropped something.* | *I'm worried that something might have happened to him.* **2 or something** a phrase used when you are not completely sure what a thing is, or are suggesting other possibilities: *It must have been eaten by a fox or something.* | *Let's go to a film or something* **3 something like: a** rather like: *It looked something like a potato.* **b** about: *There were something like 1000 people on the march.* **4 something to do with** having a connection with: *I don't know exactly what his job is, but it's something to do with oil.* **5 that's something** a phrase used to say that at least there is one good thing: *At least we didn't lose any money. That's something!*

some·time¹ /ˈsʌmtaɪm/ *adv* at some uncertain time in the past or the future: *Our house was built sometime around 1905.* | *You must come and visit us sometime.*

sometime² *adj* [only before a noun] *fml* former: *the sometime chairman of British Rail*

some·times /ˈsʌmtaɪmz/ *adv* on some occasions but not on others: *Sometimes I drive to work and sometimes I walk.*

some·what /ˈsʌmwɒt ‖ -wɑːt/ *adv fml* slightly: *He looked cold, and somewhat lonely.* | *The news somewhat surprised me.* | *The experience of being in prison has changed him somewhat.*

some·where /ˈsʌmweəʳ/ *adv* **1** in or to some place: *She's on holiday somewhere in Spain.* | *I'm looking for my bag-it must be somewhere.* **2** used when you are giving a number that is not exact: *somewhere between 40 and 60 students*

son /sʌn/ *n* a male child –compare DAUGHTER –see picture on page 343

so·na·ta /səˈnɑːtə/ *n* a piece of music for one or two instruments, one of which is a piano

song /sɒŋ ‖ sɔːŋ/ *n* **1** [C] a piece of music with words for singing: *a love song* | *a folk song* | *They're playing our song.* **2** [U] the act of singing: *After a few drinks, we burst into song.* **3** [C;U] the musical sound that a bird makes: *the song of the blackbird* **4 for a song** cheaply: *I bought that old wardrobe for a song.* **5 make a song and dance about something** to be unnecessarily annoyed or worried about something: *Stop making such a song and dance about the washing-up and do it!*

song·bird /ˈsɒŋbɜːd ‖ ˈsɔːŋbɜːrd/ *n* a bird that can sing well

son·ic /ˈsɒnɪk ‖ ˈsɑː-/ *adj* of or relating to sound waves

son-in-law /ˈ·· ˌ·/ *n* **sons-in-law** the husband of your daughter –compare DAUGHTER-IN-LAW –see picture on page 343

son·net /ˈsɒnɪt ‖ ˈsɑː-/ *n* a 14-line poem with a formal pattern of line endings

so·nor·ous /ˈsɒnərəs, səˈnɔːrəs ‖ səˈnɔːrəs, ˈsɑːnərəs/ *adj fml* having a pleasantly full sound: *a sonorous bell* | *a sonorous voice*

soon /suːn/ *adv* **1** a short time from now, or a short time after the time mentioned: *I hope to hear from him soon.* | *He died soon after he retired.* | *We should arrive soon after lunch.* **2 as soon as** after something has happened without any delay: *I'll phone you as soon as I hear any news.* **3 no sooner ... than** a phrase you use to say that after one thing has happened something else happens without any delay: *No sooner had she sat down than the phone rang.* **4 sooner or later** a phrase used to say that something is certain to happen, either soon or after a time: *Don't worry, you'll find a job sooner or later.* **5 the sooner the better** a phrase used to say that you would like something to happen as soon as possible: *The sooner she leaves home the better.* **6 would just as soon, would sooner** phrases you use to say that you would prefer to do something: *I'd sooner die than spend my life in a wheelchair.*

soot /sʊt/ *n* [U] black powder produced by fires, and often found in a chimney –**sooty** *adj* **sootier, sootiest**

soothe /suːð/ *v* **soothed, soothing** [T] **1** to make someone who is angry or anxious feel calmer: *A nice cup of tea will soothe your nerves.* | **soothing words 2** to make something less painful: *I need something to soothe my sore throat.* | *soothing cream*

so·phis·ti·cat·ed /səˈfɪstɪkeɪtɪd/ *adj* **1** experienced in social life and behaviour: *a sophisticated young woman* –opposite **unsophisticated 2** showing intelligent understanding: *a sophisticated response* **3** not simple: *sophisticated machinery* –**sophistication** /səˌfɪstɪˈkeɪʃən/ *n* [U]

sop·o·rif·ic /ˌsɒpəˈrɪfɪk ◂ ‖ ˌsɑː-/ *adj* that makes you fall asleep: *a soporific drug* | *soporific speeches*

sop·ping /ˈsɒpɪŋ ‖ ˈsɑː-/ *adv,adj* extremely wet: *Our clothes are sopping wet.*

sop·py /ˈsɒpi ‖ ˈsɑːpi/ *adj* **soppier, soppiest** *BrE infml* too full of tender feelings like sorrow and love and therefore rather silly: *a soppy film* | *You're getting soppy about him!*

so·pra·no /səˈprɑːnəʊ ‖ -ˈpræ-/ *n* **sopranos** a high singing voice of a woman or young boy

sor·cer·er /ˈsɔːsərəʳ ‖ ˈsɔːr-/ *n* a person believed to perform magic by using the power of evil spirits; a female sorcerer is called a **sorceress** –**sorcery** *n* [U]

sor·did /ˈsɔːdɪd ‖ ˈsɔːr-/ *adj* **1** unpleasant and shameful: *a sordid attempt to cheat his brother* **2** very dirty and unpleasant: *a rather sordid little house* –**sordidly** *adv* –**sordidness** *n* [U]

sore¹ /sɔːʳ/ *adj* **1** painful because of infection, hard use, or a wound: *I've got a sore throat.* | *His feet were*

sore after so much running. **2** *infml* angry and upset: *She was sore at losing to a younger opponent.* **3** very serious: *The bridge is in sore need of repair.* **4 a sore point** a subject that makes someone uncomfortable or upset: *Don't mention drinking and driving – it's a sore point with him since he lost his licence.* **–soreness** *n* [U]

sore² *n* a place on the body that is painful, often because of infection

sore·ly /ˈsɔːli ‖ ˈsɔːrli/ *adv fml or lit* greatly: *John has sorely missed since he emigrated to Australia.*

sor·row¹ /ˈsɒrəʊ ‖ ˈsɑː-, ˈsɔː-/ *n fml* **1** [U] unhappiness: *I felt great sorrow at her death.* | *He expressed deep sorrow for what he had done.* **2** [C] a situation that makes you sad: *the sorrows of old age* **–sorrowful** *adj* **–sorrowfully** *adv*

sorrow² *v* [I] *lit* to experience or express sad feelings: *The sorrowing relatives gathered around his grave.*

sor·ry /ˈsɒri ‖ ˈsɑːri, ˈsɔːri/ *adj* **sorrier, sorriest** **1** [never before a noun] sad: *I'm so sorry about your husband's death.* | *He was sorry to hear the news of the accident.* | *I'm sorry to have to tell you this.* **2** [never before a noun] unhappy about your past actions: *If you're really sorry, I'll forgive you.* | *He's sorry that he made you cry.* **3 Sorry, I'm sorry** a phrase used to tell someone that you are unhappy about the effect on them of your speech or behaviour: *Sorry, I'm late.* | *Sorry! Did I hurt you?* **4 Sorry, I'm sorry** a phrase used as a polite expression to show you do not agree with something that has been said: *Sorry but I think you're wrong.* **5 Sorry, I'm sorry** a phrase used to refuse permission politely: *Sorry but you can't go in there.* **6** a word used to ask someone to repeat what they said: *Sorry? What did you say?* **7** a word used to correct yourself when you say the wrong thing: *He's six, sorry, seven years old.* **8 be/feel sorry for someone** to feel pity for someone: *I felt so sorry for him when he failed his exams.* **9 feel sorry for yourself** to feel pity for yourself: *Stop feeling sorry for yourself and decide what you're going to do next!* **10** terrible (used of the appearance or condition of a person or thing): *He was a sorry sight in his dirty old clothes.*

■ USAGE In British English you may say **(I'm) sorry** to people when you accidentally touch them, or push against them, or get in their way (for example, if you step on someone's foot). In American English you say **Excuse me.** In both British and American English you can say **Sorry?** when you do not hear what someone says. You can also say **Pardon (me)?** but this is more common in American English.

sort¹ /sɔːt ‖ sɔːrt/ *n* **1** a type or kind of person or thing: *What sort of food do you like?* | *There were all sorts of people there.* | *It looks like an insect of some sort.* –see KIND 1 (USAGE) **2** *infml* a person of a particular type: *She's a good sort.* **3 of sorts** of poor quality: *He's a writer of sorts.* **4 out of sorts** feeling unwell or annoyed **5 sort of** *infml* used when you are saying that something is true in some way: *It's sort of round and green, a bit like a lettuce.* | *I sort of thought you might say that.* | *It was a sort of dog-like creature.*

SPELLING NOTE

Words with the sound / s /, may be spelt **c-**, like **city**, or **ps-**, like **psychology**.

---

sort² *v* [T] to put things in order or in place according to their type: *The letters are all sorted here before being sent off for repair.* | *Can you sort these clothes into two piles, please?*

sort sthg ↔ **out** *phr v* [T] **1** to put things into groups according to their type: *I'm just sorting out the papers that can be thrown away.* **2** to solve a problem or difficulty: *We've got a few little problems to sort out.*

sort through sthg *phr v* [T] to look through a number of things in order to find the ones that you want: *He was sorting through a pile of papers on his desk.*

sor·tie /ˈsɔːti ‖ ˈsɔːrti/ *n* **1** a short attack made by an army from a position of defence **2** a short trip into an unfamiliar place **3** a short experience of an unfamiliar situation: *His first sortie into the world of film-making wasn't very successful.*

SOS /ˌes əʊ ˈes/ *n* letters used as an international signal when help is needed, especially by ships in trouble

so-so /ˈ· ·/ *adj, adv infml* not very bad and not very good: *The food was good, but the room so-so.* | *"Does he play the piano well?" "So-so".*

sot·to vo·ce /ˌsɒtəʊ ˈvəʊtʃi ‖ ˌsɑː-/ *adv* in a soft voice so that other people cannot hear

souf·flé /ˈsuːfleɪ ‖ suːˈfleɪ/ *n* [C;U] a light dish made from beaten eggs, flour, and milk, and then baked: *cheese soufflé* | *a chocolate soufflé*

sought /sɔːt/ *n* the past tense and past participle of SEEK

soul /səʊl/ *n* **1** [C] the part of a person that is believed to exist even after the body has died: *She's dead, but her soul's in heaven.* **2** [U] the special quality of deep, sincere feeling: *It was a stylish performance but it lacked soul.* **3** [C] the true nature of something: *the soul of our nation* **4 the soul of something** a fine example of a quality: *Your son is the soul of charm.* **5** [U] see SOUL MUSIC: *a soul group* **6 keep body and soul together** to have enough money and food to live **7** [C] a person: *You mustn't tell this to a soul.* | *She's a dear old soul.*

soul-des·troy·ing /ˈ· ·ˌ··/ *adj* extremely uninteresting: *He's got a soul-destroying job in a factory.*

soul·ful /ˈsəʊlfəl/ *adj* full of feeling, especially great sadness: *a soulful look* **–soulfully** *adv* **–soulfulness** *n* [U]

soul·less /ˈsəʊl-ləs/ *adj* with no warm or friendly human qualities: *a soulless office building*

soul mu·sic /ˈ· ˌ··/ *n* [U] a type of popular music often sung by black musicians and that expresses strong feelings

sound¹ /saʊnd/ *n* **1** [C;U] something that can be heard: *the sound of voices* | *strange sounds from the next room* | *Does sound travel through these walls?* **2 the sound of something** an idea that you get from something you read or hear: *From the sound of it, I'd say the matter was serious.* **3** [C] a stretch of water connecting two larger areas of water **–soundless** *adj* **–soundlessly** *adv*

sound² *v* **1** [I] (of something said or heard) to produce a particular quality or effect: *Your idea sounds a good one.* | *Does this sentence sound right?* | *It sounds as if you'll need a new car if the damage is as bad as they say.* **2** [I;T] to make a noise, often as a signal: *Sound your horn to warn the other driver!* | *The dinner bell sounded.* **3** [T] to pronounce something: *Can you sound those letters?*

sound off *phr v* [I] to express a strong opinion, usually to people who are not interested (a phrase used to express disapproval): *He's always sounding off about the behaviour of young people.*

sound sbdy ↔ **out** *phr v* [T] to try to find out someone's opinion or intention

sound³ *adj* **1** in good condition: *in sound health* | *a sound construction* **2** good and dependable: *We're pleased with the company's sound performance this year.* | *a sound candidate for the job* **3** based on truth or good judgment: *sound advice* **4 sound asleep** sleeping deeply – **soundly** *adv* – **soundness** *n* [U]

sound ef·fects /ˈ··ˌ·/ *n* [pl] sounds produced to give the effect of natural noises in a broadcast, play, or film

sound·proof¹ /ˈsaʊndpruːf/ *adj* to and from or through which sound cannot pass: *a soundproof room* | *soundproof material*

soundproof² *v* [T] to make a place soundproof: *He's soundproofed the bedroom so that he can practise playing his drums.*

sound·track /ˈsaʊndtræk/ *n* the recorded sound, especially the music from a film

soup /suːp/ *n* [U] liquid food, usually containing small pieces of meat, fish, or vegetables that have been boiled

sour¹ /saʊəʳ/ *adj* **1** having a bitter taste: *sour green apples* **2** having an unpleasant taste produced by the chemical action of bacteria: *sour milk* **3** bad-tempered: *He gave me a sour look.* **4 sour grapes** the act of pretending to dislike something that you really want quite badly, because you know that you cannot have it **5 turn sour** become unpleasant: *Relationships in the office have turned sour.* [RELATED PHRASE go sour] – **sourly** *adv* – **sourness** *n* [U]

sour² *v* [I;T] **1** to make or become sour: *I added lemon juice to make soured cream.* **2** to make or become unpleasant: *His bad temper soured the atmosphere.*

source /sɔːs ‖ sɔːrs/ *n* **1** a place, person, or thing from which something comes: *Can you find the source of the engine trouble?* | *Have you any other source of income apart from your job?* | *the source of the rumour* **2** the place where a stream of water starts: *Where is the source of the River Thames?* **3** a person or book that provides information: *A government source confirmed that tax cuts were unlikely.*

south¹ /saʊθ/ *n* **1** [U] the direction to the right of a person facing the rising sun: *Is that way south?* | *It's to the south of here.* **2 the south** the southern part of a country which is further south than the rest: *The South of England is warmer than the North.* | *He lives in the South.*

south² *adj* **1** (also **South**) in the south or facing the south: *He lives on the south side of the park.* **2 south wind** a wind coming from the south

south³ *adv* (also **South**) towards the south: *Let's travel south.* | *It's south of here.*

south·bound /ˈsaʊθbaʊnd/ *adj* travelling towards the south: *To get to Oxford Circus, take the southbound train.*

south·east¹ /ˌsaʊθˈiːst◂/ *n* (also **Southeast**) **1** [sing; U] the direction that is halfway between south and east **2 the southeast** the southeastern part of a country

southeast² *adj* [only before a noun] **1** in the southeastern part of something; *the southeast corner of the park* **2 southeast wind** a wind coming from the southeast – **southeasterly** *adj*

southeast³ *adv* towards the southeast: *These windows face southeast.*

south·east·ern /ˌsaʊθˈiːstən ‖ -ərn/ *adj* in or from the southeast part, especially of a country

south·east·ward /ˌsaʊθˈiːstwəd ‖ -ərd/ *adj*,*fml* going towards the southeast –**southeastwards** (also **southeastward** *AmE*) *adv*

south·er·ly /ˈsʌðəli ‖ -ər-/ *adj* **1** towards the south: *the southerly shore of the lake* **2** coming from the south (used of a wind): *warm southerly winds*

south·ern /ˈsʌðən ‖ -ərn/ *adj* (also **Southern**) in or from the south part of an area: *the southern US* | *the warm southern sun*

South·ern·er /ˈsʌðənəʳ ‖ -ərnəʳ/ *n* a person who lives in or comes from the southern part of a country

south·ern·most /ˈsʌðənməʊst ‖ -ərn-/ *adj fml* furthest south: *the southernmost station on the railway line*

south pole /ˌ· ˈ·/ *n* **the South Pole** the point furthest south on the surface of the earth, and the land around it

south·ward /ˈsaʊθwəd ‖ -ərd/ *adj* going towards the south: *a southward journey* –**southwards** (also **southward** *AmE*) *adv* : *We travelled southwards for several days.*

south·west¹ /ˌsaʊθˈwest◂/ *n* **1** [sing; U] the direction which is halfway between south and west **2 the southwest** the southwestern part of a country

southwest² *adj* [only before a noun] **1** in the southwestern part of something: *the southwestern mountains* **2 southwest wind** a wind coming from the southwest –**southwesterly** *adj*

south·west³ *adv* towards the southwest: *We'll sail southwest.*

south·west·ern /ˌsaʊθˈwestən ‖ -ərn/ *adj* in or from the southwest part, especially of a country

south·west·ward /ˌsaʊθˈwestwəd ‖ -ərd/ *adj fml* going towards the southwest –**southwestwards** (also **southwestward** *AmE*) *adv*

sou·ve·nir /ˌsuːvəˈnɪəʳ, ˈsuːvənɪəʳ/ *n* an object bought on holiday or on a trip to remind you about it: *I bought this bag as a souvenir of my visit to London.*

sou'west·er /saʊˈwestəʳ/ *n* a hat made of shiny material, worn especially by sailors to keep their heads dry during storms

sove·reign¹ /ˈsɒvrɪn ‖ ˈsɑrv-/ *n* **1** (also **Sovereign**) a king or queen **2** a British gold coin used in the past with a value of £1

sovereign² *adj* **1** highest and greatest (used of power): *Sovereign power must lie with the people.* **2** independent and self-governing (used of a country): *a sovereign state* –**sovereignty** *n* [U]

So·vi·et /ˈsaʊviət, ˈsɒ- ‖ ˈsəʊ-, ˈsɑː-/ *adj* from or connected with the USSR: *the Soviet Union* | *a Soviet official*

sow¹ /saʊ/ *n* a fully grown female pig

sow² /səʊ/ *v* **sowed**, **sown** /səʊn/ or **sowed**, **sowing** **1** [I; T] to plant or scatter seeds: *We'll sow grass in that field.* | *It's time for sowing.* | *This land is being sown with wheat.* **2** [T] *fml* or *lit* to make an unpleasant feeling or situation develop: *The newspapers are sowing doubt and despair.*

soy·a bean /ˈsɔɪə, biːn/ *n* (also **soybean** /ˈsɔɪbiːn/) a plant native to Asia which produces oil and is eaten as food

spa /spaː/ *n* a place with a spring of mineral water where people come to be cured of disease or to improve their general health: *spa water* | *a spa town*

space¹ /speɪs/ n 1 [C;U] an empty area: *Is there enough space at the table for 10 people?* | *Keep some space between you and the car ahead.* | *a parking space* 2 [U] the area that surrounds all objects and continues outwards in all directions without limits: *the concepts of time and space* | *He was just staring into space.* 3 [U] the area outside the earth's air, where other heavenly bodies move: *The satellite is travelling through space.* | *a space station* | *in outer space* 4 [U] the feeling that a place is large and open, without too many things in it: *A wonderful sense of space was created by clever furnishing.* 5 [C;U] the amount of room that you have on a page or in a talk to deal with something: *I haven't got enough space to discuss other people's research.* 6 [sing] a period of time: *Within the space of three years, he had become champion jockey.*

space² v **spaced, spacing** [T] to arrange things with spaces or periods of time between them: *Space the desks two metres apart.* | *Space the activities through the day.*

space sthg/sbdy ↔ **out** phr v [T] to position people or things with spaces or periods of time around them: *The flowers were neatly spaced out at 6 inch intervals.* | *Space out the icecreams so that the children don't get sick!*

space·craft /'speɪs-krɑːft ‖ -kræft/ n **spacecraft** a vehicle able to travel in space

space·ship /'speɪsˌʃɪp/ n a vehicle for carrying people through space

spa·cious /'speɪʃəs/ adj large, so that there is room to move around –**spaciousness** n [U]

spade /speɪd/ n 1 a tool with a blade and a long handle, used for digging the earth –see picture on page 638 2 **spades** a set of playing cards which has one or more figures shaped like a black pointed leaf printed in black: *the six of spades*

spa·ghet·ti /spə'geti/ n [U] Italian food consisting of long strings made from a paste of flour and water: *I'll have spaghetti, please.*

span¹ /spæn/ n 1 the distance between the two limits of something: *The bird had a wing span of over a metre.* 2 a length of time during which something lasts: *I've got a very short memory span.*

span² v **-nn-** [T] 1 to stretch over a certain area: *A bridge spanned the stream.* 2 to last a certain length of time: *His army career spanned four decades.*

span·gle /'spæŋgəl/ n a small piece of shiny metal or plastic used to decorate clothes or hair –**spangled** adj

span·iel /'spænjəl/ n a type of dog with long ears and rather long hair

Span·ish¹ /'spænɪʃ/ adj from or connected with Spain: *the Spanish Civil War*

Spanish² n 1 **the Spanish** the people of Spain 2 [U] the language of Spain: *I'm learning Spanish at evening classes.*

spank /spæŋk/ v [T] to hit someone with your open hand, especially on their bottom: *Do it now, or I'll spank you!* –**spank** n –**spanking** n : *If you don't stop that noise, you'll get a good spanking!*

span·ner /'spænər/ n BrE a metal hand tool with jaws or a hollow end which you use to twist something into or out of its place –see picture on page 638

SPELLING NOTE

Words with the sound /s/, may be spelt **c-**, like **city**, or **ps-**, like **psychology**.

---

spar¹ /spɑːr/ n a thick pole, especially one used on a ship to support sails or ropes

spar² v **-rr-** [I] 1 to BOX without hitting the other person hard, usually because you are practising 2 to argue, usually in quite a friendly way: *Here the minister can be seen sparring with newspaper reporters.*

spare¹ /speər/ v **spared, sparing** [T] 1 to make someone or something free to do something or to be used: *Can you spare me five minutes?* | *We're so busy that no one can be spared for any other work.* | *Could you spare your car for a while?* 2 to leave someone or something unharmed: *Take my money but spare my life!* | *In the event of war not even children will be spared.* 3 to avoid making someone do or listen to something unpleasant: *Spare me all the details of the meeting – just tell me about what they decided.* | *He was spared having to identify the body.* 4 [usually used in negatives and questions] to avoid doing, using, or spending something: *No trouble was spared to make sure they enjoyed themselves.* 5 **something to spare** something that is not really needed but could be used: *Let's go! There's no time to spare.* | *I've got money to spare.*

spare² adj 1 kept for use when needed: *a spare tyre* | *a spare room* 2 free from other activities or uses: *It's something to do in her spare time.* | *Have you got a spare piece of paper?* 3 rather thin: *her spare figure*

spare³ n a second object of the same kind that is kept for possible use: *This tyre is damaged. Have you got a spare?*

spar·ing /'speərɪŋ/ adj using or giving little: *Be sparing in the amount of salt you add.* –**sparingly** adv: *Apply this cream sparingly.*

spark¹ /spɑːk ‖ spɑːrk/ n 1 a small piece of burning material thrown out by a fire or by the striking together of two hard objects 2 a flash of light produced by electricity 3 a very small but important amount of a quality: *a spark of intelligence* 4 **bright spark** infml a clever person (a word usually used to mean the opposite of this): *Some bright spark was caught cheating in the exam today.*

spark² v [I] to produce a spark

spark sthg ↔ **off** phr v [T] BrE to be the direct cause of something: *What sparked off the quarrel?*

spar·kle /'spɑːkəl ‖ 'spɑːr-/ v **sparkled, sparkling** [I] 1 to shine in small flashes: *a diamond that sparkled in the sunlight* 2 to be clever and full of life: *She sparkles in company.* –**sparkle** n [C;U]

spark plug /'·-·/ n a part in an engine which makes an electric spark to fire the petrol

spar·row /'spærəʊ/ n a small brown bird very common in many parts of the world

sparse /spɑːs ‖ spɑːrs/ adj limited in number or amount –**sparsely** adv: *a sparsely populated area* –**sparseness** n [U]

spar·tan /'spɑːtn ‖ -ɑːr-/ adj simple and without comfort: *spartan accommodation*

spas·m /'spæzəm/ n 1 a sudden uncontrolled tightening of the muscles 2 a sudden violent effort, feeling, or act: *spasms of pain*

spas·mod·ic /spæz'mɒdɪk ‖ -'mɑː-/ adj 1 of or like a spasm: *spasmodic pain* 2 happening for short periods of time but not continuously: *spasmodic increases in the population* –**spasmodically** /-kli/ adv

spas·tic /'spæstɪk/ n a person suffering from a disease in which some parts of the body cannot be controlled –**spastic** adj

spat /spæt/ v the past tense and past participle of SPIT

spate /speɪt/ n BrE a large number or amount of something: *There has been a spate of accidents on this bend.*

spa·tial /ˈspeɪʃəl/ adj fml connected with size, shape, or position —**spatially** adv

spat·ter /ˈspætəʳ/ v [I;T] to cover something with drops of liquid: *The car spattered my clothes with mud.* | *A little oil spattered on the wall.*

spat·u·la /ˈspætjʊlə ‖ -tʃələ/ n a tool with a wide flat blade, for spreading, mixing, or lifting soft substances

spawn¹ /spɔːn/ v 1 [I;T] (of fish and certain other creatures) to lay eggs in large quantities 2 [T] to produce something in large numbers: *The computer industry has spawned hundreds of new companies.*

spawn² n [U] the eggs of fish and certain other creatures that live in water

speak /spiːk/ v spoke /spəʊk/, spoken /ˈspəʊkən/, speaking 1 [I] to say things by using your voice: *Most children begin to speak between the ages of one and two.* | *She's been unable to speak since the accident.* | *I haven't spoken to Robert for a few months.* | *We spoke about the new contract.* 2 [T] to express or say something in words: *They were convinced the prisoner was not speaking the truth.* 3 **be on speaking terms with someone, be speaking to someone** to be friendly with someone, especially someone with whom relations are often difficult 4 **speak badly/well of someone** to say bad or good things about someone 5 **speak for yourself** a phrase used to show that you disagree with someone's opinion and are annoyed that they thought you agreed: *'I'm sure we'll do well.' 'Speak for yourself!'* 6 **speak your mind** to say exactly what you think 7 **to speak of** worth mentioning: *"Did you do anything interesting at the weekend?" "Nothing to speak of."* 8 [I] to make a speech: *She makes a lot of money speaking to groups of businessmen.* 9 [T] to be able to talk in a particular language: *She can read Italian but she can't speak it.* | *Do you speak English?* | *We need a French-speaking secretary.* 10 [I] to express thoughts, ideas or feelings in a way that does not use words: *Actions speak louder than words.* 11 **so to speak** as one might say, although it is not strictly true

speak for sbdy phr v [T] to act for a person or group by expressing their thoughts or opinions to other people: *I'm speaking for those who cannot be present at this meeting today.*

speak out phr v [I] to state your opinions freely and boldly: *The newspaper spoke out against the government's decision.*

speak up phr v [I] 1 to speak more loudly: *Please speak up so that people at the back can hear you.* 2 to state your opinions freely and boldly: *If you disagree, you should speak up.*

speak·er /ˈspiːkəʳ/ n 1 a person making a speech: *an interesting speaker* 2 a person who speaks a language: *a speaker of English* 3 see LOUDSPEAKER

speak·ing¹ /ˈspiːkɪŋ/ n **public speaking** the art of speaking formally to groups of people

speaking² adv 1 **speaking of something** a phrase used to introduce a different but related subject: *Speaking of John, is he feeling better these days?* 2 **speaking as someone** a phrase used to show that what you are saying is based on your own experience: *Speaking as a lover of poetry I have to say that I have little respect for modern poets.* 3 a word used with another adverb to make clear the limits of the subject area you are talking about: *Generally speaking, British people are quite polite.* | *Technically speaking, she's a legal adviser rather than a lawyer.*

spear¹ /spɪəʳ/ n a pole with a sharp point at one end, used in the past as a weapon

spear² v [T] to stick a pointed object into something: *He speared a piece of meat with his fork.*

spear·head /ˈspɪəhed ‖ ˈspɪər-/ n the person or group that leads an attack on something: *the spearhead of the movement* —**spearhead** v [T] : *The attack on slavery was spearheaded by William Wilberforce.*

spear·mint /ˈspɪəˌmɪnt ‖ ˈspɪər-/ n [U] a common plant used to give a strong fresh taste to sweets and other substances

spe·cial¹ /ˈspeʃəl/ adj not ordinary or usual: *A special train was provided for the football supporters.* | *a special friend of mine* | *Of course my birthday is a special occasion!*

special² n something that is not of the usual or ordinary kind: *a two-hour television special*

spe·cial·ist /ˈspeʃələst/ n a person who has particular knowledge in an area of work, study, knowledge, or training: *a heart specialist* | *He's a specialist in Roman coins.*

spe·ci·al·i·ty /ˌspeʃiˈæləti/ n specialities (**specialty** /ˈspeʃəlti/ AmE) 1 an area of work or study that someone knows a lot about: *Her speciality is ancient Greek poetry.* 2 a particularly fine product for which a person or place is known: *Fish baked in pastry is the speciality of this restaurant.*

spe·cial·ly /ˈspeʃəli/ adv 1 for one particular purpose or person: *I made a cake specially for you.* 2 more than usual: *It's not specially hot today.*

spe·cies /ˈspiːʃiːz/ n species a group of plants or animals of the same kind, which are alike in all important ways and can breed together

spe·cial·ize /ˈspeʃəlaɪz/ v **specialized, specializing** (also **specialise** BrE) [I] to limit what you do in your work or studies to particular areas or subjects: *She's a doctor who specializes in tropical diseases.* —**specialization** /ˌspeʃəlaɪˈzeɪʃən ‖ -lə-/ n [C;U]

spe·cial·ized /ˈspeʃəlaɪzd/ adj (also **specialised** BrE) developed for one particular use or in one particular field of knowledge: *specialized tools* | *specialized knowledge*

spe·cif·ic /spəˈsɪfɪk/ adj 1 detailed and exact: *You say that your factory is in the South of England. Can you be a bit more specific?* 2 particular: *The book was aimed at a specific group.* | *My research deals with customs specific to West Africa.* —**specifically** /-kli/ adv : *They specifically told us not to go there.* | *a book written specifically for schoolchildren in Nigeria*

spe·cif·ics /spəˈsɪfɪks/ n [pl] the details of a subject that need to be considered: *Could you give me a few specifics?* | *Let's talk about the specifics.*

spe·ci·fi·ca·tion /ˌspesəfəˈkeɪʃən/ n 1 [C;U] any or all of the parts of a detailed plan, description, or set of instructions: *According to the specifications, this wire should go into that hole.* | *Are you sure this was made to specification?* 2 [C] something that is stated or demanded: *None of the candidates meet our specifications.*

spe·ci·fy /ˈspesəfaɪ/ v **specified, specifying** [T; + that] 1 to mention something exactly: *Be careful to specify every relevant point.* 2 to state what is necessary: *The rules specify what must be done in cases of disagreement.*

spe·ci·men /ˈspesɪmɪn/ n 1 a single thing that is a typical example of its kind: *a fine specimen* of *a mountain lion* 2 a small amount of something that shows what the whole thing is like: *The doctor will need a specimen of your blood for testing.*

spe·cious /ˈspiːʃəs/ adj fml seeming true or correct but in fact not so: *a specious argument* –**speciously** adv –**speciousness** n [U]

speck /spek/ n a small spot or mark: *I've got a speck of dirt in my eye.*

speck·le /ˈspekəl/ n a small coloured mark, especially one of a large number of similar marks –**speckled** adj : *speckled birds' eggs*

spec·ta·cle /ˈspektəkəl/ n 1 **spectacles** (also **specs** infml) glasses that help people to see better: *I can't see a thing without my spectacles.* 2 a grand public show or scene 3 a scene that is unusual and interesting 4 **make a spectacle of yourself** to do something silly that makes people look at you

spec·tac·u·lar¹ /spekˈtækjʊlər/ adj very special and splendid –**spectacularly** adv

spectacular² n a special entertainment: *a television spectacular with lots of famous stars*

spec·ta·tor /spekˈteɪtər ‖ ˈspekteɪtər/ n a person who watches an event or sport without taking part

spec·tre /ˈspektər/ n (**specter** AmE) a spirit without a body

spec·trum /ˈspektrəm/ n **spectra** /-trə/ 1 the set of bands of coloured light into which a beam of light may be separated 2 a range of any of various kinds of waves: *a sound spectrum* 3 a range of different opinions, feelings, or subject areas: *We found a wide spectrum of opinions on this issue.*

spec·u·late /ˈspekjʊleɪt/ v **speculated, speculating** 1 [I; +that] to consider what might be true but without enough proof to be sure: *Many people have been speculating* **about** *whether the situation will lead to war.* | *He speculated that she might have gone to France.* 2 [I] to try to make money by taking a business risk: *He speculated* **in** *commercial property.* | *They made a lot of money by speculating* **on** *the price of gold.* –**speculator** n –**speculative** adj : *a speculative investment*

spec·u·la·tion /ˌspekjʊˈleɪʃən/ n 1 [U] thoughts about what might happen: *The politician's remarks gave rise to speculation* **about** *his future.* 2 [C;U] taking a risk in order to make money: *His speculations on the Stock Market led to a considerable loss.*

sped /sped/ the past tense and past participle of SPEED

speech /spiːtʃ/ n 1 [C] a formal talk to a group of listeners: *In an angry speech, the MP criticized the government's action.* | *I'm making a speech at the club dinner tomorrow.* 2 [U] the ability to speak or the act of speaking: *She is researching speech development in children.* 3 [U] way of speaking: *His speech was slow and hesitant.* 4 [U] spoken language: *That phrase sounds all right in speech but not in writing.*

speech·less /ˈspiːtʃləs/ adj unable to speak at a particular moment because of strong feeling or shock: *He was speechless with anger.* –**speechlessly** adv –**speechlessness** n [U]

SPELLING NOTE

Words with the sound / s /, may be spelt **c-**, like **city**, or **ps-**, like **psychology.**

---

speed¹ /spiːd/ n 1 [C;U] the rate at which something moves or happens: *The car was travelling at a speed of 30 mph.* | *Modern trains can achieve speeds in excess of 200 miles per hour.* | *We work at different speeds.* | *It's for measuring speed.* –see FASTNESS (USAGE) 2 [U] very fast movement: *The team won because of their speed with the ball.* 3 **at speed** very fast: *The car was travelling at speed.*

speed² v **speeded** or **speed** /sped/, **speeding** 1 [I+adv/prep] to move or happen quickly: *We were enjoying ourselves so much that the time sped quickly by.* | *He jumped into his car and sped off into the night.* 2 [T] to make something move or happen fast: *Security guards sped the President to the waiting helicopter.* 3 [I only in progressive forms] to break the speed limit: *The driver was fined for speeding.* | *She was speeding when the police stopped her.*

speed up phr v [I;T **speed** sbdy/sthg ↔ **up**] to go faster or to make something or someone go faster: *Production of the new car was speeded up.* | *We had to speed up to meet the new targets.*

speed·boat /ˈspiːdbəʊt/ n a small power boat built to travel at high speed –see picture on page 735

speed·om·e·ter /spɪˈdɒmɪtər, spiː- ‖ -ˈdɑː-/ n an instrument in a vehicle that shows how fast it is going –see picture on page 49

speed·way /ˈspiːdweɪ/ n **speedways** 1 [U] a type of motorcycle racing 2 [C] the track where this racing is done

speed·y /ˈspiːdi/ adj **speedier, speediest** 1 fast: *We wished him a speedy recovery.* 2 able to move fast: *It's a speedy little car.* –**speedily** adv –**speediness** n [U]

spell¹ /spel/ v **spelt** /spelt/ or **spelled, spelling** 1 [T] to say or write in order the letters of a word: *My surname is spelt S-M-Y-T-H.* 2 [I] to know the correct letters in words: *He writes well, but he can't spell.* 3 [T] to form a word: *B-O-O-K spells "book".* 4 [T] to mean something: *This vote spells defeat for the government.* –**speller** n

spell sthg ↔ **out** phr v [T] 1 to explain something in a very detailed way: *The government is spelling out its plans in a party political broadcast.* 2 to write or say a word letter by letter

spell² n 1 a condition caused by the use of magical power: *He put a spell on her.* 2 the words used to cause magic power 3 **be under someone's spell** to be in the power of someone 4 a period of time: *He spent a spell in prison.* | *a hot spell*

spell·bound /ˈspelbaʊnd/ adj [never before a noun] with your attention held as if by magic: *The children sat spellbound as the old man told his story.*

spell·ing /ˈspelɪŋ/ n [C;U] the way of forming words from letters: *Her spelling has improved.* | *English and American spellings of some words are different.*

spelt /spelt/ the past tense and past participle of SPELL

spend /spend/ v **spent** /spent/, **spending** 1 [I;T] to pay money: *They spent their last dollars on a good meal.* | *How much do you want to spend?* 2 [T] to pass or use time: *Come and spend the weekend with us.* | *He spent three years working overseas.* | *I spent a lot of time planning this trip.* 3 **spend a penny** a less direct expression for 'go to the TOILET'

spend·thrift /ˈspend,θrɪft/ n a person who spends money wastefully

spent¹ /spent/ adj fml used up: *a spent force*

spent² the past tense and past participle of SPEND

sperm /spɜːm ‖ spɜːrm/ n sperm or sperms 1 [C] a cell produced by the sex organs of a male animal, which is able to unite with the female egg to produce new life 2 [U] the liquid from the male sex organs in which these cells swim

spew /spjuː/ v 1 [I;T] to send out in a flood: *The burst pipe was spewing out water.* 2 [I] *infml* to VOMIT

sphere /sfɪəʳ/ n 1 a round object 2 an area of existence, action, or activity: *His main sphere of influence is the world of banking.* 3 a group of people with the same interests and activities

spher·i·cal /ˈsferɪkəl/ adj in the form of a sphere(1)

sphinx /sfɪŋks/ n an ancient Egyptian image of a lion with a human head

spice¹ /spaɪs/ n 1 [C;U] a vegetable product often used in powder form for giving a taste to other foods: *herbs and spices | a pinch of mixed spice* 2 [U] interest or excitement: *I need some jokes to add spice to the speech.*

spice² v spiced, spicing [T] to add spice to something
spice sthg ↔ **up** phr v [T] to make something interesting: *He spiced up his speech with some jokes.*

spick-and-span /ˌspɪk ən ˈspæn/ adj clean, bright, and tidy

spic·y /ˈspaɪsi/ adj spicier, spiciest 1 containing or tasting of spice¹ (1): *I don't like spicy food.* 2 exciting and perhaps slightly improper or rude: *spicy stories*

spi·der /ˈspaɪdəʳ/ n a small creature with eight legs which makes threads into nets for catching insects

spi·der·y /ˈspaɪdəri/ adj long and thin like the legs of a spider: *the old lady's spidery writing*

spike¹ /spaɪk/ n 1 a piece of metal with a point at one end: *There are spikes along the top of the fence. | I bought running shoes with spikes on the soles.* 2 something long and pointed –**spiky** adj spikier, spikiest *infml: spiky hair*

spike² v spiked, spiking [T] 1 to put a spike through something 2 to add a little alcohol to a drink

spill /spɪl/ v spilled or spilt /spɪlt/, spilling 1 [I;T] to pour out accidentally, especially over the edge of a container: *My hand slipped and I spilt my drink. | There was some spilt milk on the floor.* 2 **spill the beans** *infml* to tell a secret before you should
spill out phr v [I] (used of people) to come out of a place in large numbers: *The congregation spilled out into the street.*

spin¹ /spɪn/ v spun /spʌn/, spinning [I;T] 1 to make thread by twisting cotton or wool: *She spent her days spinning. | She spun the wool into thread.* 2 to turn round and round fast: *The child was fascinated by the spinning top. | He spun the coin on the table. | Let the washing spin before you put it out to dry.* 3 **be spinning** to feel confused and perhaps DIZZY: *My head is spinning with all this new information.* 4 **spin a yarn** to tell a story which is not completely true
spin sthg ↔ **out** phr v [T] to make something last longer than it should

spin² n 1 a short pleasure trip: *We went for a spin in the new car.* 2 **in a spin** in a state of confusion because something unexpected has happened

spin·ach /ˈspɪnɪdʒ, -ɪtʃ ‖ -ɪtʃ/ n [U] a vegetable with broad green leaves

spin·al /ˈspaɪnl/ adj relating to the row of bones in your back: *a spinal injury*

spin·dle /ˈspɪndl/ n 1 a round pointed rod around which you twist the thread when you are spinning 2 a machine part around which another part turns

spin·dly /ˈspɪndli/ adj long, thin, and weak-looking: *a young horse with spindly legs*

spin dri·er /ˌ· ˈ··/ n (also **spin dryer**) an electric machine used to get water out of wet clothes

spin-dry /ˌ· ˈ·/ v spin-dried, spin-drying [T] to remove water from wet clothes in a machine that spins them round and round

spine /spaɪn/ n 1 (also **spinal column** /ˌ·· ˈ··/, **backbone**) the row of bones down the centre of the back of humans and some animals 2 the end of a book where the pages are fastened together 3 a sharp point found on plants or animals

spine·less /ˈspaɪnləs/ adj without moral courage: *He's too spineless to protest.* –**spinelessly** adv –**spinelessness** n [U]

spin·ney /ˈspɪni/ n spinneys BrE a small area of trees and low plants

spinning wheel /ˈ·· ·/ n a small machine used in the past to make thread

spin-off /ˈ· ·/ n a useful product or result besides the main one: *The non-stick frying pan is an industrial spin-off from space research.*

spin·ster /ˈspɪnstəʳ/ n old fash an unmarried woman, especially an older one (a word sometimes used to express disapproval)

spi·ral¹ /ˈspaɪərəl/ n a curve winding round and round a central point or line: *a spiral staircase*

spiral² v -ll- BrE (also -l- AmE) [I] 1 to move up or down in a spiral: *The damaged plane spiralled towards the earth.* 2 (of an amount or level) to move up more and more quickly: *spiralling prices* 3 **spiral down** (of an amount or level) to fall more and more quickly

spire /spaɪəʳ/ n a tower rising steeply to a point, often found on a church

spir·it¹ /ˈspɪrɪt/ n 1 [C] a person's soul or mind: *His spirit was troubled.* 2 [C] a presence without physical form, often of a person who is dead: *evil spirits | the spirit of the dead man* 3 **the spirit of something** the central quality or inner nature of something: *the spirit of the age* 4 [U] great strength of purpose: *a man of great spirit* 5 a way of feeling or thinking: *He took the criticism in the right spirit. | Her spirits rose.* 6 **spirits** [pl] strong alcoholic drink: *He likes wine but never drinks spirits.* 7 **high spirits** feelings of happiness and enjoyment: *The children were in high spirits at the thought of their holiday.* [RELATED PHRASE **low spirits**] 8 **team spirit** a feeling of working for the good of a group, not just for yourself

spirit² v [T] to take a person or thing to or from a place in a secret mysterious way: *She was spirited away through the back door before her fans could see her.*

spir·it·ed /ˈspɪrɪtɪd/ adj 1 active and excited: *a spirited quarrel | He made a spirited defence of the proposal.* 2 -**spirited** having a certain kind of feeling: *high-spirited | public-spirited*

spirit lev·el /ˈ·· ˌ··/ n (also **level** AmE) an instrument that shows whether a surface is level –see picture on page 638

spir·i·tu·al¹ /ˈspɪrɪtʃuəl/ adj 1 concerning non-physical things like thoughts, feelings and beliefs: *our spiritual nature* 2 religious: *spiritual songs | an adviser in spiritual matters* –**spiritually** adv

spiritual² n a religious song sung originally by the black peoples of the US

spir·i·tual·is·m /ˈspɪrɪtʃʊlɪzəm/ n [U] the belief that dead people may send messages to living people, often through a person with special powers –**spiritualist** n

spit¹ /spɪt/ v **spat** /spæt/ (also **spit** AmE), **spitting** [I;T] **1** to force a small amount of liquid from your mouth: *She spat on the ground.* | *He's very ill and spitting blood.* **2 be spitting** to be raining very lightly: *It's still spitting outside.* **3 be the spitting image of** to look exactly like another person or thing: *She's the spitting image of her mother.* **4** infml **within spitting distance** very close: *They live within spitting distance of his office.*

spit sthg ↔ out phr v [T] **1** to force liquid or food from your mouth: *He tasted the meat and spat it out.* **2** to say something with force, because you are angry: *He spat out his criticisms of his wife.*

spit² n **1** [U] the liquid that is produced in your mouth **2** [C] a thin pointed rod which is stuck through a piece of meat before the meat is cooked over a fire

spite¹ /spaɪt/ n [U] **1** the desire to hurt someone or annoy them: *I'm sure he only told them out of spite.* **2 in spite of** although something is true: *We managed to enjoy ourselves in spite of the rain.* | *She had very little money. In spite of that, she managed to send her son to university.*

spite² v **spited, spiting** [T] to try to hurt or annoy someone: *He only did it to spite me.*

splash¹ /splæʃ/ v [I;T] **1** (of liquids) to fall or strike against something in small drops: *The rain splashed on the window pane.* | *The car drove through the puddle and splashed my legs.* | *Paint splashed onto the carpet.* **2** to move liquid in a noisy way: *The children had great fun splashing about in the pool.* | *He splashed after-shave onto his skin.*

splash out phr v infml [I] to spend a lot of money on something: *They splashed out on a video camera.*

splash² n **1** the movement or noise made by splashing: *I fell into the water with a splash.* **2** a small amount of something that has fallen or been added: *a splash of paint on the floor* | *A splash of red gave life to the picture.* | *a splash of vodka*

splat /splæt/ n [sing] a noise of something wet hitting a surface –**splat** adv

splen·did /ˈsplendɪd/ adj **1** grand in appearance: *a splendid golden crown* **2** excellent: *a splendid piece of work* | *You've got the job? Splendid!* –**splendidly** adv

splen·dour /ˈsplendər/ n (**splendor** AmE) [C;U] grand beauty: *He lived in great splendour.* | *the splendours of the autumn landscape*

splice /splaɪs/ v **spliced, splicing** [T] **1** to join two things together: *Can you splice the ends of the tape together?* **2** infml **get spliced** to get married

splint /splɪnt/ n a flat piece of wood or metal used for keeping a broken bone in position

splin·ter¹ /ˈsplɪntər/ n **1** [C] a small sharp piece that has broken off something, especially something made of wood: *I've got a splinter in my finger.* | *a splinter of glass* **2** [only before a noun] a group that has separated from a larger one: *They quarrelled with the party leader, and formed a splinter group.*

splinter² v [I;T] to break into small pieces

split¹ /splɪt/ v **split, splitting** **1** [I;T] to break apart along the whole length: *His coat had split down the back.* | *He split the wood with one blow from his axe.* **2** [I;T] to divide into separate parts or groups: *We split into two groups, and searched the forest.* | *The book is split into 12 chapters.* | *a quarrel which split the Liberal Party* | *Who was the first person to split the atom?* **3** [T] to divide something among people: *I'll come with you, and we'll split the cost of the petrol.* **4 split the difference** to fix a figure halfway between two figures already mentioned: *He wanted £60 for the chair and I offered £40, so in the end we split the difference.* **5 split hairs** to talk about something at a level of unnecessary detail **6 split your sides** to laugh a lot at something that is extremely funny

split off phr v [I;T **split** sthg ↔ **off**] to break off from the main part

split up phr v **1** [I] to end a relationship or marriage: *After two unhappy years John and Mary decided to split up.* **2** [I] to go in different directions: *The group split up to try to find food.* **3** [T **split** sthg ↔ **up**] to divide into smaller parts

split² n **1** a cut or break made when something splits: *I'm just mending a split in my trousers.* **2** a division or separation within a group: *a split in the Labour Party*

split-lev·el /ˌ· ˈ···/ adj built so that different parts of the same room or floor of a building are at different heights : *a split-level bathroom*

split sec·ond /ˌ· ˈ···/ n a very short moment: *For a split second, I thought I had made a mistake.* –**split -second** adj : *Split-second timing is crucial to the success of this operation.*

split·ting /ˈsplɪtɪŋ/ adj very painful (used of a headache)

splut·ter¹ /ˈsplʌtər/ n a noise like liquid or air being forced out of something with difficulty

splutter² v [I] **1** to speak with difficulty, as if confused: *"But-but…" he spluttered.* **2** to make a noise like liquid or air being forced out of something with difficulty: *I spent the day coughing and spluttering in bed.*

spoil¹ /spɔɪl/ v **spoiled** or **spoilt** /spɔɪlt/, **spoiling** **1** [T] to stop something being good: *The visit was spoilt by an argument.* | *He spoiled the soup by putting too much salt in it.* **2** [I] to decay or lose good qualities: *The fruit has spoilt in the hot sun.* **3** [T] to treat someone too well: *You spoil that child!* **4 spoil yourself** to treat yourself very well: *Have another chocolate. Go on, spoil yourself!* **5 be spoiling for something** to be eager for trouble or for a fight

spoil² n **the spoils** things taken without payment, usually by an army or by thieves: *I expect they are dividing up the spoils.*

spoil·sport /ˈspɔɪlspɔːt ‖ -ɔːrt/ n a person who puts an end to someone else's fun

spoilt /spɔɪlt/ the past tense and past participle of SPOIL

spoke¹ /spəʊk/ n any of the bars which connect the outer ring of a wheel to the centre, such as on a bicycle

spoke² v the past tense of SPEAK

spok·en /ˈspəʊkən/ v **1** the past participle of SPEAK **2 -spoken** speaking in a certain way: *He was well-spoken and obviously good at his job.*

spokes·man /ˈspəʊksmən/ n **spokesmen** /-mən/ a person chosen to speak officially for a group; a female **spokesperson** is called a **spokeswoman**

sponge¹ /spʌndʒ/ n 1 [C;U] A simple sea creature which grows a light frame full of small holes, or the substance which this creature consists of 2 [C;U] a piece of rubber, plastic, or sponge which is full of holes and that you use for washing your body 3 [C;U] *BrE* see SPONGE CAKE

sponge² v **sponged, sponging** [T] 1 to clean something with a soft wet cloth or sponge: *Sponge the surfaces lightly with a damp cloth.* 2 to remove liquid in this way: *I'll just sponge the blood from the wound.* 3 **sponge on/off** someone to take advantage of someone's generous nature in order to get money and other things from them as a gift (a phrase used to express disapproval): *At 25, he's still sponging off his parents.* **–sponger** n

sponge-bag /ˈspʌndʒbæg/ n a small bag that you take with you when you travel, and in which you carry the things you need to keep yourself clean and fresh

sponge cake /ˈ· ·/ n [C;U] a light cake made from eggs, sugar, and flour: *I've made a sponge cake.* | *Would you like some sponge cake?*

spong-y /ˈspʌndʒi/ adj **spongier, spongiest** soft and wet, like a sponge: *The grass is spongy after the rain.* **–sponginess** n [U]

spon-sor¹ /ˈspɒnsəʳ ‖ ˈspɑːn-/ n 1 a person or business that provides the money for something like a sports event, often in return for advertising their products at the event: *We interrupt this programme to hear a few words from our sponsor.* 2 a person or business that agrees to give money to a good cause if another person succeeds in doing something special: *I am looking for sponsors for my marathon run on behalf of the Save the Children Fund.* 3 a person that takes responsibility for formally putting forward a suggestion

sponsor² v [T] 1 to pay for something, usually in return for advertising particular products: *The research programme was sponsored by tobacco companies.* 2 to agree to give someone money for a good cause if they succeed in doing something special: *a sponsored charity run* 3 to put forward a formal suggestion

spon-ta-ne-ous /spɒnˈteɪniəs ‖ spɑːn-/ adj happening naturally, without planning: *A spontaneous cheer rose from the crowd.* **–spontaneously** adv **–spontaneity** /ˌspɒntəˈneɪəti, -ˈniː- ‖ ˌspɑːn-/ n [U]

spoof /spuːf/ n a funny false copy or description of something: *a magazine spoof of university life*

spook /spuːk/ n infml 1 a spirit, especially one that appears to frighten people 2 *AmE* see SPY

spook-y /ˈspuːki/ adj **spookier, spookiest** infml frightening: *a spooky old house* | *It gets spooky here after dark.*

spool /spuːl/ n a wheel around which things like wire, camera film, or TAPE are wound

spoon¹ /spuːn/ n 1 an object used for mixing, serving, and eating food: *a wooden spoon* 2 see SPOONFUL: *Two spoons of sugar, please.*

spoon² v [T] to use a spoon to pick something up and put it somewhere: *Spoon the mixture into individual dishes.*

spoon-feed /ˈ· ·/ v **spoonfed** /-fed/, **spoonfeeding** [T] 1 to feed someone, often a baby, with a spoon 2 to teach someone everything they need to know, or do everything for them, so that they do not need to think for themselves

spoon-ful /ˈspuːnfʊl/ n **spoonfuls** or **spoonsful** (also **spoon**) the amount that a spoon will hold: *Add two teaspoonfuls of sugar.*

spo-rad-ic /spəˈrædɪk/ adj happening for short irregular periods, but not continuously: *sporadic fighting* **–sporadically** /-kli/ adv

spore /spɔːʳ/ n a very small cell produced by some plants, which is able to develop into a new plant

spor-ran /ˈspɒrən ‖ ˈspɔː-, ˈspɑː-/ n a special kind of bag worn by men in Scotland as part of their national dress

sport¹ /spɔːt ‖ spɔːrt/ n 1 [C;U] a game or activity done for physical exercise or pleasure: *Do you think football is an exciting sport?* | *I've never been very keen on sport.* | *a sports shop* –see RECREATION (USAGE) 2 [C] a person who accepts defeat or a joke without becoming angry or upset: *You're a good sport!* 3 [U] fun: *I only said it in sport!*

■ USAGE **Game** and **match** are both used when talking about sports. Use **game** for an occasion when people meet to take part in a particular sporting activity: *Let's have a game of tennis.* | *They meet for a game of squash every Monday.* | *The children were having an informal game of cricket on the back lawn.* Use **match** for more public occasions when two people or teams are competing: *The teams are in training for the big match.* | *a cricket match on the village green* | *a football match*

sport² v [T] to wear something that you appear proud of: *She came in today sporting a fur coat.*

sport-ing /ˈspɔːtɪŋ ‖ ˈspɔːr-/ adj 1 [only before a noun] of or concerning sports: *a painter of sporting scenes* 2 fair and generous, especially in sports: *It was very sporting of them to let our team go first.* 3 **a sporting chance** a good possibility: *He stands a sporting chance of winning, I think.* **–sportingly** adv

sports car /ˈ· ·/ n a fast car, that is usually low with a roof that opens

sports-man /ˈspɔːtsmən ‖ ˈspɔːr-/ n **sportsmen** /-mən/ a person who plays a lot of sport; a woman who plays a lot of sport is called a **sportswoman**

sports-man-ship /ˈspɔːtsmənʃɪp ‖ ˈspɔːr-/ n [U] a spirit of fair play and generous behaviour when winning or losing

spot¹ /spɒt ‖ spɑːt/ n 1 [C] a small round area on a surface which is different in colour from the main area: *a white dress with blue spots* 2 [C] a raised mark on your skin, sometimes caused by disease: *I'm covered in spots.* 3 [C] a dirty mark: *He tried to remove the spot on his sweater with soap and water.* 4 [C] a place known for a particular quality or event: *For many years Spain was a favourite holiday spot.* | *This was the spot where we first met.* 5 **on the spot: a** at the place where something is happening: *He had a heart attack in the theatre but luckily there was a doctor on the spot.* **b** without stopping to consider: *Of course, I resigned on the spot.* 6 [sing] a small amount: *How about a spot of tea?* | *I felt a spot of rain.* 7 **be in a spot** to be in a difficult position: *With no electricity, we were really in a spot.* 8 **put someone on the spot** to put someone in a difficult position: *The question really put the Prime Minister on the spot.*

spot² v -tt- [T] to recognize a person or thing: *I spotted a friend in the crowd.*

spot-less /ˈspɒtləs ‖ ˈspɑːt-/ adj completely clean: *a spotless house* **–spotlessly** adv **–spotlessness** n [U]

spot-light¹ /ˈspɒtlaɪt ‖ ˈspɑːt-/ n 1 [C] a powerful lamp with a narrow beam that can be directed at a particular place, used especially in theatres 2 **in the spotlight** receiving a lot of public attention

spotlight² *v* **spotlit** *or* **spotlighted, spotlighting** [T] to direct attention towards something: *He's written an article spotlighting the difficulties of school-leavers.*

spot·ted /ˈspɒtɪd ‖ ˈspɑː-/ *adj* with a pattern of spots on it: *a spotted dress* –see picture on page 147

spot·ter /ˈspɒtəʳ ‖ ˈspɑː-/ *n* a person who keeps watch for a particular thing: *a train spotter*

spot·ty /ˈspɒti ‖ ˈspɑːti/ *adj* **spottier, spottiest** *BrE infml* with spots: *a spotty teenager* | *spotty material*

spouse /spaʊs, spaʊz/ *n law* a husband or wife

spout¹ /spaʊt/ *v* **1** [I;T] to come out or be made to come out in a forceful stream: *Water spouted from the rock.* | *The volcano erupted, spouting lava high into the air.* **2** [T] to pour out in a stream of words: *She's always spouting Shakespeare.*

spout² *n* an opening from which liquid comes out: *the spout of a teapot*

sprain /spreɪn/ *v* [T] to damage a joint in the body by twisting it suddenly: *He sprained his ankle playing football.* –**sprain** *n* : *a nasty sprain*

sprang /spræŋ/ *v* the past tense of SPRING¹

sprat /spræt/ *n* a small fish found in the sea, used as food

sprawl /sprɔːl/ *v* **1** [I] to lie or sit with your arms and legs stretched out: *She sprawled out in a comfortable chair.* **2** [I] to stretch over a large area of land, often in an unattractive way: *The city sprawls for miles in each direction.* –**sprawl** *n* : *dreadful urban sprawl*

spray¹ /spreɪ/ *n* **1** [U] water blown in very small drops: *We parked the car by the sea and it got covered in spray.* **2** [C;U] liquid in a can or container forced out under pressure: *insect spray* | *hair spray* **3** [C] a container that is used to hold this liquid: *a spray of touch-up paint for the car* **4** [C] leaves and flowers growing on a branch or arranged decoratively: *a spray of lilies*

spray² *v* [I;T] to scatter or be scattered under pressure: *to spray paint on a wall* | *spray a wall with paint* | *They sprayed the President's car with bullets.*

spread¹ /spred/ *v* **spread, spreading** **1** [I;T] to open or stretch out: *a ship with sails spread* | *He spread his hands.* **2** [I] to cover a large area or period of time: *His interests now spread over several subjects.* | *Payments will be spread over two years.* **3** [T] to put a covering on something: *to spread butter on bread* **4** [I;T] to reach or have an effect on more people or things: *The fire spread quickly.* | *The disease is spread by touch.* **5** [I;T] to make or become widely known: *If I tell you this secret, don't spread it around.* | *The news spread quickly.*

spread² *n* **1** [sing] the act or action of spreading: *the spread of a disease* | *the spread of information* **2** [C] a variety: *a spread of interests* | *The students' ages show a wide spread.* **3** [C] a newspaper or magazine article or an advertisement running across one or more pages: *a two-page spread* **4** [C] a large or grand meal: *Our host had a fine spread waiting for us.* **5** [C;U] a soft food for spreading on bread: *a tube of cheese spread*

spread-ea·gle /ˌ· ˈ·· ‖ ˈ· ˌ··/ *v* **to be spread-eagled** to be in a position with arms and legs spread out: *lying spread-eagled on the bed*

> **SPELLING NOTE**
>
> Words with the sound /s/, may be spelt **c-**, like **city**, or **ps-**, like **psychology**.

spree /spriː/ *n* a time of free and wild fun, spent enjoying yourself

sprig /sprɪg/ *n* a small end of a stem or branch with leaves: *a sprig of parsley*

spright·ly /ˈspraɪtli/ *adj* **sprightlier, sprightliest** cheerful and active: *a sprightly old man* –**sprightliness** *n* [U]

spring¹ /sprɪŋ/ *v* **sprang** /spræŋ/, **sprung** /sprʌŋ/, **springing** **1** [I] to jump: *She sprang to her feet.* **2** [T] to produce without warning: *We sprang the news on him.* **3** [I] to be the result of: *Her hatred of men springs from her childhood.* **4** [I] to start being active: *I turned the key and the engine sprang to life.* **5 spring a leak** to begin to let in water through a crack

spring up *phr v* [I] to happen or appear quickly: *A wind suddenly sprang up.* | *Towns sprang up in the desert when gold was found there.*

spring² *n* **1** [U;C] (also **Spring**) the season between winter and summer in which leaves and flowers appear **2** [C] a place where water comes up naturally from the ground **3** [C] a length of metal wound around, which returns to its original shape after being pushed: *a watch-spring* | *What an uncomfortable chair! It needs new springs.* **4** [U] the quality of this object: *There's not much spring in this old bed.* **5** [C] a sudden large jump: *The cat made a sudden spring at the mouse.*

spring·board /ˈsprɪŋbɔːd ‖ -bɔːrd/ *n* **1** a strong board which bends and helps you jump higher **2** something which makes an action or activity possible: *a springboard to success*

spring-clean /ˌ· ˈ·◄/ *v* [I;T] to give a place a thorough cleaning, especially in the spring –**springclean** *n*

spring·y /ˈsprɪŋi/ *adj* **springier, springiest** returning quickly to its original shape after being pressed

sprin·kle /ˈsprɪŋkəl/ *v* **sprinkled, sprinkling** [T] to scatter in drops or small grains: *Sprinkle sugar on the strawberries.*

sprin·kler /ˈsprɪŋkləʳ/ *n* an apparatus for scattering drops of water: *a garden sprinkler*

sprin·kling /ˈsprɪŋklɪŋ/ *n* a small quantity: *a sprinkling of snow*

sprint¹ /sprɪnt/ *v* [I] to run for a short distance at your fastest speed –**sprinter** *n*

sprint² *n* **1** a short run **2** a short race: *the 100 metres sprint*

sprite /spraɪt/ *n* a fairy, especially a playful one

sprout¹ /spraʊt/ *v* [I;T] to grow or send up new growth: *We could see the leaves sprouting on the trees.*

sprout² *n* **1** a new growth on a plant **2** see BRUSSELS SPROUT

spruce¹ /spruːs/ *n* [C;U] a tree with short needle-shaped leaves found in northern parts of the world

spruce² *adj* tidy and clean –**sprucely** *adv* : *sprucely dressed*

spruce³ *v* **spruced, sprucing: spruce yourself up** to make yourself look neat and tidy: *He spruced himself up for the interview.*

sprung /sprʌŋ/ *v* the past participle of SPRING¹

spry /spraɪ/ *adj* active (used especially of old people): *a spry old lady*

spud /spʌd/ *n* *infml* a potato

spun /spʌn/ *v* the past tense and past participle of SPIN¹

spur¹ /spɜːʳ/ *n* **1** a sharp pointed object worn on the heel of a rider's boot to help control a horse **2** something acting to encourage an activity: *The news was* *a spur to continued effort.* **3 on the spur of the moment** without preparation or planning

spur² *v* **-rr-** [T] **1** to kick a horse with spurs **2** to urge to faster action or greater effort: *She spurred on her team.*

spu·ri·ous /'spjʊəriəs/ *adj* **1** false or pretended: *a spurious signature* | *spurious sympathy* **2** based on incorrect reasoning: *a spurious argument* –**spuriously** *adv* –**spuriousness** *n* [U]

spurn /spɜːn ‖ spɜːrn/ *v* [T] to refuse: *She spurned all offers of help.*

spurt¹ /spɜːt ‖ spɜːrt/ *n* **1** a short sudden increase of effort: *a spurt of activity* **2** a sudden rush: *a spurt of blood* | *a spurt of interest* **3 put a spurt on** to hurry: *She put a spurt on and passed the other runners.*

spurt² *v* [I] **1** to flow out suddenly: *Water spurted from the broken pipe.* **2** to increase your speed suddenly and for a short time: *We spurted past the bus.*

sput·ter /'spʌtə\r/ *v* **1** [I;T] to say or speak in confusion **2** [I] to make repeated soft explosive sounds: *The car's engine sputtered for a moment and then died.* –**sputter** *n*

spy¹ /spaɪ/ *spies n* a person employed to find out secret information

spy² *v* **spied, spying 1** [I] to watch secretly: *He's always spying on his neighbours.* **2** [I] to act as a spy **3** [T] *lit* to catch sight of: *She spied her friend in the crowd.*

sq a written abbreviation for square: *6 sq metres*

squab·ble /'skwɒbəl ‖ 'skwɑː-/ *v* **squabbled, squabbling** [I] to have a quarrel over something unimportant: *What are you children squabbling about now?* –**squabble** *n*

squad /skwɒd ‖ skwɑːd/ *n* [C +sing/pl verb] a group of people working as a team: *The bomb squad has arrived.*

squad·ron /'skwɒdrən ‖ 'skwɑː-/ *n* [C; + sing/pl verb] a group belonging to the armed forces: *The squadron is ready for duty.*

squal·id /'skwɒlɪd ‖ 'skwɑː-/ *adj* very dirty or unpleasant: *squalid living conditions* –**squalidly** *adv*

squall /skwɔːl/ *n* a sudden strong wind –**squally** *adj*

squal·or /'skwɒlə\r ‖ 'skwɑː-/ *n* [U] dirty, unhealthy, and unpleasant conditions: *living in squalor in a filthy room*

squan·der /'skwɒndə\r ‖ 'skwɑːn-/ *v* [T] to use up foolishly: *The government is squandering our money on nuclear weapons.*

square¹ /skweə\r/ *n* **1** a shape with four straight sides of equal length forming four right angles: *Draw a square with sides of 10 centimetres.* | *a square of cloth* **2** an open space in a city, often in the shape of a square: *The market is held in the square.* | *He lives in Norfolk Square.* **3** a number equal to another number multiplied by itself: *16 is the square of 4.* **4** a tool with a straight edge and often in the shape of an L which is used for drawing and measuring right angles **5 square one** *BrE* the very beginning: *All my papers were lost in the fire, so now I'm back to square one.* **6 square root** the number which when multiplied by itself equals a particular number: *3 is the square root of 9.*

square² *adj* **1** having four equal sides and four right angles: *A handkerchief is usually square.* | *a square tower* **2** like a square in shape: *a square jaw* | *square shoulders* **3** being a measurement of area equal to that of a square with sides of a particular length: *144 square inches equal 1 square foot.* **4**

being the stated length on all four sides: *The room is 6 metres square.* **5** [never before a noun] paid and settled: *Our account is all square.* **6** [never before a noun] equal in points: *The teams are square at one match each.* **7 square deal** fair and honest treatment: *I don't think I'm getting a square deal at that garage.* **8 a square meal** a good satisfying meal –**squareness** *n* [U]

square³ *v* **squared, squaring 1** [T] to make something into a shape with a straight edge and right angles: *He squared off the end of the piece of wood.* **2** [T] to mark squares on: *squared paper* **3** [T] to multiply a number by itself once: *2 squared equals 4.* **4** [I;T] to fit a particular explanation or standard: *His statement doesn't square with the facts.* **5** [T] to settle: *I squared my account at the store.*

square up *phr v* [I] to settle a bill: *Let's square up – how much do I owe you?*

square⁴ (also **squarely**) *adv* directly: *He looked her square in the eye.*

squash¹ /skwɒʃ ‖ skwɑːʃ, skwɔːʃ/ *v* **1** [I;T] to force or be forced into a flat shape or a small space: *I sat on my hat and squashed it.* | *May I squash in next to you?* **2** [T] to force into silence or inactivity: *She felt squashed after so much criticism.*

squash² *n* **1** the act of being forced into a small space: *There was quite a squash in the train.* **2** [U] a game played in a walled court with rackets (RACK-ET\u00b9) and a rubber ball **3** [U] *BrE* a sweet fruit drink: *a glass of orange squash*

squat¹ /skwɒt ‖ skwɑːt/ *v* **-tt-** [I] **1** to sit with your legs bent and your weight on your feet –see picture on page 736 **2** to live in a place without permission

squat² *adj* unpleasantly short or low: *It's a rather squat building, isn't it?*

squat·ter /'skwɒtə\r ‖ 'skwɑː-/ *n* a person who lives in a building without permission

squawk /skwɔːk/ *v* [I] to make a loud rough-sounding cry, especially as made by birds: *hens squawking at the sight of a cat* –**squawk** *n*

squeak /skwiːk/ *v* [I] to make a very high sounding noise: *a squeaking door* –**squeak** *n : the squeak of a mouse* –**squeaky** *adj* **squeakier, squeakiest** *: a squeaky voice*

squeal /skwiːl/ *v* [I] to make a long very high sound or cry: *squealing tyres* | *squealing pigs* –**squeal** *n : squeals of delight from the children*

squeam·ish /'skwiːmɪʃ/ *adj* easily shocked by unpleasant things: *It's a violent film, so don't go if you're squeamish.* –**squeamishly** *adv* –**squeamishness** *n* [U]

squeeze¹ /skwiːz/ *v* **squeezed, squeezing 1** [T] to press: *to squeeze an orange* | *squeeze the water out of a wet cloth* **2** [I;T] to fit by forcing or pressing: *The train was full but I squeezed in anyway.* **3** [T] to force out by pressure: *to squeeze toothpaste out of a tube*

squeeze² *n* **1** [C] an act of pressing: *She gave his hand a gentle squeeze.* **2** [C] a small amount squeezed out: *a squeeze of lemon juice* **3** [sing] the state of being pressed together: *There's room for one more, but it'll be a squeeze.* **4** [C] a difficult state of affairs caused by short supplies or tight controls: *a credit squeeze*

squelch /skweltʃ/ *v* [I] to make a wet sucking sound, for example when stepping through mud –**squelch** *n*

squid /skwɪd/ *n* a sea creature with 10 arms at one end of a long body

squig·gle /ˈskwɪgəl/ n infml a short wavy or twisting line: *What do these squiggles on the map mean?* –**squiggly** adj

squint[1] /skwɪnt/ v [I] **1** to look at something with almost closed eyes **2** to be unable to position both eyes to look in the same direction at once

squint[2] n a disorder of the eye muscles causing the eyes to look in two different directions

squire /skwaɪəʳ/ n in the past, the main landowner in a country area of England

squirm /skwɜːm ‖ skwɜːrm/ v [I] to twist your body about, as if from discomfort or nervousness: *questions that made him squirm*

squir·rel /ˈskwɪrəl ‖ ˈskwɜːrəl/ n a small animal with a long furry tail that lives in trees and eats nuts

squirt[1] /skwɜːt ‖ skwɜːrt/ v **1** [I;T] to force or be forced out in a thin stream: *to squirt oil into a lock | The oil squirted all over his trousers.* **2** [T] to hit with a stream of liquid: *I was squirted with water.*

squirt[2] n a quick thin stream of liquid

SRN /ˌes ɑːr ˈen/ a written abbreviation for STATE REGISTERED NURSE

Ssh /ʃ/ interj see SH

St n **1** a written abbreviation for STREET: *Regent St* **2** an abbreviation for SAINT, used before the person's name: *St Andrew*

stab[1] /stæb/ n **1** a wound made by a pointed weapon: *a stab in the chest* **2** a sudden painful feeling: *a stab of guilt* **3** have a stab at to try to do something: *Have a stab at answering question 3.*

stab[2] v -bb- [I;T] **1** to strike forcefully with a pointed weapon: *Julius Caesar was stabbed to death. | The murdered girl had been stabbed with a knife.* **2** stab someone in the back to attack someone who trusted you

stab·bing[1] /ˈstæbɪŋ/ adj sharp and sudden (used of pain)

stabbing[2] n an attack when someone is stabbed

sta·bil·i·ty /stəˈbɪlɪti/ n [U] the state of being fixed and unlikely to change: *the stability of their marriage* –opposite **instability**

sta·bil·ize /ˈsteɪbɪˌlaɪz/ v stabilized, stabilizing (also **stabilise** BrE) [I;T] to make or become firm or steady: *The price of coffee has been rising and falling, but has now stabilized.* –**stabilization** /ˌsteɪbɪlaɪˈzeɪʃən ‖ -lə-/ n [U]

sta·bil·iz·er /ˈsteɪbɪˌlaɪzəʳ/ n (also **stabiliser** BrE) an apparatus or chemical that stabilizes something: *a ship's stabilizers*

sta·ble[1] /ˈsteɪbəl/ n **1** a building for keeping horses in **2** a group of racing horses with one owner

stable[2] v stabled, stabling [T] to put or keep in a stable

stable[3] adj not easily moved, upset, or changed: *a stable chair | a stable relationship* –opposite **unstable** –**stably** adv

stack[1] /stæk/ n **1** an orderly pile: *a stack of books* **2** stacks infml a large amount or number: *stacks of work to do*

stack[2] v **1** [T] (also stack sth ↔ up) to make into a neat pile: *They stacked the chairs at the back of the hall.* **2** be stacked with to be full of: *The shop was stacked with goodies.*

SPELLING NOTE

Words with the sound / s /, may be spelt **c-**, like **city**, or **ps-**, like **psychology**.

---

sta·di·um /ˈsteɪdiəm/ n **stadiums** or **stadia** /-dɪə/ a large sports ground with rows of seats built around a sports field

staff[1] /stɑːf ‖ stæf/ n **1** [C + sing/pl verb] the group of people who do the work of an organization: *The school's teaching staff is excellent. | a staff of 15 | She's on the staff of the new university.* **2** [C] a thick stick used as a support or as a sign of office

staff[2] v [T] to provide the workers for something: *a hospital staffed with 20 doctors*

stag /stæg/ n a fully grown male deer

stage[1] /steɪdʒ/ n **1** [C] a period in a course of events: *The plan is still in its early stages.* **2** [C] a part of a journey: *We travelled by easy stages, stopping often along the way.* **3** [C] the raised floor on which plays are performed in a theatre: *The actor was on stage for hours.* **4** the stage work in the theatre: *When she was five years old, she decided that she wanted to go on the stage.* **5** set the stage to carry out the preparations so that something can happen: *The stage was set for a great victory.*

stage[2] v staged, staging [T] **1** to perform or arrange for public show: *stage an art show | stage a football match* **2** to make something happen, especially for public effect: *stage a one-day strike*

stage-coach /ˈsteɪdʒkəʊtʃ/ n in the past, a closed horse-drawn vehicle for carrying passengers: *to travel by stagecoach*

stage fright /ˈ··/ n [U] nervousness felt when performing in public

stage man·age /ˌ·ˈ··/ v [T] to organize an event, often without people knowing: *The riots were stage managed by opponents of the government.*

stage man·ag·er /ˈ· ˌ···/ n a person in charge of what happens on a stage during a performance

stag·ger[1] /ˈstægəʳ/ v **1** [I] to move unsteadily on your feet: *a drunk staggering across the street* **2** [T] to arrange at different times: *Our holidays are staggered; John's off for a week, then I'm off for a week.*

stagger[2] n an unsteady movement of a person who finds it difficult to walk: *She gave a stagger as she began to feel faint.*

stag·gered /ˈstægəd ‖ -gərd/ adj very surprised: *I was staggered when I found out the truth.*

stag·ger·ing /ˈstægərɪŋ/ adj almost unbelievable: *a staggering rise in the cost of petrol* –**staggeringly** adv

stag·ing /ˈsteɪdʒɪŋ/ n **1** [C;U] the action or art of performing a play: *a new staging of "Hamlet"* **2** [U] movable boards and frames for standing on

stag·nant /ˈstægnənt/ adj **1** not flowing or moving (used of water): **2** inactive: *Business is stagnant at the moment.* –**stagnantly** adv

stag·nate /stægˈneɪt ‖ ˈstægneɪt/ v **stagnated, stagnating** [I] to stop developing –**stagnation** /stægˈneɪʃən/ n [U]

staid /steɪd/ adj serious and dull –**staidly** adv –**staidness** n [U]

stain[1] /steɪn/ v [I;T] **1** to change the colour of something, in a way that is lasting: *teeth stained by years of smoking* **2** to darken chemically: *to stain the chairs to match the dark table*

stain[2] n [C;U] **1** a stained place or spot: *blood stains on my shirt* **2** a chemical for changing the colour of wood

stained glass /ˌ· ˈ·◄/ n [U] coloured glass used to make pictures or patterns in windows

stain·less steel /ˌ·· ˈ·◄/ n [U] a type of metal not easily attacked by RUST: *a set of stainless steel knives*

stair /steə^r/ n 1 **stairs** [pl] a set of steps that go from one floor of a building to another: *Granny had difficulty climbing the stairs.* 2 [C] a step in a set of stairs

stair·case /'steəkeis ‖ 'steər-/ (also **stairway** /-wei/) n a set of stairs with its supports and side parts

stake¹ /steik/ n 1 [C] a share in something, such as a business, that gives you an interest in whether it succeeds: *Young people need the feeling that they have a stake in the country's future.* | *The company sold its 15% stake in the commercial bank.* 2 **at stake** at risk: *Hundreds of jobs are at stake if the mine closes.* 3 **stakes** [pl] the things you can win or lose when doing something risky: *They always play cards for high stakes.* 4 [C] a pointed wooden post which is driven into the ground and used as a support for something

stake² v **staked, staking** [T] 1 to risk money or your public position on the result of something: *I've staked all my hopes on you.* | *The President is staking his reputation on a successful outcome to the talks.* 2 **stake a claim** to state that you have a right to something: *He staked a claim to the land where he'd found gold.*

stal·ac·tite /'stæləktait ‖ stə'læktait/ n a sharp piece of rock which points down from the roof of a cave; a stalactite is formed over a long time by water dripping from the roof

stal·ag·mite /'stæləgmait ‖ stə'lægmait/ n a sharp piece of rock which points up from the floor of a cave, and is formed by water coming down in drops

stale /steil/ adj 1 no longer fresh (used of food or air): *stale bread* 2 not new or exciting: *She told the same stale jokes again!* 3 without new ideas or life, because you have done the same thing for too long (used of a person): *I'm getting stale in this job – I need a change.* –**staleness** n [U]

stale·mate /'steilmeit/ n [U; sing] 1 a situation in which neither side in an argument or competition can get an advantage 2 a position in the game of CHESS from which neither player can win

stalk¹ /stɔːk/ v 1 [T] to quietly follow a person or animal while staying hidden and waiting to catch or kill them: *The hunter stalked the lion for two days.* 2 [I] to walk stiffly, proudly and angrily: *She stalked out of the house in a rage.*

stalk² n 1 the main stem of a plant supporting its leaves, fruits or flowers 2 the part of a fruit or leaf which connects it to a plant or tree

stall¹ /stɔːl/ n 1 an indoor enclosure for an animal: *cattle in their stalls* 2 a large table in a public place from which you sell something or give information about something: *a market stall* 3 **the stalls** the seats on the main level of a theatre in front of the stage

stall² v 1 [I] (used of an engine) to stop suddenly because of a lack of power: *The car stalled on the hill.* 2 [T] to make an engine stop suddenly because of a lack of power: *Inexperienced pilots often stall their planes.* 3 [I] *infml* to delay doing something until a later time: *Stop stalling and answer my question!*

stal·lion /'stæljən/ n a fully-grown male horse kept for breeding

stal·wart¹ /'stɔːlwət ‖ -ərt/ adj strong and determined: *He's a stalwart supporter of the organization.* –**stalwartly** adv

stalwart² n a firm, dependable follower of an organization or political party

sta·men /'steimən/ n the male part of a flower which produces POLLEN

stam·i·na /'stæmɨnə/ n [U] the strength of body or mind to keep doing something tiring: *You need great stamina to run the 10,000 metres.*

stam·mer¹ /'stæmə^r/ v [I;T] to speak with difficulty, repeating sounds and pausing, either habitually or because of excitement or fear: *She stammers when she feels nervous.* | *He stammered his thanks.* –**stammerer** n

stammer² n [sing] the habit of stammering when you speak: *Ben's got a slight stammer.*

stamp¹ /stæmp/ v 1 [I] to walk with noisy, heavy steps: *She was stamping about in the cold trying to keep her feet warm.* | *He stamped out of the room angrily.* 2 **stamp your foot/feet** to lift your foot and bring it down forcefully: *"I won't do it", said the child, stamping her feet.* 3 **stamp on** to intentionally put your foot down hard on something: *She stamped on the bee and killed it.* 4 [T] to mark a word or sign on a paper or a letter by pressing with a special tool: *The immigration officer stamped my passport.* 5 [T] to clearly show that somebody or something has a particular quality or is of a particular type: *The roof stamps the church as Victorian in design.* | *His years in the army had stamped him with an air of brisk authority.*
stamp sth ↔ out phr v [T] to completely put an end to something bad: *The new law will help to stamp out the illegal drugs trade.*

stamp² n 1 (also **postage stamp** *fml*) a small piece of paper sold by the post office for sticking on a letter or parcel before you post it: *a twenty pence stamp* 2 a small piece of wood or metal which is covered with ink and then prints a mark on a surface, or the mark that it makes: *The stamp in the library book shows it must be returned tomorrow.* 3 a mark which shows a particular quality: *His music bears the stamp of his passionate personality.*

stam·pede¹ /stæm'piːd/ n 1 a sudden rush of frightened animals 2 a sudden rush to do something by a crowd of people: *There's been a stampede to buy gold before the price goes up.*

stampede² v **stampeded, stampeding** [I] 1 to rush suddenly and wildly: *The angry crowd stampeded through the town.* | *stampeding elephants* 2 [T] to make animals rush wildly or suddenly: *The fire stampeded the cattle.*

stance /stɑːns ‖ stæns/ n 1 a way of standing 2 a way of thinking shown in a position which you state publicly: *What's the government's stance on terrorism?*

stanch /stɑːntʃ ‖ stɔːntʃ, stɑːntʃ/ v –see STAUNCH

stand¹ /stænd/ v **stood** /stʊd/, **stood** 1 [I] to support yourself upright on your feet: *I had to stand all the way home on the bus.* | *She was standing by her desk.* 2 [I] to rise so that you are standing: *The teacher asked them to stand.* 3 [T] to make someone stand somewhere: *He stood the child on the wall.* 4 [I; + adv/prep] to move in a particular direction when you are standing: *The police told the crowd to stand back.* | *She stood aside to let me past.* 5 [I] to have a particular height: *The building stands over 200 feet high.* 6 [I] to be in an upright position somewhere: *The house stands on the corner of the High Street.* | *Few houses were left standing after the explosion.* 7 [T] to put something somewhere in an upright position: *Stand the ladder against the wall.* | *She stood the clock on the mantelpiece.* 8 [I] to be at a particular level: *Inflation now stands at 11%.* 9 [I] to remain unchanged: *My offer of help still stands.* 10 [T] to be good enough or strong enough to bear something: *This work will hardly stand close examination.* 11 **can't stand** to dislike something strongly or be unable to bear it: *I can't stand getting up early.* | *I couldn't stand listening to him any more.* | *She can't stand noise.* –see BEAR¹ (USAGE) **12 stand someone something** to pay for a meal or a drink for someone: *Let me stand you lunch.* **13** [I] to be one of the people trying to be elected in an election: *He has decided not to stand for Parliament again.* **14 stand to do something** to be likely to do something: *She stands to inherit £20,000 when her father dies.* **15 stand a chance** to have a chance of succeeding: *You don't stand a chance of getting that job!* **16 stand idle** to not be in use: *The machines have been standing idle since the strike began.* **17 stand in the way of something** to prevent something from happening: *He accused the minister of standing in the way of progress.* **18 standing on your head** very easily: *I could do that standing on my head.* **19 stand on your own two feet** to be able to live without help from other people **20 it stands to reason** = it is clear: *It stands to reason that we've got to invest in other fuel sources before oil runs out.* **21 stand trial** to be tried in a court

stand by *phr v* **1** [T **stand by** sbdy/sthg] to continue to support someone or something: *I still stand by my decision to sack him.* **2** [I] to do nothing while something unpleasant is happening: *We can't stand by and watch while people die of cold on our streets.* **3** [I] to be ready to help or do something if you are needed: *Fire and ambulance services are standing by in case the celebrations get out of hand.*

stand down *phr v* [I] to give up your position so that someone else can take it up: *He stood down in favour of a younger candidate.*

stand for sthg *phr v* [T] **1** to represent a word or phrase: *What does PTO stand for?* **2** to support an idea or set of ideas: *I am opposed to this prime minister and everything that he stands for.* **3 won't stand for something** to refuse to accept something: *I won't stand for his rudeness any longer!*

stand in *phr v* [I] to take someone's place or do their job while they are away: *I'm standing in for the chairman while he's on holiday.*

stand out *phr v* [I] **1** to have a colour or shape that can easily be seen: *The words on the sign stood out clearly.* **2** to be clearly much better than the rest: *She stands out as the best poet of her generation.*

stand up *phr v* **1** [I] to stand: *I've been standing up all day.* | *He stood up when I came into the room.* **2** [T **stand** sthg ↔ **up**] to put something somewhere in an upright position: *The dustbin had fallen over so I stood it up again.* **3** [I] to stay in good condition after hard use: *It's a good little car that will stand up to a lot of rough treatment.* **4** [I] to be accepted as true: *This evidence will never stand up in court.*

stand up for sbdy/sthg *phr v* [T] to defend someone or something against attack: *You must stand up for your rights.* | *At last he's learning to stand up for himself.*

stand up to sbdy *phr v* [T] to refuse to accept unjust treatment from someone

stand² *n* **1** a small outdoor shop: *an ice-cream stand* **2** a piece of furniture for putting something on: *an umbrella stand* | *a music stand* **3** the place in a

---

SPELLING NOTE

Words with the sound / s /, may be spelt **c-**, like **city**, or **ps-**, like **psychology**.

---

court where people stand when they are being questioned **4 stands** [pl] buildings at a sports ground; they have open fronts and rows of seats or places where people can stand **5 make a stand** to make a strong attempt to defend yourself: *The retreating army made a last stand just on the border.* **6 make a stand, take a stand** to state your ideas strongly: *The prime minister took a firm stand on the question of import controls.*

stan·dard¹ /ˈstændəd ‖ -ərd/ *n* **1** a level or degree of quality which is considered acceptable: *This teacher sets high standards for his pupils.* | *Watchmakers work to a high standard of precision.* | *I'm afraid this work is below the standard required.* **2** an accepted level used to make comparisons: *By European standards, this is a low salary.* **3 standards** [pl] principles which influence people's morals and behaviour: *I'm shocked by the moral standards of teenagers today!*

standard² *adj* **1** usual or ordinary: *It's standard practice now to search passengers at airports.* **2** [only before a noun] generally recognized as correct or acceptable: *The students want to learn standard pronunciation.* **3** widely used in order to understand a particular subject (used of books): *It's the standard text for medical students.*

stan·dard·ize /ˈstændədaɪz ‖ -ər-/ *v* **standardized, standardizing** (also **standardise** BrE) [T] to change things so that they are alike in every case: *Efforts to standardize spelling in English have not been a success.* | *The toys are produced using standardized parts.* –**standardization** /ˌstændədaɪˈzeɪʃən ‖ -dərdə-/ *n* [U]

standard lamp /ˈ·· ·/ *n BrE* a lamp on a tall stand which stands on the floor

standard of liv·ing /ˌ·· · ˈ··/ (also **living standard**) *n* the degree of wealth and comfort in everyday life that a person, group, or country has: *This region enjoys a high standard of living.* | *She had to adapt to a lower standard of living.*

stand·by /ˈstændbaɪ/ *n* **standbys** **1** a person or thing that is kept ready to be used if needed: *If the electricity fails, the hospital has a standby generator.* | *Powdered milk is a good standby in an emergency.* **2 on standby: a** ready to act at any time: *A special team of police were on standby during the game.* **b** able to travel on a plane just before it takes off if there is a seat nobody wants

stand-in /ˈ· ·/ *n* a person who takes the place or job of somebody else for a time

stand·ing¹ /ˈstændɪŋ/ *adj* [only before a noun] continuing in use or force: *We have a standing invitation: we can visit them whenever we like.* | *His meanness has become a standing joke among his friends.*

standing² *n* [U] **1** rank or position, particularly according to the opinion of other people: *a lawyer of high standing* | *The company's standing has been badly damaged by the scandal.* **2** period during which something has existed: *an agreement of several years' standing*

standing or·der /ˌ·· ˈ··/ *n* [C;U] *BrE* an instruction to your bank to pay a fixed amount of money from your account to a particular person or organization at regular times

stand-off·ish /stænd'ɒfɪʃ ‖ -'ɔːfɪʃ/ *adj* rather formal and unfriendly –**standoffishly** *adv*

stand·point /ˈstændpɔɪnt/ *n* a position from which things are seen and opinions are formed: *from the standpoint of the ordinary voter*

stand·still /ˈstændˌstɪl/ n [sing] a condition of no movement or activity: *She brought the car to a standstill.*

stank /stæŋk/ v the past tense of STINK

stan·za /ˈstænzə/ n a group of lines forming a division of a poem

sta·ple[1] /ˈsteɪpəl/ n **1** a small piece of thin wire which is pushed through sheets of paper to hold them firmly together –see picture on page 539 **2** a food that forms the regular and most important part of somebody's usual meals: *Rice is a staple in the region.* **3** a main product that is produced or sold: *Bananas and sugar are the staples of Jamaica.*

staple[2] v **stapled, stapling** [T] to fasten with wire staples

sta·pler /ˈsteɪplər/ n a small instrument used to push wire staples into paper see picture on page 539

star[1] /stɑːr/ n **1** a very large mass of burning gas in space which is seen as a bright point of light in a clear sky: *stars twinkling in the sky* **2** an object or shape with five or more points coming out of it: *The walls were decorated with gold stars.* **3** an object or sign in the shape of a star which is worn as a mark of office or rank, or as a measure of quality: *a four-star general* | *The guidebook awarded the hotel five stars.* **4** **the stars** the signs of the ZODIAC, regarded as determining your fate: *She always reads the stars in the newspaper.* **5** a famous or very skilful performer: *a film star* | *a football star* **6** see ASTERISK[1] –**starless** adj

star[2] v **-rr-** **1** [T] to have as the most important performer: *an old film starring Charlie Chaplin* **2** [I] to appear in a film or play as the most important performer: *Clint Eastwood will star in a new thriller.* **3** [T] to mark with one or more stars

star·board /ˈstɑːbəd ‖ ˈstɑːrbərd/ n [sing] the right side of a ship or aircraft as you face forward –opposite PORT[5]

starch[1] /stɑːtʃ ‖ stɑːrtʃ/ n **1** [C;U] a white tasteless substance found in food such as rice, bread, and potatoes: *Avoid eating so much starch if you want to lose weight.* **2** [U] a product used for stiffening cloth

starch[2] v [T] to stiffen with starch: *starched collars* | *starched tablecloths*

starch·y /ˈstɑːtʃi ‖ ˈstɑːr-/ adj **starchier, starchiest** **1** full of starch: *starchy foods* **2** infml stiffly correct and formal in manner

star·dom /ˈstɑːdəm ‖ ˈstɑːr-/ n [U] the state of being a very famous performer

stare /steər/ v **stared, staring** [I] **1** to look steadily at someone or something for a long time: *He sat staring into space, thinking deeply.* | *She stared at him in horror.* **2** **stare someone in the face** (used of an answer to a problem) to be very clear: *The solution is staring us in the face — let's borrow the money.* –**stare** n : *She gave him a long cool stare.*

stare sbdy **out** phr v [T] to make a person look away by looking at them steadily for a long time

star·fish /ˈstɑːˌfɪʃ ‖ ˈstɑːr-/ n **starfish** or **starfishes** a flat sea creature with five arms forming a star shape

stark[1] /stɑːk ‖ stɑːrk/ adj **1** very bare or severe in appearance: *the stark silhouette of rocks against the sky* **2** very hard and unpleasant: *The film conveys the stark realities of life for the poor.* –**starkly** adv

stark[2] adv **1** **stark naked** infml wearing nothing at all **2** **stark raving mad** infml completely mad

star·let /ˈstɑːlɪt ‖ ˈstɑːr-/ n a young actress who has had small parts in some films and hopes to become famous

star·light /ˈstɑːlaɪt ‖ ˈstɑːr-/ n [U] the light given by the stars

star·ling /ˈstɑːlɪŋ ‖ ˈstɑːr-/ n a common greenish-black European bird

star·ry /ˈstɑːri/ adj **starrier, starriest** filled with stars: *a starry winter sky*

starry-eyed /ˌ··ˈ·◄/ adj full of unreasonable or silly hopes

Stars and Stripes /ˌ·· ˈ·/ n AmE the flag of the United States of America (a phrase which sounds too solemn for ordinary use)

star-stud·ded /ˈ· ˌ··/ adj infml using many famous performers: *a star-studded cast*

start[1] /stɑːt ‖ stɑːrt/ v **1** [I;T] to begin an activity and continue doing it: *As everyone's here, can we start?* | *He started working here a week ago.* | *The bus didn't come, so we started to walk home.* | *He wants to start guitar lessons.*

□ USEFUL PATTERNS: to start something; to start to do something; to start doing something

2 [I;T] to bring or come into existence: *How did the trouble start?* | *Who started that rumour?* | *She's trying to start a sports club.* **3** [I; T] to take place or make something take place: *The concert started late.* | *We only started dinner at ten o'clock.* **4** [I; T] to begin operating or make something begin operating: *Oh no! The car won't start.* | *He's had a lot of trouble starting the truck.* **5** [I] to begin a journey: *It's a long way, so we'll have to start early.* **6** [I] to begin work: *You're hired — when can you start?* | *In this office, we start at eight every morning.* **7** [I] to go from a particular point or time: *Prices start at £5.00.* | *Starting from Monday, the lunch break will be longer.* **8** [I] to move suddenly in an uncontrolled way because of fear or surprise: *The touch on his shoulder made him start.* **9** **to start with**: a first; when there are several points you want to make, you can use this expression before or after the first one: *There were several reasons why he fell from power. To start with, there was his policy on Europe. Then there was his aggressive manner.* **b** you use this expression when you give a reason for something which has just been mentioned; you think that this reason by itself is very strong, but you are suggesting that it is not the only one: *I don't think he's got a chance. I mean, he hasn't got the right qualifications to start with, has he?* **c** first; you use this expression when you are talking about the first of several events: *We had soup to start with. Then we had a lovely piece of beef. And then for pudding we had lemon mousse.* **d** first; you can use this expression when you are going to give the first of a number of instructions: *To start with, switch on. Then key in the code word.* **e** at first; you use this expression when you say what happens at the beginning of a period of time when it is different or may be different from what happens later: *To start with, we'll use the old cooker. There's an old electric one there. Then later on, we'll probably get a gas one.*

start off phr v **1** [I] to have your first job: *Bill started off in marketing.* | *They started off as dancers.* **2** [I;T **start sthg ↔ off**] to do the first stage of an activity: *I always start off the first lesson by discussing the students' aims.*

start out phr v [I] to begin in a particular state or position which later changes: *The building started out as a library, but was then used as a school.*

start sthg ↔ **up** phr v to set up a new business or organization: *They're starting up a restaurant.*

start[2] n [C; sing] **1** the beginning of an activity or situation: *The start of the race had to be delayed.* | *It's late — we'd better make a start on the cooking.* |

From the start I disliked him. **2** the first part of something: *The start of the film was rather dull.* | *The start of the term is very tiring for teachers.* **3** a sudden uncontrolled movement because of surprise or fear: *I woke up with a start.* **4 for a start** you use this expression when you are making the first of several points you could make: *I don't think she'll get the job. She's too young, for a start.*

start·er /ˈstɑːtəʳ ‖ ˈstɑːr-/ *n* **1** the first course of a meal: *Would you like soup or melon as a starter?* **2** a person who gives the signal for a race to begin **3** an instrument for starting a car or engine

start·le /ˈstɑːtl ‖ ˈstɑːrtl/ *v* **startled, startling** [T] to make someone have a sudden surprise or shock: *You startled me! I didn't hear you come in.* –**startled** *adj* : *She looked at me startled.*

starv·a·tion /stɑːˈveɪʃən ‖ stɑːr-/ *n* [U] suffering or death caused by lack of food

starve /stɑːv ‖ stɑːrv/ *v* **starved, starving 1** [I] to die or suffer greatly from lack of food: *They got lost in the desert and starved to death.* | *Thousands could starve if the crops fail again.* **2** [T] to make a person or animal suffer or die by not giving them food: *She's ready to starve herself to lose weight.* **3** *infml* **be starving** be very hungry: *I'm starving — let's have lunch.* **4 be starved of** to not have enough of something you need: *a child starved of affection*

state[1] /steɪt/ *n* **1** [C; sing] a condition in which a person or thing is: *Doctors are worried about his state of health.* | *The survivors are still in a state of shock.* | *The room was in an awful state.* **2 in a state** *infml* to be very nervous or anxious: *Paul always got into a real state during exams.* **3 in no fit state** not healthy or calm enough to do something: *Immediately after the accident, she was in no fit state to talk to the police.* **4** [C] a country considered as a political organization: *Most former colonies have become self-governing states.* **5** [C] a smaller, partly self-governing area into which a large country is divided: *the State of California* | *Queensland is one of the states of Australia.* **6** [U] (also **State**) the government or political organization of a country: *Should industry be controlled by* **the** *state?* | *State secrets* **7** [U] the formality and ceremony connected with a ruler or head of government: *The Queen made a state visit to Canada.* **8 the States** *infml* the United States of America

state[2] *v* **stated, stating** [T+(that)] *fml* to say or express in speech or writing: *This book states the case for women's rights very clearly.* | *Please state your name and address.* | *The witness stated that he had never seen her before.*

state·ly /ˈsteɪtli/ *adj* **statelier, stateliest 1** grand, graceful and rather formal: *a row of tall, stately towers* | *a stately manner* **2 stately home** a large, old house of historical interest which can be visited by the public –**stateliness** *n* [U]

state·ment /ˈsteɪtmənt/ *n* **1** [C] a written or spoken declaration made formally: *The police took down the witness's statement.* | *In a statement made last night, the Minister announced important tax cuts.* **2** [C] a piece of paper from your bank which lists the amount of money paid or received and the total in your account **3** [sing; U] expression in words: *You need to provide a clearer statement of your goals.*

SPELLING NOTE

Words with the sound / s /, may be spelt **c-**, like **city**, or **ps-**, like **psychology.**

---

states·man /ˈsteɪtsmən/ *n* **statesmen** /-mən/ an experienced political leader who is widely respected for being wise and honourable; a female statesman is called a **stateswoman** –**statesmanship** *n* [U]

stat·ic /ˈstætɪk/ *adj* **1** not moving, changing, or developing: *Prices remained static on the stock exchange.* **2 static electricity** electricity which does not flow in a current but collects on the surface of objects

sta·tion[1] /ˈsteɪʃən/ *n* **1** a building by a railway where trains stop regularly for passengers or goods: *a station platform* | *We took a taxi to Euston Station.* –see picture on page 735 **2** a building from which buses start their journey: *a coach station* –see picture on page 735 **3** a building that is a centre for a particular service or activity: *a police station* | *a petrol station* **4** an organization that broadcasts on television or radio: *I can't get many foreign stations on this little radio.* **5** a small military establishment: *a naval station* **6** *old-fash* someone's position or rank: *She married a man beneath her station.*

station[2] *v* [T] **1** to make someone stay in a particular place so that they can stop trouble if necessary: *Guards were stationed around the prison.* **2 be stationed** to be sent to a particular place for military duty: *For most of the war, he was stationed in Europe.*

sta·tion·a·ry /ˈsteɪʃənəri ‖ -neri/ *adj* not moving: *The car was stationary when the accident happened.*

sta·tion·er /ˈsteɪʃənəʳ/ *n* a person or shop that sells stationery

sta·tion·er·y /ˈsteɪʃənəri ‖ -neri/ *n* [U] materials for writing such as paper, ink, and pencils

station wag·on /ˈ·· ˌ··/ *n* the usual American word for ESTATE CAR

stat·is·ti·cian /ˌstætɪˈstɪʃən/ *n* a person who works with statistics

sta·tis·tics /stəˈtɪstɪks/ *n* **1** [pl] facts or information based on studying a collection of numbers: *These statistics show there are 57 deaths per 1,000 of population.* | *official statistics* **2** [U] the science of studying numbers in order to get facts or information: *Statistics is a branch of mathematics.* –**statistical** *adj* –**statistically** /-kli/ *adv*

stat·ue /ˈstætʃuː/ *n* something which looks like a person or animal, made in stone or metal

stat·u·esque /ˌstætʃuˈesk/ *adj* tall, large and graceful (used of women)

stat·u·ette /ˌstætʃuˈet/ *n* a very small statue which you put on a table or shelf

stat·ure /ˈstætʃəʳ/ *n* [U] *fml* **1** a person's natural height: *She hadn't yet grown to her full stature.* **2** someone's importance, position and influence: *He's a politician of considerable stature, respected by people from all parties.*

sta·tus /ˈsteɪtəs ‖ ˈsteɪtəs, ˈstæ-/ *n* **1** [U] your social rank or position considered in relation to other people: *What's his status in the company?* **2** [U] social recognition and importance: *They think that having a big car gives them status.* **3** [U] the legal or official position of a person or organization: *What's your status in this country? Are you a citizen?* **4** [sing] the stage a situation has reached, or its importance at a particular time: *What's the status of the talks between the two countries?* **5 status symbol** something that you have which shows your social status, or what you would like it to be: *For some people a pedigree dog is more of a status symbol than a pet.*

status quo /ˌsteɪtəs ˈkwəʊ ‖ ˌsteɪ-, ˌstæ-/ *n* the status quo the existing situation at a particular time

stat·ute /ˈstætʃuːt/ *n fml* a law written down formally

stat·u·to·ry /ˈstætʃʊtəri ‖ -tʃɔːri/ *adj fml* fixed or controlled by law: *statutory control of wages*

staunch[1] /stɔːntʃ ‖ stɔːntʃ, stɑːntʃ/ *adj* dependably loyal: *a staunch friend* –**staunchly** *adv*

staunch[2] *v* (also **stanch** *AmE*) [T] to stop a flow, especially the flow of blood from a wound

stave /steɪv/ **staved, staving**
　　stave sthg ↔ **off** *phr v* [T] to prevent or keep away for a time: *They had just enough food to stave off hunger.*

stay[1] /steɪ/ *v* **1** to remain somewhere: *I stayed late at the party last night.* | *I'm sorry I can't stay, but my husband's waiting.* | *Can you stay for dinner?* **2** to live in a place for a while as a guest or visitor: *My cousin's coming to stay next week.* | *They're staying at a hotel.* **3** to continue to be in a particular place, situation or state: *Please stay where you are.* | *The price has gone down, but I don't think it'll stay down.* | *The weather stayed warm all week.* | *I can't stay awake another minute!* **4 stay away** to keep away from someone or something to avoid trouble: *Stay away from my daughter!* **5** *infml* **stay put** to remain somewhere: *Just stay put while I answer the phone.*
　　stay in *phr v* [I] to remain at home: *In the evenings, we usually stay in and read.*
　　stay on *phr v* [I] to remain after the usual or expected time for leaving: *Are you going to stay on at school after sixteen?*
　　stay out *phr v* [I] **1** to remain away from home: *Her mother was very worried when she stayed out so late.* **2** to continue to be on strike: *The miners stayed out for months.*
　　stay up *phr v* [I] to remain out of bed past the usual time: *We sometimes let the children stay up late.*
　　■ USAGE Compare **stay** and **live**. Use **stay** when you are talking about a short period of time and **live** for longer periods: *I'm going to* **live** *in London, but I'll* **stay** *at a hotel until I can find a suitable house.*

stay[2] *n* [C] a limited period of living in a place: *a short stay in hospital* | *During my stay in Paris, I went to many museums.*

stead·fast /ˈstedfɑːst ‖ -fæst/ *adj* **1** faithful and loyal: *a steadfast friend* **2** firm and unchanging: *steadfast in your beliefs* –**steadfastly** *adv*

stead·y[1] /ˈstedi/ *adj* **steadier, steadiest 1** not moving or shaking: *Keep the ladder steady.* | *His hand was steady as he lit the candle.* **2** moving or developing in an even, regular way: *a steady growth in industry* –opposite **unsteady** (for senses 1, 2) **3** staying at about the same level with few changes: *We drove at a steady speed.* **4** dependable and sensible (used of people) **5 a steady job** a job which is likely to continue –**steadily** *adv* –**steadiness** *n*

stead·y[2] *v* **steadied, steadying 1** [I;T] to make or become more calm or still: *She steadied the boat as they reached the port.* | *The pound has steadied after early losses on the market.* **2 steady yourself** to make yourself less nervous and confused: *He steadied himself before answering my question.*

steak /steɪk/ *n* [C;U] a thick flat piece of meat or fish: *How would you like your steak done, sir?* | *stewing steak* | *a salmon steak*

steal /stiːl/ *v* **stole** /stəʊl/, **stolen** /ˈstəʊlən/, **stealing 1** [I;T] to take something belonging to someone without their permission and with no intention of giving it back: *She used to steal money from her father's drawer.* | *He was sent to prison for stealing.* |

My bicycle was stolen last week. –see ROB (USAGE) –see THIEF (USAGE) **2** [I] to move secretly and quietly: *He stole out of the house without anyone seeing him.* **3 steal the scene/show** to get all the praise and attention expected by someone else at a public event

stealth /stelθ/ *n* [U] the action of acting secretly and quietly so that nobody notices you: *Stealth is something any hunter has to learn.* –**stealthy** *adj* **stealthier, stealthiest** : *She gave a stealthy glance at her watch.* –**stealthily** *adv*

steam[1] /stiːm/ *n* [U] **1** hot gas produced by boiling water: *Clouds of steam rose from the machine.* **2** power produced by putting steam under pressure: *The engines are driven by steam.* | *a steam locomotive* **3 let off steam** to get rid of strong feelings or active strength kept under control: *Young children need to let off steam by running around outside.* | *I let off steam by shouting at the dog.*

steam[2] *v* **1** [I] to produce steam: *steaming hot coffee* **2** [I] to travel by steam power: *The ship steamed into the harbour.* **3** [T] to cook by heating with steam: *Lightly steam the vegetables.* –see COOK[1] (USAGE) **4** [T] to use steam to open something: *He steamed open the letter.*
　　steam up *phr v* **1** [I] to be covered with steam: *Her glasses steamed up when she came into the warm room.* **2** *infml* **be**|**get steamed up** to be or become cross or upset: *She got pretty steamed up when I told her the news.*

steam·er /ˈstiːməʳ/ *n* see STEAMSHIP

steam·roll·er[1] /ˈstiːmˌrəʊləʳ/ *n* a heavy vehicle with very wide wheels for making road surfaces flat

steamroller[2] *v* [T] *infml* to force someone to do what you want by using all your power or influence: *He was steamrollered into signing the agreement.*

steam·ship /ˈstiːmˌʃɪp/ *n* (also **steamer**) a large ship driven by steam power

steed /stiːd/ *n lit* a horse for riding

steel[1] /stiːl/ *n* [U] a hard strong metal containing mainly iron and used for making things like tools, machines, and parts of buildings

steel[2] *v* [T] **steel yourself** to harden yourself enough to do something unpleasant: *He steeled himself to go in and say he was sorry.*

steel·works /ˈstiːlwɜːks ‖ -ɜːrks/ *n* [plural is **steelworks**] [C +sing/pl verb] a factory where steel is made

steel·y /ˈstiːli/ *adj* **steelier, steeliest 1** blue-grey in colour like steel: *steely blue eyes* **2** hard and strong: *steely determination*

steep /stiːp/ *adj* **1** rising or falling at a large angle: *This hill's too steep to ride up.* **2** showing a large increase or decrease: *a steep rise in prices* **3** *infml* unreasonably expensive: *He's asking £500 for his old car, which I think is a bit steep.* –**steeply** *adv* –**steepness** *n* [U]

steeped /stiːpt/ *adj* thoroughly filled or familiar with: *an ancient building steeped in history* | *a tribe steeped in the traditions of the past*

stee·ple /ˈstiːpəl/ *n* a church tower with the top rising to a point

stee·ple·chase /ˈstiːpəltʃeɪs/ *n* a race for people or horses in which they have to jump over fences or other objects

steer[1] /stɪəʳ/ *v* **1** [I;T] to control a ship or vehicle so that it goes in a particular direction: *He steered the car carefully into the garage.* | *Bill steered with one hand while adjusting the radio with the other.* **2** [T] to guide someone to where you want them to go: *She*

steered the visitors towards the garden. **3 steer the conversation** to try to change the subject of a conversation in a way that nobody notices: She tried to steer the conversation towards less painful topics. **4 steer clear of** to avoid

steer² n a male animal of the cattle family with its sexual organs removed

steering wheel /'··· ·/ n the wheel which you turn to control the direction in which a car or other vehicle moves –see picture on page 49

stel·lar /'stelə^r/ adj tech of or concerning the stars

stem¹ /stem/ n **1** the central part of a plant above the ground from which the leaves or flowers grow **2** the narrow upright part of a wine glass or similar container which supports the bowl: the stem of a wine glass

stem² v -mm- [T] to stop the flow or spread of: How can we stem the flow of blood?
stem from sthg phr v [T] to have as an origin or cause: This problem stems from poor management in the company.

stench /stentʃ/ n fml a strong bad smell

sten·cil¹ /'stensəl/ n a piece of card, metal, or plastic, in which patterns or letters have been cut – by putting ink or paint through these holes you make patterns or letters on the surface below

stencil² v -ll- (-l- AmE) [T] to print by using a stencil

step¹ /step/ n **1** the action of lifting one foot and putting it down in front of the other in order to move along: Take two steps forward and two steps back. | With every step I took the load got heavier. **2** the sound made when you take a step: I heard steps outside. **3** the distance covered in one step: There's a newsagent just a few steps down the road from the butcher. **4** a flat narrow surface, often one in a set of surfaces each higher than the one before, on which you put your foot for climbing up and down to different levels: Mind the step outside the door. | She was standing on the church steps. | A flight of steps led to the house. **5** an action in a set of actions which aims to produce a particular result: Our first step towards improving efficiency was to buy modern equipment. **6** a stage in a process: Scientists here are a few steps ahead of the rest of the world. **7** a movement of the feet in dancing: She learned the new steps quickly. **8 steps** a ladder which folds **9 in step** to move your left and right leg at the same time as other people: soldiers marching in step [RELATED PHRASE **out of step**] **10 step by step** gradually moving from one stage to the next: Step by step he learned the rules of the game.

step² v -pp- [I] **1** to lift one foot up and put it down in front of the other in order to move along: She stepped on a spider. | He stepped forward to receive his prize. **2 step into the breach** to do a job which someone else had said they would do but could not: When she was taken ill her son stepped into the breach and organized the event instead. **3 step out of line** to act differently from other people or from what is expected
step back phr v [I] to try to consider something in a new and different way: Let's step back a minute and think again.

SPELLING NOTE

Words with the sound / s /, may be spelt **c-**, like **city**, or **ps-**, like **psychology**.

---

step down (also **step aside**) phr v [I] to leave a job or official position: He's seventy years old and believes it's time to step down as chairman.
step in phr v [I] to begin to take part in a difficult situation in order to improve it: If the dispute gets any worse the government will have to step in.
step sthg ↔ **up** phr v [T] infml to increase in size or speed: We'll have to step up the work to finish by June.

step-broth·er /'step¸brʌðə^r/ n a male person whose father or mother has married your father or mother

step-fath·er /'step¸fɑːðə^r/ n a man who is not your natural father, but who your mother has married

step-lad·der /'step¸lædə^r/ n a ladder which folds

step-moth·er /'step¸mʌðə^r/ n a woman who is not your natural mother, but who your father has married

steppe /step/ n **the steppes** a large area of land without trees, especially in the Soviet Union

stepping stone /'··· ·/ n **1** a way of improving or becoming more successful: Are good exam results a stepping stone to a more successful job? **2** one of a row of large stones, which you walk on to cross a river

step-sis·ter /'step¸sɪstə^r/ n a female person whose father or mother has married your father or mother

ster·e·o¹ /'steriəu, 'stɪər-/ n stereos a record player or sound system which gives out sound from two different places by means of two speakers (SPEAKER)

stereo² (also **stereophonic** /¸steriəu'fɒnɪk◂, ¸stɪər- ‖ -'fɑː-/ fml) adj using a system of sound recording or broadcasting in which sound comes from two different places: a stereo recording | a stereo record player

ster·e·o·type¹ /'steriətaɪp/ n a fixed set of ideas or image which many people wrongly believe represents a particular person or thing: The characters in the film are just stereotypes, with no individuality. | racial stereotypes

stereotype² v stereotyped, stereotyping [T] to have a fixed idea or image of a general type which you wrongly believe represents a particular person or thing: You can't stereotype policemen – they're all different.

ster·ile /'steraɪl ‖ -rəl/ adj **1** unable to produce babies (used of people or animals) **2** very clean and free from harmful bacteria: The operation was performed in sterile conditions. **3** lacking new thought or imagination: His theory is based on a few sterile ideas. –**sterility** /stə'rɪlɪti/ n [U]

ster·il·ize /'sterɪlaɪz/ v **sterilized, sterilizing** (also **sterilise** BrE) [T] **1** to make clean and free from harmful bacteria **2 be sterilized** to have an operation so that you are unable to have children –**sterilization** /¸sterɪlaɪ'zeɪʃən ‖ -lə-/ n [U]

ster·ling¹ /'stɜːlɪŋ ‖ -ɜːr-/ n [U] tech the type of money used in Britain, based on the pound (£): The value of sterling has risen. | £200 sterling

sterling² adj [only before a noun] fml of the highest standard: Her sterling work was much appreciated.

stern¹ /stɜːn ‖ stɜːrn/ adj very firm and severe: a stern teacher | a stern look | stern discipline –**sternly** adv –**sternness** n [U]

stern² n the back end of a ship

steth·o·scope /'steθəskəup/ n a medical instrument which is used for listening to your heart and breathing; it consists of two tubes which go in the doctor's ears and a round part that goes on your chest

ste·ve·dore /ˈstiːvₐdɔːr/ n BrE a person whose job is loading and unloading ships

stew¹ /stjuː ‖ stuː/ n [C;U] a dish of meat and vegetables cooked together slowly in liquid

stew² v [I;T] 1 to cook slowly and gently in liquid −see COOK¹ (USAGE) 2 **stew in your own juice** infml to be left to suffer as a result of your own actions

stew·ard /ˈstjuːəd ‖ ˈstuːərd/ n 1 a man who serves passengers on a ship, train, or plane; a woman who does this is called a **stewardess** 2 one of the people who arrange a public event, such as a horse race

stick¹ /stɪk/ n 1 a long thin piece of wood which has been cut or has fallen off a tree: He drew in the sand with a stick. 2 (also **walking stick**) a thin rod of wood or metal used to support your body when walking: Since the accident she's had to walk with a stick. 3 a long thin piece of something: a stick of celery

stick² v stuck /stʌk/, **sticking** 1 [T] to push a pointed object into or through something: Don't stick pins into the chair! | She stuck her fork into the meat. 2 [T] to fix something to something else by using GLUE or a similar substance: His job is to stick labels on the boxes. 3 [I] to become or remain fixed to something or in a particular position: Oh no! This stamp won't stick! | The paint was still wet, so the handle stuck to my hand. | She couldn't get the door to open − it kept sticking. 4 [T] infml to put: He stuck his coat down on the chair. 5 **can't stick** infml to hate something or someone and feel that you cannot bear them: I just can't stick his voice. 6 **stick in your mind** infml to be remembered for a long time 7 **stick your neck out** infml to do or say something which could cause yourself harm or difficulty: I admire her for sticking her neck out and refusing to do what was expected.

stick around phr v [I] infml to wait somewhere, often because you hope something good will happen

stick at sthg phr v [T] to continue to work hard at something difficult: By really sticking at the lessons, she's improved her tennis a lot.

stick by sbdy phr v [T] infml to continue to support: She always sticks by her friends.

stick out phr v 1 [T; **stick** sthg ↔ **out**] to make something come out from inside: Don't stick your tongue out at me! 2 [I] to be positioned beyond something: The roof sticks out at least a metre in front of the door. 3 [I] infml to be clearly seen or noticed: Her unusual hairstyle makes her really stick out in a crowd. 4 **stick it out** to continue in a difficult situation without giving up: I don't like this course, but I'm determined to stick it out. 5 **stick out like a sore thumb** infml to seem very much out of place

stick out for sthg phr v [T] to refuse to accept anything less than or different from what you first asked for: In spite of management's refusal, the union are sticking out for a 10% increase in wages.

stick to sthg phr v 1 to continue to behave according to a decision, plan or agreement: I've decided to stick to my original idea. 2 to remain near to someone or something: If you stick to main roads, you won't get lost.

stick together phr v [I] to stay loyal to each other (used of two or more people)

stick sthg ↔ **up** phr v [T] to put on a wall: The room will look better if you stick up some pictures.

stick up for sbdy/sthg phr v [T] to support and defend a person or belief: Thanks for sticking up for me in the argument.

stick with sbdy/sthg phr v [T] infml to stay close or loyal to someone: Stick with me and you'll get rich!

stick·er /ˈstɪkər/ n a small piece of paper with a picture or writing on it which you stick to things: political stickers on car windows

stick-in-the-mud /ˈ· · · ˌ·/ n stick-in-the-muds infml a person who will not change or accept new things

stick·ler /ˈstɪklər/ n a person who demands a particular quality from themselves and other people: She's a stickler **for** the truth.

stick·y /ˈstɪki/ adj **stickier**, **stickiest** 1 covered with or containing a substance which sticks to anything it touches: sticky sweets | sticky labels 2 infml awkward or difficult (used of a situation): He put me in a very sticky position by telling me his secrets. 3 unpleasantly hot and wet (used of weather) 4 **come to/meet a sticky end** infml to suffer ruin, dishonour or death −**stickiness** n [U]

stiff¹ /stɪf/ adj 1 not easily bent or changed in shape: stiff paper | stiff new shoes | Beat the egg whites until stiff. 2 painful when moved (used of muscles or joints in the body): She felt very stiff the day after her first exercise class. 3 not easily moved: I couldn't turn the key − the lock's very stiff. 4 formal and not friendly (used of behaviour): a stiff smile 5 infml a **stiff drink** a drink which contains a large amount of strong alcohol 6 difficult or severe: a stiff examination | The judge gave him a stiff sentence. −**stiffly** adv −**stiffness** n [U]

stiff² adv infml extremely: scared stiff | bored stiff | frozen stiff | worried stiff

stiff·en /ˈstɪfən/ v 1 [I] to suddenly become still and tense because you are angry or afraid: He stiffened at her rude remarks. 2 [I;T] to make or become more difficult to bend or move: a shirt with a stiffened collar 3 [I;T] to make firmer or more severe (used of behaviour): Your comments will only stiffen his resolve.

sti·fle /ˈstaɪfəl/ v stifled, stifling [I;T] 1 to make or become unable to breathe properly because of heat or a lack of fresh air: The gas stifled them. | a stifling hot day 2 to prevent from happening or developing: The government stifled all opposition.

stig·ma /ˈstɪɡmə/ n stigmas a feeling of shame or dishonour: There is a stigma about having to ask for money.

stile /staɪl/ n two wooden steps which must be climbed to cross a fence or wall around a field

sti·let·to /stɪˈletəʊ/ n stilettos 1 a knife with a very sharp narrow blade, used as a weapon 2 **stiletto heel** a high thin heel of a woman's shoe

still¹ /stɪl/ adv 1 used to say that something is continuing to happen or continuing to be true: Is the secretary still here? | Do you still live in Birmingham? | Is John still working? 2 even so: I knew that I wouldn't win, but I still think it was unfair that I came last. | I know he's done a terrible thing, but he's still my father. | I'm not very happy about it. Still, it's no use worrying, is it? 3 used for making comparisons stronger: It's cold now and it will be colder still tonight.

still² adj 1 not moving: Keep still while I brush your hair. 2 quiet and calm: The house was still. 3 not containing gas (used of drinks): still orange juice −**stillness** n [U]

still³ v [T] lit to make someone quiet and calm

still⁴ n 1 [C] a photograph taken from a film 2 [U] lit quietness and calm

still·born /ˈstɪlbɔːn, ˌstɪlˈbɔːn ‖ -ɔːrn/ adj born dead

stilt /stɪlt/ n 1 a wooden or metal pole which supports a building above ground or water level 2 one of a pair of poles, with a supporting piece for your foot, with which you can walk raised above the ground –see PAIR (USAGE)

stilt·ed /ˈstɪltɪd/ adj very formal and unnatural (used of behaviour or conversation)

stim·u·lant /ˈstɪmjɡlənt/ n a drug or other substance which makes your body more active for a time: Coffee is a stimulant.

stim·u·late /ˈstɪmjɡleɪt/ v stimulated, stimulating [T] 1 to make something become more active or develop more quickly: Light stimulates plant growth. | Lowering of interest rates should stimulate the economy. 2 to fill someone with new ideas and interest: Going back to college has really stimulated her. 3 to make a part of someone's body move or behave in a particular way: It's a chemical which stimulates the production of hormones. –stimulation /ˌstɪmjɡˈleɪʃən/ n [U]

stim·u·lus /ˈstɪmjɡləs/ n stimuli /-liː/ 1 something which encourages activity or development: Building new shops will be a stimulus for business in the area. 2 something which fills you with new ideas and interest: He loves the stimulus of living in a big city. 3 something which makes a part of your body move or act

sting¹ /stɪŋ/ v stung /stʌŋ/, stinging 1 [I;T] (used of plants and insects) to hurt by pricking with a poison: He was stung by a wasp. | The leaves of these plants sting. –see BITE² (USAGE) 2 [I;T] to feel or make someone feel a sharp pain: My eyes are stinging from the smoke. | Careful – these chemicals will sting your eyes! 3 [T] to make someone feel hurt and cross: What you said so casually really stung him.

sting² n 1 the sharp organ of some animals which stings: Does a bee die when it loses its sting? 2 a sharp pain in a part of your body: the sting of salt rubbed into a wound 3 take the sting out of to remove the difficult or bad part of a situation: News of winning the competition took the sting out of her dismissal.

stin·gy /ˈstɪndʒi/ adj stingier, stingiest very mean: He's really stingy with his money. –stinginess n [U]

stink /stɪŋk/ v stank /stæŋk/, stunk /stʌŋk/, stinking [I] 1 to have a strong unpleasant smell: The room stank of garlic. –see SMELL (USAGE) 2 infml to have an unpleasant or offensive quality: Frankly, your attitude stinks! –stink n

stint¹ /stɪnt/ v [T] to give too small an amount of something: Don't stint on the cream when you make the cake.

stint² n a limited period of work: After a stint in the army, he opened a shop.

stip·pled /ˈstɪpəld/ adj painted or covered with small dots

stip·u·late /ˈstɪpjɡleɪt/ v stipulated, stipulating [T +(that)] to state clearly as a necessary condition of an agreement: The company stipulated payment in advance.

stip·u·la·tion /ˌstɪpjɡˈleɪʃən/ n [C;U] a statement of conditions: My only stipulation is that I am given a share in the profits.

SPELLING NOTE

Words with the sound / s /, may be spelt c-, like city, or ps-, like psychology.

---

stir¹ /stɜːr/ v -rr- 1 [T] to mix a liquid using a spoon or something similar: He stirred his coffee. 2 [I] to move slightly from one position to another: She stirred in her sleep. 3 [T] (used of the wind) to make something move slightly: A breeze gently stirred the surface of the lake.

stir sth ↔ **up** phr v [T] to cause trouble: Don't stir things up again by refusing to go there. 4 [T] to produce a strong feeling in someone: His speech stirred the crowd to anger. 5 **stir yourself** to make yourself move: We finally stirred ourselves from the fire and went to bed.

stir² n 1 [C] an act of stirring: Give the mixture a few stirs. 2 [sing] strong public feeling: His resignation has created quite a stir.

stir·rup /ˈstɪrəp ‖ ˈstɜː-/ n a metal piece that you put your foot in when you are riding a horse

stitch¹ /stɪtʃ/ n 1 [C] a short piece of thread sewn into a piece of material to join two edges together or for decoration: The stitches are so small and neat that you can't see them. 2 [C] a turn of the wool round the needle in knitting (KNIT): Make sure there are 20 stitches on the needles. 3 [C] a piece of thread which sews the sides of a wound together: The cut needed 15 stitches. 4 [sing] a sharp pain in your side, caused by too much exercise or laughter: She had a bad stitch from running. 5 **in stitches** infml laughing uncontrollably: His jokes had us all in stitches.

stitch² v 1 [I;T] to sew: Will you stitch a button on this shirt? 2 [T] to sew the edges of a wound together using a special needle: The doctor stitched the cut.

stoat /stəʊt/ n a small brown furry animal that eats other animals

stock¹ /stɒk ‖ stɑːk/ n 1 [C;U] money lent to a government or company, on which interest is paid: stocks and shares | government stock 2 [C] a supply of something for use: How long will the country's stocks of coal last? | We've bought a good stock of food for the weekend. 3 [U] the total supply of goods for sale in a shop: There wasn't much stock left after the sale. 4 **in stock** held ready for sale by a shop: I'm afraid we have no red ones in stock at the moment. [RELATED PHRASE **out of stock**] 5 [U] farm animals, especially cattle, sheep, or pigs 6 [U] a liquid made from the juices of meat, vegetables, or fish used in cooking 7 [U] the people from whom someone is descended: He comes from good farming stock. 8 **take stock** to stop for a while to consider a situation so you can make a decision: He took stock of his situation and decided he needed a long holiday.

stock² v [T] 1 to keep supplies of goods to sell: That shop stocks all types of shoes. 2 to fill: a shop well stocked with goods

stock up v [I] to buy a full store of goods in case you cannot get them later: Bad weather was expected, so we stocked up on food.

stock·ade /stɒˈkeɪd ‖ stɑː-/ n a wooden fence built for defence

stock·brok·er /ˈstɒkˌbrəʊkər ‖ ˈstɑːk-/ n a person whose job is buying and selling stocks (STOCK¹) and shares (SHARE¹)

stock ex·change /ˈ··ˌ·/ n 1 the place where stocks (STOCK¹) and shares (SHARE¹) are bought and sold 2 **the Stock Exchange** (also **the stock market**) the business of buying and selling stocks (STOCK¹) and shares (SHARE¹)

stock·ing /ˈstɒkɪŋ ‖ ˈstɑː-/ n 1 a close-fitting piece of clothing which covers your feet and legs; stockings are usually worn by women and made of nylon –see PAIR (USAGE) **2 in your stockinged feet** wearing stockings or socks, but no shoes

stocking cap /'·· ,·/ n the usual American word for a WOOLLY HAT

stock·ist /'stɒkɪ̱st ‖ 'stɑː-/ n a person or firm that keeps a particular sort of goods for sale: *This firm is a stockist of "Woofo" dog food.*

stock mar·ket /'· ,·/ n see STOCK EXCHANGE

stock·pile /'stɒkpaɪl ‖ 'stɑːk-/ v **stockpiled, stockpiling** [T] to keep a large store of food or weapons, especially because they might become difficult to get for future use –**stockpile** n

stock-still /,· '·◂/ adv without the slightest movement: *She stood stock-still and listened.*

stock·tak·ing /'stɒk,teɪkɪŋ ‖ 'stɑːk-/ n [U] the making of a list of all the goods held in a business or shop

stock·y /'stɒki ‖ 'stɑː-/ adj **stockier, stockiest** short, strong and solid (used of people) –see picture on page 245

stodg·y /'stɒdʒi ‖ 'stɑː-/ adj **stodgier, stodgiest** 1 unpleasantly filling and heavy (used of food) 2 dull and uninteresting: *a stodgy old schoolmaster*

sto·ic·al /'stəʊɪkəl/ (also **stoic**) adj patient and uncomplaining through suffering or difficulties –**stoically** /-kli/ adv –**stoicism** /-ɪsɪzəm/ n [U] : *He bore all his misfortunes with stoicism.*

stoke /stəʊk/ v **stoked, stoking** [T] (also **stoke up**) 1 to add wood or coal to a fire so that it burns more strongly 2 to make an unpleasant feeling or disagreement even stronger: *Your letter of complaint will only stoke up his resentment.*

stole¹ /stəʊl/ n a long straight piece of material worn on the shoulders by women at formal social occasions

stole² v the past tense of STEAL

sto·len /'stəʊlən/ v the past participle of STEAL

stol·id /'stɒlɪ̱d ‖ 'stɑː-/ adj showing no excitement when strong feelings might be expected –**stolidly** adv

stom·ach¹ /'stʌmək/ n 1 [C] the organ in the body where food is digested (DIGEST) 2 [C] the front part of your body below your chest: *He sat with his hands folded across his stomach.* | *She lay on her stomach.* 3 liking or desire for something unpleasant: *I've got no stomach for a fight.*

stomach² v [T] **can't stomach** to hate something or someone and feel that you cannot bear them: *I can't stomach his jokes.*

stom·ach·ache /'stʌmək,eɪk/ n [C;U] continuing pain in the stomach: *The pills really helped to get rid of my stomachache.* –see ACHE² (USAGE)

stomp /stɒmp ‖ stɑːmp, stɔːmp/ v [I] infml to walk with heavy steps: *He stomped up the stairs in a rage.*

stone¹ /stəʊn/ n 1 [C] a small piece of rock: *He threw a stone at the dog.* 2 [U] a solid mineral substance often used for building: *stone steps* | *walls made of stone* 3 [C] a single hard seed inside certain fruits: *She swallowed a cherry stone.* 4 [C] a jewel: *These stones are worth a lot of money.* 5 [C] (plural is **stone** or **stones**) a unit used in Britain for measuring weight, equal to 14 pounds or 6.35 kilograms: *He weighs 13 stone.* 6 **stone cold** extremely cold (used of things) 7 **stone deaf** completely unable to hear 8 **a stone's throw** a short distance: *It's only a stone's throw from his house to the station.*

stone² v **stoned, stoning** [T] to throw stones at someone, especially as a punishment: *The criminal was stoned to death.*

Stone Age /'· ·/ n the **Stone Age** the earliest period of man's history, when all tools were made of stone

stoned /stəʊnd/ adj [never before a noun] infml very drunk or under the influence of drugs

stone·ma·son /'stəʊn,meɪsən/ (also **mason**) n a person whose job is cutting stone into shape for building

stone·ware /'stəʊnweəʳ/ n [U] pots and other containers made from a special clay that contains a hard stone

stone·work /'stəʊnwɜːk ‖ -ɜːrk/ n [U] the parts of a building made of stone

ston·y /'stəʊni/ adj **stonier, stoniest** 1 containing or covered with stones: *stony ground* 2 showing no pity or feeling: *Their pleas were heard in stony silence.* –**stonily** adv

stood /stʊd/ v the past tense and past participle of STAND

stool /stuːl/ n 1 a seat without a supporting part for your back or arms: *a piano stool* 2 tech a piece of solid waste matter passed from the body

stoop /stuːp/ v [I] 1 to bend your upper body forwards and down: *He had to stoop to get through the entrance.* 2 to habitually stand or wait with your head and shoulders bent –**stoop** n [sing] : *an old woman with a stoop*

stoop to sth phr v [T] to reach a low standard of behaviour by doing something immoral: *I wouldn't stoop to stealing money.*

stop¹ /stɒp ‖ stɑːp/ v **-pp-** 1 [I;T] to no longer continue an action or activity: *Stop making such a noise!* | *Apply pressure on the wound to stop the bleeding.* | *She stopped her piano lessons because they were so expensive.* | *Stop! What do you think you're doing?*
☐ USEFUL PATTERNS to stop; to stop something; to stop doing something
2 [T] to prevent something from happening or someone from doing something: *I'm going, and you can't stop me.* | *You must try to stop her telling such lies.* | *How can I stop the dog barking all night?* | *You'd better stop Joe from telling them about it.*
☐ USEFUL PATTERNS to stop someone; to stop someone doing something; to stop someone from doing something
3 [I;T] to end or make something end: *The rain finally stopped.* | *The referee stopped the fight by sending one player off the field.* 4 [I] to interrupt a journey or activity before continuing: *We stopped for tea in a village café.* | *I don't usually stop at every word I don't recognize.* 5 [I;T] to no longer move or make someone or something no longer move: *She started to run, but then stopped.* | *Stop the bus – I want to get off.* 6 [I;T] to no longer work or to turn something off: *His watch keeps stopping.* | *Stop the video please.* 7 [T] to prevent money from being paid: *The bank stopped his cheque because he had no money in his account.* 8 **stop at nothing** to be ready to do anything, even something wrong or dangerous, in order to get what you want 9 **stop short of** to stop yourself from doing something, or before reaching a dangerous point: *He stopped short of actually accusing her of the theft.* | *She slammed on the brakes and stopped just short of the cliff edge.*

stop off phr v [I] infml to interrupt a journey to make a short visit to friends or a particular place: *Let's stop off for tea at Aunt Betty's.* | *On our way north, we stopped off in York.*

stop² n 1 an act of stopping or the state of being stopped: *We went straight there without making any stops.* | *The guide said that the next stop was the National Gallery.* | *Since the war, work on the project has come to a complete stop.* 2 a place on a road or railway line where buses or trains stop for passengers: *a bus stop* | *The next stop is Oxford.* **3** a dot used to show where a sentence ends **4 put a stop to** to prevent something undesirable from continuing: *The new law has put a stop to all the tax evasion of the last few years.* **5 pull out all the stops** to do everything possible to succeed in something: *He pulled out all the stops to complete the work in time.*

stop·cock /ˈstɒpkɒk ‖ ˈstɑːpkɑːk/ *n* a tap (TAP) which controls the flow of water or gas in a pipe

stop·gap /ˈstɒpgæp ‖ ˈstɑːp-/ *n* something that fills a need for a short time until something better can be found: *They've lent us an old bed as a stop-gap until our new one is delivered.*

stop·o·ver /ˈstɒpˌəʊvəʳ ‖ ˈstɑːp-/ *n* a short stay between parts of a journey, for example a long plane journey

stop·page /ˈstɒpɪdʒ ‖ ˈstɑː-/ *n* **1** a blocked state which stops something from moving, for example in a pipe **2** the act of stopping work in order to show disagreement with an employer: *Stoppages in the steel industry have increased.* **3** stoppages [pl] money officially taken from your pay, usually before you get it: *stoppages for tax and insurance*

stop·per /ˈstɒpəʳ ‖ ˈstɑː-/ *n* an object which fits in and closes the opening to a bottle or other container

stop press /ˌ· ˈ·◂/ *n* **the Stop Press** the latest news, added to a newspaper after the main part has been printed

stop·watch /ˈstɒpwɒtʃ ‖ ˈstɑːpwɑːtʃ, -wɔːtʃ/ *n* a watch which can be stopped and started at any time, so that you can measure exactly how long something takes

stor·age /ˈstɔːrɪdʒ/ *n* [U] **1** the act of keeping something somewhere until it is needed, or a place to keep things: *storage space* | *Her furniture is in storage until she finds a new home.* **2** the process of keeping information on a computer: *Storage on these discs is very simple.*

store¹ /stɔːʳ/ *v* **stored, storing** [T] **1** to keep something somewhere for in the future: *Washing powder is stored in the cupboard on the left.* **2** to keep information on a computer or in your memory: *I could see her storing away the details in her mind.*

store² *n* **1** a supply of something kept for use in the future: *This animal makes a store of nuts for the winter.* **2** a large building in which goods are stored **3** a large shop: *a furniture store* | *a department store* **4** the usual American word for shop: *the local village store* **5 in store** about to happen: *There's a nasty shock in store for him.* **6 set great store by** to feel that something is very important: *He sets great store by his sister's ability.*

store·house /ˈstɔːhaʊs ‖ ˈstɔːr-/ *n* a thing or person full of interesting and useful ideas or information: *The book is a wonderful storehouse of techniques for teachers.*

store·room /ˈstɔːrʊm, -ruːm/ *n* a room where goods are kept till needed

sto·rey (**story** *AmE*) /ˈstɔːri/ *n* **1** a floor or level in a building: *There are three storeys including the ground floor.* **2** -**storeyed** (-**storied** *AmE*) having

---

SPELLING NOTE

Words with the sound / s /, may be spelt **c-**, like **city**, or **ps-**, like **psychology**.

---

a certain number of storeys: *a six-storeyed block of flats*

stork /stɔːk ‖ stɔːrk/ *n* a large bird, with a long beak and legs, which lives close to water

storm¹ /stɔːm ‖ stɔːrm/ *n* **1** bad weather conditions with strong wind and often rain, lightning and thunder: *crops damaged by heavy storms* | *a sandstorm* **2** a show of strong or angry feeling: *The General's speech was greeted with a storm of abuse.* **3 storm in a teacup** *infml* a lot of trouble or worry about something unimportant **4 take by storm** (used of a performer or performance) to get the great approval of: *Her singing took New York by storm.*

storm² *v* **1** [T] to attack violently: *Angry crowds stormed the building.* **2** [I] to move violently and noisily because you are angry: *He stormed out of the room.*

storm·y /ˈstɔːmi ‖ -ɔːr-/ *adj* **stormier, stormiest** **1** very rainy and windy: *stormy weather* | *a stormy day* **2** full of strong disagreements and angry feelings: *a stormy meeting* | *a stormy relationship*

sto·ry /ˈstɔːri/ *n* **stories** **1** an account of people and events, real or imagined: *She wrote a story about space exploration.* | *an extraordinary life story* | *He promised to tell the children a story.* | *The story of our friendship began when we were students.* **2** an article in a newspaper or magazine, or a piece of news on the radio or television: *The main story this week is about Poland.* **3** a false description of events: *She told me some story about missing the train.* | *His teacher shouted at him for telling stories.* **4 it's the same story/the same old story** it's the same undesirable situation which has happened again: *It's the same old story — the addicts need money for drugs, so they steal to get it!* **5 only part of the story/not the whole story** a phrase used when you think you cannot completely understand a situation, because you don't have enough information about it

stout¹ /staʊt/ *adj* **1** rather fat and heavy: *He became stout as he grew older.* –see picture on page 245 **2** strong and thick: *a stout pair of boots* **3** [only before a noun] strong and determined: *a stout supporter of the team* –**stoutly** *adv* : *He stoutly defended her against criticism.* –**stoutness** *n* [U]

stout² *n* [U] a strong dark beer

stout·heart·ed /ˌstaʊtˈhɑːtɪd◂ ‖ -ɑːr-/ *adj lit* brave and determined

stove /stəʊv/ *n* an apparatus used for cooking or for heating a room

stow /stəʊ/ *v* [T] to put something away neatly so that it is not in the way: *The ship's cargo is stowed in the hold.* | *You can stow your bags away under the desks.*

stow·a·way /ˈstəʊəweɪ/ *n* a person who hides on a ship or plane to get a free journey or to escape from somewhere

strad·dle /ˈstrædl/ *v* **straddled, straddling** [T] **1** to have one leg on either side of something: *He sat straddling the fence.* **2** to be on either side of a place: *The village straddles the canal.*

strag·gle /ˈstrægəl/ *v* **straggled, straggling** **1** to move or spread untidily or unevenly: *A few huts straggled across the countryside.* **2** to arrive singly or in small groups separate from a main group: *Runners were still straggling in hours after the winners had arrived.* –**straggler** *n*

strag·gly /ˈstrægəli/ *adj* **stragglier, straggliest** growing or spreading out untidily: *straggly hair*

straight¹ /streɪt/ adj **1** not bent or curved: *Draw a straight line.* | *a straight road* | *I hate having such straight hair.* –see picture on page 245 **2** level or upright: *Put the mirror straight.* | *That fence post isn't straight.* **3** with no water added (used of an alcoholic drink) **4** serious: *This is his first straight play.* **5 straight answer** an honest answer **6 straight choice** a simple choice between two things **7 straight face** a serious face

straight² adv **1** in a straight line: *Go straight down this road and you'll see the school.* | *It's straight in front of you.* **2** directly and without delay: *She came in and went straight to bed.*

straight³ n **the straight** the straight part of a road or race track

straight·a·way /ˌstreɪtəˈweɪ/ adv at once and without delay: *The doctor came straightaway.*

straight·en /ˈstreɪtn/ v [I;T] to become straight or to make something straight or tidy: *There's a series of bends, and then the road straightens.* | *He straightened his tie.*

straighten out phr v **1** [I;T **straighten** sthg ↔ **out**] to become straight or to make something straight **2** [T **straighten** sthg ↔ **out**] to remove the confusions or difficulties in a situation: *It will take ages to straighten out his business affairs.*

straighten up phr v **1** [I] to stand upright from a position in which your body is bent **2** [T **straighten** sthg ↔ **up**] to make something tidy: *Straighten your room up and put your things away.*

straight·for·ward /ˌstreɪtˈfɔːwəd ǁ -ˈfɔːrwərd/ adj **1** simple and easy to do or understand: *She thought the exam questions were very straightforward.* **2** honest and open (used of a person or their behaviour): *He's always been very straightforward about what he wants.* –**straightforwardly** adv

straight·laced /ˌstreɪtˈleɪst◄/ adj having severe, rather old ideas about correct morals

strain¹ /streɪn/ n **1** [C] a breed of plant or animal: *This strain of wheat can grow during a cold spring.* **2** [sing] a particular quality in someone's character which can be passed from parents to children: *There's a strain of madness in the family.* **3** the **strains** lit notes of music: *She heard the strains of a well-known song as she approached the house.*

strain² v **1** [T] to damage or weaken a part of your body by using it awkwardly or too much: *You'll strain your eyes reading in such bad light.* | *Bob strained a muscle while gardening.* **2** [T] to separate a liquid from a solid by using a container with small holes in it: *He strained the vegetables.* **3** [T] to force something beyond usual or acceptable limits: *My patience has been strained to the limit.* | *Having two more children to feed strained their budget even further.* **4** [I;T] to make a great effort to do something: *She had to strain her ears to hear the announcement.* | *You look as if you're straining to understand me.*

strain³ n **1** [C;U] the force causing something to be tightly pulled or stretched: *The rope broke under the strain of supporting such a heavy load.* **2** [C] a state in which someone or something is forced to do more than is acceptable: *The additional work put a great strain on him.* | *Reducing the bus service has placed a great strain on the trains.* **3** [U] a state of anxiety and worry: *She's under a lot of strain at the moment; her child's very ill.* | *Strain is often caused by overwork.* **4** [U] damage to a part of the body caused by using it awkwardly or too much: *eye strain*

strained /streɪnd/ adj **1** unfriendly and lacking in trust: *Relations between the couple became strained.* **2** nervous and tired: *You're looking strained – are you working too hard?*

strain·er /ˈstreɪnəʳ/ n an instrument used for separating solids from liquids: *a tea strainer*

strait /streɪt/ n **1** a narrow passage of water between two areas of land: *the Straits of Dover* | *the Strait of Gibraltar* **2 straits** an extremely difficult situation, such as illness or lack of money: *When my father lost his job, we were in desperate straits.*

strait·jack·et /ˈstreɪtˌdʒækɪt/ n a garment which holds the arms down, preventing a mad person from harming themselves or other people

strand /strænd/ n **1** a single thin piece or thread: *Many strands are twisted together to form a rope.* **2** a part of a story, belief or situation: *At the end of the book the different strands of the plot come together.*

strand·ed /ˈstrændɪd/ adj **1** left on the shore and unable to get back to the sea: *The boat was left stranded when the tide went out.* **2** in a very difficult situation, unable to get away: *There I was, stranded in a foreign country with no money.*

strange /streɪndʒ/ adj **1** unusual, surprising, and difficult to understand: *It's strange you've never met him.* | *She's got a strange habit of stroking her nose when she's thinking.* | *The doctor thought her strange behaviour was caused by stress.* **2** unfamiliar or not known before: *Tell the children not to talk to strange people.* | *The city I grew up in, now seems very strange to me.* –**strangely** adv : *Strangely, I've never seen that television show before.* –**strangeness** n [U]

strang·er /ˈstreɪndʒəʳ/ n **1** a person who is unfamiliar to you: *A complete stranger waved to me in the street.* **2** a person in an unfamiliar place: *I'm a stranger in this town. Can you tell me the way to the station?* **3 to be a stranger to something** to feel completely unfamiliar with a particular situation: *Pam's no stranger to living abroad.*

stran·gle /ˈstræŋgəl/ v **strangled, strangling** [T] **1** to kill a person or animal by pressing on their throat **2** to prevent something from growing or developing: *The government's policies are slowly strangling the economy.* –**strangulation** /ˌstræŋgjʊˈleɪʃən/ n : *Death was caused by strangulation.*

stran·gle·hold /ˈstræŋgəlhəʊld/ n a strong control or influence which prevents development: *A few large companies have a stranglehold on the production of cars.*

strap¹ /stræp/ n a strong narrow band of leather or other material, used to fasten things together or to carry something: *a watch strap* | *The strap on my bag is broken.*

strap² v **-pp-** [T] to fasten in place with straps: *She strapped the bag onto her back.*

strap·ping /ˈstræpɪŋ/ adj [only before a noun] big, strong and healthy: *a fine, strapping man*

stra·ta /ˈstrɑːtə ǁ ˈstreɪtə/ n plural of STRATUM

strat·a·gem /ˈstrætədʒəm/ n a clever trick or plan to deceive an enemy or get what you want

stra·te·gic /strəˈtiːdʒɪk/ adj **1** done as part of a plan intended to help you succeed in something: *The union took a strategic decision to sign the agreement.* **2** connected with defence or war: *secret purchases of strategic materials* –**strategically** /-kli/ adv

strat·e·gy /ˈstrætədʒi/ n **strategies 1** [U] the art of planning something skilfully, particularly a war: *The general was a master of strategy.* **2** [C] a particular plan for gaining success in an activity: *marketing strategies* –**strategist** n

strat·i·fied /'strætɪfaɪd/ adj divided into separate levels: *The society will become increasingly stratified as more people lose their jobs.* | *stratified rock* —**stratification** /ˌstrætɪfɪ'keɪʃən/ n [U]

strat·os·phere /'strætəsfɪəʳ/ n **the stratosphere** the outer band of air which surrounds the earth, starting at about ten kilometres above the earth —compare ATMOSPHERE

stra·tum /'strɑːtəm ‖ 'streɪ-/ n **strata** /-tə/ **1** a band of one of the different kinds of rock which make up the levels of the earth's surface **2** a group of people in society similar in class or education̄: *What people eat differs widely in each social stratum.*

straw /strɔː/ n **1** [U] dried yellow stems of grain plants such as wheat: *a straw hat* **2** [C] a thin dried stem of wheat, rice, etc. **3** [C] a thin paper or plastic tube for sucking up liquid: *She drank the juice through a straw.*

straw·ber·ry /'strɔːbəri ‖ -beri, -bəri/ n **strawberries** a small red juicy fruit which is soft and grows on plants near the ground: *strawberries and cream* | *strawberry ice cream* —see picture on page 344

stray[1] /streɪ/ v **strayed, straying** [I] **1** to wander away from the proper path or place: *Some of the sheep strayed into the neighbour's field.* **2** to be unable to keep to a particular subject, and to think or talk about other things instead: *During the talk, his thoughts strayed.*

stray[2] n **strays** an animal lost from its home or having no home

stray[3] adj [only before a noun] **1** wandering or lost from home: *stray cats* **2** separated from things of the same kind: *He was hit by a stray bullet.*

streak[1] /striːk/ n **1** a thin line or band, different from what surrounds it: *Streaks of grey began to appear in her black hair.* **2** a particular quality, often bad, which sometimes appears in someone's behaviour: *There's a streak of cruelty in his character.* **3** repeated success or failure for a period: *I was on a winning streak, and made a lot of money.*

streak[2] v **1** [I+adv/prep] to move very fast: *The cat streaked across the road with the dog behind it.* **2** [T] to cover with streaks: *His face was streaked with dirt.*

streak·y /'striːki/ adj **streakier, streakiest 1** marked with streaks: *streaky paintwork* **2 streaky bacon** BACON which has lines of fat in it

stream[1] /striːm/ n **1** a natural flow of water smaller than a river: *a mountain stream* **2** a continuous flow of people or vehicles: *A steady stream of visitors came to see him in hospital.* | *a stream of traffic* **3** a large number of remarks or questions: *Her speech was followed by a stream of questions.* **4** a group of school pupils of the same age and ability who are taught together: *She's in the top stream.* **5 go with the stream** to follow what most people do or think in a particular situation [RELATED PHRASE **go against the stream**]

stream[2] v **1** [I+adv/prep] to flow fast and strongly: *The pipe broke and water streamed onto the floor.* | *Tears streamed down her cheeks.* **2** [I+adv/prep] to move quickly in a mass: *The crowd streamed out of the football stadium.* **3** [T] *BrE* to group people together according to age and ability: *The pupils are streamed into four ability groups.* **4** [I+adv/prep] (of light) to shine brightly through something: *Vera opened the curtains and the light streamed in.*

stream·er /'striːməʳ/ n a long narrow piece of coloured paper used for decorating a room when there is a party

stream·line /'striːmlaɪn/ v **streamlined, streamlining** [T] **1** to make something into a long smooth shape which moves easily through water or air: *a streamlined racing car* **2** to make a business, organization, or process simpler and able to work more effectively: *How can we streamline production?*

street /striːt/ n **1** a road in a town or village with houses or other buildings on one or both sides: *101 Oxford Street* | *a narrow street* **2** connected with activities that take place outside the house in a town: *homeless people living on the streets* | *street musicians* | *street life* **3 streets ahead** *infml* much better than something else **4 up your street** in your area of interest or activity: *Tell Tim about the book — it's right up his street.*

■ USAGE 1 A **street** is in the middle of a town, and usually has shops and buildings. A **road** can be in the town or country, and usually leads to another town, or another part of a town. 2 British speakers often say **in** a street/road: *the shops* **in** *the High Street* | *a house* **in** *Bristol Road.* American speakers often say **on** a street/road: *the stores* **on** *Main Street* | *a house* **on** *Boston Road*

street·car /'striːtkɑːʳ/ n the usual American word for TRAM

strength /streŋθ, streŋθ/ n **1** [C;U] the quality of being physically strong: *He does weight-training to build up his strength.* | *They pushed with all their strength, but the car didn't move.* **2** [U] the quality of being brave and determined in a difficult situation: *With great strength of character, she continued working throughout her illness.* **3** [U] influence or power: *the strength of the multinational companies* **4** [C] a particular quality which makes someone or something effective or forceful: *the strengths and weaknesses of the argument* | *His strength as a writer is the clarity of his style.* **5** [U] closeness in a relationship: *The strength of their marriage was badly affected by all his trips abroad.* **6** [U] the total amount of people: *Membership of the club is growing in strength.* **7 below strength** having fewer members than are needed: *The police force is 400 below strength.* [RELATED PHRASE **at full strength**] **8 from strength to strength** with continuing success: *Our new company is going from strength to strength.* **9 in strength** in large numbers: *By 10 a.m. the football supporters were arriving in strength.* **10 on the strength of** persuaded or influenced by: *We bought this car on the strength of his advice.*

strength·en /'streŋθən, 'streŋθən/ v **1** [I;T] to make or become more powerful: *If we can find more witnesses, it'll strengthen your case.* | *Last year popular feeling against the war strengthened.* **2** [I;T] (of relations between people or groups) to make or become closer: *Relations between the two countries strengthened after the treaty was signed.* | *The college wants to strengthen its links with industry.* **3** [T] to become more determined: *She felt strengthened by his support.* **4** [T] to make something physically stronger: *The bridge was strengthened with metal supports.*

stren·u·ous /'strenjuəs/ adj needing great effort or activity: *a strenuous climb* | *strenuous exercise* | *a*

SPELLING NOTE

Words with the sound / s /, may be spelt **c-**, like **city**, or **ps-**, like **psychology**.

strenuous effort -**strenuously** *adv* -**strenuousness** *n* [U]

stress[1] /stres/ *n* **1** [C;U] pressure caused by the difficulties of life which makes you feel worried or tense: *He's under stress because he has too much work to do.* | *He hated the stress of living in a big city.* | *Her headaches seem to be caused by stress.* **2** [C;U] force of weight caused by something heavy: *The old bridge collapsed under the stress of heavy vehicles.* **3** [C] the degree of force you put on something like a beat in music or a word or part of a word when you say it: *In "under", the main stress is on "un".* **4** [U] a special importance: *The stress on discipline is noticeable in the school.*

stress[2] *v* [T] **1** to give particular importance to a matter when talking or writing about it: *She stressed the need for careful spending.* **2** to give force to a beat in music or to a word or part of a word when you say it so that it sounds a little louder than what is around it: *The word "machine" is stressed on the second syllable.*

stress·ful /ˈstresfəl/ *adj* causing a feeling of stress: *a stressful job*

stress mark /ˈ··/ *n* a mark to show that stress falls on a certain part of a word

stretch[1] /stretʃ/ *v* **1** [I;T] to make or become wider or longer: *I tried stretching the shoes, but they still didn't fit.* | *Be careful the jumper doesn't stretch when you wash it.* **2** [I+adv/prep] to spread out in space or time: *The forest stretched for miles.* | *The project will now have to stretch on into the new year.* | *The desert stretched away into the distance.* **3** [I;T] to straighten your limbs or body to full length: *She got out of bed and stretched.* | *Stretch your arms above your head.* -see picture on page 736 **4** [I not in progressive forms] to be elastic: *Rubber bands stretch.* **5** [T] to pull something tightly so that it reaches its full length or width: *She stretched the rope between the two poles.* **6** [T] (of a job) to make use of all your ability and skills: *She left the company because she didn't feel she was being stretched enough.* **7** [T] to push something beyond its proper or natural limits: *His awful behaviour really stretches my patience.* | *The hospital was stretched to the limit with so few staff.* **8 stretch your legs** go for a short walk

stretch out/stretch yourself out *phr v* [I;T **stretch** sthg ↔ **out**] to lie with your legs and arms at full length: *The cat stretched out in front of the fire.* | *She stretched herself out on the couch.*

stretch[2] *n* **1** [C] an act of stretching your body: *I stood up and had a good stretch.* **2** [U] the ability to increase in length or width: *For these costumes we need fabric with plenty of stretch.* **3** [C] a level area of land or water: *a pleasant stretch of coast* **4** [C] a continuous period of time: *As part of her training she spent a stretch caring for the disabled.* **5 at a stretch** without stopping or having a break: *The prisoners were made to stand for hours at a stretch.* **6 by no/any stretch of the imagination** a phrase you use when you want to show that you find it impossible to believe that something is true: *By no stretch of the imagination could she be called a competent driver.*

stretch·er /ˈstretʃər/ *n* a long piece of thick material with poles on either side on which a sick person can be carried

strew /struː/ *v* **strewed, strewn** /struːn/ *or* **strewed** [T] **1** to scatter irregularly: *There were papers strewn all over the floor.* **2** to lie scattered: *The path was strewn with flowers.*

strick·en /ˈstrɪkən/ *adj* experiencing strongly the effects of trouble, illness or some other problem: *stricken with polio* | *stricken by doubts* | *Supplies were rushed to the drought-stricken area.*

strict /strɪkt/ *adj* **1** severe in demanding obedience to rules of behaviour: *They are very strict with their children.* | *a strict teacher* **2** which must be followed: *He had strict instructions not to tell anyone.* **3** exact: *This is a rather strict interpretation of the facts.* -**strictly** *adv* -**strictness** *n* [U]

stric·ture /ˈstrɪktʃər/ *n fml* **1** severe blame or disapproval: *The judge was severe in his strictures.* **2** something that limits both physically and morally: *Because of our religion, there are certain strictures on what we eat.*

stride[1] /straɪd/ *v* **strode** /strəʊd/, **stridden** /ˈstrɪdn/, **striding** [I; + adv/prep] to walk with long steps or cross with one long step: *She strode up to the front door and knocked.* | *He strode across the stream.* -see **WALK**[1] (USAGE)

stride[2] *n* **1** a long step in walking **2 make great strides** to improve or do well **3 take something in one's stride** to accept and deal with something easily: *Some people would have been shocked, but she takes it all in her stride.*

stri·dent /ˈstraɪdənt/ *adj* **1** with a hard unpleasant sound: *She always talks in such a strident voice.* **2** unpleasantly strong or loud in your opinions or demands: *a strident political campaign* -**stridently** *adv*

strife /straɪf/ *n* [U] trouble or disagreement between people: *family strife* | *The city was torn apart by political strife.*

strike[1] /straɪk/ *v* **struck** /strʌk/, **struck, striking** **1** [T] to hit someone or something: *He struck her several times on the face.* **2** [I] to attack someone or something: *The army struck at dawn.* **3** [I] (of something unpleasant) to happen suddenly: *Suddenly disaster struck.* **4** [T] to give you a particular feeling or idea: *How does the room strike you?* | *He strikes me as being a very clever man.* **5** [T] to come into your mind: *Suddenly a terrible thought struck me.* | *It struck me that I had made a terrible mistake.* **6** [I] to stop working because of a disagreement, usually over pay: *The unions are threatening to strike if their pay demands are not met.* **7** [T] to discover something: *The company say that they have struck oil under the Irish sea.* **8** [I+adv/prep] to start going in a particular direction: *We struck east towards the hills.* **9** [I;T] (of a clock) to make a sound to show what time it is: *The clock struck three.* **10 strike a balance** to do something that is between two extremes: *It's hard to strike a balance between caution and boldness.* **11 strike a bargain** to come to an agreement with someone **12 strike a blow for something** to do something which helps towards gaining a particular thing: *She struck a blow for women's rights.* **13 strike a chord** to give you feelings of understanding or sympathy **14 strike a light, strike a match** to light a match **15 be struck dumb** to be so shocked that you cannot speak **16 strike fear/terror into someone's heart** to make someone feel very afraid **17 strike it rich** to suddenly become very wealthy **18 strike while the iron is hot** to do something while the occasion is still favourable **19 within striking distance of** very near to a place

strike back *phr v* [I] to do something to attack someone who has attacked or harmed you

strike down *phr v* **be struck down** to be harmed by something: *We were all struck down by a strange illness.*

strike sbdy ↔ **off** phr v [T] to take someone's name off an official list so that they are no longer a member of a professional body

strike up phr v **1** [T **strike up** sthg] to start a friendship with someone: *They struck up a friendship on the plane.* **2** [I;T **strike up** sthg] to start to play music: *The band struck up a lively march.*

strike² n **1** a time when people do not work because they want more pay or better conditions of work: *The strike lasted for two months.* **2 on strike** not working because of a strike: *The workers have been on strike for three weeks now.* | *They're threatening to go on strike.* **3** an attack: *The air force has carried out dozens of air strikes against enemy targets.*

strik·er /'straɪkəʳ/ n **1** a person on strike **2** a player in football who attacks

strik·ing /'straɪkɪŋ/ adj **1** very noticeable or unusual: *There were striking similarities between the two books.* **2** beautiful in an unusual way: *What a striking woman!* **–strikingly** adv

string¹ /strɪŋ/ n **1** [C;U] narrow cord made of threads twisted together: *She tied the parcel up with string.* | *a ball of string* | *The keys are hanging on a string.* **2** [C] a thin piece of wire stretched tightly across a musical instrument to produce sound **3 the strings** [+sing/pl verb] the set of players in an ORCHESTRA who play instruments with strings **4** [C] a set of things connected together on a thread: *She wore a string of pearls.* | *a string of onions* **5** [C] a set of things or events which follow each other closely: *We've had a string of complaints about that programme.* | *He appeared in a string of horror films.* **6 no strings attached** a phrase used of something which is given to you with no conditions: *The company paid for me to do the course with no strings attached.*

string² v **strung, strung**

string sbdy **along** phr v infml [T] to falsely encourage someone's hopes: *He will never be paid the money they promised him; they're just stringing him along.*

string sthg ↔ **out** phr v [I;T] to spread out in a line: *He strung out 12 pairs of socks on the washing line.* | *Small shops were strung out along the motorway.*

string sthg ↔ **together** phr v [T] to put things together to make one thing: *She felt so tired that she could hardly string a sentence together.*

string sthg ↔ **up** phr v [T] to hang something high: *They strung up coloured lights round the room.*

string bean /ˌ· ˈ·/ n the American word for RUNNER BEAN

strin·gent /'strɪndʒənt/ adj severe (used of rules or conditions): *stringent restrictions* **–stringently** adv **–stringency** n

string·y /'strɪŋi/ adj **stringier, stringiest** containing hard narrow pieces (used of food): *The meat was so stringy we could hardly chew it.* **–stringiness** n [U]

strip¹ /strɪp/ v **-pp-** **1** [T] to remove parts of something or the covering on its surface: *Elephants stripped the leaves from the trees.* | *You'll have to strip the walls before painting.* **2** [I;T] to undress: *He stripped and jumped into the water.* | *The customs officials stripped and searched him.*

SPELLING NOTE

Words with the sound / s /, may be spelt **c-**, like **city**, or **ps-**, like **psychology**.

---

strip sbdy **of** sthg phr v [T] to remove someone's rights or possessions: *The military court stripped him of his rank and house.*

strip off phr v [I;T **strip off** sthg] to take off your clothes

strip² n **1** a narrow piece of paper or other material **2** a narrow area: *a strip of water*

strip car·toon /ˌ· ·ˈ·/ n the usual British word for COMIC STRIP

stripe /straɪp/ n **1** a long narrow band which is different in colour from what surrounds it: *She wore a sweater with red and black stripes.* **2** a narrow band of colour on someone's uniform which shows their rank **–striped** adj

strip·pa·gram /'strɪpəgræm/ n a person who is paid to visit someone on a special occasion and undress in front of them

strip·per /'strɪpəʳ/ n infml a performer in a striptease

strip·tease /'strɪptiːz, ˌstrɪp'tiːz/ n (also **strip show** /ˈ· ·/) [C;U] a performance in which someone takes off their clothes to music in a sexually exciting way

strip·y /'straɪpi/ adj **stripier, stripiest** (also **stripey**) covered in stripes of colour: *a stripy pattern* –see picture on page 147

strive /straɪv/ v **strove** /strəʊv/, **striven** /'strɪvən/, **striving** [I] fml to struggle hard to get or do something: *She strove for recognition as an artist.* | *The company is striving to improve its public image.*

strode /strəʊd/ v the past tense of STRIDE

stroke¹ /strəʊk/ v **stroked, stroking** [T] to pass your hand gently and slowly over something: *The cat likes being stroked.*

stroke² n **1** a sudden illness in part of someone's brain which can cause death or loss of movement in certain parts of their body: *She had to walk with a stick after she had a stroke.* **2** a line or mark made by a single movement of your brush or pen when painting or writing: *With a few quick strokes, she sketched his face.* **3** a movement of the arms repeated when swimming or rowing: *He swam across the lake with strong confident strokes.* **4** a method of swimming: *Breaststroke is a tiring stroke.* **5** the sound made by a clock at a given time: *At the twelfth stroke, we all started cheering.* **6** a soft, gentle movement of your hand across something: *He gave the dog a stroke.* **7 a stroke of luck** an unexpected piece of good luck: *What a stroke of luck you were still there.* **8 a stroke of genius** a very clever idea: *It was a stroke of genius to take this route.* **9 at a stroke/in one stroke** at once and with a single firm action: *Don't believe politicians who promise to improve things in one stroke.* **10 not do a stroke of work** a phrase you use to describe someone who does not do any work: *As far as I can tell, she's never done a stroke of work in her life.*

stroll /strəʊl/ v [I] to walk, especially slowly, for pleasure –see WALK 1 (USAGE)

strong /strɒŋ ‖ strɔːŋ/ adj **1** physically powerful and able to use great force or effort: *He must be very strong to be able to carry that box.* | *strong arms* **2** having great power or influence: *a strong personality* | *strong leadership* | *Before the war it was one of the world's strongest nations.* **3** not easily broken, changed or destroyed: *strong furniture* | *a strong will* | *strong beliefs* | *a strong economy* | *a strong relationship* **4** having a powerful effect on the mind or senses: *a strong smell* | *She makes a strong impression on everyone she meets.* **5** great in value or degree: *I told him in the strongest possible terms that* he needed to change his behaviour. | **strong suspicions** **6** containing a lot of the substance which gives taste or produces particular effects: *The tea is too strong for me.* | *strong drug* **7** showing a high likelihood of success: *There's a strong possibility that Spain will win the match.* | *She's a strong candidate for the job.* **8** [only after a noun] having the stated number of members: *The organization is now 500 strong.* **9** good: *One of the plan's strong points is its clarity.* | *The school's very strong* **on** *teaching reading.* **10 still going strong** still continuing actively, even after a long time: *The club's still going strong after all these years.*

strong·box /ˈstrɒŋbɒks ‖ ˈstrɔːŋbɑːks/ *n* a metal box which you can lock to keep valuable things safe in

strong·hold /ˈstrɒŋhəʊld ‖ ˈstrɔːŋ-/ *n* **1** a strongly defended place or position: *a guerilla stronghold* **2** a place where a particular way of life or belief is common: *The clubs are a stronghold of male privilege.*

strong lan·guage /ˌ· ˈ··/ *n* [U] swearing and curses

strong-mind·ed /ˌ· ˈ···◁/ *adj* firm and determined in your beliefs and opinions –**strong-mindedness** *n* [U]

strong room /ˈ· ·/ *n* a room, for example in a bank, with a special thick door and walls, where valuable objects can be kept

strove /strəʊv/ *v* the past tense of STRIVE

struck /strʌk/ *v* the past tense and past participle of STRIKE

struc·tur·al /ˈstrʌktʃərəl/ *adj* of or concerning structure: *a structural fault* –**structurally** *adv*

struc·ture¹ /ˈstrʌktʃəʳ/ *v* **1** [U] the way in which parts are arranged or organized into a whole: *the structure of the brain* | *the financial structure of the company* | *the structure of a sentence* **2** [C] something which has been built, especially a building: *The hospital is a tall, brick structure.*

structure² *v* **structured, structuring** [T] to arrange something carefully in an organized way: *You'll need to structure the argument in the report more carefully.*

strug·gle¹ /ˈstrʌgəl/ *v* **struggled, struggling** [I] **1** to make very great efforts to do something difficult: *She struggled up the stairs with her heavy bags.* | *Many young writers have to struggle* **for** *recognition.* **2** to move violently in order to get free: *He struggled* **against** *his attacker.* | *They struggled to get out of the burning car.*

struggle on *phr v* [I] to continue to do something although it is very difficult: *Hungry and exhausted, the climbers struggled on.*

struggle² *n* a great effort to do something difficult: *the nation's struggle* **for** *independence* | *With a struggle, he controlled his temper.* | *Three people were hurt in the struggle.*

strum /strʌm/ *v* **-mm-** [I;T] to play a stringed musical instrument quickly and informally: *She was strumming loudly on her guitar.*

strung /strʌŋ/ *v* the past tense and past participle of STRING

strut¹ /strʌt/ *v* **-tt-** [I] to walk proudly with your chest pushed forwards: *The male bird strutted in front of the female.*

strut² *n* a piece of wood or metal holding the weight of a part of a building

stub¹ /stʌb/ *n* **1** the short end of a cigarette or pencil which is left when the rest has been used **2** the small piece of a cheque or ticket which you keep as a record after use

stub² *v* **-bb-** [T] to hurt your toe by hitting it against something

stub sthg ↔ out *phr v* [T] to stop a cigarette from burning by pressing the end against something

stub·ble /ˈstʌbəl/ *n* [U] the short stiff remains of wheat or a man's beard after it has been cut –**stubbly** *adv*

stub·born /ˈstʌbən ‖ -ərn/ *adj* **1** determined and having a strong will: *She's so stubborn that she'll never listen to your advice.* **2** difficult to move or remove: *stubborn stains* –**stubbornly** *adv* –**stubbornness** *n* [U]

stub·by /ˈstʌbi/ *adj* **stubbier, stubbiest** short and thick: *his stubby fingers*

stuck¹ /stʌk/ *adj* [never before a noun] **1** fixed in position and impossible to move: *The door's stuck; we'll have to get out through the window.* | *His finger got stuck in the hole.* **2** *infml* unable to continue doing something: *We'll really be stuck if the bank won't lend us the money.* | *I'm stuck – can you help solve this problem?* **3** unable to get away from a place: *She's stuck at home all day with the children.*

stuck² *v* the past tense and past participle of STICK

stuck-up /ˌ· ˈ·◁/ *adj* *infml* very proud and unfriendly because you think you are very important: *She's too stuck-up to speak to her old friends.*

stud /stʌd/ *n* **1** a number of horses or other animals kept for breeding **2** a small piece of metal which sticks out from a surface and is used to prevent slipping or for decoration: *The ground's wet — you'll need boots with studs.* **3** a small piece of metal or another substance worn in the ear for decoration: *a pair of gold studs*

stud·ded /ˈstʌdɪd/ *adj* covered with studs or other small objects: *a ring studded with diamonds* | *a star-studded sky*

stu·dent /ˈstjuːdənt ‖ ˈstuː-/ *n* **1** a person who is studying at a place of education or training: *a university student* | *students at secondary school* **2** a person with an interest in a particular subject: *a student of human nature*

stud·ied /ˈstʌdid/ *adj* carefully considered or planned before being expressed: *She asked about his wife with studied informality.*

stu·di·o /ˈstjuːdiəʊ ‖ ˈstuː-/ *n* **studios** **1** a workroom for a painter or photographer **2** a room from which broadcasts are made: *a television studio* **3** a place where cinema films are made: *Pinewood studios*

stu·di·ous /ˈstjuːdiəs ‖ ˈstuː-/ *adj* fond of reading and studying: *a studious young man* –**studiously** *adv* –**studiousness** *n* [U]

stud·y¹ /ˈstʌdi/ *n* **studies** **1** [U] the act of learning about a subject: *She spent the afternoon deep in study.* **2 studies** subjects studied: *the Department of African Studies* **3** [C] a thorough enquiry into a particular subject including a piece of writing: *She's made a study of Shakespeare's comedies.* | *the latest studies on the effects of drugs* **4** [C] a room in a house used for studying or private work: *She writes all her letters in the study.* **5** a drawing or painting of a detail done to prepare for a larger work

study² *v* **studied, studying** **1** [I;T] to spend time learning a subject: *She studies French.* | *She's studying to be a doctor.* **2** [T] to examine carefully: *Before leaving they studied the map.* | *Jack studied her face closely.*

stuff /stʌf/ *n* [U] *infml* **1** a substance of any sort: *What's this sticky stuff on the floor?* | *There are one or two interesting stories, but the rest is pretty boring stuff.* **2** a group of things: *I can't carry all my*

stuff in this bag. **3 know your stuff** to be skilful in or know a lot about a particular subject: *We asked him to fix the car because we thought he really knew his stuff.*

stuff² *v* **1** [T] to fill something with a substance: *The bag was stuffed full of old toys.* | *They stuff the pillows* **with** *feathers.* **2** [T] to push something into something else quickly and untidily: *She stuffed the letter into her pocket.* **3 stuff yourself** *infml* to eat a lot of food: *The children were stuffing themselves* **with** *sweets.* **4** [T] to fill a chicken, piece of meat or vegetable with a mixture of finely cut-up food before you cook it: *In Greece, peppers are stuffed* **with** *meat and rice.* **5** [T] to fill the skin of a dead animal so that it looks real: *the stuffed head of a deer* **6 get stuffed** *BrE* a very rude phrase used when you are angry or annoyed with someone: *He wanted to borrow my car again, but I told him to get stuffed.*

stuff·ing /'stʌfɪŋ/ *n* [U] **1** material used as a filling for something: *Old clothes were used as a stuffing for the cushions.* **2** a mixture of food placed inside a piece of meat, chicken, or vegetable before cooking

stuff·y /'stʌfi/ *adj* **stuffier, stuffiest 1** unpleasantly hot with little fresh air: *a stuffy room* **2** dull and full of old ideas: *a stuffy organization* | *a stuffy person* –**stuffily** *adv* –**stuffiness** *n* [U]

stum·ble /'stʌmbəl/ *v* [I] **stumbled, stumbling 1** to put your foot down awkwardly while walking or running so you start to fall: *She stumbled in the dark and hurt her knee.* **3** to stop or make mistakes in speaking or reading aloud: *She stumbled* **over** *the long word.* –**stumble** *n*
stumble across sthg *phr v* (also **stumble on** sthg) [T] to find or discover something by chance: *Scientists have stumbled on a possible cure for the disease.*

stumbling block /'·· ·/ *n* something which prevents action or development: *The biggest stumbling block* **to** *an agreement is the attitude of the employers.*

stump¹ /stʌmp/ *n* **1** the small part of something left after the rest has been cut off or broken down: *a tree stump* | *the stump of a tooth* | *the stump of a pencil* **2 stumps** the three upright pieces of wood at which the ball is thrown in the game of cricket

stump² *v* **1** [I+adv/prep] to walk heavily: *He stumped angrily up the stairs.* **2** [T] *infml* to put an unanswerable question to someone: *He was stumped by the journalist's question.*
stump up sthg *phr v* to pay money unwillingly: *Yet again you're asking your father to stump up the money for new clothes!*

stump·y /'stʌmpi/ *adj* **stumpier, stumpiest** short and thick: *stumpy little fingers*

stun /stʌn/ *v* **-nn-** [T] **1** to make someone unconscious or confused by hitting them on the head **2** to shock or surprise someone very much: *He seemed stunned by the news.* | *a stunned silence*

stung /stʌŋ/ *v* past tense and past participle of STING

stunk /stʌŋk/ *v* past tense of STINK

stun·ning /'stʌnɪŋ/ *adj* **1** extremely attractive or beautiful: *She looks stunning in that dress.* **2** very surprising or unexpected: *a stunning result* –**stunningly** *adv*

stunt¹ /stʌnt/ *v* [T] to prevent the full growth or development of something: *A bad diet may stunt growth in children.*

stunt² *n* **1** an act of dangerous physical skill: *One of his stunts in the film was to drive a car off a mountain.* **2** an action which gains public attention: *Dressing in funny costumes was a publicity stunt to raise money for the children's hospital.*

stunt man /'· ·/ *n* a person who does dangerous acts in a film so that the actor does not have to do them; a female stuntman is called a **stuntwoman**

stu·pe·fied /'stjuːpɪfaɪd ‖ 'stuː-/ *adj* **1** very surprised: *He was stupefied to see her there.* **2** unable to think or feel: *He was in a stupefied state from all the drugs.* –**stupefaction** /ˌstjuːpɪ'fækʃən ‖ ˌstuː-/ *n* [U]

stu·pen·dous /stjuː'pendəs ‖ stuː-/ *adj* extremely large or good: *a stupendous mistake* | *We had a stupendous time at the party.* –**stupendously** *adv*

stu·pid /'stjuːpɪd ‖ 'stuː-/ *adj* **1** silly or foolish: *a stupid person* | *I think you were stupid to agree with him.* **2** [only before a noun] *infml* a word you use for a thing when you find it annoying or you do not like it: *This stupid drawer won't open.* –**stupidly** *adv* –**stupidity** /stjuː'pɪdɪti ‖ stuː-/ *n*

stu·por /'stjuːpəʳ ‖ 'stuː-/ *n* a state in which you cannot think or use your senses properly: *He lay on the bed in a drunken stupor.*

stur·dy /'stɜːdi ‖ -ɜːr-/ *adj* **sturdier, sturdiest** strong and unlikely to break or be hurt: *a sturdy horse* | *a sturdy wooden desk* –**sturdily** *adv* –**sturdiness** *n* [U]

stut·ter /'stʌtəʳ/ *v* [I] to speak with difficulty because you cannot easily say the first sound of a word: *"I c– c– can't help it"* *she stuttered.* –**stutterer** *n* –**stutter** *n*

sty /staɪ/ *n* (also **stye**) an infected swollen place on the eyelid

style¹ /staɪl/ *n* **1** [C;U] a general way of doing something which expresses the belief of the particular person or group doing it: *an informal style of management* | *African styles of leadership* **2** [C;U] someone's typical way of behaving or thinking: *I wouldn't tell you lies — that's not my style.* | *In characteristic style, he insisted on paying for everybody.* **3** [U] high quality or grace in manner, social behaviour, or appearance: *Although she has very little money, she always dresses with great style.* | *His salary allows him to live in style.* | *I hate this singer's music, but I admit she has style.* **4** [C] fashion in clothes: *The latest styles look really good on young people.* **5** [C] the way that something looks: *They sell leather jackets in different colours and styles.* | *This hotel is similar in style to the others in the chain.* | *Your new hair style really suits you.* | *a painting in the style of Picasso* **6** [C;U] a particular choice of words or manner of expression which is typical of a writer or speaker: *The letter is written in a very formal style.* | *He's an interesting writer, but I don't like his style.* **7 -style**: in the manner of a certain person or place: *I liked my hamburgers cooked American-style.*

style² *v* **styled, styling** [T] to arrange or form something in a certain pattern or shape: *She had her hair styled by a famous hairdresser.*

styl·ish /'staɪlɪʃ/ *adj* fashionable and attractive: *He's a stylish dresser.* –**stylishly** *adv* –**stylishness** *n* [U]

styl·ist /'staɪlɪst/ *n* –see HAIRDRESSER

styl·is·tic /staɪ'lɪstɪk/ *adj fml* of or concerning style in writing or art: *Can you see stylistic differences*

between the original painting and the copy?
–**stylistically** /-kli/ *adv*

styl·ize /ˈstaɪlaɪz/ *v* **stylized, stylizing** (also **stylise** *BrE*) [T] *fml* to present something in a work of art in a fixed unnatural style rather than as in real life

sty·lus /ˈstaɪləs/ *n* **styluses**, *or* **styli** /-laɪ/ the instrument on a RECORD PLAYER that looks like a needle and picks up the sound signals from a record

suave /swɑːv/ *adj* having charming manners which you sometimes use insincerely to get what you want (used of men) –**suavely** *adv*

sub /sʌb/ *n infml* **1** an abbreviation for SUBSCRIPTION **2** an abbreviation for SUBMARINE

sub·com·mit·tee /ˈsʌbkəˌmɪti/ *n* [C +sing/pl verb] a smaller group formed from a larger committee to deal with a certain matter in more detail

sub·con·scious[1] /ˌsʌbˈkɒnʃəs ‖ -ˈkɑːn-/ *adj* not fully known or understood by the conscious mind (used of thoughts and feelings) –see CONSCIOUS (USAGE) –**subconsciously** *adv*

subconscious[2] *n* (also **unconscious**) **the subconscious** the hidden thoughts and feelings you have in your mind that you are not conscious of, but which influence your behaviour

sub·con·ti·nent /ˌsʌbˈkɒntɪnənt ‖ -ˈkɑːn-/ *n* a large mass of land made up of a number of different countries

sub·di·vide /ˌsʌbdɪˈvaɪd/ *v* **subdivided, subdividing** [T] to divide something into smaller parts: *The house is being subdivided into four flats.* –**subdivision** /-dɪˈvɪʒən/ *n* [U]

sub·due /səbˈdjuː ‖ -ˈduː/ *v* **subdued, subduing** [T] **1** to bring something under your control, often by force: *Napoleon subdued most of Europe.* | *She tried to subdue her anger.* **2** to make a colour or light less bright

sub·dued /səbˈdjuːd ‖ -ˈduːd/ *adj* **1** not as bright or loud as usual: *subdued lighting* | *a subdued voice* **2** unnaturally quiet in behaviour: *You're very subdued – is anything the matter?*

sub·hu·man /sʌbˈhjuːmən/ *adj* behaving in a completely unacceptable way: *Anyone who can do such a terrible thing must be subhuman.*

sub·ject[1] /ˈsʌbdʒɪkt/ *n* **1** something which is being talked or written about: *He always tries to change the subject when I mention how dirty the flat is.* | *The subject of her book is the steel industry.* **2** a word used in grammar to describe the part of the sentence which represents the person or thing that performs the action of the verb or about which something is stated: *In the sentence "Mary hit John", "Mary" is the subject of the sentence.* **3** a branch of knowledge studied in a school, college, or university: *She's taking six subjects in her examinations.* **4** a person who lives in a particular country and owes loyalty to the state or royal leader: *British subjects* | *the King's subjects* | *a subject of the King* **5** something represented in art: *The subject of the painting is the Battle of Waterloo.*

subject[2] *adj* **1** likely to be influenced by something: *The arrangements are subject to change next year.* **2** governed by or dependent on something: *These outdoor concerts are subject to the local health regulations.*

sub·ject[3] /səbˈdʒekt/ *v* [T] to limit someone's freedom by bringing them under your control –**subjection** /-ˈdʒekʃən/ *n* [U]
subject sbdy to sthg *phr v* [T] to make someone experience something, usually something unpleasant: *He subjected us to unpleasant walks in the cold.*

sub·jec·tive /səbˈdʒektɪv/ *adj* strongly influenced by personal feelings rather than facts: *This is a very subjective judgment of her abilities.* –**subjectively** *adv* –**subjectivity** /ˌsʌbdʒekˈtɪvˌti/ *n* [U]

subject to /ˈsʌbdʒɪkt tə, tʊ, tuː/ (*as for* **to**)/ *prep* depending on: *Our plans may change subject to the weather.*

sub·ju·gate /ˈsʌbdʒʊɡeɪt/ *v* **subjugated, subjugating** [T] **1** to conquer and take control of a group of people: *The northern tribes were subjugated in the war.* **2 be subjugated** made less important than something else: *Her needs were always subjugated to those of her parents.* –**subjugation** /ˌsʌbdʒʊˈɡeɪʃən/ *n* [U]

sub·junc·tive /səbˈdʒʌŋktɪv/ *n* a special form (MOOD) of the verb used in certain languages to express doubt, wishes, a dependent verb, etc. –**subjunctive** *adj*

sub·let /sʌbˈlet/ *v* **sublet, sublet, subletting** [I;T] (of a person who rents property from its owner) to rent part of a property to someone else: *He rents the house and sublets a room to a friend.*

sub·lime /səˈblaɪm/ *adj* *lit* very noble or wonderful and causing deep feelings: *sublime music* –**sublimely** *adv*

sub·ma·rine[1] /ˈsʌbməriːn, ˌsʌbməˈriːn/ *n* (also **sub** *infml*) a type of ship which can travel under water

submarine[2] *adj* *tech* growing or used under or in the sea: *submarine plant life* | *a submarine cable*

sub·merge /səbˈmɜːdʒ ‖ -ɜːr-/ *v* **submerged, submerging 1** [I;T] to go or make something go under the surface of water: *The submarine submerged, then rose to the surface.* | *dangerous submerged rocks* | *Submerge the photographic plates in fluid.* **2 submerge yourself in something** to give all your time and attention to something: *He completely submerged himself in local politics.*

sub·mis·sion /səbˈmɪʃən/ *n* **1** [U] an acceptance of someone else's power over you: *He battered his opponent into submission.* **2** [C] the sending of an official paper or plan to someone so they can decide whether to accept it or not: *All submissions must be received by October 30.*

sub·mis·sive /səbˈmɪsɪv/ *adj* gentle and too willing to obey orders –**submissively** *adv* –**submissiveness** *n* [U]

sub·mit /səbˈmɪt/ *v* **tt 1** [I;T] to accept someone else's power over you: *He was losing the fight, but he refused to submit.* **2** [T] to offer an official paper or plan for consideration: *You'll have to submit the proposal to the committee.*

sub·nor·mal /ˌsʌbˈnɔːməl ‖ -ɔːr-/ *adj* having less ability of mind than is usual: *a school for the educationally subnormal*

sub·or·di·nate[1] /səˈbɔːdɪnət ‖ -ɔːr-/ *n fml* a person of a lower rank or position

subordinate[2] *adj* less important than something else: *Everything else is subordinate to the need for conserving heat.* | *a subordinate clause*

sub·or·din·ate[3] /səˈbɔːdɪneɪt ‖ -ɔːr-/ *v* **subordinated, subordinating** *fml* to put in a position of less importance: *He subordinated his ideas to the general good of the group.* –**subordination** /səˌbɔːdɪˈneɪʃən ‖ -ɔːr-/ *n* [U]

sub·poe·na /səˈpiːnə, səb-/ *v* **sub-poenaed, sub-poenaeing** *law* to give someone a written order to attend a court of law –**subpoena** *n* : *He received a subpoena last week.*

sub·scribe /səbˈskraɪb/ *v* **subscribed, subscribing 1 subscribe to** to agree with a particular belief or opinion: *I've never been able to subscribe to such a peculiar theory!* **2** [I] to pay money in order to regularly receive a magazine or newspaper: *I subscribe to a weekly women's magazine.* **3** [I] to regularly give money in support of some good cause: *She subscribes to a society which helps to protect animals.*

sub·scrib·er /səb'skraɪbəʳ/ *n* **1** a person who pays to regularly receive a magazine or newspaper **2** a person who pays for the use of a service over a period of time: *a telephone subscriber* **3** someone who regularly gives money to support a good cause

sub·scrip·tion /səb'skrɪpʃən/ *n* an amount of money given regularly by people who belong to an organization, support a good cause, or regularly receive a particular magazine or newspaper

sub·se·quent /'sʌbsɪkwənt/ *adj fml* existing or coming after something else, sometimes as a result of it: *We made plans for a visit, but subsequent difficulties with the car prevented it.* **–subsequently** *adv* : *An investigation revealed that some letters were taking as long as three days to arrive. Subsequently, a more efficient system was introduced.* | *She claimed to be a wealthy aristocrat, but it subsequently emerged that she was the daughter of a car salesman.*

sub·ser·vi·ent /səb'sɜːviənt || -ɜːr-/ *adj* **1** willing to do what others want (a word used to show disapproval) **2** considered as less important than another thing: *All other considerations were subservient to the need for a quick profit.* **–subserviently** *adv* **–subservience** *n* [U]

sub·side /səb'saɪd/ *v* **subsided, subsiding** [I] **1** (of a building or land) to sink gradually to a lower level **2** to become less violent or strong: *We could only go out once the storm subsided.* | *Pam's anger subsided when I explained the situation.*

sub·si·dence /səb'saɪdəns, 'sʌbsɪdəns/ *n* [U] the sinking of land or buildings to a lower level

sub·sid·i·a·ry[1] /səb'sɪdiəri || -dieri/ *adj* connected with but of less importance than something else: *The secretarial college offers a foreign language as a subsidiary subject.*

subsidiary[2] *n* **subsidiaries** a company which is part of a larger company: *British Tyres is a subsidiary of the British Rubber Company.*

sub·si·dize /'sʌbsɪdaɪz/ *v* **subsidized, subsidizing** (also **subsidise** *BrE*) [T] (of governments or large organizations) to pay part of the costs of something in order to keep prices lower or help an organization: *In our school you can buy subsidized meals.* | *Farmers have been heavily subsidized by the government.* **–subsidization** /ˌsʌbsɪdaɪ'zeɪʃən || -də-/ *n* [U]

sub·si·dy /'sʌbsɪdi/ *n* **subsidies** money paid, by a government or other organization, in order to keep prices lower or support a public service

sub·sist /səb'sɪst/ *v* [I] to stay alive on very small amounts of money or food: *They subsisted on bread and water.* **–subsistence** *n* [U]: *subsistence farming*

sub·son·ic /ˌsʌb'sɒnɪk || -'sɑː-/ *adj* flying very fast but below the speed of sound: *subsonic aircraft*

sub·stance /'sʌbstəns/ *n* **1** [C] a material or type of matter: *radioactive substances* | *Heroin is an illegal substance.* **2** [U] *fml* the truth: *There is no substance*

in these rumours. **3 the substance of** the most important part of what someone says: *The substance of their theory is given in the last chapter.*

sub·stan·dard /ˌsʌb'stændəd◄ || -ərd/ *adj* below an acceptable standard: *I'm afraid this work is substandard.*

sub·stan·tial /səb'stænʃəl/ *adj* **1** large in size or value: *The new director made substantial changes.* | *He earns a substantial amount of money.* **2** large and strongly made: *a substantial wooden desk*

sub·stan·tial·ly /səb'stænʃəli/ *adv* **1** mainly or generally: *There are one or two differences, but the plans are substantially the same.* **2** by a large amount: *Conditions in the prison have improved substantially.*

sub·stan·ti·ate /səb'stænʃieɪt/ *v* **substantiated, substantiating** [T] *fml* to prove the truth of something: *Can you substantiate your claim?* **–substantiation** /səbˌstænʃi'eɪʃən/ *n* [U]

sub·sti·tute[1] /'sʌbstɪtjuːt || -tuːt/ *n* **1** a person or thing acting or used in place of another: *If you don't have butter, you could use margarine as a substitute.* | *Our teacher was ill, so we were taught by a substitute.* **2 no substitute** a phrase used when you believe something cannot be used instead of something else in a way that is satisfactory: *Expensive toys are no substitute for a parent's love.*

substitute[2] *v* **substituted, substituting** **1** [T] to use something or someone in place of another: *They don't like potatoes, so we substituted rice.* **2** [I] to be used instead of something or someone else: *If Mary doesn't arrive I'll have to substitute for her.* **–substitution** /ˌsʌbstɪ'tjuːʃən || -'tuː-/ *n* [C;U]

sub·ter·fuge /'sʌbtəfjuːdʒ || -ər-/ *n* [C;U] a trick or dishonest way of doing something

sub·ter·ra·ne·an /ˌsʌbtə'reɪniən◄/ *adj* underground: *subterranean rivers*

sub·ti·tles /'sʌbˌtaɪtlz/ *n* [pl] words printed over a film in a foreign language to translate what is being said: *a French film with English subtitles*

sub·tle /'sʌtl/ *adj* **subtler, subtlest** **1** cleverly indirect in getting what you want: *He wasn't exactly subtle in the way he offered us a bribe.* | *a subtle plan* **2** very clever and good at noticing fine details: *a subtle mind* **3** pleasant and delicate: *a subtle taste* | *a subtle purple* **4** not easily noticed or explained: *There's been a subtle change in their relationship since she started working.* **–subtly** *adv* : *subtly different*

sub·tle·ty /'sʌtlti/ *n* **1** [U] the ability to notice fine details and to use them in a clever way: *He argued his case with great subtlety.* **2** [sing] the quality of not being easily noticed or explained: *The film is remarkable for the subtlety of its images.* **3** [C] an idea, thought, or detail which is not easily noticed: *I think the translator missed some of the subtleties of the original.*

sub·tract /səb'trækt/ *v* [T] to do a sum by taking one number or amount away from another; for example if you subtract 10 from 30 you get 20 **–subtraction** /-'trækʃən/ *n* [C;U]

sub·urb /'sʌbɜːb || -ɜːrb/ *n* an outer area of a town or city, where people live: *a suburb of London* | *I live in the suburbs.* **–suburban** /sə'bɜːbən || -ɜːr-/ *adj* : *suburban living*

sub·ur·bi·a /sə'bɜːbiə || -ɜːr-/ *n* [U] the suburbs (a word often used to show disapproval)

sub·ver·sive /səb'vɜːsɪv || -ɜːr-/ *adj* aiming to destroy established ideas and those in power: *The government wants to ban this magazine because*

SPELLING NOTE

Words with the sound / s /, may be spelt **c-**, like **city**, or **ps-**, like **psychology**.

they consider it to be subversive. | *a subversive influence* **-subversive** *n* : *The peace campaigners were regarded as subversives by the police.* **-subversively** *adv* **-subversiveness** *n* [U]

sub·vert /səbˈvɜːt ‖ -ˈɜːrt/ *v* [T] *fml* to try to destroy the power and influence of a government or established ideas **-subversion** /-ˈvɜːʃən ‖ -ɜr- / *n* [U]

sub·way /ˈsʌbweɪ/ *n* **1** a path under a road or railway by which it can be crossed safely **2** the usual American word for an underground railway: *It's quicker to go by subway.*

suc·ceed /səkˈsiːd/ *v* **1** [I] to manage to do something: *If you try hard, you'll succeed.* | *Jan finally succeeded in passing her driving test.* **2 succeed in doing something** to manage to do something: *He succeeded in putting out the fire.* **3** [I] to be done or completed with a favourable result: *If the plan succeeds, he'll be very wealthy.* –compare FAIL **4** [T] to follow after something in time: *A silence succeeded his words.* –compare PRECEDE **5** [T] to be the next person to get a particular position or job: *Mr White will succeed the chairman when he resigns.*

suc·cess /səkˈses/ *n* **1** [U] the act of getting the result you aimed for: *We had no success in finding a new flat.* | *a low success rate* **2** [C] a person or thing that is very favourably accepted or reaches a high position: *His new play was a great success.* | *I've no doubt Joyce will make a success of her new business.*

suc·cess·ful /səkˈsesfəl/ *adj* **1** having got the result you aimed for: *My attempt to make a cake wasn't successful.* | *successful peace talks* **2** having reached a high position, for example in your job: *a successful journalist* **3** very favourably accepted: *a very successful opera* –opposite **unsuccessful** **-successfully** *adv*

suc·ces·sion /səkˈseʃən/ *n* **1** [C] a number of people or things following each other closely: *A succession of visitors interrupted his work.* **2** [U] the act of being the next person with the right to a particular position: *If the king dies the succession passes to his son.* **3 in succession** following each other: *His words came out in quick succession.* | *We went to Oxford for the third weekend in succession.*

suc·ces·sive /səkˈsesɪv/ *adj* following each other: *He was late for work on three successive days.* **-successively** *adv*

suc·ces·sor /səkˈsesər/ *n* a person who takes someone's job or position when they leave: *The director's successor starts next week.*

suc·cinct /səkˈsɪŋkt/ *adj* clearly expressed in a few words **-succinctly** *adv* **-succinctness** *n* [U]

suc·cour[1] /ˈsʌkər/ *n* (succor *AmE*) [U] *fml & lit* help given in difficulty

succour[2] *v* [T] *fml & lit* to give help to someone in difficulty

suc·cu·lent /ˈsʌkjʊlənt/ *adj* pleasantly juicy (a word used to express approval): *a succulent fruit* **-succulence** *n* [U]

suc·cumb /səˈkʌm/ *v* [I] *fml* **1** to stop opposing a desire or strong influence: *He eventually succumbed to our offer to buy his company.* **2** to suffer the bad effects of an illness: *She succumbed to cholera and died.*

such /sʌtʃ/ *predeterminer, det, pron* **1** so great, or to so great a degree: *Don't be such a fool!* | *They're such nice people.* **2** like the one or ones mentioned: *We spent the money on knives, forks, plates, and other such things.* | *He shouted "Get out!" or some such remark.* **3 such as** for example: *You should take up a sport such as tennis or badminton.*

■ USAGE Compare **such** and **so**. **Such** often comes in the pattern **such** followed by an adjective, followed by a noun: **such** *interesting people.* **So** comes before an adjective alone: *The people are* **so** *interesting,* or before *much, many, few:* **so** *much money* | **so** *many people* | **so** *few inquiries*

such·like /ˈsʌtʃlaɪk/ *pron,determiner infml* things of the kind already mentioned: *Do you enjoy plays, films, and suchlike?* | *tennis, cricket, and suchlike summer sports*

suck /sʌk/ *v* **1** [I;T] to draw liquid into your mouth by using your lips and the muscles at the side of your mouth: *She was sucking milk through a straw.* **2** [I;T] to hold something in your mouth and move your tongue around it, for example in order to eat it: *Tim's always sucking a sweet.* | *The baby was sucking its thumb.* **3** [T+adv/prep] to draw something forcefully in a particular direction: *Powerful currents sucked the boat under water.* **4 be sucked into something** to become unwillingly part of something unpleasant: *He was sucked into a life of crime.*

suck·er /ˈsʌkər/ *n* **1** the organ on some animals or insects by which they can hold on to surfaces: *Flies have suckers on their feet.* **2** a small piece of rubber which sticks to a surface: *The hook is attached to the wall by means of a sucker.* **3** *infml* a foolish person who is easily cheated or deceived: *You're a sucker to believe all his stories!*

suck·le /ˈsʌkəl/ *v* suckled, suckling **1** [T] to feed a baby or young animal with milk from the breast **2** [I] (of a baby or young animal) to feed by sucking from the breast

suc·tion /ˈsʌkʃən/ *n* [U] **1** the process of removing air or liquid from a container or space so that another substance is drawn in by the resulting pressure: *Dust is drawn into a vacuum cleaner by suction.* **2** the process of making one surface stick to another by removing the air between them: *The toy sticks to tables through suction.*

sud·den /ˈsʌdn/ *adj* **1** happening or coming quickly and unexpectedly: *a sudden illness* | *a sudden increase in the price of petrol* **2 all of a sudden** unexpectedly and quickly, so that you are surprised: *All of a sudden, the lights went out.* **-suddenly** *adv* **-suddenness** *n* [U]

suds /sʌdz/ *n* (also **soapsuds**) [pl] the bubbles formed by soap when mixed with water

sue /sjuː ‖ suː/ *v* sued, suing [I;T] to bring a legal claim against someone because of some loss or damage you have suffered: *If you don't return our property, we'll sue.* | *Mr James sued him for libel.*

suede /sweɪd/ *n* (also **suède**) [U] soft leather with a slightly rough surface: *suede shoes*

su·et /ˈsuːɪt, ˈsjuːɪt ‖ ˈsuː-/ *n* [U] hard fat from an animal, used in cooking

suf·fer /ˈsʌfər/ *v* **1** [I] to experience pain, difficulty, or loss: *He died quickly, he didn't suffer very much.* | *The economy is bound to suffer if inflation increases.* | *She suffered terribly when her marriage broke up.* **2** [T] to experience a situation in which something painful or unpleasant happens to you: *If you break the law you must be prepared to suffer the consequences.* | *He suffered the humiliation of being forced to resign.* | *Doctors suffer a lot of stress at work.* **3** [I] to become gradually worse in quality through lack of care and attention: *He started to drink a lot and his work suffered.*

suffer from sthg *phr v* [T] to experience something painful or unpleasant either habitually or over a long period of time: *Pete's always suffered from*

headaches. | *The company has suffered from inefficient management.*

suf·fer·ance /'sʌfərəns/ *n* **on sufferance** with permission, though not welcomed: *He's only here on sufferance.*

suf·fer·er /'sʌfərəʳ/ *n* a person who suffers from a particular illness: *headache sufferers*

suf·fer·ing /'sʌfərɪŋ/ *n* [C;U] great pain or difficulty which someone experiences: *There was a great deal of suffering during the war.* | *She never complained about her sufferings.*

suf·fice /sə'faɪs/ *v* **sufficed, sufficing** [I; not in progressive forms] *fml* to be enough: *Her income suffices for her needs.*

suf·fi·cien·cy /sə'fɪʃənsi/ *n* [sing] *fml* enough of something for a particular need or purpose

suf·fi·cient /sə'fɪʃənt/ *adj* enough for a particular need or purpose; a rather formal word for **enough**: *The hospital have sufficient supplies of the drug.* | *This money should be sufficient to buy new furniture.* –**sufficiently** *adv* : *He wasn't sufficiently experienced to do the job.*

suf·fix /'sʌfɪks/ *n* a letter or group of letters that is put at the end of a word in order to change its meaning or use; for example if you add the suffix *-ness* to *kind* you get the word *kindness* –compare PREFIX

suf·fo·cate /'sʌfəkeɪt/ *v* **suffocated, suffocating** [I;T] to die or make someone die because of lack of air –**suffocation** /ˌsʌfə'keɪʃən/ *n* [U]

suf·frage /'sʌfrɪdʒ/ *n* [U] the right to vote for the government of your choice

suf·fra·gette /ˌsʌfrə'dʒet/ *n* a woman in Britain in the early 20th century who was a member of a group which tried to obtain for women the right to vote

sug·ar¹ /'ʃʊgəʳ/ *n* [U] a sweet white or brown substance obtained from plants and used in food: *I take sugar in tea, but not in coffee.*

sugar² *v* [T] to put sugar in: *Did you sugar my tea?*

sug·ar·y /'ʃʊgəri/ *adj* **1** containing sugar **2** too nice or kind to be sincere: *a poem full of sugary sentiment*

sug·gest /sə'dʒest ‖ səg'dʒest/ *v* [T] **1** to give someone an idea to consider: *I'd like to suggest an alternative plan.* | *I suggest that we leave now.*

□ USEFUL PATTERNS to suggest something; to suggest doing something; to suggest that someone (should) do something

2 to say that someone or something is good for a particular purpose because you know from your own personal experience: *Can you suggest a good hotel?* | *She suggested Bill for the job.* **3** to make a new thought or idea appear in someone's mind: *I'm not suggesting that you are responsible for the problem.* **4** to give signs of something: *Her expression suggested anger.* | *The figures suggest an improvement in health care.*

sug·ges·ti·ble /sə'dʒestɪbəl ‖ səg-/ *adj* easily influenced (used of people): *She's at a very suggestible age.*

sug·ges·tion /sə'dʒestʃən ‖ səg-/ *n* **1** [C] an idea given for consideration: *The teacher made some useful suggestions to help us in the examination.* | *Can I make a suggestion?* **2** [U] the act of saying what someone might do in a particular situation: *I went*

there on your suggestion. **3** [sing] a slight sign: *She speaks with a suggestion of a foreign accent.* | *There are suggestions that she might change her mind.*

sug·ges·tive /sə'dʒestɪv ‖ səg-/ *adj* **1** which makes you think of something: *The painting is suggestive of spring.* **2** showing thoughts of sex: *a suggestive remark* –**suggestively** *adv*

su·i·cid·al /ˌsuːɪˈsaɪdl◂, ˌsjuː- ‖ ˌsuː-/ *adj* **1** wanting to kill yourself: *He was feeling positively suicidal.* | *It was a hospital ward for suicidal patients.* **2** likely to lead to death or destruction: *They made a suicidal attempt to climb the mountain in a snowstorm.* –**suicidally** *adv*

su·i·cide /'suːɪsaɪd, 'sjuː- ‖ 'suː-/ *n* **1** [C;U] the act of killing yourself: *She tried to commit suicide.* **2** [U] a course of action someone chooses to follow which destroys their position in society: *It would be political suicide to hold an election now.*

suit¹ /suːt, sjuːt ‖ suːt/ *n* **1** a set of clothes made of the same material, including a short coat with trousers or skirt: *a tweed suit/a dark suit* –see picture on page 50 **2** a set of clothes used for a particular purpose: *a bathing suit* **3** one of the four kinds of cards used to play a game of cards **4** –see LAWSUIT

suit² *v* [T] **1** to be convenient or acceptable: *It's a small house but it suits our needs.* | *Would it suit you if I arrived in the evening?* **2** to match or look good on someone: *That colour doesn't suit him.* **3** to have the right qualities or be of the right kind for something: *As a couple, Steve and Mary are ideally suited.* **4** **suit yourself** *infml* to do what you like without thinking too much about other people: *"I don't feel like going out tonight." "Suit yourself."*

sui·ta·ble /'suːtəbəl, 'sjuː- ‖ 'suː-/ *adj* right or acceptable for a particular situation or purpose: *Is she suitable for the job?* | *It's a flat suitable for a large family.* –opposite **unsuitable** –**suitably** *adv*

suit·case /'suːtkeɪs, 'sjuːt- ‖ 'suːt-/ *n* a large flat box with handles which you use to carry clothes and possessions when travelling

suite /swiːt/ *n* **1** a set of rooms in a hotel **2** a set of matching furniture for a room: *a suite of dining-room furniture* **3** a piece of music with several loosely connected parts

sui·tor /'suːtəʳ, 'sjuː- ‖ 'suː-/ *n fml* a man wishing to marry a particular woman

sulk /sʌlk/ *v* [I] to be silently bad-tempered for a time because you are angry about something: *My son sulked all afternoon because I didn't buy him that toy train.* –**sulk** *n* : *She's in one of her sulks again!* –**sulky** *adj* **sulkier, sulkiest** –**sulkily** *adv*

sul·len /'sʌlən/ *adj* **1** silently showing dislike and bad temper: *She's a rather sullen-looking woman.* | *He looked at me with sullen resentment.* **2** dark and unpleasant: *a sullen sky* –**sullenly** *adv* –**sullenness** *n* [U]

sul·phur /'sʌlfəʳ/ *n* (**sulfur** *AmE*) [U] a yellow substance which smells unpleasant

sul·tan /'sʌltən/ *n* a ruler in some Muslim countries, especially in the past

sul·ta·na /sʊl'tɑːnə ‖ -'tænə/ *n* a small seedless dried GRAPE

sul·try /'sʌltri/ *adj* **sultrier, sultriest 1** hot and uncomfortable (used of weather) **2** showing strong sexual attraction or desire (used of a woman or her appearance): *a sultry smile* –**sultriness** *n* [U]

sum¹ /sʌm/ *n* **1** a simple calculation, such as adding or dividing: *The children learn to do sums at school.* **2** an amount of money: *I've spent a large sum of money on repairing the car.* | *Huge sums of money were wasted by the previous government.*

sum²

sum up phr v -mm- **1** [I;T **sum** sthg ↔ **up**] to list the main points of a formal conversation or argument that has gone before: *John, would you sum up, please?* | *Let's sum up the main arguments on each side.* **2** [T **sum** sbdy/sthg ↔ **up**] to describe a person or thing in a few words, or to make a quick judgment of them: *He summed up the situation immediately, and decided not to become involved.* **3** **to sum up** you can use this expression when you are going to give the main ideas from a talk, a piece of writing, or a meeting at the end of it: *...then in 1991 she opened her fiftieth shop. To sum up, she's an example of a thoroughly successful business woman.*

sum·mar·ize /ˈsʌməraɪz/ v **summarized, summarizing** (also **summarise** BrE) [T] to make a short account which includes only the main points out of something longer

sum·ma·ry¹ /ˈsʌməri/ n **summaries 1** a short account of something giving only the main points: *Here is a summary of the article.* **2 in summary** a phrase used to show that you are going to list the main points of the discussion or argument that has gone before

summary² adj fml done at once, without considering the matter further: *Any employee caught stealing faces summary dismissal.* –**summarily** adv

sum·mer /ˈsʌməʳ/ n (also **Summer**) [C;U] the season between spring and autumn when the sun is hot: *It was a beautiful summer.* | *summer clothes* –**summery** adj : *a summery dress*

sum·mer·house /ˈsʌməhaʊs ‖ -ər-/ n a small building in a garden where you can sit in warm weather

sum·mer·time /ˈsʌmətaɪm ‖ -ər-/ n [U] the period of summer

summing-up /ˌ··ˈ·/ n **summings-up** a speech giving the main points of a discussion or argument that has gone before, especially by a judge at the end of a court case

sum·mit /ˈsʌmɪt/ n **1** the top of a mountain: *After a 3 hour climb, we reached the summit.* **2** [sing] the highest level: *She has reached the summit of her career.* **3** a meeting between heads of state: *The leaders of six nations are attending today's summit in Moscow.*

sum·mon /ˈsʌmən/ v [T] fml to order someone to come to a certain place: *I was summoned to the manager's office.*

summon up sthg phr v [T] to find a certain quality, especially courage, inside yourself when you need it: *She summoned up all her strength and kicked the door open.*

sum·mons¹ /ˈsʌmənz/ n an official order to appear somewhere, especially in a court of law

summons² v [T] to give an official order to someone to appear in court

sump·tu·ous /ˈsʌmptʃuəs/ adj grand and expensive: *a sumptuous feast* –**sumptuously** adv –**sumptuousness** n [U]

sun¹ /sʌn/ n **1 the sun** the burning star in the sky, from which the earth receives light and heat **2** [C;U] light and heat from the sun: *Don't sit in the sun for too long.* | *Let's lie outside and get some sun.* **3** [C] a star round which other bodies turn

sun² v -nn- [T] **sun yourself** to sit or lie in the sun: *She was sunning herself in the garden.*

sun·bathe /ˈsʌnbeɪð/ v **sunbathed, sunbathing** [I] to sit or lie in strong sunlight in order to make your body brown –see BATH² (USAGE) –**sunbather** n

sun·beam /ˈsʌnbiːm/ n a thin line of sunlight

sun·burn /ˈsʌnbɜːn ‖ -ɜːrn/ n [U] sore, red skin from spending too much time in strong sunlight –**sunburnt** adj

sun·dae /ˈsʌndeɪ ‖ -di/ n a dish made from ice cream and fruit

Sun·day /ˈsʌndi/ n (also **Sun.**) the day between Saturday and Monday

Sunday school /ˈ·· ·/ n [C;U] religious education for Christian children on a Sunday

sun·dial /ˈsʌndaɪəl/ n an apparatus, used especially in former times, which shows the time when the sun shines according to where the shadow of a pointer falls

sun·down /ˈsʌndaʊn/ n see SUNSET

sun·dry /ˈsʌndri/ adj [only before a noun] various: *books, pens, and sundry other items*

sun·flow·er /ˈsʌnˌflaʊəʳ/ n a plant with a large yellow flower, and seeds which are used to make cooking oil

sung /sʌŋ/ v the past participle of SING

sun·glass·es /ˈsʌnˌɡlɑːsɪz ‖ -ˌɡlæ-/ n [pl] glasses with dark glass in them which you wear to protect your eyes from the sun

sunk /sʌŋk/ v the past participle of SINK

sunk·en /ˈsʌŋkən/ adj **1** below the surface, especially of the water: *a sunken ship* **2** below the surrounding surface: *sunken eyes*

sun·lamp /ˈsʌnlæmp/ n (also **sunray lamp** /ˈsʌnreɪ ˌlæmp/) a lamp which you can use to make your skin brown

sun·light /ˈsʌnlaɪt/ n [U] natural light from the sun

sun·lit /ˈsʌnˌlɪt/ adj brightly lit by the sun

sun·ny /ˈsʌni/ adj **sunnier, sunniest 1** full of bright sunlight: *a sunny room* | *a sunny day* **2** cheerful: *a sunny smile* –**sunnily** adv

sun·rise /ˈsʌnraɪz/ n [C;U] the time in the morning when the sun appears: *We got up at sunrise.*

sun·set /ˈsʌnset/ n **1** (also **sundown**) [U] the time when the sun disappears as night begins: *They stopped work at sunset.* **2** [C] the colours that the sun leaves in the sky as it disappears in the evening: *What a beautiful sunset.*

sun·shade /ˈsʌnʃeɪd/ n see PARASOL

sun·shine /ˈsʌnʃaɪn/ n [U] light and heat from the sun: *I was sitting in the garden, enjoying the sunshine.*

sun·stroke /ˈsʌnstrəʊk/ n (also **heatstroke**) [U] an illness caused by spending too much time in the hot sun: *If you don't come inside soon, you'll get sunstroke!*

sun·tan /ˈsʌntæn/ n (also **tan**) skin which has turned brown in the hot sun: *I'm trying to get a suntan.* –**suntanned** adj

su·per /ˈsuːpəʳ, ˈsjuː-‖ ˈsuː-/ adj **1** infml wonderful: *a super cook* | *The party was super!* **2** very large or high quality: *Oil is carried in super tankers.*

su·per·an·nu·at·ed /ˌsuːpərˈænjueɪtɪd, ˌsjuː- ‖ ˌsuː-/ adj fml old and not as useful as in the past: *superannuated ideas*

su·per·an·nu·a·tion /ˌsuːpərænjuˈeɪʃən, ˌsjuː- ‖ ˌsuː-/ n [U] fml money paid to provide an income for when you are too old to work

su·perb /sjuːˈpɜːb, suː-‖ suːˈpɜːrb/ adj excellent: *The food was superb.* –**superbly** adv

su·per·cil·i·ous /ˌsuːpəˈsɪliəs, ˌsjuː- ‖ ˌsuːpər-/ adj showing that you think other people are less important than you are (a word used to show disapproval): –**superciliously** adv –**superciliousness** n [U]

su·per·fi·cial /ˌsuːpəˈfɪʃəl, ˌsjuː- ‖ ˌsuːpər-/ adj 1 on or near the surface: *Despite all the blood, they were only superficial cuts.* 2 showing no deep understanding or serious thought (a word used to show disapproval): *His understanding of scientific laws is very superficial.* | *She's a rather superficial person.* –**superficially** adv –**superficiality** ˌsuːpəfɪʃˈælʒti, ˌsjuː- ‖ ˌsuːpər-/ n [U]

su·per·flu·ous /suːˈpɜːfluəs, sjuː- ‖ suːˈpɜːr-/ adj not necessary, or more than is needed –**superfluously** adv –**superfluousness** n [U]

su·per·hu·man /ˌsuːpəˈhjuːmən, ˌsjuː- ‖ ˌsuːpər-/ adj beyond usual human powers: *superhuman strength*

su·per·im·pose /ˌsuːpərɪmˈpəʊz, ˌsjuː-, ˌsuː-/ v superimposed, superimposing [T] to put something on top of something else, but so that you can still see what is below: *They superimposed one film image on another.*

su·per·in·tend /ˌsuːpərɪnˈtend, ˌsjuː- ‖ ˌsuː-/ v [T] to be in charge of and direct an activity

su·per·in·tend·ent /ˌsuːpərɪnˈtendənt, ˌsjuː- ‖ ˌsuː-/ n 1 a person who is in charge of a place or activity 2 a British police officer of high rank

su·pe·ri·or¹ /suːˈpɪəriəʳ, sjuː- ‖ sʊ-/ adj 1 of higher rank, class, or quality: *He is superior to me at work.* | *This is superior wool.* –opposite **inferior** 2 showing that you consider yourself better than other people: *a superior smile* –**superiority** /suːˌpɪəriˈɒrʃti, sjuː- ‖ sʊˌpɪəriˈɔː-, -ˈɑː-/ n [U]

superior² n a person of higher rank: *I'll have to ask my superiors about that.* –compare INFERIOR

su·per·la·tive¹ /suːˈpɜːlətɪv, sjuː- ‖ sʊˈpɜːr-/ n the form of a word which expresses more of a quality than anything else: *The superlative of 'good' is 'best'.* –compare COMPARATIVE –see Study Note on page 99

superlative² adj fml 1 excellent: *This wine is of superlative quality.* 2 expressing more of a quality than anything else: *the superlative form of the adjective*

su·per·man /ˈsuːpəmæn, ˈsjuː- ‖ ˈsuːpər-/ n supermen /-mən/ a man, usually in a story, who has much greater powers of mind and body than other people

su·per·mar·ket /ˈsuːpəˌmɑːkʒt, ˈsjuː- ‖ ˈsuːpərˌmɑːr-/ n a large shop where you collect the food and other goods you need, and pay for them all on your way out

su·per·nat·u·ral /ˌsuːpəˈnætʃərəl, ˌsjuː- ‖ ˌsuːpər-/ adj not explained by natural laws but by powers which cannot be completely understood: *She has supernatural powers which she uses to harm her enemies.* –compare UNNATURAL –**supernaturally** adv

su·per·sede /ˌsuːpəˈsiːd, ˌsjuː- ‖ ˌsuːpər-/ v superseded, superseding [T] to put something else in the place of something which is no longer satisfactory: *That computer has now been superseded by a smaller one.*

su·per·son·ic /ˌsuːpəˈsɒnɪk◂, ˌsjuː- ‖ ˌsuːpərˈsɑː-/ adj faster than the speed of sound: *a supersonic aircraft* –compare SUBSONIC

su·per·star /ˈsuːpəstɑːʳ, ˈsjuː- ‖ ˈsuːpər-/ n an extremely famous performer, especially a singer or a film actor

---

SPELLING NOTE

Words with the sound / s /, may be spelt **c-**, like **city**, or **ps-**, like **psychology**.

---

su·per·sti·tion /ˌsuːpəˈstɪʃən, ˌsjuː- ‖ ˌsuːpər-/ n [C;U] a belief which is not based on reason: *The 14th floor is immediately above the 12th because of superstition about the number 13.* –**superstitious** adj : *a superstitious fear of black cats* –**superstitiously** adv

su·per·struc·ture /ˈsuːpəˌstrʌktʃəʳ, ˈsjuː- ‖ ˈsuːpər-/ n something built above the main part of a building or ship

su·per·vise /ˈsuːpəvaɪz, ˈsjuː- ‖ ˈsuːpər-/ v supervised, supervising [I;T] to make sure that work or some other activity is done properly: *Who is going to supervise the examination?* –**supervisor** n –**supervisory** adj –**supervision** /ˌsuːpəˈvɪʒən, ˌsjuː- ‖ ˌsuːpər-/ n [U] : *The work was done under my supervision.*

sup·per /ˈsʌpəʳ/ n [C;U] the last meal of the day –see DINNER (USAGE)

sup·plant /səˈplɑːnt ‖ səˈplænt/ v [T] fml to take the place of another person or thing

sup·ple /ˈsʌpəl/ adj bending or moving easily: *You need to be supple to be a good gymnast.* | *a supple material* –**suppleness** n [U]

sup·ple·ment¹ /ˈsʌplʒmənt/ n a thing which is added to something else: *The colour supplement is inside the main part of the newspaper.*

sup·ple·ment² /ˈsʌplʒment/ v [T] to add something to another thing: *He supplements his wages by working as a gardener at weekends.*

sup·ple·men·ta·ry /ˌsʌplʒˈmentəri◂/ adj additional: *This water supply is supplementary to the main system.*

sup·pli·er /səˈplaɪəʳ/ n a person or firm that provides something, especially goods: *We're expecting a delivery from the suppliers.*

sup·ply¹ /səˈplaɪ/ v supplied, supplying [T] to provide something: *The council supplies free books to schools.* | *All employees are supplied with a uniform.*
□ USEFUL PATTERNS to supply something to someone; to supply someone with something

supply² n supplies 1 [C] an amount of something that can be used: *a large supply of food* 2 in short supply difficult to find: *Meat is in short supply at the moment.* 3 supplies things that are necessary for daily life, especially for a fixed period of time: *The climb will take a week, so you'll need to carry a lot of supplies with you.* 4 [U] an amount of something that can be produced and provided: *The stability of the economy depends on a balance of supply and demand.* 5 [C] a system of providing something: *We've had problems with the water supply.*

supply and de·mand /·,· · · ·ˈ·/ n [U] the relation between the amount of goods for sale and the amount that customers want to buy, which has a strong influence on prices in a free market system

sup·port¹ /səˈpɔːt ‖ -ɔːrt/ v [T] 1 to help, encourage, or approve of someone's ideas or actions because you want them to succeed: *Do you support the union's demand for higher wages?* | *Which football team do you support?* 2 to provide money or food for a person or animal to live on: *She has a large family to support.* | *Fields like these support thousands of different insects.* 3 to bear the weight of a person or thing: *Can those shelves support so many books?* 4 to help someone keep their balance: *Give your grandfather your arm and support him up those steps.* 5 to help show that something is true: *I've found historical evidence to support my ideas.*

support² n 1 [U] encouragement and help: *Thank you for all the support you have given us.* 2 **in support of** to show approval of a person, idea or action: *We are demonstrating in support of animal rights.* 3 [U] money which is provided for a person to live on or to help a business: *When his parents died he was left with no means of support.* | *Financial support to the airline will protect jobs for a while.* 4 [C] something which bears the weight of something else: *The supports under the bridge are beginning to crack.*

sup·port·er /səˈpɔːtəʳ ‖ -ɔːr-/ n a person who gives help, encouragement, or approval to a person, group, idea, or activity: *Liverpool supporters danced in the street after the match.* | *He's a loyal supporter of the Prime Minister and her policies.*

sup·pose¹ /səˈpəuz/ v supposed, supposing 1 [+(that)] to consider something to be probably true: *I suppose he's gone home.* | *Do you suppose she'll agree?* 2 **I suppose** a phrase used to show **a** that you believe something although you do not want to believe it or you are still not certain: *I suppose you're right.* **b** that you will probably agree to something although you do not like the idea: *Well, he could come with us, I suppose.* **c** that you are making a guess based on the information you have: *He must have lived here for about 3 years, I suppose.* 3 **be supposed to: a** to be expected to do something because of duty, law or custom: *You're supposed to wear a seat belt in the car.* | *We're not supposed to smoke in here.* **b** infml to be generally considered to be: *It is supposed to be a really good film.* 4 **suppose, supposing a** you use these words when you want someone to consider a particular situation and the results that would follow from it: *Suppose he refuses to help us. What are we going to do then?* | *Supposing he refused to help us. What would we do then?* **b** you can use these words when you are suggesting something: *"Suppose we meet at five o'clock. How would that be?" "Well, I think that's leaving it a bit late. Supposing we say half past four."*

suppose² conj (also **supposing**) if: *Suppose she finds out, what would we do then?*

sup·pos·ed·ly /səˈpəuzɪ̣dli/ adv according to what people believe: *Supposedly, she's a rich woman.*

sup·po·si·tion /ˌsʌpəˈzɪʃən/ n fml [C;U] a guess, or something that is believed to be true because it is probable: *The Minister's claims for the economy are pure supposition.*

sup·press /səˈpres/ v [T] 1 to stop something becoming known: *News of his arrest was suppressed by the police.* 2 to control your feelings so that they are not expressed: *She smiled, suppressing her anger.* 3 to put an end to an activity, often by force: *Armed opposition to the government was quickly suppressed.* –**suppression** /-ˈpreʃən/ n [U]

su·prem·a·cy /səˈpreməsi/ n [U] power which is greater than any other: *The country's supremacy at sea was unchallenged for fifty years.*

su·preme /suːˈpriːm, sjuː-, sə- ‖ suː-, suː-/ adj 1 highest in position and usually the most powerful: *A final decision on the case will be made by the Supreme Court.* 2 greatest or highest in degree: *This matter is of supreme importance.* –**supremely** adv

sur·charge /ˈsɜːtʃɑːdʒ ‖ ˈsɜːrtʃɑːrdʒ/ n an amount that you must pay in addition to the usual amount: *The surcharge on airline tickets is to cover increased oil prices.*

sure¹ /ʃuəʳ/ adj 1 [never before a noun] certain about something: *I think so, but I'm not absolutely sure.* | *Are you quite sure that this is the right bus?* | *I'm not sure whether he's telling the truth.* | *I'm not quite sure about that.* □ USEFUL PATTERNS be sure of/about something; be sure who, why, whether, etc.; be sure that... 2 [never before a noun] certain to happen: *It's sure to rain while we're out.* 3 **sure of something** certain to get something: *He can be sure of a warm welcome.* 4 **sure of someone** certain that someone can be trusted: *You can be quite sure of John. When he says he'll do something, he does it.* 5 **make sure: a** to find out for certain: *I'll just make sure that the car's locked.* **b** to arrange that something will certainly happen: *Make sure you get here before midnight.* 6 giving information that is certain: *It's a sure sign that he's angry with me.* 7 **sure of yourself** confident about your own abilities, actions and opinions 8 **Be sure...** Don't forget to do something: *Be sure to take an umbrella.* 9 **sure enough** as expected –**sureness** n [U]

■ USAGE Compare **sure** and **certain**. We can use **sure** in the same way as **certain** in sentences like these: *I'm* **sure**/**certain** *that he'll come tomorrow.* | *He's* **sure**/**certain** *to come tomorrow.* But we cannot use **sure** after **it** in sentences like this: *It is* **certain** *that he'll come tomorrow.*

sure² adv 1 AmE infml certainly: *Sure I will.* | *She sure is tall.* 2 **for sure** certainly true: *She won't lend you any money; that's for sure.*

sure·ly /ˈʃuəli ‖ ˈʃuərli/ adv 1 a word used to show you believe someone to be true or correct: *She's surely one of the greatest women of her time.* 2 a word used to express surprise that something might not be true: *Surely you remember him?* | *You know him, surely?* 3 AmE of course

■ USAGE In British English **surely** is often used to show in an indirect way that you disapprove of something or that you disagree with something which has been said: **Surely** *he's finished by now!* (= he's too slow?) | **Surely** *you didn't mean that.* (= I don't agree with what you said) | **Surely** *she'll write and let us know.* (= I don't agree with your suggestion that she won't write) If you do not want to give this meaning, use **I'm sure** instead: **I am sure** *he's finished by now.* (= I believe he has finished) | **I'm sure** *she'll write.* (= I believe she will write)

surf¹ /sɜːf ‖ sɜːrf/ n [U] white water formed by waves when they break on the shore or on rocks

surf² v [I] to ride on a special narrow board over breaking waves: *We could take our surfboards to the beach and go surfing.* –**surfer** n

sur·face¹ /ˈsɜːfɪ̣s ‖ ˈsɜːr-/ 1 the outside or top of something: *the earth's surface* | *Don't scratch the surface of the table!* | *The insects hovered on the surface of the pond.* 2 what is clear in a situation and not hidden: *The level of staff unhappiness only came to the surface when people started leaving the company.* 3 **on the surface** judging quickly, without careful thought or a deeper understanding: *On the surface it seems a good idea.* [RELATED PHRASES **below the surface, beneath the surface:** *Below the surface he's a very unhappy man.*]

surface² v surfaced, surfacing 1 [I] to come to the top of a body of water: *She surfaced to take in air.* 2 [I] to appear again after time has passed: *We heard no news of him for years, and then he surfaced in Hong Kong.* 3 [T] to cover something with hard material: *The roads are being surfaced.*

surface³ adj **surface mail** letters and parcels that travel by land and sea

sur·feit /ˈsɜːfɪt ‖ ˈsɜːr-/ n fml too large an amount, especially of food: *This year farmers have produced a surfeit* **of** *corn.* | *He's suffering from a surfeit* **of** *chocolate.*

surge¹ /sɜːdʒ ‖ sɜːrdʒ/ n 1 a sudden strong feeling: *He felt a surge of anger.* 2 a sudden increase in some kind of activity: *a surge in the electric current*

surge² v **surged, surging** [I: + adv/prep] to move forward like powerful waves: *The crowd surged past him.*

sur·geon /ˈsɜːdʒən ‖ ˈsɜːr-/ n a doctor who performs medical operations

sur·ge·ry /ˈsɜːdʒəri ‖ ˈsɜːr-/ n **surgeries** 1 [U] the performing of medical operations: *He needed immediate surgery to prevent another heart attack.* 2 [C] BrE a place where doctors or DENTISTs treat people 3 [C;U] a time when doctors, DENTISTs and Members of Parliament see people who need their help: *He holds a surgery every Saturday morning.*

sur·gi·cal /ˈsɜːdʒɪkəl ‖ ˈsɜːr-/ adj 1 used in operations: *a surgical knife* 2 needing an operation: *surgical treatment for cancer* **−surgically** /-kli/ adv

sur·ly /ˈsɜːli ‖ ˈsɜːrli/ adj **surlier, surliest** rude and unpleasant: *He gave me a surly look.*

sur·mise /səˈmaɪz ‖ sər-/ v **surmised, surmising** [I;T; +(that)] fml to guess that something might be true **−surmise** n

sur·mount /səˈmaʊnt ‖ sər-/ v [T] fml to deal with a problem successfully **−surmountable** adj

sur·name /ˈsɜːneɪm ‖ ˈsɜːr-/ n your family name: *Alan's surname is Smith.* −see FIRST NAME (USAGE) −compare FIRST NAME

sur·pass /səˈpɑːs ‖ sərˈpæs/ v [T] fml to do more of something or to do something better than other people or what is expected: *Her exam results surpassed all our expectations.*

sur·plus /ˈsɜːpləs ‖ ˈsɜːr-/ n an amount that is more than what is needed or used: *Some countries continue to produce an oil surplus.* **−surplus** adj : *These chairs are surplus to our requirements.* | *surplus milk*

sur·prise¹ /səˈpraɪz ‖ sər-/ n 1 [U] the feeling caused by something unexpected: *To my surprise I won the competition.* 2 [C] something unexpected which happens or is arranged by others: *Her visit was a very pleasant surprise.* | *I've got a surprise for you.* | *a surprise birthday party* 3 **take someone by surprise** to happen when a person is not expecting it: *When he offered me the job it took me completely by surprise.*

surprise² v **surprised, surprising** [T] to cause someone to feel surprise: *The taste surprised him.* | *I was surprised to hear that his wife had left him.* | *They surprised us* **with** *a visit.*

sur·pris·ing /səˈpraɪzɪŋ ‖ sər-/ adj causing a feeling of surprise: *It's not surprising that they lost.* | *He was a man of surprising youth.* **−surprisingly** adv

sur·real·is·m /səˈrɪəlɪzəm/ n [U] a modern style of art and literature in which the artist connects unrelated images and objects **−surrealist** adj, n

sur·real·is·tic /səˌrɪəˈlɪstɪk/ adj 1 (also **surreal** /səˈrɪəl/) strange, with the qualities of dreams rather than real life 2 concerning or in the style of surrealism

---

SPELLING NOTE

Words with the sound / s /, may be spelt **c-**, like **city**, or **ps-**, like **psychology.**

---

sur·ren·der /səˈrendəʳ/ v 1 [I] to admit that you have been beaten: *With no alternative left, the army surrendered.* | *They've surrendered* **to** *the enemy forces.* 2 **surrender to something** to allow something to control what you do or feel: *He surrendered to the temptation of an expensive meal.* 3 [T] fml to give up something that you value: *I surrender any claim I have to the money.* **−surrender** n [U]

sur·rep·ti·tious /ˌsʌrəpˈtɪʃəs◂/ adj done or experienced secretly: *a surreptitious kiss* **−surreptitiously** adv **−surreptitiousness** n [U]

sur·round¹ /səˈraʊnd/ v [T] 1 to be or go around something on every side of it: *The prison is surrounded* **by** *a high wall.* | *The police surrounded the house.* 2 to be near a person or thing all the time: *She was surrounded by good friends.* | *Dangers will surround us until we leave here.* 3 **to surround yourself with something** to make sure that people or things are near you: *He surrounded himself with every material comfort.*

surround² n an edge, especially a decorative one: *a surround for a fireplace*

sur·round·ing /səˈraʊndɪŋ/ adj [only before a noun] around and near a particular place: *There are few villages in the surrounding area.* **−see** ENVIRONMENT (USAGE)

sur·round·ings /səˈraʊndɪŋz/ n [pl] 1 the area around a particular place: *The castle looked out of place in its surroundings.* 2 living conditions: *She grew up in comfortable surroundings.*

sur·veil·lance /sɜːˈveɪləns ‖ sɜːr-/ n [U] a close watch kept on someone, especially someone believed to have criminal intentions: *The police have been keeping him under surveillance.*

sur·vey¹ /səˈveɪ ‖ sər-/ v **surveyed, surveying** [T] 1 to look carefully at a person or place, one part at a time: *He surveyed the surrounding countryside.* 2 to examine every area of a subject or situation: *His article surveys research findings over the last 20 years.* 3 to examine the condition of a building: *Has the house been properly surveyed?* 4 to make a map of an area of land 5 to find out what a group of people think or do, usually by asking them questions

sur·vey² /ˈsɜːveɪ ‖ ˈsɜːr-/ n 1 a general view of a place, subject or situation: *You must include a survey of the relevant literature in your essay.* 2 a careful examination of a building, especially for someone who may buy it: *We were not going to buy the house without a satisfactory survey.* 3 a careful examination of an area of land in order to make a map 4 an examination of people's behaviour or opinions, usually based on questions you ask them: *We're conducting a survey* **of** *drinking habits.*

sur·vey·or /səˈveɪəʳ ‖ sər-/ n a person whose job is to examine the condition of buildings or map areas of land

sur·viv·al /səˈvaɪvəl ‖ sər-/ n 1 [U] the state of continuing to live or exist after a difficult or dangerous situation: *We had little hope of survival.* 2 [C] something which has continued to exist from an earlier time

sur·vive /səˈvaɪv ‖ sər-/ v **survived, surviving** 1 [I;T] to continue to live or exist after a difficult or dangerous situation: *She survived the accident.* | *Four people were killed; only one survived.* 2 [T] to live longer than another person: *He survived both his children.* 3 [I;T] to live through a difficult situation without serious hurt or harm: *It's been a year of emotional ups and downs, but at least we survived!* **−survivor** n : *There were no survivors* **of** *the plane crash.*

sus·cep·ti·ble /səˈseptɨbəl/ *adj* **1** easily influenced: *He is very susceptible to other people's suggestions.* **2** likely to suffer from or as a result of something: *I'm highly susceptible to the cold.* –**susceptibility** /səˌseptɨˈbilɨti/ *n* [U]

sus·pect¹ /səˈspekt/ *v* [T] **1** [+(that)] to feel that something may exist or be true: *At first, we suspected that he was lost.* | *They suspect corruption.* **2** to believe that someone may be guilty: *They suspect him of murder.* **3** to have doubts about whether you can trust a person or way of behaving: *He helped me but I suspect his motives.*

sus·pect² /ˈsʌspekt/ *n* a person who is thought to be guilty, especially of a crime

suspect³ *adj* that is perhaps not to be trusted: *I find her loyalty increasingly suspect.*

sus·pend /səˈspend/ *v* [T] **1** to hang from above: *We could suspend a rope from that tree.* **2** to hold something still in liquid or air: *Dust remained suspended in the empty room.* **3** to delay or stop something for a period of time: *The investigation has been suspended until the autumn.* **4** to prevent someone from belonging to a group or continuing in a job for a time, usually because of bad behaviour: *She was suspended from school for taking drugs.*

sus·pend·er /səˈspendər/ *n* **1** a fastener hanging down from a belt to hold a woman's stockings up –see picture on page 50 **2 suspenders** the American English word for BRACES

sus·pense /səˈspens/ *n* [U] a state of uncertain expectation: *We waited in suspense for our test results.* | *a story of mystery and suspense*

sus·pen·sion /səˈspenʃən/ *n* **1** [U] the act of suspending a person or thing or the state of being suspended **2** [C;U] the apparatus fixed to the wheels of a vehicle to lessen the effects of rough road surfaces

sus·pi·cion /səˈspiʃən/ *n* **1** [C] a feeling that something may exist or be true: *I have a suspicion that he's right.* **2** [C;U] a feeling that someone may be guilty or that something may be wrong: *She treats us with great suspicion.* | *He has his suspicions about the company finances.* | *He's under suspicion of murder.* | *The police have their suspicions about who killed him.* **3 above suspicion** most certainly not guilty: *The dead man's family is above suspicion.* **4** [sing] a slight amount or taste of something: *There's a suspicion of onion in the soup.*

sus·pi·cious /səˈspiʃəs/ *adj* **1** not trusting a person or situation: *She was suspicious of our intentions.* | *His statement made the police suspicious.* **2** causing a lack of trust in others: *His behaviour has been very suspicious.* –**suspiciously** *adv* : *behaving suspiciously* | *suspicously well-behaved*

sus·tain /səˈsteɪn/ *v* [T] **1** to keep someone strong, alive, or happy: *A good breakfast will sustain us through the day.* **2** to continue something over a long period: *She owes her success to sustained hard work.* | *He couldn't sustain his interest in the job.* **3** to suffer something: *They sustained severe injuries in the accident.* **4** to support something heavy

sus·te·nance /ˈsʌstɨnəns/ *n* [U] *fml* food and drink, or its value to people's health and strength

svelte /svelt/ *adj* attractively thin and stylish (used especially of a woman)

SW *n,adj* a written abbreviation for SOUTHWEST(ERN)

swab¹ /swɒb ‖ swɑːb/ *n* a piece of cotton wool used to clean wounds or to hold liquid for medical tests

swab² *v* -**bb**- [T] (also **swab down**) to clean something with water, especially floors on a ship

swag·ger /ˈswægər/ *v* [I+adv/prep] to walk with a proud, swinging movement: *He swaggered down the street after his victory.* –**swagger** *n* : *He walks with a swagger.*

swal·low¹ /ˈswɒloʊ ‖ ˈswɑː-/ *v* **1** [T] to move something down your throat from your mouth: *Try to swallow a little soup.* **2** [I] to make the same movement of the throat, especially as a sign that you are nervous: *He swallowed, and then began his talk.* **3** [T] *infml* foolishly to accept something as true: *I swallowed the whole story.* **4** [T] to hide your feelings or control them with difficulty: *She swallowed her pride and apologised.*
swallow up *phr v* [T **swallow** sbdy/sthg ↔ **up**] to cause a person or thing to disappear into something larger: *Higher living costs have swallowed up our pay rise.*

swallow² *n* a small bird with pointed wings and a double-pointed tail

swam /swæm/ *v* the past tense of SWIM

swamp¹ /swɒmp ‖ swɑːmp, swɔːmp/ *n* [C;U] an area of soft, wet land –compare MARSH –**swampy** *adj*

swamp² *v* [T] **1** to fill something with water, usually causing it to sink: *The boat was swamped by high waves.* **2** to have a much larger quantity of something than you can deal with: *We've been swamped by inquiries.*

swan /swɒn ‖ swɑːn/ *n* a large white bird with a long neck, which lives on rivers and lakes

swank·y /ˈswæŋki/ *adj* swankier, swankiest *infml* too fashionable or expensive: *a really swanky party*

swap¹ /swɒp ‖ swɑːp/ *v* -**pp**- (also **swop**) [I;T] *infml* to exchange things: *The manager has agreed that we can swap jobs.* | *I'll swap any of my stamps for that one of yours.* | *Well, I prefer your coat – do you want to swap?*

swap² *n* (also **swop**) *infml* an exchange: *Shall we do a swap?*

swarm¹ /swɔːm ‖ swɔːrm/ *n* [C; + sing/pl v] **1** a large group of insects that move together: *a swarm of bees* **2** a large number of people moving at the same time: *swarms of students*

swarm² *v* [I+adv/prep] **1** to move in a large group: *People came swarming out of the building.* | *Ants swarmed all over me.* **2 swarm with something** to be full of moving crowds: *The place was swarming with tourists.*

swar·thy /ˈswɔːði ‖ -ɔːr-/ *adj* swarthier, swarthiest with a dark skin (used of a person)

swas·ti·ka /ˈswɒstɨkə ‖ ˈswɑː-/ *n* a cross with each arm bent back at a right angle, which was used as a sign by NAZIS in Germany

swat /swɒt ‖ swɑːt/ *v* -**tt**- [T] to hit an insect with a flat object, especially to kill it

sway /sweɪ/ *v* swayed, swaying **1** [I] to move slowly from side to side: *The trees swayed in the wind.* **2** [T] to influence someone: *Don't be swayed by promises that may be false.* –**sway** *n* [U]

swear /sweər/ *v* swore /swɔːr, swoːrn/, sworn /swɔːn ‖ swoːrn/, swearing **1** [I] to use bad language: *Don't swear at me!* **2** [I; T + (that)] to make a formal promise: *He swore that he would never see her again.* | *She swore to tell the truth.* **3** [T] to make a person promise something formally: *I've been sworn to secrecy.* **4 swear by something** to claim that something is particularly useful: *He swears by cold baths for keeping healthy.* **5 swear to something** to say that something is certainly true: *I couldn't swear to it, but I think he lied.*

swear in *phr v* [T **swear** sbdy ↔ **in**] to make someone promise formally that they will tell the truth or that they will be loyal and honest in their new position: *The new president was sworn in.*

swear·word /'sweəwɜːd ‖ 'sweərwɜːrd/ *n* a rude word used to express anger or lack of respect

sweat¹ /swet/ *n* **1** [U] liquid which comes out through your skin when you are hot or frightened: *Sweat was running down her face.* | **2 in a sweat, in a cold sweat** covered in sweat, usually from fear **3** [sing;U] *infml* hard work: *Digging that hole was a real sweat.*

sweat² *v* [I] to produce liquid that comes out through your skin because you are hot or frightened: *He was sweating in the intense heat.* **2** [I] to work very hard: *We sweated day and night to get the work finished in time.* **3 sweat it out** to manage in an unpleasant situation until it ends: *They had to sweat it out until help arrived.*

sweat·er /'swetər/ *n* a warm garment which covers the upper part of your body, including your arms

sweat·shirt /'swet-ʃɜːt ‖ -ɜːrt/ *n* a loose garment made of thick cotton which covers the upper part of your body, including your arms – see picture on page 50

sweat·y /'sweti/ *adj* **sweatier, sweatiest 1** wet from heat or fear (used of people): *sweaty feet* **2** unpleasantly hot, making you sweat: *sweaty weather* | *sweaty work*

swede /swiːd/ *n* [C;U] a round yellow vegetable which grows under the ground

sweep¹ /swiːp/ *v* **swept** /swept/, **swept, sweeping 1** [T] to clean something or remove it by brushing: *He swept the floor.* | *She swept the dirt into the street.* **2** [I; + adv/prep] to remove something completely: *All thought of revenge was swept from my mind.* **3** [I; + adv/prep; T; + adv/prep] to move quickly and powerfully: *The crowd swept through the gates.* | *A storm swept over the country.* | *The boat was swept out to sea.* **4** [I; T + adv/prep] to spread quickly: *The news swept across the country.* **5** [I + adv/prep] (of a person) to move with pride in a certain direction: *She swept angrily from the room.* **6** [I + adv/prep] to form a long curve: *Hills sweep round the bay.* **7** [T] to look around a place: *The security camera swept the store.* **8 sweep the board** to win almost everything in a competition **9 sweep someone off their feet** to attract someone so strongly that they fall in love with you immediately **10 sweep something under the carpet** to hide something that you want to keep secret

sweep up *phr v* [I;T **sweep** sthg ↔ **up**] to remove something from the floor by sweeping it

sweep² *n* **1** an act of sweeping: *This room needs a good sweep.* **2** a swinging movement of your arm: *with a sweep of his sword* **3** a long curved shape: *the long sweep of the distant hills* **4** the wide range of a subject: *the broad sweep of her argument*

sweep·er /'swiːpər/ *n* a person or thing that sweeps: *a road-sweeper* | *a carpet sweeper*

sweep·ing /'swiːpɪŋ/ *adj* **1** important and covering a wide range of things: *They are making sweeping changes to the health service.* **2** too general: *That's a rather sweeping statement.*

SPELLING NOTE

Words with the sound / s /, may be spelt **c-**, like **city**, or **ps-**, like **psychology**.

---

sweep·stake /'swiːpsteɪk/ *n* a way of risking money on the result of a horserace

sweet¹ /swiːt/ *adj* **1** containing or tasting of sugar: *This tea is too sweet for me.* | *I eat a lot of sweet things between meals.* –opposite **bitter 2** pleasant to your senses: *What sweet music!* | *I love the sweet smell of freshly-picked flowers.* **3** attractive (used especially of small or young people and things): *Your little boy looks sweet in his new coat.* **4** kind or gentle: *It was sweet of you to think of me.* | *She has such a sweet smile.* **5 have a sweet tooth** to enjoy eating sweet things **6 in someone's own sweet time, in someone's own sweet way** at the time or in the way that suits a person and not others: *I expect he'll do it in his own sweet time.* **7 keep someone sweet** to do something to please someone so that they don't get angry –**sweetly** *adv* –**sweetness** *n* [U]

sweet² *n BrE* **1** [C] a sweet thing such as chocolate which is eaten for pleasure –see also CANDY **2** [C;U] (also **dessert, pudding**) sweet food served at the end of a meal

sweet corn /ˈ· ·/ *n* [U] see CORN

sweet·en /'swiːtn/ *v* **1** [I;T] to make or become sweeter: *Shall I sweeten your coffee?* | *Apples sweeten as they become ripe.* **2** [T] (also **sweeten** sbdy **up**) *infml* to give something to someone or do something for them in order to persuade them to help you: *You'll have to sweeten her up before you ask her for a loan.*

sweet·ener /'swiːtnər/ *n* **1** a substance used instead of sugar to make food and drink taste sweet **2** something that you give someone to make a request or a deal more attractive

sweet·heart /'swiːthɑːt ‖ -hɑːrt/ *n* a person that you love or a way of addressing them: *Have you had a good day, sweetheart?*

sweet·meat /'swiːtmiːt/ *n* a sweet or any food in the past made of or preserved in sugar

sweet pea /ˌ· ˈ· ‖ ˈ· ·/ *n* a climbing plant with sweet-smelling flowers

swell¹ /swel/ *v* **swelled, swollen** /'swəʊlən/ *or* **swelled, swelling 1** [I] (also **swell up**) to become larger and rounder: *My ankle has swollen up.* **2** [I;T] to become or make something larger in size: *The army has swollen to twice its normal size.* | *Refugees are swelling the camps.* **3** [I;T] to fill into a curved shape: *Wind swelled the sails.* **4** [I;T] (of strong feelings) to grow suddenly or to have a sudden effect on someone: *My heart swells with pride when I hear him sing.*

swell² *n* **1** [C] the movement of large stretches of the sea up and down **2** [sing] an increase of sound

swell³ *adj AmE infml* very good or nice: *a swell teacher*

swell·ing /'swelɪŋ/ *n* [C;U] a place on your body that has become larger and rounder than usual: *I've got a nasty swelling on my foot.*

swel·ter·ing /'sweltərɪŋ/ *adj infml* very hot indeed: *It's sweltering in here!*

swept /swept/ the past tense and past participle of SWEEP

swerve /swɜːv ‖ swɜːrv/ *v* **swerved, swerving 1** [I] to move suddenly in another direction: *The car swerved to avoid the dog.* | *The ball swerved in the air.* **2** [I] to change your intentions –**swerve** *n*

swift¹ /swɪft/ *adj fml* quick: *He's a swift runner.* | *I'm hoping for a swift response.* –**swiftly** *adv* –**swiftness** *n* [U]

swift² *n* a small bird with long wings which eats insects

swig /swɪg/ v **-gg-** [T] *infml* to drink in large amounts: *He was swigging brandy straight from the bottle.* –**swig** n : *a swig of beer*

swill[1] /swɪl/ v [T] **1** to wash something by pouring large amounts of water over it **2** to drink something in large amounts

swill[2] n [U] waste food that is fed to pigs

swim[1] /swɪm/ v **swam** /swæm/, **swum** /swʌm/, **swimming 1** [I] to move through water using arms and legs or a tail: *Shall we swim to the island?* | *Fish are swimming back into the lake.* | *He goes swimming every morning.* **2** [T] to cross a certain distance by doing this: *I can swim the river twice without stopping.* | *She swam 2 kilometres.* **3** [I] to be full of or covered with liquid: *All the food was swimming in fat.* **4** [I] to seem to move or be confused: *One drink and the room was swimming.* | *My head was swimming.* –**swimmer** n

swim[2] n an act or period of swimming: *Let's go for a swim!*

swim·ming /ˈswɪmɪŋ/ n [U] the activity or sport of swimming –see picture on page 637

swimming bath /ˈ··· ·/ n (also **swimming baths**) a public place specially built for swimming, usually indoors

swimming cos·tume /ˈ·· ˌ··/ n (also **swimsuit**) a piece of clothing worn for swimming

swimming pool /ˈ··· ·/ n a pool specially built for swimming in: *They've got a swimming pool in their garden.*

swimming trunks /ˈ·· ·/ n [pl] an article of clothing worn by men for swimming

swim·suit /ˈswɪmsuːt, -sjuːt ‖ -suːt/ n see SWIMMING COSTUME

swin·dle /ˈswɪndl/ v **swindled, swindling** [T] to cheat someone, especially to get their money: *He's swindled me out of £100!* –**swindle** n : *a big bank swindle* –**swindler** n

swine /swaɪn/ n **swine 1** *old fash or tech* a pig: *swine fever* **2** *infml* a nasty, unpleasant person: *Give that back, you swine!*

swing[1] /swɪŋ/ v **swung** /swʌŋ/, **swung, swinging 1** [I;T] to move backwards and forwards from a fixed point: *They were swinging their arms as they walked.* | *The sign was swinging in the wind.* | *The children were swinging on a rope.* **2** [I;T] to move in a curve: *The door swung open.* **3 swing at something or someone** to move your arm up in an attempt to hit a person or thing: *I jumped out of the way as he swung at me.* **4** [I;T+adv/prep] to turn quickly: *He swung round and faced his attacker.* | *She swung the car into the drive.* **5** [I] (of opinions or feelings) to change from one extreme to another: *Public opinion has swung against the government.* **6** [I] *infml* (of music or parties) to be full of life **7 swing into action** to act quickly

swing[2] n **1** a swinging action or movement: *Would you like a swing on my rope?* **2** a seat hanging on ropes or chains, on which children play: *We've bought a swing for the garden.* **3** a great change in opinion or feelings: *There's been a big swing in public opinion since the election.* **4** a kind of music played by bands in the 1930s **5 get into the swing of something** to become used to a particular activity and do it well: *It took me a year to get into the swing of teaching.* **6 go with a swing** to be successful and full of life: *All our parties go with a swing.*

swing·ing /ˈswɪŋɪŋ/ adj *old fash* **1** full of life: *a swinging party* | *a swinging part of town* **2** fashionably free and active: *swinging teenagers* –**swingingly** adv –**swinger** n

swipe[1] /swaɪp/ n a sweeping blow which may or may not hit a person or thing: *He took a swipe at me with his newspaper.*

swipe[2] v **swiped, swiping 1** [I] to try to hit a person or thing with a quick swing of your arm: *He swiped wildly at the ball, and missed completely.* **2** [T] *infml* to steal: *Someone's swiped my book!*

swirl /swɜːl ‖ swɜːrl/ v [I] to move in circles: *The water swirled about his feet.* –**swirl** n : *with a swirl of her skirt* | *swirls of smoke*

swish[1] /swɪʃ/ v **1** [I;T] to move quickly through the air with a whistling sound **2** [I] (of cloth) to move with a soft sound –**swish** n

swish[2] adj *infml* fashionable and expensive: *We went to a very swish restaurant.*

switch[1] /swɪtʃ/ n **1** an apparatus for controlling the flow of an electric current: *a light switch* **2** a sudden change or exchange: *We were confused by the last-minute switch in textbooks.* **3** a small thin stick

switch[2] v [I;T] to change or exchange: *They switched places.* | *He got tired of teaching and switched to painting.*

switch off phr v **1** [I;T **switch** sthg ↔ **off**] to turn off an electric light or apparatus by pushing a switch: *Could you switch the television off?* **2** [I] to stop paying attention: *She switches off if you mention the subject.*

switch on phr v **1** [I;T **switch** sthg ↔ **on**] to turn on an electric light or apparatus by pushing a switch: *Switch on the computer!* **2** [T **switch** sthg ↔ **on**] to start showing a certain kind of behaviour: *Switch on the charm and he'll do whatever you want.*

switch over phr v [I] **1** to change a habit completely: *People are switching over to low calorie drinks.* **2** to change from one radio or television station to another: *This programme is boring – can we switch over?*

switch·board /ˈswɪtʃbɔːd ‖ -bɔːrd/ n a central board which connects different telephone lines in the same company: *a switchboard operator*

swiv·el /ˈswɪvəl/ v **-ll-** *BrE* ‖-**l-** *AmE* (also **swivel round**) [I;T] to turn round while remaining in the same place –**swivel** n : *a swivel chair*

swol·len[1] /ˈswəʊlən/ adj **1** bigger than usual: *Her foot was very swollen after her accident.* **2** [only before a noun] greater than is reasonable: *She has a swollen opinion of herself.*

swollen[2] v the past participle of SWELL

swoon /swuːn/ v [I] *old fash* to fall as you lose consciousness –**swoon** n

swoop[1] /swuːp/ v [I] **1** to descend suddenly from the sky: *The bird swooped to catch a fish.* **2** to move towards a place quickly and without warning: *The police swooped on the thieves' hiding place.*

swoop[2] n **1** a sudden movement down from the sky **2** a sudden and unexpected movement towards a place: *Five people were arrested in a dawn swoop on their houses.* **3 at one fell swoop, in one fell swoop** all at the same time

swop /swɒp ‖ swɑːp/ v,n see SWAP

sword /sɔːd ‖ sɔːrd/ n a weapon with a long sharp blade

sword·fish /ˈsɔːdˌfɪʃ ‖ -ɔːr-/ n **swordfish** or **swordfishes** a large fish with a long, thin upper jaw

swords·man /ˈsɔːdzmən ‖ -ɔːr-/ n **swordsmen** /-mən/ a person who is trained to fight with a sword

swore /swɔːr/ v the past tense of SWEAR

sworn /swɔːn ‖ swɔːrn/ v **1** the past participle of SWEAR **2 sworn enemies** people who have an extreme and long lasting dislike of each other

swot¹ /swɒt ‖ swɑːt/ n BrE infml a person who studies extremely hard and is usually disliked for this

swot² v -tt- (**grind** AmE) [I] infml to study hard, especially in preparation for an examination: I'm swotting for tomorrow's test.

swot up phr v [I] to learn as much as possible about a subject quickly: He's swotting up on international law.

swum /swʌm/ v the past participle of SWIM

swung /swʌŋ/ v the past tense form and the past participle of SWING

syc·a·more /'sɪkəmɔːr/ n [C;U] a type of tree, or the hard wood that comes from it

syc·o·phant /'sɪkəfənt/ n a person who tries too hard to please important people, especially by praising or agreeing with them, for personal advantage (a word used to show disapproval) –sycophantic /ˌsɪkə'fæntɪk◂/ adj

syl·la·ble /'sɪləbəl/ n a word or part of a word which contains one vowel sound: There are two syllables in "window". | "Exciting" is a three syllable word.

syl·la·bus /'sɪləbəs/ n syllabuses or syllabi /baɪ/ an arrangement of subjects for a particular course of study: Is Shakespeare on next year's literature syllabus?

sym·bol /'sɪmbəl/ n **1** a sign or object which represents something else: This wedding ring is a symbol of our love. | What's the symbol for a church on this map? **2** a letter or figure which represents a sound, number, or chemical substance: "H_2O" is the symbol for water.

sym·bol·ic /sɪm'bɒlɪk ‖ -'bɑː-/ adj (also **symbolical** /-lɪkəl/) used or seen as representing something else: The Queen's visit is symbolic of the friendship between the two countries. –symbolically /-kli/ adv

sym·bol·is·m /'sɪmbəlɪzəm/ n [U] the use of symbols to represent things, especially in literature, painting, and film

sym·bol·ize /'sɪmbəlaɪz/ v symbolized, symbolizing (also **symbolise** in British English) [T] to be used or seen as a symbol of something else: Cars like these symbolize capitalism at its worst.

sym·met·ri·cal /sɪ'metrɪkəl/ adj (also **symmetric**) balanced in size, shape, or arrangement: a symmetrical design –opposite **asymmetric** –symmetrically /-kli/ adv

sym·me·try /'sɪmətri/ n [U] **1** exact balance in the arrangement of one or more things **2** the pleasant effect of such a balance

sym·pa·thet·ic /ˌsɪmpə'θetɪk◂/ adj **1** feeling or showing pity for another person's problems or suffering: She was sympathetic when I explained why I hadn't done the work. **2** understanding and usually approving of someone's behaviour or opinions: He was sympathetic to my idea. –opposite **unsympathetic** –sympathetically /-kli/ adv

sym·pa·thize /'sɪmpəθaɪz/ v sympathized, sympathizing (also **sympathise** in British English) [I]

SPELLING NOTE
Words with the sound / s /, may be spelt c-, like city, or ps-, like psychology.

---

to feel or show pity for another person's problems or suffering: It's hard to sympathize with such a difficult man. **2** to understand and usually approve of someone's behaviour or opinions: I sympathize with most of her political views. –sympathizer n

sym·pa·thy /'sɪmpəθi/ n **1** [C;U] a feeling or expression of pity for the problems or sufferings of another person: She pressed his hand in sympathy. | I didn't get much sympathy from the doctor. | My sympathies are with the victim's family. **2** [U] understanding and usually approval of someone's behaviour or opinions: I have a lot of sympathy for his point of view.

sym·pho·ny /'sɪmfəni/ n symphonies a piece of music written for an ORCHESTRA

symp·tom /'sɪmptəm/ n a sign of illness or of something bad: The first symptom is a high temperature. | The number of homeless people is a symptom of social decay. –symptomatic /ˌsɪmptə'mætɪk/ adj

syn·a·gogue /'sɪnəgɒg ‖ -gɑːg/ n a place where Jews meet for religious worship

syn·chro·nize /'sɪŋkrənaɪz/ v synchronized, synchronizing (also **synchronise** in British English) **1** [T] to set clocks and watches so that they show the same time **2** [I;T] to happen or make things happen at the same time or speed: They synchronized their steps. –synchronization /ˌsɪŋkrənaɪ'zeɪʃən ‖ -nə-/ n [U]

syn·di·cate¹ /'sɪndɪkət/ n [C +sing/pl verb] a group of people or companies that come together for a particular purpose, especially a business plan: The hotel is being built by a syndicate of local businessmen.

syn·di·cate² /'sɪndɪkeɪt/ v syndicated, syndicating [T] to print something in a number of different newspapers or magazines: My article has been syndicated in local papers all over the country. –syndication /ˌsɪndɪ'keɪʃən/ n [U]

syn·drome /'sɪndrəʊm/ n a set of signs, qualities or events which are typical of a general condition

syn·o·nym /'sɪnənɪm/ n a word with the same meaning as another word: "Sad" and "unhappy" are synonyms.

sy·non·y·mous /sɪ'nɒnəməs ‖ -'nɑː-/ adj meaning the same or having a strong association with a particular thing: Football matches are becoming synonymous with crowd violence. –synonymously adv

sy·nop·sis /sɪ'nɒpsɪs ‖ -'nɑːp-/ n synopses /-siːz/ a short account of something longer, like the contents of a book or the story of a film

syn·tax /'sɪntæks/ n [U] the rules of grammar which are used for ordering words in a sentence –syntactic /sɪn'tæktɪk/ adj –syntactically /-kli/ adv

syn·the·sis /'sɪnθəsɪs/ n syntheses /-siːz/ [C;U] the combination of different things or ideas: Our beliefs are a synthesis of Eastern and Western religions. –compare ANALYSIS

syn·the·size /'sɪnθəsaɪz/ v synthesized, synthesizing (also **synthesise** in British English) [T] to produce something by combining different ideas or chemicals

syn·thet·ic /sɪn'θetɪk/ adj made by humans and not natural: I prefer cotton to synthetic material. –synthetic n –synthetically /-kli/ adv

syph·i·lis /'sɪfəlɪs/ n [U] a serious illness caught by having sex with an infected person

sy·phon /'saɪfən/ n,v see SIPHON

sy·ringe¹ /sɪ'rɪndʒ/ n a tube used in medicine for putting liquids such as drugs into your body or for removing small amounts of blood

syringe² *v* **syringed, syringing** [T] to treat a part of your body by removing something from it with a syringe

syr·up /ˈsɪrəp ‖ ˈsɜː-, ˈsɪ-/ *n* [U] thick, sweet liquid –**syrupy** *adj*

sys·tem /ˈsɪstəm/ *n* **1** [C] a group of related parts working together: *the postal system* | *London's transport system* **2** [C] your body as a whole, or certain parts of it working together: *Too many nuts are bad for your digestive system.* **3** [C] an ordered set of ideas or methods: *The problem is with the British parliamentary system.* | *We need systems that will make our work easier.* **4** [U] organization: *You need some system in your study methods.* **5 the system** the rules and methods of a society or organization: *She's trying to beat the system and avoid paying tax.* **6 get something out of your system** to express strong feelings in some way so that you do not have to continue controlling them

sys·te·mat·ic /ˌsɪstəˈmætɪk◂/ *adj* thorough and done according to a careful plan: *The police made a systematic search of the room.* –**systematically** /-kli/ *adv*

sys·te·ma·tize /ˈsɪstəmətaɪz/ *v* **systematized, systematizing** (also **systematise** in British English) [T] to arrange and order things according to a careful plan: *Our marketing strategies must be systematized.* –**systematization** /ˌsɪstəmətaɪˈzeɪʃən ‖ -mətə-/ *n* [U]

T,t

T, t /tiː/ **T's, t's** **1** the 20th letter of the English alphabet **2 to a T** *infml* exactly: *That hat suits her to a T.*

ta /taː/ *interj infml* thank you

tab /tæb/ *n* **1** a small piece of cloth or paper fixed to something and giving information about it: *We've been asked to sew name tabs into the children's school clothes.* **2** *infml AmE* a bill **3 keep tabs on** *infml* to pay careful attention to what is happening or what someone is doing: *Keep tabs on your spending.*

tab·by /'tæbi/ *n* **tabbies** a cat with dark bands on its brown or grey fur

ta·ble¹ /'teɪbəl/ *n* **1** a piece of furniture with a flat top supported by one or more legs: *a kitchen table | A table for two, please, near the back of the restaurant.* **2** [+ sing/pl verb] the people sitting at a table: *The whole table got up as she entered the room.* **3** a set of facts or figures arranged in rows across and down the page: *Table 1 shows our profits over the last 3 years.*

table² *v* **tabled, tabling** [T] to formally suggest something to be talked about in a meeting

ta·ble d'hôte /ˌtɑːbəl 'dəʊt/ *n* a fixed price meal in a hotel or restaurant

ta·ble·spoon /'teɪbəlspuːn/ *n* **1** a large spoon used for serving food **2** (also **tablespoonful** /-fʊl/) the amount that a tablespoon holds: *a tablespoon of flour*

tab·let /'tæblɪt/ *n* **1** medicine in a small, hard form: *Take two tablets before every meal.* **2** a flat piece of a hard material like stone, with words cut into it **3** *fml* a small block of soap

table ten·nis /'·· ˌ··/ *n* [U] an indoor game played on a table by two or four players who hit a small ball to each other across a net

tab·loid /'tæblɔɪd/ *n* a newspaper with small pages, a lot of pictures, and little serious news

ta·boo /təˈbuː, tæˈbuː/ *n* a strong religious or social custom which forbids certain behaviour or speech: *There is a taboo on eating meat.* **–taboo** *adj*: *Is that a taboo subject?*

tab·u·late /'tæbjʊleɪt/ *v* **tabulated, tabulating** [T] to arrange facts or figures in rows or lists **–tabular** /'tæbjʊləʳ/ ‖ -bjə-/ *adj*: *This information would be clearer in tabular form.* **–tabulation** /ˌtæbjʊ'leɪʃən/ *n* [U]

ta·cit /'tæsɪt/ *adj* shown or understood without being put into words: *We had a tacit agreement to cooperate with each other.* **–tacitly** *adv*

ta·ci·turn /'tæsɪtɜːn ‖ -ɜːrn/ *adj fml* tending to speak very little and sometimes appearing unfriendly **–taciturnity** /ˌtæsɪ'tɜːnɪti ‖ -'tɜːr-/ *n* [U]

tack¹ /tæk/ *n* **1** a small nail with a sharp point and flat head: *carpet tacks* **2** [C] *infml* a method of doing something different to one used before: *If that doesn't work, I'll try a different tack.* **3** [C;U] a course or change in direction of a sailing ship which allows the wind to fill its sails **4** [C] a long loose stitch used to fasten pieces of cloth together before sewing them properly

tack² *v* **1** [T + adv/prep] to fasten something to a solid surface with a small, sharp nail: *She tacked a notice to the board.* **2** [I + adv/prep] to sail in a particular direction so that the ship's sails catch the wind **3** [T] to fasten pieces of cloth together with long loose stitches before sewing them properly: *You tack the curtains and I'll sew them.*

tack sthg ↔ **on** *phr v* [T] *infml* to add something not originally planned to the end of something already prepared: *She tacked a few words on to her sister's letter.*

tack·le¹ /'tækəl/ *n* **1** [C] an attempt to take the ball away from an opponent in certain sports: *What a fine tackle by the England captain!* **2** [U] the apparatus used in a sport: *Don't forget to bring your fishing tackle.* **3** [U] a system of ropes and wheels for lifting or pulling things

tackle² *v* **tackled, tackling** **1** [T] to take action to deal with something: *How can we tackle this problem?* **2** [I;T] to try to take the ball away from an opponent in certain sports **3** [T] *infml* to try to stop someone, often by attacking them: *My husband tackled the burglar and made him drop everything.* **4** [T] to speak to someone directly and honestly so as to deal with a problem: *You'll have to tackle her parents about her bad behaviour.*

tack·y /'tæki/ *adj* **tackier, tackiest** **1** sticky: *The paint is still tacky so don't touch it.* **2** *infml* unpleasant and of poor quality: *Many souvenirs are really tacky.*

tact /tækt/ *n* [U] the ability to do or say the right thing at the right time so that no offence is given: *He used great tact to resolve the conflict.* **–tactful** *adj*: *I appreciate your tactful handling of a difficult situation.* **–tactfully** *adv* **–tactless** *adj*: *His tactless remark upset her greatly.*

tac·tic /'tæktɪk/ *n* **1** a means of getting a desired result: *I respect her aims but not her tactics!* **2 tactics** [pl] the organization of military forces to win a battle: *A general should be skilled in tactics.* **–tactical** *adj*: *a tactical decision | tactical skill in battle*

tac·tile /'tæktaɪl ‖ 'tæktl/ *adj fml* related to or experienced by touch

tad·pole /'tædpəʊl/ *n* a small black water creature with a long tail that grows into a FROG or TOAD

tag¹ /tæg/ *n* **1** [C] a small piece of some material fixed to something to give information about it: *Is there a price tag on that dress?* **2** [U] a chasing game played by children **3** [C] a phrase added to a sentence to give it more importance or make it a question

tag² *v* **-gg-** [T] to fasten a small piece of some material to something to give information about it: *We've tagged all our sheep.*

tag along *phr v* [I] to go with other people who often do not particularly want you to be with them: *Wherever I went, my little sister used to tag along.*

tag sthg ↔ **on** *phr v* [T] to add something to the end of something already written or said: *Her objections were casually tagged on at the end of the report.*

tail¹ /teɪl/ *n* **1** the movable part at the end of an animal's body: *The dog wagged its tail with pleasure.* **2** anything like a tail in appearance or position: *the tail of a plane* **3 tails** [pl] see TAILCOAT **4 tail end** the last part of something: *the tail end of the film* **5** *infml* a person employed to watch and follow someone: *He's got a tail on his wife.* **6 on someone's tail** close behind someone or near to finding them: *The police are on his tail.* **7 tails** [pl] the side of a coin which does not have the head of a ruler on it

tail² *v* [T] **1** to follow someone and watch what they do: *The police have been tailing me.* **2** to take the ends off small fruit and vegetables before cooking or eating them

tail off *phr v* [I] to become less in quantity, strength, or quality: *His voice tailed off as he saw his father's expression.*

tail-coat /ˌteɪlˈkəʊt, ˈteɪlkəʊt/ *n* (also **tails**) a man's formal evening coat with the lower back part divided into two

tai-lor¹ /ˈteɪləʳ/ *n* a person who makes clothes to particular measurements, especially for men

tailor² *v* [T] **1** to make or change something so that it is suitable for a particular situation: *We can tailor the insurance policy to meet your needs.* **2** to make clothes by cutting and sewing cloth to particular measurements

tailor-made /ˌ··ˈ·◄/ *adj* **1** specially made or extremely suitable for a particular purpose or person: *The job is tailor-made for John.* **2** specially made to fit the wearer (used of clothes): *a tailor-made suit*

taint /teɪnt/ *v* [T] to make a person or thing less pure and desirable: *He is tainted by his friendship with corrupt businessmen.* **–taint** *n* [sing]: *The taint of dishonesty ruined his reputation.*

take¹ /teɪk/ *v* took /tʊk/, taken /ˈteɪkən/, taking [T] **1** to put your hand round something and hold it, especially when someone has offered it to you: *She took his arm and led him across the road.* | *He held out the letter and I took it.* | *Shall I take your coat?* **2** to remove something from a place or from someone's possession: *I took the scissors out of the drawer.* | *She opened her purse and took out some money.* | *Who's taken my pen?* **3** to carry someone or something from one place to another: *I think I'll need to take some work home this evening.* | *We can take you to the station if you like.* | *It's time to take the children to school.* **4** to do something: *Let's take a walk.* | *Can I take a look at the baby?* **5 take a bus/taxi/train** to go somewhere by bus, taxi, or train: *Shall we take a taxi to the station?* **6** to travel along a particular road: *We took the motorway as far as Birmingham.* **7 take a seat** to sit down **8** to swallow medicine, especially regularly: *Take two tablets three times a day.* **9** to accept or receive something: *I offered her £1000 for the car, but she wouldn't take it.* | *You never take my advice.* | *Why should I take the blame?* **10** to need something: *It takes a lot of time to create a beautiful garden.* | *It took us three hours to get home.* | *It takes a lot of courage to do what he's done.* **11** to record or measure something: *He took my name and address.* | *The nurse took my temperature.* **12** to understand something in a particular way: *I took his remarks as a compliment.* **13** to have a particular feeling when something happens: *She took it very badly when her father died.* | *He never takes me seriously.* **14** to consider something or think about it: *Many countries in Africa regularly experience food shortages. Let's take Ethiopia, for example.* **15** to have a particular opinion about something: *She takes the attitude that people should sort out their own problems.* **16** to start renting a house or flat: *We took a small flat in London.* **17** to seize a place by force: *Troops have taken the capital city.* **18** to give someone a lesson: *I take the students for French and German.* **19** to wear a particular size of clothes or shoes: *What size do you take?* **20 be taken ill** to become ill suddenly **21 can't take** to be unable to accept or bear something: *I can't take his constant criticism.* **22 I take it** = I suppose: *I take it you know what you're doing.*

23 take it from me = believe me **24 take leave of someone** *fml* to say GOODBYE to someone **25 take something as read** to accept that something is true without questioning it **26 take place** to happen: *When did the accident take place?* **27 take your own life** to kill yourself

take aback *phr v* **be taken aback** to be very surprised and shocked

take after sbdy *phr v* [T] to look or behave like someone in your family: *She takes after her mother.*

take sthg ↔ **apart** *phr v* [T] to separate something into the small pieces that it is made of

take sthg ↔ **back** *phr v* [T] **1** to take something to the place where you got it from: *These shoes don't fit – I'll have to take them back.* **2** to agree to receive something back: *The machine was obviously faulty, but the shop refused to take it back.* **3** to admit that you were wrong in something that you said: *I'm sorry – I take that back.*

take sthg ↔ **down** *phr v* [T] **1** to separate a structure into pieces so that it is no longer standing: *Engineers are taking down the bridge.* **2** to write down a piece of information: *She took down my phone number.*

take in *phr v* **1** [T **take** sbdy ↔ **in**] to provide a home for someone: *My sister agreed to take me in for a while.* **2** [T **take** sthg ↔ **in**] to make clothes smaller or narrower **3** [T **take** sthg ↔ **in**] to understand something: *There were too many facts to take in all at once.* **4** [T **take** sbdy ↔ **in**] to deceive someone

take off *phr v* **1** [T **take** sthg ↔ **off**] to remove a piece of clothing: *She came in and took her coat off.* **2** [I] (of a plane) to rise into the air **3** [T **take** sbdy ↔ **off**] *infml* to copy someone's speech or ways of behaving **4** [T **take** sthg ↔ **off**] to not go to work for a particular period of time: *I'm taking a couple of weeks off.*

take on *phr v* **1** [T **take** sbdy ↔ **on**] to start to employ someone: *We're taking on a new secretary this week.* **2** [T **take on** sthg] to start to have a particular quality: *His face took on an expression of dismay.* **3** [T **take** sbdy ↔ **on**] to start a fight or competition with someone **4** [T **take** sthg ↔ **on**] to accept responsibility for something: *I've taken on too much work.*

take out *phr v* **1** [T **take** sthg ↔ **out**] to remove something from a place **2** [T **take** sbdy ↔ **out**] to take someone to a place such as a restaurant or theatre: *She's taking me out for a meal tonight.* **3 take out insurance** to obtain insurance: *Have you taken out life insurance yet?* **4 take it out of you** to make you feel very tired

take sthg **out on** sbdy *phr v* [T] to express your own feelings by making someone else suffer: *When he's had a bad day he takes it out on the children.*

take sthg ↔ **over** *phr v* [T] to gain control over something or responsibility for it: *The company has been taken over by a Dutch firm.* | *Sarah will take over my job when I leave.*

take to *phr v* **1** [T **take to** sbdy/sthg] to like someone or something straight away: *I took to him as soon as I met him.* **2 take to doing something** to begin doing something regularly: *He's taken to staying out late.* **3 take to your bed** to go to bed because you are ill

take sthg ↔ **up** *phr v* [T] **1** to start doing an activity, usually for pleasure: *He took up writing poetry while he was still at school.* **2** to use a particular amount of time or space: *Books take up a lot of space.* | *The visit took up the whole of Sunday.* **3** to continue something: *I'll take up the story where I left off yesterday.*

take sbdy **up on** sthg *phr v* [T] **1** to accept an offer that someone has made to you: *I'd like to take you up on your offer of a meal.* **2** to question something that someone has said: *I'd like to take you up on that last point.*

take up with *phr v* **1** [T **take** sthg **up with** sbdy] to ask someone about something: *I think I need to take this matter up with my lawyer.* **2** [T **take up with** sbdy] *infml* to become friendly with someone

take upon *phr v* **take it upon yourself to do something** to do something even though no one has asked you to do it

take² *n* a scene that is filmed as part of a film or television broadcast

take·a·way /ˈteɪkəweɪ/ *n* **1** a shop from which cooked meals are taken away to be eaten: *Let's get some food from the Chinese takeaway.* **2** a hot cooked meal which you buy in a shop but eat somewhere else: *an Indian takeaway* –**takeaway** *adj* : *a takeaway meal*

ta·ken /ˈteɪkən/ the past participle of TAKE

take-off /ˈteɪk-ɒf ‖ -ɔːf/ *n* **1** [C;U] the beginning of a flight, when a plane leaves the ground: *It was a smooth takeoff.* **2** *infml* an amusing copy of someone's behaviour: *He does takeoffs of leading politicians.*

take·over /ˈteɪkˌəʊvəʳ/ *n* [C;U] **1** an act of gaining control of a company, by buying most of its shares **2** an act of gaining control of a country or organization, often by force: *a military takeover*

tak·ings /ˈteɪkɪŋz/ *n* [pl] receipts of money from sales: *We were counting the day's takings.*

tal·cum pow·der /ˈtælkəm ˌpaʊdəʳ/ (also **talc** /tælk/ *infml*) *n* [U] very fine powder which you put on your body to dry it or make it smell nice

tale /teɪl/ *n* **1** a story of imaginary events, especially exciting ones: *She told us tales of adventure.* **2** a written or spoken account of a real situation or event: *tales of life in the desert* **3** a false or unkind story about another person, particularly a child, told so they will be punished: *How can I stop Susie telling tales?*

tal·ent /ˈtælənt/ *n* [C;U] a special natural ability: *She shows great artistic talent.* | *He's looking for a way to use his talents.* | *a talent for drawing* –see GENIUS (USAGE) –**talented** *adj* : *a very talented actor*

tal·is·man /ˈtælɪzmən/ *n* an object which is believed to have magic powers to protect people and bring them luck

talk¹ /tɔːk/ *v* **1** [I] to use words to express yourself in speech: *I want to talk to you about something.* | *The baby's just learning to talk.* **2** [T] to discuss or express something in words: *We're sick of people talking politics.* | *Talk sense!* | *Don't talk rubbish!* **3** [I] *infml* to give secret information, usually unwillingly: *The suspect refused to talk.* **4** [T] to speak a particular language: *Shall we talk French?* **5** [I] to give an informal speech about something: *She'll talk on ancient history.* **6** [I] to speak about other people's actions and private lives: *The neighbours are already talking about us.* **7 talking of something** you use this expression in conversation when you are introducing a new subject which is slightly related to the last one: *Then we had an enormous dinner and went to bed. Talking of food, did you know they've got Italian Christmas cakes in the delicatessen?* **8 talk your way out of something** to avoid something, especially trouble, by explaining or persuading someone **9 talk shop** to talk about work: *Please stop talking shop!* **10 now**

you're talking! = now you are saying something that is really interesting to me **11 talk of the devil!** an expression used when a person being discussed suddenly enters the room **12 you can talk** = you are as guilty of that as the person you mentioned: *He steals? You can talk – what's the company name on that pen you're using?*

talk back *phr v* [I] to answer someone in a rude manner

talk down *phr v* **1** [T **talk** sbdy/sthg ↔ **down**] to help the pilot of a plane to land by giving spoken instructions: *The radar has failed, so we'll have to talk the planes down.* **2** [I] to talk to someone as if you are more important than they are: *I dislike doctors who talk down to their patients.*

talk sbdy **into** sthg *phr v* to persuade someone to do something: *He talked me into selling my car.*

talk sbdy **out of** sthg *phr v* to persuade someone not to do something

talk sthg ↔ **over** *phr v* [T] to discuss something thoroughly: *Can't we talk it over without arguing?*

talk sbdy ↔ **round** *phr v* [T] to persuade someone to change their mind: *He didn't want to come but we talked him round.*

talk² *n* **1** [C] a conversation: *I had a long talk with Mrs Jones today.* **2** [C] an informal speech: *She's gone to a talk on American politics.* **3 talks** [pl] formal discussions: *Most European leaders will be attending the talks in Rome.* **4** [U] a particular way of speaking: *baby talk* **5** [U] speech which may be meaningless or give false information: *His threats were just talk.* | *There's been a lot of talk about Linda and Paul.*

talk·a·tive /ˈtɔːkətɪv/ *adj* fond of talking

talk·er /ˈtɔːkəʳ/ *n* a person who talks in a particular way: *He's a fast talker.*

tall /tɔːl/ *adj* **1** of greater than average height: *a tall man* | *a tall building* | *tall trees* –see picture on page 245 **2** used when giving measurements: *2 metres tall* | *How tall are you?* **3 tall order** a request that is difficult to carry out **4 tall story** a story that is difficult to believe

tal·low /ˈtæləʊ/ *n* [U] hard animal fat used for making candles

tal·ly¹ /ˈtæli/ *n* tallies a record of points or amounts kept as you go along: *Please keep a tally of what you spend.*

tally² *v* tallied, tallying [I] to be the same as something else in all details: *Your figures don't tally with mine.* | *The two accounts don't tally.*

tal·on /ˈtælən/ *n* one of the sharp curved nails on the feet of some hunting birds

tam·bou·rine /ˌtæmbəˈriːn/ *n* a circular frame with skin stretched over it and small metal plates round the edge, which is shaken or beaten to make a musical sound

tame¹ /teɪm/ *adj* **1** trained to live with people (used of animals): *a tame lion* **2** *infml* unexciting: *a tame football match* **3** obedient or always willing to help (a word used to express disapproval): *Haven't you got a tame politician you could ask about this?* –**tamely** *adv* –**tameness** *n* [U]

tame² *v* tamed, taming [T] **1** to train an animal to be gentle and live with people **2** to bring something dangerous or violent under control: *Scientists have not yet tamed nature.* –**tamer** *n*

tam·per /ˈtæmpəʳ/ *v* **tamper with** to touch or make changes in something without permission: *My car wouldn't start after he tampered with it.*

In order to use a word correctly you need to know what word class (or "part of speech") it belongs to. Is it a noun, a verb, an adjective etc.?

All the words in this dictionary have a label which tells you which word class they belong to. You will find a list of these labels inside the front cover.

To see some examples of the most common word classes and how they are used, look at the passages below. The passages are all the same except that a different word class has been underlined in each one.

Nouns (*n*)

Yesterday when I finished <u>work</u> I went to the <u>cinema</u> with my <u>sister</u>. We really enjoyed the <u>film</u>, which was a <u>comedy</u> and very funny. Afterwards we were incredibly hungry, so I took her to <u>dinner</u> at a Chinese <u>restaurant</u>.

Verbs (*v*)

Yesterday when I <u>finished</u> work I <u>went</u> to the cinema with my sister. We really <u>enjoyed</u> the film, which <u>was</u> a comedy and very funny. Afterwards we <u>were</u> incredibly hungry, so I <u>took</u> her to dinner at a Chinese restaurant.

Adjectives (*adj*)

Yesterday when I finished work I went to the cinema with my sister. We really enjoyed the film, which was a comedy and very <u>funny</u>. Afterwards we were incredibly <u>hungry</u>, so I took her to dinner at a <u>Chinese</u> restaurant.

Adverbs (*adv*)

<u>Yesterday</u> when I finished work I went to the cinema with my sister. We <u>really</u> enjoyed the film, which was a comedy and <u>very</u> funny. <u>Afterwards</u> we were <u>incredibly</u> hungry, so I took her to dinner at a Chinese restaurant.

Pronouns (*pron*)

Yesterday when <u>I</u> finished work <u>I</u> went to the cinema with my sister. <u>We</u> really enjoyed the film, <u>which</u> was a comedy and very funny. Afterwards <u>we</u> were incredibly hungry, so <u>I</u> took <u>her</u> to dinner at a Chinese restaurant.

Prepositions (*prep*)

Yesterday when I finished work I went <u>to</u> the cinema <u>with</u> my sister. We really enjoyed the film, which was a comedy and very funny. Afterwards we were incredibly hungry, so I took her <u>to</u> dinner <u>at</u> a Chinese restaurant.

Conjunctions (*conj*)

Yesterday <u>when</u> I finished work I went to the cinema with my sister. We really enjoyed the film, which was a comedy <u>and</u> very funny. Afterwards we were incredibly hungry, <u>so</u> I took her to dinner at a Chinese restaurant.

Read this passage. For each word, decide which word class it belongs to and write it in the correct place in the table below. The first four have been done for you.

Last weekend I went to the seaside with a group of friends. We took sandwiches with us and had a picnic on the beach. When we arrived, the weather was quite cold, so we felt rather disappointed. Fortunately it soon got warmer and we had a wonderful time.

Noun	Verb	Adjective	Adverb	Pronoun	Preposition	Conjunction
weekend	went	last		I		

tam·pon /ˈtæmpɒn ‖ -pɑːn/ n a hard mass of cotton that a woman pushes inside her to collect the blood during her PERIOD

tan[1] /tæn/ v -nn- 1 [I;T] to make or become brown as a result of being in strong sunlight: *This cream will help you to tan.* | *She lay tanning her legs.* 2 [T] to change animal skin into leather

tan[2] n see SUNTAN

tan[3] adj yellowish brown in colour –see picture on page 147

tan·dem /ˈtændəm/ n 1 a bicycle built for two riders sitting one behind the other 2 **in tandem** working closely together: *We'll be working on the project in tandem.* –**tandem** adv : *They rode tandem.*

tang /tæŋ/ n a strong taste or smell: *the tang of the sea air* –**tangy** adj

tan·gent /ˈtændʒənt/ n 1 a straight line that touches the outside of a curve but does not cut across it 2 **go off at a tangent** infml to change suddenly from one course of speech, thought, or action to another –**tangential** /tænˈdʒenʃəl/ adj

tan·ge·rine /ˌtændʒəˈriːn ‖ ˈtændʒəriːn/ n [C;U] a small sweet orange with a loose skin

tan·gi·ble /ˈtændʒəbəl/ adj clear and certain enough to be felt or noticed: *We need tangible proof of her guilt.* –**tangibly** adv –**tangibility** /ˌtændʒɪˈbɪləti/ n [U]

tan·gle[1] /ˈtæŋɡəl/ v **tangled, tangling** [I;T] 1 to make or become a mass of twisted threads: *This thread tangles easily.* –opposite **untangle** 2 **tangle with someone** infml to quarrel with someone 3 **be tangled up in** to be caught in rope or wires: *My scarf got tangled up in the barbed wire fence.*

tangle[2] n 1 a confused mass of threads: *a tangle of wool* | *Your hair's in a tangle.* 2 a state of confusion: *My business affairs are in a real tangle.*

tan·go /ˈtæŋɡəʊ/ n **tangos** a dance with a strong beat of South American origin –**tango** v [I]

tank /tæŋk/ n 1 a large container for storing liquid or gas: *a fish tank* | *There's enough petrol in the tank for the drive to Oxford.* 2 a large, military vehicle with a gun and heavy armour, which moves on metal belts

tan·kard /ˈtæŋkəd ‖ -ərd/ n a large cup with a handle, usually used for drinking beer

tank·er /ˈtæŋkəʳ/ n a ship or road vehicle specially built for carrying large quantities of gas or liquid: *an oil tanker*

tan·ner /ˈtænəʳ/ n a person whose job is making animal skins into leather

tan·noy /ˈtænɔɪ/ n BrE tdmk a system of loudspeakers (LOUDSPEAKER) for giving information to the public

tan·ta·lize /ˈtæntəl-aɪz/ v **tantalized, tantalizing** [T] to encourage a strong desire for something that you do not actually allow a person or animal to enjoy: *He's been tantalizing us with the promise of foreign travel.* | *a tantalizing smell*

tan·ta·mount /ˈtæntəmaʊnt/ adj **tantamount to** the same, in effect, as something else: *Her answer is tantamount to a refusal.*

tan·trum /ˈtæntrəm/ n a sudden uncontrolled attack of anger, especially by a child: *Does he often have these tantrums?*

tap[1] /tæp/ n 1 an apparatus for letting liquid or gas out of a pipe or container: *Could you turn the hot tap off, please?* 2 **on tap: a** from a barrel: *Is the beer on tap or in bottles?* **b** ready for use when needed: *We*
have all the information we need on tap. 3 a gentle knock on something: *I felt a tap on my shoulder.*

tap[2] v -pp- 1 [I;T] to knock gently on something: *I tapped on the window to announce my arrival.* | *She tapped her fingers impatiently on the desk.* 2 [T] to use something or take something from a supply: *The country's mineral wealth has never really been tapped.* 3 [T] to make a secret telephone connection so that you can listen to other people's conversations: *The phones of foreign diplomats have been tapped.* 4 [T] to take liquid from a tree through a hole in its trunk: *They are tapping rubber trees.*

tap danc·ing /ˈ· ˌ··/ n [U] a kind of dancing in which dancers use special shoes to beat time to the music with their feet –**tap dancer** n

tape[1] /teɪp/ n 1 [U] a special narrow plastic band on which sound or images can be recorded: *I've got the match on tape.* | *Record the opera on this blank tape.* 2 [C] a length of narrow plastic on which sound or images have been recorded: *I want to buy a tape of Michael Jackson's songs.* 3 [C;U] a long, very narrow piece of material used for tying things like parcels 4 [C] a long, narrow piece of material which is stretched across a course to show the end point of a race

tape[2] v **taped, taping** 1 [I;T] to record something on a TAPE RECORDER, CASSETTE RECORDER or VIDEO RECORDER: *He tapes a lot of business conversations.* 2 [T] to fasten or fix something using tape which sticks: *She taped the box closed.* 3 **have something or someone taped** infml to understand exactly how to deal with a person or situation: *After a month in the new job, I had it taped.*

tape deck /ˈ· ·/ n a machine that records and plays back sound –see picture on page 442

tape mea·sure /ˈ· ˌ··/ n a long narrow band of cloth or steel with centimetres marked on it, which is used for measuring things –see picture on page 638

ta·per[1] /ˈteɪpəʳ/ v [I;T] to become or to make something gradually narrower towards one end

taper off phr v [I] to gradually become less in size or quantity: *Enthusiasm for the project has been tapering off.*

taper[2] n a very long thin candle

tape re·cord·er /ˈ· ·ˌ··/ n a machine that records and plays back sound

tap·es·try /ˈtæpɪstri/ n **tapestries** [C;U] heavy cloth onto which a picture is sewn or woven: *There were beautiful tapestries on the walls.* | *tapestry chair covers*

tape·worm /ˈteɪpwɜːm ‖ -wɜːrm/ n a long flat worm that can live inside the bodies of people and animals

tap·i·o·ca /ˌtæpiˈəʊkə/ n [U] small white grains of food made from the tropical CASSAVA plant

tar /tɑːʳ/ n [U] a black substance, thick and sticky when it is hot and hard when it is cold, which is used for making roads

ta·ran·tu·la /təˈræntjʊlə ‖ -tʃələ/ n a large hairy poisonous SPIDER

tar·dy /ˈtɑːdi ‖ ˈtɑːrdi/ adj lit slow to act or happen

tar·get /ˈtɑːɡɪt ‖ ˈtɑːr-/ n 1 an object, building, or place which is aimed at, especially with a gun or bomb: *We are trained to hit moving targets.* 2 a person or thing that people blame, laugh at, or attack: *He is the target of many jokes.* 3 an amount or result which you hope to reach: *The company has failed to meet its production targets.*

tar·iff /ˈtærɪf/ n 1 a list of fixed prices charged for services, especially in a hotel: *Compare the room* *tariffs in the two hotels.* **2** a tax collected by a government, usually on goods coming into a country

tar·mac /'tɑːmæk ‖ 'tɑːr-/ *n* **1** [U] a mixture of TAR and small stones used for making road surfaces **2 the tarmac** an area covered with this substance, especially one where planes wait before taking off

tar·nish /'tɑːnɪʃ ‖ 'tɑːr-/ *v* **1** [I;T] to become or to make a metal object less bright: *These silver spoons tarnish easily unless they are polished.* | *Wet weather can tarnish brass.* **2** [T] to make something less perfect: *The scandal has tarnished the reputation of several politicians.* **–tarnish** *n* [U]

tar·ot /'tærəʊ/ *n* the telling of a person's future using a set of 22 special cards: *tarot cards*

tar·pau·lin /tɑː'pɔːlᵻn ‖ tɑːr-/ *n* [C;U] heavy material which is covered with a special substance to prevent water passing through it

tar·ra·gon /'tærəgən/ *n* [U] a plant which is used to give food a special taste

tart¹ /tɑːt ‖ tɑːrt/ *n* **1** [C;U] a circle of pastry cooked with fruit or some other filling in it: *a piece of apple tart* **2** [C] *infml* a woman or girl who is considered to be sexually immoral

tart² *adj* **1** unpleasantly sharp in taste: *These apples are too tart to eat raw.* **2** unpleasantly sharp or unkind in speech: *We were hurt by her tart comments on our efforts.*

tar·tan /'tɑːtn ‖ 'tɑːrtn/ *n* [C;U] woollen cloth woven with bands of different colours and widths crossing each other, which is typically from Scotland; many patterns have an association with a particular Scottish family

tar·tar /'tɑːtəʳ ‖ 'tɑːr-/ *n* **1** [C] a fierce person, often a woman, with a violent temper **2** [U] a hard substance that forms on your teeth

tartar sauce /ˌ·· '· ‖ '··· /*n* [U] (also **tartare sauce**) a cold, thick liquid that is eaten with fish

task /tɑːsk ‖ tæsk/ *n* **1** a piece of work, often difficult, that has to be done: *I was given the task of sweeping the floors.* | *She finds looking after her father a difficult task.* **2 take someone to task** to scold someone severely: *She was taken to task for her negative attitude.*

task force /'·· ·/ *n* [+sing/pl verb] a group of people, especially military people, who are sent to a place for a special purpose

task·mas·ter /'tɑːsk₁mɑːstəʳ ‖ 'tæsk₁mæstər/ *n* a person who gives other people a lot of work to do: *Our teacher's a hard taskmaster.*

tas·sel /'tæsəl/ *n* a bunch of threads tied together at one end and hung on things like curtains for decoration

taste¹ /teɪst/ *v* **tasted, tasting** **1** [T] to judge the taste of food or drink by putting a little into your mouth: *Do you want to taste the wine?* **2** [T] to experience the sensation of food or drink in your mouth: *After a spicy main course, I can't taste the pudding.* **3** [I] to have a particular taste: *These oranges taste nice.* | *This soup tastes of chicken.* **4** [T] to experience something for a short time: *Now that he has tasted the freedom of living alone, he doesn't want her back.*

taste² *n* **1** [C;U] the sensation of saltiness, sweetness and so on that you have when something is put in your mouth: *I like the taste of Indian food.* | *This cake has very little taste.* | *I've got a cold, so I've lost my sense of taste.* **2** [C] a small quantity of food or drink that you try: *Have a taste of the soup and tell me what you think.* **3** [C] a short experience of

something: *It was his first taste* **of** *freedom.* **4** [C;U] the ability to choose and judge things which are attractive or of good quality: *She has good taste* **in** *clothes.* **5 a taste for** a liking for something: *I am trying to develop a taste for shellfish.* **6 in bad taste** not at all suitable for a particular time or occasion: *His behaviour at the funeral was in very bad taste.* [RELATED PHRASE **in good taste**]

taste·ful /'teɪstfəl/ *adj* showing someone's ability to choose what is attractive or of good quality: *The room was decorated in tasteful shades of pink.* **–tastefully** *adv*

taste·less /'teɪstləs/ *adj* **1** providing no sensation when it is put in your mouth: *tasteless medicine* **2** showing someone's lack of ability to decide what is attractive or of good quality: *tasteless furniture* **3** offensive to other people's feelings of what is suitable: *He made a number of tasteless remarks about her sick father.* **–tastelessness** *n* [U]

tast·er /'teɪstəʳ/ *n* a person whose job is to test the quality of food and drink by tasting them: *a wine taster*

tast·y /'teɪsti/ *adj* **tastier, tastiest** **1** with a strong and pleasant taste: *a tasty meal* **2** *infml* sexually attractive

tat·tered /'tætəd ‖ -ərd/ *adj* old and torn: *tattered clothes*

tat·ters /'tætəz ‖ -ərz/ *n* **in tatters: a** torn in many places (used of clothes): *His shirt was in tatters after the fight.* **b** destroyed: *The conflict left her career in tatters.*

tat·too¹ /tə'tuː, tæ'tuː/ *v* [T] to draw pictures or write on someone's skin using a sharp tool and coloured inks: *A heart was tattooed on his chest.*

tattoo² *n* **1** words or a picture drawn on someone's skin using a sharp tool and coloured inks **2** a rapid beating of military drums played as a signal **3** an outdoor military show with music

tat·ty /'tæti/ *adj* **tattier, tattiest** *infml* untidy, dirty, and in bad condition: *tatty clothes* **–tattily** *adv* **–tattiness** *n* [U]

taught /tɔːt/ the past tense and past participle of TEACH

taunt /tɔːnt/ *v* [T] to try to make someone angry or unhappy by making unkind remarks about their weak points: *He was taunted by other children about his weight.* **–tauntingly** *adv* **–taunt** *n*

Tau·rus /'tɔːrəs/ *n* one of the signs of the ZODIAC

taut /tɔːt/ *adj* **1** stretched tight: *Pull the rope until it's taut!* **2** showing signs of anxiety: *Her face was taut and pale with worry.* **–tautly** *adv* **–tautness** *n* [U]

tau·tol·o·gy /tɔː'tɒlədʒi ‖ tɔː'tɑː-/ *n* **tautologies** [C;U] a statement in which you say the same thing twice using different words: *It is a tautology to say that he sat alone by himself.* **–tautological** /ˌtɔːtə'lɒdʒɪkəl ‖ -'lɑː-/ *adj*

tav·ern /'tævən ‖ -ərn/ *n old fash* a pub

taw·dry /'tɔːdri/ *adj* **tawdrier, tawdriest** bright and highly decorated but cheap and of poor quality: *tawdry jewellery* **–tawdriness** *n* [U]

taw·ny /'tɔːni/ *adj* brownish yellow in colour

tax¹ /tæks/ *v* [T] **1** to take a certain amount of money from income or the price of goods and services in tax: *Most luxury goods are taxed at 15%.* | *The government plans to tax small businesses more heavily.* **2** to make heavy demands on a person:

The child really taxes my patience. | *It was a long, taxing journey.*

tax² *n* [C;U] money collected by the government from your income or property, or goods and services that you pay for, which is used to support public services: *Taxes on alcohol and cigarettes have gone up again.* | *Half of my salary goes in tax.* | *a plan to impose a tax on betting*

tax·a·ble /ˈtæksəbəl/ *adj* that can or must be taxed: *taxable income*

tax·a·tion /tækˈseɪʃən/ *n* [U] **1** the collection of money in tax by the government: *We must increase taxation if we are to spend more on the health service.* **2** the amount of money that people have to pay in tax

tax-free /ˌ·ˈ·◄/ *adj* with no tax to pay: *tax-free income* –**tax-free** *adv*: *Artists can live there tax-free.*

tax·i¹ /ˈtæksi/ *n* [C;U] (also **taxicab** /ˈtæksikæb/ *fml*) **1** a car and driver which can be hired by members of the public: *Shall I call a taxi?* –see picture on page 735 **2 by taxi** travelling in a taxi: *Shall we go by taxi?*

taxi² *v* **taxied, taxiing** [I] (of a plane) to move slowly along the ground before taking off or after landing

tax·i·der·my /ˈtæksɪˌdɜːmi ‖ -ɜːr-/ *n* [U] the art of preserving and filling the skins of dead animals, so that they look like living creatures –**taxidermist** *n*

taxi rank /ˈ·· ·/ (also **taxi stand**) *n* a place where taxis wait for passengers

tax·pay·er /ˈtæksˌpeɪəʳ/ *n* a person who pays part of their income as tax

TB /ˌtiː ˈbiː/ an abbreviation for TUBERCULOSIS

tbs [plural is **tbs**] a written abbreviation for TABLESPOON

tea /tiː/ *n* **1** [U] the dried leaves of a bush grown mainly in Asia: *a packet of tea* **2** [C;U] a hot brown drink made by pouring boiling water onto these leaves: *Would you like a cup of tea?* | *Two teas with milk and sugar, please.* **3** [C;U] a small meal served in the afternoon, or a main meal served in the early evening: *What are we having for tea today?* –see DINNER (USAGE) **4** [U] a drink made like tea but using the leaves or flowers of other plants: *a glass of mint tea*

tea·bag /ˈtiːbæg/ *n* a small bag with tea leaves inside, which you put into boiling water to make tea

tea cad·dy /ˈ· ˌ··/ *n* **tea caddies** a small tin in which tea is kept

teach /tiːtʃ/ *v* **taught** /tɔːt/, **taught, teaching** [I; T; + (that)] **1** to give knowledge, training, or lessons in a particular subject or skill: *She teaches history.* | *Mary teaches politics to university students.* | *I teach young children swimming.* | *My religion teaches that war is wrong.* | *He taught the boys to play cricket.* | *I taught them what to do.*
□ USEFUL PATTERNS to teach someone; to teach something; to teach someone to do something; to teach someone that …. **2 teach someone a lesson** to punish someone so that they do not repeat what they have done: *I'm going to stop your pocket money to teach you a lesson.*

teach·er /ˈtiːtʃəʳ/ *n* a person who teaches, especially at a school or college: *He's a music teacher.* | *a secondary school teacher*
■ USAGE **Teacher** is not usually used as a form of address. It is usual for students to call their teachers by their names, either formally: *Good morning* **Ms Smith/Mr Jones**, or informally: *Good morning* **Mary/Bill**.

teach·ing /ˈtiːtʃɪŋ/ *n* **1** [U] the work of a teacher: *Most of my teaching is in the mornings.* **2** [C] the moral, political or religious beliefs taught, often by a person of historical importance: *the teachings* **of** *Confucius*

tea co·sy /ˈ· ˌ··/ *n* **tea cosies** a thick cover put over a teapot to keep the tea hot

tea·cup /ˈtiːkʌp/ *n* a cup from which you drink tea

teak /tiːk/ *n* [U] a very hard wood which is used for making furniture and ships

tea·leaf /ˈtiːliːf/ *n* **tealeaves** /-liːvz/ one of the small pieces of leaf used for making tea

team¹ /tiːm/ *n* [+sing/pl verb] **1** a group of people who work together or play a game or sport together: *He's in the school cricket team.* | *A team of management consultants has been called in to advise us.* | *Do you enjoy team games?* **2** two or more animals pulling the same vehicle: *a team of horses*

team² *v*
team up *phr v* [I] to work with another person for a particular purpose: *I've teamed up with Jane to write the book.*

team spir·it /ˌ· ˈ··/ *n* [U] the feeling of loyalty among members of a team working together for the success of the group as a whole

team·work /ˈtiːmwɜːk ‖ -wɜːrk/ *n* [U] the ability of a group to work well together

tea·pot /ˈtiːpɒt ‖ -pɑːt/ *n* a container with a handle and a SPOUT, from which tea is poured into cups –see picture on page 148

tear¹ /tɪəʳ/ *n* **1** a drop of salty liquid that runs from your eye when you are unhappy or in pain: *Tears streamed down her face.* **2 in tears** crying: *He was so upset, he was almost in tears.*

tear² /teəʳ/ *v* **tore** /tɔːʳ/, **torn** /tɔːn ‖ tɔːrn/ **1** [T] to make irregular holes in cloth or paper, or to pull material apart leaving irregular edges: *Just tear the paper down the middle!* | *You've torn your trousers again, you careless boy.* –see BREAK (USAGE) **2** [T + adv/prep] to remove a person or thing by force: *You tear the paper off the walls and I'll paint them.* | *She tore herself from his grasp and ran.* **3** [I] to split, leaving irregular holes or edges: *This material tears easily.* **4** [I + adv/prep] to move at great speed: *She tore down the road to catch the post.* **5 in a tearing hurry** in a great rush to get somewhere **6 tear a strip off someone** *infml* to scold someone severely **7 tear into someone** to express your anger with someone, usually in words **8 be torn** to be unable to choose between two or more things or courses of action: *I'm torn between going with her and staying with the children.*

tear sthg **apart** *phr v* [T] to divide an organization or country by causing great trouble: *The country was torn apart by the civil war.*

tear sbdy ↔ **away** *phr v* [T] to make someone leave a place or stop doing something although they do not want to: *He couldn't tear himself away from the T.V.*

tear sthg ↔ **down** *phr v* [T] to destroy or use force to remove a building: *All the flats are being torn down.*

tear sthg ↔ **up** *phr v* [T] to destroy something made of paper by pulling it into pieces: *He tore up every photograph he had of her.*

tear³ /teəʳ/ *n* a hole or split in cloth or paper where it has been torn

tear·a·way /ˈteərəweɪ/ *n* *infml* a wild youth who is difficult to control

tear·drop /ˈtɪədrɒp ‖ ˈtɪərdrɑːp/ n a single tear that falls from your eye when you are crying

tear·ful /ˈtɪəfəl ‖ ˈtɪər-/ adj crying or on the point of crying –**tearfully** adv –**tearfulness** n [U]

tea·room /ˈtiːruːm, -rʊm/ n a small restaurant where tea and light meals are served

tease /tiːz/ v **teased, teasing** [I;T] **1** to laugh at playfully or unkindly or make jokes about: *They teased me at school because I wore glasses.* **2** to annoy a person or animal by offering or threatening something without actually meaning it: *He doesn't mean it; he's only teasing.* **3 tease something out of someone** to persuade someone to tell you something even though they are unwilling –**tease** n : *Don't be such a tease!*

teas·er /ˈtiːzəʳ/ n infml a difficult question, for example in a competition

tea·spoon /ˈtiːspuːn/ n **1** a small spoon used for mixing sugar into tea or coffee **2** (also **teaspoonful**) the amount of something that this spoon holds: *I take two teaspoons of sugar in my coffee.*

teat /tiːt/ n **1** a rubber object with a hole in it, fixed to a bottle for a baby to suck liquids through **2** the part of the flesh on the body of a female animal through which a baby sucks its mother's milk

tea·time /ˈtiːtaɪm/ n [U] the time in the afternoon when people have tea

tea tow·el /ˈ·ˌ·/ n a cloth for drying things like cups and plates after they have been washed

tech /tek/ n see TECHNICAL COLLEGE

tech·ni·cal /ˈteknɪkəl/ adj **1** having special and usually practical knowledge, especially of an industrial or scientific subject: *technical experts | This book is too technical for a child to understand.* **2** of or related to a particular subject, especially a practical or scientific one: *technical training | The book is full of technical terms.* –**technically** /-kli/ adv

technical col·lege /ˈ··· ·ˌ·/ n (also **tech** infml) a college that provides courses in practical subjects related to particular jobs, as well as in arts and social sciences for students who have left school

tech·ni·cal·i·ty /ˌteknɪˈkælʌti/ n **technicalities 1** a detail of a rule which is carefully followed: *He could not be tried for the crime because of a technicality in the law.* **2** the **technicalities** the small details of a process or method: *He's interested in the technicalities of paper-making.*

tech·ni·cian /tekˈnɪʃən/ n a skilled worker, especially in science or industry

tech·nique /tekˈniːk/ n **1** [C] a way of doing some practical or specialist activity: *I am practising new photographic techniques.* **2** [U] skill in doing something practical, artistic, or connected with sport: *She is working with her new piano teacher to improve her technique.*

tech·nol·o·gy /tekˈnɒlədʒi ‖ -ˈnɑː-/ n **technologies** [C;U] the branch of knowledge or activity dealing with scientific and industrial methods and their practical use in industry: *We haven't got the technology to compete with the Japanese in electronics.* –**technologist** n –**technological** /ˌteknəˈlɒdʒɪkəl ‖ -ˈlɑː-/ adj : *The computer is the result of recent technological advances.* –**technologically** /-kli/ adv

ted·dy bear /ˈtedi beəʳ/ (also **teddy**) n a toy bear filled with soft material

te·di·ous /ˈtiːdiəs/ adj long and very uninteresting: *tedious political speeches* –**tediously** adv –**tediousness** n [U]

tee /tiː/ n the small object from which the player first hits the ball in a game of GOLF

teem /tiːm/ v [I] **1** to be crowded with living, moving creatures: *The river was teeming with fish.* **2** infml to rain very heavily

teen·age /ˈtiːneɪdʒ/ adj [only before a noun] **1** concerning teenagers or for teenagers: *teenage fashions* **2** (also **teenaged**) between 13 and 19 years old: *a teenage boy*

teen·ag·er /ˈtiːneɪdʒəʳ/ n a young person between 13 and 19 years old: *The audience consisted mainly of teenagers.* –see CHILD (USAGE)

teens /tiːnz/ n [pl] the period of a person's life between the ages of 13 and 19: *She's in her teens now.*

tee shirt /ˈtiː ʃɜːt ‖ -ʃɜːrt/ n see T-SHIRT

tee·ter /ˈtiːtəʳ/ v **1** [I + adv/prep] to stand or move in an unsteady way: *She teetered along the street in her high-heeled shoes.* **2 teeter on the brink, teeter on the edge** to be close to a terrible state or event: *The company is teetering on the brink of financial ruin.*

teeth /tiːθ/ the plural of TOOTH

teethe /tiːð/ v **teethed, teething** [I] (of babies) to grow teeth for the first time, often painfully: *The poor child is teething.*

tee·to·tal /ˌtiːˈtəʊtl◂/ adj never drinking alcohol: *I've been teetotal since I realised I had a drinking problem.* –**teetotaller** BrE (**teetotaler** AmE) n

tel·e·com·mu·ni·ca·tions /ˌtelikəmjuːnʌˈkeɪʃənz/ n [pl] the sending or receiving of messages by telephone, television, telegraph, or radio

tel·e·gram /ˈtelʌgræm/ n a message sent by telegraph which is delivered to someone

tel·e·graph /ˈtelʌgrɑːf ‖ -græf/ n [U] a method of sending messages along wire by electric or radio signals: *Send it by telegraph.* –**telegraph** v [T] : *We telegraphed her the news.* –**telegraphic** /ˌtelʌˈgræfɪk◂/ adj –**telegraphically** /-kli/ adv

telegraph pole /ˈ··· ·/ (also **telegraph post**) n a pole for supporting telephone and telegraph wires

te·lep·a·thy /tʌˈlepəθi/ n [U] the sending of thoughts from one person's mind to another's without speaking or writing or any ordinary use of the senses –**telepathic** /ˌtelʌˈpæθɪk◂/ adj –**telepathically** /-kli/ adv

tel·e·phone¹ /ˈtelʌfəʊn/ n (also **phone** infml) a machine used for speaking to someone who is a long way away from you: *I need to make a telephone call. | He's on the telephone to his mother. | Can I use your telephone?* –see picture on page 539

telephone² (also **phone** infml) v **telephoned, telephoning 1** [I;T] to speak to someone by telephone: *Did you telephone Bob? | I telephoned to invite them. | She telephoned the news to her brother.* **2** [T] to ring the number of a person you want to speak to by telephone: *I've been telephoning him all morning but he's not there. | You can't telephone London direct from here.*

■ USAGE If you want to **telephone** your mother (or **phone** her, or **ring** her (**up**) or **call** her) you **dial** her **number**. If you want your mother to pay for the call you ask the **operator** for a **reverse charge call** (or a **collect call** in America) and the operator will **connect** you. The phone will **ring** and your mother may **answer** by picking up the **receiver**. If she is busy she may ask you to **call back** later. When she finishes speaking to you she will **hang up** (= replace the receiver). If she is already **on the phone** when you call her, her number is **engaged** (British English) or **busy** (American English).

telephone booth /ˈ··· ·/ n a small enclosed space in a public place, where you can make telephone calls

telephone ex·change /ˈ··· ·ˌ·/ n (also **exchange**) a central place where telephone connections are made

te·leph·o·nist /tɪˈlefənɪst/ n a person who works in a telephone exchange or answers the telephone in a company or organization

tel·e·pho·to lens /ˌtelɪˈfəʊtəʊ ˈlenz/ n an additional part for a camera that allows you to take clear pictures of distant objects

tel·e·scope¹ /ˈtelɪskəʊp/ n a long scientific instrument which makes distant objects appear nearer and larger

telescope² v telescoped, telescoping [I;T] to become or to make something shorter, usually by sliding one part over another

tel·e·scop·ic /ˌtelɪˈskɒpɪk◄/ adj 1 making distant objects appear nearer and larger: a telescopic lens 2 made of parts that slide over one another to make the whole thing shorter

tel·e·van·gel·ist /ˌtelɪˈvændʒəlɪst/ n a person who tries to persuade people to become CHRISTIANS by talking to them over the television; televangelists often ask people to send them money

tel·e·vise /ˈtelɪvaɪz/ v televised, televising [T] to broadcast something on television: The whole of the World Cup will be televised.

tel·e·vi·sion /ˈtelɪˌvɪʒən, ˌtelɪˈvɪʒən/ n (also **telly**, **TV** infml) 1 [C;U] an electrical apparatus which broadcasts pictures and sound: Shall I turn the television on? | What's on television this evening? 2 [U] the things that are broadcast on television: Do you watch much television? | a television programme 3 [U] the business of recording and broadcasting pictures and sound: the television industry

■ USAGE Remember to use the preposition **on** for expressions such as: I saw it **on** television. | The Prime Minister appeared **on** television last night. | What's on **telly/on T.V.** tonight?

tel·ex /ˈteleks/ n 1 [U] a method of sending printed messages by electrical signals: Send it ¹by telex. 2 [C] a message sent in this way: A telex has arrived from Hong Kong. 3 [C] a special machine for sending these messages: The telex operator will send it for you. –**telex** v [I;T]: We'll telex our charges to you immediately.

tell /tel/ v told /təʊld/, **telling** 1 [T] to express something in words: Did you tell Joan about Paul? | John told us he'd seen you in town. | Can you tell me what time the party starts? | The children want me to tell them a story. | Are you telling me the truth? □ USEFUL PATTERNS tell someone (about) something; to tell someone that; tell someone what, why, how, etc. –see SAY¹ (USAGE) 2 [T] to advise someone to do something: I told him to see a doctor if he was worried. □ USEFUL PATTERNS to tell someone to do something; to tell someone that... 3 [T] to order someone to do something: Children should do as they're told! | I told her not to be late. –see ORDER² (USAGE) 4 [T] to let someone know something: This light tells you if the machine is on or off. 5 **I told you so** a phrase used when you warned someone that something would happen and it did: 'It didn't work.' 'I told you so.' 6 **time will tell** = we will know some time in the future: Only time will tell whether they have made the right decision. 7 **tell the time** to read the time from a clock or watch 8 **be able to tell** to recognize or

judge the truth of something: It was so dark I couldn't tell it was you. | I can't tell the difference between the twins. | "Which team will win?" "Who can tell?" 9 **there's no telling** it is not possible to know: There's no telling when the situation will improve. 10 [I] to have a bad effect on someone: The long hours of difficult work are starting to tell **on** us. 11 [I] to pass someone's secret to another person: If I show you what I did, will you promise not to tell? | You won't tell **on** me, will you? 12 **you're telling me** infml a phrase used when you agree with someone completely 13 **tell you what, I tell you what** an expression used in informal conversation when you are going to suggest a good idea you have just had: I tell you what – why don't you put the table against the other wall?

tell sbdy ↔ **off** phr v [T] to scold someone: She tells me off for the smallest mistakes.

tell·er /ˈtelər/ n 1 a person employed to receive and pay out money in a bank 2 a person who counts votes during an election

tell·ing /ˈtelɪŋ/ adj 1 very effective: a telling argument 2 showing your feelings, even if you intend to hide them: a telling remark

tell·tale¹ /ˈtelteɪl/ n infml a person who passes on other people's secrets, knowing that they will be punished

telltale² adj [only before a noun] making something clear that is intended to be hidden: A telltale look of jealousy in his eyes contradicted his calm manner.

tel·ly /ˈteli/ n [C;U] –see TELEVISION (USAGE)

te·mer·i·ty /tɪˈmerəti/ n [U] fml bold confidence which is not suitable and often not polite: He had the temerity to ask for higher wages at the end of his first week's work.

tem·per¹ /ˈtempər/ n 1 [C;U] an angry state of mind: John's in a temper. | a fit of temper 2 **fly into a temper, get into a temper, lose your temper** to become angry suddenly 3 **keep your temper** to stay calm 4 [C;U] a particular nature or state of mind, especially with regard to how easily you get angry: She has such a sweet temper. | He could never control his temper. 5 **-tempered** having a certain kind of nature or state of mind: She's a bad-tempered old lady. 6 [U] tech the degree to which a metal has been made hard or strong

temper² v [T] 1 tech to make metal harder and stronger by heating it and then making it cool 2 fml to make something less severe or difficult: His words were harsh, but he tempered them **with** a smile.

tem·pe·ra·ment /ˈtempərəmənt/ n [C;U] a person's nature, which influences their way of thinking or acting: Their marriage succeeds because their temperaments are so similar.

tem·pe·ra·men·tal /ˌtempərəˈmentl◄/ adj 1 having frequent and sudden changes of feelings: The actor was so temperamental that people refused to work with him. 2 caused by or related to a person's nature: She had a temperamental dislike of competitive sports. –**temperamentally** adv

tem·pe·rance /ˈtempərəns/ n [U] fml self-control 2 total avoidance of alcoholic drinks

tem·pe·rate /ˈtempərət/ adj 1 showing self-control: temperate behaviour 2 never very hot or cold: Britain has a temperate climate.

tem·pe·ra·ture /ˈtempərətʃər/ n [C;U] 1 the degree of heat or coldness of a person, thing, or place: The average temperature in London is 15°C. | The constant changes in temperature made me ill. 2 **have a**

temperature, run a temperature to have a higher body temperature than usual: *You're not going out while you've got a temperature!* **3 take someone's temperature** to measure the temperature of someone's body: *Get the thermometer and I'll take your temperature.*

tem·pest /ˈtempɪst/ *n lit* a violent storm

tem·pes·tu·ous /temˈpestʃuəs/ *adj* **1** stormy: *the tempestuous sea* **2** full of strong feelings and arguments: *a tempestuous meeting* –**tempestuously** *adv* –**tempestuousness** *n* [U]

tem·ple /ˈtempəl/ *n* **1** a building used for worship in certain religions: *a Buddhist temple* **2** one of the two flat places on each side of your forehead

tem·po /ˈtempəʊ/ *n* **tempos** *or* **tempi** /-piː/ **1** *tech* the speed at which music is played: *Let's try that again at a faster tempo.* **2** the speed at which something happens: *I found it difficult to adjust to the tempo of city life.*

tem·po·ral /ˈtempərəl/ *adj fml* **1** related to practical material affairs, as opposed to religious affairs: *the temporal power of the state* **2** related to or limited by time: *"When" is a temporal conjunction.*

tem·po·ra·ry /ˈtempərəri, -pəri ‖ -pəreri/ *adj* lasting only for a limited time: *a temporary holiday job* –compare PERMANENT –**temporarily** /ˈtempərərəli ‖ ˌtempəˈrerəli/ *adv* : *I was temporarily delayed.*

tempt /tempt/ *v* [T] **1** to try to persuade someone to do something which may be unwise or immoral: *He tried to tempt me to cheat in the examination.* | *Another firm is trying to tempt her away from her present job with an offer of more money.* | *Leaving your car open might tempt someone into stealing it.* □ USEFUL PATTERNS to tempt someone to do something; to tempt someone with something; to tempt someone into doing something **2** to try to attract someone to do something that you want them to do: *His mother tried to tempt him by preparing delicious meals.* **3 be tempted to do something** to want to do something but to be unsure if it is the right thing to do: *It's a very attractive offer and I'm tempted to accept.*

temp·ta·tion /tempˈteɪʃən/ *n* **1** [U] a state in which you feel persuaded to do something which may be wrong: *I resisted the temptation to smoke a cigarette.* **2** [C] a situation or thing which may persuade you to do something wrong: *the temptations of a big city*

tempt·ing /ˈtemptɪŋ/ *adj* attractive, but perhaps not the right thing to do: *It's tempting to believe that I'll be promoted soon.* | *a tempting offer* –**temptingly** *adv*

ten /ten/ *det, n, pron* the number 10

ten·a·ble /ˈtenəbəl/ *adj fml* **1** reasonable and able to be successfully defended (used of an argument or belief): *Her views are no longer tenable.* –opposite **untenable** **2** that can be held by someone for a certain length of time (used of an office or position): *How long is the post tenable for?*

te·na·cious /tɪˈneɪʃəs/ *adj* determined, and not easily accepting defeat: *She has proved a very tenacious opponent of the new road scheme.* –**tenaciously** *adv* –**tenacity** /-ˈnæsɪti / *n* [U]

ten·an·cy /ˈtenənsi/ *n* **tenancies** [C;U] the use of a room, land, or building for which rent has been paid, or the length of time you have this use for: *a tenancy agreement* | *rights of tenancy*

ten·ant /ˈtenənt/ *n* a person who pays rent for the use of a room, building, or land: *a council tenant*

tend /tend/ *v* **1** [I] to do or happen often or usually: *Janet tends to get angry if you ask her stupid questions.* | *It tends to rain here a lot in spring.*

□ USEFUL PATTERN to tend to do something **2** [T] *fml* to look after someone or something in a caring way: *She tended her husband lovingly during his illness.* | *a farmer tending his sheep*

tend to sthg/sbdy *phr v* [T] to pay attention to someone or something: *The nurses tended to the soldiers' wounds.*

ten·den·cy /ˈtendənsi/ *n* **tendencies** **1** a part of your character which makes you likely to think or behave in a particular way: *He's always had a tendency towards frivolity.* | *She has a tendency to shout when she gets angry.* □ USEFUL PATTERN have a tendency to do something **2** a general development towards a certain situation or condition: *There is a growing tendency for people to work at home instead of in offices.*

ten·der[1] /ˈtendəʳ/ *adj* **1** easy to bite through: *tender meat* **2** painful or sensitive: *His wound is still tender.* **3** gentle and loving: *tender loving care* **4** [only before a noun] *lit* young and inexperienced: *He was sent to boarding school at the tender age of eight.* –**tenderly** *adv* –**tenderness** *n* [U]

tender[2] *n* **1** a statement of the price you would charge for doing a job or providing goods **2** a vehicle carrying coal or water, pulled behind a railway engine

tender[3] *v* **1** [T] *fml* to formally offer or give something: *"Passengers must tender the exact fare."* | *The minister tendered his resignation.* **2** [I] to make a formal offer to do a job or provide goods at a certain price: *Several firms have tendered for the new road building contract.*

ten·der·heart·ed /ˌtendəˈhɑːtɪd◂ ‖ -dərˈhɑːr-/ *adj* easily made to feel love, pity, or sorrow –**tenderheartedly** *adv*

ten·don /ˈtendən/ *n* a thick strong cord that connects a muscle to a bone

ten·dril /ˈtendrɪl/ *n* a thin curling stem by which a climbing plant fastens itself to something

ten·e·ment /ˈtenɪmənt/ *n* a large building divided into flats in the poorer areas of a city

ten·et /ˈtenɪt/ *n fml* a principle or belief: *the tenets of the Christian religion*

ten·ner /ˈtenəʳ/ *n BrE infml* £10 or a ten pound note

ten·nis /ˈtenɪs/ *n* [U] a game played between two or four people who use rackets (RACKET) to hit a small ball backwards and forwards across a low net dividing a specially marked level court: *Would you like a game of tennis?* | *a tennis ball* –see picture on page 637

tennis shoe /ˈ··· ·/ *n* the usual American word for a PLIMSOLL

ten·or /ˈtenəʳ/ *n* **1** a male singer with a high voice **2** a musical instrument with quite a low range of notes **3** the **tenor** of *fml* the general meaning of: *I understood the tenor of his speech but not the details.* –**tenor** *adj*

tense[1] /tens/ *n* [C;U] any of the forms of a verb that show whether you are talking about the past, the present, or the future: *"I have eaten" is the present perfect tense.*

tense[2] *adj* **1** stretched tight or stiff: *tense muscles* **2** nervous and anxious: *I'm always tense before an exam.* **3** causing feelings of worry and nervousness: *a tense moment before we heard the news* –**tensely** *adv*

tense[3] *v* tensed, tensing [I;T] to become tight and stiff: *I saw her tense up when the phone rang.* | *Tense your muscles, please!*

ten·sion /ˈtenʃən/ n 1 [U] the degree of tightness of a wire or rope: *Don't tighten the violin strings too much as they can snap under the tension.* 2 [C;U] a feeling of anxiety or fear: *He's suffering from nervous tension.* | *racial tensions in South Africa.* | *The border dispute has been a continuing source of tension.* 3 [U] *tech* electric power: *Danger! High tension wires.*

tent /tent/ n a movable shelter made of cloth or plastic material, supported by poles and ropes and used by campers to sleep in: *Where shall we pitch the tent?*

ten·ta·cle /ˈtentəkəl/ n a long thin boneless arm on certain creatures, used for moving, seizing, or touching: *the tentacles of an octopus*

ten·ta·tive /ˈtentətɪv/ adj 1 not certain or complete: *We've made tentative plans for a holiday but haven't really decided yet.* 2 done carefully and slowly without much confidence: *a tentative smile* –**tentatively** adv

ten·ter·hooks /ˈtentəhʊks ‖ -ər-/ n **on tenterhooks** worried or excited about something that will happen soon

tenth /tenθ/ 1 det, pron, adv 10th 2 one of ten equal parts

ten·u·ous /ˈtenjuəs/ adj very thin or weak (used of an idea or connection): *There is only a tenuous link between the film and the book on which it is based.*

ten·ure /ˈtenjəʳ, -juəʳ/ n [U] fml 1 the legal right to use land or buildings: *conditions of tenure* 2 the length of time you keep a job or position

tep·id /ˈtepɪd/ adj 1 only slightly warm (used of liquids) 2 not showing much interest: *a rather tepid welcome*

term[1] /tɜːm ‖ tɜːrm/ n 1 one of the periods of time into which the school or university year is divided: *the summer term* | *Do we have end-of-term exams?* 2 a fixed or limited period of time: *The President is elected for a four-year term.* | *a term of imprisonment* 3 a word or expression used in a particular activity, profession, or subject: *a medical term* | *terms of abuse* 4 **in the long term** over a long period of time: *In the long term we will make a profit.* [RELATED PHRASE **in the short term**] 5 **terms** the conditions under which you make an agreement: *We're trying to negotiate the loan on favourable terms.* | *terms of employment* 6 **in terms of** from the point of view of: *In terms of sales, the book hasn't been successful.* | *In business terms the project isn't viable.* 7 **be on good terms with** to be friendly with someone 8 **come to terms with** to accept something unpleasant: *I think I've come to terms with losing my job now.* 9 **in no uncertain terms** clearly and angrily: *He told me in no uncertain terms to go away.* 10 **think in terms of, talk in terms of** to consider something as a possibility: *We're thinking in terms of investing the money in property.* 11 **terms of reference** the limits of an enquiry or report: *This problem is outside the committee's terms of reference.*

term[2] v [T] to name or describe someone or something as a particular thing: *The chairman of this parliament is termed the "Speaker".*

ter·mi·nal[1] /ˈtɜːmɪnəl ‖ ˈtɜːr-/ adj concerning or having an illness that will cause death: *terminal cancer* | *terminal patients* –**terminally** adv : *a hospice for the terminally ill*

terminal[2] n 1 an apparatus usually consisting of a keyboard and a SCREEN by which you can give instructions to a computer and get information from it 2 a place where people, planes, and other vehicles begin or end a journey –see picture on page 735 3 a point at which connections can be made to an electric system

ter·mi·nate /ˈtɜːmɪneɪt ‖ ˈtɜːr-/ v **terminated, terminating** [I;T] fml to bring or come to an end: *Your contract has been terminated.* | *The meeting terminated successfully.* –**termination** /ˌtɜːmɪˈneɪʃən ‖ ˌtɜːr-/ n [U]

ter·mi·nol·o·gy /ˌtɜːmɪˈnɒlədʒi ‖ ˌtɜːrmɪˈnɑː-/ n [U] a system of specialized words and expressions used in a particular science, profession, or activity: *I don't understand scientific terminology.*

ter·mi·nus /ˈtɜːmɪnəs ‖ ˈtɜːr-/ n the end of a railway or bus line

ter·mite /ˈtɜːmaɪt ‖ ˈtɜːr-/ n a tropical insect like an ant that destroys wood, and builds hills of earth

ter·race /ˈterəs/ n 1 BrE a row of houses joined to each other 2 a flat outdoor area next to a building or on the roof, where you can sit or have your meals 3 one of the wide steps from which you can watch a football match 4 a flat piece of ground cut in the slope of a hill where crops are grown

ter·raced /ˈterəst/ adj 1 having flat pieces of ground cut in the side of a hill like large steps on which crops can be grown 2 **terraced house** a house which is part of a row of houses joined together –see picture on page 441

ter·ra·cot·ta /ˌterəˈkɒtə ‖ -ˈkɑː-/ n [U] hard reddish brown baked clay

ter·rain /teˈreɪn, tɪ-/ n [U] an area of land, and whether it is rough, smooth, easy or difficult to cross: *rocky terrain*

ter·ra·pin /ˈterəpɪn/ n a type of small water TURTLE

ter·res·tri·al /tɪˈrestriəl/ adj 1 related to the Earth, rather than the moon, or space 2 tech living on land, rather than in water or in the air: *a terrestrial animal*

ter·ri·ble /ˈterəbəl/ adj 1 very serious: *a terrible accident* 2 infml very bad or of poor quality: *You look terrible – are you ill?* | *a terrible play* 3 causing great dislike or fear: *There was a terrible noise and then a loud crash.*

ter·ri·bly /ˈterəbli/ adv 1 very badly: *He played that game terribly.* 2 infml very: *I've been terribly worried about you.* | *It wasn't a terribly good film.*

ter·ri·er /ˈteriəʳ/ n a type of small dog originally used for hunting

ter·rif·ic /təˈrɪfɪk/ adj infml 1 very good or enjoyable: *a terrific party* 2 very great: *She drove at a terrific speed.*

ter·rif·i·cally /təˈrɪfɪkli/ adv infml very: *It's terrifically cold today.*

ter·ri·fy /ˈterəfaɪ/ v **terrified, terrifying** [T] to fill someone with terror or fear: *Heights terrify me!*

ter·ri·to·ri·al /ˌterəˈtɔːriəl/ adj 1 relating to the land a country controls 2 **territorial waters** the sea near a country's coast over which that country has legal control

ter·ri·to·ry /ˈterətəri ‖ -tɔːri/ n **territories** 1 [C;U] the land that the government of a country controls: *British territories* | *We travelled through unknown territory.* 2 [C;U] a piece of land which an animal defends as belonging to it alone 3 [C] an area of interest or an area for which someone is responsible: *I never deal with the engineers' salaries: that's Peter's territory.*

ter·ror /ˈterəʳ/ n 1 [U] extreme fear: *He had a look of terror on his face.* | *The children ran away in terror.* 2 [C] someone or something that makes you very frightened: *the terrors of war*

ter·ror·is·m /ˈterərɪzəm/ n [U] the use of violence or the threat of violence to obtain political demands –**terrorist** adj,n : Terrorists have claimed responsibility for the bomb blast that killed 20 people.

ter·ror·ize /ˈterəraɪz/ v **terrorized, terrorizing** (also **terrorise** BrE) [T] to frighten someone or force them into doing something by using threats or violence: The cashier was terrorized into handing over the money.

terror-strick·en /ˈ·· ˌ··/ adj (also **terror-struck** /ˈ·· ˌ·/) extremely frightened

terse /tɜːs ‖ tɜːrs/ adj using very few words, sometimes in a way which seems rude –**tersely** adv

TESL /ˈtesəl/ n [U] the teaching of English to people who live in an English speaking country and who don't speak English as their first language; an abbreviation for **the Teaching of English as a Second Language**

ter·tia·ry /ˈtɜːʃəri ‖ ˈtɜːrʃieri, -ʃəri/ adj **1** fml at a third stage of development **2 tertiary education** education at the level of college or university

test[1] /test/ n **1** a number of questions or exercises to find out how good someone is at something or how much they know: a history test | I've passed my driving test. **2** the using of something to see how it works: Before buying the car I went for a test drive. | atom bomb tests **3** a short medical check on part of your body: an eye test | a blood test **4 put something to the test** to find out the qualities of something by using it in certain conditions

test[2] v [T] **1** to find out how much someone knows by asking them questions **2** to find out what something is like or how well it works: These wet roads really test a car's tyres. | I must have my eyes tested. | He prodded the fruit, testing it for ripeness.

tes·ta·ment /ˈtestəmənt/ n fml something that shows or proves something else very clearly: The aircraft is a testament to its designer's skill.

test case /ˈ· ·/ n a case in a court of law which establishes a particular principle, which is then used as a standard for other cases

tes·ti·cle /ˈtestɪkəl/ n one of the two round organs below a man's PENIS which produce SPERM

tes·ti·fy /ˈtestɪfaɪ/ v **testified, testifying** [I +(that)] to make a solemn statement about what is true: The teacher testified to the pupil's ability. | One witness testified that he'd seen the robbery. | She can't testify against her husband.

tes·ti·mo·ni·al /ˌtestɪˈməʊniəl/ n a formal written statement about someone's character and abilities

tes·ti·mo·ny /ˈtestɪməni ‖ -məʊni/ n [C;U] a formal statement, as made by a witness in a court of law

test match /ˈ· ·/ n (also **test**) one of a group of cricket or RUGBY matches played between teams of different countries

test pi·lot /ˈ· ˌ··/ a pilot who flies new aircraft in order to test them

test tube /ˈ· ·/ n a small tube of thin glass, closed at one end, used in scientific tests

test-tube ba·by /ˈ· · ˌ··/ n a baby started outside a mother's body and then planted inside her to develop naturally

tes·ty /ˈtesti/ adj infml impatient and bad tempered –**testily** adv

tet·a·nus /ˈtetənəs/ n [U] a serious disease caused by infection in a cut or wound, which stiffens the muscles, especially your jaw

tête-à-tête /ˌteɪt ɑː ˈteɪt, ˌteɪt ə -/ adv talking together in private: We dined tête-à-tête. –**tête-à-tête** n : a cosy tête-à-tête

teth·er /ˈteðər/ n **1** a rope or chain to which an animal is tied **2 at the end of your tether** having used up all your patience and strength and unable to manage any longer –**tether** v [T] : a dog tethered to a post

text /tekst/ n **1** [U] writing, for example in a book: Children's books often have more pictures than text. | This computer prints out text very fast. **2 the text** the exact original words or printed form of a speech, article, or book: The text of the President's speech is in today's newspaper. **3** [C] a sentence from the Bible that a priest reads and talks about in church **4** [C] a book which students studying a certain subject have to read: Hamlet is a set text this year.

text·book /ˈtekstbʊk/ n a standard book for the study of a particular subject

tex·tile /ˈtekstaɪl/ n any material made by weaving: a textile factory | silk and cotton textiles

tex·ture /ˈtekstʃər/ n [C;U] how rough or smooth, coarse or fine something feels when you touch it: the delicate texture of her skin | a soil with a loose sandy texture

than /ðən; strong ðæn/ conj, prep used when you are comparing two things: She's older than me. | He's older than I am. | He earns more than I do. | They were away for more than a week.

thank /θæŋk/ v [T] **1** to show or tell someone that you are pleased that they helped you or gave you something: I thanked him for his advice. | How can I ever thank you? You've been so helpful.
□ USEFUL PATTERNS to thank someone for something; to thank someone for doing something **2 thank you** (also **thanks** infml) an expression used to show that you are grateful to someone: Thank you for the present. | Do you want some tea? No, thank you. **3 have yourself to thank** to be responsible for something bad: You've only got yourself to thank for the accident. **4 thank God, thank goodness, thank heaven** an expression of pleasure that something unpleasant or worrying has ended: Thank God my son's alive!

thank·ful /ˈθæŋkfəl/ adj glad that something good has happened or grateful for something: I was thankful to be free of the problem. | I'm very thankful that I don't have to look after elderly relatives. –**thankfully** adv –**thankfulness** n [U]

thank·less /ˈθæŋkləs/ adj not likely to be rewarded with thanks or praise: He has the thankless task of organizing the rubbish collection.

thanks /θæŋks/ n [pl] **1** words which show how pleased you are that someone has helped you or done something for you: Give thanks to God. | I'll get no thanks for all this hard work. **2 thanks to** because of: Thanks to your stupidity, we lost the game.

thanks·giv·ing /ˌθæŋksˈɡɪvɪŋ◂/ n [U] **1** an expression of gratefulness to God **2 Thanksgiving** a holiday in the U.S. in November on which God is thanked for the year's crops

thank-you /ˈθæŋkjuː/ n an expression of thanks: a special thank-you for all your help | a thank-you letter

that[1] /ðæt/ det, pron **those** /ðəʊz/ **1** the person or thing that is further away in place or time: You look in this room and I'll look in that one over there. | That's my boss over there. | What's that? **2** the person or thing already stated or known about: I've got a meeting at two o'clock, but I'll be free after that. | I never want to see that man again! | "We're getting a pay rise next month." "That's good." **3 that's it**

a phrase you use to say that something is finished **4 that's that** a phrase you use to say that there is nothing more to say or do **5 that is, that is to say:** a phrases used when you are going to explain a word that you think people may not have understood: *The wood is then decorticated. That is, the bark is all taken off the outside.* **b** phrases used when you are going to say something more exactly a second time, perhaps because you think that you were not very clear or gave the wrong idea the first time: *He's going to do the garage again. That is, he's going to change the roof.*

that² *adv infml* not that not very: *I didn't like the film that much.*

that³ *conj* /ðət; *strong* ðæt/ **1** used after certain nouns, verbs, and adjectives: *Is it true that you're leaving?* | *I think that I'd better leave now.* | *There's no proof that she was here.* **2** who or which: *It was George that told me.* | *Did you see the letter that came today?* | *Did you get the books that I sent you?* | *He's the one person that I trust completely.*

■ USAGE 1 We can only leave out the relative pronoun when it is the object of the verb: *She's the woman* (**that**) *I love.* 2 We can only use **that** instead of **who** or **which** when we limit the meaning of a noun to show which ones(s) we mean: *I'll stay with my brother – the one* **who**/**that** *lives in Leeds.* We cannot use **that** when we simply add extra information: *This is my father,* **who** *lives in London.* 3 In ordinary speech we often leave out **that** before a noun clause, especially after common verbs of saying and thinking: *She said* (**that**) *it wasn't true.* | *I think* (**that**) *you're right.*

thatch /θætʃ/ *n* [U] roof covering made of STRAW or reeds (REED) –**thatched** *adj* : *Our house has a thatched roof.* | *a thatched cottage*

thaw /θɔː/ *v* **1** [I;T] to change from a solid frozen state to become liquid or soft because of an increase in temperature: *The snow is thawing.* | *Make sure that the chicken is properly thawed* **out** *before you cook it.* **2 it's thawing** = it's becoming warm enough for snow and ice to melt: *It's starting to thaw.* **3** [I] (of a person) to become friendlier or less formal –**thaw** *n*

the¹ /ðə, ði; *strong* ðiː/ *definite article,det* **1** used before singular and plural nouns when it is understood who or what you mean: *The sun is shining.* | *I spoke to her on the telephone.* **2** used as part of some names: *the Rhine* | *the Alps* **3** used before an adjective to make it into a noun: *We must help the poor.* | *emergency aid to feed the hungry* **4** used before a singular noun when you are talking about something in general: *The lion is a wild animal.* **5** used before the names of musical instruments: *She plays the violin.* **6** each: *He's paid by the hour.* **7** used in dates: *Monday the seventh of January.* **8** used in front of numbers to talk about a period of ten years: *the 1940s* | *He was born in the fifties.* **9** most important or most fashionable: *It's the place to go!*

the² *adv* used in comparisons: *The more you eat the fatter you will get.* | *He's the cleverest child in the class.*

thea·tre /ˈθɪətər/ *n* (**theater** *AmE*) **1** [C] a building with a stage on which plays are performed: *London's theatres* | *Shall we go to the theatre?* **2** [sing;U] the study of plays and the work of people who write, produce, or act in plays: *I'm interested in the theatre.* | *modern Russian theatre* **3** [C] a large room with each row of seats placed higher than the one in front: *a lecture theatre* **4** [C] see OPERATING THEATRE

the·at·ri·cal /θiˈætrɪkəl/ *adj* **1** related to or for the theatre: *a theatrical company* **2** showy and not natural (used of behaviour) –**theatrically** /-kli/ *adv*

thee /ðiː/ *pron* you (a word which is no longer used in modern English)

theft /θeft/ *n* [C;U] the act or crime of taking something which does not belong to you: *The police reported an increase in theft.* | *the theft of a car*

their /ðər; *strong* ðeər/ *det* **1** relating to or belonging to people, animals, or things that have already been mentioned: *They went in and took off their coats.* | *Students have to work hard to pass their exams.* **2** *infml* relating to or belonging to a person who has already been mentioned, when it has not been stated whether the person is a man or a woman: *Someone had come in and left their suitcase in the hall.*

theirs /ðeəz ‖ ðeərz/ *pron* something relating to or belonging to the people, animals, or things that have already been mentioned: *Our house is very similar to theirs.*

them /ðəm; *strong* ðem/ *pron* [used as the object of a verb] **1** the people, animals, or things that have already been mentioned: *Where are my shoes? I can't find them.* –see ME (USAGE) **2** *infml* the person who has already been mentioned, when it has not been stated whether the person is a man or a woman: *Someone came into the office looking for you, so I gave them your phone number.*

theme /θiːm/ *n* **1** the subject of a talk or piece of writing **2** a simple tune on which a piece of music is based **3** an idea which is repeated a number of times in a work of art or literature

theme song /ˈ· ·/ *n* (also **theme tune**) a song or tune played often during a musical play or film

themselves /ðəmˈselvz/ *pron* **1** used as the object of a verb or a PREPOSITION when the subject of a verb is plural and the action is done to the same people: *They consider themselves to be quite well off.* | *They had bought themselves a new car.* | *They're very pleased with themselves.* **2** used to add force to the word "they", or to the names of people or animals: *They had done all the decorating themselves.* **3 by themselves** alone, with no one with them or helping them: *They had spent the day by themselves.* | *They had managed to mend the roof by themselves.*

then¹ /ðen/ *adv* **1** at a particular time in the past or the future: *We lived in the country then.* | *I'll probably be dead by then.* **2** after that: *He poured himself a drink and then sat down.* | *The letters are collected from postboxes. They are then taken to the sorting office.* **3** used in sentences with "if": *If you want to go home, then go.* | *If I get any news then I'll phone you.* **4** used when you are adding something to what you have just said: *We have to think about how to avoid such accidents in the future. Then there's the question of compensation for the victims of this accident.* **5** used when you are reminding people of the main points in what has been said, or when you are showing the real meaning of earlier points: *The main problem facing the government, then, is the economy.* **6 but then** used when you are giving a piece of information which goes against what has just been said: *We could just repair the roof, but then that won't solve the problem completely.*

then² *adj* [only before a noun] at that time in the past: *the then president of the country*

thence /ðens/ *adv fml* from there: *They travelled to Paris and thence to the South of France.*

theo·lo·gian /θɪəˈləʊdʒən/ *n* a person who has studied theology

the·ol·o·gy /θiˈɒlədʒi ‖ θiˈɑː-/ n [U] the study of God and religious beliefs –**theological** /θiəˈlɒdʒɪkəl ‖ -ˈlɑː-/ adj

theo·rem /ˈθɪərəm/ n tech a statement in the science of numbers that can be shown to be true by reasoning

theo·rize /ˈθɪəraɪz/ v theorized, theorizing (also **theorise** BrE) [I] fml to form a set of ideas about how something works

theo·ry /ˈθɪəri/ n theories **1** [C] an explanation for something which is reasonable or scientifically acceptable, but which has not yet been proved to be true: Darwin's theory of evolution | The detective's theory is that the murderer was well known to the victim. **2** [U] the general principles for the study of an art or science as opposed to practical skill in it: musical theory | There will be two chemistry exams; one on theory and one will be practical. **3 in theory** a phrase used to describe the way something should happen but may not in practice: In theory the train should arrive at 9.15, but it's usually late. –**theorist** n –**theoretical** /ˌθɪəˈretɪkəl/ adj : theoretical science | a theoretical possibility –**theoretically** /-kli/ adv : Theoretically it's my job, but in fact I don't do it.

ther·a·peu·tic /ˌθerəˈpjuːtɪk◄/ adj **1** related to the treating or curing of a disease: a therapeutic diet **2** having a good effect on your health or state of mind: I find sewing very therapeutic.

ther·a·py /ˈθerəpi/ n therapies [C;U] the treatment of illnesses of the mind or body without drugs or operations: She's going to give me some heat therapy. –**therapist** : a speech therapist

there[1] /ðeər/ adv **1** in or to that place: They've lived there for ten years. | Look over there. | Could you put it down there, please? | That man over there might know. **2** at that point: I read to the bottom of the page and decided to stop there. **3** used for drawing attention to someone or something: There goes John. **4** **there and then, then and there** at that time and place: He asked me to marry him there and then. **5** **there, there** a phrase you use to comfort someone: There, there, don't cry. **6 there you are: a** a phrase you use when you are giving someone something that they want **b** a phrase you use when you have been proved to be right: There you are. I said it wouldn't work.

there[2] pron **there is, there are** a phrase used to show that someone or something exists or happens: There's a cat on the roof. | There are some letters for you. | There was a knock on the door. | Is there a telephone near here?

there·a·bouts /ˌðeərəˈbaʊts/ adv near a particular place, time, or number: I'll see you at six o'clock or thereabouts.

there·af·ter /ðeərˈɑːftər ‖ -ˈæf-/ adv fml after a particular time or event: He left the country in 1979 and thereafter I heard nothing from him.

there·by /ðeəˈbaɪ, ˈðeəbaɪ ‖ -ər-/ adv fml by doing or saying a particular thing: He became a British citizen, thereby gaining the right to vote.

there·fore /ˈðeəfɔːr ‖ ˈðeər-/ adv for the reason that has just been stated: This engine uses less fuel and is therefore better for the environment. | You have repeatedly failed to deliver the goods on time. We therefore feel that we have no alternative but to find another supplier. –see Study Note on page 508

there·in /ðeərˈɪn/ adv fml because of the fact or situation that has just been stated

there·up·on /ˌðeərəˈpɒn, ˈðeərəpɒn ‖ -pɔːn, -pɑːn/ adv fml at the moment when something happens

and as af result of it: She told him that she was at last free, and thereupon he fell to his knees and asked her to marry him.

therm /θɜːm ‖ θɜːrm/ n tech a measurement of heat used in Britain for measuring the amount of gas people use

ther·mal /ˈθɜːməl ‖ ˈθɜːr-/ adj relating to, producing, or caused by heat: thermal energy

ther·mo·me·ter /θəˈmɒmɪtər ‖ θərˈmɑː-/ n an instrument for measuring and showing temperature

ther·mos flask /ˈθɜːməs ˌflɑːsk ‖ ˈθɜːrməs ˌflæsk/ (also **thermos** AmE) n tdmk a container used to keep drinks either hot or cold

ther·mo·stat /ˈθɜːməstæt ‖ ˈθɜːr-/ n an apparatus that keeps a room or machine at a particular temperature by disconnecting and reconnecting a supply of heat when necessary

the·sau·rus /θɪˈsɔːrəs/ n a book of words put in lists according to their meaning rather than in an alphabetical list

these /ðiːz/ det,pron the plural of THIS

the·sis /ˈθiːsɪs/ n theses /-siːz/ **1** a long piece of writing done for a university degree **2** an opinion put forward as a statement and supported by reasoned argument

they /ðeɪ/ pron [used as the subject of a verb] **1** the people, animals, or things that have already been mentioned: My parents live in Newcastle. They moved there two years ago. | Take these books – they might be useful. | These ideas aren't new. They've been around for years. **2** people in general: They say it might snow tonight. **3** infml a person who has already been mentioned, when it has not been stated whether the person is a man or a woman: I met someone the other day who said that they knew you.

they'd /ðeɪd/ **1** short for "they had": If only they'd been here. **2** short for "they would": They'd never believe you.

they'll /ðeɪl/ **1** short for "they will" **2** short for "they shall"

they're /ðər; strong ðeər, ðeɪər/ short for "they are"

they've /ðeɪv/ short for "they have"

thick[1] /θɪk/ adj **1** having a large distance between opposite surfaces: thick walls | a thick layer of snow **2** used when giving measurements: The castle walls are two metres thick. | How thick are the walls? **3** not flowing easily (used of a liquid): thick soup **4** made of many things grouped closely together: a thick forest | thick black hair **5** thick with full of or covered with: The air was thick with smoke. **6** not clear in sound (used of a voice): a thick accent **7** difficult to see through: thick mist **8** infml stupid (used of a person) **9 as thick as thieves** infml very friendly –**thick** adv : The flowers grew thickest near the wall. –**thickly** adv

thick[2] n **1** in the thick of in the middle of: in the thick of the fight **2** through thick and thin through both good and bad times

thick·en /ˈθɪkən/ v **1** [I] to become more closely packed together: The forest thickens to the north. **2** [I] (of smoke or mist) to become more solid and difficult to see through **3** [I,T] to make or become more solid: Thicken the soup by adding flour.

thick·et /ˈθɪkɪt/ n a thick growth of bushes and small trees

thick·ness /ˈθɪknəs/ n [C;U] the quality or degree of being thick: The length of nails you need depends on the thickness of the planks.

thick·set /ˌθɪkˈset◄/ adj having a broad strong body

thick-skinned /ˌ· ˈ·◂/ *adj* not easily offended by anything unpleasant said about, or to you

thief /θiːf/ *n* **thieves** /θiːvz/ a person who steals things, usually without violence

■ USAGE Compare **thief, burglar, robber, shoplifter, pickpocket. Thief** is a general word for a person who **steals**. A **burglar** steals from houses after **breaking in**. A **robber** is often more violent and steals from people, banks and organizations. A **shoplifter** takes things from shops without paying. A **pickpocket** steals from the pockets and bags of people in crowds.

thieve /θiːv/ *v* **thieved, thieving** *old fash* [I] to steal things

thigh /θaɪ/ *n* the top part of your leg between your knee and your HIP²

thim·ble /ˈθɪmbəl/ *n* a small hard cap put over your finger to protect it when you are sewing

thin¹ /θɪn/ *adj* **-nn-** **1** having a small distance between opposite surfaces: *The ice is too thin to skate on.* | *thin cloth* **2** having little fat on your body: *She looked thin after her illness.* –see USAGE –see picture on page 245 **3** watery (used of a liquid): *thin soup* **4** not very large in quantity: *Your hair's getting very thin on top.* **5** weak: *Your argument is a bit thin.* | *a thin excuse* **6 thin on the ground** *infml* not easily found because not present in large numbers **–thin** *adv*: *Don't cut the bread so thin.* **–thinly** *adv*: *Spread the butter thinly.* | *a thinly populated area* | *a thinly disguised attempt to cheat us* **–thinness** *n* [U]

■ USAGE **1 Thin** is a general word to describe people who have little or no fat on their bodies. To describe people as **thin** in a good way we use **slim** or **slender**: *I wish I were as* **slim/slender** *as you*, or **lean** (= thin in a strong and healthy way): *a* **lean**, *muscular body.* If people are too thin they are **skinny** (informal), **underweight**, or (worst of all) **emaciated**: *He looks very* **skinny/underweight** *after his illness.* | *The prisoners were* **emaciated**. **2** We can use **thin** for things: *a* **thin** *pole*, but we usually do not use it for flat surfaces or openings. Instead we say **narrow**: *a* **narrow** *road* | *a* **narrow** *bed* | *a* **narrow** *gap*.

thin² *v* **-nn-** **1** [T] (also **thin** sthg ↔ **down**) to make a liquid more watery: *You should thin the paint with turpentine.* **2 his hair is thinning** = he is starting to lose his hair

thing /θɪŋ/ *n* **1** any object, especially an object that cannot or need not be named: *What's that thing you've got on your head?* | *I opened the door and the first thing I saw was a cloud of smoke.* **2 not a thing** nothing: *I haven't got a thing to wear.* | *It's so dark I can't see a thing.* **3** a fact, statement, or idea: *What a nasty thing to say to your sister!* | *One thing is certain: I'm not lending him any money again.* | *He says the first thing that comes into his head.* **4** an action, activity, or event: *What's the next thing we have to do?* | *I hope I'm doing the right thing in accepting this job.* | *She might resign, which is the last thing I want.* **5 things** [pl] **a** your personal possessions: *Pack your things, we're going to leave.* **b** the general situation at a particular time: *Cheer up! Things could be worse.* **6** a person or animal, usually when expressing your feelings about them: *Our dog's been quite ill, poor thing.* **7 the thing** *infml* something necessary or desirable: *A glass of cold beer is just the thing on a hot day.* | *The main thing is to keep calm.* **8 do your own thing** *infml* to do what is satisfying to you personally **9 for one thing** you use this expression when you give a reason for something which has just been mentioned; you think that the reason by itself is very strong, but you are suggesting that it is not the only one: *I don't think she'll get the part. She can't sing for one thing.* | *I don't think now's a good time for expanding. For one thing, interest rates are high. And for another, wages are still rising fast.* [RELATED PHRASE **for another thing:** *For one thing, it's expensive. And for another thing, I don't think it's very good.*] **10 have a thing about** *infml* to have a strong like or dislike for **11 make a thing of** *infml* to give too much importance to something: *I disagree with you, but let's not make a thing of it.* **12 it's a good thing** = it's lucky: *It's a good thing George can't hear us!*

thing·a·ma·jig /ˈθɪŋəmədʒɪg/ *n* (also **thingumajig, thingamabob** /ˈθɪŋəmʌbɒb ‖ -baːb/, **thingummy** /ˈθɪŋəmi/) *infml* a person or thing whose name you have forgotten or do not know: *a new thingamajig for opening bottles*

think¹ /θɪŋk/ *v* **thought** /θɔːt/, **thought 1** [I;T] to use your mind to have thoughts and form opinions: *She thought for a moment before answering me.* | *Think hard before you answer.* | *I need some time to think before I can reach a decision.* | *What are you thinking about?* | *You look as though you're thinking great thoughts.* **2** [T;+(that)] to have something as your opinion: *I think he's wrong about this.* | *I think it was Jane, but I'm not sure.* | *What do you think about the plans?* | *I'm not sure what I think of Tom.* | *We didn't think we'd be this late.* | *"Do you think it will rain?" "Yes, I think so."* | *"Will she get the job?" "I don't think so."* | *I think myself very lucky.* **3 think of something: a** to have something as an idea: *I've thought of a brilliant solution to our problem.* | *I can think of two possible reasons for the delay.* **b** to remember something: *I can't think of his name at the moment.* **c** to consider that something is the thing mentioned: *I will always think of Birmingham as my home.* | *I don't think of him as a friend.* **4 be thinking about/of doing something** to be considering doing something: *I'm thinking of giving up my studies and getting a job.* | *Have you ever thought about emigrating?* **5 think about someone, think of someone** to consider someone's needs or wishes: *She never thinks about anyone but herself.* **6 come to think of it** a phrase you use when you have just remembered something or had an idea: *Come to think of it, I've met him before.* **7 think a lot of, not think much of, etc** to have a high or low opinion of someone or something: *He thinks a lot of you.* | *I don't think much of this food.* **8 think aloud** to speak your thoughts as they come **9 think better of it** to decide not to do something when you have considered it more carefully: *I was going to tell her, but I thought better of it.* **10 think nothing of doing something** to consider that something is easy or usual: *She thinks nothing of walking three miles to work every day.* **11 think the world of someone** to be very fond of someone: *He thinks the world of his children.* **12 think the worst** to believe that something bad or unpleasant has happened: *When someone's late I always think the worst.* **13 think twice** to consider carefully before you do something: *Think twice before you agree to work for her.* **14 think well/highly of** to have a good opinion of someone or something: *I think very highly of her.*

think back *phr v* [I] to remember something that happened in the past

think sthg ↔ **over** *phr v* [T] to think about something carefully: *It's a good offer but I'll have to think it over.*

think sthg ↔ **through** *phr v* [T] to consider all the details and aspects of something: *It's an interesting idea and I want to spend some time thinking it through.*

think sthg ↔ **up** *phr v* [T] to create an idea in your mind: *I haven't thought up an excuse yet.*

think² *n* **have a think** to use your mind to have thoughts and form opinions: *I need to have a think about this.*

think·er /'θɪŋkəʳ/ *n* someone who uses their mind well, often producing new and interesting ideas: *One of the great thinkers of the 18th century.*

think·ing /'θɪŋkɪŋ/ *n* [U] **1** the act of using your mind to produce thoughts: *I've been doing some thinking about our next project.* **2** a way of thinking or view of something: *What's the government's thinking on this matter? | To my way of thinking, it's all wrong.*

thin·ner /'θɪnəʳ/ *n* [U] a liquid added to paint to make it spread more easily

third /θɜːd ‖ θɜːrd/ *det, pron, adv* **1** 3rd; when you have several points you want to make, you can order them and number them "First,...", "Second,...", "Third,..." etc.: *There are several reasons why the plan will not work. First, there has not been enough preparation. Second, there is not enough money. Third, it is too complicated.* **2** *n* one of three equal parts **3** *n* the lowest class of British university degree: *She got a third in Chemistry.*

third·ly /'θɜːdli ‖ 'θɜːr-/ *adv* as the third in a set of facts or reasons; when you have several points you want to make, you can order them and number them "Firstly,...", "Secondly,...", "Thirdly,...", etc.: *There are several reasons why the plan will not work. Firstly, there has not been enough preparation. Secondly, there is not enough money. Thirdly, it is too complicated.*

third par·ty /ˌ·ˈ··◄/ *n tech* **1** a person in a law case or agreement who is not one of the two main people concerned **2 third party insurance** a type of insurance under which your insurance company will pay money to anyone or anything damaged by you

third per·son /ˌ·ˈ··◄/ *n* **the third person** a form of the verb that you use with "he", "she", "it", or "they": *"They are" is the third person plural of "to be".*

third-rate /ˌ·ˈ·◄/ *adj* of very poor quality

Third World /ˌ·ˈ·◄/ *n* **the Third World** the industrially less developed countries of the world in Asia, South America, and Africa

thirst¹ /θɜːst ‖ θɜːrst/ *n* **1** [sing] a sensation of dryness in your mouth caused by the need to drink: *Running five miles gave me quite a thirst. | a thirst-quenching drink* **2** [U] lack of drink for a long time: *They died of thirst.* **3 a thirst for** a strong desire for something: *the thirst for excitement*

thirst² *v* **thirst for/after something** to have a strong desire for something: *Our people thirst for independence.*

thirst·y /'θɜːsti ‖ 'θɜːr-/ *adj* **thirstier, thirstiest 1** feeling the need to drink something, or making you feel this need: *Salty food makes me thirsty. | Chopping firewood is thirsty work.* **2 thirsty for** having a strong desire for something: *She was thirsty for power.* **–thirstily** *adv*

thir·teen /ˌθɜːˈtiːn◄ ‖ 'θɜːr-/ *det, n, pron* the number 13 **–thirteenth** *det, n, pron, adv*

thir·ty /'θɜːti ‖ 'θɜːrti/ *det, n, pron* **1** the number 30 **2 the thirties, the Thirties** the years 1930–1939 **3**

in her thirties, in their thirties, etc. aged between 30 and 39 **–thirtieth** *det, n, pron, adv*

this¹ /ðɪs/ *det, pron* **these** /ðiːz/ **1** the person or thing that is nearer in place or time: *You look in this room and I'll look in that room over there. | I saw Mrs Jones this morning. | What's this?* **2** *infml* a certain: *This man came up to me and asked me for money.*

this² *adv infml* as much as this: *I've never been out this late before.*

this·tle /'θɪsəl/ *n* a wild plant with prickly leaves and purple flowers

thith·er /'ðɪðəʳ ‖ 'θɪðər/ *adv old fash* to that place

thong /θɒŋ ‖ θɔːŋ/ *n* a narrow length of leather used as a fastening or a whip

thorn /θɔːn ‖ θɔːrn/ *n* **1** a small sharp-pointed growth on a plant: *the thorns on a rose bush* **2 thorn in your flesh/side** a continual cause of annoyance or problems

thorn·y /'θɔːni ‖ 'θɔːrni/ *adj* **1** having sharp-pointed growths **2** difficult to deal with: *a thorny problem*

thor·ough /'θʌrə ‖ 'θʌrəʊ, 'θʌrə/ *adj* **1** complete and careful: *a thorough search* **2** very careful to cover every detail: *She's slow but very thorough.* **–thoroughly** *adv* : *We thoroughly enjoyed ourselves.* **–thoroughness** *n* [U]

thor·ough·bred /'θʌrəbred ‖ 'θʌrəʊ-, 'θʌrə-/ *n* a horse whose parents were both of very good breed

thor·ough·fare /'θʌrəfeəʳ ‖ 'θʌrəʊ-, 'θʌrə-/ *n fml* a main road in a town or city

those /ðəʊz/ *det, pron* the plural of THAT

thou /ðaʊ/ *pron biblical* you: *"Thou shalt not kill."*

though¹ /ðəʊ/ *conj* **1** in spite of something: *I recognized her at once, though I hadn't seen her for ten years. | I enjoy it even though it's hard work.* **2** but: *I think she's away at the moment, though I'm not sure.* **3 as though** as if: *She looks as though she's been crying.*

though² *adv* in spite of something: *Gardening is quite hard work. I enjoy it, though.*

thought¹ /θɔːt/ *n* **1** [U] the action of thinking: *She sat deep in thought.* **2** [U] serious consideration: *Give the matter plenty of thought before you accept.* **3** [C] an idea or opinion: *What are your thoughts on the subject? | "Yes, the thought had crossed my mind."* **4** [U] a particular way of thinking: *modern thought* **5** [sing] something that someone has done or offered to do for you: *Thank you for the flowers: it was a very kind thought. | With no thought for her own safety, she jumped in the river to help him.*

thought² the past tense and past participle of THINK

thought·ful /'θɔːtfəl/ *adj* **1** showing that you are thinking deeply: *The girl looked thoughtful and sad.* **2** paying attention to the feelings of other people: *It was very thoughtful of you to visit me. | a thoughtful present* **–thoughtfully** *adv* **–thoughtfulness** *n* [U]

thought·less /'θɔːtləs/ *adj* careless or selfish: *It was thoughtless of you to forget Mum's birthday.* **–thoughtlessly** *adv* **–thoughtlessness** *n* [U]

thou·sand /'θaʊzənd/ *det, n, pron* the number 1,000 **–thousandth** *det, n, pron, adv*

thrash /θræʃ/ *v* **1** [T] to hit someone hard with a whip or stick as a punishment **2** [T] to defeat someone thoroughly in a game **3** [I + adv/prep] to move wildly about from pain or fear: *The fish thrashed about in the net.*

thrash sthg ↔ **out** *phr v* [T] to reach agreement about a problem or produce a decision by talking about it in detail: *After a long argument we thrashed out a plan. | We need to thrash this out.*

thrash·ing /ˈθræʃɪŋ/ n a severe beating or defeat

thread¹ /θred/ n **1** [C;U] very thin cord, made by spinning cotton, wool, or silk, used in sewing or weaving **2** [C] a line of reasoning connecting the parts of an argument or story: *I've lost the thread of your argument.* **3** [C] a raised line around the outside of a screw

thread² v [T] **1** to pass a thread through something: *I can't thread this needle.* | *Let's thread the beads onto a string.* **2** **thread your way through** to move carefully and with difficulty through something where there is very little space

thread·bare /ˈθredbeəʳ/ adj worn very thin (used of material and clothes)

threat /θret/ n **1** [C;U] a warning that someone will hurt or punish you if you do not do what they say: *I obeyed, but only under threat of punishment.* | *They used the threat of strike action to enforce their demands.* **2** [C] a possible danger: *Some people see computers as a threat to their jobs.* **3** **threat of** a warning or possibility of future problems: *The clouds brought a threat of rain.* | *The threat of bankruptcy hung over the company.*

threat·en /ˈθretn/ v **1** [I;T] to say that you will do something bad or hurtful: *I was threatened with a beating if I didn't obey.* | *She threatened to murder me.*

□ USEFUL PATTERNS to threaten to do something; to threaten someone with something **2** [T] seem likely to harm, spoil, or ruin something: *The new motorway threatens the peace of the village.* | *He thinks his job is threatened.* **3** [I] seem likely to happen: *The incident threatens to ruin his chances in the election.* **4** [T] to warn that something bad may happen: *The black clouds threatened rain.* –**threatening** adj –**threateningly** adv

three /θriː/ det, n, pron the number 3

three-di·men·sion·al /ˌ·····/ adj (also **three-D, 3-D** /ˌθriː ˈdiː◂/) having length, depth, and height: *The painting gives a wonderful 3-D effect.* | *a three-dimensional model*

three-quar·ter /ˌ· ˈ···◂/ adj [only before a noun] consisting of three of the four equal parts of something: *The game lasted for 2¾ hours.*

thresh /θreʃ/ v [I;T] to separate the grain from corn or wheat by beating it

thresh·old /ˈθreʃhəʊld, -fəʊld/ n **1** the doorway or a piece of wood or stone fixed beneath the doorway which is the entrance to a building **2** the lowest level at which something begins to happen or operate: *She has a low pain threshold.* | *tax thresholds* **3** **on the threshold of** on the point of finding or starting something new: *Scientists are now on the threshold of a better understanding of how the brain works.*

threw /θruː/ the past tense of THROW

thrift /θrɪft/ n [U] wise and careful use of money and goods –**thrifty** adj

thrill¹ /θrɪl/ v [I;T] to get or give a very strong feeling of excitement, pleasure, or fear: *We were thrilled at your news.* | *I was thrilled to hear your news.* | *Fast driving really thrills me.*

thrill² n a sudden, very strong feeling of excitement, pleasure, or fear

thrill·er /ˈθrɪləʳ/ n a book, play, or film that tells a very exciting story, usually of crime and violence

thrive /θraɪv/ v throve /θrəʊv/ or thrived, thriven /ˈθrɪvən/, thriving [I] to develop well and be healthy or successful: *Business is thriving.* | *He thrives on hard work.*

throat /θrəʊt/ n **1** the passage from the back of your mouth to your lungs and stomach: *a sore throat* **2** the front of your neck: *They had cut his throat.* **3** **at each other's throats** fighting or arguing violently

throat·y /ˈθrəʊti/ adj low and rough (of someone's voice): *a throaty cough*

throb /θrɒb/ v -bb- [I] to beat strongly and regularly: *My heart was throbbing with excitement.* –**throb** n

throes /θrəʊz/ n [pl] **1** lit violent, sudden pains: *death throes* **2** **in the throes of** struggling with: *a country in the throes of war*

throm·bo·sis /θrɒmˈbəʊsɪs ‖ θrɑːm-/ n [U] tech the condition of having a thickened or solid mass of blood in a blood tube or your heart

throne /θrəʊn/ n **1** the ceremonial chair of a king or queen **2** **the throne** the position of being king or queen: *She was only fifteen when she came to the throne.* | *the power behind the throne*

throng¹ /θrɒŋ ‖ θrɔːŋ/ n [+sing/pl verb] a large crowd of people: *Throngs of people are gathering outside the palace.* | *a throng of admirers*

throng² v [I] to go in large groups of people: *People thronged to see the play.*

throt·tle¹ /ˈθrɒtl ‖ ˈθrɑːtl/ v **throttled, throttling** [T] to seize someone tightly by the throat and so stop them breathing

throttle² n a part of a pipe that opens and closes to control the flow of petrol or oil into an engine

through¹ /θruː/ adv,prep **1** adv,prep from one side of something to the other: *Water flows through this pipe.* | *We couldn't see through the mist.* | *I opened the gate and let them through.* –see picture on page 540 **2** prep by means of something: *This crisis could be solved through negotiation.* **3** adv,prep from the beginning to the end of something: *I don't think that he will live through the night.* | *I've read through the report.* | *She read the letter through.* | *She stopped the tape half way through.* **4** adv,prep successfully to the end of something: *Did you get through your exams?* **5** prep among all the parts of something: *I was looking through the papers on my desk.* **6** adv infml finished: *Are you through yet?* **7** **through and through** completely

through² adj [only before a noun] going all the way to a place: *a through train*

through·out /θruːˈaʊt/ adv,prep **1** in every part of something: *There were celebrations throughout the country.* | *The house has been recently painted throughout.* **2** from the beginning to the end of something: *The party continued throughout the night.* | *He remained loyal throughout.*

throw¹ /θrəʊ/ v **threw** /θruː/, **thrown** /θrəʊn/, **throwing** **1** [I;T] to send through the air by moving your arm back and then quickly forwards, letting go of whatever you are holding: *It's my turn to throw.* | *She threw the javelin 100 metres.* | *Someone threw a stone at me.* | *Throw the ball to Grandad.* | *Could you throw me the newspaper, please?* –see picture on page 736

□ USEFUL PATTERNS to throw something; to throw something at someone; to throw something to someone; to throw someone something **2** **throw yourself** to move suddenly and forcefully: *She threw herself down on the bed.* **3** [T + adv/prep] to put on or take off clothes quickly and carelessly: *He threw off his clothes and jumped into the water.* | *She threw a shawl around her shoulders.* **4** [T] to make someone fall to the ground: *The horse threw* *him.* **5** [T] to send light or sound in a particular direction: *The sun threw shadows on the grass.* **6** [T + adv/prep] to cause someone suddenly to be in a particular state: *The new system has thrown us all into confusion.* **7** [T] *infml* to arrange or give a party or dinner **8** [T] *infml* to confuse or shock: *His remarks threw me for a moment.* **9 throw a fit** to have a sudden attack of uncontrolled temper **10 throw the book at someone** *infml* to make all possible legal or police charges against someone **11 throw yourself at someone: a** to rush violently towards someone **b** to attempt forcefully to win the love of someone **12 throw yourself into something** to do or take part in something eagerly and actively

throw sthg ↔ **away** *phr v* [T] **1** to lose something by foolishness: *He threw away the chance of a good job.* **2** to get rid of something that you do not want: *Are you throwing all those books away?*

throw sthg ↔ **in** *phr v* [T] *infml* to supply something in addition, without increasing the price: *The room costs fifteen pounds a night, with meals thrown in.*

throw sthg ↔ **off** *phr v* [T] to free yourself from something: *It took me a week to throw off that cold.*

throw sthg ↔ **open** *phr v* [T] to allow people to enter a place: *They have decided to throw the gardens open to the public.*

throw out *phr v* **1** [T **throw** sthg ↔ **out**] to refuse to accept something: *The committee threw out my suggestions.* **2** [T **throw** sbdy/sthg ↔ **out**] to get rid of something or force someone to leave: *Why don't you throw out that old sofa and get a new one? | He was thrown out of the hotel because he was wearing jeans.*

throw together *phr v* **1** [T **throw** sthg **together**] to make something quickly: *I just threw the meal together.* **2 throw people together** to bring people together so that they get to know each other: *I think it was luck which threw us together at that party.*

throw up *phr v* **1** [I] *infml* to be sick **2** [T **throw** sthg ↔ **up**] to make something move from the ground into the air: *Mud was thrown up by the cars in front.* **3** [T **throw** sthg ↔ **up**] to produce something: *The discussion has thrown up a lot of good ideas.*

throw² *n* **1** an action of moving your arm back and then forwards quickly letting go of whatever you are holding **2** the distance to which something is thrown: *a throw of 100 metres | a record throw*

thrush /θrʌʃ/ *n* a small bird with a brownish back and a spotted breast

thrust¹ /θrʌst/ *v* **thrust, thrusting** **1** [T + adv/prep] to push something forcefully and suddenly: *We thrust our way through the crowd.* **2 thrust something on/upon someone** to force someone to accept something: *All this publicity was thrust upon her.*

thrust² *n* **1** a forceful push: *a sword thrust* **2** the thrust of the main meaning or central point of: *The thrust of her argument was that all interference in industry was wrong.*

thud /θʌd/ *n* a dull sound as caused by a heavy object falling to the ground or hitting something soft: *He fell to the floor with a thud.* –**thud** *v* [I + adv/prep]

thug /θʌg/ *n* a violent person

thumb¹ /θʌm/ *n* **1** the short thick finger which is set apart from the other four **2 thumbs up** an expression of satisfaction, victory, or approval **3 under somebody's thumb** *infml* under the control or influence of someone

thumb² *v* [I;T] *infml* to ask for a free ride from passing motorists by holding out your thumb: *He thumbed a lift to London.*

thumb through sthg *phr v* [T] to look through a book quickly

thumb·nail¹ /ˈθʌmneɪl/ *n* the nail on the upper outer edge of your thumb

thumbnail² *adj* [only before a noun] **thumbnail sketch** a very short description or account

thumb·tack /ˈθʌmtæk/ *n* the usual American word for DRAWING PIN

thump¹ /θʌmp/ *v* **1** [T] to hit someone forcefully with the hand tightly closed: *I'll thump you on the nose!* **2** [I] to produce a loud, dull sound by beating, falling or walking heavily: *The excitement made her heart thump.*

thump² *n* the dull sound of a heavy blow

thun·der¹ /ˈθʌndəʳ/ *n* [U] the loud explosive noise that follows a flash of lightning: *Can you hear the thunder? | thunder and lightning*

thunder² *v* **1 it thunders, it is thundering** = there are loud explosive noises following flashes of lightning: *Our dog is always afraid when it thunders.* **2** [I] to make a very loud deep sound: *The guns thundered in the distance. | "Get out!" he thundered.*

thun·der·bolt /ˈθʌndəbəʊlt ‖ -dər-/ *n* **1** a flash of lightning and crash of thunder together **2** a sudden event which causes great shock

thun·der·clap /ˈθʌndəklæp ‖ -ər-/ *n* a single loud crash of thunder

thun·der·ous /ˈθʌndərəs/ *adj* extremely loud: *thunderous applause*

thun·der·storm /ˈθʌndəstɔːm ‖ -dərstɔːrm/ *n* a storm of heavy rain with thunder and lightning

thun·der·struck /ˈθʌndəstrʌk ‖ -ər-/ *adj* [never before a noun] very surprised indeed

thun·der·y /ˈθʌndəri/ *adj* giving signs that thunder is likely (used of the weather)

Thurs·day /ˈθɜːzdi ‖ ˈθɜːr-/ (also **Thur** or **Thurs**) the day between Wednesday and Friday

thus /ðʌs/ *adv fml* **1** in this way or for this reason: *The new machines will work faster, thus reducing our costs. | We had been told to expect help from local people. Thus, we were quite unprepared for the hostility we found. | Put a plastic bag over the plants to keep them moist. This prevents the soil drying out and there is thus less need to water them.* **2 thus far** up until now

thwart /θwɔːt ‖ θwɔːrt/ *v* [T] to prevent someone or something from succeeding: *My plans were thwarted by the weather.*

thyme /taɪm/ *n* [U] the dried leaves of a plant, used for giving a special taste to food

thy·roid /ˈθaɪrɔɪd/ *n* (also **thyroid gland** /ˈ·· ˌ·/) an organ in your neck that controls the development of your mind and body

ti·a·ra /tiˈɑːrə/ *n* a piece of jewellery like a small crown which can be worn on the head by women on formal occasions

tic /tɪk/ *n* a sudden uncontrolled movement of the muscles, usually in your face

tick¹ /tɪk/ *n* **1** the short regularly repeated sound of a clock or watch **2** a mark ✓ put against an answer or a name on a list to show that it is correct or that a person is present **3 a tick** *BrE infml* a moment: *I'll be down in a tick.* **4** a very small insect-like creature that fixes itself to animals and sucks their blood

tick² *v* **1** [I] to make a regularly repeated short sound, for example like a clock or watch **2** [T] to mark something with a tick, to show that it is correct or has been dealt with: *All his answers had been ticked.* **3 what makes someone tick** what makes someone excited or want to live in a particular way

tick off *phr v infml* **1** [T **tick** sbdy/sthg ↔ **off**] to remove something or someone from a list by ticking that word or name: *I've ticked off everything that I've bought.* **2** [T **tick** sbdy ↔ **off**] to speak angrily to someone: *He ticked me off because I was late.*

tick over *phr v* [I] to continue working at a slow, steady rate: *The car's engine was ticking over.* | *Work in the office has been ticking over while you've been on holiday.*

tick·et /'tɪkɪt/ *n* **1** a printed piece of paper or card which shows that a person has paid for a journey on a bus or train, or entrance into something like a cinema: *a bus ticket* | *Entrance to the theatre is by ticket only.* **2** a piece of card or paper that shows the price or size of an object for sale **3** a printed notice showing that you have parked your car in a place where you are not allowed to park it: *a parking ticket* **4** a list of people put forward by one political party in an American election

tick·le¹ /'tɪkəl/ *v* **tickled, tickling 1** [T] to touch someone's body lightly with your fingers to make them laugh **2** [I;T] to touch or be touched lightly by something in a rather annoying way: *These rough sheets tickle.* **3** [T] to delight or amuse you: *I was tickled by her description of the wedding.*

tickle² *n* [C;U] a feeling of being touched lightly by something

tick·lish /'tɪklɪʃ/ *adj* **1** easily made to laugh because your body is sensitive to tickling **2** difficult (used of a problem): *a ticklish situation*

tid·al /'taɪdl/ *adj* **1** related to the tide: *tidal currents* **2 tidal wave** a very large dangerous ocean wave

tid·bit /'tɪdbɪt/ *n* the usual American word for TITBIT

tide¹ /taɪd/ *n* **1** the regular movement of the sea level up and down the shore: *The sea comes right up to the cliffs when the tide is in.* | *Strong tides make swimming dangerous.* **2** the direction in which the opinion of a lot of people is moving: *The tide of public opinion seems to be turning against the government.*

tide² *v*

tide sbdy **over** *phr v* [T] to help someone through a difficult period: *Can you lend me ten pounds, to tide me over the next few days?*

tide·mark /'taɪdmɑːk ‖ -mɑːrk/ *n* **1** the highest point reached by a tide on the shore **2** a mark round the inside of a bath that shows the level of the water before it was emptied

tid·ings /'taɪdɪŋz/ *n* [pl] *old fash* news

ti·dy¹ /'taɪdi/ *adj* **tidier, tidiest 1** neat and orderly in appearance or habits: *It's a very tidy house.* | *She's so tidy!* **2** *infml* quite large (used of amounts of money): *a tidy income* –**tidily** *adv* –**tidiness** *n* [U]

tidy² *v* **tidied, tidying**

tidy sthg ↔ **up** *phr v* [I;T] to make a place neat: *When are you going to tidy your room up?*

tidy sthg ↔ **away** *phr v* [T] to put something out of sight or out of the way: *Could you tidy away your homework so that we can have dinner?*

tie¹ /taɪ/ *n* **1** (also **necktie** *AmE*) a band of cloth worn round the neck and tied in a knot at the front **2** a cord or string used for fastening something **3 ties** [pl] something that unites people: *family ties* | *ties of friendship* **4 a tie** something that limits your

freedom: *Young children can be a tie.* **5** a result of a competition in which the competitors have the same number of points or votes: *There was a tie for first place.*

tie² *v* **tied, tying 1** [T +adv/prep] to fasten something with a cord, string, or rope: *You have to tie this label onto your suitcase.* | *She tied her horse to the gate.* **2** [I;T] to fasten by drawing together and knotting: *Can you tie your own shoe laces yet?* | *My dress ties at the back.* **3** [I] to be equal in a competition: *Two teams have tied for second place.* **4 be tied to** to be connected to: *Salary increases are tied to inflation rates.*

tie sbdy **down** *phr v* [T] **1** to limit someone's freedom: *She feels her job is tying her down.* **2** to force someone to make a decision: *She tied him down* to *a date for the meeting.*

tie in with sthg *phr v* [T] to be in agreement with something: *This story doesn't tie in with the facts.*

tie sthg ↔ **up** *phr v* [T] **1** to fasten something with cord, string, or rope: *Make sure you've tied up that parcel securely before you post it.* | *She tied it up* **with** *string.* **2** to put money into an account or business so that it cannot be used for anything else **3** to connect one fact with another one: *The police are trying to tie up his escape from prison* **with** *the murder.*

tied up /ˌ· '·/ *adj* very busy: *I'm afraid I can't come, I'm rather tied up at work this week.*

tier /tɪəʳ/ *n* one of a number of levels rising one above another: *Their wedding cake had three tiers.*

tiff /tɪf/ *n* a slight quarrel: *a lovers' tiff*

ti·ger /'taɪgəʳ/ *n* a large fierce Asian wild cat that has yellow fur with black bands; a female tiger is called a **tigress**

tight¹ /taɪt/ *adj* **1** fitting part of your body closely: *tight shoes* **2** leaving no free room or time: *The children sat in a tight little group.* | *a tight schedule* **3** firmly fixed in place: *This drawer is so tight I can't open it.* **4** well ordered or firmly controlled: *There was tight security at the airport when the President's plane arrived.* **5** stretched out as far as possible: *The cover of the drum has to be stretched until it's really tight.* **6** not generous with money **7** [never before a noun] *infml* drunk **8 in a tight corner/spot** in a difficult position –**tightly** *adv*

tight² *adv* closely or firmly: *She held the baby tight.* | *Close your eyes tight.* | *Hold tight!*

tight·en /'taɪtn/ *v* **1** [I;T] to make something more firmly fixed in place or hold it more firmly: *These screws need tightening.* | *She tightened her grip on the steering wheel.* **2** [I;T] to stretch as far as possible **3** [T] to control something more firmly: *Security at the palace has been tightened.* **4 tighten your belt** *infml* to try to live on less money: *We just can't afford to go on like this, we'll have to tighten our belts.*

tighten up *phr v* [I;T **tighten** sthg ↔ **up**] to make something firmer or more severe: *The government is tightening up on the drinking and driving laws.*

tight·fist·ed /ˌtaɪt'fɪstɪd◂/ *adj infml* very unwilling to give or share money

tight·rope /'taɪt-rəʊp/ *n* a tightly stretched rope or wire, high above the ground, on which performers walk and do tricks

tights /taɪts/ *n* [pl] a very close-fitting garment made of thin material covering the legs and lower part of the body; tights are usually worn by women –see PAIR (USAGE) –see picture on page 50

tile /taɪl/ *n* a thin square piece of baked clay or other material used for covering roofs, walls, or floors: *polystyrene ceiling tiles | slate roof tiles | white bathroom tiles* –**tile** *v* **tiled, tiling** [T]

till[1] /tɪl/ *prep,conj* until: *Let's wait till tomorrow. | Drive straight on till you get to the school.*

till[2] *n* a drawer where money is kept in a shop

till[3] *v* [T] *old fash* to cultivate the ground

til·ler /ˈtɪləʳ/ *n* a long handle fastened to the RUDDER of a boat so that it can be turned easily

tilt[1] /tɪlt/ *v* [I;T] to slope or make something slope by lifting one end of it

tilt[2] *n* **1** [C;U] a position in which one end of something is higher than the other: *She wore her hat at a tilt. | with a tilt of the head* **2** **at full tilt** *infml* at full speed

tim·ber /ˈtɪmbəʳ/ *n* **1** [U] wood or trees to be used for building **2** [C] a wooden beam

time[1] /taɪm/ *n* **1** [U] a measurable quantity that we measure in minutes, hours, days, and years: *Young children have no concept of time.* **2** [sing;U] a period of time: *It takes a long time to get there by car. | I spend quite a lot of time reading. | I never have enough time to do things properly. | I waited for a short time, then went home. | After a time the phone rang.* **3** [U] a system of measuring time: *British Summer Time* **4** [C] a particular point in the day which is stated in hours and minutes: *"What's the time?" "It's one o'clock." | What time shall we leave?" "Ten o'clock." | I must find out the times of trains to London.* **5** [C;U] a particular moment or occasion: *It's time to leave. | Do you remember the time the car broke down? | I'll tell him the news next time I see him. | I've tried to phone several times. | This is the second time this week that she's been late. | Now is the time to tackle these problems.* **6** [C] a period in history: *in ancient times | in the time of Queen Victoria* **7** [U] the rate or speed at which a piece of music is played **8 times** [pl] used when you are comparing things and saying how much bigger, smaller, etc one thing is than the other thing: *This machine is better, but it's three times more expensive. | This show is five times as popular as any other show on television.* **9 about time** a phrase you use to say that something should be done now: *Isn't it about time you got married?* **10 ahead of time** before the time when something should be done: *We finished ahead of time.* **11 ahead of your time** too modern or too original for the period of history in which you live **12 all the time** continuously: *She just works all the time.* **13 at one time** in the past: *At one time I wanted to be a dentist.* **14 at the same time** in spite of this: *I feel disappointed, but at the same time I'm determined to try again.* **15 at times** sometimes: *At times I felt very lonely.* **16 before your time** before you were born **17 for the time being** for the moment, until something else is arranged: *You can stay with us for the time being.* **18 from time to time** sometimes, but not very often: *I see Mary from time to time.* **19 have no time for something** *infml* to dislike something: *I haven't got much time for people like him.* **20 have the time of your life** to spend a very enjoyable time **21 in good time** at the right time or early: *If we set off at 9 o'clock we should get there in good time.* **22 in time** after a period of time: *She'll get over the shock in time.* **23 in a day's time, in a week's time, etc** after a day, a week, etc: *I'll see you again in two weeks' time.* **24 in time to do something** early enough to do something: *We arrived in time to see the beginning of the parade.* **25 in your own good time** when you are ready to do something: *She'll get*

in touch with me in her own good time. **26 take time** to need time in order to happen: *It takes time for people's attitudes to change.* **27 take your time** to do something slowly **time after time, time and again** repeatedly or on many occasions: *She came out with the same excuses time after time.* **28 two at a time, three at a time, etc** in groups of two, three, etc: *She ran up the stairs two at a time.* **29 work against time** to be trying to do something before a particular time

■ USAGE 1 Compare **spend time, pass time, waste time**. If we **spend** time on something we use time sensibly, or in ways that are neither good nor bad: *to* **spend** *time doing English homework.* If we have too much time which we try to fill we may **pass** the time: *Listening to the radio helped me to* **pass** *the time.* If we use time badly and without success we **waste** time: *I* **wasted** *a lot of time trying to find a parking space.* 2 At 11.45 it is *a quarter* **to** *twelve* in British English but *a quarter* **to/of** *twelve* in American English. At 12.15 it is *a quarter* **past** *twelve* in British English but *a quarter* **past/after** *twelve* in American English.

time[2] *v* **timed, timing** [T] **1** to arrange for something to happen at a particular time: *We timed our visit to coincide with the arts festival.* **2** to measure the speed with which something happened: *We timed our journey – it took two hours.*

time bomb /ˈ· ·/ *n* **1** a bomb that can be set to explode at a particular time **2** a dangerous or difficult situation: *Until we deal with unemployment properly, we are sitting on a time bomb.*

time-hon·oured /ˈ· ˌ··/ *adj fml* respected because of age or long use: *a time-honoured custom*

time-keep·er /ˈtaɪmˌkiːpəʳ/ *n* a person who records the time of competitors in a race or work done by others

time lag /ˈ· ·/ *n* the period of time between two connected events

time·less /ˈtaɪmləs/ *adj* lasting forever or not changed by time: *the timeless beauty of the stars*

time lim·it /ˈ· ˌ··/ *n* a period of time within which something must be done

time·ly /ˈtaɪmli/ *adj* happening at just the right time: *a timely warning*

tim·er /ˈtaɪməʳ/ *n* a machine that measures or records time: *Don't forget to set the timer on the video. | an egg timer*

times /taɪmz/ *prep* multiplied by a particular number: *What's thirteen times six?*

time-scale /ˈtaɪmskeɪl/ *n* the length of time during which something happens or develops

time-ta·ble /ˈtaɪmˌteɪbəl/ *n* a table of the times at which buses and trains arrive and leave or at which classes in a school or college take place –**timetable** *v* **timetabled, timetabling** [T] : *The meeting was timetabled to begin at two o'clock. | It is timetabled for two o'clock.*

time warp /ˈ· ·/ *n* a situation which seems to belong to another period of history: *Visiting these distant villages is like being in a time warp. Nothing has changed for centuries.*

time-worn /ˈtaɪmwɔːn ‖ -wɔːrn/ *adj lit* showing signs of having been used for a long time

tim·id /ˈtɪmɪd/ *adj* not confident or courageous –**timidly** *adv* –**timidity** /tɪˈmɪdɪti/ *n* [U]

tim·ing /ˈtaɪmɪŋ/ *n* [U] the choosing of exactly the right moment to do something so as to get the best effect: *a dancer with perfect timing | We must get the timing right.*

tim·o·rous /ˈtɪmərəs/ adj fml nervous and easily frightened –**timorously** adv

tin¹ /tɪn/ n 1 [U] a soft whitish metal, used to cover metal objects with a protective shiny surface 2 [C] a small metal container in which food or drink is sold or stored: a tin of beans | a biscuit tin | a tin of peaches –see picture on page 148

tin² v -nn- [T] to preserve food by packing it in a tin –**tinned** adj : tinned sardines

tinc·ture /ˈtɪŋktʃər/ n [C;U] a medical substance mixed with alcohol

tin·der /ˈtɪndər/ n [U] fml any material that catches fire easily: The plants are as dry as tinder.

tin·foil /ˈtɪnfɔɪl/ n [U] a very thin sheet of shiny metal, used as a protective wrapping for food

tinge /tɪndʒ/ n a tinge of a small amount of colour or feeling: There was a tinge of sadness in her voice. –**tinged** adj : Her black hair was tinged with grey.

tin·gle /ˈtɪŋgəl/ v **tingled, tingling** [I] to feel a slight prickly sensation: My fingers tingled with the cold. –**tingle** n : I felt a tingle of excitement.

tin·ker¹ /ˈtɪŋkər/ n a person who travels from place to place mending metal pots or pans

tinker² v [I] to try to repair or improve something by making small changes but without a fixed plan: Don't tinker with my television.

tin·kle /ˈtɪŋkəl/ v **tinkled, tinkling** [I;T] to make light ringing sounds: The bell tinkled as he opened the shop door. –**tinkle** n

tin·ny /ˈtɪni/ adj 1 cheaply and badly made (used of something metal such as a car) 2 having a thin metallic sound: a tinny bell

tin o·pen·er /ˈ· ˌ···/ n a tool for opening tins of food –see picture on page 638

tin·sel /ˈtɪnsəl/ n [U] threads of shiny metallic material on a string used for decoration at Christmas

tint¹ /tɪnt/ n a pale or delicate shade of a colour

tint² v [T] to give a slight colour to something: I'm going to have my hair tinted.

ti·ny /ˈtaɪni/ adj extremely small

tip¹ /tɪp/ n 1 the pointed or thin end of something: the tip of your nose | a town at the southern tip of India 2 a place where unwanted waste is left 3 a small amount of money given in addition to the official price to someone who has done something for you: Shall I leave the waiter a tip? 4 **on the tip of your tongue** forgotten for the moment but should soon be remembered: Oh, what's her name? It's on the tip of my tongue. 5 **the tip of the iceberg** a small part of a much larger situation or problem 6 a helpful piece of advice: Take a tip from the experts. | useful tips on gardening

tip² v -pp- 1 [I;T] to move so that something is no longer level or straight up: He tipped his chair back and looked thoughtful. 2 [T] to pour something carelessly from one container into another: She tipped the flour into the bowl. 3 [I;T] to give a small amount of money to someone for something they have done for you 4 to consider someone most likely to do something: MacTavish is widely tipped as being the next chairman.
tip sbdy ↔ **off** phr v [T] to give someone a warning or a piece of secret information: The police were tipped off that a bank robbery was being planned.
tip sthg ↔ **over** phr v [T] to move something so that it turns or leans too far: Sit down or you'll tip the boat over.

tip-off /ˈ· ·/ n a piece of secret information or warning: a tip-off about the robbery

tip·ple /ˈtɪpəl/ n infml an alcoholic drink: What's your favourite tipple?

tip·ster /ˈtɪpstər/ n a person who gives advice about the likely winner of horse and dog races

tip·sy /ˈtɪpsi/ adj slightly drunk

tip·toe¹ /ˈtɪptəʊ/ n **on tiptoe** on your toes, with the rest of the feet raised above the ground

tiptoe² v [I] to walk quietly and carefully on your toes –see picture on page 736

ti·rade /taɪˈreɪd, tɪ-‖ ˈtaɪreɪd, tɪˈreɪd/ n a long, angry speech

tire¹ /taɪər/ v **tired, tiring** 1 [I;T] to feel weak and in need of a rest: a tiring day | After walking for two hours I began to tire. 2 **tire of something** to become uninterested in something: She never tires of talking about her work.
tire sbdy ↔ **out** phr v [T] to make someone very tired: The children have completely tired me out.

tire² n see TYRE

tired /taɪəd ‖ taɪərd/ adj 1 needing to rest or sleep 2 **be tired of something** become uninterested in or annoyed by something: I'm tired of your stupid remarks. 3 **tired out** unable to do much more: I'm tired out so I'll go to bed. –**tiredness** n [U]

tire·less /ˈtaɪələs ‖ ˈtaɪər-/ adj never needing a rest: a tireless worker –**tirelessly** adv

tire·some /ˈtaɪəsəm ‖ ˈtaɪər-/ adj annoying: a tiresome child

tis·sue /ˈtɪʃuː, -sjuː ‖ -ʃuː/ n 1 [U] animal or plant cells which are similar in form and purpose and make up a particular organ: lung tissue | leaf tissue 2 [U] (also **tissue paper**) light thin paper used for wrapping or packing things which might get broken 3 [C] a piece of soft paper used for blowing your nose on: a box of tissues 4 **a tissue of lies** something that is completely untrue

tit /tɪt/ n 1 a woman's breast (a word which some people consider not to be polite) 2 a small European bird

tit·bit /ˈtɪtˌbɪt/ n (also **tidbit** AmE) a small piece of particularly nice food

tit for tat /ˌ· · ˈ·/ n infml something unpleasant you do to someone in return for something unpleasant they did to you

tit·il·late /ˈtɪtɬeɪt/ v **titillated, titillating** [T] to excite someone pleasantly, especially sexually: a titillating piece of news –**titillation** /ˌtɪtɬˈeɪʃən/ n [U]

tit·i·vate /ˈtɪtɬveɪt/ v **titivated, titivating** [I;T] infml to make yourself look pretty or tidy

ti·tle /ˈtaɪtl/ n 1 a name given to a book, painting, or play: The title of the play is "Hamlet". 2 a word or name, such as "Mr", "Lady", "Doctor", or "General", used before a person's name as a sign of their position in society or profession 3 the position of unbeaten winner in certain sports competitions: Tonight they will be fighting for the title.

ti·tled /ˈtaɪtld/ adj having a high position in society and a noble title, such as "Lord"

title deed /ˈ··· ·/ n a paper showing a person's legal right of ownership of property

title-hold·er /ˈ·· ˌ···/ n a person or team who is at present the unbeaten winner of a sports competition

title role /ˌ··· ˈ·/ n the main character in a play, after whom the play is named: He played the title role in "Macbeth".

tit·ter /ˈtɪtəʳ/ v [I] to laugh in a nervous or silly way –**titter** n

tit·tle-tat·tle /ˈtɪtl ˌtætl/ n [U] *infml* talk about other people's lives or activities (a word used to express disapproval)

tit·u·lar /ˈtɪtʃ̬ələʳ/ adj holding a title but not having the duties or power of office

T-junc·tion /ˈtiː ˌdʒʌŋkʃən/ n *BrE* a place where two roads join in the shape of a T –see picture on page 735

to¹ /tə, *before vowels* tʊ; *strong* tuː/ prep **1** towards someone or something, or in the direction of someone or something: *She threw the ball to me.* | *Is this the road to London?* | *She gave the book to me.* | *He rushed to the door.* | *I'm writing a letter to my mother.* | *My daughter will go to school next year.* –see picture on page 540 **2 to yourself** for yourself: *I want a room to myself.* **3** before a certain hour: *It's five to four.* | *We have to leave by a quarter to eleven.* **4** per: *There are 100 pence to the pound.* **5 to the left, to the right** on the left or right: *To your left you will see the Houses of Parliament.* | *Turn your head to the right.* **6** used in showing how someone feels when something happens: *To my surprise he handed me the envelope.* | *To our dismay, he still wasn't home by midnight.*

to² /tuː/ adv **1** into a position of being shut but not locked: *The wind had blown the door to.* | *Could you just close the door to?* **2 to and fro** moving backwards and forwards or from side to side: *The pendulum swung to and fro.* | *She was walking to and fro in front of the building.*

to³ /tə, *before vowels* tʊ; *strong* tuː/ used with verbs to form the INFINITIVE: *I don't want to go.* | *You ought to understand.* | *They made an attempt to land.* | *I need some scissors to cut this string.* | *I was very sorry to leave them.*

■ USAGE It is sometimes considered bad English to put any other word between **to** and the verb that follows it, making a "split infinitive": *He was wrong to suddenly leave like that.* Some people consider that this should be; to **leave** *suddenly*, or even *suddenly* to **leave**. But sometimes there is no better place to put **to**: *Your job is to really understand these problems.* | *She likes to half close her eyes and view the paintings from a distance.*

toad /təʊd/ n an animal like a large FROG

toad·stool /ˈtəʊdstuːl/ n a poisonous, uneatable type of FUNGUS that looks like the MUSHROOM

to-and-fro /ˌ· · ˈ·/ adj forwards and backwards or from side to side: *a to-and-fro movement* –**to and fro** adv : *The pendulum swung to and fro.*

toast¹ /təʊst/ v [T] to make food such as bread or cheese brown, by holding it close to heat: *toasted crumpets* –see COOK¹ (USAGE)

toast² n **1** [U] bread made brown by being heated: *toast and marmalade* **2** [C] a call on other people to drink wine together to express good wishes for someone: *He proposed a toast to the bride and groom.* **3 the toast** someone who is greatly loved and admired: *the toast of Broadway*

toast³ v [T] to drink and wish for the success and happiness of someone: *He was toasted by all his friends.*

toast·er /ˈtəʊstəʳ/ n an electric apparatus for toasting bread –see picture on page 638

to·bac·co /təˈbækəʊ/ n [U] a plant or its large leaves, prepared for smoking in cigarettes and pipes

to·bac·co·nist /təˈbækənɪst/ n **1** a person who sells tobacco and cigarettes **2 tobacconist's** a shop that sells tobacco and cigarettes: *I've run out of cigarettes and the tobacconist's will be closed by now.*

to·bog·gan /təˈbɒgən ‖ -ˈbɑː-/ n a board curved up at the front, for carrying people over snow –**toboggan** v -nn- [I] : *The children love to go tobogganning down the hill.*

today /təˈdeɪ/ adv, n **1** this present day: *Today is Tuesday.* | *Today is my birthday.* | *I've got to go shopping today.* **2** this present time: *the young people of today* | *People travel more today than they used to.*

tod·dle /ˈtɒdl ‖ ˈtɑːdl/ v **toddled, toddling** [I] to walk with short unsteady steps, like a small child does

tod·dler /ˈtɒdləʳ ‖ ˈtɑːd-/ n a small child who has just learnt to walk –see CHILD (USAGE)

toe¹ /təʊ/ n **1** one of the five parts at the end of each foot **2 on your toes** ready for action

toe² v toed, toeing **toe the line** to obey orders

toe·nail /ˈtəʊneɪl/ n the NAIL on a toe

tof·fee, toffy /ˈtɒfi ‖ ˈtɑːfi/ n [C;U] a hard brown sweet made by boiling sugar and butter: *a sticky toffee* | *toffee apples*

together /təˈgeðəʳ/ adv **1** so as to be joined or in a group: *Tie the ends together.* | *Add these numbers together.* | *The people gathered together to protest.* **2** with one another: *We went to school together.* | *Together these two companies account for 90% of all sugar production.* **3** at the same time: *Why do all the bills seem to come together?* **4** *infml* in control of life and with no problems with your feelings: *She seems to be really together.* **5 together with** as well as: *They sent me an application form, together with some leaflets telling me about the company.*

to·geth·er·ness /təˈgeðənɪs ‖ -ðər-/ n [U] a feeling of being united and friendly with other people

tog·gle /ˈtɒgəl ‖ ˈtɑː-/ n a small, shaped bar of wood used as a button

togs /tɒgz ‖ tɑːgz, tɔːgz/ n [pl] *infml* clothes

toil /tɔɪl/ v *lit* **1** [I] to work hard and without tiring –see WORK¹ (USAGE) **2** [I + adv/prep] to move with tiredness, difficulty, or pain: *The slaves toiled up the hill pulling the heavy blocks.* –**toil** n [U]

toi·let /ˈtɔɪlɪt/ n **1** [C] a large bowl connected to a pipe, used for getting rid of your body's waste matter: *Where's the toilet please?* | *Please flush the toilet.* **2** [C] a room with a toilet in **3** [U] *old fash* the act of washing, dressing yourself, and taking care of your appearance

toilet pa·per /ˈ··· ˌ··/ n [U] thin paper for cleaning your body when waste matter has been passed from it

toi·let·ries /ˈtɔɪlɪtriz/ n [pl] things you use when washing or taking care of your body, such as soap, face cream, etc.

toilet roll /ˈ··· ·/ n a roll of toilet paper

toilet wa·ter /ˈ·· ˌ··/ n [U] a pleasant-smelling but not very strong PERFUME

to·ken /ˈtəʊkən/ n **1** something which is not very large or very important in itself, but which represents something important: *All the family wore black as a token of their grief.* | *a token payment* | *a token strike* **2** a card or a piece of metal used instead of money, for a particular purpose: *a book token* | *You need to buy a token for the car-wash.*

told /təʊld/ the past tense and past participle of TELL

tol·e·ra·ble /ˈtɒlərəbəl ‖ ˈtɑː-/ adj fairly good, or good enough to be tolerated: *a tolerable heat* –**tolerably** adv

tol·e·rance /ˈtɒlərəns ‖ ˈtɑː-/ n **1** [C;U] the ability to suffer pain or hardship without being damaged: *He*

has no tolerance to cold. **2** [U] the quality of allowing people to behave in a way that may not please you, without becoming annoyed **3** [U] the quality of allowing different opinions to your own to be tolerated

tol·e·rate /ˈtɒləreɪt ‖ ˈtɑː-/ *v* **tolerated, tolerating** [T] to allow something you do not like to be practised or done: *I can't tolerate bad manners.* –see BEAR² (USAGE) –**tolerant** *adj*

tol·e·ra·tion /ˌtɒləˈreɪʃən ‖ ˌtɑː-/ *n* [U] the quality of allowing people to hold different opinions or beliefs or to behave in a way that may not please you, without becoming annoyed: *religious toleration*

toll¹ /təʊl/ *n* **1** a tax paid to use a road or bridge **2 the death toll** the number of people who have died in an accident: *The death toll has now risen to 20.*

toll² *v* [I;T] to ring slowly and repeatedly: *The bells tolled to commemorate the tragedy.* –**toll** *n* [sing] : *the toll of the bell*

to·ma·to /təˈmɑːtəʊ ‖ -ˈmeɪ-/ *n* **tomatoes 1** [C;U] a soft red fruit eaten as a vegetable: *six ripe tomatoes* | *tomato soup* –see picture on page 344 **2** [C] the plant on which this fruit grows: *This is the month to plant out your tomatoes.*

tomb /tuːm/ *n* a grave, especially a large decorated one above ground

tom·boy /ˈtɒmbɔɪ ‖ ˈtɑːm-/ *n* a young girl who likes to be rough and noisy

tomb·stone /ˈtuːmstəʊn/ *n* a stone put up over a grave bearing the name, date of birth and death of the dead person

tom·cat /ˈtɒmkæt ‖ ˈtɑːm-/ (also **tom** /tɒm ‖ tɑːm/ *infml*) *n* a male cat

tome /təʊm/ *n lit* a large book

tomorrow /təˈmɒrəʊ ‖ -ˈmɔː-, -ˈmɑː-/ *adv,n* **1** the day after today: *Tomorrow is Wednesday.* | *I'm going to London tomorrow.* | *I'll see you tomorrow evening.* **2** the future: *This could be the food crop of tomorrow.*

tom-tom /ˈtɒm tɒm ‖ ˈtɑːm tɑːm/ *n* a long narrow drum, beaten with the hands

ton /tʌn/ *n* **tons** *or* **ton 1** a unit for measuring weight equal in Britain to 2,240 pounds and in the US to 2,000 pounds **2** (also **tonne, metric ton**) a unit for measuring weight equal to one thousand kilograms **3** *infml* a very large quantity or weight: *I bought tons of food.* | *This book weighs a ton!* **4 come down on someone like a ton of bricks** to punish or speak to someone very severely

tone¹ /təʊn/ *n* **1** [C] the quality of sound of a musical instrument or singing voice: *That piano has a beautiful tone.* **2** [C] a particular manner of expression: *to speak in low tones* | *I don't like your tone of voice.* **3** [C] a variety of a colour: *a picture painted in tones of blue* **4** [U] the general quality or mood of something: *the tone of our neighbourhood* **5** [C] a fixed separation between musical notes in a scale: *There is a tone between B and C sharp.* | *a semi-tone*

tone² *v* **toned, toning**
tone sthg ↔ **down** *phr v* [T] to reduce the violence or force of something: *You must tone down your language; stop swearing.*
tone in *phr v* [I] to match: *Your hat and shoes tone in well with your dress.*
tone sbdy/sthg ↔ **up** *phr v* [T] to make stronger and more healthy: *Swimming is the best way to tone up your body.*

tone-deaf /ˌ· ˈ·◂/ *adj* unable to tell the difference between musical notes

tone·less /ˈtəʊnləs/ *adj* lacking colour and looking lifeless: *a toneless voice*

tongs /tɒŋz ‖ tɑːŋz, tɔːŋz/ *n* [pl] an instrument with two movable arms, used for holding or lifting things: *She used the tongs to put the coal onto the fire.*

tongue /tʌŋ/ *n* **1** [C] the soft part inside your mouth, used for tasting and speaking **2** [U] a cow's tongue, used as food **3** [C] an object shaped like a tongue: *tongues of flame* **4** [C] *lit* a spoken language: *My native tongue is English.* **5 hold your tongue** to be silent **6 with your tongue in your cheek** *infml* saying something without meaning it seriously

tongue-tied /ˈ· ·/ *adj* unable to speak freely because you are nervous

tongue twist·er /ˈ· ˌ··/ *n* a word or phrase difficult to say quickly

ton·ic /ˈtɒnɪk ‖ ˈtɑː-/ *n* anything which increases health or strength: *Country air is a good tonic.* | *The doctor gave me a special tonic.* | *a tonic for depression* –**tonic** *adj*

tonic wa·ter /ˈ·· ˌ··/ (also **tonic**) [U] gassy water with a slightly bitter taste, often added to alcoholic drinks: *a gin and tonic*

to·night /təˈnaɪt/ *adv,n* this present night, or the night that follows today: *It's very cold tonight.* | *I'll see you tonight.*

ton·nage /ˈtʌnɪdʒ/ *n* [U] the total weight or size of something expressed in TONS

tonne /tʌn/ *n* **tonnes** *or* **tonne** see TON

ton·sil /ˈtɒnsəl ‖ ˈtɑː-/ *n* one of two small organs at the sides of your throat near the back of your tongue

ton·sil·li·tis , tonsilitis /ˌtɒnsᵻˈlaɪtᵻs ‖ ˌtɑːn-/ *n* [U] infection of the tonsils

too /tuː/ *adv* **1** also: *She bought me a book and a box of chocolates too.* | *I was very excited and a bit nervous too.* | *"I'm absolutely fed up." "I am too."* **2** more than is needed or wanted: *You're going too fast.* | *This dress is too small for me.* | *It's too cold to go swimming.* **3 not too** not very: *He wasn't too pleased when I told him I was leaving.*

■ USAGE **1** Compare **too** and **very**. **Too** usually suggests something bad or unsuitable: *It's too cold today* (so I don't want to go out). **Very** suggests that something is neither good nor bad: *It's very cold today* (but I have a warm coat, so the temperature is no problem). **2** We can use **too** before adjectives on their own: *This coffee is too sweet.* But we cannot use **too** before an adjective followed by a noun; thus we cannot put **too** before *sweet* in *this sweet coffee.* Notice also the word order in these two sentences: *The day is too hot.* | *It's too hot a day.*

took /tʊk/ the past tense of TAKE

tool /tuːl/ *n* **1** any instrument such as an axe, hammer, or spade for doing special jobs –see MACHINE (USAGE) **2** a person dishonestly used by someone for their own purposes: *The king was just a tool of the military government.* **3 down tools** *infml* to stop working as a protest

toot /tuːt/ *v* [I;T] to make a short warning sound with a horn or whistle: *The car drivers tooted their horns.* –**toot** *n*

tooth /tuːθ/ *n* **teeth** /tiːθ/ **1** one of the small hard white bony objects in your mouth, used for biting and tearing food **2 teeth** the pointed parts on a comb, SAW or ZIP **3 long in the tooth** *infml* old **4 tooth and nail** fighting very violently

tooth·ache /ˈtuːθ-eɪk/ *n* [C;U] a pain in a tooth –see ACHE² (USAGE)

tooth·brush /'tu:θbrʌʃ/ n a small brush used for cleaning your teeth

tooth·paste /'tu:θpeɪst/ n [U] a substance used for cleaning your teeth

tooth·pick /'tu:θ‚pɪk/ n a small pointed piece of wood used for removing food stuck between your teeth

top[1] /top ‖ ta:p/ n **1** the highest or upper part of something: *at the top of the page* | *They live on the top floor.* | *the top of my desk* | *the table top* **2 the top** the best or most important position: *He started life at the bottom and worked his way to the top.* –compare BOTTOM **3** a cover: *I can't unscrew the top of this bottle.* | *I wish you'd put the top back on the toothpaste.* **4** a piece of clothing that you wear on the upper part of your body: *a skirt with a matching top* **5** a child's toy that spins and balances on its point **6 at the top of your voice** as loudly as possible **7 at top speed** very fast **8 get on top of you** *infml* to be too much for you: *This work is getting on top of me.* **9 on top** over or above: *a cake with cream on top* **10 on top of** in addition to: *She's got all this extra work to do. And, on top of that, her mother's ill.* | *On top of your basic pension you'll get a disability allowance.*

top[2] v **-pp-** [T] **1** to form or be a top for something: *a cake topped with cream* **2** to be higher, better, or more than something: *Their profits have topped ours this year.* **3 top the bill** to be the chief actor or actress in a play
top sthg ↔ **up** *phr v* [T] **1** to fill up a partly empty container: *We need to top the car up with petrol.* | *Shall I top your glass up for you?* **2** to bring an amount of money up to an acceptable level: *The director's salary is topped up by a share in the company's profits.*

top[3] adj **1** at the top: *the top step* **2** best: *Fred is our top man.* | *top of the class*

to·paz /'təʊpæz/ n [C;U] a precious stone cut from a transparent yellowish mineral

top·coat /'topkəʊt ‖ 'ta:p-/ n **1** a long, warm coat worn over other clothes in cold weather **2 the top-coat** the last covering of paint to be put on a surface

top dog /‚· '·/ n *infml* the person in the most important position

top hat /‚· '·/ n a man's tall silk hat worn only on formal occasions

top-heav·y /‚· '·‚⊲/ adj not properly balanced because there is too much weight at the top

top·ic /'topɪk ‖ 'ta:-/ n a subject for conversation, talk, or writing

top·ic·al /'topɪkəl ‖ 'ta:-/ adj related to a subject of present interest: *Recent events have made this film very topical.* –**topically** /-kli/ adv

top·less /'topləs ‖ 'ta:p-/ adj with the upper part of the body, including the breasts, bare (used of a woman or a piece of clothing): *a topless swimsuit* | *a topless dancer*

top·most /'topməʊst ‖ 'ta:p-/ adj [only before a noun] highest: *the topmost branches of the old oak tree*

to·pog·ra·phy /tə'pɒgrəfi ‖ -'pa:-/ n [U] the science of describing or mapping the character of a place, especially the shape and height of the land –**topographical** /‚topə'græfɪkəl ‖ ‚ta:-, ‚təʊ-/ adj

top·ping /'topɪŋ ‖ 'ta:-/ n [C;U] something put on top of food to make it look or taste nicer: *cream topping*

top·ple /'topəl ‖ 'ta:-/ v **toppled, toppling 1** [I] to become unsteady and fall over: *She toppled from the ladder.* **2** [I;T] to lose power, or to make someone lose their power: *a scandal that could topple the government*
topple over *phr v* [I] to become unsteady and fall over: *Watch out! The bricks nearly toppled over.*

top-se·cret /‚· '·◄/ adj to be kept very secret: *top-secret military information*

top·sy-tur·vy /‚topsi 'tɜ:vi◄ ‖ ‚ta:psi 'tɜ:rvi◄/ adj, adv in a state of confusion

torch /tɔ:tʃ ‖ tɔ:rtʃ/ n **1** *BrE* a small electric light that you carry in your hand –see picture on page 638 **2** a mass of burning material tied to a stick and carried to give light **3** the usual American word for BLOWLAMP

torch·light /'tɔ:tʃlaɪt ‖ 'tɔ:r-/ n [U] light produced by torches: *a torchlight procession*

tore /tɔ:ʳ/ the past tense of TEAR

tor·ment[1] /'tɔ:ment ‖ 'tɔ:r-/ n **1** [C;U] very great pain or suffering: *He suffered torments.* **2** [C] someone or something that causes this: *That child is a torment to his parents.*

tor·ment[2] /tɔ:'ment ‖ tɔ:r-/ v [T] to make someone suffer pain or annoyance: *The boy tormented his little sister.* –**tormentor** n

torn /tɔ:n ‖ tɔ:rn/ the past participle of TEAR

tor·na·do /tɔ:'neɪdəʊ ‖ tɔ:r-/ n **tornadoes** or **tornados** a very violent wind that spins at great speed

tor·pe·do /tɔ:'pi:dəʊ ‖ tɔ:r-/ n **torpedoes** a bomb shaped like a tube that travels under the sea and is used to destroy ships –**torpedo** v [T] : *We torpedoed the enemy ships.*

tor·pid /'tɔ:pɪd ‖ 'tɔ:r-/ adj *fml* moving slowly: *a torpid mind* –**torpor** /'tɔ:pəʳ ‖ 'tɔ:r-/ n [U]

tor·rent /'tɒrənt ‖ 'tɔ:-, 'tɑ:-/ n **1** a violently rushing stream: *The rain fell in torrents.* | *A torrent of water swept down the valley.* **2** a large amount of unpleasant language: *a torrent of abuse* –**torrential** /tɒ'renʃəl ‖ tɔ:-/ adj : *torrential rain*

tor·rid /'tɒrɪd ‖ 'tɔ:-, 'tɑ:-/ adj *lit* **1** very hot: *the torrid desert sun* **2** concerning strong uncontrolled feelings: *a torrid story of sex and violence*

tor·so /'tɔ:səʊ ‖ 'tɔ:r-/ n the human body without the head and limbs

tor·toise /'tɔ:təs ‖ 'tɔ:r-/ n a slow-moving land animal with a hard shell

tor·toise·shell /'tɔ:təsʃel, 'tɔ:təʃel ‖ 'tɔ:r-/ n [U] the hard brown and yellow shell of the tortoise or TURTLE, used for making combs and ornaments

tor·tu·ous /'tɔ:tʃuəs ‖ 'tɔ:r-/ adj **1** twisted and winding: *a tortuous mountain road* **2** not simple or direct: *They found out the truth by tortuous means.*

tor·ture[1] /'tɔ:tʃəʳ ‖ 'tɔ:r-/ n **1** [U] the act of causing severe pain, done out of cruelty or to find out information: *instruments of torture* **2** [C;U] severe pain or suffering: *the tortures of jealousy*

torture[2] v **tortured, torturing** [T] to cause great pain to a person or animal out of cruelty, or as a punishment: *The prisoner was tortured to make him admit to the crime.* –**torturer** n

To·ry /'tɔ:ri/ n, adj **Tories** a member of the British CONSERVATIVE Party: *The Tories never supported the bill.* –**Tory** adj : *Tory principles*

toss[1] /tɒs ‖ tɔ:s/ v **1** [T + adv/prep] to throw something: *He tossed the ball to me.* **2** [I] to move about rapidly or make something move rapidly: *The boat was tossed about in the stormy sea.* | *He tossed about in his sleep.* | *The horse tossed its head back.* **3** [T] to mix food lightly so as to cover it in sauce: *Toss*

the salad in the dressing. **4** [I;T] to throw a coin to decide something according to which side lands face upwards: *There's only one cake and two of us, so let's toss for it.*

toss sthg ↔ **off** *phr v* [T] to produce something quickly with little effort: *She tossed off a few ideas for advertising the new product.*

toss² *n* **1** a sudden backward movement: *She gave a quick toss of her head.* **2 the toss** an act of tossing a coin to decide something: *Our team won the toss, so we play first.*

toss-up /ˈ·-·/ *n* [sing] *infml* an even chance: *It's a toss-up between the two of them as to who will get the job.*

tot¹ /tɒt ‖ tɑːt/ *n* **1** a very small child: *a tiny tot* **2** a small amount of a strong alcoholic drink: *a tot of rum*

tot² *v*

tot sthg ↔ **up** *phr v* [T] to add up: *Now tot up the sub-totals.*

to·tal¹ /ˈtəʊtl/ *adj* complete: *the total population of Britain* | *total silence* –**totally** *adv* : *I totally agree with you.*

total² *n* **1** a number or quantity obtained by adding other amounts together: *Add these numbers together and tell me the total.* | *A total of two hundred people visited the castle.* **2 in total** as a total: *In total, there were two hundred visitors.*

total³ *v* **-ll-** (**-l-** *AmE*) [T] to add up to a particular amount: *Your debts total one thousand pounds.*

to·tal·i·tar·i·an /təʊˌtælɪˈteəriən/ *adj* based on a political system in which one political group controls everything and does not allow opposition parties to exist –**totalitarianism** *n* [U]

to·tal·i·ty /təʊˈtælɪti/ *n* [U] *fml* completeness

tot·ter /ˈtɒtəʳ ‖ ˈtɑː-/ *v* [I+adv/prep] to move or walk in an unsteady way: *The old lady tottered down the stairs.*

tot·ter·y /ˈtɒtəri ‖ ˈtɑː-/ *adj* unsteady and shaky

tou·can /ˈtuːkən, -kæn/ *n* a brightly-coloured tropical bird with a large beak

touch¹ /tʌtʃ/ *v* **1** [I;T] to feel something with your hands or another part of your body: *Visitors are asked not to touch the paintings.* | *You can look, but don't touch.* **2** [I;T] to be right next to something with no space between: *The branches were hanging down and touching the water.* | *We were standing close together with our shoulders touching.* **3** [T] to eat, drink, or take action with something: *I never touch alcohol.* | *I haven't touched my work all weekend.* **4** [T] to make you feel sad: *a very touching story* **5** [T] to make you feel grateful: *I was very touched by her kindness.* **6 touch and go** uncertain as to whether something will succeed or not: *The doctors have said it's touch and go whether she'll live.* **7 touch wood** a phrase you use when you touch something made of wood in order to avoid bad luck: *I haven't been ill at all this winter* – *touch wood.*

touch down *phr v* [I] **1** (of a plane) to land **2** to press the ball down and get a point in a game of RUGBY

touch on sthg *phr v* [T] to mention something in just a few words: *He only touched on the subject of water pollution.*

touch sthg ↔ **up** *phr v* [T] to improve something by making small changes or additions

touch² *n* **1** [U] the sense by which you know whether something is hard, smooth, rough, hot, etc: *Its fur was soft to the touch.* **2** [C] an act of touching something: *He felt the touch of her hand on his shoulder.* **3** a **touch** a small amount of something **4** [C]

a small detail that improves something: *I'm just putting the finishing touches to the picture.* **5** [sing] someone's way of doing something, especially when it shows skill: *I seem to be losing my touch.* **6 get in touch with someone** to write to someone or telephone them: *I'm trying to get in touch with my brother.* **7 in touch** speaking or writing to someone regularly: *Are you still in touch with John?* | *We must keep in touch.* **8 in touch with something** knowing the latest information about a subject: *I try to keep in touch with what's going on in Linguistics.* [RELATED PHRASE **out of touch with something**] **9 lose touch** to stop seeing someone, writing to them or telephoning them: *I lost touch with her years ago.*

touch-and-go /ˌ·-ˈ-·◂/ *adj* risky and with an uncertain result: *It was touch-and-go whether he would get there in time.*

touched /tʌtʃt/ *adj* [only after a noun] **1** feeling grateful: *I was very touched by their present.* **2** *infml* slightly mad

touch·stone /ˈtʌtʃstəʊn/ *n* something used as a test or standard

touch·y /ˈtʌtʃi/ *adj* easily offended and over-sensitive

tough¹ /tʌf/ *adj* **1** strong and not easily weakened: *Only tough breeds of sheep can live in the mountains.* | *He won't give up, he's really tough.* **2** difficult to cut or eat: *tough meat* **3** difficult to do and demanding effort: *a tough lesson* **4** rough and hard: *The government will get tough with people who avoid paying taxes.* | *a tough criminal* **5** *infml* unfortunate: *Tough luck!* | *Life is tough on single parents.* –**toughness** *n* [U]

tough² *n infml* a rough, violent person such as a criminal

tough·en /ˈtʌfən/ *v* [T] to make someone or something stronger: *toughened steel* | *The experiences of the last few months had toughened her.*

tou·pee /ˈtuːpeɪ ‖ tuːˈpeɪ/ *n* a piece of false hair that fits over a place on a man's head where his hair no longer grows

tour¹ /tʊəʳ/ *n* **1** a journey during which several places are visited: *a tour round Europe* **2 on tour** travelling to a lot of different places: *The National Theatre is on tour in the North.* **3** a short trip to or through a place: *We went on a guided tour round the castle.* **4** a period of duty at a single place, especially abroad: *a two-year tour in Germany*

tour² *v* [I;T] to travel around a particular area: *We're touring Italy on our holidays.* | *a touring holiday*

tour de force /ˌtʊə də ˈfɔːs ‖ ˌtʊər də ˈfɔːrs/ *n fml* a show of strength or skill

tour·is·m /ˈtʊərɪzəm/ *n* [U] **1** the business of providing holidays for tourists **2** travelling for pleasure

tour·ist /ˈtʊərɪst/ *n* a person travelling for pleasure: *Oxford is full of tourists in summer.* | *I'm not a tourist, I live here!*

tour·na·ment /ˈtʊənəmənt, ˈtɔː- ‖ ˈtɜːr-, ˈtʊər-/ *n* a number of competitions between players, played until the most skilful wins: *a tennis tournament* | *a chess tournament*

tour·ni·quet /ˈtʊənɪkeɪ, ˈtɔː- ‖ ˈtɜːrnɪkət, ˈtʊər-/ *n* a band of cloth or something soft, twisted tightly round a limb to stop it bleeding

tou·sle /ˈtaʊzəl/ *v* tousled, tousling [T] to make someone's hair untidy

tout /taʊt/ *v* [I] to try to persuade people to buy or use your goods or services: *touting for business* –**tout** *n* : *a ticket tout*

tow¹ /təʊ/ v [T] to pull a vehicle along by a rope or chain

tow² n **1 on tow** being towed: *a vehicle on tow* **2 in tow** *infml* following closely behind: *She arrived with her children in tow.*

to·wards /tə'wɔːdz ‖ tɔːrdz/ prep (also **toward** AmE) **1** in the direction of something: *She walked towards the door.* | *He was standing with his back towards me.* | *We are heading towards an economic crisis.* –see picture on page 540 **2** not long before a particular time: *Towards the end of the afternoon it began to rain.* **3** in relation to: *the government's attitude towards education* | *What are his feelings towards you?* **4** to pay for some of the cost of something: *We save £20 a week towards our holiday.*

tow·el¹ /'taʊəl/ n a piece of cloth or paper used for drying wet things: *a bath towel* | *paper towels* | *a linen tea towel*

towel² v -ll- (-l- AmE) [T] to rub or dry something with a towel

tow·el·ling /'taʊəlɪŋ/ n [U] (**toweling** AmE) thick, soft cloth, used for making towels: *a towelling bath robe*

tow·er¹ /'taʊəʳ/ n **1** a tall, narrow building standing alone or forming part of another building: *the Tower of London* | *the Eiffel Tower* **2 a tower of strength** a person who gives help and encouragement

tower² v [I;+adv/prep] to be very tall, especially in relation to the surroundings: *The mountains towered over the town in the valley.*

tower block /'··· ·/ n a tall building containing flats or offices

town /taʊn/ n **1** [C] a place with many buildings where people live and work; a town is larger than a village, but smaller than a city –see picture on page 246 **2** [U] the business or shopping centre of such a place: *We went to town to do some shopping today.* **3** [C +sing/pl verb] the people who live in a town: *The whole town is in agreement about the plan.* **4** [U] life in towns and cities in general: *I like the town better than the country.* | *to leave the country for the town* **5 go to town** *infml* to act freely especially by spending a lot of money **6 go out on the town** *infml* to enjoy yourself in town, especially at night

town coun·cil /ˌ· '··/ n [+sing/pl verb] BrE the people elected to govern a town: *The town council does not have support for this policy.*

town hall /ˌ· '·/ n the building used for local government offices and public meetings

town·ship /'taʊnʃɪp/ n in South Africa, a place where non-white citizens live

towns·peo·ple /'taʊnzˌpiːpəl/ n **the townspeople** the people who live in a town

tow·path /'təʊpɑːθ ‖ -pæθ/ n **towpaths** /-pɑːðz ‖ -pæðz/ a path along the side of a river or CANAL where people can walk

tow rope /'· ·/ n a rope used for pulling vehicles

tox·ic /'tɒksɪk ‖ 'tɑːk-/ adj fml poisonous: *a toxic drug* | *toxic waste from a factory* –**toxicity** /-'sɪsⱼti/ n [U]

tox·i·col·o·gy /ˌtɒksɪ'kɒlədʒi ‖ ˌtɑːksɪ'kɑː-/ n [U] the scientific and medical study of poisons –**toxicologist** n

tox·in /'tɒksⱼn ‖ 'tɑːk-/ n a poison produced by bacteria in a plant or animal body

toy¹ /tɔɪ/ n an object for children to play with: *Children love getting new toys to play with.* | *a toy shop* n [U]

toy² adj [only before a noun] **1** used to play with: *a*

toy soldier | *a toy clock* **2** smaller than the usual kind (used of dogs): *a toy poodle*

toy³ v

toy with sthg *phr v* [T] **1** to play with something without any purpose: *a child toying with its food* **2** to be considering something, but not very seriously: *She toyed with the idea of changing her job.*

trace¹ /treɪs/ v **traced, tracing** [T] **1** to look for and find something: *The criminal was traced to London.* | *I can't trace the letter you sent me.* **2** to copy the lines on a drawing, using transparent paper **3** to discover and describe the history or development of something: *It was a most interesting talk tracing the development of the Labour movement.*

trace² n **1** [C;U] a mark or sign showing the former presence or passing of something or someone: *The police found no trace of the man.* | *lost without trace* **2** [C] a very small amount of something: *Traces of poison were found in the dead man's blood.*

trac·ing /'treɪsɪŋ/ n a copy of a map or drawing made by tracing

track¹ /træk/ n **1** a rough path or road: *a farm track* –see WAY (USAGE) **2 off the beaten track** quiet and not near people or other buildings: *It's difficult to find them – they live quite off the beaten track.* **3** a line or number of marks left by a person, animal or vehicle: *The trapper followed the fox's tracks.* | *tyre tracks* **4 to be on someone's track** to be following and trying to catch someone: *The police are on his track and hope to catch him soon.* **5** an area especially prepared for running or racing: *track and field events* **6** the metal lines on which a train runs: *Something had been thrown onto the track.* –see picture on page 735 **7** one of the songs or pieces of music on a record or TAPE: *I love the last track on this album.* **8 be on the right track** to be thinking in the right way [RELATED PHRASE **be on the wrong track**] **9 cover/hide your tracks** not to leave signs of where you have been and what you have been doing **10 have a one track mind** *infml* to give all your attention to one thing only **11 keep track of sbdy/sthg** to be sure that you know what is happening or where someone is [RELATED PHRASE **lose track of sbdy/sthg**] **12 stop (dead) in your tracks** to stop suddenly

track² v [T] to follow the track of something or someone in order to catch them –**tracker** n : *police tracker dogs*

track sbdy/sthg ↔ **down** *phr v* [T] to find someone or something by hunting or searching: *I finally tracked him down in Paris.*

track and field /ˌ·· ·ˌ·/ n [sing] the usual American word for ATHLETICS

track·suit /'træksuːt, -sjuːt ‖ -suːt/ n a warm loose-fitting suit worn for informal occasions or when training for sport –see picture on page 50

tract /trækt/ n **1** *fml* a short article, especially about a religious, political, or moral subject **2** a wide stretch of land: *immense tracts of open wasteland* **3** *tech* a system of related organs in your body with one purpose: *the digestive tract*

traction en·gine /'trækʃən ˌendʒⱼn/ n a large vehicle, used in the past for pulling heavy loads

trac·tor /'træktəʳ/ n a motor vehicle with large wheels and thick tyres, used for pulling farm machinery or other heavy objects

trade¹ /treɪd/ n **1** [U] the buying and selling of goods: *a trade agreement between England and France* | *He made his money in trade.* **2 the trade** a particular business or industry: *the cotton trade* | *He's in the* *tourist trade*. –see JOB (USAGE) **3** [C] a job, especially one needing special skills: *He insisted that his son should learn a trade*. **4 do a good trade, do a roaring trade** carry out a successful business: *The shop does a good trade on Saturdays*.

trade² *v* **traded, trading 1** [I] to carry on trade: *He trades in meat*. | *Britain is now trading with Eastern Europe*. **2** [T] to buy, sell, or exchange: *They traded their clothes for food*.

trade sthg ↔ **in** *phr v* [T] to give something in part payment for something new: *He traded in his old car in for a new one*. –**trade-in** /ˈ·· ·/ *n*

trade-mark /ˈtreɪdmɑːk ‖ -mɑːrk/ *n* **1** a special mark on a product to show that it is made by a particular producer **2** a thing that is typical of a person or company

trad-er /ˈtreɪdəʳ/ *n* a person who buys and sells goods

trades-man /ˈtreɪdzmən/ *n* **tradesmen** /-mən/ a person who buys and sells goods, especially a shopkeeper

trade un-i-on /ˌ· ˈ···/ *n* (also **trades union**) an organization of workers set up to represent their interests and to deal as a group with the employers –**trade unionism** *n* [U] –**trade unionist** *n*

trade wind /ˈ· ·/ *n* a tropical wind

tra-di-tion /trəˈdɪʃən/ *n* **1** [U] the passing down of opinions, beliefs, practices, and customs from the past to the present: *respect for tradition* **2** [C] an opinion, belief, or custom passed down in this way: *It is a tradition that women get married in long white dresses*. –**traditional** *adj* : *the traditional English breakfast* –**traditionally** *adv*

traf-fic¹ /ˈtræfɪk/ *n* [U] **1** all the vehicles moving in a place: *rush-hour traffic* | *air traffic control* **2** buying and selling goods illegally: *the traffic in endangered species* | *the traffic in cocaine*

traffic² *v* **trafficked, trafficking**

traffic in sthg *phr v* [T] to carry on trade of an unlawful kind: *He was found to be trafficking in stolen goods*. –**trafficker** *n*

traffic cir-cle /ˈ·· ˌ··/ *n* the usual American word for ROUNDABOUT

traffic jam /ˈ·· ˌ·/ *n* a long line of vehicles that cannot move because the road is blocked –see picture on page 246

traffic lights /ˈ··· ·/ *n* [pl] a set of coloured lights used for controlling and directing traffic on roads: *Watch out! The traffic lights are about to change*. –see picture on page 735

traffic war-den /ˈ·· ˌ··/ *n* a person whose job is to check that vehicles are not parked in the wrong place

tra-ge-dy /ˈtrædʒɪdi/ *n* **tragedies 1** [C] a serious play that ends sadly: *Shakespeare's "Hamlet" is a very famous tragedy*. **2** [U] these plays considered as a group **3** [C;U] a terrible, unhappy, or unfortunate event: *It was a tragedy that she died so young*. –**tragic** *adj* : *a tragic hero* | *a tragic accident* –**tragically** /-kli/ *adv*

trail¹ /treɪl/ *v* **1** [I + adv/prep; T + adv/prep] to drag or be dragged behind: *Her long skirt trailed in the mud*. | *The child was trailing a toy train on a string*. **2** [T] to follow the tracks of a person or animal: *The hunters trailed the tiger for five hours*. **3** [I + adv/prep] to walk in a tired way, often behind someone else: *The defeated army trailed back to camp*. **4** [I] to grow over or along the ground **5 be trailing** to be behind in a competition: *The Conservative Party was trailing in the opinion polls*.

trail away *phr v* [I] (also **trail off**) to become slowly quieter or weaker: *He was unable to complete what he wanted to say and his voice just trailed away*.

trail² *n* **1** the track or smell of a person or animal **2** a path across rough country **3** a stream of dust or smoke behind something which is moving **4 be on the trail of someone or something** to be following or trying to find someone or something

trail-er /ˈtreɪləʳ/ *n* **1** a framework like a table with wheels onto which things can be loaded to be pulled by another vehicle: *a car pulling a boat on a trailer* **2** an advertisement for a new film, showing small parts of it **3** the usual American word for CARAVAN

train¹ /treɪn/ *n* **1** a line of connected railway carriages drawn by an engine: *I've got to catch that train!* **2 by train** travelling in a train: *It's cheaper to go by train*. **3** a chain of related events or thoughts: *The telephone rang and interrupted my train of thought*. **4** a part of the back of a long dress that spreads over the ground **5** a long line of moving people, vehicles, or animals

train² *v* **1** [I;T] to give or be given teaching and practice in a profession or skill: *The army trains soldiers to fight*. | *She is training to be a doctor*. | *He spends two hours a day training for the race*. □ USEFUL PATTERNS to train for something; to train someone for something; to train to do something; to train someone to do something **2** [T + adv/prep] to point a gun at something or someone **3** [T] to direct the growth of a plant

train-ee /treɪˈniː/ *n* a person who is being trained: *a trainee reporter* | *He's still a trainee*.

train-er /ˈtreɪnəʳ/ *n* **1** a person who trains someone: *He always follows the advice of his trainer*. **2** *BrE* **trainers** [pl] special shoes worn for running or for informal occasions –see picture on page 50

train-ing /ˈtreɪnɪŋ/ *n* [C;U] **1** instruction for a particular job or activity: *The company gave me an excellent training*. **2 be in training** to be preparing for an event by exercising and eating suitable food: *He's in training for the match next week*.

trait /treɪt/ *n* a particular quality of someone or something: *Generosity is her best trait*.

trai-tor /ˈtreɪtəʳ/ *n* someone who is disloyal, especially to their country

tra-jec-to-ry /trəˈdʒektəri/ *n* **trajectories** *tech* the curved path of an object moving through the air: *the trajectory of a bullet*

tram /træm/ *n* (also **tramcar** /ˈtræmkɑːr/) a vehicle for the public, driven by electricity, that runs along metal lines in the road

tramp¹ /træmp/ *v* [I + adv/prep; T] to walk a long way, steadily but in a tired way: *They tramped through the woods all day*. | *She tramped the streets looking for work*.

tramp² *n* **1** a person with no home or job, who wanders from place to place **2** [sing] the sound of heavy walking: *the tramp of the soldiers' feet on the road* **3** a long walk

tram-ple /ˈtræmpəl/ *v* **trampled, trampling 1** [T] to step heavily on something and damage it: *trampled grass* **2 trample on someone** *infml* to behave in an unfair or cruel way towards someone: *He trampled on people's feelings*.

tram-po-line /ˈtræmpəliːn ‖ ˌtræmpəˈliːn/ *n* an apparatus consisting of a sheet of material held to a metal frame by springs, on which people can jump up and down

trance /trɑːns ‖ træns/ *n* a condition of your mind where you are not in control of your thoughts and feelings, and may be controlled by someone else: *She was in a deep trance*.

tran·quil /'træŋkwɨl/ *adj* calm and peaceful: *a tranquil lake | a tranquil smile* –**tranquillity** (**tranquility** *AmE*) /træŋ'kwɪlɨti/ *n* [U]

tran·quil·lize /'træŋkwɨlaɪz/ *v* **tranquillized, tranquillizing** (also **tranquillise** *BrE*) [T] **be tranquillized** to be given a drug which makes you calmer and less anxious

tran·quil·liz·er /'træŋkwɨlaɪzər/ (also **tranquilliser** *BrE*) *n* a drug used for making a person calm

trans·act /træn'zækt/ *v* [T] to carry a piece of business through to an agreement

trans·ac·tion /træn'zækʃən/ *n* a piece of business

trans·at·lan·tic /ˌtrænzət'læntɪk◂/ *adj* **1** on the other side of or across the Atlantic Ocean: *a transatlantic military base | transatlantic flights* **2** concerning countries on both sides of the Atlantic Ocean: *a transatlantic agreement*

tran·scend /træn'send/ *v* [T] *lit* to go beyond the limits of something: *The wish for peace transcended political differences.*

tran·scen·den·tal /ˌtrænsen'dentl/ *adj fml* going beyond human knowledge, thought, belief, and experience: *transcendental truths*

trans·con·ti·nen·tal /ˌtrænzkontɨ'nentl, ˌtræns-ˌ-kɑːn-/ *adj* crossing a CONTINENT: *a transcontinental railway*

tran·scribe /træn'skraɪb/ *v* **transcribed, transcribing** [T] **1** to make a full written copy of something **2** to arrange a piece of music for an instrument or voice other than the original –**transcription** /-'skrɪpʃən/ *n*

tran·script /'trænskrɪpt/ *n* a written or printed copy of something that was spoken

trans·fer¹ /træns'fɜːr/ *v* **-rr-** **1** [I;T] to move from one place or job to another within the same organization: *The office was transferred from Belfast to Dublin. | He is hoping to be transferred to another team.* **2** [T] to take something from one person and give it to another: *Responsibility for staff was transferred to the company secretary.* **3** [T] to move from one place to another: *The money will be transferred to your account.* –**transferable** *adj*

trans·fer² /'trænsfɜːr/ *n* **1** [C;U] a move to another place or job: *He wants a transfer to another team. | the transfer of funds to a new account* **2** [C] a drawing or pattern for sticking or printing onto a surface: *He had a transfer of Mickey Mouse on his T-shirt.*

trans·fer·ence /'trænsfərəns/ *n fml* [U] the moving of something to a different person or place

trans·fixed /træns'fɪkst/ *adj lit* unable to move or think because of terror or shock

trans·form /træns'fɔːm ‖ -fɔːrm/ *v* [T] to change something completely in form, appearance, or nature: *The area of wasteland was transformed into a park.* –**transformation** /ˌtrænsfə'meɪʃən ‖ -fər-/ *n* [C;U]

trans·form·er /træns'fɔːmər ‖ -ɔːr-/ *n* an apparatus for changing electrical force from one VOLTAGE to another

trans·fu·sion /træns'fjuːʒən/ *n* [C;U] a medical process when the blood of one person is given to someone else: *The driver had to have a blood transfusion after the accident.*

tran·si·ent /'trænziənt ‖ 'trænʃənt/ *adj* lasting for only a short time: *transient happiness* –**transience** *n* [U]

tran·sis·tor /træn'zɪstər, -'sɪstər/ *n* **1** a small electrical apparatus, used in radios or televisions **2** (also **transistor radio**) a small radio which is easy to carry

tran·sit /'trænsɨt, -zɨt/ *n* **in transit** being moved from one place to another: *His luggage got lost in transit.*

tran·si·tion /træn'zɪʃən, -'sɪ-/ *n* [C;U] a change from one state or condition to another: *We hope there will be a peaceful transition to the new system. | a city in transition* –**transitional** *adj*: *a transitional period*

tran·si·tive /'trænsɨtɪv, -zɨ-/ *adj tech* needing a direct object (used of verbs): In the sentence *"I broke the cup"*, *"broke"* is a transitive verb. –see Study Note on page 589

trans·late /trænz'leɪt, træns-/ *v* **translated, translating** **1** [I;T] to change speech or writing from one language into another: *The book was translated from French into English.* **2** [T] to change from one form into another: *A politician should translate ideas into action.* –**translator** *n* –**translation** /-'leɪʃən/ *n* [C;U]: *I've only read Tolstoy's books in translation. | an excellent translation*

trans·mis·sion /trænz'mɪʃən ‖ træns-/ *n* **1** [U] sending or passing something to a person or place **2** [C;U] something broadcast by television or radio **3** [C] the parts of a vehicle that carry power from the engine to its wheels

trans·mit /trænz'mɪt ‖ træns-/ *v* **-tt-** **1** [I;T] to send out electric signals, messages, and news: **2** [T] to carry something from one person, place, or thing to another: *How is the disease transmitted?*

trans·mit·ter /trænz'mɪtər ‖ træns-/ *n* an apparatus that sends out radio or television signals

trans·par·en·cy /træn'spærənsi, -'speər-/ *n* **transparencies** **1** [C] a piece of photographic film, on which a picture can be seen when light is passed through **2** [U] the state of being transparent

trans·par·ent /træn'spærənt, -'speər-/ *adj* **1** able to be seen through: *Glass is transparent. | Her silk dress was almost transparent.* **2** clearly recognized: *His honesty was transparent.* –**transparently** *adv*

tran·spire /træn'spaɪər/ *v* **transpired, transpiring** *fml* **1** [+ that] to become known at a later date: *It later transpired that the minister had lied about the money in parliament.* **2** [I] to happen: *Let's wait and see what transpires.*

trans·plant¹ /træns'plɑːnt ‖ -'plænt/ *v* [T] **1** to move something from one place to another **2** to move an organ or part of the body from one person to another –**transplantation** /ˌtrænsplɑːn'teɪʃən ‖ -plæn-/ *n* [U]

trans·plant² /'trænsplɑːnt ‖ -plænt/ *n* the medical operation in which an organ or part of the body is moved from one person to another: *a heart transplant*

trans·port¹ /'trænspɔːt ‖ -ɔːrt/ *n* (also **transportation** /ˌtrænspɔː'teɪʃən ‖ -pər-/ *AmE*) **1** [U] the moving of goods or people from one place to another: *The transport of goods by air is very costly.* **2** [U] a means or system of carrying passengers or goods from one place to another: *a public transport system | I'd like to go to the concert, but I've no transport.*

■ USAGE **1** For most methods of transport use **by** when you are talking about how someone gets to a place: *She came by car/taxi/bus/tube/plane, etc.* But for walking use **on foot**: *She came on foot.* **2** When talking about events which happen while you are using a particular form of public transport use **on**: *I met Jim on the train/on the bus/on the boat/on the plane/on the tube.*

trans·port² /træn'spɔːt ‖ -ɔːrt/ v [T] to carry goods or people from one place to another –**transportable** adj

trans·pose /træn'spəʊz/ v **transposed, transposing** [T] **1** to change the order or position of two or more things: *By mistake the printers transposed the letters of that word.* **2** to change the key of a piece of music

trans·ves·tite /trænz'vestaɪt ‖ træns-/ n a person, usually a man, who likes to wear the clothes of the opposite sex –**transvestism** /-tɪzəm/ n [U]

trap¹ /træp/ n **1** an apparatus for catching and holding animals: *a mouse trap* **2** a plan for deceiving and tricking a person **3** an unpleasant or dangerous situation from which it is difficult to free yourself **4** a light two-wheeled vehicle pulled by a horse **5** *infml* your mouth: *Shut your trap.*

trap² v **-pp-** [T] **1** to catch in a trap or by a trick: *He trapped foxes and sold their fur.* | *He trapped me into admitting I had done it.* **2 be trapped: a** to be unable to move or escape from somewhere: *We were trapped in the lift for four hours.* **b** to be unable to free yourself from a difficult or unpleasant situation: *She was trapped at home with five children.*

trap·door /'træpdɔːʳ/ n a small door covering an opening in a floor or roof

tra·peze /trə'piːz/ n a short bar hung from two ropes, used by acrobats (ACROBAT) and gymnasts (GYMNAST)

trap·pings /'træpɪŋz/ n [pl] articles of dress or decoration, especially those which show someone's social position: *He possessed all the trappings of high office.*

trash /træʃ/ n [U] **1** something worthless or of low quality **2** the usual American word for RUBBISH(1)

trash·can /'træʃkæn/ n the usual American word for DUSTBIN

trash·y /'træʃi/ adj **trashier, trashiest** worthless: *a trashy novel*

trau·ma /'trɔːmə, 'traʊmə/ n **1** [U] damage to your mind caused by a sudden shock or terrible experience: *an accident resulting in great trauma and suffering* **2** [C] an extremely upsetting experience: *the trauma of her son's death*

trau·mat·ic /trɔː'mætɪk/ adj extremely upsetting –**traumatically** /-kli/ adv

trav·el¹ /'trævəl/ v **-ll-** (also **-l-** *AmE*) **1** [I] to make a journey from one place to another: *He travelled across the States on a Greyhound bus.* –see TRAVEL² (USAGE) **2** [I +adv/prep;T] to move from one place to another: *At what speed does light travel?* | *The news travelled fast.* | *We travelled thousands of miles.* **3 travel light** to travel without much LUGGAGE

travel² n **1** [U] the activity of travelling **2 travels** [pl] journeys made in foreign countries

■ USAGE Compare **travel**, **travels**, **journey**, **voyage**, **trip**. **Travel** is the general activity of moving from place to place: *He came home after years of foreign travel.* We use **travels** when a person goes to different places over a period of time: *Did you go to Rome during your travels round Europe?* We use **journey** when we think of the time spent or the distance covered in going from one particular place to another: *a 60-hour journey by train from Paris to Moscow.* We use **voyage** for a journey by sea: *The voyage from England to Australia used to take several months.* A **trip** is a short journey, or one on which you spend only a short time in another place, then come back: *We'll have time for a trip to France next weekend.*

travel a·gen·cy /'··· ,···/ n travel agencies a business that arranges people's holidays and journeys

travel a·gent /'·· ,·/ n a person who owns or works in a travel agency

trav·el·ler /'trævələʳ/ n (also **traveler** *AmE*) a person who is on a journey

traveller's cheque /'··· ,·/ n a cheque sold by a bank to a person intending to travel abroad, exchangeable at most banks for the money of the particular country

tra·verse /'trævɜːs ‖ trə'vɜːrs/ v **traversed, traversing** [T] *fml* to pass across, over, or through something

trav·es·ty /'trævəsti/ n **travesties** a copy, account, or example of something that gives a completely false idea of it: *His trial was a complete travesty of justice.*

trawl¹ /trɔːl/ v [I;T] to fish with a very large net: *boats out trawling the lake for fish*

trawl² n a large wide fishing net that is drawn along the sea bottom

trawl·er /'trɔːləʳ/ n a fishing vessel that uses a trawl

tray /treɪ/ n a flat piece of wood or metal with raised edges, used for carrying small articles: *The waitress put the plates on a tray and carried them into the dining room.*

treach·e·rous /'tretʃərəs/ adj **1** disloyal **2** full of hidden dangers: *treacherous currents* –**treacherously** adv

treach·e·ry /'tretʃəri/ n [U] disloyalty and deceit

trea·cle /'triːkəl/ n [U] a thick sticky dark liquid made from sugar

tread¹ /tred/ v **trod** /trod ‖ trɑːd/, **trodden** /'trɒdn ‖ 'trɑː-/, **treading** **1** [I] to walk or step on something: *Don't tread on the flowers!* **2** [I] to walk in a special way: *She trod carefully between the flowers.* **3** [T] to press on something firmly with your feet: *They crush the juice out of the fruit by treading it.* **4 tread on someone's toes** to offend someone **5 tread water** to stay upright in deep water with your head above the surface, by moving your legs

tread² n **1** [sing] the sound made when walking: *We recognized John's heavy tread.* **2** [C;U] the raised pattern on a tyre **3** [C] the part of a stair on which you place your foot

trea·son /'triːzən/ n [U] the crime of disloyalty to your country, for example by telling its secrets to an enemy –**treasonable** adj

trea·sure¹ /'treʒəʳ/ n **1** [U] wealth in the form of things like gold, silver, or jewels **2** [C] a very valuable object: *The gallery has many wonderful art treasures.*

treasure² v **treasured, treasuring** [T] to regard something as very valuable

trea·sur·er /'treʒərəʳ/ n a person in charge of the money belonging to an organization

trea·su·ry /'treʒəri/ n **the Treasury** the government department that controls and spends public money: *The treasury is spending less this year.*

treat¹ /triːt/ v [T] **1** to act or behave towards someone in a particular way: *She treats us like children.* **2** to handle something in a particular way: *This glass must be treated with care.* | *He treated the idea as a joke.* **3** to try to cure an illness by medical means: *a new drug to treat this disease* **4** to buy or give someone something special: *I'm going to treat myself to a holiday in Spain.* **5** to put a special substance on something to protect it or give it a special quality: *The wood has been treated to make it water-proof.* –**treatable** *adj*

treat² *n* **1** something special that gives pleasure: *It's a great treat for her to go to London.* **2 It's my treat** = I will pay for everything

trea·tise /ˈtriːtɪs, -tɪz/ *n* a book or article, written in a formal way, that examines a particular subject

treat·ment /ˈtriːtmənt/ *n* **1** [C;U] the methods used to make a sick person better: *He's gone to hospital for special treatment.* **2** [U] behaviour towards someone: *His treatment of his mother is awful.*

treat·y /ˈtriːti/ *n* **treaties** a formal agreement between countries

treb·le¹ /ˈtrebəl/ *n* **1** [C] a person with a high singing voice **2** [U] the upper half of the whole range of musical notes

treble² *adj,adv* **1** made up of three things or three parts **2** producing a high sound or able to sing in a high voice

treble³ *predeterminer* three times as much: *He earns treble my wages.* | *The house is worth treble what we paid for it.*

treble⁴ *v* **trebled, trebling** [I;T] to make or become three times as large as before: *My salary has trebled over the last ten years.*

tree /triː/ *n* a tall plant with a wooden trunk, branches, and leaves: *an apple tree* | *the trees in the wood* –see picture on page 441

trek /trek/ *v* **-kk-** [I +adv/prep] to make a long hard journey –**trek** *n*: *a long trek through the mountains*

trel·lis /ˈtrelɪs/ *n* a light upright wooden frame used as a support for climbing plants

trem·ble /ˈtrembəl/ *v* **trembled, trembling** [I] to shake because you are afraid: *You're trembling but there's nothing to be frightened of.* | *His voice trembled with fear.* –**tremble** *n*

tre·men·dous /trɪˈmendəs/ *adj* **1** very great in size, amount, or degree: *This plane travels at a tremendous speed.* | *a tremendous explosion* **2** wonderful: *We went to a tremendous party last night.*

trem·or /ˈtremər/ *n* a shaking movement: *an earth tremor* | *a tremor of fear*

trench /trentʃ/ *n* a long narrow hole cut in the ground

trend /trend/ *n* **1** a general tendency or change in direction in the way a situation is developing: *the trend of rising unemployment* | *the latest trends in women's clothes* **2 set a trend** to start a new fashion

trend·set·ter /ˈtrendˌsetər/ *n infml* a person who starts a new fashion

trend·y /ˈtrendi/ *adj* **trendier, trendiest** *BrE infml* very fashionable: *a trendy club* –**trendiness** *n* [U]

trep·i·da·tion /ˌtrepɪˈdeɪʃən/ *n* [U] *fml* a state of anxiety: *in fear and trepidation*

tres·pass /ˈtrespəs, -pæs/ *v* [I] to go onto privately owned land without permission –**trespasser** *n*

tres·tle /ˈtresəl/ *n* a wooden beam fixed to a pair of legs, used as a support for a table

tri·al /ˈtraɪəl/ *n* **1** [C;U] the legal process of hearing and judging a person or case in a court: *The murder trial lasted six weeks.* **2 on trial** being tried in court: *She's on trial for robbery.* **3 stand trial** to be tried in a court: *He stood trial for the murder of his wife.* **4** [C] a test to find out how good something is: *The car is now undergoing trials.* | *a trial period* **5 on trial** being tested: *For the first few months in my new job I was very much on trial.* **6** [C] a cause of worry or trouble: *That boy is quite a trial to his*

teachers. **7 trials** [pl] unpleasant things: *the trials and tribulations of bringing up children* **8 trial and error** a way of getting satisfactory results by trying several methods and learning from your mistakes: *learning to cook by trial and error*

tri·an·gle /ˈtraɪæŋgəl/ *n* **1** a flat shape with three straight sides and three angles **2** a small three-sided musical instrument made of steel, played by being struck with a steel rod –**triangular** /traɪˈæŋgjʊlər/ *adj*: *a triangular piece of land*

tribe /traɪb/ *n* a group of people of the same race, beliefs, and language under the leadership of a chief or chiefs: *American Indian tribes* –**tribal** *adj*: *tribal music*

tribes·man /ˈtraɪbzmən/ *n* **tribesmen** /-mən/ a male member of a tribe

trib·u·la·tion /ˌtrɪbjʊˈleɪʃən/ *n* [C;U] *fml* trouble, grief, and suffering: *the trials and tribulations of modern life*

tri·bu·nal /traɪˈbjuːnəl/ *n* a court of people officially appointed to deal with special matters: *The rent tribunal has ordered that my rent be reduced.*

trib·u·ta·ry /ˈtrɪbjʊtəri ‖ -teri/ *n* **tributaries** a stream or river that flows into a larger one: *the tributaries of the Rhine*

trib·ute /ˈtrɪbjuːt/ *n* [C;U] **1** something done, said, or given to show respect or admiration for someone: *We pay tribute to his courage.* **2 a tribute to** something which shows the excellent result or effect of something else: *Their exam results are a tribute to the school.* **3** payment made by one ruler or country to another as the price of peace

trick¹ /trɪk/ *n* **1** an act needing special skill, especially done to confuse or amuse people: *magic tricks* | *No one understood how I did the card tricks.* **2** a clever and useful skill: *John taught me the trick of getting a fire to burn well.* **3** something done to deceive someone or make them look foolish: *He got the money by a trick.* **4** the cards played or won in one part of a game of cards **5 play a trick on someone** to do something to deceive someone **6 do the trick** *infml* to fulfil your purpose: *This medicine ought to do the trick and get rid of your cough.*

trick² *adj* [only before a noun] *infml* **1** made for playing tricks: *trick photography* **2 trick question** a question which seems clear but is full of hidden difficulties

trick³ *v* [T] to deceive or cheat someone: *She tricked me into admitting responsibility.*

trick·e·ry /ˈtrɪkəri/ *n* [U] the use of tricks to deceive or cheat

trick·le /ˈtrɪkəl/ *v* **trickled, trickling** [I +adv/prep] **1** to flow in drops or in a thin stream: *Blood trickled down his face.* **2** to move gradually in small groups: *Refugees are trickling home now that the war is over.* –**trickle** *n*

trick·y /ˈtrɪki/ *adj* **trickier, trickiest** **1** difficult to handle or deal with **2** clever and deceitful: *a tricky politician* –**trickiness** *n* [U]

tri·cy·cle /ˈtraɪsɪkəl/ *n* a cycle with three wheels, two at the back and one at the front, which is often ridden by small children

tried¹ /traɪd/ *adj* found to be good by testing: *a tried and tested method*

tried² the past tense and past participle of TRY¹

tri·fle¹ /ˈtraɪfəl/ *n* **1** [C] a thing of little value or slight importance: *wasting your money on trifles* **2** [C;U] a dish made with fruit, jelly, and cream **3 a trifle** *fml* slightly: *He's a trifle angry.*

trifle² v **trifle with someone** to treat someone without seriousness or respect: *The general is not a man to be trifled with.*

tri·fling /'traɪflɪŋ/ adj of little importance or value

trig·ger¹ /'trɪgəʳ/ n the small piece of metal that you press to fire a gun

trigger² v [T] (also **trigger** sth ↔ **off**) to start a chain of events: *Price increases trigger off demands for wage increases.*

trig·o·nom·e·try /ˌtrɪgə'nɒmɪtri ‖ -'nɑː-/ n [U] the branch of MATHEMATICS that deals with the relationship between the sides and angles of triangles (TRIANGLE)

tri·lat·e·ral /ˌtraɪ'lætərəl/ adj including three groups or countries: *a trilateral agreement* **–trilaterally** adv

trill /trɪl/ n **1** tech the rapid repeating of two musical notes **2** the short, sharp, repeated sounds of a bird **–trill** v [I]

tril·o·gy /'trɪlədʒi/ n **trilogies** a group of three related things like books or plays connected by common subject matter

trim¹ /trɪm/ v **-mm-** [T] **1** to make something neat, even, or tidy by cutting: *My hair needs trimming.* | *a neatly trimmed beard* **2** to decorate the edge of something: *a coat trimmed with fur* **3** to reduce something by taking away unnecessary parts: *The theatre has to trim its costs.*
trim sth ↔ **off** phr v [T] to cut something off because it is not necessary: *She trimmed off the fat before cooking the meat.*

trim² adj **1** tidy and attractive in appearance: *trim gardens* **2** thin and fit: *a trim figure*

trim³ n **1** an act of cutting: *She gave my hair a good trim.* **2 in good trim** in good physical condition: *The team was in good trim for the match.*

tri·mes·ter /trɪ'mestəʳ ‖ traɪ-/ n the usual American word for a TERM at a school or college

trim·mings /'trɪmɪŋz/ n [pl] something added to the main thing, often for decoration: *duck served with all the trimmings*

trin·ket /'trɪŋkɪt/ n a small object or piece of jewellery of low value

tri·o /'triːəʊ/ n **trios 1** [+sing/pl v] a group of three people, especially musicians **2** a piece of music written for three singers or musicians

trip¹ /trɪp/ v **-pp- 1** [I] to catch your foot and lose your balance: *He tripped over a stone and fell to the ground.* **2** [T] to make someone lose their balance by making them fall over something, for example your foot: *He stopped the thief by tripping him.* **3** [I+adv/prep] to move or dance with quick light steps: *The little girl tripped lightly down the path.*
trip up phr v [I;T **trip** sbdy ↔ **up**] **1** to fall or to make someone fall **2** to make a mistake or make someone make a mistake: *He tripped up over the details of the contract.* | *He tripped me up by asking confusing questions.*

trip² n a journey from one place to another: *He went on a trip to Europe.* | *a business trip* | *a day trip to the country* –see TRAVEL² (USAGE)

tri·par·tite /traɪ'pɑːtaɪt ‖ -'pɑːr-/ adj having three parts or including three groups of people

tripe /traɪp/ n [U] **1** the wall of the stomach of the cow, pig or ox, eaten as food **2** infml worthless or stupid talk or writing: *Why do you read such tripe?*

trip·le¹ /'trɪpəl/ v **tripled, tripling** [I;T] to grow to or be made to grow three times greater in size or amount

triple² adj **1** having three parts **2** repeated three times: *a triple dose of medicine*

trip·let /'trɪplɪt/ n any of three children born to the same mother at the same time

trip·li·cate /'trɪplɪkɪt/ adj consisting of three parts that are exactly alike: *triplicate copies of the contract* **–triplicate** n : *The contract has been written in triplicate.*

tri·pod /'traɪpɒd ‖ -pɑːd/ n a frame with three legs, used for standing a camera on

trip·per /'trɪpəʳ/ n old fash a person on a pleasure trip

trite /traɪt/ adj used too often to be effective or interesting (used of an idea or remark)

tri·umph¹ /'traɪəmf, -ʌmf/ n **1** [C] a complete victory or success: *a triumph over the enemy* | *his examination triumph* **2** [U] a feeling of joy and satisfaction caused by success: *shouts of triumph* **–triumphant** /traɪ'ʌmfənt/ adj : *a triumphant army* **–triumphantly** adv

triumph² v [I] to gain victory or success, especially in dealing with a difficult situation or opponent: *She triumphed over a disabling illness.*

tri·um·phal /traɪ'ʌmfəl/ adj related to or marking a triumph: *a triumphal arch*

triv·i·a /'trɪviə/ n [pl] unimportant or useless things

triv·i·al /'trɪviəl/ adj of little importance: *Why do you get angry over such trivial matters?* **2** ordinary: *trivial everyday duties* **–triviality** /ˌtrɪvi'ælɪti/ n **trivialities** [C;U]

trod /trɒd ‖ trɑːd/ the past tense of TREAD

trod·den /'trɒdn ‖ 'trɑːdn/ the past participle of TREAD

trol·ley /'trɒli ‖ 'trɑːli/ n **1** a small low cart which you push by hand and use to carry heavy things **2** BrE a small table on wheels from which food and drinks are served

trol·ley·bus /'trɒlibʌs ‖ 'trɑː-/ n a bus that draws power from electric wires running above it

trom·bone /trɒm'bəʊn ‖ trɑːm-/ n a large brass musical instrument with a long sliding tube played by blowing **–trombonist** n

troop¹ /truːp/ n **1** a band of people or animals: *a troop of monkeys* **2** a group of soldiers on horses or in armoured vehicles **3 troops** [pl] soldiers: *The general inspected the troops.*

troop² v [I+adv/prep] to move together in a group: *Everyone trooped into the meeting.*

troop·er /'truːpəʳ/ n a soldier of the lowest rank, especially in the CAVALRY

tro·phy /'trəʊfi/ n **trophies 1** a prize given for winning a race or competition **2** something taken after much effort, especially in war or hunting: *Hunting trophies hung on the wall.*

trop·ic /'trɒpɪk ‖ 'trɑː-/ n **1** one of the two imaginary lines drawn around the world; the line drawn at about 23½° north of the EQUATOR is called the **tropic of Cancer** and the line 23½° south the **tropic of Capricorn 2 the tropics** the very hot area found between the tropic of Cancer and the tropic of Capricorn

trop·i·cal /'trɒpɪkəl ‖ 'trɑː-/ adj **1** relating to the tropics: *tropical flowers* | *the tropical sun* **2** very hot and wet: *tropical weather* **–tropically** /-kli/ adv

trot¹ /trɒt ‖ trɑːt/ n [sing] **1** a fairly quick movement made by a horse between a walk and a GALLOP **2** a fairly fast human speed between a walk and a run **3 on the trot** infml one after another: *She won three* *matches on the trot.* **4 be on the trot** to be very busy: *I've been on the trot since yesterday.*

trot² /v-tt-/ **1** [I+adv/prep] (of an animal, especially a horse) to move fairly fast: *The little girl trotted along behind her father.* **2** [I] (of an animal, especially a horse) to move with a movement between a walk and a GALLOP

trot·ter /ˈtrɒtəʳ ‖ ˈtrɑː-/ *n* a pig's foot eaten as food

trou·ble¹ /ˈtrʌbəl/ *v* **troubled, troubling** **1** [T] to make you feel worried or anxious: *What's troubling you?* **2** [T] to cause inconvenience to someone: *I'm sorry to trouble you, but could you possibly help me?* | *May I trouble you for the salt?* **3 not trouble to do something** to not make the effort to do something because it is inconvenient: *Don't trouble to write when you're away.* **–troubling** *adj* : *a troubling report*

trouble² *n* **1** [U] a medical condition or illness: *Her mother suffers from heart trouble.* **2 troubles** [pl] problems: *He told me all his troubles.* | *Put all your troubles behind you and make a new start.* **3 the trouble** something which causes a problem: *The trouble with you is that you believe everything people tell you.* | *What's the trouble?* **4** [U] difficulty: *I don't anticipate any trouble getting them to agree.* | *I had quite a lot of trouble finding your house.* **5** [U] fighting or disagreement: *They sent in troops to deal with the trouble at the border.* **6** [U] effort or inconvenience: *The boss took the trouble to explain the situation to me.* | *Of course I'll help – it's no trouble at all.* **7 in trouble** in difficulty, often because you have done something wrong: *Her son kept getting into trouble with the police.* **8 ask for trouble, look for trouble** to behave in a way that causes a difficulty or danger: *Driving like that he's just asking for trouble.*

■ USAGE In the phrases **to have trouble with something** and **to have trouble doing something** the word trouble is *always uncountable* (NEVER plural): *I'm having* **trouble** *with my essay.* | *I had real* **trouble** *explaining things to my friends.*

troubled /ˈtrʌbəld/ *adj* suffering from problems: *His face had a troubled look.* | *She's been troubled by a bad back for years.* | *a troubled region*

trou·ble·mak·er /ˈtrʌbəlˌmeɪkəʳ/ *n* a person who keeps on causing trouble

trou·ble·shoot·er /ˈtrʌbəlˌʃuːtəʳ/ *n* a person employed to remove causes of trouble, usually in an organization

trou·ble·some /ˈtrʌbəlsəm/ *adj* causing trouble or anxiety: *a troublesome tooth*

trough /trɒf ‖ trɔːf/ *n* **1** a long narrow container used to hold water or food for animals **2** a long narrow hollow area, for example between two waves **3** *tech* an area of lower pressure between two areas of high pressure

troupe /truːp/ *n* a group of singers, actors or dancers

troup·er /ˈtruːpəʳ/ *n* a member of a troupe

trou·sers /ˈtraʊzəz ‖ -ərz/ *n* [pl] an outer garment covering your body from the waist down, with one part for each leg: *a pair of blue trousers* –see PAIR (USAGE) –see picture on page 50 **–trouser** *adj* [only before a noun] : *a trouser leg*

trous·seau /ˈtruːsəʊ, truːˈsəʊ/ *n* **trousseaux** *or* **trousseaus** /-səʊz/ *old fash* the personal possessions, especially clothes, that a woman brings with her when she marries

trout /traʊt/ *n* [plural is **trout**] [C;U] a river fish with darkish spots on its brown skin, used for food

trow·el /ˈtraʊəl/ *n* **1** a tool with a flat blade for spreading cement or PLASTER **2** a small garden tool

with a curved blade for digging small holes –see picture on page 638

tru·ant /ˈtruːənt/ *n* **1** a pupil who stays away from school without permission **2 play truant** to stay away from school without permission: *If you saw John in town this morning he must have been playing truant.* **–truancy** *n* [U] : *We have a high level of truancy at this school.*

truce /truːs/ *n* an agreement between two enemies to stop fighting for a short time

truck /trʌk/ *n* **1** a large motor vehicle used for carrying goods in large quantities: *Heavy trucks aren't allowed to cross this bridge.* **2** *BrE* an open railway vehicle for carrying goods: *coal trucks*

truc·u·lent /ˈtrʌkjələnt/ *adj* bad-tempered and always willing to quarrel **–truculence** *n* [U]

trudge /trʌdʒ/ *v* **trudged, trudging** [I + adv/prep] to walk with heavy steps, slowly and with effort: *The soldiers trudged wearily through the mud.* **–trudge** *n*

true /truː/ *adj* **truer, truest** **1** in accordance with fact or reality: *a true story* | *Is the news true?* | *Is it true you're going away?* **2** real and sincere: *true love* | *I have a true interest in your future.* **3** faithful and loyal: *a true friend* | *He remained true to his principles.* **4** exact: *a true copy* **5** a good example of a particular thing: *a true Frenchman* | *true competition* **6** correctly fitted or placed: *If the door's not exactly true it won't close properly.* **7 come true** to happen just as you wished or expected **8 true to form/type** behaving or acting just as you would expect **9 true to your word** doing what you promised to do

true-life /ˌ· ˈ· ◂/ *adj* [only before a noun] based on fact: *a true-life adventure story*

truf·fle /ˈtrʌfəl/ *n* **1** a FUNGUS that grows underground and is considered good to eat **2** a type of soft sweet

tru·is·m /ˈtruːɪzəm/ *n* a statement that is so clearly true that there is no need to say it

tru·ly /ˈtruːli/ *adv* **1** exactly: *He cannot truly be described as stupid, but he is lazy.* **2** really: *I am truly grateful to you.* | *a truly beautiful view* **3 yours truly** a phrase used at the end of a formal letter before the signature **4** a word used to show strongly that you are telling the truth: *No, truly, I didn't break the window.*

trump¹ /trʌmp/ *n* **1** any card of a suit chosen to be of the highest value in a particular card game **2 come/turn up trumps** to behave in a generous or helpful way, especially unexpectedly **3 your trump card** the best or most effective thing you can do to gain advantage over someone

trump² *v* [T] to beat a card by playing a trump

trump sthg ↔ **up** *phr v* [T] to invent a reason or story falsely: *The President wanted to get rid of him, so he was sent to prison on a trumped-up charge.*

trum·pet¹ /ˈtrʌmpʌt/ *n* **1** a brass wind instrument, played by pressing three buttons in various combinations **2** a loud cry made by an elephant

trumpet² *v* [I] **1** to play a trumpet **2** (of elephants) to make a loud sound **–trumpeter** *n*

trun·cate /trʌŋˈkeɪt ‖ ˈtrʌŋkeɪt/ *v* **truncated, truncating** [T] *fml* to shorten something by cutting a part or end off it: *a truncated report*

trun·cheon /ˈtrʌntʃən/ *n* a short thick stick carried as a weapon by British policemen

trun·dle /ˈtrʌndl/ *v* **trundled trundling** [I + adv/ prep; T + adv/prep] to move or be made to move slowly and heavily on wheels: *An old lady was trundling a cart along the street.*

trunk /trʌŋk/ n 1 the thick main stem of a tree 2 the human body apart from the head and limbs 3 a large box in which clothes or belongings are stored or packed for travel 4 the very long nose of an elephant 5 the usual American word for the BOOT of a car 6 **trunks** a garment worn by men for swimming

trunk call /ˈ· ·/ n a telephone call made over a long distance

trunk road /ˈ· ·/ n a main road

trust¹ /trʌst/ n 1 [U] firm belief in the honesty or worth of someone or something: *I don't place any trust in his promise.* | *It took the teacher a long time to gain the children's trust.* 2 [U] responsibility for something important or valuable: *a position of trust* 3 [U] care: *After their parents' death the children were put in my trust.* 4 [C;U] an arrangement for the holding and controlling of money and property for someone else: *money held in trust for a child* | *She set up a trust for the benefit of her grandchildren.* 5 **take something on trust** to accept something as true without proof

trust² v 1 [T] to have faith in someone or something and believe in their honesty: *Don't trust him, he's dishonest.* | *Trust my judgment!* 2 [T] to believe someone or something will act properly and successfully: *That actor can always be trusted to give an excellent performance.* | *Can I trust you to look after my best interests?*
□ USEFUL PATTERNS to trust someone to do something
3 [T] to give or tell someone something important: *I trusted Tom with my secret.* 4 [+(that)] to believe that something is right or true: *She trusted her information was correct.* 5 **trust in** to have faith in someone or something 6 **Trust you!** a phrase used when someone behaves in a way that is typical of them: *Trust him to ask a question just at the wrong moment.*

trust·ee /trʌsˈtiː/ n a person or firm that legally holds and controls property for someone else

trust·ful /ˈtrʌstfəl/ adj (also **trusting**) ready to believe in the sincerity of others: *the trustful nature of a small child* –**trustfully** adv

trust·wor·thy /ˈtrʌst,wɜːði ‖ -ɜːr-/ adj dependable and responsible –**trustworthiness** n [U]

trust·y /ˈtrʌsti/ adj **trustier, trustiest** old fash faithful: *My trusty old car will get us home safely.*

truth /truːθ/ n **truths** /truːðz/ 1 [U] that which is in accordance with fact and reality: *You must always tell the truth.* 2 [U] the quality of being true: *I don't doubt the truth* **of** *his information.* 3 [C] a fact or principle accepted as true: *the truths of science* 4 **in truth** fml really 5 **to tell you the truth** a phrase to make it clear you are being honest: *To tell you the truth, I don't like him at all.*

truth·ful /ˈtruːθfəl/ adj 1 true to the facts: *a truthful account of what happened* 2 honest: *a truthful boy* –**truthfully** adv –**truthfulness** n [U]

try¹ /traɪ/ v **tried, trying** 1 [I;T] to attempt to do something: *I don't think I can do it but I'll try.* | *Please try to come.* | *Don't try and do too much at once.*
□ USEFUL PATTERNS to try something; to try to do something
2 [T] to do something or use something so that you can find out if it is effective or enjoyable: *Have you tried this new soap?* | *It seems a good idea; I'll try it.* | *I tried waterskiing on holiday but didn't like it.*

□ USEFUL PATTERNS to try something; to try doing something
3 [T] to examine a person in a court of law to decide if they are guilty: *They're going to try him for murder.* 4 [T] to go to a person or place to find out if they can give you what you want: *I tried four shops before I got the shoes I wanted.* 5 [T] to attempt to open a door or windows: *I think the door's locked but I'll try it just in case.*
■ USAGE 1 You can make **try** stronger by using *hard*: *He isn't very good at English, but he* **tries hard.** 2 Compare **try to do** *something* and **try doing** *something.* If you **try to do** *something* you make an effort to do it, but without success: *I tried to finish the work, but I didn't have enough time.* If you **try doing** *something* you do it in order to see what will happen: *If the machine doesn't work,* **try giving** *it a kick.*

try sthg ↔ **on** *phr* v [T] to put on an article of clothing to see if it fits

try² n **tries** 1 an attempt: *Let me have a try.* | *It was a good try but it didn't succeed.* 2 points that you win in a game of RUGBY by putting the ball down behind the opposing team's GOAL

tsar /zɑːʳ, tsɑːʳ/ n (also **czar, tzar**) the ruler of Russia before 1917

tset·se fly /ˈtetsi flaɪ, ˈtsetsi-, ˈsetsi-/ n (also **tsetse**) a blood-sucking African fly that causes disease

T-shirt /ˈtiː ʃɜːt ‖ -ʃɜːrt/ n (also **tee shirt**) a close-fitting piece of clothing with a round neck and short sleeves (SLEEVE) which you wear on the upper part of your body –see picture on page 50

tsp [plural is **tsps**] a written abbreviation for TEASPOON: *one tsp of salt*

tub /tʌb/ n 1 a round or OBLONG container, for packing, storing, or washing things –see picture on page 148 2 AmE a bath

tu·ba /ˈtjuːbə ‖ ˈtuːbə/ n a large brass wind instrument that produces low notes

tub·by /ˈtʌbi/ adj **tubbier, tubbiest** infml short and fat

tube /tjuːb ‖ tuːb/ n 1 a hollow round pipe of metal, glass, or rubber often used for holding liquids 2 a long thin metal container, fitted with a cap, for holding things like TOOTHPASTE or paint –see picture on page 148 3 a hollow pipe or organ in your body: *the bronchial tubes* 4 **the tube** BrE the underground railway in London: *He hates going on the tube.* 5 **by tube** travelling on the tube: *I usually go by tube.*

tu·ber /ˈtjuːbəʳ ‖ ˈtuː-/ n a fleshy swollen underground stem, such as the potato

tu·ber·cu·lo·sis /tjuːˌbɜːkjʊˈləʊsɪs ‖ tuːˌbɜːr-/ n [U] (also **TB**) a serious infectious disease that attacks the lungs –**tubercular** /tjuːˈbɜːkjʊləʳ ‖ tuːˈbɜːr-/ adj

tub·ing /ˈtjuːbɪŋ ‖ ˈtuː-/ n [U] metal or plastic in the form of a tube

tu·bu·lar /ˈtjuːbjʊləʳ ‖ ˈtuː-/ adj like a tube or made from a tube: *tubular metal furniture*

T.U.C. /ˌtiː juː ˈsiː/ an organization of TRADES UNIONS in Britain; an abbreviation for **Trades Union Congress**

tuck¹ /tʌk/ v [T + adv/prep] 1 to put something into a desired or convenient position: *a book tucked under his arm* 2 to put the end of a piece of clothing under another so that it looks tidy: *Tuck your shirt into your trousers.*

tuck sthg ↔ **away** *phr* v [T] to put something in a safe or hidden place: *She's got a lot of money tucked away.*

tuck in *phr v* **1** [I] *infml* to eat eagerly **2** [T **tuck sbdy ↔ in**] to make someone comfortable in bed by pulling the covers tight

tuck² *n* **1** [C] a flat fold of material sewn into a garment for decoration or to give it a particular shape **2** [U] *BrE old fash* food, especially cakes and sweets as eaten by school children: *a tuck shop*

Tues. an abbreviation for Tuesday

Tues·day /ˈtjuːzdi ‖ ˈtuːz-/ *n* the day between Monday and Wednesday

tuft /tʌft/ *n* a bunch of hair, feathers, or grass –**tufted** *adj*

tug¹ /tʌg/ *v* [I;T] to pull something with force or much effort: *We tugged, and the rope broke.* | *The little child tugged his mother's arm.*

tug² *n* **1** a sudden strong pull **2** see TUGBOAT

tug·boat /ˈtʌgbəʊt/ *n* (also **tug**) a small powerful boat used for guiding large vessels into or out of harbours

tug-of-war /ˌ·· ˈ·/ *n* a test of strength in which two teams pull against each other on a rope

tu·i·tion /tjuːˈɪʃən ‖ tuː-/ *n* [U] teaching, especially of people in small groups: *tuition fees* | *He needs extra tuition in physics.*

tu·lip /ˈtjuːlɪp ‖ ˈtuː-/ *n* a garden plant that grows from a BULB and has large colourful cup-shaped flowers

tum·ble /ˈtʌmbəl/ *v* **tumbled, tumbling** **1** [I] to fall or roll over suddenly, helplessly, or in a disordered way: *The child tripped and tumbled down the stairs.* | *The water tumbled over the rock.* **2 tumble to something** *infml* to understand something suddenly: *It was a long time before I tumbled to what I meant.*

tumble² *n* a fall

tumble dry·er /ˈ·· ˌ··/ *n* (also **tumble drier**) an electric machine which is used to dry washing

tum·bler /ˈtʌmbləʳ/ *n* a drinking glass with no handle or stem

tum·my /ˈtʌmi/ *n* **tummies** *infml* your stomach: *a tummy ache*

tu·mour /ˈtjuːməʳ ‖ ˈtuː-/ *n* (**tumor** *AmE*) a mass of diseased cells in your body

tu·mult /ˈtjuːmʌlt ‖ ˈtuː-/ *n* [C;U] *fml* confused noise and excitement –**tumultuous** /tjuːˈmʌltjuəs ‖ tuː-/ *adj*: *a tumultuous welcome* –**tumultuously** *adv*

tu·na /ˈtjuːnə ‖ ˈtuːnə/ *n* [C;U] a large sea fish, used for food: *a tin of tuna fish*

tun·dra /ˈtʌndrə/ *n* **the tundra** a cold treeless plain in the far north of Europe, Asia, and North America

tune¹ /tjuːn ‖ tuːn/ *n* **1** an arrangement of musical notes that form a pleasing sound: *Do you know the tune to this song?* | *a catchy tune* **2 change your tune** to change your opinion or behaviour **3 in tune: a** producing the correct musical notes: *The piano is now in tune.* | *She can't sing in tune.* **b** in agreement or sympathy: *His ideas were in tune with mine.* [RELATED PHRASE **out of tune**] **4 to the tune of** by an amount of: *We were overcharged to the tune of fifty pounds.*

tune² *v* **tuned, tuning** [T] **1** to set a musical instrument so that it produces the proper notes **2** to put an engine in good working order

tune in *phr v* [I] to set a radio to receive broadcasts from a particular radio station: *We always tune in to the BBC at nine o'clock.*

tune·ful /ˈtjuːnfəl ‖ ˈtuːn-/ *adj* having a pleasing tune –**tunefully** *adv*

tune·less /ˈtjuːnləs ‖ ˈtuːn-/ *adj* unmusical and unpleasant to listen to –**tunelessly** *adv*

tun·er /ˈtjuːnəʳ ‖ ˈtuː-/ *n* **1** the part of a radio or television that changes the signals into sound and pictures **2** a person who tunes musical instruments: *a piano tuner*

tu·nic /ˈtjuːnɪk ‖ ˈtuː-/ *n* **1** a loose outer piece of clothing without arms which reaches to your knees **2** a short coat worn by policemen or soldiers as part of a uniform

tuning fork /ˈ·· ·/ *n* a small steel instrument that produces a fixed musical note when struck, used in tuning musical instruments

tun·nel¹ /ˈtʌnl/ *n* an underground or underwater passage

tunnel² *v* **-ll-** (also **-l-** *AmE*) [I] to make a tunnel under or through a hill or river

tur·ban /ˈtɜːbən ‖ ˈtɜːr-/ *n* **1** a head-covering consisting of a long length of cloth wound round your head –see picture on page 50 **2** a woman's small tight-fitting hat

tur·bine /ˈtɜːbaɪn ‖ ˈtɜːrbɪn, -baɪn/ *n* an engine or motor driven by the pressure of liquid or gas

tur·bo·charg·er /ˈtɜːbəʊˌtʃɑːdʒəʳ ‖ ˈtɜːrˌbəʊˌtʃɑːr-/ *n* a FAN in a car which makes it work better and is driven by waste gas from the engine –**turbocharge** *v* **turbocharged, turbocharging** [T] : *My car has a small engine, but it's been turbocharged so it's very powerful.*

tur·bot /ˈtɜːbɒt, -bət ‖ ˈtɜːrbət/ *n* [plural is **turbot**] [C;U] a large fish with a flat body, used for food

tur·bu·lence /ˈtɜːbjʊləns ‖ ˈtɜːr-/ *n* [U] **1** the state of being violent and uncontrolled **2** irregular and violent movement of air or water: *The flight was very uncomfortable because of turbulence.*

tur·bu·lent /ˈtɜːbjʊlənt ‖ ˈtɜːr-/ *adj* violent and stormy: *turbulent weather* | *a turbulent period of history*

tu·reen /tjʊˈriːn ‖ təˈriːn/ *n* a large deep dish with a lid, from which soup is served

turf¹ /tɜːf ‖ tɜːrf/ *n* **turfs** or **turves** /tɜːvz ‖ tɜːrvz/ **1** [U] a surface made of soil with thick grass growing on it: *the smooth turf of a bowling green* **2** [C] a small piece of thick grass with soil: *She bought some turfs for her lawn.* **3 the turf** the sport or world of horseracing

turf² *v* [T] to cover a piece of land with turf **turf sbdy ↔ out** *phr v* [T] *infml* to throw someone out: *He's been turfed out of his house because he hasn't paid the rent.*

turf ac·coun·tant /ˈ· ·ˌ··/ *n* a BOOKMAKER

tur·gid /ˈtɜːdʒɪd ‖ ˈtɜːr-/ *adj* too solemn, uninteresting, and difficult to understand (used of a piece of writing)

tur·key /ˈtɜːki ‖ ˈtɜːrki/ *n* [C;U] a large bird bred for its meat which is used as food, particularly on special occasions

Turk·ish /ˈtɜːkɪʃ ‖ ˈtɜːr-/ *adj* from or connected with Turkey

Turkish¹ **the Turkish** the people of Turkey **2** [U] the language of Turkey

tur·moil /ˈtɜːmɔɪl ‖ ˈtɜːr-/ *n* [sing;U] a state of confusion, excitement, and anxiety: *The whole town was in turmoil.* | *I was thrown into a complete turmoil by the news.*

turn¹ /tɜːn ‖ tɜːrn/ *v* **1** [I] to move round: *The wheel turned slowly.* **2** [T] to make something move round: *She turned the key in the lock.* | *He turned the*

picture round to face the wall. | She turned the bottle upside down. **3** [I] to move your body or your head so that you can see in another direction: He turned and waved. | She turned round to look at him. **4** [I + adv/prep] to change the direction in which you are moving: She turned down a side street. | The car turned into the car park. **5** [T] to make a car or other vehicle change the direction in which it is moving: She turned the car into a narrow lane. **6 turn a corner** to move round a corner: The car turned the corner and disappeared. **7** [I] to become something different: The water had turned into ice. | Their amusement turned to horror when they realized what had really happened. | The grass had all turned brown in the dry weather. –see BECOME (USAGE) **8** [T] to make something into something different: They plan to turn the building into a hotel. | The heat had turned the milk sour. **9** [T] to reach a certain age or time: He's just turned 40. | It's just turned three o'clock. **10 turn a blind eye** to pretend not to notice something bad **11 turn tail** to run away **12 turn the tables** to change from being in a weak position to being in a strong position **13 turn your attention/thoughts to something** to start thinking about something: Now let's turn our attention to the problems of the Third World. [RELATED PHRASE **your attention/thoughts turn to something**] **14 turn your hand to something** to begin to do something that needs skill **15 turn your stomach** to make you feel sick

turn against phr v [I;T **turn** sbdy **against** sbdy/sthg] to start disliking someone or something, or cause someone else to start disliking someone or something: She seems to have turned against me.

turn away phr v **1** [I] to look in another direction so that you do not have to look at something: I tried to talk to her but she turned away. **2** [T **turn** sbdy ↔ **away**] to refuse to allow someone to enter a place

turn back phr v **1** [I] to return in the same direction that you have come from: We had to turn back because of the snow. **2** [T **turn** sbdy ↔ **back**] to make someone return in the same direction that they have come from

turn down phr v **1** [T **turn** sthg ↔ **down**] to reduce the heat produced by a heater or the sound produced by a radio or record player **2** [T **turn** sbdy ↔ **down**] to refuse a request that someone has made to you: I applied for the job but they turned me down. –see REFUSE (USAGE)

turn in phr v **1** [I] infml to go to bed **2** [T **turn** sbdy ↔ **in**] to give someone to the police

turn off phr v **1** [T **turn** sthg ↔ **off**] to cause something to stop operating by turning a button or SWITCH: Shall I turn the television off? **2** [I;T **turn off** sthg] to leave a road: We turned off the main road onto a country lane.

turn on phr v **1** [T **turn** sthg ↔ **on**] to cause something to start operating by turning a button or SWITCH: He turned on the light. **2** [T **turn on** sbdy] to attack someone suddenly **3** [T **turn** sbdy **on**] to make someone feel sexually interested **4** [T **turn** sthg **on** sbdy] to direct a weapon towards someone: He shot his wife then turned the gun on himself.

turn out phr v **1** [T **turn** sthg ↔ **out**] to cause a light to stop shining: She turned out the light. **2** [I] to gather for a public event: Crowds of people turned out to welcome the troops home. **3** [T **turn** sthg ↔ **out**] to produce something: The factory turns out 3000 cars a day. **4 turn out to be** to be shown to be in the end: His story turned out to be true. **5** [T **turn** sbdy **out**] to force someone to leave a place

turn over phr v **1** [T **turn** sthg ↔ **over**] to think about something: I've been turning the idea over in my mind. **2** [T **turn** sthg ↔ **over**] to give something to someone who has a right to have it **3** [T **turn** sbdy **over**] to give someone to the police

turn to phr v **1** [T **turn to** sbdy] to go to someone for help: I don't know who I can turn to. **2** [T **turn to** sthg] to start doing something: Some young people turn to crime. **3** [T **turn to** sthg] to go to a particular page in a book: Turn to page 27.

turn up phr v **1** [I] to be found or discovered: The missing bag turned up under an old railway bridge. **2** [T **turn** sthg ↔ **up**] to find something: Police have turned up some interesting new evidence. **3** [I] to arrive somewhere: They turned up late as usual. **4** [T **turn** sthg ↔ **up**] to increase the heat produced by a heater or the sound produced by a radio or record player **5** [T **turn** sthg ↔ **up**] to shorten a piece of clothing

turn² n **1** an act of turning: He gave the handle a couple of turns. **2** a change of direction: Take the next turn on the right. **3** a change or development: We were all surprised by this latest turn of events. | There seems to have been a turn for the worse. **4** the chance or right to do something that other people have done or are going to do: It's my turn to drive next. | Can I have a turn on your bicycle? **5** infml an attack of an illness: He's had one of his turns. **6** a short performance in a show **7 the turn of the century** the period at the end of one century and the beginning of the next **8 a good turn** a useful or helpful action **9 done to a turn** perfectly cooked **10 in turn** one after the other: Each of the candidates was interviewed in turn. **11 take turns, take it in turns** to do something one after the other: We took it in turns to carry the suitcase. | We took turns at driving the car.

turn·coat /ˈtɜːnkəʊt ‖ ˈtɜːrn-/ n someone who changes their political party, principles, or loyalty (a word used to express disapproval)

turn·ing /ˈtɜːnɪŋ ‖ ˈtɜːr-/ n a place where one road branches off from another: You'll find a telephone down the first turning on the left.

turning point /ˈ··· ·/ n a point in time when an important change takes place: a turning point in the country's industrial development

tur·nip /ˈtɜːnɪp ‖ ˈtɜːr-/ n [C;U] a round vegetable which grows underground and is used as food –see picture on page 344

turn·out /ˈtɜːnaʊt ‖ ˈtɜːrn-/ n the number of people who attend a meeting or other event: They usually get a turnout of a hundred or more at their meetings.

turn·o·ver /ˈtɜːnˌəʊvəʳ ‖ ˈtɜːrn-/ n [U] the amount of business done, workers hired, or articles sold in a particular period: a turnover of £5,000 a week

turn·stile /ˈtɜːnstaɪl ‖ ˈtɜːrn-/ n a small gate with four metal arms, spinning round on a central post, which allows people to pass one at a time

turn·ta·ble /ˈtɜːnˌteɪbəl ‖ ˈtɜːrn-/ n the flat, round, spinning surface on a record player where a record is played

turn-up /ˈ· ·/ n a narrow band of cloth turned upwards at the bottom of a trouser leg

tur·pen·tine /ˈtɜːpəntaɪn ‖ ˈtɜːr-/ n [U] (also **turps** /tɜːps ‖ tɜːrps/ infml) a thin liquid, used for making paint thin or removing it

tur·quoise¹ /ˈtɜːkwɔɪz, -kwɑːz ‖ ˈtɜːrkwɔɪz/ n [U] a bluish-green, precious stone

turquoise² adj a colour that is bluish-green –see picture on page 147

tur·ret /ˈtʌrɪt/ n a small tower, usually at a corner of a larger building

tur·tle /ˈtɜːtl ‖ ˈtɜːrtl/ n an animal that lives in water, with a soft body covered by a hard horny shell

tusk /tʌsk/ n a very long pointed tooth on certain animals such as the elephant

tus·sle /ˈtʌsəl/ v tussled, tussling [T] to fight roughly without weapons –tussle n

tut interj a sound made by sucking in air and moving your tongue behind your teeth, used to express slight disapproval or annoyance

tu·tor /ˈtjuːtəʳ ‖ ˈtuː-/ n 1 a teacher who gives private instruction to a single pupil or a very small class 2 in British universities, a teacher who directs the studies of a number of students and teaches small groups of students –tutor v [I;T] : Mr Smith is tutoring Tom in Latin.

tu·to·ri·al¹ /tjuːˈtɔːriəl ‖ tuː-/ adj related to a tutor or his or her duties

tutorial² n a lesson given by a tutor

tux·e·do /tʌkˈsiːdəʊ/ n the usual American word for DINNER JACKET

TV /ˌtiː ˈviː ◂/ n see TELEVISION

twad·dle /ˈtwɒdl ‖ ˈtwɑːdl/ n [U] infml nonsense

twang /twæŋ/ v [T] to pull the strings on a musical instrument such as a GUITAR so that they make a quick ringing sound

tweak /twiːk/ v [T] to pull and twist something, especially someone's ear or nose, with a sudden movement –tweak n

tweed /twiːd/ n [U] coarse woollen cloth: a tweed suit

tweet /twiːt/ v [I] to make the short high noise of a small bird –tweet n

twee·zers /ˈtwiːzəz ‖ -ərz/ n [pl] a small metal tool with two parts joined together at the end, used for picking up small objects or pulling out hairs

twelve /twelv/ det,n,pron the number 12 –twelfth /twelfθ, twelθ/ det,n,pron,adv

twen·ty /ˈtwenti/ det,n,pron 1 the number 20 2 the Twenties, the twenties the years from 1920 to 1929 3 in her twenties, in their twenties, etc. aged between 20 and 29 –twentieth det,n,pron,adv

twenty-one /ˌ· ˈ· ◂/ det,n,pron the number 21

twice /twais/ predeterminer, adv two times: I've read the book twice. | He eats twice the amount that I eat. | He works twice as hard as anyone else.

twid·dle /ˈtwɪdl/ v twiddled, twiddling 1 [I;T] to move your fingers to twist or turn something, often in a purposeless way: He irritated me by constantly twiddling with his pencil. 2 twiddle your thumbs to waste your time doing nothing useful

twig /twɪg/ n a small thin woody stem growing from a branch

twi·light /ˈtwaɪlaɪt/ n [U] the time when day is about to become night

twin /twɪn/ n 1 either of two children born to the same mother at the same time: Jean and John are twins. | my twin sister 2 either of two things which are closely connected or very like each other: twin towns | twin beds

twine¹ /twaɪn/ n [U] strong cord or string made by twisting threads together

twine² v twined, twining [I+adv/prep;T+adv/prep] to twist: The stems twined round the tree trunk. | She twined the ribbon in her hair.

twinge /twɪndʒ/ n 1 a sudden sharp pain: a twinge of toothache 2 a sudden unpleasant feeling: a twinge of regret

twin·kle /ˈtwɪŋkəl/ v twinkled, twinkling [I] 1 to shine with an unsteady light: stars twinkling in the sky 2 (of your eyes) to show pleasure, excitement, and amusement: Her eyes twinkled. –twinkle n [sing] : a twinkle of delight in his eyes

twin·kling /ˈtwɪŋklɪŋ/ n in a twinkling, in the twinkling of an eye infml in a moment

twirl /twɜːl ‖ twɜːrl/ v [I;T] to turn round and round quickly –twirl n

twist¹ /twɪst/ v 1 [T] to wind something in a particular direction: They made a rope by twisting threads. | She twisted her hair round her fingers to make it curl. 2 [T] to turn: Twist the handle and the box will open. | For this exercise, you need to twist your head more. 3 [T] to change the shape of something by bending it: The child twisted the wire into the shape of a star. 4 [T] to damage a part of your body by moving it suddenly or awkwardly: She's twisted her ankle. 5 [I] to bend: The river twisted through the valley.

twist² n 1 [C] an act of turning something in a particular direction: Give the lid a twist. 2 [C;U] something, such as thread or rope made by twisting two or more lengths together 3 [C] a bend: a road with a lot of twists in it 4 [C] an unexpected change or development: a strange twist of fate –twisty adj : a twisty road

twist·er /ˈtwɪstəʳ/ n a dishonest person who cheats other people

twit /twɪt/ n infml a stupid fool

twitch¹ /twɪtʃ/ v [I;T] to move or make something move suddenly and quickly: Her lips twitched nervously | The horse twitched its ears.

twitch² n 1 a repeated sudden movement of a muscle which you cannot control 2 a sudden quick pull

twit·ter /ˈtwɪtəʳ/ v [I] 1 (of a bird) to make a number of short high sounds 2 (of a person) to talk quickly and nervously: always twittering on about something unimportant –twitter n [U] : the twitter of birds in the trees

two /tuː/ det,n,pron 1 the number 2 2 in two into two parts: cut it in two

two-faced /ˌtuːˈfeɪst ◂/ adj deceitful and dishonest in the way you behave to other people

two-piece /ˌ· ˈ· ◂/ adj [only before a noun] consisting of two matching parts (used of clothes): a two-piece suit –two-piece n

two-way /ˌ· ˈ· ◂/ adj moving or allowing movement in both directions: a two-way mirror | two-way traffic

ty·coon /taɪˈkuːn/ n a businessman or industrialist with great wealth and power

ty·ing /ˈtaɪ-ɪŋ/ the present participle of TIE²

type¹ /taɪp/ n 1 [C] a particular class or group of people or things which share important common qualities and are different from those outside the group or class: What type of plant is this? | She's the type of person that I admire. | There have been several incidents of this type recently. 2 [C] a person of the stated kind: She's an odd type. | a sporty type 3 not my type a phrase you use to describe a person you do not particularly like 4 [U] the size or style of printed letters used in a piece of writing

type² v typed, typing [I;T] to write something using a machine such as a TYPEWRITER or WORD PROCESSOR

type sthg ↔ **up** phr v [T] to type something that was written by hand

type·cast /ˈtaɪpkɑːst ‖ -kæst/ v **typecast, typecast-ing** [T] to repeatedly give an actor the same kind of part: *He's always typecast as a murderer because his face looks rather evil.*

type·face /ˈtaɪpfeɪs/ n the size and style of the letters used in printing

type·writ·er /ˈtaɪpˌraɪtəʳ/ n a machine that prints letters or numbers by means of keys which you press with your fingers –see picture on page 539

type·writ·ten /ˈtaɪpˌrɪtn/ adj written using a typewriter

ty·phoid /ˈtaɪfɔɪd/ n an infectious disease causing fever and often death, caused by bacteria in food or drink

ty·phoon /ˌtaɪˈfuːn◂/ n a very violent tropical storm

ty·phus /ˈtaɪfəs/ [U] an infectious disease that causes severe fever and is carried by fleas (FLEA)

typ·i·cal /ˈtɪpɪkəl/ adj **1** showing the main signs and qualities of a particular kind, group, or class: *a typical eighteenth-century church | a typical British summer* **2** showing the usual behaviour or manner of someone: *It was typical of him to arrive so late.*

typ·i·cally /ˈtɪpɪkli/ adv **1** usually: *She typically works from six in the morning till midnight.* **2** showing the usual signs or qualities of a particular group: *a typically American solution*

typ·i·fy /ˈtɪpˌfaɪ/ v **typified, typifying** [T] to serve as a typical example: *the high quality that typifies all his work | He typifies the Englishman abroad.*

typ·ist /ˈtaɪpˌst/ n a secretary employed mainly for typing (TYPE²) letters

tyr·an·nize /ˈtɪrənaɪz/ v **tyrannized, tyrannizing** (also **tyrannise** *BrE*) [I;T] to use power over a person, country or people with unjust cruelty

tyr·an·ny /ˈtɪrəni/ n [U] **1** the use of cruel or unjust power to control a person or country **2** government by a cruel ruler with complete power –**tyrannical** /tɪˈrænɪkəl/ adj

ty·rant /ˈtaɪərənt/ n **1** a ruler with complete power, who rules cruelly and unjustly **2** a person in control of other people who behaves in a severe and unfair way to them

tyre /taɪəʳ/ n (**tire** *AmE*) a thick piece of rubber, usually filled with air, that fits round a wheel: *a car tyre* –see picture on page 49

tzar /zɑː, tsɑːʳ/ n see TSAR

U,u

U, u /juː/ U's, u's *or* Us, us the 21st letter of the English alphabet

u·biq·ui·tous /juːˈbɪkwɨtəs/ *adj fml* appearing, happening, or done everywhere

ud·der /ˈʌdəʳ/ *n* the part of a female animal like a cow where milk is produced

UFO /ˈjuːfəʊ, ˌjuː ef ˈəʊ/ *n* UFO's a mysterious object seen in the sky; some people think that UFO's are space vehicles bringing creatures from another world; an abbreviation for UNIDENTIFIED FLYING OBJECT

ugh /ʊx, ʌg/ *interj* an expression of dislike: *Ugh! This medicine tastes nasty.*

ug·ly /ˈʌgli/ *adj* uglier, ugliest **1** unpleasant to look at: *an ugly face | Some parts of the city are rather ugly.* **2** very unpleasant and sometimes violent: *An ugly scene developed in the crowd when a group of boys started fighting. | in an ugly mood* –ugliness *n* [U]

UHF /ˌjuː eɪtʃ ˈef/ *n* [U] the method used for sending television pictures; an abbreviation for ultrahigh frequency

UK /ˌjuː ˈkeɪ◂/ *n* the UK Great Britain and Northern Ireland; an abbreviation for United Kingdom

u·ku·le·le /ˌjuːkəˈleɪli/ *n* a musical instrument like a small GUITAR

ul·cer /ˈʌlsəʳ/ *n* a rough place on your skin or inside your body which may bleed or produce poisonous matter: *a stomach ulcer | mouth ulcers*

ul·te·ri·or /ʌlˈtɪəriəʳ/ an ulterior motive a reason for doing something that is not the one you say: *He has an ulterior motive for seeing her: he's going to ask for some money.*

ul·ti·mate /ˈʌltɨmɨt/ *adj* [only before a noun] **1** last: *The ultimate responsibility lies with the President.* **2** the ultimate *infml* greatest or best: *This is the ultimate bicycle. You'll never find a better one. | Her house was the ultimate in luxury.*

ul·ti·mate·ly /ˈʌltɨmɨtli/ *adv* in the end: *Many gave their opinions, but ultimately the decision lay with the President.*

ul·ti·ma·tum /ˌʌltɨˈmeɪtəm/ *n* ultimatums *or* ultimata /-tə/ a statement of something that must be done under a threat of force: *They gave us this ultimatum: if we didn't move out of the house before the end of the week, they would throw us out.*

ul·tra·ma·rine /ˌʌltrəməˈriːn/ *n* [U] a very bright blue colour –ultramarine *adj*

ul·tra·son·ic /ˌʌltrəˈsɒnɪk◂ ‖ -ˈsɑ-/ *adj* above the range of human hearing

ul·tra·vi·o·let /ˌʌltrəˈvaɪəlɨt◂/ *adj* beyond the purple end of the colour SPECTRUM and unable to be seen by human beings: *Use suncream to protect your skin from ultraviolet light.*

um·bil·i·cal cord /ʌmˌbɪlɪkəl ˈkɔːd ‖ -ˈkɔːrd/ *n* the tube of flesh which joins a baby to its mother before birth

um·brage /ˈʌmbrɪdʒ/ *n* take umbrage to show that your feelings have been hurt

um·brel·la /ʌmˈbrelə/ *n* **1** an arrangement of cloth over a folding frame with a handle, used for protection against rain **2** a single organization that includes many others

um·pire¹ /ˈʌmpaɪəʳ/ *n* a judge in charge of a game

umpire² *v* umpired, umpiring [I;T] to act as umpire for a game

ump·teen /ˌʌmpˈtiːn◂/ *det, n, pron infml* a large number: *I've seen that film umpteen times.* –umpteenth *n,det*: *That's the umpteenth time I've told you not to do that!*

UN /ˌjuː ˈen◂/ *n* an international organization that tries to help relations between different countries; an abbreviation for United Nations

un·a·bat·ed /ˌʌnəˈbeɪtɨd/ *adj* without losing force: *The storm continued unabated.*

un·a·ble /ʌnˈeɪbəl/ *adj* unable to do something not having enough power, skill, knowledge, time, or money to do something: *He was unable to open the door. | I'm afraid I'll be unable to attend the meeting tomorrow.*

un·a·bridged /ˌʌnəˈbrɪdʒd◂/ *adj* not shortened (used of a book or play)

un·ac·com·pa·nied /ˌʌnəˈkʌmpənid◂/ *adj* **1** alone: *Children unaccompanied by an adult will not be admitted.* **2** without music: *an unaccompanied song*

un·ac·coun·ta·ble /ˌʌnəˈkaʊntəbəl/ *adj* **1** not easily explained: *unaccountable behaviour* **2** not held responsible (used of people in public office) –unaccountably *adv*

un·a·dul·te·rat·ed /ˌʌnəˈdʌltəreɪtɨd/ *adj* **1** not mixed with impure substances **2** complete: *unadulterated nonsense*

un·af·fect·ed /ˌʌnəˈfektɨd◂/ *adj* **1** not changed in any way: *People in the south of the country were unaffected by the food shortages in the north.* **2** natural in behaviour or character: *the unaffected delight of a child*

un·aid·ed /ʌnˈeɪdɨd/ *adj* without help from anyone else: *It has to be your own unaided work. | He is now able to walk unaided.*

u·nan·i·mous /juːˈnænɨməs/ *adj* **1** all agreeing: *The voters were unanimous.* **2** agreed by everyone: *a unanimous decision* –unanimously *adv* –unanimity /ˌjuːnəˈnɪmɨti/ *n* [U]

un·ap·proa·cha·ble /ˌʌnəˈprəʊtʃəbəl◂/ *adj* not very friendly, and so difficult to talk to

un·armed /ˌʌnˈɑːmd◂ ‖ -ˈɑːr-/ *adj* not carrying weapons

un·as·sum·ing /ˌʌnəˈsjuːmɪŋ◂, -ˈsuː- ‖ -ˈsuː-/ *adj* quiet in manner

un·at·tached /ˌʌnəˈtætʃt◂/ *adj* **1** not connected **2** not married or in a serious relationship

un·at·tend·ed /ˌʌnəˈtendɨd◂/ *adj* without being watched: *Your car is quite likely to get damaged if you leave it unattended.*

un·a·wares /ˌʌnəˈweəz ‖ -ˈweərz/ *adv* **1** without noticing **2** take someone unawares to surprise someone

un·bal·anced /ˌʌnˈbælənst/ *adj* **1** slightly mad (used of people): *He became a bit unbalanced after his wife died.* **2** not fair and exact (used of writing and reports): *an unbalanced account*

un·bear·a·ble /ʌnˈbeərəbəl/ *adj* too bad to be put up with: *unbearable heat | The pain was unbearable.* –unbearably *adv*

un·be·lie·va·ble /ˌʌnbɨˈliːvəbəl/ *adj* **1** very surprising: *It's unbelievable how many children she has!* **2** excellent: *My weekend in Paris was unbelievable.* –unbelievably *adv*

un·bend·ing /ʌnˈbendɪŋ/ adj refusing to change opinions, or decisions

un·born /ˌʌnˈbɔːn◂ ‖ -ɔːrn◂/ adj not yet born

un·bound·ed /ʌnˈbaʊndd̩/ adj limitless: *unbounded admiration*

un·bri·dled /ʌnˈbraɪdld/ adj lit not controlled: *unbridled anger*

un·bur·den /ˌʌnˈbɜːdn ‖ -ɜːr-/ v **unburden yourself to someone** to tell someone about your secret problems so that you feel better about them

un·but·ton /ˌʌnˈbʌtn/ v [T] to unfasten the buttons on something

un·called-for /ʌnˈkɔːld fɔːr/ adj not deserved or right: *Such rudeness is quite uncalled-for.*

un·can·ny /ʌnˈkæni/ adj mysterious: *It seemed uncanny to hear her voice from the other side of the world.* –**uncannily** adv

un·cared-for /ʌnˈkeəd fɔːr ‖ -ˈkeərd-/ adj not well looked after: *His face is dirty and his clothes are uncared-for.*

un·ce·re·mo·ni·ous /ˌʌnserd̩ˈməʊniəs/ adj **1** informal: *an unceremonious but sincere welcome* **2** not done politely: *She finished the meal with unceremonious haste.* –**unceremoniously** adv

un·cer·tain /ʌnˈsɜːtn ‖ -ɜːr-/ adj **1** not sure: *I'm uncertain how to get there.* | *a man of uncertain origin* **2** undecided or unable to decide: *Our holiday plans are still uncertain.* **3** changeable: *uncertain weather* –**uncertainly** adv –**uncertainty** n [C;U]

un·char·i·ta·ble /ʌnˈtʃærd̩təbəl/ adj not kind or fair in judgments: *an uncharitable remark*

un·chart·ed /ʌnˈtʃɑːtd̩ ‖ -ɑːr-/ adj lit not known well enough for maps or other records to be made of it: *the uncharted forests of Brazil*

un·checked /ˌʌnˈtʃekt◂/ adj not prevented from developing: *The disease spread unchecked.*

un·cle /ˈʌŋkəl/ n the brother of your father or mother, or the husband of your aunt: *He's my uncle.* | *Take me swimming, Uncle Jack!* –see picture on page 343

un·clean /ˌʌnˈkliːn◂/ adj not considered pure in a religious way: *In ancient times lepers were thought to be unclean.*

un·com·for·ta·ble /ʌnˈkʌmftəbəl, -ˈkʌmfət- ‖ ˈkʌmfərt-, -ˈkʌmft-/ adj not comfortable: *an uncomfortable chair* | *I felt uncomfortable when John and Jane started arguing with each other.* –**uncomfortably** adv : *uncomfortably close to the fire*

un·com·mit·ted /ˌʌnkəˈmɪtd̩◂/ adj [to] not having given loyalty to any one thing, group or belief: *She hasn't yet decided her position and wants to remain uncommitted.*

un·com·mon /ʌnˈkɒmən ‖ -ˈkɑː-/ adj rare or unusual: *It's quite uncommon for someone not to have a television these days.*

un·com·pro·mis·ing /ʌnˈkɒmprəmaɪzɪŋ ‖ -ˈkɑːm-/ adj refusing to change ideas or decisions: *He is uncompromising in his demands.* –**uncompromisingly** adv

un·con·cerned /ˌʌnkənˈsɜːnd ‖ -ɜːr-/ adj not worried or anxious: *She seemed quite unconcerned about not having a job.* –**unconcernedly** /-nd̩li/ adv

un·con·di·tion·al /ˌʌnkənˈdɪʃənəl/ adj completely without conditions or limitations: *The rebels want unconditional freedom for all their political prisoners.* –**unconditionally** adv : *They surrendered unconditionally.*

un·con·scious¹ /ʌnˈkɒnʃəs ‖ -ˈkɑːn-/ adj **1** in a state that is like sleep when you do not know what is happening, caused by an accident or illness: *After the car crash I was unconscious for several hours.* –see CONSCIOUS (USAGE) **2** not meant intentionally: *His sexist comment was quite unconscious.* **3** without knowing about something: *Susan was unconscious of the fact that Bill was attracted to her.* –**unconsciously** adv –**unconsciousness** n [U]

unconscious² n **the unconscious** –see SUBCONSCIOUS

un·co·op·e·ra·tive /ˌʌnkəʊˈɒpərətɪv ‖ -ˈɑːp-/ adj unwilling to work with other people, or help them, or do what they want when they ask

un·cork /ʌnˈkɔːk ‖ -ɔːrk/ v [T] to open a bottle by removing the CORK

un·couth /ʌnˈkuːθ/ adj behaving and speaking in a rough and rude way

un·cov·er /ʌnˈkʌvər/ v [T] **1** to remove a covering from something **2** to discover: *The police uncovered a plan to shoot the President.*

un·crit·i·cal /ʌnˈkrɪtɪkəl/ adj not willing or able to make judgments about whether something is good or bad –**critically** /-kli/

un·cut /ˌʌnˈkʌt◂/ adj **1** not made shorter (used of books, films, or plays) **2** not having the surface cut and shaped (used of a precious stone like a diamond)

un·daunt·ed /ʌnˈdɔːntd̩/ adj not at all discouraged by danger or difficulty

un·de·cid·ed /ˌʌndɪˈsaɪdd̩/ adj in doubt and not having made a decision: *The jury were still undecided after discussing the trial for six hours.* | *A lot of people are still undecided about who they're going to vote for.*

un·de·ni·a·ble /ˌʌndɪˈnaɪəbəl/ adj certainly true: *Picasso was an undeniable genius.* –**undeniably** adv

un·der /ˈʌndər/ adv,prep **1** prep directly below something or covered by something: *There's a box of papers under the table.* | *He squeezed under the fence.* | *She was wearing a cream blouse under her jumper.* | *These animals spend most of their time under water.* –see picture on page 540 **2** adv, prep less than a particular amount: *It costs under £5.* | *children under seven years old* | *children aged eight and under* **3** prep working for someone and controlled or guided by them: *I've got three junior secretaries under me.* | *He's studying under one of the world's leading physicists.* **4** prep during the rule of someone: *What was it like living in Spain under Franco?* | *new laws brought in under the conservative government* **5** prep used to say where a piece of information is kept in a system: *It's filed under "I" for "Invoices".* **6** prep using a particular name, usually one which is not your real name: *I booked into the hotel under the name of Shaw.* | *He wrote a great many books under various names.* **7** adv not enough: *The project has been under-financed and under-staffed.* **8 under age** too young by law to do certain things such as drive a car or drink alcohol

un·der·arm /ˈʌndərɑːm ‖ -ɑːrm/ adj,adv thrown without moving your hand above your shoulder

un·der·car·riage /ˈʌndəˌkærɪdʒ ‖ -ər-/ n the wheels of an aircraft and the frame they are connected to

und·er·charge /ˌʌndəˈtʃɑːdʒ ‖ ˌʌndərˈtʃɑːrdʒ/ v **undercharged, undercharging** [I;T] to charge too little money for something: *They undercharged him by £6.*

un·der·clothes /ˈʌndəkləʊðz, -kləʊz ‖ -dər-/ n [pl]
(also **underclothing** [U]) clothes that you wear
next to your body under other clothes

un·der·coat /ˈʌndəkəʊt ‖ -dər-/ n a covering of paint
put onto a surface as a base for a top covering of
paint

un·der·cov·er /ˌʌndəˈkʌvər◂ ‖ -dər-/ adj, adv acting
secretly in order to get information: an undercover
agent | a police officer working undercover

un·der·cur·rent /ˈʌndəˌkʌrənt ‖ -dərˌkɜːr-/ n 1 a
hidden current of water beneath the sea's surface
2 a feeling or opinion that is hidden beneath the
surface of a situation: Wherever I went in the city I
felt an undercurrent of danger.

un·der·cut /ˌʌndəˈkʌt ‖ -ər-/ v undercut, undercut,
undercutting [T] to sell goods or services more
cheaply than another shop

un·der·dog /ˈʌndədɒg ‖ ˈʌndərdɔːg/ n a person or
country that is weaker and not expected to succeed

un·der·done /ˌʌndəˈdʌn◂ ‖ -ər-/ adj not completely
cooked

un·der·es·ti·mate /ˌʌndərˈestɪˌmeɪt/ v underestimated, underestimating [I;T] to think that
something or someone is not as valuable, great or
able as it really is: The builder underestimated how
much the job would cost by £200. | Don't under-
estimate a baby's ability to understand what you're
saying. **underestimate** /-tɪˌmət/ n : £1.2 m is almost
certainly an underestimate.

un·der·foot /ˌʌndəˈfʊt ‖ -ər-/ adv under your feet
when you are walking: The grass was wet underfoot.

un·der·go /ˌʌndəˈgəʊ ‖ -dər-/ v underwent /-ˈwent/,
undergone /-ˈgɒn‖ˈgɔːn/ [T] to experience something that is unpleasant or necessary: His mother
is undergoing treatment for cancer.

un·der·grad·u·ate /ˌʌndəˈgrædʒuɪt ‖ -ər-/ n a
university student who has not yet taken their first
degree

un·der·ground¹ /ˌʌndəˈgraʊnd ‖ -ər-/ adv under the
surface of the ground: an underground cave | The
waste is buried underground.

underground² /ˈʌndəgraʊnd ‖ -ər-/ adj. secret,
unofficial, or illegal: The underground political
movement opposing the government is very well
organized.

underground³ n a railway system in which the
trains run in passages below the ground, especially
the system in London: We travelled across London
on the underground. | We went by underground. | a
map of the London Underground

un·der·growth /ˈʌndəgrəʊθ ‖ -dər-/ n [U] bushes and
plants growing under the trees in a wood: thick
undergrowth | They cleared a path through the
undergrowth.

un·der·hand /ˌʌndəˈhænd◂ ‖ -ər-/ adj done
dishonestly and secretly: He acquired all that
money in a very underhand manner.

un·der·lie /ˌʌndəˈlaɪ ‖ -ər-/ v underlay /-ˈleɪ/,
underlain /-ˈleɪn/, underlying [T] to be a hidden
cause of something: Social problems and poverty
underlie much of the crime in today's cities.

un·der·line /ˌʌndəˈlaɪn ‖ -ər-/ v underlined, under-
lining [T] 1 to draw a line under a word to make
it noticeable 2 to show the importance of something: Accidents at work underline the need for better
safety standards.

un·der·manned /ˌʌndəˈmænd◂ ‖ -ər-/ adj not
having enough workers

un·der·men·tioned /ˌʌndəˈmenʃənd◂ ‖ -ər-/ adj fml
mentioned later in a letter, contract, or in legal
writing

un·der·mine /ˌʌndəˈmaɪn ‖ -ər-/ v undermined,
undermining [T] to weaken or slowly destroy: My
confidence was undermined by his constant criti-
cism. | The storm badly undermined the sea wall.

un·der·neath¹ /ˌʌndəˈniːθ ‖ -ər-/ adv, prep 1
adv,prep under or below: There was a dog under-
neath the table. | She wore a white blouse under-
neath her jumper. 2 adv used when you are describing what someone feels but does not show to other
people: She smiled, but underneath she was furious.

underneath² n [sing] the bottom or lower surface
of something

un·der·nour·ished /ˌʌndəˈnʌrɪʃt | ˌʌndərˈnɜː-, -ˈnʌ-/
adj not healthy or well developed because of lack
of food or the right kind of food
—**undernourishment** n [U]

un·der·pants /ˈʌndəpænts ‖ -ər-/ n [pl] a short piece
of clothing worn under trousers by men and boys
—see PAIR (USAGE) —see picture on page 50

un·der·pass /ˈʌndəpɑːs ‖ ˈʌndərpæs/ n a road or path
that goes under another road

un·der·priv·i·leged /ˌʌndəˈprɪvᵻlɪdʒd◂ ‖ -dər-/ adj
not having the advantages of other people

un·der·rate /ˌʌndəˈreɪt/ v underrated, under-
rating [T] to have too low an opinion of something:
We underrated his powers as a speaker. | His music
has been very underrated in the past.

un·der·shirt /ˈʌndəʃɜːt ‖ ˈʌndərʃɜːrt/ n the usual
American word for VEST

un·der·side /ˈʌndəsaɪd ‖ -ər-/ n the lower side or
surface: The underside of our car is ever so rusty.

un·der·signed /ˈʌndəsaɪnd ‖ -ər-/ n [pl] the under-
signed the people who have signed a letter or
contract

un·der·sized /ˌʌndəˈsaɪzd◂ ‖ -ər-/ adj too small or
smaller than usual

un·der·staffed /ˌʌndəˈstɑːft ‖ ˌʌndərˈstæft/ adj not
having enough workers: The office is understaffed
since the secretary left.

un·der·stand /ˌʌndəˈstænd ‖ -ər-/ v understood
/-ˈstʊd/, understood [not in progressive forms] 1
[I;T] to know or get the meaning of words or ideas:
She tried to explain the theory to me but I didn't
really understand. | I can't understand modern art. |
He can understand quite a lot of English but he can't
speak very much. | I found the lecture hard to under-
stand. 2 [T] to know someone's character and know
why they act in the way they do: I've known Emily
for 15 years but I still can't understand her. | I can
understand how you feel. 3 [+(that)] fml to know
something because you have been told: I understand you're coming to work for us. 4 [+(that)] to
think something is the case even if this has not been
stated directly: I thought it was understood that we
would get paid extra for working at the weekend. 5
make yourself understood to make your meaning clear to others: I don't really speak German but
I can make myself understood. —**understandable**
adj : I think his reaction was understandable.
—**understandably** adv : He was understandably
angry.

un·der·stand·ing¹ /ˌʌndəˈstændɪŋ ‖ -ər-/ n 1 [U]
knowledge of something or of what something
means: Helen has very little understanding of music.
2 [U] sympathy towards and knowledge of a person's character: There is a deep understanding
between them. 3 [C] a private informal agreement:
We have come to an understanding.

understanding² *adj* sympathetic and kind: *She was very understanding when I told her my problem.*

un·der·state /ˌʌndəˈsteɪt ‖ -ər-/ *v* **understated**, **understating** [T] to make something seem less important than it is: *The government understated the seriousness of the problem.*

un·der·state·ment /ˈʌndəˌsteɪtmənt ‖ -dər-/ *n* a statement which is not strong enough: *To say the film wasn't very good is an understatement: it was absolutely awful!*

un·der·stood /ˌʌndəˈstʊd ‖ -ər-/ the past tense and past participle of UNDERSTAND

un·der·stud·y /ˈʌndəˌstʌdi ‖ -ər-/ *n* **understudies** an actor who learns the part of another actor in a play and can act that part if necessary

un·der·take /ˌʌndəˈteɪk ‖ -ər-/ *v* **undertook** /-ˈtʊk/, **undertaken** /-ˈteɪkən/, **undertaking** **1** [T] to start work on: *She undertook the training of the new staff.* **2 undertake to do something** to promise or agree to do something: *She undertook to pay the money back within six months.*

un·der·tak·er /ˈʌndəteɪkəʳ ‖ -dər-/ *n* a person whose job it is to arrange funerals

un·der·tak·ing /ˌʌndəˈteɪkɪŋ ‖ ˈʌndərteɪ-/ *n* **1** a job that is started and someone is responsible for: *To start a new business can be a risky undertaking.* **2** a promise: *The council has given an undertaking to improve local services.*

un·der·tone /ˈʌndətəʊn ‖ -dər-/ *n* a quiet voice: *He spoke in an undertone.*

un·der·took /ˌʌndəˈtʊk ‖ -ər-/ the past tense of UNDERTAKE

un·der·wa·ter /ˌʌndəˈwɔːtəʳ ‖ ˌʌndərˈwɔːtər, -ˈwɑː-/ *adj* used or done below the surface of the water: *an underwater camera* | *Richard loves swimming underwater.*

un·der·wear /ˈʌndəweəʳ ‖ -dər-/ *n* [U] clothes worn next to your body under other clothes

un·der·weight /ˌʌndəˈweɪt ‖ -ər-/ *adj* weighing too little: *He is several pounds underweight.* –see THIN¹ (USAGE)

un·der·went /ˌʌndəˈwent ‖ -ər-/ the past tense of UNDERGO

un·der·world /ˈʌndəwɜːld ‖ ˈʌndərwɜːrld/ *n* **1** in ancient stories the place where the spirits of the dead live **2** the criminal world

un·de·si·ra·ble¹ /ˌʌndɪˈzaɪərəbəl/ *adj fml* **1** unpleasant with a possible bad effect: *Many drugs have undesirable side-effects.* **2** not socially acceptable

undesirable² *n* a person thought of as socially unacceptable

un·de·vel·oped /ˌʌndɪˈveləpt/ *adj* **1** without industry or modern farming (used of a place or country) **2** not built on (used of land)

un·dis·tin·guished /ˌʌndɪˈstɪŋgwɪʃt/ *adj* ordinary, without any special qualities

un·di·vid·ed /ˌʌndɪˈvaɪdɪd/ *adj* **1** complete: *The children gave me their undivided attention while I read them a story.* **2** having no divisions

un·do /ʌnˈduː/ *v* **undid** /-ˈdɪd/, **undone** /-ˈdʌn/ [T] **1** to unfasten something that is tied, sewn, or connected: *I can't undo the knot in this string.* | *He undid the buttons on his shirt.* | *I undid my sewing because it was wrong.* –opposite **do up 2** to remove the effects of something: *It will be difficult to undo your mistakes.*

un·do·ing /ʌnˈduːɪŋ/ *n* [sing] the cause of ruin or failure: *Alcohol was his undoing.*

un·done¹ /ˌʌnˈdʌn/ *adj* **1** unfastened or loose: *Your shoelace has come undone.* **2** not done: *I've got a pile of work that is still undone.*

undone² the past participle of UNDO

un·doubt·ed /ʌnˈdaʊtɪd/ *adj* known for certain to be true –**undoubtedly** *adv*: *The story is undoubtedly true.*

un·dreamed-of /ʌnˈdriːmd əv, -ɒv ‖ -əv, -ɑːv/ *adj* (also **undreamt-of** /ʌnˈdrempt/) better than could have been imagined: *undreamed-of wealth*

un·dress /ʌnˈdres/ *v* **1** [I] to take your clothes off: *The doctor asked me to undress.* **2 get undressed** to take your clothes off: *I got undressed and went to bed.* **3** [T] to take off someone's clothes: *He undressed the baby and put her in the bath.*

un·due /ˌʌnˈdjuː ‖ -ˈduː-/ *adj* [always before a noun] more than is necessary or suitable: *She left with undue haste.*

un·du·late /ˈʌndjʊleɪt ‖ -dʒə-/ *v* **undulated**, **undulating** [I] to move or have slopes like waves rising and falling: *undulating hills*

un·du·ly /ʌnˈdjuːli ‖ -ˈduː-/ *adv* too much: *His parents did not seem unduly worried.*

un·earth /ʌnˈɜːθ ‖ -ˈɜːrθ/ *v* [T] to dig up or find something: *The dog unearthed a bone in the garden.*

un·earth·ly /ʌnˈɜːθli ‖ -ˈɜːrθ-/ *adj* **1** strange and unnatural: *There was an unearthly presence in the room.* **2** *infml* very early or very late and inconvenient: *I had to get up at an unearthly hour to get to the airport.*

un·eas·y /ʌnˈiːzi/ *adj* **uneasier**, **uneasiest** uncertain, worried, or anxious: *He feels uneasy about the future.* –**uneasily** *adv* –**uneasiness** (also **unease** /ʌnˈiːz/ *lit*) *n* [U]

un·e·co·nom·ic /ˌʌniːkəˈnɒmɪk, ˌʌnekə- ‖ -ˈnɑː-/ *adj* not producing enough profit: *These old coal mines are quite uneconomic.* –**uneconomically** /-kli/ *adv*

un·e·co·nom·i·cal /ˌʌniːkəˈnɒmɪkəl, ˌʌnekə- ‖ -ˈnɑː-/ *adj* wasteful or expensive: *It's uneconomical to buy such small packets.* | *She uses no end of water. She's very uneconomical.* –**uneconomically** *adv*

un·ed·u·cat·ed /ʌnˈedjʊkeɪtɪd ‖ -dʒə-/ *adj* not having had much education

un·em·ployed /ˌʌnɪmˈplɔɪd/ *adj* **1** not having a job: *He's an unemployed actor.* **2 the unemployed** the people who do not have a job

un·em·ploy·ment /ˌʌnɪmˈplɔɪmənt/ *n* [U] **1** the number of people in a society without a job: *The level of unemployment has increased by 5000 this month.* **2** the situation of not having a job: *Unemployment can be very depressing for people.*

un·en·light·ened /ˌʌnɪnˈlaɪtənd/ *adj* not having knowledge or understanding of something: *a very unenlightened policy*

un·en·vi·a·ble /ʌnˈenviəbəl/ *adj* difficult and unpleasant: *The policeman had the unenviable job of telling the woman that her husband had been killed.*

un·e·qual /ʌnˈiːkwəl/ *adj* **1** not of equal size, value or strength: *The two bags were unequal in weight.* **2** not the same or treated fairly: *The women workers complained about unequal pay and conditions.* **3** **unequal to something** not having enough strength or ability to do something: *He was unequal to the job.* –**unequally** *adv*

un·e·qualled /ʌnˈiːkwəld/ *adj* (**unequaled** *AmE*) better than any other: *Her record as a tennis champion is unequalled.*

un·e·quiv·o·cal /ˌʌnɪˈkwɪvəkəl/ adj totally clear in meaning –**unequivocally** /-kli/ adv

un·er·ring /ʌnˈɜːrɪŋ/ adj without making a mistake: With unerring aim she hit the ball into the hole.

un·e·ven /ʌnˈiːvən/ adj 1 not smooth, flat, straight, or regular: The road surface is very uneven here. 2 not equal or balanced: The match is going to be very uneven because Jones has much more experience than Freeman. –**unevenly** adv –**unevenness** n [U]

un·fail·ing /ʌnˈfeɪlɪŋ/ adj continuous and always present: My parents' unfailing support has helped me to succeed. –**unfailingly** adv

un·faith·ful /ʌnˈfeɪθfəl/ adj having a sexual relationship with someone else when you are already married or have a partner

un·fath·o·ma·ble /ʌnˈfæðəməbəl/ adj which cannot be understood

un·fa·vou·ra·ble /ʌnˈfeɪvərəbəl/ adj (**unfavorable** AmE) 1 not good and not what you would like: The dollar's exchange is very unfavourable at the moment. 2 showing disapproval: Most of the reviews of the film were unfavourable. –**unfavourably** adv

un·feel·ing /ʌnˈfiːlɪŋ/ adj cruel and not sympathetic towards others: My old boss was horrible – totally cold and unfeeling.

un·flag·ging /ʌnˈflæɡɪŋ/ adj without getting tired or stopping: She has an unflagging interest in her work as a teacher.

un·flinch·ing /ʌnˈflɪntʃɪŋ/ adj without fear when in danger or difficulty

un·fold /ʌnˈfəʊld/ v 1 [T] to open something from a folded position: She took the letter out of the envelope and unfolded it carefully. 2 [I] to develop and become clear: The film gets more and more interesting as the story unfolds.

un·fore·seen /ˌʌnfɔːˈsiːn/ adj not expected in advance: Due to unforeseen circumstances publication has been delayed.

un·for·get·ta·ble /ˌʌnfəˈɡetəbəl/ adj not easy to forget: We had the most unforgettable holiday travelling around China.

un·for·tu·nate[1] /ʌnˈfɔːtʃənɪt/ adj 1 having bad luck which is usually not deserved: He is a poor, unfortunate man with no home or family. 2 producing a bad result: She telephoned at a rather unfortunate moment.

unfortunate[2] n someone who has an unlucky life that you feel sorry for

un·for·tu·nate·ly /ʌnˈfɔːtʃənɪtli/ adv a word used to say that you are sorry or disappointed about something: Unfortunately they've sold the house to someone else. | "Will you be there tomorrow?" "No, unfortunately not."

un·found·ed /ʌnˈfaʊndɪd/ adj without any supporting facts: The newspaper story was quite unfounded.

un·furl /ʌnˈfɜːl/ v [T] to unroll and open a flag or sail

un·gain·ly /ʌnˈɡeɪnli/ adj awkward and ungraceful in movement –**ungainliness** n [U]

un·gov·er·na·ble /ʌnˈɡʌvənəbəl/ adj fml not controllable

un·gra·cious /ʌnˈɡreɪʃəs/ adj not polite or friendly –**ungraciously** adv

un·grate·ful /ʌnˈɡreɪtfəl/ adj not showing any thanks when someone is kind or generous: Don't think I'm ungrateful, but I can't accept your offer. –**ungratefully** adv

un·guard·ed /ʌnˈɡɑːdɪd/ adj careless about what you say: an unguarded moment

un·hap·pi·ly /ʌnˈhæpɪli/ adv 1 in a sad way 2 fml unfortunately: Unhappily, we could not finish the work.

un·hap·py /ʌnˈhæpi/ adj **unhappier**, **unhappiest** 1 sad: She had an unhappy marriage. 2 worried and not pleased: She was unhappy about the children going out alone. –**unhappiness** n [U]

un·health·y /ʌnˈhelθi/ adj **unhealthier**, **unhealthiest** 1 not generally in good health: He looks thin and unhealthy. 2 likely to cause bad health: an unhealthy climate | Too much salt is unhealthy. 3 unnatural: an unhealthy interest in murder –**unhealthily** adv

un·heard /ˌʌnˈhɜːd/ adj go unheard not to be listened to: Her complaints went unheard.

unheard-of /·ˈ·ˌ·/ adj very unusual: It's unheard-of to pass the examination so young.

un·hinge /ʌnˈhɪndʒ/ v **unhinged**, **unhinging** [T] to cause someone to become unbalanced in their mind: His terrible experience unhinged him. | He's really quite unhinged.

un·hook /ʌnˈhʊk/ [T] 1 to remove something from a hook 2 to unfasten the hooks of something: She unhooked her necklace and put it in a box.

u·ni·corn /ˈjuːnɪkɔːn/ n an imaginary animal like a horse with one horn growing from its forehead

un·i·den·ti·fied /ˌʌnaɪˈdentɪfaɪd/ adj whose name or origin is not known: An unidentified man was seen near the scene of the murder.

unidentified fly·ing ob·ject /·ˌ···ˌ···ˌ ˈ·ˌ·/ n see UFO

u·ni·form[1] /ˈjuːnɪfɔːm/ n [C;U] a certain type of clothing which all members of a group wear, for example in the army, a school, or the police: British policemen wear dark blue uniforms. | Have we got to wear school uniform? –**uniformed** adj: Two uniformed policemen came to the door.

uniform[2] adj always the same and never changing: All the windows were painted a uniform colour. –**uniformity** /-ˈfɔːmɪti/ n [U] –**uniformly** adv

u·ni·fy /ˈjuːnɪfaɪ/ v **unified**, **unifying** [T] 1 to join together to make one whole: Spain was unified in the 16th century. 2 to make all the same: The company wishes to unify its computer systems. –**unification** /ˌjuːnɪfɪˈkeɪʃən/ n [U]

u·ni·lat·e·ral /ˌjuːnɪˈlætərəl/ adj 1 done by or having an effect on only one side in an agreement 2 **unilateral disarmament** one country removing its NUCLEAR weapons without waiting for other countries to do the same

un·im·pea·cha·ble /ˌʌnɪmˈpiːtʃəbəl/ adj fml that should not be doubted

un·in·formed /ˌʌnɪnˈfɔːmd/ adj showing a lack of knowledge and information: an uninformed opinion

un·in·hab·i·ta·ble /ˌʌnɪnˈhæbɪtəbəl/ adj unfit to live in

un·in·hib·it·ed /ˌʌnɪnˈhɪbɪtɪd/ adj free in what you say and do without worrying about what other people think

un·in·ter·est·ed /ʌnˈɪntrɪstɪd/ adj not interested –see DISINTERESTED (USAGE)

un·in·ter·rupt·ed /ˌʌnɪntəˈrʌptɪd/ adj continuous

u·nion /ˈjuːnjən/ n 1 [U] the act of joining or state of being joined into one: the union of East and West

Germany **2** [C] a group of countries or states joined together: *the Soviet Union* **3** [C+sing/pl v] a club or society which represents a group of workers, or a profession: *Do you belong to a union?* | *The Students' Union are holding elections today.* **4** [C] *fml* a marriage: *a union blessed by the Church*

u·nion·ize /ˈjuːnjənaɪz/ v **unionized, unionizing** (also **unionise** *BrE*) [I;T] to form a TRADE UNION or arrange a union for a particular industry –**unionization** /ˌjuːnjənaɪˈzeɪʃən ‖ -njənə-/ n [U]

Union Jack /ˌ·· ˈ·/ n the national flag of Great Britain

u·nique /juːˈniːk/ adj **1** the only one of its type: *Each person's voice is unique.* **2** related to one person, place, or thing only: *Kangaroos are unique to Australia.* **3** *infml* unusual: *She has a rather unique singing style.* –**uniquely** adv –**uniqueness** n [U] ■ USAGE Because **unique** means "the only one" many people do not consider it correct to use **unique** with the meaning "unusual", or to use expressions like *fairly/rather* **unique**.

u·ni·sex /ˈjuːnɪˌseks/ adj *infml* which can be used by both men and women: *a unisex hairdresser*

u·ni·son /ˈjuːnɪsən, -zən/ n **in unison: a** in perfect agreement **b** together: *"Yes!" they answered in unison.*

u·nit /ˈjuːnɪt/ n **1** something such as a group of things or people that forms a single and complete whole within something larger: *an army unit* | *The family is a small social unit.* **2** a piece of furniture which can be fitted with others of the same type: *a kitchen unit* **3** an amount or quantity used as a standard of measurement: *The pound is the standard unit of money in Britain.*

U·ni·tar·i·an /ˌjuːnɪˈteərɪən/ adj of a branch of the Christian church –**Unitarian** n

u·nite /juːˈnaɪt/ v **united, uniting** [I;T] to join together into one and act together: *The threat of a foreign attack united the government and its opponents.*

u·nit·ed /juːˈnaɪtɪd/ adj **1** joined in a state of agreement: *They are a very united family.* **2** all together: *We must make a united effort to help.* **3** (only before a noun) (also **United**) joined in an organization: *the United States of America* | *the United Nations*

u·ni·ty /ˈjuːnɪti/ n [U] state of being joined together in agreement: *Political leaders always try to show there is unity in their party.*

u·ni·ver·sal /ˌjuːnɪˈvɜːsəl◂ ‖ -ɜːr-/ adj **1** for or concerning all the people in the world, or everyone in a particular group: *There was universal agreement to stop the plan.* | *Love is a subject of universal interest.* **2** concerning the whole world: *The dangers of pollution are universal.* –**universally** adv –**universality** /ˌjuːnɪˌvɜːˈsælɪti ‖ -ɜːr-/ n [U]

u·ni·verse /ˈjuːnɪvɜːs ‖ -ɜːrs/ n all space and everything that exists in it: *Stars fill every part of the universe.*

u·ni·ver·si·ty /ˌjuːnɪˈvɜːsɪti◂ ‖ -ɜːr-/ n **universities** [C;U] a place of education at the highest level, where degrees are given: *Which university did you go to?* | *Jean is a university professor.* | *"Has he got a job?" "No, he's still at university."* | *They've passed their exams and they're going to university in September.* | *She went to Leeds University.* | *She went to the University of Leeds.*

un·kempt /ˌʌnˈkempt◂/ adj having very untidy clothes and hair

un·kind /ˌʌnˈkaɪnd◂/ adj cruel, unfriendly, or unpleasant to people –**unkindly** adv –**unkindness** n [C;U]

un·known /ˌʌnˈnəʊn◂/ adj **1** not known: *The cause of the disease is unknown.* **2** not famous or familiar: *Until recently these fruits were unknown outside Asia.*

un·law·ful /ʌnˈlɔːfəl/ adj against the law: *an unlawful action* –**unlawfully** adv

un·leash /ʌnˈliːʃ/ v [T] to allow strong or violent forces or feelings to come out: *Enormous forces are unleashed in a thunderstorm.*

un·leav·ened /ʌnˈlevənd/ adj made without YEAST, and therefore flat (used of bread)

un·less /ʌnˈles, ən-/ conj except if something happens: *Do not leave the building unless you are instructed to do so.* | *Unless the government agrees to give extra money, the theatre will have to close.* ■ USAGE Do not use **unless** when you are talking about imaginary events. Use *if...* **not** instead: *If we weren't so poor* (imaginary because we are poor) *we could go on holiday.* | *She would have died* (imaginary) *if the doctor had* **not** *arrived on time.* **Unless** cannot be used in these sentences.

un·like¹ /ˌʌnˈlaɪk/ adj [never before a noun] different: *She's very unlike her mother. They're completely unlike.*

unlike² prep it's **unlike him to...** = it's not typical of him to...: *It's unlike him to be late. He's usually on time.*

un·like·ly /ʌnˈlaɪkli/ adj not likely: *He may come, but it's very unlikely.* | *They're unlikely to be at home before six o'clock.* | *It seems unlikely that they'll come now.* □ USEFUL PATTERNS be unlikely to do something; it is unlikely that... –**unlikeliness** (also **unlikelihood**) n [U]

un·load /ʌnˈləʊd/ v **1** [T] to remove goods from a vehicle or container: *Can you help me unload the car?* **2** [I] to have goods removed: *The trucks unload as soon as they arrive at the warehouse.* **3** [I;T] to remove the bullets from a gun or film from a camera

un·lock /ʌnˈlɒk ‖ -lɑːk/ v [T] to unfasten the lock on something: *That door is quite difficult to unlock.*

un·looked-for /ʌnˈlʊkt fɔːʳ/ adj lit unexpected

un·loos·en /ʌnˈluːsən/ v [T] to make something less tight: *He unloosened his tie when he got outside.*

un·luck·y /ˌʌnˈlʌki/ adj **unluckier, unluckiest** not lucky: *People say it's unlucky to walk under a ladder.* | *She's been unlucky with her car – it's always breaking down.*

un·made /ˌʌnˈmeɪd◂/ adj **1** not made ready for sleeping in (used of a bed) **2** not having a hard surface, but just made of earth (used of roads)

un·mask /ʌnˈmɑːsk ‖ -ˈmæsk/ v [T] to show the hidden truth about someone or something

un·men·tio·na·ble /ʌnˈmenʃənəbəl/ adj too unpleasant to be spoken of

un·mis·ta·ka·ble /ˌʌnmɪˈsteɪkəbəl/ adj too clear and recognizable to be thought of as anything else: *the unmistakable sound of a baby crying* –**unmistakably** adv

un·mit·i·gat·ed /ʌnˈmɪtɪɡeɪtɪd/ adj [always before a noun] bad in every way and not to be excused: *I knew we should never have done it. It's been an unmitigated disaster.*

un·moved /ʌnˈmuːvd/ adj showing no sympathy or feelings

un·nat·u·ral /ʌnˈnætʃərəl/ adj **1** not what is usual, expected, or normal: *It's unnatural for him to have a rest after a meal.* **2** *It's unnatural for a child to spend so much time with adults.* | *Those tomatoes are so red they look unnatural.*

☐ USEFUL PATTERNS it is unnatural to do something; it is unnatural for someone to do something **2** false and not sincere: *an unnatural laugh* **–unnaturally** *adv* : *It was unnaturally quiet when I arrived.*

un·ne·ces·sa·ry /ʌnˈnesəsəri ‖ -seri/ *adj* not needed or more than is needed: *It's unnecessary to spend too much time on this job.* | *It was unnecessary for you to ask.* | *I want to avoid any unnecessary expenses on the trip.*
☐ USEFUL PATTERNS it is unnecessary to do something; it is unnecessary for someone to do something **–unnecessarily** /ʌnˈnesəsərɪli ‖ ˌʌn-nesəˈserɪli/ *adv* : *unnecessarily rude*

un·nerve /ˌʌnˈnɜːv ‖ -ɜːrv/ *v* **unnerved, unnerving** [T] to take away someone's courage or confidence: *The accident unnerved him and he hasn't driven since.* | *an unnerving experience* | *He seemed quite unnerved by the experience.*

un·ob·tru·sive /ˌʌnəbˈtruːsɪv/ *adj* not too noticeable and not getting in people's way; a word used to express approval: *The builders tried to be as unobtrusive as possible.* **–unobtrusively** *adv*

un·of·fi·cial /ˌʌnəˈfɪʃəl◄/ *adj* not arranged or said formally or officially: *The workers have organized an unofficial strike.* **–unofficially** *adv* : *They told her unofficially that she had got the job.*

un·or·tho·dox /ʌnˈɔːθədɒks ‖ ʌnˈɔːrθədɑːks/ *adj* not according to usual beliefs or methods: *It's an unorthodox medical treatment but it's definitely helping.*

un·pack /ʌnˈpæk/ *v* [I;T] to take things out of a case or box: *I'm just going to unpack my suitcase.*

un·par·al·leled /ʌnˈpærəleld/ *adj* so great that nothing is equal or better: *an unparalleled success*

un·pick /ʌnˈpɪk/ *v* [T] to remove the stitches from a piece of sewing

un·pleas·ant /ʌnˈplezənt/ *adj* **1** not pleasant or enjoyable: *an unpleasant smell* **2** unkind or rude and unfriendly: *My brother was very unpleasant to me when I was little.* **–unpleasantly** *adv* **–unpleasantness** *n* [U]

un·pre·ce·dent·ed /ʌnˈpresᵻdentᵻd/ *adj* never having happened or been done before: *Such winds were quite unprecedented and caused widespread damage.*

un·pre·ten·tious /ˌʌnprɪˈtenʃəs/ *adj* not trying to appear important or wealthy: *They are rich but have an unpretentious lifestyle.* **–unpretentiously** *adv* **–unpretentiousness** *n* [U]

un·prin·ci·pled /ʌnˈprɪnsᵻpəld/ *adj* done without caring about behaving honestly and morally: *He is totally unprincipled about money.*

un·prin·ta·ble /ʌnˈprɪntəbəl/ *adj* too rude or offensive to be repeated in writing (used of what someone says)

un·pro·fes·sion·al /ˌʌnprəˈfeʃənəl/ *adj* not behaving according to the standards of a particular profession **–unprofessionally** *adv*

un·pro·voked /ˌʌnprəˈvəʊkt◄/ *adj* not caused by anything that was done before: *an unprovoked attack*

un·qual·i·fied /ʌnˈkwɒlᵻfaɪd ‖ -ˈkwɑː-/ *adj* **1** not having suitable knowledge or qualifications (QUALIFICATION): *inexperienced and unqualified young people* | *She is unqualified to teach in Britain.*
☐ USEFUL PATTERNS be unqualified to do something; be unqualified for something **2** not limited: *unqualified praise*

un·ques·tio·na·ble /ʌnˈkwestʃənəbəl/ *adj* certain and not to be doubted **–unquestionably** *adv* : *She is unquestionably our best player.*

un·rav·el /ʌnˈrævəl/ *v* -**ll**- (also -**l**- *AmE*) **1** [I;T] to become or cause to become undone or untied **2** [T] to find out the truth about something when it is not simple

un·real /ˌʌnˈrɪəl◄/ *adj* seeming imaginary or unlike reality (used of an experience)

un·rea·so·na·ble /ʌnˈriːzənəbəl/ *adj* **1** beyond what is fair, acceptable, or sensible: *She claimed that her ex-husband's behaviour had been totally unreasonable.* **2** too great (used of an amount or cost) **–unreasonably** *adv* **–unreasonableness** *n* [U]

un·rea·son·ing /ʌnˈriːzənɪŋ/ *adj* not using the power of reason

un·re·lent·ing /ˌʌnrɪˈlentɪŋ◄/ *adj* continuous and often done very purposefully, without worrying about what other people feel: *a week of unrelenting activity* **–unrelentingly** *adv*

un·re·lieved /ˌʌnrɪˈliːvd◄/ *adj* continuous and never varied (used of something unpleasant): *unrelieved anxiety*

un·re·mit·ting /ˌʌnrɪˈmɪtɪŋ/ *adj* never stopping

un·re·quit·ed /ˌʌnrɪˈkwaɪtᵻd◄/ *adj fml* **unrequited** love love that is not given in return

un·re·served /ˌʌnrɪˈzɜːvd◄ ‖ -ɜːr-/ *adj* complete and without doubts or limits: *You have my unreserved admiration.* **–unreservedly** /-vᵻdli/ *adv*

un·rest /ʌnˈrest/ *n* [U] dissatisfaction and anger causing trouble in society: *Unemployment causes a lot of social unrest.*

un·re·strained /ˌʌnrɪˈstreɪnd◄/ *adj* not held back or controlled: *unrestrained anger*

un·roll /ʌnˈrəʊl/ *v* [I;T] to open from a rolled position: *They unrolled the carpet.*

un·ru·ly /ʌnˈruːli/ *adj* **unrulier, unruliest** uncontrollable and wild in behaviour: *unruly children* **–unruliness** *n* [U]

un·said /ʌnˈsed/ *adj* thought of but not spoken: *She left her criticisms unsaid.*

un·sa·vour·y /ʌnˈseɪvəri/ *adj* (**unsavory** *AmE*) unpleasant or morally unacceptable: *He's a rather unsavoury character.*

un·scathed /ʌnˈskeɪðd/ *adj* not harmed: *He escaped from the accident completely unscathed.*

un·screw /ʌnˈskruː/ *v* [T] **1** to remove something by undoing the screws that hold it in place **2** to undo a screw top by turning it: *I can't unscrew the top of this bottle.*

un·scru·pu·lous /ʌnˈskruːpjᵿləs/ *adj* not caring about honesty and fairness: *They use very unscrupulous business methods.* **–unscrupulously** *adv* **–unscrupulousness** *n* [U]

un·seat /ʌnˈsiːt/ *v* [T] to remove someone from a position of power

un·seem·ly /ʌnˈsiːmli/ *adj fml* not suitable in behaviour in a situation where politeness or seriousness is needed **–unseemliness** *n* [U]

un·set·tle /ʌnˈsetl/ *v* **unsettled, unsettling** [T] to make someone feel anxious, dissatisfied, or worried: *The sudden changes unsettled her.*

un·set·tled /ˌʌnˈsetld◄/ *adj* **1** changeable and uncertain (used of a situation): *The weather will be rather unsettled over the next few days.* **2** feeling anxious, worried, and unable to keep your mind on one thing **3** not decided or agreed: *Their argument is still unsettled.*

un·set·tling /ʌnˈsetlɪŋ/ *adj* making you feel anxious, dissatisfied, or worried: *All these changes are very unsettling.*

un·sha·kea·ble /ʌnˈʃeɪkəbəl/ adj (also **unshak-able**) firm in what you believe: *an unshakeable belief in God*

un·sight·ly /ʌnˈsaɪtli/ adj not pleasant to look at −**unsightliness** n [U]

un·skilled /ˌʌnˈskɪld◂/ adj **1** not trained for a particular type of job: *unskilled workers* **2** not needing special skill: *an unskilled job*

un·so·phis·ti·cat·ed /ˌʌnsəˈfɪstɪkeɪtɪd◂/ adj having simple likes and dislikes and not having much experience of the world and society

un·sound /ˌʌnˈsaʊnd◂/ adj **1** not healthy, strong, or in good condition: *Most of the building is in good condition but the roof is unsound.* **2** not having a firm base in reason and fact: *an unsound argument*

un·spea·ka·ble /ʌnˈspiːkəbəl/ adj very bad and totally undeserving of respect: *His behaviour has been unspeakable.* −**unspeakably** adv : *unspeakably cruel*

un·stuck /ʌnˈstʌk/ adj **come unstuck** to fail: *His plans came unstuck.*

un·stud·ied /ˌʌnˈstʌdid/ adj fml natural, and not the result of a lot of effort

un·swerv·ing /ʌnˈswɜːvɪŋ ‖ -ɜːr-/ adj firm in your aims or purpose −**unswervingly** adv

un·tan·gle /ˌʌnˈtæŋɡəl/ v **untangled, untangling** [T] to take out knots and straighten things that have been twisted together: *Can you untangle these wires?*

un·tapped /ˌʌnˈtæpt◂/ adj not yet being used: *The sea is an untapped source of power.*

un·ten·a·ble /ʌnˈtenəbəl/ adj impossible to defend (used of a belief or an argument)

un·thin·ka·ble /ʌnˈθɪŋkəbəl/ adj too terrible to imagine happening: *The prospect of a nuclear war is unthinkable.*

un·think·ing /ʌnˈθɪŋkɪŋ/ adj done or said without thinking about the effect −**unthinkingly** adv

un·ti·dy /ˌʌnˈtaɪdi/ adj **untidier, untidiest** not neat or well arranged: *His bedroom is always untidy.* −**untidiness** n [U]

un·tie /ʌnˈtaɪ/ v **untied, untying** [T] to undo something that is tied, such as a knot: *This knot is really tight. I can't undo it.*

until /ʌnˈtɪl, ən-/ prep, conj (also **till**) **1** up to a particular time: *Wait until tomorrow.* | *We'll stay here until the others arrive.* **2** **not until** only when it is a particular time: *I'm afraid your watch won't be ready until tomorrow.*

un·time·ly /ʌnˈtaɪmli/ adj fml **1** happening too soon: *Her death at the age of 29 was most untimely.* **2** not suitable for the occasion: *an untimely remark* −**untimeliness** n [U]

un·tir·ing /ʌnˈtaɪərɪŋ/ adj not stopping or showing tiredness in what you are doing −**untiringly** adv

un·told /ˌʌnˈtəʊld◂/ adj **1** too great to be counted or measured: *The war caused untold damage and suffering.* **2** not told or expressed: *The story remained untold for years.*

un·to·ward /ˌʌnˈtə ·wɔːd ‖ ˌʌnˈtɔːrd/ adj fml unexpected and unfortunate: *Nothing untoward happened on the journey.*

un·truth /ʌnˈtruːθ, ˈʌntruːθ/ n fml something that is not true

un·truth·ful /ʌnˈtruːθfəl/ adj dishonest and telling lies: *She made untruthful statements to the police.* −**untruthfully** adv

un·used[1] /ˌʌnˈjuːzd◂/ adj not used: *There was a lot of unused space in the house.*

un·used[2] /ʌnˈjuːst/ adj **unused to** having no experience of something: *He is unused to such hot weather.* | *unused to doing his own washing*

un·u·su·al /ʌnˈjuːʒuəl, -ʒəl/ adj **1** uncommon and not what is expected: *There's been an unusual amount of extra work this month.* | *It's unusual for us to go out much in the evenings.* **2** different and interesting: *What an unusual name!*

un·u·su·al·ly /ʌnˈjuːʒuəli, -ʒəli/ adv **1** in an unusual way **2** more than is common: *We had an unusually hot summer this year.*

un·veil /ˌʌnˈveɪl/ v [T] to remove a covering from a painting or sign on a building: *The Queen will unveil a plaque to open the new hospital.*

un·war·rant·ed /ʌnˈwɒrəntɪd ‖ -ˈwɔː-, -ˈwɑː-/ adj unwelcome and done without good reason: *This is a totally unwarranted use of public money.*

un·well /ʌnˈwel/ adj [never before a noun] ill

un·wiel·dy /ʌnˈwiːldi/ adj large, heavy, and awkward to move: *a large, unwieldy box*

un·wind /ʌnˈwaɪnd/ v **unwound** /-ˈwaʊnd/, **unwound 1** [I;T] to pull out or undo something wrapped round something else: *I unwound some cotton from the reel.* **2** [I] infml to do something restful after working hard: *She had a long bath to unwind after a hectic day at the office.*

un·wit·ting /ˌʌnˈwɪtɪŋ/ adj without knowing about or without intending to do something −**unwittingly** adv : *She made the mistake quite unwittingly.*

un·wound /ʌnˈwaʊnd/ the past tense and past participle of UNWIND

un·zip /ˌʌnˈzɪp/ v **-pp-** [T] to open something by undoing a long metal fastener called a ZIP

up[1] /ʌp/ adv, prep **1** adv, prep in or towards a higher place or position, away from the floor or the ground: *She lifted the box up onto the shelf.* | *The dog jumped up when it saw us.* | *He stood up.* | *I picked the letter up off the floor.* | *I wound the car window up.* | *He turned his collar up against the rain.* | *A bird was flying high up in the air.* | *He was jumping up and down.* | *He ran up the hill.* | *The water got up my nose.* | *Her office is up those stairs.* −see picture on page 540 **2** adv out of bed: *I got up quite early this morning.* | *Are you up yet?* **3** adv in or towards the North: *We're travelling up to Scotland this evening.* **4** adv showing increase: *Production has gone up this year.* | *Please turn the radio up.* **5** adv near or towards a person or thing: *He came up to me and asked my name.* | *We didn't get right up to the paintings to have a close look.* **6** adv completely finished, or so as to be completely finished: *Eat up your meat.* | *Time's up!* | *My three weeks were up and I had to go back to work.* **7** adv divided into pieces: *He tore up the newspaper.* | *They divided up the money.* **8** adv so as to be together: *Please add up these numbers.* | *Collect up the fallen apples.* **9** adv in operation (used of a computer): *Is the computer back up yet?* **10** **up the road, up the street** further along or at the far end of the road or street: *He ran up the road.* | *They live just up the road.* **11** **up a river** along a river against the direction of the current **12** **the road is up** = the road is being repaired **13** **not up to much** infml not very good: *The food's not up to much here.* **14** **up and about** no longer in bed and ill: *You'll soon be up and about again.* **15** **up and down** backwards and forwards along something: *running up and down the road* | *He was* *pacing up and down the room.* **16 ups and downs** a mixture of good and bad experiences: *We've had our ups and downs in life.* **17 up against something** having to face something: *I thought of all the problems we were up against.* **18 up against it** having a lot of problems or difficulties: *We were really up against it!* **19 up to** as much as or as many as: *He can earn up to £20,000 a year.* | *The room can hold up to 200 people.* **20 up to, up until** until: *I've never thought about it up to now.* | *She lived at home right up until she got married.* **21 up to something: a** *infml* busy doing something bad: *I think he's up to something.* | *What are they up to?* **b** *infml* good enough for something: *I'm not sure if she's really up to that job.* | *My German isn't up to translating his letter.* **22 up to someone** someone's choice or responsibility: *It's up to you to do it yourself.* | *It's up to her to decide whether or not to go on the course.* **23 what's up?** *infml* = what's the matter?

up² *adj* showing increase: *Inflation is up by 2%.*

up³ *v* **-pp-** *infml* **1** [T] to increase something: *Oil companies have simply upped the price of petrol.* **2 up and do something** to do something suddenly and unexpectedly: *She just upped and left!*

up-and-com·ing /ˌ·· '···◂/ *adj* likely to succeed in the future: *an up-and-coming actress*

up·braid /ˌʌpˈbreɪd/ *v* [T] *fml* to speak angrily to someone because they have done something wrong

up·bring·ing /ˈʌpbrɪŋɪŋ/ *n* [sing] the way someone is cared for and taught to behave by their parents: *They had a very strict upbringing.*

up·date /ˌʌpˈdeɪt/ *v* **updated, updating** [T] **1** to make something more modern or fashionable **2** to give the latest information –**update** /ˈʌpdeɪt/ *n* : *And now over to Peter Potter for an update on the travel situation in London this morning.*

up·end /ʌpˈend/ *v* [T] to make something stand on one end: *We'll have to upend the cupboard to get it through the door.*

up·grade /ˌʌpˈgreɪd/ *v* **upgraded, upgrading** [T] **1** to give someone or something a higher or more important position or rank **2** to improve the standard of something: *British Rail's decision to upgrade the track between London and Brighton*

up·heav·al /ʌpˈhiːvəl/ *n* [C;U] a great change causing worry and confusion: *Moving house will be a big upheaval.*

up·held /ʌpˈheld/ the past tense and past participle of UPHOLD

up·hill /ˌʌpˈhɪl◂/ *adj,adv* **1** going towards the top of a hill: *walking uphill* –opposite **downhill** **2** difficult and needing a lot of effort: *Teaching this class is an uphill struggle.*

up·hold /ˌʌpˈhəʊld/ *v* **upheld** /-ˈheld/, **upheld** [T] **1** to support and defend something: *We must uphold the right to free speech.* **2** to declare something to be right and correct: *The appeal judge upheld the court's decision.*

up·hol·ster /ʌpˈhəʊlstəʳ/ *v* [T] to cover furniture with soft material to make it comfortable: *an upholstered chair* –**upholsterer** *n*

up·hol·ster·y /ʌpˈhəʊlstəri/ *n* [U] material that makes a comfortable covering and filling for seats and other furniture

up·keep /ˈʌpkiːp/ *n* [U] the act or cost of keeping something repaired and in order: *We can no longer afford the upkeep of a large house.*

up·land /ˈʌplənd/ *adj* being the higher land in an area: *the upland areas of the country*

up·lifting /ˌʌpˈlɪftɪŋ/ *adj* encouraging you morally

upon /əˈpɒn ‖ əˈpɑːn/ *prep fml* on: *He lay upon the floor.* | *We acted upon your advice.*

up·per¹ /ˈʌpəʳ/ *adj* [always before a noun] **1** higher: *the upper part of the body* **2** higher than or above something else that is similar: *Passengers may smoke on the upper floor of the bus.* **3 the Upper House** the House of Lords in the British parliament **4 have/get the upper hand** to have or get control in a situation

up·per² *n* the top part of a shoe or boot

upper class /ˌ·· '·◂/ *n* [+sing/pl verb] **the upper class** or **the upper classes** a small social class of families with a lot of land and money and who often have noble titles: *The upper classes usually send their children to private school.* –**upper-class** *adj*

up·per·most /ˈʌpəməʊst ‖ -pər-/ *adv,adj* **1** facing up or in the highest position: *Insert the paper with the shiny side uppermost.* **2** being the most important thing: *Your happiness is uppermost in my mind.*

up·right¹ /ˈʌp-raɪt/ *adj* **1** standing or sitting with a very straight back: *She woke up and sat upright in bed.* **2** taller than some other kinds of the same thing: *an upright piano* | *Is it an upright freezer or a chest freezer?* **3** honest, fair, and responsible: *an upright citizen*

upright² *adv* standing in an upright position

up·ris·ing /ˈʌpˌraɪzɪŋ/ *n* an act of the ordinary people suddenly and violently opposing those in power

up·roar /ˈʌp-rɔːʳ/ *n* [sing;U] angry shouting and noise, often done as a protest

up·root /ˌʌpˈruːt/ *v* **1** [T] to pull a plant out of the earth by the roots **2 uproot yourself** to move away from your home and familiar surroundings: *The family uprooted themselves and went to live abroad.*

up·set¹ /ʌpˈset/ *v* **upset, upsetting** [T] **1** to make someone feel unhappy and anxious about something: *He didn't mean to upset you.* **2** to knock something over accidentally: *I upset a bottle of ink on the carpet.* **3** to cause something to change suddenly and become unsettled and confused: *Our plans were upset by the change in the weather.* | *The election results will upset the government's confidence.* **4** to cause a slight illness in the stomach: *That wine has upset my stomach.*

up·set² /ˌʌpˈset◂/ *adj* **1** feeling unhappy and anxious about something: *She was very upset about her parents' divorce.* **2** slightly ill: *I think it must have been that seafood that's given me this upset stomach.*

up·set³ /ˈʌpset/ *n* **1** [C;U] the act of causing sudden change and confusion **2** [C] an illness of your stomach that lasts only a short time: *a tummy upset*

up·set·ting /ʌpˈsetɪŋ/ *adj* making you feel unhappy and anxious: *If people are rude to you, it's very upsetting.*

up·shot /ˈʌpʃɒt ‖ -ʃɑːt/ *n* **the upshot** the result in the end: *The upshot of the negotiations was a new trade agreement.*

up·side down /ˌʌpsaɪd ˈdaʊn/ *adv* **1** in a position with the top facing down and the bottom facing up **2** untidy and in disorder: *Everything's upside down in this house.*

up·stage¹ /ˌʌpˈsteɪdʒ◂/ *adv* towards the back of the stage in the theatre

up·stage² /ʌpˈsteɪdʒ/ *v* **upstaged, upstaging** [T] to take attention away from someone else in order to get attention for yourself

up·stairs /ˌʌpˈsteəz◂ ‖ -ˈsteərz◂/ *adj,adv* situated on or going to an upper floor in a building: *She went*

upstairs to her bedroom. | *We could hear a party in the flat upstairs.* | *"Where is she?" "Upstairs."* | *The children watched from an upstairs window.*

up·start /ˈʌpstɑːt ‖ -ɑːrt/ *n* a person who has risen suddenly to a high position and takes advantage of their new power (a word used to express disapproval)

up·stream /ˌʌpˈstriːm◂/ *adv,adj* moving against the current of a river or stream: *We travelled upstream for a few miles.*

up·surge /ˈʌpsɜːdʒ ‖ -ɜːr-/ *n* a sudden large rise in something: *There has been an upsurge in the number of violent films on television recently.*

up·tight /ˈʌptaɪt, ʌpˈtaɪt/ *adj infml* angry and nervous about something without saying so: *He's been very uptight recently.*

up-to-date /ˌ· · ˈ·◂/ *adj* **1** modern and new: *Our school uses all the most up-to-date teaching methods.* **2** having all the latest information: *an up-to-date newspaper* **3 bring/keep someone up-to-date** to give someone all the latest information: *Peggy's letters keep me up-to-date with all the family's news.*

up·ward /ˈʌpwəd ‖ -ərd/ *adj* going up: *the upward movement of prices*

up·wards /ˈʌpwədz ‖ -ərdz/ (also **upward** *AmE*) **1** going, looking, or facing up: *The plane moved gently upwards.* | *I looked upwards towards his window.* **2 upwards of** more than: *There were upwards of 3000 people at the rally.*

u·ra·ni·um /juˈreɪniəm/ *n* [U] a heavy white metal that is a simple substance; uranium is RADIOACTIVE and is used to make NUCLEAR weapons

U·ra·nus /ˈjʊərənəs, juˈreɪnəs/ *n* the PLANET seventh in order from the sun

ur·ban /ˈɜːbən ‖ ˈɜːr-/ *adj* of a town or city: *Most people live in urban areas.*

ur·bane /ɜːˈbeɪn ‖ ɜːr-/ *adj* polite and confident in any social situation

ur·ban·i·za·tion /ˌɜːbənaɪˈzeɪʃən ‖ ˌɜːrbənə-/ *n* [U] the process of turning the country into town

urge¹ /ɜːdʒ ‖ ɜːrdʒ/ **urged, urging 1 urge someone to do something** to try very hard to persuade someone to do something: *He urged me to think again.* **2** [T] to suggest very strongly that something is important or necessary: *The committee urged the need for action to control pollution.* **3** [T + adv/prep] to encourage someone or to try to persuade them to move faster: *He urged me towards the check-in desk.*
urge sbdy ↔ on *phr v* [T] to encourage someone or to try to persuade them to do something: *Their supporters urged them on.*

urge² *n* **1** a strong desire **2 have/get the urge to do something** feel the desire to do something: *She suddenly got an urge to go back to New York.*

ur·gent /ˈɜːdʒənt ‖ ˈɜːr-/ *adj* very important and needing to be dealt with without delay: *It's not urgent. It can wait till tomorrow.* **–urgently** *adv* **–urgency** *n* [U]

u·ri·nal /ˈjʊərɪnəl, jʊˈraɪ-‖ ˈjʊərɬ-/ *n* a men's LAVATORY for urinating

u·ri·nate /ˈjʊərɬneɪt/ *v* **urinated, urinating** [I] to pass urine from your body

u·rine /ˈjʊərɬn/ *n* [U] liquid waste material passed from your body

urn /ɜːn ‖ ɜːrn/ *n* **1** a large decorative container in which the ashes of a dead person are kept **2** a large container in which large quantities of tea or coffee may be heated and kept

us /əs, s; *strong* ʌs/ *pron* [used as the object of a verb] the people who are speaking: *Did he see us?* | *That house is too small for us.* | *He bought us all a drink.* –see ME (USAGE)

US /ˌjuː ˈes◂/ *n* (also **USA** /ˌjuː es ˈeɪ/) an abbreviation for **United States of America:** *the US navy*

us·age /ˈjuːzɪdʒ, ˈjuːsɪdʒ/ *n* **1** [U] the way something is used or the degree to which something is used **2** [C;U] a generally accepted way of using a language or the way a particular word is used: *modern English usage*

use¹ /juːs/ *n* **1** [U] the act or fact of using something: *Do you approve of the use of guns by the police?* **2** [U] the ability or right to use something: *He lost the use of his legs after his accident.* | *My mother gave me the use of the car while she was away.* **3** [C;U] the purpose or reason for using something: *A food processor has several different uses.* **4** [U] the usefulness or advantage in something: *Is this book any use?* | *What's the use of worrying?* **5 in use** being used **6 of use** useful **7 make use of something** to use something in order to succeed in doing something: *I make use of my spare time by studying.*

use² /juːz/ *v* **used, using** [T] **1** to put something into action or employ it for a purpose: *The company now uses a computer to do all its accounts.* | *Do you know how to use a video camera?* | *We used the money to buy a car.* | *He never uses buses.* | *We are using the world's resources at an alarming rate.* | *The car's using too much oil.* **2** *derog* to treat someone unfairly for your own advantage without considering that person: *I realised he was just using me but I was still in love with him.* **–usable** *adj*
use sthg ↔ up *phr v* [T] to finish the supply of something completely: *Who's used up all the paper?*

used¹ /juːzd/ *adj* which has already been owned by someone else: *used cars*

used² /juːst/ *adj* **used to** accustomed to something: *to get used to English food* | *I'm not used to getting up so early.*
□ USEFUL PATTERNS be used to something; be used to doing something

used to /ˈjuːst tə, -tʊ/ *v negative short form* **usedn't to** [modal verb] used to show that something happened often, regularly, or always in the past: *I used to go swimming on Saturdays.* | *People used to think that the earth was flat.* | *I used not to like gardening, but I love it now.* | *Didn't she used to live in Germany?* | *Used you to work in a bank?* | *I don't play tennis much these days, but I used to.* | *I never used to eat cakes, but I eat a lot now.* –see Study Note on page 392

■ USAGE **1 Used to** has various negative forms. Some people think that *He* **used not to**…is the only correct form, but *He* **didn't use to**… and *He* **didn't used to**… are both very common. *He* **never used to**… is also frequently used. **2** In ordinary conversation the most natural question forms are **Did(n't) he use to**…?/**Did(n't) he used to**…? but note that the more formal form **Used(n't) he to**… also exists.

use·ful /ˈjuːsfəl/ *adj* **1** helpful and having a practical purpose: *This guide to London is a really useful book.* | *Jane gave me some useful advice.* **2** helpful: *She's a useful person to have around.* **–usefulness** [U]

use·less /ˈjuːsləs/ *adj* not of any use: *This knife is so blunt it's useless!* **–uselessly** *adv* **–uselessness** *n* [U]

us·er /ˈjuːzəʳ/ *n* a person or thing that uses something, especially a product or service: *Will users please note that from next week the photocopier will* *be switched off at 5.30 pm.* | *telephone users* | *users* **of** *large quantities of water*

us·er-friend·ly /ˌ·· ˈ··◂/ *adj* easy to understand and use (used especially of computers)

ush·er¹ /ˈʌʃəʳ/ *n* a person who shows people to their seats at a wedding, or in a cinema or theatre

usher² *v* [T + adv/prep] *fml* to bring people to a place by showing them the way: *She ushered the guests into the room.*

usher sthg ↔ **in** *phr v* to be the cause of or start of something new and important: *The bombing of Hiroshima ushered in the nuclear age.*

ush·er·ette /ˌʌʃəˈret/ *n* a woman who shows people to their seats in a cinema

USSR /ˌjuː es es ˈɑːʳ/ an abbreviation for **Union of Soviet Socialist Republics**, the Soviet Union

u·su·al /ˈjuːʒuəl, ˈjuːʒəl/ *adj* **1** as happens, or is done most often, or as is expected: *We had lunch at our usual table by the window.* **2 as usual** as is common or has happened many times before: *As usual, Marc was the last to arrive.*

u·su·al·ly /ˈjuːʒuəli, ˈjuːʒəli/ *adv* generally, or as is expected: *I'm not usually so late.* | *The baby usually wakes up at seven.*

u·surp /juːˈzɜːp ‖ -ɜːrp/ *v* [T] *fml* to take power or a position from someone without having the right to do so

u·su·ry /ˈjuːʒəri/ *n* [U] *old fash* the practice of lending money at a very high rate of interest

u·ten·sil /juːˈtensəl/ *n* a tool or object used in the kitchen: *kitchen utensils*

u·te·rus /ˈjuːtərəs/ *n* **uteruses** or **uteri** /-raɪ/ *tech* a woman's WOMB

u·til·i·ty /juːˈtɪlɨti/ *n* **utilities 1** [U] usefulness **2** [C] any useful service for the public, such as the bus service, water supply, or electricity supply

u·til·ize /ˈjuːtɨlaɪz/ *v* **utilized, utilizing** (also **utilise** *BrE*) [T] *fml* to use something in a practical way: *Solar panels utilize energy from the sun.* –**utilization** /ˌjuːtɨlaɪˈzeɪʃən ‖ -lə-/ *n* [U]

ut·most /ˈʌtməʊst/ *adj* [always before a noun] **1** of the greatest degree: *with her utmost strength* **2 do your utmost** to make the greatest possible effort: *They did their utmost to save their marriage.*

u·to·pi·a /juːˈtəʊpiə/ *n* (also **Utopia**) an imaginary perfect society –**utopian**÷ *adj*

ut·ter¹ /ˈʌtəʳ/ *adj* [always before a noun] complete and total: *It was an utter waste of time.* | *He's an utter fool.* –**utterly** *adv*

utter² *v* [T] to make sounds or speak words: *She didn't utter a word all evening.*

ut·ter·ance /ˈʌtərəns/ *n fml* **1** [C;U] the act of speaking **2** [C] something that a person says

U-turn /ˈjuː tɜːn ‖ -tɜːrn/ *n* **1** a turning movement in a car, taking you back in the direction you came from **2** a complete change in plans or actions: *a U-turn in government policy*

V,v

V, v /viː/ **V's, v's** or **Vs, vs** the 22nd letter of the English alphabet

v a written abbreviation for VERB

V[1] /viː/ n a thing shaped like the letter V: *She cut the material out in a V.*

V[2] a written abbreviation for VOLT

v. /viː/ see VERSUS

va·can·cy /'veɪkənsi/ n **vacancies** [C] **1** a room in a hotel or guest house that is not being used **2** an unfilled job or position: *We have a vacancy for a driver at the moment.*

va·cant /'veɪkənt/ adj **1** not being used or lived in (used of a seat, room, house, or space): *We looked all over town for a vacant room.* | *The toilet is vacant now.* **2** not filled at the moment (used of a job): *The job was advertised in the "Situations Vacant" section of the newspaper.* **3** showing that you are not interested in something or are not thinking about anything: *There was a vacant expression on his face.* –**vacantly** adv : *She stared vacantly into space.*

va·cate /və'keɪt, veɪ- ‖ 'veɪ-/ v **vacated, vacating** [T] to stop using or living in a place: *Guests must vacate their rooms by 11 am.*

va·ca·tion /və'keɪʃən ‖ veɪ-/ n **1** the usual American word for HOLIDAY: *We'll take our vacation in July.* **2** on vacation *AmE* on holiday **3** a period of holiday when universities are closed: *the summer vacation* –**vacation** v *AmE* [I] : *My parents are vacationing in Europe.*

vac·cin·ate /'væksɪneɪt/ v **vaccinated, vaccinating** [T] to put vaccine into someone's body as a protection against a disease –**vaccination** /ˌvæksɪ'neɪʃən/ n [C;U] : *He's had his vaccination against typhoid.*

vac·cine /'væksiːn ‖ væk'siːn/ n [C;U] a substance containing a form of a disease which is used to protect people against that disease

vac·il·late /'væsɪleɪt/ v **vacillated, vacillating** [I] to be continually changing from one opinion or feeling to another: *Charles vacillated between hope and fear.* –**vacillation** /ˌvæsɪ'leɪʃən/ n [C;U]

vac·u·ous /'vækjuəs/ adj *fml* showing no sign of ideas or thought: *a totally vacuous remark*

vac·u·um[1] /'vækjuəm, -kjum/ n **1** a space that has no air or gas in it **2** a feeling of emptiness and loss: *Her death left a vacuum in his life.*

vacuum[2] v *infml* [I;T] to clean with a vacuum cleaner: *I've been vacuuming all morning.* | *I've vacuumed the stairs.*

vacuum clean·er /'··· ˌ··/ n a machine which cleans the floor by sucking up dirt in a flow of air

vacuum flask /'··· ·/ n see THERMOS FLASK

vag·a·bond /'vægəbɒnd ‖ -bɑːnd/ n *old fash* a person who lives a wandering life and is thought to be lazy or worthless

va·ga·ries /'veɪgəriz/ n [pl] unusual or unexpected changes in a situation: *the vagaries of love*

va·gi·na /və'dʒaɪnə/ n the passage which leads from the outer sex organs of women or female animals, to the organ in which young are formed –**vaginal** adj

va·grant /'veɪgrənt/ n a person who has no home or work and goes from place to place –**vagrancy** n [U]

vague /veɪg/ adj **1** not clear in shape or easy to see: *I could see the vague shape of another car through*

the fog. **2** not clearly expressed or explained: *Her directions to the house were rather vague and we got lost.* **3** not clear or certain in your mind: *Our plans are still a bit vague.* | *I've got a vague idea who she is.* **4** not behaving or expressing yourself clearly: *John is a very dreamy, vague sort of person.* –**vaguely** adv –**vagueness** n [U]

vain /veɪn/ adj **1** full of pride and admiration for yourself, your appearance, and your abilities **2** without a successful result: *The teacher made a vain attempt to get the children to obey.* **3** in vain without success: *We tried in vain to make him change his mind.* –**vainly** adv

val·ance /'væləns/ n a pretty cover that hangs from the frame of a bed to the floor

vale /veɪl/ n *lit* a broad low valley: *the Vale of Evesham*

val·en·tine /'væləntaɪn/ n a greeting card sent to someone you love on **Saint Valentine's Day** (February 14th)

val·et /'vælɪt, 'væleɪ/ n **1** a male servant, who looks after a man's clothes, cooks his meals, etc. **2** someone who cleans and presses clothes in a hotel

val·i·ant /'væliənt/ adj *lit* very brave in a dangerous situation like a war –**valiantly** adv

val·id /'vælɪd/ adj **1** based on strong reasons: *I hope you have a valid excuse for arriving late at work.* **2** that can be legally used at a certain time: *Your train ticket is valid for three months,* –opposite **invalid** **3** *law* written or done in a proper way so that a court of law would agree with it –**validity** /və'lɪdɪti/ n : *The judge did not question the validity of the statement.*

val·i·date /'vælɪdeɪt/ v **validated, validating** *fml* [T] to make legal or prove to be correct: *In order to validate the agreement between yourself and your employer, you must both sign it.* –**validation** /ˌvælɪ'deɪʃən/ n [C;U]

Val·i·um /'væliəm/ n *tdmk* [U] a drug for making people feel calmer or less anxious

val·ley /'væli/ n the land lying between two lines of hills or mountains, often with a river running through it

val·our /'vælər/ n *lit* (valor *AmE*) [U] great bravery, especially in war

val·u·a·ble /'væljuəbəl, -jʊbəl ‖ 'væljʊbəl/ adj **1** worth a lot of money: *a valuable diamond* **2** very useful: *Your help has been very valuable.*

■ USAGE Remember that **invaluable** is NOT the opposite of **valuable**! The word **invaluable** is NOT used to talk about prices or money. It means "extremely useful": *Their advice proved invaluable to us on our journey.* | *Your assistance has been invaluable.* If you want to describe things which have no value, you can use the word **worthless**: *The metal looked like gold, but in fact it was completely worthless.*

val·u·a·bles /'væljuəbəlz, -jʊbəlz ‖ -jʊ-/ n [pl] things that you own, such as jewellery, that are worth a lot of money: *You should put your valuables in the bank.*

val·u·a·tion /ˌvæljʊ'eɪʃən/ n [C;U] a calculation of how much money something is worth: *We asked for a valuation of the house.*

val·ue[1] /'vælju/ n **1** [U] the usefulness or importance of something: *My grandmother's advice was* *of great value to me.* | *Their research is interesting but has little practical value.* **2** [C;U] The amount of money that something is worth if it is sold or exchanged: *The value of the pound has fallen recently.* | *The insurance company put a value of $1,000 on the picture.* | *The thieves took some clothes and books, but nothing of great value.* **3** [U] worth compared with the amount paid: *We offer the best value in town – only £6.50 for a three course meal.* | *The large packet of soap powder is better value than two small ones.* **4 value for money** worth the amount paid: *A weekly ticket is value for money because you can use it as often as you like.* **–valueless** *adj*

value² *v* **valued, valuing** [T] **1** to calculate how much money something is worth: *The piano is valued at £4,000.* **2** to consider something to be very important: *I've always valued your friendship very highly.*

value-ad·ded tax /ˌ··· ·· ·-/ *n* see VAT

val·u·er /ˈvæljuəʳ/ *n* a person whose work is to decide how much money things are worth

val·ues /ˈvæljuːz/ *n* [pl] principles and beliefs about what is important in life and how people should behave: *Moral values have changed a lot in the last 50 years.*

valve /vælv/ *n* **1** part of a pipe or tube which opens and shuts in order to control the flow of liquid, air, or gas passing through it: *You put air into a bicycle tyre through the valve.* **2** a closed glass tube with no air in it, used for controlling a flow of electricity, as formerly in radio or television

vam·pire /ˈvæmpaɪəʳ/ *n* an evil spirit which is believed to live in a dead body and suck people's blood while they are asleep

van /væn/ *n* **1** a road vehicle smaller than a LORRY which is used for carrying goods or people: *a delivery van* | *a police van* | *a van driver* –see picture on page 49 **2** a covered railway carriage for goods and sometimes people: *Put your bicycle in the guard's van.*

van·dal /ˈvændl/ *n* a person who intentionally damages or destroys public property: *All the seat-covers on the train were ripped by vandals.*

van·dal·is·m /ˈvændəl-ɪzəm/ *n* [U] intentional and pointless damage and destruction of public property

van·dal·ize /ˈvændəl-aɪz/ *v* **vandalized, vandalizing** (also **vandalise** *BrE*) [T] to damage or destroy a piece of public property intentionally: *We can't use any of the public telephones round here; they've all been vandalized.*

vane /veɪn/ *n* a flat blade on an instrument that makes it possible to use the force of wind or water to drive certain machines: *the vanes of a propeller*

van·guard /ˈvænɡɑːd ‖ -ɑːrd/ *n* **1** [+sing/pl verb] the soldiers marching at the front of an army **2 in the vanguard of** in the leading position in any course of development: *Scientists are in the vanguard of technological development.*

va·nil·la /vəˈnɪlə/ *n* [U] a substance obtained from a tropical plant, used to give its special taste to certain sweet foods: *vanilla ice cream*

van·ish /ˈvænɪʃ/ *v* [I] **1** to disappear suddenly: *With a wave of his hand, the magician made the rabbit vanish.* **2** to cease to exist: *Many types of animal have now vanished from the earth.* **3 vanish into thin air** to disappear suddenly and with no explanation

van·i·ty /ˈvænɪti/ *n* [U] being extremely proud of yourself, your appearance, and your abilities

van·quish /ˈvæŋkwɪʃ/ *v lit* [T] to defeat someone completely

van·tage point /ˈvɑːntɪdʒ ˌpɔɪnt ‖ ˈvæn-/ *n* a good position from which to see something

va·por·ize /ˈveɪpəraɪz/ *v* **vaporized, vaporizing** (also **vaporise** *BrE*) [I;T] to change into vapour: *Water vaporizes when boiled.*

va·pour /ˈveɪpəʳ/ *n* (**vapor** *AmE*) **1** [C;U] a liquid in the form of a gas such as mist or steam: *A cloud is a mass of vapour in the sky.* **2** [U] *tech* the gas to which a liquid or solid can be changed by the action of heat: *water vapour*

var·i·a·ble¹ /ˈveəriəbəl/ *adj* **1** likely to change at any time: *The winds today will be light and variable.* **2** that can be changed intentionally: *The speed of the toy boat is variable.* **–variability** /ˌveəriəˈbɪlɪti/ *n* [U]

variable² *n fml* something which can vary in quantity or size: *The time of the journey depends on a number of variables, such as the amount of traffic on the road.*

var·i·ance /ˈveəriəns/ *n* **at variance with** in opposition to and not in agreement with: *What he did was at variance with company policy.*

var·i·ant¹ /ˈveəriənt/ *adj* [always before a noun] different and varying: *There are many variant spellings in English.*

variant² *n* a different form, for example of a word or phrase

var·i·a·tion /ˌveəriˈeɪʃən/ *n* [C;U] a change in degree, amount, or quantity: *There are great variations in house prices in different parts of the country.* | *This story is just a variation on his last book.*

var·i·cose veins /ˌværɪkəʊs ˈveɪnz/ *n* a medical condition in which the blood vessels of the leg have become very swollen

var·ied /ˈveərid/ *adj* **1** of different kinds: *The students come from varied backgrounds.* | *The restaurant has a very varied menu.* **2** not staying the same and having changing qualities: *She has led an interesting and varied life.*

var·ie·gat·ed /ˈveərɪɡeɪtɪd/ *adj* marked irregularly in spots, lines, or areas of different colours (used of a flower or leaf)

va·ri·e·ty /vəˈraɪəti/ *n* **varieties 1** [U] difference in quality, type, or character: *You need a lot of variety in your diet.* **2 a variety of** a group containing different sorts of the same thing: *These T-shirts are available in a wide variety of colours.* **3** [C] a type which is different from others in the same group: *different varieties of bananas* **4** [U] a theatre or television show including singing, dancing, jokes, and acts of skill: *a variety show*

var·i·ous /ˈveəriəs/ *adj* **1** different from each other: *There are various ways of getting there but we always go by train.* **2** [always before a noun] several or a number of: *Various people said they had seen the accident.* **–variously** *adv*

var·nish¹ /ˈvɑːnɪʃ ‖ ˈvɑːr-/ *n* [C;U] a liquid which gives wood a hard shiny surface

varnish² *v* [T] to cover with a liquid which gives a hard shiny surface: *You should varnish the shelves to protect the wood.*

var·y /ˈveəri/ *v* **varied, varying** [I;T] to be, make, or become different: *Children need a varied, balanced diet.* | *The quality of her work never varies.*

vase /vɑːz ‖ veɪs, veɪz/ *n* a glass or clay container, used to put flowers in –see picture on page 148

va·sec·to·my /vəˈsektəmi/ n **vasectomies** [C;U] an operation for removing a man's ability to become a father by cutting the small tube that carries his SPERM

vast /vɑːst ‖ væst/ adj very large and wide or great in size or amount: *The vast plains stretch for 600 miles.*

vast·ly /ˈvɑːstli ‖ ˈvæstli/ adv very much: *That restaurant is vastly overpriced!*

vat /væt/ n a very large barrel or container for holding liquids

VAT /ˌviː eɪ ˈtiː, væt/ n [U] a tax in Britain and some other European countries added to the price of an article; an abbreviation for VALUE-ADDED TAX

vault[1] /vɔːlt/ n **1** a roof formed by a number of arches **2** (also **vaults**) an underground room in which the bodies of the dead are placed, or in which valuable things are stored **3** a jump made by vaulting

vault[2] v [I+adv/prep;T] to jump over something using your hands or a pole to gain more height: *He vaulted over the gate and ran away.*

VCR /ˌviː siː ˈɑːr/ an American word for a VIDEO recorder

VDU /ˌviː diː ˈjuː/ n an apparatus with a SCREEN which shows information from a computer or WORD PROCESSOR; an abbreviation for **visual display unit** –see picture on page 539

've /v, əv/ short for HAVE: *We've finished.*

veal /viːl/ n [U] meat from a very young cow –see MEAT (USAGE)

veer /vɪər/ v [I+adv/prep] to turn or change direction: *The car was out of control and suddenly veered across the road.*

vege·ta·ble /ˈvedʒtəbəl/ n a plant that is grown for food to be eaten in the main part of a meal, rather than with sweet things: *meat and vegetables | green vegetables such as cabbage and spinach*

veg·e·tar·i·an /ˌvedʒəˈteəriən/ n a person who does not eat meat or fish –**vegetarian** adj : *a vegetarian restaurant* –**vegetarianism** n [U]

veg·e·tate /ˈvedʒəteɪt/ v **vegetated, vegetating** [I] to live life without any interests or social activity

veg·e·ta·tion /ˌvedʒəˈteɪʃən/ n [U] plants in general: *the colourful vegetation of the tropical rainforest*

ve·he·ment /ˈviːəmənt/ adj using strong and violent words: *She made a vehement attack on the government's policies.* –**vehemently** adv –**vehemence** n [U]

ve·hi·cle /ˈviːɪkəl/ n **1** something such as a bicycle, car, or bus, which moves or carries people and goods **2** fml something which can be used to send or carry something else: *Television has become an important vehicle for spreading political ideas.*

ve·hic·u·lar /viːˈhɪkjʊlər/ adj fml concerning vehicles on roads: *vehicular traffic*

veil /veɪl/ n **1** a covering of fine cloth or net for the face, worn by women, sometimes for religious reasons **2** a **veil of** something which covers or hides something else: *a veil of mist | There was a veil of secrecy over the army's activities.*

veiled /veɪld/ adj **1** wearing a fine cloth or net over the face **2** hidden and not expressed directly: *veiled threats*

vein /veɪn/ n **1** a tube that carries blood from any part of your body to your heart **2** a thin line which runs in a pattern through leaves and the wings of certain insects **3** a crack in rock which is filled with useful metal: *a vein of silver* **4** **in the same vein** with the same general meaning or style: *The newspaper has had many letters in the same vein complaining about the article.*

TRANSPORT

Exercise 1
Which of these things can you see on a motorway?

bicycle	speedboat	crossroads
roundabout	lorry	motorbike
pelican crossing	bus stop	T – junction
zebra crossing	coach	level crossing

Exercise 2
What sort of power drives these vehicles? Put a tick in the correct boxes. Remember that some vehicles may have two or more different types of power.

	muscle power	wind power	petrol engine	diesel engine	jet engine	turbine engine
aeroplane						
bus						
car						
dinghy						
helicopter						
hovercraft						
liner						
lorry						
rowing boat						
speedboat						
train						
yacht						

lift

kneel

squat

crouch

crawl

throw

hold

bend

lean

stretch

sit

pull

push

catch

drag

fall

carry

run

punch

hit

skip

kick

walk

leap

drop

pick up

jog

march

jump

put down

hop

tiptoe

clim

ve·loc·i·ty /vɪˈlɒsɪti ‖ vɪˈlɑː-/ *n* **velocities** *tech* [C;U] speed in a certain direction, or rate of movement

ve·lour /vəˈluəʳ/ *n* [U] a heavy cloth with a soft surface

vel·vet /ˈvelvɪt/ *n* [U] a finely-woven cloth with a soft furry surface

vel·vet·y /ˈvelvɪti/ *adj* very soft and like velvet

ve·nal /ˈviːnl/ *adj fml* **1** acting unfairly or wrongly, in return for money or other rewards **2** done, not for honest reasons, but for money

ven·det·ta /venˈdetə/ *n* a long-lasting and violent argument between families

ven·ding ma·chine /ˈvendɪŋ məˌʃiːn/ *n* a machine which you can buy drinks or chocolate from by putting money into it

vend·or /ˈvendəʳ/ *n* **1** someone who sells things from a cart or small vehicle: *a street vendor* **2** *law* the seller of a house or land

ve·neer /vɪˈnɪəʳ/ *n* **1** [C;U] a thin covering of good quality wood put on the surface of a cheaper material **2** [sing] an outer appearance which hides something unpleasant: *a veneer of good manners*

ven·e·ra·ble /ˈvenərəbəl/ *adj* considered to deserve great respect or honour (used of someone or something old)

ven·e·rate /ˈvenəreɪt/ *v* **venerated, venerating** *fml* [T] to treat with great respect and honour –**veneration** /ˌvenəˈreɪʃən/ *n* [U]

ven·geance /ˈvendʒəns/ *n* [U] **1** punishment given to someone for harm they have done to you or your family: *The bombing was an act of vengeance by terrorists.* **2 with a vengeance** *infml* to a greater degree than expected or usual: *The wind's blowing with a vengeance today.*

venge·ful /ˈvendʒfəl/ *adj lit* showing a strong desire to punish someone for the harm they have done to you

ven·i·son /ˈvenɪzən, -sən/ *n* [U] meat from a deer –see MEAT (USAGE)

ven·om /ˈvenəm/ *n* [U] **1** liquid poison which certain snakes, insects, and other creatures use when they bite or sting you **2** full of hatred and bad feeling: *He spoke about his ex-boss with venom and anger.* –**venomous** *adj : a venomous insult*

vent¹ /vent/ *v* [T] to express strong feelings by directing them at someone or something: *Don't vent your anger on the children, it's not their fault!*

vent² *n* **1** a hole, opening, or pipe by which gases, smoke, air, or liquid can enter or escape from an enclosed space **2** a long narrow straight opening at the bottom of a coat, at the sides or back **3 give vent to** to express something freely: *He gave vent to his frustration by kicking the door.*

ven·ti·late /ˈventɪleɪt ‖ -tl-eɪt/ *v* **ventilated, ventilating** [T] to allow fresh air into a room or building: *The bar was smoky and badly ventilated.*

ven·ti·la·tion /ˌventɪˈleɪʃən ‖ -tl-eɪ-/ *n* [U] a way of making the air fresh in a room or building: *There was no ventilation in the office except for a small high window.*

ven·ti·la·tor /ˈventɪleɪtəʳ ‖ -tl-eɪ-/ *n* **1** a machine for ventilating a room or building **2** a machine which helps someone to breathe

ven·tril·o·quis·m /venˈtrɪləkwɪzəm/ *n* [U] the art of speaking without moving your lips so that the sound seems to come from somewhere else –**ventriloquist** *n*

ven·ture¹ /ˈventʃəʳ/ *v* **ventured, venturing 1** [I + adv/prep] to go somewhere, especially if it could be dangerous: *He hasn't ventured out of the house since*

VERBS OF MOVEMENT

Complete this passage with verbs from the illustration.

Some children are helping old Mrs Grainger in her garden. She is telling them what to do.

"Tony and Martin, ¹run down to the garden shed and get the ladder.
²C _ _ _ _ it to the apple tree. Then I'll come and tell you what to do. Don't ³w _ _ _ on the flowerbeds, ⁴j _ _ _ over them!

Sarah and Jane, there are some carrots and a lot of weeds growing here. I want you to ⁵p _ _ _ up the weeds and put them in the wheelbarrow. It's not a difficult job but I can't ⁶b _ _ _ at my age. Don't get your legs dirty, ⁷k_ _ _ _ on this board!

Mary and Colin, I want you to ⁸c _ _ _ _ under those bushes and ⁹p _ _ _ up those bits of paper.

Carol and John, can you see that old tree on the ground near the pond? Can

you ¹⁰d _ _ _ it down to the end of the garden? Don't try to ¹¹l _ _ _ it, it's very heavy. Ah, Elaine, you're a nice tall girl. You see that beautiful peach on the tree by the wall? Can you ¹²s _ _ _ _ _ _ up and get it for me?

Now, Tony and Martin, you've got the ladder, good. Now Tony, ¹³l _ _ _ the ladder against the tree. Good. Martin, you must ¹⁴h _ _ _ the ladder. Make sure it doesn't move. Tony, can you ¹⁵c _ _ _ _ the ladder and get those apples? Be careful! Don't ¹⁶f _ _ _ down! That's right, Tony. Can you get that big red apple? Good. Now ¹⁷t _ _ _ _ it to me. I'll
¹⁸c _ _ _ _ it. Be careful, don't ¹⁹d _ _ _ it! Good. Now, I'm going to ²⁰s _ _ in this nice chair and enjoy the sun."

Half an hour later, old Mrs Grainger was asleep in her chair. "We mustn't wake her up," said Elaine. "Let's ²¹t _ _ _ _ _ out of the garden and let her sleep."

his accident. **2** [T] to dare to say something you are not sure about: *If I may venture an opinion, I think we should say no and wait for a better offer.* **3 venture into something** to risk doing something that may be dangerous: *I would never venture into business without plenty of money.*

venture² *n* something you decide to do where there is a risk of failure as well as a chance of success

ven·ue /ˈvenjuː/ *n* a place where something is arranged to happen: *The venue for the talks has not been announced for security reasons.*

Ve·nus /ˈviːnəs/ *n* the PLANET second in order from the sun, and next to the earth

ve·ran·da /vəˈrændə/ *n* (also **verandah**) an open area with a floor and a roof on the outside of a house: *When the evenings were warm we sat outside on the verandah.*

verb /vɜːb ‖ vɜːrb/ *n* a word or phrase that is used to describe an action, experience, or state: In the sentences *"She wrote a letter", "He feels hungry"* and *"I get up at seven o'clock", "wrote", "feels"* and *"get up"* are verbs. –see Study Note on page 687

verb·al /ˈvɜːbəl ‖ ˈvɜːr-/ *adj* **1** spoken, not written: *a verbal agreement* **2** connected with words and their use

verb·al·ize /ˈvɜːbəlaɪz ‖ ˈvɜːr-/ *v* **verbalized, verbalizing** *fml* (also **verbalise** *BrE*) [I;T] to express something in words

verb·al·ly /ˈvɜːbəli ‖ ˈvɜːr-/ *adv* in spoken words and not in writing

verbal noun /ˌ·· ˈ·/ *n* a noun which comes from a verb, describes an action or experience, and ends in "-ing"; in the sentence *"The building of the bridge was slow work", "building"* is a verbal noun

ver·ba·tim /vɜːˈbeɪtɪm ‖ vɜːr-/ *adj, adv* repeating the actual words exactly: *She could remember his words verbatim even though it was so long ago.*

ver·bi·age /ˈvɜːbi·ɪdʒ ‖ ˈvɜːr-/ *n* [U] too many unnecessary words in speech or writing

ver·bose /vɜːˈbəʊs ‖ vɜːr-/ *adj fml* using or containing too many words: *The speech was verbose and boring.*

ver·dant /ˈvɜːdənt ‖ ˈvɜːr-/ *adj lit* covered with fresh green plants or grass

ver·dict /ˈvɜːdɪkt ‖ ˈvɜːr-/ *n* **1** the official decision made in a court of law, at the end of a trial: *Members of the jury, what is your verdict? Guilty, or not guilty?* **2** *infml* a statement giving someone's opinion or judgment of something: *What's your verdict on the film?*

verge¹ /vɜːdʒ ‖ vɜːrdʒ/ *n* **1** the edge or border of a road or path, usually covered with grass **2 on the verge of** very near to: *The two countries are on the verge of war.* | *She was very upset and on the verge of crying.*

verge² *v* **verged, verging, verge on something** to be similar to a particular quality: *His strange behaviour sometimes verges on madness.*

ver·i·fy /ˈverɪfaɪ/ *v* [T; +that] to make sure that a fact or statement is true: *The police can now verify people's personal details on their computer files.* | *We have to verify that you are the true owner of the house before lending you any money.* –**verifiable** *adj* –**verification** /ˌverɪfɪˈkeɪʃən/ *n* [U]

ver·i·si·mil·i·tude /ˌverɪsɪˈmɪlɪtjuːd ‖ -tʊrd/ *n fml* [U] the quality of seeming to be true and real

ver·i·ta·ble /ˈverɪtəbəl/ *adj* [always before a noun] a word used to make a description more forceful: *The meal was a veritable feast.*

ver·mil·ion /vəˈmɪljən ‖ vər-/ *adj, n* [U] a bright reddish-orange colour

ver·min /ˈvɜːmɪn ‖ ˈvɜːr-/ *n* [pl] **1** small animals or birds that cause damage and are difficult to control: *To a farmer foxes are vermin because they steal and kill chickens.* **2** unpleasant biting insects that live on the body of humans or animals

ver·mouth /ˈvɜːməθ ‖ vərˈmuːθ/ *n* [U] a drink made from wine with the taste of certain plants added to it

ver·nac·u·lar /vəˈnækjŭləʳ ‖ vər-/ *n* the native, spoken language of a country or area: *His poetry is written in the vernacular of the south.*

ver·ru·ca /vəˈruːkə/ *n* a small hard growth on the bottom of a person's foot

ver·sa·tile /ˈvɜːsətaɪl ‖ ˈvɜːrsətl/ *adj* **1** having many different skills and being able to change quickly from one kind of activity to another: *He's a very versatile actor.* **2** having many different uses: *Nylon is a versatile material.* –**versatility** /ˌvɜːsəˈtɪlĭti ‖ ˌvɜːr-/ *n* [U]

verse /vɜːs ‖ vɜːrs/ *n* **1** [U] written language arranged in lines, with a pattern of repeated beats as in music, and often with words of matching sound at the end of some lines: *a book of comic verse* **2** [C] a set of lines which forms one part of a poem or song: *The song has four verses.* **3** [C] a group of sentences that together form one numbered division of one of the books of the BIBLE

versed /vɜːst ‖ vɜːrst/ *adj* **well versed in** having a thorough knowledge of or skill in a subject

ver·sion /ˈvɜːʃən ‖ ˈvɜːrʒən/ *n* **1** one person's account of an event: *The two newspapers gave different versions of what happened.* **2** a slightly different form, copy, or style of something: *Monet painted many different versions of the flowers in his garden.* **3** a form of written or musical work which is different in some way from the original: *a film version of the book*

ver·sus /ˈvɜːsəs ‖ ˈvɜːr-/ *prep* (also **v., vs.**) in opposition to or against, especially in a game of sport: *The England versus Australia cricket match is starting today.*

ver·te·bra /ˈvɜːtɪbrə ‖ ˈvɜːr-/ *n* **vertebrae** /-briː, -breɪ/ one of the small hollow bones down the centre of your back, which form your SPINE

ver·te·brate /ˈvɜːtɪbrŏt, -breɪt ‖ ˈvɜːr-/ *adj, n tech* an animal, bird, or fish which has a backbone

ver·ti·cal /ˈvɜːtɪkəl ‖ ˈvɜːr-/ *adj* pointing up and down in a straight line and forming an angle of 90 degrees with a flat surface like the ground: *vertical lines* –**vertically** /-kli/ *adv*

ver·ti·go /ˈvɜːtɪɡəʊ ‖ ˈvɜːr-/ *n* [U] a feeling of sickness caused by looking down from a great height

verve /vɜːv ‖ vɜːrv/ *n* [U] a strong feeling of enjoyment

very¹ /ˈveri/ *adv* **1** to a great degree: *It's very warm today.* | *He's not very old.* | *It's a very exciting book.* | *The traffic was moving very slowly.* | *Thank you very much.* **2** used with SUPERLATIVE adjectives or with words like "same", "own", "first", and "last" to make them stronger: *It's the very best film I've seen this year.* | *He was the very last to finish.* | *I'd love to have my very own boat.* **3 very much so** a phrase you use to agree with someone strongly: *"The government seems to be in some difficulty now." "Oh, very much so."* **4 very well** a phrase you use when you are agreeing to do something that you do not really want to do

■ USAGE We can say **very** *big* or *the* **very** *biggest*, but the comparative form is **much** *bigger*.

very² adj [only before a noun] exact: *He's the very man I've been looking for.* | *I missed the very beginning of the film.* | *He was determined to climb to the very top of the mountain.*

ves·pers /ˈvespəz ‖ -ərz/ n [U] the evening service in some divisions of the Christian church

ves·sel /ˈvesəl/ n fml 1 a round container, such as a glass, pot, or bucket, for holding liquids 2 a ship or large boat: *a fishing vessel*

vest /vest/ n 1 BrE a piece of clothing worn next to the skin under a shirt – see picture on page 50 2 the usual American word for WAISTCOAT

vest·ed /ˈvestɪd/ adj fml 1 vested in given as a legal right to a person or group: *The power to make new laws is vested in the government by the people.* 2 **vested interest** a strong reason for doing something, because you will gain something from it: *The tobacco companies have a vested interest in claiming that cigarette smoking isn't harmful.*

ves·ti·bule /ˈvestɪbjuːl/ n fml an entrance area or room just inside the outside door of a building

ves·tige /ˈvestɪdʒ/ n a small part that remains of something big or important that once existed: *This stone is the last vestige of the old castle.*

vest·ments /ˈvestmənts/ n fml [pl] ceremonial clothes worn by priests for church services

ves·try /ˈvestri/ n vestries a room in a church where the priest puts on his ceremonial clothes

vet¹ /vet/ n (also **veterinary surgeon** fml) a trained animal doctor

vet² v -tt- infml [T] to examine carefully to make sure something or someone is acceptable for a particular purpose: *Everyone who works with military secrets must be thoroughly vetted.*

vet·e·ran /ˈvetərən/ n 1 someone who has a lot of experience in something, especially in war: *Grandfather is a veteran of the First World War.* 2 **veteran car** a car made before 1919 – **veteran** adj [always before a noun] : *a veteran politician*

vet·e·ri·nar·i·an /ˌvetərɪˈneəriən/ n the usual American word for VET

vet·e·ri·na·ry /ˈvetərɪnəri ‖ -neri/ adj [always before a noun] connected with the medical care and treatment of sick animals: *veterinary science*

veterinary sur·geon /ˈ····· ˌ··/ n see VET

ve·to¹ /ˈviːtəʊ/ n vetoes [C;U] the official power to refuse permission for something: *The Presidential right of veto.*

veto² v vetoed, vetoing [T] to refuse to allow something: *The President vetoed the plan.*

vex /veks/ v old fash [T] to make someone feel angry – **vexation** /vekˈseɪʃən/ n [C;U]

VHF /ˌviː eɪtʃ ˈef/ n [U] the radio wave band of 30 to 300 million HERTZ; an abbreviation for **very high frequency**

vi·a /ˈvaɪə, viːə/ prep 1 travelling or sent through a place on the way to somewhere else: *We flew to Athens via Paris and Rome.* 2 using a particular person or thing: *These television pictures came via satellite.* | *I sent Mary a message via her sister.*

vi·a·ble /ˈvaɪəbəl/ adj able to succeed without any problems: *Your idea is interesting, but not really economically viable.* – **viability** /ˌvaɪəˈbɪlɪti/ n [U]

vi·a·duct /ˈvaɪədʌkt/ n a long high bridge which carries a road or railway line across a valley

vi·brant /ˈvaɪbrənt/ adj 1 exciting and full of life: *Hong Kong is a vibrant, fascinating city.* 2 bright and strong (used of colour or light)

vi·brate /vaɪˈbreɪt ‖ ˈvaɪbreɪt/ v vibrated, vibrating [I;T] to shake quickly with a slight movement that may often be felt rather than seen: *The music was so loud, the whole house was vibrating.* | *You make the sound by vibrating the tongue against the teeth.*

vi·bra·tion /vaɪˈbreɪʃən/ n [C;U] a slight continuous shaky movement: *Can you feel the vibrations of the ship's engines?* | *If you touch the machine you will feel the vibration.*

vic·ar /ˈvɪkəʳ/ n a priest in the Church of England who is in charge of an area – see PRIEST (USAGE)

vic·ar·age /ˈvɪkərɪdʒ/ n the house of a vicar

vi·car·i·ous /vɪˈkeəriəs ‖ vaɪ-/ adj experienced indirectly through watching or reading about other people and not doing something yourself: *People can get a vicarious pleasure from reading about the lives of rich families.*

vice /vaɪs/ n 1 [U] criminal behaviour connected with sex, drugs, and immoral practices 2 [C] a bad or immoral part of a human character 3 [C] infml a bad habit: *Smoking is my only vice.* 4 (**vise** AmE) a tool with metal jaws that can be tightened, used for holding an object firmly so that you can work on it with both hands

vice-chan·cel·lor /ˌ·· ˈ···/ n the person who controls the affairs of a university

vice·roy /ˈvaɪsrɔɪ/ n a king's or queen's representative ruling for them in another country

vice ver·sa /ˌvaɪs ˈvɜːsə, ˌvaɪsɪ- ‖ -ɜːr-/ adv and the same is true in the opposite situation from the one just stated: *When she wants to go out, he wants to stay in, and vice versa.*

vi·cin·i·ty /vɪˈsɪnɪti/ n [U] 1 the surrounding area: *There were no good schools in the vicinity.* 2 **in the vicinity of** near to: *a restaurant in the vicinity of the hotel*

vi·cious /ˈvɪʃəs/ adj 1 cruel and showing the desire to hurt people: *He gave the dog a vicious blow with his stick.* 2 dangerous and likely to hurt people: *a vicious-looking knife* – **viciously** adv – **viciousness** n [U]

vicious cir·cle /ˌ··· ˈ··/ n a situation in which the effect of one problem creates another, and causes the first problem to return: *Crime leads to prison, which leads to unemployment, which leads to crime. It's a vicious circle.*

vic·tim /ˈvɪktɪm/ n 1 a person or animal that is harmed or killed by someone, or by something unpleasant happening to them: *Four people were killed in the explosion, but police have not yet named the victims.* 2 someone or something that suffers as a result of something unpleasant happening: *She was a victim of cancer.*

vic·tim·ize /ˈvɪktɪmaɪz/ v victimized, victimizing (also **victimise** BrE) [T] to cause someone to suffer unfairly: *When she lost her job, she felt she'd been victimized because of her political views.* – **victimization** /ˌvɪktɪmaɪˈzeɪʃən ‖ -mə-/ n [U]

vic·tor /ˈvɪktəʳ/ n lit a winner in a battle or competition

Vic·to·ri·an /vɪkˈtɔːriən/ adj, n 1 belonging to or living in the time when Victoria was the Queen of Britain (1837–1901): *Victorian furniture* | *Florence Nightingale was a famous Victorian.* 2 having the strong moral opinions of the society at the time of Queen Victoria, especially believing in hard work and strict sexual morals

vic·to·ry /ˈvɪktəri/ n victories [C;U] the act of winning or state of having won in war or in any kind of struggle: *We will lead our party to victory in the next election!* | *Tonight's game will see another victory for Italy over the Dutch team.* –**victorious** /vɪkˈtɔːriəs/ *adj* : *the victorious team*

vid·e·o¹ /ˈvɪdiəʊ/ *n* **1** [U] recording and showing moving pictures, film, or television using special TAPE called VIDEOTAPE: *I've got the children on video.* | *Teachers now use a lot of video in the classroom.* **2** [C;U] (also **video cassette**) a container holding videotape –see picture on page 442 **3** [C] (also **video recorder** *fml*) a machine which records pictures and sound using videotape: *You can record two programmes at the same time on this video.* | *Rewind the video.* –see picture on page 442 **4** [C] a film or television broadcast recorded on videotape: *Let's rent a video to watch tonight.*

video² *v* (also **videotape**) [T] to record something on videotape: *I must remember to video the last episode tonight.*

video cas·sette /ˌ··· ·ˈ·/ *n* see VIDEO

video re·cord·er /ˈ··· ·ˌ··/ *n* see VIDEO

vid·e·o·tape¹ /ˈvɪdiəʊteɪp/ *n* [U] a long narrow band of MAGNETIC material on which television pictures and sound are recorded

videotape² *v* [T] see VIDEO

vie /vaɪ/ *v* **vied, vying** [I] to compete against someone for something: *They are vying with each other for the job as captain.*

view¹ /vjuː/ *n* **1** [U] the ability to see something from a particular place: *My view of the harbour was blocked by the new buildings.* | *If you stand here you'll get a better view of the procession.* **2** [C] the things that you can see from a particular place: *The view from the top of the hill was superb.* | *a hotel with lovely views* **3** [U] a position in which something can be seen: *The sea was now in view.* | *A range of hills came into view.* | *The valley was hidden from view by mist.* **4** [C] a personal opinion or belief about something: *He has very strong views on education.* | *In my view, he should never have been offered the job in the first place.* **5 in view of something** taking something into consideration: *In view of his age and ill health, the police have decided not to prosecute him.* **6 on view** being shown to the public: *These paintings will be on view at the British Museum until next month.* **7 with a view to do·ing something** with the aim of doing something: *We decorated the house with a view to selling it.*

■ USAGE Compare **view, scenery, scene, landscape**. **View** is countable. We use **view** to talk about all the things we can see at a distance from a particular place: *You'll get a fine view of the town from the top of the hill.* **View** can be countable but **scenery** is uncountable. We use **scenery** to talk about the beautiful or ugly appearance of part of the country: *We passed through some magnificent scenery on our journey through Scotland.* **Scene** is countable. A **scene** is what you see both close up and at a distance, and may include people and movement: *a happy scene of children playing in the park.* **Landscape** is countable. We use **landscape** for any combination of hills, valleys, fields, etc. in a particular area: *The landscape was typical of Scotland, with high mountains, lakes, and deep valleys.*

view² *v* [T] **1** to look at or examine something carefully: *Several possible buyers have already been to view the house.* **2** to consider something in a particular way: *They viewed the future with some alarm.* | *I viewed his action as a breach of trust.*

view·er /ˈvjuːəʳ/ *n* a person watching television

view·point /ˈvjuːpɔɪnt/ *n* your general opinions and way of thinking about something

vig·il /ˈvɪdʒɪl/ *n* [C;U] **1** watching and guarding something or someone, usually at night: *There was an all-night vigil outside the prison.* **2 keep vigil** to watch and guard something or someone

vig·i·lant /ˈvɪdʒɪlənt/ *adj fml* continually watchful or on guard: *A vigilant police force helps to control crime.* –**vigilance** *n* [U]

vig·i·lan·te /ˌvɪdʒɪˈlænti/ *n* a member of an unofficial organization which keeps order and punishes crime when it thinks the police is not keeping order properly

vig·our /ˈvɪgəʳ/ *n* (**vigor** *AmE*) [U] forceful strength or activity of body or mind –**vigorous** *adj* : *She made a vigorous speech in defence of the government.* –**vigorously** *adv*

vile /vaɪl/ *adj* **1** hateful and wicked: *He was a vile man who treated everyone badly.* **2** *infml* nasty or unpleasant: *The walls were a vile shade of green.*

vil·i·fy /ˈvɪlɪfaɪ/ *v* **vilified, vilifying** *fml* [T] to say bad things about someone or something

vil·la /ˈvɪlə/ *n* a pleasant house with a garden in the country or used for holidays: *We're renting a villa in the south of France for the summer holidays.*

vil·lage /ˈvɪlɪdʒ/ *n* a small group of houses and other buildings in a country area: *She lives in a village in the mountains.*

vil·lag·er /ˈvɪlɪdʒəʳ/ *n* a person who lives in a village

vil·lain /ˈvɪlən/ *n* **1** a wicked man, or the main bad character in an old play, film, or story: *The villain always gets caught at the end of the story.* –opposite **hero** **2** *infml* a criminal

vil·lain·y /ˈvɪləni/ *n* [U] *lit* wicked behaviour

vin·ai·grette /ˌvɪnəˈgret, ˌvɪneɪ-/ *n* [U] a sharp-tasting mixture of oil and VINEGAR which is put on salads (SALAD)

vin·di·cate /ˈvɪndɪkeɪt/ *v* **vindicated, vindicating** [T] to show that someone or something is free from blame: *The report clearly vindicates the company's actions.* –**vindication** /ˌvɪndɪˈkeɪʃən/ *n* [sing]

vin·dic·tive /vɪnˈdɪktɪv/ *adj* wanting to harm someone who has harmed you

vine /vaɪn/ *n* **1** a climbing plant that produces bunches of juicy green or purple fruit **2** any creeping or climbing plant

vin·e·gar /ˈvɪnɪgəʳ/ *n* [U] an acid-tasting liquid used in preserving or adding taste to food

vine·yard /ˈvɪnjəd ‖ -jəd/ *n* a piece of land planted with vines for wine production

vin·tage¹ /ˈvɪntɪdʒ/ *adj* [always before a noun] **1** made in a particular year and of high quality (used of wines): *a bottle of vintage claret* **2** of high quality and lasting value: *a vintage silent film* **3 vintage car** a car made between 1919 and 1930

vintage² *n* a fine wine produced in a particular year: *a 1982 vintage*

vi·nyl /ˈvaɪnɪl/ *n* [U] firm plastic which you can bend; it is used for making records and floor and chair coverings

vi·o·la /viˈəʊlə/ *n* a stringed musical instrument, a little larger than a VIOLIN

vi·o·late /ˈvaɪəleɪt/ *v* **violated, violating** [T] **1** to take no notice of a promise or agreement: *This action violates the international agreements on protecting wild animals.* **2** to break into or spoil a place that should be respected –**violation** /ˌvaɪəˈleɪʃən/ *n* [C;U] : *They have been fishing in our waters, in violation of the recent agreement.*

vi·o·lence /ˈvaɪələns/ n [U] **1** very great force of feeling or action: *The violence of the storm was very frightening.* **2** the use of physical force to hurt or harm someone: *There is a lot of violence on television these days.* | *robbery with violence*

vi·o·lent /ˈvaɪələnt/ adj **1** using physical force to hurt or harm someone: *He was a violent man who had attacked his wife before.* | *a violent storm* | *There were violent clashes between police and demonstrators.* **2** produced by damaging physical force: *He died a violent death.* **3** using great force in your actions or language, especially because you are angry: *She has a violent temper.* –**violently** adv

vi·o·let /ˈvaɪəlɪt/ n **1** [C] a small plant with sweet-smelling purple flowers **2** [U] a bluish purple colour –**violet** adj

vi·o·lin /ˌvaɪəˈlɪn/ n a four-stringed musical instrument which you hold under your chin and play by drawing a BOW across the strings –**violinist** n

VIP /ˌviː aɪ ˈpiː/ n a person who is given special treatment because they are famous or important; an abbreviation for **very important person**: *the VIP lounge at the airport*

vi·per /ˈvaɪpəʳ/ n a small poisonous snake

vir·gin¹ /ˈvɜːdʒɪn ‖ ˈvɜːr-/ n a person, usually a woman or girl, who has never had sexual relations with a member of the opposite sex –**virginal** adj

virgin² adj lit untouched or unspoiled: *no footmarks on the virgin snow*

vir·gin·i·ty /vɜːˈdʒɪnɪti ‖ vɜːr-/ n [U] the state of being a virgin: *She was 19 when she lost her virginity.*

Virgin Mar·y /ˌvɜːdʒɪn ˈmeəri ‖ -ɜːr-/ n in the Christian religion, Mary, the mother of Christ

Vir·go /ˈvɜːɡəʊ ‖ ˈvɜːr-/ n one of the signs of the ZODIAC

vir·ile /ˈvɪraɪl ‖ ˈvɪrəl/ adj full of male qualities such as physical strength and sexual power (used to express approval): *a virile young sportsman*

vi·ril·i·ty /vɪˈrɪlɪti/ n [U] male sexual power or male qualities in general (used to express approval)

vir·tu·al /ˈvɜːtʃuəl ‖ ˈvɜːr-/ adj [only before a noun] in fact though not in name: *The king was so much under the influence of his wife that she was the virtual ruler of the country.*

vir·tu·al·ly /ˈvɜːtʃuəli ‖ ˈvɜːr-/ adv almost: *The dinner's virtually ready. I've only got to make the salad.*

vir·tue /ˈvɜːtʃuː ‖ ˈvɜːr-/ n **1** [U] goodness, nobleness, and worthiness: *a man of the highest virtue* **2** [C] any good quality of character or behaviour: *Among her many virtues are loyalty, courage, and truthfulness.* **3** [C;U] an advantage: *One of the virtues of this curtain material is that it's easily washable.* **4 by virtue of** as a result of: *Though she isn't British by birth, she's a British citizen by virtue of her marriage to an Englishman.*

vir·tu·o·so /ˌvɜːtʃuˈəʊzəʊ ‖ ˌvɜːrtʃuˈəʊsəʊ/ n a very skilful performer in one of the arts, especially music

vir·tu·ous /ˈvɜːtʃuəs ‖ ˈvɜːr-/ adj doing the right thing morally –**virtuously** adv

vir·u·lent /ˈvɪrɡlənt/ adj **1** full of hatred (used of a feeling) **2** very powerful, quick-acting, and dangerous to life or health (used of a poison or disease) –**virulence** n [U]

vi·rus /ˈvaɪərəs/ n a living thing even smaller than bacteria which causes infectious disease: *the common cold virus* | *virus infections* –**viral** /ˈvaɪərəl/ adj

vi·sa /ˈviːzə/ n an official mark put onto a PASSPORT giving a foreigner permission to enter, pass through, or leave a particular country: *Do Americans need a visa to visit Britain?*

vis·age /ˈvɪzɪdʒ/ n lit your face

vis-à-vis /ˌviːz ɑː ˈviː, ˌviːz ə ˈviː/ prep fml **1** with regard to **2** when compared to: *This year's profits show an improvement vis-à-vis last year's.*

vis·count /ˈvaɪkaʊnt/ n (also **Viscount**) a British nobleman

vis·count·ess /ˈvaɪkaʊntɪs/ n (also **Viscountess**) the wife of a viscount, or a woman with the rank of viscount

vis·cous /ˈvɪskəs/ adj thick and sticky and not flowing easily (used of liquids)

vis·i·bil·i·ty /ˌvɪzɪˈbɪlɪti/ n [U] the degree of clearness with which objects can be seen according to the weather: *We had a splendid view of the mountains because of the very good visibility.* | *The mist was so thick that visibility was down to only ten metres.*

vis·i·ble /ˈvɪzɪbəl/ adj able to be seen –opposite **invisible** –**visibly** adv : *He was visibly anxious about the examination.*

vi·sion /ˈvɪʒən/ n **1** [U] the ability to see: *When I had my eyes tested the optician said that my vision was perfect.* **2** [U] the ability to imagine how things could be done differently in the future: *a man of vision* | *We need someone with real vision to take over the company.* **3** [C] something seen in a dream, in your imagination, or as a religious experience: *She had a vision in which God seemed to appear before her.* | *He has a clear vision of the future he wants for his children.* **4 have visions of doing something** to think that something will happen: *There was so much traffic on the way to the airport that I had visions of missing the plane.*

vi·sion·a·ry /ˈvɪʒənəri ‖ -neri/ adj,n **visionaries** a person who has a vision of how things could be done differently in the future

vis·it¹ /ˈvɪzɪt/ v [I;T] to go and spend time with a person or in a place: *Aunt Jane usually visits us for two or three weeks in the spring.* | *While we're in Europe we ought to visit Holland.* | *When we were in London we visited the Tower twice.* | *Visiting hours in the hospital are from 4.30 to 6.00.*

visit² n an action or time of visiting: *He makes several visits back home every year.* | *We've just had a visit from the police.* | *I think you should pay a visit to the doctor about your arm.*

vis·i·ta·tion /ˌvɪzɪˈteɪʃən/ n fml a formal visit by someone in charge, usually in order to discover whether things are in good order

vis·it·or /ˈvɪzɪtəʳ/ n a person who visits: *Visitors to the castle are asked not to take photographs.*

vi·sor /ˈvaɪzəʳ/ n the part of a HELMET which is moved down to protect your face when you are doing something such as riding a motorcycle

vis·ta /ˈvɪstə/ n a distant view, to which your eyes are directed between narrow limits, for example by rows of trees

vi·su·al /ˈvɪʒuəl/ adj experienced by or connected with seeing: *a strong visual impact* | *The visual arts are painting, dancing, and the cinema, as opposed to music and literature.* –**visually** adv : *Visually the chair is very pleasing, but it's uncomfortable to sit on.*

visual aid /ˌ··· ·ˈ·/ an object such as a picture, map, or film which teachers show people to help them learn

vi·su·al·ize /ˈvɪʒuəlaɪz/ v visualized, visualizing (also **visualise** *BrE*) [T] to form a picture of something or someone in your mind: *He described the place carefully and I tried to visualize it.* | *Can you visualize living on the moon?* | *I can't visualize him as a bank clerk. He's too dreamy.*
□ USEFUL PATTERNS to visualize something; to visualize doing something; to visualize someone as something –**visualization** /ˌvɪʒuəlaɪˈzeɪʃən ‖ -lə-/ n [U]

vi·tal /ˈvaɪtl/ adj **1** very necessary or very important: *This point is vital to my argument.* | *Your support is vital for the success of my plan.* **2** *fml* full of life and force: *Their leader's vital and cheerful manner filled his men with courage.*

vital sta·tis·tics /ˌ··· ·ˈ··/ n [pl] **1** *infml* the measurements of a woman's body round the chest, waist, and hips (HIP); people use this expression when they are talking about how attractive a woman's body is **2** certain official facts about people's lives, especially their births, marriages, and deaths

vi·tal·i·ty /vaɪˈtæləti/ n [U] strength and life: *He has a pleasant voice, but his singing lacks vitality.*

vi·tal·ly /ˈvaɪtl-i/ adv **vitally important** extremely important: *It is vitally important to switch off the electricity before attempting to repair the television.*

vit·a·min /ˈvɪtəmɪn, ˈvaɪ- ‖ ˈvaɪ-/ n [C;U] a chemical substance which is present in certain foods, and is important for growth and good health: *This type of bread has added vitamins.* | *Oranges contain vitamin C.*

vit·re·ous /ˈvɪtriəs/ adj tech of or like glass: *The cooker is finished with white vitreous enamel.* | *vitreous rocks*

vit·ri·ol·ic /ˌvɪtriˈɒlɪk◂ ‖ -ˈɑːl-/ adj bitter and violent (used of a feeling or its expression): *a vitriolic attack on the Government's plans for cuts in public services*

vi·va·cious /vɪˈveɪʃəs/ adj attractively full of life (used especially of women) –**vivacity** /-ˈvæsəti/ n [U]

viv·id /ˈvɪvɪd/ adj **1** bright or strong in colour: *a vivid flash of lightning* | *vivid red hair* **2** producing sharp clear pictures in your mind: *a child with a vivid imagination* | *a vivid description* –**vividly** adv

viv·i·sec·tion /ˌvɪvɪˈsekʃən/ n [U] the practice of performing operations on living animals in order to increase medical knowledge

vix·en /ˈvɪksən/ n a female fox

viz /vɪz/ adv *fml* that is to say; you use **viz** when you have already mentioned a general group and you are now going to mention all the particular things in it: *On most English farms you'll find only four kinds of animal, viz horses, sheep, cattle, and pigs.*

vo·cab·u·la·ry /vəˈkæbjʊləri, vəʊ- ‖ -leri/ n vocabularies **1** [U] words: *After we'd done the grammar exercise, we learnt some new vocabulary.* **2** [C;U] all the words you know in a language: *Our baby's just starting to talk. He's got a vocabulary of about ten words.* | *the average vocabulary of an intermediate student* **3** [C;U] the words used in a particular subject or situation: *I find it difficult to understand the vocabulary of the lawcourts.*

vo·cal /ˈvəʊkəl/ adj **1** [only before a noun] related to your voice: *The tongue is one of the vocal organs.* | *I like instrumental music better than vocal music.* **2** *infml* expressing yourself freely and noisily in words: *She was very vocal at the meeting.* –**vocally** adv

vocal cords /ˈ··· ·, ˌ·· ·ˈ·/ n (also **vocal chords**) [pl] the pair of thin bands of muscle in your throat that produce sound when you talk or sing

vo·cal·ist /ˈvəʊkələst/ n a singer of popular songs, especially one who sings with a band

vo·ca·tion /vəʊˈkeɪʃən/ n **1** [C;U] a strong desire to do a particular kind of work, usually work that helps other people, combined with a natural ability for it: *She's a good doctor because she has a real vocation for looking after people who are ill.* **2** [C] a job that you really want to do and that you have a natural ability for, usually one that helps other people: *Teaching children is more than just a way of making money: it's a vocation.* **3** [sing] a special call from God to be a priest, NUN, or MONK

vo·ca·tion·al /vəʊˈkeɪʃənəl/ adj preparing for a particular type of job: *vocational training for pilots*

vo·cif·er·ous /vəˈsɪfərəs, vəʊ- ‖ vəʊ-/ adj *fml* noisy in the expression of your ideas: *vociferous demands for higher wages*

vod·ka /ˈvɒdkə ‖ ˈvɑːdkə/ n [U] a strong, colourless, and almost tasteless alcoholic drink, first made in Russia and Poland

vogue /vəʊg/ n **1** the fashion or custom at a certain time: *High boots were the vogue for women last year.* | *There was a vogue for painting stripes on your car.* **2 in vogue** fashionable: *Long hair for men is no longer in vogue.* [RELATED PHRASE **out of vogue**]

voice¹ /vɔɪs/ n **1** [C] the sound you hear when someone speaks: *We could hear the children's voices in the garden.* | *He spoke in a very loud voice.* **2** [C;U] an opinion: *The Government should listen to the voice of the people.* **3** [C] a person or newspaper that expresses the opinions of a group: *He became the recognized voice of the West Indian community in Britain.* **4** [C;U] in grammar, the system for choosing an active or PASSIVE verb form depending on whether the subject of the sentence does something (**active voice**) or has something happen to it (**passive voice**) **5 give voice to something** to express an idea **6 have a voice in something** to be able to say what you think about something and influence what happens: *Parents feel that they should have a voice in the school rules.* **7 in good voice** singing well **8 keep your voice down** to speak more quietly **9 -voiced** having a voice of the stated kind: *loud-voiced*
■ USAGE Notice how the preposition **in** is used in sentences such as: *She spoke in a soft/angry voice.* | *He replied in a loud/gentle voice.* | *Does he always talk in that high-pitched voice?*

voice² v **voiced, voicing** [T] to express something in words, especially forcefully: *The councillor voiced the feeling of the meeting when he demanded action to improve the water supply.*

void¹ /vɔɪd/ adj **1** [never before a noun] *fml* empty: *That part of the town is completely void of interest for visitors.* **2** *law* having no legal force (used of official agreements): *A contract signed by a child is void.*

void² n [sing] **1** an empty space, especially the space around our world and beyond the stars: *A ball of fire seemed to fall out of the void, disappearing before it reached the earth.* **2** a feeling of something lacking in your life: *The child's death left a painful void in his parents' lives.*

vol /vɒl ‖ vɑːl/ n a written abbreviation for VOLUME²

vol·a·tile /ˈvɒlətaɪl ‖ ˈvɑːlətl/ adj **1** likely to change quickly and unexpectedly: *a volatile situation* **2**

tech easily changing into a gas (used of a liquid or substance) –**volatility** /ˌvɒləˈtɪlɪti ‖ ˌvaːl-/ n [U]

vol·au·vent /ˈvɒl əu ˈvɒŋ ‖ ˌvɔːl əu ˈvaːn/ n a small very light pastry case filled with something such as meat or chicken

vol·ca·no /vɒlˈkeɪnəu ‖ vaːl-/ n volcanoes *or* volcanos a mountain with a large opening called a CRATER at the top through which melting rock called LAVA, steam, and gases escape from time to time with explosive force from inside the earth: *An active volcano may explode at any time.* | *an extinct volcano* –**volcanic** /-ˈkænɪk / adj :*volcanic rocks* | *volcanic activity*

vole /vəul/ n a small short-tailed animal of the rat and mouse family

vo·li·tion /vəˈlɪʃən ‖ vəu-, və-/ n fml [U] **of your own volition** of your own free choice in choosing a course of action: *I didn't ask him to go. He went of his own volition.*

vol·ley /ˈvɒli ‖ ˈvaːli/ n **1** a lot of shots fired at the same time: *A volley of shots was heard.* **2** continuous shouting by someone in a quarrel or attack: *a volley of abuse* **3** in tennis, a shot in which a player hits a ball which has not touched the ground first

vol·ley·ball /ˈvɒlibɔːl ‖ ˈvaː-/ n [U] a game in which a large ball is struck by hand across a net without being allowed to touch the ground

volt /vəult/ n a standard measure of the force of electrical current along wires

volt·age /ˈvəultɪdʒ/ n [C;U] electrical force measured in volts

volte-face /ˌvɒlt ˈfæs, -ˈfaːs ‖ ˌvɔːlt ˈfaːs/ n [sing] fml a change to a completely opposite opinion or course of action

vol·u·ble /ˈvɒlju̞bəl ‖ ˈvaː-/ adj talking with a great flow of words (a word often used to express disapproval)

vol·ume /ˈvɒljuːm ‖ ˈvaːljəm/ n **1** [U] loudness of sound: *The television seems a bit loud. Could you turn the volume down?* **2** [U] size or quantity thought of as measurement of the space filled by something: *The volume of this container is 100,000 cubic metres.* **3** [C] a book, especially one of a set of the same kind: *We have a set of Dickens's works in 24 volumes.* **4** [C;U] the amount of something: *The volume of passengers on the railways is increasing again.*

vo·lu·mi·nous /vəˈluːmɪ̞nəs, vəˈljuː- ‖ vəˈluː-/ adj **1** very loose and full and made using a lot of cloth (used of clothes): *a voluminous skirt* **2** containing a lot or able to hold a lot: *a voluminous shopping bag* | *a voluminous report*

vol·un·ta·ry /ˈvɒləntəri ‖ ˈvaːlənteri/ adj **1** done of your free choice and not because you are forced: *He made a voluntary statement to the police.* **2** done unpaid: *She does voluntary work with old people.* –**voluntarily** /ˈvɒlləntərɪ̞li ‖ ˌvaːlənˈteərɪ̞li/ adv : *He made the promise quite voluntarily. I didn't force him to.*

vol·un·teer¹ /ˌvɒlənˈtɪər ‖ ˌvaː-/ n **1** a person who offers to do something **2** a person who is willing to do something unpaid: *This work costs us nothing. It's all done by volunteers.*

volunteer² v **1** [I;T] to offer to do something: *He volunteered to help me move.* | *He volunteered me for guard duty!*
□ USEFUL PATTERNS to volunteer for something; to volunteer someone for something; to volunteer to do something

2 [I] to offer to join the armed forces of your own free will **3** [T] to tell someone something without being asked: *She volunteered the information.*

vo·lup·tu·ous /vəˈlʌptʃuəs/ adj suggesting or expressing sexual pleasure (used especially of women): *The dancer's movements were slow and voluptuous.* | *She had a large voluptuous mouth.*

vom·it¹ /ˈvɒmɪ̞t ‖ ˈvaː-/ v [I;T] to throw up food and drink from your stomach through your mouth: *The smell made me want to vomit.*

vomit² n [U] food and drink that has come back up from your stomach and out of your mouth

voo·doo /ˈvuːduː/ n (also **Voodoo**) [U] a set of magical beliefs and practices, used as a form of religion in the West Indies

vo·ra·cious /vəˈreɪʃəs, vɒ- ‖ vɔː-, və-/ adj fml **1** eating or desiring large quantities of food **2** very eager for something and always wanting more: *She's a voracious reader.*

vor·tex /ˈvɔːteks ‖ ˈvɔːr-/ n vortexes *or* vortices /-tɪ̞siːz/ a mass of water or air turning around a hollow central part which sucks things in; you see a vortex when water leaves a bath

vote¹ /vəut/ v voted, voting **1** [I;T; +(that)] to express your choice officially from among the possibilities offered, usually by marking a piece of paper, or by raising your hand at a meeting: *You're only 16. You're too young to vote.* | *Did you vote for Neil Kinnock at the last election?* | *The railway workers have voted to go back to work on Monday.* | *The sign said "Vote Labour".* | *The Liberal Democrats voted against closing more railway lines.* | *Parliament is to vote on dog licences again.* | *They voted that the meeting be adjourned.*
□ USEFUL PATTERNS to vote for someone; to vote to do something; to vote against something; to vote that...
2 [T] to agree to provide something as the result of a vote: *Parliament has voted the town a large sum of money for a new road.* **3** [T] infml to agree as the general opinion: *The party was voted a great success.*

vote² n **1** [C] a process of making a choice or decision by allowing people to give their opinion and then seeing which choice is most popular: *The question will be settled by a vote.* **2 take a vote on something, put something to the vote, put something to a vote** to vote on something **3** [C] an official expression of one person's opinion in an election: *There were 15 votes in favour of my suggestion, and 23 against.* | *He will certainly not get my vote at the next election.* | *The total number of votes cast was 38.* | *James Smith got 14,000 votes.* **4** [sing] the total number of votes by a particular set of people: *In elections in New York, the Irish vote is very important.* **5 the vote: a** the total number of votes in an election: *The Greens won over 10% of the vote.* **b** the right to vote in political elections: *In Britain, people get the vote at the age of 18.* **6 vote of thanks** a public expression of thanks: *Mrs Jones proposed a vote of thanks to Dr Brown for his interesting talk.*

vot·er /ˈvəutər/ n a person who votes

vouch /vautʃ/ v **vouch for: a** to say that you know from your personal experience that someone or something is dependable: *I've read this report carefully and I can vouch for its accuracy.* **b** to take responsibility for someone's future good behaviour: *I'll vouch for my son's future behaviour, officer.*

vouch·er /ˈvautʃər/ n a ticket that is used instead of money for a particular purpose: *a travel voucher* |

Some firms give their workers luncheon vouchers, which they can use to buy a meal.

vow¹ /vaʊ/ n fml a solemn promise: *All the men took a vow of loyalty to their leader.*

vow² v [T; + (that)] to declare or swear solemnly that you will do something: *When young Ernie was caught stealing he vowed he'd never do it again.*

vow·el /ˈvaʊəl/ n a speech sound in which you let your breath out without any stop or any closing of the air passage in your mouth: *The vowels in the English alphabet are* a, e, i, o, *and* u.

voy·age /ˈvɔɪ-ɪdʒ/ n a long journey made by boat or ship or in space: *The voyage from England to India used to take six months.* | *a voyage to the moon* –see TRAVEL² (USAGE)

vs. /ˈvɜːsəs ‖ ˈvɜːr-/ see VERSUS

vul·gar /ˈvʌlgəʳ/ adj 1 very rude, low, or bad-mannered and going against the accepted standards of polite society: *Putting food into your mouth with a knife is considered vulgar in Britain.* | *vulgar language* 2 showing a lack of fine feeling or good judgment in the choice of what is beautiful: *The house was full of costly, but very vulgar furniture.* –**vulgarly** adv

vul·gar·i·ty /vʌlˈgærˌti/ n **vulgarities** 1 [U] the quality of being vulgar 2 [C] an example of vulgar speech or action

vul·ne·ra·ble /ˈvʌlnərəbəl/ adj easily hurt in body or mind: *We're in a vulnerable position here, with the enemy on the hill above us.* | *She looked so young and vulnerable.* | *Your arguments are vulnerable to criticism.* –**vulnerability** /ˌvʌlnərəˈbɪlˌti/ n [U]

vul·ture /ˈvʌltʃəʳ/ n a large ugly tropical bird which feeds on dead animals

vy·ing /ˈvaɪɪŋ/ the present participle of VIE

W,w

W, w /'dʌbəlju:/ **W's, w's** *or* **Ws, ws** the 23rd letter of the English alphabet

W 1 a written abbreviation for WEST **2** a written abbreviation for WATT(s)

wad /wɒd ‖ wɑːd/ *n* **1** a thick soft mass of material: *Put wads of cotton wool in your ears to keep out the noise.* **2** a thick collection of things such as pieces of paper: *a wad of bank notes*

wad·dle /'wɒdl ‖ 'wɑːdl/ *v* **waddled, waddling** [I+adv/prep] to walk with short steps, moving your body from one side to the other, like a duck: *The fat man waddled up to her.* –**waddle** *n*

wade /weɪd/ *v* **waded, wading** [I] **1** to walk through water which is quite deep: *We had to wade across the river.* **2** **wade through something** *infml* to read a lot of writing which is not very interesting: *I waded through that report last night.*

wa·fer /'weɪfəʳ/ *n* **1** a very thin BISCUIT, eaten especially with ice cream **2** a thin round piece of bread used in the Christian religious ceremony of COMMUNION

waf·fle¹ /'wɒfəl ‖ 'wɑː-/ *n* a large light cake marked with squares, common in the US

waffle² *v* **waffled, waffling** [I] *BrE infml* to talk or write in words that may sound good but do not really say anything: *Stop waffling and answer the question!* –**waffle** *n* [U]: *The teacher said my essay was just a load of waffle.*

waft /wɑːft, wɒft ‖ wɑːft, wæft/ *v* [I + adv/prep; T + adv/prep] to move lightly: *Cooking smells wafted along the hall.*

wag /wæg/ *v* -**gg**- [I;T] to shake something quickly and repeatedly from side to side: *Look at the dog's tail wagging —he must be pleased to see us!* | *He wagged his finger at me.* –**wag** *n*

wage¹ /weɪdʒ/ *n* [sing] (also **wages** [pl]) the money you are paid each week for your work, especially if you do unskilled work: *a weekly wage of £128* | *The company's wage bill is over two million pounds a year.* | *I can't afford to do anything until I get my wages.* –see PAY² (USAGE)

wage² *v* **waged, waging** [T] *fml* to begin and continue a struggle of some kind: *The police are waging a campaign against drug-pushers in the city.* | *They are waging a war which they cannot win.*

wa·ger /'weɪdʒəʳ/ *v fml* **1** [T] to risk money on the result of a future event: *I'll wager you £5 that John fails his driving test.* | *He wagered £10 on an unknown horse.* **2** [+(that)] to be sure about something: *I'll wager he's there by now.* –**wager** *n* : *How about a wager on the final of the World Cup?*

wag·gle /'wægəl/ *v* **waggled, waggling** [I;T] to move frequently from side to side: *Can you waggle your ears?* –**waggle** *n*

wag·gon /'wægən/ *n* **1** (**wagon** *AmE*) a strong four-wheeled vehicle, mainly for heavy loads, drawn by horses or oxen: *The American pioneers crossed the continent in covered waggons.* **2** (also **goods waggon**) a railway goods vehicle with an open top

waif /weɪf/ *n lit* an uncared-for or homeless child: *a pitiful little waif*

wail /weɪl/ *v* [I] to cry out with a long sad sound suggesting grief or pain: *The wind wailed in the chimney all night.* | *"She's taken my apple," he wailed.* | *She wailed with grief.* –**wail** *n* : *with a wail of despair*

waist /weɪst/ *n* **1** the narrow part of your body just above your hips (HIP): *a slim waist* **2** the part of a piece of clothing that goes round your waist: *It's a nice skirt, but too big round the waist.*

waist·coat /'weɪskəʊt, 'weskət ‖ 'weskət/ *n BrE* a piece of clothing with buttons and no arms that you wear on the upper part of your body, usually over a shirt and under a JACKET; it is usually worn as part of a suit –see picture on page 50

waist·line /'weɪstlaɪn/ *n* **1** an imaginary line round the waist which you use to judge how fat someone is: *No sugar for me, thanks – I'm watching my waistline.* **2** the position of the waist of a piece of clothing: *Low waistlines are the fashion this year.*

wait¹ /weɪt/ *v* **1** [I] to stay without doing anything until someone comes or something happens: *Hurry up! We're waiting.* | *Try not to keep her waiting.* | *Our business can wait until after dinner.* | *I'm waiting for Jack.* | *We waited 20 minutes for a bus.* | *We're waiting to see the doctor.* | *They're waiting for the children to come home.*

☐ USEFUL PATTERNS to wait for someone/something; to wait to do something; to wait for someone to do something

2 I can't wait = I am very eager to do or experience something: *He's passed his driving test. He can't wait to tell his father.* | *"The party's tomorrow, isn't it?" "Yes. I can't wait!"* **3 wait and see** to find out soon, when it is the right time: *"What's for dinner?" "Wait and see."* | *"Do you think John will be better before Christmas?" "We'll just have to wait and see."* **4 you wait!, just you wait!** a phrase used when you are warning someone about something that will happen to them or something that they will learn soon: *I'll get even with you – you wait!* | *Just you wait! You'll find he's not nearly as easy to work for as you think.*

wait about/around *phr v* [I] to wait a long time for someone or something you are expecting, usually without having much to do: *We got everything ready sooner than we thought, so now we're just waiting around for the big day.*

wait on sbdy *phr v* [T] **1** to serve someone food in a restaurant **2** to attend someone as a servant **3** **wait on someone hand and foot** to do everything for someone, often including things they could perfectly well do for themselves: *Her children expect her to wait on them hand and foot.*

wait up *phr v* [I] *infml* to delay going to bed: *Don't wait up for me. I shall be home very late.*

■ USAGE Compare **wait for** and **expect. Waiting** is a kind of activity. If you **wait for** someone or something, you arrange your timetable or actions and perhaps stay in one place, so that you are ready: *"Why are you standing there?" "I'm waiting for John."* **Expecting** is a state of mind. If you **expect** someone or something, you think the person will come or the event will happen, but you will probably not stay in one place or make special arrangements: *I'm expecting the postman.* | *We're expecting a cold winter.*

wait² *n* **1** [sing] a period of waiting: *We had a long wait for a bus.* **2 lie in wait for someone** to hide, waiting to attack someone: *The robbers were lying in wait for him.*

wait·er /'weɪtəʳ/ *n* a person who serves food at the tables in a restaurant

waiting list /ˈ··· ·/ n a list of people who want something, such as treatment in hospital or a job: *She's on the waiting list for a kidney transplant.*

waiting room /ˈ··· ·/ n a room for people who are waiting, for example to see a doctor

wai·tress /ˈweɪtrɨs/ n a woman who serves food at the tables in a restaurant

waive /weɪv/ v waived, waiving [T] *fml* to use your power to decide to behave in a particular case as if a rule or a right did not exist: *We cannot waive this rule except in case of serious illness.*

wake¹ /weɪk/ v woke /wəʊk/ or waked, woken /ˈwəʊkən/ or waked, waking 1 [I;T] to stop being asleep: *I usually wake at eight o'clock.* | *We were woken by an almighty bang.* 2 **your waking hours** the hours you spend not in bed and asleep: *She spends all her waking hours working.*

wake up phr v 1 [I; T **wake** sbdy **up**] to stop being asleep: *I woke up at six o'clock.* | *What time shall I wake you up in the morning?* | *They were woken up by someone knocking at the door.* | *Wake up, Jimmy. It's seven o'clock!* 2 [I] to start to pay attention: *Wake up at the back there!* | *When he had his first child, he woke up to his responsibilities a bit.*

wake² n 1 a track left by a ship in water 2 **in the wake of** following as a result of: *There was a great deal of hunger and disease in the wake of the war.* 3 a gathering to watch and grieve over a dead person on the night before the burial, especially in Ireland

wake·ful /ˈweɪkfəl/ adj not able to sleep: *a wakeful night*

wak·en /ˈweɪkən/ v [I;T] *lit* to wake: *We were wakened by a loud bang.*

walk¹ /wɔːk/ v 1 [I;T] to move forward in a natural way by putting one foot in front of the other: *Do you walk to work, or do you come by bus?* | *We walked ten miles.* | *She likes walking.* | *He was walking along the rope.* –see picture on page 736 2 **go walking** to walk for pleasure in the country: *We went walking in the French Alps.* 3 [T] to walk along: *tired out after walking the streets of London all day* 4 **walk the dog** to take your dog for a walk 5 **walk someone somewhere** to walk with someone to a particular place, often to protect them on their way: *I'll walk you to the bus stop.* 6 **walk all over someone** to make someone do exactly what you want, without considering their needs and feelings

■ USAGE Compare **walk**, **stroll**, **stride**, **march**. **Walk** is the usual word for moving on foot at a normal speed. If you **stroll** you walk a short distance, slowly or lazily, probably for pleasure. If you **stride** you walk with long steps and if you **march** you walk with firm regular steps, like a soldier.

walk away with sthg phr v [T] to obtain a prize or job very easily

walk in on sbdy phr v [T] to surprise someone by going into a room unexpectedly

walk into sthg phr v [T] 1 to find yourself in a bad situation because you were not careful to avoid it: *He walked right into the trap.* 2 to obtain a job very easily

walk off with sthg phr v [T] *infml* 1 to steal something: *Someone's walked off with my bicycle.* 2 to win something easily: *She walked off with first prize.*

walk out phr v [I] 1 to leave suddenly, especially because you disapprove of something 2 (of a group of workers) to stop work and leave your workplace as a strong complaint about something

walk out on sbdy phr v [T] *infml* to leave someone suddenly, especially in a time of trouble: *He just*

walked out on his wife and family without saying a word!

walk² n 1 a journey on foot: *Let's go for a short walk.* | *Shall we have a walk this afternoon?* | *I think I'll just take a walk down to the village.* | *The station's just a ten-minute walk from here.* 2 a path for walking along: *There is a beautiful walk along the river.* 3 the particular way of walking of one person: *I recognized him quite a long way off because of his walk.*

walk·ie-talk·ie /ˌwɔːki ˈtɔːki/ n *infml* a two-way radio that can be carried, allowing you to talk as well as listen

walking stick /ˈ··· ·/ n a stick that you use to support yourself when you are walking

walk·man /ˈwɔːkmən/ n *tdmk* (also **Walkman**) a very small machine for playing music, which has small EARPHONES and is carried around by the user

walk of life /ˌ·· ·ˈ·/ n **walks of life** a position in society

walk·out /ˈwɔːk-aʊt/ n the action of leaving a meeting or organization as an expression of disapproval or complaint

walk·o·ver /ˈwɔːkˌəʊvəʳ/ n *infml* a very easy victory

wall¹ /wɔːl/ n 1 a narrow upright structure, made of stone or brick, which encloses something: *a garden surrounded by stone walls* | *the ancient city walls of Cairo* 2 the side of a building or a room: *Hang that picture on the wall.* | *They painted the walls pink.* –see picture on page 441 3 the inner surface of something hollow: *the walls of blood vessels* -**walled** adj : *an old walled town*

wall²

wall sthg ↔ **off** phr v [T] to separate a place with one or more walls: *This part of the house is walled off because it has a dangerous floor.*

wal·let /ˈwɒlɨt ‖ ˈwɑː-/ n a small flat leather case for holding cards and paper money, usually carried by a man in his pocket

wal·lop /ˈwɒləp ‖ ˈwɑː-/ v [T] *infml* to hit very hard: *I'll wallop you if you hit your sister again!*

wal·low /ˈwɒləʊ ‖ ˈwɑː-/ v [I] 1 to allow yourself to continue to experience an unpleasant feeling for longer than you need to: *I wish you'd stop wallowing in self-pity!* 2 to move or roll about happily in mud or water: *Pigs enjoy wallowing in mud.* -**wallow** n

wall·pa·per /ˈwɔːlˌpeɪpəʳ/ n [U] thick decorative paper to cover the walls of a room -**wallpaper** v [T] : *We've decided to wallpaper the bedroom.*

wal·nut /ˈwɔːlnʌt/ n 1 [C] a nut which you can eat; it has a round rough shell 2 [C;U] the tree that produces these nuts, or its wood

wal·rus /ˈwɔːlrəs ‖ ˈwɔːl-, ˈwɑːl-/ n walruses an animal which looks like a SEAL, lives in the sea, and has two long teeth which point downwards from its face

waltz¹ /wɔːls ‖ wɔːlts/ n 1 a piece of music with three beats in each bar: *a waltz by Strauss* 2 a rather slow dance for two people done in time to this music

waltz² v 1 [I] to dance a waltz 2 [I + adv/prep] *infml* to move in a particular direction easily and confidently: *Pam waltzed up to her and gave her a kiss.*

wan /wɒn ‖ wɑːn/ adj *lit* ill, weak, and tired in appearance: *The prisoners looked pale and wan.*

wand /wɒnd ‖ wɑːnd/ n a thin stick used by a person who does magic tricks: *He waved his magic wand and pulled a rabbit out of the hat.*

wan·der /ˈwɒndəʳ ‖ ˈwɑːn-/ v 1 [I;T] to walk through an area without a fixed aim: *The poor child was found wandering the streets.* | *Tourists* *wandered idly through the old city.* **2** [I] (of your thoughts) to begin to move on to other things: *I found my attention wandering.* **–wanderer** *n*

wan·der·lust /'wɒndəlʌst ‖ 'wɑːndər-/ *n* [U] a strong desire to travel to places which are far away

wane[1] /weɪn/ *v* **waned, waning** [I] **1** (of a feeling or condition) to become gradually smaller or less: *Her affection for him began to wane.* | *the waning power of the king* **2** (of the moon) to become smaller

wane[2] *n* **on the wane** becoming smaller, weaker, or less: *The government's popularity is on the wane.*

wan·gle /'wæŋgəl/ *v* **wangled, wangling** [T] *infml* to get something from someone by persuading them in a clever or dishonest way: *I managed to wangle an invitation out of George.*

wan·na /'wɒnə ‖ 'wɔː-, 'wɑː-/ **1** want to **2** want a ■ USAGE **Want to** and **want a** are sometimes pronounced in this way in informal speech. They may be written **wanna** in stories to show an informal way of speaking, especially in American English: *I don't* **wanna** *go.* (= I don't want to go.) | **Wanna** *drink?* (= Do you want a drink?)

want[1] /wɒnt ‖ wɔːnt, wɑːnt/ **1** [I;T] to feel a desire or wish for something: *Do you want a drink?* | *What do you want for your birthday?* | *He wants to leave soon.* | *Do you want me to help you?* | *I want that work finished by Tuesday.* | *She doesn't want people coming in and out all day.*
☐ [USEFUL PATTERNS to want something; to want to do something; to want someone to do something; to want something done] –see WANNA (USAGE)
2 [I] *infml* should or ought: *You want to leave early so as to miss the traffic.* | *You want to see a doctor about that cough.*
☐ USEFUL PATTERN want to do something
3 **be wanted** to be searched for by the police: *He is wanted for murder.* | *They're wanted for questioning.* **4** [T] *infml* to need: *This job wants doing this week.* | *The house wants painting.*
☐ USEFUL PATTERN want to do doing
want for *phr v infml* **want for nothing** to have everything that you need: *His children wanted for nothing except his love.*

want[2] *n* **1** **for/from want of** because of a lack or absence of something wanted or needed: *The plants died for want of water.* | *We watched television, for want of anything better to do.* **2** [U] *fml* severe lack of things necessary to life: *They had lived all their lives in want.* **3** **wants** [pl] the things you want: *My wants are few and soon satisfied.*

want·ing /'wɒntɪŋ ‖ 'wɔːn-, 'wɑːn-/ *adj fml* **be found wanting** to be considered not good enough: *Her new invention was tested and found wanting.*

wan·ton /'wɒntən ‖ 'wɔːn-, 'wɑːn-/ *adj* intentionally causing damage or harm for no reason: *wanton cruelty*

war[1] /wɔːr/ *n* **1** [C;U] a period of armed fighting between nations or countries: *He fought in both World Wars.* | *Is war ever necessary?* | *a prisoner of war* **2** **at war** fighting: *England and France were still at war with each other.* **3** **go to war** to begin fighting a war: *The navy is preparing to go to war.* **4** [C] a struggle against something bad, or a strong competition between groups: *the war* **against** *disease* | *a trade war* **5** **have been in the wars** *infml* to have been hurt or damaged: *Your car looks as if it's been in the wars!*

war[2] *v* **-rr-** [I] *lit* to fight a war: *a meeting between the generals of the warring forces*

war·ble /'wɔːbəl ‖ 'wɔːr-/ *v* **warbled, warbling** [I] (of birds) to sing with a clear, continuous, yet varied note **–warble** *n*

ward[1] /wɔːd ‖ wɔːrd/ *n* **1** a large room with beds in a hospital, usually for people all needing treatment of the same kind: *the maternity ward* **2** a division of a city, especially for political purposes: *Which ward does she represent on the council?* **3** a child who is officially under the protection of a law court or a person who is not their parent

ward[2] *v*
ward sthg ↔ **off** *phr v* [T] to protect yourself against something bad or unpleasant: *I've managed to ward off a cold this winter by taking these tablets.*

war·den /'wɔːdn ‖ 'wɔːrdn/ *n* **1** a person who looks after a place and the people in it: *the warden of an old people's home* **2** an official who helps to see that certain laws are obeyed: *a traffic warden* **3** *AmE* the head of a prison

ward·er /'wɔːdər ‖ 'wɔːr-/ *n* a prison guard

war·drobe /'wɔːdrəʊb ‖ 'wɔːr-/ *n* **1** a cupboard in which you hang up clothes **2** a collection of clothes belonging to one person: *She bought a new summer wardrobe.*

ware·house /'weəhaʊs ‖ 'weər-/ *n* **warehouses** /-haʊzɪz/ a large building for storing things, especially things that are going to be sold

wares /weəz ‖ weərz/ *n* [pl] *lit* articles for sale in the street or a market: *The baker travelled round the town selling his wares.*

war·fare /'wɔːfeər ‖ 'wɔːr-/ *n* [U] military activity against an enemy: *chemical warfare*

war·head /'wɔːhed ‖ 'wɔːr-/ *n* the explosive front end of a bomb or MISSILE

war·i·ly /'weərɪli/ *adv* in a very careful way **–wariness** *n* [U]

war·like /'wɔːlaɪk ‖ 'wɔːr-/ *adj* liking war or skilled in war: *a warlike nation*

warm[1] /wɔːm ‖ wɔːrm/ *adj* **1** having or producing heat which is pleasant, but not strong enough to be hot: *warm milk* | *a warm fire* | *a warm sunny day* **2** able to keep in the heat and protect you from the cold: *warm clothes* **3** showing very friendly feelings: *warm support for the local team* | *warm friendship* | *a warm welcome* **4** giving a pleasant feeling of cheerfulness or comfort: *warm colours* | *a warm voice* **–warmly** *adv* : *They greeted each other warmly.*

warm[2] *v* [T] to make something hotter: *They warmed their hands over the fire.*
warm to sbdy/sthg *phr v* [T] *infml* to begin to like someone or become more interested in something: *The students immediately warmed to their new teacher.* | *The more he spoke, the more he warmed to his subject.*
warm up *phr v* **1** [I;T **warm** sthg ↔ **up**] to make or become hotter: *The room soon warmed up.* | *You'll have to warm the engine up a bit first.* **2** [T **warm** sthg ↔ **up**] to reheat cooked food: *We can warm up the leftovers for supper.* **3** [I] to get ready for a performance or event by practising just before it starts: *The singers are already warming up for the concert.*

warm[3] *n* **the warm** a warm place, state, or condition: *Come into the warm, out of the cold.*

warm-blood·ed /ˌ· '··◄/ *adj tech* having a body temperature that remains fairly high whether the temperature of the surroundings is high or low

warm-heart·ed /ˌ· '··◄/ *adj* kind and friendly towards other people

war·mon·ger /ˈwɔːˌmʌŋgəʳ ‖ ˈwɔːrˌmʌŋ-, -ˌmɑːŋ-/ *n* a person who encourages people to prepare for or start a war (a word used to express disapproval)

warmth /wɔːmθ ‖ wɔːrmθ/ *n* [U] **1** the state or quality of making someone feel warm: *the warmth of the fire* | *His light jacket provided little warmth.* **2** kind, friendly, and generous behaviour: *She was loved for her warmth and humour.*

warm-up /ˈ· ·/ *n* a period of gentle exercising in preparation for a sports event: *After a 15-minute warm-up, the game began.*

warn /wɔːn ‖ wɔːrn/ *v* **1** [I;T; +(that)] to tell someone of a possible future problem or danger so they can try to prevent it or avoid it: *The morning paper warned of serious delays at the airport.* | *He warned his students that they would have to work very hard to pass.* | *I warn you it's going to be very cold.* | *Her boss had warned her about difficult customers.*
□ USEFUL PATTERNS To warn of something; to warn someone of something; to warn that...; to warn someone that...
2 [T] to advise someone not to do something because of a possible problem or danger in the future: *I warned her not to go near the dog, but she ignored me.*

warn·ing /ˈwɔːnɪŋ ‖ ˈwɔːr-/ *n* [C;U] something which tells someone of a possible problem or danger: *The enemy attacked without warning.* | *The health department have issued warnings about the disease.* | *Let this experience be a warning to you.*

warp¹ /wɔːp ‖ wɔːrp/ *v* **1** [I;T] to make or become bent and damaged, often because of heat or water: *This wood warps easily in damp conditions.* | *The record was warped from the sun.* **2** [T] to strongly influence someone or something in a bad way: *Her attitude to men was warped by several bad experiences.* **-warped** *adj* : *the warped mind of a killer*

warp² *n* a twist or fault

war·path /ˈwɔːpɑːθ ‖ ˈwɔːrpæθ/ *n* **on the warpath** *infml* angry and looking for someone to fight or punish

war·rant¹ /ˈwɒrənt ‖ ˈwɔː-, ˈwɑː-/ *n* an official order signed by a judge which allows the police to do something such as search someone's house: *The magistrate issued a warrant for his arrest.*

warrant² *v* [T] *fml* to make something seem right or reasonable: *The tiny crowd didn't warrant such a huge police presence.*

war·ran·ty /ˈwɒrənti ‖ ˈwɔː-, ˈwɑː-/ *n* under warranty covered by a GUARANTEE: *We'll repair your car without charging because it's still under warranty.*

war·ren /ˈwɒrən ‖ ˈwɔː-, ˈwɑː-/ *n* **1** a system of underground passages in which a number of rabbits live **2** a place in which too many people live, or in which you can get lost easily: *a warren of narrow old streets*

war·ri·or /ˈwɒriəʳ ‖ ˈwɔː-, ˈwɑː-/ *n lit* a soldier or experienced fighter: *a noble warrior*

war·ship /ˈwɔːˌʃɪp ‖ ˈwɔːr-/ *n* a naval ship with guns used for war

wart /wɔːt ‖ wɔːrt/ *n* **1** a small hard swelling on the skin of your face or hands **2 warts and all** not failing to mention the bad parts

war·time /ˈwɔːtaɪm ‖ ˈwɔːr-/ *n* [U] a period of time during which there is a war

war·y /ˈweəri/ *adj* **warier, wariest** careful about something because it is new or could cause problems: *The staff are wary of the new proposals.*

was /wəz; *strong* wɒz ‖ wəz; *strong* wɑːz/ the past tense of BE, 1st and 3rd person singular: *He was angry.* | *I was at home.*

wash¹ /wɒʃ ‖ wɔːʃ, wɑːʃ/ *v* **1** [T] to clean something with water and soap: *This shirt needs washing.* | *He washed his hands.* | *Can you wash those marks off the chair, please?* **2** [I] (also **wash up** *AmE*) to clean yourself or a part of your body with water and soap: *Jack washed and went to bed.* **3** [I] to be able to be cleaned with soap and water without being damaged: *These clothes only wash in cold water.* **4** [I + adv/prep] *lit* to flow over or against something: *The waves washed against the shore.* **5** [T +adv/prep] to be carried by water: *The waves washed him off the rocks into the sea.* **6 it won't wash** = I don't believe it: *It's a good story, John, but it just won't wash with me.* **7 wash your hands of** *infml* to refuse to be responsible for: *I wash my hands of you and all your wild ideas!*

wash sthg ↔ **away** *phr v* [T] to carry something away with the force of moving water: *farm animals washed away by the floods*

wash sthg ↔ **down** *phr v* [T] **1** to clean something large with a lot of water: *The walls need to be washed down.* **2** to drink something while eating or as soon as you have finished eating: *We washed our hamburgers down with some beer.*

wash out *phr v* **1** [I;T **wash** sthg ↔ **out**] to remove or be removed by washing: *Did she manage to wash that dirty mark out of her coat?* | *Do you think these ink spots will wash out?* **2 be washed out** to be prevented because of rain: *The football match was washed out.*

wash up *phr v infml* **1** [I] *BrE* to clean the dishes, knives, forks, etc., after a meal: *Who's going to wash up tonight, then?* **2** [T **wash** sbdy/sthg **up**] (of waves) to bring someone or something onto land: *The sea washed up the body of the drowned sailor.*

wash² *n* **1 have a wash** to wash yourself, especially your hands and face: *She had a quick wash.* **2 give someone/something a wash** to wash someone or something: *Give the car a good wash.* **3 in the wash** being washed: *I'm afraid all your shirts are in the wash.*

wash·a·ble /ˈwɒʃəbəl ‖ ˈwɔː-, ˈwɑː-/ *adj* able to be washed without damage: *Is this cushion cover washable?*

wash·ba·sin /ˈwɒʃˌbeɪsən ‖ ˈwɔːʃ-, ˈwɑːʃ-/ *n* (**washbowl** /-bəʊl/ *AmE*) a large bowl fixed to the wall for washing your hands and face; it is usually found in a bathroom

washed-out /ˌ· ˈ·◄/ *adj* **1** extremely tired: *She felt completely washed-out after working all night.* **2** very pale in colour: *washed-out old curtains*

wash·er /ˈwɒʃəʳ ‖ ˈwɔː-, ˈwɑː-/ *n* a ring of metal, rubber, or plastic between two pipes, which makes a better, tighter joint

wash·ing /ˈwɒʃɪŋ ‖ ˈwɔː-, ˈwɑː-/ *n* [U] clothes or things like sheets which need to be washed, or are being washed or dried: *I'll just hang the washing out to dry.* | *a pile of dirty washing*

washing ma·chine /ˈ··· ˌ·/ *n* a machine for washing clothes

washing-up /ˌ··· ˈ·/ *n* [U] the activity of washing the dirty plates, forks, knives, etc., that have been used to prepare and eat a meal: *It's your turn to do the washing-up.* | *I hate washing-up.* | *a bottle of washing-up liquid*

wash·out /ˈwɒʃ-aʊt ‖ ˈwɔːʃ-, ˈwɑːʃ-/ *n infml* a failure: *His plan was a complete washout.*

wash·room /ˈwɒʃrʊm, -ruːm ‖ ˈwɔːʃ-, ˈwɑːʃ-/ n AmE euph a room containing a TOILET (a less direct word than TOILET)

was·n't /ˈwɒzənt ‖ ˈwɑː-/ short for "was not": I wasn't at school yesterday.

wasp /wɒsp ‖ wɑːsp, wɔːsp/ n a yellow and black insect similar to the bee, which stings

wast·age /ˈweɪstɪdʒ/ n fml [sing] loss, or lack of proper use: this terrible wastage of our resources

waste¹ /weɪst/ n 1 [sing; U] a wrong or unnecessary use of something: These new weapons are a waste of public money. | The meeting was a complete waste of time. | The staff are thinking of ways to prevent waste. 2 [U] used substances, from which the valuable parts have been removed: A lot of poisonous waste from the chemical works goes into the river. | Waste from the body passes out from the bowels. | the body's waste products 3 wastes [pl] lit a large empty area of land: No crops will grow on these stony wastes. | the Arctic wastes 4 go to waste to remain unused: It's a shame to let this food go to waste.

waste² v wasted, wasting 1 [T] to use something wrongly or use too much of something: I've wasted a lot of money on that useless car. | Don't waste time on unimportant details. 2 waste a chance, waste an opportunity not to use a chance to do something 3 be wasted on someone to be too good for someone to recognize such high quality: His jokes were completely wasted on his students.

waste away phr v [I] to become very weak and thin because of illness or lack of food

waste³ adj [only before a noun] 1 got rid of because of being used, worthless, or damaged: waste material from nuclear power plants | waste paper 2 **waste land**, **waste ground** an area of land that is not being used or cared for: The waste ground beside the railway was covered with weeds.

wa·sted /ˈweɪstɪd/ adj [only before a noun] useless and unnecessary: a wasted journey

waste·ful /ˈweɪstfəl/ adj tending to waste things: wasteful habits

waste·pa·per bas·ket /ˌweɪstˈpeɪpə ˌbɑːskɪt, ˈweɪstˌpeɪpə- ‖ ˈweɪstˌpeɪpər ˌbæs-/ n (also **waste-basket** /ˈweɪstˌbɑːskɪt ‖ -ˌbæ-/ AmE) a small container on the floor of a house or office in which you put unwanted paper – see pictures on pages 148 and 539

watch¹ /wɒtʃ ‖ wɑːtʃ, wɔːtʃ/ v 1 [I;T] to look at a person or object which is doing something, or at an activity or event, for a period of time, and pay attention to it: Do you watch much television? | They watched the sun set. | Watch how to do this. | The children watched to see what would happen. – see SEE 1 (USAGE) 2 [T] to look at or follow carefully and secretly: The police have been watching the house for weeks. | I felt I was being watched. 3 [T; +(that)] to take care of or pay attention to: I'll watch the baby if you want to pop out. | Watch that the milk doesn't boil over. | You'll have to watch what you say when you talk to the general. 4 **Watch it!** infml Be careful!: Hey! Watch it! There are glasses in that box. 5 **watch your step** a phrase used to warn someone to be careful in their behaviour: You'd better watch your step, or you'll be fired! –watcher n

watch out phr v [I] infml to be careful to avoid something unpleasant: Watch out! There's a car coming.

watch over sbdy/sthg phr v [T] to protect and take care of

watch² n 1 a small clock worn on your wrist: My watch has stopped. –see picture on page 50 2 the

watch one or more guards ordered to watch a place or a person: The night watch comes on duty at six o'clock. 3 **keep watch** to look around carefully for signs of danger, so that you can warn other people 4 **keep a close/careful watch on** to carefully give your attention to something: The government is keeping a close watch on rising prices.

watch·dog /ˈwɒtʃdɒg ‖ ˈwɑːtʃdɔːg, ˈwɔːtʃ-/ n 1 a fierce dog kept to guard property 2 a person or group that tries to prevent dishonest or illegal behaviour by companies or other organizations: The government appointed a committee to act as a watchdog on the steel industry.

watch·ful /ˈwɒtʃfəl ‖ ˈwɑːtʃ-, ˈwɔːtʃ-/ adj careful to notice things: From then on, she was watchful for any sign of activity in the empty house.

watch·mak·er /ˈwɒtʃˌmeɪkə ‖ ˈwɑːtʃ-, ˈwɔːtʃ-/ n a person who makes or repairs watches or clocks

watch·man /ˈwɒtʃmən ‖ ˈwɑːtʃ-, ˈwɔːtʃ-/ n **watchmen** /-mən/ a guard of a building: Call the night watchman if there is any trouble tonight.

watch·word /ˈwɒtʃwɜːd ‖ ˈwɑːtʃwɜːrd, ˈwɔːtʃ-/ n a word or phrase that expresses a principle of a particular group of people: "Caring and sharing" is their watchword.

wa·ter¹ /ˈwɔːtər ‖ ˈwɔː-, ˈwɑː-/ n 1 [U] the most common liquid on the Earth, which falls from clouds as rain and forms rivers, lakes, and seas; people and animals need water to live: The prisoner was given only bread and water. | Turn on the hot water now. | sea water | bathwater 2 [U] a large amount or area of water: He's fallen in the water. | They ran down to the edge of the lake and dived into the water. | The flood had left most of the town under water. 3 **waters** [pl] the sea around a country which is considered to belong to it: The boat was caught fishing in Norwegian waters. 4 **in hot water** infml in trouble: We'll get into hot water if the teachers hear about this. 5 **it's water under the bridge** = you should stop worrying about it because it has already finished and there's nothing you can do about it now

water² v 1 [T] to pour water on the soil so that plants can grow: It's very dry: we must water the garden. | Mike watered the roses yesterday. 2 [I] (of your eyes) to become filled with tears: The pain made her eyes water. 3 [I] (of your mouth) to become filled with SALIVA, the liquid that helps you to eat food, usually because you have seen something that you would like to eat: The sight of the cake made his mouth water.

water sthg ↔ **down** phr v [T] 1 to weaken a liquid by adding water to it: This beer has been watered down! 2 to make a speech or report less forceful by removing any strong opinions from it: The Minister's statement had been watered down so as not to offend anyone.

wa·ter·borne /ˈwɔːtəbɔːn ‖ ˈwɔːtərbɔːrn, ˈwɑː-/ adj carried by water: waterborne diseases

wa·ter·col·our /ˈwɔːtəˌkʌlər ‖ ˈwɔːtər-, ˈwɑː-/ n (**watercolor** AmE) 1 **watercolours** [pl] coloured paints that are mixed with water and used for painting pictures: She mostly paints in watercolours. 2 [C] a picture painted using watercolours: Have you sold any more watercolours lately?

wa·ter·cress /ˈwɔːtəkres ‖ ˈwɔːtər-, ˈwɑː-/ n [U] a plant with leaves which taste hot, grown in water and used as food

wa·ter·fall /ˈwɔːtəfɔːl ‖ ˈwɔːtər-, ˈwɑː-/ n water that falls straight down over rocks, often from a great height

wa·ter·front /ˈwɔːtəfrʌnt ‖ ˈwɔːtər-, ˈwɑː-/ n [sing] a part of a town, or a piece of land, near an area of water: *We strolled along the waterfront.*

wa·ter·hole /ˈwɔːtəhəʊl ‖ ˈwɔːtər-, ˈwɑː-/ n a pool in a dry country where wild animals go to drink

watering can /ˈ··· ·/ n a container with a long SPOUT, for watering garden plants

wa·ter·logged /ˈwɔːtəlɒgd ‖ ˈwɔːtərlɔːgd, ˈwɔː-, -lɑːgd/ adj **1** full of water and so unable to float (used of boats) **2** completely full of water (used of land): *The footballers couldn't play because the ground was waterlogged.*

water main /ˈ·· ·/ n a large underground pipe carrying a supply of water

wa·ter·mark /ˈwɔːtəmɑːk ‖ ˈwɔːtərmɑːrk, ˈwɑː-/ n a mark made on paper by the maker, seen only when it is held up to the light

wa·ter·mel·on /ˈwɔːtəˌmelən ‖ ˈwɔːtər-, ˈwɑː-/ n [C;U] a large round fruit with green skin, juicy red flesh, and black seeds

wa·ter·proof¹ /ˈwɔːtəpruːf ‖ ˈwɔːtər-, ˈwɑː-/ adj which does not allow water to go through: *Is the tent waterproof?* – **waterproof** v: *The walls were waterproofed with a special material.*

waterproof² n a coat which does not let water go through

wa·ter·shed /ˈwɔːtəʃed ‖ ˈwɔːtər-, ˈwɑː-/ n a time or event which marks a very important change in a person's life or a country's history: *Leaving her first job was a watershed in her life.*

wa·ter·side /ˈwɔːtəsaɪd ‖ ˈwɔːtər-, ˈwɑː-/ n the **waterside** the edge of a river, lake, or sea

water ski /ˈ·· ˌ·/ v [I] to do the sport in which you move over water on skis (SKI), pulled by a boat: *She loves to go water skiing.* – **water skiing** n [U]: *Water skiing is becoming a popular sport.*

wa·ter·tight /ˈwɔːtətaɪt ‖ ˈwɔːtər-, ˈwɑː-/ adj **1** through which no water can go: *a watertight box* **2** produced with great care, so there is no possibility of mistakes or unintended results: *a watertight argument* | *a watertight plan*

wa·ter·way /ˈwɔːtəweɪ ‖ ˈwɔːtər-, ˈwɑː-/ n a long passage of water along which ships can travel, such as part of a river: *Canals and rivers form the inland waterways of a country.*

wa·ter·works /ˈwɔːtəwɜːks ‖ ˈwɔːtərwɜːrks, ˈwɑː-/ n [pl] a building in which supplies of water for the public are cleaned

wa·ter·y /ˈwɔːtəri ‖ ˈwɔː-, ˈwɑː-/ adj **1** containing too much water: *watery soup* **2** very pale in colour: *a watery sun*

watt /wɒt ‖ wɑːt/ n a measure of electrical power: *Put a 100 watt bulb in that lamp.*

wave¹ /weɪv/ v **waved, waving 1** [I] to hold your arm up in the air and move your hand, for example to greet someone: *She waved excitedly.* | *We waved goodbye to them.* | *He waved frantically at us to get out of the way.* **2** [T] to hold something in your hand and move it quickly from side to side: *The children waved their flags as the President's car passed.* **3** [T +adv/prep] to show someone the direction they should go by signalling with your hand: *The policeman waved the traffic on.* | *He waved his students away impatiently.* **4** [I] to move in the air, from side to side or up and down: *The branches waved in the wind.*

wave sthg ↔ **aside** phr v [T] to treat an idea or suggestion as unimportant: *She waved his objections aside.*

wave² n **1** the movement of your hand when waving: *The actress gave the crowd a wave.* **2** a raised line of water on the surface of the sea or other area of water, caused when the water rises or falls: *In bad weather, we get very large waves pounding on the shore.* **3** an evenly curved part of your hair: *natural waves in her hair* **4** a sudden increase in a particular feeling or way of behaviour which can spread uncontrollably: *The police are worried about the recent wave of violence.* | *A wave of panic spread through the crowd.* **5** a form in which some forms of ENERGY, such as light and sound, travel: *radio waves* | *sound waves*

wave band /ˈ·· ·/ n a set of sound waves of similar lengths, used especially for broadcasting by radio

wave·length /ˈweɪvleŋθ/ n **1** a radio signal sent out on radio waves that are a particular distance apart **2 on the same wavelength** to have similar opinions to someone, so that you understand each other well [RELATED PHRASE **on a different wavelength**]

wa·ver /ˈweɪvəʳ/ v [I] **1** to be unsteady or uncertain in a belief or decision: *He wavered between accepting and refusing.* | *Her confidence in his abilities never wavered.* **2** to move slightly: *The flame wavered and then went out.*

wav·y /ˈweɪvi/ adj having regular curves: *wavy hair* | *a wavy line*

wax¹ /wæks/ n [U] **1** a solid substance made of fats or oils, which changes to a thick liquid when melted; it is often used to make candles **2** the soft yellow substance found in your ears

wax² v **1** [T] to put wax on a surface as a polish: *The floor was waxed every Thursday.* **2 wax and wane** (of the moon) to gradually increase and decrease in size or amount: *The moon waxes and wanes every month.*

wax·work /ˈwækswɜːk ‖ -wɜːrk/ n **waxworks 1** a model of a famous person made in wax **2 waxworks** a place where you can see waxworks

way¹ /weɪ/ n **1** [C] a road or path that you need to follow in order to reach a place: *Is this the way to the station?* | *Could you show me the way out, please?* **2** [sing] the distance that you have to travel in order to reach a place: *Is it a long way to Manchester?* | *She complained all the way home.* **3 lose your way** to become lost and not know how to find the place that you are looking for **4 on the way** while travelling to a place: *We'll stop and have lunch on the way.* | *I was on my way to work.* **5** [C] a direction: *Come this way.* | *He was looking the other way so he didn't see me.* **6 the right way round, the right way up** facing in the right direction: *Have I got this picture the right way round?* [RELATED PHRASE: **the wrong way round/up**] **7** [C] a manner or method of doing something: *There are several ways in which you can pay.* | *What's the best way to clean leather furniture?* | *There must be a better way of keeping food fresh.*

□ USEFUL PATTERNS a way to do something; a way of doing something

8 ways [pl] small bits of behaviour that are typical of a particular person: *We were very fond of him in spite of his annoying little ways.* **9 in a way, in some ways, etc** used when you are saying that something is true partly but not completely: *In a way I think she's right.* | *I agree with you in some ways.* **10 in the way** in a place or position that prevents you from going somewhere: *I can't get past – that suitcase is in the way.* | *I got up to leave, but she stood in my way.* **11 out of the way: a** not in a place

or position that prevents you from going somewhere: *Could you move that box out of the way?* | *Get out of my way!* **b** finished: *I'll be happier once the exams are out of the way.* **12 out of someone's way** not near to a place where someone is going: *Can you give me a lift home, if it's not too far out of your way?* **13 by the way** a phrase you use when you want to talk about something that is not directly concerned with what you have just been talking about: *We'll discuss this at the meeting later. By the way, did you tell Steven about the meeting?* **14 by way of** as a way of doing something: *He handed me his card by way of introduction.* **15 can't have it both ways** a phrase you use to tell someone that they have to choose between two possibilities, but they cannot have both **16 get your own way** to do or get what you want **17 go out of your way to do something** to make a great effort to do something: *She seemed to be going out of her way to be nice to me.* **18 have a way with** to be able to form good relationships with a particular type of people: *He has a way with children.* **19 keep out of someone's way** to avoid seeing or talking to someone **20 under way** taking place: *Discussions between management and unions are now under way.* **21 No way** No: *"Are you going to help Mary again?" "No way!"*
■ USAGE 1 We do not use **way** when we are thinking of a particular **road**, **path**, or **track**: *We followed a muddy* **path** *through the forest.* | *We walked to the village along a narrow* **track** *instead of taking the main* **road**. 2 **By the way**. Although this expression seems to suggest that we are going to add unimportant information, we often use it to introduce a topic which is very important to us: **By the way**, *is it all right if I don't pay you the money I owe you just yet?*

way² *adv* far: *The film was made way back in 1929.* | *We're way behind with our work.*

way·lay /weɪˈleɪ/ *v* **waylaid** /-ˈleɪd/, **waylain** /-ˈleɪn/ [T] to wait for someone and stop them going somewhere, for example because you want to talk to them: *She waylaid me as I was leaving the meeting.*

way-out /ˌ· ˈ·◄/ *adj infml* very modern, but strange or unusual: *way-out clothes*

way·side /ˈweɪsaɪd/ *n* **the wayside** the side of the road (a word no longer used in modern English)

way·ward /ˈweɪwəd ‖ -ərd/ *adj* difficult, changeable, and not easily guided: *wayward behaviour* | *a wayward son*

WC /ˌdʌbəljuː ˈsiː/ *n* a TOILET

we /wi; *strong* wiː/ *pron* [used as the subject of a verb] the people who are speaking: *Shall we go for a drink?* | *We all enjoyed the film.*

weak /wiːk/ *adj* **1** lacking physical strength or power: *I still feel a bit weak after my illness.* | *a weak heart* | *weak eyes* **2** not firm or determined in character: *The teacher's so weak that the children do what they like.* | *a weak and indecisive leader* **3** easily broken, defeated, or destroyed: *The shelf's too weak to hold all those books.* | *a weak team* **4** containing too much water and lacking taste: *weak soup* | *weak tea* **5** lacking skill or ability in a particular area: *The article is weak on facts.* | *She's weak at maths.* **6** lacking the ability to persuade or force people: *a weak argument* **7** faint (used of light or sounds) — **weakly** *adv*

weak·en /ˈwiːkən/ *v* [I;T] **1** to make or become less powerful or less physically strong: *She weakened as the illness got worse.* | *a country weakened by war and disease* | *Years of carrying heavy boxes had* weakened his back. | *These disputes have weakened the government's position.* **2** to make or become less determined: *Nothing could weaken her resolve to become a doctor.* | *Their sense of responsibility never weakened.*

weak·ling /ˈwiːklɪŋ/ *n* a person lacking physical strength or strength of purpose

weak·ness /ˈwiːknɪs/ *n* **1** [U] the state of lacking strength in your body or character: *The symptoms are general weakness and nausea.* | *The parents accused the headteacher of weakness.* **2** [C] an imperfect part of something: *The cost of your plan is its main weakness.* | *a structural weakness in the building* **3** [C] a fault in someone's character: *His weakness is refusing to accept criticism.* **4** [C] a strong liking for something which is bad for you: *I've got a real weakness for chocolate.*

weal /wiːl/ *n* a red mark on the skin where you have been hit or beaten

wealth /welθ/ *n* **1** [U] the state of owning a large amount of money and possessions: *It was a decade of wealth and affluence.* **2** [U] money and possessions: *His wealth increased year by year.* **3 a wealth of** *fml* a large number or amount of: *a wealth of examples*

wealth·y /ˈwelθi/ *adj* **wealthier**, **wealthiest** having a lot of money or other valuable possessions: *a wealthy family* | *Nigeria was comparatively wealthy in those days.*

wean /wiːn/ *v* [T] **1** to accustom a young child to eat food instead of its mother's milk: *Most babies are weaned by the time they are one.* **2** to gradually help someone to stop doing something that is bad for them: *How can we wean him from his habit of getting drunk every night?*

weap·on /ˈwepən/ *n* an object used to attack people, such as a gun or bomb: *nuclear weapons*

wear¹ /weər/ *v* **wore** /wɔːr/, **worn** /wɔːn ‖ wɔːrn/ **1** [T] to have something on your body, especially as clothing: *He's wearing a new coat.* | *Does your brother wear glasses?* | *She's wearing a pearl necklace.* | *It is compulsory to wear seat belts when you are driving in England.* —see DRESS¹ (USAGE) **2** [T] to have your hair in a particular style: *She wore her hair tied in a ribbon.* **3** [I;T] to weaken or damage by continued use: *I like this shirt, but the collar has worn.* | *a worn carpet* **4** [T + adv/prep] to produce by continuous use: *You've worn a hole in your sock.* | *The villagers had worn a path through the fields.* **5 wear well/badly** to last in good or bad condition: *This coat will wear well if you look after it properly.* **6 wear thin** to become less acceptable because of being used too much: *I felt sorry for Jackie at first, but now all her moaning about her husband is beginning to wear a bit thin.*

wear away *phr v* [I;T **wear** sthg ↔ **away**] to gradually disappear or make something disappear from continuous use: *Over the centuries, the wind has worn the rocks away.*

wear down *phr v* **1** [I;T **wear** sthg ↔ **down**] to become, or make something become, gradually smaller or thinner: *My shoes are badly worn down at the heels.* **2** [T **wear** sbdy/sthg ↔ **down**] to gradually lessen somebody's strength or strength of purpose: *We wore down their opposition after several hours' argument.*

wear off *phr v* [I] (of a feeling or effect) to be slowly reduced until it disappears: *The pain is wearing off.*

wear on *phr v* [I] to pass slowly in time: *The day wore on.*

wear out phr v 1 [I;T **wear** sthg ↔ **out**] to be or become useless from use: *Her shoes wear out quickly when she goes walking.* | *worn-out old shoes* 2 [T **wear** sbdy ↔ **out**] to tire someone greatly: *If you don't stop working you'll wear yourself out.*

wear² n [U] 1 clothes of a particular type or for a particular purpose: *evening wear* | *footwear* 2 (also **wear and tear**) continuous use which weakens or damages something: *This carpet is already showing signs of wear.* 3 the quality of lasting in use: *There's still plenty of wear in these tyres.*

wear·ing /'weərɪŋ/ adj tiring: *It's a very wearing job.*

wear·i·some /'wɪərɪsəm/ adj making you feel tired and annoyed: *a wearisome task*

wear·y¹ /'wɪəri/ adj **wearier, weariest** very tired: *You look rather weary after your long journey.* | *a weary smile* –**wearily** adv –**weariness** n [U]

weary² v **wearied, wearying** [I] to become tired of and lose interest in something: *He soon wearied of his job at the bank.*

wea·sel /'wiːzəl/ n a small thin furry animal which can kill other small animals

weath·er¹ /'weðər/ n [U] 1 the condition of wind, rain, sunshine, snow, etc., at a certain time or over a period of time: *good weather* | *severe weather conditions* | *What will the weather be like tomorrow?* 2 **under the weather** infml not very well

weather² v 1 [T] to pass safely through difficulty: *The government will need to weather this crisis to win the next election.* 2 [I;T] to change or be changed in shape or colour because of wind or other weather conditions: *Rocks weather until they are worn away.*

weather-beat·en /'·· ,··/ adj brown and lined from being outdoors in bad weather (used of your face or skin)

weath·er·cock /'weðəkɒk ‖ -ərkɑːk/ n (also **weather vane**) a small metal object which shows the direction the wind is blowing by turning round in the wind; it is often shaped like a male chicken and fixed to the top of a building

weather fore·cast /'·· ,··/ n a description of what future weather conditions are likely to be, for example on the radio

weath·er·man /'weðəmæn ‖ -ər-/ n **weathermen** /-men/ a person whose job is to describe likely weather conditions on television and the radio

weave¹ /wiːv/ v **wove** /wəʊv/, **woven** /'wəʊvən/, **weaving** 1 [I] to make material by crossing threads under and over each other on a LOOM: *Do you know how to weave?* 2 [T] to make something by twisting parts together: *to weave a basket*

weave² v **weaved, weaving** [I; + adv/prep] to move along, changing direction frequently to avoid hitting anything: *Taxis wove through the traffic.*

weave³ n the way in which a material is woven and the pattern formed by this: *a loose weave*

weav·er /'wiːvər/ n a person whose job is to weave cloth

web /web/ n 1 a net of thin threads made by a SPIDER to catch other insects 2 a detailed arrangement or network: *a complex web of relationships*

webbed /webd/ adj **webbed feet** feet which have skin between the toes, as on a duck's foot

wed /wed/ v **wedded** or **wed, wedded** or **wed** [I;T] lit to marry

we'd /wid; strong wiːd/ 1 short for "we had": *We'd arranged to meet in town.* 2 short for "we would": *We'd love to meet him.*

wed·ded /'wedɪd/ adj **wedded to something** agreeing with something and supporting it strongly: *The government is firmly wedded to the idea of cutting taxes.*

wed·ding /'wedɪŋ/ n a marriage ceremony, especially with a party or meal afterwards: *Have you been invited to their wedding?*

wedding ring /'··· ·/ n a gold ring, used in the marriage ceremony and worn to show that you are married

wedge¹ /wedʒ/ n 1 a V-shaped piece of wood, with one thin end and one quite wide end, used for example for holding a door open 2 something shaped like a wedge: *a big wedge of chocolate cake* 3 **the thin end of the wedge** something which seems unimportant but will open the way for more serious things of a similar kind

wedge² v **wedged, wedging** [T + adv/prep] to fix something firmly into a place or a position, for example with a wedge: *Wedge the door open.* | *I was wedged into a corner.*

wed·lock /'wedlɒk ‖ -lɑːk/ n [U] old fash 1 the state of being married 2 **born out of wedlock** born of unmarried parents

Wednes·day /'wenzdi/ n (also **Wed.** or **Weds.**) the day between Tuesday and Thursday

wee /wiː/ adj dialect very small: *a wee child*

weed¹ /wiːd/ n 1 a wild plant that grows where you do not want it to grow: *The garden's full of weeds.* 2 a person who has a thin, weak body

weed² v [I;T] to remove weeds from a place: *I spent the afternoon weeding the garden.*

weed sbdy/sthg ↔ **out** phr v [T] to get rid of things or people that you do not want: *We need to weed out incompetent teachers.*

weed·y /'wiːdi/ adj **weedier, weediest** infml having a thin, weak body

week /wiːk/ n 1 a period of seven days, usually starting on Sunday or Monday: *The flight to Accra goes twice a week.* | *I'll see you next week.* 2 the period of time during which you work, for example in a factory or office: *She works a 60-hour week.* | *The five-day week is usual in most firms.* 3 **Monday week, Tuesday week, etc.** a week after Monday, Tuesday, etc: *She's coming on Sunday week.* 4 **a week on Monday, a week tomorrow, etc.** a week after the stated day: *He'll be back a week on Saturday.* | *I'll see you a week tomorrow, then.* | *a week next Tuesday* 5 **week in, week out** happening every week, without change or rest

week·day /'wiːkdeɪ/ n one of the days of the week, except Saturday or Sunday: *We're only open on weekdays.*

week·end /ˌwiːk'end◂, 'wiːkend ‖ 'wiːkend/ n Saturday and Sunday: *See you at the weekend.*

week·ly¹ /'wiːkli/ adj,adv happening or appearing once a week or every week: *my weekly visit to the hospital* | *a weekly magazine* | *We meet twice weekly.*

weekly² n **weeklies** a magazine or newspaper which appears once a week

weep /wiːp/ v **wept** /wept/, **wept** [I] lit to let tears fall from your eyes: *I could weep when I think of all the money we've lost.* –**weep** n

weep·y /'wiːpi/ adj infml feeling sad and wanting to cry

weigh /weɪ/ v 1 [T] to find the weight of something by using a special machine: *Have you weighed yourself lately?* | *The packets are all weighed before they leave the factory.* 2 [+ complement] to have a particular weight: *It weighs six kilos.* | *I weigh less than*

I used to. **3 weigh a ton** *infml* to be extremely heavy to carry **4** [T] to consider something carefully: *He weighed the ideas in his mind.* **5 weigh anchor** to raise the ANCHOR of a boat or ship so that it can move

weigh down *phr v* **1** [T **weigh** sbdy/sthg **down**] to make someone or something heavier, so that they cannot move easily: *I was weighed down with the shopping.* **2** [T **weigh** sbdy **down**] to make someone feel worried: *I was weighed down by my responsibilities.*

weigh on sbdy *phr v* [T] to make someone feel worried: *His lack of money weighed on his mind.*

weigh sthg ↔ **out** *phr v* [T] to measure an amount of something by weighing it: *I weighed out half a kilo of flour and added it to the mixture.*

weigh sbdy/sthg ↔ **up** *phr v* [T] to try to understand or form an opinion about someone or something: *She eyed him carefully for a while, weighing him up.*

weight¹ /weɪt/ *n* **1** [U] the heaviness of something, which can be measured in units such as kilos: *What's the baby's weight?* **2 put on weight** (of a person) to become heavier: *He's put on a lot of weight recently.* [RELATED PHRASE **lose weight**: *I'm trying to lose weight.*] **3** [C] a piece of metal of a standard heaviness, which can be balanced against a substance to measure an equal heaviness of that substance: *Put a one-kilo weight in the scales.* **4** [C] a heavy object: *You shouldn't lift heavy weights after an operation.* **5** [U] value or importance: *These latest findings add more weight to his theories.* | *Her ideas don't carry much weight around here.* **6 pull your weight** to join in work equally with others **7 throw your weight about/around** to give orders to other people, because you think that you are important **8 a weight off your mind** something that you do not have to worry about any more

weight² *v* [T] to put a weight on something to make it heavier: *Fishing nets are weighted so that they sink in the water.*

weight sthg ↔ **down** *phr v* [T] to make something heavier so that it cannot move easily

weight·ed /ˈweɪtɪd/ *adj* [never before a noun] giving advantage to one particular person or group: *The system of elections is weighted in favour of the main political parties.*

weight·ing /ˈweɪtɪŋ/ *n* [U] *BrE* additional pay given because of the high cost of living in a certain area, usually London: *The salary is £15,600 a year, including London weighting.*

weight·less /ˈweɪtləs/ *adj* having no weight, for example because a person or thing is flying in space –**weightlessness** *n* [U]

weight lift·ing /ˈ· ˌ··/ *n* [U] the sport of lifting specially shaped weights above your head –**weight lifter** *n*

weight·y /ˈweɪti/ *adj* **weightier, weightiest** important and serious: *weighty decisions*

weir /wɪər/ *n* a wall across a river, which stops or controls the flow of the water above it

weird /wɪəd ‖ wɪərd/ *adj* strange and unusual: *weird shapes in the mist* | *He has some weird ideas.*

weird·o /ˈwɪədəʊ ‖ ˈwɪər-/ *n infml* someone who behaves in a strange and unusual way

wel·come¹ /ˈwelkəm/ *v* **welcomed, welcoming** [T] **1** to meet or greet someone you are pleased to see: *The Queen welcomed the President when he arrived.* | *They welcomed him with flowers.* **2** to be pleased about something that has happened or has been said: *We welcome these changes in the law.* | *They welcomed my suggestion.*

welcome² *adj* **1** acceptable and received with pleasure: *You are always welcome at my house.* | *All suggestions will be welcome.* **2 make someone welcome** to behave in a friendly way towards someone, to show that you are pleased to see them **3 be welcome to do something** to be allowed to do something: *No one has ever done it before, but you're welcome to have a try.* **4 You're welcome** a polite phrase used when someone has thanked you for something: *"Thank you!" "You're welcome."*

welcome³ *interj* a word used when you want to show that you are pleased to see someone who has just arrived somewhere: *Welcome home!* | *Welcome to England.*

welcome⁴ *n* a friendly greeting given to someone who has just arrived somewhere: *We were given a warm welcome when we arrived.*

weld /weld/ *v* [T] to join metals by pressing or melting them together when they are hot –**weld** *n* : *a weld in the pipe*

weld·er /ˈweldər/ *n* a person whose job is to weld metal

wel·fare /ˈwelfeər/ *n* [U] **1** a person's general comfort, good health, and happiness: *We're only thinking of his welfare: we want him to be happy in his new school.* **2** help that is given to people who are poor or have social problems: *She's interested in doing welfare work.* **3** money that is given to poor people in the US

welfare state /ˌ·· ˈ· ‖ ˈ··· / *n* a system of health care, unemployment pay, etc., that is provided by the government

well¹ /wel/ *adv* **better** /ˈbetər/, **best** /best/ **1** in a way that is good or satisfactory: *She paints very well.* | *He was clean and well dressed.* | *I can't hear very well.* **2** thoroughly: *I don't know John very well.* | *You haven't washed that very well.* **3** very much: *I can't reach it – it's well above my head.* | *He finished well within the time allowed.* **4 as well** also: *I'd like a sandwich, please, and a cup of tea as well.* **5 as well as** in addition to something else: *I'm learning French as well as German.* **6 just as well** a phrase you use to say that it is good that something has happened: *I forgot to bring my other bag, which was just as well because it would have been heavy to carry round.* **7 well and good** satisfactory **8 well and truly** completely: *He was well and truly drunk.* **9 well done** a phrase you say to someone when they have done something successfully **10 well out of it** lucky to be free from a situation **11 well up on something** knowing a lot about something

well² *adj* **better, best** [never before a noun] **1** healthy: *My mother's not very well at the moment.* | *I don't feel very well.* **2 all is well** everything is in a satisfactory state **3 it's all very well** a phrase you use when you are annoyed about something that someone has done: *It's all very well for you to say you're sorry, but I've been waiting here for two hours!*

well³ *interj* **1** used when you are surprised by something: *Well, what a surprise.* | *So they're getting divorced, are they? Well, well.* **2** used when you are pausing before you speak, or when you are uncertain about something: *"Are you sure about that?" "Well, I think so. It's what I was told."* **3** used when you are continuing a story: *Well, then she said that they're thinking of emigrating.* **4** used when you are correcting the idea before: *There's no problem at all. Well, maybe there's a small problem.* –see Study Note on page 508 **5 oh well** a phrase you use when you are trying to be cheerful about something bad that has happened: *Oh well, things could be a lot worse, I suppose.*

well⁴ *n* **1** a hole in the ground from which water is taken **2** a hole in the ground from which oil is taken

well⁵ *v*

well up *phr v* [I] (of tears) to come into your eyes: *Tears welled up in her eyes.*

we'll /wil; *strong* wiːl/ short for "we will" or "we shall"

well-ad·vised /ₗ·ˈ·ˈ·◄/ *adj* **you would be well-advised** a phrase used when you are suggesting that someone should do something: *You would be well-advised to see the doctor about that pain.*

well-bal·anced /ₗ·ˈ·◄/ *adj* sensible and not having any unreasonable feelings of fear, jealousy, etc.: *a happy, well-balanced child*

well-be·ing /ₗwelˈbiːɪŋ, ˈwelˌbiːɪŋ/ *n* [U] a person's good health and happiness: *The warm summer weather always gives me a sense of wellbeing.*

well-bred /ₗ·ˈ·◄/ *adj old fash* polite, and having good manners

well-brought-up /ₗ·ˈ·ˈ·◄/ *adj* taught to behave in a polite and acceptable way (used of children)

well-built /ₗ·ˈ·◄/ *adj* having a strong body with large muscles –see picture on page 245

well-con·nect·ed /ₗ·ˈ·ˈ·◄/ *adj* knowing or related to people of power and social importance

well-done /ₗ·ˈ·◄/ *adj* cooked thoroughly, for quite a long time

well-earned /ₗ·ˈ·◄/ *adj* much deserved: *a well-earned rest after so much hard work*

well-es·tab·lished /ₗ·ˈ·ˈ·◄/ *adj* having existed successfully for quite a long time

well-found·ed /ₗ·ˈ·ˈ·◄/ *adj* based on facts: *Our fears proved to be well-founded.*

well-groomed /ₗ·ˈ·◄/ *adj* having a very neat clean appearance

well-heeled /ₗ·ˈ·◄/ *adj infml* rich

well-in·formed /ₗ·ˈ·ˈ·◄/ *adj* knowing a lot about several subjects or about one particular subject

wel·ling·ton /ˈwelɪŋtən/ *n* (also **wellington boot** /ₗ···ˈ·/, **welly** *infml*) a rubber boot which keeps your feet and legs dry

well-in·ten·tioned /ₗ·ˈ·ˈ·◄/ *adj* doing something in the hope of helping someone, though often failing: *It was a well-intentioned effort to help, but disaster followed.*

well-known /ₗ·ˈ·◄/ *adj* known by many people: *It's a well-known fact that too much sugar is bad for you.* –see FAMOUS (USAGE)

well-mean·ing /ₗ·ˈ·◄/ *adj* doing something in the hope of helping someone, though often failing: *a well-meaning effort*

well-meant /ₗ·ˈ·◄/ *adj* done in the hope of helping someone, but unsuccessful: *His actions were always well-meant.*

well-nigh /ˈ·ˈ·/ *adv fml* almost

well-off /ₗ·ˈ·◄/ *adj* **better-off, best-off** *infml* **1** rich: *They're very well-off.* **2** **well-off for something** having plenty of something: *We're quite well-off for space here.* **3** **you don't know when you're well-off** = you're more fortunate than you know

well-read /ₗ·ˈ·◄/ *adj* having read many books and learnt a lot from them

well-spok·en /ₗ·ˈ·◄/ *adj* speaking in a polite, correct way, like an educated person

well-thought-of /ₗ·ˈ·ˈ·◄/ *adj* liked and admired by a lot of people

well-timed /ₗ·ˈ·◄/ *adj* said or done at the most suitable time: *well-timed advice*

well-tried /ₗ·ˈ·◄/ *adj* often used before and known to work well: *well-tried methods*

well-wish·er /ˈ·ˌ·ˈ/ *n* a person who gives good wishes to another on a special occasion

well-worn /ₗ·ˈ·◄/ *adj* said too often, and so having little meaning

wel·ly /ˈweli/ *n* wellies see WELLINGTON

Welsh¹ /welʃ/ *adj* of or connected with Wales: *the Welsh mountains*

Welsh² *n* **1** **the Welsh** the people of Wales **2** the language of Wales

welt /welt/ a raised mark on your skin, for example from a hit by a whip

wel·ter /ˈweltəʳ/ *n* **a welter of things** a disordered mixture of things: *a welter of confused policies*

wench /wentʃ/ *n* a young woman (a word which is no longer used in modern English)

wend /wend/ *v lit* **wend your way** to move or travel slowly

went /went/ the past tense of GO

wept /wept/ the past tense and past participle of WEEP

were /wəʳ; *strong* wɜːʳ/ *negative short-form* **weren't** /wɜːnt ‖ ˈwɜːrənt, wɜːrnt/ the past tense of BE

we're /wɪəʳ; *strong* wiːəʳ/ short for "we are"

were·wolf /ˈweəwulf, ˈwɪə- ‖ ˈweər-, ˈwɪər-/ *n* **werewolves** /-wulvz/ a man in some stories who sometimes turns into a WOLF

west¹ /west/ *n* **1** [U] the direction in which the sun sets: *The road goes through the town centre from east to west.* **2** **the West** the western part of the world, especially western Europe and the United States: *Leaders from the West have been invited to peace talks in Moscow.* **3** **the west** the western part of a country

west² *adj* **1** in or towards the west: *West Africa* **2** **west wind** a wind blowing from the west

west³ *adv* (also **West**) **1** towards the west: *We travelled west for three days.* | *She sat facing West, watching the sun go down.* **2** from the west (used of a wind)

west·bound /ˈwestbaund/ *adj* travelling towards the west: *To get to London Airport, take the westbound train.*

West End /ₗ·ˈ·◄/ *n* **the West End** the western part of central London, where the shops and theatres are

west·er·ly /ˈwestəli ‖ -ərli/ *adj* **1** towards the west: *We set off in a westerly direction.* **2** coming from the west (used of a wind)

west·ern¹ /ˈwestən ‖ -ərn/ *adj* (also **Western**) **1** belonging to the west part or area of a country: *Western Scotland* **2** relating to the people of Europe or the United States: *the Western way of life* | *Western technology*

western² *n* (also **Western**) a story or film about life in the West of the US in the past

west·ern·er /ˈwestənəʳ ‖ -tər-/ *n* a person who lives in Europe or the United States

west·ern·ize /ˈwestənaɪz ‖ -tər-/ *v* (also **westernise** *BrE*) **be westernized** to start to use the customs and behaviour typical of Europe and the United States

West In·di·an /ˌ·ˈ···/ adj from or relating to the West Indies: West Indian cooking

westward /ˈwestwəd ‖ -ərd/ adj going towards the west: a westward journey –**westwards** (also **westward** AmE) adv :We travelled westwards for several days.

wet[1] /wet/ adj 1 covered with liquid and so not dry: My shoes had got wet in the rain. | My hair's all wet now! 2 rainy: wet weather | We can't go out, it's too wet. 3 still sticky, and not yet dry or solid: The sign said "Wet paint". | The cement's still wet. 4 infml lacking strength of mind: Don't be so wet! You can do it, if you try! 5 **wet blanket** a person who discourages other people and prevents them enjoying themselves –**wetness** n [U]

wet[2] n 1 the wet rainy weather: Don't go out in the wet. 2 infml a person in the British CONSERVATIVE Party who is not politically extreme

wet[3] v wet or wetted, wet or wetted, wetting [T] 1 to make something wet: Wet the cloth and clean the table with it. 2 **wet the bed, wet yourself** to pass water from your body, in bed or in your clothes, because you cannot control your body

wet suit /ˈ· ·/ n a piece of clothing made of rubber, worn by people who do water sports

we've /wiv; strong wiːv/ short for "we have"

whack[1] /wæk/ v [T] to hit someone or something with a hard blow

whack[2] n 1 a hard blow 2 **your whack** infml your fair share of something

whacked /wækt/ adj [never before a noun] infml very tired

whack·ing /ˈwækɪŋ/ adj infml very big: They live in a whacking great house in Hollywood.

whale[1] n 1 a very large animal which lives in the sea, and looks like a fish but is a MAMMAL 2 **have a whale of a time** infml to enjoy yourself very much

whal·ing /ˈweɪlɪŋ/ n [U] the hunting of whales

wharf /wɔːf ‖ wɔːrf/ n **wharfs** or **wharves** /wɔːvz ‖ wɔːrvz/ a place where ships can be tied up to unload goods

what /wɒt ‖ waːt, wʌt/ predeterminer,det,pron 1 used in questions about a thing that is not known: What are you doing? | What colour is it? | What time is it? | What did he say? 2 the thing or things that: She told me what to do. | I know what you mean. | Show me what you bought. | I gave her what books I had. –see WHICH (USAGE) 3 used to show surprise: What a strange thing to say! | What beautiful weather. | You did what? 4 infml used when someone has called your name and you want to show that you have heard them and are listening: "Mary?" "What?" "Have you fed the dog?" 5 **what for** infml why: "I'm going to Paris." "What for?" | What did you do that for? 6 **what if** what would happen if: What if we get delayed and miss the train? 7 **what with** infml because of something: What with all this extra work, I haven't had time to do any gardening. 8 **what's more** used to introduce an additional point which is stronger than the one before: She's just the person to help you. She's lived in Turkey. What's more, she speaks Turkish.

what·ev·er[1] /wɒtˈevəʳ ‖ waɪ-, wʌ-/det,pron 1 det, pron no matter what thing: These animals will eat whatever they can find. | Use whatever information you can find. | Whatever you do, don't be late. –see EVER(USAGE) 2 pron infml anything else like the thing mentioned: Anyone carrying bags, boxes, or

whatever was stopped by the police. 3 pron used when you are surprised and are asking "what": Whatever is it? | Whatever did you do that for? 4 pron infml it doesn't matter which: "Shall we go to a film, the theatre, or for a meal?" "Whatever."

whatever[2] adj (also **whatsoever**) none whatever, nothing whatever, etc none at all, nothing at all, etc: I know nothing whatever about it. | She had no money whatever.

wheat /wiːt/ n [U] a plant from whose grain flour is made, or its grain: a field of wheat

whee·dle /ˈwiːdl/ v wheedled, wheedling 1 **wheedle someone into doing something** to persuade someone to do something by being pleasant to them 2 **wheedle something out of someone** to obtain something from someone by pleasant persuading: He managed to wheedle five pounds out of his father.

wheel[1] /wiːl/ n 1 a circular object with an outer frame which turns around an inner part; wheels are used for making vehicles move and for making machinery work –see picture on page 49 2 the wheel used to guide and turn a car or other vehicle: She was sitting behind the wheel of her car.

wheel[2] v 1 [T +adv/prep] to move something which has wheels, by pushing it: The nurse wheeled the table up to the bed. 2 [I] (of birds) to fly round and round in circles: Birds were wheeling above us.

wheel round/around phr v [I] to turn round suddenly: He wheeled round and looked at me.

wheel·bar·row /ˈwiːlˌbærəʊ/ n a small cart with one wheel at the front, two legs, and two handles at the back for pushing: Put those stones in the wheelbarrow. –see picture on page 638

wheel·chair /ˈwiːltʃeəʳ/ n a chair with large wheels used by a person who cannot walk

wheeling and deal·ing /ˌ··· ·ˈ··/ n [U] making deals in a skilful, and perhaps dishonest, way: The issue was only decided after a great deal of political wheeling and dealing.

wheeze /wiːz/ v wheezed, wheezing [I] to make a noisy whistling sound when you breathe: By the time he reached the top of the stairs he was panting and wheezing. –**wheeze** n

wheez·y /ˈwiːzi/ adj making a noisy whistling sound when you breathe: a wheezy cough

whelk /welk/ n a sea animal which lives in a shell, and is sometimes used as food

when /wen/ adv,conj 1 at what time: When are they arriving? | She'll tell us when we can come in. 2 at a particular time: When I left school I didn't know what I wanted to do. 3 considering a particular fact: I can't explain anything when you won't listen. 4 although: She's always complaining about being hard up, when in fact she's got loads of money.

whence /wens/ adv from where (a word that is no longer used in modern English): They returned to the land whence they had come.

whenever /wenˈevəʳ/ adv 1 at whatever time: I go and visit him whenever I'm in town. | Come round whenever you like. 2 used when you are surprised and are asking "when": Whenever did you have time to do this?

where /weəʳ/ adv,conj,pron in or to which place: Where do you live? | Where are the keys? | Where are you going? | the office where I work | Sit where you like.

where·a·bouts[1] /ˌweərəˈbaʊts◂ ‖ ˈweərəbaʊts/ adv, conj used in questions when you are asking the question "where": Whereabouts do you live?

whereabouts² /'weərəbauts/ n [U + sing/pl verb] the place where someone or something is: *Nobody knows his whereabouts.*

where·as /weər'æz/ conj used when you are stating something that is opposite to what you have just said: *They spend all their money on their house, whereas we prefer to spend ours on travelling.*

where·by /weə'bai ‖ weər-/ adv fml by which or by means of which: *We need a better system by whereby we can calculate our future costs.*

where·in /weər'ın/ adv,conj fml in what or in which

where·u·pon /ˌweərə'pɒn ‖ 'weərəpɑːn, -pɔːn/ conj fml after which: *One of them called him a liar, whereupon a fight broke out.*

wher·ev·er /weər'evər/ adv,conj **1** in or to whatever place: *Sit wherever you like.* | *Wherever you go, I will go with you.* **2** used when you are surprised and are asking "where": *Wherever have you been?*

where·with·al /'weəwɪðɔːl ‖ 'weər-/ n fml **the wherewithal to do something** the money that you need to do something: *I haven't got the wherewithal to pay you.*

whet /wet/ v -tt- [T] **1** lit to sharpen something: *She whetted her knife on the stone.* **2 whet your appetite** to make you wish for more: *The experience had whetted my appetite for adventure.*

wheth·er /'weðər/ conj **1** used to show a choice between different possibilities: *He asked me whether I enjoyed my work or not.* | *I'll find out whether she's ready.* | *Tell me whether or not you like it.* **2** used to show that it does not matter which is chosen or which is true: *I'll go whether you come with me or not.* | *All couples will benefit whether they have children or not.*

whew /hjuː/ interj see PHEW

which /wɪtʃ/ det, pron **1** used in questions when there is a choice to be made: *Which shoes shall I wear, the red ones or the brown ones?* | *Which of these books is yours?* **2** used to show what thing or things someone means: *Did you see the letter which came this morning?* | *This is the book which I told you about.* **3** used to add more information to a sentence: *We went back to their house, which is lovely.* | *She said she's been waiting for half an hour, which wasn't true.*

■ USAGE Compare **which** and **what**. 1 Use **which** when the choice is from a particular group of things or people: **Which** *colour do you want, red or blue?* We use **what** when the choice is from an unknown number of things or people: **What** *colour would you like your new car to be?* 2 **Which** can be followed by *of*, but **what** cannot be followed by *of*: **Which** *of the puppies do you like best?*

which·ev·er /wɪtʃ'evər/ det, pron **1** any one whatever: *Take whichever seat you like.* | *It has the same result whichever way you do it.* **2** used when you are surprised and are asking "which": *Whichever road did you come along?*

whiff /wɪf/ n a smell which you smell for just a short time: *I caught a whiff of her perfume as she walked past me.*

while¹ /waɪl/ n a while a length of time, usually a short one: *After a while she fell asleep.* | *We had to wait a little while.*

while² conj (also **whilst** BrE) **1** during the time when something is happening: *I read a lot while I was at college.* | *I always listen to the radio while I'm cooking.* **2** although: *While I agree with a lot of what you say, I still can't accept your conclusions.*

while³ v whiled, whiling

while sthg ↔ **away** phr v [T] to spend time in a lazy way: *She whiled away the hours sunbathing in the garden.*

whim /wɪm/ n a sudden idea or wish, often one that is not reasonable: *I was tired of pandering to her whims.* | *A soldier won't fight very hard for a leader who is going to shoot him on a whim.*

whim·per /'wɪmpər/ v [I] **1** to make small weak cries of fear or pain **2** to say something in a small trembling voice: *"Don't hurt me!" he whimpered.* –**whimper** n : *The dog gave a whimper of pain.*

whim·si·cal /'wɪmzɪkəl/ adj strange and amusing –**whimsically** adv

whine /waɪn/ v whined, whining [I] **1** to make a high sad cry or sound: *The dog was whining at the door.* | *The machinery clattered and whined.* **2** to complain in an unnecessarily sad voice: *Stop whining, child!* –**whine** n : *the whine of an aircraft engine*

whinge /wɪndʒ/ v whinged, whinging or whingeing [I] infml to complain often and unnecessarily: *Stop whingeing about it and just get on with it!*

whin·ny /'wɪni/ v whinnied, whinnying [I] (of a horse) to make a gentle sound –**whinny** n

whip¹ /wɪp/ n **1** a long piece of rope or leather fastened to a handle, used for hitting animals or people **2** a member of Parliament who is responsible for making other members of his or her party attend at voting time

whip² v -pp- **1** [T] to beat someone with a whip **2** [T+adv/prep] to move something quickly: *He whipped out his gun.* | *She whipped off her coat.* **3** [I + adv/prep] (of the wind) to move very quickly across something: *The wind whipped across the fields.* **4** [T] to beat cream or eggs until they are stiff: *apple pie with whipped cream*

whip sthg ↔ **up** phr v [T] **1** to cause feelings to become stronger: *They're trying to whip up support for the new political party.* **2 whip up a meal** to make a meal quickly

whip·ping /'wɪpɪŋ/ n a beating with a whip

whip-round /'· ·/ n BrE infml a collection of money among a group of people to give to one member or to buy something for one member: *We're having a whip-round for old Fred – he's leaving, you know.*

whir /wɜː/ v -rr- [I] see WHIRR

whirl¹ /wɜːl ‖ wɜːrl/ v **1** [I;T+adv/prep] to move round and round very fast: *the whirling dancers* | *The leaves were picked up by the wind and whirled into the air.* **2 my head is whirling** = I am extremely excited and confused

whirl² n **1** very fast and rather confused movement or activity: *the whirl of the dancers* | *The sales department was a whirl of activity.* **2 in a whirl** very confused: *My head's in a whirl; let me sit down and think quietly.* **3 give something a whirl** infml to try something new and see if it works: *It's an unusual idea, but I think we should give it a whirl.*

whirl·pool /'wɜːlpuːl ‖ 'wɜːrl-/ n a place with circular currents of water in a sea or river, which can pull objects down into it

whirl·wind /'wɜːl,wɪnd ‖ 'wɜːrl-/ n **1** a tall round body of air moving rapidly forward, which can destroy things in its path **2** [only before a noun] happening very quickly: *a whirlwind romance*

whirr /wɜːr/ v (also **whir**) [I] to make a regular sound like something turning and beating against the air: *the whirring sound of the engine* –**whirr, whir** n : *the whirr of the sewing machine*

whisk¹ /wɪsk/ n **1** a small tool for beating eggs or cream: *an egg whisk* –see picture on page 638 **2** a quick light movement: *The cow brushed off the flies with a whisk of its tail.*

whisk² v **1** to move something with a quick sweeping movement: *The horse whisked its tail.* **2** [T +adv/prep] to move or remove quickly: *She whisked the cups off the table.* | *The President was whisked off to the airport.* **3** [T] to beat eggs or cream to get air into them

whis·ker /ˈwɪskəʳ/ n **1** one of the long stiff hairs that grow near the mouth of an animal such as a cat or rat **2** whiskers [pl] hair growing on the sides of a man's face

whis·key /ˈwɪski/ [U] WHISKY made in Ireland or the US

whis·ky /ˈwɪski/ n whiskies **1** [U] a strong alcoholic drink made from grain, produced especially in Scotland: *a bottle of whisky* **2** [C] a glass of whisky

whis·per /ˈwɪspəʳ/ v **1** [I;T] to speak very quietly, so that only a person very near you can hear: *The children were whispering in the corner.* | *"Listen!" she whispered.* | *He whispered a warning and then vanished.* **2** [I] (of the wind or leaves) to make a soft sound –**whisper** n : *She spoke in a whisper.*

whis·tle /ˈwɪsəl/ n **1** a simple musical instrument that makes a high clear sound when air or steam is forced through it: *The referee blew his whistle for a free kick.* **2** the high clear sound made by forcing air or steam through a whistle or through your lips: *He gave a loud whistle of surprise.*

whistle² v whistled, whistling **1** [I] to make a high clear sound by forcing air through your lips or through a whistle: *He whistled to his dog.* | *She was whistling merrily.* | *The train whistled as it left the station.* **2** [T] to produce music by doing this: *He was whistling that tune again.* **3** [I+adv/prep] to move with a whistling sound: *The wind whistled in the chimney.*

white¹ /waɪt/ adj whiter, whitest **1** of the colour of milk, snow, and salt: *white paint* | *white hair* –see picture on page 147 **2** pale in colour: *white wine* | *Her face was white with fear.* **3** belonging to a race with a pale skin **4** with milk or cream (used of tea or coffee) –**whiteness** n [U]

white² n **1** [U] the colour which is white: *a woman dressed in white* **2** [C] a person of a race with a pale skin: *There were both whites and blacks at the meeting.* **3** [C] the white part of your eye **4** [C;U] the part of an egg which is colourless but becomes white after cooking: *Beat three egg whites until stiff.*

white-col·lar /ˌ· ˈ···◂/ adj [only before a noun] concerning people who work in offices or at professional jobs, rather than doing hard or dirty work with their hands: *a white-collar union*

white el·e·phant /ˌ· ˈ···/ n something that is useless and unwanted, especially something that costs a lot of money

White·hall /ˈwaɪthɔːl, ˌwaɪtˈhɔːl/ n [+sing/pl verb] the British government, especially the government departments rather than Parliament

white-hot /ˌ· ˈ·◂/ adj extremely hot (used of metal)

White House /ˈ· ·/ n the White House [+ sing/pl verb] the official Washington home of the President of the United States, or the US government

white knight /ˌ· ˈ·/ n a person or organization that puts money into a business company to save it from being taken over by another company

white lie /ˌ· ˈ·/ n a harmless lie

whit·en /ˈwaɪtn/ v [I;T] to make or become white, or more white: *I must whiten my tennis shoes.*

white pa·per /ˌ· ˈ··/ n an official report from the British government on a certain subject: *a new white paper* **on** *education*

white spir·it /ˌ· ˈ··/ n [U] a strong liquid made from petrol, used for example for making paint thinner

white·wash¹ /ˈwaɪtwɒʃ ‖ -wɔːʃ, -wɑːʃ/ n **1** [U] a white mixture made from LIME and water, used especially for painting walls **2** [C;U] an attempt to hide a mistake or bad action: *The report was simply a whitewash.*

whitewash² v [T] **1** to cover something with whitewash: *whitewashing the farm buildings* **2** to try to hide a mistake or bad action

whith·er /ˈwɪðəʳ/ adv,conj lit to where: *Whither is he going?*

whi·ting /ˈwaɪtɪŋ/ n whiting or whitings a sea fish used for food

whit·tle /ˈwɪtl/ v whittled, whittling [T] to cut wood to a smaller size by taking off small thin pieces

whittle sthg ↔ **down** phr v [T] (also whittle sthg ↔ **away**) to reduce by a continuous and gradual process: *Can't you whittle down the wedding list any more?* | *We're whittling away at their sales figures.*

whizz¹ /wɪz/ v -zz- (also whiz) [I+adv/prep] infml to move very fast, often making a noisy sound as if rushing through the air: *Cars were whizzing past.*

whizz² n (also whiz) **1** [sing] a noisy sound like something rushing through the air **2** [C] infml someone who is very fast or skilled at the stated activity: *She's an absolute whiz* **at** *cards.*

whizz kid /ˈ· ·/ n infml (also whiz kid) a person who is very successful at an early age because of their natural skill or cleverness

who /huː/ pron **1** used in questions about a person that is not known: *Who are you?* | *Who's at the door?* | *Who won the race?* **2** used to show which person or people someone means: *The woman who wrote this letter works in a hospital.* | *Do you know the people who live here?* | *The man who I talked to had lived in the town all his life.* **3** used to add more information about a person or people: *I had lunch with my sister, who lives nearby.*

■ USAGE Except in very formal language we can use **who** instead of **whom** as an object in questions. Thus we can say **Who** *did you see?* instead of the more formal **Whom** *did you see?* or **Who** *were you dancing with?* instead of the more formal *With* **whom** *were you dancing?*

who'd /huːd/ **1** short for "who had" **2** short for "who would"

who·dun·it /ˌhuːˈdʌnɪt/ n infml (also whodunnit) a story or film about a murder that is concerned with finding out who did it

who·ev·er /huːˈevəʳ/ pron **1** whatever person: *I'll take whoever wants to come.* | *Whoever it is, I don't want to see them.* **2** used when you are surprised and are asking "who": *Whoever can that be at this time of night?*

whole¹ /həʊl/ adj **1** not divided or cut in half: *a tin of whole peaches* | *Swallow the tablet whole.* **2** [only before a noun] all the: *I spent the whole day in bed.* | *He drank a whole bottle of wine.*

whole² n **1** the whole of all of something: *The whole of the morning was wasted.* **2** something which is complete and is made up of several parts:

We must regard the education system as a whole. **3 on the whole** in general: *On the whole I agree with you.*

whole-food /ˈhəʊlfuːd/ n [C;U] food that is in a simple natural form, without anything removed or added

whole-heart-ed /ˌ·ˈ·◂/ adj giving all that you can of the stated quality: *You have my whole-hearted support.* **–wholeheartedly** adv

whole-meal /ˈhəʊlmiːl/ adj (also **wholewheat**) made without removing the covering of the grain (used of flour or bread)

whole-sale /ˈhəʊlseɪl/ adj,adv **1** related to the selling of goods in large quantities and usually at low prices: *a wholesale supplier of office machinery | She buys the materials wholesale.* **2** to a very great degree and without people troubling to make moral judgments (usually used of something bad): *wholesale slaughter*

whole-sal-er /ˈhəʊlˌseɪləʳ/ n a businessman who sells goods wholesale

whole-some /ˈhəʊlsəm/ adj **1** good for your body: *wholesome food* **2** having a good or desirable moral effect

whole-wheat /ˈhəʊlwiːt/ n see WHOLEMEAL

who'll /huːl/ short for "who will"

whol-ly /ˈhəʊl-li/ adv completely: *I don't think he was wholly to blame for the accident. | To be fair, it's not wholly her fault.*

whom /huːm/ pron the form of WHO that is used in formal English when it is the object of a verb or PREPOSITION: *Whom did you see? | a man whom she had met on holiday* –see WHO (USAGE)

whoop /wuːp, huːp/ v [I] to make a loud cry, usually a happy one: *whooping with delight* **–whoop** n

whoo-pee /wʊˈpiː/ interj old fash a word that people say when they are very happy and excited

whoop-ing cough /ˈhuːpɪŋ kɒf ‖ -kɔːf/ n [U] a disease which causes you to cough a lot and then make a lot of noise as you breathe in

whoops /wʊps/ interj (also **oops**) a word that people say when someone has fallen over, dropped something, or made a mistake: *Careful now... Whoops!*

whoosh /wʊʃ ‖ wuːʃ/ v [I+adv/prep] to move quickly with a rushing sound: *The train whooshed past.* **–whoosh** n

whop-per /ˈwɒpəʳ ‖ ˈwɑː-/ n infml **1** something which is surprisingly big: *Did you catch that fish? What a whopper!* **2** a big lie

whop-ping /ˈwɒpɪŋ ‖ ˈwɑː-/ adv, adj [only before a noun] infml extremely big

whore /hɔːʳ/ n a woman who earns money by having sex with anyone who will pay for it

who're /ˈhuːəʳ/ short for "who are"

whorl /wɜːl ‖ wɔːrl/ n the shape which a line makes when going round in a SPIRAL, for example in some seashells

who's /huːz/ **1** short for "who is": *Who's he talking about?* **2** short for "who has": *Who's he brought to the dinner?*

whose /huːz/ det, pron used when you are asking who something belongs to or stating who something belongs to: *Whose house is this? | Whose is that car? | That's the man whose house was burnt down.*

who've /huːv/ short for "who have": *I know some people who've been there. | Who've you been staying with?*

why /waɪ/ adv,conj **1** for what reason: *Why did you do it? | I don't know why he got so angry. | I can see now why it won't work. | There must be a reason why he refused.* **2 why not** a way of suggesting to someone what they should do: *If your car's broken down, why not go by bus? | Why don't you phone him?*

wick /wɪk/ n **1** a piece of twisted thread in a candle, which burns as the WAX melts **2** a piece of material in an oil lamp which burns and gives light **3 get on someone's wick** infml to annoy someone

wick-ed /ˈwɪkɪd/ adj **1** extremely bad morally: *a wicked man | the wicked witch | a wicked waste of money* **2** playful in a rather troublesome or bad way: *a wicked smile* **–wickedly** adv **–wickedness** n [U]

wick-er-work /ˈwɪkəwɜːk ‖ ˈwɪkərwɜːrk/ n (also **wicker**) [U] objects made from weaving together thin branches or reeds (REED): *wickerwork furniture*

wick-et /ˈwɪkɪt/ n **1** the set of three sticks at which the ball is thrown in cricket **2** the area of grass between the two wickets in a cricket match

wide¹ /waɪd/ adj wider, widest **1** measuring a large amount from side to side or from edge to edge: *a wide road | The gate isn't wide enough for me to drive the car through.* **2** used when giving measurements: *How wide is the doorway? | The river is about ten metres wide.* **3** covering or including a large range of things: *She has very wide interests. | books on a wide variety of subjects* **4** (also **wide open**) fully open: *wide eyes* **5 wide of the mark** very far from being correct

wide² adv **1** to a great distance from side to side, or to the greatest distance possible: *He stood with his legs wide apart. | Spread your arms wide. | "Open wide," said the dentist. | The window was wide open.* **2** far away from the right point (used in sport): *The ball went wide. | His shot was wide of the goal.*

wide-a-wake /ˌ·ˈ··◂/ adj fully awake

wide-eyed /ˌ·ˈ·◂/ adj **1** with your eyes fully open because you are very surprised **2** showing a willingness to accept or admire things without questioning them: *He found her wide-eyed innocence very appealing.*

wide-ly /ˈwaɪdli/ adv **1** over a wide range of things or places: *She has read widely. | They have travelled widely.* **2** by many people: *It's widely believed that the government will lose the election.* **3** to a large degree: *widely different opinions*

wid-en /ˈwaɪdn/ v [I;T] to make or become wider: *They're widening the road. | The river widens out here. | We'll have to widen the scope of our operation.*

wide-spread /ˈwaɪdspred/ adj existing or happening in many places or among many people: *The disease is becoming more widespread. | a widespread belief in his innocence*

wid-ow /ˈwɪdəʊ/ n **1** a woman whose husband has died **2** a woman whose husband is often away doing the stated activity: *a golf widow*

wid-owed /ˈwɪdəʊd/ adj left alone after the death of your husband or wife

wid-ow-er /ˈwɪdəʊəʳ/ n a man whose wife has died

wid-ow-hood /ˈwɪdəʊhʊd/ n [U] the state or period of being a widow

width /wɪdθ/ n [C;U] size from one side to the other side: *What is its width? | The garden is six metres in width.*

wield /wiːld/ v [T] **1** to carry a weapon and be prepared to use it: *They rushed at him, wielding their knives.* **2** to have and use power or influence: *She wields a lot of power in the government.*

Many English nouns, verbs and adjectives are commonly followed by prepositions. If you do not know which preposition to use with a particular word, look it up in this dictionary. The dictionary helps you in two main ways:

1 *Many words can be used either alone or together with a preposition. When this is the case the dictionary tells you which prepositions you can use by showing them in the examples in special dark print.*

This entry tells you that the adjective **bored** can be used alone. But it can also be used with the preposition **with.**

---
bored /bɔːd ‖ bɔːrd/ *adj* **1** tired and uninterested: *The students all looked bored.* | *She was bored* **with** *her job.*

This entry tells you that the verb **borrow** can be used alone. But it can also be used with the preposition **from.** The examples show that you usually **borrow** a thing **from** a person.

---
bor·row /ˈbɒrəʊ ‖ ˈbɑː-, ˈbɔː-/ *v* [T] **1** to take something for a certain time, intending to return it: *Can I borrow your dictionary for a moment?* | *I borrowed £5* **from** *my mother.*

This entry tells you that the verb **console** can be used alone. But it can also be used with the prepositions **for** and **with.** The examples show that you usually **console** somebody **for** something bad that has happened to them. And that you **console** them **with** something nice that you give them or do for them.

---
con·sole[1] /kənˈsəʊl/ *v* **consoled, consoling** [T] **1** to give comfort or sympathy to someone in times of disappointment or sadness: *Nothing will console her* **for** *the loss of her dog.* | *She tried to console me* **with** *a cup of tea.*

This entry tells you that the noun **risk** can be used alone. But it can also be used with the preposition **of.** The examples show you that you should use **of** in order to give more details about the risk.

---
risk[1] /rɪsk/ *n* **1** [C;U] a possibility something bad may happen: *He was taking a risk by overtaking on a bend.* | *There was no risk* **of** *infection.*
---

2 *Some words are never used alone but are always used with particular prepositions. Some other words are nearly always used with particular prepositions in order to express particular meanings. When this is the case the dictionary shows both the main word and the preposition in special dark print.*

This entry tells you that the adjective **riddled** is always used with the preposition **with.**

---
rid·dled /ˈrɪdld/ *adj* [only before a noun] **riddled with** full of holes: *The man's body was riddled with bullets.* | *The beam was riddled with woodworm.*

This entry tells you that when the verb **consist** means "to be made up of a number of things" it is used with the preposition **of.** But when it means "to be really" it is used with the preposition **in.**

---
con·sist /kənˈsɪst/ *v* **1** **consist of something** to be made up of a number of things: *The city of New York consists of five boroughs.* | *a delivery of supplies, consisting mainly of food and medicines* **2** **consist in something** to be really: *For me, the pleasure of the meal consisted entirely in the conversation – the food was terrible.*

This entry tells you that the noun **search** is followed by the preposition **of** when it is in the fixed phrase **in search of.**

---
search[2] *n* **1** an act of searching: *a long search for the lost treasure* **2** **in search of** looking for: *in search of happiness* | *He went in search of his long-lost brother.*

NOTE Remember that there are also many verbs where a word which looks like a preposition makes up part of the meaning, for example **come across** (= discover), **look into** (= investigate) etc. These are considered to be *phrasal verbs* and are listed in this dictionary as separate headwords in alphabetical order under the main verb.

(See STUDY NOTE: **Phrasal verbs** on page 475)

wife /waɪf/ n wives /waɪvz/ the woman to whom a man is married: *This is my wife, Jenny.* | *the President and his wife* –see picture on page 343

wife·ly /ˈwaɪfli/ adj having or showing the good qualities of a wife (a word which is usually used humorously in modern English)

wig /wɪg/ n a covering of hair for someone's head, used because they no longer have any hair or to hide their real hair: *I'm sure she's wearing a wig.*

wig·gle /ˈwɪgəl/ v wiggled, wiggling [I;T] to move in small side-to-side, up-and-down, or turning movements: *She wiggled her fingers to check they were OK.* | *a rabbit wiggling its nose* –**wiggle** n : *with a wiggle of her hips* | *writing full of strange wiggles*

wig·wam /ˈwɪgwæm ‖ -wɑːm/ n a tent of the type used by some North American Indians

wild¹ /waɪld/ adj **1** living or growing in natural conditions and having natural qualities, and not bred, grown, or produced by humans: *wild animals in the jungle* | *a bunch of wild flowers* | *wild honey* **2** violent and uncontrollable in behaviour: *A wild man leapt out of the bushes at them.* | *She rushed out with a wild look in her eyes.* | *a pop star who drives women wild with desire* **3** violent (used of weather or the sea): *a wild wind* **4** showing strong feelings: *His speech was greeted with wild applause.* **5** having or showing lack of thought or control: *a wild guess* | *a wild throw* **6** be wild about *infml* to like very much: *My son's absolutely wild about racing cars.* –**wildness** n [U]

wild² adv **run wild** to behave as you like, without any control over you: *Some parents just seem to let their children run wild.*

wild³ n **the wild** the natural state in which an animal usually lives: *The lion escaped and returned to the wild.*

wil·der·ness /ˈwɪldənɪs ‖ -dər-/ n **1** any place where there is no sign of human presence or control: *a city which is fast becoming a lawless wilderness* **2** **the wilderness** an area of land with little natural life, especially a desert **3** **in the wilderness** far from the centre of an activity: *Churchill spent years in the political wilderness before he led Britain through the war.*

wild·fire /ˈwaɪldfaɪəʳ/ n **like wildfire** extremely fast: *The news spread like wildfire.*

wild-goose chase /ˌ· ˈ· ·/ n *infml* a completely useless search

wild·life /ˈwaɪldlaɪf/ n [U] animals and plants which live in natural conditions: *The island is full of interesting wildlife.*

wild·ly /ˈwaɪldli/ adv **1** in a way that shows a lack of thought or control: *He ran wildly down the street.* | *His answer was wildly wrong.* **2** *infml* extremely: *I'm afraid I'm not wildly enthusiastic about the idea.*

wil·ful /ˈwɪlfəl/ adj **1** showing the intention of doing exactly what you want: *a wilful child* **2** done on purpose: *wilful damage to the farmer's crops* –**wilfully** adv –**wilfulness** n [U]

wi·li·ness /ˈwaɪlinɪs/ n [U] cleverness at using tricks and deceit to get what you want

will¹ /wɪl/ v *negative short form* **won't** [modal verb] **1** used to show that something is going to happen in the future: *It will probably rain tomorrow.* | *What will you do if you lose your job?* | *I won't be at home this evening.* –see 's (USAGE) **2** used to show that someone is willing to do something: *I won't go!* | *No one will take the job.* | *The door won't shut.* **3** used

to show that something always happens or can happen: *Oil will float on water.* | *Accidents will happen.* | *Will your car hold six people?* **4** used to show that you think something is very likely or certain: *That will be Jack at the door.* | *They will be in France by now.* **5** used to show that someone often or always does something unpleasant or annoying: *She will keep talking when I'm trying to work!* –see Study Note on page 392 **6** **will you** a rather direct way of asking someone to do something: *Will you post a letter for me, please?* | *Shut the door, will you?* | *You won't tell him, will you?* | *Will you be quiet!* **7** **will you have** a polite way of offering something to someone: *Will you have a cup of tea before you go?* **8** **you will** a way of ordering someone to do something: *You will do as you are told!*

will² v [T] **1** **will someone to do something** to try to make someone do something by using the power of your mind: *I was willing him to stop but he walked straight past.* **2** to leave money or possessions to someone when you die, by writing it in your will

will³ n **1** [C;U] the strength of purpose to do something and the power or ability to do it: *He no longer has the will to live.* | *a battle of wills* | *She didn't believe in free will.* **2** [U] what is wished or intended by someone who has power: *He saw her death as God's will.* **3** [C] a written statement in which a person says what should happen to their money and property after they die: *He decided that it was time he made a will.* | *She left me £5000 in her will.* **4** **at will** when and how you want: *She can turn on the tears at will.*

will·ing /ˈwɪlɪŋ/ adj **1** ready to do something: *We can start right now, if you're ready and willing.* | *Is she willing to help?*
□ USEFUL PATTERN be willing to do something **2** acting eagerly and without being forced: *a willing helper* –**willingly** adv –**willingness** n [U]

wil·low /ˈwɪləʊ/ n a tree which grows near water, with long thin branches

wil·low·y /ˈwɪləʊi/ adj pleasantly tall, thin, and graceful: *a girl with a willowy figure*

will·pow·er /ˈwɪlˌpaʊəʳ/ n [U] strength of purpose: *He keeps saying he'll stop smoking, but he hasn't got any willpower.*

wil·ly-nil·ly /ˌwɪli ˈnɪli/ adv even though most people may not want it: *They introduced the new law willy-nilly.*

wilt /wɪlt/ v [I] **1** (of a plant) to become less fresh, bend, and start to die: *The flowers are wilting.* **2** (of a person) to become tired and weaker: *I'm wilting in this heat.*

wil·y /ˈwaɪli/ adj **wilier, wiliest** very clever in using tricks, especially for getting what you want: *a wily negotiator*

wimp /wɪmp/ n *infml* a weak or useless person, especially a man –**wimpy, wimpish** adj

win¹ /wɪn/ v **won** /wʌn/, **won, winning 1** [I;T] to be the best or first in a struggle, competition, or race: *Who won?* | *She won the race.* | *I never win at cards.* | *The winning team got a silver cup.* **2** [T] to be given something because you are successful in any kind of competition: *She won a prize for the painting.* | *He won a gold medal in the 100 metres.* | *Congratulations! You've won a chance to meet your favourite pop star.* **3** [T] to gain something by effort or ability: *The scheme eventually won the support of the city council.* | *By her hard work she won herself a place.* **4** **I can't win** = I will not get what I want whatever

I do **5 you win** *infml* a phrase used when you are admitting, rather unwillingly, that someone is right, or agreeing in the end to do what they want **6 win the day** to be successful after a lot of argument

■ USAGE Compare **win, gain, earn.** You can **win** or **gain** something as a result of great effort or ability: *He won/gained everyone's approval by his hard work.* You can **gain** something useful or necessary whether or not you deserve it: *He gained everyone's attention by banging the table with his fist.* You can **earn** something which you deserve: *Take a rest now. You've earned it!* You can also **earn** money for work you do: *She's earning £300 a week at present.*

win sbdy ↔ **over** *phr v* (also **win** sbdy ↔ **round**) [T] to gain someone's support by persuading them: *I'm sure we'll be able to win him round to our way of thinking in the end.*

win² *n* a victory or success: *Our team's had three wins and two defeats this season.*

wince /wɪns/ *v* **winced, wincing** [I] to move the top of your body back a little bit suddenly, often making a twisted expression with your face, as if drawing away from something painful or unpleasant: *She touched the snake, wincing slightly.* | *He winced when I told him how much the repairs would cost.* –**wince** *n*

winch /wɪntʃ/ *n* a machine for pulling up heavy objects by means of a rope or chain that is wound around a turning part –**winch** *v* [T+adv/prep] : *They winched the car out of the ditch.*

wind¹ /wɪnd/ *n* **1** [C;U] a strongly moving current of air: *The bridge is closed due to high winds.* | *a 70-mile-an-hour wind* | *The clothes on the washing line flapped in the wind.* | *A sudden gust of wind blew the door shut.* **2 get your wind** to breathe properly or regularly again **3** [U] air or gas in the stomach: *Small babies often get wind.* **4** [U] *infml* words without meaning **5 get wind of** *infml* to hear about something, especially accidentally or unofficially: *If anyone gets wind of our plans, we'll be in trouble.* **6 there is something in the wind** something that people are trying to keep secret is about to happen or is being done **7 put the wind up someone** *infml* to make someone become afraid or anxious

■ USAGE **Wind** is a general word for a moving current of air. A **breeze** is usually a pleasant, gentle wind: *A light, summer breeze was blowing.* A **gust** is a strong, sudden rush of air: *A sudden gust blew the door shut.* A **gale** is a very strong wind: *Our chimney was blown down in a gale.*

wind² /wɪnd/ *v* [T] to cause someone to be breathless or to have difficulty in breathing: *He was badly winded by the fall.*

wind³ /waɪnd/ *v* **wound** /waʊnd/, **wound 1** [T + adv/prep] to turn or twist something repeatedly around something else: *The nurse wound the bandage round his arm.* | *He wound the wool into a ball.* **2** [T + adv/prep] to move something by turning a handle or pressing a button: *She wound down the car window.* | *Can you wind the video forward again, please?* | *The film had finished, so he wound it back.* **3** [T] to turn part of a machine round and round, in order to make it work: *Can you wind that clock for me?* **4** [I+adv/prep] to follow a twisting course, with a lot of changes of direction: *The path winds through the woods.*

wind down *phr v* **1** [T **wind** sthg ↔ **down**] to bring something to an end gradually: *The company is winding down its business in Hong Kong.* **2** [I] (of a clock or machine) to work more slowly before at last stopping **3** [I] (of a person) to rest and become calmer or less active after work or excitement

wind up *phr v* **1** [I;T **wind** sthg ↔ **up**] to bring something to an end: *I think we should wind up the meeting now.* | *The company's being wound up.* **2** [T **wind** sthg ↔ **up**] to turn part of a machine round and round, in order to make it work: *He wound up his watch.* **3** [I+adv/prep] *infml* to put yourself in a certain state or place accidentally: *You'll wind up in hospital if you drive so fast.* **4** [T **wind** sbdy ↔ **up**] *infml* to annoy someone on purpose, usually playfully: *Don't take any notice – she's just trying to wind you up.*

wind·bag /ˈwɪndbæg/ *n infml* a person who talks too much, especially about uninteresting things

wind·break /ˈwɪndbreɪk/ *n* a fence, wall, or line of trees intended to give some protection from the wind

wind·fall /ˈwɪndfɔːl/ *n* **1** an unexpected lucky gift, especially of money **2** a piece of fruit that has fallen off a tree

wind·ing /ˈwaɪndɪŋ/ *adj* having a twisting turning shape: *a winding road through the old town* | *winding stairs*

wind in·stru·ment /ˈwɪnd ˌɪnstrʊmənt/ *n* any musical instrument played by blowing air through it

wind·mill /ˈwɪndˌmɪl/ *n* a building containing a machine that crushes grain, provides electricity, or pumps water; it is driven by large sails which are turned round by the wind

win·dow /ˈwɪndəʊ/ *n* **1** a glass-filled opening in the wall of a building or in a vehicle, to let in light and air: *Open the bedroom window.* | *looking in all the shop windows* –see picture on page 441 **2** *tech* one of the number of areas into which a computer's SCREEN can be divided, each of which is used to show a particular type of information

window box /ˈ·· ·/ *n* a box full of earth outside a window, in which plants can be grown

window dress·ing /ˈ·· ˌ··/ *n* [U] **1** arranging goods in a shop window to attract customers **2** something that tries to attract people to an idea or activity in a rather dishonest way, by giving special attention only to the good things about it

win·dow·pane /ˈwɪndəʊpeɪn/ *n* a single whole piece of glass in a window

window-shop·ping /ˈ·· ˌ··/ *n* [U] looking at the goods in shop windows without intending to buy anything: *We wandered along Oxford Street, just window-shopping.*

win·dow·sill /ˈwɪndəʊˌsɪl/ *n* the flat shelf formed by the piece of wood or stone below a window –see picture on page 441

wind·pipe /ˈwɪndpaɪp/ *n* the tube which forms an air passage from your throat to the top of your lungs

wind·screen /ˈwɪndskriːn/ *n* (**windshield** *AmE*) the piece of glass or transparent material across the front of a vehicle, which the driver looks through –see picture on page 49

windscreen wip·er /ˈ·· ˌ··/ *n* (also **wiper, windshield wiper** *AmE*) a thin piece of metal with a piece of rubber along it, which clears rain from a windscreen –see picture on page 49

wind·shield /ˈwɪndʃiːld/ *n* the usual American word for a WINDSCREEN

wind·sock /ˈwɪndsɒk ‖ -sɑːk/ *n* a tube-shaped piece of material, fastened to a pole at airports to show the direction of the wind

wind·surf /ˈwɪndˌsɜːf ‖ -ˌsɜːrf/ *v* [I] to move along on the water on a flat board with a sail –**windsurfing** *n* [U] –**windsurfer** *n*

wind·swept /ˈwɪndswept/ adj 1 open to the wind (used of a place): *a bare windswept plain* 2 untidy, as if blown by the wind (used of a person): *her windswept appearance*

wind tur·bine /ˈwɪnd ˌtɜːbaɪn ‖ -ˌtɜːrbɪ̩n, -baɪn/ n a machine with large flat sails which are turned by the wind to produce electricity

wind·y /ˈwɪndi/ adj windier, windiest with a lot of wind: *windy weather* | *a windy hillside*

wine /waɪn/ n [C;U] an alcoholic drink made from grapes (GRAPE) or other fruit: *I'd like a glass of red wine, please.* | *a dry white wine* | *the wines of Alsace* | *home-made apple wine*

wine bar /ˈ· ·/ n BrE a place where you can buy wine and light meals

wing /wɪŋ/ n 1 a movable part of the body of a bird or insect, which it uses for flying: *The parrot flapped its wings noisily.* 2 one of the large flat parts which stand out from each side of a plane and support it in flight 3 a part of a structure which stands out from the main or central part: *the west wing of the hospital* 4 BrE the side part of a car that covers the wheels: *a badly dented wing* –see picture on page 49 5 the position or player on the far right or left of the field in a game such as football: *He came racing down the right wing.* 6 a group within a political party or organization, whose members have aims or opinions that are different from the main part of the organization: *The government will have to change their plans to satisfy the right wing of the party.* 7 the wings [pl] the sides of a stage, where an actor is hidden from the people watching the play 8 under someone's wing being protected or helped by someone: *The older boys took the new pupils under their wing.*

wing·er /ˈwɪŋəʳ/ n a player who attacks down one side of the field, in games such as football

wing·span /ˈwɪŋspæn/ n the distance from the end of one wing to the end of the other, when both of them are stretched out

wink¹ /wɪŋk/ v [I;T] 1 to close and open one eye rapidly, usually as a signal between people, especially of amusement or a shared secret: *He winked at her, and she realized he was only pretending to be angry.* 2 (of a light) to flash on and off: *The driver winked his lights at us.* | *fireflies winking in the dark* 3 wink at something to pretend that you have not noticed something bad or illegal

wink² n 1 a winking movement: *with a wink of approval* | *She gave me a knowing wink.* 2 not get a wink of sleep, not sleep a wink not to be able to sleep at all: *I didn't get a wink of sleep last night.*

win·ner /ˈwɪnəʳ/ n a person or animal that has won or that people think is likely to win

win·ning /ˈwɪnɪŋ/ adj very attractive: *a winning smile*

win·nings /ˈwɪnɪŋz/ n [pl] money which has been won

win·ter¹ /ˈwɪntəʳ/ n (also Winter) [C;U] the coldest season of the year, between autumn and spring: *a very cold winter* | *We went skiing last winter.* | *Does it snow here in winter?*

winter² v [I+adv/prep] to spend the winter in a particular place: *to winter in a warm country*

win·ter·time /ˈwɪntətaɪm ‖ -ər-/ n [U] the winter: *Heating bills are highest in the wintertime.*

win·try /ˈwɪntri/ adj (also wintery) very cold, like it is in winter: *wintry clouds* | *a wintry scene*

wipe /waɪp/ v wiped, wiping 1 [T] to rub a surface in order to remove dirt or liquid: *Wipe your shoes on the mat.* | *He wiped the table with a damp cloth.* |

Come on, stop crying and wipe your eyes. | *Let's do the dishes – you wash and I'll wipe.* 2 [T+adv/prep] to remove something by doing this: *She wiped the tears away.* | *Wipe the crumbs off the table onto the floor.* 3 wipe a tape, wipe something off a tape to remove the sounds or pictures that were recorded on a TAPE¹ (2): *I'm afraid I wiped your film off that video.*

wipe sthg ↔ **down** phr v [T] to rub a large surface with a cloth in order to remove dirt or liquid: *Wipe down the walls before you start painting.*

wipe sbdy/sthg ↔ **out** phr v [T] to destroy or remove completely: *The cost of the new machinery has wiped out all our profits this year.*

wipe sthg ↔ **up** phr v [T] to remove liquid or dirt from something with a cloth: *Wipe up that mess!* | *Please wipe that milk up.*

wipe² n a movement in which something is rubbed against something else: *Give the baby's nose a good wipe.*

wip·er /ˈwaɪpəʳ/ n see WINDSCREEN WIPER

wire¹ /waɪəʳ/ n 1 [C;U] a piece of thin metal in the form of a thread: *a wire fence* | *The string wasn't strong enough, so we used wire.* 2 [C;U] a piece of metal like this used for carrying electricity from one place to another: *Connect the blue wires together.* 3 [C] the usual American word for a TELEGRAM

wire² v wired, wiring [T] 1 (also wire sthg ↔ up) to connect up wires in something, especially in an electrical system: *I've wired that plug up.* 2 AmE to send a TELEGRAM to someone: *He wired me the results of the examination.*

wire·less /ˈwaɪələs ‖ ˈwaɪər-/ n [C;U] old fash a radio

wire-tap·ping /ˈ· ˌ··/ n [U] listening secretly to other people's telephone conversations

wir·ing /ˈwaɪərɪŋ/ n [U] the arrangement of the wires that form the electrical system in a building: *This old wiring needs replacing.*

wir·y /ˈwaɪəri/ adj wirier, wiriest rather thin, but with strong muscles: *a wiry body* –wiriness n [U]

wis·dom /ˈwɪzdəm/ n [U] 1 knowledge, experience, and good judgment: *an old man respected for his great wisdom* 2 good sense and judgment: *They questioned the wisdom of going to a country that was at war.*

wisdom tooth /ˈ· ·/ n wisdom teeth one of the four large back teeth in humans, which do not usually appear until the rest of the body has stopped growing

wise /waɪz/ adj 1 having or showing good sense and judgment, and the ability to understand what happens and to decide on the right action to take: *a wise old woman* | *a wise decision* | *It was wise of you to leave when you did.* 2 get wise to infml to begin to understand that someone is being dishonest 3 get wise AmE infml to find out about something 4 none the wiser unable to understand something even though someone has tried to explain it: *He went into how it worked in great detail, but I was still none the wiser!* –wisely adv

wise-crack /ˈwaɪzkræk/ n a clever joking remark

wise guy /ˈ· ·/ n infml a person who thinks he knows more than other people

wish¹ /wɪʃ/ v 1 [+(that)] to want a particular situation to exist, when this is either impossible or very unlikely: *I wish I could fly.* | *I wish I were a bird.* | *He wished he'd never mentioned it.* | *I wished that the ground would open and swallow me up.* 2 wish for something to think of something that you would like very much and hope to get it, or that it will happen: *"I made a wish." "What did you wish for?"* **3** [I;T] *fml* to want: *The newspapers can print whatever they wish.* | *Do you wish to see the wine list, sir?* **4 wish someone something** to hope that someone has something: *We wish you a merry Christmas.* | *I wish you luck!* **5 I would not wish something on someone** = I would not want someone else to have to suffer the same experience that I have suffered: *It was a terrible ordeal, one that I wouldn't wish on my worst enemy.*

wish² *n* **1** a feeling of wanting something: *I am sure everyone shares my wish for these peace talks to succeed.* | *He asked me to respect her last wishes and not tell her parents.* **2** an attempt to make a particular thing happen by thinking about it very hard, especially when it could only happen by magic: *Blow out the candles and make a wish.* **3** a thing that you wish for: *I'm sure you'll get your wish one day.* **4 best wishes** hopes that someone is well and happy: *Please give your parents my best wishes.* | *She sends her best wishes to you both.*

wishful think·ing /ˌ·· '··/ *n* [U] a strong belief that something you want very much to happen will happen, when in fact it is very unlikely to: *He's convinced she thinks he's wonderful — talk about wishful thinking!*

wish·y-wash·y /ˈwɪʃi ˌwɒʃi ‖ -ˌwɔːʃi, -ˌwɑːʃi/ *adj* without clear aims and principles: *rather wishy-washy ideas*

wisp /wɪsp/ *n* **1** a thin or delicate untidy piece of something: *a wisp of hair* **2** a small thin twisting bit of smoke or steam – **wispy** *adj*

wist·ful /ˈwɪstfəl/ *adj* thoughtful and rather sad, especially because of a wish which may not be satisfied, or thoughts of past happiness which may not return: *She left, with a wistful glance over her shoulder.* – **wistfully** *adv* : *He thought wistfully of days gone by.*

wit /wɪt/ *n* **1** [U] the ability to say things which are both clever and amusing **2 have the wit to do something** to be clever or sensible enough to do something: *He hadn't the wit to say no.* **3 at your wits' end** made too worried by difficulties to know what to do next **4 frighten/scare someone out of their wits** to frighten someone very much **5 have/keep your wits about you** to be ready to act sensibly: *You need to keep your wits about you when you're driving in London.* **6 -witted** having a particular type of ability or understanding: *quick-witted* | *dim-witted*

witch /wɪtʃ/ *n* a woman who is believed to have magic or evil powers

witch·craft /ˈwɪtʃkrɑːft ‖ -kræft/ *n* [U] the performing of magic to make things happen

witch·doc·tor /ˈwɪtʃ ˌdɒktəʳ ‖ -ˌdɑːk-/ *n* a person in some societies who is believed to have magical powers and be able to cure people: *the tribe's witch-doctor*

witch-hunt /ˈ· ·/ *n* a search for people whose political views are disliked or who are thought, sometimes falsely, to be responsible for something that has gone wrong, so that they can be made to suffer or be removed from power

with /wɪð, wɪθ/ *prep* **1** by or next to something, or among or included in something: *Put this book with the others.* | *Connect this wire with the other one.* | *Mix the flour with some milk.* | *He was sitting with his friends.* **2** used to show that people do something together: *He never plays with his brother.* | *Girls rarely fight with each other.* **3** using something: *Cut it with scissors.* | *This photo was taken with my new camera.* **4** having something: *a man with a beard* | *a book with a green cover* **5** showing a particular way of behaving: *Please handle the box with care.* | *He fought with great courage.* **6** supporting a person or an idea: *We're all with you in this.* **7** able to understand what someone is saying: *I'm not quite with you.* **8** relating to something: *What's the problem with the car?* | *Be patient with them.* **9** because of something: *With John away at university we've got more room in the house.* **10** in the same direction as the wind or the movement of water: *sailing with the wind*

with·draw /wɪðˈdrɔː, wɪθ-/ *v* **withdrew** /-ˈdruː/, **withdrawn** /-ˈdrɔːn/ **1** [T] to take away or take back: *The drug has been withdrawn from the market.* | *I'd like to withdraw some money, please.* **2** [T] to take back something that was said or offered because it was wrong or must be changed: *I think you should withdraw that last remark.* **3** [I;T] to move away or move back: *The two men withdrew from the room while the others voted for who should be chairman.* | *He has withdrawn his armies.* **4** [I;T] to decide that you or someone else will not take part in something: *She withdrew from the election.* | *He withdrew his horse from the race.*

with·draw·al /wɪðˈdrɔːəl, wɪθ-/ *n* **1** [C;U] the taking or moving away of something: *a gradual withdrawal of troops* | *withdrawal of financial support* **2** [C] an amount of money that you take out of your bank account **3 withdrawal symptoms** the unpleasant effects suffered by someone when they stop taking a drug

with·drawn /wɪðˈdrɔːn, wɪθ-/ *adj* quiet and thoughtful and not very willing to meet or talk to other people

with·er /ˈwɪðəʳ/ *v* [I] **1** (of a plant) to become dry and then to die **2** (of a part of your body) not to have grown and developed properly **3** to get weaker and, in the end, die away: *Our hopes of being rescued gradually withered.*

with·er·ing /ˈwɪðərɪŋ/ *adj* **withering look** a way of looking at someone which is intended to make them feel ashamed: *The teacher gave me a withering look.*

with·hold /wɪðˈhəʊld, wɪθ-/ *v* **withheld** /-ˈheld/, **withheld** [T] to refuse to give something to someone: *He was accused of withholding information from the police.*

with·in /wɪðˈɪn ‖ wɪðˈɪn, wɪθˈɪn/ *adv,prep* **1** *fml* inside something: *They have an important role within the community.* | *A voice came from within the house.* **2** not going beyond something: *We must keep within these spending limits.* **3** before a particular amount of time is finished: *We should be there within an hour.* | *You should hear something within a day or two.*

with·out /wɪðˈaʊt ‖ wɪðˈaʊt, wɪθˈaʊt/ *adv,prep* **1** not having or not using something: *Don't go out without your coat.* | *I managed to do it without any help.* | *There's no milk, so we'll have to manage without.* **2 without doing something** not doing something: *He left without saying goodbye.* | *Can you clean it without breaking it?*

with·stand /wɪðˈstænd, wɪθ-/ *v* **withstood** /-ˈstʊd/, **withstood** [T] to remain unharmed or unchanged by something: *Children's furniture must withstand rough treatment.*

wit·ness¹ /ˈwɪtnʌs/ *n* **1** a person who sees something happen and can describe it to other people:

There were no witnesses to the accident. **2 be witness to something** *fml* to see something happen **3** a person who tells in a court of law what they saw happen or what they know about someone: *a witness for the prosecution* **4** someone who is present at the signing of an official paper and who also signs it, to show that they saw it being signed

witness² *v* [T] **1** to see something happen: *Did anyone witness the accident?* **2** to be present when an official paper is being signed and then to add your signature to show this: *Will you witness my signature?*

witness box /'···/ *n* (also **witness stand** *AmE*) the raised area where witnesses stand in court when they are being questioned

wit·ter /'wɪtəʳ/ *v* [I] to talk for a long time about something unimportant or uninteresting: *What are you wittering on about?*

wit·ti·cis·m /'wɪtɨsɪzəm/ *n* a clever and amusing remark

wit·ty /'wɪti/ *adj* **wittier, wittiest** having or showing a clever mind and an amusing way of expressing your thoughts: *a witty speaker | a witty remark* **–wittily** *adv*

wives /waɪvz/ the plural of WIFE

wiz·ard /'wɪzəd || -ərd/ *n* **1** a man in children's stories who has magic powers **2** someone who is very good at something: *He's a financial wizard.*

wiz·ened /'wɪzənd/ *adj* old and dried up, with lines in the skin: *wizened apples | a wizened old lady*

wk a written abbreviation for WEEK

wob·ble /'wɒbəl || 'wɑ:-/ *v* **wobbled, wobbling** [I;T] to move unsteadily from side to side: *Who's wobbling the table? | The jelly wobbled about.* **–wobble** *n* : *with a wobble in his voice*

wob·bly /'wɒbli || 'wɑ:-/ *adj* moving unsteadily from side to side: *wobbly handwriting*

woe /wəʊ/ *n lit* **1** [U] great sorrow: *a tale of woe* **2 woes** [pl] problems: *He poured out all his woes.*

woe·ful /'wəʊfəl/ *adj* **1** very sad: *woeful eyes* **2** *fml* very bad: *a woeful lack of understanding* **–woefully** *adv*

woke /wəʊk/ the past tense of WAKE

wok·en /'wəʊkən/ the past participle of WAKE

wolf¹ /wʊlf/ *n* **wolves** /wʊlvz/ a wild animal of the dog family which hunts other animals in a group

wolf² *v* [T] (also **wolf sth** ↔ **down**) to eat food very quickly: *He wolfed his meal down.*

wom·an /'wʊmən/ *n* **women** /'wɪmɪn/ **1** [C] a fully grown human female: *Is your doctor a man or a woman?* **2** [U] women in general **3** [C] a man's wife or girlfriend, in some societies; this use is considered offensive in most Western countries **4 woman** a rude way of speaking to a woman when you are angry: *Sit down, woman.*

wom·an·hood /'wʊmənhʊd/ *n* [U] the time when someone is considered a woman and not a girl

wom·an·izer /'wʊmənaɪzəʳ/ *n* (also **womaniser** *BrE*) a man who likes to have sexual relationships with a lot of women **–womanizing** *n* [U]

wom·an·ly /'wʊmənli/ *adj* having or showing the qualities suitable for a woman: *She showed a womanly concern for their health.*

womb /wuːm/ *n* the part of a woman's body where a baby develops before it is born

wom·en·folk /'wɪmɪnfəʊk/ *n* [pl] *infml* women or female relatives

won /wʌn/ the past tense and past participle of WIN

won·der¹ /'wʌndəʳ/ *v* **1** [I;T] to express a wish to know something, silently or in words: *I wonder if she knows we're here. | "Do you think they'll get married?" "I wonder." | I wonder what really happened. | I was just wondering about my car. Will it be fixed by Thursday?*
□ USEFUL PATTERNS to wonder if/whether...; to wonder who, what, why, etc.; to wonder about something
2 [I; + that] to be surprised about something: *I wondered at his rudeness. | I wonder that he can come back here after what happened.* **3 I wonder if** a phrase you use when you want to ask politely for something: *I wonder if I could have some more tea? | I was wondering if you could give me a lift.*
■ USAGE Compare **wonder** and **admire**. You can **wonder at** (= be very much surprised at) both good and bad things: *We wondered at the magnificent buildings/the dreadful poverty in the city.* You admire good things, without being surprised by them: *I have always admired Shakespeare's plays.*

wonder² *n* **1** [U] a feeling of strangeness, surprise, and admiration: *She gazed in wonder, seeing snow for the first time. | He was filled with wonder at the sight of his newly-born son.* **2** [C] someone or something that makes you feel surprise and admiration: *the wonders of modern science* **3 it's a wonder** *infml* it's surprising: *It's a wonder that you recognized me after all these years.* **4 no wonder, it's no wonder, it's small wonder** it's not surprising: *"I got to bed at 5 a.m." "Well, no wonder you're so tired."* **5 work wonders, do wonders** to bring extremely good results: *He looked so tired before, but his holiday has worked wonders.*

wonder³ *adj* [only before a noun] extremely good: *a new wonder drug which they hope will cure cancer*

won·der·ful /'wʌndəfəl || -dər-/ *adj* **1** causing great pleasure: *wonderful news* **2** deserving admiration: *a wonderful advance in computer science* **–wonderfully** *adv*

won·der·ment /'wʌndəmənt || -dər-/ *n* [U] *lit* a feeling of strangeness, surprise, and admiration

won·drous /'wʌndrəs/ *adj* causing great admiration

won·ky /'wɒŋki || 'wɑːŋki/ *adj BrE infml* unsteady and likely to break, fall, or fail: *That table's a bit wonky!*

wont¹ /wəʊnt || wɔːnt/ *n fml* **as is someone's wont** as someone often does: *He spoke for too long, as is his wont.*

wont² *adj* **be wont to do something** to be in the habit of doing something: *He is wont to express himself rather forcefully on that subject.*

won't /wəʊnt/ short for "will not": *I won't go!*

woo /wuː/ *v* **wooed, wooing** [T] **1** to try to get someone's support: *Politicians try to woo voters before an election.* **2** (of a man) to try to persuade a woman into love and marriage (a word no longer used in modern English, except humorously)

wood /wʊd/ *n* **1** [U] the substance of which trees are formed, which is cut and used for various purposes, for example, burning, making paper, or making furniture: *Put some more wood on the fire. | a polished wood floor* **2** [C] (also **woods** [pl]) a place where a lot of trees grow together, smaller than a forest: *We went for a walk in the woods.*

wood·cut·ter /'wʊd,kʌtəʳ/ *n* a man whose job is to cut down trees

wood·ed /ˈwʊd̬d/ adj covered with trees: a densely wooded hillside

wood·en /ˈwʊdn/ adj **1** made of wood: a wooden spoon **2** stiff and expressionless: I thought her performance was rather wooden.

wood·land /ˈwʊdlənd, -lænd/ n [U] an area of land covered with trees: large areas of woodland | woodland birds

wood·peck·er /ˈwʊdˌpekəʳ/ n a bird with a long beak, with which it can make holes in trees and pull out insects

wood·wind /ˈwʊdˌwɪnd/ n [U+sing/pl verb] the set of tube-shaped musical instruments which are played by blowing

wood·work /ˈwʊdwɜːk ‖ -wɜːrk/ n [U] **1** the parts of a house that are made of wood **2** the skill of making wooden objects

wood·worm /ˈwʊdwɜːm ‖ -wɜːrm/ n **1** [C] the small wormlike young of certain beetles (BEETLE), which eat holes in wood **2** [U] the damage done by these creatures

wood·y /ˈwʊdi/ adj **1** having a lot of trees: a woody valley **2** like wood: plants with woody stems

woof /wʊf/ n, interj infml a word used for describing the sound made by a dog

wool /wʊl/ n [U] **1** the soft thick hair which sheep and some other animals have on their bodies **2** thick thread or cloth made from this: another ball of wool for my knitting | a wool suit **3 pull the wool over someone's eyes** to trick someone or hide the facts from them

wool·len /ˈwʊlən/ adj (also **woolen** AmE) made of wool: a woollen coat

wool·lens /ˈwʊlənz/ n (also **woolens** AmE) [pl] clothes made of wool

wool·ly¹ /ˈwʊli/ adj **1** made of wool or like wool: woolly socks **2** showing a lack of clear thinking (used of people or their thoughts)

woolly² n **woollies** infml a piece of clothing made of wool: winter woollies

woolly hat /ˌ··ˈ·/ n BrE a close-fitting hat worn to keep the head and ears warm – see picture on page 50

woolly-head·ed /ˌ···ˈ···/ adj tending not to think clearly or have sensible ideas

woo·zy /ˈwuːzi/ adj infml unsteady or confused

word¹ /wɜːd ‖ wɜːrd/ n **1** [C] the smallest piece of a language which has a meaning; the letters or sounds of a word do not usually change and in English a written word has a space on either side: What's the French word for "mouse"? | For homework I'd like you to write an essay of about 500 words. **2 put something into words** to express something clearly **3 in your own words** not repeating what someone else has said **4 in other words** a phrase used when you are repeating an idea in other words because you think that people may not have understood the real meaning behind the words and you need to explain it: It goes on horizontally. In other words, it goes from side to side, not from top to bottom. | The company has to reduce labour costs. In other words, some of us are going to lose our jobs. – see Study Note on page 539 **5 in a word** making a short general statement of the main points of something: It's a long story. In a word, I quit. **6 not in so many words** not expressed clearly and directly, but only suggested [RELATED PHRASE **in so many words**] **7 word for word**: a in exactly the same words: Tell me what she said, word for word. **b** by translating each word of one language into a word in another language, rather than giving the meaning of whole phrases and sentences **8**

get a word in edgeways to manage to say something: She went on and on about her holiday, and I couldn't get a word in edgeways. **9 have a word with, have a few words with** to have a short conversation with someone, usually in private and about something you do not want other people to hear: Peter, could I have a word with you after class, about your homework? **10 have a good word for** to say pleasant things about: She never has a good word for her brother. **11 put in a good word for** to say something good about someone to someone who is important: Could you put in a good word for me with the headmaster? **12 have words** to argue angrily **13 have the last word** to make the last decision or remark in a conversation or argument **14 not a word** nothing at all of what has been said or written: I don't believe a word of what she says. | The music was so loud that I couldn't hear a word of what he was saying. **15 a word of advice** some advice: Let me give you a word of advice. [RELATED PHRASE **a word of warning**] **16** [U] a message or piece of news: The hostage sent word that he was alive and well. **17 give the word, say the word** to tell someone to start doing something: When I give the word, you may open your exam papers. **18** [sing] a promise: I give you my word that I won't tell anyone. | She always keeps her word. **19 take someone's word for it** to accept what someone says as correct without any other proof **20 by word of mouth** in speech rather than in writing **21 from the word go** from the beginning **22 my word, upon my word** expressions of surprise (phrases no longer used in modern English) **23 too...for words** infml a phrase you use when you want to say that a quality is very strong; it is usually a quality you disapprove of: Honestly, the government's thinking on this is too muddle-headed for words.

word² v [T] to choose particular words to express something: He worded the explanation well. | a carefully-worded apology

word·ing /ˈwɜːdɪŋ ‖ ˈwɜːr-/ n [U] the words and phrases chosen to express something: Let's discuss the wording of the advertisement.

word-per·fect /ˌ· ˈ··/ BrE (**letter-perfect** AmE) adj repeating or remembering every word of some thing completely correctly: Her speech was word-perfect.

word pro·cess·or /ˈ· ˌ···/ n a small computer used for typing (TYPE) letters and reports, and storing information – see picture on page 539 – **word processing** n [U]

word·y /ˈwɜːdi ‖ ˈwɜːrdi/ adj using or containing too many words: a wordy explanation

wore /wɔːʳ/ the past tense of WEAR

work¹ /wɜːk ‖ wɜːrk/ n **1** [U] activity which uses effort and is done for a particular purpose, not for pleasure: It was hard work digging the garden. | I've been busy doing work in the house. **2 at work** doing some work: He was sitting watching some men at work on the roads. **3 get to work, set to work** to start doing some work: We'd better set to work on this decorating. **4** [U] a job: What work do you do? | He's not home from work yet. | She's still at work. | Do you enjoy your work? – see JOB (USAGE) **5 in work** with a job: The number of people in work has increased over the last three years. **6 out of work** with no job but wanting a job: Many people have been out of work for more than a year. **7** [U] the tasks that you have to do in your job: I've had to bring some work home with me this evening. | I've got a lot of work to do at the moment. **8** [U] something that a person has produced by working or by doing their job: *The garden looks lovely – and it's all my own work.* **9** [U] a study that has been done on a particular subject: *Recent work in this area suggests that men are more likely to get this disease than women.* | *A lot of work has been done on this subject.* **10** [C] a piece of art produced by writing, painting, etc.: *the works of Shakespeare* **11 have your work cut out** to have something very difficult to do: *You'll have your work cut out to get that job finished by next week.*

■ USAGE Compare **work, labour, toil.** We can use **work** as a general word for all activities of the mind or body, pleasant or unpleasant. For unpleasant and tiring work we can use **labour** or (more literary) **toil**: *Clearing the field of stones took ten days of backbreaking* **labour**/**toil.**

work sthg ↔ **off** *phr v* [T] to get rid of by work or activity: *He worked off his anger by going for a run.*

work on sthg *phr v* [T] to give your attention to doing something: *I haven't found out her name yet, but I'm working on it.*

work out *phr v* **1** [T **work** sthg ↔ **out**] to find by reasoning or calculating: *Have you worked the answer out?* | *The police can't work out how the thieves entered the building.* | *She'd worked out that it would cost over £100.*

work² *v* **1** [I] to be active or use effort in order to do something: *I've been working in the garden all afternoon.* | *He's working on a new book at the moment.* **2** [T] to make someone be active or use effort: *The teachers work us far too hard.* **3** [I] to be employed: *She works in an office.* | *He works as a salesman.* | *She works for a large computing firm.* **4** [I] to operate properly: *This light doesn't work.* **5** [T] to make a machine operate: *He showed us how to work the coffee machine.* **6** [I] to be successful: *I'm sure her plan won't work.* **7** [+complement] to become: *The handle had worked loose.* **8 work against the clock** to work quickly because you have to finish a job by a particular time **9 work your way** to manage to get somewhere gradually by using a lot of effort: *He managed to work his way to the front of the crowd.* **10 work yourself into a rage/temper** to become very angry **11 work to rule** to obey exactly the rules of your work but do nothing more, as a way of showing that you are unhappy about something **12 work wonders** to have very good results

□ USEFUL PATTERNS to work something out; to work out how, why, who, etc. to work out that... **2** [I] to have an answer which can be calculated: *The cost works out at £6 a night.* **3** [I] to be successful or develop: *I hope the new job works out for you.* | *I wonder how their ideas worked out in practice.* **4** [T **work** sthg ↔ **out**] to plan or decide something: *I've drawn up the main outlines but we'll work out the details later.* **5** [I] *infml* to exercise: *She's working out in the gym.*

work up *phr v* **1** [T **work** sbdy **up**] to make someone angry or upset: *She's worked herself up into a terrible state about her exam.* **2** [I;T **work** sthg ↔ **up**] to develop or move towards: *I've worked up quite a thirst playing tennis.* | *I'm not ready to give blood yet, but I'm working up to it.*

work·a·hol·ic /ˌwɜːkəˈhɒlɪk ‖ ˌwɜːrkəˈhɔː-/ *n* a person who likes to work too hard or who is unable to stop working

work·bench /ˈwɜːkbentʃ ‖ ˈwɜːrk-/ *n* a table with a hard surface for working on with tools: *a carpenter at his workbench*

work·day /ˈwɜːkdeɪ ‖ ˈwɜːrk-/ *n* (also **working day** /ˌ·· ˈ·/) **1** a day which is not a holiday **2** the amount of time during which you work each day

worked up /ˌ· ˈ·◂/ *adj* [never before a noun] unhappy, angry, and worried: *Don't get so worked up about it!*

work·er /ˈwɜːkəʳ ‖ ˈwɜːr-/ *n* **1** someone who does a particular type of job: *office workers* | *farm workers* **2** someone who works in a particular way: *She's a hard worker.* **3** someone employed by other people, usually to do physical work and not management: *a factory worker*

work·force /ˈ··-/ *n* [sing+sing/pl verb] all the people who work in an industry or a factory: *The entire workforce is out on strike.*

work·ing /ˈwɜːkɪŋ ‖ ˈwɜːr-/ *adj* [only before a noun] **1** relating to or used for work: *The diplomats had a working breakfast with the President.* | *working clothes* | *working capital* **2** having a job that is paid: *childcare facilities for working mothers* **3** **the working day, the working week** the number of hours that you spend each day or week at work: *How long is your working day?* **4** used as a base for planning how to do something (used of an idea): *a working theory* **5 a working knowledge of** enough practical knowledge to do something: *I have a working knowledge of car engines and can do most repairs.* **6 be in working order** to be operating properly

working class /ˌ··· ˈ·◂/ *n* **the working class, the working classes** the social class to which people belong who work with their hands, for example in factories or mines – **working-class** *adj*

working par·ty /ˈ·· ˌ··/ *n* a committee which examines a particular subject and reports what it finds

work·ings /ˈwɜːkɪŋz ‖ ˈwɜːr-/ *n* [pl] the way in which something works or operates: *I shall never understand the workings of her mind.*

work·load /ˈwɜːkləʊd ‖ ˈwɜːrk-/ *n* the amount of work you are expected to do in a particular period of time: *She has a very heavy workload.*

work·man /ˈwɜːkmən ‖ ˈwɜːrk-/ *n* **workmen** /-mən/ a man who works with his hands, in a particular skill or trade: *The workmen fixed the water system.*

work·man·like /ˈwɜːkmənlaɪk ‖ ˈwɜːrk-/ *adj* having or showing the qualities of a good workman: *her workmanlike methods*

work·man·ship /ˈwɜːkmənʃɪp ‖ ˈwɜːrk-/ *n* [U] skill in making things: *good workmanship* | *Look at the workmanship on this carved desk.*

work of art /ˌ·· · ˈ·/ *n* **works of art** **1** something, for example a painting, which is produced by an artist: *Rodin's "The Thinker" is one of many works of art in the museum.* **2** something which has been produced with great skill: *Did you see her wedding dress? It was a real work of art.*

work·out /ˈwɜːkaʊt ‖ ˈwɜːr-/ *n infml* a period of physical exercise and training

works /wɜːks ‖ wɜːrks/ *n* [plural is **works**] a factory or other industrial place of work: *a gas works*

work·shop /ˈwɜːkʃɒp ‖ ˈwɜːrkʃɑːp/ *n* **1** a room or place where machines are built or repaired **2** an occasion when a group of people meet and work together in order to share and develop ideas about a subject: *a two-day workshop on management techniques*

work·shy /ˈ·· ·/ *adj* not liking work and trying to avoid it (a word used to express disapproval)

work·top /ˈwɜːktɒp ‖ ˈwɜːrktɑːp/ *n* a flat surface on top of a piece of kitchen furniture where you can prepare food

work-to-rule /ˌ· · ˈ·/ *n* a form of working which causes activity to become slower, because attention is paid to every point in the rules, even when unnecessary, and no additional work is done, in order to support a claim for more money

world /wɜːld ‖ wɜːrld/ n **1 the world** the Earth, on which we live: *the richest man in the world* | *I'd love to sail round the world.* –see EARTH¹ (USAGE) **2 the world** people generally: *We don't want the whole world to know about it.* **3 the...world** a group of living things: *the animal world* **4 the...** **world** a part or area of the world that has a particular character: *the developing world* | *the industrialized world* **5 the world of...** a particular area of human activity: *the world of football* | *the football world* **6** the way someone thinks and lives: *He's in a world of his own.* | *a glimpse into my son's world* **7** a PLANET or star system which may contain life: *a strange creature from another world* **8 a world of** *infml* a large amount of: *That holiday did me a world of good.* | *There's a world of difference between thinking about it and doing it.* **9 for all the world as if** exactly as if **10 in the world** a phrase used to make your question or statement more forceful: *What in the world are you doing?* **11 not for the world** a phrase used to say that you certainly do not want to do something: *I wouldn't hurt her for the world.* **12 out of this world** *infml* wonderful **13 the best of both worlds** the advantages which each choice offers, without having to choose between them **14 worlds apart** completely different: *Their ways of life are worlds apart.*

world-class /ˌ·'·◄/ *adj* among the best in the world: *a world-class footballer*

world-ly /'wɜːldli ‖ 'wɜːr-/ *adj* **1** related to the pleasures of this physical life, rather than the things of the spirit **2** knowing a lot about life **3 worldly goods** the things that you own –**worldliness** *n* [U]

worldly-wise /ˌ·'·◄ ‖ '·· ·/ *adj* experienced and knowing a lot about the way people can behave

world pow·er /ˌ·' ·'··/ *n* a powerful country whose trade and politics have an effect on other parts of the world

world-wide /ˌwɜːld'waɪd◄ ‖ ˌwɜːr-/ *adj,adv* in or over all the world: *French cheeses are famous worldwide.*

worm¹ /wɜːm ‖ wɜːrm/ *n* **1** a small thin tube-like creature with no backbone or legs which lives in the earth **2 have worms** to have a small worm or worms living in your body and possibly causing illness

worm² *v* **1** [I+adv/prep] (also **worm your way**) to move slowly and with difficulty, often by twisting: *We wormed our way through the crack in the wall.* **2 worm your way into something** to make yourself accepted by someone, gradually and sometimes dishonestly: *He wormed his way into her confidence.* | *worming their way into fashionable society* **3** [T] to give an animal medicine to get rid of worms in its body

worn /wɔːn ‖ wɔːrn/ the past participle of WEAR

worn-out /ˌ·'·◄/ *adj* **1** no longer usable because of so much use in the past: *worn-out shoes* **2** [never before a noun] very tired: *She was worn-out after three sleepless nights.*

wor·ried /'wʌrid ‖ 'wɜːrid/ *adj* anxious: *a worried frown on her face* | *He seems worried* **about** *something.* | *They are worried that the hijackers will make further demands.* –**worriedly** *adv*

wor·ry¹ /'wʌri ‖ 'wɜːri/ *v* **worried, worrying 1** [T] to make someone anxious or uncomfortable: *It worries me that he's working so hard.* | *a very worrying*

state of affairs **2** [I] to be anxious about something: *Worrying* **about** *your health can make you ill.* | *Don't worry!* **3 not to worry** = it doesn't matter **4** [T] (of a dog) to chase and bite an animal

worry² *n* **worries 1** [U] a feeling of fear and uncertainty about something: *She is a great source of worry to her parents.* **2** [C] something that makes you anxious: *The profit and loss figures have prompted worries over the company's future.*

worse¹ /wɜːs ‖ wɜːrs/ *adj* **1** [comparative of BAD] less good: *The weather was much worse than we had expected.* **2** [never before a noun] more ill: *He's worse than he was last week.* **3 none the worse for something** not harmed by something

worse² *adv* [comparative of BADLY] in a way that is less good or less satisfactory: *You're behaving worse than an animal!*

worse³ *n* [U] **1** something that is worse: *I thought that what had happened was bad enough, but worse was to follow.* **2 change for the worse** a bad change

wors·en /'wɜːsən ‖ 'wɜːr-/ *v* [I;T] to make or become more difficult, worrying, or unpleasant: *The situation has worsened.* | *the worsening economic crisis*

wor·ship¹ /'wɜːʃɪp ‖ 'wɜːr-/ *n* **1** strong feelings of love, respect, and admiration for someone, usually God: *They bowed their heads in worship.* **2** a religious service: *They attended worship.* **3 Your Worship** the polite way of addressing a MAYOR or MAGISTRATE

worship² *v* **-pp- (-p-** *AmE*) **1** [I;T] to show great respect, admiration, and love for someone: *He worships the ground she walks on.* | *His admirers worshipped at his feet.* | *Let us worship God by singing hymn number 23.* **2** [I] to attend a church service: *They worship regularly at this church.* –**worshipper** *n*

worst¹ /wɜːst ‖ wɜːrst/ *adj* [superlative of BAD] [only before a noun] most bad: *This is the worst accident for years.* | *He's the worst driver I know.*

worst² *adv* [superlative of BADLY] the most badly: *Who suffered worst?* | *He must be the worst dressed man I've ever met.*

worst³ *n* **1 the worst** the thing or part that is most bad: *The worst is yet to come.* | *Go on, tell me the worst.* **2 at worst** if the worst thing happens **3 if the worst comes to the worst** if the worst situation happens

wor·sted /'wʊstɪd/ *n* [U] wool cloth: *a worsted suit*

worth¹ /wɜːθ ‖ wɜːrθ/ *prep* **1** having the value mentioned: *This house is worth a lot of money.* | *a necklace worth £2000* **2** having possessions and money with the value mentioned: *She's worth at least a million pounds.* **3** good enough or useful enough for you to do the thing mentioned: *It's a film that's really worth seeing.* | *It's well worth making the effort to learn to drive.* | *I suppose it's worth a try.* **4 worth it** good, useful, or enjoyable: *Don't lock the door – it's not worth it.* | *The food is expensive there, but it's worth it.* **5 worth your while** useful or helpful to you and so deserving the effort that is needed: *It would be worth your while to write to companies asking if they have any job vacancies.*

worth² *n* [U] **1** value: *Most of the jewellery was of little or no worth.* **2** the quantity that a particular amount of money will buy or pay for: *Several thousands of pounds' worth of clothing was ruined in the fire.* | *The storm did thousands of pounds' worth of damage.* **3** the amount of something that will last for a particular time: *I've only got two weeks' worth of work left on this project.*

worth·less /ˈwɜːθləs ‖ ˈwɜːrθ-/ adj **1** of no value or use: *I'm afraid it's completely worthless.* | *a worthless action* **2** with no good qualities: *a worthless member of society*

■ USAGE Compare **worthless** and **priceless**. We use **worthless** about things that are of no value: *The stone looked like a diamond, but it was completely* **worthless**. But we use **priceless** about things that are very valuable indeed: *a priceless painting by Van Gogh*

worth·while /ˌwɜːθˈwaɪl◂ ‖ ˌwɜːr-/ adj deserving the effort needed, or the time and money spent: *I think "Save the Children" is a worthwhile charity to support.* | *We queued for ages, but it was worthwhile. The concert was fantastic!*

wor·thy /ˈwɜːði ‖ ˈwɜːrði/ adj **1** [only before a noun] deserving respect or serious consideration: *a worthy opponent* | *worthy aims* **2** deserving: *worthy of admiration* | *I don't feel worthy to receive all this praise.* **3** -**worthy** deserving of something: *a praiseworthy action* | *a newsworthy event*

would /wʊd/ v *negative short form* **wouldn't** [modal verb] **1** used when someone said or thought that something was going to happen, or when they intended to do something: *They said it would be fine.* | *She said that she would come.* | *I knew she would be annoyed.* –see 's (USAGE) **2** used when you are talking about what is likely or possible: *I would be very surprised if he came now.* | *A fall in the price of oil would have serious consequences for our economy.* **3** used to say that you are willing to do something: *She would do anything for her parents.* **4** used to show that something happened regularly in the past: *We used to work in the same office and we would often have coffee together.* –see Study Note on page 392 **5** would like, would love a polite way of saying that you want something: *I would love a cup of tea!* | *Would you like a biscuit?* **6** would you a polite way of asking someone to do something: *Would you post this for me, please?* | *Shut the door, would you?* **7** wouldn't, would not used to say that someone refused to do something: *I tried to talk to her, but she wouldn't listen.* **8** I would a phrase you use when you are giving advice to someone: *"What shall I do about the cat?" "I would have it put down."* | *I would get rid of that car if I were you.* **9** I would think, I would have thought a phrase you use when you are giving your opinion: *I would think that the company must be in financial difficulty.* | *I would have thought that she would be pleased to get the job.*

wound¹ /waʊnd/ the past tense and past participle of WIND³

wound² /wuːnd/ n a damaged place in your body, usually a hole or tear through your skin made by a weapon such as a gun or knife: *a bullet wound* | *The wound is healing fast.*

wound³ /wuːnd/ v [T] **1** to damage someone's body with a weapon such as a gun or knife: *Was he badly wounded?* **2** to hurt someone's feelings and make them feel unhappy: *He has really wounded her pride.*

■ USAGE Compare the use of **wound, injure,** and **hurt** when we talk of damage to the body. You can be **wounded** from an attack in which a gun, a sword, or a knife is used. You can be **injured** when any other weapon is used (such as a heavy stick or a bomb), or in an accident: *He was injured in a car crash.* Both **wound** and **injure** are more serious than **hurt**: *She slipped and hurt her knee.*

wove /wəʊv/ the past tense of WEAVE

wov·en /ˈwəʊvən/ the past participle of WEAVE

wow /waʊ/ *interj infml* an expression of surprise and admiration: *Wow! Look at her new car!*

W.P.C. /ˌdʌbəljuː piː ˈsiː/ a female member of the British police force having the lowest rank; an abbreviation for **Woman Police Constable**

wran·gle /ˈræŋgəl/ v wrangled, wrangling [I] to have an angry or noisy argument: *The boys were wrangling over whose turn it was.* –**wrangle** n

wrap¹ /ræp/ v [T+adv/prep] -pp- to put something around something else to cover or protect it: *I wrapped the book in brown paper before I posted it.* | *I wrapped the rug around his legs to keep him warm.*
wrap up phr v **1** [T wrap sthg ↔ up] to put paper around a parcel or present **2** [I] to wear warm clothes: *It's cold outside. Wrap up well.* **3** [T wrap sthg ↔ up] *infml* to complete a meeting or an agreement

wrap² n a piece of material which is worn around a woman's shoulders

wrapped /ræpt/ adj **wrapped up in** giving all your attention and care to something: *She's wrapped up in some project at work at the moment.*

wrap·per /ˈræpəʳ/ n a piece of paper or plastic which covers a book or sweet when you buy it

wrap·ping /ˈræpɪŋ/ n [C;U] **1** paper or other material used for covering and protecting something: *Don't take the wrapping off. It might get damaged.* **2** **wrapping paper** coloured paper that you put around a present

wrath /rɒθ ‖ ræθ/ n [U] *lit* great anger: *the wrath of God* –**wrathful** adj

wreak /riːk/ v *lit* **1** **wreak havoc** to cause a lot of damage **2** **wreak vengeance on someone** to make someone suffer because they have harmed you in some way

wreath /riːθ/ n **1** a circular arrangement of flowers or leaves, especially one put on a grave **2** a curling piece of smoke, mist, or gas

wreathe /riːð/ v wreathed, wreathing [T] *lit* **1** **wreathed in, wreathed with** completely covered or surrounded by something **2** **wreathed in smiles** smiling very happily

wreck¹ /rek/ n **1** [C] a ship which has sunk or been partly destroyed on rocks: *Divers went down to the wreck.* | *You can see the wreck when the tide's out.* **2** [C;U] the destruction of a ship by sinking or by crashing into rocks: *There have been hundreds of wrecks on that coast.* | *The wreck of the Titanic shocked everyone.* **3** [U] the state of being ruined or destroyed: *the wreck of all our plans* **4** [C] something or someone in a very bad state: *She's a complete wreck after her illness.* | *He's still driving round in that old wreck.*

wreck² v [T] to destroy something: *The ship was wrecked on the rocks.* | *The weather has completely wrecked our plans.*

wreck·age /ˈrekɪdʒ/ n [U] the broken parts of something that has been destroyed: *The wreckage of the car lay all across the road.*

wren /ren/ n a very small brown European bird

wrench¹ /rentʃ/ v [T] **1** to pull something hard with a twisting or turning movement: *He slammed the door so hard that he wrenched the handle off.* **2** to twist and damage a joint of your body: *She fell awkwardly and wrenched her ankle.*

wrench² n **1** an act of twisting and pulling **2** **be a wrench** to be painful or difficult because you have to leave someone or something **3** a metal tool for turning and undoing nuts

wrest /rest/ v [T+adv/prep] *fml* to pull something away from someone roughly: *She wrested the gun out of his hands.*

wres·tle /ˈresəl/ v **wrestled, wrestling 1** [I;T] to fight by holding on to someone and trying to throw them to the ground: *She wrestled with her attacker.* **2 wrestle with something** to try to deal with something difficult

wres·tling /ˈreslɪŋ/ n [U] a sport in which two people wrestle and each tries to throw the other to the ground **–wrestler** n

wretch /retʃ/ n **1** a poor or unhappy person: *unlucky wretches with no homes* **2** someone, especially a child, who has done something bad

wretch·ed /ˈretʃɪd/ adj **1** very poor or unhappy **2** unpleasant and annoying: *Wretched child! Why can't she behave?*

wrig·gle /ˈrɪgəl/ v **wriggled, wriggling 1** [I] to twist your body from side to side: *He wriggled uncomfortably on the hard chair.* | *They wriggled through the gap.* **2** [T] to move a part of your body from side to side or up and down: *Wriggle your toes.* **3 wriggle out of something** *infml* to avoid doing something unpleasant or taking the blame for something **–wriggle** n

wring /rɪŋ/ v **wrung** /rʌŋ/, **wrung 1** [T] (also **wring** sthg ↔ **out**) to twist and press something to remove water from it: *Wring those wet things out.* **2 wring your hands** to twist your hands together as though washing them, as a sign of worry or grief **3 wring something's neck** to kill something by twisting its neck **4 wringing wet** extremely wet **–wring** n

wrin·kle[1] /ˈrɪŋkəl/ n **1** a line in something which is folded or crushed **2** a line on an old person's skin **–wrinkly** adj

wrinkle[2] v **wrinkled, wrinkling** [I;T] to form into lines or folds: *the wrinkled face of the old man*

wrist /rɪst/ n the joint between your hand and the lower part of your arm

wrist·watch /ˈrɪstwɒtʃ ‖ -wɑːtʃ, -wɔːtʃ/ n a watch made to be fastened on a person's wrist

writ /rɪt/ n an official legal paper telling someone to do or not to do a particular thing

write /raɪt/ v [I;T] **wrote** /rəʊt/, **written** /ˈrɪtn/, **writing 1** to make letters or words, especially by using a pen or pencil on paper: *The children are learning to write.* | *Write the address on the envelope.* **2** to make something, such as a book or play, by writing: *She's written several books already.* | *Have you written that report yet?* | *She writes for the stage.* **3** to produce and send a letter to someone: *She wrote to me last month.* | *I've written a letter to the local newspaper.* | *He wrote me a letter.* | *I wish he would write more often.* | *He wrote to tell me the news.* | *She wrote asking for money.*
□ USEFUL PATTERNS to write to someone; to write a letter to someone; to write someone a letter; to write to say, ask, etc.; to write saying, asking, etc.
write back phr v [I;T **write** sthg ↔ **back**] to write a letter replying to one you have received
write sthg ↔ **down** phr v [T] to record information or speech by writing it: *Write your idea down while it's clear in your mind.* | *I wrote down everything you told me.*
■ USAGE In informal American English you can say: *I'll write you next week.* | *Please write me soon.* This is NOT generally acceptable in British

English. Instead you should say: *I'll write to you.* | *I'll write you a letter.* | *Please write to me.* | *Please write me a letter soon.*
write in phr v [I] to send a letter to a firm, asking for something or giving an opinion: *We wrote in for a free book, but the firm never replied.*
write off phr v **1** [T **write** sbdy/sthg ↔ **off**] to regard someone or something as being lost or having failed: *The newspapers wrote him off as a failure, but he proved them wrong.* | *We'll have to write our holiday off. We can't afford it now.* **2** [I] to write to a firm, especially to buy something: *She wrote off for the book, because the shop didn't have it.*
write out phr v [T] **1** to write something in full: *to write out a report* **2** to write something official: *to write out a cheque*
write sthg ↔ **up** phr v [T] to write something again in a complete and useful form: *to write up your notes*

write-off /ˈ· ·/ n a vehicle that has been so badly damaged that it cannot be repaired

writ·er /ˈraɪtə[r]/ n a person who writes, especially as a job

write-up /ˈ· ·/ n *infml* a written report which gives a judgment about a play or a new product: *The concert got a good write-up in the local paper.*

writhe /raɪð/ v **writhed, writhing** [I] to twist your body because you are in great pain: *writhing in agony*

writ·ing /ˈraɪtɪŋ/ n **1** [U] the activity of writing, especially books: *Writing is a difficult way of earning a living.* **2** [U] the style which a person writes by hand: *I can't read the doctor's writing.* **3** [U] something that has been written: *There was writing all over the walls.* **4 in writing** written on paper: *You must get the agreement down in writing.* **5 writings** [pl] all the books and other things that someone has written: *Darwin's scientific writings*

writing pa·per /ˈ·· ···/ n [U] smooth, good quality paper for writing letters on

writ·ten /ˈrɪtn/ the past participle of WRITE

wrong[1] /rɒŋ ‖ rɔːŋ/ adj **1** not correct: *the wrong answer* | *That clock's wrong.* | *You're completely wrong.* **2** not suitable: *That style is wrong for your hair.* | *This is the wrong time to ask for a pay rise.* **3** [never before a noun] not morally acceptable: *It's wrong to tell lies.* | *Stealing is wrong.* **4 get the wrong end of the stick** to understand something wrongly **–wrongly** adv

wrong[2] adv **1** wrongly: *You've spelt the word wrong.* **2 get it wrong** to misunderstand something **3 go wrong: a** to make a mistake: *This sum isn't right, but I can't see where I went wrong.* **b** to develop in an unsatisfactory way: *After five years, their marriage suddenly went wrong.* **c** to stop working properly: *The car's gone wrong.* | *Something's gone wrong with the car.*

wrong[3] n **1** [U] behaviour that is not morally acceptable: *You're old enough to know right from wrong.* **2** [C] *fml* a very bad or unjust action: *He did you a terrible wrong.* **3 in the wrong** mistaken or deserving blame: *Which of the two drivers was in the wrong?*

wrong[4] v [T] *lit* to treat someone very unfairly

wrong-do·ing /ˈrɒŋˌduːɪŋ ‖ ˌrɔːŋˈduːɪŋ/ n [U] *fml* bad, evil, or illegal behaviour **–wrongdoer** n

wrong·ful /ˈrɒŋfəl ‖ ˈrɔːŋ-/ adj *fml* unjust or illegal: *wrongful imprisonment* **–wrongfully** adv

wrote /rəʊt/ the past tense of WRITE

wrought /rɔːt/ *adj lit* made or done

wrought i·ron /ˌ· '···◄/ *n* [U] iron shaped into a useful form or pleasing pattern: *a wrought-iron gate*

wrung /rʌŋ/ the past tense and past participle of WRING

X,x

X, x /eks/ **X's, x's** *or* **Xs, xs** the 24th letter of the English alphabet

x *n* a sign used in MATHEMATICS for a quantity that is not known but which can be calculated: *If 3x =6, x=2.*

X *n* **1** [U] a letter that you use instead of a name when you do not want people to know the name: *the victim, whom we shall call Mrs X* **2** [C] a film which is considered unsuitable for young people under 18: *"Terrors of the Grave" is an X.*

xen·o·pho·bi·a /ˌzenəˈfəʊbiə/ *n* [U] unreasonable fear and dislike of foreigners or strangers –**xenophobic** *adj*

xe·rox /ˈzɪərɒks, ˈze-‖ ˈzɪərɑːks, ˈziː-/ *v* [T] *tdmk* (also **Xerox**) to make a photographic copy of something printed or written on a special electric copying machine –**xerox** *n* : *Copy the letter on the xerox.* | *Make a xerox of the letter.*

X·mas /ˈkrɪsməs, ˈeksməs/ *n* [U] *infml* Christmas

x-ray /ˈeks reɪ/ *v* [T] (also **X-ray**) to photograph, examine, or treat someone by means of x-rays: *They x-rayed her leg to find out if the bone was broken.*

X-ray *n* **1** a powerful unseen beam of light which can pass through substances that are not transparent, and which is used especially for photographing medical conditions inside your body **2** a photograph taken using this

xy·lo·phone /ˈzaɪləfəʊn/ *n* a musical instrument made up of a set of flat wooden bars which produce musical notes when struck with small wooden hammers

wry /raɪ/ *adj* showing that you do not like a situation very much, or that you do not really believe something, or find it slightly amusing: *a wry expression* | *"I'm not invited," he said with a wry smile.* –**wryly** *adv*

Y,y

Y y /waɪ/ **Y's, y's** or **Ys, ys** the 25th letter of the English alphabet

yacht /jɒt ‖ jɑːt/ n a boat with sails or a motor, used for pleasure –see picture on page 735

yacht·ing /'jɒtɪŋ ‖ 'jɑːtɪŋ/ n [U] the sport or activity of sailing or racing in a yacht: *Yachting can be very expensive.* –**yachting** v [only in progressive forms]: *We're going yachting next weekend.*

yam /jæm/ n a tropical climbing plant whose root is eaten as a vegetable

yank /jæŋk/ v [I] infml to pull something suddenly and sharply: *He yanked the rope.* –**yank** n : *Give it a yank.*

Yank n infml (also **Yankee** /'jæŋki/) a citizen of the United States of America (a word which is considered slightly offensive)

yap /jæp/ v -pp- [I] **1** (of dogs) to make short sharp excited noises **2** infml to talk noisily and about unimportant things –**yap** n

yard /jɑːd ‖ jɑːrd/ n **1** a unit for measuring length, equal to 3 feet or about .914 metres: *The target was about 100 yards away.* **2** AmE a garden behind a house **3** an enclosed or partly enclosed area next to a building: *a churchyard* **4** an enclosed area used for a particular business: *a shipyard* | *a coalyard*

yard·stick /'jɑːd‚stɪk ‖ 'jɑːrd-/ n a standard of measurement or comparison: *Is money the only yardstick of success?*

yarn /jɑːn ‖ jɑːrn/ n **1** [U] thread made of wool or cotton **2** [C] infml a long story, often one that is not true

yawn /jɔːn/ v [I] **1** to open your mouth wide and breathe in deeply, because you are tired **2** (of a hole) to become wide open: *The hole yawned before him.* | *a yawning crack* –**yawn** n : *I gave a loud yawn, but he just kept on talking.*

yd a written abbreviation for YARD

yeah /jeə/ adv infml yes

year /jɪəʳ, jɜːʳ ‖ jɪər/ n **1** a period of 365 or 366 days, divided into 12 months, beginning on January 1st and ending on December 31st **2** a period of 365 days measured from any point: *He's three years old.* | *I arrived here two years ago today.* | *I've known him for years.* **3** a period of about a year in the life of an organization or system: *We take our examinations in June, at the end of the school year.* | *the financial year* **4** all the year round, all year round during the whole year **5** the year dot infml a very long time ago: *That hat went out of fashion in the year dot!*

year·ling /'jɪəlɪŋ, 'jɜː- ‖ 'jɪər-/ n a young horse between one and two years old

year·ly /'jɪəli, 'jɜː- ‖ 'jɪərli/ adj [only before a noun] **1** every year or once a year: *a yearly meeting* **2** concerning or lasting for a period of one year: *a yearly season ticket* –**yearly** adv : *We meet twice yearly.*

yearn /jɜːn ‖ jɜːrn/ v [I] lit **yearn for something, yearn to do something** to have a strong, loving, or sad desire for something: *They yearned to return home.* –**yearning** n [C;U]

yeast /jiːst/ n [U] a form of very small plant life that is used in making bread, and for producing alcohol in beer and wine

yell /jel/ v [I;T] to say, shout, or cry something loudly: *He yelled out orders.* | *Don't yell at me like that!* –**yell** n : *yells of excitement*

yel·low /'jeləʊ/ adj of a colour like that of butter, gold, or the middle part of an egg: *a yellow flower* –see picture on page 147 –**yellow** n [U] : *dressed in yellow* –**yellow** v [I] : *The paper had yellowed with age.*

yelp /jelp/ v [I] to make a high sharp sound, especially because of pain or excitement: *The dog yelped when I hit it.* –**yelp** n : *He gave a yelp of delight.*

yen /jen/ n **1** [plural is **yen**] the standard unit of money in Japan **2** [sing] a strong desire: *He has a yen to travel.* | *a sudden yen for some chocolate*

yes /jes/ adv **1** used when you are agreeing with someone or agreeing to do something: *"Do you like him?" "Yes."* | *"I think these people should be locked up." "Yes, I agree."* | *"Lock the door when you leave." "Yes, alright."* **2** used to show that you are listening to someone and want them to continue speaking: *"John?" "Yes?" "Have you got my scissors?"*

yes-man /'jes mæn/ n **yes-men** /-men/ a person who always agrees with their employer or leader (a word used to express disapproval)

yes·ter·day /'jestədi/ adv, n **1** the day before today: *Yesterday was Sunday.* | *I saw her yesterday afternoon.* | *Did you go to the meeting yesterday?* **2** the past: *the fashions of yesterday*

yet¹ /jet/ adv **1** used in questions to ask if something has happened already? *Is she home yet?* –see JUST² (USAGE) –see ALREADY (USAGE) **2** not yet: a not up till now: *He's not home yet.* | *I haven't finished yet.* b not now, but later: *Don't tell anyone yet.* **3** in the future: *We may win yet.* | *The plan may yet succeed.* **4** used to make a word stronger: *He made yet another mistake.* | *I had to listen to his story yet again.*

yet² conj even so: *She's a funny girl, yet you can't help liking her.*

yew /juː/ n a tree with small leaves that are always green and small red berries

yield¹ /jiːld/ v **1** [T] to give or produce something: *His business yields big profits.* **2** [I;T] to admit defeat or give up control of something: *The government will yield under pressure from the opposition.* | *We were forced to yield our position to the enemy.* **3** [I] to bend or break because of a strong force: *The shelf was beginning to yield under the weight of the boxes.*

yield² n the amount of something that is produced: *the yield per acre is very small* | *a yield of 5p per share*

yip·pee /jɪ'piː ‖ 'jɪpi/ interj infml a word that you say when you are delighted, happy, or successful: *"You've won." "Yippee!"*

yo·del /'jəʊdl/ v -ll- (also -l- AmE) [I] to sing with many rapid changes between your natural voice and a very high voice

yo·ga /'jəʊgə/ n [U] a system of exercises which help you to control your body and your mind

yog·hurt /'jɒgət ‖ 'jəʊgərt/ n (also **yogurt, yoghourt**) [C;U] milk that has turned thick and slightly sour through the action of certain bacteria; yoghurt is eaten, not drunk

yoke¹ /jəʊk/ n **1** a wooden frame used to fasten animals together when they are pulling a vehicle **2** a frame worn across a person's shoulders and used for carrying things **3 the yoke of** the cruel or hard rule or control of: *freed from the yoke of military government*

yoke² v **yoked, yoking** [T] to join two animals together with a yoke

yo·kel /ˈjəʊkəl/ n a simple or foolish country person (a word usually used in a humorous way)

yolk /jəʊk ‖ jəʊk, jelk/ n [C;U] the yellow central part of an egg

yon·der /ˈjɒndəʳ ‖ ˈjɑːn-/ adj,adv over there (a word which is no longer used in modern English): *Walk to yonder hill.* | *the house yonder*

yonks /jɒŋks ‖ jɑːŋks/ n [U] *infml* a long time: *I haven't seen him for yonks.* | *That was yonks ago!*

you /jə, jʊ; *strong* juː/ *pron* [used as the subject or object of a verb] **1** the person or people who are being spoken to: *You must all listen carefully.* | *Shall I get you a drink, John?* **2** people in general: *It's not good for you to eat too much meat.* | *You can't believe what politicians say.*

you'd /jəd, jʊd; *strong* juːd/ short for "you had" or "you would"

you'll /jəl, jʊl; *strong* juːl/ short for "you will" or "you shall"

young¹ /jʌŋ/ adj **younger** /ˈjʌŋgəʳ/, **youngest** /ˈjʌŋgəst/ **1** in an early stage of life, growth, or development: *a young girl* | *They have three young children.* | *Most of the teachers here are quite young.* | *These young plants are doing well.* **2** related to or suitable for young people: *That style's too young for her.*

young² n [pl] **1 the young** young people considered as a group **2** young animals: *The lion fought to protect her young.*

young·ster /ˈjʌŋstəʳ/ n a young person

your /jəʳ; *strong* jɔːʳ ‖ jər; *strong* jʊər, jɔːr/ det **1** relating to or belonging to the person or people who are being spoken to: *Your hands are dirty.* | *Could you all leave your books on that table?* **2** relating to or belonging to people in general: *These boots really keep your feet warm.*

you're /jəʳ; *strong* jɔːʳ ‖ jər; *strong* jʊər, jɔːr/ short for "you are"

yours /jɔːz ‖ jʊərz, jɔːrz/ *pron* **1** something related to or belonging to the person or people who are being spoken to: *Our house is very similar to yours.* **2** **Yours, Yours faithfully, Yours sincerely** a polite phrase that you write at the end of a letter before your name: *Yours sincerely, John Brown.* ■ USAGE **Yours faithfully/Yours truly** are used to end a formal letter that begins *Dear Sir/Madam* etc. **Yours sincerely** is very commonly used to end a less formal letter that begins *Dear Mr Smith/Ms Jones* etc. In informal letters many endings are possible, for example **Yours** and **Best wishes**.

your·self /jəˈself ‖ jər-/ *pron* **yourselves** /-ˈselvz/ **1** used as the object of a verb or a PREPOSITION when the subject of a verb is the person who is being spoken to and the action is done to the same person: *You'll hurt yourself.* | *You should look at yourself in the mirror!* | *Why don't you buy yourself some new clothes?* **2** used to add force to the word "you": *You admitted yourself that you hadn't been very successful.* | *I'm afraid you'll have to carry your bags yourselves.* **3 by yourself** alone, with no one with you or helping you: *You'll have to spend quite a lot of time by yourself.* | *Can you manage to lift that box by yourself?*

youth /juːθ/ n **youths** /juːðz‖juːðz, juːθs/ **1** [U] the period of time when you are young: *In my youth I used to play football.* –see CHILD (USAGE) **2** [C] a young man (a word often used to express disapproval): *a gang of youths* **3 the youth** [pl] young men and women considered as a group: *The youth of today are better educated.*

youth·ful /ˈjuːθfəl/ adj **1** having the qualities of young people: *his youthful enthusiasm* **2** young: *our youthful prime minister* –**youthfully** adv

youth hos·tel /ˈ· ˌ··/ n a place where young people can stay cheaply when they are travelling around on holiday

you've /jev; *strong* juːv/ v short for "you have"

yo-yo /ˈjəʊjəʊ/ n a toy made of a thick circular piece of wood, metal, or plastic, which can be made to move up and down a piece of string which is tied to it

yule /juːl/ n *lit* (also **Yule**) Christmas

yule·tide /ˈjuːltaɪd/ n *lit* (also **Yuletide**) the Christmas season

yup·pie /ˈjʌpi/ n (also **yuppy**) a young person in a professional job with a high income, especially one who enjoys having an expensive and fashionable way of life (a word often used to express disapproval)

Z, z

Z, z /zed ‖ ziː/ **Z's, z's** or **Zs, zs** the 26th and last letter of the English alphabet

za·ny /ˈzeɪni/ adj strange, foolish, and amusing

zap /zæp/ v infml **1** [T] to attack or destroy someone or something **2** [I + adv/prep] to move somewhere quickly or forcefully

zeal /ziːl/ n [U] great eagerness: carried away by revolutionary zeal

zeal·ous /ˈzeləs/ adj very keen: zealous in doing his duty | zealous supporters of the government –**zealously** adv

ze·bra /ˈziːbrə, ˈze- ‖ ˈziːbrə/ n an African animal that looks like a horse and has black and white lines all over its body

zebra cross·ing /ˌ·· ˈ··/ n a set of black and white lines painted on a road in Britain, to show that people have the right to cross the road in that place –see picture on page 735

zen·ith /ˈzenɪθ ‖ ˈziː-/ n [sing] the point at which something is at its most successful: Rome's power reached its zenith under the emperor Trajan.

ze·ro[1] /ˈzɪərəʊ ‖ ˈziːrəʊ/ n zeros or zeroes **1** the name of the sign 0 and of the number it stands for **2** the point between + and – on a scale. **3** the temperature on the CENTIGRADE scale at which water freezes: It was five below zero last night. –**zero** adj [only before a noun]: conditions of zero gravity | Our target is zero inflation.

■ USAGE In British English **zero** is NOT used when saying telephone numbers. Use **0** (pronounced "oh"/əʊ/) instead.

zero[2] v

zero in on sthg phr v [T] **1** to aim a weapon directly at something **2** to give all your attention to something

zest /zest/ n [U] a feeling of eager excitement: She entered into the work with zest. | a zest for life

zig·zag[1] /ˈzɪgzæg/ n a line shaped like a row of touching w's: a zigzag path

zigzag[2] v -gg- [I] to go in a zigzag: The path zigzags up the hill.

zinc /zɪŋk/ [U] a bluish-white metal that is used in the production of other metals

zip[1] /zɪp/ n (also **zip fastener** /ˌ· ˈ···/ BrE, **zipper** /ˈzɪpər/ AmE) a fastener made of two sets of metal or plastic teeth and a sliding piece that draws them together; zips are often used to fasten clothes: Do my zip up, would you? –see picture on page 50

zip[2] v -pp- **1** [T] to put something into a particular condition using a zip: Zip the sleeping bag together. **2** [I + adv/prep] to move quickly and forcefully: The bullet zipped past my head.

zip up phr v **1** [T **zip** sthg ↔ **up**] to fasten something with a zip: He zipped the bag up. | She zipped up her dress. –opposite **unzip 2** [T **zip** sbdy **up**] to fasten someone into something with a zip: Would you zip me up? I can't reach.

zip code /ˈ· ·/ n AmE a series of numbers and letters that is part of an address

zo·di·ac /ˈzəʊdiæk/ n **the zodiac** a picture which shows an imaginary belt through space along which the sun, the moon, and the planets (PLANET) travel; the zodiac is divided into 12 equal parts, which each have names, and is used by people who believe that the stars influence a person's character and fate: "Which sign of the zodiac are you?" "I'm a Gemini."

zom·bie /ˈzɒmbi ‖ ˈzɑːm-/ n a person who does not seem to know where they are or what they are doing: I was so tired I was wandering about like a zombie.

zone /zəʊn/ n a division or area marked off from others by particular qualities: a war zone | the US postal zones

zoo /zuː/ n zoos a park where many kinds of living animals are kept for people to look at or study

zo·ol·o·gy /zuːˈɒlədʒi, zəʊˈɒ- ‖ -ˈɑːl-/ n [U] the scientific study of animals, and of where and how they live –**zoologist** n –**zoological** /ˌzuːəˈlɒdʒɪkəl, ˌzəʊə- ‖ -ˈlɑː-/ adj

zoom /zuːm/ v [I+adv/prep] **1** to increase rapidly: Prices have zoomed up in the last year. **2** infml (of a driver or vehicle) to go quickly and noisily: Jack went zooming past in his new car.

zoom in phr v [I] (of a camera) to move quickly from a distant view to a close view of something: The camera zoomed in on the child's face.

zoom lens /ˈ· ·/ n a camera LENS which can move quickly between a distant and a close-up view

zuc·chi·ni /zʊˈkiːni/ n [plural is **zucchini**] the usual American word for a COURGETTE

Answer Key

Workbook exercises

Exercises 1
1. animal 2. happy 3. jug 4. queen 5. well
6. zoo

Exercise 2
1. abacus 2. about 3. absent 4. actor
5. address 6. animal

Exercise 3
photograph, calendar, knife, circle, cinema, gentleman, writer, chauffeur

Exercise 4
1. admire 2. craftsman 3. explore 4. forcible
5. hijack 6. kind-hearted 7. lively 8. poison²

Exercise 5
adamant ... adapt, crown jewels ... crucial, eagle ... ear, half-sister ... half-timbered, personal column ... personal organizer, semi colon ... semi-final

Exercise 6
pianist, pick, pick out, pick up, picket, pick-me-up, pickpocket, picnic

Exercise 7
1. hand 2. eye 3. teach 4. field¹ 5. sell
6. back¹

Exercise 8
1. airport 2. air hostess 3. air force 4. air terminal 5. airline

Exercise 9
1. a critic 2. a yacht 3. astrology, wildlife, architecture etc. (almost anything, according to your interests) 4. windy 5. money, characteristics etc. 6. food

Exercise 10
1. 1 2. 4 3. 5 4. 1 5. 6 6. 4

Exercise 11
abacuses, grouse, phenomena, tomatoes, cargoes *or* cargos, indexes *or* indices, skies, wives

Exercise 12
1. adv, prep 2. n, v 3. adv, prep, adj
4. n, v, adj 5. adj, n, adv 6. adv, prep, adj

Exercise 13
attack, apple, adventure

Exercise 14
1. My father arrived at the station
5. They opened the door/window etc.

Exercise 15
1. ... of having 2. going 3. ... to see
4. to drink ... 5. steal/stealing

Exercise 16
1. with 2. on 3. from 4. with 5. through

Exercise 17
1. fml 2. infml 3. old fash 4. AmE 5. tech, fml
6. infml

Exercise 18
begin, look for, television, succinct, wrong

Exercise 19
1 syllable: and, axe 2 syllables: address, angry
3 syllables: alphabet, animal

Exercise 20
letters, elephant, useful

Exercise 21
a**bove**, **act**ion, ac**cept**, ad**dress**

Exercise 22
1a. in**crease** b. **in**crease 2a. per**mit** b. **per**mit

Exercise 23
/iː/ – field, key, people, scene, sheep, team
/e/ – bed, bread, bury, friend, said
/ɒ/ – cough, pot, watch
/uː/ – blue, boot, do, group, move, shoe

Study Note exercise

WORD CLASSES OR 'PARTS OF SPEECH'

noun	verb	adjective	adverb
weekend	went	last	quite
seaside	took	cold	rather
group	had	disappointed	fortunately
friends	arrived	warmer	
sandwiches	was	wonderful	
picnic	felt		
beach	got		
weather	had		
time			

pronoun	preposition	conjunction
I	to	and
We	with	When
us	of	so
we	with	and
we	and	
it		
we		

Picture exercises

CAR

1. (back) door 2. ignition 3. clutch pedal
4. rear-view mirror 5. headlights 6. fuel gauge 7. indicators 8. brake 9. petrol cap

CLOTHES

Exercise 1
1. red t-shirt 2. green slippers 3. blue raincoat
4. red dressing gown 5. red tie

Exercise 2

	belt	collar	sleeves	pockets	lapels	buttons
jeans	?	✗	✗	✓	✗	✓
raincoat	?	✓	✓	✓	✓	✓
nightdress	✗	?	?	✗	✗	?
tracksuit	✗	?	✓	?	✗	✗
waistcoat	✗	✗	✗	✓	✗	✓
gloves	✗	✗	✗	✗	✗	✗
sandals	✗	✗	✗	✗	✗	✗
scarf	✗	✗	✗	✗	✗	✗

COLOURS AND PATTERNS

black [7], blue [5], green [6], grey [3], pink [4], red [1], white [8], yellow [2]

CONTAINERS

Exercise 1
1. bucket 2. churn 3. bottles 4. crates 5. kettle
6. teapot 7. cups 8. saucers 9. jug

Exercise 2

	wood	plastic	glass	china	paper	metal
bag	✗	✓	✗	✗	✓	✗
bottle	✗	✓	✓	✗	✗	✗
crate	✓	✓	✓	✗	✗	✗
cup	✗	✓	?	✓	✓	✗
saucepan	✗	✗	✗	✗	✗	✓
box	✓	✓	✗	✗	✗*	✗
jug	✗	✓	✓	✓	✗	?
vase	✗	✗	✓	✓	✗	✗
tube	✗	✓	✗	✗	✗	✓

*Note that boxes are often made of CARDBOARD, a sort of thick, stiff paper.

ENVIRONMENTAL PROBLEMS

Exercise 1
1. mixture 2. smog 3. power 4. chimneys
5. clouds 6. rain 7. forests 8. spray 9. pesticides
10. chemicals 11. blood

FAMILY TREE

Exercise 1
1. father 2. father in law 3. wife 4. husband
5. grand daughter 6. daughter in law 7. aunt
8. parents

Exercise 2
1H, 2I, 3J, 4B, 5D, 6F, 7G, 8C, 9G, 10A

Puzzle
His son

FOOD

Exercise 3
1. eggs 2. milk 3. butter 4. mushrooms
5. cheese 6. ham 7. onions 8. bananas

LIVING ROOM

Exercise 1
armchair, kettle, washbasin, wardrobe, mantelpiece, lamp, towel, cushion, tap, bath, saucer, pillow

living room	kitchen	bathroom	bedroom
armchair	kettle	washbasin	wardrobe
lamp	towel	towel	lamp
cushion	tap	tap	cushion
mantelpiece	saucer	bath	pillow

OFFICE

Exercise 1
1. answering machine 2. fax machine 3. waste paper basket 4. photocopier 5. disk drive 6. calculator 7. stapler 8. printer 9. pencil sharpener 10. VDU

Exercise 2
1. both show the days and dates of the year; a calendar usually shows a month at a time, and is hung on a wall, and a diary usually shows a week at a time, and is in the form of a book.
2. both are devices used in a COMPUTER to store data; a floppy disk can be removed from the computer, but a hard disk cannot.
3. both are metal devices for holding sheets of paper together; paper clips are more easily removable and reusable than staples, which make holes in the paper.

PREPOSITIONS

1. into 2. into 3. under 4. inside 5. out of 6. to 7. on 8. along 9. in 10. into 11. under 12. beside 13. next to 14. out of 15. through 16. outside 17. towards 18. near 19. under

SPORTS

Exercise 1

Individual	team
athletics	rugby
boxing	American football
cycling	basketball
golf	cricket
skiing	soccer
horse racing	
swimming	
tennis	

Exercise 2
1. rugby, American football
2. cricket, golf, tennis
3. swimming
4. horse racing
5. rugby, soccer, American football

Exercise 3
pitch – cricket, American football, soccer, rugby
track – cycling, athletics
court – tennis, basketball

course – horse-racing, golf
pool – swimming
slope – skiing
ring – boxing

TOOLS AND EQUIPMENT

Exercise 1
1. These are all items used for opening things
2. These are all items used for cutting things
3. These are all items used for digging in the ground.

Exercise 2
1. hose 2. lawnmower 3. axe 4. potato peeler
5. potato masher 6. iron 7. corkscrew 8. toaster
9. hammer 10. tin opener

Exercise 3
1. hammer 2. drill 3. screwdriver 4. spanner
5. tape measure 6. saw   7. chisel   8. mallet

TRANSPORT

Exercise 1
Things you can see on a motorway – lorry, coach, motorbike (only if it is very powerful)

Exercise 2

	muscle power	wind power	petrol engine	diesel engine	jet engine	turbine engine
aeroplane	✗	✗	✗	✗	✓	✗
bus	✗	✗	✓	✓	✗	✗
car	✗	✗	✓	✓	✗	✗
dinghy	✓	✗	✗	✗	✗	✗
helicopter	✗	✗	✗	✗	✓	✓
hovercraft	✗	✗	✗	✗	✓	✓
lorry	✗	✗	✓	✓	✗	✗
rowing boat	✓	✗	✗	✗	✗	✗
ship	✗	✗	✗	✓	✗	✓
speedboat	✗	✗	✓	✗	✗	✗
train	✗	✗	✗	✓	✗	✗
yacht	✗	✓	✗	✗	✗	✗

VERBS OF MOVEMENT

1. run 2. carry 3. walk 4. jump 5. pull 6. bend
7. kneel 8. crawl 9. pick 10. drag 11. lift
12. stretch 13. lean 14. hold 15. climb 16. fall
17. throw 18. catch 19. drop 20. sit 21. tiptoe.

Word building

Word beginnings

a-¹ /ə/ (*makes adjectives and adverbs*) **asleep** sleeping | **alive** living

a-² /eɪ, æ, ə/ not: **atypical** not typical

aero- /ˈeərəʊ, ˈeərə/ relating to air: **aerodynamics** the study of forces on a body moving through air

Afro- /ˈæfrəʊ/ relating to Africa: **Afro-Asian** relating to both Africa and Asia

ambi- /ˈæmbɪ, æmˈbɪ/ both; double: **ambiguous** having more than one possible meaning; unclear | **ambidextrous** able to use both hands equally well

Anglo- /ˈæŋgləʊ/ relating to England: **Anglo-American** relating to both England and America

ante- /ˈæntɪ/ before: **antenatal** relating to the time before birth −compare **post-**

anti- /ˈæntɪ ‖ ˈæntaɪ, ˈæntɪ-/ **1** having a feeling or opinion against: **antinuclear** opposing the use of nuclear weapons and power −compare **pro- 2** opposite to or of: **anticlimax** a much less satisfying end (CLIMAX) than expected | **anticlockwise** in the opposite direction to the movement of the hands of a clock **3** preventing or acting against: **antifreeze** a liquid put into water in a car to stop it from freezing

arch- /ɑːtʃ, ɑːr- ‖ ɑːr-/ chief; first: **archbishop** a chief bishop

astro- /əˈstrɒ, ˈæstrəʊ, ˈæstrə ‖ əˈstrɑː/ relating to the stars, planets, and space: **astronomy** the study of the planets and stars

audio- /ˈɔːdiəʊ/ *also* **audi-** /ˈɔːdi/ relating to sound and hearing: **audiovisual** using or relating to both sound and sight

auto- /ˈɔːtəʊ, ˈɔːtə/ **1** self: **autobiography** a book about one's own life written by oneself **2** without help: **automatic** working by itself without human operation

be- /bɪ/ (*makes verbs*) to make; become; treat as: **belittle** to say that a person or thing is small or unimportant

bi- /baɪ/ two; twice: **biplane** a plane with two wings | **bilingual** able to speak two languages equally well | **biweekly** happening once every two weeks, or twice a week

bio- /ˈbaɪəʊ/ relating to life and living things: **biochemistry** the scientific study of the chemistry of living things | **biodegradable** able to be broken down into harmless products by the action of living things

by- /baɪ/ **1** less important: **by-product** something formed in addition to the main product **2** near: **bypass** a road near a city or town so that drivers can go around it rather than through it

centi- /ˈsentɪ/ *also* **cent-** /ˈsent/ 100; 100th: **Centigrade** a scale of temperature in which water boils at 100° | **centimetre** a measurement of length = 0.01 metres

co- /kəʊ/ together; with: **co-worker** a person with whom one works

contra- /ˈkɒntrə ‖ ˈkɑːn-/ opposite; against: **contradict** to say the opposite of (a statement, opinion, etc.)

counter- /ˈkaʊntər/ opposite; against: **counterrevolution** a movement opposing a revolution | **counterattack** an attack opposing another attack

cross- /krɒs ‖ krɔːs/ going across or between: **cross-Channel** going across the Channel | **cross-cultural** going between two or more cultures

de- /diː, dɪ/ the reverse or opposite of: **de-emphasize** to make less important | **devalue** to make (the value of something such as a currency) less

deca- /ˈdekə/ *also* **dec-** /dek/ ten: **decade** a period of ten years

deci- /ˈdesɪ/ a tenth part: **decilitre** 0.1 litres

dis- /dɪs/ **1** the opposite of: **discontented** not happy; not contented | **disagree** to have a different opinion; not agree **2** to change back; remove: **disconnect** to remove a connection of (something, especially something electrical)

en- /ɪn/ *also* **em-** /ɪm; *strong* em/ (*makes verbs*) **1** to put in, on, or around: **encase** to cover completely (as) with a case | **enclose** to put a wall or fence around **2** to make; cause to be: **enlarge** to make larger | **empower** to give (someone) the right or power to do something

equi- /ˌekwɪ, iːkwɪ/ equal: **equidistant** equally distant | **equivalent** (of amount, number, etc.) same; equal

Euro- /ˈjʊərəʊ/ European: **Eurovision** an organization for exchanging television and radio programmes in Europe

ex- /eks/ no longer being; former: **ex-husband** a man who was a woman's husband, but who is now DIVORCEd from her

extra- /ˈekstrə/ beyond; outside: **extrasensory** beyond the five senses of sight, smell, taste, and touch

fore- /fɔːr/ **1** earlier; before: **foresee** to guess what is going to happen in the future **2** placed in front of; before; front part of: **forearm** the front part of the arm, below the elbow | **forefront** the most forward place

geo- /dʒiːəʊ/ relating to the earth: **geology** the study of the materials (soil, rocks, etc.) which make up the earth | **geography** the study of the seas, rivers, towns, etc., on the surface of the earth.

hecto- /ˈhektəʊ/ 100: **hectolitre** 100 litres

hetero- /ˈhetərə, -rəʊ/ other; different: **heterogeneous** of (many) different kinds | **heterosexual** attracted to people of the opposite sex −compare **homo-**

homo- /ˈhəʊməʊ, ˈhɒmə- ‖ ˈhəʊməʊ, ˈhɑːmə/ same; like: **homogeneous** formed of parts of the same kind | **homosexual** attracted to people of the same sex −compare **hetero-**

hyper- /ˈhaɪpər/ above or too (much): **hypercritical** too critical

in- /ɪn/ **1** *also* **il-** /ɪl/, **im-** /ɪm/, **ir-** /ɪr/ not: **inexact** not exact **2** in; into; on: **inset** something put in as an addition into something else

■ USAGE **in-** meaning "not" usually changes to **il-** before *l*: **illegal** not legal; **im-** before *b, m,* or *p*: **imbalance** lack of balance | **immobile** not mobile | **impatient** not patient; **ir-** before *r*: **irregular** not regular or even; not usual

inter- /ˈɪntər/ between; among: **international** ̶ ing to do with more than one nation | **inter** ̶ **age** marriage between members of ̶ groups, families, etc.

intra- /ˌɪntrə/ *also* **intro-** /-trəʊ/ inside: **introspection** looking into one's own thoughts and feelings | **intravenous** inside a VEIN

kilo- /ˈkɪlə/ 1,000: **kilogram** 1,000 grams; **kilometre** 1,000 metres

macro- /ˈmækrəʊ/ large; great: **macroeconomics** the study of the economics of a country or countries

mal- /mæl/ bad; wrong: **malformation** the condition of being shaped wrongly | **malfunction** a fault in the operation of a machine

mega- /ˈmegə/ 1 million: **megawatt** 1,000,000 watts (WATT) of electricity 2 *infml* unusually large or great: **megastar** a star who is extremely famous and popular

micro- /ˈmaɪkrəʊ/ 1 very small: **microcomputer** a very small computer 2 a millionth: **microsecond** a millionth (0.000 000 1) of a second

mid- /mɪd/ middle: **midpoint** a point at or near the centre or middle | **midway** halfway or in a middle position

milli- /ˈmɪlɪ/ a thousandth: **milligram** 1,000th (=0.001) of a gram (a measurement of weight) | **millimeter** 1,000th (=0.001) of a meter (a measurement of length)

mini- /ˈmɪnɪ/ *infml* very small: **minibreak** a short holiday

mis- /mɪs/ 1 bad; wrong: **misspelling** a wrong spelling | **misjudge** to have a wrong opinion of 2 the opposite of: **mistrust** not to trust

mono- /ˈmɒnəʊ, ˈmɒnə ‖ ˈmɑː-/ one; single: **monorail** a railway with only one rail | **monopoly** a situation where only one person or group sells a particular thing, produces something, etc. | **monosyllabic** (of a word) having one syllable

multi- /ˈmʌltɪ/ many; more than one: **multicoloured** having many colours | **multistorey** (of a building) having many levels or floors

neo- /ˈniːəʊ, ˈniːə/ new; a later kind of: **neoclassical** a new or later kind of classical style: *the neoclassical architecture of America*

non- /nɒn ‖ nɑːn/ not: **nonstop** without stopping before the end | **nonpayment** not having paid: *He is in trouble for nonpayment of taxes.*

out- /aʊt/ 1 outside: **outdoors** in the open air 2 more than; beyond: **outgrow** to grow too big for: *The girl has outgrown her clothes.*

over- /ˈəʊvər/ 1 too much: **overexcited** too excited | **overpopulation** the condition of having too many people (in a country) 2 across; above: **overland** across or by land

photo- /ˈfəʊtəʊ/ 1 light: **photoelectric cell** an instrument which starts an electrical apparatus working by means of light 2 photography: **photocopy** (to make) an exact copy of (a letter, drawing, etc.) using a special machine (PHOTOCOPIER)

post- /pəʊst/ after; later than: **postwar** belonging to the time after a war | **postpone** to put off to a later time

pre- /priː/ before: **prewar** before a war | **preschool** relating to children who are too young to go to school

pro- /prəʊ/ in favour of: **pro-education** in favour of education –compare **anti-**

pseudo- /ˈsjuːdəʊ ‖ ˈsuː-/ not real; false: **pseudonym** a false name, used especially by a writer of

books | **pseudomodern** seeming to be (but not) modern

psycho- /ˈsaɪkəʊ/ *also* **psych-** /saɪk/ relating to the mind: **psychotherapy** the treatment of disorders of the mind | **psychology** the study of the mind and of behaviour

quadri- /ˈkwɒdrɪ ‖ ˈkwɑː-/ *also* **quadr-** /ˈkwɒdr ‖ kwɑːdr/ four: **quadrilateral** (a figure) with four sides

quasi- /ˈkwɑːzi, ˈkweɪzaɪ/ seeming or like: **quasi-scientific** seeming to be scientific

quin- /kwɪn/ five: **quintet** (music for) five players or singers together

re- /riː, rɪ/ again: **remake** to make (especially a film) again | **rethink** to think about again
    ■ USAGE When **re-** means "again", it is pronounced /riː/. In other words beginning with **re-**, it is usually pronounced /rɪ/ (or /riː/ before a vowel). Compare **recover** (to get better) /rɪˈkʌvər/ and **re-cover** (to cover again) /ˌriːˈkʌvər/

self- /self/ of or by oneself, independent: **self-explanatory** that explains itself | **self-control** control of oneself | **self-employed** working for oneself

semi- /ˈsemɪ/ 1 half: **semicircle** half a circle 2 partly: **semisolid** partly solid and partly liquid | *a* **semi-detached** *house* a house partly joined to another house by one shared wall

sub- /sʌb/ 1 under: **submarine** a ship which can travel under water 2 a smaller part of: **subregion** a small part of a region 3 less than: **subhuman** having less than human qualities

super- /ˈsuːpər, ˈsjuː- ‖ ˈsuː/ greater or more than: **supersonic** faster than the speed of sound | **superstar** a very famous and popular performer

tele- /ˈtelɪ/ 1 at or over a long distance: **telescope** an instrument for looking at objects that are far away | **telephone** an electrical apparatus for talking to other people a long distance away 2 using a telephone: **telesales** the sale of goods by telephone 3 using or for television: **televangelism** trying to convert people to religion by means of television

thermo- /ˈθɜːməʊ ‖ ˈθɜːr-/ heat: **thermometer** an instrument for measuring temperature | **thermodynamics** the study of the relationship between heat and mechanical energy

trans- /træns, trænz/ 1 across; on the other side of: **transatlantic** crossing, on the other side of, or concerning countries on both sides of the Atlantic 2 change: **transform** to change completely in form, appearance, or nature

tri- /traɪ/ three: **triangle** a flat figure with three straight sides

ultra- /ˈʌltrə/ 1 beyond: **ultrasonic** (of sound waves) beyond the range of human hearing 2 very; excessively: **ultramodern** very modern | **ultramarine** a very bright blue colour

un- /ʌn/ 1 (*makes adjectives and adverbs*) not: **uncomfortable** not comfortable | **unhappy** not happy | **unwashed** not washed 2 (*makes verbs*) to make the opposite of; reverse: **undress** to take one's clothes off | **unlock** to unfasten the lock of | **untie** to undo (a knot or something tied)

vice- /vaɪs/ next in rank or importance: **vice-president** the person next in official rank below a president: *the Vice-President of the United States*

Word endings

-ability, -ibility /ə'bɪlᵻti/ (*makes nouns from adjectives ending in* -able, -ible) **flexibility** the quality of being flexible (= easy to bend or change) | **reliability** the quality of being reliable; able to be trusted

-able, -ible /əbəl/ (*makes adjectives*) **1** able to be ...ed: **washable** able to be washed | **drinkable** that can be drunk **2** showing or having: **knowledgeable** having a good deal of knowledge | **reasonable** showing or having reason or good sense

-age /ɪdʒ/ (*makes nouns*) **baggage** all the bags and containers with which a person travels | **storage** a place for storing goods | **passage** the action of going across, by, over, etc.

-al /əl/ *also* -ial **1** (*makes adjectives*) **political** of or concerning politics **2** (*makes nouns*) **arrival** the act of arriving | **refusal** the act of refusing

-an /ən/ *also* -ian, -ean **1** (*makes adjectives and nouns from names of places or people*) **American** a person belonging to or connected with America | **Christian** a person who believes in the teachings of Jesus Christ **2** (*makes adjectives*) **Dickensian** of or like Dickens or his books **3** (*makes nouns from words ending in* -ic, -ics, *and* -y) **historian** a person who studies and/or writes about history

-ance, -ence /əns/ (*makes nouns*) **1** **importance** the quality or state of being important | **patience** the quality of being patient **2** an example of: **performance** an act of PERFORMING in a play, film, etc.

-ant, -ent /ənt/ **1** (*makes adjectives*) **pleasant** pleasing to the senses, feelings, or mind | **different** unlike; not of the same kind **2** (*makes nouns*) **servant** a person who works for another in the other's house | **student** a person who is studying at a school, college, etc. | **disinfectant** a chemical used to DISINFECT | **deodorant** a substance that removes unpleasant smells (ODOURS)

-ar /əʳ/ **1** (*makes nouns*) see -ER² **2** (*makes adjectives*) **muscular** having big muscles; strong-looking

-arian /eərɪən/ (*makes nouns and adjectives*) **vegetarian** someone who does not eat meat or fish | **librarian** a person who is in charge of or helps to run a library

-ary /əri ‖ eri/ **1** (*makes nouns*) a person or thing connected with or a place for: **library** a building or room which contains books that can be read and usually borrowed **2** (*makes adjectives*) **customary** established by custom; usual

-ate /ᵻt, eɪt/ **1** (*makes adjectives*) showing; full of: **considerate** showing consideration for **2** (*makes verbs*) to act as; cause to become: **activate** to cause to be active | **regulate** to bring order or method to; make REGULAR **3** (*makes nouns*) a group of people: **electorate** all the people in a place or country who can vote

-ation /eɪʃən/ (*makes nouns*) **declaration** an act of declaring | **hesitation** an act of hesitating (= pausing in or before an action) | **exploration** the act or an action of exploring (EXPLORE) (= to travel to a place for the purpose of discovery)

-ative /ətɪv/ (*makes adjectives*) **imaginative** using or having imagination | **talkative** liking to talk a lot

-ator /eɪtəʳ/ (*makes nouns*) a person or thing that does something: **narrator** a person who NARRATES | **generator** a machine which makes energy, usually electricity

-cide /saɪd/ (*makes nouns*) kill: **suicide** the act of killing oneself | **insecticide** a chemical substance made to kill insects

-cracy /krəsi/ (*makes nouns*) a government or class characterized by ...: **democracy** a government that is DEMOCRATIC; government by elected representatives of the people

-cy /si/ (*makes nouns*) **accuracy** the quality of being ACCURATE (= exact and correct)

-d /d, t/ see -ED

-dom /dəm/ (*makes nouns*) **1** the state of being (something): **boredom** the state of being BORED (= uninterested because something is dull) **2** **kingdom** the country ruled by a king or queen: *the United Kingdom*

-ean /ɪən/ see -AN

-ed, -d /d, ᵻd, t/ **1** (*makes regular past tenses and past participles*) *we* **laughed** | *I have* **waited** | *a man* **wanted** *by the police* **2** (*makes adjectives*) *a* **bearded** *man* (= a man with a beard) | *a long-*tailed *cat*

-ee /iː/ (*makes nouns*) **1** somebody to whom something is done: **employee** a person who is employed | **trainee** a person who is being trained | **refugee** a person who has been driven from his/her country **2** somebody who is or does something: **absentee** a person who is absent from work, etc.

-eer /ɪəʳ/ (*makes nouns*) a person who does an activity: **mountaineer** a person who climbs mountains | **profiteer** someone who makes large profits in times of war or difficulty

-en /ən/ **1** (*makes adjectives*) made of: **golden** of or like gold | **wooden** made of wood **2** (*makes verbs*) to cause to be or to have: **darken** to make or become dark: *The sky darkened after sunset.* | **soften** to make or become soft

-ent /ənt/ see -ANT

-er¹, -r /əʳ/ (*makes the comparative of short adjectives and adverbs*) **hotter** more hot | **safer** more safe –see Study Note on page 99

-er², -ar, -or, -r /əʳ/ (*makes nouns*) **1** a person who does an activity: **footballer** a person who plays football | **teacher** a person who teaches | **liar** a person who tells lies | **actor** a person who acts | **writer** a person who writes **2** a person who lives in (a place): **Londoner** a person who lives in London | **villager** a person who lives in a village **3** a thing that does something: **cooker** an apparatus on which food is cooked under direct heat | **heater** a machine for heating air, water, etc.

-ery, -ry /əri/ (*makes nouns*) **1** the art or quality of: **cookery** the art of cooking | **bravery** the quality of being brave **2** a place where something is done: **bakery** a place where bread is baked and/or sold

-es /ᵻz/ see -S

-ese /iːz/ (*makes adjectives and nouns*) relating to a country, its language or people, or a style: **Japanese** of or relating to the people, language, or country of Japan | **journalese** in the style of the language used in newspapers

-esque /esk/ having a manner or style like: **picturesque** looking like a picture: *a picturesque old village*

-ess /ᵻs, es/ female: **actress** a woman who acts in plays and films | **lioness** a female lion

-est, -st /ɪst/ (*makes the superlative of many short adjectives and adverbs*) **highest** the most high: *Mount Everest is the highest mountain in the world.* | **hottest** the most hot: *the hottest day of the year* – see Study Note on page 99

-ette /et/ (*makes nouns*) small: **kitchenette** a small kitchen

-fold /fəʊld/ (*makes adjectives*) times; multiplied by: **fourfold** four times (an amount)

-ful¹ /fəl/ (*makes adjectives*) **delightful** causing delight; highly pleasing | **painful** causing pain

-ful² /fʊl/ (*makes nouns*) the amount that a container holds: **cupful** the amount held by a cup | **spoonful** the amount held by a spoon

-fy /faɪ/ see -IFY

-gram /græm/ (*makes nouns*) a message delivered by a person as an amusing surprise, often on someone's birthday: **kissagram** someone paid to deliver a message and also to kiss the person they are delivering it to

-hood /hʊd/ (*makes nouns*) the state or period of being: **childhood** the time or condition of being a child | **womanhood** the state or period of being a woman

-ial /iəl/ see -AL

-ian /iən/ see -AN

-ibility /əˈbɪlɪti/ see -ABILITY

-ible /ɪbəl/ see -ABLE

-ic /ɪk/ (*makes adjectives*) **poetic** of, like, or connected with poets or poetry – see -ICAL (USAGE)

-ical /ɪkəl/ (*makes adjectives*) connected with: **historical** connected with history
■ USAGE Some pairs of words ending in **-ic** and **-ical** have different meanings. For example, **historic** means 'having a long history' or 'being remembered in history', but **historical** means 'something that happened in the past' or 'relating to the study of history'.

-ics /ɪks/ (*makes nouns*) a science or particular activity: **economics** the scientific study of the way industry and trade produce and use wealth | **athletics** the sport of exercising the body by running, jumping, etc.

-ie /i/ see Y (2)

-ify /ɪfaɪ/ *also* **-fy** (*makes verbs*) to make or become: **purify** to make pure | **simplify** to make simple | **clarify** to make clearer or easier to understand

-ing /ɪŋ/ 1 (*makes the present participle of verbs*) *she's* **sleeping** | *I'm* **waiting** *for you.* 2 (*makes nouns from verbs*) **Running** *keeps you healthy.* | *a* **sleeping** *pill* (= a pill to make a person sleep) | *a beautiful* **painting** | **Painting** *is fun.*

-ise /aɪz/ see -IZE

-ish /ɪʃ/ (*makes adjectives*) 1 relating to a country, its language, or people: **British** of Britain | **Swedish** of Sweden 2 like; typical of: **childish** (a word often used to express disapproval) of or typical of a child | **foolish** like a fool; without good sense; stupid | 3 rather: **reddish** slightly red | **smallish** rather small 4 approximately: **fortyish** about forty | **sixish** at about 6 o'clock

-ism /ɪzəm/ (*makes nouns*) 1 the ideas, principles, or teaching of: **socialism** a belief in equality and in public ownership | **Buddhism** a religion of east and central Asia, based on the teachings of the Buddha 2 a practice or activity: **terrorism** the practice of using violence to obtain political demands 3 a quality or characteristic: **heroism** the quality of being a HERO (= someone who acts with great courage)

-ist /ɪst/ 1 (*makes nouns and adjectives*) a follower of a movement: **socialist** a person who believes in SOCIALISM 2 (*makes nouns*) someone who studies, produces, plays, or operates: **guitarist** someone who plays the guitar | **pianist** someone who plays the piano | **machinist** a person who operates a machine | **linguist** someone who studies language | **novelist** someone who writes NOVELS

-ite /aɪt/ (*makes nouns and adjectives*) a follower of a movement: **Trotskyite** a supporter of Trotsky's ideas

-ity /ɪti/ *also* **-ty** (*makes nouns*) the quality or an example of: *It was an act of* **stupidity** *to drive so fast.* | **cruelty** *to animals*

-ive /ɪv/ (*makes adjectives*) having a tendency, character, or quality: **creative** creating new ideas and things | **descriptive** that describes | **explosive** that can explode

-ize, -ise /aɪz/ (*makes verbs*) **popularize** to make popular | **legalize** to make legal | **criticize** to find fault with; judge severely
■ USAGE Both **-ize** and **-ise** are used in British English, but only **-ize** is generally used in American English.

-less /ləs/ (*makes adjectives*) 1 without: **hopeless** without hope | **painless** causing no pain | **careless** without taking care | **powerless** without power or strength 2 that never …s; that cannot be …ed: **tireless** never getting tired | **countless** that cannot be counted

-let /lɪt/ (*makes nouns*) small: **booklet** a small book, usually with paper covers | **piglet** a young pig

-like /laɪk/ (*makes adjectives*) like or similar to: **childlike** of or typical of a child

-logy /lədʒi/ see -OLOGY

-ly /li/ 1 (*makes adverbs from adjectives*) *Please drive* **carefully**. | *The man was walking very* **slowly**. 2 (*makes adjectives and adverbs*) happening regularly: **hourly** happening every hour | **daily** happening each day 3 (*makes adjectives*) having the manner of: **motherly** having or showing the love, kindness, etc., of a mother 4 (*makes adverbs*) from a particular point of view: *Some people didn't like the film, but* **personally** *I thought it was very good.*

-ment /mənt/ (*makes nouns from verbs*) 1 the act or result of: **government** the act or method of ruling a country | **encirclement** the action or result of making a circle around something | **development** the action or result of developing 2 the condition of: **confinement** the state of being CONFINED (enclosed within limits); the time during which a woman about to give birth has to stay in bed

-most /məʊst/ (*makes the superlative of some adjectives and adverbs*) most: **topmost** nearest the top | **northernmost** nearest the north

-ness /nɪs/ (*makes nouns*) **goodness** the quality of being good | **loudness** the quality of being loud

-ology /ɒlədʒi/ (*makes nouns*) the science or study of: **geology** the study of the materials which make up the earth | **sociology** the scientific study of societies and human groups

-or /əʳ/ see -ER

-ory /əri ‖ ɔːri, ɔːri/ 1 (*makes adjectives*) **satisfactory** causing SATISFACTION; good enough 2 (*makes nouns*) place or thing used for: **observatory** a place where scientists look at stars, etc.

-ous /əs/ (*makes adjectives*) **dangerous** able to or likely to cause danger | **spacious** having a lot of space

-phile /faɪl/ (*makes nouns*) a person who is attracted to: **Anglophile** a person who likes England

-philia /ˈfɪliə/ (*makes nouns*) love of: **Anglophilia** a love of England –compare **-phobia**

-phobia /ˈfəubiə/ (*makes nouns*) very strong fear or dislike: **Anglophobia** a dislike of England | **claustrophobia** a fear of being in a closed space –compare **-philia**

-ry /ri/ see -ERY

-s, -es /z, s, ᵻz/ **1** (*makes the plural of nouns*) one **cat**, three **cats** | one **glass**, two **glasses** **2** (*makes the third person singular of the present tense of verbs*) she **sings** | He likes reading. | He watches television.

-ship /ʃɪp/ (*makes nouns*) **1** the state or condition of having or being: **friendship**: the condition of having a friendly relationship | **partnership**: the state of being a partner, especially in business. **2** skill; craft: **scholarship** the knowledge, work or method of SCHOLARS | **workmanship** skill in making things | **musicianship** skill in performing or judging music

-some /səm/ **1** (*makes nouns*) **twosome** a group of two people or things **2** (*makes adjectives*) causing; producing: **fearsome** causing fear | **troublesome** causing trouble

-ster /stəʳ/ (*makes nouns*) a person who does an activity or who is of a certain group: **youngster** a young person

-th /θ/ (*makes adjectives from numbers, except for those ending in 1, 2, or 3*) **sixth** | **hundredth** | **fortieth**

-ty /ti/ see -ITY

-ule /juːl/ a small kind of: **globule** a drop of liquid

-ure /jəʳ/ (*makes nouns from verbs*) **closure** the act of closing | **failure** lack of success; failing

-ward /wəd ‖ wərd/ also **-wards** /wədz ‖ wərdz/ (*makes adjectives and adverbs*) in the direction of: **backward** directed toward the back, the beginning, or the past | **homeward** going toward home

-ware /weəʳ/ (*makes nouns*): **hardware** metal goods for the home and garden, such as pans, tools, etc. | **ironware** goods made from iron

-ways /weɪz/ see -WISE

-wise /waɪz/ also **-ways** **1** (*makes adjectives and adverbs*) in the manner or direction of: **lengthways** in the direction of the length | **clockwise** in the direction in which the hands of a clock move **2** (*often infml*) (*makes adverbs*) with regard to: **moneywise** with regard to money: I'm having a lot of problems moneywise.

-y /i/ **1** (*makes nouns*) **jealousy** a JEALOUS feeling | **sympathy** pity for the suffering of another **2** also **-ie** (*infml*) (*makes nouns*) names for people: **granny** grandmother | **Jamie** James **3** (*makes nouns*) names for animals, used especially by small children: **doggy** dog **4** (*makes adjectives*) **noisy** making a lot of noise | **sunny** having bright sunlight

List of irregular verbs

The list below shows those verbs that have irregular past tense, PAST PARTICIPLE, or PRESENT PARTICIPLE forms (see page 8 of the workbook at the front of this dictionary)

The INFINITIVE form is shown first, e.g. **begin**

2 = past tense, e.g. *As I was walking home it* **began** *to rain.*

3 = past participle, e.g. *It had already* **begun** *to rain before I left home.*

4 = present participle, e.g. *It is just* **beginning** *to rain now.*

The number 2/3 means that the past tense and past participle are the same form. The pronunciation of each form is shown at its own place in the dictionary.

abide¹ 2/3 abided 4 abiding
abide² 2 abode 3 abided 4 abiding
arise 2 arose 3 arisen 4 arising
awake 2 awoke *or* awaked 3 awaked *or* awoken 4 awaking
be – see BE
bear 2 bore 3 borne 4 bearing
beat 2 beat 3 beaten *or* beat 4 beating
become 2 became 3 become 4 becoming
befall 2 befell 3 befallen 4 befalling
begin 2 began 3 begun 4 beginning
behold 2/3 beheld 4 beholding
bend 2/3 bent 4 bending
bereave 2/3 bereaved *or* bereft 4 bereaving
beseech 2/3 besought *or* beseeched 4 beseeching
beset 2/3 beset 4 besetting
bet 2/3 bet *or* betted 4 betting
bid¹ 2/3 bid 4 bidding
bid³ 2 bade *or* bid 3 bidden *or* bid 4 bidding
bide 2 bode *or* bided 3 bided 4 biding
bind 2/3 bound 4 binding
bite 2 bit 3 bitten 4 biting
bleed 2/3 bled 4 bleeding
bless 2/3 blessed *or* blest 4 blessing
blow 2 blew 3 blown 4 blowing
break 2 broke 3 broken 4 breaking
breed 2/3 bred 4 breeding
bring 2/3 brought 4 bringing
broadcast 2/3 broadcast ‖ *also* broadcasted *AmE* 4 broadcasting
build 2/3 built 4 building
burn 2/3 burnt *or* burned 4 burning
burst 2/3 burst 4 bursting
buy 2/3 bought 4 buying
cast 2/3 cast 4 casting
catch 2/3 caught 4 catching
chide 2 chided *or* chid 3 chid *or* chidden ‖ *also* chidded *AmE* 4 chiding
choose 2 chose 3 chosen 4 choosing
cleave 2 cleaved *or* cleft *or* clove 3 cleaved *or* cleft *or* cloven 4 cleaving
cling 2/3 clung 4 clinging
clothe 2 clothed ‖ *also* clad *AmE* 3 clad ‖ *also* clothed *AmE* 4 clothing
come 2 came 3 come 4 coming
cost 2/3 cost 4 costing
creep 2/3 crept 4 creeping
cut 2/3 cut 4 cutting
dare 2/3 dared 4 daring
deal 2/3 dealt 4 dealing
dig 2/3 dug 4 digging
dive 2 dived ‖ *also* dove *AmE* 3 dived 4 diving
do – see DO
draw 2 drew 3 drawn 4 drawing
dream 2/3 dreamed *or* dreamt 4 dreaming
drink 2 drank 3 drunk 4 drinking
drive 2 drove 3 driven 4 driving

dwell 2/3 dwelt *or* dwelled 4 dwelling
eat 2 ate 3 eaten 4 eating
fall 2 fell 3 fallen 4 falling
feed 2/3 fed 4 feeding
feel 2/3 felt 4 feeling
fight 2/3 fought 4 fighting
find 2/3 found 4 finding
flee 2/3 fled 4 fleeing
fling 2/3 flung 4 flinging
fly 2 flew 3 flown 4 flying
forbear 2 forbore 3 forborne 4 forbearing
forbid 2 forbade *or* forbad 3 forbidden *or* forbid 4 forbidding
forecast 2/3 forecast *or* forecasted 4 forecasting
foresee 2 foresaw 3 foreseen 4 foreseeing
foretell 2/3 foretold 4 foretelling
forget 2 forgot 3 forgotten 4 forgetting
forgive 2 forgave 3 forgiven 4 forgiving
forsake 2 forsook 3 forsaken 4 forsaking
forswear 2 forswore 3 forsworn 4 forswearing
freeze 2 froze 3 frozen 4 freezing
get 2 got 3 got *esp. BrE* ‖ gotten *AmE* 4 getting
gild 2/3 gilded *or* gilt 4 gilding
give 2 gave 3 given 4 giving
go 2 went 3 gone 4 going
grind 2/3 ground 4 grinding
grow 2 grew 3 grown 4 growing
hang¹ 2/3 hung 4 hanging
hang² 2/3 hanged 4 hanging
have – see HAVE
hear 2/3 heard 4 hearing
heave¹ 2/3 heaved 4 heaving
heave² 2/3 hove 4 heaving
hew 2 hewed 3 hewed *or* hewn 4 hewing
hide 2 hid 3 hidden 4 hiding
hit 2/3 hit 4 hitting
hold 2/3 held 4 holding
hurt 2/3 hurt 4 hurting
keep 2/3 kept 4 keeping
kneel 2/3 knelt ‖ *also* kneeled *AmE* 4 kneeling
knit 2/3 knit *or* knitted 4 knitting
know 2 knew 3 known 4 knowing
lay 2/3 laid 4 laying
lead 2/3 led 4 leading
lean 2/3 leant *esp. BrE* ‖ leaned *esp. AmE* 4 leaning
leap 2/3 leapt *esp. BrE* ‖ leaped *esp. AmE* 4 leaping
learn 2/3 learned *or* learnt 4 learning
leave 2/3 left 4 leaving
lend 2/3 lent 4 lending
let 2/3 let 4 letting
lie¹ 2 lay 3 lain 4 lying
lie² 2/3 lied 4 lying
light 2/3 lie *or* lighted 4 lighting
lose 2/3 lost 4 losing
make 2/3 made 4 making
mean 2/3 meant 4 meaning
meet 2/3 met 4 meeting

mislay 2/3 mislaid 4 mislaying
mislead 2/3 misled 4 misleading
misspell 2/3 misspelt *or* misspelled 4 misspelling
misspend 2/3 misspent 4 misspending
mistake 2 mistook 3 mistaken 4 mistaking
misunderstand 2/3 misunderstood 4 misunderstanding
mow 2 mowed 3 mown *or* mowed 4 mowing
outbid 2 outbid 3 outbid || *also* outbidden *AmE*
  4 outbidding
outdo 2 outdid 3 outdone 4 outdoing
outshine 2/3 outshone 4 outshining
overcome 2 overcame 3 overcome 4 overcoming
overdo 2 overdid 3 overdone 4 overdoing
overhang 2/3 overhung 4 overhanging
overhear 2/3 overheard 4 overhearing
override 2 overrode 3 overridden 4 overriding
overrun 2 overran 3 overrun 4 overrunning
oversee 2 oversaw 3 overseen 4 overseeing
overshoot 2/3 overshot 4 overshooting
oversleep 2/3 overslept 4 oversleeping
overtake 2 overtook 3 overtaken 4 overtaking
overthrow 2 overthrew 3 overthrown 4 overthrowing
partake 2 partook 3 partaken 4 partaking
pay 2/3 paid 4 paying
prove 2 proved 3 proved *or* proven 4 proving
put 2/3 put 4 putting
quit 2/3 quit 3 quit *or* quitted 4 quitting
read 2/3 read 4 reading
rebuild 2/3 rebuilt 4 rebuilding
redo 2 redid 3 redone 4 redoing
relay 2/3 relayed 4 relaying
remake 2/3 remade 4 remaking
rend 2/3 rent || *also* rended *AmE* 4 rending
repay 2/3 repaid 4 repaying
rewrite 2 rewrote 3 rewritten 4 rewriting
rid 2 rid *or* ridded 3 rid 4 ridding
ride 2 rode 3 ridden 4 riding
ring² 2/3 ringed 4 ringing
ring³ 2 rang 3 rung 4 ringing
rise 2 rose 3 risen 4 rising
run 2 ran 3 run 4 running
saw 2 sawed 3 sawn || *also* sawed *AmE* 4 sawing
say 2/3 said 4 saying
see 2 saw 3 seen 4 seeing
seek 2/3 sought 4 seeking
sell 2/3 sold 4 selling
send 2/3 sent 4 sending
set 2/3 set 4 setting
sew 2 sewed 3 sewn || *also* sewed *AmE* 4 sewing
shake 2 shook 3 shaken 4 shaking
shave 2/3 shaved 4 shaving
shear 2 sheared 3 sheared *or* shorn 4 shearing
shed 2/3 shed 4 shedding
shine¹ 2/3 shone 4 shining
shine² 2/3 shined 4 shining
shoot 2/3 shot 4 shooting
show 2 showed 3 shown || *also* showed *AmE* 4 showing
shrink 2 shrank *or* shrunk 3 shrunk *or* shrunken
  4 shrinking
shut 2/3 shut 4 shutting
sing 2 sang 3 sung 4 singing
sink 2 sank || *also* sunk *AmE* 3 sunk || *also* sunken *AmE*
  4 sinking
sit 2/3 sat 4 sitting
slay 2 slew 3 slain 4 slaying
sleep 2/3 slept 4 sleeping
slide 2/3 slid 4 sliding

sling 2/3 slung 4 slinging
slink 2/3 slunk 4 slinking
slit 2/3 slit 4 slitting
smell 2/3 smelt *esp. BrE* || smelled *esp. AmE* 4 smelling
smite 2 smote 3 smitten || *also* smote *AmE* 4 smiting
sow 2 sowed 3 sown *or* sowed 4 sowing
speak 2 spoke 3 spoken 4 speaking
speed 2/3 sped || *also* speeded *AmE* 4 speeding
spell 2/3 spelt *esp. BrE* || spelled *esp. AmE* 4 spelling
spend 2/3 spent 4 spending
spill 2/3 spilled *or* spilt 4 spilling
spin 2/3 spun 4 spinning
spit 2/3 spat || *also* spit *AmE* 4 spitting
split 2/3 split 4 splitting
spoil 2/3 spoiled *or* spoilt 4 spoiling
spread 2/3 spread 4 spreading
spring 2/3 sprang || *also* sprung *AmE* 3 sprung
  4 springing
stand 2/3 stood 4 standing
steal 2 stole 3 stolen 4 stealing
stick 2/3 stuck 4 sticking
sting 2/3 stung 4 stinging
stink 2 stank *or* stunk 3 stunk 4 stinking
strew 2 strewed 3 strewn *or* strewed 4 strewing
stride 2 strode 3 stridden 4 striding
strike 2 struck 3 struck || *also* stricken *AmE* 4 striking
string 2/3 strung 4 stringing
strive 2 strove 3 striven || *also* strived *AmE* 4 striving
swear 2 swore 3 sworn 4 swearing
sweep 2/3 swept 4 sweeping
swell 2 swelled 3 swollen *or* swelled 4 swelling
swim 2 swam 3 swum 4 swimming
swing 2/3 swung 4 swinging
take 2 took 3 taken 4 taking
teach 2/3 taught 4 teaching
tear 2 tore 3 torn 4 tearing
tell 2/3 told 4 telling
think 2/3 thought 4 thinking
thrive 2 throve *or* thrived 3 thrived *or* thriven 4 thriving
throw 2 threw 3 thrown 4 throwing
thrust 2/3 thrust 4 thrusting
tread 2 trod 3 trodden *or* trod 4 treading
unbend 2/3 unbent 4 unbending
undergo 2 underwent 3 undergone 4 undergoing
understand 2/3 understood 4 understanding
undertake 2 undertook 3 undertaken 4 undertaking
undo 2 undid 3 undone 4 undoing
unwind 2/3 unwound 4 unwinding
uphold 2/3 upheld 4 upholding
upset 2/3 upset 4 upsetting
wake 2 woke *or* waked 3 woken *or* waked 4 waking
waylay 2/3 waylaid 4 waylaying
wear 2 wore 3 worn 4 wearing
weave¹ 2 wove 3 woven 4 weaving
weave² 2/3 weaved 4 weaving
wed 2/3 wedded *or* wed 4 wedding
weep 2/3 wept 4 weeping
wet 2/3 wet *or* wetted 4 wetting
win 2/3 won 4 winning
wind² 2/3 winded 4 winding
wind³ 2/3 wound 4 winding
withdraw 2 withdrew 3 withdrawn 4 withdrawing
withhold 2/3 withheld 4 withholding
withstand 2/3 withstood 4 withstanding
wring 2/3 wrung 4 wringing
write 2 wrote 3 written 4 writing

Sound/pronunciation

The symbols used to show pronunciation in this dictionary are those of the International Phonetic Alphabet (IPA), and are the same as those used in the *Longman Dictionary of Contemporary English*, and in the *English Pronouncing Dictionary* by Professor A. C. Gimson (Dent, 14th Edition, 1977). We use these symbols to show both British and American pronunciation.

British pronunciation The type of British speech described in this dictionary is called Received Pronunciation, or RP. It is the speech common among educated English speakers especially in the south of England, and is the type of British English pronunciation that is usually taught to students of English.

American pronunciations The type of American English described in this dictionary is one of the more common accents of American English.

The pronunciation of many words is the same in both British and American English. Whenever they are different, we show the American pronunciation following the British one, after the sign ||, like this:

   pot /pɒt||pɑːt/

This means that the British pronunciation is /pɒt/ and the American pronunciation is /pɑːt/.

When the British and American pronunciations are very similar, we only show the part of the American pronunciation that is different. For example:

   abnormal /æb'nɔːməl || -'nɔːr-/

This means that the British pronunciation is /æb'nɔːməl/ and the American pronunciation is /æb'nɔːrməl/.

Abbreviations Abbreviations which are only used in writing, such as **mm** or **lb**, are not given pronunciations. But pronunciations are shown for abbreviations commonly used in speech, such as: BA /ˌbiː'eɪ/ VAT /ˌviː eɪ 'tiː, væt / NATO /'neɪtəʊ/

Strong and weak forms Many common words, like **am**, **of**, **to**, etc., can be pronounced in more than one way:

   am /m, əm; *strong* æm/

This means that **am** is usually pronounced /m/ or /əm/ in conversation:

   I'm /aɪm/ *going to the shops*
   I am /əm/ *going soon*

But when **am** is used at the end of a sentence, or when it is stressed, we use the strong form /æm/:

   Who's going to the shops? I am /æm/.

SPECIAL SIGNS

/ə/ means that the sound /ə/ may be pronounced or may be left out. For example: **memory** /'meməri/ may be pronounced /'meməri/ or /'memri/.

/ɓ/ means that some speakers use the sound /ə/ and some use the sound /ɪ/. For example: **sensible** /'sensɓəl/ may be pronounced /'sensəbəl/ or /'sensɪbəl/.

/ʊ̈/ means that some speakers use /ə/ and some use /ʊ/. For example: **regular** /'regjʊ̈ləʳ/ may be pronounced /'regjʊləʳ/ or /'regjələʳ/.

/i/ shows that many British speakers use /ɪ/ but many American speakers us /iː/. In both varieties of English it can also represent a sound somewhere between /ɪ/ and /iː/ **happy** /'hæpi/ **happiness** /'hæpinɪ̈s/ **deviate** /'diːvieɪt/ **deviation** /ˌdiːvi'eɪʃən/

/u/ represents a sound similar to /uː/ but shorter. It usually appears in an unstressed syllable when the syllable which follows starts with a vowel: **punctual** /'pʌŋktʃuəl/ **punctuality** /ˌpʌŋktʃu'ælɪ̈ti/

/ʳ/ at the end of a word means that in American English the /r/ sound is always pronounced while in British English it is pronounced only when the next word begins with a vowel sound. For example: **far** /fɑːʳ/ is usually pronounced /fɑː/ in British English, but **far away** would be pronounced /fɑːrə'weɪ/.

/'/ shows that the SYLLABLE after this sign is said with more force and STRESS (main stress) than the other syllables in the word. For example: **able** /'eɪbəl/ is pronounced <u>a</u>ble, with the main stress on the first syllable, and **ability** /ə'bɪlɪ̈ti/ is pronounced a<u>bil</u>ity, with the main stress on the second syllable.

/ˌ/ shows that the syllable after this sign is said with some stress, but not as much as main stress. For example: **agriculture** /'ægrɪˌkʌltʃəʳ/ is pronounced <u>ag</u>ri<u>cul</u>ture, with the main stress on the first syllable, and less stress (secondary stress) on the third syllable.

/◄/ shows stress shift. The main stress of some words changes when they are used before a noun. For example: **independent** /ˌɪndɪ-'pendənt ◄ / means that we say: *She is very inde<u>pend</u>ent.* but: an <u>inde</u>pendent <u>wom</u>an.

/···/ When an entry is made up of two or more words, like **alarm clock**, with the pronunciations shown at **alarm** and **clock**, we do not repeat them at **alarm clock**. Instead we show you how the phrase **alarm clock** is stressed by using a dot for each syllable /·/, and the stress marks /'/ and /ˌ/. for example: **alarm clock** /·'··/ means that the main stress is put on the second syllable of **alarm**: a<u>larm</u> clock.

/-/ A hyphen has two uses. In **nighttime** /'naɪt-taɪm/ it is used to show that the /t/ sound is pronounced twice. In **mosaic** /məʊ'zeɪ-ɪk/ it is used to show that there are two separate vowel sounds in the middle of the word, /eɪ/ and /ɪ/. The hyphen is also used in alternative pronunciations to replace any part which has been omitted because it is the same as in the pronunciation just given. For example: **abduct** /əb'dʌkt, æb-/ means that there are two possible pronunciations: /əb'dʌkt/ and /æb'dʌkt/.